ENGLISH VERSE
1701-1750

A CATALOGUE OF SEPARATELY PRINTED POEMS
WITH NOTES ON CONTEMPORARY
COLLECTED EDITIONS

VOLUME 1: CATALOGUE

D. F. FOXON

Whoever thinks a faultless piece to see,
Thinks what ne'er was, nor is, nor e'er shall be.
Pope, Essay on criticism

CAMBRIDGE UNIVERSITY PRESS

Published by the Syndics of the Cambridge University Press
Bentley House, 200 Euston Road, London NW1 2DB
American Branch: 32 East 57th Street, New York, N.Y.10022

© Cambridge University Press 1975

Library of Congress Catalogue Card Number: 70-152637

ISBN: 0 521 08144 0 (set of two volumes)

First published 1975

Printed in Great Britain
at the University Printing House, Cambridge
(Euan Phillips, University Printer)

CONTENTS OF VOLUME 1

CONTENTS OF VOLUME 2

PREFACE

Not long after I had joined the Department of Printed Books at the British Museum, Sir Frank Francis, then Keeper there as well as secretary of the Bibliographical Society, followed the tradition established by A. W. Pollard in pointing out to me the opportunities that a post in the Museum offered for undertaking some systematic bibliographical research. Although I was not attracted by the particular project he suggested, the general idea took root, and this is the place to record my gratitude to him as well as to the Museum and my colleagues there. I was particularly fortunate in spending a few years working on the revision of the General Catalogue before it finally ground to a halt; and the experience thus gained in dealing with the books of all periods and many languages that made up a series of several hundred consecutive entries would be hard to achieve in other ways. One was faced with many bibliographical problems and learnt the use of numerous reference books; and then in revising the entries for authors like Defoe and Dickens I began to feel some confidence in dealing with more extensive groups of material. There was also a negative reaction: like many users of the catalogue we were frustrated by those rules which we nevertheless had to follow for the sake of consistency, and it was a relief to dream of how one could organize a catalogue if one were not fettered by precedent, except in those general conventions which have become familiar over the past century and a half. At this time Donald Wing had recently completed his *Short-title catalogue, 1641–1700*, and the eighteenth century lay waiting for the bibliographer; but again there was a negative reaction: when cataloguing or dealing with accessions one wished for collations to identify imperfections, and to know whether entries with different imprints represented variant title-pages, reissues, or new editions. So there grew the idea of a short-title catalogue with rather more bibliographical sophistication, though necessarily limited in its scope. The most sensible limitation seemed to be one of form, and to me verse was the obvious choice.

Soon afterwards I heard Fredson Bowers read a paper to the Bibliographical Society[1] on his bibliography of the Restoration drama, in which he described his technique of comparing as many copies as possible of each edition with a control copy on microfilm. The points that impressed me most were the number of unrecorded variants, issues, and even editions which could be found only by personal examination of multiple copies, and his argument that the more copies a bibliographer has examined, the more safely can his descriptions be condensed. It became clear to me that though my catalogue could not provide full bibliographical descriptions, any attempt to produce a reliable work must involve seeing as many copies as possible myself and not relying on published catalogues or other second-hand sources. As a check against concealed editions, reset sheets, and reissues I decided to adopt Falconer Madan's practice of recording the position of signature letters relative to the text above them, a method of identification I had already come to trust and one which was far cheaper and easier than the use of microfilm. Needless to say, it cannot provide the precision of Bowers's technique, and the user of this catalogue will soon become irritated by the frequency of notes like 'apparently a reimpression' or 'sheet B is apparently reset' which are based on the evidence of signatures. But I would justify this by my early experience with Charlton Hinman's collating machine which has, it seems to me, changed the whole balance of bibliographical investigation. I would now be unwilling to attempt to define the relationship between two copies printed from the same types unless I could compare them (or xeroxes of them) on the Hinman collator, since only this can reveal, for example, whether or not the type-pages have been removed from the forme between impressions.[2] And I have recently argued in more general terms[3] that now that editors collate multiple copies of a text by machine, they have the materials for a more complete bibliographical

---

[1] 'Purposes of descriptive bibliography, with some remarks on methods', *The Library* V. 8 (1953) 1–22.
[2] D. F. Foxon, 'Modern aids to bibliographical research', *Library trends* 7 (1959) 574–81. This is, of course, a typically eighteenth-century problem.
[3] *Thoughts on the history and future of bibliographical description* (1970).

analysis than the descriptive bibliographer could attempt – unless he were to duplicate that laborious process. In short, I feel that in so far as Bowers has established textual study based on machine collation, he has rendered his own principles of bibliographical description less relevant; but I have the greatest respect for his work in both fields as well as a personal debt for his inspiration, encouragement, and kindness.

It is, however, unlikely that my ideas would have been translated into action without the example of the late William A. Jackson whom I met on his annual visits to England in search of untraced works and copies for the revision of the *Short-title catalogue, 1475–1640*. There can have been few bibliographers so devoted to the pursuit of completeness, and I was fortunate in catching something of that spirit of the chase from him, though I could never have hoped to emulate his devotion over so many years. Quite apart from the example he set, his advice and help encouraged me to make concrete plans for my work; and it was his practical experience and assistance in the United States that enabled me to make a good start on this catalogue.

Having paid tribute to this scholarly inspiration, I must make it plain that I have reconciled myself to something less than the perfection at which the scholar aims. Although I have tried to achieve more bibliographical sophistication than earlier short-title catalogues, my primary concern has been to record where copies of poems can be found so that the scholar may have ready access to them; and if that scholar is a bibliographer or a textual critic, I can only hope to have helped him on his way.

As work proceeded, I added information that was not in my original plan. Originally I had not even thought of quoting first lines, and I am most grateful to whoever it was that first pointed out this defect. I gradually came to realize that the evidence of authorship which came my way should be recorded, however imperfect and incomplete it might be, since attributions pass from catalogue to catalogue until they are taken for granted though their origin is lost. I later decided to do what I could to date the publication of the poems and (when possible) to record their entry in the Stationers' Register, transfers of their copyrights, and details of their printing. Finally I compiled the indexes which produced new information about relationships and publication. Yet all these signs of activity should not lead the user to think that the last word has been said.

Perhaps the clearest way to express the problem of compiling a work like this is to say that it contains some ten thousand entries and represents some ten thousand hours of work. An average entry thus represents an hour's work, which must include making a description of the first copy, comparing that with other copies, consulting reference books, establishing publication dates, considering authorship and subject, preparing copy for the typist, editing for the press, and making the entries in the indexes. Clearly such a time limit is incompatible with the highest standards of scholarship. Two specific problems may be mentioned under this head. As I travelled the British Isles and the United States, I began to pride myself on the accuracy with which I had estimated the time I would need in each library. I now realize that there is a converse of Parkinson's Law, and that work done contracts to fill the time available for it – when time was short, familiar works were not properly examined and the description of new ones was skimped. Again, the speedy way of using reference books was to work right through each and make what seemed the relevant notes on my slips, rather than to consult them separately for each work. It is now clear that what seemed irrelevant at first might have solved a problem at a later stage; but there was rarely time to go back. I am aware that there are many outstanding problems to be solved and errors to be corrected, some no doubt from obvious sources; but conscious of the limited time available I have only pursued what seemed the obvious leads to a quick answer.

A related problem is my neglect of library catalogues.[1] One good reason for this is that one cannot look up unrecorded authors or anonymous books, because they are as yet unknown. So my practice has been to make straight for the book stacks and record what I found there. As a result I have not only missed

---

[1] I have at various times checked the catalogues of the British Museum, Bodleian, Folger, Harvard, Huntington, University of Texas, and Yale libraries, as well as the National Union Catalog in the Library of Congress.

PREFACE

works (such as translations) that are not in the main sequences and those which were out on loan at the time, but I have missed information that cataloguers have provided. As an ex-cataloguer I am ashamed of this slight; I also fear that both libraries and myself will be embarrassed by my recording works that do not appear in their catalogues. My catalogue is also out of date; it roughly represents American library holdings in 1960 and British holdings in 1965.[1]

Worst of all, this is the work of one pair of eyes and one brain. I have a prejudice against co-operative bibliography, because I value the memories that are evoked and the connections that are made when one person sees all the material. But in a work like this, accuracy is most easily achieved when each description is checked against the original by another person, and another person will also be a safeguard against those inconsistencies and rash judgements which will undoubtedly be found here. As for the tasks of editing, indexing, and proof-reading which have occupied me for the last eight years, they proved far more demanding than the collecting of materials, and the strain was greater than I (knowing my limitations) had feared. Again, I do not believe that these functions can simply be delegated, but I should not now be prepared to undertake them single-handed.

I can now turn to the more cheerful subject of those who have helped me, and first must come the generous North American foundations without whose help this work could never have been carried out. I had been able to build a skeleton of the catalogue from various bibliographical sources, but it was not until a Harkness Fellowship from the Commonwealth Fund enabled me to work and travel in the United States for eighteen months in 1959–61 that it began to be fleshed out with detail. The help and understanding of Lance Hammond and Martha English need no tribute from me, but I shall never forget how readily problems were solved so that one's work could also be a pleasure. After this interlude progress was again slow until by leaving the British Museum in 1965 I was able to spend six months working in the major libraries of the British Isles before going to Queen's University at Kingston, Ontario. Here, as well as the steady encouragement of George Whalley, I found new sources of finance for the task of supplementing, typing, and indexing my material; and I am grateful to the American Council of Learned Societies, the Arts Research Committee of Queen's University, the Canada Council, and the Humanities Research Council of Canada for their subventions. Finally I must confess that far more of my time as a Guggenheim Fellow in 1967–68 was spent in completing this catalogue than I had anticipated; and – I suspect in good company – I have to thank Gordon Ray for his forbearance as well as his faith in my work.

When I turn to the scholars who have helped me at every need, enumeration becomes impossible. All those who have engaged in research will know how much unexpected and undeserved help one receives from fellow scholars, but only those who have tried to produce a work like this can know how limitless that help can be. My greatest debt is naturally to librarians, who must have been sorely tried by my demands but yet were always ready to do more than I asked. I only hope that in so far as this catalogue helps them, they may be in some part repaid for their kindness. It is impossible to thank them enough; and as a token I name some of my most tried correspondents: Robert Donaldson, Mary Isabel Fry, Desmond Neill, Mary Pollard, Julian Roberts, the late Daniel Whitten, and Marjorie Wynne.

I have in general restricted this catalogue to copies in public collections, but I have received every possible help as well as hospitality from those private collectors whom I have consulted. They include the Duke of Devonshire, Lord Bath, Lord Crawford and Balcarres, Lord and Lady Rosebery, Lord Rothschild, John Brett-Smith, H. B. Forster, John R. Hetherington, Robert Horn, Mary Hyde, Wilmarth Lewis, Kenneth Monkman, Lois Morrison, Arnold Muirhead, A. N. L. Munby, J. M. Osborn, William Rees-Mogg, John Sparrow, Robert A. Taylor; and the late W. N. H. Harding, Geoffrey Tillotson, d'Alté A. Welch, and Sir Harold Williams. I have also had generous assistance from many booksellers as well as from the auction houses.

---

[1] I have been able (with varying completeness) to add accessions to the British Museum, Bodleian, Harvard, and Yale. When I have not examined a particular copy, the symbol for its library is printed in italic.

PREFACE

For help in the production of the printer's copy I am particularly indebted to Marion Armstrong who had the greatest share in the typing and not only set the standards but also made the task seem possible; to Valerie Brown who sorted the slips for the subject index and the index of first lines, and to Juliet Grindle who did the same for the chronological index and the index of imprints. Kathleen Coburn, Ruth Mortimer, Desmond Neill, Simon Nowell-Smith, and Mary Pollard did more than they perhaps realize in clarifying my ideas about the way the catalogue and indexes should be arranged. Desmond Neill has done more than friendship could ask in reading the whole of the proofs, and Enid Nixon checked the subject index for me; neither can be held responsible for the inaccuracies, inelegancies, and inconsistencies that remain. I am appreciative of the burden that the Cambridge University Press has borne, and am particularly indebted to Diane Speakman for her ready and continual help.

For the future, I shall be glad to receive corrections, additions, and enquiries; and though I cannot face with enthusiasm the prospect of publishing a volume of revisions, I can at least undertake that these records will in some way be made available to other scholars.

DAVID FOXON

Oxford
1974

INTRODUCTION

In trying to describe how this work has been prepared and presented, I find myself somewhat encouraged by a paragraph in Sir Walter Greg's introduction to *A bibliography of the English printed drama to the Restoration* which explains better than I can the shortcomings to which a work of this scope is subject. It concludes, 'lest anyone should think that looking back on my work I feel any complacency over the manner of its execution, I here admit that I can hear the caustic critic who ever sits like a familiar imp at my elbow maintaining that my problem in writing this introduction has been threefold: first to discover what I have done, next why I did it, and lastly how best it may be defended.' A similar caustic critic has caused me increasing disquiet in the final stages of preparing this volume, and with far more justification.

That this is not a descriptive bibliography but a short-title catalogue with frills is no defence against charges of inconsistency and inaccuracy, nor does it weaken the conviction that it would have been a better book if I had been able to visualize its final form more clearly before I started collecting the material on which it is based. I can only comfort myself with the thought that much of the inconsistency is due to attempts to make it more informative, and more of the inaccuracy to a desire to make it available as soon as possible. One personal circumstance may be mentioned in extenuation: as a British Museum cataloguer I found it impossible to eradicate certain conventions, especially since I was at first writing catalogue entries both for the Museum and for this work; and I also expected that the preparation of my final typescript would be carried out with the resources of the Museum at hand.

It may be useful to give some idea of how the material was collected. I have worked with 5 × 8 in. slips of bond paper printed with compartments for the categories of information to be recorded, the author, title, date, and format of each item running along the top of the slip so that it could easily be found in the filing boxes. (The fact that the compartment for the title was somewhat restricted may account for some regrettable abbreviation of titles.) Apart from what is regularly printed in the catalogue I recorded three things: the watermark of the paper and the size of any uncut copy; the position of a number of signature letters relative to the last line of the text above them, or press-figures when they were present; and the pages on which printers' ornaments appeared. I had hoped to collect information on ornaments and thus identify the printer of each work concurrently with this catalogue, but this soon proved impossible, though ornaments led to the discovery of many Edinburgh piracies. The noting of watermarks brought to light many unrecorded fine-paper issues as well as revealing some bibliographical anomalies; the signature positions made it possible to identify concealed editions or to suggest that so-called editions were from the same setting of type as their precedessors. I have come to regret that I have not been able to make this information available so that unknown issues might be readily identifiable when they appear.

The slips were filed in two series, those where the author's name appeared in the work and those which were anonymous – whether or not the author was known. This not only enabled me to turn directly from each anonymous work to its slip, but it saved the bulk of individual cross-references for each title to its author. Instead, one reference slip could usually list all the works attributed to an author, with whatever degree of certainty; on another reference slip I made notes of the collected editions of the author. These latter notes were originally intended only for my own use; only at a late stage did I realize how useful they might be to users of the catalogue.

When I started work the modern xerographic copying machines were not available; they might well have caused me to adopt different methods, just as they are, I believe, a challenge to some traditional bibliographical procedures. Xerox enlargements of microfilm were available, however, and it was possible to make reproductions of most of the half-sheets. These provide almost a quarter of the catalogue entries, and descriptions of them are accordingly more accurate than for other works (which is fortunate because of their rarity), while many unsuspected editions have been revealed which normal methods of description could not have distinguished.

The boxes of slips and the xerox enlargements were the materials I carried with me from library to library, and though they fitted into one large suitcase, their weight made me glad I had kept their bulk to the minimum. I relied in part on comparing multiple copies with my slips to bring to light my errors as well as variants; but I have learnt for myself the lesson that once an error is made, it is hard to eradicate. There is no substitute for a second pair of eyes to check one's work at every stage. Unnoticed errors aside, I have no regrets about the method I employed; in particular I was gratified that when I prepared my final text it was not necessary to engage in a great deal of correspondence, and what questions had to be asked could normally be brief.

SCOPE

The catalogue attempts to list all separately published verse written in English, as well as works written in other languages and printed in the British Isles, but it omits all works printed in America since they have already been catalogued.[1] It is, however, primarily a catalogue of verse written between 1701 and 1750, and it excludes poems by authors who died before 1701 with two main exceptions: it seemed desirable to list all the poems piratically printed by Henry Hills between 1708 and 1710 (when the first copyright act came into force), and also some anonymous works whose earlier origins might not be recognized (e.g. B485, C429, J99) or which were related to other works of this period (e.g. A182–3, S639–46). It excludes works only published in miscellanies and in periodicals, with the exception of the very rare and short-lived *Daily Slip*, some numbers of which consisted of a single poem (J56, M159, M538).

Collections of verse by a single author are included in a much abbreviated form, but the dividing line is not always easy to draw. I have treated as single works small collections where the title takes a form like Swift's *Baucis and Philemon... Together with Mrs. Harris's earnest petition... As also an ode against solitude*. Works like George, lord Lyttelton's *The progress of love, in four eclogues* or James Thomson's *The seasons* can reasonably be regarded as having a unity which is manifest in their titles. I feel more doubt about the collections of political fables which will be found under Aesop and under William Pittis – it is not even certain that one author was responsible for each of them – but since they have a unifying title I have treated them as single works.

Since I did not originally intend to print entries for the collected poems of authors, my materials were collected according to subjective rather than critical principles. I hope I have included all collections of poems by living authors in the period 1701–1750, except for some cases where poems form a very minor part of the author's works in prose and verse. I also include collections published after 1750 which contain poems which appeared earlier, but these are usually restricted to those prepared by the author or his executors; collections of poems written after 1750 and those prepared by later editors are excluded. Where an author's collected poems appeared before 1750 I sometimes list later editions which contain additional material.

Translations and versifications have been included as though they were original works, and they appear either under the translator's name or under their title when the translator is not known. A few works in foreign languages have been included although they were published abroad. Latin poems by Britons (e.g. Dibben, D296; Flemyng, F167) which were also printed in Britain deserved entry, as did an Amsterdam edition of a poem by J. G. Pritz originally printed in London (P1101·5). On the other hand I have followed the rule and excluded the works of two Irish Latinists, D. McEnroe and P. St. John, which seem to have been printed in France; there are probably others of which I know nothing. I feel least justification in including a number of Jacobite poems in French written to celebrate the invasion of

---

[1] In Oscar Wegelin, *Early American poetry* (1930), supplemented by R. E. Stoddard, *A catalogue of books and pamphlets unrecorded in Oscar Wegelin's Early American poetry* (1969), and in Charles Evans, *American bibliography* (1903–59). For two exceptional cases, see L165 and W256.

1745; although one or two claim to have been printed 'à Edimbourg' I have little doubt of their continental origin (see A1, C131, C383, I67, N302·5, O22, O58, O172). Nevertheless they are both rare and relevant, and they take their place here with the caution that others may exist in French libraries.

The following classes of material are excluded[1] with the exceptions noted:

1. Popular broadside ballads, slip songs, and chap-books, which have no author or reference to current events. The extent of this material is enormous and it is usually undated and undatable; I am pleased to feel that it is very properly a separate field of study. At the same time it does have links with what I include; Jacobite satires used the slip song form extensively, while political works like Richard Glover's *Hosier's ghost* were reprinted for the popular market. In the same way Walter Pope's *The wish* appeared both as a black-letter ballad and as a normally published pamphlet poem. Some songs by authors included here were certainly disseminated in popular form (e.g. C51, G62), and others remain to be identified, though the date of surviving editions may often be later than 1750. In general I have tried to include all those works which refer to historical and political events, deaths, executions, and wonders, as well as those few songs where I have identified the author and the date appears to lie within my period. Chap-books often took the form of 'garlands' or collections of songs which fall outside my terms of reference, but I have included a number of single poems in this format (e.g. B200, B201, C160, G309, L41, N51). I am, however, certain that my record of this ephemeral material is neither complete nor consistent.[2] Frost-fair and bellman's verses are excluded; and, at the other extreme, tripos verses.

2. Engraved sheets or half-sheets, typically songs with music and political cartoons with engraved verses below. The songs call for no comment except that many were written by authors included here; I have sometimes noted the existence of engraved musical versions of a printed text, but I have made no search for them. The cartoons are sometimes found with the text engraved below and sometimes with it printed by letterpress; I have included only the latter type, except for a few works where the author is known (e.g. B402). Engraved verses without music or pictures are included, but coverage of all this material is weak since it is usually found in print rooms rather than in libraries; the only collection that I have searched systematically is in the Department of Prints and Drawings of the British Museum.

3. Oratorios and opera libretti. The dividing line is difficult here, because I include odes which were set to music and these are sometimes in dialogue form. The terminology of the author is not always helpful; one 'lyric poem' was subsequently printed as an 'oratorio' (L212–14). I have tried to exclude works which were performed in the theatre, but a cantata (M157), an epithalamium (H47), and a masque (R66) remain. Dialogue poems like Edward Ward's *Honesty in distress... A tragedy, as it is basely acted by her majesty's servants upon god's stage the world* are included since they were not intended for performance.

4. Works consisting of prose and verse are excluded when the prose precedes the verse, unless it can be considered merely as an introduction (as in F172). This is an arbitrary rule based on British Museum practice, but to the best of my knowledge its only serious effect it is to exclude some editions of *The ballad... answered stanza by stanza. With the Memorial, alias Legion, reply'd to paragraph by paragraph* (B34–7).

ARRANGEMENT

Entries are made under either the author or the first word of the title; noblemen are entered under their family name.[3] Cross-references are made from the titles of poems to their authors when they are anonymous or when the author's name does not appear on the title-page; they are also made from initials or from pseudonyms to the main entry under author or title. (In cases where it is not clear whether an

---

[1] Compilers of catalogues of verse have tended to include unmetrical epitaphs, whether in English or in Latin, and liturgical parodies such as *Old England's Te deum*; I exclude both categories.

[2] I am comforted that the publishers had the same problems; the 1754 catalogue of William and Cluer Dicey in the Bodleian has a note on p. 56, 'There are near Two Thousand different sorts of SLIPS; of which the New Sorts coming out almost daily render it impossible to make a Complete Catalogue.'

[3] Noblemen are entered under their titles in the subject index, since where they are the subjects of poems it seemed more useful to keep the form the poet used.

author's name is real or pseudonymous, the entry is made under the name.) As has been said above, translations are entered not under the original author but under the translator or (if he is unknown) under the title; again cross-references are made from the original author or title (versifications of parts of the Bible being grouped under that heading). Where attributions of anonymous works to an author have been rejected, cross-references have been made from the author to their titles. A note on the principles of attribution forms the next section of the introduction.

Under an author, the abbreviated entries for collected works stand first in chronological order, and are followed by separate works in alphabetical order. (I have, however, brought together editions of the same work with different titles, and have also grouped the separate parts of (for example) Thomson's *Seasons* under the collective title.) Cross-references to works attributed to him or written jointly by him are inserted in this alphabetical sequence as are supposititious works, though here the author's name (or the dash that represents it) is printed within inverted commas. Works published anonymously have the name or the dash in square brackets.

Other anonymous works are entered under the first word of their title (other than the definite or indefinite article) which is used as a heading in its modern spelling; with proper names I have usually kept the form that is used, though I have brought together Chloe and Cloe, Volpone and Vulpoon with appropriate cross-references.

The serial number of each new work is printed in bold type in the hope that it may make it easier to find the first of a series of editions. I have given a serial number to works which I have not seen but which appear to be reliably reported, but have withheld them from those which may well be 'ghosts'. Where I have had to add entries after the initial numeration was complete I have used decimal points: B101·5 stands between B101 and B102, though a fine-paper issue of B101 would normally appear as B101·1 to leave the maximum space for new works. The order of a series of editions is first by year, and within that year (1) authorized editions at the place of first publication, (2) unauthorized editions at that place, (3) reprints elsewhere – normally, in the case of London works, Scottish reprints precede Irish ones. This system has been modified in some cases; for example Defoe's *Mock mourners* (D132–42) has a series of numbered editions of both authorized and unauthorized editions including Dublin editions with a false London imprint, and it seemed likely that the user would find a single sequence easier to use. I must stress that my arrangement does not represent the transmission of the text, which can only be determined by textual collation; in some cases it is quite arbitrary. Where there were independent London and Dublin editions of a text I have often added a note that the priority is not determined, but the situation is more complex when a popular satire appeared in four or five half-sheet editions. These may well stem from different manuscripts, sometimes with different titles, and the problem of priority is acute. I have tended to rely on certain rules of thumb, and where a copy is dated (typically by Narcissus Luttrell) I have put that edition first as some sort of anchor; similarly I have given preference to an edition with a book-seller's name to one without, to a known bookseller against a probable pirate, and to a well-printed edition against a badly printed one. I have sometimes been able to add notes on the relationship of these editions, but the problems need further study and no priority should be assumed from the order I give.

In listing a series of editions, I have tried to use the prefix [another edition] as little as possible. Following normal practice, a first dash represents the heading, while a second may represent either a part or the whole of a title (including minor variations of spelling or punctuation):

Baker, Abel. The temple, a poem. *London*, 1710.
— — *Dublin*, 1710.
— — The second edition. *London*, 1712.

I use [another edition] only when there is no distinction between editions as they are normally described; distinguishing features are then added in the form of a note. When an entry has a prefix like [reimpression], [fine paper], [reissue], I have not thought it necessary to use a dash as well; the title is to be understood

INTRODUCTION

as repeated. Where a new edition has a quite different title I have introduced the prefix [*idem*] to show the identity of the work with its predecessor.

Finally, it will be seen that cross-references vary in the form they take. This is partly the result of the way the catalogue has been assembled, but I hope the variation may be useful to the user. The broad distinction is that the cross-reference from the title of an anonymous work to its author is to the author's name rather than to its serial number; the reader thus knows at once what attribution is made. But when a cross-reference is made from an author to a work he may have written, the title is already known and the reference is to the serial number and not the heading; since collections have no serial number, references for them have to be made to the heading. Under authors whose works are translated (or versified), the translator's name is given first, so the reference can be to serial number – except, again, in the case of collections where the translator's name has to be sufficient guide.

ATTRIBUTION

The decision whether or not to enter a work under an author to whom it has been attributed is always difficult, and I have not allowed myself the escape of printing the entry under both author and title. I have felt that to enter a tentative attribution under the author might lead the careless to assume that his authorship is certain, and might possibly discourage the scholarly from further examination of the problem. At the same time it has clearly been impossible for me to enter at all deeply into the canon of any author either by biographical research or by internal evidence of style – in itself often a dangerous criterion. I have therefore been reduced to employing a rule of thumb which lays me open to the charges of being both credulous and over-sceptical. My chief reason for acceptance has been contemporary evidence, which is of varying kinds. The subsequent inclusion of a poem in an authorized collection of an author's works (and I have found many hitherto unrecognized examples) is clearly the best evidence. Entries to authors in the Stationers' Register or in printers' accounts are almost equally good, though there may be problems (e.g. G162·5, P475). Booksellers' advertisements should normally be reliable, though I have attributed a number of new works to Edward Ward on their authority with some hesitation. Contemporary manuscript attributions on title-pages inevitably vary in authority, from those clearly made by a friend of the author to those which may be merely the product of coffee-house gossip;[1] the problem may be seen in the varying attributions of *Faction display'd* (which I give to William Shippen), and the unreliable are common (as I have realized too late) in manuscript commonplace books. Where there is an unresolved conflict of evidence or an obscure attribution which might have far-reaching effects (e.g. C207) I have held my hand, but otherwise I have followed contemporary sources or what have seemed to me obvious links between works.

When on the other hand the attribution is merely an unsupported statement in the catalogue of a library or a modern bookseller I have normally recorded but not accepted it, even though it may originally be based on exactly the same sort of evidence.[2] (Some individual cases have escaped my vigilance, e.g. F187, J16.) I do, however, give weight to cumulative authority – even though, as in the case of Swift, successive editors can be shown to have been united in misjudgement. Thus, under Defoe I accept *A hymn to the mob* which has been in the canon for a century though external evidence is lacking, while I reject *A hymn to the funeral sermon* because it rests on the authority of the late J. R. Moore alone. I personally feel that this and similar attributions to Defoe are probably correct, but the final decision must rest with other students of Defoe and not with me. In the absence of external evidence,

---

[1] A volume in the library of Lambeth Palace with Archbishop Cornwallis's bookplate is the only case I know of a series of apparently wild attributions of pamphlet poems; though they are in an eighteenth-century hand I suspect they may not be contemporary with the poems (see E2, F104, G10).

[2] I have usually ignored the attributions of the Wrenn Catalogue, the irresponsibility of which has been shown by W. B. Todd in 'Some Wiseian attributions in the Wrenn Catalogue', *The Library* V. 23 (1968) 95–107. I have also ignored some clearly incorrect attributions from modern secondary sources.

INTRODUCTION

I ask for a consensus of scholarly opinion; and a poem which has been printed by editors with hesitation is banished.

Considerations of space have prevented detailed discussion of authorship, and I have frequently limited myself to recording the earliest piece of evidence I have found. Thus if I have found copies with early manuscript ascriptions I may quote these without referring to the poem's subsequent inclusion in the author's works. Quite often I have found early evidence of some sort, and it seemed preferable to record such new information rather than familiar and easily accessible sources.

FORM OF ENTRY – COLLECTIONS

It was no part of my original design to include the collected poems of authors; I was innocent enough to believe that they were readily available. For my own purposes I kept rough notes of them, including any peculiarities I became aware of, but without any systematic attempt at bibliographical investigation. When it became clear to me that some of these collections were hard to trace, I decided to include them in an abbreviated form. The title and imprint is given in my usual way, but the collation is restricted to the traditional record of pagination which merely gives the last page of each numbered series – convention which is of more use in distinguishing editions than is often realized nowadays. These descriptions are often based on a single copy, and should be treated with appropriate caution. I list only four copies, two in Britain and two in America, but without necessarily having seen them all; nor do I distinguish those I have not seen, as I do elsewhere. Normally the preference is given to copies at the British Library and Bodleian, Harvard and Yale; my records for these libraries are the most complete. I have not consistently searched the National Union Catalog, and American copies may often be found there when I give no location. I have added some notes on publication and authorship, but again these are not to be considered exhaustive.

FORM OF ENTRY – SINGLE WORKS

A full entry consists of six sections: heading, title, and imprint; collation; bibliographical note; first line; notes on authorship and subject; locations.

Title

The titles are quoted with no attempt to represent the capitalization of the title-page; this is (it seems to me) a hopeless pursuit, and I have reduced capitalization to a minimum. Punctuation follows the original as closely as possible, though occasionally a stop has been added to indicate a break which is provided by the typography of the original. Titles are abbreviated more than I would now wish, omissions being represented by three stops except for mottoes and authors' names which (following British Museum practice) are silently omitted. Restored readings in mutilated copies are enclosed in angle brackets. Peculiarities of spelling are normally copied without comment, but I use [!] in cases where the reader might suspect that a typographical error is in the catalogue rather than the original – though doubtless errors of transcription are present and unnoticed.

Where there is no title-page to a pamphlet and the title is taken from the drop-head or caption title, it has [dh] prefixed;[1] in broadsides, half-sheets, and slips where this is necessarily the source of the title, it is omitted. Imprints given in a colophon similarly have [col] prefixed to them.

Imprint

Any attempt to abbreviate imprints involves some rationalization, and that in its turn creates problems. I regretfully omitted addresses from my notes except where I was aware that they might be significant, and having thus departed from direct transcription I was influenced by the common misconception about imprints of the form 'London: printed and sold by J. Jones'. In such cases it is unusual for Jones to be

[1] I should perhaps have followed Greg in using [ht] for head-title, but in this period it could be thought to stand for half-title.

the printer; indeed it is probable he is not the copyright owner but rather a distributor of pamphlets – a 'mere publisher' in eighteenth-century usage. I have therefore rationalized this form of imprint as *London printed, and sold by J. Jones* in the hope that those unfamiliar with eighteenth-century usage may not be misled. Having gone so far, I have normalized other regular imprints to the form *London, printed by X, for Y; sold by Z*, 1725. In this I have been influenced by British Museum practice as in the substitution of the ampersand for 'and' – little imagining that it would be printed in a type-face with such a conspicuous *&*. More complex imprints keep their original punctuation as far as abbreviation admits, particularly those such as *London: printed; and re-printed in Dublin by X*.

When there is no place of publication or date in the work, it is supplied (where possible) in square brackets, while false imprints are enclosed in quotation marks. This sounds simple, but it is necessary to give a warning that the supplying of imprints is a subjective matter and necessarily somewhat arbitrary; cataloguers will understand this, but other scholars may not. There are many occasions when one writes [*London*, 1713.] or [*Dublin*? 1727?] or [*London*? 174–?] without being able to give the evidence, at least in a form sufficiently concise for a catalogue such as this. In the absence of external evidence of publication, an unqualified date will usually be the product of internal evidence, a tentative date may be deduced from dated works on the same theme, a decade perhaps suggested by the typography. The place of publication may also be suggested by the typography, the subject matter, or the company in which the poem is found.[1] To some extent these judgements are all subjective, and the cataloguer has no option but to follow his hunch and lay his head on the block; indeed in this context too much thought paralyses judgement. What must be said is that square brackets themselves should suggest a caution; if I write [1710] I think the odds are ten to one that I am right, whereas with [1710?] the odds may be no better than even.[2]

In the form of supplied dates I follow the old Library of Congress rules by trying to establish terminal dates. Accordingly a poem which refers to Anne as queen will be dated [1702/14], not [*c*. 1710] or in the misleading British Museum form of [1710?]. Only when no terminus seems available do I fall back on a decade, [170–?]; I hope this sensible but uncommon convention will cause no confusion.

Wherever possible I have added information about the precise date of publication in parentheses after the imprint. Again this was not part of my original intention, nor have I searched all the newspaper files. Where monthly catalogues were available – either separately published or in periodicals like the *Gentleman's Magazine* – I have been content to give the month unless a more precise date came to hand. Only for the periods 1701–1714 and 1717–1723 have I systematically read the Burney newspapers in the British Museum. I have freely taken newspaper dates from other authorities without acknowledgement; in all cases I have tried to give the earliest advertisement which says 'This day is published', but earlier advertisements may come to light. Advertisements that a book *will* be published on a certain day have been recorded in that form, since performance did not always meet promise. Newspapers dated, like the *Post-Man*, 22–24 May are recorded as 24 May, the publication day.

Monthly catalogues (including the book lists in the *History of the Works of the Learned*) have their pitfalls. They were all published in the following month – the January issue in February – but whereas in the first quarter of the century catalogues might be published quite late in the following month and so might include books appearing in the first days of that month, the competition between the *Gentleman's Magazine* and the *London Magazine* to appear first may have led to the omission of publications of the last day or two of the preceding month. I have recorded conflicts of evidence as (*GM* March; *LM* April), but would guess that the publication date is here late March.

[1] It is worth mentioning here that the main collection of Dublin half-sheets at Trinity College, Dublin, appears to have been bound in the early nineteenth century, one volume to a year, in an attempt at chronological order. A few of the implied dates are clearly incorrect, but I have normally followed the year as [1727?] and recorded that the work is bound in a volume with that date.

[2] I fear that the presence or absence of the query is scarcely rational either. There is a series of Jacobite slip songs of 1715–20 which I have attributed to [*London*?]; the typography and press-work is so good that I feel sure this is their source... but could there have been a secret press elsewhere?

INTRODUCTION

It has been difficult to be consistent in the treatment of purchase dates added in manuscript. It might seem logical to put them on a par with newspaper dates and record them as the earliest date so far known, but whereas a newspaper date like (*PM* 29 July) is recognizable for what it is, a date repeated baldly from a manuscript note suggests a settled publication date when it may be the date of a copy presented before publication or purchased months afterwards. As a result I have tried to discriminate, doubtless inconsistently. For the first fifteen years of the period Narcissus Luttrell regularly dated each pamphlet he bought, and I have recorded these dates as (25 May, Luttrell); they can seldom be shown to be incorrect, though they may precede or follow newspaper advertisements by a day or two. After the reign of Queen Anne his interest seems to have slackened and he often records only the month, sometimes several months after the advertisements; these dates are rarely of use, but I record them for completeness in the list of copies. Other dates that have some authority are those found in copies from Tom's Coffee House[1] and some notes on Edinburgh half-sheets of the form 'Edinburgh printed 29 May 1721'; I usually accept these as firm evidence. I record other manuscript dates either in the notes or in the list of copies, but if they are the only evidence of publication the date is given as (15 Nov?).

The entries of works in the Stationers' Register were at this period frequently made on the same day as the newspapers announced publication and since here the source can be easily revealed I record (*SR* 14 April). It should be noted that the copyright act of 1709 required registration before publication and Pope in particular seems to have had his copies entered a day or two before publication. In such cases I have given the date of publication according to the newspapers and reserved the entry for a note, but there are probably more cases of entry before publication than I have distinguished. Some copies were entered after publication, but this is unusual.

In studying the printers' ledgers that survive, one again frequently finds a correlation between the date a work is entered and the date of newspaper advertisements. Closer study is needed, but it seems probable that topical pamphlets would go to the distributors for immediate publication and the job would be entered as completed that day. It is equally clear that new editions of established works might be printed and charged for before stocks of the old were exhausted, or that works printed for the author might be delivered and privately circulated a week or two before publication – if they were to be published at all (cf. P10). I have therefore treated dates from this source with caution, but have used them to provide a tentative date in the absence of other evidence.

Frequently there are dates from a number of sources, and where they conflict a choice has to be made. But except for recording only the earliest newspaper advertisement, I give all the evidence either in the bibliographical note or (in the case of manuscript dates) in the list of copies. The reader may therefore make his own decision.

Collation

I have generally tried to follow the Greg–Bowers formulary, though with some minor modifications which arise from the nature of my material and of the catalogue. Little need be said of format except that I have followed Bowers's suggestion of using 1°, $\frac{1}{2}^o$, $\frac{1}{4}^o$ and $\frac{1}{8}^o$ for unfolded single, half, quarter and eighth-sheets; when printed with the longer side horizontal, I have called them *obl* $\frac{1}{2}^o$. My one departure from strict bibliographical terminology is the use of the term *slip*. Slip songs came into popularity in this period and were printed in four columns parallel to the shorter side of the sheet, though they may normally have been produced by half-sheet imposition. In either case the correct term would seem to be *long* $\frac{1}{4}^o$, but slip was what the trade called them, and it seemed a more readily comprehensible term. I have occasionally used the term (again following trade practice) for other irregular bits of paper, but I hope that I have differentiated these from the normal slip by a note. In all these cases I record whether one or both sides is printed (unless pagination reveals this) and also whether the text is in one or more columns.

[1] See Paul Kaufman, 'Coffee houses as reading centres', in his *Libraries and their users* (1969) 115–27.

INTRODUCTION

In the collation proper I have deviated from the norm in three main respects. The most heretical is in the use of an odd superior figure for a single leaf. While A^3 is certainly ambiguous, A^1 is not, and I think a collation A^1 B–D^2 E^1 is typographically clearer than A1 B–D^2 E1. The fact that single folio leaves are common among these poems, sometimes clearly printed by half-sheet imposition (e.g. E430, P984), has encouraged me in this practice; there are indeed a number of folio half-sheet poems signed 'A'.

The second results from a collation, common in the seventeen-forties, of a two-sheet folio in fours which would normally be A^4, but where the outer sheet is unsigned and the inner is signed B. I have represented this by the convention $A^2 < B^2$ which probably represents what the printer had in mind.[1] Sometimes he signed the fourth leaf C, and I then write A^1 B^2 C^1, leaving it to be understood that A1 and C1 are conjugate. Where a sheet acts as a wrapper round a larger pamphlet I follow this more conventional practice, though I then record in a note cases where I have actually seen the conjugacy.

A more tricky problem of wrappers is found typically in half-sheet octavos where the title is printed as part of the last section. It is commonly said that the title is printed on the final leaf and folded back, and the collation then is clearly $A^1[=E4]$ B–D^4 $E^4(-E4)$. However, it seems to have been equally common to print the title on the first leaf of the last section so that, together with its conjugate final leaf, it forms a perfect wrapper. This can readily be expressed as $A^1[=E1]$ B–D^4 $E^4(-E1)$, but one should then record the 'mis-signing' (E2 as 'E', E3 as 'E2'). I have, however, allowed this collation to stand without recording the fact that the final leaves are technically mis-signed.[2] It is often impossible in the absence of watermarks to determine which practice was followed and one has to write E(3 ll); I leave it to be implied that the title probably formed part of E without thinking it necessary to make a note to that effect.

As to pagination, I have followed Bowers's example of inferring the beginning and end of numbered sequences, but I have gone one step further.[3] As I wished for my own purposes to note where all ornaments occurred, it seemed easiest to record them as well as the contents by pagination. Since for eighteenth-century books Bowers permits the use of inferred pagination for references to unnumbered preliminary sequences,[4] it seemed to be logical to use that inferred pagination in the collation. Accordingly I write *i–viii, 1 2–23 24* rather than *[8] 1 2–23 24*, and only use a bracketed total when there is already a sequence of roman numeration or there are other disturbances to be recorded. In most straightforward cases this works well and makes it easy to correlate signatures and pagination; there are some cases where it would have been wiser to use the bracketed total. I am less sure now that this provides a satisfactory method for recording contents, and I suspect that I would now mix signatures for unpaginated preliminaries with pagination for the text.

To the very limited extent that I refer to contents, inconsistency of this kind will be found. I decided from the first to record any frontispiece, half-title, errata, or advertisement (as frt, hft, err, advt), as well as final blanks which I include in the pagination formula as *1–22 23–24 blk*. With the errata and the advertisements I was particularly concerned to find variants, but I was also anxious to identify those leaves which were most likely to be missing. Thus, if I record a copy as (–A1, D4), having noted that A1 is a half-title and D4 an advertisement leaf, the user knows precisely what is missing. I have accordingly tended to refer to these leaves by signatures when they stand alone; but when the final leaf has text on the recto and an advertisement on the verso I revert to pagination and write '24 advt'. The mixture may look untidy, but I hope it will prove serviceable in use.

When frontispiece and plates are insert   rather than printed in the signatures of the book I have recorded them on the periphery of the collation as '(frt+) A–K^4 (+3 plates)'; they are, of course, excluded from the pagination in such a case.

---

[1] Philip Gaskell in *The first editions of William Mason* (1951) viii suggested the use of the term 'outset', preferring to write 'π^2 (outset) A–B^4', rather than to invent a new hieroglyph'. Neither solution is impeccable.

[2] Compare the similar problem of $M^8(-M1.8)$ in Bowers, *Principles of bibliographical description* (1949) 252, n. 6; a precise parallel is found in his description on p. 321 (but read '*vol. 8*' for '*vol. 6*').

[3] I have on occasion used inverted commas to distinguish mispagination (1–20 '23–25' 24) where it seemed to give greater clarity. The record of mispagination is, however, far from complete.

[4] *Principles* p. 316.

INTRODUCTION

Bibliographical note

I have tried to keep different sorts of information in a standard order. First comes any distinguishing feature necessary to identify a concealed edition, impression, or fine-paper copy. For the last, it may be useful to list certain common watermarks with references to illustrations of them in Edward Heawood's *Watermarks* (1950) and Philip Gaskell's *New introduction to bibliography* (1972).

	Heawood	Gaskell
Amsterdam arms	342–438	fig. 34
Dutch lion	3136–54	fig. 38
London arms	454–77	fig. 42
Pro patria	3696–718	fig. 37
Royal arms	441–50	fig. 35
Strasburg bend	58–118	fig. 30

The other watermarks recorded are, I hope, self-descriptive.

The other element that is given preference is reference to standard bibliographies. I have made no attempt at inclusiveness; apart from author bibliographies such as Griffith's *Pope* or Teerink's *Swift* I have systematically listed all the works in R. P. Bond, *English burlesque poetry 1700–1750* (1932) and Milton Percival, *Political ballads illustrating the administration of Sir Robert Walpole* (1916) since they are both detailed and informative. I have also made references to *The Rothschild Library* (1954) for the sake of its full descriptions, though when I give Rothschild as a location I have not felt it necessary to make a reference as well: in almost all cases these are half-sheets where that catalogue has little to add. References to other authorities are only made for specific reasons. I have not thought it necessary to note when I differ from an authority I have referred to.

Next come bibliographical notes on features common to all copies, followed by peculiarities found in some copies only. Finally come notes giving evidence of printing and publication: these may supplement the date of publication given after the imprint. In the case of works entered in the Stationers' Register I record the owner of the copyright only when it differs from the imprint of the work; I have tried to list the surviving deposit copies in the nine copyright libraries established by the act of 1709. Where information about the printing has come to light from the ledgers of Ackers, Bowyer, Ruddiman, Strahan, and Woodfall[1] I have noted it briefly, but I make no claim to completeness; I have also tried to record sales of copyright.

First line

This is quoted without any terminal punctuation except for exclamation marks, question marks, or dashes. Capitalization has been normalized and occasional typographical accidents such as turned letters have been silently corrected, but the original spelling is preserved. I have normally added the first lines of supplementary poems, and when there may be difficulty in identifying them with their titles I have prefixed a brief title in italics to each.

Notes on authorship and subject

If the author's name is not on the title-page but he signed a preface or dedication, that information is given here; if he only used his initials they are recorded. Evidence for the authorship of anonymous or pseudonymous works is then given; as noted above (p. xvi) I have often confined myself to the earliest evidence I have traced except where disagreement exists between authorities.

I originally had no thought of printing any information on the subject matter of the poems, but for my own benefit I made brief notes where the title of the poem was uninformative or misleading, or where contemporary annotation revealed the object of a satire. I had, however, reproductions of most of the half-sheets, and many of these had to be dated from their subject matter. Considering how rare most of these

---

[1] Known only from the extracts printed in *N&Q* I. 11–12 (1855).

INTRODUCTION

are and that I had the texts before me, I decided to do what I could to record their subject when the titles were unhelpful. I have similarly used what notes I had for other minor verse, but with better-known authors and poems I have made little attempt to elucidate the subject. The result is again inconsistency, but I hope the information is given where it is most needed. It must be added that many political and social satires have a wide range of targets, and one can only say (if the title does not reveal the fact) 'a satire on the whigs' or 'a political fable'. Mainly for this reason I have added a chronological index, hoping that the historian will thus be enabled to find his way to material that will interest him; it is also a gesture to those distinguished advocates of the chronological arrangement of catalogues with whom I cannot agree.

I have tried to record the titles of related works, typically when one answers another, except when they are already given in the title. These works are usually in verse and will be found elsewhere in the catalogue; those in prose (when I have identified them) I have tried to distinguish and to give a location for them when they are rare.

Locations

I have followed the policy of W. A. Jackson in the revised *Short-title catalogue, 1475–1640*, in limiting the number of locations recorded to five in the British Isles and five in the United States of America, adding a plus sign when further copies are known to me. I have come to feel some regret at this limitation, but I shall be happy to supply additional locations on request. On the other hand the locations I give are primarily those of copies I have examined, though I may add others in italic. I have made no attempt to list further American copies from the National Union Catalog; since this is now in course of publication, the reader can consult it himself. I do not list copies in private collections or in the trade except when no copy can be found in a public library. I have made an exception of half-sheets, normally rare, and have listed all copies I know; this reveals, for example, the high survival rate of some of Swift's works in this format.

In selecting copies to record, I have tried to give a wide geographical spread. The ideal for British libraries is British Library, Bodleian, Cambridge University Library, National Library of Scotland, and Trinity College, Dublin (L, O, C, E, DT); this order is maintained for other libraries in these cities, and other locations are arranged alphabetically after them. In the absence of a generally accepted list of symbols I have based mine on a list which the late L. W. Hanson was compiling at the time of his death, in which the first component represents the place (B = Birmingham, Ba = Bath, Br = Bristol) and the second the library; though I believe the system is sound, I claim no authority for its application. For American libraries I use the accepted National Union Catalog symbols (except that I have used the obsolete NNP, not NNPM, for the Pierpont Morgan Library). Here the preferred libraries are at Harvard, Yale, Chicago, University of Texas, and Los Angeles (MH, CtY, ICN or ICU, TxU, CSmH or CLU-C) and as far as possible gaps have been filled from the same geographical areas.

I have tried to add brief notes on copies where they may be of service. Imperfections are noted in Greg's way: where a missing leaf such as a half-title, advertisement leaf, or blank does not affect the text or title, it is recorded as (–A1); more serious imperfections are noted as (lacks D⁴). An attempt has been made to record uncut copies, though where they are common not all are listed; 'cropt' copies are so noted, using Greg's term. Copies of pamphlets in original condition are recorded as 'stitched, uncut'. Manuscript notes of date are recorded if they have not previously been noted in the entry; when the date has been given as (12 April, Luttrell) after the imprint, the relevant copy is merely identified as (Luttrell). In some cases I note copies with useful or important annotations, but this was an afterthought and many are regrettably unidentified.

There remains the problem of finding the copies recorded. I have tried to side-step the pitfalls of the British Museum catalogue by giving the press-mark of each copy (though I have avoided the use of double parentheses by referring to a pamphlet bound in a volume of tracts as 11641.e.20/3 instead of 11641.e.20 (3)). Many accessions of the last decade are merely recorded as (1962); they are doubtless catalogued by now, but I was not able to trace them when I was preparing my copy. I wish it had been possible to give press-marks for other libraries, but it puts heavy pressure on space. I am now aware that some half-sheets and slips in the Bodleian are not in the general catalogue (notably the Jacobite satires in MS. Rawl. poet. 203, 207), nor is the magnificent and little-known Madden collection of slip songs at Cambridge (which I have only skimmed). Other libraries have their failings, in the United States as well as Britain; and the very generosity of librarians in showing me uncatalogued material may rebound upon their own heads. Users of this catalogue may save time and trouble if they remember that many anonymous works entered here under authors will only appear under their title in library catalogues.

ABBREVIATIONS

GENERAL

advt	advertisement
blk	blank
col	colophon
dh	drop-head title (caption title)
err	errata
frt	frontispiece
hft	half-title

PERIODICALS

Modern periodicals are abbreviated according to the conventions of the MLA; eighteenth-century periodicals known by one-word titles are entered accordingly as Bee, Craftsman, Review, Tatler, *etc.*

BA	Bibliotheca Annua
BM	British Magazine
DA	Daily Advertiser
DC	Daily Courant
DG	Daily Gazetteer
DJ	Daily Journal
DP	Daily Post
DPB	Daily Post-Boy
EP[1]	English Post
EvP	Evening Post
FP	Flying Post
GA	General Advertiser[2]
GEP	General Evening Post
GM	Gentleman's Magazine
GSJ	Grub-Street Journal
HM	Miscellany ('by Richard Hooker')
LaM	Lady's Magazine[3]
LDP	London Daily Post and General Advertiser
LEP	London Evening Post
LG	London Gazette
LJ	London Journal
LM	London Magazine
LP	London Post
MC	Monthly Catalogue
MChr	Monthly Chronicle
Mist	Mist's Weekly Journal
OE	Old England
PB	Post Boy
PM	Post-Man
PPB	Protestant Post-Boy
PSGB	Political State of Great Britain
SJEP	St. James's Evening Post
SJP	St. James's Post
SM	Scots Magazine
SR[4]	Stationers' Registers
TC	Term Catalogues ('A catalogue of books...' ed. Arber, 1903)
WEP	Whitehall Evening-Post
WL	History of the Works of the Learned
WM	Weekly Miscellany

OTHER WORKS

This list contains those works which have been systematically consulted, as well as standard reference books which are occasionally cited. Specialized monographs, to which only a few references have been made, are often named in the text rather than abbreviated. This is not a complete list of works consulted.

Ackers's ledger   *A ledger of Charles Ackers*, ed. D. F. McKenzie and J. C. Ross, 1968.

Aldis   H. G. Aldis, *A list of books printed in Scotland before 1700*, 1904 (reprinted with additions, 1970).

Allibone   S. A. Allibone, *A critical dictionary of English literature and British and American authors*, 1899.

Anderson   John Anderson, *Catalogue of early Belfast printed books*, 1890 (*Supplement*, 1894; *Second supplement*, 1902).

Aubin   R. A. Aubin, *Topographical poetry in XVIIIth-century England*, 1936.

---

[1] There may be some entries where this abbreviation is used in error for *EvP*.

[2] Before 10 March 1744 the title was *London Daily Post and General Advertiser*; some entries before that date may be abbreviated as *GA*, following Ralph Straus, *Robert Dodsley* (1910).

[3] March–July 1733, in the collection of J. R. Hetherington.

[4] Not a periodical, but listed here since its abbreviation is of that form. Printed as *A transcript of the registers...1640–1708*, ed. G. E. B. Eyre (1913–15); subsequent entries are taken from the mss.

ABBREVIATIONS

Ault Norman Ault, *New light on Pope*, 1949.

Baker Frank Baker, *A union catalogue of the publications of John and Charles Wesley*, 1966.

Ball F. Elrington Ball, *Swift's verse: an essay*, 1929.

Blanchard Rae Blanchard (ed.), *The occasional verse of Richard Steele*, 1952.

Bond R. P. Bond, *English burlesque poetry, 1700–1750*, 1932.

Bowyer's ledgers Seven ledgers are the property of the Grolier Club, New York; I have used xerox prints of these in the Bodleian, which also owns his paper stock ledger (MS. Don. b. 4). Information is mainly taken from the two general printing ledgers (I, IV) supplemented by the detailed ledger for 1730–39 (II) and the paper stock ledger.

Bradner Leicester Bradner, *Musae Anglicanae: a history of Anglo-Latin poetry, 1500–1925*, 1940 (supplement in *The Library* V. 22 (1967) 93–103).

Bradshaw *A catalogue of the Bradshaw collection of Irish books in the University Library, Cambridge*, 1916.

Bushnell N. S. Bushnell, *William Hamilton of Bangour*, 1957.

Case A. E. Case, *A bibliography of English poetical miscellanies 1521–1750*, 1935.

CBEL *The Cambridge bibliography of English literature*, ed. F. W. Bateson, 1940.

Cibber Theophilus Cibber, *The lives of the poets of Great Britain and Ireland, to the time of Dean Swift*, 1753.

Crum Margaret Crum (ed.), *First-line index of English poetry 1500–1800 in manuscripts of the Bodleian Library, Oxford*, 1969.

Dobell P. J. Dobell, *A catalogue of XVIIIth century verse*, 1933 (a reissue of his catalogues 99, 102, 122, 128, 133, and 105).

Dodsley [Robert Dodsley, ed.] *A collection of poems. By several hands*, 1748 (and later eds.).

Evans Charles Evans, *American bibliography: a chronological dictionary*, 1903–59.

Faber G. C. Faber (ed.), *The poetical works of John Gay*, 1926.

Gaskell, Foulis Philip Gaskell, *A bibliography of the Foulis Press*, 1964.

Gaskell, Mason Philip Gaskell, *The first editions of William Mason*, 1951.

Gibson Andrew Gibson, *New light on Allan Ramsay*, 1927.

Green Richard Green, *The works of John and Charles Wesley, a bibliography*, 1896.

Griffith R. H. Griffith, *Alexander Pope: a bibliography*, 1922–27.

Halkett & Laing Samuel Halkett and John Laing, *Dictionary of anonymous and pseudonymous English literature*, 1926–62.

Hanson L. W. Hanson, *Contemporary printed sources for British and Irish economic history, 1701–1750*, 1963.

Haslewood Joseph Haslewood's collections in the British Library, particularly his interleaved copy of Jacob's *Poetical register* (C.45. d.17–19) recording Luttrell copies then in the Heber collection, and the newspaper advertisements in C.45.d.9–11.

Hazen, Walpole A. T. Hazen, *A bibliography of Horace Walpole*, 1948.

Heawood Edward Heawood, *Watermarks, mainly of the 17th and 18th centuries*, 1950.

Jacob Giles Jacob, *The poetical register*, 1719–20.

Lee William Lee, *Daniel Defoe: his life, and recently discovered writings*, 1869.

Lowndes W. T. Lowndes, *The bibliographer's manual of English literature… New edition… by G. H. Bohn*, 1857–64 (and reprints).

Macdonald Hugh Macdonald, *John Dryden: a bibliography of early editions and of Drydeniana*, 1939.

McKenzie D. F. McKenzie, *The Cambridge University Press, 1696–1712: a bibliographical study*, 1966.

Maidment [Maidment, James, ed.] *Scotish elegiac verses, MDCXXIX–MDCCXXIX*, 1842.

Martin Burns Martin, *A bibliography of the writings of Allan Ramsay*, 1931.

Moore J. R. Moore, *A checklist of the writings of Daniel Defoe*, 1960.

Morgan W. T. (and C. S.) Morgan, *A bibliography of British history (1700–1715)*, 1934–42.

Nichols John Nichols, *Literary anecdotes of the eighteenth century*, 1812–16.

Nichols, Collection John Nichols (ed.), *A select collection of poems: with notes, biographical and historical*, 1780–82.

Nichols, Illustrations John Nichols, *Illustrations of the literary history of the eighteenth century*, 1817–58.

O'Donoghue D. J. O'Donoghue, *The poets of Ireland*, 1912.

Pearch [George Pearch, ed.] *A collection of poems in four volumes. By several hands*, 1770.

Percival Milton Percival, *Political ballads illustrating the administration of Sir Robert Walpole*, 1916.

Pettit Henry Pettit, *A bibliography of Young's Night thoughts*, 1954.

Plomer H. R. Plomer (*et al.*), *A dictionary of the printers and booksellers...from 1668 to 1725*, 1922; *...from 1726 to 1775*, 1932.

POAS VI *Poems on affairs of state... Volume 6: 1697–1704, edited by Frank H. Ellis*, 1970.

Rawlinson Richard Rawlinson's ms. collections for a new edition of Wood's *Athenae Oxonienses*, in the Bodleian (indexed by S. and M. A. Gibson in Oxford Bibliographical Society, *Proceedings and papers* I (1924) 67–95).

Reed, Repository [Isaac Reed, ed.] *The repository, a select collection of fugitive pieces of wit and humour*, 1777–83.

Rogers R. W. Rogers, *The major satires of Alexander Pope*, 1955.

Rothschild *The Rothschild Library. A catalogue*, 1954.

Ruddiman's ledger The ledger of Thomas Ruddiman's printing shop, giving detailed accounts for 1710–1715; National Library of Scotland MS. 763.

Sale W. M. Sale, jr, *Samuel Richardson: master printer*, 1950.

Smith Joseph Smith, *A descriptive catalogue of Friends' books*, 1867 (*Supplement*, 1893).

Smith, Anti-quakeriana Joseph Smith, *Bibliotheca anti-quakeriana: or, a catalogue of books adverse to the Society of Friends*, 1873.

SR The registers of the Stationers' Company, edited by G. E. B. Eyre to 1708 (1913–15); subsequently from the mss.

Strahan's ledger The first of William Strahan's printing ledgers, starting in 1738; B.M. Add. MS. 48800.

Straus, Curll Ralph Straus, *The unspeakable Curll*, 1927.

Straus, Dodsley Ralph Straus, *Robert Dodsley: poet, publisher and playright*, 1910.

Teerink Herman Teerink, *A bibliography of the writings in prose and verse of Jonathan Swift*, 1937. (Second edition ed. A. H. Scouten, 1963; this edition omits much peripheral material to which reference is made, but its additions have been incorporated.)

Thomas M. G. Lloyd Thomas (ed.), *The poems of John Philips*, 1927.

Thorn-Drury Notes, particularly on Luttrell copies, in Thorn-Drury's copy of Jacob's *Poetical register* in the Bodleian (Thorn-Drury d.1–4).

Troyer H. W. Troyer, *Ned Ward of Grubstreet*, 1946.

Waller A. R. Waller (ed.), *Matthew Prior: Poems on several occasions*, 1905.

Watt Robert Watt, *Bibliotheca Britannica*, 1824.

Wegelin Oscar Wegelin, *Early American Poetry ... Second edition*, 1930.

Whincop 'A compleat list of all the English dramatic poets' in Thomas Whincop, *Scanderbeg: or love and liberty*, 1747.

Wiley A. N. Wiley, *Rare prologues and epilogues, 1642–1700*, 1940.

Williams Harold Williams (ed.), *The poems of Jonathan Swift... Second edition*, 1958.

Williams, Points I. A. Williams, *Points in eighteenth-century verse*, 1934.

Wing D. G. Wing, *A short-title catalogue... 1641–1700*, 1945–51.

Woodfall's ledger Extracts from the ledger of Henry Woodfall senior, covering 1734–1747, and of Henry Woodfall junior, covering 1737–1748, printed by P.T.P. in *N&Q* I. 11 (1855) 377–8, 418–20, and I. 12 (1855) 217–19.

Wrenn *A catalogue of the library of the late John Henry Wrenn. Compiled by H. B. Wrenn. Edited by Thomas J. Wise*, 1920. (The attributions of authorship in this catalogue are unreliable, and have usually been ignored; cf. p. xv, n. 2.)

Wright & Spears H. B. Wright and M. K. Spears (ed.), *The literary works of Matthew Prior*, 1959 (second edition, 1971).

LIBRARY SYMBOLS

The symbol is printed in italic when the copy at that library has not been examined.

LIBRARY SYMBOLS

PrP	Harris Public Library, Preston
RP	Reading Public Libraries
SaU	St Andrews University Library
ShU	Sheffield University Library
SrS	Shrewsbury School Library
WaP	Warrington Public Library
WcC	Winchester College Library
WgP	Wigan Public Library
WrP	Worcester Public Library
YM	York Minster Library
YP	York City Library
YU	York University Library

Broxbourne   Broxbourne Library (on deposit at the Bodleian Library)

Chatsworth   Chatsworth House Library, Bakewell, Derbyshire

Forster   H. B. Forster, Woodstock, Oxon.

Longleat   The Marquis of Bath, Longleat

Madan   The late F. F. Madan (on deposit at the British Library)

Rosebery   The Earl of Rosebery, South Queensferry, West Lothian

Rothschild   Lord Rothschild (at Trinity College, Cambridge)

USA

CCC	Honnold Library, Claremont Colleges, Claremont
CLU	University of California at Los Angeles
CLU-C	— William Andrews Clark Memorial Library
CLSU	University of Southern California, Los Angeles
CSmH	Henry E. Huntington Library, San Marino
CU	University of California, Berkeley
CtY	Yale University, New Haven
CtY-D	— Divinity School Library
CtY-M	— Medical School Library
DFo	Folger Shakespeare Library, Washington
DLC	Library of Congress, Washington
DNLM	National Library of Medicine, Bethesda, Md.
GEU	Emory University, Atlanta
ICN	Newberry Library, Chicago
ICU	University of Chicago, Chicago

IEN	Northwestern University, Evanston
IU	University of Illinois, Urbana
IaU	University of Iowa, Iowa City
InU	Indiana University, Bloomington
KU	University of Kansas, Lawrence
MB	Boston Public Library
MBAt	Boston Athenaeum, Boston
MH	Harvard University, Cambridge
MH–AH	— Andover–Harvard Theological Library
MH–BA	— School of Business Administration Library
MWA	American Antiquarian Society, Worcester
MWiW-C	Williams College, Williamstown, Chapin Library
MdBJ	Johns Hopkins University, Baltimore
MeWC	Colby College, Waterville, Maine
MiU	University of Michigan, Ann Arbor
MiU-C	— William L. Clements Library
MnHi	Minnesota Historical Society, St Paul
MnU	University of Minnesota, Minneapolis
NBuG	Buffalo and Erie County Public Library, Grosvenor Reference Division
NN	New York Public Library
NN-A	— Arents Collection
NN-B	— Berg Collection
NNC	Columbia University, New York
NNH	Hispanic Society of America, New York
NNP	Pierpont Morgan Library, New York
NNUT	Union Theological Seminary, New York
NcD	Duke University, Durham
NcU	University of North Carolina, Chapel Hill
NjP	Princeton University, Princeton
NjR	Rutgers University, New Brunswick
OCU	University of Cincinnati, Cincinnati
OCl	Cleveland Public Library
OO	Oberlin College, Oberlin
OU	Ohio State University, Columbus
OrU	University of Oregon, Eugene
PBL	Lehigh University, Bethlehem
PBm	Bryn Mawr College, Bryn Mawr
PHC	Haverford College, Haverford

LIBRARY SYMBOLS

PHi   Historical Society of Pennsylvania, Philadelphia

PP   Free Library of Philadelphia

PPL   Library Company of Philadelphia

PSC   Swarthmore College, Swarthmore

PSC-Hi   — Friends Historical Library

PU   University of Pennsylvania, Philadelphia

RPB   Brown University, Providence

RPBJCB   John Carter Brown Library, Providence

TxHR   Rice University, Houston

TxU   University of Texas, Austin

ViU   University of Virginia, Charlottesville

ViW   College of William and Mary, Williamsburg

WaU   University of Washington, Seattle

Brett-Smith   J. R. B. Brett-Smith, Princeton, N.J.

Harding   The late W. N. H. Harding, Chicago (now Bodleian Library, Oxford)

Horn   R. D. Horn, Eugene, Oregon

Institute for Sex Research   Institute for Sex Research (at Indiana University)

Lewis Walpole Library   Lewis Walpole Library, Farmington, Conn.

Rosenbach   Rosenbach Foundation, Philadelphia

A

A., B. Buds and blossoms of piety, 1716–. *See* Antrobus, Benjamin.

A., H., *gent.* The court convert, 1698–. *See* Waring, Henry.

A., J. In luctuosum & nunquam satis deflendum obitum... [1727.] *See* Anderson, James, *D.D.*

— In luctuosum & præmaturum obitum..., [1724.] *See* Anderson, James, *D.D.*

A., R. A remark upon the baths, in the city of Bath, 1715. *See* Ashby, Richard.

A., R., *shoemaker.* A satyr on the journey-men taylors, [172–.] *See* Ashton, Robert.

A1 **A.** [dh] A son altesse royale monseigneur le Prince de Galles. [1745.]
4°: *A²*; *1–3; 4 blk.*
>   Probably printed on the continent.

'Cher & brillant espoir d'un peuple malheureux'
>   At end, 'Par un officier irlandais étant à Ostende'. Cf. *Les Irlandois,* [1745.]

E.

A2 **Abbott, William.** An elegy on the much lamented death of Sir Walter St. John, baronet, who departed this life July the 2d, 1708. at his dwelling-house in Battersea. [*London,* 1708.]
1°: 1 side, 2 columns.
>   Mourning borders.

'Gone! and no omen to portend thy fall'
MH.

Abelard. Abelard to Eloisa, 1725. *See* Barford, Richard.

— Abelard to Eloisa, 1747. *See* Cawthorn, James.

— Abelard to Eloisa, in answer to Mr. Pope's, 1730. *See* Dalacourt, James.

A3 **Abigail.** Abigal's lamentation for the loss of secretary H - - - - -y. Translated from the Greek of Homer. [*London,* 1708.]
½°: 1 side, 1 column.
'Now Phœbus did with frowns the world survey'
>   *Crum* N545: 'Asgill's lamentation for the losse of Mr. Harley. From the Greek of Homer left imperfect by Mr. Walsh', 11 Feb 1708. The reference to Walsh (who died on 18 March 1708) is paralleled in other mss. 'Asgill' is an error for Abigail (Masham).

MH.

A4 — [*idem*] The prophesy: or, M——m's lamentation for H——y. Translated from the Greek of Homer. [*London*] *Printed for Abel Roper,* 1710. (18 Oct, Luttrell)
½°: 1 side, 1 column.
>   Above imprint, 'Done on such another paper and letter, and may therefore be bound up with the *Impartial account* in *folio*'.

L(C.121.g.9/156, Luttrell),O; *Harding.*

Abramideis. Abramideis: or, the faithful patriarch, 1705. *See* Coward, William.

Absalom. Absalom and Achitophel. A poem, 1708–. *See* Dryden, John.

Absalon. Absalon et Achitophel, 1723. *See* Coward, William.

Academia. Academia: or, the humours of the university of Oxford, 1716. *See* D'Anvers, Alicia.

Access. The access or permitted approach of a court penitent, 1703. *See* Waring, Henry [The coronation].

— The access to virtue, 1704. *See* Waring, Henry [The coronation].

A5 **Accident.** The accident; a pastoral essay. *London, printed by J. Chaney; sold by M. Cooper,* 1746 [1747?]. (*SR* 31 Oct 1747)
2°: *A²* B²; *1–3* 4–8.
>   Advertised in *BM, GM, LM* Nov 1747; possibly the date is a misprint. Deposit copies at L,O,E.

'From rosy fingers, morning shook the dew'
>   A love story of Damon and Phillis.

L(643.m.14/16),O,E; CSmH,NN,NjP.

A6 **Accomplished.** The accomplish'd hero: or, the Caledonian songsters. From the French of Francis Salignac de la Motte Fenelon... *London, printed for C. Corbett,* 1748. (*BM, GM* April)
2°: *A⁴*; *1–3* 4–8.
>   Horizontal chain-lines, with watermark placed as in a normal folio.

'On the green borders of the silver Tweed'
L(11630.h.45); IU,TxU.

A7 — The accomplish'd leader: a poem. Being an emblematical essay upon the first clause of Cant. viii. 5... By the author of the Summum bonum. *London, printed in the year* 1733.
8°: *A⁴* B–C⁴; *i–ii* iii–iv, 5–24. 24 advt of books printed for Aaron Ward.
'When radiant Sol in occident declines'
>   A devotional poem.

O.

A8 **Account.** An account of a great fight, between the Christians, and the quakers, and also how they blew themselves up, with a magazine of there own

An **account** of a great fight

Accurate

gunpowder. [*London*] *Printed for the author, T. H.,* [1701.] (13 March, Luttrell)
obl 1°: 1 side, 3 columns.
'There was a fight which held out very long'
>   On the attacks by Francis Bugg, George Keith, and Charles Leslie against the quakers.
MH(Luttrell).

— An account of a strange and wonderful apparition lately seen, 1734. *See* Dunkin, William.

A9 — An account of Mr Cuiscard [!], with the fifteen plagues of a French-man. Written by an English gentleman lately broke upon the wheel in France, for the same. *London, printed and re-printed in Dublin,* [1711.]
8°: *A*⁴; *1–2* 3–8.
>   Only the *Fifteen plagues* are printed in the copy seen.
'Upon that happy nation lies a curse'
>   Written after the attempt by Guiscard on Harley's life.
DA.

A10 — An account of the dreadful apparition of Mr. G------e the usurer and pawn broker, that appear'd to blind T---m the bookseller, at his lodgings the 3d. night after his death. [*Dublin*, 172–?]
½°: 1 side, 1 column.
'T----m H----d awake! and listen well my tale!'
>   A ms. note in the DN copy reveals the bookseller's name as Tom Hurd. The apparition confesses himself a book thief.
DN.

A11 — An account of the life and actions of Mrs. M'Leod. [*Edinburgh*, 1727.]
½°: 1 side, 2 columns.
'Since nought can satisfy the wrath'
>   Margaret M'Leod was hanged for forgery, 8 March 1727.
E.

A12 — An ⟨ac⟩count of the life and tragical end of Alaster Mackalaster, ⟨w⟩ho was hanged at Aberdeen the 31st of May, 1723. To the tune of, Captain Johnston's lament. [*Edinburgh?* 1723.]
½°: 1 side, 2 columns.
>   The foot of the second column adds 'A new song. To the tune of Lochaber no more' by Allan Ramsay.
'Into a place in Argile shire'
New song: 'Farewel to Lochaber, and farewel my Jean'
E.

A13 — An account of the most horrid and unchristian actions of the grave makers in Edinburgh, their raising and selling of the dead, abhorred by Turks and heathens, found out in this present year 1711, in the month of May. [*Edinburgh*, 1711.]
½°: 1 side, 2 columns.
'Dear friends and Christians, what shall I say'
E.

A14 **Accurate.** An accurate tho' compendious encomium on the most illustrious persons, whose monuments are erected in Westminster-abbey. An heroic poem, in Latin and English... By a gentleman, late of Baliol College, Oxford. *London, printed for the author,* 1749. (*GM* April)
4°: *A*⁴ B–E⁴; *1–7* 8–39 *40 blk.* A1 engraved frt.
>   Subsequent edition 1755, with title *A compendious encomium...,* copy at L.
'Sacra deo magno, multos venerata per annos'
'By zealous Edward built, for length of years'
O; *MH*(in contemporary wrappers).

A15 **Achates.** Achates to Varus. An epistle: describing some late wonderfull appearances that ensued from a touch of Ithuriel's spear. Together with a large preface... *London, printed for E. Curll,* 1746. (*SR* 20 Aug)
8°: *A*² B–I⁴; *[4] i* ii–xxiii *xxiv blk, 1* 2–40. A1 advt.
>   On p. 21, 'An elegy, sacred to the memory of an illustrious divine, deceas'd'. Deposit copies at O, SaU. An abbreviated version of the first poem was published as *Dissenting piety,* [1747?]
'See, dearest Varus, at thy strange command'
Elegy: 'Lo! the tall column lifts its head'
>   Both poems are satires on Isaac Watts, who did not die until 1748; the elegy is on his loss of sense.
L(1465.f.23),O,SaU; IU(lacks A1, all after G1).

A16 **Achilles.** Achilles to Chiron. By the right honourable the Lady **** Occasion'd by reading a poem, call'd Chiron to Achilles. *London, printed for Jacob Robinson,* 1738. (*GM, LM* July)
2°: *A*² B² C¹; *i–iii* iv, *3* 4–8.
>   Also printed with an Edinburgh piracy of Jacob's *Chiron to Achilles,* dated 1732; that may well be the first edition.
'Accept that tribute which I justly owe'
>   *Chiron to Achilles,* 1732, is by Hildebrand Jacob.
L(643.m.16/3),O,C; CSmH,CtY,DFo,ICN, TxU+.

A17 **Acquittal.** The acquital. [*London*] *Printed for T. Cooper,* 1741. (*LDP* 30 March)
obl 1°: 1 side, 3 columns.
>   Large engraving at head.
'Who be he dat stand alone-a'
>   On Walpole's defeat of the motion for his removal. Advertised as a sequel to *The motion.*
L(P&D 2486),O(cropt).

A18 **Acrostic.** Acrostic. [*Edinburgh?* 171–?]
½°: 1 side, 1 column.
>   At foot, 'The [k]ey will be published in a few days'.
'Dear Davy, my dear, how comes it to pass'
>   The acrostic reads, 'David Perpendicular'.
E.

Acrostic

A19 — An acrostick upon the name of Dr. Henry Sacheverell, the church's champion. Humbly presented to his grace, John, ld arch bishop of York. *London, printed in the year* 1710.
½°: 1 side, 1 column.
'Distrest Ecclesia from the pulpit groans'
In praise of Sacheverell.
L(1875.d.6/110).

Actum. Actum fidei, 1725. *See* 'Vigaeus, Tranquillus'.

Ad. Ad Annam britannam, [1712?/13.] *See* Pitcairne, Archibald.

— Ad Annam Pitcarniam, [1710?/13.] *See* Pitcairne, Archibald.

— Ad Archibaldum Reidium, [1713.] *See* Pitcairne, Archibald.

— Ad Bertramum Stotum equitem anglum, [1712?/13.] *See* Pitcairne, Archibald.

— Ad Caesarem britannicum e Germania redeuntem ode, 1724. *See* Greer, John.

— Ad Calvini discipulos, [1712.] *See* Pitcairne, Archibald.

— Ad Cyclopas alpinos, [1712?/13.] *See* Pitcairne, Archibald.

— Ad G.B., [1710.] *See* Pitcairne, Archibald.

— Ad Georgium Kirtonum, Proserpinae a potione, [1708?/13.] *See* Pitcairne, Archibald.

— Ad Gilb. Burnet. scotum, A.P. scotus, [1710/13.] *See* Pitcairne, Archibald [Ad G.B.].

A20 — Ad Gulielmum Cumbriae ducem ode. [*Glasgow, Foulis press,* 1748?]
4°: A–B²; *1–3* 4–8.
Gaskell, *Foulis* 114; possibly related to the 'Odes by a lady, inscribed to the Duke of Cumberland' advertised in Wardlaw's *Hardyknute,* 1748. Title in half-title form.
'Quo non cruentos papicolas agit'
L(11408.bb.49).

— Ad Haium comitem Kinulium, [1712?/13.] *See* Pitcairne, Archibald.

— Ad Homerum, Catulli carmen ex Graeco Sapphus versum, [1711.] *See* Pitcairne, Archibald.

— Ad Hugonem Dalrimplium, [1712?/13.] *See* Pitcairne, Archibald.

A21 — Ad illustrissimum & potentissimum principem Jacobum Hamiltoniæ ducem in Caledoniam ab Anglia pro secundo reducem gratulatio. *Edinburgi, ex officina hæredum Andreæ Anderson,* 1702.
4°: *A⁴*; *1–2* 3–7 *8 blk.*
'In patriam, dux magne, tuam redis unus in ore'
E.

— Ad Jacobum Andraeas Pitcarnius Archibaldi filius, [1712?/13.] *See* Pitcairne, Archibald.

— Ad Jacobum gallovidium equitem, caledonium, [1712?/13.] *See* Pitcairne, Archibald.

— Ad Jacobum Magnum, [1711?] *See* Pitcairne, Archibald.

— Ad Janum, [1712?] *See* Pitcairne, Archibald.

— Ad Joanetam Pitcarniam, [1712?/13.] *See* Pitcairne, Archibald.

— Ad Johannem Calvinum, [1712.] *See* Pitcairne, Archibald.

— Ad Jonathem - - - - - - - - - - - - - - - - - -Novembris anni MDCCXII, [1712.] *See* Pitcairne, Archibald.

— Ad Josephum Scaligerum, [1710.] *See* Pitcairne, Archibald.

— Ad Junium anni MDCCXII, [1712.] *See* Pitcairne, Archibald.

— Ad Lodoicam Stuartam, ipso suo natali, [1710?] *See* Pitcairne, Archibald.

— Ad Margaritam Pitcarniam, [1712?/13.] *See* Pitcairne, Archibald.

— Ad Phoebum, [1710?/13.] *See* Pitcairne, Archibald.

— Ad Phoebum Apollinem, [1712?/13.] *See* Pitcairne, Archibald.

A22 — Ad priscos Scotos, scilicet montanos, in praelia apud Gladsmuir, xxi Septembris, MDCCXLV, et apud Falkirk, xvii Januarii, MDCCXLVI, sub ductu et exemplo Caroli principis, et Scotiæ senescalli. [*Edinburgh?* 1746.]
½°: 1 side, 1 column.
With an English imitation. The L copy is ruled in red.
'Praeclarum specimen nuper dedit insita virtus'
'That virtue Scotia's sons doth own'
In praise of the Young Pretender's victories.
L(C.115.i.3/92).

— Ad Robertum Lindesium, [1710?/13.] *See* Pitcairne, Archibald.

A23 — 'Ad versutum cardinalem. Carmen νουθετικον. Cum prefatione expostulatoria. *Londini, prostant venales apud Gul. Parker, & J. Roberts.* Price 6d.' (*LEP* 5 Aug 1742)

— Ad virum ornatissimum...D. Jacobum Astley, [1710?] *See* Monsey, R.

A24 **Adams,** —, *Dr.* 'To the queen upon the peace. A poem in Latin and English. [*London*] *Printed for E. Curll.* Price 4d.' (*PB* 7 July 1713)
This is the form of title quoted by Straus; *PB* 7 July reads 'This day is publish'd Dr Adams's poem to the queen upon the peace'; the title may be generalized. Straus tentatively identifies the author as Dr. Samuel Adams, but there seems no evidence for this. The only

Adams, *Dr.* To the queen

possible candidate seen is *A poem dedicated to the queen...upon declaration of the peace, 1713,* published in April.
(*Straus, Curll* 223.)

A25 Adams, —, *Mr.* The brave Englishman: or the vision. Aug. 19. 1710. N.S. [*London*] *Sold by S. Popping,* [1710.]
½°: 1 side, 1 column.
'By Ebro's streams the British general sate'
In praise of General James Stanhope, subsequently earl Stanhope.
O.

A26 Adams, George. Vera fides: a poetical essay, in three cantos... The whole being designed as a useful lesson for our modern atheists, deists and infidels. *London, printed for J. Roberts, 1731.* (*GSJ* 29 May)
8°: A–E⁴; *1–2* 3–40. 40 err & advt.
'Sing muse the malice of that impious man'
WcC; ICU.

Adams, Jane. Miscellany poems. *Glasgow, printed by James Duncan, 1734.*
8°: pp. 189.   L,E; CLU-C,IU.
Some copies contain an errata slip. The dedication is signed 'Jean Adams'.

Addison, John. The works of Anacreon translated into English verse, with notes... To which are added the odes, fragments, and epigrams of Sappho... *London, printed for John Watts, 1735.*
12°: pp. 279.   L,O; CtY,IU.

Addison, Joseph.
The authorized collection of Addison's poems forms part of the first volume of The works of the right honourable Joseph Addison, *edited by Thomas Tickell in four quarto volumes, 1721. A selection from this collection, including the poems, appeared as* The miscellaneous works in verse and prose of the right honourable Joseph Addison, *first published in three duodecimo volumes, 1726; a fourth was added in 1728 (copy at OCU).*

— Poems on several occasions. With a dissertation upon the Roman poets. *London, printed for E. Curll, 1719* [1718]. (Aug?)
8°: pp. xvi, 162 + 53.   L,O; CtY,MH.
Addison's eight Latin poems reprinted with English translations by Thomas Newcomb, George Sewell, and Nicholas Amhurst. The dissertation appears to be a reissue of a separate edition of 1718 with its own title-page. Some copies add *Scating: a poem, 1720.* Dated Aug 1718 in *Haslewood;* 'second edition corrected' advertised in *PB* 28 May 1719.

— — The second edition. *London, printed in the year 1724.*
12°: pp. x, 60.   L,O; CtY,KU.
The dissertation is not mentioned on the title-

Addison, J. *Collections*

page, though it may have been bound with some copies. Reissued in Addison's *Miscellanies, 1725.*

— Miscellanies in verse and prose. *London, printed for E. Curll, 1725.*
12°: pp. x, 60 + 72 + 75 + 51.   L,O; CtY,IU.
A nonce collection, containing *Poems on several occasions, 1724;* Thomas Foxton's *Serino, 1723; Mr. Addison's Dissertation, 1721;* and Robert Young, *An essay upon Mr. Addison's writings* (no title-page).

— The Christian poet. A miscellany of divine poems, all written by the late Mr. Secretary Addison... With memoirs of Mr. Addison's life and writings. *London, printed for E. Curll, 1728.* (*MC* April)
8°: pp. 24 +.   L,O; CSmH,CtY.
A nonce collection; despite the title, only the first 24 pages contain Addison's poems, though the price of the volume is 4s. The additional contents vary from copy to copy.

— The poetical works. *Glasgow, printed by Robert Urie, 1750.* (*SM* Aug)
8°: pp. 241.   L,O.
The rival Glasgow edition entitled *Poems on several occasions* was published by Foulis in 1751.

———————

A27 — The campaign, a poem, to his grace the Duke of Marlborough. *London, printed for Jacob Tonson, 1705* [1704]. (*PM* 14 Dec)
2°: A² B–G²; *i–iv,* 1–23 *24.* A1 hft; 24 advt.
Watermark: DP. Luttrell copy dated 14 Dec recorded in *Haslewood.* The bibliography of the early editions is discussed by R. D. Horn in *SB* 3 (1950) 256–61.
'While crouds of princes your deserts proclaim'
Translated into Latin as *Expeditio militaris Addisoniana, 1708.*
L(Ashley 5154, hft supplied),O(−A1),E,DT,LdU-B + ; CSmH,CtY,IU,MH,TxU + .

A28 — [fine paper]
Watermark: star. No advertisements on p. 24. Margins altered.
OW,LdU-B; DFo,*NN-B.*

A29 — — The second edition. *London, printed for Jacob Tonson, 1705.*
2°: A² B–G²; *i–iv,* 1–23 *24 blk.* A1 hft.
Apparently reset.
L(1476.dd.31; 1481.f.19/2, uncut),LDW(−A1),O,OW,DG + ; CtY,KU,MH,TxU(2).

A30 — — The third edition. *London, printed for Jacob Tonson, 1705.* (*LG* 15 Feb)
2°: A–B² C–F²; *i–iv,* 1–20. A1 hft.
Reset, and revised by Addison.
O,DN; MH(−A1).

Addison, J. The campaign

A31 — — *Edinburgh reprinted according to the London copy*, 1705.
4°: A–B⁴; *1–2* 3–16.
E(uncut),ES; MH,NjP.

A32 — — [*Dublin*, 1705?]
8°: A⁴ ⟨B²⟩; *1* 2–12.
Drop-head title. Printed by John Brocas on the evidence of a faulty titling capital, according to Miss Mary Pollard.
DT(slightly cropt).

A33 — — *London printed, and sold by H. Hills*, 1710.
8°: A⁸; *1–2* 3–16.
P. 3 line 12 reads '...Compaign'.
L(11631.b.2),O(2),C,E,DT+; ICN,IU,MH(2),TxU+.

A34 — [another edition]
P. 3 line 12 reads '...Campaign'. Reissued with other remaindered Hills poems in *A collection of the best English poetry*, 1717 (*Case* 294).
L(C.124.b.7/56),LVA-F,O; CtY,MH.

A35 — — With remarks thereon, and a true account of his life, and all the famous transactions of that British general. *London, printed for T. Warner*, 1713.
8°: *A⁴* B–C⁴; *1–4* 5–24. A1 woodcut frt.
O; CtY,DFo.

A36 — — The fifth edition. *London, printed for Jacob Tonson*, 1713. (*DC* 10 Nov)
12°: A–C¹² D² E¹; *i–iv*, *1* 2–74. A1, B1 frt.
Printed with *Rosamond... The third edition*, which occupies B1 onwards; copies of *The campaign* are found alone, but may have been separated in recent times.
O(2, 1 *Campaign* only); CtY(*Campaign* only, uncut, −A1),MH.

A37 — — The fifth edition. *London, printed for Jacob Tonson*, 1713.
12°: A–C¹² D⁶; *i–iv*, *1* 2–76 *77–80*. A1, B1 frt; D5–6 advt.
In some copies B3 is signed 'B2'.
L(1346.d.33/1),LDW,O(2, 1 *Campaign* only, −A1),OW,EtC; TxU(*Campaign* only).

A38 — — The sixth edition. *London, printed for J. Tonson; sold by J. Brotherton*, 1725.
12°: A¹²; *i–iv*, *1* 2–19 *20 blk*. A1 frt.
Without *Rosamond*.
L(1962),LG,O; MH.

'—' Colin's complaint... By Mr. Addison [actually by Rowe], [171–?] *See* Rowe, Nicholas.

[—] A description of the play-house in Dorset-garden, 1706. *See* D236.

— Expeditio militaris Addisoniana [Latin translation of *The campaign*], 1708. *See* E603–4.

A39 — A letter from Italy, to...Charles, lord Halifax. By Mr. Joseph Addison. 1701. Together with the Mourning muse of Alexis... By Mr. Congreve. 1695. To which is added the Despairing lover. *London printed, and sold by H. Hills*, 1709.

Addison, J. A letter from Italy

8°: A⁸; *1–2* 3–16.
P. 4 line 16 reads 'O'er the warm bed'. Some copies (O,CT,ICU) have variant '1669' for '1695' in title. Congreve's poem was first published in 1695.
'While you my lord the rural shades admire'
L(1486.aa.36; C.109.aaa.1, unopened),LG,O(2), CT(3),E+; CtY,ICN,MH,OCU,TxU+.

A40 — [another edition]
P. 4 line 16 reads 'O're the warm bed'. Re-issued with other remaindered Hills poems in *A collection of the best English poetry*, 1717 (*Case* 294).
L(C.124.b.7/31),LDW,O,OC(uncut),C+; CtY, MH(2),TxU.

— Mr. Addison's fine ode to Dr. Thomas Burnet ...Done into English, 1727. *See* M287–8.

[—] Pygmaïogeranomachia: or, the battel of the pygmies and cranes. Done from the Latin original, 1715. *See* P1179.

— The resurrection. A poem. Written by Mr. Addison [in Latin; here translated by Nicholas Amhurst], 1718. *See* A204–6.

'—' Scating: a poem. By Mr. Addison [or rather, by Philip Frowde, translated by Thomas Newcomb], 1720. *See* N270.

A41 [—] To her royal highness the Princess of Wales, with the tragedy of Cato. Nov. 1714. To Sir Godfrey Kneller, on his picture of the king. *London, printed for J. Tonson*, 1716 [1715]. (*SR* 20 Dec)
2°: π¹ A–B² C¹; *i–ii*, *1–9 10 blk*.
Watermark: HT. *Rothschild* 8. π1 and C1 are conjugate. The Luttrell copy dated 23 Dec is recorded in H. G. Commin cat. 136/69. Deposit copies at L,LSC,O,EU,AdU,SaU.
'The muse that oft, with sacred raptures fired'
'Kneller, with silence and surprize'
Collected in Addison's *Works*, 1721.
L(643.m.13/10; Ashley 4681),O,EU,LdU-B, SaU+; CSmH,CtY,DFo,MH,TxU+.

A42 [—] [fine paper]
Watermark: IL.
TxU.

A43 [—] — The second edition. *London, printed for J. Tonson*, 1716.
2°: π¹ A–B² C¹; *i–ii*, *1–9 10 blk*.
Apparently a reimpression, at least in part.
L(11660.g.4); CtY(uncut),TxU.

A44 [—] — The third edition. *London, printed for J. Tonson*, 1716.
2°: A–C²; *i–ii*, *1–9 10 blk*.
L(1970),OC(uncut),OW; MH.

A45 [—] — The fourth edition. *London, printed for J. Tonson*, 1716.
2°: A–C²; *i–ii*, *1–9 10 blk*.
Apparently a reimpression of the preceding.
PBL,TxU.

Addison, J. To her royal highness

A46 [—] — *London: printed for J. Tonson, and reprinted in Dublin by S. Powell, for G. Risk*, 1716.
4°: A⁴; *1* 2–8. 8 advt.
DT(2); MH.

A47 — To Sir Godfry Kneller, on his picture of the king. A poem. By the right honourable Joseph Addison esq; *Dublin, printed by A. Rhames, for E. Dobson*, 1716.
2°: A²; *1–2* 3–4.
    First published with *To her royal highness*, 1716, above.
DT.

A48 — [dh] To Sir Godfrey Kneller, on his picture of the king. [col] *A la Haye, chez T. Johnson*, 1716.
4°; A⁴; *1–8*.
    Followed by a French imitation.
'Que tu sçais bien, Kneller, à l'aide des couleurs'
DLC; *Biblioteca Nazionale, Milan.*

— Two poems viz. I. On the deluge... II. In praise of physick and poetry... Written by Mr. Addison [in Latin; here translated by Thomas Newcomb], 1718. *See* N275.

A49 Address. [dh] The address. [col] *London, printed in the year* 1704.
4°: A⁴; *1–4*, 2 columns.
    Reprinted with a verse answer in *The whigs scandalous address answered stanza by stanza*, 1704.
'Ye men of might, and muckle power'
    Apparently first attributed to Defoe in *Moore* 77; the first line appears in his *An elegy on the author of the True-born-English-man*, 1704. The preface to *The whigs scandalous address answered* refers to 'our Legionite'; it is largely a versification of *Legion's humble address to the lords*. See F. H. Ellis, in *POAS* VI. 633.
L(806.k.16/66),O(uncut); ICU(2).

A50 — The address, a new ballad. Tune of, Ye commons and peers, &c. *London, printed for J. Smith*, 1727. (*Mist* 25 March)
2°: A⁴; *1–3* 4–8.
'Price four pence'. *Percival* appendix 2.
'Believe us, dread sir,/We come whip and spur'
    A satirical versification of the Totnes address.
CSmH,CtY,MH,NjP,OCU.

A51 — — *London, printed for J. Smith*, 1727.
2°: A²; *1–2* 3–4.
    Horizontal chain-lines, poor paper. 'Price two pence'.
MH(uncut).

— An address humbly inscribed to his grace, the Duke of Devonshire, 1737. *See* Ward, John.

A52 — An address of part of the Ch—sh—re grand-j—y, to Sr. J—ph J—l. [1710/11.]
½°: 1 side, 1 column.
    The order of editions has not been determined, but this is clearly the correct form of the first line.

An address of part

'Good sir, sin the queen has done with addresses'
    Crum S611: 'The address of 8 of the grand jury...' The Cheshire grand jury to Sir Joseph Jekyll; satirizing the low church congratulations on Sacheverell's trial at which he was manager. Written in dialect.
OW.

A53 — [*idem*] An address to Sir Joseph Jekyll, lord chief justice of Chester. [*London?* 1710/11.]
½°: 1 side, 1 column.
    Variant first line:
'Sin' the queen has doon with addresses'
L(C.20.f.2/336), Rothschild; MiU, *Harding.*

— An address of thanks from the society of rakes, 1735. *See* Ramsay, Allan.

— An address to his majesty King George, 1714. *See* Pennecuik, Alexander, *1652–1722.*

A54 — The address to Mr. G- - Gr- -n- -ll upon his retiring from court. Written by an unknown hand. [*London*, 1712.]
slip: 2 sides, 1 column.
    The address is followed by 'The changeling: being Mr. G- Gr-n-ll's answer. Now dedicated to my Ld. L-ds-d-n. Written by his own hand', and by a final couplet 'In usum Lansdunum'.
'Why, Gr- - - - -ill, is thy life confin'd'
Changeling: 'Who e'er thou art, who tempts in such a strain'
    Crum W2358, W2225. A republication of the poem by Elizabeth Higgons and George Granville's reply of 1690 renouncing public life, now issued with ironic application after his return to power and acceptance of the title Baron Lansdowne in Dec 1711.
O; *Harding.*

A55 — An address to our sovereign lady. [*London*, 1704.] (5 April, Luttrell)
½°: 1 side, 1 column.
    The paper has horizontal chain-lines, and the format could be ¼°.
'We address you to day in a very new fashion'
    The authorship is discussed by F. H. Ellis in *POAS* VI. 618; he favours Arthur Mainwaring. A satire on the address of the Commons to the queen, 23 Dec 1703, on the Scottish conspiracy.
L(1475.c.2/32),O,DA,Crawford; ICN(Luttrell).

— An address to Sir Joseph Jekyll, [1710/11.] *See* An address of part of the Ch—sh—re..., [1710/11.]

A56 — An address to the ladies of St. Warborough's parish. *Dublin, printed in the year* 1724.
½°: 1 side, 2 columns.
'Ladies, to you a suppliant lo I come'
    A request that they should plead Harry's suit to Arabella.
Rothschild.

Address

A57 — An address to the worshipful company of barbers in Oxford; occasioned by a late infamous libel, intitled, The barber and fireworks, a fable, highly reflecting on one of the honourable members. By a barber. *Oxford, printed in the year* 1749.
4°: B–D² (B2 as 'B'); *1–2* 3–12.
'What, shall a saucy rhyming dunce, sirs'
In defence of the barbers. Cf. *The trimmer trimm'd*, 1749. A heavily annotated copy of [John Sampson] *The intrigue*, 1750, in the possession of Mr. John Sparrow refers to 'Bilstone's Answer to the Address to the Oxford Barber's suppo⟨sed⟩ to be wrote by Web the barber'. Web has not been identified.
L(11630.e.5/18),*OQ*; CtY(uncut),MH.

A58 — — The second edition. *Oxford, printed in the year* 1749.
4°: B–D² (B2 as 'B'); *1–2* 3–12.
O; CSmH,CtY(2, 1 uncut),OCU.

A59 — — The third edition. *Oxford, printed in the year* 1749.
4°: A⁴ B²; *1–2* 3–12. 12 advt.
P. 2 records the thanks of the company to the author, dated 2 June 1749.
O(2); CtY,InU.

A60 [**Adee, Swithin.**] The Craftsman's apology. Being a vindication of his conduct and writings: in several letters to the king. *London, printed for T. Cooper*, 1732.
8°: A–D⁴; *1–2* 3–32.
'Great sir, if your highness is pleas'd to peruse'
A nineteenth century ms. note in the L copy records that the authorship is revealed in 'Isaac Reed's ms.' A satire against Bolingbroke in five verse letters.
L(11644.eeee.20),O.

Admiral. Admiral Haddock: or the progress of Spain, 1739. *See* Boyd, Elizabeth.

— Admiral Hosier's ghost, 1740. *See* Glover, Richard.

A61 — Admiral Matthews engagement against the combin'd fleets of France and Spain. [*London?* 1744?]
slip: 1 side, 1 column.
Woodcut at head. Another song is printed on the reverse of the slip, which is so mounted that it cannot be identified.
'Brave Admiral Matthews has been on the main'
On Thomas Mathews's action off Toulon, 12 Feb 1744. It claims to have been written on board his ship.
L(C.20.f.9/384).

A62 Adollizing. Adollizing: or, a lively picture of adoll-worship. A poem in five cantos. *London, printed for A. Dodd*, 1748. (*BM, LM* Feb)

Adollizing

4°: A⁴ B–C⁴ D²; *i–ii* iii–iv, 5–28.
'Fav'rite of gods and men! spirit refin'd!'
On a disappointed lover who made a full-size female doll as a substitute.
L(11630.c.8/9; 11630.e.3/5, cropt).

A63 Adultery. Adultery a-la-mode. An epistle from Lady Traffick to Sir John. *London, printed for R. Thomas*, [1746.] (*BM, GM* June)
2°: A² B–C²; *1–3* 4–12.
'Severe's the charge against all womankind'
L(1973); ICN,MiU(cropt).

A64 Adventure. The adventure of a German knight: or, the scuffle-royal, between a foreigner, the devil, and a lawyer. Written by Count Monteego. Upon the ill treatment he met with on the Mall on George's-hill, after his arrival from Germany. *London printed; and re-printed and sold in Dublin*, 1733.
8°: A⁶; *3–4* 5–12 *13–14*.
A woodcut printed on p. 14 was possibly intended to be a frontispiece.
'Kind reader, pray, my heat excuse'
A satire on 'Count Monteego's' behaviour. His identity has not been established. Probably a piece of Dublin origin, with no London original.
L(11633.bb.1/3).

A65 — The adventure of the bee and the spider. A tale…To which are added, the thirty marks of a fine woman. From the Latin of Franciscus Cornigerus. *London, printed for T. Payne*, 1722. (*DJ* 13 Aug)
8°: A⁴ B–C⁴; *1–4* 5–24. A1 hft.
Entered in *SR* 15 Aug; no deposit copy traced.
'In days of yore, when beasts could speak'
A bawdy poem. The author also wrote *A description of Bedlam* in prose.
Brett-Smith.

A66 — — The second edition. *London, printed for T. Payne*, 1722. (*PB* 25 Aug)
8°: A⁴ B–C⁴; *1–4* 5–24. A1 hft.
Probably from the same setting of type as the preceding; the title is not a cancel.
L(164.1.24, Luttrell, Nov).

A67 Adventures. 'The adventures of Esquire Twiford in his trip to the Fleet, a poem. [*London*] *Sold by A. Baldwin.* Price 3*d*.' (*PM* 21 April 1711, 'just published')
Listed again in *PM* 10 Nov 1711 with expanded title 'with some merry observations by the way; concluding with seasonable advice to such young gentlemen…' The words 'a poem' are omitted from this entry, but probably the original description is correct.

A68 — The adventures of Telemachus. Attempted in English blank verse, from the Archbishop of Cambray. *London, printed for J. Roberts*, 1729. (*MChr* 19 Sept)

The **adventures** of Telemachus

8°: *A*⁴ a¹ B–H⁴ I¹; [*8*] *i* ii, *1* 2–58. A1 hft.
'Still fond Calypso, pensive and forlorn'
  Books I and II only of Fénelon's *Télémaque*.
L(992.h.7/8); *CLU-C*.

A69 — The adventures of Telemachus. In English
verse. Book I. *London printed, and are to be sold by
J. Morphew, 1712.* (1 Aug, Luttrell)
8°: A–M⁴ N²; *i–iv*, 1–96.
  Entered in *SR* 8 Feb 1712 by Dorman New-
man and George Harris; deposit copies at
E,EU. Advertised in *PB* 29 July for 'Thurs-
day next' [31 July].
'When first Ulysses from Calypso fled'
  A translation of book I of Fénelon's *Télémaque*.
L(239.k.1, Luttrell),C,E,EU; *MiU*.

— The adventures of Telemachus, son of Ulysses,
1738. *See* Manning, Francis.

Advice. Advice: a satire, 1746. *See* Smollett,
Tobias.

A70 — Advice from C - - - -b S - - - - - -y to his daughter.
[*Dublin*] *Printed in the year* 1730.
slip: 1 side, 1 column.
'From darkest shades, behold I rise'
  From Caleb Smalley to his daughter Molly;
replied to in *M- - -y S- - - -y's answer*, 1730.
CtY.

A71 — Advice from fairyland. An imitation of our
present Irish poetry. Inscrib'd to the poetasters of
Dublin. But more particulary [!], several reptiles
of T.C. Being K. Oberon's declaration. *Dublin,
printed by G.N.* [*Gwyn Needham*] & *R.D.* [*Richard
Dickson*] *in Dame-street,* 1726.
½°: 1 side, 2 columns.
  Bond 90; *Rothschild* 1893; *Teerink* 1205.
'Little lads of Dublin town'
  Early ms. note in the Rothschild copy (which
has a Dublin collector's mark 'F') 'By Dean
Smedley'; but in *The Grubstreet cavalcade,*
1727, 'News from fairyland' ('printed by
D-cks-n under-hand') is attributed to Eyre.
Reprinted in *Gulliveriana,* 1728. Said by
Teerink to be occasioned by the answers to
Smedley's *A satyr,* 1725, but it is a general
satire on Dublin poetasters.
L(1890.e.5/5; C.121.g.8/147, mutilated), Roths-
child.

A72 — Advice from the stars. In a letter to the
pretending doctor, Whaley. *Dublin, printed by
C. Carter,* 1714.
½°: 1 side, 1 column.
'To let you know I am your friend'
  On John Whalley, the quack astrologer.
Answered by John Whalley's *A decree of the
stars for Cornelius Carter,* [1714], which
attributes the authorship of this to Carter.
C.

A73 — Advice to a certain dean. [*Dublin*] *Printed in the
year* 1730.

Advice to a certain dean

½°: 1 side, 1 column.
  Teerink 1297.
'O S—t! why shou'd you who art wiser indeed'
  Advising Swift not to join in Delany's search
for preferment.
L(C.121.g.8/180),C,DT.

— Advice to a friend on his marriage, 1735. *See*
Blyth, Francis.

— Advice to a lady, 1733. *See* Lyttelton, George,
baron Lyttelton.

A74 — Advice to a poet, designiug [!] to write on the
Duke of Marlborough's return to England. In
imitation of Waller. [*London*] *Printed for C. Cross
near Westminster,* [1714.]
slip: 1 side, 1 column.
  The imprint is fictitious: 'C. Cross' stands for
Charing Cross. First line misprints 'let let...'
'First, let thy piece, address the mighty man'
L(C.121.g.9/167).

A75 — [another edition, title reads:] Advice to a poet,
designing...
  The copy seen was reissued in a collection of
slip poems entitled *State poems. Being a
collection of choice private pieces,* 1715.
Brett-Smith.

— Advice to a son, 1736. *See* Hammond, William.

A76 — Advice to a widow. *London, printed for M.
Cooper,* [1747.] (*GM,LM* Feb)
2°: *A*⁴; *1–2* 3–7 *8 blk.*
'What means that quick repeated sigh?'
  Against marrying again.
O,E.

A77 — Advice to an aspiring young gentleman of
fortune. In imitation of the fourth satyr of Perseus.
London, printed for T. Cooper, 1733. (*GSJ* 15 June)
2°: *A*² B–C²; *1–3* 4–11 *12 blk.*
  With the Latin text.
'Affairs of state (your garter'd friend suppose'
L(1482.f.26),O,LdU-B; CSmH,CtY,ICN,MH(2),
OCU+.

A78 — Advice to Dr. Harry Gambol, upon the
pulling down of his stage, given by his abused
patient. To the tune of, Which nobody can deny.
*London, printed for A. B—tr, one who has had
expensive experience of the doctor's barbarous
practice,* [1714?]
slip: 1 side, 1 column.
'Harry Gambol at last, is gone packing his ways'
  On the fall of Bolingbroke.
Harding.

A79 — Advice to England; or resolution. A poem.
Occasioned by the late earthquake... *London,
printed for John Hinton,* 1750. (*GM* March)
8°: A–B⁴ C²; *1–3* 4–20.
'Tho' the hoarse accents of the trumpet's voice'
O,*LdU-B*; NN,OCU.

Advice to Great Britain

A80 — Advice to Great Britain, &c. A poem. By a hearty lover of his country. *London, printed for Richard Mount; sold by J. Nutt*, 1701. (20 Oct, Luttrell)
2°: A–B²: *1–2* 3–8.
    Watermark: Dutch lion. The Luttrell copy is in the collection of R. D. Horn.
'A time there was e're itch of pow'r began'
LLP; TxU.

A81 — [fine paper]
    Watermark: fleur-de-lys on shield.
LdU-B.

A82 — Advice to Mr. Handel: which may serve as an epilogue to Israel in Egypt. [*London*, 1739?]
½°: 1 side, 1 column.
'Griev'st thou, my friend, that harmony has foes?'
    In praise of Handel.
MH.

A83 — Advice to Mr. L---------n, the dwarf fan painter, at Tunbridge-Wells. *London, sold by H. Carpenter*, 1748. (*GM, LM* Aug)
2°: A⁴; *1–2* 3–8.
'Painting and poetry, you know'
    Crum P16. Addressed to Thomas Loggan. A satire on society persons, identified in ms. in L,LdU-B,O copies. Cf. [John Kidgell] *An answer to the advice*, [1748.]
L(C.57.g.7/25, Horace Walpole's),O,OW,LdU-B; MH,OCU.

A84 — Advice to Mr. Vario the painter. A poem. On the defeat of the French and Bavarians, by the confederate forces, commanded by his grace, the Duke of Marlborough. *London, printed by R. Tookey; sold by S. Malthus*, [1704.]
½°: 1–2, 1 column.
'Vario, no more thy sacred skill prophane'
    In praise of Marlborough's victory at Blein-heim.
Crawford.

A85 — — [*London?*] *Reprinted in the year* 1709.
½°: 1–2, 1 column.
MH,TxU.

— Advice to new-married husbands, 1712. *See* Plaxton, —, *Mr.*

A86 — Advice to Sappho. Occasioned by her verses on the imitator of the first satire of the second book of Horace. By a gentlewoman. *London, printed for the authoress, near White's Chocolate-house; sold by J. Roberts*, 1733. (*GSJ* 13 April)
2°: A² B²: *1–2* 3–7 *8 blk.*
    Some copies (O,ICN,IU) have a ms. correction in p. 6 line 12, changing 'hope' to 'home'. Other copies have the correction made in type.
'When Rome was lash'd by Juvenal's sharp lines'
    A reply to *Verses addressed to the imitator...* [1733], here assumed to be by Lady Mary Wortley Montagu.
L(11641.l.1/2),O(Harley, 'R April 12'); CSmH, CtY,MH,ICN,TxU+.

An advice to Scribogg hare

A87 — An advice to Scribogg hare, on the approach of the craps of Hoath. By a famous master of the game. [*Dublin?* 173–?]
½°: 1 side, 1 column.
'Scribogg vornou look about/The craps of Hoath are coming out'
    A hunting piece, addressed to the hare on Scribogg Hill. The pack presumably belonged to William St. Lawrence, Lord Howth.
OW.

A88 — Advice to the author of a late poem, entituled, The British court. *Printed for the booksellers of London and Westminster*, 1707.
½°: 1–2, 1 column.
'For shame give or'e/And write no more'
    The British court, 1707, was written by Joseph Browne.
MC,Crawford.

A89 — Advice to the clergy. A poem. Inscribed to the celebrated tutor, of a more celebrated peer. *Dublin: printed; and re-printed at London by E. Holloway, near Hungerford-market*, 1734. (*GSJ* 17 Jan)
4°: A² B–C²; *1–2* 3–12.
    No Dublin edition has been traced.
'Start not, ye sons of crape---nor think I mean'
    Dedicated to 'the reverend Doctor S—'; if the Dublin origin is correct, Sheridan is presumably intended.
L(11660.f.8); CtY,TxU.

A90 — Advice to the fair: an epistolary essay, in three parts: on dress, converse, and marriage: address'd to a sister. *London, printed for J. Wilford*, 1738. (*GM, LM* April)
2°: A² B–E²; *1–3* 4–20.
'To thee! lov'd maid, with whom I joy to share'
L(11660.g.5),O,LdU-B; CSmH,CtY,IU,MH, TxU+.

— Advice to the fair-sex, 1736. *See* Free, John.

A91 — Advice to the high-church. [*London?*] *Printed in the year* 1711.
½°: 1 side, 2 columns.
'You talk of your high-church addresses'
    Against a peace with France.
Crawford,Rothschild.

— Advice to the Kentish long-tails, 1701. *See* Brown, Thomas.

— Advice to the ladies, 1745. *See* Poole, —, *Alderman.*

A92 — Advice to the ladies of Great Britain; a new court ballad. *London, printed for A. Moore*, 1730.
2°: A² B²; *1–2* '1' 4–8.
'Ye ladies fair, of Britain's isles'
    On their amours; the advice is to beware of servants talking.
L(163.n.29, ms. notes),O,OW(2); CLU-C,CtY, IU(uncut),MH,TxU(2, ms. notes)+.

Advice to the ladies

A93 — — 'London, *printed for A. Moore*', 1730.
4º; *A²*; *1* 2–4.
A pedlar's version.
L(C.40.m.10/175).

A94 — — 'London, *printed for the author; and to be
sold by the booksellers, and the several pamphlet-
sellers*' [*Dublin*], 1730.
8º: *A⁴*; *1–3* 4–8.
DT(3); IU.

A95 — Advice to the ladies of Michael's parish. Or, a
satyr on the publisher of the fourth part of the
Ladies library. By Miss Sh——ny M----r---n.
[*Dublin*, 1722.]
½º: 1 side, 1 column.
'What senseless scribler, did presume to write'
There is a copy of *The ladies' fourth library*
[1722] at L.
DN.

A96 — ⟨Advice to th⟩e l⟨adies,⟩ or, an answer to the
court and city beauties: in a dialogue between two
young ladies, whose characters are drawn. *London,
printed in the year* 1707.
8º: *A⁴*; *1–2* 3–⟨8⟩.
'Oh my Belinda! prithee tell me true'
Occasioned by [Joseph Browne] *The British
court*, 1707, and *The London belles*, 1707.
LG.

A97 — Advice to the muse, on the king's landing.
Perth re-printed by Mr. Robert Freebairn, 1716.
½º: 2 sides, 1 column.
No earlier edition is recorded.
'Hail god-like youth! whom Britain's angry stars'
In praise of the Old Pretender.
L(C.115.1.3/40).

— Advice to the poets. A poem, 1706. *See* Blackmore, *Sir Richard*.

A98 — Advice to the q--n. [*London*, 1710.] (12 May,
Luttrell)
½º: 1 side, 1 column.
No brace against lines 30–32.
'O A---a! think, thou poor unhappy qu---'
Advice to dismiss her whig ministers.
ICN(Luttrell).

A99 — [another edition]
Brace against lines 30–32.
O,OW,Crawford; MH.

A100 — [another edition, title reads:] Advice to the
q---n.
InU,MH.

A101 — Advice to the saylors, in an epistle to honest
Ned Whipstaff. *London, printed in the year* 1704.
(20 Jan, Luttrell)
½º: 2 sides, 1 column.
'I heard, dear friend, this morn by crony Tom'
ICN(Luttrell).

A102 — Advice to the tories: a ballad. By a friend to the
German Doctor. [*London*, 1714.]
slip: 1 side, 1 column.

Advice to the tories

'To you, ye tories, I address'
L(C.121.g.9/164).

A103 — [another edition, title reads:] Advice to the
tories; ...
In this edition there is no spacing between the
verses.
L(C.121.g.9/170),O.

A104 — Advice to the true representatives of old England. [*London*, 1703?/04?]
½º: 1 side, 1 column.
'Ye Commons of England, who are on the scent'
LLP; MH.

A105 — Advice to whiggs: or, a challenge to the
Jacobites; and all such as are ill-affected to the
present government, and endeavour the ruine of
the protestant interest, to muster up their argu-
ments, and vindicate themselves, if they can.
London, printed in the year 1702 [1701]. (9 Dec,
Luttrell)
1º: 1 side, 3 columns.
'Come hither you that would our land enthrall'
MH(Luttrell, 'A silly poem').

A106 — An advice to young-men: or, a dialogue betwixt
youth and conscience. *Glasgow, printed by Robert
Sanders*, 1701.
8º: A⁴; *1–2* 3–8.
'Young youth, O tell me! whither art thou bound?'
E.

A107 **Advocate.** The advocats complaint, or a survey of
the uneasiness, of that employment. [*Edinburgh*,
170–.]
½º: *1–2*, 1 column.
'Last night, as I lay tossing on my bed'
ES.

Aedes. Ædes Badmintonianæ, 1701. *See* Trapp,
Joseph.

A108 **Aesculapius.** Æsculapius: a poem. Humbly
inscribed to the honble Sir Hans Sloane, bar't,
president: the fellows and the rest of the members
of the Royal College of Physicians. *London, printed
by Allan Clark*, 1721. (*DP* 25 April)
4º: *A²* B–E²; *1–2* 3–19 *20 blk*.
All copies seen have a ms. note on p. 19
apologizing for the errata, due to 'the author
not having an opportunity of attending the
press'.
'The chaos lay in wild confusion hurl'd'
L(841.b.84/4),DG,*MR*; CtY-M.

Aesop.
*The following are apparently translations or
adaptations of Aesop's fables:*

'Æsop naturalized, and exposed to the publick
view in his own shape and dress; by way of essay.
One hundred fables. The second edition corrected.

Aesop. *Collections*

[*London*] *Printed for D. Midwinter & T. Leigh.'*
(*TC* Michaelmas 1702)

First published at Cambridge, 1697 (*Wing* A744).

[*idem*] Æsop naturaliz'd: in a collection of fables and stories from Æsop, Locman, Pilpay, and others. The third edition; with the addition of above 50 new fables. *London, printed for D. Midwinter*, 1711. (*SR* 27 Feb)
8°: pp. 160.   L,O; MH.

A radical revision of the preceding.

— The fifth edition... *London, printed for D. Midwinter, & A. Ward*, 1743.
8°: pp. 160.   O; IU.

———————

A new translation of Æsop. In a hundred select fables, burlesqu'd, 1705. *See* N236.

[*reissue*] The fables of Æsop, in English verse, [1705/10?] *See* N237.

———————

Arwaker, Edmund: Truth in fiction: or morality in masquerade. A collection of two hundred twenty five select fables of Æsop, and other authors, 1708.

———————

Stacy, Edmund: Sir Roger L'Estrange's fables, with morals and reflections, in English verse, 1717.

[—] [*reissue*] Æsop's fables, with morals and reflections, 1720.

———————

Æsop unveil'd, or the beauties of deformity; being a poetical translation of several curious fables out of Æsop, and other approv'd mythologists, equally as diverting and beneficial to the English reader, as his comic shape and instructive morals were to the ancients. *London, A. Bettesworth & C. Hitch*, [1730?]

MH.

Listed in *MChr* Dec 1730 as sold by J. Clarke, H. Cooke, T. Warner; possibly this is another issue.

———————

The collections entered or cross-referenced below are collections of political fables after the manner of Aesop; and they have been catalogued as single works rather than as collections because in most cases they appear to have been designed as a unified work. Similar works where Aesop is not the first word of the title should be sought in the index.

A109 — Æsop at Barcelona: or, several select fables, relating to the times. *London, printed in the year* 1705.
8°: *A*⁴; *1* 2–8.
Fable 1: 'Two men to Jove their prayers made'
11 fables.
CT.

Aesop at court

— Æsop at court, 1702. *See* Yalden, Thomas.

— Æsop at Oxford: or, a few select fables in verse, 1709. *See* Pittis, William.

— Æsop at Paris, his letters and fables, 1701. *See* Ward, Edward.

A110 — Æsop at Portugal: being a collection of fables, apply'd to the present posture of affairs... *London, printed in the year* 1704. (*TC* Easter)
8°: A–E⁴; *i–iv*, 1–36.
Fable 1: 'An old baboon, who long had been'
MH(uncut).

— Æsop at St. James's, 1729. *See* Freeman, Isaac.

— Æsop at the bear-garden: a vision, 1715. *See* 'Preston, —, *Mr.*'

— Æsop at the Bell-tavern in Westminster, 1711. *See* Pittis, William.

A111 — Æsop at Utrecht. *London printed, and sold by the booksellers*, 1712. (11 March, Luttrell)
4°: A⁴; *i–ii*, 1–6.
Rothschild 199.
Fable 1: 'A stately lioness with prudent skill'
Two fables. 'Upon the French king under the characters of the wolf and the hawk', Luttrell.
L(164.m.61, Luttrell); TxU.

A112 — [*dh*] Æsop at Westminster, or, a tale of the jack-daws. [*London*, 1710?]
4°: A²; *1–4*.
'A cook, who once, had for his guest'
On the Sacheverell affair?
MH.

A113 — Æsop in Europe. Or a general survey, of the present posture of affairs... By way of fable and moral... *London printed, and sold by B. Bragg*, 1706. (*PM* 12 Jan)
8°: A–K⁴; *i–viii*, 1–71 72 *blk*.
Fable 1: 'Two weasels had once got an egg by a wile'
Dedication signed 'N.R.'
O,DT; *NcD*.

— Æsop in masquerade, 1718. *See* Pittis, William.

A114 — Æsop in mourning; or, five select fables, relating to the times... With a choice receipt to cure dim'd sighted Christians. *London, printed for J. Brooks*, 1714.
8°: A⁴; *1* 2–8.
Fable 1: 'A certain lady of renown'
O; OCU.

A115 — Æsop in Scotland, exposed in ten select fables relating to the times... *London, printed in the year* 1704.
8°: *A*⁴; *1* 2–8.
Fable 1: 'Some crafty curs, who had abused their master'
O; MH,*RPJCB*.

A116 — Æsop in Spain. Or, a few select fables in verse, translated from the Spanish. *London printed, and*

Æsop in Spain

are to be sold by A. Baldwin, 1701. (*PM* 14 Jan)
8⁰: A–E⁴; *1–2* 3–37 '*40–41' 40 blk.*
Fable 1: 'There was a monarch, whose imperial sway'
    8 fables, certainly not translated from the Spanish. Against the Jacobites.
L(12305.ccc.11/1),LLP,O,DrU; CtY,IU,NjP.

A117 —— *London, printed in the year* 1701.
8⁰: A⁸; *1* 2–16.
    Presumably this is the 'sham edition' denounced in *FP* 25 Jan.
MH.

A117·2 — [*idem*] Eight fables on the present posture of affairs in Europe... To which is prefix'd, Esop's advice both to the princes and people of Europe. *London, printed for Eliz. Mallet,* 1703.
8⁰: A⁴(±A1) B–E⁴; *1–2* 3–37 '*40–41' 40 blk.* 2 err.
    A reissue of the original edition, A116.
L(12305.f.14).

A118 — Æsop the wanderer; or, fables relating to the transactions of Europe; occasionally writ since the late battle at Bleinheim... *London printed, and sold by the booksellers of London and Westminster,* 1704. (31 Aug, Luttrell)
8⁰: *A*⁴ B–D⁴ '*D*'⁴ (D2 as 'C2'); *i–viii,* 1–31 *32 blk.*
A1 hft.
    Advertised in *FP* 5 Sept.
Introduction: 'A courtier once, a man of fame'
L(164.1.8, Luttrell); IU(−A1),MH(−A1).

A119 Aethiops. Æthiops: a poem. The second edition. *Norwich, printed by S. Collins, near the Red-Well, for the author,* 1713.
2⁰: *A*² B–C²; *i–ii,* 1–10.
    No first edition has been traced.
'In times when sordid int'rest rul'd the roast'
    A satire on Norwich politics.
NwP(uncut).

A120 — Æthiopides: a poem. Being the second part of Æthiops. *Norwich, printed by S. Collins, near the Red-Well, for the author,* 1713.
2⁰: *AA*² BB–DD²; *i–ii,* 1–14.
'Revolving time in circling years does show'
NwP(uncut).

African. The African prince now in England, 1749.
See Dodd, William.

A121 After-thought. The after-thought: or, a review of the late terrible fire in Cornhill. A political essay by an inhabitant near the Royal-Exchange. *London, printed for R. Griffiths, & J. Swan,* 1748. (*GM* April)
2⁰: *A*⁴; *i–ii,* 1–6.
    Horizontal chain-lines.
'Am I thus favour'd! Is my dwelling sav'd!'
OCU.

Against. 'Against ingratitude. A satyr. [*London*] *Sold by B. Bragg.*' (*WL* April 1706)

Against ingratitude

    Presumably the same work as 'A satyr against ingratitude. Printed for S. Sturton, and sold by B. Bragg' advertised in *PM* 20 April; possibly the same work as 'Satire the second' below, which was dated 20 April by Luttrell. If this identification is correct, the first satire remains unidentified; the only possible candidate appears to be *A satyr against ingratitude,* 1699 (copy at MH).

A122 — Against ingratitude. Satire the second. *London, printed for Samuel Sturton,* 1706. (20 April, Luttrell)
2⁰: A–G²; *i–iv,* 1–24.
    Mixed watermarks in both copies seen; that at OCU is possibly on fine paper. 'Against ingratitude. A satyr' was listed in *WL* April 1706 as sold by B. Bragg; see above.
'None mourn his death whom living all admir'd'
ICN(Luttrell),OCU.

A123 Age. Age in distress: or, Job's lamentation for his children. A poem in blank verse... By a gentleman. *London, printed for J. Fuller,* 1750. (*LM* March)
4⁰: A–C² D¹; *1–2* 3–11 *12–14.*
    The final leaf D1 contains 'A poem on the earthquake' which was possibly published separately and is also entered separately. Vertical chain-lines.
'No sooner has Aurora shed her rays'
    Dedication signed 'Eugenio'.
L(1465.i.12/8, lacks D1),O; OCU.

A124 — The age of mad-folks. [*London,* 1710.] (May?)
½⁰: 1 side, 2 columns.
    'The' of title on separate line. Recorded by Hearne on 31 May 1710.
'These nations had always some tokens'
    A satire on the Sacheverell affair.
L(Lutt.II.2),OW,Rothschild.

A125 — [another edition, title all on one line.]
O,C.

A126 — The age of wonders: to the tune of Chivy chase. [*London*] *Printed in the year* 1710.
½⁰: 1 side, 2 columns.
    The rule above the imprint is in two parts. *Morgan* M14 records a London quarto edition of eight pages, 1710, possibly in error.
'The year of wonders is arriv'd'
    Attributed to Defoe in *Moore* 169; he gives no evidence. Defoe quotes two lines in the *Review* 27 March 1711. A satire on the tories. Replied to by *Wonders upon wonders,* [1710.]
L(112.f.44/26),LLP,O,Rothschild; IU,NjP.

A127 — [another edition]
    The rule above the imprint is apparently composed of 18 short rules.
O-JJ,Chatsworth,Rothschild; OCU.

A128 — [another edition]
    The rule above the imprint is composed of 14 short rules.
InU.

The **age** of wonders

A129 —— *London printed, and Edinburgh reprinted by John Reid junior*, 1710.
$\frac{1}{2}$°: 1 side, 2 columns.
L(C.20.f.9/673),E(2, 1 dated in ms. Sept).

A130 Aged. The aged father's blessing or a choice catalogue of divine lessons excellently express'd and set forth in six pious and profitable poems... *Edinburgh, printed by Mr. Andrew Symson*, 1708.
8°: A^4; *1–8*.
> Printed in chap-book style. There are numerous reprints in the second half of the century, and there must have been earlier editions.

'You sons and daughters view my hoary head'
L(1076.1.18/20).

A131 Agent. [dh] An agent turn'd inside out: or, a peace officer with his heels upwards. [col] [*London*] *Printed in the year* 1709, *and sold by the booksellers*.
4°: A^2; *1–4*.
'Good people attend, while I sing you a song'
DT,*MR*.

'Agricola Candidus.' The high mass, 1746. *See* H201.

A132 [**Ainsworth, Robert.**] [dh] An epicedium sacred to the memory of the late Revd Mr. Thomas White, M.A. prebendary of Lichfield...who deceased Feb. 25, $17\substack{09\\10}$. [*London?* 1710.]
2°: A^2; *1–4*.
> The copy seen possibly lacks a title-leaf.

'Ah! rev'rend friend, since thou art gone, I'll try'
> Ms. note in O-JJ copy 'By the ingen: Mr. Robt: Ainsworth'.

O-JJ.

Ajax. Ajax his speech to the Grecian knabbs, 1748. *See* Forbes, Robert.

[**Akenside, Mark.**] Odes on several subjects. *London, printed for R. Dodsley; sold by M. Cooper*, 1745. (*SR* 26 March)
4°: pp. 54.   L,O; CtY,MH.
> *Williams, Points* 44 discusses the cancel B1, printed as G4; some copies are said to have B1 uncancelled with the corrected text. Copies at LdU-B, TxU may represent this state. Deposit copies at L,E,EU,AdU. Revised edition 1760.

[—] — '*London, printed for R. Dodsley; sold by M. Cooper*' [*Edinburgh?*], 1745.
8°: pp. 44.   L,LVA-D; MH,TxU.
> Probably an Edinburgh piracy.

— The poems of Mark Akenside. *London, printed by W. Bowyer & J. Nichols*, 1772.
4°: pp. xi, 380.   L,O; CtY,MH.

Akenside, M.

> According to *Lowndes* there are fine-paper copies; all copies seen have Strasburg bend watermark. Subsequent editions are not listed here.

———————

A133 [—] A British philippic: a poem, in Miltonic verse. Occasion'd by the insults of the Spaniards, and the preparations for war. *London, printed by J. Chaney, for A. Dodd*, 1738. (Sept)
2°: A^1 B–C^2; *1–5 6–12*.
> *Williams, Points* 41–3. Probably the frontispiece was not yet ready for this impression.

'Whence this unwonted transport in my breast?'
> Signed 'Britannicus'. First published in *GM* Aug 1738, and the separate edition announced there. On the publication of *The pleasures of imagination*, 1744, *GM* announced it as by the same author as this. The copy at E has a later ms. ascription 'By Israel Wilkes'.

L(643.m.16/4),E.

A134 [—] [*idem*] The voice of liberty; or, a British philippic: a poem in Miltonic verse. Occasion'd by the insults of the Spaniards, and the preparations for war. To which is prefix'd a copper-plate... *London, printed by J. Chaney, for A. Dodd*, 1738. (*GM,LM* Sept)
2°: A^2 B–C^2; *1–5 6–12*. A1 frt.
> Apparently from the same setting of type, though corrected and rearranged.

L(643.m.16/1,–frt),O; CtY(–frt),DFo,MH.

A135 [—] — By a free-born Briton. *London: printed; and, Dublin reprinted and sold by Edward Waters*, 1738.
4°: A^4; *1–3 4–8*.
DG.

A136 [—] An epistle to Curio. *London, printed for R. Dodsley; sold by M. Cooper*, 1744. (*SR* 14 Nov)
4°: A^4 B–C^4 D^2; *1–7 8–27 28*. A1 hft; 28 advt.
> Listed in *GM,LM* Nov; deposit copies at L,E,EU.

'Thrice has the spring beheld thy faded fame'
> Collected in Akenside's *Poems*, 1772, as 'Ode to Curio'; addressed to William Pulteney, earl of Bath.

L(840.1.7/5; 644.k.16/1; 11630.d.3/4,–A1; Ashley 2299),O(2, 1 –A1),CT,E,LdU-B +; CSmH(–A1),CtY(–A1),ICN,MH(2, 1 uncut), TxU(–A1)+.

A137 — An ode to the right honourable the Earl of Huntingdon. *London, printed for R. Dodsley; sold by M. Cooper*, 1748. (19 Jan)
4°: A–C^4 D^2 (A3 as 'A2'); *1–4 5–26 27–28*. A1 hft; D2 advt.
> Imprint reads 'Pall-mall'. *Rothschild* 23; *Williams, Points* 45–6. The order of editions is not determined. The first edition is dated as 19 Jan in *Straus, Dodsley*; the second edition was advertised in *GA* 9 Feb.

Akenside, M. An ode

'The wise and great of every clime'
L(840.l.4/1,−A1,D2;643.k.5/9,−A1,D2),O,EU,
AdU,LdU-B+; CLU,CtY(−A1,D2),ICU,MH,
TxU(−D2)+.

A138 — — *London, printed for R. Dodsley; sold by M. Cooper*, 1748.
4⁰: A–C⁴ D² (A3 as 'B2'); *1–4* 5–26 *27–28*. A1 hft; D2 advt.
　　Imprint reads 'Pall-Mall'. The outer forme of B and sheet D are from the same setting of type as the preceding.
L(11630.c.8/3,−A1, lacks D²; 11630.c.9/13, lacks A1-2, D²; Ashley 2300,−D2),O,LdU-B; CSmH (−A1,D2),CtY-M(−A1),ICN,KU(−A1),TxU+.

A139 [—] The pleasures of imagination. A poem. In three books. *London, printed for R. Dodsley,* 1744. (*SR* 14 Jan)
4⁰: *A*⁴ B–Q⁴; *1–4* 5–125 *126–128* (20 as '22'). A1 hft; Q4 advt.
　　With a five-line note on p. 9; press-figures 21–1, 30–1, 32–1 . . . For the priority of editions see Foxon in *Book Collector* (Spring 1956) 77–8. Advertised in *DP* 16 Jan; deposit copies at E,EU.
'With what attractive charms this goodly frame'
　　Collected in Akenside's *Poems*, 1772.
L(840.l.7/3; 840.l.2/2,−A1; 671.h.15, presentation copy; Ashley 2298,−Q4),O(−Q4),E, DT(−A1),LdU-B(uncut)+; CtY(uncut,−Q4), ICN,IU(−Q4),MH(−A1),TxU(2, 1 uncut).

A140 [—] [another edition]
　　No note on p. 9; press-figures 15–2, 22–1, 30–2, 32–2 . . .; p. 22 correctly numbered. Reset except for O,P,Q, and parts of N and A.
L(11659.d.1; Ashley 4682,−Q4)LVA-D(−A1, Q4),O(2,1−Q4,1−A1,Q4),OW,C; CtY,IU(−A1), MH(−Q4),TxU(uncut,−A1).

A141 — — By Mark Akinside, M.D. (The third edition.) *London, printed for R. Dodsley,* 1744. (20 May?)
8⁰: A–I⁸; *i–iv* v–xi *xii–xiv,* 15–142 *143; 144 blk.* A1 hft; I8 advt.
　　'The third edition' on half-title. A second edition octavo was listed in *GM* May, and by *Straus, Dodsley* from *GA* 20 May. It is not clear whether a 'second edition' is missing or whether this was misdescribed in the advertisements.
L(11609.c.34,−A1,I8),LVA-D,O(−I8),SaU; CtY,MH.

A142 — — (The fourth edition.) *London, printed for R. Dodsley,* 1744.
8⁰: A–I⁸; *i–iv* v–xi *xii–xiv,* 15–142 *143–144.* A1 hft; I8 advt.
　　'The fourth edition' on half-title.
LVA-D,O,C(−A1); CtY(−I8),MH(−I8).

A143 [—] — '*London, printed for R. Dodsley*', 1744.
8⁰: π⁴ A–M⁴ N¹; *1–2* 3–7 *8, 1* 2–98.

Akenside, M. The pleasures of imagination

　　This appears to be a piracy, probably of Scottish origin.
GU; MH.

A144 [—] — '*London, printed in the year* 1744.'
8⁰: π¹[= M4] ²π⁴ A–L⁴ M⁴(−M4); *i–ii, 1–2* 3–102. π1 hft.
　　Almost certainly a piracy; the same ornaments are found in piratical editions of Pope's *Essay on man.* Possibly of Newcastle origin. The L copy has an errata leaf bound at end.
L(1488.bb.27),NeU(−π1); ICU.

A145 [—] — *Dublin, printed by and for George Faulkner,* 1744.
12⁰: A–D¹² E⁸; *1–2* 3–100, *1–3* 4–11 *12 blk.*
　　In some copies A6 is signed 'B'. E3–8 contain Pope's 'Verses on the grotto at Twickenham' with separate title and pagination.
O,DA,DN,DT,GU+.

A146 [—] — The fifth edition. *Dublin, printed by and for George Faulkner,* 1748.
12⁰: A–D¹² E⁶ F²; *1–2* 3–100, *1–3* 4–11 *12.* ²12 advt.
L(1484.ee.2/2,3),DN; MH.

— A song by Mr. Akinside, 1745. *In* F270.

A147 Alarm. The alarm. A poem, addressed to all lovers of our constitution in church and state: occasioned by the present rebellion in Scotland, and the approaching invasion. *London, printed for M. Cooper,* 1745. (*GM,LM* Sept)
2⁰: *A*² C–E²; *1–5* 6–15 *16 blk.* A1 hft.
　　Horizontal chain-lines.
'Why stands so long the nation in amaze'
L(643.l.28/14),GM; CSmH,InU(−A1),KU,MH (−A1),OCU.

A148 — — The second edition, with above one hundred additional lines. *London, printed for M. Cooper; sold at the pamphlet shops of London & Westminster,* 1745.
2⁰: *A–B*² C–D²; *1–3* 4–16.
　　Horizontal chain-lines.
E.

A149 — [dh] An alarm, to Scotland. Or some observations upon the lightning that was upon the eighteenth of May 1710; the sun being the culler [!] of blood the day before. [*Edinburgh?* 1710.]
8⁰: *A*⁴; *1–7 8 blk.*
'Great Britain, I invite you to repent'
L(11623.aa.36).

A150 — [dh] An alarm to the seceders with a receipt of their doctrine. Being an account of the fall, of their Babel that was lately builded by them in Scotland. [*Edinburgh?* 174–?]
8⁰: *A*⁴; *1* 2–8.
'Thou art the seed, of a seditious weed'
　　Apparently a satire on the secession from the presbyterian church led by Ebenezer Erskine.
GM.

A151 — [dh] An alarm to the wits. Being an hymn on the death of t⟨he⟩ late reverend father in god, Pet⟨er⟩ lord bishop of Cork. Occasion⟨ed⟩ by the delay of his elegy. [col] [*Dublin*] *Printed by S. Powell*, 1735.
4°: *A*²; *1 2–4*.
    Vertical chain-lines.
'He's gone! But, still shall nature stun'd'
O.

A152 Albania. Albania: a poem, addressed to the genius of Scotland. Dedicated to General Wade... *London, printed for T. Cooper*, 1737. (*GM,LM* March)
2°: π¹ A–E² *F*¹; [2] *i* ii–iv, *5* 6–21 *22*.
    Rothschild 208.
'Howe'er important in the high debate'
    An 'advertisement' on p. 22 says it was 'wrote by a Scots clergyman, since dead.' Cf. *TLS* 21 Sept 1940 for Sir Walter Scott's notes on it.
L(643.m.15/30),LVA-D(2),OW,LdU-B; CSmH, IU,NN-B,OCU.

A153 Albertus. Albertus the second: or, the curious justice. [*London?* 174–?]
slip: 1 side, 1 column.
'Assist me, a rustick, O muse, to indite'
L(C.121.g.9/129).

A154 Albina. Albina: or a poem on the death of his late sacred majesty William III. *London, printed for Joseph Wild*, [1702.] (9 April, Luttrell)
2°: *A*² B–D²; *i–iv, 1–11 12 blk*.
'O! My Alexis, prithee tell'
L(11631.i.15/7); CLU-C,*NjP*(Luttrell),OCU.

A155 — Albina, the second part. Or, the coronation. A poem on her present majesty's happy accession to the crown. By the author of Albina... *London, printed for Joseph Wild*, 1702. (28 April, Luttrell)
2°: *A*² B–C²; *1–2 3–12*.
    The Luttrell copy is recorded in *Haslewood*.
'Awake my Chloris, hast and dress'
O; TxU.

Albion. Albion, a poem, 1720. *See* Theobald, John.

A156 — Albion's glory: a pindarique ode on the royal train that attended the happy coronation of her most sacred majesty Queen Ann. Written by the authors of Britannia's loss. *London printed, and sold by John Nutt*, 1702. (7 May, Luttrell)
2°: π¹ A–B² C²; *i–ii, 1–11 12. 12* advt.
    The Luttrell copy is recorded in *Haslewood*.
'Arise my muse, thy sable weeds throw by'
O.

— Albion's naval glory, 1705. *See* Browne, Joseph.

— Albion's triumph. An ode, 1743. *See* Boyse, Samuel.

A157 — Albion's triumph: or, Roman bravery. A congratulatory poem, to his grace John, duke of Marlborough: on his return to England, from his late glorious victory...at Bleinheim... By a gentleman of the university of Cambridge. *London, printed by R. Tookey; sold by S. Malthus*, 1705. (*WL* Jan)
4°: *A*²B–*F*² (B2 as 'B'); *i–ii* iii–v *vi blk*, *1–18. 18* advt.
'Thrice hail great sir, thrice welcome to the land'
    Probably by the same author as *Luctus Britannici*, 1705, who describes himself thus and used the same printer and bookseller a month earlier.
LDW.

A158 Alcander. Alcander: a poem, occasion'd by the victories of his grace the Duke of Marlborough. *London, printed for J. Morphew*, 1709. (24 May, Luttrell)
2°: *A*¹ B–E² *F*¹; *i–ii, 1–17 18 blk*. 17 err.
'Alcander wise by long experience grown'
Horn(Luttrell, xerox at L).

[Alcoforado, Marianna.]
Love without affectation, in five letters from a Portuguese nun [sometimes identified as M. Alcoforado], to a French cavalier. Done into English verse, 1709. *See* L287.

Aldenardum. Aldenardum carmen Duci Malburiensi, [1708.] *See* Wilson, Bernard.

A158·5 Alderman. The alderman's advice to his daughter; being a medicine or, cure for the scolding ladies. In answer to the Scourge for ill wives. To which is added, a satyr upon an ignorant quack, that murder'd a friends child, which occasion'd the mother (upon the news of it,) to miscarry. *Dublin, printed, anno dom.* 1737.
8°: *A*⁴; *1–8*
'Miss Molly, a fam'd toast, was fair and young'
Satyr: 'Tho' 'twas thy luck to cheat the fatal tree'
    The *Scourge for ill wives* has not been identified.
MH.

— The alderman's guide, [1732.] *See* Sterling, J.

A159 Alexis. Alexis, a pastoral to the memory of Alexander Innes P.P. in Marishal-College Aberdeen. *Aberdeen, printed by J. Chalmers*, 1744.
4°: A(4 ll) B²; *1–3 4–12*.
    The collation is obscure. Apparently a small quarto, though the copy seen is cut to octavo size; the watermark suggests A1, 2 are conjugate.
'Come weeping friendship! to these mournful plains'
GM.

— Alexis: or, the distrest shepherd, [1743.] *In* Dorinda... The third edition, 1743.

Alexis

'**Alexis.**' The amour of Cytherea, 1724. *See* Morrice, Bezaleel.

— The present state of poetry, 1726. *See* Morrice, Bezaleel.

A160 All. All hands to a court martial: being a true description of the court-martial to be held, for the trial of the admirals Matthews and Lestock, &c. By a state-boatswain. [*London*, 1745.]
$\frac{1}{2}$°: 1 side, 2 columns.
     Large woodcut at head, copied from engraved print dated 26 April 1745 (L, P&D 2682).
'Shall British glory rise again'
     The two admirals had quarrelled and failed to collaborate off Toulon.
L(P&D 2683).

— All men mad, 1704. *See* Ward, Edward.

A161 — All out at last, or, the whigs farewel to Westminster. *London, printed in the year* 1710.
$\frac{1}{2}$°: 1 side, 1 column.
'Farewel, farewel, to rump and good old cause'
InU.

A162 — All prophecy's at an end. Or, an elegy on the much lamented death, of Dr. John Whally... Thursday 16th of January 1723–4... [*Dublin*, 1724.]
$\frac{1}{2}$°.
L (1964).

A163 All-devouring. The all-devouring monster; or new five per c------t. A ballad. By Trojanus Laocoon. '*Pandæmonium, printed for Venerable Merlin, at the Memento Mori*' [*London*], 1748.
4°: *A*⁴; *1–2* 3–7 *8 blk.*
'Ye Britons! who hate to be led by the nose'
     A modern ms. ascription to John Lockman in the MH copy is thought to be by G. L. Kittredge; its reliability is not known.
L(11630.c.9/5; 11630.c.6/21, cropt); MH.

A164 Allan. [dh] Allan Ramsay metamorphosed to a hather-bloter poet, in a pastoral, between Ægon and Melibiæ. [*Edinburgh?* 1720?]
4°: *A*²; *1* 2–4.
     The date of publication is suggested by the poems of Ramsay referred to in the pastoral.
'What swain is he, who merits double praise'
     Attributed in the GM catalogue to William Forbes of Disblair, perhaps because of other satires by him in the same volume; no authority for the attribution is known.
GM.

Allan, —.
Modern catalogues tend to give this author's name as Allan Pierce, but early ms. ascriptions are of the form '*By Allan*' *or* '*By   Allan*'; *cf.* Bang the brocker, or Bully Pierce alias A-----n the turncoat, [*1705.*] *His real name may well have been J. Pierce; he was an associate of Defoe.*

Allan, —.

A165 [—] A curb for a coxcomb, or, an answer to the Renagado whip'd, written by F--s of D--r, in defence of his lewd practices, after he was devorc'd, and excommunicated for the same. *Edinburgh, printed in the year* 1704.
4°: A–B²; *1–2* 3–8.
'What ails thee Forbes that thou canst not bear'
     Early ms. attribution to Allan in a copy at E. A reply to [William Forbes] *The renegado whip't*, 1704; followed by further satires against Allan, *A new year's gift for the renegado*, 1705, [Forbes] *Mack-faux*, 1705, and *Bang the brocker*, [1705.]
E(5),GM.

A166 [—] A satyre on F---s of D---r, by way of return for his Essay on marriage. [*Edinburgh*, 1704.]
$\frac{1}{2}$°: 2 sides, 1 column.
'Teach me my muse to check with keenest pen'
     Early ms. attribution to Allan in a copy at E. An attack on [William Forbes] *An essay upon marriage*, [1704]; replied to by [Forbes] *The renegado whip't*, 1704.
E(3).

A167 Allegro. L'allegro ed il penseroso in sonno: or, the power of sleep. An ode. *London, printed for J. Roberts*, 1742. (*LEP* 18 Feb)
2°: *A*² B² C¹; *1–3* 4–10.
'Hence airy empty pleasure'
O; CtY,DFo,OCU.

Alleine, Jos. Epigrams on subjects divine and moral, for the entertainment of youth: chiefly intended as an exercise for children that learn to write. With a recommendatory poem by N. Tate... *London, printed for John Lawrence*, 1706.
4°: pp. 28.   E.

[**Allen, Thomas.**] An epitaph upon Mrs. Frances Kentish, [1721/22.] See E445.

[—] An epitaph upon the late Mrs. Anne Hales, [1720?/22.] See E446.

[—] To Venus upon the charms of music, [1722?] *See* T399.

A168 [**Allett, Thomas.**] Oxford act: an epistle to a noble lord. *London, printed for John Morphew*, 1714.
8°: *A*² B–C⁴; [4] i–vii *viii*, 1–7 *8 blk.* A1 hft.
'When Greece, my lord, with tides of glory swoll'n'
     Listed in *Rawlinson* under Allett with title 'A poem on the accession of K. George 1st. dedicat. to Ld Hallifax', quoting this first line.
O.

Allibond, John.
[*Rustica academiæ Oxoniensis nuper reformatæ descriptio*] [*Ward, Edward:*] A seasonable sketch

Allibond, J. A seasonable sketch

of an Oxford reformation...now reprinted, with an English version, 1717. *See* W175–6.

A169 Allt, William. The Gibeonites of this day discover'd... In a letter and poem to a gentlewoman, from Joshua ix. 3, 4, 5. *London, printed for the author; sold by J. Lewis, and by R. Palmer in Hinkley, Leicestershire,* [1746?]
8°: A⁶; *i–ii* iii–iv, 5–12.
> Date from ms. in the L copy. The prose letter is an introduction to the poem.
'Come, ye souls, who are returning'
> Preface and letter signed. A methodist poem.
L(11631.a.70).

Allusion. An allusion to Horace's Integer vitæ, 1716. *See* Hughes, John.

— An allusion to the bishop of Cambray's supplement of Homer, 1706. *See* Cavendish, William, *duke of Devonshire*.

A170 — An allusion to the third ode of the first book of Horace. On his excellency Philip earl of Chesterfield, lord lieutenant of Ireland, leaving Great-Britain. *London, printed, Dublin, reprinted by Ed. Bate, for Chas. Leslie,* 1745.
4°: *A*⁴; *1–2* 3–8.
> No London edition traced.
'As some fond parent, tho' with reason blest'
> The poem is signed 'A. Mills' on p. 8.
> He has not been identified, but the poem should be entered under him.
KU.

A171 Alma. Alma mater: a satirical poem. Designed to have been published in March last. By a gentleman of New Inn Hall. *London, printed for Richard Wellington,* 1733 [1732?]. (*LM* Dec 1732)
4°: *A*⁴ B–D⁴ E²; *1–4* 5–36. A1 hft.
'Since int'rest, vanity, and spite combine'
> The CtY copy contains an early ms. key. A letter of De Blossiers Tovey, principal of New Inn Hall, in *Rawlinson* claims the authorship statement is false; 'it is generally supposed to be written by one that had formerly been of St. Johns, he having published two or three things of that nature before'.
L(11630.e.9/11),O,*LdU-B*; CtY,ICN(–A1),NjP, OCU,TxU+.

A172 — Alma's complaint. An ode in imitation of the second of the first book of Horace. Adress'd to... John lord bishop of Clogher, vice-chancellor... *Dublin, printed by George Faulkner,* 1735.
8°: *A*⁴; *1–3* 4–8.
'Urg'd by the growing vices of the time'
DA.

Almeria. Almeria, 1730. *See* Turner, Joseph.

A173 Almonds. Almonds for parrots: or, a soft answer to a scurrilous satyr, call'd, St. James's Park. With

Almonds for parrots

a word or two in praise of condons. Inscrib'd to the worthy gentlemen at Wills. *London printed, and are to be sold by the booksellers,* 1708. (Aug)
2°: A–C²; *1–2* 3–12.
> Advertised in *DC* 7 Aug for 'next week' [9–14 Aug], and listed in *WL* July, which is not inconsistent with a date in early August. Luttrell dated his copy 10 May, but this must be an error; his copy of *St. James's Park* to which this is a reply was dated 8 June.
'Arise, my muse; expand thy soaring wing'
> A satire on current sexual practices, in answer to Joseph Browne's poem.
LG; CLU-C(Luttrell, 10 May),OCU.

A174 — — *London, printed in the year* 1708.
8°: A⁴; *1* 2–8.
> A piracy.
L(1079.m.22),LdU-B.

Alney, John. The hymns of Callimachus, translated from the Greek. *London, printed for the author; sold by C. Davis, C. Hitch, & R. Dodsley,* 1744. (17 April)
4°: pp. 101.   CtY,ICN.
> Errata slip on p. 102. Publication date from *Straus, Dodsley.* Entered in Strahan's ledger to Joseph Barnardiston under April 1744, 1000 copies.

———

[—] A paraphrase on the creation, 1744. *See* P54.

A175 Aloe. 'The aloe tree, a tale. [*London*] *Printed for J. Roberts.* Price 6d.' (*GA* 9 May 1746)
> Classified under 'poetry' in *BM* May.

Alsop, Anthony. Antonii Alsopi...Odarum libri duo. *Londini,* 1752.
4°: pp. 88.   L,O; CtY,MH.
> Watermark: fleur-de-lys on shield. A prospectus dated 27 July 1748 is in *Rawlinson.* A copy at L (11409.h.30) has sixty pages of ms. additions; there is further additional ms. material at MH.

— [fine paper]   L,O.
> Watermark: Strasburg bend.

———

A176 [—] Charissimo suo duci de Vendosme. Tallardus. [*London*] *Printed for John Morphew,* [1708?]
½°: *1–2,* 1 column.
'Spes erat nuper mihi te videndi'
> Included in the ms. additions to Alsop's *Odarum,* 1752, at L; cf. *Bradner* 235n. Marshal Tallard (a prisoner at Nottingham) to the Duc de Vendôme after his failures against Marlborough.
MC,Chatsworth.

A177 [—] Charlettus Percivallo suo. Percivallus Charletto suo. *Væneunt Londini anno* 1706. (*DC* 3 April)
½°: 1 side, 2 columns.

Alsop, A. Charlettus Percivallo suo

Two poems, one to each column. Advertised in *DC* as sold by B. Bragg.
Charlettus: 'Hora dum nondum sonuit secunda'
Percivallus: 'Qualis ambabus capiendus ulnis'
Printed in Alsop's *Odarum*, 1752, and a ms. copy ascribed to him among Charlett's mss. at O. Erroneously printed in Edmund Smith's *Works*, 1714–. The pretended authors are Arthur Charlett and archdeacon William Percival.
L(835.m.8/14),O,Chatsworth,Crawford; CLU-C, MH(Luttrell, '1706').

Altamira. Altamira's ghost, 1744. *See* Boyd, Elizabeth.

'Altior, J.' The theatrical volunteer, 1741. *See* T128.

Ambitious. The ambitious father, [1730?/31.] *See* Ward, Edward.

A178 Amelia. Amelia to Mallamour. An epistle. Translated from the original Greek. *London, printed for A. Miller*, 1743 [1746?].
8°: A–B⁴ C²; *1–3* 4–20.
The O copy changes the date in ms. to 'MDCCXLVI'.
'Read o'er these lines, the records of my woes'
From Betty Rochfort, lady Bellfield, to her brother-in-law Arthur Rochfort.
O,LdU-B; *MdBJ*,OCU.

A179 Ames, Henry. A new translation of Horace's Art of poetry, attempted in rhyme. *London, printed for W. Pepper; sold by J. Roberts, W. Meadows, A. Dodd, J. Graves*, 1727. (*MC* Nov)
8°: A–F⁴; *i–ii* 3 iv–viii, 1–40.
Watermark: nil. Because of the difficulty of checking watermarks, some fine-paper copies may wrongly be included here. Uncut copy measures 8¼ × 5½ inches.
'Should some unskilful painter undertake'
L(161.k.30); CSmH,*CtY,DLC*,ICU,MH(uncut)+.

A180 — [fine paper]
Watermarks: BF and animal. Cut copy 8½ × 5½ inches.
E,LdU-B.

A181 — 'A poem on the birth of the young prince. [*London*] *Printed for S. Baker*. Price 3*d*.' (*DC* 6 Dec 1717)
Compare Edward Biddle, *A poem on the birth of the young prince*, published by S. Baker 23 Nov 1717; possibly this is a separate publication of his poem.

A182 [Ames, Richard, *d. 1693.*] The folly of love. A new satyr against woman. Together with the batchelors lettany, by the same hand. The fifth edition,

Ames, R. The folly of love

corrected and enlarged. *London, printed for E. Hawkins*, 1701.
4°: A–G²; *i–iv*, 1–24. iv advt.
A variant state of the title in the copy at CSmH reads 'bachelors'. First published 1691, fourth edition 1700. These reprints are included because of their relationship to Gould's poems referred to under A183.
'Happy was man, when first by nature made'
L(840.h.4/4); CSmH,ICN,NN.

A183 [—] Sylvia's revenge, or, a satyr against man: in answer to the satyr against woman. The eleventh edition corrected. *London, printed for Susanna Battersby*, 1707 [1706]. (*PB* 9 Nov)
4°: A² B–F²; *i–iv*, 1–19 20. 20 advt.
First published in 1688. Reprinted with [Robert Gould] *Love given over*, 1709, 1710.
'Then must it thus, ye heavens for ever be'
Ascribed to Ames by *CBEL*, but not listed among his works in *The folly of love*, 1693; it is, however, entered as by Ames in *SR* 22 May 1688. Apparently an answer to [Robert Gould] *Love given o're*, 1683–, and answered by him in *A satyrical epistle*, 1691, subsequently entitled *The poetess*, [1706.]
DLC,ICN.

A184 [—] — The twelfth edition corrected. *London, printed for Susanna Battersby*, 1720.
4°: A² B–F²; *i–iv*, 1–19 20. 20 advt.
L(840.h.4/8).

[Amhurst, Nicholas.] Political poems. Viz. I. Protestant popery... II. An epistle from the pope to Dr. Snape. III. An epistle to the Chevalier... IV. An epistle to Mr. Addison. Written by a student at Oxford. *London, printed for E. Curll*, 1719. (*PB* 21 April)
8°. AdU,LdU-B; CtY.
A nonce collection.

[—] Poems on several occasions. To which is added, A letter to Mr. Law. By a student of Oxford. *London, printed for E. Curll*, 1720.
8°. KU.
A nonce collection, adding *An epistle from the Princess Sobieski* and *The protestant session*, together with the prose *A letter to the Revd Mr. Law*.

— Poems on several occasions. Dedicated to the reverend Dr. Delaune... *London, printed for R. Francklin*, 1720. (*PB* 14 May)
8°: pp. xxxvi, 118. L,O; ICN,MH.
No watermark.

— [fine paper] CLU-C,MH.
Watermark: Strasburg bend.

— — The second edition, in which is inserted the Test of love. *London, printed for R. Francklin*, 1723. (*MC* March)
12°: pp. xxviii, 1–72 61–84. L,O; KU.

Amhurst, N. *Collections*

— [reissue] The third edition, in which is inserted the Test of love. *London, printed for R. Francklin,* 1724.

> L; CSmH,DLC.
> Cancel title.

See also the pseudonym under which Amhurst edited The craftsman: 'D'Anvers, Caleb'.

[—] The art of beauty: a poem. Humbly address'd to the Oxford toasts, 1719. *See* A317.

A185 [—] The bottle-scrue: a tale. *London, printed, and Dublin, reprinted, in the year* 1732.
8°: *A*⁴; *1 2–8*.
> Apparently reprinted from Amhurst's *Poems,* 1720; no separate London edition is recorded.
'The patten, fan, and petticoat'
L(11601.d.28/4),DA,DG,DK,DT+; ICU,PU, TxU.

A186 [—] — The second edition. *London, printed, and Dublin, reprinted, in the year* 1732.
8°: *A*⁴; *1 2–8*.
> *Rothschild* 205.
Rothschild.

A187 — The British general; a poem, sacred to the memory of his grace John, duke of Marlborough. Inscribed to the right honourable William, earl Cadogan. *London, printed for R. Francklin,* 1722. (7 Aug?)
8°: *A*⁴ B–E⁴; *i–viii, 1 2–31 32 blk*. A1 hft.
> Advertised in *DP* 3 Aug 1722 for 'Tuesday next' [7th] as on 'superfine imperial paper'; apparently all copies are on the same size of paper, though many are cut down and some (e.g. CtY) appear to be on inferior stock.
'Churchill is dead! and in that word is lost'
L(1465.f.62, −A1; 161.l.3, Luttrell, August; G.14129/5),O(−A1),C,LdU-B; CSmH,CtY,ICN (uncut),MH,TxU+.

A188 [—] A congratulatory epistle from his holiness the Pope, to the reverend Dr. Snape. Faithfully translated... By the author of Protestant popery. *London, printed for E. Curll,* 1718. (*PB* 29 May)
8°: A–D⁴; *i–x, 1 2–18 19–21; 22 blk*. D4 advt.
> No watermark; advertised at 6*d*.
'To thee, my Snape, in these reforming times'
> Reissued in Curll's nonce-collection *Poems,* 1720.
L(164.n.14),O,E,DT,AdU+; CSmH,CtY(−D4), ICN,IU,MH+.

A189 [—] [fine paper]
> Watermark: Strasburg bend; advertised at 1*s*.
L(1077.k.23/3); CtY(−D4).

A190 [—] A congratulatory epistle to the right honourable Joseph Addison, esq; occasioned, by his being made one of his majesty's principal secretaries of state. By a student at Oxford. *London, printed for E. Curll,* 1717. (*PB* 10 Aug)
8°: A–B⁴; *1–3 4–15 16 blk*.

Amhurst, N. A congratulatory epistle

> One copy at CtY 'ex dono authoris' is apparently on fine paper, but there is no watermark or difference in price to distinguish ordinary and fine paper, which are therefore listed together.
'While half the globe is shook with wars and arms'
> Reissued in Curll's nonce-collection *Poems,* 1720.
LG,LVA-F,O,AdU; CtY(2, 1 presentation copy), KU(2),MH,TxU.

A191 [—] Congratulatory verses to Edward Biddle, gent. occasion'd by his poem on the birth of the young prince. With some remarks critical, hypercritical, satyrical, and panegyrical. By the old three. *London, printed for James Knapton; sold by Stephen Kiblewhite, bookseller in Oxford,* 1718. (*DC* 8 Jan)
8°: π¹ A–C⁴ D² E¹; *[2] i–viii, 1–22*. π1 hft.
'From Isis banks three kindred bards unknown'
> *Rawlinson* attributes to Amhurst, 'all the verse part by him'; it is not clear whether there was a syndicate which produced other works.
L(11641.bbb.39, −π1),O,OW(−π1); ICN(−π1), IU(−π1),OCU.

A192 — The conspiracy. Inscribed to the right honourable William earl Cadogan. *London, printed by W. Wilkins; sold by J. Peele,* 1723. (*MC* May)
2°: *A*² B–C²; *1–3 4–12*.
> Listed in *MC* as printed for J. Peele and R. Francklyn.
'In times, when faction plumes her drooping wing'
MH.

A193 [—] An epistle from a student at Oxford to the Chevalier. Occasioned by his removal over the Alps, and the discovery of the Swedish conspiracy. *London, printed for E. Curll,* 1717. (*MC* April)
8°: A–C⁴; *1–3 4–20, 1–4*. C3, 4 advt.
> *Straus, Curll* records a 'second edition' advertised in May 1718, presumably one of Curll's fictions. Advertisement in *PB* 30 Dec 1718 records copies at 6*d*. and 1*s*.; copies at CtY,AdU are probably on fine paper, but there is no watermark or difference in price to distinguish ordinary and fine paper, which are therefore listed together.
'While you, dread sir, whom partial heav'n denies'
> Reissued in Curll's nonce-collection *Poems,* 1720.
LG,LVA-F,O(2,1 − C3,4),DN,AdU(2)+; CtY('ex dono authoris'),KU,MH(−C3,4),TxU.

A194 — An epistle from the Princess Sobieski to the Chevalier de St. George. *London, printed for E. Curll,* 1719 [1718]. (*PB* 30 Dec)
8°: A–C⁴; *1–3 4–22 23–24*. C4 advt.
> Watermark: initials; 'Price six pence' on title.
'To thee, dear James, my lover and my friend'
LG,LVA-F,O,E,AdU(2); CSmH,CtY,IU,KU, NNC.

A195 — [fine paper]
> No watermark; price deleted from title, '1*s*.'

Amhurst, N. An epistle from the Princess

substituted. The advertisement leaf C4, missing from copy seen, may have been cancelled for this issue. Advertised in *PB* 30 Dec 1718 as on 'Royal paper for the curious'.
MH(−C4).

A196 — An epistle (with a petition in it) to Sir John Blount, bart. one of the directors of the South-Sea Company. *London, printed for R. Francklin*, 1720. (*DP* 1 Aug)
4⁰: *A*² B–D²; *1–3* 4–15 *16 blk*.
'Wonder not Blount, whose magick hand'
　　Replied to by *An epistle from Dick Francklin*, 1721.
L(161.k.1),LDW,O,OW,DrU; CtY(uncut),DFo, ICN(Luttrell,August), IU,MH.

A197 — — The second edition. *London, printed for R. Francklin*, 1720. (*DP* 10 Aug)
8⁰: *A*⁴ B–C⁴; *1–5* 6–18 *19–23; 24 blk*. A1 hft; C2–4 advt.
L(1077.k.37,−A1),DA(uncut); CSmH(−A1, C2–4),IU(−A1),MB,MH,TxU(−A1).

[—] Eubulus Oxoniensis discipulis suis, 1720. *See* E483.

A198 — A familiar epistle from Tunbridge-Wells to a gentleman at Oxford. *London, printed for R. Francklin*, 1720. (*DP* 2 Sept)
2⁰: *A*² B² C¹; *1–3* 4–10.
　　No watermark seen in any copy except Amsterdam arms in sheet B of copy at OW; probably an accidental mixing of paper.
'Tho' proud Del—ne, for nameless, partial ends'
O,OW; CtY(Luttrell, Sept),TxU.

[—] A mock epithalamium upon the fictitious marriage of the Pretender, 1718. *See* M351.

A199 [—] Oculus Britanniæ: an heroi-panegyrical poem on the university of Oxford... *London, printed for R. Francklin*, 1724. (*MC* July)
8⁰: A–I⁴; *i–viii, 1* 2–64.
　　Engraving on title.
'Matron of arts, and to the british youth'
　　Dedication signed 'Philo-musus'. Ascribed to Amhurst by *Cibber* V. 337.
L(11607.c.24/1),O(2, 1 uncut),OW,C,LdU-B; CSmH,CtY,ICN,MH,OCU+.

[—] The Oxford criticks. A satire, 1719. *See* O268.

[—] A poem upon his majesty's late journey to Cambridge and Newmarket [actually by Eustace Budgell], 1728. *See* B557.

A200 [—] Protestant popery: or, the convocation. A poem. In five cantos. Address'd to the...lord bishop of Bangor. *London, printed for E. Curll*, 1718. (*PB* 22 April)
8⁰: *A*⁴(A2+a⁴ b²) B⁴ D–K⁴ L²; *1–4* [12] 5–74 *75–76*. A1 frt; L2 advt.
　　No watermark; 'Price 1s. 6d.' on title. a⁴ b² add a preface and postscript.
'A priestly-war I sing, and bloodless field'

Amhurst, N. Protestant popery

Reissued in Curll's nonce-collection *Poems*, 1720. Apparently George Sewell was thought to be the author on publication; he issued a denial in *PB* 17 May.
L(1465.f.2,−A1;164.n.16,−L2),O(3),C,AdU, WcC+; CLU-C,CtY(2, 1−A1, 1−L2),KU,MH, TxU(−A1)+.

A201 [—] [fine paper]
Watermark: Strasburg bend; no price on title. Advertised in *PB* 22 April, 'Some are done on a superfine Royal paper, price 3s. gilt on the leaves'.
L(1077.k.12); CSmH,KU.

A202 [—] The protestant session, a poem. Addressed to the right honourable Earl Stanhope. By a member of the Constitution Club at Oxford. *London, printed for E. Curll*, 1719. (*PB* 21 April)
8⁰: A–C⁴; *1–7* 8–24.
　　No watermark; 'Price six-pence' on title.
'At length the great decisive year is come'
　　Reissued in Curll's nonce-collection *Poems*, 1720. Early ms. ascription to Amhurst in fine-paper copy at L.
LG,LVA-F,O,OW,AdU; DFo,ICU,IU,KU,MH.

A203 [—] [fine paper]
Watermark: Strasburg bend; no price on title. Advertised as 'Royal paper' price 1s. in *PB* 21 April.
L(11633.d.5, early ms. 'Mr. Amhurst').

A204 [—] The resurrection. A poem. Written by Mr. Addison. *London, printed for E. Curll*, 1718. (*PB* 30 Jan)
8⁰: (frt+) A⁴ ˣB² B⁴ C⁴(−C4); *i–ii* iii–xii, *1* 2–8 *17–21 22. 22 advt*.
　　Latin text followed by English translation.
'Egregios fuci tractus, calamique labores'
'The pencil's glowing lines and vast command'
　　The Latin text is by Addison; the translation is attributed to Amhurst in Addison's *Miscellanies in verse and prose*, 1725.
O(2, 1 uncut); CLU-C,CSmH,MH,NN,TxU.

A205 [—] The second edition. *London, printed for E. Curll*, 1718.
8⁰: (frt+) A⁴ a² B⁴ C⁴(−C4); *i–ii* iii–xii, *1* 2–13 *14. 14 advt*.
　　Apparently a reimpression, with the type rearranged.
L(1465.f.44); DFo,ICN.

A206 [—] The third edition. *London, printed for E. Curll*, 1718. (*PB* 11 March)
8⁰: (frt+) A⁴ a² B⁴ C⁴(−C4); *i–ii* iii–xii, *1* 2–13 *14. 13–14 advt*.
　　Apparently a reimpression. Subsequently reprinted in editions of Gilbert Burnet's *The state of those that are to rise*, 1728–.
DrU(uncut),WcC; CtY,ICU,IU(2),MH.

A207 [—] Strephon's revenge: a satire on the Oxford toasts. Inscrib'd to the author of Merton walks.

Amhurst, N. Strephon's revenge

London, printed for R. Francklin; sold by J. Bettenham, 1718.
8⁰: π² A–G⁴; [4] i–viii, 1–47 *48 blk.* π1 hft; viii err. Watermark: initials, ? MW. Half-title 'The Oxford toasts', by which it is commonly known. Engraving on title, missing in one copy at CtY.
'At length with vengeance bursts my raging vein' Ascribed to Amhurst by *CBEL, DNB; Haslewood* records a ms. attribution in a copy of the fourth edition. Addressed to John Dry.
L(C.70.bb.3),O(2,1 uncut,1−π1),OW,C,LdU-B; CLU-C,CSmH,CtY(2, 1 lacks π1, A4).

A208 [—] [fine paper]
Watermark: Strasburg bend.
OCU.

A209 [—] — The second edition corrected. *London, printed for R. Francklin; sold by J. Bettenham, 1718.*
8⁰: π² A–G⁴; [4] i–viii, 1–48. π1 hft; 48 advt.
L(11631.bb.81),O(2); CtY,MH(−A1).

A210 [—] — The third edition corrected. *London, printed for R. Francklin, 1720 [1719]. (PB 10 Dec)*
8⁰: A–G⁴ H²; i–ii iii–viii, 1–52. 52 advt.
With 'An appendix. Being a collection of verses', and so recorded as a miscellany in *CBEL* II. 196.
O(uncut),OW,C,LdU-B; DFo,MH,TxU.

A211 [—] — The fourth edition. *London, printed for R. Francklin, 1724.*
8⁰: A–H⁴; i–iii iv–viii, *1 2–54 55–56.* H4 advt.
O,*HU*; NjP.

A212 [—] The test of love. A poem. *London, printed for T. Cooper, 1737. (GM,LM Sept)*
2⁰: A¹ B–C² D¹; *3–5 6–14.*
'Oft' hast thou told me, Jack, in friendly part' A revised version of the text first printed in Amhurst's *Poems*, 1723.
L(11602.i.11/3),AN,*DrU-U*; OCU.

A213 [—] — An epistle to a friend. *London, printed for E. Comyns, J. Robinson, J. Jackson, & A. Dodd, 1742. (17 April)*
2⁰: A¹ B–C² D¹; *1–3 4–11 12 blk.* 11 advt.
Copy from Tom's Coffee House in Lewis Walpole Library dated 17 April; listed in *GM,LM* April. Substantially revised from the text of 1737. Listed again in *GM,LM* Jan 1749 as published by Sheepey; possibly that refers to a new edition.
O; CSmH,DLC,OCU.

A214 [—] — *Edinburgh, printed in the year 1742.*
8⁰: A⁴; *1–2 3–8.*
GM; CtY,MH.

A215 [—] A view of the Duke of Marlborough's battles, painted by Mr. Leguerre, in his grace's house at St. James's. Inscrib'd to the Duke of Montague. *London, printed for E. Curll, 1717. (PB 10 Aug)*
8⁰: [? A¹ B²] C⁴; *3–4 5–16.*
The collation is obscure.

Amhurst, N. A view

'While the great-vulgar shine with borrow'd rays' The CtY copy is stabbed with presentation copies of other Amhurst poems; the LVA-F copy is bound in a collection of Amhurst poems.
LVA-F,O; CtY,KU,TxU.

Aminadab. Aminadab's courtship: or, the quaker's wedding, 1717. *See* Bockett, Elias.

Amorous. The amorous d---h--ss, 1733. *See* Phino-Godol, 1732–.

A216 — The amorous jilt, or a trip from Beavis Marks to Mincing Lane. A tale. On the late marriage of a celebrated Jew lady. *London, T. Fox, 1747. (BM Dec)*
4⁰.
(Pickering & Chatto cat. 272/14615.)

A217 — The amorous nun; or, the cloyster'd beauty; being good luck at last. A poem. *London printed, and sold by S. Malthus, 1705. (WL July)*
4⁰: A–F² (A2 as 'A'); *i–ii, 1–22.*
'Where Isis's streams in pleasing murmurs glide' An Oxford love story, possibly adapted from a continental tale.
DT.

— The amorous soldiers, 1741. *See* A poem on the taking St. Mary's, [170–.]

A218 — The amorous war: or, a duel with the passions. A poem. In a letter to a friend. By a gentleman of the university of Oxford. To which is added, the defeat: or, the lover vanquish'd... *London, printed by Tho. Darrack; sold by John Morphew, 1709. (Tatler 3 Sept)*
8⁰: A–B⁴; *1–2 3–16.*
With three other short poems.
'Convinc'd by reason, I her laws obey' L(164.l.50, Luttrell, 9 Sept; 11631.d.57); OCU,TxU.

Amory, Thomas. 'A poem in praise of Taunton, 1724.'
Quoted by various authorities, the earliest traced being *Watt*; the reference probably stems from the statement in Amory's *Sermons* (1775) 527, 'Dr. Amory...in the year 1724, published a poem on the praises of Taunton, the place of his birth'. No evidence of separate publication has been found.

Amour. The amour of Cytherea, 1724. *See* Morrice, Bezaleel.

A219 **Amyntar.** [dh] Amyntar: a pastoral elegy bewailing the death, and sacred to the memory of the right honourable, John earl of Rothes...who died on Tuesday the 9th of May, 1722. [*Edinburgh?* 1722.]
4⁰: A²; *1 2–4.*
'Why weeps Mylindor in this gloomy grove?'

Amyntar: a pastoral elegy

>Very similar first line to *The shepherd's tears*, 1724, by Alexander Pennecuik (d. 1730), but a quite different poem; it is possibly by the same author.
>GM; CtY.

Amyntor. Amyntor and Theodora, or the hermit, 1747. *See* Mallet, David.

Anacreon.
Addison, John: The works of Anacreon translated into English verse, 1735.

Rolli, Paolo Antonio: Delle ode d'Anacreonte Teio traduzione, 1739.

Anatomy. An anatomy of atheisme, 1701–. *See* Dawes, *Sir* William, *bart.*

A220 **Ancient.** The ancient philosophers vindicated against tipling. Written by a young lady. *Dublin, printed in the year* 1721.
½°: 1 side, 1 column.
'Diogenes sober and wise, is said to have liv'd in a tub'
>Apparently a reply to Edward Ward's *The tipling philosophers*, 1720.
CLU-C.

'Anderson, Henry.' *See* Waring, Henry.

A221 **Anderson, James,** *D.D., minister of the presbyterian church in London.* Ad reverendissimum in Christo patrem, Gulielmum, archiepiscopum Cantuariensem totius Angliæ primatem; in luctuosum & nunquam satis deflendum obitum, nobilissimæ generosissimæ amantissimæ ornatissimæq; conjugis. [*London,* 1731.]
½°: 1 side, 1 column.
Mourning borders.
'Flevimus, o utinam possent, Gulielme, dolores'
>At foot, 'Posuit dolens J. Anderson'.
L(835.m.8/3).

A222 — In luctuosum & nunquam satis deflendum obitum reverendissimi doctissimi dilectissimi dignissimi piissimiq; Dom. Henrici, episcopi Londinensis, qui Fulham septimo Julij die, anno salutis humanæ MDCCXIII. ætatis suæ LXXXI fatis succubuit epitaphium. [*London?* 1713.]
½°: 1 side, 1 column.
Mourning borders. With two shorter epitaphs.
'Hei mihi quod non sum permagnos aptus ad ausus'
>At foot, 'Posuit dolens J. Anderson'.
E.

A223 [—] In luctuosum & nunquam satis deflendum obitum, serenissimi augustissimiq principis, Georgii Ludovici, Magnæ Britanniæ Franciæ & Hiberniæ regis, fidei defensoris, &c. carmen pastorale. [*London,* 1727.]
½°: 1 side, 1 column.
Mourning borders.

Anderson, J. In luctuosum

>'Cur solus, Melibæe, sedes, mœstusq sub umbra'
>At foot, 'Posuit dolens J.A.'
L(835.m.8/18).

A224 [—] In luctuosum & præmaturum obitum, reverendissimi in Christo patris, Gulielmi, archiepiscopi Eboracensis. [*London,* 1724.]
½°: 1 side, 1 column.
Mourning borders.
'Tristia cum nati ploraret funera Phœbus'
>At foot, 'Posuit dolens J.A.'
L(835.m.8/4).

A225 **Anderson, James,** *minister of the evangile at Collass.* The winter night, showing plainly the blindness wherein were misled of [!] in popery... *Glasgow, printed by Robert Sanders,* 1713.
12°: A⁸ B⁴; *1*–2 3–24.
'The winter night I think it lang'
E.

'Andrew, *Merry.*' Merrie Andrews remarks, [1715.] *See* M198.

Anglia. Anglia triumphans, 1703. *See* Harris, Joseph.

Angling. Angling, 1741. *See* The innocent epicure, 1713–.

'Anglipoloski.' The dyet of Poland, a satyr, 1705. *See* Defoe, Daniel.

A226 **Anna.** Anna in anno mirabili: or, the wonderful year of 1702. A rehearsal. [*London*] *Printed for B. Bragg,* 1702. (15 Dec, Luttrell)
2°: *A*² B²; *1*–2 3–8.
>Copies seen have different watermarks, possibly representing different impressions.
'At length day breaks, and shades of night give way'
MH(Luttrell),TxU.

A227 — Anna triumphans. A congratulatory poem on the peace. *London, printed for R. Gosling,* 1713. (22 May, Luttrell)
2°: *A*² B–C²; *1*–2 3–12.
>Advertised in *PB* 23 May. The Luttrell copy is in the possession of J. R. B. Brett-Smith.
'Whilst heav'n alone, which laid the prosp'rous train'
CtY(uncut),MH,TxU.

A228 **Anniversary.** An anniversary ode on her majesty's birth-day, being the sixth day of February, 170⅔. *London, printed by R. Janeway; sold by B. Bragg* 1703. (8 Feb, Luttrell)
2°: *A*² B–C²; *1*–2 3–12.
'Hail sacred spirits of ætherial frame'
MR-C; MH,OCU(Luttrell).

Anno

Anno. Annoque domini 1732. The Irish bishops, 1732. *See* Swift, Jonathan.

Annotations. The annotations of the Grub-street society, 1731. *See* Bockett, Elias.

A229 **Anointment.** The anointment. A poem. *Dublin, printed in the year* 1742.
8°: A–B⁴; *1–3 4–15 16 blk.*
'The night, in clouded majesty array'd'
An Irish Dunciad.
LVA-F,DA.

'Anonymus.' A hymn to money, 1704. *See* H453.

Another. Another original canto of Spencer, 1714. *See* Croxall, Samuel.

A230 **Answer.** An answer from S——a F——a to S——r S——o. *London, printed for J. Roberts,* 1727. (*MC* March)
2°: *A² B²; 1–4 5–8. A1 hft.*
'Your sad complaints no sooner I receiv'd'
Signed 'F——a'. A bawdy reply to *An epistle from S——r S——o,* 1727. The author is intended to be Faustina B. Hasse, the singer, writing to Senesino.
C(lacks A²); PPL.

A231 — 'An answer from the King of Sweden to the British lady's epistle to him. Writ by Mrs. Centlivre. [*London*] *Printed for James Roberts, & Nath. Travis.* Price 6d.' (*DC* 24 June 1717)
Presumably a verse answer to Susanna Centlivre, *An epistle to the King of Sweden,* 1717.

A232 — An answer from the Lord ***** in Ireland, to a letter sent by E——ce B——ll, esq; in England. *London, printed for J. Roberts,* 1718 [1717]. (*PB* 9 Dec)
8°: *A² B–C⁴; 1–4 5–18 19–20 blk.* A1 hft.
'Your friends receiv'd with aking hearts'
A satirical reply to Eustace Budgell's prose *A letter to the Lord ****.*
L(116.g.2); OCU(–A1).

A233 — An answer to a late abusive pamphlet, intituled, The true-born Englishman, &c. Together with the true character of a true Englishman. *London, printed by, and for Benj. Harris,* 1700 [1701]. (31 Jan 1701, Luttrell)
½°: *1–2, 1 column.*
'A certain barber, fraught with much ill nature'
An attack on Defoe's poem. The first line suggests the author attributed it to Dr. Barber.
MH(Luttrell).

A234 — An answer to a late scurrilous pamphlet, intitled The countess's speech to her son Roderigo... To which is subjoin'd, an introduction by way of reply to the vile preface annex'd to the said scurrilous pamphlet. *London, printed for*

An **answer** to a late scurrilous pamphlet

A. Moore, and sold by the booksellers of London & Westminster, [1731.] (*MC* Feb)
2°: A–B².
Luttrell's copy is recorded in *Haslewood;* at that time it was perfect, and the first line is quoted thence.
'When faction late Britannia's isle o'erspread'
A reply to the satire on John, lord Hervey and the Countess of Bristol.
Lewis Walpole Library (Luttrell, May, lacks B²).

— An answer to a scandalous poem, 1733. *See* Swift, Jonathan.

— An answer to Dr. D-----y's fable, 1730. *See* Swift, Jonathan.

A235 — An answer to Duke upon duke, &c. With a key. Set to musick by the same hand. *London, printed for B. Moor; sold by the booksellers,* 1720. (*DP* 22 Aug)
2°: *A¹ B²; i–ii, 1 2–4.*
Printed music at head of p. 1. The advertisements give the publisher as A. Moor or Moore.
'Thou Pope; oh popery burning hot'
Crum T2235. A mock reply by Nicholas Lechmere to Pope.
L(1876.f.1/81, lacks A1); MH,OCU(Luttrell, Aug).

A236 — — *London, printed by F. Clifton, where may be had the right and true Duke upon duke,* [1720.]
½°: *1–2, 2 columns.*
Four staves of woodcut music after the title. The 'key' is a woodcut of a key below the imprint.
L(C.116.i.4/54).

A237 — [dh] An answer to Hamilton's Bawn: or, a short character of Dr. S—t. [*Dublin,* 1732.]
4°: *A²; 1–2.*
Teerink 1612; *Williams* 1123. Printed on one side of the leaf only. The copy at DA is bound with pamphlets of 1732.
'Is S—'s ingratitude proclaim'd again?'
Swift's letter to Henry Jenney of 8 June 1732 was occasioned by this poem; he had thought William Tisdall was the author, 'but I hear he hath utterly denied it, and I believe him, for I am confident he is an honest man'. An answer to Swift's *The grand question debated,* 1732.
DA.

A238 — An answer to High church loyalty, or, prosperity to old England. *Cambridge, printed in the year* 1710.
½°: *1 side, 1 column.*
The imprint is probably false, and London the place of publication.
'You pinacle flyers, where would you advance'
An attack on the Jacobites.
L(C.20.f.2/230), Rothschild.

A239 — [dh] An answer to John Brigs's ballads. By C—d and S—t, May 29. 1729. [*Edinburgh?* 1729.] (16 June?)
8°: *A²; 1–4.*

An **answer** to John Brigs's ballads

'When abandoned mockers and scriblers conspire'
A ms. note in the E copy expands the names
in the title to 'Crawferd' and 'Stewart'; they
have not been identified, and it is not clear if
they are the true authors. On John Simson's
suspension, attacking *A ballad by J--n B--s*,
[1729], which was pro-Simson.
E(ms. date 16 June).

— An answer to Miss Prue, 1706. *See* The city
madam, 1702–.

A240 — An answer to Mr. Leech. [*Hereford?* 1741.]
obl ⅛°: 1 side, 1 column.
'My Grubstreet bard, your reasons nought avail'
An epigram on the Hereford election.
O.

A241 — 'An answer to Mr. Pope's ballad, entituled,
News from court; to the tune of, To all ye ladies
now at land. [*London*] *Printed for, and sold by
S. Huddlestone, & J. Roberts.*' (*PB* 31 Jan 1719)
Possibly a half-sheet. The attribution of
News from court to Pope is not accepted,
thought it was published with his name.

A242 — An answer to Polly Peachum's ballad. The following lines being sent to the author as an answer
to the foregoing ballad, he to shew what he publish'd
was not done out of malice to Polly Peachum, has
annex'd them to this edition... *London, printed by
A. Moore,* [1728.]
½°: 1 side, 2 columns.
'Pray, sir, who are you'
A reprint of the reply included in *A new
ballad, inscrib'd to Polly Peachum*, [1728],
which satirized Lavinia Fenton's lovers.
L(C.116.i.4/40).

A243 — — *London, printed for M. Robinson, on Saffron
Hill,* [1728.]
½°: 1 side, 2 columns.
O; MH.

— An answer to the Advice to Mr. L-g-n, [1748.]
See Kidgell, John.

A244 — An answer to the Assembly of bum-bees.
[*Edinburgh?* 1729?].
½°: 1 side, 1 column.
'As snarling Momus sung descenting bees'
An attack on the general assembly of the
Church of Scotland's leniency to the heretical
John Simson, in reply to *The bum-bees
assembly*, [1729?]
E.

— An answer to the Ballyspellin ballad, 1728. *See*
Swift, Jonathan.

A245 — ⟨An⟩ answer to the Band-ballad, by a milliner.
[*Dublin*, 1731.]
½°: 1 side, 1 column.
'The town is alarm'd and seems at a stand'
A reply to *The band*, 1731, on the fashion of

An **answer** to the Band-ballad

lawyers wearing bands reintroduced into
Ireland by John Bowes.
L(C.121.g.8/190).

A246 — An answre [!] to the Christmas-box. In defence
of Docter [!] D—n—y. By R—t B—r. *Dublin,
printed in the year* 1729 [1730?].
8°: *A*⁴; *1–2* 3–7 *8 blk.*
'Ye damnable dunces, ye criblers what mean ye'
The author intended is Rupert Barber,
husband of the poetess Mary Barber. Ascribed
to Thomas Sheridan by *Ball* 250, but evidence
is wanting. Occasioned by Swift's *An epistle
upon an epistle*, 1730.
LVA-F,DG,DT; MH(cropt).

A247 — An answer to the Curious maid. A tale. *London,
sold by T. Bickerton,* [1721.] (*PB* 11 Feb)
2°: *A*² B¹; *1–2* 3–6.
'Thy muse, O bard, that wonders tells'
Waller prints this as attributed to Prior; but
since *The curious maid* is by Hildebrand Jacob,
not Prior as sometimes suggested, there is no
evidence for that attribution; rejected by
Wright & Spears, 810. It is an answer to
Jacob's poem.
L(Ashley 4981),O(uncut),OW; CLU-C(Luttrell,
Feb).

A248 — [dh] An answer to the Great noise about
nothing: or, a noise about something. [col] *Printed
in the year* 1705.
4°: *A*²; *1–4*.
'When noise and clamour gets the upper hand'
Crum W1342. A tory reply to *A great noise
about nothing*, 1705.
L(164.m.42),E; CtY,ICU,IU,MB,MH.

A249 — — [*Edinburgh?* 1714?]
4°: *A*²; *1–4*.
Presumably a new edition to accompany the
1714 edition of *A great noise*.
L(11626.c.44/5),O,*E*,ES.

A250 — An answer to the Hymn to the victory in
Scotland. By an officer in his majesty's fleet.
*London, 'printed by W. Mallard near the May-pole
in the Strand',* [1719.]
½°: 1 side, 2 columns.
The imprint is apparently fictitious.
'I tell the deeds of great bravadoes'
A reply to *A hymn to the victory*, [1719.]
L(1872.a.1/183).

A251 — [dh] An answer to the letter pretended to be in
commendation of the reverend Mr. M--w F--h's
speech. In a letter to himself. [*Dublin*, 1712?]
4°: *A*²; *1* 2–4.
'Were I at rhyme as great a witch'
In answer to *A letter to the reverend Mr.
M---w F---h*, [1712?].
L(11630.bbb.3).

A252 — An answer to the Mock mourners, by way of
reflection on a late satyr. Pretended to be written

An **answer** to the Mock mourners

by the author of the True-born English-man.
London, printed 1702.
8°: *A*⁴; *1–2* 3–8.
'Such always was the nature of a fool'
> The address 'To the reader' signed 'R.B.';
> conceivably by Richard Burridge. An answer
> to Defoe's poem.

CtY.

A253 — An answer to the Pleasures of a single life: or,
the comforts of marriage confirm'd and vindicated.
London, printed for M. Goodwin, 1701.
8°: A⁴; *1* 2–8.
'When from dark nothing heaven the world did
make'

CLU-C.

A254 — An answer to the Six save-alls: or, the extraordinary proporty [!] of good save-alls. *London,
printed in the year* 1710.
½°: 1 side, 2 columns.
'Since save-alls are so much the mode of the
nation'
> A reply to *The save-alls,* 1710; an attack on
> the bishops who voted for Sacheverell.

NN.

— An answer to the Tale of a nettle, 1710.
See 'Defoe, D.'

'Anthony, *Doctor.'*
*'Doctor Anthony' has not been further identified,
and it is not clear whether any of the poems listed here
were written by him; some at least appear to be
attributed to him in jest.*

A255 — [dh] Dr. Anthony turn'd poet and astrologer.
[*Dublin,* 172–.]
8°: A⁴; *1–8.*
'Planets and aspects I will sour'
L(993.e.49/9).

A256 — Doctor Anthony's advice to the Hibernian Æsop:
or, an epistle to the author of the B—s w—g.
Dublin, printed in the year 1729.
½°: 1 side, 2 columns.
'Faith, sir, it's strange, and somewhat sad'
> A satire on Charley Coffey, author of the play,
> *The beggar's wedding,* 1729.
L(1890.e.5/106).

A257 — Dr. Anthony's description of the coronation.
[*Dublin,* 1727?]
(Dobell cat. 105/294.)

A258 — Dr. Anthony's lamentation for the loss of all
his patients. *Dublin, printed in the year* 1725–26.
(Dobell cat. 105/294.)

A259 — Doctor Anthony's last will, with his legacies to
all the poets and physicians. Written by himself in
a convulsion fit, mistaken by him for a furor
poeticus. [*Dublin,* 172–.]
½°: 1 side, 1 column.
'My brother poets and physicians'
L(1890.e.5/103).

'Anthony, *Doctor.'*

A260 — Doctor Anthony's new year's-gift. [*Dublin,*
1726?]
½°: 1 side, 1 column.
> The DT copy is bound with half-sheets of
> January 1726.
'All you who wou'd feign live a life that is long'
DT.

A261 — Dr. Anthony's petition. [*Dublin,* 1725/30.]
½°: 1 side, 1 column.
'Then if by chance I could'
L(C.121.g.8/99).

A262 — Doctor Anthony's poem in praise of the pox.
[*Dublin,* 1725/30.]
½°: 1 side, 1 column.
> *Bond* 81.
'Great pox, thou noble sire of the gout'
L(C.121.g.8/105).

A263 — Pride will have a fall. Or, the hue and cry after
E—s. A new ballad by Doctor Anthony, esq;
[*Dublin*] *Printed in the year* 1730.
½°: *1–2,* 2 columns.
> P. 2 headed 'The second part'.
'To this new ballad lend an ear'
> The object of the satire is possibly Mr. Eames.
DT; CtY.

A264 — A satyr on a clyster-pipe, or a clyster-pipe satyr.
Written by Doctor Anthony. [*Dublin,* 1727?]
½°: 1 side, 1 column.
> The DT copy is bound with half-sheets of 1727.
'Behold a satyr, on a pinch'
DT.

Anti. 'The anti Orpheus; or an epistle to Mr.
A——n H——ll. [*London*] *Sold at the pamphlet
shops.* Price 3*d.*' (*MC* Dec 1726)
> Listed in *MC* among the prose pamphlets, but
> possibly in verse. Probably addressed to
> Aaron Hill.

Antidote. The antidote; being a poem of reflection
on the late epithalamium, 1713. *See* Crispe, Henry.

A265 Anti-priapeia. Anti-priapeia: or, an answer to
Priapeia presbyteriana, or the presbyterian peezle.
In a letter from the general assembly of Scotland,
to their missionary in London, intercepted and
paraphrased by Ille ego qui quondam. [*London?*]
Printed in the year 1720.
8°: *A*² B–D⁴ (D2 as 'D3'); *i–iv,* 1–24. A1 hft.
'With woful phyz, and doleful greeting'
> A satire on the presbyterians, occasioned by
> the fact that James Anderson, D.D., of the
> presbyterian church in Swallow Street,
> London, was known to have caught the pox.
> *Priapeia presbyteriana* has not been traced; it
> may be an invented title.

CSmH.

A266 —— [1720?]
8°: π¹ A–B⁴; *i–ii,* 1 2–16.

Anti-priapeia

Possibly an Edinburgh reprint.
L(1079.m.23).

'Antiquæ.' A poet's impartial reply, 1744. *See* P696.

A267 Antisatirist. The antisatyrist. A dialogue. To which is prefixed, a short dissertation on panegyric, and satyr. *Dublin, printed by George Faulkner*, 1750.
8°: *A*⁸; *1–2 3–15 16 blk.*
The verse begins on p. 9.
'What object tempts my serious friend to smile?'
L(992.g.1/1),DA(2),DT(uncut); IU.

A268 Antoeus. Antœus. A tale. [1742?]
½°: 2 sides, 1 column.
The use of rules composed of type flowers below the title suggests a possible Dublin origin.
'Antœus was a might lord'
A very generalized account of a struggle between two politicians, variously identified. *Crum* A1356: 'Antaeus and Alcides: Pultney and Walpole', 1742, is probably correct.
L(1850.c.10/51),O,C,LdU-B.

Antonietti. Antonietti, ducis Corsorum, 1744. *See* King, William, *principal of St. Mary Hall*.

[**Antrobus, Benjamin.**] Buds and blossoms of piety, with some fruits of the spirit of love, and directions to the divine wisdom. Being a collection of papers written by B.A. The third edition. *London printed, and sold by the assigns of J. Sowle*, 1716.
8°: pp. 128.   L,LF; MWiW-C.
First published 1684.

[—] — The fourth edition. *London printed, and sold by T. Sowle Raylton & L. Hinde*, 1743.
8°: pp. 128.   LF; DLC,PSC-Hi.
Sheets B–H have horizontal chain-lines.

Apollo. Apollo: or a poetical definition of the three sister-arts, poetry, painting and musick. By Hybernicus. *London, printed for J. Roberts*, 1729. (*MChr* 23 Dec)
8°: pp. 26.   O; TxU.
A prose introduction on pp. 1–5, followed by a collection of songs, and 'The eunuch. A tale'. It may be a miscellany, but I suspect the hand of Bezaleel Morrice who wrote elsewhere on the parallels of painting and poetry, and had Irish connections.

— Apollo outwitted, [c. 1720.] *See* Swift, Jonathan.

A269 — [dh] Apollo's advice to all freeholders and freemen of the kingdom of Ireland, in reference to the ensuing elections... [col] *Dublin, printed by William Forrest*, 1727.
4°: *A*²; *1 2–3 4 blk.*
''Tis so long since from me you have heard, that, God-wot'
DLC.

Apollo

— Apollo's edict, [1725?] *See* Barber, Mary.

— Apollo's maggot in his cups, 1729. *See* Ward, Edward.

— Apollo's stratagem, or Button unmask'd, 1721. *See* Jacob, Hildebrand.

Apology. An apology to the Lady C—r—t, 1730. *See* Swift, Jonathan.

A270 — An apology to the town, for himself and the bottle, by J. Nick-all. [*London*] *Printed for B. Dickinson*, [1749.] (*GA* 8 Feb)
½°: 1 side, 3 columns.
Engraving at head, dated 8 Feb 1748/9.
'Ye English sages grave and wise'
On the bottle hoax.
L(P&D 3025).

Apostates. The apostates, 1701. *See* Tutchin, John.

Apostles' creed.
Sedgwick, Ralph: A paraphrase, or, an explanation of the apostles creed, [173–?] *See* S186.

A271 Apothecary. The apothecary in the sheet, or Ad---m's repentance, truely delineated by D. M. [*Dublin*, 1726.]
slip: 1 side, 1 column.
'God wott, great cause I have to weep'
On Mordecai Adam, caught in bed with two whores who were sisters, Mrs. A——rsh and Miss ——.
DN; CSmH(mutilated).

A272 — The apothecary's petition to a canonical judge. *Dublin, printed* 1726.
½°: 1 side, 2 columns.
'I humbly request who am cited as wencher'
A satire on Mordecai Adam.
DN.

A273 Apotheosis. Apotheosis basilike: or, a pindarick ode, upon the pious and blessed transit of that most excellent prince James the II... Written at the court of St. Germains in the same year, 1701. And printed in this present year, 1708. [*London*?] 1708.
4°: *A*² B–C⁴ D²; *i–iv, 1–20. A1 hft.*
'Upon the borders of eternity'
L(11631.d.29),OW; DFo,TxU.

A274 Apparition. The apparition. [*London*, 1711?]
¼°: 1 side, 1 column.
'As Mort—r lay pensive and with pains'
Crum A1600. A satire on Robert Harley, addressed by Guiscard's ghost.
L(C.121.g.9/161).

A275 — The apparition. *Edinburgh, printed by James Ross*, [1727.] (May)
½°: 1 side, 1 column.
'At mid-night hours, when nature seems to nod'

The **apparition**

A ms. note in the E copy gives the date as May 1727 and identifies the subject as Margaret M'Leod, hanged for forgery 8 March 1727 and said to appear as a ghost.
E.

— The apparition. A poem, 1710. *See* Evans, Abel.

— The apparition: a poem. Address'd to...James earl of Caernarvan, 1718. *See* Gildon, Charles [Canons].

— The apparition of Donald Macdonald's ghost, 1746. *See* Macdonald, Donald.

A276 — The apparition; or Grigg's ghost to the E--l of Ox---d. [*London*] *Printed in the year* 1715.
slip: 1 side, 1 column.
Beneath the poem, 'An epitath [!] design'd for the Earl of Ox—d'.
'From the dark caverns of the earth I come'
Crum F761. The ghost of William Gregg, the conspirator in Harley's office in 1706, to Harley.
Herts CRO(Panshanger box 46); *Harding*.

A277 — The apparition: or, the late b---p of E---n's ghost's alarum to the d---n of Ch-----r. *London, printed for S. Baker,* 1718.
2°: *A*² B¹; *1-2* 3-6.
'Sherl--k, thy doom is sign'd, fate presses on'
An attack on Thomas Sherlock, dean of Chichester, caused by the Bangorian controversy; the ghost is perhaps Andrew Snape, 'bishop' of Eton.
MR-C; MB.

Appeal. An appeal to the people of Great Britain, [1716.] *See* Garth, *Sir* Samuel.

'Aquila.' The old wife's tale, 1742. *See* O129.

A278 Ar. Ar ddydd-gwyl Ddewi, ag ar anedigaeth Twysoges Gymry. [1715?]
½°: 1 side, 1 column.
Six lines of Welsh verse on St. David's day, followed by a French paraphrase, titled 'Sur la naissance de la Princesse de Galles, & a l'honneur de Saint David'.
'Y Cymru Mwynion Medrys, mewn donniau dawn a dysc'
'Enfans d'Albion qui tenez le sang'
Anti-Jacobite verses in honour of Caroline of Ansbach, princess of Wales, born on St. David's day, 1 March 1683.
CtY.

Arbiter. Arbiter Europæ, mandato Brittonis Annæ, [1712?] *See* Pitcairne, Archibald.

A279 Arbuckle, James. An epistle to the right honourable Thomas earl of Hadington, on the death of Joseph Addison, esq; *London, printed for T. Cox,* 1719.
8°: A–C⁴; *1-3* 4-23 *24 blk*.

Arbuckle, J. An epistle

'To you, my lord, whose goodness could excuse'
LVA-F,E(2),GM; CtY,IU,MH.

A280 — [variant imprint:] *London, printed for J. M'Euen in Edinburgh, and for T. Cox, London,* 1719.
O(2),E,AN; DLC.

A281 — Glotta a poem humbly inscribed to the right honourable the Marquess of Carnarvon. *Glasgow, printed by William Duncan, and are to be sold in his shop in the Salt-Mercat,* 1721.
8°: A–C⁴; *1-3* 4-22 *23-24 blk*.
Reprinted in Dublin with Lord Hervey's *Monimia to Philocles*, 1728.
'Sacred, O Glotta, be the following strains'
A topographical poem on the Clyde, with a description of the game of golf on pp. 10-11.
L(1077.c.68),O(—C4),E(2,1—C4),DA(uncut), LdU-B+; MH.

A282 — Momus mistaken: a fable. Occasioned by the publication of the works of the revd. Dr. Swift, D.S.P.D. in Dublin. *Dublin, printed in the year* 1735.
½°: 1 side, 2 columns.
Teerink 1313.
'One day, as is his wont, the Dean'
L(C.121.g.8/192).

[A283–4 = H157·5–6]

A285 [—] A new prologue, on the anniversary of his majesty K. George. Spoke by Mr. Griffith. *Dublin, printed by J. Carson,* 1725.
½°: 1 side, 1 column.
'Since virtue first inspir'd harmonious lays'
The Rothschild copy has a ms. note 'By Mr. Arbuckle' by the contemporary Dublin collector who marked his broadsides 'F'.
L(C.121.g.8/47),Rothschild.

[—] A panegyric on the reverend D--n S----t. In answer to the libel on Dr. D--y, and a certain great l--d, 1729-30. *See* P36.

A286 — A poem inscribed to the Dublin Society. *Dublin, printed by R. Reilly, for George Ewing,* 1737.
4°: A⁴ B²; *1-3* 4-11 *12 blk*.
'When Rome was rising into pow'r and fame'
Inscribed to a society for promoting Irish manufactures.
L(11660.e.64),DK.

A287 — Snuff a poem. *Glasgow, printed in the year* 1717.
8°: A⁸ B⁴; *1-5* 6-24. A1 hft.
Bond 58.
'To snuff the muse her grateful homage brings'
L(11660.e.63),O(uncut),E; *MH*.

A288 —— *Edinburgh, printed by Mr. James M'Euen and company for the author, and to be sold by Mr. James M'Euen bookseller in Edinburgh, and by the booksellers in Glasgow,* 1719.
8°: A–B⁸ C⁴; *i-vi, 1-32* 33-34 *blk*.
L(1162.e.23,—C4),O,CT(—C4),E,AN+; MH, NN-A(—C4).

Arbuckle, J. Snuff

A289 [—] — *London, printed for F. Cogan*, 1732. (*GSJ* 9 Nov)
4⁰: A–D⁴; *1–2* 3–32.
>Entered to Cogan in Bowyer's ledgers under 12 Nov 1732, 500 copies printed.
L(11630.d.14/13; 11656.r.7/9),O.

[**Arbuthnot, John.**] The ball. Stated in a dialogue betwixt a prude and a coquet, 1724. *See* B20.

A290 [—] Γνωθι σεαυτον. Know yourself. A poem. *London, printed for J. Tonson*, 1734. (*GSJ* 10 May)
4⁰: A² B⁴; *i–iv, 1* 2–8.
'What am I? how produc'd? and for what end?'
>Printed as Arbuthnot's in *Dodsley* I (1748) 196; ms. in Arbuthnot's hand at L.
L(11630.d.18/11; 11633.h.5; T.655/24),O; CSmH,CtY,ICU,IU,TxU +.

[—] An heroi-comical epistle from a certain doctor, [1716.] *See* H155.

[—] A poem address'd to the Quidnunc's, at St. James's Coffee-house London, 1724. *See* P518.

[—] Several copies of verses on occasion of Mr. Gulliver's travels, 1727. *See* S356.

[—] Whiggism laid open: and the loyal churchman's health, [1712.] *See* W391.

Archimedes. Archimedes regi Geloni, [1712?/13.] *See* Pitcairne, Archibald.

Are. Are these things so? 1740. *See* Miller, James.

Argus. 'Argus, a ballad. With the political beggar. To the tune of the Jovial beggar. Price 6*d*.' [1741.]
>Advertised for publication 'in a few days' in *The compleat history of Bob of Lyn*, [1741]; possibly it never appeared.

A291 **Ariel.** [dh] Ariel and Mirza: an eclogue, to the pious memory of the right reverend father in god, Alexander lord bishop of Edinburgh. [*Edinburgh*, 1720.]
2⁰: A²; *1–4.*
'What weighty charge, O Mirza, 'mongst these towers'
>Alexander Rose or Ross died in 1720.
E.

Arimant. Arimant and Tamira: an eastern tale, 'MDCCVII'.
>The date is an error for MDCCLVII; listed in *LM* Dec 1757.

Ariosto, Lodovico.
[*Orlando furioso*] The landlord's tale: a poem. From the twenty-eighth book of Orlando furioso, 1708. *See* L44.

Armour. Armour. A poem. An imitation of Milton, 1723. *See* Kennett, White.

A292 **Arms.** Arms and the man. A new ballad. *London, printed for L. Raymond; sold by A. Moore*, 1746.

Arms and the man

2⁰: A⁴; *1–2* 3–7 *8 blk.*
>12 stanzas.
'God prosper the king and the king's noble sons'
>A satire on the Jacobite rebellion, making fun of both sides. Cf. *The sequel of Arms and the man*, 1746.
L(C.57.g.7/16; 643.l.28/17, lacks A1),O,AdU, LdU-B,*MR-C*; CSmH,CtY,NN,MH,OCU +.

A293 —— *London, printed for W. Baker, in the Strand*, [1746.]
½⁰: 1 side, 2 columns.
>Three rough woodcuts above the text.
O(crop); CSmH.

A294 — [*idem*] Arms and the man, I sing. A ballad. [*Edinburgh?* 1746.]
½⁰: 1 side, 1 column.
>Stanzas 1–12, as the preceding. '[To be continued.]' at foot.
E(3, 1 mutilated),AdU; ICN.

A295 — [part 2] Arms and the man, I sing. A ballad. [*Edinburgh?* 1746.]
½⁰: 1 side, 1 column.
>Stanzas 13–22. '[Part II. To be continued.]' at foot; no more seen. Some copies (O, E) have variant first word, 'Ancore'.
'Encore; now let's have th' other touch of the song'
L(1875.d.6/12),O,E(2),AdU; ICN.

Armstrong, John. The miscellaneous works of John Armstrong, M.D., in verse and prose... *Dublin, printed for L. Flin*, 1767.
12⁰: pp. xxiv, 208.   O.
>Clearly an unauthorized collection.

— Miscellanies. *London, printed for T. Cadell*, 1770.
8⁰: 2 vol.   L,O; CtY,MH.
>There is also a Scottish piracy (at L) and a Dublin reprint (at O) in this year.

A296 [—] The art of preserving health: a poem. *London, printed for A. Millar*, 1744. (*SR* 10 April)
4⁰: A¹[= S4] B–R⁴ S⁴(–S4); *i–ii, 1* 2–134.
>Watermark: fleur-de-lys; 'Price four shillings sewed' on title. *Rothschild* 56. Listed in *GM,LM* April. Entered in *SR* to Armstrong by Millar; deposit copies (fine paper) at L,O,E,EU,GU. Entered in Strahan's ledger to Millar under April 1744, 1250 coarse and 50 fine. Reissued in 1747.
'Daughter of Pæon, queen of every joy'
>Subsequently published under Armstrong's name.
L(11630.c.5/9; 840.l.2/1),OC,C,E,EU +; CSmH, CtY(uncut),ICN,MH(2),TxU(2) +.

A297 [—] [fine paper]
>Watermark: Strasburg bend; no price on title.
L(11602.gg.24/10; 11642.h.43/4),O,E,EU,GU; NjP.

Armstrong, J. The art of preserving health

A298 [—] — *Dublin, printed for John Smith, & William Powell*, 1744.
12°: A–F⁶ G²; *1–3* 4–76.
L(C.71.bb.15/9),O,C,DG,DN(2)+; CSmH, CtY-M,*MH*.

A299 — — The second edition. *London, printed for A. Millar*, 1745. (*DA* 30 April)
8°: *A*⁴ B–Q⁴; *1–5* 6–128. A1 hft.
No watermark. Entered in Strahan's ledger to Millar under April 1745, 1000 copies, together with '2 quires medium for do.' Possibly the latter provided six fine-paper copies.
L(T.299/1),O(2),C,E,LdU-B+; CU,CtY, CtY-M,IU,MH.

A300 — [fine paper]
Watermark: Strasburg bend.
L(1162.i.6, presentation copy).

A301 [—] — *London, printed for A. Millar*, 1747. (Sept?)
4°: *A*¹(±) B–R⁴ S⁴(–S4); *i–ii, 1* 2–134.
A reissue of the quarto edition of 1744, with cancel title. 'Title to Health, no. 200' entered to Millar in Strahan's ledger under Sept [1747] must refer to these cancels.
C.

A302 — — The third edition. *London, printed for A. Millar*, 1748 [1747?].
8°: *A*⁴ B⁴(±B3) C–Q⁴; *1–5* 6–128. A1 hft.
Cancel B3 has not been observed in all copies. Entered in Strahan's ledger to Millar under Nov 1747, 1000 copies. A fiftieth share of the copyright formed part of lot 23 of the trade sale of Thomas Woodward, 12 March 1752 (cat. at O-JJ).
L(1485.fff.28),O(2,–A1),C(2),E(2),LdU-B+; CtY,DFo.

A303 [—] The oeconomy of love: a poetical essay. *London, printed for T. Cooper*, 1736. (*SR* 2 March)
8°: A² B–F⁴ G²; *i–iii* iv, 1–43 *44 blk.*
Watermark: unicorn; 'Price one shilling' on title. Entered in *SR* to A. Millar; deposit copies not traced, possibly fine-paper issue below. Listed in *GM,LM* Feb.
'Thy bounties, love, in thy soft raptures when'
Subsequently published under Armstrong's name.
LVA-D,O,E,LdU-B; CSmH,CtY,IU,MH,TxU+.

A304 [—] [fine paper]
Watermark: bird with crown; no price on title.
L(Tab.603.a.14).

A305 [—] — The second edition. *London, printed for T. Cooper*, 1737. (*GM,LM* Aug)
8°: A² B–F⁴ G²; *i–iv*, 1–43 *44 blk.* A1 hft.
LVA-D(2),OW,E(–A1); CtY(–A1).

A306 [—] — The third edition. *London, printed for T. Cooper*, 1739.
8°: A² B–F⁴ G²; *i–iv*, 1–43 *44 blk.* A1 hft.
L(11659.bb.45),E; CLU-C,ICN.

Armstrong, J. The oeconomy of love

A307 — — The fourth edition. '*London, printed for T. Cooper*,' 1742.
8°: A–D⁴; *1–3* 4–32.
Almost certainly the Scottish piracy which formed part of the case of Millar and others against Kincaid and others which started in 1743.
DNLM.

A308 — — The fifth edition. *Dublin, printed in the year* 1742.
8°: *A*⁴ B–C⁴ D²; *1–3* 4–28.
DN(2, 1 uncut).

A309 [—] — A new edition. *London, printed for M. Cooper*, 1745. (*GM* Jan)
8°: *A*² B–F⁴ G²; *i–iv*, 1–43 *44 blk.* A1 hft.
L(1489.tt.19),O.

A310 [—] — A new edition. *London, printed for M. Cooper*, 1747. (*LM* March)
8°: *A*² B–F⁴ G²; *i–iv*, 1–43 *44 blk.* A1 hft.
Some textual changes have been observed from 1745.
L(1961),O(–A1),C,E,GU(–A1)+.

A311 [—] — A new edition. *London, printed for M. Cooper*, 1749.
8°: *A*² B–F⁴ G²; *i–iv*, 1–43 *44 blk.* A1 hft.
O,C(–A1),CT,LdU; DFo,OCU.

A312 Army. Army proceedings or the conjunct expedition. [*London*, 1741.]
obl ½°: 1 side, 5 columns.
Engraved title and large engraving at head.
'What do me see! what do me read!'
On the failure of Admiral Edward Vernon and Brigadier-general Wentworth at Cartagena.
NNP.

Arnold, Cornelius. Poems on several occasions. *London, printed in the year* 1757.
4°: pp. 240. L,O; CtY,MH.

———————

A313 — Distress. A poetical essay. Humbly inscribed to the right honourable John earl of Radnor. *London, printed for the author; sold by John Swan*, [1750.] (*GA* 10 July)
8°: *A*⁴ B⁴ C⁴(–C4); *1–5* 6–21 *22 blk.* A1 hft.
C4, missing from the copy seen, was possibly blank.
'Where Thames profuse, and lavish of his charms'
L(11632.g.5),*MR*; *MH*.

A314 Arnot, Samuel. A theoretick view of eternity... To which a poem is subjoyned, on the four-fold state of man... *Edinburgh, printed by Mr. Andrew Symson*, 1711.
8°: *²* A–F⁴ G²; *i–iv, 1* 2–⟨52⟩. 52 err.
The second leaf is signed '**'. The poem on the four-fold state of man begins on p. 23.
'It is the statute law of heav'n above'
'When god created th' earth, and ev'ry thing'
GM(slightly cropt).

Arrian. *For the* Enchiridion *of Epictetus, collected by Arrian, see* Epictetus.

A315 Arrival. The arrival. Inscrib'd to the Duke of Cambridge. A pindaric essay. '*Printed for C. Cross near Westminster*', 1714. (13 Sept)
slip: 2 sides, 1 column.
    The daily slip, no. 1, for Monday, 13 Sept 1714. The imprint is fictitious; 'C. Cross' stands for Charing Cross. The copy seen was reissued in *State poems. Being a collection of choice private pieces*, 1715.
'Advent'rous muse! too daring in thy theme'
    On the arrival of the future Prince of Wales.
Brett-Smith.

A316 — The arrival of the king. A poem. Inscrib'd to Sir Andrew Fountaine. London, *printed for J. Roberts*, 1714. (25 Sept, Luttrell)
2°: *A*² B–C² *D*¹; *i–iv*, *1*–9 *10 blk.*
    Luttrell's date from *Haslewood.*
'On lofty Cooper's hills aerial brow'
CSmH(uncut).

Art. The art of acting, 1746. *See* Hill, Aaron.

— The art of architecture, 1742. *See* Morris, Robert.

— The art of beauing, 1730. *See* 'Gulliverianus, Martinus'.

A317 — The art of beauty: a poem. Humbly address'd to the Oxford toasts. London, *printed for R. Francklin; sold by J. Bettenham*, 1719 [1718]. (*DC* 28 Dec)
8°: *A*⁴ B–C⁴ *D*²; *i–iv* v–viii, 9–22 *23*–28. A1 hft, C4 advt for cream cosmetic, D² advt of Francklin's books.
    Watermark: initials. Engraved vignette on title-page, not printed in LdU-B copy. The MH copy is reissued in *The Oxford miscellany*, 1720. The Luttrell copy, dated Dec, is recorded in Pickering & Chatto cat. 351/48.
'Attend, ye fair, whilst, anxious for your praise'
    Dedication signed 'J.B.' According to *Rawlinson*, by Nicholas Amhurst and James Welton.
L(11631.d.5),O,OW,LdU-B; CSmH(uncut), MH(–D²),NjP,OCU,TxU +.

A318 — [fine paper]
8°: *A*⁴ B–C⁴.
    Watermark: Strasburg bend. The copy seen lacks D² of advertisements, probably intentionally; the price is partly erased from the half-title.
CtY.

— The art of cookery, 1708–. *See* King, William, *the gazeteer.*

A319 — The art of courtship. A poetical essay. London, *printed for M. Cooper, & W. Owen*, 1748. (*GM, LM* Dec)
4°: *A*⁴ C⁴; *1*–3 4–16.

'Come, blooming Venus, beauteous goddess, come'
OCU.

— The art of dancing, 1729–. *See* Jenyns, Soame.

— The art of decyphering discovered, 1727. *See* Davys, John.

— The art of dress, 1717. *See* Breval, J. D.

A320 — The art of intriguing: or the various ways of making love. A poem. In two books. London, *printed for Tho. Warner*, 1718. (*PB* 4 March)
8°: *A*–D⁴; *i–viii*, *1* 2–24.
'Intriguing arts I sing, let none disdain'
    Ovidian in tone; a satire on contemporary society.
CtY,NjP.

A321 — The art of life; an epistle to J---. R---. esq;... To which is added, some other select pieces... With a translation of a Latin poem, entitled, Abramis. Publish'd in the year 1735. London, *printed for L. Gilliver and J. Clarke; sold by J. Roberts...also by Mr. Thurlbourn at Cambridge, and Mr. Fletcher at Oxford*, 1737. (*LM* June, *GM* Aug)
8°: π¹[= G4] A–F⁴ G⁴(–G4); *1*–3 4–55 *56 blk.*
    An 'advertisement' on p. 15 says the additional poems are by another hand or hands.
'Thou blest with ev'ry choicest gift in life'
    The Latin poem *Abramis* is by Robert Luck, and the translation is said to be by 'Philomusus'.
L(11631.d.42),C; *ICN.*

A322 — The art of love. London, *printed for R. Dodsley; sold by M. Cooper*, 1745. (*GM,LM* Jan)
2°: π¹ *A*² B–C² *D*¹; *1*–5 6–16. π1 hft.
'O thou, to whom ten thousand altars smoak'
    Sometimes ascribed to Charles Hopkins, by confusion with his work of this title.
L(1962,–π1),LdU-B(–π1); CLU(–π1),CtY, OCU(–π1),TxU(uncut).

A323 — The art of love. Paraphrased from Ovid. London, *printed in the year* 1701. (20 Sept, Luttrell)
8°: A–F⁴; *i–ii*, *1*–6 9–48. 48 err.
    Bond 5.
'To all the lovers in the city'
    A burlesque.
L(161.k.34, Luttrell).

A324 — [reissue] The poet banter'd: or, Ovid in a visor A burlesque poem on his Art of love... The second edition with additions. London, *printed for A. Baldwin*, 1702 [1701]. (*WL* Nov)
8°: A⁴(±A4) B–F⁴; *1*–2 3–48. 48 err.
    A reissue with a new sheet A and changed first line.
'To lovers all, in town or city'
L(11601.dd.17/1; 11641.de.21),DT; DFo.

A325 — The art of poetry. London, *printed for R. Dodsley*, 1741. (19 March)
2°: *A*¹ B–D² E¹; *i–ii*, *1* 2–14.

The **art** of poetry

Rothschild 225. Dated from *Straus, Dodsley*; listed in *GM, LM* March.
'Scarce in Parnassus shall we find one peer'
L(163.n.52),O,C; CSmH,CtY,IU,MH,OCU.

— The art of poetry, in four cantos, 1715. *See* Soames, *Sir* William.

— The art of politicks, 1729–. *See* Bramston, James.

— The art of preaching, [1738.] *See* Dodsley, Robert.

— The art of preserving health, 1744–. *See* Armstrong, John.

A326 — The art of scribling, address'd to all the scriblers of the age. By Scriblerus Maximus. *London, printed for A. Dodd,* 1733. (*GSJ* 1 Nov)
2°: *A*¹ B–F²; *i–ii, 1–20.*
     Half-title possibly missing from copies seen.
'Whoe'er ye be, that scribling can't refrain'
CtY,MH.

A327 — The art of stock-jobbing: a poem, in imitation of Horace's Art of poetry. By a Gideonite. *London, printed for R. Baldwin, & J. Jefferys,* 1746. (*GM, LM* April)
8°: A–C⁸; *i–v vi–xi xii blk, 13–47 48 blk.* A1 hft.
'If Hogarth a Change stock-jobber should draw'
L(11650.cc.19/3),O; IU,MH-BA(−A1),*MnU.*

A328 — The art of wenching, a poem. *Dublin, printed by George Faulkner,* 1737.
8°: A–B⁴ C² (C1 as 'D'); *1–3 4–19 20 blk.*
     Williams 1138.
'O my lamented Susan, while with thee'
     Williams says that the attribution to Swift 'may readily be dismissed'.
L(C.71.bb.15/5),C,DG(uncut); PU.

A329 **Artful.** The artful priest: or, the virgin sacrifice. An humorous tale. By the late celebrated J.J. H---d--g--r, esq; Now first printed from his original manuscript. *London, printed 'for John of Gaunt', near Charing Cross in the Strand, & W. Webb, junior, in St. Paul's Church Yard,* 1749. (*BM* Nov)
4°: *A*¹ B–D²; *3–4 5–16.*
     Half-title probably missing from the copy recorded.
'What various wiles, what diff'rent schemes are try'd'
     The implied attribution to Heidegger is surely made in jest.
MnU.

A330 **Articles.** [dh] Articles of peace, or a parcel of safe resolutions over a glass of claret. [col] *London, printed in the year* 1701. (20 Aug, Luttrell)
2°: A²; *1–4.*
''Z—nds what a bustle is here between kings'
CLU-C(Luttrell).

Artless. The artless muse: being six poetical essays on various subjects. By a person in obscure

The **artless** muse

life... *London, printed for D. Farmer, J. Robinson, H. Whitridge, & A. Dodd,* 1737. (*LM* May)
8°: pp. 72.   O; MH.
     Collected from previous publications of the author.

A331 **Arundell,** —, *Mr.* The directors, a poem: addressed to Mr. Stanhope. Occasioned by his epistle to his royal highness the Prince of Wales. *London, printed for E. Curll,* 1720. (*DP* 11 Nov)
8°: *A*⁴ B–D⁴ E²; *1–4 5–35 36 blk.* A1 hft.
'Ingenious Stanhope, if you can, excuse'
     On the South Sea bubble.
O; KU(−A1),MH-BA,NN(−A1).

A332 —— The second edition. *London, printed for E. Curll,* 1720. (*PB* 24 Nov)
8°: *A*⁴ B–D⁴ E²; *1–4 5–35 36 blk.* A1 hft.
     Apparently a reimpression or press-variant title. *Straus, Curll* dates as 15 Nov.
L(161.k.3, Luttrell, Nov),C; CU,TxU.

Arwaker, Edmund. Pia desideria: or, divine addresses... Written in Latin by Herm. Hugo. Englished by Edm. Arwaker. The third edition, corrected. *London, printed for Henry Bonwicke,* 1702.
8°: pp. 238.   L,O; CtY,MH.
     This translation was first published in 1686.

—— The fourth edition, corrected. *London, printed for R. & J. Bonwicke,* 1712. (*PB* 14 June)
8°: pp. '268' [238].   L,O; NN.

— Divine entertainments: in English and Latin. Selected from the works of the learned Hermanius Hugo; and translated by the revd. Mr. Edmund Arwaker, M.A. Fit for the use of schools... *York, printed and sold by Tho. Gent,* [1727?]
8°: pp. 16.   L.
     Printed in two columns for the English and Latin, with the woodcut blocks familiar from Gent's other religious works. The copy seen has an added quarter-sheet as a wrapper with the title 'Divine emblems and conferences: or, the learned and pious youth's recreation' and advertisements for other pious works below; while on the recto of the second leaf is a letter of approval to Gent from 'J.P.' dated 4 Sept 1727.

— Truth in fiction: or morality in masquerade. A collection of two hundred twenty five select fables of Æsop, and other authors. Done into English verse. *London, printed for J. Churchill,* 1708. (*DC* 10 April)
8°: pp. xvi, 326.   L,O; CtY,MH.
     The copyright formed lot 22 of the trade sale of Awnsham Churchill, 26 July [1720] (cat. at O-JJ), sold with 15 books to Wyat for £2. In Wyat's sale, 19 Feb [1733] (cat. at O-JJ), it formed part of lot 2, sold to A. Ward.

Arwaker, E.

A333 — The birth-night, a pastoral. *London, printed for H. Bonwicke*, 1705. (*PM* 6 Feb)
2°: *A*¹ B–D² *E*¹; *i–ii*, 1–13 *14 blk*.
'Defensive folds our midnight flocks inclose'
L(11642.i.6),O; CLU-C(Luttrell, 7 Feb),*ICN*,
MH,NjP,TxU(2).

A334 — An embassy from heav'n: or, the ghost of Queen Mary. A poem. *London, printed for, and sold by S. Malthus*, 1704. (*DC* 24 Oct)
4°: *A*² B–F²; *i–iv*, 1–20.
'Damon and Thirsis from a mossy rock'
L(161.1.6, Luttrell, 24 Oct),LDW,LG,O,DT;
CSmH,CtY,ICN(uncut),InU,MH.

A335 As. As bob as a robin: or, all's well that ends well. [*London*] *Printed in the year* 1712.
½°: 1 side, 1 column.
    The title is in two lines, the first ending
    '...or,'.
'A robin red-breast that had long'
    A political fable in favour of Robert Harley
    and the dismissal of Marlborough.
L(C.20.f.2/300).

A336 — [another edition]
    The title is in three lines, 'or,' having a line to
    itself.
L(G.1390/17).

A337 Ascent. The ascent of the separate soul, a poem. *London, printed by S. Palmer, for J. Morley*, 1723. (*MC* May)
4°: *A*² B–C²; *1–3* 4–12.
'Oh happy hour, when the unshackled soul'
L(163.m.5, Luttrell, May),O,*LdU-B*; IU.

A338 —— *Dublin, printed by and for J. Carson, & S. Fuller*, 1724.
4°: *A*⁴; *1–3* 4–8.
DA.

A339 [**Ashby, Richard.**] A remark upon the baths, in the city of Bath in Somersetshire. With a word of tender caution and admonition to the inhabitants thereof. *London, printed by the assigns of J. Sowle, in White-hart-court, and at the Bible in George Yard*, 1715.
½°: 1 side, 2 columns.
    First published in 1699 (*Wing* A3940).
'I've travel'd far and near'
    Signed 'R. A.'; ascribed to Ashby by *Smith* I.
    138.
LF.

A340 — A tender greeting and exhortation to youth. *London, printed by J. Sowle*, 1707.
½°: 1 side, 2 columns.
'Give ear O youth, and bow to truth'
    Signed 'Richard Ashbey', from Worcester,
    1 Dec 1706.
LF.

Ashton, R.

A341 Ashton, Robert. A congratulary poem to the reverend Daen [!] Swift. *Dublin, printed* 1725.
½°: 1 side, 2 columns.
    Teerink 1209.
'Whilst others write of heroes and renown'
L(C.121.g.8/64).

A342 — An historical poem in honour of the loyal society of journeymen shoemakers, who are to dine at the Bull's-Head in Fish-shamble Street; on Wednesday the 25th of this instant October, 1727. being the anniversary of St. Crispin. *Dublin, printed by Thomas Walsh*, [1727.]
½°: 1 side, 2 columns.
'To day ye tunefull nine, who dwell upon'
DT.

A343 — A new elegy on the unfortunate death of Henry Nelson, bricklayer, who was carry'd away in a whirl wind, on the second day of November, one thousand, seven hundred and twenty six. [*Dublin*, 1726.]
½°: 1 side, 2 columns.
'Proceed my pen and reach the glorious end'
    A mock elegy, attacking Ashton's rival poet.
DT(imprint cropt).

A344 — A poem in honour of the loyal society of journeymen shoe-makers, who are to dine at the Castle in Castle-street, on Monday October the 25th, 1725. Being the anniversary of St. Crispin. [*Dublin*, 1725.]
½°: 1 side, 2 columns.
'My infant muse, assist my tender pen'
L(C.121.g.8/88).

A345 — A poem in honour of the loyal society of journeymen shoe-makers, who are to dine at the Bull's-Head in Fishamble-street, on Tuesday October the 25th 1726. Being the anniversary of St. Crispin. [*Dublin*, 1726.]
½°: 1 side, 2 columns.
    Printed in dirty red ink.
'Apollo now or never shew your art'
L(C.121.g.8/155),DT.

A346 — A poem on the birth day of her late majesty Queen Anne, of ever glorious memory, dedicated to the reverend Dean Swift, writ by Rob. Aston. *Dublin, printed by C.C. [Cornelius Carter]*, 1726–7.
½°: 1 side, 2 columns.
    Teerink 1276.
'With joy great Swift, we view the breaking morn'
L(1890.e.5/63).

A347 [—] A satyr on the journey-men taylors, written by R.A. shoemaker. [*Dublin*, 172–.]
½°: 1 side, 1 column.
'Why silent Clio dost the pomp dispise?'
L(1890.e.5/171),DT.

A348 Ashwick, Samuel. The eighth book of the Iliad of Homer; attempted by way of essay. By Samuel Ashwick... The second edition. *London, printed for J. Brindley, M. Sheepey, & G. Keith*, 1750. (*GM* Aug)

Ashwick, S. The eighth book

4°: A^1 B–N^2 O^1; *i–ii*, 1–50. 50 err.
    The entry in *GM* does not specifically refer to a second edition; no first edition has been traced.
'Aurora, saffron rob'd, in glory flames'
L(832.i.28).

Asiniad. The Asiniad, 1730. *See* 'Gulliver, Martin.'

A349 Ass. The ass age, or the world in hieroglyphick. An amusement, agreeably resembling the humour of the present times. [*London*] *Sold by J. Morphew,* [1712?]
1°: 1 side, 4 columns.
    Large multiple engraving at head, including the title. After imprint, 'Beware of paultry wooden-cutts', suggesting the existence of an earlier state which was pirated. Printed in Grover's scriptorial type.
'Poets before, have brought upon the stage'
L(P&D 1475); MH(Luttrell, undated).

A350 — [variant]
    '(Price three-pence.)' added after imprint. Luttrell paid fourpence for the preceding.
DFo.

A351 — [*idem*] The ass age: or, the fools in fashion: being a comical description of the times... *London, printed by J. Bradford,* 1711–2.
1°: 1 side, 4 columns.
    Large woodcut between title and text.
DFo.

Assassination. Assassination display'd, 1711. *See* Stacy, Edmund.

Assembled. The assembled patriots, 1732. *See* Weston, James.

A352 Aston, —, *Mr.* 'An eclogue after Virgil's manner on the Duke's being expected at Bath. [*London*] *Cooper.* Price 1*s*.' (*GM* Feb 1747)
    Slightly different forms of the title are quoted in *BM, LM*.
    Presumably on the Duke of Cumberland.

Aston, Anthony. The Medley songs, as they have been successfully receiv'd written and sung by Tony Aston, and dispos'd of by him only. *Edinburgh, printed for the author by Mr. Thomas Ruddiman,* 1726.
12°: pp. 36.
    Recorded in *Haslewood*. Probably related to an imperfect collection of twenty pages at L (12331.ee.31/7*) with drop-head title 'The prologue, epilogues, and songs performed in Tony Aston's Medley'.

Aston, A.

A353 — A new South-Sea ballad, made and sung by Mr. Anthony Aston, in the Magician: or, Harlequin director. [*London*, 1721?]
slip: 1 side, 1 column.
    Woodcut at head.
'Here's a whim wham new come over'
    The magician, 1721, was by John Rich.
C.

A354 [—] The pleasures of the Bath: with the first and second part of the Tipling philosophers. *Bristol, printed by S. Farley,* 1721.
$\frac{1}{2}^o$: 1 side, 3 columns.
    Engraved editions with music at L, dated [1715?], with titles *The Bath medley* and *The medley or the humours of the Bath*.
'The spring's a coming'
    Attributed to Aston by the L music catalogue. *The tipling philosophers* is a reprint of selected stanzas from the work of Edward Ward, 1710.
L(1872.a.1/166).

A355 Aston, Miles. An elegy on the lamented death of John Mullen, doctor of physick, deceas'd July 11th, 1729. *Dublin, printed by E. Waters,* 1729.
$\frac{1}{2}^o$: 1 side, 2 columns.
    Mourning headpiece.
'The thirsty tyrant, active in our woe'
DT.

A356 — An heroick poem, on the powerful and commanding art of brewing. Tho' of later invention than other crafts; yet far superior to the most ancient occupations of men, in the great utility it brings to princes, as well as peasants in the British Isles. *Dublin, printed by Edward Waters,* 1728.
$\frac{1}{2}^o$: 2 sides, 1 column.
'A modern art, throughout the globe renown'd'
L(1890.e.5/49); C.121.g.8/166).

A357 — An heroick poem on the weaving trade setting forth 'its antiquity and use, humbly inscribed to 'its great patron Doctor Swift... *Dublin, printed by J. Gowan,* [1734?]
4°: A^2 B^2; *i–ii*, 1–6.
    Date from *Hanson* 4682.
'Cease heathen muse in thy Sicilian hill'
L(11632.bb.56),C(uncut).

A358 — Hibernia out of mourning. A congratulatory poem on the happy arrival of his excellency the Lord Carteret, lord lieutenant of Ireland. Humbly inscrib'd by that antient and necessary branch of the cloathing-trade, call'd scriblers, alias spinsters. *Dublin, printed by Edward Waters,* 1727.
$\frac{1}{2}^o$: 1–2, 1 column.
'Awake old Neptune from thy watry bed'
DT.

A359 — ⟨Peace and plenty.⟩ An historical poem on the useful art of baking, which was practised and taught by the greatest of kings and queens. *Dublin, printed by Edward Waters, in the year* 1727.
$\frac{1}{2}^o$: 2 sides, 1 column.

Aston, M. Peace and plenty

'When furious Gauls attempted to consume'
DT(cropt).

A360 — Virtue and industry. An historical poem on the art of spinning (alias) scribling, shewing it's antiquity, and how it was practised by men and women of the highest rank in all ages, as appears in sacred and prophane writings. *Dublin, printed by Christopher Dickson, '2727' [1727].*
½°: 2 sides, 2 columns.
'When royal Jason and the Aragonauts'
DT.

Aston, Robert. *See* Ashton, Robert.

A361 **Astraios.** 'Αστραιος: humbly dedicated to his excellency the Lord Carteret. [*Dublin, 1725/30.*]
½°: 1 side, 1 column.
'Fly forked satyr, turn your ill tun'd lays'
In praise of Carteret's administration of justice in Ireland.
L(C.121.g.8/128); CtY,PU.

Astrea. Astræa: or, the composition, 1720. *See* Morrice, Bezaleel.

— Astræa: or, the dream, and Composition, 1719. *See* Morrice, Bezaleel.

A362 — Astrea triumphans. The temple of gratitude, and the trophies of Vigo; being a congratulatory poem to his grace the Duke of Ormond, on his happy accession to the lieutenancy of the kingdom of Ireland. *London, sold by A. Baldwin, 1703.* (23 March, Luttrell)
2°: A–D²; *i–iv, 1–12.*
The Luttrell copy is in the collection of R. D. Horn; listed in *WL* March.
'The bright Astrea now no longer driven'
L(1482.f.4),DA,LdU-B,*MR-C*; CtY(2).

A363 — [dh] Astrea's commission to the complaining ghost. [*17––.*]
4°: B⁴; *1 2–8.*
The copy seen perhaps lacks the title.
'From Hades, with the rich-man's wish, I'm sent'
OCU.

A364 — [dh] Astræa's congratulation. An ode upon Alderman Henry French being elected representative for the city of Dublin... [col] [*Dublin*] *Printed [by J. Hoey] in the year 1733.*
4°: A²; *1 2–4.*
'What! is there yet a place below'
C.

[**Atterbury, Francis.**] Absalon et Achitophel. Carmine latino-heroico [actually by William Coward], 1723. *See* C476.

A365 **Atwood, George.** The CXIXth psalm paraphras'd in English verse. *London, printed for William Innys, 1730.* (*MChr* 4 March)
4°: A–D⁴ E²; [4] *i* ii–iv, *1 2–28.* A1 hft.

Atwood, G. The CXIXth psalm

'What num'rous blessings does god's law bestow'
L(11630.d.12/9; 1465.i.12/16,–A1; 162.1.7), AdU; MH(–A1),NjP.

A365·5 [**Atwood, William.**] A modern inscription to the Duke of Marlborough's fame. Occasion'd by an antique, in imitation of Spencer. With a preface unveiling some of the beauties of the ode, which has pass'd for Mr. Prior's. *London, printed in the year 1706.* (*DC* 29 Aug)
2°: A¹ a–b² c¹ B–C²; *i–xii, 1–8.*
Advertised in *DC* as printed for Jonathan Robinson.
'As of his faction's downfal P---r sings'
Elizabeth Thomas's copy, now at BlU, is a presentation copy inscribed 'By Wm. Atwood esqr.' The preface attacks Prior's *Ode...to the queen,* 1706.
O,*BlU*; CtY,MH(Luttrell, 18 Sept),OCU,TxU.

A366 **Aubin, Penelope.** The extasy: a pindarick ode to her majesty the queen. *London, printed for the author, 1708.*
4°: A⁴ B⁴; *1–4 5–16.* A1 hft.
'Rouzed by the inchanting sounds of joy'
L(11643.h.26/2).

A367 — The Stuarts: a pindarique ode. Humbly dedicated to her majesty of Great Britain. *London, printed for John Morphew, 1707.* (27 Nov, Luttrell)
2°: A–C²; *1–2 3–12.*
'When bounteous heaven with such a lib'ral hand'
L(643.l.25/12); ICU(Luttrell).

A368 — The wellcome: a poem, to his grace the Duke of Marlborough... *London, printed for John Morphew, 1708.*
4°: A–B⁴ C²; *1–4 5–19 20 blk.* A1 hft.
'From distant climes, and long fatigues return'd'
DLC.

A369 **Audenarde.** Audenarde, a poem, inscrib'd to the right honourable the Earl of Bridgwater. *London, printed for Henry Clements, 1708.* (*DC* 13 Aug)
2°: A² B–C²; *1–2 3–12.*
The Luttrell copy, dated 13 Aug, is in the collection of R. D. Horn. *WL* Aug 1708 records 'The 2d edition', not traced.
'Leave for a while, my lord, th' affairs of state'
O,*MR-C*; InU(uncut),MH(uncut),OCU.

'Audley, Henry.' *See* Waring, Henry.

A370 **August.** August the second, one thousand seven hundred and thirty eight. A prediction; in the manner of many. By Bickerstaff the younger. *London, printed for T. Cooper, 1738.* (*GM, LM* Aug)
2°: A² B²; *1–2 3–8.*
'In this great year our master Pope'
Occasioned by Pope's *One thousand seven hundred and thirty eight.*
IU,OCU,TxU.

Augusta

A371 Augusta. Augusta: or the city's triumph. A poem. Inscrib'd to the right honourable Humphrey Parsons esq; on his being elected lord mayor. *London, printed for A. More,* 1730. (*MChr* Oct)
2°: A² B¹; *1–3* 4–6.
'Forgive, my lord, that mine, an artless muse'
TxU.

— Augusta triumphans, 1707–. *See* Settle, Elkanah.

— 'Augusta triumphans: or London and liberty. Verses occasion'd by the citizen's petition on Tuesday the 3d of Aprill 1733 against the bill for the further extension of the excise. [*London*] *Printed on a broadside for frames, for J. Wilford. Price 6d.*' (*GSJ* 24 April; *LM* May 1733)
Possibly this refers to the large sheet B465, recorded under *Britannia excisa.*

Augusta, *princess of Wales.* Copy of a letter from Lady D------------ at London, to Miss B-------- at Dublin. *Dublin, printed by M. Rhames,* [1736/–.]
8°: pp. 12.   DN; CU.
A series of six translations from Latin and French, said in the introductory letter to be by the Princess of Wales. Their authenticity has not been confirmed.

A372 Auricula. The auricula. [*Dublin,* 1727?]
½°: 1 side, 1 column.
Date suggested by the L catalogue.
'Old Florio pore'd with eager eyes'
In praise of Grace Carteret.
L(1890.e.5/91).

A373 Austin. Austin, and the monks of Bangor. *London, printed for J. Roberts,* 1718. (*PM* 25 Feb)
2°: A² B²; *1–2* 3–8.
'When Saxon princes England's sceptres bore'
Listed in *Waller* as attributed to Prior; rejected in *Wright & Spears* 806. A defence of Hoadly.
L(643.l.24/40; Ashley 5662/1),O; CLU-C, CSmH,MH,*PBL*,TxU.

Auther, John. Divine poems on several occasions. *London, printed by J. Darby & T. Browne; sold by J. Noon, & J. Chandler, Caleb Ratten in Harborough, and Tho. Ryles in Hull,* 1727.
8°: pp. 83.   L; CSmH.
Listed in *MC* April 1728, possibly subsequent to provincial publication.

Author. The author of a Character, &c, 1717. *See* Bockett, Elias.

Authors. The authors of the town; a satire, 1725. *See* Savage, Richard.

Avianus, Flavius.
Pennecuik, Alexander, *d. 1730*: An ancient pro-

Avianus, F.

phecy concerning stock-jobbing... Written, a thousand years ago, in the form of a parable, by the famous Avian, 1721. *See* P149.

Ayloff, William. Marvil's ghost, 1709. *In* F248.

A374 Ayre, William. The saint: a tale. From the original Italian of Boccace. *London, printed for J. Roberts,* 1734. (*GM* Oct; *LM* Nov)
2°: A–E²; *1–3* 4–20.
'Distinguish'd praises mark that gracious day',
From the first tale of the first day of the *Decameron.*
L(11642.i.10/2),LdU-B; CtY,DFo,*ICN.*

A375 — Truth. A counterpart to Mr. Pope's Essay on man, epistle the first. *London, printed for R. Minors,* 1739. (*DA* 13 March)
4°: A² B–D²; *i–iv, 1* 2–11 *12 blk.*
'Price 6d.' on title.
'Though Pope has said it, must the world submit?'
L(11630.c.13/15),LdU-B(uncut); MH.

A376 — [reissue] Truth. A counterpart to Mr. Pope's Essay on man. Epistle the first, opposing his opinions of man with respect to the universe. *London, printed in the year* 1739.
4°: A²(±A1) B–D²; *i–iv, 1* 2–11 *12 blk.*
Reissue with cancel title bearing no price, possibly intended for presentation; compare the second epistle below.
LVA-D,O(uncut).

A377 — Truth. A counterpart to Mr. Pope's Essay on man. Epistle the second, opposing his opinions of man as an individual. *London, printed for the author; sold by Mrs. Dodd, Mrs. Nutt, Mr. Chapelle, & R. Minors,* 1739. (*DA* 13 June)
4°: A² B–D²; *i–iv, 1–12.*
'Price 6d.' on title.
'Know all thou canst, nor timorously go'
MiU.

A378 — [variant imprint:] *London, printed in the year* 1739.
No sign of cancel title; probably a press-variant title with changed imprint and no price, possibly intended for presentation.
LVA-D.

Ayres, Philip. Emblems of love, in four languages. *London printed, and sold by Hen. Overton,* [170–?]
8°.   GU; DFo,IaU.
A collection of emblems with engraved text, apparently first issued in 1683.

— [*idem*] Emblemata amatoria: or Cupid's address to the ladies. *London printed, and sold by W. Likely, & L. Stokoe,* 1714.
8°.   L.
With a printed title added, from which the description is taken.

Ayres, P.

— Emblems of love... *Printed for J. Osborn, London*, [173–?]

8°.   L,GU; DFo,NcD.

    The engraved title again. The copyright and 44 copper plates were sold as lot 22 of the trade sale of John Osborn senior of Horsley Downs, 11 Nov 1746, to Wren (cat. at O-JJ).

Ayres, P. Emblems of love

— — [*London*] *Printed for John Wren*, [175–?]

8°.   L,O; CtY,MH.

    The engraved title has been reworked to change the imprint.

B

B., A. Elegie on the much to be lemented death of the right honourable Sir William Anstruther, [1711.] *See* E47.

— The farce is over, 1742. *See* F58.

— The happy bride, 1730. *See* H39.

— Histrio theologicus, 1715. *See* H262.

— The Phœnix of Claudian, 1731. *See* P264.

— To the memory of the truly pious Sir George Freeman, [171-/22.] *See* Bonwick, Ambrose.

— Ward's downfall, 1734. *See* W42.

B., B. A congratulatory letter from one poet to another, 1747. *See* C345.

B., C. Monsieur Rapin's Latin heroick poem on Christ's-passion, 1717. *See* Beckingham, Charles.

B., E. Altamira's ghost, 1744. *See* Boyd, Elizabeth.

— Truth, a poem, 1740. *See* Boyd, Elizabeth.

B., G. Tres libri Solomonis, 1708. *See* T470.

B., H. The holy Bible in verse, 1701–. *See* Harris, Benjamin.

'B., H., *poet-laureat*.' The Pretender's declaration, 1716. *See* P1035.

B., J. The art of beauty, 1719. *See* A317.

— Bartholomew-fair, 1729. *See* B91.

— Honesty yet to be found, 1721. *See* H301.

— A spiritual poem, 1728. *See* Besse, Joseph.

B., J., *esq.* Henry and Minerva, 1729. *See* Breval, John Durant.

B., J., *gent.* An elegy on the death of our late sovereign King George, [1727.] *See* E128.

B., J., *writing-master.* In praise of tea, 1736. *See* I32.

B., J.D. The art of dress, 1717–. *See* Breval, John Durant.

B., J.J. An ode on the happy marriage of... Philip David Kræuter, 1749. *See* O47.

B., L., *W.* A new song to the honourable Miss C——t, 1726. *See* N216.

B., M. An elegy on the universally lamented death of the right honourable Robert lord vis. Molesworth, [1725.] *See* E192.

— The ladies answer, [1703.] *See* L8.

— To the citizens, 1724. *See* T362.

— The widows address, 1725. *See* Barber, Mary.

B., M., *gent.* An elegy upon his late majesty James II, 1701. *See* E160.

B., N. The royal conqueress, 1704. *See* R306.

B., R. An answer to the Mock mourners, 1702. *See* A252.

— The duty of a husband, 1707. *See* D563.

— The Hell-fire-club, 1721. *See* H136.

— The vanity of the life of man, 1708–. *See* Crouch, Nathaniel.

— Wedlock vindicated, 1702. *See* W268.

— Youth's divine pastime, [1710?]–. *See* Crouch, Nathaniel.

B————, S————. A city intrigue, 1714. *See* C205.

B., S. Mons Alexander, [1731/32.] *See* M405.

B———, T——. Poems and odes, after the manner of Anacreon, 1746. *See* Brecknock, Timothy.

B., T., *a rum duke.* A new song upon a new subject, [1736.] *See* N225.

B., T., *e C.C.C. Oxon. discipulo.* Lusus poetici, 1720. *See* Bisse, Thomas.

B., T., *fellow of the Sisyphian society of weavers.* The black-bird, 1741. *See* Collier, John.

B., T., *gent.* Miscellany poems on several subjects, 1702. *See* Miscellany.

— A poem on the drawing room, 1716. *See* P611.

B., T., *minister of the gospel.* The vagabond tories, [1714/15?] *See* V6.

B., W. An epistle of his grace the Duke of Grafton, 1736. *See* E399.

— The Lamentations of Jeremiah, 1708. *See* Brown, William.

— Laugh upon laugh, 1740. *See* Brownsword, William.

B., W., *gent.* Impiety and superstition expos'd, 1710. *See* Brown, William.

B1 **Babel.** Babel inspected. *Glasgow*, 1749. 12°.
GM(missing 1967).

Baboon

B2 Baboon. The baboon a-la-mode. A satyr against the French. By a gentleman. *London, printed for, and sold by S. Malthus*, 1704 [1705]. (25 Jan, Luttrell)

4°: *A*² B–F²; *i–ii*, 1–22. 22 advt.

Listed in *WL* Jan.

'Speak thou sweet solace of my vacant hours'

L(164.1.66, Luttrell),O,DG.

Bacchanalia. Bacchanalia: or, a description of a drunken-club, 1746. *See* Darby, Charles.

Bacchanalians. The Bacchanalians: or, a midnight modern conversation, 1733. *See* Bancks, John.

B3 Bachelor. The batchelor's choice, or, the happy wish. A poem. *London printed, and sold by J. Morphew*, 1707.

4°: *A*² B–E²; *i–ii*, 1–18.

'Assist me heav'n, direct me in my choice'

Pickering & Chatto cat. 256/644, 'on the last page is written "Moses Brown London"; this is probably the poet'. But Moses Browne the poet was born in 1704, so this can only be a sign of subsequent ownership.

ICU.

B4 — The bachelor's dream. *Dublin, printed in the year* 1725.

½°: 1 side, 2 columns.

The lower half of the sheet contains 'The maiden-dream', which was also printed separately.

'When in sweet slumbers on my bed I lay'

Maiden-dream: 'One night extended on my downy bed'

Two erotic dreams.

L(C.121.g.8/61).

B5 Bachelors. The batchelors and maids answer to the Fifteen comforts of matrimony. Being real encouragements for all single people to marry... *London printed, and sold by Henry Hills*, [1706?]

8°: *A*⁴; *1* 2–8. 8 advt for patent medicine.

Date suggested by *The fifteen comforts of matrimony*, 1706.

'But why shou'd marriage render man undone?'

CLU-C.

Backgammon. Back-gammon: or, the battle of the friars, 1734. *See* Bellamy, Daniel, *the elder*.

B6 [Bacon, Phanuel.] The kite. An heroi-comical poem. In three canto's. *Oxford, printed by L. Lichfield*, 1722. (18 Dec?)

8°: π⁴ A–D⁴ (π2 as '*₊*'); *i–viii*, 1–31 *32 blk*.

Bond 69. Apparently all copies are printed on large paper, probably royal, but the Strasburg bend watermark seen at L, CLU-C has not been found in all copies. A copy at O bears the receipt of Walter Wyatt, distributor of stamps for the county of Oxford, for 5s. pamphlet

Bacon, P. The kite

duty under the stamp acts; it records the payment by Bacon, 18 Dec 1722.

'Dian knew well to chace the tim'rous hare'

Bacon's authorship is confirmed by the receipt mentioned above.

L(11631.c.28),LG,O(2),*DrU*,LdU-B; CLU-C, MH(uncut),OCU,TxU(lacks π2–4).

B7 [—] — *London, printed for J. Walthoe*, 1729. (*SR* 18 July)

4°: *A*² B–C⁴ D²; *1–4* 5–24.

Printed by Samuel Richardson (*Sale* 71). Deposit copies at O,SaU; listed in *MChr* 19 July.

L(163.1.72;C.70.f.1/1),O,E,LdU-B,SaU;CSmH (uncut),CtY,IU,MH,NjP + .

B8 Baffled. The baffled hero: an heroic poem, in three books, on a memorable engagement. Humbly inscribed to his excellency Sir John Cope... *London, printed for J. Collier*, 1746 [1745]. (*GA* 4 Nov)

4°: *A*² B–H²; *1–3* 4–32.

Bond 189. Vertical chain-lines.

'Let others sing how Dettingen records'

A burlesque. Cope was routed at the battle of Prestonpans, 21 Sept 1745.

L(11630.c.1/15; 11630.c.13/17); IU.

Bagpipes. Bag-pipes no musick, [1720?] *See* 'Couper, John'.

Baker, Daniel.

There is a ms. collection of Baker's poems at L (Add. MS. 11723).

B9 — The history of Job: a sacred poem. In five books. *London, printed for Robert Clavel*, 1706. (*TC* Easter)

8°: A–S⁴; *i–viii*, 1–135 *136*. 136 advt.

'You that at ev'ry trifling cross repine'

L(11631.bb.3),LDW,O,AdU,NwP; CU,NjP.

Baker, Henry. Original poems, serious and humorous. *London, printed for the author; sold by J. Roberts*, 1725. (*MC* Feb)

8°: pp. xiv, 87.   L,O; CtY,MH.

— [fine paper] *London, printed for the author*, 1725.   L,O; CtY,IU.

Watermark: Strasburg bend.

— The second part of original poems. *London, printed for the author; sold by J. Parker, T. Wotton, & T. Worral, R. Franklin, J. Brotherton, & J. Roberts*, 1726. (*MC* Feb)

8°: pp. 103.   O; CSmH,MH.

— [fine paper] *London, printed for the author*, 1726.   LdU,LdU-B; CtY.

Watermark: Strasburg bend.

— Medulla poetarum Romanorum: or, the most beautiful and instructive passages of the Roman poets... With translations of the same in English verse. By Mr. Henry Baker. *London, printed for*

Baker, H.

D. *Midwinter, A. Bettesworth & C. Hitch, J. & J. Pemberton, R. Ware [and others], 1737.*
8°: 2 vol.   L,O; MH.

The translations are mainly selected from other authors, sometimes revised by Baker.

B10 — An invocation of health. A poem. *London, printed for the author; sold by J. Parker, J. Woodman, A. Dodd, & S. Nut, 1723. (DP 19 Feb)*
2°: *A² B²; 1–2 4–8.*

Entered to Henry Baker in *SR* 1 March; deposit copies at L,E,SaU.

'Health! good supreme! offspring of heaven! divine'
L(643.m.13/19),C,E,SaU; CtY,CtY-M,TxU(2).

[—] The labyrinth, a tale, 1734. *See* L3.

B11 — The universe. A poem. Intended to restrain the pride of man. *London, printed for T. Worrall,* [1734.] *(GM April)*
8°: *A–G⁴; 1–5 6–8, 1 2–40 41–48.* A1 frt; G1–4 advt.

'300 Universe, a poem, with the whole of the copy' formed lot 59 of the trade sale of Thomas Worrall, 10 Nov 1737 (cat. at O-JJ), sold to Gosling for £4; presumably the copyright was subsequently repurchased by his brother John.

'Thy works, eternal power by whom she sings!'
L(T.197/2, – G⁴),O(– G⁴),CT(lacks A⁴, – G⁴),E, LdU-B+; CLU,*CtY*,IEN(– G⁴),IU,MH(uncut) +.

B12 — — A philosophical poem...The second edition. *London, printed for J. Worrall,* [1746.] *(GA 4 Aug)*
8°: *A–F⁴; 1–5 6–8, 1 2–40.* A1 frt.
L(11631.e.2),O(2, 1–A1),OW,CT; CtY,TxU.

B13 — — The third edition. *London, printed for J. Worrall,* [1746/–.]
8°: *A⁴ B–F⁴; 1–5 6–8, 1 2–40.* A1 frt.

No date has been assigned to this edition; it may well be later than 1750, but it may also be related to the Dublin third edition of 1749.
L(11643.bbb.13/3),E; ICN,*MiU*,MH.

B14 — — The third edition. *Dublin, printed by R. James, 1749.*
12°: *A⁶ B–C⁶; 1–3 4–36.*
DN.

B15 'Baker, *Sir* James.' Horace, epod. IV. imitated, by Sir James Baker, kt. to Lord Cad––––n. [*London?* 1717?]
slip: 1 side, 1 column.

Printed with *An excellent new ballad* ['Of all the days in the year'], [1717?]; the O,IU copies are not divided.

'As tender lambs with wolves agree'
Crum A1673. Tentatively attributed to Gay by *Faber* xxxi, 638; the pseudonym seems to have been used by Pope (*Twickenham Pope*, VI,

'**Baker,** *Sir* **J.**' Horace, epod. IV.

136 n.) though there may have been a real James Baker. A satire on William Cadogan, earl Cadogan.
O; IU.

B16 — [another edition, title reads:] Horace...imitated. By...to Lord Cad------n.
O.

[**Baker, Thomas.**] Miscellany poems on several subjects...By T. B. gent, 1702. *See* Miscellany.

[—] A long vacation prologue. Writ by Mr. B---k--r, 1708. *See* L246.

[—] A poem on the drawing room: together with three epilogues, 1716. *See* P611.

'**Baker, Thomas.**' A new song, warbled out of the oracular oven of Tho. Baker, [1714.] *See* N228.

B17 **Balguy, John.** The fast-day. A poem. *London, printed for J. & H. Pemberton; sold by J. Roberts, 1741. (DP 2 Feb)*
2°: *A² B²; 1–2 3–8.*
'O thou, truth's fairest off-spring! Heav'nly bred!'
O; CU,CtY,ICN,*PHi*,TxU.

B18 — — The third edition, corrected and enlarged. *London, printed for J. & H. Pemberton; sold by J. Roberts, 1741.*
4°: *A⁴ B⁴; 1–4 5–15 16 blk.* A1 hft.

No second edition traced.
E; NjP.

B19 **Ball.** The ball; or, un passo tempo: a poem. Displaying the vices, follies, extravagances, amours, and intrigues of our modern gentry... Particularly the ridotto-ladies, at the Opera-theatre. *London, printed for A. Dodd, 1723. (MC March)*
2°: *A² B²; 1–2 3–8.*
'In modern days it is become no crime'

Attributed to Edward Ward by *Wrenn*, which is usually unreliable; *Troyer* 278 admits a similarity of style but finds no evidence to support the attribution.
TxU(2).

B20 — The ball. Stated in a dialogue betwixt a prude and a coquet, last masquerade night, the 12th of May. *London, printed for J. Roberts, 1724. (MC June)*
2°: *A¹ B–C²; i–ii, 1 2–8.*

Reissued in *A collection of original poems,* 1724 (*Case* 329).

'O Jesu!–Coz!– why this fantastick dress?'
T. J. Wise in *Ashley Catalogue* IX, 80 says it was 'credited to Gay by Mr. George Aitken ... However there is...no direct evidence to support the attribution. The dialogue may quite well have been Arbuthnot's.' Rejected by *Faber* xxxiii.
L(11661.dd.10; Ashley 4839); CtY,MH(Luttrell, June),TxU.

Ballad

B21 Ballad. A ballad by J-----n B-----s. [*Edinburgh?* 1729.] (14 May)
½°: 1 side, 1 column.
 Stanzas 1–8. Date from ms. note in a copy at E.
'When W——on cants, and L——g bauls'
 Ms. notes in copies at L and E expand the name in the title to 'John Brigs', but it is not clear if he is the true author; possibly the Edinburgh publisher of that name is intended, but cf. D397. A satire on the suspension of John Simson by the general assembly of the Church of Scotland. Cf. *An answer to John Brigs's ballads*, [1729.]
L(Rox.III.736),E(2).

B22 — [part 2] J------n B-------s's ballad continued. [*Edinburgh?* 1729.] (23 May)
½°: 1 side, 1 column.
 Stanzas 9–16. 'More a-coming yet' at foot. Date from ms. note in a copy at E.
'Do ye appear in any page'
L(Rox.III.428),E(2).

B23 — A ballad in honour of the present regency. [*London?* 1719.]
slip: 1 side, 1 column.
 In this edition, over-run lines are preceded by a square bracket.
'Tho' great George be gone o'er, yet to shew his love to us'
 On the regency set up in May 1719. Very similar in format to Jacobite propaganda of this period.
MH.

B24 — — [another edition]
 Over-run lines are preceded by a parenthesis.
L(MS Landsdowne 852, fol. 282); CSmH.

B25 — Balad [!] made on the present election. In the behalf of Squire H-----d. Tune of, You commons and peers, &c. [*Dublin,* 1727.]
½°: 1 side, 1 column.
 'Balad' in title printed from five woodcut initials, the fourth being a V reversed.
'Freemen far and near, I pray you come here'
 In favour of William Howard.
DT.

B26 — A ballad: occasion'd by some ladies wearing ruffs at court on the anniversary of his m——y's birth-day, the 29th of May, 1727. *London, printed for A. Moore; sold by the booksellers of London & Westminster,* 1727. (*MC* June)
2°: A² < B¹; *i–ii*, *1* 2–4.
 Percival appendix 4.
'Ye lords and ladies of this isle'
 The ladies are identified in a ms. note in the LdU-B copy as 'Lady Denbigh, Lady Dudley, and Mrs. Berkley'; there is a *double-entendre* on pubic hair.
O(2),OW(2),LdU-B; CLU-C,CtY,InU(Luttrell, July)MH,NjP+.

A ballad: occasion'd by

B27 — [*idem*] The courtiers new ruff and the ladies in buff, a new ballad. Occasion'd by some ladies wearing ruffs at court on the anniversary of his M----y's birth-day, the 29th of May, 1727. *London, printed by William Fowler, in Fleet Street,* [1727.]
½°: 1 side, 2 columns.
NjP.

B28 — [*idem*] A new ballad on the ladies wearing ruffs in the drawing-room at St. James's. *Dublin, printed in the year* 1735.
½°: 1 side, 2 columns.
 An earlier Dublin edition was advertised in a Dublin edition of Savage's *The bastard*, 1728.
NN.

— The ballad of the cloak: or, the cloak's knavery, [172–?] *See* The cloak's knavery, [1718–.]

B29 — A ballad on Lord Pelham's birth-day, July 24, 1714. To the tune of, London is a fine town, &c. [*London?*] *Printed in the year* 1714.
½°: 2 sides, 1 column.
'Come bring the liquor hither'
 On the coming of age of Thomas Pelham-Holles, subsequently duke of Newcastle.
O-JJ, Crawford.

— A ballad on the battle of the two dukes, [1720?] *See* Duke upon duke, 1720–.

B30 — A ballad on the Junto. To the tune of Lilly bullero. [*London,* 1710?]
½°: 1 side, 1 column.
'Now Britains mourn,/Your liberty's torn'
 A tory attack on the Junto and the Duke and Duchess of Marlborough.
O-JJ, Rothschild.

B31 — — [another edition]
 The second line reads 'Your liberty torn'.
InU.

B32 — A ballad on the most renowned Shuff of Newbury... To the tune of Chevy Chase. *London, printed in the year* 1707.
½°: 1 side, 2 columns.
 Two woodcuts in title.
'In bloody town of Newbury'
 Crum I11250, dated 1664. Ostensibly a popular ballad, but a witty work on Shuff who died of eating custard for a wager.
L(1876.f.1/39).

B33 — A ballad on the taking of Bergen-op-zoom. *London, printed for M. Cooper,* 1747. (*SR* 16 Oct)
2°: A² B¹; *1–2* 3–6.
 Deposit copy at L. Listed in *GM* Oct.
'Han't you heard of a fortress, renowned in fame'
L(643.m.14/21); NN.

B34 — The ballad, or some scurrilous reflections in verse, on the proceedings of the honourable house of commons: answered stanza by stanza. With the Memorial, alias Legion, reply'd to paragraph by

The **ballad**, or some scurrilous reflections

paragraph. *London, printed by D. Edwards; sold by the booksellers of London & Westminster, 1701.* (*LP* 27 June)

8⁰: π² A–E⁴; *i–iv, 1–38 39–40 blk.*

A reprint of *Ye true-born Englishmen*, [1701] with a verse answer. There are various impressions and probably various mixtures of the resulting sheets. The following groups of copies have each similar peculiarities in the use of italic parentheses round the page numbers:

(3) (4) (6) LU,O(2),LdU-B; TxU.
(3) (4) (6) L(523.a.49/4),LU,O; CLU-C, CSmH.
(3) (4) (6) C; MH.
(3) *(9)* O.
(3) *(9)* L(1077.c.53),DT; MB,TxU.

Ballad: 'Ye true-born Englishmen proceed'
Answer: 'Ye slaves who make it your pretence'
Williams 1073 records Ball's suggestion that the answer was written by Swift and Charles Davenant. The imprint is the same as Pittis's *Chaucer's whims* of July 1701; he seems a more likely author.

L(1077.c.53, –E4; 523.a.49/4),LU(2, 1–E4), O(4, 1 uncut),C,DT+; CLU-C,CSmH,MB,MH, TxU(2, 1 uncut, 1–E4)+.

B35 —— The 4th edition. *London, printed by D. Edwards; sold by the booksellers of London & Westminster, 1701.*

8⁰: π² A–E⁴; *i–iv, 1–38 39–40 blk.*

A reimpression.

C(uncut),CT,EN,EtC; MB,NjP.

B36 —— *London printed, and sold by the booksellers of London & Westminster, 1701.*

8⁰: A–B⁴; *1–2 3–16;* pp. 2–7 in 2 columns.

A piracy.

AdU; IU,TxU.

B37 —— The ballad...answered and confuted; as also the Legion, alias Memorial. Particularly reply'd to. *London, printed for John Wells; sold by the booksellers of London & Westminster, 1701.*

8⁰: A⁴; *1 2–8.*

Replies only, without the originals. Reprinted in *The memorial, alias Legion, answered... with a reply to the scurrilous reflections in verse;* since this puts the prose first, editions are excluded from this catalogue.

TxU.

B38 —— A ballad sung by the English grenadiers in their camp on the Rhine. To the tune of, The cuckoo. [*London, 1743.*]

½⁰: 1 side, 1 column.

'When British horse, but chiefly blue'
Crum W925: 'On the battle of Dettingen'. On the alleged cowardice of Ilton, the Hanoverian general who commanded the Horseguards at Dettingen.

OCU.

A **ballad**. To the tune

B39 —— A ballad. To the tune of Chevy Chase. *London, printed for H. Carpenter, 1749.* (*BM* Nov; *GM* Dec)

2⁰: A²<B¹; *1–2 3–6.*

'God prosper long our patriot cause'
A satire on George Bubb Dodington and James Ralph.

L(C.57.g.7/26, Horace Walpole's ms. notes); CSmH,DFo,DLC.

B40 —— A ballad. To the tune of, On the fourteenth of August. *London, printed for J. Millan, 1741.* (*LDP* 15 Jan)

2⁰: A⁴; *1–4 5–8.* A1 hft.

'While your comrades abroad/Are plowing the main'
A recruiting ballad for the navy.

L(1484.m.25); CtY.

B41 —— A ballad, upon a gentleman's sitting upon the Lady W-----'s Cremona fiddle. To the tune of King John, and the abbot of Canterbury. *London printed, and sold by J. Roberts, 1720.* (*DC* 19 Jan)

2⁰: A²<B¹; *i–ii, 1–3 4 blk.*

'Ye lads and ye lasses that live at Longleat'
An accident at Longleat to Lady Weymouth's fiddle.

L(11602.i.6/8, lacks A1); OCU,MH,TxU.

B42 —— A ballad, wrote in the time of Queen Elizabeth, on occasion of a duel fought between two peers, in the reign of King Edward III. *London, printed for A. Moore,* [1723.] (*MC* April)

½⁰: 1 side, 2 columns.

Luttrell's copy, dated May, is recorded in *Haslewood.*

'God prosper long the commonweal'
A satire on a duel between Nicholas Lechmere, baron Lechmere and William Cadogan, earl Cadogan. Cf. *A fight and no fight,* [1723], and the new edition of *Duke upon duke, 1723.*

L(1876.f.1/103); DFo.

B43 Ballard, John. Honour. A poem. Humbly inscrib'd to, and friendly recommended by the rev. Dr. Swift, D.S.P.D. *Dublin, printed by Sam. Dalton, 1739.*

8⁰: A⁴ B–C⁴; *1–2 3–21 22–23; 24 blk.* 23 advt.

Advertisement on p. 23 for a subscription edition of *Orbis in urbe,* an anthology with the addition of the compiler's poetical works and a tragedy *The royal sin.*

'Not all the threats or favours of a crown'
Apparently the same work as Charles Montagu, earl of Halifax's *The man of honour,* 1690–. A note on p. 22 records that Swift corrected this poem, but the whole publication appears to be fraudulent.

DA; CLU-C.

B44 Bally, George. The loves of Hero and Leander. Translated from the Greek of Musæus. *London, printed for, and sold by, T. Osborne, M. Nutt, M.*

Bally, G. The loves of Hero and Leander

Cooper, J. Robinson, G. Woodfall, H. Chapelle, and at the pamphlet shops in the court of requests, 1747. (GM, LM Jan)
4°: a⁴ B–D⁴ E¹; [2] i–vi, 1–26.
'Sing, muse, the lamp that shed its conscious light'
L(11630.e.1/14; 161.m.75); ICN,*MH*,NjP.

B45 — Solomon de mundi vanitate, liber secundus... poema Matthæi Prior latine traductum...cui adjicitur Alexandri convivium, Drydeni... lingua eadem donata a Georgio Bally. *Cantabrigiæ, typis academicis excudebat J. Bentham. Veneunt apud J. et R. Tonson, P. Vaillant, et R. Dodsley, Londini; Corn. et J. Crownfield, et Gul. Thurlbourn Cantabrigiæ; J. Fletcher Oxonii, et J. Pote Etonæ*, 1743. (GM Aug)
4°: ᵖA⁴ B², A–P⁴; i–xii, 1–5 6–119 120 blk. vii err.
Rothschild 1688. List of subscribers, pp. ix–xii.
'Sollicitos age falle dies vitæque labores'
L(11626.g.11; 79.d.8),O,C,CT,*MR*(2); CLU-C,CtY,KU,NjP.

Ballyspellin. Ballyspellin, [1728.] *See* Sheridan, Thomas.

B46 Balsam. A balsom for backsliders, or some hints anent the oath of abjuration. [*Edinburgh, 1712?*]
½°: 1 side, 2 columns.
'Although the news be spread of late'
Encouraging presbyterians to accept the oath of abjuration, and against the Pretender.
E.

B47 Bambridge. Bambridge and H--g---n's petition, to a certain great knight. [*London*] *Printed for J. Thompson*, [1729/–.]
½°: 1 side, 2 columns.
'Good Sir R——t serene'
An act was passed in 1729 disabling Thomas Bambridge from continuing in his post as warden of the Fleet prison; John Huggins was the former warden. The petition is doubtless to Walpole.
Harding.

Bancks, John. The weavers miscellany: or, poems on several subjects. By John Bancks, now a poor weaver in Spittle-fields. *London printed, and sold by the author at John Knotts at the Queen's-Arms in Dorset-street Spittle-Fields; S. Hester of White-Fryars-Gate; and by the book-sellers and pamphlet-sellers of London, & Westminster*, 1730. (MChr Dec)
8°: pp. 24.   L,O; CtY,MH.
The L copy has a ms. note and corrections by the author.

— Poems on several occasions: consisting of tales, epistles, songs, odes, epigrams... None of them ever before printed. *London, printed for the author*, [1733.] (GSJ 10 May)
12°: pp. 184.   L,O; CtY.

Bancks, J. *Collections*

— Miscellaneous works in verse and prose... *London, printed by T. Aris, for the author; sold by C. Corbett, J. Brindley, Mess. Gilliver & Clarke, J. James, Mess. Ward & Chandler, and at their shops in Coney-street, York, and at Scarborough Spaw*, 1738. (LM Nov)
8°: 2 vol.   L,O; CtY.
There are *Proposals* dated 17 Sept 1737 at L. In a trade sale of C. Corbett, 23 Feb 1738 (cat. at O-JJ), lot 56 is 'Bancks's Poems, 2 vols. now printing, C. C. has advanced on this work fifty-two pounds ten shillings', sold to Cooper for £42.

— [reissue] The second edition, corrected. *London, printed for James Hodges*, 1739.
8°: 2 vol.   O; IU, NjP.
Cancel title to each volume.

[—] [reissue] Miscellaneous works, in verse and prose, of Mr. William Cartaret... *London, printed for the author*, 1748.
8°: 2 vol.   Forster.
Cancel title to vol. I; no title to vol. II. The copy seen is in a contemporary binding, labelled 'Cartaret's Works'. Pp. 147–150, 215–218, 265–274 of vol. I have been cancelled.

———

B48 [—] 'The Bacchanalians: or, a midnight modern conversation. A poem. Address'd to the ingenious Mr. Hogarth. Describing each particular gentleman which he has introduc'd in that merry conversation piece, lately publish'd by him. To which is prefix'd, a frontispiece, fit to be fram'd, neatly engrav'd, from his original. [*London*] *Sold by Mr. Jolliff, Mrs. Nutt, Mrs. Dodd, & Mr. Dickenson.* Price 6d.' (DJ 13 March 1733, 'this day at 10 o'clock')
The advertisement suggests a normal pamphlet edition, though Bancks in a note to his 1738 reprint (see below) records that he wrote the poem at the request of a friend who was copying Hogarth's plate. 'This piece, as it now stands (except a very few alterations and additions) was publish'd entire under the said copy: but was afterwards mangled by other print-sellers, and even by the same, to put under several copies of different sizes, where scraps of it were sometimes inserted among verses by other hands.' Possibly there were both engraved and letterpress editions. Probably the edition to which Bancks refers is that by R. Sayer (L, P&D 2124), where the verses are engraved on a separate plate printed below the picture. Another larger version by John Bowles (L, P&D 2126) has a modified text.
'Sacred to thee, permit this lay'
Reprinted, with a small engraving, in Bancks's *Miscellaneous works* (1738) I. 87.

B49 [—] 'The game of put: a tale. [*London.*] Price 6d.' (GM April 1737)

Bancks, J. The game of put

Probably the poem with this title collected in Bancks's *Miscellaneous works* (1738) I. 293, with first line:
'Dick serv'd a widow of no mean esteem'

B50 [—] 'Nature will prevail: an apology for a darling passion, in an epistle to a friend; with explanatory notes. [*London*] *Printed for T. Cooper.* Price 6d.' (*GM, LM* May 1736)
Listed in *LM* under 'poetry, plays, novels &c.' The similarity of their titles makes it probable that this is an earlier version of Bancks's *Love atones for little crimes*, 1738.

B51 [—] [*idem*] Love atones for little crimes: an ethic epistle, by way of apology for a darling passion. Cum notis variorum. *London, printed for J. Torbuck; sold by the booksellers & pamphlet-shops*, 1738. (*GM, LM* Jan)
4°: *A*² B–D²; *1–2* 3–15 *16 blk.*
''Tis true, I said in amorous rhymes'
Reprinted in Bancks's *Miscellaneous works* (1738) I. 202.
L(11630.c.13/22).

B52 [—] 'The royal guardian. A poem. [*London*] *Printed for B. Dickinson.* Price 6d.' (*DP* 23 June 1732, 'This day at ten')
'If virtue ever were the poets' care'
Reprinted in Bancks's *Miscellaneous works* (1738) II. 147. In praise of Queen Caroline's regency after George II's departure for Hanover.

B53 Band. The band. Inscrib'd to the gentlemen of the long robe. [*Dublin*] '*Printed by A. Moore*', 1731.
½°: 1 side, 1 column.
A. Moore is normally a London imprint (though a false one), but the subject matter and provenance of copies is Dublin.
'Ye sages that would have both law and good conscience'
On the re-introduction to Ireland of the fashion of lawyers wearing bands, by John Bowes, solicitor-general. Cf. *An answer to the band-ballad*, [1731.]
L(C.121.g.8/188),C.

B54 Bang. Bang the brocker, or Bully Pierce alias A-----n the turncoat. A new song. [*Edinburgh*, 1705.]
½°: 1 side, 2 columns.
Engraved plate of music above text, titled 'Bang the broker'.
'When Pierce Renegado came first to the town'
The copy at E has a nineteenth century ms. attribution to William Forbes. It is certainly related to his attacks upon Pierce, alias Allan.
L(1871.f.3/17, cropt),E.

B55 Banished. The banish'd beauty: or, a fair face in disgrace, a poem. *London, printed for A. Moore; sold by the booksellers of London & Westminster*, 1729. (*DJ* 4 March)

The **banish'd** beauty

2°: *A*² B²; *1–2* 3–8.
Printed on a mixed stock of paper. Listed in *DJ* 4 March as printed for A. Moore; in *MChr* 4 March as printed for J. Roberts.
'Let jarring realms, and Europe's doubtful state' Catalogued as by Gay in T. J. Wise, *Ashley Library* II. 142, but doubted by *Faber*. Verses in *DJ* 7 March 'On reading a poem call'd, The banish'd beauty' begin 'G—y bids a banish'd beauty brighter shine...', but the poem does not read as though Gay were the author. On the Duchess of Queensberry's banishment from court.
L(Ashley 4840),LdU-B; CSmH,ICN,MH.

B56 — [reimpression] *London printed, and sold by T. Read, and by the booksellers of London & Westminster*, 1729. (*DJ* 5 March)
2°: *A*² B²; *1–2* 3–8.
Printed on a mixed stock of paper. Listed in *DJ* 5 March as printed for T. Read.
L(1489.d.21); MH,TxU(2).

B57 — [reimpression] The second edition. *London printed, and sold by T. Read, and by the booksellers of London & Westminster*, 1729.
2°: *A*² B²; *1–2* 3–8.
One copy at OW apparently has sheet B from the preceding impression.
O,OW(2); CtY,MH.

B58 — [reimpression] The third edition. *London printed, and sold by T. Read, and by the booksellers of London & Westminster*, 1729. (*DJ* 14 March)
2°: *A*² B²; *1–2* 3–8.
Advertised in *DJ* as 'with alterations and additions occasioned by some lines inserted in the Daily Journal of Friday March 7'. With a textual change in p. 7, line 17, and the addition of eight lines 'occasioned by reading some verses printed in the Daily-Journal...' on p. 8.
O; OCU(uncut),MH.

B59 — The banish'd beauty... To the D------ss of Q--------. [*Dublin*] *Printed by Rich. Dickson*, [1729.] (*Silver Court gazette*, 20 March)
½°: 1 side, 2 columns.
Advertised as 'The third edition, with alterations and additions, occasion'd by some lines inserted in the Daily-Journal, of Friday March 7... Written by Mr. Gay' in the *Silver Court gazette*, following the London *DJ* advertisement of 14 March.
C(cropt),DT; CSmH(cropt).

B60 Bank. The bank thrown down. To an excellent new tune. *Dublin, printed by John Harding*, [1721.] (Dec?)
½°: 1 side, 1 column.
Rothschild 2069; *Teerink* 630; *Williams* 286.
'Pray, what is this bank of which the town rings?'
Attributed to Swift by *Ball* 164, and accepted in *Williams* 'with some hesitation, as probably

The **bank** thrown down

    authentic'. On the rejection of a scheme for a national bank.
    L(C.121.g.8/93,cropt),C,DG(cropt),DT; CtY.

B61 —— *Dublin, reprinted in Mountrath-street, 1721.*
    ½°: 1 side, 1 column.
      Teerink 630A.
    DN.

[**Banks, John.**] The prologue and epilogue to the last new play of the Albions queens, 1704. *See* P1121.

[**Bannatyne, George.**] The resurrection: a poem, 1747. *See* D414.

B62 **Ban——ry.** Ban——ry grumblers. [*London?* 1710?]
    ½°: 1 side, 2 columns.
    'To our mayor 'twas bruited'
      On Sacheverell's visit to Banbury.
    Harding.

B63 **Barbarous.** The barbarous and bloody murder of Mr. E——re of T. C. who in a poetick rapture lept out of his garret window and unfortunately broke his neck. [*Dublin, 172–?*]
    ½°: 1 side, 2 columns.
    'Alas! how fragil and uncertain'
      A satire on Mr. Eyre, a Trinity College poetaster; possibly the Henry Eyre who entered in 1725.
    Rothschild.

Barbarus. Barbarus exclusit tumulo me Nassus avito, [1712?/13.] *See* Pitcairne, Archibald, P377.

B64 **Barber.** The barber and fireworks. A tale. *London, printed for J. Davis, near St. Paul's, and may be had at the Royal Exchange; and of all the booksellers in Oxford,* [1749.]
    4°: A² B²; 1–2 3–7 8 blk.
      An 'advertisement' on the title refers to a 'curious print', not identified.
    'Ambition fires the meanest breast'
      On a barber (apparently Laury Horner) who planned an abortive firework display in Oxford for the thanksgiving day. Replied to by *An address to the worshipful company of barbers,* 1749.
    O; NjP.

B65 —— The barber turn'd packer. A new ballad. To the tune of Packington's pound. *London, printed for A. Moore; sold at the pamphlet shops of London & Westminster, 1730.* (*MChr* 8 Jan)
    2°: A² < B¹; 1–2 3–5 6 blk.
      Percival XII.
    'No writer of scandal doth Caleb excell'
      Percival (p. li) suggests John, lord Hervey was the author, but there is no external evidence for this. An attack on John Barber for packing

The **barber** turn'd packer

    the jury which acquitted Richard Francklin in Nov 1729 for publishing a libel in *The Craftsman* no. 140.
    O; MH.

B66 —— *London, printed for A. Moor,* [1730.]
    ½°: 1–2, 1 column.
    L(1876.f.1/115); MH.

B67 [**Barber, Constantine.**] To the right honourable the Lady Elizabeth Boyle, daughter to the right honourable John earl of Orrery, on her birth-day, May the 7th, 1733. *Dublin, printed by George Faulkner, 1733.*
    4°: A²; 1–3 4.
    'May each new year some new perfection give'
      Printed as Constantine Barber's in Mary Barber's *Poems,* 1734.
    DA.

Barber, James. The poetical works of the reverend Mr. James Barber. *London, printed for J. Torbuck, 1739.*
    8°: 3 pt.   L; IU,MH.
      Reissues of *The farmer's daughter, The law suit,* and *Tom K---g's.*

    —— The second edition. *London, printed for J. Torbuck, J. Hodges, & F. Noble, 1740.* (*GM, LM* Oct)
    12°: pp. 90.   O.

———————

B68 [—] The farmer's daughter: or, the art of getting preferment... To which is added, the female skirmish: or, the tripple plea. *London, printed for J. Torbuck, & W. Smith,* [1738.] (*GM, LM* Jan)
    8°: (frt +) π² B–G⁴ (frt 2 before F3); i–iv, 1–47 48. π1 hft; 48 advt.
      'The female skirmish' occupies pp. 37–47, and has a separate frontispiece. Reissued in Barber's *Poetical works,* 1739.
    'Thee sacred prophet I invoke'
    Female skirmish: 'Three buxom dames, of portly size'
      A modern ms. note in the copy at YM reads 'The scene of this satire is laid at Bishopsthorpe nr. York, and it is not improbable that the archbishop mentioned is Lancelot Blackburne...'
    L(1077.k.11),O(lacks π², F3–G4),YM; CSmH, MH(— frt 2),NjP(lacks F3–G4).

B69 [—] The law suit: or the farmer and fisherman. A poem. In which is contained, the polite speech of the chairman of a bench of justices...and the various artifices made use of in the several courts ... *London, printed for G. Spavan; sold at the pamphlet shops of London & Westminster, 1738.* (*GM, LM* March)
    8°: A⁴ B–G⁴; i–viii, 1–46 47; 48 blk. A1 frt; G4 advt.

Barber, J. The law suit

'Since right and wrong, the stated case'
The 'second edition' was reissued in Barber's *Poetical works*, 1739.
O,C; CU,CtY,MH(2),NjP.

B70 [—] [reissue] The law suit or the farmer and fisherman. A poem in hudibrastick verse... The second edition corrected. *London, printed for G. Spavan*, 1739.
8°: $A^4(\pm A2)$ B–G^4; *i –viii,* 1–46 *47; 48 blk.* A1 frt; G4 advt.
Reissued in Barber's *Poetical works*, 1739.
L(992.k.23; 1077.k.11),EN; MH(–A1).

B71 [—] Tom K----g's: or, the Paphian grove. With the various humours of Covent Garden, the theatre, L---d M——ton's, &c. A mock-heroic-poem, in three cantos. *London, printed for J. Robinson; sold at the pamphlet-shops at the Royal-Exchange, Temple-Bar, and Charing-Cross,* 1738. (*GA* 10 Feb)
8°: A^1 B–I^4 (+3 plates); *i–ii,* 1 2–64.
Bond 166. Reissued in Barber's *Poetical works*, 1739.
'Kind Venus goddess of the Paphian grove'
L(11633.e.22); CtY.

B72 [—] [variant title, reads:] the theatre, the gaming-table, &c...
O; DFo,MH(–1 plate).

B73 [—] [reissue] The second edition. To which is added, a dedication to Mrs. K----g, and the author's apology... *London, printed for John Torbuck, J. Robinson, G. Spavan, and sold at the pamphlet shops...,* 1738.
8°: A^2 B–I^4 (+3 plates); *i–iv,* 1 2–64.
Title cancelled, replaced with new A^2 which includes the dedication.
L(1077.k.11,–2 plates); CLU-C,CU(–1 plate), DFo,ICN.

B74 [—] [reissue] *London, printed for P. Sambroke, under the Piazza's, Covent Garden,* 1741.
8°: A^2 B–I^4 (+3 plates); *i–iv,* 1 2–64.
No statement of edition on title. Another reissue with new A^2.
L(1465.e.28),O; InU.

Barber, Mary. Poems on several occasions. *London, printed for C. Rivington,* 1734 [1735?].
4°: pp. xlviii, 283.   L,O; CtY,MH.
Printed by Samuel Richardson (*Sale* 135). Entered to Mrs. Barber in *SR* 17 May 1735, transferred to C. Rivington 12 June 1735, and deposit of copies recorded there; they are to be seen at L,O,E. Presentation copy at CtY.

—— *London, printed for C. Rivington,* 1735.
8°: pp. lxiv, 290.   L; IU,NcD.
Printed by Samuel Richardson (*Sale* 165).

— [reissue] *London, printed for the author; sold by C. Rivington, J. Walthoe, J. Stagg, D. Browne, J.*

Barber, M.

Parkes, & T. Jackson, J. Brindley, & J. Leake, at Bath, 1736.
O; CtY,TxU.
Cancel title.

———————

B75 [—] [dh] Apollo's edict. [*Dublin,* 1725?]
4°: A^2; 1 2–4.
Teerink 904; *Williams* 269, 355. The copy at DT is bound with poems of 1725.
'Ireland is now our royal care'
Reprinted in Mary Barber's *Poems,* 1734. Sometimes attributed to Swift (as in *Williams*) but the evidence seems insufficient to overcome its inclusion in Mrs. Barber's poems; it may well have been revised by Swift. See O. W. Ferguson in *PMLA* 70 (1955) 433–40. Related in some way to Swift's 'Apollo to the dean' and Delany's *News from Parnassus,* 1721.
DT; ICN.

B76 [—] The prodigy: or, the silent woman. In a letter from a lady in town to a friend in the country. *Dublin, printed by E.S.* [*Elizabeth Sadleir*] *on the Blind-key,* [1726?]
$\frac{1}{2}$°: 1–2, 1 column.
The DT copy is bound with half-sheets of 1726.
'Tho' rhyme serves the thoughts of great poets to fetter'
Printed in Mary Barber's *Poems,* 1734.
DT; CSmH,CtY.

B77 [—] A tale being an addition to Mr. Gay's Fables. *Dublin, printed by S. Powell, for George Ewing,* 1728.
8°: A^4; *1–2* 3–7 *8.* 8 advt.
'A mother, who vast pleasure finds'
Printed in Mary Barber's *Poems,* 1734. An appeal for Queen Caroline to provide a pension for Gay; see E. L. Gay in *N&Q* 10 July 1915.
O,DN; CtY,MH.

B78 [—] To his excellency the Lord Carteret, occasion'd by seeing a poem intitul'd, The birth of manly virtue. [col] *Dublin, printed by S. Harding* 1725.
2°: A^2; *i–ii,* 1–2.
Teerink 1200.
'The picture strikes. – 'Tis drawn with wondrous art!'
Printed in Mary Barber's *Poems,* 1734. In praise of the poem usually ascribed to Swift, and of Carteret.
L(1890.e.5/100; C.121.g.8/71); CtY(lacks A1).

[—] To the citizens, 1724. *See* T362.

B79 [—] [dh] Verses occasion'd by seeing the captives, who were lately redeem'd by his majesty, from Barbary. [*London?* 1734/35.]
2°: A^2; 1 2–3 *4 blk.*
'A sight like this, who can unmov'd survey?'

Barber, M. Verses occasion'd

Printed in Mary Barber's *Poems*, dated 1734 but not published before May 1735. The captives arrived in London 11 Nov 1734.
OCU.

B80 [—] The widows address to the rt. hon. the Lady Carteret. By M.B. *Dublin, printed by C.C.* [*Cornelius Carter*], 1725.
½⁰: 1 side, 1 column.
Two poems, 'To the honble. Miss Carteret' and 'To the right honble. the Lady Carteret'.
'Fair innocence, the muses loveliest theme'
'Wearied with long attendance on the court'
Printed in Mary Barber's *Poems*, 1734.
L(C.121.g.8/72).

[**Barber, Rupert.**] An answre [!] to the Christmas-box. In defence of Docter [!] D——n—y. By R——t B——r, 1729. *See* A246.

B80·5 Barbon, —, *Dr*. Magna Britannia triumphans: or, the coronation of the high and mighty Anne, by the grace of god of England, Scotland, France and Ireland, queen, defender of the faith, &c. who was crowned at Westminster Abby, on Thursday the 23d of April, 1702. *London printed, and are to be sold by E. Mallet,* 1702. (24 April, Luttrell)
1⁰: 1 side, 3 columns.
Large woodcut at head. Towards the foot of the second column, 'The Te deum', a separate work.
'When glorious Anna's happy reign began'
Te deum: 'To thee, O lord, we chearful praises sing'
At the foot of the first poem, 'By Dr. Barbon'.
MH(Luttrell).

B81 [**Barford, Richard.**] Abelard to Eloisa. *London, printed by J. Bettenham; sold by T. Warner,* 1725. (*MC* Feb)
8⁰: *A*² B–D⁴ E²; *i–iv*, 1–26 27–28. E2 advt.
'Whilst in her cell sad Eloisa mourns'
A copy at ICU has an early ms. note 'By Mr. Bareford – now a parson'.
L(11631.d.1),O; CtY(−E2),ICU(2),MH,TxU.

B82 — The assembly. An heroi-comical poem. In five cantos. *London, printed for B. Lintot,* 1726. (*SR* 13 May)
8⁰: A–H⁴; *i–viii*, 1 2–54 55–56. A1 hft; H4 advt.
Bond 91. Deposit copies at L,LSC,O,E,EU, SaU; listed in *MC* May. The copyright was purchased by Lintot, 26 April 1726, for fifteen guineas (*Nichols* VIII. 293) and formed part of lot 50 in a trade sale attributed to Lintot, 27 Nov 1739 (cat. at O-JJ); it was repurchased by Lintot.
'Say, ye recording nine! blest maids that rove'
L(992.h.6/6),O,OW,E,SaU+; CSmH(−A1), CtY,*ICN*,MH,TxU+.

B83 — An epistle to the right honourable Philip Dormer, earl of Chesterfield. Occasion'd by the

Barford, R. An epistle

late and present situation of affairs in Europe... *London, printed for Lawton Gilliver,* 1730. (*SR* 15 April)
8⁰: A–C⁴; *1–3* 4–23 *24*. 24 advt.
Deposit copies at E,EU; listed in *MChr* April.
'While anxious Europe trembled with alarms'
L(E.2021/12),O(2),E,EU,WcC; CtY,MH.

B84 — A poem on Knolls-Hill in Essex, the seat of the honourable Sir Jonh [!] Fortescue Aland... *London, printed for R. Dodsley; sold by M. Cooper,* 1745 [1744]. (13 Nov)
2⁰: A¹ B–C² D¹; *1–3* 4–11 *12 blk*.
A1 and D1 have been seen to be conjugate. Date of publication from *Straus, Dodsley*; listed in *GM,LM* Nov.
'Deign, vocal sisters, ever-tuneful maids'
L(1489.m.5),O(2).

Barker, George. 'England's glory in the declaration of war. Compos'd by George Barker.' [1739.] *Percival* appendix 69, referring to Sir Charles Firth's *Naval songs* where it is printed 'from a broadside in the possession of the author' which cannot now be traced in the Firth collection at O. Possibly from an engraved song, with Barker as the composer rather than author.

[**Barker, Thomas.**] Miscellany poems on several subjects... By T. B. gent, 1702. *See* Miscellany.

Barkshire. *See* Berkshire.

B85 Barnard Castle. The Barnard-Castle tragedy, shewing how one John Atkinson... servant to Thomas Howson, miller, at Barnard-Castle Bridge End, courted the said Howson's sister; and... broke her heart... Tune of, Constant Anthony. [*Newcastle?*] *Printed for the author, in the year* 1718.
½⁰: 1 side, 2 columns.
A popular broadside, with two rough cuts above text. Subject and provenance suggest a northern printer.
'Young men and maidens all, I pray you now attend'
L(Rox.III.797).

Barnes, Joshua. Ἀνακρεων Χριστιανος. Anacreon Christianus, hoc est parodiæ duæ Anacreonticæ, & alia poemata, psalmi aliquot Davidici, omnia Anacreontis stylo & metro Græce & Latine, donata per Josuam Barnes. *Cantabrigiæ, recentioribus typis academicis,* 1705.
8⁰: pp. 35.   L,LVA-D.

B86 Barrett, M. & Rayner, William. An ode, humbly inscrib'd to his royal highness the Prince of Orange, on his landing to espouse the Princess Royal of England. *London, printed for W. Rayner; sold by A. Dodd, & J. Jolliffe,* 1733.
2⁰: 8 pp.

From the description it seems that the dedication is signed by the authors from the King's Bench prison.
(Pickering & Chatto cat. 192/783; also in their *An illustrated catalogue*, 5508.)

B87 Barrett, Stephen. The battle of the giants. A poem. To the Duke. By S. Barret, M.A. *London, printed by E. Cave; sold by M. Cooper*, 1746. (*GM,LM* July)
2°: A² < B²; *i–ii, 1* 2–6.
'Sing, muse, how rebel Titans rose'
A eulogy to the Duke of Cumberland on his campaign in Scotland.
L(1959); CtY.

B88 — Bucolica Alexandri Popii, (quatuor anni temporum inscripta titulis) latine reddita: interprete S. Barrett... *Londini, excudebat E. Cave, ibidemq; prostant, nec non apud R. & J. Tonson & S. Draper; R. Fletcher, & S. Parker, Oxon. & J. Thurlbourn, Cantab.*, 1746. (*GM,LM* April)
4°: A² B–M²; *i–iv, 1–3* 4–43 *44 blk.* iv err.
English and Latin text; engraving at head of each season (not printed in one copy at L).
Spring: 'Primus ego his arvis musam meditabar agrestem'
L(11630.f.44; 11630.c.5/10, cropt),O,C,*MR*; CLU-C,CSmH,IU,MH.

B89 [—] War, an epic satyr. Setting forth the nature of Fr--ch policy, and the true cause of the present commotions in Europe. In four canto's. *London, sold by S. Birt; T. Smith, in Canterbury; and S. Parker in Oxford*, 1747. (*GM,LM* March)
8°: A–L⁴ M¹; *i–ii* iii–ix *x, 3* 4–80 *81–82.* 81 err; 82 advt.
'War is my theme; celestial maids! retire'
For Barrett's authorship, see *GM* 71 (1801) 1152.
L(11657.c.84; T.1551/1, lacks A1); CtY(−M1).

B90 Bartholomew-fair. Bartholomew Fair: an heroicomical poem. *London printed, and sold by S. Baker*, 1717. (*PB* 27 Aug)
8°: A–E⁴; *i–viii, 1–29* '33' *31–32.* E4 advt.
'While busy mortals, with the worthless crowd'
L(1969, −E4); CLU-C,MH(−E4).

B91 — Bartholomew-fair: or, a ramble to Smithfield. A poem in imitation of Milton. *London, printed for J. Roberts*, 1729. (*MChr* 26 Aug)
2°: A¹ B²; *1–3* 4–6.
Bond 99.
'Scarce had the burning Phoebus roll'd his carr'
A letter to the publisher is signed 'J.B.'; it is doubtful whether it is by the author.
MH.

[**Barton, Richard.**] Farrago: or miscellanies in verse and prose. *London, printed in the year* 1739.
8°: pp. 181. L,O; CtY,MH.
Watermark: crowned initials. Barton's author-

ship is revealed in an acrostic on b1ᵛ. Printed by Samuel Richardson (*Sale* 242).
[—] [fine paper] DM; CSmH,IU.
Watermark: Strasburg bend.

Basia. Basia Joannis Secundi Nicolai Hagensis: or the Kisses, 1731. *See* Ogle, George.

— Basia: or, the charms of kissing, 1719. *See* Tooly, Thomas.

Basin. The bason: a poem, 1727. *See* Coffey, Charles.

[**Basset, J.**] Sodoms catastrophe [!], a poem, with the addition of other pieces of poetry, 1748. *See* S543.

B92 Batavia. Batavia in tears: or, an elegy from the Dutch, upon the melancholy news, of the ever to be lamented death of that glorious monarch, William III. king of Great Britain. *London, printed by Benj. Harris*, 1702. (31 March, Luttrell)
1°: 1 side, 3 columns.
Mourning cuts at head with texts printed in Dutch, and mourning borders. Variant at O(1971), 'Geschreeven door B.H.'
'Ye liquid streams, which thro' our sluces glide'
The same 'author' (translator?) wrote *The solemnity of the muses at the funeral of King William III*, 1702.
MH(Luttrell).

B93 Bath. Bath. A poem. *Printed for Messrs Longman and Shewell, London; J. Leak, in Bath; and M. Lewis, in Bristol*, 1748. (*GM, LM* Feb)
4°: A–D⁴ (B2 as 'B3'); *1–3* 4–32.
Possibly printed at Bath, from the cut on p. 3.
'Thee, Bath, and flutt'ring belles and beaus I sing'
A satire.
L(11630.c.4/3, ms. date 1 March; 11630.c.8/24), O(2).

B94 — The Bath toasts for the year 1715. Inscrib'd to Mr. Pope. To which is added, exact descriptions of the Bath and Tunbridge-Wells. *London, printed for E. Curll*, 1715. (*PB* 22 Oct)
8°: A⁴, C2–4, A2–4, [ ]⁴; *1–4* 5–8, *19* 20–24, [6], *1* 2–8. A1 hft, advt on verso; [ ]⁴ advt.
Apparently a new poem with two prose pieces reissued from previous works: C2 'A description of the Bath by Nestor Ironside, esq;' A2 'A letter from Tunbridge' dated 25 July 1714.
'Is this the spring renown'd for radiant dames'
LG.

Bath, William Pulteney, *earl of. See* Pulteney, William, *earl of Bath*.

Batrachomuomachia. Batrachomuomachia: or the battle of the frogs and mice, 1736. *See* Price, Henry.

Batt

Batt. Batt upon Batt, 1706–. *See* Speed, John.

Battel. *See* Battle.

Battiad. The Battiad, 1750. *See* Mendez, Moses.

B95 **Battle.** A battle fought with the boasters: or, Patroclus's weak defence by force defeated; and H-lm-s, S-mp-n, E-gl-d . . . cast headlong into the sea of ignorance. By Philomathematicus's army of arguments. *London, printed in the year* 1738 *and sold by the booksellers in town & country.*
8°: *A*⁴ B–D⁴ E² (D2 as 'D'); *1–2* 3–36.
　　List of subscribers on pp. 3–4, mainly from Norfolk. Other poems and letters on the same subject and mathematical solutions, pp. 16–36.
'Boasts, and the man I sing, whose fame of late'
　　An attack on *The Greek grammar* (1735–) of John Holmes, and on his supporters, Thomas Simpson and Daniel Eagland, as dunces.
O; InU.

B95·5 — [reissue] The dunces of Norfolk, a satire. Or, Patroclus and his clan, lately assembled at H**** truly delineated . . . The second edition. *London, printed for J. Cooper,* 1740 [1739]. (*GM, LM* Sept)
8°: *A*⁴(±*A*1) B–D⁴ E²; *1–2* 3–36.
OCU.

B96 — The battle of Almanza. [*London?* 1707/–.]
slip: 1 side, 1 column.
　　Rough cut of two musicians at head.
'Down by a chrystal river clear'
C.

B97 — [another edition]
　　Rough cut of fighting at head. Many textual variations suggest oral transmission.
'Down by a chrystal river side'
C.

B98 — The battel of Audenard. A poem. Occasion'd by the glorious victory obtain'd over the French near that place . . . With the characters of the general officers, who were present in the engagement. *London printed, and are to be sold by J. Morphew,* 1708. (20 July, Luttrell)
2°: A–C²; *1–4* 5–12.
'Cœlestial maid, now touch thy golden lyre'
O; CLU-C(Luttrell).

B99 —— Also a new copy of verses of Jack Frenchman's lamentation. *London, printed and sold by H. Hills, for the benefit of the poor,* 1708.
8°: A⁸; *1–3* 4–15 *16.*
　　Jack Frenchman's lamentation on p. 16, printed in two columns.
L(11631.b.31),O,C,EU,DT+; CSmH,CtY,ICN, MH(2),TxU+

B100 — 'The battle of Culloden. A poem. By a gentleman of the Inner Temple. Price 6*d.*' (*BM* May 1746)

Battle

B101 — 'The battle of Dettingen. An ode. [*London*] *Printed for M. Cooper.* Price 6*d.*' (*DA* 4 Aug 1743)

[**B102** = E8] — The battle of Oudenarde, 1709. *See* Earbery, Matthias.

B103 — The battle of Preston. To the tune of Killie-cranky. [*Edinburgh?* 1745.]
½°: 1 side, 2 columns.
'The Chevalier being void of fear'
　　A Jacobite song.
MC.

B104 — The battle of the bards: a poem. [*Dublin*] *Printed in the year* 1734.
8°: *A*⁴; *1–2* 3–8.
　　On p. 8, 'The end of the first canto'.
'When first poetick broils grew high'
　　The battle is between Carthy and Dalacourt against Dunkin and Sican.
LVA-F,DN.

B105 — The battle of the colliers: an excellent new ballad. To the tune of King John, and the abbot of Canterbury. *London, printed for H.D. and T.C. in Fleetstreet,* [172–.]
slip: 1 side, 1 column.
'I tell not, as whilom did merry Mat. Prior'
　　On a fight between two City coal-merchants, Sir T[homa]s of Fleetstreet and Sir H[ug]h of Fleetditch.
L(C.116.i.4/23).

— The battle of the poets, 1725. *See* Cooke, Thomas.

— The battle of the sexes, 1723–. *See* Wesley, Samuel, *the younger.*

— The battel: or, morning-interview, 1716. *See* Ramsay, Allan.

— Battel without bloodshed, 1701. *See* Ward, Edward.

B106 **Battles.** The battles. A poem. On the late successes of her majesty's arms by sea and land. *London, printed for John Nutt,* 1705. (16 Jan, Luttrell)
2°: A–D²; *1–2* 3–13 '10–11' *16.* 16 advt.
　　Watermark: small fleur-de-lys on shield. Advertised *DC* 17 Jan.
'Ye sacred muses whose exalted lays'
LDW,DG,*MR-C*; MH(Luttrell),TxU.

B107 — [fine paper]
　　Watermark: Amsterdam arms.
O.

B108 **Bauble.** The bauble, a tale. *London printed, and sold by T. Edlln* [!], *& N. Cox,* 1721. (*DP* 13 April)
2°: *A*² B²; *1–2* 3–7 *8 blk.*
'Cloe, a nymph, divinely fair'
　　A tale of a dildo user.
O; CtY,*NjR.*

Baucis. Baucis and Philemon, 1709–. *See* Swift, Jonathan.

Bawdy-house

B109 Bawdy-house. 'The bawdy-house: a poem. *London, printed for Jacob Gibbs; and sold at the London Gazette, a pamphlet-shop, Charing Cross*. Price 6d.' (*DC* 28 Jan 1723, 'this day will be publish'd')
> *Ridotto*, 1723 is (ironically?) dedicated to 'the suppos'd author of... The bawdy house', identified as 'H----y M-----t, esq;'

B110 [Baynard, Edward.] Health; a poem. Shewing how to keep and preserve it in a sane and sound state. As also to restore it when low and diminish'd. To which is annex'd the Doctor's decade. By Dabry Dawne M.D. *London, printed for J⟨ohn⟩ Roberts*, [1716.] (28 April, Luttrell)
8°: π⁴ A–F⁴; [4] i–iv, 1–46 *47–48 blk*. π1 hft.
> 'ohn' of 'John Roberts' obliterated from imprint. Listed in *MC* April.
'If twice man's age, you would fulfil'
L(161.1.31, Luttrell, –π1, F4),O(–π1),GM(–π1, F4); CtY-M(–F4),*DNLM*.

B111 [—] Health, a poem. Shewing how to procure, preserve, and restore it. To which is annex'd the Doctor's decade. The second edition, corrected. By Dabry Dawne, M.D. *London printed, and sold by James Bettenham*, 1719. (*PB* 21 April)
8°: A–G⁴ H¹; i–x, 1–48.
> Entered to William & John Innys in Bowyer's ledgers under 17 April, 750 copies printed.
L(1494.aa.10),O,*DrU*; CtY,*DNLM*.

B112 — — The third edition, corrected. By Edward Baynard. *Dublin, printed by and for George Grierson*, 1721.
8°: A–C⁸ D⁴; i–x, 1–46.
DG,DN.

B112·5 — — The fourth edition, corrected. *Dublin, printed by and for George Grierson*, 1722.
8°: A–D⁴ E²; i–x, 1–26.
O.

B113 [—] — By Darby Dawne, M.D. The third edition, corrected. *London printed, and sold by J. Roberts*, 1724. (*MC* May)
8°: A–G⁴ H²; i–v vi–xii, 1–48. A1 hft.
> A 'fourth edition' was printed in Boston, 1724.
L(1038.g.39),O,CT(–A1),LdU-B.

B114 — — The fourth edition, corrected. *London printed, and sold by J. Roberts*, 1731 [1730]. (*MChr* Nov)
8°: *A*⁴ B–G⁴ H²; i–v vi–xii, 1–48. A1 hft.
L(T.1056/12),O,DT,*BrP*; CtY-M,*MB*,MH.

B115 — — The fifth edition, corrected. *Dublin, printed by and for George Grierson*, 1732.
8°: *A*⁴ B–D⁴; i–viii, 1–24.
> Imprint date of DN copy corrected in ms. to 1733. A reference has been seen to a Dublin fourth edition of 1732, not traced.
C(lacks A1),DA,DN.

B116 — — The fifth edition, corrected. *London printed, and sold by J. Roberts*, 1736 [1737]. (*LM* Jan)

Baynard, E. Health

8°: A–G⁴ H²; i–v vi–xii, 1–48. A1 hft.
L(11631.bbb.8); CtY,MH(–A1).

B117 — — The sixth edition corrected. *London printed, and sold by J. Roberts*, 1740.
8°: A–G⁴ H²; i–v vi–xii, 1 2–48. A1 hft.
L(1961),O; CLU-C,CtY,*IEN*.

B118 — — The seventh edition corrected. *London printed, and sold by J. Roberts*, 1742.
8°: A–G⁴ H²; i–v vi–xii, 1 2–48. A1 hft.
L(551.a.26/3),LVA-D(–A1),OW; *DNLM,WaU*.

B119 — — The eighth edition. *Manchester, printed by R. Whitworth, bookseller*, [1742/–.]
8°: A–E⁴; i–iii iv–ix, 1–31.
> *Morgan* S21 records a 1748 edition as '9th ed., corrected, ix, 27 pp., 8°, Manchester (R. Whitmath [!])', probably in error for the 1758 edition listed in Emmanuel Green, *Bibliotheca Somersetensis* (1902) I.60. This edition may well be later than 1748.
MP.

B120 — — The eighth edition, corrected. *London printed, and sold by J. Roberts*, 1749.
8°: A–G⁴ H²; i–v vi–xii, 1 2–48. A1 hft.
L(11631.bbb.48),O,*BrP*; CtY-M(–A1),*DNLM*.

B121 — — The sixth edition. '*London printed, and sold by J. Roberts*', 1750.
8°: a² b⁴ A–C⁴ D²; i–v vi–xii, 1 2–28. a1 hft.
> A piracy; the copy at O is bound with Scottish pamphlets.
L(1964, uncut),O,EU(stitched, unopened); CtY-M.

Bays. The Bays miscellany, or Colley triumphant, [1730.] *See* Cooke, Thomas.

B122 [Beach, Thomas.] Eugenio: or, virtuous and happy life. A poem. Inscrib'd to Mr. Pope. *London, printed for R. Dodsley*, 1737. (*GM* April; *LM* May)
2°: *A–B*² C–E² (E1 as 'D'); *1–5* 6–20. A1 hft.
> The order of this and the following edition has not been established; the collations suggest a close relationship.
'Ye venerable sages of the schools'
> For Beach's authorship see Swift's letter to him of 12 April 1735 recommending revisions which Beach adopted.
L(11651.m.88),LVA-D,O(–A1); CtY,ICN(uncut,–A1),ICU,MH(2, 1–A1),TxU(–A1).

B123 [—] — *London, printed for R. Dodsley*, 1737.
4°: *A*⁴ C⁴ D²; *1–5* 6–20. A1 hft.
CLU-C,CSmH,IU,NjP,TxU.

B124 Bear. The bear-garden in mourning. Or, an elegy on the death of Mr. Christopher Preston, master of her majesties bear-garden, at Hockley in the Hole, who was torn to pieces last night, being Sunday, the 18th of September, by one of his own

The **bear**-garden in mourning

bears, in the 81st year of his age. *London, printed for the Bear-Garden Society*, 1709.
1°: 1 side, 2 columns.
    Within woodcut mourning borders.
'Hear me ye Hockley valleys make my moan'
O.

Beast. The beasts confession to the priest, 1738. *See* Swift, Jonathan.

B125 Beasts. The beasts in power, or Robin's song: with an old cat's prophecy. Taken out of an old copy of verses, suppos'd...by John Lidgate... *London, printed in the year* 1709. (*DC* 9 March)
8°: A⁴; *1–2* 3–8.
    First line on p. 3 ends 'some'. *DC* advertises it as sold by J. Morphew; listed in *WL* Feb. Reprinted in an edition by Hills of *The eagle and the robin*, 1709.
'One that had in her infant state'
    Printed in *Nichols, Collection* III.13–18 as by William King (1663–1712), probably because it was reprinted by Hills with *The eagle and the robin* which Nichols (wrongly?) attributed to King. The chain of evidence is very weak, and though Nichols was the editor of King's works, the attribution should be treated with suspicion; it has apparently been overlooked hitherto. Harley warns the queen against Marlborough.
L(11631.d.33; 164.m.48),O(2),CT,E,DG+; CSmH,CtY,ICN,MB,MH+.

B126 — [another edition]
    First line on p. 3 ends 'very'.
O-JJ,OW; CtY,IU,MH.

Beata. Beata Maria virgo ab angelo Gabriele salutata, 1729. *See* Tilly, William.

Beatific. The beatific vision: a poem, 1735. *See* Codrington, Samuel.

Beau. The beau and the academick. A dialogue in imitation of Bellus homo and academicus, 1733. *See* Bowyer, William.

B127 — The beau in a wood: a satyr. With his last will and testament: and also his elegy and epitaph. *London, printed for John Willis; sold by John Nutt*, 1701. (*PM* 29 April)
4°: A–C²; *i–viii*, 1–16.
'Heav'ns! to what height our follys now arise'
    Dedication signed 'M.S.'
MH(mutilated).

— The beau philosopher. A poem, 1736. *See* Bennet, Philip.

B128 — The beau-thief detected: a poem, inscribed to the fair m---ds of h---n---r... By J. W. *Westminster, printed by, and for, A. Campbell; sold by the booksellers of London & Westminster*, 1729. (*MChr* 13 May)

The **beau**-thief detected

2°: A⁴ (A2 as 'B2'); *1–3* 4–7 *8 blk*.
'Say, muse, how Damon, in St. James's Park'
    On Damon's theft of the maids of honour's shifts.
LdU-B; MH.

B128·1 — [fine paper?] *Westminster, printed in the year* 1729.
    Watermark: London arms.
O(uncut, ms. corrections).

B129 Beaumont, *Sir* **John.** Bosworth-field: a poem written in the year 1629... *London printed, and sold by H. Hills*, 1710.
8°: A–B⁸ C⁴; *1–2* 3–39 *40. 40 advt*.
    First published 1629; Beaumont died in 1627. Reissued with other remaindered Hills poems in *A collection of the best English poetry*, 1717 (*Case* 294), and included here to complete the list of Hills reprints.
'The winters storm of civil war I sing'
L(11626.d.6; C.124.b.7/48; G.18914/1),O(2), CT,AdU,WcC; CtY,MH,TxU.

Beaumont, Joseph. Original poems in English and Latin... *Cambridge, printed by J. Bentham; sold by W. Thurlbourn in Cambridge; and C. Bathurst, in London*, 1749.
4°: pp. xlix, 139.   L,O; CtY,IU.
    A frontispiece is found in some copies, but a note at IU records 'The plate...was published separately'.

B130 — Psyche, or love's mystery, in XXIV. cantos: displaying the intercourse betwixt Christ, and the soul... The second edition, with corrections throughout, and four new cantos, never before printed. *Cambridge, printed at the University-Press, for Tho. Bennet, London*, 1702. (*LG* 5 March)
2°: (frt+) a–b⁴ A–2Z⁴ 3A² (a3 as 'b3'); *i–xvi*, 1–370 *371–2*; 2 columns. 3A2 advt.
    McKenzie 56; 750 copies printed. First published 1648. *TC* Easter 1707 records a remainder issue at 3s. 6d.
'Eternal love, of sweetest poetry'
    Edited by Joseph's son, Charles Beaumont.
L(840.m.9),O,C(2),DT,*WcC*+; CLU-C,CtY, DFo,ICN,*MH*+.

Beauties. The beauties, 1746. *See* Walpole, Horace.

B131 — The beauties of the universe. A poem. By a gentleman of the navy. *London printed, and sold by J. Roberts*, 1732. (*GM* 24 Jan)
8°: A–E⁴; *i–x, 1* 2–30.
'When universal nature I survey'
    Dedication signed 'R.G.' Ascribed by *Dobell* 541 to Robert Gambol, but no evidence for the attribution is known.
O,LdU-B; CtY,MH,TxHR,TxU.

Beautiful. A beautiful young nymph going to bed, 1734. *See* Swift, Jonathan.

Beauty

B132 Beauty. The beauty and excellence of charity. A poem. Most humbly presented to the Lady Dutry. *London, printed for the author,* [1737?]
4°: π¹ A–C² (A1 as 'A2'); *1–2* 3–13 *14 blk.*
> Probably issued with variant title-pages with alternative dedicatees. The NjP copy is bound with part of the original wrapper bearing a poem addressed to Lady Dutry and part of a letter dated 27 April 1737.

'Let charity be now the muse's care'
> What is apparently the author's name in the NjP letter is partly cropt, but probably 'John Peter C⟨oæt?⟩'. See *A divine poem on the creation,* 1718, and other poems listed there. For other poems issued in this way, see W. Howard, H. Nevil, R. Spencer.

NjP.

B133 — Beauty and proportion. A poem. *London, printed for T. Astley,* [1733.] (*GSJ* 20 March)
2°: *A²* B–D²; *1–3* 4–15 *16 blk.*
'How strange a thing, ye pow'rs is beauty grown!'
IU,OCU.

— Beauty: or the art of charming, 1735. *See* Dodsley, Robert.

B134 — Beauty's advocate. A poem... Written by a gentleman of the university of Cambridge. *London printed, and sold by B. Bragg,* 1705 [1704]. (*FP* 14 Dec)
2°: *A²* B–D²; *i–vii,* 1–9.
'When the Almighty, from his heav'nly throne'
DFo(Luttrell, 14 Dec).

B135 [Beckingham, Charles.] An epistle from Calista to Altamont. *London, printed for A. Moore; sold by the booksellers of London & Westminster,* 1729. (*MChr* 12 Dec)
2°: *A²* B²; *1–2* 3–8.
> Reprinted in *The whole tryal between...the Lord Abergavenny and Richard Liddell, esq;...* [1730] (copy at EtC).

'To jealous love, and injur'd honour's ear'
> Ascribed to Beckingham by *Whincop.* The adulterous Lady Abergavenny's apology to her husband. See *An epistle from Altamont to Lorenzo,* 1730.

L(163.n.28),O,LdU-B; CSmH,CtY,MH,OCU, TxU.

B136 [—] — The second edition. *London, printed for A. Moore; sold by the booksellers of London & Westminster,* 1729.
2°: *A²* B²; *1–2* 3–8.
> Apparently a reimpression.

MR(cropt); National Library of Australia, Canberra.

B137 [—] — The third edition. *London, printed for A. Moore; sold by the booksellers of London & Westminster,* 1729.
2°: *A²* B²; *1–2* 3–8.

Beckingham, C. An epistle

> Apparently a reimpression.

L(11647.g.75); NjP.

B138 [—] — *London: printed, and Dublin re-printed, and sold by James Hoey, & George Faulkner,* 1730.
8°: *A⁴;* *1–3* 4–8.
L(1960),DA.

B139 — The lyre. A tale. Inscrib'd to Doctor Towne. *London, printed for Edward Symon,* 1726. (*MC* Feb)
2°: *A²* B–D²; *1–3* 4–15 *16 blk.*
'Shall letter'd spleen still grow upon our clime'
O; MH,NN,TxU.

B140 [—] Monsieur Rapin's Latin heroick poem on Christ's-passion. Translated into English blank verse. *London, printed for J. Morphew,* 1717. (*MC* April)
8°: *A²* B–E⁴ F²; *i–iv,* 1–36.
> Some copies (O,AN) have an engraved frontispiece, apparently from a set of Bible illustrations.

'Let others sing of arms, of lawrels bought'
> Dedication signed 'C.B.' Ms. note in AN copy 'By Charles Beckingham. Author of Scipio Africanus, a tragedy'.

O,AN; CtY.

B141 — [*idem*] Christus patiens: or the sufferings of Christ an heroic poem. In two books. Made English from the Latin original of Rapin. *London, printed for E. Curll, C. Rivington, J. Brotherton, & W. Lewis,* 1720. (*PB* 8 March)
8°: *a⁴* b⁴ B–N⁴; *i–xvi,* 1 2–95 *96 blk.* a1 frt.
> Dedication signed. A revised version.

'Let others swell their mercenary lays'
L(701.d.12/2),LVA-D; CtY,KU,*NNUT,*TxU.

B142 — — The second edition. *London, printed for E. Curll,* 1737. (*GM* March)
8°: *A²* B–D⁸ E⁶; *i–iv,* 1–60. A1 frt.
O(2),C; CtY,*ICN,MiU.*

B143 — An ode to the right honourable Sir Robert Walpole, knight of the most noble order of the Garter. On his installation. *London, printed for and sold by J. Millan, J. Roberts, N. Blandford, A. Dodd, E. Nutt, J. Millar,* [1726.] (*MC* June)
2°: *A¹* B–C²; *i–ii,* 1 2–7 *8.* 8 advt.
'Whence, Windsor, this diffusive grace'
L(162.n.3),O; TxU.

B144 — A poem on his most sacred majesty King George the Second, his accession to the throne. Addressed to the right honourable the Earl of Peterborow. *London, printed by J. Read; sold by T. Warner,* [1727.]
2°: *A²* B²; *1–3* 4–8.
'For her departed lord, does Britain show'
O-*JJ*; TxU.

B145 — — *London: printed, and Dublin: re-printed by J. Gowan,* 1727.
½°: 1 side, 2 columns.
L(C.121.g.8/161),C,DT.

Beckingham, C.

B146 [—] Sarah, the quaker, to Lothario, lately deceased, on meeting him in the shades. *London, printed for A. Moore; sold at most of the pamphlet-shops in London & Westminster*, 1728. (*MChr* 19 Dec)

2°: A–B²; *1–2* 3–8.

'No respite from my tortures can I have?'

> *Crum* N251. Attributed to Beckingham by *Whincop*. On Spencer Cowper, justice of common pleas 1727, who was acquitted of the murder of Sarah Stout in 1699. Cf. *Lothario's answer to Sarah the quaker*, 1729.

L(11630.f.54),O,LdU-B;   CLU-C,CSmH(Luttrell, Dec),MH(uncut),TxU.

B147 [—] — The second edition. *London, printed for A. Moore; sold at most of the pamphlet-shops in London & Westminster*, 1728.

2°: A–B²; *1–2* 3–8.

> Watermark: pro patria, as the preceding. Apparently a reimpression or press-variant title.

LF,LSC.

B148 [—] — The second edition. *London, printed for A. Moore; sold at most of the pamphlet-shops in London & Westminster*, 1728.

2°: A–B²; *1–2* 3–8.

> Page 3 is reset. Most copies are on unwatermarked paper, but that at CU has Amsterdam arms, and is possibly on fine paper.

L(642.l.28/1),O,OW,BaP; CU,CtY,NN,OCU.

B149 [—] — The third edition, with additions. *London, printed for A. Moore; sold at most of the pamphlet-shops in London & Westminster*, 1729.

2°: A–B²; *1–2* 3–8.

> Revised, and apparently reset.

L(1970); PHC.

B150 [—] Sarah the quaker to Lothario, alias S——C—— judge, lately deceased, on meeting him in the shades. *London: printed for A. Moore: and Dublin: reprinted by Christopher Dickson*, 1728–9.

8°: A⁴; *1–2* 3–8.

L(1963).

B151 — Verses occasion'd by the death of the Czar of Muscovy, humbly inscrib'd to the right honourable the lord Viscount Townsend. *London, printed for J. Roberts*, 1725. (*MC* March)

2°: *A*² B² C¹; *1–3* 4–10.

'Whilst Europe trembling for its doubtful state'
Chatsworth.

B152 — Verses on the death of Mr. Prior, humbly inscrib'd to the right honble the Lady Henrietta Cavendish, Holles, Harley. *London, printed for J. Roberts, & J. Graves*, 1721. (*PB* 12 Oct)

2°: *A*² B–C²; *1–5* 6–11 *12 blk*. A1 hft.

'Whilst Wimple's dome its envy'd guest resigns'
L(1959),O; DFo(–A1),MH.

B153 Bed. The bed of honour. To which is annex'd, the Seasons: a poem. Inscribed to the...Earl of

The bed of honour

Albermarle, &c. By the author of the Temple of war and Review. [*London*] *Printed for the author*, 1732.

8°: A⁴(A1 + *a1) B–C⁴ D⁴(–D4); *i–ii* iii–iv, 3–30.

> *a1 bears a list of subscribers, largely military men.

'Once more, stern god of war, once more inspire'
Seasons: 'When thro' the Ram, Sol takes his swift career'
L(11631.d.7).

B154 — The bed-tester-plot, a ballad. Tune, Ye commons and peers, &c. *London, printed in the year* 1718.

½°: 1 side, 2 columns.

> One copy at O is conjugate with 'Cibber', *The following address*, [1718.]

'At St. James's of late,/On a great bed of state'

> *Crum* A1840b, dated '1717'. On the collapse of a bed on George I and his mistress Baroness Schulenberg, subsequently Duchess of Kendal.

L(Cup.600.b.1/15),O(2, 1 cut and mounted),C; CSmH.

B155 Bedlam. Bedlam: a poem on his majesty's happy escape from his German dominions, "and the great wisdom of his conduct there. *London, printed for J. Huggonson*, 1741. (*GM, LM* Nov)

2°: *A*² B–C²; *1–3* 4–12.

> Horizontal chain-lines.

'What mean these loud aërial cracks I hear?'

> Said in the preface to be a genuine mad poem on George II's return.

L(11602.i.11/4; 162.n.51),O,LdU-B; CSmH, NjP,MH(uncut),OCU,TxU +.

B155·5 — — '*London, printed for J. Huggonson*' [*Edinburgh*], 1741. (*SM* Oct)

8°: A² B⁴; *1–3* 4–12.

> The C copy is in a volume of Edinburgh tracts. The *SM* for October was presumably printed fairly late in November.

C; ICU,MH.

B156 — — *London, 'printed for Lord Flame, at Hurlothrumbo's Head, in the Strand'*, 1741.

12°: *A*² B⁴; *1–2* 3–12.

> The imprint is clearly fictitious. The format is uncertain; A has vertical chain-lines, B horizontal.

L(1969).

B157 Beef. Beef and butt beer, against mum and pumpernickle. H--n--r scrubs, or; a bumper to old England, -- Huzza. A drinking song. [*London*] *Printed for B.C.* [*B. Cowse*] *in Pater-noster-row*, 1742. (*LDP* 11 Nov)

2°: *A*⁴; *1–2* 3–8.

> Two poems.

'In good King G---'s golden days,/Whoe'er advis'd the king, sir'

Beef and butt beer

'Here's a health to the king and speedy peace'
Anti-Hanoverian satires.
L(163.n.4; C.57.g.7/7),O,AdU; CtY,MH,OCU.

B158 —— *London, printed for T. Davis in Shorts-Gardens,* [1742.]
½°: 1 side, 2 columns.
One song to each column, with a woodcut at the head of each and 'Tune, of Charles of Sweeden', and 'Tune, Down among the dead men.'
O.

B159 Beelzebub. Beelzebub's advice to his club at the Devil. [*London,* 1712?]
½°: 2 sides, 1 column.
'To sink that state the senate does support'
A tory poem attacking the whigs' attitude to peace.
Chatsworth.

B160 Beeriad. The Beeriad or progress of drink. An heroic peom, in two cantos. The first being an imitation of Mr. Pope's Dunciad; the second a description of a ram feast... By a gentleman in the navy. To which is annex'd a figurative moral tale upon liberty... *Gosport, printed by J. Philpot,* 1736.
4°: π¹ A–L⁴ M²; *i–iii* iv–x, *1* 2–56 55–82.
Bond 146. Philpot's name in the imprint is genuine.
'Beer and the men (a mighty theme!) I sing'
Dedication signed 'R.C.'
DFo,MH,NjP.

B161 Beggar. [dh] The beggar on horseback: or, the old proverb made true. [col] [*London?*] *Printed in the year* 1706.
4°: *A²*; *1–4*, 2 columns.
'As I have heard, in times of yore'
MH,TxU.

B162 [Behn, Aphra.] The land of love. A poem. *London, printed by H. Meere, for C. King, & A. Bettesworth,* 1717. (*MC* March)
12°: (frt+) A–F⁶; *1–2* 3–72.
'I should have dy'd silent, as flow'rs decay'
Printed as 'A voyage to the isle of love' in Aphra Behn's *Poems,* 1684, 1697.
L(11632.a.24); CSmH,ICU(−frt).

B163 [Belcher, James.] A cat may look upon a king. An epistolary poem, on the loss of the ears of a favourite female cat. To ****** *Dublin, printed in the year* MDXXXII [i.e. 1732].
½°: 1 side, 1 column.
'Thou enemy, who e'er thou art'
Early ms. note in CSmH copy 'By Ia. Belcher Esqr'.
CSmH.

B164 Belgrade. Belgrade. A poem. *London, printed for J. Roberts,* 1717. (*PM* 19 Sept)

Belgrade. A poem

2°: *A²* B–C²; *1–3* 4–12.
The E and one O copy have a variant in the outer forme of C, with the pagination in parentheses, not brackets; possibly this indicates a reimpression.
'If brave heroic acts a place can claim'
On Prince Eugene's victory over the Turks.
L(11631.k.5/2),O(2),E.

B165 Belhaven. Belhaven's vision: or, his speech in the union-parliament. November 2. 1706. *London, printed for A. Beets, over against St. Clement's Church in the Strand,* 1729.
8°: *A⁴*; *1–2* 3–8.
The imprint is possibly false.
'While all the world to this day'
A lament for the fate of Scotland under the Union, presumably versifying the speech of John Hamilton, lord Belhaven.
L(11626.aa.42),E(2).

B166 — [*idem*] Belhaven's vision: or the present state of Scotland. [*Glasgow?*] *Printed in the year* 1731.
8°: *A⁴*; *1–2* 3–8.
Possibly an Irish, not a Scottish edition; the ornament on p. 3 is copied from an Edinburgh original.
E,DA,GM.

B167 — Belhaven's vision: or, his speech in the union-parliament. November 2. 1706. *Edinburgh, printed in the year* 1732.
8°: *A⁴*; *1–2* 3–8.
O(uncut).

B168 — [*idem*] The Lord Belhaven's vision and prophesy of the present times, past present and to come. *Printed in the year* 1737.
8°: *A⁴*; *1–2* 3–8.
Horizontal chain-lines.
ICN.

Belhaven, John Hamilton, *baron. See* Hamilton, John, *baron Belhaven.*

B169 Belief. I. The belief of the divinity of Jesus Christ necessary to salvation. II. The doctrines of transubstantiation and the trinity not equally credible. Being theses maintained in the university of Cambridge, anno 1696. By Robert Moss, D.D. *London, printed for E. Curll,* 1728. (*MC* July)
8°: A–D⁴; *1–8* 9–32.
The translations are anonymous; the original Latin texts on pp. 25–32. A 'second edition' was advertised in *SJEP* 28 Sept 1728.
'Reason, tho' bright, yet when survey'd with pride'
'Reason's bright power exalts us from the ground'
C.

B170 Believer. The believer's farewel to the world, or, an elegie on the death of...Sir Robert Hamilton son to Sir Thomas Hamilton, of Prestoun who dyed upon the 21st. of October 1701. aged 51 years. [*Edinburgh?*] *Printed in the year* 1701.

The **believer's** farewel

4°: A–E²; *1–3* 4–19 *20 blk.*
'What can so many heavy deaths portend!'
L(11631.c.26),E,EU,GM.

— The believer's dowry, 1708. *See* Erskine, Ralph.

B171 Belisarius. [dh] Belisarius and Zariana. A dialogue. [col] *London, printed for J. Morphew,* 1710.
8°: A⁸; *1–16. 16 advt.*
Also advertised by Henry Hills; it resembles his productions.
'Welcome, my lord, thrice welcome from afar'
A satire on the Duke and Duchess of Marlborough.
O,DT,AdU; CtY,ICU,*MB.*

B172 — [*idem*] Bellisarius a great commander; and Zariana his lady. A dialogue. *London printed, and sold by J. Morphew,* 1710.
8°: π² A⁸; *i–iv, 1–16. 16 advt.*
Presumably a reissue adding title-leaf and preface.
L(1077.k.27, made-up),LG,CT,E; ICN,NN, OCU,TxU.

B173 [Bell, Beaupré.] The osiers. A pastoral translated from the Latin of Sannazarius. With some account of Sannazarius, and his piscatory eclogues. *Cambridge, printed for the author, at the University-Press in the year* 1724.
4°: π¹ A² χ¹ B–E²; *i–ii, 1–21 22 blk.*
π1 and χ1 (title and fly-title) have been seen to be conjugate.
'If yet, dear friend, the goddess fans the fire'
The copy at O has a ms. note recording its presentation by Bell.
O.

Bell, Joseph. Spring flowers, or poems, treating 1. On passing pleasure. 2. Concerning the blessed deity. 3. On the creation. 4. On man in paradise, &c. Being the puerilia of Joseph Bell printer. *Edinburgh, printed by Joseph Bell, and sold at the printing house in Craig's closs; also sold by Patrick Bell at his lodgings in Perth, and by David Bell at his house in Lednock,* 1731.
8°: pp. 52. L,E.

'Bellamant.' The beau and the academick, [1733.] *See* Bowyer, William.

Bellamy, Daniel, *the elder.* Love triumphant: or, the rival goddesses. A pastoral opera... To which are added, some original poems, and translations. Never before publish'd. *London, printed for, and sold only by Mrs. Bellamy, at her school in Old Boswel-court,* 1722. (*SR* 13 June)
8°: pp. 72. L,O; CtY.
Horizontal chain-lines; possibly a duodecimo in fours. Deposit copy at O.

— The young ladies miscellany: or, youth's innocent and rational amusement... *London, printed by E. Say, for the author; and sold only by Mrs.*

Bellamy, D. *Collections*

Bellamy, at her school; and Mrs. Wood, at the College, in Bury, in the county of Suffolk, 1723.
12°: pp. x, 216. L,O; CtY,ICU.
Dedication signed. Largely dramatic.

— — The second edition. Adorn'd with cuts. *London, printed by E. Say, for Thomas Corbet,* 1726.
12°: pp. x, 216. DFo.

— Gay's Fables epitomiz'd; with short poems applicable to each occasion, extracted from the most celebrated moralists antient and modern, for the use of schools. *London, printed for B. Creak,* [1733.] (*GSJ* 8 March)
8°: 34 ll. L,CT.
Engraved title; engraved scene and fable on each verso; verse applications on each recto. Only the themes are taken from Gay.

— The dramatick pieces, and other miscellaneous works in prose and verse, of D. Bellamy, formerly of St. John's College, Oxford. Adorned with sculptures. In which are introduced, several select essays, never before published, by D. Bellamy, jun. of Trinity-College, Cambridge. *London, printed for the author,* 1739.
12°: pp. 37, 83, 105. DFo,MH.
The plays have a separate collation.

— [reissue] Miscellanies in prose and verse, consisting of dramatick pieces, poems, humorous tales, fables, &c... Vol. I... By D. Bellamy, some time since of St. John's-College, Oxford, and D. Bellamy, jun. of Trinity-College, in Cambridge. *London, printed for J. Hodges,* 1739. (*GM* July)
L; CtY.
Cancel title.

— — The second edition. *London, printed for J. Hodges,* 1741.
12°: pp. xii, 228. O; ICU.

— Miscellanies in prose and verse... Vol. II... By D. Bellamy, sometime since of St. John's College, Oxford. *London, printed for J. Hodges,* 1740. (*GM* July)
12°: pp. 228. L,O; CtY,ICU.
There is no verse in this volume.

———————

B174 [—] Back-gammon: or, the battle of the friars. A tragi-comic tale. To which is added, a short essay on the folly of gaming, by way of application. *London, printed for J. Wilford,* 1734. (*GSJ* 2 Feb)
8°: (frt+) A¹ B–C⁴ D⁴(–D1); *i–ii, 1 2–22.*
Bond 136.
'Of two battalions set in rank and file'
Reprinted in Bellamy's *Dramatic pieces,* 1739.
L(T.902/7, cropt); CtY,MnU.

B175 — An elegiac poem, in commemoration of his late most sacred majesty, King George. *Sold by George Bickham at his drawing school, against King's Gate Street in High Holborn, & by the print-sellers of London,* [1727.]
obl 1°.

Bellamy, D. An elegiac poem

An engraved sheet, with portrait in centre engraved by G. Bickham jr. and verses on each side engraved by J. Bickham.
'In a dark vale, where melancholy yew'
LDW.

B176 [—] Taffy's triumph: or, a new translation of the Cambro-muo-maxia: in imitation of Milton. By a gentleman of Oxford. *London printed, and sold by J. Morphew,* 1709. (8 Feb, Luttrell)
2°: *A*² B–D²; *1–2* 3–16.
Advertised in *DC* 10 Feb. This translation was reprinted in an edition of *The eagle and the robin,* 1709.
' – Sing, heav'nly muse,/The Cambro-Britain, whose prolifick brain'
The revised version, *The Cambro-Britannic engineer,* was printed in Bellamy's *The young ladies miscellany,* 1723.
DA,*DrU*; Cty,TxU(Luttrell).

B177 [—] — '*London printed, and sold by J. Morphew,*' 1709.
8°: *A*⁸; *1–2* 3–16.
Presumably a piracy, possibly printed in London by H. Hills.
L(161.m.74),EU,DT,LdU-B,WcC+ ; CSmH, MH,NN.

B178 [—] [*idem*] The Cambro-Britannic engineer: or the original mouse-trapp-maker... By a gentleman of Oxford. To which are added, some occasional and humorous Bubble-letters: written...1720... By the same hand. *London printed, and sold by J. Roberts,* 1722. (March, Luttrell)
8°: A–D⁴ E²; *1–2* 3–36.
Revised text.
'Sing, heav'nly muse, in lays harmonious sing'
L(161.m.76,Luttrell,March),O,E,WcC;MH,NN.

B179 — Two court fables, apply'd to the late glorious coronation: with a short ode, on the first of March, being the anniversary of her majesty's birth-day. *London, printed for Joseph Marshal; sold by J. Roberts,* 1728. (*MChr* 1 March)
2°: *A–C*²; *1–3* 4–11 *12.* 12 advt.
'A pelican, belov'd by Jove'
'One cloudy day, a drop of rain'
'Had great Apelles once beheld that face'
PPL.

B180 Belle. La belle assemblée; or, the Tinmouth bathers. A poem, humbly inscribed to the ladies of Newcastle, &c. By G.K. *Newcastle upon Tyne, printed by Isaac Lane, and company, at the head of the Side,* [1734?]
'I raise the strain – genius of verse draw near'
Written in reply to John Duick's poem on the Scarborough belles, published in 1734.
(From a reprint by J.S., Newcastle, 1828.)

Bellman. The bellman and the captain, 1749. *See* Byrom, John.

Bellman

B181 — The bellman of St. James's verses extraordinary. *London, printed for J. Oldcastle,* 1746. (*GM* Jan)
2°: *A*² < B²; *1–3* 4–8.
The order of editions has not been established. 14 short poems.
Prologue: 'Attend, my friends, attend, and ye shall hear'
Dedication signed 'John Trot'. Sophisticated verses, largely satirizing the court and politics, in imitation of the annual bellman's sheet of verses; probably by one pseudonymous author.
L(1973), O,OA; CtY,MH.

B182 — — To the nobility, gentry, and all my good masters and mistresses of the parish of St. James's, and without, these lines are humbly presented by John Trot, voluntier bellman. [*London*] *Printed for J. Oldcastle,* 1746.
1°: 1 side, 3 columns.
Engraving of bellman at head.
DFo,*MH*.

B183 Bellows, Thomas. To each gentleman soldier, in the company of Capt. Matthew Belcher, captain in the yellow regiment of train'd-bands of the city of London. [*London,* 1714/–.]
½°: 1 side, 1 column.
Verses enclosed in emblematic woodcut border.
'In times of old, immortal Homer sung'
Signed 'Thomas Bellows, Marshal'; but possibly written for him. See John Browne and Jacob Hall for similar productions.
L(C.20.f.2/354).

Bellus. Bellus homo et academicus, 1733. *See* Hasledine, William.

B184 Belphegor. Belphegor: or the marriage of the devil. A burlesque poem. *London, printed for A. Dodd,* 1714.
8°: A–C⁴; *1–4* 5–24. A1 hft.
Reissued in *A new collection of miscellany poems, for the year 1715* (copy in W.N.H. Harding's collection).
'The chronicles of Florence tell'
Reprinted in *A new collection of miscellany poems, for the year, 1718,* edited and perhaps written by George Davis. A version of Machiavelli's *Belfagor.*
O,CT(title cropt); TxU.

B185 [**Belsham, James.**] Mors triumphans: ode lyrica. Carmine alcaico. *Londini, prostant apud R. Dodsley, et apud J. Buckland,* 1744 [1743]. (*GM,LM* Dec)
4°: A–E²; *1–2* 3–19 *20.*
Entered in Strahan's ledger to Buckland under Nov 1743, 250 copies printed.
'Mortalis ævi gaudia lubrica'
Attributed to James Belsham in the LDW

Belsham, J. Mors triumphans

    copy, which is bound in a volume from the Belsham family.
L(11630.d.6/4),LDW,C.

B186 Belsize. Belsize-house. A satyr, exposing I. The fops and beaux... II. The characters of the women... III. The buffoonry of the Welsh ambassador. IV. The humours of his customers... By a serious person of quality. *London, printed for T. Warner,* 1722. (*DJ* 3 Sept)
8°: $A^4(-A2)$ B–D⁴; [2] 5–32.
    The Luttrell copy, once in the possession of Dobell, was dated Dec.
'Some angry muse assist my nimble pen'
    The 'Welsh ambassador', who was proprietor of Belsize-house, was William Howell.
L(1077.c.52),LG.

B187 Belvedere. Belvedere: a poem. [173–?]
8°: A⁸; *i–ii, 1–13 14 blk.*
    Title in half-title form; three short poems added at end. The typography suggests a date after 1730, and possibly after 1750.
'From gentle skies, and ever blooming plains'
LVA-F.

B188 — The belvidere: a poem. Inscrib'd to Joseph Grove, esq. of Richmond, in the county of Surry. *London, printed in the year* 1749.
8°: A⁸($\pm$A2); *1–2 3–14 15–16 blk.*
    Dated from Richmond, 31 May 1749.
'The sweets of nature, – the disclosing spring'
L(993.b.37); CtY.

B189 Bench. The bench. An eclogue. Occasioned by the war between England and Spain. *London, printed for Josiah Graham,* 1741 [1740]. (*GM,LM* Oct)
8°: π^2 A–E⁴; *i–xii, 1–29 30–31; 32 blk.* π1 hft.
'As on a bench near Isis'-banks I sat'
    A postscript on pp. 30–31 reveals that this is a translation of William King (1685–1763), *Scamnum,* 1740; it expresses the intention of translating his *Miltonis epistola* and *Sermo pedestris.*
O; CSmH(lacks E4).

B190 — [reissue] The Oxford shepherds. A political pastoral on the present posture of affairs. Translated from the Latin original... The second edition. *London, printed for J. Graham; sold by the booksellers of London & Westminster,* 1741.
8°: π^1 A–D⁴ E⁴(–E3, 4 +E3); *i–x, 1 2–29 30 blk.*
    Cancel title (with erratum on verso) replaces title and half-title; E3,4 cancelled to remove postscript.
O; CtY,DLC,*PBL.*

B191 — [reissue] Scamnum, ecloga: or, the pastoral politicians. Translated from the Latin of Dr. King... The second edition. To which is added, Mr. Pope's description of his grotto at Twickenham. *London, printed for E. Curll,* 1744.
8°: π^1($\pm$) A⁴χ¹ B–E⁴; *i–x, 1 2, 1 2–29 30–31; 32 blk.*

The bench. An eclogue

    New cancel title (with erratum on verso) conjugate with χ¹ bearing Pope's verses; the postscript is preserved.
CtY,KU,*OCU,*TxU.

Benedicite.
Foxton, Thomas: A poetical paraphrase on the universal hymn of praise to the creator, entitled Benedicite, 1727. *See* F226.

Bennet, Benjamin. Occasional hymns: chiefly for the lord's day and lord's table. Being a collection from others. With an addition of new hymns. *Newcastle, printed by John White, for J. Button, R. Akinhead, and M. Brison,* 1722.
12°: pp. xvi, 84.   L.
    The first twenty-one hymns are by Bennet; the rest are collected and altered by him.

B192 Bennet, George. 'Pamela versified: or, virtue rewarded. An heroick poem... Done from the originals. [*London*] A. Ilive.' (*DA* 24 July 1741)
    To be printed in fifteen numbers 'with copper-plate cuts' at 2*d.* a part. Part 2 was announced for 18 August in *DA* 12 Aug. *SM* Oct 1741 reports that it 'began to be published lately at London in numbers, but the work now seems dropt'; the text quoted there (possibly the beginning of the poem) starts:
'Sacred to beauteous virtue be the lay'
    A versification of Richardson's novel.
(W.M. Sale, *Samuel Richardson* (1936) 129f.)

B193 [Bennet, Philip.] The beau philosopher. A poem. By a gentleman of Cambridge. *London, printed for the author, and sold by J. Roberts; C. Crownfield, & W. Thurlbourn, Cambridge,* 1736. (*GM,LM* Jan)
8°: (frt+) A–D⁴ E¹; *1–3 4–34.*
'Philosophers, unpolish'd creatures, foes'
    Bennet's authorship is recorded in Baker's *Biographia dramatica,* 1812.
C,LdU-B; CSmH,CtY(uncut, – frt),NN,TxU.

[Bennet, *Sir* William.] A tale of three bonnets, 1722. *See* R96.

B194 [Bennison, J.] Ode ad honorabilem Thomam Parkyns, baronettum. *Nottinghamiæ apud Johannem Collyer,* 1724.
2°: A²; *1 2–4.*
    Both copies seen have been cut down to quarto size.
'Oras per Anglorum undique fertiles'
    The copy at O is signed in ms. 'J. Bennison'.
O,NtP.

B195 [Benson, William.] Virgil's husbandry, or an essay on the Georgics: being the first book translated into English verse. To which are added the Latin text, and Mr. Dryden's version. With notes critical, and rustick. *London, sold by William &*

Benson, W. Virgil's husbandry

> *John Innys, & John Pemberton,* 1725. (*MC* June)
> 8°: π²(π1 + frt) A⁴ a⁴(a4 + plate) B–G⁴ H¹ ²a–b⁴;
> [*4*] *i* ii–xv *xvi, 1* 2–50 *51–65; 66 blk.* π1 hft.
> Engraved ornaments throughout.
> 'What may delight the plains, beneath what signs'
>> Ms. ascription to Benson in the C copy; a copy
>> at L has an early label on the binding, 'Benson's
>> Virgil'.
> L(1487.b.12/1; 1000.i.4),O(2,–π1, 1–plates),C,
> DK,LdU-B(–π1)+; CLU-C,CSmH,DFo(2),
> MH,NjP.

B196 [—] Virgil's husbandry, or an essay on the Georgics:
being the second book translated into English
verse... *London, sold by William & John Innys,*
1724. (*MC* May)
> π²(π1 + frt) A⁴ a–b⁴ c²(c2 + plate) B–G⁴ ˣH¹ H–I⁴
> K²; [*4*] *i* ii–xxviii, *1* 2–50 *51–70.* π1 hft.
> 'Thus far of plains manur'd, and heav'nly signs'
> L(1487.b.12/2),OW,C,CT(–π1, frt),LdU-B;
> CLU-C(uncut), CSmH,DFo,NjP(–π1).

B197 [—] — The second edition. *London, sold by
William & John Innys,* 1724.
> Apparently a variant title-page.
> O(–π1),DT; DFo,MH.

Bentham, Edward. A certain proposal of a certain
little tutor, [1749?] *See* C99.

B198 [**Bentley, Richard,** *1708–1782.*] A petition to the
right hon. Mr. — —, in favour of Mr. Maclean. By
a lady. *London, printed for G. Smith,* 1750.
> 2°: A⁴ < B¹; *1–3* 4–10.
> The pamphlet is formed of two sheets folded
> round a half sheet; A2 and B are signed. Pp.
> 7–9 contain a mock index.
> 'If ever statesman melted at distress'
>> Early ms. ascription to Bentley by Horace
>> Walpole in the L copy. A mock petition to
>> Henry Pelham on behalf of James Maclean,
>> 'gentleman highwayman'.
> L(1347.m.13, Walpole's ms. notes),LdU-B(–A4);
> MH.

B199 **Berington, Simon.** [dh] To his most excellent
majesty James III. king of England... [*Douai?*
1710?/16.]
> 4°: A⁴; *1–8.*
> L dates as [1721?] and wrongly suggests it is a
> fragment; but Berington came on the mission
> 1716, and the date is probably soon after
> James's service at Oudenarde and Malplaquet.
> 'When brooding fates design'd to bless the earth'
>> Signed at end, from 'the English Colledge at
>> Doway'.
> L(11632.f.4),O.

[**Berkenhout, John.**] Three original poems; being
the posthumous works of Pendavid Bitterzwig, esq;
to which is added, the...last will and testament of
that well-known author. *Oxford, printed for T.*

Berkenhout, J. Three original poems

> *Carnan in St. Paul's Church-yard; and may be had
> of the booksellers at York, Leeds, and Wakefield,*
> [1751.] (*LM* March)
> 8°: pp. vii, 47. L,LdP; OCU.
> Usually dated 1750, but the date of 1751 is
> confirmed by an advertisement in the *Leeds
> Mercury* 5 March 1751. Reprinted in *Thoresby
> Society* 22 (1915) 58ff, and there attributed to
> Francis Fawkes; but the copy at LdP has a
> ms. life of John Berkenhout prefixed and is
> attributed to him.

B200 **Berkshire.** The Barkshire tragedy: being a true
account of a barbarous murther, committed on the
body of an infant, about half a year old; by John
Tubb...who was executed at Abington...on the
24th of March, 1711–12... *Printed for W. Royce
in St. Clements, near Oxford,* [1712?]
> 8°: A⁴; *1* 2–8.
> A chap-book.
> 'Come lend an ear good people'
> L(1077.d.67/9, lacks A2.3).

B201 — The Berkshire tragedy, or the Whittam miller
who most barbarously murder'd his sweet-heart...
Edinburgh, printed for John Keed, 1744.
> 8°: A⁴; *1* 2–8.
> A chap-book.
> 'Young men and maidens all give ear'
>> The miller's name was John Mauge; his dying
>> words and confession are printed on p. 8.
> L(1078.k.26/13).

B202 [**Besse, Joseph.**] A spiritual poem: or Christian
counsel to youth. Formerly compos'd and pub-
lish'd in English by Richard Claridge. Now turn'd
into Latin by J.B. *London printed, and sold by the
assigns of J. Sowle,* 1728.
> 8°: A–C⁴; *1–3* 4–23 *24 blk.*
> Title taken from p. 2; p. 3 has Latin title
> 'Carmen spirituale: monita Christiana...'
> and imprint. Pp. 16–23 contain 'Carmen
> spirituale construed'.
> 'Sit deus ipse timor vester; quæ jussit, agatis'
>> Translator's name from LF.
> L(11408.aa.17),LF(3); CtY,*PHi,PSC-Hi.*

Bessy. Bessy Bell and Mary Gray, [1720.] *See*
Ramsay, Allan.

Bethlem. Bethlem Hospital, 1717. *See* Rutter,
John.

B203 **Better.** The better sequel better'd. In a dialogue
betwixt the oak and the dunghill. *London printed,
and sold by A. Dodd, E. Nutt, & A. Smith, and by
the booksellers of London & Westminster,* 1729.
[1728]. (*MChr* 12 Dec)
> 2°: A² B–C²; *1–3* 4–12.
> 'Thou scoundrel dunghill, hence, avaunt'
>> A sequel to [William Broome] *The fable of the*

The **better** sequel better'd

> *oak and the dunghill*, 1728, and *The dunghill and the oak*, [1728.]
> O(uncut): MH,OCU(uncut),TxU(3, 2 uncut).

B204 [**Betterton, Thomas.**] The royal conquest, or, the happy success against a potent enemy. As it was sung in the Prophetess at the Queens theatre. To a new play-house tune... [*London*] *Printed for Charles Bates*, [1705.]
½°: 1 side, 2 columns.
> Two lines of printed music above text.
'Let the souldiers rejoyce'
> *Crum* L295. The first three stanzas were printed in Betterton's *Prophetess*, 1690, and the rest of the text apparently dates from the reign of William III; but the reference to the Queen's theatre must relate this to the performance of 23 May 1705. Betterton's authorship is not certain; a ms. at O is subscribed 'M.N.'
MH.

B205 [**Bettesworth, John.**] The judgment of Paris. A poem. By a student of Christ-church College, Oxford. *London, printed for W. Webster, near St. Paul's*, 1743. (*DA* 23 July)
2°: *A*² B–C² D¹ (B2 as 'C'); *1–3* 4–14.
> *Rothschild* 240. From the date, this must be the 'Judgment of Paris' entered in Strahan's ledger to John Duncan under 22 July, though it is recorded as '2 sheets folio no. 500'.
'Daughters of Jove, immortal nine, inspire'
> Attributed to Bettesworth in *Rawlinson*.
O; IU,OCU.

B206 **Beware.** Beware of lakey vessels: or, the down-fall of hoopt petticoats. A new song. [*Dublin*, 173–?]
½°: 1 side, 1 column.
'The lasses of Dublin, in sorrowful dumps'
C.

Bewick, William. Miscellany poems by way of letters to several eminent persons. *Newcastle upon Tyne, printed for the author, by Tho. Middleton*, 1741.
8°: pp. 316.   L,NeP.

— [reissue] Several letters and miscellany poems... The second edition... *Newcastle, printed for the author; and are to be sold by James Fleming*, 1742.
8°: pp. 316, 107.   L,NeP; ICU.
> Cancel title and 'an appendix of several letters...'

B207 — Alphus: or, the fourth eclogue of Baptist Mantuan, a carmelite; being a satyr against women. Done into English verse by William Bewick... *London, printed for T. Warner*, 1718.
8°: *A*² B–D⁴ E²; *i–iv*, *1* 2–27 *28 blk*.
'Janus, your silly goat (I see) looks thin'
CU,MiU.

Bewick, W.

B208 — Faustus, Fortunatus, and Amyntas: or, three eclogues of Baptist Mantuan. Done into English verse by William Bewick. *London, printed for T. Warner*, 1718. (*PB* 21 Jan)
8°: *A*² B–G⁴ H²; *i–iv*, *1–51 52 blk*.
'Come Faustus, in this cool and shady wood'
CSmH.

B209 — A poem on tobacco, from the original Latin of Raphael Thorius... By the reverend William Bewick. *London, printed by J. Read; sold by J. Harris, A. Dodd, and the booksellers of London & Westminster*, 1725. (*MC* Feb)
8°: *A–C*⁴ D²; *1–2* 3–27 *28 blk*.
'I sing the harmless pipe, the fragrant herb'
L(11631.b.67).

Bible.

Bible summaries

Bilcliffe, J.: The holy Bible; containing the old and new testaments, with apocripha. Done into verse for the benefit of weak memories, 1703, [17––.] *See* B213–14.

[Harris, Benjamin:] The holy Bible in verse, containing the old and new testaments with the apocrypha, 1701, 1715, 1724. *See* H61–3.

The history of the old and new testaments: or, an epitome of the sacred writings, [1726.] *See* H259.

Massey, William: Synopsis sacerrima: or, an epitomy, of the holy scriptures, in English verse, 1719. *See* M135.

Wesley, Samuel, *the elder*: The history of the new testament... attempted in verse, 1701, 1715, 1717. *See* W325–7.

— The history of the old testament in verse, 1704, 1715. *See* W328–9.

— The history of the old and new testament attempted in verse, 1716. *See* W330.

I Corinthians

Morell, Thomas: The Christian's epinikion, or song of triumph. A paraphrase on ch. XV of St. Pauls' 1st epistle to the Corinthians, attempted in blank verse, 1743. *See* M438.

Ecclesiastes

Hill, Andrew: The book of Ecclesiastes paraphrased. A divine poem, 1712. *See* H234–5.

Esdras

Collier, Mary: The three wise sentences taken from the first book of Esdras, ch. III. and IV., 1739. *In* C288.

Hebrews

Wesley, Charles: The life of faith, exemplified in the eleventh chapter of St. Paul's epistle to the Hebrews, [1740.] *See* W318.

The triumphs & excellency of faith, as described

by the apostle Paul, Heb. xi. versified, [174–?]
See T505.

Isaiah

A paraphrase on the fourteenth chapter of Isaiah,
in English verse, 1706. *See* P56.

A paraphrase on the fourteenth chapter of Isaiah,
only appropriating what is there meant of the King
of Babylon to Oliver the Protector, 1710. *See* P57.

A paraphrase on part of the fourteenth chapter of
Isaiah, in English verse, 1712. *See* P52.

[Wesley, Charles:] 'The paraphrase on Isaiah 14
[? for 64]', [1742.] *See* W321.

Jeremiah

[Brown, William:] The Lamentations of Jeremiah,
paraphras'd, 1708. *See* B516.

Erskine, Ralph: A short paraphrase upon the
Lamentations of Jeremiah, 1750. *See* E459.

Job

Young, Edward: A paraphrase on part of the book
of Job, 1719, 1726, 1732. *See* Y100–7.

Thompson, William, *fellow of T.C.D.*: A poetical
paraphrase on part of the book of Job, 1726, 1727.
See T168–70.

A paraphrase on the book of Job in verse, with
reflections, 1748. *See* P53.

Jonah

Mitchell, Joseph: Jonah: a poem, 1720. *See*
M309–11.

— [*idem*] Jonah, a poetical paraphrase, 1724. *See*
M312.

Joshua

A paraphrase on part of the book of Joshua, 1724.
See P51.

Judges

Bouchery, Weyman: Hymnus sacer: sive paraphrasis in Deboræ et Baraci canticum, alcaïco
carmine expressa. E libro Judicum. Cap. V, 1706.
See B325.

Part of the song of Deborah and Barak paraphras'd,
from Judges v, 1732. *See* P95.

Proverbs

Tres libri Solomonis, scilicet, Proverbia, Ecclesiastes, et Cantica, carmine latino redditi, 1708, 1709.
See T470–1.

Psalms

Boyse, Joseph: Family hymns for morning and
evening worship... All taken out of the psalms of
David, 1701.

Gibbs, James: The first fifteen psalms of David,
translated into lyric verse, 1701.

— [reissue] Part of a new version of the psalms,
1712.

Darby, Charles: The book of psalms in English
metre, 1704.

Kennett, Basil: An essay towards a paraphrase of
the psalms, in English verse, 1706.

Squire, Joshua: Select psalms of David. Translated anew into English meter, 1707.

Watts, Isaac: The psalms of David imitated in the
language of the new testament, 1719, 1722, 1725,
1727, 1729, 1734, 1736, 1737, 1744, 1747, 1748.

Daniel, Richard: A paraphrase on some select
psalms, 1722.

[Hanway, John:] Psalmi Davidis quinquaginta
priores versibus elegiacis latine rediti, 1723, 1726.

Twenty six chosen psalms of thanksgiving and
praise, love and glory, 1725.

Daniel, Richard: The royal penitent: a paraphrase
on the seven penitential psalms, 1727.

— A paraphrase on some select psalms, and upon
the seven penitential psalms, 1737.

[**1**] The first psalm, [1714?] *In* C458.

Pope, Alexander: A Roman catholick version of the
first psalm, 1716. *See* P953–4.

[**2**] Brereton, Thomas: An English psalm. Or, a
hymn on the late thanksgiving day: being a
protestant version of the second psalm, 1716. *See*
B416.

[**20**] The XX psalm, imitated from Buchanan,
[1711.] *See* T581–2.

[**23**] Part of the 23d psalm taken out of the new
version, [1732.] *See* P96.

[**29**] A paraphrase on the XXIXth psalm, occasioned
by the prospect of peace, 1713. *See* P61.

[**41**] Part of the XLI psalm, to be sung, [1726.]
See P91.

[**45**] Stennett, Joseph: A version of...the XLVth
psalm, 1709. *In* S746.

[**77**] The mourner: a sacred poem. In imitation of
the lxxviith psalm, 1740. *See* R336.

[**78**] Three verses of the 78th psalm, in the new
translation, [1714?] *See* T258.

[**82**] A paraphrase on the lxxxii psalm, [1725?]
See P55.

The original of government, and duty of magistrats. A paraphrase on the LXXXII psalm, [17––.]
See O245.

[**104**] A paraphrase on the hundred and fourth
psalm, in verse, 1741. *See* P58.

Henderson, Andrew: Psalmi centesimi quarti
paraphrasis poetica, 1745. *See* H143·5.

[Burgh, James:] An hymn to the creator of the
world. The thoughts taken chiefly from Psal. civ,
1750. *See* B575–6.

Bible. Psalms

[**112**] Part of the 112th psalm, taken out of the new version, [1728, 1734.] *See* P93–4.

[**119**] Atwood, George: The CXIXth psalm paraphras'd in English verse, 1730. *See* A365.

[**137**] [Hamilton, William, *of Bangour*:] An imitation of the 137. psalm, [1746?] *See* H16.

[**138**] Part of the CXXXVIIIth psalm, the new version, [1742/43]. *See* P92.

[**139**] A paraphrase on the CXXXIX psalm, 1730. *See* P59.

Song of Solomon

[Simson, Patrick:] The Song of Solomon, called the Song of songs. In English meeter, 1701, 1716. *See* S467–8.

[Clark, James:] The wise or foolish choice… In a paraphrase on the Song of Solomon, 1703. *See* C229.

Stennett, Joseph: A version of Solomon's Song of songs, 1709. *See* S746.

[Croxall, Samuel:] The fair Circassian, a dramatic performance [from the Song of Solomon], 1720. *See* C520.

Ker, John, *d. 1741*: Cantici Solomonis paraphrasis gemina, 1727. *See* K20–1.

Erskine, Ralph: A paraphrase, or large explicatory poem upon the Song of Solomon, 1736, 1742. *See* E457–8.

Bland, John: A grammatical version from the original Hebrew, of the Song of Solomon, into English blank verse, 1750. *See* B280.

Song of the three children

[Le Pla, Mark:] A paraphrase on the Song of the three children, 1724. *See* L105–6.

— [*idem*] The Song of the three children paraphras'd, 1728. *See* L107.

Bibliotheca. Bibliotheca: a poem, 1712. *See* Newcomb, Thomas.

Bickerstaff. Bickerstaff's Æsop, [1709.] *See* Pittis, William (P424).

'**Bickerstaff,** *Esquire*.' The dog-kennel to be lett: or, Esquire Bickerstaff's prophecy, 1709. *See* D392.

'**Bickerstaff,** *Squire*.' Squire Bickerstaffe's elegy on…John Dolben, 1710. *See* S671.

'**Bickerstaff** *the younger*.' August the second, 1738. *See* A370.

B210 Bickerstaff, Ezra. England's doom. A prophecy. By Ezra Bickerstaff, esq; Giving an account of strange things that shall befal England, unless timely prevented by our amendments. *London, printed for T. Rogers in Fleet-street*, 1709.
½°: 1 side, 1 column.
'Britons! these lines I lately took'

Bickerstaff E. Englands doom

The author is probably pseudonymous, but the prophecy is not a satirical one. Cf. *The dog-kennel to be lett: or, Esquire Bickerstaff's prophecy*, 1709.
Rothschild.

'**Bickerstaff, Isaac.**' Bickerstaff's Æsop, [1709.] *See* Pittis, William (P424).

'**Bickerstaffe, Jacob.**' A letter from Mr. Jacob Bickerstaffe…occasion'd by the death of Queen Anne, [1714.] *See* L130.

B211 Bickham, George. 'A poem on writing; dedicated to the six most eminent writing-masters of Great Britain, with each of their pictures, adorned with great variety of flourishes and designs. Invented, written, and engraven by George Bickham. [*London*] *Sold by H. Overton, I. King, & J. Barnes*. Price 2s. 6d.' (*Tatler* 2 Nov 1710)
Advertised as 'This day is published, on a sheet of royal paper'.

B212 Biddle, Edward. A poem on the birth of the young prince… To which is added, Augustus. A tragedy. Both written by Edward Biddle, gent. *London, printed for S. Baker*, 1717. (*PB* 23 Nov)
8°: A² B–E⁴ F²; *i–ii, 1* 2–37 *38 blk.*
Only the first act of the tragedy is printed.
'Start up my muse, shake off thy sable gloom'
See [Nicholas Amhurst] *Congratulatory verses to Edward Biddle*, 1718, and cf. A181.
CSmH,*Ct Y*,DFo,ICN.

B213 Bilcliffe, J. The holy Bible; containing the old and new testaments, with the apocripha. Done into verse for the benfit [!] of weak memories. The whole containing above one thousand lines, illustrated with twenty cuts. *London printed, and sold by J. Bradford*, 1703.
32°: A–D⁸; *i–v, ⟨1–2⟩* 3–36 *40–62.*
Title on A2 in woodcut border 'The holy Bible, in verse. 1703.' Possibly the versification entered in *SR* 6 April 1711 to William Marshall as old copy.
'Here god by Moses gave to man'
'The introduction' on A1ᵛ signed 'J. Bilcliffe B.A.' An imitation of Benjamin Harris's versification with the same title, and denounced by him in a caution (dated 15 March 1712) found in his editions after that date.
The late d'Alté A. Welch (lacks B4.5; xerox at L).

B214 —— The forty first impression. *Newcastle upon Tine, printed and sold by John White, at his house at the head of the Painter-Heugh*, [17––.]
18°: A¹² B⁶; *1–2* 3–36.
E.

B215 Billingsgate. The Billingsgate fray: or, a way to set matters right at home. [*London*] *Printed for J. Wilford*, 1734.

The **Billingsgate** fray

4°: A–B^4 C^2; *1–3* 4–18 *19; 20 blk.* 19 advt.
  The copy seen (watermark: Strasburg bend) is almost certainly a fine-paper copy.
'Mankind can never live at ease'
  An entertaining low life poem, with Billingsgate abuse.
E.

B216 [**Billingsley, Nicholas.**] Carmen lugubre. A mournful poem. On the death of a dear and useful relative, Mrs. Grace Billingsley, who departed this life, April 13. 1701. aged 67 years. [*London?* 1701.]
1°: 1 side, 2 columns.
  Mourning borders.
'Earth, keeps the relicts of a choice dear wife'
  Apparently written by her husband Nicholas.
LDW.

[**Bilstone, —.**] The trimmer trimm'd; or the wash-ball and razor used to some purpose, 1749. *See* T481.

B217 [**Bingley, John.**] The fair quakers: a poem. *London, printed for J. Morphew,* 1713. (*SR* 28 Oct)
2°: A–D^2; *i–iv,* 1–12.
  Rothschild 392. Entered in *SR* to John Phillips by Edward Symon; deposit copies at L,LSC, O,EU,AdU. Advertised in *Examiner* 30 Oct.
'Aid sacred nymphs of the Pierian spring'
  For Bingley's authorship, see the reissue below; the publisher's note on A2 makes it clear that it was published without his knowledge. Answered (in prose) by [Josiah Martin] *Remarks on a poem,* 1714. *The second part of the Fair quakers,* 1714, *is by another hand; they were advertised together in PB 15 Jan as printed for John Philips, sold by J. Morphew.*
L(643.1.26/9),LF,O,EU(uncut),AdU + ; CtY, ICU(lacks D^2),TxU(2, uncut).

B218 — [reissue] The fair quaker: or, the seraphick amours of John Bingley with a female Friend. And his poetical lamentation just before his death. To which is prefix'd his funeral elegy. By a lover of truth. *London, printed for R. Burleigh,* 1715. (*MC* May)
2°: A^2(–A1 + $^\pi$A^2) B–D^2; *1–2* 3–4 *iii–iv,* 1–12.
  The funeral elegy was also published separately as *A funeral poem, inscrib'd to the memory of J--n B----y,* [1715.]
Elegy: 'No longer muse, no longer take thy flights'
L(11602.i.15/2),LF(–A2); TxU.

Bion.
Cooke, Thomas: The Idylliums of Moschus and Bion, translated from the Greek, 1724.

B219 Birds. The birds and beasts, a fable... *London, printed for Edw. Lewis,* 1710. (*SR* 10 June)
$\frac{1}{2}^o$: 1 side, 1 column.
  Entered to Lewis in *SR*; deposit copy at E.

The **birds** and beasts

'And such are those whose wiley waxen mind'
  An attack on time-servers.
LSA,E.

B220 Birkhead, Mathew. The enter'd prentices song. By our late brother Mr. Mathew Birkhead, deceas'd. To be sung when all grave business is over, and with the master's leave. *Dublin, printed by George Faulkner,* [1725/30.]
$\frac{1}{2}^o$: 1 side, 2 columns.
  On the other side, Charles Delafaye, *The fellow crafts song,* [1725/30.] The copy at L forms part of a collection of Dublin half-sheets of 1725/30.
'Come let us prepare'
L(C.121.g.8/90),C.

Birmingham. The Birmingham blind man's meditation and diversion. Being a collection of plain poems upon several occasions. With a copy of verses upon his own blindness. Compos'd by himself, since it hath pleased god to take his sight from him. *London, printed for the author in Birmingham,* 1734.
12°: pp. 84.   BP.

'**Birnie, Pate.**' Grubstreet nae satyre, [1720.] *See* Ramsay, Allan.

B221 Birth. The birth of manly virtue from Callimachus. [col] *Dublin, printed by George Grierson,* [1725.]
2°: A–C^2; *i–iv,* 1 2–8.
  Rothschild 2097; *Teerink* 653A; *Williams* 381. Title in half-title form. Reprinted with Roberts's third edition of Swift's *Cadenus and Vanessa,* 1726.
'Once on a time, a righteous sage'
  Reprinted in Cogan's *Supplement to the works of Dr. Swift,* 1752. *Ball* 124–5 considered the poem Swift's, but that he intended it to be attributed to Delany. Williams thought Delany might have had some part in its composition; his copy (now at C) was bound with Delany's *To the right honourable Arthur, earl of Anglesey,* 1721. Swift's authorship needs confirmation. See also [Mary Barber] *To his excellency the Lord Carteret,* 1725, and *A poem inscrib'd to the author of the Birth of manly virtue,* 1725.
C; CSmH,CLU-C.

B222 —— *Dublin, printed by and for George Grierson,* 1725.
8°: A^4; *i–iv,* 1 2–4.
  Teerink 653.
L(995.a.17),LVA-F,C(uncut),DN; CSmH.

B223 Birthday. The birth-day. June 10. 1715. [*London?* 1715.]
obl $\frac{1}{4}^o$: 1 side, 2 columns.
'Let Britain now a grateful homage pay'

The **birth-day.** June 10

> *Crum* L158. Jacobite verses on the Old Pretender's birthday.
> L(1973),O(2).

B224 — The birth-day ode. [*Edinburgh,* 1745.]
½°: 1 side, 1 column.
'Fame! let thy trumpet sound'
> In praise of George II and William duke of Cumberland, with a prayer for victory.
> E.

B225 — [dh] A birth-day ode. [*Edinburgh?* 1746?]
2°: *A*²; 1–4.
'Awhile forget the scenes of woe'
> A Jacobite poem on the Young Pretender.
> LG,E.

B226 Bishop. The bishop of Ely's thanksgiving-sermon, preach'd on the seventh of June, 1716. Done into verse. *London, printed for Tho. Corbet; sold by J. Roberts,* 1716. (*PM* 7 Aug)
8°: *A*¹ B–E⁴ F⁴(–F4); *i–ii,* 1 2–37 *38 blk.* 37 err.
'It is not certain what deliverance made'
> The bishop was William Fleetwood.
> L(11632.b.24); CSmH,TxU.

B227 — The bishop of Rochester's case; or an hymn to the Tower. *London printed, and reprinted in Dubling* [!] *by John Harding,* [1722/23.]
½°: 1 side, 1 column.
'Hail mighty fabrick! England's magazine'
> On Francis Atterbury's imprisonment in the Tower before his trial.
> L(C.121.g.8/19).

B228 — The bishop or no bishop; or, the disappointed doctor. *London, 'printed for Caveat Proctor, near Doctors' Commons'. And sold by T. Reynolds, and the booksellers of London & Westminster,* [1734?]
2°: *A*² B²; *1–3* 4–8.
'A truth there was in times of old'
> On the cancellation of Thomas Rundle's appointment to the see of Gloucester.
> *MR-C*; CLU-C,ICN,KU,MH,NjP.

B229 — — *London, printed by James Harris, near Dr. Cimmons* [!], [1734?]
8°: *A*⁴; *1* 2–8.
> A rough piracy.
> L(1078.h.16).

B230 — Bishop Ridly's ghost: a poem occasioned by the present unnatural rebellion, in favour of a Popish pretender. *London, printed for M. Cooper,* 1745. (*GM,LM* Dec)
2°: *A*¹ B–E²; *i–ii,* 1–'17' *18 blk.* 17 err.
'While, mad with vengeance, on th'Albanian hills'
> AdU; CtY.

B231 Bishop, Samuel. Ode honorabilis Caroli Hanbury Williams... ad honoratissimum Stephanum Poyntz ...latine reddita, a Sam. Bishop, scholæ Mercatorum Scissorum, alumno. *Londini:* [1746/50.]
4°: *A*⁴ B²; *1* 2–11 *12 blk.*
> Latin and English text.

Bishop, Samuel

'Dum sic Wilhelmum laudibus evehit'
L(T.662/3),O.

[**Bisse, Thomas.**] Lusus poetici olim conscripti, a T.B. e C.C.C. Oxon. discipulo. *Londini, typis Gul. Bowyer,* 1720. (25 June?)
8°: pp. 32.   L,EtC.
> Entered to Bisse in Bowyer's ledgers under 25 June, '4 half-sheets & one reprinted no. 150 & 50 large'; large-paper copies have not been identified.

———

B232 [—] Microscopium, & Certamen glaciale. [*London,* 1716?] (31 Aug?)
2°: π¹ *A*² B² C²; *i–ii,* 1–11 *12 blk.*
> Title in half-title form. 'Finis' on p. 8 suggests that C² containing 'Certamen glaciale' was added. Probably the 'Latin poems in 3 sheets in folio' entered to Bisse in Bowyer's ledgers under 31 Aug 1716, 50 copies printed.
'Dædaleas naturæ artes, quas prodiga rebus'
'Isis, quæ fluvios prona dea fundis ab urna'
> Reprinted in Bisse's *Lusus poetici,* 1720; the text of 'Microscopium' is apparently revised from *Musæ Anglicanæ* II, 1699. *Rawlinson* records other 'Latin poems in fol. without date printed I think at Oxford entit. *Machina pneumatica—Gallorum pugna—Funambuli...*' They have not been traced.
L(11631.h.7).

B233 Bisset, William. Verses compos'd for the birth-day of our most gracious Queen Caroline: the first birth-day of a protestant queen consort for one hundred and ten years. Repeated the same day in the great drawing-room... *London, printed for J. Roberts,* 1728. (*MChr* 19 March)
2°: A–C²; *i–iii* iv–vi, 7 '2' 9 10–12. 12 err.
> Poems 'To the King', 'To the Queen', and 'Postscript...The British jubilee; or, carmen sæculare'.
'Great, good, and just; and no less brave and wise!'
'Best of your sex that ever wore a crown!'
'With joy we see the times, most gracious queen'
L(643.l.24/50),O.

B234 — [*idem*] The British jubilee: or, carmen sæculare. Verses compos'd for the birth-day of our most gracious Queen Caroline... The second edition. *London, printed for J. Roberts,* 1728.
2°: A–C²; *i–iii* iv–vi, 7 '2' 9 10–12.
> Apparently partly reset.
CtY(Osborn collection).

'**Bitterzwig, Pendavid.**' Three original poems, 1751. *See* Berkenhout, John.

B---k--r, *Mr.* A long vacation prologue, 1708. *See* L246.

B235 Black. The ⟨black⟩ procession. Or, a description of C---r H---d's funeral. [*Dublin,* 1728.]

The **black** procession

½°: 2 sides, 1 column.
Reprinted in *Crumbs of comfort*, 1728.
'Melpomene, thou patroness'
A satirical funeral poem on William Howard.
DT(cropt).

B236 — Black upon blue: or a purging potion for Father Ch--pp--n. *Dublin, printed by E. Waters, in the year* 1728.
½°: 2 sides, 1 column.
Reprinted in *Crumbs of comfort*, 1728.
'Well Ch--pp---n, is it come to this'
A satire against Richard Choppin's electioneering.
Crawford.

Blackbird. The black-bird: a poem, 1741. *See* Collier, John.

B237 — The black-bird, or the flower of England flown. [*Edinburgh*, 1716/19.]
½°: 1 side, 2 columns.
Two rough woodcuts at head.
'Into a fair morning, for fresh recreation'
A Jacobite ballad in praise of the Old Pretender.
L(1876.f.1/86).

— The blackbird's song, 1715. *See* Stacy, Edmund.

— The black-bird's tale, [1710.] *See* Stacy, Edmund.

— The black-bird's second tale, 1710. *See* Stacy, Edmund.

— The black-bird's third tale, 1710. *See* Stacy, Edmund.

— The blackbird's winter song, [1715?] *See* Stacy, Edmund [The blackbird's song].

Blacklock, Thomas. Poems on several occasions. *Glasgow, printed for the author; sold by the book-sellers in town & country,* 1746.
8°: pp. 88.   L,O; CtY,TxU.
Most copies contain an errata slip.

—— *Edinburgh, printed by Hamilton, Balfour & Neill,* 1754.
8°: pp. xvi, 181.   L,O; DLC,IEN.
A much larger collection than the preceding; a second edition, quarto, was published by Dodsley in 1756.

Blackmore, Sir Richard. A paraphrase on the book of Job: as likewise on the songs of Moses, Deborah, David, on six select psalms, some chapters of Isaiah, and the third chapter of Habakkuk... The second edition revised. *London, printed for Jacob Tonson,* 1716. (*EvP* 28 June)
12°: pp. lxxxiii, 312.   L,O; DLC.
First published in 1700.

— A collection of poems on various subjects. *London, printed by W. Wilkins, for Jonas Browne, & J. Walthoe,* 1718 [1717]. (*DC* 9 Dec)
8°: pp. xvi, 477.   LWS,O; CtY,MH.
Presentation copy at LWS.

Blackmore, *Sir* **R.**

— A new version of the psalms of David, fitted to the tunes used in churches. *London, printed by J. March, for the Company of Stationers,* 1721. (*LG* 5 Dec)
12°: pp. 330.   L,E; MH,TxU.

B238 [—] Advice to the poets. A poem. Occasion'd by the wonderfull success of her majesty's arms, under the conduct of the Duke of Marlborough, in Flanders. *London, printed by H.M. for A. & J. Churchill,* 1706. (23 July, Luttrell)
2°: A–I²; *1–2* 3–34 *35; 36 blk.* I2 err.
In some copies (ICU,TxU), sheet F is unsigned. Advertised in *LG* 25 July.
'Oh! let the conqueror stop his swift career'
Reprinted in Blackmore's *Collection*, 1718.
Cf. *A panegyrick epistle... to S.R—B—,* 1706.
L(643.l.25/10, −I2),LLP,O,DG,WcC+; CLU-C (Luttrell),DFo,ICU,MH(uncut),TxU(4)+.

B239 [—] — The second edition corrected. *London, printed for A. & J. Churchill,* 1706.
2°: A–H²; *1–2* 3–32.
L(11630.g.21),O; CtY(2),ICN,MH.

B240 — Alfred, an epick poem. In twelve books. Dedicated to the illustrious Prince Frederick of Hanover. *London, printed by W. Botham, for James Knapton,* 1723. (*MC* July)
8°: a⁴ b–d⁸ B–2F⁸ 2G⁴; [*8*] i–xlviii, 1–456. xlviii err; 456 advt.
Watermark: S.
'I sing the man, who left fair Albion's shore'
L(11633.bb.7; 993.h.7),O,C,LdU-B,SaU+; CSmH,CtY,ICU,MH,TxU+.

B241 — [fine paper]
Watermark: fleur-de-lys on shield.
L(80.i.14, dedication copy); ICN.

B242 — Creation. A philosophical poem. In seven books. *London, printed for S. Buckley, & J. Tonson,* 1712. (*LG* 28 Feb)
8°: A⁸ a–b⁸ c⁴ B–Z⁸ Aa⁴; [*2*] i ii–lii *liii–liv*, 1–359 *360 blk.* liv err.
Watermark: monogram PH; cut copies 7½ × 4¾ inches. Entered in *SR* 1 March 1712 in equal shares to Tonson and Buckley; no deposit copies traced.
'No more of courts, of triumphs, or of arms'
L(994.l.2),LVA-D,O,*MR*; CSmH,ICU,MH,NjP,TxU+.

B243 — [fine paper]
No watermark; cut copies 8¾ × 5½ inches.
C; CtY.

B244 —— Demonstrating the existence and providence of a god... The second edition. *London, printed for S. Buckley, & J. Tonson,* 1712.
8°: A⁸ a–b⁸ c⁴ B–Z⁸ Aa⁴; [*2*] i ii–lii *liii–liv*, 1–359 *360 blk.*
Advertisement of 23 May recorded in *Haslewood.*
L(991.f.29),O,E; CLU-C,CU,IU,*InU*,MH.

Blackmore, *Sir* **R.** Creation

B245 —— The third edition. *London, printed for J. Tonson, J. Brown, & O. Lloyd, 1715.*
12°: A¹² a–b¹² B–L¹²; [2] *i* ii–lxvi *lxvii–lxx,* 1–237 *238–240.* 238–240 advt.
L(1486.a.2),LVA-D,O; CLU-C,*CtY*,IU,MH, *PU*+.

B246 —— The fourth edition. *London, printed for A. Bettesworth, & J. Pemberton, 1718.* (*PB* 7 Aug)
12°: A¹² a–b¹² B–L¹²; [2] *i* ii–lxvi *lxvii–lxx,* 1–237 *238–240.* 238–240 advt.
     Reissued in 1736, B248.
L(994.b.3),*LVA-F*,O,EU; CLU-C,CSmH,*DLC*, *MB*,MH.

B247 —— The fifth edition. *Dublin, printed by S. Powell, for G. Risk, G. Ewing, & W. Smith, 1727.*
12°: A–I¹²; [2] *i* ii–xxxvii *xxxviii–xxxx,* *1* 2–174.
O,DN.

B248 —— The fourth edition. *London, printed for J. & J. Pemberton, 1736.*
12°: π² A¹²(−A1) a–b¹² B–L¹²; [4] *i* ii–lxvi *lxvii–lxx,* 1–237 *238–240.* π1, 238–240 advt.
     A reissue of the edition of 1718, with cancel title. A half-share of the copyright appeared in lot 18 of the trade sale of Henry Pemberton, 25 Oct 1748 (cat. at O-JJ).
TxU.

B249 — Eliza: an epick poem. In ten books... *London, printed for Awnsham & John Churchill, 1705.* (*DC* 19 July)
2°: A¹ B–4M² 4N¹; *i–ii,* 1–305 *306–322.* 322 err.
     Watermark: fool's cap. Many copies add four pages of advertisements of books published by the Churchills, dated 1700.
'Let, heav'nly muse, enthusiastick fire'
L(641.m.12),O,C,EU,DT+; CSmH(in contemporary morocco),DFo,ICN,MH,TxU+.

B250 — [fine paper]
     Watermark: fleur-de-lys on shield.
L(11626.k.3, presentation copy to Duke of Marlborough; 75.i.4, presentation copy to Queen Anne).

B251 — [reissue] Second edition. *London, printed for W. Chetwood, T. Jauncy, & S. Chapman, 1721.*
2°: A¹(±) B–4M² 4N¹; *i–ii,* 1–305 *306–322.* 322 err.
DLC.

B252 [—] A hymn to the light of the world. With a short description of the cartons of Raphael Urbin, in the gallery at Hampton-Court. *London, printed for Jacob Tonson, 1703* [1702]. (7 Dec, Luttrell)
2°: A¹ B–G² H¹; *i–ii,* 1–26.
     Watermark: crown. Paste-on slip reading 'Cartons' for 'Chartones' in drop-head title, p. 16. The Luttrell copy is recorded in Pickering & Chatto cat. 284/25. Listed in *WL* Dec 1702.
'Hail radiant off-spring, emanation bright!'
     Reprinted in Blackmore's *Collection,* 1718.
L(1970),O,DT,*WgP*; CSmH,CtY,ICN,MH,TxU (2)+.

Blackmore, *Sir* **R.** A hymn

B253 [—] [fine paper]
     Watermark: X (cf. *Heawood* 3116).
LLP; TxU.

B254 [—] Instructions to Vander Bank, a sequel to the Advice to the poets: a poem, occasion'd by the glorious success of her majesty's arms, under the command of the Duke of Marlborough, the last year in Flanders. *London, printed for Egbert Sanger, 1709.* (*PB* 10 March)
2°: A–C²; *1–2* 3–12.
     No watermark.
'Have all thy bards, Britannia, spent their vein'
     Reprinted in Blackmore's *Collection,* 1718.
O(2, 1 uncut); CLU-C(Luttrell, 10 March),CtY, DFo,KU,TxU.

B255 [—] [fine paper]
     Watermark: monogram PH.
LLP; MH.

B256 [—] — *London printed, and sold by H. Hills, 1709.*
8°: A⁸; *1–2* 3–16.
     Some copies (L,C,E,InU) have a misprint in title 'Flandres' for 'Flanders'. Reissued with other Hills poems in *A collection of the best English poetry,* 1717 (*Case* 294).
L(1466.b.47; 1346.b.45; C.124.b.7/10),O(2),C, E,LdU-B+; CtY,ICN,InU,MH,TxU+.

B257 [—] The Kit-Cats. A poem. *London, printed for E. Sanger & E. Curll, 1708.* (*DC* 22 May)
2°: A² B–F²; *i–iv,* 1–19 *20.* A1 hft; 20 advt.
     No watermark. *Bond* 20. The poem was re-advertised by Curll with Blackmore's name in *PB* 7 March 1717; *Straus, Curll* suggests it was a new octavo edition, but the reference to fine-paper copies on royal paper makes it probable that this edition is in question.
'I sing the assembly's rise, encrease and fame'
     Reprinted in Blackmore's *Collection,* 1718. A satire on Jacob Tonson and his poets.
L(11630.g.19; 11602.i.14/4),O(−A1),OC,DG, LdU-B+; CLU-C(Luttrell,22 May),CSmH,CtY, KU(uncut),TxU+.

B258 [—] [fine paper]
     Watermark: J.
MH(−A1),TxU.

B259 [—] — *London printed, and sold by H. Hills, 1708.*
8°: A⁸; *1–2* 3–16.
     A2, A3, A4 signed. The order of this and the following edition is undetermined.
L(992.h.3/3); MH,TxU.

B260 [—] [another edition]
8°: A⁸; *1–2* '2' 4–16.
     A3 only signed.
OC(uncut).

B261 [—] — To which is added the Picture, in imitation of Annacreon's Bathillus. As also the Coquet beauty, by...the Marquis of Normandby. *London printed, and sold by H. Hills, 1708.*

Blackmore, *Sir* **R.** The Kit-Cats

8º: A⁸; *1–2* 3–16.
O(2),OW,C,EU,DT; CSmH,CtY,IU,MH.

B262 [—] — *London printed, and sold by H. Hills,* 1709.
8º: A⁸; *1–2* 3–16.
Reissued with other remaindered Hills poems in *A collection of the best English poetry,* 1717 (*Case* 294).
L(11632.aaa.16; C.124.b.7/34),LVA-F,O(2),E, WcC; CtY,ICN,ICU,MH,TxU.

B263 [—] The nature of man. A poem. In three books. *London, printed for Sam Buckley; sold by the booksellers of London & Westminster,* 1711. (*DC* 6 April)
8º: A⁴ B–H⁸ I¹; *[4]* i–iv, *1*–113 *114 blk.* A1 hft.
Watermark: star. Some copies (e.g. L,ICN) have A3 signed 'A2' and p. iv numbered 'vi'.
'Superiour bards, the pride of ancient days'
Reprinted in Blackmore's *Collection,* 1718.
L(11632.bb.31),O,LdU-B; CLU-C,CtY,ICN, MH,TxU+.

B264 [—] [fine paper]
Watermark: Strasburg bend. A3 unsigned, p. iv correctly numbered.
IU.

B265 — [reissue] By Sir Richard Blackmore. *London, printed for John Clark, & A. Dodd,* 1720. (*PB* 1 March)
8º: A⁴(−A1–3,+A2.3) B–H⁸ I¹; *[2]* i–iv, *1*–113 *114 blk.*
No half-title in copies seen.
L(11645.ee.46/2),C,E; *IU,MH,TxU.*

[—] The Pretender's declaration...turn'd into verse...by the most ingenious Richardo Mauro, 1708. *See* M140.

B266 — Prince Arthur. An heroick poem... The fourth edition revised... *London, printed for J. Tonson,* 1714.
12º: A–Q¹²; *i–xxiv,* *1* 2–341 *342–360.* Q11–12 advt.
'I sing the Briton, and his generous arms'
The title of the copy seen may have escaped cancellation, and the book not intended for issue in this form. First published in 1695.
L(1076.a.27).

B267 — [another issue] *London, printed for J. Tonson, and are to be sold by J. Knapton & D. Midwinter, A. Betsworth, W. Taylor, N. Cliff & D. Jackson, T. Varnam & J. Osborn, J. Browne,* 1714. (*Englishman* 28 Jan)
12º: A¹²(±A1) B–Q¹²; *i–xxiv,* *1* 2–341 *342–360.* Q11–12 advt.
The title is clearly a cancel in the AdU copy, probably so in all copies.
LVA-D,O,AdU; CtY,ICU,IU(−Q12),NNP (−Q11,12),*NjP+*.

B268 — Redemption: a divine poem, in six books... *London, printed for A. Bettesworth, & James Mack Euen,* 1722. (*DP* 7 May)
8º: A–Bb⁸; *i–ii* iii–xxxi *xxxii,* *1* 2–143 160–368.
Title in red and black.

Blackmore, *Sir* **R.** Redemption

'I who have sung, how from the realms of night'
L(03440.i.29; 994.l.3),LVA-D(2),O,E,LdU-B; CtY,MH,*OCU*,TxU+.

B269 Blacksmith. The blacksmith's recreation; or the triumphant maid. To the tune of Twangdillo, &c. [*Dublin*] *Printed in the year* 1725.
½º: 1 side, 1 column.
'Come hither ye maidens of country and town'
On an amorous encounter between the blacksmith, All-n, and Miss R—by.
L(C.121.g.8/49).

[**Blackstone, Henry.**] The pantheon: a vision, 1747. *See* P45.

B270 '**Blackwell, James,** *operator for the feet.*' A friendly apology for a certain justice of peace; by way of defence of H—y H—n, esq; [*Dublin*] *Printed in the year* 1730.
8º: A⁴; *1–3* 4–7 *8 blk.*
Williams 1134.
'I sing the man, of courage try'd'
Included in Nichols's *Supplement* to Swift's Works, 1779, but not by him. A satire on Hartley Hutchinson.
L(11601.ccc.38/2),LVA-F,DA,DT(uncut); MH.

[**Blair, Hugh.**] A poem sacred to the memory of the reverend Mr. James Smith, 1736. *See* P657.

[—] The resurrection: a poem. In three parts, 1747. *See* D414.

B271 Blair, Robert. The grave. A poem. *London, printed for M. Cooper,* 1743. (*GM,LM* March)
4º: A⁴ B–E⁴; *1–3* 4–39 *40 blk.*
'Whilst some affect the sun, and some the shade'
L(11630.d.15/5),LSC,O,E,LdU-B+; CSmH, CtY,ICN,MH,TxU+.

B272 — — The second edition. *London, printed for M. Fenner; sold by M. Cooper,* 1743. (*LDP* 5 Nov)
8º: A–F⁴; *1–3* 4–45 *46; 47–48 blk.* 46 err.
C(−F4); CLU-C(−F4),CSmH,InU,KU(−F4), NN(−F4).

B273 — — *Edinburgh, printed by R. Drummond, for the employer, and sold by most of the booksellers in town and country,* 1747.
8º: A⁴ B–E⁴; *1–2* 3–39 *40 blk.*
Horizontal chain-lines.
CtY.

B274 — — The third edition. *London printed, and sold by J. Waugh,* 1749.
8º: A–F⁴; *1–3* 4–45 *46–48.* 46–48 advt.
A fifth edition with imprint 'Edinburgh, printed for William Gray junior, 1751' (copy at E) was listed in *SM* Dec 1750.
L(11631.d.8),*LVA-D*,O; IU,NjP.

B275 [—] [dh] A poem dedicated to the memory of the late learned and eminent Mr. William Law, professor of philosophy in the university of Edinburgh. [*Edinburgh,* 1728?]

Blair, R. A poem

4°: A⁴; 1–8.
　　Date from Robert Anderson's life of Blair; the
　　CSmH copy is bound with poems of the 1740s.
'In silence to suppress my griefs I've try'd'
　　Collected in Anderson's edition of Blair, 1826.
L(11631.f.20),E; CSmH.

B276 Blair, Thomas. Gibbie and Wattie. A pastoral on
the death of Alexander Maben organ-maker in
Edinburgh. *Edinburgh, printed for, and sold by the
author,* 1734.
4°: A–C²; 1–2 3–12.
'Come, Wattie, while our hirsels feed thegither'
L(11632.df.10).

B277 — — *Edinburgh, printed in the year* 1734.
8°: A⁴ B²; 1–2 3–12.
GM.

B278 — — *Edinburgh printed, and sold in Swan-Close
[by R. Drummond?],* 1749.
8°: *A⁴*; *1* 2–8.
L(1077.c.6/2),O.

B279 Blake, Elizabeth. England's glory: or, a trium-
phant loyal health to the queen, church, Doctor
Sacheverell, and the new loyal members of parlia-
ment. To that noble and heroick tune of, Huzza!
Bomb. *London, printed by Edward Midwinter,* 1710.
½°: 1 side, 1 column.
'To the church and great Anne'
Rothschild.

[**Blakiston, —, *Mr.*]** The pantheon: a vision, 1747.
See P45.

[**Bland, —, *Mr.*]** The constellation: poems, on
several occasions. *London printed, and sold by
S. Keimer,* 1715. (*MC* April)
8°: pp. 40.　ICN,MH.
　　According to *Rawlinson* this was written by
　　'Mr. Bland' with the exception of a few
　　pieces by John Locker.

[**Bland, James.]** An essay in praise of women:
containing nine poems. *London, printed for the
author; sold by J. Roberts, J. Batley, J. Jackson,
C. King, T. Cox, C. Corbet, & J. Batson,* 1735.
8°: pp. 16.　DLC,IU.
　　Apparently a supplement to the second edition
　　of Bland's prose *An essay in praise of women,*
　　1735; possibly also published separately.

B280 Bland, John. A grammatical version, from the
original Hebrew; of the Song of Solomon, into
English blank verse... The whole being a drama,
in seven scenes... *London, printed for, and sold by
J. Wren,* 1750.
8°: A⁴ b² B–G⁴ H²; *i–iii* iv–x *xi–xii,* 1–52.
'With kisses of his mouth, let him kiss me'
L(T.1941/1),O,E; ICU,NN(lacks G4–H2).

Blasphemy. Blasphemy as old as the creation,
1730. *See* Newcomb, Thomas.

B281 Blasted. The blasted laurel. A poem. *London
printed, and are to be sold by A. Baldwin,* 1702.
(19 Jan, Luttrell)
2°: A–D²; *i–ii,* 1–14.
　　The Luttrell copy is recorded in *Haslewood;*
　　listed in *WL* Jan.
'In ancient days, had Roman rage run down'
　　A satire on the poets, with a particular attack
　　on Prior.
LG,O; DFo,IU(B2 mutilated),MH(uncut),TxU.

[**B282 = C55·5] Blatant.** The blatant-beast, 1742. *See*
Carte, Thomas.

B283 Blazing. 'The blazing star. An ode. Humbly
address'd to the Princess Royal. [*London*] *Sold by
Miss Reason at the Wells.*' (*LaM* June 1733)

B-----le, *Madam.* The fifteen plagues of a
maiden-head, 1707. *See* F135.

— The fifteen pleasures of a virgin, 1709. *See* F136.

Blenheim. Bleinheim, 1728. *See* Lyttelton, George.

— Bleinheim, a poem, inscrib'd to the right
honourable Robert Harley, 1705–. *See* Philips,
John.

B284 Blessings. The blessings attending George's
accession and coronation. [*London?* 1715.]
⅛°: 1 side, 1 column.
　　Originally conjugate with *Let each have his
　　own.* Also printed in *On the thanksgiving-day,*
　　[1715.]
'The golden age is now again restor'd'
　　Crum T695: 'On the thanksgiving day the
　　20th March 1714/5'; one ms. marked 'R.C.'
　　A Jacobite satire against George I.
CtY.

[**B285 = O224·2] Bl--ke--y.** Bl--ke--y's prologue and
epilogue; or, the Theatre-royal in Drury-lane,
the grand lodge for free masons, 1729. *See* On the
27th of January, [1730.]

B286 Block. A block for Allan Ramsay's wigs, or, the
famous poet, fall'n in a sleep. [*Edinburgh,* 172–?]
½°: 1 side, 2 columns.
'Vow Allie, what's come ore ye now'
　　Complaining of Ramsay's silence.
E.

B287 Blockade. The blockade of Edinburgh castle; or,
Captain Taylor in Livingston's yards. A poem.
[*Edinburgh,* 1745.]
½°: 1 side, 1 column.
'Where wholesom pot-herbs flourish all around'
L(C.115.i.3/74),E.

B288 Blot. A blott is no blott, 'till it is hott; or, among
all the funds the worst fund is refund. The few
following lines, writ extempore, on occasion of

A blott is no blott

C—n B—h his book, entitled, A method of determining the areas of right lined figures universally, by T—s B—h, esq; s--rv--r and ing--eer g--n--l. [*Dublin*] *Printed in the year* 1725.
½°: 1 side, 1 column.
'Cou'd a surveyor! think this a mystery?'
Signed 'A, B, C, D, &c. philo-mats.' A satire on Thomas Burgh's book of 1724.
CtY.

Blue. 'Blue-ey'd Nancy; or, the disappointed lovers. An excellent new ballad. To the tune of Fair Rosamond; or to any other better tune, to which the lovers of musick shall set it. [*London*] *Printed, and sold by J. Roberts, & T. Griffith.* N.B. To prevent counterfeits, they are stamp'd.' (*DP* 24 Jan 1722, 'to-morrow')
There is no evidence that this was published; it might possibly have been an engraved sheet with music. A stanza quoted in the advertisement is probably the first; it opens 'All in Soho, there liv'd a toast'.

B289 — [dh] The blue garter no more a sign of honesty than a gilded bush is of good wine. [col] *London, printed* [!] *Newcomb in Wine-court, Fleetstreet,* 1713. (*SR* 13 Feb)
2°: *A*² < *B*¹; ff. *1 2–3.*
Printed on one side of the leaf only, the third leaf on the verso. Entered in *SR* by Michael Holt to John Baber (? for Barber) and Richard Newcomb; deposit copies at L,EU.
'In antient times when Britain's warlike sons'
L(11602.i.12/7***, uncut; C.20.f.2/238),O,EU.

Blue-skin. Blue-skin's ballad, 1724–5. *See* Newgate's garland, [1724/25.]

B290 Blunder. The blunder of all blunders,|On the wonder of all wonders.|Or, Gulliver devour'd by butterflies: or, the fops observation on Lilliput, &c. *Dublin, printed in the year* 1726.
½°: 1 side, 2 columns.
Teerink 1217.
'As mercenary canting quacks'
An attack on the commentators on *Gulliver's Travels.*
L(C.121.g.8/54),DT.

Blunderella. Blunderella: or, the impertinent, 1730. *See* Carey, Henry.

Blunt. Blunt to Walpole: a familiar epistle in behalf of the British distillery, 1730. *See* Bockett, Elias.

'Blunt, Alexander.' Geneva: a poem, 1729. *See* Bockett, Elias.

Blyth, Francis. 'Poems on various subjects.'
There are proposals dated 16 Nov [174–?] at

Blyth, F.

O-JJ; a reference to previous proposals suggests a chronic state of impending publication.

———————

B291 [—] Advice to a friend on his marriage, a poem. *London, printed for T. Cooper, Mrs. Nutt, Cooke, & Charlton, Mrs. Dodd, and at the pamphlet shops of London & Westminster,* 1735 [1736]. (GM,LM Jan)
2°: *A*¹ B–F² *G*¹; *i–ii, 1 2–21 22 blk.*
'Cease, Drusus, cease; make thy strong transports less'
Attributed to 'Francis Blythe esq;' in subsequent listing in *GM,LM* Feb 1736.
CLU.

'B—m, B., *esq;*' To the right honourable Lady Mary, vis. T—y, 1732–3. *See* T390·5.

B292 Bo---. Bo---'s in disgrace,|With the bells of this place.|Or|As every one thinketh,|It's so the bell clinketh. [*Dublin,* 1740?]
½°: 1 side, 2 columns.
'War may bring better times'
An attack on Walpole.
C.

B293 Boarding-school. The boarding-school. A new ballad. Tune Chivy-chaise. [*Dublin*] *Printed for P. Neal in Georges Lane,* 1725.
slip: 1 side, 1 column.
'Ye ladies that in Y---- street dwell'
On Parson Creed chasing Jack Passionate away from the school.
C.

B294 Bob. Bob Booty's lost deal, or, the cards shuffled fair at last. *London, printed by John Jones, in the Strand,* [1742.]
½°: 1 side, 2 columns.
Percival LXXIV. Woodcuts at head.
'You honest hearts, that wish'd fair play'
On the fall of Walpole. According to Percival, an adaptation of [Laurence Price] *A knave at the bottom.*
L(1876.f.1/126).

B295 — A Bob for the court; or, Prince Eugene's welcome. [*London*] *Printed in the year* 1712. (2 Jan, Luttrell)
½°: 1 side, 1 column.
After imprint, 'Price One Peny'.
'To cure the nation of the rot'
A tory poem in praise of Harley's peace moves. Reprinted and answered in *Honest Tom's resentment,* 1712.
O,*Chatsworth*; ICN(Luttrell),TxU.

B296 — [another edition]
No price after imprint.
MH.

A **Bob** for the court

B297 — [another edition]

No price after imprint. On the other side, *A vindication of the Duke of Marlborough*, 1712; possibly a Dublin reprint.

Harding.

'**Bobbin, Timothy.**' The black-bird, 1741. *See* Collier, John.

Boccaccio, Giovanni.

[*Decameron*, day 1, tale 1] Ayre, William: The saint, 1734. *See* A374.

[day 2, tale 6] Taubman, Nathaniel: Virtue in distress: or, the history of Mindana [based on Boccaccio], 1706. *See* T93.

[day 2, tale 8] [Pix, Mary:] Violenta, or the rewards of virtue, 1704. *See* P463–4.

[day 5, tale 4] The nightingale, 1721. *See* N301–2.

[day 6, tale 10] Fra Cipolla, 1737. *See* F228–9.

[*idem*] The popish impostor, [1740], 1748. *See* F230, 230·5.

───────────

Humphreys, Samuel: The amorous groom, and the gossips wager: two novels from Boccace, 1735. *See* H401.

B298 [**Bockett, Elias.**] Aminadab's courtship: or, the quaker's wedding. A poem...Written by a Friend. *London, printed for J. Roberts*, 1717. (*DC* 27 Sept)

12°: A–D⁶ E⁴; *1–5* 6–54 *55–56 blk.* A1 frt.

'Aminadab, a well-enlighten'd Friend'

Authorship from *Smith* I. 289; no confirmation found.

LF,GU(uncut, −E4),LdU-B; DFo,MH.

B299 [—] The annotations of the Grub-street society on Mr. Bowman's sermon, in a letter from Parson Orthodox to Mother Bavius... To which is added, the sorrowful lamentation of Parson Orthodox. Done into English metre, after the manner of Thomas Sternhold. By the author of Geneva: a poem. *London, printed for, and sold by T. Warner, and the pamphlet-shops in London & Westminster*, [1731.] (*GSJ* 5 Oct)

8°: A⁴(−A4) B–C⁴ ²C⁴ D¹; *iii–v* vi–viii, *9* 10–34.

'Dear Goody! you have seen, no doubt'

For Bockett's authorship, see *Geneva* below.

LF(2),O; MH.

B300 [—] The author of a Character, &c. to the author of a letter, dated, Enfield, Feb. 18, 1717. [*London*] *Printed in the year* 1717.

8°: A⁸ B²; *1–2* 3–20.

''Tis strange! Must nonsense flow without constraint?'

Cf. *A character*, 1717, below. A reply to *A letter from a friend in the country to his friend in London*, 1717, written in prose in defence of William Gibson.

LF(2); MH.

Bockett, E.

B301 [—] Blunt to Walpole: a familiar epistle in behalf of the British distillery. *London, printed for J. Wilford, & E. Bockett*, 1730. (*MChr* 27 Jan)

8°: A² B–D⁴ E²; *1–5* 6–31 *32.* A1 hft, err; 32 advt.

'Sir Robert, tho' at your levee'

Signed on p. 31 'A. Blunt', 20 Dec 1729. A copy at LF is in a contemporary volume labelled 'Bockett's Miscellanies'; note his name in imprint. On the effects of the gin act.

L(11631.e.6,−A1),LF(2, 1 uncut, 1−A1), O(−A1); IU.

B302 [—] A character. [*London*] *Printed in the year* 1717.

8°: A⁸; *1–2* 3–13 *14–16.*

Reprinted in *A complete collection of pamphlets, pro and con*, no. 1, 1727 (copy at LF); revised first line there, 'Why G— first a preacher did commence'.

'Satyr, audacious G—n's wiles reherse'

Early ms. attribution to Bockett in a copy at LF. A satire on William Gibson. This and *A character defended* were replied to in *A letter to the author of a Character*, 1717.

LF(2, 1 uncut),O; MH.

B303 [—] A character defended. [*London*] *Printed in the year* 1717.

8°: A⁸; *1–2* 3–15 *16 blk.*

Reprinted in *A complete collection of pamphlets, pro and con*, no. 1, 1727.

'As long as C—le can write, and G—n rage'

LF(2, 1 uncut); MH.

B304 [—] Geneva: a poem. Address'd to the right honourable Sir R— W—. By Alexander Blunt, distiller. *London, printed for T. Payne; sold by the booksellers of London & Westminster*, 1729. (*MChr* 16 April)

8°: A⁴ B–D⁴; *1–15* 16–32. A1 hft.

Bond 104. Most copies have misprint 'booksellesr' in imprint.

'Thy virtues O Geneva! yet unsung'

For the authorship, cf. *Blunt to Walpole* above. A defence of gin in blank verse, occasioned by the presentment of the Middlesex grand-jury.

L(161.k.7,−A1),LF(2, 1−A1); CSmH,CtY(−A1),DLC,MH,TxU+.

B305 [—]— In Miltonic verse. *London: printed, and Dublin re-printed by James Hoey & George Faulkner*, 1729.

8°: A⁴; *1–3* 4–8.

C,DA.

[—] The London clergy's petition against the quakers affirmation, answer'd, paragraph by paragraph, 1722. *See* L236.

B306 — A poem to the memory of Aquila Rose, who dy'd at Philadelphia, August the 22d, 1723. ætat. 28. *London, printed for the author*, 1723–4.

8°: A⁴ B²; *1–5* 6–12. A1 hft.

Bockett, E. A poem to the memory

> Reprinted in Rose's *Poems*, Philadelphia, 1740.
> 'Marino!–– welcome from the western shore'
> L(G.13782/4),LF(2, 1–A1); NN,*PHi*,PU(–A1).

B307 [—] A return to the author of a Letter to the author of a Character. [*London*] *Printed in the year* 1717.
8°: A⁸; *1–2* 3–16.
'And must we calmly hear his nonsense still'
> Signed 'The author of a Character'; cf. *A character*, 1717, above. A reply to *A letter to the author of a Character*, 1717.
> LF(2, 1 uncut); MH.

B308 [—] The yea and nay stock-jobbers, or the 'Change-alley quakers anatomiz'd. In a burlesque epistle to a friend at sea. *London, printed for J. Roberts, A. Dodd, & J. Billingsly*, 1720. (*DP* 5 Dec)
8°: *A⁴* B–D⁴; *1–5* 6–32. A1 hft.
'Whilst thou my friend with sails unfurl'd'
> Poem signed 'Damon'. A copy at LF is in a contemporary volume labelled 'Bockett's Miscellanies'.
> L(G.13782/3),LF(2,–A1),O(–A1); CtY,OCU (–A1).

B309 [—] — The second edition. *London, printed for J. Roberts, A. Dodd, & J. Billingsly*, 1720. (*PB* 6 Dec)
8°: *A⁴* B–D⁴; *1–5* 6–32. A1 hft.
> The title is not a cancel; either a reimpression or press-variant title, probably the latter.
> LF.

Bockett, Richard. Fruits of early piety, consisting of several Christian experiences, meditations, and admonitions. Written in verse... Very profitable for the perusal of youth. *London, printed by the assigns of J. Sowle*, 1722.
8°: pp. 50.   LF; CLU-C,CtY.

— — The second edition. *London, printed by the assigns of J. Sowle*, 1735.
8°: pp. 40.   LF; MH,PSC-Hi.
> An undated third edition (copies at L,NN) was probably published after 1767.

B310 Boeoticorum. Bœoticorum liber. Or, a new art of poetry. Containing the best receipts for making all sorts of poems according to the modern taste. In two canto's. *London: printed. Dublin: re-printed by and for George Faulkner*, 1732.
8°: *A⁴* B⁴ C²; *1–3* 4–18 *19–20*. C2 advt.
> *Rothschild* 204. The order of editions is uncertain, though the following appears to be one of a group of reprints of Dublin poems produced by Bowyer and partners.
'Oft Bardus to Apollo pray'd'
DA,DG; OCU.

B311 — — *Dublin, printed: London, reprinted and sold by J. Roberts*, 1732. (3 May?)
4°: A–B⁴ C²; *1–3* 4–20. 20 advt.

Boeoticorum liber

> The date of publication is obscure: listed in *GM,LM* April, and in *GSJ* 8 May 1732. Entered in Bowyer's ledgers to 'WB & partners' under 3 May, 750 copies printed.
> L(11630.d.15/7, title cropt),O; ICN,IU.

Boileau. Boileau's Lutrin: a mock-heroic poem, 1708. *See* Ozell, John.

Boileau-Despréaux, Nicolas.
[*Art poétique*] Soames, *Sir* William: The art of poetry, 1710, 1715. *See* S540–1.

— [reissue] The true περι βαθους, 1728. *See* S542.

[*Lutrin*] Ozell, John: Boileau's Lutrin: a mock heroic poem, 1708. *See* O282–3.

— [*idem*] The Lutrin, 1714, 1730. *See* O284–5.

Denne, Henry: Love alone: or, the star that leads to Christ...written in French by Mr. Boileau, 1703. *See* D217.

[Southcott, Thomas:] Monsieur Boileau's epistle to his gardiner, 1712. *See* S615.

B312 [**Bold, Michael.**] Paradisus amissa. Poema, anglicè scriptum Johane Milton. Nunc autem ex auctoris exemplari Latinè redditum. Per M. B. Liber primus. *Londini: typis J. G.*, 1702.
4°: *A⁴*(±A1) B–O⁴; *1–3* 4–109 *110–112 blk*.
> Latin title from p. 2; English title 'Paradise lost... Book the first' and imprint on p. 3. Text in Latin and English.
'Quo primævus Adas temerato fœdere numen'
> Ms. notes on the author in the CtY copy.
> L(11626.c.13),LVA-D; CSmH,CtY.

B313 [—] — Poema, a Joanne Miltono conscriptum. Latinitate donavit M. B. Liber primus. *Londini, typis J. Hughs*, 1736.
4°: *A⁴* B⁴ C⁴(±C4) D–N⁴ O⁴(–O4); *1–3* 4–109 *110*. 110 err.
> L(1162.e.41).

B314 [**Boldero, John.**] In illustrissimum infantem nuper natum. [*London*, 1717.]
½°: 1 side, 1 column.
'Juno potens uteri, ad mortales non voco nixus'
> Ms. note in L copy, 'per Ioh. Baldero Cantab.'
> On the birth of Prince George William.
> L(Cup.651.e/217),O.

B315 [**Bolton, J.**] Prince Eugene: an heroic poem on the victorious progress of the confederate arms in Italy; under the conduct of his royal highness the Duke of Savoy, and Prince Eugene. *London, printed for Edmund Curll, & Egbert Sanger*, 1707 [*1706*]. (19 Oct, Luttrell)
2°: A–C²; *i–ii*, 1–10. 10 advt.
> The Luttrell copy is recorded in Blackwell cat. 390/63; advertised in *DC* 30 Oct as sold by J. Morphew.

Bolton, J. Prince Eugene

'O! lend, Pierian virgins, lend your aid'
  Ms. attribution in O copy 'By Mr. Bolton of
  Ch. Church'; he has not been identified.
  Readvertised in *PM* 6 Feb 1707 as 'by J.B. of
  Christ Church College, Oxford'.
O(uncut); KU,TxU(2).

Bond, William.
*'H. Stanhope is usually considered to be a pseudonym
of Bond, since Curll in* The Curliad *(1729) 24–5
coupled them as responsible for* The progress of
dulness, *1728 (a work chiefly in prose, and excluded
here). Poems by Stanhope are entered under his
name.*

[—] The epistles of Clio and Strephon, 1720–. *See*
Fowke, Martha.

[—] The thresher's miscellany, 1730. *See* 'Duck,
Arthur'.

———————

[—] Buckingham House.
  An edition of this poem was issued without
  preliminaries in [John Markland] *Three new
  poems,* 1721. It seems probable that it was
  previously issued separately.

B315·5 [—] Cobham and Congreve. An epistle to lord
  Viscount Cobham, in memory of his friend, the
  late Mr. Congreve. *London, printed for E. Curll,*
  1730. (*MChr* April)
  8°: π¹[=F4] A–E⁴ F⁴(–F4); *i–ii, 1–2* 3–46. π1
  hft.
  'Since my weak voice in Congreve's praise
  preferr'd'
    Ascribed to Bond under the title 'Congreve
    and Cobham' in Curll's advertisement in
    Margaret, lady Pennyman's *Miscellanies,* 1740.
  L(11631.d.52),O.

B316 [—] A description of the four last things, viz.
  death, judgment, hell, & heaven; in blank verse.
  London, printed for John Clark, 1719. (*PB* 17 Feb,
  'Monday next' [23])
  12°: A–N⁶; *i–iii* iv, *5* 6–154 *155–6*. N6 advt.
  'When by th' assistance of some heavenly ray'
    Ascribed to Bond by LDW.
  O.

B317 [—] — The second edition. To which is added
  three Spectators printed in the year 1715... *London,
  printed for John Clark,* 1719.
  12°: A⁶(±A1) B–N⁶, ²A–B⁶; *i–iii* iv, *5* 6–154 *155–6,
  1–3* 4–23 *24*. N6, ²B6ᵛ advts.
    A reissue with the addition of ²A–B⁶ in prose.
    Advertised in *DJ* 31 Jan 1723.
  L(11630.bb.10),LDW.

B318 [—] — An odaic essay in commemoration of the
  nativity of our lord. *London, printed for J. Battley,
  T. Buttler, T. Franclin; sold by T. Payne,* 1724
  [1723]. (*MC* Dec)
  2°: a² b¹ B–D²; *i–v* vi, *1* 2–11 *12 blk.*
  ''Tis well and wisely done, my muse'
  DT; TxU(uncut).

Bond, W.

B319 — The third book of Tasso's Jerusalem. Written
  originally in Italian. Attempted in English. By
  Mr. Bond. *London printed, and sold by W. Lewis,
  H. Clements, & T. Warner,* 1718. (*DC* 2 May)
  8°: a⁴ b² A–G⁴ H²; *i–ii* iii–xii, *1–3* 4–59 *60 blk.*
  59 err.
    Printed with Fairfax's translation on facing
    pages. The advertisement in *DC* reveals that
    this was 'published, by way of specimen';
    Bond proposed to translate all twenty books.
  'Now sparks of light shoot streaming thro' the
  air'
  MH.

B320 — 'Verses sacred to the memory of the most noble
  Henrietta, late duchess of Grafton... [London]
  Printed for A. Bettesworth. Price 6d.' (*MC* Feb
  1727)
    Clearly the ordinary issue (on paper) of the
    following.
  'O Grafton, Suffolk's lord, who are'

B321 — [on satin] Verses sacred to the memory of the
  most noble Henrietta, late duchess of Grafton.
  Humbly inscrib'd to the most illustrious prince,
  Charles, duke of Grafton. [London, 1727.]
  2°: A–D²; *1–2* 3–15 *16 blk.*
    Title in form of a dedication. Printed on satin,
    with black borders sewn on.
  L(C.43.h.14).

Bonefonius, Joannes.
The Basia *were translated by several hands in*
Pancharis queen of love, *1721–, and in other
miscellanies.*

Pancharilla, from Bonefonius. A new ballad,
[1725/30.] *See* P27.

B322 [**Bonwick, Ambrose.**] [dh] To the memory of the
  truly pious Sir George Freeman knight of the Bath,
  his ever honour'd godfather. [London, 171–/22.]
  2°: A²; *1–4.*
  'Blest soul! Thou [who] were wont to be'
    Signed 'A. B.', expanded in the copy seen to
    'Ambrose Bonwicke'. According to *Rawlinson,*
    by the elder Bonwick, 1652–1722.
  O(MS. Rawl. J fol. 2/223).

B323 **Bookey, Sacheverell.** In congratulation to Sir
  John Lake, on the conclusion of the war. A poem.
  London, printed for Henry Clements, 1713. (*PB*
  2 June)
  4°: A² B–C²: *1–2* 3–12.
  'Ere (cursed instance!) as the poets feign'
  CtY.

Booth, Barton. Memoirs of the life of Barton
  Booth, esq; with his character. To which are
  added several poetical pieces, written by himself,
  viz., translations from Horace, songs, odes &c...
  London, printed for John Watts, 1733.
  8°: pp. 58.   L,LdU-B; CtY.
    Verse on pp. 37–58.

Boots. 'Boots and saddles.' [*Dublin*, 1726?]
The existence of this work, presumably a half-sheet, is suggested by *Horse and away. Being the second part of Boots and sadles* [!], [1726?]

B324 Bordman, T. In obitum illustrissimi Georgii I. et in successionem & inaugurationem serenissimi Georgii II... *Londini, typis J. Darby & T. Browne; prostant apud J. Osborn, & T. Longman, G. Hinchcliffe, & R. King,* 1727.
2°: A–B²; *1–2* 3–8.
'Scandit odoratum quando Phœbeius ales'
Dedication signed.
O.

Bottle-screw. The bottle-scrue: a tale, 1732. *See* Amhurst, Nicholas.

B325 Bouchery, Weyman. Hymnus sacer: sive paraphrasis in Deboræ et Baraci canticum, alcaïco carmine expressa. E libro Judicum. Cap. V... *Cantabrigiæ, typis academicis, impensis Edm. Jeffery. Prostant venales Londini apud Jac. Knapton,* 1706. (*PM* 6 July)
4°: π² A–D⁴; *i–iv,* 1–30 *31; 32 blk.* 31 err.
McKenzie 153; 500 copies printed.
'Insigne victis hoc super hostibus'
L(837.h.19),O(uncut),*C; PU.*

Boulter. Boulter's monument, 1745. *See* Madden, Samuel.

B326 Bounce. Bounce to Fop. An heroick epistle from a dog at Twickenham to a dog at court. By Dr. S—t. *Dublin, printed, London, reprinted for T. Cooper,* 1736. (*GM* May)
2°: *A²* B–C²; *1–4* 5–11 *12 blk.* A1 hft; 11 'err'.
Teerink 976; *Williams* 1135; *Rothschild* 1628.
'To thee, sweet Fop, these lines I send'
It is generally agreed that the original idea was Swift's, but that the writing is largely by Pope.
L(11602.i.16/6; Ashley 5067),O(2, 1 Harley's 'much altered by mr Pope', −A1),C,E,LdU-B+; CSmH,IU,MH,PU,TxU.

B327 — — The second edition. *Dublin, printed, London, reprinted for T. Cooper,* 1736.
2°: *A²* B–C²; *1–4* 5–11 *12 blk.* A1 hft; 11 'err'.
A reimpression.
L(11646.w.15),O,DN; CtY,MH,PU,TxU.

B328 — — *London: printed, and Dublin re-printed by George Faulkner,* 1736.
8°: *A⁴;* 1–2 3–7 *8.* 8 advt.
Without the attribution to 'Dr. S—t'.
DA,DG(uncut, A4 mutilated); MH.

Boureau Deslandes, A. F.

[**Boureau Deslandes, André François.**] Poetæ rusticantis literatum otium. *Londini, impensis Bernardi Lintot,* 1713. (*PB* 24 Jan)
12°: pp. 43. L; ICN.
Presentation copy at L. Deslandes's poems seem not to have been published in France until after 1740. The advertisement in *PB* reads 'Written at Paris by one of the Ambassador's retinue'.

— Poetæ rusticantis literatum otium: sive, carmina Andreæ Francisci Landesii. Secunda editio priori auctior. *Londini, impensis Bernardi Lintott,* 1713.
8°: pp. 52. L; NjP.
The copyright formed part of lot 29 of a trade sale of Bernard Lintot, 27 Nov 1739 (cat. at O-JJ); it is listed as out of print. A half-share re-appeared in lot 11 of the sale of W. Hinchliffe & J. Carter, 2 Dec 1742.

Bourne, Vincent. Poematia, latine partim reddita, partim scripta... *Londini, sumptibus authoris, typis J. Watts; væneunt apud B. Barker,* 1734. (*GSJ* 11 May)
12°: pp. 148. L,O; CSmH,MH.
Entered in *SR* 15 July 1734; deposit copies at L,EU.

— — Iterum edita. *Londini, typis J. Bettenham, sumptibus B. Barker, apud quem prostant, & apud R. Ware,* 1735.
12°: pp. 136. L,O; CSmH,CtY.

— — Tertio edita. *Londini, typis J. Bettenham, sumptibus B. Barker, apud quem prostant, & apud R. Ware,* 1743.
12°: pp. 252. L,O; CtY,MH.

— — Quarto edita. *Londini, typis J. Bettenham, sumptibus B. Barker,* 1750.
12°: pp. 246. L,O; CSmH,CtY.

[—] Three songs in English and Latin. [*London, B. Barker,* 1746.] (*BM* Dec 1746; *GM,LM* Jan 1747)
2°: pp. 7. L; CU.
Title in half-title form; note 'The musick to the songs in English, as set by Dr. Greene, is to be had at Mr. Walsh's...' The first two songs, 'The fly' and 'The invitation to a robin-red-breast', were printed in Bourne's *Poematia,* 1743; the third, 'The snow-drop' was added in the edition of 1750. Listed in *GM, LM* as published by Barker, and again in *GM,LM* Dec 1748, 'by the late Mr. Vincent Bourne', as published by Owen.

B329 [—] Corydon querens; carmen pastorale latine redditum. Editio altera. *Londini, typis E. Say; prostant venales apud B. Barker, T. Combes, J. Clarke, & J. Lacy,* 1722.
2°: *A²* B²; *1–3* 4–7 *8 blk.*

Bourne, V. Corydon querens

Latin and English texts. The first edition was probably that in *Comitalia Cantabrigiensia*, 1721.
'Deceptos pastor secum meditatus amores'
Collected in Bourne's *Poematia;* a translation of Rowe's *Colin's complaint.*
CtY,*MH.*

B330 — — carmen pastorale, tertio editum. Latine reddidit V. Bourne... *Londini, sumptibus B. Barker, apud quem prostant; & apud J. Roberts,* 1726.
8°: *A*⁴ B⁴ C²; *1–7* 8–19 *20 blk.* A1 hft.
With the addition on pp. 17–19 of 'In obitum Roussæi, anno MDCCXXI...editio altera', with title on p. 15. Reissued with *Thyrsis & Chloe,* 1728.
L,O,CT(−A1); CtY,IU,MH.

B331 — Gulielmus Susannæ valedicens. *Londini, typis J. Bettenham; sumptibus B. Barker,* 1731.
8°: *A*⁸; *1–7* 8–15 *16 blk.* A1 hft.
Latin and English texts. The copy at O was issued with *Thyrsis & Chloe,* 1728.
'In statione fuit classis; fusisque per auras'
Dedication to Gay signed; a translation of Gay's 'Sweet William's farewell to black-ey'd Susan'.
L(993.e.46),O(−A1),CT(−A1); MH(uncut,−A1).

B332 [—] In obitum Roussaei, anno 1721, carmen elegiacum. *Londini, typis J. Redmayne,* 1724.
2°: *A*²; *i–ii, 1* 2.
Latin text only; reprinted with Bourne's *Corydon querens,* 1726.
'Alme Charon, (nam tandem omnes, qui nascimur & qui'
Rouse (?) was apparently a college servant and boatman at Trinity College, Cambridge.
CtY.

B333 [—] Thyrsis & Chloe, William and Margaret; Votum Dris Gualteri Pope, The old man's wish; & Corydon querens, Colin's complaint: tres cantilenæ Anglicæ celebratioris nominis Latine redditæ. *Londini, sumptibus B. Barker,* 1728. (*MChr* 15 May)
8°: *A*⁴(−A1) B⁴; *A–B*⁴; *A*⁴ B⁴ C²; *i, 1–5* (twice) *6 7 8 blk; i–iv* v–vii *viii, 9* 10–16; *1–7* 8–19 *20 blk.*
To *Thyrsis & Chloe* are added *Votum,* 1728 (possibly not separately published) and *Corydon querens,* 1726, which are also listed separately. The copy at O was issued with *Gulielmus Susannæ valedicens,* 1731, stabbed with it.
'Omnia nox tenebris, tacitaque involverat umbra'
A translation of David Mallet's poem. Bourne's name appears in the added poems.
L(11405.e.10/3, lacks general title A2 and *Thyrsis & Chloe*),O; IU.

B334 — Votum Dris Gualteri Pope latine redditum. *Londini: anno* 1728. *Impensis B. Barker, & F. Fayram.*

Bourne, V. Votum

8°: *A–B*⁴ (A3 as 'a'); *i–iv* v–vii *viii, 9* 10–16.
All copies seen were issued with *Thyrsis & Chloe,* 1728. Latin text only.
'Si senii descendam, & cœpi vergere, ad annos'
Dedication signed; a translation of Walter Pope's *The wish.*
L(11405.e.10/3),O; IU.

Bowden, Samuel. Poetical essays on several occasions... Vol. I. *London, printed for J. Pemberton, & C. Davis,* 1733. (*GSJ* 18 Aug)
8°: pp. xxxv, 159.   L,O; DFo,ICU.

— — Vol. II. *London, printed for J. & J. Pemberton,* 1735.
8°: pp. xii, 188.   L,O; PU,ICU.
The two volumes are sometimes found bound together; the O copy is in a presentation binding.

— Poems on various subjects; with some essays in prose... *Bath, printed by T. Boddely, for the author; sold by Mr. Leake & Mr. Frederick, Bath; Messrs. Cadell, Hickey, & Palmer, Bristol; Mr. Raikes, Gloucester; Mr. Collins, Salisbury; Mr. Goadby, Sherborne; and by Messrs. Hitch & Hawes, London,* 1754.
8°: pp. xxi, 390.   L,O; ICU.

———

B335 [—] A poem on the new method of treating physic. Inscribed to Dr. Morgan, on his Philosophical principles of medicine. *London, printed for S. Chandler,* 1726. (*MC* Jan)
2°: A–C²; *1–3* 4–12.
'Distinguish'd worth demands the poet's lays'
Reprinted in Bowden's *Poetical essays* I, 1733. On Thomas Morgan's *Philosophical principles,* 1725.
*DNLM,*MH,OCU.

B336 **Bowl.** A bowl of punch upon the peace. *London, printed for John Morphew,* 1713.
½°: *1–2, 1* column.
'The gods and the goddesses lately did feast'
Cf. *Crum* T692: 'A bowl of punch'; ascribed in L (Add. MS. 23904, fol. 91) to 'Capt. Ratcliffe'. This version apparently adds six lines in praise of Harley and the Stuarts, but whether Alexander Radcliffe was still alive and responsible for them is not known.
TxU.

Bowling. 'Bowling. A poem. With miscellaneous translations... [*London*] *Printed for J. Knapton.*' (*MC* May 1716)
See Miscellaneous translations from Bion, 1716.

[**Bowman,** —, *Mr., 'a Scots gentleman'.*] The last guinea, a poem, 1720. *See* L51.

Bowman, W.

Bowman, William. Poems on several occasions. *London, printed for the author*, 1727.
8°: pp. 106.   O; CtY,MH.
　　Also issued in *The altar of love*, 1727.

—— The second edition, corrected. *London, printed for E. Curll*, 1732. (*GM* 15 Jan)
8°: pp. 80.   L,O; ICU.

B337　[Bowyer, William.] The beau and the academick. A dialogue in imitation of Bellus homo and academicus, spoken at the late publick act at Oxford. Address'd to the ladies. *London, printed for J. Roberts*, [1733.] (*GM* Sept)
4°: A² B⁴ C² (A2 as 'A'); *i–iv, 1–12*.
　　Entered in Bowyer's ledgers below the entry for *Bellus homo* to 'Messrs Innys & Bowyer partners in Bellus Homo &c' of 20 Sept, 500 copies printed; the detailed accounts suggest it may have still been printing after that date.
'At study still! still mad! come, take the air'
　　Preface signed 'Bellamant'; Bowyer's authorship from *Nichols* II. 37n. A translation of William Hasledine's *Bellus homo et academicus*, 1733.
O; CtY,OCU.

[Boyd, Elizabeth.] The humorous miscellany; or, riddles for the beaux. Humbly inscribed to the right honourable the Earl of Cardigan. By E— B—. *London, printed for S. Slow; sold by the booksellers of London & Westminster*, 1733.
4°: pp. 32.   L; ICN.
　　Attributed to Eustace Budgell in an early ms. note in the copy at ICN, but clearly by a female author; attributed to Boyd by L.

————————

B338　[—] Admiral Haddock: or, the progress of Spain. A poem. *London printed, and sold by J. Applebee, C. Corbett, E. Nutt, E. Cook, & M. Bartlett, & A. Dodd*, 1739 [1740]. (*GM,LM* Feb)
2°: π¹ A² B–C² D¹; *i–ii, 1–2 3–14.* π1 hft, advt.
'When great Eliza fill'd the British throne'
　　For authorship, see the following issue.
L(1961); MH,NjP,TxU(uncut).

B339　— [another issue] By Eliz. Boyd. *London, sold by Elizabeth Boyd, at a cook's-shop, the sign of the Leg of Pork and Sausages, in Leicester-street, by Swallow-street, St. James's*, [1740.]
2°: A²(? ±A1) B–C² D¹; *1–2 3–14.*
　　Title apparently a cancel; no half-title seen in this issue.
LdU-B; InU.

B340　[—] Altamira's ghost; or, justice triumphant. A new ballad. Occasion'd by a certain nobleman's cruel usage of his nephew. Done extempore. By E. B. *London printed, and sold by Charles Corbett*, 1744. (*LEP* 24 April)

Boyd, E. Altamira's ghost

2°: A¹ B² C¹; *1–3 4–8.*
　　A1 and C1 have been seen to be conjugate.
'All in the dark and dolesome hour'
　　Entered in the ledger of Henry Woodfall jun. to Mrs. E. Boyd in Jan 1744, 500 copies (*N&Q* I. 12 (1855) 217).
L(1489.m.4); CtY,DFo,KU(uncut),MH.

B341　— Glory to the highest, a thankgiving poem, on the late victory at Dettingen. To which is subjoin'd a sacred hymn, on the same occasion, both done extempore. *London printed, and sold by the author, at the new pamphlet shop over-against the Crooked-Billet in Leicester-street, near Burlington-gardens*, 1743.
4°: A⁴; *1–2 3–8.*
'Victorious heroe's, learned bards excite'
L(C.118.c.2/10); NN.

B342　— The happy North-Briton. A poem. On the marriage of his grace the Duke of Hamilton and Brandon, with Miss Spencer. *London, printed for the author*, 1737.
2°: A²; *1–3 4.*
'Wake sprightly muse, wake sweetly warbling lyre'
IU(uncut).

B343　[—] A poem on the arrival of the right honourable William earl Cowper, after a dangerous illness. Against his birth-day. By Louisa. *London, printed by T. Edlin*, 1730.
2°: A² B²; *1–3 4–5 6 blk, 1 2. ²2 err.*
　　Two poems.
'Sing Clio, the ador'd, the god-like youth'
'Say muse, how shall I sing the lovely pair'
　　Although only the second poem is unambiguously by 'Louisa' (Elizabeth Boyd), Edlin printed her poems at this period and both are almost certainly hers.
CtY,OCU.

B344　[—] To the right honourable William lord Harrington, on his late return from Paris. A poem. By Louisa. *London, Tho. Edlin*, 1730.
2°: 6 pp.
(Pickering & Chatto cat. 267/11064.)

B345　[—] Truth, a poem. Address'd to the right honourable William lord Harrington. By E----. B----. *London printed, and sold by the author, & C. Corbett, and at the pamphlet shops of London & Westminster*, 1740. (*GM,LM* Dec)
4°: π¹ A⁴; *i–ii, 1–3 4–8.* π1 hft, advt; 2 advt.
'Wake vocal shell, awake melodious muse'
CtY.

B346　— [another issue] By E----. Boyd. *London printed, and sold by the author, at the new pamphlet shop over-against the Crooked Billet in Leicester-street, near Burlington-gardens*, 1740.
4°: A⁴; *1–3 4–8.* 2 advt.
　　No cancel title seen; no half-title in copy seen.
L(1959).

Boyd, E.

B347 [—] Variety: a poem, in two cantos. Humbly offer'd to the god of change. To which is annex'd, an answer to an Ovid's epistle. By Louisa. *Westminster, printed for T. Warner, & B. Creake, 1727* [1726]. (*MC* Nov)
8⁰: A–M⁴ N²; *i–vi, 1 2 1 2–92.*
> On p. 77 'Macareus to Æolus. Done in imitation of Dryden's Canace to Macareus', and on p. 87 'Æolus to Pluto'. The copyright with 300 books was sold in lot 19 of the trade sale of B. Creake, 21 April 1727 (cat. at O-JJ) to John Osborn of Horsley Downs.
'Of all that heightens, or formations mirth'
'Canace murther'd; – Ha! What is't I hear?'
> 'Louisa' was the pseudonym of Elizabeth Boyd.
L(11632.bb.26); CSmH,CtY,DFo,OCU.

B348 — Verses congratulatory, on the happy marriage of the right honourable the Lady Diana Spencer with the Lord John Russel. *London, printed by T. Edlin, 1731.*
2⁰: A²; *1–3 4.*
'Raise high my muse, bold soar thy tow'ring wing'
O-JJ.

B349 — Verses most humbly inscrib'd to his majesty King George IId. on his birth-day. *London, printed by Tho. Edlin,* [1730.] (*MChr* Nov)
2⁰: A² B¹; *1–3 4–6.*
'When heaven reveals it self to mortal eyes'
ICU.

B350 — [another issue?] *London, printed by Tho. Edlin, 1730.*
2⁰: A² B¹; *1–3 4–6.*
> Apart from the date in the imprint, the copy seen appears to have a variant sheet B.
CtY.

Boyer, Abel. 'Recueil de divers sonnets faits sur les Camisars & la victoire remportee par le Duc de Marlborough, sur les bouts-rimez donnez, par M. Boyer. *Sold by all the French booksellers in London & Westminster.*' (*PM* 19 Sept 1704)
> It is not clear whether Boyer was the author or editor of this collection.

B351 **Boyle, John,** *earl of Cork & Orrery.* The first ode of the first book of Horace imitated, and inscribed to the Earl of Chesterfield. *London, printed for C. Bathurst, & G. Hawkins, 1741.* (*GM,LM* April)
2⁰: *A²* B–C² D¹; *1 2–13 14 blk.*
> *Rothschild* 1487. The precedence of London & Dublin editions is not clear. All copies have ms. correction in p. 7 line 9, in different hands. Apparently the 'Ode in Imitat. of Horace' in 3 sheets entered to Hawkins & Bathurst in Bowyer's ledgers about April 1741; 500 copies printed.

Boyle, J. The first ode

'O thou, whose virtues Albion's sons can trace'
L(840.m.1/51; 162.n.37),LVA-D,O,DrU; CSmH, CtY,IU,MH,TxU(2)+.

B352 — The first ode of the first book of Horace. Inscribed to the Earl of Chesterfield. *Dublin, printed by and for George Faulkner, 1741.*
8⁰: A⁸ B² (A3 as 'A4'); *i–iii, 1–14 15–17.* B2 advt. Watermark: IA.
L(1000.k.22/3),LVA-F,DA,DG; CtY,NN,NjP (Orrery's interleaved and annotated copy, – B2),PP.

B353 — [fine paper]
Watermark: Strasburg bend.
C,DG.

B354 [—] [A poem, sacred to the memory...] [dh] Verses by a young nobleman, on the death of his grace the Duke of B—. [*London, 1736?*]
8⁰: A⁴; *1–8.*
> The status of this edition is uncertain, but presumably it precedes the editions which reveal Boyle's authorship. The copy seen is on good paper, watermarked with Strasburg bend, which suggests an authorized version possibly intended for private circulation.
'Must then my heart familiar long with grief'
> On the death of Edmund Sheffield, duke of Buckingham.
OCU.

B354·5 — A poem, sacred to the memory of Edmund Sheffield, duke of Buckingham... *London, printed for J. Brindley, 1736* [1737]. (*GM,LM* March)
2⁰: *A²* B–C²; *1–5 6–12.*
> *Rothschild* 1486.
L(643.1.28/30),O,LdU-B; CSmH,CtY,NN-B, NjP,TxU(uncut)+.

B355 — A poem to the memory of Edmund Sheffield... *Dublin, printed by George Faulkner, 1741.*
8⁰: A⁸; *i–vi, 1 2–8 9–10.* A1 hft; A8 advt.
L(992.h.11/1),O; NjP(Orrery's interleaved, annotated copy, – A8),PP.

B356 — Pyrrha: an imitation of the fifth ode of the first book of Horace. *London, printed for R. Dodsley; sold by T. Cooper, 1741.* (28 Nov)
2⁰: *A²* B² C²; *1–2 3–11 12 blk.*
> Horizontal chain-lines. Date from *Straus, Dodsley*; listed in *GM* Nov, *GM,LM* Dec.
'When to that dear, but inauspicious bow'r'
> Cf. *Pyrrha a cantata... Not by John earl of Orrery, 1741.*
L(643.m.16/12; 162.n.40),LVA-D,O,DrU,LdU-B; CSmH,CtY,MH,PP(Orrery's annotated copy), TxU(2)+.

B357 — Pyrrha. The fifth ode of the first book of Horace imitated. *Dublin, printed by and for George Faulkner, 1742.*
8⁰: *A⁴* B⁴ *C²*; [2] *i* ii–vii, *1–8 9–11.* C2 advt.
L(1000.k.22/2),LVA-F,DA(– C2),DN(uncut); NjP(Orrery's interleaved and annotated copy, – C2).

Boyle, J.

[—] To the reverend Doctor Swift... With a present of a paper-book, 1733. *See* T390.

Boyse, Joseph. Family hymns for morning and evening worship. With some for the lord's-days... All taken out of the psalms of David. *Dublin, printed at the back of Dick's coffee-house; and are to be sold by Matth. Gunne,* 1701.
8°: pp. 116.   EN.

[—] A collection of divine hymns upon several occasions, suited to our common tunes... The second edition corrected. *London, printed for Tho. Parkhurst,* 1704.
8°: pp. 102.   O.

Boyse, Samuel. Translations and poems written on several subjects. *Edinburgh, printed by Mr. Thomas & Walter Ruddiman,* 1731.
8°: pp. xviii, 195.   L,O; CtY,MH.

— [reissue] *London, printed for the author; sold by John Gray,* 1734. (*GM* Feb)
CtY.
Cancel title, and list of subscribers cancelled.

— Translations and poems, written on several occasions. *London, printed for the author,* 1738. (*LM* March)
8°: pp. viii, 322.   L,O; IU,TxU.
The dedication copy to the Duke of Buccleuch at LVA-D has an engraved coat of arms at head of the dedication.

[—] Miscellaneous works, serious and humorous; in verse and prose. Design'd for the amusement of the fair sex. *Reading, printed by J. Carnan; sold by R. Ware, London; J. Newbery, Reading; & J. Wimpey, Newbury,* 1740.
8°: pp. 144.   O,RP.

B358 [—] Albion's triumph. An ode, occasioned by the happy success of his majesty's arms on the Maine. In the stanza of Spencer. *London, printed for J. Robinson,* 1743. (*DA* 2 July)
2°: B⁴; *1–2* 3–8.
Two errata are noted in the advertisement in *DA* 4 July.
'Immortal maid, fair daughter of the skies!'
Attributed to Boyse by *Cibber* V. 174, and *Annual Register* (1764) 54f. On the victory at Dettingen.
MH,OCU,PU,TxU.

B359 [—] Deity: a poem. *London, printed for J. Roberts,* 1739 [1740]. (*GM,LM* Feb)
8°: A¹ B–G⁴ H⁴(–H4); *i–ii*, 1–54.
'From earth's low prospects and deceitful aims'
A note in Chalmers *English Poets* XIV (1810) 517 refers to a letter from Boyse to Sir Hans Sloane of 14 Feb. 1739/40, clearly soliciting a present in return for a presentation copy.
L(992.h.10/6),LVA-D,O; CtY,IU,MH.

Boyse, S. Deity

B360 [—] — The third edition. *London, printed for J. Roberts,* 1740.
8°: A¹ B–G⁴ H⁴(–H4); *i–ii*, 1–54.
Clearly from the same setting of type; whether a reissue or reimpression is not clear. No 'second edition' traced.
CtY,TxU.

B361 [—] — *London, printed for C. Corbett,* 1749. (*GM,LM* March)
8°: A–G⁴; *1–2* 3–56.
L(T.1638/5),O(2),OW,*MR*; CLU-C(uncut),CtY, ICU,*MB*,NjP+.

B362 [—] — *Dublin, printed by R. James,* 1749.
12°: A–C⁶; *1–2* 3–36.
C,DA,BaP,*WgP*; MH,PP.

B363 [—] An ode, inscribed to the Royal Company of Archers, on their march, July 8. 1734. *Edinburgh, printed by W. Cheyne,* 1734.
8°: A⁴; *1–2* 3–8.
'Ye martial breasts, the pride of Scotia's plain'
Printed in Boyse's *Translations and poems,* 1738.
E.

B364 [—] The olive: an ode. Occasion'd by the auspicious success of his majesty's counsels, and his majesty's most happy return. In the stanza of Spenser. *London printed, and sold by R. Amey,* 1737. (*GM,LM* March)
4°: A² B–C⁴ D²; *1–5* 6–24. 4 err.
'Long had Bellona rais'd her furious hand'
Collected in Boyse's *Translations and poems,* 1738; according to *Annual Register* (1764) 54f. its dedication to Walpole procured Boyse ten guineas.
L(1962),LDW; KU(uncut),MH.

B365 — The praise of peace. A poem. In three cantos. From the Dutch of M. Van Haren... By Mr Boyse. *London, printed for A. Dodd,* 1742. (*GM,LM* Sept)
8°: π¹ A² B–F⁴ G² H¹; *i–vi*, *1* 2–44 *45–46*.
π1 and H1 have been seen to be conjugate. Dated 1749 by *CBEL* in error; but listed in *BM,GM* May 1748 for Dodd & Payne. Chalmers *English Poets* XIV (1810) 518–9 quotes a letter of Boyse to Cave, 21 July 1742, delivering the ms.
'Daughter of Jove! Calliope divine'
L(11555.d.18; 992.h.11/2),O; CSmH.

B366 — Retirement: a poem, occasioned by seeing the palace and park of Yester. *Edinburgh, printed anno* 1735.
8°: a⁴ A–B⁴ C²; *i–viii*, 1–20.
'O thou, who in eternal light, unseen'
Dedication signed.
MH(lacks a4),NN.

B367 — The tears of the muses: a poem, sacred to the memory of the right honourable, Anne late viscountess of Stormont. *Edinburgh, printed anno* 1736.

Boyse, S. The tears of the muses

8°: π^4 A⁴ B²; *i–ii* iii–vii *viii*, 1–12. viii err.
'As late the thoughtful muse, in pensive mood'
Dedication signed.
L(11645.ee.44/2),GM; CtY,ICN,NN.

B368 [—] To the memory of the late reverend Mr. John Anderson, minister of the gospel at Glasgow. By a student of philosophy in the university. *Glasgow, printed by William Duncan*, 1721.
2°: *A²*; *1* 2–4.
'Shall streaming tears a nations eyes o'erflow'
Printed in Boyse's *Translations and poems*, 1731.
E(2, 1 uncut),EU.

B369 [—] Verses occasioned by seeing the palace and park of Dalkeith, anno MDCCXXXII. Humbly inscrib'd to his grace the Duke of Buccleugh. *Edinburgh, printed anno* 1732. (Oct?)
8°: *A⁴*(−A1) B⁴(−B4); *3–4* 5–14.
Precedence of this edition and the following has not been finally established, but this is in larger type and on better paper. The copy seen probably lacks half-title and final leaf. In a letter of 20 Nov 1732 to Sir John Clerk (SRO, GD 18/4517) Boyse refers to sending 'as you were pleased to desire...one hundred copies to Mr. Lesly' and speaks of his great concern at hearing 'the verses were reprinted on a half sheet of brown paper by a noted ballad-printer in town and sold for halfpence a piece in the market at Dalkeith'. He also expresses surprise at the London reprint.
'I ask not Phoebus, nor the fabled nine'
Collected in Boyse's *Translations and poems*, 1738.
L(11631.aaa.56/19).

B370 [—] Verses occasioned by seeing the palace, park, school, and town of Dalkeith, anno MDCCXXXII. *Edinburgh, printed in the year* 1732.
8°: *A⁴*; *1–2* 3–8.
Possibly the piratical half-sheet referred to above, though certainly not on 'brown paper'.
L(1078.k.26/14),E.

B371 [—] [*idem*] Dalkeith. A poem. Occasion'd by a view of that delightful palace and park, the seat of his grace the Duke of Buccleugh... By a Scotch gentleman. *London, printed for T. Worrall*, 1732. (*GSJ* 3 Nov)
2°: *A¹* B² C¹; *i–ii*, *1* 2–5 '4'. '4' advt.
A1 and C1 have been seen to be conjugate.
E; CtY,OCU.

B372 — Verses, sacred to the memory of the right honourable, Charles, earl of Peterborough, and Monmouth. *Edinburgh, printed by W. Cheyne*, 1735.
8°: *A⁴* B⁴; *i–ii* iii–iv, 5–16.
'When press'd by fate inferior mortals bow'
Dedication signed.
O,E; CtY.

Br., J.

Br., J. A letter to Mareschal Tallard, 1706. *See* L146.

— Lettre au Marechal de Tallard, 1706. *See* L158.

B----r, Tom. Miscellany poems on several subjects, 1702. *See* Miscellany.

B373 [**Brady, Nicholas.**] A song compos'd by Mr. Henry Purcell; and to be performed at St. Mary-Hall, in Oxon, on St. Cecilia's-day, 1707. By Mr. Saunders and Mr. Court, assisted by the best voices and hands. [*Oxford*, 1707.]
½°: 2 sides, 1 column.
'Hail, bright Cecilia, hail!'
Crum H43: 'St. Cecilia's song', 1692. See F. B. Zimmermann, *Purcell* (1963) no. 328.
O.

B374 — Proposals for publishing a translation of Virgil's Æneids in blank verse. Together with a specimen of the performance. *London, printed for the author*, 1713.
8°: *A⁴* B–C⁴; *i–vii*, 1–8(twice) [*1 blk*]. A1 hft.
Latin and English text on facing pages, numbered concurrently 1–8.
'Arms, and the hero, who from ruin'd Troy'
L(11375.bb.8; G.18423/7),O,O-*JJ*; CtY,*MH*, TxU.

B375 — Virgil's Æneis translated into blank verse. [Book 1] *London, printed for the author*, 1714.
8°: *A²* B–D⁸ E⁸(±E2) F⁸(±F2) G–H⁸ I⁴ (H3 as 'H4'); *i–iv*, *1* 2–56(twice) [*1 blk*], i–viii. A1 blk; viii err.
Latin and English text on facing pages, numbered concurrently 2–56. Book 1 only.
L(1001.g.24),O(2, 1 −A1); CtY(−A1),DFo (−A1),*MH*,NjP(−A1).

B376 — — [Books 1–3] *London, printed for Bernard Lintott*, 1716.
8°: *A²* B–L⁸ M⁶. A1ᵛ advt; M6ʳ err.
Separate pagination for each book. English text only of books 1–3.
L(78.a.27),O; CtY,NjP.

B377 — — Volume II. [Books 4–6] *London, printed for Robert Gosling*, 1717.
8°: *A²* B–M⁸ N². A1ᵛ advt; N2ᵛ err.
Separate pagination for each book. English text only.
L(78.a.27); NjP.

B378 Bragge, Francis. The passion of our saviour. ⟨To which is added⟩ A pindarick ode on the suffering god. In imitation of Rapin's Christus patiens. [*London*] *Engraved on ⟨ plates⟩ and sold by John Sturt in Golden-Lion Court in Aldersgate Street*, [1703/–.]
Title and twenty single oblong leaves of text, numbered 1–20.
Printed from engraved plates on rectos only, with a separate engraved border round each.

Bragge, F. The passion

> According to *DNB* (followed by *Wing*), published in 1694. That date may be correct for an earlier printing, but this must be dated after 10 Dec 1702 when Sturt was still at the Cross, Red Cross St.; he is recorded at the Golden Lion by 25 March 1706; these dates come from advertisements in *LG*.
> 'What dark and dismal shade is this'
> L(11626.a.8).

B379 — — *[London] Sold by J. Tinney engraver at the Crown in Great East Cheap Cannon Street,* [1730?/–.]
> 45 oblong single leaves, numbered 1–45.
> The text from the same plates as the preceding, with illustrations added on facing pages; different engraved borders to the leaves.
> L(220.b.23).

B380 — Two odes from the Latin of the celebrated Rapin, imitated in English pindaricks. By a gentleman at Cambridge. *London, printed by J. M. [John Matthews?] for Robert Mawson,* 1710. (*DC* 2 March)
> 8°: A–D⁴; *i–viii, 1–23 24. 24 advt.
> Watermark: ? initials.
> 'O! Tell me who's this lovely child?'
> 'What dark and dismal shade is this?'
> Dedication signed.
> O,DrU.

B381 — [fine paper]
> Watermark: fleur-de-lys on shield.
> L(11403.b.43).

B382 **Brailsford, John.** Derby silk-mill. A poem. Attempted in Miltonick verse. To which is added, a particular description of the machine, or silk mill, erected at Derby. *Nottingham, printed for the author by George Ayscough,* 1739.
> 2°: (6 pp.)
> Pagination from S. F. Creswell, *Collections towards the history of printing in Nottinghamshire,* 1863.
> Presumably on the silk mill built by Sir Thomas Lombe in 1719.
> O-JJ(title only).

B383 [**Bramston, James.**] The art of politicks, in imitation of Horace's Art of poetry. *London, printed for Lawton Gilliver,* 1729. (*MChr* 8 Dec)
> 8°: (frt+) *A¹[= G4] B–F⁴ G⁴(–G4); i–ii, 1 2–45 46 blk.*
> Watermark: FS. No engraving on title. For a discussion of this and subsequent editions see *Williams, Points* 63–7. *SR* 4 Dec 1729 records assignment of copy to Gilliver; deposit may have been later. Deposit copies (fine paper) at O,EU.
> 'If to a human face Sir James should draw'
> Printed as Bramston's in *Dodsley* I. John Lloyd's *The play,* 1730, claims on the title that he wrote *The art of politicks,* but this is clearly erroneous.

Bramston, J. The art of politicks

> L(C.133.c.2/4),O(2, 1 uncut),OW(2),C(2), LdU-B+; CLU-C,ICU,MH.

B384 [—] [fine paper]
> Watermark: eagle with crown. 'There's for the curious a small number on royal paper. Price 1s. 6d.' (*MC* Dec 1729).
> O,EU; CtY,IU,KU,MH.

B385 [—] — *London, printed for Lawton Gilliver,* 1729.
> 8°: (frt+) A–F⁴; *1–3 4–47 48. 48 advt.*
> Engraved Homer in oval frame on title, ten books advertised on p. 48 in this and the following entry; they are different impressions from the same type with minor changes. This impression on paper watermarked with grapes; single rule above imprint.
> O,C(–frt).

B386 [—] [another impression]
> Two rules above imprint. Copies contain variant readings which are probably related to two impressions on paper watermarked with grapes or with a horse respectively; but so many copies have mixed sheets that they cannot readily be distinguished.
> L(1486.ee.17),C(2),CT,E,EtC; CtY,DFo,ICN, MH(2, 1 lacks C⁴),TxU+.

B387 [—] [another edition] *London, printed for Lawton Gilliver,* 1729.
> 8°: (frt+) A–F⁴ (B1 as 'C'); *1–3 4–47 48. 48 advt.*
> Engraved Homer in scrolled frame on title; seven books advertised on p. 48.
> L(161.m.69),LG,C,LdU-B; CLU-C,ICN.

B388 [—] — '*London, printed for Lawton Gilliver'* [*Edinburgh*], 1729.
> 12°: (frt+) A –C⁶; *1–3 4–36.*
> Printed in Edinburgh by Ruddiman on the evidence of the ornaments.
> L(11631.aa.46/4),LVA-F,AdU; CtY.

B389 [—] — *Dublin, printed by S. Powell, and sold at the corner of Sycamore-alley, in Dame's Street, and by Stearne Brock,* 1729.
> 8°: (frt+) *A¹ B–F⁴ G⁴(–G4); i–ii, 1 2–45 46 blk.*
> Many copies lack the frontispiece, which may not have been ready at time of first publication.
> L(1481.b.20,–frt),C,DA(2,1–frt),DN(2,1–frt), DT+; DLC(–frt),PP(–frt).

B390 [—] — Humbly address'd to the right honourable ***** ***** and James duke Heidegger. esq; Written by Messieurs A. Pope and J. Gay. *London: printed, and Dublin re-printed, and sold by James Hoey, & George Faulkner,* 1729.
> 8°: A⁴ B⁸; *1–3 4–24.*
> C,DA,DT.

B391 [—] — *London, printed for Lawton Gilliver,* 1731.
> 8°: (frt+) A–F⁴; *1–3 4–47 48. 48 advt.*
> L(992.h.9/3; 12274.h.2/7,–frt),O,C(–frt),*MR*; CSmH,MH,TxU.

Bramston, J. The crookcd six-pence

B392 [—] The crooked six-pence. With a learned preface found among some papers bearing date the same year in which Paradise lost was published by the late Dr. Bently... The original manuscript will be deposited in the Cotton-library. *London, printed for R. Dodsley; sold by M. Cooper*, 1743. (*LDP* 4 Nov)
4°: *A*⁴ B–C⁴; *i–ii* iii–x, *11* 12–24.
   Bond 179. With a reprint of John Philips, *The splendid shilling*.
'Happy the maid, who from green sickness free'
   Attributed to Bramston in Isaac Reed's *Repository* I (1777) 129f. The mock-scholarly preface attributes the poem to Katherine Philips ('the matchless Orinda'), and suggests that *The splendid shilling* was written by Grub-street hacks who had heard of it; it was then mistakenly attributed to John Philips.
L(11630.f.42; 11631.g.30/5; 643.k.5/3; 11630.c.14/4, mutilated),LVA-D,O,C,CT; IU, MH.

B393 [—] The gardener's congratulatory poem to the Prince and Princess of Orange. Written in the month of March, 1734. *London, printed for T. Cooper*, 1734. (March?)
2°: *A*² B–C²; *i–iv*, *1* 2–7 *8 blk.* A1 hft.
   Listed in Hooker's *Miscellany* 6 April 1734 as published 'last month'.
'Welcome the month whose kalends bring'
   Advertised in Hooker's *Miscellany* 27 April as 'By the author of the Man of taste'. Bramston's authorship has not been generally noticed, and the attribution should perhaps be treated with reserve.
IU.

B394 [—] Ignorami lamentatio supra legis communis translationem ex latino in anglicum... *Londini, vendit hunc librum Gilliverus cujus insigne est Homerus*, 1736. (*SR* 5 May)
2°: *A*² B–F²; [2] i–ix *x*, 1–9, i–iii.
   Listed in *GM,LM* May. Deposit copies at L,O,E,AdU.
'Est currens mundus demens, ego credo, rotundus'
   Attributed to Bramston by *Rawlinson*.
L(643.m.14/11),O(2),E,DT,AdU;CSmH,IU,NjP, OCU.

B395 [—] — *Londini: vendit hunc librum Gilliverus cujus insigne est Homerus. Et Dublini: vendit Georgius Faulknerus, cui patronus est Draperus*, 1736.
8°: A⁸ B⁴; [2] i–viii, 1–9, i–v.
C,DA,DG,DN.

B396 [—] The man of taste. Occasion'd by an epistle of Mr. Pope's on that subject. By the author of the Art of politicks. *London, printed by J. Wright for Lawton Gilliver*, 1733. (*SR* 5 March)
2°: *A*² B–E²; *1–4* 5–19 *20* advt. A1 hft & frt; 20 advt.
   No advertisement at foot of title; 15 books advertised on p. 20. The two following entries are partly reimpressions, partly reset. Some copies (e.g. at MH, CSmH) are

Bramston, J. The man of taste

probably from mixed sheets, but may represent a third reimpression. W. B. Todd in *Library* V. 8 (1953) 186 argued that this was the last impression; I have placed it first on the evidence of the deposit copies. Advertised in *GSJ* 8 March. Deposit copies at L,O,E,EU,GU, SaU.
'Whoe'er he be that to a taste aspires'
   Collected as Bramston's in *Dodsley* I. Imitated by [Thomas Newcomb] *The woman of taste*, 1733. Satirized in *The modern poet*, 1735.
L(643.m.14/8; 163.n.7; C.59.h.9/7),O(2),C,E, LdU-B(uncut)+; CSmH(2, 1 with 'A. Pope – Twikenham' on title),CtY(2),IU,MH(2),TxU+.

B397 [—] [another impression]
   Advertisement for *The art of politicks* at foot of title; 16 books advertised on p. 20. Italic parentheses round pagination on pp. 6,7,11, 12,13,15.
LSC,LVA-D,O,C; CtY(2),ICN,OCU.

B398 [—] [another impression]
   Advertisement for *The art of politicks* at foot of title; 16 books advertised on p. 20. Italic parentheses round pagination on pp. 7,8,11, 12,15,16,19.
L(12273.m.1/18; 1484.m.7/6, –A1; C.57.g.7/2), LVA-D,OA,LdU-B(uncut),WcC; CLU,ICU(3), MH(2),TxU.

B399 [—] — '*London, printed by J. Wright, for Lawton Gilliver*' [*Edinburgh*], 1733.
(frt+) *A*⁴ B⁴ C² (A2 as 'B'); *1–2* 3–19 *20 blk.*
   One copy at TxU is reissued in a collection of Edinburgh piracies, *Poems, a chosen collection*.
L(1488.c.39, –frt),LVA-D,EN; CLU-C(–frt), IU,MH,MiU,TxU(2)+.

B400 [—] — *London: printed, Dublin, re-printed by and for George Faulkner*, 1733.
8°: *A*⁴ B⁴ C² (B1 as 'C'); *1–5* 6–19 *20*. A1 hft; 20 advt.
   Five books advertised on p. 20.
L(1961),O(–A1),DK(3),LdU; IU,MH(2),TxU.

B401 [—] — *London: printed, Dublin, re-printed by and for George Faulkner*, 1733.
8°: *A*⁴ B⁴ C²; *1–5* 6–19 *20*. A1 frt; 20 advt.
   Nine books advertised on p. 20. Woodcut frontispiece. A copy at DN mixes sheets of this and the preceding.
O; CtY.

B402 [—] Scotch tast [!] in vista's. [*London*, 1741/42.]
obl ¼°: 1 side, 1 column.
   Engraved print with short engraved text below. Dated as 1741 in L (P&D) catalogue, but see below.
'Old I—y to show a most elegant tast'
   A longer form of the text is quoted (and ascribed to Bramston in a note) in a letter of Horace Walpole to Mann, 3 June 1742. A satire on Archibald earl of Islay, subsequently duke of Argyll.
L(P&D 2510).

Brand, *Sir* A.

Brand, *Sir* **Alexander.** A true collection of poems on the several birth-days of his majesty King George, and of their royal highnesses the Prince and Princess of Wales. From the 1st of March 1724–5, to the 1st of March 1727. [*London*, 1727.]
2⁰: pp. 10. L,O.
> Watermark: Amsterdam arms. The O copy has remains of blue ribbon used to stab the pamphlet.

— [reimpression?] *London, printed for the author; sold by A. Dodd, and the booksellars* [!] *of London & Westminster,* 1727. (*MC* May)
2⁰: pp. 11. CtY.
> A poem to the Duke of Argyll is added on pp. 10–11; printed on different paper, water-marked with London arms.

[**Brayer, Thomas.**] Miscellany poems on several subjects... By T.B. gent., 1702. *See* Miscellany.

B403 Brazen. [dh] The brazen age banish'd. [*Dublin,* 1725?]
4⁰: *A²; 1 2–4.*
'Hibernia hard beset with gloomy cares'
> A welcome to Lord Carteret as lord lieutenant of Ireland.
O,C,DT; MH,OCU.

B404 Br—d-street. The Br—d-street patriots; or, the impartial judge. A canto in imitation of Hudibras. *London, printed in the year* 1717.
8⁰: A–C⁴; *1–2 3–22 23–24 blk.*
> *Bond* 52.
'When Britain's isle was over-run'
> A whig satire against the tory alderman for Broad Street ward, 'Sir Jocky'.
O; MH(uncut).

Breathings. The breathings of a pious soul, [174–?] *See* Hawksworth, Abraham Richard.

[**Brecknock, Timothy.**] Poems and odes, after the manner of Anacreon. By T------ B-------. *London, printed in the year* 1746. (*GA* 5 March)
4⁰: pp. 64. L,CT.
> Advertised in *GA* as by Brecknock, and as published by Dodsley.

B405 [—] The important triflers. A satire: set forth in a journal of pastime a-la-mode... (To which is added, a whimsical piece of poetry.) By Captain Cockade. *London, printed for M. Cooper,* 1748. (*BM,GM* April)
4⁰: *A⁴(−A4)* B–C⁴ D¹[= A4]; *i–ii, 1–5 6–22.* A1 hft; 4 err.
> *Rothschild* 848. Also listed in *BM* April 1749.
'I rise about seven, and read till tow'rds nine'
> A copy at L has a ms. note after 'Captain Cockade': 'als Tim: Brecknock author of the

Brecknock, T. The important triflers

Anacreonti⟨   ⟩ since hanged'; Breck-nock was executed *c.* 1786. Sometimes ascribed to Fielding because his name was added to the Dublin reprint below.
L(11602.gg.24/15; 11630.c.6/18,−A1; 11630.c.8/18,−A1),O(2,−A1),*BrP*; CtY(uncut),KU, OCU.

B406 [—] — By Henry Fielding, esqur; author of Tom Jones. *Dublin, printed by James Hoey,* 1749.
12⁰: *A⁶ B²; 1–5 6–16.* 16 advt.
BaP; *CLU-C*,NjP,*NjR*.

B407 Breeches. The breeches, a tale. Inscribed to the fair of Great-Britain. With a satyrical introduction. *London, printed for the author; sold by W. Lloyd & J. Wygate,* 1738. (*GM, LM* Oct)
2⁰: π¹ *A²* B–G² H¹; [2] *i–iii iv–ix, 1 2–10, 1 2–11.* π1 hft.
Introduction: 'As Stephen, in his happy state'
Breeches: 'A certain pair, who late were ty'd'
> A satire on James Miller.
L(643.1.28/28, mutilated, lacks π1, H1); CtY, DLC(−π1),ICU(−π1),MH(−π1),OCU(−π1).

Brereton, Jane. Poems on several occasions... With letters to her friends, and an account of her life. *London, printed by Edw. Cave,* 1744 [1745?]. (7 Jan 1745?)
8⁰: pp. lxviii, 303. L; NcU,MnU.
> *GM* Dec 1744 announces delivery to sub-scribers for 7 Jan 1745.

— [large paper] LVA-D,O.
> Reimposed as a quarto.

B408 [—] The fifth ode of the fourth book of Horace, imitated: and apply'd to the king. By a lady. *London, printed for William Hinchliffe; sold by J. Roberts,* 1716. (*MC* Nov)
2⁰: *A–B²; 1–3 4–8.*
> On pp. 3–4, 'Verses occasion'd by reading the following ode'.
'O thou! whom heav'n's propitious pow'r'
Verses: 'When fam'd Augustus rul'd the Roman state'
> Printed in Jane Brereton's *Poems,* 1744; the introductory verses are by William Hinchliffe.
C; MH.

B409 [—] Merlin: a poem. Humbly inscrib'd to her majesty. To which is added, The royal hermitage: a poem. Both by a lady. *London, printed by Edward Cave,* 1735. (*GM,LM* Dec)
4⁰: (frt+) *A²* B–D²; *1–3 4–16.*
> 'Price Six-pence' on title. *Merlin* introduces two short poems, 'To the queen' (p. 9) and 'Merlin's prophecy' (p. 11); the added poem (p. 13) is titled 'On the bustoes in the royal hermitage'.
'Illustrious queen! The loyal zeal excuse'

Brereton, J. Merlin

'While to our queen each duteous bard conveys'
Signed 'Melissa'; printed in Jane Brereton's
Poems, 1744.
L(11632.f.42; 11630.e.18/14,–frt; 642.1.28/3),
O; CtY,ICU(–frt),OCU,TxU.

B410 [—] [fine paper] *London, printed by Edward Cave,*
'MDCCXXV' [1735].
4°: (frt+) *A*²(±A1) B–D²; *1–3* 4–16.
No price on title, which is a cancel with the
erroneous date corrected in ms. With a
fleur-de-lys watermark as the preceding, but
probably the large-paper issue listed at 1*s.* in
LM Dec 1735.
CSmH.

B411 Brereton, Robert. A dialogue between Menalcas
and Palæmon; being an exercise for Christmas-day,
1738. *London, printed for the author; sold by T.
Cooper,* [1739.] (*GM,LM* Feb)
2°: *A*² B–C²; [*4*] 9 10–16. A1 hft.
'What pleasing harmony invite's the ear'
LdU-B; ICU,NN-B.

B412 [—] [another issue] By ‒‒‒‒‒‒‒‒‒‒ Coll. Camb.
No cancel has been seen, nor has any explana-
tion of this variant title-page been found.
MP.

B413 [Brereton, Thomas.] Charnock's remains: or,
S‒‒‒‒l his coronation. A satyr: being a parody
upon Dryden's Mac-Fleckno. *London, printed for
J. Baker,* 1713. (14 April, Luttrell)
8°: A–C⁴; *1–2* 3–23 *24 blk.*
Bond 32.
'Mankind must die; nor good from ill can save'
Reprinted with Brereton's name, below.
Rawlinson notes under the 1719 edition 'This
had been ill printed in 1710 [!] without the
author's knowledge, and is a burlesque on
Dr Sacheverell's progress after his tryal'.
Dryden's satire adapted to fit Sacheverell.
L(161.k.8, Luttrell),O(uncut),AdU; CLU-C,CtY,
MH.

B414 — [*idem*] Charnock junior: or, the coronation.
Being a parody upon Mac-Flecknoe. In three
cantos. Now first publish'd correct and intire.
London, printed for William Chetwood, 1719.
8°: *A*⁴ B–D⁴; *1–5* 6–31 *32.* 31 err; 32 advt.
A revised text.
O; DFo,ICN,MH.

B415 — A day's journey, from the vale of Evesham to
Oxford: in a familiar epistle, to N. Griffith, esq; To
which are added two town-eclogues. *London
printed, and sold by R. Burleigh,* [1717.] (*DC* 29
June)
8°: A–B⁸; *1–3* 4–29 *30; 31–32 blk.* 30 advt.
P. 19 is fly-title 'Two town-eclogues: in
allusion to the ninth and part of the second of
Fontenelle'; one is titled 'Poor Suky' and the
other 'The crisis'.
'Since woolly Cotswold is no more in view'

Brereton, T. A day's journey

Suky: 'One ev'ning fair, fast by the Bird-cage side'
Crisis: 'Three weeks, three melancholy weeks had
past'
O,AdU(–B8); CtY(–B8),ICU,MH.

B416 — An English psalm. Or, a hymn on the late
thanksgiving-day: being a protestant version of the
second psalm. *London, printed for Jonas Brown, &
J. Roberts,* 1716. (*MC* Sept)
2°: *A*² B–C²; *i–iv,* 1–8. A1 hft.
'Why rage the papist thus combin'd'
The title is perhaps occasioned by Pope's
A Roman catholick version of the first psalm,
1716.
L(11602.i.26/4, uncut).

B417 — George: a poem. Humbly inscrib'd to the...
Earl of Warrington. *London, printed for Jacob
Tonson,* 1715. (*MC* Feb)
12°: A¹²; *i–ii,* 1 2–21 *22 blk.*
'Him, whose sad absence thou hast long condol'd'
In praise of King George.
L(11632.aaa.4),O,E.

[**Breval, John Durant.**] Military and other poems
upon several occasions... By an officer in the army,
1716. *See* Military.

[—] Miscellanies, upon several subjects; occasionally written. By Mr. Joseph Gay, 1719. *See*
'Gay, Joseph'.

*The pseudonym 'Joseph Gay' was used by both Breval
and Francis Chute when writing for Curll, with
consequent problems of who wrote what.*

────────────

B418 [—] The art of dress. A poem. *London, printed for
R. Burleigh,* 1717. (*MC* Feb)
8°: *A*⁴(A1 + frt) B⁴ C⁴(–C4) D–F⁴; *i–viii,* 1 2–35,
1 2–3. A1 hft; ²1–3 advt.
On pp. 27ff. 'Apple-pye. A poem. By Dr.
King'. *Straus, Curll* quotes the assignment of
copy from Breval to Curll, 13 Feb 1717; he
dates publication as 7 March. Reissued in
The ladies miscellany, 1718.
'In antient times, before this isle was known'
Apple-pye: 'Of all the delicates which Britons try'
Dedication signed 'J.D.B.'; cf. the assignment
referred to above. 'Apple-pye' is by Leonard
Welsted; printed in his *Epistles,* 1724.
L(992.h.3/11; 164.1.15,–A1),O(3, 2–A1),
C(–A1, frt),LdU-B(–A1); CLU-C,CtY,IU,MH,
TxU(–A1, frt)+.

B419 [—] [reissue?] An heroi-comical poem... The
second edition. *London, printed for E. Curll,* 1717.
(*PB* 23 June)
No cancel title seen; possibly a press-variant
title.
MH(–A1),TxU.

B420 [—] Calpe, or Gibraltar. A poem... By the author
of the Art of dress. *London printed, and sold by R.
Burleigh,* '1708' [for 1718; but 1717]. (*DC* 14 Nov)

Breval, J. D. Calpe

8⁰: A–C⁴ D²; *i–viii, 1* 2–16 *17–19; 20 blk.* 19 err.

'In fair Hesperia's utmost southern shore'
O; CtY,MH,NN.

B421 [—] [reissue] The second edition. *London printed, and sold by J. Roberts,* 1720. (*DC* 25 Jan)
8⁰: A⁴(–A1, +π²) B–C⁴ D²; [2] *i–viii, 1* 2–16 *17–19; 20 blk.* π1 hft; 19 err.
Cancel title with conjugate half-title.
DFo,IU,KU,MH.

B422 [—] [*idem*] Gibraltar; a poem. Most humbly inscrib'd and address'd to the right honourable the Earl of Portmore. *London, printed for H. Noorthouck; sold by J. Roberts, W. Meadows, T. Worrall, S. Austen, J. Millan,* 1727. (*MC* July)
4⁰: A² a² B–F²; *i–viii, 1* 2–20.
L(643.k.3/3; 163.m.1, Luttrell, July); CSmH (uncut).

B423 [—] Calpe, or Gibraltar. A poem... By a gentleman, now residing there. *London: printed, and Dublin reprinted by S. Powell, for Richard Norris,* 1727.
8⁰: A–C⁴; *i–viii, 1* 2–13 *14–16.*
L(11774.aaa.9/7),DA(uncut),DN(3).

B424 [—] The church-scuffle: or, news from St. Andrew's. A ballad. To the tune of A begging we will go, &c. Written by Mr. Joseph Gay. *London, printed for E. Curll,* 1719. (Feb?)
2⁰: A¹ B²; *i–ii,* 1–3 *4. 4* advt.
The 'second edition' advertised in *PB* 28 Feb 1719 is really a reprint in *The court miscellany,* 1719.
'Have you not heard of a pious fray'
Ascribed to Breval in *CBEL*; but since the pseudonym of Joseph Gay was also used by Francis Chute, the attribution should be regarded with caution. On Sacheverell's proceedings against William Whiston.
OC(uncut),MC(lacks A1); CtY(Luttrell, March), MH.

[—] An epistle to the right honourable Joseph Addison, [1717.] *See* E420·5.

B424·5 [—] Henry and Minerva. A poem. By J.B. esq; *London, printed for J. Roberts,* 1729. (*MChr* 1 April)
8⁰: A⁴ B–F⁸; *1–9* 10–87 *88 blk.* A1 hft.
Printed by Samuel Richardson (*Sale* 72).
'Beaufort, great heir of that distinguished blood'
Ascribed to Breval in the advertisements in Mary Chandler's *The description of Bath,* 1738, 1741. A poem on the introduction of polite learning to England at the Reformation.
L(11643.b.25,–A1),LVA-D,O(uncut),*MR*; CtY, ICN,IU(–A1),MH.

B425 [—] Mac-Dermot: or, the Irish fortune-hunter. A poem. In six canto's. By the author of the Art of dress. *London, printed for E. Curll,* 1717. (*PB* 13 Aug)

Breval, J. D. Mac-Dermot

8⁰: A–G⁴; *i–viii, 1* 2–48. viii err.
PB 29 Aug announces 'A complete key' for next week.
'Of all the youths, whom Munster's fruitful soil'
L(164.l.22),DK,LdU-B; DFo,ICN,KU,MH, TxU+.

B426 [—] Morality in vice: an heroi-comical poem. In six cantos. By Mr. Joseph Gay. Founded upon Mr. Hogarth's six prints of a Harlot's progress; and illustrated with them. Necessary for all families... *London, printed in the year* 1733.
8⁰: A⁴ B–H⁴ (+6 plates); [4] i–iii *iv,* 1–56. A1 hft; iii advt.
This issue with uncancelled title may not have been intended for publication.
'The various scenes of vicious loves I sing'
Ascribed to Breval by *CBEL* (as *The lure of Venus*) and *DNB* (as *The harlot's progress*). The advertisement on p. iii is for Chute's *The petticoat,* and the attribution should be regarded with caution.
CtY.

B427 [—] [reissue] The lure of Venus: or, a harlot's progress. An heroi-comical poem. In six cantos. By Mr. Joseph Gay. Founded upon Mr. Hogarth's six paintings; and illustrated with prints of them. *London, printed in the year* 1733. (*DJ* 1 May)
8⁰: A⁴(±A2) B–H⁴ (+6 plates); [4] i–iii *iv,* 1–56. A1 hft; iii advt.
Listed in *LM* April as printed for J. Wilford.
L(11661.b.27; 992.k.8/1, lacks A2),LdU-B; CLU-C(lacks plates),CtY,ICN,KU,MH.

B428 [—] [*idem*] The harlot's progress. An heroi-comical poem. In six cantos. By Mr. J. Gay. Founded upon Mr. Hogarth's six paintings. *Dublin, printed by S. Powell, for Edward Exshaw,* 1739.
12⁰: A² B–E⁴/²; *1–4* 5–28.
DG; CtY.

B429 [—] [reissue] The harlot's progress. Founded upon Mr. Hogarth's six paintings. *Dublin, printed by S. Powell, for Edward Exshaw,* 1739.
12⁰: A²(±A1) B–E⁴/²; *1–4* 5–28.
L(11602.bb.33/2, title cropt, preface from *The spleen* inserted); CSmH,MH.

B430 [—] Ovid in masquerade. Being, a burlesque upon the xiiith book of his Metamorphoses, containing the celebrated speeches of Ajax and Ulysses... By Mr. Joseph Gay. *London, printed for E. Curll,* 1719 [1718]. (*PB* 20 Dec)
8⁰: A–G⁴; *i–viii,* 1–48. vi advt.
Bond 57.
'The roaring dons of Greece sat down'
Ascribed to Breval by *Nichols, DNB, CBEL.* Since the pseudonym Joseph Gay was also used by Francis Chute, the attribution should be regarded with caution.
L(11355.e.21),OW,DK; CLU-C,CtY,IU,KU, MH+.

Breval, J. D. Ovid in masquerade

B431 [—] [reissue] The force of eloquence illustrated, in two witty orations, spoken before the nobles of Greece...merrily translated into burlesque verse from the 13th book of Ovid's Metamorphoses. By Mr. Joseph Gay... The second edition. *London, printed for E. Curll, 1721.* (*DP* 6 Feb)
8°: A⁴(±A1) B–G⁴; *i–viii*, 1–48. vi advt.
> The title is presumably a cancel, but has not been verified as such.
University of Otago (microfilm at L).

[—] The progress of a rake: or, the templar's exit, 1732. *See* P1106.

[—] The rake's progress; or, the humours of Drury-lane, 1735. *See* R10.

[**Brewer, Thomas.**] Miscellany poems on several subjects... By T.B. gent., 1702. *See* Miscellany.

Brewster, S. The young club a congratulatory poem, [1713.] *See* D298.

B432 [**Brewster, Thomas.**] The satires of Persius, translated into English verse... Satire the first. *London, printed by J. Bettenham; sold by T. Cooper, 1741.* (10 Feb?)
4°: A² B–D⁴ E²; *i–iv*, *1* 2–28.
> Listed in *GM,LM* Feb.
'Vain cares of man! All earthly things how vain!'
> Early ms. note in the KU copy 'By Thomas Brewster M: D fellow of Snt. John's College Oxford and physician at Bath'.
L(11630.c.10/8, ms. date 10 Feb; 11630.d.16/2, mutilated),O,LdU-B; CtY,IU,KU,*MH.*

B433 [—] — Satire the second. *London, printed by J. Bettenham; sold by T. Cooper; Mess. Clements at Oxford; Thurlbourne at Cambridge; Leake & Frederick at Bath, 1741.* (23 March?)
4°: B⁴ C⁴; *1–3* '6' *5* 6–16.
> Listed in *LM* March.
'Again, Macrinus, comes the genial day'
> Rewritten from Brewster's translation of 1733, B437.
L(11630.c.10/8, cropt, ms. date ? 23 March),O, OW(lacks B1),LdU-B; CtY,IU,KU,*MH.*

B434 [—] — Satire the third and fourth. *London, printed by J. Bettenham; sold by T. Cooper; Mess. Clements at Oxford; Thurlbourne at Cambridge; Leake & Frederick at Bath, 1742.* (*GM* April)
4°: A² B–E⁴; *i–iv*, *1* 2–30 *31–32 blk.* 30 err.
'So! Sure as morning comes, the trade's the same'
''Twas thus, of old, the bearded awful sage'
L(11630.c.10/8, cropt),O,OW(lacks A1),LdU-B; CtY,IU,KU,*MH.*

B435 [—] — Satire the fifth. *London, printed by J. Bettenham; sold by T. Cooper; Mess. Clements at Oxford; Thurlbourne at Cambridge; Leake & Frederick at Bath, 1742.*

Brewster, T. The satires of Persius

4°: A⁴ B–D⁴ E¹; *1–4* 5–34. 34 err.
'O for a hundred pair of brazen lungs'
L(11630.c.10/8, cropt),O,OW(lacks A1),LdU-B; CtY,IU,KU,*MH.*

B436 [—] — Satire the sixth. *London, printed by J. Bettenham; sold by T. Cooper; Mess. Clements at Oxford; Thurlbourne at Cambridge; Leake & Frederick at Bath, 1742.*
4°: A⁴ B⁴ C²; *1–5* 6–20.
'Has winter drawn thee, say, poetic friend'
L(11630.c.10/8, cropt),O,OW(lacks A1),LdU-B; CtY,IU,KU,*MH.*

B437 — A translation of the second satyr of Persius. *London, printed by W. Bowyer, for J. Roberts, and the booksellers of Oxford & Cambridge, 1733.* (*GM* July)
2°: A² B–C²; *1–2* 3–12.
> Entered to Brewster in Bowyer's ledgers under 24 June and 5 July 1733, 500 copies printed. 1000 proposals for a translation of Persius, ⅛°, were entered under 18 July 1733 but have not been traced.
'The sacred dawn of this auspicious light'
L(1484.m.7/3; 11386.m.9),BaP,LdU-B; CSmH, CtY,ICN,NjP.

Bribery. Bribery, a satire, 1750. *See* Missy, César de.

— Bribery and simony, 1703. *See* Ward, Edward.

B438 **Brice, Andrew.** Freedom: a poem, written in time of recess from the rapacious claws of bailiffs, and devouring fangs of goalers, by Andrew Brice, printer. To which is annexed the author's case. *At Exon, printed by and for the author, at his printing-office opposite to St. Stephen's church, in the High-street, 1730.* (June)
8°: a–b⁴ c² A–Q⁴ (L2 as 'L3'); [*10*] *i* ii–vi *vii–x*, *1* 2–128.
> Bond 108. Advertised in *Brice's Weekly Journal* 6 March 1730 as 'to be printed by subscription, and publish'd with speed if suitable encouragement be given'; the dedication is dated 18 June 1730, and it was advertised as 'just publish'd' 26 June 1730. There is a 'List of such subscribers as disdain'd not to have their names appear' on p. x.
'Rich freedom's joys I sing; unparallel'd'
L(11641.df.29),EtC,ExI,ExP; DFo.

B439 **Brickenden, Francis.** Advice to a young gentleman. An epistle. *London, printed for T. Cooper, 'MDCCXXXII' [1742].* (*GM,LM* July 1742)
2°: A² B²; *1–2* 3–8.
'To guide the wand'ring step, and sketch the plan'
O; ICN.

Bricklayer. The bricklayer's poem, 1745. *See* Jones, Henry.

Bridgeroom

B440 Bridgeroom. The bridegroom at his wit's end. Or an el-e-gy on Miss G-a-f-f-e-n-y's me-dn--h-d by Mr. W-d. [*Dublin*, 1727.]
½°: 1 side, 1 column.
> Mourning borders.

'Tell me no more who is my freind'
> A poem in praise of friendship, with no apparent relationship to the title.

DT(ms. date 1727).

B441 Bridge. The bridge of life, an alegorical poem. In imitation of the 159th. Spectator. By the author of the Battle of the sexes. *Dublin, printed by Richard Dickson,* 1724.
4°: π¹ A² B² C¹; *i–ii, 1–2* 3–10. π1 hft, err and advt on verso.
> π¹ and C¹ have been seen to be conjugate.

'Unhappy state of all things here below'
> The author intended is Samuel Wesley junior, but the poem is not collected in his works. Dublin attributions are unreliable, and Wesley's authorship awaits confirmation.

DA,DG,LdU-B; ICN,*RPB*.

B442 Bridge, William. In obitum regis Georgii I. [*Oxford*? 1727.]
½°: 1 side, 1 column.
'Pars immortalis, deserta carne, Georgi'
> At foot 'Guil. Bridge S. Th. D. Coll. di. Jo. Bapt. soc.'

O.

B443 [**Bridges, —, *Mr.***] Divine wisdom and providence; an essay. Occasion'd by the Essay on man. *London, printed by J. Huggonson; sold by J. Roberts,* 1736. (*LDP* 31 March)
2°: A² B–F²; *1–5* 6–24.
'E'er time first mov'd, or e'er the youthful sun'
> The author is identified by TxU as Robert Bridges, but this has not been confirmed.

LVA-D(2, 1 uncut),O(2),LdU-B; CLU-C,CtY, MH,NjP,TxU.

B444 —— The second edition, corrected. By Mr. Bridges. *London, printed by J. Huggonson; sold by J. Roberts,* 1737. (*LEP* 19 April)
2°: π¹ A² B–E² F¹; [2] *i* ii–iii *iv, 5* 6–22.
O; CSmH,MiU,TxU(2).

B445 —— The third edition, corrected. *London, printed for T. Worral,* 1738.
4°: π¹ A–C⁴ D⁴(–D4); [4] *i* ii–v *vi, 1* 2–21 '23'. π1 hft.
> In the O copy π1 is bound as a fly-title after the preliminary leaves; this may be correct.

O,LdU-B(–π1).

B446 — An hymn to the supreme being. With a preface on the general design of it. *London, printed for T. Cooper,* 1739. (*GM* May)
2°: π¹ A–D² E¹; *i–vi, 1–13* 14. 14 err.
> Entered to Mr. Bridges in Bowyer's ledgers under 12 April, 250 copies printed; a note that

Bridges, —, *Mr*. Divine wisdom

one sheet was reprinted possibly belongs to the next entry in the ledger.
'Parent of all things! Cause supreme!'
O; NN-B,TxU.

[**Bridges, J.**] Homer in a nutshell [actually by Thomas Tooly], 1715–. *See* T420.

B447 Bridle. A bridle for the French king; or, an emblem of that tyrant's downfal. Done from the original, &c. [*London*] *Printed and sold by H. Hills,* [1706/07.]
½°: 1 side, 2 columns.
> Large allegorical woodcut at head. On the other side, *The infallible mountebank,* 1707.

'Tyrant! if man cannot thy power asswage'
> In praise of England's victories over France.

L(Harley 5931, fol. 251),O.

B448 Brigadier. Brigadier M'Intosh's farewel to the highlands, to an excellent new tune. [*Edinburgh*? 1716/–.]
½°: 1 side, 2 columns.
> No woodcut at head.

'M'Intosh is a soldier brave'
> William Mackintosh, the Jacobite, escaped to France in 1716.

MC.

B449 — [another edition]
> Rough woodcut at head.

E.

Brigs, John. A ballad by J-----n B-----s, [1729.] *See* B21.

[**B450 = L240·2**] **Bristol.** The Bristol merchants triumphant, [1733.] *See* The London merchants triumphant, 1733.

B451 — The Bristol-wells. A poem. For the year 1749. By a gentleman at the wells. *Bristol, printed for Thomas Cadell; sold by W. Frederick, at Bath,* 1749.
2°: A² B–D²; *i–iii* iv, *1* 2–11 *12* blk.
'Where Avon rolls its brown unsettled flood'
> In praise of the ladies at the wells.

O(uncut); TxU(uncut).

B452 Britain. Britain made free. A poem on his royal highness the Duke of Cumberland. *Edinburgh,* 1746.
8°: A⁴; *1–2* 3–8.
'If joy which now presents before mine eyes'
EU(cropt).

— Britain's consolation, in triumph after lamentation, 1747. *See* Don, James.

— Britain's hero, 1722. *See* Jacob, Giles.

B453 — Britain's joy, for the noble victory obtained by their forces over the French and Bavarians, August 13th 1704. To its own proper tune. [*London*? 1704.]
slip: 1 side, 1 column.

Britain's joy

'Hark, I hear the cannon roar'
A song on the victory at Blenheim.
E(cropt).

B454 — 'Britain's joy; or, King George return'd.
A poem to his majesty, on his arrival from beyond
sea. [*London*] *Printed for J. Roberts.* Price 4*d.*'
(*MC* Jan 1717)

— Britain's lamentation, and hopes of triumph,
[1745/46.] *See* Don, James.

B455 — 'Britain's ode of victory. On the expected happy
triumphant return of the illustrious Duke of
Cumberland, and his suppression of the horrid
rebellion. [*London*] *Printed for M. Cooper.* Price 1*s*'.
(*GA* 14 June 1746)

— Britain's palladium, 1712. *See* Browne, Joseph.

B456 — Britains rejoiceing at the coronation of his royal
majesty King George, to the tune of my Nanny O.
[*Edinburgh?* 1714.]
½°: 1 side, 2 columns.
'What blessed legacy was this'
E.

B457 — Britain's triumph, or, Monsieur defeated.
London, printed by W. Hughs, in Fleet-street,
[1743.]
½°: 1 side, 2 columns.
'Noble Britons raise your voice'
On the victory at Dettingen.
O.

B458 — Britain's wrongs. A new ballad. On the
m------ry. *London, printed for G. Lion,* [1743.]
(*GM, LM* April)
2°: A⁴; *1–2* 3–8.
Horizontal chain-lines.
'Ye true-hearted Britons, draw near to my ditty'
An attack on the ministry.
AdU; MH,OCU.

Britain, John. 'The amoret, or love poems. By
John Britain, M.A. Price 6*d.*'
Listed among poems published by John
Wilford in *Thesaurus Ænigmaticus* III, 1726.

Britannia. Britannia. A poem, 1729–. *See* Thomson,
James.

— Britannia: a poem. With all humility inscrib'd..., 1710. *See* Ward, Edward.

B459 — Britannia excisa: Britain excis'd. A new ballad
to be sung in time, and to some tune. *London,
printed by T. Reynolds,* 1733. (*LM* Jan)
2°: A⁴; *1–3* 4–8.
Percival p. 63. Large cut of the excise-monster
on title; small landscape headpiece on p. 3.
The order of this and the following (possibly
another impression) has not been determined.
'Folks talk of supplies'
Percival p. xlvii suggests William Pulteney's
authorship of both parts on the evidence of

Britannia excisa

style. Against Walpole's excise bill. Cf.
A sequel to Britannia excisa, 1733, and *The
countryman's answer,* 1733.
LSC,O,*MR*; KU,MH.

B460 — [variant]
No headpiece on p. 3; head-title in large
capitals in its place.
L(162.m.71),LU,O(3),OW,C; CSmH,MH(uncut),NNC(uncut),NjP,OCU+.

B461 —— *London, printed by T. Raynolds* [!], [1733.]
2°: A²; *1* 2–4.
A piracy.
L(C.116.i.4/18),LSA.

B462 — Britannia excisa: Britain excis'd. Part II. Tune
of, Packington's pound. [*London,* 1733.]
½°: *1–2,* 1 column.
The C copy is stabbed with the folio edition of
part I, to which it was presumably added. The
same setting of type but without numeration
of stanzas is printed as C2 of *The lords protest in
the late session of parliament,* 1733, with part I
as C1; these leaves are often found detached.
'Ye knaves and ye fools, ye maids, widows and
wives'
Crum Y72: 'The excise...'
L(112.f.44/20),OW,C; DLC.

B463 — [*idem*] A new song. Tune of Packington's
pound. [*London?* 1733.]
½°: 1 side, 2 columns.
Allegorical woodcut at head.
O-JJ.

B464 — Britannia excisa; Britain excis'd. A new
ballad... [parts 1 & 2] [1733.]
4°: A⁴; *1* 2–8.
Presumably a piracy, possibly of Scottish
origin.
AdU; InU.

B465 — Britannia excisa. [*London,* 1733.] (April)
1°: 1 side, 4 columns.
A large sheet with three large woodcuts over
columns 2 & 3. Column 1 contains 'Britannia
excisa'; columns 2 & 3 'Britannia excisa.
Part II'; column 4 'Excise congress' (first
published as *The congress of excise-asses,*
[1733]). *The projector's looking-glass,* 1733
(April) advertises this as given away *gratis*
with *The state juggler... A new excise opera.*
L(P&D 1937),LU.

B466 — Britannia invicta: or Britain's apology. A poem...
By W.R. M.D.R. *London, printed for J. Robinson,*
1745. (*GA* 11 Oct)
4°: ⟨A–E² F¹⟩; *1–3* 4–22.
'To what a height, O Britain, grew thy fame'
L(11630.b.4/9, cropt).

B467 — Britannia: or the contrast between Robert
W— and William P—. A pastoral dialogue, by way
of allegory. *London, printed for T. Taylor,* 1741.
2°: A¹ B² C¹; *1–2* 3–8.

Britannia: or the contrast

'Robert and William both were jolly swains'
On Walpole and Pulteney.
L(1962),LG,LdU-B; CSmH(uncut),KU,MH,NjP.

— 'Britannia's address to her sons, on their late behaviour in parliament. [*London*] *Printed for J. English. Price 6d.*' (*DA* 16 May 1745)
It is not clear whether this work is in verse or prose.

— Britannia's gold mine, 1750. *See* Lockman, John.

B468 — Britannias lamentation for the loss of Mustapha, one of the two Turks. A ballad. To the tune of Chivey Chase. [*London*] *Printed by Ed. Holloway, near Fleet Ditch,* [*c.* 1718.]
slip: 1 side, 1 column.
'O weep Britannia and lament'
A Jacobite mock lament for the death of Mustapha, one of George I's pages of the back stairs.
CSmH.

B469 — Britannia's loss. A poem on the death of England's Cæsar. *London, printed for J. Nutt,* 1702. (16 March, Luttrell)
2°: π^1 A–C²; *i–ii, 1–2* 3–12.
'A voice arose from sorrow's dusky cave'
The same authors also wrote *Albion's glory,* 1702, and *A poem on the late glorious success,* 1702. A lament for William III.
MH,*NjP*(Luttrell).

— Britannia's memorial, 1715. *See* Stacy, Edmund.

B470 — Britannia's precaution to her sons the gentlemen, clergy, and freeholders of England, against the approaching general election. Most humbly inscribed to the honourable Edward Vernon... By the author of Seventeen hundred and thirty-nine: and the Hibernian politicians. *London, printed for W. Owen, and R. Goadby in Sherborne,* [1741.]
2°: A–D² (A2 as 'A'); *1–2* 3–16.
'To you, O Vernon, whom a patriot zeal'
The author of *The Hibernian politicians,* 1740, was possibly called Gardiner.
L(11602.i.15/4).

B471 — Britannia's summons to the old genius of the nation. Or, glorious candidates for the new elections. *London printed, and sold by John Morphew,* 1710.
8°: A–B⁴; *1–2* 3–16.
'Rowse up, old genius of my fruitful isles'
LLP,O(2); CtY,ICN.

B472 — Britannia's tears: a satyrical dirge by way of a lamentation on the deplorable death of... Queen Anne... and as a chastisement to all her merry mourners. *Dublin, printed in the year* 1714.
8°: A–B⁴; *1–2* 3–16.
'The gleamy morn had scarcely shook off night'
L(523.a.49/1),DA,DN; InU.

— Brittania's tears: or, England's lamentation, 1701/2. *See* Harris, Benjamin.

Britannia's triumph

B473 — 'Britannia's triumph. Humbly inscribed to the Duke of Cumberland. [*London*] *Cooper. Price 1s.*' (*GM* Feb 1747)

Britanniae. Britanniæ lætantis exultatio, [1714.] *See* Perkins, Joseph.

'Britannicus.' A letter from Don Blas de Lezo, 1740. *See* L126.

— A letter from Don Thomas Geraldino, 1740. *See* L128.

B474 British. The British admiral: a poem. Inscrib'd to Edward Vernon, esq; *London, printed for John Osborn; sold by the booksellers in town & country,* 1740. (*GM* July; *GM, LM* Aug)
2°: *A¹* B–D² E¹; *1–3* 4–16.
'Awake, ye nine harmonious maids, who dream'
ICN.

B475 — British bravery. A poem. Dedicated to the right honourable the Earl of Stair. *London, printed for Jacob Robinson,* 1743. (*DA* 6 Nov)
2°: *A²* B–C² D¹; *i–vi, 1* 2–8. A1 hft.
'Now, when fierce discord rages, and the sword'
On the victory at Dettingen.
O; CtY,KU,MH,OCU,TxU.

B476 — The British censor. A poem. *London, printed for J. Baker,* 1712. (23 Dec, Luttrell)
4°: A–C²; *1–5* 6–12.
'While thy most fruitful labours pass about'
A satire on Addison's journalism.
L(164.n.77, Luttrell),LLP,GU,*MR-C*.

— The British court, 1707. *See* Browne, Joseph.

B477 — 'The British court; or, poetical characters of the royal family; also, of the Dukes of Marlborough, Bedford, Devonshire, Montague, and the Bp. of Bangor. By a person of quality. [*London*] *Printed for E. Curll. Price 6d.*' (*PB* 23 July 1717)

B478 — British frenzy: or, the mock-Apollo. A satyr. *London, printed for J. Robinson,* 1745. (*GM, LM* Feb)
2°: *A¹* B–C²; *1–2* 3–10.
Horizontal chain-lines.
'The curse, Apollo, why wilt thou prolong?'
Against the harlequinade and John Rich.
L(1962),O; DFo,KU,MH.

B479 — The British heroe, a new ballad, on the valiant Duke of Cumberland's journey to Scotland. By a star. *London, printed for, and sold by A. Moore,* 1746. (*GM* Feb)
2°: *A²* B¹; *1–2* 3–5 6 blk.
'Since William the great,/ The defence of the state'
CSmH(uncut),OCU.

— The British hero; or the vision, 1733. *See* Manning, Francis.

— The British muse, 1702. *See* Tutchin, John.

British

B480 — The British ode: to his grace the Duke of Marlborough. [*London*, 170–?]
2°: 4 ll.
> In Welsh. Possibly the 'Cywydh i clod y fawr lwyddianus Duke o Marlbrow' reprinted in Lintot's *Miscellaneous poems* II, 1720 (*Case* 260(2)b). See E. D. Jones, 'A Welsh poem in an English anthology' in *Journal of the Welsh bibliographical society*, July 1948.

(*Dobell* 2397.)

— A British philippic: a poem, in Miltonic verse, 1738. *See* Akenside, Mark.

— British piety display'd in the glorious life, [1742.] *See* Gent, Thomas.

— The British warriour, [1706.] *See* Daniel, Richard.

— British wonders, 1717. *See* Ward, Edward.

— The British worthies, [1729.] *See* Smith, Joseph.

B481 Britons. Britons thanksgiving. A poem, on our happy deliverance from the fears of the plague. [col] April the 25th, 1723. *By W.S.*
½°: 1 side, 2 columns.
'Britons, my muse once more inclines to sing'
> W.S. in the colophon is possibly the author rather than printer or publisher. Religious verses.

O.

Brittain, Thomas. A collection of plain and necessary poems, viz. 1. The cold season. On the late severe and hard frost... *Northampton, printed for the author*, 1740.
8°: pp. vi, 18.　L.
> A collection of five poems.

B482 Britton. Britton's consort: or, the musick-meeting. A satyr. Written by S.P. gent. *London printed, and are to be sold by the booksellers of London & Westminster*, 1703. (13 April, Luttrell)
2°.
> Advertised in *Observator* 14 April as 'by the ingenious T.P. gent'.
> Entered in *Morgan* F299 as by Samuel Phillips; the attribution is plausible but not confirmed. On Thomas Britton, the 'musical small-coal man'. Answered by *The satyrizer satyriz'd*, 1703.

(*Thorn-Drury*.)

'**Brocade, Timothy.**' A genuine epistle from M—w P—r, 1714. *See* G125.

B483 [**Brodie, Joseph.**][dh] *Scribimus indocti doctique poemata passim.* Le repos. An epistle to the publick. [*Edinburgh*, 1737.]
12°: A⁴; 1–8.

Brodie, J. Le repos

'The town has been so plagu'd of late'
Signed 'Fidelio F,A,C., Edinbr. 24. August 1737'. This pseudonym was used by Brodie for his prose pamphlets relating to the Porteous riots.
EN,EP.

Broke, Richard Verney, *lord Willoughby de. See* Verney, Richard, *baron Willoughby de Broke.*

Broken. The broken mug. A poem, [172–.] *See* Whyte, Laurence.

B484 — The broken-pipkin: a tale, dedicated to the citts. *London printed, and sold by Ben. Bragge*, 1705. (1 March, Luttrell)
½°: 1 side, 2 columns.
'As story goes, some sage wisakers'
> Apparently a satire on the expense involved in the war with France.
Rothschild; ICN(Luttrell).

B485 [**Brome, Alexander.**] The record of a famous action upon the case. In rythme. Wherein Priscilla Morecrave, widow, was the plaintiff, and Roger Pricklove was the defendant... Written by some man of the law... And now reprinted, with a preface, for the benefit of students and professors of the law in the present age. *London, printed for J. Roberts*, 1727.
2°: A² B² C²; 1–4 5–12.
> Originally printed *c.* 1660 (*Wing* R630); included here lest its anonymity should lead it to be thought to be an eighteenth-century work.
'Be it remembred now that formerly'
> Included in the third edition of Brome's *Songs and other poems*, 1668.
DFo(Luttrell),MH.

B486 Bromwich, John. The good shepherd: a sacred eclogue on the birth of Christ. *Birmingham, printed by T. Aris for the author*, 1743.
2°: A² B–C²; i–ii, 1–2 3–10.
'Ye swains of Solyma! where-e'er ye lead'
L(11630.h.8),BP.

B487 Brooke. Brooke and Hellier. A satyr. *London printed, and sold by J. Baker*, 1712. (*Spectator* 12 March)
8°: A–D⁴; 1–2 3–32.
''T has been observ'd of human nature'
> Apparently in favour of Thomas Brooke and John Hellier, the wine merchants, who started a big advertising campaign in Aug 1711, and petitioned parliament in 1712 (*Hanson* 1727). Apparently in reply to [Edward Ward] *The quack-vintners*, 1712. Cf. *Brooks and Hellier, a poem*, 1712.
L(164.1.65, Luttrell, 13 March),O; ICU,OCU, TxU.

Brooke, H.

[**Brooke, Henry,** *1694–1757, master of Manchester Grammar School.*] The quack-doctor. A poem, 1745. *See* Q1.

Brooke, Henry, *1703?–1783.* A collection of the pieces formerly published...to which are added several plays and poems. *London, printed for the author,* 1778.
8°: 4 vol.   L,O; CSmH,CtY.

— The poetical works... The third edition. *Dublin, printed for the editor,* 1792.
8°: 4 vol.   L.

B488 — Tasso's Jerusalem, an epic poem. Translated from the Italian. By Henry Brooke, esq; Book I. *London, printed by J. Hughs, for R. Dodsley,* 1738. (*SR* 27 Jan)
4°: *A*¹ B–F⁴ G⁴(−G4); *1–3* 4–47 *48 blk.*
In some copies (O,TxU) C2 is signed 'D2'. Dated by *Straus, Dodsley* 28 Jan; listed in *GM, LM* Feb. Entered in *SR* to Brooke; deposit copies at E,EU,GU,SaU.
'Of arms, devote to heav'n's eternal king'
L(11630.c.10/12, ms. date 31 Jan; C.70.f.1/5), O,E,DG,LdU-B+; *ICN*,MH,TxU.

B489 — — Book II. *London, printed by J. Hughs, for R. Dodsley,* 1738. (*SR* 5 April)
4°: A–F⁴; *1–3* 4–48.
Listed in *GM,LM* April. Entered in *SR* to Brooke; deposit copies at E,EU,GU,SaU.
'The king, in each anticipating thought'
L(11630.c.10/12, ms. date 6 April; C.70.f.1/5), O,E,DG,LdU-B+; *ICN*,KU,TxU.

B490 — — Book III. *London, printed by John Hughs, for R. Dodsley,* 1738. (*SR* 18 Aug)
4°: A–D⁴ E²; *1–3* 4–35 *36 blk.*
Listed in *GM,LM* Aug. Entered in *SR* to Brooke; deposit copies at E,EU,GU,SaU.
'The eastern breeze, fresh harbinger of dawn'
L(11630.c.10/12; C.70.f.1/5),O,E,DG,LdU-B+; *ICN*,KU.

B491 [—] Universal beauty a poem. *London printed, and sold by J. Wilcox,* 1735. (*GM* Jan)
2°: *A*² B–F²; *i–iv, 1* 2–20.
Printed by Samuel Richardson (*Sale* 166). Listed in *GM* as 'To be continued, 6 sheets at a time, price 1s.'
'Tritonia! Goddess of the newborn skies'
Reprinted in Brooke's *Collection,* 1778.
L(641.m.13/1; 643.1.28/31; 75.h.18, ? presentation copy),O,OA,OW; CtY(2),ICN,ICU,IU,MH.

B492 [—] — Part II. *London printed, and sold by J. Wilcox,* 1735. (*GM* March)
2°: *A*² B–F²; *i–iv, 1*–20.
'Thus does the maz'd inexplicable round'
L(641.m.13/1; 643.1.28/31; 75.h.18, ? presentation copy),O,OA,OW; CtY(2),ICN,ICU,IU,MH.

Brooke, H. Universal beauty

B493 [—] — Part III. *London printed, and sold by J. Wilcox,* 1735. (*LM* April)
2°: *A*² B–F²; *1–2* 3–24. 24 err.
'Thus beauty, mimick'd in our humbler strains'
L(641.m.13/1; 634.1.28/31; 75.h.18, ? presentation copy),O,OA,OW; CtY(2),ICN,ICU,IU,MH.

B494 [—] — Part IV. *London printed, and sold by J. Wilcox,* 1735.
2°: *A*² B–F²; *1–2* 3–24.
Printed by Samuel Richardson (*Sale* 166).
'Fresh from his task, the rising bard aspires'
L(641.m.13/1; 643.1.28/31; 75.h.18, ? presentation copy),O,OA,OW; CtY(2),ICN,ICU,IU,MH.

B495 [—] — Part V. *London, printed for J. Wilcox,* 1735. (*LM* July)
2°: *A*² B–F²; *1–2* 3–24.
Printed by Samuel Richardson (*Sale* 166).
'Thus nature's frame, and nature's god we sing'
L(641.m.13/1; 643.1.28/31; 75.h.18, ? presentation copy),O,OA,OW; CtY(2),ICN,ICU,IU,MH.

B496 [—] — Part VI. *London, printed for J. Wilcox, & L. Gilliver,* 1735 [1736]. (*GM,LM* March)
2°: *A*² B–F²; *1–2* 3–23 *24 blk.*
Printed by Samuel Richardson (*Sale* 166).
'Ye human offsprings! of distinguish'd birth'
L(641.m.13/1; 643.1.28/31),O,OW; CtY(2),ICN, ICU,IU,MH.

B497 [—] Universal beauty. A poem. *London: printed. And, Dublin re-printed by George Faulkner,* 1736.
8°: *A*⁴ B–C⁴; [2] *i* ii, *1* 2–20.
Below imprint 'To be continued'. Part 1 only.
L(1963).

B498 **Brookes, Henry.** Daphnis. A pastoral poem. To the most illustrious his grace the Duke of Marlborough, &c... *London, printed by J. Darby, for Bernard Lintot,* 1707.
2°: *A*² B–C²; *1–2* 3–11 *12 blk.*
'Well met Alexis! 'tis a glorious day'
CSmH,NNC.

B498·5 **Brooks.** Brooks and Hellier, a poem: [followed by epigram from Martial.] *London printed, and sold by J. Baker,* 1712.
½°: *1–2,* one column.
Below the title and the epigram from Martial, an English translation of the epigram, apparently as an introduction to the poem on p. 2, 'Great news from Oporto'.
'To balderdash his old Falernian'
Great news: 'I sing of jolly Bacchus, and the wine'
In praise of the wines of Brooke and Hellier; possibly the publication which provoked [Edward Ward] *The quack vintners,* 1712, answered by *Brooke and Hellier. A satyr,* 1712.
MH.

Broome, William. Poems on several occasions. *London, printed for Bernard Lintot,* 1727. (*SR* 9 March)

Broome, W. *Collections*

8°: pp. xiii, 248. L,O; CLU-C,MH.
Lintot paid £35 for the copyright, 22 Feb 1727 (*Nichols* VIII. 294); see also the agreement at L (Add. MS. 38729, fol. 50).

— — The second edition, with large alterations and additions. *London, printed for Henry Lintot,* 1739. (*GM* July)
8°: pp. xxiii, 280. L,O; CLU-C,MH.
There are two presentation copies at L.

— — The second edition, with large alterations and additions. *London, printed for Henry Lintot; sold by J. Wren,* 1750.
8°: pp. xiii, 248. L,O; CtY,MH.
A reissue of the 1727 edition with a cancel title.

_____

B499 [—] The oak, and the dunghill. A fable. *London printed, and sold by J. Roberts,* 1728. (*MChr* 15 Oct)
2°: A–B² C¹; *i–iv, 1 2–5 6 blk.* A1 hft.
No watermark.
'On a fair mead a dunghill lay'
Ascribed to 'Broome' in L copy C.59.h.9, bound in a volume well annotated throughout in a contemporary hand. Not included in Broome's *Poems,* 1735, and the attribution has been questioned. Answered by *The dunghill and the oak,* [1728], and *The better sequel better'd,* 1729; ms. reply in copies at O,CtY.
L(840.m.1/46,–A1; C.59.h.9/12),O(2, 1–A1), OW,C,LdU-B; CtY(2),MH(2),NjP,TxU(2, 1–A1).

B500 [—] [fine paper]
Watermark: fleur-de-lys.
CSmH,IU.

B501 Brown. Brown bread and honour, a tale. Moderniz'd from an ancient manuscript of Chaucer. *London, printed for John Morphew,* 1716. (*MC* June)
2°: *A² B²; 1–2 3–8.*
'In days of old, so poets feign'
L(C.131.h.1/1*),O(uncut); IU.

Brown, James. The dying heathen. A poem. Compos'd by Edward Stephens, and translated into Latin by James Brown, [1745.] *See* S749.

B502 [**Brown, John.**] An essay on satire: occasion'd by the death of Mr. Pope. *London, printed for R. Dodsley,* 1745. (*DA* 24 April)
4°: A–D⁴; *i–ii iii–iv, 5 6–32.*
Engraving on title.
'Fate gave the word, the cruel arrow sped'
The second edition was printed under Brown's name.
L(12273.m.1/19),O,*HU*,LdU-B; CSmH,CtY, ICN,MH(uncut),TxU(2)+.

B503 — — Inscribed to Mr. Warburton. The second edition; corrected and enlarged by the author, in

Brown, J. An essay on satire

the same manner in which it is inserted in the new edition of Mr. Pope's works, now in the press. *London, printed for R. Dodsley; sold by M. Cooper,* 1749. (*GA* 17 March)
4°: A–D⁴; *1–3 4–32* (14, 15 as '13, 14').
Title in red and black. A copy at L has a state of sheet B with p. 16 misnumbered '19'; both copies at L have p. 27 misnumbered '72'.
L(11630.b.7/12; 161.1.15),*LVA-D,MR*; MH.

B504 [—] Honour. A poem. Inscribed to the right honble the lord Viscount Lonsdale. *London, printed for R. Dodsley; sold by M. Cooper,* 1743. (*LDP* 20 Dec)
4°: *A⁴* B–C⁴; *1–5 6–23 24.* A1 hft; 24 advt.
Brown's correspondence with Dodsley (at O) reveals the existence of fine-paper copies; none has been identified. The watermark in copies seen is a fleur-de-lys.
'Yes: all, my lord, usurp fair honour's name'
Printed as Brown's in *Dodsley* III (1748). Horace Walpole's copy at MH has Walpole's ms. ascription to Robert Nugent, but this is clearly erroneous.
L(11630.c.9/10),O,OC,LdU-B; CSmH,CtY,ICN, MH(uncut),NjP+.

B505 — On liberty: a poem, inscribed to his grace the Chancellor and to the University of Cambridge, on occasion of the peace. *London, printed for C. Davis; sold by M. Cooper,* 1749. (*DA* 26 April)
4°: *A⁴* B⁴; *1–5 6–16.* A1 hft.
Title in red and black. Recorded in Bowyer's ledgers under 7 April 1749; 750 copies printed.
'At length the hostile din of war is o'er'
L(11630.b.6/15, Bank Coffee House, 29 April; 161.1.14,–A1),C; *MB*,MH(uncut),TxU.

B506 [**Brown, Nicholas.**] The north-country-wedding, and the fire, two poems in blank verse. *Dublin, printed by A. Rhames, for J. Hyde,* 1722.
4°: A–D²; *1–2 3–16.*
Errata slip on page 2 in CtY, DG copies. Watermark only seen in some copies, possibly because of the use of half-sheets.
'Now through the welkin wide the rosy morn'
'Happy the man, who void of care and strife'
Printed as Brown's in Concanen's *Miscellaneous poems,* 1724.
O,DG(2),DN; CtY.

Brown, Thomas.
The works *in two volumes octavo were first published in 1707; a third volume dated 1708 (WL Aug 1707) and a fourth dated 1709 were added. The first duodecimo edition in four volumes appeared in 1715 and was supplemented by a volume of* Remains *in 1720. The full bibliography of these editions has never been unravelled.*

_____

B507 [—] Advice to the Kentish long-tails, by the wisemen of Gotham. In answer to their late sawcy

Brown, T. Advice to the Kentish long-tails

petition to the parliament. *London, printed for A. Baldwin,* 1701. (May?)
½⁰: 1–2, 1 column.
    Dated 12 May at foot of p. 2.
'We, the long heads of Gotham, o'er our merry cups meeting'
    Printed in Brown's *Works* I. Occasioned by the Kentish petition of 8 May.
CtY.

B508 [—] [variant imprint:] *London, printed in the year* 1701.
CSmH.

B509 [—] — *London, printed in the year* 1701.
½⁰: 1 side, 1 column.
LG(cropt), Crawford.

B510 [—] — [*Edinburgh,* 1701.]
½⁰: 1 side, 1 column.
L(11602.i.6/13).

[—] The city madam, and the country maid, 1702. *See* C207.

B511 [—] A dialogue between the pillory and Daniel Defoe. [*Edinburgh,* 1706.] (11 Dec?)
½⁰: 1 side, 1 column.
    The two copies at E suggest an Edinburgh origin; possibly reprinted there to embarrass Defoe.
'Awake, thou busie dreamer, and arise'
    Printed in Brown's *Works* I; apparently written in 1703, but its first appearance not identified.
E(2, 1 dated in ms. 11 Dec 1706); TxU.

B512 [—] An elegy upon the lamented death of Edward Millington, the famous auctioneer. [*London*] *Published by John Nutt,* 1703. (1 Sept, Luttrell)
½⁰: 2 sides, 1 column.
'Mourn! – mourn! you booksellers, – for cruel death'
    Collected in Brown's *Remains,* 1720.
L(C.20.f.2/217; Harley 5947, fol. 175), O(Luttrell), Chatsworth, Crawford; CSmH, *MH*.

B513 [—] The last Observator: or, the devil in mourning. A dialogue between John Tutchin and his countryman. [*London,* 1704.]
½⁰: A¹; 1–2, 1 column. 2 advt.
'Come, honest country-man, what news dost bring?'
    Printed in Brown's *Works* I. A satire against Tutchin.
Crawford.

B514 [—] The mourning poet: or the unknown comforts of imprisonment, calculated for the meridian of the three populous universities of the Queen's Bench, the Marshalsea, and Fleet... Written by a poor brother in durance. *London, printed in the year* 1703. (20 May, Luttrell)
2⁰: A² B–D²; i–iv, 1–11 12. 12 advt.
    A ms. note in Gill's poems at E(Cwn. 301) refers to a catalogue of Rodd, *c.* 1850, listing an 8⁰ edition printed at Bury St. Edmunds.

Brown, T. The mourning poet

'Tho' Phœbus does his kindlier warmth refuse'
    Printed in Brown's *Works* IV.
O; CSmH, CtY, ICN(Luttrell, uncut).

[—] The pleasures of a single life, or, the miseries of matrimony, 1701. *See* P488.

B514·5 — Tom. Brown's letter from the shades, to the French king in purgatory. *London,* '*printed for Will ⟨Jack-about⟩*', [1713?]
½⁰: 1 side, 2 columns.
    Wing T1782, in error.
'And wilt thou leave young Jemmy in the lurch?'
    A reprint of Brown's *A satyr upon the French king,* [1697], adapted to refer to Louis XIV's deserting the cause of the Pretender as a result of the treaty of Utrecht. See F. H. Ellis in *POAS* VI. 713.
L(1850.e.10/55, cropt).

B515 [**Brown, William.**] Impiety and superstition expos'd: a poetical essay... By W.B., gent. *Edinburgh, printed by John Moncur; sold by John Vallange,* 1710.
4⁰: π² *–4*⁴ 5*² A–K⁴; i–xxxx, 1–79 80 blk. π1ᵛ err.
'Th' impious quaff off sin, ev'n till they burst'
    Ascribed to Brown by *Watt.*
L(11632.df.7); DFo, IU, *MnU.*

B516 [—] The Lamentations of Jeremiah, paraphras'd. By W.B. *Edinburgh, printed by John Moncur,* 1708.
4⁰: A–C⁴; 1–2 3–24. 24 err.
'How doth the city solitary sit'
    Ascribed to Brown in a nineteenth-century ms. note (? by Maidment) in the L copy.
L(1104.b.34/10).

Browne, Isaac Hawkins. Poems upon various subjects, Latin and English. By the late Isaac Hawkins Browne, esq; Published by his son. *London, printed for J. Nourse, & C. Marsh,* 1768.
8⁰: pp. 160.   L, O; CtY, MH.

———

B517 [—] The fire side: a pastoral soliloquy. On the E--- of G----- taking the s---ls. *London, printed for Henry Carpenter,* [1746.] (*GM, LM* May)
2⁰: A⁴; 1–5 6–8. A1 hft.
    Printed on mixed paper, some with horizontal chainlines.
'Thrice happy, who free from ambition and pride'
    Collected in Browne's *Poems,* 1768; a ms. version at MC is ascribed to 'Sr Hanbury Williams'. A satire on John Carteret, earl of Granville's inability to form a ministry.
L(1965), C(lacks A1.4), LdU-B; CLU, CtY, ICN, MH, TxU+.

B518 [—] The fire side: a pastoral soliloquy. *London, printed for G. Hawkins; sold by M. Cooper,* [1746.] (*BM* June)
2⁰: A⁴; 1–5 6–8.

Browne, I. H. The fire side

Browne, John

A prefatory note on p. 3 claims greater correctness for this edition. The notes added throughout are said to be by John Upton.
L(840.m.1/11),OA; CSmH,CtY,IU.

B519 [—] On design and beauty. An epistle. *London, printed for J. Roberts,* 1734. (*GM* Jan)
2°: *A²* B–C²; *i–ii, 1* 2–10. 10 err.
'Highmore, you grant, that in the painter's art'
Printed in Browne's *Poems,* 1768.
L(643.m.15/23),O(uncut),OW; CSmH(lacks A1), CtY,ICN,MH,TxU(2)+.

B520 [—] A pipe of tobacco: in imitation of six several authors. *London, printed for L. Gilliver,* 1736. (*GSJ* 15 Jan)
8°: *A⁴* B–C⁴; *1–7* 8–23 *24 blk.* A1 blk; A2 hft.
Bond 151. According to Brett-Smith's edition of 1924, blank A1 is sometimes found after C4. Entered in *SR* 15 Jan; deposit copies at O,EU, AdU.
'Old battle-array, big with horror is fled'
Reprinted in Browne's *Poems,* 1768.
L(11631.bb.68,−A1),O(−A1,2),EU,AdU(−A1), LdU-B(2, 1 uncut, 1−A1)+; CSmH(−A1),CtY (−A1),MH(2, 1−A1, 1−A1, 2),*MnU*,NN-A(−A1).

B521 [—] — The second edition. *London, printed for L. Gilliver,* 1736.
8°: *A⁴* B–C⁴; *1–7* 8–23 *24 blk.* A1 blk; A2 hft.
A reimpression, with some corrections.
LVA-D(−A1),OW(−A1); MH(−A1, 2),NN (−A1),TxU(−A1).

B522 [—] — The third edition, with notes. *London, printed for W. Bickerton,* 1744. (*DA* 4 May)
8°: π¹[= C1] *A⁴* B⁴ C⁴(−C1) (B1 as 'A'); *i–ii, 1–5* 6–21 *22 blk.* π1 hft.
L(11631.e.48),O(−π1),LdU-B; ICN(−π1),IU(uncut),MH(−π1),NN-A,NjP.

B523 [—] — The fourth edition, with notes. *London, printed for W. Bickerton,* 1744.
8°: π¹[= C1] *A⁴* B⁴ C⁴(−C1) (B1 as 'A'); *i–ii, 1–5* 6–21 *22 blk.* π1 hft.
Apparently from the same setting of type as the preceding.
L(1962,−A1),O(−A1); DLC,NN-A(−A1).

B524 [—] [*idem*] Of smoking. Four poems in praise of tobacco... With an ode, on the same subject, to Lord Bolingbroke. *London, printed for E. Curll,* 1736.
8°: A–C⁴ (A2 as 'A', A3 as 'A2'); *1–3* 4–23 *24 blk.*
The added ode is John Philips's *Ode to Henry St. John* in Latin and English. This edition is usually considered a piracy of the preceding, but all the poems had been printed in newspapers by 2 Dec 1735, and Curll may have been the first to print these four. Reissued in [Giles Jacob] *The rape of the smock,* 1736, with the other two poems added.
L(Tab.603.a.17/1),O,GU; CtY(2),KU(−A1), MH(−A1),*NN-A.*

Browne, John

B525 Browne, John. [first line:] Sir, with submission, I humbly crave... [*London,* 1706/07?]
½°: 1 side, 1 column.
Verses enclosed in emblematic woodcut border.
'Sir, with submission, I humbly crave'
Signed 'your trusty marshal, John Browne'; but possibly written for him. See Thomas Bellows and Jacob Hall for similar productions.
L(C.20.f.2/355).

B526 — To each gentleman soldier in the company of Captain Christopher Parkinson, captain in the yellow regiment of train'd-bands of the city of London. [*London,* 1709/11.]
½°: 1 side, 1 column.
Verses enclosed in the same emblematic woodcut border.
'Rouse up my British muse, and sing once more'
Signed 'your trusty marshal, &c. John Browne'.
L(C.20.f.2/353).

B527 — To each gentleman soldier in the company of Captain Samuell Robinson, captain in the yellow regiment of trained-bands of the city of London. [*London,* 1712/14.]
½°: 1 side, 1 column.
Verses enclosed in emblematic woodcut border.
'Hail sons of war, accept the muses praise'
Signed 'Your trusty marshal, John Browne'.
L(C.20.f.2/356).

Browne, Joseph. 'Several odes of Horace translated into English verse, by way of specimen to the whole version. Done with the notes... Corrected and enlarged, with several new additions, to be printed by subscription in folio. [*London*] *Sold by B. Bragg...where proposals may be had.*' (*FP* 26 May 1705)
A translation of Book 1, odes i–xv, as is known from *A letter from a gentleman in town to a friend in the country concerning Dr. Joseph Browne's new translation,* 1705 (copy at DT).
A set of proposals 'corrected and enlarged' dated 10 Nov 1704 is at L (Harley 5946, fol. 238–9).

[—] State and miscellany poems; compos'd occasionally, according to the circumstances of the author, and the difficulty of the times. Consisting of fables, satyrs, panegyricks, &c. By the author of the Examiner. Vol. II. *London printed, and sold for the benefit of the author, by G. Sawbridge, R. Knaplock & H. Clements, A. Bettesworth & J. Baker, Will. Mears & Jonas Brown, R. Richardson, W. Lewis, S. Chapman, & J. Greaves,* 1715.
8°: pp. 384.   O; CLU-C,MH.
A continuation of *State tracts... By the author of the Examiner,* 1715. Rawlinson's copy (at O) is lettered on the spine, 'Dr. Ios. Brown's Works'. Ascribed to William Oldisworth in

Browne, Joseph.

DNB (and thence in library catalogues), possibly by confusion with Oldisworth's *State tracts*, 1714. Both writers appear to have written *The examiner*, Browne being the later of the two. It is just conceivable that more than one author is represented in this collection, but the references in the prefaces to the author's imprisonment in 1706 seem to fit Browne.

———

B527·1 [—] Albion's naval glory, or Britannia's triumphs: a poetical essay towards a description of a sea fight. Occasion'd by the late engagement between the English, Dutch, and French fleets... *London, printed by H. Meere, for Francis Fawcet; sold by Benj. Bragg,* 1705 [1704]. (6 Nov, Luttrell)
2°: *A*² B–D²; *1–4* 5–16. 16 err.
The Luttrell copy is recorded in *Haslewood.* Advertised in *DC* 10 Nov.
'I sing the pride of Albion, and the pow'r'
Reprinted in Browne's *State and miscellany poems,* 1715, as 'A poetical essay on the last sea-fight with the French, August 12. 1704.'
O; *NcD.*

B527·2 [—] Britain's palladium: or, my Lord Boling-broke's welcome from France. *London, printed for J. Morphew,* 1712. (*PB* 16 Sept)
2°: *A*² B–C²; *1–2* 3–12.
Advertised in *Examiner* 11 Sept for 'Saturday next' [13 Sept]; the Luttrell copy dated 17 Sept is recorded in *Haslewood.*
'What noise is this, that interrupts my sleep?'
Reprinted in Browne's *State and miscellany poems,* 1715. Ascribed to William King (1663–1712) in his *Remains* (1732) 161; King was a friend of Browne, which may account for the confusion.
ICU,MH,TxU.

B527·3 [—] — *London: printed for John Morphew, and re-printed in Dublin by Cornelius Carter,* 1712.
4°: *A*² B²; *1–2* 3–8.
DA.

B527·4 [—] The British court: a poem. Describing the most celebrated beauties at St. James's, the Park, and the Mall... *London, printed for [Samuel Bunchley], and sold at the Publishing-office in Dove Court, near Bearbinder Lane,* 1707. (May?)
2°: *A*² B–D²; *i–ii, 1–2* 3–14. A2 advt.
The advertisement leaf A2 was presumably intended to follow the poem, but is not normally bound there. Advertised in *DC* 26 May as just published.
'Give me a genius, fill'd with soft delight'
Reprinted in Browne's *State and miscellany poems,* 1715; continued by his *The London belles,* 1707. See *Advice to the ladies,* 1707, and *Advice to the author of a late poem,* 1707.
L(1959),LdU-B; *CLU-C,ICN,MH,PBL.*

Browne, Joseph. The British court

B527·5 [—] — The second edition, with additions. *London, printed for [Samuel Bunchley], and sold at the Publishing-office, in Dove Court,* 1707. (*DC* 4 June)
2°: *A*² B–D²; *1–2* 3–16.
O; CtY,NjP,TxU(mutilated).

B527·6 [—] — *London, printed for, and sold at the Publishing-office,* 1707.
8°: *A*⁸; *1–2* 3–16.
Possibly a piracy.
Institute for Sex Research.

B527·7 [—] — [*London*] *Printed in the year* 1707.
8°: *A*⁴; *1* 2–8.
A piracy.
LG,O,DrU; NN.

B527·8 [—] The circus: or, British olympicks. A satyr on the ring in Hide-Park. *London printed, and sold by the booksellers of London & Westminster,* 1709. (*DC* 22 June)
8°: *A–D*⁴; *1–8* 9–30 *31–32 blk.*
'From vulgar eyes, on plains exalted high'
Reprinted in Browne's *State and miscellany poems,* 1715.
C; CLU-C(−D4),OCU.

B527·9 [—] — *London printed, and sold by the booksellers of London & Westminster,* 1709.
8°: *A*⁸; *1–3* 4–15 *16.* 16 advt.
A piracy by Henry Hills; advertisement on p. 16 for his poems. Murray Hill cat. 91 (1965) 642 reports that A7 is a cancel, but this has not been confirmed. Reissued with others Hills piracies in some copies of *A collection of the best English poetry,* 1717 (*Case* 294).
L(11601.dd.17/4; 1078.l.15; C.124.b.7/40*), O(6),CT,E,LdU-B+; CtY(uncut),DFo,ICN,MH, TxU+.

B528 [—] The country parson's honest advice to that judicious lawyer, and worthy minister of state, my lord keeper. [*London,* 1706.] (30 Jan, Luttrell)
½°: *1–2, 1 column.*
'Be wise as Somerset, as Somer's brave'
Browne was convicted of publishing this poem, though he consistently denied his authorship; see *DNB* and refs. A satire on William Cowper. See *The lawyer's answer,* 1706, and *The country parson's advice to those little scribblers,* [1706.]
L(C.20.f.2/303),O,MC,Chatsworth, Crawford; ICN(Luttrell),InU,MH,NN.

B529 [—] — [*London,* 1706.]
½°: *1 side, 1 column.*
Ms. note in PPL copy 'This was cryed about streets by the hawkers in January 1705 [/06]'.
L(112.f.44/39),O(2),MC,Crawford;CtY,MH,NN, PPL.

B530 [—] The country parson's honest advice to...my l. k—r. With a reply, how to become a bishop. [1706/–.]

91

Browne, Joseph. The country parson's

½°: 1 side, 1 column.

The reply suggests a somewhat later date than 1706.

Reply: 'That lowly vicar may in order rise'
LSA; TxU.

B530·1 [—] The fox set to watch the geese: a state-paradox. Being a welcome from Newmarket, by way of fable. *London, printed for Benj. Bragg*, 1705. (*DC* 26 April)

4°: A^2 B–F^2; *i–iv*, 1–19 *20 blk*. A1 hft.

'In times of yore, when brutes were speakers'
Reprinted in Browne's *State and miscellany poems*, 1715, as 'Volpone'; also ascribed to him in *N&Q* III. ii (1862) 14.

L(1077.k.24/3); CSmH,CtY,IU,TxU(–A1).

B530·15 [—] [reissue] Volpone, or the fox. By way of fable, very applicable to the present times. *London printed, and sold by Benj. Bragg*, 1706 [1705]. (*DC* 15 Nov)

4°: $A^2(\pm)$ $B^2(-B1)$ C–F^2; *i–ii*, 1–19 *20 blk*.

Original A^2 and B1 cancelled, replaced by new title and first leaf of text. The printer is identified as 'Mr. Grantham' by Robert Clare, one of Harley's informers; see H. L. Snyder in *The library* V. 22 (1967) 339. The reliability of these identifications is uncertain, and Clare records the printer of the previous issue as unknown; he attributes the poem to Pittis.

O,DT; CLU-C,CtY,ICU,MH.

B530·2 [—] The Gothick hero. A poem, sacred to the immortal honour of Charles XII. king of Sweden... *London printed, and sold by B. Bragge*, 1708 [1707]. (27 Nov, Luttrell)

2°: 8 ll.

The Luttrell copy is recorded in *Haslewood* and by Pickering & Chatto cat. 248/13920. Listed in *WL* Nov and *DC* 2 Dec 1707.

'I sing not of Bellona's praise, or war'
Reprinted in Browne's *State and miscellany poems*, 1715.

(*Haslewood*.)

B530·3 [—] The insect war: or, a battle between the high-church hornets, the scribbling wasps, the canting catterpillars, and the state butter-flies. A parable. *London printed, and sold by B. Bragge*, 1706. (9 May, Luttrell)

2°: A^2 B–D^2; *1–2* 3–16.

The Luttrell copy is in the possession of J. R. B. Brett-Smith.

'In old, and modern fables I have read'
Reprinted in Browne's *State and miscellany poems*, 1715.

LLP; IU(uncut).

B530·4 [—] Liberty and property. A satyr. *London printed, and sold by B. Bragg*, 1705. (*FP* 29 March)

4°: A^1 B–F^2 G^1; *i–ii*, 1–22.

'My muse attempts no vain heroick skill'

Browne, Joseph. Liberty and property

Reprinted in Browne's *State and miscellany poems*, 1715.
DT,*MR*; CtY.

B530·5 [—] The London belles: or, a description of the most celebrated beauties in the metropolis of Great Britain. The ladies names [listed]... *London, printed for [Samuel Bunchley], and sold at the Publishing office, in Dove Court, near Bearbinder Lane*, 1707. (26 June, Luttrell)

2°: A–D^4; *1–2* 3–16. 16 advt.

The Luttrell copy is recorded in *Thorn-Drury*; advertised in *DC* 28 June as 'just publish'd'.

'Tho' greater stars, plac'd in a higher sphere'
Reprinted in Browne's *State and miscellany poems*, 1715 as 'The city beauties, &c'. See *Advice to the ladies*, 1707.

L(11630.f.35; C.66.f.27, inserted in a Settle funeral binding); CLU-C,NN.

B530·52 [—] — *London, printed in the year* 1707.

8°: A^4; *1* 2–8.

A piracy. The typography is regular throughout.

L(12330.f.26/1),LG; OCU.

B530·55 [—] — *London, printed in the year* 1707.

8°: A^4; *1* 2–8.

Another piracy. Pp. 7 and 8 are in smaller sizes of type, p. 8 partly in two columns.

LG; CtY,DLC.

B530·6 [—] The patriots of Great Britain: a congratulatory poem to those truly noble and illustrious peers who happily united the two kingdoms... *London, printed by R. J. [Richard Janeway]; sold by J. Morphew*, 1707. (14 May, Luttrell)

2°: A^2 B–D^2; *i–iv*, 1–12.

The Luttrell copy is in the collection of R. D. Horn; advertised as 'just published' in *PM* 17 May.

'How shall my muse express thy pow'r or praise'
Reprinted in Browne's *State and miscellany poems*, 1715, as 'On the union...'

MH.

B530·7 [—] The royal prophetess: or, Israel's triumphs over Jabin king of Hazor. An heroick poem. Written after the manner of the antients; and now publish'd upon the occasion of the unparallell'd success of her majesty's forces, under...Marlborough. *London printed; sold by A. Baldwin*, 1706. (31 May, Luttrell)

4°: A^4 B–G^4; *i–viii*, 1–48. A1 hft.

Listed in *WL* May.

'When pious Joshua Israel's people led'
Reprinted in Browne's *State and miscellany poems*, 1715.

AdU,*MR*; CLU-C(Luttrell, uncut, –A1),ICN, OCU.

B530·8 [—] St. James's Park: a satyr. *London printed, and sold by John Morphew*, 1708. (8 June, Luttrell)

2°: A–D^2; *1–2* 3–16.

The Luttrell copy is recorded in *Haslewood*.

Browne, Joseph. St. James's Park

'In days of yore, when vertue was in vogue'
Reprinted in Browne's *State and miscellany poems*, 1715. A satire on the amours of the beaux and belles. Answered by *Almonds for parrots*, 1708.
L(1972), LG,*MR*,YU; CSmH,IU(title cropt),*MB*.

B530·82 [—] — [*London?* 1708?]
4°: *A*²; *1–4*, 2 columns.
Drop-head title only. A piracy.
O; TxU.

B530·84 [—] — *London printed, and sold by H. Hills, 1708.*
8°: A⁸; *1–2* 3–16.
A piracy.
L(11633.bb.1),CT; CtY,IU,MH,OCU,TxU.

B530·86 [—] — *London printed, and sold by H. Hills, 1709.*
8°: A⁸; *1–2* 3–16.
Reissued with other Hills piracies in *A collection of the best English poetry*, 1717 (*Case 294*).
L(11601.dd.17/6; C.124.b.7/35),LG,O(4),E, WcC+; CtY,ICU,IU,MH,TxU.

B530·9 [—] The singing-bird's address to the eagle: being a complaint against the owls, the kites, the crows, and the cuckoe's. Imitated from an old fable of Phædrus; not in any edition... *London printed, and sold at the Publishing-office [of Samuel Bunchley], in Dove-court near the back-door of the General Post-Office*, 1707.
8°: A⁸; *1–2* 3–16.
'Somewhere about the sun, as I have read'
Reprinted in Browne's *State and miscellany poems*, 1715. A political fable about the persecution of authors.
EU.

B530·95 [—] The splitter of freeholds: with a Search for religion. A satyr. *London printed, and sold by the booksellers of London & Westminster*, 1708. (*WL* April)
4°: *A*² B–G⁴; *i–iv*, 1–47 *48 blk.*
The splitter of freeholds is possibly the same work as was published anonymously in 1705 (S659).
'Long has the city been the scene of vice'
Search: 'Tell me, you glorious shades, where I may trace'
Both poems were reprinted in Browne's *State and miscellany poems*, 1715.
E.

[—] Useful and delightful instructions, by way of dialogue between the master & his scholar [probably by Thomas Gill], 1712. See G162·5.

Browne, Moses. Poems on various subjects. Many never printed before. *London, printed by and for Edward Cave*, 1739. (*GM* 1 Oct)
8°: pp. x, 460.   L,O; CtY,MH.

Browne, M.

— The works and rest of the creation: containing I. An essay on the universe... II. Sunday thoughts... In three parts. *London, printed for A. Millar*, 1752.
12°: pp. xiv, viii, 240.   L,O.

[—] The coquets: or, a convert and a half, 1750. *See* C434.

B531 [—] Piscatory eclogues: an essay to introduce new rules, and new characters, into pastoral... *London, printed by C. Ackers, for John Brindley*, 1729. (*MChr* 18 April)
8°: A⁴ b⁴(–b4) B–R⁴ S¹; *i–xiv, 1* 2–129 *130. 130* advt.
'Since Maro in divine Augustus' days'
Dedication signed 'Immerito'. Reprinted in Browne's *Poems*, 1739.
L(992.k.24/2),LdU-B; CSmH,CtY(2, 1 stitched, uncut),ICN,IU,MH(2)+.

B532 — The Richmond beauties. A poem. Inscribed to their royal highnesses the young princesses. *London, printed for E. Curll*, 1722 [1721]. (*PB* 16 Dec)
8°: A–D⁴ (C2, D2 as 'C3', 'D3'); *1–2* 3–32.
Including three other poems, two by Browne and one by William Derham. Reissued in *The altar of love*, 1727.
'Whilst the glad muse exults her strains'
L(11632.e.10; 161.l.16, Luttrell, 26 Dec); CLU-C,ICN,IU,MH,NjP+.

B533 — Sunday thoughts. Part I. Containing the publick, family, and solitary duties. *London, printed for J. Payne & J. Boquet* [!], 1749. (*GM,LM* May)
12°: (frt+) π¹ A–E⁶ F¹; *i–iii* iv–xiv, *1* 2–49 *50 blk.*
The frontispiece represents a church.
'Mute with conceal'd distress, joy-widow'd long'
Dedication signed.
MR; OO.

B534 — Sunday thoughts. Containing the publick, family, and solitary duties... Part I. The second edition. *London, printed for J. Payne & J. Bouquet; sold also by Mr. Sandby, Mr. Millar, Mr. Barnes, Mr. Jackson, Mr. Chapelle, Mr. Trye, Mr. Cook*, 1750. (*GA* 23 March)
12°: (frt+) π¹ A–E⁶ F¹; *i–iii* iv–xiv, *1* 2–49 *50 blk.*
Copies seen are bound with part II; the portrait frontispiece is referred to in the advertisement in *GA*. Entered in Strahan's ledger to Payne & Bouquet, 500 copies. A further entry in Sept 1750 '200 titles for Sunday thoughts' suggests a cancel title (possibly for parts 1 & 2 together), though it may merely have been for advertisement.
O(–frt),*MR-C*; DLC.

B535 — Sunday thoughts. The morning's meditating walk. Containing the internal, early, and preparatory duties... Part II. *London, printed for J. Payne*

Browne, M. Sunday thoughts

& *J. Bouquet; sold also by Mr. Sandby, Mr. Millar,
Mr. Barnes, Mr. Jackson, Mr. Chapelle, Mr. Trye,
Mr. Cook, 1750. GM,LM* June)
12°: *A*² B–E⁶ F⁴; *i–iv, 1* 2–56.
> Entered in Strahan's ledgers to Payne &
> Bouquet, 500 copies.
'As one belated on some perilous road'
O; DLC.

B536 — The throne of justice; a pindaric ode; humbly
dedicated to...lord Viscount Molesworth. *London,
printed for T. Edlin, 1721. (DP* 26 May)
2°: A–C²; *i–iv, 1* 2–8.
> Some copies have a ms. correction on p. 5,
> stanza X, line 1.
'Restor'd to ancient rule begin my verse'
CtY,*CU*,IU,MH.

[—] Verses on the late earthquakes, 1750. *See*
V64.

B537 [—] Verses to the right honourable the Earl of
Scarborough. Upon the death of the late glorious
king, and his present majesty's most happy
accession. *London, printed for J. Millan, and at his
shop by the Horse-Guards, 1727. (MC* July)
8°: *A*¹ B–C⁴ D²; *3–4* 5–24. 24 err.
> Copies seen probably lack half-title, A1 of *A*².
'Permit, my lord, a grateful muse to sing'
O; OCU.

B537·1 — [variant title:] By Moses Browne.
> Possibly intended for presentation, but not
> apparently on fine paper.
O.

Browne, Simon. Hymns and spiritual songs. In
three books... *London, printed for Eman. Matthews,
1720. (PB* 14 April)
12°: pp. 368.   L,O; CtY-D,MH.
> A set of tunes, engraved by Francis Hoffman,
> is bound between preliminaries and text in
> both editions.

—— The second edition. *London, printed for
James Hodges, 1741.*
12°: pp. 289.   L,O; NNUT.

B538 [**Brownsword, William.**] Laugh and lye down;
or, a pleasant, but sure, remedy for the gout,
without expence or danger... In a poem serio-
comic. Humbly inscribed to Sir Hans Sloane...
[*London*] *Printed for Lawton Gilliver, 1739.
(GM,LM* July)
8°: π¹[= F1] A–E⁴ F⁴(–F1); *i–ii, 1* 2–46.
'To all the hobling generation'
> Ascribed to Brownsword in *Rawlinson* where
> it is noted of his poems 'these 3 sd. to be
> printed for Lawton Gilliver...but are the
> authors own ⟨ ?⟩'.
L(1188.d.5/3); CSmH,MH.

B539 [—] Laugh upon laugh, or, laughter ridicul'd.
A poem, ethi-comico-satyrical... With some
other pieces by the same hand... By the author of

Brownsword, W. Laugh upon laugh

Laugh and lye down... *London, printed for Lawton
Gilliver, 1740.* (28 March?)
8°: A–G⁴ H² (A2 as 'A'); *i–iii* iv–viii, 9–58 *59;
60 blk.* H2 advt.
> Publication date from *Rawlinson*; listed in
> *GM,LM* April.
'Some prelude here the muse advises'
> Dedication signed 'W. B.' The advertisement
> on p. 59 lists Brownsword's *On prophecy* as
> well as *Laugh and lye down.*
L(11631.c.1),LdU-B; ICN(–H2),ICU,IU(–H2),
TxU.

B540 — On prophecy, as pointing out the Messiah.
A divine ode. Humbly inscrib'd to the right
reverend father in god, Francis lord bishop of
Chichester. To which are annexed some suitable
notes both explanatory and instructive. *London, printed for L. Gilliver & J. Clarke, 1739. (GM* March)
2°: π¹ A² B² C–E²; *1–3* 4 *5* vi 7 8–22.
'When man became impure and fell'
O(uncut); CtY.

B541 [**Broxholme, Noel.**] A letter from a lady to her
husband abroad. *London, printed for J. Roberts;
sold by A. Dodd, & E. Nutt, 1728. (MChr* 3 Sept)
2°: *A*² B–D² *E*¹; *i–iv, 1*–13 *14 blk.* A1 hft.
'To thee, dear youth, in sacred wedlock ty'd'
> Early ms. note in CLU copy 'Dr. Hollins
> daughter to Edward Walpole esq; by Dr.
> Broxholme'. Edward Walpole (the second son
> of Sir Robert) had apparently deserted John
> Hollings's daughter (Margaret?). Abridged
> and altered as *A letter from a lady to her
> husband,* [1740?].
L(1484.m.4; 1489.d.44),O,LdU-B; CLU,CSmH,
NjP,OCU,TxU(2, 1 uncut)+.

B542 [—] — *London, printed for a company of of* [!]
stationers, [1728?]
2°: *A*²; *1* 2–4.
> Apparently a piracy.
CtY.

B543 [—] — *Dublin, printed by S. Powell, for George
Risk, George Ewing, & William Smith, 1728.*
8°: A⁸; *1–3* 4–15 *16 blk.*
CT,DN,DT(2); CtY.

B544 [—] — The second edition. *London, printed for
J. Roberts; sold by A. Dodd, E. Nutt, 1729* [1728?].
2°: *A*² B–D² *E*¹; *i–iv, 1*–13 *14 blk.* A1 hft.
> Largely reset.
L(163.n.18),C,LdU-B,*MR-C*; CtY,IU,MH.

B545 [—] — The third edition. *London, printed for
J. Roberts; sold by A. Dodd, E. Nutt, 1729* [1728?].
2°: *A*² B–D² *E*¹; *i–iv, 1*–13 *14 blk.* A1 hft.
> A reimpression.
L(11647.g.76),O,BaP(–A1),EtC(–A1),WcC.

B546 [—] — The fourth edition, corrected. *London,
printed for J. Roberts; sold by A. Dodd, E. Nutt,
1729. (MChr* 6 Jan)

Broxholme, N. A letter

    2º: *A*² B–D² *E*¹; *i–iv*, 1–13 *14 blk*. A1 hft.
      In part, at least, a reimpression.
    O,C; IU,TxU(uncut).

B547 [—] — The fifth edition, corrected. *London, printed for J. Roberts; sold by A. Dodd, E. Nutt,* 1729.
    2º: *A*² B–D² *E*¹; *i–iv*, 1–13 *14 blk*. A1 hft.
      Apparently a reimpression.
    CSmH.

B548 **Br—sh.** The Br—sh embassadress's speech to the French king. [*London,* 1713.] (March)
    slip: 1 side, 1 column.
      No comma at end of line 14, 'done'. Swift's *Journal to Stella* on 23 March 1713 reports 'It has been printed in 3 or 4 different ways, & is handed about, but not sold: it abuses the Qu— horribly'. One printer, William Hart, was tried and sentenced at Queen's Bench, 27 June 1713.
    'Hail tricking monarch! more successful far'
      Crum H131. An attack on the ministry for making peace with France. Put into the mouth of Adellinda Talbot, wife of the Duke of Shrewsbury, ambassador to France. Cf. *The em--ss----ss's sp--ch,* [1713?].
    LSA,*C*.

B549 — [another edition]
      Comma at end of line 14, 'done,'
    Herts CRO (Panshanger box 46).

B550 **Brush.** A brush to the Curry-comb of truth, &c. or, the Drapier. An eclogue in imitation of Virgil's Silenus... *Dublin, printed in the year* 1736.
    8º: A⁴; *1–2* 3–8.
      Teerink 980. The title-page has a warning to beware of counterfeit editions.
    'At first our muse in Syracusian strains'
      A satire on Swift, in reply to [William Dunkin] *A curry-comb of truth,* 1736.
    LVA-F,*C*,DA(2),DN; CtY,MH.

B551 [**Bryan, —.**] The temple of fame, a poem occasion'd by the late success of the Duke of Ormond, the Duke of Marlborough, Sir George Rook &c. Against France and Spain. Inscrib'd to Mr. Congreve. *London, printed for John Nutt,* 1703. (30 Jan, Luttrell)
    2º: *A*² B² C¹ D²; *i–ii*, 1–12.
      Listed in *WL* Feb.
    'Till now of late, we thought the loud report'
      Dobell 2665 quotes a ms. note 'Wrote by one Bryan a worthy chaplain to Bp. of Norwich'. Sometimes confused with Yalden's poem of this title, published in 1700; a ms. note in the EU copy of the following makes that error.
    MR-C; CtY(Luttrell).

B552 [—] The temple of fame. A poem. Inscrib'd to Mr. Congreve. *London printed, and sold by H. Hills,* 1709.

Bryan, —. The temple of fame

    8º: *A*⁸; *1–2* 3–15 *16*. 16 advt.
      Reissued with other remaindered Hills poems in *A collection of the best English poetry,* 1717 (*Case* 294).
    L(11631.b.64; C.124.b.7/40),O,E,EU,LdU-B+; ICN,ICU,MH,OCU,TxU.

Bubb, George. *See* Dodington, George Bubb.

Bubble. The bubble: a poem, 1721. *See* Swift, Jonathan.

B553 **Bubblers.** The bublers medley, or the d--l will have his own. [*London,* 1721.]
    ½º: 1 side, 2 columns.
      Large rough woodcut at head.
    'Ye fools in Great-Britain, repent in your folly'
      Reflections on the South Sea bubble.
    MH-BA.

Buchanan, George.
Monteith, Robert: The very learned Scotsman, Mr. George Buchanan's Fratres fraterrimi, three books of epigrams, and book of miscellanies, in English verse, 1708.

———

The prince. An epigram, originally written by George Buchanan to Thomas Randolph, 1711. *See* P1056.

The XX psalm imitated from Buchanan, [1711.] *See* T581–2.

The poor client's complaint. Paraphrased out of Buchanan, [173–?] *See* P753.

B554 '**Buck, Stephen,** *of Stocks-Market.*' Geneva. A poem in blank verse. Occasioned by the late act of parliament for allowing liquors compound of English spirits. Written in imitation of Philips's Splendid shilling. With a dedication to all gin-drinkers. *London, printed for T. Cooper,* 1734 [1733]. (*GM* Dec)
    4º: A–B⁴; *1–2* 3–16.
      Bond 139.
    'Bless'd be the man! forever bless'd his name!'
      Stephen Buck is almost certainly a pseudonym inspired by Stephen Duck. In praise of gin.
    O; CSmH.

B555 [**Buckeridge, Bainbrigg.**] On her majesty's grant of Woodstock park, &c. to his grace the Duke of Marlborough, 1704. In a letter to Signior Antonio Verrio at Hampton-court. [*London,* 1704/05.]
    ½º: 2 sides, 1 column.
    'Renown'd in arms, when mighty heroes rise'
      Printed as Buckeridge's in *Nichols, Collection* V. 165. *Jacob* II. 22 gives the title as 'A letter to Signior Verrio, at Hampton-Court, upon a sketch drawn by him of the battle of Blenheim...' See also a letter from Buckeridge to Ralph Palmer in *HMC* 6 (1877) 391 quoting the poem.
    MC,Crawford; CSmH.

Buckingham

Buckingham. Buckingham House. *See* Bond, William.

Buckingham, John Sheffield, *duke of. See* Sheffield, John, *duke of Buckingham.*

[Budgell, Eustace.] The humorous miscellany... By E— B—, 1733. *See* Boyd, Elizabeth.

—————

[—] The counterpart of the State-dunces. By a native of New-York, 1733. *See* C442.

B556 [—] Desolation: or, the fall of gin. A poem. To which is added, a new ballad, on the same subject. Both by Timothy Scrubb, of Ragg-Fair, esq; *London printed, and sold by J. Roberts,* 1736. (6 May?)
4°: A–B⁴; *1–3* 4–16.
    Percival appendix 62. Listed in *GM,LM* May.
'Thy son, Melpomine, inspire'
Gin: 'What mean these sad looks and this sighing'
    The preface to *The contrast to the Man of honour,* 1737, refers to the death of 'Timothy Scrub', clearly identifying him with Eustace Budgell; it appears to be a pseudonym he used at other times.
L(11630.c.13/6, ms. date 6 May); TxU.

[—] An epistle to the egregious Mr. Pope... By Mr. Gerard, 1734. *See* G130.

[—] The London merchants triumphant, 1733. *See* L239.

[—] Magnanimity. A poem, 1735. *See* M397.

[—] Mr. B-----ll's farewel to the ladies of Dublin, [1719.] *See* M291.

B557 — A poem upon his majesty's late journey to Cambridge and Newmarket. *London, printed for Benj. Motte,* 1728. (*PB* 30 May)
2°: A² B–E²; *1–5* 6–20. A1 hft; 20 err.
'Britannia's king in arms in arts renown'd'
    Rawlinson listed 'Budgell's Poem to the K. at Newmarket' as one of Nicholas Amhurst's works; probably he intended the 'observations' of Caleb d'Anvers in the following edition.
L(11642.i.10/1),O,C(lacks A²),LdU- B;CtY(2, 1 cropt),MH,TxU(2).

B558 —— To this new edition is added, some observations on the said poem by Caleb D'Anvers esq; of Gray's Inn. *London, printed for J. Wilford; sold by the booksellers of London & Westminster,* 1730. (*MChr* June)
4°: A⁴ B–E⁴; *1–3* 4–40.
L(161.l.17),O.

B559 [—] Verres and his scribblers; a satire in three cantos. To which is added an examen of the piece, and a key to the characters and obscure passages. *London, printed for C. Browne, near Moorfields,* 1732. (*GM* 17 Jan)

Budgell, E. Verres

8°: π¹[= F4] A⁴ B–E⁸ F⁴(–F4); *i–ii* iii–x, 1–70. x err.
    In some copies (e.g. L,MH) B3 is signed 'A3'.
Introduction: 'And shall I then for ever silent stand'
    Ms. attribution to 'Eust: B—ll' by Thomas Davison in a copy belonging to Mrs. Lois Morrison, now at San Antonio College, Texas. A satire on Walpole and his journalists.
L(11602.ee.15/1),O,E,LdU-B; CtY,ICU,IU,MH (uncut),TxHR+.

Buds. Buds and blossoms of piety, 1716–. *See* Antrobus, Benjamin.

B560 **Buggin, R.** The inchanted garden, a vision. *Limerick, printed by Thomas Brangan,* 1716.
8°: A–D⁴; *1–5* 6–31 *32 blk.*
'Guide me, O Venus, darling of mankind'
MH.

B561 **[Bulkeley, John.]** The last day. A poem. Book the first. *London, printed for J. Stagg, J. Roberts, & E. Berrington,* [1717.] (*MC* Feb)
2°: *A² B–F²; [2] i ii, 1 2–20.*
    Advertised in *PB* 3 Dec 1717 as printed for Jonas Browne.
'All bounteous sire, author of good, whose name'
    For Bulkeley's authorship, see the revised edition below.
DN; CSmH,MH.

B562 — The last day. A poem in XII. books. By the late J. Bulkeley... *London, printed for J. Peele, R. King, C. Rivington, & W. Chetwood,* 1720 [1719]. (*PB* 15 Dec)
8°: π² A–Bb⁸ Cc⁴; *[4] i* ii–xvi, *1–2* 3–389 *390–392 blk.* π1 frt.
    In some copies (LVA-D,CSmH) the preface is signed in type by Thomas Purney, the editor. These do not appear to be on fine paper, but may be presentation copies. Book I is largely rewritten from the preceding.
'That day, when golden trumps awake the dead'
L(11631.bb.10, – frt, Cc4),LVA-D,O,LdU-B; CSmH,CtY(– Cc4),IU,TxU.

B563 — [reissue] *London, printed for T. Corbet,* 1722.
8°: π²(±π2) A–Bb⁸ Cc⁴; *[4] i* ii–xvi, *1–2* 3–389 *390–392 blk.* π1 frt.
    DP 1 Feb 1723 advertised a '2d edition... for J. Peele', possibly a further reissue.
BU.

Bulkeley, Richard. Poems on several occasions, viz. The Limerick beauties... *Limerick, Andrew Welsh,* 1739.
4°: pp. 12.   City Library, Limerick.

[Bulkeley, *Sir* Richard.] Luctus Britannici, a poem, to the memory of Sir Roger L'Estrange, 1705. *See* L319.

Bull, R.

B564 Bull, Roger. Grobianus; or, the compleat booby. An ironical poem. In three books. Done into English from the original Latin of Friderick Dedekindus, by Roger Bull, esq; *London, printed for T. Cooper*, 1739. (*GM,LM* April)
8°: A–T⁸; *i–v* vi–xiii *xiv–xvi*, *1* 2–276 277–287; *288 blk.*
'Whoe'er thou art, tho' hating rigid rules'
Roger Bull has not been identified; it may be a pseudonym.
L(991.1.1; G.18968),O,DG,LdU-B; CtY,*ICN*, MH,*NN*,OCU+.

B565 — [reissue] Grobianus; or, the compleat gentleman. An ironical poem... The second edition, to which is added, a receipt to make maw wallop. *London, printed for T. Cooper*, 1739.
8°: A⁸(±A1) B–T⁸ χ²; *i–v* vi–xiii *xiv–xvi*, 1–276 277–287; *288 blk*, 5–7 *8 blk*.
A reissue with a cancel title; χ², paged 5–7, contains the receipt to make maw wallop 'By a young lady of quality'. These leaves are found as described here, after T8, in the IEN copy; after T2 in the L copy; and after A2 in the PU copy. They were reprinted in *LM* July 1740 and as a broadside *c.* 1800 titled 'Dean Swift's Maw-wallop...'; see Falkner Grierson cat. 5 (1967) 189.
L(11410.a.89); *IEN,PU*.

Bullock, Charles. 'Original miscellany poems. To which is added, the Covent-Garden heiress, describing the ladies and beaus near the Theatre, Drury Lane. Also Adventures of half an hour, a farce... By Charles Bullock. [*London*] *Sold by J. Morphew*.' (*PB* 21 June 1720)
One wonders if this could possibly be the work of Christopher Bullock, the dramatist.

B566 Bum-bees. [dh] The bum-bees assembly: a poem. [*Edinburgh?* 1729?]
8°: A²; *1–4.*
'Of all things that are known in nature'
A satire on Professor John Simson's suspension by the general assembly. See *An answer to the Assembly of bum-bees*, [1729?]
E,GM.

Bumography. Bumography: or, a touch at the lady's tails, 1707. *See* Dunton, John.

'**Bunch,** *Mother*.' Mother Osborne's letter, 1733. *See* M524.

Bundle. A bundal [!] of spirituall meditations, for the souls advantage, of all those who would rightly improve them: Collected together in metre. By one, who wisheth god to be glorified in the salvation of souls. *Glasgow, printed by James Duncan, and are to be sold in his shop*, 1734.
12°: pp. 12.   L.

Bung

B567 Bung. Bung's address. To the tune of, Chevy-chase. [*London*, 1727.]
½°: 1 side, 2 columns.
At foot, 'The Totness address to his new majesty King George II...'
'Old Bung a second summons sent'
Totness address: 'We, who not long ago profest'
'On Sir Gilbert Heathcot', Luttrell. 'The Totness address' is a different work from *The Totness address versified*, 1727; Crum W165.
Rothschild(Luttrell); InU.

Bunyan, John.
[Hoffman, Francis:] The pilgrim's progress... By John Bunyan. And now done into verse, 1706, 1723. *See* H268–70.

B568 Burch, J. The impartial Englishman: or, the joyful Briton. Humbly inscrib'd to all lovers of their country. *London, printed for the author in the year* 1739.
2°: (3 ll); *1–3* 4–6.
'Now Briton's rejoice, and chear up your hearts'
A patriotic ballad against Spain.
L(1482.g.14).

B569 Burchett, Josiah. The ark. A poem. In imitation of Du Bartas. *London, printed for Edward Castle*, 1714. (*DC* 2 March)
4°: A² B–C⁴; *i–iv*, 1–16. A1 hft.
No watermark. *DC* 9 March notes an erratum. Entered in *SR* 19 March to Ferdinando Burleigh; deposit copies at O,E, SaU.
'The doom on parents for orig'nal sin'
L(1465.f.2,–A1; 841.i.21/2; 162.l.9, Luttrell, 2 March),O,E,SaU; CtY(–A1),DFo,MH.

B570 — [fine paper]
Watermark: fleur-de-lys.
OW('Donum autoris'),C.

B571 — Mr. Burchett's farewel to Sandwich. [*London*, 1741?]
½°: 2 sides, 1 column.
On the other side, 'The answer to Mr. Burchett's farewel to Sandwich.'
'Thou most distress'd, infatuated town!'
Answer: 'Your leaving our gates, to shake off the dust'
Burchett was M.P. for Sandwich until 1741; his authorship of this poem has not been confirmed.
InU.

— Patie and Roger: a pastoral, by Mr. Allan Ramsay... To which is added, an imitation of the Scotch pastoral: by Josiah Burchett, 1720. *See* R77.

— Richy and Sandy, a pastoral [by Allan Ramsay, with an imitation by Burchett], [1720?] *See* R86.

Burchett, J.

B572 — Strife and envy, since the fall of man. A poem. *London, printed for Edward Castle*, 1716. (*MC* April)
2⁰: *A¹ B–C² D¹*; *1–2 3–11 12 blk.*
> Watermark: Amsterdam arms. A1 and D1 have been seen to be conjugate. Listed in *MC* as 'printed for R. Burleigh'.
'E'er the most high and undistinguish'd light'
CtY(Luttrell, 5 May),MH.

B573 — [fine paper?]
> Watermark: fool's cap.
L(1480.d.17),O.

Burgess, Daniel. Psalms, hymns, and spiritual songs. By the late reverend Mr. Daniel Burgess. *London, printed for John Clark*, 1714.
12⁰: pp. viii, 312.   L,E; ICU.

B574 'Burgess, Daniel.' A new elegy upon the death of the late p—t, which departed this life at the palace of Kensington on Thursday the 21st of this instant September, 1710, to the universal grief of low church, fanaticks, whiggs and dissenters. Written by Dr. Burggess [!]. [*London*] *Printed in the year* 1710.
½⁰: 1 side, 2 columns.
> Mourning headpiece and borders.
'Mourn each dissenting babe of grace'
> Satirically ascribed to Burgess; a satire on the regrets of whigs and dissenters for the fall of the whig ministry.
Rothschild.

B575 [**Burgh, James.**] An hymn to the creator of the world. The thoughts taken chiefly from Psal. civ. To which is added in prose, an idea of the creator from his works. *London printed, and sold by M. Cooper, and the pamphlet shops in London & Westminster*, 1750. (*LM* April)
8⁰: A–F⁴ G²; [2] *i ii–iii iv–vi, 1* 2–44.
'Awake, my soul! with joy thy god adore'
> The dedication in a copy at O is signed by Burgh in ms.
L(117.f.63),O(2),CT(uncut),E,LdU-B+; *CLU-C*, MH,*NN*,NjP.

B576 [—] — The second edition. *London, printed in the year* 1750.
8⁰: A–F⁴ G²; [2] *i ii–iii iv–vi, 1* 2–44.
O; CU,CtY,IU,NNUT,*PHi*.

B577 Burgundy. Burgundy bewitch'd: or, Vendome in a trance. In a dialogue between the French generals, after the battle of Audinarde. *London, printed by H. Hills*, 1708.
4⁰: *A²*; *1* 2–4.
'Unhappy minute to us, 'twas that sent'
> On Louis, duke of Burgundy, and Vendome.
L(11631.e.38).

Burley. Burley on the Hill, [170–?] *See* Wright, James.

Burnbank

B578 Burnbank. Burnbank and George Fachney's last shift: or, a strange plot at a dead lift. [*Edinburgh*, 1722.] (23 Feb)
½⁰: 1 side, 1 column.
'Whileom I sung two memorable men'
> On James Campbell of Burnbank and George Fachney, two Edinburgh criminals. Possibly by Alexander Pennecuik the younger.
E; CSmH(ms. 'This came out 23 Febry 1722').

— Burnbank's farewel to Edinburgh, [1722?]
See Pennecuik, Alexander, *d. 1730.*

B579 'Burnet, Gilbert.' An elegy on the death of the illustrious monarch William the third, late king of England, Scotland, France, and Ireland… Written by the reverend Dr. Burnet. *London, printed for E. Hawkins*, 1702.
1⁰: 1 side, 2 columns.
> Mourning headpiece and woodcut borders.
'Alas! 'tis so; no virtue can withstand'
> The attributions of elegiac broadsides are unreliable.
L(C.20.f.2/223).

B580 — — *Edinburgh. Re-printed by the heirs and successors of Andrew Anderson*, 1702.
1⁰: 1 side, 2 columns.
> Mourning borders.
E(2).

B581 '—' A new elegy on the much lamented death of his royal highness Prince George of Denmark, who departed this life at the palace of Kensington, on Thursday the 28th of October, 1708. in the 55th year of his age, to the great grief of her majesty, and the whole nation in general. Written by D. Burnet. *London, printed by J. Read*, 1708.
1⁰: 1 side, 2 columns.
> Mourning headpiece and woodcut borders. The order of impressions is uncertain.
'Be hush'd ye gentle winds, nor breath aloud'
> The attributions of elegiac broadsides are unreliable; and see the impression below which omits his authorship.
MWiW-C.

B581·5 [—] [another impression] The court in tears: or, a new elegy on the much lamented death of his royal highness Prince George of Denmark… *London, printed by J. Read*, 1708.
1⁰: 1 side, 2 columns.
> Mourning headpiece and woodcut borders. In this impression the line 'The court in tears:' compensates for the omitted line 'Written by D. Burnet.'
Formerly A. N. L. Munby, Cambridge.

[**Burnet,** *Sir* **Thomas.**] 'The new-year's miscellany: consisting of satyrs, sonnets, epigrams, &c. never before published. [*London*] *Sold by A. Dodd.* Price 6d.' (*MC* Jan 1715)
> Referred to in Burnet's letters as a shilling volume.

Burnet, *Sir* **T.**

[—] Verses written on several occasions, between the years 1712 and 1721. *London, printed for T. Becket,* 1777.
4°: pp. iv, 71.   L,O; MH.

———

B582 [—] The flying general: or, Ormond at Paris. An excellent new ballad, to the tune of To you fair maidens now at land. *London printed, and sold by A. Boulter,* 1715. (Aug?)
½°: 1 side, 1 column.
'To you, dear Ormond, cross the seas'
    Referred to in a letter of Burnet's, dated by Nichol Smith (ed. 1914, 91–2) 7 Aug 1715.
Harding.

[—] Homerides: or, Homer's first book moderniz'd. By Sir Iliad Doggrel [the verse by George Duckett], 1716. *See* D485.

B583 [—] A second epistle to Mr. Tickell, author of the incomparable ode, call'd A voyage to France, &c. *London, printed for J. Roberts,* [1718.] (*PM* 8 July)
½°: 2 sides, 1 column.
'O Tickell, greatly fated to inherit'
    A continuation of *The tickler tickell'd* below; see Nichol Smith's edition of Burnet's letters (1914) 284.
Crawford.

B584 [—] The tickler tickell'd: being an epistle to the author of the incomparable ode, call'd, A voyage to France, &c. *London, printed for J. Roberts,* 1718. (*PB* 24 June)
2°: A² < B¹; *1–2* 3–5 *6 blk.*
'Well, Tickell! thou has found it out'
    Burnet in a letter of 29 June wrote 'It is said by the town to be Mat. Prior's', but in spite of Nichol Smith's caution in his edition of Burnet's letters (1914) 305, certainly by him. A draft of another poem begins 'Epistles two already have I writ/To thee, O Tickell...' A satire on Tickell's *Ode. Occasion'd by...the Earl Stanhope's voyage to France,* 1718.
L(1485.dd.3; 11795.k.31/4),LVA-F,O; CtY (uncut),MH,*PBL,*TxU.

———

Burnt. 'Burnt children dread the fire. [*London*] *Printed for J. Roberts.* Price 6*d.*' (*GSJ* 6 Nov 1732)
    Listed in *LM* Nov under 'plays, poetry, and entertainment'; it is not certain that it is in verse.

———

[Burridge, Richard.] An answer to the Mock mourners, by way of reflection on a late satyr, 1702. *See* A252.

B585 — A congratulatory poem, on the coronation of Queen Ann; as it was presented to her most serene majesty. *London, printed by James Read; sold by the booksellers of London & Westminster,* 1702. (9 May, Luttrell)
2°: A–D²; *i–iv, 1–12.*

Burridge, R. A congratulatory poem

'Hail! blessed queen, the guardian of our laws'
L(1963, Luttrell).

[—] The fifteen comforts of a Dutch-man, 1707. *See* F124.

B586 [—] Hell in an uproar: occasion'd by a scuffle that happen'd between the lawyers and the physicians for superiority. A satyr. [*Dublin*] *Printed in the year* 1725.
8°: A⁸; *1–2* 3–15 *16 blk.*
    First published in London, 1700 (copies at L,ICU).
'Vext with damn'd law-suits all my abject life'
L(993.e.49/5),DT; CtY-M.

B587 [—] — *London, printed for T. Watkins; sold by the booksellers at Charing-Cross; the Royal-Exchange; and the universities of Oxford & Cambridge,* 1750.
8°: A¹ B–C⁴ D⁴(–D4) (B1 as 'A'); *i–ii, 1–22.*
DNLM.

B588 — The recantation. Written by the author of the Dutch catechism. *London, printed in the year* 1703.
2°: A² B–D²; *i–iv, 1–12.*
'A lonesome, rude, and indigested heap'
    The dedication is signed 'Richard Burridge', but possibly not his poem; *The Dutch catechism* has not been identified.
CLU-C,NNC.

———

B589 **Burroughs, Lewis.** An ode, to be performed at the castle of Dublin, on the 30th of October, being the birth-day of...George II... Set to musick by Mr. Matthew Dubourg... *Dublin, printed by S. Powell, for George Ewing,* 1743.
4°: A⁴; *1–3* 4–7 *8 blk.*
'Be present, ev'ry guardian pow'r'
DA.

B590 — An ode to be performed at the castle of Dublin, on the 30th of October, being the birth-day of his...majesty George II... Set to music by Mr. Matthew Dubourg... *Dublin, printed by S. Powell, for G. & A. Ewing,* 1745.
4°: A⁴; *1–3* 4–8.
'In ev'ry field, on ev'ry wave'
DA,DN,LdU-B.

B591 — ⟨An⟩ ode to be performed at the castle of Dublin, on the 30th of October, being the birth-day of his...majesty George II... Set to music by Mr. Matthew Dubourg... *Dublin, printed by S. Powell, for G. & A. Ewing,* 1747.
4°: A⁴; *1–3* 4–⟨8⟩.
'While Britain hears the trump of fame'
DT(slightly cropt).

———

[Burton, John.] [dh] A miscellany of poems. [*London?* 173–?]
8°: pp. 32.   O.
    An imperfect collection containing four Bible paraphrases included in the following. It collates A–D⁴, with a catchword on the last page showing it to be incomplete. The flyleaf

Burton, J.

of the pamphlet volume in which it is bound describes it as 'Burton's Misc. of Poems'; the other pamphlets in the volume are from the period 1729–31.

— Sacræ scripturæ locorum quorundam versio metrica... *Oxoniæ, e theatro Sheldoniano*, 1736.
8°: pp. 79.   L,O; *CtY,DLC*.
Dedication signed.

'Burton, Robert.' The vanity of the life of man, 1708–. *See* Crouch, Nathaniel.

— Youth's divine pastime, [1710?]–. *See* Crouch, Nathaniel.

Bury. Bury, and its environs, 1747. *See* Winter, John.

Bury, Samuel. A collection of psalms, hymns, and spiritual songs, fitted for morning and evening worship in a private family. *London, printed by Tho. Bunce, for Tho. Parkhurst*, 1707.
12°: pp. 146.   L.
Errata slip on final leaf.

B592 Busby, Richard. Grammatica Busbeiana auctior & emendatior, i.e. Rudimentum grammaticæ græco-latinæ metricum. In usum nobilium puerorum in schola regia Westmonasterii. *Londini, ex officina Eliz. Redmayne*, 1702.
8°: A–N⁸ O⁴; *i–ii*, 1–214.
Signature A2 under n and ax of 'Syntax'. The order of editions has not been established, though the L copy of the following has addenda which were subsequently incorporated in the edition of 1722. One of the editions is probably misdated. First published in this form in 1689 as *Rudimentum grammaticæ græco-latinæ metricum* (copies at O,MH).
'Visum est grammaticæ metricis lenire laborem'
Busby was clearly responsible for the production of this work, 'tho' probably written by some of his ushers' (Wood, *Athenæ Oxonienses* (1820) IV. 418); it has been included here because of its doubtful status.
O.

B593 — [another edition]
Signature A2 under S and n of 'Syntax'. The copy at L adds A⁸; 1–15 *16 blk*, headed 'Addenda & corrigenda' and also in verse; this was apparently incorporated in the 1722 edition. It also adds A–C⁴, a prose work on Greek, reprinted in 1721 and subsequently as *Græcæ grammaticæ compendium*, and frequently found bound with later editions.
L(624.c.23),LWS; *IU*.

B594 — — Quæ in prioribus editionibus ad calcem adjecta, suis jam locis inseruntur. *Londini, typis J. Redmayne, apud quem prostant; & apud B. Barker*, 1722.

Busby, R. Grammatica Busbeiana

8°: A–O⁸; *i–ii, 1* 2–222.
Title in red and black.
L(625.d.2),O; *NN*.

B595 — — *Londini, typis J. Bettenham; sumptibus B. Barker*, 1732.
8°: π¹ A–O⁸ P¹; *i–ii, 1* 2–176 173–222.
L(lacks π1),O; *PPL*.

B596 — — *Londini, typis J. Bettenham; sumptibus B. & B. Barker*, 1743.
8°: A–O⁸ P²; *i–ii, 1* 2–226.
MB,MnU.

B597 [—] Rudimentum grammaticæ latinæ metricum. In usum nobilium puerulorum in schola regia Westmonasterii. *Londini, ex officina E. Redmayne*, 1702.
8°: A–C⁸ D²; *1–2* 3–52.
Horizontal chain-lines. First published in 1688 (copies at LG,MH).
'Visum est grammaticæ metricis lenire laborem'
Apparently an earlier work than the preceding; the relationship between the two has not been studied: they have the same first line, but this is limited to Latin grammar. Like the preceding, this was probably written by the ushers under Busby's direction, and is included here for the same reason.
LWS,C(uncut).

B598 [—] — contractum et emendatum. *Londini, impensis P. Redmayne, & B. Barker*, 1720.
8°: *A²* B–D⁸; *i–ii* iii–iv, *1* 2–48.
This and subsequent editions omit the introductory verses and begin with 'Orthoepeia literæ'.
'Litera, si præeat vocalis, pura vocatur'
LWS(2).

B599 [—] — *Londini, sumptibus B. Barker*, 1729.
8°: A–C⁸ D² (A3 as 'B3'); *1–3* 4–50 *51; 52 blk*. 51 advt.
O,*SrS*.

B600 [—] — *Londini, sumptibus B. Barker*, 1734.
8°: A–C⁸ D² (A3, 4 as 'B3, 4'); *1–3* 4–52. 52 advt.
IU.

B601 [—] — *Londini, sumptibus B. & B. Barker*, 1742.
8°: A–D⁸; *1–3* 4–60 *61–63; 64 blk*. 61–63 advt.
O; *ICU,IU*.

B602 Butchers. The butchers answer to the taylors poem: or, their whole profession unmask'd. [*Dublin*, 1725/30.]
½°: 1 side, 2 columns.
On the other side, *The tradesman's hue and cry*, [1725/30.] The copy at L forms part of a collection of Dublin half-sheets of 1725/30.
'Ingenious Stitch, I've read your rhymes'
A reply to *A poem in praise of the journey-men taylors*, [1725/30.]
L(C.121.g.8/91).

Butchers

B603 — The butchers letter of advice to the weavers. *Dublin, printed in the year* 1723.
$\frac{1}{2}$°: 1 side, 1 column.
'Dear brother weavers, late of no renown'
Crawford.

B604 'Butler, Jemmy.' The strolling hero, or Rome's knight errant. A hudibrastick poem on the Young Chevalier's expedition... By Jemmy Butler. *London, printed for M. Cooper,* 1744. (*GM,LM* March)
8°: A–C⁴; *1–2* 3–24.
Bond 210.
'Assist, O muse! the bard who racks'
The intended author is James Butler, duke of Ormonde; but this is, of course, a joke.
E,AdU; CtY,ICN.

B605 Butler, Richard. The British Michael, an epistolary poem, to a friend in the country. *London, printed by J. Matthews; sold by William Lewis,* 1710 [1709]. (*PB* 6 Dec)
2°: π² A² B–L²; *i–viii,* 1–39 40 blk. π1 hft.
Watermark: fool's cap. Advertised in *Review* 6 Dec as printed for W. Lewis; sold by J. Woodward, & J. Morphew.
'To you, dear Damon, long my faithful friend'
O(Luttrell, 7 Dec); MiU.

B606 — [fine paper]
Watermark: fleur-de-lys on shield.
L(11630.h.55, ? presentation binding); MH.

B607 'Butler, Samuel.' Dildoides. A burlesque poem. By Samuel Butler, gent. With a key explaining several names and characters in Hudibras. Never before printed. *London printed, and sold by J. Nutt,* 1706. (1 Nov, Luttrell)
2°: A–C² D¹; *1–2* 3–14.
In the DT copy, Nutt's name is deleted.
'Such a sad tale prepare to hear'
Crum S1276. Although the poem is commonly ascribed to Butler in seventeenth century ms. miscellanies, his authorship remains unconfirmed. *Crum* also records an attribution to Sir Charles Sedley.
DT(uncut); CSmH,MH(Luttrell).

B608 '—' The morning's salutation: or, a friendly conference between a puritan preacher and a family of his flock, upon the 30th of January. By Mr. Butler. Author of Hudibras. *Dublin, re-printed by Daniel Tompson,* 1714.
8°: A⁴ (A1ᵛ as 'A2'); *1* 2–8.
No previous edition has been traced.
'Good morrow to thee: how dost do?'
Wrongly ascribed to Butler according to L catalogue.
L(11631.a.63/11),O.

B608·5 [—] [*idem*] ⟨A⟩ dialogue between a dissenting minister and the Calves-head-club. On the 30th of

Butler, S. The morning's salutation

January, being the martyrdom of King Charles. *Dublin, re-printed* 1721.
$\frac{1}{2}$°: 2 sides, 2 columns.
Butler's name is omitted from this edition.
L(C.121.g.8/16).

B609 Buttered. The butter'd apple-pye. [*London*] *Printed in the year* 1711. (1 Sept, Luttrell)
$\frac{1}{2}$°: 1 side, 2 columns.
'Sir Gravity well grown in years'
A tale of strife between a female poet and her husband.
O; ICN(Luttrell).

B610 Button. Button, and button-hole: with a character of the drabs, and the change of old-hat. In three familiar epistles in verse. *London, printed for A. Moore,* 1723. (*DP* 19 Feb)
2°: A² B²; *1–2* 3–8.
On a drab: 'Our old friend, as I've heard, is now pretty hoddy'
Upon another drab: 'You have, my dear coz (as now 'tis the fashion)'
Old-hat: 'On Friday last, as we were at dinner'
Double entendres on clothes and sex.
L(11630.h.10, ms. date 19 Feb),LdU-B.

B—y, *Mr.* An ode occasion'd by the battle of Rammelies. By Mr. B—y, [1706.] *See* O37.

'Byfielde, —, *Dr.*' The devil and the doctor, 1719. *See* M80.

Byrom, John. Miscellaneous poems. *Manchester, printed by J. Harrop,* 1773.
8°: 2 vol.   L; MH.
Watermark: post-horn on shield.

— [fine paper]   L,O; MH.
Watermark: Strasburg bend.

———

B611 [—] The bellman and the captain. [*London,* 1749.] (Aug)
obl $\frac{1}{2}$°: 1 side, five columns.
Engraved title and engraving at head.
'An arch and sturdy bellman of the town'
Reprinted in Byrom's *Poems* III (1912) 18 from ms. First printed in *Chester courant* 25 July 1749, where it is dated from Manchester, 14 July. Reprinted in *London evening post* 1 Aug 1749. This edition is referred to as taken from the newspaper in a letter of Byrom, 19 Aug 1749.
L(P&D 3039).

B612 [—] An epistle to a friend; occasioned by a sermon intituled, The false claims to martyrdom consider'd: a sermon preach'd at St. Anne's church, Manchester, November 2, 1746... By Benj. Nichols, M.A. assistant-curate of the said church... *London, printed for M. Cooper,* 1747. (*LM* Aug)

Byrom, J. An epistle to a friend

4⁰: A^4 B–D^4; *1–5* 6–32. A1 hft.
'Dear sir,/I'm really sorry that our friend'
Printed in Byrom's *Poems* I. ii (1894) 332ff, and referred to in his correspondence. Against the harshness of Nichols's sermon about the execution of the rebels of 1745.
L(11602.gg.29/1),O,MP(stitched, uncut),*NeU*, PrP; MH-AH(−A1).

B613 [—] An epistle to a gentleman of the Temple. Occasioned by two treatises just published, wherein the fall of man is differently represented; viz. I. Mr. Law's Spirit of prayer, II. The Bishop of London's Appendix... *London, printed for R. Spavan*, 1749. (*LM* Aug)
2⁰: A^1 B–F^2; *i–ii, 1* 2–19 *20 blk.*
Printed by Samuel Richardson (*Sale* 366).
'Sir, upon casting an attentive look'
Reprinted in Byrom's *Poems* II, 1773.
L(1489.m.38),O,MP,*MR*; CtY,MH,*RPJCB*,TxU (2, 1 uncut).

B614 [—] A full and true account of an horrid and barbarous robbery, committed on Epping-Forest, upon the body of the Cambridge coach. In a letter to M. F. esq; *London printed, and sold by J. Roberts*, 1728. (*MChr* 20 March)
2⁰: A^1 B–C^2 D^1; *i–ii, 1* 2–9 *10 blk.*
No watermark.
'Dear Martin Folkes, dear scholar, brother, friend'
Reprinted in Byrom's *Poems* I, 1773.
L(11602.i.10/7); CtY,MH.

B615 [—] [fine paper]
Watermark: fleur-de-lys. Margins altered.
MP; MH.

B616 [—] A genuine dialogue between a gentlewoman at Derby and her maid Jenny in the beginning of December, 1745. Taken from the Chester Journal. [1747/48.]
¼⁰: 1 side, 2 columns.
Vertical chain-lines. Printed in the *Chester courant* 10 Nov 1747.
'Jenny come here: I'm told that you have been'
Printed in Byrom's *Poems* I. ii (1894) 324; this edition referred to in a letter of Byrom to his wife, 17 March 1748. In praise of the Young Pretender's appearance.
L(C.38.g.14/18),OJJ; CSmH,CtY.

B617 [—] [first line:] Good people, I, El'sabeth dowager Ad-ms... *Chester, 'printed by a true blue'*, [1748.]
½⁰.
'Communicated to [A.W. Ward] by Mr. C.W. Sutton, who found them on an old broad-

Byrom, J. Good people

sheet... endorsed in ms: "1748. Verses by Dr Byrom on Adams's Recantation".'
'Good people, I, El'sabeth dowager Ad-ms'
Elizabeth Adams, publisher of *Adams's weekly courant* and her son John apologize for a libel on Bishop Samuel Peploe printed in August.
(Byrom, *Poems* II. ii (1895) 574.)

[—] The prologue and epilogue to the new tragi-comical-farcical opera, call'd Hurlothrumbo [the epilogue by Byrom], [1729.] *See* M187.

B618 [—] Sir Lowbred O - - - n: or, the Hottentot knight. A new ballad, to the tune of The abbot of Canterbury. Occasion'd by a pamphlet lately publish'd, intitled Jacobite and nonjuring principles freely examin'd... By J. Owen. *London, printed for M. Cooper; sold by the booksellers in Manchester*, [1748.] (March)
2⁰: π^2 A–D^2 E^1; *i–ii, 1–2* 3–19 *20 blk.* π1 hft.
All copies seen appear to have been printed as folio but cut down to quarto size.
'When Lowbred of Rochdale, good people, sat down'
The publication is referred to in a letter of Edward Byrom to John Byrom, 23 March 1748. An attack on Josiah Owen's pamphlet of 1747 (copy at MP).
O,MP(−π1, lacks E1),PrP.

B619 [—] Sir Lowbred O..n, or, the Hottentot knight. [1748?]
½⁰.
Rough woodcut at head. Recorded by A. W. Ward as possibly the first edition.
(Byrom, *Poems* ed. A. W. Ward I. ii (1894) 358.)

B620 [—] Tunbridgiale, a poem: being a description of Tunbridge. In a letter to a friend at London. By the author of My time O ye muses, &c. Spectator, vol. VIII. *London, printed for W. Meadows*, 1726. (21 Oct?)
4⁰: A^2 B–C^2; *1–5* 6–11 *12 blk.* A1 hft.
Listed in *MC* Oct.
'Dear Peter, whose friendship I value much more'
Reprinted in Byrom's *Poems* I, 1773.
L(840.h.4/11),LVA-F(−A1),O(ms. date 21 Oct) *LdU-B,MR*; CtY(−A1),DFo.

B621 Bystander. The by-stander. A poem. *London, printed for T. Cooper; sold at the pamphlet shops of London & Westminster*, 1741. (*GM,LM* Dec)
2⁰: A^2 B–D^2; *1–2* 3–16.
'With some, there seems a doubt, how first began'
CtY.

C

C., A., *gent.* A cynic laughing, 1706. *See* C555.

C., B. Cupid in quest of beauty, 1709. *See* C540.

C., C. A familiar epistle to Mr. Mitchell, 1720. *See* F54.

— A prologue spoken by Mr. Elrington, 1725. *See* Coffey, Charles.

— The true great man, 1737. *See* T527.

C., F., *gent.* An elegy on John Tutchin, 1707. *See* E262.

— A poem on the death of the Countess of Sunderland, 1716. *See* P601.

C., H., *of the Custom House.* The antidote, 1713. *See* Crispe, Henry.

— An elegy on the lamented death..., 1713. *See* Crispe, Henry.

— An epithalamium, 1712. *See* Crispe, Henry.

— Some verses sent to the...Earl of Oxford, 1712. *See* Crispe, Henry.

C., J. De pace, 1713. *See* D74.

— An essay, upon Polemo-medinia, 1704. *See* E476.

— Nobilissimo domino Roberto domino Harley, 1712. *See* N311.

— On the death of Mr. Brand, [1717.] *See* O196.

— A poem on the blessed nativity, [1717.] *See* Colme, John.

— Poems, paraphrases and translations, 1736. *See* Crackanthorp, John.

— Sacred hymns for the children of god in the days of their pilgrimage, 1741–. *See* Cennick, John.

— Spiritual life. Poems on several divine subjects, 1727. *See* Craig, James.

C., M. Χοιροχωρογραφια, 1709. *See* Richards, Thomas.

— A match at foot-ball, 1720. *See* Concanen, Matthew.

— Poems divine, moral, and philosophical, 1746. *See* Poems.

C., R. The Beeriad or progress of drink, 1736. *See* B160.

— The blessings attending George's accession and coronation, [1715.] *See* B284.

— Illustrissimo ac nobilissimo Georgio comiti de Cromartie, [1703/04.] *See* I6.

— In dolendum obitum docti & pii viri magistri Joannis Cunninghamii, [1710.] *See* I18.

— Nobilissimo & illustrissimo Jacobo comiti de Seafield, [1705?] *See* N312.

C——, R——, *Mr.* A just character of the revd. Mr. Boyce, [1728.] *See* Choppin, Richard.

C., R., *of the Middle Temple.* The female apologist, 1748. *See* F85.

C., S. Mock poem: or, whiggs supplication, 1702–. *See* Colvil, Samuel.

— A new copy of verses on the nativity, 1715. *See* N120.

C., S., *M.A.* A psalm of thanksgiving, 1703–. *See* Cobb, Samuel.

C., T. The convert, 1749. *See* Cooke, Thomas, *vicar of Bayton.*

C., T., *rector of Sevenoke in Kent.* Eirenodia, 1728. *See* Curteis, Thomas.

C., W. A congratulatory poem: on his grace the Duke of Ormond, 1703. *See* C352.

— The friendship of Christ, 1718. *See* Cheyn, William.

— The Preston prisoners to the ladies about court and town, 1716. *See* Wogan, Charles.

C., W., *A.M.* The reformer's ghost, [1725/30.] *See* R151.

———

C1 **C——.** The c—— unmasqu'd: or, the state puppet-shew. *London, printed for J. Irons,* 1734. (*GM* March)
2°: *A*² B–C² *D*²; *1–2* 3–16.
'Thanks to the gods, who've crown'd my elder days'
　　A satire on politics, in dramatic form with exits and entrances.
CSmH,CtY,MH,OCU,TxU + .

C1·5 **Cade, Thomas.** A divine poem on the redemption of mankind, by the coming of our blessed saviour... *London, printed for Joseph Turner, bookseller in Sheffield; sold by J. & B. Sprint,* 1709.
4°: A–C⁴; *1–2* 3–23 *24 blk.*
'Come ye kind angels, and declare the love'
TxLL.

Cadenus. Cadenus and Vanessa, 1726–. *See* Swift, Jonathan.

Cæcilia. *See* Cecilia.

Cælia. *See* Celia.

'Calder, Robert.' Calderus Visharto qui se moderatorem...vocat [probably by Archibald Pitcairne], [1713?] *See* P345.

— 'Poem on Dr Pitcairn.' [*Edinburgh*, 1713.]
Entered in Ruddiman's ledger for the week ending 26 Dec 1713 as '2 pages pot'; there is another entry of 'Poem for Mr Calder, press' in the week ending 16 Jan 1714. The first is clearly one of Calder's poems on Pitcairne's death printed in the *Selecta poemata, Archibaldi Pitcarnii* (1727) 94–8, but no separate edition has been traced.

Caledonia. Caledonia, &c. A poem in honour of Scotland, 1706–. *See* Defoe, Daniel.

C2 — Calidonia rediviva: or, the Scotch riddle. Being a new description of a port in North Britain. *London printed, and sold by J. Baker*, 1711.
8°: A⁸; *1–2* 3–16.
'A port in North-Britain lies south of the Clide'
A rather bawdy satire.
E; MB.

Calender, John. Lugubres cantus. Poems on several grave and important subjects, 1719. *See* Mitchell, Joseph.

———

[—] On the death of Mr. Brand, student of philosophy... By J.C. one of his fellow students, [1717.] *See* O196.

———

[**Caley,** —, *Mr.*] News from court. A ballad... By Mr. Pope, 1719. *See* P903.

C3 Call. A call to the guard by beat of drum. *Dublin, printed in the year* 1725.
½°: 1 side, 2 columns.
'Rat too, rat too, rat too, rat tat too, tat rat too'
Apparently a London satire on the footguards.
L(C.121.g.8/58).

Callimachus.
Alney, John: The hymns of Callimachus, translated from the Greek, 1744.

———

The birth of manly virtue from Callimachus, [1725.] *See* B221–2.

Callipaedia. Callipædia; or, the art of getting pretty children, 1710–. *See* Oldisworth, William.

C4 Callipaediae. Callipædiæ; or, an art how to have handsome children: written in Latin by the abbot

Quillet. To which is added, Pædotrophiæ... written in Latin by Monsieur St. Marthe... Now done into English verse. *London, printed for John Morphew*, 1710. (*PB* 7 March, 'just publish'd')
8°: A⁴ B–R⁸ S⁴; *i–viii, 1* 2–264.
Entered in *SR* 12 April 1710 to Jacob Tonson, apparently as 'old copy'.
'I sing the pleasures of the nuptial bed'
Pædotrophiæ: 'Tho', sacred nymphs, you're free from fond desires'
A different translation from those by Rowe and Oldisworth.
L(11405.bb.30),OW,E,*NeU*; CLU-C,MH,*NNC, PU*.

C5 — — The second edition. *London, printed for J.T.* [Tonson] *and sold by J. Peele*, 1718. (*PB* 5 Aug)
12°: A–G¹² H⁶; *i–xvi, 1* 2–'163' (163,164 as '164,163'). A1 frt.
L(11409.ccc.24),O,*NeU*.

Callistia. Callistia; or the prize of beauty, 1738. *See* Jacob, Hildebrand.

Calpe. Calpe, or Gibraltar, [1718]–. *See* Breval, J. D.

Calpurnius Siculus, Titus.
[Mawer, John:] The happy reign. An eclogue. Imitated from Calpurnius Siculus, [173–.] *See* M145.

C6 Cam. Cam and Isis. Address'd to Charles D—, esq; *London, printed for W. Owen*, 1749. (*GM* June)
2°: (3 ll); *1–2* 3–6.
'Since furious Cam/Fam'd Isis does damn'
Apparently occasioned by William Mason's *Isis*, 1749.
O; CtY,OCU.

C7 Cambridge. The Cambridge election. A new ballad. Tune of, King John and the abbot. *London, printed for A. Moore*, 1729. (*MChr* 31 Dec)
2°: A⁴; *1–3* 4–7 *8 blk*.
The OW copy has watermark of Amsterdam arms, the others of London arms.
'Ye regents, non-regents, and men of the gown'
On Thomas Gooch and others.
L(1968),O,OW; CLU-C.

C8 — — Tune of, King John and the abbot of Canterbury. *London, printed for A. Moor*, 1729.
2°: A²; *1–3* 4.
Probably a piracy.
MH(uncut).

Cambro-britannic. The Cambro-britannic engineer, 1722. *See* Bellamy, Daniel.

Cambro-Briton. The Cambro Briton robb'd of his bauble, 1727. *See* Stanhope, Philip Dormer, *earl of Chesterfield*.

Cameronian

C9 Cameronian. The Cameronian address to King George. [*Edinburgh*, 1715?]
½°: 2 sides, 2 columns.
'Illustrious prince of high renown'
Against the Jacobites.
E.

C10 [**Campbell, Archibald,** *duke of Argyll.*] A pastoral elegy on the death of the Lady Hilaretta. In a dialogue between two lords. *London, printed for A. More,* [1729/30.]
2°: *A*² *B*¹; *1–3* 4–6.
'Say, my Toupet, whence all this grief appears?'
Ascribed in a ms. note in J. R. B. Brett-Smith's copy to 'Ld Isla', i.e. Archibald Campbell, subsequently 3rd duke of Argyll. On Katherine, lady Abergavenny who married both 15th and 16th barons and committed adultery with Richard Lyddel; she died 4 Dec 1729.
OW; MH.

C11 Campbell, Duncan. A poem upon tea. Wherein its antiquity, its several virtues and influences are set forth... Also the objections against tea, answered, and the best way of proceeding in love-affairs: together with the sincere courtship of Dick and Amy &c. *London printed, and sold by Mrs. Dodd, J. Roberts, J. Wilcox, J. Oswald, W. Hinchliffe, J. Cocks, J. Parker, W. Wyatt, R. Downes, R. Viney,* 1735 [1734]. (*LM* Nov)
8°: A–D⁴; *1–8* 9–32. 7 advt.
'Tea is the sparkling subject of my song'
L(1077.k.36),E(stitched, uncut); IU.

C12 Campbell, Duncan, *junior.* The Perkinade, an heroic poem; containing some curious and authentick memoirs of that egregious hero... *London, printed for J. Collyer,* 1745. (*GA* 20 Nov)
8°: A–C⁴; *1–2* 3–24.
'When whimsy got into the head'
The author may well be pseudonymous.
Against the Young Pretender.
L(1484.cc.3).

Campbell, Kenneth. [A small collection of Latin poems.] [*London?* 1711/14.]
24°: pp. 12.   L.
No title; signed on p. 12. Cf. *The Huth Library* (1880) I. 256 for another collection.

C13 — Ad nobilissimos Anglos consolidantes. [*Edinburgh?* 1705?]
¼°: 1 side, 1 column.
One copy seen is conjugate with Campbell's *Ad serenissimam reginam*, each being printed on one recto of a quarto half-sheet.
'Dicite jam, Britones, quo Mæcenate poeta'
Signed 'Kenethus Campbell'.
O,Herts CRO (Panshanger box 46).

C14 — Ad serenissimam reginam. Ode. [*Edinburgh?* 1705?]

Campbell, K. Ad serenissimam reginam
¼°: 1 side, 1 column.
One copy seen is conjugate with Campbell's *Ad nobilissimos Anglos consolidantes*, each being printed on one recto of a quarto half-sheet.
'Nympha, Peterboreis quæ nunc fæliciter ausis'
Signed 'Kenethus Campbell'.
O,Herts CRO (Panshanger box 46).

C15 — Carmen Rammeliense. [*Edinburgh?* 1706.]
½°: 1 side, 1 column.
'Quicquid deorum, motibus inclytis'
Signed 'Kenethus Campbell de montibus'.
In praise of Marlborough's victory at Ramillies.
Chatsworth.

C16 — Faciam eos in gentem unam. [1707?]
½°: 1 side, 1 column.
'Dicite jam, Britones, quo successore beata'
Signed 'Ken. Campbell.' On the union with Scotland. There is a ms. continuation 'Feci eos in gentem unam' by Campbell at O, Herts CRO (Panshanger box 46).
C,Chatsworth.

C17 — In obitum eruditissimi et colendissimi D. Georgij Campbell s.s. theologiæ professoris, apud Edinburgenses. [*Edinburgh?* 1701.]
½°: 1 side, 1 column.
'Unde repentino luimus commissa dolore?'
Signed 'Ken: Campbell'.
E.

[—] In palatium sancti Jacobi die natali serenissimæ Annæ, [1712.] *See* I31.

C18 Canary. Canary-birds naturaliz'd in Utopia. A canto. *London printed, and sold by the booksellers,* [1709.] (*DC* 15 June)
8°: A–D⁴; *1–6* 7–30 *31–32 blk.*
'In our unhappy days of yore'
A modern note in a copy at PPL attributes the poem to Francis Hare. The attribution seems very improbable. Against the Huguenots in England, and Defoe; occasioned by the act for naturalizing foreign protestants, 7 Anne c.5.
L(164.m.47, Luttrell, 15 June, –D4),LLP(–D4); CLU-C(–D4),PPL.

C19 — — *London printed, and sold by the booksellers of London & Westminster,* [1709.]
8°: A⁸ B⁴; *1* 2–24.
Pp. 23–24 are printed in a smaller type. Probably one of Henry Hills's piracies; reissued with other Hills poems in *A collection of the best English poetry,* 1717 (*Case* 294).
L(11633.b.56; 1488.de.26; 1078.l.11; C.124. b.7/44),O,EU,DT,LdU-B+; CSmH,CtY,ICN, MH(2),TxU(2)+.

C20 — — *London printed, and sold by the booksellers of London & Westminster,* 1709.
8°: A⁸; *1–2* 3–16 (14,15 as '15,14'). 2 columns on p. 16.
O(3),EN(cropt); InU(uncut),TxU(cropt).

Canary birds naturaliz'd

C21 —— The contents of this romantick canto. *London, printed in the year* 1709.
8°: A⁸; *1* 2–16.
Pp. 14–16 are printed in a smaller type.
PPL.

C22 Candidates. The candidates. *London, printed for J. Baker,* 1713.
8°: A–C⁴; *1–2* 3–24.
'While distant climates mourn their fate'
An election satire.
LDW,DG; IU,InU(uncut),OCU.

—— The candidates for the bays, 1730. *See* Cooke, Thomas.

'Candidus, Gulielmus.' Elegy on the never enough to be lamented death of Lord John Hamilton of Balhaven, 1708. *See* Whyte, William.

C23 Candour. Candour: or, an occasional essay on the abuse of wit and eloquence. *London printed, and sold by M. Watson,* 1739. (*GM,LM* May)
4°: *A¹ B² C–E² F¹; 1–3* 4–20.
The order of editions is obscure. Though the poem was entered in *SR* 10 April to Patrick Guthrie and the deposit copies are of the folio edition below, they contain an editor's preface referring to an incorrect edition. Probably this is the 'incorrect' edition, perhaps issued with the author's connivance.
'Enough has satire vicious times bewail'd'
Probably by Patrick Guthrie to whom the poem was entered in *SR*.
L(11630.c.4/7); MH,TxU.

C24 —— *London, printed by M. Watson,* 1739.
2°: π² χ¹ B–E²; [6] *5* 6–19 *20 blk.*
π2 is dedication to the Duke of Newcastle, χ1 preface by the author, verso blank. Apparently the first state of the folio edition. The copy seen is fine paper, watermark fleur-de-lys on shield.
TxU.

C25 —— [another issue] *London, printed by M. Watson,* 1739.
2°: π¹ A–E²; [6] *5* 6–19 *20 blk.*
A1ʳ–A2ʳ preface by the editor, A2ᵛ preface by the author; no dedication. The copy seen is on ordinary paper, no watermark. The preface by the editor refers to an incorrect edition, and says this is to be sold at a guinea a copy.
TxU.

C26 —— [another issue] *London, printed by M. Watson,* 1739.
2°: π² A–E²; [8] *5* 6–19 *20 blk.*
This issue (on fine paper) has the dedication to Newcastle on π2. Most copies have the words 'Candour' and 'abuse' on the title apparently painted in red over a blind impression, and 'essay' painted in blue over

Candour

black; but a copy at O has the title in black throughout. Deposit copies at O,E,GU.
O(2),E,GU; IU,NN.

C27 —— [another issue] *London, printed by M. Watson,* 1739.
π²(π1 + χ¹) A–E²; [*10*] *5* 6–19 *20 blk.*
This issue (on fine paper) adds a leaf after the title, paged 1–2, 'An imitation of the XIIIᵗʰ epistle of the first book of Horace to the editor of a poem called Candour'. Title in red, blue, and black as preceding.
LLP.

C28 Cannon, Thomas. Apollo; a poem: or the origin of the world assign'd. With reflections upon human nature. *London, printed for J. Roberts, A. Dodd, & J. Fox,* 1744. (1 Dec)
2°: *A¹ B–E² F¹; i–ii, 1* 2–18.
Listed in *GM* Dec. Entered in Woodfall's ledger to Cannon under 20 Nov 1744.
'Forsook by fortune, unemploy'd by power'
L(1962),O(2); CSmH(uncut),CtY(ms. date 1 Dec).

Canons. Canons: or, the vision, 1717. *See* Gildon, Charles.

C29 Canterbury. The Canterbury tale: or story of the wandering turtle. In twelve canto's... Scriptum Cantaur' [!] 17. maii, 1712. Anna philo. *London, printed in the year* 1712.
8°: A–B⁴ (A2 as 'A3'); *1–2* 3–16.
'In that kind season of the year'
A political fable: a satire on whig opposition to the Treaty of Utrecht.
O; MH.

—— Canterbury tales, rendered into familiar verse, 1701. *See* Pittis, William.

Canto. A canto of the Fairy queen, 1739. *See* West, Gilbert.

C30 Captain. Captain Gordon's welcome home, a new song in praise of his taking the French privateers, and a rich prize. A new song, to an excellent new tune, Hark I hear the cannons roar. [*Edinburgh,* 170–?]
½°: 1 side, 2 columns.
'Now brave Captain Gordon's come'
Probably in praise of Thomas Gordon, one of the few captains in the Scots navy. In favour of independence from England.
E.

C31 —— Captain Green's last conference with Captain Madder, his first mate, in the Tolbooth of Edinburgh. *Edinburgh, printed by James Watson,* 1705.
4°: A⁴; *1–2* 3–8.
'Is this the vast advantage we propos'd?'
Thomas Green was executed for piracy, 11 April 1705.
E(2); RPJCB.

Captain

— Captain John Peddie, 1741. *See* Martin, Thomas.

C32 — Captain Porteous's ghost; giving an account how he was dragged from the Tolbooth of Edinburgh by the outragious mob, and hung up by the neck like a dog... With many other pleasant jests relating thereunto; all in elegiack verse. *Edinburgh, printed in the year* 1738.
8°: A⁸; *1* 2–16.
Preface: 'It is not good to raise the dead'
'What din and noise is this I hear'
EP.

C33 — Captain Thomas Green's last farewell to the ocean and all the world, who was execute with two more of his crew at Leith within the flood-mark, 11 April 1705, for piracie and murder. *Edinburgh, printed by G.J. [George Jaffray] in the year* 1705.
½°: 1 side, 2 columns.
'Adieu fair ocean, on thee long I liv'd'
E.

C34 — Captain Tom's ballad... A pleasant new song, to the tune of, Packington's pound. [*London*] *Printed in the year* 1710. (10 April, Luttrell)
obl ½°: 1 side, 3 columns.
Old worm-eaten woodcut above text.
'Now all you good Britains from Dover and Fife'
On the Sacheverell riot in London.
L(C.121.g.9/158, Luttrell).

C35 — Capt. Wel—he's answer to Miss Molly War---rt--on. [*Dublin*, 1726/28.]
slip: 1 side, 1 column.
'I the dapper spark, so smart'
Clearly intended for Paddy Walsh, 'the Little Beau', and perhaps a reply to 'Ambrose Philips', *A new poem*, 1726.
L(C.121.g.8/140).

C36 Cardinal. The cardinal's coach couped. Or the whigs lamentation for the episcopal toleration. '*London, printed by John Morphew*', 1711.
½°: 1 side, 2 columns.
14 stanzas. The style and subject are Scottish, and the printing far inferior to anything produced for Morphew. Probably an Edinburgh work with a false imprint.
'The ca——l has got a scoup'
A satire on presbyterian whigs.
E.

C37 — [another edition]
18 stanzas, with considerable revisions. By the same printer as the preceding.
'Alas! our kirk has got a scoup'
L(1876.f.1/58, cropt),E.

C38 — — [*Edinburgh*, 1711?]
½°: 1 side, 2 columns.

The **cardinal**'s coach couped

21 unnumbered stanzas. By a different printer from the preceding editions.
E.

Carey, Henry. Poems on several occasions. *London printed, and sold by J. Kent, A. Boulter, & J. Brown*, 1713. (*DC* 20 Jan, 'yesterday')
8°: pp. 86.   L,O; CSmH,TxU.
Entered in *SR* to Carey 13 Feb 1713; deposit copies at L,E,EU.

— — *London, printed in the year* 1720. (*SR* 17 March)
12°: pp. 88.   L,O.
Entered in *SR* to Carey; deposit copies at L,O,E,EU. *MC* Aug 1726 invited subscriptions for an octavo edition; probably the following took its place.

— — The third edition, much enlarged. *London, printed by E. Say*, 1729. (*SR* 4 April)
4°: pp. 226.   L,O; CtY,MH.
P1 is a cancel for O4. Copies have a portrait frontispiece. Entered in *SR* to Carey; deposit copies at L,O,E,SaU.

C39 [—] Blunderella: or, the impertinent. A tale... To which is added the Beau monde, or, the pleasures of St. James's. A new ballad. *London, printed for A. Dodd; sold by the booksellers of London & Westminster*, 1730. (*MChr* 17 March)
2°: A–C²; *1–3* 4–12. 12 err.
Some copies (e.g. O,MH) have a corrected state of B outer forme, reading 'Speech' for 'Spech' in p. 8 line 7. Entered to Carey in SR 17 March; deposit copies at L,EU.
'The tea was drank and ta'en away'
Beau monde: 'Oh! St. James's is a lovely place'
Reprinted in Carey's *Poems*, 1729.
L(644.m.14/18; 163.n.26),LSC,O(2),EU(uncut); CSmH,CtY,MH,TxU(2).

C40 [—] — The second edition. *London, printed for A. Dodd; sold by the booksellers of London & Westminster*, 1730.
2°: A–C²; *1–3* 4–12. 12 err.
A reimpression or a press-variant title. The title reads 'Blundrella...'
OW; MH.

C41 [—] The downfall of Bartholomew fair. Sung by Mr. Este, in the Honest Yorkshire man. To the tune of, Bartholomew fair. [*London?*] *Given gratis at the theatre*, [1735?]
⅛°: 1 side, 1 column.
'O Bartledom fair,/Since thy lord mayor'
The honest Yorkshire man, 1735, was by Henry Carey.
O.

C42 [—] Faustina: or the Roman songstress, a satyr, on the luxury and effeminacy of the age. *London, printed for J. Roberts*, [1726.] (*SJEP* 10 May)

Carey, H. Faustina

4⁰: A⁴ B²; *1–3* 4–11 *12 blk.*
'Britons! for shame, give all these follies o'er'
> Printed in Carey's *Poems*, 1729, as 'A satyr on the luxury...' Occasioned by the debut of Faustina B. Hasse, 5 May 1726.

L(840.h.4/9),O(uncut),E; CSmH,MH,OCU.

C43 [—] The Grumbletonians: or, the dogs without-doors. A tale. *London, printed for J. Peele, 1727.* (*MC* March)
2⁰: A⁴; *1–3* 4–8. 8 advt.
'A wealthy farmer in the west'
> Reprinted in Carey's *Poems*, 1729.

L(1959),O(uncut); DFo.

C44 [—] — *London, printed by K. Clifton, in Hanging-Sword Court in Fleet-street,* [1727.]
2⁰: *A²*; *1* 2–3 '5'.
> Horizontal chain-lines. Presumably a piracy.

O.

[—] A hue and cry after M—k... By the author of Namby Pamby, [1726?] *See* H355.

C45 [—] A Lilliputian ode on King George the IId's and Queen Caroline's happy accession to the throne. [*Dublin*] *Printed by J. Gowan, 1727.*
½⁰: 1 side, 2 columns.
'Smile, smile,/ Blest isle'
> Reprinted in Carey's *Poems*, 1729.

L(C.121.g.8/156).

C46 [—] [*idem*] A poem to his majesty King George, II. on the present state of affairs in England, with remarks on the alterations expected at court, after the rise of the parliament. By the rev. Dr. J. Swift, dean of St. Patrick's. In Lilliputian verse. *Dublin, printed by little George Faulkner, 1727.*
slip: 1 side, 1 column.
> *Teerink* 1230.

CSmH.

C47 [—] Mocking is catching, or, a pastoral lamentation for the loss of a man and no man. In the simple stile. By the author of Namby Pamby. *London, printed for N. Blandford; sold by J. Roberts, A. Dodd, & E. Nutt,* [1726.] (*SR* 11 June)
½⁰: 2 sides, 1 column.
> Entered to Carey in *SR*; deposit copy at O. Listed in *MC* June.

'As musing I rang'd in the meads all alone'
> Reprinted in Carey's *Poems*, 1729. A satirical comment on Senesino's leaving England.

L(C.121.g.9/189),O.

C48 [—] — *London: printed and Dublin re-printed by George Faulkner, 1726.*
½⁰: 2 sides, 1 column.

L(1890.e.5/122),DG,DT; CtY,NjP.

C49 [—] Namby Pamby: or, a panegyrick on the new versification address'd to A----- P----. [*Dublin,* 1725.]
½⁰: 1 side, 2 columns.

Carey, H. Namby Pamby

> *Bond* 83; *Teerink* 923. The order of editions has not been determined.

'All ye poets of the age'
> Reprinted in Carey's *Poems*, 1729. A satire on Ambrose Philips.

CSmH,MH.

C50 [—] — to A--- P--- esq; ... By Capt. Gordon, author of the Apology for Parson Alberony, and the Humourist. [*Dublin,* 1725.]
½⁰: 1 side, 2 columns.
> A variant copy at DT has 'Finis' at end; others have not. The attribution to Thomas Gordon is false, possibly a deliberate misattribution.

L(1890.e.5/126; C.121.g.8/186),O,DT; MH.

C51 — A new song in the Honest Yorkshireman. Composed by Mr. Carey. [*London?* 1735/–.]
slip: 1 side, 1 column.
'Come hither, my country 'squire'
C.

C52 — Of stage tyrants. An epistle to the right honourable Philip earl of Chesterfield. Occasion'd by the Honest Yorkshire-man being rejected at Drury-Lane... *London, printed for J. Shuckburgh, & L. Gilliver, J. Jackson, and J. Leake at Bath. And sold by A. Dodd, E. Nutt, & E. Cook, 1735.* (*LM* Nov)
2⁰: *A¹* B–C² D¹; *i–ii,* 1–8 *9; 10 blk.* 9 advt.
> There appear to be variant states of the outer forme of C.

'O Chesterfield! my patron and my pride'
L(11630.f.9,–D1; 643.l.25/22; 643.l.28/16, –D1); CLU-C,CtY(–D1),DLC,KU,TxU(2, 1 –D1).

C53 — A pastoral, by Mr. Cary. [*London?* 173–?]
slip: 1 side, 1 column.
> Probably an unauthorized edition.

'Flocks are sporting, doves are courting'
C.

Carmen. Carmen coronarium, 1727. *See* Roach, Richard.

C54 — Carmen elegiacum in mortem clarissimi ducis Malborough, romani imperii principum collegio, pro meritis suis, aggregati. *Londini, typis Tho. Edlin, 1723.*
8⁰: A–B⁴; *1–2* 3–16.
'Proh dolor! Extincta est Malburgæ gloria gentis'
C.

— Carmen epinicium augustissimæ Russorum imperatrici sacrum, [1737.] *See* Maittaire, Michael.

— Carmen irenicum, 1707. *See* Settle, Elkanah.

— Carmen lugubre. A mournful poem, 1701. *See* Billingsley, Nicholas.

— Carmen natalitum, 1714. *See* Settle, Elkanah.

— Carmen rhythmicum, 1749. *See* Wilmot, George.

Carmen

— Carmen seculare, for the year 1720. *See* Sewell, George.

— Carmen seculare, for the year 1735. *See* Parratt, William.

C55 — Carmen seculare, or a new year's gift for the city of London. With impartial characters of the principal magistrates. *London, printed by J. How*, [1709.] (6 Jan, Luttrell)
2°.
>Advertised in *PB* 8 Jan 1709, where it is listed as sold by J. Morphew.
>(*Thorn-Drury*.)

— Carmen seculare, presented to the...king, [1720?] *See* Newcomb, Thomas.

Carmina. Carmina sacra de omnibus festis ecclesiae anglicanae, 1748. *See* Pigott, Samuel.

Carole. Carole Gothorum longe fortissime ductor, [1711?] *See* Pitcairne, Archibald.

— Carole, si similis fratris..., [1711?] *See* Pitcairne, Archibald.

'Cartaret, William.' Miscellaneous works, in verse and prose, 1748. *See* Bancks, John.

C55·5 [**Carte, Thomas.**] The blatant-beast. A poem. *London, printed for J. Robinson*, 1742. (*GM, LM* Dec)
2°: *A² B–C²; 1–3 4–12.*
>Entered in Strahan's ledger to Mr. Carte under 20 Nov 1742, 250 copies printed. Some payment was received from Robinson.
>'Beauty, the fondling mother's earliest pray'r'
>Other works entered to Carte in Strahan's ledger were certainly written by him, and it is therefore probable that he is the author of this. A satire on Pope.
L(1973); CtY,DFo,MH,TxU(2).

[**Carter, Cornelius.**] Advice from the stars. In a letter to the pretending doctor, Whaley, 1714. *See* A72.

[**Carter, Elizabeth.**] Poems upon particular occasions. *London, printed in the year* 1738.
4°: pp. 24.   L,LdU-B; MH.

— Poems on several occasions. *London, printed for John Rivington*, 1762. (*GM, LM* Jan)
8°: pp. vi, 104.   L,O; CtY,MH.
>Dedication signed. There are a number of subsequent editions.

C56 Carthage. Carthage reveng'd. *London, printed in the year* 1712.
8°: *A–B⁴ C²; i–ii, 1–16 17–18 blk.*
>Watermark: fleur-de-lys on shield, which suggests a fine-paper copy.

Carthage reveng'd

'Now had imperial Rome confirm'd her sway'
A political satire on Marlborough.
L(1962).

Carthy, Charles.
A translation of the second book of Horace's epistles. Together with some of the most select in the first, with notes. A pastoral courtship, from Theocritus. One original poem in English, and a Latin ode spoken before the government on his majesty's birth-day, 1730. *Dublin, printed by Christopher Dickson*, 1731.
4°: pp. 116.   L,O; CSmH,IU.
>The O copy is apparently in a presentation binding.

―――――――

C56·5 [—] The gift of Pallas. A poem. Occasioned by a fine piece of linnen lately sent from Ireland, as a present to her royal highness the Princess Ann. *Dublin, printed by James Hoey*, 1733.
4°: *A⁴ B²; 1–2 3–12.* 12 advt.
>The copies at O,NN have the Amsterdam arms watermark, that at L has post-horn; possibly there are fine-paper copies. The copies at L,O add two leaves, 'An ode. In imitation of the third ode of the third book of Horace... By the same hand.', which is paged *1 2–4*; it was previously published separately in 1732.
>'The gods were round imperial Jove'
>The advertisement on p. 12 invites subscriptions to the author's translation of Longinus; an epigram against Carthy printed by *Williams* 667 makes it clear that Carthy was issuing proposals for his translation. Wrongly ascribed to William Dunkin by the O catalogue (and thence in *Halkett & Laing*) by confusion with his *The lover's web*, 1734, which was written on the same occasion.
L(11631.e.44),O; NN.

C56·7 [—] [dh] An ode. In imitation of the third ode of the third book of Horace. Address'd to the city of Dublin. [*Dublin*, 1732.]
4°: *A²; 1 2–4.*
>Reprinted as a supplement to Carthy's *The gift of Pallas*, 1733.
>'The man that's obstinately just'
>In praise of Humphry French, lord mayor of Dublin.
L(C.121.g.8/191),C,*DG*.

C57 [—] An ode on the present war with Spain. *Dublin, printed by and for Geo. Faulkner*, 1740.
8°: *A–B⁴; 1–2 3–14 15–16.* B4 advt.
>The order of editions has not been determined.
>'When justice holds no more the scales'
>The edition below is attributed to Carthy by E. R. McC. Dix, *List of books and pamphlets printed in Armagh* (1910); he had not seen the

Carthy, C. An ode on the present war

> book, but took the entry from 'an old cata-
> logue'. *O'Donoghue* makes the same attribu-
> tion, probably from the same source.
> DA(2, – B4); NN,NjP,*RPJCB.*

C58 [—] — [col] *Armagh, printed by William Dickie,*
1740.
4⁰: *A⁴; 1 2–8.*
> Drop-head title only. Apparently composed of
> two half-sheets one within the other.
> PU.

[—] A prologue, spoken by Mr. Elrington...
Written by C.C. [i.e. Charles Coffey], 1725. *See*
C277.

C59 [—] The third ode, of the third book of Horace,
imitated. On occasion of the French fortifying
Dunkirk. *Dublin, printed by R. Reilly,* 1740.
8⁰: A⁴; *1–3 4–8.*
> The order of editions has not been deter-
> mined.
> 'The man, who stedfastly adheres'
> Ascribed to Carthy by E.R. McC. Dix from
> the Armagh edition on the same evidence as
> C57.
> L(1963),DG.

C60 [—] — [col] *Armagh, printed by William Dickie,*
1740.
4⁰: *A⁴; 1 2–8.*
> Drop-head title only.
> DFo.

[—] To his excellency John, lord Carteret, 1729.
See T332.

C61 Castle-Howard. Castle-Howard, the seat of the
right honourable Charles earl of Carlisle. To whom
this poem is humbly inscribed. *London, printed by
E. Owen in Amen-corner,* [1732.] (*GSJ* 12 Sept)
2⁰: *A² B–E²; 1–2 3–20.*
'When happy plenty, the effect of peace'
L(163.n.44),O; CSmH(uncut),CtY.

Castleton, Nathaniel. Several preparatory instances of Mr. Castleton's way of writing, produc'd
against the intricate representation of him in the...
Spectator [17 Sept 1714]. *London, printed for John
Morphew,* 1715.
4⁰: pp. 27+.   O.
> A collection of verse. Continued by *An essay
> towards a coalition of parties,* 1715, and *An
> explanatory supplement,* 1715, both in prose.
> It is not clear whether parts 1 and 2 were
> issued separately; the pagination is continuous.

[—] The antidote; being a poem of reflection
[actually by Henry Crispe], 1713. *See* C508.

[—] An epithalamium [actually by Henry Crispe],
1712. *See* C510.

Castleton, N.

C62 [—] [dh] An ode to the most honourable the lord
high-treasurer of Great-Britain. [col] *London,
printed by W. Bowyer,* 1713.
2⁰: A²; 1–4.
> The priority of this and the following has not
> been established. There may be fine-paper
> copies; the watermark of the copy seen is pro
> patria. It bears a penny tax stamp.
> 'What man? What heroe praise attains'
> Almost certainly by Castleton, whose poems to
> Harley were printed by Bowyer for Richard
> Sare. In praise of Harley and the peace with
> France.
> C.

C63 [—] [*idem*] [dh] The olive, an ode. [*London,
printed for Richard Sare; sold by John Morphew,*
1713.] (*DC* 29 April)
2⁰: A²; *1–3 4 blk.*
> Apparently from the same basic setting of
> type as the preceding, but with much revision,
> including alternative stanzas. The watermark
> of the copy seen, fleur-de-lys on shield,
> suggests a fine-paper copy. Imprint from *DC,*
> presumably advertising ordinary paper copies;
> there is none in the copy seen.
> C.

[—] Some verses sent to the right honourable the
Earl of Oxford [actually by Henry Crispe], 1712.
See C514.

C64 [—] [dh] To the right honourable Mr. Harley.
[col] *London, printed for Richard Sare,* 1711.
(28 April, Luttrell)
2⁰: A²; *1–3 4 blk.*
> No watermark; '(Price Twopence)' in colo-
> phon. Entered in Bowyer's ledger, 30 April
> 1711, as 'Mr Castleton's poem to Mr Harley';
> it went through five impressions, a total of
> 1025 copies. Wrongly identified by *Nichols*
> with [Henry Crispe] *Some verses sent...* 1712.
> The five impressions have not been differen-
> tiated.
> 'Once more, by you inspir'd, my muse'
> L(1481.f.19/9, uncut),O,C,*MR*; TxU(Luttrell).

C65 [—] [fine paper?]
> Watermark: Amsterdam arms; no price in
> imprint.
> MH.

C66 [—] [dh] To the right honourable the Lord
Harley, on the promotion of his father to the
nobility. [col] *London, printed for Richard Sare,*
1711. (June)
2⁰: A²; *1–3 4 blk.*
> No watermark. Entered in Bowyer's ledger
> 18 June 1711 as 'Mr Castleton's poem to Ld
> Harley on his father's promotion'; 325 copies
> printed.
> 'While Oxford's name from clouds of danger
> breaks'
> C; MH,TxU.

Castleton, N. To...the Lord Harley

C67 [—] [fine paper]
    Watermark: fleur-de-lys.
    Chatsworth.

Cat. A cat may look upon a king, [1732.] *See* Belcher, James.

C68 Catch. The catch sung by the journey-men weavers to the tune of —— This great world is a bubble. [*Dublin*] *Printed by J. Gowan, 1726.*
½°: 1 side, 1 column.
    The verso bears *An account of the journey-men weavers grateful congratulation of the Rev. Dr. Swift...Sep. the 5th 1726* in prose.
'Now all danger's over'
Rothschild.

C69 Catcott, Alexander Stopford. The court of love, a vision from Chaucer. *Oxford, printed at the Theater for Anthony Peisley; and are to be sold by James Knapton, William Taylor, Henry Clements, William Meadows, & John Morphew, booksellers in London, 1717.*
8°: A–D⁴; *1–2* 3–32.
'As once I lay with thoughts of love possess'd'
L(11631.d.10),O; CLU-C,*CtY*,ICN,*IU*,MH+.

C70 —— The poem of Musæus, on the loves of Hero and Leander, paraphras'd in English, heroick verse. *Oxford, printed at the Theater for Anthony Peisley; and are to be sold by James Knapton, William Taylor, Henry Clement, William Meadows, & John Morphew, booksellers in London, 1715.*
8°: π² A–C⁴ D²; *i–iv*, 1–28.
'Sing, muse, of hidden love the conscious flame'
    Dedication signed.
L(11335.c.48/1, with a later ms. dedicatory poem), O; CtY,NjP.

C71 —— *Dublin: reprinted by S. Powell, for G. Risk, 1716.*
12°: A–C⁶; *1–6* 7–35 *36 blk*.
    Also issued with the Dublin reprint of Thomas Tickell's *The first book of Homer's Iliad*, 1716.
O, CT,DK,DN,DT.

C72 Catherall, Samuel. Cato major. A poem. Upon the model of Tully's Essay of old age. In four books. *London, printed for J. Roberts, 1725.* (*MC* Sept)
8°: *A*⁴ a⁴ B–M⁴; *i–v* vi–xvi, 1–88. A1 frt.
    Printed by Samuel Richardson (*Sale* 35).
'*Scipio.* Cato! Well met. *Cato.* Hail vertuous, hopeful youths!'
    In dialogue.
L(1465.f.47),O(–A1),LdU-B; CSmH,CtY(uncut),ICN,MH,TxU+.

C73 — Εἰκὼν Σωκρατικη. Or, A portraiture of Socrates, extracted out of Plato. In blank verse. *Oxford, printed by L. Lichfield, for A. Peisley; and are to be*

Catherall, S. Εἰκὼν Σωκρατικη
sold by J. Knapton, H. Clements, J. Morphew, & W. Meadows, booksellers in London, 1717.
8°: *A*⁴ B–H⁴; *i–viii*, 1–53 *54–56 blk*. A1 frt.
'Simplicity of speech, and naked truth'
L(11631.c.9,–A1),O('Ex dono A. Peisley'),OW (–H4),DT,WcC+;CSmH(–A1,H4),CtY(–H4), ICN(–H4),MH(–H4),TxU(–H4).

C74 —— The second edition [imprint as C73].
    Apparently a press-variant title.
CtY.

C75 — An epistle humbly inscrib'd to the university of Oxford, occasion'd by the death of the ld. bishop of Durham. Written in imitation of Waller's style. *Oxford, printed at the Theatre for Anth. Peisley; and are to be sold by J. Knapton, W. Meadows, W. Taylor, & T. Combes, booksellers in London, 1721.* (*DP* 7 Oct)
2°: A–C² (A2 as 'A'); *i–ii*, 1–10.
'Waller, as sweet a bard, as ever sung!'
O,DN; CtY,DFo(Luttrell, Oct).

C76 — An essay on the conflagration in blank verse. *Oxford, printed for Anthony Peisley; and are to be sold by James Knapton, William Meadows, & John Morphew, booksellers in London, 1720.* (18 Jan?)
8°: (frt+) A–I⁴ K¹; *i–viii*, 1–66.
'A godlike man encount'ring hellish foes'
    On the last judgement.
L(1465.f.3; 1465.f.27,–frt; 161.k.9),O(2, 1 'Ex dono A. Peisley', 1 –A1, lacks K1),C; CLU-C (Luttrell, Feb),CtY,ICN,IU,MH(ms. date 18 Jan) +.

Catholic. The catholick poet, 1716. *See* Oldmixon, John.

Cato. Cato's ghost, [1715?] *See* Meston, William.

Cato, Dionysius.
Dionysius Cato his four books of moral precepts, 1714. *See* D317.

C77 Cause. The cause of liberty. Addressed to the British senate. *London, printed by, and for, J. Chrichley, 1734* [1735?]. (*GSJ* 27 Jan)
2°: *A*¹ B–E² F¹; *3–4* 5–21 *22 blk*.
'From week to week, while venal pens essay'
    In praise of George II and Walpole.
O,*LdU-B*; IU,InU.

Causidicade. The Causidicade, 1743. *See* Morgan, Macnamara.

C78 Causton, Peter. Tunbridgialia: or, the pleasures of Tunbridge. A poem. In Latin and English heroic verse. Written by Peter Causton. *Mount Sion: printed and sold at the end of the Upper Walk, at Tunbridge-Wells, 1705.*
4°: A–C⁴; *i–vi*, 1–17 *18 blk*. A1 hft.
    First published 1686.

Causton, P. Tunbridgialia

'Prime poëtarum, præclara gente Frohocka'
'Thou best of poets, and thou best of friends'
The form of the title suggests that Causton also wrote the English version, but this has not been confirmed.
L(11602.f.24/4),O,DT,EtC.

C79 — Tunbrigialia. Authore P. Causton. *Londini, anno* 1709.
8°: A(6 ll); *1–2* 3–12.
Although signed on A2, A3, A4, the collation appears to be A² B⁴. Similar in appearance to the publications of Henry Hills. Latin text only.
L(11408.aaa.25),O(2),EU; CtY,ICN,IU,TxU.

C80 **Caution.** A caution to the burgesses; or the bottle conjurer. [*London?* 1749?]
½°: 1 side, 1 column.
'From Blossoms Inn when Bob came down'
Harding.

Cavalcade. The cavalcade: a poem on the riding the franchises, [172–.] *See* Nelson, Henry.

C81 [**Cavendish, William,** *duke of Devonshire.*] [dh]
An allusion to the bishop of Cambray's supplement of Homer. [col] [*London*] *Printed in the year* 1706.
2°: A²; *1–4.*
The first line is apparently misprinted; subsequent editions read '...love you write'.
'Cambray, whilst of seraphick love you set'
Attributed to Cavendish in Walpole's *Noble authors* (1759) 99; early ms. ascription in a copy at TxU.
L(840.m.1/10),LLP,DA,DT,MC+; CSmH,CtY, MH,TxU(2).

C82 [—] [*idem*] The charms of liberty: a poem. By the late Duke of D—. To which is added, The battle of Audenard; Royal health and wise: ingenuous poems. Written by several hands. *London, printed by Benj. Bragg,* 1709.
8°: A⁸ (A2ᵛ as 'A3'); *1* 2–16.
The other poems are by Edward Ward and Tom Brown.
DA(−A3.6).

C83 [—] — To which is added, epigrams, poems and satyrs. Written by several hands. *London, printed in the year* 1709.
8°: A⁸; *1–2* 3–16.
The drop-head title reads 'THE *Charms* of *Liberty*...' Possibly published by Henry Hills.
L(12331.ee.31/9),LG,O,LdU-B; CU,ICU,NjP.

C84 [—] [another edition]
The drop-head title prints 'Charms of Liberty' in black letter. Reissued with other remaindered Hills poems in *A collection of the best English poetry,* 1717 (*Case* 294).
L(C.124.b.7/42),O,E,WcC; CtY(2),IU,MH,TxU.

Cawthorn, J.

Cawthorn, James. Poems. *London, printed by W. Woodfall; sold by S. Bladon,* 'MDDCLXXI' [1771].
4°: pp. 226. L,O.

C85 [—] Abelard to Eloisa. *London, printed for M. Cooper,* 1747. (*GM,LM* Nov)
4°: *A*(2 ll) B–C⁴ D(2 ll); *i–iii* iv, 1–19 20 *blk.*
The two leaves of A appear to be conjugate with those of D.
'Ah, why this boding start? this sudden pain'
Ms. note in the OCU copy 'By Mr Cawthorne master of Tunbridge school'; printed in Cawthorn's *Poems,* 1771.
L(1960, title mutilated); CtY(title mutilated), OCU.

C86 [—] [reissue] The second edition. *London, printed for M. Cooper,* 1748.
4°: *A*(2 ll, ± A1) B–C⁴ D(2 ll); *i–iii* iv, 1–19 20 *blk.*
TxU.

C— — —d, *E—l of.* The Gymnasiad, 1744. *See* Whitehead, Paul.

C—d & S—t. An answer to John Brigs's ballads, [1729.] *See* A239.

Cebes. Cebes's Table never before translated into English verse. By a lady, 1707. *In* P998.

C87 **Cecilia.** Cæcilia's song. [*Dublin,* 1704.]
½°: 1 side, 1 column.
'Awake, awake, whose harmonious souls'
A hymn for St. Cecilia's day.
DG.

C88 **Celadon.** Celadon, or, the bright example; a pastoral on the death of his royal highness the P. of Denmark. Inscrib'd to the court and quality of Great Britain. *London, printed in the year* 1708 [1708/9]. *For the author.* (*PB* 8 Feb 1709)
2°: A–C² *D*¹; *1–2* 3–13 *14 blk.* 13 err.
Engraving on p. 3.
'No more, my Thyrsis, lay thy pipe aside'
L(11602.i.26/1); InU(Luttrell, 8 Feb), MH.

C89 **Celebrated.** The celebrated beauties: being an heroick poem, made on the Colledge Green and Queen's Square ladies. *Bristol, printed by Joseph Penn, bookseller, in Wine-street,* 1720.
8°: *A*⁴ B²; *1* 2–12.
'Ye sacred dryads, who adorn the woods'
L(11630.bbb.5).

C90 **Celia.** Cælias complaint: or, love's looking-glass. Dedicated to the boarding-schools. *London, printed for John Nutt,* 1704. (29 July, Luttrell)

Celia's complaint

2°: *A²* B–C² D¹; *i–iv*, 1–10. 10 advt.
'Beneath the shade of a cool cypress grove'
DFo(Luttrell).

C91 Celibacy. Celibacy: or, good advice to young fellows to keep single... Being an answer to Matrimony; or, good advice to the ladies, &c. *London, printed for T. Read, 1739.* (*GM* Sept)
2°: *A¹* B–E² F¹; *i–ii, 1 2–17 18 blk.*
'And have the fates, my Strephon, then decreed'
L(1962); CSmH,IU,MH,NN-B,OCU.

[Cennick, John.] Sacred hymns for the children of god in the days of their pilgrimage. By J.C. *London printed, and sold by B. Milles, 1741.*
12°: pp. xxxii, 220.   L,O; CtY-D,NNUT.
There is an errata slip in the copy at NNUT.

[—] — The second edition. *London printed, and sold by B. Milles, 1741.*
12°: pp. xxxii, 243.   L,BrP; ICN(impft),NcD.
In some copies (e.g. Moravian Archives, London) p. 243 is numbered '143'.

[—] — *London, printed by John Lewis; sold for the author at the Tabernacle,* [1741?]
12°: pp. xii, 117.   Moravian Archives, London.
A different collection from the preceding.

[—] — *London, printed by John Lewis; sold by the author, 1742.*
12°: pp. x. 117.   L,BrP; ICN,NNUT.

[—] — Part II. *London, printed by John Lewis; sold by the author, 1742.*
12°: pp. 196.   L,BrP; ICN,NNUT.

— Sacred hymns for the use of religious societies. Generally composed in dialogues. Part I. *Bristol, printed by Felix Farley, 1743.*
12°: pp. 52.   L,DT; NNUT.

—— Part II. *Bristol, printed by Felix Farley, 1743.*
12°: pp. 96.   L,DT; NNUT.

—— *London, printed by John Hart; sold by J. Lewis, 1744.*
12°: pp. 96.   Moravian Archives, London.

— [reimpression or variant date:] 1745.
Moravian Archives, London.

—— Part III. *London, printed by John Hart; sold by J. Lewis, 1744.*
12°: pp. 240.   Moravian Archives, London, DT.

— [reimpression or variant date:] 1745.
Moravian Archives, London; NNUT.

There is said to be a Dublin collection of Cennick's hymns, 1747, and a third edition of 1749; but I have been unable to trace copies or details of them.

Censoriad. The Censoriad, 1730. *See* 'Gulliver, Martin.'

Centlivre, S.

[Centlivre, Susanna.] The catholick poet; or Protestant Barnaby's sorrowful lamentation [probably by W. Oldmixon], 1716. *See* O165.

C92 — An epistle to Mrs. Wallup, now in the train of her royal highness the Princess of Wales. As it was sent to her to the Hague. *London printed, and sold by R. Burleigh, & A. Boulter, 1715* [1714]. (*DC* 14 Oct)
2°: *A–B²; 1–4 5–8.* A1 hft.
'Madam, what muse can speak, what pen display'
O; IU(–A1),MH.

C93 **[—]** An epistle to the King of Sweden from a lady of Great-Britain. *London, printed for J. Roberts, & Arabella Morris, without Temple-Bar, 1717.* (*MC* March)
2°: *A²* B–C²; *1–4 5–11 12 blk.* A1 hft.
A second edition 'by Mrs. Susan Centlivre' was advertised in *PB* 4 June 1717.
'To thee rude warrior, whom we once admir'd'
Mrs. Centlivre's authorship is revealed in the advertisement quoted above. Cf. *An answer from the King of Sweden to the British lady's epistle to him,* 1717.
L(1959),O,DT;   CSmH(uncut),MH,OCU(–A1), PBL,TxU(2).

C94 **[—]** — *Dublin: re-printed by Samuel Fairbrother, 1717.*
8°: *A⁴* (A1ᵛ as 'A2'); *1 2–8.*
DN,DT; TxU.

C95 **[—]** The masquerade. A poem. Humbly inscribed to his grace the Duke d'Aumont. *London, printed for Bernard Lintott, 1713.* (*DC* 3 Sept)
2°: *A²* B²; *1 2–7 8 blk.*
With a French prose version.
'The globe with wond'rous pains men traverse o'er'
Attributed to Mrs. Centlivre by *Whincop*; see also Jane Norton in *Book collector* 1957.
MR-C; CtY,ICU(uncut, ms. date 18 Sept).

C96 — A poem. Humbly presented to his most sacred majesty George...upon his accession to the throne. *London, printed for T. Woodward, 1715* [1714]. (*MC* Oct)
2°: *A²* B²; *1–5 6–8.* A1 hft.
'The lark, while she her gratitude to prove'
L(11631.h.1, title cropt),O,DT,*MR-C*.

C97 — A woman's case: in an epistle to Charles Joye, esq; deputy governor of the South-Sea. *London, printed for E. Curll, 1720.*
8°: *A²* B–C⁴; *i–iv, 1–13 14–16.* A1 hft; C4 advt.
'Oh Joye! thy name I never knew'
DLC(–A1, C4),MH.

Cerealia. Cerealia: an imitation of Milton, 1706. *See* Fenton, Elijah.

C98 Certain. A certain dutiful son's lamentation for the death of a certain right reverend... To which is added a certain funeral poem upon a very uncertain

A **certain** dutiful son's lamentation

most honourable... *London, printed for J. Mor-*
phew, & S. Jeeves, 1715.
8⁰: *A⁴* B–C⁴ D²; *1–4* 5–27 *28 blk.* A1 hft.
    All copies seen have a ms. correction of the
    price from '*6d.*' to '*4d.*'
'Well, since my venerable dad is'
ICU,IU,NjP(–A1).

C99 — A certain proposal of a certain little tutor, for
making certain reformations in a certain method of
education, most certainly practis'd in a certain
university. *London, printed for M. Cooper,* [1749?]
8⁰: A⁴; *1–2* 3–7 *8 blk.*
'What all concerns I advertise'
    Purporting to be written by Edward Bentham,
    but a satire on him. Closely related to William
    King's attacks on Bentham, and possibly
    written by him.
O; CtY.

Cervantes Saavedra, Miguel de.
Ward, Edward: The life and notable adventures of
that renown'd knight, Don Quixote de la Mancha.
Merrily translated into hudibrastick verse, [1710]–
1714. *See* W103–111.

Chace. *See* Chase.

[**C100** = O168·2] **Chain.** A chain of providence, 1705.
See Oldmixon, John [A pastoral poem].

Chaloner, Thomas. The merriest poet in
Christendom: or Chaloner's miscellany, being a
salve for every sore... Publish'd and recommended to the world by Robert Hartley... *London*
printed, and sold for the benefit of the author by
Henry Bulley, and by George Lee, printer, 1732.
8⁰: pp. 113.   L,O; ICN.

C101 — The true Briton. Or, a new health. Compos'd by
Tho Chaloner, gent. [*London?* 1729/36.]
slip: 1 side, 1 column.
'Since our king to his German dominions is gone'
C.

Chamberlaine, Walter. *For a group of pseudony-*
mous poems in which Chamberlaine may have had a
share, see 'Gulliver, Martin'.

[—] A poem occasioned by a view of Powers-court
House, 1741. *See* P548.

[—] A Tartarean tale... By W.C. A.M., 1746.
See T43.

C102 [—] The three travellers. A tale. *Dublin, printed by*
S. Powell, for T. Thornton, 1733.
8⁰: A⁴; *1–2* 3–7 *8 blk.*
'A good repute, a virtuous name'
    Printed as Chamberlaine's by Alicia Lefanu
    in her *Memoirs...of Mrs. Sheridan,* 1824.
L(11631.a.63/7),LVA-F,DA,DG(2),DN+.

Chamberlen, —, *Mr.*

C103 Chamberlen, —, *Mr.* News from hell: or, a
match for the directors; a satire. Humbly inscribed
to the honourable members of the secret committee:
with a dedication to the Emperour of the Moon.
By Mr. Chamberlen. *London, printed for the author;*
sold by J. Roberts, 1721. (*DP* 24 Feb)
2⁰: A–D²; *i–ii* iii–v '*iv*', *1–10.*
'Ill-fated Albion! once the happy seat'
    The author has not been identified; possibly
    Hugh Chamberlen, the man-midwife and
    projector, is intended. An attack on specula-
    tion.
L(1487.d.7),LVA-F; CtY,MH-BA(Luttrell, May).

C104 [**Chamberlen, Paul.**] The perspective, or Calista
dissected. To which are prefixed, a lock and key to
the late opera of Calista. *London, printed for J.*
Dicks; sold by the booksellers of London & West-
minster, 1731.
4⁰: A–B⁴; [2] i–v *vi,* 1–8.
'The hero feels a fertile skull'
    Ms. attribution to Chamberlen by John
    Henley in the L copy.
L(643.k.3/8, ms. notes by John Henley).

C105 Chambermaid. The chamber-maid's policy; or,
a certain priest outwitted. *Dublin, printed in the year*
1736.
8⁰: 7 pp.
(Pickering & Chatto cat. 260/3912.)

C106 Champion. The champion's defeat. An excellent
new ballad. To its own tune. *London, printed for*
T. Cooper, 1739. (*GM* Oct)
2⁰: A² B¹; *1–3* 4–5 *6 blk.*
'O London is a brave town'
    Crum O571. On the city of London's rejection
    of Sir George Champion as candidate for lord
    mayor.
LG; CSmH,CtY.

C107 [**Chandler, Mary.**] A description of Bath: a poem.
In a letter to a friend. *London, printed for J. Roberts,*
J. Jackson, J. Gray; and J. Leake, & S. Lobb,
booksellers in Bath, [1733.] (*GSJ* 24 Feb)
2⁰: A² B–E²; *i–ii, 1–3* 4–18. A1 hft.
'Whilst you, my friend, with anxious cares attend'
    Subsequent editions published under Mary
    Chandler's name.
L(643.m.15/5),LDW(–A1),O,LdU-B;   CLU-C
(–A1),CU,MH,OCU,TxU(2).

C108 [—] A description of Bath. A poem. Humbly
inscribed to her royal highness the Princess Amelia.
London, printed for J. Leake, bookseller in Bath; and
J. Gray, bookseller in the Poultry, 1734. (*GM,LM*
Sept)
2⁰: A² B–E²; *1–2* 3–19 *20 blk.*
    Revised text, variant first line. Printed by
    Samuel Richardson (*Sale* 136).
'Amelia, beauteous princess, deign to view'
L(11630.h.7),O(2),BaP(2),LdU-B,WcC(ms.
corrections); CU(uncut),CtY,IU,MH,NjP+.

Chandler, M. A description

C109 — — The third edition. To which are added, several poems by the same author. *London, printed for James Leake, bookseller in Bath,* 1736.
8°: A^4 a^2 B–F^8 G^4; *i–xii, 1 2–77 78–88.* A1 hft; F8–G4 advt.
        Printed by Samuel Richardson (*Sale* 190).
L(11632.bb.8),O,*BaP,BrP*(2); *CLU-C*,CtY(uncut),ICU,*NN.*

C110 — — The fourth edition. To which are added, several poems by the same author. *London, printed for James Leake, bookseller in Bath,* 1738. (*GM,LM* Oct)
8°: A^4 a^2 B–F^8 G^4; *i–xii, 1 2–77 78–88.* A1 hft; $F7^v$–G4 advt.
        Printed by Samuel Richardson (*Sale* 228).
L(11632.bb.9),*BaP,BrP*(2); CU(–A1),CtY (–F8–G4),MH.

C111 — — The fifth edition. To which are added, several poems by the same author. *London, printed for James Leake, bookseller in Bath,* 1741.
8°: A^4 a^2 B–F^8 G^4; *i–xii, 1 2–77 78–87; 88 blk.* A1 hft; $F7^v$–G4 advt.
        Half-title not in copies seen, but present in the reissue below. Printed by Samuel Richardson (*Sale* 272).
L(11632.aaa.11,–A1); CSmH(–A1),MH(–A1).

C112 — [reissue] The sixth edition. To which is added, a true tale, by the same author. *London, printed for James Leake, bookseller in Bath,* 1744.
8°: $A^4(\pm A2)$ a^2 B–E^8 $F^8(\pm F7,+\chi^4)$ G^4; *i–xii, 1 2–85 78–87; 88 blk.* A1 hft; $\chi4^v$–G4 advt.
        F7 is cancelled to remove the beginning of the advertisements on p. 78, and χ^4 contains 'A true tale'.
True tale: 'Why, madam, must I tell this idle tale?'
L(11632.aaa.12),O; *Lewis Walpole Library.*

C113 **Change.** A change at court: or, he's out at last. '*Oxford*', *printed in the year* 1714. (30 July, Luttrell)
½°: 1 side, 1 column.
        Probably printed at London.
'How often do's Dame Fortune man beguile'
        On the dismissal of Robert Harley.
MH(Luttrell).

Changes. The changes: or, faction vanquish'd, 1711. *See* Hamilton, Newburgh.

C114 **Chapman, Richard.** Britannia rediviva: or, Britain's recovery. An heroick poem humbly inscrib'd to the king's most excellent majesty. *London, printed for Bernard Lintott,* 1714. (18 Sept, Luttrell)
2°: A^2 B^2 C^1; *1–4 5–10.* A1 hft.
        Listed in *MC* Sept.
'Tho' god in wrath did first a king ordain'
        Cf. *An elegy on the heroic poem lately publish'd by the vicar of Cheshunt,* 1715.

Chapman, R. Britannia rediviva

L(643.1.25/14; 162.n.4,–A1),LLP,O,AdU (Luttrell); CLU-C,DFo.

C115 — An essay on the judgment of Paris. Most humbly inscrib'd to his highness the Prince of Orange, &c. and occasion'd by his intending marriage with... the Princess Royal. *London, printed in the year* 1733.
2°: A^2 B^2 (A2 as 'A'); *1–3 4–8.*
'Once, on a time, Queen Hecub's boy'
CLU-C.

[—] Le feu de joye: or, a brief description of two most glorious victories, 1705. *See* F115.

C116 — The new-year's gift: being a seasonable call to repentance... In a poem, moral and divine. [*London*] *Printed in the year* 1731.
4°: A^2 B–C^2; *i–iv, 1 2–8.*
'Such desperadoes sure were never known'
L(161.1.23, slightly cropt),O(uncut, in wrappers), LdU-B.

[—] To his grace the Duke of Marlborough, a poem. By a gentleman of the church of England, [1712.] *See* T337.

C117 **Chapman, Thomas.** The winter campaign. A poem. *London, printed for R. Dodsley; sold by M. Cooper,* 1746. (*GA* 15 Nov)
2°: A^2 B–C^2 D^1; *i–ii iii–vi, 7 8–14.*
'Sweet as it is to view our dangers past'
O,AdU; CtY,NjP.

'**Chapmanno-Wiskero.**' An elegy on the heroic poem lately publish'd by the vicar of Cheshunt, 1715. *See* E145.

Chappel, Sarah. [dh] Divine poems, composed by Sarah Chappel, belonging to the Tabernacle. [*London,* 1741/–.]
8°: pp. '8' [4].   L.
        Two poems only, by a convert of George Whitefield; possibly an incomplete copy.

Chappelow, John. The Christian's life is a piece of chequer work, made up of sorrow and joy. Or, the believers ground of joy under sorrowful dispensations. Being a comfortable poetical paraphrase on several selected texts of scripture... *London, printed for the anthor* [!], *in the year* 1724.
8°: pp. xii, 82.   L,LDW.

Character. A character, 1717. *See* Bockett, Elias.

C118 — A character. [*Dublin, printed by Aaron Rhames,* 1722?]
½°: 1 side, 1 column.
        The printer is identified from the ornaments.
'As various arts do shine in various men'

A **character**

> In praise of Swift.
> TxU.

— A character defended, 1717. *See* Bockett, Elias.

C119 — The character of a certain whigg. [*London*] *Printed in the year* 1712 [1711]. (31 Dec, Luttrell)
½°: 1 side, 1 column.
> Some copies have horizontal chain-lines. Line 19, 'P------x'.
'Industrious, unfatigu'd in faction's cause'
> *Crum* I1676. An attack on Thomas Wharton, marquis of Wharton.
L(11630.h.59),O(cropt and mounted), Crawford; ICN(Luttrell),InU,MH,NNP,OCU,TxU(2).

C120 — [another edition]
> Line 19, 'P----x'.
O.

— The character of a covetous citizen, 1702. *See* Ward, Edward.

C121 — 'A poem entitled, The character of a freeman. [*London*] *Sold by J. Chrichly*. Price 6d.' (*GM* April 1736)

C122 — The character of a master of a vessel. [*Dublin*] *Printed in the year* 1729.
½°: 1 side, 1 column.
'A brawny lump, that scarce knows good from ill'
DT.

C123 — A character of a turn-coat: or, the true picture of an English monster. [*London*] *Printed in the year* 1707.
½°: 1 side, 2 columns.
> Two woodcut heads in the centre which change from male to female when reversed. Text runs from both head and foot. Title in 4 lines.
'If kings are gods, as scripture say they be'
O,OW; MH(Luttrell).

C124 —— *Printed in the year* 1707.
½°: 1 side, 2 columns.
> A reprint with rough copies of the woodcuts. Title in 2 lines.
L(1871.f.3/18).

C125 — The character of a turn-coat…a British monster. [*London?* 1714/20?]
½°: 1 side, 2 columns.
> Text abbreviated and revised to include George I as king; new copies of the woodcuts.
'Some angry muse direct my pen'
Crawford.

C126 — The character of a Welsh-man, or, a poem in praise of St. David. *Dublin: printed by C.C.* [*Cornelius Carter*], 1721.
½°: 1 side, 1 column.
'David was king, after god's heart anointed'
CtY.

C127 — A character of Anselmus: or, a view of Parnassus. A poem. In two parts. Written in the year

A **character** of Anselmus

> MDCCXXXI, occasioned by a libel called, Christianity as old as the creation… *London, printed for J. Clarke*, 1732. (*GSJ* 11 Jan)
12°: A–E⁶; *1–4* 5–60. A1 hft; 4 err.
'In this rank age with mad ambition fir'd'
> A reply to Matthew Tindal's book, 1730.
DFo.

C128 **Characteristics.** Characteristicks: a dialogue. *London, printed for Charles Corbett*, 1741. (*GM, LM* Feb)
2°: A² B² ˣB² C² D¹; *i–iv, 1* 2–14.
'Says Juvenal, "In every clime, and state'
> A satire on poets and their political writings.
L(1482.f.39),O,LdU-B(ms. notes); CSmH,CtY, ICN,MH,TxU+.

C129 **Characters.** Characters: an epistle to Alexander Pope esq; and Mr. Whitehead. *London, printed for T. Cooper; sold by the booksellers of London and Westminster*, 1739. (*LDP* 1 March)
2°: A² B–D²; *1–5* 6–15 *16 blk*. A1 hft.
'Shall Pope and Whitehead, with the rankest hate'
> An attack on both. According to *A dialogue which lately pass'd between the Knight and his man John*, [1739], Thomas Odell 'answer'd Wh[itehea]d's satire'; possibly this is the poem intended.
L(11630.h.42),O,OW,C,LdU-B+; CSmH,CtY (−A1),IU,MH,TxU+.

C130 — Characters in dancing, drawn from real life. Concluding with a rhapsody in the Miltonic stile. Address'd to Lælius. *London, printed for W. Owen, at Homer's Head, near Temple-Bar; and at Tunbridge-Wells*, 1749. (*LM* Sept)
4°: A⁴ B²; *1–4* 5–12.
'Does Maurus move? who would not laugh to see'
CtY.

— 'Characters of an October (like) club at E—d's.'
> An attack on Elias Bockett's feud with William Gibson; replied to incidentally in Bockett's *The author of a Character*, 1717, and listed in *A complete collection of pamphlets*, 1727. Possibly not printed.

— The characters of the age, 1743. *See* The modern Englishman, 1738.

Charissimo. Charissimo suo duci de Vendosme. Tallardus, [1708?] *See* Alsop, Anthony.

C131 **Charles.** [dh] Charles Edouard en Ecosse. Ode. Imprimée à Dublin le ¹⁹⁄₃₀ Août 1475 [!]. [1745.]
4°: A⁴; *1* 2–8.
> No trace has been found of a Dublin edition. Probably printed in France.
'Sanglant théâtre de la guerre'
E.

C132 — Charles of Sweeden. [*London?* 1718/19.]
slip: 1 side, 1 column.
'Glorious hero are you dead'
C.

'**Charles Edward Stuart,** *the Young Pretender.*'
The poetical works of the inimitable Don Carlos,
commonly called the Young Chevalier. With an
introductory letter from a gentleman in Edinburgh
to his friend at London... *London, printed for
J. Oldcastle,* 1745. (*GA* 29 Nov)
2°: pp. 16.   O.
    Two libertine French poems, 'L'ode priapique'
and 'Epitre à Uranie'. The attribution may
well be false.

Charlettus. Charlettus Percivallo suo, 1706. *See*
Alsop, Anthony.

C133 Charley. Charley in the chair. *Dublin, printed in the
year* 1748.
½°: *1–2*, 2 columns.
'My honest friend, I'll tell you news'
    A satire on Charles Lucas.
C.

C134 Charmers. The charmers. A poem. Humbly
inscrib'd to the hon. Lady Gore. *Dublin, printed for
Peter Wilson,* 1743.
4°: *A*² B–C⁴ D²; *i–ii* iii–iv, *5* 6–24.
    A poem to the author is signed 'J. Marshall'.
'Now surly winter shews his furrow'd face'
L(11602.gg.24/8),O,DA.

Charmes. 'Les charmes de Stow; ou description
de la belle maison de plaisance de my lord Cobham,
avec une traduction angloise. [*London*] *Nourse.*
Price 1*s.*' (*BM, GM* June 1749)
    Listed in *GM* under 'Poetry and plays', but
in *BM* under 'Miscellanies'; it seems probable
that it is a prose work.

C135 Charmion, John. Æ. M. S. eximii pietate, eruditione, prudentia' viri D. Ebenezræ Pembertoni,
apud Bostonienses Americanos prædicatoris vere
evangelici. Epitaphium. [*Edinburgh,* 1717?]
½°: 1 side, 1 column.
    Dated as 1717 in printed catalogue of E;
bound with other material of 1724–27.
'Hic jacet ereptus medijs, proh fata! trophæis'
    At end: 'Posuit Jo. Charmion in literas|Litera-
tosque affectu percitus.'
E.

Charms. The charms of liberty, 1709. *See*
Cavendish, William *duke of Devonshire.*

Charnock. Charnock's remains, 1713. *See* Brereton, Thomas.

C136 Chase. 'The chace: a poem. In heroick verse.
[*London*] Printed for B. Dickenson. Price 1*s.*'
(*LM* Aug 1735)

    A rhyming version of Somervile's *The chace.*
'The gently warbling lyre no more I string'

C137 —— Written originally in four books in blank
verse, by William Somervile, esq; *London, printed
for B. Dickinson,* 1749.
8°: (frt+) A–H⁴; *1–5* 6–64.
NN.

C138 Chase, J. The sixth epistle of the first book of
Horace, imitated by J. Chase. *London, printed for
D. Browne,* 1740. (*GM,LM* April)
2°: *A*² B–C²; *1* 2–11 *12 blk.*
'Would you be happy and continue so'
    The identification of this author with the
following is uncertain.
LdU-B; CtY,KU.

C139 Chase, John. An ode. On the success of her
majesty's arms, under his grace the Duke of
Marlborough. *London, sold by John Morphew,* 1706.
(17 Dec, Luttrell)
2°: A–C²; *1–4* 5–12.
'I never slept on fam'd Parnassus head'
OW,LdU-B; CtY(+half-title from another poem),
DFo(Luttrell),MH,TxU.

C140 Chaucer. 'Chaucer's Farmer and fryar modernized. [*London*] *Cooper, Jones, G. Woodfall.* Price
6*d.*' (*BM, GM* June 1746)

—— Chaucer's whims, 1701. *See* Pittis, William.

Chaucer, Geoffrey.
Ogle, George: The Canterbury tales of Chaucer,
moderniz'd by several hands, 1741, 1742.

———

Cobb, Samuel: The carpenter of Oxford, or, the
Miller's tale from Chaucer, 1712. *See* C245.

—— [*idem*] The miller's tale from Chaucer, 1725.
See C246.

[Prior, Matthew:] Earl Robert's mice. A poem in
imitation of Chaucer, 1712. *See* P1073–5.

The miller of Trompington: being an exercise
upon Chaucer's Reeve's tale, 1715. *See* M233.

Brown bread and honour, a tale. Moderniz'd from
an ancient manuscript of Chaucer, 1716. *See*
B501.

Catcott, A. S.: The court of love, a vision from
Chaucer, 1717. *See* C69.

Dart, John: The complaint of the black knight from
Chaucer, 1718, 1720. *See* D48–50.

Sewell, George: The proclamation of Cupid...
A poem from Chaucer, 1718. *See* S372.

[Markland, John:] Three new poems, viz. I. Family
duty: or, the monk and the merchant's wife. Being
the Shipman's tale from Chaucer. Moderniz'd,
1721. *See* M104.

Chaucer, G.

[Philips, *Captain*:] The romance of the rose. Imitated from Chaucer, 1721. *See* P202.

Ogle, George: Gualtherus and Griselda: or the Clerk of Oxford's tale. From Boccace, Petrarch, and Chaucer, 1739, 1741. *See* O95-6.

Chaucer's Farmer and fryar modernized, 1746. *See* C140.

[Jackson, Andrew:] Matrimonial scenes: consisting of the Seaman's tale, the Manciple's tale, the character of the Wife of Bath, the tale of the Wife of Bath, and her five husbands. All modernized from Chaucer, 1750. *See* J9.

'**Chaunter, Humphrey.**' King George for England, 1745. *See* K47.

C141 Chelsea. The Chelsea monarch: or, money rules all. A new court ballad. *London, printed for C. Davies; sold by the booksellers of London & Westminster*, 1731. (*MChr* May)
2°: A² B²; *1-2* 3-7 *8 blk.*
　　Percival XX. Copies at O, CtY are on paper watermarked with the royal arms; others with pro patria.
'Tho' money thus reigns ---- as by title divine'
　　A satire against venal politicians. Walpole had a house in Chelsea.
L(11602.i.26/6),O(uncut); CSmH(uncut),CtY (uncut),DLC(uncut),*MH-BA*,TxU.

C142 Chetwood, William Rufus. Kilkenny: or, the old man's wish. *Dublin, printed for the author; sold by G. Faulkner, G. & A. Ewing, P. Wilson, J. Esdall,* 1748.
4°: A-B⁴ C²; *1-2* 3-20.
'Since man is surely born to die'
L(11643.bbb.20/3); *NjP.*

Chevalier. The Chevalier de St. George: an heroi-comick poem, 1718. *See* Purney, Thomas.

— The Chevalier de St. Patrick, 1734. *See* Dalacourt, James.

C143 — The Chevaliers market or highland fair. [*London*] *Sold* [*by George Bickham?*] *in May's Buildings, Covent Garden,* [1745.]
obl ½°: 1 side, 4 columns.
　　Large engraving with title engraved below; the letterpress text is not present in the L copy and is mounted separately in NNP. The engraved imprint is found in the L copy only; the date is given in the engraved publication statement.
'Here, loyal subjects, I am come'
　　A satire against the Young Pretender.
L(P&D 2660, print only); NNP.

C144 [Cheyn, William.] The friendship of Christ: to which is added a description of charity... By a true

Cheyn, W. The friendship of Christ

son of the church of Scotland. *Edinburgh, printed by Robert Brown for the author, and are to be sold at Mr. John Macky's shop,* 1718.
8°: π⁴ A-R⁴ ²A-B⁸; *1-8* 9-142 *143-144 blk,* 1-32.
　　Folding table between pp. 44/45; p. 83, title to 'Adam's dream'; ²A-B⁸, 'The old man's warning to the young; as an appendix to Adam's dream'.
'Oh, how sweet must the meditation be'
　　Dedication signed 'W.C.' Copies are found bound with the other poems by Cheyn below.
L(11631.b.12),O,E; NNUT.

C145 — God's glorious perfections shining in Christ, with the blessed uses of those in three parts... [*Edinburgh*] *Printed in the year* ⟨1718⟩.
8°: A-O⁴ P¹; *i-xii,* 1 2-'92' [102]. '92' err.
　　Folding plate between pp. 10/11; all copies seen have title cropt.
'Sure I have read of many wonder'
　　Dedication signed.
L(11631.b.12),O,E(lacks plate); NNUT.

C146 [—] Some pressing motives, to the cheerful performance of these four Christian dutyes... [*Edinburgh,* 1718?]
8°: A-F⁴ G²; *1-2* 3-52. 52 err.
'Upon the lord thy burden cast'
　　Copies are found bound with the other poems by Cheyn above.
L(11631.b.12),O,E; NNUT.

Chichlaeus. Chichlæus, [1716?] *See* Randolph, Herbert.

C147 Chicken, Edward. ⟨The collier's wedding; a poem.⟩ ⟨*Newcastle upon Tyne, printed and sold by John White,*⟩ [173-?]
2°: A-I²; *1-3* 4-36.
　　The copy seen has A1, I2 supplied in facsimile by John Bell; the title and imprint are taken from that source. The ms. described in the edition of 1829 had an author's note 'written in the year 1729'.
'I sing not of great Cæsar's might'
NeU(mutilated, lacks A1, I2).

C148 [—] No; -- this is the truth. A poem. *Sold by the booksellers in Newcastle upon Tyne,* [1741.]
2°: A-C²; *1-3* 4-11 *12 blk.* 11 err.
　　In spite of the signatures, the watermarks suggest the true collation is A⁶.
''Midst all the clamours, noise, and false alarms'
　　Ascribed to Edward Chicken, apparently on the evidence of a manuscript described in the 1829 edition of *The collier's wedding.* A reply to *Is this the truth?* [1741], attacking Richard Ridley, father of Matthew Ridley, a candidate in the Newcastle election, and recommending Walter Blackett. Answered by *No -- that's a mistake,* [1741.]
L(11631.h.22),NeA,NeP; MH.

Chicken, E.

[—] A Sunday evening's conversation at Benwell [actually by Taylor Thirkeld], 1726. *See* T154.

C149 Chimerical. The chymerical patriot: or, Lucas awake. *Dublin, printed by T. Knowles,* 1749.
8⁰: A⁴; *1–3* 4–8.
'One morn serene, ere Phœbus had display'd'
A satire on Charles Lucas.
L(11631.bb.55),O(2).

C150 Chimney-sweeper. The chimney-sweeper in disgrace: or, a dialogue between the lord bishop of — and T.N. chimney-sweeper in St. Margaret's parish. To the tune of Chivy-chace. [*London,* 1708.]
½⁰: *1–2,* 1 column.
'All-in the city West-minster'
Crum A964a: 'A dialogue...' A satire on John Moore, bishop of Ely, canvassing 'Tom Negro' for Henry Boyle in the Westminster election.
O,MC,Chatsworth(ms. date 1708); TxU.

C151 Chinese. A Chinese tale. Written originally by that prior of China the facetious Sou Ma Quang...under the title of Chamyam tcho chang, or, Chamyam with her leg upon a table. First translated by a famous missionary: and now re-translated by a society of linguists. Inscribed to Thomas Dawson esq;... *London, printed for J. Cooper; sold by the pamphlet-sellers of London & Westminster,* [1740.] (*GM,LM* Feb)
4⁰: A¹ B–G² H¹; *i–ii,* 1–25 *26 blk.*
The title gives the price as 'one shilling. With a curious frontispiece, taken from a large China punch-bowl just come over, in that gentleman's [Thomas Dawson's] possession; design'd and engrav'd by Mess. Gravelot and Scotin. Price one shilling... N.B. The print will be sold for 2s. 6d. singly.' The copy seen has no frontispiece.
'Say, muse! what has the largest share'
An erotic tale. *A court lady's curiosity,* advertised in *LDP* 29 Jan 1741, is clearly related to this work.
L(1967).

C151·5 —— *London printed, and sold by the pamphlet-sellers of London & Westminster,* 1740.
8⁰: (frt+) A¹ B–C⁴ D¹; *1–2* 3–19 20.
With a very free folding frontispiece.
Institute for Sex Research.

Chiron. Chiron to Achilles, 1732. *See* Jacob, Hildebrand.

C152 Chivalry. Chivalrie, no trifle --- or, the knight and his lady: a tale. *Dublin, printed in the year* 1746.
8⁰: A⁴; *1* 2–8.
'No packet arriv'd? and the wind still at east---'
Attributed to 'a young parson named Stevens' in Sir John Gilbert *History of the city of Dublin*

Chivalry, no trifle

(1861) II.33, and to 'Stevens or Stephens' by by *O'Donoghue.* There is no reason to doubt the attribution, but it has not been possible to identify the author. A satire occasioned by George Faulkner's refusal of a knighthood and his wife's regrets.
L(1959),O,DA,DN,DT(2)+; NN.

C153 — Chivalry, no trifle... *Dublin, printed in the year* 1747.
8⁰: A⁴; *1* 2–8.
C.

C154 —— Address'd to the Earl of Chesterfield. *Dublin, printed: London, reprinted for A. Freeman, and to be had at all the booksellers and pamphlet-shops,* 1747 [1746]. (*GM* Nov)
2⁰: *⁴; *1–3* 4–8.
The collation is uncertain, but the second leaf is signed '*2'. The 'London bookseller's preface' identifies Faulkner as the subject.
L(1973); IU(2),MH,TxU.

C155 — [*idem*] Knighthood, no trifle----or, Lady Wou'd-be; a tale...The second edition. *Dublin, printed: London, reprinted for A. Freeman, and to be had of all the booksellers and pamphlet-shops,* 1747.
2⁰: *⁴; *1–3* 4–8.
Apparently a reimpression.
LVA-D(presentation to Garrick, Feb); ICN,OCU.

C156 Chloe. 'Cloe convinc'd: or, seeing's believing. A tale. To which is added, An English padlock. By Mr. Prior.' [*London, printed for W. Shaw.*] (*SJEP* 13 Feb 1733)
Listed in *SJEP* with an advertisement for *Good goose don't bite,* 1733; also in *LM* Feb. Possibly a new edition of [Hildebrand Jacob] *The curious maid,* 1720.

C157 — Chloe monita. [*London?* 173–?]
8⁰: A⁴; *1* 2–7 *8 blk.*
Title in half-title form. English and Latin text on facing pages. The English text was printed in *GM* March 1735.
'Dum fastu me, chara Chloe, fas præter & æquum'
'Dear Chloe, while thus beyond measure'
O.

— Chloe surpriz'd, 1732. *See* Shepherd, Samuel.

Choice. The choice. A poem, 1701–. *See* Pomfret, John.

C158 — A choice new song, call'd, She-land, and Robinocracy. To all sorts of tunes. [*London*] *Printed in the year* 1711.
½⁰: 1 side, 2 columns.
26 numbered stanzas.
'She-land, the praise of all the earth'
A satire on Robert Harley.
L(112.f.44/31; G.559/6),LLP,E,DT,Crawford.

A choice new song

C159 —— [*London?* 1711.]
½°: 1 side, 2 columns.
Stanzas not numbered.
'The [!] land, the praise of all the earth'
MH.

C160 — A choice penny-worth of wit: or, clear distinction between a virtuous wife, and a wanton horlot [!]. In three parts... [*London*] *Printed for S. Wates in Fleetstreet*, [1707?]
8°: *A*⁴; *1* 2–8.
A chap-book.
'Here is a penyworth of wit'
The story of William Lane.
L(1076.1.22/42, ms. date 1707).

Choirochorographia. Χοιροχωρογραφια: sive, Hoglandiæ descriptio, 1709. *See* Richards, Thomas.

[**Cholmondeley, Charles.**] Taffi's masterpiece: or, the Cambro-British invention, 1709. *See* T3.

C161 [**Choppin, Richard.**] A just character of the revd. Mr. Boyce. Written by Mr. R— C—. [*Dublin*, 1728.]
½°: 1 side, 2 columns.
'A goodly teacher of the holy train'
Richard Choppin is certainly the author intended; he preached a funeral sermon on Boyse, 8 Dec 1728. This could conceivably be a versification by another hand.
L(1890.e.5/16).

C162 **Chorley, Josiah.** A metrical index to the Bible: or alphabetical tables of the holy scriptures, in metre. Composed I. To help the memory. II. To con-note with the letters, the numbers, of the several chapters. III. And to supply the want of a small concordance... *Norwich, printed by W. Chase for Tho. Goddard*, 1711. (*SR* 17 July)
8°: π⁴ *A*–*D*⁸; *i–viii*, 1–64.
Entered in SR to Josiah Chorley by Henry Chorley; deposit copy at EU.
'All things created Moses writes'
A revision of Chorley's *A brief memorial of the Bible*, 1688 (*Wing* C3926).
L(1017.k.18/2),O,E,EU,NwP(3)+; *MB*(presentation copy, 19 July 1711)

C163 —— The second edition. *Norwich*, 1714. (23 Feb?)
Probably the edition advertised in *DC* 23 Feb 1714 as 'this day is published... Sold by T. Goddard in Norwich, and E. Matthews [*London*]'.
NwP(mislaid 1966).

Christ. Christ's kirk on the green, 1718–. *See* Ramsay, Allan.

C164 **Christening.** The christening. A satirical poem. In which are contain'd the humorous transactions,

The christening

speeches, and behaviour of the guests who were present at the ceremony and entertainment. *London, printed for W. James*, 1732. (*GSJ* 6 July)
2°: *A*(2 ll) B–C²; *1–4* 5–12. A1 frt.
The frontispiece is titled 'The court gossips', and the work was advertised with that title. Listed in *GM*, *LM* July as printed for S. Slow.
'When nature prompts, and all the world's on fire'
A satire on Anne Vane's illegitimate child by Frederick, prince of Wales.
L(643.m.14/3),O; CSmH(–A1),DLC(–A1), ICU(–A1),MH(cropt),OCU+.

C165 —— [*Dublin*] *Printed by T. Walsh*, 1733.
8°: *A*⁴; *1–2* 3–8.
DA; IU.

C166 **Christian.** The Christian hero. A poem. [*Dublin?*] *Printed in the year* 1746.
4°: *A*⁴; *1–2* 3–8.
'From those bright mansions of eternal day'
On the Young Pretender.
DK.

— 'The Christian hero's martial looks here shine', [1745?] *See* On seeing the prince's picture, [1745?]

— The Christian muse: or, second gift of Theophilus Philanthropos, 1740. *See* Poole, Robert.

C167 — The Christian priest. A poem sacred to the memory of the truly reverend, learned, and pious Dr. Samuel Clarke... *London, printed for B. Creake*, 1729. (*MChr* 19 June)
8°: A–C⁴; *i–viii*, 1–11 *12–16*. 16 advt.
'Ye sons of sacred truth exalt your lays'
Dedication signed 'R.W.'
L(11631.e.67).

— Christian songs, 1749. *See* Glas, John.

C168 — The Christian test: or, the coalition of faith and reason. A sacred poem. Submitted to the candid censure of the friends, and to the chicane and caville of the enemies of Christianity. In two books. Book 1. *London, printed for R. Amey*, 1742. (*LM* Feb)
2°: *A*² B–D²; *[2] i* ii, *5* 6–16.
'Among the various notions of mankind'
Dedicated to Lord Charles Noel Somerset.
O.

— The Christian's epinikion, or song of triumph, 1743. *See* Morell, Thomas.

C169 — The Christian's exercise. A poem. *London, printed in the year* 1712.
12°: A–D⁶; *1–4* 5–48.
'Oh! that I had the pinions of a dove'
Dedication to the treasurer and governors of Christ's Hospital signed 'N.M.', apparently by an ex-pupil.
L(11660.de.4).

Christianity

Christianity. Christianity without persecution, 1719. *See* Waldron, George.

C170 Christmas. A Christmas box for Namby Pamby, or, a second part to the same tune. [*Dublin*, 1725.]
slip: 1 side, 1 column.
    Teerink 924, *Williams* 1125, *Bond* 80.
'Now the day is almost peeping'
    Ball 202 tentatively ascribes this to Swift, but the attribution is not accepted by Williams. A satire on Ambrose Philips.
L(1890.e.5/128).

— A Christmas carol, 1715. *See* Edwards, Thomas.

— A Christmas invitation to the Lord Carteret, 1725. *See* Smedley, Jonathan.

C171 Christus. Christus natus est. Christ is born. The sinners redemption: wherein is described the nativity of Lord Jesus Christ... *London printed, and sold by J. Bradford*, 1701. (15 May, Luttrell)
1°: 1 side, 4 columns.
    Large woodcut at head. This title entered in *SR* by Charles Brown and Thomas Norris, 20 Sept 1712, as 'old copy'.
'All you that are to mirth inclin'd'
MH(Luttrell),MWiW-C.

— Christus patiens: or the sufferings of Christ an heroic poem, 1720–. *See* Beckingham, Charles [Monsieur Rapin's Latin heroick poem].

Chudleigh, Mary, *Lady*. Poems on several occasions. Together with the Song of the three children paraphras'd. *London, printed by W.B. for Bernard Lintott*, 1703.
8°: pp. 126, 75.   L,O; CtY,MH.

—— The second edition. *London, printed by D.L. for Bernard Lintott*, 1709. (*DC* 17 Aug)
8°: pp. 126, 75.   L,O; ICU,TxU.
    Issued with *The ladies defence*, 1709, added.

— [reissue] The second edition. *London, printed for Bernard Lintott; sold by Charles Rivington*, 1713.
    L.
    Cancel title.

—— The third edition, corrected. *London, printed for Bernard Lintot*, 1722.
12°: pp. 269.   L,O; ICU,MH.
    The copyright appeared in a trade sale of Lintot, 8 Nov 1743 (cat. at O-JJ).

—— The fourth edition, corrected. *London, printed for J. Wren*, 1750.
12°: pp. 269.   MiU.
    Probably a reissue of the preceding; the title is a cancel.

— Essays upon several subjects in prose and verse. *London, printed by T.H. for R. Bonwicke, W. Freeman, T. Goodwin, J. Walthoe, M. Wotton,*

Chudleigh, M., *Lady*

S. Manship, J. Nicholson, R. Parker, B. Tooke, & R. Smith, 1710.
8°: pp. 240.   L,O; CtY,TxU.
    A few poems are imbedded in a prose structure.

———————

C172 [—] The ladies defence: or, the bride-woman's counsellor answer'd: a poem. In a dialogue between Sir John Brute, Sir William Loveall, Melissa, and a parson. Written by a lady. *London, printed for John Deeve*, 1701. (*PM* 22 Feb)
2°: A² a² B² C–G²; *i–viii, 1–23 24 blk*. 23 advt.
Watermark: London arms.
'Welcome, thou brave defender of our right'
    Dedication signed 'M---y C-------'; the following edition usually bound with her *Poems*, 1709.
L(11630.g.6),O; CSmH,DFo,ICN,MH(uncut, ms. date 22 Feb),NN+.

C173 [—] [fine paper?]
Watermark: Amsterdam arms.
CtY.

C174 [—] — *London, printed by D. L.* [*Dryden Leach?*] *for Bernard Lintott*, 1709.
8°: A*–B*⁸; *i–ii 3 iv–xxix xxx–xxxii*. xxx–xxxii advt.
    Issued with her *Poems*, 1709. Lintot paid Cox a guinea for the copyright, 30 July 1709 (*Nichols* VIII. 295).
L(11631.e.9/2; 11659.aaa.91/2),O; ICN,ICU, OCU,TxU.

Church. The church and monarchy secur'd, [1711.] *See* Trapp, Joseph.

C175 — The church in no danger. A new song. [*London*, 1707?]
½°: 1 side, 1 column.
    Wing C3994A, misdating it 1689. Four lines of ms. music between title and text.
'While fanaticks, and papists, and quakers agree'
    Crum W1829, dating it 1707. A tory song.
MH.

C176 — The church militant, or the whigs triumphant. Being the ch------ of En------ds lamentation for the contempt of her Memorial. An iambick poem. *London, printed for Benjamin Bragge*, 1705. (*WL* July, Aug)
4°: A–D⁴; *1–2 3–32*.
'Since the sons of the church'
    Attributed to Defoe by Robert Clare, one of Harley's informers; see H. L. Snyder in *The library* V. 22 (1967) 337. His attributions seem in many cases to be wild guesses.
DT; IU,InU.

C177 —— [*London?* 1705.]
4°: A²; *1–4*, 2 columns.
    Drop-head title only. Presumably a piracy.
L(11660.bb.20).

The **church** of England martyr

C178 — The church of England martyr. A poem. Inscrib'd to all loyal church-men. *Dublin, printed by E. Waters,* [1710?]
4°: *A*⁴; *1–3* 4–7 *8 blk.*
'This day for solemn sorrow set apart'
On the martyrdom of Charles I, probably in connection with the Sacheverell affair.
DFo.

C179 — The church of England's address to the members of her communion. Especially to such as have laid down their offices at this critical juncture... *London, printed in the year 1704.* (*TC* Trinity)
2°: *A*² B–C²; *1–2* 3–12.
'Ye sons that at my altars fall'
Crum Y133.
MR-C; TxU.

C180 — The church of England's joy on the happy accession of her most sacred majesty Queen Anne, to the throne... *London printed, and sold by John Nutt, 1702.* (22 April, Luttrell)
2°: *A*² B–C²; *i–iv*, 1–8.
'My muse, thy ambition cease; beware'
ICN(Luttrell),MH.

— The church of England's new hymn, to the state scaffold, 1710. *See A hymn to the scaffold,* 1710.

— The church of England's new toast, 1710. *See A toast for all true hearts,* 1710.

C181 — The church of Scotlands lamentation concerning the setting up of plays and commedies. March 1715. [*Edinburgh,* 1715.]
½°: 1 side, 2 columns.
'Let not the news in Gath be told'
A presbyterian attack on the theatre in Edinburgh.
L(Rox.III.553).

— The church-scuffle, 1719. *See* Breval, J. D.

C182 — The church too hard for the state, or the knight overthrown, a poem. *London, printed for A. Moore; sold by the booksellers of London & Westminster,* 1729. (*MChr* 3 Feb)
2°: *A*² B²; *1–2* 3–8. 8 advt.
'Of ev'ry realm how hard's the fate'
L(11630.h.57/1),LSC; OCU,TxU.

C183 — — '*London*' [*Dublin*], *printed in the year* 1729.
8°: *A*⁴; *1–3* 4–8.
L(11633.b.8),DA; CtY,ICU.

C184 — The church yard: a satirical poem. *London, printed for T. Cooper; sold by the booksellers of London & Westminster,* 1739. (*GM, LM* May)
2°: *A*² B–E²; *1–5* 6–19 *20 blk.* A1 hft.
'Are there such bards, who, fond on courts to wait'
Largely a satire on contemporary poets, comparing them with the dead.

The **church** yard

L(11630.h.12),O,LdU-B,BaP; CSmH,CtY,MH, OCU(uncut, −A1),TxU+.

C185 [**Churchill, William.**] October; a poem: inscrib'd to the fox-hunters of Great-Britain. In two books. *London, printed by Richard Harbin,* 1717. (25 July)
8°: *A*⁴ B–G⁴; *1–5* 6–55 *56 blk.* A1 hft.
Advertisement in *DC* 22 July for publication on 'Thursday next' [25 July]; subscribers to send for their books to Mr. Halford's. This issue without a bookseller's name is clearly the subscribers' issue.
'Let Gallic bards, inspir'd with genuine wines'
Early ms. ascription to Churchill in TxHR copy.
YU; NN,TxHR.

C186 [—] [another issue] *London, printed by Richard Harbin; sold by J. Morphew,* 1717.
8°: *A*⁴ B–G⁴; *1–5* 6–55 *56 blk.* A1 hft.
Advertised in *PB* 12 Oct 1717 with this imprint, but possibly originally published with the subscribers' issue. Copies seen apparently have a variant sheet B from the preceding.
O; CSmH(−A1),CtY.

C187 [—] A poem humbly inscrib'd to his grace the Duke of Marlborough, occasion'd upon his repeated victories in Flanders... Wrote in the camp by W. C. an officer of Major General How's regiment. *London, printed for Benjamin Bragg,* 1709. (*DC* 19 May)
2°: A–D²; *i–iv*, 1–12.
'Ye tuneful nine, that drink the purling stream'
Early ms. attribution to Churchill in L copy.
L(11642.i.9/1); DFo(Luttrell, 19 May).

[**Chute, Francis.**] Miscellanies, upon several subjects; occasionally written. By Mr. Joseph Gay, 1719. *See* 'Gay, Joseph'.

The pseudonym 'Joseph Gay' was used by both J. D. Beval and Chute when writing for Curll, with consequent problems of who wrote what.

C188 — Beauty and virtue. A poem sacred to the memory of Anne, late countess of Sunderland. Humbly inscrib'd to his grace the Duke of Marlborough. *London, printed for R. Burleigh,* 1716. (25 July, Luttrell)
8°: *B*⁴ C–D⁴; *1–4* '1' 5–20, 1–4. B1 hft; D3–4 advt.
The Luttrell copy is recorded in Pickering & Chatto cat. 289/63. Listed in *MC* July as by 'Mr. Chale'. Reissued in *The ladies miscellany,* 1718. A half share of the copyright formed part of lot 37 in the trade sale of John Hooke, 31 May 1731 (cat. at O-JJ), sold to Osborn.
'What bounds to sorrow shall the muse propose'

Chute, F. Beauty and virtue

L(701.d.12/4,−B1),O,LdU-B(−B1); CSmH
(−D3-4),DFo,InU(−B1),MH(−D3-4),TxU
(−D3-4)+.

C189 [—] The petticoat, an heroi-comical poem. In two
books. By Mr. Gay. *London, printed for R. Burleigh,*
1716. (28 June)
8°: *A*⁴ B–F⁴; [4] i–iii iv, 1–39 40 blk. A1 hft;
iii err.
> Bond 48. Dated 28 June by *Straus, Curll*;
> listed in *MC* June '... N.B. Not written by
> Mr. Gay'.
'Since in such odd fantastick times as these'
> Frequently attributed to Breval, who also used
> the pseudonym of Joseph Gay; but the assign-
> ment of title at L (Add. MS. 38728, fol 41)
> dated 4 July is between Chute and Curll &
> Hooke, for six guineas.
L(11631.d.21),O,CT(−A1),E(−A1),LdU-B+;
CSmH,CtY,ICN,KU(stitched, uncut),TxU+.

C190 [—] — The second edition corrected. *London,
printed for R. Burleigh,* 1716. (9 July)
8°: *A*⁴ B–F⁴; [4] i–iii iv, 1–39 40 blk. A1 hft.
> Dated 9 July by *Straus, Curll.* Reissued in
> *The ladies miscellany,* 1718.
L(11602.e.1/2),O(−A1),OW(2),CT(−A1);
CSmH(−A1),CtY,IU,MH(uncut),TxU+.

C191 [—] — By Mr. Gay. *Dublin, printed for G. Risk,*
1716.
12°: A–B⁶; 1–2 3–23 24 blk.
L(1481.aa.1/2),DN,AdU; CtY,MH.

C192 [—] [idem] The hoop-petticoat... By Mr. Gay...
The third edition. *London, printed for E. Curll &
J. Hooke, & W. Taylor,* 1720.
8°: A–F⁴; i–iv v–vii viii, 1–39 40 blk. A1 hft,
advt.
> A third share of the copyright 'with about 200
> books' formed part of lot 37 of the trade sale of
> Hooke, 31 May 1731 (cat. at O-JJ), sold to
> Osborn.
L(11631.c.22, title mutilated),LG(−A1),O(2,
−A1),C; CSmH,CtY(−A1),ICN,MH,TxU
(−A1)+.

C193 'Cibber, Colley.' The following address, from the
hundreds of Drury, was this day presented to his
majesty by Mr. Cibber... To the king's most
excellent majesty, the humble address of the mayor,
aldermen, and common-council... [*London,* 1718.]
¼°: 1 side, 2 columns.
> Dated at head 'St. James's, Jan. 1. 17¹⁷⁄₁₈.'
> Printed with *The bed-tester-plot,* [1718]; the
> O copy is not divided.
'Sir,/Since the scum of these three nations'
> A Jacobite satire, written as though by Cibber,
> but in fact satirical of him.
O,Crawford; CSmH,MH(cropt).

C194 — An ode for his majesty's birth-day, October 30,
1731. By Mr. Cibber, servant to his majesty.

Cibber, C. An ode for his majesty

London, printed for John Watts, 1731. (*MChr* Oct)
4°: *A*² B² *C*¹; 1–5 6–9 10 blk. A1 hft.
'When Charles, from anarchy's retreat'
L(11630.d.12/16).

C195 '—' An ode for the new year. Written by Colley
Cibber, esq; poet laureat. [*London?* 1731?]
½°: 1 side, 2 columns.
> No type flowers at head. *Percival* appendix
> 29.
'God prosper long our gracious k—'
> A ms. version at L(Add. MS. 28095, fol 69) is
> endorsed 'Westley's Ode for Cibber, 1731'.
> *Ault, New Light* 316 suggests Pope's author-
> ship. Samuel Wesley and Pope were in asso-
> ciation in 1730, and they may have been
> jointly concerned in it.
CtY (Osborn collection).

C196 '—' — [*London?* 1731?]
¼°: 1 side, 2 columns.
> Double row of type-flowers at head, arranged
> in pairs about a horizontal axis.
L(C.40.m.10/176),LSA.

C197 '—' [another impression?]
> Double row of type-flowers at head, arranged
> in symmetrical groups of four.
TxU.

C198 — An ode to his majesty, for the new-year, 17³⁰⁄₃₁.
London, printed for John Watts, 1731. (*GSJ* 7 Jan)
4°: *A*² B² *C*¹; 1–5 6–9 10 blk. A1 hft.
'Once more, the ever-circling sun'
L(11630.c.9/8); CSmH.

C199 — 'An ode to his majesty, on new-year's-day, 1732.
[*London*] Sold by J. Roberts.' (*GSJ* 1 Jan 1732;
MChr Jan)
> The imprint is taken from *MChr,* which gives
> the price as 1s. against 6d. in *GSJ.* The text
> is printed in *GM* Jan with first line:
'Awake with joyous songs the day'

[—] The prologue and epilogue of George Barnwell [the epilogue by Cibber], [1731?] *See*
P1120.

C200 — A prologue in the opera call'd Camilla. Written
and spoke by Mr. Cibber at the Theatre Royal in
Drury-lane, July the 5th 1706. *London, printed for
Bernard Lintott,* 1706. (10 July, Luttrell)
½°: 1 side, 1 column.
> Advertised in *DC* 12 July; listed in *WL* June
> (probably published later in July).
'While frowning Mars our smiling isle surrounds'
> Reprinted with commentary by E. L. Avery
> in *SEL* 5 (1965) 455f.
ICN(Luttrell).

C201 **Cibber, Theophilus.** The association: or, liberty
and loyalty. Verses occasion'd by the present
unnatural rebellion. *London, printed for W.
Bickerton,* 1745. (*GM* Oct)
2°: *A*² B² *C*¹; 1–2 3–9 10 blk.

Cibber, T. The association

L copy from Tom's Coffee House, possibly dated 28 Oct.
'Wrongs to redress, and justice to maintain'
L(1962),AdU.

Cicero, Marcus Tullius.
Denham, *Sir* John: Cato major of old age, 1710. *See* D213.

Catherall, Samuel: Cato major. A poem. Upon the model of Tully's Essay of old age, 1725. *See* C72.

Cider. Cyder. A poem. In two books, 1708–. *See* Philips, John.

Cinquième. Cinquième dialogue entre deux freres, [1707.] *See* Dialogue entre deux freres, 1707.

C202 **Circumvention.** The circumvention, or, the amorous successful politician; a tale... Render'd into English. *London, printed for A. Moore; sold by the booksellers of London & Westminster*, [1727.] (*MC* April)
4°: A–B⁴; *1–2* 3–16.
'There liv'd a great and mighty prince'
Clearly not a translation; on Lord Crafty's amorous success.
L(1077.k.39); ICN,*OCU*.

Circus. The circus: or, British olympicks, 1709. *See* Browne, Joseph.

C203 **Citizen.** The citizen's procession, or, the smugler's success and the patriots disappointment. Being an excellent new ballad on the excise-bill. *London, printed for A. Dodd*, 1733. (*GM* July)
2°: *A*² B²; *1–3* 4–8.
Percival appendix 50.
'You puts that have land, and you cits that have none'
In defence of the defeated excise bill.
L(162.n.69),LSC,LU,O(4),*MR*; CSmH,CtY, InU,MH,OCU+.

C204 **City.** The city, in glory: or Downing-street, in the dumps. [*London*, 1740.]
slip: 1 side, 1 column.
Percival LIX.
'Good people give attention now'
On the election of Sir Humphrey Parsons as lord mayor of London, instead of the expected Sir Robert Godschall.
C.

C205 — A city intrigue: or, the sick lady's cure. A poem. With the comical adventure between Strephon and Sylvia. *London printed, and sold by J. Roberts*, 1714.
8°: *A*⁴ B–C⁴; *i–viii, 1* 2–14 *15–16 blk*. A1 hft.
'On Monday, August twenty seven'
Dedication signed 'S-------- B--------'.
O(–A1); OCU.

City

C206 — The city lady's choice of a new standing member, in the room of the late fallen one. A new ballad. *London, printed for W. Webb*, 1742.
2°: *A*² < B²; *1–2* 3–7 *8 blk*.
Rothschild 226. Compare *The ladies choice for new members*, advertised in 1747.
'Some coblers turn poets, to serve their best friends'
The poem has only a sexual, no political, significance.
O; IU(uncut).

C207 — The city madam, and the country maid: or, opposite characters of a virtuous housewifely damsel, and a mechanick's town-bred daughter. By the author of The pleasures of a single life, &c. *London, printed for John Nutt*, 1702.
2°: *A*² B–D²; *i–iv, 1–12*.
Half-bred-gentlewoman: 'Proud, lazy, lustful, ignorant and vain'
Rural virgin: 'Modest, engaging, innocent and fair'
The MH copy has an early ms. attribution 'Mr More', not further identified. Listed in *Rawlinson* under Thomas Brown, together with an incomplete entry for *The pleasures of a single life*; Rawlinson apparently had doubts. Brown can scarcely have written *The grand mistake*, 1705, which claims to be by the same author; he died in 1704. Sometimes attributed to Edward Ward, following *Lowndes*.
O; CLU-C,CtY,ICN,MH,TxU(2).

C208 — [*idem*] Miss Prue, in her tempting pinner; or, the true character of a citizen's daughter. *London, printed by E.B. near Ludgate*, [1706?]
8°: *A*⁴; *1* 2–8.
A reprint of 'The city madam', the first poem above.
'Proud, lazy, lustful, ignorant and vain'
Arnold Muirhead, St. Albans.

C209 — An answer to Miss Prue, in her tempting pinner: or, a true description of a maid, bred up in the country at her rock and reel. A poem. *London, printed by Henry Hills*, 1706.
8°: *A*⁴; *1* 2–8.
A reprint of the second poem in C207.
'Modest, engaging, innocent and fair'
Forster.

C210 — The city ramble: or, the wolf turn'd shepherd. To the tune of, As down in a meadow, &c. [*London*, 1737.]
slip: 1 side, 1 column.
'As lately through London I rambl'd along'
Crum A1586: 'On the 3 per cent scheme 1737'. A satire against Sir John Barnard's scheme for reducing the national debt.
O.

C211 — The city struggle. A satire. Occasion'd by the late election of a lord mayor. *London, printed for T. Robins; sold at the Royal Exchange, St. James's, Bond St., Charing Cross*, 1740. (*GM, LM* Oct)

The **city** struggle

4⁰: *A*⁴ B⁴; *1–5* 6–15 *16 blk*. A1 hft.
'Whoever hopes, fair peace! to see thee more?'
> On the election of Sir Humphrey Parsons
> instead of Sir Robert Godschall.

CtY(uncut).

C212 — The city triumphant: or, the burning of the excise-monster. A new ballad. To the tune of, King John and the abbot of Canterbury. *London, printed for T. Reynolds; sold by the booksellers and pamphletsellers of London & Westminster, 1733.* (*GM* April)
2⁰: *A*² B²; *1–2* 3–8.
> *Percival* appendix 51.

'Historians relate that in Afric are bred'
L(840.m.1/23),LU,C(uncut); CSmH,NNC(uncut).

C213 — — '*London, printed for T. Reynolds...*', 1733.
8⁰: A⁴; *1–2* 3–8.
> A piracy; just possibly from Edinburgh.

L(1961),*LdU-B*; ICN.

C214 Clancy, Michael. A poem inscribed to his excellency the Earl of Harrington, lord lieutenant of Ireland. *Dublin, printed by George Faulkner, 1749.*
8⁰: A⁴; *1–2* 3–8.
'When shrewd star-gazers chance to spy'
O,DN.

C215 — Templum Veneris, sive amorum rhapsodiæ... Cecinit Michael Clancy, M.D... For the benefit of the author. *London, printed for R. Dodsley; sold by M. Cooper, 1745.* (*GM,LM* Nov)
4⁰: A⁴ b⁴ B–D⁴ E² (A3 as 'A2'); [2] *i–iii* iv–x [*1*] x–xi *xii blk*, *1* 2–28. A1 hft.
> Both copies at L have ms. errata on a blank leaf bound after the text.

'Deliciæ Veneris Cnidus, hos Cytherea recessus'
L(11408.f.19,–A1; T.662/4).

C216 Clans. The clans lamentation, against Mar and their own folly. To the tune of, Bony Katharine Ogie. [*Edinburgh?* 1715/–.]
½⁰: 1 side, 2 columns.
'As I did travel in the north'
L(Rox.III.336).

C217 Clare, R. The English hero: or, the Duke of Marlborough. A poem upon the late glorious victory over the French and barbarians at Hochstetten. Dedicated to her grace the Dutchess of Marlborough. *London printed, and are to be sold by B. Bragg, [1704.]* (*PM* 19 Aug)
2⁰: *A*² B²; *i–iv*, *1–4*.
> The Luttrell copy dated 19 Aug is recorded in *Haselwood.*

'Rouze up, ye drowsie mortals! at the call'
> Dedication signed.

L(11626.i.6); CtY,MH.

Claremont. Claremont. Address'd to the right honourable the Earl of Clare, 1715. *See* Garth, *Sir* Samuel.

Claridge, R.

C218 Claridge, Richard. Carmen spirituale: **or**, Christian counsel to youth. *London printed, and sold by T. Sowle, 1703.*
1⁰: 1 side, 2 columns.
'Fear god, and his commandments keep'
> At foot, 'By Richard Claridge'. Translated into Latin by Joseph Besse as *A spiritual poem, 1728.*

L(C.121.g.9/139, title cropt),LF(2).

C219 — — 'Reprinted 8vo. 1707. ½ [sheet].'
(*Smith* I.411.)

C220 — — The third edition. To which are added, morning and evening meditations. *London printed, and sold by the assigns of J. Sowle, 1716.*
8⁰: A⁴; *1–3* 4–8.
Meditations: 'With pious thoughts, do thou begin the day'
LF; *PSC-Hi.*

Clarinda. Clarinda: or the fair libertine, 1729. *See* Ralph, James.

C221 Clarissa. Clarissa: or, the courtezan. An heroic poem. *Dublin, printed in the year 1749.*
8⁰: A⁴; *1–3* 4–8.
'While from their lays our modern bards exclude'
> A satire on a Dublin whore.

DG.

C222 Clark, Hugh. Meditations upon the love of Christ, in the redemption, of elect-sinners... Now published at the desire, of his near and dear relations and Christian friends, and that by way of elegy. [*Glasgow?*] *Printed in the year 1727.*
4⁰: A–C⁴; *1* 2–24.
> Pp. 23–24 printed in two columns.

'Crost in a meaner theam, I mind to prove'
L(11631.e.12),O,E(2),GM(2).

C223 — — [*Glasgow?*] *Printed in the year 1740.*
8⁰: *A*⁴ B–C⁴; *1–2* 3–24.
E(lacks A1, supplied in ms.)

C224 — — *Edinburgh, printed by Thomas Lumisden & company, 1748.*
8⁰: A–C⁴ D²; *1–2* 3–28.
> The format is uncertain; the leaves show horizontal chain-lines, and the work is possibly a duodecimo.

GM.

C225 Clark, J. Bethlem a poem. By a patient. Humbly inscrib'd to the honble. Edwd. Vernon...by... J. Clark. *London, sold by Saml. Lyne, [1744.]*
1⁰: 1 side, 2 columns.
> Engraved throughout, with a view of the hospital at head. Dated at head, 1 May 1744. At foot, 'Proper to be had and read, by all when they go to see Bedlam'.

'Good sir, I pardon beg for this address'
LG.

Clark, J.

C226 [**Clark, James.**] The cross and the crown, or, a cluster of cordials...in way of dialogue betwixt Ben-oni and Barnabas. Composed in England anno 1685, printed at Edinburgh anno 1686; and now revised by the author, one of the ministers of the gospel in Glasgow. *Edinburgh, printed by the heirs and successors of Andrew Anderson, and to be sold by James Stuart, Glasgow*, 1705.
8⁰: A⁸; *1* 2–15 *16 blk*.
    Earlier edition not traced.
'This day when Phœbus, with his ruddie rays'
    For Clark's authorship of this and the following, see W. J. Coupe rin *Records of the Glasgow Bibliographical Society* 11 (1933) 73f.
E.

C227 [—] Gratulatio Britannica, ob exoptatum & pergratum adventum, serenissimi & augustissimi Georgii...in Britanniam. *Glasguæ, excudebat Hugo Brown, academiæ typographus*, 1714. (24 Sept?)
8⁰: A⁴; *1*–2 3–7 *8*.
    Dated at end 13 Sept; a presentation copy at E has ms. date 24 Sept.
'Pleridum sacrata cohors canit ore rotundo'
    A copy at E has the inscription 'Ex dono reverendi authoris J. Clk. V.D.M.Gl:'
E(2).

C228 [—] The practical atheist: or blasphemous clubs taxed. The second edition corrected by the author, a lover of poetry. *Edinburgh reprinted* 1721.
8⁰: A⁴; *1*–2 3–8.
    First edition not traced.
'Had I Heraclitus his faculty'
    Wrongly ascribed to James Porterfield by *Halkett & Laing*, following Maidment's note in the L copy. The E copy has early ms. notes 'By Mr J.C.' and 'To the revd Mr Robt. Woddrow'; Wodrow was a friend of Clark, and this is clearly the right attribution.
L(11631.a.5),E.

C229 [—] The wise or foolish choice: or the wisdom of choosing Christ... In a paraphrase on the Song of Solomon, and an abstract of... Ecclesiastes... Both done in metre by one of the ministers of the gospel in Glasgow. *Edinburgh, printed by J. W. [James Watson] for James Wardlaw*, 1703.
8⁰: A¹ B–H⁴ I⁴(–I4); *i*–*ii*, 1–62.
'This sacred Song of Songs was penn'd'
'Fond man! Why charm'd? Why wheedled so?'
    Early ms. in the E copy 'I. Clerk'.
E.

C230 Classic. The classic quarrel. A tale. Very useful to be read by all young gentlemen of parts and learning. By the author of a Proper reply to a lady. [*London*] *Printed for T. Osborne*, [1733.] (*GSJ* 5 May)
2⁰: A² B–D²; *1*–3 4–16. *16 advt*.
'Swords, and the swords-men, muse, I sing'
OA; MH(uncut),NjP(uncut),TxU.

Claudian

C231 Claudian. Claudian's Rufinus: or, the court-favourite's overthrow. Being a curious and correct Grub-street edition of one of the best satyrical poems, of one of the best poets, on one of the worst statesmen that ever liv'd. *London, printed for C. Guest*, 1730. (*MChr* 12 Feb)
8⁰: π¹ a–b⁴ c² A–C⁴; [2] *i* ii–xix *xx blk, 9* 10–30 *31–32*.
'Oft has this thought perplex'd my wav'ring mind'
    The satire appears to be intended against Walpole. The preface is satirically addressed to Pope, and signed 'Nameless Name'.
L(T.1056/11); TxU.

C232 — — The second edition. *London, printed for E. Smith; sold by the book-sellers, and pamphlet-sellers in London & Westminster*, 1730.
8⁰: π¹ a–b⁴ A–C⁴ D¹; *i*–*iii* iv–xvi, *1* 2–26 *27–28*.
    D1 which bears an 'After-thought' was printed with the title π1, and is sometimes bound immediately after the title.
L(011388.bb.19),O(2),LdU-B; CSmH,CtY,MH, TxU.

Claudianus, Claudius.

[*De raptu Proserpinæ*] Hughes, Jabez: The rape of Proserpine, from Claudian, 1714, 1716, 1723. *See* H368–370.

[*In Rufinum*] Claudian's Rufinus: or, the court-favourite's overthrow, 1730. *See* C231–2.

The stumbling-block. From Claudian against Rufinus [parody of first 23 lines], 1711. *See* S775.

———————

The Phœnix of Claudian. Translated into English verse, 1731. *See* P264.

C233 [**Clay, Stephen.**] An epistle from the elector of Bavaria to the French king: after the battel of Ramillies. *London, printed for Jacob Tonson*, 1706. (*DC* 26 Nov)
2⁰: π² A–F²; *i*–*viii*, 1–20. *π1 hft*.
    No watermark. Pp. 17–20 'To the Duke of Marlborough'. The Luttrell copy dated 26 Nov was formerly in the collection of C. H. Wilkinson.
'If yet, great sir, your heart can comfort know'
To the Duke: 'Pardon, great duke, if Britain's stile delights'
    For Clay's authorship see R. W. Chapman in *RES* 1.92; there are early ms. attributions in the CSmH, Wilkinson copies, and see the fine paper entry below. Wrongly ascribed to Prior by *Waller, CBEL*.
O(2, 1 uncut, –π1),OW,LdU-B; CSmH,CtY,ICU, NjP,TxU(3, 1 uncut)+.

C234 [—] [fine paper]
    Watermark: X. The dedication copy to William Cowper in contemporary morocco

Clay, S. An epistle

(sold Christie's 18 April 1961, lot 211) had the dedication signed in type; the blind impression can be seen in the L copy at 1347.m.60.
L(1347.m.60; Ashley 4968),O; MH.

C235 [—] [dh] An epistle from the elector of Bavaria to the French king. [col] [*London*] *Printed by H. Hills*, [1706/08?]
8°: A⁴; *1* 2–8.
LG; CSmH,TxU.

C236 **Clear.** A clear stage, and no favour: or, tragedy and comedy at war. Occasion'd by the emulation of the two theatric heroes, David and Goliah. Left to the impartial decision of the town. *London, printed for J. Huggonson*, [1742.] (Nov)
2°: A–C²; *1–2* 3–12.
A copy from Tom's Coffee House in the Lewis Walpole Library is dated Nov.
'Long in suspence the tattling gossip stood'
David and Goliah are said to represent David Garrick and James Quin, but Charles Macklin might be a more appropriate Goliah.
L(11630.f.74); *MH.*

Cleio. *See* Clio.

Clergy. The clergy of the city of London and liberty of Westminster's address to the queen... paraphras'd, [1710.] *See* The London address, [1710.]

C237 **Clergyman.** The clergyman and goldsmith, in the trap; or, a new hymn to the pillory. *London, printed by J. Williams, Southwark*, [1703/–.]
½°: 1 side, 2 columns.
Large cut of pillory above text.
'Hail! thou great engine that for shew'
O.

— The clergyman's choice of a wife, 1738. *See* Legh, George.

C238 — The clergyman's daughter's new annual book. Consisting of justice and jnjustice [!]... Written by this author, who brings a small tract of her own work once a year, and no more... *London, printed in the year* 1735.
12°: A⁶; *1–2* 3–12.
'Grant aid to me, Jehovah, I require'
Clearly a begging poem. The author describes herself as 'descended from eminent clergymen, from the third generation, all in and near the city of York'.
L(11631.b.27; 1488.aa.8).

Clinch, William. Poems on several occasions. Consisting of odes, epigrams, pastorals, &c. Together with remarks on the memoirs of the young prince of Anamboe, in a poetical epistle to the author... *London, printed for the author; sold by G. Jones*, [1749.] (*GM* Dec)
4°: pp. 51.   DFo.

Clio

C239 **Clio.** Clio. A poem humbly inscrib'd to his grace the Duke of Bedford, by T---- F----. *London, printed for A. Millar; sold by M. Cooper*, 1748. (*GM, LM* March)
2°: π¹ A² B–D² E¹; *i–ii, 1–5* 6–17 *18 blk.* π1 hft.
Entered in Strahan's ledger to Millar, 29 Feb 1748, 500 copies.
'Whilst cool philosophy sat musing'
Possibly by the same author, T.F., as *The puppet shew*, 1748.
CtY.

— Clio and Strephon: being, the second and last part of the Platonic lovers, 1732. *See* Fowke, Martha.

— Cleio. Poetical meditations upon sundry parts of scripture, and moral phrases... By W. D. gent. *Edinburgh, printed by John Reid junior, and are to be sold by John Vallange*, 1711.
4°: pp. 46.   GM.

C240 **Cloak.** The cloak's knavery. ['*Edinburgh, printed by Mr Wm. Adam* May 1718'.]
½°: 1 side, 2 columns.
Engraved music above title. Imprint in ms. in the E copy, possibly added by its purchaser. What is apparently an earlier edition is recorded in Ruddiman's ledger for the week ending 12 June 1714, 'The Cloak a Ballad 1 page... 300 copies.'
'Come buy my new ballad'
An attack on the presbyterians' part in the commonwealth. Cf. *Wing* B603–4, *The ballad of the cloak.*
E.

C241 — — [*Dublin*, 172–?]
½°: 1 side, 2 columns.
CtY.

C242 — [*idem*] The ballad of the cloak: or, the cloak's knavery. Tune of, Packington's pound. [*Newcastle, printed by John White*, 172–?]
The L copy is cut apart and mounted; its original format was probably 1 side, 3 columns. The woodcut at head was used by John White at this period.
L(LR.31.b.19/1.112).

C243 — [*idem*] The cloak's knavery. A new song. [*Dublin*] *Printed for Paddy Droghedy, and sold at his lodging's opposite to Madam Violante's booth in Dames-street*, 1732.
½°: 1 side, 2 columns.
The imprint is possibly fictitious.
L(1871.f.3/26).

Cloe. *See* Chloe.

Cloister. The cloyster in Bartholomew Fair, 1707. *See* Massalina, 1707.

C—m, C. A familiar epistle to Mr. Mitchell, 1720. *See* F54.

Coachman

C244 Coachman. The coachman's wish: or, a familiar epistle by way of dialogue between Thomas and Grizel. *Dublin, printed in the year* 1729.
8°: A⁴; *1–2* 3–8.
'Grizel, thou charmer of our isle'
L(992.a.39/1).

[**Coæt, John Peter.**] The beauty and excellence of charity, [1737?] *See* B132.

Cobb, Samuel. Poems on several occasions. With imitations... *London, printed for R. & J. Bonwick,* 1707. (*PM* 7 Jan)
8°: pp. 264.   LVA-D,O; ICN,MB.

— [reissue] The second edition, with additions. *London, printed for E. Curll, & E. Sanger,* 1709.
8°: pp. 283.   O.
    Cancel title and eleven leaves added at end.

— [reissue] The third edition. *London printed, and sold by James Woodward,* 1710. (*DC* 2 March)
8°: pp. 283.   L,LdU-B; DFo.
    New cancel title.

———————

— Callipædia. A poem. In four books [in part translated by Cobb], 1712–. *See* R280.

C245 — The carpenter of Oxford, or, the Miller's tale, from Chaucer. Attempted in modern English, by Samuel Cobb... To which are added two imitations of Chaucer... By Matthew Prior, esq; *London, printed for E. Curll, R. Gosling, & J. Pemberton,* 1712.
8°: π¹ B–G⁴ H⁴(–H1); *i–ii,* 1–46 *47–54.* 54 advt.
    The Prior poems start on p. 47. Some copies (e.g. MH) add a four leaf catalogue of Curll's books. *Nichols* VIII.294 records the payment of five guineas by Lintot to 'Betterton', 7 April 1712, for 'The Miller's tale, with some characters from Chaucer'.
'Whilom in Oxford, an old chuff did dwell'
L(1078.l.12/2; 992.h.3/5),O; CSmH,KU,MH,TxU.

C246 — [*idem*] The Miller's tale, from Chaucer. Inscrib'd to N. Rowe, esq; 'London' [*Dublin*], *printed in the year* 1725.
8°: A–C⁴; *1–2* 3–23 *24 blk.*
L(012330.ee.32/2),O,DA.

C247 — The female reign: an ode, alluding to Horace, B. 4. Od. 14... attempted in the style of Pindar. Occasion'd by the wonderful successes of the arms of her majesty and her allies. With a letter to a gentleman in the university. *London, printed for J. Woodward,* 1709. (*DC* 8 Sept)
2°: A–D²; *1–4* 5–15 *16 blk.*
    The Luttrell copy (dated 1 Sept) appears to precede all advertisements, and is possibly wrongly dated; but cf. C249.

Cobb, S. The female reign

'What can the British senate give'
    In honour of Queen Anne.
LVA-F; ICN,ICU(presentation copy, 13 Sept), MH(Luttrell, 1 Sept),TxU.

C248 —— *London, printed by H. Hills; sold by the booksellers of London & Westminster,* 1709.
8°: A⁸; *1–4* 5–16.
    Reissued with other Hills poems in *A collection of the best English poetry,* 1717 (*Case* 294).
L(1078.l.12/1; C.124.b.7/16),O(2),C,E,LdU-B+; CtY,IU,MH,TxU.

C249 — Honour retriev'd. A poem. Occasion'd by the late victories obtain'd over the French and Bavarians... *London, printed for William Turner, & John Nutt,* 1705 [1704]. (20 Dec, Luttrell)
2°: A² B–G²; *i–iv,* 1–24. A1 hft.
    The Luttrell copy is recorded in *Haslewood.* Advertised in *PM* 4 Jan.
'Scarce had we time allow'd our thanks to yield'
LDW(–A1),O; CSmH,CtY,ICN,MH,TxU.

C250 — The mouse-trap: a poem. Written in Latin by E. Holdsworth... Made English by Samuel Cobb... *London, printed for E. Curll, & E. Sanger,* 1712. (*PB* 17 July)
8°: π¹(+frt) A–C⁴ D⁴(–D1); *i–viii,* 1 *2–23 24.* π1 hft; 24 advt.
    English text only.
'Sing muse, the Briton, who on mountains bred'
L(161.k.35),LLP,O(3, 1 uncut, 1–π1),C; ICU, MH,TxU.

C251 — [*idem*] Muscipula: or, the mouse-trap: a poem in Latin and English... Translated by Samuel Cobb... The second edition. *London, printed for E. Curll,* 1720.
8°: A–D⁴ (A3 as 'A2'); *i–viii,* 1–23 *24 blk.* A1 frt.
    It is clear from the form of title and the price (1*s.* as opposed to 6*d.* for the preceding) that the intention was to issue the Latin text with this, and many copies are found with the 1709 edition for Curll & Sanger.
L(1486.r.7),O(–A1),OW,C,E+; CLU-C,CtY, ICN,ICU,KU(3)+.

C252 — The mouse-trap: a poem... Made English by Samuel Cobb... *London, printed for J. Torbuck,* 1738 [1737]. (*GM* Oct)
8°: π¹ A⁸(–A8); *1–2* 3–15 *16.* 16 advt.
    The collation is tentative; the final part of J. T[orbuck], *A collection of travels,* 1738. *CBEL* records an edition of 1731, not traced, possibly in error for this.
L,O; MH,PU.

C253 —— *London, printed for J. Torbuck,* [174–?]
8°: A⁸; *1–2* 3–15 *16 blk.*
O,DT.

C254 — The mouse-trap: a poem. Translated from the Latin by Samuel Cobb... *London, printed for the booksellers in town & country,* [174–?]
4°: (frt+) A–B⁴ C²; *1–3* 4–20.

Cobb, S. The mouse-trap

Clearly a piracy; the date is very tentative. Vertical chain-lines, but the copy seen is apparently a small quarto.
NN.

C255 — News from both universities. Containing, I. Mr. Cobb's tripos speech at Cambridge, with a complete key inserted. II. The brawny priest: or, the captivity of the nose. A poem. *London, printed for J. Roberts*, 1714.
8°: *A*² B–D⁴; *i–iv, 1* 2–24. A1 hft, advt.
Cobb's speech is dated 19 Feb 1702; 'Nasus prehensus', dated 20 Jan 1714, has an English imitation. The copy at OCU has a fleur-de-lys watermark not seen elsewhere; it is possibly on fine paper.
''Twas well, when our forefathers did agree'
Nasus prehensus: 'Clystere nuper duriusculam paulo alvum'
Imitated in English: 'Fat Buphalus, his o'er-fed paunch to ease'
The author and translator of 'Nasus prehensus' have not been identified.
L(11626.bb.14,–A1),O(2, 1 uncut,–A1, 1–A1, lacks D4); CtY,InU,KU,OCU.

C256 [—] A poem on Prince Eugene. *London, printed for J. Baker*, 1712.
½°: A¹; *1–2, 1* column.
'So Tydeus look'd, when, single, he oppos'd'
Reprinted in the additions to Cobb's *Poems*, 1709.
L(Cup.645.e.1/23),LLP,Crawford; MH.

C257 — The Portugal expedition. To which is added, Dr. G—h's epigram on the same subject. *London, printed for R. Basset; sold by John Nutt*, 1704.
4°: A⁴; *1–2* 3–8. 8 advt.
Pp. 6–7 contain 'In Caroli III. iter lusitanum', a Latin version of the English poem; p. 8 has both Garth's epigram and a translation by Cobb.
'At length auspicious blasts are heard to blow'
'Ventus, hyperboreo qui congeminatur ab axe'
L(1077.k.29/4); TxU.

C258 [—] A psalm of thanksgiving to be sung by the children of Christ's-Hospital on Monday, Tuesday and Wednesday, in Easter-week...1704. Composed by Mr. Barrett... The words by S. C. M.A. *London, printed by Fr. Leach*, 1703 [1703/4].
1°: 1 side, 2 columns.
Woodcut borders. Typeset music with first verse at head. The verse is followed by an annual report of the charities. See Susi Jeans 'The Easter psalms of Christ's Hospital', *Proceedings RMA*, 1961/62.
'Awake! ye drowsie mortals rise!'
Authorship from Christ's Hospital minutes.
L(Music I.600.g/15).

C259 [—] A psalm of thanksgiving to be sung by the children of Christ's-Hospital, on Monday, Tuesday,

Cobb, S. A psalm of thanksgiving

and Wednesday of Easter-week...Composed by Mr. Barrett... [*London*] *Printed by Fr. Leach*, 1705.
1°.
(*Morgan* H39; *Britwell Handlist*, I. 203.)

C260 [—] A psalm of thanksgiving to be sung by the children of Christ's-Hospital, on Monday, Tuesday and Wednesday in Easter-week...1706. Composed by Mr. Barrett... The words by S.C. A.M. *London, printed by Fr. Leach*, 1706. (26 March, Luttrell)
1°: 1 side, 2 columns.
Format and authorship as 1703 edition.
'The morning's up, the sun prepares'
L(10350.g.12/14; Music I. 600/6, Luttrell).

C261 [—] A psalm of thanksgiving...1709. Composed by Mr. Barret... The words by S.C. M.A. [*London*] *Printed by John Barber*, 1709.
1°: 1 side, 2 columns.
Format and authorship as preceding.
'Behold the man whom the Judæan race'
Christ's Hospital office.

C262 [—] A psalm of thanksgiving...1712. Composed by Mr. Barret... The words by S.C. A.M. [*London*] *Printed by John Barber*, 1712.
1°: 1 side, 2 columns.
Format and authorship as preceding.
'Lo, the bless'd morning is begun'
Christ's Hospital office.

C263 [—] A psalm of thanksgiving...1713. Composed by Mr. Barret... The words by S.C. M.A. [*London*] *Printed by John Barber*, 1713.
1°: 1 side, 2 columns.
Format and authorship as preceding.
'Begin, let ransom'd man rejoyce'
Christ's Hospital office.

Cobbler. The cobler, a tale, [173–.] *See* Wesley, Samuel, *the younger*.

C264 — The cobler of Gloucester, and his wife Joan's new litany; to be said or sung by all true Englishmen... *London, printed for A. Moore*, [173–?]
2°: (3 ll); *1–2* 3–6.
'O heavenly Father, from thy mansions bright'
InU.

— The cobler's poem, 1745. *See* Weeks, James Eyre.

Cobden, Edward. Poems on several occasions. *London, printed for the benefit of a clergyman's widow, and sold by W. Innys, J. & P. Knapton, S. Austen, J. & J. Rivington, & R. Dodsley*, 1748. (*GM* Feb)
8°: pp. x, 352.   L,O; MH,TxU.
Entered to Cobden in Bowyer's ledgers, no date, 1000 copies printed; 25 copies of one sheet were apparently re-imposed (or re-impressed) and another 25 'workt without taking off'. This collection includes Cobden's

Cobden, E.

translation of Holdsworth's *Muscipula* which was made in 1718 and sometimes recorded as though published then.

***

C265 [—] On Miss Forrester playing with her shadow. By Dr. D-----, chaplain to his majesty. *London, printed for R. Dodsley; sold by M. Cooper*, 1743. (25 March)
2°: $A^2 < B^2$; *1-3* 4-8.
Copy from Tom's Coffee House, dated 25 March, in Lewis Walpole Library; listed in *GM* March.
'Nature, which purest prospects gives'
Printed in Cobden's *Poems*, 1748; the reference to 'Dr. D—' is unexplained, but there was no royal chaplain with such a name at this time.
L(1484.m.14),O; CtY(uncut),MH.

C266 — A poem on the death of the right honourable Joseph Addison, esq; *London, printed for A. Bettesworth, J. Brotherton, E. Curll, & J. Graves*, 1720. (*DP* 18 Jan)
8°: A^1 B–D^4 E^1; *i–ii, 1–3* 4–26. A1 hft.
Some copies (O,IU) have B2 signed 'B'. Luttrell's copy, now in the Osborn collection at CtY, is dated Feb.
'O Addison! were none your worth to sing'
L(11631.d.12),LVA-F(−A1),O(−A1),OW(−A1); CtY,DFo,IU(−A1),MH,TxU+.

C267 [—] A religious ode, occasioned by the present rebellion. Written Oct. 11, 1745. By a clergyman. *London, printed for R. Dodsley; sold by M. Cooper*, 1745. (*GM* Nov)
4°: A^4 B^4; *1–4* 5–16. A1 hft.
'Jehovah, whose almighty will'
Printed in Cobden's *Poems*, 1748.
L(11630.b.4/8),O,AdU,*MR*; NN(−A1).

[C268 = B315·5] **Cobham.** Cobham and Congreve, 1730. *See* Bond, William.

Cobler. *See* Cobbler.

C269 **Cock.** Cock-fighting display'd: or, Lucas cut down. *Dublin, printed by T. Knowles*, 1749.
½°: 2 sides, 2 columns.
'Ye commons, and peers,/Pray, lend me your ears'
On Charles Lucas's election fight.
C.

C270 **Cock, John.** A [p]rophesie for the year one thousand seven hundred and fifteen years. [*Edinburgh*, 1714/15.]
½°: 1 side, 1 column.
'In seventeen hundred and fifteen years'
E.

'Cockade, *Captain*.' The important triflers, 1748. *See* Brecknock, Timothy.

Cockburn, Catharine. *See* Trotter, Catharine.

Cockburn, R.

C271 [**Cockburn, Robert.**] Vice triumphant: or, the world run mad. A satyre. *Edinburgh, printed in the year* 1719.
8°: A–B^4; *1-2* 3–15 *16 blk.*
'Now men with an unblushing face begin'
Early ms. attribution to Cockburn in the copy at E.
E.

C272 **Cocken, David.** To the worshipful Company of Frame-work-knitters. [*London*] *Printed by W. Downing*, [171–?]
½°: 1 side, 1 column.
Engraving of knitting frame at head.
'Of all the engines humane wit can boast'
Signed 'David Cocken, Beadle'; but possibly written for him. In praise of William Lee's invention of the stocking-frame.
L(C.121.g.9/184),O.

'Codex, *Dr*.' Dr. Codex's fifth pastoral, 1734. *See* D352.

— Dr. Codex's pastoral letter versified, 1739. *See* D352·5.

C273 **Codrington, Samuel.** The beatific vision: a poem. *London, printed for R. Hett*, 1735.
4°: A^2 B–D^2; *1–5* 6–16.
'Forgive the muse, that boldly dares to roll'
Dedication signed.
L(1465.i.12/6); CtY,NjP(uncut).

[**Coetlogon, Dennis de.**] Plain truth, or downright Dunstable, 1740. *See* P475.

C274 **Coffee.** Coffee: a tale. *London, printed for H. Curle*, 1727. (*MC* July)
8°: A^4(−A4) a^4 B–E^4 F^1[= A4]; [2] *i* ii–iv vii–xiv, *1* 2–33 *34 blk.*
'According to custom,/Which verse-mongers use'
The same author translated *Mr. Addison's fine ode*, 1727. A satire.
DFo,KU(uncut),TxU(stitched, uncut).

C275 — The coffee-women turn'd courtiers. An excellent new ballad. To the tune of, Ye commons and peers. [*London*? 1714/15.]
slip: 1 side, 1 column.
'For an apple of gold'
Crum F436: 'Strange news from St James's... 1714'. An anti-Hanoverian satire, apparently based on a practical joke when three women of the town were presented to George I. One was apparently Anne Rochford.
O.

Coffey, Charles. Poems and songs upon several occasions, with love letters, and a novel, nam'd Loviso. To which is added a diverting farce, call'd Wife and no wife... *Dublin, printed by Edward Waters*, 1724.
8°: pp. 48+44+38.   DN.

***

Coffey, C.

C276 [—] The bason: a poem. Inscrib'd to Samuel Burton, esq; In three cantos. *Dublin, printed in the year* 1727.
8°: A^8; *1–2* 3–16.
'Apollo, patron of the muse's song'
Ms. attribution to Coffey in one DN copy, signed 'J.A. Jany. 19th. 1727' (possibly James Arbuckle, and probably 1727/8). On a new reservoir and pleasure garden in Dublin.
L(1963),DN(2); OCU.

C277 [—] A prologue, spoken by Mr. Elrington, on the 22d of April, being the birth-day of his excellency the Lord Carteret. Written by C. C. *Dublin, printed by Pressick Rider & Thomas Harbin*, 1725.
½°: 2 sides, 1 column.
On the verso 'Epilogue, spoken by Mr Griffith, who play'd the part of Ben. By the same'.
'As when a pregnant cloud dissolv'd to showers'
'Thus do we sailors spend our merry lives'
Contemporary ms. ascription to Coffey in the Rothschild copy, which bears the Dublin collector's mark 'F'. Sometimes ascribed in error to Charles Carthy. Satirized in *A satyr ascrib'd to his excellency, L— C—t*, [1725.]
L(C.121.g.8/74),Rothschild; MH,TxU.

C278 [—] Temple-Oagg: or, the spaw-well. A new poem, in three canto's. *Dublin, printed by E. Waters*, 1723.
8°: $A^8(-A8)$; *1–5* 6–13 *14 blk.*
'Let bards invoke the sacred nine t' inspire'
Dedication signed 'C.C'; Charles Coffey is almost certainly the author.
L(11631.bb.84); CtY.

C279 Cogitations. Cogitations upon death: or, the mirrour of mans misery. Being very choice and profitable lessons, for putting all Christians in a prepared condition for mortality. *Edinburgh printed, and sold by Robert Brown*, 1719.
8°: A^8; *1* 2–16.
Two additional poems on pp. 13–16.
'I have such dread when I should die'
GM(uncut).

C280 —— *Glasgow, printed by James Duncan*, 1722.
12 pp.
GM(missing 1967).

C281 Co-gr-ss. The co-gr-ss of asses. *London, 'printed for Baalam, and sold by the tribe of Isachar'*, [1721?]
2°: A^2; *1–2* 3–4.
'In days of yore, when beasts and birds'
MH suggests this may be a satire on the Congress of Brunswick.
O; InU,MH.

C282 Colcannen. The Colcannen match: or, the belly duel. A poem. In three canto's. *[Dublin] Printed in the year* 1730.
8°: A^4; *1–2* 3–8.
Teerink 956.

The **Colcannen** match

'On Faughan's banks a little village stands'
LVA-F,DA,DK; IU.

C283 [Cole, John.] To the memory of the revd. Mr. Mordecai Andrews. A monody. *London, printed for the author; sold by Vertue & Goadby, stationers, at the Royal Exchange*, 1750. (*GM,LM* March)
4°: A^4; *1–2* 3–8.
'Once and again, the fault'ring muse has try'd'
Early ms. attribution to Cole in the CU copy.
L(11631.bbb.4),LDW(2); CU.

C284 Colin. Colin Clout's madrigal, on the auspicious first of March, 1727–8. Being the anniversary of her majesty's birth-day. *London, printed for W. Mears*, 1728. (*MChr* 29 Feb)
2°: $A–B^2$ C^1; *1–2* 3–9 *10 blk.*
'Wou'd our druid but lend me'
OCU.

— Colin's mistakes, 1721. *See* Prior, Matthew.

Collection. A collection of divine hymns upon several occasions, suited to our common tunes, 1704. *See* Boyse, Joseph.

— A collection of new state songs, in old popular tunes... By Jeremiah van Jews-Trump, esq; *London, printed for J. Chrichley*, 1732.
8°: pp. 30. L.
Percival p. 191; listed with the miscellanies in *CBEL* II.202 as 'possibly by one hand'.

— A collection of poems. By the author of a poem on the Cambridge ladies. *Cambridge, printed by W. Fenner*, 1733. (*GM* Feb)
8°: pp. 120. C,CT; CtY.
Listed as a miscellany in *CBEL* II.203; some poems by other hands are added, but it is essentially the work of one author, apparently from Catherine Hall. His name is given in cipher in the CtY copy as 'Gigd 3829'. The same author wrote *Poems on several occasions. By the author of the poem on the Cambridge ladies*, 1736, and see P535 for the poem on the Cambridge ladies.

— A collection of poems; consisting of odes, tales, &c... By the author of the Duel a poem. *London, printed for J. Roberts*, 1731. (*GSJ* 15 April)
8°: pp. 55. L,O; CtY,MH.
The author also wrote *A poem sacred to the memory of...Dan Poulteney*, 1731.

— [reissue] The honeysuckle. A curious collection of poems... *London, printed for A. Dodd, E. Nutt, J. Critchley, J. Jolyffe*, 1731.
8°: pp. 60. O.
Cancel title, and *The duel* added at the end.

C285 — A collection of state flowers. *London printed, and sold by J. Dormer*, 1734.
2°: A^2 $B–C^2$; *1–4* 5–12. A1 frt.
'Whilst fierce Bellona threatens loud alarms'
Politicians satirized as flowers.

A **collection** of state flowers

L(11602.i.17/1),O,E,LdU-B; *CLU-C*,MH,OCU, TxU.

— A collection of the writings of the author of the True-born English-man, 1703. *See* Defoe, Daniel.

College. The college-examination, 1731. *See* Percival, William, *barrister*.

C286 — College-wit sharpen'd: or, the head of a house, with, a sting in the tail: being, a new English amour, of the epicene gender, done into burlesque metre, from the Italian. Adress'd to the two famous universities of S-d-m and G-m-rr-h. *London, 'printed for J. Wadham, near the Meeting-house in Little Wild-street', where the supplement, which will shortly be published, may be had; and sold at the pamphlet-shops of London & Westminster,* 1739. (*GM* June; *LM* July)
8°: *A*¹[= D1] B–C⁴ D⁴(–D1); *i–ii, 1–22*.
The drop-head title is 'The Wadhamites'.
'At length, the quære is decided'
A satire on the homosexual scandal concerning John Swinton and Robert Thistlethwayte of Wadham.
L(1080.m.31),O(2),EN; CtY,TxU.

C287 [**Collier, John.**] The black-bird: a poem. By T. B. fellow of the Sisyphian society of weavers. *'Amsterdam': printed for the author; in the year* 1741.
8°: *A*⁸; *1–5 6–16*.
The imprint is false; certainly printed in England, possibly in Manchester, though the ornaments appear to be of London origin.
'When bright Apollo's flaming car had run'
Dedication signed 'Timothy Bobbin', 15 Jan 1739. Collected in Collier's works, but this earliest publication not recorded. A satire on Mr. Samuel Chetham of Castleton.
C(ms. corrections),PrP; *InU*.

Collier, Mary. Poems on several occasions, by Mary Collier, author of the Washerwoman's labour, with some remarks on her life. *Winchester, printed by Mary Ayres, for the author,* 1762.
8°: pp. 62.   L,O; IU.

C288 — The woman's labour: an epistle to Mr. Stephen Duck; in answer to his late poem, called The thresher's labour. To which are added, the three wise sentences taken from the first book of Esdras, ch. III. and IV. *London, printed for the author; sold by J. Roberts, and at the pamphlet shops near the Royal Exchange,* 1739. (*GM,LM* Aug)
8°: *A² B–D⁴ E²*; *1–5 6–32*.
'Immortal bard! thou fav'rite of the nine!'
Mary Collier is described on the title as 'now a washer-woman, at Petersfield in Hampshire'.
L(1346.f.17),O; CtY,MiU.

C289 — — The second edition. *London, printed for the author,* 1739.

Collier, M. The woman's labour
8°: 16 ll.
(*Dobell* 306.)

C290 — — The third edition. *London,* 1740.
8°: 16 ll.
(*Dobell* 307.)

C291 Collier, Samuel. On discontent: by Samuel Collier, labourer. [1743.]
½°: *1–2*, 1 column.
'Of all the evils that befal mankind'
Ms. note in the O copy 'By a labourer that worked at the revd Mr Welchman at Preston Baggot near Henley 174²⁄₃'.
O.

C292 Collier, William. A congratulatory poem on his majesty's happy return to England. *London, printed for J. Roberts,* 1732. (*GSJ* 11 Oct)
2°: *A² B–C²*; *1–3 4–12*.
'Who that e'er felt the poet's sacred fire'
O; CLU.

[—] A poem humbly address'd to his highness the Prince of Orange, 1734. *See* P527.

C293 Collins, Richard. Nature display'd. A poem. *London, printed for J. Crokatt,* 1727. (*MC* June)
12°: *A⁶(–A6+χ²) B–G⁶*; *1–9 10–12 *11–12 13–82 83–84*. G6 advt.
'Hail! sacred sons of wisdom! whilst I choose'
Dedication signed.
L(11645.ee.55),O(uncut); CtY,*InU*,MH,TxHR, TxU+.

Collins, William. Odes on several descriptive and allegoric subjects. *London, printed for A. Millar,* 1747 [1746]. (*SR* 19 Dec)
8°: pp. 52.   L,O; CtY,MH.
Deposit copies at O,E,SaU. Entered in Woodfall's ledger under 15 Dec 1746; 1000 copies printed.

— The poetical works of Mr. William Collins. With memoirs of the author... By J. Langhorne. *London, printed for T. Becket & P. A. Dehondt,* 1765.
8°: pp. 184.   L,O; MH.

— [another edition]
8°: pp. 132.   O.
Apparently a Scottish piracy.

— 'An epistle to the editor of Fairfax his translation of Tasso's Jerusalem. [*London*] *Printed for R. Manby, & H. S. Cox*.' (*GA* 27 March 1750, 'on Saturday next' [31 March].)
Previously advertised for publication 'in a few days' in *WEP* 3 Feb 1750. According to A. D. McKillop in *TLS* 6 Dec 1928 (p. 965), 'it is safe to say it was never published'.

C294 — Ode occasion'd by the death of Mr. Thomson. *London, printed for R. Manby & H. S. Cox,* 1749. (*GM* June)

Collins, W. Ode

2°: *A² B²*; *1–4 5–8*.
   Rothschild 659.
'In yonder grave a druid lies'
L(Ashley 4782),LVA-D.

C295 — The passions, an ode. Written by Mr. Collins. Set to musick by Dr. Hayes. Performed at the Theatre in Oxford, July 2, 1750. [*Oxford? 1750?*]
4°: *A¹ B⁴ C¹*; *1–2 3–10 11–12 blk.*
   Rothschild 660. A1 and C1 have been seen to be conjugate. The Rothschild copy is described as large paper; there is no watermark in the copies seen.
'When music, heavenly maid, was young'
O,OM,OW; MH(in contemporary marbled wrappers).

C296 —— Set to musick by Dr. Hayes. *Winchester, printed by W. Greenville, 1750?*]
4°: *A² B²* (A2 as 'B'); *1–3 4–8.*
LVA-D.

C297 —— [*London? 1750/–.*]
8°: *A⁴*; *1–2 3–8.*
   Title in half-title form, with woodcut head-piece above and below.
L(1346.b.46).

C298 [—] Persian eclogues. Written originally for the entertainment of the ladies of Tauris. And now first translated, &c. *London, printed for J. Roberts,* 1742. (*DP* 6 Jan)
8°: *A² B–C⁴ D²*; *i–iii iv, 5–24.*
   Rothschild 653. Entered in Woodfall's ledger under 10 Dec 1741; 500 copies, with a half-sheet reprinted.
'Ye Persian maids, attend your poet's lays'
   Reprinted in Collins's *Poetical works,* 1765.
L(Ashley 2908),LVA-D(2, 1 lacks A2, has ms. corrections by Collins); CSmH,CtY,NN-B.

— 'A poem on the same occasion [i.e. on the royal nuptials]. By Wm Collins. [*London*] *Printed for J. Roberts.* Price 6d.' (*GM* March 1734)
   No poem by Collins on this subject has been traced, and I. A. Williams, *Seven eighteenth-century bibliographies* (1924) 107 suggests a misprint for William Collier. Possibly the work listed is *A poem humbly address'd to his highness the Prince of Orange, and the Princess Royal,* published by Roberts on 13 March 1734.

C299 [—] Verses humbly address'd to Sir Thomas Hanmer. On his edition of Shakespear's works. By a gentleman of Oxford. *London, printed for M. Cooper,* 1743. (*GM,LM* Dec)
2°: *A¹ B–C² D¹*; *1–3 4–12.*
   Rothschild 655.
'While, own'd by you, with smiles the muse surveys'
L(11764.m.4),LVA-D(title cropt); DFo,MH.

C300 — [*idem*] An epistle: addrest to Sir Thomas Hanmer, on his edition of Shakespear's works. The second edition. To which is added, a song from the Cymbeline of the same author. By Mr. William

Collins, W. Verses

Collins... *London, printed for R. Dodsley, & M. Cooper,* 1744. (*GA* 9 May)
2°: *A–D²*; *1–2 3–15 16 blk.*
   Rothschild 656. Revised text.
'While born to bring the muse's happier days'
Song: 'To fair Fidele's grassy tomb'
L(1874.d.33),LVA-D; CtY(uncut),DFo,*MB.*

Colme, John.
Possibly the Joannes Colme who graduated from Edinburgh in 1691. He addressed manuscript poems to various notables, doubtless in hope of reward; there are examples to William earl Cowper (Herts CRO, Panshanger papers, box 46) and to Sir John Clerk of Pennycuik (SRO GD 18/4403, 4407–8).

C301 — De ætate, & vita humana, carmen elegiacum, ex lingua vernacula, in Latinam rythmice, & ad verbum fere redditum... [*Edinburgh? 171–?*]
½°: 1 side, 2 columns.
'Tres quinquaginta, ac sexcentos circiter annos'
   Signed 'Jo. Colme'.
E.

[—] De pace...carmen gratulatorium, 1713. *See* D74.

[—] Nobilissimo domino Roberto Harley... De Dunquerca recepta, 1712. *See* N311.

[—] On the death of Mr. Brand, student of philosophy... By J.C. one of his fellow students, [1717.] *See* O196.

C302 — A poem on the blessed nativity, 25th. December, 1716. [*Edinburgh,* 1716.]
½°: 1 side, 1 column.
'Whil'st such as would all order disapprove'
   Signed 'Jo. Colme'.
E.

C303 [—] A poem on the blessed nativity, 25th December, 1717. [*Edinburgh,* 1717.]
¼°: 1 side, 1 column.
'Hail, glorious day! Does yet my life remain'
   Signed 'J.C.'
NN.

C304 [—] A poem on the 30th of January 1716. [*Edinburgh,* 1716.]
¼°: 1 side, 1 column.
'What thought, far less expression, can I find'
   The E copy signed in ms. 'Jo: Colme.' On the martyrdom of Charles I.
E.

C305 **Colpas, Andrew.** A brief rhythmical composition: of some conspicuous affairs of this world. *Winchester, printed by Isaac Philpot, for the author,* 1⟨732⟩.
4°: *A⁴*; *1 2–8.*
   Date completed in ms. in the copy seen.
'This mortal state is full of care, and of perplexity'
L(11631.f.8).

Coluthus, *Thebaeus*

Coluthus, *Thebaeus*.
The rape of Helen. Translated from the Greek of
Coluthus Thebaeus, 1731. *See* R118.

C306 [**Colvil, Samuel.**] Whiggs supplication, a mock-
poem. In two parts. By S. C. [*Edinburgh?*] *Printed
in the year* 1702.
8⁰: A–H⁸; *1–10* 11–128.
First published 1681 as *Mock poem*, in 1687
as *Whigs' supplication*, and in 1692 as *The
Scotch Hudibras*. An edition was advertised
with other Edinburgh books in *DC* 25 March
1709.
'After invoking of the muse'
DLC.

C307 — The whiggs supplication, or, the Scotch-
Hudibras, a mock poem. In two parts. *London,
printed for James Woodward, & John Baker,* 1710.
(*PB* 13 April)
12⁰: A–Q⁶; *i–xii,* 1–178 *179–180 blk.*
L(1078.a.5),O,E,*DrU*,GM + ; CLU-C(–Q6),
CSmH(–Q6),DFo(–Q6),IU(–Q6),*MiU*.

C308 [—] [*idem*] Mock poem: or, whiggs supplication.
*Edinburgh, printed by James Watson, and sold at his
shop,* 1711.
8⁰: A–G⁸ H⁴; *i–x,* 1–110.
The apology signed 'S.C.' Some copies
(O,GM,GU) appear to have a variant sheet H.
L(11633.a.61),O,E,GM,GU; CtY,TxU.

C309 — The whiggs supplication, or, the Scotch-
Hudibras. A mock-poem. In two parts. *Belfast,
printed by and for Samuel Wilson & James Magee,*
1741.
12⁰: A–O⁶; *i–xii,* 1–153 *154–156. 154–156 advt.*
O,C,E,GM,BlL + .

C310 **Comberbach, Roger,** *junior*. A poem, upon his
sacred majesty King George, and the royal family.
Chester, printed in the year 1715.
4⁰: *A²* B–C²; *1–4* 5–12.
'The youthful muse that long unmark'd has play'd'
Dedication signed.
O,DT; DLC.

C311 **Come.** Come on then. – Occasioned by a pam-
phlet lately published, intituled, Have at you all. By
the author of, They are not. *London, printed for
T. Cooper,* 1740. (Dec?)
2⁰: *A²* B²; *1–2* 3–7 *8 blk.*
'What the dire itch of scribbling can restrain?'
A reply to Robert Morris's poem.
MH.

C312 **Comical.** A commical dialogue between R.
F--------ne, and Madam B-------ly, that met in
the shades below. [*Dublin,* 1729?]
½⁰: 1 side, 1 column.
The copy at L forms part of a collection of
Dublin half-sheets of 1725/30.
'Welcome dear madam to our gloomy shead'

A comical dialogue

Probably referring to Madam Bently, died
2 Aug 1729 (cf. E56).
L(C.121.g.8/92).

C313 — A comical history of the Bible and stick. Or, a
new way to cheat the devil. *Printed at the request
of the generous electors of Westminster, as a warning-
piece to fools,* [1749.]
½⁰: 1 side, 2 columns.
Two acrostics and prose introduction above
the text.
'Oh! that I had ne'er subscribed'
An election squib against Granville Leveson-
Gower, viscount Trentham.
L(1876.f.1/141),O(crop't).

C314 — A comical sonnet,|On Ch-------s blue
bonnet;|Being a sequel to the Merry new joke,|
That was lately written on Joseph's old cloak.
[*Dublin,* 1729?]
½⁰: 2 sides, 1 column.
Woodcut at head, titled 'The wonderful
bonnet'. The DT copy is bound with half-
sheets of Feb 1729.
'Of all the blue bonnets, that came on the stage'
A continuation of *A merry new joke,* [1729?],
satirizing Richard Choppin.
DT.

C315 **Comi-farci-operatical.** A comi-farci-operatical
humorous and political burlesque scene between the
King and Queen of Spain, an English sailor, and
Farinelli, on the present posture of affairs. *Dublin,
printed by James Hoey,* 1741.
8⁰: A⁸; *1–5* 6–15 *16 blk.*
'Briton's rejoice, for Vernon is decreed'
It is doubtful if this was ever intended for
theatrical production.
C,DA.

Comitia. Comitia lyrica, 1707. *See* Maidwell,
Lewis.

C316 **Commendatory.** A commendatory poem to the
honourable city of Dublin, in the behalf of William
Howard esq; anno 1727. By R.V. [*Dublin,* 1727.]
½⁰: 1 side, 1 column.
'A man by his birth and education'
DT.

Commercium. Commercium ad mare australe,
1720. *See* Randolph, Herbert.

C317 **Committee.** A committee of rats, on the down-fall
of catts. [*Dublin,* 1727?]
½⁰: 1 side, 1 column.
The DT copy is bound with half-sheets of 1727.
'One Rhodilard by name,/A cat of wond'rous fame'
C,DT.

C318 **Common.** [dh] The common-hunt, or, the pursute
of the pope. [*London?* 17––.]
2⁰: A²; *1* 2–4.

The **common** hunt

Horizontal chain-lines. Dated by L as [1720?]; but probably earlier.
'Religion having suffer'd long'
Against popery.
L(1850.c.10/58); CLU-C,CSmH,CtY,InU,TxU.

'**Common, Rose,** *shameless woman.*' On wisdom's defeat, [1725.] *See* O230.

C319 Commoner. The commoner, a poem. *London printed, and sold by H. Hills,* 1710.
8º: A⁸; *1–4* 5–14 *15–16.* A8 advt.
Possibly a piracy of an untraced edition. Reissued in *A collection of the best English poetry,* 1717 (*Case* 294).
'When Titan with his splendid rays had blest'
Preface signed 'Incognito'.
L(1875.d.6/178; C.124.b.7/49),LVA-F,O,AdU, WcC; CSmH,CtY,ICN,MH(2),TxU+.

C320 Companion. A companion to the bottle; or, Don Jumpedo in the character of Harlequin jumping down his own throat. *London, printed for B. Dickinson,* March 20, 174⁸₉.
½º: 1 side, 3 columns.
Large engraving at head, which bears the date of publication.
'Howe'er impossible the feat may seem'
A harlequinade inspired by the bottle hoax.
L(P&D 3024); NNP.

C321 Complaint. The complaint of a family, who being very rich, turn'd away a good steward, and afterwards became miserable. [*London*] *Printed by J. Williams, in the Strand,* [1715?]
½º: 1 side, 2 columns.
'A potent family once we were'
A Jacobite ballad lamenting the loss of the Stuarts.
L(1876.f.1/73).

C322 — The complaint of Job. A poem. *London, printed for Richard Wellington,* 1734. (*GM* April)
2º: A² B–D² E¹; *i–iii* iv, *5* 6–18. ii, *18* advts.
'Oh! that the voice of grief had pow'r to raise'
L(1490.f.12),OA; CSmH,CtY,ICN,TxU.

C323 — The complaint of the poor, being deprived of their former way of living, by the uncharitable laws, lately made against begging. The first cry. [*London?*] *Printed for the godly to consider the poors case,* 1711.
8º: A⁸ B⁴; *1–2* 3–24.
A chap-book.
'Ye rulers all, both great and small'
L(11644.ee.22).

— The complaint: or, night-thoughts on life, death, & immortality, 1742–. *See* Young, Edward.

C324 Complete. The compleat art of painting. A poem. Translated from the French of M. du Fresnoy. By D.F. gent. *London, printed for T. Warner,* 1720. (25 March?)

The **complete** art of painting

8º: π¹ A–F⁴ G⁴(–G1); *i–ii,* *1–53* *54 blk.*
Lee 208; *Moore* 430, dating it as 25 March. π1 appears from the CtY copy to have been printed as G1, but it is disjunct, not wrapped round.
'Painting and poetry two sisters are'
Traditionally accepted as Defoe's translation, but apparently on no other grounds than the initials, which are not in the form normally used by Defoe.
LU,O; CLU-C,CtY(stitched,uncut),MB,TxU(uncut).

C325 — The compleat history of Bob of Lyn. A new ballad. To the tune of Bonny Dundee. Proper to be sung at elections. *London, printed for Jacob Lock,* [1741.] (28 Feb)
2º: A⁴ (A2 as 'A'); *1–2* 3–8. *8* advt.
Percival LXVII. A copy from Tom's Coffee House, dated 28 Feb 1741, is in the Lewis Walpole Library.
'Good people of England! give ear to my song!'
A satire on Walpole.
L(11626.h.12/3); IU(uncut).

— The complete vintner, 1734. *See* Ward, Edward [The delights of the bottle].

C326 Compliment. The compliment. Addressed to his royal highness the Duke of Cumberland. Containing, I. An invitation to the Lodge in Windsor Great-Park. II. A new order of knighthood... III. The sweet William. By the author of the Two lurchers, &c. *Eton, printed for J. Pote; sold also by M. Cooper,* [*London,*] 1746. (*GM, LM* Nov)
4º: A² B–D² E¹; *1–2* 3–17 *18 blk.*
The sweet William was also published separately.
'Great Duke! from conquests here retreat'
'William the brave, a fav'rite name'
'The pride of France is lilly white'
The two lurchers has not been identified.
AdU.

Compter. *See* Counter.

Concanen, Matthew. Poems upon several occasions. By the author of, The match at foot-ball. *Dublin, printed by A. Rhames, for E. Dobson,* 1722.
8º: pp. xx, 99.   O,DN; CtY,MH.
No watermark. Dedication signed.

— [fine paper]   L.
Watermark: fleur-de-lys on shield; L copy in presentation binding.

_____

C327 [—] A match at foot-ball: a poem. In three cantos. *Dublin, printed for the author,* 1720.
8º: A⁴ B–E⁴ F²; *1–2* 3–42 *43–44 blk.* 2 err.
Bond 63. List of subscribers on pp. 3–6.
'I sing the pleasures of the rural throng'

Concanen, M. A match at foot-ball

Dedication signed 'M.C.'; printed in Concanen's *Poems*, 1722.

DA(2, – F2),DT(lacks A2.3); *CLU-C*,CSmH,CU, MH.

C328 [—] A match at foot-ball; or the Irish champions. A mock-heroick poem, in three canto's. *London, printed for R. Francklin, W. Chetwood & J. Woodman, & J. Graves, 1721. (DP 27 March)*
8°: π² A–F⁴; i–iv, 1 2–44 45–48. F3–4 advt.
Advertised in *DP* 17 March for publication 'to-morrow' [18 March], but perhaps delayed.
L(11633.e.45/2; 1078.h.12/1; 164.m.1, Luttrell, April),O,DA(–F3–4); CtY,ICN,IU,*MB*,NN+.

C329 — [*idem*] The Fingallians exercise or, the Soards match at foot-ball. A poem. In three cantoes... By Mat Concanen, gent. *Dublin, printed at the Rein Deer, in Montrath-street where printing are done reasonably by C. Hicks,* [1726/36.]
8°: *A*⁸; 1–2 3–16.
LVA-F.

C330 [—] Meliora's tears for Thyrsis: a pastoral lamenting the death of the late Lord Southwell: humbly inscribed. to the right honourable Thomas now Lord Southwell. *Dublin, printed for James Fitz-Symons,* 1720.
8°: A⁴; 1–2 3–8.
'Now crimson blushes stain'd the western sky'
Printed in Concanen's *Poems*, 1722.
DN.

[—] A prologue to the Conscious lovers, 1723. *See* P1133.

C331 **Conclave.** The conclave dissected: or, the character of the f—s of T—y C—e. [*Dublin*, 1725/26.]
½°: 1 side, 1 column.
'When B—n will not with the laws dispense'
Characters of the fellows of Trinity College, Dublin. Attributed in *Advice from fairyland*, 1726, to 'Ph—pps & Dun—can'.
L(C.121.g.8/102),C,DT; CtY.

Conclusion. 'The conclusion, a poem.'
Referred to in *Remarks on the pamphlets lately published, on occasion of the late act of parliament, for bringing to justice the murderers of Captain John Porteous,* [1737?]; this is the final entry, and is possibly meant humourously.

C332 **Condemned.** The condemn'd bridegroom or, the sorrowful lamentation of Mr. Hogan Swanson, who was arraigned at Westminster for stealing Pleasant Rawlings an heiress, and...executed on Wednesday the 9th of December, 1702 at St. Thomas's Watering's near Kent-street-end, in South-wark. To the tune of Johnson's farewel. [*London*, 1702.] (Dec)
½°: 1 side, 2 columns.
'You that have courted women-kind'
L(C.121.g.9/135).

Condolatory

C333 **Condolatory.** A condolatory poem humbly inscrib'd to her most sacred Britannick majesty, occasion'd by the much lamented death of her late royal consort Prince George... By T------s S--------on. *London, printed for the author,* 1708.
½°: 1 side, 2 columns.
Mourning headpiece.
'Of all Great Britain's losses, this alone'
Probably the same author wrote *The Scheld*, [1709.]
L(C.121.g.9/151).

Condom. Condom. A poem, [1723?] *See* Kennett, White [Armour].

Conduitt, John. 'A copy of verses on Mr. Philips's poem on the victory at Bleinheim... To the commons.'
A manuscript, written in pen-and-ink facsimile of type ('a most inimitable piece of penmanship of the famous Chester writing master Thomasin') is at O; there was apparently no printed edition.

C334 [—] A poem upon the late glorious successes, &c. Humbly inscrib'd to his grace the Duke of Marlborough. *London, printed for Jacob Tonson,* 1707 [1706]. (*DC* 30 Dec)
2°: A–C²; i–ii, 1–10.
'Oh! when together will one age afford'
Dobell 2595 quotes a contemporary ms. ascription to Conduitt; a similar attribution is in a copy at Chatsworth.
O,*MR-C*; CLU,CSmH(Luttrell, 30 Dec),CtY, *InU*,OCU.

Coney, Thomas. The devout soul: or an entertainment for a penitent, 1722, 1731.
The verse forms a very small proportion of this devotional work.

———

C335 — A pindarique ode upon her majesty's happy accession to the crown... *London, printed for R. Wilkin,* 1702. (*TC* Trinity)
2°: *A*² B–C²; 1–2 3–12.
'No more, my muse, let worldly toys'
O; CtY.

C336 **Confederacy.** 'The confederacy: or, a welcome to victory; a poem on the several successes of the confederate forces under the command of his grace the Duke of Marlborough. [*London*] Sold by A. Baldwin.' (*WL* Aug 1705)

C337 **Confederates.** The confederates joy, for the taking of Landau. To the tune of, Sound the trumpet. [*London?*] *Printed and sold by T. Moore,* 1704.
½°: 1 side, 2 columns.
Two rough cuts above text.

The confederates joy

'Hark the bells ring, hark the bells ring'
Rothschild.

C338 Conference. A conference concerning transubstantiation. Versify'd by A.N. Address'd to J.M. author of the Conference on the meaning of the word transubstantiation. [*Dublin*] *Printed in the year* 1730.
8°: *A*⁴; *1–4* 5–8.
Dedication signed 'A.N.' The prose *Conference* was also published in Dublin, 1730
'Employ'd in learned dissertation'
L(1606/790).

C339 — A conference in rime betwixt one of the Duke of Argyles men, and the Earl of Mars, taking their chappen. To be sung to the tune of Lilibelaro bulina law. [*Edinburgh*, 1715?]
½°: 1 side, 2 columns.
'Poor Scotland the seat of war is become'
E.

C340 Confession. A confession and lamentation, recomended to Mr. Madder to subscribe before his death that thereby he may appease his countrey mens wrath thats hot against him for his unaccountable hardness. To the tune of, Captain Johnstons lament. [*Edinburgh*, 1705.]
½°: 1 side, 2 columns.
'My countrey men come here I'le tell'
John Madder was first mate to Thomas Green the pirate; they were executed in 1705.
E.

C341 — 'The confession of Peter Hough, proprietor of Sadler's Wells, to a muse. An ode. [*London*] *Milford.* Price 6*d*.' (*BM*,*GM* July 1750)

C342 Confessor. The confessor. A tale. *London printed, and sold by J. Roberts,* 1724. (*MC* April)
2°: 5 ll.
'A cavalier, as story says'
(*Haslewood*, describing Luttrell's copy dated 'April'.)

Confondant. Confondant du passé le leger souvenir... [1731?] *See* Swift, Jonathan.

Congratulary. A congratulary poem on Dean Swift's return to town, 1725. *See* C350.

Congratulatio. Congratulatio Roffensis, 1701. *See* Williams, Bartholomew.

C343 Congratulation. Congratulation for the happy arrival of his grace the Duke of Argile, her majesties high commissioner for the kingdom of Scotland. *Edinburgh, printed by George Jaffrey in the year* 1705.
½°: 1 side, 1 column.
'As when a missive to poor Ovid came'
E.

Congratulation

C344 — The congratulation. Humbly inscrib'd to his grace the Duke of Ormond. *London, printed in the year* 1712.
½°: 1 side, 1 column.
Possibly a Dublin publication; so catalogued by C.
'At length propitious heav'n begins to smile'
L(1850.e.10/25),O,C.

Congratulatory. A congratulatory epistle from his holiness the Pope, 1718. *See* Amhurst, Nicholas.

— A congratulatory epistle to the right honourable Joseph Addison, esq, 1717. *See* Amhurst, Nicholas.

C345 — A congratulatory letter from one poet to another, on the divorcement of his wife. Written some years since... To which is annex'd, an humorous new ballad, called the Female combatants. By B.B. *Dublin, printed by Richard James,* 1747.
8°: *A*⁴ B–*C*⁴; *i–ii* iii–iv, 5–24.
'While you, dear sir! from marriage bonds enlarg'd'
Female combatants: 'Ye lasses and lads, if to listen you'll come'
The first poem is to Matthew Pilkington; the second is on a fight between Lady Pendergrass and Mrs. Phips which took place in 1745, according to a ms. note in the O copy.
L(11631.e.1; 11632.aaa.63),O; CSmH.

C346 — A congratulatory ode, most humbly inscribed to a certain very great man, on his becoming greater. *London, printed for John Warner; sold by the booksellers in Ludgate-street...,* 1744 [1743]. (*GM, LM* Dec)
2°: *A*⁴; *1–2* 3–8.
'O muse, to laureat Cibber dear'
A satire on Samuel Sandys's elevation to the peerage.
L(162.n.57),O(2); CSmH(uncut),MH,OCU(uncut),PU,TxU+.

C347 — A congratulatory ode, most humbly inscribed to the statesman on his travels. By Joshua Jingle, esq; poet laureat to the Pelemites, Selemites, and other great personages. *London, printed for W. Webb,* 1748. (*GM,LM* Aug)
2°: *A*⁴ (A3 as 'B'); *1–4* 5–8. A1 hft.
'Old Eng----d mourns her past disgrace'
Printed with Sir Charles Hanbury Williams's *Odes,* 1768, but the attribution seems improbable. Addressed to the Duke of Cumberland.
CSmH(–A1),IU(cropt),MH(–A1),OCU.

C348 — A congratulatory poem, humbly inscrib'd to the right honourable Francis Child, esq;...October 29. 1731. By an old citizen, but a young poet, alias poetaster... *London, printed for the author,* 1731.
2°: *A*² < B²; *1–3* 4–8.
'Hail! happy Child! thrice happy be the day'
On Child's election as lord mayor. An attack on whig financial policy.
O.

A **congratulatory** poem, humbly inscrib'd

C349 — A congratulatory poem: humbly inscribed to the right honourable Sir Robert Walpole, on the conclusion of the convention between their majesties of Great-Britain and Spain. *London, printed for J. Brett; sold by the booksellers of London & Westminster*, 1739. (*GM* Feb)
2°: A² B²; *1–3* 4–8.
'While faction rages with envenom'd spite'
L(11630.h.57/4),O,OW; CLU,CSmH,TxU.

C350 — A congratulary poem on Dean Swift's return to town. By a member of the club, held at Mr. Taplin's in Truck-street, October, 7th. 1725. *Dublin, printed in the year* 1725.
½°: 1 side, 1 column.
Teerink 1210.
'Welcome! thou guardian genius of our isle'
L(C.121.g.8/48).

C351 — A congratulatory poem, on his grace, James, duke of Ormond. Written by a lady of quality, and presented to his grace, by her own hand. *London printed, and sold by H. Hills,* 1712.
8°: A⁴; *1–4* 5–8.
'Welcome brave warrior, welcome to the name'
MH.

C352 — A congratulatory poem; on his grace the Duke of Ormond. Lord lieutenant of Ireland, &c. *Dublin, printed* 1703.
8°: A⁴(−A1) B–D⁴ E⁴(−E4); *i–ii*, 1–34. ii err.
E3 was apparently wrongly imposed; the leaf has been reversed in binding. Possibly A1 and E4 are missing from the copy seen.
'Let others with loud Iö's fill the skies'
Dedication signed 'W.C.'
DN.

C353 — A congratulatory poem on his majesty King George's safe and happy return to his British dominions, Dec. 30, 1723. By the company of grey-headed gentlemen... *London, printed by R. Tookey,* 1724.
2°: A¹ B²; *i–ii*, 1 2–4.
Copies seen may lack a half-title.
'Receive, great sir, with a propitious smile'
Compare *Right Brunswick-mum...being the white-hair'd gentlemen's congratulation,* 1715.
CtY(lacks A1),OCU.

C354 — 'A congratulatory poem on his majesty's safe arrival in England. [*London*] *Printed for the author; sold by J. Janeway, and by the pamphletsellers of London & Westminster.* Price 6d.' (*DJ* 27 Sept 1732).

C355 — A congratulatory poem, on the anniversary-day of his majesty King George's coronation, being Monday October 20. 1718. These lines are humbly inscrib'd to all the worthy, loyal gentlemen of Kent... By T.H. gent. *Canterbury, printed by J. Abree,* 1718.
2°: A²; *1–2* 3–4.
'Phospher, drive on, and usher in this day'
The author also wrote *A panegyrical poem on*

A **congratulatory** poem, on the anniversary

the fair and celebrated beauties, 1718, variously ascribed to T. Harrison or T. Hardres.
InU.

C356 — A congratulatory poem on the happy accession to the throne of the high and mighty Princess Anne, our most gracious queen. *London, printed by I. Dawks; sold by John Nutt,* [1702.] (23 March, Luttrell)
1°: 1 side, 2 columns.
'When sable clouds on racking winds do fly'
MH(Luttrell).

— A congratulatory poem on the happy prospect of peace, [1736.] *See* A gratulatory poem, [1736.]

C357 — A congratulatory poem on the happy recovery of the Earl of Stair from his late illness. Humbly address'd to her grace the Dutchess dowager of Marlborough. *London, printed for J. & H. Pemberton; sold by W. Bickerton,* 1744. (*GM, LM* June)
2°: A⁴; *1–3* 4–8.
Horizontal chain-lines.
'Dear to bright honour, to thy country dear'
O.

— A congratulatory poem, on the most auspicious birth-day of his majesty King George, 1723. *See* Nevil, Henry.

C358 — A congratulatory poem on the translation of the right reverend father in god, Edmund, from the see of Lincoln, to the see of London. *London, printed for J. Roberts,* 1724.
4°: A² B–D²; *1–2* 3–16.
The watermark of the copy seen, fleur-de-lys on shield, suggests fine paper.
'As diff'ring parties once did all agree'
On Edmund Gibson.
L(11631.f.13).

C359 — A congratulatory poem to his grace the D. of Argyle, on his late victory over the rebels in Scotland. *London, printed for Edward Symon,* 1716 [1715]. (*MC* Dec)
2°: A(3 ll); *1–2* 3–6.
Watermark: fool's cap. A2 signed.
'Whilst great Argyle, allur'd with worthy views'
Possibly the 'poem to the Duke of Argyle, upon his obtaining a victory over the rebels' attributed to Samuel Croxall in *Cibber* V. 292.
PPL.

C360 — [fine paper]
Watermark: fleur-de-lys on shield.
L(163.n.36).

— A congratulatory poem to his grace the Duke of Marlborough, &c. upon his safe return, 1704. *See* Smallwood, James.

C361 — A congratulatory poem to his grace the Duke of Marlborough, on his glorious success and victories over the French and Bavarians. *London, printed by R. Janeway; sold by B. Bragg,* 1704. (12 Aug, Luttrell)
½°: *1–2*, 1 column.

A **congratulatory** poem to his grace

'Brave general, whose conduct in the field'
R. D. Horn in *Huntington Library Quarterly*
24 (1961) ascribes this to James Smallwood,
but the evidence is not conclusive.
MH.

C362 — A congratulatory poem to the right honourable,
Sir E.S. &c. [*London*? 1702?]
½°: 2 sides, 1 column.
The date is suggested by the references to the
Duke of Ormond's victories by sea and land.
'The poets praise those most who need it least'
Longleat.

C363 — A congratulatory poem upon his most sacred
majesty's happy arrival from his German domi-
nions... A pindaric. By T.G. M.D. in Suffolk.
London, printed by R.T. [*R. Tookey*?]; *sold by S.
Popping,* 1719. (Nov, Luttrell)
2°: A–B² C²; *1–6 7–12.* A1 hft.
'All hail! to Britain's monarch; view nature's act!'
TxU(Luttrell).

— A congratulatory poem upon the coronation of
his majesty King George, 1714. *See* Erskine, Ralph.

C364 — A congratulatory poem, upon the safe arrival of
his grace the Duke of Shrewsbury in Ireland.
Dublin, printed by E. Waters, 1713.
½°: 1 side, 1 column.
'Welcome, great hero! from the best of queens'
Rothschild.

— A congratulatory verse, to her grace the
Dutchess of Marlborough, 1704. *See* Johnson,
Charles.

— Congratulatory verses to Edward Biddle, 1718.
See Amhurst, Nicholas.

C365 — Congratulatory verses to the reverend Mr.
Thomas Wharton... occasioned by the death of the
celebrated Matthew Prior esq; *London, printed for
J. Peele,* 1722 [1721]. (*DP* 17 Nov)
2°: A² B¹; *1–3 4–6.*
'Pox on these senseless, whining sonneteers'
Ms. 'Risdale' at head of title in the O copy;
the O catalogue suggests his authorship, but
it is almost certainly an owner's name. The
congratulations are due to Prior's death leaving
some scope for lesser poets.
O,OW; CtY(Luttrell, Jan).

C366 Congress. The congress. A poem. Inscribed to the
right reverend John, lord bishop of London.
London, printed for J. Roberts, 1714. (*PB* 9 March)
8°: A–C⁴ D²; *1–3 4–27 28.* 28 advt.
'To hush the melancholy voice of war'
With characters of the ministry.
O; CtY(cropt),MH,OCU.

C367 — The congress of beasts. To which is annex'd,
Advice to Sir Bob. A new ballad. Dedicated to a
certain she monster. *London, printed for A. More,*
[1728.] (*MChr* 21 Dec)
4°: A⁴ B–C⁴; *i–v vi–vii viii blk, 9–24.* A1 hft.

The **congress** of beasts

'When beasts could speak in times of yore'
Advice: 'Whilst doubty Bob with muckle might'
Dedication signed 'Bestia de Silva'. Against
Walpole and his administration.
L(164.n.62, Luttrell, undated),C(−A1).

C368 — The congress of excise-asses. Or, Sir B--ue
S--ng's overthrow: a new ballad. To the tune of,
I'll tell thee, Estcourt, a pleasant tale. *London,
printed for Mr. Nichols, and sold at the pamphlet
shops,* [1733.] (*GM, LM* Feb)
2°: A² B²; *1–2 3–8.*
Percival XXVI. Two large woodcuts on title.
Reprinted on a large sheet with *Britannia
excisa,* [1733.]
'All good Christian people'
Percival p. xlvii suggests William Pulteney's
authorship on the evidence of style. On the
fall of the excise scheme, planned by Walpole,
Sir William Yonge, and Sir John Randolph.
L(P&D 1937*),O(cropt),C(uncut); MH,NNC
(uncut),TxU.

C369 — The congress of the beasts. To the tune of, Lili
bulera buling a la. [*London*? 1748.]
½°: 1 side, 1 column.
'O brother Tom, do you hear the event?'
A beast fable about the congress of Aix-la-
Chapelle.
E.

Congreve, William.
*Congreve's poems were collected in the third volume
of his* Works, *1710; most copies have a second title
'Poems upon several occasions' and a table of contents,
the preliminaries collating A⁴ a²; another issue (copy
at MH) omits these and the preliminaries are
apparently A⁴(−A1).*

— The poetical works of Mr. William Congreve...
*Dublin, printed by J. Jones, for George Risk, George
Ewing, & William Smith,* 1736.
12°: pp. [97]–328.　O.
A reissue of sheets E–O of volume 2 of the
Dublin 1736 edition of Congreve's *Works.*

———

C370 — A hymn to harmony, written in honour of
St. Cecilia's day, MDCCI... Set to musick by
Mr. John Eccles... *London, printed for Jacob
Tonson,* 1703 [1702]. (*PM* 10 Dec)
2°: A² B–C²; *i–iv, 1–7 8.* A1 hft; 8 advt.
Watermark: crown. The Luttrell copy, dated
11 Dec, is in the Pforzheimer collection.
'O harmony, to thee we sing'
L(C.59.i.9),O,*MR*; CLU-C,CSmH,CtY,MB,
MH.

C371 — [fine paper]
Watermark: X (cf. *Heawood* 3116); no adver-
tisement on p. 8, which is blank.
CSmH,TxU.

C372 [—] An impossible thing. A tale. *London printed,
and sold by J. Roberts,* 1720. (*DC* 25 March)

Congreve, W. An impossible thing

    4⁰: $A^4(\pm A2)$ B⁴ C²; *i–iv, 1* 2–16. A1 hft.
        Watermark: ? ID. Half-title 'Two tales'; on
        p. 14 'The peasant in search of his heifer...'
    'A goblin of the merry kind'
    Peasant: 'It so befell: a silly swain'
        Printed in Congreve's *Works*, 1720; sometimes
        wrongly attributed to Prior. Imitated from
        La Fontaine.
    L(163.1.55, Luttrell, 25 March); CtY.

C373 [—] [fine paper]
        Watermark: fleur-de-lys. The copy at O
        appears to have a cancel B3.4.
    O(−A1); CSmH.

C374 [—] [*idem*] Two tales. First, an Impossible thing.
    Second, the Peasant in search of his heifer. After
    M. De la Fontaine. [*Dublin*, 1722?]
    8⁰: A^8; *1–3* 4–15 '14'.
        Title in half-title form. The DA copy is
        catalogued as 1722, but no authority for this
        date has been traced.
    DA.

    [—] Jack Frenchman's lamentation. An excellent
new song, 1708. *See* J1.

C375 — A letter from Mr. Congreve to the right
honourable the lord Viscount Cobham. *London,
printed for A. Dodd, & E. Nutt*, 1729. (*MC* March)
    2⁰: A^2 B¹; *1–3* 4–6.
        Reprinted with the Dublin edition of Pope's
        Dunciad, 1729.
    'Sincerest critick of my prose, or rhime'
    L(162.n.5, Luttrell, March; Ashley 5177),O,OW,
    LdU-B; CSmH,CtY,KU,MH,TxU+.

    — The mourning muse of Alexis, 1709. *In* A39.

C376 — A pindarique ode, humbly offer'd to the queen,
on the victorious progress of her majesty's arms...
To which is prefix'd, a discourse on the pindarique
ode. *London, printed for Jacob Tonson*, 1706. (*LG*
19 Aug)
    2⁰: π¹ A–C² D¹; *i–vi*, 1–10.
        There are undoubtedly fine-paper copies (e.g.
        DK,ICU) but as there are no watermarks to
        distinguish them, they are not separately
        recorded. π1 and D1 have been seen to be
        conjugate.
    'Daughter of memory, immortal muse'
    L(840.m.1/5; Ashley 4786),O(2),C(2, 1 uncut),
    DT,LdU-B+; CLU-C(uncut),CtY,ICN,MH,
    TxU(2, 1 uncut)+.

C377 [—] A prologue spoken by Mrs. Bracegirdle, at the
entertainment of Love for love. [column 2:]
Epilogue spoken by Mrs. Barry, April the 7th, 1709.
at a representation of Love for love: for the benefit
of Mr. Betterton, at his leaving the stage. *London,
printed for J. Smith near Fleetstreet*, 1709.
    ½⁰: 1 side, 2 columns.
        Prologue and epilogue in two columns, with
        title at head of each.
    'Custom, which every where bears mighty sway'

Congreve, W. A prologue

    'As some brave knight, who once with spear &
shield'
        The prologue is by Congreve, originally
        published in 1695 (copy at LVA-F); the new
        epilogue is by Rowe, published separately in
        1709.
    MH.

C378 [—] Prologue to the court; on the queen's birth-
day, 1704. *London, printed for J. Tonson*, 1705.
(6 Feb, Luttrell)
    ½⁰: 1–2, 1 column.
        Advertised in *DC* 8 Feb.
    'The happy muse, to this high scene preferr'd'
        Printed in Congreve's *Works*, 1710.
    Crawford; CSmH,ICN(Luttrell),MB,MH,TxU.

    [—] A satyr against love. Revis'd and corrected by
Mr. Congreve, 1703. *See* S43.

C379 — The tears of Amaryllis for Amyntas. A pastoral.
Lamenting the death of the late lord Marquis of
Blandford... *London, printed for Jacob Tonson*,
1703. (2 July, Luttrell)
    2⁰: A–C²; *i–iv*, 1–8.
        Watermark: fool's cap. Listed in *WL* June.
        Morgan F86 records a 1705 quarto edition, not
        traced.
    ''Twas at the time, when new returning light'
    LDW,O; CLU-C(Luttrell),CtY,DFo,ICU,TxU
    (2)+.

C380 — [fine paper]
        Watermark: ID.
    L(1346.m.33); CSmH.

C381 **Conjuring.** The conjuring whig or the hanging
sails man. '*London, printed for Evan Jones near Shon
ap Morgan Row*', [1716?]
    ½⁰: 1 side, 2 columns.
        The imprint is probably false.
    'Come listen a while and I will unfold'
        The tale of a Welshman hanged as the Pretender.
    L(1876.f.1/80).

C382 **Connoisseur.** The connoisseur. A satire on the
modern men of taste. *London, printed for Robert
Turbutt; sold by the booksellers in town & country*,
[1735.] (*GM* March)
    2⁰: A^2 B–F²; *1–5* 6–22 *23*; 24 blk. A1 hft; F2 advt.
    'Why sleeps the muse, whilst blund'ring Dorus
lives'
    L(11630.h.15,−F2),O(−A1),*DrU-U*,WcC(uncut);
    CSmH,CtY(−A1,F2),ICU,MH,TxU(2)+.

C383 **Conquerant.** Le conquerant d'Ecosse. '*A Edimbourg*', 1745.
    8⁰: A^8; *1–3* 4–14 *15–16*.
        The typography seems almost certainly
        continental. A8 not seen.
    'Le crime assez longtems gouverna⟨it⟩ l'Angle-
terre'
    Jacobite propaganda.
    E(−A8).

Consequence

Consequence. The consequence of a late famous treaty, 1749. *See* The hostages, 1749.

Consolation. The consolation, 1745. *See* Young, Edward (Y54).

C384 — Consolation to Mira mourning. A poem. Discovering a certain governor's intreigue [!] with a lady at his court. [*London*] *Printed, and sold by the booksellers of London & Westminster*, 1710.
8⁰: A⁸; *1–2* 3–16.
'Why thus disguis'd? Ah! why's thy lovely face'
> *Wright & Spears* 800 quote T. J. Wise's suggestion of Prior or Settle's authorship; they reject Prior's, and Settle's authorship seems extremely improbable.

L(1488.aa.18),O(2),AdU,LdU-B; CLU-C,CtY, ICN,MH,TxU+.

Consolatory. 'A consolatory epistle to the author of the Curious maid, occasion'd by his awkward answerers, and imitators.'
> Advertised for publication 'in a few days' in *PB* 18 April 1721; there is no evidence that it ever appeared.

C385 — A consolatory epistle to the Jacks of Great Britain. Written originally in Spanish, on occasion of the taking of Vigo; by an Irish, Romish, Spanish, runaway, rebel-captain. Made English by a gentleman of Oxford. *London printed, and sold by W. Boreham*, [1719.] (28 Nov, Luttrell)
8⁰: A–B⁴ C² (A2 as 'A'); *i–ii* iii–viii, 1–12.
'No doubt you've heard, his excellence'
> The Spanish original is surely fictitious; against the Jacobites.

L(164.k.42, Luttrell),DN.

C386 — A consolatory ode. Inscrib'd to the Marquis de la Chetardie, on his disgrace, and return from the Russian court. *London, printed for M. Cooper*, [1744.] (*GA* 29 Aug)
4⁰: A–B⁴; *1–3* 4–15 *16 blk*.
'Who's that in melancholy dumps?'
L(11630.c.4/4; 11630.c.13/12, lacks B4),CT.

C387 — A consolatory poem in praise of retirement. Spoke to the late King James, at his arrival at St. Germains, in the year 1688. By Father L. *London, printed for A. Baldwin*, 1701. (30 Oct, Luttrell)
2⁰: A² B–C² D¹; *i–ii*, 1–12.
'How easy 'tis to prove that all is vanity'
AdU(Luttrell); CLU,CLU-C,CSmH,MH.

C388 — A consolatory poem on the death of a young lady, in a dialogue between Calophilus and Theophilus. Humbly address'd to all persons, who are under any dejection of spirit upon the death of a... friend. *Reading printed, and sold by J. Newbery & C. Micklewright; and by T. Cooper, London*, 1742. (21 June)
2⁰: A² B–C²; *i–iv*, 1–8. A1 hft.
> Listed in *GM, LM* June as 'printed for T. Cooper'.

A **consolatory** poem on the death

'What hideous shrieks are these, which pierce mine ears'
Lewis Walpole Library (Tom's Coffee House, 21 June).

C389 — — The second edition. *London, printed for James Fletcher in the Turl, Oxford*, 1746.
2⁰: A¹ B–C²; *i–ii*, 1–8.
> Apparently a reissue of the preceding with a cancel title-leaf; the copy seen possibly lacks a half-title.

L(11630.g.27).

C390 **Conspiracy.** The conspiracy. A poem. Part I. *London, printed for B. Couse*, 1744. (*GM,LM* Nov)
8⁰: A–G⁴ H²; *1–3* 4–60.
'Where erst Knight-Templars made their fam'd abode'
NN.

C391 **Constable.** The constable's trip from Turn-stile to Hick's-Hall. *London, printed by T. Jarriot*, [1714.] (14 July, Luttrell)
½⁰: 1 side, 1 column.
'Within the space of less than half a mile'
> 'Upon Mr John Mills', Luttrell.

ICN(Luttrell).

C392 **Constant.** The constant lovers: or, the pleasures of matrimony. A new ballad. Dedicated to Sir Robert Walpole and his new-married lady. *London, printed for C. Patterson, in the Strand*, [1738.]
½⁰: 1 side, 2 columns.
> *Percival* appendix 64. Large woodcut above text.

'Lucinda the lovely,/The joy of her swain'
> On Maria Skerret's marriage to Walpole.

L(1876.f.1/110); *Harding*.

Constellation. The constellation: poems, on several occasions, 1715. *See* Bland, —, *Mr*.

C393 **Consultation.** The consultation. [*London*] *Printed in the year* 1712.
½⁰: 1 side, 1 column.
'At dead of night when midnight hags prepare'
> Marlborough and Godolphin plotting their restoration to power.

L(1850.e.10/24).

C394 **Consummation.** Consummation: or, the rape of Adonis. *London, printed for E. Curll*, 1741. (*Craftsman* 7 Nov)
8⁰: A⁴ B–F⁴; [4] *i* ii–iii *iv*, 1 2–38 *39–40*. A1 hft; F4 advt.
> With 'The resurrection, a tale' on p. 24 and 'The dispute' on p. 30. Reissued in *The Merryland miscellany*, 1742 (DLC).

'While some with Cæsar's praise defile the page'
L(P.C.20.b.7/4); CSmH(–A1),DLC,KU.

Contemplation. Contemplation: or, the triumph of love, 1747. *See* Hamilton, William, *of Bangour*.

Contending

Contending. The contending candidates, 1722.
See Ward, Edward (W122).

C395 Contest. A contest between Mars and Jupiter. A
serenade to be represented on the birth-day of his
most sacred majesty George...at the castle of
Dublin the 28th of May, 1721... Prepar'd by
Mr. John Sigismond Cousser... *Dublin, printed by
Thomas Hume*, 1721.
4°: *A*⁴; *1–3* 4–8.
'Pernicious peace! fair but illusive syren'
DT.

C396 — A contest between Marsyas and Apollo, to be
represented on the birth-day of his most sacred
majesty George...at the castle of Dublin the 28th
of May, 1723...Set by Mr. John Sigismond
Cousser... *Dublin, printed by Thomas Hume*, 1723.
4°: *A*⁴; *1–3* 4–8.
'Forbear, unskillful mortal'
Apparently translated from the Italian.
DG,DT.

C397 — The contest decided, address'd to Mrs. Woffington. [*Dublin*, 174-/5-.]
½°: *1–2*, 1 column.
'The muses having lately met'
Margaret Woffington settles the dispute
between Tragedy and Comedy.
L(1890.e.5/177).

C398 Contrast. [dh] The contrast. [*Edinburgh?* 1746?]
8°: *A*²; *1–4*.
On pp. 2–4, 'An epitaph in imitation of Dr.
Arbuthnot's on Colonel Charteris', which is
not in verse.
'Happy the man, and worthy so to be'
A Jacobite attack on William duke of Cumber-
land.
E(2).

C399 — The contrast to the Man of honour. *London,
printed for J. Morgan*, 1737. (*LM* May; *GM* June)
2°: *A*² B–E²; *i–ii* iii *iv*, 5–19 *20 blk*.
'Must smiling innocence, and well-try'd worth'
The preface refers to the death of 'Timothy
Scrub' or Eustace Budgell; he and the tories
are attacked.
L(11630.h.22),LVA-D,O,*DrU-U*; CSmH,CtY,
MH,OCU,TxU.

C400 Contretemps. The contre temps; or, rival queans:
a small farce. As it was lately acted, with great
applause, at H—d—r's private th—re near the
H---y m---t. *London, printed for A. Moore*, 1727.
4°: *A*² B–D²; *1–5* 6–16. A1 hft.
'Dread queen and princess, hail! we thus are met'
A satire in dramatic form on Heidegger,
Cuzzoni, Senesino, Faustina, and Handel. Not
to be confused with Cibber's burlesque, *The
rival queans.*
O; *DFo,MH,NN.*

Convent

C401 Convent. The convent. A tale. *London, printed for
M. Cooper*, 1749. (*GM, LM* Feb)
8°: A–C⁴; *1–2* 3–23 *24 blk*.
'As a long sword and scarlet cloaths'
OCU.

C402 Convention. The convention. An excellent new
ballad. To which is added, The King of Spain's
protest, and a new epitaph. *London, printed for
T. Reynolds*, 1739.
2°: A⁴; *1–3* 4–5 6–7; *8 blk.*
Percival XLIII.
'Ken ye, sirs, for as much as some small differences'
An epistle from a n--ble l--d, 1740 suggests
Pulteney's authorship. A satire on the con-
vention between England and Spain.
O; MH(lacks A1.4),MH-BA(lacks A4),TxU(2, 1
uncut).

C403 — — *London, printed for T. Reynolds*, 1739.
2°: A⁴; *1–3* 4–78 *blk.*
Probably another impression, with pagination
added to pp. 6–7.
CLU(uncut),CtY(uncut),InU,KU(cropt).

C404 — 'The convention. [*Edinburgh.*] Price 3d.' (*SM*
Feb 1739)
Probably an Edinburgh piracy of the preceding.

Conversation. The conversation. A tale, 1720. See
Prior, Matthew.

Convert. The convert: a poem, 1749. See Cooke,
Thomas, *vicar of Bayton.*

C405 Cook, Ebenezer. The sot-weed factor: or, a
voyage to Maryland. A satyr. In which is describ'd,
the laws, governments, courts and constitutions of
the country... In burlesque verse. *London printed,
and sold by B. Bragg*, 1708. (15 Jan, Luttrell)
4°: *A*¹ B–F² G¹ (F1 as 'E'); *i–ii*, 1–21 *22 blk.*
Bond 21. Listed in *WL* Dec 1707. Reprinted as
Sotweed redivivus at Annapolis, 1730.
'Condemn'd by fate to wayward curse'
L(1077.c.59, imprint cropt; 161.l.24, Luttrell);
MH,*MnHi*,NN,*PP,RPJCB.*

Cooke, Thomas, *1703–1756*. The Idylliums of
Moschus and Bion, translated from the Greek.
With annotations. To which is prefixed an account
of their lives... *London, printed for J. Brotherton, &
Jer. Battley*, 1724. (*MC* April)
8°: pp. 100.   L; CSmH.
The price below the imprint is usually deleted
in ms.

— [variant: no date or price on title]   L.
The copy seen is in a contemporary morocco
binding; clearly this issue is for presentation,
but it does not appear to be on fine paper.

— The works of Hesiod translated from the Greek.
London, printed by N. Blandford, for T. Green, 1728.
4°: 2 vol.   L,O; IU,MH.

Cooke, T. *Collections*

There are possibly fine-paper copies. The copyright and 80 books were sold in Green's trade sale, 13 March 1732 (cat. at O-JJ) for £6. 2s.

— — The second edition. *London, printed by John Wilson, for John Wood & Charles Woodward*, 1740. 12°: pp. lv, 240.   L,O; IU,MH.

— [reissue] The second edition. *London, printed for T. Longman, J. Osborn, S. Birt, & C. Hitch*, 1743.
L.
Cancel title.

— Tales, epistles, odes, fables, &c. With translations from Homer and other antient authors. To which are added proposals... *London, printed for T. Green*, 1729. (*MChr* 3 April)
8°: pp. iv, 214.   L,LVA-D; CtY,MH.
The copyright was sold in Green's trade sale, 13 March 1732 (cat. at O-JJ).

[—] The Bays miscellany, or Colley triumphant... Written by Scriblerus Quartus. *London, printed for A. Moore; sold by the booksellers of London & Westminster*, [1730.] (*MChr* Dec)
8°: pp. 38.   L; DFo,MH.
Apparently all by Cooke, but possibly others may have assisted.

— Mr. Cooke's original poems, with imitations and translations... *London, printed for T. Jackson, & C. Bathurst*, 1742. (*GM* April)
12°: pp. vi, 311.   L,O; CLU-C,MH.

C406 — The bath. A tale. Addressed to his grace the Duke of Montague. *London, printed for J. Roberts*, 1726. (*MC* Jan)
2°: A² B–D²; *1–5* 6–15 *16 blk*. A1 hft.
Printed by Samuel Richardson (*Sale* 43).
'Say, shall the brave like common mortals dye'
CLU(−A1),CtY,MH.

C407 — — To which is added, the Scandalous chronicle: or, ballad of characters. Written for the use of the poets... *Dublin, re-printed in the year* 1726.
8°: A⁴ B²; *1–2* 3–12.
'The scandalous chronicle' occupies pp. 9–12.
Scandalous chronicle: 'Young Flash, a bard, and eke a beau'
'The scandalous chronicle' is assumed to be by Cooke in *DNB*, but no confirmation of this has been found.
L(993.e.49/3; 11631.a.63/9, lacks B²).

C408 [—] The battle of the poets. An heroick poem. In two canto's. *London, printed for J. Roberts*, 1725. (*MC* May)
2°: A² B–E²; *1–3* 4–20.
'Thy forest, Windsor, and the dreadful day'
Early ms. attribution in the O copy; a revised version printed in Cooke's *Tales*, 1729. Not to be confused with the play of this title, published in 1731.
L(12273.m.1/10; 643.m.12/34),O; CtY,DFo, TxU.

Cooke, T.

[—] The battle of the sexes: a poem [by Samuel Wesley, preface by Cooke], 1723. *See* W333.

C409 [—] The candidates for the bays. A poem... Written by Scriblerus Tertius. *London, printed for A. Moore, and sold at the White-hart, next E. Lynn's, whip-maker, over against Devereux-Court, without Temple-Bar*, 1730. (*MChr* Dec)
4°: A–B⁴; *i–ii*, 1–13 *14*. 14 advt.
'Britannia long since was the muses retreat'
Ascribed to Cooke by *CBEL*, doubtless on account of the pseudonym which was used by Cooke; the attribution should be treated with caution until it is confirmed.
O; CtY,MH.

C410 — An epistle to the right honourable the Countess of Shaftesbury, with a prologue and epilogue on Shakespeare and his writings. *London, printed for T. Cooper*, 1743. (*GM,LM* Jan)
2°: A² B²; *1–2* 3–8.
The prologue on p. 5, epilogue on p. 7.
'Fair patroness of long departed worth'
Prologue: 'The sun without a rival guides the day'
Epilogue: 'An antient bard, Simonides his name'
L(1347.m.20),O; CSmH,CtY,IU,MH,TxU+.

C411 — An essay on nobility, addressed to his grace the Duke of Somerset. [*London*] *Printed in the year* 1736.
4°: A¹ B²; *1–3* 4–6.
Possibly this separate edition was intended for private circulation only.
'Glory by few is rightly understood'
O.

C412 [—] Essays. I. On nobility. To his grace the Duke of Somerset. II. On the antient and modern state of Britain... To his grace the Duke of Marlborough. *London, printed, and sold by J. Huggonson*, 1737.
2°: A² B–C² D¹; *1–3* '2' 5–13 *14 blk*.
'Price six-pence' on title. The additional poem has first line:
'Shall France triumphant over Europe ride'
Reprinted in Cooke's *Poems*, 1742.
O; CSmH,CtY,MH,OCU(uncut),TxU+.

C413 [—] [reissue] *London, printed for T. Cooper*, 1739.
2°: A²(±A1) B–C² D¹; *1–3* '2' 5–13 *14 blk*.
'Price one shilling' on cancel title. *Rothschild* 218.
CSmH,CtY,ICN,NN.

C414 [—] An hymn to liberty. *London, printed for R. Francklin, R. Dodsley, & M. Cooper*, 1746. (13 Feb)
2°: A¹ B–D² E¹; *1–3* 4–16.
Date from *Straus, Dodsley*; listed in *GM,LM* Feb.
'Of reason and of virtue born'
Early ms. ascription to Cooke in a TxU copy; *GM* Jan 1792 quotes a letter from Ambrose Philips to Cooke, 11 June 1746, in praise of the poem.
L(1347.m.40),O,LdU-B(2); CSmH,CtY,IU,MH, TxU(2)+.

Cooke, T. Immortality reveal'd

C415 — Immortality reveal'd. A poem. In four epistles. To a friend. *London, printed by W. Bowyer, for the author,* 1745.
2°: π^1 a² b¹ c² B–U²; *i–ii* iii–viii *ix–xii,* 1–76. viii err. List of subscribers in c².
'Studious and grave has ever been thy mind'
Preface signed, p. viii.
L(11657.m.12),O; TxU(ms. errata).

C416 — Marlborough, a poem in three cantos. Occasion'd by the death of the late Duke of Marlborough. *London, printed for T. Payne,* 1722. (Aug?)
8°: A^4 B–D⁴; *i–viii,* 1 2–24. A1 hft.
Listed in *DJ* 30 Aug as 'just publish'd'.
'Fair Cytherea, and her lovely train'
Dedication signed.
L(1077.i.33/3),*HU*; IU,MH(–A1).

C417 [—] An ode on beauty, to which are prefixed some observations on taste, and on the present state of poetry in England. *London, printed for M. Cooper, & R. Dodsley,* 1749. (21 Nov)
2°: A² B–C² (A2 as 'A'); *1–2* 3–11 *12 blk.*
Horizontal chain-lines. Date from *Straus, Dodsley*; listed in *GM, LM* Nov. A second edition was published in 1756.
'Direct thine eye to yonder plains'
Cooke's authorship is recorded in *GM* Jan, March 1792.
L(11630.h.49),O(2); CtY(2),ICN,MH,NjP,TxU
+.

C418 [—] An ode on martial virtue, to which are prefixed observations on taste, and the present state of poetry in England. *London, printed for M. Cooper,* 1750. (*LM* March)
2°: A^2 B–C²; *1–2* 3–12.
'Go, says the centaur to Pelides, go'
Cooke's authorship is recorded in *GM* Jan, March 1792.
L(11630.h.31),O; CSmH,CtY(2),ICN,MH,TxU
+.

C419 — Petworth. A poem. To his grace the Duke of Somerset. *London, printed in the year* 1739.
2°: A^2 B²; *1–2* 3–7 *8 blk.*
'From town retir'd, where vice and folly reign'
O; CtY,NjP.

C420 [—] 'Philander and Cydippe. A love tale, address'd to the hon. the Marchioness of Annandale. [*London*] *Printed for J. Brotherton.* Price 6d.' (*MC* May 1727)
Listed in *CBEL* with date 1726.
'In that fair isle, the garden of the main'
Reprinted in Cooke's *Poems,* 1742, as 'third edition'.

C421 — A poem occasion'd by the late conspiracy. By Mr. Cooke. *London, printed for J. Roberts,* 1723. (Jan, Luttrell)
2°: A^2 B²; *i–iv,* 1 2–4.
'Albion, the glory of her sister isles'
Probably by Thomas Cooke, though not

Cooke, T. A poem

collected in his *Tales,* 1729. On the Atterbury plot?
AdU(Luttrell).

C422 [—] A rhapsody on virtue and pleasure. To the right honourable James Reynolds esq;... *London, printed for T. Cooper,* 1738 [1739?]. (*GM, LM* Feb 1739)
2°: A^2 B–D²; *1–2* 3–16.
Watermark: T; 'Price one shilling' on title. *Rothschild* 216.
'When virtue from the busy world retires'
The fine-paper copies below are not anonymous.
O,C,LdU-B; *CLU-C,*IU,MH,OCU,TxU.

C423 — [fine paper]
Watermark: fleur-de-lys on shield; no price on title. Cooke named as author.
CSmH,CtY,MH,TxU.

C424 [Cooke, Thomas, *vicar of Bayton.*] The convert: a poem. *Birmingham, printed for the author; sold by H. Moseley, in Kidderminster; J. Cotton, in Shrewsbury; R. Bailey, in Lichfield; & T. Aris, in Birmingham,* 1749.
4°: A^2 B–H²; *1–5* 6–31 *32 blk.*
'Awak'd at last, thanks to thy gracious call'
Dedication signed 'T. C.', expanded in ms. in the ShU copy to 'Cooke'.
BP(uncut, ms. notes),*ShU.*

C425 — A cursory view of the creation; in a hymn to the all-gracious, wise and powerful creator. In four parts. *London, printed for the author; sold by W. Innys & R. Manby,* 1739.
2°: A–B² b² c¹ C–Y²; [2] *i–v* vi–xiv, 1 2–78.
No watermark; horizontal chain-lines. List of subscribers, pp. vii–xii. Listed in *GM, LM* Nov 1740.
'When with attentive thought and curious eye'
CLU,IU(ms. corrections).

C426 — [fine paper]
Watermark: fleur-de-lys on shield.
O(marbled wrappers),BP(marbled wrappers).

[**Cooke, William,** *dean of Ely.*] Musæ juveniles. *Londini, typis H. Parker; cura Josephi Pote, bibliopolæ Etonensis,* 1732.
8°: pp. 104.   O,LdU-B.
Watermark: crowned initials. Early ms. attribution in the L copy of following issue.

[—] [fine paper]   L.
Watermark: ? dagger.

[**Cooper, John Gilbert.**] Poems on several subjects... By the author of the Life of Socrates. *London, printed for R. & J. Dodsley,* 1764.
12°: pp. 139.   L,O; MH.

C427 [—] The power of harmony: a poem. In two books. *London, printed for R. Dodsley,* 1745. (*GM, LM* Nov)

Cooper, J. The power of harmony

4°: A^4 B–F^4 G^2; 1–4 5–52. A1 hft.
'Of harmony, and her cœlestial pow'r'
Reprinted in Cooper's *Poems*, 1764.
L(11630.b.4/7; 11630.e.6/4,−A1; 1465.k.7, −A1),O,OC,OW,LdU-B; CtY(−A1),DFo,ICN, IU,NN.

C428 [**Cooper, William.**] Præhonorabili domino, ------ comite [!] de ------, &c. &c. [1749.]
obl ¼°: 1 side, 2 columns.
'Huc, venerande! tuæ mihi pervenere tabellæ'
Dated, 'Talacre, in com. Flint. x cal. Jan. 1749.' and the L copy signed in ms. 'Will. Cooper MD.' Addressed to John Boyle, fifth earl of Orrery, on his country seat.
L(840.k.4/8).

C429 Coppinger, Matthew. A session of the poets, by Matthew Coppinger. Design'd to be published before his execution. *London, printed for Tho. Atkinson; sold by Benj. Bragge*, 1705. (*DC* 20 Feb)
2°: A^2 B–D^2; 1–6 7–15 16 blk. A1 hft.
Previously published in *Poems on affairs of state* III (1698) 304.
'Now had Apollo heard in verse and prose'
Coppinger was executed 27 Feb 1695.
OW(Luttrell, 20 Feb),CJ,DG,*MR-C*.

Copy. Copy of a letter from Lady D------ at London, to Miss B------ at Dublin, [1736/−.]
See Augusta, *princess of Wales*.

— Copy of the paper..., [1712?] *See* The true copy of a paper, 1712.

C430 — A copy of verses, design'd to have been presented to the Duke of Cambridge, on his arrival in Great-Britain. By a gentleman, who is much a lover of the Reformation and the Revolution. *London, printed for J. Roberts*, 1714. (*MC* Aug)
2°: A^2 B^1; 1–2 3–6.
Pp. 5–6 contain 'The first psalm'.
'Amidst the off'rings of the tuneful throng'
O(lacks B1); CtY.

— A coppy of verses, expressing the peoples dissatisfaction, 1701. *See* Ye true-born Englishmen proceed, [1701.]

C431 — A copy of verses made on the publick fire-works, in honour of peace, exhibited on Thursday, the 27th, of April 1749. in St. James's Park. Tune – Charles of Sweeden. [*London*, 1749.]
½°: 1 side, 2 columns.
Large woodcut at head.
'Come free Brittons lets all rejoice'
L(C.116.i.4/116).

C432 — A copy of verses sent in a letter to A.C. on the 13th November, 1716, being the anniversary of the victory obtain'd at Dunblane. [*Edinburgh*, 1716?]
½°: 1 side, 1 column.
'If I, who wont to sing (supinely laid'
In praise of the Campbells, both the earl of

A copy of verses sent
Islay and the duke of Argyll; presumably addressed to a Campbell.
E.

C433 — A coppy of verses writt in a common-prayer-book, presented to a lady in 1644. Upon her building a closet for her books. *London, printed for, and sold by H. Hills, & J. Baker*, 1710. (*SR* 12 June)
½°: 1 side, 1 column.
Entered in *SR* by Hills and Baker; deposit copy at LSC?
'Since it has lately pleas'd our new born state'
On the presbyterians' suppression of the *Book of common prayer*, applied to the case of Sacheverell.
LSC; MH.

— A copy of verses wrote by a gentleman lately deceased, 1735. *See* Green, Matthew.

C434 Coquets. The coquets: or, a convert and a half. Occasioned by the late earthquakes. *London, printed for J. Payne & J. Bouquet*, 1750. (*GM* March)
4°: A^1 B–D^2 E^1 (C1 as 'D'); 3–5 6–17 18 blk.
Two poems, on Myrtilla the half-convert and Constantia the complete convert. Entered in Strahan's ledger to Payne & Bouquet, 500 copies.
Myrtilla: 'Two sisters, young and gay, yet chaste'
Constantia: 'Before her glass, in rapture high'
Possibly by Moses Browne, whose *Sunday thoughts* were printed and published by the same hands this month.
O; CtY(uncut),IU,MH.

Cornish, Philip. 'Poems on several occasions. By Philip Cornish, comedian. Price 6*d*.'
Advertised in *The curiosity: or, gentlemen and ladies repository* (Lynn, 1740; copy at O).

C435 Cornwall, C. Homeros, Homoros. The third book of Homer's Ilias burlesqu'd. *London, printed by S. Richardson, for C. Stokes; sold by the booksellers of London & Westminster*, 1722. (*DC* 2 March)
8°: A^4 B–K^4; i–xvi, 1 2–63 64 blk. A1 hft.
Advertised in *DC* as sold by J. Roberts and C. Stokes.
'Nine years consum'd, in noise, and follys'
CT; CtY,*DLC*,*IEN*,IU.

Corona. Corona civica, 1706. *See* Vernon, —, *Rev. Mr.*

C436 — Corona Cupidinis: or the effigies of love, a poem. *London, printed for the author*, 1743.
8°: A^8; 1–2 3–16.
'Mount, mount thy silver streams, Idalia, fair'
University of Otago (microfilm at L).

C437 Coronation. The coronation. A poem. *London, printed for J. Roberts*, 1714. (21 Oct, Luttrell)
2°: A^2 B^2 C^1; 1–2 3–10.

The **coronation**

Listed in *MC* Oct 1714.
'In times tyrannic, when despotic pow'r'
CtY,IU(Luttrell).

— The coronation, or, England's patroness, 1702.
See Waring, Henry.

Corydon. Corydon and Cochrania, 1723. *See*
Pennecuik, Alexander, *d. 1730.*

— Corydon querens; carmen pastorale, 1722. *See*
Bourne, Vincent.

C438 Costeker, John Littleton. Κοστιαχον: or, wit
triumphant over beauty. A poem. *London printed,
and sold by Mrs. Dodd, Mr. Crichley, Mr. Hinchliffe,
Mr. King, & Mr. Jackson,* 1731.
8°: A⁴(A1 + a²) B–C⁴; *i–ii* iii–v *vi,* 3–24.
a² contains the dedication to the Duchess of
Richmond.
'Man was an embryo in great chaos' womb'
O; CtY.

Couch, Thomas. Poems on several occasions.
London printed, and sold by B. Bragge, 1708. (*DC*
6 Feb)
8°: pp. 96. CtY.

C439 Council. The council of hell. '*Printed at you may
go look*', [*London?* 1715.]
slip: 1 side, 1 column.
'A council below,/Summon'd not long ago'
A Jacobite attack on the whigs.
O(divided and mounted).

C440 Councillor. Councillor Layer's last farewell to the
world who was executed for high-treason, on
Friday the 17th of May 1723. To the tune of John-
son's farewell. [*London?* 1723.]
½°: 1 side, 2 columns.
Rough woodcut above text.
'This day I am ordain'd to die'
A popular ballad on Christopher Layer.
L(1872.a.1/167*).

Counter. The Counter scuffle, 1708–. *See* Speed,
Robert.

C441 Counterpart. [dh] The counterpart of the Elegy
on the Philadelphian society: in answer to the
scoffers. [col] *London, printed for, and are to be sold
by John Nutt,* 1703.
2°: A²; *1* 2–4, 2 columns. 4 advt.
Reprints *An elegy upon the Philadelphian
society,* [1703] and intersperses a verse reply.
Response: 'If English folk should laugh, and god
should speak'
L(Harley 5946, fol. 246–7).

C442 — The counterpart of the State-dunces. By a
native of New-York. *London, printed for W. Mears,*
1733. (*GSJ* 7 July)
2°: *A²* B² C¹; *1–2* 3–10.

The **counterpart** of the State-dunces

'While disappointed Caleb swells with rage'
The attribution to a native of New York is not
necessarily to be taken seriously. Mrs. Lois
Morrison suggests (privately) that Eustace
Budgell was the author.
L(1484.m.7/13),LSC; *DLC,*MH,OCU.

C443 Countess. The countess's epistle to her lover,
Polyarchus. *London, printed for T. Boreman; sold
by the booksellers of London & Westminster,* 1735.
(*LM* Jan)
2°: π¹ A–B²; *i–ii,* *1* 2–8.
'To thee, I send, my Polyarchus, this'
L(11657.m.22); DLC,OCU.

C444 — The countess's speech to her son Roderigo,
upon her first seeing him, after he was wounded in
a late duel... To which is prefixed, some curious
observations... *London, printed by R. Walker, for
the author; sold by the booksellers of London &
Westminster,* [1731.] (*GSJ* 4 Feb)
2°: A–B²; *1–2* 3–8.
'When first this duel reach'd the tender ears'
Possibly by Robert Drury, whose *Pulteney,*
[1731] was also 'printed by R. Walker, for the
author'. A mock address from the Countess
of Bristol to John lord Hervey after his duel
with William Pulteney. See *An answer to a late
scurrilous pamphlet, intitled The countess's
speech,* [1731.]
MH,CSmH.

C445 — — The second edition. *London, printed by R.
Walker, for the author; sold by the booksellers of
London & Westminster,* [1731.]
2°: A–B²; *1–2* 3–8.
Apparently a reimpression.
L(11626.h.12/1); *CLU-C,*CtY.

C446 — — The third edition. With an addition of some
lines that were not in the two former editions.
*London, printed by R. Walker, for the author; sold
by the booksellers of London & Westminster,* [1731.]
2°: A–B²; *1–2* 3–8.
L(643.m.15/12, uncut),O; OCU.

C447 — — The fourth edition, with the addition of
some lines... *London, printed by R. Walker for the
author; sold by the booksellers of London & Westminster,* [1731.] (May, Luttrell)
2°.
(*Haslewood,* describing Luttrell's copy.)

Country. The country bard, 1739–. *See* Morgan,
David.

C448 — The country beau, or, a struggle for a kiss.
Dublin, printed in the year 1749.
½°: 1 side, 2 columns.
'Soon as the sun began to peep'
L(1890.e.5/178).

C449 — The country courtship, or, the maiden's choice.
Who prefer'd a moderate man before a whig or

tory. To a pretty French tune. [*London?*] *Printed in the year* 1713.
½°: 1 side, 2 columns.
'A tory, a whig and a moderate man'
L(1876.f.1/65).

— The country girl: an ode, 1742. *See* Williams, *Sir* Charles Hanbury.

C450 — The country hobb upon the town mobb: or, the party scuffle. In hudibrastick verse. *London printed, and sold by Edm. Powell,* 1715. (29 July, Luttrell)
4°: A–C²; *i–ii, 1–9 10 blk.*
'A doctor, all inspired with love'
   The struggle between high and low church will be ended by King George I.
L(164.l.63, Luttrell).

C451 — [dh] The country lamentation. [*Edinburgh?* 173–?]
8°: *A⁴*; 1–8.
   The L copy is bound with Edinburgh and Glasgow poems of the 1730s.
'A cloud of folk met all at once'
   On hard times in the Scottish countryside.
L(1078.k.26/4).

[C452–3 = W566, 566·5] — The country life; or an invitation of the soul to retirement, 1717–. *See* Wren, John.

C454 — The country parson's advice to those little scriblers, who pretend to write better sense than great secretaries: or, Mr. Stephens's triumph over the pillory. [*London,* 1706.] (11 May, Luttrell)
½°: 1–2, 1 column.
'Be wise as Ad—n, as Br—ne be brave'
   Occasioned by [Joseph Browne] *The country parson's honest advice,* [1706.] Luttrell annotates 'Upon Secretary Harley'.
ICN(Luttrell).

C455 — The country parson's advice to the little scriblers...or, Mr. Stevens's triumph over the pillory. [*London?* 1706.]
½°: 1 side, 1 column.
MiU.

— The country parson's honest advice to that judicious lawyer, [1706]. *See* Browne, Joseph.

C456 — The country peoples recreation, the king's landing at Rye. [*London?* 1714.]
½°: 1 side, 2 columns.
   Popular half-sheet, two rough cuts above text.
'Let every Brittish heart rejoyce'
L(1850.e.10/44).

C457 — The country priest. A satyr... By T. W. gent. *London, printed for J. Robinson,* 1746. (*GM, LM* Oct)
4°: A–B⁴ C¹; *1–3 4–18.*
   Vertical chain-lines.
'A neighbouring priest near Hackney lives'
L(11630.c.1/2),O.

C458 — The country squire's ditty. A ballad. To the tune of To you fair ladys, &c. [*London?* 1714?]

slip: 1–2, 1 column.
   On p. 2, 'The first psalm'.
'To you, dear topers, at the court'
First psalm: 'The man is blest that hath not lent'
   Two anti-jacobite songs.
Crawford.

C459 — The country vicar, or, Alkibla burlesqued. *London, printed in the year* 1729.
8°: A⁴; *1–2 3–8.*
'A country vicar growing lazy'
   A satire on William Asplin, author of *Alkibla. A disquisition upon worshipping towards the east,* 1728.
O.

C460 — The country vicar's address to her majesty. *London, printed in the year* 1707.
4°: A–C⁴ D²; *1–4 5–27 28 blk.*
'To you this humbly I address'
   Preface signed 'Philometrius'. For a moderate religious policy.
O,DT; MH.

C461 Countryman. The country-man and his wife Joan in mourning. Being an elegy, on the much lamented death of Mr. John Tuchin, the late famous author of the Observator. Who departed this life, at his lodgings in the Mint in Southwark; on Tuesday the 23d of September, 1707. in the forty-seventh year of his age. [*London*] *Priuted* [!] *by D.R.* [*D. Richmond*] *in Half-pav'd Court, Salsbury-court,* [1707.]
½°: 1 side, 1 column.
   Mourning headpiece and borders.
'What tongue can tell or pen express the pain'
CSmH.

C462 — The countryman's answer to the ballad, call'd, Britannia excisa. [*London*] *Printed in the year* 1733. (*LM* April)
½°: 2 sides, 1 column.
'Folks are mad with the cries'
   A whig defence of Walpole's excise proposals.
L(162.m.70/10); NNC.

— 'The countryman's miscellany; or, reflections on the glorious planet of the sun, with other poems, wrote by a person who took the hint from a request made to Mr. Stephen Duck to write something on that subject, which he declin'd. [*London*] *Sold at St. John's Gate* [*by E. Cave*], *by Mr. Roberts, and the booksellers of London & Westminster.* Price 6d.' (*GM* July 1732)

— 'The countryman's true tale, or right will take place at last. A satyr. [*London*] *E. Powell.* Price 6d.'
   Advertised as in the press in *Illia's plain,* [1714?]; by the same author, W.M. There is no evidence that it ever appeared.

C463 'Couper, John.' Bag-pipes no musick: a satyre on Scots poetry. An epistle to Mr. Stanhope. [*Edinburgh,* 1720?]

Couper, J. Bag-pipes no musick

½°: 1 side, 1 column.
> Apparently first published in Arundell, *The directors*, 1720 (advertised in *DP* 11 Nov) pp. 33–5, as 'To Mr. Stanhope, upon reading his epistle to his royal highness the Prince of Wales', signed 'John Cowper'. This is undoubtedly an Edinburgh edition published by Allan Ramsay. Reprinted as a supplement to Ramsay's *Fables and tales*, 1722 (R33).

'As Dryden justly term'd poetick sound'
> Signed 'John Couper' and dated 'Oxford, Novemb. 4. 1720'. A satire on the publication of Ramsay's poems in England. Ramsay's reply as 'Pate Birnie', *Grubstreet nae satyre*, [1720?] treats this author as the ghost of John Cowper, kirk-treasurer's man, whose elegy Ramsay wrote (prematurely) in 1714. It is probably pseudonymous, and may well be by a friend of Ramsay's.

E.

C464 Court. The court broker. A description of an anti-patriot: in a conference between Sir Thomas Gresham's statue, in the Royal Exchange; and its near neighbour. *London, printed for T. Fox*, 1747.
4°: A^1 B–C^2 D^1 (D_1 as 'C'); *1–2* 3–12.
> Vertical chain-lines.

'Silence ye cits, let patriots be dumb'
L(11630.c.6/16; 840.k.4/2),LG; CLU(uncut), CSmH.

C465 — — *London, printed by A. More*, [1747?]
8°: A–B^4; *1* 2–16.
> Possibly a provincial piracy. Horizontal chain-lines, blue paper. Title-page to the second part on p. 9, and large woodcut on p. 10.

O.

— The court convert: or, a sincere sorrow for sin, 1698–. *See* Waring, Henry.

— The court gossips, 1732. *See* The christening, 1732.

[C466 = B581·5] — The court in tears, 1708. *See* 'Burnet, Gilbert' [A new elegy].

C467 — The court lady's tale, or, a tale from the D— of M—. [*London*] *Printed in the year* 1710. (*SR* 18 May)
½°: 1 side, 1 column.
> Entered in *SR* to Andrew Hinde; deposit copy at E. On the other side of the MH copy, an illiterate naval ballad, *The English salours* [!] *triumph, over the French fleet where ere they meat* [!] *them*, 1710.

'Since tales are so much the new mode of the city'
> In defence of Sacheverell.

E; MH.

C468 — The court monkies. Inscrib'd to Mr. Pope. *London printed, and sold by J. Dormer*, 1734. (*GSJ* 14 Feb)
2°: (frt +) A^2 B^2; *1–2* 3–8.
> The frontispiece is a folding plate.

The **court** monkies
> 'Since various subjects various pens employ'
> An attack on the court and on Cibber; no direct references to Pope.

L(11630.h.38, – frt),O(– frt),LdU-B; CSmH, ICN(– frt),IU,MH,TxU(2).

— Court poems, '1706' [1716] –. *See* Montagu, *Lady* Mary Wortley.

C469 — The court spy; or the starling's song. To which is added, the disguis'd statesman's ramble, a fable. *London, printed for R. Franklin*, 1730.
8°: π^1 A^4 B^4; *i–ii, 1–3* 4–16. π1 hft.
> Horizontal chain-lines except for the half-title π1. The added poem occupies pp. 15–16. A small and badly printed octavo in spite of the price of 6*d*. on the title.

'A rev'rend starling, learn'd and bold'
Ramble: 'Sly Mercury, once had a whim in his head'
> The starling, displaced by Walpole, warns George II against him.

YU.

C470 — The court visit; to a great lady at her country-seat, who lately remov'd her habitation, because the air of St. James's did not agree with her constitution. *London, printed in the year* 1710.
½°: 1 side, 1 column.
'I'm sorry, madam, at my heart to see'
> In defence of Sarah, duchess of Marlborough.

Rothschild.

Courtier. The courtier, [1712?] *See* The reward of ambition, 1712.

Courtiers. The courtiers new ruff, [1727.] *See* A ballad: occasion'd by some ladies, 1727.

C471 Courtship. The courtship. A pastoral, in imitation of Mr. Gay. By J.W. *London, printed for W. Owen*, 1748. (*GA* 14 April)
4°: A^4 B^4; *1–3* 4–16.
'The weary sun had ta'en his leave of day'
L(11630.c.8/17); CSmH,CtY,IU,MH.

C472 Cousteil, Isaac. Woman's prerogative. A poem. As it was presented to her most sacred majesty Queen Caroline. *London, printed for S. Slow*, 1736. (*LM* March; *GM* April)
4°: A–D^2; *1–2* 3–14 *15–16 blk*.
> Title-page in red and black.

'Woman's prerogative, the theme I chuse'
LdU-B; CSmH(– D2),MH(– D2),NjP(– D2).

C473 Covent Garden. Covent Garden in mourning, a mock heroic poem. Containing some memoirs of the late celebrated Moll King... *London, printed for the author; sold by B. Dickinson*, 1747. (*BM* Oct)
2°: A^2 < B^2; *1–2* 3–8.
'Soon as the dreadful busy search was o'er'
KU,OCU.

Coventry. The Coventry ballad, 1705. *See* A health to the tackers, 1705.

Coventry, F.

C474 [**Coventry, Francis.**] Penshurst. Inscribed to William Perry, esq; and the honble. Mrs. Elizabeth Perry. *London, printed for R. Dodsley; sold by M. Cooper*, 1750. (9 Feb)
4°: *A*² B–C⁴ D²; *1–2* 3–22 *23–24*. D2 advt.
> Publication date from *Straus, Dodsley;* listed in *GM* Feb.
> 'Genius of Penshurst old!'
>> Coventry's authorship noted in a presentation copy to W. V. Lisburne at LdU-B; printed as Coventry's in *Dodsley* IV.
L(11630.c.5/13,–D2; 840.k.4/21,–D2),O(–D2), C(–D2),LdU-B,*MR*; CSmH,CtY(–D2),IU,MH (–D2),TxU+.

C475 [**Coward, William.**] Abramideis: or, the faithful patriarch. Exemplify'd in the lives of Abraham, Isaac, Jacob and Joseph. An heroic poem. *London, printed for Abel Roper, & J. Chantry*, 1705. (*DC* 8 March)
8°: A⁸ a⁴ B–X⁸ Y⁴; *i–xxiv*, 1–326 *327–328*. 326 err; Y4 advt.
> Title in red and black.
> 'Æternal spirit of that bless'd abode'
>> For Coward's authorship see *GM* (1787) 100.
L(11631.d.2,–Y4),O,WcC; CtY,ICN,MH.

C476 [—] Absalon et Achitophel. Carmine latino-heroico. Editio secunda. *Londini, anno salutis* 1723.
8°: *A*² B–E⁴ F¹; *1–2* 3–38.
> First edition 1682. This edition was issued by Curll with Atterbury's *Maxims*, 1723.
> 'Cognovere pias nondum pia secula fraudes'
>> A translation of Dryden's poem, first published in 1682, as was a translation by Francis Atterbury; Curll clearly reprinted this in error for Atterbury's. See *Macdonald, Dryden* pp. 25, 26n.
L(T.933/9),O; DFo.

C477 — Licentia poetica discuss'd: or, the true test of poetry... To which are added, critical observations on the principal, antient and modern poets... A poem. *London, printed for William Carter*, 1709. (*PB* 14 April)
8°: *⁴ A⁸(–A1) B⁸ C⁴, C⁸(–C6–8) χ⁸(–χ8) D⁸(–D1–4) E–H⁸ I⁸(±I2) (*2 as '*'); [*46*] 1–107 *108–112*. I8 advt.
> The original title A1 (preserved at TxU) was the same as *1. The cancels replace pages 11–24. There are errata on the first C4ᵛ. Horizontal chain-lines in the text of the poem.
> 'All labouring to reform must miss their aim'
L(1162.h.18),O,C(lacks H2–I8),E; CtY,MH,TxU.

[**Cowper, Ashley.**] The Norfolk poetical miscellany. To which are added some select essays and letters in prose. Never printed before. By the author of the Progress of physick. *London, printed for the author; sold by J. Stagg*, 1744. (*GM* Dec)
8°: 2 vol. L,O; IU,MH.
> The dedication is signed 'Timothy Scribble'.

Cowper, A. *Collections*

> A collection of poems by various authors, including Cowper the editor. A copy at L (992.k.20,21) has many early ms. attributions. Reissued with cancel titles in 1754 as 'The poetical miscellany...' (copies at L,CtY).

[—] Poems and translations. By the author of the Progress of physic. *London, printed for W. Brown*, 1769.
8°: pp. ix, 234.   L; ICU.

___

C478 [—] The faction, a tale. Humbly inscrib'd to Messrs. Craftsman and Compy. By Timothy Scribble esq; *London, printed for J. Roberts*, 1740. (17 Nov)
2°: *A*² B²; *1–2* 3–8. 8 advt.
> Copy from Tom's Coffee House dated 17 Nov in Lewis Walpole Library; listed in *GM,LM* Nov.
> 'In ages past when men did prize'
>> Collected in Cowper's *Poems*, 1769.
L(1484.m.19); CtY,MH,TxU.

C479 [—] High boys up go we! or, a rod for somebody. An excellent new ballad, occasion'd by a late poem, entitled An ode to mankind. By Timothy Scribble esq; *London, printed for J. Roberts*, 1741. (17 Feb)
2°: *A*² B²; *1–3* 4–8.
> Copy from Tom's Coffee House, dated 17 Feb, in Lewis Walpole Library.
> 'Come hither bold Britons, and I will disclose'
>> Collected in Cowper's *Poems*, 1769. Occasioned by [Robert Nugent, earl Nugent] *An ode to mankind*, 1741.
L(1961),MC; CU,*CtY*,OCU,MH,TxU+.

C480 [—] The progress of physic. By Timothy Scribble, esq; *London, printed for J. Stagg; sold by J. Roberts*, 1743.
2°: *A*² B–E²; *1–3* 4–20.
> 'Long ere physicians knew the healing art'
>> Early ms. attribution to 'Ant: Ashely Cooper' in LdU-B copy; collected in his *Poems*, 1769.
LdU-B; CtY-M,DFo,IU,KU,TxU+.

C481 [—] — The second edition, corrected, and considerably enlarged. *London, printed for J. Stagg; sold by J. Roberts*, 1743.
2°: *A*² B–F²; *1–3* 4–24.
> No reference to 'Timothy Scribble'. Early ms. attribution 'By Mr Ashley Cooper' in the L copy. An edition was listed in *BM,GM* Jan 1750 'with notes and observations from ancient authors: by a physician', published by Corbett. It is possibly a reissue of this edition.
L(163.n.54).

Cowper, John. *See* 'Couper, John'.

C482 [**Cowper, Joseph.**] Τεχνηθυραμβεια or, a poem upon Paddy Murphy, porter of Trin. Coll. Dublin. Translated from the original in Latin. *Dublin printed, and sold by Edward Waters*, 1728.

Cowper, J. Τεχνηθυραμβεια

8⁰: *A²* B–C²; *1–2* 3–12.
> Below imprint, 'At the aforesaid place, gentlemen may have the Latin one, stitch'd up with the English...'

'Behold Apollo's youngest son'
> Though the following is different in metre and in mock-heroic form, parallel passages suggest that it is a reworking of this version, and by the same author. Ms. note 'By Dr Duncan' in DT copy refers to the author of the Latin, William Dunkin.

C,DA,DT; CtY.

C483 — Technethyrambeia: or, a poem on Paddy Murphey, under-porter of T. C. Dublin. Translated from the original in Latin. By Joseph Cowper, A.B. *Dublin printed, and sold by George Faulkner*, 1730.
8⁰: *A⁴* B⁴; *1–3* 4–16.
'Transported with the muses softer charms'
L(11623.aaa.25),O,C,DA(2),DT+.

[Cowper, Spencer, *dean of Durham*.] Of good nature. An epistle humbly inscrib'd to his g--ce the D-ke of C---s, 1732. *See* O82.

[Cox, *Sir* **Richard.]** Faction display'd, in answer to Faction display'd, a poem, 1704. *See* F24.

Coxwell, Henry. The Odes of Horace. Translated into English verse. *Oxford, printed for the author*, 1718.
4⁰: pp. 116.   L,O; CLU-C,CtY.

C484 Crab. The crab-tree a tale. *London, printed for J. Johnson, near London-bridge*, [172–?]
½⁰: 1 side, 2 columns.
> Large wood-engraving above text, with title above it. The order of editions is uncertain. Reprinted in *Wisdom revealed*, [1732.]

'The moon was pendulous above'
> A bawdy tall story.

L(C.116.i.4/49).

C484·5 — The crabb-tree. A tale. [*London*, 172–?]
½⁰: 1 side, 2 columns.
> In this edition the title is below the wood-engraving, which is a different block from the preceding.

CLU-C.

C485 — The crab-tree a tale. [*Dublin*, 172–?]
½⁰: 1 side, 1 column.
CSmH.

Crabb, John. Georgiana: sive tentamina poetica in Georgium serenissimum... *Londini, ex officina Jacobi Knapton*, 1725.
8⁰: pp. vii, 44.   O,GM.

— [reissue] Quibus adjicitur Georgianorum incrementum novum... Editio secunda. *Londini, ex officina Jacobi & Johan. Knapton*, 1726.
8⁰: pp. vii, 52.   CtY.

Crabb, J.

C486 — In Georgium reducem carmen θριαμβευτικον. *Oxoniæ, typis Lichfieldianis*, 1719. (*DC* 12 Dec)
2⁰: *A²* B²; *1–2* 3–8.
'Salve pater patriæ, summorum gloria regum'
O(uncut).

C487 [—] A poem to the king. *London, printed for J. Roberts*, 1717. (*MC* Feb)
8⁰: A–B⁴ C²; *1–2* 3–19 *20 blk*.
'We Persians like, the rising sun adore'
> Ms. note in the GM copy 'Ex dono authoris – Johan: Crabb A: M:' A whiggish poem.

L(164.n.9, Luttrell, April),GM; MH.

C488 — A poem upon the late storm and hurricane. With an hymn. Dedicated to the queen. *London, printed for John Wyat*, 1704. (*PM* 18 Jan)
2⁰: *A²* B–D²; *i–iv*, 1–12.
'When the almighty went out of his place'
L(689.eee.31, Luttrell, 18 Jan),LDW,O(uncut), DG; CLU-C,CSmH,DFo,MH,TxU.

C489 [—] Quadriennium Jacobi, sc. secundi: or, a poetical amusement on the reign of James the second. By a country curate. *London, printed for J. Roberts*, 1722 [1723?]. (Jan 1723, Luttrell)
8⁰: *A⁴* B–C⁴; *1–6* 7–23 *24 blk*. A1 hft.
'Loe! Charles at length is dead; and James proclaim'd'
> Early ms. attribution to Crabb in the GM copy.
> In praise of the Hanoverian succession.

L(164.m.35, Luttrell),GM.

C490 [—] A tale, and no tale: that is to say, a tale, and no tale of a tub. *London, printed for J. Roberts*, 1715. (23 Dec, Luttrell)
8⁰: A–C⁴; *1–4* 5–24.
> Listed in *MC* Dec.

'When Rome took thought, and her no god nor man'
> Early ms. attribution to Crabb in the GM copy, where it is bound with other poems by him. On the struggles between high and low church.

L(164.l.64, Luttrell),DT,DrU,GM; DLC.

[Crackanthorp, John.] Poems, paraphrases and translations. By J.C. *London printed, and sold by the assigns of J. Sowle*, 1736.
8⁰: pp. 60.   LF,CT.
> Authorship from *Smith* I.459.

C491 Craft, James. The Saphirah in triumph: or, British valour display'd. Compos'd by James Craft, who lost his arm in the action. [1744/45?]
obl ½⁰: 1 side, 4 columns.
> Rough woodcut at head of first two columns; a hawker's broadside.

'Come you jovial British fellows'
L(L.R.31.b.19/I.224)

Craftsman. The Craftsman's apology, 1732. *See* Adee, Swithin.

Craftsman

C492 — The Craftsman's business. Being, an explanation and description of I. Several sorts of dogs... II. Several sorts of uncommon animals... III. The original of French asses...as promised in the Country-journal, or Craftsman, Sept. 13, 1729. The whole interspers'd with an account of a large mackay, party-colour'd with red and blue. *London, printed for the author, and sold by R. Walker, C. Marsh, and by the book-sellers and pamphlet-sellers,* [1729.]
8°: *A*⁴ B–C⁴; *1–4 5–19 20–23; 24 blk.* A1 hft; 21–23 advt.
'You true-born Englishmen proceed'
A political satire: the mackay is Walpole.
L(Burney 273),O(–A1).

C493 Crafty. The crafty courtier: or the fable of Reinard the fox: newly done into English verse, from the antient Latin iambics of Hartm. Schopperus... *London, printed for John Nutt,* 1706. (*DC* 10 April 'lately publish'd')
8°: *A*⁴ B–V⁸ X⁴; *i–viii, 1–311 312.* A1 hft; X4 advt.
'Nor arms I sing, nor of adventurous deeds'
L(11501.b.19),O,C; *CLU-C,CtY,ICN,MH, NjP+*.

C494 [**Craggs, James,** *the younger.*] King Edward's ghost: or, the king and the cobler. [*London?* 1712?]
slip: 1 side, 1 column.
'I'll tell you a story, a story most merry'
Printed in *GM* XI (1741) 213 as 'A song. By Mr. Craggs in 1713; afterwards Secretary of State'. A whig satire on the six knights of the garter, created 12 Oct 1712. See *The second part of King Edward and the cobler,* [1712?]
O; *OCU,Harding.*

Craig, —, *Mr.* A translation of Vida's three pastoral eclogues, 1736. *In* E460.

[**Craig, James.**] Spiritual life. Poems on several divine subjects... *Edinburgh, printed by Mr. James Davidson & company,* 1727.
8°: pp. xxv, 214.   L,O; *IU,TxU.*
Dedication signed 'J.C.' A new edition appeared in 1751.

C495 Crambo. Crambo's elopement. Or the austere poetaster's ramble; his adventures in St. James's Park; and a trip to Chelsea. A poem. With moral reflections by way of epilogue. In imitation of Rochester. Written by a private gentleman. *London, printed by B. Baddam & M. Carter, in Well-Close-square; sold by the booksellers of London & West-minster,* 1720.
8°: *A*⁴ B–C⁴; *1–3 4–23 24 blk.*
''Twas in that season when you've seen'
NN.

'**Crambo, Christopher.**' Mr. Bowman's sermon, 1731. *See* M292.

Crauford, D.

C496 Crauford, David. Ovidius Britannicus: or, love-epistles. In imitation of Ovid. Being an intreague betwixt two persons of quality. To which are added. Phaon's answer to Sapho and Theseus answer to Ariadne, which are wanting in Ovid's epistle. *London, printed for John Chantry,* 1703.
8°: (frt+) A⁶ B–D⁸ χ² E–L⁸; *i–xii, 1–52 41–152.* xii err.
'What yet in tears? The fair Amestris still'
The dedication to David lord Boyle of Kelburn, subsequently earl of Glasgow, is by Charles Gildon.
L(1077.k.42,–frt),DT,GM,WgP; CLU-C(–frt), *DFo,ICN,MiU,NNC.*

Crawley, Constantia. *See* Grierson, Constantia (*née* Crawley).

C497 C—rd-n-l. The c—rd-n-l dancing-master, or pl—ce-m—n in leading-strings. [*London*] *Published according to act of parliament,* February 18, 1742. *By J. Huggonson.*
obl 1°: 1 side, 4 columns.
Two engravings and tunes at head, with engraved title. Printed verses below, 'The c—rd—l's dancing-song' and 'The pl—n's ballad', with imprint at foot of col. 4. Advertised in *LEP* 6 March.
'Make de Spanish step'
'How charm'd! with leading-strings'
Satires on Walpole's foreign policy.
L(P&D 2530, imprint cropt),O-JJ; NNP.

C498 — The c-rd-n-ls master-piece, or Europe in a flurry. [*London*] *Publish'd* October 1741, *according to act of parliament, by T. Cooper.*
1°: 1 side, 3 columns.
Large engraving with title at head; imprint at foot.
'Who see my raree shew, come from Prague'
A satire on Cardinal Fleury dismembering Europe.
L(P&D 2503); NNP.

C499 Creagh, *Sir Michael.* Poem presented by Sir Michael Creagh, to their present majesties the King and Queen of Great Britain, &c. when Prince and Princess of Wales, upon her majesties birthday, being the first of March, 1717–18. [*Dublin*] *Printed in the year* 1727.
½°: 1 side, 1 column.
'Pardon great princess, this liberty I take'
Signed 'Michael Creagh, knight'.
DT.

Creation. The creation. A pindaric illustration of a poem, 1720. *See* Hill, Aaron.

C500 — The creation of women; a poem. *London, printed for T. Warner,* 1725. (*MC* March)
2°: *A*¹ B–C² D¹ (D1 as 'C'); *i–ii, 1–10.*
'When Jove had measur'd out the spacious earth'

The **creation** of women

A satire against women.
O; CSmH.

C501 —— *Dublin, printed by J. Watts, for J. Thompson, 1725.*
8°: A–B⁴; *1–3* 4–14 *15–16 blk.*
LdU-B; CtY.

Credidimus. Credidimus terras Hydram liquisse Britannas, [1710?] *See* Pitcairne, Archibald.

C502 Credit. The credit and interest of Great Britain consider'd: or, the way to live above want. Wherein temperance is commended for her decency, and being provident. *London, printed for P.G. [Philip Gwillim]; sold by J. Morphew, 1710. (SR 28 April)*
1°: 1 side, 3 columns.
Entered in *SR* to Philip Gwillim as 'a broad sheet'; deposit copy at E.
'What is the thing our natures doth require'
E.

C503 —— *London, printed and sold at the Bible in George-yard, Lombard-street,* [173–?]
1°: 1 side, 3 columns.
The address is that of T. Sowle Raylton.
LF.

C504 — [reissue] *London, printed and sold at the Bible in George-yard, Lombard-street. Sold also by Benjamin Middleton in Wellingborough,* [173–?]
1°: 1 side, 3 columns.
The Wellingborough imprint has apparently been printed subsequently.
O-JJ.

C505 —— [174–?]
1°: 1 side, 3 columns.
Bands of type flowers at head and foot. A shortage of certain sorts suggests a provincial printer.
LF.

Cricket. Cricket. An heroic poem, 1744–. *See* Dance, James.

C506 Cries. The cries of the oppressed. Or, Herod's cruelty display'd, at the taking of Bergen-op-Zoom by the French... *London, printed in the year 1747.*
4°: *A⁴*; *1–2* 3–8.
A chap-book. The format is uncertain.
'Kind tender hearted people all'
E.

Criminal. The criminal stirling, [172–?] *See* Pennecuik, Alexander, *d. 1730.*

C507 Crisis. The crisis upon crisis. A poem. Being an advertisement stuck in the lion's mouth at Button's: and addressed to Doctor S----t. *London, printed for J. Morphew, 1714. (14 April, Luttrell)*
4°: A–E²; *i–ii, 1* 2–18.
Advertised in *PB* 15 April.
'As Temple notes, not meaning evil'

The **crisis** upon crisis

Against Richard Steele's *The crisis*.
L(164.n.4, Luttrell),LLP,O; MH.

C508 [**Crispe, Henry.**] The antidote, being a poem of reflection on the late epithalamium on the most auspicious nuptials of...the Marquess of Carmarthen, and the Lady Elizabeth Harley, &c... By Mr. H. C. of the Custom House. *London, printed for John Morphew, 1713. (23 Feb, Luttrell)*
2°: A⁴; *i–ii, 1–6.*
Advertised in *PB* 26 Feb.
'Hymen, disturb'd his song was disallow'd'
The poems below by 'H. Crispe of the Custom House' make the attribution clear, though *Nichols* I. 69 wrongly ascribes it to 'Henry' (for Nathaniel) Castleton. Occasioned by Crispe's own *An epithalamium,* 1712.
O(uncut); CSmH(Luttrell, cropt).

C509 [—] An elegy on the lamented death of the right honourable, and vertuous lady Elizabeth late marchioness of Carmarthen... Humbly inscrib'd to...the Marquess of Carmarthen...the Earl of Oxford, and earl Mortimer, and...Peregrine duke of Leeds... By Mr. H. C. of the Custom House. *London, printed for John Morphew, 1713. (DC 16 Dec)*
2°: A⁴; *i–ii, 1–6.*
At head of title, 'Colles lamentis, lamentis implet & urbes'.
'Carmarthen, Oxford, Leeds, great names, and great'
Lady Carmarthen died 20 Nov 1713.
MR-C; TxU(uncut).

C510 [—] An epithalamium. Being stanzas on the most auspicious nuptials of the... Marquess of Carmarthen, and the Lady Elizabeth Harley... The 15th day of December, anno 1712... By Mr. H. C. *London, printed for John Morphew, 1712 [1713]. (DC 7 Jan)*
2°: A⁴; *i–ii, 1–6.*
The Luttrell copy, recorded in *Haslewood,* was dated 8 Jan.
'Stoutly fought, and bravely won!'
L(11632.i.3); NjP,TxU.

C511 — On the honourable board of commissioners of her majesty's Custom-House, London; in the year of peace, 1713. *London, printed for J. Morphew, 1713. (Examiner 17 July)*
2°: A⁴; *i–ii, 1–6.*
No watermark seen.
'Can there within these walls pretend to dwell'
O(uncut); NN.

C512 — [fine paper]
Watermark: fleur-de-lys.
L(840.m.18); TxU.

C513 — A poem on occasion of the promotion of the right honourable the Lord Keeper Harcourt to be lord high chancellor of Great Britain. The 7th of April 1713. And on the peace. Inscribed to John

Crispe, H. A poem

Barlow, esq;. *London, printed for John Morphew,*
1713. (*PB* 7 July)
2°: A–H² I²(I1 + χ1); *i–ii,* 1–35 *36 blk.*
'Permit, my condescending friend, permit'
O(uncut, ms. date 18 Sept).

C514 [—] Some verses sent to the right honourable the
Earl of Oxford, lord high-treasurer of Great-
Britain; on occasion of a late subtil and barbarous
machination against his lordship's valuable life...
on the 4th of November 1712. *London, printed for
John Morphew,* 1712. (8 Nov?)
2°: A–B² (A2 as 'A'); *i–ii,* 1–5 *6 blk.*
Advertised in *PB* 10 Jan 1713 with Crispe's
Epithalamium.
'Still injur'd, still forgiving hero, where'
Early ms. on title of the NjP copy 'By Mr.
H. C.' Clearly another of Crispe's poems to
Harley, though wrongly ascribed by *Nichols*
to Castleton (cf. C508).
O(Luttrell, 7 Jan 1713); CtY,MH(uncut, ms. date
8 Nov),NjP,TxU.

C515 — To the honourable Matthew Prior, esq; on his
promotion to the commission of her majesty's
customs, and first coming to the board. January 28.
1711. *London, printed for E. Curll,* 1712.
4°: *A²;* 1–2 3–4.
No watermark seen; 'Price two pence' on title.
'Will then the muse, the great Priorian muse'
CSmH,KU,TXU.

C516 — [fine paper, in folio]
Watermark: royal arms; no price on title.
C.

Crooked. The crooked six-pence, 1743. *See*
Bramston, James.

Cross. The cross and the crown, 1705. *See* Clark,
James.

C517 Cross-grove, Henry. Britannia. Anna's glory: or
the happy union. A poem. Humbly dedicated to...
William Cooke, esq; mayor. *Norwich, printed in
Magdalen-street by the author,* 1707.
2°: A²; 1 2–4.
'When raging vice and restless discord reign'd'
O.

Crouch, Nathaniel. Choice emblems, divine and
moral, ancient and modern: or, delights for the
ingenious, in above fifty select emblems. *London,
printed for Edmund Parker,* 1721.
12°: pp. 207.   GU.
Apparently a reissue of *Delights for the ingenious,* 1684.

— — The sixth edition. *London, printed for Edmund
Parker,* 1732.
12°: pp. 207.   O,GU; DFo,MH.

[—] The vanity of the life of man... To which are
added, several other poems upon diverse subjects

Crouch, N. *Collections*

and occasions. By R.B... The third edition.
London, printed for Nath. Crouch, 1708.
12°: pp. 92.   L.
First published in 1688 (copy at L).

[—] — By Robert Burton... The fifth edition.
London, printed for A. Bettesworth, & J. Batley,
1729.
12°: pp. 92.   L; CLU-C.

[—] Youth's divine pastime. Containing forty
remarkable scripture histories turned into English
verse. With forty pictures... In two parts. Part
I... The twelfth edition. *Printed for the booksellers
of London & Westminster,* [1710?]
12°: pp. 94.   L(2).
The prefatory epistle is signed 'R.B.' The
earliest recorded edition is the third, 1691.
This may be a piracy. One copy at L has ms.
date '1710' on title, but this may be too early;
compare part 2 below.

[—] — The fifteenth edition. *London, printed for
A. Bettesworth & C. Hitch, & J. Batley,* 1732.
12°: pp. 96.   E.

[—] Youth's divine pastime. Part II... By R.B.
author of the first part. The second edition. *Printed
for the booksellers of London & Westminster,* [1710?]
12°: pp. 96.   L(2).
The copies seen are bound with the twelfth
edition of part 1, one of which is dated in ms.
'1710'. The woodcuts are inferior copies of
those in the authorized edition below, and it is
probably a piracy. The date is suspect, though
part 2 was in print by 1708.

[—] — The second edition. *London, printed for
Thomas Crouch,* 1723.
12°: pp. 96.   CLU.

[—] — The fifth edition. *London,* 1737.
NNC.

[—] — By R. Burton... The sixth edition. *London,
printed for C. Hitch, & James Hodges,* 1749.
12°: pp. 96.   L,E; DLC,NNUT.

C518 [Crow, Isaac.] A psalm of thanksgiving to be sung
by the children of Christ's-Hospital on Monday,
Tuesday, and Wednesday, in Easter-week... 1716.
Composed by Mr. Barret... [*London*] *Printed by
John Barber,* 1716.
1°: 1 side, 2 columns.
Woodcut borders. Typeset music with first
verse at head. The verse is followed by an
annual report of the charities.
'Descend angelick choir again, adorn'
Authorship from Christ's Hospital minutes.
Christ's Hospital office.

C519 [—] A psalm of thanksgiving... 1718. Composed
by Mr. Barret... [*London*] *Printed by John Barber,*
1718.
1°: 1 side, 2 columns.
Format and authorship as preceding.

Crow, I. A psalm of thanksgiving

'Ride now triumphant through the sky'
Christ's Hospital office.

[**Croxall, Samuel.**] The fair Circassian, a dramatic performance... The second edition corrected. To which are added several occasional poems, by the same author. *London, printed for J. Watts; sold by Samuel Chapman, & William Chetwood*, 1721.
12°: pp. 59.   O,LdU-B; CSmH,TxU.
The first edition, which contains *The fair Circassian* only, is entered as a separate work below. The added poems occupy pp. 29-59.

[—] — The third edition, 1723.
A copy was recorded in the Mercantile Library, Philadelphia, now defunct. Probably it had the same imprint as the following.

[—] — The fourth edition. '*London, printed for J. Watts; sold by W. Meres*' [*Dublin*], 1723.
DA,DN; NNC.
The copies I believe I have seen at DA, DN cannot now be traced.

[—] — The fourth edition corrected. *London, printed for J. Watts*, 1729.
12°: pp. 57.   L,LVA-D; IU.

[—] — The fifth edition corrected. *London, printed for J. Watts*, 1732.
12°: pp. 49.   O; CtY,ICN.

[—] — The sixth edition corrected. *London, printed for J. Watts; sold by B. Dod*, 1743.
12°: pp. 49.   O,E; MH,TxU.
Reissued as 'The seventh edition', [1756?/–], copy at O.

[—] — The tenth edition. '*London, printed for J. Watts; sold by B. Dod*', 1750.
8°: pp. 40.   O,AdU.
Apparently a Scottish piracy.

———————

[—] Colin's mistakes. Written in imitation of Spenser's style [actually by Prior], 1721. *See* P1065.

[—] A congratulatory poem to his grace the D. of Argyle, on his late victory over the rebels in Scotland, 1716. *See* C359.

C520 [—] The fair Circassian, a dramatic performance. Done from the original by a gentleman-commoner of Oxford. *London, printed for J. Watts*, 1720. (*SR* 24 May)
4°: A⁴ a² B–D⁴ E²; *i–xii, 1* 2–28.
Deposit copies at O,E,EU. Subsequent editions containing a collection of Croxall's poems are entered above.
'Virgins of Albion, ye fair female kind'
The dedication is signed 'R. D.' and the authorship is heavily disguised; early ms. note in the CtY copy 'really by Parson Croxall'. A versification in dialogue of the *Song of Solomon*, clearly not intended for performance.
L(164.i.54; 161.h.69, Luttrell, May),O,E,EU, BaP; CtY,*CLU-C*,CSmH,DFo.

Croxall, S.

C521 — An ode humbly inscrib'd to the king, occasion'd by his majesty's most auspicious succession and arrival. Written in the stanza and measure of Spencer. By Mr. Croxall, author of the two original canto's, &c. *London, printed for Bernard Lintott*, 1714. (*SR* 5 Oct)
2°: A–E² F¹; *i–ii* iii–iv, *1–18*.
Listed in *MC* Sept. Lintot paid Croxall twelve guineas for the copy on 22 Sept (*Nichols* VIII. 295). Deposit copies at L,LSC,O,EU,AdU.
'Now could I wish for that fam'd golden lyre'
L(643.m.13/6),LSC,O(2),EU(uncut),AdU(uncut)+; CSmH,CtY(2),ICN,MH(Luttrell, 8 Oct), TxU(2, 1 uncut)+.

C522 [—] An original canto of Spencer: design'd as part of his Fairy queen, but never printed. Now made publick, by Nestor Ironside, esq; *London, printed for A. Baldwin*, 1714 [1713]. (1 Dec?)
4°: A–D⁴; *1–2* 3–30 *31–32 blk.*
Vertical chain-lines, with foolscap watermark. Advertised in *DC* 1 Dec 1713 as 'just published'.
'Fair liberty, bright goddess, heavenly-born'
Early ms. attribution to Croxall in the L copy; subsequently acknowledged by him. A political allegory attacking Harley.
L(11630.b.5/6),E(2),*MR*; ICN(−D4),ICU,MH (uncut),TxU(2).

C523 [—] [fine paper]
Watermark: star.
ICU.

C524 [—] — The second edition. *London, printed for James Roberts*, 1714 [1713]. (*DC* 3 Dec)
4°: A–D⁴; *1-2* 3–30 *31–32 blk.*
Apparently a reimpression; vertical chain-lines as the first impression. Some copies (e.g. CtY) have some sheets from the following.
L(11631.f.37/2,−D4; 11633.bbb.42/1,−D4; 841.c.9/12),LDW(−D4),O(−D4),C,DK+; CtY(−D4),DFo,ICN,IU.

C525 [—] — The third edition. *London, printed for James Roberts*, 1714.
4°: A–D⁴; *1–2* 3–30 *31–32 blk.*
Sheets B and C are apparently partly reset. Horizontal chain-lines.
L(11631.f.37/3,−D4),C; CtY(−D4),ICN(−D4), MH(−D4).

C526 [—] — The second edition. '*London, printed for James Roberts*' [*Edinburgh*], 1714.
8°: A⁴ B⁸; *1–2* 3–24.
The printer's ornaments are of Edinburgh origin.
NjP,TxU.

C527 [—] Another original canto of Spencer: design'd as part of his Fairy queen, but never printed. Now made publick, by Nestor Ironside, esq; *London, printed for James Roberts*, 1714.
4°: A–D⁴; *1–2* 3–32.

Croxall, S. An original canto

'Ay me! what aking thoughts possess my mind'
L(11630.b.5/7; 11631.f.37/1; 841.c.9/13),O,
C(uncut); CSmH,DFo,ICN,MH.

[—] To his grace the Duke of Argyle, after the
defeat of the Northern rebellion, 1716. *See* T335.

C528 — The vision. A poem. By Mr. Croxall, author of
the two original cantos of Spenser. *London, printed
for J. Tonson*, 1715. (*SR* 6 July)
2°: *A*² B–F²; *i–iv, 1–20*.
    Listed in *MC* July; deposit copies at L,LSC,
    O,EU,AdU,SaU.
'The man, whose life by virtue's model fram'd'
L(643.m.13/7),O(2),EU,AdU,LdU-B+; CtY,
ICN(uncut),IU(Luttrell, 8 July),MH,TxU+.

C529 Cruel. A cruel and bloody declaration, publish'd
by the cardinals at Rome, against Great-Britain,
and Ireland. '*Rome printed, and re-printed in*'
Dublin, Nov. 12, 1725.
½°: 1 side, 1 column.
    The Rome imprint is clearly false.
'Heu dolor anxietas! Suspiria rumpite pectus'
    Macaronic verses against the Roman church.
CSmH.

C530 Crumbs. Crumbs of comfort for a reverend, aged,
and greatly mortified lover. In a letter from a fellow
of a certain college in Oxford, to the rev. Dr.
W—son, to console him under his affliction for a
late unfortunate verdict, given against him in
Westminster-Hall. *London, printed for T. Ward*,
1747.
8°: A–B⁴ C²; *1–2 3–19 20 blk*.
'Most reverend sir, and *quondam* chum'
    Nathaniel Wilson, prebendary of Worcester,
    was found guilty of breach of promise to Miss
    Davids, 5 June 1747, with damages of £7,000.
O.

C531 — Crumbs of comfort: or, hymns of consolation;
recommended by the synod to all pious families
under their present afflictions. *Dublin printed, and
sold by E. Waters*, 1728.
8°: *A*⁴ B⁴ C² D⁴; *i–ii iii–v vi, 1–21 22*.
    In the CtY copy the pagination is irregular. This
    should probably be considered a collection;
    it reprints at least three separately published
    poems, *The black procession*, [1728]; *Black upon
    blue*, 1728; *The last speech to the election*, 1728.
'Melpomene, thou patroness'
    This appears to be a series of satires by one
    author relating to the death of William
    Howard M.P. and the election campaign of
    Richard Choppin.
DA; CtY.

C532 Crutch. A ⟨c⟩rutch for a lame conscience, or, a
satyr on a certain society. [*Dublin*, 1728?]
½°: 1 side, 2 columns.
    The MH copy has a Dublin collector's initial, F.
'You men of quick sight,/That pretend to new light'

A crutch for a lame conscience

    A satire against the 'new light' sect which was
    active in Dublin from 1715. Compare
    Swaddling John's address, 1728.
MH.

C533 — [*idem*] New light. [*Dublin*, 1728?]
½°: 1 side, 2 columns.
L(C.121.g.8/98).

C534 Cruttenden, Robert. Pindar's ode to Proserpina.
Translated from the French of Monsieur De la
Motte. And humbly addressed to...the Lord
Hardwick... *London, printed for T. Cooper*, 1738.
(*GM,LM* May)
2°: *A*² B–E²; *1–11 12–19 20 blk*. A1 hft.
    Errata slip on p. 19 in most copies; in TxU
    between pp. 4/5.
'Queen of the gloomy king, whose awful sway'
O; CLU-C,CU(no errata slip),CtY,DFo,TxU.

C535 C----t. The c----t candidate and the cobler. A
true tale. [*London*? 174–?]
obl ¼°: 1 side, 1 column.
    The copy seen contains two settings above one
    another, printed by half-sheet imposition to
    make four copies on a sheet.
'While Bribewell every art with Jobson us'd'
    A tale of election bribery.
O-JJ.

C536 — The c—t sermon. A new ballad. Dedicated to
the reverend Dr. C—. *London printed, and sold by
H. Carpenter*, [1748.] (*GM, LM* Dec)
2°: *A*⁴; *1–6 7–8*. A1 hft.
'Ye beaux and ye belles, both in court and in city'
    Dedication signed 'Joseph'. A reply to
    Cobden's sermon *A persuasive to chastity*.
L(T.13*/6, –A1),O(2, 1 –A1); CSmH(–A1),IU,
MH(–A1).

C537 Cuckold. The cuckold in purgatory: or, the fall of
the second man, Adam. [*London*, 1712.] (21 Feb?)
½°: 1 side, 1 column.
    The copies at O, MH have an incorrect variant
    in line 4, 'C— –pel' for 'C— –nel'.
'Adam the first on apple made his meal'
    On the expulsion of Adam de Cardonnel from
    the house of commons.
L(1850.c.10/34),O,Chatsworth (ms. date 21 Feb
1712),Crawford; MH(both states),*Harding*.

Cuckoo. The Cuckow's song anent the election of
peers, [174–?] *See* Davidson, William.

Cudgel. The cudgel, 1742. *See* Ward, Edward
[*Durgen*].

C538 Cullin, Michael. Ode in pacem. *Dublinii, typis
Jacobi Hoey*, 1749.
8°: *A*⁴; *1–3 4–8*.
'Huc ferte gressus, culmina linquite'
O.

Culloden

C539 Culloden. 'Culloden, or loyalty triumphant. [*London*] *Mrs. Dod*. Price 6d.' (*BM* June 1747)
   Listed in *BM* under the heading 'Poetry and plays'.

C540 Cupid. Cupid in quest of beauty: or, Venus at Stratford. A lampoon. By the author of the British-Apollo. *London printed, and sold by most booksellers of London & Westminster,* 1709. (*Tatling Harlot* 26 Aug)
8°: A⁴; *1–2* 3–8.
   'Nature while Tempest liv'd, by her took aim'
   Preface signed 'B.C.' *The British Apollo,* 1708–1711, was a periodical.
   L(1481.aaa.3).

C541 Cupulo. The cupulo. A poem. Occasion'd by the vote of the house of commons, for covering that of St. Paul's with British copper... *London printed, and sold by J. Morphew,* 1708. (*DC* 3 April)
2°: A–C²; *1–4* 5–12.
   Thorn-Drury records the Luttrell copy dated 1 April.
   'Westward from fair Augusta's city, lies'
   L(643.1.24/31),O,*MR-C*.

C542 Cur. The cur and the lap-dog, a poem. Inscrib'd to her grace the Dutchess of Manchester. *London, printed for J. Brindley, & C. Corbett,* 1737. (*LM* May)
2°: A² B–C²; *1–3* 4–12.
   Teerink 981; *Rothschild* 2246.
   'Bright was the morn, the hemisphere'
   Not discussed in *Williams*; there seems no reason to attribute the work to Swift.
   L(11642.i.10/3; Ashley 5253),LVA-D,O(uncut), DN,LdU-B; CLU-C,CtY,MH,OCU,TxU+.

— Cur tibi natalem felix Heriote quotannis, [*1712?/13.*] *See* Pitcairne, Archibald.

C543 Curatical. The curatical battle for Q. Chappel: address to the reverend parsons, D---k and M----l. *London, printed for H. Carpenter,* 1746. (*BM* Dec)
2°: (3 ll); *i–iii* iv–vi.
   'Quoth Stephen D--k to Tom of K--w'
   A satire on Stephen Duck and Thomas Morell.
   CSmH.

Curb. A curb for a coxcomb, 1704. *See* Allan, —.

C544 Cure. 'A cure for a scold: a poem. [*London*] Printed for J. Lewis. Price 2d.' (*GM* July 1736)
   Possibly a half-sheet from the price.

C545 — A cure for the cow. Inscribed to the author of the Tale of a cow and her keepers. [*London?* 173–?]
16 pp.
   (Pickering & Chatto cat. 259/2861.)

Curiosity. The curiosity: or, the gentleman and lady's general library, 1738–. *See* Dorman, Joseph.

Curious

C546 Curious. The curious females, a tale. [*London,* 172–?]
slip: 1 side, 1 column.
   Reprinted with *The man of honour,* Dublin 1737, and, as 'The female contest', with *Kick him Jenny,* 1737.
'Four lovely lasses, gay and bright'
   A comparison of their pubic hair.
Herts CRO (Panshanger box 46).

— The curious maid, 1720–. *See* Jacob, Hildebrand.

C547 — The curious maid, continu'd. A tale. *London printed, and sold by J. Roberts,* 1721. (*PB* 28 March)
2°: A² B²; *1–2* 3–8.
   A 'second edition' was advertised in *DC* 31 March.
'And having, with a careless lift'
   There is no reason to believe that this continuation is by Hildebrand Jacob; the style is much inferior.
L(Ashley 4980, Luttrell, April),O; CSmH.

[Curll, Edmund.] A just imitation of the first satire of the second book of Horace, [1733.] *See* J116.

C548 Curry, J. Courtship: an heroi-comical poem. In five cantos. *Dublin, printed by S. Powell, for Thomas Lawrence,* 1727.
8°: A–E⁴ F¹; *1–5* 6–42.
'I sing the wiles that artless lovers cheat'
GU; DFo.

C548·5 [—] [reissue?] The miser turn'd courtier: an heroi-comical poem. In five cantos. *London printed, and Dublin reprinted by S. Powell, for Philip Crampton,* 1727.
8°: A–E⁴ F¹; *1–5* 6–42.
   Probably the title is a cancel; the drop-head title is 'Courtship', showing that was the earlier issue.
DA(2, 1 lacks A1); DFo,OCU,TxU.

Curry-comb. A curry-comb of truth for a certain dean, 1736. *See* Dunkin, William.

C549 — A curry-comb of truth for the a--------n and c---------s of the city of Dublin. A new song. To the tune of, There was a jovial beggarman, &c. *Dublin, printed in the year* 1749.
½°: 1 side, 2 columns.
'Of all the trades of Dublin'
   In praise of Charles Lucas against the aldermen and councillors of the city of Dublin.
C.

C550 Curses. [dh] Curses against the stars: or, the French-king's lamentation to the Pope for his ill success this war...with the Pope's answer and advice: together with a new health sung on her majesties birth-day... [col] *London printed: and re-printed in Channel-row, Dublin,* 1709–10.
4°: A²; *1–4.*
   No London edition has been traced.

Curses against the stars

    'Most pious sir, complaint to you I send'
    L(11631.bb.54).

C551 Curteis, Thomas. Eirenodia: a poem sacred to peace, and the promoting of human happiness... By T. C. rector of Sevenoke in Kent. *London, printed for R. Wilkin, 1728* [1727]. (*MC* Nov)
    8°: A–H⁴ (F1 as 'E'); *i–vi* vii–xx, 21–64.
        Watermark: T.
    'Celestial dove; by whose enlivening warmth'
        Dedication signed. The relationship between this poem and C553 has not been determined.
    NNC.

C552 — [fine paper]
        Watermark: Strasburg bend.
    CtY.

C553 [—] Genethlia: a poem on the blessed nativity. Design'd to excite an awful sense of religion both in the indolent and unbelieving part of mankind. *London, printed for W. Wilkin, 1727* [1726]. (*MC* Dec)
    2°: A² B–F²; *i–ii*, 1–22.
    'Celestial dove, by whose enliv'ning warmth'
        Remains of presentation inscription from Curteis in the CtY copy.
    CtY.

C554 C---y. The c---y e---on. Occasion'd by this passage out of the Observator of Wednesday, June 13. 1705... [*London, 1705.*]
    ½°: 1–2, 1 column.
    'When the grave saints had wisely fix'd on three'

The c---y e---on

    A satire on the members of parliament for the city of London.
    Rothschild.

Cyder. *See* Cider.

Cynegetica. Cynegetica, 1718. *See* Morgan, H.

C555 Cynic. A cynic laughing: or, the gentleman in a garret. A poem. Recommending the vertues of the place. By A.C. gent. *London printed, and sold by J. Morphew,* 1706. (*WL* Aug)
    ½°: 2 sides, 2 columns.
    'Thou grand disposer of all humane things'
    CtY.

Cynthiad. The Cynthiad; or, man in the moon, 'MDCCXLV'.
    The date, found in copies at LG,IU, is clearly a misprint for MDCCLXV; the correct form is in a copy at NN.

Cynthio. Cynthio, 1727. *See* Young, Edward.

Cyprian, *Saint*.
[*Epistolae*] [Tunstall, William:] St. Cyprian's Discourse to Donatus. Done into English metre, 1716, 1717. *See* T548–50.
    — [reissue] St. Cyprian's description of the pagan age, 1725. *See* T551.

Cythereia. Cythereia: or, new poems upon love and intrigue, 1723. *See* Markland, John.

D

'D-----, *Dr.*' On Miss Forrester playing with her shadow, 1743. *See* Cobden, Edward.

D., A. A narration of the wonders of grace, 1734. *See* Dutton, Anne.

D., C. Iter boreale, [1708.] *See* I73.

D., C., *rector of K—— in S——*. A poem upon our unhappy loss of Sir Cloudesly Shovel, 1708. *See* Darby, Charles.

— The union a poem, 1707. *See* Darby, Charles.

D——., H——. Monsieur Pretendant, 1745. *See* M411.

D., H., *philogram*. Love alone: or, the star that leads to Christ, 1703. *See* Denne, Henry.

D., H., *Ripensis*. De senectute, 1746. *See* Dering, Heneage.

— Reliquiae Eboracenses, 1743. *See* Dering, Heneage.

D., J., *esq*. The match, [1730?] *See* Dalacourt, James.

D---, J---, *T.C.D.* Abelard to Eloisa, 1730. *See* Dalacourt, James.

D., J., *S.I.D.* Britain's lamentation, and hopes of triumph, [1745/46.] *See* Don, James.

D., O., *broguemaker*. A dialogue between the brogue-makers, [1725/30.] *See* D266.

D., R. The fair Circassian, 1720–. *See* Croxall, Samuel.

— The footman's friendly advice, [1730.] *See* Dodsley, Robert (D389).

— On the death of Sir William Sharp, [1706?] *See* O199.

D., W., *gent*. Cleio. Poetical meditations upon sundry parts of scripture, 1711. *See* Clio.

D., *Sir* W. An elegy on the much lamented death of her most sacred majesty Queen Anne, [1714.] *See* E45–6.

D1 D----. The D---- deputies. A satyr. *London, printed in the year* 1705.
4°: *A*² B–F²; *1–2* 3–24.
'Now, satyr, raise thy forked sting, strike deep'
Attributed to Defoe by Robert Clare, one of Harley's informers; see H. L. Snyder in *The library* V.22 (1967) 333. His attributions seem in many cases to be wild guesses, but this is perhaps more plausible than usual. An attack on the Dutch in general and their deputies in particular for their opposition to Marlborough.
L(1077.k.24/2),LLP,C,E,DT(uncut)+; CtY.

D2 — The D--- of M----- turn'd conjurer. Or the history of the golden apple. *London, printed by J. Cramphorn, in Fleet-street,* 1712.
½°: 1 side, 2 columns.
'Licensed and entered according to act of parliment' below title; but not traced in *SR*.
'When Juno, Venus, Pallas, strove'
An attack on Marlborough, suggesting that if he had been in Paris's situation, he would have sought bigger bribes from the goddesses.
LSA.

D3 — The D----- of M---- turn'd conjurer... [*London?*] *Printed in the year* 1712.
½°: 1 side, 2 columns.
Crawford,Rothschild.

D4 — [*variant title:*] The history of the three goddesses, and the golden apple of Prince Paris and Prince Avaro. [*London?*] *Printed in the year* 1712.
½°: 1 side, 2 columns.
The text is from the same setting of type as the preceding.
L(1876.f.19/23); MH.

D5 — The D...s hue and cry after an old turnip man. [*London*] *Printed for R. Thomas,* [1719.] (Aug, Luttrell)
½°: 1 side, 2 columns.
'O! yes, O! yes, if any man or woman'
Apparently a satire on George I.
ICN(Luttrell).

Dalacourt, James. *This is the form of name he used in this period; subsequently he changed it to Delacour.*

— Poems by the Revd. James De-La-Cour, A.M. *Cork, printed by Thomas White,* 1778.
8°: pp. 110.   L; ICU,MH.

— *For a group of pseudonymous poems in which Dalacourt may have had a share, see* 'Gulliver, Martin'.

D6 [—] Abelard to Eloisa, in answer to Mr. Pope's fine piece of Eloisa to Abelard. By J--- D---, T.C.D. *Dublin, printed by S. Powell, for Abraham Bradley,* 1730.
8°: A–B⁴; *1–6* 7–16.
'From shades as deep, and gloomy as the bow'rs'
Reprinted in Dalacourt's *Poems,* 1778; ms. attribution in the LVA-F copy.
L(11602.bb.33/8),LVA-F,O,DA(2).

Dalacourt, J.

D7 [—] The Chevalier de St. Patrick. Or, the Irish Pretender's character. *Dublin, printed in year* 1734. ½°: 1 side, 2 columns.
'To thee O D—n, be these truths addrest'
Ms. note in the NN copy, 'Supos'd to be wrote by Iˢ Dalacourt T.C.D. on Mr. Dunkin A.M.'
NN.

D8 [—] The match, a poem. In three heats----------
By J. D. esq. *Dublin printed, and sold by George Faulkner,* [1730?]
8°: *A⁴; 1–2* 3–8.
Copies at DA, DT are bound with poems of 1730.
'Speed and the games I sing, where counties meet'
Dalacourt's authorship seems almost certain from the initials and the publication by Faulkner.
DA,DT(2),LdU-B.

D9 [—] The progress of beauty. A poem. *Dublin printed, and sold by George Faulkner,* 1732.
8°: *A⁴* B–C⁴; *1–3* 4–23 *24.* 24 advt.
'Say muse, what next, what high immortal theme'
Attributed to Dalacourt in [William Dunkin] *An account of a strange and wonderful apparition,* 1734. Tentatively ascribed to George Granville, lord Lansdowne, in Elizabeth Handasyde, *Granville the polite* (1933) 282.
C,DN.

D10 [—] — *Dublin, printed. London, reprinted and sold by J. Roberts,* 1732. (*GSJ* 28 April)
4°: A–D⁴ E²; *1–3* 4–36.
Entered to 'WB & Partners' in Bowyer's ledgers under 26 April 1732, 500 copies printed.
O; CSmH,CtY,IU,KU,TxU.

D11 — A prospect of poetry: address'd to the right honourable John, earl of Orrery. To which is added, a poem to Mr. Thomson on his Seasons. *Dublin, printed by S. Powell, for William Heatly,* 1734 [1733?].
8°: A–H⁴; *1–2* 3–64.
Watermark: Amsterdam arms. 'To Mr. Thomson, on his Seasons' occupies pp. 59–64.
'What various styles to diff'rent strains belong'
To Thomson: 'From sunless worlds, where Phœbus seldom smiles'
L(11631.a.63/2),O,DG,DN,DT; CSmH,CtY.

D12 — [fine paper]
Watermark: fleur-de-lys.
DA,DN(presentation binding); CLU-C.

D13 —— *Dublin printed: London reprinted, for J. Roberts,* 1734 [1733]. (*GSJ* 27 Dec)
8°: A–H⁴; *1–2* 3–64.
Also listed in *GSJ* as published 10 Jan 1734.
L(1966),LVA-D,O,C; CtY,DFo,ICN,MH(uncut),TxU+.

D14 —— *Dublin, printed for Peter Wilson,* 1743.
8°: A⁴(±A1) B–H⁴; *1–2* 3–64.

Dalacourt, J. A prospect of poetry

A reissue of the Dublin edition of 1734. C,DA.

[—] The tea-kettle a poem humbly inscrib'd to Miss H------lt, 1730. *See* T112.

[**Dale, Thomas.**] An epistle to Alexander Pope, esq; from South Carolina [actually by James Kirkpatrick], 1737. *See* K88·5.

'**Dalgleish, John.**' Huy and cry for apprehending George Fachney, [1721/22.] *See* Pennecuik, Alexander, *d.1730.*

Dalkeith. Dalkeith. A poem, 1732. *See* Boyse, Samuel [Verses occasion'd by seeing the palace].

D15 [**Dalton, John.**] An epistle to a young nobleman from his præceptor. *London, printed for Lawton Gilliver, & Robert Dodsley,* 1736. (*SR* 16 March)
2°: *A–B² C–E²; i–ii, 1–2* 3–17 *18 blk.* A1 hft.
Listed in *GM, LM* March. Entered in *SR* to Lawton Gilliver alone; deposit copies at L,O, E,AdU.
'"What is nobility?" – Wou'd you then know'
For Dalton's authorship, see the following.
To Viscount Beauchamp.
L(11630.h.57/3; 643.m.14/10),O(3, 1–A1),C,E, LdU-B+; CSmH,CtY,ICN,MH,TxU+.

D16 — Two epistles. The first, to a young gentleman from his preceptor. Written in the year 1735–6. The second, to the right honourable the Countess of Hartford, at Percy-Lodge: in the year 1744. *London, printed for R. Dodsley,* 1745. (*GM,LM* March)
4°: A–E⁴; *i–iii* iv–vi *vii–viii, 1* 2–32.
To Lady Hartford: 'You ask me, madam, if the muse'
L(11630.c.5/1; 840.l.7/7; 161.l.29),O(lacks E4), OW,LdU-B,*MR*; CSmH,CtY,ICN,IU,MH+.

D17 **Dalton, Oliver.** An elegy on the much lamented death of the reverend Father James Fitzsimons a Romish priest, who departed this life the first inst. June, 1726. at his late dwelling-house in Dirty-lane near Thomas-street...Written by his friend Oliver Dalton. [*Dublin,* 1726.]
½°: 1 side, 2 columns.
Mourning borders.
'Cease bright Sol, your resplendent rays obscure'
DT(imprint cropt).

[**D18 = G138**] **Damned.** The damneds doom, 1701. *See* Gibson, William, *licensed schoolmaster.*

D19 **Damocles.** Damocles. [*London?* 172–?]
½°: 1 side, 2 columns.
'Happy! thrice happy is his fate!'
On the uncertain position of the politician; there is no indication of its particular subject, but it is possibly Walpole.
CSmH,MH.

Damon

D20 Damon. Damon and Amarillis: a pastoral eclogue. Humbly inscribed to the right honourable the Lady Cowper on her marriage. *London, printed for H. Chapelle,* 1750. (*BM* May)
2°: *A*² B²; *1–3* 4–8.
'Damon, this morn, methought the god of day'
L(1890.c.1/2).

D21 — Damon's case and resolution, a poem. *Dublin, printed by John Harding,* [1724?]
½°: 1 side, 2 columns.
CSmH copy bound with half-sheets of 1724.
'Damon, unhappy Damon! sure'
A pastoral.
CSmH.

'**Damon.**' The yea and nay stock-jobbers, 1720. *See* Bockett, Elias.

Dance, James. *Dance subsequently assumed the name of Love.*

[—] Poems on several occasions. By James Love, comedian. *Edinburgh, printed by R. Fleming,* 1754.
8°: pp. xii, 115.   L; CtY,MH.

D22 [—] Cricket. An heroic poem. Illustrated with the critical observations of Scriblerus Maximus. *London, printed for W. Bickerton,* [1744.] (*LEP* 5 July)
4°: *A*⁴(–A4) B–D⁴ *E*¹; [2] *i* ii–iii *iv, 1* 2–25 *26 blk.*
Bond 184.
'While others, soaring on a lofty wing'
Reprinted in Dance's *Poems,* 1754. Dedicated to John, earl of Sandwich. The poem describes the match between Kent and England played on 18 June 1744.
L(11602.gg.1/9),CT; MCC library, London.

D23 [—] — The second edition. *London, printed for W. Bickerton,* 1745. (*DA* 4 July)
4°: *A*⁴(–A4) B–D⁴ *E*¹; [2] *i* ii–iii *iv, 1* 2–25 *26 blk.*
From the same type as the preceding, but with revisions to sheet D including the addition of four lines on p. 23 celebrating a catch by Lord John Sackville. It is not clear whether the remainder of the pamphlet is reissued or reimpressed.
MCC library, London.

[—] Yes they are: being an answer to Are these things so? [actually by Robert Morris], 1740. *See* M511.

Dancing. The dancing devils, 1724. *See* Ward, Edward.

D24 — The dancing-master. A satyr. Canto I. *London, printed for A. Moore; sold by the booksellers of London,* 1722. (*PB* 2 June)
8°: A–B⁴ C²; *1–2* 3–20.
'Of all the plagues with which poor England's curst'
L(164.l.47, Luttrell, June); OCU.

Danger

D25 Danger. The danger is over: or, all parties agreed. *London, printed in the year* 1710.
½°: 1 side, 2 columns.
'Ye peers, and seers; of gracious ears'
Crum Y103: 'A song'. Occasioned by the sentence on Sacheverell.
OW; MH.

D26 Daniel. Daniel the prophet no conjurer: or, his scandal club's scandalous ballad, called the Tackers; answer'd paragraph by paragraph. [*London*]...*sold by B. Bragg,* 1705. (*DC* 14 April, 'yesterday')
4°: A⁴; *1–2* 3–8, 2 columns.
The original poem is reprinted together with the answer.
Tackers: 'In vain of the battle we boast'
Answer: 'The battle had never been gain'd'
A reply to *The tackers,* 1705, which was probably by Charles Darby: the 'scandal club' is Defoe's.
L(11626.e.22, cropt),O,*MR*; MB,TxU(2).

Daniel, Richard. A paraphrase on some select psalms. *London, printed for Bernard Lintot,* 1722. (*SR* 17 Aug)
8°: pp. 112.   L,O; CtY.
Deposit copies at L,O. The sequence of editions is uncertain. Entered to Lintot in Bowyer's ledgers under 1 Aug 1722, 500 copies printed.

— — *Dublin, printed by George Grierson,* 1722.
8°: pp. 131.   L,DA.
No watermark.

— [fine paper]   O.
Watermark: Strasburg bend.

— The royal penitent: a paraphrase on the seven penitential psalms. *London, printed for Bernard Lintot,* 1727. (*MC* Feb)
8°: pp. 63.   L,O; CtY.
The sequence of editions is again uncertain. See *A Paraphrase on the seven penitential psalms,* [1727?] for a skit on Daniel's paraphrase.

— — *Dublin, printed by George Grierson,* 1727.
4°: pp. 64.   DT; CSmH.

— A paraphrase on some select psalms, and upon the seven penitential psalms, entitled the Royal penitent. *London, printed by H. L. for Joseph Fisher,* 1737. (*LM* April)
8°.   (Pickering & Chatto cat. 259/2909.)

D27 [—] The British warriour. A poem. In a letter to his excellency the Lord Cutts, occasion'd by the late glorious success of her majesty's arms. *London, printed for Benj. Bragg,* [1706.] (*DC* 24 Oct)
2°: *A*¹ B–D² *E*¹; *i–ii, 1–*14. 14 advt.
'The British muse in Chaucer first began'

Daniel, R. The British warrior

Printed as Daniel's in Lintot's *Miscellany poems and translations*, 1720. On the victory at Ramillies.
O; CtY,DFo(uncut),ICN(Luttrell, 30 Oct),MH, TxU.

D28 [—] — *London: printed for B. Bragg; and re-printed for M. Gunne, Dublin*, 1706.
4°: *A*² B–C²; *1–2* 3–12. 12 advt.
L(1966),DA,DG,DN,DT(3); CtY,DLC.

D29 [—] The dream: a poem occasion'd by the death of his late majesty, William III. *London printed, and sold by John Nutt*, 1702. (21 May, Luttrell)
2°: *A*² B–G²; *i–iv*, 1–24. A1 hft.
Listed in *WL* May 1702. The priority between London and Dublin editions has not been established.
'The shades of waneing night had now begun'
Daniel's authorship is stated in the Dublin edition below.
O,*MR-C*; CLU-C,*NjP*(Luttrell).

D29·2 [—] — The second edition. *London printed, and sold by John Nutt*, 1702.
2°: *A*² B–G²; *i–iv*, 1–24. A1 hft.
Apparently from the same setting of type as the preceding.
L(11631.k.5/1),LDW(–A1); MH.

D29·5 — A dream; or, an elegiack poem, occasion'd by the death of William III. king of Great Britain, France and Ireland. *Dublin, printed by John Brocas, and are to be sold by Matthew Gunn*, 1702.
4°: A–F²; *1–2* 3–24.
L(11632.f.16),DG,DT(2); ICN,IU.

D30 — God the creator, and the preserver: a poem. *London, printed for W. Taylor*, 1714. (*MC* Sept)
2°: *A*² B–C²; *i–iv*, 1–8.
'Offspring of heav'n, celestial flame'
Dedication signed.
L(11633.i.5).

D31 — A poem on the return of his majesty King George from Hanover: inscrib'd to her royal highness the Princess of Wales. *London, printed for Bernard Lintot*, 1717. (*MC* Jan)
2°: *A*² B²; *1–2* 3–8.
The priority of this and the Dublin edition has not been determined. Entered to Lintot in Bowyer's ledgers under 24 Dec 1716, 250 copies printed.
'Britain arise, in all your glory smile'
O-*JJ*,DN; CLU,CSmH,TxU.

D32 — — *Dublin, printed by J. Carson, for Jer. Pepyat*, 1717.
2°: *A*² B²; *1–2* 3–7 *8 blk.*
DT.

D33 — [*idem*] Great Britains triumph. A poem on his majesty's return, by the reverend Mr. Archdeacon Daniel. [*London*] *Sold by J. Clark engraver, & the printsellers*, [1720.] (*PB* 12 Nov)
½°: 1 side, 3 columns.

Daniel, R. A poem on the return

Engraved throughout, with portrait headpiece signed 'J. Clark sc. 1720'.
L(112.f.44/38, Luttrell, Nov),LDW,O-JJ.

Danniston, Walter. *Danniston's name was apparently used by Archibald Pitcairne in a number of his Latin poems; whether Walter Denneston, the schoolmaster at Musselburgh who died c.1703, is intended is not clear.*

— Archibaldo Pitcarnio Gualterus Dannistonus εὐχαιρειν, [1710?/13.] *See* P341.

— Dannistonus Pitcarnio s.d., [1710?/13.] *See* P354.

— Gualteri Dannistoni ad Georgium Buchanum epistola, [1706?] *See* P364.

— Gualterus Dannistonus ad amicos, [1710?] *See* P366.

— Gualterus Danistonus, scotus, Sannazario veneto, [170–?] *See* P369.

D34 [**D'Anvers, Alicia.**] Academia: or, the humours of the university of Oxford. In burlesque verse. *London, printed for J. Morphew*, 1716. (*SR* 20 June)
12°: A–D⁶ (C2,3 as 'D2,3'); *i–iv*, 1–41 *42–44.* 42–44 advt.
First published in 1691 as 'By Mrs. Alicia D'Anvers' (*Wing* D220). Listed in *MC* June. Entered in *SR* to James Knapton; deposit copies at E,EU; EU has Knapton's name substituted in ms. for Morphew in the imprint.
'I intend to give you a relation'
L(11646.bbb.21, Luttrell, 27 June),O(2),E,EU, LdU-B; CLU-C,CtY,*NNC*,TxU.

D35 [—] [reissue] *London, printed for James Roberts*, 1730. (*MChr* 22 Jan)
12°: A⁶(±A1) B–D⁶; *i–iv*, 1–41 *42–44.* 42–44 advt.
O.

D36 **D'Anvers, Arthur.** The funeral. A poem, in memory of the late Duke of Marlborough. *Dublin, printed by Thomas Hume*, 1725.
2°: A–B² C–D²; *i–iv*, 1–12.
'Not rival chiefs engag'd in bloody strife'
L(1347.m.24).

D37 — The invasion, a poem, most humbly inscribed to his royal highness Prince William, duke of Cumberland... *Dublin, printed by S. Powell*, 1746.
8°: A–B⁴; *1–5* 6–14 *15–16 blk.*
Dedication dated 25 Jan 1746.
'The muse who sung the flight at Dettingen'
O,DN,DT.

D38 — 'The invasion, a poem. [*London*] *Cooper, Woodfall.* Price 6*d*.' (*BM, GM* Feb 1746)

D39 — A poem on the glorious victory obtain'd by the king of Great Britain, at the head of the allies, over the French commanded by Marshall Noailles, June 16, 1743, near Dettingen. *Dublin printed, and sold by Christopher Dickson*, 1743.

D'Anvers, A. A poem on the glorious victory

8°: A^4 B^4; *1–5* 6–16.

The title appears to be a cancel in the LVA-F copy but has not been confirmed elsewhere.
'Say, goddess muse, what caus'd that fatal day'
L(1490.pp.78),LVA-F,LdU-B; MH.

'D'Anvers, Caleb.' A collection of poems on several occasions; publish'd in the Craftsman. *London, printed for R. Francklin, 1731.*
8°: pp. 76.   L,O; CtY,MH.

A miscellany of poems contributed to the paper, often attributed to Nicholas Amhurst who edited the *Craftsman* under this pseudonym.

'—' The Craftsman's poems on several occasions ... By the reputed Caleb D'Anvers, author of the Craftsman, and other eminent hands. *Dublin, printed by and for James Hoey, 1732.*
8°: pp. 32.   L,DA.

A different collection from the preceding.

D40 '—' King Cock-lorrel's treat, or, a feast for the devil. By Calib D'Anvers of the Peak, esq; Dedicated to the right hon. S. R. S. W. '*London, printed by J. Tonpson* [!], *and sold by the booksellers*' [*Dublin*], [1729?]
slip: 1 side, 1 column.

The DT copy is bound with Dublin half-sheets of 1729.
'King Cock-lorrel once, had the devil his guest'
DT; NN.

D41 '—' ⟨A new⟩ ballad. By Caleb D'Anvers, esq; To the tuno [!] of, —Ye commons and peers. *London, printed for J. Johnson, near London-bridge,* [1731.]
½°: 1 side, 2 columns.

Percival, appendix 30. Published in *DC* 10 Feb 1731.
'Ye roundheaded tories, and longheaded Jacks'
A satire on *The Craftsman's* attacks on Walpole's government.
L(1876.f.1/114, title cropt).

D42 **D'Anvers, Griffith Morgan.** Persius Scaramouch: or, a critical and moral satire on the orators, scriblers, and vices of the present times. In imitation of the first satire of Persius. By way of dialogue betwixt the said Mr. D'Anvers, and Mr. Orator Henley of Lincoln's-Inn-Fields. By Griffith Morgan D'Anvers, M.A. formerly of Jesus-College in Oxford. *London, printed for J. Wilford, 1734.* (*HM* 27 April)
2°: A–B^2 C–E^2; *i–ii* iii–iv, *5* 6–19 *20 blk.*
Latin and English texts.
'I never din'd with Dennis or with Pope'
D'Anvers has not been traced in *Alumni Oxonienses;* he is possibly pseudonymous.
O; CSmH,KU,MH,NjP,TxU.

D43 **Danvers, Joseph.** Tipping tipt justice: or, the rev. Mr. Silvester's Critical dissertation, &c.

Danvers, J. Tipping tipt justice

wherein he pretends to confute Mr. Foster's notion of heresy, versified. *London, printed for the author; sold by the booksellers and pamphletsellers of town & country,* [1735.] (*GM* Nov)
8°: A–D^4; *1–3* 4–31 *32 blk.*
'St---ng with courage fresh assail'

'Joseph Danvers' is possibly a pseudonym. A versification of Tipping Silvester's *A critical dissertation on Titus iii. 10, 11. Wherein Mr. Foster's notion of heresy is consider'd and confuted,* 1735.
L(11633.f.46),O,LdU-B; CtY.

Daphnis. Daphnis and Chloe. A ballad, [1720.] *See* Gay, John.

— Daphnis: or, a pastoral elegy, 1701–. *See* Froud, John.

Darby, Charles. The book of psalms in English metre. The newest version fitted to the common tunes. *London, Tho. Parkhurst, 1704.*
12°: pp. 352.   L.

D44 [—] Bacchanalia: or, a description of a drunken-club. A poem. *London, printed for M. Cooper, 1746* [1745]. (*GM* Oct)
2°: A^2 B–D^2 E^1; *1–2* 3–18.

First published in 1680 (*Wing* D243). The copyright of 'A Description of a Drunken Club' with 179 books was sold as part of a lot in the trade sale of Francis Cogan, 10 July 1746 (cat. at O-JJ), to Waller for 18*s.* 6*d.*
'It was my hap spectator once to be'
L(11631.k.7/5),OA; CtY,DFo,TxU.

[—] Oxfordshire, 1704. *See* O276.

[—] The Oxfordshire nine, 1705. *See* O277.

D44·5 [—] A poem upon our unhappy loss of Sir Cloudesly Shovel, admiral of the British fleet; who was cast away upon the rocks near Scilly, called, the Bishop and his clerks, and not one man saved. By C.D. rector of K—— in S——. *London printed, and sold by Ben Bragge, 1708* [1707]. (29 Nov, Luttrell)
2°: A^2; *1–4.*
'Who could suspect his fate so hard should prove?'

Charles Darby was rector of Kedington in Suffolk; cf. *The union* below.
MH(Luttrell).

D45 [—] The tackers. By a church of England minister. [*London*] 1705. (April ?)
½°: 1 side, 2 columns.
Column two contains 'A postscript'.
'In vain of the battel we boast'

Contemporary ms. note in the PPL copy 'Mr Darby of Suffolk'. See *Daniel the prophet no conjurer,* 1705, a reprint of *The tackers* with a verse reply which suggests the author is part of Defoe's 'scandal club'. This has led to its

Darby, C. The tackers

being attributed to John Tutchin. See also
*The tackers vindicated...with a word to Mr.
John Tutchin about his scandalous ballad,*
1705 (copy at L), a prose work which includes
a verse parody of this.
O,Rothschild; PPL('Aprill 1705').

D46 [—] The tackers. [*London?* 1705.]
½°: 1 side, 2 columns.
LSA.

D46·5 [—] The union a poem humbly dedicated to the
queen. By C.D. rector of K---- in S----. *London,
printed for John Wyat,* 1707. (27 March, Luttrell)
2°: A–B²; *1–2* 3–7 *8 blk.*
Advertised in *DC* 2 April.
'At length, great queen, that glorious work is done'
Charles Darby was rector of Kedington in
Suffolk, and signed his *An elegy on the death
of the queen,* 1695, in this way. An illegible
note of authorship in the copy at InU is
perhaps 'Charles Dabry'.
O,*MR-C*; CLU-C(Luttrell),InU(uncut).

D47 Darius. Darius's feast: or, the force of truth.
A poem, addressed to the right honourable the
Earls of Salisbury and Exeter. *London, printed for
Lawlon* [!] *Gilliver,* 1734. (*GM* Dec)
2°: *A²* B–E²; *i–iv, 1* 2–15 *16.* 16 advt.
''Twas on a joyful day; the gorgeous feast'
L(11602.i.17/2),O(2),E,DT(lacks A1),LdU-B;
CSmH,CtY(2),ICN,MH,TxU +.

Dark. The dark penitent's complaint, 1712. *See*
Waring, Henry.

Dart, John. The works of Tibullus, containing
his four books of love-elegies. Translated by Mr.
Dart. To which is prefix'd, the life of the author...
*London, printed by T. Sharpe, for W. Newton, A.
Bettesworth & J. Batley, and W. Mears & T.
Jauncey,* 1720. (*DP* 1 July)
8°: pp. xxxix, lii, 264.   O; CLU-C,MH.
Watermark: initials. There are cancels and an
errata leaf not traced in all copies.

— [fine paper] *London, printed by T. Sharpe, for
A. Bettesworth, W. Newton, W. Mears & T.
Jauncy,* 1720.
L; CtY,MH.
Watermark: Strasburg bend.

D48 — The complaint of the black knight from
Chaucer. *London, printed by R. Redmayne; sold by
J. Morphew,* 1718. (*PB* 2 Sept)
8°: π² A⁴ χ¹ B–E⁴ F²; *i–xiv,* 1–36. π1 hft.
No watermark.
'In that soft time when nature youthful grows'
LVA-D(−π1),LdU-B; CSmH,CtY(−π1),MH
(−π1).

D49 — [fine paper]
Watermark: fleur-de-lys on shield.
L(1465.f.9,−π1).

Dart, J. The complaint

D50 — [reissue] The complaint of the black knight:
an elegiack poem from Chaucer. *London, printed
for Jer. Batley,* 1720. (*PB* 18 Aug)
8°: π²(±) A⁴ χ¹ B–E⁴ F²; *i–xiv,* 1–36. π1 hft.
ICN,IU,*MnU.*

D51 — A poem on Chaucer and his writings. Written
at the request of the lord bishop of Rochester...
London printed, and sold T. Paine, 1722. (*DJ*
10 Oct)
2°: π¹ A–C²; *[2]* i–iv, 1–8.
In the ICU copy, sheet B is unsigned.
'When in some curious gallery we stand'
CtY(uncut),ICU,IU,*MH.*

D52 [—] Westminster Abbey: a poem. *London, printed
for J. Batley,* 1721. (*DJ* 28 April)
8°: *A⁴* B–I⁴; *i–viii, 1* 2–64 (17–24 as '33–40').
A1 hft; 64 err.
'Muse, leave a while soft Venus and her joys'
Ms. note by Pope in the LVA–D copy 'By
John Dart'.
L(11658.g.46,−A1),LVA-D(Pope's copy),O,
LdU-B; CSmH,CtY(−A1),ICU,MH(−A1),TxU
(−A1)+.

D53 Dartington. Dartington. A poem. Inscrib'd to
A.C. esq;. *Exon, printed by Philip Bishop,* 1714.
8°: A⁸; *1–3* 4–16.
'Britannia, famous isle, that all admir'd'
University of Otago (photocopy at L).

D'Assigny, F. Poems on several occasions...
*London printed, and sold by J. Roberts, E. Nutt,
A. Dodd, and by the booksellers of London &
Westminster,* 1730.
8°: pp. 32.   MH.
No watermark.

— [fine paper]   CtY.
Watermark: fleur-de-lys.

— [variant title?] The second edition.
O; CtY.

— [reissue?] The ladies miscellany: or, a curious
collection of amorous poems, and merry tales.
*London, printed for A. More; sold by E. Nutt,
A. Dodd, and at the pamphlet shops in London &
Westminster,* 1730. (*MChr* June)
8°: pp. 32.   CtY.
Apparently a reissue with a cancel title.

[Davenant, Charles.] A dialogue between the
cities of London and Paris, 1701. *See* D267.

David. David Veneri, [1710?/13.] *See* Pitcairne,
Archibald.

— David's lamentation over Saul and Jonathan,
1736–. *See* Lockman, John.

D53·5 [Davidson, —, tailor.] The taylor's vindication.
[*Edinburgh,* 17––?]
slip: 1 side, 1 column.
Dated as [1670?] in the L catalogue, but

Davidson, —. The taylor's vindication

probably its primitive appearance is due to its Edinburgh origin; a seventeenth-century date is not impossible.

'There was a simple Adamite'
Clearly the poem answered by *The merchants and hammer-mens complaint against the taylors. Or, a hot goose for poet Davidson, the taylor; author of, The taylors vindication,* [17––?]. Davidson has not been identified.
L(C.121.g.9/30).

D54 Davidson, George. [dh] Georgius Davidsonus Comiti Aboinio, vicesimo secundo Aprilis die, ipsius natali, anno 1717. S.P.D. [*Edinburgh,* 1717.]
4°: *A*⁴; *1–7 8 blk.*
'Qui ferant fulmen creat ales acer'
L(11408.e.13),E(2); TxU.

D55 — Joanni Voluseno matheseos professori Georgius Davidsonus, de morte Archibaldi Pitcarnii Scoti. [*Edinburgh,* 1713.] (Oct)
½°: 1 side, 1 column.
Entered in Ruddiman's ledger, both for case and press, for the week ending 31 Oct 1713, 'Mr Davidson's poem on the Doctor 150 copies'; apparently entered again in the following week both for case and press, 100 copies, though another work by Davidson may conceivably be intended.
'Quando prisca fides, omnes & Apollinis artes'
E(2, 1 cropt); TxU.

D56 Davidson, William. Carthagena, a new poem, containing a true and particular relation of every thing material in that fatal expedition. *Edinburgh, printed and sold in the Swan-close* [*by R. Drummond?*], 1741.
8°: *A*⁸; *1 2–16.*
'Thou first born sister of the sacred nine'
E,GM.

D57 — The Cuckow's lamentation for our loss at Carthagena. [*Edinburgh?* 1741.]
slip: 1 side, 1 column.
'Now mourn, each peer, renowned knight'
Signed 'William Davidson'.
Rosebery.

D58 [—] The Cuckow's song anent the election of peers. [*Edinburgh,* 174–?]
½°: 1 side, 1 column.
'Great Hamilton and Scot of royal blood'
'The Cuckow' was apparently Davidson's nom-de-plume.
Rosebery.

D59 — In mrum. Georgium Livingston, coram suprema curia juridica, clerum probum, celebrem, epitaphium. [*Edinburgh?* 1744.]
¼°: 1 side, 1 column.
'Insignis clericus, patriæ pater atque columna'
The date of Livingston's death is given in a ms. note in the TxU copy as 31 Dec 1743.
TxU.

Davies, J.

Davies, J. Select fables, tales &c. in English verse... By J. Davies, late schoolmaster of Sandbach in Cheshire. *London, printed for the author,* 1738. (*GM* Aug)
8°: pp. 127. ICN.
Perhaps a different author from the following.

D60 Davies, John, *1704–1735.* Bury-fair: a poem... With three other copies of verses. Viz. I. A South-Sea couple. II. On a microscope. III. Vanity and worth, a fable. All by John Davies, late of St. Peter's College Cambridge. *London, printed for E. Curll,* 1724 [1723]. (*MC* Aug/Sept)
8°: *A*¹ B–C⁴ D⁴(–D4); *i–ii, 1 2–22.*
Reissued in *The altar of love,* 1727 (copies at L,MH), without title-leaf.
'Tell me, my muse! (if thou wilt deign to lend'
CLU-C,CtY,DFo,ICN.

D61 [**Davies, Samuel.**] [dh] The following verses were composed by a pious clergyman in Virginia... as he was returning home in a very gloomy and rainy night. [*London,* 175-.]
2°: *A*²; *1 2–4.*
On p. 3, 'A clergyman's reflections on the death of one of his pious parishioners', in this edition with spaces between the stanzas.
'Come, heavn'ly pensive contemplation, come'
'Of my dear flock one more is gone'
Ascribed to Samuel Davies by MiU-C on the authority of S. Foster Damon; the second poem is printed in Davies's *Sermons on important subjects* (Boston, 1811). A manuscript of the first poem in the Osborn collection at CtY dates the occasion as 16 Sept 1750.
*MiU-C,*NjP.

D62 [—] [another edition]
In this edition by the same printer there are no spaces between the stanzas of the second poem.
L(840.l.10/9); *MH.*

D63 [—] — [*London?* 175–?]
4°: 4 pp.
Without 'A clergyman's reflections'.
MiU-C.

Davies, Sneyd. *Poems by Sneyd Davies are included in John Whaley's* A collection of poems, *1732.*

Davis, George. A new collection of miscellany poems, for the year, 1718. *London, printed for W. Boreham,* 1718.
8°: pp. 58. L.
A reissue of an unidentified collection, with additions; the drop-head title is 'New miscellany poems'. The dedication is signed 'George Davis', but it is questionable if he is the author. A related work, *A new collection of miscellany poems, for the year 1715,* (copy

Davis, G. A new collection

belonging to W. N. H. Harding) has the imprint 'printed for G. Davis; sold by E. Lewis', suggesting that he is the publisher or editor of a miscellany. The following separately published poems are reprinted in the 1718 collection: *Belphegor*, 1714; *The farthingale reviv'd*, 1711; *The signior in fashion*, 1711.

Davis, Richard. Hymns composed on several subjects, and on several occasions... In five parts... The fifth edition corrected. *London, printed by T.R. in the year 1738.*
12°: pp. vi, 200.   L,DT; NNUT.
  The earliest edition traced is the second, of 1694. The fourth edition was listed in *TC* Trinity 1707.

—— The seventh edition, corrected... *London, printed for J. Ward, 1748.*
12°: pp. viii, 184.   L,LDW; DLC,NNUT.

D64 [**Davys, Edward,** *viscount Mountcashel.*] A poem delivered to the reverend Doctor Swift, dean of St. Patrick's, Dublin; by a young nobleman, November 30. 1725. Being the dean's birth-day. [*Dublin, 1725.*]
½°: 1–2, 1 column.
  Teerink 1211. One copy at L has a slip with ms. date '1730' pasted over 1725 in title.
'In sixteen hundred sixty eight'
  Ms. ascription to Mountcashel in the C copy and index to the DT volume; wrongly ascribed to Lord Orrery in PU.
L(1890.e.5/57; C.121.g.8/124),C,DT; PU,TxU.

D65 — To his excellency our Lord Carteret lord lieutenant of Ireland: the humble petition of Lord Viscount Mont-Cashel, and the rest of his schoolfellows. [*Dublin, 1725.*]
½°: 1 side, 1 column.
'With greatest respect and most awful submission'
  Appealing for a week's summer holiday from Thomas Sheridan's school, after his appointment as Carteret's chaplain.
L(1890.e.5/99, ms. date '7bre 13th 1725'; C.121.g.8/126); CSmH,PU.

[—] To the honourable Master Henry Barry, [*1725/30.*] *See* T372.

D66 [**Davys, John.**] The art of decyphering discovered: in a copy of verses to a lady, upon sending her an ænigma, written in cyphers. *London, printed for Step. Fletcher, bookseller in Westminster-hall; and are to be sold at his shop in Oxford, 1727.* (*MC* June)
2°: A² B²; *1–3* 4–8.
'If for a while you can sit still'
  Ascribed to Davys by *Rawlinson.*
OW,MP; MH,TxU(uncut).

D67 [**Dawes,** *Sir* **William,** *bart.*] An anatomy of atheisme: a poem. By the author of the Duties of

Dawes, *Sir* **W.** An anatomy of atheisme

the closet... The second edition, revis'd. *London, printed for Thomas Speed, 1701.*
8°: A–D⁴; *i–viii*, 1–24. ii advt.
  Below imprint, 'Price 3d. or 20s. a hundred to those who give them away'. First published 1694. Horizontal chain-lines; possibly printed as a quarto. Entered as 'old copy' in *SR* 8 June 1710 to Tho. Speed.
'Since some with bare-fac'd impudence deny'
O,GM; MH.

D68 —— The fourth edition, revis'd. *London, printed for John Wilford, 1731.*
8°: (frt+) A–D⁴; *i–viii*, 1–24.
  Dawes's name on portrait frontispiece. Third edition not traced.
L(11631.d.16),O,E; CtY,MH,NN,PU.

D69 **Dawley.** Dawley, D'Anvers, and Fog's triumph; or, the downfall of Belzabub, Bell, and the dragon: a new ballad. *London, printed for J. Roberts; sold by the booksellers of London & Westminster, 1734.*
2°: A² B²; *1–2* 3–7 *8 blk.*
  Percival appendix 59.
'Dear wise-headed friends, of the Jacobite clan'
  A satire against the high church tories, put into the mouth of Bolingbroke.
O.

D70 **Dawn.** The dawn of honour; or, fountain of liberty. *London, printed for J. Huggonson, 1742.* (*GM* May)
2°: A² B–C²; *1–2* 3–12.
  Horizontal chain-lines.
'Depress'd, desponding Britain's genius lay'
MH.

'Dawne, Dabry, *M.D.*' Health; a poem, [1716]–. *See* Baynard, Edward.

Dawson, William. Miscellaneous poems on several occasions. By Mr Dawson, &c... *London, printed for J. Roberts, A. Dodd, T. Payne, & J. Fisher, 1735* [1734]. (*GM* Dec)
8°: pp. 64.   L,O; CtY,MH.
  A subsequent collection, *Poems on several occasions*, was published at Williamsburg, Virginia, in 1736. The identity of this Dawson and the William who wrote the poems below needs confirmation.

D71 — The atheist, a philosophical poem, representing and confuting the arguments brought in favour of their tenets. *London, printed for the author, 1723.*
4°: A² B–E² F¹; *1–4* 5–22. A1 hft.
'When Maro's lyre was in fame's temple hung'
L(840.h.7/7),LVA-F.

D72 — The British swain. In five pastorals. To which are added some miscellaneous poems, design'd as a specimen of a larger work. *London, printed for J. Noon, 1724.* (*MC* April)

Dawson, W. The British swain

8°: *A*¹ B–I⁴ K¹; *i–ii*, *1* 2–66.
'Close by the entrance of the woodland plain'
CtY,IU.

D73 Day. A day spent in Dublin. To the right honourable Lady B————. *Dublin, printed in the year* 1746–7.
½°: 1 side, 2 columns.
'The labour of a Dublin day'
    According to a ms. note in the DT copy, addressed to Margaret, lady Barrymore; possibly a satire on her social life.
DT(ms. notes).

D74 De. De pace ab optima & augustissima nostra regina felicissime constituta, carmen gratulatorium. *Londini, apud Johannem Morphew,* 1713. (*PB* 11 April 'in a few days')
4°: A–C² D²; *i–vi*, 1–8 *9; 10 blk.*
'Albion, æquoreis circumdata fluctibus ora'
    Dedication and poem signed 'J.C.'; possibly by John Colme. Cf. N311.
L(837.h.34, with a ms. dedicatory poem to Hans Sloane).

— De senectute, 1746. *See* Dering, Heneage.

D———e. The D———e of Marlborough's fine show, [1712?] *See* An excellent new song, call'd, The full tryal, [1712?]

D75 Dead. The dead emperor: or, reviving peace. Being some deep coffee-house speculations on these important subjects. *London, printed for M. Cooper,* 1745.
2°: *a*² < b²; *1–2* 3–8.
'I saw, one day, as people pass'd'
    On the death of Charles VII.
L(1962); CtY,OCU.

D76 Deal. Deal in an uproar. A satyr. In memory of some late proceedings of the mayor, jurats, and common-council...for erecting a chappel of ease there, &c. Written by a very good acquaintance of Esq; Toby. *London, printed for J. Baker,* 1713. (31 March, Luttrell)
2°: *A*² B–C²; *1–2* 3–12.
'In sight of treacherous Goodwin's faithless sands'
MH(Luttrell).

D77 Dean. Dean Swift for ever: or, Mary the cookmaid to the Earl of Orrery. To which are added, thoughts on various subjects, from the Dean's manuscript in Mrs. Mary's possession. *London, printed for J. Robinson,* [1745?/–.]
2°: *A*² B² C¹; *1–4* 5–10. A1 hft.
    The copy seen at CtY lacks the 'thoughts'; its half-title is bound as A2.
'My lord, finding your lordship's letters on a stall'
    Apparently an imitation of Swift's 'Petition of Frances Harris'.
CtY(impft?).

Dean

D78 — [dh] The Dean's answer to David Mullan's letter. [col] *Dublin, printed in the year* 1735.
4°: *A*²; *1–4*.
'From lofty garret comes your thund'ring verse'
    Signed 'Draper'. Not recorded by the bibliographers of Swift, but it is unlikely to be by him.
CtY.

[**D79** = M416·5] — The Dean's provocation for writing the Lady's dressing-room. A poem, 1734. *See* Montagu, *Lady* Mary Wortley.

'**Dear-heart, Philo.**' A paraphrase on the fourteenth chapter of Isaiah, 1710. *See* P57.

Dearing, Heneage. *See* Dering, Heneage.

D80 Death. Death. A poem. In two books. *Dublin, printed by and for J. Carson, & Syl. Pepyat,* 1731.
8°: A–F⁴; *i–ii* iii–vi, 7–48.
'Whilst other theams superior bards employ'
O,C,DN(2),DT; TxU.

— The death and burial of John Asgill, 1702. *See* Stearne, John.

D81 — The death and burial of the new-coin'd halfpence. [*Dublin,* 1725.]
½°: 1 side, 1 column.
'Well then it's o'er, and all the tricks undone'
    On William Wood's surrender of his patent.
Rothschild.

D82 — Death to believers a passage to glory; or an elegie to the memory of...James Curry, son of James Currie merchant in Pentland who dyed the 19 of January 1701, and of his age the 13th year. *Edinburgh, printed for William Swanstoun,* 1704.
4°: *A*⁴ B²; *1–12*.
'O cruel death! can neither youth nor age'
E,EP(cropt); TxU.

— Death's vision represented in a philosophical, sacred poem, 1709–. *See* Reynolds, John.

D83 Deborah. Deborah: a sacred ode. *London, printed for Richard Sare,* 1705. (*DC* 13 Jan)
2°: *A*² B–C² D¹; *i–iv*, 1–10.
'Æthereal ray that didst inspire'
LDW; CLU-C(Luttrell, 13 Jan),CSmH,MH.

D84 — Deborah and Barak: a poem. *London, printed for A. Baldwin,* 1705 [1704]. (*DC* 9 Dec)
4°: A–B⁴ C²; *1–2* 3–19 *20 blk.*
'The mighty Shamgar dy'd, Shamgar the brave'
    Apparently in praise of Queen Anne and Marlborough.
EtC; InU,TxU.

Decadem. Decadem alteram, ex probatissimis auctoribus, 1738. *See* Meston, William.

D85 Declaration. A declaration without doors. [*London,* 1705?]

A **declaration** without doors

$\frac{1}{2}^o$: 1 side, 2 columns.
> *Moore* 108.
'O ye Britains draw near'
> *The Review* 25 Oct 1705 advertised 'A declaration without doors; by the author of, &c.' and on 30 Oct 'There will be speedily publish'd An answer to that scurrilous and reflecting pamphlet, entituled, A declaration without doors'. Wilson, Lee, and Dottin attribute to Defoe an untraced quarto with this title; the two latter had not seen it, and Dottin conjectured it was in prose. Moore identifies this as Defoe's but it does not appear to be the work advertised, and there is no other evidence of Defoe's authorship. An attack on William Bromley.

LDW,Rothschild; MH,NN.

Dedekind, Friedrich.
Bull, Roger: Grobianus; or, the compleat booby ... Done into English from the original Latin, 1739. *See* B564–5.

D86 Defection. The defection: or, the patriot prostituted. A poem. *London, printed for W. Webb,* 1742.
4°: A–B⁴; *1–3* 4–16.
> Vertical chain-lines.
'That subjects love from rev'rence, hate from fear'
OCU.

D87 Defence. A defence for the ladies: or, the virtues of the broad brim'd hat, in answer to the hoop'd petticoats. *London, printed for F.C. [Francis Clifton?] near Black Fryars,* [171–?]
$\frac{1}{2}^o$: 1 side, 2 columns.
'When rebellious usurpation'
> Ironic defence of the hats; a tory poem. Possibly related to *The farthingale reviv'd,* 1711.
L(1876.f.1/91).

D88 — A defence of the church of England, in answer to the Oliverian's low-church ballad. To the tune of, Ye rebells of England, you have murder'd your king: or, the high church health. *London, printed at the sign of the Star in Pye-corner,* 1710.
$\frac{1}{2}^o$: 1 side, 1 column.
'Ye bold presbyterians what is it you mean'
Rothschild.

[Defoe, Daniel.] A collection of the writings of the author of the True-born English-man... *London, printed in the year* 1703.
8°: pp. 289.   L,O; CtY,MH.
> An unauthorized collection.

[—] A true collection of the writings of the author of the True born English-man. Corrected by himself. *London printed, and are to be sold by most booksellers in London & Westminster,* 1703.
8°: pp. 465.   L,O; CtY,MH.

Defoe, D. *Collections*

[—] — The second edition corrected and enlarg'd by himself. *London printed, and are to be sold by most booksellers in London & Westminster,* 1705.
8°: pp. 470.   L; CtY,MH.

[—] A second volume of the writings of the author of the True-born Englishman. Some whereof never before printed. Corrected and enlarged by the author. *London printed, and sold by the booksellers,* 1705.
8°: pp. 479.   L,O; CtY,MH.

— [reissue] The genuine works of Mr. Daniel D'Foe... Containing thirty nine scarce and valuable tracts, upon many curious and uncommon subjects. To which is added a complete key to the whole... *London printed, and sold by the booksellers,* [1721?] (*SJP* 4 Oct)
8°: 2 vol.   L; CtY,MH.
> A reissue of both volumes with cancel titles and a printed 'key' at end, pp. 1–8. They were previously advertised as 'third edition' in 1710, 1713.

[—] The address, 1704. *See* A49.

[—] The age of wonders: to the tune of Chivy chase, 1710. *See* A126.

— 'Defoe's answer to the quaker's catechism; or a dark lanthorn for a friend of the light, a poem follow'd by prose. 8 pp., 1706.'
> Listed in *Morgan* 1100, but not identified; not in *Moore*.

D89 '—' An answer to The tale of a nettle. Written by D. D'Foe. 'Oxford', *printed in the year* 1710.
$\frac{1}{2}^o$: 1 side, 1 column.
> The imprint is probably false.
'When the good man was won to so gracious a deed'
> Not discussed by any bibliographer of Defoe, but most improbably by him.
MH.

D90 — Caledonia, &c. A poem in honour of Scotland, and the Scots nation. In three parts. *Edinburgh, printed by the heirs and successors of Andrew Anderson,* 1706. (Dec?)
2°: π² ¶² ¶¶¹ A–P²; *i–x,* 1–60.
> Watermark: French arms (3 fleur-de-lys on shield). *Lee* 96; *Moore* 129, 'about the beginning of December'. Privilege from Scottish privy council, dated 3 Dec, on verso of title.
'In northern hights, where Nature seldom smiles'
> Dedication to the Duke of Queensberry and preface signed.
L(G.13436); CLU-C,ICN,InU,MB,MH.

D91 — [fine paper?]
> Watermark: Amsterdam arms and fool's cap, mixed. It has been impossible to decide with certainty which watermarks represent the better paper.
L(599.i.22/2),O,E(2),EU; CSmH,TxU.

Defoe, D. Caledonia

D92 —— *London, printed by J. Matthews; sold by John Morphew*, 1707. (*Review* 28 Jan)
8°: A⁴ B–D⁸ E⁴; *i–viii*, 1–55 56 blk.
L(1077.h.12; G.13509),LU,O(uncut),E(2),LdU-B+; CSmH,CtY,ICN,MB,MH,TxU(2).

D93 —— *London, printed. Dublin: re-printed by Francis Dickson for John Ware*, 1707.
8°: A⁸ B⁴ ²B⁴ C⁴ ²C² (²B1, 2 as 'B3, B4'; ²C1 as 'C3'); *i–iv*, 1–40.
DA(lacks B2.3),DN(cropt),DT(2).

D94 [—] Caledonia: a poem in honour of Scotland, and the people of that nation... Dedicated to the Duke of Argyll. *London, printed for W. Owen; sold at the pamphlet-shops at the Royal-Exchange, Ludgate-street, and Charing-Cross*, 1748. (*BM* May; *GM, LM* June)
8°: A(3 ll) B–G⁴ H¹; *3–8* 9–58.
LU,GU; CSmH(ms. date 4 July, lacks H1),CU, CtY.

[—] The church militant, or the whigs triumphant, 1705. *See* C176.

[—] The compleat art of painting. A poem. Translated from the French of M. du Fresnoy. By D.F. gent, 1720. *See* C324.

[—] The D---- deputies. A satyr, 1705. *See* D1.

[—] A declaration without doors, [1705?] *See* D85.

[—] The devil upon dun... By the author of the True born Englishman [actually by William Shippen], [1705.] *See* S442.6.

[—] Dissectio mentis humanae: or a satiric essay on modern critics [actually by Bezaleel Morrice], 1730. *See* M477.

D95 [—] The double welcome. A poem to the Duke of Marlbro'. *London printed, and sold by B. Bragg*, 1705. (*Review* 9 Jan)
4°: A–D⁴; *i–ii*, 1–30.
Lee 65; *Moore* 90. Luttrell's copy is dated 22 Jan, the date it was advertised in *DC*.
'The muse that by your victory's inspir'd'
Advertised in the *Review* as 'by the author of the True-born English man', and collected by Defoe in *A second volume*, 1705.
L(164.m.36, Luttrell, 22 Jan),O,C; CLU-C, CSmH (2, 1 stitched, uncut),CtY,ICU,MB,TxU.

D96 [—] — *London, printed in the year* 1705.
4°: A–D⁴ (A2 as 'B2'); *i–ii*, 1–30.
Part from standing type, part reset. In some copies (e.g. LdU-B,MH) D1 is signed 'E'.
LDW,LU,LdU-B; CLU-C,CtY,InU,MB,MH+.

D97 [—] The dyet of Poland, a satyr. '*Printed at Dantzick*' [*London*], *in the year* 1705. (July?)
4°: A² B–H⁴ I²; *i–iv*, 1–60 (57 as '56'). iv err.
Lee 74; *Moore* 100; *Rothschild* 738. Publication dated by *Lee* as May 1705. Attacked in the *Whipping-post* 10 July 1705 and a reply advertised there 17 July. *The case of the*

Defoe, D. The dyet of Poland

Church of England's memorial fairly stated (1706) refers to its clandestine printing and circulation some months before publication. Possibly generally published early in July.
'In northern climes when furious tempests blow'
Preface signed 'Anglipoloski'. Referred to as unperfected and unpublished in a letter of Defoe tentatively dated by Healey as June 1704 (*Letters*, p. 19).
L(840.h.7/4; Ashley 3037; G.13506; 161.1.4), O,C,E(3),DT+; CSmH,CtY,InU,MB(2),TxU+.

D98 [—] — '*Printed at Dantzick*' [*London*], *in the year* 1705.
8°: *A*⁴ B–D⁴; *i–ii*, *1* 2–30.
Possibly a piracy.
O(2),AdU; CLU-C,CtY,DFo,MB,Rosenbach.

D99 [—] — To which is added A memorial to the Tantivy-high-flyers of England... '*Printed at Dantzick*' [*Dublin?*], *in the year* 1705.
8°: π¹[= D4] A–C⁴ D⁴(–D4); *i–ii*, 1–30.
The copies at Dublin suggest this is an Irish edition. The only addition is on p. 30, a key and some 20 lines of additional verse headed: 'The poet-laureat of England to the two roaring St. Germain-bulls, La--ly and Sachev---ll...'
O,DA,DT(2, 1 lacks D1–3); CtY.

D100 [—] The dyet of Poland, a satyr. Consider'd paragraph by paragraph. To which is added a key to the whole... *London printed, and sold by Ben. Bragg*, 1705. (*DC* 13 July)
8°: A–I⁴; *i–viii*, 1–64.
Prose commentary, with the text of Defoe's poem. Previously announced in *DC* 7 July as 'This day will be publish'd The Polish dyet answer'd...'
The commentary is probably by William Pittis; see T.F.M. Newton in *MP* 33 (1935–6) 175, and the *Whipping-post* 2 Oct 1705.
O,CT,EU,DT; CtY,MH,TxU.

D101 [—] — The second edition. *London printed, and sold by Ben. Bragg*, 1705. (*DC* 24 July)
8°: A–I⁴; *i–viii*, 1–64.
Apparently a reimpression.
MB.

D102 [—] An elegy on the author of the True-born-English-man. With an essay on the late storm. By the author of the Hymn to the pillory. *London, printed in the year* 1704. (*Review* 15 Aug)
4°: A² B–H⁴; *i–iv*, 1–56.
Lee 60; *Moore* 83 (refers to the verses on A1ᵛ as signed J.L. in some copies; only the L copy has been seen with the verses signed, and there in ms. 'J.P.').
'Satyr sing Lachrime, thou'rt dead in law'
Storm: 'I'm told, for we have news among the dead'
Reprinted by Defoe in *A second volume*, 1705.

Defoe, D. An elegy

L(G.13504),O(2, 1 lacks A²),C,E,DT(cropt)+;
CSmH,DFo(2),ICU,MB(2),MH,TxU+.

D103 [—] — ⟨*London, printed in the year* 1704.⟩
4⁰: ⟨A²⟩ B–H⁴; ⟨*i–iv*⟩, *1–56*.
B–E⁴ are apparently the same setting as the preceding, corrected; the rest is reset.
O(lacks A²).

D103·5 [—] [*idem*] [dh] The live man's elegy: or, a hymn among the dead. By the author of the True-born-English-man. [*London*] *Printed for the booksellers of London & Westminster*, 1704.
4⁰: A²; *1–4*.
Page 4 is set in smaller type. Apparently a piracy, omitting many passages of personal satire, though the variant title might imply an independent source.
CLU-C(A2 cropt).

D104 [—] An elegy on the author of the True-born-English-man. With an essay... '*London*' [*Dublin*], *printed in the year* 1704.
8⁰: A⁸ B–C⁴; *1–2 3–32*.
The CtY copy was previously bound with the 1704 Dublin edition of *The true-born Englishman. A hymn to the pillory* is added, starting on p. 25.
L(1970); CtY.

D105 [—] — *London, printed* [*by H. Hills*] *in the year* 1708.
8⁰: A–C⁴; *1–2 3–24*.
Reissued with other remaindered Hills poems in *A collection of the best English poetry*, 1717 (*Case* 294).
L(C.124.b.7/2),O,C,AdU(2),LdU-B+; CLU-C, CtY,IU,MB(2),MH,TxU.

[—] An elegy on the death of the late famous Observator... Written by the author of the Review, 1707. *See* E264.

[—] England's late jury: a satyr, 1701. *See* E320.

[—] An epistle from Jack Sheppard to the late l—d c—ll—r of E--d, 1725. *See* E369.

D106 [—] An essay on the great battle at Ramellies. By the author of the Review. *London, printed in the year* 1706. (May?)
½⁰: *1–2*; 1 column.
Not in *Moore* or other Defoe bibliographies.
'Say, Britains! felt you nothing in your souls'
Printed in the *Review*, 21 May 1706, and acknowledged by Defoe, 'the birth of three hours'. There entitled 'On the fight at Ramellies'.
CLU-C.

[—] Faction display'd. The second part, 1704. *See* F25.

D107 '—' The fifteen comforts of a Scotch-man. Written by Daniel D'Foe in Scotland. *London, printed in the year* 1707. (Feb?)
8⁰: A⁴; *1 2–8*.
Moore 143, suggesting date of Feb.

Defoe, D. The fifteen comforts

'Be dumb ye beggars of the rhiming trade'
All authorities have regarded Defoe's authorship as doubtful. A congratulatory poem on the Union.
L(1078.g.11),O; MB.

D108 '—' — *London printed, and reprinted at the Old Post-Office in Fish-Shamble-street, Dublin*, 1707.
8⁰: A⁴; *1 ⟨2⟩–7 8 blk*.
DT(slightly cropt).

[—] Good advice to the ladies...By the author of the True born Englishman, 1702–. *See* G219.

[—] High-church miracles, or, modern inconsistencies, 1710. *See* H196.

D109 — Daniel Defoe's Hymn for the thanksgiving. *London, printed for the author*, 1706. (June?)
½⁰: 1 side, 1 column.
Moore 119.
'When Israel's army pass'd the dreadful stream'
Printed in the *Review* for 27 June 1706 in similar typography, which confirms the attribution to Defoe.
Rosenbach.

D110 [—] A hymn to peace. Occasion'd by the two Houses joining in one address to the queen. By the author of the True-born-English-man. *London, printed for John Nutt*, 1706. (8 Jan, Luttrell)
4⁰: A–G⁴ H² (A2 as 'B2'); *1–2 3–60*.
Lee 79; *Moore* 109. Advertised in *Review* 12 Jan. All copies seen of this state have ms. corrections on pp. 3, 19, 35, 48, presumably by the printer.
'Hail image, of th' eternal mind'
The only external evidence for Defoe's authorship is the statement of the title-page. 'A scandalous abusive thing on the Churchmen', Luttrell.
L(1103.f.74, uncut, Luttrell; 1103.f.52, ms. date 10 Jan); MB.

D111 [—] — [variant imprint:] *London, printed in the year* 1706.
Some copies (e.g. ICN) have no ms. corrections.
LLP,LU,DT; CLU-C,CtY,ICN,MB,MH+.

D112 [—] — [col] *London, printed by Henry Hills*, [1706?]
4⁰: A⁴; *1–8*; 2 columns.
Drop-head title only. Probably a piracy contemporary with the first edition.
L(11631.f.35).

D113 [—] — *London, printed* [*by H. Hills*] *in the year* 1709.
8⁰: A–B⁸; *1–2 3–32*.
Reissued with other remaindered Hills poems in *A collection of the best English poetry*, 1717 (*Case* 294).
L(C.124.b.7/16),O(lacks B⁸),C; CSmH,CtY,MB, MH,Rosenbach+.

Defoe, D. A hymn to the funeral sermon

[—] A hymn to the funeral sermon, [1703.] *See* H458.

D114 [—] A hymn to the mob. *London printed, and sold by S. Popping, J. Fox, S. Boulter, A. Boulter, & J. Harrison, 1715.* (*DC* 14 July)

8⁰: A⁴ C–G⁴; [2] i–vi, 1–40.

Lee 170; *Moore* 324. Some copies (e.g. E,MB) have D2 signed 'D3'. Entered in *SR* to Bryan Mills, 15 July; deposit copies at L,O,E,EU,AdU.

'Hail! ancient gentry, nature's eldest line'

Moore quotes passages from the *Review* of 1710 apparently foreshadowing this work.

L(992.h.6/3; G.18423/2),O(2),E,DT,AdU+; CSmH,CtY(lacks A2–4),InU,MB(2),MH+.

D115 [—] A hymn to the pillory. *London, printed in the year 1703.* (2 Aug, Luttrell)

4⁰: A² B–D⁴; i–iv, 1–24 (12,13 as '13,12'). A1 hft.

Lee 41; *Moore* 59. Copies asterisked have a variant sheet B. Listed in *WL* Aug; there is evidence that it was published on 29 July, the first day Defoe stood in the pillory.

'Hail hi'roglyphick state machin'

Reprinted by Defoe in *A second volume, 1705.* A 'sequel' was published as *A hymn to Tyburn, 1703*; Defoe's authorship of that does not seem to have been investigated. See also [Thomas Brown] *A dialogue between the pillory and Daniel Defoe,* [1706] and *Remarks on the author of the Hymn to the pillory,* 1703.

L(164.m.31, Luttrell; Ashley 584; G.13500*), LVA-F(–A1),O(2, 1–A1),C,DK*+; CSmH (uncut),MB,MH,MiU,TxU+.

D116 [—] — The second edition corrected, with additions. *London, printed in the year 1703.*

4⁰: A² B–D⁴; i–iv, 1–24. A1 hft.

Sheet B is (at least in part) from standing type.

L(1973),DG,DT(2).

D117 [—] — The third edition corrected, with more additions. *London, printed in the year 1703.*

4⁰: A² B–D⁴; i–iv, 1–24. A1 hft.

Verses 'A.D.D.F' added on A1ᵛ; apparently a reissue or reimpression. Listed in *TC* Trinity 1704.

OW; CtY,MB(–A1),MH,Rosenbach,TxU.

D118 [—] — [*London,* 1703?]

4⁰: *A²*; 1–4; 2 columns, not divided by rule.

Drop-head title only. *Rothschild* 776 (either this or the following edition). Presumably a piracy.

LSC,LU,O,C; MB,TxU.

D119 [—] — [*London,* 1703?]

4⁰: A²; 1–4; 2 columns, divided by rule.

Drop-head title only.

C(uncut).

D120 [—] — by the author of the True-born Englishman. Upon his standing in the pillory, the thirty first of July, 1703. [*Dublin?* 1703?]

Defoe, D. A hymn to the pillory

8⁰: A–B⁴; *1–2* 3–15 *16 blk*.

The Dublin origin is suggested by the copy at DA as well as by the watermark and typography.

DA; ICN,MB(uncut).

D121 [—] A hymn to the pillory. *London, printed [by H. Hills] in the year 1708.*

8⁰: A⁸; *1–2* 3–15 *16*. 16 advt of Hills.

Reissued with other remaindered Hills poems in *A collection of the best English poetry,* 1717 (*Case* 294).

L(C.124.b.7/3),LU,O,AdU,*MR*; CLU-C,CtY, IU,MB,MH,TxU(2, 1 uncut)+.

D122 [—] — [*London,* 1721.]

Lee quotes under 25 Feb 1721 'Reprinted and sold in the streets'; the source has not been identified, but the reason was clearly the two occasions in the week ending 25 Feb when Nathaniel Mist stood in the pillory. Defoe was associated with him in the editorship of *The weekly journal.* An edition was also advertised by Wilford in *The true born Englishman,* 1748.

D123 — A hymn to victory. *London, printed for J. Nutt, 1704.* (*Review* 29 Aug)

4⁰: A–G⁴ H²; i–viii, 1–52.

Lee 62; *Moore* 85. The quality of the paper seems to vary (e.g. in the copies at O), but in the absence of watermarks it has been impossible to distinguish fine-paper copies. All copies have a ms. deletion in p. 6, line 9.

'Hail, victory! thou stranger to our land'

Dedicatory poem signed.

L(11626.bb.17),LU(uncut),O(2),C,DT(2, 1 uncut)+; CLU-C,IU,MB(2, 1 uncut),MH,TxU+.

D124 — — The second edition. *London, printed for J. Nutt, 1704.* (*Review* 9 Sept)

4⁰: A–G⁴ H²; i–viii, 1–52.

Parts of F, G, H, and A are from standing type. Verses to the author added on A1ᵛ.

L(1077.k.24/1),DA; CSmH,MB,MH.

D125 [—] — [*London,* 1704?]

4⁰: A⁴; 1–8; 2 columns.

Drop-head title only. An advertisement in the *Review* 5 Sept refers to 'three sorts of counterfeits, or shams...one is a half sheet, another a whole sheet, and the third a sheet and half'. This is presumably the sheet and the following the sheet and half.

CtY,MB.

D126 — — *London, printed in the year 1704.*

4⁰: A–C⁴; *1–3* 4–11 *12 blk*; 2 columns.

L(164.n.78),*MR*; TxU.

D127 — — By the author of the True-born Englishman. '*London, printed for J. Nutt*' [*Edinburgh?*], 1704.

4⁰: A⁴ *B⁴* C–E⁴ F²; i–viii, 1–36.

Defoe, D. A hymn to victory

Probably a piracy; the three copies at E suggest an Edinburgh origin.

L(11631.e.81),E(3); CSmH,CtY,MB,*NjP*,TxU.

D128 [—] Jure divino: a satyr. In twelve books. By the author of the True-born-Englishman. *London, printed in the year* 1706. (*Review* 18 July, 'Saturday next', i.e. 20 July)

2°: (frt+) π² a–h² ²a–b² B–H² 2B–2I² 3B–3G² 4B–4H² 5A–5H² 6A–6E² 7A–7G² 8A–8I² 9B–9G² 10B–10G² 11A–11H² 12A–12F². (Each book has a set of signatures of the form 'B2–I2²' reversed here to 2B–2I², &c. Where a new book begins on the second leaf of a bifolium, that leaf is signed as the first of the new series: thus 2I2 is signed as 'A3'. Separate pagination for each book, not quoted here.) h1ᵛ err.

Watermark: fool's cap. *Lee* 93, *Moore* 115. A Defoe letter of 24 May (ed. Healey, p. 124) announces readiness for distribution to provincial booksellers, says the frontispiece will cost one shilling extra and is optional.

'Instructing satyr, tune thy useful song'
Preface signed 'D. F.'

LU(2),O,OW,C,E+; CSmH,CtY(2),IU,MB,MH, TxU+.

D129 [—] [fine paper]
Watermark: fleur-de-lys on shield.
L(G.560),DM; MB.

D130 [—] — *London, printed in the year* 1706. (*DC* 24 July)

8°: (frt+) A–U⁸ Y⁸; [4] i–xlii [2], i–ii, i–v *vi*, 1–8, 7–23 *24*, 1–24, 1–19, 68–93, 1–26, 1–15, 135–278.

Moore dates as 19 July, preceding the authorized edition. Denounced as a piracy in *Review* 3 Aug, and attributed to B. Bragg, 'publisher in ordinary to the pyrates'. The irregular pagination no doubt results from haste in attempting to precede the authorized edition. The price is said in the following to have been 5*s*. as against 13*s*. for the folio.

L(1078.m.3),*LVA-D*,C,EU,DT; CSmH,CtY, IU(2),MB(2),MH+.

D131 [—] Jure divino: a satyr. The first [*etc.*] book. By the author of the True-born-Englishman. *London, printed by P. Hills,* [1706.]

8°: 12 parts, described below.

A piratical reprint in twelve parts. The first five parts exist in different forms, the relationship of which, though close, has not been determined. The first five parts appeared in 16-page form, part 1 promising 12 parts at 1 penny. Part 4a advertised that this penny edition would include the notes, and promised a new edition of part 2 with these added as soon as the rest were published. They also appeared as octavo half-sheets paged *1* 2–8 like the remaining parts, and an advertisement in one issue of part 1 announces that each book will be sold at ½*d*. and the whole will be sold stitched for 6*d*.

Defoe, D. Jure divino

L(11631.c.14; 11632.de.10),LU(uncut),O(2); CLU-C,CtY,InU,*MB*(2),MH(bk.1–9),TxU+.

1a *London, printed in the year* 1706.
pp. *1–2* 3–15 *16*. 1 woodcut portrait of Defoe; 16 advt.
O(2); MB.

1b *London, printed by P. Hills,* [1706.]
pp. *1* 2–8. 1 woodcut portrait; 8 advt.
L(11631.c.14),LU,O; *MB*,MH,TxU.

1c *London, printed by P. Hills,* [1706.]
pp. *1* 2–8. 1 woodcut of Defoe in pillory; 8 no advt. Apparently from the same type as 1b.
CLU-C,CtY,InU,Rosenbach.

1d [As 1c except:] woodcut portrait of Defoe pasted over the pillory cut.
L(11632.de.10); *MB*,KU.

2a *London, printed by P. H.* [1706.]
pp. *1–2* 3–16.
O(2).

2b *London, printed in the year* 1706.
pp. *1* 2–8. In part from the same type as 2a.
LU; CtY,Rosenbach.

2c *London, printed by P. Hills,* [1706.]
pp. *1* 2–8.
L(2),O; CLU-C,InU,KU,*MB*(2),MH.

3a *London, printed in the year* 1706.
pp. *1–2* 3–16 (3 reversed).
O(2); MB,MH.

3b *London, printed by P. Hills,* [1706.]
pp. *1* 2–8.
L(2),LU,O; CLU-C,CtY,InU,*MB*(2), MH,TxU.

4a [no title, 1706.]
pp. 1–16. 16 advt.
O.

4b *London, printed by P. Hills,* [1706.]
pp. *1* 2–8.
All copies except 4a & 4c.

4c *London printed, and sold by H. Hills,* 1710.
MB.

5a [no title, 1706.]
pp. 1–16.
O.

5b *London, printed by P. Hills,* [1706.]
pp. *1* 2–8.
All copies except 5a.

[—] Lewis in a sweat: or, a dry clout for the King of Spain... By the author of the True-born English-man, 1702. *See* L162.

[—] The London ladies dressing-room... Written by the author of the True-born Englishman, 1705. *See* L238.

D132 [—] The mock mourners. A satyr, by way of elegy on King William. By the author of the True-born Englishman. *London, printed* 1702. (12 May, Luttrell)

4°: *A*² B–E⁴; *i–iv*, 1–32.

Defoe, D. The mock mourners

Lee 28; *Moore* 42. Varying press figures:
17–¶, 18–¶, 29–¶, 31–¶: LDW,LU,E; CSmH.
17–¶, 18–¶, 29–†, 31–¶: L(164.m.27),C; MB.
17–¶, 18–¶, 29–†, 31–†: LdU-B; CLU-C, InU.
17–†, 18–†, 29–¶, 31–¶: CtY.
17–†, 18–†, 29–†, 31–¶: DA; ICN,TxU.
17–†, 18–†, 29–†, 31–†: L(1482.bb.2/7; 11631.bb.91),O.
'Such has been this ill-natur'd nations fate'
Reprinted by Defoe in *A true collection*, 1703.
Luttrell attributed the work to 'Dr. Barber'.
See *An answer to the Mock mourners*, 1702.
L(164.m.27, Luttrell; 1482.bb.2/7; 11631.bb.91),O,C,E,DA+; CSmH,CtY,ICN,MB,TxU+.

D133 [—] — The second edition corrected... *London*, printed 1702.
4°: *A*² B–E⁴; *i–iv*, 1–32.
Apparently a reimpression with textual revisions. Varying press figures:
iii–†, 22–†, 31–¶: EU,EtC; CtY,MH,TxU.
iii–†, 22–†, 31–†: O; DFo.
iii–†, 17–¶, 18–¶, 31–†: CLU-C.
The CLU-C copy may have sheet D from the preceding.
O,EU,EtC,*MR-C*; CLU-C,CtY,DFo,MH,TxU.

D134 [—] — The second edition corrected... '*London*' [*Dublin*], printed 1702.
4°: *A*² B–C⁴ D²; *i–iv*, 1–20.
In most copies B2 is signed 'A2'. Copies at L,LDW are from Dublin tract volumes.
L(C.131.de.11),E,DK(2),DN(3),DT(3)+; IU, MB,Rosenbach.

D135 [—] — [variant imprint:] '*London*' [*Dublin*], printed for M. Gunne in Essex-street, 1702.
L(G.13495),DK.

D136 [—] — The third edition corrected... *London*, printed 1702.
4°: *A*² B–E⁴; *i–iv*, 1–32.
Apparently a reimpression of D133. Press figures iii–†, 29–†, 30–¶.
C,DG; CtY,MB,TxU.

D137 [—] — The fourth edition corrected... *London*, printed 1702.
4°: *A*² B–E⁴; *i–iv*, 1–32.
Apparently a reimpression. Press figures 18–†, 21–†.
MB(uncut),MH,MiU,Rosenbach.

D138 [—] — The fifth edition corrected... *London*, printed 1702.
4°: *A*² B–E⁴; *i–iv*, 1–32.
Apparently a reimpression. Press figures iii–†, 18–†, 21–†. Sheet E is wrongly perfected in all copies seen. *Morgan* E152 records '6th ed. 36 pp., 4°, 1702', not traced.
L(1968); MB,Rosenbach(lacks 2 leaves of E).

D139 [—] — The fifth edition corrected... *London*, printed 1702.
8°: B⁸; *1–2* 3–16.

Presumably a piracy, like subsequent octavos.
E; CSmH,CtY,MB,NN.

D140 [—] — The seventh edition corrected... *London*, printed 1702.
4°: A–D⁴; *1–4* 5–32.
Apparently reset. Press figures 4–*, 11–*. An advertisement by B. Bragg in *PM* 23 Feb 1703 may refer to this or to the following seventh edition.
LSC; InU,MB.

D141 [—] — The seventh edition corrected... *London*, printed 1702.
8°: B⁸; *1–2* 3–16.
Apparently a reimpression of the octavo 'fifth edition', D139.
CtY,IU,MB,*PU*.

D142 [—] — The ninth edition corrected... *London*, printed 1702.
8°: B⁸; *1–2* 3–16.
Apparently a reimpression.
O; MB.

D143 [—] — The eighth edition corrected... *Edingburgh* [!], printed in the year 1703.
8°: A–C⁴; *1–4* 5–24.
Apparently set from D140.
E; MB.

D144 — More reformation. A satyr upon himself. By the author of the True born English-man. *London*, printed in the year 1703. (16 July, Luttrell)
4°: A–E⁴ F² G–H⁴; *i–viii*, 1–52 (38,39, 42, 43 as '34, 35, 38, 39' in most copies).
Lee 38; *Moore* 56. Listed in *WL* July.
'He that in satyr dips his angry pen'
Defoe's authorship is revealed in the 'advertisement' on the verso of the title. Reprinted in *A second volume*, 1705.
L(164.m.30, Luttrell; C.40.g.7; G.13493/3),O(2),C(2), EU,DT(2)+; CLU-C,CtY,InU(2),MB, MH,TxU+.

[—] A new elegy on the death of trade. By the author of the True-born English-man, 1706. *See* N132.

[—] The new wonder, or, a trip to St. Paul's. By the author of the True-born Englishman, 1710. *See* N241.

[—] Now is the time. A poem. By the author of the, True born English-man, 1706. *See* N331.

[—] A poem to the author of the Scots answer to the Brittish vision, [1706.] *See* D150.

D145 [—] Reformation of manners, a satyr. [*London*] *Printed in the year* 1702.
4°: *A*² B–I⁴; *i–iv*, 1–64.
Motto on title 'Væ Vobis Hypocritè'. *Lee* 29; *Moore* 43; *Rothschild* 733.
'How long may heaven be banter'd by a nation'
Reprinted by Defoe in *A true collection*, 1703.

Defoe, D. Reformation of manners

L(11630.b.5/5; 11631.e.54; Ashley 3035;
G.13493/2),LU,O,C,E+; CSmH,ICN(2),MB,
MH(2, 1 uncut),TxU+.

D146 [—] — [*London*] *Printed in the year* 1702.
4°: A² B–I⁴; *i–iv*, 1–64.
Motto on title 'Væ Vobis Hipocritè'. Apparently a new setting of type throughout. In some copies (O,DT) sheet D is wrongly perfected, and one (InU) has a variant sheet D, possibly reprinted to replace faulty sheets.
LSC,O,C,DT; CtY,IU,InU.

D147 [—] — [*London?*] *Printed in the year* 1702.
4°: *A⁴* B–D⁴; *1–4* 5–32.
Motto on title 'Væ Vobis Hypocrite'.
L(11631.f.31; Ashley 3036); DFo,ICU.

D148 [—] A reply to the Scots answer to the British vision. [*Edinburgh*, 1706.] (Nov?)
½°: 1 side, 1 column.
Title reads '... Answer, To...' *Moore* 128.
'Hail noble lord of parts immense'
Defoe's letter to Harley of 28 Nov 1706 refers to his circulating a reply to Lord Belhaven's *A Scots answer to a British vision*, and this is almost certainly it. Answered by Belhaven's *An equivalent for Defoe*, [1706?] and also *A second defence of the Scotish vision*, [1706.]
L(8142.k.1/17, mutilated),E.

D149 [—] [another impression?]
Title reads '... Answer to...' There is no clear priority between this and the preceding, and they may represent press-variants rather than impressions.
E(2); CSmH.

D150 [—] [*idem*] A poem to the author of the Scots answer to the Brittish vision. [*Edinburgh*, 1706.]
½°: 1 side, 1 column.
Peter Murray Hill cat. 67 (1959) 13 claimed this was the first edition, printed by the Heirs of Andrew Anderson. It is likely that Defoe's poem was circulated in ms., and printed by anyone who wished. This edition is probably from a different ms. copy from the preceding.
MH.

[—] A Scots poem: or a new-years gift, 1707. *See* S145.

D151 [—] The Spanish descent. A poem. By the author of the True-born Englishman. *London, printed in the year* 1702. (Nov?)
4°: *A⁴* B–C⁴ D²; *1–2* 3–27 *28 blk.*
Lee 32; *Moore* 47. Some copies (e.g. L,CLU-C) have ms. corrections on pp. 3, 8. Dated by *Lee* as Nov.
'Long had this nation been amus'd in vain'
Reprinted by Defoe in *A true collection*, 1703.
L(11601.ff.1/2),O,C,DT,LdU-B+; CLU-C,
CSmH,ICN(2),MB,TxU+.

Defoe, D. The Spanish descent

D152 [—] — *London, printed in the year* 1703.
8°: A⁸; *1–2* 3–16.
Probably a piracy.
MH,Rosenbach.

[—] The true-born Britain. Written by the author of the True-born Englishman, 1707. *See* T513.

D153 [—] The true-born Englishman. A satyr. [*London*] *Printed in the year* 1700. (Jan 1701?)
4°: *A²* B–K⁴; *i–iv*, 1–71 *72 blk.*
Lee 16; *Moore* 28. According to an answer advertised in *PB* 30 Jan, issued by 'Captain Darby'. In the preface to *A second volume*, 1705, Defoe says 'A book that besides nine editions of the author, has been twelve times printed by other hands; some of which have been sold for 1d. others 2d. and others 6d.... 80000 of the small ones have been sold in the streets for 2d. or at a penny...' It has not been possible to distinguish nine authorized printings or twelve piracies; for clarity, however, the two classes are separated below.
'Speak, satyr; for there's none can tell like thee' Defoe's authorship is acknowledged in many of his writings. Cf. *An answer to a late abusive pamphlet*, 1700, *The English gentleman justified*, 1701, *English men no bastards*, 1701, and *The fable of the cuckoo*, 1701.
L(C.95.c.28; Ashley 581),LU,O,LdU-B; *CSmH, CtY*,DFo(with 9th ed. prelims added),MB(2), MH,TxU(uncut)+.

D154 [—] — [*London*] *Printed in the year* 1701. (23 Jan?)
4°: A–H⁴; *i–iv*, 1–60.
p. 35 numbered at inner margin. Corrected text, probably reset page by page in A–D, thereafter compressed.
O,C,E; CLU-C(uncut),CtY(ms. date 23 Jan),KU.

D155 [—] [another impression]
p. 35 numbered normally; pp. 48,49 as '58, 59'. In some copies (e.g. O,MB) the numbers of pp. 30, 31 are reversed, possibly representing another printing.
L(840.h.7/3),O(lacks A1),E(2); CSmH,ICN,MB (2),Rosenbach.

D156 [—] — The ninth edition. With an explanatory preface. [*London*] *Printed in the year* 1701.
4°: ᵖA⁴ A⁴(–A1) B–H⁴; *i–x*, 1–60.
The presence of the same pagination errors as in the preceding suggests this is a reissue.
L(1481.aaa.38; 1482.bb.2/6, lacks ᵖA1),OC(uncut),DK; CLU-C,MB.

D157 [—] — The tenth edition. With an explanatory preface. [*London*] *Printed in the year* 1701.
4°: ᵖA⁴ A⁴(–A1) B–H⁴; *i–x*, 1–60.
A–F are reset.
L(G.13493/1),LDW,C,E,EU; CLU-C,MH,TxU.

Defoe, D. The true-born Englishman

Piracies

D158 [—] — [*London?*] *Printed in the year* 1700 [1701].
8⁰: A–D⁴; *1–4* 5–32.
CtY.

D159 [—] — [*London*] *Printed in the year* 1701.
8⁰: A–C⁴; *i–ii*, 1–22.
    This fits the description of the piracy referred to in *PB* 30 Jan 'in three half-sheets only', said to be put out by the 'White-Friars sham-printer'. F. H. Ellis in *POAS* VI.763 records variants which suggest two impressions.
O(3),CT,E,LdU-B,NeU; CtY,IU,MB,MH,TxU.

D160 [—] — [*Edinburgh*] *Printed in the year* 1701.
4⁰: A–D² *†*² [ ]²; *i–ii*, 1–22.
    The page division follows the preceding.
E(4, 1 uncut),LdU-B; CtY,MB.

D161 [—] — Note, this is printed word for word from the shilling book. [col] [*London*] *Printed in the year* 1701.
8⁰: A–B⁴; *1* 3–16 (2 possibly cropt in copies seen); pp. 10–15 in 2 columns.
    Drop-head title only.
L(1490.m.37); TxU.

D162 [—] — The tenth edition. With an explanatory preface. [*London?*] *Printed in the year* 1701.
4⁰: A–C⁴ D–E² F⁴; *i–vi*, 1–32 *33–34 blk.*
O; MB(−F4),Rosenbach(−F4),TxU(−F4).

Answers

D163 [—] The true-born Englishman: a satyr, answer'd, paragraph by paragraph. *London, printed in the year* 1701. (*FP* 1 Feb)
8⁰: A–L⁴ *L⁴; *i–viii*, 1–88.
    The paper has horizontal chain-lines. The text of Defoe's poem is printed with a prose commentary by William Pittis; he appears to have thought John Toland was the author. The Luttrell copy dated 1 Feb is recorded in Pickering & Chatto cat. 259/3063.
L(8122.aa.35),O,C; CtY,DFo,ICU,MB,MH.

D164 [—] [fine paper]
    Printed on heavy unwatermarked paper. The epistle dedicatory has printed signature 'W. Pittis'.
CLU-C.

D165 [—] — The 2d edition corrected. *London, printed in the year* 1701. (*PB* 6 Feb)
8⁰: A–M⁴; *i–viii*, 1–88.
O(uncut),AdU; CtY,MB,TxU.

———

D166 [—] The true-born Englishman a satyr. *London, printed in the year* 1702.
12⁰: A–C⁶ D⁶(−D6); *1–3* 4–46.
    D6 not in copies seen, probably blank.
L(11630.a.9, lacks A1); CtY(uncut).

D167 [—] — The nineteenth edition with large additions... Unto which is added A prologue to Tamer-

Defoe, D. The true-born Englishman

lan... By Dr. Garth. '*London*' [*Dublin*] *printed for M.G.* [*Matthew Gunne*] *at Essex-street-gate*, 1704.
8⁰: A–B⁸ C⁴ (C2 as 'C3'); *i–vii*, 1–33.
    Pp. 1–9 numbered at inner margin.
CtY,MB,MH.

D168 [—] — [*London*] *Printed* [*by H. Hills*] *in the year* 1708.
8⁰: A–B⁸ C⁴; *1–2* 3–39 *40.* 40 advt of Hills's poems.
    Reissued with other remaindered Hills poems in *A collection of the best English poetry*, 1717 (*Case* 294).
L(C.124.b.7/1),LDW,O,CT; CtY,MB,MH.

D169 [—] — [*London?*] *Printed in the year* 1708.
8⁰: A–D⁴; *1–2* 3–32.
    Horizontal chain-lines.
L(1489.t.3); CSmH.

D170 [—] — [col] *London, printed in the year* 1708.
4⁰: A⁴; *1–8*; 2 columns.
    Drop-head title only. A half-sheet edition was entered in the Stationers' Register as 'old copy' by Edward Midwinter, 26 Feb 1711.
L(11631.f.11); MB.

D171 [—] — *Printed for, and sold by J. Baker, London,* 1713.
8⁰: A–F⁴; *i–xii*, 1–34 *35; 36 blk.*
MB.

D172 [—] — *Printed in the year* 1713.
8⁰: A–B⁸ (A3 as 'A4'); *1–2* 3–32.
L(164.k.40),LU; CLU-C.

D173 [—] — Corrected and enlarg'd by the author. *London printed, and sold by James Roberts*, 1716. (16 March, Luttrell)
12⁰: A–H⁴/²; *i–xii*, 1–36.
    Entered in *SR* 5 March by Roberts as 'old copy'. With a new 'preface by the author'. Subsequently advertised in *DP* 9 Oct 1719.
L(164.k.41, Luttrell); MB.

D174 [—] — *Edinburgh, reprinted by Robert Brown, and are to be sold at his printing-house*, 1717.
8⁰: A–B⁸ (A3 as 'A4'); *1–2* 3–32.
    Possibly reprinted from D172.
L(1488.c.36),E; MB.

D175 [—] — Corrected and enlarged by the author. *London, J. Wilford*, [1721?]
12⁰: 25 ll. including advt.
    An edition was advertised in *DJ* 10 March 1721 'at the Three flower-de-luces in Little-Britain' which was Wilford's address; it was also frequently advertised by Wilford in *DJ* in July & Aug 1722. Possibly this is a reissue of James Roberts's 1716 edition.
(*Dobell* 391.)

D176 [—] — The one and twentieth edition. *Dublin, printed by and for Sam Fuller*, 1728.
8⁰: A–D⁴; *1–4* 5–32.
L(1488.de.21),O,C,DK; MB.

Defoe, D. The true-born Englishman

D177 [—] — The two and twentieth edition. *Dublin, printed by and for Sam. Fuller, 1730.*
8°: A–D⁴; *1–4* 5–32. 32 advt.
There appear to be variant states of B2, with and without footnote.
L(MS.Eg.158),DG,DK; *MB,TxU.*

D178 [—] — Corrected and enlarg'd by the author. *London printed, and sold by J. Wilford, 1731.* (*MChr* Aug)
12°: A–E⁶; *i–xii,* 1–2 3–46 *47–48.* E6 advt.
CLU-C,MB.

D179 [—] — The three and twentieth edition. *Dublin, printed by and for James Hoey, 1733.*
8°: A–D⁴ (A2 as 'A3'); *1–4* 5–32. 32 advt.
DA(2); MB.

D180 [—] — The three and twentieth edition. *Dublin, printed by and for Isaac Jackson, 1743.*
12°: A–D⁴/² E⁴; *1–4* 5–32. 32 advt.
O,DN,BaP; CtY,MB.

D181 [—] — Corrected and enlarg'd by the author. *London, printed by J. Wilford; sold by A. Dodd, & E. Cooke, 1748.* (*LM* Jan)
12°: A–E⁶; *i–xii,* 1 2–45 '44' *47–48.* E6 advt.
L(1960),C; MB.

D182 [—] — The five and twentieth edition. *Dublin, printed by Isaac Jackson; sold by most of the booksellers in city and country, 1749.*
8°: A–B⁸; *1–4* 5–32. 32 advt.
L(11657.i.114),O,DA(uncut),DG,DN.

D183 [—] — [175–?]
12°: B–F⁶; *i–iii* iv–xiv, 1 2–45 *46 blk.*
The L copy is bound in a volume of plays dated 1754–61.
L(642.k.49/7),O.

D184 —— By Daniel D'Foe. *London, printed for the booksellers in town and country, [175–?]*
8°: *A*⁴ B–E⁴; *i–iii* iv–v, 6–38 *39–40 blk.*
Possibly a provincial reprint, in spite of the 'London' imprint. Horizontal chain-lines.
MB; *Bibliothèque Publique, Nantes.*

D185 [—] [dh] The the [!] vision, a poem. [*Edinburgh,* 1706.] (Nov?)
4°: *A*²; 1 2–4.
Moore 123, as before 28 Nov. The first 'THE' in roman caps is followed on the next line by 'The Vision,' in black letter. P. 1, line 2 reads 'Withches.' Priority of the printings of this poem is uncertain.
'Come hither ye dreamers of dreams'
Defoe's letters (ed. Healey, pp. 148, 162) show his authorship and that John Hamilton, baron Belhaven, whom it attacked, believed Lord Haddington to be the author. Answered by Hamilton's *A Scots answer to a British vision,* [1706.] For Hamilton's original speech, see *Belhaven's vision,* 1729.
E(2); CSmH,CtY.

Defoe, D. The vision

D186 [—] [variant]
The redundant 'THE' has been removed and p.1, line 2 corrected to read 'Witches'.
MB.

D187 [—] [another edition]
Partly reset. Empty parentheses above title. The L copy has a variant position of the page number 4.
L(1475.c.2/6),O,E(4).

D188 [—] [dh] The vision, a poem. Being an answer to the Lord Beilhaven's speech. By a person of quality. [col] *Printed at Edinburgh; and reprinted at London for Benjamin Bragg, 1706.* (7 Dec?)
4°: A²; 1–4.
Dated as 7 Dec in *Moore.*
L(806.k.16/67*),DG; NN.

[—] Ye true-born Englishmen proceed, [1701.] *See* Y7.

D189 **Deist.** The deist's creed, with the free-thinker's annext. By a gentleman of Trinity College, Cambridge. *London printed, and sold by J. Roberts, 1731.* (*GM* 13 March)
8°: A–E⁴; *1–3* 4–40.
''Tis sweet, when furious storms plough up the mayn'
O,WcC.

Deity. Deity: a poem, 1739–. *See* Boyse, Samuel.

Delacour, James. *See* Dalacourt, James.

D190 **Delafaye, Charles.** The fellow crafts song. By our brother Charles Delafaye esq, To be sung and play'd at the grand-feast. [*Dublin, printed by George Faulkner, 1725/30.*]
½°: 1 side, 2 columns.
On the other side, Matthew Birkhead, *The enter'd prentices song,* [1725/30.] The copy at L forms part of a collection of Dublin half-sheets of 1725/30. The ornament at foot belonged to Faulkner.
'Hail masonry! thou craft divine!'
L(C.121.g.8/90),C.

D191 **De la Garde, Martin.** The adventures of three hundred years; between Prince Florio and Princess Clelia, in the Happy Island. *London, printed for the author; sold by C. Corbett, 1736.*
4°: *A*¹ B–D⁴ E¹; *i–ii,* 1–26. 26 advt.
'Of time's effects, assist me muse to sing'
CtY,DLC.

D192 — An essay on real felicity. *London, printed for the author; sold by Charles Corbett,* [1736.] (*GM* Feb)
4°: *B*² C–H² *I*¹; *5–9* 10–34. 6 err.
With a congratulatory poem by John Hill.
'Since thou my soul, of pure celestial birth'
L(11631.g.33/3),O; CU,CtY,KU,*PU.*

D193 — 'The vision. A poem. [*London*] *Withers, Cooper.* Price 1s.' (*BM,GM* Dec 1746)

De la Mayne, T. H.

D194 De la Mayne, Thomas Hallie. Love and honour. A dramatick poem, taken from Virgil. In seven cantoes. *Dublin, printed by S. Powell, for the author,* 1742.
12⁰: π¹ a⁶ A–O⁶ P⁴; *i–xiv, 1–2* 3–176.
    The order of editions has not been determined. Subscribers on a1–3.
'Beneath the shelter of these woody hills'
DA(uncut),DN.

D195 — — *London, printed by T. Gardner, for the author,* 1742. (*GM,LM* Dec)
12⁰: (frt+) π² a⁴ A–O⁶ P⁴; *i–xii, 1–2* 3–176. π1 hft.
L(238.c.4),O(−frt),C(−π1),LdU-B; CSmH (−π1),*DLC*,ICN,ICU,IU+.

[**Delany, Patrick.**] An apology to the Lady C—r—t [actually by Swift], 1730. *See* S799.

[—] The birth of manly virtue from Callimachus, [1725.] *See* B221.

D196 [—] An epistle to his excellency John lord Carteret lord lieutenant of Ireland. [col] *Dublin, printed by George Grierson. Where a small edition of this poem may be had,* [1729.]
2⁰: A–B²; *1–8.*
    Teerink 1609; *Williams* 471. Title in half-title form; engraved ornament on p. 3. Reprinted in the London editions of Swift's *A libel on Dr. D—ny,* 1730.
'Thou wise and learned ruler of our ile'
    For Delany's authorship see *Williams;* answered by Swift's *An epistle upon an epistle,* 1730, and *A libel on D-- D-----,* 1730.
C,DN.

D197 [—] — *Dublin, printed by and for George Grierson,* 1730 [1729].
8⁰: A⁴; *1–8.*
    Teerink 1610.
C,DA,DG,DN,DT; MH.

D198 [—] — To which is added, an Epistle, upon an epistle; being a Christmas-box for Doctor D------ny. *Dublin, printed in the year* 1730.
8⁰: A⁴; *1–8.*
    Teerink 686. Swift's *An epistle upon an epistle* was separately printed in 1730.
L(11601.cc.38/4, lacks A3, 4),LVA-F,DA(2), DT(2, 1 lacks A1, 2); CSmH.

[—] Ireland's black day... By D. D——y, [1730.] *See* I58.

D199 [—] Longford's Glyn: a true history. Faithfully translated from the Irish original. *London, printed by W. Bowyer, for J. Roberts,* 1732. (*GSJ* 3 April)
2⁰: A² B–D²; *i–iv, 1–11* 12 blk.
    Rothschild 791. Entered in Bowyer's ledgers under 3 April 1732; 1000 copies printed. The paper ledger under 6 May records 75 copies, gilt, delivered 'to Dr. Delany & others by his order'.
'In fair Tyrone, for fruitful fields renown'd'
    The Rothschild copy has a ms. note 'the gift

Delany, P. Longford's Glyn

of the author the revd. Dr. Delane⟨ ⟩'; though the attribution is there considered conjectural, the evidence seems conclusive.
L(11626.h.11/1),O,C(2),DA(uncut),LdU-B+; KU,MH,NjP,OCU,TxU.

D200 [—] — *London: printed. And, Dublin, re-printed by and for George Faulkner,* 1732.
8⁰: A⁴ B–C⁴; *i–v* vi–viii *ix–x, 11* 12–22 *23–24* blk. A1 hft.
L(1488.a.34),DT(−C4); CtY,IU.

D201 [—] — The second edition. *London, printed for Charles Bathurst,* 1739. (17 Jan?)
2⁰: A²(±) B–D²; *i–iv, 1–11* 12 blk. A1 hft.
    A reissue of the London edition of 1732 with new half-title and title replacing title and dedication. The cancel is entered in Bowyer's ledgers under 17 Jan 1739, 500 copies printed.
O(uncut),DN(uncut); CtY(−A1),ICN,KU(−A1), NjP.

D202 [—] News from Parnassus. *Dublin, printed by John Harding,* 1721.
½⁰: 2 sides, 1 column.
    Williams 260.
'Parnassus February the twenty seventh'
    See *Williams* for the attribution to Delany. In reply to Swift's 'Apollo to Dean Swift' (not, apparently, separately published); cf. [Mary Barber] *Apollo's edict,* [1725?].
CSmH,TxU.

D203 [—] The pheasant and the lark. A fable. *Dublin, printed in the year* 1730.
8⁰: A⁴; *1–3* 4–8.
    Rothschild 788; *Williams* 507.
'In ancient times, as bards indite'
    For Delany's authorship see *Williams;* answered by Swift's *An answer to Dr. D-----y's fable,* 1730.
L(11601.ccc.38/10),LVA-F,DA,DN,DT(3); CtY.

D204 [—] — The second edition with editions [!]. *Dublin, printed in the year* 1730.
8⁰: A⁴; *1–3* 4–8.
L(Ashley 1836),DA; MH.

D205 [—] A riddle by the revd. Doctor D-----y, inscrib'd to the Lady C--------t. [*Dublin*] *Printed in the year* 1726.
½⁰: 1 side, 1 column.
    Teerink 656; *Williams* 937. Reply below in two columns, headed 'Answered by the reverend Dean S----t'.
'I reach all things near me, and far off to boot'
'With half an eye/Your riddle I spy'
    Delany, Carteret and Swift are clearly the missing names; reprinted as by Delany and Swift by Cogan, 1752; see *Williams.* All these riddles are of doubtful authorship, but those published as if by Delany are all included here.
DT; CtY.

Delany, P.

D206 [—] A riddle by the revd. Doctor D-----y, inscrib'd to the Lady C--------t. [*Dublin*] *Printed in the year* 1726.
½°: 1 side, 2 columns.
> *Teerink* 656; *Williams* 936. By the same printer as the preceding; early ms. on DT copy, 'No. 2'.
'Of all inhabitants of earth'
> Delany's authorship is clearly intended, and the attribution is probably as reliable as the preceding.

DT.

D207 [—] A third riddle. By the revd. Doctor D----y. [*Dublin*] *Printed in the year* 1725-6.
½°: 1 side, 2 columns.
> *Teerink* 656; *Williams* 915.
'In youth exalted high in air'
> Printed as by Delany in *Whartoniana*, 1727.

C(2),DT.

D208 [—] A fourth riddle. By the rv. D. D——y. [*Dublin*] *Printed by R. Dickson*, 1726.
slip: 1 side, 1 column.
> *Teerink* 656. Below, 'A receipt for cuckolding. By a female physician.'
'I am a thing--- esteem'd by all'
Receipt: 'Two or three visits, 2 or 3 bows'
> This is an inferior publication by a different printer, and less likely to be an authentic work of Delany. The *Receipt* is by Pope; see Twickenham ed. VI (1954) 104-5.

L(1890.e.5/9; C.121.g.8/144, cropt).

D209 [—] To the Dutchess of Grafton. *Dublin, printed by Aaron Rhames*, 1723.
½°: 1 side, 1 column.
'Once Pallas did her form disguise'
> Printed as Delany's in *Miscellaneous poems* (ed. Concanen), 1724.

C; TxU.

D210 [—] To the right honourable Arthur, earl of Anglesey, and viscount Valencia. September 25th, 1721. [*Dublin*, 1721.]
½°: 1 side, 1 column.
'If th' old Samian doctrine of spirits be true'
> Reprinted in *Miscellaneous poems* (ed. Concanen), 1724, as 'supposed to be written by Dr. Delany'; the attribution has been generally accepted.

C; CtY,IU.

[—] The true character of the Intelligencer. Written by Pady Drogheda [i.e. William Tisdall], 1728. *See* T319.

[—] Verses left with a silver standish, 1733. *In* T390.

Delectable. A delectable little history in metre: of a lord and his three sons...
> A doggerel poem of Scottish origin, apparently first printed in 1692 (*Aldis* 3220). No attempt

A **delectable** little history

has been made to locate copies, but there are Edinburgh editions of 1705 (noted in 1708), 1708 (E), and 1725 (L).

Delights. The delights of the bottle, 1720–. *See* Ward, Edward.

Delphinis. Delphinis quanto balaena britannica fertur, [1710?/13.] *See* Pitcairne, Archibald.

D211 **Deluge.** The deluge: or, cautious old-woman. A tale. *London, printed by T.W.; sold by J. Roberts*, 1723. (*MC* May)
2°: A² B–D²; *1-3* 4-16.
> Reissued in *A collection of original poems*, 1724 (*Case* 329).
'In days of yore, as antient legends speak'
> By the same author as *The longitude discover'd*, 1726.

L(Ashley 5662/2),O; CSmH,CtY,DFo,TxU.

D212 **Demas.** [dh] Demas chastis'd: or, the Buxsted advocate for tythe-hops display'd. [col] *London, printed in the year* 1708. (29 May, Luttrell)
2°: A²; *1-4*.
'Let treach'rous Demas never more pretend'
LU(Luttrell),*MR-C*.

Denham, *Sir John.* A version of the psalms of David *was published posthumously in 1714; it is probably from this that* A hymn to be sung by the charity-children, [1714] *is taken; see* H449.

The following poems are included here despite Denham's death in 1669 in order to complete the list of piracies by Henry Hills.

D213 — Cato major of old age. A poem. *London printed, and sold by H. Hills*, 1710.
8°: A–B⁸; *1-4* 5-32.
> First published 1669. Reissued with other remaindered Hills poems in *A collection of the best English poetry*, 1717 (*Case* 294).
'Though all the actions of your life are crown'd'
L(C.124.b.7/47),LVA-F,O,C,WcC; *CtY,ICN, IU*,MH,*NN*.

D214 — Coopers-Hill. A poem... *London printed, and sold by H. Hills*, 1709.
8°: A⁸; *1-4* 5-16.
> Type-flowers at head of p. 5. First published 1642.
'Sure there are poets which did never dream'
O,CT(2); ICN,IU,MH.

D215 — [another edition]
> No type-flowers at head of p. 5; imprint divides 'near/the water-side'.
L(1162.d.18),O(2),CT,E,EU + ; CtY,MH,TxU.

D216 — [another edition]
> No type-flowers at head of p. 5; imprint divides 'Black-Fryers,/near the water-side'. Reissued with other remaindered Hills poems in *A collection of the best English poetry*, 1717 (*Case* 294).
L(C.124.b.7/26),O(2),C,CT,AdU + ; MH.

Denham, *Sir* **J.**

D216·5 '—' The true presbyterian without disguise: or, a character of a presbyterian's ways and actions. By Sir John Denham, knight. *London, printed in the year* 1730.
8°: A⁴; *1–2* 3–8.
 Apparently first printed as Denham's in 1680.
'A presbyter is such a mon'strous thing'
 Denham's authorship is generally considered to be a fiction.
MR-C.

D217 Denne, Henry. Love alone: or, the star that leads to Christ. An epistolary poem, written in French by Mr. Boileau. Done into English by way of imitation, by H. D. philogram. *London, printed by J. How; sold by B. Bragg,* 1703 [1702?]. (*WL* Dec 1702)
2°: *A*² B–D²; *i–iv,* 1–11 *12 blk.*
 The listing in *WL* does not necessarily preclude a date in January 1703.
'Doctor, you're right, love only works the cure'
 Dedication signed.
CtY.

D218 — Marlborough. An heroic poem. *London, printed by W. Downing, and are to be sold by B. Bragge,* 1704. (*FP* 21 Nov)
4°: *A*² B–D⁴; *i–iv,* 1–24.
'Fame, for a while, 'till British arms appear'
C(uncut); ICN,*ViW.*

Denneston, Walter. *For the possible use of Denneston's name in Archibald Pitcairne's Latin poems, see* Danniston, Walter.

D219 — [dh, p. 2] Mytilopolis sive Musselburgi, oppidi antiquissimi, elogium. [dh, p. 3] A panegyrick, on the most antient town of Musselburgh. [*Edinburgh?* 1703?]
4°: *A*² B² C⁴; *1* 2–15 *16 blk.*
 P. 1 bears a dedication to the bailies of Musselburgh from Christian Denneston, the author's widow, in which she says she has 'caus'd [the Latin poem] to be turn'd to English'. Text in Latin and English. James Bain was appointed schoolmaster in Denneston's place in 1703.
'Forte sub Auroram (quamprimum Phœbus Eoo'
'Once in a morning (when the sun did rise'
L(1480.aa.34).

Dennis, John. The select works of Mr. John Dennis. *London, printed by John Darby,* 1718.
8°: 2 vol. O; CtY,MH.
 Watermark: fleur-de-lys. Proposals were issued in 1717 (*CBEL* II.572).

— [fine paper] L.
 Watermark: Strasburg bend.

— [reissue] The select works of Mr. John Dennis, in two volumes: consisting of plays, poems, &c... To which is added, Coriolanus, the invader of his country... *London, printed for J.D.; sold by*

Dennis, J.

D. Browne, W. Mears, S. Illidge, F. Clay, T. Bickerton, T. Corbet, W. Chetwood, & T. Payne, 1721.
8°: 2 vol. L; PU,ViU.
 Cancel title found in vol. 2 only of the copy at L; *The invader of his country,* 1720, is added to that volume.

D220 — The battle of Ramillia: or, the power of union. A poem. In five books. *London, printed for Ben. Bragg,* 1706. (*DC* 30 Dec)
8°: A⁸ a⁶ B–I⁸ K²; *i–xxviii,* 1–132. a6 blk.
 Watermark: post-horn on shield. Errata slip on p. 132.
'Of Belgian provinces by unions pow'r'
O; CSmH,*DLC.*

D221 — [fine paper?]
 Watermark: initial at centre of sheet. Some ordinary paper copies may be wrongly entered here.
L(11632.df.2); CtY,DFo,ICN,MH.

D222 — Britannia triumphans: or the empire sav'd, and Europe deliver'd... A poem. *London, printed for J. Nutt,* 1704. (*PM* 28 Nov)
8°: *A*⁴(±A1) a⁴ B–G⁴ H⁴(±H1.4) I–K⁴; *i–xvi,* 1–72 (30 as '03').
 Watermark: cartouche with initials. Ms. corrections in many copies.
'Up, rouze your selves, ye nations, praise the lord'
 On the battle of Blenheim.
L(161.1.33, Luttrell, 1 Dec),LDW,O,OC; ICN (lacks A1),*MnU*,NjP(lacks A3–a4, preface).

D223 — [fine paper]
 Watermark: star. Apparently H1.4 are not cancelled in fine-paper copies: two lines from p. 49 are misplaced on p. 50.
OW('Donum autoris'); CLU-C(presentation binding),CtY,MH(presentation binding).

'—' John Dennis, the sheltring poet's invitation to Richard Steele...to come and live with him in the Mint, 1714. *See* J69.

D224 — The monument: a poem sacred to the immortal memory of the best and greatest of kings, William the third, king of Great Britain, &c. *London, printed for D. Brown, & A. Bell,* 1702. (18 June, Luttrell)
4°: A² a⁴ B–G⁴; *i–ii* iii–xii, 1–48.
 Watermark: Dutch lion. Listed in *WL* June.
'What sudden damp has seiz'd upon my soul'
L(161.1.34, Luttrell),O,C,DT,LdU-B+; CLU-C,CtY(2),ICN,MH,TxU+.

D225 — [fine paper]
 Watermark: fleur-de-lys.
CSmH.

D226 — A poem upon the death of her late sacred majesty Queen Anne, and the...accession of his sacred majesty King George... *London, printed by H. Meere; sold by J. Baker,* 1714. (*SR* 2 Oct)

Dennis, J. A poem upon the death

8°: *A*⁴ B–D⁴; *1–4* 5–30 *31–32 blk*. A1 hft.
Entered to John Dennis by John Brightland
in *SR*; deposit copies at O,E,AdU,SaU.
'Those British bards appear to me to have sunk'
L(992.h.3/9,—A1, D4; Ashley 626,—A1, D4),O,
E,AdU,SaU; CtY,IU(Luttrell, 9 Oct),InU,MH,
TxU+.

D227 Denny, Glover. Sexus invicem depraeliantes: ex
anglico latine redditum. Per Glo: Denny, esq;
Londini, impensis C. Corbett, 1740.
4°: π¹ *A*² B–G⁴ H⁴(–H4); *i–ii* iii–v *vi blk*, *1* 2–53
54 blk.
The collation given is tentative. English and
Latin texts.
'Tu suaves mirare modos, numerosq; decentes'
A translation of Samuel Wesley's *The battle
of the sexes*.
L(11630.c.3/13).

D228 Departure. The departure. To his excellence,
Lord Carteret. A poem. [*Dublin*] *Printed by
Richard Dickson, 1726.*
½°: 1 side, 1 column.
Printed in a red-brown ink.
'Shall then in vain such streams of sorrow flow'
L(C.121.g.8/152),C,DT,Rothschild.

D229 Dependant. The dependant. An epistle to the
honourable Sir George Oxenden bart… *London
printed, and sold by A. Dodd, J. Roberts, E. Nutt,
and by the book-sellers of London & Westminster,
1734.* (*GM* Feb)
2°: *A*² B–E²; *1–4* 5–18 *19; 20 blk*. A1 hft; E2 advt.
No watermark.
'While Nassau's most auspicious name'
On being a suppliant for office.
O,LdU-B,*MR-C*; CSmH,CtY(–E2),ICU(–E2),
MH(–A1),TxU+.

D230 — [fine paper]
Watermark: post-horn on shield. Advertise-
ment leaf E2 possibly cancelled.
O(–E2).

Derham, William. The pastoral muse, 1722. *In*
B532.

Dering, *Sir* Edward. Several poems and elegies
in Latin as well as English, in memory of the most
excellent Maria. To which is added, a pindarick
poem, on the blessings of adversity. [*London*] 1701.
8°: pp. 44. O.
Edited and in part written by Dering in
memory of his wife.

D231 [Dering, Heneage.] De senectute. Per H. D.
Ripensem. *Eboraci: impensis Joannis Hildyard, 1746.*
2°: π² <A²; *3–5* 6–8 *9; 10 blk*. 9 advt.
'Flentis hamadryadis luctum, quercumq; dolen-
tem'
For Dering's authorship, see *DNB*.
L(11409.h.20).

Dering, H.

D232 [—] Reliquiæ Eboracenses. Per H. D. Ripensem.
*Eboraci: typis Cæsaris Ward et Ricardi Chandler.
Prostant venales apud Johannem Hildyard, biblio-
polam, 1743.* (4 June?)
4°: π² A–M⁴ (B2 as 'C2'); *i–iv*, 1–95 *96 blk*. iv err.
Of the five copies at YM, three are in identical
presentation bindings in mottled calf, and
three have a ms. addition to the errata.
'Eboracæ peragro fines; lustroque viator'
A copy at YM is interleaved with a ms. trans-
lation into English verse by Thomas Gent
which reveals Dering's name.
L(11630.b.7/3, Tom's Coffee House, 4 June, lacks
A4; 837.g.37, 'ex dono authoris'; 78.d.36;
G.17791),DrU(2, 1 presentation, 1 in wrappers
uncut),LdP,YM(5),YP; CtY,*ICU*,MH.

D233 Dermot. Dermot and Cicely: or, the Irish gimb-
let. A tale, in three canto's, in the manner of
Hudibras. *London, printed for W. Trow, 1742.*
8°: A–C⁴ (+1 plate); *1–3* 4–23 *24 blk*.
Title in red and black. A stub between C2.3
in the ICU copy and an offset on C1ᵛ of the
MCC copy are clearly the remains of an
erotic plate.
'In Munster once, as legends tell'
An erotic pastoral with references to cricket.
MCC library, London (–plate); ICU (–plate).

D234 Desaguliers, John Theophilus. The Newtonian
system of the world, the best model of government:
an allegorical poem… With copper plates. To
which is added, Cambria's complaint against the
intercalary day in the leap-year. *Westminster,
printed by A. Campbell, for J. Roberts; sold by the
booksellers of London & Westminster, 1728.* (*MChr*
15 Feb)
4°: A–G⁴ (+3 plates); *i–iii* iv–vi *vii–viii*, *1* 2–46
47–48. 47 advt; 48 err.
'In ancient times, ere bribery began'
'Three winters Cambria had with pleasure view'd'
A note by Desaguliers in *Rawlinson* records
that 'Cambria's complaint' was written by a
friend. Cf. Samuel Edwards, *The Copernican
system*, 1728.
L(643.k.3/5),O,CT(2),E,LdU-B; CtY,CtY-M,
DLC,MH,TxU.

Descazeaux, Michel Du Halley. Œuvres choisies
de Mr. Descazeaux. [*London, 1745?*]
8°: pp. 31. O.

Description. A description in answer to the
Journal, 1722. *See Percival, William, dean of Emly.*

— A description of Bath, [1733]–. *See Chandler,
Mary.*

D235 — The description of Dunkirk with Squash's
and Dismal's opinion. How easily Prince Eugene
may retake it, and many other matters of the last
importance. [*London?*] *Printed in the year 1712.*
½°: 1 side, 2 columns.

The **description** of Dunkirk

Teerink 869; *Williams* 1098.
'Harley at length has reapd the fame'
    In praise of Harley's efforts for peace, against the whigs. Ascribed to Swift by *Ball* 130, but not accepted by Williams.
L(11602.i.12/4).

— A description of the four last things, 1719. *See* Bond, William.

D236 — A description of the play-house in Dorset-garden. [*London*] *Sold by B. Bragg*, 1706. (23 July, Luttrell)
½°: 1 side, 2 columns.
'Where gentle Thames thro' stately channels glides'
    Crum W1707: 'The play house'; one ms. dated 1699, one attributing the poem to Addison. Printed in Sedley's *Poetical works*, 1707 as 'By J. Addison' and thence collected in Johnson's *Poets*. But see C. N. Greenough in *Harvard Studies* 17 (1935) 55–65, quoting other ascriptions and doubting Addison's authorship. An earlier text is printed as Addison's by F. H. Ellis in *POAS* VI. 29.
Crawford; ICN(Luttrell),MH.

D237 — A description of the young a-------s cavalcade, on circuit. *Dublin, printed in the year* 1747.
½°: 1 side, 2 columns.
'When our gallants are preparing'
    A satire on the Irish attorneys.
L(1890.e.5/3).

D238 — The description, or the matchless-fair-one. A poem. *London, printed for S.S.* [*Samuel Sturton?*] *and are to be sold by B. Bragg*, 1706. (*WL* April)
2°: *A*¹ B²; *i–ii*, 1 2–4.
'The eager merchant does in vain sail o'er'
O; CSmH.

Desolation. Desolation: or, the fall of gin, 1736. *See* Budgell, Eustace.

D239 Devil. The devil a barrel better herring; or, a merry dialogue between in and out. *Printed and sold by the booksellers of London & Westminster*, 1710. (*PB* 4 Nov)
½°: 1 side, 1 column.
    Advertised in *PB* by J. Baker.
'As once two knights, tho' lords by being m——rs'
    A dialogue between successive lord mayors of London, Sir Samuel Garrard and Sir Gilbert Heathcote, contrasting their attitudes to Sacheverell.
MH,OCU,*Harding*.

D240 — — [*London?* 1710.]
½°: 1 side, 1 column.
Harding.

D241 — — [*Dublin*, 1710.]
½°: 1 side, 1 column.
    On the other side, Swift's *The virtues of Sid Hamet*, 1710.
O; *CSmH*,TxU.

Devil

— The devil and the doctor, 1719. *See* Mandragora, 1717–.

D242 — The devil in a whirl-wind at Westminster-hall. Being a comical relation of the great fright the lawyers and others were put in, last Wednesday, by a storm blowing down old Bradshaw's head, and breaking into Westminster-hall. [*London*] *Printed by R.N.* [*Richard Newcomb*] *in Fleetstreet*, 1712.
½°: 1 side, 1 column.
'Upon the southern end of that great hall'
    On the fall of the head of John Bradshaw the regicide.
L(11602.i.12/5).

D243 — The devil knows what. A poem. To which is annex'd, the Compromise; or, a dialogue between W. and P. in imitation of the 9th ode of Horace, book the 3d. Both written by a state lunatick. *London, printed for E. Rayner; sold by the booksellers of London & Westminster*, [1731.] (*GSJ* 9 March)
2°: A–B²; *1–2* 3–7 *8 blk.*
    'The compromise' was published separately as *A dialogue between the right honourable . . .* [1731?].
'Geneva's a subject long since out of date'
Compromise: 'Whilst you and I were cordial friends'
    Political satires, the second on Walpole and Pulteney.
DrU,LdU-B; CSmH,OCU(cropt).

D244 — The devil repriev'd from the jaws of death and --------, &c. &c. &c. An heroic tale. After the manner of Machieval's Belphegor. *London, printed for J. H. Hubbard*, 1742. (*GM, LM* Oct)
8°: A–C⁴; *1–3* 4–24.
'Strange uproars shook the regions all below'
    A satire on Sir Thomas De Veil.
L(11633.b.14),O.

D245 — The devil to do about Dunkirk, in burlesque verse. Wherein the several conjectures of different parties and perswasions, concerning that intended expedition, are set forth. *London printed, and sold by J. Morphew*, 1708. (11 March, Luttrell)
4°: *A*² B–G²; *1–4* 5–28.
    Teerink 838; not in *Williams*.
'Muse, if thou can'st a while assist'
L(164.m.44, Luttrell),O,C; CtY.

D246 — [*idem*] The Gottenburgh frolick: or, the Swedish invasion burlesqu'd. Wherein the several conjectures of men of different parties . . . are set forth in very merry metre. *London, printed by N.M. for J. Morphew*, 1717.
8°: A⁴ C–E⁴ F¹; *1–3* 4–34.
    Text slightly revised to adapt it to the new subject.
O,*MR-C*; CLU-C,MB,MH,OCU.

D247 — The devil to do on the death of Old-Nick. A new poem. *Dublin, printed by Gwyn Needham*, [1727?]

The **devil** to do on the death

½°: 1 side, 2 columns.
The DT copy is bound with half-sheets of 1727.
'A month ago, that rogue, Old-Nick'
The death of an unsuccessful courtier.
DT; CtY.

[D248–50 = S442·2–6] — The devil upon dun: or, moderation in masquerade, 1705. *See* Shippen, William [The sequel].

D251 — The devil upon two sticks. Or, a hue and cry after the Drapier's club. Written by the clerk of the parish. *Dublin printed, and sold by E. Waters, 1736.*
8°: A⁸(−A4.5); *1–2* 3–12.
'Poor Tom an honest country swain'
Tom keeps an alehouse at the sign of the Drapier; but fashions change and the house is neglected. Possibly Mr. Taplin's club which flourished in 1725 is intended.
DA(2),DN.

D252 Deviliad. The Deviliad. An heroic poem. *London, printed for W. Bickerton, 1744.* (*GM,LM* May)
4°: *A⁴* B–D⁴; *i–v* vi–x, *11* 12–32. A1 hft.
In some copies (L,CT,DFo,MH) sheet C is wrongly perfected.
'Arms, and the knighted col'nel, muse, relate'
Ascribed to — Taswell by *Halkett & Laing* on the authority of the L catalogue. No evidence remains at L for the attribution, and the Taswell intended has not been identified. A satire on a riot at Sir Thomas De Veil's house.
L(11630.b.5/8; 11630.c.5/8; 1465.k.11,−A1), O,CT; CtY,DFo,ICN,IU,MH+.

Devonshire, William Cavendish, *duke of. See* Cavendish, William, *duke of Devonshire.*

Dewar, —, *Mr.* 'Poem on Duke Hamilton.' [*Edinburgh,* 1713.]
Entered in Ruddiman's ledger for the week ending 9 May 1713.

'**Diagoras.**' War with priestcraft, 1732. *See* W40.

Dialogue. A dialogue between a depending courtier, 1735. *See* Ward, Edward [Nuptial dialogues, W133].

[D253 = B608·5] — A dialogue between a dissenting minister and the Calves-head-club, 1721. *See* 'Butler, Samuel' [The morning's salutation].

D254 — A dialogue between a secretary of state and a Connaught squier; or, a satyr in imitation of Horace Ibam forte via &c. *Dublin, printed 1714.*
4°: A⁴; *1–2* 3–8. 8 'advt'.
'As I on Stephens Green was taking air'
L(1960),C; CtY.

— A dialogue between a surly husband, [172–]. *See* Ward, Edward [Nuptial dialogues, W132].

D255 — A dialogue between Captain Tom and Sir H——y D——n C——t. [*London*] *Printed for the*

A **dialogue** between Captain Tom

consolation of those who can bear a cross in the year 1710. (*SR* 9 Oct)
½°: 1 side, 2 columns.
Entered in *SR* by John Morphew. This and the following are apparently by the same printer.
'Come, fair muse, of Grub-street'
A satire against Sir Henry Dutton Colt, whig candidate in the Westminster election.
C,Chatsworth,Rothschild.

D256 — [another edition, title reads:] ...Sir H--y D--n C--t.
L(C.121.g.9/159).

D257 —— [*Dublin*] *Re-printed for the consolation of those who can bear a cross in the year,* 1710.
½°: 1 side, 2 columns.
C,DG; CSmH.

D258 — A dialogue between George Fachney and Alexander Pennicuik. [*Edinburgh,* 1722?]
½°: 1 side, 2 columns.
'Ae time our poet met wi' Fackney'
A satire on Pennecuik, challenged on the inaccuracy of his verses on Fachney.
CSmH.

— A dialogue between G--s E---e and B--b D---n, 1741. *See* Williams, *Sir* Charles Hanbury.

D259 — A dialogue between Hermodactyl and Gambol, on Tuesday, Aug. 31. 1714. '*Printed for C. Cross near Westminster*', [1714.]
slip: 1 side, 1 column.
The imprint is fictitious; 'C. Cross' stands for Charing Cross. The copy seen was reissued in *State-poems. Being a collection of choice private pieces of the year 1714,* 1715.
'How strangely times are alter'd, Hall!'
A satire on Bolingbroke and Harley.
Brett-Smith.

D260 — A dialogue betvven [!] his grace the Duke of Argyle, and the Earl of Mar. Or an excellent new song, to the tune of the Hare merchants rant, &c. [*Edinburgh,* 1715?]
½°: 1 side, 2 columns.
Two rough cuts at head.
'Argyle and Mar are gone to war'
A popular ballad, on Argyll's side.
L(Rox. III. 329).

D261 — [dh] A dialogue between Martin Luther, and Jack Calvin. [*London?* 1713?]
4°: *A²*; *1–4*.
The date is suggested by DFo.
'Peace brother Jack, I'm glad to see ye'
DFo.

— A dialogue between Menalcas and Palaemon, [1739.] *See* Brereton, Robert.

D262 — A dialogue between Pasquin and Morforio, two statues in Rome. [*London,* 1701?]
½°: 1 side, 1 column.
Line 2, 'I thought you'd no business...'

A dialogue between Pasquin

'Why how now Pas--- since the last election'
A satire on the power of the leading politicians.
LLP.

D263 — — [*London?* 1701?]
½°: 1 side, 1 column.
Line 2, 'I thought you'd had no business...'
apparently the correct reading; but this edition is very inferior typographically.
L(112.f.44/43, cropt).

D264 — A dialogue between Pasquin and Porforio [!]...
[*Dublin?* 1701?]
½°: 2 sides, 1 column.
The copy at DK is bound with Dublin half-
sheets, many of 1701.
DK.

D265 — A dialogue between St. Peter and a low-church-
man. *London printed and re-printed in Dubiin* [!],
[1710?]
½°: 2 sides, 1 column.
No London edition has been traced.
'Why, how now friend, I prithee of what church'
A high-church satire.
MH.

D266 — ⟨A⟩ dialogue between the brogue-makers and
journey-men shoe-makers. By O. D. broguemaker.
[*Dublin*, 1725/30.]
½°: 1 side, 1 column.
The copy at L forms part of a collection of
Dublin half-sheets of 1725/30.
'Thy aid divine, Apollo I implore'
L(C.121.g.8/101, ms. date 6 Oct).

D267 — A dialogue between the cities of London and
Paris, in relation to the present posture of affairs,
rendred into verse... Written by a person who has
no mony to pay taxes in case of a war. *London
printed, and are to be sold by the booksellers of
London & Westminster*, 1701. (2 Oct, Luttrell)
2°: A² B–D²; i–iv, 1–4 7–13 14 blk.
Teerink 831; *Williams* 1073. Listed in *WL*
Sept.
'Thou city whose aspiring turrets rise'
Ball 49–50 suggests that this was written in
collaboration between Swift and Davenant;
Williams considers this 'no more than a
guess'.
LG,LVA-D,LVA-F,O,*CJ*+; CLU-C(Luttrell),
ICU,TxU.

D268 — A dialogue between the French standards in
Westminster-hall, and the guns on the Tower-
wharf, on the anniversary of her majesty's birth,
suppos'd to be occasioned by their then firing.
London, printed for John Wickins; sold by J. Nutt,
1705. (6 Feb, Luttrell)
2°: A² B–C²; 1–2 3–12.
'Sons of the Thunderer, and Bellona's care'
O(2),E,DG,*MR-C;* CLU-C,MH(Luttrell).

D269 — A dialogue between the miller and his dogg.
[*Dublin?* 1712?]
½°: 1 side, 2 columns.

A dialogue between the miller

'A miller once of note and might'
Apparently an attack on Marlborough, though
the L copy is bound with Dublin half-sheets
of 1725/30.
L(C.121.g.8/106, imprint cropt).

D270 — A dialogue between the old black horse at
Charing Cross, and the new one, with a figure on it
in H---er Square. To the tune of the Abbot of
Canterbury. [*London*, 1718?]
½°: 1 side, 2 columns.
13 stanzas.
'In London late happen'd a pleasant discourse'
A satire occasioned by George I's statue in
Hanover Square.
L(1876.f.1/87),O(2).

D271 — [*idem*] Here is a dialogue that passed between
the poor beast at Charing-Cross, and the strange
beast in G---- S------. [*London?*] '*Printed for
Mary Nortin and Sguire* [!] *Jump*', [1726?]
½°: 1 side, 2 columns.
Small woodcut of horses at head. A 9-stanza
version, referring to the statue of George I in
Grosvenor Square.
NNP.

— A dialogue between the pillory and Daniel
Defoe, [1706.] *See* Brown, Thomas.

D272 — A dialogue between the right honourable Sir
Robert Walpole, and William Poultney esq; In
imitation of Horace's ninth ode, book 3. [*London*,
1731?] (16 Jan?)
4°: A²; 1–2; 3–4 blk.
Also printed in *The devil knows what*, [1731.]
In the L copy the blank leaf A2 has been
folded round to make a cover for the post.
Probably the work variously listed in Bowyer's
ledgers as 'Advice to Poultney', 'A letter a
poem', 'A poem in defence of Ld Walpole',
and 'a poem in imitation of Horace'; listed
under 16 Jan 173[1] for T. Woodward, half a
sheet demy 4°, 100 copies and 12 royal; no
fine-paper copies have been identified.
'While you and I were cordial friends'
L(11631.g.46).

— A dialogue between two free electors, 1749.
See Missy, César de.

— A dialogue between two noted horses, 1736.
See Marvell, Andrew.

D273 — A dialogue between two sisters and a certain
apothecary. [*Dublin*, 1726.]
½°: 1 side, 2 columns.
'A wolf and bear did often meet'
In defence of Mordecai Adam, charged with
fornication with two whores.
DN.

D274 — A dialogue between whigg and whigg: or, Tom
Double's rogueries discovered. *Dublin printed, and
sold by John Haite, at the back of Dick's-Coffee-
house, in Skinner-row*, [1710?]

A dialogue between whigg

½°: 1 side, 1 column.
'There came a Scot of late I hear, to wait upon
Tom Double'
    A Scotsman's complaint against Sacheverell
and the lack of toleration for presbyterians.
MH.

D275 — A dialogue between Windsor Castle, and
Blenheim House, the seat of the Duke of Marlborough; formerly call'd Woodstock-Bower. *London, printed in the year* 1708.
8°: *A*⁴; *1* 2–8.
'Twas in St. Edward the confessor's days'
    On Marlborough.
L(164.k.29).

[**D276** — A dialogue betwixt Lewis and the devil in the
last year of his puissance: with his last will and
testament. *London, printed by John Wallis, near the
Green Dragon tavern in Fleet-street,* [1690.]
½°: 1 side, 2 columns.
'What shrill and eccho'd groans possess my
soul?'
    Wrongly dated as 1715 by MH; Luttrell's copy,
    dated 13 Sept 1690, is at ICN.]

D277 — A dialogue betwixt Satan and a young man: or,
Satan's temptations to delay repentace [!] answered.
By J.J. a pious young divine, at Aberdeen. *Edin-
burgh printed, and sold by John Reid,* 1716.
½°: 1 side, 2 columns.
'What haste! young man, why up so soon i' th'
morn?'
E.

— A dialogue betwixt William Lick-ladle,
[1715/–.] *See* A new Scotch song, [1715/–.]

D278 — [dh] Dialogue entre deux freres, touchant les
prophetes cevenois. [col] *A Londres, l'an de grace*
1707.
8°: A⁴; 1–8.
'A vôtre nez, mon frere, on rit partout de vous'
O.

D279 — [dh] Second dialogue entre deux freres.
Touchant les prophetes cevenois. [*London,* 1707.]
8°: A⁴; 1–8.
'Mon frere, enfin, je viens vous demander pardon'
O.

D280 — [dh] Troisième dialogue entre deux freres...
Du XXX. may. [*London,* 1707.]
8°: A⁴; 1–8.
'Mon frere, auriez vous crû que parmi les chrétiens'
O.

D281 — [dh] Quatrième dialogue entre deux freres...
Extrait du procez qui a été intenté contre les
pretendus profetes...le 4 juillet 1707... [*London,*
1707.]
8°: A⁴; 1–8.
'Je viens de rencontrer au milieu de la ruë'
O.

Dialogue entre deux freres

D282 — [dh] Cinquième dialogue entre deux freres, &
Timante leur ami...Du 23. juin 1707. [*London,*
1707.]
8°: A⁴; 1–8. 8 advt.
'Vous avez trés-bien fait, mon frere, & sagemēt'
O.

D283 — [dh] Sixième dialogue entre deux freres...Du
8. juillet 1707. [*London,* 1707.]
8°: A⁴; 1–8. 8 advt.
'Eh! bien mon frere, eh! bien, nôtre troupe
sacrée'
O.

D284 — [dh] Finis coronat opus. Septième et dernier
dialogue entre deux freres...Du 30. juillet 1707...
[*London,* 1707.]
8°: A⁴; 1–8. 8 advt, err.
    The advertisement lists the seven dialogues
    bound together and a forthcoming 'Ode à la
    gloire...de...Mr. Maximilien M——'.
'Voila vos inspirez qui sans l'avoir predit'
O.

D285 — A dialogue in burlesque verse, between Parson
Betty and Parson Bowman, in justification of their
sermons. By Timothy Tagg, of Tingle-lane, poet-
taster. *London, printed for H. Cooke,* 1731. (*GSJ*
23 Sept)
8°: A–D⁴; *1–2* 3–32.
'Since men in faith were so divided'
    A satire on the sermons of Joseph Betty and
    William Bowman.
L(4455.b.28/3, lacks D4),O,E,LdU-B(uncut); IU,
PU.

D286 — A dialogue on one thousand seven hundred and
thirty-eight: together with a prophetic postscript
as to one thousand seven hundred and thirty-nine.
London, printed for T. Cooper, 1738. (*LM* Aug)
2°: *A*² B–D²; *1–3* 4–15 *16 blk.*
'If I mistake not, sir, there was a time'
    On the state of satire, with an attack on
    Pope's *One thousand seven hundred and thirty
    eight.*
L(11642.i.10/5; 11602.i.20/3),O(uncut),LdU-B
(uncut); CLU-C,CtY,MH,OCU,TxU.

D287 — A dialogue which lately pass'd between the
knight and his man John. *London, printed by
W. Lloyd; sold by the booksellers & pamphlet-shops,*
[1739.] (*GM* July)
2°: *A*² B–D²; *1–3* 4–16.
    Horizontal chain-lines.
'With rosy fingers, see the morn'
    A satire on Walpole.
L(1973),O; TxU(uncut).

D288 —— '*London, printed by W. Lloyd; sold by the
booksellers & pamplet-shops* [!]' [*Edinburgh,* 1739.]
8°: A–B⁴; *1–2* 3–16.
    The copies at C,CtY,IU are bound with
    Edinburgh piracies.
L(11631.bb.46),C; CtY(uncut),IU,OCU.

Diamond

D289 Diamond. Diamond cut diamond: the lamentations of the nonjuring clergy, &c. An historical poem, from the reformation to this present year... *London printed, and sold by J. Peele, & J. Marshall,* 1724.
8°: π¹ A–M⁴ O–P⁴ Q²; *i–x, 1–88, 81–97 98–100.*
π1 hft; 98 err; Q2 advt.
'In pious times, e'er heaven's fav'rite nation'
Brett-Smith.

D290 — — The second edition. *London printed, and sold by J. Marshall, & J. Peele,* 1724.
8°: π¹ A⁴(±A1) B–M⁴ O–P⁴ Q²; *i–x, 1–88, 81–97 98–100.* π1 hft; 98 err; Q2 advt.
A reissue with a cancel title (and possibly a new half-title).
L(11601.d.20/3; 11631.aaa.8,−Q2),AdU.

D291 Diaper, William. Brent a poem. By the rev. Mr. William Diaper, some time curate of the parish of Brent. *Sarum, printed for William Collins at the Bible and Crown in Silver Street, and sold by T. Astley and R. Baldwin in St. Paul's Churchyard, London,* [1732?]
2°: A² B–C² D¹; *i–ii iii–iv, 1–9 10. 10 advt.*
The date is suggested by the works advertised; the copy at WcC is bound with poems of 1729–33.
'Happy are you, whom Quantock overlooks'
A manuscript version of 1709 is in the Osborn collection at CtY; Diaper died in 1717.
WcC.

— Callipædia. A poem. In four books [in part translated by Diaper], 1712–. *See* R280.

D292 — Dryades; or, the nymphs prophecy. A poem. *London, printed for Bernard Lintott,* 1713 [1712]. (*Examiner* 29 Dec)
2°: A¹ B–I² K¹; *i–ii, 1–34.*
Entered in *SR* 31 Dec; deposit copies at L,LSC,O,EU,AdU,SaU.
'Forgive, ye nereids, if I sing no more'
L(643.1.26/10),LSC,O(2),EU,AdU + ; CSmH (uncut),*CtY*,MH(uncut),*PBL*,TxU.

D293 — An imitation of the seventeenth epistle of the first book of Horace. Address'd to Dr. S——ft. *London, printed for John Morphew,* 1714. (*PB* 2 Feb)
4°: A–B⁴; *1–2 3–16.*
Rothschild 796a; *Teerink* 1083.
'Tho' you conversant are at court'
L(11641.h.8/1),O(uncut),C,GU,LdU-B + ; CtY, IU(uncut),PU,TxU.

D294 [—] Nereides: or, sea eclogues. *London, printed by J. H. for E. Sanger,* 1712. (*DC* 15 March)
8°: A⁴ χ¹[=K4] B–I⁴ K⁴(−K4); *i–ii iii–x, 1–69 70 blk.*
Presentation copy at NNC to Mrs. Frances Palmer dated 12 March; referred to in Swift's *Journal to Stella* under the same date.
'Think, Glaucus, you were once a fishing swain'

Diaper, W. Nereides

The authorship is revealed in Swift's *Journal to Stella*, and the poem referred to in Diaper's *Dryades*.
L(11641.df.26),O,OW,DT,LdU-B + ; CtY,ICN, MH,NNC,TxU + .

— Oppian's Halieuticks of the nature of fishes and fishing [books 1–2 translated by Diaper], 1722. *See* O236.

D295 Dibben, Thomas. Carmen sæculare to the king. *London, printed for Jacob Tonson,* 1701.
8°: A–E⁸; *i–ii, 1 2–75 76–78 blk.*
The Latin title on A1ᵛ reads 'Carmen sæculare serenissimo principi Gulielmo III° inscriptum ... T. Dibben...' Text in Latin and English. There may be fine-paper copies (e.g. LLP,CtY) but the watermark evidence has been insufficient to distinguish them.
'Jane bifrons, priscos a tergo respice lapsi'
A translation of Prior's poem of 1700.
LLP(−E8),O,DT; CSmH,CtY,IU,MH,NN + .

D296 [—] Excellentissimo domino, domino Johanni episcopo Bristoliensi... hoc in Mosam recepto gratulatorium carmen kalendis Januarii S.V. inscribit servorum devinctissimus. [*Utrecht?* 1712.]
4°: A⁴; *1–6; 7–8 blk.*
Title in half-title form.
'O decus Angliaci nautæ, pulcherrima sylvæ'
A copy at O has an accompanying letter from William Ayerst at Utrecht to Dr. Charlett explaining the origin of the poem.
O(2).

D297 — Excellentissimo dom°. dom°. Johanni, episcopo Bristol. sigilli privati custodi, & reginæ Magnæ Britanniæ a secretioribus consiliis, in Mosam fluvium accepto gratulatorium carmen. Kalendis Januarij inscribit Tho. Dibben. *Londini, impensis Bernardi Lintott,* [1712.] (23 Jan, Luttrell)
½°: *1–2,* 1 column.
Listed in *PB* 5 Feb.
L(Cup.645.e.1/17; 1865.c.8/122),LLP,Chatsworth; MH(Luttrell).

D298 [—] The young club a congratulatory poem to his excellency John lord bishop of Bristol... upon the peace signed at his lordships house April 11. 1713. Humbly presented by G. Hastings, S. Brewster, & T. Dibben, his lordships pages. [*Utrecht?* 1713.]
4°: A⁴; *1–7; 8 blk.*
Title in half-title form.
'Amidst the crowds, that joyn in verse & prose'
Ms. attribution to Dibben in the O copy.
L(1479.dd.15/2),O('ex dono authoris').

D299 [—] — *London, printed for Bernard Lintott,* 1713.
½°: *1–2,* 1 column.
L(C.121.g.8/7),Crawford.

D300 Dick. Dick, or devil, or the devil upon Dick. A hudibras---tic, poem inscrib'd to --------. [*Dublin,* 1735.]

Dick, or devil

$\frac{1}{2}$°: 1 side, 2 columns.
''Till now, 'twas thought Sir Isa'c Newton'
Signed, 'W.M. Essex-street. 18th March.
1735.' An attack on an author who used
dashes in his verses.
C.

D301 Dick, David. True Christian love. To be sung
with any of the common tunes of the psalms of
David. *Edinburgh, printed in the year* 1701.
8°: A–C⁴ D⁴(–D4) (D2 as 'D3'); *1–2* 3–29
30 blk.
'I have a heart for love, and love'
L(3438.e.28),E.

D302 Dickinson, William. [dh] Ode gratulatoria, in
Magnæ Britanniæ imperium fauste & feliciter
adunatum, honoratissimo illustrissimoq; Wil-
lielmo domino Cowper... a Gulielmo Dickinson,
chirurgo, humillime dicata. [col] *Londini, impensis
Tim. Child,* 1707. (*DC* 29 April)
2°: *A²*; *1–4.*
'Et me Latine, non solitum, loqui'
Ascribed to John Philips in *CBEL*, probably
following *Dobell* 1246. The cause of this error
has not been determined.
O; TxU.

D303 — 'Ode in artem anatomicam. Ornatissimo doctis-
simoque viro D. Ricardo Mead, M.D. dicata.
[*London*] *Sold by Tim Childe.*' (*DC* 21 Nov 1710)

D304 Dickson, David. Georgio dei gratia... In regna
sua feliciter redeunti David Dicksonus medicus
Edinensis gratulatur. [*Edinburgh,* 1717/–.]
2°: *A²*; *1–4.*
'Cum, varios mundi solis radiantis adinstar'
E,EU; TxU.

Die. Die xxv. Decembris anni MDCCXII, 1712.
See Pitcairne, Archibald.

— Die xxx Novembris, anni MDCCXII, [1712].
See Pitcairne, Archibald.

Diet. The dyet of Poland, 1705. *See* Defoe, Daniel.

D305 Difference. The difference between keeping and
marriage. An heroic epistle from Edoarda to
Hamillio, on his late nuptials at Bath. *London,
printed for W. Webb,* 1743. (12 Jan?)
2°: *A²* B–C²; *1–2* 3–12.
Rothschild 238. Horizontal chain-lines. Listed
in *GM, LM* Jan.
'Swift, swift, good John, another bottle--fly-'
From Miss Edwards to Lord Anne Hamilton,
married in late 1742.
L(163.n.31); CtY,MH(ms. date 12 Jan).

— The difference between verbal and practical
virtue, 1742. *See* Hervey, John, *baron Hervey.*

'Digbeye, Glubech.' Robin's pathetick tale, 1727.
See R239.

Diggon

Diggon. Diggon Davy's resolution on the death
of his last cow, 1747. *See* Dodd, William.

[**D306** = R264·5] [**Dillingham, William.**] A true ecclesiastical history... By Thomas Hobbes... Made
English, 1722. *See* Rooke, John.

'Dillon, John, *kt.'* The pleasures of a single life,
[1726/36.] *See* P503.

Dillon, Wentworth, *earl of Roscommon. The
following poems are included here despite Dillon's
death in* 1685 *in order to complete the list of
piracies by Henry Hills.*

D307 — An essay on translated verse. *London printed,
and sold by H. Hills,* 1709.
8°: A⁸; *1–2* 3–16.
Pagination in parentheses. First published in
1684.
'Happy that author, whose correct essay'
L(1485.w.31),O(3),EU; CtY,MH,OCU,TxU.

D308 — — *London printed, and sold by H. Hills,* 1709.
8°: A⁸; *1–2* 3–15 '15'.
Pagination in square brackets. Reissued with
other remaindered Hills poems in *A collection
of the best English poetry,* 1717 (*Case* 294).
L(C.124.b.7/8),O,E; CtY,*ICU*,IU(2),MH.

D309 — Horace: Of the art of poetry: a poem. *London
printed, and sold by H. Hills,* 1709.
8°: A⁸; *1–2* 3–16.
A2 unsigned. First published in 1680.
'If in a picture (Piso) you should see'
L(11388.aaa.15),O(3),OW,C,E+; CtY,ICU,MH,
OCU.

D310 — [another edition]
A2 signed.
AdU; CtY,MH.

D311 — Horace's Art of poetry. Made English by the
right honourable the Earl of Ros-common.
London: printed, and re-printed for G. Grierson,
[*Dublin,*] 1711.
12°: A–D⁶; *i–viii,* 1–37 *38–40 blk.*
L(1958,–D6),DA.

D312 — Q. Horatii Flacci De arte poetica liber. Ad
Pisones. Horace's treatise concerning the art of
poetry... By the Earl of Roscommon. *Dublin,
printed for William Heatly,* 1733.
8°: *A²* B–K⁸ L²; *i–iv,* 1 *2–147* 148 *blk.*
Watermark: Amsterdam arms. Latin and
English texts.
DN; IU.

D313 — [fine paper?]
Watermark: fleur-de-lys.
L(11385.aaa.19).

D314 — [reissue] The second edition. *Dublin, printed
for Peter Wilson,* 1743.
8°: *A²*(±A1) B–K⁸ L²; *i–iv,* 1 *2–147* 148 *blk.*

Dillon, W. *earl.* Horace

The copy seen has the Amsterdam arms as watermark.

DN.

'—' An ode upon solitude, 1709. *In* S801.

'—' A prospect of death: a pindarique essay. Written by the right honourable the late Earl of Roscommon [actually by John Pomfret], 1704. *See* P733.

D315 [**Dinsdale, Joshua.**] The dove-cote: or, the art of breeding pigeons, a poem. *London, printed for Joseph Davidson,* 1740. (*GM,LM* March)
8°: A–D⁴; *1–3* 4–31 *32 blk.*
Entered in Strahan's ledger to Davidson under 8 Jan 1740, 500 copies.
'What care and industry the dove requires'
Not previously attributed to Dinsdale, but the conjunction of date, publisher, and subject with his *The modern art of breeding bees* makes the attribution hard to resist.
L(11632.aaa.19),O,LdU-B; CU,NN,OCU.

D316 — The modern art of breeding bees, a poem. *London, printed for Joseph Davidson,* 1740. (*GM, LM* Oct)
8°: A–C⁴ D²; *1–3* 4–26 *27–28.* D2 advt.
Entered in Strahan's ledger to Davidson under 13 Oct, 500 copies.
'Immortal bard! that on Italian plains'
L(1465.f.52),O(−D2).

D317 Dionysius. Dionysius Cato his four books of moral precepts. Translated out of Latine hexameter, into English meeter: by J.M. *Edinburgh, printed by Robert Brown,* 1714.
8°: A⁴ B–C⁴; *i–iv,* 1–20.
Previously published at Edinburgh in 1700 (copy at L).
'If god almighty be a sp'rit'
E.

D318 Directions. 'Directions how to gain by losses. Delivered in a poem occasioned by the late dreadful fire at Blandford, which happen'd at the time when the small pox rag'd over a great part of that town. [*London*] *Printed for J. Roberts; sold by J. Pemberton, & J. Oswald.* Price 6d.' (*LM,LaM* April 1733)

D319 — Directions to a painter. [*London?* 1716?]
slip: 2 sides, 1 column.
'Painter: your colours and your pencils get'
Crum P14: 'Directions to a painter writ in 1660 by Sir Jno: Denham kt', dated as [1716?]. A Jacobite attack on George I.
L(11626.i.11/6).

D320 Disappointed. The disappointed marriage, or an hue and cry after an outlandish monster. *London, printed for S. Gardiner, in the Strand,* 1733.
½°: 1 side, 2 columns.
'O yes, O yes, I want to know'

The **disappointed** marriage

A satire against William prince of Orange on occasion of his marriage with the Princess Royal.
L(1876.f.1/106; C.20.f.2/184, mutilated).

D321 Discarded. The discarded country gager: a poem. By T.L. late one of that fraternity. Inscribed to the gagers of Great-Britain. *London, printed in the year* 1718.
8°: A–B⁴; *1–3* 4–15 *16 blk.*
'Let poet's fam'd and poet's laureat sing'
On the hard state of the excise gaugers.
O.

D322 — The discarded fair-one. An heroick epistle from Hamilla to Cesario. In the Ovidian stile. *London, printed for M. Cooper,* 1745. (*GM, LM* July)
2°: A⁴; *1–3* 4–8.
'At length 'tis done---Hamilla's from you thrown'
On Lady Archibald Hamilton's dismissal from the household of Frederick, prince of Wales. Answered by *From Cæsario to Hamilla,* 1745.
L(1962),O,LdU-B; CSmH,ICN,KU,MH,OCU.

D323 Discontent. Discontent; or, an essay on faction: a satire. Address'd to the writers of the Craftsman, and other party papers. *London, printed for W. Warner; sold by T. Cooper, & J. Jolliffe,* [1736.] (*LM* Sept)
2°: π¹ A–C² D¹; *1–3* 4–16.
'What! must poor harrass'd Britain never rest'
Particularly on Bolingbroke, Amhurst and Budgell.
L(1489.m.15); OCU(uncut).

D324 — Discontent the universal misery. In an epistle to a friend. *London, printed for T. Cooper,* 1734. (*GM, LM* June)
2°: A¹ B–D² E¹; *1–2* 3–16.
'While you, my Lollius, amidst cares and strife'
A ms. note in the TxU copy signed 'B: J: U, 1778' records that these verses were written by his father at Oxford. The author has not been identified; possibly James Upton. John Upton seems improbable, since according to *DNB* he died unmarried; Francis Upton did not matriculate until 1737.
L(11630.h.16),O,LdU-B; CSmH,CtY,ICU,MH (2),TxU+.

D325 Discontented. The discontented virgin. *London printed, and sold by A. Moore,* 1727. (*MC* March)
½°: 2 sides, 1 column.
'What tho' I am a courtly lass'
In spite of fashionable distractions, her maidenhead plagues her.
L(C.121.g.9/190).

D326 Discord. Discord, or, one thousand seven hundred forty four. By a great poet lately deceased.

Discord

Printed from the original MSS. Permissu superiorum. *London, printed for B. Cowse,* [1744.] (*GA* 19 June)
2°: *A*¹ B–E² *F*¹; *i–ii,* 1–17 *18 blk.*
In some copies (e.g. L, TxU) sheet E has horizontal chain-lines. A and F have been seen to be conjugate.
'In meditation wrapp'd! absorb'd in thought!'
A dialogue between Pope and Warburton in which Pope confesses the self-love that dominated his life.
L(12273.m.1/17),LVA-D,O,BaP; CLU-C(uncut),CtY,ICU,TxU(2, 1 uncut).

D327 —— '*London, printed for B. Cowse*' [*Edinburgh*], 1744.
8°: A–B⁴ C² (A2 as 'A'); *1–3* 4–20.
Printed by Ruddiman on the evidence of the ornaments.
L(1486.s.11),EN,LdU-B(uncut); IU,MH,NN, OCU.

D328 **Discovery.** The discovery: or, the squire turn'd ferret. An excellent new ballad. To the tune of High boys! up go we; Chevy Chase; or what you please. *Westminster, printed by A. Campbell, for T. Warner; sold by the booksellers,* 1727 [1726]. (20 Dec)
2°: A⁴; *1–3* 4–8.
Publication date from *Twickenham Pope* VI. 259–64.
'Most true it is, I dare to say'
Crum M504. Almost certainly the ballad on Mary Toft (who claimed to have given birth to rabbits) which Pope told Spence had been written 'by him and Mr. Pulteney'.
L(643.1.24/49; 163.n.13),O,OW,AdU.

D329 —— The second edition. *Westminster, printed by A. Campbell, for T. Warner; sold by the booksellers,* 1727 [1726]. (24 Dec)
2°: A⁴; *1–3* 4–8.
Publication date from *Twickenham Pope.*
Apparently a reimpression.
L(1178.h.4/14; C.116.i.4/30); MH,OCU,TxU.

D330 —— The third edition. *Westminster, printed by A. Campbell, for T. Warner; sold by the booksellers,* 1727.
2°: A⁴; *1–3* 4–8.
Apparently a reimpression.
L(1850.c.10/60); CtY.

D331 **Diseases.** The diseases of Bath. A satire, unadorn'd with a frontispiece. *London, printed for J. Roberts,* 1737. (*LM* Feb)
2°: *A*² B–E²; *1–3* 4–20.
Rothschild 209.
'My friend! I've heard you often plight your faith'
A satire on both physical and moral diseases.
L(11602.i.17/5),LVA-D,O(2, 1 uncut),OA,LdU-B+; CSmH,CU(uncut),NjP,OCU,TxU.

Dispensary

Dispensary. The dispensary, 1703–. *See* Garth, *Sir* Samuel.

D332 —— The Dispensary transvers'd: or, the consult of physicians. A poem. In six canto's. Occasion'd by the death of his late h. the D. of G——r. *London, printed for John Nutt,* 1701. (*PB* 22 April)
8°: A⁴ a⁴ B–L⁴ M² (H2 as 'H3'); *i–xvi,* 1–84. 84 err.
'Tell me, Apollo, for thou best dost know'
Occasioned by Sir Samuel Garth's *Dispensary* and the death of the Duke of Gloucester.
DT; CtY-M,MH,TxU.

Dissectio. Dissectio mentis humanae, 1730. *See* Morrice, Bezaleel.

Dissenter. The dissenter, 1704. *See* Ward, Edward.

D333 **Dissenters.** The dissenters triumph: or, a universal joy for the rebuilding and furnishing Doctor Burgess's sanctified synogue [!]. *Dublin, re-printed* 1710.
½°: 1 side, 2 columns.
On the other side, *Win first, lose last,* [1710.] A variant text from *Jack Presbiter's triumphant rejoycing* (London, 1710); possibly there was a London edition of this text which has not been traced.
'Dear sisters come see you how fine'
A satire against Daniel Burgess.
OCU.

D334 **Dissenting.** Dissenting piety. [*London,* 1747?]
½°: 1 side, 2 columns.
Engraved portrait at head by Ravenet, dated 1747. Conceivably the same work as 'Non con parson a poem', entered to Manby & Cox in Bowyer's ledgers, possibly on 16 Sept 1746; the price suggests that was a half-sheet.
'Oh, thou, long trusted with each gift divine'
A satire against Isaac Watts, abbreviated from *Achates to Varus,* 1746.
O.

D335 **Dissertator.** The dissertator in burlesque. *London, printed for Bernard Lintott,* 1701. (*PB* 5 July)
8°: A–C⁸ D⁴; *i–viii,* 1–48 (6, 7 as '34, 35').
Bond 6. The paper has horizontal chain-lines, with a watermark in the normal octavo position.
'Tho' fashions in apparel change'
O,LdU-B; DFo(uncut),IU,TxU.

D336 **Dissolution.** The dissolution. *London, printed in the year* 1710.
½°: 1 side, 2 columns.
'A chymist that had long essay'd'
On the fall of Godolphin and dissolution of parliament as a result of the Sacheverell affair.
MC.

Distaff, J.

'**Distaff, J.**' Monarchy and church, 1710. *See* M396.

D337 Distressed. The distress'd maid being put to her last shift,|Maketh her petition to the reverend Dr. Swift. In imitation of Frances Harris's petition. [*Dublin*, 172–?]
½°: 1 side, 1 column.
'That your petitioner being about twenty-five years of age, has never yet been a bride'
In imitation of Swift's poem, originally written in 1701 (*Williams* 68). See *The revd. Dr. S---- answer*, [172–?]
C; *CtY*.

D338 Dive, Charles. On the Duke of Marlborough. A poem. [*London*] *Printed for E. Curll*, 1712. (7 Feb?)
½°: 2 sides, 1 column.
Curll advertisements at foot of verso.
'As late I walk'd beside that silver spring'
LLP,Crawford; *MH*,TxU(ms. date 7 Feb).

D339 — To the queen, upon the death of his royal highness. *London printed for Benjamin Barker; sold by J. Morphew*, 1709 [1708]. (*DC* 16 Nov)
2°: *A²; i–ii, 1–2.*
'Whilst tears o'erflow the royal widow's bed'
Listed in *Blanchard* 112, as a poem possibly by Steele; she had been unable to trace a copy of this text.
DG.

D340 Diverting. A diverting dialogue between a state black-a-more and a young lady in Ab--y - S----t. *Dublin, printed in the year* 1⟨727?⟩
½°: 1 side, 2 columns.
The copy at DT is bound with half-sheets of 1727.
'Come sweet fair maid and grant me love'
DT(cropt); CtY(imprint mutilated).

Divine. The divine or hypostatical union, 1707. *See* Waring, Henry.

— A divine poem dedicated to the memory of... Richard Claridge, [1723.] *See* Ellis, William.

D341 — A divine poem on the creation, redemption by and sufferings of, our lord and saviour Jesus Christ: applicable to this holy time of lent. Humbly presented to the Lady Cowper. *London, printed for the author*, 1718.
4°: *A¹ B–D²; i–ii, 1 2–11 12.*
Probably issued with variant title-pages with alternative dedicatees.
'Arise my soul with hov'ring wing'
Almost certainly by the same author as *Faith and practice*, 1717, *The Lord's day*, 1720, *The nature, necessity, use...*, 1720, and *On the nativity*, 1717; cf. also *A funeral poem, sacred to the memory of...John Churchill*, 1722. *On the nativity* has the same imprint as

A **divine** poem

a presentation poem of the same year by Henry Nevil, and he could be the author of them all. See also *The beauty and excellence of charity*, [1737?]. For other poems issued in this way, see W. Howard, H. Nevil, R. Spencer.
CtY.

D342 — [reissue] On the creation of the world, the birth and sufferings of, and redemption by, our lord and saviour Jesus Christ: a divine poem. Applicable to this holy time of lent. Humbly presented to Mrs. Millington. *London, printed for the author*, 1719.
4°: *A¹(±) B–D²; i–ii, 1 2–11 12.*
With a cancel title-leaf; presumably there were other states with alternative dedicatees.
L(11601.ff.1/3).

— Divine songs: occasionally compos'd on variety of subjects, fitted to the meanest capacity... The second edition. *London, printed for John Marshall*, 1735.
12°: pp. *1–16*, 13–30. E.
The epistle to the reader is signed 'F.H.' Possibly by Francis Hoffman, whose versification of the *Pilgrim's Progress* was published by Marshall.

— Divine wisdom and providence, 1736. *See* Bridges, —, *Mr.*

[**Dixon, Sarah.**] Poems on several occasions. *Canterbury, printed by J. Abree*, 1740.
8°: pp. xxvi, 203. L,O; CtY,MH.
A copy at L has ms. additions.

D——k, S——n. The year of wonders, 1737. *See* Y14.

D---l, R---d. A paraphrase on the seven penitential psalms, [1727?] *See* P60.

D-----n. D-----n S------t's prologue to Hyppolitus, [1721.] *See* Helsham, Richard.

D343 D—n—l. D—n—l B—g—s his circular letter, to his loving congregation. To the tune of Hey boys up go we. [*London*, 1710.]
½°: 2 sides, 1 column.
'To all my holy sisterhood, these do with greeting come'
A satire against Daniel Burgess after his meeting house was sacked by the Sacheverell mob.
O.

D344 Dobson, William. Paradisus amissus. Poema Joannis Miltoni. Latine redditum a Gulielmo Dobson. *Oxonii, e theatro Sheldoniano*, 1750.
4°: π⁴(−π1?) A–Pp⁴; *i–vi, 1 2–304.*
No watermark. Copies seen apparently lack a

Dobson, W. Paradisus amissus

leaf before title, possibly blank. The imprimatur is dated 'Mar. 12. 1749–50.' A second volume was published in 1753.
'Primam hominis noxam, vetitaque ex arbore fœtus'
O.

D345 — [fine paper]
Watermark: Strasburg bend.
L(77.k.6),*MR*.

D346 — Solomon de mundi vanitate. Poema Matthæi Prior arm. latine redditum, per Guil. Dobson... [Book I.] *Oxoniæ, e theatro Sheldoniano*, 1734.
4°: π² A–I⁴; *i–iv, 1 2–71 72 blk.*
Rothschild 1687. Latin and English text.
'Audite, O gentes; linguis animisque favete'
L(11630.e.27),O(2),OW,*MR; CLU-C*,CSmH, CtY,IU,TxU.

D347 — — [Book II.] *Oxoniæ, e theatro Sheldoniano*, 1735. (*LM* May)
4°: π² A–L⁴ M²; *i–iv, 1 2–91 92 blk.*
'I nunc, disce moras & tædia longa dierum'
L(11630.e.27),O(3),OW(2, 1 presentation copy?); CLU-C(2),CtY,IU,TxU.

D348 — — [Book III.] *Oxoniæ, e theatro Sheldoniano*, 1736.
4°: π² A–K⁴ L²; *i–iv, 1 2–83 84 blk.*
'Ergo age, pars nostri melior, vis vivida, vitæ'
L(11630.e.27, lacks π1),O(2),OW,C; CLU-C, CtY,IU,TxU.

D349 Doctor. The doctor and Bess. A satyr. *London, printed for J. Roberts*, 1736.
2°: A² B²; *1–3 4–8.*
'Lafeinte, a true sprout of the hipocrite race'
LVA-D; IU,MH,TxU(uncut).

— Doctor Anthony's... *For poems titled thus, see* 'Anthony, *Doctor*'.

D350 — Dr Bungey's recantation. [*London*] *Printed for J. Spoorn, near the Strand*, [1710.]
slip: 1 side, 1 column.
'Long I liv'd in dark privation'
A satire on Sacheverell.
L(C.121.g.9/154),Crawford; *MH,Harding*.

D351 — — [*London?* 1710.]
slip: 1 side, 1 column.
L(C.121.g.9/153).

D352 — Dr. Codex's fifth pastoral: humbly address'd to the people of every diocese in Great-Britain and Ireland. *London, printed for T. Cooper*, 1734. (*LM* June)
2°: A² B² C¹; *1–3 4–9 10 blk.*
'Ye moral cattle of my plains'
A satire on Edmund Gibson for his opposition to the nomination of Thomas Rundle to the see of Gloucester.
O.

D352·5 — Dr. Codex's pastoral letter versified; by way of caution against lukewarmness on one hand and enthusiasm on the other. To which is prefix'd an introduction fairly stating the case between both.

Dr. Codex's pastoral letter

London, printed for and sold by J. Brett, 1739. (*LM* Sept)
8°: A² B–D⁴ E²; *i–iv, 1 2–27 28 blk.* A1 hft.
'Extremes on either side are wrong'
Subscribed 'Edm' L——'; a satire on Edmund Gibson's pastoral letter.
MR.

— Dr. Crofts's exercise, 1713. *See* Trapp, Joseph.

D353 — Dr. Croxall to Sir Robert Walpole. *London, printed for Timothy Atkins, and sold by the booksellers of London & Westminster*, 1730. (*MChr* 19 Feb)
2°: A¹ B²; *i–ii, 1 2–4.*
Some copies were possibly issued without the title-leaf, including the Luttrell copy (dated Feb, 'gratis') sold at Sotheby's 16 Oct 1961. *Plomer* suggests the imprint is fictitious.
'If a truth may be ask'd, sir, pray what did it mean?'
A satire on Croxall's sermon of 30 Jan attacking the government; suggesting it was caused by Walpole's having refused his promotion.
L(C.131.h.1/4),O(lacks A1),OW(lacks A1), LdU-B(uncut); MH.

D354 — The doctor militant, or church-triumphant. To the tune of Packington's pound: By N.F.G. gent. [*London*, 1710.]
½°: *1–2,* 1 column.
'Bold whiggs and phanaticks, now strive to pull down'
In praise of Sacheverell.
MH, *Harding*.

D355 — Dr. Pepusche's song perform'd for his exercise in the Theatre at Oxford July 13. 1713. [*Oxford*, 1713.]
½°: 2 sides, 1 column.
'Hail queen of islands! hail illustrious fair'
Pepusch was the composer; the exercise was for the degree of Doctor of Music. Whether he wrote the words himself is uncertain.
LLP,O.

D356 — Dr. Radcliffe's advice to the ladies, and Dr. Garth's opinion to the beaux. With the ladies answer. *London, printed for M. Barrington*, 1711.
½°: 1 side, 2 columns.
'Cloe in love's affairs grown nice'
'Doctor, pray give a repetition'
Harding.

D357 — Dr. Woodward's ghost. Occasion'd by a passage in Dr. Mead's preface to his treatise of the small-pox and measles, severely reflecting on that gentleman's memory... By Dr. Andrew Tripe, nephew to the late doctor. *London, printed for Jeremiah Reason*, 1748 [1747]. (9 Dec)
4°: A² B–C²; *i–iv, 1 2–8.*
'From soft Elysium's fair retreats'
The same pseudonymous author wrote *The small-pox*, 1748.

Dr. Woodward's ghost

L(11630.c.13/21, ms. date 9 Dec 1747; 840.k.4/3; 841.b.84/6); KU.

D358 — The doctor's decade; | Or the ten utensils of his trade. | For in ten words, the whole art is compriz'd; | For some of the ten are always advis'd... [*Dublin*, 172–?]
½°: *1–2*, 2 columns.
'These few evacuations'
L(C.121.g.8/12).

Doctors. The doctors miscellany... or, a curious collection of wondrous cures, amorous poems, sonnets and translations. *London, printed for W. Trott; sold by the booksellers of London & Westminster, 1731.*
12°: pp. vi, 66.   EU.
The dedication is signed 'your wou'd be doctor, J.M.' Listed with miscellanies in *CBEL* II. 201 as 'possibly by one hand'.

D359 Dodd, J., *philomathes.* The irresistible fair, a poem. Humbly inscrib'd to that incomparable, and celebrated beauty Miss F--y Be--l. *London, printed for the author; sold by A. Dodd, E. Cook, and by the pamphlet-sellers of London & Westminster, 1739. (LM* March)
4°: A–B⁴; [2] i–iv, *1–10.*
'When souls are struck with beauteous heav'nly forms'
L(11630.c.4/9); CSmH,CtY(uncut).

Dodd, James. The trooper's merry miscellany. Or poems on several occasions. *London, printed for the author, and sold by him only at the Bull-Head Pale-Ale-House in Fleet-street, 1727.*
8°: pp. *1–56* '55–57'.   L.

— [reissue] The second edition. *London, printed for the author; sold by the booksellers of London & Westminster, 1729.*
8°: pp. 61.   L; DFo.
Cancel title, and three leaves substituted for I².

D360 — Tragedy speeches burlesqu'd. [*London?* 172–?]
slip: 1 side, 1 column.
Five short burlesques, with the original passages from Lee and Young.
Burlesque 1: 'Collected in myself I'll rule alone'
Signed 'James Dodd'.

O-JJ.

Dodd, William. The African prince... and Zara's answer. An elegy on the death of his royal highness Frederick prince of Wales. And Diggon Davy's resolution... The second edition. *London, printed for Mr. Waller, & Mr. Ward, 1755.*
4°: pp. 44.   O; ICN.

— Poems. *London, printed by Dryden Leach, for the author, 1767.*
8°: pp. viii, 271.   L,O; CtY,MH.

Dodd, W.

D361 [—] 'The African prince now in England, to Zara at his father's court, a poetical epistle. [*London*] Payne, Bouquet. Price 6d.' (*BM* July 1749)
'Princes, my fair, unfortunately great'
Reprinted in Dodd's *Poems*, 1767. Continued by *Zara, at the court of Annamboe,* 1749.

D362 [—] Diggon Davy's resolution on the death of his last cow. A pastoral. *London, printed by J. Oliver; sold by M. Cooper, 1747. (BM,GM* Sept)
2°: *A*² B²; *1–3* 4–8.
'Beneath an hawthorn's bush, secreted shade'
Printed in Dodd's *Poems*, 1767. Apparently the same work as *A pastoral on the distemper* listed by *CBEL, Halkett & Laing.*

L(1973),O.

D363 [—] A new book of the Dunciad: occasion'd by Mr. Warburton's new edition of the Dunciad complete. By a gentleman of one of the Inns of Court... *London, printed for J. Payne & J. Bocquet* [!], 1750. (*GM* July)
4°: A–D⁴ E²; *i–v* vi–viii, *1* 2–27 *28 blk.* A1 hft.
Some copies (e.g. LVA-D) correct the name in the imprint to 'Bouquet'.
'Of revolutions in that state I sing'
Listed among Dodd's writings in his *Thoughts in prison.* An attack on Warburton.
L(12273.m.1/21; 11630.c.6/6; 11630.d.2/8, —A1; 11630.e.13/1, —A1; 840.k.4/17, —A1), O(—A1),OW,E,LdU-B + ; CSmH(uncut),CtY (uncut),ICN,MH(ms. date 30 July),TxU + .

D364 [—] — *Dublin, printed by James Esdall, 1750.*
12°: A–C⁶; *i–ii* iii–vi, 7 8–34 *35–36.* C6 advt.
C,DK,DN; IU.

D365 [—] Zara, at the court of Annamaboe, to the African prince, now in England. *London, printed for J. Payne and J. Bouquet, 1749. (SR* 30 Aug)
4°: *A*¹ B–D² E¹; *1–3* 4–15 *16 blk.*
Deposit copies at O,GU,SaU. Listed in *GM* Aug.
'Should I the language of my heart conceal'
Reprinted in Dodd's *Poems*, 1767. A continuation of *The African prince* above.
L(C.70.f.1/9),O,GU,SaU.

Doddridge, Philip.
Doddridge's Hymns were published posthumously (edited by J. Orton) at Shrewsbury in 1755.

D366 — 'The principles of Christian religion, expressed in plain and easy verse, and divided into short lessons for the use of little children. [*London*] *Printed and sold by M. Fenner.* Price 4d.' (*LDP* 6 Dec 1743)
'Now for a while aside I'll lay'

D367 — — divided into short lessons for the use of children and youth... The second edition. *London printed, and sold by J. Waugh, 1748.*
12°: A–C⁶; *i–iii* iv–vi, 7 8–35 *36 blk.*
Divided into 24 lessons.
LDW.

Dodington, G. B. *baron*

D368 Dodington, George Bubb, *baron Melcome*. Ad somnum. [*Oxford*, 1708.]
½°: 2 sides, 1 column.
> Reprinted from *Exequiæ celsissimo principi Georgio*, 1708. With engraved head- and tail-piece, used elsewhere in that volume.
'O somne, blandum numen amantibus'
Signed 'Geo. Bubb'.
L(C.38.1.6/25).

D369 [—] An epistle from John More, apothecary of Abchurch-lane to L--- C-------, upon his treatise of worms. *London, printed for W. Webb*, [1743.] (*LDP* 29 Nov)
2°: *A*⁴; *1–2* 3–7 *8 blk.*
'The learned hold, that worms in time'
> Attributed to Dodington in Horace Walpole's copy at L, and in his ms. life of Sir Charles Hanbury Williams. A satire on Lord Carteret and the treaty of Worms.
L(163.n.2;C.57.g.7/13, Walpole's copy),O,O-*JJ*; CSmH,CtY.

D370 [—] — To which is subjoin'd, a letter from the Constitutional journal. '*London, printed for W. Web* [!]' [*Edinburgh*, 1743].
8°: A–B⁴; *1–2* 3–15 *16 blk.*
> Printed in Edinburgh by Robert Fleming on the evidence of the ornaments.
CtY,OCU.

D371 [—] An epistle to the right honourable Sir Robert Walpole. *London, printed for J. Walthoe*, 1726 [1725]. (*MC* Dec)
2°: *A*² B–C²; *1–3* 4–11 *12.* 11 err; 12 advt.
'Tho' strength of genius, by experience taught'
> Attributed to Dodington in the *European Magazine*, June 1784. There are ms. attributions to Dodington in three copies of the fourth edition below.
L(162.n.67),C; MH.

D372 [—] — The second edition. *London, printed for J. Walthoe*, 1726. (*SR* 4 Jan)
2°: *A*² B–C²; *1–3* 4–11 *12.* 12 advt.
> Deposit copies at L,O,E,EU.
L(643.m.13/23),O(2),E,EU,EtC+; CSmH,CtY, ICN(uncut),MH,TxU(cropt)+.

D373 [—] — The third edition. *London, printed for J. Walthoe*, 1726.
2°: *A*² B–C²; *1–3* 4–11 *12.* 12 advt.
L(1962); NjP.

D374 [—] — The third edition. *Dublin, printed in the year* 1726.
8°: *A*⁴; *1–2* 3–8.
O,DN; ICN,MH,PU.

D375 [—] — The fourth edition. *London, printed for T. Cooper*, 1741.
2°: π¹ A–B²; *i–ii, 1* 2–8.
> Ms. attributions to Dodington in the copies at L,LdU-B,CtY.
L(11651.m.80),LdU-B; CtY,MH,NN-B.

Dodsley, R.

Dodsley, Robert. A muse in livery: or, the footman's miscellany. *London, printed for the author*, 1732. (*GSJ* 25 April)
8°: pp. 151.   L,O; CtY,MH.
> Dedication signed.

[—] A muse in livery. A collection of poems. *London, printed for J. Nourse*, 1732.
8°: pp. 102.   O; CtY,MH.
> The relationship between this and the following issue is obscure, but this title-page was clearly printed on the final leaf of H⁴. Many copies lack the frontispiece.

— [another issue] The muse in livery... The second edition. By R. Dodsley. *London, printed for T. Osborn, & John Nourse*, 1732.
L; CtY,MH.
> This issue has a list of subscribers added on A2–4. A third of the copyright formed part of lot 50 of a trade sale attributed to Lintot, 27 Nov 1739 (cat. at O-JJ), was re-purchased by him and reappeared in a sale of 8 Nov 1743.

— Colin's kisses. Being twelve new songs design'd for music... *London, printed for R. Dodsley; sold by T. Cooper*, 1742. (*LM* Nov)
4°: pp. 16.   L; DLC,MH.
> An engraved edition with the music was published in Dec, copy at L.

D376 [—] The art of preaching: in imitation of Horace's Art of poetry. *London, printed for R. Dodsley*, [1738.] (18 April)
2°: *A*¹ B–E² F¹; *i–ii, 1*–18.
> Date from *Straus, Dodsley*; listed in *LM* April.
'Should some strange poet, in his piece, affect'
> Reprinted in Dodsley's *Trifles*, 1745; *Straus* quotes an advertisement from *LEP* 24 Aug 1738 giving Dodsley's name.
L(643.1.28/25; 643.m.15/4),O(2),OW(2, 1 uncut),C,LdU-B+; CtY(2),DFo,ICN,MH,TxU+.

D377 [—] — '*London, printed for R. Dodsley*' [*Edinburgh*, 1738].
8°: A–C⁴; *1–2* 3–22 *23–24 blk.*
> Printed in Edinburgh on the evidence of the ornaments.
L(1966,–C4),EN; CSmH,MH.

D378 [—] — '*London, printed for R. Dodsley*' [*Glasgow?* 1738/42].
8°: π² A–B⁴ C²; *i–iv, 1*–19 *20.* π1 hft.
> The ornament on p. iii was used by Robert Sanders in Glasgow, 1713; the TxU copy is bound with Edinburgh piracies.
L(11660.aa.10),C,GU(ms. date 1742); KU,MH, TxU.

D379 [—] — *London, printed: Dublin re-printed by and for Sylvanus Pepyat, and for Oliver Nelson*, 1738.
8°: A–C⁴ (A2 as 'B2'); *1–2* 3–22 *23–24 blk.*
DK,DN(–C4),DT(–C4).

Dodsley, R. The art of preaching

D380 [—] — *London, printed: and Belfast, re-printed by Francis Joy,* 1738.
8⁰: A–B⁴ C⁴(−C4); *1–2 3–22.*
    C4 not seen, possibly blank. Reprinted by Franklin in Philadelphia, 1739 and 1741.
    PU.

D381 [—] Beauty: or the art of charming. A poem. *London, printed for Lawton Gilliver,* 1735. (6 Jan)
2⁰: *A² B–E²; i–iv, 1 2–12 17–18 19–20.* A1 hft; E2 advt.
    Date from *Straus, Dodsley;* listed in *LM* Jan.
    'What gives the maiden blush its loveliest dye'
    L(11657.m.23; 11630.h.54, −A1, E2),LG(−A1, E2),O,E,LdU-B; CSmH(2, 1 uncut),CtY(2),ICN, MH,TxU(2)+.

D382 [—] — [*Dublin, printed for Edward Exshaw,* 1735.]
8⁰: *A⁴; 1 2–8.* 8 advt.
    Drop-head title only. Advertisements on p. 8 for Exshaw's publications, including the *London Magazine* for Dec 1734.
    LVA-F,DA; IU.

D383 [—] An epistle from a footman in London to the celebrated Stephen Duck. *London, printed for J. Brindley; sold by J. Roberts, J. Wilford, E. Nutt, & A. Dodd,* 1731. (*GSJ* 27 Feb)
2⁰: A–B²; *1–3 4–8.*
    'To thee, the happy fav'rite of the nine'
    Reprinted in Dodsley's *A muse in livery,* 1732.
    O,OW.

D384 — An epistle to Mr. Pope, occasion'd by his Essay on man. *London, printed for L. Gilliver,* 1734. (*LM* Nov)
2⁰: *A² B²; 1–3 4–8.*
    'Great bard! in whom united we admire'
    L(1961),O,LdU-B; CSmH,MH,TxU(2).

D385 [—] The modern reasoners: an epistle to a friend. *London, printed for Lawton Gilliver,* 1734. (*LEP* 31 Jan)
2⁰: *A² B² C¹; 1–3 4–10.*
    'Whence comes it, *** that each pretending fool'
    Reprinted in Dodsley's *Trifles,* 1745.
    L(11630.h.44),O(2),LdU-B(uncut); CSmH,CtY, ICU,MH(2),TxU(3)+.

D386 [—] — '*London, printed for Lawton Gilliver*' [*Edinburgh*], 1734.
8⁰: *A⁴ B²; 1–4 5–12.* A1 hft.
    Printed by Robert Fleming on the evidence of the ornaments.
    L(1488.bb.29),O; MH,NN(uncut).

D387 — Pain and patience. A poem. *London, printed for R. Dodsley; sold by M. Cooper,* 1742 [1743]. (*LDP* 25 Nov 1743)
4⁰: *A⁴ B⁴; 1–6 7–15 16 blk.* A1 hft.
    Rothschild 801. The date in the imprint is apparently misprinted.
    'To scourge the riot and intemperate lust'
    Dedicated to Dodsley's physician, Peter Shaw, after Dodsley's recovery; a discussion

Dodsley, R. Pain and patience

of the illnesses caused by excess and the role of patience in cure.
L(11630.b.7/11*),O(uncut),LdU-B; CSmH,CtY (−A1),ICN,MH,NN(−A1).

D387·2 [—] Pain and patience a poem on the indisposition of her [ladyship] the Countess of Y---th. *London, printed for A. More,* [1743?]
4 pp.
    Maurice Johnson's copy, sold as recorded below, was annotated as being by Dodsley. This edition seems likely to be unauthorized, possibly satirizing the Countess of Yarmouth; and there is no certainty that the text is the same.
    (*Sotheby's,* 23 March 1970, lot 26A.)

D388 [—] Servitude: a poem. To which is prefix'd, an introduction... Also a postscript... Written by a footman. In behalf of good servants, and to excite the bad to their duty. *London, printed for T. Worrall,* [1729.] (*MChr* 20 Sept)
8⁰: A–D⁴; *1–5 6–32.* 26 advt.
    In some copies (e.g. L,CtY) p. 6 is misnumbered '5'.
    'Brothers in servitude attend the song'
    The preface and postscript are said to have been written by Defoe.
    L(11631.bb.26),O; CLU-C,CtY,ICN,InU,TxU.

D389 [—] [reissue] The footman's friendly advice to his brethren of the livery... To which is prefix'd, an introduction... Also a postscript... By R. D. now a footman. *London, printed for T. Worrall,* [1730.] (*DJ* 13 Feb)
8⁰: A⁴(±A1) B–D⁴ E¹; *1–5 6–32 33–34.* E1 advt.
    Advertisement leaf E1 conjugate with cancel title, sometimes bound before the title.
    L(8407.ccc.33/1, −E1),MR-C; CLU-C(+cancelland title),CtY,IU.

D390 [—] Verses on the grotto at Twickenham. By Mr. Pope. Attempted in Latin and Greek. To which is added Horti Popiani: ode sapphica. Also the cave of Pope. A prophecy. *London, printed for R. Dodsley; sold by M. Cooper,* 1743. (13 Oct)
4⁰: *A⁴ B⁴; 1–5 6–16.*
    There appear to be minor movements of the type between copies, and most have the pressfigure 2 on p. 4. The variations are not consistent from copy to copy, but they may represent a reimpression with subsequent mixing of sheets. Date from *Straus, Dodsley;* listed in *GM,LM* Oct.
    'Hic ubi sublustri sylvae nutantis in umbra'
    L(11656.r.7/10),LVA-D,O,C,LdU-B; CtY,ICN, IU,MH(2, 1 uncut),TxU(2)+.

D391 **Dog.** The dog in the wheel. A satyr. With the character of a disinterested, peaceable and loyal stat----n, in opposition to that of a busy, turbulent, sp---hing p---r. *London, printed in the year* 1705. (18 Dec, Luttrell)
4⁰: *A² B–D²; 1–4 5–15 16 blk.* A1 hft.

The **dog** in the wheel

On pp. 11–15, 'The man of honour', by Charles Montagu, earl of Halifax.
'Once in a certain family'
Against John Thompson, lord Haversham.
L(164.n.75, Luttrell),OW; TxU.

D392 — The dog-kennel to be lett: or, Esquire Bicker-staff's prophecy concerning the downfal of the sharpers. *London, printed in the year* 1709.
½°: 1 side, 2 columns.
Large cut of named animals at head.
'O yes, if in country or town'
Harding.

'**Dogerel, Daniel.**' The life of Cato the censor, 1714. *See* L181.

'**Doggrel, Humphrey,** *esq;*' The old fox chas'd, 1742. *See* O112.

'**Doggrel,** *Sir Iliad.*' *Used as a joint pseudonym by Sir Thomas Burnet and George Duckett for their mixture of prose and verse,* Homerides: or, a letter to Mr. Pope, 1715, *and for* Homerides: or, Homer's first book moderniz'd, 1716; *for the latter, see* Duckett, George.

D393 Doleful. The doleful complaint of Sir Humphry Mac-----h, on the loss of his election at Oxford. *London, printed in the year* 1705.
½°: 1 side, 2 columns.
'Ye freeholders most dear/Of Cardigan-shire'
A satire on Sir Humphry Mackworth.
DG.

D394 Don. Don, a poem. *London, printed in the year* 1655. *Re-printed with additions,* 1742.
4°: π⁴(−π1) A–T² U¹[=π1]; *i–vi, 1* 2–78.
The 1655 edition is not recorded by *Wing*; reprinted again in 1814.
'Pallas, immortal maid, thy succour bring'
On the river and the seats it runs by.
E.

D395 — Don Francisco Sutorioso. A poem. *London, printed for, and sold by H. Hills,* 1710.
12°: A⁸ B⁴; *1–4* 5–24. A1 hft.
'We sing the man, who from clove-pudding'
A satire on Francis Taylor; cf. *The upstart,* 1710.
L(11601.dd.11/2),O(2, 1 uncut, −A1),DT; *CU,* NN,NjP.

D396 — Don Francisco's descent to the infernal regions, an interlude. *London, printed for S. Slow, and sold [by R. Walker] next E. Lynn's, a whipmaker, over-against Devereux-court, without Temple-Bar,* 1732. (*GM* 26 Feb)
4°: A–B⁴; *1–2* 3–14 *15–16.* B4 advt.
'What means this dreadful bustle on the shore'
A dialogue between Colonel Francis Charteris and Mother Needham.
L(C.118.c.2/4).

Don

D397 — Don Poetastro's epistle to J--n B--ggs, in hudibraick [!] verse. *[Edinburgh] Printed in the year* 1735.
8°: A⁴; *1–2* 3–8.
'Altho' (my trusty friend) the muses'
To John Briggs, the bookseller?
LdU-B.

D398 Don, James. Britain's consolation, in triumph after lamentation... *Printed for the author, in the year* 1747.
8°: A⁸; *1–2* 3–16.
Rough provincial printing, probably Scottish.
'In Britain's lamentation'
James Don's name is given in the opening lines. Celebrating the Duke of Cumberland's defeat of the Jacobites.
E.

D399 [—] [dh] Britain's lamentation, and hopes of triumph. [1745/46.]
8°: A⁴; *1–8.*
'Don Carolus, my namesake's son'
Signed 'J.D.S.I.D.'. For Don's authorship see the preceding. A lamentation for the early Jacobite successes.
E.

D400 Donaldson, James. A panegyrick upon the most ancient, curious, honourable and profitable art of weaving. *Edinburgh, printed by John Moncur,* 1712.
4°: A⁴; *1* 2–8.
'From what bewitch'd unhappy ignorance'
L(11632.df.8/1).

D401 — A panegyrick upon the most honourable, ancient and excellent art of wright-craft. *Edinburgh, printed by John Moncur,* 1713.
4°: A–C⁴ (A1ᵛ as 'A2'); *1* 2–24. 24 err.
'Wright-craft, this art who rightly would define'
L(11632.df.8/2).

D402 — A panegyrick upon the mysterious art of malting and brewing. *Edinburgh, printed by John Moncur,* 1712.
4°: A–C²; *1–2* 3–11 *12 blk.*
'In ancient times whilst sublime arts did ly'
L(11631.bb.95).

D403 Donore. The Donore ballad. Inscrib'd to the praise of the worthy M.B. Drapier. Written on the occasion of putting up his head in Truck-street. ⟨*Dublin, printed by C. Carter,* 1724–5.⟩
½°: 1 side, 1 column.
'Ye loving Hibernians come listen a while'
In praise of Swift.
L(C.121.g.8/38, cropt); CtY(mutilated).

D404 Dorinda. Dorinda: or, the grove in tears. A pastoral elegy towards the character of that excellent, and universally lamented lady, the... Countess of Euston. *London, printed for the author,* 1743. (*LDP* 4 April)

Dorinda: or, the grove in tears

   2°: *A*² B–D²; *1–3* 4–15 *16 blk.*
   Rothschild 232. A copy from Tom's Coffee
   House dated 5 April is in the Lewis Walpole
   Library.
   'O'erwhelm'd in grief, with horrid thoughts
   opprest'
   L(11651.m.90),O; DFo,ICN,MH(uncut),NjP.

D405 — — A pastoral elegiac essay... The second
edition, with the addition of a poem, in Miltonic
verse, to her immortal memory. *London, printed for
the author, and sold by M. Cooper, and at the
pamphlet shops in Pall Mall, St. James's Street, and
Charing Cross, &c.,* 1743. (*LDP* 12 April)
   2°: *A*¹ B–C² D¹; *1–3* 4–12.
   A and D have been seen to be conjugate.
   Addition: 'Could piety or virtue ought avail'
   L(1489.d.40); CSmH,MH.

D406 — — The third edition, with the addition...
*London, printed for the author, and sold by M.
Cooper...,* 1743. (*LDP* 20 April)
   2°: *A*¹ B–C² D¹; *1–3* 4–12.
   From the same setting of type as the second
   edition, revised. The KU copy adds D²,
   pp. *1* 2–4, containing 'Alexis: or, the distrest
   shepherd. A complaint for the loss of Belinda.
   In imitation of that celebrated poem in the
   six-hundred and third Spectator'; another
   copy, bound separately, is at L(1870.d.1/25).
   Alexis: 'My time, O ye muses! was happily spent'
   'Alexis' is an imitation of John Byrom's poem,
   which does not appear to have been published
   separately.
   L(643.l.25/24); CtY,KU,OCU.

[Dorman, Joseph.] The curiosity: or, the gentleman and lady's general library. *York, printed by
Alexander Staples,* 1738.
   8°: pp. 151.   L; CLU-C,CtY.
   The volume contains a ballad opera, 'The
   woman of taste' (otherwise known as 'The
   female rake') which is generally attributed to
   Dorman, as well as a good deal of prose.

[—] — The second edition much improved.
London, printed for James Hodges, 1739.
   12°: pp. 201.   L,O; CtY,MH.
   There are additional poems not by Dorman.

D407 **[—]** The female rake: or, modern fine lady. An
epistle from Libertina to Sylvia. In which is
contain'd, the a-la-mode system. *Dublin, printed:
London, reprinted; and sold by J. Wilford,* [1735.]
(*GM,LM* Sept)
   2°: *A*² B–E²; *i–iv, 1* 2–16. A1 frt.
   There was probably no Dublin edition.
   'While you, my dear, with philosophic eyes'
   Reprinted in Dorman's *The curiosity,* 1738.
   Answered by *True taste,* 1735.
   L(163.m.59),LVA-D,O(2),LdU-B; CU(–A1),
   CtY,ICN,MH(2, 1 dated 29 Sept, 1–A1),TxU+.

Dorman, J.

D408 **[—]** Folly. A poem. Written by the author of the
Female rake, and Rake of taste. *London, printed for
T. Cooper,* 1737. (*GM,LM* Feb)
   2°: *A*² B–E²; *1–5* 6–19 *20 blk.* A1 hft.
   'Enough, my muse, 'tis time to lay aside'
   LVA-D,O; IU(uncut),MH,OCU(–A1),TxU(2,
   1 lacks E2).

D409 **[—]** The rake of taste. A poem, dedicated to
Alexander Pope, esq. *Dublin printed: London
reprinted; and sold by Mrs. Dodd, Mrs. Nutt, and by
the booksellers in town & country,* [1735.] (*DG*
3 Nov)
   2°: (frt+) *A*² B–D² E¹; *i–iv, 1* 2–14.
   There was probably no Dublin edition.
   'In vain, dear Jack, dost thou employ thy youth'
   Reprinted in Dorman's *The curiosity,* 1738.
   L(1482.f.35),LVA-D(2),O(2, 1–frt),OA; CSmH,
   CtY,ICN,MH(–frt),TxU(2)+.

Dorrington, Theophilus. Devotions for several
occasions, ordinary and extraordinary, in psalms,
and hymns, and spiritual songs; collected from the
holy scriptures. *London, printed for J. Wyat,* 1707
(*WL* July)
   12°: pp. xx, 346.   L,O.

[—] A poem on the arrival of the king, 1714. *See*
P584.

'Dorset, *Earl of.*' The new court, [1714/15.] *See*
N125–6.

D410 **Dotage.** Dotage. A poem, inscrib'd to a gentle-
man within a few years of his grand-climacterick
... By J.W. *London, printed for A. Moore; sold by
the pamphlet-shops of London & Westminster,* 1728.
   8°: B–E⁴; *1–2* 3–32.
   'Full five and fifty winters o'er thy head'
   On love and marriage.
   O,*LdU-B.*

D411 — — *London, printed for W. Mears, J. Brindley;
sold by the booksellers of London & Westminster,*
1729. (*MChr* 1 April)
   8°: B⁴(±B1) C–E⁴; *1–2* 3–32.
   A reissue with a cancel title.
   O; CtY.

D412 — Dotage. A poem. Written in imitation of Mr.
Dryden's style. *London, printed by J. Leake,* 1717
[1716]. (*PM* 6 Nov)
   8°: *A*⁴ B–D⁴; *1–7* 8–31 *32 blk.*
   A1 not seen, probably half-title.
   'Is there, in friendship, yet, a dearer name'
   L(11631.e.74,–A1).

'Dothat, Andrew.' A satyr on the Kentish-men,
1701. *See* S56.

Double. The double captive, or chains upon
chains: containing the amorous poems and letters
of a young gentleman, one of the Preston prisoners
in Newgate... *London, printed by J. Churchil, and*

The **double** captive

sold only at the Bluecoat Coffee-house...for the benefit of the author, 1718. (*PB* 1 Feb)
8°: pp. viii, 79.　　MH.
　　No price on title: no watermark.

— [fine paper]　L.
　　Watermark: fleur-de-lys on shield. The copy seen has no dedication leaf.

— [another issue]　CLU-C.
　　Cancel title, with 'Price one shilling' after imprint; no watermark.

D413 — [dh] The double-shaver, or, an advice to the barbers. [*Dublin*, 1725?]
4°: *A²*; 1–4.
　　The DT copy is bound with pamphlets of 1725.
'A scall'd sorry thing, assuming human shape'
　　A satire on a pimping barber.
DT.

— The double welcome. A poem to the Duke of Marlbro', 1705. *See* Defoe, Daniel.

[**Douglas, John.**] Pandæmonium: or a new infernal expedition. Inscrib'd to a being who calls himself William Lauder. By Philalethes, 1750. *See* P28.

D414 '**Douglas, William.**' The resurrection: a poem. In three parts. *London, printed for, and sold by G. Strahan, R. Hett, R. Dodsley, G. Lewis, & J. Brindley*, 1747. (*GM* April)
2°: *A²* B–G²; *i–iv*, 1–24.
　　Errata slip on p. 24.
'Whilst others sing the various chance of arms'
　　Clearly the poem written by Hugh Blair and his cousin George Bannatyne and then published by Douglas as his own; cf. Boswell's *Life of Johnson*, ed. Birkbeck Hill, I. 360.
CSmH.

'**Douglass, Gawin.**' A poem to the memory of the famous Archibald Pitcairn, [1713.] *See* Ramsay, Allan.

Dove. The dove. A poem, 1717. *See* Prior, Matthew.

Dovecote. The dove-cote: or, the art of breeding pigeons, 1740. *See* Dinsdale, Joshua.

Dower, E. The Salopian esquire: or, the joyous miller. A dramatick tale... To which are added, poems... *London, sold at Mr. Warren's, Mrs. Riggall's, Messieurs Thomas & Loyde, and at the Angel near Clerkenwell church*, 1738. (*GM* July)
8°: pp. 95.　　O; CSmH,CtY.
　　The play (in prose) was not acted. The poems occupy pp. 57–74. Apparently reissued in 1739 (copies at L,ICU).

D415 Dowglass, R. [An elegy] upon the much to be lamented death of her grace the Dutches of

Dowglass, R. An elegy

Queensberry and Dover, &c.; who departed this life October 20, 1709. [*Edinburgh*, 1709.]
½°.
'Amazing stroak! A princess great this day'
(*Maidment* 168.)

D416 Dowie, Thomas. The country man's companion: or, some meditations on the valuableness of a precious soul... Composed to common metre... *Edinburgh, printed by Thomas Lumisden & John Robertson, for the author*, 1743.
8°: A–E⁴ F²; *i–ii* iii–v vi, 7–44.
'O blessed life, where gospel-light'
L(11631.b.65),O,E.

D417 [—] A poem on regeneration, or, the new birth: composed into common metre...To which are added, a few remarks on the present rebellion. By the author of the Country-man's companion. *Edinburgh, printed by T. Lumisden & J. Robertson*, 1746.
8°: A–H⁴; *i–ii* iii–vi, 7–63 *64 blk*.
　　The 'Remarks' on the rebellion, starting p. 54, are in verse.
'The sov'reign lord of heav'ns and earth'
L(1960); OCl.

— 'A poem on the sufferings of Christ.'
　　On the title of Dowie's *The country man's companion*, 1743, he is described as 'author of a poem on the sufferings of Christ, printed about twenty years ago'; it has not been traced.

D418 Downes, James. A pindarick sacred to the memory of the illustrious James earl Stanhope... *London, printed for B. Cowse*, 1721. (April, Luttrell)
8°: *A⁴* B–C⁴; *i–viii*, 1–16.
'Ye sacred nine, from Helicon'
Murray Hill cat. 81/322 (Luttrell).

Downfall. The downfall of Bartholomew fair, [1735?] *See* Carey, Henry.

D419 — The down-fall of Cockburn's meeting-house. To the tune of, Come sit thee down my Phillis. [*Edinburgh?* 1714.]
½°: 1 side, 2 columns.
'We have not yet forgot sir'
　　According to a ms. note in the L copy, the meeting house collapsed at Glasgow in Aug 1714.
L(Rox.II.705),E.

— The down-fall of S——n and W——r, [1741/42.] *See* The independent Westminster electors toast, [1741/42.]

D420 — The down-fall of the counts. A new ballad. To the tune of Derry down, &c. *Dublin, printed in the year* 1746–7.
½°: 1 side, 2 columns.
'Oh! Conaught, dear Conaught, how it grieves me to tell'

The **downfall** of the counts

> On the aftermath of the riot at the Theatre Royal led by E. Kelly against Thomas Sheridan, when the members of Trinity College took their revenge on the young bloods Martin, FitzGerald, and Kelly.
> DT(ms. notes); CtY.

D421 — The downfall of Wrstminster-bridge [!]; or, my lord in the suds. A new ballad. To the tune of King John, and the abbot of Canterbury. *London, printed for H. Carpenter,* [1747.] (*GM, LM* Nov)
2°: *A*² < *B*¹; *1–3* 4–6.
'I sing not of battles, nor do I much chuse'
L(11626.h.11/7; T.13*/3),LG; CLU-C,CtY, MH,OCU,TxU +.

Drake. Drake upon Duck, 1735. *See* 'Drake, Benjamin'.

D422 '**Drake, Benjamin.**' 'Drake upon Duck. A poem on the celebrated Stephen Duck's Shunamite, Thresher's labour, Poverty, Cumberland, Royal marriage, and Queen's grotto. By Benjamin Drake, yeoman. [*London*] *Printed for J. Roberts.* Price 1s.' (*LM* Oct 1735)
> Printed in *GM* July 1735 (p. 383) with first line:
> 'Hail! Stephen Duck, with praise around begirt'
> The author's name must surely be pseudonymous.

Drake, James. The humours of New Tunbridge Wells at Islington. A lyric poem. With songs, epigrams, &c. Also imitations... *London, printed for J. Roberts,* 1734. (*GM* Feb)
8°: pp. 96.   L,O; CtY,MH.
> Treated as a miscellany by *Case* 393, though the preface is written in terms of a single author. Drake's name is revealed there; but it is possible that the preface is a hoax and the author a pseudonym mocking Stephen Duck.

D423 '**Drake, James,** *a sailor.*' The complaint. A lyric rhapsody; address'd to his genius, by James Drake, a sailor, now on board a small English ship. *Dublin, printed by James Hoey,* 1730.
8°: *A*⁴; *1–3* 4–8.
'Leave, teizing principle, my breast'
> The author is surely pseudonymous; a satire on Stephen Duck's success in a letter from Richard Love-Merit to Mr. Bavius.
DA; CSmH.

D424 **Drake, James,** *the late Dr., of Salisbury.* The lover. A poem. *London, printed for T. Cooper, W. Shropshire, & T. Gardner,* 1739. (*GM,LM* Dec)
2°: *A*² B–D²; *1–5* 6–15 *16 blk.* A1 hft.
'No more by fame mislead or glory fir'd'
SrS; CtY.

'**Drake, Peter,** *fisherman, of Brentford.*' The grotto, a poem, 1733. *See* Green, Matthew.

Dramatic

D425 **Dramatic.** The dramatic poetaster a vision. Humbly inscrib'd to the most illustrious the Viscount Nessuno. *London, printed for T. Cox, T. Astley, & S. Harding,* 1732. (*GSJ* 9 May)
2°: *A*² Aa¹ B–G² H¹; *i–ii, 1* 2–30. 4 err.
> Watermark: circular snake (cf. *Heawood* 3786–92).
'Pensively musing on the wayward fate'
L(643.m.15/16),*MR*; IU,MH(2, 1 uncut),OCU.

D426 — [variant paper]
> Watermark: star. Possibly another impression.
DFo,DLC.

D427 — The dramatick sessions: or, the stage contest. *London, printed for A. Moore,* 1734. (*GM* July)
2°: *A*² B–G²; *1–3* 4–28. 28 advt.
> Pp. 17–28 contain 'A dedication to a certain great man', in prose. Listed again in *GM* March 1735.
'Mighty nonsense, the goddess that reigns o'er the stage'
> A satire on contemporary dramatic writers.
O,OW(uncut); CSmH,CtY(lacks A1, G2),DFo (lacks E-G²),MH,TxU(lacks E-G²).

D428 **Draper.** [column 1] The Drapier anatomiz'd: a song. [column 2] A new song sung at the club at Mr. Taplin's, the sign of the Drapier's Head in Truck-street. To the tune of the Apprentices song in massonary [!]. *Dublin, printed in the year* 1724.
½°: 1 side, 2 columns.
'The Drapier I swear,/I love and revere'
New song: 'With brisk merry lays/We'll sing to the praise'
> In praise of Swift. 'The second song was reprinted in *Fraud detected* and in *The Hibernian patriot*, where it is attributed to Mr. Witheral' (*Drapier's Letters*, ed. Davis, 382).
L(C.121.g.8/35),LVA-F,C,DT.

D429 — The Draper's apparition to G-----e F-----r, a new poem. *Dublin, printed in the year* 1745.
8°: *A*⁴; *1–3* 4–7 *8 blk.*
'Whilst F——r without slumber lay'
> An attack on George Faulkner's editing of Swift's works, for including 'half-form'd embryo works'.
DK,DT.

— The Drapier's ballad, 1724–5. *See* Sheridan, Thomas.

'**Draper.**' The Dean's answer to David Mullan's letter, 1735. *See* D78.

D430 **Dream.** The dream, a poem... By Semper Anonimus. *London printed, and sold by S. Popping,* 1715. (11 May, Luttrell)
8°: *A*² B–D⁴ E²; *i–iv, 1*–28.
> Listed in *MC* May.
'One day, as I sat musing, all alone'

The dream, a poem

A naive attack on political life.
L(164.k.39, Luttrell); CLU-C,CtY.

[D431-2 = D29, 29·2] — The dream: a poem occasion'd by the death of... William III, 1702. *See* Daniel, Richard.

D433 — The dream. A poem, sacred to the blessed and glorious memory of her late majesty Queen Caroline. *London, printed for J. Roberts,* 1737 [1738?]. (*GM, LM* Jan 1738)
4°: A–C²; *1–2* 3–12.
'(Price Four Pence)' deleted from title of L copy. Listed in *LM* at 4*d.*, *GM* at 6*d.*
'How vain is grief, amidst the pomps of woe'
L(11630.c.1/5),LDW.

D434 — The dream of the Solan goose, with advice to robin red-breast, sent in a packet from Leith. *London, printed in the year* 1709. (*DC* 16 March)
8°: A⁴; *1–2* 3–8.
At head of p. 3, a bold leaf-patterned wood block (a variant block in one TxU copy). Advertised in *DC* as 'sold by J. Morphew'.
'I'm one of those who in Basse Isle'
Signed 'Thine own/Solan Goose'. A political fable, addressed to Harley.
L(1077.c.45),O,C,AdU,LdU-B(uncut)+; CSmH, CtY,IU,MB,TxU(2)+.

D435 — [another edition]
At head of p. 3, 15 type flowers grouped 3, 3, and 9.
OW,EU; ICN.

D436 — [another edition]
At head of p. 3, two rows of type flowers divided by a rule. Probably a piracy.
MH.

D437 — A dream: or, the force of fancy. A poem, containing characters of the company now at the Bath. With a key incsrted [!]. *London, printed for Edmund Curll,* 1710. (9 Oct, Luttrell)
8°: A⁴; *1–2* 3–8. 1, 8 advts.
''Twas now high noon,/The sun in all his warmer glories shone'
L(164.k.38, Luttrell),O,BaP,BrP; CtY,InU,NN.

D438 — The dream; the 24th. Sept. 1710. Occasion'd by the D--- of Sh---- leading the Qu---, and the L---- N---- G---- bearing the sword. [*London,* 1710.]
½°: 1 side, 1 column.
'Thrice did I hear Britannia's genius shriek'
Fears of doom under a tory government, with Charles Talbot, duke of Shrewsbury as lord chamberlain.
Rothschild.

D439 Dreamer. The dreamer's dream. *Dublin, printed by E. Waters,* 1713.
½°: 1 side, 1 column.
'Hey day, what's this? 'Tis very strange'
A satire on the Dublin election of 1713.
DG.

Drinking

D440 Drinking. Drinking by authority. Now who'd be sober? A new ballad. Occasion'd by the encouragement given to drinking in several late G--z--ttes. *London, printed for G. Lyon,* 1743. (*LDP* 21 April)
2°: A⁴; *1–2* 3–8.
Rothschild 234.
'The statesmen in or out declare'
O; MH,OCU.

— The drinking match, 1722–. *See* 'Wharton, Philip, *duke of Wharton*'.

D441 Drive. Drive on coachman. An humorous tale. Occasion'd by an affair lately discover'd in a family of quality. *London, printed for and sold by J. Brett,* 1739.
8°: A¹ B–C⁴ D²; *i–ii, 1* 2–20.
The copy at L may lack a half-title. A copy at Chatsworth has an erotic plate facing p. 17 which is probably original.
'Who woman would debar from ill'
An erotic tale.
L(P.C.31.f.9).

'Drogheda, Pady.' The true character of the Intelligencer, 1728. *See* T319.

Dromgold, Jean. An ode, to his eminence the Cardinal de Fleury [by John Lockman, with French translation by Dromgold], [1741.] *See* L219.

Drummond, Thomas. Poems sacred to religion and virtue. *London, printed for D. Wilson & T. Durham,* 1756.
8°: pp. xvi, 175.   L,O.

———————

[—] A letter to a friend: with two poems sacred to the memory of... Thomas Rattray, 1743. *See* L144.

D442 [—] A poem to the memory of the right reverend father in god, Dr. Thomas Rattray of Craighall. *Edinburgh, printed in the year* 1743.
8°: A⁴ B¹; *1–2* 3–9 *10 blk.*
'O! for a muse like his, that mourn'd in strains'
Reprinted in Drummond's *Poems,* 1756.
L(11631.d.46).

D443 [—] [dh] To the memory of Mr. David Drummond: addrest to a friend. [*Edinburgh,* 1741.]
4°: A²; *1–4.*
Printed by Ruddiman on the evidence of the ornaments.
'Forgive the muse, that, with a heart sincere'
Reprinted in Drummond's *Poems,* 1756. Erroneously attributed to Allan Ramsay in *Book collector* 10 (1961) 433.
E(3); NN-B.

[Drummond, William, *of Hawthornden.*] An essay, upon Polemo medinia [usually ascribed to Drummond] or the midden-fight, 1704. *See* E476.

Drunkard

Drunkard. The drunkard's looking-glass, [1711?]
See Ellis, William.

D444 Drury. The Drury-lane monster. Humbly inscrib'd to the old woman in Hand-alley. [*London*]
Printed for J. Roberts, [1717.] (*PB* 22 Jan)
½°: 1 side, 1 column.
'Near the hundreds of Drury a monster was
shown'
    A satire on Pope, Gay and Arbuthnot as
    authors of *Three hours after marriage*.
L(C.20.f.2/326),LSA,Rothschild.

[Drury, Robert.] The countess's speech to her
son Roderigo, [1731.] *See* C444.

D445 — Pulteney: or, the patriot. A poem. *London,
printed by R. Walker, for the author, and sold at the
White Hart, next E. Lynn, whip-maker, over-against
Devereux-Court without Temple-Bar*, [1731.] (*GSJ*
15 Feb)
4°: A–D²; *i–ii* iii–iv, 5–14 *15*; *16 blk*. 15 advt.
    The address is Walker's.
'Say oh! my muse, the glorious cause declare'
    In praise of Pulteney.
L(1485.fff.30),O.

[Dry, John.] Miscellaneous translations from
Bion, Ovid, Moschus, and Mr. Addison, 1716.
See Miscellaneous.

D446 [—] Merton walks, or the Oxford beauties, a poem.
*Oxford, printed for Edw. Whistler, and are to be
sold by J. Knapton, H. Clements, W. Smith, in
London*, 1717.
8°: A–D⁴; *1–2* 3–31 *32 blk*.
'Long in Augusta's courts had Venus reign'd'
    Ascribed to John Dry by the O catalogue.
    The attribution to George Woodward in
    CBEL is apparently an error resulting from a
    different 'The Oxford beauties' in his *Poems*,
    1730. See [Nicholas Amhurst], *Strephon's
    revenge: a satire on the Oxford toasts. Inscrib'd
    to the author of Merton walks*, 1718.
L(11631.bb.60),O(3, 1 with ms. notes),OW(3),
LdU-B; CSmH(uncut),CtY,ICN,MH,NjP+.

D447 [—] — The second edition. *Oxford, printed for
Edw. Whistler, and are to be sold by J. Knapton,
H. Clements, W. Smith, in London*, 1717.
8°: A–D⁴; *1–2* 3–31 *32 blk*.
    Apparently a reimpression, with some resett-
    ing of sheet A.
L(11641.bbb.39/1); CtY,MH.

Dryden, John.
*Some poems of Dryden are included here, despite his
death in 1700, in order to complete the account of the
piracies by Henry Hills.*

D448 [—] [dh] Absalom and Achitophel. A poem.
[*London*, 1708?]
4°: A⁴; *1*–8, 2 columns.

Dryden, J. Absalom and Achitophel

Macdonald 121. First published in 1681.
The relationship between this edition and the
following is obscure; this may be earlier than
1708, and it is not clear which edition is
referred to on p. 24 of the Hills editions
below: 'the book lately published in 4to is
very imperfect and uncorrect'. With a key
between the title and the text. *The second part
of Absalom and Achitophel*, 1709, 'printed and
sold by J. Read', is entered under Nahum
Tate.
'In pious times, e'er priest-craft did begin'
    Translated into Latin by William Coward as
    Absalon et Achitophel, 1723.
O; DFo(cropt),*MH*.

D448·5 [—] — The eight [!] edition. [col] *London,
printed by J. Read*, 1708.
4°: A⁴; *1*–8, 2 columns.
    Drop-head title only.
MR.

D449 [—] — *London printed, and sold by H. Hills*, 1708.
8°: A–C⁴; *1–2* 3–24. 24 advt.
    Signature C under 'his'. The advertisement
    says 'the book lately published in 4to is very
    imperfect and uncorrect in so much that
    above thirty lines are omitted in several
    places, and many gross errors committed...'
L(11650.cc.20/1),O.

D450 [—] — *London printed, and sold by H. Hills*, 1708.
8°: A–C⁴; *1–2* 3–24. 24 advt.
    Signature C under 'Trade'. Reissued with
    other Hills poems in *A collection of the best
    English poetry*, 1717 (*Case* 294).
L(C.124.b.7/4),O(5),C,EU,DA+; CtY,IU,MH,
TxU(2).

D451 [—] — To which is added an explanatory key
never printed before. *Dublin, printed by James
Hoey & George Faulkner*, 1727.
8°: *A⁴* B–D⁴ E²; *i–iii*, *1* 2–29 33–36. 36 advt.
DA,DN; DFo,TxU.

D452 — — Written by Mr. Dryden. To which is
added an explanatory key... *Dublin, printed by
James Hoey, & George Faulkner*, 1729.
8°: *A⁸* B⁸ C²; *1–4* 5–36.
DA.

D453 — — *Dublin, printed by and for James Hoey*, 1731.
8°: A–B⁸ C²; *1–2* 3–35 *36*.
DG.

D454 — — *Dublin, printed by and for James Hoey*, 1735.
8°: *A⁴* B–C⁴ D²; *1–3* 4–27 *28*.
DA,DK,DN.

D455 — Eleonora: a panegyrical poem, dedicated to the
memory of the late Countess of Abingdon. *London
printed, and sold by H. Hills*, 1709.
8°: A⁸; *1–2* 3–16.
    First published in 1692. Reissued with other

Dryden, J. Eleonora

remaindered Hills poems in *A collection of the best English poetry*, 1717 (*Case* 294).
'As, when some great and gracious monarch dies'
Dedication signed.
L(C.124.b.7/23),O,AdU; CtY,IU,MH,TxU.

D456 — The hind and the panther. A poem, in three parts... [*Dublin*] *Re-printed in the year 1725.*
8⁰: A⁴ B–H⁴ I(3 ll); *1–7 8–70*.
First published in 1687. No London edition of this period has been traced. I4 is possibly missing from the copy seen.
'A milk-white hind, immortal and unchang'd'
DA.

D457 —— *London, printed in the year 1742.*
8⁰: A⁴ B–G⁸; *i–iii iv–viii, 1 2–96.*
L(11634.aa.3); CLU-C.

D458 [—] Lucretius: a poem against the fear of death. With an ode in memory of ...Mrs. Ann Killigrew ... *London printed, and sold by H. Hills,* 1709.
8⁰: A⁸; *1 2–16.*
Two poems, originally printed in Dryden's miscellanies, 1685 and 1693. Reissued with other remaindered Hills poems in *A collection of the best English poetry*, 1717 (*Case* 294).
'What has this bugbear death to frighten man'
L(C.124.b.7/22),O,C,E; CSmH,CtY,MH.

D459 — Mac Flecknoe: a poem. By J. Dryden. With Spencer's ghost: being a satyr concerning poetry. By J. Oldham. *London, printed by H. Hills; sold by the booksellers of London & Westminster,* 1709.
8⁰: A⁸; *1–2 3–16.*
Dryden's poem first published in 1682.
'All humane things are subject to decay'
L(1485.w.32),O(2),CT(2),E,AdU+; CtY,MH, IU,TxU.

D460 [—] The medal. A satyr against sedition. By the author of Absalom and Achitophel. *London printed, and sold by H. Hills,* 1709.
8⁰: A⁸; *1–2 3–16.*
First published in 1682. Reissued with other remaindered Hills poems in *A collection of the best English poetry*, 1717 (*Case* 294).
'Of all our antick sights, and pageantry'
L(11657.i.2; C.124.b.7/18),O,E,LdU-B; CtY(2), IU,MH,TxU.

D461 — Religio laici: or, a layman's faith. A poem. *London printed, and sold by H. Hills,* 1710.
8⁰: A⁸ B⁴; *1 2–24.*
First published in 1682. Reissued with other remaindered Hills poems in *A collection of the best English poetry*, 1717 (*Case* 294).
'Dim, as the borrow'd beams of moon and stars'
L(C.124.b.7/54),O,C,AdU; CtY,IU,MH,TxU.

D...s. The D...s hue and cry, [1719.] *See* D5.

Du Bartas, Guillaume de Saluste, *seigneur.*
Burchett, Josiah: The ark. A poem. In imitation of Du Bartas, 1714. *See* B569–70.

Dublin

D462 **Dublin.** The Dublin-ballad. [*Dublin,* 1713/14.]
½⁰: 1 side, 2 columns.
'Come listen good people and I will relate'
On the disputed election of the lord mayor of Dublin. Answered by *Tit for tat,* 1714.
C; MH.

D463 — The Dublin intelligence. [*Dublin?* 1713?]
½⁰: 1 side, 1 column.
'Here's a house to be let'
C,Rothschild.

— The Dublin-jubilee, a new poem, 1725. *See* Nelson, Henry.

— The Dublin scuffle, 1729. *See* The Grubstreet cavalcade, 1727–.

D464 **Duchess.** The Dutchess of C——'s memorial. To the tune of, The dame of honour. [*London,* 1706.]
½⁰: 1 side, 2 columns.
On the other side, *General Fielding's answer,* [1706.]
'What tho' my name is toss'd about'
A satire on Barbara, duchess of Cleveland's bigamous marriage with Robert Feilding.
L(1872.a.1/158).

D465 — The dutchess's epistle to her son Don Pedro; occasion'd by his late promotion at court. *London, printed for T. Reynolds,* 1734. (*GM* March)
2⁰: A¹ B² C–D² E¹; *3–4 5–17 18 blk.*
'While vice and folly bear imperial sway'
DLC,ICN,OCU.

D466 **Duck.** The duck drowned in Parnassus or, the goose triumphant. Containing Philip Goose the Berkshire thatcher's poem. Presented to her majesty by...Lord Townshend, on Thursday the 29th of October, 1730. *London, printed for T. Roberts near Warwick Lane,* 1730.
4⁰: A²; *1–3 4.*
The imprint is probably fictitious.
'When Juno, Pallas and the Cyprian queen'
A satire on Stephen Duck's reception at court.
O.

'Duck, Arthur.' The thresher's miscellany: or, poems on several subjects, written by Arthur Duck. Now a poor thresher...though formerly an Eton-scholar... *London, printed for A. Moore,* 1730. (*MChr* Oct)
8⁰: pp. 24.   L,C; MH,TxU.
The copy at C has a note (? by Thomas Martin, 1697–1771) 'This all invention by Mr Curl to put off some odd pieces given him by WB & others, many years ago'; the poems by W.B. are noted in ms. Clearly inspired by Stephen Duck; 'W.B.' is probably William Bond, one of Curll's authors.

— [variant title?] The second edition.
L,LdU-B; ICU,IU.

—— The third edition. *London, printed for A. Moore*, 1731.

8º: pp. 24.   O; KU.

— [variant title?] The fourth edition.
      E; ICN.

Duck, Stephen. Poems on several subjects... which were publickly read by the right honourable the Earl of Macclesfield, in the drawing-room at Windsor-Castle, on Friday the 11th of September, 1730... *London, printed for J. Roberts; sold by the booksellers of London & Westminster*, 1730. (*DP* 28 Sept)

8º: pp. 32.   L,YU; IU.

> The first seven editions are mainly from standing type. Editions 1 & 2 have the same press-figures (4–3, 16–1, 23–3) and may represent merely a press-variant title; similarly, editions 3 to 6 have the same press-figures (10–1, 23–1, 28–2) except that copies of 5 and 6 sometimes have press-figures 28–1 or 28–3.

—— The second edition. (*DP* 30 Sept)
      O; CtY.

—— The third edition, corrected. (*DP* 2 Oct)
      L,O; CtY,MH.

—— The fourth edition, corrected.
      O; ICN,ICU.

—— The fifth edition, corrected.
      O; MH.

—— The sixth edition, corrected. (*DP* 5 Oct)
      O,LdU-B; InU.

> A copy at CtY, which adds the life of Duck (a²) after the title as in the following editions, probably represents a mixture of sheets.

The following account of the various states or impressions of the 'seventh edition' is highly tentative. One or two of the early states may be the result of binders' errors or mixed sheets. On the other hand, a few copies have been seen with anomalous press-figures, not recorded here; they may suggest piecemeal reprinting of some sheets.

— Poems on several subjects... read by the right honourable... The seventh edition, corrected. To which is added, some account of the author. *London, printed for J. Roberts; sold by the booksellers of London & Westminster*, 1730. (*DP* 9 Oct)

8º: pp. vi, 32.   OW; TxU.

> The 'account' is added as a² after the title. No frontispiece; ornament on p. 30. Probably sheet D of the preceding impression has been used in error.

—— [2]   O,WcC; DFo.

> No frontispiece. Sheet D has been rearranged to include two congratulatory poems on pp. 31–32; there is no ornament on p. 30.

—— [3]   OW; CtY,ICN.

> Frontispiece added, found in all subsequent issues by Roberts.

—— [4; title reads 'read in the drawing-room']
      L,LG; NN.

> This reading is found in subsequent London issues of 1730.

—— [4a; fine paper]
      Chatsworth.

> Watermark: fleur-de-lys on shield.

—— [5; reimpression]
      L,E; ICU,NN.

> Signature C under 'as' (previously under 'much'). This is by far the most commonly found state.

—— [6]   C; TxU.

> Signature D after 'blindly', not under it as in previous issues. Possibly this sheet only has been reimpressed.

—— The seventh edition, corrected. To which is added, some account... '*London, printed for J. Roberts; sold by the booksellers of London & Westminster*' [*Edinburgh*], 1730.

8º: pp. vi, 32.   L,GU.

> Printed by R. Fleming on the evidence of the ornaments.

—— The tenth edition, corrected... '*London, printed for J. Roberts; sold by the booksellers of London & Westminster*', 1730.

8º: pp. vi, 20.   L.

> Clearly a piracy.

— Poems on several occasions. By Stephen Duck, thresher. *Dublin, printed by S. Powell, for George Ewing*, 1730.

8º: pp. 31.   DG,DT.

> Contains only 'The thresher's labour' and 'The Shunamite'.

— Poems on several subjects... The eighth edition, corrected... *London, printed for J. Roberts; sold by T. Astley*, 1731. (*DP* 4 June)

8º: pp. 32.   Foxon.

—— The eighth edition, corrected... *Dublin, printed by and for J. Watts*, 1731.

8º: pp. vi, 31.   DA.

—— The eighth edition... *Dublin, printed by S. Powell, for George Ewing*, 1731.

8º: pp. 32.   DN.

—— The ninth edition. To which are added, several poems by the same author, not in any former editions. Also a copy of verses from a miller in Ireland to Stephen Duck. *London, printed for J. Roberts; sold by T. Astley*, 1733. (*LM* June)

8º: pp. 31.   O,DN; NN,TxU.

> Press-figures 7–5, 12–3, 23–4, 32–†. The order of the three editions listed here has not been determined, but the date 1733 is suspect for the later ones; an entry in Ackers's ledger

Duck, S. *Collections*

25 Jan 1742 for Astley, 'a new edition of Duck's poems, containing two sheets' probably relates to one of them.

— [another edition]
DFo,TxU.
Press-figures 10–2, 18–2, 26–1.

— [another edition]
CtY.
Press-figures 7–3, 12–3, 23–1, 29–3.

— Poems on several occasions. *London, printed for the author*, 1736. (*GM* May)
4°: pp. xl, 334.   L,O; CtY,MH.
Copies are normally watermarked with an eagle, but there are possibly fine-paper copies with no watermark (e.g. BaP). Printed (for the subscribers) by Samuel Richardson (*Sale* 192).

—— *London, printed for W. Bickerton*, 1736. (*LM* June)
8°: pp. xxxix, 312.   O,LdU-B; CtY,DFo.
Printed by Samuel Richardson (*Sale* 211).

— [reissue] To which is prefixed, an account of the author. By J. Spence... The second edition. *London, printed for W. Bickerton*, 1737.
L,O; CtY,DFo.
Two fourth-shares of the copyright appeared in the trade sale of Bickerton [1737?], and all four shares in the sale of C. Corbett, 23 Aug 1737 (cats. at O-JJ).

— Poems on several occasions. *London, printed for John Osborn, Samuel Birt, & James Hodges*, 1738. (*GM* Aug)
12°: pp. xlviii, 239.   LVA-D,O; CtY,DFo.
Shares of the copyright appeared in the trade sales of John Osborn, father and son (11 Nov 1746, 19 Nov 1751) and of S. Birt (5 Feb 1756).

— Curious poems on several occasions. Viz. I. On poverty. II. The thresher's labour. III. The Shunamite. All newly corrected, and much amended, by the author Stephen Duck. *London printed, and sold by John Lewis*, 1738.
8°: pp. 28.   L.

D467 — Alrick and Isabel: or, the unhappy marriage. A poem. *London, printed for J. Roberts*, 1740. (*GM,LM* April)
2°: *A*² B–E²; *i–ii* iii iv, *1*–16.
Printed by Samuel Richardson (*Sale* 261).
'In vain we forge coercive chains, to bind'
L(643.m.16/9),O; CLU-C,CtY(uncut),MH,MiU, TxU(2)+.

D468 —— *Dublin, reprinted by and for Geo. Faulkner*, 1740.
8°: *A*⁴ B⁴ C²; *i–ii* iii iv, *1*–16.
DA(2); CSmH,TxU.

Duck, S. *Every man in his own way*

D469 — Every man in his own way. An epistle to a friend. *London, printed for J. Roberts, & R. Dodsley*, 1741. (*LDP* 10 March)
2°: *A*¹ B–E² F¹; *i–ii*, *1* 2–18.
Printed by Samuel Richardson (*Sale* 274).
''Twere well, my Lælius, if I could pursue'
O; CtY,DFo,ICN,MH,TxU(2).

D470 — Hints to a schoolmaster. Address'd to the revd. Dr. Turnbull. *London, printed for J. Roberts, & R. Dodsley*, 1741. (13 Feb)
2°: *A*¹ B–C² D¹; *i–ii*, *1* 2–9 *10*. 10 advt.
Copy from Tom's Coffee House dated 13 Feb in Lewis Walpole Library; listed in *LM* Feb.
'Should you, my friend, employ your time'
MH,*NcU*,TxU.

D471 — An ode on the battle of Dettingen. Humbly inscrib'd to the king. *London, printed for R. Dodsley; sold by M. Cooper*, 1743. (*LDP* 15 Nov)
2°: *A*⁴; *1*–2 3–7 *8 blk.*
'Illustrious prince! by heav'n design'd'
L(C.57.g.7/9),O; CtY,MH.

D472 — A poem on her majesty's birth-day. *London, printed for J. Jackson, & T. Cooper*, 1735. (*LM* March)
2°: *A*² B²; *1*–4 5–8. A1 hft.
'O you the monarch's bliss, the muse's friend!'
CLU-C(–A1),MH.

D473 — A poem on the marriage of his serene highness the Prince of Orange, with Ann princess-royal of Great Britain... To which are added, verses to the author, by a divine. With the author's answer. *London, printed for Weaver Bickerton*, 1733–4. (*DJ* 15 March 1734)
2°: *A*² B–E²; *i–iv*, *1* 2–7 *8*, *1* 2–8.
Verses to the author and his reply on D–E².
Ms. corrections on pp. 1, 6 in all copies seen.
'Illustrious prince, forgive the feeble lay'
Verses: 'Who hopes to rival Milton's flame'
Reply: 'When I, in feeble verse, essay'd'
CLU-C,CtY,ICN(uncut),MH,TxU+.

D474 —— With the author's answer, and his poem on Truth and falsehood. *Printed in the year* 1734.
8°: A–C⁴; *i–ii*, *1* 2–8, *1* 2–8, *1* 2–6.
Clearly a piracy; its place of printing is obscure.
L(11602.ee.1/4),O.

D475 —— The second edition. To which are added, an imitation of Horace's Ode on Pindar, in a letter to the author, by a clergyman. With the author's answer. *London, printed for W. Reason*, 1735. (*DC* 23 Jan)
2°: *A*¹ B–E²; *i–ii*, *1* 2–7 *8*, *1* 2–8.
A reissue of the first edition of 1734 with a cancel title; no half-title seen.
TxU(uncut).

D476 — A poem written by Stephen Duck, esq; *Printed in the year* 1731.
8°: *A*⁴; *1* 2–8.
A piratical reprint of 'The thresher's labour',

Duck, S. A poem

printed in Duck's *Poems*, 1730. Possibly printed at Northampton; the copy seen belonged to Thomas Brittain of Chatton, Bedfordshire, whose own poems were printed there in 1740; the *Northampton mercury* projected an edition of Stephen Duck, 26 Oct 1730.
'The grateful tribute of these rural lays'
L(1965).

D477 — Royal benevolence. A poem. Most humbly address'd to... Queen Caroline. As it was presented... by the author, on Friday, the 2d of October, 1730... To which is annexed, a poem on providence... *London printed, and sold by W. Harris, and by the booksellers & pamphletsellers of London & Westminster*, 1730. (*MChr* Oct)
2°: A² B²; *1-2* 3-8.
Listed in MChr as sold by A. Dodd.
'Most bounteous queen, my grateful thanks I pay'
Providence: 'Could mortals taste of heavenly bliss and joy'
R. M. Davis, *Stephen Duck, the thresher poet* (1926) 43f. suggests that these poems, which were not collected in Duck's works, may not be authentic.
MH,TxU.

D478 — — The second edition. *London printed, and sold by W. Harris, and by the booksellers & pamphletsellers of London & Westminster*, 1730.
2°: A² B²; *1-2* 3-8.
Apparently a reimpression or a press-variant title.
OW.

D479 — — The third edition. '*London printed, and sold by W. Harris, and by the booksellers and pamphletsellers of London & Westminster*' [*Edinburgh*], 1730.
8°: A⁴; *1-2* 3-8.
Printed by R. Fleming on the evidence of the ornaments.
GU.

D480 — — *London: printed and, Dublin: re-printed and sold by George Faulkner*, [1730?]
8°: A⁴; *1-3* 4-8.
L(1961),C,DT.

D481 — To his royal highness the Duke of Cumberland, on his birth-day. April the 15th, 1732. *London, printed for J. Jackson*, 1732. (*GSJ* 18 April)
2°: A¹ B² (B1 as 'B2'); *3-4* 5-7 *8 blk.*
A half-title is possibly missing from the copies seen.
'Twelve times hath Sol his annual race begun'
L(11632.i.4),OW(uncut); ICN,MH.

D482 — Truth and falshood. A fable. *London, printed for J. Watts*, 1734. (*GSJ* 17 Jan)
2°: A² < B² < C¹; *i-iv, 1* 2-6.
Entered in *SR* 17 Jan; deposit copies at L,O,E,EU,AdU. Reprinted with a piratical edition of *A poem on the marriage*, 1734, D474.
'Soon as the iron age on earth began'

Duck, S. Truth and falshood

L(643.m.14/5),O(2),E,EU,LdU-B(uncut) + ; CLU-C,CtY,ICN,MH,TxU(2)+.

D483 — The vision. A poem on the death of her most gracious majesty Queen Caroline. *London, printed for J. Roberts, & J. Jackson*, 1737. (*GM,LM* Dec)
2°: A² B-C²; *i-iv, 1-7 8 blk.* A1 hft.
Printed by Samuel Richardson (*Sale* 212).
''Twas on the fatal day that claims a sigh'
L(643.l.28/29; 603.k.28/2),O(3, 1-A1),C, LdU-B; CSmH,CtY,ICN,MH,TxU(2)+.

D484 — — The second edition. *London, printed for J. Roberts, & J. Jackson*, 1737.
2°: A² B-C²; *i-iv, 1-7 8 blk.* A1 hft.
Apparently a reimpression. What appears to be a provincial piracy was advertised in *The curiosity: or, gentlemen and ladies repository* (Lynn, 1740; copy at O).
O.

[—] The year of wonders... By S——n D——k, 1737. *See* Y14.

D485 [**Duckett, George.**] Homerides: or, Homer's first book moderniz'd. By Sir Iliad Doggrel. *London, printed for R. Burleigh*, 1716. (*PM* 29 May)
12°: A-D⁶; *i-ii* iii-vi, 7-45 *46; 47-48 blk.* 46 advt.
Bond 46. Printed by John Darby according to the correspondence referred to below.
'O goddess! sing Achilles' choler'
The correspondence of Sir Thomas Burnet and Duckett makes it clear that Duckett wrote the poem and Burnet the preface. Early ms. note in the O copy 'by Mr. Thomas Burnet', in GM 'by Duccet'.
L(12247.h.2/1,-D6),O,GM(uncut); CSmH(uncut),CtY,MnU,TxU(uncut).

D486 [—] The Northumberland prophecy: with an introduction and a postscript. By Andrew Schethrum, esq; *London, printed for R. Burleigh*, 1715. (*DC* 21 Nov).
8°: A⁴ B-C⁴; *1-5* 6-23 *24 blk.* A1 hft.
The text of the prophecy only occupies pp. 13-14.
'Fre seventeen hondred twenty yere'
Sir Thomas Burnet's letter of 14 Dec 1715 to Duckett refers to 'my introduction to your prophecy'; for the identification see *The letters of Thomas Burnet to George Duckett, 1712-1722*, ed. Nichol Smith (1914) 259, 307.
AdU; *ICN*.

D487 **Dudley,** —, *Mr.* The first satire of Persius, translated into English verse by Mr. Dudley. *London, printed for J. Catterns*, 1739. (*GM,LM* March)
8°.
Listed in *Straus, Dodsley* under 3 April with a reference to *GA*; it has not been traced there,

Dudley, —. The first satire

> but presumably Dodsley's name appeared in an advertisement.
> (Pickering & Chatto cat. 259/3567.)

D488 Duel. The duel; a poem: inscribed to the right honourable W------ P-----y esq; *London, printed for A. Moore; sold by A. Dodd, E. Nutt, & J. Joliffe,* [1731.] (*GSJ* 1 Feb)
2°: *A*² B²; *1–2* 3–8.
'Forgive the daring rashness of the muse'
> The author wrote *A collection of poems,* 1731, and *A poem sacred to the memory of . . . Dan Poulteney,* 1731. In praise of Pulteney after his duel with John, lord Hervey.
O; CSmH,MH.

D489 — — The second edition. *London, printed for A. Moore; sold by A. Dodd, E. Nutt, & J. Joliffe,* [1731.]
2°: *A*² B²; *1–2* 3–8.
> Apparently a reimpression.
L(1489.d.39),O; CtY,NjP,OCU.

D490 — — The third edition. *London, printed for A. Moore; sold by A. Dodd, E. Nutt, & J. Jolliffe,* [1731.]
2°: *A*⁴; *1–2* 3–8.
> A new edition.
L(643.m.15/11).

D491 — — The fourth edition. *London, printed for A. Moore; sold by A. Dodd, E. Nutt, & J. Jolliffe,* [1731.]
2°: *A*⁴; *1–2* 3–8.
> Apparently a reimpression.
L(1489.d.38).

D492 — — *London,* ⟨*printed*⟩ *for A. Moore,* [1731.]
4°: *A*²; *1–2* 3–4.
> A piracy.
L(C.116.i.4/58).

D493 — — '*London: printed by A. Moore*' [*Dublin*], 1731.
8°: *A*⁴; *1–3* 4–8.
> A Dublin reprint; the DFo and IU copies are in Dublin pamphlet volumes.
DA; DFo,IU.

D494 — A duel and no duel; or, the skirmish of the West-India heroes. A burlesque account of the . . . quarrel between Sir C——r O——le, and Governor T——ey . . . By an honest sailor. *London, printed for G. Foster,* 1743.
8°: A–C⁴ D¹; *1–2* 3–26.
'When sea and land shall disagree'
> On Sir Chaloner Ogle's assault on Edward Trelawny, governor of Jamaica.
MH,NN.

D495 — — *London, printed for T. Davis,* 1743.
8°: *A*⁸; *1* 2–16.
NN.

Du Fresnoy, C. A.

Du Fresnoy, Charles Alphonse.
The compleat art of painting. A poem. Translated from the French, 1720. *See* C324.

Du Halley Descazeaux, Michel. *See* Descazeaux, Michel Du Halley.

Duick, John. A memorial for Britons. Verses written by J. Duick, during the course of the rebellion, and published in the London Courant, according to the following dates. [*London*] *Published according to act of parliament by Tho. Bakewell,* [1746.] (*BM* July)
½°. L(P&D).
> Engraving at head, the poems in letter-press.

— 'Scarborough: a poem in imitation of Mr. Gay's Journey to Exeter.'
> Listed in Richard Gough, *British topography* (1780) II. 456, almost certainly from Moses Browne, *Poems on various subjects* (1739) 205n, 'Written by Mr. John Duick, and printed in the year 1733.' In fact, first printed in *GM* 4 (1734) 155f, and see also p. 268n, 'now enlarged . . . and published in a miscellany, nam'd from it', i.e. *The Scarborough miscellany for the year 1733.*

D496 Duke. Duke Hamilton and Lord Moon. [*London,* 1712/–.]
slip: 1 side, 1 column.
> Rough woodcut at head.
'Duke Hamilton was as fine a lord'
> A popular ballad on the duel between James Douglas, duke of Hamilton and Charles, baron Mohun, 15 Nov 1712.
C.

D497 — [dh] Duke H——ton's ghost to the Duke of Sh----ry. [col] *London, printed by R. Newcomb,* 1713.
2°: *A*²<*B*¹; ff. 1–3.
> Printed on one side of the leaf only.
'From peaceful bowers, and from silent shades'
> The Duke of Hamilton's ghost to Charles Talbot, duke of Shrewsbury. A tory satire in favour of D'Aumont and peace.
OW(lacks B1); *TxU.*

D498 — The Duke of Anjous farewel to Spain: or, a hue and cry after a little stray king, that was lately lost in a fog: with a reward of ten thousand pistoles, for any one that will bring him to his grandfather the French king. *London, printed by B. Taylor, near Fleetstreet,* [1709?]
½°: 1 side, 2 columns.
> Rough woodcuts above text.
'To all forreign nations now under the sun'
> The Duke of Anjou was Philip V of Spain.
MH.

The **Duke** of Marlborough

D499 — The Duke of Marlborough and the court's new toast. [*London?* 1714/15?]
½⁰: 1 side, 1 column.
'A health to Great Britain, and long may she flourish'
    Whig propaganda.
LSA.

— The Duke of Marlborough's arrival, 1709. *See* Welsted, Leonard.

D500 — The Duke of Marlborough's delight or his honours cordial advice to his fellow soldiers. To h [!] new tune. [*London?* 1712?]
½⁰: 1 side, 2 columns.
    Very badly printed.
'Set the glass round,/about you have a care sir'
    The date is suggested by O, but there are no specific references.
O.

D501 — The Duke of Marlborough's welcome to England. [*London?* 1709?]
½⁰: 1 side, 1 column.
    Woodcut trophy with Queen Anne at head.
'Welcome great hero from the Belgick plains'
DG(cropt).

D502 — Duke upon duke, an excellent new play-house ballad. Set to musick by Mr. Holdecombe. *London, printed for A. Moor near St. Paul's Church, and sold by the booksellers,* 1720. (*DP* 15 Aug)
2⁰: A¹ B²; *i–ii, 1* 2–4.
    Typeset music at head of p. 1. The order of editions has not been determined. There was also at least one engraved music edition, not listed here. An advertisement in *PB* 18 Aug reads 'The great demand there is for this ballad has tempted some pyrates to print a Grub-street copy of it; but gentlemen will easily distinguish the right copy, by the musick printed at the head of it, and by the goodness of the paper and character.'
'To lordings proud I tune my song'
    Clearly 'the ballad on Lechmere and Guise', a 'good part' of which is ascribed to Pope by Spence on Pope's authority; see *Twickenham Pope* VI. 217–24 and references. Another edition below, *A ballad on the battle,* has an early ms. attribution to Prior. *An answer to Duke upon duke,* 1720 is addressed to Pope as the author. A satire on the quarrel between Nicholas Lechmere, subsequently first baron Lechmere, and Sir John Guise.
L(1876.f.1/94, lacks A1),O,LdU-B; CtY(B² from 1723),IU,MH(2, 1 lacks A1),TxU(lacks A1).

D503 — — [*London,* 1720.] (24 Aug, Luttrell)
½⁰: *1–2,* 2 columns.
    Woodcut melody printed with first verse; the rough woodcut at head was also used in *A fight and no fight,* [1723].

Duke upon duke

MH(Luttrell, 'An abusive thing on Mr. Lechmere', cropt).

D504 — — [*London, printed by F. Clifton,* 1720.]
½⁰: *1–2,* 2 columns.
    Very rough woodcut music at head; no woodcut. The same music appeared in *An answer to Duke upon duke,* [1720], 'London: printed by F. Clifton...where may be had the right and true *Duke upon duke.'*
L(C.116.i.4/52, mutilated),O.

D505 — [*idem*] An excellent old ballad, called Pride will have a fall, as set forth in the true and delectable history of the deadly strife between the dukes of Guise and Lancastere which fell out in the reign of Richard Cœur de Lion. [*London*] '*Printed for J. Blare on London-Bridge*', [1720?]
obl 1⁰: 1 side, 4 columns.
    Large and well-cut woodcut at head of the first two columns; 'The end of the first part' at the foot of column four. Blare, the ballad publisher, died in 1706; this is a sophisticated imitation of a ballad printing.
L(1871.f.3/25),O; NjP.

D506 — [*idem*] A ballad on the battle of the two dukes. [*London,* 1720?]
slip: *1–2,* 1 column.
    Woodcut at head in popular style; but both the woodcut and the typography suggest a sophisticated imitation of a slip ballad. Early ms. title at head, 'Duke upon duke. An excellt new play house ballad' and (? in another hand) 'made... by Mat Prior'. Some ms. corrections to text.
Crawford.

D507 — Duke upon duke, an excellent new play-house ballad... *London, printed for A. Moor; sold by the booksellers,* 1723. (*DJ* 3 April)
2⁰: A¹ B²; *i–ii, 1* 2–4.
    Typeset music at head of p. 1. Advertised in *WEP* 6 April as 'An account of a late re-encounter. Duke upon duke'. A new edition of D502 on occasion of the quarrel between Nicholas baron Lechmere and William earl Cadogan. See also *A ballad, wrote in the time of Queen Elizabeth,* [1723] and *A fight and no fight,* [1723].
L(1970); InU,MH,OCU(Luttrell, April).

D508 Dulcinead. The Dulcinead variorum: a satyrical poem, in hudibrastick verse. *London, printed for A. Moore,* 1729. (*MChr* 16 May)
4⁰: A–B⁴; [2] i–iv, 1–9 *10.* 10 advt.
    Bond 103.
'Near T----b----r, as stories tell us'
    A tale of four beaux who love Dulcinea.
L(840.h.4/12),LDW; CtY.

Dullardiad. The Dullardiad, 1730. *See* Wagstaff, Humphry.

Dulness

D509 Dulness. Dulness cherish'd, or a burlesque on the epistle address'd to the town poets, with additional notes... By a lady of quality. *Dublin, printed in Dame-street, opposite Eustace-street, 1730.*
8°: *A⁴; 1–2 3–8.*
'Thus in a Grub Street state, how happy I'
A burlesque of *The inspir'd poet, 1730.*
LVA-F.

'**Dunbo,** *Mrs.*' A genuine epistle written sometime since, *1735. See* Jacob, Hildebrand.

Duncan, John. A poem on the proceedings, *[1726] is ascribed in a contemporary hand to 'John Dunkan of T.C.D.', and* Helter skelter, *[1726/27?] to 'John Duncan of T.C.D.' by the same hand. No one of this name is recorded in the registers of Trinity College Dublin. Possibly Jacob Duncan (matriculated 1725) or William Dunkin (B.A. 1729) was intended; the latter's name was sometimes spelt 'Duncan' by contemporaries.* Advice from fairyland, *1726, refers to* The conclave dissected, *[1725/26] and* Namby Pamby's lamentation, *[1726] as by 'Ph—pps & Dun—can'.*

[D510–11 = B95·5] **Dunces.** The dunces of Norfolk, a satire, *1740. See* A battle fought with the boasters, *1738.*

Dunciad. The Dunciad. An heroic poem, *1728–. See* Pope, Alexander.

D512 Duncombe, William. The Carmen sæculare of Horace. Translated by Mr. William Duncombe. *London, printed for John Watts, 1721. (DC 6 June)*
2°: *A² B–C²; i–vi, 1 2–5 6 blk. A1 hft.*
'Hear, Phœbus, source of light, heav'n's brightest grace!'
L(643.1.24/43),O; TxU.

D513 Dunghill. The dunghill and the oak. A fable; occasioned by the fable of the Oak and the dunghill. *London, printed for R. Walker and W.R., [1728.] (MChr 6 Dec)*
2°: *A–B²; 1–2 3–7 8 blk.*
W.R. in the imprint possibly stands for William Rayner.
'In Hedden fields, for curious pasture fam'd'
Occasioned by William Broome's poem; followed by *The better sequel better'd, 1729.*
TxU(ms. date, 9 Dec).

Dunkan, John. *See* Duncan, John.

Dunkin, William. Select poetical works of the late William Dunkin... *Dublin, printed by W. G. Jones, 1769, 70.*
4°: 2 vol. DN,DT; DLC,MH.
The second volume is 'printed by S. Powell'.

— [another edition, in 8°]
L,DN; DLC,MH.

Dunkin, W.

— [*idem*] The poetical works... *London, printed for W. Nicoll; sold by T. Beckett, 1774.*
4°: 2 vol. L,DN; CtY,TxU.

For poems attributed to 'John Duncan', 'John Dunkan', or 'Dun—can', by which names Dunkin is perhaps intended, see Duncan, John.

D514 [—] An account of a strange and wonderful apparition lately seen in Trinity-College, Dublin. Or, a dialogue between a poet and his grandmother's ghost. *[Dublin] Printed in the year 1734.*
12°: *A⁶ (A3 as 'B'); 1–2 3–12.*
On p. 12 'The end of the first part'; continued by *Mezentius on the rack,* D523.
'Her heavenly form shall with Belinda's live'
Mezentius on the rack seems to be clearly Dunkin's and this must be by the same author. A satire on Dalacourt with epigrams on Charles Carthy.
LVA-F,DA,DT.

D515 — Bœotia, a poem. Humbly addressed to his excellency Philip earl of Chesterfield... *Dublin, printed by George Faulkner, 1747.*
8°: *A–C⁴ (A2 as 'B2'); 1–2 3–22 23–24 blk.*
Rothschild 824. Separate title on p. 13, The story of Daphne.
'As late I mus'd upon the fates'
Daphne: 'The candid muse, ambitious to record'
L(1465.f.51,–C4),C,DA,DN,DT+; CtY,ICN (lacks B3–C4),MH,TxU.

D516 [—] A curry-comb of truth for a certain dean: or, the Grub-street tribunal. *Dublin, printed in the year 1736.*
8°: *A⁴ (A1ᵛ as 'A2'); 1 2–8.*
Teerink 979; Williams 1137. Reprinted in the miscellany *S—t contra omnes, [1736.]*
'Dean, Drapier, Tatler, Gulliver'
The IU copy of the second edition has an early ms. attribution to Dunkin. A review of Swift's activities. Answered by *A brush to the Curry-comb of truth, 1736.*
LVA-F,DA(2),DN,DT(2); MH.

D517 [—] — *Dublin, printed by Ebenezer Rider, 1736.*
8°: *A⁴ (A1ᵛ as 'A2'); 1 2–8.*
Possibly a variant impression of the preceding.
CtY.

D518 [—] A curry-comb of truth for a certain dissembling dean... The second edition revis'd and corrected by the author. *Dublin, printed in the year 1736.*
8°: *A⁴; 1 2–8.*
Signature possibly cropt in the copy seen.
IU.

D519 — An epistle to the right honourable James lord visct. Charlemont. With a translation of the sixth satire of the second book of Horace. *Dublin, printed by and for George Faulkner, 1744.*
8°: *A–F⁴; 1–2 3–44 45–48.* F3–4 advt.

Dunkin, W. An epistle

P. 27 is a fly-title to the 'sixth satire'.
'As errant knights by cross indentures'
Satire VI: 'I often wish'd, I had a farm'
DA(2, 1 – F3–4),DG; CtY(– F3–4),ICN,MH,PP.

D520 [—] Epistola ad Franciscum Bindonem, arm. cui adjiciuntur quatuor odæ. *Dublinii, typis Georgii Faulkneri, 1740.*
8⁰: *A⁴* B–G⁴; *1–2* 3–56.
Teerink 1323. Second title on p. 25, 'An epistle to Francis Bindon esq; to which are added an ode to the... Earl of Orrery, and one on Mr. Pope. Translated from the Latin by different hands.'
'Ingens artis opus manus est aggressa, parentem'
'Whilst on the canvas, by your matchless hands'
Occasioned by Bindon's portrait of Swift.
DG.

D521 —— Authore Gulielmo Dunkin A. M. *Dublinii, typis Georgii Faulkneri, 1741.*
8⁰: *A⁴* B–G⁴; *1–2* 3–56.
Apparently a new edition of the Latin poems in A–C⁴, but the title to the translations on D1 is dated 1740 as in the preceding, and the English text is apparently from the same type.
L(1213.m.16/4),C(presentation copy to Lord Orrery, 1741),DA,DN(presentation copy to Lord Orrery, 7 Feb 1742),LdU-B; CtY,PU.

[—] The gift of Pallas. A poem [actually by Charles Carthy], 1733. *See* C56·5.

D522 — The lover's web. A poem. Inscribed to the Lady Caroline Sackville. *Dublin, printed by George Faulkner, 1734.*
4⁰: *A²* B–D²; *1–2* 3–16.
Rothschild 823. Errata slip on verso of title of the ICN copy; others have ms. corrections.
'To thee, blest nymph, whom princely courts refine'
On the presentation of a piece of Irish linen to Anne, the princess royal, on her marriage. Cf. [C. Carthy], *The gift of Pallas*, 1733.
L(11642.bbb.51),DA,DT(2),LdU-B; ICN,MH (uncut).

D523 [—] Mezentius on the rack. [*Dublin*] *Printed in the year 1734.*
12⁰: A⁸ B⁴; *1–2* 3–23 *24*.
A continuation of *An account of a strange and wonderful apparition*, D514.
'Horace advises bards in vain'
The 'advertisement' on p. 24 is by Dunkin (see D526), and his authorship is assumed in such satires as *A libel upon the Dublin dunces*, 1734. A satire on Charles Carthy, with a second set of epigrams against him.
LVA-F,DA,DT.

[—] An ode. In imitation of the third ode of the third book of Horace [actually by Charles Carthy], [1732.] *See* C56·7.

D524 — An ode, to be performed at the castle of Dublin, on the 1st. of March, being the birth-day

Dunkin, W. An ode

of... Queen Caroline... Set to musick by Mr. Matthew Dubourg... *Dublin, printed by S. Powell, for G. Ewing, 1734.*
4⁰: *A⁴*; *1–3* 4–8.
From the watermarks in the C copy, this appears to have been printed on two separate half-sheets.
'If conscious of thy ancient fire'
C,DG; CtY.

D525 [—] The poet's prayer. A poem. *Dublin, printed by George Faulkner, 1734.*
4⁰: *A²*; *1–2* 3–4.
'If e'er in thy sight I found favour, Apollo'
Printed in Dunkin's *Poetical works*, 1769–70.
O; DLC.

D526 '—' A proclamation from Parnassus. Being the substance of a second advertisement lately published in prose, but now turned into metre, and considerable improved by me William Dunkin... [*Dublin*] *Printed in the year 1734.*
8⁰: *A⁴* B²; *1–2* 3–11 *12*.
'Whereas some friends of mine, confess'd'
A satire on Dunkin occasioned by the 'advertisement' in his *Mezentius on the rack*, 1734.
L(C.71.bb.15/8),LVA-F.

D527 [—] Τεχνηθυραμβεια. Sive poema in Patricium Murphæum, S.S. & ind. Trin. Collegii, Dublinii. subjanitorem. *Dublinii, typis Edvardi Waters, 1728.*
8⁰: *A²* B² C²; *1–2* 3–12.
'En! ego musarum blando perculsus amore'
Reprinted in 1730 with Dunkin's name; an English translation by Joseph Cowper was published in 1728, 1730, and was probably intended to accompany these editions.
DA(2),DT(2); CtY,NcU.

D528 — Technethyrambeia: sive poëma in Patricium Murphæum... Authore Gulielmo Dunkin, A.B. *Dublinii, ex officina Georgii Faulkneri, 1730.*
8⁰: *A⁴* B⁴; *1–3* 4–15 *16 blk*.
L(11623.aaa.12),O,C,DA(2),DT +.

D529 — The vice-roy: a poem. To his grace the Duke of Dorset. *Dublin, printed by George Faulkner, 1735.*
4⁰: A⁴ B² C⁴; *1–3* 4–19 *20 blk*.
The copy at DFo has Amsterdam arms watermark; those at C,DT, have GR crowned in circle. Possibly there are fine-paper copies.
'While, active for the public weal'
C,DT,*MR*; DFo.

D530 [—] A vindication of the libel: or, a new ballad; written by a shoe-boy, on an attorney, who was formerly a shoe-boy. [*Dublin*] *Printed in the year, 1729–30.*
½⁰: 1 side, 1 column.
Rothschild 822; *Teerink* 954; *Williams* 1133.
'With singing of ballads, and crying of news'
For Dunkin's authorship see *Nichols, Illustrations* V. 384, quoting Deane Swift: 'That poem was, I know, written by my very worthy friend Dr. Dunkin'. A satire against Hartley

Dunkin, W. A vindication

Hutchinson, occasioned by his arrest of two newsboys for selling Swift's *Libel on D——D——*, 1730.
L(1890.e.5/84),DT; CtY.

D531 [—] A vindication of the libel on Dr. Delany, and a certain great lord. Together with a panegyric on Dean Sw--t... To which is added I. The said libel... *Dublin: printed, London: re-printed for J. Wilford, and sold at the pamphlet shops*, 1730. (*MChr* April)
8°: A–C⁴ D²; *1–3* 4–27 *28 blk.*
Five poems in all, by various authors.
C; CLU-C.

D532 Dunkirk. Dunkirk deliver'd: or, the devil and the D---ch disappointed. [*London?*] *Printed in the year* 1712.
½°: 1 side, 1 column.
On the other side, in prose, *A full and true account of a...murder...of my Lord Wharlen* [!], 1712.
'Amongst the unwholsome Belgick bogs'
A tory attack on the Dutch.
Rothschild.

D533 Dunoscope. The dunoscope. In imitation of the Splendid shilling. Address'd to the three learned universities of Dublin, Oxon, and Cambridge. *London: printed, and Dublin reprinted by E. Rider*, 1736.
8°: A–B⁴; *1–2* 3–15 *16.* 16 advt.
No London edition has been traced.
'Whilom in strain Miltonic Christ-Church bard'
In imitation of John Philips. It claims to have been written at Magdalen-Hall, Oxford.
O; OCU.

Dunton, John. Neck or nothing in verse: or, a complete collection of all the treasonable poems... in favour of the Pretender. With answers to 'em in rhime... Part I... *London, printed for the author, and are to be sold by S. Popping*, 1719. (*PB* 26 May)
8°: pp. 25. DT.
Clearly intended to be continued.

———

Dunton lists a number of poems as published in An appeal to his majesty, [1723] and was continually announcing works as forthcoming which do not seem to have appeared. Some of these poems may well have formed part of larger works. No attempt has been made to list them; the situation is further complicated because 'panegyrick' and 'satyr' are often used by Dunton to refer to prose works.

D534 [—] Bumography: or, a touch at the lady's tails, being a lampoon (privately) dispers'd at Tunbridge-Wells, in the year 1707. By a water-drinker ... Also, a merry elegy upon Mother Jefferies, the antient water-dipper. *London, printed in the year* 1707. (29 Nov, Luttrell)
8°: a–c⁴ B–I⁴; [2] i–vi v–xviii *xix–xx*, 1–64.

Dunton, J. Bumography

The elegy begins on p. 55. Advertised as 'just published' in *PM* 13 Dec.
'Ye sons of women hither throng'
Elegy: 'Soft elegy, design'd for grief and tears'
Dunton's authorship is revealed in advertisements for the second edition, *The rump.* Compare *A rod for Tunbridge beaus*, 1701.
L(164.1.36, Luttrell, lacks I⁴),CT,DT.

D535 [—] [*idem*] 'The rump: or, a touch at the lady's tails: being a lampoon privately dispers'd at Tunbridge-Wells, in the year 1707. By a water-drinker...As also, a merry elegy upon Mother Jefferies, the antient water-dipper. The 2d edition. To which is added, the Lady's dressing-room; or the morning conference... [*London*] *Sold by J. Morphew.*' (*DC* 16 July 1708, 'just publish'd')

D536 [—] 'The he-strumpets: a satyr on the sodomite club. [*London*] *Printed for B. Bragge.*' (*PM* 7 Oct 1707)
'The fourth edition, alter'd and much enlarg'd', is printed in Dunton's *Athenianism* (1710) II. 93ff. It there has the first line: 'Having giv'n all the whores a touch'

D537 — 'King George for ever; or the celestial coronation, a poem. By Mr. John Dunton. To which is annexed his dying groans from the Fleet Prison. [*London*] *Sold by J. Roberts.* Price 6d.' (*MC* Oct 1727)

D538 [—] The pulpit-fool. A satyr. *London, printed in the year* 1707. (*DC* 20 May)
4°: A⁴(–A4) B–I⁴ K¹; *i–vi*, 1–66.
'How stupid, jackish, and how vile, at best'
Referred to, and extracts reprinted in Dunton's *Athenianism* I, 1710.
L(11630.c.13/19, Luttrell, 22 May),O,DT,*MR*; CSmH,CtY,DFo,*MH*.

D539 [—] The second part of the Pulpit-fool. A satyr. Containing a distinct character of the most noted clergy-men in the queens dominions, both churchmen and dissenters. *London, printed for B. Bragge, of whom is to be had the first part*, 1707. (15 July, Luttrell)
4°: A–L² (K1 as 'L'); *1–3* 4–40. 40 advt.
Advertised in *Observator* 16 July.
'I have (already) nam'd the pulpit-fool'
L(11630.c.13/19, Luttrell),DT; CtY,*MB,MH*.

D540 [—] Stinking fish: or, a foolish poem, attempted by John the Hermit. Part I. To be continu'd 'till the Hermit has cry'd all his stinking fish... *London, printed by R. Tookey, and are to be sold by John Morphew... Of whom also is to had the Tunbridge lampoon, entitled the Rump... The second edition; written by the same author*, 1708. (*DC* 26 July)
8°: A–M⁴ N¹; [2] i–ix *x*, 1–44 49–89 *90.* 89–90 advt.
'When god almighty had his palace fram'd'

Dunton, J. Stinking fish

The preface and advertisements are clearly Dunton's.
L(1077.k.13),O(uncut, title partly in facsimile); MH.

D'Urfey, Thomas. Tales tragical and comical... Done into several sorts of English verse, with large additions and improvements. *London, printed for Bernard Lintott,* 1704.
8°: pp. 295.   L,O; CtY,TxU.

— Stories, moral and comical...done into several sorts of English verse and prose, with large additions and embellishments. *London, printed by Fr. Leach; sold by Isaac Cleave,* [1706.]
8°: pp. 257.   L,O; CtY,TxU.

Advertised in *PM* 11 Dec 1705 as 'in the press' and listed as published in *PM* 14 Feb 1706.

— 'Musa & musica, or humour and music. Being an extraordinary collection of pleasant and merry humours, with Scotch and love songs, the words by Mr. D'Urfey. Never before printed. [*London*] *Printed for L. Pippard.*' (*PM* 13 June 1710)

Entered in *SR* 10 June 1710; copies at L are recorded in W. C. Smith, *A bibliography... of John Walsh 1695-1720* (1948) no. 358. An engraved collection with music.

— New opera's, with comical stories, and poems, on several occasions, never before printed. Being the remaining pieces, written by Mr. D'Urfey. *London, printed for William Chetwood,* 1721.
8°: pp. 382.   L,O; CtY,MH.

Many of D'Urfey's songs were published with music as engraved half-sheets; these are excluded.

D541 — The authentick letter of Marshal de Boufflers to the French king, on the late unfortunate, but glorious battel, (as he calls it) near Mons. Paraphrastically done into English metre, and set to the famous tune of Old Simon the king. Written by Mr. Durfey. [*London*] *Printed for J. Walter,* [1709/10.]
½°: 1 side, 2 columns.
On the other side of the Chatsworth copy, *A new copy of verses, sung in triumph,* [1711.] Two lines of printed music with first stanza.
'Me send you, Sir, one letter'
Chatsworth.

D542 — [*idem*] An excellent new song, on the authentick letter of Marshal D'Bouffler's to the French king, on the late unfortunate, but glorious, battle (as he calls it) fought near Mons; paraphrastically done into metre, in broken English. Written by Mr. Durffey. To a famous tune on the Welsh-harp, call'd, Of a noble race was Shinkin [*Dublin*] *Printed for Eliphal Dobson, junior,* 1710.
½°: 1 side, 2 columns.
TxU.

D'Urfey, T.

D543 — The French pride abated; or, a friendly admonition to lowly humility. The words by Tho Durfey. To a new tune. [*London*] *Printed for S. Deacon,* [1708.]
½°: 1 side, 2 columns.
First verse printed with six lines of typeset music.
'Grand Lewis let pride be abated'
L(1876.f.1/41).

D544 — Honor & opes: or, the Brittish merchant's glory. A poem, congratulatory. On the happy decision and conclusion of all differences between the old and new companies, united in trade to the East-Indies... *London, printed in the year* 1708.
2°: A–B² C–E²; *i–iv,* 1–15 *16 blk.*
'Long in a baleful cave, by nature made'
Dedication signed.
O.

D545 — The hubble bubbles. A ballad. To the tune of, ----O'er the hills, and far away. By Mr. D'uffey. *London, printed for J. Roberts,* 1720.
½°: 2 sides, 1 column.
Elegant woodcut of man in the stocks blowing bubbles above imprint.
'Ye circum, and uncircumcis'd'
Crum Y23. On the bubble speculations.
L(1876.f.1/90).

D546 [—] — [*London?* 1720.]
½°: 1 side, 2 columns.
Rough woodcut at head. A piracy.
O.

D547 [—] The hubble bubble. To the tune of O'er the hills and far away. [*Edinburgh?* 1720.]
½°: 1 side, 2 columns.
A variant text. The E copy is bound with Edinburgh half-sheets.
'Jews, Turks, and Christians, hear my song'
E.

D548 [—] [*idem*] The hue and cry after the South-Sea, or, a new ballad call'd the Hubble bubbles. To the tune of, O'er the hills and far away. [*Dublin,* 1720.]
½°: 1 side, 1 column.
On the other side, [E. Ward] *A South Sea ballad,* 1720. The earlier version of the text.
TxU.

D549 — A new ode. Or, dialogue between Mars, the god of war, and Plutus, or Mammon god of riches. Perform'd in an entertainment made for his grace the Duke of Marlborough... at Vintners-Hall, in the city. The words by Mr. Durfey, set to musick by Mr. Weldon, and sung by Mr. Elford and Mr. Leveridge, December, the 19th, 1706. *London, printed by J. Bland,* 1706.
½°: 1 side, 2 columns.
The priority of editions is uncertain, and they are arranged by the date they bear; probably the following is the only authorized edition.

D'Urfey, T. A new ode

'From glorious toyls of war'
L(1870.d.1/97; C.116.i.4/34, cropt),DG(cropt).

D550 — — [col] *London, printed by Fr. Leach, for the author; sold by B. Bragg,* 1707.
2°: *A²*; 1–4. 4 advt.
Drop-head title only.
MC,*MR*; TxU.

— 'A new song in honour of the glorious assembly at court on ye queen's birthday; made to a pretty Scotch tune by Mr. Durfey, 1 p., folio, 1712.'
Morgan O495, possibly recording an engraved song.

D551 [—] The progress of honesty: or, a view of the court and city. *London, printed for J. Brett; sold by the booksellers of London & Westminster,* 1739. (*GM,LM* Nov)
2°: *A¹* B–E²; *1–3* 4–18.
First published 1681.
'One summer evening, when the wearied sun'
L(1962),O; CtY(uncut),KU.

D552 — Titus and Gissippus: or, the power of friendship. A moral story, in heroick verse... By Mr. D'Urfey. [*London, printed by Fr. Leach,* 1706.]
8°: *A¹* B–E⁸; 1–48 153–167 *168 blk.*
Another impression of K–M⁸ 'E'⁸ of D'Urfey's *Stories moral and comical,* [1706]; B–D have changed signatures and pagination, but E is common to both.
'When fam'd Augustus did Rome's empire bless'
O.

D553 — The trophies: or, Augusta's glory. A triumphant ode, made in honour of the city, and upon the trophies taken from the French at the battel of Ramellies... *London, printed by Fr. Leach, for the author; sold by B. Bragg,* 1707 [1706]. (24 Dec)
2°: *A²* B–E²; *i–iv,* 1–15 *16 blk.*
Advertised in *DC* 27 Dec as published on 'Tuesday', 24 Dec; Luttrell's copy dated 24 Dec is recorded by *Thorn-Drury.*
'To sing Augusta's glory in extreme'
O; CLU-C,CtY.

D554 Durgen. Durgen, a satyr, to the celeberted [!] Mr. P--------pe, on his Dunciad: By Namby Pamby. *Dublin, printed by Rich. Dickson,* [1729.] (*Silver Court Gazette,* 1 Jan)
slip: 1 side, 1 column.
'Seraphic brute! How else shall I address'
An attack on Pope. Probably not by Ambrose Philips, and not apparently related to Edward Ward's *Durgen,* 1729.
C.

— Durgen. Or, a plain satyr, 1729. *See* Ward, Edward.

D555 Durston, John. [dh] Illustrissimo domino, et heroi vere magnanimo, Domini Joanni, duci Marlboriensi, de Gallis & Bavaris ab ipso, pugna

Durston, J. Illustrissimo domino

ad Bleinheim inita, strenue debellatis, epinicium... [1704/05.]
2°: *A²*; 1–4.
Possibly printed at Oxford.
'Attonitus tandem respirat Phœbus, & inquit'
L(1970),O.

D556 Dutch. The Dutch are come in at last. Or, a new-years-gift for the whiggs. With the Pretender's letter to a whigg l--d in England. *London, printed by J. Read,* 1712.
2°: *A² < B¹*; *1–2* 3–4 *5* 6.
The inner forme of A is blank; an inexpensive sheet-and-a-half avoiding the use of stamped paper. The 'Pretender's letter' precedes the verse.
'Are all the Dutch at length come in'
InU.

D557 — The Dutch bribe, a ballad. [17--.]
½°: 1 side, 1 column.
'Your cheese we have eat, and a toast with it drank'
A satire on the excise of cheese, apparently directed against John Cooper of Fife, who has not been identified.
MH.

D558 — The Dutch embassy. [*London?* 1714/15.]
8°: A–B⁴; *1–2* 3–15 *16 blk.*
'When George, the great elector of Hanover'
Crum W1096. An anti-Hanoverian account of the Dutch embassy to congratulate George I after his accession.
O,C; CSmH(uncut),MH,NjP.

— 'The Dutch riddle: or, a character of a h——y monster, 1708.' *See* Ward, Edward (W164).

Dutchess. *See* Duchess.

D559 Duties. 'The duties of servants to their masters...' [*Worcester?* 171–?]
Title taken from *A supplement to the verses, entitul'd, The duties...,* a single sheet printed at Worcester. This presumably had the same format and was by the same author.

D560 Dutton, Anne. A narration of the wonders of grace, in verse... To which is added, a poem on the special work of the spirit... As also sixty one hymns... *London, printed for, and sold by the author, in the year* 1734.
8°: A–R⁴ S²; *i–iii* iv–viii, *9* 10–139 *140 blk.*
'The wonders of god's ancient love'
L(11631.bbb.12),O,*LdU-B*; ICN,NNUT.

D561 [—] — The second edition, corrected by the author, with additions. *London, printed for the author; sold by John Oswald,* 1734.
8°: A–S⁴; *i–iii* iv–viii, *9* 10–143 *144 blk.*
The preface is signed 'A. D.'
L(1162.l.42); CLU-C.

Duty

D562 Duty. The duty of a husband: or, the lady's answer to the Duty of a wife. [*London*] *Printed and sold by D. Richmond, in Salisbury-court,* [1707?]
8°: A⁴; *1* 2–8.
'When god in Eden's happy shade'
A reply to Samuel Jackson's poem.
CLU-C.

D563 — The duty of a husband, written in answer to the Duty of a wife. By R.B. *London, printed in the year* 1707.
8°: *A⁴; 1–2* 3–8.
'The man whom heaven has dispos'd to bless'
A reply to Samuel Jackson's poem.
University of Otago (photocopy at L).

— The duty of a wife, 1707. *See* Jackson, Samuel.

D564 Duumvirate. [dh] The duumvirate. [1705?]
4°: A²; *1–4*
The O copy is among the Carte papers (208, fol. 397); probably printed in France.
'Our floating isle allmost an age has spent'
Jacobite propaganda, particularly directed against Godolphin and Marlborough.
O.

D565 Dux. Dux Britannicus, or the Duke of Marlborough. A poem. By a Shrewsbury scholar. Together with a prophecy by another hand. *Salop, printed by Thomas Jones,* 1704.
4°: A⁴; *1–4* 5–8.
'May Marlborough such loud acclamations see'
MB.

D——y, *D.* Ireland's black day, [1730.] *See* I58.

D-----y, *Doctor.* A riddle by the revd. Doctor D-----y, 1726. *See* Delany, Patrick.

— A third riddle. By the revd. Doctor D-----y, 1725–6. *See* Delany, Patrick.

— A fourth riddle. By the rv. D. D——y, 1726. *See* Delany, Patrick.

Dyer, John. Poems... Viz. I. Grongar Hill. II. The ruins of Rome. III. The fleece, in four books. *London, printed by John Hughs, for Messrs. R. & J. Dodsley,* 1761.
8°: pp. 188. L,O; CtY,MH.
Reprinted as *The poetical works of John Dyer,* 1765 (copies at L,O), probably a Scottish piracy.

Dyer, J.

D566 [—] The ruins of Rome. A poem. *London, printed for Lawton Gilliver,* 1740. (*SR* 27 Feb)
4°: *A² B–D⁴ E²; i–iv, 1* 2–28.
Engraving on title. Listed in *GM,LM* March. Deposit copies at EU,AdU,GU. An edition by Russel, price 6*d.*, was listed in *LM* April/May 1748; it was possibly a reissue.
'Enough of Grongar, and the shady dales'
Reprinted in Dyer's *Poems,* 1761.
L(840.k.3/13; C.70.f.1/8),O(2),C,E,LdU-B(2, 1 uncut)+; CLU-C,CtY,IU,MH,TxU(2).

D567 Dyer, Robert. An epistle humbly addressed to the honourable Mrs. Elizabeth Trevor, daughter of the late Sir Richard Steele, upon her marriage with the honourable John Trevor esq;... *London, printed for Lawton Gilliver,* 1732. (*GSJ* 20 July)
4°: *A⁴ B⁴ C²; 1–7* 8–20.
'Accept, bright fair! with native smiles, my zeal'
O; CtY.

Dyet. *See* Diet.

D568 Dyke, Ann. The female muse. A poem on the coronation of her sacred majesty Queen Ann. *London printed, and are to be sold by J. Nutt,* 1702. (1 May, Luttrell)
2°: *A² B–C²; i–iv, 1–7* 8 *blk.*
The Luttrell copy is recorded in *Haslewood.*
'Once more our most dear indulgent heaven'
Dedication to Marlborough signed.
O.

D569 [**Dykes, Oswald.**] 'Good manners for schools; being a paraphrase upon Qui mihi, in English verse. Dedicated to all masters for the use of their scholars; fit to be bound up either with Lily's Grammar or the Accidence...The third edition. [*London*] *Printed for A. Bettesworth, & M. Corbett; sold by J. Morphew.* Price 2*d.* or 10*s.* a hundred.' (*PB* 19 July 1709, 'this day will be publish'd'.)
Apparently first published in 1700; there are both folio and half-sheet editions at L. The Luttrell copy of the folio, dated 29 June and with an attribution to Dykes, is in the possession of Arnold Muirhead. The half-sheet edition bears Dykes's name. The first line is quoted from the folio of 1700. The copyright formed part of lot 146 of the trade sale of Arthur Bettesworth, 18 Jan 1759.
'Boys, that wou'd scholars be, your minds dispose'

E

E., S.F. Poems on several occasions, together with a pastoral, [1703.] *See* Egerton, Sarah Fyge.

E1 Eagle. The eagle, a fable on the times. With an essay on fable in verse, inscrib'd to Josiah Burchett esq; *London, printed for J. Pemberton, 1723 [1722].* (*DP* 28 Dec)
8°: A–B⁴ C²; *1–4* 5–19 *20 blk.*
A1 not seen, possibly half-title.
'A mother eagle, weak and blind'
L(11649.d.42/2, –A1).

E2 — The eagle and the robin. An apologue. Translated from the original of Æsop... By H.G. L. Mag. *London printed, and sold by J. Morphew, 1709.* (*DC* 1 Feb)
2°: A² B–C²; *i–iv,* 1–8.
Some copies (O,DT,MH, and one at TxU) have a variant outer forme of B, and possibly represent another impression.
'A lady liv'd in former days'
Preface signed 'Horat. Gram.' presumably standing for Horace the schoolmaster. There is no evidence that it is translated from Aesop. Printed in *Nichols, Collection* III.1–13 as by William King (1663–1712), almost certainly on the evidence of a ms. note in the LLP copy which was known to him. The ms. notes in this volume are erroneous, and though Nichols was the editor of King's works, the attribution should be treated with suspicion; it has apparently hitherto been overlooked.
L(1481.f.19/3, uncut),LLP,O,DT; *CU*,ICU,MH, TxU(2, 1 Luttrell, 1 Feb).

E3 — — *London, printed by J. Read, behind the Green-Dragon-tavern in Fleet-street, 1709.*
8°: *A⁴; 1* 2–8.
A piracy.
O(2),OC(uncut); IU.

E4 — — *London printed, and sold by J. Bradford, in Fetter-lane, [1709.]*
8°: *A⁴; 1* 2–8.
A piracy.
C(uncut),DN(cropt),DT(cropt),LdU-B.

E5 — — Together with Taffey's triumph... By a gentleman of Oxford. *London printed, and sold by Henry Hills, 1709.*
8°: A⁸; *1–2* 3–16.
'Taffey's triumph' is Daniel Bellamy's translation of Edward Holdsworth's *Muscipula.*
L(12306.ppp.51; 1077.k.23/1; G.1390/5),OW, CT(2),EU; CLU-C,CtY,ICN,MH.

E6 — — With an old cat's prophecy... suppos'd to be writ by John Lidgate... *London printed, and sold by H. Hills, 1709.*
8°: A⁸; *1–2* 3–16.
The 'old cat's prophecy' was previously published as *The beasts in power,* 1709.

Reissued with other remaindered Hills poems in *A collection of the best English poetry,* 1717 (*Case* 294).
L(C.124.b.7/15),O(2),EU,AdU; CtY,IU,MH.

E7 — [The eagle, falconer, and hawk...] '*London, printed for M. Cooper.* Price 1*s.*' (*DA* 7 April 1743)
A continuation of *The old fox and his son,* 1742; advertised there with this title for the first of the three fables it would contain. Advertised in *DA* as 'Three fables, viz. Preferment despis'd, the usurper punish'd, and liberty esteem'd...'

E8 [Earbery, Matthias.] The battel of Oudenarde. A poem in two canto's. *Norwich, printed by Henry Cross-grove, 1709.* (*PB* 2 April)
2°: π(2 ll) A² B–E²; [4] iii–iv [2], 5–20.
The preliminaries are irregular and the collation given is hypothetical. The second leaf bears a dedication to Queen Anne, the third to Charles, viscount Townshend, the fourth 'the printer to the reader'. Advertised in *PB* as 'sold by J. Morphew'. The Luttrell copy, dated 2 April, is in the collection of R. D. Horn.
'What man with thirst of glorious acts would burn'
L(11632.h.24); CLU-C.

E8·1 — [another issue, with the author's name.]
MH.

Earl. Earl Mortimer's speech, [1711.] *See* Jonson, Benjamin.

— Earl Robert's mice, 1712. *See* Prior, Matthew.

Earle, Jabez. Verses upon several occasions. *London, printed by W.D., 1723.*
12°: pp. '93' [83].   O; DLC.
The copy at O is in a presentation binding.

— — The second edition with additions. *London, printed by J. Humfreys, for S. Chandler, 1724.*
12°: pp. 120.   L,O; CtY,NNUT.

— Sacred poems. *London, printed in the year 1726.*
12°: pp. 37.   L,O.

[—] Umbritii Cantiani poemata. *Londini, impensis Joannis Graii, 1729.*
12°: pp. [1]–34, 45–150.   L,O.
A copy at LDW has a ms. attribution to Earle.

E9 [—] ⟨Umbritii Cantiani Rus. Satira nata ex tertia Juvenalis.⟩ ⟨*Londini, prostat apud J. Osborne, & S. Chandler,*⟩ [1724.] (*MC* Dec 1724)
8°: A–C⁴; *1–3* 4–23 *24 blk.* 23 err.
The copy seen lacks the title-leaf A1; the title is quoted from the drop-head title on p. 3 which corresponds with the entry in *MC*; the imprint is taken from that. Possibly printed as a duodecimo with three signatures.
'Felicem censes, vetus, o! et fide sodalis'

Earle, J. Rus

For Earle's use of this pseudonym, see his *Poemata* above.

Ct Y(lacks A1).

E10 Early. Early soliloquies. *Edinburgh, printed in the year* 1711.

4°: A^4; *1–3* 4–7 *8 blk.*

The copy at GM has A2 signed.

'In silent waiting while I muse'

A devotional poem.

E(2),GM.

E11 — Early soliloquies, as also the Daily sacrifice: or, the Lord's prayer paraphrased. *Edinburgh printed, and sold by Robert Brown,* 1719.

8°: A^4; *1–2* 3–7 *8.*

E.

E12 — Early soliloquies. *Edinburgh, printed in the year* 1722.

4°: A^4; *1–3* 4–8.

E.

'Easy, Charles.' The siege of Carlisle, 1746. *See* S459.

E13 Ecclesia. Ecclesia & reformatio. Or, a dialogue between St. Patrick's-church and Wood-street meeting-house. *Dublin, printed for John Afleck,* [1728?]

8°: A^4 B^4; *1–3* 4–16.

The DA copy is tentatively dated 1728; references on p. 12 suggest the reign of George I.

'Tell me great fabrick! tho' our distance seems'

A dialogue between the church and the dissenters.

L(11631.e.46),C(2, 1 uncut),DA.

E14 Eclipse. The eclipse, a poem, in commemoration of the total eclipse of the sun, April 22. 1715 . . . By W.W. *London, printed for J. Baker,* 1715. (*MC* May)

2°: A–C^2; *1–2* 3–12.

'Thou globe of fire intense, amazing vast'

The initials and the subject suggest that William Whiston was the author.

MH.

Economy. The oeconomy of love: a poetical essay, 1736–. *See* Armstrong, John.

Edgcumbe, Richard, *baron Edgcumbe.* Labour in vain, 1742. *In* W494.

E15 Edinburgh. The Edinburgh cuckolds: or the history of horns. Written by the author of the Roman relique. *Edinburgh, printed and sold for the author,* 1722.

4°: A^4; *1–2* 3–8.

'The pow'rs above on fair Britannia smile'

The Roman relique has not been identified.

A modern ms. note in the GM copy suggests

The **Edinburgh** cuckolds

William Forbes as author, but no evidence to support the attribution has been traced.

GM.

— Edinburgh's address to the country, [1718.] *See* Ramsay, Allan.

E16 — Edinburgh's observator or observations upou [!] the ladys of Edinburgh. [*Edinburgh,* 171–.]

½°: 1 side, 2 columns.

'Unto you wanton Edinburgh sparks'

Apparently one of the poems replied to in Allan Ramsay's *The scriblers lash'd,* 1718.

L(1850.e.10/6).

— Edinburgh's salutation to the most honourable, my lord marquess of Carnarvon, [1720.] *See* Ramsay, Allan.

E17 Edrisa. Edrisa: or, an elegiac poem on the death of a fine lady in Pall-Mall. In which are contained her principal amours and adventures. *London, printed for M. Cooper,* 1743. (1 Sept?)

2°: π^1 A^2 B^1; *1–2* 3–8.

Rothschild 239. Listed in *GM* Sept.

'As when of old the prince of Roman rakes'

On Miss Edwards.

O; MH,OCU(uncut, dated 1 Sept; ms. notes).

E18 — Edrisa. An elegiac poem on the death of the Lady E------ds . . . *Dublin, printed in the year* 1743.

8°: A^8; *1–3* 4–16.

DA.

E19 Edwards, Samuel. The Copernican system, a poem . . . *Cambridge, printed at the University-Press,* 1728. (*MChr* 21 Feb)

4°: π^2 A–B^4; *i–iv, 1* 2–16.

Listed in *MChr* as sold by J. Stagg.

'Assist, Urania, the advent'rous song'

Possibly occasioned by J. T. Desaguliers, *The Newtonian system,* 1728.

L(11656.r.7/12, uncut; 1465.i.12/4),O,*CQ*; ICN (uncut),ICU,*MiU*.

E20 [Edwards, Thomas.] [dh] A Christmas carol. Dedicated to the ancient Britons that understand English, by a country parson. [col] *London, printed for J. Roberts,* 1715. (*MC* Dec)

4°: A^4; *1* 2–8, 2 columns.

'This is the most joyful time'

Early ms. note in the L copy 'By Edwards, rector of Aldwinde in Northamptonshire'. Apparently written in a Welsh metrical form.

L(11631.f.6).

E21 Eelbeck, Henry. [dh] Epinicion anglicanum ad illum magnanimum ac equitem illustrissimum D. Georgium Bingium (arrogantium de clade Hispanorum) cui munus classis præfecti sacro jure delatum erat . . . [*London,* 1718?]

8°: A^4; 1–8.

'Æquorei Mavortis opus sulcantia pontum'

Eelbeck, H. Epinicion

Admiral George Byng destroyed the Spanish fleet off Cape Passaro, 31 July 1718.
L(1213.m.16/2).

E22 Effigies. [dh] The effigies of the Legion. [col] *London, printed for John Nutt*, 1701. (30 July, Luttrell)
2°: *A²*; *1–4*.
Woodcut above text.
'Long had the rebel monster strove to rear'
MH(Luttrell).

[Egerton, Sarah Fyge.] Poems on several occasions, together with a pastoral. By Mrs. S.F. *London printed, and are to be sold by J. Nutt*, [1703.] (*TC* Trinity 1703)
8°: pp. 15, 117.   L,O; DFo,MH.
Large unidentified watermark. Dedication signed 'S.F.E.' In most copies B1–4 are cancels.

[—] [fine paper]   MH.
No watermark seen. The copy at MH was presented and has ms. corrections; the preliminaries differ from the preceding.

— [reissue] A collection of poems on several occasions... By Mrs. Sarah Fyge Egerton. *London printed; sold by the booksellers of London & Westminster*, 1706 [1705]. (*DC* 20 Dec)
DFo,TxU.
Cancel title.

––––––––––

E23 [—] The female advocate: or, an answer to a late satyr against the pride, lust and inconstancy of woman. Written by a lady in vindication of her sex. *London, printed for J. Taylor*, 1707 [1706]. (*DC* 5 July)
8°: *A–D⁴*; *i–vi, 1–25 26*. 25–26 advt.
First published in 1686.
'Blasphemous wretch! How canst thou think or say'
Advertised in *DC* with Mrs. Egerton's poems. A reply to [Robert Gould] *Love given over*.
LdU-B.

E24 E———h. E———h's instructions to their member. *Printed for Patrick Ramsay, in London*, 1739. (*GM, LM* Dec)
2°: *A² < B²*; *1–3 4–7 8 blk*.
Some copies (L,CtY) have a variant page 7, which may represent a reimpression. The imprint is probably fictitious.
'When Keen and Quadra club'd their wits'
Edinburgh ironically recommending adhesion to Lord Islay (subsequently duke of Argyll) and Sir Robert Walpole in support of the place bill.
L(1962),E; CtY,DLC,MH,OCU.

E25 — [dh] E––––––––h's instructions to their member. [*Edinburgh*, 1739.]
4°: *A²*; *1–4*.
L(11630.b.8/6).

Eight

Eight. Eight fables on the present posture of affairs in Europe, 1703. *See* Æsop in Spain, 1701–.

Eighteenth. The eighteenth epistle of the second book of Horace, 1737. *See* Hamilton, William, *of Bangour*.

E26 Eikones. Εἰκόνες ἰατρικαι, or a visionary discourse with Hippocrates. *London, printed for T. Warner*, 1726.
2°: *A² < B²*; *1–2 3–8*.
'Just was the sun in his swift chariot hurl'd'
An ironic poem on the medical profession; Hippocrates sends messages to leading practitioners.
L(643.m.12/35).

Eirenodia. Eirenodia: a poem sacred to peace, 1728. *See* Curteis, Thomas.

E27 Eis. Εἰς την του Χριστου σταυρωσιν μονοσροφικα. An ode on the crucifixion of Christ. Being a paraphrase of a Greek hymn...at the end of Bishop Andrews's Devotions. By R—t T—r, A.M. *Edinburgh, printed by T. W. & T. Ruddimans*, 1742.
8°: *A⁴*; *1 2–7 8 blk*.
With the Greek text.
'Of trivial rhimes enough! – let's now'
Tentatively ascribed to Robert Trotter by E catalogue.
L(11631.c.4),E,EN,SaU.

E28 E—l. The E—l of G—d—n to D—ct—r G—th, upon the loss of Miss Dingle: in return to the D—ct—r's consolatory verses to him, upon the loss of his rod. [*London*] *Printed in the year* 1711.
½°: 2 sides, 1 column.
Teerink 859.
'Thou, who the pangs of my embitter'd rage'
Early ms. in the DG copy, 'A ridicule on Godolphin & Garth by Dean Swift'. Not discussed by *Williams*. A reply to *A poem to the Earl of Godolphin. By Dr. G—h*, 1710.
L(1876.f.1/57),O,DG,Chatsworth,Crawford;MH,TxU.

E29 Election. The election. A poem. *London, printed in the year* 1701. (*PM* 8 Feb)
4°: *A–B⁴*; *1–2 3–15 16 blk*.
'The day was come when all the folk in furs'
On the city of London election.
L(11631.c.18),LG,BrP; CLU-C,OCU.

E30 — The election. To the tune of the Cobler. [17––.]
½°: 1 side, 1 column.
'I sing of electors, but not of a king'
Harding.

E31 Elections. The elections. A proper new ballad. By a candidate. – To the tune of Ye commons and peers. [*Dublin*] *Printed by R. Dickson*, [1727?]

The elections

½⁰: 1 side, 2 columns.
'Come, all ye freeholders'
DT.

Elegia. Elegia. In obitum reverendi Henrici
Alderich, [1710/11.] *See* Percival, William, *dean of
Emly.*

E32 — Elegia in præmaturum obitum nobilissimi, &
maximæ spei adolescentis Johannis, marchionis de
Blancford. Illustrissimi ducis de Marlborough filii
unici, mortui Cantabrigiæ, dum literis præclaram
operam daret. Die 20. mense Februar. *Londini,
imprimebat Richardus Janeway, anno* 170⅔. (March?)
½⁰: 1 side, 2 columns.
Mourning borders.
'Huc adsint sacræ, mœstissima turba, sorores'
L(C.40.m.11/99).

E33 — [on vellum]
L(835.m.8/11).

E34 — Elegeia Popi in memoriam infelicis nymphæ, in
latinum versum reddita. *Londini, impensis M.
Fletcher, in Oxon, & M. Cooper, in vico vulgo dicto
Paternoster-row,* 1744. (28 July)
2⁰: *A*(2 ll) B²; *i–ii, 1 2–5 6 blk.*
The collation appears to be irregular; possibly
the title is a cancel. A copy from Tom's Coffee
House dated 28 July is in the Lewis Walpole
Library.
'Ecquid adest spectrum, fallacis lampade lunæ'
A translation of Pope's *Elegy to the memory of
an unfortunate lady.*
L(11630.g.32),OW; TxU.

E35 **Elegiac.** An elegiack ode on the right honourable
James, earl Stanhope. [*Dublin?* 1722.]
½⁰: 1 side, 1 column.
The L copy is bound with Dublin half-sheets.
On the other side, *In Johannem Churchill...
epitaphium,* [1722.]
'Thou Stanhope, whom no earth cou'd bear'
L(1890.e.5/26).

E36 — An elegiac pastoral on the death of the Duke of
Marlborough, who dy'd on Saturday, the 16th of
June, 1722. [*London,* 1722.]
½⁰: 2 sides, 1 column.
'Sicilian muse, exalt thy rural strain'
MC.

[E37 = E456] — An elegiack poem. To the memory
of...Mr. James Cuthbert, 1739. *In* Erskine,
Ralph [An elegy].

E38 — An elegiac poem to the memory of the rev. Mr.
John Hubbard, who departed this life July 13, 1743.
Composed by a young gentleman. *London, John
Oswald,* [1743.]
4⁰: 10 pp.
(Pickering & Chatto cat. 261/5457.)

E39 **Elegiae.** Elegiae tristes, ad pudicitiam adhortantes.
Cantabrigiae: impensis Cornelii Crownfield; prostant

Elegiae tristes

*apud Jacobum Knapton, & Rob. Knaplock, biblio-
polas Londinenses,* 1719. (*DC* 1 Jan)
8⁰: *A⁴* B–E⁴ F²; *i–viii, 1–36.* A1 hft.
'Si non impediant lacrymarum flumina quicquid'
C(2, 1 – A1, uncut),CT(– A1),EtC,NwP.

E40 **Elégie.** Elégie sur la mort de son altesse royale le
Prince George de Danemarc décédé à Kensington,
le jeudi 28. octobre 1708... *A Londres, par J.
Delage,* 1708.
½⁰: 1 side, 2 columns.
Mourning borders.
'Princesse vous pleurez vôtre deüil est extréme'
O.

E41 — Elégie sur la mort du trés-puissant prince,
Guillaume III. roy d'Angleterre...décédé en son
palais de Kensington, le dimanche 8. de mars
1702... *A Londres, par J. Delage,* 1702.
½⁰: 1 side, 2 columns.
Mourning borders.
'Hélas! il ne vit plus, ah! perte irreparable'
Crawford.

Elegy.

*Elegies are arranged in alphabetical order by their
subjects, whose names are printed in bold type.
Noblemen are entered under their territorial designa-
tion, since their surnames are seldom given.*

E42 — An elegy on the much lamented death of the
right honourable the Lord **Altham,** who departed
this life this present Friday being the 17th of this
instant November 1727. At his late dwelling house
near Chapel-zod. [*Dublin,* 1727.]
½⁰: 1 side, 1 column.
Mourning borders. The same text and setting
of type as *An elegy on...Robert Rochford,*
[1727.]
'What sacred pomp is this invades my eye'
DT.

E43 — An elegy on the death of her most gracious
majesty Queen **Anne,** who dy'd at her palace in
Kensington, on the first of August 1714. By a late
fellow of New-College in Oxford. *London printed,
and sold by H. Meere,* 1714.
2⁰: *A² B¹; 1–2 3–6.*
'Amidst the tears that dutifully flow'
L(1484.g.5/28); InU.

E44 — An elegy on the death of her sacred majesty
Queen **Anne.** In a pastoral dialogue between Doron
and Alexis. By a gentlewoman. *London, printed for
J. Morphew,* 1714. (24 Aug, Luttrell)
2⁰: *A² B–C²; 1–2 3–12.*
Listed in *MC* Aug.
'Doron, methinks this lovely, gloomy shade'
O(2, 1 Luttrell),OW.

E45 — An elegy on the much lamented death of her
most sacred majesty Queen **Anne:** who departed
this mortal life at her palace at Kensington, on
Sunday the 1st of this instant August, 1714. in the

An **elegy** on...Queen Anne

50th year of her age. *London, printed by J. Read,* [1714.]
1°: 1 side, 2 columns.
 Mourning headpiece and woodcut borders.
'Britannia's children! now bewail the day'
L(KTC.126.c.1/8).

E46 — [variant title:]...Writen [!] by Sir W.D.
MWiW-C.

E47 — Elegie on the much to be lemented [!] death of the right honourable Sir William **Anstruther**, of that ilk; one of the lords of the session, and member of justiciary, who departed this life the 22. day of January; 1711. [*Edinburgh,* 1711.]
½°: 1 side, 1 column.
 Mourning borders.
'Mourn, O! North Brittian! and ye judge's all'
 Signed 'Mr. A.B.'
E.

E48 — [An elegy] on the death of his grace Archibald duke of **Argyle**, who departed this life the 28th day of Sept. 1703, in the flower and strength of his age... [*Edinburgh,* 1703.]
½°.
'Man's life's a flying vapour, which doth rise'
(*Maidment* 148, 'from a broadside...now in the possession of Charles Kirkpatrick Sharpe, esq.')

E49 — An elegy on the much lamented death of his grace, John, duke of **Argyle**; who departed this life, on the third of October, 1743. [*Edinburgh?* 1743.]
½°: 1 side, 1 column.
 Mourning borders.
'Weep, Scotland, weep! great cause thou hast to mourn!'
L(1880.b.29/5).

E50 — An elegy on the much lamented death of his grace the Duke of **Argyle** and Greenwich, who departed this life, on Monday the 3d of this instant October at his grace's seat at Sand-brook near Petersham in Surry in the 78th. year of his age. *London, printed for T. Davis, in Fleet-street,* [1743.]
½°: 1 side, 2 columns.
 Mourning headpiece and borders. L copy has ms. note, 'By subscription. No. 1000'.
'Ye muses nine, put on your sable dress'
L(112.f.44/42).

E51 — Elegy upon the much to be lamented death ef [!] her grace the Dutchess af [!] **Athol**, who departed this life January 9th. 1707. [*Edinburgh,* 1707.]
½°: 1 side, 1 column.
 Mourning borders.
'Death as a champion bold, a gyant feirce'
E.

— An elegy on the **author** of the True-born-English-man, 1704–. *See* Defoe, Daniel.

E52 — An elegy on Willy **Bald**| Who was long porter in Traquaire:| Tho' he's now dead he was not

An **elegy** on Willy Bald

auld;| Alas for him my heart is saire. [*Edinburgh,* 171–?]
½°: 1 side, 2 columns.
'And has auld death that bloody knave'
E.

E53 — An elegy on the much lamented death of John Hamilton lord **Balhaven**, &c. who departed this life, at London, June 21. 1708. *Edinburgh, printed by John Reid,* 1708.
½°: 1 side, 1 column.
 Mourning borders.
'Ah! cruel death, why dost thou us deprive?'
L(11633.i.9/13),E(2).

E54 — Elegy on the much to be lamented death of Lord John Hamilton of **Balhaven**. *Edinburgh, printed by John Reid,* 1708.
½°: 1 side, 1 column.
 Mourning borders.
'O! who their eyes from weeping can refrain?'
E.

E55 — An elegy on the much lamented death of the reverend Mr. James **Bathgate**, late minister of the gospel at Orwel. Who died the 30 day of March 1724. [*Edinburgh*] *Printed in the year* 1724.
8°: A⁴; *1–2* 3–8.
'What means this tyrant, death, to trample down'
E.

E56 — An elegy on the much lamented death, of Madam **Bently**, who broak her neck rideing towards Doney-brook, on Saturday the 2d of this inst. August 1729. [*Dublin,* 1729.]
½°: 1 side, 1 column.
 Mourning borders.
'Since its a fashion grown so common'
 In part the same text as *An elegy on the much lamented death of Mr. W— T—r,* [1726].
DT.

E57 — An elegy on the death of James, duke of **Berwick**, who was kill'd one [!] the 11th of April, N.S. in a battle fought between him and the Earl of Galway, near Aryo de Puerci in Spain, where the French and Spanish army were totally defeated by the confederate forces. *London, printed by Thomas Johnson, near the Royal-Exchange,* 1706.
½°: 1 side, 2 columns.
 Mourning headpiece and borders.
'Alas what dismal news of late affrights'
 A false alarm; the Duke of Berwick did not die until 1734.
MH.

E58 — An elegy on the much lamented death of the **bill** to prevent occasional conformity, that departed this life the third time at Westminster, December the 15th. 1704. *London, printed in the year* 1704. (Dec)
1°: 1 side, 2 columns.
 Mourning headpiece and borders.
'Once more kick'd out and hurried to her grave'
L(KTC.126.c.1/2),OW; CSmH.

An elegy on Patie Birnie

— An elegy on Patie **Birnie**, [1721.] *See* Ramsay, Allan.

E59 — An elegy on the much lamented death of Mother **Blackham**, the late college-tart-woman, who departed this life the first of November, 1730. Written by a well-wisher of her's in Trinity. *Dublin, printed in the year* 1730.
½°: 1 side, 2 columns.
'Ungrateful death! an apple gave thee birth'
DT.

E60 — Elegy, upon the much to be lamented death, of Sir Robert **Blacwood**, late provost in Edinburgh. Who departed this life Aprile the 24th 1720. [*Edinburgh*, 1720.]
½°: 1 side, 1 column.
Mourning borders.
'Oh! death, thou conquerour of men'
E.

E61 — An elegy on the much lamented death of Quarter-master Brice **Blare**; who died at Strabane. By a northern bard. *Dublin, printed by J. Carson*, 1734.
½°: 1 side, 2 columns.
'Scarce had the bells the news began'
C.

E62 — An elegy on the great and famous **Blew-stone**, which lay on the Castle-hill of Edinburgh, and was buried therein. [*Edinburgh*, 171–?]
½°: 1 side, 1 column.
'What place is this I've fixt my feet upon?'
E.

E63 — An elegy on the much lamented death of the honble Christian **Borr**, esq; who departed this life the 10th inst. June, 1733. [*Dublin*, 1733.]
½°: 1 side, 1 column.
Mourning headpiece and borders.
'What grief and wo do's now my soul oppress'
CSmH.

E64 — An elegie on the never enough lamented death, of the right honourable John Murray lord **Bowhill**, one of the senators of the colledge of justice; who departed this life upon the 26th March 1714. [*Edinburgh*, 1714.]
½°: 1 side, 1 column.
Mourning borders.
'O! thou my muse, that's now bedew'd with tears'
E.

E65 — An elegy on the much lamented death of the revd. Mr. Joseph **Boyss**, who departed this life on Friday the 22d of November, 1728. [*Dublin*, 1728.]
½°: 1 side, 2 columns.
Mourning borders. The O copy is bound next to a Dublin half-sheet, and a copy was listed with Dublin elegies in Dobell **cat.** 105/296.
'Death who regards not wealth or blood'
O.

E66 — An elegie upon the never enough to be lamented death, of the right honourable Adam **Brown**, esq;

An elegy upon...Adam Brown

lord provost of Edinburgh, who departed this life the 16 of October; 1711. [*Edinburgh*, 1711.]
½°: 1 side, 1 column.
Mourning borders.
'As soon as death by sin was usher'd in'
E(2),GM.

E67 — An elegy on the much lamented death of Matthew **Buckinger**, the famous little-man (without arms or legs) who departed this life at Cork, Sept. 28. 1722. [*Dublin*, 1722.]
½°: 1 side, 2 columns.
Mourning borders. Later reprinted in *The Drapier's miscellany*, 1733. Probably the same work as *A serio-comical elegy, on the much lamented death of Matthew Buckinger* [London, 1722.]
'Poor Buckinger at last is dead and gone'
A punning elegy, attributed to Swift as 'suppos'd' author in *Two elegies on the much to be lamented death of Matthew Buckingher* (Edinburgh, 1723).
C.

E68 — — who departed this life at Edinburgh. [*Edinburgh*? 1722?]
½°: 1 side, 2 columns.
Presumably reprinted at Edinburgh, to judge from the change of title.
L(1876.f.1/108),E(title cropt).

E69 — An elegy on the death of Francis **Burgersdicius**, burnt in the College-parks Monday the 26th of October, 1730. [*Dublin*] *Printed in the year* 1730.
½°: 1 side, 1 column.
'We must resign (heav'n his great soul does claim)'
Apparently on the abandonment of Franco Burgersdijk's *Institutionum logicarum libri duo* as a text book at Trinity College Dublin. Written in imitation of Waller's poem on the death of Cromwell.
C; CSmH.

E70 — Elegy on the much to be lamented death of the reveren [!] Doctor Gilbert **Burnet**, bishop of Salisbury, who departed this life March 17th. 1715, in the 73 year of his age. [*Edinburgh*, 1715.]
½°: 1 side, 1 column.
Mourning borders.
'Here is a loss to church state & to all'
E.

E71 — [An elegy...] on my lord New Town **Butler**, 10th March, 1724. [*Dublin*, 1724.]
½°.
(Dobell cat. 105/296.)

E72 — An elegy on the very much lamented death, of Sir Toby **Buttler**, knight barrister at law, how [!] departed this life this 11th of March 1720–21. In the 78 year of his age. [*Dublin*, 1721.]
½°: 1 side, 1 column.
Mourning headpiece and borders.

An **elegy** on…Sir Toby Buttler

'To day as great a soul is fled'
L(11602.i.1/2).

E73 — ⟨An elegy⟩ on the lamented death of the right hon. William Cadogan, earl **Cadogan**, viscount Caversham, baron of Reading and of Oakley, general of the foot forces in South Britain, master of the robes, colonel of the first regiment of foot guards, governor of the Isle of Wight, knight of the most noble order of the Thistle, and one of his majesty's most hon. privy councill. *Dublin, re-printed in the year* 1726.
½°: 1 side, 1 column.

On the other side of the DT copy, *A poem on the proceedings, at the annual meeting,* [1726.]
'Mourn! Britain! mourn! thy captain general's fled'
DT(title cropt).

E74 — An elegy on the much lamented death of Charles **Campbel** esq; who departed this life the 29th inst. October 1725. [*Dublin, printed by C. Carter,* 1725.]
½°: 1 side, 1 column.
Mourning headpiece and borders. Printed by Carter on the evidence of the headpiece.
'What tho' no pious tears nor vows can save'
L(11602.i.1/19, imprint cropt).

E75 — Elegie on the death of Mr. George **Campbell**, professor of divinity in the college of Edinburgh. [*Edinburgh,* 1701.]
½°: 1 side, 1 column.
Mourning borders.
'Assist Melpomene, thou doleful muse'
L(11633.i.9/2).

E76 — Elegy on the mournful banishment, of James **Campbell** of Burnbank, to the West-Indies. [*Edinburgh,* 1721/22.]
½°: 1 side, 2 columns.
19 stanzas.
'Now let salt tears run down our cheeks'
L(11602.i.6/4, mutilated),E.

E77 — Elegy on the murnful banishment of James Campbel… [*Edinburgh,* 1721/22.]
½°: 1 side, 2 columns.
23 stanzas and 3 stanzas of epitaph.
E; CSmH.

E78 — [*idem*] The life and conversation of James Campbell of Burnbanck. Published from the original coppy. [*Edinburgh,* 1721/22.]
½°: 2 sides, 2 columns.
Over 30 stanzas.
CSmH.

— An elegy on the lamented death of the right honourable…Elizabeth late marchioness of **Carmarthen,** 1713. *See* Crispe, Henry.

E79 — ⟨An elegy…**Cathcart**…⟩ an account of his strange life and wonderful actions, &c. [*Edinburgh,* 172–?]
½°: 1 side, 2 columns.
'Oh! Edinburgh the muses seat'

An **elegy**…Cathcart

A mock elegy on James Cathcart, the astrologer. Answered by *The restoration of the famous Cathcart,* [172–?].
E(title cropt).

E80 — An elegy on the much lamented death of the right honourable William Caulfield, lord viscount **Charlemont**, who departed this life, on Thursday the 21st of this instant July, 1726… [*Dublin*] *Printed by Elizabeth Sadleir,* 1726.
1°: 1 side, 2 columns.
Mourning borders.
'Oh! cruel death can nothing stop thy rage'
DT.

E81 — An elegy on the much lamented death of the rt. hon. William Caulfield, lord viscount **Charlemont** who departed this life on Thursday the 21st of this inst. July 1726. at his house on College-green. *Dublin, printed by* ( ), 1726.
½°: 1 side, 1 column.
Mourning borders.
'Thou best of lords, and thou of mortals best'
DT.

E82 — An elegy on the death of Capt. Edward **Charleton,** who departed this life on Thursday the 13th inst. December, 1722. in the 53d year of his age. *Dublin, printed* ⟨in⟩ *the year* 1722.
½°: 1 side, 2 columns.
Mourning borders.
'And thus you leave us noble captain'
CtY(mutilated).

E83 — An elegy on the burning of the **Church memorial**. [*London,*] 1705.
½°: 1 side, 1 column.
'No! sacred pages, never more repine'
Crum N254: 'An elegy on the burning of the Memorial by order of the court at the Old Bailey upon the presentation of a very whiggish grand jury. Sep. 4. 1705'. *The memorial of the church of England* was by James Drake.
O,*MR*,Chatsworth,Crawford; *NjP*.

E84 — [*idem*] Fire and faggot: or the bishop of St. Asaph's bonfire, on Thursday last, in the palace-yard in Westminster. [*London*] *Printed in the year* 1712.
½°: 1 side, 1 column.
Reprinted on the occasion of the burning of the preface to William Fleetwood's *Four sermons,* 1712, on 12 June 1712. Apparently not the *Fire and faggot* written by Pittis in 1705.
L(1850.c.10/26),LLP,O,*O-JJ*; MH.

E85 — An elegy on the reverend Dean **Clayton**, who departed this life on Friday the 24th inst. Septemb. 1725. [*Dublin, printed by C. Carter,* 1725.]
½°: 1 side, 1 column.
Printed by Carter on the evidence of the mourning headpiece.
'O rev'rend dean, since death has been so kind'
L(11602.i.1/16).

An **elegy** on...Jack Clifford

E86 — An elegy on the much lamented death of Jack **Clifford**, the news-cryer, formerly packet-carrier to B—y Wh—ch—t. [*Dublin*, 1727?]
½°: 1 side, 1 column.
　　Mourning headpiece and borders. The DT copy is bound with half-sheets of 1727.
'What, Clifford dead! no poet to rehearse'
L(11602.i.1/28),DT.

E87 — Elegy on the much lamented death of Ch-----les **Co-----ey**, the poet. [*Dublin*] *Printed in the year* 1725.
½°: 1 side, 2 columns.
'Shall Co—ey die, and yet not have'
　　A mock elegy, satirizing Charles Coffey.
L(11602.i.1/23).

E88 — An elegy on the much to be lamented death, of William **Connelly**, esqr; late speaker to the honourable house of commons, who departed this life, this present Thursday being the 30th inst. October, 1729. At his house in Caple-street Dublin. [*Dublin*, 1729.]
½°: 1 side, 1 column.
　　Mourning borders.
'Grim cruel death, how fatal is thy blow'
DT.

E89 — [An elegy...] on Alderman **Constantine**, 15th March, 1724. [*Dublin*, 1724.]
½°.
(Dobell cat. 105/296.)

E90 — An elegy on the universally lamented death of the right honourable Sir. Samuel **Cook**...who departed this life...yesterday being Snuday [!] the 27th of this instant August, 1726... [*Dublin*, 1726.]
½°: 1 side, 1 column.
　　Mourning borders.
'When saints depart, and leave their earthly bed'
DT.

E91 — [An elegy] on the death of the right honourable George earl of **Cromarty**, lord Tarbat, &c. who departed this life 27th August 1714, about the 90th year of his age. [*Edinburgh*, 1714.]
½°.
'Mourn all ye loyalists in Britain's isle'
(*Maidment* 206, communicated by David Haig.)

E92 — An elegy on the much lamented death of Mr. Aaron **Crossly**, herald-painter of Dublin, who departed this life, on Friday the first of this instant October, 1725. *Dublin, printed by W. Wilmot*, 1725.
½°: 1 side, 2 columns.
　　Mourning headpiece.
'How few surviving mortals warning take'
L(11602.i.1/17).

E93 — An elegy, inscrib'd to the Duke of **Cumberland**. *Edinburgh, printed for Hamilton & Balfour*, 1746.
4°: A–B⁴ (A2 as 'A', A4 as 'B2'); *1–2* 3–15 *16 blk*.
　　The watermark varies; most copies have the royal arms, a copy at E has pro patria, the copy at L has none. Possibly one represents fine paper.

An **elegy**...Duke of Cumberland

'Why swells my heart? Why flows the painful tear?'
　　Written on his reported death at the battle of Falkirk.
L(11631.d.61),E(2, 1 in original wrappers),GM, LdU-B; *CU*,MH.

E94 — An elegy on the much-lamented death of Mr. George **Curtis** of the city of Dublin, banker. [*Dublin*, 1727.]
½°: 1 side, 1 column.
　　Mourning headpiece and borders.
'Nature demands it from us all'
　　The first half of the text is substantially the same as *A funeral elegy on...Mr. Richard Johnson and Mr. John Porter*, [1730.]
L(11602.i.1/27),DT.

E95 — An elegy on the much lamented death of Father Nicholas **Dalton**, who departed this life on Wednesday the 17th of this instant November 1725. At his late lodging in Bridge Street. [*Dublin*, 1725.]
½°: 1 side, 1 column.
　　Mourning head- and tailpieces.
'Ye learned doctors, on whose brows sits grief'
L(11602.i.1/21).

E96 — An elegy on the much lamented death of Denis **Daly**, one of the late King James's judges in this kingdom, who departed this life, at his lodgings in High-street Dublin, on Saturday the 11th of this instant March 1720–21. [*Dublin*, 1721.]
½°: 1 side, 1 column.
　　Mourning borders.
'Come help me now ye muses, to deplore'
L(11602.i.1/3).

E97 — An elegie, on, the never enough to be lamented death, of the reverend Mr. William **Delape** preacher of the gospel, who departed this life October 30, 1720. Aged 28 years. [*Edinburgh*, 1720.]
½°: 1 side, 1 column.
　　Mourning borders.
'O great, eternal, high and mighty one'
E.

E98 — An elegy on the much lamented death of Richard **Delemar** esq; council at law, who departed this life, at his lodgings in St. Michael's Lane Dublin, on Wednesday the 22d. of this instant February 1721–22. [*Dublin*, 1722.]
½°: 1 side, 1 column.
　　Mourning borders.
'You students of the Temple, now bewaile'
L(11602.i.1/3*).

— An elegy on the much lamented death of Mr. **Demar**, [1720.] *See* Swift, Jonathan.

E99 — An elegy on the much lamented death of Sir Thomas **De Veil**, knt. who departed this life on Tuesday the seventh of October at his house in Bow-street, Covent-garden, at three o'clock in the morning. [*London*, 1746.]
1°: 1 side, 2 columns.
　　Mourning headpiece and woodcut borders.

An **elegy** on . . . Sir Thomas De Veil

'What's this I hear, great De Veil breath'd his last'
O; MWiW-C.

E100 — [*idem*] An elegy on the much lamented death of Sir Thomas De Veil, knt. who departed this life at one o'clock this morning. [*London*, 1746.]
½º: 1 side, 2 columns.
    Mourning headpiece and borders. An inferior production to the preceding, but possibly an earlier edition to judge from the title.
    O.

E101 — An elegy on the much lamented death of William duke of **Devonshire**; lord steward of the household to the late King William . . . who departed this life in the 64th year of his age, at his house at St. James's, on Monday the 18th of August, 1707. *London, printed by J. Read*, 1707.
½º: 1 side, 2 columns.
    Mourning headpiece and borders. The MH copy has a ms. correction to '68th year'.
'No more!---Alas, that bitter word, no more!'
MH.

— An elegy on **Dicky** and Dolly, 1732. *See* Swift, Jonathan.

E102 — An elegy on the untimely death of Mr. Benjamin **Dod**, late linen-draper in Cornhill, who unfortunately fell from his horse, coming from Oxford, on Fryday the 7th of June, 1706. In answer to his last will and testament lately publish'd. *London, printed by E.B. near Ludgate*, [1706.]
½º: 1 side, 2 columns.
    Mourning headpiece.
'Attend, while I relate the fall'
MH.

E103 — An elegy on the lamented death of John **Dolben**, esq; (one of the chief managers against Dr. Henry Sacheverel, at his late tryal at Westminster) who departed this life on Monday the 29th of May, 1710. *London, printed in the year* 1710. (*SR* 30 May)
½º: 1 side, 2 columns.
    Mourning headpiece and borders. Entered in *SR* to Will Wise.
'Lament, lament, ye champions of the laws'
L(C.20.f.2/229),DA(mutilated),Madan.

E104 — An elegy on the much lamented death of the revern'd father in god, Sir Daniel **Dowdwel**, who departed this life, on Sunday the 4th of this inst May 1729. Near his chappel on Arron's Key, Dublin. [*Dublin*, 1729.]
½º: 1 side, 1 column.
    Mourning headpiece and borders.
'Dead? and I live to hear it and not dye'
    Almost identical text and setting of type as *An elegy on the much lamented death of William King*, [1729.]
DT.

E105 — An elegy on the much lamented death of Henry Moore, earl of **Drogheda**, who departed this life on Sunday being the 28th of this instant May 1727.

An **elegy** on . . . earl of Drogheda

At his late lodgings on the Batchalers Walk, and in the 27th year of his age. [*Dublin*, 1727.]
½º: 1 side, 1 column.
    Mourning headpiece.
'My mournful muses guide this pen of mine'
    Substantially the same text as *An elegy on . . . Mr. John Parnel*, [1727.]
DT.

E106 — An elegy, on the never enough to be lamented death of that vertuous and worthy gentleman Capt: Geo: **Drummond**. Who dyed at Edinburgh, September 26, 1720. [*Edinburgh*, 1720.]
½º: 1 side, 1 column.
    Mourning borders.
'How frail, how vain, momentainous man?'
E.

E107 — [An elegy] on the much to be lamented death of Mr. Charles **Dunbreck**, captain of the city guard of Edinburgh, &c. who died the 31st of October 1717. [*Edinburgh*, 1717.]
½º.
'What means the warlike Mars thus to appear'
(*Maidment* 216, from David Haig's copy.)

E108 — An elegy on the much lamented death of Sir John **Eccles** knight bar. who departed this transitory life, on Sunday the 2d of this instant April 1727. [*Dublin*, 1727.]
½º: 1 side, 1 column.
    Mourning borders.
'Since god decreed, all men shou'd turn to dust'
DT.

E109 — An elegy on the much lamented death of Sir Henery **Echlin**, bart. late seccond baron of his majesty's court of exchequer, in Ireland, who departed this life the 29th. of this instant November 1725. [*Dublin*, 1725.]
½º: 1 side, 1 column.
    Mourning borders.
'Mourn! mourn! ye nine your Echlin now is gone'
L(11602.i.1/22).

E110 — An elegy on the lamented death of Miss **Edwards**, who departed this life at her house in Pall-Mall; on Tuesday the 23d, of Angust [!], in the 27th year of her age. *London, printed for T. Davis in Black-Horse-alley in Fleet-street*, [1743.]
½º: 1 side, 2 columns.
    Mourning headpiece and borders.
'Ye muses strike the trembling string'
L(C.121.g.9/119).

E111 — An elegy on **eighteen aldermen**; who were prevented by death, from assisting at the ceremonies of proclaiming the peace between her majesty, and the catholick king of Spain. *Dublin, printed by E. Waters*, [1713?]
½º: 1 side, 1 column.
'You sons of faction, who from truth dissent'
    Occasioned by the dispute over the Dublin mayoralty.
L(1890.e.5/28),C(imprint cropt).

E112 — An elegy on the much to be lamented death of Mary **Eriskine** relick of James Hair, late drugist in Edinburgh. Who departed this life, July 2d. 1707. [*Edinburgh*, 1707.]
½º: 1 side, 1 column.
    Mourning borders.
'If they did Dorcas for her thrift bemoan'
L(11633.i.9/10).

— Elegie on the death of...Sir James **Falconer** of Phesdo, [1705.] *See* Whyte, William.

E113 — Elegy on the death of Handsome **Fealding**, who departed from a sober life, on the very day that he bid adieu to good manners, to the great grief of those peaceable people, call'd quakers, who have often invited him to enter into their mortifying congregation. [*London*, 1712?]
½º: 1 side, 2 columns.
    Mourning borders.
'Each matron, consecreated in the trade'
    A satirical elegy.
O.

— [An elegy] on the death of the incomparable Thomas **Fisher**, [1711.] *See* Monteith, Robert.

E114 — An elegy on the much lamented death of Mr. Prime Serjeant **Fitz-Gerald**; who unfortunately fell off his horse yesterday, being the 21st of this instant January, 1724–5. Of which fall he soon dy'd. [*Dublin*, 1725.]
½º: 1 side, 1 column.
    Mourning borders.
'Surprizing dangers apt to startle more'
L(11602.i.1/8).

E115 — An elegy on the much to be lamented death, of the reverend, Mr. Joseph **Foord**. minister of the gospel at Edinburgh, who departed this life July the 15th, 1719. In the 26th, year of his age. [*Edinburgh*, 1719.]
½º: 1 side, 1 column.
    Mourning borders.
'O death, why tyrranisest thou in thy might?'
E.

E116 — An elegy on the much lamented death of Alderman **Ford**, who departed this life the 25th of this instant August, 1725. *Dublin, printed by C.C.* [*Cornelius Carter*], 1725.
½º: 1 side, 1 column.
    Mourning headpiece and borders.
'Almighty death, by whose decessive blow'
L(11602.i.1/14, imprint cropt),C.

E117 — Elegy on the never enough to be lamented death, of the Earl of **Forquar**, who departed this life: December the 7th, 1715. The twenty one year of his age. [*Edinburgh*, 1715.]
½º: 1 side, 1 column.
    Mourning borders.
'Ah! Scotland, ah! why are thy muses dumbe?'
    Archibald Douglas, the earl of Forfar, was fatally wounded at Sherrifmuir.
Crawford.

E118 — An elegy on the much lamented death of Mr. Robert **Fortune**, our lord mayor's clerk, who departed this life on Monday the 18th of this instant December 1727. At his house in Loftis's Lane. [*Dublin*, 1727.]
½º: 1 side, 1 column.
    Mourning borders.
'Know all men in the name of god'
DT.

E119 — An elegy on the much lamented death of Robert **Fortune**, gent. who departed this life, on Sunday 17th inst. December. 1727. *Dublin, printed in the year* 1727.
½º: 1 side, 1 column.
    Within woodcut arch. A ms. correction in the DT copy changes the date to the 18th.
'Oh fortune! fortune, thou hast done thy worst'
DT.

E120 — An elegy on the royal family of **France**. [*London*, 1712.] (20 March, Luttrell)
2º: A²; 1–4.
'Nor shall they fall unmourn'd--- Nor dare we pry'
    The copy at CtY has an early ms. note 'writ by Mr. Westl⟨ ⟩', unfortunately cropt; possibly by Samuel Wesley the elder.
CtY,InU(Luttrell),MH,OCU(ms. date 22 March).

E121 — An elegy. On the death of the most ingenious, good natur'd, loyal, undesigning, compassionate, virtuous, and facetious, Ma----w **Fr----ch**, senior fellow of Trinity-College, Dublin. [*Dublin*, 1714.]
½º: 1 side, 1 column.
    Mourning headpiece and borders.
'Mourn all you whigs, with deepest anguish mourn'
    On the death of Matthew French, 12 March 1714.
Rothschild.

E122 — An elegy on the much lamented death of the right honourable R. **Freeman**, one of the lords justices, and lord high chancellor of her majesty's kingdom of Ireland: who departed this life the 20th of this inst. Novemb. 1710. [*Dublin*, 1710.]
½º: 1 side, 1 column.
    Mourning borders.
'O tyrant death! O hard result of fate'
DT.

E123 — An elegy, on the death of the **French king**, who departed this life on Wednesday March 27th, 1709. About eight at night, of an appaplex. *London printed: and re-printed in Channel-row, Dublin*, 1709.
½º: 1 side, 2 columns.
    Mourning headpiece and borders.
'Just ripe for vengance, and diviner wrath'
    Louis XIV did not in fact die until 1715.
DT.

E124 — An elegy on the death of Mr. Joseph **Fuller**, late minister of the gospel at Reading...who departed this life March the 9th, 1712. in the 38th year of his age. *London, printed in the year* 1713.

An **elegy** on... Joseph Fuller

1°: 1 side, 2 columns.
  Mourning borders.
'Sit down, sad muse! and thy free thoughts apply'
LDW.

E125 — An elegy on the downfall, ruin and destruction of a **fur-bush**, that was kindled at the Rose-Tavern in Castle-street, on Monday the first day of January, 1727–8, at five a'-clock in the afternoon; and continued burning at the Tholsel, where it is likely to be consumed. [*Dublin*, 1728.]
½°: 1 side, 2 columns.
'Weep ye mountains and ye vallies'
  The 'fur-bush' appears to have been a parliamentary candidate, possibly Forbes.
CtY.

E126 — An elegy on the much lamented death of Harry **Gambol**, who dy'd of a pleuresy, Aug. 31. [*London*] *Printed by John Nichols near Charing Cross*, [1714.]
slip: 1 side, 1 column.
'How vain, delusive, and how transitory'
  A mock elegy on the fall of Bolingbroke.
MH.

E127 — An elegy on the memory of the honourable Colonel James **Gardner**, who was cruelly murdered by the antichristian mob near Tranent, Sept. 21. 1745. [*Edinburgh*, 1745.]
½°: 1 side, 2 columns.
  Mourning headpiece.
'Who can but ly in sable weed'
O.

E128 — 'An elegy on the death of our late sovereign King **George**, of glorious memory. By J.B. gent. [*London*] *Sold at the pamphlet shops*. Price 4*d*.' (*MC* Aug 1727)

E129 — 'An elegy on the much lamented death of his royal highness Prince **George** of Denmark... Who departed this life October 28. 1708. [*London*] *Printed, and sold by B. Bragge*.' (*Observator* 30 Oct 1708)
  Listed at 1*d*. in *Observator* 10 Nov, suggesting that it is a half-sheet. Possibly the same work as B581, *A new elegy... Written by D. Burnet*, (printed by J. Read, 1708).

E130 — An elegy on Lucky **Gibson**, who departed this life January 20th, 1718. [*Edinburgh*, 1718.]
½°: 1 side, 1 column.
'Why, why dull poets of this canker'd age'
  Lucky Gibson was an Edinburgh bawd.
E.

E131 — An elegy on the much lamented death of that pious and laborious minister of Jesus Christ, the rev. Mr. Andrew **Giffard**, late pastor of a baptized congregation of believers in the city of Bristol; who departed this life Novem. the 6th, 1721, in the 80th year of his age. *Bristol, printed by Henry Greep, in Lewin's-Mead*, 1721.
1°: 1 side, 2 columns.
  Mourning borders.

An **elegy** on... Andrew Giffard

'When I beheld the sad procession go'
LDW.

E132 — An elegy on the much lamented death of the most excellent... Madam **Gineva**. Worthy to be perused by all distillers, whether simple or compound. *London, printed for T. Cooper*, 1736. (*LM* April)
2°: *A*¹ *B*² *C*²; *1–3 4–9 10 blk*.
'Pope I ne'er grudg'd his own Pierian stream'
  A mock elegy satirizing gin-drinking.
L(11630.h.27),LU,LdU-B; TxU(uncut).

E133 — An elegy upon the much lamented death of that religious and virtuous gentlewoman, Mrs. Mary **Gordan**... *Edinburgh, printed in the year* 1723.
8°: *A*⁸; *1–2 3–16*.
'What dismal sound strikes mine affrighted ears!'
NN.

E134 — An elegy on the much lamented death of Captain Thomas **Green**; who was executed with others of his crew, under the pretence of being a pirate, &c. in Scotland, April the 11th 1705. *London printed, and sold by the booksellers of London & Westminster*, 1705.
½°: 1 side, 2 columns.
  Mourning borders.
'Presumptuous arrogance! inhumane rage!'
  Crum P377.
L(C.20.f.2/225).

E135 — An elegy on the death of M. de **Guiscard**, who died in Newgate the 17th of March; which was found near Tyburn, in a letter directed to a gentleman living in Wolverhampton. [*London*] *Sold by J. Morphew*, 1711.
½°: 1 side, 1 column.
'Has then the villain's neck deceiv'd our hope'
MH.

E136 — Elegy on the deplorable death of Margaret **Hall**, barbarously murder'd by her husband Nicol Mushet of Boghall, Mondays night the 17 October 1720, in the 17th year of her age. [*Edinburgh*, 1720.]
½°: 1 side, 1 column.
'All hearts be swell'd with grief, with tears all eyes'
  Possibly by Alexander Pennecuik (d. 1730); it is very similar in typography to his *Elegy on the death of Nichol Muschet*, [1721.]
E; OCU.

E137 — An elegy upon the exceeding much to be lamented death of the illustrious princess Anne dutches of **Hamilton**, who departed this life the 16th. of October 1716, in the 96th. year of her age. [*Edinburgh*, 1716.]
½°: 1 side, 1 column.
  Mourning borders.
'This noble princess of immortal fame'
E.

E138 — An elegie on the much lamented death of the right honourable and most hopeful young noble hero, Lord Basil **Hamilton** youngest son to his grace William late duke of Hamilton, who was

An **elegy** on…Lord Basil Hamilton

unfortunatly drownd, endeavouring to save the life of a French peasant who served his lordship. [*Edinburgh*, 1701.]
½°: 1 side, 1 column.
 Mourning borders.
'Ah! cruel and untimely death'
L(11633.i.9/5).

E139 — Elegie on the universally lamented death of the right honourable Lord Basil **Hamilton**, brother german to his grace the Duke of Hamiltoun. (Being a short hint of his heroick life, and fatal death.) Who dyed August 27th. 1701. Ætatis 27. [*Edinburgh*, 1701.]
½°: 1 side, 1 column.
 Mourning borders.
'Ah! how all elements conspire with death'
E(cropt).

E140 — An elegy on the death of his grace James duke of **Hamilton** and Brandon. [*Edinburgh*, 1743?]
½°: 1 side, 1 column.
'Rouse! rouse! my muse, in justice let me say'
E.

E141 — An elogie on the much lamented death of Mr. John **Hamilton**, minister of the gospel in the Gray-friars parish of Edinburgh; and sometime, formerlie in Ireland. [*Edinburgh*, 1702.]
½°: 1 side, 1 column.
 Mourning borders.
'Come citizens, and mourne with me a part?'
E; *MB*.

E142 — Elegy on the death of Patrick **Hamilton** younger of Green, who was beheaded at the Grass-merkat of Edinburgh, upon the 5th of September 1716. [*Edinburgh*, 1716.]
½°: 1 side, 1 column.
 Mourning borders.
'My weeping muse proceed with murnful tone'
E.

E143 — Elegy on the much-lamented death of John **Harding** printer, who departed this transitory life, this present Monday being the 19th of this instant April 1725. [*Dublin*, 1725.]
½°: 1 side, 1 column.
 Mourning borders.
'When heav'n corrects, shall man complain'
 Williams 1109 remarks in refuting Swift's authorship of another poem on Harding that this bears more resemblance to Swift's style; but there is no evidence that it is by him.
L(11602.i.1/11).

E144 — An elegy on the much lamented death of Mr **Harrison**, the banker who departed this life the 4th. day of July 1725. [*Dublin*, 1725.]
½°: 1 side, 1 column.
 Mourning borders.
'Great Harrison is dead, lament Hibernians all'
L(11602.i.1/13),O.

E145 — An elegy on the **heroic poem** lately publish'd by the vicar of Cheshunt. By Chapmanno-Wiskero.

An **elegy** on the heroic poem

London printed, and sold by J. Morphew, 1715 [1714]. (*MC* Nov)
2°: A–B² C¹; *1–2* 3–10.
'God the first poet was, and poets made'
 A satire on Richard Chapman's *Britannia rediviva*, 1714.
L(643.1.25/15); MH.

E146 — An elegy on the much lamented death of the reveren'd Dr. Francis **Higgin's** who departed this life on Tuesday the 3d. of this instant September, 1728. at his late lodging in Mary's-street. [*Dublin*, 1728.]
½°: 1 side, 1 column.
 Mourning borders.
'Nay, now forbear, for pity's sake give o're'
 Apparently related to *An elegy on the much lamented death, of the reverend Doctor Trever*, [1727], which has the same first line.
CtY.

E147 — An elegy on the death of **high-church** passive-obedience and non-resistance: which departed this life on the 22d of this instant March 17$\frac{09}{10}$, much lamented. *London printed, and sold by B. Bragge*, 1710. (*Observator* 25 March)
1°: 1 side, 2 columns.
 Mourning headpiece and woodcut borders.
'Weep all you passive slaves, no more repine'
 On the conviction of Sacheverell.
L(KTC.126.c.1/5).

E148 — An elegy upon the much lamented death of Janet **Hill**, spouse to the famous Tinclarian Doctor William Mitchell, who departed this life, 13th of October 1716. [*Edinburgh*, 1716.]
½°: 1 side, 1 column.
 Mourning borders.
'The defunct has obtain'd a name'
E.

E149 — An elegy on the much lamented death of Thomas **Hogg**; who departed this life on Thursday, the 13th of this instant January, 1725–6. [*Dublin*, 1726.]
½°: 1 side, 2 columns.
 Mourning headpiece.
'I am told my honest friend Tom Hogg'
DT(imprint cropt).

E150 — An elegy on the much lamented death, of the reverend divine Dr. John **How**, minister of the gospel, to a pious congregation in Silver-street, who departed this life at his dwelling house in St. John's⟨ ⟩ on Monday morning last, being the 2d instant, 1705, in the 72 year of his age. *London, printed by J. Read*, 1705.
½°: 1 side, 2 columns.
 Mourning headpiece and borders.
'Lament, lament, for learned How that's gone'
O(slightly cropt).

E151 — An elegy on the much lamented death of William **Howard** esq; one of his majesty's counsel's at law, and one of the representatives in parliament

An **elegy** on...William Howard

for the honourable city of Dublin, who departed this life, at his house in Chancery-lane, on Saturday December the 30th 1727. [*Dublin*, 1728.]
½°: 1 side, 1 column.
    Mourning headpiece and borders.
'Great god how shall my trembling tongue declare'
    Substantially the same text as *An elegy on the much lamented 'Squire Roberts*, [1727] and other elegies listed there.
DT.

E152 — An elegy on the much lamented death of the right honourable --------- lord of **Howth**, who departed this life this present Tuesday May the thirtieth, 1727. [*Dublin*, 1727.]
½°: 1 side, 1 column.
    Mourning headpiece.
'Thus sets the shining planet of the day'
    On Thomas St. Lawrence, Lord Howth.
DT.

E153 — An elegy on the much lamented death of Doctor Richard **Hoyle**, who departed this life the 1st. of this instant September 1730. at the place call'd Dorrow, near Tallimoor in the King's county, to the unspeakeable loss of the poor. [*Dublin*, 1730.]
½°: 1 side, 1 column.
    Mourning borders.
'And must our deaths be silenc'd too! I guess'
DT.

E154 — An elegy upon the much to be lamented death, of the right honourable Sir David **Hume** of Crossrig, one of the seuators [!] of the college of justice; who departed this life April 13. 1707. [*Edinburgh*, 1707.]
½°: 1 side, 1 column.
    Mourning borders. On the other side of the E copy, *A true account of a great engagement*, [1706?] in prose.
'True grace and vertue are such special things'
L(11633.i.9/9),E.

E155 — An elegy on the death of **James** the second, late king of England, who departed this mortal life, on Wednesday the 3d of Septemb. at St. Germains-en Lay, at 3 a clock in the morning in the sixty eight year of his age, 1701. *London, printed by H.H.* [*Henry Hills*] *in Black-fryers*, 1701.
1°: 1 side, 2 columns.
    Royal arms as headpiece, woodcut mourning borders.
''Tis true---when death, fate's minister does call'
L(C.20.f.2/215).

E156 — An elogie on the death of **James** the seventh and second, late king of Great Britain, France and Ireland, &c. who departed this life at St Germans in France, the 14th. day of September N.S. 1701... [*Edinburgh*, 1701.]
½°: 1 side, 1 column.
'What eyes o'reflow with tears! that he is gone'
    Signed, 'A Vero Scoto'.
E.

An **elegy** on...King James

— An elegy on the death of King **James**, [1701?] *See* On the death of King James, [1701?]

E157 — An elegy, on the death of the late King **James**, who departed this life, at his pallace of St. Germains in France, on Wednesdny [!] the 3d of September 1701, in the 68th year of his age. *London, printed by J. Wilkins, near Fleet-street*, 1701. (8 Sept, Luttrell)
1°: 1 side, 2 columns.
    Mourning headpiece and woodcut borders.
'What rumour's this, as does our ears amuse?'
L(KTC.126.c.1/3); MH(Luttrell).

E158 — — '*London, printed by J. Wilkins*', [1701.]
½°: 1 side, 2 columns.
    Probably an Edinburgh reprint.
E.

E159 — [*idem*] On the much lamented death, of the most serene and illustrious prince, James VII. and II. late king of Scotland, England, France and Ireland, who departed this life in the royal palace of St. Germans in France, upon Saturday, the 6th of September 1701. in the 68th year of his age. [*London?* 1701.]
½°: 1 side, 2 columns.
    A more sophisticated text and better printed sheet; the priority of editions has not been established.
'What rumour's this that does our ears amuse?'
E.

E160 — An elegy upon his late majesty **James** II. (of ever blessed memory) king of Great Britain, &c. By M.B. gent. [*Paris?*] *Printed in the year* 1701. *And are to be sold by Mr.*   *at St. Germains.*
4°: *A*² B–E²; [2] i–ii, 1–16.
    The blank in the imprint is completed in ms. 'W. Weston' in the copy seen. The preface complains of the failures of the author's friends in Paris and St. Germains who were responsible for having it printed.
'If so! good angels! take his precious soul!'
O.

E161 — An elegie upon the much lamented death of the most serene and potent prince, **James** VII: late of Scotland, England, France and Ireland, king. Who departed this life at St. Germans in France, September 14: N.S: 1701. [*Edinburgh*, 1701.]
1°: 1 side, 2 columns.
    Mourning borders.
'Before sin tainted the pure universe'
E(2, 1 cropt).

E162 — An elegy on the much lamented death of **Jaquo'** the monkey keeper of the Black-dogg, who was barbarously murther'd last night by a hard hearted gentlewoman. *Dublin, printed in the year* 1725.
½°: 1 side, 1 column.
'Hark! hark the noise, the sorrows, and the eccho!'
L(1968, mutilated),C.

E163 — An elegy on the much lamented death of **Jenny** the fish, which departed this life at Rings-End the

An **elegy** on . . . Jenny the fish

19th. of Jan. 1718. [*Dublin*] *Printed at the request of her lamenters*, [1718.]
½°: 2 sides, 1 column.
   Mourning headpiece.
'If ladies weep when petted lap-dogs die'
   Reprinted in *Poems written occasionally by John Winstanley . . . interspers'd with many others*, 1742; the authorship is not made clear.
IU.

— An elegy on the death of Robert **Jones**, 1748. *See* Wesley, Charles.

E164 — An elegy on the much lamented death of **Joseph** emperor of Germany, who departed this life the 17th of April, N.S. 1711, in the 33d year of his age, the 21st of his reign as king of the Romans, 23d of Hungary, and 6th as emperor. *London, printed; and re-printed by F. Dickson, Dublin*, 1711.
½°: 1 side, 1 column.
   Mourning headpiece and borders. No London edition has been traced.
'Can Christendom's great champion sink away'
   Cf. *Crum* C41: 'On the death of King James', 1625.
DT.

E165 — An elegy on the much lamented death of that faithful and laborious minister of the gospel, Mr. Benjamin **Keach**, late pastor of a church of Christ, meeting on Horsly-down, Southwark: who departed this life, July the 18th, 1704. In the sixty fourth year of his age. Written by a member of his congregation. *London, printed by R. Tookey; sold by S. Malthus*, [1704.]
1°: 1 side, 2 columns.
   Mourning borders.
'Oh! what convulsions seize my tender breast'
L(C.20.f.2/219).

E166 — An elegy upon the moeh [!] to be lamented death of Commissioner **Kello**, who departed this life the 2d. of October 1716. [*Edinburgh*, 1716.]
½°: 1 side, 1 column.
   Mourning borders.
'Abimalech a champiou [!] bold and stout'
   'Commissioner Kello', otherwise John Cayley.
E.

— An elegy, sacred to the memory of Dr. Thomas **Kenn**, [1711.] *See* Stacy, Edmund.

E167 — An elegy on the much lamented death of A - - - l B - - - g - - - m, the passau countess of **Kerry**, one of the western islands of this kingdom. [*Dublin*, 1727.]
½°: 2 sides, 1 column.
   A ms. note in the DT copy gives her date of death as 30 April 1727.
'If we may credit what royal David said'
DT(cropt).

E168 — An elegy on the death of Capt. William **Kidd**, who was executed at Execution-dock, on Friday the 23d of this instant May, 1701. *London printed, and sold by A. Baldwin*, [1701.] (24 May, Luttrell)
½°: 1 side, 1 column.

An **elegy** on . . . William Kidd

Mourning borders.
'When any great and famous man does die'
MH(Luttrell).

E169 — An elegy on the much lamented, and ever to be recorded death of Mr. Daniel **Kimberly**, who unfortunately resign'd his breath near St. Stephens Green, on Wednesday the 27th of this instant May 1730. for procureing a husband to Miss Reading, contrary to her will. [*Dublin*, 1730.]
½°: 1 side, 1 column.
   Mourning borders.
'Who wo'd not both this age and country dread'
   Apparently Kimberly was executed for rape.
CtY.

E170 — An elegy on the much lamented death of Sir John **King** bar. who departed this life the 19th of this inst. March, 172²⁰. [*Dublin*, 1721.]
½°: 1 side, 1 column.
   The date in the title is presumably intended for 172$\frac{0}{1}$.
'Begin ye sweet melodious heav'nly choir'
C.

E171 — An elegy on the most reverend father in god, his grace, William [**King**], late lord archbishop of Dublin. Who departed this life, May the 8th. 1729, in the 80th. year of his age. *Dublin, printed by James Carson*, 1729.
1°: 1 side, 3 columns.
   Mourning borders. The order of editions is uncertain.
'Complaints like ours, in Ramah's vale were heard'
   Cf. *Crum* C677, Nahum Tate's 'Elegy on Dr. Tillotson pub. 1695'; probably an adaptation of Tate's poem. On William King.
DT.

E172 — — *Dublin, printed by J. Carson*, 1729.
½°: 1 side, 2 columns.
   Mourning borders. Variant first line:
'The like complaints, in Rama's vale were heard'
C,DT.

E173 — An elegy on the much lamented death of William **King**, bishop of Dublin, primate of Ireland, and one of the lords justices of this kingdom; who departed this life this present Wednesday being the 8th of this instant May 1729. at his house in Cavens Street, Dublin. [*Dublin*, 1729.]
½°: 1 side, 1 column.
   Mourning headpiece and borders.
'Dead? and I live to hear it and not dye'
   Almost identical text and setting of type as *An elegy on the much lamented death of the revern'd father in god, Sir Daniel Dowdwel*, [1729.]
DT.

E174 — An elegy on the much lamented loss of his grace William **King** lord arch-bishop of Dublin, primate and metropolitan of all Ireland, who died, May 8, 1729. At his palace of St. Sepulchre's in Kevan's

An **elegy** on...William King

Street, Dublin. *Dublin, printed by J.K. and sold by the stationers*, 1729.
½°: 1 side, 1 column.
> In woodcut arch.

'Oh! blackest day that e're the sun 'rose on'
DT.

E175 — An elegy made on the **Last speech** and dying words of the ever to be forgotten Bank of Ireland, which was executed at Colledge-green on Saturday the 9th instant. [*Dublin*, 1721.]
½°: 1 side, 1 column.
> Mourning borders.

'Oh! unlucky bank, art thou now condemn'd'
> *The last speech and dying words of the Bank of Ireland*, [1721] is a prose broadside.

CtY.

E176 — An elegy on Mr. George **Lauder**. [*Edinburgh*, 17--.]
½°: 1 side, 1 column.
'Dull is the muse that aids the servile pen'
E.

E177 — Elegy upon the much lamented death of Lucky **Law**. [*Edinburgh*, 1714?]
½°: 1 side, 2 columns.
'Since the raign of King Solomon'
> Lucky Law was a fruit-wife.

EP.

E178 — An elegy on that worthy patriot of his country, Sir Roger **L'Estrange**. *London, printed in the year* 1705.
½°: 1 side, 2 columns.
'D'ye hear the news! Sir Roger he's retir'd'
> A satire against him.

Crawford.

E179 — An elegy on the much lamented death of Sir Roger **L'Estrange**, who departed this life on Monday the 11th. day of December 1704. In the 88th year of his age. *London, printed by D. Edwards in the year* 1704. (Dec)
1°: 1 side, 2 columns.
'L'Estrange departed! and no mourning muse'
L(C.20.f.2/218),LLP; CSmH.

E180 — An elegy on the very much lamented death of that truely noble and pious lady the Countess of **Leven**. Daughter to the right honourable, the Lord Bruntisland and Margaret countess of Weems, snatch'd away by a sudden death, January 9th. 1702. *Edinburgh, printed by James Watson*, 1702.
1°: 1 side, 2 columns.
> Mourning borders.

'As sudden claps of thunder strikes the ear'
E(2).

E181 — An elegy on the much lamented death of Dr. Dennis **Mc.Carthy** priest of Corke who lately departed this life, in the 80th year of his age, 1725–6. [*Dublin, printed by C. Carter*, 1726.]
½°: 1 side, 2 columns.
> Mourning headpiece and borders. Printed by Carter on the evidence of the headpiece.

An **elegy** on...Dennis Mc.Carthy

'Shall feeble mortals in their low estate'
DT.

E182 — An elegy on the much-lamented death of the reverend father in god, Dr. Thaddeus **Mc.Dermot**, priest of St. Francis's chappel: who departed this transitory life, on Monday the 12th of this inst. April, 1725, and was interr'd in St. James's church yeard with great solemnity. [*Dublin*, 1725.]
½°: 1 side, 1 column.
> Mourning borders.

'O happy shade! if thou can'st now attend'
L(11602.i.1/10).

E183 — An elegy on the never to be lamented death of Mirs. **M'Leod**, who was execute on Wednesday the 8th of March, 1727. [*Edinburgh*, 1727.]
½°: 1 side, 2 columns.
'O curs'd Atropus, thou cancard wife'
E.

E184 — Elegy on the much to be lamented death, of loyal **Margaret**. Who departed this life June the 6th 1717. [*Edinburgh*, 1717.]
½°: 1 side, 2 columns.
'Ye loyalists your weeds put on'
L(1876.f.1/95),E.

E185 — An elegy or a poem upon the death of his grace John duke of **Marlebourgh**. [1722.]
½°: 1 side, 2 columns.
> A poor piece of printing, possibly re-introducing a poem written at the time of his dismissal.

'Who can cndole [!] this hero's loss? who can?'
O.

E186 — An elegy on the much to be lamented death, of Francis **Masterton** apothecary. [*Edinburgh*, 171–?]
½°: 1 side, 1 column.
> Mourning borders.

'Come thou my mournful muse to his great name'
E.

E187 — An elegy, on the right honourable Edward earl of **Meath**; who dy'd on Tuesday the 22d of February, 1709 [!]. [*Dublin*, 1708.]
½°: 1 side, 2 columns.
> Mourning headpiece and borders.

'Retir'd from business in a dark alcove'
> The Earl of Meath's death seems without doubt to have been on 22 Feb 1707/8.

MH.

E188 — Elegie on the much to be lamented death, of the good and great Mr. George **Meldrum**, professor of divinity, and one of the ministers of the gospel in Edinburgh. [*Edinburgh*, 1709.]
½°: 1 side, 1 column.
> Mourning borders.

'Could I, great Meldrum! thy great worth proclaim'
E.

E189 — An elegy on the much unlamented death of Mathias **Merrideth** govenour of St. Giles work

An elegy on...Mathias Merrideth

house; who departed this life, at Tottenham Court on Saturday the 14th, of February 1732. Being a mornfull dirge or poem made by a poor man in the work-house, shewing all his barbarities to the poor, also how he was frightn'd to death by the ghost or appari,on [!] of the woman that he last starved to death in the darke-hole. *London, printed for D. Smith*, 1732.
½°: 1 side, 2 columns.
  Mourning headpiece.
'Merridieth's gone, but where there's none can tell'
L(C.20.f.2/244).

E190 — An elegy on the much to be lamented death, of Mr. John **Merry** surgeon apothecary. [*Edinburgh*, 171–?]
½°: 1 side, 1 column.
  Mourning borders.
'Is Merry dead, his active spirit flown?'
E.

— An elegy upon the lamented death of Edward **Millington**, 1703. *See* Brown, Thomas.

E191 — An elegy on **moderation**. [*London*, 1710?]
½°: 1 side, 1 column.
  Mourning borders.
'Offspring divine! parent of peace and love!'
  Apparently inspired by the Sacheverell affair.
L(112.f.44/45),LLP,Crawford; TxU.

E192 — An elegy on the universelly lamented death of the right honourable Robert lord vis. **Molesworth**, a lover, protector, and the best of friends to poor Irelands rights, liberties, and church; who departed this life at his country seat at Brackanstown, on Sunday morning about one of the clock, May the 23d. 1725. In the 80th year of his age. By M.B. [*Dublin*, 1725.]
½°: 1 side, 1 column.
  Mourning borders.
'Tho' death has done his worst you cannot die'
L(11602.i.1/12).

E193 — An elegy on the death of Colonel Alexander **Montgomery**, knight of the shire for the county of Donnegal. [*Dublin*, 1729?]
½°: 1 side, 1 column.
  The DT copy is bound with half-sheets of 1729.
'Once mighty Rome, the ruling sceptre sway'd'
DT.

E194 — [An elegy] on the much lamented death of the most noble lady Christian marchioness of **Montrose**; who departed this life the 21st of April 1710, about the flower of her age. [*Edinburgh*, 1710.]
½°?
'O what a change in few days hath death made'
  Elegy on ... the reverend Mr. Thomas Wilkie, [1711] has a very similar first line.
  (*Maidment* 173.)

E195 — Elegy upon the death of Mrs. **Motly**. [*Dublin*, 1727.]

Elegy upon...Mrs. Motly

½°: 1 side, 1 column.
  Mourning borders. A ms. note in the DT copy gives the date of this whore's death as 26 March 1727.
'Ye tender nymphs who strive to please the town'
DT.

E196 — [dh] An elegy upon the much lamented death of a wise, mild, pious, sober, and hopeful youth Samuel **Murray**...at Glasgow...January 1st 1715. being eldest son to Mr. J.M. minister at P------t. [1715.]
4°: A⁴; 1 2–8.
  With other poems in Latin and English on Murray's death.
'Time-comforts are like grass; death hath bereav'd'
CtY(uncut).

— Elegy on the death of Nicol **Muschet**, [1721.] *See* Pennecuik, Alexander, *d. 1730*.

E197 — An elegy on the much lamented death of John lord, viscount **Nettervill** of Douth, who departed this life, December 1727. [*Dublin*, 1727.]
½°: 1 side, 1 column.
  Mourning headpiece and borders.
'Great god how shall my trembling tongue declare'
  Substantially the same text as *An elegy on the much lamented 'Squire Roberts*, [1727] and other elegies listed there.
DT.

E198 — An elegy on the much lamented death of the right honourable the Countess of **Neuburgh**. [*Dublin*, 1736.]
½°: 1 side, 1 column.
  Mourning borders.
'Begin my muse, begin your mournful strains'
C.

E199 — An elegy to the lasting memory, and upon the much to be lamented death of the pious, and well accomplished gentleman, and much honoured, William **Nisbet** of Dirletoun. Obiit, 20. October 1724, ætatis 60. [*Edinburgh*, 1724.]
½°: 1 side, 1 column.
  Mourning borders.
'There is no truth more evident to sense'
E.

E200 — Elegy on the much lamented death of Mr. **No Body**. [*Dublin*, 1727?]
½°: 1 side, 1 column.
  The DT copy is bound with half-sheets of 1727.
'Since the sad news has reach'd my ears'
  Mr. No Body's name is given in the text as 'B--y', but the nickname was used for Marcus Dowley.
DT.

E201 — An elegy on the sudden and much lamented death of his grace, Henry duke of **Norfolk**, and earl marshal of England, who departed this life at his house in St. James's-square, on Wednesday

An **elegy** on…duke of Norfolk

last, near 11 a clock in the morning, being April the 2d 1701, in the 48th year of his age. *London, printed by Jer. Wilkins, near Fleet-street*, 1701. (3 April, Luttrell)
½⁰: 1 side, 2 columns.
　　Mourning headpiece and borders.
'Oh! mornful muse, let me with tears rehearse'
O; MH(Luttrell).

E202 — An elegy on the much lamented death of Richard **Nuttley** esq; council at law, and one of the judges of his majesty's court of king's bench, in the reign of the late Queen Anne; who departed this life this present Tuesday being the 11th of this instant November 1729. At his house in Mary's Street Dublin. [*Dublin*, 1729.]
½⁰: 1 side, 2 columns.
　　Mourning headpiece and borders.
'Let each great genius of the tuneful nine'
DT.

E203 — An elegy on the death of the late famous Doctor Titus **Oates**; who departed this life, at his house in Ax-yard, Westminster, on Thursday the 12th of July, 1705. in the 68th year of his age. Written by the Observator. *London printed, and sold by the booksellers of London & Westminster*, [1705.]
½⁰: 1 side, 2 columns.
　　Mourning headpiece and borders.
'The plot is spoild and we are all undone'
　　The attribution to the Observator, i.e. John Tutchin, is false: it is an attack on him, as well as on Oates.
CSmH,MH.

E204 — An elegy upon the much unlamented death of Dr. Titus **Oates**. Who departed this life on Thursday the 12th of this instant July, at his house in Ax Yard, Westminster. *London printed, and sold by the booksellers*, [1705.]
1⁰: 1 side, 2 columns.
　　Mourning borders.
'Gone! and no comet to portend thy fall?'
CSmH.

E205 — An elegy on the death of that great peer, the right honourable Lord George Hamilton, earl of **Orkney**, one of the marishals of Great Britain, lord governor of Edinburgh-castle and Virginia, colonel of his majesty's two batallions of Scots royal, one of his majesty's most honourable privy council, &c. [*Edinburgh*, 1737.]
½⁰: 1 side, 2 columns.
'Great Orkney's dead, what news is this we hear'
　　Signed, J.G. *C.S.*
E.

E206 — Elegy on the death of Hary **Ormiston**, late hangman in Edinburgh. [*Edinburgh*, 1715?/22.]
½⁰: 1 side, 2 columns.
　　Below, 'Another elegy done by another hand'.
'O curs'd Atropus cruel wife!'
'An has ald death come in his rage'
E(2).

An **elegy** on…duke of Ormonde

E207 — An elegy on his grace James duke of **Ormonde**, who departed this life the 12th of November, 1730. at Valedolid in Spain. [*Dublin*, 1730.]
½⁰: 1 side, 1 column.
'Has death at last or'ecome that libral soul'
　　A false alarm; the Duke of Ormonde did not die until 1745.
DT.

E208 — An elegy on the much lamented death of Mr. John **Parnel** one of his majesty's judges of the king's bench who departed this life at his country seat near Maryborough in the Queen's county, on Sunddy [!] the 2d of this instant July 1727. [*Dublin*, 1727.]
½⁰: 1 side, 1 column.
　　Mourning headpiece.
'My mournful muses guide this pen of mine'
　　Substantially the same text as *An elegy on… Henry Moore, earl of Drogheda*, [1727.]
DT.

E209 — An elegy upon the death of the famous Dr. John **Partridgd** [!], the great astrologer, who departed this life (according to Esq; Biggerstaff's prediction) this morning between the hours of one and two a clock, being the 29th of March, at his house near Covent-Garden. *London, printed in the year* 1708.
½⁰: 1 side, 2 columns.
　　Mourning headpiece and borders.
'O Partridge! art thou gone, and we in tears?'
　　The relationship of this broadside to Swift's mock elegy of the same date is obscure.
Crawford.

— An elegy on Mr. **Patrige**, 1708. *See* Swift, Jonathan.

E210 — [An elegy] on the much to be lamented death of the right honourable the Lord **Pencaitland**, one of the senators of the college of justice, who departed this life, May 30, 1729. *Edinburgh, printed by William Adams*, 1729.
½⁰?
'Empress of Islse [!], who rules the rolling Forth'
(*Maidment* 255.)

E211 — An elegy, upon the **Philadelphian society**: with the false oracles, last speech, and confession. [*London*, 1703.]
½⁰: 2 sides, 2 columns.
'Good English folk, come shake both sides and head'
　　Cf. *The counterpart of the Elegy*, 1703.
L(Harley 5946, fol. 245),LLP.

E212 — An elegy on the death of Sir Constantine **Phipps**, who in the reign of the late Queen Ann, was lord chancellor of this kingdom; and in the year 1710. was councel for Dr. Sachveral [!], and also for the late lord bishop of Rochester the last session. Who departed this life the 9th of this inst. October 1723. at his sate [!] in London. [*Dublin*, 1723.]

An **elegy** on...Sir Constantine Phipps

½º: 1 side, 1 column.
Mourning borders.
'To mournful plaints Brittania turn your muse'
CtY.

E213 — An elegy on the much lamented death of that honourable and charitable Lady Grace **Pierpoint**; who departed this life at her house in So-hoe Square on the 25th of March being lady day 1703, in the 60 year of her age. *London, printed for J. Wilkins,* [1703.]
½º: 1 side, 2 columns.
'You widdows, orphans, and each needy soul'
CSmH.

E214 — Elegy on the much to be lamented death of Doctor Archibald **Pitcairn.** [*Edinburgh,* 1713.]
½º: 1 side, 1 column.
Mourning borders.
'Lament you muses, mourn you sacred sheed'
E.

E215 — Elegie on the never enough to be lamented death of the much honoured Doctor Archibald **Pitcarne**, who departed this life the 23d of Occober [!] 1713. [*Edinburgh,* 1713.]
½º: 1 side, 1 column.
Mourning borders.
'Let muses mourn, and physitians condole'
TxU.

E216 — An elegy on the death of Mr. Jo. **Poe**, who unfortunately departed this life at Kilmainham Gallows, October the 20th. 1725. with a concise character of his life, &c. Written the day before his execution. [*Dublin,* 1725.]
½º: 1 side, 1 column.
Mourning borders.
'Just heaven at length, indulgent to mankind'
L(11602.i.1/18).

E217 — An elegy on Mr. **Pope**. Humbly inscrib'd to H. St John, l. Bolingbroke. By a friend. *London, printed for Lawton Gilliver; sold by J. Roberts,* 1744. (*GA* 5 June)
2º: π¹ A¹ B² C¹; *1–2* 3–10.
π1, C1 seen to be conjugate in the O copy.
Horizontal chain-lines.
'I can't forbear---not tears alone shall flow'
L(515.1.11/9),O; CtY,IU,TxU(uncut).

E218 — An elegy on the death of Mr. Alexander **Pope**. Being an imitation of the ninth elegy in the third book of Ovid. *London, printed for R. Dodsley; sold by M. Cooper,* 1744. (*GA* 22 June)
2º: A⁴; *1–5* 6–8. A1 hft.
'If e'er soft numbers grac'd the royal hearse'
O; CLU-C,IU,MH,NN.

E219 — Elegy on the much lamented death of those excellent patriots and lovers of their country the family of the **potatoes** in the kingdom of Ireland, who fell by a general massacre, being confined and starved alive by cold and hunger (cruellest of deaths!) between the 26th day of December, and the 18th of January in the year 1739, to the

Elegy on...the potatoes

inexpressible loss and grief of their weeping, bleeding country. *Dublin, printed by George Faulkner,* 1739–40.
½º: 1 side, 2 columns.
Bond 171, from *Gentleman's Magazine,* Jan 1740.
'If ever grief was great without disguise'
The L copy has two early ms. attributions in the same hand to Dean Swift. Not known to *Teerink* or *Williams*, and very improbably by Swift. See *The resurrection of the potatoes,* 1739. L(1489.m.17),Crawford.

E220 — Elegie on John **Pringle**, town-piper of Lauder. To the tune of, Lang unken'd. (Done by Maggie Riddel's son.) [*Edinburgh,* 172–?]
½º: 1 side, 2 columns.
'O gosh! what will come o' us now?'
The authorship is certainly false; it resembles both in style and typography Alexander Pennecuik's *Elegy on the much lamented death of merry Maggie Wilson... (Done by Rorie Pringle...),* [172–], and is possibly by him.
E.

E221 — [*idem*] An elegy of John Pringle, the famous piper of Lawder, written in imitation of...Lord Belhaven's speech...By a gentleman near the town of Lawder. *Edinburgh, printed in the year* 1732.
8º: A⁴; *1–2* 3–8.
E.

E222 — An elegy on the much lamented death of the Rev. Charles **Proby** minister of Lockrue, who departed this life Jan. the 3d 1726–7. By R.G. [*Dublin,* 1727.]
½º: 1 side, 1 column.
Mourning borders.
'Triumphant nine, prepare your cymbals, raise'
DT.

E223 — [An elegy...] on the death of Thomas **Putland**, banker in Dublin, 30 March, 1721. [*Dublin,* 1721.]
½º.
(Dobell cat. 105/296.)

E224 — An elegy on the much to be lamented death of Lady Jean **Ramsay**, only daughter to the late General George Ramsay, who departed this life the day of October 1707. [*Edinburgh,* 1707.]
½º: 1 side, 1 column.
Mourning borders.
'The pearl of Caledon is gone'
L(11633.i.9/11).

E225 — [An elegy...] on Sir John **Rawdon**, 1st Feb. 1723–24. [*Dublin,* 1724.]
½º.
(Dobell cat. 105/296.)

E226 — An elegy on the much to-be-lamented death of the right worshipful Sir Thomas **Rawlinson**, knight. Late alderman of the city of London... Who departed this life, on Thursday the 11th of November, 1708. in the 62d year of his age. [*London,* 1708.]

An **elegy** on…Sir Thomas Rawlinson

1°: 1 side, 2 columns.
Mourning headpiece and borders. The chain-lines in the paper run vertically, and it has a foolscap watermark in one quarter.
'Lament my muse, beneath thy mournful weeds'
O.

[E227 — [An elegy] on the much to be lamented death of the much honoured Sir John **Riddel** of that ilk, knight-baronet. [*Edinburgh*, 1700.]
'Ah cruel death! it's time to give it o'er'
Printed by *Maidment* 204 from a broadside, and dated between 1699 and 1713; but Riddel died 1 Apr 1700.]

E228 — An elegy on the much lamented 'Squire **Roberts**, overseer of his majesty's custom-house, who departed this life on Monday the 18th of this instant December 1727. At his house near the Round Church. [*Dublin*, 1727.]
½°: 1 side, 1 column.
Mourning headpiece and borders. The DT copy has a ms. correction of the date to Sunday the 17th.
'Great god how shall my trembling tongue declare'
Substantially the same text as the elegies on John, viscount Nettervill, [1727] William Howard, [1728] and Frances, countess of Tirconnel, [1731.]
DT.

E229 — An elegy on the much lamented death of Robert **Rochford**, lord chief baron of his majesty's court of exchequer, who departed this life at his country seat in Gawl's Town in the county West-meath, on Wednesday the 11th of this instant October 1727. [*Dublin*, 1727.]
½°: 1 side, 1 column.
Mourning borders. The same text and setting of type as *An elegy on…the right honourable the Lord Altham*, [1727.]
'What sacred pomp is this invades my eye'
DT.

E230 — Elegy on the much to be lamented death, of Lord Alexander **Ross**, bishop of Edinburgh, who departed this life March the 20th, 1720. [*Edinburgh*, 1720.]
½°: 1 side, 1 column.
Mourning borders.
'Oh cruel death, what's thy rage or intent?'
E.

E231 — Elegie on the never enough to be lamented cruel death, of the most hopeful and gallant young gentleman, Mr. William **Rue**, of Chesters, who was barbarously murdered by George Ballantine… Musgrave Mackgie…and William Hamilton… In Febr. 1710. With brief description of his penitentials. [*Edinburgh*, 1710.]
½°: 1 side, 1 column.
Mourning borders.
'O fatal death! thou many methods takes'
E.

Elegy on…Gilbert Rule

E232 — Elegie on the death of Mr. Gilbert **Rule**, principal of the college of Edinburgh. Who departed this life, June 7th. 1701. Aged 72 years. [*Edinburgh*, 1701.]
½°: 1 side, 1 column.
Mourning borders.
'Full fraught with years and knowledge doth resort'
L(11633.i.9/3).

E233 — An elegy on the much lamented death of Henry **Sacheverel**, D.D. Who departed this life, on Friday June the 5th, 1724. In the 51st year of his age. *London printed: and re-printed in Dublin, by John Harding*, [1724.]
½°: 1 side, 2 columns.
Mourning borders. Probably the same elegy as listed in Dobell cat. 105/296.
'What mournful muse, who knows so well'
Madan.

E234 — An elegie, upon the much to be lamented death of Colonel **Sara**, who departed this life, at Leith, the 28th. of August 1718. [*Edinburgh*, 1718.]
½°: 1 side, 1 column.
Mourning borders.
'What mournful sound is this doth reach mine ears'
E.

E235 — An elegye upon the never enough to be lamented decease of that antient ilustrious and venerable lady Princess **Scocia**. [*Edinburgh*, 1707.]
½°: 1 side, 1 column.
Mourning borders.
'This princess rare, of ancient pedigree'
On the union with England.
E(3).

E236 — An elegie on the much to be lamented death of the right honourable Sir John **Shaw** of Greenock, knight, one of her majesties principal tacksmen, for the customs and excise of Scotland, who departed this life the 17th. of April, 1702. [*Edinburgh*, 1702.]
½°: 1 side, 1 column.
Mourning borders.
'Ah! now the joy of Greenock's banks is gone?'
E.

E237 — An elegy on the deplorable death of Mr. Thomas **Sheridan**, author of Alexander's-overthrow or, the down fall of Babilon, who departed this mortal life, on Thursday the 8th of March, 172½. [*Dublin* 1722.]
½°: 1 side, 1 column.
Mourning borders.
'Assist with mournful strains, assist my muse'
A mock elegy.
C,DT.

E238 — An elegy on the much lamented death of Sr. Bartholomew **Shower** knight, late famous councelor at law, and one of the late members of parliament; who departed this life at his house in the Inner-Temple-lane, on Thursday the 4th of December 1701, in the 40th year of his age. *London, printed by J. Wilkins*, 1701. (6 Dec, Luttrell)

An elegy on…Sr. Bartholomew Shower

½°: 1 side, 2 columns.
Mourning headpiece and borders.
'If ever England mourn'd for man of sence'
L(KTC.126.c.1/7),Crawford; CSmH,MH(Luttrell).

E239 — Ane elegy, occasion'd by the death o' the revd. Mess Alexander **Sinclare**, wha departed this warld the first day o' Appril, 1722. [*Dublin*, 1722.]
½°: 1 side, 2 columns.
Mourning headpiece and borders. The L copy is bound with Dublin half-sheets.
'Their harts mun be as hard as stean'
L(11602.i.1/4).

E240 — An elegy on the much lamented, and never to be forgotten death of the right honourable Christopher Fleming lord barron of **Slain**, and viscount Longford, who departed this life, (at his late lodgings on the Inns) on Thursday the 14th of this instant July, 1726. and in the 45th year of his age. [*Dublin*, 1726.]
½°: 1 side, 1 column.
Mourning headpiece and borders.
'Hark how the bells his fatal loss deplore'
Christopher Fleming forfeited his peerage in 1691, but the attainder was reversed 21 April 1709. There seems some doubt as to whether his patent as Viscount Longford was ever enrolled.
DT.

E241 — An elegy upon the death of Mr. Aaron **Smith**, who departed this life on the 28th of June, 1701. [*London*] *Printed for R. Barnham*, 1701. (2 July, Luttrell)
½°: 1 side, 2 columns.
Mourning headpiece and borders.
'Now vill—ns weep! since you have lost your head'
On Aaron Smith, solicitor to the treasury; *DNB* gives his date of death as '1697?'.
MH(Luttrell).

E242 — [An elegy] on the death of the right honourable and truly pious George earl of **Southerland**, who departed this life the 4th of March 1703, and of his age the 70th year. [*Edinburgh*, 1703.]
½°?
The similarity of this title to the following makes one suspect a possible confusion by Maidment.
'Almighty power at length in love doth call'
(*Maidment* 146.)

E243 — An elegie upon the very much lamented death of the right honourable and truly pious Georgf [!] earl of **Southerland**, who departed this life the 4th March 1703, & of his age the 70 year. [*Edinburgh*, 1703.]
1°: 1 side, 2 columns.
Mourning borders.
'Fly swift wing'd godess messenger of death'
E.

Elegy on…earl of Stairs

E244 — Elegy on the much to be lamented death of the right honourable John earl of **Stairs**. Who departed this life upon Wednesday, the 8th of January, anno 1707. [*Edinburgh*, 1707.]
½°: 1 side, 1 column.
Mourning borders.
'The sovereign beeing who doth beeing give'
L(11633.i.9/8),E(2); NjP.

E245 — [dh] An elegy upon the much lamented death of the right honourable, John earl of **Stair's**. [*Edinburgh*, 1707.]
2°: A²; 1 2–3 4 blk.
'Is't the reward of the ungrateful age'
E.

E246 — [dh] An elegy on the death of Mrs. Elizabeth **Staples**, late wife of Mr. Robert Staples…who died the 19th of May 1729, in the 42d year of her age. By a divine of the church of England. [col] *Norwich, printed by Henry Cross-Grove*, 1729.
2°: A²; i ii–iii iv blk.
'Oh! may the fear of heaven's avenging hand'
NwP.

E247 — An elegy sacred to the memory of Mr. Samuel **Stockell**, who departed this life May the 3d. 1750. in the 49th. year of his age. *London printed, and sold by L. How, in Petticoat-lane*, [1750.]
½°: 1 side, 2 columns.
Mourning borders. Printed on a half-sheet of very large paper.
'Stockell is dead, no more you hear him groan'
L(C.20.f.2/249).

E248 — An elegy. On the much lamented death of Alderman John **Stoyte**, esq; member of parliament for this city; who departed this life, on Tuesday the 2d of July, 1728. *Dublin, printed in the year* 1728.
½°: 1 side, 2 columns.
'Come bright Urania, nay come all the nine'
L(11602.i.1/25).

E249 — [An elegy] on the right honourable William lord **Strathnaver**, who died 13th July 1720, aged 32. [*Edinburgh*, 1720.]
½°?
'Sing muse (if grief allow) in softest lays'
(*Maidment* 223.)

E250 — An elegie, on the much to be lamented death, of Sir James **Stuart**. of Goodtrees her majesty's advocat, who departed this life, May 1st. 1713. In the 78 year of his age. [*Edinburgh*, 1713.]
½°: 1 side, 1 column.
Mourning borders.
'Mourn northern parts of the Great Britain's isle'
E(cropt),Rosebery.

E251 — An elegy on the much lamented death of Charles earl of **Sunderland**, who died April, 1722. *Dublin, printed by John Harding*, [1722.]
½°: 1 side, 1 column.
Mourning headpiece.
'Long since the pacquet brought the dismal news'

An **elegy** on...earl of Sunderland

L(11602.i.1/5, imprint cropt), OC(Wake letters XXII.127.)

— An elegy on the King of **Sweden**, [1718/19.] *See* Meston, William.

E252 — An elegy on the late Mass John **T——**, minister of the gospel at M——. [*Edinburgh?*] *Printed in the year* 1749.
8°: *A*⁴ B⁴; *1–5* 6–16.
'I warn you a' wi' mony a groan'
An 'advertisement' on A2 says it was composed about twelve years ago. On a whiggish minister who had a dispute with the parish schoolmaster called Sword.
GM,LdU,*MR-C*.

E253 — [An elegy...] on the hon. —— **Talent**, esq., 17 June, 1724. [*Dublin*, 1724.]
½°.
(Dobell cat. 105/296.)

E254 — An elegy upon **Tiger**; her dear lady's joy and comfort, who departed this life, the last day of March, 1727. To the great joy of Bryan, that his antagonist is gone. [*Dublin*, 1727.]
½°: 1 side, 1 column.
   Bond 208; *Teerink* 662; *Williams* 1130.
Mourning borders.
'And is poor Tiger laid at last so low!'
   Swift's authorship was suggested by *Ball* 227, but is rejected by Williams.
DA,DT(cropt).

E255 — An elegy on the much lamented death, of Frances countess of **Tirconnel**, who departed this life at her lodgings on Ormonds Key Dublin. On Sunday the 7th inst March 1730. (Aged 102 years.) [*Dublin*, 1731.]
½°: 1 side, 1 column.
   Mourning borders.
'Great god how shall my trembling tongue declare'
   Substantially the same text as *An elegy on the much lamented 'Squire Roberts*, [1727] and other elegies listed there.
DT.

E256 — An elegy upon the late ingenious Mr. **Toland**. *London, printed for T. Payne*, 1722. (*PB* 27 March)
2°: *A*² B¹; *1–2* 3–6.
'O Toland! mighty friend to nature's laws'
OCU.

E257 — An elegy. On the much lamented death of Mr. **T———r**, the famous occulist, who was suffocated by a new method of fumigation at the College, the first of this instant April, 1732. [*Dublin*, 1732.]
½°: 1 side, 1 column.
'Oh! cruel death we know that thou'
   A mock elegy on John Taylor.
C,DT.

E258 — An elegy on the much lamented death of Mr. **W—— T——r**, an attorney, who departed this life on Saturday the 1st. of October, 1726. [*Dublin*, 1726.]
½°: 1 side, 2 columns.
'Since its a fashion grown so common'
   On William Taylor. In part the same text as *An elegy on the much lamented death, of Madam Bently*, [1729.]
L(11602.i.1/24),DT.

E259 — An elegy on the death of **trade**. *London, printed by W.H. for J. Thorpe; sold by the booksellers of London & Westminster*, 1720. (*DP* 11 May)
8°: *A*(3 ll) B–E⁴; *i–vi, 1* 2–31 *32 blk*.
   Possibly a cancel title, the collation being *A*⁴(−A1,2 +A2).
'An honest old dame/Mother Trade was her name'
O.

E260 — ⟨An⟩ elegy on the much lamented death, of the reverend Doctor **Trever**, who departed this life at his late dwelling house on Sunday the 17th of this instant September 1727. [*Dublin*, 1727.]
½°: 1 side, 1 column.
   Mourning borders.
'Nay, now forbear, for pitty sake give o're'
   Apparently related to *An elegy on the much lamented death of the reveren'd Dr. Francis Higgin's*, [1728], which has the same first line.
DT.

— An elegy on the lamented death of poor **truth** and honesty, 1705. *See* Pittis, William.

E261 — An elegy on the much lamented death of the rt. hon. —— ld. visc. **Tullemoore**, who departed this life the 8th of this inst. September, 1725. at his country seat. ⟨*Dublin, printed by C. Carter*,⟩ 1725.
½°: 1 side, 1 column.
   Mourning headpiece and borders.
'Retire ye graces, quit the flowery plain'
   On John Moore, lord (not viscount) Tullamore.
L(11602.i.1/15, mutilated).

E262 — An elegy on John **Tutchin**, the Observator, who departed this life at the Rummer in St. Georges-street in the Mint in Southwark, on Tuesday the 23d of this instant September, 1707. at 7 of the clock in the evening, in the 60th year of his age. Written by F.C. gent. [*London*] *Printed in the year* 1707.
½°: 1 side, 1 column.
   Mourning headpiece and borders.
'When blazing stars, or comets in the skies'
   Against Tutchin.
CSmH.

E263 — An elegy on Mr. John **Tutchin**, author of the Observator, who departed this life on Tuesday, the 23d of this instant September, 1707. in the 44th year of his age. Who dy'd a martyr for the publick cause. *London printed, and sold by B. Bragge*, [1707.] (*PM* 25 Sept)
1°: 1 side, 2 columns.
   Mourning headpiece and borders.

An **elegy** on Mr. John Tutchin

> 'Dismiss'd from life, and from life's anxious cares'
> L(KTC.126.c.1/1).

E264 — An elegy on the death of the late famous Observator, Mr. John **Tutchin**; who departed this life, at his lodgings in the Mint, on Tuesday the 23d of September, 1707. in the 47th year of his age. Written by the author of the Review. *London, printed for R. Phillips, near West-Smithfield*, 1707.
½°: 1 side, 2 columns.
> Mourning headpiece and borders. On the other side of the O copy, *The infallible mountebank*, 1707.
> 'Mourn, mourn, ye presbyterians, all undone'
> The author intended is Defoe; not in *Moore* or other Defoe bibliographies. The attributions of elegiac broadsides are unreliable.
> O; MH.

E265 — An elegy on the much lamented death of Alderman Paeter **Verdoen**, kt. who departed this life the first of January, one thousand seven hundred thirty oue [!]. [*Dublin, printed by E. Waters*, 1731.]
½°: 1 side, 1 column.
> Printed by Waters on the evidence of the mourning headpiece.
> 'Mourn all ye city patriots, Verdoen's dead'
> DT.

E266 — An elegy on the death of the Lady **Walpole**... who departed this life on Sunday the fourth day of June, 1738. *London, printed for R. White, near Smithfield Bars*, [1738.]
½°: 1 side, 2 columns.
> 'When death prepares to strike his fatal dart'
> LdU-B.

E267 — An elegy on the death of John **Wat** grieve to the Laird of Culquhalzie, who served that family upwards of 40 years. [*Edinburgh*, 172–?]
½°: 1–2, 1 column.
> 'With drooping head I now bemoan'
> E.

E268 — An elegy on A—r—n **W—e**, who flew from hence the other night. *Dublin, printed in the year* 1735.
½°: 1 side, 1 column.
> Mourning borders.
> 'Let quakers weep and builders now rejoice'
> Crawford.

E269 — Elegy, on the much to be lamented death of David earl of **Weems**. Who departed this life March the 13th, 1720. [*Edinburgh*, 1720.]
½°: 1 side, 1 column.
> Mourning borders.
> 'Ah! fatal stroak, that from us has remov'd'
> E.

E270 — Elegy on the much lamented death of his excellency Richard **West**, esq; lord high chancellor of Ireland, and one of the lords justices of this kingdom, who departed this life the third of this instant December, 1726. *Dublin, printed in the year* 1726.

Elegy on...Richard West
½°: 1 side, 2 columns.
> 'At this unwelcome news lament you nine'
> The first half of the poem is substantially the same as an elegy on Henry, viscount Dillon (1714) in Laurence Whyte's *Poems*, 1740. Probably rewritten by Whyte for this occasion.
> DT(mutilated).

— An elegy on Dr. John **Whalley**, 1724. *See* Swift, Jonathan (S834).

E271 — Elegy, on the much to be lamented death of James **Whetty** taylor and free-man in the Pattaraw who departed this life Apprile the 5th, 1720 about the 69. of his age. With a caution to his successors. [*Edinburgh*, 1720.]
½°: 1 side, 1 column.
> 'And has old death that bloody knave'
> E(2).

E272 — An elegy on the little lamented death of Mr. James **Whiston**, alias the devils change-broker: who departed this life, near the Custom-house, on Friday the 28th of November, 1707. In the seventyeth year of his age. *London, printed for Simon Ager, near the Royal Exchange, Cornhill*, [1707.]
½°: 1 side, 2 columns.
> Mourning headpiece and woodcut borders.
> 'Mourn Britains, mourn, your careful doctor's gone'
> CtY.

E273 — An elegy on the much lamented death of Mr. Jeremiah **White**, the late fanatick minster [!], who was chaplain once to that most discreet, pio⟨us⟩ and sanctified usurper Oliver Cromwell; having departed th⟨is⟩ life on Friday the 14th of this instant March, at his house in Jerusalem-court ⟨in⟩ St. John's, in the 78th year of his age. [*London*, 1707.]
½°: 1 side, 2 columns.
> Mourning headpiece and borders.
> 'What muse shall I invoke, to help me sing'
> DG(cropt).

E274 — An elegy, sacred to the memory of that excellent father in god, and eminent apostle of Jesus Christ, Mr. George **Whitehead**, who (in full assurance of a blessed resurrection) departed this life, on Friday, the 8th of Mar, 1723. Æt. 87. *London, printed by S. Gilbert & R. Phillips*, 1723.
1°: 1 side, 2 columns.
> Mourning borders.
> 'Is worthy Whitehead dead, that godly seer?'
> L(KTC.126.c.1/6),O(cropt).

E275 — — *London printed, and Dublin re-printed, by Elizabeth Sadleir*, 1723.
1°: 1 side, 2 columns.
> Mourning borders.
> LF.

E276 — — *Kendal, printed and sold by Thomas Ashburner*, [1723.]

An **elegy**...George Whitehead

    1°: 1 side, 2 columns.
      Mourning borders.
    LF.

E277 —— [1723.]
    1°: 1 side, 2 columns.
      Printed within a border of texts.
    LF.

E278 — Elegy on the much lamented death of the right honourable William **Whitshed**, lord chief justice of his majesty's court of common-pleas, who departed this life at his country seat at Stormonstown, on Saturday the 26th of this instant August 1727. [*Dublin*, 1727.]
    ½°: 1 side, 1 column.
      Mourning borders. The DT copy has a ms. correction of the date to 25th.
'Still we do find, black cloath wears out the first'
    An abridgement of 'Upon the death of so many reverend ministers of late' by Robert Wild (printed in his *Iter boreale*, 1668), with minor adaptations to fit the subject.
    DT.

E279 — Elegy on the much lamented death of the reverend Mr. Thomas **Wilkie**, minister of the gospel in the Cannongate church of Edinburgh, who departed this life 19th of March 1711. [*Edinburgh*, 1711.]
    ½°: 1 side, 1 column.
      Mourning borders.
'O what a change hath death in few days made!'
    The *Elegy on the much lamented death of...Christian marchioness of Montrose*, [1710] has a very similar first line.
    E.

E280 — An elegy, from the mercers, lacemen, milliners, weavers and wyerdrawers, upon the death of the late King **William**... As likewise an humble address, to her present most sacred majesty Queen Ann... *London, printed in the year* 1702. (19 March, Luttrell)
    ½°: 1 side, 1 column.
      Mourning borders.
'All pious, loyal souls, who love the truth'
MH(Luttrell).

E281 — Elegie on the death of our late soveraign King **William**. [*Edinburgh*, 1702.]
    ½°: 1 side, 2 columns.
      Mourning borders.
'What direful, dismal, mourning's this doth fill'
L(11633.i.9/7).

E282 — Elogie on the ever to be lamented death of **William**, the thrid [!], king of Great Brittan, France and Ireland. [*Edinburgh*, 1702.]
    ½°: 1 side, 1 column.
      Mourning borders.
'Proud and imperious fate, what is thy hate?'
L(11633.i.9/6).

— An elegy on the most reverend father in god,

An **elegy** on...William

his grace, **William**, late lord archbishop of Dublin, 1729. *See* E171 *under* King.

E283 — Elegie on the much lamented death of the reverand Mr. David **Williamson**, one of the ministers of the West-kirk at Edinburgh, who dyed the 6 of August 1706. [*Edinburgh*] *Printed by G.J.* [*George Jaffrey*], 1706.
    ½°: 1 side, 1 column.
      Mourning headpiece and borders.
'When god decreed the higher orbs above'
E.

E284 — An elegy sacred to the memory of the reverend Mr. Samuel **Willson**, who died October 6, 1750. in the 49 year of his age. [1750.]
    1°: 1 side, 2 columns.
      Mourning borders.
'O'er gracious spirit – sadness that is spread'
LDW.

— Elegy on the much lamented death of merry Maggie **Wilson**, [172–.] *See* Pennecuik, Alexander, *d. 1730*.

E285 — An elegy on the much lamented deaths of Edward **Winfield** esq; who departed this life on Thursday last, and yesterday being the 12th of this instant January 1728–9. died his lady at their house in William-steet [!]. [*Dublin*, 1729.]
    ½°: 1 side, 1 column.
      Mourning borders.
'O muse the mournful scene'
DT.

— Elegy on Lucky **Wood**, [1718?] *See* Ramsay, Allan.

E286 — An elegy on the lamented death of —— **Worth** esq. who depart'd this life at Rathfarnham on Sunday the 7th of Nov. inst. 1725. [*Dublin*, 1725.]
    ½°: 1 side, 1 column.
      Mourning borders.
'Thou pride of villages whose ponds and groves'
L(11602.i.1/20).

E287 — An elegy on the much lamented death of Sir Watkin Williams **Wynn**, bart. Who died by a fall from his horse in hunting, near Wrexham, in Denbighshire, on Tuesday the 26th. of September, 1749. *Salop, printed by I. Cotton & I. Eddowes*, 1749.
    8°: *A*⁴; *1* 2–8.
      The format is uncertain. A Welsh translation on pp. 5–8.
'Mourn, mourn ye Britons all, for cruel death'
'Chwi-soneddigion mawrion mwyn'
    The elegy is attributed to Richard Rolt in the CdP catalogue, but his *Poem sacred to the memory* is apparently quite a different work.
CdP.

— An elegy to a **young lady**, 1733. *See* Hammond, James.

E288 — An elegy upon the **young prince**. To the tune of the Children in the wood. [*London?* 1717/18.]

An **elegy** upon the young prince

slip: 1 side, 1 column.
> Printed with *To the soldiers of Great Britain*; the NjP copy is undivided.

'Come muses all/Lament the fall'
> *Crum* C549. A Jacobite satire on the quarrel between George I and the Prince of Wales over the christening of his son.

O; NjP.

Eleonora. Eleonora: a panegyrical poem, 1709. *See* Dryden, John.

Eleventh. The eleventh epistle of the first book of Horace, 1749. *See* Pullein, Samuel.

E289 **Elias.** Elias and Enoch. A dialogue on the death of the right reverend Alexander, late lord bishop of Edinburgh. [*Edinburgh*, 1720.]
'Enough, my soul, let's quit this cool retreat'
> (*Maidment* p. 220, reprinting a copy in the Diocesan Library, Edinburgh.)

Elisae. Elisae Havartae principi Gordoniae, A.P. scotus s.d., [1712.] *See* Pitcairne, Archibald.

E290 **[Ellis, John.]** The surprize: or, the gentleman turn'd apothecary. A tale written originally in French prose; afterwards translated into Latin; and from thence now versified in hudibrastics. *London printed, and sold by the booksellers of London & Westminster*, 1739. (*GM,LM* Jan)
8°: π²(π1 + frt) A–H⁸ I⁸(–I4.5) (G4 as 'C4'); i–iv, 1–3 4–139 140 blk.
> Title from π2ʳ; π1ᵛ is Latin title, 'Nobilis pharmacopola...' Latin prose and English verse on facing pages. Many copies have a manuscript correction to the last line of p. 105.

'Beauty's of health the offspring fair'
> A presentation copy at CtY has a ms. note of authorship. Originally written by Jacob de Villiers as *L'apoticaire devalisé*, 1660; translated into English as *The gentleman apothecary*, 1670; translated into Latin as *Nobilis pharmacopola*, 1693. A curious tale.

L(P.C. 19.a.14, presentation copy),LG,O(– frt); CtY,ICN,MH(lacks π1,– frt).

E291 — — *Dublin printed, and sold by the booksellers*, 1739.
12°: A–F⁶; 1–2 3–71 72 blk.
> English translation only.

DA,DG,DN.

E292 **[Ellis, William.]** A divine poem dedicated to the memory of that faithful servant and minister of Christ, Richard Claridge, who departed this life the 28th day of the month called April, 1723. Ætatis suæ 74. *London, printed for, and sold by William Ellis, at the Queen's-Head, the corner of Crown-court in Grace-church-street*, [1723.]
1°: 1 side, 2 columns.
'What! though we justly fun'ral pomp disuse'

Ellis, W. A divine poem
> Ellis's name in the imprint makes his authorship nearly certain.

L(1870.d.1/46),LF.

E293 — The drunkard's looking-glass: or, the picture of a sot drawn to the life. Wherein he may plainly see, that he is a spoiler of wealth, a destroyer of health, the sorrow of his family... [*London*, 1711?]
½°: 1 side, 2 columns.
> Woodcut scenes at head; on the other side a mock invitation by Ellis, *You are welcome all, to Fumblers Hall*, dated 14 Oct 1711.

'Drunkard, stand, if thou canst, and see within this glass'
> At end of 'The conclusion', 'Now can you say I have spoke a word amiss? | No surely, says your friend Will-Ellis'.

L(1870.d.1/99*, mutilated).

E294 — [*idem*] The true emblem of a sot: or, a looking-glass for all drunkards, wherein the pot-valiant-hero may see what a fine figure he makes when he's in Sir John Barleycorn's custody. [*London*, 171–?]
½°: 1 side, 2 columns.
> Three woodcuts at head, one at foot. 12 lines added beneath the lower cut. On the other side of the Harding copy, *Proposals for improving money*, in prose. Apparently a variant text of the preceding, with first line:

'Alas, how beast-like the drunkard wallowing lies'
> Signed like the preceding.

Harding.

E295 — A poem on the high-church champion Dr. Sacheverell. [*London*, 1710?]
½°: 1 side, 2 columns.
> Woodcut of Sacheverell at head, flanked by two couplets at right angles to the main text; one reads 'This is the tenth edition of this noble print, | Which hath a reverend doctor's picture in't'.

'For speaking gospel-truth, it shakes my reason'
> Ellis's name in the other couplet at head, and in the last line. In praise of Sacheverell.

Madan.

E296 **[—]** The queen of Great Brittain's royal bounty to the distressed Palatines, 1709. *London, printed for William Ellis*, 1709.
½°: 1 side, 1 column.
'French tyranny to such a height is grown'
> Ellis's authorship is deduced from the imprint.

O.

E297 — A welcome to the high and mighty hero George, by the grace of god, king of Great Britain, France and Ireland, defender of the faith. I W. Ellis (her late majesty's poet) wisheth all joy and happiness, and a long and prosperous reign over his numerous people. [*London*, 1714.]
½°: 1 side, 2 columns.
> Rough woodcut at head.

'Welcome great George, unto the British crown'
Crawford.

Ellison, W.

E298 [**Ellison, Cuthbert.**] A most pleasant description of Benwel village, in the county of Northumberland. Intermix'd with several diverting incidents, both serious and comical. Divided into two books. By Q. Z. late commoner of Oxon. *Newcastle upon Tyne, printed and sold by John White*, 1726.
12°: A–K¹² L¹²(L2+χ¹) M–Z¹² Aa¹² Bb⁶ (L3 as 'L2'); *i–ii* iii–iv, 5–581 *582–589; 590 blk.* 589 err.
> The inserted leaf after L2 is a dedication of the second part to Ralph Jenison.
'Speak, goddess muse! / As wond'rous news'
> Ascribed to Ellison by William Upcott, *Bibliographical account of works relating to English topography* II (1818) 1045, and by the Newcastle antiquarians. Cf. [Taylor Thirkeld] *A Sunday evening's conversation at Benwell*, 1726.
L(238.g.27, lacks χ1),O(2),NeP; CtY,*DFo*,ICN, ICU.

Ellwood, Thomas. A collection of poems on various subjects. *London printed, and sold by Luke Hinde*, [175–?]
8°: pp. 62. L,LF; MH.

———

E299 — Davideis. The life of David king of Israel: a sacred poem: in five books. *London printed, and sold by the assigns of J. Sowle*, 1712. (*SR* 12 Nov)
8°: a⁸ A–T⁸ U⁴; [*2 blk*] *i–ii* iii–xiv, 1–310 *311–312 blk.* 310 err.
> No watermark. Many copies (but not those deposited at Stationers' Hall) have 5 advertisement leaves at end, the first four signed *4. Entered in *SR* to Edward Sanders; deposit copy at EU, probably also at L,O,E,SaU.
'After King Saul had (by the sin he wrought'
L(994.l.8,–a1),LDW(–a1, U4),O,EU,SaU+; CtY(–a1, U4),DFo,ICN,IU(–a1, U4),MH(–a1, U4).

E300 — [fine paper]
> Watermark: star. The watermark is difficult to see, and some of the copies above may be fine paper.
LF(–a1,U4).

E301 — — The second edition with additions. *Dublin, printed by Sam. Fairbrother; sold by S. Fuller*, 1722.
8°: A(3 ll) B–N⁸ O⁴ P²; [6] 17–219 *220 blk.*
> The collation of the preliminaries is obscure, but A2.3 appear to be conjugate.
L(1966),LF,LVA-D,O,DN(lacks P2); MH.

E302 — — The second edition. *London printed, and sold by the assigns of J. Sowle*, 1727.
8°: A⁴ a⁴ B–U⁸ W²; *i–ii* iii–xiv, 1–310.
> Most copies add *4 of advertisements.
L(11631.c.19),LF,*LVA-D*,O; IU,*PSC-Hi*.

E303 — — The third edition, corrected. *London printed, and sold by T. Sowle Raylton, & Luke Hinde*, 1749.

Ellwood, T. Davideis
8°: A–O⁸ P²; *i–ii* iii–viii, *1* 2–217 *218–220.* 218–220 advt.
LF,O; *PHC*.

Elogie. *See* Elegy.

Elogium. Elogium famæ inserviens Jacci Etonensis, 1750. *See* King, William, *principal of St. Mary Hall.*

Elsum, John. A description of the celebrated pieces of paintings; of the most eminent masters ancient and modern, with reflections upon the several foreign-schools of painting. *London, printed for D. Brown, S. Clark, & C. King*, 1704.
8°: pp. 133. O; CtY,IU.
> A reissue of *Epigrams upon the paintings of the most eminent masters*, 1700. The copy at O is very heavily corrected, apparently for a new edition.

Embarassed. The embarrass'd knight, [1748.] *See* Jenyns, Soame.

E304 Emblem. An emblem of the South Sea; or, the poor mans hue and cry after money. *London, 'printed by Sir John Would-have-all in Fleet-lane'*, 1720.
1°: 1 side, 3 columns.
> Series of popular woodcuts at head with appropriate captions.
'O money, O money, where hast thou been'
O.

[**Emerson, —, *Mr.*]** Trick upon trick, 1732. *See* T479·5.

E305 Emma. Emma, carmen, Matth. Prior, arm. latine redditum. *London, printed for H. Lintott, J. & R. Tonson & S. Draper; sold by J. Shuckburgh*, 1748. (*GM,LM* March)
4°: A–H⁴ I²; *1–3* 4–67 *68 blk.* 67 err.
> With the English text of Prior's poem.
'Candida nympha Chloë, cujus perstringor ocellis'
MR; CtY,NjP,*OO*.

Emmanuelis. Emmanuelis Alvari Regulae de syllabarum quantitate, 1730. *See* Vaslet, Louis.

E306 Empty. The empty purse. A poem in Miltonics. Dedicated to the thrice worthy person that fills it. *London, printed for W. Owen, & G. Woodfall*, 1750. (*GM,LM* April)
2°: A² B–D²; *i–ii* iii–iv, 1–12.
'Hail, gentle purse! that erst wert lib'ral wont'
L(643.l.25/27),*DT*; CtY,IU(cropt),TxU.

E307 Em--ss----ss. The em..ss....ss's sp..ch to the Fr..ch k..g. *London, printed by J. Read*, [1713?]
2°: A² < B¹; *1–2* 3–6.
> Printed on one side of the paper only.
'Hail sacred king, now wars and discord cease'
> Presumably the Duchess of Shrewsbury

The **em..ss....ss**'s sp..ch

addressing Louis XIV, and apparently related to *The Br—sh embassadress's speech to the French king,* [1713.]
CSmH.

E308 Emulation. The emulation of the insects: or, a minister chosen. A fable. Inscribed to his grace John, duke of Argyle. *London, printed for T. Cooper,* 1742. (17 Dec)
8°: A–D⁴; *1–3 4–29 30–31; 32 blk.* D4 advt.
Listed in *GM,LM* Jan 1743.
'Seldom the man, whose word's sincere'
Continued by *The old fox and his son,* 1742.
L(11631.d.19, Tom's Coffee House, 17 Dec); CtY,IU.

E309 Encomium. The encomium, a poem: humbly inscrib'd to the...lord high chancellor of Great Britain. Occasion'd chiefly by the successes of the last campaign, and his lordship's speech thereupon *... London, printed by J. Darby; sold by J. Morphew,* 1710. (*Tatler* 14 March)
2°: *A*² B² C(3 ll); *1–2 3–14.*
Horizontal chain-lines, with foolscap watermark in the centre of the leaf. The second leaf of C is signed 'C2' and inset. The Luttrell copy, dated 14 March, is in the collection of R. D. Horn.
'Long has injurious satyr vex'd the town'
Addressed to William Cowper, earl Cowper.
O; CSmH,CtY,TxU(uncut).

E310 — [fine paper]
Watermark: London arms.
TxU.

Encouragement. ⟨Incouragement⟩ for sinners; or, instructions for saints. *London, printed for the author, by R. Tookey,* 1719.
8°: pp. iv, 55.   E.
The title-leaf of the copy seen is imperfect, and the title is completed from the drop-head. A collection of poems by a lady.

— The encouragement of the ladies of Ireland, [1721.] *See* Swift, Jonathan (S840).

E311 England. England in miniature, or truth to some tune. A new ballad. *London, printed for T. Payne; sold at the pamphlet shops of London & Westminster,* 1729. (*MC* June)
2°: *A*² B² C¹; *1–3 4–10.*
'All you that are willing your cares to beguile'
MH,TxU.

E312 —— *Dublin, printed by James Hoey & George Faulkner,* ⟨1729?⟩
½°: 1 side, 2 columns.
L(1968, imprint cropt).

E313 — England triumphant, or, the King of France, in a violent passion, being a dialogue that past between the French king rnd [!] his secatary [!] of war, in a secret conference, relating to the French

England triumphant

kings present state of affairs. Tune, the King of Frances lamentation. *London, 'printed for Mounsier de Garlick Pinch, at de Tree flying Frog, in Spiter de field',* [1708?]
½°: 1 side, 2 columns.
Two rough woodcuts above text.
'Sir, here's de express'
L(1876.f.1/42).

E314 — England's alarum-bell: or, give not up Gibraltar. A new ballad. The tune, ––Come and listen to my ditty, &c. *London, printed for A. Price,* 1749. (*GM* Feb)
2°: *A*² B²; *1–2 3–7 8 blk.*
'Pale her looks, and clad in mourning'
L(11630.h.30),O; CSmH(uncut),KU.

— England's danger and duty, 1745. *See* Scott, Thomas.

E315 — England's doom; as debated in a junto of infernal spirits... A poem. Wherein the notorious increase of atheism, immorality, and prophaneness ...is boasted of by the evil, and lamented by the good spirits... *London, printed for the author; sold by R. Amey, and at the pamphlet-shops of London & Westminster,* 1736. (*GM, LM* April)
8°: *A*¹ B–E⁴ *F*¹; *i–ii, 1 2–33 34 blk.*
A note on A1ᵛ records that pen corrections have been made throughout the edition.
'Thus far, with arms triumphant, have we gain'd'
L(11631.bb.24); IU,OCU,TxU.

E316 — England's exhortation: or, a warning-piece to sinners. [*London*] *Printed by and for T. Norris,* [1715.] (29 April, Luttrell)
½°: 1 side, 1 column.
'Let every mortal Christian now awake'
ICN(Luttrell).

E317 — England's glory: a poem. Perform'd in a musical entertainment before her majesty, on her happy birth-day. *London, sold by Richard Harrison,* 1706. (7 Feb, Luttrell)
2°: (frt +) *A*² B² C¹; *i–iv, 1–6.*
Listed in *WL* Feb as sold by B. Bragg.
'Lov'd Britannia! Heav'n allows thee'
Dedication signed by James Kremberg, the composer.
L(11626.k.7),O(Luttrell); MnU.

— England's glory. Being an excellent new ballad on the fleet at Spithead, [1729.] *See* Great Britain's glory, 1729.

E318 — England's glory: or, the march of the British forces into Flanders. Tune of Preston fight. [*London?* 174–?]
slip: 1 side, 1 column.
'Our troops of Great-Britain are now gone from home'
C.

E319 — England's ingratitude: or, Jonathan Wild's complaint. *Dublin, printed by Thomas Hume,* 1725.
½°: 1 side, 2 columns.

England's ingratitude

'Within the confines of that dreary cell'
L(C.121.g.8/57); CtY.

E320 — England's late jury: a satyr. *London, printed for the information of the free-holders of England*, 1701. (Nov?)
½º: A¹; 1–2, 2 columns.
No rule above 'Conclusion' on p. 2.
'Wisely an observator said'
A satire on the ministry. Tentatively attributed to Defoe by F. H. Ellis in *POAS* VI. 344.
MC,*Chatsworth*,Crawford,Rothschild; MH,TxU.

E321 — [another edition]
Rules above 'Conclusion' on p. 2.
L(G.559/4),LLP.

E322 —— A satyr: with the counter-part, in answer to it. To which is added, a scandalous dialogue between Monsieur Shaccoo, and the Poussin doctor: with the vindication of those two worthy persons... [*London*] *Printed in the year* 1702 [1701]. (*PB* 4 Dec)
8º: A–E⁴ (A2 as 'A'); 1–2 3–39 40 blk.
The 'scandalous dialogue' is in prose.
Answer: 'That observator whom you name'
L(11631.bb.23),O(2, 1 lacks B⁴).

E323 — England's most humble address to her lawful sovereign, of all princes the most accomplish'd, and eminently endow'd with all manner of vertues, yet exiled! [*London?* 1714/18?]
slip: 1 side, 1 column.
'Great monarch, hasten to thy native shore'
Crum G528. Jacobite verses to the Old Pretender.
CSmH.

E324 — England's passing-bell. Written at the university of Oxford. *Oxford, printed in the year* 1710.
½º: 1 side, 1 column.
The Oxford imprint is possibly false.
'Oh fam'd Britania, whither wilt thou run?'
In praise of Sacheverell and high church.
O.

E325 — England's resolution to down with popery, in spite of France and Spain. [*London?* 174–.]
slip: 1 side, 1 column.
Rough woodcut at head.
'True Britons come hither, let's all join together'
C.

E326 — Englands sorrow, and the soldiers in tears for the loss of their king and general, William the IIId. who departed this life at his palace at Kensington on Sunday the 8th of March 1701. Aged 52. To the tune of, The bleeding heart. *Dublin, printed by Francis Dickson*, [1702.]
½º: 1 side, 2 columns.
Mourning headpiece and borders.
'Mourn England mourn, the loss is great indeed'
DT.

E327 — England's surprize; or, the French king's joy for the Duke of Marlborough's being turn'd out of favour. To the tune of, Now now comes on the

England's surprize

glorious year. [*London*] *Printed for J. Nickolson, near West-Smithfield*, [1712.]
½º: 1 side, 2 columns.
'What news is this flys up and down'
Crawford.

E328 — England's triumph in the joyful coronation of a protestant queen: or an acrostick... *London, printed by W. Onley; sold by J. Nutt*, [1702.] (24 April, Luttrell)
½º: 1 side, 1 column.
'Aurora, the bright usher of the morn'
ICN(Luttrell).

E329 — England's triumph, or an occasional poem on the happy coronation of Anne queen of England, &c. [*London*, 1702.] (3 June, Luttrell)
1º: 1 side, 3 columns.
Very large woodcut at head.
'Brave subjects of England rejoice and be glad'
MH(Luttrell).

E330 **English.** The English beautys. A poem. *London, printed for J. Roberts; sold by the booksellers of London & Westminster*, [1728.] (*MChr* 29 Nov)
2º: A¹ B² C¹; 1–2 3–8.
'Tho' god a paradise had given'
In praise of the ladies of the court, by name.
O(lacks A1),OW; CSmH,MH,NjP,OCU,TxU(2).

E331 — English courage display'd, or, brave news from Admiral Vernon: being a copy of verses giving an account of the taking Porto Bello, the 22d of Nov last, written by a seaman on board the Burford the admiral ship, and sent here from Jamaica [!]. Tune of, Glorious Charles of Sweeden. [1740?]
slip: 1 side, 1 column.
Percival appendix 80. Rough woodcut at head.
'Come loyal Britains all rejoyce, with joyful acclamations'
C.

E332 — English courage display'd: on Admiral Vernon's taking of Carthagena. To the tune of, Glorious Charles of Sweeden. [*London?* 1741.]
½º: 1 side, 2 columns.
Percival LXVIII. Woodcut of ships at head.
'Brave loyal Britons all rejoice'
Crum B531. A revision of the preceding, applied to Cartagena in anticipation of a victory there.
C.

— English credulity; or ye're all bottled, [1749.]
See The magician, or bottle cungerer, 1748/9.

E333 — The English gentleman justified. A poem. Written on the occasion of a late scurrilous satyr, intituled, the True-born-Englishman. *London, printed for J. Nutt*, 1701. (*EP* 26 Feb)
4º: A² B–H⁴ (C1ᵛ as 'C2'); [4] 9–63 64 blk. 63 err.
The CtY copy has vertical chain-lines.
'To search for times in dark oblivion cast'
Against Defoe's poem.
L(1972),O,C; CLU-C,CtY,ICN,IU,MB+.

The **English** gentleman justified

E334 — — *Dublin, re-printed for Matthew Gunn, 1701.*
8°: A⁸ B–C⁴; *1–4* 5–30 *31–32 blk.*
C.

E335 — The English Haddock, not to be caught in a
Spanish nett. Tune of, The king and the miller of
Mansfield, &c. [1740?]
slip: 1 side, 1 column.
Rough woodcuts at head and foot.
'How happy a state did the Spaniard possess'
On Admiral Nicholas Haddock.
C.

— The English hero, [1704.] *See* Clare, R.

E336 — English men no bastards: or, a satyr against the
author of The true-born English-man. *London
printed, and are to be sold by A. Baldwin, 1701.*
(17 May, Luttrell)
½°: 2 sides, 2 columns.
Advertisement for the *New state of Europe*
after imprint.
'What makes an English sat'rist loosely write'
Against Defoe.
O; CtY,ICN(Luttrell),Rosenbach.

E337 — [*idem*] A satyr upon thirty seven articles.
London, printed in the year 1701.
½°: 2 sides, 2 columns.
L(C.121.g.9/132),Rothschild; CLU-C,CSmH.

E338 — The English muse: or, a congratulatory poem
upon her majesty's accession to the throne of
England. *London printed, and are to be sold by J.
Nutt, 1702.* (9 April, Luttrell)
2°: A–D²; *1–2* 3–16.
The Luttrell copy is recorded in *Haslewood.*
'Let grief no more our English hearts untune'
MH,TxU(2).

— An English padlock, 1705. *See* Prior, Matthew.

E339 — The English padlock unlock'd. [*London, 1705?*]
½°: *1–2*, 1 column.
Wing E3107, in error.
'The Spanish dons, as authors tell us'
An imitation of Prior's *An English padlock,*
1705; comparing the padlock on the mind with
Spanish girdles of chastity.
L(C.20.f.2/301),OW,Crawford.

E340 — The English sailors resolution to fight the
Spaniards. [*London?* 1739.]
slip: 1 side, 1 column.
Percival appendix 68.
'Come all you jolly sailors bold'
C.

E341 — The English salours [!] triumph, over the
French fleet where ere they meat [!] them. To the
tune of the Sailers delight. *London prited* [!] *for
John Smith, near Fleetstreet, 1710.*
½°: 1 side, 2 columns.
'The wind blows a loft boys'
An illiterate naval song with no particular
historic reference.
MH.

Englishman

E342 **Englishman.** The Englishman's answer to the
magick lanthorn. [*London?* 1740.]
slip: 1 side, 1 column.
Percival appendix 81. Rough woodcut of ship
at head.
'Where now be dose brag-boasters'
In praise of Admiral Vernon, in answer to
*The raree-show-man. Or, his box and magick
lanthorn expos'd,* [1740.]
C.

E343 — An English-man's thought on the fourth of
November. *London printed, and sold by J. Roberts,
1715.* (*DC* 4 Nov)
2°: A–B²; *i–iv*, *1–3* 4 blk.
'Welcome the day which gave the hero birth'
On King William's birthday, in thanks for his
ensuring the protestant succession of George I.
O.

Enquiry. An enquiry after virtue, [173–]–. *See*
Morris, Robert.

Enthusiasm. The enthusiasm, 1739. *See* Hiffernan,
Paul.

Enthusiast. The enthusiast, 1744. *See* Warton,
Joseph.

[E344 = H147·5] **Eosphoros.** Ἑωσφόρος: or, the morning
star, 1746. *See* Heosphoros.

Epicedium. An epicedium sacred to the memory of
the late revd Mr. Thomas White, [1710.] *See*
Ainsworth, Robert.

Epictetus. Epictetus: a poem, 1709. *See* The porch
and academy open'd, 1707–.

Epictetus.
Walker, Ellis: Epicteti Enchiridion made English.
In a poetical paraphrase, 1701, 1702, 1708, 1709.
See W13–17.

— [*idem*] Epicteti Enchiridion. The morals of
Epictetus, 1716, 1724. *See* W18–19.

— [*idem*] The morals of Epictetus; made English,
1737. *See* W20.

The porch and academy open'd, or Epictetus's
manual newly turn'd into English verse, 1707. *See*
P998.

[*idem*] Epictetus: a poem, 1709. *See* P999.

Ivie, Edward: Epicteti Enchiridion latinis versibus
adumbratum, 1715, 1723, 1744. *See* I74–6.

E345 **Epidemical.** Epidemical madness: a poem in
imitation of Horace. *London, printed for J. Brindley;
sold by Mrs. Dodd, and the booksellers of London &
Westminster, 1739.* (*GM, LM* March)
2°: *A²* B–D²; *1–3* 4–16.
'You write so seldom, and are so severe'
A general satire on society.
O(2),OW,LdU-B; CSmH,CtY,MH,NN-B,TxU.

Epigram

Epigram. 'An epigram on Dan de F—: a poem. 1710.'

    Listed in *Morgan* M180; no evidence of publication has been found.

— An epigram on the Spectator, 1712. *See* Tate, Nahum.

Epigrammata. Epigrammata anti-Gallica. Sive epigrammata quædam quibus conscribendis fuerunt occasioni. Et pugna ad Blenheim, & vallum in Flandria perruptum. *Londini, prostant venales apud B. Bragg*, 1705. (*DC* 27 Nov)
2⁰: pp. 11.   O; CtY.

— Epigrammata de quibusdam summis hujus seculi viris, 1737. *See* Forbes, John.

— 'Epigrammata tria.' [*London*, 1727.] (21 Oct?) 4⁰.

    Entered in Bowyer's ledgers to Fletcher Gyles under 21 Oct 1727, one sheet in quarto, fine paper, 50 copies printed.

Epigrams. Epigrams in distich. *London, printed for J. Stagg*, 1740. (*GM* Feb)
2⁰: pp. 20.   L,O; CSmH,NjP.
    Clearly by one author.

Epilogue. An epilogue, as it was spoke by Mr. Griffith [1721.] *See* Swift, Jonathan.

E346 — Epilogue. Designed to be spoken by Alonzo, at the acting of the Revenge by some school-boys. [*Dublin*, 1727?]
½⁰: 1 side, 1 column.
    The DT copy is printed on the reverse of *A riddle by the reverend Dean S—y*, [1726/27?]
'Since none in virtue to perfection rise'
    Possibly written by Thomas Sheridan for his school.
DT.

E347 — 'An epilogue intended to be spoken by Mr. Estcourt to the Recruiting officer, a comedy, written by Mr. George Farquhar. [*London*] *Printed for B. Lintott; sold by A. Baldwin*. Price 1*d*.' (*DC* 28 Sept 1710)
    Presumably a half-sheet.

E348 — An epilogue recommending the cause of liberty to the beauties of Great Britain. Spoken by Mrs. Oldfield. At the Theatre-Royal. [*London*] *Printed for Beruard* [!] *Lintott*, [1716.] (16 March, Luttrell)
2⁰: A¹ B²; i-ii, 1-4.
    Listed in *MC* March. Entered to Lintot in Bowyer's ledgers under 15 March, 500 copies.
'Now since the force of rude rebellion's fled'
LSA(lacks A1); ICN(Luttrell),OCU.

E349 — — The second edition. *London, printed for Bernard Lintott*, [1716.] (17 March?)
2⁰: A¹ B²; i-ii, 1-4.
    Entered in Bowyer's ledgers under 17 March; a reimpression, as is shown by the charge.

An epilogue recommending

    A subsequent duplicate entry under 26 March shows 1000 copies in all were printed.
O,OC(uncut); CSmH,MH(uncut).

E350 — — [*Edinburgh*] *Printed in the year* 1716.
4⁰: A²; 1 2-4.
E.

— An epilogue spoke to a play call'd the Alchymist, [1721.] *See* Pack, Richardson.

— Epilogue spoken by Mrs Barry, April the 7th, 1709, 1709. *See* Rowe, Nicholas.

E351 — Epilogue: spoken by Mrs. Mountfort at the Theatre Royal in Drury Lane. [*London*] *Printed for Bernard Lintott*, 1705.
½⁰: A¹; 1-2, 1 column.
'As a young lawyer many years will drudge'
O,Crawford; MH.

E352 — Epilogue. The last comic epilogue, spoken to the town, by the famous comedian, Mr. William Pinkeman, published at the request of several persons of quality, by permission of the author. *London, printed for J.W.* [*Jeremiah Wilkins?*] *in Fleet-street*, [1701.]
½⁰: 1 side, 1 column.
'This long vacation how we've thrash'd in vain'
    Also published in *The last new prologue and epilogue*, [1701.]
O.

— Epilogue, to be spoke at the Theatre-Royal, [1721.] *See* Swift, Jonathan.

E353 — The epilogue, to be spoken before the four Indian kings, at the Queen's theatre in the Haymarket, this present Monday, being the 24th of April. *London printed, and sold by B. Bragg*, [1710.] (*Supplement*, 24 April)
½⁰: A¹; 1-2, 1 column.
    Entered in *SR* to James Read, 24 April 1710.
'As Sheba's queen with adoration came'
LSA; MH.

E354 — The epilogue to his grace James duke of Ormond's last speech to her majesty, at his departure for Flanders. *London, printed* April the 22d 1712.
½⁰: 1 side, 1 column.
'In due obedience to your sacred will'
    An indirect attack on Marlborough.
O; ICN(Luttrell),MH.

— Epilogue to Tamerlane, [1746.] *See* Walpole, Horace.

E355 — An epilogue to the court, on the queen's birthday. By Roger, the Observator's country-man. *London printed, and sold by B. Bragg*, 1705. (14 Feb, Luttrell)
½⁰: 1-2, 1 column.
'The rustick muse thus having chang'd the scene'
Crawford; ICN(Luttrell).

Epinikion

E356 Epinikion. Epinikion Marlburiense Bleinhemianum: 2° Agusti [!] 1704. [*London?*] *Parlamento pio convento*, 24 Octobris 1704.
4°: A⁴; *i–ii*, *1–5* 6 *blk*.
Dedication to Marlborough on A1ᵛ.
'Before the queen o' th' French was grown mis-spir'd'
Signed 'R.R.' at end of text.
O.

E357 — 'Epinicion sacro nomini Annæ Magnæ Britanniæ, &c. reginæ. [*London*] *Sold by A. Baldwin.* Price 2*d*.' (*DC* 27 March 1707)

Episcopade. The 'Episcopade, 1748. *See* Morgan, Macnamara [The 'Piscopade].

E358 Epistle. An epistle address'd to a friend. [*Edinburgh?*] *Printed in the year* 1740.
8°: A–B⁴ C²; *1–2* 3–19 20 *blk*.
'Shall the gay beauties of this charming seat'
A tribute to Robert Dundas the elder, lord Arniston. Dated from Arniston 23 Oct 1739.
E; CtY,IU,MH.

— An epistle from a footman in London to the celebrated Stephen Duck, 1731. *See* Dodsley, Robert.

E359 — An epistle from a gentleman at Twickenham, to a nobleman at St. James's. Occasion'd by an Epistle from a nobleman, to a doctor of divinity. *London, printed for William Guess; sold at the pamphlet-shops*, [1734.] (*GSJ* 14 March)
2°: *A²* < B²; *1–2* 3–8.
The imprint is possibly pseudonymous. Reprinted in K99.
'Kindly accept what kindly I indite'
Written as if from Pope to Lord Hervey, in reply to Hervey's *Epistle from a nobleman*, 1733.
O,OW,E,WcC(uncut); CLU-C(uncut),CtY,IU, MH(2),TxU.

— An epistle from a lady in England, 1717. *See* Tickell, Thomas.

E360 — An epistle from a merchant's clerk to his master, on his being discharg'd the compting-house, &c. *London, printed for S. Clements; sold by the booksellers of London & Westminster*, [172–/3–?]
2°: *A²* B²; *1–5* 6–8. A1 frt.
'Great sir, (as great as Cæsar's son)'
From a dismissed minister to the king, with some satire on Walpole.
L(643.m.15/14, uncut); CtY(lacks frt),*MH-BA*, OCU(uncut).

E361 — An epistle from a n--ble l--d to Mr. P--y. *London, printed for T. Cooper*, 1740 [1741?]. (*LDP* 13 Jan)
2°: *A⁴*; *1–3* 4–8.
'Happy the man who with such ease'
Addressed to William Pulteney on his satires;
'Old topics in his hands are new,│Spithead

An **epistle** from a n--ble l--d

and *Hounslow* we *Review*,│And start at the *Convention*.'
L(11661.dd.4, uncut),O; CSmH,DLC,InU,MH, OCU(uncut)+.

— An epistle from a nobleman to a doctor of divinity, 1733. *See* Hervey, John, *baron Hervey*.

E362 — An epistle from a royalist to a young lady, written before the restoration. Now publish'd on the twenty ninth of May. *London, printed for William Falstaff*, 1750. (*LM* June)
2°: *A¹* B²; *1–2* 3–6.
The collation is tentative. The imprint is possibly pseudonymous.
'I question now, so well you act your part'
MH,OCU.

— An epistle from a student at Oxford to the Chevalier, 1717. *See* Amhurst, Nicholas.

E363 — An epistle from Altamont to Lorenzo. *London printed, and sold by T. Read, and the booksellers of London & Westminster*, 1730. (*MChr* 2 March)
2°: *A²* B²; *1–2* 3–8.
'When injur'd honour bids its vengeance rise'
Probably occasioned by [Charles Beckingham] *An epistle from Calista to Altamont*, 1729; Lord Abergavenny to his wife's lover, Richard Lyddel.
TxU.

E364 — An epistle from an English jesuit, to the Pope, concerning the present affairs of Europe. *London, printed for J. Roberts, & E. Berrington*, 1718.
2°: *A²* B–C²; *1–2* 3–12.
'Whilst restless kings ambitious of renown'
A satire on the Jacobites.
L(643.m.12/29),DT; MH.

E365 — An epistle from an half-pay officer at the tilt-yard, to his friend at Jenny Man's. *London printed, and sold by Ferd. Burleigh*, [1714.] (25 June, Luttrell)
4°: *A²* B⁴; *1–4* 5–10 *11–12 blk*. A1 hft.
'Indulge no more (dear angry friend) the spleen'
The retired soldier must now turn to love.
L(164.m.73, Luttrell),LdU-B(uncut),AN(−B4); CtY,ICN.

E366 — An epistle from an half-pay officer in the country, to his friend in town, occasion'd by the late conspiracy, and the birth of the young princess. *London, printed for J. Peele*, 1723. (May, Luttrell)
2°: *A²* B–C²; *1–3* 4–12.
The Luttrell copy is in the collection of R. D. Horn.
'From woods and lawns, serene and hush'd retreats'
On the Atterbury plot and the birth of Princess Mary.
L(11661.dd.5); MH,TxU.

— An epistle from Calista to Altamont, 1729–. *See* Beckingham, Charles.

E367 — An epistle from D--ct--r R--ck to Mr. Or--t--r H--n--y; containing several curious particulars: and including a panegyric on the

An **epistle** from D--ct--r R--ck

celebrated Mr. M--k--n. *London, printed for
J. Evans; sold at the pamphlet-shops in London &
Westminster,* 1746.
2°: *A*² B² C¹; *1-3* 4–10.
'While with our names the world's so free'
    From Doctor Rock to John Henley.
CtY.

E368 — An epistle from Dick Francklin, bookseller; to
Nick Amhurst, poet, up three-pair of stairs.
Occasion'd by his epistle to Sir J—n Bl—t. *London,
printed for J. Roberts; sold by J. Graves, & J.
Woodman,* 1721. (*DP* 14 Jan)
8°: *A*⁴ B–C⁴; *1-4* 5–23 *24 blk.* A1 hft.
'Wonder not, Nick, whose magick feather'
    Occasioned by Amhurst's *An epistle (with a
    petition in it) to Sir John Blount,* 1720.
O; CSmH,CtY,MH.

E369 — An epistle from Jack Sheppard to the late l—d
c—ll--r of E--d, who when Sheppard was try'd,
sent for him to the chancery bar. [*Dublin*] *Printed
in the year* 1725.
½°: 1 side, 1 column.
    The InU copy has a Dublin collector's initial,
    F; the L copy is bound in a collection of Dublin
    half-sheets.
'Since your curiosity led you so far'
    Crum S659. *Moore* 470 tentatively ascribed
    this to Defoe; the Dublin origin, not known to
    him, makes the attribution more unlikely.
    Printed as by Philip duke of Wharton in
    'Lewis Melville', *The life and writings of
    Philip duke of Wharton* (1913) 149; no
    evidence is quoted. An attack on the Earl of
    Macclesfield who was convicted by the house
    of lords on 27 May 1725.
L(C.121.g.8/109, imprint cropt); CSmH,InU.

— An epistle from John More, apothecary, [1743.]
See Dodington, George Bubb, *baron Melcome.*

E370 — An epistle from Jonathan Wild to Colonel
Chartres. *London printed, and sold by A. Moore, and
the booksellers of London & Westminster,* 1730.
(*MChr* 13 March)
2°: *A*² B²; *1-2* 3–8.
'From the dark realms of lowest hell I come'
ICN.

E371 — An epistle from little Captain Brazen to the
worthy Captain Plume. To which is added, an
answer to the said epistle... *London, printed for
A. Moore; sold by the booksellers of London &
Westminster,* [1731.] (*GSJ* 1 Feb)
2°: A–B²; *1-2* 3–8.
'Vaunt not thyself, good Capt. Plume'
Answer: 'I read, sir, your polite epistle'
    Occasioned by the duel between Pulteney and
    John, lord Hervey.
L(11657.m.29); DFo,MH(uncut).

— An epistle from London, to Richardson Pack,
1722. *See* Sewell, George.

An **epistle** from Lord L---l

— An epistle from Lord L---l to Lord C---d,
1740. *See* Pulteney, William, *earl of Bath.*

E372 — An epistle from Matt of the Mint, lately
deceased, to Captain Macheath. *London, printed for
A. Moore; sold by the booksellers of London &
Westminster,* 1729. (*Craftsman* 1 March)
2°: *A*² B²; *1-2* 3–8.
'From those dire realms of everlasting gloom'
O(uncut),LdU-B; ICN,MH.

[E373 = F272]

E374 — An epistle from Sapho to Philenis. With the
Discovery; or, paradise review'd. *London, printed
for W. Trott; sold by the booksellers of London &
Westminster,* 1728. (*MChr* 9 Jan)
2°: *A*–B² C²; *i-iv,* 1–8.
    A2, C1 are fly-titles to the two poems. A
    Dublin edition was advertised for speedy
    publication in *A modest praise of pritty Miss
    Smalley,* 1730.
'Where is th' asswaging pow'r that verse is said'
Discovery: 'In summer's season, at the noon of day'
    Two erotic poems.
Turnbull Library, Wellington, N.Z.

E375 — An epistle from Sempronia to Cethegus. To
which is added Cethegus's reply. *London, printed
for John Holmes,* 1713.
8°: *A*¹[=D4] B–C⁴ D⁴(–D4) (D2 as 'C2'); *i-ii,*
1–22.
    R. D. Horn reports that the Luttrell copy was
    dated 26 Nov, but the copy cannot now be
    traced.
'Such eyes as Somerset's; imperious dame!'
    The L catalogue tentatively ascribes this to
    George Sewell; but at this date he was writing
    flattering poems to Marlborough. This appears
    to be a vicious attack on the Duchess of Marl-
    borough and Thomas, marquis of Wharton(?).
    On the other hand, a copy forms part of the
    nonce collection of Sewell, *Miscellanies in verse
    and prose,* 1714, at ICN.
L(T.1787/9),MR-C; CtY,IU,MH,NN,TxU(un-
cut)+.

E376 — An epistle from Signora F----a to a lady.
'*Venice*' [*London*], *printed in the year* 1727.
2°: *A*²; *1* 2–4.
'Condemn not, madam, as I write in haste'
    A lesbian poem, intended for Faustina B.
    Hasse, the singer.
L(841.m.26/2; 163.n.21); DFo(ms. notes).

E377 — An epistle from S------o, to A------a
R------n. *London, printed for M. Smith; sold by
the booksellers of London & Westminster,* 1724.
2°: (3 ll); *i-ii,* 1 2–3 *4 blk.*
    '[Price 4d.]' after imprint. Apparently com-
    posed of three separate leaves.
'Hail angry maid! – at sight of this don't frown'
    From the castrato Senesino to Anastasia

An **epistle** from S------no

Robinson, afterwards Countess of Peter-borough; apologizing for his impotence.
O,OA(lacks title); CSmH,MH,NjP,OCU.

E378 —— *London, printed in the year* 1724.
2⁰: (3 ll); *i–ii, 1 2–3 4 blk.*
No price on title. A different setting of type. Reissued in *A collection of original poems,* 1724 (*Case* 329).
CtY,MH.

E379 — An epistle from S——r S——o to S——a F——a. *London, printed for J. Roberts,* 1727. (*MC* March)
2⁰: *A² B²; 1–5 6–8. A1 hft.*
Engraving of two singers on title.
'While rival queens disturb the peaceful stage'
From the castrato Senesino to Faustina B. Hasse. Cf. *An answer from S—a F—a to S—r S—o,* 1727, and *F—na's answer to S—no's epistle,* 1727.
L(11630.h.62); MH,NjP,OCU(−A1),PPL,TxU (uncut).

— An epistle from the elector of Bavaria, 1706. *See* Clay, Stephen.

E380 — An epistle from the late Lord Bo------------------ke to the Duke of W----------n. *London, printed for A. Moor,* 1730. (*MChr* May)
8⁰: A–C⁴; *1–2 3–24.*
'To read these lines a pensive eye prepare'
Bolingbroke to the Duke of Wharton. A satire on Jacobite tories and *The Craftsman.*
L(11631.bbb.9),O,OW,EtC; CtY,NN,OCU.

E381 — An epistle from the platonick Madam B---ier, to the celebrated Signor Car---ino. *London, printed for R. Smith,* 1734. (*GM* March)
2⁰: *A² B–C²; 1–4 5–11 12 blk. A1 hft.*
'Pardon, from one scarce known, this rude address'
A castrato poem from Mme Barbier to Carestini.
MH.

— An epistle humbly address'd to the right honourable the Earl of Oxford, [1732?] *See* Mawer, John.

[E382 = C75]

E383 — An epistle in behalf of our Irish poets. To the right hon. Lady C——t. *Dublin, printed by E. Needham,* 1726.
½⁰: 1 side, 2 columns.
Teerink 1212.
'Dear madam./Before you depart from this nation'
To Lady Carteret.
L(C.121.g.8/153),C,DT(2).

E384 — An epistle in verse to a friend, in imitation of the second epistle of the first book of Horace. *London, printed for J. Robinson; sold by the booksellers of London & Westminster,* 1739. (*GM,LM* April)
2⁰: *A² B–D²; 1–5 6–15 16 blk. A1 hft.*
Latin and English texts.
'While you, perhaps, sage Littleton explore'

An **epistle** in verse

O(−A1, uncut),LdU-B; CSmH,DFo(uncut),NN, TxU.

— The epistle of Yarico to Inkle, 1750. *See* Moore, Edward [Yarico to Inkle].

— An epistle on preferment, 1744. *See* An essay on preferment, 1736–.

E385 — An epistle to * * * * * *, doctor of physick, and fellow of the Royal College of Physicians, London, and of the Royal Society, f---- and s----. On his plan of his present method of practice. *London, printed for the author; sold by the booksellers in London & Westminster,* 1744. (*DA* 27 Aug)
2⁰: *A¹ B–C² D¹; i–ii, 1 2–10.*
Horizontal chain-lines.
'Finish'd the stage, the croud collected round'
Tentatively ascribed to Sir James Stonhouse by NN; but his name on that copy appears to be a mark of ownership. On Cromwell Mortimer's system of payments (cf. *Nichols* V. 424).
L(777.1.1/57),O,LdU-B; CtY-M,NN,OCU.

E386 — An epistle to a certain dean, written originally in Italian, by Carlo Monte Socio...and translated from the Vatican manuscript. By a student in philosophy. *London: printed, and Dublin re-printed in the year* 1730.
8⁰: *A⁴; 1–3 4–8.*
Teerink 1300. There may have been no London edition.
'To wake the soul by tender strokes of art'
Teerink's entry implies that the poem is addressed to Swift, but this is not certain. It is a satire on a sermon preached by 'C----e', probably Henry Clarke, professor of divinity at Trinity College, Dublin.
L(11601.ccc.38/9),DG,DT; MH.

E387 — An epistle to a fellow commoner at Cambridge. Occasioned by the present disputes there. *London, printed for Charles Corbett,* [1750.] (*LM* Dec)
2⁰: A(4 ll) (A2 as 'A'); *1–2 3–8.*
'True, wou'd but all with thee, my Lollius, join'
O,C; OCU.

E388 — An epistle to a friend. *Dublin, printed by and for George Faulkner,* 1733.
8⁰: *A⁴; 1–3 4–8.*
'The wisest are by narrow bounds confin'd'
L(11631.a.63/13),LVA-F,*LdU-B*; IU.

— An epistle to a friend; occasioned by a sermon, 1747. *See* Byrom, John.

— An epistle to a gentleman of the Temple, 1749. *See* Byrom, John.

— An epistle to a lady, who desired the author to make verses on her, 1734. *See* Swift, Jonathan.

— An epistle to a person of quality, 1735. *See* Jacob, Hildebrand.

E389 — An epistle to a worshipful gentleman, who designs to stand candidate for a worshipful place;

An **epistle** to a worshipful gentleman

occasioned by a sort of advertisement penn'd in a very odd sort, by a gentleman of some sort, when perhaps he was out of sorts. Written by the author of the Totness and Sailor's address, and revis'd by the Revd. D. J------- S----. [*Dublin?*] *Printed in the year* 1727.
½°: 1 side, 2 columns.
'Forgive me, worthy sir, if I'
> *The Totness address versify'd*, 1727, was by Joseph Mitchell; the author of *The saylors address*, 1727, is unknown. There seems no reason to take the present attribution of authorship seriously, any more than Swift's revision.

Crawford.

— An epistle to a young nobleman, 1736. *See* Dalton, John.

E390 — An epistle to a young student at Cambridge; with the characters of the three great quacks, M--pp, T---l--r, and W----d... *London, printed for J. Jones; sold by the booksellers & pamphlet-shops in town & country*, 1737.
2°: *A²* B²; *1–3* 4–8.
'Whilst you, dear Harry, sweat and toil at college'
> Two of the quacks are presumably John Taylor and Joshua Ward.

OCU.

[E391 = K88·5] — An epistle to Alexander Pope, esq; from South Carolina, 1737. *See* Kirkpatrick, James.

E392 — An epistle to Alexander Pope, esq; occasion'd by some of his late writings. *London, printed for J. Wilford*, 1735. (*DJ* 4 Feb)
2°: *A¹* B² C¹; *i–ii*, *1* 2–6.
> '(Price Sixpence.)' on title. No watermark.

'Tir'd with my spleen tho' with thy numbers pleas'd'
> Ms. note in Lady Mary Wortley Montagu's copy (below), 'Not by me except a correction or two'.

O(uncut),OA,LdU-B; CLU-C,CSmH,CtY,DFo.

E393 — [fine paper]
> No price on title. No watermark, but good paper; margins altered.

CtY(Lady Mary Wortley Montagu's).

E394 — An epistle to Archibald Hutcheson, esq; By a freeholder of Great-Britain. *London, printed for T. Payne*, 1722. (*PB* 7 July)
2°: (3 ll); *1–3* 4–6.
'To you, great sir, in character and fame'
MH-BA(Luttrell, Aug).

— An epistle to Curio, 1744. *See* Akenside, Mark.

E395 — An epistle to Dean Swift. A poem... By a gentleman in the army. *Hereford, printed: and sold by the booksellers of London & Westminster and most book-sellers in the country*, 1739.
2°: *π²* A–D²; [2] ii–iii, *1*–16.

An **epistle** to Dean Swift

> *Teerink* 1319. π2 in the L copy appears to be a cancel; possibly that is another issue.

'Whilst on Parnassus top, inthron'd you sit'
L(11631.i.8); MH,TxHR.

E396 — An epistle to D—n S—t. In answer to a Lible [!] on D— D——. and a certain great lord. [*Dublin*] *Printed in the year* 1730.
8°: *A⁴*: *1–2* 3–7 *8 blk*.
> The CtY copy was originally bound in a Dublin pamphlet volume.

'Attend malicious S—t si vous plait'
> A reply to Swift's *A libel on D— D—*, 1730.

CtY.

— An epistle to Dr. Young, [1734.] *See* Turner, Joseph.

E397 — An epistle to Eustace Budgell, esq; occasioned by the death of the late Dr. Tindall. [*London*] *Printed by John Hughs*, 1734 [1733]. (*GM* Dec)
2°: *A²* B–D²; *1–3* 4–15 *16 blk*.
> Most copies have a ms. deletion on p. 5, line 5.

'Budgell! thy Tindall's death demands thy muse'
O; CtY,ICN,MH,OCU.

— An epistle to Florio, 1749. *See* Tyrwhitt, Thomas.

E398 — An epistle to Ge--ge Ch--ne, M.D. F.R.S. upon his Essay of health and long life. With notes... By Pillo-Tisanus... *London, printed for J. Roberts*, 1725.
8°: *A⁴* B–I⁴; [4] *i* ii–iv, 1–62 *63–64*. A1 hft.
> I4 not seen.

'Dear Doctor! – While the road to health you shew'
> To George Cheyne.

OCU(−I4).

— An epistle to his excellency John lord Carteret, [1729]–. *See* Delany, Patrick.

— An epistle to his grace the Duke of Grafton, 1724. *See* Smedley, Jonathan.

E399 — An epistle to his grace the Duke of Grafton. With stanza's on the marriage of the Prince of Wales with the Princess of Saxe-Gotha. *London, printed for A. Dodd*, 1736. (*GM* April)
2°: *A²* B–D²; *1–3* 4–5 *6*, *1–3* 4–10.
> With a separate title to the 'Stanzas', with imprint 'Printed by E. Cave'.

'While much distinguish'd you, my lord, support'
Stanza's: 'Whene'er my muse attempts to sing'
> The epistle signed 'W.B.' The entry in *GM* refers to poems by the author printed in *GM* July 1734 and Jan 1736.

O-JJ; CSmH.

E400 — An epistle to John James H--dd--g--r, esq; on the report of Signior F—r—n—lli's being with child. *London printed, and sold by E. Hill, near St. Paul's*, 1736. (*LM* Jan)
2°: *A²* B²; *1–2* 3–8.
'Say, my dear count, and, with thy solemn face'

An **epistle** to John James H--dd--g--r

Addressed to Heidegger, on the castrato Farinelli.

O; CtY,OCU.

— An epistle to Joseph Addison, 1715. *See* Sewell, George.

E401 — An epistle to MacD—d, b—r. Occasion'd by a certain very remarkable advertisement repeated in the D----y J--------l several times. By Timothy Meanwell, attorney at law. *London printed, and sold by A. Moore, and the booksellers of London & Westminster, 1730.* (*MChr* April)

2⁰: *A² B²*; *1–2* 3–8.

'To thee, dear Mac! whose ev'ry wish succeeds'
According to *MChr*, 'to MacDrummond, banker'; apparently he had been complaining of the poets' satires on women.

E.

E402 — An epistle to Mr. Handel, upon his operas of Flavius and Julius Cæsar. *London, printed for J. Roberts, 1724.* (*MC* April)

2⁰: (3 ll); *i–ii*, *1* 2–3 *4 blk*.

The Luttrell copy dated May is recorded in *Haslewood*. Reissued in *A collection of original poems*, 1724 (*Case* 329).

'Crown'd by the general voice, at last you shew'
CtY,MH,OCU,TxU.

— An epistle to Mr. P - - in anti-heroicks, 1738. *See* Paget, Thomas Catesby, *baron Paget*.

[E403 = T565·5] — An epistle to Mr. Pope, 1732. *See* Turner, Joseph.

E404 — An epistle to Mr. Pope. By the author of the letter to the patron of the Trip to Barleduc. *Edinburgh, printed in the year 1716.*

8⁰: *A⁴*; *1–3* 4–8.

'While you, in fair Augusta, justly great'
Dedication signed 'Scoto-Britannus' and dated 2 Feb 1716. Probably by John Steddy, who wrote *A trip to Bar-le-Duc*, 1715; the 'letter' has not been identified.

IU.

— An epistle to Mr. Pope, from a young gentleman at Rome, 1730. *See* Lyttelton, George, *baron Lyttelton*.

— An epistle to Mr. Pope. Occasioned by Theobald's Shakespear, 1733. *See* Mallet, David [*Of verbal criticism*].

— An epistle to Mr. Pope, on reading his translations of the Iliad, 1731. *See* Morrice, Bezaleel.

E405 — An epistle to Mr. Pope, on the death and ensuing funeral of the Duke of Marlborough. *London, printed for F. Clay, 1722.* (*DJ* 8 Aug)

2⁰: *A² B–C²*; *1–3* 4–12.

'While Britain mourns, and pays her grateful tears'
L(643.l.24/45); CtY,MH.

— 'An epistle to Mr. T— L— at the Golden Anchor in Cornhill. [*London*] *Printed for A. Moor.* Price 6d.' (*MChr* July 1730)

An **epistle** to Mr. T— L—

Listed in *MChr* under 'poetry, and books of entertainment'; quite likely a prose work.

E406 — An epistle to Mr. Thomas Elrington, occasion'd by the murder of the tragedy of Cato last Monday night. [*Dublin*] *Printed in the year 1730.*

8⁰: *A⁴*; *1–3* 4–7 *8 blk*.

'"To wake the soul by tender stroaks of art'
A satire on Elrington's production of Addison's *Cato*; Pope's prologue is quoted in the first two lines. The author is satirized in *The inspir'd poet*, 1730.

L(11602.bb.33/3).

— An epistle to Mr. Welsted, 1721. *See* Morrice, Bezaleel.

E407 — An epistle to Mistress N---v---l. Being a love-letter from a young gentleman in town, to his mistress in the country. *London, printed for J. Duncan, 1743.* (*GM* May; *LM* Sept)

2⁰: *A² B–E²*; *i–iv*, *1–16*.

Entered in Strahan's ledger to Duncan under 7 May 1743, 500 copies.

'Queen of my heart, dear charmer of my soul'
The same author wrote *Sephalissa to Sylvius*, 1743. The addressee is expanded in *LM* as 'Mrs. Nevil'.

O(3); CtY,DFo.

E408 — An epistle to R--- W---, esq; occasion'd by a pamphlet, entitul'd, The defection consider'd, &c. By the author of a late poem, call'd The woful treaty: or, unhappy peace. *London printed, and sold by J. Billingsley, & S. Baker, 1718.* (April, Luttrell)

4⁰: *A–C⁴* (B2 as 'C2'); *1–2* 3–24.

'The muse, who touch'd with Catalonia's wrong'
A eulogy on Walpole, occasioned by Matthew Tindal's pamphlet.

L(162.l.70, Luttrell; T.9*/1); InU.

E409 — — The second edition. *London printed, and sold by J. Billingsley, & S. Baker, 1718.*

4⁰: *A–C⁴*; *1–2* 3–24.

Apparently a reimpression.

O.

E410 — An epistle to Sir J--r--y S---b----k. By a gentleman at the university of Cambridge. *London, printed for R. Dodsley, 1735.* (*GM* May)

2⁰: *A² B–C²*; *i–ii*, *1–2* 3–10. A1 hft.

'Wilt thou peruse what I indite'
A ms. note in the copy at C identifies the addressee as Sir Jeremy Sambrooke; the author was a friend of his at Cambridge.

L(11602.i.11/2),O(–A1),C; CLU,CtY(–A1, uncut),KU,MH,TxU.

E411 — [dh] An epistle to Sir Richard Blackmore, kt. on occasion of the late great victory in Brabant. [col] *London, printed for John Chantry, 1706.* (20 July, Luttrell)

2⁰: *A²*; *1–4*.

'Oh Blackmore! Why do'st thou alone refuse'

An **epistle** to Sir Richard Blackmore

'A banter on Sir Richard' (Luttrell), occasioned by the battle of Ramillies.
O,DG,MC,*MR-C*; CtY(uncut),ICN(Luttrell), IU,TxU(2, uncut).

E412 — An epistle to Sir Samuel Garth. Occasion'd by the landing of the Pretender, and the report of his royal highness the Prince of Wales's going to Scotland. *London, printed for Bernard Lintott,* 1716. (2 Feb, Luttrell)
2°: *A*² B–C²; *1–4* 5–12.
The Luttrell copy is recorded in Pickering & Chatto cat. 245/12472; listed in *MC* Feb.
'O Garth! to whom thy own Apollo gave'
L(643.1.25/16),OW,AdU; CtY-M,PPL.

E413 — An epistle to Sir. Scipio Hill, from Madam Kil——k. [*London?* 1715/20.]
slip: 1 side, 1 column.
'To thee, Oh knight! in hopes of aid, I send'
A Jacobite satire against George I and his mistress Baroness Kielmansegge, subsequently countess of Darlington.
NN,*Harding*.

E414 — An epistle to the author of the Essay on reason. *London, printed for T. Cooper,* 1735. (*GM* June)
2°: *A*² B–C²; *1–3* 4–12.
'Long has the poet's lawful claim been known'
An attack on Walter Harte's poem.
O,LdU-B,WcC(uncut); IU,TxU.

— An epistle to the heritors of the West-kirk parish, 1732. *See* Preston, William.

— An epistle to the King of Sweden, 1717. *See* Centlivre, Susanna.

E415 — An epistle to the little satyrist of Twickenham. *London, printed for J. Wilford,* 1733. (*GSJ* 30 March)
2°: *A*² B² C¹; *1–3* 4–10.
'By sleep deserted, when for rest reclin'd'
A sober attack on Pope and his pride.
L(1346.m.39),LVA-D(2),O,LdU-B; CLU-C, CtY,ICN,MH,TxU(2)+.

— An epistle to the lord Viscount Bolingbroke, 1714. *See* Young, Edward.

E416 — An epistle to the most learned Doctor W--d----d; from a prude, that was unfortunately metamorphos'd on Saturday December 29, 1722. *London, printed by T.W.; sold by J. Roberts, B. Creak, & S. Chapman,* 1723. (*DJ* 4 Feb)
2°: *A*² B²; *1–3* 4–8.
Reissued in *A collection of original poems,* 1724 (*Case* 329).
'O son of Galen, lend your friendly aid'
Signed 'Prudentia'. T. J. Wise suggested Gay's authorship; *Faber* xxxi rejected Gay but suggested Arbuthnot; L. M. Beattie (*John Arbuthnot,* 1935) and *CBEL* do not accept it. The epistle is addressed to John Woodward; the prude changed her sex on seeing Senesino at the opera.

An **epistle** to the...Doctor W--d----d

L(643.1.25/19; Ashley 5189, uncut),O,OW,LdU-B; CSmH(uncut),CLU-C(Luttrell, Feb),CtY,IU, MH,TxU+.

E417 — — 'London, printed by T.W. and sold by J.R.' [*Edinburgh*], 1723.
8°: A⁴; *1–2* 3–8.
Printed by Ruddiman on the evidence of the ornament.
TxU.

E417·2 — — metamorphos'd on Monday the 25th. day of March, 1723. *Dublin, printed by J. Carson,* 1723.
½°: *1–2,* 1 column.
IU.

E418 — An epistle to the rev. Mr. Tho. G-bb-ns, on his Juvenilia: or, poems on several occasions. [*London*] *Printed for M. Cooper,* 1750. (*GM* Sept)
2°: A⁴; *1–3* 4–8.
'Dear friend, whose elegiack vein'
To Thomas Gibbons.
O; CLU-C,CtY.

E419 — An epistle to the Rev'd. --- occasioned by a long sermon preach'd at St. M-----s-church, October the 20th, 1734. *Dublin, printed in the year* 1734.
½°: 1 side, 2 columns.
'Dear reverend sir,/ In your epistle'
Signed, 'Roger'.
L(C.121.g.9/199).

E420 — An epistle to the righgt [!] honourable Charles Montague, baron of Halifax. Writ upon occasion of the signal successes of her majesties arms in the last summers campaign. 1706. *London, printed for Sam Crouch, Tim. Goodwin, & Jos. Fox,* 1707.
4°: A–E⁴; *1–2* 3–38 *39–40 blk.*
'Shall Anna's arms extend from pole to pole'
P. J. Dobell, *Literature of the restoration,* 1918 (no. 1135), 'This looks like one of Nahum Tate's productions'.
L(11632.cc.13); InU,MH.

E420·5 — ⟨An epistle to the right honourable Joseph Addison, esq;⟩ [*London, E. Curll,* 1717.]
8°: ⟨ ⟩ B–C⁴ D²; ⟨ ⟩ *1* 2–19 *20.* 20 advt.
The copy seen lacks the preliminary leaves; the title is quoted from the drop-head title.
'To thee once more, by duteous raptures prest'
The copy seen is bound with two poems by J. D. Breval, who is probably the author.
MH(lacks preliminaries).

E421 — An epistle to the right honourable Philip earl of Chesterfield. *London, printed for M. Cooper,* 1745. (*GM, LM* May)
4°: A–B⁴; *1–2* 3–15 *16 blk.*
Watermark: fleur-de-lys.
'When first the muses deign'd t' inspire'
In praise of Chesterfield.
L(11630.e.4/10),O; MH,*NcD*,OCU.

E422 — [fine paper]
Watermark: Strasburg bend.
CtY.

An **epistle** to the rt. hon. Sir Robert Walpole

[E423 = W538]
— An epistle to the right honourable Sir Robert Walpole, 1726–. *See* Dodington, George Bubb.

E424 — An epistle to the right honourable Sir Robert Walpole. *London, printed for W. Mears,* 1728. (*MC* Feb)
2°: *A*² B²; *i–iii* iv, 5–8.
'Whilst venal poets in unbidden lays'
IU,*MH*,TxU(cropt).

E425 — An epistle to the right honourable Sir Robert Walpole. *London, printed for J. Walthoe,* 1730. (*MChr* April)
2°: *A*⁴; *1–2* 3–8.
'Whate'er to private offices we owe'
CSmH,NN.

E426 — An epistle to the right honourable Sir Robert Walpole. *London, printed for R. Dodsley,* 1739. (*LDP* 10 May)
2°: *A*² B–D²; *1–5* 6–14 *15–16 blk.* A1 hft.
'In thy calm intervals of social peace'
 The ms. note in the O copy 'By Robert Nugent Esq. Member of Parl.' cannot be contemporary with publication, since Nugent was not returned as an MP until 1741. The attribution is accepted by *Halkett & Laing*, but the poem is not printed with Nugent's poems in *Dodsley* or elsewhere. Although addressed to Walpole in friendly terms, it advises him to retire and praises Cobham, a position not inconsistent with Nugent's politics.
L(643.m.16/6,–D2),O,C(2),BaP,LdU-B(–D2); CSmH(–D2),CtY,ICN(–D2),MH(–A1),TxU+.

E427 — — '*London, printed for R. Dodsley*' [*Edinburgh*], 1739.
8°: π¹ A⁴ B¹; *1–3* 4–12.
 The printer has not been identified, but the copy at E is bound with thirty tracts all of which are Edinburgh piracies.
L(1972),E; CLU-C,IU,InU,MH.

E428 — An epistle to the right honourable Sir Robert Walpole; occasion'd by the writings of the Craftsman, and the late peace concluded with Spain. *London, printed for J. Roberts,* 1730. (*MChr* 2 Feb)
4°: A–B⁴; *1–3* 4–16.
'Great, brave, and faithful! let the proud disdain'
O,EtC; CSmH.

E429 — An epistle to the right honourable William Pultney, esq; upon his late conduct in publick affairs. *London, printed for B. Dod,* 1742. (*LM* July)
2°: *A*¹ B–D² E¹; *i–ii,* 1 2–14. ii err.
 Rothschild 2572. 'To the reader' on A1ᵛ.
''Twas Heav'n's decree ---- 'tis seal'd ---- the moment's past'
 Ascribed to Sir Charles Hanbury Williams by *CBEL,* apparently in error.
L(11602.i.20/5),O; CSmH,CU,InU,OCU,TxU+.

An **epistle** to the rt. hon. William Pultney

E430 — An epistle to the right honourable William Pultney, esq; now earl of Bath... The third edition. *London, printed for B. Dod,* 1742.
2°: *A*² B–D² E¹; *i–iv,* 1 2–14.
 Apparently a reimpression; no 'second edition' identified. The copy seen has A1ᵛ, A2ʳ blank, probably due to a failure to perfect a sheet in half-sheet imposition; the correct collation is probably that of the first edition.
Forster.

E431 — An epistle to the supposed author of the paraphrastical hudibrastick verses in the magazine. *Nottingham, printed by George Ayscough,* 1740.
2°: *A*¹ B²; *1–2* 3–6.
'Why son of ------- shou'd thy metre'
 A reply to *The instructors instructed,* 1739, which was reprinted in the *Daily gazetteer* 14 Dec 1739 and thence in the *Gentleman's magazine* for Dec 1739.
MC.

E432 — — Together with a burlesque upon, an imiation [!] of, and an answer to the said epistle...by the author of the Instructors instructed, or have at you, blind harpers. *Nottingham, printed by George Ayscough,* 1740.
8°: *A–B*⁴; *1–3* 4–15 *16 blk.*
 The epistle is printed on the versos and the answer on the rectos.
Answer: 'Tell me (for sure some devil did)'
CSmH(ms. corrections).

E433 — An epistle to William Morley esq; one of the directors of the South-Sea company. *London, printed for J. Roberts,* 1720. (*DP* 6 Aug)
8°: *A*(3 ll) B⁴ C(3 ll); *i–iv* v–vi, 1–14. A1 hft.
'Since all, in these harmonious times'
 'Bantering him for a subscription', Luttrell.
L(164.k.46, Luttrell, August).

E434 — An epistle to William Pitt esq; *London, printed for R. Dodsley; sold by M. Cooper,* 1746. (*GA* 13 March)
2°: *A*² < B²; *1–2* 3–8.
'Since one there is, who with uncommon art'
 A eulogy of Pitt. Satirized in *Short verses, in imitation of long verses,* 1746, which suggests the author is 'Ly—on', or George Lyttelton; but not included in his collected works.
L(11657.m.9),O,AdU; CSmH,MH(uncut),OCU.

E435 — An epistle to young gentlemen. A poem. With other miscellany pieces. By a young gentleman going abroad. *London printed, and sold by J. Roberts,* 1718 [1717]. (*DC* 28 Nov)
8°: A–C⁴ D²; *1–3* 4–28.
'To you, who know, as yet, no anxious hours'
CtY,InU(uncut).

— An epistle upon an epistle, 1730. *See* Swift, Jonathan.

— An epistle with some odes, 1746. *See* Fortescue, James.

Epistles

Epistles. Epistles and poems by Clio and Strephon, 1729. *See* Fowke, Martha.

— The epistles of Clio and Strephon, 1720–. *See* Fowke, Martha.

E436 — The epistles of Penelope to Ulysses, and Phyllis to Demophoon. Newly translated from Ovid. *London, printed for the author; sold by J. Robinson,* 1748. (*GM, LM* March)
4⁰: *A*¹ B–D² E¹; *i–ii, 1* 2–14.
'Your consort grieves at slow Ulysses' stay'
OCU.

Epistola. Epistola ad amicum familiaris, 1740–1. *See* Joy, James.

— Epistola ad Franciscum Bindonem, 1740. *See* Dunkin, William.

E437 Epistolary. An epistolary letter from T----- H----- to Sr H-----s S------e; who saved his life, and desired him to send over all the rarities he could find in his travels. *Printed at Dublin, and reprinted at London for T. Payne,* 1729. (*MChr* 4 Nov)
2⁰: *A*² B²; *1–2* 3–7 *8 blk.*
There was probably no Dublin edition. Reprinted by E. A. B. Mordaunt, 1904.
'Since you, dear doctor, sav'd my life'
A satirical letter from Thomas Hearne to Sir Hans Sloane. Printed in Sir Charles Hanbury Williams *Works* (1822) I. 124 as 'Sir Charles Hanbury Williams to Sir Hans Sloane'; dated by *DNB* as 1739–40, and accepted by Lord Ilchester in his life, though redating it as 1732. None knew of this edition, the date of which makes a doubtful attribution even less probable.
L(713.m.29/19; 643.1.24/51),OA,OW; CSmH, MH.

— An epistolary poem to a lady, on the present expedition of Lord Cathcart, 1740. *See* Rogers, Thomas.

E438 Epitaph. Epitaph on Alexander Robertson of Struan, esq; [*Edinburgh*? 1749?]
8⁰: *A*²; *1–4*.
Title in half-title form.
'Here, in cold earth, wrapt in eternal sleep'
CtY.

E439 — An epitaph on Bona-fide. [*London*?] *Printed in the glorious year* 1715.
½⁰: *1–2*, 1 column.
'Here lies an old man of seventy-seven'
On the death of Louis XIV.
Rothschild.

E440 — An epitaph on his grace James duke of Hamilton, who was basely and treacherously murder'd by George Maccartney, an Irish-man, second to the Lord Mohun, in Hyde-park the 15th of November 1712. *Edinburgh, printed by James Watson,* 1712.
½⁰: 1 side, 1 column.

An **epitaph** on...James duke of Hamilton
Mourning borders.
'Stranger! this stately monument contains'
E.

E441 — An epitaph on Mr Samuel. Smith, minister of Newgate. *London printed and Edinburgh reprinted [by Margaret Reid?] at the foot of the Horse-weynd,* [171–?]
½⁰: 1 side, 2 columns.
No London edition has been traced.
'Under this stone/Lies a reverend drone'
E.

E442 — An epitaph on Mrs. Marjory Scott. Who died at Dunkeld, Feb. 26. 1729. aged one hundred and twenty five. [1729/–.]
½⁰: 1 side, 1 column.
Mourning borders.
'Stop passenger, until my life you read'
Crum S1218: 'An inscription on the tomb stone of one Margaret Scot...'
LDW.

E443 — An epitaph on the French prophet, who was to make his resurrection on the 25th of May. *Edinburgh, printed by James Watson, and sold at his shop,* 1709.
½⁰: 1 side, 1 column.
Mourning borders.
'Here lies a prophet, who, as people say'
Apparently on Thomas Emes; there is a reference to John Lacy, another Camisard 'prophet'.
E.

E444 — Epitaph on the much lamented death of Mr. David Crawfurd of Drumsuy, her majesty's historiographer, who died the 16th of January 1708. [*Edinburgh*, 1708.]
½⁰: 1 side, 1 column.
'The gods resolv'd a master-piece to show'
According to *DNB*, David Crawford the historiographer died in 1726.
E.

E445 — An epitaph upon Mrs. Frances Kentish, who died at London in 1721, and was buried at Northall in Middlesex upon St. Thomas's day... [*Canterbury*? 1721/22.]
½⁰: 1 side, 1 column.
The O copy was given to Thomas Hearne on 25 June 1722 with the following, printed at Canterbury. The typography of the two is very similar.
'Her soul's above, her mortal part's here laid'
Given to Hearne by Thomas Allen, rector of Thurston, who may possibly be the author.
O.

E446 — An epitaph upon the late Mrs Ann Hales, a nun of the order of St. Austin, and door-keeper of the nunnery. *Printed at Canterbury,* [1720?/22.]
½⁰: 1 side, 1 column.
'Locks, bars and walls too weak to bind'
The O copy was given to Hearne (with the

An **epitaph** upon the late Mrs Ann Hales

preceding) by Thomas Allen, rector of Thurston, who may possibly be the author.

O.

Epitaphium. Epitaphium Annæ reginæ Magnæ Britanniæ, Franciæ, & Hiberniæ reginæ tumulo inscribendum, 1714.

Listed by Leicester Bradner in '*Musae Anglicanae*: a supplemental list', *Library* V. 22 (1967) 97; but it is a prose inscription.

— Epitaphium viri reverendissimi D. Georgii Meldrumii, [1709.] *See* Scott, *Sir* William.

Epithalamium. An epithalamium address'd to Mrs. Cox, 1715. *See* Hinchliffe, William.

— An epithalamium. Being stanzas..., 1712. *See* Crispe, Henry.

E447 — An epithalamium on the jovial nuptials of Capt. James Donaldson gazetteer and observator: with the meritorious lady Mrs. Jean Reid, alias Mrs. Scot. [*Edinburgh*, 170–?]
½°: 1 side, 2 columns.
'In compensation of your vademecum'
At foot: 'Composed by a Lady of Honour'.
E.

E448 — An epithalamium on the king's marriage. [1719?]
2°: *A*²; 1 2–3 *4 blk.*
With two other poems, 'Sobieskia' and 'The bonny black laddie'.
'O sacred James, listning with ravish'd ear'
On the Pretender's marriage to Princess Sobieski.
L(1876.f.1/85; C.115.i.3/54).

— An epithalamium, or poem, on the marriage of Robert Rochfort, 1737. *See* Gahagan, Usher.

E449 **Equity.** The equity of Parnassus: a poem. *London, printed for C. Corbett; sold by Mrs. Nut & Mrs. Cooke, Mrs. Dodd, & at Mrs. Haywood's*, 1744. (*OE* 11 Feb)
2°: *A*² B–D²; 1–5 6–16. A1 hft.
Engraving on title.
'No longer now the criminal of state'
A bitter satire on Walpole and Pulteney.
L(162.n.50,–A1); CSmH,CtY(–A1),MH,OCU (uncut, –A1),TxU+.

Equivalent. An equivalent for Defoe, [1706?] *See* Hamilton, John, *baron* Belhaven.

E450 — The equivalent for fasting: or, consecration-fee. Tune of, King John and the abbot of Canterbury. [*London*, 1727/30.]
½°: 2 sides, 2 columns.
With three other satirical poems.
'I'll tell you a story, and warrant it true'
On the consecration of St. George's, Hanover Square.
MH.

Erasmus, D.

Erasmus, Desiderius.
[*Colloquia*] [Forbes, William:] Xantippe, or the scolding wife, done from the Conjugium of Erasmus, 1724. *See* F196.

Errington, Prideaux. Copies in verse, for the use of writing schools, and hymns for charity-schools. Never before extant. *Newcastle upon Tyne, printed for the author, and sold by Mr. Shaw*, 1723.
4°: pp. iv, 40.   L,NeP.
The copy at L has corrections by the author for the 1734 edition.

— New copies in verse, for the use of writing schools: consisting of fifty-three alphabets... *Newcastle upon Tyne, printed by Isaac Lane, and company, for the author, and sold by the booksellers in town*, 1734.
8°: pp. xi, 162.   L,NeP.

[**Erskine, Ralph.**] Gospel canticles: or, spiritual songs. In five parts... By a minister of the gospel in the church of Scotland. *Edinburgh, printed by Mr. James M'Ewen and company, and to be sold by the said Mr. James M'Ewen and other booksellers*, 1720.
8°: pp. 100.   L,E.
Errata slip in some copies.

— [*idem*] Gospel sonnets, or, spiritual songs. In six parts... The 2d edition (of that book formerly intituled, Gospel canticles) corrected and amended ...with the addition of the sixth part... *Edinburgh, printed for John Briggs*, 1726.
8°: pp. xiv, 170.   L,E.

— — The 3d edition... *Edinburgh, printed for John Briggs*, 1732.
12°: pp. xiv, 170.   L,E.

— — The fourth edition, with large additions and great improvements. *London, printed for J. Oswald; sold by the booksellers of Edinburgh & Glasgow*, 1734.
12°: pp. xviii, 270.   L,C; NNUT.

— — The fifth edition... *Edinburgh, printed by Thomas Lumisden & John Robertson*, 1736.
12°: pp. xxiv, 264.   E.

— — The fifth edition... *London, printed for J. Oswald; sold by the booksellers of Edinburgh & Glasgow*, 1741.
12°: pp. xviii, 270.   MH-AH.

— — The sixth edition... *London, printed for J. Oswald*, 1750.
12°: pp. xviii, 270.   L; CtY-D,NN.

E451 [—] The believer's dowry. Or, a poem upon Isa: 54. 5. .... The author is one who seeks the prayers of the godly reader. *Edinburgh, printed by John Moncur at his printing house at the foot of the Bull Closs*, 1708.
8°: *A*⁸ B⁴; 1–4 5–24.
'Christ is the husband, saints the bride'

Erskine, R. The believer's dowry

Later incorporated in revised form in Erskine's *Gospel sonnets*.
L(1487.ee.15),E.

E452 [—] — *Edinburgh, printed and sold by Robert Brown in Forrester's-Wynd, 1720.*
8°: A⁸; *1–4* 5–16.
L(1076.1.10/3).

E453 [—] — To which is added, the Christian's daily practice of piety. *Glasgow, printed by Robert Sanders, and are to be sold in his shop, 1723.*
12°: A⁸; *1–4* 5–16.
L(11631.a.6).

E454 [—] A congratulatory poem upon the coronation of his majesty King George; with Dunfermline's address to his majesty for redressing Scotland's grievances. *Edinburgh, printed by John Reid, 1714.*
4°: A⁴; *1–3* 4–8.
'Hail mighty monarch, welcome to the throne'
The attribution to Erskine in *Halkett & Laing*, doubtless based on the E catalogue, probably stems from the fact that Erskine was minister at Dunfermline.
L(11630.b.8/4),E(2).

E455 [—] — *Glasgow, printed in the year 1714.*
4°: A⁴; *1–3* 4–8.
O,E(2).

E456 — An elegy: or funeral poem on the much lamented death of...Mr. Alexander Hamilton, late minister of the gospel in Stirling. To which is prefix'd, an elegiack poem, to the memory of...James Cuthbert...in English and Latin... Also, Smoaking spiritualiz'd: a short poem. *Edinburgh, printed for David Duncan, 1739.*
8°: π⁴ A⁴ C–D⁴; *i–viii*, 1–24.
There are separate titles on π2, C3 to the elegies on Cuthbert and Hamilton; 'Smoaking spiritualiz'd' is printed on D4.
Cuthbert: 'Long did my muse expectant wish to see'
Hamilton: 'Death, dost thou difficult us now to know'
Smoaking: 'This Indian weed now wither'd quite'
E(lacks π1),GM; MH(uncut),NN-A.

E457 — A paraphrase, or large explicatory poem upon the Song of Solomon... *Edinburgh, printed by Tho. Lumisden & Jo. Robertson, for James Beugo bookseller in Dunfermline; and sold by him, and by Gideon Crawfurd, 1736.*
12°: A–X⁴; *i–ii* iii–xvi, 17–166 *167–168 blk.*
Note on copyright on verso of title, 'The author expects that none will presume to reprint this book without his advice and consent first had and obtained thereto'.
'The choice of anthems exquisite'
L(11632.aa.6,–X4),E(–X4),EN,GM.

E458 — — *London, printed for John Oswald, 1742.*
12°: A¹² B–N⁶; *i–ii* iii–xvi, *17* 18–166 *167–168 blk.*
Strahan's ledger records printing for John Oswald on or after 15 June 1742 '1250 titles

Erskine, R. A paraphrase

for Erskine's Poetical paraphrase with a catalogue...8 quires of paper...' Presumably these were a conjugate pair of 12° leaves, possibly for advertising. Reprinted in Boston, 1743.
L(11631.b.8,–N6),E; NN(–N6).

E459 — A short paraphrase upon the Lamentations of Jeremiah. Adapted to the common tunes... *Glasgow, printed for John Newlands, and sold by him at his shop, 1750.*
8°: A–D⁴ E²; *i–iii* iv–vi, 7–36.
Errata slip on p. 36.
'Ah how so populous of late'
L(1023.a.27/6, cropt),O(uncut),E.

E460 **Erskine, William.** Scacchia ludus: or, the game of chess. A poem. Written originally in Latin by Marcus Hieronymus Vida... Translated into English by Mr. Erskine. With...a translation of Vida's three pastoral eclogues. By Mr. Craig. The whole adorn'd with a handsome frontispiece, and a curious head of Vida. *London, printed for A. Millar, 1736.* (*GM* April)
8°: (frt+) A⁴ B–P⁸ (+1 plate); *i–viii, 1* 2–219 *220; 221–224 blk.* 220 err.
Folding plate facing p. 1. Title-pages to separate parts dated 1735. Latin and English texts.
'We trace war's image thro' its various scenes'
The identity of Mr. Craig has not been determined.
L(11405.e.40,–frt,P8),O(–P8),DG(–plate,P8), *DrU*,LdU-B(–P8); CtY(–plate, P8),MH,NN (–plate, P8),*NjP*,PU.

Esq. Esq; S---ys's budget open'd, 1743. *See* Williams, *Sir* Charles Hanbury.

Essai. Essai sur la critique; imité de l'Anglois, 1717. *See* Robethon, John.

E461 **Essay.** An essay by way of elegy, on the hon^d: Arthur Upton esq; of Castle Upton, of ever-pious memory. Written Nov. – 1706. *Belfast, printed by James Blow, 1707.*
4°: A⁴; *1–2* 3–8.
'Great Upton to the highest bliss is born'
Ascribed to James Kirkpatrick of Belfast by *Anderson* (1890) 7, possibly because almost all early Belfast books were written by him. No other evidence has been found.
C.

— An essay in praise of women, 1735. *See* Bland, James.

— An essay on calumny, 1744. *See* Saunders, —, *Mr.*

— An essay on conduct and education, 1738–. *See* Fry, John.

— An essay on conversation, 1737. *See* Stillingfleet, Benjamin.

An **essay** on criticism

— An essay on criticism, 1711–. *See* Pope, Alexander.

— An essay on design and beauty, 1739. *See* Leslie, Charles.

E462 — An essay on faction. *London, printed for J. Peele, 1733. (GSJ* 13 Nov)
2⁰: *A*² B–D²; *1–2* 3–16.
No watermark.
'Shall baleful hate unwearied vigour use'
LdU-B; CSmH,IU,MH,OCU.

E463 — [fine paper]
Watermark: fleur-de-lys.
TxU.

— An essay on happiness, 1737. *See* Nugent, Robert, *earl Nugent.*

— An essay on human life, 1734–. *See* Paget, Thomas Catesby, *baron Paget.*

— An essay on man, [1733]–. *See* Pope, Alexander.

E464 — An essay on preferment. By the author of the Rapsody on the army. *Dublin, printed in the year 1736.*
8⁰: *A*⁴ B⁴; *1–2* 3–16.
Teerink 1316.
'Run, run, the levee opens, cry the slaves'
Ends in praise of Swift.
L(11659.df.3),C,DA(2, 1 uncut),DK; CtY,ICN.

E465 — [*idem*] An epistle on preferment, inscribed to the rev. Dr. Swift, D.S.P.D. Found among the papers of a great author. *London, printed for Joseph Collyer; sold by the booksellers in London and Westminster,* 'D.DCC.XLIV' [1744]. (31 Oct)
2⁰: *A*¹ B–E² *F*¹; *i–ii, 1 2–17 18 blk.*
Horizontal chain-lines. Listed in *GM* Oct.
L(1962, Tom's Coffee House, 31 Oct),O,DN; CLU-C(uncut),CtY(uncut),MH,OCU,PU.

E466 — An essay on Prince Eugene's success in Italy. By way of epistle to the honourable G.G. esq; *London, printed for M. Wotton, 1702. (WL* Sept)
4⁰: *A*² B–C²; *1–4* 5–12. A1 hft.
'Let haughty victors boast of conquests won'
DT(2); CSmH,*ICN.*

— An essay on reason, 1735. *See* Harte, Walter.

— An essay on satire, 1745. *See* Brown, John.

— An essay on the character of Sir Willoughby Aston, 1704. *See* Yalden, Thomas.

E467 — 'An essay on the death of our late most gracious queen. [*London*] *Printed for John Morphew.* Price 2*d.*' (*PB* 24 Aug 1714)
Possibly a half-sheet from the price, and probably in verse.

— An essay on the different stiles of poetry, 1713. *See* Parnell, Thomas.

— An essay on the great battle at Ramellies, 1706. *See* Defoe, Daniel.

— An essay on the poets, 1712–. *See* Morrice, Bezaleel.

An **essay** on the soul of man

E468 — An essay on the soul of man. *London printed, and sold by Jacob Robinson, 1744.* (1 Feb?)
2⁰: A–F² (F2 as 'E2'); *i–iv, 1 2–20.*
Listed in *GM, LM* Feb.
'Genius of verse! with ardour fill my breast'
By the same author as *A poetical and critical essay on Homer,* 1744.
L(11630.h.21),C; CSmH,IU,MH(ms. date 1 Feb), OCU.

E469 — An essay on the theatres: or, the art of acting; a poem. In imitation of Horace's Art of poetry. *London printed, and Dublin re-printed by and for J. Kinneir, & A. Long, 1745.*
12⁰: *A*² B⁶ C⁴ (B3 as 'B5'); *i–iii* iv, *5* 6–24. C4 advt.
'Should Hogarth, with extravagant conceit'
DN.

— An essay on the universe, 1725. *See* Morrice, Bezaleel.

E470 — An essay on the universe: a poem. *London, printed for John Oswald, 1733. (GSJ* 18 April)
8⁰: *A*⁴ B–C⁴; *1–4* 5–24. A1 hft.
'Oh, thou, whose bold and penetrating eye'
Dedicated to Pope. Apparently a different work from B. Morrice's poem of this title, 1725.
L(11631.b.17); CtY(−A1),MH.

— An essay on the vicious bent and taste of the times, 1737. *See* Manning, Francis.

E471 — An essay on victory. Being a congratulatory poem, on the happy successes of his majesty's councils and conduct. Interspers'd with memoirs of the principal generals and ministers, concern'd in those great events. To which is prefix'd, a preface, (by a friend of the author's)... By a person altogether independent of ministerial influence... *London, printed for the author; and are to be sold by the booksellers of London & Westminster; and for the conveniency of those who attend the houses of lords and commons, at Waghorn's, and other coffee-houses, and at the pamphlet-shops in and about the court of requests, 1744.*
2⁰: *A*² b² B–F² *G*¹; *i–viii, 1 2–21 22 blk.*
'[Price two shillings.]' below imprint.
'If you great guardian of Britannia's fate'
The essay is partly composed of extracts from previously published poems by various authors.
OO.

E472 — — Interspers'd with memoirs of the heroick bravery... To which is prefix'd, a preface, (by a friend of the author's)... By a lover of his country, and of the protestant succession... *London, printed for J. Roberts, and are to be sold by the booksellers of London & Westminster, 1744. (GM, LM* March)
2⁰: *A*² b² B–F² *G*¹; *i–viii, 1 2–21 22 blk.*
'[Price one shilling and six-pence.]' below imprint. Apparently a reissue or reimpression.
InU.

An **essay** to the memory

E473 — An essay to the memory of John, lord Cutts, &c. Who died January the twenty sixth 170$\frac{6}{7}$. *Dublin, printed for M. Gunne*, 1707.
4°: *A*² B–C²; *1–3* 4–11 *12 blk.*
'When Cutts is dead, shall none but ballad verse'
LDW,O,C.

— An essay, to the pious memory of...Mr. George Trosse, 1713. *See* Mortimer, J.

E474 — An essay upon friendship. A poem. Inscrib'd to the right honourable the Earl of Mar... By a gentleman of Scotland. [*London?*] *Printed for the author in the year* 1714.
2°: *A*² B–D²; *i–iv, 1–12.*
'Whilst sacred friendship, I thy virtues sing'
Dedication signed 'W.F.' Probably by the same author as *The triumph of virtue... by a gentleman of North-Britain*, 1713.
E.

E475 — An essay upon lineage and succession... Written by a person of honour. *Edinburgh, printed* 1746.
8°: *A*⁴; *1–2* 3–8. 8 advt.
Horizontal chain-lines. Previously printed (as *A*⁴, and with colophon 'Edinburgh, printed by John Moncur 1713') as part 2 of *The protest of the Chevalier St. George; with a poem concerning hereditary right, anexed.*
'Vain carnal men make carnal policy'
An attack on the divine right of kings.
CSmH,NN.

— An essay upon marriage in a letter adress'd to a friend, [1704.] *See* Forbes, William.

E476 — An essay, upon Polemo medinia or the midden-fight. Between Vitarva & Neberna. *Edinburgh, printed by John Reid younger*, 1704.
4°: *A*⁴; *1–3* 4–8.
The order of editions is not established.
'Ye nymphs who in Fifes highest mountains dwell'
The author's dedication signed 'J.C.' and addressed to George Drummond; J.C. was a prisoner in the Tolbooth. A translation of the poem generally ascribed to William Drummond of Hawthornden.
E; MH.

E477 — — *Edinburgh, printed by George Jaffrey*, 1704.
4°: *A*⁴; *1–3* 4–8.
CtY.

Essays. Essays, 1737. *See* Cooke, Thomas (C412).

— Essays in sacred poetry. Viz. I. The blessing. II. Power and love. III. Dependance and repentance. IV. Of the resurrection. *London, printed for J. Roberts; sold by J. Harrison*, 1716. (*MC* April)
8°: pp. 31.   CtY.

E478 Estcourt, Richard. Britain's jubilee: a new congratulatory ballad, on the glorious victories obtain'd by the Duke of Malborough, over the

Estcourt, R. Britain's jubilee

French: writ by the famous comedian, Mr. Escourt, and sung by him to most of our nobility, with great applause. *London printed, and sold by J. Morphew*, [1707?]
½°: 1 side, 2 columns.
First verse printed with five lines of typeset music. Also published as an engraved sheet. Reprinted in H. Hills's edition of *Windsor Castle*, 1708.
'You tell me Dick you've lately read'
MC; TxU,*Harding.*

[—] An excellent new song, call'd, The full tryal and condemnation of John duke of Marlborough, [1712.] *See* E578.

[—] On the jewel in the Tower, 1712. *See* O205.

E479 Et. Et tu Brute? or, the m--'d c--l. [*London*, 1704?]
4°: *A*⁴; *1–2* 3–8.
Title in half-title form.
'To give the last amendments to the bill'
Crum T2961: 'A confutation of the bishops about the occasion bill'; attributed in a ms. at L (Add. MS. 25490, fol. 13) to H. Hall, organist of Hereford. See F. H. Ellis in *POAS* VI. 508. The CLU-C copy of the following edition has an early ms. note 'Suppos'd by Prior'. The mitre'd cabal: a satire on the bishops concerned with the bill against occasional conformity.
L(164.n.61, Luttrell, no date),O; CLU-C,DFo, TxU.

E480 — [*idem*] The m—'d c—b: or, the L——th. consultation. Et tu Brute?... From a correct copy. *London, printed in the year* 1704.
4°: *A*⁴; *1–2* 3–8.
'M—'d c—b' printed with continuous rules. This is a corrupt text, though it may be printed from a better ms. tradition.
O; CLU-C(ms. corrections),ICU,IU,InU,*MB.*

E481 — The m—'d c—b; or, the L—th consultation... '*London*', *printed in the year* 1704.
4°: *A*⁴; *1–2* 3–8.
The rules in 'M—'d c—b' are each composed of three short sections, though the inking sometimes obscures this. Probably an Edinburgh reprint from the location of copies.
L(11626.c.44/6; 11643.i.23),E(3),ES; CtY,NjP, OCU.

E482 Eternity. 'Eternity: a poem. By T.R. gent. [*London*] *Printed by S. Lee for the author; sold by J. Morphew.*' (*MC* Aug 1716)
Possibly by the same author as *The true state of mortality*, 1708, also by T.R.; that has been ascribed to Thomas Rogers.

E483 Eubulus. Eubulus Oxoniensis discipulis suis. Being an imitation of the celebrated Qui mihi. In praise of drunkenness. In Latin and English .

Eubulus Oxoniensis

London, printed for J. Roberts, 1720 [1719]. (Dec, Luttrell)
8°: A–C⁴ (B signed as 'A'); *i–ii* iii–viii, *1–2* 3–8, *1* 2–8.
> Reissued in *The Oxford miscellany,* 1720. Latin and English text.
'Qui mihi combibulus puer es, cupis atque jocari'
'Thou chief companion of my cup'
> Early ms. note in the TxU copy, 'What follows is the joint composition of N. Amhurst & John Wynne. Two most abandon'd scoundrels. By Eubulus & his pupil are meant Dr Thelwal & Tom Williams'.
L(161.m.67, Luttrell),O(2),OW; MH,OCU,TxU.

E484 Eucharist. The eucharist. A poem. *Edinburgh, printed by T. & W. Ruddimans,* 1737.
8°: A–D⁴; *1–3* 4–32.
'Arise, my muse, from low pursuits arise'
GM; *DLC*,MH,OCU.

— The eucharist. Or the holy sacrament, 1717. *See* Settle, Elkanah.

E485 Eugenio. Eugenio: or, the disconsolate shepherd. A dirge on the death of Dorinda. *London, printed for M. Cooper,* 1743. (*LDP* 23 April)
2°: A⁴; *1–2* 3–7 *8 blk.*
Rothschild 233.
'In a lone vale, which nature made'
> On the death of the Countess of Euston. A reply to *G----e and D----y,* 1743.
L(11630.h.22),O; CtY,DFo,IU,MH,OCU +.

E486 — — The second edition. *London, printed for M. Cooper,* 1743.
2°: A⁴; *1–2* 3–7 *8 blk.*
> Apparently a reimpression or variant title.
KU.

— Eugenio: or, virtuous and happy life, 1737. *See* Beach, Thomas.

'**Eugenio.**' Age in distress: or, Job's lamentation, 1750. *See* A123.

E487 European. The European mourners: or, the emperor's funeral. With Marshal Bellisle's progress to captivity. *London, printed for W. Webb,* [1745.]
obl ½°: 1 side, 3 columns.
> Large woodcut with 3 verses below. Originally published as an engraved sheet (L, P&D 2619).
'For what have these gentry these four years been fighting?'
> On the choice of a successor to Charles VII.
L(P&D 2620); NNP(imprint cropt).

E488 Eusden, Laurence. An epistle to the noble, and right honourable Sir Robert Walpole... *London printed, and sold by J. Roberts,* 1726.
2°: A–B² C²; *1–3* 4–12.
'From Cam's fam'd banks, and Granta's green retreats'
MH,TxU(2, 1 uncut).

Eusden, L. An epistle

E489 — — The second edition. *London printed, and sold by J. Roberts,* 1726.
2°: A–B² C²; *1–3* 4–12.
> Apparently a reimpression or press-variant title.
TxU(2).

E490 — Hero and Leander: a poem by Musaeus, translated from the Greek by L. Eusden... *Glasgow, printed by Robert & Andrew Foulis, and sold by John Ross, in Edinburgh,* 1750. (*SM* Sept)
8°: A–D⁴; *1–3* 4–32.
> No watermark. *Gaskell, Foulis* 163. Previously published in miscellanies.
'Sing, muse, the conscious torch, whose nightly flame'
O.

E491 — [fine paper]
> Watermark: fleur-de-lys.
L(11340.c.20/1),DK; MH.

E492 — A letter to Mr. Addison, on the king's accession to the throne. *London, printed for J. Tonson,* 1714. (*SR* 12 Oct)
2°: A–D² (A2 as 'B'); *i–ii,* 1–13 *14 blk.*
> Entered in *SR* to Jacob Tonson by Isaac Miller; deposit copies at L,O,EU,AdU,SaU. Listed in *MC* Oct.
'While to new honours you, unenvy'd, soar'
L(643.m.13/5; 162.n.7),LVA-F,O,EU,SaU +; CSmH,CtY(uncut),ICN,MH,TxU(2, 1 uncut) +.

E493 — [*idem*] The royal family! A letter to Mr. Addison, on the king's accession to the throne. *London: printed for J. Tonson: and re-printed and sold by E. Waters,* [Dublin,] 1714.
8°: A–B⁴; *1–2* 3–15 *16 blk.*
L(12274.e.1/5),DA,DN.

E494 — An ode for the birthday, as it was sung before his majesty. *London, printed for Jacob Tonson,* 1720. (*DC* 2 June)
2°: A² < B¹; *i–ii,* 1 2–4.
> Watermark: fleur-de-lys.
'A hero scarce could rise of old'
LVA-F,AdU; CSmH,CtY.

E495 — An ode for the birthday, MDCCXXI. As it was sung before his majesty. *London, printed for Jacob Tonson,* 1721.
2°: A² < B¹; *i–ii,* 1 2–4.
> Watermark: fleur-de-lys.
'When the great Julius on Britannia's strand'
L(840.m.1/27),O,*LdP*; TxU.

E496 — The ode for the birth-day, MDCCXXIII. In English and Latin. *Cambridge, printed at the University-Press, and sold there by Corn. Crownfield; and by Jacob Tonson, & John Graves, London,* 1723. (*MC* May)
4°: π¹ A⁴; *i–ii,* 1 2–7 *8 blk.*
'Hail to the lov'd, returning, glorious day!'
'Salve, chara dies, redeuntis tu decus anni!'
L(161.l.39, Luttrell, May),LVA-D.

Eusden, L. An ode for the new year

E497 — An ode for the new year, as it was sung before his majesty. *London, printed for Jacob Tonson,* 1720. (*DC* 6 Jan)
2°: *A*² *B*²; *i–iv, 1 2–3 4 blk.* A1 hft.
Watermark: fool's cap.
'Lift up thy hoary head, and rise'
L(643.l.24/41).

E498 — [fine paper]
Watermark: fleur-de-lys.
ICN.

E499 — An ode for the new-year, as it was sung before his majesty. *London, printed for Jacob Tonson,* 1721.
2°: *A*² < *B*¹; *i–ii, 12–4.*
The collation is tentative. Watermark: fleur-de-lys.
'Say, gen'rous parent of the vine'
O.

E500 — The origin of the knights of the Bath, a poem, humbly inscrib'd to his royal highness Prince William Augustus. *London, printed for Jacob Tonson,* 1725. (*MC* July)
2°: *A*² *B*²; *1–3 4–8.*
No watermark.
'Hail glorious off-spring of a glorious race!'
L(643.l.24/47),DT; CtY,TxU(3, 1 uncut).

E501 — [fine paper]
Watermark: fleur-de-lys.
O.

E502 — The parallel. With a dedication to the right honourable the Lord Carteret, one of his majesty's principal secretaries of state. *London, printed for Jacob Tonson,* 1722.
2°: *A*² < *B*²; *i–ii, 1 2–6.*
'Alcides once on Mauritanian ground'
CtY,ICN.

E503 — A poem humbly inscribed to his royal highness Prince Frederic, on his safe arrival in Great Britain... *London printed, and sold by J. Roberts,* 1729. (*MChr* 22 Jan)
2°: *A*² *B–C*²; *1–3 4–11 12 blk.*
'While British crowds their loyal tongues employ'
O,OA; CtY,MH,NjP,TxU(2).

E504 — A poem on the marriage of his grace the Duke of Newcastle to the right honourable the Lady Henrietta Godolphin, inscrib'd to his grace. *London, printed for J. Tonson,* 1717. (*MC* April)
2°: *A–C*² *D*¹; *1–3 4–14.*
No watermark.
'While Gothick arms begin t' infest the times'
L(643.l.24/38),O; *CLU-C*,CSmH,CtY,MH,MiU.

E505 — [fine paper]
Watermark: star.
LVA-F; TxU.

E506 —— The second edition. *London, printed for J. Tonson,* 1717.
2°: *A–C*² *D*¹; *1–3 4–14.*

Eusden, L. A poem on the marriage

Apparently a reimpression or press-variant title. No watermark.
L(1959),O.

E507 — A poem to her royal highness on the birth of the prince. *London, printed for Jacob Tonson,* 1718 [1717]. (*DC* 25 Nov)
2°: *A*² *B*²; *i–iv, 1 2–4.* A1 hft.
Watermark: O.
'While ev'ry British heart a tongue employs'
L(162.n.9),LVA-F,O; CSmH,IU,MH.

E508 — [fine paper?]
Watermark: fleur-de-lys.
L(643.l.24/39),LdU-B.

E509 — Three poems. I. To the right honourable the lord high-chancellor...on his lordship's being created earl of Macclesfield. II. To...the Lord Parker; on his return from his travels. III. To...the Lord Parker; on his marriage with Mrs. Mary Lane. *London, printed for Jacob Tonson,* 1722. (*PB* 15 Nov)
2°: *A*² *B–C*² *D*¹; *1–3 4–14.*
'Desert, oft hid in shades, when monarchs trace'
'The muse, that trac'd thee in far distant climes'
'Again, my muse, the lyre to Parker string'
L(643.l.24/44; 162.n.8),O(2),*LdP*,WcC(uncut); CtY,TxU.

E510 — Three poems; the first, sacred to the immortal memory of the late king; the second, on the happy succession...and a third humbly inscrib'd to the queen. *London, printed for J. Roberts,* 1727. (*MC* Nov)
2°: *A*² *B–F*² *G*¹; *1–3 4–25 26 blk.*
''Tis not enough in secret to lament'
'As when learn'd sages optic arts display'
'With his great fathers when great Brunswic slept'
L(643.m.12/36); CtY,MH,TxU(3, 1 uncut).

E511 —— The second edition. *London, printed for J. Roberts,* 1727.
2°: *A*² *B–F*² *G*¹; *1–3 4–25 26 blk.*
Apparently a reimpression or press-variant title.
O,C,WcC(uncut); DLC.

E512 — To her highness the Princess Anne, on her recovery from the small-pox. *London, printed for J. Tonson,* 1720. (*DC* 29 July)
2°: *A*² *B*¹; *1–3 4–5 6.*
'Young, beauteous pride of a long-glorious race'
TxU(Luttrell, July).

E513 — To Mr. John Saunders, on seeing his paintings in Cambridge. [*London?* 1725.]
½°: *1–2,* 1 column.
'Welcome, nice artist, to these learn'd retreats'
Signed from Trinity College, 22 Nov 1725, 'Laurence Eusden'.
L(1970),C.

E514 — Verses at the last publick commencement at Cambridge. Written and spoken by Mr. Eusden. *London, printed for J. Tonson,* 1714. (*SR* 15 July)
2°: *A–C*² *D*¹; *i–ii, 1–12.*

Eusden, L. Verses

No watermark. Entered in *SR* to Tonson by Isaac Miller; deposit copies at L,LSC,O,EU, AdU,SaU. Listed in *MC* July.
'Hail, British fair ones, who in silence sit'
L(643.m.13/1),O,C,EU,DN(lacks A1)+; CLU-C, CtY(uncut),ICN,NjP,TxU(3)+.

E515 — [fine paper]
Watermark: London arms.
LVA-F; MH.

E516 — — The second edition. *London, printed for J. Tonson, 1714.*
2⁰: A–C² D¹; *i–ii*, 1–12.
Apparently the early sheets are reset, the rest reimpressed.
L(11632.i.5),O(2),C; CSmH,DFo,TxU(uncut).

Eusebia. Eusebia triumphans, 1702–. *See* Settle, Elkanah.

E517 [**Evans, Abel.**] The apparition. A poem. [*Oxford*] *Printed in the year 1710. And are to be sold by the booksellers of London & Westminster.* (*PB* 24 Jan 1710)
8⁰: A–E⁴; *1–2* 3–38 *39–40 blk.*
Watermark: initial. Some variant copies (e.g. at L,O,MH,TxU) have no footnote on p. 21. Advertised in *PB* as 'Printed for A. Peasly at Oxford; and sold by Bernard Lintott'; Hearne on 19 Jan recorded it as just published, printed by Leonard Lichfield; the date given above is that of its London publication.
'Begin my muse: the dire adventure tell'
Early ms. attributions to Evans in copies at LdU-B and OW (a fine-paper presentation copy). A satire on Matthew Tindal's *The rights of the Christian church asserted*, 1706. For a satirical continuation, see *The second part of the Apparition*, 1710.
L(11623.d.2,–E4; 164.m.55; G.18423/3),LDW, O(5),OW,LdU-B+; CSmH,CtY,IU(2, 1–E4), MH(2),TxU(2)+.

E518 [—] [fine paper]
Watermark: fleur-de-lys on shield.
OW('Donum autoris').

E519 [—] — Or, A dialogue betwixt the devil and a doctor, concerning the rights of the Christian church. The second edition. *Printed in the year 1710. And are to be sold by the booksellers of London & Westminster.* (29 June?)
8⁰: A–C⁴; *1–2* 3–23 *24 blk.*
It has not been determined whether this edition was also printed in Oxford, but the changes to the title make it clear that it is the authorized second edition. This form of title was advertised in *PM* 29 June without the words 'The second edition', and adding Mrs. Baldwin to the general booksellers' imprint.
L(T.756/12),O(3),OW,DG,DT; CSmH,CtY,KU, MH,TxU+.

Evans, A. The apparition

E520 [—] [variant, title reads:] concerning a book falsly call'd the Rights of the Christian church. The second edition. *Printed in the year 1710. And are to be sold by the booksellers of London & Westminster.*
The first line has also been changed to read 'Begin, my muse! the dire adventure tell'. Possibly another impression.
O; KU.

Piracies

E521 [—] The apparition. A poem. *London printed, and sold by H. Hills, 1710.*
8⁰: A–C⁴; *1–2* 3–24.
L(1960),O,C,EU,AdU(2)+; CtY,DFo,IEN.

E522 [—] The appa.tion [!]. A poem. *Oxford printed, and sold by the booksellers of London & Westminster, 1710.*
8⁰: A⁸; *1* 2–16.
A copy belonging to F F. Madan had corrected title reading 'apparition'. The Oxford imprint in this and the following edition is suspect.
L(11642.bb.58),O(cropt); ICN(cropt).

E523 [—] — The second edition. *Oxford printed, and sold by the booksellers of London & Westminster, 1710.*
8⁰: A⁸; *1* 2–16.
Apparently a reimpression.
O(2).

E524 [—] — The second edition. *Printed in the year 1710. And are to be sold by the booksellers of London & Westminster. The whole 6 penny poem verbatim.*
8⁰: *A⁴* B⁴; *1* 2–16.
The C copy is treated as a Dublin reprint, but the reference to the '6 penny poem' suggests an English origin.
C; DLC.

E525 [—] — [*Dublin*] *Printed in the year 1710.*
8⁰: A–C⁴ (C2 as 'C3'); *1–2* 3–23 *24 blk.*
The NN copy is bound in a collection of Dublin tracts.
IU,NN.

———————

E526 [—] The apparition. A poem. Or, a dialogue betwixt the devil and a doctor... The third edition. *Printed in the year 1726. And are to be sold by the booksellers of London & Westminster.*
8⁰: A⁴(±A1) B–C⁴; *1–2* 3–23 *24 blk.*
A reissue of the authorized second edition of 1710, E519.
O; *CtY*,ICN.

E527 [—] [reissue] The fourth edition. *Printed in the year 1726. And are to be sold by the booksellers of London & Westminster.*
8⁰: A⁴(±A1) B–C⁴; *1–2* 3–23 *24 blk.*
L(1961),WcC.

E528 [—] Præ-existence. A poem, in imitation of Milton. *London, printed for John Clark, 1714.*
8⁰: *A⁴* b⁴ B–D⁴ (B as 'C'); *i–xvi*, 1–24. A1 hft.
'Now had th' archangel trumpet, rais'd sublime'

Evans, A. Præ-existence

Printed as by Evans in *Dodsley* I.
L(11631.bbb.39/7),O(2, 1–A1),DT(2); CtY,IU
(–A1),MH(–A1),TxU.

E529 [—] — *London, printed for Thomas Osborne, 1740.*
(*GM,LM* Oct)
4⁰: A² B–E²; *i–viii, 1 2–12.*
L(11631.f.29),*MR-C*; ICN,IU,MH(uncut),NjP.

E530 [—] Vertumnus. An epistle to Mr. Jacob Bobart,
botany professor to the university of Oxford... By
the author of the Apparition. *Oxford, printed by
L.L. [Leonard Lichfield] for Stephen Fletcher, and
are to be sold by John Morphew, London, 1713.* (*PB*
25 June)
8⁰: π² A–D⁴; [2] *1–2 3–33 34 blk.* π1 frt; 33 advt.
'Thank heav'n! at last our wars are o'er'
Early ms. attribution in a copy at O.
L(992.h.3/7; B.700/1),O(4, 2–π1),WcC; CSmH,
CtY(2),ICN,MH,TxU(2)+.

E531 **Evening.** An evening thought. *London printed, and
sold by J. Roberts, 1715.* (*MC* June)
8⁰: A–C⁴; *i–vi, 1 2–17 18.* 18 advt.
'When evening shades invite to open fields'
L(11643.f.1); OCU.

E532 **Exact.** An exact list of the battle of Dyesart, which
was fought by King Georges forces, and the saltors
and suttors and coliars, with a list of the killed and
wounded. Or the furious march at the battle of
Dyesart. *Edinburgh, printed in the year 1720.*
½⁰: 1 side, 2 columns.
'Upon the twenty eight of January'
A tenants' revolt against their laird at Dysart.
E.

E533 **Exaltatio.** Exaltatio cleri. Or, the honour and
usefulness of the clergy vindicated... Per W.H.
clericorum minimum. *London, printed for the author,
1701.*
4⁰: A–B⁴; *i–ii, 1–13 14 blk.*
'Were I some raking wit, whose talent lyes'
CtY,IU.

E534 **Excellency.** ⟨The⟩ excellency of a holy life, and
the vanity of carnal and sensual delights; plainly
shewed in the happy end of the righteous, and the
miserable end of the wicked: with the wicked man's
lamentation at the hour of death. *London, printed in
the year 1702 [1701].* (16 Dec, Luttrell)
1⁰: 1 side, 3 columns.
'How is the anxious soul of man betray'd'
CLU-C(Luttrell).

E535 **Excellent.** An excellent ballad of the Lord
Mohun and Duke Hamilton. With an exact account
of their melancholy deaths. [*London?* 1712.]
obl ½⁰: 1 side, 3 columns.
Large woodcut above text.
'Come all ye people far and near'
L(Rox.III.390).

An **excellent** new ballad

E536 — An excellent new ballad. [I'le tell you a story...]
Dublin, printed for T. Harbin, 1725-6.
½⁰: 1 side, 1 column.
'I'le tell you a story a story most merry'
A satire on Francis Hutchinson, bishop of
Down & Connor.
L(1890.e.5/32; C.121.g.8/40),C,DN,DT(2); CU,
PU.

E537 — An excellent new ballad. [Now Britain, now...]
[*London?* 1714.]
slip: 1 side, 1 column.
Stanza 3, line 2, 'Our Merchants...'
'Now Britain, now hold up thy head'
A whig welcome for King George and the
new ministry.
DA,*Crawford*(title cropt).

E538 — [another edition]
Stanza 3, line 2, 'Onr Merchant's...'
O.

E539 — [another edition, title reads:] An excellent new
badlad.
L(C.121.g.9/166).

E540 — An excellent new ballad. [Of all the days...]
[*London?* 1717?]
slip: 1 side, 1 column.
Printed with 'Sir James Baker', *Horace, Epod.
iv. imitated*, [1717?] The O,IU copies are not
divided.
'Of all the days in the year'
A Jacobite song in praise of the Pretender.
The date is suggested by a reference to the
tenth of June falling on a Monday.
O; CSmH,IU.

E541 — An excellent new ballad. [The christ'ning...]
[*London?* 1717/18.]
½⁰: 1 side, 2 columns.
'The christ'ning was not yet begun'
A satire on the quarrel between George I and
the Prince of Wales at the baptism of his son
George William.
O,Herts CRO (Panshanger box 46); MH,*Harding.*

E541·5 — An excellent new ballad against Wood's half-
pence, &c. To the tune of, Lillibolero, &c. *Dublin,
printed by John Harding, 1724.*
½⁰: 1 side, 2 columns.
'Now Woods and his half-pence are all gone to pot'
CtY

E542 — An exelent [!] new ballad ascrib'd to the ladies
of Munster. By the h---- J.S. [*Dublin*, 173–?]
½⁰: 1 side, 1 column.
'Ye ladies of Munster, come listen a while'
An ascription to Swift may be intended, but it
is clearly not his.
Crawford.

E543 — An excellent new ballad: being the second part
of the Glorious warriour. Writ by an eminent
soldier at home. [*London*, 1710.]
½⁰: 1 side, 2 columns.

An **excellent** new ballad: being

Teerink 844; Williams 1087.
'Ye citizens of Westminster'
A mock second part to The glorious warrior, 1710; supposed to be written by General Davenant, who represented James Stanhope at the Westminster election. Ball, 110–11, suggests this is the ballad known to have been written by Swift on the election; Williams rejects it.
L(Cup.645.e.1/22),O,Chatsworth; Harding.

E544 — An excellent new ballad. By the author of Mr. W------ S---'s ballad. Edinburgh, printed in the year 1742.
8°: A²; 1–2 3–4.
'O am not I a weary wight'
According to L, a political satire with reference to the Chippenham election petition.
L(11631.aaa.56/18).

E545 — An excellent new ballad, called Illustrious George shall come. To the tune of, The king shall enjoy his own again. [London? 1713?]
slip: 1 side, 1 column.
'Tho' Britain on to ruin runs'
A whig ballad against Jacobite tories. Cf. Crum T2332 which appears to be a related Jacobite ballad.
LLP.

E546 — An excellent new ballad, giving a full and true account of a terrible fray that happen'd lately at Squire --------'s in Berry street, between Jo. Rigat, (commonly call'd the Doctor) and one Sarah Lewis, a maid-servant... (To the tune of Chivy-chase.) [London, 172–?]
½°: 1 side, 2 columns.
''Twixt Sally born in Lambeth town'
Although printed in black-letter to represent a popular ballad, this appears to be a sophisticated imitation.
LVA-F.

E547 — An excellent new ballad, giving a full and true relation how a noble lord was robb'd of his birthday cloaths, and how the same afterwards appeared, and were burn'd on the Pretender's own back at Charing Cross, February 6th, 1713. To the tune of, To you fair ladies now at land, &c. [London, 1713.]
½°: 1–2, 1 column.
'Ye weavers all of Spittle Fields'
On the fate of some silk suits imported after the treaty of commerce with France.
O-JJ; OCU.

E548 —— [London, 1713.]
slip: 2 sides, 1 column.
Date and tune omitted from title.
LLP; OCU,Harding.

E549 — An excellent new ballad in praise of Monaky Gall; in imitation of Molly Mogg... To the tune of, The frolicksom lord Duke of Buckingham, &c. [Dublin, 1726?]
½°: 1 side, 1 column

An **excellent** new ballad in praise

'While dull poetasters are chiming'
L(C.121.g.8/80).

E550 — An excellent new ballad inscrib'd to the Irish Polly Peachum, on her benefit of the Beggar's opera: given, at the general desire of the nobility and gentry of Dublin, April, XI. MD,CC,XXVIII. By a person of honour. Tune. Pretty Polly say, &c. [Dublin] Printed by Rich. Dickson, [1728.]
½°: 1 side, 2 columns.
'Since evr'y scribbling Bays'
On Lavinia Fenton, who played Polly.
L(C.121.g.8/167).

E551 — An excellent new ballad, intituled the New way of the turn coat. To the tune of, John Anderson my joe. [Edinburgh, 1715.] (Feb)
½°: 1 side, 2 columns.
Two rough woodcuts at head. Ms. in L copy, 'Edr febr 1715'.
'I loved no king in fortie one'
An adaptation of The turncoat, [1712/14.]
L(C.121.g.9/175).

E552 — An excellent new ballad on the fall of guinea's. [London? 1717/18.]
slip: 1 side, 1 column.
Last stanza, line 1, '...Hannover'.
'One and twenty and six-pence, not three weeks ago'
A Jacobite satire on the devaluation of the guinea from £1.1s.6d. in December 1717.
O; CSmH.

E553 —— [another edition]
Last stanza, line 1, '...Hanover'. Printed with A new ballad, [1717/18]; the O copy is not divided.
O.

E554 — An excellent new ballad, on the modesty of the bankers of Dublin, who are content to loose three halfpence, and let the rest of the kingdom loose no more than two shillings and six pence in every four pound piece, by the late reduction of the coin. To the tune of the Abbot of Canterbury. [Dublin] Printed by James Carson, [1737.]
½°: 1 side, 1 column.
Hanson 5069.
'With Irish assurance let England no longer'
LU.

E555 — An excellent new ballad on the wedding of pritty Miss S--lly to jolly old J---o. By Captain Gulliver. [Dublin] A.D. 1730.
½°: 1 side, 1 column.
Teerink 1239.
'Ye gallants of Dublin, come listen a while'
Probably on Molly Smalley, the subject of other Dublin poems this year.
L(C.121.g.8/175, imprint cropt),DT.

— An excellent new ballad: or the true En---sh d---n to be hang'd for a r-----pe, [1730.] See Swift, Jonathan.

An **excellent** new ballad, or

— An excellent new ballad, or, the whigs lamentation, 1711. *See* The new Kilmainham ballad, [1711/12.]

E556 — An excellent new ballad, shewing how Mr. Mor—cai Ad—d—m's, pothecary, was catch'd in bed with Miss — and Miss', 2 sisters, by Mr. C— an honest constable . . . To the tune, of You commons and peer's, &c. *Dublin, printed for J. Car, & Ja. Pattin, in Coles-alley in Castle-street, 1726.*
½°: 1 side, 1 column.
'An apothecary cloathed in black'
    On Mordecai Adams, found in bed with two whores.
L(C.121.g.8/145).

E557 — An excellent new ballad, to a new tune. [*Dublin*, 1727?]
½°: 1 side, 2 columns.
''Tis no wonder if all honest men should be sower'd'
    A tory election ballad against William Howard.
O-JJ.

E558 — An excellent new ballad. To the tune of, A begging we will go, &c. [*London?* 1715/20.]
slip: 1 side, 1 column.
    Stanza 3, line 1, '. . . Hannover'.
'I am a turnip ho-er'
    Probably the poem attributed to Thomas Warton the elder by Hearne, 31 Jan and 17 July 1718: 'There is a ballad handed about, both in ms. & print, called *The Turnip Hoer.* The author is said to be one Mr. Wharton . . .'
A Jacobite satire on George I.
CSmH.

E559 — [another edition]
    Stanza 3, line 1, '. . . Hanover'.
O.

E560 — An excellent new ballad. To the tune of Chivy Chace. [*London?* 1718?]
slip: 1 side, 1 column.
    Two rules in title; '*FINIS.*' at end. Printed with *The petition*, [1718?]; the NjP copy is not divided.
'God prosper long our noble king'
    Crum G299: 'A ballad on the christening 1718'. A Jacobite satire occasioned by the quarrel between George I and the Prince of Wales at the christening of his son George William.
NjP.

E561 — [another edition]
    No rules in title; '*FINIS.*' at end. Printed with *The petition*, [1718?]; the O copy is not divided.
O.

E562 — [another edition]
    No rules in title; no '*FINIS.*' at end.
L(MS.Eg.1717, fol. 66),O.

E563 — An excellent new ballad. To the tune of D'Urfey's Fart. [*London?* 1715/20.]
½°: 1 side, 2 columns.

An **excellent** new ballad. To the tune of

'Of late, as they say,/On a Christmas day'
    Crum O118: 'A tragi-comical farce as it is acted at St. James's'. A Jacobite satire.
O; NjP.

E564 — An excellent new ballad. To the tune of, Let the soldiers rejoyce, &c. [*London?* 1718?]
slip: 1 side, 1 column.
    Printed with *An excellent new ballad. To the tune of, Of noble race was - -*, [1718?]; the NjP copy is not divided.
'Let the soldiers rejoyce,/With a general voice'
    A Jacobite satire resulting from the consideration of the articles of war by parliament, in imitation of the song from Betterton's *Prophetess*, 1690.
CSmH,NjP.

E565 — An excellent new ballad. To the tune of, Of noble race was --. [*London?* 1718?]
slip: 1 side, 1 column.
    No '*FINIS.*' at end.
'Of doubtful race was Georgy'
    A Jacobite satire on George I, put into a Welshman's mouth.
O; CSmH.

E566 — [another edition]
    '*FINIS.*' at end. Printed with *An excellent new ballad. To the tune of, Let the soldiers rejoyce, &c,* [1718?]; the NjP copy is not divided.
NjP.

E567 — An excellent new ballad, to the tune of, The bonny black ladie. [*Edinburgh?* 1745?]
½°: 1 side, 2 columns.
'To all loyal subjects glad tidings I bring'
    A Jacobite song.
CSmH.

E568 — An excellent new ballad. To the tune of You cut purses all, &c. [*Dublin*] *Printed by G. Needham & R. Dickson,* [1727?]
½°: 1 side, 2 columns.
    The DT copy is bound with half-sheets of 1727.
'The physitians of late/Held a learned debate'
    A satire on a bill prepared by the medical profession.
L(1890.e.5/241, cropt),DT; CtY.

E569 — An excellent new ballad. Tune of King John and the abbot of Canterbury. [*London*, 1737.]
½°: 1 side, 2 columns.
'Tho' Ovid has given us so many relations'
    Crum T2389: 'On Sr Tho: Abney's appearing [at] Queen Caroline's funeral 1737 . . .'
CSmH.

E570 — An excellent new ballad upon the new half-pence. To the tune of, Which no body can deny. *Dublin, printed by John Harding,* [1724.]
½°: 1 side, 1 column.

An **excellent** new ballad upon the new halfpence

'You subjects of Ireland come all and rejoice'
A satire on William Wood's coinage.
DT.

E571 — An excellent new ballad upon the present grnd-jury [!]. *Dublin, printed in the year 1724.*
½°: 1 side, 1 column.
Teerink 1111.
'No thanks to our foes, our cause it is clear'
On the grand jury which refused to make a presentment of Swift's *Seasonable advice.*
Rothschild; *Ct Y.*

E572 — An excellent new copy of verses, being the sorrowful lamentation of Mrs. Cooke, for the loss of her husband Thomas Cooke, the famous butcher of Gloucester, who was executed at Tyburn on Wednesday the 11th of August 1703. To the tune of, Forgive me if your looks I thought. *London, printed for C. Barnet, in Fleet-street, 1703.*
½°: 1 side, 1 column.
On the other side of the L copy, *A most strange, but true account of a very large sea-monster* (printed for R. Smith, 1704), a prose work.
'Unto my sad complaint give ear'
L(C.40.m.9/89).

E573 — An excellent new hymn, composd by the priests of the order of St. Perkin, for the use of high-church, upon their approaching day of humiliation, being the coronation-day of his truly protestant majesty King George. *[London? 1714.]*
slip: 1-2, 1 column.
Part I on recto, Part II on verso.
'Oh! why dost thou forsake us thus?'
A mock-Jacobite lament.
Crawford(pagination cropt); *Harding.*

E574 — [another edition, title reads:] An excelleut [!] new hymn...King Georeg [!].
O.

E575 — An excellent new song: being a brief account of the rebels molestations, and how they were chased back from England. *Printed in the year 1746.*
8°: A⁴; *1-2* 3-8.
Either printed in Edinburgh or the north of England.
'Come and give good attention; for my song it is true'
CSmH.

— An excellent new song, being the intended speech of a famous orator against peace, [1711.] *See* Swift, Jonathan.

E576 — An excellent new song, called, An end to our sorrows. To the tune of, I laugh at the Pope's devises. *[London] Printed in the year 1711.*
½°: 1 side, 2 columns.
Some copies (e.g. OCU) omit the word 'tune' in title.
'Sing praise to our grac'ous Queen Anne'
An ironic poem on Harley's ministry.

An **excellent** new song, called, An end

L(112.f.44/33; C.20.f.9/646; G.559/12); NNP, OCU,PPL,TxU,*Harding.*

— An excellent new song, called, Credit restored, 1711. *See* Mainwaring, Arthur.

E577 — An excellent new song call'd Loyalty restored. To the tune of Remember ye whigs what was formerly done. *London, printed for John Morphew, 1711.*
½°: 1 side, 2 columns.
A different text with the same first stanza was published as *Vulpoon in the snare,* 1712.
'All Britains rejoice/With a general voice'
A tory reply to whig satires like the preceding.
LLP; MB(imprint cropt).

— An excellent new song, called, Mat's peace, 1711. *See* Mainwaring, Arthur.

E578 — An excellent new song, call'd, The full tryal and condemnation of John duke of Marlborough. *[London, 1712?]*
½°: 1 side, 2 columns.
Two lines of typeset music printed between title and text. 20 stanzas. A shorter version was printed in the *Observator* 28 June 1712.
'I now have an ambition'
Crum I364: 'John duke of Marlborough'. A. T. Hazen in *A catalogue of Horace Walpole's library* (1969) no. 2446 records Horace Walpole's attribution of this work to Richard Estcourt. A defence of Marlborough in the form of an ironic attack.
L(11602.i.12/34),DT,Crawford,Rothschild; MH (cropt).

E579 — [idem] The Flanders ballad: or, the D---e of Marlborough's rare show, with a true discovery of all his covetuous [!] actions against his q---n and country. *London, printed by J. Collicoat, near West-Smithfield, [1712?]*
½°: 1 side, 2 columns.
16 stanzas. Variant first line:
'Most men have an ambition'
L(C.20.f.2/367,cropt),MC,Rothschild;MH,TxU.

E580 — [idem] The D---e of Marlborough's fine show, with his conduct and management when in Flanders. *London, printed by J. Collicoat, near West-Smithfield, [1712?]*
½°: 1 side, 2 columns.
DA.

E581 — [idem] An excellent new song on the huffing, heathen, covetous, quarrelsome, uncivil, hot-headed, slovenly, bold, meddlesome, heinous John duke of M--------. To some tune! *London, printed by Will. Hart, 1713.*
½°: 1 side, 2 columns.
17 stanzas.
TxU.

E582 — — *Dublin, printed by Elizabeth Dickson, [1713.]*
½°: 1 side, 2 columns.

An **excellent** new song, call'd, The full tryal

>From the same setting of type as the preceding,
but with Marlborough's name printed in full.
Possibly this imprint is false.
C.

E583 — [idem] The trial and condemnation of John
duke of Marlborough. To the tune of, And as I was
going to Derbey. *London, printed in the glorious
year of liberty*, 1715.
½°: 1 side, 2 columns.
>20 stanzas. First line reverts to the form:
'I now have an ambition'
Rothschild.

E583·5 — An excellent new song call'd the Irish-man's
joy, for the downfall of Woods and his brass half-
pence & farthings. To the tune of Randel a
Barnaby. &c. [*Dublin*, 1724/25.]
½°: 1 side, 2 columns.
'My dear loving country-men listen a while'
>References to the Drapier and the grand-jury
suggest that this poem dates from a time before
the patent was formally revoked.
CtY.

E584 — An excellent new song, call'd the Trusty and
true English-man. [*London*, 1712.] (2 Jan, Luttrell)
½°: 2 sides, 2 columns.
Teerink 867; *Williams* 1096.
'Poor England's condition/By sons of perdition'
>A satire against the whigs. *Ball* 125 suggested
that Swift had a share in its composition;
Williams doubts it.
L(162.m.70/13, Luttrell; G.559/3),C,*LdU-B*,
Chatsworth; CSmH,CtY,MH,TxU.

E585 — [idem] The trusty and true English-man.
[*London?* 1712.]
½°: 2 sides, 2 columns.
Rothschild.

E586 — An excellent new song lately composed. To the
tune of the Bony broom. [*Edinburgh*, 1716?]
½°: 1 side, 2 columns.
>Rough woodcut at head. In column 2, 'An
answer to the above lines'.
'Hard fate that I should banish't be'
Answer: 'Well fix King George upon the throne'
>A Jacobite ballad and reply.
L(L.23.c.1/11),E.

[E587 cancelled]

E588 — An excellent new song made by a lover of his
country; against Woods's brass half-pence. To the
tune, We have catcht you in the nick. [*Dublin*,1724.]
½°: 1 side, 2 columns.
'Last week as I was walking'
CtY.

— An excellent new song on the huffing...John
duke of Marlborough, 1713. *See* E581–2.

E589 — An excellent new song, to a good old tune.
[*Dublin?*] *Printed in the year* 1726.
½°: 1–2, 1 column.
Teerink 926; *Williams* 1128.

An **excellent** new song, to a good old tune

'I synge of a sermon, a sermon of worth'
>On Edward Synge's sermon on toleration.
Ball 225 suggested Swift's authorship;
Williams thinks it unlikely.
OW,DT; CSmH.

E590 —— [*Dublin*] *Printed in the year* 1726.
½°: 1 side, 1 column.
L(C.121.g.8/157).

E591 — An excellent new song, to the memorable tune
of Lillibullero. [*London*] *Printed in the year* 1711.
½°: 1 side, 2 columns.
>No rules in title.
'Oh! brother Tom, dost know the intent'
>Against the tories and peace with France.
Continued by *A new song. Being a second part*,
[1711/12.]
O,DT,Crawford,Rothschild; PU.

E592 — [another edition]
>Two rules in title.
L(112.f.44/29, title cropt).

— An excellent new song, to the tune of, Old long
syne, [1746/–.] *See* A song, to the tune of Auld lang
syne, [1746/–.]

— An excellent new song upon his grace our good
lord archbishop of Dublin, 1724. *See* Swift,
Jonathan.

E593 — An excellent new song upon the declarations of
the several corporations of the city of Dublin;
against Woods's half-pence. To the tune of London
is a fine town &c. [*Dublin*, 1724.]
½°: 1 side, 2 columns.
Teerink 1149; *Williams* 1110.
'O Dublin is a fine town'
>Conjecturally ascribed to Swift by Scott
(1814,X.486); not accepted by Williams. Most
of the declarations date from late August and
September 1724.
LVA-F; CtY.

E594 — An excellent new song upon the late grand-jury.
Dublin, printed in the year 1724.
½°: 1 side, 1 column.
Teerink 1155; *Williams* 1110.
'Poor monsieur his conscience preserv'd for a year'
>On the jury that refused to make a presentment
of Swift's *Seasonable advice*, and on John
Vereilles, a juror of French extraction. Con-
jecturally ascribed to Swift by Scott (1814, X.
581); not accepted by Williams.
L(C.121.g.8/37),LVA-F,C,E,DT; CSmH(2),*CtY*.

— An excellent old ballad, called Pride will have a
fall, [1720?] *See* Duke upon duke, 1720–.

E595 — An excellent old ballad, made at the restauration
of K. Charles II. With a second part to the same
tune, by a modern hand. *London, printed in the
year* 1711.
½°: 2 sides, 2 columns.
Teerink 868.
'Rebellion has broken up house'

An **excellent** old ballad

Second part: 'The Juncto has broken up house' *Ball* 145, n. 5, 'probably Arbuthnot, if not Swift, had some part in' this; but there is no evidence for this assertion. The second part is a tory attack on the defeated whigs.
L(1876.f.1/55).

E596 —— *London, printed in the year* 1712.
½⁰: 2 sides, 2 columns.
L(11602.i.12/32***; 1850.c.10/33),O,OW,MR, Rothschild; MH.

—— An excellent song, intituled, Fy gar rub her o're wi strae, [172–.] *See* Ramsay, Allan (R54).

E597 —— An excellent song on the present times, by a country hind. To the tune of Killycranky. [*Edinburgh?* 1745.]
½⁰: 1 side, 2 columns.
'In this auld year, whose end is near'
Against the Jacobites.
E; CSmH.

Excellentissimo. Excellentissimo domino, domino Johanni episcopo Bristoliensi, [1712.] *See* Dibben, Thomas.

E598 **Excise.** The excise-bill versify'd. To which is subjoin'd curious and particular remarks. *London, printed for W. James*, 1733. (*GSJ* 12 July)
8⁰: A–E⁴ F⁴(–F4); *1–2* 3–46.
F4 not seen, possibly blank.
'A junto lately, or committee'
CtY,OCU.

E599 —— An excise elegy: or, the dragon demolish'd. A new ballad. To the tune of Packington's pound. *London, printed for W. James; sold by the booksellers & pamphletsellers of London & Westminster*, 1733. (*GM* April)
2⁰: A² B²; *i–ii* iii–iv, 5–8.
Percival XXVII.
'Good people of England, I pray ye draw near'
The dedication signed 'Philalethes'. Against the excise bill.
LU,C(uncut); CSmH,CtY,KU,MH,TxU+.

E600 —— —— The second edition with additions. *London, printed for W. James; sold by the booksellers & pamphletsellers of London & Westminster*, 1733.
2⁰: A² B²; *i–ii* iii–iv, 5–8.
Apparently from the same setting of type as the preceding.
LSC(lacks B²),O.

E600·5 —— 'The excise sermon versified. Price 6d.' (*Bee* April 1733)
Listed in the *Bee* (I.ix) as published between 29 March and 5 April 1733. Clearly related to *A very long, curious and extraordinary sermon*, 1733, by 'Robert Winer' or 'Robert Vyner', which is a satire on Walpole's excise proposals. There are editions of this work, printed in white on black paper, at L.

Excursion

Excursion. The excursion, 1728. *See* Mallet, David.

E601 **Excursory.** An excursory view on the present state of men and things. A satire. In a dialogue between the author and his friend. *London, printed for C. Corbett*, 1739. (*GM* Aug)
2⁰: A¹ B–D² E¹; *1–3* 4–15 *16 blk.*
'Writing a satire?/If I am, what then?'
L(1482.f.41); CSmH,CtY,IU,MH(uncut),TxU(2, 1 uncut).

E602 **Exequiae.** Exequiæ Carolinæ: or, a poem on the martyrdom of King Charles I. *London, printed in the year* 1710.
2⁰: A²; *1–2* 3–4.
'Faction and schism that ope' the dreadful way'
OW; MH.

E603 **Expeditio.** Expeditio militaris Addisoniana, poema, duci de Malborough inscriptum. Latinè reddidit, T.G. *Londini, impensis R.G.*, 1708 [1709]. (*PB* 19 Feb)
8⁰: B–E⁸ F⁸(–F8); *1–3* 4–75 *76–78 blk.* 75 err.
Latin and English text and titles; English title on B1ᵛ 'The campaign. A poem...'
'Dum tua Teutonici proclamant facta dynastæ'
L(161.l.1, Luttrell, 19 Feb, –F7),EU(lacks B1), DT,LdU,WcC+; CLU-C,MH(–F7).

E604 —— [reissue] *Londini, impensis autoris*, 1717 [1718].
8⁰: A² B⁸(–B1) C–E⁸ F⁸(–F8); [4] 3 4–75 *76–78 blk.*
In the copy seen an additional I has been stamped in the imprint of the new titles A1ᵛ and A2ʳ to make the date 1717 into 1718; an extra X is added to the original imprint on B2ʳ to change 1708 to 1718.
DK.

Expedition. The expedition: a poem, on the duke's going to Flanders, 1747. *See* Fortescue, James.

E605 —— The expedition. An ode. Written in October, 1740. *London, printed for T. Cooper*, [1741.] (*LM* July)
2⁰: A² B–C²; *1–2* 3–12.
'From the charm'd port escap'd at last'
On the expedition to Cartagena.
L(643.m.16/10); CSmH(uncut),*NNH*,TxU.

E606 —— —— '*London, printed for T. Cooper*' [*Edinburgh*, 1741.] (*SM* July)
8⁰: A² B⁴; *1–2* 3–12.
Copies at C,E bound in Edinburgh pamphlet volumes.
O,C,E(2); CtY,OCU.

E607 **Experienced.** The experienc'd student, a poem. Shewing the nature and causes of the miserable condition of chaplains and teachers, in this age and nation. *Edinburgh, printed by William Brown &*

The **experienced** student

> *John Mosman, and sold by the said W. Brown, 1716.*
> 8°: ^πA⁴ A–B⁴ C⁴; *i–ii, 1–6, 1–21 22–23; 24 blk.*
> 22–23 advt.
>> The collation is uncertain. Four congratulatory
>> poems on ^πA2–4.
> 'The chaiplain and the teacher that's confin'd'
> GM(slightly cropt).

E608 Explanation. ⟨An⟩ explanation of a tale of a
tale: humbly inscribed to *.*.*.*.*.*.*.*.*. *[Dublin]*
Printed in the year 1731.
½°: 1 side, 2 columns.
'I own dear D—— your tale is true'
> Apparently an attack on Swift, on the assump-
> tion that he wrote *A tale in allusion to a certain
> tale,* 1731.
L(C.121.g.9/195).

—— An explanation of the Tale of a nettle, 1710. *See*
The tale of a nettle, 1710.

E609 Expostulation. The expostulation or the disconsolate shepherd. *Dublin, printed by John Gowan,*
[1725/30.]
½°: *1–2,* 2 columns.
> The L copy forms part of a collection of
> Dublin half-sheets of 1725/30.
'Laura, thy humours so perverse'
L(C.121.g.8/117).

Expostulatory

Expostulatory. An expostulatory epistle to Sir
Richard Steele, 1720. *See* Rowe, Elizabeth.

E610 Express. An express from Parnassus, to the
reverend Dr. Jonathan Swift dean of St. Patrick's.
[Dublin, 1724.] (Nov)
½°: 2 sides, 1 column.
> *Teerink* 1197.
'From the mount of Parnassus November the fift'
> In praise of Swift's attacks on Wood's half-
> pence.
LVA-F,C,DT,Rothschild; CSmH,CtY.

E611 Extravagant. The extravagant wish: a dream.
Dublin, printed by George Faulkner, 1749.
8°: *A⁴ B⁴; 1–2 3–15 16 blk.*
> No watermark.
'I lately read, and read in print'
O,C(2),DA.

E612 —— [fine paper]
> Watermark: fleur-de-lys on shield.
TxU.

[**Eyre, Henry.**] Advice from fairyland. An
imitation of our present Irish poetry, 1726. *See* A71.

F

F., B., *gent.* A plot discover'd against the trade and industry of Great-Britain, [1714?] *See* P506.

F., D. Jure divino: a satyr, 1706. *See* Defoe, Daniel.

F., D., *gent.* The compleat art of painting, 1720. *See* C324.

F——, G——, *gent.* A prophetick congratulatory hymn, [1718/19.] *See* P1138.

F., J. Epigrammata de quibusdam summis hujus seculi viris, 1737. *See* Forbes, John.

— An essay on conduct and education, 1738–. *See* Fry, John.

F., R., *gent.* Ajax his speech to the Grecian knabbs, 1748. *See* Forbes, Robert.

F., S., *Mrs.* Poems on several occasions, together with a pastoral, [1703.] *See* Egerton, Sarah Fyge.

F——, T——. Clio. A poem, 1748. *See* C239.

F., W. An essay upon friendship, 1714. *See* E474.

F., W., *of D.* Xantippe, or the scolding wife, 1724. *See* Forbes, William.

'F——a.' An answer from S——a F——a, 1727. *See* A230.

F1 Fable. A fable of an old woman and her doctor. [*London,* 1718/19.]
slip: 1 side, 1 column.
    Communicated to Thomas Hearne 14 Feb 1719.
'Dame Briton of the grange, once fam'd'
    Crum D9b: 'A fable thought to be wrote by Mr. Prior'; rejected by *Wright & Spears* II. 808. A Jacobite satire.
CSmH,*MH.*

F2 — The fable of Bubo and Turturella, which takes in all manner of cuckoldome, with a good variety of cases. *Dublin, printed by and for J. Gowan,* 1726.
8°: *A*⁴ B⁴; *i–ii, 1* 2–14.
'Once on a time by stress of weather'
L(11632.a.57),O.

— The fable of Midas, 1712. *See* Swift, Jonathan.

F3 — The fable of the beasts and their king. By an unknown hand. *London printed, and sold by B. Bragg,* 1703. (12 Nov, Luttrell)
4°: A–B⁴; *1–4* 5–16.
'A time there was in ages that have been'

L(164.m.29, Luttrell; 840.h.4/5, lacks B3, 4), O,E; IU,InU,NjP,OCU.

F4 — The fable of the blackbird and kite. *London, printed for John Moor,* 1723.
2°: π¹ A²; *i–ii,* 1–4.
'There is a place in London-town'
GU(title cropt); CSmH(lacks π1),IU,InU(lacks π1),OCU,TxU(2, 1 lacks π1).

F5 — The fable of the cocks and ganders. [*London,* 1712?]
½°: 1 side, 1 column.
'Some cocks of the game'
    On the way in which military supplies are diverted from the fighting men, probably with reference to Marlborough and *A fable of the housewife and her cock,* 1712.
MH.

— The fable of the cods-heads, 1712. *See* Pittis, William.

F6 — The fable of the cuckoo: or, the sentence on the ill bird that defiled his own nest. Shewing, in a dissenter's dream, some satyrical reflections, on a late infamous libel, call'd, The true-born Englishman. *London, printed in the year* 1701. (*PB* 27 Feb)
4°: π² A(2 ll) B–F⁴ H–N⁴ O² (H2 as 'F2'); [4] i–iv, 1–40 49–99 *100 blk.* π1 hft; 99 err.
    The errata record the omission of signature G. π² may be cancels for two leaves of A⁴.
'A princely eagle, that had long been crown'd'
    An attack on Defoe's poem.
L(991.b.31,–π1); CtY,DFo,MH.

F7 — A fable of the dogs. *London printed, and sold by T. Bickerton, & E. Smith,* [1719.] (16 Oct, Luttrell)
2°: *A*² B¹; *1–3* 4–6.
    The Luttrell copy is recorded in Pickering & Chatto cat. 247/13282.
'Two dogs from diff'rent litters come'
CSmH.

F8 — A fable of the housewife and her cock. *London, printed in the year* 1712, *and sold by the booksellers.*
½°: *1–2,* 1 column.
    Teerink 864.
'There was a housewife kept a cock'
    On Queen Anne and Marlborough's dismissal. There is no reason to attribute it to Swift, though it is doubtless related to *A fable of the widow and her cat* which is possibly by him.
L(G.1390/11),LSA; MH.

F9 — The fable of the lyon and the fox. *London, printed in the year* 1712. *and sold by the booksellers.*
8°: *A*⁴; *i–ii,* 1–5 *6 blk.*
    Rothschild 1692. Horizontal chain-lines.
'A lyon by his valiant deeds preferr'd'
    Printed by *Waller* as attributed to Prior, following T. J. Wise; rejected by *Wright & Spears* 801. A defence of Harley, in favour of Marlborough's dismissal.
L(Ashley 1330),O; InU.

The **fable** of the shepherd

F10 — The fable of the shepherd and his dog, in answer to the fable of the widow and her cat. *London, printed in the year* 1712. (28 Jan?)
$\frac{1}{2}$°: 1 side, 1 column.
    Teerink 863. Title in three lines.
'An honest shepherd on the wolds'
    In defence of Marlborough, in answer to the fable possibly written by Swift.
L(G.1390/12); PU(ms. date, 28 Jan).

F11 — [another edition]
    Title in four lines.
TxU.

F12 —— *London: printed and re-printed in Dublin*, 1711 [i.e. 1711/2].
$\frac{1}{2}$°: 1 side, 1 column.
    On the other side, *A fable of the widow and her cat*, [1712.]
CtY.

F13 — A fable of the widow and her cat. [*London*] *Printed for John Morphew*, 1712. (16 Jan, Luttrell)
$\frac{1}{2}$°: 2 sides, 1 column.
    Teerink 862; *Williams* 151. Luttrell's copy is of the issue below.
'A widow kept a favourite cat'
    For a discussion of Swift's authorship, see *Williams* and references; he prints it 'with some hesitation'. The date of publication disproves the contention that it is the piece referred to in Swift's *Journal* under 4 Jan; but there is evidence that contemporaries thought it was by Swift – see *When the cat's away... humbly inscrib'd to Dr. S—t*, [1712.] An attack on Marlborough. For other related poems see *The fable of the shepherd and his dog*, 1712, *A fable of the housewife and her cock*, 1712, *The fable of the cocks and ganders*, [1712.]
L(Ashley 4972),LLP,LSA,O,OW,C; CtY,TxU.

F14 — [variant imprint:] [*London*] *Printed in the year* 1712.
    Possibly copies with this imprint were intended for free distribution, not for sale.
C(2),MC(2),Chatsworth (ms. date 18 Jan), Crawford, Rothschild (ms. date 22 Jan); ICN(Luttrell, 16 Jan),MH,TxU.

F15 —— *London, printed for Philpot near Charing-Cross*, 1711 [i.e. 1711/2].
$\frac{1}{2}$°: 1 side, 2 columns.
L(Ashley 4971),O.

F16 —— [*London*] *Printed in the year* 1712.
$\frac{1}{2}$°: 1 side, 2 columns.
    The copies seen are variant; one has 'Price one peny' after imprint. They may represent different impressions.
L(Ashley 4975); G.1390/9).

F17 —— *London printed; and re-printed in ⟨Dublin?⟩*, [1712.]
$\frac{1}{2}$°: 1 side.

A **fable** of the widow

    Recorded in *Williams* 151 from Dobell cat. 105/299.

F18 —— [*Dublin*, 1712.]
$\frac{1}{2}$°: 1 side, 2 columns.
    On the other side, *The fable of the shepherd and his dog*, 1711 [i.e. 1711/2].
CtY.

F19 — 'A fable translated out of Phædrus. Humbly inscribed to the directors and members of the South-Sea Company. [*London*] *Printed, and sold by Ferd. Burleigh*. Price 2d.' (*DC* 18 Jan 1714)
    Possibly a half-sheet from the price, and probably in verse.

F20 — A fable; with a word of advice to blind Elymas the sorcerer. *Dublin, printed in the year* 1735.
4°: *A*²; *1–2* 3–4.
'As once through a village a carrier drove'
    A satire on Elymas Clark.
C.

Fables. Fables and tales for the ladies. To which are added, miscellanies, by another hand. *London, printed for the proprietor; sold by C. Hitch & L. Hawes, & H. Whitridge*, 1750. (*SR* 2 Nov)
8°: pp. 196.   L,EU; CtY,IU.
    Entered in *SR* to John Rockall, who is possibly the author of the main series of poems. Reissued as 'written by a country book-seller. The second edition, with additions...' in 1754 (copies at L,O).

— Fables for the female sex, 1744–. *See* Moore, Edward.

F21 — Fables, in English and French verse. Translated from the original Latin of Gabriel Faerno. With one hundred copper-plates. *London, printed for Claude Du Bosc; sold by C. Davis*, 1741. (*GM*, *LM* April)
8°: 2 vol: (frt+) A–N⁸, A⁸(A1+*A²) B–M⁸; *i–iii* iv–xvi, *1–2* 3–190 *191–192 blk*, *i–iii* iv–vi, *3–191 192 blk*.
    The plates are by Claude du Bosc.
'As round their dying parent's bed'
    The French translation is that of Charles Perrault.
L(12305.cc.35,–¹N8),C; CSmH,IU,*PBm,RPB*.

— The fables of Æsop, in English verse, [1705/10?] *See* A new translation of Æsop, 1705–.

F22 **Facetious.** A facetious poem in imitation of the Cherry and slae, giving account of the entertainment, love and despare got in the Highlands of Scotland... By G.G. of S. *Edinburgh, printed in the year* 1701.
8°: A–B⁴; *1* 2–16.
'It was in August, on a night'
    The E catalogue says 'erroneously ascribed to Gilbert Gordon by Dr. Irving'.
E.

Faction

F23 Faction. The faction: a poem on the new Jacobite and Swedish conspiracy. *London, printed for S. Popping, J. Harrison, & A. Dodd,* 1717.
2°: *A² B¹*; *1–2* 3–6.
'Despair, when sprung from great and just disgrace'
L(11631.k.8),AdU.

— The faction, a tale, 1740. *See* Cowper, Ashley.

— Faction display'd, 1704. *See* Shippen, William.

F24 — Faction display'd, in answer to Faction display'd, a poem. [*London*] *Printed in the year* 1704. (22 April, Luttrell)
½°: 2 sides, 1 column.
'Good people give ear, I'll declare to you all'
> A reply to William Shippen's poem. H. L. Snyder in *The Library* V. 22 (1967) 327n attributes it to Sir Richard Cox on the evidence of *The letter-books of John Hervey, first earl of Bristol* (1894) I. 205–7.

L(C.121.g.9/112),Longleat,Rothschild; MH (Luttrell).

F25 — Faction display'd. The second part. *London, printed in the year* 1704. (*WL* April)
4°: *A¹ B–F² G¹*; *i–ii, 1–22.*
'Distant a little from the Gallick shore'
> A continuation of William Shippen's *Faction display'd,* 1704. There is no evidence that it is by the same author; indeed, it appears to turn the satire against the high church party. Defoe writes of the author in *The protestant jesuite unmask'd* (1704) and may conceivably have himself been the author as suggested (privately) by F. Bastian.

LLP,LVA-F,O,OC(uncut),C+; InU.

Faerno, Gabriello.
Fables, in English and French verse. Translated from the original Latin, 1741. *See* F21.

F26 Fagg. Fagg him Salley: so I will, when my month's up. Being the case of a certain famous Sussex baronet...To which is added, the Fox caught in his own trap: or, the Jew roasted... *London printed, and sold by J. Dormer,* 1734. (*GSJ* Feb)
2°: *A² B²*; *1–2* 3–8.
'I sing of a batter'd old knight'
Fox: 'A Jew that's well noted for money golore'
> The first poem is on Sir Robert Fagge and his sexual misadventures; the second on M——z D- C——a (Mendez Da Costa?) and his attempt to win a paternity case.

L(163.n.23); TxU.

F27 — ⟨F⟩agg him Sally... [1734.]
½°: 1 side, 2 columns.
> Without the second poem.

L(C.116.i.4/26).

Fair. The fair assembly, 1723. *See* Ramsay, Allan.

Fair

— The fair Circassian, 1720–. *See* Croxall, Samuel.

F28 — The fair court: or, a library of all the select ladies, in the Earl of Meath's liberty, and parts thereto adjoin'd. By an admirer of the fair sex. [*Dublin*] *Printed by Elizabeth Sadlier,* 1726.
½°: 2 sides, 2 columns.
> On the recto, 'St Katherine's Parish'; on the verso, 'The beauties of St. Mary's Parish'.

'Thou sacred queen of Helicon descend'
St. Mary's: 'Outliv'd in splendor, by the subsequent'
> Congratulatory verses on the ladies.

CtY.

F29 — The fair in an uproar, or, the dancing-doggs. As they perform in Mr. Pinkeman's new opera in Bartholomew Fair. *London printed, and sold by J. Morphew,* [1707.] (30 Aug, Luttrell)
½°: 1 side, 2 columns.
> Large engraving at head. Note after imprint, 'Beware of wretched halfpenny wooden cuts'.

''Tis well we live in such a fickle place'
ICN(Luttrell).

— The fair quakers: a poem, 1713. *See* Bingley, John.

F30 — The fair question, or who deserves an impeachment now? *London, printed in the year* 1710. (*PB* 14 Oct, 'just published')
8°: *A–C⁴*; *1–4* 5–23 24 blk.
> Advertised in *PB* by J. Baker.

'In times of old, when beasts could prate'
> For Sacheverell and against the whigs.

L(164.k.64, Luttrell, 15 Nov),O,C,AdU,LdU-B (uncut); MB.

[**F31** — Fair Rosamund, to the fair Hibernian. An epistle. *London, printed for T. Howard in Fleet-street,* [1752.] (*LM* Jan)
2°: *A⁴*; *1–2* 3–8.
'Model of Venus! and most fam'd of any'
> Included in error.]

F32 — The fair sex turn'd Amazons: or, a new poem made on the lady's hatts, &c. By Mr. E.R. [*Dublin?* 172–?]
½°: 1 side, 1 column.
'Immortal gods, shall woman still invaid'
MH.

— A fair shell, but a rotten kernel, 1705. *See* Ward, Edward.

F33 — The fair suicide: being an epistle from a young lady, to the person who was the cause of her death. *London, printed for Richard Wellington,* 1733. (*LM* April)
2°: A–C²; *1–2* 3–12.
'To thee, O ——, my greatest, cruell'st foe'
LdU-B; CSmH,ICN,IU(2),OCU,TxU.

F34 —— The second edition. *London, printed for Richard Wellington,* 1733.

The **fair** suicide

    2°: A–C²; *1–2* 3–12.
    MH.

F35 — The fair thinker, or reason asserted: in a dissection of bigottry and devotion. A satire. *London, printed for T. Robins; sold at the Royal Exchange, St. James's, Bond-street, and Charing-cross, 1740.* (*GM, LM* Nov)
    8°: *A²* B–E⁴; *i–ii* iii–iv, *5* 6–36.
'Satire! ascend, with good intention fir'd'
    A freethinking poem.
L(11661.aa.22),O,CT,EU(uncut); CLU-C(uncut),MH,OCU,TxU.

F36 — Fair warning. *London, printed for, and sold by John Baker, 1710.* (5 April, Luttrell)
½°: 1 side, 1 column.
    Printed in Grover's scriptorial type. Entered in *SR* 26 April; deposit copy at E. Reprinted with an answer as *The whiggish fair warning,* 1711.
'Madam, look out, your title is arraign'd'
    Crum M28: 'To the queen'. A whig address to the queen, against Sacheverell.
L(C.38.1.6/27),LSA,E,Crawford,Rothschild; CSmH,MH(Luttrell).

    Fairy. The fairy feast, 1704. *See* King, William, *the gazetteer.*

F37 — The fairy-king a poem. By Mr. —— P. ——. [*Dublin*] *Printed in the year 1726.*
slip: 1 side, 1 column.
'Upon a time the fairy elves'
    The attribution intended is probably to Ambrose Philips.
L(C.121.g.8/146; 1890.e.5/187).

F38 — [variant]... By Mrs. Peggy — With——rs.
DT.

F39 **Faith.** Faith and practice: or, the necessity of a worthy reception of the blessed sacrament of the Lord's supper. A sacred poem. Humbly presented to the honourable the Lady Prichard. *London, printed by John Cluer, 1717.*
4°: π¹ A–B²; *1–2* 3–10.
    Probably issued with alternative title-pages with different dedicatees.
'Was ev'ry Christian's conduct open laid'
    For other poems by the same author, see *A divine poem on the creation,* 1718; possibly Henry Nevil was the author.
DT.

F40 **Faithful.** The faithful few. An ode, inscribed to all lovers of their country. *Edinburgh, printed by W. Cheyne, and sold at most booksellers shops in town, 1734.*
8°: *A⁴*; *1–2* 3–8.
'While pow'r triumphant bears unrival'd sway'
    Ascribed to William Hamilton of Bangour by *Halkett & Laing* II. 256 as 'in his collected

The **faithful** few

poems'; not traced in the collections of 1748, 1760, and 1850; rejected by *Bushnell* 50.
O,E,LdU-B; CSmH,CtY,MH.

F41 —— *Edinburgh, 1734.*
8°: *A⁴*; *1–3* 4–8.
    Possibly a piracy.
L(164.n.25).

    — The faithful sheepherd, a funeral poem, [1726.] *See* Pennecuik, Alexander, *d. 1730.*

F42 **Fall.** The fall and restoration of man. A poem, occasion'd by St. Paul's words... Address'd to a lady. *London, printed for E. Curll, 1710 [1711?].* (*PB* 15 Feb 1711)
4°: *A⁴*; *1–2* 3–8.
'Believe me madam, since the fig leaf's on'
IU.

    — The fall of virtue, 1738. *See* Leslie, Charles.

F43 **Fall, James.** The protestants charge against the church of Rome, maintained: or, an antidote against popery. *London, printed for Aaron Ward, 1746.*
8°: (frt+) A–E⁴; *i–ii* iii–viii, *1–32.*
    Four other poems on pp. 8–18, and a prose summary on pp. 19–32.
'O gulph of horror! O profound abyss!'
L(108.f.32),BP(–frt).

F44 **Falling.** The falling out. To the tune of Hey boys up goe wee. [*London?* 1717/18.]
slip: 1 side, 1 column.
    Printed with *The pretender,* [1717/18]; the NjP copy is not divided.
'An old man, and his graceless young'
    A Jacobite satire, on the dispute between George I and the Prince of Wales at the christening of Prince George William.
O; CSmH,NjP.

F45 **False.** False happiness: a satire addressed to a friend; and humbly inscrib'd to the right honourable Sir John Barnard, knt. lord-mayor. *London printed, and sold by J. Purser, and by the booksellers & pamphlet-shops of London & Westminster, 1738.* (*GM, LM* Oct)
2°: *A²* B² C¹; *1–4* 5–10.
'Attend my V——n, while the daring muse'
    The dedication is signed 'A citizen'.
LDW; CtY,NN-B,NjP,TxHR.

F46 — False honour: or, the folly of duelling expos'd. A poem, in hudibrastics. Occasioned by the late unhappy affair between Capt. Clarke and Capt. Innes. *London, printed for A. Type, near Cheapside; sold at the pamphlet-shops in London & (especially) Westminster, 1750.* (*GM* May)
4°: A–C²; *1–2* 3–12.
    The imprint is possibly fictitious.
'While venal pens and factious scribes'

False honour

Captain Edward Clarke was sentenced to death for killing Captain Thomas Innes in a duel.

O.

F47 — The false patriot: a satire. *London, printed for C. Corbett, 1739.* (*LM* Aug)

2⁰: *A*² B²; *1–3* 4–8.

'I wou'd, by heav'n, abolish public wrong'

TxU.

F48 — The false patriot: a satyrical epistle to W——P——y, esq; on his being created E----1 of B---th, &c. *London, printed for T. Johnson; sold at the Royal Exchange, St. James's and Charing-cross, 1742.*

4⁰: *A*⁴ B⁴; *1–5* 6–15 *16 blk.* A1 hft.

'Stars, robes, and the various colour'd strings'

On William Pulteney being made earl of Bath.

L(11630.b.7/4, −A1),O; MH(uncut, −A1).

F49 —— 'London' [Edinburgh], *printed in the year 1742.*

8⁰: *A*⁴; *1–2* 3–8.

Printed by Ruddiman on the evidence of the ornaments; note below imprint 'N.B. Sold in London at 6d.'

E,GU,LdU-B; CtY,MH.

F50 — The false patriot. An epistle to Mr. Pope. *London, printed for James Roberts, 1734.* (*GM, LM* March)

2⁰: *A*² B–C²; *1–3* 4–12.

'Him, who reviles your muse, pronounce at sight'

O,LdU-B;DFo(uncut),ICN,MH,OCU,TxU(2)+.

[F51 = H157·2] — The false patriot's confession, 1737. *See* Hervey, John, *baron Hervey.*

F52 Famed. The famed hero, or, the Duke of Argyll's welcome to London. A congratulatory poem upon his grace's happy reduction of the rebels. [*Edinburgh?* 1716.]

1⁰: 1 side, 2 columns.

'Deborah did a divine song compose'

E.

F53 Familiar. A familiar answer to a familiar letter. '*London', printed in the year 1720.*

4⁰: *A*⁴; *1–3* 4–7 *8 blk.*

Very roughly printed, probably at Dublin.

'Dr. Smed altho' I'm press'd with cares'

A satirical reply to [Jonathan Smedley] *A familiar epistle to his excellency Charles earl of Sunderland, 1720.* The possibility of Swift's authorship is suggested in Murray Hill cat. 109 (1969) 46.

L(11602.ee.10/5); NjP.

— A familiar discourse between a Jacobite and a French Hugonot, 1702. *See* The grand affairs of Europe, 1702.

— A familiar epistle to his excellency Charles earl of Sunderland, 1720. *See* Smedley, Jonathan.

Familiar

F54 — A familiar epistle to Mr. Mitchell. Containing a seasonable satire, written in the fashionable style of modern poetick beggars. By a money'd man. *London, printed for T. Jauncy, 1720.* (*DP* 26 Sept)

8⁰: *A*² B–D⁴ E²; *i–ii* iii *iv,* 1–27 *28 blk.*

'Whilst I, a foe to stocks and bubbles'

The 'advertisement' is signed 'C.C.', the poem 'C. C——m.' A satire on Joseph Mitchell.

CSmH,NN,OCU.

— A familiar epistle to the right reverend the ld. bp. of Bangor, 1720. *See* Smedley, Jonathan.

— [dh] Familiar epistles between W-- H--- and A-- R--, [1719.] *See* Ramsay, Allan.

Family. Family duty: or, the monk and the merchant's wife, 1721. *In* Markland, John (M104).

Famous. A famous prediction of Merlin, 1709. *See* Swift, Jonathan.

F55 Fan. The fan: a heroi-comical poem, in three canto's. *Printed for James Carlos, bookseller, in the Dove-lane in Norwich, 1749.*

4⁰: *A*² B–E²; *i–iii* iv, *5* 6–20.

'Ye gentlest powers! of musick, who inspire'

According to ms. notes in the copies seen, on the loss of her fan by Lydia lady Pettus at a Norwich assembly.

O,NwP(lacks A²).

F56 —— *Printed for James Carlos, bookseller, in the Dove-lane in Norwich, 1749.*

8⁰: *A*⁴ B⁴ C⁴(−C4); *i–iii* iv, *5* 6–22.

L(1465.g.25/1); CtY,DFo,OCU.

F57 Fanatical. Fanatical doctrine. In a sermon preach'd in D-----, January 30th, 1728. [*Dublin,* 1728/29.]

½⁰: 1 side, 1 column.

'When I beheld the royal martyr slain'

L(1890.e.5/110),C,DT; MH.

Fanciad. The Fanciad, 1743. *See* Hill, Aaron.

F58 Farce. The farce is over; or, the plot discover'd without an enquiry, a poem. Dedicated to the rt. hon. R. e. of O------d. *London printed, and sold by the booksellers & pamphlet-shops in London & Westminster, 1742.*

4⁰: *A*² B–C²; *1–4* 5–12.

'Sing, honest muse, nor fruitless be thy song'

Dedication to Robert Walpole, earl of Orford, signed 'A.B.'

CSmH,CtY.

F59 Farewell. A farewel to passive-obedience and non-resistance. *London, printed in the year 1710.*

½⁰: 1 side, 1 column.

A **farewell** to passive obedience

'Let passive-slaves contented be'
A tory satire on the Sacheverell affair.
MH,OCU.

— A farewel to the world, 1725. *See* Wotton, *Sir Henry.*

[**Farewell, George.**] Farrago. [*London*] *Printed for the author; to be sold only by Lawton Gilliver,* 1733 [1734?]. (*SR* 15 March 1734)
8°: pp. iv, 188.   L,O; CtY,ICN.
    Preface signed 'Pilgrim Plowden'; note in an interleaved copy at L, 'Writ by Mr. Farewell at Bulloigne in France', and entered to him by Gilliver in *SR*. Presentation copy at ICN; deposit copy at E.

Farmer. The farmer's daughter: or, the art of getting preferment, [1738.] *See* Barber, James.

F60 — The farmer's yard; a new fable for Æsop. [*Dublin?*] *Printed in the year* 1747.
8°: A⁴; *1–2* 3–8.
'Once on a time, in farmer's yard'
DA(2); ICU.

F61 Farmer, Peter. A new model for the rebuilding masonry on a stronger basis than the former; with a sound constitution, and a curious catechism ...teaching the whole world to be masons... To which is added, several diverting songs by celebrated masons of the old order, and some new ones... By Peter Farmer esq; Dedicated to Mr. Orator Henley. *London, printed for J. Wilford,* 1730. (*MChr* Nov)
8°: A–D⁴; *i–ii* iii–vi, 7–32.
    The 'new model' appears to consist of the verse catechism printed on pp. 8–15; the remainder of the pamphlet is occupied with a miscellany of masonic songs.
'Are you a brother mason?'
    The author's name is possibly a pseudonym inspired by Stephen Duck. A satire on the freemasons and on John Henley.
L(161.1.40).

Farquhar, George. Love and business: in a collection of occasional verse, and eipistolary [!] prose... *London, printed for B. Lintott,* 1702. (*PM* 25 Nov)
8°: pp. 159.   L,O; CtY,DFo.
The collection contains very little verse.

F62 — Barcellona. A poem. Or, the Spanish expedition, under the command of Charles earl of Peterborough... [*London*] *Publish'd for the benefit of the author's widow and children,* 1710.
4°: A² B–G⁴; *i–iv,* 1–48.
    Watermark: grapes; poor paper. No price on title. The relationship of the two issues is obscure.

Farquhar, G. Barcellona

'Now had those fleets once rivals in dispute'
L(Ashley 3210),O; CSmH,CtY.

F63 — [another issue] *London, printed for John Smith, & Richard Standfast,* 1710. (*Tatler* 11 May)
4°: A–G⁴; *i–viii,* 1–48.
    Watermark: fleur-de-lys/FH; this paper is also of poor quality. 'Price 1s.' on title. Printed from the same setting of type as the preceding, with the addition of a dedication to Charles earl of Peterborough on A2.3, signed 'Marg. Farquhar'.
L(11633.df.27),O,E; MWiW-C,NN.

F64 — The prologue spoken by Mr. Wilks, at the opening of the theatre in the Hay-market, October the 15th, 1706. [*London*] *Printed for B. Bragg,* 1706.
½°: 1 side, 1 column.
    The Chatsworth copy appears to be a variant with the date in the title '5th' corrected in ms. to '15th'. On the other side of the MH copy, *A list of the names of the prisoners...*, printed by Henry Hills, 1708.
'Great revolutions crown this wond'rous year'
Chatsworth; MH.

[—] The trifle, a new song, 1714. *See* T480.

Farrago. Farrago, 1733. *See* Farewell, George.
— Farrago: or miscellanies in verse and prose, 1739. *See* Barton, Richard.

Farther. A farther hue and cry after Dr. Sw----t, 1714. *See* A genuine epistle from M——w P——r, 1714.

F65 Farthingale. [dh] The farthingale reviv'd: or, more work for the cooper. A panegyrick on the late, but most admirable invention of the hoop-petticoat: written at the Bath in the year 1711. [col] [*London*] *Sold by John Baker,* 1711. (*SR* 13 July)
2°: A²; *1–4.*
    Entered in *SR* to John Darby; deposit copy at L. Advertised in *DC* 14 July.
'There's scarce a bard, that writ in former time'
    Printed in *A new collection of miscellany poems, for the year,* 1718, edited and perhaps written by George Davis. *Female folly,* 1713, 'By the author of the satyr upon hoop'd petticoats' is possibly by the same author.
L(C.20.f.2/236),LSA.

F66 — — [*Edinburgh,* 1711.]
4°: *A²; 1–4.*
    Drop-head title, ending with '...petticoat'. With an Edinburgh printer's ornament on p. 1.
ES,GM.

F67 Fashion. Fashion: a poem. By a young gentleman. *London, printed for T. Worrall; sold by J. Roberts,* 1733 [1734?]. (*LM* Jan 1734)
2°: B–C² D¹ (B2 as 'B'); *1–3* 4–10.

Fashion: a poem

'I sing of fashion: come, ye modish throng'
ICN,IU,OCU.

— Fashion: an epistolary satire to a friend, 1742.
See Warton, Joseph.

F68 Fatal. Fatal love or, the young maiden's tragedy: being a sad and dismal relation, of one Mary Low, late cook maid to Esq; Fansaw in St. James's Park, who drowned her self in Rosamonds Pond, on Wednesday night last, for the love of a young man who was her fellow servant. To the tune of, Johnson's farwel. *London, printed for John Wiseman, near the Royal-Exchange,* 1704.
½⁰: 1 side, 2 columns.
'You maidens who intend to wed'
    A popular ballad.
L(C.40.m.9/87).

F69 — The fatal union of France and Spain. A satyr. By H.J. esq; *London printed, and sold by A. Baldwin,* 1701. (*PM* 12 April)
4⁰: *a*² b² B–D²; *i–viii*, *1–12*. a1 hft.
'When Charles the fifth, so glorious for renown'
O(2, 1 lacks a²).

F70 — — *London printed, and sold by the booksellers of London & Westminster,* 1701.
4⁰: A–B²; *1–2* 3–8.
L(11631.c.54); MH.

F71 Fatality. The fatality of forc'd marriage. Exemplified in some circumstances of the life of a Neapolitan woman of quality. With additional poems by the same hand. *London, printed in the year* 1741.
8⁰: A–D⁴; *1–4* 5–31 *32 blk.* 31 err.
    The CSmH copy has a frontispiece portraying the interior of a church; it may not be original.
'The tenant of a hut that fac'd the sea'
CSmH,IU.

F72 Fate. The fate of an Hibernian muse, a true tale. In an epistle to R--- N--- esq; with a postscript, occasioned by the arrival of his excellency Philip earl of Chesterfield... *Dublin, printed by Oli. Nelson,* [1745.]
8⁰: *A*⁴ B⁴; *1–5* 6–16. A1 hft.
    The postscript is dated 31 Aug 1745.
'Believe me, sir, however strange, 'tis true'
L(1959),LVA-F(–A1),O.

F73 — The fate of courtezans and their enamerato's. A new ballad. Inscrib'd to Mrs C--- P------- and the angelick Signor F-----lli. *London, printed for F. Cook, in Black-fryars; sold at the pamphlet-shops of London & Westminster,* 1735.
2⁰: *A*²; *1* 2–4.
        Horizontal chain-lines; printed on half a double-sized sheet (16″ × 25″ approx), bearing a halfpenny stamp.
'To you, fair nymphs of Venus' train'
        A warning to Farinelli to keep away from Constantia Phillips lest she pox and ruin him.

The fate of courtezans

        Cf. *The happy courtezan,* 1735, and *The secrets of a woman's heart,* 1735.
L(1876.f.1/109).

F74 — The fate of traytors. A poem upon the rebellion. *London, printed for E. Curll,* 1716. (2 April, Luttrell)
8⁰: A–C⁴; *i–ii* iii–vi, 7–24.
        Listed in *MC* April; dated by *Straus, Curll* 5 April.
'Are these the Britons, whom ye stil'd the bold'
        Dedication signed 'W.H.'
L(164.n.8, Luttrell),O,E; MH.

F75 Father. A father's advices to his children. To which are added, religious and useful poems on various subjects. By D.H. presbyter of the church of England. *London, printed for the author,* 1740.
12⁰: A–O⁸/⁴ (D2 as 'D3'); *1–5* 6–166 *167–168*.
'Dear children, whom the Lord to me hath giv'n'
LdU-B.

— The father's blessing, [170–?] *See* Jole, William.

— A father's instructions to his son, 1748. *See* Scott, Thomas.

F76 Fatigues. The fatigues of a great man, or, the plague of serving one's country. A satyr. *London, printed for A. Dodd; sold by the booksellers of London & Westminster,* [1730.] (*MChr* July)
2⁰: A–C²; *1–3* 4–12.
'Let peasants rise at morn, 'tis more polite'
        A satire on Walpole.
CSmH(uncut),InU(Luttrell, July),NjP.

F77 — — '*London, printed for A. Dodd; sold by the booksellers of London & Westminster*' [*Dublin*], 1730.
8⁰: *A*⁴; *1–2* 3–8.
DA; ICU.

F78 — — The second edition. *London, printed for A. Dodd; sold by the booksellers of London & Westminster,* [1733.] (*LM* March)
2⁰: A–C²; *1–3* 4–12.
L(C.131.h.1/10).

F79 — — '*London, printed for A. Dodd; sold by the booksellers of London & Westminster*' [*Edinburgh*], 1734.
8⁰: A–B⁴ (some copies B2 as 'C2'); *1–2* 3–14 *15–16 blk.*
        Printed by Robert Fleming on the evidence of the ornaments.
O(–B4),LdU-B; CtY(–B4),InU,MH,OCU.

F80 Fatio de Duillier, Nicolas. [dh] Nicolai Facii Duillierii Neutonus ecloga. [col] [*Oxford*] *Editio ab auctore recognita. Anno* 1728. Pridie ante Paschatis diem. (20 April)
8⁰: *A*²; *1–4*.
        Ms. note in the O copy (inserted in a presentation copy to Fatio de Duillier from Newton of his *Principia,* 1726) 'Oxoniæ ad Isin, e Theatro Sheldoniano'.

Fatio de Duillier, N. Neutonus

'Natura omniparens cunctis præfecta creandis'
L(11405.e; 161.m.20),LDW,O(ms. corrections).

Faustina. Faustina: or the Roman songstress, a satyr, [1726.] *See* Carey, Henry.

Favourite. The favourite, a simile, 1712. *See* Sewell, George.

Fawkes, Francis. Original poems and translations. *London, printed for the author; sold by R. & J. Dodsley, J. Newbery, L. Davis & C. Reymers, T. Davies, and by H. Dell, 1761.*
8°: pp. xix, 281.   L,O; CtY,MH.

———

[—] Bramham Park. To Robert Lane esq; ... Written in May 1745.
> Listed as a separate work in *CBEL*, presumably from the catalogue at O; but the copy there is merely extracted from Fawkes's *Original poems*, 1761.

F81 Fear. Fear and interest makes the harvest. A dialogue between a lawyer and a church-warden. Or fear and interest are the motives of papists conforming to the church of England... [*Dublin*] *Printed in the year 1732.*
8°: A⁴; *1–8*.
'Ring your bells, beat your drums'
DK.

F82 Feilding, Robert. An elegy on the death of the Dutchess of Cleveland, who died on Sunday night last October, 9. 1709. at her house at Chiswick, in the 65th year of her age. Written by Beau Fielding. *London, printed for J. Dutton,* [1709.]
1°: 1 side, 2 columns.
> Mourning headpiece and woodcut borders.
'Be husht ye silent winds and gently breath'
> The attributions of elegiac broadsides are unreliable, and Feilding's authorship must be doubted.
CSmH.

F83 — General Fielding's answer to the Dutchess of C——'s memorial. To the tune of, The dame of honour. [*London,* 1706.]
½°: 1 side, 2 columns.
> On the other side, *The Dutchess of C——'s memorial,* [1706.]
'If I was by misfortune sent'
> An answer to Barbara, Duchess of Cleveland, whom Feilding bigamously married; but probably satirically attributed to him.
L(1872.a.1/158).

F84 — Handsome Fealding's letter to his first wife, Madam Wadsworth, occasionally written on her personating Madam Deleau. *London, printed for T. Bland, near Fleet-street,* [1706.]
½°: 1 side, 1 column.
'Go shameful model of a cursed w-----e!'

Feilding, R. Handsome Fealding's letter

> Signed 'R.F. From the Jelly House in Pall Mall, Friday December 13th 1706'; but, like the other poems here, possibly falsely attributed to him. Feilding was tricked into marrying Mary Wadsworth 9 Nov 1705, believing her to be the rich widow Mrs. Deleau.
DG,Rothschild.

Felicity. 'The felicity of a country life. In an epistle from the country to a friend in London. [*London*] *Printed for J. Janeway.* Price 6*d.*' (*LM* Dec 1732)
> Listed in *LM* under 'plays, poetry, and entertainment'; it is not certain that it is in verse, but it is very tempting to relate it to [Bezaleel Morrice] *On rural felicity; in an epistle to a friend,* published in Dec 1733; Morrice's *Amour of Venus,* 1732, was published by Janeway.

Female. The female advocate: or, an answer to a late satyr, 1707. *See* Egerton, Sarah Fyge.

F85 — The female apologist. A satire. Occasion'd by the monthly memoirs of a celebrated British lady. By R.C. of the Middle Temple, esq. *London printed, and sold at the pamphlet-shops at the Royal Exchange, Temple-Bar, & Charing-Cross, 1748.* (*GM, LM* Aug)
4°: A⁴ B⁴; *1–4* 5–15 *16 blk.* A1 hft.
> Colophon, p. 15, 'Printed for H. Stibbs, near Cornhill'.
'How early did love's flame inspire'
> A satire on Teresia Constantia Phillips.
L(11630.c.8/16,−A1); TxHR,TxU.

F86 — 'Female apostacy: or, the true-born Englishwoman: a satyr. [*London*] *Sold by S. Malthus.*' (*WL* Aug 1705)
'How doubly blest was man in paradise'

F87 — — [*London?* 1705?]
4°: A²; *1–4*, 2 columns.
> This edition is probably a piracy.
CtY.

F88 — Female chastity, truth and sanctity: a satire. *London, printed for M. Harris, 1734.* (*GM, LM* Dec)
2°: A–D² E¹; *1–4* 5–18.
> The date in the CSmH copy has been altered by erasure and pen to 1735. Possibly a revision of *Female piety and virtue,* 1725.
'The truth of womankind is all a cheat'
> A satire on the falsity of women.
L(1482.f.32); CSmH,TxU.

F89 — [*idem*] Woman unmask'd, and dissected; a satire. *London printed, and sold by J. Brett, & Mrs. Bartlett, 1740.* (*GM, LM* June)
8°: A² B–G⁸ H¹ (C2 as 'C3', F2 as 'E2'); *i–iv, 1* 2–98.
> Apparently a much enlarged version of the preceding.
DFo.

Female chastity

F90 — [reissue] Female qualifications: or, jilts and hypocrites portray'd. A satire, chiefly occasion'd by two pieces, publish'd not long since. The one entitled, Woman not inferior to man; and the other Woman's superior excellence to man. *London printed, and sold by J. Brett, & M. Bartlet,* 1741. (*LDP* 15 Jan)

8°: A^2 B–G^8 H^1 (C2 as 'C3', F2 as 'E2'); *i–iv,* *1* 2–98.

> A1 is probably a cancel. Listed in *GM, LM* Jan as sold by A. Dodd.

E; ICN.

F91 — The female dunces. Inscrib'd to Mr. Pope. *London printed, and sold by J. Dormer,* 1733. (*GSJ* 7 July)

2°: A^2 B^2; *1–2* 3–8.

'When women deviate from strict virtue's rules'
CtY,DLC,MH,TxU.

— Female empire, 1746. *See* Hawkins, William.

F92 — The female faction: or, the Gay subscribers. A poem. *London, printed for J. Roberts; sold by the booksellers of London & Westminster,* 1729. (*MChr* 25 March)

2°: A^2 B^2; *1–2* 3–8.

> *Bodleian Quarterly Record* (VII. 332) quotes an advertisement in the *Daily Post Boy* 26 March 1729 giving a correction 'sleeps' for 'smiles' in the last line but four.

'D'Anvers! no more in weekly libels deal'
> On the subscribers to Gay's *Polly.*
L(163.n.16, ms. notes),LVA-D,O(2, 1 uncut),C (uncut); CSmH,CtY,MH,OCU,TxU.

F93 — — *London, printed: and Dublin re-printed and sold by James Hoey, & George Faulkner,* 1729.

8°: A^4; *1–3* 4–7 *8.* 8 advt.
DA,DG,*MR-C.*

F94 — Female folly: or, the plague of a woman's riding-hood and cloak. By the author of the satyr upon hoop'd petticoats. *London, printed by R. Newcomb,* 1713.

2°: (3 ll); ff. *1* 2–3.
> Printed on one side of the leaf only.

'How strangely woman kind did first begin'
> Possibly the 'satyr upon hoop'd petticoats' is *The farthingale reviv'd,* 1711. The L copy has a nineteenth-century ms. attribution to Sir Richard Steele, which is absurd. On the cloak as a cover for thieving or immorality.
L(1870.d.1/23).

F95 — Female honour. An epistle to the lady in favour from the lady lately kick'd-out. *London, printed for J. Huggonson,* 1742. (*LM* Oct)

2°: A^2 B–C^2; *1–2* 3–12.
> *Rothschild* 228, 229. Horizontal chain-lines.

'With sullen spleen devour'd, and gloomy thought'
> From Henrietta Howard, countess of Suffolk, to the Duchess of Yarmouth.
O,LdU-B; MH,OCU.

Female honour

F96 — — *London printed: and Dublin re-printed in the year* 1742.

8°: A^4; *1* 2–8.
O,DG,DN.

F97 — The female monster or, the second part of the world turn'd topsy turvey. A satyr. *London printed, and sold by B. Bragg,* 1705. (5 March, Luttrell)

4°: A^2 B–F^2; *i–iv,* 1–18 *19–20 blk.* A1 hft.
> Advertised in *FP* 17 Feb for 'Tuesday next' [20th] and in *PM* 6 March as 'yesterday'.

'If man the greatest brute on earth was made'
> A continuation of *The monster,* 1705. A vicious satire on women.
L(643.k.2/2, – A1,F2, Luttrell); CtY,NjP(– F2).

F98 — The female moralist. A poem. *London, printed for J. Robinson, & R. Dodsley,* 1744. (*GM* Sept)

4°: π^1 A^2 B–F^2 G^1; *i–vi,* *1* 2–22. π1 hft.

'Thy furrow'd brow, my Pylades, unbend'
L(11630.c.10/11; 11630.d.15/10, –π1; 11630. e.6/8, –π1),O(–π1),CT,LdU-B; DLC,NN,OCU (–π1),TxHR.

— The female muse, 1702. *See* Dyke, Ann.

F99 — Female piety and virtue. A poem. *London, printed for J. Roberts, J. Billingsley, A. Dodd, J. Stagg, &. H. Whitridge,* 1725 [1724]. (*MC* Nov)

8°: A–D^4; *1–3* 4–32.
> What appears to be a revised version was printed as *Female chastity,* 1734.

'Virtue or piety is all a cheat'
> A satire against women.
O; IU.

— Female piety exemplify'd, [1743/–.] *See* Gent, Thomas (G112).

F100 — The female proselyte a sad back-slider: a burlesque poem, in hudibrastick verse. Humbly inscribed to the reverend Dean Swift. *London, printed for T. Cooper,* 1735. (*GM* Dec)

2°: A–E^2; *1–3* 4–20.

'Ye toping cits, by morn who whet'
DrU-U; KU,MH.

— Female qualifications, 1741. *See* Female chastity, 1734–.

— The female rake: or, modern fine lady, [1735.] *See* Dorman, Joseph.

F101 — The female speaker; or, the priests in the wrong: a poem. Being an epistle from the celebrated Mrs. D--mm--d to Dr. St---b---g and Mr. F---t---r. Occasioned by their dispute on the subject of heresy. *London, printed for B. Dickinson,* 1735. (*GM* Sept)

2°: (frt +) A^2 B–E^2 F^1; *1–3* 4–22.

'From the remotest banks of northern Tay'
> A bawdy epistle from May Drummond, the quaker, to Henry Stebbing and James Foster.
L(11602.i.16/5),LVA-D,C; OCU,TxU.

The **female** tumbler

— 'The female tumbler. A tale. With a curious frontispiece. [*London*] *Printed for G. Foster*. Price 6d.' (*GM, LM* Sept 1737)

Listed in *LM* under 'entertainment and poetry'; it is not clear whether it is in verse.

F102 — The female volunteer: or, an attempt to make our men stand. An epilogue intended to be spoken in Drury-lane playhouse by Mris. Woffington, in the habit of a volunteer, upon reading the Gazette extraordinary, containing an account of the battle of Falkirk, fought January 17. 1746. [*London?* 1746.] (Feb?)

½°: 1 side, 1 column.

GA 26 Feb 1746 advertises 'The female volunteer. Being a curious print of Mrs. Woffington in the habit of a soldier. With an epilogue intended to be spoke by her in that character...' Possibly this is the text, separated from the print.

'Plague of all cow'rds, I say – Why, bless my eyes –'

AdU.

F103 — The female worthies: or, a catalogue of vertuous women, recorded in Scripture. Now recommended for examples to both rich and poor women, in our days. *York, printed by J. White & R. Ward*, 1725.

12°: A–C⁴; *1* 2–24.

The format is uncertain; the chain-lines are vertical but the chap-book appearance and size suggests it is 12°.

'Eve, the mother of all living'

YM.

Fénelon, François de Salignac de la Mothe.

[*Télémaque*] The adventures of Telemachus. In English verse. Book I, 1712. *See* A69.

The adventures of Telemachus. Attempted in English blank verse [books 1, 2], 1729. *See* A68.

[Manning, Francis:] The adventures of Telemachus, son of Ulysses. The first book, 1738. *See* M83.

———

The portrait of a just and honourable man, a poem, written originally in French, by the archbishop of Cambray, 1731. *In* H388.

The accomplish'd hero: or, the Caledonian songsters. From the French, 1748. *See* A6.

Fenton, Elijah. Poems on several occasions. *London, printed for Bernard Lintot*, 1717. (*SR* 18 March)

8°: pp. 224.   L,O; CtY,MH.

Watermark: initials. Q⁴ of Lintot advertisements usually at end; but Hannas cat. 20/706 records a copy with advertisements of John Darby. Deposit copy at O. Entered in Bowyer's ledgers under 19 Feb 1717, 1,000 copies and 25 large paper.

Fenton, E.

— [fine paper]   DFo.
Watermark: Strasburg bend.

———

F104 [—] Cerealia: an imitation of Milton. *London, printed for Thomas Bennet*, 1706. (*DC* 21 Feb)

2°: B² C–D²; *i–ii*, 1–10. 10 err.

Bond 15.

'Of English tipple, and the potent grain'

Early ms. attribution to Fenton in the CLU-C, CtY copies, and in the L copy of the second edition. Usually ascribed to John Philips on the evidence of a ms. attribution in the LLP copy, adopted in *Nichols, Collection* IV. 274. According to Nichols the attribution is in Archbishop Tenison's handwriting, but this is almost certainly incorrect. Cf. *Thomas* xxv, who prints it as Philips's.

LLP,O,OW,C(lacks B1),DT+; CLU-C,CtY,IU (Luttrell, 21 Feb),MH,TxU(2, 1 uncut).

F105 [—] — The second edition with additions. *London printed for Thomas Bennet*, 1706.

2°: B² C–D²; *i–ii*, 1–10.

L(11645.i.35).

F106 — An epistle to Mr. Southerne, from Mr. El. Fenton. From Kent, Jan. 28. 17¹⁰⁄₁₁. *London, printed for Benj. Tooke, & Bernard Lintott*, 1711. (*DC* 2 June)

8°: A⁴ B–C⁴; *i–iv*, 1–19 *20 blk*. A1 hft.

There are fine-paper copies, which have not been identified; the normal watermark is initials. Press-figure 11-1 is found in many copies, not in EU,CtY,IU. Listed in Bowyer's ledgers to 'Partners' under 26 May 1711, 1100 copies 'with margins altered for fine'.

'Bold is the muse to leave her humble cell'

L(992.h.5/1; 161.k.11,–A1),O(2,–A1),EU; CSmH,CtY(–A1),ICN,MH,TxU+.

F107 [—] A letter to the knight of the sable shield. *London, printed for Bernard Lintott*, 1716. (25 June?)

2°: A² B²; *1–2* 3–8.

Entered to Lintot in Bowyer's ledgers under 25 June, 500 copies printed. Listed in *MC* June.

'Sir knight, who know with equal skill'

Ascribed to Fenton in a Lintot catalogue of c.1725; included with Fenton's poems in Johnson's *Poets*. Listed by *Waller* as attributed to Prior; rejected by *Wright & Spears* 805. A satire on Blackmore and Tonson.

LVA-F; DFo,OCU,TxU.

F108 [—] M. Manlius Capitolinus. [*London*] *Sold by John Morphew*, 1712. (15 Jan, Luttrell)

½°: 1 side, 1 column.

Advertised in *PB* 19 Jan.

'Ambition is a plant, that's always found'

Ms. note in the Chatsworth copy 'R/ Jan: 10: 1711/12. Mr Fenton'. On the dismissal of Marlborough.

Fenton, E. M. Manlius Capitolinus

O,C,MC, *Chatsworth*, Crawford; ICN(Luttrell), MH,NjP,TxU.

F109 [—] [variant imprint:] [*London*] *Printed in the year* 1711 [i.e. 1711/2].
L(Cup.645.e.1/9).

F110 [—] An ode to the sun, for the new-year. *London, printed for Jacob Tonson*, 1707. (*DC* 11 Jan)
2°: *A*¹ B–D² *E*¹; *i–ii*, 1–13 *14*. 14 advt.
　　Watermark: WC. A1 and E1 have been seen to be conjugate. Copies have variant states of the advertisement for *A defence of plays* at the foot of p. 14. L(840.m.1/25) reads 'To morrow...'; CtY,DFo,ICU 'On Tuesday, Jan. 7. was publish'd...'; other copies are just headed 'Advertisement' with no dates given.
　　'Begin, celestial source of light'
　　Reprinted in Fenton's *Poems*, 1717; early ms. attribution in the TxU copy.
L(840.m.1/25; Ashley 5662/4),LLP,O,*MR-C*; CSmH(Luttrell, 11 Jan),CtY,DFo,IU(uncut), TxU(2)+.

F111 [—] [fine paper]
　　Watermark: HD. Advertisement on p. 14 in third state with no dates given.
L(643.1.25/13, title cropt, ms. revisions); MH.

F112 [—] On the first-fit of the gout. By a person of honour. [*London*] *Sold by John Morphew*, 1706. (*DC* 2 July)
½°: 1–2, 1 column.
　　'Welcome thou friendly earnest of fourscore'
　　Crum W242. Printed and ascribed to Fenton in Dr. Johnson's *Life;* it was earlier printed in *Oxford and Cambridge miscellany poems*, [1708] edited by Fenton, but was not there identified as his. The attribution is possibly suspect.
Crawford; MH(Luttrell, 2 July),TxU.

F113 — To the queen, on her majesty's birth-day. *London, printed for Benjamin Tooke*, [1712.] (6 Feb, Luttrell)
2°: *A*²; 1–2 3–4.
　　No watermark. The Luttrell copy is recorded in *Haslewood*.
　　'From this auspicious day three kingdoms date'
L(1481.f.19/5),LLP; CSmH,MH(ms. date 7 Feb).

F114 — [fine paper]
　　Watermark: pro patria.
O.

F115 Feu. Le feu de joye: or, a brief description of two most glorious victories obtain'd by her majesty's forces and those of her allies, over the French and Bavarians...at Schellenbergh and Blainheim... Under the magnanimous and heroick conduct of his grace the Duke of Marlborough. A poem. By a British muse. *London, printed by Freeman Collins,*

Le **feu** de joye

for W. Henchman, 1705 [1704]. (*PM* 30 Nov)
4°: A–D⁴ (C as 'D'); *i–vi*, 1–26.
　　Ms. correction to p. 15, line 5.
　　'Musing one night in bed what I shou'd do'
　　A letter of William Cowper to Thomas Park, 17 May 1793 (William Hayley, *Life and letters* (1835) V. 147), referring to Chapman's Homer, reads 'He cannot surely be the same Chapman who wrote a poem, I think, on the battle of Hochstadt, in which, when I was a very young man, I remember to have seen the following lines...'; he then quotes from this poem. (Park's copy with his notes is at InU.) Richard Chapman is clearly intended.
L(11631.bb.12),O; InU.

F116 Fickle. The fickle courtier, or, love in a quandary. A poem. *London, printed in the year* 1710. (*PB* 5 Aug)
8°: A⁸; *1–3* 4–16.
　　'In a May-morning, on a meadow green'
L(1477.aa.3/4); CtY,ICN,IU(2, 1 uncut),OCU, TxU(2).

F117 Fiddler. The fidler's fling at roguery. (Canto verace odioso) Divided into several canto's. To be successively continued. *London, printed for W. Smith, at Corelli's Head (a musick-shop) against Norfolk-street, in the Strand*, 1730. (*SR* 8 May)
8°: A–D⁸ E⁴; *1–9* 10–72. 72 advt.
　　Entered in *SR* to Susannah Fox; listed in *MChr* May as sold by J. Jackson, J. Hooke, C. Rivington. A2–3 contain a preface on the inadequacies of copyright protection, and the intention of signing copies to prevent infringement; the O copy is signed 'S. Fox' and numbered 276; the MH copy is unsigned. The deposit copies at L,E,EU,SaU are unsigned but numbered respectively 8, 1, 7, 5.
　　'The fidler h's lost his fiddle, – hoe'
　　Ascribed by *Lowndes* to Edward Ward, very improbably; the author is most likely Susannah Fox, whose address is given on p. 72 as 'At Mr. Francis's, in Fountain Court'. Cf. *The rival lapdog*, 1730. A satire on Walpole.
L(992.h.8/5),O,E,EU,SaU; MH.

F118 — [reissue] Canto I. *London, printed for W. Smith; (musician,) at Corelli's Head in the Strand*, 1734.
8°: π² A⁸(–A1–3) B–D⁸ E(5 ll, 4th as '*A2') F–M⁴ N¹; [4] 7–9 10–67 *68*, i–iii iv–v *vi*, 69 70–71 '82–136'.
　　Canto II is added with a separate title-page dated 1734; the original E4 is cancelled and replaced by a new conclusion to canto I and prelims to canto II. The new dedication on π2 is signed 'Frank'.
L(1966); CSmH,ICN,NjP.

'Fidelio F, A, C.' Le repos, [1737.] *See* Brodie, Joseph.

Field

The **fifteen** comforts of a Dutch-man

Field. The field-spy, 1714. *See* Ward, Edward.

F119 Fielding, Henry. 'The coronation. A poem. And an ode on the birth-day. By Mr. Fielding. [*London*] *Printed for B. Creake; sold by J. Roberts.* Price 6*d*.' (*DJ* 10 Nov 1727).

There seems no reason to doubt that this is by Henry Fielding, and his first published work.

F120 [—] Τῆς Ὁμήρου Vερνον-ιαδος . . . The Vernoniad. Done into English, from the original Greek of Homer. Lately found at Constantinople. With notes in usum, &c. Book the first. *London, printed for Charles Corbett, 1741.* (*LDP* 21 Jan)

4°: π¹[=E1] A–D⁴ E⁴(–E1); *i–ii, 1 2–37 38 blk.*

Bond 174; *Rothschild* 842. '100 Vernoniad by Fielding, and one eighth of the copy' formed lot 3 of an anonymous trade sale (probably of C. Corbett) of 23 Dec 1742 (cat. at O-JJ), sold to Lintot for £1. 14*s*.

'Arms and the man I sing, who greatly bore'

L(1465.f.50; 11630.b.1/13, title mutilated),E; CLU-C,CSmH,CtY,MH(uncut).

F121 [—] — *Dublin printed, and sold by the booksellers,* 1741.

8°: A–F⁴; *1–3 4–46 47–48 blk.*

Printed by George Faulkner, according to *Bradshaw* 1119.

L(11659.c.59, –F4),C(2),DA(–F4),DG,DN+; ICN,MH(–F4),PP(–F4).

'—' The important triflers. A satire [actually by T. Brecknock], 1749. *See* B406.

F122 [—] The masquerade. A poem. Inscrib'd to C------t H-----d------g-----r . . . By Lemuel Gulliver, poet laureat to the king of Lilliput. *London printed, and sold by J. Roberts, & A. Dodd,* 1728. (*MChr* 30 Jan)

4°: A² B–C⁴; *i–iv, 1–15 16 blk.*

'Some call curiosity an evil'

Reprinted with Fielding's *The Grub-street opera,* 1731. Addressed to J. J. Heidegger.

CtY.

F123 — Of true greatness. An epistle to the right honourable George Dodington, esq; *London, printed for C. Corbet,* 1741. (*LDP* 7 Jan)

2°: π² A–C²; *1–3 4–16.*

Rothschild 841.

''Tis strange, while all to greatness homage pay'

L(Ashley 4830),O,C; CLU-C(uncut),CtY,ICN, IU,MH.

[—] The puppet shew, 1748. *See* P1170.

Fielding, Robert. *See* Feilding, Robert.

F124 Fifteen. The fifteen comforts of a Dutch-man. Written by the author of the Dutch-catechism. *London, printed in the year* 1707.

8°: A⁴; *1 2–8.*

'You may talk of haughty France, and boast of Spain'

A whiggish poem. *The recantation,* 1703, is also 'by the author of the Dutch catechism', and is entered under Richard Burridge who signs the dedication. *The Dutch catechism* has not been traced. Probably all these works are by Burridge.

Horn (xerox at L).

F125 — [dh] The fifteen comforts of a lawyer: or a dialogue between the flying-horse in the Temple, and the rose at the Counter-gate. [col] *London, printed in the year* 1707.

4°: A²; *1–4.*

'Thou more than awful house, where crouds resort'

L(164.1.27).

F126 — The fifteen comforts of a wanton wife: or, the fool well fitted. Dedicated to the London cuckolds. *London, printed in the year* 170⁶₇.

8°: A⁴; *1 2–8.*

'Unhappy man! yoak'd with a wanton wife'

CLU-C.

F127 — The fifteen comforts of cuckoldom. Written by a noted cuckold in the New-Exchange in the Strand. [*London*] *Printed in the year* 1706.

8°: *A⁴; i ii, 3–8.*

'As I last night in bed lay snoring'

L(1076.1.22/7).

F128 — The fifteen comforts of matrimony. Or, a looking-glass for all those who have enter'd in that holy and comfortable state. Wherein are sum'd up all those blessings that attend a married life. Dedicat [!] to batchelors, maids & widdowers. *London, printed in the year* 1706.

8°: *A⁴; 1 2–8.*

'Happy were man, when born as free as air'

The fifteen comforts of whoring, 1706, is attributed to the same author. Replied to in *The batchelors and maids answer,* [1706?].

L(11644.eee.61; 1076.1.22/6).

F129 — — Dedicated to batchelors and widdowers. *London, printed in the year* 1706.

8°: *A⁴; 1 2–8.* 8 advt. for patent medicine.

CLU-C.

F130 — — Dedicated to batchelers and widowers. *Edinburgh printed, and sold by Robert Brown,* [1706/–.]

8°: *A⁴; 1 2–8.*

E.

F131 — The fifteen comforts of whoring, or, the pleasures of a town-life. Dedicated to the youth of the present age. By the author of the Fifteen comforts of matrimony. *London, printed in the year* 1706.

8°: *A⁴; i ii, 3–8.*

'No sooner youth throws off his infant plays'

Cf. *The whores and bawds answer,* 1706.

CLU-C.

The **fifteen** plagues

F132 — The fifteen plagues of a coach-man, foot-man, and a butler, in their several stations and places, with the forty five plagues of their own confessions, in a comical dialogue... *London, printed for J. Smith, near Fleet-street,* [1711.] (*SR* 25 May)
8⁰: *A*⁴; *1* 2–8.
    Entered in *SR* by Stephen Gilbert to John Bradford; deposit copy at EU.
'Three jolly lads as ere was seen on earth'
EU.

F133 — The fifteen plagues of a cook-maid, chamber-maid, and nursery-maid, in their several places; with the 45 plagues of their own confessions, in a comical dialogue... *London, printed for J. Smith, in the Strand,* [1711.] (*SR* 16 May)
8⁰: *A*⁴; *1* 2–8.
    Entered in *SR* by Stephen Gilbert to John Bradford; deposit copy at EU.
'Three jolly lasses strapping brisk and gay'
EU.

F134 — The fifteen plagues of a lawyer, a quack doctor, a recruiting captain...To which is added, the fifteen plagues of a foot-man, coach-man... *London, printed by H. Goodwin, in the Strand,* [1711?]
8⁰: *A*⁴; *1* 2–8.
    List of 29 professions in two columns on title.
    Date suggested by other works of similar title.
'If there on earth be one that has not met'
L(1077.i.33/2),LG(cropt).

F135 — The fifteen plagues of a maiden-head. Written by Madam B-----le. *London, printed by F.P. near Fleet-street,* 1707. (19 March?)
8⁰: *A*⁴; *1* 2–8.
    James Read was indicted at Guildhall quarter sessions, 21 April 1707, for causing this work to be printed on 15 March. (Angell Carter was indicted for publishing it, 19 March.) 'Read's case' at the Queen's Bench is reported in John lord Fortescue, *Reports of select cases* (1748) 98f.; Read was found guilty of the publication, but the indictment quashed after legal argument. What is probably a provincial reprint was advertised in *The curiosity: or, gentlemen and ladies repository* (Lynn, 1740; copy at O).
'The woman marry'd is divinely blest'
    Madam B-----le was a noted bawd. For an answer, see *The maids vindication,* 1707.
L(1076.l.22/8); CLU-C.

F136 — The fifteen pleasures of a virgin. Written by the suppos'd author of the Fifteen plagues of a maidenhead. *London, printed in the year* 1709.
8⁰: *A*⁴; *1* 2–8 (5 as '6').
'In these unhappy and more wretched days'
    The fifteen plagues of a maiden-head claimed to be 'Written by Madam B-----le'; but that attribution to a noted bawd was clearly humorous.
L(1076.l.22/37).

Fifth

F137 Fifth. The fifth ode of the first book of Horace imitated. *London, printed for J. Webb, near St. Paul's,* 1745. (*DA* 31 Jan)
2⁰: *A*² B²; *1–3* 4–8. A1 hft.
    Listed in *GM, LM* Feb 1745.
'Prithee, dear D---, what statesman now'
    Against Thomas Pelham-Holles, duke of Newcastle.
L(1493.c.17/62, Tom's Coffee House, 31 Jan),O (lacks A²),LdU-B(uncut); CtY(−A1),OCU.

F138 — 'The fifth ode of the fourth book of Horace, apply'd to the king on his return from Hanover to Great Britain. [*London*] Printed for J. Roberts. Price 4d.' (*PB* 25 Oct 1720)
'King of the British isles, from heroes sprung!'

F139 —— The second edition. *London, printed for J. Roberts,* 1720. (*DP* 7 Nov)
2⁰: *A*² B¹; *1–3* 4–6.
MH(Luttrell, Oct).

— The fifth ode of the fourth book of Horace, imitated: and apply'd to the king, 1716. *See* Brereton, Jane.

— The fifth ode of the fourth book of Horace imitated: and inscrib'd to the king, 1714. *See* Needler, Henry.

F140 Fight. A fight and no fight, or the mock-duel in St. James's-park. *London, printed by A. Moore; sold by the booksellers of London and Westminster,* [1723.]
½⁰: 1 side, 2 columns.
    Rough cut (used in *Duke upon duke,* 1720, D503) at head.
'Two doughty ——s the other day'
    Ms. note in the MH copy, 'Lord Lechmere & Cadogan 1722'. A satire on a duel between them, probably in March 1722/3. Cf. *A ballad, wrote in the time of Queen Elizabeth,* [1723.]
L(1876.f.1/102); MH.

[**Finch, Anne,** *countess of Winchilsea.*] Miscellany poems, on several occasions. Written by a lady. *London, printed for John Barber; sold by John Morphew,* 1713.
8⁰: pp. 390. L.
    Watermark: star. E8, G1, 3 are usually cancels.

[—] [fine paper] L,Rothschild.
    Watermark: fleur-de-lys on shield.

[—] [variant imprint:] *London, printed for J.B.; sold by Benj. Tooke, William Taylor, & James Round,* 1713.
    L,O; DFo,MH.
    This is the normal issue, deposit copy at O; it was entered in *SR* to Barber by Morphew, 18 June.

Finch, A., *countess*

— [variant title] Written by the right honble Anne, countess of Winchilsea. *London, printed for J.B.; sold by Benj. Tooke, William Taylor, & James Round, 1713.*

L,LVA-D.

— [cancel title] *London, printed for J.B.; sold by Benj. Tooke, William Taylor, James Round, & John Morphew, 1713.*

CtY.

— [reissue] Poems on several occasions... *London, printed by J.B.; sold by W. Taylor, & Jonas Browne, 1714.*

LVA-D,OW; MH,TxU.

———

[—] Free-thinkers. A poem in dialogue, 1711. *See* F247.

F141 [—] The spleen, a pindarique ode. By a lady. Together with A prospect of death: a pindarique essay. *London printed, and sold by H. Hills, 1709.*
8°: A⁸; *1-2* 3-16.
'What art thou, spleen, which everything dost ape?'
> *The spleen* was published in Lady Winchilsea's *Miscellany poems,* 1713; *A prospect of death* is by Pomfret.

L(11644.bbb.16; G.18423/4),O(2),C,E,LdU-B+; CSmH,CtY,ICN,MH,TxU+.

F142 [—] The Tunbridge prodigy. *London, sold by A. Baldwin, 1706.* (DC 7 Nov)
½°: 1-2, 1 column.
'Protect our state, and let our Marlbro' thrive'
> Printed as Lady Winchilsea's by Thomas Birch in *A general dictionary, historical and critical,* 1734-41, from a manuscript in the possession of Lady Hertford.

MC,Rothschild.

F143 [—] — Written by a lady. *London printed, and sold by J. Morphew,* [1706.]
½°: 1-2, 1 column.
> On p. 2 'To the author of the Tunbridge prodigy'.

To the author: 'When tuneful ladies strike the trembling lyre'
L(1850.e.10/49).

Finis. Finis coronat opus. Septième et dernier dialogue entre deux freres, [1707.] *See* Dialogue entre deux freres, 1707.

F144 Fire. Fire and faggot, or; an ellegy on Dr. S---ch---ls two sermons, which were burnt on Monday the 27th of March, 1710. *London printed, and are to be sold by the booksellers of London & Westminster,* [1710.]
8°: A⁴; *1-3* 4-8. 8 advt.
'Oh cursed fate those sacred books are burnt'
> Suggests the ashes of Sacheverell's sermons should be preserved in a memorial.

C; ICN(cropt).

Fire

— Fire and faggot: or the Bishop of St. Asaph's bonfire, 1712. *See* An elegy on the burning of the church memorial, 1705– (E84).

— Fire and faggot or the city bonfire, 1705. *See* Pittis, William.

Fireside. The fire side: a pastoral soliloquy, [1746.] *See* Browne, Isaac Hawkins.

F145 Fireworks. The fire-works. A poem. In Miltonic verse. By a young gentleman of Trinity College. *Dublin, printed by Augustus Long, 1749.*
8°: A⁴ B⁴; *1-3* 4-14 *15-16* blk.
'In eastern courts (from Britain's gentler sway'
> The fireworks were at Stephen's Green, in celebration of the peace.

O(−B4).

First. The first epistle of the second book of Horace, imitated, 1737. *See* Pope, Alexander.

F146 — First oars to L--m--th; or, who strives for preferment. *London, printed for J. Thompson, in the Strand,* [1731.] (May)
½°: 1 side, 3 columns.
> *Percival* XXI. Large woodcut at head of text. No type flowers between columns.

'At L—m—th dwells as fame reports'
> On the contention of Edmund Gibson, Benjamin Hoadly and Lancelot Blackburne for the see of Canterbury on Wake's illness. Cf. *The mitre,* [1731.]

L(643.1.24/30); MH(ms. date, May 1731), Harding.

F147 — [another edition]
> Rows of type flowers between columns.

L(C.20.f.2/291; P&D 2867, cropt); MH,NNP.

— The first ode of the second book of Horace paraphras'd, 1714. *See* Swift, Jonathan.

F148 — 'The first ode of the third book of Horace. Inscrib'd to the Earl of Chesterfield. [*London*] *Sold by Jacob Robinson.* Price 6d.' (GM,LM Jan 1745)

F149 — The first of April: a blank poem, in commendation of the suppos'd author of a poem lately publish'd, call'd Ridotto, or downfal of masquerades. *London, printed for, and sold by J. Graves,* [1723.]
4°: a⁴ b²; *i-ii* iii-viii, 9-11 *12* blk.
> The collation is tentative. The poem is indeed blank; all that is printed is a dedication to 'No Body' on pp. iii-viii, and footnotes on pp. 9-11. Dated 1723 (doubtless 1 April) from the reference to *Ridotto,* published 4 March 1723.

PU.

— The first of April: a poem, [1723/24?] *See* Swift, Jonathan.

— The first of August, 1716–. *See* Nevil, Henry.

First

— The first satire of Juvenal imitated, 1740. *See* Gilbert, Thomas.

F150 — The first satire of the second book of Horace, imitated. *London, printed for M. Cooper, 1745.* (*GM* Oct)
2°: π² A–C²; *i–ii, 1–2* 3–14. π1 hft.
'Some think my satires (this is what I hear)'
    Early ms. attribution to Thomas Gilbert in the TxU copy, but not reprinted in his *Poems, 1747.*
L(1962),GM; ICU,TxU.

F151 **Fishery.** Fishery, a poem: or a letter to C.L. esq; *London, printed by J.M. [John Matthews?]; sold by J. Baker, 1714.* (*MC* Sept)
2°: A¹ B²; *i–ii, 1–4.*
    Engraving on title.
'The volume, sir, so kindly lent by you'
    Signed 'A.M.' *Morgan* Q430 (following Pickering & Chatto cat. 284/171) interprets the initials as Arthur Maynwaring to Charles Leslie; but Maynwaring died in 1712 and Leslie was in the Pretender's household by 1713. Encouraging the building of a large fishing fleet.
O(Luttrell, 16 Oct),*MR-C*; CSmH.

F152 **Fitchett, John.** The hero reviv'd; or, a poem on the glorious successes and victories obtain'd by the Duke of Marlborough at Bleinheim. *London, printed for John Barnes, 1705.* (*DC* 26 March)
2°: A(2 ll) B–C²; *1–4* 5–12.
    The two leaves of A are not conjugate; A2 is the dedication.
'As, when in antient times to mighty Jove'
DT; TxU(Luttrell, 27 March).

F153 **'Fitzcotton, Henry.'** A new, and accurate translation of the first book, of Homer's Iliad. By Henry Fitzcotton, esq; *Dublin, printed by George Faulkner, 1749.*
8°: A–F⁴ G²; [2] *i* ii–x xi–xiv, *1* 2–35 *36.* 36 advt. No watermark. *Bond* 202.
'Come, Clio, sing (if such your will is)'
    The author is clearly pseudonymous, possibly basing his name on Charles Cotton. A burlesque paraphrase, satirizing the lord lieutenant, William Stanhope, first earl of Harrington.
O,DA,DG(uncut),DN; DLC,MH.

F154 — [fine paper]
    Watermark: fleur-de-lys on shield.
DN; TxU.

F155 — — *Dublin printed: London reprinted for W. Owen, 1749.* (*GM,LM* March)
8°: A–E⁴; *i–iii* iv–x xi–xiv, *15* 16–40.
L(11315.c.11),DT; CtY,IU,TxU.

F156 [**Fitzgerald, —, *Mr.*]** Mendico-hymen seu,tuphlo-pero-gamia. The beggar's match. Translated from

Fitzgerald, —. Mendico-hymen

the Latin. *Dublin, printed by Tho. Hume, for Jer. & Sil. Pepyat, 1723.*
8°: A⁸; *1–3* 4–16.
'Say gentle Hymen, god of chaste delights'
    Dedicated to William Thompson, author of the Latin; a copy of the 1730 edition at DN has an early ms. note 'By Mr. Fitzgerald'. Of the several Fitzgeralds at Trinity College, Dublin, Shorthall Fitzgerald is perhaps the most probable candidate.
C,DA,DG; CtY.

F157 [—] — The second edition. *Dublin, printed for J. & S. Pepyat, 1723.*
8°: A⁸; *1–3* 4–16.
CLU-C,OCU.

F158 [—] — *London printed, and sold by J. Roberts, A. Dodd, & J. Billingsley, 1724.* (Feb, Luttrell)
8°: A² B–D⁴; *1–4* 5–27 *28 blk.* A1 hft.
    Listed in *MC* April.
L(11633.e.45/7),O,LdU-B; CtY,MH(Luttrell).

F159 [—] — *Dublin printed, and sold by George Faulkner, 1730.*
8°: A⁴ B–C⁴; *1–3* 4–23 *24.* 24 advt.
L(11631.a.34/2),O,C,DA(2),DN(2)+.

F160 [—] — By a gentleman of the university of Dublin. *Dublin, printed by and for M. Pepyat, 1734,*
8°: A–C⁴; *1–2* 3–23 *24 blk.*
O,DA.

Fitzgerald, Thomas. Poems on several occasions. *London, printed by J. Watts, 1733.* (*GSJ* 24 Sept)
8°: pp. 112.   L,O; CtY,MH.
    Errata slip at end of preliminaries in some copies; dedication signed.

— — The second edition. *London, printed by J. Watts, 1736.*
8°: pp. 112.   L,O; CLU,MB.

[—] Georgia, a poem. Tomo Chachi, an ode. A copy of verses on Mr. Oglethorpe's second voyage to Georgia, 1736. *See* G128.

[**F161** = **W245·5**] **Five.** Five pastoral eclogues, 1745. *See* Warton, Thomas, *the younger.*

'Flamingo.' A shorter and truer advertisement, 1727. *See* S453.

Flanders. The Flanders ballad, [1712/13.] *See* An excellent new song, call'd, The full tryal, [1712?]– (E579).

'Flash, Timothy.' A panegyrick on the reverend father John Baptist Girard, 1731. *See* P38.

F162 **Flavia.** Flavia to Fanny, an eipstle [!]. From a peerless poetess, to a peerless p—— in immortal dogrill. Occasioned by a late epistle from Fanny to her governess. *London, printed for T. Reynolds;*

sold by the booksellers of London & Westminster,
[1733/34.]
2°: *A*² B²; *1–3* 4–8.
'Dear sister, of the rhyming tribe'
As from Lady Mary Wortley Montagu to
John, lord Hervey, occasioned by his *An
epistle from a nobleman, 1733.*
MR-C; MH,TxU(2, 1 uncut).

F163 Fleming, Robert. Fame's mausoleum: a pindarick poem, with a monumental inscription,
sacred to the glorious memory of William the
great. Humbly offer'd as an essay. *London, printed
for Andrew Bell, 1702.*
8°: A–B⁸ C⁴ Dd²; *i–ii* iii–v *vi blk,* 7–37 *38–44.*
38–44 advt.
Signature B2 entirely under 'Birds'. The
order of editions has not been determined.
Issued with Fleming's *Practical discourse...
King William,* 1702, 1703; possibly not published separately.
'What, William dead! – Unthinking man forbear'
L(10806.b.5),E(–C4–Dd2).

F164 — — *London, printed for Andrew Bell, 1702.*
8°: A–B⁸ C⁴(–C4); *i–ii* iii–v *vi blk,* 7–37 *38.*
38 advt.
Signature B2 under 'Birds do'. The copy
seen may lack C4, Dd² of advertisements.
LdU-B.

F165 Flemyng, Malcolm. Neuropathia: sive, de mor-
bis hypochondriacis, et hystericis, libri tres, poema
medicum. Cui praemittitur dissertatio epistolaris
prosaica ejusdem argumenti. *Eboraci, excudebant
Cæsar Ward, et Ricardus Chandler, sumptibus
autoris, 1740.*
8°: π⁴(–π4) a–i⁴ k(2 ll) A–I⁴ K¹; [6] *i* ii–lxxiv
lxxv–lxxvi, 1–73 *74.* π1 hft; π3, k2 fly-titles; 74 err.
Watermark: fleur-de-lys. Possibly the fly-
title k2 was printed as π4, and k1 and K1
printed as a conjugate pair. Advertised in
GM,LM July 1741. Possibly the 'Proposals
for Latin poem' 1 sheet, 400 copies entered
to Ward & Chandler in Bowyer's ledgers
under 9 March 1738 are related to this work.
'Casta animi Pallas; puræ rationis amatrix'
O.

F166 — [fine paper]
Watermark: fleur-de-lys on shield. In one
copy at L, h3 is a cancel.
L(1190.i.1/1, ms. corrections; 78.e.7, presentation
copy to Joseph Smyth),YM; CtY-M.

F167 — — *Amstelaedami, apud Henricum Boussiere,
1741.*
8°: a–k⁴ A–I⁴ (a3 as 'a2'); [6] *i* ii–lxxiv, 1–72.
MH.

F168 Flight. A flight from Westminster. Norfolk in
tears, or the Tower in mourning, for the loss of a

Robin. '*Printed by Hugo de Burgo, for the company
of flying stationers*', [*c.* 1730?]
½°: 1 side, 2 columns.
Clearly a satire on Walpole. The date is
suggested by Pickering & Chatto, but a
reference to Walpole's imprisonment in the
Tower in 1712 could be intended.
(Pickering & Chatto cat. 269/12459.)

F169 — [dh] The flight of religious piety from Scotland,
upon the account of Ramsay's lewd books, &c.
and the hell-bred play-house comedians... [*Edinburgh,* 1736?]
8°: A⁸; *1–16.*
Three poems. On p. 9 'A looking-glass for
Allan Ramsay', and on p. 15 'The dying
words of Allan Ramsay'.
'When as Aurora did dispel'
Looking-glass: 'When god at first was Israel's king'
Dying words: 'Unhappy fate, and woful time'
Chalmers in his edition of Ramsay (1800)
suggested Alexander Pennecuik the younger
as author; but he died in 1730. An attack on
Allan Ramsay, who opened his playhouse in
1736 and closed it in 1737.
L(11631.aaa.56/12).

F170 — The flight of the Pretender, with advice to the
poets. A poem, in the Arthurical,-Jobical,-Eliza-
bethical style and phrase of the sublime poet
Maurus. *London, printed for Bernard Lintott,*
[1708.] (*DC* 28 April)
8°: A⁸; *i–vi,* 1–8 *9–10 blk.*
Bond 19. The watermark in the MH copy, a
small fleur-de-lys, has not been identified in
other copies; possibly that is on fine paper.
'Oh! thou Pretender stop thy swift career'
A parody of Blackmore's style. Cf. M140.
L(11631.e.32,–A8),OW,CT,E(–A8),DG+;
CLU-C,CSmH,DFo,MH,TxU+.

F171 — — *London printed, and sold by H. Hills, 1708.*
8°: π² A⁴; *i–iv,* 1–8.
L(1078.i.12/1),O,E,AdU,LdU-B+; CtY,DFo,
ICN,IU,OCU.

F172 Flint, George. The lunatick; or, great and
astonishing news from Bedlam. *London, printed for
the author; sold by the booksellers of London &
Westminster,* [1728.] (*MChr* 18 May)
8°: B–F⁴; *1–2* 3–40.
A prose work, but followed by 'A lunatick
paraphrase on the fable of Ulysses his men
transform'd to beasts' on pp. 18–40.
'To paths untrod our humour leads'
A satirical poem.
L(11643.bbb.23/2); *CSmH.*

F173 Flora. Flora triumphans. Wanstead garden. An
heroick poem most humbly addrest to the honourable Sir Richard Child, bar. *London, printed by
William Redmayne; sold by John Morphew, 1712*
[1713?]. (*PB* 17 Jan 1713)

Flora triumphans

  4⁰: *A*¹ B–E²; *1–2* 3–17 *18 blk.*
  'As wit some mighty product to essay'
  L(163.m.55, Luttrell, 21 Jan),O; MH,TxU.

F174 [**Floyd, Philip.**] Prosperity to Houghton... To the tune of, An ape, a lion, a fox and an ass, &c. [*London*, 1728/29?]
  ½⁰: 1 side, 1 column.
    Percival appendix 20.
  'Some bards of old times much delighted with sack'
    Floyd's authorship is revealed in a related poem, *Houghton hare-hunting*, [1729?]. In praise of Walpole's hospitality.
  L(1876.f.1/111),MC,Rothschild; MH,NN,Lewis Walpole Library (Horace Walpole's, ms. notes).

Flying. The flying general, 1715. *See* Burnet, *Sir* Thomas.

F175 **F——na.** F——na's answer to S——no's epistle. *London, printed for A. Moore,* 1727.
  2⁰: A⁴; *1–3* 4–8.
  'Base and ungrateful to my proffer'd love'
    From Faustina B. Hasse to the castrato Senesino, in answer to *An epistle from S——r S——o to S——a F——a,* 1727.
  L(11602.i.12/9).

Foedus. Fœdus spirituale. In usum extranei lectoris. A sacerdote in ecclesia anglicana. *Londini, prostant venales apud L. Stokoe,* 1713.
  2⁰: pp. 15.   O.
    A collection of Latin poems. The imprint is quoted from a cancel slip over the original.

Following. The following address, from the hundreds of Drury, [1718.] *See* 'Cibber, Colley'.

— The following fable is most humbly inscribed, 1725. *See* To the honourable Mr. D.T., 1725.

— The following humble address, 1727. *See* The saylors address, 1727.

— The following verses were composed by a pious clergyman in Virginia, [175–.] *See* Davies, Samuel.

F176 **Folly.** Folly. A poem. *London, printed for B. Barker; sold by J. Roberts,* 1727. (*MC* Feb)
  8⁰: A–C⁴; *i–ii* iii–v *vi,* 1–18. 18 advt.
  'Long with licentious pow'r and gen'ral sway'
  IU,TxU.

— Folly. A poem. Written by the author of the Female rake, 1737. *See* Dorman, Joseph.

— The folly of industry, 1704. *See* Wycherley, William.

— The folly of love, 1701. *See* Ames, Richard.

F177 — Folly triumphant; or, an humorous epilogue to the beaux of the town. [*London*] *Printed in the year* 1749.

Folly triumphant

  ½⁰: 1 side, 2 columns.
    Engraving at head.
  'Too long provok'd in these censorious times'
  L(P&D 3068).

  '**Foly**, *the rake.*' The geneology [!], a poem. Humbly inscrib'd to the Dutchess of Puddle-dock, by Foly the rake, 1726. *See* G99.

Fontenelle, Bernard de.
  [*Poésies pastorales*] Brereton, Thomas: Two town eclogues: in allusion to the ninth and part of the second of Fontenelle, [1717.] *In* B415.

F178 **Fontenoy.** Fontenoy, a new satiric ballad. To the tune of Bumpers 'Squire Jones. *London, printed for J. Collyer,* [1745.] (*GM* May)
  2⁰: A⁴; *1–8.*
    Horizontal chain-lines.
  'Ye brave Britons all,/Who rejoice to be told of your country's fame'
  L(C.57.g.7/11); DFo,MH,OCl.

F179 —— *Dublin, printed by Kinneir & Long,* 1745.
  8⁰: A⁴; *1–8.*
  DA.

F180 **Fools.** [dh] Fools have fortune: or, a guinea gave for an oyster. Being Gogmagog's confession. With an exact copy of the letter of license granted to the whimsical lawyer of Chancery-lane. Written by W.S. a brother of the quill. [col] *Printed for F. ⟨   ⟩ near Temple-Bar,* 1707.
  4⁰: A²; *1* 2–4.
  'Since true content doth such a treasure bring'
  L(11631.f.33).

Footman. The footman's friendly advice to his brethren of the livery, [1730.] *See* Dodsley, Robert [Servitude].

F181 **For.** ⟨   ⟩ for the death of Mr. Curtis the banker. [*Dublin*] *Printed in the year* 1727.
  ½⁰: 1 side, 2 columns.
  'Oh! Betty, Betty I'm undone'
    From the subject matter, the title might well be 'Miss ——'s lament for the death...'.
  DT(title cropt).

F182 — [dh] For the fifth of November, 1747. The fate of popes and tyrants; a tale, addressed to the good people of Great Britain, on the report of a second rebellion. [*London?* 1747.]
  2⁰: A²; *1* 2–4.
  'Never cry, popes and tyrants all go to the devil'
  TxU.

F183 **Forbes, Francis.** Suite de la satyre de Boileau sur la ville de Paris. Par Forbes. *A Edimbourg, de l'imprimerie de R. Fleming,* 1750 [1749?]. (*SM* Dec 1749)
  8⁰: (6 ll); *i–ii,* 1 2–10.

Forbes, F. Suite de la satyre

'Que veut dire ceci? quelle ville est la nôtre?'
L(11481.d.14).

[Forbes, John.] Epigrammata de quibusdam summis hujus seculi viris. *Londini, apud Tho. Smith,* 1737.
4⁰: pp. 20.   L,O.
    Signed on p. 20 'J.F.'
—— Auctore Johanne Forbes. *Londini,* 1739.
4⁰: pp. 8.   L,O.

F184 [Forbes, Robert.] Ajax his speech to the Grecian knabbs. From Ovid's Metam. lib. XIII... Attempted in broad Buchans. By R.F. gent. *[Edinburgh] Printed in the year* 1748.
12⁰: π^1 A–B⁴; *1–2* 3–17 *18 blk.*
    Bond 175.
'The wight an' doughty captains a''
    Attributed to Forbes by James Maidment in *Scotish ballads and songs* I. 215. Notes in Maidment's copy at E refer to a second edition of 1748 with Forbes's name given in full, but the edition of 1755 is still by 'R.F.'
L(11631.aaa.56/13),E(2, 1 uncut, 1 lacks π1); CSmH.

[Forbes, William.] Allan Ramsay metamorphosed to a hather-bloter poet, [1720?] *See* A164.

[—] Bang the brocker, or Bully Pierce alias A-----n the turncoat. A new song, [1705.] *See* B54.

[—] The Edinburgh cuckolds: or the history of horns, 1722. *See* E15.

F185 [—] An essay upon marriage in a letter adress'd to a friend. *[Edinburgh?* 1704.]
4⁰: A–C² D¹; *1–2* 3–13 *14 blk.*
    Title in half-title form.
'Dear friend,/'Tis talk'd which I scarce can think true'
    Early ms. attribution to Forbes in a copy at E. Answered by [Allan] *A satyre on F——s of D——r,* [1704.]
E(3); CSmH.

F186 [—] Mack-faux the mock-moralist or Pierce the traitor unmask'd and hang'd, a satyre on A——n the renegado. *[Edinburgh?] Printed in the year* 1705.
4⁰: A⁴; *1–4* 5–8.
'Lampoon'd and hiss'd, and damn'd the thousandth time'
    Early ms. attribution to Forbes in a copy at E. A reply to [Allan] *A curb for a coxcomb,* 1704, though an early hand in the GM copy notes 'Des Blair on Dan: Defoe'.
L(11626.c.44/1),E(4),GM; CSmH,CtY,IU.

F187 [—] The patriots, a satyr, written on the 12th of October, 1734. *[London] Printed for S. Berkley* [!], 1734.
8⁰: 12 ll, inc. last blank.
    The publisher is unknown; possibly an error of transcription for 'Buckley'.

Forbes, W. The patriots

    The evidence for Forbes's authorship is not known, and the date and place of publication (if it be London) suggest a doubt.
(*Dobell* 2901.)

F188 [—] A pil for pork-eaters: or, a Scots lancet for an English swelling. *Edinburgh, printed by James Watson,* 1705.
4⁰: A⁴ B² (A3 as 'A2'); *1–2* 3–12.
    No watermark.
'Heavens! are we such a servile nation grown'
    Attributed to Forbes in David Laing's *Various fugitive pieces of Scotish poetry,* [1825.] Also attributed to Alexander Pennecuick (d. 1730) but this attribution, which results from its being reprinted in his *A compleat collection,* [174–], was known to and rejected by Laing; the date is clearly too early.
L(1076.m.13; 1104.b.34/9, cropt),E(4),GM,*MR-C*; CtY(cropt).

F189 [—] [fine paper]
    Watermark: three circles.
E.

F190 [—] A pill for pork-eaters... *[Edinburgh] Printed [by James Watson] in the year* 1705.
4⁰: A⁴; *1* 2–8.
    P. 8 is printed in smaller type.
E; MH.

F191 [—] A pil for pork-eaters... To which is added the Englishman's grace over his pock pudding, with Robert the third's answer to Henry the fourth of England. *Edinburgh, printed in the year* 1705 [reprinted 173–?].
8⁰: A⁴ B⁴(B1+χ^2); *1–2* 3–10, *1–3 4 blk,* 1–6.
    The 'Englishman's grace' in χ^2 refers to King George, Walpole and war with Spain.
Englishman's grace: 'Joy of my heart, and comfort of my life'
Robert the third: 'During the reign of the royal Robert'
E.

F192 [—] The rattle-snake, or, a bastonado for a whig. *London, printed by Richard Gunning... Register'd in the Stamp-office, according to the act of parliament, and enter'd in the Hall-book,* 1712–13.
4⁰: (11 ll); *i–iv,* 1–17 *18 blk.* i hft.
    The collation is obscure. Not traced in *SR.*
'For which of all our gross enormous crimes'
    Early ms. attribution to Forbes in the E copy.
E.

F193 [—] [variant imprint:] *London, printed by Richard Gunning; sold by J. Morphew,* 1712–13.
TxU.

F194 [—] The renegado whip't. A satyre in answer to A----n's lybel on the author of the Essay on marriage. *[Edinburgh] Printed in the year* 1704.
4⁰: A⁴; *1–2* 3–8.
'If his abused case revenge doth crave'

Forbes, W. The renegado whipt

> Early ms. attributions to Forbes in copies at E,GM. A reply to [Allan] *A satyre on F——s of D——r,* [1704.]
>
> L(11643.h.26/1),E(3),GM; IU,TxU.

F195 [—] The true Scots genius, reviving. A poem. Written upon occasion of the resolve past in parliament, the 17th of July 1704. [*Edinburgh*] *Printed in the year* 1704.

4°: A⁴; *1–3* 4–8.

'Rous'd from a lethargy of hundred years'

> A tentative attribution to William Forbes in the hand of Alexander Gardyne (before 1885) in a copy at E has a later pencil note 'It *is* by Forbes'. No evidence has been adduced, and the attribution should be received with caution.
>
> L(11631.b.66; 11632.cc.20; 11622.bb.1/2),E(4), *GM*; CtY,NjP.

F196 [—] Xantippe, or the scolding wife, done from the Conjugium of Erasmus, by W.F. of D. *Edinburgh, printed in the year* 1724.

4°: *A*(3 ll) B–D⁴; *i–ii,* 1–27 *28 blk.*

'Now welcome, dear Xantippe, prithee tell'

> The author intended is clearly Forbes of Disblair, but it may not be by him; there are illegible ms. alterations to the statement of authorship in the copy at E.
>
> E,GM.

Ford, Simon.
Silvester, Tipping: Piscatio. Or, angling. A poem. Written originally in Latin by S. Ford... Translated from the Musæ Anglicanæ, 1733. *See* S464–5.

Foreign. The foreign address, 1735. *See* Young, Edward.

F197 Forger. The forger's doom: or, John Currie's last speech. [*Edinburgh,* 1728.]

½°: 1 side, 2 columns.

'I find I was a fool to mock the laws'

> He was scourged 3 April 1728, exposed at the Tron, and banished.
>
> E.

Forgiving. The forgiving husband, and adulterous wife, 1709. *See* Ward, Edward.

Former. The former, present, and future state of the church of England, 1715. *See* Stacy, Edmund [The picture of a church militant].

F198 [**Forrest, Theodosius.**] The roast beef of Old England. A cantata. [*London,* 1749/–.]

½°: 1 side, 3 columns.

> Engraving after Hogarth at head. The original print was advertised in *GA* 8 March 1749. According to R. E. Moore, *Hogarth's literary relationships* (1948) 61n, probably published in 1749; a later date seems more probable.

Forrest, T. The roast beef

> Reprinted for R. Withy [175–] and for Robert Sayer [176–].

''Twas at the gates of Calais, Hogarth tells'

> For Forrest's authorship, see Nichols & Steevens, *Genuine works of Hogarth* (1808) I. 147–8.
>
> L(P&D 3053).

F199 Forsaken. The forsaken fair. An epistle from Calista in her late illness at Bath, to Lothario on his approaching nuptials. *London, printed for B. Dickinson,* 1736.

2°: *A*¹ B–D² E¹; *i–ii,* 1 2–14.

> Copies at NN, TxU have an engraved frontispiece which is possibly original.

'Forgive dear faithless youth my errors past'

> Anne Vane to Frederick prince of Wales.
>
> L(11602.i.17/4),BaP; CSmH,CtY,MH,NN, TxU +.

— The forsaken lover's letter to his former sweetheart, [1722.] *See* Gent, Thomas.

Fortescue, James. Essays moral and miscellaneous. *Oxford, printed for W. Owen, M. Cooper, & R. Baldwin,* [*London,*] 1754.

8°. L,O; CtY,ICU.

> A nonce collection.

F200 [—] An epistle with some odes on love, virtue, and other subjects. *London, printed for S. Birt,* 1746. (*SR* 7 April)

4°: *A*² B–H²; *1–2* 3–31 *32 blk.*

> The odes begin on p. 12. Entered to Birt in SR; deposit copies at E,EU,AdU, and probably L,O. Listed in *LM* April.

'Cloe, I can, with half an eye'

> Listed by Fortescue in *Rawlinson,* as 'Printed for Cooper in 1746'.
>
> L(644.k.16/5),O,E,EU,AdU +; IU,OCU.

F201 [—] The expedition: a poem, on the duke's going to Flanders. *London, printed for M. Cooper,* 1747. (*GM,LM* Feb)

2°: *A*² B–C² D¹; *1–3* 4–13 *14 blk.*

'Let others sing the hero bold, as great'

> Listed as his by Fortescue in *Rawlinson;* advertised in Fortescue's *A view of life,* 1749. In praise of William Augustus, duke of Cumberland.
>
> O,OA; CtY,MH.

F202 [—] Nature, a poem. Tending to shew, that every part in the moral world is, in a beautiful variety, regularly ordered and adjusted... With a particular view to the inequalities of life... With some reflections on the late, and present times. *London, printed for M. Cooper; sold by J. Fletcher, in Oxford,* 1747. (*GM,LM* Sept)

4°: *A*⁴(–A4) B–C⁴ D¹; [2] *i–ii* iii–iv, *5* 6–22. A1 hft.

Fortescue, J. Nature

Drop-head titles, 'Nature'; 'Part the second'; 'Essay the second'. A copy at O adds a fourth section, headed 'Part the second', collating a² E–G²; *i–iv*, 23–34, and prefaced by a dedicatory poem 'To a lady'.
'Few of themselves, of nature all complain'
Advertised (as in five parts) in Fortescue's *A view of life*, 1749.
L(11630.c.1/20; 11631.g.30/7; 11630.e.18/2, lacks D1),O(2, 1 – A1).

F203 [—] Nature a poem; being an attempt towards a vindication of providence, in the seemingly most exceptionable things of the natural world. *London, printed for M. Cooper; sold by J. Fletcher, in Oxford,* 1748.
4°: *A*⁴ B–C⁴; [2] *i–ii* iii–v *vi*, 7 8–22. A1 hft.
A continuation of the preceding. Vertical chain-lines.
'Look through all nature, this one maxim's plain'
O(–A1); CtY,*OCU*.

[—] A poetical essay on the equal distribution of happiness among mankind, [1746.] *See* P704.

F204 [—] Science: an epistle on it's decline and revival. With a particular view to the seats of learning, and a virtuous, philosophical life. *Oxford, printed for J. Fletcher; sold by M. Cooper & W. Owen in London, and J. Leake at Bath,* 1750. (*GM* April)
4°: *A*² B–E⁴ F²; *i–ii* iii–iv, 1–36.
Also issued in Fortescue's *Essays*, 1754, despite its octavo format; that issue normally bears Fortescue's name on the title. The two issues are not distinguished here. Pagination and signatures are continued by *An essay on sacred harmony*, 1753.
'From gloomy horrors, big with black despair'
L(11631.b.52),O(2),C,DrU; CtY,*DFo*,ICU,IU.

F205 [—] A view of life in its several passions. With a preliminary discourse on moral writing. *London, printed for M. Cooper; sold by W. Owen; J. Fletcher at Oxford; and J. Leake at Bath,* 1749. (*LM* Oct)
8°: A–C⁴; *i–ii* iii–vii *viii*, 9–23 *24 blk*. 23 advt.
Title in red and black. Reissued in Fortescue's *Essays*, 1754.
'Of man, his progress, and his end'
L(11631.b.52/2),O,C,E,LdU-B; CtY,*DFo*,ICU, IEN,IU.

Fortunate. The fortunate complaint, 1709. *See* Pomfret, John.

F206 Fortune. Fortune not blind: a serenade to be represented on the birth-day of...George...king of Great Britain, &c. at the castle of Dublin, the 28th of May, 1715... Set by Mr. John Sigismond Cousser... *Dublin, printed by Daniel Tompson,* 1715.
4°: A⁴; *1–2* 3–8.
'Awake, desponding fair one!'
L(1960).

Fortune

— Fortune's bounty, [1705.] *See* Ward, Edward.

F207 Forty-one. Forty-one. [*London?* 1719.]
slip: 1 side, 1 column.
The last word of the first line over-runs. Printed with *A pastoral letter*, [1719]; the O copy is not divided.
'When on us heav'n show'r'd blessings down'
A Jacobite attack on dissenters.
O; CSmH.

F208 — [another edition]
The first line does not over-run. Printed with *A pastoral letter*, [1719]; the L copy is not divided.
L(1876.f.1/83).

F209 — Forty one in miniature: an elegiack poem. Inscrib'd to the honourable Matthew Prior, esq; *London, printed in the year* 1711.
4°: *A*² B–D²; *1–2* 3–15 *16 blk*.
'Prepare, my muse, the wond'ring world to tell'
On the death of General Daniel Parke in Antigua.
O; CSmH,OCU.

F210 Foster, R. The restauration. A poem. *London, printed for E. Berington, & J. Morphew,* 1718.
2°: *A*² B–C²; *i–iv*, 1–8.
'When first the pow'r eternal brought to light'
DrU; TxU.

F211 Four. Four hudibrastick canto's, being|Poems on four the greatest heroes | That liv'd in any age since Nero's, | Don Juan Howlet, Hudibras | Dicko-banes and Bonniface. *London, printed for J. Roberts,* 1715. (21 May, Luttrell)
8°: A–D⁴ E²; *1–3* 4–36.
Bond 42. Listed in *MC* May.
'In W——d a while ago/Was rara s——t and rara show'
L(1959),CT,AdU; CSmH,CtY,MH,OCU(Luttrell),TxU(2)+.

[**F212** = H20·5] — Four odes. I. On sleep. II. On beauty..., 1750. *See* Hamilton, William Gerard.

— Four satires: translated from the Latin, into English verse, 1743. *See* Major, William.

F213 — Four satires. Viz. I. On national vices... II. On writers... III. On quacks... IV. On religious disputes... *London, printed for T. Cooper,* 1737 [1736]. (*GM,LM* Nov)
8°:a⁴ A⁴(–A1) B–G⁴ H²; *i–iii* iv–viii, 3 4–59 *60 blk*. 59 err.
'Tho' with Herculean toil a wit'
O(2),C,CT; CtY,*DFo*,IU,OCU.

Fournier, A. G. The glory of France. Avis a Monsieur de *** premier peintre de sa majesté [signed 'A. G. Fournier']... Advice to the French king's chief painter, 1747. *See* G184.

Fourteenth. The fourteenth chapter of Isaiah in English verse, [1706.] *See* A paraphrase on the fourteenth chapter, [1706.]

Fourth. The fourth book of Virgil's Æneid. In four cantos, with notes, [1739.] *See* Theobald, John.

F214 — The fourth ode of the fourth book of Horace, imitated and applied to his royal highness the Duke of Cumberland. *London printed, Armagh re-printed by William Dickie, in the year* 1746.
2°: *A–B²; 1–2 3–8.*
The London edition has not been traced.
'As that imperial bird employ'd by Jove'
L(11602.i.14/8),C(uncut).

— A fourth riddle, 1726. *See* Delany, Patrick.

F215 — The fourth satire of the first book of Horace, imitated. Address'd to Alexander Pope esq; *London, printed for J. Roberts,* 1733. (*LaM* June)
2°: *A² B–F²* (D1 as 'E', E1 as 'E2'); *1–5 6–23 24 blk.*
'In virtue's cause our old comedians wrote'
In defence of Pope's satires.
O,OW; CSmH,TxU.

[**Fowke, Martha.**] The epistles of Clio and Strephon, being a collection of letters that passed between an English lady, and an English gentleman in France... *London, printed for J. Hooke, F. Gyles, & W. Boreham,* 1720. (*PB* 26 March)
8°: pp. lxviii, 131.   L,O; TxU.
The title is a cancel. Letters in prose and verse between Martha Fowke and William Bond, edited by John Porter.

[—] [another cancel title, undated]
L,O; CtY,MH.

[—] — The second edition. *London, printed for J. Hooke,* 1729 [1728]. (*MC* Nov)
12°: pp. xxiv, 176.   L,LdU-B; NcD.

[—] [reissue] The platonic lovers: consisting of original letters in prose and verse... The third edition, corrected. *London, printed for John Wilford, & Richard Chandler,* 1732.
12°: pp. xxiv, 176.   L,LdU-B; CtY,ICN.
Cancel title, G3, I3–4; two leaves of contents added. Ackers's ledger under 15 April 1732 records 'printing 1500 of a half sheet of the Platonic Lovers' for Wilford.

———

[—] Epistles and poems by Clio and Strephon. With the Parson's daughter, a tale. The third edition. *London, printed for E. Curll,* 1729 [1728].
12°: pp. 36.   ICU,KU.
An unauthorized collection.

— [reissue] Clio and Strephon: being, the second and last part of the Platonic lovers... By William Bond...and Mrs Martha Fowke... *London, printed for E. Curll,* 1732.
MH.

[**Fowler, John.**] The last guinea; a poem, 1720–. *See* L51.

F216 — On the queens most glorious victories over the French king. [*and*] On the happy situation of the British isle. [*London,* 1707?]
2°: *A¹ B²; 1–5; 6 blk.*
Two conjugate half-sheet poems, each printed on the recto, preceded by a dedication leaf 'To the queen's most excellent majesty, and to the right honourable the lords commissioners for the union of both kingdoms', signed 'John Fowler'. The dedication leaf is not always found with the poems, which have sometimes been separated.
'The Macedonian youth, whose mighty name'
'Bless'd British isle, by heavens propitious hand'
LLP(dedication separated from poems), Crawford (*On the happy situation* only); CtY,MH(*On the happy situation* only),OCU(no dedication),TxU (*On the queens* only).

[F217–18 = P461·5–6]

[F219 = H80] **Fox.** The fox, a fryar, 1719. *See* Harris, Timothy.

— The fox and monkey, [1740.] *See* Gibbons, Thomas.

F220 — The fox in mourning, for the loss of his tail. [*London?* 1740?]
slip: 1 side, 1 column.
Percival appendix 89. Rough woodcut at head.
'A sly and crafty fox B—b tail'd'
Percival suggests this is in praise of Sir Humphrey Parsons's election as lord mayor of London, contrary to Walpole's wishes.
C.

— The fox set to watch the geese, 1705. *See* Browne, Joseph.

— The fox unkenell'd: or, the sham memorial, [1710.] *See* Pittis, William.

F221 — The fox unkennel'd; or, the whiggs idol. By a young nobleman of the university of Oxford. *London, printed by J. Benson, in the Strand,* [1715.]
½°: 1 side, 2 columns.
Wing F2032, in error. On the other side of the O copy, *The lord chancellor's speech in council,* in prose.
'If men are deem'd for loyalty'
Attacking Marlborough in contrast to the Duke of Ormonde.
L(Lutt.II.83),O.

Fox, John. Motto's of the Wanderers; in Latin and English: several of which are paraphras'd in heroick verse. By the author of the Wanderer. *London, printed by H. Meere,* 1718 [1717].
8°: pp. 37.   L; IU,MH.
Apparently intended to be bound with *The wanderer,* and usually so found; they were advertised together in *DC* 11 Nov 1717. The

Fox, J.

dedication copy at MH to Mr. Byrd contains a letter of protest from him; in other copies the dedication is cancelled.

F222 [—] The publick spirit; a poem. [*London*] *Printed in the year* 1718 [1717]. (Nov?)
8°: A² B–D⁴; *i–iv*, *1–24*. iv err.
> Usually found bound with Fox's *The wanderer*; it is mentioned on the title of that collection, which was advertised in *DC* 11 Nov 1717.

'I who, e'er while, unequal numbers chose'
> A panegyric on Sir Francis Nicholson.

L(245.k.15); IU,MH,NNC.

[Fox, Stephen, lord Ilchester.] The rival lap dog and the tale, 1730. *See* R214.

[Fox, Susannah.] The fidler's fling at roguery, 1730–. *See* F117.

[—] The rival lap dog and the tale, 1730. *See* R214.

Foxton, Thomas. Moral songs composed for the use of children. *London, printed for Richard Ford,* 1728. (*SR* 14 March)
12°: pp. x, 58.   L,O.
> Deposit copy at O.

— — *London, printed for Richard Ford,* 1737.
12°: pp. 57.   David McKell Library, Chilicothe, Ohio.
> *CBEL* II. 556 records a fourth edition as c.1745. At Richard Ford's trade sale, 14 Nov 1738 (cat. at O-JJ) the copyright formed lot 27 and was sold (with 470 books) to Richard Hett for £10; the assignment from Catherine Ford is listed in Dobell cat. 66 (1941) 45. Hett assigned a quarter share to Aaron Ward at the same time (Dobell 66/46). Another quarter share formed part of lot 26 in Hett's sale, 9 May 1745 (cat. at O-JJ).

F223 — Jesina: or, delusive gold. A pastoral. Lamenting the misfortunes of a lady of quality, ruined by South-Sea stock. *London, printed for E. Curll,* 1721 [1720]. (Dec?)
8°: A¹ B⁴ C⁴(−C4); *i–ii*, *1 2–13 14 blk.*
> The copy at KU has two Curll catalogues at the end of four leaves each, one of poems and one of divinity: their presence suggests that this is not an imperfect copy of the following, but an earlier issue. The advertisement in *PB* 29 Dec includes 'The czar' as in the following.

'The chearful morn adorn'd each purple cloud'
LdU-B; KU.

F224 — [reissue] *London, printed for E. Curll,* 1721 [1720]. (*PB* 29 Dec)

Foxton, T. Jesina

8°: A¹ B⁴ C⁴(−C4) D⁴; *i–ii*, *1 2–22.*
> The added D⁴ has fly-title D1 'The czar. A poem. Inscribed to Sir John Norris, upon his return from the Baltick. By Mr. Hastings'. Copies seen have Curll's catalogue of poems at end, signed A⁴.

The czar: 'Norris, renown'd for actions good and great'
L(1972),E; CLU-C,DFo,MH(lacks B2.3).

F225 — The night-piece. A poem. *London, printed for W. Hinchliffe,* 1719.
8°: A–D⁴; *i–ii iii–viii*, *1 2–22 23–24 blk.*
> Advertised in *PB* 14 Jan 1720 as printed for J. Roberts.

'From lonely vaults can blooming landskips rise'
> Dedication signed.

L(1959,−D4),LDW(−D4),O; ICU.

F226 — A poetical paraphrase on the universal hymn of praise to the creator, entitled Benedicite. [*London*] *Printed for J. Pemberton,* 1727.
8°: A–B⁴ C²; *1–2 3–20.*
'O all ye works of the almighty king!'
> Dedication signed.

L(1959),O.

F227 — The tower. A poem. *London, printed in the year* 1727 [1726]. (20 Aug)
12°: A–D⁶; [4] *i ii–vi*, *1 2–34 35–38*. A1 frt; D5–6 advt.
> Publication date from *Straus, Curll*; listed in *MC* Aug as printed for H. Curll. Foxton's receipt for a guinea 'and several books' from Curll in payment for the copyright is at L (Add. MS. 38728, fol. 102).

'When beauty shines with a triumphant air'
L(11630.aa; 11626.aaa.18,−A1, D5–6),O(in contemporary morocco),LdU-B; ICN,KU,MH(−D5–6).

F228 Fra. Fra Cipolla. A tale. In Boccace. Translated from the original manuscript, with notes historical, critical and moral. *London, printed for T. Read,* 1737. (*GM,LM* Feb)
2°: A² B–E²; *1–5 6–19 20 blk.* 19 err.
> No watermark; 'Price One Shilling.' on title.

'Boccace, the scourge of wicked monk'
> Apparently a free version of the tenth story of the sixth day of the *Decameron*.

CSmH.

F229 — [fine paper]
> Watermark: fleur-de-lys; no price on title.

L(11630.h.9).

F230 — [*idem*] The popish impostor: a narrative. Faithfully translated from the original manuscript. Setting forth the frauds and artifices of the Romish clergy, to impose upon the laity. With explanatory notes. By a country curate. *London, printed for T. Cooper; sold at the pamphlet-shops in London & Westminster,* [1740.] (19 Nov)
2°: A² B–E²; *1–3 4–19 20 blk.*

Fra Cipolla

Basically the same text as the preceding, with revisions and omissions. Copy from Tom's Coffee House in the Lewis Walpole Library dated 19 Nov; listed in *GM, LM* Nov.
'Boccace, the scourge of lech'rous monk'
L(1484.m.22); MH,OCU.

F230·2 — The popish impostor: a narrative very proper to be read in protestant families of all denominations. *London, printed for M. Cooper, 1748.* (*GM* May)
8⁰: π¹ A–C⁴ D¹; [2] *i–ii* iii–vii *viii blk, 9–25 26 blk.*
MR.

Francis, Philip. The odes, epodes, and Carmen seculare of Horace. In Latin and English. With critical notes... *London, printed for A. Millar, 1743.* (*GM* Jan)
8⁰: 2 vol.   L,O; CtY,NjP.

— The satires of Horace. In Latin and English. With critical notes... Vol. III. *London, printed for A. Millar, 1746.* (*GM* Jan)
8⁰: pp. xvi, 349.   L,O; ICN,NjP.

— The epistles and Art of poetry of Horace. In Latin and English. With critical notes... Vol. IV. *London, printed for A. Millar, 1746.* (*GM* Jan)
8⁰: pp. 313.   L,O; ICN,NjP.

— A poetical translation of the works of Horace... The second edition. *London, printed for A. Millar, 1747.*
12⁰: 4 vol.   L,O; IU,NjP.
This is the title of vol. 1; the other volumes have the same individual titles as above.

—— The third edition. *London, printed for A. Millar, 1749.*
4⁰: 2 vol.   O; MH,NjP.
The copy at NjP is 'the gift of the ingenious translator'.

—— The fourth edition, revised and corrected. *London, printed for A. Millar, 1750 [1749].* (*LM* Nov)
12⁰: 4 vol.   O; ICU,NjP.
The volumes have individual titles like the second edition; vol. 4 is 'the third edition' with imprint dated 1749.

'**Franciscus**, *Cornigerus*.' The adventure of the bee and the spider. A tale... From the Latin of Franciscus Cornigerus, 1722. *See* A65.

'**Frank**.' The fidler's fling at roguery, 1734. *See* F118.

F231 **Fraser, Peter.** Iniquity display'd: or, the happy deliverance. A poem. Humbly inscrib'd to the right honourable the Lord Finch. *London, printed for the author, 1729.* (April, Luttrell)
2⁰: A⁴ (A3 as 'B'); *1–4 5–8.*
The relationship and order of issues is obscure; that with the imprint of J. Roberts was listed in *MChr* 7 April.

Fraser, P. Iniquity display'd

'Like the unhappy Israelites distress'd'
Dedication signed from the Fleet Prison, 30 March 1729. Thanking Lord Finch for his intervention in the rogueries and villanies of the prison.
L(1484.m.24),O; CLU,CtY,MH(Luttrell).

F232 — [variant imprint:] *London printed, and sold by T. Read, and by the booksellers of London & Westminster, 1729.*
Possibly a new impression.
OW; TxU.

F233 — [variant imprint:] *London, printed for J. Roberts, and sold by the booksellers of London & Westminster, 1729.* (*MChr* 7 April)
E.

F234 **Frederick.** Frederick and Augusta. An ode. By one of the people called quakers. *London, printed for J. Roberts, & Tho. Payne, 1736.* (*GM, LM* June)
4⁰: A–B⁴; *1–2 3–15 16 blk.*
'Hail Britannia, queen of isles'
Congratulations on the Prince of Wales's marriage.
O; MH,*MWA*.

Free. The free masons, 1723. *See* F244.

— Free thoughts upon faith, 1746. *See* Hill, Aaron.

Free, John. Poems, and miscellaneous pieces formerly written by John Free... *London, printed by W. Bowyer for the author, 1751.*
8⁰: pp. 165.   L,O; MH.
Entered to Free in Bowyer's ledgers under 15 Feb 1751; 500 copies printed, with a dedication quarter-sheet entered separately.

————

F235 [—] Advice to the fair-sex. A poem translated from the Greek of Naumachius. *London, printed in the year 1736.*
2⁰: A² B–C²; *1–2 3–11 12 blk.*
With the Greek text.
'Happy the maid, whose body pure and chaste'
Collected in Free's *Poems*, 1751.
L(11626.h.11/3),LdU-B.

F236 — The guardian: an imitation of Horace, ode V. book IV humbly addressed to his royal highness the Duke of Cumberland, upon his defeat of the rebel army in Scotland. *London, printed for R. Dodsley; sold by M. Cooper, 1746.* (*GA* 30 April)
2⁰: A⁴; *1–2 3–8.*
'Oh! at a lucky hour for Britain born'
AdU; CSmH,MiU.

F237 — Stigand: or, the antigallican. A poem, in Miltonic verse. *London, printed for Marshall Sheepey, 1750.* (*LM* Dec)
4⁰: A² B–E² F¹; *i–iv, 1 2–16 17–18.* F1 advt.
Vertical chain-lines.
'Untinsel'd be this verse, nor tagg'd with rhime'

Free, J. Stigand

L(1465.i.12/9; 11630.c.8/19, lacks E–F); ICU
(–F1),MH,*NN*.

F238 [—] The story of Susanna: a poem. *London,
printed in the year* 1730.
8°: A–B⁴ C²; *1–3* 4–20.
　　Ms. corrections in most copies change the
first line to 'Sublimer themes to epic...'
'Sublime themes do to epic strains belong'
　　Early ms. ascription to Free in the MH copy;
reprinted in his *Poems,* 1751.
CT; CSmH,MH,OCU.

F239 Freeholder. The freeholder. An excellent new
ballad, tune, King John and the abbot. [*London?*
1741.]
½°: *1–2,* 1 column.
'You gallant freeholders, now lend us a hand'
　　Crum Y257: 'A song for the general election'.
O-JJ.

F240 — — [*London?* 1741.]
½°: 1 side, 1 column.
OCU.

F241 Freeman. The freeman's litany. *Dublin, printed
in the year* 1749.
½°: 1 side, 2 columns.
'From villainy dress'd in the doublet of zeal'
　　Cf. *Crum* F788: 'A new litanie', printed 1656.
Two stanzas (including the first) are the same
as *A litany for lent,* 1714.
CtY.

F242 [**Freeman, Byam.**] Southampton; a poem. In-
scrib'd to a lady. By a gentleman of Oriel-College,
Oxford. *Oxford, printed by Leon. Lichfield, for
William Hayes,* 1748.
4°: *A*⁴ B⁴(–B4); *1–4* 5–14. A1 hft.
'As some faint new-born plant which scarce
sustains'
　　Ascribed to Freeman by *Rawlinson.*
CtY.

F243 Freeman, Isaac. Æsop at St. James's. By Isaac
Freeman, esq; *London, printed for the author; sold
by A. Dodd, E. Nutt, & A. Smith, and most booksellers in London & Westminster,* 1729. (*MChr*
9 Jan)
2°: A–B²; *1–2* 3–8.
'Æsop, a keen satyrick name'
　　'Isaac Freeman' is probably a pseudonym.
L(840.m.1/4); KU,MH,TxU.

F244 Freemasons. The free masons; an hudibrastick
poem... With their laws, ordinances, signs,
marks... and the manner of their installation
particularly describ'd. By a free mason. *London,
printed for A. Moore,* 1723. (*DP* 15 Feb)
8°: A–C⁴; *1–2* 3–24.
'All kingdoms have their mason-free'

The freemasons

　　The poem claims to reveal the secrets of the
masons, with much sexual detail.
O.

F245 — — The second edition. *London, printed for
A. Moore,* 1723. (*DP* 18 Feb)
8°: A–C⁴; *1–2* 3–24.
　　Probably a reimpression or a press-variant
title.
L(164.1.25, Luttrell, Feb).

F246 — — The third edition. *London, printed for A.
Moore,* 1723.
8°: A–C⁴; *1–2* 3–24.
　　Probably a reimpression or a press-variant
title.
C.

F247 Freethinkers. Free-thinkers. A poem in dialogue.
*London printed, and sold by the booksellers of London
& Westminster,* 1711. (7 March, Luttrell)
8°: A–C⁴ D² (D1 as 'C'); *1–2* 3–28.
　　Bond 28.
'Friend! if I'm late, excuse the failing'
　　Tentatively ascribed to Anne Finch, countess
of Winchilsea by *Halkett & Laing* and by
CBEL; early ms. attribution 'By Lady
Whinchesea' in a copy in the possession of
W. Rees-Mogg (now at NN-B). The attribu-
tion remains doubtful; not included in her
poems or mss.
L(164.1.19,Luttrell),C;DFo,MH,NN,OCU,TxU.

[**Freind, John.**] The devil and the doctor... By
Doctor Byfielde, 1719. *See* M80.

F248 [**Freke, John.**] The history of insipids, a lampoon,
by the Lord Roch—r. With his Farewell. 1680.
Together with Marvil's ghost. By Mr. Ayloff.
London printed, and sold by H. Hills, 1709.
8°: A⁸; *1–2* 3–16.
　　Pattern of 14 type-flowers on title-page.
'Chaste, pious, prudent, C—— the second'
Farewell: 'Tir'd with the noysome follies of the
age'
Marvil's ghost: 'From the dark Stygian lake I
come'
　　The author intended is Rochester, but John
Freke was the true author. A warrant was
issued 12 May 1676 against him for dispersing
this libel; see F. H. Ellis in *PQ* 44 (1965) 472f.
L(11631.aaa.38),O,CT,E,DrU+; CLU-C,CtY,
ICN,MH(2),TxU+.

F249 [—] [another edition]
　　Pattern of 6 type-flowers on title-page.
Reissued with other remaindered Hills poems
in *A collection of the best English poetry,* 1717
(*Case* 294).
L(C.124.b.7/32),LVA-F,DrU,WcC; CtY,ICU,
MH.

F250 — A poem on the safe arrival of the Spanish
monarch, Charles III. to the British shoar. With

Freke, J. A poem on the safe arrival

Great Britains wishes for his prosperous voyage to his royal throne. *Sold by the booksellers of London & Westminster,* 1704. (21 March, Luttrell)
½⁰: 2 sides, 1 column.
'Arise, behold the royal fleet, whose name'
L(C.121.g.9/141, Luttrell).

F251 French. The French invasion. To the tune of, Prety parrot say, &c. *London, printed in the year* 1708.
½⁰: 1 side, 2 columns.
'Have you heard of late,/How affairs of state'
    On Abigail Masham's communications with Harley.
DT; CSmH.

F252 — [dh] The French king distracted; or his sad lamentation, for the late defeat of his forces in Bavaria, by the Duke of Marlebrough... [col] *London, printed for C. Green,* 1704.
4⁰: *A*²; *1* 2–4.
'What must I do alas? I am undone!'
TxU.

F253 — The French king's advice to the late high-flying m--b-rs. To the tune of Lillibullero. [*London*] 1705. (*DC* 26 April)
½⁰: 1 side, 2 columns.
'Well play'd, my dear friends, (for the catholick cause)'
    A satire against the high church tories.
O,Crawford,*Longleat*; CSmH.

F254 — — [*London?* 1705.]
½⁰: 1–2, 1 column.
Rothschild.

F255 — The French king's lamentation for the miscarriage of Monsieur Guiscard. Being a new song, to an excellent new tune, sung at the opera theatre in Covent-garden. [*London*] *Printed in the year* 1711.
½⁰: 1 side, 2 columns.
'When Lewis the great/Had heard of the fate'
    A whig song.
O,Crawford; InU.

F256 — The French king's rhodomontade... Rochester's prophetick answer... [1706.]
½⁰: 2 sides, 1 column.
    The L copy is bound with Dublin half-sheets, but is possibly of London origin.
'Thus Rochester's song,/Which he prophecy'd long'
    In praise of Marlborough.
L(C.121.g.8/3); MH.

F257 — The French marshal catch'd in a trap. A new ballad, to the tune of A cobler there was, &c. *London, printed for J. Collyer, & Mr. Chapelle; sold at the pamphlet-shops of London & Westminster,* 1745. (*GM* Feb)
2⁰: *A*² *B*¹; *1–2* 3–5 *6 blk.*

The **French** marshal

'Ye Britons, delighted attend to my theme'
    Crum Y12.
MC; CSmH.

— The French pedlar, [1713.] *See* The pedlar, [1713.]

F258 — The French preliminaries. A new ballad to the old tune of Packingtons pound. '*Amsterdam*' [*London*], *printed in the year* 1712.
½⁰: 1 side, 2 columns.
'All you that have stock, and are mad for a peace'
    A whig attack on peace negotiations.
L(112.f.44/37),LLP,DT,Crawford; MH-BA,NN.

F259 — [another edition, title reads:]... Packington's pound.
Rothschild; MH,TxU.

F260 — The French prophet's resurrection: with his speech to the multitude that behold the miracle. *London printed, and sold by J. Morphew,* 1708. (May?)
½⁰: 1–2, 1 column.
'From the cold grave, where kings and prophets sleep'
    The 'French prophet' was Thomas Emes, whose resurrection on 25 May 1708 was prophesied by John Lacy.
DG.

F261 — French sincerity exemplified in the surrender of Dunkirk to her Britannick majesty Queen Anne. Interspers'd with a medley of whigg loyalty and low ch--h moderation. Compil'd to expose the moderate faction, by an arch anti-whigg. [*London?* 1712?]
½⁰: 1 side, 2 columns.
    Rough woodcut of ship at head.
'Now Dunkirk's surrendred no room's left to fear'
    Tory verses.
L(1850.e.10/11; C.121.g.9/163); *Harding.*

F262 — The French tyrant, or the royal slave. A poem containing the most remarkable occurences of his reign, with his character; maxims; his dream of hell, and Mazarin's ghost. *London, printed for J. Nutt,* 1702. (5 Feb, Luttrell)
2⁰: *A*² *B–G*²; *1–2* 3–28.
''Twas in the solemn silence of the night'
    On Louis XIV.
LG,DK,*LdU-B*; InU(Luttrell).

F263 Frenchman. The French-man letter to his friend in England. Tune of the Rare-show, &c. [*London?* 1741.]
slip: 1 side, 1 column.
    Rough woodcut at head.
'Se de great and mighty war'
    An attack on Walpole and English naval incompetence.
C.

F264 — The Frenchman's lamentation for the loss of the Earl of Gallway. [*Dublin?*] *Printed in the year* 1716–17.

The **Frenchman's** lamentation

$\frac{1}{2}$°: 1 side, 1 column.
'Ye pow'rs who watch o'er sublunary things'
Addressed to Henri de Massue de Ruvigny, earl of Galway, possibly on his retirement from Ireland.
MH.

F265 Freshman. The fresh-man's entry into the university, a satyr... By a bachelor in the college. *Dublin, 'printed by Timothy Telltruth', 1736.*
8°: A^8; *1–2* 3–16.
'From school and mamma a coxcomb I came'
A satire on Trinity College, Dublin.
DA.

Fribbleriad. The Fribbleriad, 'MDCCXLI'.
The date is a misprint for MDCCLXI, which is so printed in some copies.

F266 Friend. A friend in need is a friend in deed: or, a project, at this critical juncture, to gain the nation a hundred thousand pounds per annum from the Dutch; by an Irish whale fishery. Inscrib'd to Arthur Dobbs esq;... *Dublin, printed in the year 1737.*
8°: A^4; *1–2* 3–8.
'Nor songs, nor tales of love delight the muse'
Attributed to James Sterling by the catalogue of RPJCB, probably on account of his *An epistle to the Hon. Arthur Dobbs, 1752.* The attribution is unconfirmed.
DG,DN; *RPJCB.*

F267 Friendly. A friendly admonition to all persons of the Romish persuasion in Ireland, being a 2d extract from Reasons tribunal. *Armagh, printed in the year 1745.*
$\frac{1}{2}$°: 2 sides, 1 column.
'O say, when William from Bovinda's flood'
Reason's tribunal was published in Dublin, 1735.
C.

F268 — Friendly advice to a child unborn. A little piece of poetry, with very long notes. By a person of learning, as you may see by the motto. *London, printed for M. Cooper, [1750.]* (*BM* March)
2°: A^2 B–C^2; *1–2* 3–11 *12 blk.*
'O thou that art the lord alone knows what'
MR; IU,MH.

F269 — A friendly epistle to the author of the State dunces. *London, printed for E. Nutt & E. Cooke; sold at the pamphlet-shops of London & Westminster, 1733.* (*GSJ* 22 June)
2°: A^2 B^2 C^1; *1–2* 3–10.
'Whoe'er thou art, who, without grace of god'
Quoted in an article in *Fog's Weekly Journal* 20 July 1734 as from the 'Friendly Epistle by Mr. M——ll'; Joseph Mitchell is clearly implied, but there is nothing to confirm the attribution. *The state dunces* is by Paul Whitehead.

A **friendly** epistle

L(11602.i.16/3),LSC,O(3),LdU-B,WcC(uncut)+; CtY,ICU(uncut),MH,NjP,OCU.

F270 Friendship. Friendship and love. A dialogue. Addressed to a young lady... To which is added, a song by Mr. Akinside... *London, printed for G. Steidel; sold by M. Cooper, 1745.* (*GM,LM* Jan)
2°: A^2 B^2; *1–2* 3–8.
The Tom's Coffee House date in the L copy is cropt, possibly Jan 16.
'In vain thy lawless fires contend with mine'
Song: 'The shape alone let others prize'
The song is well known as Akenside's; 'Friendship and love' is probably by another hand.
L(1962).

— The friendship of Christ, 1718. *See* Cheyn, William.

Frisky. The frisky muse. Humbly dedicated to the choice spirits of the age. By Rigdum Funnidos, their ballad-master in ordinary, and composer extraordinary. *London printed, and sold by the author, 1749.*
8°: pp. 56.   L(impft).
By one author, except for a contribution from a friend. A perfect copy was offered in Pickering & Chatto cat. 259/2872.

F271 From. From Cæsario to Hamilla an answer. *London, printed for M. Cooper, 1745.* (*LM* July)
2°: A^2 < B^2; *1–2* 3–7 *8 blk.*
''Tis even so, the false Hamilla's gone'
From Frederick, prince of Wales, to Lady Archibald Hamilton; in answer to *The discarded fair-one, 1745.*
L(1962),LdU-B; ICN.

F272 — From Pope Benedict XIV. to Lewis XV. of France. A burlesque poem. *London, printed for R. Lee, 1744.* (*GM, LM* June)
8°: A^1[= G_1] B–F^4 G^4(– G_1); *i–ii, 1* 2–46.
Also advertised in *DA* 12 Jan 1745.
'To Lewis, my most Christian son'
CtY,OCU.

— From W.T. in the Marshalsea, 1716. *See* Tunstall, William.

F273 [Froud, John.] Daphnis: or, a pastoral elegy upon the unfortunate and much-lamented death of Mr. Thomas Creech. The second edition, corrected. *London, printed for John Deeve, 1701.*
2°: π^2 A–C^2 (C_1 as 'D'); *i–iv, 1–12. π_1 hft; 12* advt.
First published 1700 (*Wing* D240). This is a reimpression.
'The rosie morning with prevailing light'
Froud's authorship is deduced from *The grove*, 1701 'by the author of a Pastoral elegy...'
L(1489.m.6, uncut),O; IU.

Froud, J. Daphnis

F274 [—] — With a poem on the despairing lover, and the despairing shepherd. *London printed, and sold by H. Hills*, 1709.
8°: A⁸; *1–2* 3–16.
    Reissued with other remaindered Hills poems in *A collection of the best English poetry*, 1717 (*Case* 294).
L(C.124.b.7/11),O,E,AdU; CSmH,CtY,IU,MH, TxU+.

F275 [—] The grove: or, the rival muses. A poem. By the author of a Pastoral elegy on the death of Mr. Creech. *London, printed for John Deeve*, 1701. (*PM* 15 March)
2°: *A*² B–E²; *i–iv*, 1–16. 16 advt.
    The Luttrell copy, dated 15 March, is recorded in *Haslewood*.
'Divine Thalia! charmer of my breast'
    A copy at ICU with ms. corrections has the dedication signed in ms. Elizabeth Thomas's copy at BlU is annotated and some lines attributed to a Mrs. Field. Wrongly ascribed to Oldmixon by P. B. Anderson in *PQ* 11 (1932) 406.
LDW,O(2),*BlU*; *DFo*,ICN,ICU(uncut),IU,MH.

F276 — Musa gratulatrix or a congratulatory poem to her majesty, on her coming to the Bath. *Bristol, printed for the author, and are to be sold by W. Bonny*, 1703.
2°: *A–B*² C²; *i–iv*, 1–7 8 blk.
'As when the queen of gods and wife of Jove'
LdU-B.

F277 — [dh] A prologue at the opening of the theatre in Bristol. Written by Mr. John Froud, and spoken by Mr. Geo. Powel. [*Bristol*, 1705.]
4°: A²; *1* 2–4.
    On p. 3 'The epilogue...spoken by Jacobella Power'.
'When pompous luxury and lazy pride'
'For fear our play and prologue both should fail'
DG.

F278 **Frowd, R.** A poem on Prince Eugene's victory over the Duke of Orleans. Humbly inscribed to the commissioners chosen for managing the 250000*l.* remitted to Prince Eugene... *London, printed for Isaac Cleave*, 1706. (20 Nov, Luttrell)
2°: *A*² B²; *1–2* 3–8.
'At length old time brings forth th' important hour'
TxU(Luttrell).

Frowde, Philip.
[*Cursus glacialis*] [Newcomb, Thomas:] Scating: a poem. By Mr. Addison [!] [Latin text, with English translation by Newcomb], 1720. *See* N270.

F279 — Verses on her majesty's birth-day. *London, printed for J. Watts*, 1728. (*MChr* 29 Feb)
2°: A¹ χ¹ B² C¹; *i–iv*, *1* 2–6. A1 hft.
    The half-title, signed 'A', has been seen to be conjugate with C1; the title-page is on the added leaf χ1.

Frowde, P. Verses
'Rise sweet, Aurora, rise; propitious morn'
O(−A1); CSmH(uncut),CtY(lacks χ1),MH (−A1),TxU(2, 1 uncut).

Fry, John. Select poems, containing religious epistles, &c. occasionally written on various subjects... *London printed, and sold by Mary Hinde*, 1774.
8°: pp. viii, 83.   L,O.

———————

F280 [—] An essay on conduct and education. By J.F. *London printed, and sold by the assigns of J. Sowle*, 1738.
8°: A–E⁴; *i–ii* iii–iv, 5–40.
'Whoe're attempts men's morals to reclaim'
    Ms. note in the L copy, 'By my grandfather John Fry Sutton Benjar Wiltshire'.
L(11645.ee.44/3),LF(2); *PHC*.

F281 [—] — Recommended to the people called quakers, by J. F... The second edition, with an addition of a postscript... *London printed, and sold by T. Sowle Raylton & Luke Hinde*, 1741.
8°: A⁴ B–E⁴; *i–ii* iii–iv, 5–40.
    Signed from Sutton Benjar, '11th of 2d month' (11 April).
L(11645.ee.44/4),LF(2); IU,*PHC*.

F282 **Full.** A full and ample explanation, of one King James's declaration. *Dublin, re-printed in the year* 1716.
½°: 1 side, 2 columns.
'With all the charms of France and Rome'
    An anti-Jacobite satire.
MH.

F283 — A full and true account of a curious dialogue between one Mr. D'Anvers, and one Mr. Cut, a great tobacco-merchant; and one Mr. Dash, a rich vintner... *London, printed for J. Roberts*, 1733. (*GM, LM* Feb)
2°: *A*² B²; *1–3* 4–8.
'Have you heard the report,/Quoth D'Anvers, at court'
    On the excise bill.
OW; MH,NN-A,NNC(uncut).

F284 — A full and true account of a dreadful fire that lately broke out in the Pope's breeches. *London printed, and sold by J. Baker*, 1713.
2°: *A*² B¹; *1–2* 3–6.
'The town and nation know Camilla'
    A bawdy tale of how Catherine Tofts the opera singer (subsequently wife of Joseph Smith) gave Pope Clement XI the clap.
L(C.131.h.1/5); MH,TxU.

— A full and true account of an horrid and barbarous robbery, 1728. *See* Byrom, John.

— A full and true account of the ghost of Sir J....h J...l, [1743.] *See* Williams, *Sir* Charles Hanbury (W510).

Full

F285 — Full moon. A new city ballad. Occasion'd by the late election of members of parliament for the city of London. Tune, To you fair ladies, &c. [*London*, 1741.]
½°: 1 side, 2 columns.
'To you sad wights of Crown and Fleece'
OCU.

F286 **Funeral.** A funeral apotheosis on the Tribunes, which departed this life from time to time, as they were publish'd. *Dublin, printed in the year 1729–30.*
½°: 1 side, 2 columns.
    Williams 1133.
'To what a dull and dismal pass'
    Ball 207 suggested Swift's authorship, which was suspected at the time of publication; but Williams considers it unlikely. A satire on James Arbuckle's periodical *The tribune* (ascribed in *CBEL* II. 663 to Delany).
L(1890.e.5/14),DT.

F287 — Funeral discipline; or, the character of Strip-Corps the dead-monger. Written according to the instructions of Paul Meagre, once mourner in chief to the funeral undertaker. *London printed, and are to be sold by the booksellers of London & Westminster*, 1701. (22 Dec, Luttrell)
2°: *A*² B–C²; *i–ii*, 1–10.
'Paul Meagre, you thin-gutted whelp, what a pox-is'
L(643.l.24/21),LG; CLU-C,InU(Luttrell),MH, TxU.

F288 —— *London, printed for J. Roberts, & A. Dodd*, 1725 [1724]. (*MC* Dec)
2°: A–C²; *1–3* 4–12.
MH.

F289 — A funeral elegy on the ever to be lamented deaths of Mr. Richard Johnson and Mr, John Porter; who were both unfortunately hang'd and quarter'd on Saturday the 12th of this instant December 1730. For the murder of Patrick Murphy, the 21st. of October last. [*Dublin*, 1730.]
½°: 1 side, 1 column.
    Mourning borders.
'Nature demands it from us all'
    The first half of the text is substantially the same as *An elegy on...Mr. George Curtis*, [1727.]
DT.

F290 — A funeral elegy on the father of his country, the rev. Dr. Jonathan Sw⟨ift,⟩ dean of St. Patrick's Dublin, who departed this life, at ⟨the⟩ deanery house Kev. street. On Saturday the 19th inst. Octob. ⟨1745.⟩ By J——n N——n. [*Dublin*, 1745.]
1°: 1 side, 2 columns.
    Woodcut borders.
'The royal harp, unstrung must ever lye'
DN(title mutilated, imprint cropt).

F291 — A funeral elegy on the much lamented death of Jacob Peppard esq, a member of parliament, and

A **funeral** elegy on...Jacob Peppard

clerk of the Tholsel, who died the 17th of this inst. March 172⁴⁄₅. *Dublin, printed by C.C.* [*Cornelius Carter*], [1725.]
½°: 1 side, 1 column.
    Mourning headpiece and borders.
'Where is your mourning Tholsel, where is your sable hue'
L(11602.i.1/9).

F292 — A funeral elegy on the much lamented death of John Farquarson, esq; consort to the rt. hon. the Lady Mountjoy, who departed this life, April, 3d. 1733. [*Dublin*, 1733.]
½°: 1 side, 1 column.
'Almighty tyrant death whose pow'rfull sting'
C.

F293 — A funeral elegy, on the much lamented death of Sir Samuel Cooke kt. who departed this life on Sunday the 28th of this inst. August. 1726. *Dublin, printed by C.C.* [*Cornelius Carter*], [1726.]
½°: 1 side, 2 columns.
    Mourning headpiece and borders.
'As lowring lights forebode unwelcome news'
DT.

F294 — A funeral elegy on the much lamented death of the honourable Countess of Antrim. who departed this life, at her late dwelling house in Dawson-street on Friday March the 18th. 1736–7. [*Dublin*, 1737.]
½°: 1 side, 2 columns.
    Woodcut borders.
'Come hither you who the fair sex reproach'
Crawford.

— Funeral hymns, [1746]–. *See* Wesley, John & Charles.

F295 — The funeral of faction. [*London*] *Printed for T. Cooper*, 1741. (*LDP* 1 April)
obl 1°: 1 side, 3 columns.
    Large engraving above text, dated 26 March.
    After imprint, 'Price Six-Pence.'
'God prosper long our noble king'
    A satire on the failure of Samuel Sandys's motion to dismiss Walpole.
O,O-JJ; MH.

F296 — [another edition]
    After imprint, '(Price Six-pence.)'.
L(P&D 2487); NNP.

F297 — The funeral of the low-church: or, the whigs last will and testament. [*Dublin?* 1711.]
½°: 1 side, 2 columns.
    Mourning headpiece encircling funeral ticket for 16 June 1711.
'What! is the parliament dissolv'd at last?'
    A tory satire. Cf. *The funeral-ticket of Mr. Hypocrite Low-church*, 1711.
DT.

A funeral poem

— A funeral poem, humbly offer'd to the pious memory of... Mr. Saml Pomfret, [1722.] *See* Lodge, Edward.

F298 — [dh] A funeral poem, inscrib'd to the memory of J..n B....y, author of The fair quakers, &c. [*London*? 1715.]
2°: A²; *1–4*.
    Also printed in the reissue of John Bingley, *The fair quaker*, 1715.
'No longer muse, no longer take thy flights'
    On the death of John Bingley.
O.

F299 — A funeral poem occasion'd by the re-interment of the sculls of five of those noble martyrs, who suffered for the truth at Edinburgh...now accidently dug up, and decently buried in the Gray-friers church-yard, October the 19th 1726. [*Edinburgh*, 1726.]
½°: 1 side, 1 column.
'When for our fathers sins, by angry heaven'
MH.

F300 — 'A funeral poem, on the death of the honourable Sir Cloudesly Shovel, vice admiral of Great Britain, &c. [*London*] *Sold by Mary Edwards.* Price 1*d*.' (*PB* 23 Dec 1707)
    Probably a half-sheet, judging from the price.

— A funeral poem on the death of the right honourable William Conolly, 1729. *See* Sterling, James.

F301 — A funeral poem; sacred to the memory of the late Earl of Lincoln. *London, printed for W. Meadows,* 1728. (*MChr* 11 Oct)
2°: *A²* B–C² D¹; *1–5* 6–13 *14 blk*.
'Transient, and vain is fickle fortune's smile'
IU.

F302 — A funeral poem, sacred to the memory of the most noble John Churchill, duke and earl of Marlborough... Humbly presented to Sir Hans Sloan, bart. *London, printed for the author,* 1722.
8°: A⁸(±A2); *1–4* 5–14 *15–16*. A1 hft.
    Probably issued with variant cancel title-leaves with alternative dedicatees. A8 not seen.
'Death, that the fort of life had long assail'd'
    Ascribed to Amhurst in error by L; probably by the author of *A divine poem on the creation,* 1718, who may have been Henry Nevil. The L copy was originally bound with his *On the nativity,* 1717.
L(11631.e.11,−A8).

[**F303** = S265]

F304 — A funeral poem upon the much lamented death of Lieutenant-general Wood, who departed

A funeral poem upon...Wood

this life at his house at Kensington the 17th of May, 1712. Humbly address'd to her majesty. Written by a female. A.H. *London printed, and sold by John Morphew,* 1712. (30 June, Luttrell)
4°: *A⁴*; *1–4* 5–8.
'What noise is this? Sure 'tis Wood's dismal knell'
L(162.1.39, Luttrell),LLP; DFo.

F305 — A funeral satyr in memory of the worthy treatment of the late Mr. Anthony Bowyer, of Camberwell. By a friend to Dr. Sacheverell's club. *London, printed in the year* 1709.
4°: A⁴ B²; *1–2* 3–12.
'Let him that would his doubting thoughts convince'
L(1077.k.24/4).

F306 — A funeral tear, to the blessed memory of the reverend Mr. Daniel Wilcox, late minister of the gospel. Who departed this life April the 11th. 1733. In the 57th year of his age. [*London*? 1733.]
1°: 1 side, 2 columns.
    Mourning headpiece and borders.
'What mournful scene is this which doth appear?'
LDW.

F307 — The funeral-ticket of Mr. Hypocrite Lowchurch, who gave up the ghost on the anniversary of the restoration of King Charles II. May the 29th, 1711. *London, printed in the year* 1711.
½°: 1 side, 2 columns.
    Mourning headpiece encircling funeral ticket for 'the 12th instant'.
'Alas, the very man, whose life we sought'
    A tory satire. Cf. *The funeral of the low-church,* [1711.]
LLP.

'Funnidos, Rigdum.' The frisky muse, 1749. *See* Frisky.

F308 Fustiad. The Fustiad; or, cudgel-match. A poem. In two books. *Yeovil, printed for the author, by R. Goadby and Comp.,* 1747. (*GM,LM* Dec)
4°: π² A–D⁴ E²; *i–iv,* 1–35 *36.* 35 advt.
    Book I only; p. 35 announces Book II if this succeeds. The catalogue of the Bibliothèque publique, Nantes, records a copy as '1748'. Listed in *GM* as published in London by Owen, later associated with Goadby.
'Arms and the man I sing, who gain'd renown'
CU.

Fy. Fy gar rub her o'er wi' strae, [172–.] *See* Ramsay, Allan.

Fyge, Sarah. *See* Egerton, Sarah Fyge.

G

G., *Colonel.* A new song, to the tune of To you, fair ladies, now at land, [1740/41.] *See* N219.

G., A., *gent.* The rake reform'd, 1718. *See* Glanvill, Abraham.

G., C. Threnodia virginea, 1708. *See* T261.

G., C.P. Truth and moderation, 1741. *See* T537.

G., D. Satyrae quatuor, 1735. *See* S39.

G., G., *of S.* A facetious poem in imitation of the Cherry and slae, 1701. *See* F22.

G., H. Poems on several occasions, 1748. *See* Poems.

G., H., *L. Mag.* The eagle and the robin, 1709. *See* E2.

G., J., *C.S.* An elegy on the death of that great peer...George Hamilton, earl of Orkney, [1737.] *See* E205.

G., N. Magdalen-grove, [1714.] *See* M14.

G., N.F. The answer. *In* The whiggish fair warning, 1711.

G., N.F., *gent.* The doctor militant, [1710.] *See* D354.

— Poor England bob'd, 1712. *See* P754.

— The triumph of monarchy, [1710.] *See* T500.

G., R. The beauties of the universe, 1732. *See* B131.

— An elegy on the much lamented death of the Rev. Charles Proby, [1727.] *See* E222.

G., T. Expeditio militaris Addisoniana...Latine reddidit, T.G., 1708-. *See* E603.

G., T., *M.D. in Suffolk.* A congratulatory poem upon his most sacred majesty, 1719. *See* C363.

G., T., *physician in Essex.* Scipio Britannicus: the scourge of France, 1709. *See* S137·5.

G., U., *gent.* An epithalamium...on the marriage of Robert Rochfort, 1737. *See* Gahagan, Usher.

— Palæmon, 1730. *See* Gahagan, Usher.

G1 Gagnier, John. Carolina. Ecloga in diem natalem Willielminæ Carolinæ, serenissimæ principis Walliæ... Auctore Johanne Gagnier, A.M. *Londini, typis J. Watts, apud P. Du-Noyer,* 1719. (*PM* 5 May)
4°: A–D⁴; *i–viii, 1* 2–24. viii err.

No watermark; 'Pret. 1*s.*' on title. Dedication in French, signed 'Jean Gagnier'.
'Thyrsis adest, Melibœe; venit quoque ab urbe Menalcas'
O; CtY.

G2 — [fine paper]
Watermark: fleur-de-lys; no price on title.
L(161.n.23).

G3 [Gahagan, Usher.] An epithalamium, or poem, on the marriage of Robert Rochfort...to the honourable Mrs. Mary Molesworth... By U. G. gent. *Dublin, printed by J. Gowan,* 1737.
8°: A⁸; *1–3* 4–16.
'Hark! o'er Hesperian Midia's plains around'
Authorship deduced from the unusual initials.
DA.

G4 — Mr. Pope's Temple of fame. And his Messiah ...translated into Latin. With the English prefix'd to each poem... By Usher Gahagan. Done since his confinement... *London, printed for B. Dickinson,* 1748 [1749]. (*GM,LM* Feb)
8°: A–K⁴ L²; *i–ii* iii–vii *viii, 1* 2–72 '59 68 62' 76 *blk.* viii err.
Griffith 634. English and Latin texts. Dedication dated from Newgate, 16 Feb 1749; Gahagan was hanged for coining 20 Feb 1749.
'Molle id tempus erat, crebris quo lapsibus imbres'
'Pangite, quæ Solymam colitis, jam carmina, musæ'
L(11602.ee.1/5),LG,O,C,AdU; CSmH,ICN,IU, MH.

G5 [—] Palæmon; or, a pastoral in imitation of Mr. Pope's first pastoral. Inscribed to the Reverend D---n S------t. By U. G. gent. [*Dublin*] *Printed in the year* 1730.
8°: A⁴; *1–3* 4–8.
'Here will I first invoke the sylvan muse'
Authorship from the unusual initials; inscribed to Swift.
DT,*MR-C.*

G6 — Tentamen de re critica. Anglice prius celeberrimo Alexandro Pope, Latine nunc emittente Ushero Gahagan... *Londini, prostant apud M. Cooper, apud J. Hinton, et passim apud bibliopolas. Anno* 1747.
8°: π² a–b ⁴B–M⁴; [4] *i* ii–xv *xvi blk,* 1–88. π2ᵛ err.
Latin text only. Listed in *GM* Jan 1749.
'Num, male scribendo, censendone, proditur artis'
L(11633.df.2),O,AdU; IU,TxU.

G7 Gale, Oliver. Oliver Gales, speech to his illustrious excellency John, lord Carteret, lord lieutenant general, and general governor of Ireland. As it was spoken by himself on the stage at the theatre, on Monday night, the 4th, inst. March, 1727–8. Before most of our nobility, and gentry. [*Dublin,* 1728.]
½°: 1 side, 2 columns.

Gale, O. Oliver Gale's speech

'Since you, my lord, our glorious vice-roy reign'
O; CtY.

'Gall, Monakey.' Miss Gall's letter to a certain
c-o-l-l beau, 1728. *See* M281.

Galloper. The galloper, 1710. *See* Ward, Edward.

Gallus, Gaius Cornelius.
The impotent lover describ'd in six elegies on old-
age. In imitation of Cornelius Gallus, 1718. *See*
I14.

[Gambol, Robert.] The beauties of the universe.
A poem. By a gentleman of the navy, 1732. *See* B131.

Game. The game of put, 1737. *See* Bancks, John.

G8 Gamester. The gamster prosecuted: or, poor Billy
in a peck of troubles. [London] Printed in the year
1705.
½°: 1 side, 1 column.
    On the other side, *His grace the Duke of
    Marlborough's welcome*, [1705.]
'What! Billy, still alive, who thought to meet'
Crawford.

G9 Garbott, William. New-River, a poem. *London,
printed for the author; sold by J. Hooke*, [1728.]
(*MChr* 10 May)
8°: *A*⁴ B–E⁴ 'E'⁴; *i–viii*, 1–38 *39–40 blk*. A1 hft.
'Destructive wars some may delight to sing'
    In praise of Sir Hugh Middleton's con-
    struction of the New River.
L(11643.b.30, −A1, E4),O.

G10 Garden. The garden plot. *London, printed in the
year* 1709.
½°: 1–2; 1 column.
'When Naboth's vineyard look'd so fine'
    Crum W1327. Added to the works of William
    King, the gazetteer, in Johnson's *Poets*, prob-
    ably by John Nichols on the evidence of a ms.
    note in the LLP copy which was known to
    him. The attributions in this volume are
    erroneous (cf. *The eagle and the robin*, 1709),
    and King's authorship is doubtful. For an attri-
    bution to Swift, see *Williams* 1082.
LLP, Chatsworth, Crawford.

Gardener. The gardener's congratulatory poem,
1734. *See* Bramston, James.

[Gardiner, —, Mr.] Britannia's precaution to her
sons, [1741.] *See* B470.

[—] The Hibernian politicians; an epistle from a
gentleman in the country, to his friend in town,
1740. *See* H175.

[—] Seventeen hundred and thirty-nine. Or, the
modern p---s, 1739. *See* S354.

Gardiner, —.

[—] The squib. An epistle from a gentleman in the
country to his friend in town, 1743. *See* S667.

G10·5 [Gardiner, E., *Mrs*.] A poem occasion'd by the late
thanksgiving. By a lady. *London, printed for R.
Burrough, & J. Baker*, 1707. (7 March, Luttrell)
2°: *A*² B–C²; *1–2 3–12*.
    The Luttrell copy is in the collection of R. D.
    Horn.
'Could woman's pen attain to Dryden's wit'
    A manuscript version at Blenheim Palace has a
    preface to the Duchess of Marlborough signed
    'E. Gardiner'.
CtY,DFo.

G11 Gardiner, James. Rapin of gardens. A Latin
poem. In four books. English'd by Mr. Gardiner.
London, printed by W. Bowyer, for Bernard Lintott,
[1706.] (18 July?)
8°: A⁸ a⁸ b⁴ B–N⁸ O⁴ (+4 plates); *i–xl*, 1–195
196–200 (119 as '116'). A1 frt; 196–200 advt.
    Watermark: grapes. Advertised in *DC* 16 July
    for publication on 'Thursday' [18 July].
'What with new charms the flow'ry race improves'
L(1213.1.34),EU,DT,AdU; *CSmH*,CtY,MH(2),
OCU,TxU+.

G12 — [fine paper]
    Watermark: fleur-de-lys.
LVA-D.

G13 — — The second edition, revised and finish'd.
London, printed by W. Bowyer, for Bernard Lintot,
[1718.] (*PM* 17 May)
8°: A⁸ a–b⁸ c⁴ B–O⁸ (+4 plates); *i–lvi*, *1* 2–199 '100'
201–208. A1 frt; c4 advt.
    Watermark: initial I or T. Entered to Lintot in
    Bowyer's ledgers under 8 April, 500 copies
    and 25 large paper with margins opened. The
    delay before publication may have been due to
    the plates and binding. Revised text.
'What culture best the flow'ry race improves'
L(237.h.10, −c4),LVA-D,AdU(presentation copy),
LdU-B; *CtY*,DFo(−c4),*IU,MB*,TxU+.

G13·5 — [fine paper]
    Watermark: Strasburg bend.
LVA-D; ICU.

G14 — — The third edition, revised and finish'd.
London, printed for Bernard Lintot, 1728. (*MChr* 14
March)
8°: A⁸ a–b⁸ c⁴ B–O⁸ P⁴; *i–iv v–liii liv blk*, 1–200
201–210. A1 frt; P4 advt.
    The plates to each book are printed on c4, F1,
    I1, L5; they are excluded from the pagination.
    Most copies have an additional folding plate
    before p. 1.
L(11403.b.3, −A1),LVA-D(−A1),O,OW,LdU-B
(−A1); *CtY*,NN(−A1),*NjP*.

G15 Garland. A garland for a fraudulent bankrupts
brow or a panegyrick on Robert Cowan's trip to the
Tron, who should have been exposed there, with

A **garland** for a fraudulent bankrupt

his ditty on his breast, Wednesday 22d, January 1724, by sentence of the senators of the college of justice, for defrauding his creditors of vast sums. [*Edinburgh*, 1724.] (Jan)
½°: 1 side, 2 columns.
'What moonshine or trade-wind hath blown thee here'
A ms. note in a copy at E records that he was exposed on 29 Jan.
E(2, 1 cropt).

[**Garrick, David.**] Prologue and epilogue, spoken at the opening of the theatre in Drury-lane [the epilogue by Garrick], 1747. *See* J85.

G16 Garter. The garter: a poem on the six lords made knights-companions of the noble order of the Garter. *London, printed for John Morphew*, 1712. (*PB* 20 Nov)
2°: π¹ A²; *1–3* 4–6.
'I sing not chiefs associated of old'
L(11630.g.19/1),O(Luttrell, 21 Nov),*O-JJ*; CtY.

G17 [**Garth,** *Sir* **Samuel.**] An appeal to the people of Great Britain, on the report of a new conspiracy. [*London?* 1716?]
½°: 1 side, 1 column.
'Where, where, degen'rate country-men – how high'
Reprinted with Garth's poems in *The works of celebrated authors*, 1750, with title 'On the new conspiracy, 1716'; one of the attributions there is erroneous, and this should be received with caution. Against the Jacobites.
O,E(2).

G18 [—] Claremont. Address'd to the right honourable the Earl of Clare. *London, printed for J. Tonson*, 1715. (5 May, Luttrell)
2°: *A² B–E² F¹*; *i–iv, 1–17 18 blk.*
Watermark: HT. Entered in *SR* 7 April, possibly before publication; deposit copies at L,LSC,O,EU,AdU,SaU. Listed in *MC* May.
'What frenzy has of late possess'd the brain'
Early ms. attribution to Garth in the MH copy of the fine-paper issue.
L(643.m.13/8; 163.n.43),LSC,O(3),EU,DT+; CLU-C,CSmH,CtY,CtY-M(Luttrell),TxU(2, 1 uncut).

G19 [—] [fine paper]
Watermark: fleur-de-lys.
LVA-F,LdU-B; IU,MH,NjP(2).

G20 [—] — With remarks and annotations variorum. *London, printed for J. Roberts*, [1715.] (*MC* June)
8°: A–H⁴; *1–2* 3–63 *64 blk*.
Garth's text with a satirical prose commentary.
L(11643.bbb.7; 1465.f.45); NjR,OCU.

G21 [—] The dispensary. A poem. In six canto's... The fifth edition. *London printed, and sold by John Nutt*, 1703.
8°: *A⁴* a⁸ B–G⁸; *i–xxiv*, 1–96. A1 frt.

Garth, *Sir* **S.** The dispensary

First published in 1699. Some copies (LG,O) apparently have sheets of the fourth edition of 1700 with the new preliminaries.
'Speak, goddess! since 'tis thou that best canst tell'
See *The Dispensary transvers'd*, 1701.
L(991.k.26; 991.k.27),LVA-F(presentation copy to Pope, annotated by him),C,CT,E; *CLU-C*, CtY-M(2, 1 interleaved and corrected),*IU,MH*, TxU.

G22 [—] — The sixth edition, with several descriptions and episodes never before printed. *London printed, and sold by John Nutt*, 1706. (*DC* 12 April)
8°: A⁸ a⁸ B–H⁸ I⁴; *i–xxxii*, 1–120. A1 frt.
There are fine-paper copies (CtY-M, ?CT), cut size 8½ × 5½ in. as opposed to the normal 7½ × 4½ in.; but since there is no watermark to distinguish them with certainty they are not listed separately here.
L(1162.h.17/1,–A1, ms. notes),O(2),CT,E,DT+; CSmH(Pope's copy, annotated),CtY-M(presentation copy to Orrery),ICU,MH,TxU+.

G23 — — *London, printed by H. Hills; sold by the booksellers of London & Westminster*, 1709.
8°: A–D⁸ E⁴; *[4]* i–iv *v–xii*, 1–55 *56*. A1 hft, frt; 56 advt.
Garth's name on half-title; woodcut frontispiece. Some copies (e.g. O,CtY-M) have a key added, signed F⁴, pp. 57–64; this is probably a later addition, possibly pirated from the key of 1718.
L(1485.w.34),LG,O(3, 1–A1),C,*MR*; CLU-C (–A1),CtY,ICN,MH,TxU+.

G24 — — *London, printed by J. Bradford; sold by the booksellers of London & Westminster*, 1709.
8°: *A⁴* B–G⁴; *i–iv*, 1–52. A1 hft, frt.
The half-title reads 'Dr. Garth's Dispensary'; woodcut frontispiece.
L(1162.h.17/2),O(2, 1–A1); CtY-M(–A1),IU (2),*MiU,NN,NjP*.

G25 [—] — The seventh edition. With several descriptions and episodes never before printed. *London, printed for Jacob Tonson*, 1714. (*MC* June)
12°: A–D¹² E⁶; *i–xxiv*, *1–3* 4–84. A1 frt.
No watermark. Frontispiece and six plates included in the collation. Many cancels have been seen but not fully investigated; possibly B3, 5, 7, 8; C4,6; D1, 4,10; E3. The copyright was entered to Tonson in *SR* 12 April 1710.
L(1162.f.15/1; 1346.d.33/2, lacks C6; 238.g.28), O(2),OW,*MR*; CLU-C,CtY-M,DFo,*MH,MiU*+.

G26 [—] [fine paper]
Watermark: Strasburg bend.
L(1481.aa.6),C,BaP.

G27 [—] — The eighth edition. With several descriptions and episodes never before printed. *London, printed for Jacob Tonson*, 1718.
12°: A–D¹² E⁶; *i–xxiv*, *1–3* 4–84. A1 frt.
L(11630.bb.7),O,BaP,*MR*; CLU-C,CtY-M,ICN, KU,MH+.

Garth, *Sir* **S. The dispensary**

G28 [—] — The ninth edition. To which is added, several verses omitted in the late editions, and a compleat key to the whole. *Dublin, printed by Pressick Rider, & Thomas Harbin, for Pat. Dugan,* 1725.
12°: *A*⁶ B–I⁶; *i–xx, 1 2–71 72 blk, 1 2–16.*
L(11633.aa.11),CT,DG,DN.

G29 [—] — The ninth edition. With several descriptions and episodes never before printed. *London, printed for J. T. [Jacob Tonson]; sold by Tho. Astley,* 1726. (*MC* June)
12°: A–D¹² E⁶; *i–xxiv, 1–3 4–84.* A1 frt.
L(11632.aa.24/1),LG,O(2),CT,*MR*; CtY-M, *DLC*,MH,*NjP*,TxU+.

G30 [—] — The tenth edition. To which is added, several verses…and a compleat key to the whole. *Dublin, printed by and for Sam. Fuller,* 1730.
12°: A–H⁶; *i–xix, 1 2–62 63, 1 2–14.* 63 advt.
A copy at DN was reissued with Ozell's translation of Boileau's *Lutrin*, with the imprint of Powell, Risk, Ewing, & Smith (as in the following).
L(11631.a.24),C,DN(2),*MR*; CtY-M,PP,TxU.

G31 [—] — With a compleat key to the whole… The twelfth edition. With several descriptions and episodes never before printed. *Dublin, printed by S. Powell, for George Risk, George Ewing, & William Smith,* 1730.
12°: (frt+) A–F⁸ᐟ⁴ G⁴ H–I²; *i–xvi, 1 2–72.*
I² contains 'A continuation of the key' and the prologue to *Tamerlane.* The copy at CtY-M was reissued with Boileau's *Lutrin,* 1730.
O,C,DN,AdU; CtY-M,IU(–frt),MH.

G32 [—] — The tenth edition. *London, printed for J. & R. Tonson,* 1741.
12°: A–D¹² E⁶; *i–xxiv, 1–3 4–84.* A1 frt.
L(11643.aa.52/1),O(2, 1 uncut, 1–A1),LdU-B, *MR-C*; CLU-C,CtY-M,*ICN*,IU,MH.

G33 —— The fourteenth edition. *Glasgow, printed and sold by Robert & Andrew Foulis. Edinburgh, sold by John Rosse,* 1750.
8°: A–L⁴ M²; *i–iii iv–xvi, 17 18–92.*
Watermark: pro patria in all copies. Two qualities appear to have been used, the better indicated by an asterisk in the direction-line. For this practise see *Gaskell, Foulis* p. 22; his entry 150 does not record the variant copies of this edition. No asterisk found in the copies here.
O,GM(2),*MR*; *WaU.*

G34 — [fine paper]
Asterisk in direction-line.
O,E.

[G35 = N13·5] [—] Near to the sacred and immortal frame, [1712?] *See* N13·5.

G36 [—] A poem to the Earl of Godolphin. By Dr. G—h. [*London*] *Printed in the year* 1710. (*FP* 5 Sept)

Garth, *Sir* **S. A poem to the Earl**

½°: 1 side, 1 column.
'Whilst weeping Europe bends beneath her ills'
Garth is clearly intended as the author; see Pope's correspondence (ed. Sherburn) I. 101. Answered by *The E—l of G--d—n to D—ct—r G—th,* 1711, and *Verses upon Dr. G--'s verses to the E. of G---n,* [1710/11.]
LLP,O,Crawford,Rothschild; CSmH,CtY-M, DFo,MH,TxU+.

[—] A poem upon his majesties accession [actually by George Sewell], 1714. *See* S371.

G37 — A prologue for the 4th of November, 1711. Being the anniversary for the birth-day of the late K. William… [*Dublin?*] *Printed in the year* 1711.
4°: *A*²; *1–2 3–4.*
The L copy is bound with Dublin poems; previously published with the Dublin 'nineteenth edition' of Defoe's *The true-born Englishman,* 1704.
'To day a mighty hero, comes to warm'
Crum T2929. Rowe's *Tamerlane,* published in 1702, was regularly performed on 4 November in memory of William III; the prologue was written for that occasion.
L(11631.bb.28); CtY-M(uncut).

G38 [—] [*idem*] The prologue that was spoke at the Queen's theatre in Dublin, on Tuesday the 4th of November, 1712. Being the anniversary of the late King William. *Dublin, printed by E. Waters,* 1712.
½°: 2 sides, 1 column.
On the verso, 'The answer to the prologue', previously published as *The shortest way to peace,* [1711.]
Answer: 'When Bajazet was quell'd by Tamerlane'
The answer is a tory reply.
L(1890.e.5/174).

G39 [—] Prologue spoken at the first opening of the Queen's new theatre in the Hay-market. *London printed, and sold by John Nutt,* 1705.
½°: 1 side, 1 column.
'Such was our builder's art, that soon as nam'd'
Reprinted with Garth's poems in *The works of celebrated authors,* 1750. The prologue was spoken by Mrs. Bracegirdle, 9 April 1705.
L(C.20.f.2/222),O; MH.

G40 [—] — *London printed, and sold by B. Bragg,* 1705.
½°: 2 sides, 1 column.
On the verso, 'The opening prologue paraphras'd in a familiar stile…for the particular use of Mr. Jer. Collier', a prose satire.
L(C.20.f.2/221),Crawford; CSmH.

G41 '—' A prophecy written in the Roman language, above seventeen-hundred years ago, lately found, and faithfully translated by Sir Samuel Garth, M.D. [*London?* 1714/–.]
slip: 1 side, 1 column.
A small piece of paper, possibly part of a normal slip, containing ten lines of verse.
'If augurs can foresee, a wretch is come'

'Garth, *Sir* S.' A prophecy

Garth's responsibility for this Jacobite prophecy seems very improbable.
CSmH.

[—] To his grace the Duke of Marlborough, on the report of his going into Germany [actually by George Sewell], 1713. *See* S373.

[—] Verses written to the Duke of Marlborough upon his leaving England, 1715. *See* V77.

G42 Gates. The gates of hell opend: in a dialogue between the Observator, and Review. Dedicated to Aminadab... By a friend of the light. *London printed, and sold by J. Morphew,* 1711. (16 March, Luttrell)
8°: A⁴(–A4) B–C⁴ D¹[= A4]; *1–6* 7–24.
'Tell me, Review, what hast thou late survey'd'
A satire on the periodicals.
L(164.m.58, Luttrell),O; InU,MB,NN,OCU.

G43 Gawler, William. Dorchester: a poem. *London printed, and sold by M. Cooper,* 1743. (*LDP* 26 Nov)
2°: A² B–D²; *i–vi, 1* 2–10. A1 frt.
'The distant muse with filial duty fir'd'
L(162.n.10),LG,O; CU,IU.

Gay, John. Poems on several occasions. *London, printed for Jacob Tonson, & Bernard Lintot,* 1720. (*PM* 14 July)
4°: 2 vols; pp. 546.   L,O; CtY,MH.
Gay's agreement with Tonson and Lintot, dated 28 Jan 1719[/20] was offered in Dobell cat. 66 (1941) 9. In return for the new copyrights they allowed use of the old and 250 free copies; Gay was to pay 11s. 6d. each for 500 more.

—— *Dublin, printed by S. Powell, for George Risk, George Ewing, & William Smith,* 1729.
12°: pp. 410.   O; CtY,MH.
Copies seen also have added title-leaves for a two-volume issue, dated 1730.

—— *London, printed for J. Tonson, & B. Lintot,* 1731. (*MChr* May)
12°: 2 vol.   L,O; MH.
The text of this edition is said to be revised.

—— *London, printed for H. Lintot, and J. & R. Tonson,* 1737.
12°: 2 vol.   L,O; CtY,MH.

—— *London, printed for H. Lintot, J. & R. Tonson, & S. Draper,* 1745.
12°: 2 vol.   L,O; CtY,MH.

———

— Fables. *London, printed for J. Tonson & J. Watts,* 1727. (*SR* 27 May)
4°: pp. 173.   L,O; CtY,MH.
Deposit copies at L,O.

— Fables. Invented fo the amusement of his highness William duke of Cumberland. *London: printed,*

Gay, J. *Collections*

and Dublin reprinted for G. Risk, G. Ewing, & William Smith, 1727.
12°: pp. 109.   L,O; MH.

— Fables. The second edition. *London, printed for J. Tonson & J. Watts,* 1728. (*MChr* 13 Feb)
8°: pp. 194.   L,O; CtY,MH.

—— The third edition. *London, printed for J. Tonson & J. Watts,* 1729.
8°: pp. 194.   C; CtY,MH.

— Fables. Invented for the amusement of his highness William duke of Cumberland... The second edition. *Dublin, printed by S. Powell, for George Risk, George Ewing, & William Smith,* 1730.
12°: pp. 84.   O; MH.

— Fables. By the late Mr. Gay. The fourth edition. *London, printed for J. Tonson & J. Watts,* 1733. (*LM* Nov)
8°: pp. 194.   L,O; IU,MH.

— [*idem*] Fifty-one fables, by the late Mr. Gay... '*Amsterdam, printed for J. Jones*', 1734.
12°: pp. 96.   L.
Possibly an English piracy. A J. Jones was publishing in London in 1729 and 1737.

— Fables. By the late Mr. Gay. The fifth edition. *London, printed for J. & R. Tonson & J. Watts,* 1737.
8°: pp. 194.   L,O; CtY,MH.

— Fables... The seventh edition. *Dublin, printed for G. Risk, G. Ewing, & W. Smith,* 1737.
12°: pp. 144.   MH.
The title is engraved.

— Fables by the late Mr. Gay... Containing fifty fables on the most curious subjects. Dedicated to his highness Prince William, and invented for his amusement. Revised and corrected by a gentleman at the university of Oxford. The fifth edition. *Oxford, printed for T. Wilson; sold by the booksellers of Bath, Bristol, London & Westminster; and by T. Hinton, Southwark,* 1741.
12°: pp. 90.   CtY.
Presumably an unauthorized edition.

—— The sixth edition. *London, printed for J. & R. Tonson & J. Watts,* 1746.
8°: pp. 194.   L,BaP; CtY,MH.

———

— Fables. By the late Mr. Gay. Volume the second. *London, printed for J. & P. Knapton, & T. Cox,* 1738. (*SR* 25 Nov)
4°: pp. 155.   L,O; CtY,MH.
Deposit copies at L,O.

—— *London, printed for J. & P. Knapton, & T. Cox,* 1738. (*GM,LM* Dec)
8°: pp. 155.   L,O; CtY,MH.

— The second edition. *London, printed for J. & P. Knapton, & T. Cox,* 1742.
8°: pp. 155.   L,O; CtY,MH.

Gay, J. *Collections*

—— *Dublin, printed for Peter Wilson, 1743.*
12°: pp. 73. L; CtY,MH.

—— The third edition. *London, printed for J. &*
P. Knapton, 1747.
8°: pp. 155. L; CtY,MH.
> Two fourth-shares of the copyright formed
> lots 133–4 of John Knapton's trade sale of
> 25 Sept 1755, sold for £27 and £27 10s; four
> eighth-shares formed lots 45–8 in the sale of
> Samuel Birt, 7 Oct 1756 (cats. at O-JJ).

— Fables. In two parts. [*Glasgow*] *Printed in the*
year 1750.
8°: pp. viii, 192. L; MH.
> *Gaskell, Foulis* 152. An edition of the two parts
> in one volume for S. Crowder, C. Ware, &
> J. Payne is misdated '1736' for 1786 (copies at
> CtY,MH).

[—] The ball. Stated in a dialogue betwixt a prude
and a coquet, 1724. *See* B20.

[—] The banish'd beauty: or, a fair face in disgrace, 1729. *See* B55.

[—] Blue-skin's ballad. To the tune of Packington's
pound, 1724–5. *See* N289.

G44 [—] Daphnis and Chloe. A ballad. *London, printed*
for J. Tonson, & B. Lintot, where subscriptions are
taken in for Mr. Gay's poems . . . [*1720.*] (*DC* 6 Jan)
½°: *1–2*, 1 column.
> First verse accompanied by type-set music.
> There are editions engraved throughout which
> are excluded here.
'Daphnis stood pensive in the shade'
> Reprinted in Gay's *Poems*, 1720.
MC; CSmH.

G45 — An epistle to her grace Henrietta, dutchess of
Marlborough. *London, printed for Jacob Tonson,*
1722. (*DC* 11 July)
2°: *A*² B² C¹; *i–iv, 1–5* 6 *blk*. A1 hft.
> No watermark. Entered in *SR* 11 July;
> deposit copies at L,O,E,EU.
'Excuse me, madam, if amidst your tears'
L(643.m.13/18; Ashley 5188),O,E,EU,LdU-B;
CSmH,ICN,MH.

G46 — [fine paper]
> Watermark: fleur-de-lys.
CtY.

[—] An epistle to the most learned Doctor
W--d----d, 1723. *See* E416.

G47 — The fan. A poem. In three books. *London,*
printed for J. Tonson, 1714 [1713]. (*SR* 8 Dec)
2°: A–H²; *1–2 3–32.*
> No watermark. *Rothschild* 912. Copies at OW,
> CSmH have a reset and reprinted sheet B with
> horizontal chain-lines and foolscap watermark;
> p. 5 line 4 reads 'rally'd' for 'railly'd'.
> Advertised in *DC* 9 Dec 1713 as published
> 'yesterday'. Deposit copies at L,LSC,O,EU,

Gay, J. *The fan*

AdU,SaU. The assignment of copyright from
Gay to Tonson for 14 guineas, dated 17 Nov
1713, was listed in Dobell cat. 66 (1941) 8.
'I sing that graceful toy, whose waving play'
L(643.m.13/2; 162.n.11; Ashley 4837),O,C,EU,
LdU-B+; CSmH(uncut),CtY,ICN,MH,TxU+.

G48 — [fine paper]
> Watermark: monogram PH.
DFo,NN-B,TxU.

G49 — [reissue] The second edition. *London, printed*
for J. Tonson, 1714.
2°: A²(±A1) B–H²; *1–2 3–32.*
> The copy at OW has the reprinted sheet B
> described in the entry for the first edition.
L(1961),OW,YU; ICN,MH,PPL.

G50 —— To which is added, the Smock-race, at
Finglas. *Dublin, re-printed by E. Sandys, for G.*
Grierson, 1714.
12°: A–C⁶; *1–2 3–36.*
> 'The smock-race' by James Ward was re-
> printed separately in 1716.
Smock-race: 'Now did the bag-pipe in hoarse notes
begin'
L(1971),DA,DT; CLU-C,MH.

G51 —— To which is added, the Smock-race at
Finglas. *Dublin, printed by and for A. Rhames,* 1727.
12°: A⁸ B⁴; *1–3 4–24.*
DG; MH.

[—] Homer in a nutshell [actually by Thomas
Tooly], 1715. *See* T420.

[—] Horace, epod. IV. imitated, by Sir James
Baker, kt. to Lord Cad----n, [1717?] *See* B15.

G52 [—] A letter to a lady, occasion'd by the arrival of
her royal highness the Princess of Wales. *London,*
printed for Bernard Lintott, 1714. (*DC* 20 Nov)
2°: *A*² B–C²; *i–iv, 1–8*. A1 hft.
> *MC* Nov lists editions 1, 2, 3, 4; the fifth edition
> in *Two epistles*, 1717.
'Madam, to all your censures I submit'
> Gay's authorship is given in *MC* Nov.
L(C.131.h.1/6; 643.l.25/29, lacks A²); CSmH,
CtY,MH,NN-B,TxU(lacks A²).

G53 [—] — The second edition. *London, printed for*
Bernard Lintott, 1714. (*PB* 25 Nov)
2°: *A*² B–C²; *i–iv, 1–8*. A1 hft.
> Apparently a reimpression.
L(11602.i.10/5); CtY,MH(uncut),NjP.

G54 [—] — The third edition.
> Listed in *MC* Nov 1714 with editions 1, 2, & 4.

G55 [—] — The fourth edition. *London, printed for*
Bernard Lintott, 1714. (*MC* Nov)
2°: *A*² B–C²; *i–iv, 1–8*. A1 hft.
> Apparently a reimpression or press-variant
> title.
LVA-F.

G56 [—] — To which is added, verses occasion'd by
the storm of rain, &c. the night before King

Gay, J. A letter to a lady

George's coronation. *Dublin, re-printed by A. Meres & T. Humes, and sold by the booksellers,* 1714.
8°: A⁴; *1-2* 3-8.
The 'verses' are two-line epigrams on p. 8.
DK.

G57 — [*idem*] A poem: in a letter to a lady, occasion'd by the arrival... By Mr. Gay... The third edition. *Dublin, re-printed by Daniel Tompson,* 1714.
8°: *A⁴; i-ii,* 1-6.
O.

G58 [—] The mad dog, a tale. By H----------J---------, esq; *London, printed for A. Moore; sold by the booksellers of London & Westminster,* 1730. (*MChr* 21 Jan)
2°: *A² B²; 1-2* 3-8.
Rothschild 929.
'A prude, at morn and ev'ning pray'r'
The author intended is Hildebrand Jacob, as a notable writer of bawdy verse; but the poem was collected in Gay's *Poems,* 1720.
L(11630.h.1; Ashley 5192, uncut),O; CSmH, DLC,MH,TxU(3).

G59 [—] Molly Mog: or, the fair maid of the inn. A ballad. [*London,* 1726.]
½°: 1 side, 2 columns.
Williams 1129. Printed by John Watts on the evidence of the ornament at foot; Watts printed Gay's *Poems,* 1720, and this may be an authorized edition. Published in *Mist's Weekly Journal* 27 August 1726. There are engraved editions with music, not included here.
'Says my uncle, I pray you discover'
There seems no doubt that Gay was the main author, though possibly assisted by Pope and Swift. Cf. *Munster Juggy preferr'd,* 1727.
L(1876.f.1/96, with two ms. verses); MH.

G60 — Molly Mogg or the fair maid of the inn. By Mr. Gay. [*Dublin*] *Printed by J. Gowan,* 1726.
½°: 1 side, 2 columns.
Columns separated by 28 fleur-de-lys.
MH.

G61 — [*idem*] The famous poem of Molly Mogg or the fair maid of the inn. By Mr. Gay. [*Dublin*] *Printed by J. Gowan,* 1726.
½°: 1 side, 2 columns.
Columns separated by 15 type ornaments, but apparently from the same setting of type as the preceding.
CSmH.

G62 [—] [*idem*] A new song, in praise of if [!] Molly Mogg. Tune of The city ramble... [*London?* 1726/-.]
slip: 1 side, 1 column.
A popular slip song, with a battered woodcut at head.
C.

[—] Newgate's garland: being a new ballad, shewing how Mr. Jonathan Wild's throat was cut, [1724/25.] *See* N288.

Gay, J. On Monday

G63 — On Monday next the 14th of August, at the Marlborough Bowling-green, will be perform'd (for the first time) in the 3d act, the following ode, the words by the late John Gay...set to musick by Mr. Lampe, as it is to be perform'd for the benefit of Mr. Jackson and Mr. Kountze, kettle-drummer. [*Dublin?* 1732/-.]
slip: 1 side, 1 column.
The copy seen is bound with Dublin half-sheets.
'Beneath the shadow of a beaver-hat'
Selected from Gay's 'The espousal. A sober eclogue'.
L(1890.e.5/127).

G64 [—] A panegyrical epistle to Mr. Thomas Snow, goldsmith, near Temple-Barr: occasion'd by his buying and selling the third subscriptions, taken in by the directors of the South-Sea company, at a thousand per cent. *London, printed for Bernard Lintot,* 1721. (*DC* 28 Feb)
2°: A-B²; *i-ii,* 1-5 *6 blk.*
Rothschild 921. Entered in *SR* 28 Feb; deposit copies at L,LSC,O,E,EU.
'Disdain not, Snow, my humble verse to hear'
L(643.m.13/17; Ashley 5187),LU,O(2),E,DT+; CtY(uncut),DLC,MH(uncut),TxU(2).

G65 [—] — The second edition. *London, printed for Bernard Lintot,* 1721. (*DC* 18 March)
2°: A-B²; *i-ii,* 1-5 *6 blk.*
LG,OW; MH(2).

[—] A poem address'd to the Quidnunc's, at St. James's Coffee-house London, 1724. *See* P518.

G66 — Rural sports. A poem. Inscribed to Mr. Pope. *London, printed for J. Tonson,* 1713. (*PB* 15 Jan)
2°: *A² B-F²* (A2 as 'B'); *i-ii,* 1-22.
No watermark. *Rothschild* 910. The Luttrell copy, dated 21 Jan, is recorded in *Haslewood.* Entered in *SR* 15 Jan; deposit copies at L,LSC,O,EU,AdU,SaU. Gay received 14 guineas for the copyright according to the assignment of *The fan* recorded above.
'You, who the sweets of rural life have known'
L(643.1.26/4; Ashley 4836),LVA-F,O(uncut),EU, LdU-B+; CLU-C,CSmH,CtY,MH(2, 1 uncut), TxU.

G67 — [fine paper]
Watermark: O.
CtY(presentation copy to Mrs. Arscott).

G68 — — The second edition. *London, printed for J. Tonson,* 1713.
2°: A-F²; *i-ii,* 1-22.
Revised text. An advertisement of 5 April in *Haslewood* records it as 'lately printed'.
L(11646.w.14),O; CtY,ICN,MH,TxU(uncut).

[—] Several copies of verses on occasion of Mr. Gulliver's travels, 1727. *See* S356.

G69 — The shepherd's week. In six pastorals. *London printed, and sold by Ferd. Burleigh,* 1714. (*PB* 15 April)

Gay, J. The shepherd's week

8⁰: A–E⁸; *i–xvi*, *1–3* 4–60 *61–64*. A1 frt.
No watermark. Plates included in collation. Some copies (e.g. C,MH) omit the apostrophe in title. Entered in *SR* 27 April to Tonson by Ferdinando Burleigh; deposit copies at LSC, E,EU,AdU. Gay's assignment of copyright to Tonson for twenty guineas, dated 9 March, was sold at Sotheby's, 1964.
'Thy younglings, Cuddy, are but just awake'
L(11632.cc.19; Ashley 768; G.18423/8),OW,CT (2, 1 uncut),E,LdU-B+; CLU-C,CtY,ICN,IU, MH(2)+.

G70 — [fine paper]
Strasburg bend. Apostrophe in title in all copies seen.
LVA-D,O(–A1); CSmH,MH,NN-B.

G71 — [reissue] The second edition. *London, printed for J. T. [Jacob Tonson]; sold by W. Taylor*, 1714. (*MC* Aug)
8⁰: A⁸(±A2) B–E⁸; *i–xvi*, *1–3* 4–60 *61–64*. A1 frt.
Some copies (C,DFo) have a leaf of Taylor's advertisements after E8; in the copy at EtC it is clearly conjugate with the cancel title A2 and is bound before A3. Probably the intended collation would make it *F*1.
L(11632.aaa.24; 11631.bbb.39/3),O,C,EtC,*MR*; CLU-C,*CtY*,DFo,MH.

G72 — — *Dublin, printed by S. Powell, for G. Grierson*, 1714.
12⁰: A–D⁶ (C2 as 'C3'); *i–iii* 'v' v–vii, 8–48.
Possibly not separately published; issued with other pastorals signed E–L⁶ with the general title *Miscellany pastorals*.
L(1966),DN; CtY.

G73 — — *London printed, and sold by R. Burleigh in Amen-corner*, 'MDCCXIV' [1716?].
8⁰: A–E⁸; *i–xvi*, *1–3* 4–60 *61–64*. A1 frt.
The date is possibly a misprint for 'MDCCXVI'; the textual evidence and the plates show it precedes the 1721 edition. The ornaments of John Watts suggest a date not before 1716; R. Burleigh published verse 1714–17. The title-leaves at O,LdU-B appear to be cancels.
O(2),LdU-B; CtY(made-up),*DLC*,MH(2),*TxU*.

G74 — — *London, printed for Jacob Tonson*, 1721.
8⁰: A–E⁸; *i–xvi*, *1–3* 4–60 *61–64*. A1 frt.
Rothschild 922.
L(11631.bbb.15),O(2),C,WcC; CLU-C,CtY,MH, TxU.

G75 — — The fourth edition. *London, printed for Jacob Tonson*, 1728.
8⁰: A–E⁸; *i–xvi*, *1–3* 4–60 *61–64*. A1 frt.
Listed in *MC* Sept 1728 as just re-printed, sold by Thomas Astley; in *MC* May 1729 as the fourth edition for T. Astley; and as a new edition in *MChr* 5 Feb 1730, again for T. Astley.

Gay, J. The shepherd's week

L(1162.g.30, uncut, lacks A1, E7–8),LG,O(2, –A1, plates),LdU-B; CtY,IU,MH,MiU,*TxU*+.

G76 — — *Dublin, printed by J. Watts; sold by J. Thompson*, 1728.
8⁰: A–E⁴; *1–7* 8–39 *40 blk*.
L(1481.aa.1/3; 11779.a.15/2),C; IU,MH,TxU (uncut).

G77 — — *Dublin, printed by S. Powell, for George Risk, George Ewing, & William Smith*, 1729.
8⁰: A–C⁸; *i–x*, *1* 2–32 *33–38*. C8 advt.
L(1487.a.6),O; *CtY*.

G78 — — The fifth edition. *London, printed for J. & R. Tonson*, 1742.
8⁰: A–E⁸; *i–xvi*, *1–3* 4–60 *61–64*. A1 frt.
L(11643.g.5); CtY,MH,TxU.

[—] 'Sweet William's farewell to black-ey'd Susan. A ballad. [*London*] *Printed for Bernard Lintot*. Price 2*d*.' (*PB* 10 Jan 1719)
This presumably refers to one of the engraved editions with music which are not included here. Subsequently advertised in *DC* 25 March 1719 as 'set to musick by Mr. Leveridge. The 3d edition'. Translated by Vincent Bourne as *Gulielmus Susannæ valedicens*, 1731.

G79 **[—]** To a lady on her passion for old china. *London, printed for J. Tonson*, 1725. (*DC* 12 May)
4⁰: A² B⁴; *i–iv*, *1* 2–5 *6–8 blk*. A1 hft.
'What ecstasies her bosom fire!'
Advertised in *DC, MC* as 'By Mr. Gay'; not collected in his works until 1767.
L(11656.r.7/13; 163.l.57, Luttrell, May, –B4; Ashley 3254); MH(–B4).

G80 **[—]** — [*Dublin*, 1725?]
4⁰: A²; *1* 2–4.
Drop-head title only.
DT.

[—] The triple alliance, [1724/27]. *See* T498.

G81 — Trivia: or, the art of walking the streets of London. *London, printed for Bernard Lintott*, [1716.] (25 Jan, Luttrell)
8⁰: A² B–F⁸ G⁶; *i–iv*, 1–80 *81–92*. iv err.
No watermark. *Rothschild* 916. One would expect A² to have been printed with G⁶, but the fine-paper copy at L has two watermarks in G⁶; possibly the sheets were divided before collation. The Luttrell copy is recorded in Blackwell's cat. 407/1568. Advertised in *DC* 26 Jan. Entered in *SR* 25 Jan; deposit copies at O,E,EU. Entered to Lintot in Bowyer's ledgers under 19 Jan 1716, 2000 copies and 250 fine, margins altered. Lintot paid Gay forty guineas for the copyright, 22 Dec 1715 (*Nichols* VIII. 296).
'Through winter streets to steer your course aright'
L(992.k.9/1, lacks A1; Ashley 770),LG(2),O(3, 1 imperfect),C(uncut),E+; DFo,ICN,IU,MH(2), TxU+.

G82 — [fine paper]
    Watermark: Strasburg bend. *Rothschild* 914, 915. Engraved headpieces substituted on pp. 1, 21, 53.
L(11626.f.4),O,C,LdU-B; CSmH,CtY,MH,NN-B(presentation to William Colman),TxU(2)+.

G83 —— The second edition. *London, printed for Bernard Lintot,* [1716.] (*DC* 9 June)
8°: A² B–C⁸ D⁸(±D2) E⁸ F¹; *i–iv, 1–56 57–66.*
    Rothschild 917. D2 is uncancelled in some copies (e.g. L,MH). The copy at TxU has two leaves of advertisement after F1. Apparently the edition listed as 'reprinted' in *MC* Oct 1726. Entered in Bowyer's ledgers under 7 June, 1000 copies printed.
L(12330.f.26/4),O,OW,C,E(lacks D2); CtY,*ICN,*IU,MH,TxU.

G84 —— *London: printed for Bernard Lintott: and reprinted in Dublin, by S. Powell, for G. Risk,* 1716.
12°: A² B–F⁶; *i–iv, 1–50 51–60.*
L(1966),O(title cropt),DT(2); MH.

G85 —— To which is added Rural sports. A poem. Inscribed to Mr. Pope. *Dublin, printed by S. Powell, for George Risk,* 1727.
12°: A⁶ B–C¹² D⁶; *i–xii, 1–60.*
L(1481.aa.1/1),O,C,DN(2),DT+; CtY,MH.

G86 —— The third edition. *London, printed for Bernard Lintot,* 1730. (*MChr* 25 Feb)
8°: A–D⁸ E⁴; *1–5 6–66 67–72.*
L(11631.e.25),O,C,CT(2); *CtY,*IU,MH.

G87 —— *London, published by Mrs. Newcomb, at the Naked Boy, near Temple Bar,* [175–?]
8°: A² B–H⁴ I²; *i–iv, 1–50 51–60.*
    Horizontal chain-lines. Dated 1740 by *CBEL,* but probably a piracy after 1750.
L(T.854/2),C; MH.

G88 — Two epistles; one, to the right honourable Richard earl of Burlington; the other to a lady. *London, printed for Bernard Lintot,* [1717.] (*DC* 18 Feb)
8°: *B⁸* C⁸ D⁴; *1–7 8–36 37–40.* B1 hft; D3–4 advt.
    Rothschild 913. The second poem, here printed as 'the fifth edition', is *A letter to a lady.* Entered in *SR* 19 Feb; deposit copy at EU. Lintot paid Gay ten guineas for the copyright (*Nichols* VIII. 296).
'While you, my lord, bid stately piles ascend'
    The epistle to Burlington is also known as 'A journey to Exeter'.
L(11631.d.22,–D3; Ashley 772),O(2),C(2),E, LdU-B+; CSmH,CtY(uncut),ICN,MH,TxU(2, 1–D3–4)+.

G89 [—] Wine a poem. *London, printed for William Keble,* 1708. (22 May, Luttrell)
2°: A–D²; *1–2 3–14 15; 16 blk.* 15 err.
    Bond 22. Listed in *DC* 22 May as 'just publish'd'.
'Of happiness terrestrial, and the source'
    First published with Gay's poems in Bell's

British Poets; according to *Faber* xxx the attribution was made by Aaron Hill in 1736. Some doubt has been cast upon Gay's authorship. Doubtless inspired by Fenton's *Cerealia,* 1706, and John Philips's *Cyder,* 1708.
L(Ashley 4835),O,OW; CSmH(Luttrell),CtY,MH, MWiW-C,TxU(2).

G90 [—] — *London printed, and sold by H. Hills,* 1708.
8°: A⁸; *1–2 3–15 16 blk.*
L(11632.bb.47),CT; MH,TxU.

G91 [—] — To which is added Old England's new triumph: or, the battel of Audenard. A song. *London, printed by Henry Hills,* 1708.
8°: A⁸; *1–2 3–16.*
    Old England's new triumph was separately published in 1708.
L(G.18914/2),O,C,CT,DT; CtY,ICN,IU,MH, TxU.

G92 [—] — *London printed, and sold by H. Hills,* 1709.
8°: A⁸; *1–2 3–16.*
    Reissued with other remaindered Hills poems in *A collection of the best English poetry,* 1717 (*Case* 294).
L(11657.l.1; C.124.b.7/36),LDW,LVA-F,O, WcC; CLU-C,CtY,MH(2),TxU.

'Gay, Joseph.'
A pseudonym applied by Edmund Curll to works written by John Durant Breval and by Francis Chute, doubtless in the hope of confusion with the works of John Gay. The attribution of these works between Breval and Chute is far from clear; in this catalogue all are entered under Breval except for The petticoat, *1716–, which is under Chute. It is possible that the pseudonym was used by other of Curll's authors.*

— Miscellanies, upon several subjects; occasionally written. By Mr. Joseph Gay. *London, printed for E. Curll,* 1719.
8°. L.
    Title for a nonce collection containing reissues of poems by both Breval and Chute.

G93 **Gaynam, John.** Marlborough still conquers: or, union hath got the day. A poem, upon the late victory obtained by the Prince and Duke of Marlborough; and union of the two kingdoms. *London, printed by D. Rogers,* 1708. (*DC* 16 July)
2°: *A²* B–C²; *1–2 3–12.* 12 err.
    Advertised as sold by J. Morphew.
'Lolling upon the ground, as stragglers do'
O.

G94 —— *London, printed by H. Hills,* 1708.
8°: A⁸; *1–4 5–16.*
L(1467.c.20; G.1390/4),O,E,EU,DT; CSmH, *CtY,*ICN,MH,TxU(2)+.

G95 [—] 'The tories looking-glass: a congratulatory poem in commemoration of his majesty's birth-day, May 28, 1718. [*London*] Sold by *J.* Roberts. Price 6d.' (*DC* 28 May 1718)

Gaynam, J. The tories looking-glass

John Gaynam's authorship is revealed by a statement he made to John Clarke when arrested for libel at the suit of A. Wilkinson; the statement is printed in *PB* 10 July 1718.

G96 G----e. G----e and D----y: or, the injur'd ghost. A true tale. In imitation of William and Margaret. By a young lady of quality. *London, printed for W. Webb,* 1743. (*LDP* 14 April)
2°: *A⁴*; *1–2* 3–8.
Rothschild 235, 236.
'When all was wrapt in sable night'
Dorothy, countess of Euston, reproaches her husband George Fitzroy for his infidelity and for causing the miscarriage which killed her. Replied to by *Eugenio,* 1743.
L(11621.k.2/115; 163.n.51),O,LdU-B; CSmH, DFo,MH,OCU,TxU+.

G97 — [variant title:] By a lady of quality.
CtY.

G98 — G***e and D**y or the jnjur'd [!] ghost. A true tale... By a lady of quality. *London, printed for A. Moore,* 1743.
4°: *A²*; *1* 2–4, 2 columns.
A piracy. Vertical chain-lines.
LG; CSmH.

G99 Genealogy. The geneology [!], a poem. Humbly inscrib'd to the Dutchess of Puddle-dock, by Foly the rake. *Dublin, printed in the year* 1726.
½°: 1 side, 1 column.
'Oh thou, who'rt sprung of pure thick blood!'
L(1890.e.5/191).

— The genealogy of Christ, 1729. *See* Lowth, Robert.

G100 General. The general assembly of the brewers. In modren [!] dogrill. [*Dublin*] *Printed in the year* 1729.
½°: 1 side, 1 column.
'Our brewers alledge they have suffer'd much some years past'
DT.

G101 — The general casher'd: or, a prologue between fame and envy: as it was spoken before his highness Prince Eugene of Savoy, at the play-house. *London, printed in the year* 1712.
½°: 1 side, 2 columns.
On the other side, *An account of the tryal...of Joseph Reader,* 1712, in prose.
'Thou great disturber of heroick songs'
On the dismissal of Marlborough.
NN.

G102 — [dh] The general deception. A satire upon a certain l------. [*Dublin,* 1736?]
8°: A⁴; *1* 2–8.
The printer's ornament is identical with one in the following edition; presumably both are authorized editions. The order of editions has not been determined.

The **general** deception

'Fabricius to my numbers lend thy ear'
L(900.g.30/3),DA; IU(cropt).

G103 — [*idem*] The general deception in four satires. Satire I. inscrib'd to the honourable Sir *******, bart. *Dublin printed, and sold by Ebenezer Rider,* 1736.
8°: A–B⁴; *1–6* 7–16.
L(1959),DK,*MR-C*; DFo,OCU.

— The general mistake, [1725/26.] *See* Ramsay, Allan.

G104 Generous. A generous exhortation to undertakers and journeymen-weavers, &c. *Dublin, printed by R. Dickson,* ⟨1726.⟩ (Jan)
½°: 1 side, 1 column.
Woodcut arms of the weavers at head.
'Rouse lab'ring weavers, never be dismay'd'
DT(dated in ms., Jan 1725/6).

G105 — The generous muse. A funeral poem, in memory of his late majesty K. James the II. Humbly dedicated to her royal highness. *London, printed for William Turner,* 1701. (23 Sept, Luttrell)
2°: A–D² (A2 as 'B2'); *i–iv,* 1–11 *12 blk.*
Listed in *WL* Sept. The Luttrell copy is in the collection of J. R. B. Brett-Smith.
'What, shall the croud his injur'd name blaspheme'
The loyalist, 1702, is by the same author. *Rawlinson* records 'A poem on K. James 2 death, fol & 8°' under William Pittis, and this is the only poem that fits his description; Pittis's authorship seems very plausible.
C*J*,AdU,EtC(uncut),*MR-C*; CLU-C,CSmH,CU, DFo,TxU.

G106 — — The second edition, corrected. *London, printed for William Turner,* 1701.
2°: A² B–D²; *i–iv,* 1–11 *12 blk.*
Apparently a reimpression, with A2 unsigned.
O(uncut),OC; NjP(uncut),OCU.

G107 — — The second edition, corrected. *London, printed for William Turner,* 1701.
8°: A⁴ B–C⁴; *1–4* 5–23 *24 blk.*
MR-C; CtY(uncut).

G108 — — *London, printed: and re-printed in Dublin, at the Post-office-Coffee-house,* 1701.
4°: A² B² C¹; *i–ii,* 1–8.
DA.

Genethlia. Genethlia: a poem on the blessed nativity, 1727. *See* Curteis, Thomas.

Geneva. Geneva. A poem in blank verse, 1734. *See* 'Buck, Stephen'.

G109 — The Geneva ballad. To the tune of 48. *London, printed in the year* 1705.
½°: 1 side, 2 columns.
'Of all the factions in the town'
Crum O38. Originally published in 1674 (*Wing* G515–17). A later edition is attributed to Samuel Butler by L, apparently in error. This

The **Geneva** ballad

edition was answered by *The tacker's ghost*, 1705.

L(C.40.m.9/78); CLU-C,CSmH,*MH*,*Harding*.

G110 — [*idem*] The Kentish ballad, or, the good old cause reviv'd. To the tune of, Forty eight. '*Oxford*', *printed in the year* 1710.
½°: 1 side, 2 columns.

On the other side, *Love and dignity united*, 1710, bearing a London imprint.

O.

Gent, Thomas. 'A collection of songs proper for the summer's entertainment.'

Recorded in Gent's *Life* and probably printed about 1724; there is no evidence of the exact title, or whether Gent was the author.

— Divine entertainments: or, penitential desires, sighs and groans of the wounded soul. In two books. Adorned with suitable cuts. *London, printed for M. Hotham, & T. Gent*, 1724.
12°: pp. xiv, 152.   L,YM; CLU-C.

Based on Hugo's *Pia desideria*, with woodcuts (apparently by W. Pennock) copied from those designs. Gent's *Life* records printing a thousand copies. *Divine entertainments, or spiritual comforts to the wounded mind* (York, 175–?) is an essentially different and shorter work.

— The pious and poetical works of Mr. Thomas Gent, &c. [*York*, 1772/–.]
8°.   L.

Title for a nonce collection.

———

G111 [—] British piety display'd in the glorious life, suffering, and death of the blessed St. Winefred... Part the first [*etc*]. York, *printed by Thomas Gent*, [1742.]
12°: A–C⁴, D–F⁴, G–I⁴, K–M⁴, N–P⁴, Q–S⁴; *i–ii* iii–iv, 5–24, *1–2* 3–24, *1–2* 3–24, *1–2* 3–24, *1* 2–24, *1* 2–24. A1 frt; S1ᵛ err; S2–4 advt.

Printed in six parts, the sixth unnumbered; parts 3–6 are dated 1742 and have imprint 'printed and sold by the author Tho. Gent.' There are occasional errors in the signatures. A woodcut frontispiece on A1ᵛ which was used by Gent as early as 1724 is signed 'W Pennock F'. Advertisement for subscribers, *York Courant* 2 Nov 1742; advertised as published 21 Dec 1742, price bound 1s. 6d. Also reissued in *The pious and poetical works...*
'Long after Merlin had strange things foretold'
L(G.13222),O,*MR*,YM(2).

G112 — [reissue] The holy life and death of St. Winefred; and other religious persons. In five parts... Done into verse: with an epitome in prose... Written by Thomas Gent. York, *printed by the author, and sold by John Hopkins, in Preston, and other booksellers in the country*, 1743. (21 Dec 1742?)
Six unnumbered preliminary leaves added for

volume issue. The two leaves of contents and subscribers are also bound in the L copy above, and that may be an intermediate state. A copy at YM has an extra title-leaf, possibly of later date, reading 'Female piety exemplify'd: or, the heav'nly virgin celebrated... Written by the author of the History of York, &c. ⟨871 ?⟩'.
L(G.18859/1),YM(2).

G113 [—] 'The forsaken lover's letter to his former sweetheart... Tune of Such charms has Phillis.' [*London*, 1722.]

The life of Thomas Gent (1832) 130–4 prints this poem on the occasion of his sweetheart Alice Guy of York marrying Charles Bourne, and records 'I gave the above copy, except the last stanza, to Mr. Dodd, who, printing the same, sold thousands of them, for which he offered me a price'. This entry appears under the year 1722 in Gent's ms. of his life. The poem is printed as the first work in *The forsaken lover's garland* of which there is an early edition at L(C.116.bb.11/15); it is possible that it was originally published in this form.
'What means my dearest, my sweet lovely creature'

G114 — God's judgments shewn unto mankind. Being a true and sorrowful relation of the sufferings of the inhabitants of the city of Marseilles in France, now under the dreadful calamity of the plague, pestilence and fevers... Tune of, Aim not too high. [*London*, 1720/21.]
1°: 1 side, 3 columns.

Mourning borders, and a collection of rough woodcuts at head.
'Lament, good Christians, when you hear this thing'
L(C.20.f.2/335).

G115 [—] The history of the life and miracles of our blessed saviour, Jesus Christ... Done into verse, for the delight and improvement of the weakest capacity... York, *printed and sold by Tho. Gent*, [174–?]
12°: A⁸ B⁴; *1–2* 3–23 *24*.
'Almost four thousand years had past'

Reissued in *The pious and poetical works of Mr. Thomas Gent*, [1772/–.]
L(G.18859/2),O,YM(2).

G116 — Pater patriæ: being, an elegiac pastoral dialogue occasioned by the most lamented death of... Charles Howard, earl of Carlisle...1738... [*York*] *Printed, and sold, by the author*, [1738.]
8°: A–C⁴; *i–iv*, 1–19 *20*.

Horizontal chain lines, no watermark. Possibly ordinary paper copies were printed in 12°.
'Why, Strephon, why, do you desert the plain?'
L(G.18859),*MR*,YM(2, 1 cropt),YP.

G117 — [fine paper]
Watermark: pro patria.
L(1162.f.18/1).

Gent, T.

G118 — The pattern of piety: or, tryals of patience. Being the most faithful spiritual songs of the life and death of the once afflicted Job. In five books... *Scarborough, printed by Thomas Gent, in the year of our blessed lord,* 1734.
12º: *A*¹²; *1* 2–24.
Reissued in *The pious and poetical works...* [1772/–.]
'In Idumea's land, or Uz by name'
Dedication signed.
L(G.18859),O,YM(2).

G119 [—] 'Teague's ramble.' [*London,* 1719.]
The life of Thomas Gent (1832) 96: 'He [Francis Clifton] had...obliged me in printing a little book I wrote, intitled, "Teague's Ramble", a satire I had written on some of our profession...' That this work was in hudibrastic verse seems clear from a passage on p. 51: 'I became the ludicrous sport of common Irish journeymen...which usage I afterwards remembered in an Hudibrastic poem, of which I shall take notice in another place.' A marginal note in the ms. of Gent's *Life* (at YM) records that it was printed in 1719, and refers to a reprint mentioned in the *Universal Magazine* (1747) 194: 'if not the same, yet this title'. The title *Teague's ramble at Charing Cross* is, however, listed in *BM* Sept 1747 under the heading 'Prints'; it presumably is a different work.

— [Verses printed on the ice at York, 8 Jan 1740.] There is a souvenir of eighteen lines of verse, headed 'Mr. Nicholas Hailstone' at YM. Gent's name appears in the last line. It was presumably printed with the name of any customer at head. Such souvenirs are excluded from the catalogue.

G120 Gentleman. The gentleman. An heroic poem. In two cantos. *Dublin, printed in the year* 1747.
8º: A–C⁴; *1–3* 4–22 *23–24 blk.*
'The rough designs in gentle bosoms cloak'd'
DA(–C4),DN(2, 1–C4),DT; OCU(–C4).

G121 — — The second edition. *Dublin, printed in the year* 1747.
8º: A–C⁴; *1–3* 4–23 *24 blk.*
ICN.

G122 — The gentleman commoner: a poem. By J.L. A.B. author of the Servitor. *London, printed for John Morphew,* 1716. (*MC* Nov)
12º: *A*² B⁴ C⁴(–C4); *1–4* 5–17 *18 blk.* A1 hft.
'My young esquire by mamma sage'
L(164.k.58, Luttrell, Dec),DrU.

G123 — The gentleman's study, in answer to the Lady's dressing room. *London, printed, and Dublin, re-printed, in the year* 1732.
8º: A⁴; *1–2* 3–8.
Teerink 1304. There was probably no London edition.

The gentleman's study

'Some write of angels, some of goddess'
The title of [Samuel Shepherd] *Chloe sur-priz'd,* 1732, attributes this poem to 'Miss W——'. An answer to Swift's poem.
L(11630.bb.34, title cropt),LVA-F,DA,DK; CtY, TxU.

G124 Genuine. A genuine copy of two excellent court ballads dedicated to the right honourable Sir Robert Walpole. Admiral Vernon's resolution... Argyle's advice to Sir R----t W--p--e... [1741?]
½º: 1 side, 2 columns.
'Prithy Robin say, make no more delay'
'In days of yore, when statesmen wore'
Attacks on Walpole.
L(Rox.III.629).

— A genuine dialogue between a gentlewoman at Derby, [1747/48.] *See* Byrom, John.

G125 — A genuine epistle from M——w P——r, esq; at Paris, to the reverend J——n S——t, D.D. at Windsor. With a letter to Sir Patrick Lawles... Publish'd from the original manuscripts, by Timothy Brocade... *London, anno salutis* 1714. (6 Sept, Luttrell)
8º: *A*⁴ B⁴ C²; *1–4* 5–20.
Teerink 882. With a colophon, 'Printed for A. Boulter'. Some copies (e.g. LLP,DT) are bound with [Francis Reynardson] *An ode to the Pretender,* 1713, which was reprinted for the issue below.
'Since you, dear Jon----an, alone best know'
A whig satire in the form of a mock letter from Prior to Swift.
L(164.m.71, Luttrell),LLP,O,DT; CtY,MH,*PU.*

G126 — [reissue] *London, anno salutis* 1714.
8º: π¹[= ²B1] *A*⁴ B⁴ C², ²A⁴ B⁴(–B1); *i–ii, 1–4* 5–20, *1–13 14 blk.* π1 hft.
A reissue with a half-title reading 'A farther hue and cry after Dr. Sw----t. Being a collection of curious pieces found since his departure'. *Case* 273. With the addition of a new edition of 'An ode to the Pretender' and 'Mortimer his fall'. *MC* Sept 1714 probably refers to this edition.
LVA-F(–π1),DA(lacks part 2),LdU-B; CtY(uncut),NjP,TxU(part 2 bound separately).

G127 — [*idem*] A farther hue and cry after Dr. Sw----t. Being a collection of curious pieces...Published by Timothy Brocade, esq;... The second edition. *London, printed for A. Boulter,* 1714.
8º: π¹ A–B⁴, ²A⁴ B⁴(–B1); *i–ii, 1–2* 3–16, *1–13 14 blk.* π1 hft.
Case 273c. A new edition, subsequently reissued in *Who runs next,* 1715, not listed here.
C; *CtY,*DLC.

— A genuine epistle written some time since, 1735. *See* Jacob, Hildebrand.

Georgia

G128 Georgia. Georgia, a poem. Tomo Chachi, an ode.
A copy of verses on Mr. Oglethorpe's second
voyage to Georgia. *London printed, and sold by J.
Roberts*, 1736. (*GM,LM* March)
2°: *A*² B–E²; *1–3 4–19 20 blk.*
'Whilst Europe round us pants with dread alarms'
Tomo Chachi: 'What stranger's this? and from what
region far?'
Copy of verses: 'Of heart so dauntless, of such firm
good-will'.
　　Edited by J. C. Stevens, Atlanta, 1950. *Tomo-
chachi* is printed from ms. in Wintour's edition
of Thomas Fitzgerald's *Poems* 1781; Stevens
regards his authorship of that poem as certain,
and suggests all three poems are by him. But
the edition of Samuel Wesley the younger's
Poems, 1862, by James and William Nichols,
refers twice (pp. 13, 18) to his poem *Georgia* as
published separately in 1736. Possibly this is a
joint publication, since Wesley and Fitzgerald
were friends. Tomo-chachi was the Indian
chief brought to London by Oglethorpe.
L(163.n.41); *GEU,MH,NcD.*

G129 Georgics. The Georgics of Virgil attempted in
English verse, &c. *London, printed for R. Dodsley;
sold by M. Cooper, & W. Owen*, 1750. (27 Feb)
4°: A–E⁴ F²; *1–2 3–41 42–44.* F2 advt.
　　Dated 27 Feb in *Straus, Dodsley*. Listed in
GM, LM March.
'How (under heav'n) to make with little toil'
Georgic I only.
L(11630.c.12/10, –F2; 840.k.4/22, –F2),O,CT.

G130 Gerard, —, *Mr.* An epistle to the egregious Mr.
Pope, in which the beauties of his mind and body
are amply display'd. By Mr. Gerard. *London,
printed for the author; sold by M. Harris, at the Bee-
hive*, 1734. (*LEP* 14 Feb)
2°: *A*² B–D² *E*¹; *1–2 3–17 18 blk.*
　　One copy at LVA-D is bound with a frontispiece, presumably from another work. Listed
again in *GM* April as 'with a new preface', and
so advertised in *DPB* 11 April; this has not
been traced.
'Vouchsafe, distinguish'd poet, to excuse'
　　Gerard has not been identified; Mrs. Lois
Morrison has suggested privately that the
name is a pseudonym for Eustace Budgell.
LVA-D(2); CSmH,IU,KU,MH(2),TxU(2)+.

G131 [Geree, John.] A poem to his grace the Duke of
Marlborough, on the glorious successes of the last
campaign. [*London*] *Printed in the year* 1705.
2°: *π*¹ A–C² *D*¹; *i–ii, 1–13 14 blk.*
'O thou renown'd in war, whose godlike deeds'
　　Early ms. attribution to 'Mr Gery of C.C.C.
Oxon' in the L copy; 'Geree' seems the
accepted spelling. Early ms. in the TxU copy,
'By R N A M' remains unexplained.
L(11602.i.13/3); TxU.

German

G132 German. The German doctor's cure for all
diseases. *London, printed for A--- B---r* [*A.
Boulter?*], *without Temple-Bar*, [1714?]
½°: 1 side, 1 column.
'Welcome brave monarch to this happy isle'
　　On the arrival of George I in England.
Harding.

G133 Ghastly. The ghastly wound. A tale. Inscribed to
the celebrated Mrs. S—— S——. From Monsieur
De La Fontaine. *London printed, and sold by T.
Payne*, 1723. (*PB* 14 Feb)
2°: *A*² B²; *i–ii, 1–6.*
　　The Luttrell copy is recorded in *Haslewood*
as dated April.
'In ancient legends we may find'
　　Inscribed to Sally Salisbury.
OA; OCU,TxU.

G134 Ghost. 'The ghost and the miller. A merry tale.
[*London*] *Published by C. Corbett.* Price 6d.' (*LDP*
11 July 1740)
　　Advertised with a verse quotation beginning
'A ghost I am, of awful worth'.

[Gibbons, Thomas.] Poems on several occasions.
London, printed for J. Brackstone, & R. King, 1743.
(*LDP* 4 Oct)
8°: pp. 36.　　LDW,O; CtY,NN.
　　Entered in Strahan's ledger to Gibbons under
4 Oct 1743, '2½ sheets no.750... For reprinting ¼ sheet... For stitching 50 copies in blue
and marble paper'.

— Juvenilia: poems on various subjects of devotion
and virtue. *London, printed for J. Buckland, & J.
Ward; sold also by Mr. Oswald, Mr. Gardner, &
Mrs. King*, 1750. (*LM* Aug)
8°: pp. 288.　　L,O; CtY,MH.
　　Strahan's ledger under Feb 1750 records
'Proposals for Mr. Gibbon's Poems no.
2000... Do. no. 500', entered to James Buckland; 800 copies of the edition are entered
under August.

———————

G135 — Britannia's alarm: a poem occasioned by the
present rebellion. To which is added, A fable of the
vine and bramble. *London, printed for R. King,
J. Buckland & M. Cooper, & M. Marshal*, 1745.
(*GM* Dec)
8°: *π*¹[= D4] A–C⁴ D⁴(–D4); [2] *i–ii iii–iv, 5–24*
[2] *25–28.* *π*1 hft; 28 err.
　　The unnumbered leaf D1 is a fly-title to the
fable.
'A trivial theme no more demands the lay'
Fable: 'Is there a Briton hopes to see'
L(11631.bb.30, –*π*1, D1),O(2, 1–*π*1, 1 lacks
D1–3),E,AdU(–*π*1); CSmH(presentation copy),
CLU-C,CtY,MH(–*π*1),TxU(–*π*1)+.

Gibbons, T.

G136 — An elegiac poem, to the memory of the Rev. Isaac Watts, D.D. who departed this life November 25, 1748... *London, printed for J. Oswald, J. Buckland, M. King, J. Ward, & E. Gardner*, 1749. (*GA* 10 Feb)

8º: *A*² B–D⁴ E²; *i–iii* iv, *1* 2–27 *28*. 28 advt.

Entered in Strahan's ledger to James Buckland under Feb 1749, 1000 copies, and also '500 single titles'; similar entries are frequently found to Buckland. Cf. *Plomer* for his use of titles for advertising purposes.

'Fair science blasted in its num'rous growth'

L(T.1697/4),LDW,O,C; CSmH,IU,MH,NN,NjP+.

G137 — An elegy on the death of the reverend Mr. Peter Goodwin, who departed this life November 27, 1747. in the LXIVth year of his age. *London, printed for J. Oswald*, 1748 [1747]. (*GM,LM* Dec)

8º: *A*⁴ B⁴; *1*–4 5–16. A1 hft; 16 advt.

'While other poets, hir'd to sing'

L(1415.h.53),LDW(2); CSmH(−A1).

G137·2 — 'An elegy sacred to the memory of William Beldam.' [*London*, 1742.] (March)

The title and first line are taken from Thomas Gibbons senior, *The mourner's complaint considered, and applied. In a funeral discourse for Mr. William Beldam*, second edition, 1746. The first edition of the sermon is entered in Strahan's ledger under 20 March [1742], 'a funeral sermon 2 sheets and a poem one sheet 150 copies', and under 27 March is entered 'An elegy' 100 copies. Only the one poem appears in the second edition of the sermon, and it seems possible that this elegy was first issued with the sermon and then separately.

'The muse, that once in raptures us'd to pay'

(Strahan's ledger.)

G137·5 [—] 'A poem (the fox and monkey).' [*London*, 1740.] (Oct)

Entered in Strahan's ledger to Thomas Gibbons under 17 Oct [1740], '½ sheet, 100 copies'.

(Strahan's ledger.)

Gibbs, James. The first fifteen psalms of David, translated into lyric verse: propos'd as an essay... *London, printed by J. Matthews, for John Hartley*, 1701.

4º: pp. 35. O,AdU.

Watermark: fleur-de-lys on shield.

— [fine paper] L.

Watermark: Strasburg bend. The copy seen adds 'The two first psalms corrected and improv'd', signed B⁴.

— [reissue] Part of a new version of the psalms... The second edition corrected. *London, printed for John Hartley, ⟨R. Simpson, and P. Yeo, bookseller in Exon*, 1712.⟩

O.

Gibbs, J.

Cancel title cropt in the copy seen, but the imprint supplied in ms. B1, 2 bearing the two first psalms are cancelled, and a congratulatory poem is added.

Gibeonites. The Gibeonites of this day discover'd, [1746?] *See* Allt, William.

Gibraltar. Gibraltar; a poem, 1727. *See* Breval, John Durant.

G138 [**Gibson, William**, *licensed schoolmaster*.] The damneds doom, or some meditations in verse, upon the last great sentence, at the day of judgment. *Edinburgh, printed in the year* 1701.

8º: *A*⁴ B–C⁴; *1*–4 5–22 *23–24 blk*. A1 hft.

'Heark! heark! the trumpet sounds, the court is met!'

Ascribed to Gibson on the evidence of the following edition, and Gibson's Edinburgh connection. There are probably intermediate editions, now lost, which would clarify the relationship.

O.

G138·5 — [*idem*] An essay. Being a new choice warning to sinners. With the Damned's doom: or, some meditations in verse...upon the day of judgment. *Norwich, printed and sold by F. C. [Freeman Collins] near the Red-Well*, 1712.

8º: *A*⁸; *1* 2–16.

Printed in chap-book style; it contains only *The damneds doom*.

NwP.

G139 — An elegy upon the much to be lamented death of the reverend Mr. John Wilson, minister of the gospel at North Lieth, who departed this life the 1st. of September, 1724. [*Edinburgh*, 1724.]

½º: 1 side, 1 column.

Mourning headpiece and woodcut borders.

'Still we do find, black cloth wears out the first'

At foot, 'Composed by William Gibson licensed schoolmaster'. The first six lines are quoted from Robert Wild's 'Upon the death of so many reverend ministers of late', printed with his *Iter boreale*, 1668.

E.

[**Gibson, William**, *quaker*.] A letter to the author of A character, 1717. *See* L153.

Gideon. Gideon, [1720]–. *See* Hill, Aaron.

[**G140** = C56·5] **Gift.** The gift of Pallas, 1733. *See* Carthy, Charles.

Gilbert, Thomas. Poems on several occasions. *London, printed for Charles Bathurst*, 1747.

8º: pp. viii, 264. L; CtY,IU.

G141 [—] The first satire of Juvenal imitated. *London, printed for H. Goreham*, 1740. (*GM,LM* Feb)

Gilbert, T. The first satire of Juvenal

2⁰: *A*² B–E²; *1–3* 4–20.
'Shall every pension'd scribbler draw his pen'
Reprinted in Gilbert's *Poems*, 1747.
L(1875.d.6/175); CtY,*MH*,OCU,TxU(2, 1 uncut).

[—] The first satire of the second book of Horace, imitated, 1745. *See* F150.

G142 [—] A panegyric on a court. By the author of the World unmask'd. A satire. *London, printed by and for J. Mechell,* 1739. (*GM,LM* Feb)
2⁰: *A*¹ B–E² F¹; *3–5* 6–22.
    Rothschild 220.
'Since none but flatterers to ―― resort'
    The world unmask'd is certainly by Gilbert (see below).
L(11602.1.17/8),O(uncut),DG,LdU-B(uncut); CU,DFo,ICN,TxU(2).

G143 [—] A satire on all parties: a poem. *London, printed for W. Owen,* 1749. (*GA* 16 Feb)
2⁰: A–D²; *i–ii* iii–iv, *5* 6–15 *16 blk.*
'Awake, my friend! and strike the sounding lyre!'
    The third edition, 1750, was published with Gilbert's name.
CtY,MH.

G144 [—] ― The second edition. *London, printed for W. Owen,* 1749.
2⁰: A–D²; *i–ii* iii–iv, *5* 6–15 *16 blk.*
    Apparently a reimpression or press-variant title. The L copy has an errata slip on the verso of the title.
L(643.1.28/11),SrS; KU.

G145 [—] ― *London: printed, and Dublin, re-printed in the year* 1749.
12⁰: A⁶; *i* ii–iv, *5* 6–12.
CtY.

G146 ―― The third edition, revis'd and corrected, with several additions. *London, printed for W. Owen,* 1750. (9 April?)
4⁰: A–C⁴ D²; *i–ii* iii–viii, 9–28. *28 err, advt.*
CSmH(ms. date 9 April),CtY.

G147 ― The second epistle of the first book of Horace imitated. *London, printed for T. Cooper,* 1741. (*GM,LM* March)
2⁰: *A*² B–E²; *1–5* 6–19 *20 blk.*
    Rothschild 1013.
'While you, dear Paulus, sacrifice your rest'
CtY,ICN,IU.

G148 [—] A view of the town. In an epistle to a friend in the country. A satire. *London, printed by R. Penny, for the author, and sold by A. Dodd,* 1735.
2⁰: *A*² B–F²; *i–iv, 1* 2–20. *iv err.*
    75 copies and the whole of the copyright formed part of a lot in the trade sale of Thomas Worrall, 10 Nov 1737 (cat. at O-JJ).
'To you who love to range the sylvan scene'
    Reprinted in Gilbert's *Poems*, 1747.
O,LdU-B(uncut); CSmH,ICN,MH,OCU,TxU(2, 1 uncut)+.

Gilbert, T. A view of the town

G149 [—] ― 'London, printed by R. Penny, for the author, and sold by A. Dodd' [*Edinburgh*], 1735.
8⁰: a⁴ B–C⁴ D²; *i–vi, 1–20* 21–22 *blk.*
    Printed by R. Fleming on the evidence of the ornaments.
L(11630.bbb.42/7),LVA-D,O(–D2); CtY,IU (–D2),MH(–D2),NjP(–D2),TxU+.

G150 [――] The world unmask'd. A satire. *London, printed for J. Mechell,* 1738. (*GM* March)
2⁰: *A*² B–E²; *i–iii* iv, *5* 6–16 21–24. *iv err.*
    Ms. corrections on pp. 7, 21 in all copies seen. Also listed in *GM* Dec 1746.
'Your spleen is vain! take counsel of a friend'
    Reprinted in Gilbert's *Poems*, 1747.
L(643.m.16/2),O(uncut),LdU-B(uncut); CSmH, CtY,IU,MH,TxU(uncut)+.

G151 [**Gildon, Charles.**] Canons: or, the vision. A poem. Address'd to the right honourable James earl of Caernarvan, &c. *London, printed for J. Roberts,* 1717.
8⁰: π¹ A⁴ a² B–D⁴ E¹; [2] *i–ii* iii–xii, 1–26. *π1 hft.*
'Tyr'd with the nauseous follies of the age'
    Ascribed to Gildon by *Cibber* III. 329.
L(992.h.3/12, –π1); OCU.

G152 [—] [reissue] The apparition: a poem. Address'd to the right honourable James earl of Caernarvan, &c... The second edition. *London, printed for S. Baker,* 1718 [1717]. (*PB* 19 Nov)
8⁰: π²A⁴(–A1)a²B–D⁴E¹; [2] *i–ii* iii–xii, 1–26. *π1 hft.*
    Cancel title and half-title. Advertised in *PB* as 'By Mr. G――'.
L(1966),O(–π1); DFo.

G153 ― Libertas triumphans: a poem, occasion'd by the glorious victory obtain'd near Odenard, by the forces of the allies under the command of his highness John duke of Marlborough...on the first of July, 1708. *London, printed for Tho. Bullock; sold by J. Morphew,* 1708. (*DC* 21 July)
2⁰: *A*² B–E²; *1–4* 5–20.
    Watermark: initial.
'An impious doubt did oft my mind invade'
    Dedication to George Augustus of Hanover signed.
CSmH(Luttrell, 22 July),CtY,ICN,MH,TxU.

G154 ― [fine paper]
    Watermark: Amsterdam arms.
O.

[—] Threnodia virginea: or, the apotheosis, 1708. *See* T261.

[**G155** = R334·5] [**Gill, John.**] The junto. A poem [actually by Richard Russell], 1712. *See* Russell, Richard.

G156 **Gill, Thomas.** Advice to youth: or, instructions for young men and maids. By Thomas Gill, the blind man of St. Edmonds-Bury, Suffolk. *London, printed in the year* 1708 [1709?]. (1 March, Luttrell)
8⁰: A⁸; *1–4* 5–16.

Gill, T. Advice to youth

'Young man attend a while to what I say'
L(161.k.12, Luttrell).

G157 — [variant imprint?] *London, printed in the year 1709.*
E.

G158 — The blind man's case at London: or, a character of that city. Sent in a letter to his friend in the country. By Thomas Gill the blind man of St. Edmond's-Bury, Suffolk. *London, printed in the year 1711.*
8°: A⁴; *1–2* 3–8.
'Oppress'd with cares, fatigu'd with labours'
E.

G159 —— *London, printed in the year 1712.*
8°: A⁴; *1–2* 3–8.
CtY.

G160 — Instructions for children, in verse. By Thomas Gills... *London, printed in the year 1707.*
8°: A⁸; *1–4* 5–16.
Horizontal chain-lines, but apparently octavo in format.
'From whence, dear child, does all that's good proceed?'
For a suggestion that Joseph Browne may have had a hand in the authorship, see G162·5 below.
L(12331.ee.31/10).

G161 —— *London, printed in the year 1709.* (12 March, Luttrell)
8°: A⁸; *1–4* 5–16.
L(161.k.13, Luttrell),E.

G162 — [*idem*] [dh] A practical catechism: or, instructions for children, in verse. By Thomas Gill... [*London, 171–?*]
8°: A⁴; *1–8.*
E.

G162·5 [—] [*idem*] Useful and delightful instructions, by way of dialogue between the master & his scholar, containing the duty of children. Composed in verse...and humbly recommended to the use of children of both sexes, train'd up in the charity-schools. *London printed, and sold by J. Downing,* 1712. (*SR* 8 April)
8°: A⁸; *1–2* 3–16.
Entered in *SR* to Joseph Browne; deposit copy at EU. No bookseller of that name is known, and possibly it refers to Browne the author who may have written, corrected, or entered the copy on Gill's behalf. A revised version, with first line:
'From whence, dear child, does all that's good descend?'
L(11602.e.1/1),EU.

G162·6 [—] — The second edition enlarg'd. *London printed, and sold by J. Downing,* 1716.
8°: A–C⁴; *1–2* 3–23 *24 blk.*
'Price *2d.* or *12s.* per hundred.'
L(11630.bb.32),O.

Gill, T.

G163 — [dh] Lamentation on the death of his grace Duke Hamilton. [*London, 1712?*]
8°: A²; *1–4.*
'The brave Duke Hamilton, alas is kill'd'
E.

G164 — A new-year's-gift: or, a poem upon the circumcision of our blessed lord and saviour Jesus Christ. *London, printed by R. Janeway,* [171–?]
8°: A⁴; *1–3* 4–8.
'On new-year's-day our blessed lord began'
E.

G165 — A poem upon the apparition and ascension of our blessed saviour. [*London*] *Printed at the corner of Dogwell Court, in White Fryars,* [17––?]
8°: pp. 8.
(Ms. quotation from C. J. Stewart's catalogue of 1858 in E(Cwn 301); there dated c.1660.)

G166 — Questions and answers in verse, upon the creation of the world, the fall of man, the flood, and several other passages out of the Old Testament. *London, printed in the year* 1712.
8°: A⁴ (A2 as 'A3'); *1–2* 3–8.
'Who made the world, and everything therein?'
E.

G167 — [dh] Thomas Gills of Edmund's Bury in Suffolk, upon the recovery of his sight, and the second loss thereof. [*London?* 171–?]
8°: A⁴; *1–7* 8 *blk.*
'Long had I languish'd in continual night'
L(11643.bb.32/1).

G168 — [dh] Upon the nativity of our blessed saviour. [*London,* 171–?]
8°: A⁴; *1* 2–8.
'Glory to god on high, and peace on earth'
E.

G169 **Gillmertoun.** The Gillmertoun Vulcan gone, who hew'd seven fire-rooms in a single stone: or, an elegy on George Paterson smith, good-man of the famous Gillmertoun caves. [*Edinburgh,* 172–?]
½°: 1 side, 2 columns.
'Ingenious George, at last alace thou'rt gone'
E.

Gills, Thomas. *See* Gill, Thomas.

'**Gingle, Jacob.**' The Oxford sermon versified, 1729–. *See* O270.

G170 **Glance.** A glance upon his spent time. By T.L. 1714. [1714.]
short slip: 1 side, 1 column.
'A young man I have been, & now old at last'
T.L. was eighty when he wrote this.
MH.

G171 [**Glanvill, Abraham.**] The rake reform'd: a poem. In a letter to the rakes of the town... By A. G. gent. *London, printed in the year* 1718 [1717]. (*SR* 18 Oct)
8°: *A*⁴ B–D⁴; *i–iv,* '1' 6–32. A1 *hft.*

Glanvill, A. The rake reform'd

Entered in *SR* to Abraham Glanvill; deposit copies at LSC,EU, the latter with ms. date 27 Oct.
'From verdant meads, where Isis gentle waves'
L(11659.aaa.87),LSC,O(2),EU,LdU-B+;CSmH.

G172 [—] — *London, printed for A. Dodd, 1718.*
8º: *A*⁴ B-D⁴; *1-4* 5-32. A1 hft.
A different edition, possibly mis-dated; the Luttrell copy at CtY is dated Feb 1721.
L(11659.bb.81),*MR-C*; CtY(Luttrell),DFo (–A1),MH,*NcD*,TxU.

Glanvill, John. Poems: consisting of originals and translations. *London, printed for Bernard Lintot, J. Osborn & T. Longman, & W. Bell, 1725.*
8º: pp. 298.   L,O; ICN,MH.
Some copies have a cancel C2 with enlarged errata (23 lines), and add 2Q⁴ with additional poems; both states are at MH. A copy at ICN has ms. corrections and additions by the author. Entered to Glanvill in *SR* 27 July 1725 (deposit copy at O), but not listed in *MC* until Jan 1726.

— [reissue] The second edition. *London printed, and sold by G. Strahan, J. Clark, J. Roberts, & N. Blandford, 1726.*
NjP.
Cancel title.

———————

[—] The happy pair; a new song.
There are four popular half-sheet editions of this song at L, one titled 'The loyal swain...' Though dated by *CBEL* as [1706?], they may well represent varying dates over a considerable period. They have been excluded from this catalogue like other popular songs.

G173 — A poem, occasion'd by the successes of the present war: and calculated for the beginnings of the present year. *London, printed for Egbert Sanger, 1707.*
2º: A-C²; *i-ii,* 1-10.
Watermark: Amsterdam arms. Presumably this precedes the Morphew issue which is dated 25 March.
'Years have their glory, ages have their fame'
O(author's ms. corrections),*MR-C*; CSmH.

G174 — [fine paper]
Watermark: fleur-de-lys.
DFo.

G175 — [another issue] *London printed, and sold by J. Morphew, 1707.* (25 March, Luttrell)
2º: A²(±A1) B-C²; *i-ii,* 1-10.
Advertised in *DC* 27 March.
LdU-B; CSmH,MH(Luttrell),TxU.

[Glas, John.] 'Christian songs. To which is added, the evidence and import of Christ's resurrection, versified, for the help of the memory. Price 6*d*.' (*SM* May 1749)
There is a copy of the fifth edition, 1775, at L.

Glasgow

G176 **Glasgow.** Glasgow's parrad. To the tune of, The winter is cold, my cleeding is thin. [1714.]
½º: 1 side, 2 columns.
Proper names printed in italic capitals.
'Come all ye protestants give ear to my song'
In honour of George I's coronation.
NjP.

G177 — [another edition]
Proper names printed in italic lower-case.
E.

G178 **Glass.** Glass excised; or, the schemer's mirror. A ballad. To the tune of the Leather bottel. *London, printed for W. Webb, 1746.* (*BM, GM* April)
2º: *A*¹ B²; *1-2* 3-5 *6 blk.*
'What say you to our schemer fine?'
O; MH,TxU.

G179 **Glimpse.** A glimpse of hell: or a short description of the common side of Newgate. *London, printed in the year 1705* [1704]. (*DC* 14 Dec)
4º: *A*² B-C⁴ D²; *i-iv,* 1-19 *20 blk.*
'How oft in these misjudging times'
Dedication signed 'T.H.'
L(11631.bb.100),O(Luttrell, 14 Dec).

Gloria. Gloria patri, &c. or hymns to the trinity, 1746–. *See* Wesley, John & Charles.

G180 **Glorious.** The glorious campaign, or, Jannes tou me aperdu tou pucellage. Carv'd in gold letters on the gates of Tournay. In English, She never lost her maiden-head. The tune. Ye commons and peers. [*London,* 1709.]
½º: 1 side, 2 columns.
'Alack and a day/Poor Monsieur they say'
On Marlborough's victory at Tournai.
TxU.

G181 — The glorious warriour: or, a ballad in praise of General Stanhope; dedicated to all who have votes for parliament-men in the city of Westminster. To the tune of Fair Rosamund. *London, printed for S. Popping, 1710.* (*SR* 3 Oct)
½º: 1-2, 2 columns.
Deposit copy at L.
'When Anne, a princess of renown'
Crum W888. An election ballad, answered by *An excellent new ballad, being the second part,* [1710.]
L(C.20.f.2/234),LLP,O,Crawford; InU.

G182 — The glorious works of creation and providence. A poem. To which is added, a prospect of the future state of mankind... By J.W. *London, printed for John Morphew, 1707.*
4º: *A*² B-D⁴ (B2 as 'A2'); *i-iv,* 1-23 *24 blk.*
'Just as the sun shone on our hemisphere'
L(164.k.72).

G183 — The glorious year. By J.P. To the tune of Now, now comes on the glorious year. [*London,* 1714/15.]
slip: 1 side, 1 column.

The **glorious** year

'Now, now is come the glorious year'
In praise of George I and his new ministry.
C,Crawford; *Harding.*

G184 Glory. The glory of France. Avis a Monsieur de
*** premier peintre de sa majesté...Advice to the
French king's cheif [!] painter, how to represent in
in its true light, the glory of his master... *London,
publish'd by D. Fournier,* Feb 14 1747.
½°: 1 side, 2 columns.
> Large engraving at head. French text in column
> 1, signed 'A.G. Fournier'; English text in
> column 2. The imprint is taken from the
> engraving.
'Peintre, pour bien tracer, la gloire de la France'
'Painter, display, in honour of the state'
> A satire against Louis XV.
L(P&D 2849); NNP.

G185 — The glory of his royal highness the Duke of
Cumberland, in the battle of Culloden... By ——
—— puerulus. *Printed in the year* 1747.
4°: A–C⁴; *1–5* 6–23 *24 blk.*
> Apparently a piece of provincial printing.
'I sing the man, who, when he takes the field'
E.

— The glory of Spain subdu'd by British valour,
1748. *See* McKinstry, H.

G186 [Glover, Richard.] Admiral Hosier's ghost. To
the tune of, Come and listen to my ditty. *London,
printed for Mr. Webb, near St. Paul's,* 1740. (21
May?)
2°: *A²* <B²; *1–3* 4–7 *8 blk.*
> *Percival* LVII, dating it 21 May on the evi-
> dence of *The champion* 22 May. Reprinted
> with an answer in Henry Price, *The spectre,*
> 1740.
'As, near Porto-Bello lying'
> *Crum* A1609. For Glover's authorship see
> *DNB* and refs.
L(162.n.59),O; *CLU-C,CSmH,TxU.*

G187 [—] — [*London*] *Publish'd according to act of
parliament* July 1740. (*LDP* 23 July)
> A large engraving at head, signed 'C. Mosley
> sculp.', with eleven stanzas of engraved text
> below, running in two lines from left to right.
> Two copies seen (L,O) are on half-sheets of
> large paper, one at O on a smaller whole sheet.
L(P&D 2422),O(2).

G188 [—] — [1740?]
½°: 1 side, 2 columns.
> A hawkers' broadside with a rough cut of a
> flood at head.
L(1876.f.1/121); *Harding.*

G189 [—] Admiral Hosier's ghost. [1740/–.]
slip: 1 side, 1 column.
> Possibly a later reprint; patriotic slip-songs
> had a long popularity.
C.

Glover, R.

G190 — Leonidas, a poem. *London, printed for R.
Dodsley,* 1737. (*SR* 29 March)
4°: π² A⁴(±A3) a⁴ B–Uu⁴; [4] i–xvi, *1* 2–335 *336.*
π1 blank; 336 err.
> Watermark: crowned eagle; cut copies 9¾ × 7½
> in. Entered in *SR* to Glover; deposit copies
> (fine paper) at O,E,EU,SaU.
'Rehearse, O muse, the deeds and glorious death'
> Preface signed.
O(−π1),CT(−π1),BaP(−π1); CLU-C,ICU,IU
(−π1),MH(3),TxU.

G191 — [fine paper]
> Watermark: TM; cut copies 11½ × 9 in.
L(642.1.4; 83.k.8, −π1),O,E,EU(−π1),SaU.

G192 — — *Dublin, printed by R. Reilly, for J. Smith &
W. Bruce,* 1737.
12°: A–K¹²; *i–ii* iii–xi *xii,* *13* 14–240.
C,DT; NN.

G193 — — The second edition. *Dublin, printed by R.
Reilly, for J. Smith & W. Bruce,* 1737.
12°: A–K¹²; *i–ii* iii–xi *xii,* 13–240.
L(11633.aa.20),O,C,DN,LdU-B+; CtY,*MB.*

G194 — — The second edition. *London, printed for R.
Dodsley,* 1738. (*LM* April)
12°: A–M¹²; *i–iv* v–xxii *xxiii–xxiv blk,* *1* 2–262 *263;
264 blk.* A1 hft; 263 err.
L(993.g.12),O(−A12),C; NN.

G195 — — The third edition. *London, printed for R.
Dodsley,* 1738. (*LDP* 30 May)
12°: A–M¹²; *i–iv* v–xxii *xxiii–xxiv blk,* *1* 2–262 *263;
264 blk.* A1 hft; 263 err.
L(1489.p.19),EU; CLU-C(−A1),MH.

G196 — — The fourth edition. *London, printed for R.
Dodsley,* 1739. (2 June?)
12°: A–M¹²; *i–iv* v–xxii *xxiii–xxiv blk,* *1* 2–262 *263;
264 blk.* A1 hft; 263 err.
> Dated 2 June by *Straus, Dodsley.* Expanded
> from 9 to 12 books in the fifth edition, 1770.
L(993.g.13),LVA-D,O; *MBAt,NN.*

G197 — London: or, the progress of commerce. A poem.
London, printed for T. Cooper, 1739. (*SR* 10 Nov)
4°: A–D⁴; *1–3* 4–30 *31–32 blk.*
> Some copies (L,C,CLU-C) have an added leaf
> of 'argument' after the title. This was printed
> for the second edition, and copies may have
> been produced for the remainder of this
> edition. Entered in *SR* to Glover; deposit
> copies at L,O,E,EU,GU.
'Ye northern blasts, and Eurus, wont to sweep'
L(11630.c.5/3, −D4; 11630.d.12/18, −D4;
840.k.3/11, −D4; C.70.f.1/7, −D4),O(2),CT,E,
GU+; CLU-C,CtY,ICU,MH,TxU+.

G198 — — The second edition. *London, printed for T.
Cooper,* 1739.
4°: A(5 ll) B–D⁴; *i–ii,* 1–30 *31–32 blk.* 30 err.
> The collation of A is obscure; apparently the
> fourth leaf is separate. Possibly A2 (the first
> leaf of text) was cancelled and replaced by a

Glover, R. London

fold containing the 'argument' and a new first leaf of text.
L(11602.gg.24/6,−D4),LG(−D4),LVA-F; ICN(−D4),KU(2),TxU(−D4).

G199 — — The second edition. '*London, printed for T. Cooper*' [*Edinburgh*], 1739.
8°: A⁴ B–D⁴; *1–3* 4–32.
Copies at E are bound with Edinburgh pamphlets.
E(2).

G200 — — *Dublin, re-printed by and for George Faulkner*, 1739.
8°: A–D⁴; *1–3* 4–30 *31–32*. D4 advt.
L(C.71.bb.15/1,−D4),DN(2),DT.

G201 — — The fourth edition. *Dublin, re-printed by and for George Faulkner*, 1739.
8°: A–D⁴; *1–3* 4–30 *31–32 blk*.
Apparently another impression of the preceding.
L(1493.d.12),C; CtY,*InU*,TxU.

G202 **Glukopikra.** Γλυκοπικρα: or, miscellanies melancholly and diverting. Occasioned chiefly by the death of a late incomparable and truly noble lady. By way of pastoral. *London printed, and are to be sold by A. Baldwin*, 1704. (20 Dec, Luttrell)
4°: A–D⁴; *i–ii*, 1–30.
'Under a lonely yew as Thyrsis lay'
A pastoral dialogue ranging over various subjects but chiefly concerned with lamenting Lady Brooke, apparently Ann Dodington, afterwards Brooke, afterwards Hoby, who died in Feb 1691. Luttrell notes 'A whiggish tract at last'.
O; CtY,ICN,IU(Luttrell),InU.

G——n, H——. A panegyrick in answer to a lible [!], 1730. *See* P32.

Gnothi. Γνωθι σεαυτον. Know yourself. A poem, 1734. *See* Arbuthnot, John.

Goakman, Simon. The religious magazine: or, the soul's harbour for divine entertainments. Containing, pious verses on these following subjects... *York, printed by Thomas Gent*, 1736.
12°: pp. 12. YM.

G203 **[Goatley, John.]** To the author of the panegyrick on the Canterbury ladies. *Printed for the author*, 1718.
½°: 1 side, 1 column.
Possibly printed at Canterbury.
'Hear, thou vile scribbler! of the rhiming trade'
Early ms. attribution to Goatley in L copy. Occasioned by *A panegyrical poem*, 1718.
L(11633.i.17/2).

God. God the creator, and the preserver, 1714. *See* Daniel, Richard.

God

— God's glorious perfections shining in Christ, 1718. *See* Cheyn, William.

G204 — God's judgment upon hereticks, or the infidel's overthrow; being a full and true account of Mr. Woolstain's being carried away by the devil... *London, printed (by order of his executor An————y C———ns, esq;) for Mr. E. C————l; sold by A. Moore*, 1729. (*MChr* 24 April)
2°: A² < B² (B2 as 'B'); *1–3* 4–8.
'Good people all I pray give ear'
From the text, Woolstain was a papist; but possibly referring to Thomas Woolston, the freethinker, being imprisoned in 1729. A mock popular ballad.
O; OCU.

G205 **Goddess.** The goddess Envy to Doctor D--l--y. [*Dublin*] *Printed in the year* 1730.
8°: A⁴; *1–3* 4–6 *7–8 blk*.
Teerink 952.
'Admire not sir, that I so long unseen'
In praise of Delany, occasioned by the attacks started by Swift's *Epistle upon an epistle*, 1730.
LVA-F,DA(−A4),DT,*MR-C*.

Goddolphine. Goddolphine Stygem potas et Averna fluenta, [1712?] *See* Pitcairne, Archibald.

G206 **Godly.** Godly Sarah, or, the sighing sister; a pastoral dialogue between Andrew Clubson and Tho. Woolrich... Written first in the year 1716, and now corrected and enlarged. Never before printed. *Edinburgh, printed in the year* 1737.
8°: A⁴ B–D⁴; *i–ii* iii–xii, 13–32.
'You're welcome, Woolrich, from Dunfermline fair'
Dedication and preface signed 'Ned Scrawl', clearly a pseudonym.
E(2),GM(ms. notes, lacks D4); MH,NNC.

G207 **Gods.** The gods in debate: or, no bribe like beauty. A new ballad, on the Prince of Orange's arrival. *London, printed for J. Roberts; sold by W. Waring*, [1733.] (*GM* Nov)
2°: A² < B²; *1–3* 4–8.
'Stern Æole of late'
A eulogistic poem; the gods debate on how the prince shall cross the sea, since Aeolus has locked up the winds.
L(1970),O.

Godwin, Edward. Hymns for Christian societies. *Bristol, printed by Felix Farley; sold at Smiths-Hall, Bristol; at the Tabernacle, London; at Gloucester, by Mr. G. Harris; at Northampton, by Mr. H. Walker*, 1744.
12°: pp. 24. GT.

— — Part II. *Bristol, printed by Felix Farley*... [as preceding], 1744.
12°: pp. 24. GT.

Godwin, E.

—— Part III. *Bristol, printed by Felix Farley . . .* [as preceding], 1744.
12°: pp. 24. GT.

— 'Hymns for the love-feast. Price 1*d.*'
Advertised in *Christian tales,* 1746.

— Hymns. *Bristol, printed by Sam. Farley; sold at Smith's-Hall, Bristol; at the Tabernacle, and at Mr. Pitman's, at the Tabernacle House, London,* 1747.
12°: pp. 168. O.

[—] Hymns for the festivals, and on other solemn occasions, 1748. *See* Hymns.

———————

G208 — A brief account of god's dealings with Edward Godwin. Written by himself. With a letter from Mr. John Cennick, and another from the author, by way of preface . . . The second edition, corrected. *Bristol, printed by Felix Farley,* 1744.
12°: *A*⁶ B⁶; *i–iii* iv–vi, 7 8–24.
> The drop-head title to the verse account is 'Experience'. A hymn is added on pp. 22–24. Cennick's letter is dated 20 Oct 1743, which may suggest a date for the first edition which has not been traced.

'Does any weary soul thro' sin despair'
Moravian archives, London.

G209 — Christian tales. Containing, I. The band. II. The test of self-righteousness. III. The parents instructor. IV. A supposed conference between a king and a christian. *Exon, printed by Mark Farley,* 1746.
8°: A–F⁴; *1–5* 6–46 *47; 48 blk.* 47 advt.
'Some happy souls who Jesus knew'
L(4414.cc.30),O,GT.

G210 — The death-bed: a poem. Containing the joyful death of a believer, and the awful death of an unbeliever. *Bristol, printed by Felix Farley,* 1744.
12°: A–B⁶; *1–7* 8–22 *23–24 blk.*
'Of conquering faith, my pen attempts to tell'
'Another scene my pen attempts to show'
L(1961),GT.

Goff. The goff. An heroi-comical poem, 1743. *See* Mathison, Thomas.

G211 Golden. The golden age from the fourth eclogue of Virgil, &c. *London, printed in the year* 1703.
4°: A–B²; *i–ii,* 1–6.
'Sicilian muse, thy voice and subject raise'
> Wrongly ascribed to Walsh in *CBEL;* Walsh's reply, 'The golden age restor'd', does not seem to have been published separately. The same author wrote *The leaden-age,* 1705.

L(11385.e.16),LVA-F,O,OW,C; CtY,IU.

G212 — — [*London?*] *Printed in the year* 1703.
4°: *A*⁴; *1–2* 3–8.
> This edition makes substantial additions to the text; see F. H. Ellis in *POAS* VI. 778f.

L(11375.ee.37); CSmH.

The Golden age

G213 — — [col] *London, printed in the year* 1703.
4°: *A*²; 1–4.
> Drop-head title only.

MH.

Goldwin, William. Musae juveniles. *Londini, prostant venales apud A. Baldwin,* 1706. (29 March, Luttrell)
2°: pp. 28. L.

———————

G214 — Europe. A poem. *London printed, and sold by A. Baldwin,* 1706. (*PM* 27 April)
2°: *A*² B–D²; *i–ii,* 1–13 *14 blk.*
'Tho' Europe groans, distress'd with clam'rous din'
L(1347.m.52/2, Luttrell, 27 April).

G215 — Great Britain: or, the happy isle. A poem. *London, printed by Fr. Leach; sold by B. Bragg,* 1705. (*PM* 5 June)
2°: *A*¹ B–C² *D*¹; *1–2* 3–11 '10'.
'To sing of Albion's great and happy isle'
L(1347.m.52/1, Luttrell, 5 June); CtY(uncut), DLC.

[—] An hymn to the redeemer, 1713. *See* H81.

G216 — A poetical description of Bristol. *London, printed for, and are to be sold by Joseph Penn, Bristol, and sold by Sam. Crouch, Cornhil,* 1712. (*PM* 24 May)
2°: *A*² B–G²; *i–vi,* 1–21 *22 blk.*
'Tho' muses court the shady groves and greens'
L(11602.i.10/4),O(uncut),*BrP;* CSmH,CtY.

Golf. The goff. An heroi-comical poem, 1743. *See* Mathison, Thomas.

G217 Good. Good advice if rightly take· . A ballad. *London, sold by A. Baldwin,* 1710. (*DC* 11 July)
½°: 1 side, 1 column.
'What strange confus'on at this time'
> Against 'domestic war' caused by Sacheverell.

L(1876.f.1/54, mutilated),Crawford; InU.

G218 — [dh] Good advice to beaus and batchelours, in answer to Good advice to the ladies. By the author of, A tale of a tub. [col] *London, printed in the year* 1705.
4°: *A*²; 1–4.
'Thrice happy yet, (if they the blessing prize,)'
> The implied attribution to Swift may be disregarded. Works by William King, the gazetteer, were also published with this formula, and his authorship is perhaps more possible. An answer to the following poem.

TxU.

G219 — Good advice to the ladies: shewing, that as the world goes, and is like to go, the best way for them is to keep unmarried. By the author of the True born Englishman. *London, printed in the year* 1702. (3 Sept, Luttrell)
4°: A–C⁴ (A2 as 'A'); *i–viii,* 1–16.
'I hear, my Lesbia, you must be a wife'

Good advice to the ladies

Lee 31 and *Moore* 46 attribute to Defoe; Defoe in his *Little review* 20 June 1705 apparently disowned the second edition. Subsequent opinion has fluctuated; A. M. Wilkinson in *N&Q* (24 June 1950) is cautious. Answered by *Good advice to beaus and batchelours . . . By the author of a Tale of a tub*, 1705.
L(164.1.62, Luttrell),LG,LU,C; IEN,InU,*MH*, TxU,Rosenbach.

G220 — — With the character of a beau. By the author of the True born Englishman. The second edition corrected. *London, printed for R. Smith; sold by J. Nutte*, 1705. (*WL* June)
4°: A–C⁴; *i–vi*, 1–16 *17–18*. C4 advt.
'The character of a beau' is not a separate addition.
CtY.

G221 — — *London, printed in the year* 1709.
8°: A⁴; *1* 2–8.
Similar in appearance to the chap-book poems of Henry Hills.
Rosenbach.

G222 — [*idem*] 'A timely caution; or good advice to the ladies. By a true Briton. [*London*] *Sold at the pamphlet shops. Price 6d.*' (*MC* Aug 1727)

G223 — A timely caution; or, good advice to the ladies. By a true Briton. The second edition. *London, sold by A. Dodd, E. Smith, & Mrs. Graves*, 1728.
4°: A²(±A1) B–D²; *i–iv*, 1–12.
Presumably a reissue of the preceding.
'I hear, my Cælia, you must be a wife'
CtY.

G224 — [*idem*] Matrimony; or, good advice to the ladies to keep single. In which are painted, in very lively colours, the pictures of many terrible husbands . . . particularly of one whose wife is now suing for a divorce, on account of his unnatural abuses. *London, printed for T. Read*, 1739. (*GM* July)
2°: A² B–D²; *i–iv*, *1* 2–12. A1 hft.
Rothschild 219. An added passage on pp. 6–7 attacks individuals. Answered by *Celibacy: or good advice to young fellows*, 1739.
L(11631.k.5/9,—A1),LdU-B; *CLU*-C,ICN, IU(2),MH(uncut),OCU.

G225 — Good goose don't bite; or, the city in a hubbub. A new ballad. To the tune of, Joan stoop'd down to buckle her shooe, &c. *London, printed for W. Shaw; sold by the pamphlet sellers of London & Westminster*, 1733. (*SJEP* 13 Feb)
2°: A² B²; *1–3* 4–7 *8 blk*.
Percival appendix 49.
'All to the Swan beside the Change'
On Walpole's excise proposals.
MR(2); CtY.

— A Good-Friday ramble, ⟨1707?⟩. *See* Ward, Edward.

— Good manners for schools, 1709. *See* Dykes, Oswald.

Good nature

G226 — Good-nature. A poem. By a young gentleman. *London, printed for M. Cooper*, [1744.] (*GM, LM* March)
4°: A² a⁴ B–D⁴; *i–iv* v–xii, 1–23 *24 blk*. A1 hft.
'Descend ye nine, assist me while I sing'
Possibly by the same author as *A paraphrase on the creation*, 1744, also 'by a young gentleman' and published by Cooper.
L(1485.e.6; 11630.d.3/2, lacks A1, a⁴),O(uncut), OC,CT; DFo,TxU.

— The good stewards, 1730. *See* Howard, W.

[**Goodbarn**, —, *Mr.*] Hog-land: or a description of Hampshire, 1728. *See* H275.

G227 **Goose**. The goose pye, a poem. [*Dublin*, 173–.]
½°: 1 side, 1 column.
Title in two lines.
'When Liffey backward rolls her muddy streams'
On the Irish parliament.
C.

G228 — [another impression]
Title in four lines.
C(cropt).

'**Goose, Philip**.' The duck drowned in Parnassus, or, the goose triumphant. Containing Philip Goose the Berkshire thatcher's poem, 1730. *See* D466.

'**Goosequil, Timothy**, *of the Custom-house*.' The unfortunate ramble, 1709. *See* U6.

[**Gordon, Gilbert**.] A facetious poem in imitation of the Cherry and slae, 1701. *See* F22.

Gordon, Thomas. *A Dublin edition of* Namby Pamby, [*1725*] *is ascribed to 'Capt. Gordon', and thence other works 'By the author of Namby Pamby'. For these, see the true author, Henry Carey.*

Gordon, William. Poems on several occasions. *London, printed for the author; sold by W. Needham, & Mr. Strahan*, 1750.
4°: pp. 63.   O.
The preface speaks of the author appearing in print for the first time; clearly he is not the author of the following.

G229 **Gordon, William**, *A.M.* Epistles translated from the French of Mr. Voltaire. On happiness, liberty and envy. Inscrib'd to John Comins, esq; *London, printed for J. Roberts*, 1738.
8°: A¹ B–D⁴ E(3 ll); *i–ii*, *1* 2–29 *30 blk*.
'Hermotimus, you're newly come abroad'
Translated from *Discours en vers sur l'homme*.
L(992.h.10/5),O; DLC.

Gospel. Gospel canticles: or, spiritual songs, 1720. *See* Erskine, Ralph.

Gothenburg. The Gottenburgh frolick, 1717. *See* The devil to do about Dunkirk, 1708–.

Gothic. The Gothick hero, 1708. *See* Browne, Joseph.

Gould, Robert. The works of Mr. Robert Gould... *London, printed for W. Lewis,* 1709. 8º: 2 vol.   L,O; DFo,MH.
> Watermark: crowned initials. Some copies (e.g. MH) have errata leaves in each volume.
— [fine paper]   CLU-C.
> Watermark: monogram PH; the copy at CLU-C is the dedication copy.

G230 [—] Love given over: or, a satyr against the pride, lust, and inconstancy, &c. of woman. With Sylvia's revenge, or, a satyr against man... Amended by the author. *London printed, and sold by H. Hills,* 1709.
8º: A⁸ B⁴; *1* 2–24.
> Some copies (e.g. O) have a variant state of the title reading 'With the Sylvia's revenge...' First published in 1682 (*Wing* G1422), though the first edition is usually dated 1683. *Sylvia's revenge* was first published in 1688, and separate editions of 1707, 1720 are entered under Richard Ames.
'At length from love's vile slav'ry I am free'
Answered by E23.
L(11601.dd.17/5),O(2),OW,C,CT(3); CSmH,IU, *MiU,*NjP,*TxU* +.

G231 [—] — *London printed, and sold by H. Hills,* 1710.
8º: A⁸ B⁴; *1* 2–24.
> Reissued with other remaindered Hills poems in *A collection of the best English poetry,* 1717, (*Case* 294).
L(C.124.b.7/19; G.18914/4),LG,LVA-F,AdU, LdU-B; CSmH,CtY,IU,MH.

G231·5 [—] 'The poetess, a satyr. Being a reply to the female-author of a poem call'd, Silvia's revenge. By the author of the Satyr against woman. [*London*] *Printed, and sold by the booksellers of London & Westminster.*' (*DC* 17 Dec 1706)
> Subsequently advertised in *PM* 18 Feb 1707 as 'sold by J. Morphew'. This is the title under which Gould's *A satyrical epistle to the female author of a poem, call'd Silvia's revenge,* 1691 (*Wing* G1436) appears in his *Works,* 1709, and it seems clear that this must be at least a reissue, if not a new edition. The first line in 1709 reads:
'Why, foolish woman, are you so enrag'd'
> A reply to Richard Ames's *Sylvia's revenge,* first published in 1688, and reprinted with the date 1707 though published 9 Nov 1706.

G232 Government. The government of the human body. A tale. Address'd to the freeholders of Great-Britain. Not improper to be read before the ensuing election. *London, printed for J. Roberts, & R. Dodsley,* 1741. (*LM* April)
2º: A¹ B–C² D¹; *i–ii,* *1* 2–9 *10 blk.*
'Whatever wicked atheists teach us'
CSmH(uncut),CtY,MH.

G233 Gracchus. 'Gracchus. A poetical character. [*London*] *Printed for M. Cooper.* Price 6*d.*' (*GA* 1 Feb 1749)

G234 Grace. Grace. A poem. In two books. *London, printed for George Keith,* 1749. (*GM* Feb)
4º: π¹ A⁴ B⁴(–B1); *i–ii,* *1–2* 3–14.
'The need of grace (a solemn theme) I sing'
ICU.

Graces. Graces before meat, [1746?]–. *See* Wesley, John & Charles.

Graham, D. The battle of Drummossie-Muir: containing three excellent new songs... Composed by the poet D. Graham. [*Glasgow?*] *Printed in the year* 1746.
8º: pp. 8.   E.
> A garland of loyal rejoicing.

G235 — A full, particular and true account of the rebellion in the years 1745–6... To the tune of, The gallant Grahams. To which is added, several other poems by the same author. *Glasgow, printed and sold by James Duncan,* 1746. (Oct?)
12º: A–F⁴/² I–K⁴/² G–H⁴/² L–Q⁴/² (B unsigned; F1 as 'E'); *i–ii* iii–xii, *1*–84.
> Dedication dated 29 Sept 1746, the date it was advertised in the *Glasgow courant.* Additional poems on pp. 75–84.
'We had great wars with France and Spain'
GM.

G236 [Graham, James, *marquis of Montrose.*] I'le never love thee more. To be sung with its pleasant new tune. [*Edinburgh?* 17––.]
½º: 1 side, 2 columns.
> Divided into two parts: five stanzas in the first, thirteen in the second. Although these editions are properly outside the scope of this catalogue, it seemed worth recording them.
'My dear and onely love I pray'
E(crop).

G237 [—] [*idem*] A proper new ballad, to the tune of I'le never love thee more. [*Edinburgh?* 17––.]
½º: 1 side, 2 columns.
> This edition has not been collated with the preceding, but they seem very closely related typographically. Dated by L catalogue [c. 1690]; not in *Wing.*
L(Rox. III. 579).

G238 — [*idem*] The brave Montross to his country. [*Dublin?* 172–?]

Graham, J. *marquis*

$\frac{1}{2}$°: 1 side, 2 columns.
    A different version of the text from the preceding. Eight stanzas only, with two other occasional verses.
'My dear, and only joy, I pray'
Rothschild.

G239 — Verses composed by James marquis of Montrose. [*Edinburgh*, 174–?]
8°: A^2; 1–4.
'This world's a tennis-court, and man's the ball'
CtY.

Grain. A grain of gratitude: or, historical and poetical fragments, in commemoration of the pious life and blessed death of Mr. John Eccles... By a friend and intimate acquaintance of the deceased. *London, printed for Eben. Tracy*, 1712.
8°: pp. 31.   CtY.

Gram., Horat., *L. Mag.* The eagle and the robin, 1709. *See* E2.

Grammatica. Grammatica Busbeiana, 1702–. *See* Busby, Richard.

G240 Grand. The grand affairs of Europe, discuss'd. In a dialogue between Louis a French marquis, and Marcellus a German of quality. Translated out of the original French, by an English lord. [*London*] *Printed for A. Banks; sold by the booksellers of London & Westminster*, 1702 [1701]. (20 Nov, Luttrell)
2°: A–B^2 C–D^2; i–iv, 1–12.
    Morgan D181 records a 1701 edition, probably in error from the Luttrell copy.
'Marcellus, too tedious have been our discourses'
L(11630.ff.2/14),LVA-D,DK; InU(Luttrell), TxU(2).

G241 — [reissue] A familiar discourse between a Jacobite and a French Hugonot, concerning the succession to England and Spain. *London, printed in the year* 1702.
2°: A^2($\pm A1$) B^2 C–D^2; i–iv, 1–12.
O.

G242 — The grand defeat: or, the downfall of the S---d---an party. To the tune of, Chevy Chace... *London, printed in the year* 1741. (5 March)
2°: A–B^2; 1–2 3–7 8 blk.
    Percival LXVI. Colophon 'Printed for J. Roberts'. The copy from Tom's Coffee House, dated 5 March, is in the Lewis Walpole Library. Listed in *GM*, *LM* March.
'Mark well our sad and dismal tale'
    On the defeat of Samuel Sandys's motion for the removal of Walpole, 13 Feb 1741.
O(uncut),LdU-B(uncut); CtY,ICN,KU,MH.

G243 — The grand enquiry, or, what's to be done with him? *London, printed in the year* 1712. (4 Feb, Luttrell)

The grand enquiry

$\frac{1}{2}$°: 1 side, 2 columns.
    Double rule between columns.
'When beasts could every office do'
    A fable, against Marlborough.
L(Cup.645.e.1/19; 1850.c.10/35, cropt; 1876.f.1/63, cropt),LSA,O(mutilated),Rothschild; CtY,*ICN*(Luttrell),MH(cropt),NjP.

G244 — [another edition]
    Single rule between columns.
L(1850.e.10/36).

G245 — The grand mistake: or, all men happy if they please... By the author of the Pleasures of a single life. *London printed, and sold by J. How*, 1705. (19 June, Luttrell)
2°: A^2 B–D^2; 1–2 3–16.
'Vain restless man, insatiate in desire'
    The author also wrote *The city madam*, 1702, a copy of which is attributed to 'Mr More', not further identified.
MH(Luttrell, uncut),IU.

G246 — — [*London?* 1705?]
4°: A^2; 1–4, 2 columns.
    Apparently a piracy.
CtY(cropt).

— The grand question debated, 1732. *See* Swift, Jonathan (S908).

G247 — The grand removal. Inscribed to his grace John duke of Argyle, in commemoration of the late glorious struggle for liberty... *London, printed for T. Cooper*, [1742.] (*LEP* 23 March)
2°: A^2 B–C^2; 1–2 3–12.
    Horizontal chain-lines.
'When will corruption cease? the nation cries'
    On the fall of Walpole's ministry.
L(1875.d.6/175),DT,*LdU-B*; CSmH,CtY,ICN, NjP,OCU+.

G248 — Grand sale at Westminster, being an inventory of the houshold goods and rich furniture, belonging to the house of R-- W--... *London, 'printed for James True, auctioneer'*, [1741?]
$\frac{1}{2}$°: 1 side, 2 columns.
'Foremost and first, a broken scraper'
    Another version of *An inventory of the goods and chattels of P---r W----s*, 1741, applied to Sir Robert Walpole.
OCU.

G249 Grandsire. Grandsire Hambden's ghost. And Peace, or, no peace. Two poems. Together with a prefatory answer, to some late whiggish scurrility, especially, a certain dedication. *London, printed for J. Woodward*, 1712. (19 June, Luttrell)
8°: A–F^4; i–ii, 1–43 44–46 blk.
    Entered in *SR* 20 June; deposit copies at O,E,EU,SaU. Advertised in *PB* 21 June.
'From dusky mansions, where misguided souls'
Peace: 'Must we to further mis'ries still be brought'
    The prefatory answer quotes from the dedication of Griffith Williams's *The great antichrist reveal'd*, 1660.

Grandsire Hambden's ghost

> L(164.m.64, Luttrell, —F4),O,E,DrU,SaU+;
> CSmH(—F4),CtY(—F4),MH,NjP(uncut),OCU.

G250 — [dh] The grandsir's ghost, or, a satyre on the luxury of the present age. [*Edinburgh*, 171–?]
4°: A⁴; 1–8.
> The date is suggested by neighbouring pamphlets of the volume in which the ES copy is bound. The volume does, however, cover the whole period from 1680–1720.
> 'Rous'd from the grave by the loud cries'
> ES.

G251 Grant, John. Alpheus, or a pastoral elegy on his royal highness Prince George of Denmark... *Dublin, printed by C. Carter*, 1708.
4°: A–B²; 1–2 '2–3' 5–8.
> 'Ah! nymph your brow and heavy looks declare'
> DLC.

Granville, George, *baron Lansdowne.* Poems upon several occasions. *London, printed for J. Tonson*, 1712. (*SR* 27 Sept)
8°: pp. 267.   L,O; CtY,MH.

—— The second edition. *London, printed for J. Tonson*, 1716.
12°: pp. 206.   L,O; CLU-C,MH.

—— The third edition. *London, printed for J. Tonson*, 1721.
12°: pp. 206.   L,O; CtY,IU.

—— The fourth edition. *London, printed for J. Tonson*, 1726.
12°: pp. 206.   L,O; CLU-C,IU.

—— *Dublin, printed by S. Powell, for George Risk*, 1726.
8°: pp. 92.   C,DN; PU.

—— Lately revis'd and enlarg'd by the author. *Dublin, printed by S. Powell, for George Risk*, 1732.
12°: pp. 166.   O; IU.
> Possibly based on the following collection.

— The genuine works in verse and prose. *London, printed for J. Tonson, & L. Gilliver*, 1732.
4°: 2 vol.   L,O; CtY,MH.

—— *London, printed for J. & R. Tonson, L. Gilliver, J. Clarke*, 1736.
12°: 3 vol.   L,O; CtY,MH.
> The imprint to vol. 3 is 'London, printed for J. Walthoe.' Some copies (O,MH) have an additional title to vol. 1 with imprint 'London printed, and sold by J. Osborn, 1736.'

[—] The changeling: being Mr. G- Gr-n-ll's answer, [1712.] *In* A54.

[—] The progress of beauty. A poem [actually by James Dalacourt], 1732. *See* D9.

'Gratian, Theodorus.' The Richardiad, 1743. *See* R192.

Gratulatio

Gratulatio. Gratulatio Britannica, ob exoptatum & pergratum adventum, 1714. *See* Clark, James.

G252 Gratulatory. 'A gratulatory poem on the happy prospect of peace. [*London*] *Sold by J. Roberts.* Price 6*d*.' (*GM,LM* April 1736)
> *GM* reads 'A congratulatory poem...'

G253 Gray. Gray's ellegie with his own conceity answer. [*Edinburgh*? 171–?]
½°: 1 side, 2 columns.
'And has ald death e'n come at last'
Answer: 'What raskal's this dar be so bold'
> Gray was apparently a drunken shoemaker from Montrose.
> E(2).

G254 [Gray, Thomas.] An ode on a distant prospect of Eton College. *London, printed for R. Dodsley; sold by M. Cooper*, 1747. (30 May?)
2°: A⁴; 1–3 4–8.
> Dated 30 May by *Straus, Dodsley*; listed in *LM* June.
'Ye distant spires, ye antique towers'
> Ms. attribution to Gray by Horace Walpole in the L copy.
> L(C.57.g.7/12, Horace Walpole's; Ashley 4845), LVA-D,EtC(uncut); CtY,*InU*,NNP(uncut).

G255 Great. Great Britain in danger. A poem. [*London*, 1745?]
½°: 1 side, 2 columns.
'Rouze, rouze dear Britons, is it time to slumber'
> Against the Jacobites.
> MH.

[G256 = H68]

G257 — Great-Britain's glory. Or, the stay-at-home fleet: tune of Packington's pownd. *London, printed for A. Moore*, 1729.
2°: A²; 1–3 4.
> *Percival* X. The order of editions is uncertain.
'Come, ye lovers of peace, who are said to have sold'
> *Crum* C657, 661: 'England's glory being an excellent new ballad on the fleet of Spithead'. On the inactivity of the fleet; against the efforts that culminated in the peace of Seville.
> OCU.

G258 — [dh] Great Britain's glory... A new ballad... [col] [*London*] *Printed for A. Moore*, [1729.]
½°: 3–4, 1 column.
> In spite of the pagination, this was probably intended as a half-sheet edition.
> L(1875.d.6/30; 1876.f.1/124).

G259 —— To which is added, The pacifick fleet. *London, printed for A. Moore*, 1729.
2°: A² B²<C¹; 1–3 4, 1–3 4–5 *6 blk.*
> *The pacifick fleet*, 1729, has a separate title on B1, but is apparently a different impression from that published separately.
> O(uncut); CLU-C(lacks *The pacifick fleet*),MH.

Great Britain's glory

G260 — [*idem*] England's glory. Being an excellent new ballad on the fleet at Spithead. To the tune of, The cut-purse. [*Dublin*, 1729.]
$\frac{1}{2}$°: 1 side, 2 columns.
'Come you lovers of peace, who are said to have sold'
C,DT,Crawford; CtY(mutilated).

G261 — Great-Britain's happiness: a poem on the passing of the union, to which her majesty was most graciously pleas'd to give her royal assent on Thursday the 6th of March, 170$\frac{6}{9}$. [*London*, 1707.] (7 March, Luttrell)
$\frac{1}{2}$°: 1 side, 1 column.
'Sing, sing, ye swains, in joyful strains express'
MH(Luttrell).

G262 — Great Britains hope, in an address to my lord Pembroke. By the author of the Merchants advocate. *London printed, and sold by most of the booksellers in London & Westminster*, [1708.] (3 Feb, Luttrell)
2°: *A*² B–C²; *i–iv*, 1–8.
'A nations sense, in humble lines contain'd'
LdU-B; IU(Luttrell).

G263 — Great Brittain's joy for her most gracious majesty Queen Ann's being unanimously proclaim'd through England, Scotland, and Ireland; with the loyalists health. To the tune of an Orange. *London, printed by J. Read*, [1702.]
$\frac{1}{2}$°: 1 side, 2 columns.
Rough woodcuts at head.
'Now England be merry, and ever rejoyce'
CM-P.

G264 — Great Britain's joyful triumph, for the happy union on the first of May, 1707. *London printed, and sold by John Morphew*, 1707. (5 May, Luttrell)
$\frac{1}{2}$°: 1 side, 2 columns.
'Great Britain now hath baffled France and Rome'
ICN(Luttrell).

G265 — Great Britain's union; or Litchfield races transpos'd. A new print, and ballad, to the tune of the First of August, or, &c. [*London*, 1747?]
$\frac{1}{2}$°: 1 side, 2 columns.
Large engraving at head.
'Ye subjects of true British race'
For national unity.
L(P&D 2864).

G266 — Great-Britain's welcome to his sacred majesty King George. A poem, occasion'd by his successful and glorious negotiations this summer. *London, printed for T. Warner*, 1719 [1718?]. (Nov, Luttrell)
8°: *A*⁴ B–C⁴; *1–5* 6–23 *24 blk*. A1 hft.
From the subject matter one would expect the year to be 1718, but Luttrell left the date 1719 without correction.
'Amidst the waves and raging billows tost'
L(164.n.17, Luttrell); OCU.

G267 — Great cry and little wooll: or a few verses bestow'd on Dr. Cl-----t----n, for his liberality

Great cry and little wooll

to the poets of Trinity-College, for their late occasional compositions. [*Dublin*, 1727?]
$\frac{1}{2}$°: 1 side, 2 columns.
'Poets and poetry, in spight of fate'
A satire on Robert Clayton's prizes for poetry; cf. M356, T363.
CtY.

— The great example, 1735. *See* Munns, Nathaniel.

G268 — [dh] The great hero, and the little one: or, a dialogue between Prince Eugene, and Marshal Boufflers, on the surrender of Lisle. [col] *London printed, and Edinburgh reprinted by John Reid junior*, 1708.
4°: *A*²; *1–4*.
Pagination possibly cropt in the copy seen. No London edition has been traced.
Introduction: 'Eugene and Boufflers, now contending are'
GM.

G269 — — [col] *Dublin re-printed by C. Carter*, 1708.
4°: *A*²; *1–4*.
Drop-head title only.
DLC.

— The great man's answer to Are these things so?, 1740. *See* Miller, James.

G270 — A great man's speech in Downing-street against the enquiry. To the tune of Packington's pound. *London, printed for W. Webb*, 1743. (*GM, LM* Jan)
2°: *A*² B²; *1–3* 4–8.
Rothschild 237.
'Ye old whigs, met here my new honours to grace'
On the enquiry into Walpole's administration.
L(162.n.74),LdU-B; CSmH,CtY,KU,TxU.

G271 — — '*London, printed for W. Webb*' [*Edinburgh*], 1743.
8°: *A*⁴ B²; *1–2* 3–12.
Printed by Ruddiman on the evidence of the printer's ornaments.
C,E.

G272 — Great news from St. James's or, a dialogue that passed between M——a W——le, and Madam Y——h, concerning the white horse, who broke loose, and run away with another man's dun mare. *London*, '*printed by Tanteribobus, and sold by Quibus*', [1738?]
$\frac{1}{2}$°: 1 side, 2 columns.
Percival appendix 65. Rough woodcut at head.
'O good neighbours have you not hear'd the news'
Maria Walpole and Amalie Wallmoden, countess of Yarmouth; presumably concerning George II.
L(1876.f.1/119).

G273 — [dh] A great noise about nothing: or the church's danger. A satyr. [col] [*London?*] *Printed in the year* 1705.
4°: *A*²; *1–4*.
Vertical chain-lines. A revised version was printed as *Monarchy and church*, 1710.

A **great** noise about nothing

'Of all the cheats and shams that have of late'
The same author wrote *Rime and reason*,
[1705/–.] Against the tories; cf. *An answer to
the Great noise*, 1705.
L(164.m.41), E,DT,AdU.

G274 —— [col] '*London*' [*Edinburgh?*], *printed in the
year* 1714.
4°: *A*²; 1–4.
Drop-head title only.
E,ES.

G275 — A great overthrow at court. [*London*, 1714.]
½°: 1 side, 1 column.
On the other side, *The trifle*, 1714.
'Fortune, that blind, unconstant devil'
Harding.

G276 **Green**. The green-cloth: or, the verge of the court.
An epistle to a friend. By Mr. Wh----d. *Londn* [!],
printed for F. Noble, & J. Boydel, 1739. (*LM* March)
2°: *A*² B–D² E¹; 1–3 4–18.
'A journal of my life you urge'
Sometimes ascribed to William Whitehead in
error; Paul Whitehead is probably intended,
though whether he wrote it remains obscure.
L(11602.i.17/7),C,LdU-B; CSmH(stitched, uncut),CtY,ICU,MH,TxU +.

G277 — The Green-park folly, or the fireworks blown
up: a satire. *London, printed for A. Proud*, 1749.
(*GM* May)
8°: *A*¹[=E1] B–D⁴ E⁴(–E1) (C2 as 'B2'); *i–ii*,
1–30.
'No more of bottles, or their corks'
On the fireworks celebrating the peace.
L(11642.cc.43/1),O,LdU-B(uncut); CtY,MH.

G278 —— *London, printed for A. Proud*, 1749.
8°: *A*¹ B–C⁴ D⁴(–D4); *i–ii*, 1–21 *22 blk*.
OCU.

G279 **Green**, —, *Mr.* 'An ode to his royal highness the
Duke of Cumberland. By Mr. Green. [*London*]
Printed for G. Woodfall. Price 6*d*.' (*GA* 20 April
1749)

Green, George Smith. Wisdom: or the second
book of the chronicles of the wise-women of the
city of Lulcaster. To which are added, a choice
collection of poems... [*Leicester?*] *Printed in the
year*, 1750. *And sold at the East-Gate in Leicester,
and by most booksellers.*
8°: pp. 41.   L.
The printing is very provincial.

G280 [**Green, Matthew**.] A copy of verses wrote by a
gentleman lately deceased, occasion'd by his
reading Robert Barclay's Apology. *London printed,
and sold at the Bible in Georg-yard* [!] *Lombard-
street*, 1735.
1°: 1 side, 3 columns.
The address is that of T. Sowle Raylton.

Green, M. A copy of verses

'These sheets primeval doctrines yield'
Printed with Green's poems in *Dodsley* I;
Green did not in fact die until 1737, but this
poem has been regularly attributed to him,
and the TxU copy has an early ms. attribution.
LF; TxU.

G281 [—] — *London printed, and sold at the Bible in
George-yard Lombard-street*, [1735/40?]
1°: 1 side, 3 columns.
With the addition, in column 3, of lines headed,
'The following lines were lately writ by another
gentleman on the same subject...'
LF.

G282 [—] The grotto, a poem. Written by Peter Drake,
fisherman, of Brentford. In the year of our lord
1732. *London*, 1733.
8°: *A*⁸(–A8); 1–3 4–14.
Copies seen possibly lack blank A8; both have
ms. corrections.
'Adieu a while forsaken flood'
Attributed to Green by Isaac Reed in a ms.
note in the O copy; printed as Green's in
Dodsley V: 'Printed in the year 1732, but
never published'. The pseudonym is occasioned
by Stephen Duck.
L(11631.b.14),O.

G283 — The spleen. An epistle inscrib'd to his particular
friend Mr. C. J.... By the late Mr. Matthew Green.
*London printed, and sold by A. Dodd, and at all the
pamphlet-shops in town*, 1737. (*GM,LM* Feb)
8°: *A*² B–D⁸; *i–ii* iii–iv, 1–46 *47–48 blk*.
Many copies (e.g. O,CT,MH,TxU) have an
errata slip, usually on p. iv.
'This motly piece to you I send'
A ms. note in Malone's copy at O records his
being told by Richard Glover that he wrote the
preface.
L(992.h.10/1,–D8),O(3, 2–D8),C,EU(–D8),
LdU-B+; CSmH,ICU,IU,MH(2, 1–D8),
TxU+.

G284 —— '*London printed, and sold by A. Dodd, and at
all the pamphlet-shops in town*', 1737.
8°: A–C⁴ D²; *i–ii* iii–iv, 1–24.
Probably an Edinburgh piracy.
O,C,E; ICN.

G285 —— The second edition, corrected. *London
printed, and sold by A. Dodd, and at all the pamphlet-
shops in town*, 1737.
8°: *A*² B–D⁸; *i–ii* iii–iv, 1–46 *47–48 blk*.
L(11631.d.23,–D8),LVA-F,O(–D8),EtC,
LdU-B; CtY,ICN(–D8),MH(–D8).

G286 —— *London printed: and Dublin re-printed, by and
for Sylvanus Pepyat*, 1737.
8°: *A*⁴ B–D⁴; *i–ii* iii–iv, 5–31 *32 blk*.
L(11602.bb.39/9),CT,DA; CtY.

G287 —— The third edition, corrected. To which is
added, some other pieces by the same hand. *London
printed, and sold by A. Dodd, and at all the pamphlet-
shops in town*, 1738.

Green, M. The spleen

8°: A–D⁸ E⁴; *i–ii iii–iv, 1–67 68 blk.*
In some copies (e.g. O,MH) A4 is signed 'B4'.
'Poems on several occasions' on pp. 47–67.
The copyright, with 360 books, formed lot 13
of the trade sale of William Hinchliffe and
John Carter, 2 Dec 1742; it reappeared, with
50 books, in the sale of John Osborn, 11 Nov
1746, and was purchased by Dodsley for
£3. 5s. (catalogues at O–JJ).
L(11659.b.76),O(2),C,E,LdU-B+; CtY(3),ICN,
IU,MH,*NN.*

G288 —— *London printed: and, Dublin: re-printed, by
and for Mary Pepyat, 1743.*
8°: *A⁴* B–D⁴; *i–ii iii–iv, 5–31 32 blk.*
O.

G289 **Greene, Thomas.** Threnodiæ Britannicæ. A
funeral poem to the memory of the right honourable
John lord Cutts. *London, printed for Edmund Curll,*
1707.
8°: A⁸; *1–2 3–14 15; 16 blk.* 15 advt.
'O Phœbus! father of immortal verse'
O,CT,EU; DFo,KU(uncut).

Greenwich. Greenwich-Park, 1728. *See* Howard,
Leonard.

G290 **Greer, John.** 'Ad Cæsarem Britannicum e Germania redeuntem ode. *Londini, typis Thomæ Gent,
pro usu authoris,* 1724.'
Thomas Gent records 'I printed for him this
year an ode thus entitled...'
(*The life of Mr. Thomas Gent* (1832) 143.)

G291 — A poem upon the advancement of the rt. hon.
Allen Broderick lord high-chancellor of Ireland.
*Dublin, printed by Dr. John Whalley in Arrundel-
court just without St. Nicholas Gate,* 1714.
4°: *A²; 1–2 3–4.*
'While some in tuneful numbers sound the praise'
L(11621.h.1/9).

G292 **Grief.** The grief and lamentation of Auld-Reeky,
for the loss of the twenty penny ale, occasioned by
the avarice, greed, and pride of some of the brewers
in Edinburgh. [*Edinburgh,* 1725?]
½°: 1 side, 2 columns.
'Vow, sirs, what's a this now come amang us'
The Edinburgh brewers combined against the
malt tax in 1725.
EP.

[**Grierson, Constantia,** *née* Crawley.] A poem on
the art of printing, [1728.] *See* P585.

G293 **Grierson, George Hamilton.** [dh] A prophecy
and poem...upon Britain's arms conquering their
enemies, printed May the 5th, 1743. [*London*] 1743.
8°: *A⁴; 1 2–8.*
The poem occupies pp. 2–5; the rest is
prophecy.

Grierson, G. H. A prophecy

'His grace Duke Cumberland must go'
O.

G294 **Grievous.** The grievous complaint of the beaux
and the bads, | And a the young widows, and lasses
and lads, | For death's taking Mas: James Crouck-
shanks awa, | Who buckl'd the beggers at Mount-
ounha. | Interr'd in the church-yeard of Inverask,
the 29. of March 1724. [*Edinburgh,* 1724.]
½°: 1 side, 2 columns.
'Death, ye're a slimm and packy lown'
E.

G295 **Griffith, Nehemiah.** The leek. A poem on St.
David's day. Most humbly inscrib'd to the
honourable society of Antient Britons... *London,
printed by W. Wilkins, for W. Hinchliffe,* 1717. (*MC*
Feb)
2°: *A¹* B–H² I¹; *i–ii, 1–29 30 blk.*
'Hail to the day, that crown'd with David's name'
L(11631.h.5),LVA-F,O,*AN.*

G296 — [reissue] The second edition. *London, printed by
W. Wilkins, for W. Hinchliffe,* 1718. (*DC* 26 Feb)
2°: *A²* B–H² I¹; *i–iv, 1 2–29 30 blk.* iv err.
Cancel title with engraving and conjugate A2
bearing congratulatory poems, a note, and
errata. Also advertised in *DC* 27 Feb 1719,
possibly another reissue, untraced. 'The leek:
or, the antient Briton. A poem on St. David's
day' was listed as printed for J. Wilford in
MChr 2 March 1730; possibly it was yet
another reissue. The copyright formed part of
lot 9 of the trade sale of William Hinchliffe &
John Carter, 2 Dec 1742 (cat. at O–JJ).
O,*AN;* KU.

[—] Magdalen-grove: or, a dialogue between the
doctor and the devil, [1714.] *See* M14.

G297 — An ode to the honourable Sir William Morgan,
knight of the Bath. *London, printed for J. Peele,*
1725. (*MC* June)
½°: 1 side, 1 column.
'No more, illustrious chief! disclaim'
MB.

G298 **Grigg, J.** The saviour. A poem. In two books...
Book the first. *London, printed for M. Cooper,* 1745.
(*DA* 10 April)
4°: *A⁴* B–D⁴; *i–iv v–vii viii, 1 2–23 24 blk.* A1 hft.
Entered to Cooper in Bowyer's ledgers, no
date, 500 copies printed.
'The fruit was tasted, and the threat fulfill'd'
L(11630.c.13/10),O(2,–A1); CSmH.

'**Grim,** *Old Mother.*' Old Mother Grim's tales,
1737. *See* Meston, William.

[**Grimston, William,** *viscount Grimston.*] Thalia:
or the sprightly muse. Poems on several occasions
... By a nobleman of fifteen, who designs shortly to
appear in print. *London, printed by R. Tookey; sold
by S. Malthus,* 1705 [1704]. (31 Oct, Luttrell)

Grimston, W., *viscount*

2⁰: pp. 36.   L,OA.

> Generally ascribed to Grimston; there are some difficulties about the attribution. The poems appear to have been written about 1699 when Grimston was the right age. A ms. note on the title of the L copy 'Ch: Ba——e' may possibly suggest another author.

G299 Grinstead. The Grinsted ballad. *London, printed for S. Freeman,* 1750. (*BM* Dec)

2⁰: *A*² < *B*¹; *1–3* 4–5 *6 blk.*

'Long time, by court tricks, had poor Grinsted been charm'd'

> For the East Grinstead by-election, against Joseph Yorke (later baron Dover) who was the successful candidate.

L(11602.i.15/6),O; CSmH,MH.

G300 Groans. Groans from the grave: or, a melancholy account of the new resurrection, practised in and about Edinburgh. *Edinburgh, printed in the year* 1742.

8⁰: *A*⁴; *1–2* 3–8.

'Spectators of all ranks, come and behold'

> A different work from Pennecuik's poem of this title. On the medical resurrection-men in Edinburgh.

L(1078.k.26/7).

— Groans from the grave: or, complaints of the dead, [1725.] *See* Pennecuick, Alexander, *d. 1730.*

G301 — The groans of the people at the transportation of her grace the Dutchess of Hamilton's ⟨coffin⟩ from Holy-rood-house to Hamiltoun, Thursday, 20th August, 17⟨24.⟩ [*Edinburgh,* 1724.]

½⁰: 1 side, 2 columns.

'Cochrania dead! we did almost adore'

> Anne, duchess of Hamilton, died 14 Aug 1724.

E(cropt).

Grotius, Hugo.

[*Baptizatorum puerorum institutio*] The whole duty of a Christian, both in faith and practice...from the Latin catechism of Hugo Grotius, 1711. *See* W443.

[*Eucharistia*] Lauder, William: A poem of Hugo Grotius on the holy sacrament, 1732. *See* L69–70.

———

[Rooke, John:] Eclogues translated from the Latin of Hugo Grotius [and others], 1725.

Grotto. The grotto, a poem, 1733. *See* Green, Matthew.

G302 Grounds. The grounds. *Sold at the print and pamphlet-shops of London and Westminster,* March 7, 1741.

obl 1⁰: 1 side, 3 columns.

> Title from the large engraving at head. Advertised in *LDP* 20 March as published by G. Foster.

The grounds

'Vat be dat machine do make de folk groan-é?'

> Justifying the impeachment of Walpole.

L(P&D 2484); NNP.

Grove. The grove: or, the rival muses, 1701. *See* Froud, John.

G302·5 — The grove's complaint; and the owner's reply. A poem. *Salisbury, printed for the author; sold by B. Collins,* 1745.

8⁰: A–C⁴ D⁴(−D4); *1–2* 3–30.

> D4 is probably missing from the copy seen.

'Where's now the venerable oak'

CU.

Grove, Henry. Miscellanies in prose and verse. Most of them formerly published, and now collected into one volume... *London, sold by John Gray,* 1739. (*LM* May)

8⁰: pp. 119.   L,MP; CtY.

G303 Grubb, John. The British heroes: or, a new ballad in honour of St. George, &c. *London printed, and are to be sold by John Morphew, and H. Clements in Oxford,* 1707. (*DC* 19 Aug)

4⁰: A–B⁴ C²; *i–ii,* 1–17 *18 blk* (14 as '13').

> Reprinted (as by Grubb) in John Smith's *Poems,* 1713.

'The story of King Authur [!] old'

> Burlesque verses.

L(161.l.49, Luttrell, 19 Aug),O,OW(2),DG,*MR*; CtY(3, 1 ms. corrections),MH.

G304 —— [col] *London, printed by J. Bradford,* [1707?]

4⁰: *A*²; *1–4,* 2 columns.

> Drop-head title only. A piracy.

O.

G305 Grubstreet. The Grubstreet cavalcade, or, the hungry poets petition, humbly dedicated to a certain great man... By a well-wisher of the society. *Dublin, printed by Edward Waters,* 1727.

8⁰: *A*⁴ B–D⁴; *1–2* 3–31 *32.*

> With an 'advertisement' for a Grubstreet garret on p. 32.

'Ye sober sad and merry dames'

> A satire on Eyre, Coffey, Arbuckle, Sterling, and Miss Crawley.

LVA-F.

G306 — [*idem*] The Dublin scuffle, or, the hungry poets petition, humbly dedicated to a certain great man... By a well-wisher of the society. *Dublin, printed by E. Waters,* 1729.

8⁰: *A*⁴ B–D⁴; *1–2* ⟨*3–6*⟩ 7–31 *32. 32* 'advt'.

> Possibly a reissue of the preceding.

DN(lacks A2.3).

— Grubstreet nae satyre, [1720?] *See* Ramsay, Allan.

Grumbletonians. The Grumbletonians: or, the dogs without-doors, 1727. *See* Carey, Henry.

Grumbling

Grumbling. The grumbling hive, 1705. *See* Mandeville, Bernard.

G307 Grunters. The grunters' request, to take off the test. A poem. [*Dublin*] *Printed* [*by George Faulkner*] *in the year* 1733.
8°: *A*⁴; *i–ii*, *1–6*.
    Rothschild 206.
'My lords and lairds wha represent'
    Written in Scots dialect, addressed to the Irish.
C.

G308 Grunting. The grunting ale-wife; a new ballad. (Tune, A begging we will go. &c.) *Dublin, printed in the year* 1737.
½°: 1 side, 2 columns.
'I am a swell'd-cheek ale-wife'
Rothschild.

Gualteri. Gualteri Dannistoni ad Georgium Buchananum epistola, [1706?] *See* Pitcairne, Archibald.

Guide. A guide for malt-worms. The second part, [1720.] *See* A vade mecum for malt-worms, [1720.]

G309 — A guide from the cradel [!] to the grave. Being a companion for young and old... [*London*] *Printed in the year* 'DMCCXXXII' [1732].
12°: *A*⁸; *1* 2–12 *13–16*. A7–8 advts of Edward Midwinter.
    Also issued with *The history of the five wise philosophers*, 1732, copy at L.
'Lord, what is man! a sigh a cry'
L(11631.a.25).

G310 Guido. Guido's ghost: a tale. By J.H. esq; *London, printed for John Brindley, A. Dodd; sold by the booksellers and pamphlet-shops of London & Westminster*, 1738. (*GM,LM* Jan)
2°: *A*² < B²; *1–3* 4–7 *8 blk*.
    The normal watermark is royal arms; the L copy has pro patria, but is not apparently fine paper.
'Goupy, my brother, in virtù'
    In praise of Joseph Goupy and his copying of Guido Reni.
L(1484.m.28); CtY,MH,TxU(uncut).

G311 Guiscard. Guiscard's ghost to Lord B-------ke. [*London*] *Printed for J. York near Temple-Bar,* [171–.]
slip: 1 side, 1 column.
    With 'A stanza put upon Tyburn' and 'The constitution'.
'Hail noble lord! my knife had err'd indeed'
Stanza: 'Hail reverend tripos! guardian of the law'
Constitution: 'Happy the people where no priest gives rules'
Harding.

Gulielmus

Gulielmus. Gulielmus Susannæ valedicens, 1731. *See* Bourne, Vincent.

'**Gulliver**, *Captain*.' An excellent new ballad on the wedding of pritty Miss S--lly to jolly old J---o, 1730. *See* E555.

— The Totness address transversed, 1727. *See* T427.

'**Gulliver, Lemuel,** *poet laureat to the king of Lilliput*.' The masquerade, 1728. *See* Fielding, Henry.

'**Gulliver, Martin.**'
The following poems which share the pseudonym of 'Martin Gulliver' were probably written either by one author or a small coterie, and they are therefore kept together under the pseudonym.
The Censoriad is attributed to Walter Chamberlaine by D. J. O'Donoghue in The poets of Ireland *(1912) 65, but no evidence is given. Copies of* A letter from Martin Gulliver *and* The art of beauing... By Martinus Gulliverianus *at LVA-F have pencil ascriptions to James Dalacourt.* A satyr. By way of reply, to Martin Guilliver, alias Murtagh Mc.-Dermot, *1730, suggests another author, but McDermot is perhaps another pseudonym.*

G312 — The Asiniad: a second satire upon a certain wooden-man revived. By Martin Gulliver. [*Dublin*] *Printed in the year* 1730.
8°: A⁴; *1–2* 3–8.
    Teerink 1244.
'Arms and the man of upper room'
    A satire on Hugh Graffan; possibly the first satire was *The Heraldiad* below.
CSmH,CtY.

G313 — The Censoriad. A poem. Written originally by Martin Gulliver. The second edition. Illustrated with sundry curious annotations... *London: printed, and Dublin re-printed, and sold by James Hoey & George Faulkner*, 1730.
8°: *A*⁴ B⁴ C¹; *1–4* 5–17 *18 blk*.
    Presumably no earlier London edition existed; no Dublin first edition has been traced.
'Shou'd the old censor of imperial Rome'
    A satire on Hugh Graffan. Cf. *A modest defence of Mr. Gr——n,* 1730 *and* A panegyrick in answer to a lible [!], 1730.
DT; IU.

G314 —— The third edition... *London: printed, and Dublin re-printed, and sold by James Hoey & George Faulkner*, 1730.
8°: *A*⁴ B–C⁴; *1–3* 4–22 *23*; *24 blk*.
    The fourth edition, 1730, appears to have been part of the collection *Graffanio-mastix*, 1730 (copies at C,DN,MH).
DT.

G315 —— *London; re-printed from the Dublin third edition, for Weaver Bickerton*, 1730. (*MChr* 19 Feb)
8°: A–D⁴; *1–2* 3–32.

'Gulliver, M.' The Censoriad

> Teerink 690. With a reprint of Swift's *A libel on Dr. D——y* on pp. 25–32.
> L(11633.bbb.21),LDW,CK,DN,LdU-B(lacks D⁴)+; CtY,ICN,IU(uncut),OCU,TxU.

G316 — The Heraldiad; a satyr upon a certain philosopher. Containing a description of the Grub-street debate held the 22d of this present month. By Martin Gulliver. [*Dublin*] *Printed in the year* 1730.
½⁰: 1 side, 2 columns.

> Teerink 1243.

'I sing the man with shallow head'
> See 'Humphry Wagstaff', *The Dullardiad; or, the author of the Heraldiad satyriz'd*, 1730.

L(C.121.g.8/181),C.

G317 — A letter from Martin Gulliver, to George Faulkner, printer. [*Dublin*] *Printed in the year* 1730.
8⁰: A⁴; *1–3* 4–8.

'Why, Faulkner, shou'd you be surpriz'd'
> Teerink 1240. Pencil attribution to James Dalacourt in LVA-F copy. Possibly the work answered in *A satyr. By way of reply, to Martin Guilliver, alias Murtagh Mc.Dermot*, 1730.

LVA-F; CtY(uncut),MH.

G318 — The proctor's banquet. A pindarick ode. By Martin Gulliver. *Dublin, printed in the year* 1731 [1730?].
8⁰: A⁴; *1–2* 3–8.

> Teerink 1246. The DG copy has the date apparently changed in ms. to 1730.

''Twas at the proctor's feast from folly won'
> A further satire on Hugh Graffan.

DG; CSmH,CtY.

G319 — Threnodia: or, an elegy on the unexpected and unlamented death of the Censor: together with some account of his last will and testament... Written originally by Martin Gulliver, and now revis'd and publish'd by the commentator on the Censoriad. [*Dublin*] *Printed in the year* 1730.
8⁰: A⁴; *1* 2–7 *8 blk.* 7 advt.

> Teerink 1241. Apparently reissued as part I of *Graffanio-mastix*, 1730. An advertisement on p. 7 reports that the last will and testament will appear in a forthcoming publication, presumably *Graffanio-mastix*.

'Ye writers of satire, ye whips of the times'
> A satire on Hugh Graffan.

L(11601.ccc.38/7),DA,DT; CSmH,MH.

G320 **'Gulliverianus, Martinus.'** The art of beauing: in imitation of Horace's Art of poetry. Address'd to a certain lord. By Martinus Gulliverianus... The third edition. *London printed, and Dublin: reprinted by J. Watts & W. S. Anburey; sold by J. Thompson,* 1730.
8⁰: A–C⁴ (A3 as 'A2'); *i–vi,* 1–17 *18 blk.* A1 hft.

> Bond 107; Teerink 1245. Presumably no London edition existed; no earlier Dublin edition seen. Verses to the author dated 13 Jan 1730 and signed 'C.W.'.

'Suppose Belinda painted to a hair'

'Gulliverianus, M.' The art of beauing

> Pencil attribution to James Dalacourt in LVA-F copy.
> L(11601.ccc.38/8),LVA-F,DA(2),DN,DT+; CSmH.

'Gundy, *Sir Solomon.'* The muse's vagaries, 1743. *See* Muse.

'Gunson, Gamaliel.' The progress of wit, 1730. *See* Hill, Aaron.

[Guthrie, Patrick.] Candour: or, an occasional essay on the abuse of wit and eloquence, 1739. *See* C23.

Guthry, —, *Mr.* A just imitation of the first satire of the second book of Horace, 1733. *See* J116.

Gutteridge, Thomas. 'Bragg's elegy.'
> Referred to as 'by the author of this' in a note to G324.

G321 — An elegy, in memory of the reverend Mr. Daniel Wilcox; who departed this life, April 11th 1733. In the 57th year of his age. [*London*, 1733.]
1⁰: 1 side, 2 columns.

> Mourning borders.

'O drop drop briny tears from pious eyes'
> The epitaph signed 'T. Gutteridge'.

LDW(2).

G322 — An elegy, in memory of the reverend Mr. John Newman, who departed this life, July the 25th. 1741. [*London*, 1741.]
1⁰: 1 side, 2 columns.

> Mourning headpiece and borders.

'Children of god, that's by the spirit led'
> The epitaph signed 'T. Gutteridge'.

L(C.20.f.2/246).

G323 — An elegy, sacred to the memory of the late learned and rev. Mr. John Hubbard, who departed this life July 13, 1743, in the 51st year of his age... [*London*, 1743.]
½⁰: 1 side, 2 columns.

> Mourning borders. Apparently printed on a half-sheet of very large paper with repeated watermarks.

'It's sweet to stand about a dying-bed'
> The epitaph signed 'T. Gutteridge'; he advertises himself as a teacher of shorthand at the foot.

L(C.20.f.2/248),LDW.

G324 — An elegy sacred to the memory of the reverend Mr. James Wood. [*London*, 1742.]
½⁰: 1 side, 2 columns.

> Mourning borders. Printed on a very large half-sheet.

'Alass, alass! I can't forbear to speak'
> The epitaph signed 'T. Gutteridge'; advertisement for his shorthand teaching at foot.

L(C.20.f.2/247).

Gutteridge, T.

G325 — An elegy sacred to the memory of the reverend
Mr. Mordecai Andrews: who departed this life
February the 16th. 1750. in the 34th. year of his age.
[*London*, 1750.]
1°: 1 side, 2 columns.
Mourning borders.
'Andrews is dead, over's his dying moan'
Note at foot 'this elegy to be sold by its author,
Thomas Gutteridge, at numb. 47 in Newing-
Yard Shoreditch'.
L(C.20.f.2/250).

— 'Hussey's elegy.'
Referred to in the title of G327.

— 'Man of wit...founded upon Mr. Lock's
sentiments.'
Referred to as 'by the author of this' in a note
to G324.

G326 — The royal wedding. A poem in praise of the
marriage between the illustrious William Nassau,
prince of Orange, and the lady Ann, the illustrious
princess royal of Great Britain. [*London*, 1734?]

Gutteridge, T. The royal wedding

'Folio broadside.'
(Pickering & Chatto cat. 271/14020.)

— 'Smith's elegy.'
Referred to as 'by the author of this' in a note
to G325.

G327 — The universal elegy, or a poem on Bunhill
burial ground: in which are...particularly describ'd the characters of [24 names]... By T.
Gutteridge, author of Hussey's elegy. *N.B. The
author teacheth short-hand...near the sign of the
Ship in Sun-street, in Bishopsgate-street...where
this is sold: and at Mr. Cooper's, at the Artillery
Coffee-house in Chiswell-street,* [173–?]
8°: A–D⁴ E¹; i–ii, 1–6 9–34. 34 err.
'When winter's midnight darkness spreads the
skies'
L(11602.ee.22/6).

Gymnasiad. The Gymnasiad, 1744. *See* Whitehead, Paul.

H

H., Mr. Four odes, 1750. *See* Hamilton, William Gerard.

H., A. A funeral poem upon the much lamented death of Lieutenant-general Wood, 1712. *See* F304.

H., B. Brittania's tears, 170½. *See* Harris, Benjamin.

H——, C——. A poem. Inscrib'd to the right honourable Sir Robert Walpole, on the success of his majesty's arms in America, 1741. *See* P546.

H., D., *presbyter of the church of England.* A father's advices to his children, 1740. *See* F75.

H., F. Divine songs: occasionally compos'd on variety of subjects, fitted to the meanest capacity, 1735. *See* Divine.

— The patch, 1724. *See* Hauksbee, Francis.

H., F., *gent.* Love drowned in the South-sea, [1721.] *See* L282.

H., G. A poem upon the noble company of young archers, [171–?] *See* P684.

H., J. Anglia triumphans, 1703. *See* Harris, Joseph.

— Leighton-stone-air, 1702. *See* Harris, Joseph.

— Marlborides, sive bellum Britannicum, 1707. *See* Harris, Joseph.

H., J., *esq;* Guido's ghost, 1738. *See* G310.

H——, J——, *esq;* The national alarm, 1745. *See* N6.

H., J., *Scriblerus secundus.* News from Borrows-tounness, 1745. *See* N294.

H., J., *triginta fere annos domi forisque in re militari occupatus.* Psalmi Davidis quinquaginta priores versibus elegiacis latine rediti, 1723. *See* Hanway, John.

H., P. The enthusiasm, 1739. *See* Hiffernan, Paul.

— The poet, 1739. *See* Hiffernan, Paul.

H., S., *M.A.* A psalm of thanksgiving to be sung by the children of Christ's Hospital, 1729. *See* Hetherly, Seawell.

H., T. An account of a great fight, between the Christians, and the quakers, [1701.] *See* A8.

— A glimpse of hell, 1705. *See* G179.

— Italian policy, 1744. *See* I72.

— The methodists, a satirical poem, [1739.] *See* M225.

H., T., *Cantabr.* Nundinæ Sturbrigienses, 1709. *See* Hill, Thomas.

H., T., *gent.* A congratulatory poem, on the anniversary-day of his majesty, 1718. *See* C355.

— A panegyrical poem on the fair and celebrated beauties, 1718. *See* P43.

— A tale of the lady's bodkin, [1721.] *See* T28.

H., W. Exaltatio cleri, 1701. *See* E533.

— Familiar epistles between W-- H--- and A--R--, [1719.] *See* Ramsay, Allan.

— The fate of traytors, 1716. *See* F74.

— Thura Britannica, 1702. *See* T267.

H1 Habbiac. An habbiack elegy on the untimely and deplorable death of Robert F------s kirk treasurer's man, who dy'd November 3d. 1724. [*Edinburgh*, 1724.]
½°: 1 side, 2 columns.
'Greet a ye bairns and bearded fo'k'
> On Robert Forbes. Attributed to Alexander Pennecuik (d. 1730) in the E catalogue, possibly by confusion with his elegy on Forbes in the Pennecuik ms.

E.

H2 — ⟨An habbyac on the death of Allan Ramsay.⟩ [*Edinburgh*, 1720/25?]
8°: 8 pp.
> A copy was formerly in the Signet Library, Edinburgh, but cannot now (1967) be traced. It lacked the title-leaf, and the title quoted here is from the drop-head title on page 3. There is a copy of a transcript by Burns Martin at E.

'God safe's is this auld Reeky's bard'

H3 Habby. An habby on the death of Mis. James Cruickshanks in Mountounha, alias Buckle the Begars marry them aa. *Edinburgh printed* ⟨*at the foot of the* ⟩ [1724?]
½°: 1 side, 3 columns.
'Meikle sorrow dole and care'
> Presumably the James Cruikshanks of Monktonhall deprived of his living 16 July 1702 'for prophane swearing', who died 29 March 1724.
E(mutilated).

Habert, Philippe.
[*Le temple de la mort*] Sheffield, John, *duke of Buckingham*: The temple of death...a translation out of French, 1709. *See* S390–1.

Hac. Hac Jovis Hammonis cineres conduntur in urna, [1710?/13.] *See* Pitcairne, Archibald.

Hacket, George. Occasional poems upon several subjects, viz. I. Advice to youth. II. Good-Friday.

Hacket, G.

III. Easter-day. IV. A pastoral. *Aberdeen, printed for the author*, 1737.
8°: pp. 24. GM.

Haddington, Thomas, *earl of. See* Hamilton, Thomas, *earl of Haddington*.

Halifax, Charles Montagu, *earl of. See* Montagu, Charles, *earl of Halifax*.

H4 [**Hall, David.**] Upon the anniversary held at Preston in Lancashire, by the people called quakers. 19th and 20th 2d mo, 1738. [1738.]
½°: 1 side, 1 column.
'To Preston's solemnity many repair'
   Ascribed to Hall in *Smith* I. 904; ms. note in the LF copy to the same effect.
LF.

[**Hall, Henry,** *organist of Hereford.*] Et tu Brute? or, the m--'d c--l, [1704?] *See* E479.

H5 **Hall, Jacob.** The marshal's humble offering to each gentleman soldier, in the company commanded by Lieut. col. Ellis, esq; lieut. col. in the blue regiment of Middlesex, whereof the hon. Sir Thomas Medlicott, kt. is colonel. *London, printed by R. Phillips*, [1729/37.]
½°: 1 side, 1 column.
   Verses enclosed in emblematic woodcut border.
'Since the black storms, which threat'nd hard our trade'
   Signed 'Jacob Hall, listed drum'; but possibly written for him. Cf. Thomas Bellows and John Browne for similar productions.
L(C.20.f.2/357).

H6 **Hallam, Isaac.** The cocker: a poem. In imitation of Virgil's third Georgic. Humbly inscrib'd to the honourable society of sportsmen at Grantham. *Stamford, printed by Francis Howgrave*, 1742.
4°: (frt+) π² A–H⁴ G¹; *i–viii, 1–61 62 blk.*
   Subscribers' list on π2. Advertised in *GM* Aug 1746, for M. Cooper.
'Ye British sons, and all ye tuneful nine'
L(11633.f.43); CLU-C,CtY.

Hallows, Daniel. Poems on the principal festivals and fasts of the church of England... *London, printed for J. Wilford*, 1733. (*GSJ* 26 April)
12°: pp. 120. O,WcC.
   Presentation copy at O, with ms. corrections.

— [reissue] The sacred miscellany: or poems on divine subjects... *London, printed for J. Wilford, C. Corbett, & J. Cox*, 1734. (*GM* Dec)
   L.
   Cancel title.

H7 **Halter.** A halter for rebels: or, the Jacobites downfall. A most excellent ballad to a merry old tune,

A halter for rebels

call'd--The old wife she sent to the miller her daughter. *London printed, and sold by A. Boulter*, 1715.
½°: 1 side, 1 column.
'A juncto of knaves met at Paris together'
Harding.

[**Hamilton, John,** *baron Belhaven.*] Belhaven's vision: or, his speech in the union-parliament, 1729–. *See* B165.

H8 [—] An equivalent for Defoe. [*Edinburgh*, 1706?]
½°: 1 side, 1 column.
'Let banter cease, and poetasters yield'
   Ms. attribution 'The Lord Balhaven's Answer' in a copy at E; in answer to Defoe's *A reply to the Scots answer*, [1706.]
L(8142.k.1),E(3); TxU.

H9 [—] A Scots answer to a British vision. [*Edinburgh*, 1706.] (Nov)
½°: 1 side, 2 columns.
'Two British wits conspir'd'
   An answer to Defoe's *The vision*, [1706]; in a letter to Harley of 28 Nov 1706, Defoe speaks of this as by Lord Belhaven. Defoe answered with *A reply to the Scots answer*, [1706.] See also *She put her hand upon his scull*, [1706?].
E(5); MH(2).

H10 [**Hamilton, Newburgh.**] The changes: or, faction vanquish'd. A poem. Most humbly inscrib'd to... the not guilty lords. *London printed, and sold by John Morphew*, 1711. (16 May, Luttrell)
2°: A² B–D²; *1–2 3–16.*
   Advertised in *Examiner* 17 May.
'When Anna first (the glory of our isle)'
   Hamilton's authorship is revealed in the following entry.
L(1481.f.19/8, uncut),LU,O(Luttrell); CLU-C, CSmH,MH(ms. date 25 May).

H11 — [variant title:] Most humbly inscrib'd to...the not guilty lords. By their lordships most devoted and most obedient servant, Newburgh Hamilton.
   No sign of a cancel has been seen.
NN.

H12 — The power of musick. An ode for St. Cæcilia's day. Written by Mr. Hamilton. Sett to musick by Mr. Woodcock. *London, printed for Jacob Tonson*, 1720. (*DC* 22 Feb)
4°: A² B⁴; *i–iv, 1 2–8.*
   The statement of authorship is engraved within an ornamental border.
'Tune ev'ry string, your voices raise'
L(161.l.50, Luttrell, April).

Hamilton, Thomas, *chaplain to his majesty.* Divine paraphrases. *Westminster, printed by A. Campbell, and sold at the London-Gazette, near Charing-Cross*, [1730/33.]
8°: pp. 23. O,WcC.

Hamilton, T., *chaplain*

Title in half-title form; dedication to Edward
Young signed 'Tom. Hamilton'.

H13 — Sanguine lovers: or, the Irish cry. A poem. By
the author of a Divine paraphrase. *London, printed
for the author,* 1733.
8°: π⁴ A⁴ B–E⁴; i–iii iv–v vi–viii, 1–39 *40 blk.*
List of subscribers on π4.
'Love once was nature, artless and untaught'
Dedication signed.
L(11631.d.26),DN.

H13·2 [—] [reissue] Ub-bub-a-boo: or, the Irish-howl.
In heroic verse. By Dean Swift. *London, printed for
J. James; sold by the booksellers of London & Westminster,* 1735. (*GM* May)
8°: π¹ A⁴ B–E⁴; i–ii, 1–39 *40 blk.*
Teerink 975. Cancel title replaces π4. Mentioned by *Ball* 298, as 'unlikely to have had any
connection with Swift', and the attribution
ignored by *Williams*; it has apparently never
been accepted as Swift's.
L(11601.d.28/6),O,DA; CSmH,CtY.

H13·5 [—] — *London, printed for J. James,* 1735.
8°: A–G⁴; 1–55 *56 blk.*
(Dobell cat. 16 (1936) 657, lacking A1.)

[Hamilton, Thomas, *6th earl of Haddington.*]
Forty select poems, on several occasions, by the
right honourable the Earl of -----------.
[*London*] *Printed in the year* 1753.
12°: pp. 204.   L,O.
This collection was certainly intended to be
attributed to the Earl of Haddington (see the
titles listed below), but the extent of his
authorship has never been determined; it
seems clear that some at least of the poems are
by other hands. It may be analogous to the
editions of *Poems by the E— of R—,* largely by
Rochester, but more in the nature of an
erotic miscellany. Because of the rarity of
editions and uncertainty about their relationship, I briefly list those eighteenth-century
editions known to me.

[—] Poems on several occasions. By the right
honourable the Earl of Ha—ton. The second
edition. Carefully corrected. 1756.
Lewis Walpole Library.

[—] 'Select tales in verse, by the right hon. the late
Earl of H-d-g-n. Never before printed.' [1758.]
(Advertisement of Oct 1758 in *Haslewood*.)

[—] 'Select tales in verse... The second edition.'
[1759.]
(Advertisement of 29 March 1759 in
Haslewood.)

[—] Poems on several occasions... The fifth
edition. Carefully corrected. 1764.
LVA-D.

Hamilton, T., *6th earl*

[—] Poems on several occasions... The fourth
edition. Carefully corrected. 1765.
(Pickering & Chatto cat. 260/3899.)

[—] Forty select poems on several occasions, by
the right honourable the Earl of H*******n. To
which is added, the Duke of Argyle's levee. 1769.
2 vol.   O; NN.
An edition of 1767 with this title is listed by
Halkett & Laing from Walpole's *Royal and
noble authors.*

[—] The flowers of gallantry, by the Earl of
Rochester, and other wits of the court of King
Charles the II. Correctly printed from the very
rare Antwerp edition. 1773.
CtY.
The title is false; the spine of the copy seen is
labelled 'Haddington's Poems'. Twenty-eight
tales only.

[—] New crazy tales; or ludicrous stories face-
tiously told, for the entertainment of young gentlemen and ladies. 1783.
L; CtY.

[—] Monstrous good things!! Humorous tales in
verse for the amusement of leizure minutes.
Written by the late ingenious Earl Hadding—n.
1785.
L; CtY.
A continuation of the preceding.

[—] The fortunate complaint [actually by Pomfret],
1709. *See* P731.

[—] Love triumphant over reason [actually by
Pomfret], 1709. *See* P732.

[—] Strephon's love for Delia, justify'd [actually
by Pomfret], 1709. *See* P737.

[—] The vision, a poem [actually by Defoe],
[1706.] *See* D185.

[Hamilton, William, *of Bangour.*] Poems on
several occasions. *Glasgow, printed and sold by
Robert & Andrew Foulis,* 1748.
8°: pp. 148.   O (CtY,DFo,IU,MH, paper undetermined).
Gaskell, Foulis 110.

[—] [fine paper]   L,E.
Asterisk added to signatures.

[—] — *Glasgow, printed by Robert & Andrew
Foulis,* 1749.
8°: pp. 148.   L,O; DFo,MH.
Gaskell, Foulis 131. There are two settings of
the preliminaries; one has the preface on one
page, the other on two; copies of both at GM,
DFo.

H14 [—] Contemplation: or, the triumph of love.
Edinburgh, printed for Messrs. Hamilton & Balfour,
1747. (*SM* Feb)

Hamilton, W., *of Bangour*

8⁰: π¹ A–B⁴ (A1 as 'A2'); *1–2* 3–18.
'No longer contemplation dwell'
    Printed in Hamilton's *Poems*, 1748.
L(11631.c.11),E(3),EP,EU,LdU-B; CtY,MH,*NN*.

H15 [—] The eighteenth epistle of the second book of Horace to Lollius imitated. *Edinburgh, printed in the year* 1737.
8⁰: π² A–C⁴ D¹; *i–iv, 1* 2–26.
'Dear R******, if I know thy soul aright'
    Printed in Hamilton's *Poems*, 1748. To Allan Ramsay.
O(uncut),E,*GM*,GU; MH,NN(2),OCU.

[—] The faithful few. An ode, inscribed to all lovers of their country, 1734. *See* F40.

H16 [—] An imitation of the 137. psalm. [*Edinburgh?* 1747?]
½⁰: 1 side, 1 column.
'On Gallia's shore we sat and wept'
    For the attribution to Hamilton see Bushnell in *SP* 35 (1938) 139n. A Jacobite lament.
O,E.

H17 [—] [engraved title] An ode on the victory at Gladsmuir 21 Septem^r. 1745. [*Edinburgh?* 1745?]
4⁰: *A²*; *1–2.*
    The copy seen is mutilated and has been mounted, but was apparently printed on the two inner pages, the first stanza engraved with title and music on A1ᵛ, stanzas 2–12 printed in two columns on A2ʳ. Said in James Paterson's edition of Hamilton (1850) to have been 'printed, and copies of it distributed, soon after the battle of Gladsmuir'.
'As over Gladsmuir's blood staind field'
E(mutilated).

H18 [—] A soliloquy. [*Edinburgh*, 1746.] (June?)
½⁰: 1 side, 1 column.
    According to *Bushnell*, printed in June 1746.
'My anxious soul is tore with doubtful strife'
    Printed in Hamilton's *Poems*, 1748.
CSmH.

H19 [—] Three odes. To which is added, the miss and the butterfly, a fable, in the manner of the late Mr. Gay. *Edinburgh, printed in the year* 1739.
8⁰: A–C⁴ D²; *1–2* 3–28.
'Fancy, bright and winged maid'
    Printed in Hamilton's *Poems*, 1748.
L(1485.pp.11),E(2),GM(uncut),MP; CtY-M,IU, MH,OCU,TxHR(uncut)+.

[—] Two odes of Horace imitated, 1737. *In* P897.

[**Hamilton, William,** *of Gilbertfield*.] Familiar epistles between W-- H--- and A-- R--, [1719.] *See* R51.

H20 — A new edition of the life and heroick actions of the renoun'd Sir William Wallace... Wherein the old obsolete words are rendered more intelligible; and adapted... *Glasgow, printed by William Duncan*, 1722.

Hamilton, W., *of Gilbertfield*

8⁰: *a⁴* b–d⁴ e² A–Y⁸ Z⁸(−Z8); *i–iii* iv–xxxvi, *1* 2–365 *366 blk.*
    Z8 not seen, possibly blank. Title in red and black. The preface shows it was published by subscription.
'Of our ancestors brave true, ancient Scots'
    Dedication signed; a modernized version of the poem by Henry the minstrel.
L(11644.c.59),O,C,E.

H20·5 [**Hamilton, William Gerard.**] Four odes. I. On sleep. II. On beauty. III. On taste. IV. To the right hon. the Lady **** on the death of her son. *London, printed for R. Manby & H. S. Cox*, 1750. (*GM* April)
4⁰: *A²* B–F⁴ G²; *i–iv*, 1–43 *44 blk.* A1 hft; iv err.
    The price on the half-title is altered in ms. from one shilling to one shilling 'and 4 pence'. Entered in Bowyer's ledgers to Manby & Cox, no date, as 'Four Odes...Hamilton's, 1 sheet twice composed, No 250'.
'Friend to the gloomy shade of night!'
    Ms. on title of the E copy 'by Mr. H.', and so printed in *Pearch* I. 115ff; this fits the reference to Hamilton in Bowyer's ledgers. The *Edinburgh review* Oct 1809 records that Hamilton 'about the age of twenty-one, appears to have indited various dull odes, which he forthwith printed in a handsome quarto pamphlet; but prudently abstained from publishing'.
O(−A1), E; DFo(−A1),IU(−A1),MH.

[**Hammond, Anthony.**] An ode upon solitude, 1709–. *In* S801.

H21 [**Hammond, James.**] An elegy to a young lady, in the manner of Ovid. By ------. With an answer: by a lady, author of the Verses to the imitator of Horace. *London, printed for J. Roberts*, 1733. (*DP* 28 March)
2⁰: *A²* B²; *1–3* 4–8.
'Oh! say, thou dear possessor of my breast!'
Answer: 'Too well these lines that fatal truth declare'
    Printed as Hammond's in *Dodsley* IV; the lady was Catherine Dashwood. The intended author of the answer is Lady Mary Wortley Montagu, but the poem is printed as Lord Hervey's in *Dodsley* IV.
L(1346.m.34),O(uncut),OA,LdU-B; CSmH,CtY, MH,OCU,TxU+.

H22 [—] Love elegies. Written in the year 1732. *London, printed for G. Hawkins; sold by T. Cooper*, 1743 [1742]. (*LM* Nov)
2⁰: *A²* B–F²; *i–iii* iv, *1* 2–20.
    In some copies (e.g. L,DFo) the 'end' of 'The end' has failed to print.
'Farewel that liberty our fathers gave'
    Hammond's authorship was widely known: cf.

Hammond, J. Love elegies

the following. The preface is by Lord Chester-field.
L(840.m.17; 163.n.22),LVA-D,O,*DrU-U*,LdU-B; CLU-C(uncut),CtY,DFo,ICN,ICU.

H23 [—] — By Mr. H-----nd. Written in the year 1732. With a preface by the E. of C—d. '*London, printed for G. Hawkins; sold by T. Cooper*' [*Edinburgh*], 1743.
8⁰: A–C⁴ D² (A2 as 'A3', B2 as 'C2', B3 as 'B2', C2 as 'B2'); *i–ii iii–iv, 1 2–23 24 blk.*
Printed by Ruddiman on the evidence of the ornaments. In the CtY copy, C2 is correctly signed.
L(11631.d.25),O,E,GU,MP+; CtY,IU.

H24 [—] — The second edition. *London, printed for G. Hawkins; sold by M. Cooper*, 1745.
2⁰: A² B–F²; *i–iii iv, 1 2–20.*
Horizontal chain-lines.
L(643.1.25/25),O(2),C; CtY,MH,MiU(2).

H25 [—] — *London printed, and Dublin re-printed for Edward & John Exshaw*, 1747.
12⁰: A–B⁶; *i–iii iv, 5 6–24.*
L(1962, cropt),DN; ICU.

Hammond, William, *1719–1783*. Psalms, hymns, and spiritual songs... *London, printed by W. Strahan; sold by J. Oswald*, 1745.
12⁰: pp. xxiv, 318.   L,O; NNUT.

H26 **Hammond, William,** *of Dublin?* Advice to a son. A poem. *Dublin, printed by R. Reilly, for A. Bradley*, 1736.
4⁰: A² B–E² F¹; *1–5 6–22.*
Watermark: Strasburg bend.
'Now you, my Delius, are dismiss'd the schools'
Dedication signed.
DA.

H27 — [fine paper?]
Watermark: fleur-de-lys on shield.
DN.

H28 — — The second edition corrected. To which are added, poems upon several occasions. By the same author. *Dublin, printed by R. Reilly, for A. Bradley*, 1736.
8⁰: A–F⁸ G⁴; *1–7 8–98 99–104.* 101 err; *102–104* advt.
Watermark: Amsterdam arms.
DN; InU.

H29 — [fine paper?]
Watermark: pro patria.
IEN.

H30 **Hampstead.** The Hampstead congress: or, the happy pair. *London printed, and sold by M. Cooper, A. Dodd, & G. Woodfall*, 1745. (*GM* Oct)
4⁰: A⁴ B–C⁴; *1–5 6–23 24 blk.* A1 hft.
Vertical chain-lines.
'If ancient sages well advise'
L(11630.c.4/11; 11630.c.1/16, –A1); IU(–A1).

Hampstead

H31 — Hampstead-Wells. [*London*] *Printed in the year* 1706. (26 Sept, Luttrell)
½⁰: 1–2, 1 column.
'Hail! fairest wells, tho' late the muses deign'
Crawford; MH(Luttrell).

H32 — Hampstead-Wells. Part II. *London printed, and sold by B. Bragge*, 1706. (10 Oct, Luttrell)
½⁰: 1–2, 1 column.
'Nor all deserve the biting satyr's sting'
Crawford; MH(Luttrell).

Handley, Knightly. Universal gallantry: or, the amours of the gods... *London, printed for the author; sold by J. Penn, and also by Felix Farley, printer in Bath*, 1722.
12⁰: pp. 119.   LdU-B; DLC.
The copy at LdU-B appears to be on fine paper, watermarked with fleur-de-lys on shield.

H33 **Handsome.** 'The handsome Arabian; or, a trip to the Board, the Court, and the Temple. To which is annex'd, Fog's delirium; or, a pill for the Craftsman. A poem on the times, by way of dialogue. [*London*] *Printed for R. Walker*. Price 6d.' (*MC* June 1729)
Listed in *MC* under 'new poetry', though the title might suggest that only 'Fog's delirium' was in verse.

H34 **Hannes, William.** Ode ad insignissimum virum, Matthæum Frampton, M.D. Oxon. [*Oxford*] *Typis Lichfieldianis*, 1724 [1725?].
2⁰: A² < B¹ (B1 as 'A2'; A2 as 'B'); *1–2 3–6.*
Dedication signed Jan 1724, possibly 1724/5; listed in *MC* Aug 1725 as sold by T. Warner.
'O qui salutem rite sciens, manu'
L(1970),O,C.

H35 **Hanover.** The Hanover gardiner. [1714/–.]
slip: 1 side, 1 column.
'An out landish gard'ner as we do hear tell'
A Jacobite satire.
O.

H36 **Hanoverian.** The Hanoverian leeches. To the tune of Hosier's ghost. [*London*, 1741?]
slip: 1 side, 1 column.
'Hark! ye citizens of London'
A tory election ballad.
C.

H37 — The Hannoverian torrie and whig at their bottle. To the tune of Come lay the down my Phillis. [*Edinburgh*, 1714.]
½⁰: 1 side, 2 columns.
'Since Nassau bravely freed us'
On King George's coronation, against the Pretender.
E.

Hanway, J.

[**Hanway, John.**] Psalmi Davidis quinquaginta priores versibus elegiacis latine rediti... Interprete J.H. triginta fere annos domi forisque in re militari occcupato [!]. *Londini, impensis autoris, & typis S. Palmer,* 1723. (*SR* 13 Oct)
4⁰: pp. 66.   L,O; KU.
> Deposit copies at O,E. A copy at KU 'For his grace the Archbishop of Canterbury' has many ms. corrections (some are found in all copies) and 'Ex dono autoris' printed on the title.

— Nova editio Psalmorum Davidis quinquaginta priorum, una cum nonnullis aliis selectis, versibus elegiacis latine redditorum... *Londini, prostant venales apud Tho. Edlin,* 1726 [1725]. (*SR* 9 Dec)
8⁰: pp. 82.   L,O; MH,NNUT.
> Deposit copies at L,O,SaU.

— Translations of several odes, satyrs, and epistles of Horace... With some versions out of Catullus, Martial, and the Italian poets. As likewise several occasional copies of verses by the author. *London, printed by W. Burton; sold by Mr. Stokoe,* 1730 [1729]. (*SR* 21 Nov)
8⁰: pp. 264.   L,O; CtY,IU.
> Deposit copy at O.

[**Hanway, William,** *of the navy office.*] Poems upon several occasions, chiefly publick; and on some important subjects. By a gentleman. *London, printed in the year* 1745.
8⁰: pp. 86.   O.
> Ms. attribution and other notes in O copy.

Happiness. Happiness: a poem, 1737–. *See* Ward, John.

H38 — The happiness of retirement: in an epistle from Lancashire, to a friend at court... To which is added, an encomium on the town of Preston. *London, printed for J. Oswald,* 1733. (*GSJ* 21 Feb)
8⁰: A–C⁴; *i–ii* iii–v *vi*, 7–24.
'All men to compass happiness essay'
LG; OCU.

H39 Happy. The happy bride: a poem. In three canto's. *London, printed for D. Browne,* 1730. (*MChr* June, Nov)
8⁰: A–H⁴; *i–v* vi–viii, *1* 2–55 *56*. A1 blank; 56 advt.
Other poems on pp. 44–55.
'Aid me, O Venus! beauty's pow'rful queen'
> Dedication signed 'A.B.'
L(11633.cc.2/4,–A1),O(2,–A1),LdU-B; CSmH (–A1),CtY(–A1),ICN(–A1),OCU(–A1).

H40 — The happy coalition. A poem. Humbly address'd to his royal highness the Prince of Wales on the present conjuncture and joyful reconciliation. By a gentleman of the Inner Temple. *London, printed for J. Huggonson,* 1742. (*LM* March)
2⁰: A² B–C²; *1–2* 3–12.
> Horizontal chain-lines; watermark in the fold.

The **happy** coalition

'Stay, sacred goddess, we thy aid implore'
WrP; CSmH,CtY.

H41 — The happy conquest: or, the true method, and unspeakable pleasure, of having the mind well fortify'd against all the disappointments of life. *London, printed in the year* 1719.
8⁰: A⁴ B²; [2] i–ii, 1–8.
'With utmost diligence I sought to find'
L(1477.d.19/6).

H42 — The happy courtezan: or, the prude demolish'd. An epistle from the celebrated Mrs. C— P—, to the angelick signior Far--n--li. *London, printed for J. Roberts,* 1735. (*GM* April)
2⁰: A² B–E²; *i–iv, 1* 2–16. A1 hft.
'Thou! who dost every thought and wish controul'
> A bawdy epistle from Constantia Phillips to the castrato Farinelli. Cf. *The secrets of a woman's heart,* 1735, and *The fate of courtezans,* 1735.
L(C.131.h.1/4**; 163.n.34,–A1),O,OA,*LdU-B, MR-C*; CSmH,CtY(–A1),ICN,MH,TxU(uncut) +.

— The happy government, 1734–. *See* Howard, W.

H43 — The happy life. An epistle to the honourable Lieutenant general Wade. *London, printed for T. Green,* 1733. (*GM, LM* Jan)
2⁰: A² B–C²; *1–2* 3–11 *12* blk.
'Where can the muse a sure protection find'
> *Crum* W1696.
DLC,ICN,IU,MH,OCU.

H44 — The happy marriage: an eclogue. In imitation of Virgil's Tityrus. With other poems. *London, printed for J. Duke, & B. May,* 1733. (*GM, LM* Oct)
8⁰: A⁴ B–C⁴; *i–ii, 1–3* 4–21 *22.* 22 advt.
With the Latin text of *Tityrus.*
'You, Damon, in your tender bride's embrace'
> The advertisement is for Robert Hay's *Odæ aliquot*; possibly this is by the same author.
OCU.

H45 — A happy memorable ballad, on the fight near Audenarde, between the Duke of Marlborough, of Great-Britain, and the Duke of Vendome, of France. As also the strange and wonderful manner how the princes of the blood royal of France were found in a wood. In allusion to the unhappy memorable song commonly call'd Chevy-chace. *London printed, and sold by John Morphew,* [1708.]
½⁰: 1 side, 2 columns.
> Reprinted in a Hills piracy of Tate's *A congratulatory poem to his royal highness,* 1708.
'God prosper long our gracious queen'
> *Crum* G295: 'On the battle of Audenard'.
CtY,NNP,TxU,*Harding.*

H46 —— *London, printed by J. Bradford,* [1708.]
½⁰: 1 side, 2 columns.
> Rough woodcut at head. A piracy?
L(C.40.m.10/104).

Happy

H47 — The happy nuptials, a pastoral epithalamium: as it is performed at the theatre in Goodmans-fields. By a gentleman. *London, printed by H.W.* [*Henry Woodfall?*] *and given gratis at the aforesaid theatre,* 1733.

4°: *A*⁴; *1–2* 3–8.

The performance took place on 12 Nov 1733, and while the nature of the work is not clear, it probably falls outside the scope of this catalogue.

'How comes it, Daphnis, that our nymphs and swains'

The prologue is by William Havard, but the text may be by another hand.

OCU.

— The happy reign, [173–.] *See* Mawer, John.

— The happy rival or Venus mistaken, 1711. *See* Newcomb, Thomas.

[**Harcourt, Simon.**] The female Phaeton [by Prior?], [1718.] *See* P1094.

— Three poems viz... II. The female Phaeton. By Mr. Harcourt. III. The judgment of Venus. By the same, 1720. *See* Three.

[—] Upon Lady Katherine H-de's first appearing at the play-house in Drury-lane [by Prior?], 1718. *See* P1093.

H48 Hard. The hard-us'd poet's complaint: inscrib'd to the theatric-managers and bibliopolians, of the great, little world. By Scriblerus Tertius, esq. of neither university, and indeed barely of grammatical erudition. *London, printed for the author, published by G. Woodfall, and the following booksellers of the body-politick, J. Brindley's, H. Chapelle's, J. Jackson's, H. Dunoyer's, J. Millan's, S. Harding, F. Noble's, G. Bickham's, J. Robinson's, S. Baker's, Mr. Slater's, H. Pier's, W. Owen, Wm. Reeve's, & R. Spavan,* [1750.] (*LM* Sept)

2°: *A*⁴ B²; [6] *i* ii, *5* 6–8. A1 frt.

The collation is obscure; A2.3 bearing title and preface have been seen to be conjugate. The frontispiece, A1, and the 'list of friends, non subscribers' A4 may have been separately printed. Though all copies are bound in this order, the catchwords suggest that the list of subscribers should precede the preface.

'Full twenty times hath Phœbus' car gone round'

Ascribed to Paul Whitehead by the L catalogue because his *The Gymnasiad*, 1744 was 'with the prolegomena of Scriblerus Tertius'. The attribution seems unreliable; the poem was never included among Whitehead's works.

L(11630.f.76),GM(−frt); DFo(−frt),*MH*(−frt).

[**Hardres, T.**] A congratulatory poem, on the anniversary-day of his majesty King George's coronation, 1718. *See* C355.

Hardres, T.

[—] A panegyrical poem on the fair and celebrated beauties in and about the city of Canterbury, 1718. *See* P43.

Hardy, William. Poems on several subjects. By William Hardy, a poor groom in Oxford. [*Oxford?*] 1737.

8°: pp. 28.   O; CtY.

Title in half-title form.

Hardyknute. Hardyknute, a fragment, 1719–. *See* Wardlaw, Elizabeth, *Lady.*

Hare, Thomas. A translation of the odes and epodes of Horace into English verse. Attempted by T. Hare... *London, printed for the author in the year* 1737.

8°: pp. xvi, 311.   L,O; CtY,IU.

Some copies have an errata leaf. Proposals were advertised 10 Feb 1736 (*Haslewood*).

Haren, Willem van.

Boyse, Samuel: The praise of peace. A poem. In three cantos. From the Dutch of M. Van Haren, 1742. *See* B365.

H49 [**Harison, William.**] On his grace the Duke of Marlborough going for Holland. In imitation of the third ode of the first book of Horace. *London, printed for Jacob Tonson,* 1707. (*DC* 7 April)

½°: *1–2*, 1 column.

'Thrice happy barque, to whom is giv'n'

Ascribed to Harison by *CBEL*.

LSA,DG,Crawford.

H50 — The passion of Sappho, and feast of Alexander. Set to musick by Mr. Thomas Clayton. As it is perform'd at his house in York-Buildings. *London, printed for Jacob Tonson,* 1711. (*SR* 16 May)

4°: A–C⁴; *i–viii*, 1–15 *16 blk.*

The passion of Sappho 'By Mr. Harrison'; Alexander's feast 'By Mr. Dryden'. Deposit copy at E.

'Hail sacred muse, and vocal shell'

O,E; CLU-C.

H51 — Woodstock Park. A poem. *London, printed for Jacob Tonson,* 1706. (*DC* 16 March)

2°: A–C²; *i–ii*, 1–10.

No watermark. The Luttrell copy dated 16 March is recorded in *Haslewood*.

'Kind heav'n at length, successfully implor'd'

LVA-F,O,*MR*,WcC; CtY,ICN,IU,MH,TxU+.

H52 — [fine paper]

Watermark: serpent (cf. Heawood 3766).

L(643.1.24/27).

H53 — — The second edition revis'd. *London, printed for Jacob Tonson,* 1706.

2°: A–C²; *i–ii*, 1–10.

O; CtY,TxU.

Harlequin. Harlequin-Horace: or, the art of modern poetry, 1731–. *See* Miller, James.

Harlot. The harlot's progress. An heroi-comical poem, 1739. *See* Breval, J.D. [Morality in vice].

H54 — The harlot's progress: or, the humours of Drury-lane. In six cantos. Being the tale of the noted Moll Hackabout, in hudibrastick verse... which is a key to the six prints lately publish'd by Mr. Hogarth... *London, printed for B. Dickinson, & R. Montague; sold by J. Brotherton, R. Ware, A. Dodd, J. Brindly, J. Jolliff, J. Stagg,* 1732. (*DP* 27 April)
8°: (frt+) A–H⁴; *1–2* 3–63 *64 blk*.
> *DP* 22 April advertised publication for 'Monday next' [24 April]; *GSJ* lists it as 27 April.
'I sing no songs of Alexander's'
> The same author wrote *The progress of a rake*, 1732.
OCU.

H55 — — The second edition. *London, printed for B. Dickinson, & R. Montague...*[as preceding], 1732. (*DP* 4 May)
8°: A–H⁴; *1–2* 3–64.
> No frontispiece in the copies seen. An epistle to Hogarth is added.
CtY,MH.

H56 — — The third edition. *London, printed for B. Dickinson, & R. Montague...*[as preceding], 1732.
8°: (frt+) A–H⁴; *1–2* 3–64.
> Probably a reimpression.
MH,*OrU*.

H57 — — In six cantos, illuminated with cuts to each... The fourth edition with additions: particularly an epistle to Mr. Hogarth. *London, printed for B. Dickinson, & R. Montague; sold by E. Nutt, & J. Brotherton, A. Dodd, J. Brindly, J. Jolliff, Mr. Critchly, & J. Stagg,* 1732. (*DJ* 11 May)
8°: (frt+) A–H⁴; *1–2* 3–64.
> Probably largely a reimpression; signatures B and C show some differences. After imprint '[Price two shillings, and without cuts one shilling.]' The copy seen has 5 mezzotints in green ink.
Institute for Sex Research.

H58 — — The fifth edition. To which is now first added, a curious riddle... N.B. Those who have had of the former impressions, may have the riddle singly, at the price of six pence. *London, printed for R. Montagu; sold by Mrs Nut, Mrs Dod, Mr. Brindley, Mr. Jollife, & Mr. Stag,* [1732.] (*DJ* 29 Nov)
8°: (frt+) A–H⁴ [I⁴] (+6 plates); *1–2* 3–64 [*65–72*].
> Possibly a reissue of the fourth edition with a cancel title, and with the addition of I⁴ containing [Edward Ward] *A riddle* (first published 1706), though copies seen lack that; it is found in the reissue below.
LG(−frt, plates; lacks I⁴); CSmH(lacks I⁴).

H59 — — Being the life of the noted Moll Hackabout, in six hudibrastick canto's... The sixth edition. Whereunto is prefix'd, never before printed... Satan's defeat; or Jack Presbyter triumphant. *London, printed for and sold by R. Montagu, likewise sold by C. Corbett,* 1740.
8°: (frt+) π² A⁴(−A1) B–I⁴ (+6 plates); *i–ii*, *1–72*.
> A reissue, with 'Satan's defeat' on π2.
Satan's defeat: 'Instead of a song, if 'twill make you amends'
L(Tab.603.a.22/1, lacks I⁴),O; CtY.

H60 [**Harris, Benjamin.**] Brittania's tears: or, England's lamentation. In an elegy occasion'd by the death of our so much beloved monarch, and deliverer, his late most gracious majesty, King William III. Who departed this life, for the obtaining a crown of glory, from the hands of his blessed redeemer, March the 8th. 170½. *London, printed by Benj. Harris,* 170½. (March)
1°: 1 side, 2 columns.
> Mourning headpiece and borders.
'No longer, O thou god of heav'n and earth'
> The epitaph signed 'Mœstus composuit, B.H.'; almost certainly the publisher, Benjamin Harris, who also wrote a poem on William's accession.
MH.

H61 [—] ⟨The holy Bible in verse, containing the old and new testaments with the apocrypha. The whole containing above one thousand lines...⟩ *London printed, and sold by Benj. Harris,* 1701. (*LP* 21 Feb)
32°: *A*⁸ B–D⁸; *1–64*.
> The copy described is imperfect; the title is taken from the *LP* advertisement, the imprint from the title to the new testament. First published 1698 (copy at David M. McKell Memorial Library, Chillicothe, Ohio) and reprinted with cuts 1698 (copy in the collection of the late d'Alté A. Welch).
'This book contains a full relation'
> In later editions, the letter to the reader is signed 'B. H.', i.e. Benjamin Harris.
MWA(lacks A1–4, B8, D7–8).

H62 [—] The holy Bible; containing the old and new testaments, with the apocrypha. Done into verse for the benefit of weak memories. The whole containing above one thousand lines with cuts... *London printed, and sold by B. Harris,* 1715.
32°: *A*⁸ B–⟨D⁸⟩; *1–64*.
> The copy seen has sheet D from *The parents gift to their children* bound in error for the correct sheet D. The advertisement on C2ᵛ, signed by B. Harris junior and dated 15 March 1712, warns against a spurious book 'printed by one Bradford', presumably the versification by J. Bilcliffe.
L(1962, lacks D⁸).

Harris, B.

H63 — The holy Bible; containing...with the apocrypha...above one thousand lines. *Edinburgh, printed in the year 1724.*

12°: A–B¹²; *1–3* 4–46 *47–48 blk.*

    Letter to the reader signed 'B. Harris'.

E.

Harris, Joseph.

Some of Joseph Harris's poems were made use of by Timothy Harris after 1717; the relationship between the two is obscure. Joseph appears to have been a schoolmaster at Leightonstone; see H77·2 below for his apparent use of the name Haestrect James. A begging letter to Thomas Coke referring to Anglia triumphans *and* Luzara *is quoted in G. M. Trevelyan,* Blenheim *(1930) 88 from H.M.C. Coke (1889) 178.*

H64 [—] Anglia triumphans. A pindarique ode, on his grace, the Duke of Marlborough, and his glorious campaign in the Spanish low-countries... *London, printed for the author,* 1703. (16 Feb, Luttrell)

2°: *A² B–F²; i–iv, 1–19 20 blk.* ii err.

    The Luttrell copy is recorded in *Haslewood*; listed in *WL* Feb.

'So, having ended his campaigns in Gaul'

    Dedication signed 'J. H.'; according to *Haslewood* the dedication is so similar to that of *Luzara* below that the author's identity is certain.

O(title cropt, lacks A2); CtY,TxU.

H65 — A congratulatory ode, on his royal highness, the most illustrious George Augustus, prince of Wales, his happy birth-day, Saturday, October 30. 1714. Humbly and dutifully devoted and inscrib'd to... Wilhelmina Charlotta, princess of Wales, by... Joseph Harris. [*London*, 1714.]

2°: *A–B²; i–iv, 1–4.*

    Title in the form of a dedication.

'Wake all thy fire, celestial muse'

L(162.m.45); CtY.

H66 — A congratulatory poem most humbly offer'd to his grace the Duke of Queens-berry...on his being install'd a knight of the...Garter...July the 10th, 1701... By your grace's...Joseph Harris. [*London*, 1701.]

2°: (3 ll); *i–ii, 1–4.*

    Title in the form of a dedication.

'When Dædalus of old with wings display'd'

E; *CtY.*

H67 — A funeral-pindarique ode, sacred to the happy memory of our late gracious sovereign Queen Anne, &c. With a congratulary poem, on our present most illustrious King George...inscrib'd and dedicated to...the lords justices and lords regents of the kingdom...by...Joseph Harris. [*London*, 1714.]

2°: *A² B–C²; i–ii, 1–10.*

    Title in the form of a dedication, within mourning borders. Variant dedicatee in the L copy: 'Dedicated to his grace Charles, duke of Shrewsbury'.

Harris, J. A funeral-pindarique ode

'Sad was the hour, the sadder morn began'

L(11630.g.35),LLP; CtY.

H67·5 — A funeral poem on the much lamented death of the right honourable...Elizabeth countess of Bridgewater... This elegy is...dedicated to... Mary dutchess of Mountague, by...Joseph Harris. *London, printed in the year* 1714.

2°: *A² B–C²; i–iv, 1–8.*

'Come fairest of our isle, ye graces come'

L(1972),MR-C.

H68 — Great Britain's glory: or, the loyal subjects praise for his sacred majesty King George, and his royal highness, the Prince of Wales, their safe arrival and welcome into England. Humbly inscrib'd...to [various dedicatees]...by...Joseph Harris. [*London*, 1714.]

2°: *A–B²; i–iv, 1–4.*

    Title in the form of a dedication, with different dedicatees: Daniel, earl of Nottingham (L); James Stanhope (E); Thomas, lord Pelham (O); Thomas, earl of Pembroke (CtY). The copy at CtY has fleur-de-lys watermark, others London arms; it is not clear whether there are fine-paper copies, or whether odd lots of paper were used.

'Aspiring muse, commence a noble flight'

L(643.1.24/32),LLP(lacks A²),O,E; CtY.

[—] An hymn to the redeemer, 1713. *See* Harris, Timothy.

H69 — An Indian pastoral eclogue. [*London*] *Printed in the year* 1717.

2°: *A–B² C–D²; i–iv, 1–12.*

    The dedication is signed. The copy at LdU-B has the printed signature cut away, and ms. signature 'Timothy Harris' substituted; the date is changed in ms. to 1718.

'Some leagues remote from where fam'd Ganges flows'

LdU-B; CU.

H70 [—] Leighton-stone-air, a poem. Or a poetical encomium... Also a pindarick ode on Prince Eugene of Savoy. Humbly dedicated to the worthy encouragers of the Latin boarding-school, newly erected in Leighton-stone; by the author, J.H. M.A. *London, printed for A. Baldwin,* 1702 [1701]. (23 Dec, Luttrell)

2°: A–K²; *1–2* 3–39 *40 blk.*

    The Luttrell copy is recorded by *Thorn-Drury.*

'O may I, fam'd delicious villa, be'

Pindarick: 'Hast, potent genius, hast away!'

    A copy at L is bound with Harris's *Luzara*, making the expansion of the initials almost certain.

L(11626.h.13/6; 643.1.24/25).

H71 — Luzara. A pindarique ode, on Prince Eugenius of Savoy: and his late victory over the French and Spaniards, in Italy. Most humbly dedicated, to his

Harris, J. Luzara

    grace, the Duke of Somerset. *London, printed for the author,* 170⅔ [1702?].

    2°: A–D²; [2] *i* ii, *1–12*.

        Watermark: foolscap. Ms. corrections in most copies.

    'Hail great Eugenius! more renown'd'

    Dedication signed in full.

    L(643.1.24/26),LDW,O,*MR-C*.

H72 — [fine paper]

    Watermark: Dutch lion.

    TxU.

H73 [—] [another issue] *London printed, and sold by B. Bragg,* 1702. (21 Nov, Luttrell)

    2°: A²(±A2) B–D²; [2] *i* ii, *1–12*.

        Apparently a variant imprint and a cancel dedication, replacing Harris's name with initials 'J.H.' In some copies (LLP,O,MC) the date is altered in ms. to 1703. Ms. corrections in most copies. The Luttrell copy is recorded in *Haslewood*.

    LLP,LVA-F,O,MC; CLU,CSmH,CtY,KU(lacks A2),MH.

H74 [—] Marlborides, sive bellum britannicum. Carmen heroicum lingua romana susceptum. Liber primus. Ab authore J.H. A.M. scholæ grammaticæ commensalis in vico Leighton-stone...moderatore. [*London*] *Prostant venales apud Johannem Darby,* 1707. (*DC* 4 March)

    2°: A–I²; *i–ii* iii–iv, *1–31* 32. iv err; 32 advt.

    'Arma virumque cano redivivi stemmatis Angli'

        For Harris's authorship compare *Leighton-stone-air* above.

    O.

H75 — An ode most humbly inscribed to the queen's most excellent majesty, on her happy birth-day. Febr. 6. 171¾. [*London*] *Printed in the year* 1714.

    2°: A²; *1–2* 3–4.

    'Wake all thy fire, cœlestial muse'

    O.

H76 — [dh] On the anniversary of his majesty K. George's coronation. By Mr. Joseph Harris. On the occasion of his being appointed president of the society of gentlemen, assembled at the Half-Moon Tavern in the Strand, to solemnize this happy commemoration. On Saturday, October 20, 1716. [*London,* 1716.]

    4°: A²; *1–4*.

    'Unworthy as I am, how must I boast'

    Herts CRO (Panshanger box 46, uncut).

H77 — A poem humbly offer'd to the pious memory of his late sacred majesty King William III. who died at Kensington, March the eighth, 170½... By Joseph Harris gent. [*London*] *Printed in the year* 1702.

    2°: A¹ B–C²; *i–ii*, *1–8*.

        In this issue Harris's name appears on the title; there is no dedication leaf. The order of issues is uncertain; all are apparently on the same foolscap paper.

Harris, J. A poem

    'That Græcian bard who sweetly sung of old'

    MR-C; TxU.

H77·1 — [another issue] Dedicated to the right honourable the Earl of Pembroke... [*London*] *Printed in the year* 1702.

    2°: *A*² B–C²; *i–iv*, *1–8*.

        This issue omits Harris's name from the title, but has a signed dedication to the Earl of Pembroke.

    CtY.

H77·2 [—] [another issue] By Haestrect James, esquire. [*London*] *Printed in the year* 1702.

    2°: *A*¹ B–C²; *i–ii*, *1–8*.

        No dedication. The attribution to Haestrect James is obscure; *A poem upon the conclusion of the peace of Europe,* 1698, appeared over this name, but it is perhaps a pseudonym of Harris. Compare Henry Waring for an author who used several names for his presentation copies.

    CtY.

Harris, Timothy.

Some of the poems issued over Timothy Harris's name were previously published by Joseph Harris; the relationship between the two is obscure. See also Elkanah Settle, The eucharist, 1717, apparently taken over by Harris after Settle's death, and Harris's A pindarique ode, on...Madam Howland, 1719, subsequently used by Mrs. Randolph.

H78 — Augusta lachrymans, or Belvoir in tears. Occasion'd by the much lamented death of the most noble John Manners, late duke of Rutland, &c... *London, printed for the author,* 1721.

    2°: *A*² B²; *1–3* 4–8.

    'To a thick shade, but such as ne'er inspir'd'

    CtY.

[H79 = S252·2] [—] The eucharist, [1725.] *See* Settle, Elkanah.

H80 [—] The fox, a fryar; an allusion to mankind. More particularly, and most religiously address'd to his eminency Charles, cardinal Alberoni. *London, printed for J. Roberts,* 1719. (Jan, Luttrell)

    8°: A–C⁴; *1–4* 5–24.

        The watermarks are hard to distinguish, but the CSmH copy is possibly on fine paper.

    'Aquarius ebb'd, and Pisces caught i' th' wile'

    L(164.n.19, Luttrell),LdU-B,*MR*; CSmH.

H80·2 — [another issue] By Timothy Harris, gent. *London, printed for J. Roberts,* 1719.

    8°: A–C⁴; *1–4* 5–24.

        Apparently a press-variant title.

    L(1509/1094),O.

H81 [—] An hymn to the redeemer. *London printed, and are to be sold by J. Morphew,* 1713. (*PB* 5 Feb)

    2°: *A*² B–D²; *i–iv*, *1–12*.

    'Angelic host! in form and essence bright'

        The same work as the following which bears

Harris, T. An hymn to the redeemer

Timothy Harris's dedication. Considering its date, one may suspect that Joseph Harris was the author, and that Timothy subsequently made use of it.(Cf. Elkanah Settle, *The eucharist*, 1717, apparently taken over by Harris after Settle's death.) The Luttrell copy at L is in a modern binding with three other Luttrell poems, all by William Goldwin; it has a pencil attribution to Goldwin. *Haslewood* (II. 317c) recorded these Luttrell copies and ascribed this poem to Goldwin; it may be his pencil attribution, but the authority for the attribution is not known. W. A. Oxford who owned these poems and published *William Goldwin*, 1911, does not refer to it, and presumably doubted his authorship.

L(11602.i.23/2; 1347.m.52/4, Luttrell, 6 Feb), O,OW; CLU-C(uncut),CSmH,CtY,IU,TxU(uncut)+.

H81·5 — [*idem*] An hymn on Christ's nativity, and man's redemption. By Timothy Harris... This hymn is most humbly inscrib'd and dedicated to the right honourable Thomas lord Parker... *London, printed for the author*, 1722.
4°: A^2 B–I²; *i–ii* iii–vii *viii*, *9* 10–32 '*32–34*' *36 blk.*
The copy at KU has the date altered in ms. to 1724. Ms. correction on p. 9.
O,DG,LdU-B; KU,MH.

H82 — [reissue] A sacred hymn on Christ's nativity and man's redemption. By Timothy Harris, most dutifully inscrib'd and dedicated, to her royal highness the Princess of Wales. *London, printed for the author*, [1722/27.]
4°: A^1 C–I²; *i–ii*, *9* 10–32 '*32–34*' *36 blk.*
New title, dedication cancelled.
NjP.

[—] An Indian pastoral eclogue, 1717. *See* Harris, Joseph.

H83 [—] Melazzo, and it's brave defence: a poem. *London, printed for W. Mears; sold by J. Roberts*, [1719.] (*PM* 21 Feb)
2°: A² B¹; *i–ii*, *1–4*. 4 advt.
The relationship between this and the following is obscure. The text on p. 2 is correct in the copy seen, and is in the same forme as the title-page; possibly this is the later state.
'Melazzo! Thou lasting monument of fame'
O.

H83·2 — [another issue] By T. Harris, gent. *London, printed for W. Mears; sold by J. Roberts*, [1719.]
2°: A² B¹; *i–ii*, *1–4*. 4 advt.
Apparently a variant state of the title. Corrections apparently made on p. 2 by stamping with type.
L(1501/153).

H84 — A pindarique ode, on the much lamented death of that incomparable good lady, Madam Howland;

Harris, T. A pindarique ode

who died at Streatham, on Sunday, April 19th, 1719... These lines are...inscrib'd to...her grace, the Dutchess of Bedford, &c. By... Timothy Harris. *London, printed for the author*, 1719.
4°: A^2 B^2 C^1; [2] *i* ii, *1* 2–5 *6 blk.*
Also published in a slightly revised form as *On the much lamented death of...Lady Oxenden... By Mrs. Randolph*, [1735] (R110).
'Ah! 'tis too much, relentless fate!'
L(643.m.12/30).

H85 — A poem on the death of the king of Sweden, who was kill'd before Fredrickshall, December 11. 1718. *London, printed for T. Warner; sold by E. Berrington*, 1719. (*PB* 24 Jan)
2°: A² B¹; *1–2* 3–5 *6 blk.*
Price deleted from the title of L copy. The advertisement in *PB* is anonymous, and possibly there was also an anonymous issue.
'A glorious prince he was! whose godlike breast'
L(1959).

H86 — The pomp of death. A panegyrical elegy on the illustrious John duke of Marlborough... *London, printed for the author*, 1722.
2°: A² B–D²; *i–iv*, *1* 2–12.
'When fate some mighty genius has design'd'
Dedication signed.
AN.

H87 — The skreen, detected: or, riddle, upon riddle: being a wheel, within a wheel. Recommended to all loyalists...and inscrib'd to his grace Phillip, duke of Wharton, by T. Harris, gent. *London, printed for the author*, 1721.
2°: A² B²; *1–4* 5–8.
'As on my bed, restless I museing lay'
Against Walpole.
O.

H88 — To her royal highness, the Princess of Wales; an humble oblation, on this her happy and auspicious birth-day, March the 1st, 171⅞. *London, printed in the year* 1719.
2°: A² B²; *1–4* 5–8.
'As when the heav'ns are clear, the rising sun'
L(1489.f.28).

H89 Harrison, H. A tragicomic, heroical, satyrical burlesque poem in three canto's on the hyperbole. The first canto being a brief account of taste a-la-mode... The second and third canto's contain the...customs of persons in the lowest state of life... *London, printed for J. Robinson*, [1748.] (*GM,LM* Sept)
4°: A^2 B–H²; *1–7* 8–32. A1 hft.
'I sing the buzzing follies of the town'
Dedication to Mr. Francis Hammond, anaglyphist, signed 'H. Harrison, A.S.'.
L(11630.f.25, –A1),PrP; CtY.

Harrison, J.

H90 Harrison, John. A poem, occasion'd by the much lamented death of the late reverend Mr. Robert Bragge... *London, printed for J. Oswald, 1738.* (*GM,LM* March)
4°: A–B⁴; *1–2 3–14 15–16 blk.*
No watermark; 'Price 4*d.*' on title.
'No airy theme my pensive muse employs'
LDW; CU(–D4),TxU(–D4).

H91 — [fine paper]
Watermark: fleur-de-lys on shield; 'Price 6*d.*' on title.
LDW(–D4).

[**Harrison, T.,** *of Canterbury.*] A congratulatory poem, on the anniversary-day of his majesty King George's coronation, 1718. *See* C355.

[—] A panegyrical poem on the fair and celebrated beauties in and about the city of Canterbury, 1718. *See* P43.

Harrison, Thomas. Poems on divine subjects. In two parts. To which is added a poem to the memory of the rev. Mr. Benjamin Stinton. *London, printed for, and sold by John Clark, E. Matthews, & T. Sanders, 1719.* (*DC* 9 May 'next Monday')
12°: pp. xxii, 84.   L; CLU-C.

—— The second edition. *London, printed for John Clark, 1721.* (*DJ* 2 Aug)
12°: pp. xv, 79.   L,DT.

[—] Belteshazzar; or, the heroic Jew: a dramatic poem, 1727.
According to ms. notes in the copy at IU this work was actually performed, and is therefore outside the scope of this catalogue.

Harrison, William, *d. 1713. See* Harison, William.

Hart, John. Miscellaneous translations from Bion, Ovid, Moschus, and Mr. Addison. With an original poem on bowling, 1716. *See* Miscellaneous.

H92 — Ποιημα νουθετικον: or, the preceptive poem of Phocylides, translated into English. To which are subjoin'd notes... By J. Hart. *London, printed for J. Robinson, 1744.* (*GM,LM* May)
8°: A–C⁸ D¹; *i–iii iv–vi, 1 2–44.*
'Let no adult'rous love pollute thy soul'
The identification with the John Hart whose translations from the Greek appeared in *Miscellaneous translations from Bion, 1716,* is tentative.
C; CtY,IU,PU.

Harte, Walter. Poems on several occasions. *London, printed for Bernard Lintot, 1727.* (*SR* 28 June)
8°: pp. xxx, 244.   L,O; CtY,MH.

Harte, W.

A3 is usually cancelled; both states are present in the copy at CSmH. Deposit copies at L,O.

— [reissue] *London, printed for John Cecil, 1739.*
O; ICU,TxU.
Cancel title.

[—] An epistle to Mr. Pope, on reading his translations of the Iliad and Odyssey of Homer [actually by Bezaleel Morrice], 1731. *See* M479.

H93 [—] An essay on reason. *London, printed by J. Wright for Lawton Gilliver, 1735.* (*SR* 7 Feb)
2°: A² B–I²; *i–iv, 1 2–30 31; 32 blk.* iv err; I2 advt.
Griffith 359. Entered in *SR* to Gilliver; deposit copies at L,SaU. Harley's copy at O with date of receipt 6 Feb was possibly presented before publication.
'From time's vast length, eternal and unknown'
Later editions were published under Harte's name. See *An epistle to the author of the Essay on reason,* 1735.
L(840.m.1/49; 643.m.14/9; 163.n.53),O(6),OW(3),LdU-B(uncut),SaU+;   CSmH,CtY(2),ICN, MH,TxU(2)+.

H94 [—] — The second edition. *London, printed by J. Wright for Lawton Gilliver, 1735.*
2°: A² B–I²; *i–iv, 1 2–30 31; 32 blk.* I2 advt.
The order of the two 'second' editions has not been determined; this omits line 504.
L(11657.m.31,–I2;   1490.f.19,–I2),O(2,–I2), EU,DG; CtY,KU,MH,TxU.

H95 [—] [another edition]
This edition includes line 504.
L(1489.m.32),LdU-B; CU,CtY,ICN,IU,TxU.

H96 [—] — *London: printed: Dublin: re-printed by George Faulkner, 1735.*
8°: A⁴ B–C⁴ D²; *i–iv, 1 2–26 27; 28 blk.* 27 advt.
The advertisement for Swift's works on p. 27 is dated 25 March.
O,DK; CSmH.

H97 —— The third edition, corrected. By the Reverend Walter Harte... *London, printed by J. Wright for Lawton Gilliver, 1736.*
2°: A² B–G² H²(±H2); *i–iv, 1 2–28. 28 err.*
H2 is uncancelled in the O copy, which has a ms. correction in p. 28 line 2 'expuere' for 'exupere'.
LVA-D,O,WcC(uncut); DFo,IU,MH,*OCU*,TxU.

H98 — An essay on satire, particularly on the Dunciad... To which is added, a discourse on satires, arraigning persons by name. By Monsieur Boileau. *London, printed for Lawton Gilliver, 1730.* (*SR* 11 Jan)
8°: π⁴ A⁴(–A1, 2) B–F⁴; *i–viii, 5–46 47–48.* π1 hft; π2,F4 advt.
A copy at CtY without π⁴ has A1, 2 (half-title and title) uncancelled; this original title has no reference to Boileau's discourse. Listed in *GSJ* 14 Jan. Deposit copies at L,O,EU,SaU.

Harte, W. An essay on satire

> Reissued in *A collection of pieces...on occasion of the Dunciad*, 1732.
> 'T' exalt the soul, or make the heart sincere'
> L(C.59.ff.12/2),O(2, 1−π1−2, F4),CT,E,SaU + ; CSmH,DFo,ICN,MH(−π2),TxU(2) + .

H99 — Part of Pindar's first Pythian ode, paraphrased, by the revd. Mr. Walter Harte. Set to musick by Mr. William Boyce. *London, printed in the year* 1749.
4°: A⁴; *1−2* 3–8.
> Originally published in Harte's *Poems*, 1727.
> 'Gentle lyre, begin the strain'
> L(643.k.25/12); MH.

H100 — — Set to musick by Mr. William Boyce, composer to his majesty. [*London?* 1755/−.]
8°: A⁴ B²; *1−2* 3–11 *12 blk.*
DFo.

— Verses presented to his highness the Prince of Orange. On his visiting Oxford [by Mallet and Harte], 1734. *See* M58.

H101 **Hartlib, John.** To Mr. Samuel Moore, on his arch-types, or most accurate drawings with his pen. [*London*, 170–?]
½°: 1 side, 1 column.
'How does thy wond'rous art our eyes deceive'
> Signed 'John Hartlib'.
L(Harley 5949, fol. 348).

Harvey, John. A collection of miscellany poems and letters, comical and serious. *Edinburgh, printed for the author*, 1726.
8°: pp. x, 92.   L,O; CSmH,CtY.
> The copy at CSmH is apparently in a presentation binding.

H102 — The life of Robert Bruce king of Scots. A poem... *Edinburgh, printed by John Catanach*, 1729.
4°: π¹ a–b⁴ c¹ A–Ff⁴; *i–xx*, *1*–232.
> List of subscribers on pp. x–xix; *Proposals* dated Oct 1727 at E.
> 'Whilst I, unequal, tempt the mighty theme'
> L(G.19014),O,E(2, 1 uncut, lacks b⁴ c¹),EP,GM + ; CLU-C,DLC,MH.

H103 [—] To the memory of the right honourable William, late earl of Kintore. A poem humbly inscrib'd to the right honourable John, present earl of Kintore. [*Edinburgh?*] *Printed in the year* 1719.
4°: A–D²; *1−2* 3–16.
> 'Whilst thou, great soul, pursu'st thy airy way'
> Reprinted in Harvey's *Collection*, 1726.
> L(11631.e.34),EP; CtY(uncut).

H104 **[Hasledine, William.]** Bellus homo et academicus. Recitarunt in theatro Sheldoniano apud comitia Oxoniensia MDCCXXXIII, Lodovicus Langton, et Thomas Baber...Accedit oratio Petri Francisci Courayer...habita in iisdem comitiis, quint. Id. Julii. *Londini, prostant venales, apud J. Wilford*, 1733. (*GSJ* 25 Sept)
2°: A–D²; *1−3* 4–16.

Hasledine, W. Bellus homo

> Entered to 'Messrs Innys & Bowyer Partners in Bellus Homo &c' in Bowyer's ledgers under 20 Sept, 1000 copies printed.
> 'Usque adeo insano juvat indulgere labori?'
> Ascribed to William Hasledine in *Nichols* II. 39; Langton and Baber appear only to have spoken the dialogue. Translated into English by William Bowyer as *The beau and the academick*, [1733.]
> L(C.57.g.7/3),O(2); CSmH,CtY.

Hastings, —, *Mr.* The czar. A poem. Inscribed to Sir John Norris, 1721. *In* F224.

Hastings, G. The young club a congratulatory poem, [1713.] *See* D298.

H105 **Hasty.** The hasty wedding: or the Saint Giles's fortune. An heroi-comical poem. In six canto's. *London, printed for T. Warner*, 1720. (*DC* 12 Oct)
8°: A–H⁴; *1−2* 3–64.
> The Luttrell copy dated October is recorded by *Thorn-Drury*.
> 'Near to a certain pound a church there stands'
> OCU.

H106 **Hatton, Henry Charles.** An occasional satyr. *London, printed for J. Jackson; sold by J. Peele*, 1725 [1724]. (*MC* Nov)
2°: A²(A1 + χ¹) B–C²; *i–ii*, *1−2* 3–12. 2 err.
> The collation of the preliminaries is tentative; the second leaf is a dedication leaf, not found in the CtY, TxU copies which were possibly issued without it.
> 'Tis granted, sir, you've basely been accus'd'
> Dedication signed when present.
> L(840.m.1/50); CtY(2, no dedication leaf),MH, TxU(no dedication leaf).

H107 **[Hauksbee, Francis.]** The patch. An heroi-comical poem... In three cantos. To which is added, the Welch wedding. A poem... By a gentleman of Oxford. *London, printed for E. Curll*, 1724 [1723]. (*EvP* 29 Aug)
8°: A⁴ B–F⁴; *i–iv* v–viii, *1* 2–39 *40 blk.* A1 hft.
> Reissued in *The altar of love*, 1727. 'The Welch wedding' was reprinted in Giles Jacob, *The rape of the smock*, 1736.
> 'Say, gentle muse, whence all this mighty care'
> *Welch wedding*: 'Taff boasted not of learning much, or arts'
> Dedication signed 'F.H.' Reprinted as by Hauksbee in *The school of Venus*, 1739.
> L(11658.f.53, −A1),O(−A1),E,AdU,LdU-B (−A1) + ; CLU-C,CtY(−A1),ICN,MH(−A1), OCU.

[Havard, William.] The happy nuptials, a pastoral epithalamium, 1733. *See* H47.

Have. Have at you all, 1740. *See* Morris, Robert.

Have

H108 — Have at you blind harpers. Three ballads concerning the times. Consisting of, I. The royal embassy... II. A humoursom ditty to Dr. Sacheverell's back friends. III. A cure for religious disputes... To the tune of, A soldier and a sailor, &c. *London printed, and sold by J. Baker, and by all her majesty's running-stationers*, [1710.] (*SR* 26 April)

8°: A⁴; *1–2* 3–8.
> Deposit copies at LSC,C,E,EU.

'Four kings, each god's viceregent'
'A bailiff and a boat-man'
'A dean and a prebendary'
> On the Indian kings, the Sacheverell mob, and the Socinian controversy.

LSC,O,C,E,EU.

H109 Hawke, Edward. A poem upon the law. Occasioned by a late act of parliament, entituled, An act for the amendment of the law... Together with a character of, and a panegyrick upon my lord keeper and the twelve judges. By a gentleman of the Inner-Temple. *London, printed in the year* 1707.

4°: π⁴ *A*² B–E⁴ E*¹ F–G⁴ H¹; *i–xii*, 1–34 33–50. π1 hft.
> The copy at DT has the added leaf E*1 unsigned.

'From Sala's banks our constitutions came'
> Dedication signed.

L(11631.e.27, −π1),DT,LdU-B.

H110 Hawkers. The hawkers new-year's gift; to all their worthy masters and mistresses. [*London*] *Printed by H. Buckeridge in Baldwins Gardens*, 1727. (Jan)

½°: 1 side, 2 columns.

'This new year's paper comes to kiss your hands'
> Apparently for the benefit of the hawkers of *Buckeridge's Best Intelligence*, an unrecorded newspaper.

L(1870.d.1/115).

Hawkins, William. Dramatic and other poems, letters, essays, &c... Vol. II. *Oxford, printed by W. Jackson; sold by R. & J. Dodsley, J. Rivington & J. Fletcher, & W. Owen, London; J. Fletcher & S. Parker, Oxford*, 1758.

8°: pp. 442.   O; CtY,MH.
> There are no general titles for the three-volume set of Hawkins's works.

H111 [—] Female empire: or, winter celebrated at London. *London, printed for M. Cooper*, 1746 [1747?]. (*GM,LM* Jan 1747)

2°: *A*² B–D²; *i–iv*, 1 2–3 8–16. A1 hft.

'Where proud Augusta, empire of the great'
> The copy at E has an early ms. attribution to Hawkins.

LG,E(−A1); CSmH,TxU(−A1).

H112 [—] The thimble. An heroi-comical poem. In four cantos. Dedicated to Miss Anna Maria Woodford.

Hawkins, W. The thimble

Canto the first and second... By a gentleman of Oxford. *London, printed for J. Roberts*, 1743. (*GM, LM* Feb)

2°: *A*² B–D²; *1–7* 8–16.
> Bond 187. Two cantos.

'The thimble's first original rehearse'
> An expanded version in five cantos was printed in Hawkins's *Works*, 1758.

L(1958),O(2); ICN,OCU,PU,TxU(2).

H113 [—] The thimble, an heroi-comical poem, in four cantos. Dedicated to Miss Anna-Maria Woodford. By a gentleman of Oxford. *London, printed for J. Shuckburgh; sold by M. Cooper*, 1744.

4°: A–D⁴ E²; *i–iii* iv–viii, 1 2–27 28 blk.
> Four cantos; early ms. attributions seen in copies at L,O,C. Revised text, including new first line:

'What art divine the shining thimble found'
L(11602.gg.24/9; 11630.d.16/1; 11630.b.4/6, imperfect; 840.k.2/3),O(2),OW,C; CSmH,CtY, ICN(2),ICU,MH.

H114 [**Hawksworth, Abraham Richard.**] The breathings of a pious soul, one of the people called quakers. [*Bristol?* 174–?]

½°: 1 side, 2 columns.

'Why droops the head? Why languishes the eye?'
> Ascribed to Hawksworth by *Smith* I. 925, and in a ms. note on a copy at LF.

LF(2).

Hawling, Francis. A miscellany of original poems on various subjects... Part I. *London, printed for S. Austen, J. Wood, & J. Crockat*, 'MDCCILI' [1752?].

8°: pp. 225.   L; CtY,DFo.

H114·5 [—] 'The Richmond beauties. A poem. In an epistle to J.M. esq; [*London*] *Sold by J. Roberts*. Price 6d.' (*MChr* Sept 1730)

> Printed as 'Richmond beauties, 1741. In an epistle to I.M. esquire' in Hawling's *Miscellany*, but listed in the index as 'written in the year 1728'. The addressee makes the identification clear. Printed in the *Miscellany* with first line:

'Why is it in our nature to be poor'

H115 [—] The signal: or, a satyr against modesty. *London printed, and sold by J. Roberts*, 1727. (*MC* Jan)

2°: *A*² B–D²; *1–3* 4–16.
> Also listed in *MC* Feb.

'Whether by fame or inclination drove'
> Collected in Hawling's *Miscellany*, [1752?].

MH,OCU,TxU.

H116 [—] Verses upon the much-lamented death of her sacred majesty Queen Caroline. Humbly inscrib'd to her royal highness the Princess Amelia. *London,*

Hawling, F. Verses

printed for R. Dodsley; sold by the pamphlet-sellers of London & Westminster, 1737.
2⁰: A⁴(−A1); *3–5* 6–7 *8 blk.*
　　Copies seen probably lack half-title, A1.
'Amelia! deign upon thy muse to shine'
　　Reprinted in Hawling's *Miscellany*, [1752?].
O; CSmH.

Hay, Robert. 'Odæ aliquot celebriores anglicanæ: latine redditæ.' (*GSJ* 23 June 1733)
　　Listed anonymously in *GSJ*, but advertised as by Hay in *The happy marriage*, 1733.

———

[—] The happy marriage: an eclogue. In imitation of Virgil's Tityrus. With other poems, 1733. *See* H44.

H117 Hay, William. Mount Caburn. A poem. Humbly inscrib'd to her grace the Dutchess of Newcastle. *London, printed for J. Stagg*, 1730. (*MChr* April)
2⁰: A² B–F²; *1–2* 3–24.
　　No watermark; 'Price 1*s.*' on title. Printed by Samuel Richardson (*Sale* 82).
'Poets, who mean to soar no common height'
L(11631.k.1),O(2, 1 uncut),OA,C(uncut),LdU-B; CLU,CtY(3),MH(uncut),TxU(uncut).

H118 — [fine paper]
　　Watermark: star; no price on title.
L(643.m.15/3, lacks A²); CSmH.

[Haywood, Eliza.] [dh] Poems on several occasions. [*London*, 1724?]
8⁰: pp. 16.
　　Issued in vol. 4 of a nonce collection *Works*, 1724; possibly not separately published. A 'second edition' is found in *Secret histories* (1725) II.261–80.

Hazard, Joseph. 'A collection of occasional poetical pieces in prose and verse'. (*GM* Jan 1731)

H119 He. He has kept his word. A poem. To perpetuate the memory of...Porto Bello. Written by a gentleman on board that fleet. *London, printed for R. Richards*, 1740. (*GM, LM* Nov)
2⁰: A² B²; *1–5* 6–8. A1 hft.
'When Britain's lyon lull'd supinely lay'
L(1484.m.27, lacks A2); OCU,TxU.

H120 — — *London, printed for C. Brown, in the Strand, and to be had of the persons who carry the news,* [1740.]
8⁰: A⁴ B²; *1–2* 3–4 *5–6* 7–11 *12 blk.*
　　A3 is a title-leaf to 'The weather-menders... By Mr. Spiltimber...London, printed for T. Carpenter, 1740', which occupies pp. 7–11. A piracy.
L(164.k.1, 26),O.

H121 — 'He, who worst, may still hold the candle: or, the country gentleman's address to the grumbling

traders in London. A new ballad. To the tune of, But we'll be as merry with our comrades, &c. [*London*] *Printed for T. Towers*. Price 4*d.*' (*GM* Feb 1733)
　　Listed in *LM* Feb at 2*d.*, which could suggest a half-sheet.

— The he-strumpets, 1707. *See* Dunton, John.

H122 — He's wellcome home: or, a dialogue between John and Sarah. *London, printed in the year* 1711.
½⁰: 1 side, 2 columns.
'Wellcome home, from wars alarms'
　　In praise of the Duke and Duchess of Marlborough.
L(112.f.44/32; G.1390/5).

Health. Health, a poem, [1716]–. *See* Baynard, Edward.

H123 — A health to be sung and drank by all honest Britons, upon the arrival of his sacred majesty King George, and his royal highness the prince, at Greenwich, and forever after... To the tune of, Fye soldiers, fye, why so melancholy, boys. [*London?* 1714.]
slip: 1 side, 1 column.
'Our glorious monarch's come'
Harding.

H124 — A health to honesty or, the tackers character. [*London*, 1704/05.]
½⁰: 1 side, 1 column.
　　Royal arms above title.
'He that owns with his heart, and helps with his hand'
　　Crum H446: 'The Welch health'; at L (MS. Egerton 924, fol. 31ᵛ) titled 'Oxford health'. Against occasional conformists.
MC.

H125 — A health to the Northamptonshire sneakers. [*London*] *Printed for Will. Hawkes and Tom Ponder, couriers,* [1705.] (*TC* Easter)
½⁰: 1 side, 1 column.
　　Below, 'The reply'. Listed as printed for J. Nutt in *TC*.
'We'll remember the men'
Reply: 'Here's a health to the knight'
　　Crum W287: 'The Northamptonshire toast' and H1154: 'The reply'. For and against Sir Justinian Isham and Thomas Cartwright, members for Northampton.
Crawford; CSmH,MH,*Harding.*

H126 — A health to the tackers. A new song. '*Oxford*', *printed* 1705.
½⁰: 1 side, 1 column.
　　Three lines of music above text. The Oxford imprint is suspect.
'Here's a health to the tackers, my boys'
　　A tory election ballad.
O; CSmH.

A **health** to the tackers

H127 — [*idem*] The Coventry ballad, &c. To an excellent new tune. The second edition. 'Norwich', *printed 1705.* (*DC* 14 April)
½⁰: 1 side, 1 column.
> No music. On the other side, *The messenger defeated*, 1705. The imprint is probably false.
L(1872.a.1/157*),Rothschild; CLU-C.

H128 Heany, James. Oxford, the seat of the muses: a poem... To which are added some original pieces by the same hand; with a preface, giving some account of the author. *Oxford, printed by L. Lichfield, for the author, and sold by him at Mr. Tubb's in the East-gate, and by Mr. Broughton, 1738.*
4⁰: a⁴ A–B⁴; *i–viii*, 1–14 15–16 blk.
'Could my Hibernian muse but soar on high'
L(11631.f.15,−B4),O,OW; CtY.

H129 — [reissue] The second edition. To which are added some other pieces by the same hand; with a preface, giving some account of the author. *London, printed for T. Cooper, 1738.* (*LM* April)
4⁰: a⁴(±a1) A–B⁴; *i–viii*, 1–14 15–16 blk.
> Listed in *LM* April as the second edition.
O; CU(−B4).

Heard, William. Hymns, or spiritual songs. *London, printed by J. Hart; sold by the author, J. Lewis, J. Butler, & J. Lucas, 1746.*
8⁰: pp. 33.   O.

H130 Heaven. Heaven invaded. Or, a contest between Jupiter and the giants; being a musical entertainment, to be represented on the birth-day of his most sacred majesty George... at the castle of Dublin, the 28th of May, 1727... Compos'd by Mr. John Sigismond Cousser... *Dublin, printed by George Faulkner, [1727.]*
4⁰: *A⁴*; 1–2 3–8.
'Since we first fram'd that scale of various beings'
O.

H131 Heaven-drivers. The heaven-drivers. A poem. *London, printed in the year 1701.* (7 Nov, Luttrell)
2⁰: A–D²; *i–ii*, 1–14.
> The Luttrell copy is recorded by *Dobell* 2500. All copies seen have a ms. correction to the motto on the titlepage.
'In pious times when great divisions'
> Against the Societies for Reformation of Manners.
L(1347.m.6),O; CtY,InU,MH,OCU,TxU(2).

H132 Hebrew. The Hebrew campaign: to which is annex'd, the Review in Hyde-park. *London, printed for the author, 1730.*
8⁰: *A² B–D⁴ E²*; *i–iv*, 1–27 28 blk.
> A2 bears a list of subscribers, all army officers.
'Of tribes in arms, encroaching fear'
Review: 'The theme's resolv'd: the glittering files appear!'

The **Hebrew** campaign

> The author also wrote *The temple of war*, 1731 and *The bed of honour*, 1732.
O; CtY.

Hectoris. Hectoris exuvias indutum cernite Mosen, [1712?/13.] *See* Pitcairne, Archibald.

[Heidegger, John James.] The artful priest: or, the virgin sacrifice, 1749. *See* A329.

— *See also* Heydegger.

Heliocrene. Heliocrene a poem in Latin and English, 1725–. *See* Merrick, John.

Hell. Hell in an uproar, 1725–. *See* Burridge, Richard.

H133 — Hell in epitome: or, a description of the M--sh--sea. A poem. *London, printed for J. Moore; sold by the booksellers of London & Westminster, 1718.* (*PB* 19 Aug)
8⁰: *A² B–E⁴*; *i–ii* iii–iv, 1 2–32.
> The imprint is given by *PB* as 'printed for the author, and sold by J. Bettenham'.
'Describe, my muse; in epic numbers tell'
> The imprint in *PB* suggests J. Moore could be the author. On the debtor's prison in the Marshalsea.
L(11633.cc.2/1),LG; TxU(uncut).

H134 — Hell upon earth: or, the character of the Poultrey compter. By a late prisoner confin'd in that place. *London, printed for the author, 1703.* (25 Feb, Luttrell)
½⁰: 2 sides, 1 column.
'From 'mongst the noisey crew, where devils resort'
MH(Luttrell).

H135 — Hell upon earth, or the devil tir'd with matrimony. *London, printed for F.C. [Francis Clifton?] near Fleet-street, 1718.*
½⁰: 1 side, 2 columns.
'In Florence liv'd a venerable sage'
> A tale.
L(1876.f.1/84).

H136 Hell-fire. The Hell-fire-club: kept by a society of blasphemers. A satyr. Most humbly inscrib'd to the right honourable Thomas baron Macclesfield... With the king's order in council, for suppressing immorality and prophaneness. *London, printed for J. Roberts, & A. Dodd, 1721.*
8⁰: A–C⁴; 1–9 10–23 24 blk.
'God! great and just, omnipotent and high'
> Dedication signed 'R.B.' A pietistic attack on the Hell-fire Club.
L(1077.c.51),O.

H137 Help. Help to patience under affliction. In a poem written upon occasion of the late accidental death of a worthy venerable gentleman... *Edinburgh, printed in the year 1742.* (*SM* April)

Help to patience under affliction

8º: A–G⁴; *1–2* 3–56. 56 err.
'Once in a morning, e'er the circling sun'
E.

H138 [**Helsham, Richard.**] D-----n S------t's pro-
logue to Hyppolitus, spoken by a boy of six years
old. [*Dublin*, 1721.]
½º: 1 side, 1 column.
Teerink 897.
'Ye sons of Athens, grant me one request'
Helsham's authorship is recorded in *Williams*
1023n, based on the 1765 additions to Swift's
Works. Substituted for *Mr. Sheridan's prologue
to the Greek play of Phædra and Hyppolitus*,
1721, by Tom Putland, the six-year-old, on
Helsham's instigation.
L(C.121.g.8/13),OC(Wake letters XIV. 335),
C(uncut); TxU.

Helter skelter. Helter skelter: or, the devil on
two sticks, 1704–. *See* Ward, Edward.

H139 — Helter skelter, or the hue and cry after the
attornies, going to ride the circuit. [*Dublin*, 1726/27?]
½º: 1 side, 1 column.
Teerink 712; *Williams* 572. Usually dated 1731,
when it was reprinted with Swift's *A proposal
humbly offer'd to the p—t*; but the DT copy
is bound with half-sheets of 1727, and a
related poem (referred to below) is certainly
1726.
'Now the active young attornies'
Printed with Swift's works by Hawkesworth
in 1775 and accepted as his by subsequent
editors, no doubt because it was printed with
works by him. A copy at MH has a contemporary ms. note 'By John Duncan of T.C.D.'
but no such person is known in the records.
Cf. *A poem on the proceedings*, [1726] ascribed
in the same hand to 'John Dunkan'. Possibly
Jacob Duncan (matriculated 1725) or William
Dunkin (B.A. 1729) is intended; the latter
is the more likely candidate.
L(1890.e.5/4),DT; MH.

H140 — ⟨He⟩lter skelter, the devil in a frying-pan, or
a ⟨s⟩atyr on a certain young gentleman and lady.
[*Dublin*, 1725/30.]
½º: 1 side, 2 columns.
The copy at L forms part of a collection of
Dublin half-sheets of 1725/30.
'Satyr, you can't be too severe'
L(C.121.g.8/95).

H141 **Hemp.** Hemp. A poem. Humbly inscribed to the
honourable Martin Bladen, esq;... *London, printed
for C. Corbett; sold by E. Nutt, J. Chrichley, and by
the booksellers of London & Westminster*, 1739.
(*GM, LM* Sept)
2º: A² B²; *1–3* 4–8.
'If Ariconian swains with pleasure see'
CSmH,OCU.

Henderson, A.

H142 **Henderson, Andrew.** Cumbrius triumphans carmen ob victoriam partam ad vicum Cullodenensem,
16to Aprilis 1746. *Edinburgi*, 1746.
8º: A⁴; *1–2* 3–8.
'Fama cum patrem varii sacelli'
E(title mutilated); NN.

H143 — Expeditio militaris, sive Britannia liberata,
carmen in honorem Cumbriæ ducis illustrissimi.
Edinburgi, 1746.
8º: A⁴; *1* 2–8.
'Cura quæ vatum, titulis, sacrorum'
L(11409.b.44),O,EU,AdU.

H143·5 — Psalmi centesimi quarti paraphrasis poetica.
Edinburgi, A.D. 1745.
8º: A⁴; *i–iv*, 1–4.
Horizontal chain-lines.
'Mens domino benedic mea, mi pater alme, deus-
que'
EU.

[**Henderson, Robert.**] A hymn on the sufferings
and death of our blessed lord and saviour, Jesus
Christ, 1735. *See* H426.

H144 **Henley, John.** Esther queen of Persia. An historical
poem in four books. *London, printed for E. Curll &
J. Pemberton, & A. Bettesworth*, 1714. (June?)
8º: A⁸ a⁸(±a8) B–D⁸ E⁴ F⁴(–F4); [6] *i* ii–ix *x blk*,
i–xii, 1–60 *61–66*. A1 frt.
In some copies (e.g. MH) a8 (p. 3) has press-
figure 2; this is probably the uncancelled state.
Listed in *MC* June as reprinted, probably in
error.
'While fancy leads her gayer sons astray'
L(11631.e.28),LVA-D(2),BlL; IU,KU,MH,TxU.

H145 — [reissue] The history of Queen Esther. A poem
in four books. Wherein is describ'd... The second
edition. *London, printed for A. Bettesworth, E.
Curll & J. Pemberton*, 1715. (*PB* 1 Sept)
8º: A⁸(±A2) a⁸ B–D⁸ E⁴ F⁴(–F4); [6] *i* ii–ix *x blk*,
i–xii, 1–60 *61–66*. A1 frt.
a8 is apparently uncancelled in the copies seen.
O,OW,C,E.

H145·5 [—] Tom o' Bedlam's Dunciad: or, Pope,
Alexander the pig. A poem. *London, printed for M.
Turner, at the Post-office, corner of Bow-street,
Covent-Garden; sold at the booksellers in London &
Westminster*, 1729. (*MChr* 14 May)
2º: A² B²; *1–2* 3–8.
'No muse I seek, but summon to my aid'
Rogers 138: 'The pamphlet has many of the
marks of John ("Orator") Henley's style.' The
Oratory advertisement in *DP* 29 April 1729
announces that 'Tom o' Bedlam's Dunciad'
will be held forth on the following day
(J. V. Guerinot, *Pamphlet attacks on Alexander
Pope* (1969) 170). The concurrence of evidence
makes Henley's authorship almost certain.
IU.

Henriade

Henriade. Henriade. An epick poem, 1732. *See* Lockman, John.

H146 Henry. Henry and Blanche: or, the revengeful marriage. A tale: taken from the French of Gil Blas. *London, printed for R. Dodsley; sold by M. Cooper*, 1745 [1746]. (13 Feb)
4°: *A*⁴ B–H⁴ I²; *1–4* 5–67 *68 blk.* A1 hft.
    Publication date from *Straus, Dodsley*; listed in *GM, LM* Feb.
'Tancred, the ruler of Sicilia's land'
L(11630.c.4/12, –A1),O,BaP,*LdU-B*; CLU-C (in presentation morocco),CtY,DLC,ICN,OCU+.

[H147 = B424·5] — Henry and Minerva. A poem. By J. B. esq; 1729. *See* Breval, John Durant.

H147·5 Heosphoros. Ἑωσφόρος: or, the morning star. A poem. Humbly inscribed to his royal highness the Duke of Cumberland. *London, printed for M. Cooper*, 1746. (*GM* Feb)
4°: A–B⁴; *i–iii* iv–vi, 7–16.
    Vertical chain-lines.
'William, that name's joy's essence, pleasing sound'
    The dedication signed 'S.Y.'
AdU.

Hepburn, —, Mr.
Ruddiman's ledger for the week ending 20 June 1713 records setting and printing sixty copies of 'A poem of Mr Hebpurn [!] Younger of Bearford.' Robert Hepburn died in 1712 and, unless this is a posthumous work, the author is unidentified.

H148 Hepburn, Robert. Ad Georgium Makenzium, regium, olim, apud Scotos, advocatum, Roberti Hepburnij, scoti, carmen sapphicum. [*Edinburgh*, 1711?]
½°: 1 side, 1 column.
'Te sequor læta calidus juventa'
    Possibly written by Archibald Pitcairne as if by Hepburn, like the following. The copy seen is bound with Hepburn's *Tatler.*
EU.

'—' Ricardio Stilio anglo, viro hujus sæculi maximo, Robertus Hepburnius scotus. S.D. [but probably by Pitcairne], [1713?] *See* P400.

H149 Her. Her majesties welcome to St. Paul's cathedral. A poem. *London printed, and sold by H. Hllis [!]*, [1702.]
½°: 1 side, 1 column.
    Woodcut portrait at head.
'O glorious show! See England's queen appears'
    At the thanksgiving for Marlborough's victories, 12 Nov 1702.
Crawford.

Heraldiad. The Heraldiad, 1730. *See* 'Gulliver, Martin'.

Here. Here is a dialogue that passed... [1726?]
See A dialogue between the old black horse, [1718?]

Here

H150 — Here's coming and going; or, going and coming: or, hey for Litchfield races! To the tune of the King shall enjoy his own again. [1747?]
½°: 1 side, 2 columns.
    Large rough woodcut at head.
'Ye plaids and greens, now in this place'
    A tory election ballad for Lichfield.
L(806.k.16/54).

H151 Hereditary. Hereditary right exemplified: or, a letter of condolance from Mr. Ed---d C--l to his son H--y, upon his late discipline at Westminster. *London, printed for A. More, near St. Paul's*, 1727.
8°: *A*⁴ B–C⁴ D⁴(–D4) (B2 as 'B3'); *1–5* 6–29 *30 blk.*
    A1, not seen, is probably a half-title, as in the following issue. D4 has been seen in neither.
'Fir'd by the laudable example'
    A pretended letter from Edmund Curll to his son Henry, recalling his own sufferings at Westminster (recorded in [Samuel Wesley] *Neck or nothing*, 1716); satirizing Curll's trade.
CT(–A1).

H152 — [reissue] *London, printed for A. Moor*, 1728. (*MChr* 21 June)
8°: *A*⁴(±A1, 2) B–C⁴ D⁴(–D4) (B2 as 'B3'); *1–5* 6–29 *30 blk.* A1 hft.
    It appears that A1 and 2 are a conjugate pair of leaves cancelling the original title and half-title.
L(12274.h.2/4),LVA-D; MH(–A1).

Hermit. The hermit a poem, 1748. *See* Parnell, Thomas.

H152·5 Hero. The hero in blue. A new song for the tories to put a tune to, &c. *London, printed for J. Harrison*, 1717.
slip: 1 side, 1 column.
'I sing the bold man, that sleeps in his boots'
    A satire on Charles XII of Sweden.
MB.

H153 — The heroe in miniature: or, an historick poem on Prince Eugene. *London printed, and sold by J. How, & B. Bragg*, 1702. (1 Sept, Luttrell)
2°: *A*² B–C²; *1–2* 3–12.
'Darling of men, and patron o' the wars'
O,MC; CtY(Luttrell),TxU.

— The hero of the age: or, Duke of Marlborough, 1705. *See* Robins, Jasper.

Heroes. The heroes: a new ballad, 1745. *See* Williams, *Sir* Charles Hanbury.

H154 Heroic. An heroick essay upon the unequal'd victory obtain'd by Major-general Webb over the Count de la Motte, at Wynendale. *London printed, and sold by A. Baldwin*, 1709. (*DC* 22 Feb)
2°: *A*² B–C²; *1–2* 3–11 *12 blk.*
'Delia, who once of courts and empires sung'
L(1481.f.19/4, uncut),O; CSmH,MH,TxU.

Heroic

— An heroic poem on the memorable battle fought at Bleinheim, 1741. *See* Ormsbye, Robert.

— Heroick poems on several subjects: viz. Upon the safe arrival of his majesty... By a true lover of his king and country. *London printed, and sold by J. Nutt*, 1701. (10 Nov, Luttrell)
2°: pp. 8. MH.
> The Luttrell copy is in the collection of W.N.H. Harding.

H155 Heroi-comical. An heroi-comical epistle from a certain doctor to a certain gentle-woman, in defence of the most antient art of punning. *London, printed for J. Harrison, L. Stokee* [!], *J. Stagg, E. Berrington, J. Roberts*, [1716.] (*MC* Nov)
2°: A–B²; *i–ii*, 1–6.
'Dear Nanny, all the world are running'
> 'Not improbably by Arbuthnot', according to N. Ault, *Prose works of Alexander Pope* (1936) cxiii. An answer to the prose *God's revenge on punning*, 1716, probably by Pope.
L(11602.i.10/7; 11602.i.26/3),LdU-B; CtY(uncut),DFo(Luttrell, no date),TxU.

[**Hervey, John,** *baron Hervey*.] The barber turn'd packer, 1730. *See* B65.

H156 [—] The difference between verbal and practical virtue...With a prefatory epistle from Mr. C---b---r to Mr. P. *London, printed for J. Roberts*, 1742. (*LEP* 24 Aug)
2°: A² B–C²; *i–iv*, 1 2–7 *8 blk*.
'What awkward judgments must they make of men'
> Attributed to Hervey in Walpole's *Royal and noble authors*. The epistle is supposedly from Cibber to Pope.
L(840.m.1/15),O(uncut),E; CLU-C,CtY(2),IU, MH,TxU.

[—] An elegy to a young lady... By ------. With an answer, 1733. *See* H21.

H157 [—] An epistle from a nobleman to a doctor of divinity: in answer to a Latin letter in verse. Written from H-----n-C----t, Aug. 28. 1733. *London, printed for J. Roberts*, 1733. (*GSJ* 10 Nov)
2°: A² B²; *1–2* 3–8.
> Reprinted in some editions of *Tit for tat*, 1734.
'Suppliant your pardon first I must implore'
> Attributed to Hervey in Walpole's *Royal and noble authors*. A copy at Ickworth has ms. additions and corrections, apparently by Hervey. Addressed to William Sherwin. Replied to in *An epistle from a gentleman at Twickenham*, [1734]; *Flavia to Fanny*, [1733/34]; *Tit for tat*, 1734; *The tryal of skill*, 1734.
L(12273.m.1/8),O(3, 1 Harley's with ms. notes), OW,LdU-B; CSmH,CtY,ICU(2),MH,TxU(3)+.

H157·2 [—] The false patriot's confession; or, B-----k's address to ambition. In imitation of the first ode, of

Hervey, J., *baron*. An epistle

the fourth book of Horace. *London, printed for R. Charlton*, 1737. (*GM* April)
2°: A² B²; *1–4* 5–8.
'O cease ambition to molest'
> Clearly the poem ascribed to Hervey in Walpole's *Royal and noble authors* as 'Bolingbroke's address to ambition...1737.' An attack on Bolingbroke.
O; IU.

[—] The journalists displayed, [1731.] *See* J103.

H157·5 [—] Monimia to Philocles: being a letter from an unfortunate lady, after her retirement from court to one of the most remote and solitary parts of England, to a young nobleman who, after a long courtship, had not only basely forsaken, but also treated her in a most cruel and inhuman manner. *Dublin, printed in the year* 1726.
8°: A⁴; *1–3* 4–8.
'Since language never can describe my pain'
> Printed as Lord Hervey's with other epistles in the manner of Ovid in *Dodsley* IV, and also attributed to him by Horace Walpole (Yale ed. XXXIV. 256). The implied attribution to Arbuckle in the following edition must be due to an ambiguity of grammar, but the reason for a Dublin first edition has not been explained. Concerning Sophia Howe and Anthony Lowther; see 'Lewis Melville', *Maids of honour* (1927) 210.
DA,*MR-C*.

H157·6 [—] — To which is added, Glotta a poem... By Mr. Arbuckle... *Dublin, printed by S. Powell, for J. Thompson*, 1728.
12°: A–D⁴/²; *1–2* 3–24.
> C4–D2 contain 'A poem on the taking Port St. Mary's... By an unknown hand', previously published [170–]. *Glotta* was previously published at Glasgow in 1721.
E(lacks C4–D2),DA(lacks C4–D2); TxU.

H158 [—] The patriots are come; or, a new doctor for a crazy constitution. A new ballad. To the tune of Derry down. *London, printed for W. Webb, and may be had at the booksellers, and pamphlet shops in London & Westminster*, [1742.] (*DA* 18 Oct)
2°: A¹ B–C² D¹; *i–ii*, 1 2–10.
> Rothschild 231. A1 and D1 have been seen to be conjugate.
'Oh! E—g—d attend whilst thy fate I deplore'
> Hervey's authorship is mentioned in a letter of Horace Walpole to Mann, 16 Oct 1742. The new doctor is John Carteret, earl Granville.
L(643.m.15/9),O,*DrU-U*; MH,OCU,TxU(uncut).

H159 [—] [*idem*] A new c-----t ballad. '*Dublin, printed by James Stone, in High-street*' [*London?*], 1742.
2°: A⁴; *i–ii*, 1–6.
> No James Stone is recorded as a Dublin printer, and all the indications are that this is a London edition. Variant first line:

Hervey, J., *baron.* The patriots are come

'Old England attend, whilst thy fate I deplore'
L(11632.h.20),O(uncut); IU,TxU(2).

H160 [—] — '*Dublin, printed by James Stone, in High-street*' [*Edinburgh*], 1742.
8°: *A*⁴ B²; *1–2* 3–12.
Printed by Ruddiman on the evidence of the ornaments.
L(11631.e.3),E; MH,TxU.

H161 [—] [*idem*] The s---te m—r's are come; or a new doctor for a crazy constitution... [*London?* 1742.]
½°: 1 side, 2 columns.
L(1876.f.1/127),O,C; CSmH,MH.

H161·5 [—] A satyr. In the manner of Persius. In a dialogue between the poet and his friend. By a certain English nobleman. '*London printed, and sold by the booksellers of London & Westminster*' [*Dublin*], 1730.
8°: *A*⁸; *1–3* 4–15 *16 blk.*
Rothschild 202. There is no evidence that the date is a misprint for 1739; copies at CT,DT and Rothschild are bound with contemporary Dublin pamphlets.
'Why wears my pensive friend that gloomy brow' Printed in *Dodsley* V as 'by the late Lord Hervey'; it is transcribed in a commonplace book of his son, General William Hervey (Suffolk Record Office MSS 941/53/1). The curious fact that the first edition was published in Dublin finds a parallel in his *Monimia to Philocles*, 1726. A copy of the 1739 edition at TxU has an early ms. attribution to Lord Paget. It is also reprinted as 'A dialogue between the poet and his friend' in *The Norfolk poetical miscellany*, 1744; in the well-annotated copy at L it is ascribed to the editor, Ashley Cowper, but it was not collected in his *Poems*, 1769. Despite the conflicting evidence, Hervey's authorship is much the most likely.
L(1606/788),O,CT,DK,DT(uncut); IU.

H161·6 [—] A satire in the manner of Persius: in a dialogue between Atticus and Eugenio. By a person of quality. *London, printed for J. Clarke, & J. Robinson*, 1739. (*SR* 10 Sept)
2°: *A*² B–D² *E*¹; *1–5* 6–17 *18 blk.* A1 hft.
Listed in *GM,LM* Sept; deposit copies at O,E.
O(–A1),E; CSmH(uncut),CtY,IU,MH,TxU(2, 1 uncut)+.

[—] To the imitator of the satire of the second book of Horace, 1733. *See* V46.

[—] Verses address'd to the imitator of the first satire of the second book of Horace, [1733.] *See* V39.

Hesiod.

Cooke, Thomas: The works of Hesiod translated from the Greek, 1728, 1740, 1743.

H162 **Hesperi-neso-graphia.** Hesperi-neso-graphia: or, a description of the western isle. In eight canto's.

Hesperi-neso-graphia

By W.M. *London printed, and sold by J. Baker*, 1716.
12°: A–D⁶ E² (A3 as 'A2'); *1–2* 3–52.
Bond 79. The same title was listed as printed for T. Warner in *MC* Aug 1726; possibly that was a reissue.
'In western isle renown'd for bogs'
The initials are expanded in the edition of 1755 (titled *The Irish Hudibras*) as 'William Moffett, schoolmaster'. J. C. Walker, *Historical memoirs of the Irish bards* (1786) 149n. records it as 'from the pen of the late — Jones esq. father of the right hon. Theophilus Jones, now Collector of the port of Dublin'. *O'Donoghue* suggests Walter Jones (1693?–1756) as the author, but apparently he was born c. 1700 since he entered T.C.D. in 1712 aged 12. The Dublin edition of 1724 was the earliest known to earlier authorities. Probably written by a Jones, but the identification with Walter seems doubtful.
L(1485.tt.13),O(uncut).

H163 —— *Dublin, printed by and fot* [!] *J. Carson, & W. Smith*, 1724.
12°: A–H⁴/² I² (C3 as 'B3'); *1–2* 3–52.
L(11633.a.27),LVA-F,DN,DT.

H163·5 —— *Dublin, re-printed by Theo. Jones, for William Smith*, 1735.
8°: A–C⁸ D⁴; *1–2* 3–56.
O(uncut),DG(uncut),DN(2, 1 uncut).

Hester. Hester, a poem, 1714. *See* Pearson, Thomas.

H164 [**Hetherly, Seawell.**] A psalm of thanksgiving to be sung by the children of Christ's Hospital on Monday, Tuesday and Wednesday, in Easter-week... Composed by Mr. Horwood... The words by S.H.M.A. [*London*] *Printed by John Wright*, 1729.
1°: 1 side, 2 columns.
Woodcut borders. Typeset music with first verse at head. The verse is followed by an annual report of the charities.
'Silence, ye jarring elements, be still'
Authorship from Christ's Hospital minutes.
LG.

H165 —— Composed by Mr. Horwood... The words by S. Hetherly M.A. [*London*] *Printed by John Wright*, 1735.
1°: 1 side, 2 columns.
Woodcut borders. Typeset music with first verse at head. The verse is followed by an annual report of the charities.
'When Judah's stubborn race disdain'd to own'
Christ's Hospital Office.

H166 —— [*London*] *Printed by John Wright*, 1736.
1°: 1 side, 2 columns.
Woodcut borders. Typeset music with first verse at head. The verse is followed by an annual report of the charities.
'Hail heav'nly muse, prepare, prepare'
Christ's Hospital Office.

Hewitt, —, *Mr*.

H167 Hewitt, —, *Mr*. Alexis to Celia: or, the power of love. A poem. Written by Mr. Hewitt. *Dublin, printed by S. Powell, for James Thompson, 1726.*
8°: A–B⁴; *1–5* 6–16.
'What tender language, can my fancy find?'
DA(title-leaf only); *IU*.

Hewitt, John. Miscellanies in prose and verse, consisting of poems, gay, humorous, divine, and moral. With letters of love and gallantry. *Bristol, printed by the Widow Penn, 1727.*
8°: pp. viii, 87.   L; CLU-C,CtY.
Pp. 67–87 contain poems by other authors.

H168 Hext, Francis. A pindarique ode, sacred to the memory of William III...who dyed March the eighth 170½ in the fourteenth year of his reign, at his palace at Kensington. *London, printed for J. Nutt, 1702.* (19 March, Luttrell)
2°: A² B–C²; *i–ii, 1–9 10 blk.*
Morgan *E230a records a 14 page edition, presumably in error.
'How vast's the power of all-commanding fate'
AdU; CtY(Luttrell).

H169 Heydegger. Heydegger's letter to the bishop of London. *London, printed for N. Cox in Story's-passage, going out of St. James's-park, 1724.* (*MC* April)
2°: A² B²; *1–3* 4–8.
B2 bears a prose 'account of Don Ramiro'. The Luttrell copy, dated April, is recorded in *Haslewood.*
'My lord, your sermon, preach'd at Bow'
In defence of masquerades.
L(11631.k.6),OA,DrU; CtY(lacks B2),ICU.

Heywood, James. Original poems on several occasions. *London, printed for J. Bateman, & J. Nicks, 1721.* (*PB* 6 July)
8°: pp. 32.   L,O; CtY,IU.
— Poems and letters on several subjects: viz. I. Poems... *London, printed for J. Bateman, 1722.* (*DP* 4 June)
12°: pp. xii, 198.   L,O; CLU-C,ICU.
— [reissue] *London, printed for W. Meadows, J. Stagg, & T. Worral, 1724.*
12°: pp. xii, 217.   ICN,MH.
Cancel title; additions at end.
— [reissue] Letters and poems on several subjects, viz. I. Familiar letters... The second edition with additions. *London, printed for W. Meadows, T. Worral, J. Ashford, 1726.*
12°: pp. 249.   O; CtY,MH.
Cancel title and dedication; further additions.

Heywood, John. Hymns or spiritual songs, chiefly taken from the holy scriptures. *London, printed for the author, 1740.*
8°: pp. xxii, 58.   L,O; NNUT.

Hi

H170 Hi. Hye, for cakes and ale; a new poem on a certain young miss lady in F— st---t and a brewers son call'd W—d of the city of Dublin, writ by a wel-wisher of 'em both. *Dublin, printed in the year 1726.*
½°: 1 side, 1 column.
'Alass! too oft have I invok'd my muse'
The brewer's son was Ward; the lady, Miss Gaffney?
L(1890.e.5/116; C.121.g.8/150).

H171 Hibernia. Hibernia in universal morning [!] ⟨or a royal⟩ elegy on the much lamented death, of his most sacred majesty King George, who departed this life, at his royal pallace in Hannover, on Wednesday being the 12th of this instant June 1727. And in the 68. year of his age. [*Dublin, 1727.*]
½°: 1 side, 1 column.
Mourning borders.
'Oh! wofull news, O most unhappy day'
DT(title cropt).

H172 — Hibernia in universal mourning: or, a royal funeral elegy on the much lamented death of his most sacred majesty King George, who departed this life...the 14th of this instant June 1727. And in the 68th year of his age. [*Dublin, 1727.*]
1°: 1 side, 2 columns.
Woodcut borders.
'At this unwelcome news lament you nine'
The first third of the poem is substantially the same as an elegy on Henry, viscount Dillon (1714) in Laurence Whyte's *Poems,* 1740. Probably rewritten by Whyte for this occasion.
DT.

H173 — Hibernia resurgens. To my lord bishop of Derry upon the publication of his Irish historical library. [*Dublin*] *Printed by J. Carson, 1724.*
½°: 1 side, 1 column (verso advt).
'As when of old the proud Egyptian land'
Rothschild.

H174 — Hibernia's lamentation. An elegyack poem; occasioned by the much lamented death of... Thomas, lord Southwell, who departed this life the 4th. of August, 1720. *Dublin, printed by J. Carson, 1720.*
4°: A⁴; *1–3* 4–7 *8 blk.*
'Assist me muse, in mournful notes to sing'
DT,LdU-B.

H175 Hibernian. The Hibernian politicians; an epistle from a gentleman in the country, to his friend in town. *Isle-of-Man, printed in the year 1740.*
4°: π¹ A² B–D² E¹; *1–2* 3–20.
The last line of p. 15 reads 'Unmask the *Villians*'. This appears to be the earlier of the two editions of part I, since copies are found with the earlier (1740) edition of part II. The imprint may be false.
'While you in town your precious moments spend'
The O copy of part II has a ms. identification of the gentleman in the country as 'Gardiner'

The **Hibernian** politicians

and his friend in town as 'James Wynne esqr';
it is not certain that Gardiner is actually the
author. A further satire on Dublin politicians,
The squib, 1743, is clearly a continuation,
probably by the same hand. *Bradshaw* 7359
compares the style of printing with *The
narrative*, [174–?] which may be a related work.
Britannia's precaution, [1741] claims to be by
the author of this and *Seventeen hundred and
thirty-nine*, 1739; but as these are English
works, another work with the same title may
be referred to.
C(uncut),*MR*; DFo,MH.

H176 — [another edition]
The last line of p. 15 reads 'Unmask the
Villains'.
DA(2),DG,*MR*; DFo.

H177 — The Hibernian politicians; part the second. An
epistle... *Isle-of-Man, printed by C.N. in the year
1740.*
4°: *A² B–E²; 1–2 3–20.*
'Say, my dear friend; for you without disguise'
C(uncut); DFo.

H178 —— *Isle-of-Man, printed by C.N. in the year 1741.*
4°: *A² B–F²; 1–2 3–24.*
O(ms. identifications),DA(2),DG; DFo.

H179 — The Hibernian politicians; part the third. An
epistle... [*Isle-of-Man?*] *Printed in the year 1741.*
4°: *A² B–D²; 1–2 3–16 (4 as '5').*
'Can I, unmov'd, like a Marpesian rock'
MR; DFo,MH.

H180 Hickeringill, Edmund. A burlesque poem in
praise of ignorance. The greatest part thereof
composed eight and fifty years ago. *London printed,
and sold by Benj. Bragge,* 1708. (29 Jan, Luttrell)
4°: A–I⁴; *i–x, 1–62.*
Bond 18. Advertised in *DC* 12 Feb.
'Can any knowledge wisemen please'
L(161.l.55, Luttrell),O,C,EU; TxU.

Hiffernan, Paul. Miscellanies in prose and verse.
*London, printed by H. Woodfall, for the author; and
publish'd by G. Woodfall,* 1755.
4°: pp. 168.   L.
The copy seen, which is a presentation copy
from the author, has the date altered in ms. to
either MDCCLIX or MDCCLX; but there
is reason to think the original date of publication was correct.

H181 [—] The enthusiasm. A poem. With a character
of Dr. Jonathan Swift. And of Pope's translated
Iliad, &c. Address'd to the young gentlemen of the
university of Dublin... By Mr. P.H. author of the
Poet. *Dublin, printed by James Hoey,* 1739.
8°: A⁴; *1–3 4–7 8 blk.*
Teerink 1320.
'What uncouth ardour in my bosom grows?'

Hiffernan, P. The enthusiasm

For Hiffernan's authorship, see *The poet*
below.
C,*DT*.

H182 [—] The poet. A poem... By Mr. P.H. *Dublin,
printed by James Hoey,* 1739.
8°: A⁴; *1–3 4–8.*
'Happy the youth, whose nobly thinking mind'
'The poet' as printed in Hiffernan's *Miscellanies*, 1755, differs from this, but he is clearly
the author.
DA.

H183 Higgons, Bevil. A poem on nature: in imitation
of Lucretius. To which is added, a description of
the fœtus in the womb... By the late Bevil Higgons,
esq; *London, printed for P. Meighan; sold by G.
Strahan & E. Nutt, L. Gilliver & F. Cogan, Mrs.
Dodd, J. Stagg, & J. Brindley,* 1736 [1735]. (*GM*
Nov)
2°: *A² B–E²; 1–3 4–20.*
Cancel slip over catchword on p. 4. *Rawlinson*
records a prospectus of 6 Dec 1724 for 'A
poem on nature in six books in imitation of
Lucretius, to which will be added occasional
verses on several occasions in two vol. oct.';
that venture presumably failed.
'O muse, who chief of the Castalian choir'
L(1482.f.30),O(3),LdU-B; CSmH,CtY,MH.

H184 — A poem on the peace: inscribed to the most
honble Robert, earl of Oxford, and earl Mortimer,
lord high-treasurer... *London, printed by John
Barber, and are to be sold by John Morphew,* [1713.]
(*LG* 28 April)
2°: *A² B–E²; i–iv, 1–15 16 blk.* A1 hft.
No watermark. The Luttrell copy dated 29
April is in the possession of J. R. B. Brett-
Smith.
'While no repulse thy courage can abate'
O,LdU-B; CSmH,CtY,ICN,MH,TxU(2, 1 uncut)
+.

H185 — [fine paper]
Watermark: star.
L(1482.h.1/2).

H186 — [*idem*] A poem on the glorious peace of Utrecht:
inscrib'd in the year 1713, to... Robert late earl of
Oxford... Now publish'd and most humbly
dedicated to... Edward earl of Oxford... *London,
printed for P. Meighan; sold by the booksellers of
London & Westminster,* 1731. (*GSJ* 15 May)
8°: A² B–C⁴ D²; *i–iii iv, 1 2–19 20 blk.*
O(2); CtY,*ICN*,TxU.

H187 —— The second edition. *London, printed for P.
Meighan; sold by the booksellers of London & West-
minster,* 1731.
8°: A² B–C⁴ D²; *i–iii iv, 1 2–19 20 blk.*
Apparently a variant title or a reimpression.
NN.

Higgons, E.

[**Higgons, Elizabeth.**] The address to Mr. G--Gr--n--ll upon his retiring from court, [1712.] *See* A54.

H188 High. High boys and low boys; or, a new tale of a tub. By a gentleman of the Temple. *London, printed for J. Smith, near Fleet-street*, 1710.
½°: 1 side, 2 columns.
    On the other side, *The Earl of P—brookes speech*, 1710, in prose.
'In days of old when curs did bark'
Rothschild.

— High boys up go we! or, a rod for somebody, 1741. *See* Cowper, Ashley.

H189 — High-church and the doctor out of breath: or, a seasonable stop to the high-flying squadron. *London, printed in the year* 1711. (14 April, Luttrell)
½°: 1 side, 1 column.
'Now let all true loyal subjects rejoice'
    In praise of low church against Sacheverell.
ICN(Luttrell),MH.

H190 —— *London printed, and Edinburgh re-printed by J.M.* [*John Moncur*], [1711.]
½°: 1 side, 1 column.
E,Rothschild.

H191 — The high-church bully: or, the praises of Mr. Higgins. [*London*, 1707?]
½°: 2 sides, 1 column.
'Had I but, sir, ability and skill'
    Francis Higgins was arrested for seditious preaching, 28 Feb 1707.
L(162.m.70/1),Crawford; MH.

H192 — The high church health: to the loyal good cause; being a noble copy of verses, compos'd at the university of Oxford, to the honour and glory of the queen, the church, and the renown'd Dr. Henry Sacheverell...To the tune of, The fisherman. '*Cambridge*', *printed in the year* 1710.
½°: 1 side, 1 column.
    The imprint is probably false.
'How sly the dissenters have acted of late'
L(1876.f.1/48),AdU.

H193 — The high-church hieroglyphick represented in the sign of the embleme, put up at an inn in Stoke by Naland, in Suffolk. *London, printed in the year* 1706. (16 July, Luttrell)
1°: 1 side, 2 columns.
    Large engraving at head. Advertised in *Observator* 17 Aug by J. How & B. Bragge.
'Behold the church, which some men say has stood'
    Against the high church.
L(P&D 1465),O(Luttrell).

H194 — High church in its glory, or truth oppos'd to falshood. In answer to a low church whim intituled High church miracles &c. *Printed and sold by Sutton Nicholl, London*, [1710.]
½°: 1 side, 1 column.

High church in its glory
    Engraved throughout.
'High church ne'er claim'd a right divine from Jove'
O.

H195 — The high church lovers: or, a general resolution made by young and old, rich and poor, handsome and homely to be married by Dr. Sacheverel, that true son of the protestant church, who we wish long to prosper in the works of piety. Tune of, Golden hair, &c. *London, printed in the year* 1710.
½°: 1 side, 2 columns.
'Young lovers pray be of good chear'
    A satire on Sacheverell.
L(1872.a.1/159; 1876.f.1/47),O.

— 'High church loyalty, or, a tale of tory rebellion.' One of 'Three loyal songs...Price one penny each' advertised in *Rebellious fame*, 1717.

H196 — High-church miracles, or, modern inconsistencies. *London printed, and sold by A. Baldwin*, 1710. (9 June, Luttrell)
½°: 1–2, 1 column.
'That high-church have a right divine from Jove'
    Moore 182, 'very probably, not certainly Defoe's'; there is no clear evidence for his authorship. An attack on the high church party after Sacheverell's trial. Replied to in *High church in its glory*, [1710.]
L(C.121.g.8/4),O,MC(Luttrell); MH,NN.

H197 —— *London printed, and sold by T. Harrison*, [1710.]
½°: 1–2, 1 column.
DA.

H198 — The high church spectakles, for the dim sighted low church men. *London, printed in the year* 1710.
½°: 1 side, 2 columns.
    On the other side, [William Pittis] *Vulpone's tale*, 1710.
'When I took in hand a pen for to write'
    Against the whigs.
L(Cup. 645.e.1/22).

H199 — High church, with a demonstration. On occasion of these words, (like two parallel lines meeting in the same centre.) In a sermon preach'd at Oxford, by Dr. S.L. *London, printed in the year* 1709.
½°: 1 side, 1 column.
'As Creech swang away in a sanctify'd twine'
    Presumably directed against Sacheverell.
O.

H200 — The High German doctor. To the tune of, Diogenes surly and proud. *London, printed for W. Taylor*, 1720.
½°: 1 side, 1 column.
'Præstigius Legerdemain, with strange artificial slights'
    On the disputed election at St. Andrew's Holborn, Henry Sacheverell's church. Cf. *The lecturers combat*, 1720.
L(1850.c.10/54); InU,MH.

H201 — The high mass. A poem...By Agricola Candidus, gent. author of the Latin Mercury. *London printed, and sold by J. Hart*, 1746.
8⁰: *A*⁴ B–C⁴; *i–viii*, *1–15 16*. A1 hft; 16 advt.
Horizontal chain-lines.
'What favourite muse shall I invoke'
The author of *Mercurius latinus* is not known. A satire on the Roman church.
O; OCU.

H202 Highland. The highland invasion. A new ballad. To the tune of Gossip Joan. Taken from the Westminster Journal of September 28, 1745. [*London*] *Printed for J. Mechell*, [1745.]
½⁰: 1 side, 2 columns.
Reprinted from the standing type of the *Westminster Journal*, reimposed.
'I bring you news. – From Rome'
A satire on the Young Pretender.
L(1487.w.5/2).

H203 — — In which is humourously described, the romantic views of the Pretender: being an epitome of facts relating to him and his expedition... *London, printed for J. Robinson*, 1745. (*GM* Oct)
2⁰: *A*⁴; *1–3 4–8*.
Horizontal chain-lines.
E,GM,*MR-C*; CSmH,ICU,KU.

— The highland laddie, [1723?] *See* Ramsay, Allan.

H204 — The heighland man. To the tune of the Heighland rant. [1746/–.]
slip: 1 side, 1 column.
Rough woodcut at head.
'In 17 hundred and forty-five, as plainly did appear man'
On the victory at Culloden.
C(mutilated).

H205 — The highland-man upon the overture, called nagetive [!]. [*Glasgow?* 1721.] (20 March)
½⁰: 1 side, 1 column.
'Right reverent fathers her nain-sell did hear'
Concerning a proposal of the General Assembly that the pastor should have a right of veto over the presbytery. The controversy seems to have centred in Glasgow.
E(ms. date 20 March 1721).

H206 — The highland man's lament, for the death of Donald Bayn, alias M'evan Vanifranck, who was execute in the Grass Market of Edinburgh, on Wednesday the 9th day of January 1723. [*Edinburgh*, 1723.]
½⁰: 1 side, 2 columns.
'Tonald Bayn her nane dear shoy'
E.

H207 — The highland reformation. [*Edinburgh*, 1713/14?]
1⁰: 1 side, 3 columns.
The E copy is bound with pamphlets of 1713/14; possibly a reprint of an earlier edition.

'While sable night on the star sprangled skies'
On the highland raids on the western shires of Scotland organized by Lord Lauderdale in 1677–78.
E.

H208 Highmore, John. Dettingen. A poem. Humbly inscribed, in particular, to...the Earl of S----ir, and...the Duke of M--lbor--gh. And, in general, to every gallant British officer... *London, printed for M. Cooper*, 1743. (*DA* 11 July)
2⁰: *A*² B–C²; *1–5 6–11 12 blk*. 4 err.
Horizontal chain-lines.
'Metre, than prose, we evidently find'
The dedication to Marlborough refers to earlier poems by Highmore, not specified or traced.
O(2).

Hill, Aaron. The works of the late Aaron Hill... *London, printed for the benefit of his family*, 1753.
8⁰: 4 vol. L; CtY.
No watermark.

— [fine paper] O.
Watermark: Strasburg bend.

— — The second edition. *London, printed for the benefit of his family*, 'MDCCLIIV' [1754].
8⁰: 4 vol. O; MH.
Watermark: fleur-de-lys.

— [fine paper] L.
Watermark: Strasburg bend.

H209 — Advice to the poets. A poem. To which is prefix'd, an epistle dedicatory to the few great spirits of Great Britain. *London, printed for T. Warner*, 1731. (*DJ* 13 March)
4⁰: A–E⁴; *i–ii iii–xvi*, *17–39 40 blk*.
Title in red and black. Printed by Samuel Richardson (*Sale* 98).
'Too long provok'd, immortal muse! forgive'
L(643.k.3/9),LDW,LVA-F,O; CSmH,CtY(uncut),IU,MH(uncut),TxU.

H210 — The art of acting. Part 1. Deriving rules from a new principle, for touching the passions in a natural manner... *London, printed for J. Osborn*, 1746. (*SR* 7 Nov)
2⁰: *A*² a² B–E² F¹; *i–iii iv–viii*, *5 6–22*.
Some variant press-figures. Printed by Samuel Richardson (*Sale* 339); Hill had received some proof by 29 July. Deposit copies at L,O.
'Why sleep the silent powers, that guard the stage'
Dedication signed.
L(643.m.14/18),O,*MR*; CtY(2),DFo,IU,MH, NN.

H211 — Camillus: a poem humbly inscrib'd to the right honourable Charles earl of Peterborough and Monmouth. *London, printed for Tho. Bickerton; sold by B. Bragg*, 1707. (*DC* 24 Dec)
2⁰: A–D²; *1–2 3–16*.

Hill, A. Camillus

'When injur'd heroes suffer in their fame'
O,LdU-B; CtY,MH,TxU(uncut, ms. date 13 Jan).

— The celebrated speeches of Ajax and Ulysses, for the armour of Achilles... Essay'd in English verse by Mr. Tate...and Aaron Hill, 1708. *See* T49.

H212 — The creation. A pindaric illustration of a poem, originally written by Moses, on that subject. With a preface to Mr. Pope, concerning the sublimity of the ancient Hebrew poetry... *London, printed for T. Bickerton,* 1720. (2 Aug?)
2°: A^1 B–F^2; *i–iii* iv–xiv, *1* 2–7 *8 blk.*
Advertised in *DP* 1 Aug for 'to-morrow'.
'In the beginning, the almighty god'
Preface signed.
L(11657.m.16),O(uncut); CSmH,DFo,ICU,NNP, TxU(2)+.

H213 — The dedication of the beech-tree, to the most honourable the Earl of Oxford... occasion'd by the late discovery of making oil from the fruit of that tree. [*London*] Sold by *John Morphew,* 1714. (*PB* 20 April)
2°: A(2 ll) B–C^2; *1–2* 3–11 *12 blk.*
The copy at O has a watermark in both leaves of A; possibly the title is a cancel.
'High, in thy starry orb'
O,C; *NcD*.

H214 [—] The Fanciad. An heroic poem. In six cantos. To his grace the Duke of Marlborough, on the turn of his genius to arms. *London, printed for J. Osborn,* 1743. (*GM,LM* May)
8°: A–D^8 E^4; [2] *i* ii–viii ix–xiv, *1* 2–54 *55–56 blk.*
Watermark: fleur-de-lys. Printed by Samuel Richardson (*Sale* 306), to whom Hill offered the copyright as an 'Easter offering'.
'Poets whom truth inspires, and genius draws'
Ascribed to Hill in *Cibber* V. 271.
L(992.h.11/4, – E4; 164.n.27, – E4),O(– E4), LdU-B; CtY,DFo(– E4),ICN(– E4),MH(– E4), OCU(– E4).

H215 [—] [fine paper]
Watermark: Strasburg bend.
IU.

H216 [—] Free thoughts upon faith: or, the religion of reason. A poem. *London, printed for J. Osborn,* 1746. (*SR* 18 July)
2°: A^2 B–F^2; [2] *i* ii, *1* 2–20.
Printed by Samuel Richardson (*Sale* 340).
Listed in *GM* July. Deposit copies at L,O.
'Oh, thou! — who-ere, what-ere, where-ere, thou art'
Reprinted in Hill's *Works* IV, 1753.
L(644.m.14/16),O; CtY,IU,KU,MH,NN+.

H217 [—] [dh] Gideon, or the restoration of Israel. [Books 1, 2.] [*London,* 1720.] (*PB* 26 Jan, 30 April)
2°: A^1 B–M^2 N^1, O–Z^2 (+2 plates); *i–ii,* *1–45* *46 blk,* 47–88.
Advertisement on A1^r, 'The poem of which the following pages compose the first book,

Hill, A. Gideon

will be publish'd, one book every month, the whole containing twelve books... The price of each book is *2s. 6d.*'
'Glowing, pure, with hallow'd fire'
Attributed to Hill by *Cibber* V. 261; there are many contemporary references to this poem as unpublished.
L(1963).

H218 [—] A specimen; consisting of extracts and episodes from a poem call'd Gideon; or, the restoration of Israel. Printed, and given gratis, that a judgment may be form'd of the twelve books in general; which are once every month publish'd separately... *Book I. is now publish'd. Book II. just ready for publication...may be had at most booksellers in London & Westminster,* [1720.]
8°: A–B^8 (B1 as 'C'); *1–2* 3–32.
Extracts from books 3, 4, 6, 7, 8. *PB* 30 April, 'A specimen may be had gratis'. The copy at LDW has a ms. correction to show book 2 is published, adds booksellers' names, J. Morphew, Geo. Strahan, R. Gosling; the rest cropped.
L(1346.c.12),LDW,O,CT.

H219 [—] Gideon; or, the patriot. An epic poem: in twelve books...[Books 1–3.] *London, printed for A. Millar,* 1749. (*GM* May)
4°: A^4 B–T^4 U^2; *1–5* 6–147 *148 blk.* A1 hft.
GM May lists as 'in 12 books'; the remainder were apparently not published. Printed by Samuel Richardson (*Sale* 369).
L(840.k.4/16; 162.1.22),O(– A1),OW,*MR*; CtY, MH,*MiU*.

H220 [—] The impartial. An address, without flattery. Being a poet's free thoughts on the situation of our public affairs, anno 1744. *London, printed for M. Cooper,* 1744. (*GM* April)
2°: A^2 B–C^2; *i–iii* iv, 5–12.
Printed by Samuel Richardson (*Sale* 320).
'Are these the marks, then, of our promis'd shame!'
Dedicated to John Carteret, earl Granville. Reprinted in Hill's *Works* III, 1753. Answered by *A poet's impartial reply,* 1744.
L(162.n.44); MH(uncut),OCU.

H221 — The invasion: a poem to the queen. *London, printed for Tho. Bickerton,* 1708. (*DC* 26 April)
2°: A–D^2; *1–2* 3–16.
'Pride of the world, permit an humble muse'
CtY,DLC,MH.

H222 — The judgment-day, a poem. *London, printed for T. Jauncy,* [1721.] (*PB* 9 March)
2°: π^1 A–D^2 E^1; [2] i–iv, 1–14.
Watermark: R. No fine-paper copies seen of this state.
'Hover no more, my muse! o'er idle themes'
DFo,MH.

H223 —— The second edition. *London, printed for T. Jauncy,* [1721.]
2°: π^1 A–D^2 E^1; [2] i–iv, 1–14.

Hill, A. The judgment-day

Watermark: R. Apparently a press-variant title.
L(643.m.15/2).

H224 — [fine paper] The second edition.
Watermark: fleur-de-lys on shield.
CtY.

H225 — The northern star. A poem. *London, printed for E. Berington, & J. Morphew,* 1718.
2°: *A*² B–F² (F1 as 'E'); *i–iv,* 1–20.
'Born in an age, when virtue's vigour fails'
InU,MH,TxU.

H226 — — a poem: on the great and glorious actions of the present czar of Russia; in English and Latin. The second edition. *London, printed for T. Payne,* 1724. (*PB* 14 Jan)
8°: a–b⁴ c² B–G⁴ H² (B2 as 'B'); *i–v* vi–xi, *i–ii* iii–vi [*1 blk*] vii *viii blk,* 1–3 4–51 *52 blk.*

The pagination and signatures of the preliminaries are irregular. The Latin translation is by Gilbert Hill, who signs the dedication; Aaron signs the preface.
'Aevo nata, labat quo vis probitatis, & æqui'
O; IU.

H227 — — A poem sacred to the name and memory, of the immortal czar of Russia. The third edition. *London, printed for W. Mears,* 1725.
8°: A–D⁴; *i–viii,* 1–23 *24 blk.*
English only. Preface signed. Printed by Samuel Richardson (*Sale* 39).
L(992.h.7/2),O; CtY(uncut),IU.

H228 — — The fifth edition. Revised, and corrected, by the author. *London, printed for T. Cooper,* 1739.
8°: *A*⁴ B–D⁴; *i–iv* v–viii, 1–22 *23; 24 blk.* A1 hft; 23 advt.
The 'advertisement' is signed. No fourth edition has been traced. Printed by Samuel Richardson (*Sale* 246).
WrP; MH.

H229 [—] The picture of love. A poem. To which is prefix'd an epistle dedicatory to the right honourable William Pulteney, esq; *London printed, and are to be had only at Old Man's Coffee-house, at Charing-Cross,* 1731.
4°: *A*² a² B–H²; *i–iii* iv–viii, *1* 2–28.
English text followed by Latin translation of dedication (pp. 13–16) and poem (pp. 17–28).
'Love is a passion, by no rules confin'd'
'Vis amor est animi, quam lex non ulla coercet'
The English is by Aaron Hill, reprinted in his *Works,* 1753; the Latin by Gilbert Hill, who signs the dedication.
L(11631.g.31/19, lacks F–H²),O(lacks E–H²);CtY, OCU.

H230 [—] The progress of wit: a caveat. For the use of an eminent writer. By a fellow of All-Souls. To which is prefix'd, an explanatory discourse to the reader. By Gamaliel Gunson, professor of physick and astrology. *London, printed for J. Wilford,* 1730. (*DJ* 4 April)

Hill, A. The progress of wit

8°: *A*⁴ B–D⁴ (C2 as 'C3'); *i–iv* v–xiii *xiv blk,* 15–31 *32 blk.* A1 frt.
Printed by Samuel Richardson (*Sale* 84).
'Tuneful Alexis, on the Thame's fair side'
Reprinted in Hill's *Works,* 1753.
L(C.116.b.4/5, Pope's copy),O(2, 1–A1),OW, LdU-B; CtY,ICU,MH(2),TxU(uncut).

H231 [—] The tears of the muses; in a conference, between Prince Germanicus, and a male-content party. *London, printed for T. Ward,* 1737. (5 Nov)
4°: A–E⁴; *i–iii* iv–viii, 9–40. 40 advt.
Title in red and black. Listed in *GM,LM* Nov. Printed by Samuel Richardson (*Sale* 214); Hill returned the final proof on 28 Oct.
'Germanicus, for love, and empire, born'
Reprinted in Hill's *Works,* 1753. A dialogue of Frederick prince of Wales and the muses.
L(11630.c.4/1, Tom's Coffee House, 5 Nov; 840.k.3/7; 643.k.3/14),O; TxU.

H232 [—] [reissue] The tears of the muses. A satire. The second edition. *London, printed for T. Cooper,* 1738.
4°: A⁴(±A1) B–D⁴ E⁴(±E4); *i–iii* iv–viii, 9–40.
No advertisement on p. 40.
L(1487.fff.21); CtY,NcD.

H233 Hill, Alexander. To the memorie of Sir Charles Maitland of Pittrichie. Who departed this life March 20th 1704. [*Edinburgh,* 1704.]
½°: 1 side, 1 column.
Mourning borders.
'What melancholy rumor's this I hear?'
At foot, 'Posuit Alexander Hill vestiarius in Pittrichie'.
E.

H234 Hill, Andrew. The book of Ecclesiastes paraphrased. A divine poem. *Newcastle upon Tine, printed and sold by J. White,* 1712.
8°: π⁴ A–F⁴; [2] *i* ii–vi, 1–47 *48 blk.*
Watermark: H; horizontal chain-lines in sheets E,F.
'All here below's inconstant, empty, vain'
O,CT,NeP.

H235 — [fine paper]
Watermark: fleur-de-lys on shield.
L(11631.aaa.3).

Hill, Gilbert. The northern star: a poem [Latin translation by Gilbert Hill], 1724. *See* H226.

— The picture of love. A poem [Latin translation by Gilbert Hill], 1731. *See* H229.

H236 Hill, The. Stoic philosophy; or, the praise of poverty. A poem. By The. Hill, M.B. *London printed, and sold by J. Roberts,* 1720. (*DP* 25 Feb)
8°: A–G⁴; *i–iii* iv–viii, *1* 2–46 *47–48 blk.* viii err.
'Hail goddess Poverty, my suit regard'
L(1466.g.64),O,CT(–G4),LdU-B; CtY,IU.

Hill, T.

H237 Hill, Thomas. Nundinæ Sturbrigienses. *Londini, prostant venales apud Bernardum Lintott,* 1709.
8⁰: π¹ A–B⁴ C¹ (A2 as 'B2'); *i–ii, 1–2* 3–18.
'Expositas late Cami prope flumina merces'
    See *A translation of Mr. Hill's Nundinae Sturbrigienses,* 1709.
Longleat.

H238 [—] Nundinæ Sturbrigienses, anno 1702. In fine adjiciuntur duo alia poemata. Authore T. H. Cantabr. *Londini, impensis Jacob Tonson,* 1709. (*DC* 15 Feb)
8⁰: *A²* B–C⁴ D²; *i–iv, 1* 2–20.
    Title in red and black. The preface says this is the authorized and corrected edition. Additional poems are 'Rationes' and 'Ideæ innatæ'.
L(1213.k.22/3),CT,*MP*; CtY.

H239 — Nundinæ Sturbrigienses, anno 1702. Authore, T. Hill, e Coll. S. Trin. soc. *Londini, typis J. Tonson, impensis E. Curll,* 1709. (*PB* 17 Feb)
8⁰: *A¹* B⁴ C⁴(C2+*D⁴) D–F⁴; *i–ii, 1* 2–20 [5] 18–40. 12, 13 err.
    With P. Causton's *Tunbrigialia* and *Incendium Palatinum* on C3–F4; *D⁴ contains the other poems by Hill added to the authorized edition, presumably inserted here together with additional errata at the head of p. 13 (*D1ʳ) after the publication of that edition on 15 Feb.
O(lacks C3–F4),OW,C,CT; *CLU-C*,CtY(lacks C3–F4),NNC.

H240 — Nundinæ Sturbrigienses. Authore T. Hill... *Londini, anno* 1709.
8⁰: A(6 ll); *1–2* 3–12.
    Signed on A2, A3, A4, but actually collating A² B⁴. Apparently one of H. Hills's piracies.
L(78.c.26),OW,C(2),E,AdU+; CtY,ICN,IU(2),InU,TxU.

H241 [—] Nundinæ Sturbrigienses, anno 1702. In fine adjiciuntur duo alia poemata, authore T. H. Cantabr. *Dublinii, typis A. Rhames, impensis Jer. Pepyat,* 1709.
8⁰: A–C⁴; *i–iv, 1* 2–20.
    Title in red and black.
C(2),DG,DK(uncut),DT; CtY.

[Hinchliffe, William.] Poems; amorous, moral, and divine. *London, printed for Jonas Brown, & Jer. Batley,* 1718.
8⁰: pp. 205.   L; IU.
    No watermark; dedication unsigned.

— [fine paper] *London, printed for W. Hinchliffe,* 1718.
        CtY,MH.
    Watermark: fleur-de-lys. Dedication signed in type; frontispiece added.

[—] — The second edition. *London, printed for W. Hinchliffe,* 1726. (*MC* Feb)
8⁰: pp. 205.   DLC.

Hinchliffe, W.

    Apparently a reissue of the ordinary-paper edition of 1718.

H242 [—] An epithalamium address'd to Mrs. Cox, on her marriage with Mr. Gardiner. *London, printed in the year* 1715.
4⁰: A⁴ B⁴(−B4) (A3 as 'B3'); *1–4* 5–13 *14 blk.* A1 hft.
    B4 not seen, possibly blank.
'Divinest Clio, strike the trembling strings'
    Printed in Hinchliffe's *Poems,* 1718.
L(11602.f.24/5); OCU.

H243 [—] An ode presented to the king, upon his majesty's arrival at Greenwich. *London, printed for William Hinchliffe,* 1714. (*MC* Sept)
2⁰: A(3 ll, second 'A2'); *1–2* 3–6.
'While widow'd nations your protection court'
    Printed in Hinchliffe's *Poems,* 1718.
L(1476.dd.14),LDW,O; CtY.

H244 [—] Stanza's to the lord treasurer, upon the peace. *London, printed by H. Meere, for E. Curll,* 1713. (*PB* 4 Aug)
2⁰: A(3 ll, second 'A2'); *1–2* 3–6.
    A1.3 are conjugate.
'Say, queen of harmony, celestial muse'
    Printed in Hinchliffe's *Poems,* 1718.
CtY.

H245 His. His catholic majesty's most Christian manifesto, and reasons for not paying the ninety-five thousand pounds; faithfully rendered into English metre...*London, printed for C. Corbett,* 1739. (12 Sept)
4⁰: A¹ B–D² E¹; *i–ii, 1–13 14 blk.*
    A1 and E1 are conjugate. Listed in *GM, LM* Sept.
'I Philip the king, and Queen Betty my wife'
    A travesty on Philip V's manifesto.
L(11630.d.15/3, Tom's Coffee House, 12 Sept; 11630.e.3/7; 163.m.53),LU,LdU-B; *CSmH,* DLC.

H246 — His grace the Duke of Argyle's welcome to Edinburgh, June 16th 1738. [*Edinburgh,* 1738.] (4 July?)
½⁰: 1 side, 2 columns.
'Hail glorious man! the muse her tribute brings'
E(ms. date 4 July 1738).

H247 — His grace the Duke of Marlborough's welcome into the city of London, January the 6th 1705. *London printed, and sold by H. Hills,* [1705.]
½⁰: 1 side, 2 columns.
    Woodcut portrait at head. On the other side, *The gamster prosecuted,* 1705.
'Thrice welcome home, thou mighty conqueror'
Crawford.

H248 — His grace the great Duke of Argyl's welcom to Scotland or the Scots mens great joy and Edinburghs great glory... To the tune of the Drums and the trumpets commands me from Shear. [*Edinburgh,* 1719?]

His grace the great Duke of Argyl

½°: 1 side, 2 columns.
'Scotland rejoyce, with a chearfull smile'
> After John Campbell, duke of Argyll's restoration to favour in 1719.

E.

— His grace's answer to Jonathan, 1724. *See* Swift, Jonathan.

H249 — His highness's speech to his mirmidons. [*London*, 1719?]
½°: *1–2*, 2 columns.
'My l--ds and gent--men to you'
> A satire on the king's speech to Parliament.

CSmH.

H250 — His majesty's request. [*London?* 1715.]
slip: 1 side, 1 column.
> Below, 'A litany for the present year'.

'Our gracious sov'reign condescends'
Litany: 'From all the mischiefs I shall mention here'
> *Crum* O1274. A Jacobite satire on the election of 1715. The litany is *Crum* F649: 'Litany for the year 1715'.

MH.

H251 Hist. [dh] Hist: a ballad, inscribed to the Revolution-club, Edinburgh, 3d November, 1747. (To the tune of, A cobler there was, &c.) [*Edinburgh?* 1747.]
4°: A²; *1–4*.
'In Edina's fair city, you have heard how of late'
L(C.38.g.14/23),E; CSmH.

Historical. 'An historical and poetical description, of the ancient town, and castle of Nottingham. Humbly presented to Peter Worsley, gent.' [*Nottingham, printed by John Collyer*, 1724.]
> Listed by W. J. Clarke, *Early Nottingham printing and publishing*, 1953; apparently not seen by him. It might seem from the title that a prose account precedes the verse.

H252 — An historical ballad. Humbly inscribed to the duumviri. [*London*, 1730?]
½°: 1 side, 2 columns.
> Title in four lines. *Percival* XVI, from *Robin's panegyrick*, part 2.

'Full forty years has old England complain'd'
> A satire on the policies of Sir Robert Walpole and Horatio Walpole.

MH.

H253 — — [1730?]
¼°: 1 side, 2 columns.
> Title in two lines, below type flowers.

L(11626.i.11/27).

H254 — An historical poem upon his late majesty King James II. *London, printed for A. Baldwin*, 1701. (17 Oct, Luttrell)
2°: *A² B–C² D¹; i–iv, 1–9 10 blk.*
> Listed in *WL* Oct; the Luttrell copy was in the collection of C. H. Wilkinson.

An **historical** poem

'Unhappy prince! born to be fortunes jest'
L(643.1.24/19),LLP,O,AdU; CLU-C.

History. The history and fall of the conformity bill, [1704.] *See* Mainwaring, Arthur.

— The history of David's troubles, 1741. *See* Wallis, John.

— The history of insipids, 1709. *See* Freke, John.

— The history of Joseph. A poem, 1736–. *See* Rowe, Elizabeth.

— The history of Joseph. In verse, 1736. *See* Notcutt, William.

H255 — The history of the bob tails. To the tune of the Blacksmiths. [*London?* 1715/20.]
slip: 1 side, 1 column.
'Come listen awhile, and I'll tell you strange tales'
> A Jacobite satire against the whigs.

O(cut and mounted).

H256 — The history of the famous may-pole at Ewelm in Oxfordshire: or, a true and exact relation, how it was first begg'd, then brought home; how it was set up, and how immediately it fell down again... [*London?*] *Printed in the year* 1702. (27 July, Luttrell)
12°: A–C⁶; *1–2* 3–34 *35–36 blk.*
> Vertical chain-lines.

'At Ewelm-town in Oxford-shire'
> On a local squabble: the maypole was in honour of Queen Anne.

O(Luttrell, uncut).

— The history of the grand rebellion, 1713. *See* Ward, Edward.

H257 — The history of the Guelphs. To the tune of, O London is a fine town. [*London?* 1715/20.]
slip: 1 side, 1 column.
'A country knight of German race'
> A Jacobite satire against the Hanoverians.

O(cut and mounted).

— The history of the life and miracles of our blessed saviour, [174–?] *See* Gent, Thomas.

H258 — The history of the most famous and most renowned Janny Geddes. [*Edinburgh*, 1737?]
½°: 1 side, 2 columns.
> Probably the same work as '*Jenny Geddes*, a scurrilous ballad' listed in *Remarks on the pamphlets lately published, on occasion of the late act of parliament, for bringing to justice the murderers of Captain John Porteous*, [1737?].

'When Janny Geddes, well did mark'
> A satire on those clergy who refused to read the Porteous act and who joined Ralph and Ebenezer Erskine's secession.

E,EP.

H259 — The history of the old and new testament: or, an epitome of the sacred writings of the prophets, evangelists, and holy apostles. *Dublin, printed by C. Hicks*, [1726?]

The **history** of the old and new testament

1⁰: 1 side, 5 columns.
  Rough woodcuts at head.
'Jehovah here of nothing all things makes'
DT.

H260 — The history of the secret expedition. [*Edinburgh*, 1736?]
½⁰: *1–2*, 1 column.
'No more shall Scotland now in sadness mourn'
  On the death of a redcoat named Campbell after an encounter with a sheep. In favour of the mob hanging John Porteous, 7 Sept 1736.
Crawford.

— The history of the three goddesses, 1712. *See* The D--- of M----- turn'd conjurer, 1712.

H261 — The history of the 29 years rebellion and usurpation. To a new pleasent play-house tune. Never before printed. [*London?* 1717?]
slip: 1 side, 1 column.
  Printed with *The loyal resolution*, [1717?]; the NjP copy is not divided.
'Nine tripled and two are the years'
  A Jacobite ballad.
O; CSmH,NjP.

H262 Histrio. Histrio theologicus: or, an historical-political-theological poetical account of the most remarkable passages...in the life of the late B—p of S—m... *London printed, and sold by John More*, 1715.
8⁰: *A*⁴ B–E⁴; *i–viii*, *1–32*. A1 hft; 32 advt.
'If to subvert, destroy, if to confound'
  Dedication signed 'A.B.' A satire on Gilbert Burnet.
L(G.14173),CT,AdU,DrU; CtY,*InU*.

H---n, Fr----, *gent.* Vulpoon in the snare; or a hue and cry, 1712. *See* V111.

H263 Hob. Hob turn'd courtier. A satyr. *London, printed in the year* 1703 [1702]. (19 Dec, Luttrell)
2⁰: A–D²; *1–2* 3–15 '20'.
  Advertised in Defoe's *Review*, 18 July 1704.
'Friend Ralph (for that I think's thy name'
  Attributed to Edward Ward in 1705 by Robert Clare, one of Harley's informers; see H. L. Snyder in *The library* V. 22 (1967) 337. His attributions seem in many cases to be wild guesses, but the same suggestion is made in Pickering & Chatto cat. 284/450. 'Upon some ministers of the last reign', Luttrell.
IU(Luttrell),MH,OCU,TxU.

Hobbes, Thomas.
[Rooke, John:] A true ecclesiastical history, from Moses, to the time of Martin Luther, in verse. By Thomas Hobbes of Malmesbury. Made English from the Latin original, 1722. *See* R264·5.

H264 Hobson, Thomas. Christianity the light of the moral world: a poem. *London, printed by John Lewis, in the year* 1745 [1746]. (3 Jan?)

Hobson, T. Christianity the light

4⁰: *A*⁴ B–H⁴; *1–5* 6–64. A1 hft; 64 err.
  Engraving on title, not printed in the L copy at 643.k.5/6. Publication date from *Rawlinson*; listed in *GM,LM* Jan.
'Not from eternity, mysterious name!'
L(11630.e.5/1,–A1; 643.k.5/6,–A1),OW, LdU-B; CSmH,CtY,ICN,KU,MH+.

[**H265** = N296·5] **Hodge.** Hodge and the devil: a tale, [1737.] *See* Nicoll, J.

[**Hoffman, Francis.**] Divine songs: occasionally compos'd on variety of subjects, 1735. *See* Divine.

H266 — The creed of Francis Hoffman, most humbly dedicated to the almighty Georgos. [*London*, 172–?]
1⁰: 1 side, 3 columns.
  Hoffman woodcut of a man between initials F H at head.
'I sing the faith, which all must once confess'
L(478.a.2/2).

H267 [—] [The new theory of the orbs of heaven: or, the most excellent way to sanctify our violent fits of passion.] [*London*, 172–?]
8⁰: A–B⁴ (+plate); *1* 2–16.
  The title quoted is from the drop-head on p. 4; p. 1 has a drop-head title to the prose introduction 'The right notion of an eclipse'. The copy seen was issued in *A curious uncommon account of the great eclipse of the moon*, 1725; its collation suggests an earlier separate existence, possibly with an added title-leaf.
'Bely'd and slander'd by a fiend'
  The L copy is bound in a volume of Hoffman pamphlets.
L(478.a.2/5).

H268 [—] The pilgrim's progress... By John Bunyan. And now done into verse. *London, printed by R. Tookey, and are to be sold by the booksellers of London & Westminster*, 1706. (3 April?)
12⁰: (frt+) A¹²(±A1) B–F¹² G⁶; *i–xii*, *1* 2–143 *144 blk*.
  The title is cancelled to remove Hoffman's name; the issue below has the original title. The frontispiece is a copper engraving; there are illustrative wood-engravings by Hoffman in the body of the book. Advertised in *PM* 2 April 1706 for publication 'tomorrow'.
'As thro' the world's wide wilderness I past'
L(11623.a.5),O(–frt); NN.

H269 — — And now done into verse by Francis Hoffman. *London, printed by R. Tookey, and are to be sold by Tho. Davis*, 1706 [1723/–].
12⁰: (frt+) A–F¹² G⁶; *i–xii*, *1* 2–143 *144 blk*.
  This state probably exists by accident, but since copies are comparatively common it is listed separately here. It apparently represents copies of the 1723 reissue with the original title-leaf of 1706 uncancelled. Sheet G is of

Hoffman, F. The pilgrim's progress

the edition found below, and copies at L, CSmH, NjP have the additional 12 pages advertising books printed for John Marshall. The copy at L has a wood-engraving as frontispiece, the others a copper engraving.

L(04411.c.34); CSmH(−frt),ICU,NN,NjP.

H270 — — The third edition. And now done into verse by Francis Hoffman. *London, printed for John Marshal*, 1723.

12⁰: A¹²(±A1) B–F¹² G⁶; *i–xii, 1* 2–143 *144 blk.*

A reissue of the edition of 1706 with a new cancel title. The inner forme of G is from a different setting of type from that found in 1706, though the outer forme appears to be the same; this problem has not been resolved. A six-leaf catalogue of books printed for John Marshall, paged *1* 2–12, is added to the copy seen; it has no frontispiece, and is probably imperfect in this respect.

MiU(−frt?).

H271 — A poem on the mannour of Woodstock... Now made thrice renown'd by being setled on his grace the Duke of Marlborough... Made written and engraven by F. Hoffman. [*London*, 1704/−.]

2⁰: (frt+) 7 single leaves; ff. [*1*] I–VI.

Engraved throughout on one side of the leaf.

'When France near pierc'd the empire to the heart'

O(2).

H272 — The real door, celebrated by Francis Hoffman. [*London*, 172–?]

½⁰: 1 side, 2 columns.

Hoffman woodcut of a man between initials F H at head.

'I sing who's who in this our generation'

Christ is the door to eternal life.

L(478.a.2/6).

H273 — The true protestant director: or, an alarm against popery; being the right song of St. George and the dragon... *London, printed by and for R. Phillips; sold by W. Boreham*, [1721.] (Feb, Luttrell)

2⁰: A²...; *1–2* 3– .

'Cease, Britain, from intestine jarrs'

ICN(Luttrell, lacks all after A2).

Hofman, John. Some poems on the welcome arrival, entry and coronation of the most illustrious elector of Brunswick; George, Lewis... Design'd for a new-year's gift... *London, printed by B. Mills; sold by Joseph Marshall, and the booksellers of London & Westminster*, 1715. (12 Jan, Luttrell)

4⁰: pp. 24.   L,O.

The epistle to the reader records that the poems are translated out of Dutch.

H274 **Hog.** The hog toss'd in a blanket, by the Observator and his country-man. [*London*] '*Printed for Honest Roger, country-man to the Observator*', 1705. (14 Feb, Luttrell)

4⁰: A²; *1–4*.

The **hog** toss'd in a blanket

'Troth, master, nothing could have pleas'd me more'

Apparently in defence of Tutchin against Robert Stephens, messenger to the press, known as 'Robin Hog'.

LLP; MH(Luttrell).

H275 **Hog-land.** Hog-land: or a description of Hampshire. A mock heroic poem in answer to Mr. Holdsworth's Muscipula. By Mr. Richards... *London, printed in the year* 1728 [1727]. (SJEP 7 Nov)

8⁰: *A*¹ B–D⁴ E⁴(−E4), ²A–B⁴; *i–ii, 1* 2–38 '37–44'.

Latin text on ²A–B⁴, with title on p. 31 and imprint, 'Londini: impensis H. Curll'.

'I sing the man whose warlike force subdu'd'

The original Latin was published by Richards as Χοιροχωρογραφια, 1709. A letter about Richards from John Jones in *Rawlinson* records 'The author of this translation, as I have been informed, was one Mr. Goodbarn, educated at Cambridge'; he has not been traced in *Alumni Cantabrigienses*, and confirmation seems necessary.

L(1960, ²A–B⁴ only),O(²A–B⁴ only),LdU-B; CtY, ICN,MH.

H276 **Hogg, William.** [dh] Ad augustissimam, serenissimamque Annam, Magnæ Britanniæ, &c. reginam, cum publico suffragio regina declararetur. Προσφωνητικον hexametrum. [*London*, 1702.]

4⁰: A⁴(−A4); *1–6*.

On p. 5 'Ad augustissimam, serenissimamque Annam...cum coronaretur. Προσφωνητικον. Sapphicum'.

'Qua celebrem te, diva, lyra? Quo carmine pangam'

'Anna regali serie creata'

Signed on p. 6 'Gulielmus Hogæus'.

L(837.h.33).

H277 — Ad virum nobilissimum, illustrissimumque, Robertum Harlæum, armigerum, senatus concilij Anglicani oratorem, cum primum ad hoc munus honorificum obeundum eligeretur. Carmen προσφωνητικον. Autore Gulielmo Hogæo. [*London*, 1701.]

4⁰: *A*⁴; *i–iv, 1–3* '5'.

'Nunc age, siquid habes, mea musa, O nobile carmen'

Harley was elected speaker 10 Feb 1701.

LLP,C.

H278 — In obitum augustissimi invictissimique Magnæ Britanniæ, &c. regis, Gulielmi tertii. Θρηνητικον. Autore Gulielmo Hogæo. *Londini, impensis autoris, anno salutis*, 1702.

4⁰: A⁴; *i–ii, 1–6*.

'Qua plangam tua fata lyra? Queis prosequar umbras'

L(837.h.31),DA; CtY(in mourning wrappers).

H279 [**Holdsworth, Edward.**] Muscipula: sive Cambro-muo-μαχια. *Londini, veneunt Bernardo Lintott*, [1708/09.] (DC 23 Nov 1708)

Holdsworth, E. Muscipula

8°: A⁴ C⁴ D²; *1–2* 3–19 *20 blk.*
> The order of these unauthorized printings of Lintot has not been determined; they were advertised as late as April 1709. Holdsworth disclaimed them (e.g. in *Tatler* 19 May 1709) in preparation for the authorized Curll edition.
> 'Monticolam Britonem, qui primus vincula Muri' Subsequently acknowledged by Holdsworth. Answered by [Thomas Richards] Χοιρο-χωρογραφια, 1709. Imitated in *The louse-trap*, 1723.

L(11408.e.33),OW,WcC; MH,TxU.

H280 [—] — *Londini, veneunt Bernardo Lintott,* [1708/09.]
8°: B–C⁴ D²; *1–2* 3–19 *20 blk.*
> Press-figures 5–2, 10–2; the figure on p. 5 is sometimes absent (e.g. in the L copy at T.1812/14). In part, at least, from the same type as the preceding.

L(11626.bbb.26/1, frt added from Curll edition; T.1812/14),O,EtC.

H281 [—] — *Londini, veneunt Bernardo Lintott,* [1708/09.]
8°: A–B⁴ C²; *1–2* 3–19 *20 blk.*
> Press-figures 8–3, 10–4.

WcC; CLU-C,CtY.

H282 [—] Muscipula, sive Cambro-muo-machia. *Londini, anno* 1709.
8°: A⁴; *1* 2–8.
> Clearly a piracy.

L(1103.c.33/7),O,AdU; CtY,DFo(2),ICN,MH.

H283 [—] Muscipula: sive Cambro-muo-maxia. *Apud Londini, anno domini* 1709.
8°: *A⁴*; *1–2* 3–8.
> Another piracy.

L(11408.e.60/1),O,C,E; CSmH,IU.

H284 [—] Muscipula: sive Cambro-muo-machia. *Dublinii, typis A. Rhames, impensis Jer. Pepyat,* 1709.
8°: A⁴; *1–2* 3–8.
> Apparently a reprint of the unauthorized text.

DA(uncut),DT; *DLC.*

H285 — Muscipula, sive Καμβρομυομαχια. *Londini, impensis E. Curll, & E. Sanger,* 1709. (*PB* 9 June)
8°: (frt+) A–C⁴; *i–iii* iv–viii, *1* 2–16.
> Authorized edition, advertised in *Tatler* 4 June for Monday [6 June] 'adorn'd with a cut curiously engraven'. The number of copies lacking the frontispiece prompts the thought that early copies may have been sold without it. Dedication signed. Holdsworth's receipt for five guineas from Curll for the copyright, with fifty copies for his own use, is dated 30 May 1709 (L, Add. MS. 38728, fol. 120). Reissued with Samuel Cobb's translation *The mouse-trap*, 1712, 1720; the frontispiece is then bound before the translation.

L(11408.bbb.18, originally with ms. note by Curll, now missing, —frt; 161.k.36, —frt),O(2, 1—frt), C(2, 1—frt),CT(2, 1—frt),DrU+; CU,KU.

Holdsworth, E. Muscipula

H286 — [variant imprint:] *Londini, impensis E. Curll, & E. Sanger. Veniunt* [!] *apud J. Stephens, bibliopol. Oxon.,* 1709.
O(imperfect, —frt); CtY,ICU.

H287 — — *Londini, anno* 1709.
8°: *A⁴* B⁴; *1–4* 5–15 *16.* A1 frt; *16* advt of Hills poems.
> A piracy, published by Henry Hills. Dedication and frontispiece copied from Curll's edition.

L(1078.m.6/1),OW,CT,EU,WcC(2)+; CtY,ICN, NN.

H288 — — *Londini, impensis* [!] 1709.
8°: *A⁴* B⁴; *1–4* 5–15 *16.* A1 frt; *16* advt of Hills poems.
> Additional poems added to advertisement; certainly the later edition.

O,C(2, 1 uncut); CSmH,CtY,ICN,IU,MH.

Translations, arranged alphabetically
[Bellamy, Daniel:] Taffy's triumph: or, a new translation...in imitation of Milton, 1709. *See* B176–7.

[—] [*idem*] The Cambro-britannic engineer: or the original mouse-trapp-maker, 1722. *See* B178.

Cobb, Samuel: The mouse-trap: a poem, 1712. *See* C250.

— [*idem*] Muscipula: or, the mouse-trap, 1720. *See* C251.

Cobden, Edward: The mouse-trap. A translation in the year 1718. *In* his *Poems on several occasions,* 1748.

Lewis, Richard: The mouse-trap, or the battle of the Cambrians and mice, 1728. *See* L165.

The mouse-trap. A new poem, translated from the Latin, 1710. *See* M550.

The mouse trap, a poem, done from the original Latin in Milton's stile, 1715. *See* M551.

The mouse-trap: or, the Welshmen's scuffle with the mice, 1709. *See* M552.

[Quincy, John:] The mouse-trap: or, the Welsh engagement with the mice, 1709. *See* Q15.

— [*idem*] The mouse-trap, a poem, 1714. *See* Q16.

Taffi's master-piece: or, the Cambro-British invention, 1709. *See* T3.

[Taswell, William:] Muscipula: or, the mouse-trap. Attempted in English burlesque, 1725. *See* T47.

The Welsh mouse-trap. Translated from the Latin. By F.T., 1709. *See* W283.

H289 **Holiday.** The holiday ramble: or, a walk to Pancridge. *London, printed in the year* 1703.
8°: A⁴; *1* 2–8.
> 'In the holiday time when those evils betide'
> A trip to St. Pancras, after the manner of Edward Ward.

L(1077.c.47).

Holt, —, *Mrs*

H290 Holt, —, Mrs. A fairy tale inscrib'd, to the honourable Mrs. W------ With other poems, by Mrs. Holt. *London, printed for R. Burleigh, & Arabella Morrice*, 1717. (*MC* March)
8⁰: *A*¹ B–D⁴ E⁴(–E1); *i–ii*, 1–30.
'For fear your ladyship mistake'
L(1466.b.42/1),O(remboîtage in morocco binding); DFo.

Holy. 'The holy Bible; containing the old and new testament epitomiz'd in verse, the 2d edition with cutts.'
> Entered in *SR* to William Marshall as old copy, 6 April 1711. Possibly the versification by J. Bilcliffe first printed in 1703 and 'sold by J. Bradford'; or possibly another versification.

— The holy Bible; containing the old and new testaments, with the apocripha. Done into verse, 1701–. *See* Harris, Benjamin.

—— 1703–. *See* Bilcliffe, J.

H291 — The holy Parnassus: or, advice to the poets. [*Dublin*?] *Printed in the year* 1739.
12⁰: A–B⁶ (B2 as 'B3'); *1–2* 3–24.
'Had I the parts of Pope or Swift'
> The advice is to write religious verse.

C.

H292 — 'A holy poem: or Christmas carrol on the blessed nativity of...Jesus Christ, proper for Christmas-day. *Printed for the author*, 1714.'
2⁰.
> Entered by *Morgan* under the initials 'K., A.' (*Morgan* Q356.)

Homer. Homer in a nutshell, 1715. *See* Tooly, Thomas.

— Homer travestie, 1720. *See* Tooly, Thomas [Homer in a nutshell].

— Homer's Battle of the frogs and mice, 1717. *See* Parnell, Thomas.

Homer.
The translation of the Iliad by Ozell, Broome and Oldisworth, and the translations of the Iliad and Odyssey by Pope and his assistants are not included here.

[*Iliad*] Tickell, Thomas: The first book of Homer's Iliad, 1715, 1716. *See* T281–2.

Ashwick, Samuel: The eighth book of the Iliad of Homer; attempted by way of essay, 1750. *See* A348.

[*Iliad – burlesque*] [Tooly, Thomas:] Homer in a nutshell: or, the Iliad of Homer in immortal doggrel, 1715. *See* T420.

[—] [reissue] Homer travestie: being a new translation of that great poet, 1720. *See* T421.

[Duckett, George:] Homerides: or, Homer's first book moderniz'd, 1716. *See* D485.

Cornwall, C.: Homeros, Homoros. The third book of Homer's Ilias burlesqu'd, 1722. *See* C435.

Homer.
'Fitzcotton, Henry': A new, and accurate translation of the first book, of Homer's Iliad, 1749. *See* F153–5.

[*Odyssey*] Theobald, Lewis: The Odyssey of Homer. Book I. Translated from the Greek, 1717. *See* T145.

[*Batrachomyomachia*] [Parnell, Thomas:] Homer's Battle of the frogs and mice, 1717. *See* P73–6.

Wesley, Samuel: The Iliad in a nutshell: or Homer's Battle of the frogs and mice, 1726. *See* W342.

Price, Henry: Batrachomuomachia: or the battle of the frogs and mice. Translated from Homer, 1736. *See* P1039.

'Homer.' Abigal's lamentation for the loss of secretary H-----y. Translated from the Greek of Homer, [1708.] *See* A3.

[*idem*] The prophesy: or, M—m's lamentation, 1710. *See* A4.

[Fielding, Henry:] The Vernon-iad. Done into English, from the original Greek of Homer. Lately found at Constantinople, 1741. *See* F120–21.

Homerides. Homerides: or, Homer's first book moderniz'd, 1716. *See* Duckett, George.

Homerou. Της Ὁμηρου Νερνον-ιαδος, 1741. *See* Fielding, Henry.

H293 Homunculus. Homunculus: or, the character of Mezereon, the High-German doctor. An hudibrastick poem. By Van Hugo Gasper Lunatus. *London printed, and sold by Edm. Powell*, 1715.
4⁰: *A*² B–C²; *i–ii*, 1–10.
'Is justice dead, or gone astray?'
L(11631.bb.56),*MR*; OCU.

H294 Honest. The honest citizens wish. *Dublin, printed by E. Waters*, [1710/14.]
½⁰: 1 side, 1 column.
'I much have wondred what they mean'
> In praise of Queen Anne, against party faction.

C.

H295 — Honest Clodd's advice to his countrymen, how to chuse such members of parliament in the next election, as may preserve their liberties and estates. [*London*] *Printed in the year* 1710. (*PM* 16 Sept)
½⁰: 1 side, 1 column.
> Advertised in *PM* by J. Baker.

'To open all your eyes, and let you know'
> Against the tories.

L(1876.f.19/48),MC(Luttrell, Sept),Rothschild; InU,OCU.

H296 — An honest elegy. On the lamented death of Councellor Howard. [*Dublin*, 1728.]
½⁰: 1 side, 1 column.
'When death appears, the stoutest man's a coward'
CtY.

— The honest jury; or, Caleb triumphant, 1729. *See* Pulteney, William, *earl of Bath*.

The **honest** man

— The honest man at court, 1712. *See* Montagu, Charles, *earl of Halifax.*

H297 — The honest man is worth a kingdom. [*London?* 1720?]
slip: 1 side, 1 column.
　Rough woodcut at head and foot.
'O! that it was but the laws of the land'
　Inspired by the South Sea bubble.
C.

H298 — Honest Tom's resentment of a pamphlet, entitul'd, A Bob for the court: or, Prince Eugene's welcome. *London*: April, *printed in the year* 1712.
½°: 1 side, 2 columns.
　The columns are headed 'Bob's allusions', 'Tom's resentment'. Column 1 reprints the original edition of 1712 (B295).
Tom's resentment: 'To cure the nation from relaps'
　An attack on Harley's peace moves by 'Tom Whig'.
LLP; MH.

— 'The honest voters; or, Robin's downfal.'
Percival p. 15 quotes the *Craftsman* 12 Aug 1727: 'On Thursday night last [10 Aug] some persons were seized and carried before the Lord Townshend for uttering scandalous and seditious ballads; one of which is said to be intitled *The honest voters...*' The other weekly papers have the same paragraph except for quoting this title, and one wonders if the *Craftsman* is making a political point.

H299 Honesto. Honesto Willo: a cant | In great Hudibras's strain, | Of adventures huge in the last reign; | ... Printed for the buyers, | And sold by the cryers.
Newcastle upon Tyne, printed by T. Goolding, 1715.
8°: *A*⁴ B–D⁴; *1–2* 3–31 *32 blk.*
　Horizontal chain-lines; the format is possibly duodecimo.
'As men sit under nobles chair'
　A satire on the Jacobite politicians of Queen Anne's reign, particularly Bolingbroke and Harley.
NeP.

Honesty. Honesty in distress, 1705–. *See* Ward, Edward.

H300 — Honesty the best policy... Also the Country seat, or a description of Langdon, one of the seats of Shilston Calmady, esq; situate near Plymouth... *London, printed for James Roberts,* 1715. (1 April, Luttrell)
4°: *A*² B–E² *F*²; *1–4* 5–21 *22–24.* A1 hft; F2 advt.
　Listed in *MC* April 1715.
'Blest are the men, in virtuous paths that tread'
Country-seat: 'Prepare, my muse, a country-seat to sing'
L(161.1.42, Luttrell),LdU-B,*MR*; InU,NN.

Honesty yet to be found

H301 — Honesty yet to be found, a poem in praise of Leicester-shire. By J.B. *Printed at Stamford, Lincolnshire,* 1721.
4°: A–B⁴; *1–4* 5–16.
'The grateful Trojan when kind fortune bore'
　In praise of Sir Wolstan Dixie, bart. (the dedicatee), and other Leicestershire worthies.
O; *MH.*

Honeysuckle. The honeysuckle. A curious collection of poems, 1731. *See* A collection of poems; consisting of odes, tales, &c, 1731.

Honor. Honor & opes: or, the Brittish merchant's glory, 1708. *See* D'Urfey, Thomas.

Honoratissimo. Honoratissimo viro, Henrico St.-John, 1707. *See* Philips, John.

Honori. Honori sacellum, 1707–. *See* Settle, Elkanah.

Honour. Honour. A poem, 1743. *See* Brown, John.

H302 Hooke, Thomas. The Jerusalem of Torquato Tasso. Translated by Mr. Thomas Hooke. [Book 1.] *London, printed by James Bettenham; sold by George Hawkins,* 1738. (30 Jan?)
4°: A–E⁴; *1–2* 3–39 *40 blk.* 39 err.
　Entered in *SR* 31 Jan to Hooke; deposit copies at L,O,E,EU,GU,SaU. Listed in *GM,LM* Feb as to be continued.
'The pious armies, and the chief I sing'
L(11630.c.10/13, ms. date 30 Jan; C.70.f.1/4),O, C(imperfect),E,GU + ; CtY.

H303 Hoop. An hoop for the broken mugg. A poem. *Dublin, printed in the year* 1727.
slip: 1 side, 1 column.
　Originally printed with *A new war,* [1727] according to a ms. note in the L copy.
'Me great Gambrivius [!] inspire'
　In praise of beer. The title is presumably occasioned by [Laurence Whyte] *The broken mug,* [1725?].
L(1890.e.5/50).

H304 Hoop-petticoat. The hoop-petticoat. An heroicomical poem; in four cantos. Address'd to the ladies of Great-Britain. By a young gentleman of Oxford. *London, printed for C. Corbett; sold by J. Fletcher, in the Turle, Oxford,* 1748. (*GM* May)
4°: *A*² B⁴ D–E⁴ F(3 ll); *1–3* 4–34.
　Bond 211.
'Accept, ye fair, the tribute of a muse!'
L(11630.c.8/10); DLC.

H305 — 'The hoop-petticoat... Address'd to the ladies of Ireland. By a young gentleman. *Dublin, Augustus Long',* [1748.]
　Advertised in *The true patriot,* 1749, and other Dublin pamphlets of 1748 and 1749. Probably a reprint of the preceding.

Hope.

Hope. Hope: a poetical essay on that Christian grace, 1745. *See* Morell, Thomas.

H306 Hopeful. A hopeful convention agreed upon, and design'd for the benefit of trade. An inconceivable curious medley. *London, printed for M. Watson, next the King's Arms tavern*, [1739.]
2°: *B*² C–D² *E*²; *3–7* 8–18.
'Whence is the cause Britannia droops her head?'
An attack on the convention with Spain.
O(uncut); CtY,OCU.

'Hopewell, Frank.' The oddity, 1740. *See* O15.

H307 Hopkins, Charles. The art of love: in two books dedicated to the ladies. A poem. The second edition, enlarged... *London, printed for R. Wellington*, 1704. (*PM* 18 Jan)
8°: A⁴ *a*⁴ *b*² B–G⁸ *H*², ²B–D⁴ E²; i–xx, 1–98 [2] 1–44. A1 advt.
The two books have separate collations. First published 1700. The 'second edition' is not specifically mentioned in *PM* 18 Jan: listed in *TC* Hilary 1705. Reissued in *Five love letters from a nun to a cavalier*, 1714. Ninth shares of the copyrights of both books appeared in the trade sales of William Feales, 17 Nov 1737, and C. Corbett, 22 Dec 1737 (cats. at O–JJ).
'Let lovers now bless their perplexing chains'
L(11631.aaa.19,–A1),LG,DT,LdU-B; CLU-C (–A1, H2),CtY,DFo,ICN,MH+.

H308 [—] A satyr against confinement. *London, printed for A. Baldwin*, 1702 [1701]. (27 Oct, Luttrell)
2°: A–D²; *i–iv*, 1–12.
The Luttrell copy is recorded in Pickering & Chatto cat. 247/13348; listed in *WL* Oct.
'Had I deserv'd to be severely curst'
Third edition 'By Mr. Hopkins'; presumably Charles is the Hopkins intended.
DFo,MH,TxU.

H309 — — By Mr. Hopkins... The third edition. *London printed, and sold by the booksellers of London & Westminster*, 1710.
4°: A⁴; *1* 2–8.
No second edition has been traced.
DT.

H310 [Hopkins, Thomas.] The lawyers disbanded: or, the Temple in an uproar. *London, printed for J. Perry*, [1745.] (*GM* Dec)
2°: (3 ll); *1–2* 3–6.
'Oh ye muses I 'nvoke, now I sing the law scheme'
The copy at O has an early ms. attribution 'By Mr. Thomas Hopkins of the excise office'. On a volunteer regiment raised and then disbanded.
L(11602.i.10/8),O; CLU-C,MH,TxU.

Horace. Horace book I. ode XIV, [1730.] *See* Swift, Jonathan.

Horace.

H311 — Horace, book IV. ode V. imitated. *London, printed for T. Cooper*, 1740. (*GM, LM* Oct)
2°: *A*² B²; *1–2* 3–7 *8 blk*.
'Thus anxious for her lord's return'
An ironic request for the return of George II from Hanover.
DrU-U; MH(2, 1 uncut),TxU.

H312 — [*idem*] Rare feasting at H— being a mouldy crust for poor England which was dropt by an old w— that is lately run after a white horse. [*London?* 1740?]
½°: 1 side, 2 columns.
Apparently a piratical reprint of the preceding.
MC.

— Horace, epod. IV. imitated, 1717. *See* 'Baker, Sir James'.

— Horace lib. I. epistle the ninth, [1711.] *See* Prior, Matthew.

— Horace, lib II. ode IV. imitated, [1705/07.] *See* Rowe, Nicholas.

— Horace lib. III. ode III. imitated, 1706. *See* Walsh, William.

H313 — Horace Of the art of poetry, in English numbers, with an attempt to explain the more difficult and material passages... *London, printed for J. Roberts*, 1735. (*LM* Oct)
8°: A–I⁴; *i–iii* iv–viii, *1* 2–64.
'If a painter should the fancy take'
The translation has been ascribed to Henry Ames, but appears to be a different work from his translation of 1727.
MH.

H314 — Horace Of the art of poetry, translated. *London, printed for J. Robinson*, [1746.] (*GA* 5 March)
4°: π¹ *A*² B–C² D¹; *1–3* 4–16.
Vertical chain-lines.
'If you a painter, Piso, busy saw'
L(11630.c.12/18, title mutilated).

— Horace to Scaeva, 1730. *See* Savage, John.

H315 — [dh] Horace turn'd whigg: or, a low-church ode. Horatii epodon septimum imitated. [col] *London printed, and sold by A. Baldwin*, 1710. (*SR* 23 June)
4°: A²; *1–4*.
Entered in *SR* to Bryan Mills, deposit copies at E,EU,SaU.
'What madness, countrey-men, inspires?'
Against the heat of the Sacheverell controversy.
O,C,E,DK,SaU+; OCU.

H316 — — *London, A. Baldwin, and reprinted in Dublin*, 1710.
4°: 4 pp.
(Pickering & Chatto cat. 206/15422).

H317 — Horace's allegorical advice to the people of Rome; at this time seasonable for England. Being an essay on the fourteenth ode of the first book of

Horace's allegorical advice

Horace. With the allegory explain'd. *London printed, and sold by R. Burleigh,* [1714/17.]
8°: *A*⁴ B⁴ C²; *1–4* 5–19 *20.* 20 advt.
> A1 not seen, probably half-title. The Latin text is in sheet A, the English in B, and the allegory in C. The date is suggested by Burleigh's publishing career.
'O ship new billows which around thee roar'
NN(–A1).

H318 — Horace's instructions to the Roman senate: and character of Caius Asinius Pollio. In two odes. *London, printed for R. Amey,* 1740. (*GM,LM* Jan)
8°: A–D⁴; *i–ii* iii–v, 6–31 *32 blk.*
'My honour'd friends, in senate now assembl'd'
'Illustrious C——l, ancient Scotia's boast'
> Odes III. 2 and II. 1. The second poem is in praise of John Campbell, 2nd duke of Argyll.
L(11375.c.16),GU.

Horatian. The Horatian canons of friendship, 1750. *See* Smart, Christopher.

Horatii. Horatii ep. I. lib. II. ad Augustum, 1749. *See* Jenyns, Soame.

Horatius. Horatius ad Luciferum, [1712?/13.] *See* Pitcairne, Archibald.

Horatius Flaccus, Quintus.

Works

Francis, Philip: The odes [etc; 4 vol.], 1743–46.
— A poetical translation of the works of Horace, 1747, 1749, 1750.

Partial collections

[Oldisworth, William:] The odes, epodes, and Carmen seculare of Horace, in Latin and English, 1713.
— — Translated from Dr. Bentley's Latin edition, 1719, 1737.
Hanway, John: Translations of several odes, satyrs, and epistles of Horace, 1730.
Hare, Thomas: A translation of the odes and epodes of Horace into English verse, 1737.
Francis, Philip: The odes, epodes, and Carmen seculare of Horace. In Latin and English, 1743.
— The epistles and Art of poetry of Horace. In Latin and English, 1746.

Odes

Coxwell, Henry: The odes of Horace. Translated into English verse, 1718.

Odes – smaller collections

Browne, Joseph: Several odes of Horace [i.e. book I, no. 1–15] translated into English verse, by way of specimen to the whole version, 1705.

Horatius Flaccus, Q.

[Morrice, Bezaleel:] Two odes of Horace, with a description of Fame or Report from Virgil. Attempted in English verse, 1721. *See* M498.

Welsted, Leonard: An ode to the honourable Major-general Wade...Imitated from Horace. To which is added, the fourth ode, translated from the fourth book, 1726. *See* W297.

[Manning, Francis:] The two first odes of Horace imitated, 1738. *See* M91.

Three odes from the second book of Horace imitated, 1739. *See* T255.

Horace's instructions to the Roman senate: and character of Caius Asinius Pollio. In two odes, 1740. *See* H318.

Martin, Thomas: Imitations and translations of several odes of Horace: being an essay towards a translation of that part of the author's works, 1743.

Single odes

[I. 1] The scrutiny: with a further dissertation upon Horace, the first ode, 1708. *See* S157.

To Robert Ch-ster, esq; in imitation of the first ode of Horace, [1720.] *See* T357.

Ode after the manner of the first of Horace, 1732. *See* O21.

Theobald, John: A new translation of the first ode of Horace, agreeably to its original pointing, now first restored, [1739/46.] *See* T131.

Boyle, John, *earl of Cork & Orrery*: The first ode of the first book of Horace, 1741. *See* B351–2.

[I. 2] The scrutiny: with the second ode, first satyr, and a short dissertation upon Horace, 1708. *See* S158.

Alma's complaint. An ode in imitation of the second of the first book of Horace, 1735. *See* A172.

[I. 3] [Harison, William:] On his grace the Duke of Marlborough going for Holland. In imitation of the third ode of the first book of Horace, 1707. *See* H49.

An allusion to the third ode of the first book of Horace, 1745. *See* A170.

[I. 5] Boyle, John, *earl of Cork & Orrery*: Pyrrha: an imitation of the fifth ode of the first book of Horace, 1741, 1742. *See* B356–7.

Pyrrha a cantata: being an imitation of the fifth ode of the first book of Horace. Not by John earl of Orrery, 1741. *See* P1181.

The fifth ode of the first book of Horace imitated, 1745. *See* F137.

[I. 6] [Steele, *Sir* Richard:] An imitation of the sixth ode of Horace, apply'd to his grace the Duke of Marlborough, 1704. *See* S737.

Welsted, Leonard: An ode to the honourable Major-general Wade... Imitated from Horace, 1726. *See* W297.

[**I. 9**] [Ramsay, Allan:] Fy gar rub her o'er wi' strae. An Italian canzone...imitated in braid Scots, [172–.] *See* R53–4.

[**I. 14**] Horace's allegorical advice to the people of Rome... Being an essay on the fourteenth ode of the first book of Horace, [1714/17.] *See* H317.

[Swift, Jonathan:] Horace book I. ode xiv. O navis, referent, &c. Paraphrased and inscribed to Ir——d, 1730. *See* S859.

[**I. 15**] [Welsted, Leonard:] The prophecy, or an imitation of the 15th. ode of the first book of Horace, 1714. *See* W311.

[Tickell, Thomas:] An imitation of the prophecy of Nereus. From Horace book I. ode xv, 1715, 1716. *See* T283–6.

[—] [*idem*] The Scotch prophecy, 1716. *See* T287.

An ode occasion'd by some late successes at sea. Imitated from Horace, 1747. *See* O36.

[**I. 22**] [Hughes, John:] An allusion to Horace, book I. ode xxii, 1715. *See* H372.

[—] An allusion to Horace's Integer vitæ, &c. Book I. ode xxii, 1716. *See* H373.

[**I. 37**] Neale, Thomas: An ode occasion'd by the battle of Ramelies. In imitation of Horace, lib. I. ode 37, 1706. *In* N13.

[**II. 1**] [Swift, Jonathan:] The first ode of the second book of Horace paraphras'd, 1714. *See* S854–5.

[**II. 4**] [Rowe, Nicholas:] Horace, lib. II. ode iv. imitated, [1705/07?] *See* R291.

[**II. 11**] [Pulteney, William, *earl of Bath*:] An ode, imitated from ode xi. book 2d. of Horace, 1745. *See* P1166.

[**II. 16**] Men and measures characterised from Horace. Being an imitation of the xvith ode of his second book, 1739. *See* M168–70.

The sixteenth ode of Horace, book III [for II] imitated, 1741. *See* S484.

[Jenyns, Soame:] An ode to the hon. Philip Y--ke, esq; imitated from Horace lib. II. ode xvi, 1747. *See* J65.

[**III. 1**] The first ode of the third book of Horace, 1745. *See* F148.

[**III. 3**] [Walsh, William:] Horace lib. III. ode iii. imitated, 1706. *See* W33.

[—] [*idem*] To the queen, on her coronation-day, 1706. *See* W34.

[Carthy, Charles:] An ode. In imitation of the third ode of the third book of Horace, [1732.] *See* C56·7.

[—] The third ode, of the third book of Horace, imitated, 1740. *See* C59–60.

[**III. 6**] An ode to the inhabitants of Great-Britain; in imitation of Horace, book III. ode vi, 1747. *See* O70.

[**III. 9**] The ninth ode of the third book of Horace, imitated, [1719.] *See* N304.

A dialogue between the right honourable Sir Robert Walpole, and William Poultney esq; In imitation of Horace's ninth ode, book 3, [1731?] *See* D272.

['**III. 16**'] The sixteenth ode of Horace, book III [for II] imitated, 1741. *See* S484.

[**IV. 1**] Pope, Alexander: Horace his ode to Venus. Lib. IV. ode i, 1737. *See* P896–7.

[Hervey, John, *baron Hervey*:] The false patriot's confession... In imitation of the first ode, of the fourth book of Horace, 1737. *See* H157·2.

[**IV. 2**] [Hyde, Henry, *viscount Cornbury*:] An ode to the Earl of Chesterfield... In imitation of Horace. Ode ii. book IV, 1737. *See* H419.

[**IV. 4**] The fourth ode of the fourth book of Horace, imitated and applied to...the Duke of Cumberland, 1746. *See* F214.

[**IV. 5**] [Needler, Henry:] The fifth ode of the fourth book of Horace imitated: and inscrib'd to the king, 1714. *See* N15.

[Brereton, Jane:] The fifth ode of the fourth book of Horace, imitated: and apply'd to the king. By a lady, 1716. *See* B408.

In imitation of the 5th ode of Horace. Lib, 4, [1716/20?] *See* I21.

The fifth ode of the fourth book of Horace, apply'd to the king on his return from Hanover, 1720. *See* F138–9.

Horace, book IV. ode v. imitated, 1740. *See* H311.

The Jubilade. An ode. In a paraphrastical imitation of the 5th ode of Horace, book IV, 1743. *See* J109.

Free, John: The guardian: an imitation of Horace, ode v. book IV, 1746. *See* F236.

[**IV. 9**] [Somerville, William:] An imitation of the ninth ode of the fourth book of Horace, 1715. *See* S577.

To his excellency John, lord Carteret... An imitation of Horace, ode ix. lib. IV, 1729. *See* T332.

The patriot, an ode...in imitation of the 9th of the 4th book of Horace, 1734. *See* P124.

[**IV. 14**] Cobb, Samuel: The female reign: an ode, alluding to Horace, B.4. od. 14, 1709. *See* C247–8.

Epodes

[3] Mitchell, Joseph: A curse upon punch; in imitation of the third epode of Horace, [1735.] *In* M328.

[4] Horace, epod. IV. imitated, by Sir James Baker, kt, [1717?] *See* B15–16.

[7] Horace turn'd whigg: or, a low-church ode. Horatii epodon septimum imitated, 1710. *See* H315–16.

The invasion, a poem in allusion to the VIIth epode of Horace, 1717. *See* I50.

[**16**] The sixteenth epode of Horace imitated; and addressed to the people of England, 1739. *See* S483.

[Turner, *Sir* Edward:] An imitation of Horace's 16th epode, 1739. *See* T562.

[**17**] [King, William, *principal of St. Mary Hall*:] An ode to Mira, 1730. *See* K71.

[—] Ode to Myra. In imitation of Horace's ode to Canidia. Lib. ep. od. XVII, 1730. *See* K72.

Carmen sæculare

Horneck, Philip: A votive ode for the happy delivery of her royal highness...imitated from the Carmen seculare of Horace, 1716. *See* H322.

Duncombe, William: The Carmen sæculare of Horace. Translated, 1721. *See* D512.

Satires

Francis, Philip: The satires of Horace. In Latin and English, 1746.

Single satires

[**I. 1**] The scrutiny: with the second ode, first satyr, and a short dissertation upon Horace, 1708. *See* S158.

[Minshull, —:] The miser, a poem: from the first satire of the first book of Horace, 1735. *See* M270.

[**I. 2**] [Pope, Alexander:] Sober advice from Horace to the young gentlemen about town. As deliver'd in his second sermon, [1734, 1735,] 1735, 1737. *See* P968–72.

[—] [*idem*] A sermon against adultery: being sober advice from Horace, [1738.] *See* P973.

[**I. 3**] [Smart, Christopher:] The Horatian canons of friendship. Being the third satire of the first book of Horace imitated, 1750. *See* S493–4.

[**I. 3, 4**] [Miller, James:] Seasonable reproof, a satire, in the manner of Horace, 1735, 1736. *See* M258–60.

[**I. 4**] The fourth satire of the first book of Horace, imitated, 1733. *See* F215.

The satirist: in imitation of the fourth satire of the first book of Horace, 1733. *See* S81–2.

[**I. 6**] [Walpole, Edward:] The sixth satire of the first book of Horace imitated, 1738. *See* W30.

[**I. 9**] A dialogue between a secretary of state and a Connaught squier; or, a satyr in imitation of Horace Ibam forte via &c, 1714. *See* D254.

[**II. 1**] Pope, Alexander: The first satire of the second book of Horace, imitated in a dialogue, 1733. *See* P886–92.

A just imitation of the first satire of the second book of Horace, 1733. *See* J116.

The first satire of the second book of Horace, imitated, 1745. *See* F150.

[**II. 1, 2**] Pope, Alexander: The first satire of the second book of Horace... To which is added the second satire, 1734. *See* P893–5.

[**II. 2**] Pope, Alexander: The second satire of the second book of Horace paraphrased, [1734,] 1735. *See* P961–4.

[**II. 5**] [Ogle, George:] Of legacy-hunting. The fifth satire of the second book of Horace imitated, 1737. *See* O101–2.

[**II. 6**] Swift, Jonathan: An imitation of the sixth satire of the second book of Horace, 1738. *See* S860.

Dunkin, William: A translation of the sixth satire of the second book of Horace, 1744. *In* D519.

[**II. 8**] Ogle, George: The miser's feast. The eighth satire of the second book of Horace imitated, 1737. *See* O100.

Epistles – collections

Carthy, Charles: A translation of the second book of Horace's epistles. Together with some of the most select in the first, 1731.

[Melmoth, William:] Two epistles of Horace [I.18 & II.1] imitated, 1736. *See* M165.

Single epistles

[**I. 1**] Ogle, George: Epistles of Horace imitated, 1735. *See* O93.

Pope, Alexander: The first epistle of the first book of Horace imitated, 1737, 1738. *See* P877–80.

Turner, Joseph: The first epistle of the first book of Horace imitated, 1738. *See* T566.

[**I. 2**] Ogle, George: The second epistle of (the first book of) Horace imitated, 1735, 1738. *See* O103–4.

An epistle in verse to a friend, in imitation of the second epistle of the first book of Horace, 1739. *See* E384.

Gilbert, Thomas: The second epistle of the first book of Horace imitated, 1741. *See* G147.

[**I. 3**] Ogle, George: The third epistle of the first book of Horace imitated, 1738. *See* O105.

[**I. 5**] [Swift, Jonathan:] T--l--nd's invitation to Dismal... Imitated from Horace, epist. 5. lib. 1, [1712.] *See* S911–12.

John Dennis, the sheltring poet's invitation to Richard Steele... In imitation of Horace's fifth epistle, lib. I, 1714. *See* J69.

[Sheridan, Thomas:] The invitation in imitation of Horace's epistle to Torquatus, 1720. *See* S407.

Ogle, George: The fifth epistle of the first book of Horace imitated, 1738. *See* O94.

[**I. 6**] Pope, Alexander: The sixth epistle of the first book of Horace imitated, 1737, 1738. *See* P965–7.

Chase, J.: The sixth epistle of the first book of Horace, imitated, 1740. *See* C138.

Horatius Flaccus, Q.

[**I. 7**] [Swift, Jonathan:] Part of the seventh epistle of the first book of Horace imitated, 1713. *See* S891–3.

[—] [*idem*] The seventh epistle…imitated, 1713. *See* S894.

[**I. 8, 9**] Ogle, George: The eighth [and ninth] epistle of the first book of Horace imitated, [1739.] *See* O91.

[**I. 9**] Prior, Matthew: Horace lib. I. epistle the ninth, [1711.] *See* P1078.

[**I. 11**] Ogle, George: The eleventh epistle of the first book of Horace imitated, 1738. *See* O92.

[Pullein, Samuel:] The eleventh epistle of the first book of Horace, imitated, 1749. *See* P1157.

[**I. 12**] Ogle, George: The twelfth epistle of the first book of Horace imitated, [1739.] *See* O106.

[**I. 17**] Diaper, William: An imitation of the seventeenth epistle of the first book of Horace, 1714. *See* D293.

[Savage, John:] Horace to Scaeva. Epist. xvii. book I. imitated, 1730. *See* S88.

[**II. 1**] A translation of Horace's epistle to Augustus, 1730. *See* T440–1.

[Pope, Alexander:] The first epistle of the second book of Horace, imitated, 1737. *See* P881–5.

[—] [*idem*] The second book of the epistles of Horace, imitated, 1737. *See* P882.

[Jenyns, Soame:] Horatii ep. i. lib. II. ad Augustum. The first epistle of the second book of Horace, imitated, 1749. *See* J62.

[**II. 2**] Pope, Alexander: The second epistle of the second book of Horace. Imitated, 1737. *See* P955–60.

[**II. 18**] [Hamilton, William:] The eighteenth epistle of the second book of Horace to Lollius imitated, 1737. *See* H15.

Ars poetica

Dillon, Wentworth, *earl of Roscommon*: Horace: Of the art of poetry: a poem, 1709. *See* D309–10.

— [*idem*] Horace's Art of Poetry. Made English, 1711. *See* D311.

— [*idem*] Q. Horatii Flacci De arte poetica liber, 1733, 1743. *See* D312–14.

Ames, Henry: A new translation of Horace's Art of poetry, attempted in rhyme, 1727. *See* A179–80.

Horace Of the art of poetry, in English numbers, 1735. *See* H313.

Horace Of the art of poetry, translated, [1746.] *See* H314.

Ars poetica – imitations

[King, William, *the gazetteer*:] The art of cookery: a poem. In imitation of Horace's Art of poetry, 1708, [1712.] *See* K55–9.

Horatius Flaccus, Q.

[Bramston, James:] The art of politicks, in imitation of Horace's Art of poetry, 1729, 1731. *See* B383–91.

'Gulliverianus, Martinus': The art of beauing: in imitation of Horace's Art of poetry, 1730. *See* G320.

[Miller, James:] Harlequin-Horace: or the art of modern poetry, 1731, 1735. *See* M251–4.

[Dodsley, Robert:] The art of preaching: in imitation of Horace's Art of poetry, [1738.] *See* D376–80.

Miller, James: The art of life. In imitation of Horace's Art of poetry, 1739. *See* M246–8.

[Morris, Robert:] The art of architecture, a poem. In imitation of Horace's Art of poetry, 1742. *See* M503.

An essay on the theatres: or, the art of acting; a poem. In imitation of Horace's Art of poetry, 1745. *See* E469.

The art of stock-jobbing: a poem, in imitation of Horace's Art of poetry, 1746. *See* A327.

Weeks, James E.: A rhapsody on the stage or, the art of playing. In imitation of Horace, 1746. *See* W274.

Other imitations, apparently of no specific poem

Horace to Fannius, 1734. *In* T474.

[Miller, James:] Seasonable reproof, a satire, in the manner of Horace, 1735, 1736. *See* M258–60.

Pope, Alexander: One thousand seven hundred and thirty eight. A dialogue something like Horace, [1738.] *See* P932–7.

Epidemical madness: a poem in imitation of Horace, 1739. *See* E345.

H319 Horler, Joseph. [dh] Hymn on the nativity; designed for the church. Anno salutis MDCCXXXI. [col] *Sarum, printed for the author*, [1731?]
2°: *A²*; 1–4.
'Descend ye angels, heavenly choir'
DT.

'Horncastle, Aesop.' Volpone disappointed, 1746. *See* V110.

Horneck, Anthony.
Munns, Nathaniel: Horneck's Fire of the altar versified, 1735. *See* M558.

H320 Horneck, Philip. An ode. Inscrib'd to his excellency the Earl of Wharton: lord lieutenant of Ireland. *London, printed for J. Baker; sold by E. Sanger, & E. Curl*, 1709. (*DC* 18 March)
8°: A–B⁴; 1–2 3–14 15–16 blk.
Advertised in *DC* as sold by J. Round, E. Sanger, A. Collins, J. Atkinson, E. Curll, J. Baker.
'May sprightly Venus with her watchful eye'
O,CT(2, 1 – B4).

Horneck, P. An ode

H321 — — *London printed, and sold by H. Hills*, 1709.
8°: A⁸; *1–2* 3–14 *15–16 blk.*
A piracy.
OW,CT,DG,*DrU*,LdU-B; DFo,IU,MH(cropt).

H322 — A votive ode for the happy delivery of her royal highness the Princess of Wales...imitated from the Carmen seculare of Horace. Humbly inscrib'd to her royal highness. By Mr. Horneck. *London, printed in the year* 1716. (*MC* Feb)
2°: A–B²; *1–2* 3–7 *8 blk.*
Listed in *MC* as printed for J. Baker.
'Phœbus! thou radiant honour of the sky'
Wrongly ascribed in the L catalogue to Anthony Horneck.
L(11602.i.15/3).

H323 **Horrid.** The horrid murther committed by Captain Green and his crue, on Captain Drummond and his whole men, under design of friendship by cutting off their heads, and tying them back to back, and throwing them into the sea, and sold their ship unto the Indians. [*Edinburgh*, 1705.]
½°: 1 side, 2 columns.
'Come hearken now unto my song'
Captain Thomas Green was executed in 1705.
L(Rox.III.398).

H324 **Horse.** Horse and away. Being the second part of Boots and sadles [!]. — — Raree-show. [*Dublin*, 1726?]
½°: 1 side, 1 column.
The DT copy is bound with half-sheets of July 1726.
'A quarter-brother barber surgeon'
No edition of *Boots and saddles* has been traced.
DT(title cropt).

H325 — The horse and the flies. A tale. *London, printed by Charles Corbett*, [1746.] (*GM* May)
2°: A² B²; *1–5* 6–8. A1 hft.
'Of spirit high, and matchless might'
A political fable.
L(11631.k.7/2, uncut),O; CtY(2).

H326 — The horse and the monkey. A fable. Humbly inscribed to Mr. C-----s L---s, freeman. *Dublin, printed in the year* 1749.
8°: A⁴; *1–3* 4–8.
'In days of yore, when beasts could speak'
On Charles Lucas's election candidature for the city of Dublin.
L(11631.bb.37),O.

— The horse and the olive, [1713.] *See* Parnell, Thomas.

H327 **Hortensius.** Hortensius sibi constans. [*Dublin*, 1721.]
½°: 1 side, 1 column.
'Ex schismatico fit Hortensius'
An epigram against Josiah Hort's dissenting

Hortensius sibi constans

background, on his being made bishop of Ferns and Leighlin, 1721.
DN.

Hoskins, Edward. Poems on several occasions. Never before printed, 1733. *See* Poems.

H328 **Hostages.** The hostages: an historico-satirical poem. *London, printed for T. Fox*, 1749. (*GM, LM* Jan)
4°: A¹ B² C–D² E¹; *1–4* 5–16. A1 frt.
Vertical chain-lines.
'O fair Britannia! genius of this isle'
Against the peace of Aix-la-Chapelle.
NeL; National Library of Australia.

H329 — [*idem*] The consequence of a late famous treaty concluded at Aix la Chapelle: or, the hostages, a pledge; an historico-satirical poem... The second edition. *London, printed for T. Fox*, 1749. (*BM* Jan)
4°: A¹ B² C–D² E¹; *1–4* 5–16. A1 frt.
Apparently a reimpression or variant title.
Vertical chain-lines.
O.

H330 — The hostages: an historico-satirical poem. *Dublin, printed by James Esdall*, 1748–9.
8°: A⁴ B⁴; *1–4* 5–16. A1 hft.
CtY.

H331 **Houghton.** Houghton hare-hunting. Tune ---- And a begging we will go. [*London?* 1729?]
½°: 1 side, 1 column.
Percival, appendix 21.
'Come all ye gallant knights and 'squires'
A sequel to [Philip Floyd] *Prosperity to Houghton*, [1728?], and [Sir William Yonge] *The Norfolk garland*, [1728?].
L(1876.f.1/112),Rothschild; NN,NjP, Lewis Walpole Library (Horace Walpole's, with ms. notes).

Hounslow. Hounslow-Heath, a poem, 1747–. *See* Wilkes, Wetenhall.

[**Howard, Edward,** *8th earl of Suffolk.*] Miscellanies in prose and verse, by a person of quality. *London printed, and sold by G. Strahan, C. King, & S. Briscoe*, 1725 [1724]. (*MC* Dec)
8°: pp. vii, 264.   O; CtY,NjP.
Watermark: initials.

[—] [fine paper] *London printed, and sold by Jacob Tonson*, 1725.
L.
Watermark: Strasburg bend; probably a cancel title.

[—] [reissue] The second edition, corrected by the author. *London, printed for J. Crockatt*, 1725.
DFo.
There are cancel preliminaries, including errata. The copy seen is bound with *The shepherdess's golden manual*, 1725, which advertises this second edition.

Howard, E., *8th earl*

[—] [*idem*] Musarum deliciæ: containing essays upon pastoral; ideas...sapphick verse... By a nobleman. *London, printed for S. Billingsley, 1728.* 8°: pp. xv, 221.   L,O; CLU-C,ICN.

Howard, Leonard. [dh] The poetical and other works of Dr. Howard. [*London,* 1765?] 4°: pp. 64.   MH.

> Possibly not regularly published in this form; the sheets are used in the following work.

Miscellaneous pieces in prose and verse... To which are added, the letters &c. of...Henry Hatsell...and several tracts, poems, &c... *London, printed in the year 1765.* 4°: 2 vol.   L(vol. 1 only),O(vol. 1 only); ICU, MH.

> The make-up of the volumes is highly irregular.

H332 [—] Greenwich-Park: humbly inscribed to his grace the Duke of Montagu. To which are added, poems, &c. on several occasions. *London, printed for A. Moore, 1728.*
4°: a⁴ A–K⁴ L²; i–viii, *1* 2–83 *84 blk* (23 as '11').
The added poems begin on p. 21.
'Whilst you, my lord, forsake, a while, your seat'
> Howard's authorship is clear from the reprinting of some of these poems in his *Miscellaneous pieces,* 1765. It was also referred to as to be published by subscription within a month in the advertisement for the following work in *DJ* 24 May 1728.

L(78.i.16, in presentation binding to Walpole), O(uncut),LdU-B; ICU.

H333 — 'A poem sacred to the immortal memory of King William III. To which are added, verses on the recovery of...Lord Townshend. Humbly inscribed to...Sir Robert Walpole. [*London*] *Printed for T. Edlin; sold by J. Roberts.* Price 6d.' (*DJ* 24 May 1728)
> The poem to the memory of William III is possibly that by Joseph Stennett (1702) which Howard reprinted in a shortened form in his *Miscellaneous pieces,* 1765, at the request of a friend. The verses on Townshend were reprinted and satirized in the *Craftsman* 15 June 1728; the first line there is:

'Our fears for Townshend now are gladly o'er'

H334 Howard, *Sir* **Robert.** The duel of the stags, a poem... Together with an epistle to the author, by Mr. John Dryden. *London printed, and sold by H. Hills, 1709.*
8°: A⁸; *1–2* 3–16.
> P. 9, last line '...bred'; A3 only signed. The O copy has A3 mis-signed 'A2'. First published 1668, and included here to complete the tally of Hills piracies. The order of these first two editions has not been determined.

'In Windsor forest, before war destroy'd'
O,CT; CSmH,MH.

Howard, *Sir* **R.** The duel of the stags

H335 — [another edition]
> P. 9, last line '...bred'; A2–4 signed.

L(11626.e.33),O(2),CT,E,AdU; IU,OCU,TxU.

H336 — [another edition]
> P. 9, last line '...bread'. Reissued with other remaindered Hills poems in *A collection of the best English poetry,* 1717 (*Case* 294). Reprinted with Pope's *Windsor-Forest* (Dublin, 1713).

L(C.124.b.7/27),LVA-F,O,EU,WcC; CSmH, CtY(2),MH,TxU.

H337 [**Howard, W.**] The good stewards: or, the rewards of benevolence. Humbly presented to the right honourable Peter lord King... *London, printed for the author, 1730.*
4°: π¹ A–C²; i–ii, *1*–11 *12 blk.*
> Probably issued with variant title-pages with alternative dedicatees.

'Such is the course of providence below'
> The copy addressed to Sir Hans Sloane below has a begging letter from W. Howard inserted.

MH.

H338 [—] [reissue] Humbly presented to Sir. Hans Sloane, bart... *London, printed for the author, 1730–31.*
> New title π1.

L(840.h.7/8).

H339 [—] [reissue] Humbly presented to Mr. Howe. *London, printed for the author, 1731.*
> New title π1.

O.

H340 [—] The happy government: or, the constitution of Great Britain. Humbly presented to... *London, printed for the author, 1734.*
4°: π¹ A–C²; i–ii, *1* 2–11 *12 blk.*
> Issued with variant title-pages with alternative dedicatees: 'the honourable Sir Hans Sloane' (L); 'his grace William Bentinck, duke of Portland, &c.' (NNC); 'Richard Coope, esq;' (CtY).

'The pow'r supreme, creator of mankind'
> The L copy is bound with another Howard poem presented to Sloane.

L(C.118.c.2/8); CtY,NNC.

H341 [—] [reissue] Humbly presented to his grace Francis, duke of Buccleugh... *London, printed for the author, 1747.*
> New title π1.

E.

[—] The original of apparel: or, the ornaments of dress, 1732. *See* O244.

H342 — A paraphrase in verse, on part of the first book of Milton's Paradise lost. Humbly presented to... *London, printed for the author, 1738.* (March?)
4°: *A²* B–E²; i–iv, *1*–15 *16 blk.*
> Issued with variant title-pages with alternative dedicatees: 'the honourable the Lady Evelyn' (L); 'the right honourable Lady Jane Scott and Lady Margaret [ms. correction 'Mary'] Scott' (E). Entered in the ledger of Henry

Howard, W. A paraphrase

Woodfall, jun. (*N&Q* I. 12 (1855) 217) to 'Mr. Howard, Poet' under 3 March 1738, 500 copies printed; the Apology is entered on 5 March. Another entry under 13 Jan 1739 records 'Printing three half sheets of quarto poem, no. 500... Title, etc., extra' for him; this work has not been identified. Both were included among bad debts in Dec 1742.
'Of man's first crime, and that forbidden tree'
Apology on A1^v signed (in type) 'W. Howard'.
L(11626.f.12),E.

H343 [—] The universal doom: or, the state of mortality. Humbly presented to...*London, printed for the author*, 1732.
4°: π1 A–C²; *i–ii, 1* 2–12.
Issued with variant title-pages with alternative dedicatees: 'the honourable Sir Hans Sloane' (L); 'the honourable Thomas Hope, esq;' (O); 'the right reverend father in god Thomas Tanner' (O). For other poems issued in this way, see *The beauty and excellence of charity*, [1737?] and *A divine poem on the creation*, 1718.
'Why all mankind to death should subject be'
The Tanner copy at O is accompanied by a letter signed by W. Howard.
L(C.118.c.2/6),O(2).

H344 [—] [reissue] Humbly presented to Edward Bumpstead, esq; *London, printed for the author,* 1733.
New title π1.
E(cropt).

[**H345** = M254·5] **H------r.** The H------r heroes: or, a song of triumph, [1744.] *See* Miller, James.

H346 **H----ss----y.** H------ss----y to Sir C---H----W----s: or, the rural reflection of a Welch poet. *London, printed for A. Moore,* 1746. (*GM* Sept)
2°: *A²* < B²; *1–2* 3–8.
'Stop, stop, my steed! hail Cambria, hail'
Collected in Sir Charles Hanbury Williams, *Works* (1822) I. 167 and accepted by *CBEL*, but almost certainly not by him. The author intended is Edward Hussey. Reprinted in *The foundling hospital for wit* IV (1747) 5; the CtY copy has a ms. attribution to Robert Nugent, earl Nugent.
L(11602.i.14/7),E,DT,*Dr*U-U,LdU-B; CSmH, CtY,MH,OCU,TxU+.

H347 — [another edition, title reads:] H-----ss----y to Sir C---- H---- W-----s...
O,OA; CSmH.

Hubble. The hubble bubbles, [1720.] *See* D'Urfey, Thomas.

H348 **Huddesford, William.** A congratulatory letter written from Oxford to the right honourable Joseph Addison, esq; upon his being appointed one of his majesty's principal secretaries of state. *Oxford, printed at the Theater for E. Whistler*

Huddesford, W. A congratulatory letter

bookseller of Oxford; and are to be sold by J. Knapton, J. Tonson, H. Clements, & W. Smith, London, 1717.
2°: A–C²; *1–2* 3–12.
'While you, great sir, our sovereign's counsels share'
L(1959),O(2),OW; CtY('ex dono authoris'),ICN, InU,MH,TxU(uncut).

H349 — — The second edition. *Oxford, printed at the Theater for E. Whistler bookseller in Oxford; and are to be sold by J. Knapton, J. Tonson, H. Clements, & W. Smith, London,* 1717.
2°: A–C²; *1–2* 3–12.
DFo(uncut).

Hudibras. Hudibras redivivus, 1705–. *See* Ward, Edward.

Hudibrastic. The Hudribrastick [!] brewer, 1714. *See* Ward, Edward.

Hudson, Thomas, *of Blakiston.* Poems on several occasions. In two parts. *Newcastle upon Tyne: printed by I. Thompson and Company,* 1752.
8°: pp. xxiv, 228.   L,O.

H350 [—] A naval panegyric: addressed to his excellency the Earl of Sandwich. *London, printed for M. Sheepey,* 1749. (*GM,LM* Jan)
4°: A–D²; *1–2* 3–16.
Vertical chain-lines.
'Daughter of Doris, whose earth-hidden stream'
Reprinted in Hudson's *Poems,* 1752.
L(1465.i.12/3); CtY.

H351 **Hue.** A hue and cry after a c-----y m---------te. [*Dublin,* 1726?]
½°: 1 side, 1 column.
The DT copy is bound with half-sheets of 1726.
'This alderman in pomp of late'
Signed 'S------ge J----o'. The city magistrate, apparently named 'B----n', went to Spain.
DT; NN.

H352 — A hue and cry after Daniel de Foe, for denying the queen's hereditary right. By Robin-Hog. *London, printed in the year* 1711.
½°: 1 side, 2 columns.
'Now Daniel De-Foe, now run for thy life'
An attack on Defoe, put into the mouth of Robert Stephens, messenger to the press, who pursued seditious libels.
L(1876.f.1/60).

H353 — A huy and cry after George Macartney, who killed his grace the Duke of Hamilton, &c. In Hide-Park, the 15th of November 1712. *Edinburgh, printed by John Moncur,* 1712. (5 Dec)
½°: 1 side, 1 column.

A **hue** and cry after George Macartney

'The worlds pomp, is an ambitious state'
E(ms. date 5 Dec).

H354 — An hue and cry after M----- Y----h's white-horse, who this day stray'd out of the Mews stables, and is now gone over the water... *London, printed for T. Querit, in the Strand*, 1743.
4°: *A²*; *1* 2–4, 2 columns.
The imprint is probably fictitious. Vertical chain-lines.
'Strange! who can call the course their home?'
On George II leaving A. S. M. Wallmoden, countess of Yarmouth, in order to command the allied troops.
MH(uncut).

H355 — A hue and cry, after M—k, late master to a corporation in the city of Dublin. By the author of Namby Pamby. [*Dublin*, 1726?]
½°: 1 side, 2 columns.
The DT copy is bound with half-sheets of 1726.
'A master of late/Ah! hear the sad fate'
The author intended is presumably Henry Carey, but it is not collected in his poems, nor is it reminiscent of his style or subjects.
L(C.121.g.8/77),DT.

— A huy and cry after Sir John Barlycorn, [1725.] *See* Pennecuik, Alexander, *d. 1730*.

H356 — A hue and cry after the eclipse: or, how the sun scorn'd to be Jet-Black. [*Dublin*, 1724?]
½°: 1 side, 1 column.
'Ye wise astronomers that pry'
Related to the satires on Jonathan Smedley as 'Jet Black'.
CtY(imprint cropt).

H357 — A hue and cry after the Letter to the lord-mayor of the city of Dublin. *Dublin, printed by E. Waters*, 1729.
½°: 1 side, 2 columns.
Column 1, 'A letter from a country gentle-mam [!]...', column 2, 'The answer to the letter...'. At foot, 'N.B. That I have taken the above scurvy letter, exactly from Mrs. Hussey, alias Harding's print'.
Letter: 'Of all the sports beneath the sun'
Answer: 'The lordly lion, by mishap'
In defence of Henry Burrowes, the lord mayor, against *A letter from a country gentleman*, 1729.
L(C.121.g.8/171),DN.

H358 — A hue and cry after the Lord B-k, or young Perkin glad to see his friends. *London, printed in the year* 1715.
½°: 1 side, 1 column.
'When guilty consciences do knaves accuse'
An attack on Bolingbroke.
O.

H359 — A hue and cry after the Observator: or; an enquiry after a scandalous fellow that writes it.

A **hue** and cry after the Observator

London, printed in the year 1702. (4 Aug, Luttrell)
½°: *1–2*, 1 column.
'If any good Christian, or pagan, or Jew'
A satire against John Tutchin.
CLU-C,MH(Luttrell).

— The hue and cry after the South-Sea, [1720.] *See* D'Urfey, Thomas (D548).

H360 — Hue and cry after them brewrs[!], who raise their rates on drink. *Dublin, printed* 1725.
½°: 1 side, 1 column.
'Ye injur'd sons of Grubstreet, all combine'
L(C.121.g.8/66).

— Huy and cry for apprehending George Fachney, [1721/22.] *See* Pennecuik, Alexander, *d.1730*.

H361 — The hue and cry, or Ox---ds farewel to Ireland. With his confession and advice to all priest-catchers. [*Dublin?* 1713/14.]
½°: 1 side, 1 column.
'Oh stubborn mobbs that ever did me hate'
Oxenard was a priest-catcher under Thomas, lord Wharton, lord lieutenant of Ireland. Cf. *Oxenard reviv'd*, [172–.]
MH.

H362 — A hue and cry, or the citizens lamentation after the downfall of B— and — bank: together with the lamentations of several honest men, who got daily bread by the late A--------n P-----e, the breaking up of said bank, being the cause of breaking his heart. (Tune, Now ponder well, &c.) [*Dublin*, 1733?]
½°: 1 side, 1 column.
'Now ponder well you merchants all'
A ms. note in the C copy identifies the persons as Samuel Burton, Daniel Falkiner, and Alderman Page. The bank stopped in 1733; cf. H. R. Wagner, *Irish economics, 1700–1783* (1907).
C.

'Huff, Hermanus van.' The mock magistrates: a Dutch tale, written originally in High Dutch, by the exquisite pen of Hermanus van Huff, 1721. *See* Pennecuik, Alexander, *d.1730*.

H363 Huggins, Anthony. To each gentleman soldier in the company of the honourable Paul Ferris, esq; lieut col of the Blue regiment of train'd bands of the city of London... [*London*, 1743/–.]
½°: 1 side, 1 column.
Verses enclosed in emblematic woodcut border.
'Great Britain's warlike arms do loudly ring'
Signed 'Anthony Huggins, marshal'; but possibly written for him. See John Browne and Jacob Hall for similar productions.
MWiW-C.

Hughes, Jabez. Miscellanies in verse and prose. *London, printed by John Watts*, 1737.
8°: pp. 292. L; CtY,IU.

Hughes, Jabez.

— [reissue] Claudian the poet, his elegant history of Rufinus... *London, sold by Jacob Robinson*, 1741. (*LM* April)

    O; CSmH,CtY.

Cancel title.

———————

H364 [—] An ode on the incarnation. *London, printed for John Clark*, 1709. (12 Nov, Luttrell)

2°: A^2 B–D^2; *i–ii*, 1–13 '10'.

Advertised in *DC* 15 Nov.

'Wake all thy fire, cœlestial muse'

    Collected in Hughes's *Miscellanies*, 1737.

InU(Luttrell),MiU,*PU*.

H365 [—] — To which is added The true state of mortality... By T.R. *London, printed for, and sold by H. Hills*, 1709.

8°: A^8 B^4; 1–2 3–23 24. 24 advt.

    The true state of mortality was first published in 1708; T.R. is the author of that alone. Reissued in *A collection of the best English poetry*, 1717 (*Case* 294).

L(C.124.b.7/37),LVA-F,O,EU,LdU-B+; CtY, DFo,ICN,OCU,TxU+.

H366 [—] On November 4. 1712. the anniversary of the birth of his late majesty, King William the third, of glorious memory. [*London*, 1712.]

$\frac{1}{2}$°: 1 side, 1 column.

'As with cherubic hosts and choirs divine'

    Ms. attribution to Hughes in the NjP copy. Reprinted in Hughes's *Miscellanies*, 1737.

L(1850.c.10/29); NjP.

H367 — [*idem*] Verses on November the 4th, the anniversary of the birth of his late majesty King William III. Written in the year 1712. *London, printed for William Hinchliffe*, 1715. (*MC* Dec)

2°: A^2 B^2; *i–iv*, 1 2–4.

    Subsequently advertised in *DC* 4 Nov 1717 and *MC* Nov 1723.

ICN,TxU.

H368 — The rape of Proserpine, from Claudian. In three books. With the story of Sextus and Erichtho from Lucan's Pharsalia, book 6. Translated by Mr. Jabez Hughes. *London, printed by J.D.; sold by Ferd. Burleigh*, 1714. (*MC* June)

8°: A^4 a^2 B–P^4 Q^2; *i–ii* iii–xii, 1–116. 116 err.

'The horrid horses and sulphureous car'

L(11631.bbb.39/6),O; CSmH,ICU.

H369 — [reissue] The second edition. *London, printed by J.D. for J. Osborne, A. Bettesworth & W. Taylor, J. Browne, & J. Graves*, 1716.

8°: π^2 A^4(–A1) a^2 B–P^4 Q^2; [2] *i–ii* iii–xii, 1–116. π1 frt; 116 err.

    Cancel title conjugate with frontispiece.

CT,DT.

H370 — — The second edition, corrected, and enlarg'd with notes. *London, printed for J. Watts; sold by W. Meres*, 1723. (*MC* Dec)

12°: A^6 a^6 B–F^{12} G^6; *i–xxiv*, 1 2–92 *93–132*. A1 frt.

L(1067.e.6/1); CtY,DFo.

H371 — Verses occasion'd by reading Mr. Dryden's Fables. Inscrib'd to his grace the Duke of Buckinghamshire. *London, printed for John Watts*, 1721. (*PB* 28 Feb, 'just publish'd')

2°: A^2 B–C^2; *i–iv*, 1 2–8.

'Our great fore-fathers in poetic song'

O(2); *CLU-C*,CtY,*ICN*,MH(Luttrell, March), TxU.

Hughes, John. Poems on several occasions. With some select essays in prose... *London, printed for J. Tonson & J. Watts*, 1735. (*LM* May)

12°: 2 vol.   L,O; CtY,MH.

    No watermark. List of 'subscribers to the royal paper'.

— [fine paper]   LVA-D.

    Watermark: Strasburg bend.

———————

H372 [—] An allusion to Horace, book I. ode XXII. *London printed, and sold by R. Burleigh*, 1715. (*MC* Oct)

$\frac{1}{2}$°: 1–2, 1 column.

'The man that loves his king and nation'

    Printed in Hughes's *Poems*, 1735, 'Printed at the breaking out of the rebellion, in the year 1715'. On loyalty to King George.

Herts CRO (Panshanger box 46).

H373 [—] [*idem*] An allusion to Horace's Integer vitæ &c. Book I. ode XXII. *London printed, and sold by R. Burleigh*, 1716 [1715?].

$\frac{1}{2}$°: 1–2, 1 column.

L(C.121.g.8/8).

H374 — The ecstasy. An ode. *London printed, and sold by J. Roberts*, 1720. (*PB* 17 May)

2°: A^2 B–C^2; *i–iv*, 1 2–8.

    The Luttrell copy, dated May, is in the possession of H. B. Forster.

'I leave mortality's low sphere'

L(162.n.12),O(2),LdU-B; CSmH,CtY,ICN,MH, TxU(2)+.

H375 — The house of Nassau. A pindarick ode. *London, printed for D. Brown, & A. Bell*, 1702. (1 June, Luttrell)

2°: A–D^2; *i–iv*, 1–12.

    Listed in *WL* June.

'Goddess of numbers, and of thoughts sublime!'

L(11641.h.10/9),LDW,O,LdU-B,*MR-C*; CLU-C,CtY,ICU(uncut),MH(Luttrell),TxU+.

H376 [—] An hymn, to be sung by the work-house children. [*London*, 1714.]

$\frac{1}{2}$°: 1 side, 1 column.

'Hear us, O god! this joyful day'

    Printed in Hughes's *Poems*, 1735, as 'Hymn. Sung by the children of Christ's Hospital, at the entry of King George into London, 1714'.

Crawford.

Hughes, John. An ode

H377 — An ode for the birth-day of her royal highness the Princess of Wales, St. David's day, the first of March, 171⅚. Set to musick by Dr. J. C. Pepusch ... *London, printed for Jacob Tonson, 1716. (MC April)*
4°: *A*⁴ B²; *1–7* 8–12. A1 hft.
    Watermark: post-horn on shield.
'To joy, to triumphs dedicate the day!'
AN; CtY,DFo,DLC(presentation copy).

H378 — [fine paper]
    Watermark: fleur-de-lys.
L(161.1.62).

H379 [—] [*idem*] An ode for the second of March next (St. David's day being on a Sunday)...the societies of Ancient Britons, established in honour to her royal highness's birth-day... By Dr. J. C. Pepusch. Set to musick by himself. [*London? 1719?*]
4°: *A*⁴; *1–3* 4–8.
    The same text as the preceding, apparently ascribed to Pepusch in error.
MR; DFo.

H380 — An ode in praise of musick, set for variety of voices and instruments by Mr. Philip Hart... *London, printed for B. Lintot; sold by J. Nutt, 1703. (DC 23 Feb)*
4°: *A*² B–D²; *i–iv,* 1–11 *12 blk.* A1 hft.
    Watermark: Amsterdam arms. Printed in advance of the performance of 3 March.
'Awake, celestial harmony!'
L(840.h.4/6),C; DFo(−A1),DLC,MH.

H381 — [fine paper]
    Watermark: star.
National Library of Australia, Canberra.

H382 [—] An ode to the creator of the world. Occasion'd by the fragments of Orpheus. *London, printed for J. Tonson, 1713 [1712]. (PB 27 Nov)*
2°: *A*² B–C²; *i–iv,* 1–8.
    No watermark. Entered in *SR* 27 Nov 1712; deposit copies at L,LSC(? this and second edition),O,EU,AdU.
'O muse unfeign'd! O true cælestial fire'
    Reprinted in Hughes's *Poems, 1735.*
L(643.1.26/8; 163.n.37),O(uncut),EU,AdU, LdU-B+; CSmH,CtY,ICU,MH,TxU(2)+.

H383 [—] [fine paper]
    Watermark: O.
OC,LdU-B.

H384 [—] — The second edition. *London, printed for J. Tonson, 1713 [1712]. (DC 20 Dec)*
2°: *A*² B–C²; *i–iv,* 1–8.
    A copy at LSC is bound with pamphlets deposited at Stationers' Hall.
L(11588.h.2),O,C,EU,DT+; CtY,*RPB*.

Hugo, Hermann.
Arwaker, Edmund: Pia desideria: or, divine addresses...Englished by Edm. Arwaker, 1702, 1712.

Hugo, H.

— Divine entertainments: in English and Latin. Selected...and translated by...Edmund Arwaker, [1727?]

Gent, Thomas: Divine entertainments: or, penitential desires, sighs and groans of the wounded soul [based on Hugo], 1724.

H385 **Hullin,** —, *Mr.* Discours chrêtien contre les impies, à Monsieur *****. *A Londres, par J. Delage, 1704.*
4°: *A*² B–G² H¹; *1–2* 3–29 *30 blk.*
    An Amsterdam edition of 1704 is in the Bibliothèque nationale, Paris.
'Alcipe, il est un dieu. Son pouvoir fit le monde'
L(1073.i.27).

H386 — Ode, sur les glorieux succés de monseigneur le Duc de Marlborough en Allemagne. *A Londres, par J. Delage, 1705.*
2°: *A*¹ B–C²; *1–2* 3–10.
'Dans les soudains transports que m'inspire ta gloire'
LLP.

Human. Human happiness, 1721. *See* Jacob, Giles.

H387 — Human passions: a satyr. To which is added, an ode to impudence. *London, printed for J. Roberts; sold by the booksellers of London & Westminster, 1726. (MC May)*
2°: *A*¹ B–C² D¹; *i–ii,* 1 2–10.
'Is this, O man, thy boasted excellence?'
Ode: 'Goddess, whom antient Athens knew'
L(11657.m.21),O,AdU; CtY,MH,OCU,TxU.

H388 — Human wisdom displayed: or, a guide to prudence and virtue. In two parts. I. Containing, The portrait of a just and honourable man, a poem, written originally in French, by the Archbishop of Cambray...II. A fragment on tranquillity of mind, from Pythagoras... By an old gentleman, of Gray's Inn, lately retired to a country-life. *London, printed for Thomas Corbett, 1731. (MChr May)*
8°: *A*² a–b⁴ B–F⁴; [4] i–xiv *xv–xvi blk,* 1 2–40. A1 hft.
    The second part is in prose.
'The being that's omnipotent, and said'
L(722.f.6/1).

Humble. The humble address of the muses to his majesty, 1701. *See* Tate, Nahum.

H389 — The humble address of the quakers in Scotland, to his majesty King George. [*Edinburgh, 1714/15.*]
½°: 1 side, 1 column.
'O king live thou for ever, and assure'
E.

H390 — The humble address of the wine-merchants, brewers, bakers, butchers, &c. of the city of York, to their worthy patrons, Hippocrates Obstetricus... and the worshipful Pharmacopola Caducifer Algebraicus. [*York? 1745/–.*]
slip: 1 side, 1 column.

The **humble** address of the wine-merchants

'Hail! doughty chiefs, great props of trade'
Against their sponsorship of a rich election candidate.
L(1875.b.35/3).

H391 — The hnmble [!] address of the wives of the bow, to his majeity [!] King George, their thanks for his majestys gracious answer, to the ministers address. [*Edinburgh*, 1714/15.]
½°: 1 side, 2 columns.
'Altho not common for our sex'
Against the Jacobites.
E(mutilated).

— A humble address to his majesty, from the Orford man of war, [1727.] *See* The saylors address, 1727.

H392 — An humble address, to the right reverend and honourable general assembly anent catching of foxes. [*Edinburgh*] *Printed by Margaret Reid, at the foot of the Horse Wyend*, [171–.]
½°: 1 side, 1 column.
'Pray, catch the foxes, cubs of lesser size'
Encouraging the assembly to defend the tender vines of the church from intruders.
E.

H393 — A humble advice to the loyal Scots and English. To the tune of, Old long syne. [*Edinburgh*, 1746.]
½°: 1 side, 2 columns.
'All British men that's loyalists'
Probably by the same author as *The original and conduct of the Young Pretender*, [1746], which it closely resembles.
AdU.

H394 — The humble petition of a beautiful young lady. To the reverend Doctor B---rkl---y. [*Dublin*, 1725?]
½°: 1 side, 1 column.
The O copy contains variants which are apparently later than the readings in CSmH.
'Dear doctor, here comes a young virgin untainted'
A witty mock request to accompany George Berkeley to his college in the Bermudas for which a charter was granted in 1725. Answered by Samuel Owens, *Remarks on the young ladies petition*, [1725?].
O,DT; CSmH.

H395 — — [*Dublin*, 1725?]
½°: 1 side, 1 column.
Below, 'The rvnd. Dr. B—rkl--y's answer to the young ladies petition'.
Answer: 'Dear miss, I thank you for your kind surrender'
L(C.121.g.8/86).

H396 — The humble petition of his grace Ph—p d. of Wh—n to a great man. *London, printed for A. Brooks, near St. Paul's*, 1730.
8°: A⁴ B² (A2 as 'B2'); *1-3* 4-12.
Horizontal chain-lines.
'Sir, may it please you but to hear'

The **humble** petition of his grace

A satire on Philip duke of Wharton, addressing Walpole.
O.

H397 — The humble petition of his grace P---p d. of W---n to the right hon. Sir R----t W-----e. *London printed: and Dublin: re-printed*, 1730.
8°: A⁴; *1-3* 4-8.
DK(2),DN,DT(2).

Humorous. The humorous miscellany; or, riddles for the beaux, 1733. *See* Boyd, Elizabeth.

— Humorous reflections of an antient Briton. [173–?] *See* The Welchman-s last will and testament, 1719-.

H398 Humours. The humours of a country election... To which are added the following songs... *London, printed for J. Roberts*, 1734. (GM, LM June)
8°: A⁴ B-E⁴; *1-4* 5-40. A1 frt.
The collation of the preliminaries is tentative. Treated as a miscellany in *Case* 392.
'At the time of the year when the citizens wives'
L(1971),O; MH,TxU.

H399 — — *London, printed for J. Roberts*, 1741.
8°: (frt+) A(3 ll) B-E⁴; *1-4* 5-40.
Another edition, with similarly puzzling preliminaries.
L(11633.bb.23),LG.

— The humours of New Tunbridge Wells at Islington, 1734. *See* Drake, James.

— The humours of the Black-dog, 1737. *See* Wilkes, Wetenhall.

— The humours of the Fleet, 1749. *See* Paget, William.

H400 — The humours of the present Irish clowns. A pastoral. Inscribed to George Jones, esquire. *Dublin, printed [by James Hoey] in the year* 1738.
8°: A⁴; *1-3* 4-8.
'Here will I sport a while on native plains'
A pastoral dialogue between Murtagh and Laughlin.
C.

Humphreys, Samuel. Tales and novels in verse. From the French of La Fontaine. By several hands. Published and compleated by Samuel Humphreys... *London, printed in the year* 1735.
8°: pp. xii, vii, 252.   L,O; CtY,ICN.
Five of the fourteen tales translated by Humphreys; the others by Cobb, Congreve, Fenton, Prior, etc. The agreement between Humphreys and Curll at L (Add. MS. 38728, fol. 121) is dated 6 Sept 1734 and promises the translator two guineas for each sheet of the French. A receipt for these five tales is dated 21 Dec 1734.

Humphreys, S.

H401 — The amorous groom, and the gossips wager: two novels from Boccace. *Dublin, printed by S. Powell, for William Heatly, 1735.*
8°: A–C⁴; *1–3* 4–24.
'A king in youthfull charms array'd'
'Three dames, when wine, at a collation'
CtY.

H402 — Cannons. A poem. Inscrib'd to his grace the Duke of Chandos. *London printed, and sold by J. Roberts, 1728.*
2°: *A*¹ B–F² G¹; *i–ii, 1* 2–21 *22 blk.*
'Whilst you, my lord, acquire a deathless name'
L(643.m.12/39),O; CSmH,CtY,KU,TxU.

H403 — A congratulatory poem, humbly address'd to his royal highness Frederick, prince of Wales, upon his arrival in Great Britain. *London, printed for B. Creake; sold by J. Roberts, 1729.* (*MChr* 15 Jan)
2°: *A*¹ B–C²; *1–3* 4–9 *10 blk.* 9 advt.
'Since heav'n propitious to our isle has sent'
L(1972),OW.

H404 — Malpasia. A poem, sacred to the memory of the right honourable the Lady Malpas. *London, printed for John Watts, 1732.* (*GSJ* 14 Jan)
4°: A–C²; *1–5* 6–11 *12 blk.* A1 hft.
'When heav'n has once with rich profusion join'd'
L(642.1.28/2).

H405 Hundred. [dh] An hundred godly lessons, that a mother on her death-bed gave to her children... To the tune of, Wigmore's galliard. [col] *Edinburgh, printed by William Adam's junior, 1715.*
8°: A⁴; *1* 2–8.
'My children dear, mark well my words'
L(11623.aa.19).

H406 Hunter. The hunter hunted; or, entertainment upon entertainment. A new ballad. To an old tune — — God prosper long, &c. *London, printed for the author, 1728.* (16 Dec?)
2°: *A*² *B*¹; *1–2* 3–6, 2 columns.
Percival appendix 15. Horizontal chain-lines.
'Come all you sportsmen far and near'
A satire on Walpole, relating to his hunting at Houghton.
L(1875.d.6/32; Burney 267, uncut, ms. date 16 Dec),O(2, 1 lacks A1); CtY,*MB.*

H407 Hunter, John. The wanderer and traveller. In form of a dramatick composition. *Glasgow, printed in the year 1733.*
8°: A–N⁴; *i–ii* iii–ix *x,* 1–94.
'Who's this I see,/That walks so sad'
Dedication signed. Attributed to John Wallace (another minister at Ayr) by *Halkett & Laing,* but with no authority given; the dedication is quite unambiguously by the author. A religious work in dialogue form.
SaU.

Hunter, R.

H408 Hunter, Robert. Θρηνος ἐπικηδειος ἐπι τω θανατω του πανυ Καδκαρτος... Questus funebris in obitum summi viri Cathcartis... Qui obiit... Jan. 1740. Idem latino carmine redditus. *Edinburgi, apud T. W. & T. Ruddimannos, 1741.*
8°: π¹ A⁸ B⁴(–B4); *i–ii, 1* 2–22.
'Ἀιαζω τον ἀρειον ὁλωλοτα ὠλετο Καδκαρς'
'Lamentor Mavortium peremptum: periit Cathcars'
'Ploro, musa, viri casum: cadis inclite Cathcars!'
There appears to be an error in the title: Charles, baron Cathcart died in Dec 1740.
E.

H409 Hunting. The hunting after money. *London printed, and sold by Edward Midwinter,* [1709.] (27 Aug, Luttrell)
1°: 1 side, 3 columns.
Large engraving at head, signed 'Cross sculpsit'. The style of the costumes suggests a seventeenth-century plate, presumably by Thomas Cross the elder, now re-used.
'When the bright world was fram'd, and all things plac'd'
On money 'the glittering source, whence all our evils spring'.
MH(Luttrell).

H410 — The hunting of the stag: a poem. *London, printed for J. Wilford,* [1731.] (*GSJ* 16 Sept)
2°: *A*² *B*²; *1–2* 3–8.
'Tho' Homer in heroic sings'
An attack on Walpole.
CSmH,OCU.

H411 — [*idem*] The knave of trumps fell into the dumps: Caleb turn'd physician, or a new receipt for the gripes. *London, 'printed for uhe* [!] *auther* [!] *of the Craftsman',* [1731?]
½°: 1 side, 2 columns.
Apparently a piratical reprint.
L(C.116.i.4/58).

H412 Hurst, B. 'A poem to Florinda singing, written by Mr. B. Hurst at Tunbridge. *Sold by the booksellers at Tunbridge.* Price 2d.' (*DC* 26 Aug 1706)
Subsequently (e.g. *DC* 14 Nov 1706) listed with [Richard Daniel] *The British warrior* as 'sold by B. Bragg'.

H413 Husband. The husband, a poem. Expressed in a compleat man. *London printed, and sold by H. Hills, 1710.*
8°: A⁸; *1–2* 3–16.
Originally published in 1614, *STC* 14008. Reissued with other Hills poems in *A collection of the best English poetry,* 1717 (*Case* 294).
'Life was inspir'd, the first life was divine'
L(11631.bb.40; C.124.b.7/50),O,CT,AdU, LdU-B+; CSmH,CtY,ICN,MH(2),TxU+.

Husbandmen

H414 Husbandmen. The husbandmens humble petition, to both houses of parliament. *London, printed in the year* 1711.
½°: 1 side, 1 column.
'We that farm your honours ground'
That taxation should be levied on corrupt placemen.
Crawford; MH,PU,*Harding.*

H415 — — or, the country-men's observations on those grand cheats put upon her majesty and government. [*London,* 1711.]
½°: 1 side, 2 columns.
InU.

H416 — The husband-man's petition (and the country-man's wish) to both houses of parliament. *London, printed in the year* 1711. (May?)
½°: 1 side, 2 columns.
In column 2, 'The country-man's wish for the present parliament'.
Wish: 'When rogues of all sorts are thus fairly discarded'
O(ms. date May),Crawford,Rothschild.

Huy. *See* Hue.

H417 Huy, Alexander. A new-year's gift, being a divine poem. Humbly address'd to...William Conolly, esq;...*Dublin, printed for the author, by Christopher Dickson,* 1729–30.
8°: *A*⁴; *1–4* 5–7 *8 blk.*
'The Christian world's redeemer blest we see'
O.

'Hybernicus.' Apollo: or a poetical definition of the three sister-arts, 1729. *See* Apollo.

Hyde, Edward, *earl of Clarendon.*
[Ward, Edward:] The history of the grand rebellion... Digested into verse [3 vol.], 1713, 1715. *See* W80–1.

H418 [Hyde, Henry, *viscount Cornbury.*] The judgment of the muse: or, advice to the people. A poem. Occasioned by some late writings. *London, printed for T. Cooper,* 1742. (*GM* Oct)
2°: *A*¹ B² C¹; *1–2* 3–8.
A1 and C1 have been seen to be conjugate.
'How few with serious joy behold the train'
Early ms. attribution in the IU copy to Lord Cornbury. In praise of Pulteney.
O; CtY,DFo,IU(uncut),*MH,*TxU.

H419 [—] An ode to the Earl of Chesterfield, imploring his majesty's return. In imitation of Horace. Ode II. book IV. *London, printed for T. Cooper,* 1737. (*LM* Jan)
2°: *A*² B–C²; *1–5* 6–11 *12 blk.* A1 hft.
Rothschild 214.
'For me how vain to urge my vent'rous flight'
Early ms. attribution in the CtY copy to Lord Cornbury.

Hyde, H., *viscount Cornbury.* An ode
L(840.m.1/30, −A1),O,LdU-B; CSmH,CtY, ICU,OCU(−A1),TxU+.

Hye. *See* Hi.

H420 Hymenaeus. Hymenæus, a poem. *London, printed by Benj. Motte; sold by John Morphew,* 1707. (11 Aug, Luttrell)
2°: A–D²; *1–2* 3–16.
The Luttrell copy is recorded in *Haslewood;* advertised in *LG* 14 Aug.
'If love and beauty can inspire the tongue'
LVA-F,DT,LdU-B; MB.

Hymn. A hymn at the sacrament, [1744/45.] *See* Wesley, Charles.

H421 — A hymn, fit to be sung on days of humiliation and prayer. [*Glasgow, Foulis Press,* 174–?]
½°: 1 side, 1 column.
Gaskell, Foulis 706.
'When Abrah'm, full of sacred awe'
L(11602.i.5/7, imprint cropt).

H422 — A hymn for Christmas. *London printed, and sold by J. Nutt, & Mrs. Bond next door to Old Man's coffee-house at Charing-Cross,* [170–?]
½°: 1 side, 2 columns.
'Arise my soul, and put on strength'
MC.

— A hymn for Christmas day, 1743. *See* Wesley, Charles.

H423 — An hymn for the charity-schools, to be sung on Thursday in Whitsun-week, to a psalm tune. *London printed, and sold by Joseph Downing,* 1709.
½°: 1 side, 1 column.
Watermark: fleur-de-lys on shield; possibly a fine-paper copy.
'To thee, O father of mankind'
L(1855.c.4/23).

— Hymn for the condemned prisoners, 1742. *See* Wesley, Charles.

H424 — 'A hymn for the use of the m—d—n b—ds. [*London*] Cooper. Price 6*d.*' (*BM* June 1748)

H425 — A hymn of thanksgiving for his m—-y's return to St. J——s's; a recital of the marvellous things perform'd abroad... *London, printed for A. Type, near Cheapside; sold at the pamphlet-shops in London and (especially) Westminster,* 1750. (*LM* Nov)
4°: A–C²; *1–2* 3–12.
The imprint is probably fictitious.
'What thanks to thee, supreme above'
A political satire on foreign policy.
DT; IU,OCU,TxU.

H426 — A hymn on the sufferings and death of our blessed lord and saviour, Jesus Christ... *Edinburgh, printed by Alexander Alison; sold by Robert Henderson bookseller in Coupar of Fife,* 1735.
8°: A–C⁴; *i–ii* iii–vi, 7–24.
'Of heav'ns and earth O blessed be/the supreme lord and head'

A **hymn** on the sufferings

> The introductory poem, 'The publisher to the reader' is signed 'Robert Henderson'; he may also be the author.
> L(3436.d.14),E.

H427 — A hymn preparatory to some electors, to be sung at the Scotch ambassadors on the Comb, to the tune of Old Noll. [*Edinburgh*, 1713.]
½º: 1 side, 1 column.

> On the other side of the copy seen, *A strange and wonderful relation...29th of September, 1713*, in prose, signed 'J. Maclatchy.
> 'Great Beelzebub, patron of whiggs'
> An Edinburgh election ballad.
> Crawford.

H428 — A hymn to Alderman Parsons our lord-mayor. [*London*, 1730?]
½º: 1 side, 2 columns.

> *Percival* LX. Rough woodcut portrait at head.
> 'Come loyal churchmen'
> On the election of Humphrey Parsons. Usually dated 1740, his second term of office; but 1730 seems more appropriate.
> L(1872.a.1/177).

No attempt has been made to identify the authors of the following charity-school hymns, since it seems desirable that they should stand together. Only a very small proportion of the total output survives. The Bowyer ledgers record the regular printing of hymns for charity children at St. Andrew's Holborn (1735–1748, 2000 copies twice a year, sometimes with 100 fine copies), St. Dunstan's (1724–1744, 1000 copies and 500 fine once a year), St. George's Chapel (1710–1744, 500 copies twice a year), and St. John's Chapel (1740–1749, 1000 copies once a year). There are other occasional printings, such as for St. Anne's Kew Green, for Chelmsford, and for Writtle in Essex. Similarly Ackers's ledger records printing hymns for the charity children of Clerkenwell (1744–1747, 600 copies twice a year).

H429 — A hymn to be sung at the anniversary-meeting of the charity-schools, on Thursday in Whitson-week, 1710. To a psalm-tune. *London, printed by Joseph Downing*, 1710.
½º: 1 side, 1 column.

> There is some movement of type between copies, but they are apparently all from the same setting.
> 'On this returning happy day'
> L(Cup.645.e.1/35),MC(ms. statistics on verso); MH.

H430 — A hymn to be sung at the anniversary-meeting of the charity schools, on Thursday in Whitson-week, 1711. To a psalm tune. *London, printed by Joseph Downing*, 1711.
½º: 1 side, 1 column.

> The third stanza, titled 'Chorus', is in roman type.

A **hymn** to be sung

> 'When to the temple we repair'
> L(1855.c.4/26).

H431 — [variant]
> The third stanza is in italic type.
> MC,Crawford; CtY.

H432 — An hymn, to be sung by charity-children in St. Bride's church, on Sunday the 10th of February, 1711, at the opening of a charity-school in the said parish... [*London*, 1712.]
½º: 1 side, 1 column.
'Lift up your heads, ye lofty gates'
MC.

H433 — A hymn to be sung by the charity boys and girls belonging to the ward of Farringdon within. At the parish-church of ___ on Sunday, the ___. [*London*, 171–?]
½º: 1 side, 1 column.

> Two small woodcuts at head. Clearly intended for use on successive occasions.
> 'Lift up your heads, ye lofty gates'
> MC.

H434 — Hymn, to be sung by the charity-boys of St. George's chapel in Ormond-street, upon the fourth Sunday in Advent; being Christmas-eve, 1710. When there will be publick collections for the said school. To a psalm tune. [*London*, 1710.]
½º: 1 side, 1 column.
'The day draws near, the joyful day'
MC(ms. note on verso).

H435 — An hymn, to be sung by the charity-boys of the society of St. Anns, Aldersgate, ___ at the parish church of ___ on Sunday the ___ of ___ 171 . [*London*] *Cut and printed by J. Cluer, in Bow Church-yard, printer and engraver on wood, &c.* [171–.]
½º: 1 side, 1 column.

> Large woodcut at head. Clearly intended for use on successive occasions. The CSmH copy is completed in ms. for 1713.
> 'Triumphal notes and hymns of joy'
> CSmH.

H436 — An hymn to be sung by the charity-children at Bath, upon the 7th of July, 1713. The thanksgiving-day for the peace. Being the words appointed to be sung by above four thousand charity-children at London, on the same day, as her majesty goes to, and returns from St. Paul's cathedral. [1713.]
½º: 1 side, 1 column.

> The minutes of the SPCK record that John Leason of Bath acknowledged receipt of a copy of this hymn on 29 June. One would expect this to be a Bath reprint, but the typography resembles that of Joseph Downing, the printer to the SPCK. Compare *A poem on the peace, sung by the children of the charity schools in Bath*, [1713.] Reprinted in H473.
> 'Lord, give the queen thy saving health'
> MH.

An **hymn** to be sung

H437 — An hymn, to be sung by the charity-children belonging to the ward of Farrindon within, at the parish-church of St. Martin's Ludgate. On Sunday the 29th of May, 1715... [*London*, 1715.]
$\frac{1}{2}$°: 1 side, 1 column.
'How sweet, how charming is this place'
LG.

H438 — A hymn to be sung by the charity children of Popler and Blackwall. In Popler chappel: on Sunday May the 10th 1713... To a psalm tune. [*London*, 1713.]
$\frac{1}{2}$°: 1 side, 1 column.
Two small woodcuts at head.
'To thee, O Lord, our god and king'
MC.

H439 — A hymn to be sung by the charity children of Popler. In Popler chappel: on Sunday February the 8th 1713... To a psalm tune. [*London*, 1713.]
$\frac{1}{2}$°: 1 side, 1 column.
Two small woodcuts at head.
'Let the approaching holy time'
E,MC.

H440 — An hymn to be sung by the charity-children, of St. Andrew's parish, on Sunday the 24th of this instant, April 1726. [*Dublin*, 1726.]
$\frac{1}{4}$°: 1 side, 1 column.
'Happy the man, whose tender care'
DT.

H441 — An hymn to be sung by the charity-children of St. Brides, on Sunday the 17th of Jan. 1713... [*London*, 1714.]
$\frac{1}{2}$°: 1 side, 1 column.
'Ascribe to god most solemn praise'
MH.

H442 — An hymn, to be sung by the charity-children of St. Brides, on Sunday the 13th day of June, 1714. To a psalm tune. [*London*, 1714.]
$\frac{1}{2}$°: 1 side, 1 column.
'What tribute to thy temple, Lord'
MH.

H443 — A hymn to be sung by the charity children of St. Dunstan's in the west, on Sunday the 17th of February, 17$\frac{11}{12}$. To a psalm tune. [*London*, 1712.]
$\frac{1}{2}$°: 1 side, 1 column.
Ms. note in the MC copy, 'There were 1500 of these given away'.
'Father of lights! to thee, from whom'
MC.

H444 — An hymn to be sung by the charity children of St. George the martyr, at the parish church of St. Clement Eastcheap, on Sunday the 30th of May, 1714... [*London, printed by J. Cluer, 1714.*]
$\frac{1}{2}$°: 1 side, 1 column.
Large wooduct of Cluer's at head.
'To thee, O father of mankind'
L(11602.i.12/18).

An **hymn** to be sung

H445 — An hymn to be sung by the charity-children of St. Giles Cripplegate without, on Sunday the 7th of December, 1712, at the parish-church of St. Clement Eastcheap... [*London*, 1712.]
$\frac{1}{4}$°: 1 side, 1 column.
'To god, the world's great patron, first'
MC(two further verses in ms.).

H446 — An hymn to be sung by the charity children of St. James Clerkenwell, at St. Brides-church in Fleet-street, on Sunday, November 11, 1711... [*London*, 1711.]
$\frac{1}{2}$°: 1 side, 1 column.
'To Jacob god commandment gave'
CSmH.

H447 — An hymn to be sung by the charity-children of the parish of St. Bride's, on Sunday the 14th of December 1712... [*London*, 1712.],
$\frac{1}{2}$°: 1 side, 1 column.
'While shepherds watch'd their flocks by night'
The hymn is by Nahum Tate.
MH.

H448 — An hymn, to be sung by the charity-children of the parish of St. Brides, on Sunday the 25th of March 1716... [*London*, 1716.]
$\frac{1}{2}$°: 1 side, 1 column.
'Thro' all the changing scenes of life'
From Tate & Brady's *Psalter*.
MH.

H449 — An hymn to be sung by the charity-children when his majesty King George makes his entry into the city of London: being the first six verses of the twenty first psalm. From the version of the honourable Sir John Denham... [*London*, 1714.]
$\frac{1}{2}$°: 1 side, 1 column.
'The king whom thy support has blest'
Crawford.

— An hymn to be sung by the work-house children, [1714.] *See* Hughes, John.

H450 — A hymn, to be sung in Poplar chappel, on Sunday April the 29th, 1711. At the first opening of a charity school for 30 boys, and 20 girls. To a psalm tune. [*London*, 1711.]
$\frac{1}{2}$°: 1 side, 1 column.
'To thee, O father of mankind'
MC.

H451 — A hymn, to be sung on the thanksgiving day. Before sermon. After sermon. *London, printed for J. Roberts, J. Harrison, & A. Dodd*, 1715.
$\frac{1}{2}$°: 1 side, 2 columns.
Each column contains a separate hymn, the first verse set to music.
Before: 'Come Britons rejoice, indulge holy mirth'
After: 'In lofty strains, ye grateful Britons sing'
Ms. note in the PPL copy 'This was sung in some dissenting meetings & made by a dissenting minister as I hear'. For the thanksgiving day, 20 Jan 1715.
PPL(title cropt).

An **hymn,** to be sung

H451·2 —— *Bristol, printed by W. Bonny,* [1715.]
½⁰: 1 side, 2 columns.
   No music.
L(Rox.III.881).

— A hymn to confinement, 1705. *See* Pittis, William.

H452 — An hymn to god. *London, printed for R. Dodsley; sold by M. Cooper,* 1746. (*GA* 30 March)
4⁰: *A*⁴ B–C⁴ D²; *i–v* vi–xii, *13* 14–26 *27*; *28 blk.*
A1 hft.
'Broke from its charge, my genius flies'
L(11630.c.9/12),O,CT,*MR*; CSmH,CU,IU,*NN*, NjP.

— A hymn to harmony, 1729. *See* Jortin, John.

— An hymn to liberty, 1746. *See* Cooke, Thomas.

H453 — A hymn to money. A satyr. *London printed, and are to be sold by S. Malthus,* 1704. (15 Dec, Luttrell)
8⁰: *A*² B–G²; *i–viii,* *1–19 20 blk.* A1 hft; *12 advt.*
   Pp. 13–19 contain an added 'Postscript by way of advice . . .' Advertised as 'just publish'd' in *DC* 22 Dec.
'Where is't thou darling of the world'
   Dedication signed 'Anonymus'.
L(164.l.13, Luttrell),DT(–A1); DFo,TxU(–A1).

— A hymn to Neptune, 1705. *See* Pittis, William.

— A hymn to peace, 1706–. *See* Defoe, Daniel.

H454 — A hymn to St. Tack, sung at the election of the new vice-chancellour of Oxford. [*London*] *Printed for J. Morphew,* 1706. (*DC* 30 Oct)
½⁰: *1–2,* 1 column.
'Hail thou resplendent source of high-church light!'
   A satire on tory high-churchmen.
O(2),DG(cropt),MC; TxU.

H455 — A hymn to the birth-day. [*London?* 1728?]
½⁰: 1 side, 2 columns.
   Rough woodcut portrait at head.
'Come all you loyal Welchmen'
   Addressed to the Welsh on Queen Caroline's birthday, which was St. David's day.
L(1872.a.1/168).

H456 — A hymn to the chair: or lucubrations, serious and comical, on the use of chairs, benches, forms, joint-stools, three-legged stools, and ducking-stools . . . *London, printed for B. Dickinson, Tho. Corbet, & R. Montague; sold by E. Nutt & J. Brotherton, A. Dodd, J. Brindly, J. Jolliff, Mr. Critchly, & J. Stagg,* 1732. (*GSJ* 20 May)
8⁰: A–D⁴; *1–2* 3–32.
'Hail! chair of state; thy praise I sing'
L(1973); CtY,ICN,MH,TxU(uncut).

— A hymn to the creator, 1727. *See* Welsted, Leonard.

— An hymn to the creator of the world, 1750. *See* Burgh, James.

H457 — An hymn to the deity: designed to check the reigning infidelity, and to improve some late awakening calls of providence to a reformation.

An **hymn** to the deity

London, printed for W. Meadows, 1750. (*GM, LM* April)
4⁰: A–C⁴; *1–3* 4–24.
   Vertical chain-lines.
'O thou, whom all the cherubims adore'
L(840.k.4/14; 161.m.77).

H458 — [dh] A hymn to the funeral sermon. [*London,* 1703.] (2 Oct, Luttrell)
4⁰: A²; *1–4.*
   Moore 61. The order of editions is not determined; this stands first because of Luttrell's dated copy.
'Thou great preserver of men's fame'
   Attributed to Defoe by Moore; Defoe was in Newgate at the time, and the poem is linked with Defoe in *Remarks on the author of the Hymn to the pillory,* 1703. An attack on Paul Lorrain's sermon *Walking with god,* 1703, on the execution of Thomas Cook, 11 Aug 1703.
L(162.l.43, Luttrell),LLP.

H459 —— [col] [*London*] *Printed in the year* 1703.
4⁰: A²; *1–4.*
O.

H460 —— [*London?* 1703.]
4⁰: *A*²; *1–4.*
   The text on p. 4 is printed in italic, suggesting a piratical printer with little type. The signature is possibly cropt from the copy seen.
O(slightly cropt).

H461 — An hymn to the great creator. [*Dublin,* 17––.]
½⁰: 1 side, 1 column.
   Stanza 1 only. The L copy is from a Dublin collection.
'Whilst Sol with jocund toe doth trip upon the misty mountains' top'
L(1890.e.5/51).

— A hymn to the light of the world, 1703. *See* Blackmore, *Sir* Richard.

— A hymn to the mob, 1715. *See* Defoe, Daniel.

H462 — A hymn to the new laureat. By a native of Grub-street. *London, printed for L.G.* [*Lawton Gilliver*]; *sold by A. Dodd, & E. Nutt,* 1731 [1730]. (*MChr* Dec)
2⁰: A⁴; *1–2* 3–8.
'O C——r darling of the tuneful nine!'
   A satire on Colley Cibber.
L(C.131.h.1/8, uncut),O; DFo,IU(uncut).

— A hymn to the pillory, 1703–. *See* Defoe, Daniel.

H463 — A hymn to the pope. Proving that Saint Peter never was at Rome; and that the pope's chair has no bottom, nor tyranny any foundation. In plain verse, for the information of the young and unlearned. *London, printed for the author; sold by J. Roberts, and at the pamphlet-shops in London & Westminster,* 1735. (*GSJ* 15 Sept)
8⁰: A–C⁴; *1–2* 3–23 *24 blk.*
'God is the bless'd foundation sure'

An **hymn** to the pope

Advertised as 'By the author of an essay on free-thinking', which was listed in *GM* Aug 1735 but has not been traced. Possibly a versification of [Christopher Carlile] *A discourse, wherein is plainly proved...that Peter never was in Rome*, 1572–.

IU.

[H464 = H81] — An hymn to the redeemer, 1713. *See* Harris, Timothy.

H465 — A hymn to the scaffold, in Westminster-hall. *London, printed in the year* 1710.
½°: 1 side, 2 columns.
'Thou muse of state hast mourned a banish'd race'
In praise of Sacheverell.
L(1876.f.1/52); CSmH(2),MH.

H466 — [*idem*] The church of England's new hymn, to the state scaffold in Westminster-hall: occasion'd by the tryal of skill thereon, in February the 27th, 1709... By Theophylus Phylanglus. *London, printed in the year* 1710.
8°: A⁸; 1–2 3–16.
With 'The additional litany' on pp. 13–16. A revised and enlarged version of the preceding.
O(2, 1 lacks A1.8).

H467 — A hymn to the victory in Scotland. *London, printed by R. Thomas, behind the Royal Exchange,* [1719.] (25 June, Luttrell)
½°: 1 side, 2 columns.
Imprint in roman type throughout.
'I sing the praise of heroes brave'
Crum I480. A satire on the half-hearted victory at Glenshiel. Cf. *An answer to the hymn*, [1719.] The author also wrote *A true touch of the times*, 1719.
L(C.20.f.9/498); MH(Luttrell).

H468 — [another edition]
Imprint in roman and italic type.
L(C.20.f.2/312),E; MH.

H469 — [dh] Hymn to the victory in Scotland 10th of June, 1719. [*Edinburgh,* 1719.] (10 July?)
4°: A²; 1 2–3 4 blk.
E(2, 1 dated 10 July)

H470 — [*idem*] A poem, to the victory at Glenshiel in Scotland. *London printed, and Edinburgh re-printed in the year* 1719.
½°: 1 side, 2 columns.
E.

H471 — A hymn to Tyburn. Being a sequel of the Hymn to the pillory. *London, printed in the year* 1703. (12 Aug, Luttrell)
4°: A–B⁴; i–ii, 1–14.
'Hail, venerable shade, to whom'
A sequel to Defoe's poem; the possibility of Defoe's authorship does not seem to have been investigated.
L(164.m.32, Luttrell),C; CtY,Rosenbach.

A **hymn** to Tyburn

H472 — — [*London?* 1703.]
4°: A²; 1–4, 2 columns.
Drop-head title only. A piracy.
MB.

H472·2 — [dh] A hymn to Tyburn. [*London?* 1703.]
4°: A²; 1–4, 2 columns.
Rothschild 201. Another piracy.
C.

— A hymn to victory, 1704. *See* Defoe, Daniel.

Hymns. Hymns composed for the use of the brethren, 1749. *See* Zinzendorf, N.L. von, *count.*

— Hymns for ascension day, 1746–. *See* Wesley, John & Charles.

— Hymns for children, [1746?] *See* Wesley, John & Charles.

— Hymns for Christmas day, [1744.] *See* Wesley, John & Charles [Hymns for the nativity].

— Hymns for new year's day, [1749–.] *See* Wesley, John & Charles.

— Hymns for our lord's resurrection, 1746–. *See* Wesley, John & Charles.

— Hymns for the festivals, and on other solemn occasions. *Portsmouth, printed by G. Jones,* 1748.
8°: pp. 40, ii.   L; NNUT.
Attributed to John & Charles Wesley by NNUT, but the attribution is not plausible. Edward Godwin is perhaps a more likely candidate.

— Hymns for the nativity of our lord, [1745]–. *See* Wesley, John & Charles.

— Hymns for the public thanksgiving-day, October 9, 1746. *See* Wesley, John & Charles.

— Hymns for the watch-night, [1749?] *See* Wesley, John & Charles.

— Hymns for times of trouble, [1744.] *See* Wesley, John & Charles.

— Hymns for times of trouble and persecution, 1744–. *See* Wesley, John & Charles.

— Hymns from Jeremiah, [1745.] *See* Wesley, John & Charles.

— Hymns occasioned by the earthquake, 1750. *See* Wesley, John & Charles.

— Hymns on god's everlasting love, 1741–. *See* Wesley, John & Charles.

— Hymns on the great festivals, and other occasions, 1746. *See* Wesley, John & Charles.

H473 — Hymns sung by the charity--children. Upon the occasion of the peace, July the 7th 1713. *London printed, and Edinburgh reprinted by John Reid,* [1713.]
½°: 1 side, 1 column.
'Lord give the queen thy saving health'
'Glory to god who reigns on high'
E; NN.

Hyp-doctor

H474 Hyp-doctor. 'The Hyp-doctor in tune; or the free-mason a poet. Being the bard's maggot: occasion'd by a furious string of epithets, in a late protestation versify'd in its ain style, and in stanza's of various metres... [*London*] *Sold at Mrs. Dodd's.* Price 2d.' (*DJ* 12 March 1734)

    Possibly a half-sheet from the price.

    Probably a satire on John Henley, the editor of *The hyp-doctor.* 'The subject is, the bill that officers shall only be depriv'd of their commissions by parliament, or court-martial' (*DJ*).

H475 Hypochondria. Hypocondria. A poem. In five canto's. With some prefatory reflections on discontent, natural, moral, and political... *London printed, and sold by T. Warner,* 1726. (*LJ* 12 Feb)

12°: A–I⁶; *i–iii* iv–xi *xii*, *1* 2–72 61–82 *83–84 blk.* err slip on viii.

'When whimsy got into the head'

IU(–I6),OCU(–I6).

Hypochondria.

H476 — [*reissue*] The hyp, a burlesque poem in five canto's. Including the adventures of Sir Valetude Whim, and his retinue... *London, printed for J. Batley,* 1731. (*GSJ* 26 March)

12°: A⁶(±A1) B–I⁶; *i–iii* iv–xi *xii*, *1* 2–72 61–82 *83–84 blk.* err slip on viii.

    Bond 113.

L(11607.b.26, –I6),O(–I6); CSmH,ICN.

H477 Hypocrites. The hypocrites: a satyr. *London, printed in the year* 1703. (29 June, Luttrell)

2°: *A*² B–G²; *i–iv*, *1*–23 *24 blk.* A1 hft.

    The Luttrell copy is in the possession of R. D. Horn.

'They who have best succeeded in their rhimes'

O(–A1),*LdU-B*; MH.

'Hywgi ap Englyn Margonwe.' The Taffydeis, 1746. *See* T4.

I

I. I'le never love thee more, [17––.] *See* Graham, James, *marquis of Montrose.*

I1 — I'm a fit fellow to ask questions indeed? But I hope you'll excuse me. [*Oxford*] *Printed by T. Williams,* [1718.] (17 Dec)
½°: 1 side, 2 columns.
> Large woodcut above text. Hearne's ms. note in O copy, 'This silly paper was cryed about Oxford streets on Wednesday Dec. 17. 1718, being the day when there was a meeting in the Apodyterium about [Peter] Maurice of Jesus College's sermon'.

'My lads, what do you mean?'
> Hearne, 'This paper relates to Mr. Edward Biss that was put in the pillory'.

O.

I2 Iambic. An iambick ode, upon an iambick match being an epithalamium to the Little Beau, wedded to a tall belle. *Dublin, printed for Ed. Brian & Den. Kelly,* 1728.
slip: 1 side, 1 column.
'What gentle muse, Shall I use'
> The Little Beau was Patrick Walsh.

L(1890.e.5/94).

Iberia. Iberia liberata: a poem, 1706. *See* Oldmixon, John.

I3 Idol. The idol of Paris, with what may be expected, if ever the high-flying party should establish a government agreeable to that pernicious doctrine of absolute passive obedience, &c. Written by a young lady, now upon her departure for the New Atlantis. *London printed, and sold by J. Baker,* [1710.] (May?)
8°: A⁴; *1–2* '1' 4–8.
> Advertised by Baker in May 1710 according to F.F. Madan.

'Sing, mystick muse, and with a fluent strain'
> Occasioned by the Sacheverell affair.

L(11646.d.61/1),O,E; ICN,IU,OCU.

I4 Idyll. An idylle on the peace, concluded, between the most serene Anne...and the most Christian and catholick kings, of France and Spain, &c...Set by Mr John Sigismond Cousser...and perform'd at the Theatre-Royal in Dublin, the sixteenth day of June, 1713. *Dublin, printed by Edwin Sandys,* 1713.
4°: *A*² B–C²; *1–2* 3–12.
'Happy queen, in whose calm bosom'
DK; CSmH,DLC.

Ignorami. Ignorami lamentatio supra legis communis, 1736. *See* Bramston, James.

Iliad. The Iliad in a nutshell, 1726. *See* Wesley, Samuel, *the younger.*

I5 Illia. Illia's plain: or the happy-flock. A poem. *London, printed for, and sold by Eliz. Powell, at the Prince of Wales's Arms, in Black-Fryars, near Ludgate. And by the booksellers of London & Westminster,* [1714?]
8°: A–C⁴; *i–iv, 1* 2–19 *20.* 20 advt.
> The advertisement lists 'The countryman's true tale' by the same author as in the press; it has not been traced.

'Upon a time, when poets durst not sing'
> Dedication signed 'W.M.' A fable in praise of Queen Anne and mourning her death.

L(11650.cc.19/1),O.

Illustrious. 'The illustrious couple; or, the wedding night. Sack-posset, a poem on the succeeding morning. The knight and the purse, or a mitre in dispute. [*London*] *Sold at the pamphlet shops.* Price 6d.' (*GM* March 1734)
> The title suggests that this is a small miscellany. *The knight and the purse* was published separately in the preceding year.

I6 Illustrissimo. Illustrissimo ac nobilissimo heroi Georgio comiti de Cromartie, vicecomiti de Tarbat, domino de M'Leod & Castlehaven, &c. Nunc vero serenissimæ reginæ a secretis, congratulatio. [*Edinburgh,* 1703/04.]
½°: 1 side, 1 column.
'Gaudia mirifice perfundunt pectora honesta'
> Signed 'R.C.' On George Mackenzie, created earl of Cromarty 1703, secretary of state 1702–4.

TxU.

I7 — 'Illustrissimo, potentissimoq; principi, Jacobo duci de Chandos recens creato, carmen. To his grace the Duke of Chandos, upon his late creation, an epick poem. [*London*] *To be had of Mr. Woodman's.*' (*PB* 4 July 1721)

Imitation. An imitation of Horace's 16th epode, 1739. *See* Turner, *Sir* Edward.

I8 — An imitation of Ovid Metamorphosis; inscribed to his excellency the Earl of Gallway one of the lords justices of Ireland. *Dublin, printed* 1716.
4°: *A*²; *1–2* 3–4.
'I sing of bodies shap'd to various forms'
DT.

— An imitation of the 137. psalm, [1747?] *See* Hamilton, William, *of Bangour.*

— An imitation of the ninth ode of the fourth book of Horace, 1715. *See* Somervile, William.

— An imitation of the prophecy of Nereus, 1715–. *See* Tickell, Thomas.

— An imitation of the sixth ode of Horace, 1704. *See* Steele, *Sir* Richard.

'Immerito.' Piscatory eclogues, 1729. *See* Browne, Moses.

Immobilia.

Immobilia. Immobilia sanctorum festa, 1716. *See* Skene, Robert.

Immortality. Immortality reveal'd, 1745. *See* Cooke, Thomas.

Impartial. The impartial, 1744. *See* Hill, Aaron.

I9 — [dh] An impartial narrative of the Pretender's god-son nailing up the church, and persecuting the parson. [*Dublin?* 1742?]
4°: *A*² B²; 1–8.
'When he that ought the halcyon laws to guard'
    A satire on James King, baron Kingston.
L(11632.df.48).

I10 — The impartial satyrist. A poem. *Norwich, printed by H. Collins, near the Red-Well,* 1715.
4°: ⟨A–B⁴⟩; 1–2 3–16.
'I sing no foreign bloody wars'
    A satire on Norwich characters.
L(11659.bb.43, cropt).

I11 Impeachment. The impeachment. *Printed in the year* 1710. *and sold by the booksellers of London and Westminster.* (*SR* 25 July)
½°: 2 sides, 1 column.
    Entered in *SR* to George Parker by Ann Newcomb. Advertised in *PB* 5 Aug. Deposit copies at L,E.
'A nightingale whose warbling tongue'
    Since Parker is not recorded by *Plomer*, he might be the author, not the publisher; but cf. S702. A fable about the impeachment of Sacheverell and the consequent fall of the whig ministry.
L(C.20.f.2/233),E; *Harding.*

I12 — The impeachment of his grace the D. of Marlboro', on his coming openly to town, attended by many of the nobility. [*London,* 1712.]
slip: 1 side, 1 column.
'Knows not your grace, when merit soars too high'
LSA.

— The impeachment: or, the church triumphant, 1712. *See* Russell, Richard.

I13 Imperious. The imperious beauty: or, a letter from a lover and a friend to Miss S——. *Dublin, printed in the year* 1730.
½°: 1 side, 1 column.
'To paint the various charms, of various fair'
    Reprinted in *Poems written occasionally by the late John Winstanley…interspers'd with many others,* II (1751). Probably on Molly Smalley.
CtY.

Imperium. Imperium pelagi, 1730. *See* Young, Edward.

Impertinent. The impertinent, or a visit to the court, 1733. *See* Pope, Alexander.

Impiety.

Impiety. Impiety and superstition expos'd, 1710. *See* Brown, William.

Impossible. An impossible thing, 1720. *See* Congreve, William.

I14 Impotent. The impotent lover describ'd in six elegies on old-age. In imitation of Cornelius Gallus. With a satyr on our modern letchers; shewing the many new inventions they have to raise their lust, viz. flogging &c. By the author of the Letters from a nun to a cavalier. In verse. *London, printed for J. Sackfield, & T. Warner,* 1718. (*SR* 5 July)
8°: *A*⁴(±A2) B-L⁴ *M*²; i–iv v–viii, 1 2–24 17–24 33–56 73–96, 3 4–6 (91 as '89'). A1 frt; iv err; M² advt.
    L⁴ contains the 'satyr on our modern letchers' with a separate title-page, possibly added as an afterthought, thus explaining the cancel title. Entered in SR to I. Sackfield; deposit copies at O,E,EU. Advertised in *PB* 10 July. The copyright formed part of lot 16 in the trade sale of B. Creake, 21 April 1727 (cat. at O-JJ).
'Why, envious age, wilt thou with lingring pain'
Satyr: 'Leave off your railing, you old envious wretch'
    The Latin is actually by Maximianus Etruscus. The translation appears to be based on that published in 1688 as *Elegies of old age* (*Wing* G181A) and reissued in 1689 with the present title as 'by H. Walker, gent.' (*Wing* G181B). That translation is attributed by *Watt* to Sir Hovenden Walker; but *DNB* rightly considers the attribution highly improbable. 'The author of the *Letters from a nun to a cavalier*' presumable refers to the translation in *New miscellaneous poems,* 1713, in which case the author may be Morgan Keene.
O(lacks L⁴),E(−M²),EU; *CU.*

I15 In. In and out and turn about, a new c-----t-dance. To the tune of John bob'd in, and John bob'd out: or, Bob in Joan: or, The miller of Mansfield. [*London*] *Printed for W. Webb,* 1745. (*DA* 17 Jan)
2°: *A*⁴; 1 2–8.
    After imprint, 'N.B. For the curious, The c——t bargain is annex'd'; it occupies six lines on p. 8.
'Ye people at home/Who H---n---r hate'
    On changes in the ministry.
L(1879.cc.7/32),O(2),LdU-B; CSmH(lacks A2.3), CtY,MH,NjP,OCU.

I16 — — [*London?* 1745.]
½°: 1 side, 3 columns.
L(1890.c.1/5; C.121.g.9/204); OCU.

I17 — In answer to the Le H——p's ballad in a dialogue which passed between Sr. R——t, Mr. H——re, and Mr. Le H---p's, at Sir R---t---'s, house. *London, printed for R. More, near St. Pauls,* [1727.]

In answer to the Le H—p's ballad

½°: 1 side, 2 columns.
Percival appendix 5. On the other side of the
O copy, *The maids christmas box.*
'In good faith Mr. H---p'
A further satire on Isaac Le Heup.
L(1875.d.6/30),O.

— In Barbaram & Margaritam Caroli Stuarti,
[1712?/13.] *See* Pitcairne, Archibald.

— In diem illum auspicatissimum, 1719. *See*
Monsey, R.

I18 — In dolendum obitum docti & pii viri, magistri
Joannis Cunninghamii legum professoris, qui obiit
Edinburgi 1mo die Maii, anno dom. 1710. [*Edin-
burgh*, 1710.]
½°: 1 side, 1 column.
With 'An English paraphrase on the Latin
funeral elegy...'.
'Natus patre pio, patrem sequitur sua proles'
'The genuine off-spring of a worthy sire'
At foot, 'Posuit R.C.'
E,Rosebery.

— In D. Archibaldi Pitcarnii medici...bibliothe-
cam, [1713?] *See* Kincaid, Thomas.

I19 — In honour to the king and parliament, who are
to assemble on the sixth of this instant February.
By a lover of his king and country. *London, printed
by R. Janeway*, 1701. (Feb)
½°: 2 sides, 1 column.
'May heaven shine upon our parliament'
InU.

— In illustrissimum infantem nuper natum,
[1717.] *See* Boldero, John.

— In imitation of Hudibras, 1704. *See* Ward,
Edward.

I20 — [dh] In imitation of Lucretius. Suave mari
magno, &c. [col] *London, printed for Tim. Goodwin*,
1707.
2°: A²; 1–4.
'How are we pleas'd, when from the distant shore'
MC,*MR-C.*

I21 — In imitation of the 5th ode of Horace. Lib. 4.
[*London*? 1716/20?]
½°: 1 side, 2 columns.
'When, royal youth, must we be blest again'
Crum W1425. Jacobite propaganda.
L(C.121.g.9/185),E; CSmH,MH.

— In Jacobum principem Hamiltonium, [1712.]
See Pitcairne, Archibald.

— In Jacobum secundum, Britanniae regem,
[1710?/13.] *See* Pitcairne, Archibald.

I22 — In Johannem Churchill ducem Marlburiensem
epitaphium. (Insculpatur aquila e rogo emicans,
more romano.) [*Dublin*? 1722.]
½°: 1 side, 1 column.
The L copy is bound with Dublin half-sheets.
On the other side, *An elegiack ode on the right
honourable James, earl Stanhope*, [1722.]

In Johannem Churchill

'En Jovis alta ales, quam a terra Marlburus armis'
L(1890.e.5/26).

— In laudem Edvardi Vernoni, 1740–. *See* Upton,
Francis.

— In luctuosum & nunquam satis deflendum
obitum..., [1727.] *See* Anderson, James.

— In luctuosum & præmaturum obitum...,
[1724.] *See* Anderson, James.

I23 — In Magnæ Britanniæ reginæ mortem. [*London*?
1714.]
obl ½°: 1 side, 1 column.
'Hic regina jacet, nec magnis regibus impar'
C.

— In Maij vigesimam nonam, anno MDCCXII,
[1712.] *See* Pitcairne, Archibald.

— In Maii xxix, sive Juni x, anni MDCCXII,
[1712.] *See* Pitcairne, Archibald.

I24 — In memoriam amici mihi longe charissimi, viri
vere eruditi & admodum juxta generosi Roberti
Gardiner J.C. threnodia fratri fraterrimo Gulielmo
Gardiner inscripta. [*Edinburgh*? 170–?]
1°: 1 side, 1 column.
Mourning borders.
'Discite quam rapidæ vanescunt ludicra vitæ'
MH.

— In memory of the right honourable John earl of
Strathmore, [1715/16?] *See* Meston, William [To
the memory of...].

I25 — In obitum clarissimi domini domini Jacobi
Steuarti, equitis, & Causidici regii, epicedium.
[*Edinburgh*, 1714?] (May?)
½°: 1 side, 1 column.
'Ergo jaces perdocte senex? Virtutibus annos'
The date of Stewart's death is given in another
elegy as 1 May 1713, and this may be wrongly
dated in ms.
E(ms. date, May 1714).

I26 — In obitum desideratissimi V.D.M. Edinburgen-
sis. D. Gul. Crechton. [*Edinburgh*, 1709?]
obl ½°: 1 side, 2 columns.
Mourning borders. The second column is
headed, 'The same paraphrased in English'.
Maidment 180 suggests the date 1709 from the
materials the E copy was associated with when
originally bound in a volume of newspapers.
'Saturni infausta, cras signo ad sacra vocandus'
'Compos'd to sleep on Saturn's ominous night'
E.

— In obitum illustrissimi Georgii I, 1727. *See*
Bordman, T.

I27 — In obitum illustrissimi principis Jacobi ducis de
Hamilton, Chatelrault, & Brandon, proditorie
occisi, die 15to. Nov. ann. 1712. Carmen elegiacum.
Edinburgi, typis ac impensis Jacobi Watson, 1712.
½°: 1 side, 1 column.
Mourning headpiece and borders.

In obitum illustrissimi principis

'Heu! jacet indigna Hamiltonus cæde peremptus'
L(1489.gg.1/13),Crawford.

I28 — In obitum ornatissimi viri, D. Georgii Camp-
belli, s.s. theologiæ professoris apud Edinburgenses,
epicedium. [*Edinburgh*, 1701.]
½°: 1 side, 1 column.
'Musa gemens hæret, (nil mirum) dira verendi'
L(11633.i.9/1).

I29 — In obitum piæ ac generosissimæ dominæ D.A.
Fountainhall, elegidium ad usum & captum
adolescentuli ejusdem filij Alexandri Lauder ex
industria accommodatum. April: 18. 1713. [*Edinburgh*, 1713.]
obl 1°: 1 side, 2 columns.
Mourning borders. Column 2 is headed 'The
same Englished'.
'An quia matrona es, generoso stemmate nata'
'Fall'n! by the dismal stroak of harshest fate'
On the death of the wife of Sir John Lauder,
lord Fountainhall.
E.

— In obitum Roussæi, 1724. *See* Bourne, Vincent.

I30 — In obitum summe deplorandum augustissimi
invictissimiq; monarchæ Guilielmi III. nuper
Magnæ Britanniæ, &c. regis, carmen lugubre. Hoc
porro sub finem gratulatorium propter illustris-
simæ reginæ successionem. [*London?* 1702.]
1°: 1 side, 2 columns.
'Angligenis lugenda dies! Cur solis ab ortu'
O.

I31 — In palatium sancti Jacobi die natali serenissimæ
Annæ reginæ, 1712. Magnæ Britanniæ primoribus,
humillime oblatum. Carmen. [*London*, 1712.]
½°: 1 side, 1 column.
'Hæc domus augusta est, magni nam conscia
partus'
The copy at C is bound next to Kenneth
Campbell, *Faciam eos in gentem unam*, [1707?];
possibly it is by the same author.
C.

I32 — In praise of tea. A poem. Dedicated to the
ladies of Great Britain. By J. B. writing-master.
*Printed for the author, and sold at the printing-office,
Canterbury, and by the men who carry about the news,
1736.*
4°: A–C²: *1–4* 5–11 *12 blk.*
'Tea, thou delightful innocent repast!'
L(11633.b.5).

— In Regiam Sagittariorum Scotorum cohortem,
[1713/14.] *See* Kincaid, Thomas.

— In undecimum Martii, quo ante annos octoginta
natus est Archibaldus Stevensonus, [1710.] *See*
Pitcairne, Archibald.

'Incognito.' The commoner, 1710. *See* C319.

Incouragement. *See* Encouragement.

Independent.

I33 **Independent.** The independent Westminster
choice: or, Perceval and Edwin. To the tune of The
free masons. [*London*, 1741.] (Dec?)
½°: 1 side, 2 columns.
Percival LXXXII.
'Ye Westminster boys,/With one common voice'
After the Westminster election of 1741, and
before the ensuing inquiry, in favour of
Edward Vernon and Charles Edwin.
L(8133.i.33).

I34 — The independent Westminster electors toast. In
memory of the glorious two hundred and twenty.
To the tune of, Come let us prepare, &c. [*London*,
1741/42.]
½°: 1 side, 2 columns.
Percival LXXIII.
'My Westminster friends/Now we've gained our
ends'
On the Westminster election of 1741, when
the results were declared void by a vote in the
commons of 220, 22 Dec 1741.
L(8133.i.33).

I35 — [*idem*] A new song. To the tune of, Come let us
prepare, &c. [*London*, 1741/42.]
½°: 1 side, 2 columns.
Rough woodcut at head. A variant text.
'Ye Westminster boys/By your freedom of choice'
L(8133.i.33).

I36 — [*idem*] The down-fall of S——n and W——r;
or the independant [!] Westminster electors
triumph. To the tune of, Come let us prepare, &c.
[*London*, 1741/42.]
½°: 1 side, 2 columns.
L(8133.i.33).

Indian. An Indian pastoral eclogue, 1717. *See*
Harris, Joseph.

I37 **Infallible.** An infallible cure for the gout. [*Dublin*]
Printed in the year 1726.
½°: 2 sides, 1 column.
The OCU copy has a Dublin collector's initial,
F.
'The gout I think, remains as yet unsung'
OCU.

I38 — The infallible Dr Anthony. *Printed and sold by
Tho. Fleming, at the Salmon in High Street, Dublin,*
[1726?]
½°: 1 side, 2 columns.
Engraved throughout; picture at head and
music at foot. The DT copy is bound with
half-sheets of 1726.
'From France from Spain from Rome I come'
A satire on Dr. Anthony's claims.
DT.

I39 — The infallible mountebank, or, quack doctor.
London, printed by H. Hills, 1707.
½°: 1 side, 2 columns.
Large woodcut above text. On the other side

The **infallible** mountebank

of the L and one O copy, *A bridle for the French king*, [1706/07]; on the other O copy, *An elegy on the death of the late famous Observator*, 1707.

'See sirs, see here!/A doctor rare'
  Apparently a satire on quacks, with no political references.
L(Harley 5931, fol.175),O(2, 1 cropt).

I40 — An infallible recipe to make a wicked manager of a theatre... Wrote by a member of the company of players of which Mr. xxxxxxxx was manager. *Chester*, Augt. 20 1750. *Publish'd according to the act by Monsr. Verité.*
½°: 1 side, 2 columns.
  Engraved throughout; portrait of Thomas Hallam at head.
'Take of every thing odious that's under the sun'
  Against Charles Macklin, who poked out the eye of Thomas Hallam; he died of the injury, 1735.
L(Crach.Tab.4.b.4, vol.1.fol.59).

Iniquity. Iniquity display'd, 1729. *See* Fraser, Peter.

I41 **Innocent.** The innocent epicure: or, the art of angling. A poem... The second edition. *London, printed by H. Meere, for R. Gosling*, 1713.
8°: A–M⁴; *i–viii*, 1–87 *88 blk.*
  First published in 1697; *Wing* T191, wrongly ascribing it to Nahum Tate who signed the preface of that edition.
'Of arts I sing; mysterious things explore'
  The dedicatory poem is headed 'From J.S. to O.S.'
L(993.d.48),LdU-B; CtY,DFo(uncut).

I42 — [reissue] Angling: a poem... The second edition. *London, printed for H. Slater, & F. Noble*, 1741. (*DP* 11 April)
8°: π² A⁴(−A1) B–M⁴; *i–viii*, 1–87 *88 blk.* π1 frt.
  The frontispiece is conjugate with the cancel title. Copies at L,CtY preserve the cancelland.
L(11633.a.38; 1486.pp.19),O,WaP; CtY(2),DLC, ICN,*NN*.

I43 — The innocent lampoon: or, the devotee turn'd lover. Dedicated and presented to the queen, for entertainment of her majesty and her honourable attendance at the Bath. *London, printed for J. Nutt*, 1702. (*WL* Nov)
4°: A–C⁴ D²; *i–viii*, 1–20.
'Stand off! and hold your dull impertinence'
ICN.

Insect. The insect war, 1706. *See* Browne, Joseph.

Insinuating. The insinuating bawd, [170–.] *See* Ward, Edward.

I44 **Inspired.** The inspir'd poet, or an epistle to the young poets and authors of the city of Dublin.

The **inspir'd** poet

Inscrib'd to the reverend Dean Swift. *Dublin, printed in Dame-street, opposite Eustace-street*, 1730.
8°: A⁴; *1–5* 6–8.
  Teerink 1296.
'Thus in my humble state how happy I'
  Burlesqued in *Dulness cherish'd*, 1730, where it is said to be a satire on the author of *An epistle to Mr. Thomas Elrington*, 1730.
LVA-F.

Institution. The institution of the order of the Garter, 1742. *See* West, Gilbert.

I45 **Instructions.** Instructions to a painter. A poem ... By a young gentleman. *London, printed by J. Jones, for the author*, 1714.
4°: A² B–D²; *i–iv*, 1–12.
'Assist, my muse, with brisk satyrick rage'
  In defence of Harley against Toland and Steele.
O,WgP.

I46 — Instructions to a painter on the birthday of his most sacred majesty King George. A poem. *London, printed for the author*, 1721.
4°.
(Elkin Mathews, list 69, 1960.)

— Instructions to Vander Bank, 1709. *See* Blackmore, *Sir* Richard.

I47 **Instructors.** The instructors instructed or have at you blind harpers, being a paraphrastical versification of the instructions given by some of Nottingham to their representatives in Parliament. To which is added, a faithful copy of the original instructions... To which is prefixed, an epistle... *Nottingham, printed by Tho. Collyer*, 1739.
8°: A–B⁴ C²; *1–2* 3–18 *19; 20 blk.* 19 err. & advt.
  Also printed as 'A paraphrastical, hudibrastical versification...' in the *Daily Gazetteer* 14 Dec 1739, and reprinted from there in *GM* Dec 1739. The prose epistle occupies pp. 3–11, the versification pp. 12–15, and the prose original pp. 16–18.
'To you two 'squires whom we have sent'
  A satire on the instructions sent to the Nottingham MPs, John Plumptre and Borlace Warren. Answered by *An epistle to the supposed author of the paraphrastical hudibrastick verses in the magazine*, 1740. The same author also wrote a burlesque of that work, printed with it as E432.
K. Monkman, Coxwold, York.

I48 **Intended.** The intended city's address paraphras'd. *Dublin, printed in the year* 1727.
½°: 1 side, 2 columns.
'We the lord mayor of —— town'
  A satire on Dublin's address on the accession of George II.
L(1890.e.5/196; C.121.g.8/159),Crawford.

Intrigue. The intrigue. A college eclogue, 1750. *See* Sampson, John.

Intriguing. The intriguing milliners and attornies clerks, 1738. *See* Robinson, William, *of Kendal*.

I49 Introduction. An introduction of the ancient Greek and Latin measures into British poetry. Attempted in the following pieces, viz. A translation of Virgil's first eclogue…fourth eclogue. Jacob and Rachel: a pastoral. With a preface in vindication of the attempt. *London, printed for T. Cooper, 1737.*
8⁰: π² A–G⁴ H²; [4] i ii–xvii, 18–19 20–59 60 blk. π1 hft.
> The first two poems are printed in Latin and English.

'You, Tityrus, canopy'd by a broad beech, softly reclining'
'Sicilian muses, to a strain more noble ascend we'
'In Syrian pastures, on a flowery bank by a fountain'
L(833.h.32; 161.m.78, –π1),O;DLC(–π1),MH (–π1).

I50 Invasion. The invasion, a poem in allusion to the VIIth epode of Horace. *London, printed for S. Popping, 1717.*
2⁰: A² B¹; 1–2 3–6.
'Ye impious Britons, whether will ye fly?'
NcU.

I51 — The invasion; a satyr. Or, the French king's expostulation on the Pretender's return to Dunkirk. With his last will. *London, printed by H. Hills, 1708.*
8⁰: A⁴; 1–2 3–8.
'Know all men by these, that a grand preparation'
CLU-C.

I52 Inventory. An inventory of the goods and chattels of P---r W----s, esq; from the threshold to the study inclusive. *London, printed for T. Taylor, 1741.*
2⁰: A²<B²; 1–2 3–8.
'Foremost and first, a broken scraper'
> On the distinguished money-lender, Peter Walter or Waters. Another version was applied to Walpole as *Grand sale at Westminster*, [1741?].

L(1959),O(2, 1 uncut),OA,C(uncut); CSmH,DFo, MH.

I53 — An inventory of the manuscripts, papers, poems, books, etc., to the value of £20, which were stolen out of the Chevalier de St. Patrick's study in Trinity College – but, when he really confesses, he does not know. A lame account of this loss was formerly issued in prose. [*Dublin*, 1734?]
½⁰.
'Whereas a tribe of young backbitters'
> Ms. note 'on Mr. Dunkin, A.M.'

(Dobell cat. 105/259.)

I54 Invictae. Invictæ fidelitatis præmium. [*Hereford*? 1741.]
⅓⁰: 1 side, 1 column.
'True to thy motto glorious city hail!'
> An election verse. The people of Hereford live up to their city motto in refusing bribery.

O.

I55 Invincible. The invincible hero' Arthure Dillon's sword place'd amidst the stars. A poem translatated into Englih[!] by R: N: from the ori'ginal Lattin writ by Mr. P: St. John poet lawreat. The sword speaks. [1724.]
4⁰: pp. 7.
> Continental printing, as the misprints suggest.
> Date from Bibliothèque nationale.

'Whilst bloody wars by myghty chifes [!] ware wag'd'
> A translation of St. John's *Invicti herois Arthuri Dillon*, etc. *ensis inter astra relatus. Ensis loquitur.*

Bibliothèque nationale, Paris.

Invitation. The invitation in imitation of Horace's epistle to Torquatus, 1720. *See* Sheridan, Thomas.

Io. Io! Triumphe! A poem upon Admiral Vernon, 1741. *See* Jones, Lewis.

I56 Ireland. Ireland in mourning: or, a funeral elegy on the much lamented death of the reverend father in god William King, lord archbishop of Dublin… *Dublin, printed by N. Hussey,* [1729.]
1⁰: 1 side, 2 columns.
> Mourning headpiece and woodcut borders.

'Oh! woefull news, O most unhappy day'
DT.

I57 — Ireland in universal mourning. Or, an elegy on the much lamented, and never to be forgotten death of the right honourable the Earl of Antrim, who departed this life, on Thursday the 19th of this instant October 1721 at his lodgings near the Round Church in Dublin. [*Dublin*, 1721.]
½⁰: 1 side, 1 column.
'Hibernia now condole the fatal stroke'
MH.

I58 — Ireland's black day. Or, a farewell to his excellency the Lord Carteret… By D. D——y. *Dublin, printed* [*by C. Hicks*] *at the Rein-Deer, in Mounthrath street,* [1730.]
½⁰: 1–2, 1 column.
'Wherein, great Jove, have we thy anger mov'd'
> The author intended is presumably Patrick Delany, but it appears to be a Grub-street production.

DT.

I59 — Ireland's blessing on her hopeful squires. *Dublin, printed in the year 1738.*
⅓⁰: 1 side, 1 column.
'In dead of night appear'd a form, tho' fair'

Ireland's blessing

A satire against their drunkenness and impiety.
Rothschild.

I60 — [dh] Ireland's happiness compleated: or, a new poem on his grace the Duke of Grafton...speech to both houses of parliament, the 5th of September, 1723. [*Dublin*, 1723.]
4°: A²; *1–4*.
'As in those frozen climes, where tedious night'
DT.

I61 — Ireland's lamentation, or, a new ballad on Capt. Mooney, the kid-napper. To the tune of, Horse, foot and dragoons. [*Dublin*, 172–?]
½°: *1–2*, 1 column.
'Good folks of this isle,/Pray listen a while'
CtY.

I62 — Ireland's mourning flagg. *Dublin*, *printed in the year* 1737.
½°: 1 side, 2 columns.
Mourning borders. A short poem, followed by 'Some queries occasion'd [!] by the lowering of the gold coin' in prose.
Hibernia droops her flag now waves in air'
LU.

I63 — Ireland's prospect of happiness; or a congratulatory poem on the arrival of...the Earl of Pembroke... Written by a well-wisher to this country... *Dublin*, *printed* [*by Stephen Powell?*] *at the Crown in Fishamble Street*, 1707.
4°: A⁴; *1–2* 3–7 *8 blk.*
Watermark: initials.
'Hibernia! raise again thy drooping head'
C.

I64 — [fine paper]
Watermark: post-horn.
DM.

I65 — Ireland's universal loss, or the nations moan, and complaint, for the removal of Allan Broderick lord viscount Middleton, lord high chancellor of Ireland. [*Dublin*, 1725.] (21 May?)
½°: 1 side, 1 column.
'While Europ's menac'd with disputes & jar'
L(C.121.g.8/130, ms. date 21 May 1725).

I66 — Ireland's warning, being an excellent new song, upon Woods's base half-pence. To the tune of Packinton's pound. *Dublin*, *printed by John Harding*, [1724.]
½°: 1 side, 2 columns.
Teerink 1147; *Williams* 1109.
'Ye people of Ireland both country and city'
Reprinted as by Swift in *Whartoniana*, 1727, and by Nichols; Ball suggests Swift had some share, but Williams rejects it.
L(C.121.g.9/188),*LVA-F*,DN,DT.

Irene. Irene triumphans, 1713. *See* Settle, Elkanah.

Irish.

Irish. An Irish ballad, [1712.] *See* The new Kilmainham ballad, [1711/12.]

— The Irish bishops, 1732. *See* Swift, Jonathan [Annoque domini 1732].

— Irish legs a match for English brains, 1746. *See* Williams, *Sir* Charles Hanbury (W491).

I67 **Irlandais.** [dh] Les Irlandois. Poëme. Dedié à... Edouard Stuard, prince de Galles. [1745.]
4°: *A²*; *1* 2–4.
Probably printed in France.
'Par le zéle inspiré je vais dans la carriere'
Cf. *A son altesse royale monseigneur le Prince de Galles*, [1745.]
E.

'**Ironside, Nestor.**' An original canto of Spencer, 1714. *See* Croxall, Samuel.

— Another original canto of Spencer, 1714. *See* Croxall, Samuel.

I68 **Irregular.** An irregular ode, being the first poem made on the coronation of his most sacred majesty King George...October 20th 1714. and then inscribed to...Mr. Addison...The second editon [!]. *London*, *printed for W. Boreham*, 1720. (*DP* 31 Aug)
4°: *A²* B–C²; *1–3* 4–12.
Morgan Q343 refers to an edition of [1714?]; that is presumably conjectural.
'Albion, thou art the world's epitome'
'A silly fulsome thing', Luttrell.
L(162.1.44, Luttrell, no date).

I69 **Is.** Is this the truth? A poem. *Sold by Joseph West, in the Groat-market, Newcastle*, [1741.]
2°: *A²* B²; *1–2* 3–8.
'Is there, who breathes on this terraqueous ball'
A political satire against Walter Blackett, a candidate in the Newcastle election of 1741. Answered by [Edward Chicken] *No; – this is the truth*, [1741], and *No – that's a mistake*, [1741.] The titles are clearly suggested by James Miller's *Are these things so?*, 1740.
L(11661.dd.9),NeA(uncut),NeP.

I70 **Isidora.** Isidora to Casimir: an epistle. *London*, *printed for J. Roberts*, 1735. (*GM, LM* May)
4°: *A⁴* B–C⁴; *1–4* 5–23 *24 blk.* A1 hft.
Listed again in *LM* April 1736.
'If to the priest's ideal schemes we trust'
L(11633.bbb.42/6),LVA-F,O(uncut),LdU-B; CSmH,OCU.

I71 **It.** It's come home to him at last, or the Little Whig's trip to Newgate. Being a new ballad on Mr. George Matthews, printer, who was lately committed to New- [!] for counterfeiting two notes of a thousand pounds each. To the ancient and celebrated tune of, Chevy Chase. [*London?* 1720?]
½°: 1 side, 2 columns.

It's come home at last

'God prosper long our noble king'
George Matthews was brother to John 'lately
executed for high-treason' in 1719.

O.

I72 Italian. Italian policy in the misterious journey of
the Pretender's son: an hudibrastic poem. In a
letter from a gentleman in town to his brother in
the country. By T.H. *London, printed for C.
Corbett*, 1744.

2⁰: *A⁴; I–2 3–8.*
'The ninth of last came hot from Rome'
KU,NjP(uncut).

I73 Iter. Iter boreale: or, a voyage to the north. A
poem. By C.D. *London, sold by A. Baldwin*, [1708.]
(*DC* 24 June)

2⁰: A–C² (A2 as 'A'); *I–2 3–10 11–12 blk.*
'Of labours in vain many stories are told'
A satire on the Pretender invading Scotland.
O(Luttrell, 24 June).

I74 Ivie, Edward. Epicteti Enchiridion latinis versibus

Ivie, E. Epicteti Enchiridion

adumbratum. *Oxoniæ, e theatro Sheldoniano,
impensis H. Clements, Londini*, 1715. (*MC* April)
8⁰: π⁴ A–O⁴; *i–viii, 1–109 110–111; 112 blk.* π1 frt;
O4 err.

Text in Greek prose and Latin verse.
'Res rebus quantum distant! Sunt, quæ penes
ipsos'
L(674.c.15; 52.n.3),O; *IU,MB,MH,NjP.*

I75 —— Editio secunda priori emendatior. *Oxoniæ, e
theatro Sheldoniano, impensis Steph. Fletcher*, 1723.
12⁰: a⁴ A–D¹² E⁸; *i–viii, 1–109 110–112.* a1 blk;
110–112 advt.
L(11409.b.32),O; *CtY,ICU,IU,PPL(2).*

I76 —— *Glasguae, in aedibus academicis excudebat
Robertus Foulis*, 1744.
12⁰: π² A–C⁶; *i–iv, 1–36. iv advt.*
Watermark: post-horn, apparently fine paper.
Gaskell, Foulis 48. Ordinary-paper copies were
also listed in the Foulis stock catalogue *Books
in quires*, 1777.

GM.

J

J., B., *gent.* A poem occasion'd by the rise and fall of South Sea stock, 1720. *See* P561.

J., G. Britain's hero, 1722. *See* Jacob, Giles.

— Human happiness, 1721. *See* Jacob, Giles.

J., H., *esq;* The fatal union of France and Spain, 1701. *See* F69.

J---------, H----------, *esq;* The mad dog, a tale, 1730. *See* Gay, John.

J., J., *of Aberdeen.* A dialogue betwixt Satan and a young man, 1716. *See* D277.

J., T. A pastoral in imitation of Virgil's first eclogue, 1730. *See* P110.

J., W., *A.M.* The father's blessing penn'd for the instruction of his children, [170–?] *See* Jole, William.

Jack. Jack French-man's defeat, [1708.] *See* Jack Frenchman's lamentation, 1708 (J5).

J1 — Jack Frenchman's lamentation. An excellent new song, to the tune of I'll tell thee Dick, &c. *London printed, and are to be sold by John Morphew,* 1708.
½°: 1 side, 2 columns.
> *Rothschild* 2194; *Teerink* 503; *Williams* 1078. Reprinted in *The battel of Audenard,* 1708.

'Ye commons and peers,/Pray lend me your ears'
Crum Y24: 'Jack French-man's defeat'. For the authorship of this ballad, see *Williams* and references. It was added to Swift's works by Scott in 1814 on the strength of its publication by Morphew (which is very inconclusive), and Williams finds the style appropriate. Lady Cowper ascribed it to Congreve, which Williams considers unlikely; he prefers an attribution to Prior found in a ms, but it is rejected in *Wright & Spears*. There seems no reason to assume the author was a major poet.
C,Rothschild; *MH.*

J2 — — The second edition. *London printed, and are to be sold by John Morphew,* 1708.
½°: 1 side, 2 columns.
> A reimpression; the words 'The second edition' follow the imprint.

O.

J3 — — [*Edinburgh?* 1708.]
½°: 1 side, 2 columns.
> *Teerink* 507. The L copy is bound with Edinburgh half-sheets. This and the following editions are ordered by their text rather than by publication date.

L(12350.m.18/3).

J4 — — To the tune of, I'll tell the [!] Dick, &c. Or, Who can but love a seaman, &c. [*London,* 1708.]
½°: 1 side, 2 columns.
> *Teerink* 504. Battered and worm-eaten woodcut of soldiers at head; a popular printing, adding two stanzas after the sixth.

L(1876.f.1/40).

J5 — [*idem*] Jack French-man's defeat: being an excellent new song, to a pleasant tune, called, There was a fair maid in the North-country... [*London, sold by Benj. Bragg,* 1708.] (*DC* 20 July)
obl ½°: 1 side, 4 columns.
> *Teerink* 505. Printed in black-letter in traditional broadside style, with the title and a large woodcut over the first two columns of text, but uncharacteristically paged 1–2 as though it were meant to be folded. Almost certainly the edition advertised in *DC* as sold by B. Bragg 'with a fair representation of the battle curiously engraven... price a halfpenny'. This edition has the two additional stanzas.

L(C.40.m.10/103).

J6 — Jack Presbyter's downfal: or, the church in glory: occasion'd by the dissolution of the late parliament. To an excellent new tune. *London, printed in the year* 1710.
½°: 1 side, 2 columns.
> *Teerink* 843.

'Pray lend me your ears if you've any to spare'
> For the suggestion of Swift's authorship, ignored by Williams, see *Ball* 145 n.5. On the downfall of the whig ministry.

L(1876.f.1/45).

J7 — Jack Presbiter's triumphant rejoycing: or, a general joy at the rebuilding of the old Doctor Burgess's meeting: with a brief description of all the pious relicts and necessaries lately bought, being more splendid than before. To the tune of, The Scotch wedding... *London, printed in the year* 1710.
½°: 1 side, 2 columns.
> For a variant text, see *The dissenters triumph,* 1710.

'Dear brethren do ye hear how fine'
> A satire against Daniel Burgess.

L(1876.f.1/46),O.

J8 Jacks. The Jacks put to their trumps. A tale of King James's Irish shilling. *London printed, and sold by R. Burleigh,* 1714. (*SR* 3 Dec)
4°: A^2 B^4; *1*–4 5–12. A1 hft.
> Deposit copy at E; listed in *MC* Nov.

'How wond'rous fickle is the world!'
> Attributed to Swift by Thomas Roscoe in his edition of 1841; rejected by *Williams* 1098 on several counts.

L(11631.bb.42),E,DN(–A1); NN,NNC.

J9 [Jackson, Andrew.] Matrimonial scenes: consisting of the Seaman's tale, the Manciple's tale, the

Jackson, A. Matrimonial scenes

character of the Wife of Bath, the tale of the Wife of Bath, and her five husbands. All modernized from Chaucer. *London, printed for the author; sold by A. Jackson, T. Payne, W. Shropshire, and all other booksellers,* 1750. (*LEP* 1 Feb)
8°: *A*¹ B–I⁴; *i–ii, 1 2–64.*
'Long since, a merchant, where St. Dennis lies'
'When bright Apollo, exil'd from the sky'
'Of marriage, love, contention, joys and woes'
Jackson's authorship is recorded in *Nichols* III.625–6.
L(993.e.41).

J10 [—] Paradise lost: a poem. Attempted in rhyme. Book I. *London, printed for the author; sold by A. Jackson, Mrs. Dodd, Mrs. Nutt, and by the booksellers in town and country,* 1740 [1739]. (*GM* Dec)
8°: A–D⁴; *1–2 3–32.*
'Of man's first disobedience, and repast'
Jackson's authorship is recorded in *Nichols* III.625n.
L(79.c.28); IU,MH,NN.

J11 Jackson, Joseph. 'A funeral tear to the pious memory of that eminent and laborious preacher of the gospel Dr. William Russel, who died March 6th 1702. [*London*] *Printed for Sam. Drury.* Price 6d.' (*WL* July 1702)

J12 [**Jackson, Samuel.**] ⟨The⟩ duty of a wife. *London printed, and sold by Mary Edwards,* 1707.
8°: A⁴ (A2 as 'A3'); *1 2–8.*
The order of editions has not been determined. A chap-book; large woodcut on title.
'Both antient and modern authors do say'
An edition below (J14) bears Jackson's name; he has not been identified.
O.

J13 [—] The duty of a wife. A poem. *London, printed for C. C. near Fleet-street,* 1707.
8°: *A*⁴; *1 2–8.*
University of Otago, N.Z.

J14 — — By Samuel Jackson. [*London?* 170–?]
8°: *A*⁴; *1 2–8.*
The imprint and signatures are possibly cropped in the copy seen.
CLU-C(cropt).

J15 Jackson, William. Maxims for the conduct of life, by the reverend Doctor William Jackson, late minister of St. Michan's, writ during his illness; and recommended to a friend, beseeching him at the same time to have them made publick soon after his decease. *Dublin printed, and sold by E. Waters,* 1736.
½°: 1 side, 2 columns.
Note after imprint, 'This paper is printed thus purly for pasting up in the several appartments in houses, being worthy the perusal of old and young, who have a desire to live and die well'.

Jackson, W. Maxims

'From the creation let the day begin'
C.

'**Jacob,** *door-holder to the Kit-cat club.*' The Kit-cat clubs lamentation, for the loss of the pope, the devil, and the pretender, 1711. *See* K94.

Jacob, Giles. A miscellany of poems. *London, printed for Tho. Warner,* 1718. (*PB* 4 March)
8°: pp. 64.   O; MnU,TxU.

[—] The lover's miscellany: or, poems on several occasions, amorous and gallant. In imitation of Mr. Prior... *London, printed for J. Roberts,* 1719.
8°: pp. 59.   O; CSmH.
Dedication signed 'Philemon'; listed in *Jacob* II. 299.

————

J16 [—] Britain's hero: a poem, on the death of his grace John, duke of Marlborough. *London, printed for H. Cole; sold by J. Peele,* 1722. (*PB* 11 Aug, 'just publish'd')
2°: *A*² B–C²; *1–4 5–12.*
'As when some earthquake in a distant land'
Dedication signed 'G.J.'; ascribed to Jacob by DLC, but no evidence is known except for the initials.
DLC.

J17 — The court beauties: a poem. Humbly inscrib'd to her grace the Duchess of Bolton. *London, printed for Tho. Warner,* 1718.
8°: *A*² B–C⁴; *i–iv, 1–16.* A1 hft.
A copy in the Lewis Walpole Library has Walpole's ms. notes.
'I sing of beauty, O! ye gods inspire'
L(11644.cc.19).

J18 [—] Human happiness. A poem. Adapted to the present times. With several other miscellaneous poems... *London, printed for T. Jauncy, & J. Roberts,* 1721. (*PB* 10 Jan)
8°: A–E⁴ F⁴(–F4) G⁴ (E2 as 'D2'); *i–iii iv–viii, 1–46.*
'Awake, my muse, in strains melodious show'
Dedication to Prior signed 'G.J.'; listed in *Jacob* II. 300 as still in ms.
L(164.1.76, Luttrell, Feb); ICU.

J19 [—] A journey to Bath and Bristol: an heroi-comic-historic-, and geographical poem. To which are added, the following love poems; I. Choice of a mistris... V. The fair innocent... *London, printed for J. Roberts, & Arabella Morrice, without Temple-Barr,* [1717.] (*PB* 4 June)
8°: A–E⁴ F¹ (A2 as 'A3'); *1–3 4–42.*
'In long vacation, when gay cit's repair'
The authorship is revealed in *Jacob* II. 299.
BaP(lacks C3).

J20 [—] — The second edition, corrected. To which is added, a journey from Bath and Bristol, by the way of Salisbury and Winchester. And to those are

Jacob, G. A journey to Bath

added the following love-poems... *London, printed for J. Roberts,* 1717. (*PB* 6 July)
8°: A–D⁴ E...; *1–3* 4–35 *36 blk*...
The copy seen lacks the love-poems.
Journey from Bath: 'I now in Bristol had regardless stay'd'
BrP(lacks all after E2).

J21 [—] A poem on the happy reconciliation of his most excellent majesty and his royal highness the Prince of Wales. *London, printed for T. Bickerton,* 1720. (*PB* 19 May)
2°: *A²* B¹; *1–2* 3–6.
'When two great friends are once to passion prone'
The authorship is revealed in *Jacob* II. 299.
InU(Luttrell, May),OCU.

J22 [—] — *London, printed for T. Bickerton, and reprinted in Dublin, by C. Carter,* 1720.
½°: 1 side, 1 column.
L(C.121.g.8/9).

J23 [—] The rape of the smock. An heroi-comical poem. In two books. *London, printed for R. Burleigh,* 1717.
8°: *A⁴* B–F⁴; *i–viii, 1* 2–39 *40.* A1 frt; 40 advt.
Bond 54. Four added poems by various authors, pp. 27–39. Advertisements on p. 40 for Curll's books. Reissued in *The ladies miscellany,* 1718.
'I sing a virgin's smock, the direful cause'
Subsequently published with Jacob's name.
L(011650.ee.70/2),O,LdU-B; ICU,IU,MH,OCU, TxU.

J24 — — By Mr. Jacob. The second edition. *London, printed for H. Curll,* 1727 [1726]. (1 Nov)
8°: A–E⁴ (A3 as 'A2'); *i–viii, 1* 2–32. A1 frt.
Only the first two of the added poems are reprinted here. Date from *Straus, Curll.* Reissued in *The altar of love,* 1731.
L(11631.bb.41),O(2),E(−A1); CLU-C,CSmH, IU,MH(−A1),TxU.

J25 — — The third edition. With other miscellanies. *London, printed for E. Curll,* 1736.
8°: A–D⁴, ²A–C⁴; *1–7* 8–32, *1–3* 4–23 *24 blk.* A1 frt.
The additional poems are quite different from those in the preceding editions. Pp. 24–28 contain 'The Welch wedding' by Francis Hauksbee. ²A–C⁴ is a reissue of Isaac Hawkins Browne, *Of smoking,* 1736; the title ²A1 was perhaps intended to be cancelled. Pp. 29–32 of the first part add the other two of Browne's parodies omitted from that edition.
L(Tab.603.a.17/1,−A1); KU(lacks ²A1),MH (lacks ²A1).

J26 [—] [*idem*] The thief slain: or the linen vail restored. An heroi-comic poem. In two canto's. *London, printed for J. Brown, J. Swan, and sold by all the booksellers in town & country,* [175–?]
8°: *A²*(A1 + frt) B–D⁴; *i–iv, 1* 2–22 *23; 24 blk.* A1 hft; D4 advt.
Variant first line; it is not known whether Jacob revised the text.

Jacob, G. The thief slain

'I sing a linen vail, the direful cause'
L(11631.aaa.43); ICN(−D4),MH(−D4).

Jacob, Hildebrand. The works...containing poems on various subjects, and occasions... *London, printed for W. Lewis,* 1735. (*GM, LM* Feb)
8°: pp. 461.   L,O; CSmH,IU.
Entered in Bowyer's ledgers under 21 Jan; 500 copies printed. Presentation copy to Lord Orrery at MWiW-C.

J27 [—] 'Apollo's stratagem, or Button unmask'd.' [*London, printed for A. Dod; sold by Tho. Edlin.*] (*DC* 11 Jan 1721)
Listed in the *DC* advertisement for *The curious maid,* 4th edition, as by the same author. Probably a half-sheet; the poem has only 43 lines.
'Apollo, kindly looking down'
Printed in Jacob's *Works,* 1735.

J28 — Bedlam, a poem. *London, printed for W. Lewis, & Tho. Edlin,* 1723 [1722]. (*PB* 6 Dec)
4°: A–B⁴; *1–2* 3–16.
'You who, like Proteus, in all shapes appear'
L(11602.gg.24/3; C.118.c.2/2),O; CLU-C,CtY-M,ICN,IU,MH.

J29 — Brutus the Trojan; founder of the British empire. An epic poem. *London, printed for William Lewis,* 1735.
8°: A–F⁸ G⁴ H⁸ I⁴; *i–xiv, 1*–113 *114 blk.* A1 hft.
Half-title reads 'The first five books'. Entered in Bowyer's ledgers under 28 Oct 1735; 250 copies printed. Listed in *LM* Jan 1736; the date of the ICN copy is changed in ms. to 1736. Possibly first circulated privately.
'I sing the founder of the British throne'
O(−A1); ICN,MH.

J30 [—] Callistia; or the prize of beauty. A poem. *London, printed for W. Lewis; sold by the booksellers in London & Westminster,* 1738. (*GM,LM* March)
2°: *A²* B–C²; *1–2* 3–12.
Bowyer's ledgers record 500 copies printed.
'Now the long wish'd for morning gilds the east'
Entered to Jacob in Bowyer's ledgers, 20 March 1738. The winner of the golden heart is Miss Molesworth; she and the other competitors are identified in ms. in the O copy.
L(11630.h.11),O(uncut); CSmH,CtY,IU,MH, TxU(uncut)+.

J31 — Chiron to Achilles. A poem. *London, printed for John Watts,* 1732. (*GSJ* 25 May)
4°: *A²* B–D²; *1–3* 4–16.
Entered in *SR* 25 May; deposit copies at L,O,E,EU,AdU.
'Old Chiron to his pupil thus began'
L(11602.gg.24/2, cropt; C.70.f.1/2),O(2),E, AdU,LdU-B+; CSmH(uncut),CtY,ICN,MH, TxU(2)+.

Jacob, H. Chiron to Achilles

J32 [—] — 'London, printed for J.R. in Warwick-lane' [Edinburgh], 1732.
8°: A⁸; 1–2 3–15 16 blk.
Printed by Ruddiman on the evidence of the ornaments. Possibly an imperfect copy.
MH.

J33 [—] [reissue]
8°: A⁸(A8+²A⁴); 1–2 3–15 16–18 19–24. 18 advt.
With the addition of an answer. P.17 is half-title, 'Achilles's answer to Chiron'; p. 18 is an advertisement for books sold by Allan Ramsay. From the advertisement it seems probable that this issue also dates from 1732, and that this is the first edition of *Achilles to Chiron*, which was published separately in London in 1738.
Achilles: 'Accept that tribute which I justly owe'
L(1961),O,GU; CtY,MH,NjP,TxU.

J34 [—] The curious maid. A tale. *London, sold by A. Dodd*, 1720. (Dec?)
2°: A(3 ll); 1–2 3–6.
Rothschild 1192. There are probably several impressions which have not been distinguished. All seen have the second leaf signed 'A', but the collation appears to be A² B¹.
'Beauty's a gaudy sign, no more'
Printed in Jacob's *Works*, 1735. Sometimes wrongly ascribed to Prior on the evidence of a letter from Chesterfield to Prior, 25 Jan 1721. See *The curious maid, continu'd*, 1721, *An answer to the Curious maid*, [1721], and *The peeper*, 1721.
L(Ashley 5240, uncut),OW,LdU-B; CSmH,CtY (Luttrell, Jan 1721),TxU.

J35 [—] [reimpression] *London, sold by A. Dodd, & T. Edlin*, 1720 [1721?]. (11 Jan?)
'The 4th edition' was advertised in *DC* 11 Jan 1721, for A. Dod, sold by Tho. Edlin.
L(840.m.1/42),O; CLU-C.

J36 [—] [reimpression] *London, sold by A. Dodd, T. Edlin, & J. Roberts*, [1721.] (22 Feb?)
Pp. 5–6 are reset. 'The 5th edition' was advertised in *DC* 22 Feb, sold by A. Dodd, T. Edlin, J. Roberts.
CsmH.

J37 [—] — [*London*? 1721/–.]
¼°: 1 side, 2 columns.
No rules.
O-JJ.

J38 [—] — [*Dublin*? 1721?]
½°: 1 side, 2 columns.
Two rules above text, one between columns.
L(Cup.600.b.2/6); TxU.

J39 [—] — *London, printed for W. Lewis, & Tho. Edlin*, 1723.
2°: A² B¹; 1–2 3–6.
For a possible new edition with changed title, see *Cloe convinc'd: or, seeing's believing*, 1733.

Jacob, H. The curious maid

Reprinted in a Dublin edition of *Kick him Jenny*, 1734 (K33·5).
O(uncut).

J40 — Donna Clara to her daughter Teresa: an epistle. Occasioned by a genuine letter to a young Spanish lady, from her mother, who had been long confined to a convent thro' the discovery of her intrigue with a Sicilian count. *London, printed for W. Lewis*, 1737. (4 Feb?)
2°: A² B²; 1–2 3–8.
Entered to Jacob in Bowyer's ledgers under 4 Feb 1737; 75 copies printed. Listed in *LM* Feb.
'From solitude, which ne'er must know an end'
CSmH.

J41 — — The second edition. *London, printed for W. Lewis*, 1737. (12 Feb?)
2°: A² B²; 1–2 3–8.
Entered in Bowyer's ledgers under 12 Feb, 100 copies, one sheet standing; apparently A was reset.
L(11630.h.29),E.

J42 [—] An epistle to a person of quality. (Exposing the vain pursuits of mankind.) By the author of several late epistles. *London, printed for J. Roberts*, 1735. (*GSJ* 2 May)
2°: A¹ B–C²; 1–2 3–10.
Entered to Jacob in Bowyer's ledgers under 23 April 1735; 250 copies printed.
'How hard, my lord, is it to find'
Attributed to Jacob (from Bowyer's ledgers) in *Nichols* II. 61. The 'several late epistles' have not been identified, but the following poems published by Roberts might be possible candidates: *Taste and beauty*, 1732; *The false patriot*, 1734; *The ladies of pleasure*, 1734; *The happy courtezan*, 1735.
O; MH,NjP(uncut).

J43 [—] A genuine epistle written some time since to the late famous Mother Lodge. *London, printed for J. Roberts, for the use of her creditors*, 1735. (*GM* May)
2°: A² B–C²; 1–4 5–12.
Bowyer's ledgers record 250 copies printed.
'Dear Lodge, you know my love for rhime'
Entered to Jacob in Bowyer's ledgers under 5 May 1735. According to the preface, from 'Mrs Dunbo'. The poetical autobiography of a whore.
O; NjP(uncut),TxU(uncut).

J44 — Hymn to the goddess of silence. *London, printed for J. Watts*, 1734. (*GM* Jan)
2°: A² B²; 1–2 3–7 8 blk.
'All hail! O awful, sage divinity'
L(162.n.13),O; CLU-C,DFo,RPB,TxU.

[—] The leaky vessel, a tale, 1721. See L90.

[—] The mad dog, a tale. By H----------J---------, esq, 1730. See G58.

Jacob, H.

J45 [—] The members to their soveraign... By the author of the Curious maid. [*Dublin*] *Printed in the year* 1726.
½°: 2 sides, 1 column.
> This is clearly a Dublin edition (the copy seen bears a Dublin collector's initial 'F'), but one would expect it to be a reprint of a London edition. Possibly the date is a misprint for 1729.
'O thou design'd by nature to controul'
> Printed as Jacob's in the miscellany section of Prior's *Poems*, 1733; excluded from his *Works*, 1735 (the dedication speaks of poems he wished to disown). Sometimes ascribed to Prior on the assumption that he wrote *The curious maid*.
CLU-C.

J46 [—] [*idem*] The silent flute, a poem. Being the members speech to their sovereign... By the author of the Curious maid. *London, printed for A. Moore; sold by the booksellers of London & Westminster*, 1729. (*MChr* 27 Jan)
2°: A–B²; *1–2* 3–8. 8 advt.
> Pp. 7–8 contain 'Horace, ode xxx, book I. Paraphras'd'. A song 'The silent flute' is a different work; there is an engraved edition and a slip song (at C) excluded from this catalogue.
Horace: 'Cælia this night has promis'd I'
L(Ashley 4985),OW; MH,TxU(2, 1 uncut).

J47 [—] — '*London, printed for A. Moore; sold by the booksellers of London & Westminster*' [*Dublin*], 1729.
8°: A⁴; *1–3* 4–8.
DA.

J48 [—] Patriotic love; an ode. Chiefly occasioned by some late acts of parliament: and humbly inscribed to the true friend of his country. *London, printed for W. Lewis*, 1737. (13 Jan?)
2°: A² B²; *1–2* 3–7 *8 blk*.
> Entered to Jacob in Bowyer's ledgers under 13 Jan 1737; 75 copies printed. Listed in *LM* Jan.
'Poor, hapless bird, who haunt'st the vale below'
> Attributed to Jacob in *Nichols* II. 83, doubtless from Bowyer's ledgers.
O; CSmH(uncut).

J49 — The progress of religion. A poem. *London, printed for J. Roberts*, 1737.
2°: A² B–C²; *i–iv*, 1–8. A1 hft.
'When first religion triumph'd o'er the mind'
O(2),LdU-B; CtY,MH(uncut),*NjP*,TxU.

J50 [—] 'The prude's purgatory.' [*London*, 1736.]
> Entered to Jacob in Bowyer's ledgers under 24 May 1736; a quarter sheet, 60 copies.
(*Nichols* II. 83n.)

[—] The tit-bit. A tale, 1738. *See* T320.

Jacob, H.

J51 [—] The unequal match: a tale. By the author of the Curious maid. *London, printed for W. Lewis*, 1737. (26 Feb?)
2°: A² B²; *1–2* 3–7 *8 blk*.
> Variant watermarks in copies seen. Entered to Jacob in Bowyer's ledgers under 26 Feb, 150 copies printed. Listed in *LM* March.
'Two against one, when well agreed'
> Ascribed to Jacob by *Nichols* II. 83, doubtless from Bowyer's ledgers.
L(840.m.1/43; Ashley 5242); CLU-C,CSmH, OCU.

J52 [—] — The second edition. *London, printed for W. Lewis*, 1737. (5 March?)
2°: A² B²; *1–2* 3–7 *8 blk*.
> Apparently a reimpression; Bowyer's ledgers record 100 copies as reprinted under 5 March.
MH.

Jacobi, John Christian. Psalmodia Germanica; or, a specimen of divine hymns, translated from the high Dutch. Together with their proper tunes and thorough bass. *London printed, and sold by J. Young, Mr. Smith at Bishop Beveridge's Head in Patermoster-row, W. Smith at the Orange-tree near St. Clement's Church*, 1722.
8°: pp. 144. L,O.
> Both copies seen are probably on fine paper, watermarked with fleur-de-lys on shield; they are in contemporary morocco bindings. The tunes are added on engraved plates. Jacobi is apparently the editor and translator.

J53 Jacobites. The Jacobites coat of arms. *London printed, and sold by H. Hills*, [1710?]
½°: 1 side, 2 columns.
> Large heraldic woodcut at head.
'Per fess sable and gules in chief he bears'
> Possibly occasioned by the Sacheverell affair.
L(C.20.f.2/310).

J53.5 — [dh] The Jacobites lamentation for the death of the late King James, who deceased at St. Germains, September the 4th, 1701. In a dialogue between two Jacobites, meeting together at the Devils Tavern near T.B. in Fleet Street... [col] *London, printed for Robert Johnson*, 1701.
4°: A²; *1–4*.
'Well met, right noble sir: what do you ail?'
MR-C.

Jacobo. Jacobo septimo ejus nominis, [1712?/13.] *See* Pitcairne, Archibald.

Jam. Jam te, dive, tenent Homius, [1712?] *See* Pitcairne, Archibald.

[J54 = H77.2] James, Haestrect. A poem humbly offer'd to the pious memory of his late sacred majesty King William III, 1702. *See* Harris, Joseph.

James, N.

James, Nicholas. Poems on several occasions. *Truro, printed by Andrew Brice*, 1742.
8°: pp. 148.   L,O; CtY,MH.

J55 Jane. Jane Shore to the Duke of Gloster, an epistle. *London, printed for R. Dodsley; sold by M. Cooper*, 1749. (9 May)
4°: *A*⁴ B–C⁴ D²; *1–6 7–27 28 blk*. A1 hft.
Date from *Straus, Dodsley;* listed in *GM* May.
'Just when emerging from that gloomy shade'
L(840.k.4/13,−A1),CT; CSmH,CtY(−A1),
DFo,MH,OCU.

J56 Janus. Janus. A tale. '*Printed for C. Cross near Westminster*', 1714.
slip: 2 sides, 1 column. 2 advt.
The daily slip, no 2, for 14 Sept 1714. The imprint is fictitious; 'C. Cross' stands for Charing Cross. The copy seen was reissued in *State poems. Being a collection of choice private pieces*, 1715.
'Of late within a northern town'
Against Robert Harley.
Brett-Smith.

— Janus, did ever to thy wond'ring eyes, [1704/05.]
See Smith, Edmund.

Jeffreys, George. Miscellanies in verse and prose. *London, printed for the author*, 1754.
4°: pp. xxviii, 436.   L; CtY,MH.
No watermark. List of subscribers.

— [fine paper]   O.
Watermark: Strasburg bend.

J57 — Father Francis and Sister Constance, a poem, from a story in the Spectator. And Chess: a poem. Translated into English from Vida. *London, printed for Lawton Gilliver & John Clarke*, 1736. (*SR* 1 July)
4°: *A*² B–I⁴; *i–iv, 1–64*. iv err.
Entered in *SR* to Jeffreys by Gilliver; deposit copies at L,O,E,SaU. Listed in *LM* July.
'Constantia, now a saint, was heavenly fair'
Chess: 'A sportive image of the martial race'
L(11642.h.43/2),O,E,LdU-B,SaU; CLU,CSmH,
CtY,MH,TxU +.

J58 Jemmy. Jemmy's pedigree. [*London?* 1745.]
slip: 1 side, 1 column.
Rough woodcut at head.
'Oh! vain pretender, you are come'
Against the Young Pretender.
C.

[Jenyns, Soame.] Poems. By * * * * *. *London, printed for R. Dodsley*, 1752.
8°: pp. 194.   L,O; CtY,MH.

[—] Miscellaneous pieces, in two volumes... *London, printed for R. & J. Dodsley*, 1761.
8°: 2 vol.   L,O; CtY,MH.

Jenyns, S.

[—] Miscellaneous pieces, in verse and prose. The third edition. *London, printed for J. Dodsley*, 1770.
8°: pp. 452.   L,O; CtY,MH.

— The works... *London, printed for T. Cadell*, 1790.
8°: 4 vol.   L,O; MH.

J59 [—] The art of dancing, a poem, in three canto's. *London, printed by W.P.; sold by J. Roberts*, 1729. (*MChr* 8 March)
8°: *A*² B–H⁴; *i–iv, 1–55 56 blk*. A1 hft.
The copyright formed part of lot 50 in a trade sale attributed to Henry Lintot, 27 Nov 1739 (cat. at O-JJ); it was bought in by Lintot.
'In the smooth dance to move with graceful mein'
Reprinted in Jenyns's *Works*, 1790.
L(11631.d.4; G.18967/2),O(−A1),OW; CSmH,
CtY,DFo,ICN(uncut),MH+.

J60 [—] — The second edition. *London, printed for M. Cooper*, 1744 [1743]. (*DA* 7 Nov)
8°: *A*¹ B–H⁴; *i–ii, 1–55 56 blk*.
A reissue with cancel title; no half-title in the copy seen.
O.

J61 [—] The embarrass'd knight. A satire. Occasion'd by seeing an ode inscrib'd to L——d Ch——d. *London, printed for J. Purser*, [1748.] (*GM, LM* Jan)
2°: A(3 ll); *1–2 3–6*.
A1 and 3 are conjugate; A2 is signed 'A2'.
'Who's this? what! Ha----y the lyrick'
Horace Walpole's 'Account of Sir Charles Hanbury Williams' (*Correspondence* XXX. 318) records 'Soame Jennings wrote a miserable, and abusive ode on seeing this [i.e. an ode by Williams to Chesterfield, not identified], and published it'.
MH,OCU.

— 'An epistle to Lord Lovelace, 1735.'
Listed in *CBEL* in this form, but there is no evidence that it was separately published. The error probably arises from the fact that it was printed in *Dodsley* III (1748) 153 as 'Written in the year 1735'.

J62 [—] Horatii ep. I. lib. II. ad Augustum. The first epistle of the second book of Horace, imitated. To...Philip, lord Hardwicke... *London, printed for R. Dodsley; sold by M. Cooper*, 1749. (*GA* 2 Feb)
4°: *A*⁴ B–D⁴; *1–5 6–30 31–32*. A1 hft; D4 advt.
'Whilst you, my lord, such various toils sustain'
Early ms. attributions to Jenyns in ICN,IU, KU copies; reprinted in his *Works*, 1790.
L(T.653/4),MR; CtY(uncut),ICN,ICU,IU,KU (−A1).

J63 [—] The modern fine gentleman. *London, printed for M. Cooper*, 1746. (*BM* March)
2°: *A*² <B²; *1–3 4–8*.
'Just broke from school, pert, impudent and raw'

Jenyns, S. The modern fine gentleman

        Horace Walpole's ms. ascription to Jenyns in the L copy; reprinted in his *Works*, 1790. See *The modern fine lady*, 1746; Jenyns published another poem with this title in 1751.

        L(C.57.g.7/15, Horace Walpole's copy),O(uncut); CSmH,MH,NN.

J64 [—] — '*London, printed for M. Cooper*' [*Edinburgh*], 1746.

        8°: A^4; *1–3* 4–8.

        Copies at EN,LdU,MH are bound with Edinburgh piracies.

        EN,LdU; ICN,MH.

[—] A new song to the honourable Miss C———t, 1726. *See* N216.

[—] An ode, in answer [to Sir Charles Hanbury Williams, *An ode to the honourable H---y F--x*], 1746. *In* W491.

J65 [—] An ode to the hon. Philip Y--ke, esq; imitated from Horace, lib. II. ode XVI. By S--- J--- esq; To which is added, the same ode imitated and inscribed to the Earl of B--- on his creation. *London, printed for A. Moore*, 1747. (*GM,LM* Nov)

        2°: A^4; *1–2* 3–8.

        'For quiet, Y——ke, the sailor crys'

        'In each ambitious measure crost!'

        The first poem is clearly by Jenyns; it is reprinted in his *Works*, 1790. The author of the second poem has not been identified.

        L(1959),E; CtY,DFo.

J66 [—] The 'squire and the parson: an eclogue. *London, printed for R. Dodsley*, [1749.] (11 Dec)

        2°: $A^2 < B^2$; *1–2* 3–8.

        Date from *Straus, Dodsley;* listed in *GM* Dec 1749.

        'By his hall chimney, where in rusty grate'

        Reprinted in Jenyns's *Works*, 1790.

        L(11602.i.14/12); CSmH,CtY,MH(ms. alterations).

[—] Tar water, a ballad, 1747. *See* T39.

'Jereboam, Orthodox.' The London clergy's petition, [1722/23.] *See* L237.

Jest. Jest and earnest, 1703. *See* Pittis, William [Chaucer's whims].

Jesus. Jesus. A poem. In blank verse, 1745. *See* Reynolds, John.

'Jews-Harp, Nahum, *esq;*' Monsieur Ragoo, 1749. *See* M412.

'Jews-Trump, Jeremiah van.' A collection of new state songs, 1732. *See* Collection.

'Jingle, Jeremy.' Spiritual fornication, 1732. *See* S655.

'Jingle, Joshua, *esq;*' A congratulatory ode, 1748. *See* C347.

J---l

J67 **J---l.** J---l's wife. A new ballad. In answer to one, intituled, S-----s and J----l. *London, printed for G. Foster*, 1743. (*GM, LM* Feb)

        2°: A^4; *1–2* 3–8.

        'Around th' infernal plain she rov'd'

        A reply to [Sir Charles Hanbury Williams] *S——s and J——l*, 1743.

        L(1484.m.13),O(2, uncut),LdU-B; CSmH,CU, MH,NN-B.

J------n. J------n B-------s's ballad continued, [1729.] *See* A ballad by J-----n B-----s, [1729.]

'Jo., *Honest.*' An excellent new song upon his grace our good lord archbishop of Dublin, 1724. *See* Swift, Jonathan.

J----o, S------ge. A hue and cry after a c-----y m---------te, [1726?] *See* H351.

J68 **John.** John and Betty. A tale. *Hereford, printed for the author*, 1746.

        2°: $A^1 B^2 C^2 D^1$; *1–2* 3–11 *12 blk.*

        A1 and D1 have been seen to be conjugate. According to HrP, 'almost certainly printed by W. Smith of Bye Street'.

        'I sing the loves of John and Betty'

        Attributed to — Sherborne in Pickering & Chatto cat. 266/10331, describing this copy; the origin of the identification was unknown to them at the time of its sale in 1933. *Poems and versions by the author of John and Betty*, 1754, is known from a cutting from a bookseller's catalogue, but has not been traced. No suitable Sherborne has been identified in Hereford.

HrP(uncut).

J69 — John Dennis, the sheltring poet's invitation to Richard Steele, the secluded party-writer, and member; to come and live with him in the Mint. In imitation of Horace's fifth epistle, lib. I. and fit to be bound up with the Crisis. *London, printed for John Morphew*, 1714. (*PB* 27 April)

        4°: A–C²; *1–2* 3–12.

        Teerink 604; *Williams* 1098.

        'If thou can'st lay aside a spendthrift's air'

        Printed as Swift's by Nichols (*Supplement*, 1779) and subsequent editors. Dismissed by Williams. A satire on Dennis and the whigs.

        L(11633.df.25),LLP,*CQ*; InU,MH.

J70 — John High-land-man's remarks upon the ladyes of Edinburgh. Togather with other wonderfull rareaties seen there by him, delivered in his own dialact... [*Edinburgh*, 170–?]

        1°: 1 side, 3 columns.

        The L copy is bound with Edinburgh broadsides of 170–, but the dates and the order of editions are uncertain; some may be of the seventeenth century.

        'When her nain shell to Edinburgh went'

        L(12350.m.18/1).

John

J70·2 — [*idem*] Iohn Highlandmans remarks. [*Edinburgh*, 17--?]
½°: 1 side, 3 columns.
    Title in roman capitals.
E.

J70·4 —— John Highland-man's remarks. [*Edinburgh*, 17--?]
½°: 1 side, 3 columns.
    Title in black-letter.
E.

'**John,** *the hermit.*' Stinking fish, 1708. *See* Dunton, John.

J71 Johnson, Charles. A congratulatory verse, to her grace, the Dutchess of Marlborough: on the late glorious victory, near Hochstet in Germany... *London, printed for Robert Battersby*, 1704. (*PM* 16 Sept)
2°: A–B²; *i–iv, 1–4*.
'Madam, amidst the numerous crouds that wait'
    Signed on p. 4.
InU,MH(Luttrell, 18 Sept).

J72 — The queen: a pindarick ode. *London, printed for Nicholas Cox*, 1705. (19 March, Luttrell)
2°: A² B–G²; *i–iv, 1–23 24 blk.* A1 hft; 23 err.
    Advertised in *PM* 20 March as published 'yesterday'.
'Touch, my muse, the jarring string'
MH,TxU(2, 1 Luttrell).

J73 [—] Ramelies. A poem. *London, printed for Ben. Bragg*, 1706. (*DC* 10 June)
2°: A² B–D²; *i–iv, 1–12.*
    The Luttrell copy, dated 11 June, was in the collection of C. H. Wilkinson.
'Hail goddess to our isle propitious'
    The copy at C has the dedication signed in ms; compare the following issue.
L(1347.m.29),O,C.

J74 — [another issue]
    Dedication signed in type. All copies appear to be on the same good paper.
LLP.

J75 Johnson, Richard. Cursus equestris Nottinghamiensis. Carmen hexametrum, autore Ricardo Johnson, ludi literarii ibidem magistro, commentariorum grammaticorum scriptore. *Londini, typis Johan. Matthews*, 1709. (*PB* 24 May)
4°: A–E²; *1–4 5–19 20 blk.*
    The copies at L have watermark of Amsterdam arms, those at O of Dutch lion. Possibly the latter are fine paper. Advertised in *PB* as sold by John Morphew.
'Fert animus, quo non aliud præstantius ullum'
L(837.f.36; G.9906/1),O(2),*DrU*.

J76 [Johnson, Samuel.] London: a poem, in imitation of the third satire of Juvenal. *London, printed for R. Doddesley*, 1738. (13 May)

Johnson, S. London

2°: A¹ B–E² F¹; *1–3 4–19 20 blk.*
    Rothschild 1216. Date of publication from Nichol Smith & McAdam's edition of John son's *Poems*, 1941.
'Tho' grief and fondness in my breast rebel'
L(162.n.14; Ashley 5195),O,C,EU,LdU-B+; CSmH,CtY,IU,MH,TxU+.

J77 [—] — The second edition. *London, printed for R. Dodsley*, 1738. (20 May?)
2°: A¹ B–E² F¹; *1–3 4–19 20 blk.*
    Sheets B, C, and part of D are reset. Date from *Poems*, 1941.
L(11630.h.30; 643.m.16/5),LVA-D(2),O; CSmH,CtY,MH,*NjP*,TxU.

J78 [—] — The second edition. '*London, printed for R. Dodsley*' [*Edinburgh*], 1738.
8°: B–C⁴ D²; *1–3 4–20.*
    Printed by Ruddiman on the evidence of the ornament.
O,E,*BP*; CtY,CtY-M,*NN*.

J79 [—] — The third edition. *London, printed for R. Dodsley*, 1738. (15 July)
2°: A¹ B–E² F¹; *1–3 4–19 20 blk.*
    Rothschild 1217, recorded as lacking half-title, surely in error. Partly from standing type of the second edition. Date of publication from *Straus, Dodsley.*
L(11631.i.9),LVA-F,O,BaP; CtY(2).

J80 [—] — *Dublin, reprinted by and for George Faulkner*, 1738.
8°: A–B⁴ C²; *1–3 4–19 20 blk.*
L(1963),O(uncut),C,DN; *CtY,IEN*,TxU.

J81 [—] — The fourth edition. *London, printed for R. Dodsley*, 1739.
2°: A¹ B–E² F¹; *1–3 4–19 20 blk.*
    A reissue or reimpression of the third edition.
L(840.m.1/7),O,*ShU*; MH(uncut).

J82 [—] — The fifth edition. *London, printed by E. Cave; sold by R. Dodsley*, 1750.
4°: A¹ B–F² G¹; *1–3 4–23 24 blk.*
L(11602.gg.24/18),O,*MR*; TxU.

J83 [—] A new prologue spoken by Mr Garrick, Thursday, April 5, 1750. at the representation of Comus, for the benefit of Mrs Elizabeth Foster... *London, printed for J. Payne & J. Bouquet*, 1750. *For Mrs Elizabeth Foster.* (*SR* 7 April)
2°: A² B¹; *1–3 4–5 6 blk.*
    Deposit copies at L,O,SaU. Ms. correction to p. 4 line 17 'Bust' for 'Dust' in most copies.
'Ye patriot crouds, who burn for England's fame'
    Horace Walpole's ms. attribution to Johnson in his copy at L.
L(11630.d.12/8, cropt; 643.m.14/20; C.57.g.7/28, Horace Walpole's copy),O(uncut),LdU-B, SaU; *CSmH,CtY,DFo,NN-B.*

J84 [—] — *London printed, and Edinburgh reprinted*, 1750. *For Mrs Elizabeth Foster.*
8°: A²; *1–3 4.*
CtY.

Johnson, S.

J85 [—] Prologue and epilogue, spoken at the opening of the theatre in Drury-lane 1747. *London, printed by E. Cave; sold by M. Cooper, & R. Dodsley, 1747.* (*GA* 8 Oct)
4°: *A*² B–C²; *1–3* 4–12.
    The L copy is a variant with '(Price 6*d*.)' on title; others have no price.
'When learning's triumph o'er her barb'rous foes'
'Sweet doings truly! we are finely fobb'd!'
    The prologue is by Johnson, the epilogue by Garrick.
L(C.71.ff.5),LVA-D; CtY,*MBAt*,MH, Rosenbach.

J86 [—] — *London, printed by W. Webb,* [1747.]
4°: *A*²; *1* 2–4.
    A piracy.
CSmH,CtY.

J87 — The vanity of human wishes. The tenth satire of Juvenal, imitated by Samuel Johnson. *London, printed for R. Dodsley; sold by M. Cooper, 1749.* (9 Jan)
4°: *A*⁴ B–C⁴ D²; *1–3* 4–28.
    Rothschild 1233. Date from *Poems,* 1941.
'Let observation with extensive view'
L(840.k.4/6; Ashley 3414),O,OC,E,LdU-B+; CSmH(original wrappers, uncut),CtY,ICN,MH, *TxU*+.

Johnson, Thomas. An epitaph upon his grace John, duke of Marlborough... Written by a monk of the order of St. Dominic. And translated into English by a member of the Marlborough-Club, 1714.
    Listed by *Dobell* 769, but a prose epitaph; there are copies at O,InU.

J88 **Johnston, —, Mr.** A poem humbly inscrib'd to the Lord Sunbury on his birth-day. By Mr. Johnston. *London, printed for John Bateman, 1720* [1721?]. (*DP* 4 Jan)
2°: *A*¹ B² C¹ (C1 as 'B'); *1–2* 3–6 '5–6'.
    From the evidence of the watermarks, A1 and C1 are not conjugate. The Luttrell copy, dated January, was in the collection of C. H. Wilkinson.
'Whilst we, illustrious child, attendance pay'
EtC.

[**Jole, William.**] The father's blessing penn'd for the instruction of his children. Containing godly and delightful verses... Adorn'd with 24 cuts. By W.J. A.M. *London, printed for G. Conyers,* [170–?]
12°: pp. 20.   L.
    Thirteen lessons; *cf.* William Ronksley, *The child's weeks-work,* 1712. An earlier edition is listed with Jole's name in *TC* Michaelmas 1674.

J89 **Jolly.** The jolly patriots: a new ballad. To the tune of How pleasant a sailor's life passes! *London, printed for W. Webb, 1744.* (*LEP* 10 March)

The jolly patriots

2°: *A*⁴; *1–5* 6–8. A1 hft.
'How jolly a patriot's life passes'
    A political satire.
O; CtY,InU(–A1),NN.

J90 — The jolly soldier, being a song over a bottle, to an well known tune. The Campbels are coming, aha, aha... [*Edinburgh,* 1716.]
½°: 1 side, 1 column.
'Here's a health to the noble and valiant Argyle'
    On the victory of John, duke of Argyll, at Sheriffmuir.
E.

Jonah. Jonah: a poem, 1720. *See* Mitchell, Joseph.

[**Jones, —, esq.**] Hesperi-neso-graphia: or, a description of the western isle, 1716–. *See* H162.

Jones, Henry. New poems on several occasions... *Dublin, printed by Christopher Dickson, 1735–6.*
8°: pp. 40.   DA; CSmH.
    In the copy at DA the date is overprinted '1736–7'. The author is clearly not the bricklayer. The work is dedicated to Mervyn Pratt esq.

Jones, Henry, *the bricklayer, 1721–1770.* Poems on several occasions. *London, printed for R. Dodsley, & W. Owen, 1749.* (*LM* June)
8°: pp. 31, 212.   L,O; CtY.
    Watermark: fleur-de-lys.

— [fine paper]   LVA-D; MH.
    Watermark: Strasburg bend.

— — *Dublin, printed by and for S. Powell, 1749.*
12°: pp. 136.   L,DN; DFo.

— Poems. *Dublin, printed by Richard James, 1756.*
4°: pp. 4, 141.   O; CtY.
    Separate titles dated 1756 to several of the poems.

J91 [—] The bricklayer's poem. Presented to his excellency the lord lieutenant. On his arrival in this kingdom. *Dublin, printed in the year 1745.*
8°: *A*⁴; *1–3* 4–7 *8 blk.*
'Amidst th' applause which art and learning brings'
    Reprinted in Jones's *Poems,* 1749. See [James Eyre Weeks] *The cobler's poem,* 1745.
LVA-F,O,C,DN,DT+; CU,*MB*,PP.

J92 [—] The bricklayer's poem to the Countess of Chesterfield, on her ladyship's saving the soldiers from being shot. *Dublin, printed in the year 1745.*
8°: *A*⁴; *1–2* 3–7 *8 blk.*
'What means this dismal sound, that march so slow'
    Reprinted in Jones's *Poems,* 1749.
DG,DK(2),DN,DT; CSmH,MH.

J93 — On seeing a picture of his royal highness the Prince of Wales. Which was presented to the university of Dublin. A poem. *Dublin printed:*

Jones, H. On seeing a picture

> *London reprinted; for W. Owen, & G. Woodfall,*
> *1749. (GM April)*
> 4°: *A² B–F²; i–iv, 1–19 20 blk.* A1 hft.
> No Dublin edition has been traced.
> 'In time's wide wasting walk with backward tread'
> MH.

J94 [—] Philosophy. A poem address'd to the ladies
who attend Mr. Booth's lectures. By the Bricklayer.
Dublin, printed by and for S. Powell, 1746.
8°: *A⁴; 1–3 4–8.*
'To science sacred, muse, exalt thy lays'
> Reprinted in Jones's *Poems,* 1749. Ms. note in
> the DA copy, 'Revised I am told by Baron
> Mountney [Richard Mountney, baron of the
> Irish exchequer]'; Booth 'is anglice a Mr.
> King'.

L(11631.e.7),DA,DT; MH.

J95 'Jones, Jasper.' 'The secret history of bubbies.
Written for the use of a certain great lady of the
last century, by Jasper Jones, of Llanarth... And
now communicated to the world, with a copious
index, by his executor Thomas Man. [*London*]
Printed for D. Gardiner; sold by S. Slow. Price 1s.'
(*SJEP* 27 Feb 1733)
> Also advertised as forming part of *Sylvia's*
> *study; or, the lady's magazine,* a miscellany of
> about the same date. The advertisement in
> *SJEP* quotes six lines which suggest that the
> work was in verse; they are presumably its
> opening passage:
> 'Bubbies of every form my plume portrays'
> The author is probably pseudonymous.

Jones, John. Oppian's Halieuticks of the nature of
fishes and fishing [books 3–5 translated by Jones],
1722. *See* O236.

J96 [Jones, Lewis.] Io! Triumphe! A poem upon
Admiral Vernon. By an undergraduate of Jesus-
College, Oxon. *London, printed for T. Taylor, 1741.*
(*GM, LM* Dec)
4°: *A¹ B–F²; 3–5 6–23 24.* 24 advt.
> The copy seen probably lacks the half-title,
> A1 of *A²*.
'Arms and the man I sing, the first who rose'
> Attributed to Jones in *Rawlinson.*
L(11630.f.65).

Jones, Mary. Miscellanies in prose and verse.
Oxford printed, and delivered by Mr. Dodsley, Mr.
Clements in Oxford, and Mr. Frederick in Bath,
1750.
8°: pp. lv, 405.   L,O; CtY,MH.
> Watermark: fleur-de-lys. A letter from Mary
> Jones to Dodsley dated 9 March 1755 in a
> copy at LVA-D suggests that now subscribers
> have had time to call for the book, it should be
> advertised as 'now publish'd'.

Jones, M.

— [fine paper]   L,LVA-D.
Watermark: Strasburg bend.

[—] The lass of the hill.
> A slip song, of which there is a copy at L,
> dated by *CBEL* as [*c.* 1740]. The date could
> well be much later, and it is excluded here like
> other popular songs. *A letter to Dr. Pitt,* listed
> by *CBEL* as a separate poetical work, is in
> prose.

J97 Jones, Richard. Britannia triumphans: a poem,
humbly inscrib'd to the worshipful Sir Richard
Steel, kt. *London printed, and sold by J. Baker, 1717.*
4°: *A–B⁴; 1–2 3–16.*
'As when bright Sol extends his glitt'ring stage'
MH.

Jones, Samuel. Poetical miscellanies on several
occasions. *London, printed for A. Bettesworth, &*
E. Curll; sold by Mrs. Lucas and T. Hammond, jun.
at York, T. Ryles at Hull, W. Freeman at Durham,
and J. Button, New-Castle, 1714. (*MC* July)
12°: pp. 24.   L,O; ICN,KU.

J98 — Whitby. A poem. Occasioned by Mr. Andrew
Long's recovery from the jaundice by drinking of
Whitby spaw-waters. *York, printed by Grace*
White, for T. Hammond, junior; sold by A. Bettes-
worth, A. Dodd, London, 1718.
8°: *A⁴ B⁴; 1–4 5–13 14–16 blk.* A1 hft.
'The learn'd inventers of each lib'ral art'
L(1488.gg.27).

[Jones, Walter.] Hesperi-neso-graphia: or, a
description of the western isle, 1716–. *See* H162.

J99 [Jonson, Benjamin.] Earl Mortimer's speech.
[*London,* 1711.] (2 June?)
½°: 1 side, 1 column.
> Listed in Bowyer's ledger under 2 June 1711
> as printed for Mr. Lintott, 1000 copies.
'This rise is made, yet! and we now stand, rank'd'
> Reprinted from Jonson's *The fall of Mortimer;*
> on Harley's creation as earl of Oxford and
> Mortimer, 1711.
O(cropt),Rothschild; MH,NN,*Harding.*

Jortin, John. Lusus poetici. [1722?]
4°: pp. 24.   O.
> Title in half-title form; dedication signed. The
> copy seen is inscribed 'Ex dono authoris.
> 1722.'

— Joannis Jortini Lusus poetici. Editio secunda
auctior. *Londini, impensis J. Stephens, juxta ædem*
D. Clementis, 1724.
8°: pp. 19.   CtY.

Jortin, J.

[—] Lusus poetici. Editio tertia, emendatior. *Londini, excudit Gulielmus Bowyer,* 1748. (*LM* Jan) 4°: pp. 56. L,O; CtY,TxU.

> Entered to Jortin in Bowyer's ledgers, no date, 250 copies printed *gratis* (the paper being paid for), and sewed in blue and marbled paper.

J100 [—] A hymn to harmony. *London, printed for Abraham Vandenhoek, & Lawton Gilliver,* 1729. (*MChr* 20 June) 2°: *A*² B²; *1–3* 4–8. 'Queen of sweet numbers and resistless sound'

> The copy at Shrewsbury School has a ms. ascription to Jortin by John Taylor. Advertised as 'in imitation of Spencer'.

LDW,LdU-B,SrS(uncut); CtY,IU,MH,TxU.

'Joseph.' The c——t sermon. A new ballad, [1748.] *See* C536.

J101 Joshua. Joshua: a poem in imitation of Milton: humbly inscrib'd to the Duke of Marlborough. Occasioned by Mr. Stephens's Letter to the author of the Memorial of the state of England. *London, printed for John Lawrence,* 1706. (2 May, Luttrell) 2°: *A*² B–G²; *i–vi,* 1–22. A1 hft.

> The Luttrell copy is in the collection of R. D. Horn; advertised in *DC* 8 May.

'Of glorious arms, and of their blest effects'

> Occasioned by William Stephens's *Letter* in reply to John Toland's *Memorial.*

LDW(−A1),O(uncut); ICN,InU,NjP,OCU.

Journal. The journal, [1721/22.] *See* Swift, Jonathan.

J102 — The journal of a Dublin beau. Written by a young lady. *Dublin, printed by Nicholas Hussey,* 1728–9. 8°: A⁸; *1–2* 3–15 *16 blk.* 'Basely ungenerous mankind deal'

> An answer to Swift's *Journal of a Dublin lady,* [1729.]

DA(2).

— The journal of a Dublin lady, [1729.] *See* Swift, Jonathan.

J103 Journalists. The journalists displayed. A new ballad. To the old tune of Lilleburlero. *London, 'printed by Peter Wiseacre in the Old-Baily',* [1731.] ½°: 1 side, 1 column. 'Dear friend, have you heard the fantastical chimes'

> *Percival* (p. li) suggests Lord Hervey's authorship on grounds of style; it is unconfirmed. A satire on the *Craftsman*; printed in the *London Journal,* 6 Feb 1731.

L(1875.b.35/6; G.559/10),C; *Harding.*

J104 — — *London, printed for J. Johnson, near London-Bridge,* [1731.] ½°: 1 side, 1 column. MH.

Journey

Journey. A journey to Bath and Bristol, [1717.] *See* Jacob, Giles.

— A journey to h-ll, 1705. *See* Ward, Edward.

J105 Jove. Jove's ramble: a tale shewing how the moon was made of a green cheese. *Dublin, printed in Big Ship-street,* 1723. ½°: 1 side, 2 columns.

> *Teerink* 918; *Williams* 1102.

'That gods sometimes, incognito'

> *Crum* T201: 'A tale'. Ascribed to Swift by *Ball* 171–2, but Williams feels the need for more evidence.

C,DT.

Jovi. Jovi eleutherio: or, an offering to liberty, 1745. *See* Ridley, Glocester.

J106 Joy. Joy upon joy: or, here's all in a hurry, horse and away, helter schelter, the devil in a fish kettle. Being a full and true account of a hundred and thirty thousand scolding wives, carry'd away in one night's time... *London, printed for Mary Hollingworth,* [17—.] 8°: A⁴; *1* 2–8.

> Printed in chap-book style. Dated in Murray Hill cat. 30/552 as *c.* 1710.

'You wives that are lately married'

Institute for Sex Research(uncut).

J107 [Joy, James.] Epistola ad amicum familiaris. *Londini, apud T. Cooper, et Oxoniæ, apud Jacobum Fletcher,* 1740–1. (*GM,LM* April 1741) 2°: *A*² B² C¹; *1–4* 5–9 *10 blk.* 'Dum prius cunctis mihi chare, Juli'

> Early ms. attribution to Joy in the O copy.

O; CtY,OCU.

J108 Joyful. A joyful ode: inscribed to the king, on the late victory at Dettingen. *London, printed for M. Cooper,* 1743. (*DA* 2 July) 2°: *A*⁴; *1–3* 4–8. 'From gentler notes of peace and love'

O; KU,MH,MiU.

J109 Jubilade. The Jubilade. An ode. In a paraphrastical imitation of the 5th ode of Horace, book IV. with additions. Humbly addressed to his majesty on his absence abroad, and the glorious success of his arms. *London, printed for B. Couse,* 1743. (*LDP* 16 Nov) 4°: A–B⁴; *1–2* 3–15 *16 blk.* 'Great monarch! sprung from ancient British kings'

L(11630.c.12/16); MH(uncut).

Judgment. The judgment of Hercules, 1727. *See* Mitchell, Joseph.

— The judgment of Hercules, 1741. *See* Shenstone, William.

Judgment

— The judgment of Hercules, 1743–. *See* Lowth, Robert.

— The judgment of Paris, 1743. *See* Bettesworth, John.

— The judgment of the muse, 1742. *See* Hyde, Henry, *viscount Cornbury*.

J110 Judoign. Judoign. A poem on the late victory in Brabant. *London printed, and are to be sold by B. Bragge, 1707 [1706]*. (14 Dec, Luttrell)
2°: *A*²; *1–2* 3–4.
'Rise sacred queen, Apollo's darling muse'
CLU-C(Luttrell, uncut).

J111 June. June 10th, 1745. Being the anniversary of his majesty's birth. [*Edinburgh?* 1745.]
¼°: 1 side, 1 column.
On the other side, *A poem upon the 29th of May*; originally conjugate with *Prince Charles his welcome*.
'Shall Britons still at feeble wishes stay'
A Jacobite poem.
L(C.38.g.14/11),E; CSmH.

J112 Junto. The junto. [*London?* 1710.]
½°: 1 side, 1 column.
Printed in italic type; no 'Finis' at end; first line ends '...*Spirits sleep*'.
'At dead of night when peaceful spirits sleep'
A satire on the members of the whig junto.
O,Crawford; InU,NN,*Harding*.

J113 — [another edition]
Printed in italic type; no 'Finis' at end; first line ends '...*Spirits Sleep*'.
Crawford.

J114 — [another edition]
Printed in italic type; 'Finis' at end.
L(1850.c.10/31).

J115 — [another edition]
Printed in roman type; no 'Finis' at end.
MH.

— The junto. A poem, 1712. *See* Russell, Richard [The impeachment].

Jure. Jure divino: a satyr, 1706. *See* Defoe, Daniel.

Just

Just. A just character of the revd. Mr. Boyce, 1728. *See* Choppin, Richard.

J116 — 'A just imitation of the first satire of the second book of Horace. In a dialogue between Mr. Pope and the ordinary of Newgate. With Achilles dissected, &c. [*London*] *Printed for W. Mears*. Price 6d.' (*GM,LaM* April 1733)
This is clearly the same work as 'The first satire of the second book...' printed with the prose *Achilles dissected*, 1733 (2 March), by Alexander Burnet. It seems possible that this represents a new advertisement for that work. The first line in *Achilles dissected* is:
'There are (whate'er you think sir) I am told'
The poem is signed 'Guthry' from Bolt-Court, Fleet-street, 26 Feb. 1732–3, in *Achilles dissected*; Pope's letter to Fortescue of 8 March 1733 records 'Curll has printed a parody on my own words which he is proud of as his own production...' Curll reprints so much of Pope's version of *The first satire* that there is little for him to take credit for. Cf. *The sequel of Mr. Pope's law-case*, 1733.

Juvenal.
[*Satire* 1] [Gilbert, Thomas:] The first satire of Juvenal imitated, 1740. *See* G141.

[*Satire* 3] [Earle, Jabez:] Rus. Satira nata ex tertia Juvenalis, [1724.] *See* E9.

[Johnson, Samuel:] London: a poem, in imitation of the third satire of Juvenal, 1738, 1739, 1750. *See* J76–82.

[*Satire* 7] The seventh satyre of Juvenal imitated, 1745. *See* S355.

[*Satire* 10] Johnson, Samuel: The vanity of human wishes. The tenth satire of Juvenal, 1749. *See* J87.

[*Satire* 13] The merchants advocate, a poem, in imitation of Juvenals XIII. satyr, [1708.] *See* M184.

The thirteenth satyre of Juvenal imitated, 1745. *See* T155.

'**Juvenal & Persius,** *Messrs*.' The state of Rome, under Nero and Domitian... By Messrs. Juvenal and Persius, 1739. *See* S725.

K

K., A. A holy poem: or Christmas carrol, 1714. *See* H292.

K., G. La belle assemblée, [1734?] *See* B180.

K., H., *gent.* The presbyter unmask'd, 1724. *See* P1024.

K., I. Serenissimo et invictissimo principi, [1718/20?] *See* Ker, John, *chaplain to the fleet.*

K., M. The life and actions of W.S., 1750. *See* L179.

'Kara Mustapha, *Bashaw Reis Effendi.'* The mock senator; a pleasant Arabian tale. Written originally in Arabick by Kara Mustapha, [1717/22?] *See* M357.

K1 Kaven-bail. The Kaven-bail poem: or, Tom Turd-man's epistle, address'd to Charles C---y. *Dublin, printed in the year* 1734.
8°: *A*⁴; *1–2* 3–8.
'Say, great Pythagoras of our happier days'
    An attack on Charles Carthy.
DA.

'K--ch, J--ck.' The reprieve, 1730. *See* R160.

K2 Keach, Benjamin. War with the devil, or the young man's conflict with the powers of darness [!] ... The eleventh impression. *London printed, and sold by Benj. Harris,* 1705.
8°: A–K⁸; *1–160.*
    Apparently first published in 1673 (copy at CtY). Keach died in 1704; these editions are included though they are probably of no textual significance.
'The naturalists most aptly do compare'
NNUT(lacks A2, H4–8, K6).

K3 —— *Edinburgh, printed by the heirs and successors of Andrew Anderson,* 1709.
12°: A–G¹²; *i–ii* iii–vi, 7–167 *168 blk.*
L(11631.a.67).

K4 —— The eighteenth impression. *London, printed for H.P.; sold by V. Harris at the Golden Boar's Head Grace-church Street,* [171–?]
8°: A–K⁸ (A3 as 'A5'); *1–4* 5–128 133–164.
    Horizontal chain-lines.
L(11626.aa.16).

K5 — [reissue?] The eighteenth impression. *London, printed for H.P.; sold by Han. Tracy, at the Three Bibles on London-Bridge,* [172–?]
8°: π² A–K⁸ (A3 as 'A5'); *i–iv, 1–4* 5–128 133–164. π1ᵛ, π2ʳ frts.
    π² consists of two conjugate leaves with facing woodcuts before title. Apparently from the same type as the preceding; their relation needs further investigation.
GU; *DFo.*

K6 —— The nineteenth impression. *London, printed for John Clarke,* 1728.
12°: π² A–F¹² G⁸ H²; *i–iv, 1–4* 5–161 *162–164.* π1ᵛ, π2ʳ frts; 162–164 advt.
    The collation is tentative, and based on the following edition; probably the copy seen lacks the first and last leaves.
L(1481.a.32, −π1, H2).

K7 —— The twentieth impression. *London, printed for John Clarke,* 1737.
12°: π² A–F¹² G⁸ H²; *i–iv, 1–4* 5–161 *162–164.* π1ᵛ, π2ʳ frts; 162–164 advt.
    π² and H² were probably printed with G⁸ as a duodecimo sheet.
L(11631.a.32),DM; *IaU.*

[Keene, Morgan.] New miscellaneous poems. With five love-letters from a nun, to a cavalier, 1713–. *See* New.

[—] The impotent lover describ'd in six elegies on old-age, 1718. *See* I14.

[—] Love-letters between a nobleman and his sister, 1734–. *See* L284.

K8 Keimer, Samuel. 'The platonick courtship. A poem. By Keimer Samuel, a hearty lover of honesty, sincerity and truth. Author of the Brand snatch'd from the burning... [*London*] *Printed for J. Bettenham.* Price 6d.' (*PB* 19 March 1719)

K9 — A search after religion, among the many modern pretenders to it... To which is added, an address and petition to King Jesus. *London, printed for the author, and sold at the Cheshire-Coffee-house in Kings-Arms-court on Ludgate-hill,* [1718.]
12°: *A*⁶ B–C⁶; *i–iii* iv–vi, 7–34 *35–36.* C6 advt.
'To you my friends, this book is recommended'
Address: 'Hail mighty monarch, glorious king of kings'
    A religious autobiography, written in a debtor's prison.
L(4152.aa.56/1).

K10 Keinton, Martha. A poem. *London, printed by S. Holt,* 1716.
2°: A(3 ll); *1–2* 3–6.
    A2 and A3 signed; probably a half-sheet is inserted within the fold A1.3.
'I sing the man, that Britain's crown now wears'
    Dedication signed.
L(11602.i.14/6).

Ken, Thomas, *bishop.* The works... Published from original manuscripts, by William Hawkins. *London, printed for John Wyat,* 1721.
8°: 4 vol.   L,O.
    Containing poetical works only.

Ken, T., *bishop*

[—] A paraphrase upon the hymn of St. Ambrose. Together with morning, evening, and midnight hymns. By the bishop of Bath and Wells. *Edinburgh, printed in the year* 1732.
8⁰: pp. 15.   L,GM.

> The three hymns were added to the 1695 edition of Ken's *Manual of prayers for Winchester scholars.*

[**Kennedy,** —, *Dr.*] Plain truth, or downright Dunstable, 1740. *See* P475.

[—] A short critical poem on poets and poetry, 1750. *See* P476.

K11 Kennedy, H. The comical revenge, or the friendly cuckolds. A tale. *Dublin, printed in Big Ship-street,* 1724.
8⁰: A⁴; *1* 2–8.
'Of all the passions, love we find'

> An erotic tale.

MC.

Kennett, Basil. An essay towards a paraphrase of the psalms, in English verse... *London, printed by J.H. for B. Aylmer,* 1706.
8⁰: pp. 105.   L,O; MH,NN.

> The copy at MH is in presentation morocco, and possibly on fine paper.

K12 [Kennett, White.] 'Armour. A poem. An imitation of Milton. [*London*] *Printed for E. Curll.* Price 6d.' (*DJ* 3 April 1723)
4⁰.

> The advertisement, which merely lists the poem, should perhaps read 'In imitation...' *Straus, Curll* quotes *EvP* 10 Nov 1724 as advertising 'Armour, or the never failing engine'. Subsequently reprinted in William Pattison, *Cupid's metamorphoses,* 1728; *The cabinet of love,* 1731; *The potent ally,* 1741. *Bond* 77. Rewritten as *The machine,* 1744.

'O all ye nymphs, in lawless love's disport'

> Ascribed to Kennett in *The potent ally,* 1741; see also the account of Kennett in *Rawlinson:* 'edidit sine nomine Condom a Poem Lond... 4⁰. a name which gave so just offence that the author republished it under the title of Armour...4to. Wrote in the stile of the Splendid shilling in Miltonick verse, of which about 200. were sold, as the undertaker informed me, and the rest made wast paper.'

K13 [Kennicott, Benjamin.] A poem on the recovery of the honble. Mrs. Eliz. Courtenay from her late dangerous illness. *Exon, printed by Andrew & Sarah Brice, at the sign of the Printing-press in Gandy's Lane,* 1743.
2⁰: π² A–D²; *i–iv,* 1–16.

> π2 is a dedication leaf; the copy at ExI was possibly presented without π1.

Kennicott, B. A poem

'Pardon the bold intrusion of a swain'

> The copy at ExI is bound with a collection of Kennicott's works.

ExI(lacks π1),ExP.

K14 [—] — humbly inscrib'd to Kellond Courtenay, of Painsford, esq; and his lady. Written in the year 1743... The second edition. [*Oxford*] 1747.
8⁰: A–B⁴; *i–ii* iii–iv, 5–16.

> Rough cut of the Sheldonian Theatre on title.

L(11631.e.83),LDW,O(2, 1 uncut),ExI; CtY, DLC,ICN,OCU.

[Kenrick, William.] Epistles, philosophical and moral. *London, printed for T. Wilcox,* 1759.
8⁰: pp. xxiv, 336.   L,O; CtY,ICN.

> A work designed in this form, rather than a collection.

— Poems; ludicrous, satirical and moral. *London, printed for J. Fletcher,* 1768.
pp. viii, 307.   L; CtY,MH.

K15 — The town. A satire. *London, printed for R. Griffiths,* 1748. (22 March?)
4⁰: A–C⁴; *1–3* 4–24.

> Listed in *GM,LM* March. Probably the same work listed anonymously in *BM* Dec 1748, 'The town, a satire, on Mr. G. Mr. F. Dr. D. Mrs. W. &c.'

'Wise was the clown who, when he first descried'
L(11630.c.8/21; 11630.c.9/4, ms. date 22 March), LG,O; CSmH,CU,InU,TxU.

Kensington. Kensington Garden, 1722. *See* Tickell, Thomas.

Kentish. The Kentish ballad, 1710. *See* The Geneva ballad, 1705–.

K16 — The Kentish men. A satyr. Occasion'd by the late treat at Mercer's Hall, and the publication of their five several effigies. Written by a commoner. *London, printed in the year* 1701. *And sold by the booksellers of London & Westminster.* (16 July, Luttrell)
2⁰: A–D²; *i–iv,* 1–12.

> The Luttrell copy is recorded by *Thorn-Drury*. Advertised in *PB* 17 July. A 'second edition', not seen, was advertised in *PB* 22 July.

'When men, for want of courage and of sense'

> There is a copy of the 'effigies' in L(P&D).

L(C.131.h.1/9),LG,LVA-F,O,C*J*+; CLU-C, CSmH,CtY,MH,NjP.

K17 Ker, John, *d. 1741.* [dh] Ad cives Edinburgenses, de pompa Regiorum Sagittariorum habita Junii xiv. MDCCXIV. [*Edinburgh,* 1714.] (July?)
2⁰: *A²*; 1–3 *4 blk.*

Ker, J. Ad cives Edinburgenses

A poem of 64 lines, with two sets of introductory verses to the citizens and to David Drummond, with concluding verses 'De certamine ipso & triumpho'. Probably the 'Poem on the Archers 3 pages Gr. primer' entered in Ruddiman's ledger for the week ending 17 July 1714, '12 quires (paper Mr Freebairn's)'.
'Quis canat arma, viros? Ranas cecinisset Homerus'
Signed on p.3 'Jo. Ker'.
E; NjP.

K18 — [dh] Ad D. D. Gul. Bennettum de Grubbet, equitem; de morte D. D. Gul. Scot de Thirlestane ...qui obiit Edini 8vo Octobris, 1725. Jo. Kerrus. [*Edinburgh*, 1725.]
2⁰: A²; *1*–4.
'An imitation of the Latin poem on the death of Sir Will. Scot of Thirlestane' on pp. 3–4.
'Mi Bennette, tuus jacet sodalis'
'Bennet, the muses ornament, and friend'
O,E; TxU.

K19 — [dh] Ad illustrissimum atque ornatissimum virum, Robertum marchionem de Bowmont...de nobilissimo Joanne domino Ker, ipsius filio...xxiii. die Aprilis A. Æ. C. MDCCXL nato, genethliacon. [*Edinburgh?* 1740.]
2⁰: A²; *1–2* 3–4.
The poem on p. 1 is followed by an epigram 'In eundem xxiii. diem Aprilis...', signed 'Jo. Ker'; p. 2 is blank; pp. 3–4 contain English imitations 'To the most honourable, Robert marquis of Bowmont...a poem, congratulatory... Paraphrased from the Latin' and 'An hexastichon...', signed 'William Lauder'.
'Kerrorum soboles avita, supplex'
'My lord! sprung from the antient race divine'
There is, perhaps, some question as to whether the author is identified with the correct Ker.
TxU.

K20 — Cantici Solomonis paraphrasis gemina; prior vario carminum genere, altera sapphicis versibus perscripta. Notis criticis & philologicis illustrata. *Edinburgi, in ædibus Tho. Ruddimanni, impensis auctoris*, 1727.
8⁰: †⁸ A–F⁸; *i–ii* iii–xiv *xv–xvi*, 1–96. xv err.
Watermark: Amsterdam arms.
'Nobile carmen habes, merito cui cantica cedant'
'Canticum quod rex Solomon canoræ'
L(3020.a.14, presented to the Duke of Roxburgh), O,E,AdU(4),GM(2)+.

K21 — [fine paper]
Watermark: fleur-de-lys. All copies seen are in morocco presentation bindings.
O,E(2).

K22 — Donaides: sive musarum Aberdonensium de eximia Jacobi Fraserii, J.U.D. in academiam regiam Aberdonensem munificentia, carmen eucha-

Ker, J. Donaides

risticum. Notis illustratum... *Edinburgi, in ædibus Tho. Ruddimanni*, 1725.
4⁰: A–B⁴ C–E²; *1–2* 3–28. 28 err.
Watermark: eagle. Copies are usually found bound with David Mallet's translation, *A poem in imitation of Donaides*, [1725]; there are fine-paper copies of that also, and it is difficult to correlate the two and be sure which copies are on fine paper.
'Eia alacres hilaresque virum cantemus, amœnos'
O,AdU(2, 1 with ms. corrections, contemporary gilt edges, to 'Mr. Hay of Dalgalie'); MH.

K23 — [fine paper?]
No watermark.
L(837.h.35),LVA-D,E; CtY.

K24 [—] Pitcarnium morientem. [*Edinburgh*, 1713.] (Nov)
¼⁰: 1 side, 1 column.
Below, 'Pitcarnius respondet'. Probably the 'Poem of Mr Ker' entered in Ruddiman's ledger for the week ending 7 Nov 1713, 200 copies printed.
'Quid te, Pitcarni, juvat has nunc linquere terras'
'Terras purgabam monstris: fatalia terris'
Both the address and reply are ascribed to Ker in Pitcairne's *Poemata*, 1727.
L(1185.k.2/23, cropt).

K25 Ker, John, *chaplain to the fleet*. Excellentissimæ regis majestati, petitio Joannis Ker, clerici. [1717/21.]
1⁰: 1 side, 2 columns.
'Quandoquidem celebres regiones tum boreales'
E(ms. dedication to the Duke of Roxburgh).

K26 [—] Serenissimo et clementissimo principi Georgio ...in illud Ciceronis, O tempora! O mores! carmen. *Londini, typis H. Woodfall*, 1723.
2⁰: A² B²; *1–2* 3–8.
With an English verse translation on pp. 5–8.
'Conqueritur siquis mores mala tempora culpans'
'Of evil times if any do complain'
Later ms. ascription to John Ker in the L copy. The L catalogue ascribes it to John Ker M.D., but as his library was sold in 1714 he was presumably dead by this date. This work seems to be consistent with the chaplain's verse.
L(162.n.52).

K27 [—] Serenissimo et invictissimo principi, clementissimoque nostro regi et domino, Georgio, in suam Britanniam reditum felicem gratulans ode. [1718/20?]
½⁰: 1 side, 2 columns.
'Luget heu Arctos quia Phœbus Austrum'
At foot, 'I   K   jam sexagenarius, et in classe regia ann. 28. plus minus a sacris'; ms. expansion in O copy, 'Iohannes Ker'.
O(presented to the Duke of Roxburgh).

Ker, R.

Ker, Robert, *of Gilmerton.* The serious fears of some judgments approaching upon Scotland... [*Edinburgh?*] *Printed in the year* 1717.
12°: pp. 86.   E.
> A collection of poems and prose pieces. It is not certain that the following poems are by the same author.

K28 — A short but true account of the nobility and representatives of that ancient realm and kingdom of Scotland... Written by an impartial pen, collected and drawn up by Robert Ker, in 1705... [*Edinburgh?*] *Printed in the year* 1712.
8°: A^8; *1–2* 3–16.
'To think on our ancestors brave'
E.

K29 — The true church of Scotland's lamentation, dedicated to Heu Aitkin, of Stirstrachen... Composed in the prison house of Dalkeith... *Edinburgh, printed by John Reid,* 1711.
8°: A^8; *1–2* 3–16.
'Alace! Zion! go weep and mourn'
E.

K30 **Kerry.** The Kerry cavalcade: or, the high sheriff's feast. [*Dublin*] *Printed in the year* 1733.
½°: 1 side, 2 columns.
> On the other side, a prose account headed 'Dublin, March the 24th, 1732–3'.
'Assist me, ye muses, F——ce to sing'
> A satire on the high sheriff.
CSmH.

K31 **Key.** A key to the whole state of Europe. [*London,* 1741.]
½°: 1 side, 1 column.
> Printed text to accompany a large engraved plate, also at L.
'A cub of France th' imperial eagle tears'
L(P&D 2502).

K32 **Kick.** 'Kick him Jenny. A tale. [*London*] Price 6*d*.' (*GM* Sept 1733)
'A valiant and virtuous dame'
> The same author wrote *Kick him Nan,* 1734.
> A bawdy tale.

K33 —— 'The second edition. [*London*] *Sold by J. Gover.*' (*LM* Oct 1733)

K33·5 — Kick him Jenny, a merry tale. *London: printed for Roger Clevercock: and Dublin: reprinted for Dorothy Kilcock, near Lucas's Coffee-house on Cork-hill,* 1734.
8°: A–C^4; *1–2* 3–24.
> The imprint is fictitious. Hildebrand Jacob's *The curious maid* is reprinted on pp. 22–4.
O.

K34 — Kick him Jenny, a tale... The eleventh edition. To which is added, the Female contest, a merry

tale. *London, printed for W. France near Leicest⟨er⟩ Fields,* 1737.
12°: A^6 B^6; *1–5* 6–24. A1 frt.
> 'The female contest' was separately published as *The curious females,* [172–?].
Contest: 'Four lovely lasses, gay and bright'
L(P.C.26.a.11).

K35 — Kick him Nan: or, a poetical description of a wedding night. By the author of Kick him Jenny. *London, printed for T. Reynolds,* 1734. (*GM* March)
2°: A^2 B^2; *1–2* 3–8.
> Engraving on title.
'When flesh and blood are in their prime'
L(1965),O; MH.

K36 [**Kidgell, John.**] An answer to the Advice to Mr. L—g—n, the dwarf fann-painter at Tunbridge-Wells. To which is added, Table-talk, in the modish taste. *London, printed for H. Carpenter,* [1748.] (*GM, LM* Sept)
2°: A^4; *1–3* 4–8.
'Had fate propitious made it mine'
> Ascribed to Kidgell in *Reed, Repository* III. 185f where it is reprinted with *Table-talk.* The fan-painter was Thomas Loggan; a reply to *Advice to Mr. L---------n,* 1748.
L(1489.m.20),O(2); CtY,DFo,MH.

K37 [—] Table-talk. September 1745. *London, printed for M. Cooper,* 1747. (*BM* May)
4°: A^1 B^4 C^1; *1–2* 3–11 *12 blk.*
'When lovely Cælia had resign'd'
> Attributed to Kidgell in *Rawlinson,* who has an uncompleted note that it was reprinted with a Tunbridge lampoon. A satire on polite conversation.
L(11630.c.7/4; 11630.b.6/2; 11602.gg.24/12),E; CLU-C,ICU.

K38 [—] — *London,* 1748.
4°: A^4 B^2; *1–2* 3–11 *12 blk.*
> Blank space left before date in imprint.
O.

K39 **Killiecrankie.** [dh] Killychrankie. To be sung with its own proper tune. [col] *Edinburgh, printed and sold by John Reid,* 1713.
2°: A^2; *1–2.*
> Two poems on the facing inner pages, the second headed '⟨The a⟩nswer to Killychrankie. To be sung with the same tune of Killychrankie'; the other side of the sheet is blank.
'Clavers and his Highlandmen'
Answer: 'You Highlandmen with tongue and pen'
E.

Killpatrick, Jac. *See* Kirkpatrick, James, *M.D.*

K40 **Kincaid, Thomas.** [dh] In Archibaldi Pitcarnii medici dissertationes & poemata. [*Edinburgh,* 1713.]
2°: A^2; *1–2.*

Kincaid, T. In Archibaldi Pitcarnii

Two facing pages on the inner side of the sheet. The last line on p. 1 begins 'Mortis quos avidis...'. The order of impressions has not been established. Ruddiman's ledger records the printing of 'Poem for Mr Kincaid on Dr Pitcairn' in the week ending 24 Oct; 100 copies of 'Mr Kincaid's poem on the Doctor' in the week ending 31 Oct; and 100 copies of 'Poem for Mr Kincaid' in the week ending 7 Nov. The last could conceivably refer to the following work.

'Pitcarnus sophiæ est cultor amabilis'

At foot, 'Posuit sodalis Tho. Kinkaid'. A ms. version at E is dated 6 Sept 1713, six weeks before Pitcairne's death.

L(1185.k.2/23*); TxU.

K41 — [another impression]

The last line on p. 1 begins 'Vita ut det...'. The same setting of type as the preceding, with two lines moved over to p. 2.

E.

K42 [—] In D. Archibaldi Pitcarnii medici, & philosophi, doctissimi bibliothecam instructissimam. [*Edinburgh*, 1713?]

½°: 1 side, 1 column.

'Bibliotheca bonis multisque repleta libellis'

Printed as Kincaid's in Pitcairne's *Poemata*, 1727; ms. in the E copy, 'T:K: authour'. Pitcairne's library was purchased by the Emperor of Russia in 1713 after Pitcairne's death.

L(1185.k.2/24),E; TxU.

K43 [—] [dh] In Regiam Sagittariorum Scotorum cohortem. [*Edinburgh*, 1713?] (March)

2°: A²; 1–2.

The first line of the last stanza reads 'Tali juventa, si LEO FERVIDUS'. Two facing pages on the inner side of the sheet; page 2 has the English text, headed 'On the Royal Company of Scottish Archers'. The order of editions is uncertain. Ruddiman's ledger for the week ending 7 March 1713 records setting and printing 150 copies of 'Mr Kincaid's poem', and under 28 March 'A poem on the Archers by Mr Kincaid Engl. & Lat 2 pages pot, case...Paid before'.

'Scotos pharetris quis sine gaudio'

'Who can with so much envy be possest'

The Latin text is signed 'T.K.' in *Poems...on the Archers*, 1726. Another (and later?) version of the English text is entered separately as *A poem on the Royal Company of Scottish Archers*, [1713/–.]

E(ms. 'Wm Bennett of Grubet').

K44 [—] — [*Edinburgh*, 1714?]

2°: A²; 1–2.

The first line of the last stanza reads 'Tali juventa si LEO FERVIDUS'. Ms. date 1714 in the TxU copy. Possibly the poem entered in Ruddiman's ledger for the week ending 12

Kincaid, T. In Regiam

June 1714, 'Poem on the Royal Company of Archers 2 pages pot...press 300 copies. (paper Mr Freebairn's)'.

E; TxU.

K45 [—] — [*Edinburgh*, 1714?]

½°: 1 side, 1 column.

The first line of the last stanza reads 'Tali Juventa, Si LEO FERVIDUS'. Possibly the copy seen lacks the facing page with English translation; or the Latin text may have been printed separately.

E.

K46 [—] — [*Edinburgh*, 1713/–.]

4°: A²; 1–2.

Two facing pages on the inner side of a half-sheet. P. 2 has a different English text, headed 'A poem on the Royal Company of Archers'. Another edition of the Latin with another English translation (in 2 columns on a folio half-sheet, at E) was almost certainly originally conjugate with *A list of the Royal Company of Scottish Archers*; it has the imprint 'Edinburgh, printed for David and James Adams, 1715.'

English: 'What true born Scot, but will be glad to see'

MH.

Kind. A kind of a dialogue in hudibrasticks, 1739. *See* Paget, Thomas Catesby, *baron Paget*.

King. King Cock-lorrel's treat, [1729?] *See* 'D'Anvers, Caleb'.

— King Edward's ghost, [1712?] *See* Craggs, James, *the younger*.

K47 — King George for England. A new ballad, to an old tune: necessary to be sung by all true and loyal Englishmen... To the tune of the second part of St. George for England. By Humphrey Chaunter, esq; poet laureat to Mumpsimus the IIId. king of the Gipsies. *London printed, and sold by J. Collyer, & G. Woodfall*, 1745. (GA 12 Nov)

2°: A⁴; 1–3 4–8.

Horizontal chain-lines.

'Of all the kings, or old, or new, that bear such mighty fame'

L(1962).

K48 — King Harry the eighth's ghost at the inst-----n. '*Windsor, printed for Timothy Star at the Blue Ribband*', *and sold by the booksellers of London & Westminster*, [1741.]

2°: B² (B2 as 'B'); 1–2 3–4.

Horizontal chain-lines.

'As A----s was trotting away from the chapter'

Crum A1441: 'An excellent new ballad, April [21] 1741'. A satire on the Garter installation of 1741 of the Dukes of St. Albans, Marlborough, Kingston-upon-Hull, and Portland. Ms. identifications in the L copy.

L(11630.h.28),O; DFo,InU,TxU.

K49 — King Harry the IXth, teaching L——d C——t his political alphabet. [*London*] *Printed for W. Webb*, [1743?]

½°: 1 side, 1 column.

> Engraved throughout. Possibly this was only a frontispiece to another work, for *DA* 5 April 1745 advertises *K. Harry the ninth teaching E——l G—— his political alphabet ABC*, 'with a curious frontispiece of Harry seasonably taking John by the ear'. This edition is earlier than Carteret's succession to the title in 1744, but the description is otherwise apt.

'Great A stands for army and B begins battle'

> Those intended are probably Henry Pelham and Lord Carteret, subsequently Lord Granville.

L(P&D 2588).

K50 — [*idem*] King Harry the IX, teaching G—— R—— his political alphabet A, B, C. Being a court, lesson. [*London?* 1743/–.]

½°: 1 side, 1 column.

> Large woodcut above text.

O.

K51 — King John: a poem. In answer to the Lilliputian queen, a poem address'd to the Chester ladies. With a dedication to the ladies of Chester. *London, 'printed for John Lilliput in the Little-Minories'*, 1729.

8°: A–C⁴ D⁴(–D4); 1–7 8–30.

'The pointed satyr, and the genial fire'

> Dedication signed 'Lilliputian Kate'. MR suggests that Nathaniel Lancaster might be the author. From the rhymes, it appears that the author of *The Lilliputian widow* which it answers was John Squire.

O,*MR*.

K52 — The King of St. Germains, a poem, in burlesque. *London, printed in the year* 1701. (6 Nov, Luttrell)

2°: A–D²; 1–2 3–12 17–20.

> The Luttrell copy is recorded in *Haslewood*. Listed in *WL* Nov.

'In troth, brother Lewis, who ever denies'

> Against the Pretender.

LG,E,AdU; CLU-C,OCU.

K53 — King Satan: or, the hunting of the senator. A New Market tale, told by an old fox hunter, and address'd to all true sportsmen. *London, printed for J. Roberts*, 1724 [1723]. (*MC* Oct)

8°: *A*² B–G⁴ H²; i–iv, 1–51 52 blk.

'There goes a tale of antient date'

> A satire on politicians.

L(164.n.20, Luttrell, Oct),O,C,*LdU-B;* CSmH, ICU(uncut).

K54 — King Theodore's defeat, or Neptune's triumph. [*London?* 1718?]

slip: 1 side, 1 column.

> Printed with *The petition*, [1718?]; the L copy is not divided.

'As Neptune with his watery train'

> A satire on George I meeting a storm at sea. The L catalogue identifies the subject as King Theodore of Corsica, but the associated poem rebuts that suggestion.

L(C.116.i.4/5).

King, Charles. An ode in praise of musick. Composed by Mr. Charles King, [1707.] *See* O34.

King, William, *the gazetteer, 1663–1712.* Miscellanies in prose and verse. *London, printed for B. Lintott, & H. Clements*, [1709.] (*PB* 3 March)

8°: pp. 536.　　L,O; CtY,MH.

> Watermark: star. A second volume of reissues with no general title is often found in a matching binding; it is not mentioned in the proposals (copy at O), but in *WL* Feb 1709 the works are listed as two volumes. See C. J. Horne in *The Library* IV. 25 (1944) 37–45.

— [fine paper] OW; CtY,IU.

> No watermark.

— Remains of the late learned and ingenious Dr. William King... *London, printed for W. Mears*, 1732. (*LM* July)

8°: pp. 168+166.　　L,O; CtY,IU.

— [reissue] Posthumous works of the late learned William King, L.L.D. in verse and prose... *London, printed for E. Curll, & W. Mears*, 1734.

　　CtY.

> Cancel title.

— [reissue] *London, printed in the year* 1739.

　　MH.

> Cancel title.

———

K55 [—] The art of cookery: a poem. In imitation of Horace's Art of poetry. By the author of a Tale of a tub. *London printed, and are to be sold by the booksellers of London & Westminster*, 1708 [1707]. (18 Dec, Luttrell)

2°: A–F²; i–ii, 1–22.

> *Teerink* 839. An unauthorized edition. In some copies (e.g. O,DT,CSmH) F1 is unsigned. The Luttrell copy is recorded in *Haslewood*; listed in *WL* Nov (but this often includes books of the following month).

'Ingenious Lister! were a picture drawn'

> Reprinted in King's *Works*, 1776; and see Lintot's payment for the copyright in his authorized edition below. The reference to the *Tale of a tub* may be due to King's authorship of *Some remarks on the Tale of a tub*, 1704.

L(11633.h.7),LLP,O(uncut),DT(2),LdU-B+; CSmH,CtY,MH,TxU.

K56 [—] — *London printed, and are to be sold by the booksellers ⟨of London & Westminster*, 1708.⟩

8°: A⁸; 1 2–16.

King, W., *gazetteer.* The art of cookery

A piracy, in chap-book style.
L(1077.c.44, cropt).

K57 [—] The art of cookery, in imitation of Horace's Art of poetry. With some letters to Dr. Lister... To which is added, Horace's Art of poetry in Latin. By the author of the Journey to London... *London, printed for Bernard Lintott,* [1708.] (*DC* 8 Jan)
8°: *A*⁴ B–L⁸; *i–viii,* 1–160. A1 hft.
According to *Nichols* VIII. 297, Lintot paid King 30 guineas for the copyright, 18 Feb 1708. Also listed in *WL* May.
L(11388.c.8; 1036.c.36; 94.b.11/1),O,OW,C, EU+; CSmH,DFo,IU,MH(2),TxU+.

K58 [—] — *London: printed for B. Lintott; and, reprinted for M.G.* [*Matthew Gunne*], *Dublin,* 1708.
8°: *A*⁴(−A4) B–I⁴ K¹; *i–ii,* 1–4 5–70.
L(1476.b.33, headlines cropt),DN; PP.

K59 [—] — The second edition. *London, printed for Bernard Lintott,* [1712.] (*Medley* 18 April)
8°: (frt+) A–G⁸ H⁴; *i–iv,* 1–112 *113–116.* H3–4 advt.
L(632.g.24/1),O; CU(lacks frt, A1–2),CtY(−frt), DFo,TxU.

[—] — [1725?]
A copy collating A–B⁸ and with only a half-title is at CT; it might have formed part of one of Curll's nonce collections. Possibly it is the 1725 edition recorded by *Nichols* I. 327.

K60 — The art of love: in imitation of Ovid De arte amandi. With a preface containing the life of Ovid. *London, printed for Bernard Lintott,* [1708.] (April?)
8°: (frt+) A⁴ a–b⁸ B–N⁸ O⁴ (A4 as 'a'); *i–vi* vii–xl, 1–195 *196–200.* O3–4 advt.
Advertisements seen all refer to the imprint below: this form with the title uncancelled may be aberrant. Some copies of both issues were bound up as part of a second volume to King's *Miscellanies in prose and verse,* [1709.] *LG* 29 April 1708 announces 'a small number are printed on a royal paper'; these have not been identified. Ordinary copies are printed on a very good paper with a watermark which is small and difficult to see; possibly fine-paper copies have no watermark and have been overlooked. Some copies (e.g. L) have A2 unsigned and no press-figure 5 on p. v. Lintot paid King 30 guineas for the copyright (*Nichols* VIII. 297).
'Whoever knows not what it is to love'
L(632.g.24/2),LVA-F; CSmH,ICU,MH,TxU.

K61 — [another issue] *London, printed for Bernard Lintott; sold by William Taylor, & Henry Clements,* [1708.] (*LG* 29 April)
8°: (frt+) A⁴(±A1) a–b⁸ B–N⁸ O⁴ (A4 as 'a'); *i–vi* vii–xl, 1–195 *196–200.* O3–4 advt.
L(833.g.36; 94.b.11),LVA-D,O,OW(−frt), LdU-B; CLU-C,CtY(−frt),DFo,ICN,TxU+.

[—] The beasts in power, 1709. *See* B125.

King, W., *gazetteer*

[—] Britain's palladium: or, my Lord Bolingbroke's welcome from France, 1712. *See* B527·2.

[—] The eagle and the robin. An apologue, 1709. *See* E2.

K62 [—] The fairy feast, written by the author of A tale of a tub, and the Mully of Mountown. *London, printed in the year* 1704. (11 July, Luttrell)
2°: B–D² (B2 as 'B'); *1–2 3–12.*
Teerink 834. The Luttrell copy is recorded in *Haslewood*; listed in *WL* July. An unauthorized edition.
'As poets say, one Orpheus went'
Reprinted in King's *Miscellanies* [1709] I. 367–96 with title 'Orpheus and Euridice'.
L(11602.i.14/2),O(uncut); CLU-C,CSmH,TxU.

[—] The garden plot, 1709. *See* G10.

[—] Good advice to beaus and batchelors... By the author of, A tale of a tub, 1705. *See* G218.

K63 [—] [dh] Mully of Mountown. A poem. By the author of the Tale of a tub. [col] *London, printed in the year* 1704. (23 June, Luttrell)
2°: A² (A2 as 'B'); *1–4.*
Teerink 833; *Williams* 1074. Some copies (e.g. TxU) have misprint '1702' in title. The Luttrell copy was in the possession of John Fleming in 1960. Advertised in *PM* 1 July 1704 as 'printed for the author, and sold by S. Malthus', but possibly an unauthorized edition.
'Mountown! thou sweet retreat from Dublin cares'
Reprinted in King's *Miscellanies* [1709] I. 357–66. Mully was the name of King's cow at Mountown.
LSC,O,MC; CLU-C,CSmH,CtY,MH,TxU(ms. date June 1704).

K64 [—] — *London printed, and are to be sold by the booksellers of London & Westminster,* [1705.] (25 Jan, Luttrell)
½°: 2 sides, 1 column.
MH(Luttrell).

K65 [—] The old cheese: a poem. *Dublin, printed in the year* 1725.
½°: 2 sides, 1 column.
'Young Slouch the farmer had a jolly wife'
Printed in King's *Miscellanies,* [1709.] A tale of a hen-pecked husband.
L(C.121.g.8/53); CtY.

[—] The tripe club. A satyr... By the author of the Tale of a tub, 1706. *See* T495.

King, William, *principal of St. Mary Hall, Oxford, 1685–1763.* Opera Gul. King, LL.D... [*London,* 1763?]
4°. L,O; CtY,MH.
Half-title only; partly composed of reissues,

and different copies vary slightly. Usually dated as 1760 because that date appears on the title of *Aviti epistola ad Perillam*, but it was not published in King's lifetime. King's executors burnt all but 50 of 500 copies left ready for binding at his death, according to a letter from Richard Bullock, one of the executors, in a copy at CtY.

K66 [—] Antonietti, ducis Corsorum, epistola ad Corsos de rege eligendo. *Londini, apud M. Cooper*, 1744. (27 April)
2°: *A*² B–D²; *1–4* 5–16.
    Copy from Tom's Coffee House, dated 27 April, in the Lewis Walpole Library; listed in *GM* May.
'Nobile si carmen mihi musæ, quale Maroni'
    Reprinted in King's *Opera*, [1763?].
O(2),OW,C; CLU-C,CtY,NjP,OCU.

[—] Carmen rhythmicum, monachicum, Momo dicatum [actually by George Wilmot], 1749. *See* W517.

[—] A certain proposal of a certain little tutor, for making certain reformations in a certain method of education, [1749?] *See* C99.

K67 [—] Elogium famæ inserviens Jacci Etonensis, sive gigantis; or, the praises of Jack of Eton... collected into Latin and English metre, after the manner of Thomas Sternhold, John Hopkins, John Burton, and others. To which is added a dissertation on the Burtonic style. By a Master of Arts. *Oxford, printed for S. Parker; sold by W. Owen, London*, 1750.
8°: A–N⁴; *i–ii* iii–viii, *1* 2–96. 96 err.
'Tu Sternholde, mi adspira!'
'Spirit of Sternhold me inspire'
    Referred to in King's *Anecdotes*. A satire against John Burton.
L(1465.d.9; 161.m.65),O(5),C(3),CT,*DrU*+; CtY(2),ICN,IU(2),MH(uncut),OCU+.

K68 [—] Miltonis epistola ad Pollionem. Edidit & notis illustravit F.S. Cantabrigiensis. *Londini, apud T. Cooper*, 1738. (*SR* 10 Nov)
2°: *A*² B–D²; *i–iv*, *1–11* 12 blk.
    Listed in *GM,LM* Nov. Entered in *SR* to George Hawkins; deposit copies at O,E,AdU. Entered to Mr Haw⟨kins⟩ in Bowyer's ledgers under 4 Nov, 500 copies printed; sheet A was reprinted 'being workt wrong'.
'Si vis ingenii, mihi si concessa potestas'
    Early ms. attribution to King in the C copy; listed among King's Latin poems in *The bench*, 1741. An attack on the whigs and Hanoverians.
L(11409.h.22),O(3, 1 uncut),C(uncut),E,DG+; CLU-C,CtY(2),IU,MH,*NN*.

K69 [—] — Editio altera. *Londini, apud T. Cooper*, 1738. (23 Dec?)
2°: *A*² B–D²; [2] i–ii, *1–11* 12 blk.

Entered in Bowyer's ledgers under 23 Dec, 500 copies printed. Listed in *LM* Dec.
L(11409.i.6),O,OA,C(2, 1 lacks A2, ms. notes), E(2); CtY(uncut),IU(2, 1 uncut),MH,TxU.

K70 [—] Milton's epistle to Pollio. Translated from the Latin, and illustrated with large explanatory notes. *London, printed in the year* 1740. (1 March)
2°: *A*² B–E²; *1–3* 4–19 20 blk.
    Copy from Tom's Coffee House, dated 1 March, in the Lewis Walpole Library; listed in *GM* March.
'Illustrious Pollio! were thy friend adorn'd'
    This English translation is generally assumed to be by King; I have found no direct evidence, though the way it is produced lends weight to the attribution.
L(11631.i.5),O,C,E,LdU-B; CtY(uncut),MH, OCU.

K71 [—] An ode to Mira. [*Dublin*] *Printed in the year* 1730.
½°: *1–2*, 2 columns.
'Cease! thy direful vengeance cease!'
    A forerunner of King's *The toast*, satirizing Frances, countess of Newburgh.
L(C.121.g.8/179); CSmH.

K72 [—] Ode to Myra. In imitation of Horace's ode to Canidia. Lib. ep. od. XVII. *Dublin, printed. London, reprinted* 1730.
8°: A(6 ll); *1–3* 4–12. 12 advt.
    On p. 9, 'Myra's answer. An ode, in imitation of Horace, lib. ep. ode XVIII.', reprinted in the Dublin edition of *The toast*, 1732. Advertisement on p. 12 for forthcoming *The hermaphrodite* 'By Mr. Donald', i.e. *The toast*.
Answer: 'And art thou a convert grown!'
O(lacks A4),C(pp. 9–12 only),DA.

K73 [—] A poetical abridgement, both in Latin and English, of the reverend Mr. Tutor Bentham's Letter to a young gentleman of Oxford. To which are added some remarks on the Letter to a fellow of a college. By the author of the Proposal, &c. *London, printed for W. Owen*, 1749. (*GA* 25 Feb)
8°: π¹[= H1] *A*⁴ B–G⁴ H⁴(–H1); *i–ii*, *1–5* 6–61 62 blk. π1 hft; 61 err.
'Græce loqui, & Latine'
'Little B——, who writes (and who doubts his ability?)'
    King's *A proposal for publishing a poetical translation*, 1748 (and 1749), was another satire on Edward Bentham's *Letter to a young gentleman*.
L(11632.c.3,–π1),O(2, 1–π1),C,AdU(–π1); CLU-C(–π1),CtY,MH,*NjP*,OCU(–π1).

K74 [—] Scamnum, ecloga. *Londini, apud T. Cooper*, 1740. (14 April?)
2°: *A*² B–D²; *i–iii* iv, *1–10* *11–12 blk*.
    Press-figures on pp. 8, 9 are not present in all copies. Entered to George Hawkins in

King, W., *principal.* Scamnum

Bowyer's ledgers under 4 [April], 500 copies printed. Copy from Tom's Coffee House, dated 14 April, in the Lewis Walpole Library; listed in *GM,LM* April.

'Dum fagus (namq; æstus erat) me protegit umbra' Reprinted in King's *Opera*, [1763?]. Translated into English as *The bench, An eclogue*, 1741, subsequently reissued as *The Oxford shepherds*, 1741, and as *Scamnum, ecloga: or, the pastoral politicians*, 1744.

L(11408.g.24,−D2),O,C(3, 1−D2); CSmH, CtY(uncut),IU,MH,OCU+.

K75 [—] Sermo pedestris. *Londini, apud T. Cooper*, 1739. (*GM* June)

2°: *A*² B–D²; *i–iv*, 1–12.

Entered twice in Bowyer's ledgers, under May and 14 June, 525 copies printed.

'Sunt queis displicuit Miltonis epistola; quippe' Reprinted in King's *Opera*, [1763?].

L(11409.i.8; 11630.d.1/3),O,OW,C; CSmH,IU, MH,TxU.

K76 [—] — Editio altera. *Londini, apud T. Cooper*, 1739. (23 Aug?)

2°: *A*² B–D²; *i–iv*, 1–12.

Entered in Bowyer's ledgers under 23 Aug, 500 copies printed.

O,OA,C(ms. notes); CtY.

K77 [—] Templum libertatis. Liber primus. *Londini, apud C. Bathurst, & G. Hawkins*, 1742. (*DP* 8 Jan)

2°: *A*¹ b–c² B–H² I¹; [2] *i* ii–viii, *1* 2–30. viii err.

Some copies (CSmH, CtY) have an enlarged list of errata pasted over the errata on p. viii.

'Diva potens, cœli proles pulcherrima, cujus' Reprinted in King's *Opera*, [1763?].

L(11661.dd.3),O; CSmH,CtY,ICN,IU,MH+.

K78 [—] — Liber secundus. *Londini, apud C. Bathurst, & G. Hawkins*, 1743. (*GM,LM* Jan)

2°: *A*² B–H² I¹; *i–ii* iii–iv, *1* 2–29 *30 blk*. 29 err.

One leaf of F is apparently a cancel from the evidence of watermarks. Errata for Liber I on p. 27.

'Hactenus Aonides cecinerunt omnia læta' L(11661.dd.3),O; CtY,IU,NjP.

K79 [—] The toast, an epic poem... Written in Latin by Fredrick Scheffer, done into English by Peregrine O Donald, esq; Vol. I. '*Dublin*' [*London*], *printed in the year* 1732. (*GSJ* 20 Nov)

8°: *A*² B–G⁸; *i–iv*, 1–96. iv err.

Copies in this state have pp. ii–iii blank. *Bond* 126. Advertised in November as sold by H. Lintot, but clearly distributed privately before then. A letter of Swift to Ford of 14 Oct 1732 records 'A printer brought it to me, and said a hundred of them were sent to him from England to give about'.

'Sing, O muse, Phœbus' wrath! say what cause could persuade'

The enlarged version of *The toast* was reissued with King's *Opera*, [1763?]; his authorship is

King, W., *principal.* The toast

widely referred to. A satire on Frances, countess of Newburgh.

C,ĐA; CU,MH.

K80 [—] [variant]

8°: *A*¹ B–G⁸; *i–ii*, 1–96. ii err.

In this state the errata are printed directly on the verso of the title.

OW,C; IU,TxU.

K81 [—] — *Dublin, printed in the year* 1732.

8°: *A*⁴ B–L⁴ (A2 as 'B2'); *1–7* 8 *9–16* 17–88 (3 as '1'). 88 advt.

This seems a genuine Dublin edition. It adds on pp. 82–8 'An ode to Myra', 'Myra's answer', and the advertisement for *The hermaphrodite ...with the life of Myra* from K72.

L(900.f.2/5),O,C,DN,DT(2)+; CLU-C.

K82 [—] The toast. An heroick poem in four books written originally in Latin by Frederick Scheffer: now done into English...by Peregrine O Donald esq; *Dublin: printed. London: re-printed in the year* 1736.

4°: (frt+) *A*⁴ a–g⁴ h² B–P⁴ Q⁴(Q3+*Q⁴(−*Q4)) R–Z⁴ Aa–Bb⁴ Cc⁴(±Cc2) Dd–Gg⁴ (+2 ll); *i–iii* iv–lxvi *lxvii–lxviii*, *1* 2–118 *113–*118 119–232 [*4*]. (Final leaves bear music and errata respectively.)

Listed in *GM* Jan 1737 as printed for L. Gilliver & J. Clarke, but this issue was apparently suppressed. Reissued with additions and the date changed in ms. to 1747, and also with the original date in King's *Opera*, [1763?]. (There may well be occasional copies issued at other times in various states.). The errata leaf is sometimes (e.g. L) bound after A1. Ms. note in Falconer Madan's copy at CtY, 'In a cancelled title of the Toast, after P. O'Don esq; were two lines "Pus atque venenum/Rabies armavit".' The title is not a cancel in the copies seen, and Madan is perhaps recording a proof.

L(1466.k.21),LdU-B; NNC.

K83 [—] [reissue, 1747.]

4°: (frt+) *A*⁴ a–g⁴ h² B–L⁴ M⁴(−M4,+*M–*N⁴ *O¹) N–P⁴ Q⁴(Q3+*Q⁴(−*Q4)) R...; *i–iii* iv–lxvi *lxvii–lxviii*, *1* 2–88 *89–*104 89–118 *113–*118 119...

Date altered in ms. to 1747; presentation copy at E dated May. Probably privately circulated; in most copies the errata have been corrected by hand and the errata leaf suppressed. The additional leaves *89–*104 have press-figures *98–1, *100–1; leaves *113–*118 are a different edition from the preceding. Some of the copies reissued with King's *Opera*, [1763?] (e.g. DFo,MH) have a new edition of pp. *89–*104 with no press-figures, and (apparently) leaves *113–*118 from the preceding edition. The two editions of these leaves can be compared in copies at DG,CtY,DFo.

King, W., *principal*. The toast

> L(642.1.5; 441.f.15),O,E,DG,DT+; CtY,DFo, NN.

Kinkaid, Thomas. *See* Kincaid, Thomas.

K84 Kirk. The kirk and covenant, with light foot. To which is added, Scotch margenal notes. [17––?]
½°: 1 side, 1 column.
'Alak, alas and a-walla-day'
DG (imprint cropt).

> Kirkham. 'Kirkham hunt.'
>> *On the peace proclaim'd in the year 1748* (Preston, 1748) is 'By the author of Kirkham hunt'; no evidence of its publication has been found.

K85 Kirkham, Charles. Philanglus and Astræa: or, the loyal poem. *Stamford, printed for the author*, 1712.
2°: *A*² B–D² ⟨E¹⟩; *1–4* 5–⟨18⟩.
> Watermark: London arms. Printed in black throughout. The order of what may be different editions is not known, but this is certainly on inferior paper.
'Astræa, I implore thee, tell me why'
Dedication to the queen on A2 signed.
O(lacks E1).

K86 —— *Stamford, printed for the author*, 1712.
2°: *A*² B–D² E¹; *1–4* 5–18.
> Watermark: Amsterdam arms. Very good paper. Printed in black throughout.
L(11630.g.7).

K87 —— ⟨*Stamford, printed for the author*, 1712?⟩
2°: ⟨*A*²⟩ B–D² E¹; ⟨*1–4*⟩ 5–18.
> Large unidentified watermark. Text printed in red and black except pp. 17–18.
L(C.131.h.1/8***, uncut, lacks A²).

[**Kirkpatrick, James**, *of Belfast*.] An essay by way of elegy, on the honᵈ: Arthur Upton, 1707. *See* E461.

Kirkpatrick, James, *M.D.* A. Popii excerpta quædam... Latine reddidit Jac. Kirkpatrick, M.D. *Londini, typis J. Purser*, 1749. (*GM* March)
4°: pp. xii, 122.   L; MH,TxU.
> There is a prospectus of 26 September 1747 at O-JJ, and an undated prospectus at L. The fine-paper copies referred to there and in the list of subscribers have not been identified.

K88 —— Celeberrimi Popii Tentamen de modis criticis scripta dijudicandi. Latine tentatum. Jac. Killpatrick. *Londini, typis Joh. Purser; prostant apud R. Dodsley, & Jac. Robinson*, [1745.] (*GM,LM* July)
8°: A⁴ χ⁴(−χ4) B–F⁴ G¹; [2] i–x *xi–xii*, *1* 2–41 *42 blk*.
> Latin text only.
'Pluribus ambigitur, num vere inscitior audit'
L(11633.df.3),C,CT,E; CLU-C,IU.

Kirkpatrick, J.

K88·5 [—] An epistle to Alexander Pope, esq; from South Carolina. *London, printed for J. Brindley, & C. Corbett*, 1737. (*LM* June)
2°: *A*² B–D² E¹; *1–5* 6–18. A1 hft.
'From warmer lands, ally'd to latest fame'
> The attribution is listed in *Annals of medical history*, n.s. 10 (1938) 308; no details are given, but there seems no reason for doubt. Tentatively ascribed to Thomas Dale in *CBEL* II. 302; apparently that suggestion was due to R. H. Griffith.
L(12273.m.1/14),LVA-D; ICN,KU,MH(uncut), TxU(uncut).

K89 [—] The sea-piece, a poetical narration of a voyage from Europe to America. Canto II. *London, printed for M. Cooper*, 1749. (*GM* April)
2°: *A*² B–F²; *1–5* 6–24.
> The preface reveals that the poem consists of five cantos, 'of which this is the second, tho' first publish'd'. Listed in *GM* April as well as May; the latter specifically as 'Canto 2'.
'Drayton, sweet antient bard, his Albion sung'
L(11602.i.15/5); MH.

K90 —— The sea-piece. A narrative, philosophical and descriptive poem. In five cantos. *London, printed for M. Cooper, & J. Buckland, & J. Robinson*, 1750. (*LM* Feb)
8°: A⁴ a–e⁴ f² B–T⁴ U²; *i–iii* iv–xlii *xliii–xliv blk*, *1* 2–148.
> Watermark: fleur-de-lys. In most copies B2 is signed 'B3'; those at L,NN are correctly signed. The blank f2 is often removed.
'Ye fabled deities, and fictious train'
L(11632.bb.5),C; CtY-M,ICN,MH,NN,TxU (uncut).

K91 —— [fine paper?]
> No watermark. The copies seen are presentation copies, though bound in poor calf.
O; CtY.

Kiss. Kiss me if you dare, 1710. *See* Pittis, William.

K92 —— Kiss my a-se is no treason or a new way of selling bargains. [*London*] *Sold by A. Davis, near St. Paul's*, [1727/28.]
½°: 1 side, 2 columns.
'In antient days as poets tell'
> A satire on Le Heup as ambassador.
L(1872.a.1/15).

K93 —— —— *London printed, and Dublin re-printed in the year* 1727–8.
½°: 1 side, 2 columns.
NN,OCU.

K94 Kit-cat. The Kit-cat clubs lamentation, for the loss of the pope, the devil and the pretender, that were taken into custody on Saturday last by the secretary of state. Writen [!] by Jacob door-holder to that society. [*London*] *Printed in the year* 1711.
½°: 1 side, 1 column.
'Alas! and well-a-day! our hopes are lost'

The **Kit-cat** club's lamentation

> The supposed author is Jacob Tonson, secretary to the club. William Legge, earl of Dartmouth, seized the effigies which were to have been burnt by the whigs in November 1711.

MH.

Kit-cats. The Kit-cats. A poem, 1708. *See* Blackmore, *Sir* Richard.

Kite. The kite. An heroic-comical poem, 1722–. *See* Bacon, Phanuel.

K95 Kitty. Kitty and Dick: or, the nightingale. A tale. To which is added, the Milk-maid, or the heifer; a tale. Isabella's sparrow, a ballad. An epigram... [and 3 others]. *London, printed for M. Cook, E. Nutt, & A. Dodd*, 1734.
12º: A–B⁶ C¹; *1–3* 4–26.
> In the copy seen, p. 25 has not been printed.
'A virgin's pretty toy to guard'
> Probably this should be considered a miscellany, but it is not so listed in *CBEL*.

L(1078.e.11).

— Kitty: or the female Phaeton, [174–?] *See* 'Prior, Matthew' (P1095).

Knapp, Francis. Taurus in circo. The bullbaiting. A poem in Latin [from *Musæ Anglicanæ*] and English, 1716. *See* T95.

Knave. A knave at the bottom, [17––.] *See* Price, Laurence.

— The knave of trumps fell into the dumps, [1731?] *See* The hunting of the stag, [1731.]

Knight. The knight, 1723. *See* Meston, William.

K96 — The knight and the cardinal. A new ballad. Addressed to the kings of England and France. Tune of, The king shall enjoy his own again. *London, printed by R. Walker; sold by the booksellers*, [1731.] (*GSJ* 17 June)
2º: *A²* B²; *1–2* 3–8.
'In time's remembrancers we find'
> An attack on Walpole's negotiations with Cardinal Fleury.

CSmH(uncut),MH.

K97 — The knight and the prelate: a new ballad. To the tune of King John and the abbot of Canterbury. *London, printed for P. Holder*, 1734. (*GM* March)
2º: *A²* < B²; *1–2* 3–8.
Percival XXXIV.
'In the island of Britain I sing of a k----t'
> A satire on Walpole's alliance with Edmund Gibson, bishop of London.

O; CSmH,CtY,InU(uncut),MH,OCU+.

K98 — — [*Edinburgh*] *Printed in the year* 1734.
8º: A⁴; *1–2* 3–8.
E; ICN,ICU.

The **knight** and the prelate

K99 — — To which is added, an Epistle from a gentleman at Twickenham to a nobleman at St. James's. '*London*', *printed in the year* 1734.
8º: A–C⁴; *1–3* 4–23 *24 blk.*
> P. 13 is a separate title to the *Epistle*. Clearly a piracy, possibly of Dublin origin.

L(1486.df.34),O,LdU-B,*MR-C*; CSmH.

K100 — The knight and the purse or a mitre in dispute. *London, printed for R. Amey; sold by the booksellers of London & Westminster*, [1733.] (20 March?)
2º: *A–B²*; *1–3* 4–8.
'Some by the title led astray'
CSmH(ms. date 20 March 1733),KU.

— The knight of the kirk, 1728. *See* Meston, William.

K101 — The knight outrid or, the postilion in his masters saddle, a new ballad. Occasioned by a baronet's lady, being caught in bed with her postilion. *London, printed for R. Amey; sold by the booksellers of London & Westminster*, [1734?]
2º: (4 ll); *1–2* '*2*' 4–8.
> Date suggested by poems bound with the copy recorded.
'Of late there is nothing at all will go down'
NN-B.

Knighthood. Knighthood, no trifle, 1747. *See* Chivalrie, no trifle, 1746–.

K102 Knights. The knights of the horn orders address to the fruit maids of Edinburgh. [*Edinburgh*, 1707.] (Feb)
slip: 1 side, 1 column.
> The E copy has a ms. note 'Edr. printed Febr. 1707'.
'This nations sins are many fold'
> Against the changes in sexual behaviour.

E.

K103 Knox, Thomas. Philopolites. His grace the Duke of Argyle's speech to the parliament of Great-Britain, in defence of the rights and royal prerogatives of...Edinburgh. To which is subjoin'd, an heroi-protrepticon; together with a panegyrick upon his grace... *Edinburgh, printed in the year* 1738.
4º: A–D²; *1–2* 3–16.
'After the Duke declar'd, with joynt applause'
'Arise, dead muse, in strains seraphick rise'
'Exert, my muse, in more transcendent strain'
> A versification of Argyle's speech against the penalties imposed following the Porteous riots.

EP(2).

K104 K-ntish. The K-ntish spy: or, a memorial of the C--ves H--d club: particularly of three members of the said society that absented themselves from the parish church of W-st--ham in Kent, the 30th day of January last... Turn'd into hudibrastick

The **K-ntish** spy

Korath

verse. Inscrib'd to the K-ntish petitioner. By T. W.
an enemy to faction. *London, printed in the year
1712.* (*PB* 17 April)
8°: *A*⁴ B–C⁴; *1–6 7–23 24 blk.* A1 hft.
'Since human folly first began'
   Modern pencil note in the TxU copy 'Thomas
   Wood, of Hardwick'; the authority for this
   attribution is unknown.
L(11633.e.45/4; 164.m.68, Luttrell, 17 April);
ICN,NN,TxU.

K105 Korath. Korath: or the danger of schism. A satyr.
By a gentleman. *London printed, and sold by B.
Bragg, 1705.*
4°: A⁴; *1–2 3–8.*
'Of all those sins that heat our northern clime'
   A tory attack on occasional conformists and
   presbyterians.
O.

L

L., *Father.* A consolatory poem in praise of retirement, 1701. *See* C387.

L——, ——, *gent.* A paraphrase on the lxxxii psalm, [1725?] *See* P55.

L., C., *a true Briton.* St. Taffy's day, 1724. *See* S22.

L., F., *the reverend.* Menalcas, or a pastoral, 1726. *See* M171.

L., J., *A.B.* The gentleman commoner, 1716. *See* G122.

— The servitour, 1709. *See* S222.

L., R., *gent.* Pride's exchange broke up, 1703. *See* P1051.

L., T. The discarded country gager, 1718. *See* D321.

— A glance upon his spent time, [1714.] *See* G170.

L., W. A pindarick ode on his excellency John duke of Marlborough, [1706?] *See* P287.

L., W., *junior.* A lamentation over Sion, [172–?] *See* Lamboll, William.

L1 L--. L-- H---p's embassy to H----r. Interspers'd with Brotherhood-in-law... By the author of L—h—p's ballad. *London, printed for George Read,* [1728.] (*MChr* 21 Sept)
2°: *A*² B²; *i–ii, 1–5* 6 *blk.*
'When matters grew ripe for grave consultation'
    A satire on Isaac Le Heup, by the author of *Le H-----p at Hanover* (L94·3).
OW.

L2 Labour. Labour lost: or, a new ballad upon the abdication of three blunderbus a------n, and a scurvy r------r; together with their wives, who are gone to the Bath, to improve their tails, as their husbands are gone to London, to improve their understandings. To some tune. [*Dublin,* 1709/10.]
½°: 1 side, 2 columns.
'God prosper long our noble queen'
    A tory poem against John Allen, Joseph Deane, Benjamin Burton, and John Forster, three aldermen and the recorder of Dublin.
L(1890.e.5/120),C,DG,Rothschild.

L3 Labyrinth. The labyrinth. A tale. Humbly inscrib'd to the right honourable *****. *London, printed for T. Cooper,* 1734. (*GSJ* 8 Feb)
2°: *A*² B² C¹; *1–3* 4–10.

'To list'ning crowds, in former ages'
    Ascribed to Henry Baker in *Wrenn;* the attribution can probably be safely ignored.
O,*BP;* ICN,KU,MH,OCU,TxU.

L4 Lacaux, P. Charles I. martir, poëme. *A Londres, par J. Delage,* 1703.
4°: A–D⁴; *i–viii, 1–22* 23–24 *blk.*
'Du bon Charles premier, des bons rois le modele'
    Dedication signed.
Longleat.

L5 — Poëme pour le jour de la naissance de la reine. *A Londres, chez Robert Roger, dans les Black-Fryers, prés de l'imprimerie royale,* 1705.
4°: A–B⁴; *1–2* 3–14 *15–16 blk.*
'Muse, voici le jour où nâquit nôtre reine'
LLP.

L6 Lacrimae. Lachrymæ Academiæ Jacobi regis Edinburgenæ, in obitum venerandi viri Jacobi Smithæi, ornatissimi sui gymnasiarchæ; qui ab Anglia rediens, Coldstremæ, postridie idus sextiles, A. Æ. C. MDCCXXXVI, aetatis LVI, multum desideratus interiit. [*Edinburgh,* 1736.]
½°: *1–2,* 1 column.
'Hei mihi! perpetuæ lachrymæ, sine fine dolores'
TxU.

'La Croix, Demetrius de.' *See* McEncroe, D.

Lacy, B. Miscellaneous poems compos'd at Newfoundland, on board his majesty's ship the Kinsale. By B. Lacy, A.M. then chaplain to the said ship. *London, printed for the author,* 1729.
8°: pp. vi, 128.   O; DLC,RPJCB.

[Lacy, Francis.] Menalcas, or a pastoral upon the death of a roman catholick clergy-man of distinction, 1726. *See* M171.

Lacy, J., *merchant.* Tobacco, a poem, [1733.] *See* T404·5.

L7 Lacy, John. The Steeleids, or, the tryal of wit. A poem, in three cantos. *London printed, and sold by J. Morphew,* 1714. (28 July, Luttrell)
8°: A–H⁴ (B2 as 'B3'); *i–viii, 1–53* 54–56.
    Title in red and black. Listed in *MC* Aug.
'If I no falshod in my life design'd'
    A satire on Steele and the whig poets.
L(992.h.3/8; 161.1.74, Luttrell; G.18423/6),OW, DrU; CU,CtY,DFo(ms. notes),ICN,*MH*+.

Ladies.
No attempt has been made to determine whether this word represents 'lady's' or 'ladies'' in individual poems.

L8 — The ladies answer to the True born Englishwoman, a satyr... Written by a city lady. *London, printed for the city ladies,* [1703.]

The **ladies** answer

8°: A^4; *1* 2–8.
'When fools and knaves in scandals do unite'
Epistle to the reader signed 'M.B.' *The true born English-woman*, 1703, is in prose (copy at L).

O.

L9 — The ladies choice: a poem. *London printed, and sold by J. How, & B. Bragg*, 1702. (21 July, Luttrell)
2°: A–D²; *1–2* 3–16.
The Luttrell copy is in the possession of J. R. B. Brett-Smith.
'Prithee, Belinda (for thou know'st I'm young'
Serious advice on the choice of a husband, apparently occasioned by *The pleasures of a single life*, 1701.
L(163.n.24),*MR-C*; OCU,TxU(2).

L10 —— In answer to the Pleasures of a single life. [*Dublin, printed by C. Hicks*, 1726/36.]
8°: A^8; *1* 2–15 *16*. 16 advt for C. Hicks's chapbooks.
A chap-book edition. Large cut on title.
LVA-F,O.

L11 — [*idem*] The lady's defence. In answer to the many scandalous libels lately publish'd, in a letter to the afflicted ladies. *Dublin, printed at the Rein Deer in Montrath-street, where printing is done reasonably by C.H.* [*Hicks*], [1726/36.]
8°: A^4; *1* 2–8.
DA.

L12 — 'The ladies choice for new members of parliament at the general election. A ballad. [*London*] *Webb*. Price 6d.' (*BM* June; *GM,LM* July 1747)
Probably related to *The city lady's choice of a new standing member*, 1742.

— The ladies defence, 1701–. *See* Chudleigh, Mary, *Lady*.

— The ladies delight. Containing, I. An address to all well provided Hibernians. II. The arbor vitæ... III. The natural history of the arbor vitæ... IV. Ridotto al'fresco... *London, printed for W. James*, 1732. (*GM* June)
8°: pp. 32. L,O; KU.
Listed with the miscellanies in *CBEL* II.202 as 'possibly by one hand'. Only items II and IV are in verse; it seems more likely that it is a collection of erotic pieces, some at least of which were separately published. An erotic frontispiece in the copy at KU seems from the stab-holes to be original.

—— V. Arbor vitæ, or the tree of life, versify'd and explain'd...The second edition, corrected... *London, printed for W. James*, 1732.
8°: pp. 34.   KU.

— The ladies exercise at tea, [1729?] *See* Tea. A poem, 1729.

L13 — The ladies frolick: or the spy in armour. A new ballad. To that excellent old tune of King John,

The **ladies** frolick

and the abbot of Canterbury. *London, printed for J. Roberts*, 1731. (*GSJ* 14 Dec)
2°: A^1 B–C² D^1; *1–4* 5–12. A1 hft.
A1 and D1 have been seen to be conjugate.
'Let the smiles, and the loves, and the muses draw nigh!'
A bawdy tale.
CSmH.

L14 — The ladies of pleasure. In a familiar epistle. From Beau Dapper to Miss Witless. *London printed, and sold by J. Roberts*, 1734. (*GM* March)
2°: A^2 B²; *1–3* 4–8.
'Ever did the muse the female sex befriend'
L(162.n.6); MH.

L15 — The ladies opera. [*Dublin*, 1728?]
½°: 1 side, 2 columns.
'How long, dear Puss, how long, how long'
A series of songs in imitation of *The beggar's opera*, on the court at Dublin.
L(C.121.g.8/168),DT; CSmH,CtY.

— The ladies skreen, [1727/28.] *See* A new ballad. Tune of, To you fair ladies, [1727/28] (N108).

L16 — [dh] The ladies tutor: or, the art of visiting. [*London*] *Printed for P. Hills in Cornhil*, [170–?]
4°: A^2; *1* 2–4.
'If there be any, whether maid or wife'
A satire on tea-table conversation.
L(164.1.46),DG.

L17 **Lady.** The lady and the linnet. A tale. *Dublin, printed by S. Powell, for the author*, 1741.
8°: A^4 B⁴; *1–5* 6–15 *16* blk.
'To lift the low, the proud depress'
O(2),*MR-C*.

— Lady A—s—n weary of the Dean, 1730. *See* Swift, Jonathan.

L18 — The Lady Kilmarnock and Lady Balmerino's sorrowful lamentation for the death of their lords, who were beheaded for high-treason on Towerhill, on Monday, August 18th, 1746. [*Edinburgh*, 1746.]
½°: 1 side, 2 columns.
Mourning headpiece. Separate lamentation in each column.
Kilmarnock: 'You ladies fair, in pity with me join'
Balmerino: 'Pity my mournful case, you ladies fair'
L(C.115.i.3/78); MH.

L19 — Lady Mary: a dialogue between the author and a lady at court. *London, printed for T. Cooper; sold by the booksellers of London & Westminster*, 1742. (*LM* March)
2°: A^4; *1–2* 3–8.
'Whence, madam, all this indignation now?'
L(1959),O,*MR-C*; CSmH,KU,NjP.

L20 — The lady of Brumpton and knight of Malta. A gallant tale. *London, printed for J. Roberts*, 1721. (March, Luttrell)
8°: A^2 B⁴ C⁴(– C4?); *i–iv*, 1–14. A1 hft.

The **lady** of Brumpton

    C4 not present in the copy seen.
'A certain knight of Maltan standard'
    On 'Sir Testo's' successful courtship of the heiress Katherine Field.
L(164.1.42, Luttrell).

L21 — [A lady's answer] To Mr. Ambrose Philips. [col] *Dublin, printed in the year* 1725.
2°: A⁴; *1–3* 4–7 *8 blk.*
    Bond 82. Title in half-title form; drop-head title on p. 3, 'A lady's answer to Mr. Ambrose Philips's poem'.
'Bloom of wit, and choicest flow'r'
    An elegant parody on Philips's *To the honourable Miss Carteret*, [1725.] Answered by *A new poem ascrib'd to the lady*. . .[1725.]
O; CtY(uncut).

L22 — [dh] A lady's answer to Mr. Ambrose Philips's poem. [col] *Dublin, printed in the year* 1725.
4°: *A²*; *1* 2–4.
DT.

L23 — — [*Dublin,* 1725.]
½°: 1 side, 2 columns.
    On the other side, Philips's *A new poem ascrib'd to the honourable Miss Carteret*, [1725.]
L(C.121.g.8/127),Rothschild; CtY(mutilated), NjP.

L24 — A lady's answer to Mr. Ambrose Philip's poem to the honourable Miss Carteret. *Printed at Dublin, and reprinted at London, for T. Warner,* 1725. (*MC* July)
2°: *A² B²*; *1–3* 4–8.
O(uncut); TxU.

L25 — The lady's answer, to the sev'ral little satyres on the hoop'd petticoats. [*Edinburgh,* 171–?]
½°: 1 side, 1 column.
    The Edinburgh origin seems clear from the typography and the location of copies.
'Provock'd at length by such unhumane spite'
    For satires on hoop petticoats, see the subject index.
E(2).

L26 — The lady's decoy: or, the man-midwife's defence: occasion'd by the revival of a bill of indictment against the famous Doctor D-----. *London, printed for S. Slow; sold at the pamphlet-shops of London & Westminster,* 1733. (*GM* Nov)
2°: *A² B²*; *1–2* '7' 4–8.
    In the copies at L and the Institute for Sex Research, the date has been altered to 1738.
'Ye maidens and wives,/Who lead honest lives'
    On James Douglas. An answer to *The man-midwife unmasqu'd*, 1733, which has the date similarly altered to 1738.
L(163.n.35); DLC,Institute for Sex Research.

— The lady's defence, [1726/36.] *See* The ladies choice, 1702–.

The **lady**'s dressing room

— The lady's dressing room, 1732. *See* Swift, Jonathan.

L27 — ⟨The⟩ lady's last shift: or, a cure for shame. A tale. Address'd to a certain Dublin lady. [*Dublin*] *Printed in the year* 1732.
½°: 1 side, 2 columns.
'Venus of love and beauty queen'
    On a betrayed lady; the last line suggests a reference to Anne Vane.
CSmH.

L28 — The lady's letter to the freeholders, to beware of their votes. [*Dublin,* 1727?]
½°: 1 side, 2 columns.
    The DT copy is bound with half-sheets of 1727.
'At length for those a satyr's found'
DT.

L29 — [dh] The lady's ramble: or, the female night-walker. [*London,* 170–?]
4°: A²; *1–4.*
    Dated by L [1720?], but certainly earlier, and possibly from the seventeenth century; compare *Wing* F1154–5, F1157 for works of 1682–83 on this subject.
'When Sol with his beams, had the meadows adorn'd'
L(806.k.16/66); IU,TxU.

L30 — ⟨The⟩ lady's watch. By the author of the Prude. [*Dublin?* 1722?]
½°: 1 side, 1 column.
'A fair one sought the silent poplar shade'
    A bawdy poem.
MH.

La Fontaine, Jean de.
Humphreys, Samuel: Tales and novels in verse. From the French of La Fontaine. By several hands. Published and compleated by Samuel Humphreys, 1735.

[Congreve, William:] An impossible thing. A tale [and 'The peasant in search of his heifer'; both imitated from La Fontaine], 1720, [1722?] *See* C372–4.

The ghastly wound. A tale. . .From Monsieur De La Fontaine, 1723. *See* G133.

The wonder: or, the devil outwitted [from La Fontaine], 1736. *See* W552.

L31 [**Lamboll, William.**] [dh] A lamentation over Sion, on the declension of the church. By W. L. junior. [172–?]
8°: A⁴; *1* 2–7 *8 blk.*
    Roughly printed, possibly at Reading, Lamboll's home. An engraved broadside version (without title, and anonymous) of 1747 is also at LF.
'Oh! Sion, how thy beauty fades away'
    Attributed to Lamboll in *Smith* II. 76.
LF(2).

Lamentable

Lamentable. A lamentable ballad of the tragical ends of William and Margaret, [1723/–.] *See* Mallet, David [William and Margaret].

L32 Lamentation. The lamentation, and last farewel of Serjeant William Ainslie, who was executed over the castle-wall of Edinburgh, for high treason and treachery, on Monday the 24th of December, 1716. [*Edinburgh*, 1716.]
½°: 1 side, 1 column.
'Let all bold soldiers far and near'
E.

L33 — Lamentation from the Drury-lane play-house. A new ballad. Giving a true relation of an ingenious lady, who after she had lost, and found her maiden-head nine times, is now brought to bed of a jolly black, fair, brown boy... To the tune of the Fine ladies airs. [*London*, 1743?]
½°: 2 sides, 1 column.
'How unhappy are we, by this unjust decree'
A satire on Peg Woffington and her amours with Garrick and Edward earl of Darnley [?].
MH.

L34 — The lamentation of a sinner. In imitation of the stile of Hopkins and Sternhold. *London*, '*printed for A Man near St. Clements*', [1714.]
slip: 1 side, 1 column.
Stanzas numbered. The copy seen was reissued in *State poems. Being a collection of choice private pieces*, 1715.
'How very wicked have I been'
A satire on Harley.
Brett-Smith.

L35 — Eht [!] lamentation of a sinner... *London*, '*printed for A Man near St. Clements*', [1714.]
slip: 1 side, 1 column.
First line misprinted 'How very wickey...'.
Stanzas numbered.
O.

L36 — [another impression]
Stanzas unnumbered; the same misprint in first line.
L(1871.f.3/23, title cropt).

L37 — The lamentation of the butchers wives in Musleburgh for weighting of the flesh. [*Edinburgh*, 172–?]
½°: 1 side, 2 columns.
'Some boutcher's wives got a fine soup'
E.

L38 — The lamentation of the fruit wives over their bicker,| On the news of raising the price of their liquor. In a drunken dialogue betwixt Nanny Whitie, and Lucky Robertson. [*Edinburgh*, 1725?]
½°: 1 side, 2 columns.
'Whitie what gars ye hing your lips'
Possibly occasioned by the troubles over the malt tax in 1725. Replied to in *The taverners answer*, [1725?].
E.

Lamentation

— A lamentation over Sion, [172–?]. *See* Lamboll, William.

L39 — A lamentation over the sad changes incident to believers, while inhabitants of this changeable world: together with a sad soliloquie upon the sudden news of the death of Mr. John Gillespie... *Glasgow*, *printed by Robert Sanders*, 1716.
12°: A¹²; *1–2* 3–24.
'Oh! that it were with me as in'
L(11622.bb.1/4).

Lamentations. The Lamentations of Jeremiah, paraphras'd, 1708. *See* Brown, William.

L40 — The lamentations of Mary Magdalene: on her missing the body of our Lord out of the sepulchre. Together with her exultation on the angel's appearing... *Dublin*, *printed by George Grierson*, 1724.
8°: A–B⁴ C²; [2] i–v *vi*, 1–12.
'Where is our Lord! – 'twas here our Lord was laid'
DG.

L41 Lancashire. The Lancashire garland or, Sir William Stanley's travels. *Manchester*, *printed in the year* 1731.
8°: *A⁴*; *1* 2–8.
A chap-book ballad.
'In Lancashire there liv'd a lord'
Arnold Hyde, Manchester.

Lancaster, Nathaniel. King John: a poem, 1729. *See* K51.

L42 Land. The land-leviathan; or, modern hydra: in burlesque verse, by way of letter to a friend. *London*, *printed for John Morphew*, 1712. (5 Feb, Luttrell)
8°: A–C⁴; *1–3* 4–24.
Advertised in *Examiner* 7 Feb.
'Since people now with bus'ness mix'
Against Marlborough and the whigs.
L(164.m.67, Luttrell),LLP,O,CT,DT; CtY,ICU, MH,OCU,TxU+.

— The land of love. A poem, 1717. *See* Behn, Aphra.

Landesius, Andreas Franciscus. *See* Boureau Deslandes, André François.

L43 Landing. The landing. [*London?* 1715?]
slip: 1 side, 1 column.
'Appear O James! aproach they native shore'
Crum A1367: 'The invitation', dated as 30 Jan 1715. Jacobite propaganda.
MH.

L44 Landlord. The landlord's tale: a poem. From the twenty-eighth book of Orlando Furioso. In two canto's. *London printed, and are sold by Benj. Bragge*, 1708. (*Observator* 7 Feb)

The **landlord**'s tale

2°: A–G²; *1–2* 3–27 *28 blk*.
    The Luttrell copy dated 10 Feb is listed in *Haslewood*.
'A gracious prince as ever people bless'd'
O,DT,LdU-B.

L45 Landscape. The landscape. *Dublin, printed for Peter Wilson,* 1746.
    8°: A⁴; *1–3* 4–8.
        According to *Bradshaw* 1338, printed at the University Press.
    'In blooming youth and virgin beauty gay'
    L(11631.e.36),C.

L46 —— A poem. *London, printed for John Wood, under the Royal Exchange,* 1748. (*SR* 20 April)
    2°: *A²* B–C²; *1–3* 4–12. *12 err.*
        Deposit copy at O, probably L,E. Listed in *GM* April.
    L(643.m.16/16),O,E; CtY.

L47 —— The third edition, revised and improved by the author. Together with some occasional verses by the same hand, not hitherto published. *Dublin, printed for E. & J. Exshaw,* 1748.
    8°: A–B⁴; *1–4* 5–16.
        P. 3 records that these lines 'have been lately printed in a most incorrect manner in London'.
    L(1489.p.8),DA.

Langford, Abraham. Bellaria; or the fair unfortunate: a romance. To which is added, miscellaneous works, in prose and verse. *London, printed in the year* 1730.
    8°: pp. 110.   O; CSmH,CtY.

Langley, R. 'Miscellanies in prose and verse. [*London*] *Sold by J. Robinson.* Price 2s.' (*GM,LM* Sept 1745)

Lansdowne, George Granville, baron. *See* Granville, George, *baron Lansdowne.*

'**Laocoon, Trojanus.**' The all-devouring monster, 1748. *See* A163.

Laodamia. Laodamia to Protesilaus, 1743. *See* Price, Henry.

L48 Lash. A lash for the laureat: or an address by way of satyr; most humbly inscrib'd to the unparallel'd Mr. Rowe, on occasion of a late insolent prologue to the Non-juror. *London, printed for J. Morphew,* 1718. (*PB* 4 Feb)
    2°: *A²* B–C²; *i–iv,* 1–8.
    'A foe to flatt'ry needs no patron seek'
        Rowe wrote the prologue for Cibber's *Non-juror,* first performed 6 Dec 1717.
    L(11795.k.31/3),LVA-F,O; DFo,MH,TxU(2).

Last. The last day, 1717. *See* Bulkeley, John.

The **last** farewel

L49 —— The last farewel and lamentation of Mrs. M'Leoid, who was execute in the Grass-market of Edinburgh on the 8th of March 1727, for the crime of forgery, with her last farewel to the world. [*Edinburgh,* 1727.]
    ½°: 1 side, 2 columns.
        Rough woodcut at head, mourning borders.
    'All people now both far and near'
    E.

L50 —— A last farewell, to Dolly. [*Dublin,* 1725?/30?]
    slip: 1 side, 1 column.
    'I'm sure you'le think it strange Dr. Dolly'
        The author complains of the satires they are both subject to.
    DN.

L51 —— The last guinea; a poem. *London, printed for T. Jauncy,* 1720. (*DP* 9 Sept)
    8°: ᵖA⁴ A–B⁴ C²; *i–ii* iii–viii, 1–19 *20. 20 advt.*
    'Poor relict of my once known yellow store'
        Generally ascribed to John Fowler following *Halkett & Laing,* who apparently based their attribution on the entry in the Advocates' Library catalogue for a copy of the 1759 edition, now missing. The copy at L is bound with a ms. poem and a begging letter from the author which lacks the signature. It may well be by Fowler, but it is reprinted in William Pattison, *Cupid's metamorphoses,* 1728, and indexed there as 'By Mr. Bowman, a Scots gentleman' – this attribution is presumably by Curll. This Bowman has not been identified, but is not, apparently, the William Bowman whose poems were published by Curll.
    L(1077.c.30, mutilated),O; CSmH(Luttrell, Sept), CtY,MH,TxU.

L52 —— The second edition corrected. *London, printed for T. Jauncy,* 1720.
    8°: A–C⁴ ²C²; *i–iii* iv–viii, 1–18 *19–20.* ²C2 *advt.*
    L(11602.ee.1/2),O,WcC; IU,NjP.

L53 —— *Edinburgh, reprinted, and sold by most booksellers in town,* 1727.
    8°: *A⁴* B⁴ C² (A4 as 'B'); *i–ii* iii–v *vi blk,* 1–14.
    L(11631.d.4),E.

L54 —— The last new prologue and epilogue spoken by the famous commedian Mr. William Pinkeman, touching on the humours of the age. *London printed, and are to be sold by John Nutt,* [1701.] (6 Nov, Luttrell)
    ½°: 2 sides, 1 column.
        Prologue on recto, epilogue on verso. The epilogue was published separately as *Epilogue. The last comic...* [1701.]
    'The prologue over, few regard the play'
    'This long vacation, how we've thrash'd in vain'
    L(C.124.g.2/10); ICN(Luttrell).

—— The last new prologues and epilogues, 1703. *See* Pittis, William.

— The last Observator, [1704.] *See* Brown, Thomas.

L55 — The last speech and confession of Jannet Riddle, who was execute, for murthering her own child, in the Grass Market of Edinburgh, January 21st. 1702. [*Edinburgh*, 1702.]
½°: 1 side, 2 columns.
'Oh! Oh! did ever any hear'
E.

— The last speech and dying words of John Dalgleish, [172–.] *See* Pennecuik, Alexander, *d. 1730.*

L56 — The last speech and dying words of Thomas Vert, who was execute at Durham the 12th August 1730, for the murdering of his own sister... [*Edinburgh*, 1730.] (19 Dec)
½°: 2 sides, 2 columns.
The E copy has a ms. note, 'Edr printed 19 Decr 1730'.
'You tender parents all both far and near'
E.

L57 — The last speech of the statue at Stock's-market, on it's being taken down the 17th of March, 1737. To the tune of, Ye lads and ye lasses, &c. [*London?* 1737.]
slip: 1 side, 1 column.
Percival appendix 63.
'Ye whimsical people of fair London town'
Crum Y157b.
C.

L58 — The last speech of Thomas and Robert Moore's, who was execute at Ayr, the 19th of November 1728. [*Glasgow?* 1728.]
½°: 1 side, 2 columns.
The E copy is bound with a number of Glasgow pamphlets.
'And must we die? ah wretched fate!'
E.

L59 — The last speech of Wisdom's defeat. &c. A scandalous libel, burnt this second day of October, 1725 by the common hangman. *Dublin, printed by W.P. in Skinnerrow*, 1725.
½°: 1 side, 1 column.
'I repent, that, my wisdom hither should bring me'
The libel was *On wisdom's defeat in a learned debate*, 1725, for which Sarah Harding, the printer, was apparently imprisoned.
L(1890.e.5/199); CtY,MH.

L60 — The last speech to the election: or, the fanaticks, now-or-never. Being a burlesque on a second advertisement, by the author of the first. *Dublin, printed by Edward Waters*, 1728.
½°: 1 side, 2 columns.
Reprinted in *Crumbs of comfort*, 1728.
'To all his brethren, whether sitting'
A burlesque of an election advertisement distributed through the Dublin meeting-houses, apparently satirizing an advertisement by

Forbes, standing against Stoyte, possibly relating to Richard Choppin. The reference to a first advertisement possibly relates to *An epistle to a worshipful gentleman*, 1727.
Crawford.

L61 — The last will and testament of the High-German doctor, who sicken'd on the 27th of July, and departed this life soon after. To the tune of – Why, this is the devil, &c. [*London*, 1714.]
slip: 1 side, 1 column.
'Being now on my tour/For higher or lower'
A satire on Harley's dismissal, 27 July 1714.
OCU,*Harding.*

L62 Late. A late dialogue between Dr. Burgess and Daniel d'Foe, concerning Dr. Sacheverel's trial, and the present times. [*Dublin*, 1710.]
½°: 1 side, 1 column.
On the other side, *The narrative of high and low*, [1710.]
'Quoth Daniel the doctor, to Daniel d'Foe'
A high church satire after Sacheverell's trial.
DG.

L63 — The late English p----t's elogy. [*Dublin, printed by John Harding*, 1722.]
½°: 1 side, 1 column.
Mourning headpiece and borders.
'Time no doubt, all things wears out'
On the dissolution of parliament.
L(11602.i.1/6, ms. date).

L64 — The late gallant exploits of a famous balancing captain: a new song. To the tune of the King and the miller. *London, printed for J. Huggonson*, 1741. (GM, LM Nov)
2°: A² < B²; 1–2 3–7 8 blk (4, 5 as '8, 9').
Line 2 reads '...will allow to be true'.
'I'll tell you a story as strange as 'tis new'
A satire on Horatio Walpole, baron Walpole of Wolterton.
L(11630.h.23),O,AdU,LdU-B; MH.

L65 — [another impression]
Line 2 reads '... will allow but too true' and the pagination is corrected; probably this is the revised state of sheet B. One copy at L has the old reading but correct pagination.
L(840.m.1/47; 163.n.15); CSmH,CtY,DFo, OCU,TxU+.

L66 —— '*London*' [*Edinburgh*], *printed in the year* 1741. (SM Oct)
2°: A²; 1–4.
Drop-head title only. Printed by Ruddiman on the evidence of the ornament.
E.

Latin. Latin and English poems. By a gentleman of Trinity College, Oxford, 1738–. *See* Loveling, Benjamin.

Latin

L67 — The Latin dedication of the honourable Mr. Alexander Hume-Campbell, with a literal translation thereof by Cardinal Alberoni; and the same translation again versified by another hand. '*London, printed for A. Moore*' [*Edinburgh?*], 1729.
4°: π² A–B²; *i–iv, 1* 2–8.
'Prince Frederick, and then for a''
 A satirical versification of Hume-Campbell's dedication of his thesis to Prince Frederick.
L(11631.bbb.11),E,GM; *CU*.

L68 — The (Latin) description of Hogland: with its dedication: imitated in English. *London, printed in the year* 1711. (*SR* 19 March)
8°: *A*⁴ B–D⁴; [*4*] i–iv, 1–23 *24*. A1 hft; 23, 24 advt.
 Woodcut hog on title; mock advertisements on p. 23. Entered in *SR* to Abigail Baldwin; deposit copies at O,E,AdU.
'The man's auspicious conduct, that subdu'd'
 A translation of [Thomas Richards] Χοιρο-χωρογραφια, 1709.
L(11631.aaa.29),O,E,AdU,DT; CtY,IU,TxU.

[**Lauder, William**.] A pindarick ode on his excellency John duke of Marlborough, [1706?] *See* P287.

L69 — A poem of Hugo Grotius on the holy sacrament, translated into English verse. *Edinburgh, printed by R. Fleming and company, for the author, and sold by most booksellers in town,* 1732.
8°: π⁴ A–D⁴; *i–viii, 1–30 31–32* blk.
 Watermark: grapes. With the Latin of Grotius on pp. 18–26.
'All hail! mysterious; hail! religious rites!'
 Dedication signed.
L(C.58.d.30,–D4),O,E,GM; DLC,MH(–D4).

L70 — [fine paper]
 Watermark: fleur-de-lys. The copy seen has gilt edges.
GU.

— To the most honourable, Robert marquis of Bowmont...a poem, congratulatory... Paraphrased from the Latin, [1740.] *In* K19.

Lauderdale, Richard Maitland, *earl of. See* Maitland, Richard, *earl of Lauderdale.*

L71 Laugh. Laugh and be fat, or a merry tale of my grandmothers cat, or the Drury Lane cats in an uproar. *London, by William Fowler, in Hanging Sword Court Fleet Street,* [1727.] (June, Luttrell)
½°: 1 side, 2 columns.
 Rough woodcut above text.
'O yes, O yes I cry'
 A satire against the Duchess of Kendal.
MH(Luttrell).

— Laugh and lye down; or, a pleasant, but sure, remedy for the gout, 1729. *See* Brownsword, William.

Laugh

— Laugh upon laugh, or, laughter ridicul'd, 1740. *See* Brownsword, William.

L72 Laurel. [dh] The lawrel and the ox: a fable. [*London,* 1710?]
2°: *A²*; 1–4.
'A venerable lawrel stood'
 A political fable.
DG.

[**Laurence, John.**] Paradice regain'd: or, the art of gardening. A poem [actually by Nicholas Zinzano], 1728. *See* Z2.

Lavergne, Gabriel Joseph de.
Love without affectation, in five letters from a Portugueze nun, to a French cavalier. Done into English verse, 1709. *See* L287.

L73 Law. The law corrupted; a satire. *London, printed for S. Sturton,* 1706. (*PM* 7 March)
2°: *A¹* †² B–F² G¹; *i–vi, 1–12 17–24 21–22*.
 A1 and G1 have been seen to be conjugate.
'O seed divine, by heavn's great sower sown!'
L(1959); CSmH,DFo(uncut),MH,TxU.

— The law suit: or the farmer and fisherman, 1738–. *See* Barber, James–.

L74 [**Lawson, John.**] The upper gallery. A poem... Inscribed to the revd. Dr. Swift, D.S.P.D. *Dublin, printed by George Faulkner,* 1733.
8°: *A⁴*; *1* 2–8.
'Amidst the noisy town's tumultuous scenes'
 Early ms. attributions to Lawson in the DN,MiU copies.
DG,DN; *CSmH*,DFo,*MiU*.

L75 [—] — *Dublin, printed. London, re-printed, and sold by J. Roberts,* 1733. (*GSJ* 21 Feb)
4°: B–C⁴; *1–3 4–16*. 16 advt.
 Entered in Bowyer's ledgers to 'WB & partners' under 20 Feb 1733, 750 copies printed.
L(1961),O; CtY,DFo,TxU.

L76 Lawyer. The lawyer turn'd butcher, and the physician, cook: or, hungry dogs will eat dirty pudding. *London, printed in the year* 1702 [1701]. (27 Nov, Luttrell)
2°: A–D²; *i–ii, 1–14*.
 The Luttrell copy is recorded in *Haslewood*.
'One night when that salubrious cordial, wine'
 Listed in *Waller* as attributed to Prior; rejected by *Wright & Spears*. On the killing and roasting of a cat.
L(643.1.24/22),LG; CLU-C,TxU.

L77 — The lawyers answer to the Country parson's good advice to my lord keeper. *London, printed in the year* 1706.
½°: 1 side, 1 column.
 'The Lawyers' is in roman type.
'Learnedly wise, and prudent as the rest'

The **lawyer**'s answer

Leaden

A whig reply to [Joseph Browne] *The country parson's honest advice,* [1706.]
L(1489.gg.1/14),LSA,O,MC,Rothschild; MH.

L78 — [another edition]
'The Lawyers' is in black letter.
L(C.20.f.2/226),O(cropt),Crawford.

Lawyers. The lawyers disbanded, [1745.] *See* Hopkins, Thomas.

Layng, Henry. Several pieces in prose and verse. *London, printed for the author; sold by J. Brindley,* 1748. (*GM, LM* June)
4°: pp. 168.   L,O; MH,NjP.
Watermark: pro patria. In some copies B2 is a cancel; two leaves are added after E3, and also *H–K⁴.
— [fine paper]   MH.
Watermark: royal arms.

L79 **Layng, Peter.** The judgment of Hercules, imitated from the Greek of Prodicus. Also, a metrical paraphrase on the forty-third chapter of Ecclesiasticus. *Eton, printed for J. Pote,* 1748. (*GM,LM* Jan)
4°: *A*² B–C²; *1–2 3–11 12 blk.*
Vertical chain-lines.
'Perplext in thought, as young Alcides lay'
L(11630.c.1/23; 11630.c.9/7; 840.k.4/4; T.969/9),LdU-B; CU.

L80 **L--d.** L--d B-------ke's speech upon the convention. To the tune of A cobler there was. *London, printed for Jacob Littleton, in Fleet-street,* 1739. (*GM* March)
2°: *A*⁴; *1–2 3–7 8 blk.*
Percival XLV.
'A famous assembly was summon'd of late'
A satire on Bolingbroke and the convention with Spain, in imitation of John Sheffield, duke of Buckingham's poem 'The election of a poet laureat'.
L(1347.m.15; 643.l.28/23),O,C,DT,AdU+; CSmH,CtY,ICN(2),MH,TxU(2)+.

L81 — The l——d m——r's farewel: or, the truth discover'd. To the tune of, Which no body can deny. *London, printed in the year* 1710.
½°: 1 side, 2 columns.
'You citizens all pray lend me an ear'
A satire on the lord mayor of London, Sir Samuel Garrard, for denying to the house of commons that he had supported Sacheverell's sermon at St. Paul's.
Herts CRO (Panshanger box 46).

— The l——d t——rs out at last, 1710. *See* Pittis, William.

[L82 = L93·5]

[L83–8 = L94·3–94·8]

L89 **Leaden.** The leaden-age. A poem. By the author of the Golden age. [*London*] *Printed, and sold by the booksellers of London & Westminster,* 1705 [1704]. (2 Nov, Luttrell)
4°: *A*² B⁴ C–E²; *i–iv,* 1–20.
Advertised in *DC* 6 Nov 1704 as 'just publish'd'.
'Sicilian muse, from lofty flights descend'
L(1493.m.16/2); CtY(Luttrell),MH(uncut).

L90 **Leaky.** The leaky vessel, a tale. *London, printed for J. Roberts,* 1721. (*DJ* 31 March)
2°: *A*² B² C¹; *1–3 4–10.*
One copy at O has C unsigned. The Luttrell copy recorded in Pickering & Chatto cat. 245/12341 was dated April.
'Hirco, an old, but amorous blade'
Haslewood has a newspaper advertisement pasted with the entries for Hildebrand Jacob; probably this merely represents a guess at the authorship. A bawdy tale.
L(11661.dd.6),O(2); CSmH.

Leapor, Mary. Poems upon several occasions. *London printed, and sold by J. Roberts,* 1748. (*GM* April)
8°: pp. 15, 282.   L,O; CtY,MH.
There are proposals dated 1 Jan 1747 at O; the poems were published for the benefit of the author's father, a gardener at Brackley.

—— The second and last volume. *London printed, and sold by J. Roberts,* 1751. (*GM* March)
8°: pp. xxxv, 324.   L.
Printed by Samuel Richardson (*Sale* 388).

L91 **Lecture.** A lecture in verse: or, a scourge for the town. A new ballad. To the tune of Packington's pound. *London, printed for, and sold by, S. Slow, and at the pamphlet-shops,* 1734. (*GM* Jan)
2°: *A*² B²; *1–2 3–8.*
'Come, ye sparks of St. James's who grandeur admire'
L(11657.m.36),LdU-B; MH,OCU.

— A lecture to the ladies, [1726.] *See* Pennecuik, Alexander, *d. 1730.*

L92 **Lecturers.** The lecturers combat for the parish of St. Andrew Holborn. To the tune of, Ye commoners and peers. *London, printed for T. Turner, in the Strand,* 1720. (July?)
½°: 1 side, 2 columns.
'No sooner there came/From Kingston on Thame'
A satire on the dispute caused by Sacheverell's appointment of a lecturer in his parish.
L(1850.c.10/56); MH(ms. date July).

Lee, George Henry, *earl of Lichfield.* The screen. A simile, [1742.] *See* S151.

L93 **Lee, John.** A love-letter: or, an address to maidens. Wherein the best match is offered to their choice

Lee, J. A love-letter

and acceptance... Written in familiar verse, by
John Lee. [*London?*] *Printed in the year* 1733.
8°: A–B⁴; *i–iii* iv, *5* 6–16.
'May it please thee to admit me'
    Religious advice.
L(1965).

L93·5 [Le Franc de Pompignan, Jean-Jacques.] La
prière universelle. Traduite de l'Anglois de M.
Pope. Par l'auteur de la tragedie de Didon, & du
discours sur l'interêt public. *A Londres, chez Paul
Vaillant,* [1740.]
4°: A–B²; *1–3* 4–7 *8 blk.*
    Date from E. Audra, *Les traductions françaises
    de Pope* (1931) 24. Audra suggests that this
    may be a French edition with a false imprint,
    but the evidence is inconclusive.
'O toy que la raison, que l'instinct même adore'
    Le Franc de Pompignan was the author of
    Didon.
MH; *Bibliothèque nationale, Paris.*

L94 [Legh, George.] The clergyman's choice of a
wife, delineated. In a letter to Dr. C. in England.
Wherein are several important queries. By a
foreign bishop, now residing and preaching in his
diocese in Terra incognita. *London, printed in the
year* 1738.
4°: A–B⁴; *1–4* 5–16.
'You tell me of a female pair'
    Attributed to George Legh in J. H. Turner,
    Halifax books (1906) 138, recording a Halifax
    reprint of 1776. Legh, who was vicar there,
    died in 1775.
L(11661.c.3),O; CtY,*DLC*,NN.

L94·3 Le H-----p. Le H-----p at Hanover. A new
song. [*London,* 1727.]
½°: 1 side, 2 columns.
    Stanza 3, line 3, '*Ho——ce Made Suit...*';
    stanza 11, line 4, '*Vous foutez tout cela*'.
    Percival VII. The following two entries may
    represent new impressions.
'When Robin rul'd the British land'
    Crum W1419. A satire on Isaac Le Heup's
    indecent behaviour at the Hanoverian court.
    L-- H---p's embassy, [1728], *A new ballad,
    inscrib'd to Polly Peachum,* [1728] and *The
    martin and the oyster,* 1727, are 'by the author
    of Leheup's ballad'.
CSmH.

L94·4 — [variant]
    Stanza 3, line 3, '*Ho——ce made Suit...*';
    stanza 11, line 4, '*Vous foutez tout cela*'.
CSmH.

L94·5 — [variant]
    Stanza 3, line 3, '*Ho——ce made Suit...*';
    stanza 11, line 4, '*** * * * * * * ***'.
TxU.

Le H-----p at Hanover

L94·6 — [another edition]
    Stanza 3, line 3, '*Ho---ce made Snit...*'.
L(1872.a.1/168**; G.559/14).

L94·65 — [another edition, title reads:] Le H---p at
Hanover, a new song.
    Stanza 3, line 3, '*Ho——ce made Suit...*'.
O.

L94·7 — [another edition, title reads:] Le H----p at
Hanover/a new song. [1727.]
½°: 1 side, 2 columns.
    Band of type flowers above title; rule between
    columns.
Crawford.

L94·8 — Le H——p's epistle to P. F——k. [*London,*
1727.]
½°: 1 side, 1 column.
'Think not your friend Le H--p to free, sir'
    A satire on Le Heup's behaviour to Prince
    Frederick at the Hanoverian court.
CSmH.

L95 Le-Hunt, Alexander. A poem addressed to the
Lord and Lady Brudenall, upon their marriage.
*London, printed by R. Walker, for J. Brindley; sold
by J. Roberts, A. Dodd & W. Harris, E. Nutt &
E. Smith, and by the booksellers of London & West-
minster,* [1730.] (*MChr* July)
2°: A² B²; *i–ii* iii–iv, 5–8.
'Descended from a race renown'd for arms'
L(1489.d.17),OW; CLU-C.

L96 — A poem address'd to the right honourable
Richard, earl of Burlington, upon his being
install'd knight of the most noble order of the
garter... *London, printed by Tho. Edlin; sold by
J. Roberts,* 1730. (*MChr* July)
2°: A–B²; *1–3* 4–8.
    Watermark: H.
'Since the third Edward pois'd the vengeful lance'
L(1489.d.18),O,OW; CSmH,DFo.

L97 — [fine paper]
    Watermark: fleur-de-lys on shield.
SrS.

L98 — Verses occasioned by the death of the most
noble William duke of Devonshire; and inscribed
to the honourable Lord Charles Cavendish.
London, printed for J. Roberts, 1729.
2°: A¹ B–C²; *1–2* 3–9 *10 blk.*
'Forgive, my lord, the fond officious muse'
O.

L99 — Verses on the safe arrival of his royal highness
in Great Britain. *London, printed for Benj. Motte,*
1729. (*MChr* 23 Jan)
2°: A² B–C²; *i–iv,* 1–8.
    Watermark: GF.
'From Granta's stream the loyal muse is come'
CtY,TxU.

Le-Hunt, A. Verses on the safe arrival

L100 — [fine paper]
Watermark: Strasburg bend. Cancel slip pasted over price on title.
Chatsworth.

L101 Leicestershire. The Leicestershire freeholder's song, to the tune of, Ye commons and peers, pray lend me your ears, &c. [*London*, 1715.]
½°: 1 side, 2 columns.
'Ye blades of our shire'
A tory song against the invalidating of the Leicestershire election on account of a riot on 2 Feb 1715.
O.

L102 Leigh, —, *Mr.* An epilogue, to her grace the Dutchess of Shrewsbury, May 29, 1714. Written by Mr. Leigh, and, spoke by Mr. Elrington. *Dublin, printed in the year* 1714.
4°: *A*²; *1–2* 3–4.
'Like wretches thrown on Greenland's fatal coast'
DK.

Leightonstone. Leighton-stone-air, 1702. *See* Harris, Joseph.

L103 Leixlip. Leixlip: a poem. To a young gentleman, on his painting a prospect of the River Liffy at Leixlip. *Dublin, printed by and for Oli. Nelson,* 1746.
4°: *A*² B²; *1–2* 3–8.
'The muse, tho' conscious of her feeble lays'
Tentatively ascribed to Samuel Shepherd by the DG catalogue, probably by association with his *Leixlip*, 1747. Not in Shepherd's poetical works, 1790.
DG.

[Lely, Richard.] Original poems and translations on several occasions. *London, printed in the year* 1723.
8°: pp. 87.   O.
Watermark: IV. Ms. attribution in the L copy below.

[—] [fine paper]   L.
Watermark: fleur-de-lys on shield.

— Poems and translations, on several occasions. *London, printed for J. Batley, J. Woodward, C. King, J. Jackson, & R. Franklin,* 1727. (*MC* Nov)
8°: pp. viii, 138.   L,O; CtY,MH.
Watermark: eagle. F5 and K7 are cancels. A copy at ICU has a ms. note 'Printed by John Willis stationer & printer at the Angel & Bible in Great Tower-street'.

— [fine paper]   CSmH.
Watermark: Strasburg bend. The copy seen is in a presentation binding.

L104 [Lenthall, William.] A trip to Leverpoole, by two of fate's children, in search of Fortunatus's

Lenthall, W. A trip to Leverpoole

purse. A satyre. Address'd to the honourable the commissioners of her majesties customs... By a gentleman of Lincoln's-Inn. *London, printed for Richard Croskill,* 1706 [1705]. (*DC* 29 Nov)
2°: *A*² B–F² *G*²; *i–iv, 1–21 22–24 blk.* A1 *blk.*
Advertised in *DC* as sold by John Nutt. The printer is identified as 'Mr. Thompson' by Robert Clare, one of Harley's informers; see H. L. Snyder in *The Library* V. 22 (1967) 342. The reliability of these identifications is uncertain.
'A by-blow struck from Nature's center'
William Lenthall made a public apology for his 'scandalous reflections on Mr. Manley and Mr. Walker' in this poem; it was published in *LG* 3 Dec 1705.
L(11602.i.25/9),MP(−A1); CSmH.

Leonidas. Leonidas, a poem, 1737–. *See* Glover, Richard.

L105 [Le Pla, Marc.] A paraphrase on the Song of the three children. In irregular stanzas. *London, printed for Edward Lathbury; sold by J. Roberts,* 1724 [1723]. (*SR* 6 Dec)
2°: *A*¹ B–H²; *3–4* 5–32. 32 err.
The deposit copies at L,O,E,EU and Luttrell's copy all lack a dedication leaf, and presumably represent a first issue.
'Beings, who meerly being have'
The dedication in the following issue (signed by Edm. Massey, 5 Dec 1723) records Le Pla's authorship.
L(643.m.13/20),O,E,EU; CLU-C(Luttrell, Dec).

L106 — [reissue] *London, printed for Edward Lathbury; sold by J. Roberts,* 1724.
2°: *A*¹ χ¹ B–H²; *1–4* 5–32.
Dedication leaf χ1 added, signed by Edm. Massey.
L(11657.m.20); CtY(uncut).

L107 — The song of the three children paraphras'd. By Marc Le Pla... Revis'd and publish'd by S. Wesley, A.M. *London, printed by E. Say, for W. Meadows, & T. Worrall,* 1728. (*MChr* 15 May)
8°: (frt+) *A*⁴(−A4) a⁴ B–F⁴ G¹[= A4]; *i–v* vi–xiii *xiv, 1* 2–42.
Later further rewritten by Wesley, and reprinted in James Nichols's edition of his poems, 1862.
'Beings, that lifeless meerly being have'
O,CT(−frt); CSmH(uncut),CtY,NNC(−frt).

Le Sage, Alain René.
Henry and Blanche: or, the revengeful marriage. A tale: taken from the French of Gil Blas, 1745. *See* H146.

Leslie, Charles. *Often referred to as 'Lesley', and noted as 'Charles Schaw Leslie' by Anderson (L110 below). He has not been further identified.*

Leslie, C. • **Leslie, C.** Mum

L108 [—] An essay on design and beauty. *Edinburgh, printed by R. Fleming, for A. Kincaid, and sold at his shop, and by the other booksellers in town*, 1739.
8º: *A*⁴ B–D⁴; *i–iv*, *1–27 28 blk*.
　　Some copies (e.g. GM,LdU-B) appear to be on very crisp heavy paper, but there are no watermarks to aid the identification of fine-paper copies and all may be on good stock.
'All must allow, that in the painter's art'
　　Ms. attribution to 'Lesley' in the DLC copy.
L(11632.cc.2, uncut),E,GM,GU,LdU-B; DLC, OCU.

L109 [—] — The second edition. *Edinburgh, printed by R. Fleming, for A. Kincaid, and sold at his shop, and by the other booksellers in town*, 1739.
8º: *A*⁴ B–D⁴; *i–iv*, *1–27 28 blk*.
　　Apparently a press-variant title; on the same good paper as the preceding.
GM.

L110 — [*idem*] 'A philosophical poem (Design and beauty). *Belfast, James Magee*, 1748.'
　　Anderson gives the author's name as Charles Schaw Leslie; this edition was perhaps not anonymous.
(*Anderson*, supplement 6, from private collection.)

L111 [—] The fall of virtue: or, the iron-age. A poem. *Edinburgh, printed by R. Fleming, for A. Kincaid*, 1738.
8º: a⁴ B–C⁴; *i–vi*, *1–18*.
'Awake, ye nine, and, with superiour art'
　　Dedication signed 'C.L'. A ms. attribution in the MH copy also refers to 'Lesley' as author of *An essay on design and beauty*.
L(11602.ee.1/6),O,E,GM; DLC,IU,MH,NN, OCU.

L112 [—] — The second edition. *Edinburgh, printed by R. Fleming, for A. Kincaid*, 1738.
8º: a⁴ B–C⁴; *i–vi*, *1–18*.
　　Apparently a press-variant title or a reimpression.
CtY.

L113 [—] Masonry: a poem. To which are added several songs. *Edinburgh, printed by W. Sands, A. Brymer, A. Murray & J. Cochran; sold by the booksellers in town*, 1739. (*SM* April)
8º: a² A–C⁴; *i–iv*, *1–24*.
'Immortal genius! that alone inspires'
　　Ms. note in the GM copy 'By Charles Lesley, a deistical loose thinking young man, author of "The fall of virtue..."'
E,GM,GU.

L114 [—] Mum. A political ballad, for the present times: with annotations political, critical, and historical. *Edinburgh printed, and sold by the book-sellers in town*, 1740. (*SM* Sept)
8º: *A*⁴ B–C⁴; *1–2 3–24*.
'Brave Bacchus by all is adored'
　　Attributed to Leslie by *Halkett & Laing*, giving no authority; a copy in the possession of Arnold Muirhead (1962) had an early ms. ascription. Leslie's authorship was doubted by Professor Nichol Smith in *Transactions of the Edinburgh Bibliographical Society* III (1957) 251, but he did not know of this author or his poems. A satire on Walpole and the whigs.
L(1485.c.26),O,C,E(2),GM; ICN,MH,OCU, TxU.

L115 [—] — An excellent new ballad to its own proper tune. *London, printed for Thomas Robins*, 1740. (*GM,LM* Nov)
2º: *A*² B² (A2 as 'B'); *1–3 4–8*.
　　The collation is obscure; both the second and third leaves are signed B. This edition omits the annotations.
O,C; TxU.

L115·2 [—] [*idem*] Mum is the word: or advice to the freemen of Dublin. An excellent new ballad. To its own proper tuue [!]. *Dublin, printed in the year* 1749.
½º: 1 side, 2 columns.
　　Eight stanzas are omitted, as are the notes.
C.

L116 [—] On the scarcity of the copper coin. A satyr. [*Edinburgh*] *Printed in the year* 1739. (*SM* Jan)
8º: π¹ *A*⁴ B⁴ C¹; *i–ii*, *1–3 4–16 17–18 blk*.
　　π1 and C1 have been seen to be conjugate.
'Now, barbers, bakers, coblers, buyers, sellers'
　　Ms. attribution to 'Lesley' in the MH copy, in the same hand as ascribed *The fall of virtue* to him.
L(1486.dd.5,–C1),LVA-D(–C1),O(–C1), E(–C1),*LdU-B*; CtY,MH(2,–C1),NN(–C1), NjP,OCU(–C1).

L'Estrange, *Sir* **Roger.** A poem upon imprisonment, written by Sir Roger L'Estrange, 1705. *In* P442.

L117 Let. Let each have their own. [*London?* 1715.]
⅛º: 1 side, 1 column.
　　Originally conjugate with *The blessings attending George's accession*, [1715.]
'When his lov'd Germans George was forc'd to leave'
　　Crum W1137: 'On the lamentation of the Hannoverians, for the absence of their prince, now King George of England'. A Jacobite satire against George I.
Herts CRO (Panshanger box 46); CSmH,CtY.

L118 Letter. A letter from a cobler in Patrick's-street to Jet Black. [*Dublin*] *Printed in the year* 1724.
½º: 1 side, 2 columns.
'If any line I write's a hobler'
　　A satire on Jonathan Smedley.
C,Rothschild.

L119 — A letter from a country gentlemam [!], to the honourable the lord mayor, of the city of Dublin, 1729. *Dublin, printed in the year of our lord* 1729.

A **letter** from a country gentleman

½°: 1 side, 2 columns.
'Of all the sports beneath the sun'
A satire on Henry Burrowes; reprinted and answered in *A hue and cry after the Letter*, 1729, which refers to this as 'Mrs. Hussey, alias Harding's print'.
CtY.

L120 — A letter from a friend to Miss M---y S----y. [*Dublin*] *Printed in the year* 1730.
8°: A⁴; *1–3* 4–8.
'Fair nymph, who hast with such applause so long'
To Molly Smalley. A ms. note in the copy seen suggests that Mary Smedley, daughter of Jonathan Smedley, was intended; but related poems of 1730 give the name as Smalley, and her father's name as Caleb. Cf. *A letter to Miss S-----y*, 1730.
LVA-F.

L121 — A letter from a lady to her husband. [1740.]
½°: 1 side, 2 columns.
'To thee, dear youth, in wedlock ty'd for life'
Ms. note in the OCU copy, 'Supposed to be writt by Isaac Norris – as a sayter on C. Plumstead. Introduced as a letter from his daughter in law to her husband in London – anno 1740'. Abridged and altered from [Noel Broxholme] *A letter from a lady to her husband abroad*, 1728.
OCU.

— A letter from a lady to her husband abroad, 1728–. *See* Broxholme, Noel.

L122 — A letter from a member of parliament to his friend in the country. *London, printed for John Roberts*, 1741.
8°: *A⁴*; *1–2* 3–8.
The imprint is possibly false, and the work not a London publication.
'Dear J——n, I congratulate'
OCU.

L123 — A letter from a young lady, to the revd. D----n S----t. [*Dublin*] *Printed in the year* 1724.
8°: *A⁴*; *1–2* 3–8.
Teerink 1626.
'When ought such observation draws'
In praise of Swift's campaign against Wood's halfpence.
DA,DN; CSmH.

L124 — A letter from Aminadab Firebrass quaker merchant, to M.B. drapier. *Dublin, printed by John Harding*, [1724.]
½°: 1 side, 1 column.
'My dearest friend M.B. I hope thou't excuse'
In praise of Swift's *Drapier's Letters*.
LVA-F,DT.

— A letter from D. S——t. to D. S——y, [1725.]
See Swift, Jonathan.

L125 — A letter from Doctor Dalgleish to his patient Mrs. M'Leod, and her answer. [*Edinburgh*, 1727.]
(16 Feb)

A **letter** from Doctor Dalgleish

½°: 1 side, 2 columns.
Ms. note in the E copy, 'Edr 16. febr 1727 published'.
'M Leod, you vild adulterous jad'
Possibly by Alexander Pennecuik (d. 1730); it is reprinted in his *A compleat collection*, [174–?], but that contains some poems by other hands. John Dalgleish was the Edinburgh hangman who executed Margaret M'Leod for forgery.
E.

L126 — A letter from Don Blas de Lezo, the Spanish admiral at Carthagene, to Don Thomas Geraldino. *Jamaica, printed by John Letts, for Peter & Robert Baldwin*, 1740.
2°: *A–B²*; *i–ii*, 1–6.
'To thee, my friend, though now perhaps disgrac'd'
'To the publisher' signed 'Britannicus'.
L(11626.h.11/4); *West India Reference Library, Jamaica.*

L127 — [*idem*] The letter sent from Don Blass de Lezo, the Spanish admiral at Carthagena, to Don Thomas Geraldino, versify'd. To which is added the literal translation...also the translation of another sent from Don Blass to Admiral Vernon. [*London*] *Published from the copy printed at Jamaica, and now reprinted for T. Gardner*, 1740. (*GM, LM* Aug)
2°: *A²* B–C²; *1–3* 4–11 *12* blk.
L(1973); CSmH; *West India Reference Library.*

L127.5 —— *London, publish'd from the copy printed at Jamaica*, 1740.
8°: A⁴; *1–2* 3–8.
A piracy, possibly of Edinburgh origin. The copy seen lacks the prose passages, and may be imperfect.
L(11645.ee.46/5).

L128 — A letter from Don Thomas Geraldino, in answer to Don Blas de Lezo's at Carthagene. Faithfully translated by Britannicus. *Jamaica, printed by John Letts, for Peter & Robert Baldwin*, 1740.
2°: pp. *1*–15.
'If, yet, confin'd within thy walls O chief'
West India Reference Library, Jamaica.

L129 — A letter, from J—n W—d, to J— L—n. [*Dublin*] *Printed in the year* 1736.
½°: 1 side, 2 columns.
'My silence, pardon, dearest Jo'
A mock letter from a usurer, John Wade [?] who died on 9 October.
C.

— A letter from Martin Gulliver, to George Faulkner, 1730. *See* 'Gulliver, Martin'.

L130 — A letter from Mr. Jacob Bickerstaffe, nephew to Isaac Bickerstaffe, esq, occasion'd by the death of Queen Anne. To a gentleman in Holland. *London, printed for S. Popping; sold by the*

A **letter** from Mr. Jacob Bickerstaffe

booksellers of London & Westminster, [1714.] (*PB* 19 Aug)
4°: A–C²; *1–2* 3–11 *12 blk*.
'While you require, I dare not, sir, refuse'
L(161.1.9, Luttrell, Aug).

L131 —— The second edition. *London, printed for S. Popping; sold by the booksellers of London & Westminster*, [1714.]
4°: A–C²; *1–2* 3–11 *12 blk*.
Probably a reimpression or press-variant title.
O.

L132 — A letter from the B. of S—— to the A.B. of Paris. Dated, London, Dec. 31. 1706. [*London*] *Sold by John Morphew*, 1707. (31 Dec 1706?)
½°: *1–2*, 1 column.
Luttrell underlined the date in the title of his copy as if it were the date of publication.
'Since news at Paris grows so wondrous scarce'
From Gilbert Burnet, bishop of Salisbury, to the archbishop of Paris, praising Queen Anne and exulting over the French.
O,DG; ICN(Luttrell).

L133 —— [*Edinburgh*, 1707.] (9 Jan)
½°: *1–2*, 1 column.
E(2, 1 ms. date 9 Jan).

L134 — A letter from the city mumpers, to the liberty-beggars, on the coronation of their King Clause. [*Dublin*] *Printed in the year* 1735.
½°: *1–2*, 1 column.
'Since you, poor knaves, have scrap'd some pence and pity'
NN.

L135 — A letter from the late revd. Mr. Sewel, from the other world. To a certain alderman. *Dublin, printed in the year* 1741.
4°: A² B–D²; *1–2* 3–15 *16 blk*.
'While in the realms of everlasting night'
Possibly William Sewel, the quaker (d. 1720) is intended.
PP.

L136 — A letter from the Quidnunc's at St. James's coffee-house and the Mall, London, to their brethren at Lucas's coffee-house, in Dublin... [*Dublin?* 1724?]
½°: *1–2*, 2 columns.
Teerink 1096. Reprinted in *Gulliveriana*, 1728.
'Sir, having nothing else to do'
Signed, 'R,S,T,U,W,X,Y,Z,&'. Cf. *A poem addressed to the Quidnunc's*, 1724; there is no direct connection between them.
CSmH.

L137 — A letter of advice to a friend in London: written by the Observator in the country. *London printed, and sold by J. How*, 1704. (4 March?)
2°: A² B–D²; *1–2* 3–15 *16 blk*.
'You may expect, my friend, that I should be'
Signed 'Observator' and dated 2 Feb 1704; John Tutchin is clearly intended.
L(11630.g.11),O; CtY(ms. date 4 March),MH.

A **letter** of advice

L138 — A letter of advice to the revd. D--r. D---la---y, humbly propos'd to the consideration of a certain great lord. [*Dublin*, 1730.]
½°: 1 side, 1 column.
Teerink 950; cf. *Williams* 487.
'What doctor, if great Carteret condescends'
A reply to [Patrick Delany] *An epistle to his excellency John lord Carteret*, [1729.]
L(1890.e.5/92;C.121.g.8/84),C,Rothschild;CtY.

L139 — A letter of serious advice to a young poet. *Dublin, printed* [*by Richard Reilly*] *in the year* 1735.
8°: A–C⁴; *1–3* 4–22 *23–24 blk*. 22 err.
Printer identified by *Bradshaw* 1430.
'What, shall I always hear, and never write?'
C(2),DA(uncut, –C4).

L140 — Letter of thanks, from the king of the dark regions, to the honest-jury of Guilford, who acquitted Mrs. L--g--y of the murther of her husband. *London, printed for J. Sheron*, 1732.
½°: 1 side, 2 columns.
'I Pluto king of the dark regions'
A satire on the bribed jury.
L(1871.e.1/188).

— The letter sent from Don Blass de Lezo, 1740. *See* A letter from Don Blas de Lezo, 1740.

— A letter. Sir, there having been... 1726. *See* Sheridan, Thomas (S419).

L141 — A letter to a friend in the country. *London, printed for T. Cooper*, 1740. (*GM, LM* April)
4°: B–E⁴; *1–3* 4–31 *32 blk*. 31 err.
'That all is vanity below'
L(11630.c.4/6),O; CtY.

L142 — A letter to a friend, upon the successes of the year M.DCC.VIII. *London, printed for Tho. Ward, and are to be sold by J. Morphew*, 1709. (*Tatler* 20 Oct)
2°: A¹ B–D²; *i–ii*, 1–12.
The Luttrell copy, dated 20 Oct, is in the collection of R. D. Horn.
'Tho' Flandria calls our glorious chief away'
MH(cropt).

L143 — [*idem*] [dh] A letter to a friend, on the late successes of the Duke of Marlbro'. A poem. [col] *London, printed by A. Hinde in the year* 1710.
8°: A⁴; 1–8.
Printed in two columns on pp. 3, 4, 8.
O-JJ.

L144 — A letter to a friend: with two poems sacred to the memory of the late R.R. Dr. Thomas Rattray of Craighall, bishop of Edinburgh. *Edinburgh, printed in the year* 1743.
4°: π¹ A–B² C¹; *1–2* 3–12.
The letter is purely introductory to the poems in Latin and English.
'Dum numerat doctam renitens ecclesia prolem'
'And is it so? Is then great Rattray gone?'
Ascribed to Thomas Drummond by *Halkett & Laing*; but his memorial verses in *Poems*,

A letter to a friend

1756, are quite different. A ms. note in the GM copy (probably by Maidment) suggests the letter is addressed *to* Drummond.

L(11630.b.8/10),GM.

— A letter to a lady, 1714. *See* Gay, John.

L145 — A letter to a member of the town council of Edinburgh. [*Edinburgh*, 1736.]
½⁰.
'You know, dear friend, and doubtless do lament' (*Trial of Captain Porteous*, ed. William Roughead (1909) 362.)

L146 — A letter to Mareschal Tallard. Made English out of French, by J.Br. *London, printed for Anthony Feltham*, 1706.
4⁰: A⁴ B²; *1–2* 3–12.
'It's true, Tallard, when fickle chance deny'd'
In praise of Marlborough, suggesting the surrender of the French. A translation of *Lettre au Marechal de Tallard*, 1706.
LdU-B.

L147 — A letter to Miss S——y. Written by one of her admirers. *Dublin, printed in the year* 1730.
½⁰: 1 side, 1 column.
Below, in two columns 'An answer to the above short letter of the pretended admirer of Miss S——y.'
'Th' unnumbred charms that in thy person shine'
Answer: 'Call it not love, for love to heaven is fled'
To Molly Smalley. Possibly related to *A letter from a friend to Miss M——y S——y*, 1730.
CtY.

L148 — A letter to Mr. Prior, discovering a secret of vast importance. By a fellow sufferer. *London printed, and sold by J. Roberts*, 1715. (10 Sept, Luttrell)
4⁰: π¹ A–C²; *i–ii* iii–iv, 5–14.
'When angry death glares in your face'
Written from the King's Bench prison whence Prior wrote his letter to Sir Fleetwood Sheppard.
L(164.m.7, Luttrell),O,AN.

L149 — A letter to Mr. Prior, occasion'd by the Duke of Marlborough's late victory at Ramilly, and glorious successes in Brabant. *London, printed by W.D.* [*William Downing?*] *for Edmund Curll; sold by Benj. Bragge*, 1706. (18 June, Luttrell)
2⁰: A² B–C²; *1–2* 3–12. 12 advt.
Advertised in *DC* 22 June.
'Shall Marlbro' still new victories obtain?'
L(643.l.24/28),O; CSmH,CtY,ICU(Luttrell), OCU,TxU+.

L150 — A letter to Mr. William Whiston, relating to his account of the late meteor. *London, printed for T. Bickerton*, 1719. (Aug, Luttrell)
2⁰: A¹ B²; *1–2* 3–6.
The watermark varies; that at O (fleur-de-lys) possibly represents a fine-paper copy.

A letter to Mr. William Whiston

'Since letters are grown/So frequent in town'
O; MnU(Luttrell).

— A letter to Monsieur Boileau Depreaux, 1704. *See* Prior, Matthew.

L151 — A letter to Polly. To one of her own tunes. *London, printed for A. Moore*, 1728. (*MChr* 2 April)
2⁰: A–B²; *1–4* 5–8. A1 hft.
With the air on p. 5.
'O Polly, speak thy resistless charm'
To Polly Peachum.
LdU-B; ICN,MH.

L152 — A letter to Sir R—— W—— with the characters of these five sectaries, which ought not to be trusted in troublesome times (viz.) presbyterian, independent, anabaptist, quaker and fifth monarchy-men. Concluding with advice to the K... *London, printed in the year &c.* [1714/41.]
12⁰: 8 pp.
Apparently addressed to Walpole.
(Pickering & Chatto cat. 269/12460.)

L153 — A letter to the author of A character. *London, printed for the author, and sold only by G. Rogers, stationer, just within Bishopsgate*, 1717.
8⁰: A⁴ B²; *1–3* 4–11 *12 blk*.
'If thou from heav'n art sacredly inspir'd'
Smith I. 51 'In reply to Elias Bockett, by William Gibson'. It is certainly a reply to Bockett's attack *A character*, 1717, but the specific references to Gibson in the text make his authorship seem improbable. Answered by Bockett's *A return to the author of a letter*, 1717.
LF(2); MH.

L154 — [dh] A letter to the author of the Speaker. A poem. [col] *Dublin, printed by E. Waters*, [1713/14.]
4⁰: A²; *1* 2–4.
'What a diverting sight it wou'd have been'
CSmH,CtY.

L155 — A letter to the bishop of M. by Dr. Sw—t, being a faithful inventory of the furniture of a certain gentleman in T.C. [*Dublin*, 1726.]
½⁰: 1 side, 1 column.
Teerink 932. On the other side of the PU copy, *A new ballad in praise of the ancient...city of Londonderry*, 1726.
'Imprimis, there's a table blotted'
Written in imitation of [Thomas Sheridan] *A true and faithful inventory*, [1726], and applied to a member of Trinity College. Not by Swift. Reprinted in *Poems written occasionally by John Winstanley...interspers'd with many others*, 1742.
C; PU.

— A letter to the knight of the sable shield, 1716. *See* Fenton, Elijah.

— 'Letter to the patron of the Trip to Barleduc.' *An epistle to Mr. Pope. By the author of the*

Letter to the patron

Letter to the patron of the *Trip to Barleduc* (Edinburgh, 1716) is in verse, and so may this be; it has not been traced. Probably the author was John Steddy, who wrote *A trip to Bar-le-Duc* (Edinburgh, 1715).

L156 — A letter to the reverend Mr. M---w F----h, in commendation of his speech. [*Dublin*, 1712?]
½°: *1–2*, 1 column.
'Were I, dear M-----w, who am none'
A satire on a speech of Matthew French. The date appears to be 1712, but the work is related to *The r-----r's s-----ch explain'd*, [1711], on John Foster's speech welcoming the Duke of Ormonde as lord lieutenant.
C,Crawford.

L157 — [dh] A letter to Tom Punsibi. Occasion'd by reading his excellent farce, call'd, Alexander's overthrow, or, the downfall of Babylon. [*Dublin*, 1721?]
4°: *A²*; *1 2–3 4 blk*.
'Nor turkey fat, nor goose from country-hut'
To Thomas Sheridan.
ICN.

Letters. Letters and poems on political subjects. Witten [!] by a hearty whig, and dedicated to the Earl of Oxford. *London, printed for R. Burleigh, & A. Dodd*, 1716. (*MC* Jan)
8°: pp. *1–16, 25–31*.   L,DrU; CtY.
Mainly in prose.

L158 Lettre. [dh] Lettre au Marechal de Tallard. [col] *A Londres, chez J. Cailloué, libraire, au coin de Beauford-buildings, dans le Strand*, 1706.
4°: *A–C²*; *1–12*.
'Illustre infortuné, le ciel enfin te vange'
Signed 'Br.' In praise of Marlborough and suggesting the surrender of the French. Translated as *A letter to Mareschal Tallard*, 1706, by J.Br., possibly the same author.
O.

L159 Leviathan. Leviathan, or, a hymn to poor brother Ben. To the tune of the Good old cause reviv'd. *London, printed in the year* 1710.
½°: 1 side, 2 columns.
Stanza 1, line 3 has the overrun of line 2 '[Pen,'.
'Why now so melancholy Ben?'
A high church satire against Benjamin Hoadly's doctrine of resistance in his controversy with Offspring Blackall.
O,Rothschild.

L160 — [another edition]
Stanza 1, line 3 has the overrun '(Pen,'.
LLP; MH.

L161 Levy. The levy-haunter, a satire. *London, printed for J. Roberts; sold at the booksellers and pamphlet-*

The **levy**-haunter

shops in London & Westminster, 1729. (*MChr* 27 Feb)
2°: A–C²; *i–iv, 1–7 8 blk*.
'The grey-ey'd morn, now, eastward breaks its way!'
A satire on parasites, dedicated to Walpole.
O(2, 1 uncut),OW; CSmH,MH.

L162 Lewis. Lewis in a sweat: or, a dry clout for the King of Spain. A satyr. Wherein Ignatius's ghost is brought in, discoursing with the Duke of Vendosme, concerning the victory obtained by Prince Eugene in Italy. By the author of the True-born English-man. *London, printed for R. Brigs in Holbourn*, 1702.
8°: A⁴; *1–2 3–8*.
The copy recorded in the printed catalogue of E is now at O.
'Hail, hail, auspicious Eugen, whose brave hand'
Not recorded by any Defoe bibliographer; chapbook verses of the kind specifically disowned by Defoe.
O(uncut).

L163 — Lewis upon Lewis: or, a snake in the grass. A satyrical ballad. 1712–13. To the tune of a country dance, call'd, Green sleeves. [*London*, 1713.]
½°: 1 side, 2 columns.
'Whilst peace is brewing, like good strong beer'
A whig ballad occasioned by a Jacobite 'spy' called Skelton who came from France to London and was driven to the house of 'Lewis the whig' instead of 'Lewis the scribe'.
DT.

L164 Lewis, E. The weeping muse. A poem. Sacred to the memory of his late majesty. *London, printed for Tho. Hodgson*, 1702.
2°: A–C²; *i–iv, 1–8*.
'Oh muse! my only, and my last relief!'
L(11630.g.8).

L165 Lewis, Richard. The mouse-trap, or the battle of the Cambrians and mice. A poem. Translated into English, by R. Lewis. *Annapolis, printed for the author, by W. Parks*, 1728.
8°: a² b⁴ c² B⁴ C–G⁴ H²; *i–iv v–xvi, 1 2–52*.
Included here to complete the record of translations of Holdsworth's *Muscipula*, [1708]; other American poems by Lewis are excluded. The Latin title-page has the imprint 'Annapoli: impensis R.L., typis W.P.' Title-pages in red and black; subscribers on pp. xiv–xvi.
'The mountain-dwelling Briton who design'd.'
O(presentation copy to Hearne from B. L. Calvert, governor of Maryland; original marbled wrappers, gilt),WcC; CSmH,DLC(impft).

Libel. A libel on D-- D----- and a certain great lord, 1730. *See* Swift, Jonathan.

Libel

L166 — A libel upon the Dublin dunces. In an epistle to Mr. William Dunkin. [*Dublin*] *Printed in the year* 1734.
8⁰: A⁴; *1–3* 4–8. 8 advt.
''Tis true, the wretch that dares to write'
    A satire on Charles Carthy, Dalacourt, and others.
LVA-F,DA,DN.

Libertas. Libertas triumphans, 1708. *See* Gildon, Charles.

L167 Libertatis. Libertatis amator; a litany. [*London*, 1713/14.]
slip: 1 side, 1 column.
'From the lawless dominion of mitre and crown'
    Apparently a revision of *Crum* F771: 'The antiphone to the late protestant petition', 1680. Against the high church party.
L(C.121.g.9/157).

L168 — [another edition, title reads:] Libertatis amator: a litany.
OCU, *Harding*.

Libertine. The libertine's choice, 1704–. *See* Ward, Edward.

L169 Liberty. Liberty. A poem. *London, printed for Tim. Goodwin*, 1705. (*PM* 1 Dec)
2⁰: A–C²; *1–2* 3–11 *12 blk.*
    The Luttrell copy, dated 1 Dec, is in the collection of R. D. Horn. The copy at O is in contemporary marbled wrappers with gilt edges, apparently added after its original stabbing. The printer is identified as Midwinter by Robert Clare, one of Harley's informers; see H. L. Snyder in *The Library* V. 22 (1967) 342. The reliability of these identifications is uncertain.
'Hail beauteous goddess! hail harmonious pow'r'
O; CtY,MB,MH,TxU.

L170 — Liberty: a poem. [*Dublin*, 1727.]
¼⁰: 1 side, 1 column.
'Hail liberty! thou beatific grace'
    In praise of George II's accession.
DT.

— Liberty. A poem. To the queen, 1729. *See* Stammers, William.

L171 — Liberty: an ode; occasion'd by the happy victory obtain'd by his royal highness the Duke of Cumberland. *London, printed by E. Cave; sold by M. Cooper*, 1746. (*GM, LM* July)
2⁰: A¹ B–D² E¹; *i–ii, 1* 2–14.
'Daughters of Jove, and source of sacred song'
O,*AdU*; OCU.

— Liberty and property, 1705. *See* Browne, Joseph.

L172 — Liberty: or, the meeting of the parliament. A poem. *London, printed for T. Warner; sold by A.*

Liberty: or, the meeting

Dodd, C. King & J. Stagg, & J. Jackson, 1728. (*MChr* 23 Jan)
2⁰: A² B–C²; *1–5* 6–11 *12 blk.*
    What was possibly a reissue was listed by *MChr* Jan 1732, as published by T. Warner.
'O liberty! the tribute of a breast'
    Dedication signed 'Philo-patris'.
MH.

L173 — — *Dublin, printed by and for A. Rhames*, 1728.
8⁰: A⁴; *1–4* 5–8.
CtY.

L174 — Liberty regain'd. A poem. In imitation of Milton's Paradise lost. *London, printed in the year* 1740. (28 April)
2⁰: A¹ B–E² F¹; *1–2* 3–18 *19; 20 blk.* 18 err.
    The copy from Tom's Coffee House, dated 28 April, is in the Lewis Walpole Library. Listed in *GM, LM* May as sold by M. Dodd. Part of the 'L' in the date failed to print, making the date resemble MDCCXI.
'To thee, great author of my infant muse'
    Largely an attack on Walpole.
MH(uncut),OCU.

L175 Lichfield. The Litchfield squabble. An humorous poetical narration of the several transactions at the elections for the county of Stafford, and city of Litchfield... By Peter Plain-Truth, not Lord Puff. *London, printed for the author; sold by B. Dickinson*, 1747. (*LEP* 15 Oct)
4⁰: A¹ B–H² I¹; *1–2* 3–31 *32 blk.*
    Bond 194. Vertical chain-lines.
'Assist me, muse, who did inspire'
L(11630.c.6/15),O,E; *InU*,MH(cropt).

L176 — — 'The second edition. [*London*] *Printed for the author; sold by B. Dickinson, and the booksellers & pamphletsellers.*' (*LEP* 10 Nov 1747)

L177 — — The third edition. *London, printed for the author; sold by B. Dickinson*, 1747.
4⁰: A¹ B–H² I¹; *1–2* 3–31 *32 blk.*
    Largely reset.
L(11659.cc.1).

Lichfield, George Henry Lee, *earl of. See* Lee, George Henry, *earl of Lichfield.*

L178 Liddell, George. The swan's song: or, pleasant meditations on the way... The tenth edition corrected. *London, printed for the author, and sold by John & Joseph Marshall*, 1710.
12⁰: A–D⁶; *1–3* 4–48. 2 advt.
    No earlier edition has been traced.
'O why are we afraid of man'
L(C.58.a.25/4); NNUT.

L179 Life. The life and actions of W.S. A poem. (Written by himself,) during his confinement at Liverpool, in the year, 1747. From which place he was transported... Being a proper warning for

The **life** and actions of W.S.

> youth... *London, printed for Abr. Clark, bookseller, near the Exchange, Manchester*, 1750.
> 8°: A–B⁴ C²; *1–2* 3–20.
>> *The Manchester press before 1801* (Manchester Public Library publication, new series 6) suggests it was printed in Manchester by R. Whitworth, but the London imprint is in no way impossible. Added poems by M.K. on pp. 17–20.
> 'The bard who sought e'erwhile in sportive strains'
>> W.S. had apparently been a gay poet and scholar, then a merchant abroad.
> MP(2).

— The life and conversation of James Campbell of Burnbanck, [1721/22.] *See* Elegy on the mournful banishment of James Campbell, [1721/22.]

— The life and genuine character of the rev. Dr. S--t, 1733. *See* Swift, Jonathan.

L180 — The life and history of Robert the raven. [*Edinburgh*, 1742?]
> ½°: 1 side, 1 column.
> 'The British birds of late call'd over'
>> An attack on Walpole, apparently after his resignation.
> E.

L181 — The life of Cato the censor. Humbly dedicated to R. S---le, esq; *London printed, and sold by J. Woodward, & J. Baker*, 1714.
> 8°: A–E⁴; *i–vi*, 1–34.
> 'When Rome was Rome, and in its glory'
>> Dedication signed 'Daniel Dogerel'. To Richard Steele.
> O; CtY,IU,MH,TxU.

Liffy. The Liffy: a fable, 1726. *See* Ogle, George.

Light. Light extinguish'd, [171–?] *See* Waring, Henry [The dark penitent's complaint].

Lilliputian. A Lilliputian ode, 1727. *See* Carey, Henry.

L182 — The Lilliputian widow. A poem addressed to the Chester-ladies. *London, printed by John Brown in the Strand*, 1729.
> 8°: A–C⁴; *1–2* 3–24.
> 'O Cestrian dames, your humble servant'
>> Answered by *King John*, 1729, which suggests that the author was John Squire.
> L(11631.bb.51, cropt).

[**Lillo, George.**] The prologue and epilogue of George Barnwell, the London merchant, [1731.] *See* P1120.

L183 Limerick. Limerick to Kilmallock. Sendeth greeting. To the tune of, To you fair ladies now at land. [*Dublin*, 1727?]
> ½°: 1 side, 2 columns.
>> The DT copy is bound with half-sheets of 1727.

Limerick to Kilmallock

> 'Kilmallock, my dear, neighbour town'
>> A satire on the local politicians.
> DT.

L184 Lincoln's Inn. The Lincoln's-Inn 'squire; or the protestant turn'd papist. A new ballad. To the tune of, The king and the abbot of Canterbury. *London, printed for James Moore; sold by the booksellers and pamphlet-sellers of London & Westminster*, [1730.] (*MChr* Dec)
> 2°: A² B²; *1–2* 3–7 *8 blk*.
>> *Percival* appendix 28. Also printed with *The lunatick*, 1730.
> 'I'll tell you a story, a story anon'
>> On John Shorter, Walpole's brother-in-law, who turned papist.
> OCU,TxU(2).

L185 — — [*Dublin*, 1730/31.]
> ½°: 1 side, 2 columns.
> C; CSmH.

L186 Lincolnshire. Lincolnshire. A poem. *Bury St. Edmunds, Suffolk, printed for the author*, 1720.
> 2°: A–B²; *1–3* 4–8.
>> The drop-head title on p. 3 reads 'A letter from a gentleman in Lincolnshire to his friend at Wolverhampton in Staffordshire'.
> 'Happy are you that breathe the Hampton air'
> O.

L187 — [*idem*] A satyr on Lincolnshire, in a letter from a gentleman in Lincoln⟨shire⟩ to his friend in Wolverhampton, Staffordshire... The second edition. *London, printed for and sold by M. Cooper at the Globe in Pater-noster-row*, 1736.
> 8°: *A²* B⁴ C²; *5–8* 9–20. A1 frt.
>> Possibly a false imprint and date for a piece of provincial printing; Mary Cooper did not succeed her husband at this address until 1743. The 'frontispiece' is a chap-book woodcut on the recto of A1.
> L(11601.ccc.38/13).

L188 Line. The line of beauty: or the fair quakers of Bristol. A poem. *Bath, printed by Felix Farley*, 1732.
> 2°: *A²* B–C²; *1–3* 4–12.
> 'Attend, Calliope; to whom belongs'
> DFo.

Lintoun. Lintoun-address to his highness the Prince of Orange, 1714. *See* Pennecuik, Alexander, *1652–1722*.

L189 — Lintoun's lamentation, occasioned by the death of... Mr. Alexander Pennicuick of Romanno ...who was translated from his country seat at Romanno, to the mansions of glory, 7th July 1722. [*Edinburgh?* 1722.]
> 4°: *A²*; *1–4*.
> 'Just as revolting angels did resign'
> CtY.

Lion

L190 Lion. The lion and fox, or, the Matchievelian; a satire... *London, printed for, and sold by the author,* 1735.
4°: *A*⁴(−A1) B–C⁴ D⁴(−D4); *3–5* 6–30.
   The copy seen probably lacks a half-title and final blank.
'When Æsop's eldest born, first took his birth'
O.

L191 — The lion's proclamation. *London, printed in the year* 1715.
½°: 1 side, 1 column.
   Rule above imprint in two sections.
'The lion, 'tis no matter how'
   A Jacobite satire on the need for innocent tories to flee.
L(1850.c.10/46; C.116.i.4/50, cropt),O; CSmH.

L192 — [another edition]
   Rule above imprint in one piece.
MH.

L193 Litaneia. [dh] Λιτανεια τεσσαρακοστη. Or, a lenten litany, compiled for the use of the reverend clergy of the English convocation, and the rest of their worthy brethren. [col] *London, printed in the year* 1701.
4°: *A*²; *1–4*.
'From religion dress'd up like a miss for the game'
   Against the religious establishment.
L(806.k.16/69*).

L194 Litany. [dh] A litany for lent. [col] [*Dublin*] *Printed in the year* 1714.
4°: *A*²; *1–4*.
   On p. 4, 'The end of the first part'.
'From villainy dress'd in the doublet of zeal'
   Cf. *Crum* F788: 'A new litanie', printed 1656.
   Two stanzas (including the first) are repeated in *The freeman's litany*, 1749.
L(11631.bb.52),DK.

Litchfield. *See* Lichfield.

L195 Little. The Little Beau's lamentation. For the loss of Miss C-----t. [*Dublin*] *Printed by J. Mason,* [1727?]
slip: 1 side, 1 column.
'To lonely shades and discontented groves'
   A supposed lament by Patrick Walsh for Grace Carteret's departure from Dublin.
L(1890.e.5/93; C.121.g.8/136),C.

L196 — The Little Beaus petition, to his ex---y the L. C---t. Against the young ladies of Dublin. *Printed for James Nicholson, Dublin,* March 25th, 1728.
slip: 1 side, 1 column.
''Tis hard my lord that every flirt'
   A satire on Patrick Walsh's flattery of Lord Carteret.
L(1890.e.5/96, imprint cropt);CtY.

Little

L197 — The Little Beaus, speech to his ex--y the Lord Lieu-t, and Lady C——r——t, on their late arrival. Paraphras'd. [*Dublin*] '*Printed for John Little, book-seller in Christ-Church-lane*', 1727.
slip: 1 side, 1 column.
'Most mighty lord,/I'm come on board'
   A satire on Patrick Walsh's welcome to Lord and Lady Carteret.
L(1890.e.5/95),C,DT(cropt).

L198 — Little-John's answer to Robin-Hood and the Duke of Lancaster. A ballad, to the tune of, The abbot of Canterbury. *London, printed by T. White, in Chancery-lane,* [1727.]
2°: *A*²; *1–3* 4.
   Percival appendix 1.
'Here's a story reviv'd from twelve hundred & two'
   A reply to *Robin-Hood and the Duke of Lancaster,* 1727.
MH.

L199 — [dh] The little junto. In the year 1732. [*London?* 1732.]
8°: *A*⁴; *1* 2–8.
'Tom and Harry and Kentish Tottie'
   A satire on a party attempting to reunite the dissenters with the church of England.
L(11661.c.25).

— Little Merlin's cave, 1737. *See* Ward, Edward [A riddle].

L200 — Little Preston: an heroi-comick poem, upon the late action at Holywell. To which is added the Chester lady's congratulation to the hero Ashy. *London printed, and sold by J. Roberts,* 1717. (*DC* 16 Dec)
8°: *A*⁴ B⁴ C²; *1–5* 6–20. A1 hft.
   Bond 53.
'I sing the doughty blades of dauntless might'
   On a Jacobite brawl by Ashy F——d and his friends at Holywell, North Wales.
L(164.n.12),O,AdU; CSmH,CtY,*MH*.

L201 Littlemore, S. A poem on the death of the celebrated Mrs. Oldfield, who dy'd October 23. 1730 ... Inscrib'd to the hon. Brigadier Churchill, by S. Littlemore gent. *London, printed for A. Moore, and sold at the White Hart...and by the booksellers of London & Westminster,* 1730. (*GSJ* Oct)
2°: *A*² B²; *i–iv*, *1* 2–4.
   The White Hart is Robert Walker's address; cf. C409, D445.
''Tis done: death, stern destroyer, wins the day'
   Erroneously attributed to Richard Savage by W. R. Chetwood in 1749; Littlemore's dedication is quite explicit about his authorship.
CLU,MH,TxU(uncut).

Live. The live man's elegy, 1704. *See* Defoe, Daniel [An elegy on the author].

Liveryman

L202 Liveryman. The livery-man's answer to a letter, dated at White-hall, January, 22d. 1727–8. [*London,* 1728.]

½°: 1 side, 1 column.

　　Stanza 2, line 1, 'If E——s harangue...'.

'My lord, I just receiv'd, I own'

　　Expressing the city of London's independence of Whitehall.

OCU.

L203 — [another edition]

　　Stanza 2, line 1, 'If Eyles harangue...'.

LSA.

[**Lloyd, —.**] An ode on Saint Cæcilia's day, adapted to the ancient British musick [actually by Bonnell Thornton], 1749. *See* T249.

L204 Lloyd, John. The blanket. A poem, in imitation of Milton. *London, printed for J. Batley,* 1733. (*GSJ* 11 Aug)

2°: *A*² B² C¹; *1–3* 4–9 *10.*

'Of woman's disobedience, and the fruits'

WcC; TxU.

L205 — 'Deus. Poema. Auctore Johanne Lloyd, A.M. [*London*] *Impensis Bernardi Lintott; prostant venales apud Johannem Peele.* Price 6*d.*' (*DP* 12 Aug 1721)

　　See *GM* 61 (1791) i. 502, apparently describing a later edition.

L206 — The play, a satire: upon our late dramatick pieces, the Beggars opera, Timoleon, the Humours of Oxford, &c. By John Lloyd, M.A. minister of Gilden Sutton in Cheshire, and author of The art of politicks, &c...*Printed in the year* 1730.

8°: *A*⁴ B²; *1–2* 3–12.

　　The collation is uncertain; horizontal chain-lines. Apparently a piece of provincial printing.

'To win your hearts, and gain inglorious praise'

　　The reference to Lloyd as author of *The art of politicks* is clearly erroneous; Bramston was the author.

DFo,ICU.

L207 — [*idem*] A satyr on the times: and some of the modern plays, viz. Beggars opera, Timoleon, Humours of Oxford, Cheshire comicks, &c. By John Loyd, M.A. minister of Gilden Sutton in Cheshire, and author of The art of politicks, &c... [*Dublin*] *Printed in the year* 1730.

8°: *A*⁸; *1–5* 6–15 *16 blk.* A1 hft.

L(992.a.39/2); MH.

L208 Lloyd, Robert Lumley. To King William. Written in the year 1689... [*London*] *Printed for A. Baldwin,* 1712.

½°: *1–2,* 1 column.

'When England was not safe in its own strength at home'

C,Crawford; MH.

Lloyd, W.

Lloyd, William, *bishop of Worcester.* An elegy on the much lamented death of Wriothseley duke of Bedford... By the reverend Dr. Loyd, [1711.] *See* L312.

L209 Lock, —, *Mr.* The temple of love. A vision. By Mr. Lock. *London, printed for Robert Willoughby,* 1717. (*MC* Feb)

8°: π² A–G⁴ H²; *i–iv, 1–8* 9–60. π1 hft.

'To shun the jarring tumults of the town'

O(2),LdU-B(−π1); ICN,ICU,MH,NN,TxU.

L210 — — The second edition. *London, printed for R. Willoughby; sold by J. Morphew,* 1717.

8°: π¹ A–G⁴ H²; *i–ii, 1–8* 9–60.

　　Cancel title, printed in red and black. No half-title has been seen in this issue.

L(11601.d.22/2),O,AdU; CLU-C,CtY.

Locker, John. The constellation: poems, on several occasions [in part by Locker], 1715. *See* Bland, —, *Mr.*

Lockman, John.

There are a number of theatrical pieces (prologues, epilogues, etc.) of uncertain date which were printed as slips and are bound with other works by Lockman at L,NN. Possibly they are offprints from periodicals; compare the entry for '500 songs' for 'Mr Lookman' under the account for the London Magazine, *Dec 1740, in Ackers's ledger.*

[—] The all-devouring monster; or new five per c——t, 1748. *See* A163.

L211 [—] 'Britannia's gold mine: or, the herring fishery for ever. A new ballad. [*London*] Owen. Price 6*d.*' (*LM* July 1750)

　　The entry in *LM* is presumably for the first edition, entered in Strahan's ledger to Lockman as 'Herring fishery a ballad, one sheet no. 250' under July 1750.

'Ye lovers of your freedom'

　　The OCU copy of the second edition has a dedication inscription from Lockman to his daughter.

L211·2 [—] — The second edition. To which is added, another new ballad, on the same subject. *London, printed for W. Owen; sold at the pamphlet-shops,* 1750.

4°: *A*⁴ *B*²; *1–3* 4–8 *9–11* 12. 12 advt.

　　B1 is title to 'Flourish the herring fishery'. Entered in Strahan's ledger under the preceding, 'For 250 more... For 250 of a half sheet addition...'

Flourish the herring fishery: 'O the mighty fishery!'

L(11631.g.2/2),LU,CT; CSmH,OCU,PU.

L212 [—] David's lamentation over Saul and Jonathan. A lyric poem. *London, printed in the year* 1736. (April?)

4°: A⁴; *1–3* 4–8.

Lockman, J. David's lamentation

Variant watermark, O: star; OCU: fleur-de-lys on shield. The latter may well be a fine-paper copy.

'Sing, sacred prophet, the defeat of Saul'

Lockman's name is in later editions; subsequently called an oratorio, but included here because of its ambiguous status.

O; OCU.

L213 —— A lyric poem... Set to music by Mr. Boyce. And performed in the Apollo-society, April 16, 1736. *London, printed for R. Dodsley*, 1736. (*GSJ* 12 June)

4°: A⁴ B²; *i–ii* iii–v *vi, 7* 8–12.

The text of the poem on pp. 7–12 is from the same setting of type as the preceding; the copy at LVA-F still has the signature A2 from that impression on p. 7.

L(643.k.3/12),LVA-F,O.

L214 —— An oratorio... The music by Mr. Smith... The fifth edition. *London, printed for the author, by H. Woodfall, jun.*, 1740.

4°: A¹ B–C² D¹; *1–2* 3–12.

The sixth edition was listed in *LM* April 1740 as sold by C. Corbet.

L(T.655/16); CU.

L215 [—] Henriade. An epick poem. In ten canto's. Translated from the French into English blank verse... *London, printed for C. Davis*, 1732. (*GSJ* 18 July)

8°: (frt+) A⁸ B⁴ *C¹, B–P⁸ Q⁴ R–X⁸; *i–xxvi, 1* 2–311 *312*. xxvi, 312 err.

Entered to Pemberton & Davis in Bowyer's ledgers under 12 July; the paper ledger records 1000 copies. A half-share of the copyright formed part of lot 25 of the trade sale of Pemberton, 8 Jan 1741 (cat. at O-JJ); it is there ascribed to Oldmixon.

'I sing the hero, who by right of arms'

For Lockman's translation, see *DNB*; Voltaire's authorship of the original is revealed within the book.

L(86.c.4),O(2, 1 – frt),E(2),LdU-B,WcC; CSmH, CtY,*DLC,MH*.

L216 —— An ode for St. Cecilia's-day. The words by Mr. Lockman. The musick by Mr. Boyce. [*London*] *Printed in the year* 1739.

8°: A⁴; *1–2* 3–8.

'See fam'd Apollo and the nine'

DFo,MH.

L217 —— An ode: inscrib'd to his grace the Duke of Buckingham, on his embarking for France. *London, printed for L. Gilliver*, 1730. (23 July?)

2°: A² B¹; *1–3* 4–6.

Advertisement of 23 July quoted in *Haslewood*; listed in *MChr* July.

'Strike up, my unambitious lyre'

MH.

L218 —— An ode, on the crushing of the rebellion, anno MDCCXLVI. Presented to his majesty at Ken-

Lockman, J. An ode, on the crushing

sington, and humbly inscrib'd to his royal highness the duke. *London, printed for the author; sold by M. Cooper. Likewise by H. Chapelle, G. Woodfall, P. Russell, and at the several pamphlet-shops*, 1746. (*GM,LM* Aug)

4°: A² B–E²; *1–5* 6–18 *19–20*. E2 advt.

A presentation inscription dated 21 Aug 1746 in a copy at Chatsworth refers to 'this yet unpublish'd poem'. Probably the 'Ode to the Duke of Cumberland' entered in Strahan's ledger to Lockman under Aug 1746, '2½ sheets no. 500'.

'O let me strike my boldest lyre!'

L(T.655/9),O(–E2),E(–E2),AdU(–E2); CLU, CSmH,MH.

L219 —— An ode, to his eminence the Cardinal de Fleury... *Paris, printed for Piget*, '1761' [1741].

4°: (6 ll); *1–3* 4–5 *6* blk, *1* 2–5 *6* blk.

The collation is obscure. English text, followed by French translation by 'M. l'abbé Dromgold'. Colophon 'de l'imprimerie de Prault pere'; licence of 21 Nov 1741.

'Call'd, by a heroine, from our isle'

'Appellé sur les pas d'une illustre princesse'

L(T.655/5,6),O; CLU,CSmH,MH,NN(presentation copy).

L220 —— An ode to the memory of his grace the Duke of Buckinghamshire. *London, printed for R. Dodsley*, [1736.] (*GM,LM* Jan)

2°: A² B²; *1–3* 4–8.

The order of editions is obscure; the following may be an edition for presentation.

'Oh! how chang'd is the gay scene'

O(uncut); MH,NjP.

L221 —— [*London*, 1736.]

8°: A⁴; *1–2* 3–8.

Title in half-title form: heavy paper.

CtY.

L222 —— Pastoral stanzas. Written on occasion of the marriage of C. Phipps, esquire, with the honourable Miss Lepel Hervey. *London*, 1743. (March?)

4°: A⁴; *1–3* 4–6 *7–8 blk*.

Most copies have fleur-de-lys watermark: that at MH has none. Entered in Strahan's ledger to Lockman under March 1743, 600 copies.

'Ægon, who lov'd the green retreat'

L(T.655/8; 643.k.5/2,–A4); CSmH,MH,NN, TxU.

L223 —— To her grace the Dutchess of Buckingham: with the Jesuits travels. *London, printed in the year* 1743.

8°: π² a²; *i–iv, 1* 2–4. π1 blk.

The copy seen has a ms. imprint 'Printed for J: Noon, in the Poultry'. An offprint of the dedicatory verses to vol. II of *Travels of the Jesuits*, 1743.

'Thou, on whose praises I delight to dwell!'

Signed by Lockman.

L(1961).

Lockman, J.

L224 — To the long conceal'd first promoter of the cambrick and tea-bills: an epistle. Writ at the close of last session of parliament. *London, printed for the author; sold by M. Cooper,* 1746. (*GM,LM* April)
4°: A–D⁴ E²; *1–3* 4–34 *35; 36 blk.* 35 advt.
> Entered in Strahan's ledger to Lockman under March 1746 as 'A poem on smuggling', 500 copies.

'Whilst numbers, to destructive pleasures prone'
> To Sir Stephen Theodore Janssen; on smuggling.

L(T.655/10),O; CLU,CSmH,IEN(–E2),MH.

L225 — To the right honourable the Earl and Countess of Middlesex. An ode. *London, printed in the year* 1746. (April?)
2°: *A²; 1–3* 4.
> Presumably the 'Poem on Middlesex' entered in Strahan's ledger to Lockman under April 1746, 'one sheet no. 150'.

'O! thou, in ev'ry science skill'd'
CLU.

L226 [—] Verses to a lady of quality, insulted by the rabble of writers. *London, printed for the author,* 1741. (March?)
4°: A⁴; *1–3* 4–7 *8 blk.*
> Various watermarks. Entered in Strahan's ledger to Lockman under 26 March 1741, '500 coarse and 175 fine'; there are also entries for 'a ream of coarse paper...2 quires fine... 6 quires finest'. The paper deserves further examination.

'Blest in thy rank, and in each winning grace'
> The L copy is bound with a collection of Lockman's poems. To the Duchess of Buckingham.

L(T.655/7),O; CtY,MH,NN.

L227 [—] [fine paper]
> Watermark: Strasburg bend.

TxU(Lord Orrery's copy).

L228 — Verses to his royal highness the Duke of Cumberland: on his being wounded, at the repulse of the French, near Dettingen. *London, printed for H. Chapelle; sold by J. Robinson,* 1743. (*DA* 9 July)
2°: A¹ B²; *1–2* 3–5 *6 blk.*
> Entered in Strahan's ledger to Lockman under 8 July; 250 copies printed.

'Malice, no more, thy conduct shall upbraid'
L(11631.g.2/1, cropt),O; MH.

— 'A vision.' [*London,* 1739.]
> Entered in Strahan's ledger to Lockman under 24 Nov 1739, 'a Vision, &c. 1½ sheets Great Primer Quarto 100 copies', and under 30 Nov 'To printing 200 more of Do with the paper'. It is not clear whether the work was in verse.

L229 Locusts. The locusts: or, chancery painted to the life, and the laws of England try'd in forma

The locusts

pauperis. A poem. *London, printed in the year* 1704. (*WL* May)
4°: *A² B–D⁴ E²; i–iv,* 1–28.
'How this sad change of state Apollo tell'
> A satire on the court of chancery.

DG,DT,*MR*; DFo,NN,OCU.

L230 — The second part of the Locusts: or, chancery painted to the life, and the laws of England try'd in forma pauperis. *London printed, and sold by J. Nutt...where is to be had the first part,* 1704.
4°: A–D⁴; *1–2* 3–30 *31–32 blk.*
'Satyr proceed, raise thy poetick rage'
O(–D4),DG; OCU(–D4).

L231 Lodge, Edward. A funeral poem, humbly offer'd to the pious memory of the reverend Mr. Saml Pomfret... To which is added, his late annual hymns. The second edition, with large additions. [*London*] *Printed for John Marshall... Where is sold Mr. Pomfret's Works,* [1722.] (Feb)
8°: A–D⁴; *i–vi,* 1–25 *26.* 26 advt.
> First edition not seen. Pomfret's hymns (an incomplete collection) occupy pp. 16–25. The copy at LDW has remains of a paste-on slip at foot of title with another imprint.

'Hence from my breast I banish every joy'
LDW,O.

Lodoix. Lodoix Maria Stuarta, [1712?] *See* Pitcairne, Archibald.

L232 Logico. The logico-astrologico-physico-mathematician: or, the grand mystery found out. A poem on Mr. D---s, f---l--w of T.C. Dublin. *Dublin, printed in the year* 1729.
8°: *A² B⁴; 1–2* 3–12.
'One morning taking pen and ink'
> Probably a satire on Richard Dobbs.

DN.

London. London: a poem, in imitation of the third satire of Juvenal, 1738–. *See* Johnson, Samuel.

L233 — The London address. [*London,* 1710.]
½°: 1 side, 1 column.
> Line 3 is contained in one line of type.

'We the hundred and fifty elect of the gown'
> *Crum* W152b: 'The clergy's address in plain English meeter'. A whig satire on the London clergy's address to Queen Anne, approved 21 Aug 1710.

O,E; MH.

L234 — [another edition]
> Line 3 runs over into two lines of type. The penultimate line reads 'We'l drive...'

Crawford; NN.

L234·2 — [another edition]
> Line 3 runs over into two lines of type. The penultimate line reads 'We'll drive...'

MH.

The **London** address

L234·5 — [*idem*] The clergy of the city of London and liberty of Westminster's address to the queen, presented on the 23d of Aug. 1710. Paraphras'd. A poem. [*London*, 1710.]
½°: 1 side, 1 column.
   A variant text.
MC; InU.

L235 — The London address: or, magistrates against the muses. A poetical paraphrase. *London, printed for C. Chartres*, 1730. (*MChr* May)
2°: *A*¹ B–C² D¹; *3–4* 5–14.
   Percival appendix 25.
'Most gracious king, the nation's father'
   A satirical paraphrase of the city's petition against the theatre in Goodman's Fields, April 1730. Since the theatre was Thomas Odell's, the MH catalogue suggests him as possible author.
SrS(uncut); MH.

— The London Æsop, 1702. *See* Pittis, William [Chaucer's whims].

— The London belles, 1707. *See* Browne, Joseph.

L236 — The London clergy's petition against the quakers affirmation, answer'd, paragraph by paragraph. [*London*] *Printed in the year* 1722.
8°: A–D⁴; *1–2* 3–32. 32 err.
'A late petition of the clergy'
   Smith I. 53 tentatively suggests that Elias Bockett was the author, probably on the grounds that he was the only quaker poet of the period; there seems to be no other evidence for the attribution. Cf. *The parsons compassion*, 1722.
LF(2, 1 stitched, uncut).

L237 —— corrected and very much inlarged... *London, printed for A. Moore*, [1722/23.]
8°: A–G⁴ H(2 ll) I⁴; *i–viii*, 1–60.
   With a preface signed 'Orthodox Jereboam'.
CtY,MH.

— London in mourning, 1710. *See* A new elegy on the death of trade, 1706–.

L238 — The London ladies dressing-room: or, the shop-keepers wives inventory. A satyr. Written by the author of the True-born Englishman. *London, printed for the booksellers of London & Westminster*, 1705.
8°: *A*⁴; *1* 2–8.
   The copy recorded in the printed catalogue of E is now at O.
'He that wou'd sail in troubl'd seas'
   Not recorded by any Defoe bibliographer; chap-book verses of the kind specifically disowned by Defoe.
O; *MWiW-C*.

L239 — The London merchants triumphant: or sturdy beggars are brave fellows. A new ballad proper to be sung on the 12th of June... *London, printed for*

The **London** merchants triumphant

T. Reinshau; sold by the booksellers of London & Westminster, 1733. (*GSJ* 9 June)
2°: *A*² B²; *1–3* 4–8.
   Percival appendix 52.
'I am a sturdy beggar'
   An attack on Walpole's excise bill. For the possibility of Budgell's authorship, see the following entry.
L(1489.d.37; 162.n.73),LG,LU; CSmH(uncut), CtY,ICN,NNC,OCU+.

L240 —— a new ballad proper to be sung at this time. [*London*, 1733.]
½°: 1 side, 2 columns.
   Eustace Budgell in the *Bee* II. 890 (14 July 1733) reprints this from the broadside, 'printed on a course [!] blue paper, like a common Grub-street production', and notes it 'is very far from wanting wit'. Percival suggests he may be praising a ballad of his own composition.
C.

L240·2 — [*idem*] The Bristol merchants triumphant: or, sturdy beggars are brave fellows. A new ballad, proper to be sung on the 12th of June. Humbly inscribed to the worthy merchants and citizens of Bristol. *London, printed for T. Reinshau; sold by the booksellers of London & Westminster*, [1733.]
2°: *A*² B¹; *1* 2–6.
O.

L241 — The London tale. By the author of the Tale of a nettle. *London, printed in the year* 1710. (*SR* 13 May)
½°: 1 side, 2 columns.
   Williams 1084. Entered in *SR* by William Wise; deposit copies at O,E.
'In fickle days, when grave divines'
   An attribution to Swift has been suggested on the grounds of his possible authorship of *The tale of a nettle*, 1710. Williams finds no support for the attribution. Against the low-church attackers of Sacheverell.
L(Ashley 5252),LSA,O,E; MH,TxU.

L242 **Lonergan, Edward.** The dean and the country parson. An imitation of the first eclogue of Virgil. *Dublin, E. Waters*, 1739.
4°: 16 pp.
   With the Latin text.
(*Teerink* 1322, from unidentified Quaritch catalogue.)

L243 **Long.** The long vacation: a satyr. Address'd to all disconsolate traders. *London printed, and sold by John Morphew*, 1708. (*PM* 22 June)
4°: A–F²; *1–4* 5–23 *24 blk*.
'Bless us! how silent is the noisy gown?'
DFo,OCU.

L244 —— *London printed, and sold by H. Hills*, 1708.
8°: *A*⁸; *1–4* 5–16.
L(1486.eee.13),O; CSmH,ICN,MH,OCU,TxU.

The **long** vacation

L245 — — *London printed, and sold by H. Hills*, 1709.
8º: A⁸; *1–2* 3–16.
> Reissued in *A collection of the best English poetry*, 1717 (*Case* 294).

L(1485.t.9; 11601.dd.10/1; C.124.b.7/20), LVA-F,O,*LdU-B*; CtY,IU,InU,MH.

L246 — A long vacation prologue. Writ by Mr. B---k--r and spoke by Mr. Es-----t, at the Theatre-Royal in Drury-lane. *London printed, and sold by J. Morphew*, 1708. (25 Sept, Luttrell)
½º: *1–2*, 1 column.
'You've wondered, perhaps, and been in great rage'
> The speaker was Richard Estcourt; the author was probably Thomas Baker, playwright and possible author of *A poem on the drawing room*, 1716, which includes three epilogues. Reprinted with commentary by E. L. Avery in *SEL* 5 (1965) 464f.

ICN(Luttrell).

L247 Long, Roger. The music speech, spoken at the public commencement in Cambridge, July the 6th, 1714. *London printed, and sold by J. Morphew, and C. Crownfield in Cambridge*, 1714. (*PB* 22 July)
8º: *A*⁴ B–D⁴ E²; *1–5* 6–34 *35–36 blk*. A1 hft.
> Latin prose introduction; the verse on pp. 15–34.

'The humble petition of the ladies, who are all ready to be eaten up with the spleen'
L(1413.e.12/15),O(−A1, E2),C(−E2),LdU-B (uncut); CSmH(−E2),CtY(−A1, E2),IU,MH, TxU+.

L248 — — The second edition. *London printed, and sold by J. Morphew, and C. Crownfield in Cambridge*, 1714.
8º: *A*⁴ B–D⁴ E²; *1–5* 6–34 *35–36 blk*. A1 hft.
> Either a reimpression or a press-variant title.

OC(uncut).

L249 — — The third edition. *London printed, and sold by J. Morphew, and C. Crownfield in Cambridge*, 1714.
8º: *A*⁴ B–D⁴ E¹ (D2 as 'D'); *1–5* 6–34. A1 hft.
> E2 possibly missing from copies seen. Perhaps in part from standing type.

CSmH,MH.

L250 — — The third edition. *London, printed for T. Payne, and W. Thurlbourn in Cambridge*, [1730.] (*MChr* June)
8º: A–D⁴; *1–2* 3–32.
> This new edition is perhaps related to John Taylor, *The music speech*, printed by Bowyer in July 1730; there may have been an attempt to confound the two.

O(3),C(2); CtY,ICU(lacks D4),IU,TxU(2).

Longford. Longford's Glyn: a true history, 1732–. *See* Delany, Patrick.

Longitude

L251 Longitude. The longitude discover'd; a tale. By the author of the Deluge, and Bottomless tub; tales. *London, printed for J. Roberts*, 1726. (*MC* May)
2º: *A*² B–C²; *1–2* 3–12.
> *Teerink* 920; *Williams* 1154.

'In an old author once I found'
> William reports that this 'has been ascribed to Swift on internal evidence, but it is most unlike his style'. The 'Bottomless tub' is *A tale of a bottomless tub*, 1723. A bawdy tale of an old astronomer and his young wife.

CLU-C,CtY,KU,TxU.

L252 — — *Dublin, printed by Tho. Hume*, [1726.]
8º: A⁸; *1–3* 4–15 *16 blk*.
NN.

L253 — The longitude found out: a tale. *London, printed for Thomas Edlin*, 1721. (*DP* 21 March)
2º: *A*¹ B² C¹; *1–2* 3–8.
> A '2d edition' was advertised in *DP* 13 April.

'Nature on all some gift bestows'
> A bawdy tale of the bashful poet and the nymph.

O,DT; *CLU-C*,TxU(Luttrell, April).

[Lonsdale, M.] The loss of liberty: or fall of Rome, 1729. *See* L270.

L254 Looking-glass. 'The looking-glass. A pindarick poem. Occasion'd by reading a few pages in an excellent book, intitled, the Procedure, extent and limits of human understanding, viz. pages 111 and 119. [*London*] Sold by the booksellers. Price 1s.' (*MChr* July 1730)
> The procedure...is by Peter Browne, bishop of Cork and Ross.

— A looking-glass for England, 1720. *See* Ward, Edward [A south-sea ballad] (W182).

L255 Lord. The lord and no lord, and Squire Squat. An exrellent [!] new ballad to an old tune. *London, printed by A. Moore*, [1728.]
½º: 1 side, 2 columns.
> Stanza 3, line 3 '...let *A——s* decide'. *Percival* appendix 7. Printed in *The British Journal*, 6 Jan 1728.

'I sing an old proverb that's very well known'
> A satire on Bolingbroke and Pulteney, with reference to the relationship between Bolingbroke and Pulteney's wife.

L(1872.a.1/167).

L256 — — [*London*? 1728.]
> Stanza 3, line 3 '...let *Anstis* decide'.

L(C.116.i.4/44, imprint cropt?).

L256·2 — The lord or, no lord, or the history of 'Sqire [!] Squatt... *Printed in the year* 1727–8.
O-JJ.

— The Lord Belhaven's vision, 1737. *See* Belhaven's vision, 1729–.

L257 — The Lord Bollingbrooke prov'd guilty of high-treason. [*London?* 1715?]
½°: 1 side, 1 column.
'When Torrington, to save our fleet'
 Crum W1584: 'To the Lord Bolinbroke upon his impeachmt', dated as June 1715.
Harding.

L258 — The Lord Bol------ke's epistolary canto to Dr. Sach----rell. Translated from the original French. *London printed, and sold by R. Burleigh,* [1715.] (*MC* May)
8°: A–C⁴; *1–3* 4–23 *24 blk.*
'Dear doctor, I send/To you as a friend'
 Bolingbroke to Sacheverell. There was presumably no French original.
O,AdU; CtY,IU.

— Lord Lovat's last legacy, [1748.] *See* To Mr. S-------- M-----, 1747– (T346).

L259 — [dh] The Lord M——n's ghost to the D---- of R---nd, on Sunday night last: concerning the murder of Duke Hamilton, and the peace. [col] [*London*] *Printed by Rich. Newcomb,* 1712. *And entred in the Stamp-office.*
2°: A² < B¹; ff. *1* 2–3.
 Printed on one side of the paper only, the third leaf on the verso.
''Twas in the midst of a dark gloomy night'
 Lord Mohun's ghost to the Duke of Richmond.
L(1870.d.1/24; 806.k.16/107),O(lacks B1).

L260 — Lord Pole translated; or the d----l turn'd chimney-sweeper: a ballad. To which is added, Bob's soliloquy...with an elegy upon a meeting-house... *London, printed for T. Warner; sold at the pamphlet shops in London & Westminster,* 1731. (*GSJ* 16 March)
8°: A–D⁴; *1–3* 4–31 *32.*
 'Lord Pole translated' occupies pp. 3–12; the rest is apparently a miscellany. Reissued with a cancel title as *The London medley: or, the humours of the present age* (London, printed for S. Slow & W. Harris, 1732; copy at O). Since that is titled as the miscellany it is, no separate entry is made for it here.
'All in the late great winter snow'
 A satire on a drunken whig lord.
O(lacks D4),CT.

L261 — Lord upon knight; and knight upon squire. *London, printed for A. More,* [1727/28.]
½°: 1 side, 2 columns.
 Percival appendix 6.
'A lord, and no lord, once did dwell'
 A satire on the quarrel between Bolingbroke, Walpole, and Pulteney. Cf. *The lord and no lord,* [1728.]
L(1850.e.10/58*; 1872.a.1/169).

L262 — Lord Wharton's puppies: or, just as they were sinking, their eyes open'd. An excellent new

Lord Wharton's puppies

ballad. *London, printed for M. Pike,* 1734. (*LM* May)
2°: A² B²; *1–2* 3–8.
'To all those liv'ry-men of London'
 A story originally told by Lord Wharton to Archbishop Sharp. Now retold in verse for the livery-men of London who voted blindly in the election.
E.

— The Lord Whiglove's elegy, 1715. *See* Ward, Edward.

L263 — The Lord's day: or, the Christian sabbath. A sacred poem. Humbly presented to John Boulter, esq; *London, printed for the author,* 1720.
4°: π¹ A–B²; *1–2* 3–10.
 Probably issued with variant title-pages with alternative dedicatees.
'That glorious great and memorable day'
 Probably by the same author as *A divine poem on the creation,* 1718, and other works listed there; possibly Henry Nevil was the author.
NNUT.

L263·5 — [reissue] Humbly presented to the right honourable the lord Viscount Fermanagh. *London, printed for the author,* 1729.
4°:π¹(±) A–B²; *1–2* 3–10.
O-JJ.

L264 —— Humbly presented to Mrs. Brace. *London, printed for the author,* 1729.
4°: A¹ B–C²; *1–3* 4–10.
 A different edition of the text from the preceding, but with the title in part from standing type.
O.

L265 — The lord's lamentation; or, the Whittington defeat. *London,* '*printed for John Litchfield*', [1747.] (*GM* Oct)
2°: A² < B¹; *1–3* 4–6.
'God prosper long our noble king!'
 On the Duke of Bedford, assaulted at Lichfield races.
L(C.57.g.7/18, Horace Walpole's annotations); KU(lacks B1).

L266 —— [*London?* 1747.]
½°: 1 side, 2 columns.
 Woodcut of horse race above text.
L(1871.e.1/4; 1876.f.1/153),O (mutilated).

L267 —— [*Edinburgh?* 1747.]
½°: 1 side, 2 columns.
 Columns divided by rule. No woodcut.
L(Rox.III.440),E.

Lord's prayer.
Sedgwick, Ralph: A divine poem: or, a paraphrase on the Lord's prayer, [173–?] *See* S181–2.

L268 [**Lorleach, —, *Mr.***] The muff, or one good turn deserves another; a court tale. Humbly inscribed to Madame de W——lm——n. By Mr. W——.

Lorleach, *Mr.* The muff

Sold by the booksellers and pamphlet-shops in
London & Westminster, 1740. (20 March?)
4°: A^4 B–D^4; *1–4* 5–31 *32 blk.* A1 hft.
Listed in *GM, LM* April. Entered in Wood-
fall's ledgers (*N&Q* I. xi. 378) 13 March to
Mr. Lorleach; 500 copies 'on a fine large
paper'.
'Let others muse, in numbers sing'
A satire on Frau A.S.M. Wallmoden, mistress
of George II, created Countess of Yarmouth
24 March 1740.
L(11630.c.4/5, ms. date 20 March; 11630.c.1/1;
840.1.3/4, uncut),O,DN,LdU-B(–A1); CtY,MH
(uncut),NjP(–A1).

L269 [—] A satirical epistle to Mr. Pope. *London,
printed for the author; sold at the pamphlet-shops,
1740. (DP* 14 April)
2°: A^2 B^2; *1–3* 4–8.
Entered in Woodfall's ledgers (*N&Q* I. xi.
378) 5 April to Mr. Lorleach; 500 copies
printed.
'Dear Pope, the muses' favourite, and friend!'
L(12273.m.1/15),LVA-D; DFo,DLC,TxU(2).

L270 Loss. The loss of liberty: or fall of Rome. *London,
printed by C. Ackers, for J. Brindley, 1729. (MChr*
3 May)
2°: A^2 B–F^2; *1–5* 6–24.
'When dread Tiberius sway'd the Roman world'
A modern ms. note in the O copy attributes
the poem to M. Lonsdale; the attribution is
not accepted by the O catalogue.
L(643.m.12/40),O,OW,*LdU-B*; CU,MH,OCU,
TxU(2, 1 uncut).

L271 — [reissue] The loss of liberty. A poem. *London,
printed for J. Roberts; sold by the booksellers of
London & Westminster, 1733. (GSJ* 18 June)
2°: $A^2(\pm A1)$ B–F^2; *1–5* 6–24.
Acker's ledger under 12 May 1733 records
the printing for Brindley of 400 cancel titles.
L(1484.m.3, uncut),O,LdU-B,*MR-C*; CSmH,
DLC,MH.

L272 Lost. The lost maidenhead restor'd, in reviving
the farthingale; or more work for the cooper.
A panegyrick on the late, but most admirable
invention of the hoop-petticoat. [171–?]
4°: 4 pp.
Dated as [c. 1700] by Pickering & Chatto; but
it appears to be related to *The farthingale
reviv'd,* 1711.
(Pickering & Chatto cat. 259/2867.)

L273 Lothario. Lothario's answer to Sarah the quaker,
in the shades. *London, printed for A. Moore; sold
by the booksellers of London & Westminster, 1729.*
(*MChr* 10 Feb)
2°: A^2 B^2; *1–3* 4–8.
In some copies (CtY,MH) B1 is unsigned.
'When, from unruly passions, women rail'

Lotharo's answer

Spencer Cowper's answer to Sarah Stout; in
reply to [Charles Beckingham] *Sarah, the
quaker,* 1728.
L(11657.m.14),LF,LSC,E; CtY,MH,OCU.

L274 Lottery. The lottery, a poem. *London printed, and
sold by H. Hills, 1711.*
$\frac{1}{2}^o$: A^1; *1–2,* 1 column.
Morgan N375 records two editions, probably
in error.
'Do thou, great goddess, whose superiour sway'
On the lottery at the Guildhall.
L(Cup.645.e.1/21)LLP; *Harding.*

L275 Louis. Louis le rampant; or, Argenson in his
altitudes. An heroical epistle, to be learn'd by heart,
by all non-associators; and all who are bashful in
the day of battle. *London, printed for the author;
sold by G. Lyon, and at the pamphlet-shops,* [1746.]
(*GM* July)
2°: $A^2 < B^2$; *1–2* 3–8.
'Lewis our common lord's compassion'
A satire on the letter of R.L. Voyer de Paulmy,
marquis d'Argenson, to Abraham van Hoey.
On the defeat of the Young Pretender.
L(11651.m.89).

'Louisa.' A poem on the arrival of the right
honourable William earl Cowper, 1730. *See*
Boyd, Elizabeth.

— To the right honourable William lord Harrington, 1730. *See* Boyd, Elizabeth.

— Variety: a poem, 1727. *See* Boyd, Elizabeth.

L276 Louse. The louse-trap a poem. In imitation of the
Mouse-trap. *London, printed for T. Warner, 1723.*
(*DJ* 7 Feb)
4°: A^2 B–C^2; *1–3* 4–12.
Bond 72.
'Long have I wish'd renowned heroe's praise'
In imitation of Edward Holdsworth's *Mus-
cipula,* [1708.]
MH.

L277 Lovat. Lovat's ghost: or, the courtier's warning-
piece. A ballad. To the tune of William and
Margaret. *London, printed for B. Moore, 1747.*
(*BM* May; *GM* June)
8°: π^1 A–B^4 $C^4(–C1)$; *i–ii,* *1–3* 4–21 *22 blk.* π1 hft.
''Twas at the silent midnight-hour'
E(–π1),AdU; CtY(–π1),OCU(–π1).

L278 — — *Dublin, printed by James Esdall,* [1747.]
8°: A^4; *1–2* 3–8.
L(1971),C,DT; *MH.*

L279 Love. Love after enjoyment, in two epistles from
Alexis to Vanella, and Vanella to Alexis. *London,
printed for T. Dormer; sold at the pamphlet shops
of London & Westminster, 1732. (GSJ* 4 March)
2°: π^1 A^2 B^2 χ^1 C^2 (C1 as 'C3'); *i–ii,* *1–2* 3–14.
π1, χ1 hfts.

πI and χI, the half-titles to the two epistles, have been seen to be conjugate.
'Accept, Vanella, what Alexis owes'
'While dear Alexis strives in tuneful strain'
    On Frederick prince of Wales and Anne Vane. *MR*; CtY(uncut),IU($-\pi$I),KU,MH($-\pi$I, χI), TxU+.

L280 — Love and courtship, a poem. In three cantos. *London, printed in the year* 1727.
2°: A^1 B–E^2 F^1; *i–ii*, *1–18*.
'Arms not the warriors, but the lovers care'
L(11657.m.37); OCU.

L281 — Love and divinity united. Being a true copy of verses on a young lady of quality that fell in love with Dr. Sacheverel at his tryal in Westminster-Hall. To the tune of, What is greater joy and pleasure. *London, printed by W. Wise in Fetter-lane*, 1710.
$\frac{1}{2}$°: 1 side, 2 columns.
    Rough woodcuts at head. On the other side, *The Kentish ballad*, 1710 (G110).
'Near Saint Jame's a young lady'
O.

— Love and folly. A poem. In four canto's, 1749. *See* Selden, Ambrose.

— Love and resentment, 1717. *See* Morrice, Bezaleel.

— Love atones for little crimes, 1738. *See* Bancks, John.

L282 — Love drowned in the South-Sea: or, Cymena's epistle to the perfidious Cratander, on his marriage to Cælia... By F.H. gent. *London printed, and sold by J. Roberts*, [1721.] (*PB* 11 March)
2°: A^2 B^2; *1–2* 3–8.
'O! thou cool traytor! Why am I reproach'd?'
    The metamorphosis, 1721, is probably a satire on this poem and its author.
Sotheby's 27 March 1961, lot 1157 (Luttrell, March).

— Love elegies, 1743–. *See* Hammond, James.

L283 — Love for love: or, a dialogue between a loving husband and a virtuous wife... *London, printed by Rich. Newcomb*, [170–?]
8°: A^4; *1* 2–8.
'Let others boast of an unlawful flame'
CLU-C.

— Love given over, 1709–. *See* Gould, Robert.

L284 — Love-letters between a nobleman and his sister: viz. F---rd lord Gr--y of Werk, and the Lady Henrietta Berk---ley, under the borrowed names of Philander and Silvia. Done into verse, by the author of the Letters from a nun to a cavalier. The second edition. *London, printed for Charles Corbett*, 1734.
12°: A^6 b^2 B–G^{12} H^{10}; *i–xvi*, *1* 2–162 *163–164*. A1 frt; H10 advt.
    No earlier edition has been traced, but a half share of the copyright of 'Ld Gray's

love-letters in verse, 1st vol.' formed part of a lot in the trade sale of Jonas Brown, 21 Oct 1718, and was bought by Clay. The whole copyright was sold as lots 10 and 11 of a trade sale ascribed to W. Mears, 7 June [1728], to Corbett for a guinea; it is described as 'out of print'. Third shares, each with 200 books, were sold at Mrs Bowyer's sale, 18 May 1736, and resold on 11 Jan 1737 (copies of all catalogues at O-JJ).
'When last I parted, tho' I seem'd t' agree'
    A versification of Aphra Behn's novel with this title, first published in 1683; the lovers were Forde Grey (later earl of Tankerville) and Lady Berkeley. 'The author of the Letters from a nun...' probably refers to the versification in *New miscellaneous poems*, 1713–, possibly by Morgan Keene. Three versified letters among Robert Samber's mss. at O appear to be a different version.
L(11626.a.24).

L285 — — The third edition. *Dublin, printed for James Dalton, & for James Kelburn*, 1739.
12°: A–H^6 I^4; *i–ii*, *1* 2–96 97–102. I4 advt.
DN($-$I4); CtY.

— Love of fame, the universal passion, 1728–. *See* Young, Edward [The universal passion].

— Love triumphant over reason, 1709. *See* Pomfret, John.

L286 — Love verses, by an officer in the Duke of Argyle's army. With an epistle dedicatory to Sir Richard Steele. *London, printed for R. Burleigh*, 1716. (*MC* March)
4°: A^4 B^4; *1–3* 4–16.
    Two short poems to Cælia, with a long dedicatory epistle.
'Pray, madam, let not India boast'
'Welcome ye shades, and ev'ry darker grove'
    Epistle dedicatory signed 'Phil. Sprightly'. Possibly by John Thornycroft, 'officer in the army', one of whose poems was published by Burleigh later in the year.
E(uncut),AN.

L287 — Love without affectation, in five letters from a Portugueze nun, to a French cavalier. Done into English verse, from the newest edition lately printed at Paris. To which is added a prefatory discourse... *London, printed by H. Meere; sold by J. Woodward, & J. Morphew*, 1709.
12°: A–K^6; [*10*] i–xiii *xiv*, *1*–96. A1 woodcut frt.
'Oh! rash, unhappy, and too thoughtless love!'
    A versification of the *Lettres portugaises*, commonly attributed to the nun, Marianna Alcoforado, but perhaps originally written by G. J. de Lavergne, comte de Guilleragues. The preface suggests the 'author' was M. de Vervac, but probably only in the sense that he provoked the letters. Apparently a

Love without affectation

different translation from that printed in *New miscellaneous poems*, 1713.
L(1085.d.25).

L288 — Love's invention: or, the recreation in vogue. An excellent new ballad on the masquerades. To the tune of, O! London is a fine town. *London, printed for E. Curll, & R. Francklin*, 1718.
8°: π^1[= C4] A–B^4 C^4(−C4); *i–ii, 1–3 4–22.* π1 hft.
Griffith 98. The half-title reads: 'Mr. Pope's Worms: and a new ballad on the masquerades'. Pope's poem, first published as *To the ingenious Mr. Moore*, 1716, is printed at the end. Reissued in *The Oxford miscellany*, 1720.
'O! a masquerade's a fine place'
LVA-D,O,NeU; CLU-C,CSmH(−π1),ICU,MH, NNC.

L289 —— The second edition. *London, printed for E. Curll, & R. Francklin*, 1718. (*EvP* 5 July)
8°: A^4 B–C^4; *1–5 6–24.* A1 hft, advt.
Griffith 99.
O,CT(−A1),LdU-B; CtY,ICN,KU,OCU.

L290 —— a new ballad: to the tune of, O London is a fine town &c... To which is added, A cure for cuckoldom; or, the miseries of matrimony. *London, printed for W. Cook in the Strand*, 1746. (*GA* 28 June)
8°: A–C^4 D^1; *1–2 3–26.*
'A cure for cuckoldom' was printed as *The pleasures of a single life*, 1701–.
'O Ranelagh's a fine place'
Cure: 'Wedlock, oh! curs'd uncomfortable state'
A reworking of the preceding.
L(1485.c.12).

— 'Love's last shift; or, the mason disappointed. To which is added several curious pieces... [*London*] *Sold by T. Warner*. Price 6*d*.' (*MC* June 1723)
Probably a poetical miscellany, though not listed in *Case* or *CBEL*.

'Love, James, *comedian.' See* Dance, James.

[**Loveling, Benjamin.**] Latin and English poems. By a gentleman of Trinity College, Oxford. *London, printed in the year* 1738. (*SR* 29 July)
4°: pp. iii, 136.   L,E; CSmH,CtY.
A copy at DrU has an early ms. attribution to 'B. Lovelin'. A few poems by friends are included. *Rawlinson* records proposals of 10 March 1738.

[—] — *London, printed for C. Bathurst*, 1741.
12°: pp. 179.   L,O; CtY,ICU.

L291 — The first satire of Persius imitated. *London, printed for John Brett; sold by the booksellers of London & Westminster*, 1740. (*GM,LM* April)
2°: A^2 B–E^2; *1–5 6–19 20 blk.*

Loveling, B. The first satire

'Deluded man, by flatt'ring hopes betray'd'
L(1482.f.33),LdU-B; CSmH,DFo,MH,TxU.

Lover. The lover's miscellany: or, poems on several occasions, amorous and gallant, 1719. *See* Jacob, Giles.

L292 [**Lowth, Robert.**] The genealogy of Christ; as it is represented in the east-window in the college chappel at Winchester. A poem. By a young gentleman of Winchester School. *London, printed for J. Jackson*, 1729. (*MChr* 15 May)
8°: A^4 B–C^4; *i–iv v–vi, 7–22 23–24 blk.* A1 hft.
Asterisked in *MChr* as a new edition, probably in error.
'At once to raise our rev'rence and delight'
Attributed to Lowth in *Rawlinson*; ms. attribution in the ICN copy.
L(11601.ddd.7/2),O(2),C(−A1, C4),EU(−A1, C4),WcC(2); ICN,IU(uncut),NjP,OCU.

L293 [—] The judgment of Hercules, a poem. By a student of Oxford. To which is subjoined, the golden verses of Pythagoras, translated from the Greek by Mr. Rowe. *Glasgow, printed and sold by Robert Foulis*, 1743. (*Glasgow Journal* 25 July)
8°: π^1 A–C^4 D^1; *1–2 3–28.*
Gaskell, Foulis 39. 'Price three pence' on title; no watermark. Some fine-paper copies may be wrongly entered here. π1 and D1 have been seen to be conjugate.
'Now had the son of Jove, mature, attain'd'
Translated from the Greek of Prodicus in Xenophon's *Memorabilia* by Robert Lowth; printed in his *Sermons*, 1834. Sometimes confused with Shenstone's poem of this title.
L(1485.tt.10),E(2),EN,LdU; DLC,IU(uncut), MH.

L294 [—] [fine paper]
'Price four pence' on title; watermark: posthorn.
O,GM(uncut).

L295 [—] The judgement of Hercules, from Xenophon's Memoirs of Socrates, lib. ii. Tat. no. 97. *Dublin, printed in the year* 1746.
4°: A^4 B^2; *1–2 3–12.*
O; OCU.

L296 **Loyal.** The loyal address of the clergy of Virginia. '*Williamsburgh, printed for Fr. Maggot, at the sign of the Hickery-tree in Queen-street*' [*London*], 1702.
½°: 1 side, 1 colunm.
Teerink 832; *Williams* 1074; *Bond* 204; W. S. Powell 'A Swift broadside from the opposition', *Virginia magazine of history and biography* 67 (1959) 164–9.
'May it please you dread sir, we the clerks of Virginia'
Printed by *Ball* as Swift's, but not accepted by Williams. A parody on the address presented to William III by James Blair.
L(C.20.f.2/224).

Loyal

L297 — The loyal Britain: or, George for ever. [*London?* 1744?]

slip: 1 side, 1 column.

Rough woodcuts at head and foot. On the other side, *A new song of the warrs*, [1744?].

'Your laddy can't fight, but your laddy may sing'

A typographical error in J. J. McAleer, *Ballads and songs loyal to the Hanoverian succession* (Augustan reprint society 96, 1962) has led to a false attribution to Allan Ramsay; the passage should read 'This ballad was ⟨meant to be sung to the tune of "The widow can bake, and the widow can brew",⟩ written by Allan Ramsay'. On the abortive Jacobite expedition from Dunkirk in Feb 1744.

L(Rox. III. 753).

L298 — The loyal Calves-head-club: or, commonwealths-men, who meet every night at the sign of the Tatler, Newgate-street; | To settle affairs of church and state, | Just as before, in forty eight. | Tune, A soldier and a sailor. [*London*, 1712?]

½°: 1 side, 2 columns.

The MH copy was originally bound next to *The Mohocks revel*, 1712.

'A seditious old cowardly prater'

MH, *Harding*.

L299 — The loyal church-man's triumph on the coronation of Queen Anne, on the 23d of April, being St. George's day. To the tune of Set the glass round. [*London?* 1715/–.]

½°: 1 side, 2 columns.

Two rough woodcuts at head.

'This is the day / Our glorious Anne was crown'd'

L(1876. f. 1/69, cropt).

— 'The loyal consort of musick.'

One of 'Three loyal songs... Price one penny each' advertised in *Rebellious fame*, 1717.

L300 — The loyal Irish man, or the high-church will get the day. To the tune of the Irish trot. *London, printed by J. Godfree, in Fleet-street*, [171–.]

½°: 1 side, 2 columns.

The printer is possibly pseudonymous.

'My bony dear soney'

An attack on the dissenters.

O.

L301 — The loyal resolution &c. [*London?* 1717?]

slip: 1 side, 1 column.

Printed with *The history of the 29 years*, [1717?]; the NjP copy is not divided.

'Dear royal youth I'll nere repent'

A Jacobite resolution.

O; CSmH, NjP.

L302 — The loyal trimmer. *London, printed in the year* 1712.

½°: 1 side, 1 column.

'From Sc——th depositions, and gre——ing of men'

L(1876. f. 19/26); MH.

Loyal

L303 — The loyal-wish. *London, printed in the year* 1711. (3 July, Luttrell)

½°: 1 side, 1 column.

'Free from all the fears'

ICN(Luttrell), InU, MH.

L304 — The loyal worthies. In an epistle to the right honourable the Earl of S------r. *London, printed for T. Reynolds; sold by the booksellers of London & Westminster*, 1735. (*LM* Feb)

4°: *A*² B²(−B1) C–D² (A2 as 'B'); *3–4* 5–'10' *16 blk* (13,14,15 as '11,12,10').

The cancelled B1 was the first leaf of text.

'Like the meridian sun tho' merit shines'

Presumably addressed to John Dalrymple, earl of Stair.

E; CSmH, CtY, MH, TxU.

L305 **Loyalist.** The loyalist: a funeral poem in memory of William III. late king of Great Britain... By the author of the Generous muse. *London, printed for and sold by Nich. Cox*, 1702. (28 April, Luttrell)

2°: A–D²; *i–iv*, 1–12.

'Shall heav'n too, make resumptions of its grants'

The author of *The generous muse*, 1701, was probably William Pittis.

O; CLU-C, MH, *NjP*(Luttrell).

L306 —— *Dublin, re-printed and sold by C. Carter*, 1702.

4°: *A–B*² C²; *i–iv*, 1–8.

DT.

L307 — The loyalist. A poem. Humbly inscrib'd to his grace the Duke of Hamilton. *London, printed for John Friend in Westminster-Hall; sold by J. Morphew*, 1711. (16 March, Luttrell)

2°: A–C²; *i–ii*, 1–10.

Advertised in *DC* 19 March.

'In times e'er faction did embroil the state'

O(uncut), E; CLU-C(Luttrell), CSmH, CtY(uncut), MH(uncut).

L308 **Loyalty.** Loyalty display'd: or, an answer to the factious and rebellious song, call'd, Welcome to the medal; or, the constitution restor'd in 1711. To the tune of Mortimer's hole. [*London*] *Printed by H. Smith in Holborn*, 1711.

½°: 1 side, 2 columns.

'Confound all the medals of James the third's face'

Against the Pretender, in answer to *A welcome to the medal*, 1711.

LLP.

L309 — Loyalty honour'd, or a welcome to... James duke of Ormonde. By F. Mc.D. student in the mathematicks. *Dublin, printed by Francis Dickson*, 1711.

4°: A⁴; *1–3* 4–8.

'Smile (gentle Neptune) by Jove early sent'

L(11631. bb. 57).

L310 — Loyalty reviv'd, a song. [*London?* 1715?]

slip: 1 side, 1 column.

Loyalty reviv'd

'What Booker doth prognosticate'
Crum W389. A Jacobite song.
O(cut and mounted).

L311 — 'Loyalty triumphant in bonds; or, a poetical essay on the peace. By Phileirene. [*London*] *G. Woodfall*. Price 6*d*.' (*BM* Jan 1749)
Listed in *GM,LM* Feb as 'A poetical essay...'

L312 '**Loyd,** *the reverend Dr.*' An elegy on the much lamented death of Wriothseley duke of Bedford, and son of the honourable lord Russel...who being lately ill of the small-pox, departed this life at Southampton-House, in Bloomsbury-square, on Saturday the 26th of May 1711, in the 31st year of his age. By the reverend Dr. Loyd. [*London*] *Printed for J. Smith, in Fleet-street,* [1711.]
1°: 1 side, 2 columns.
Mourning headpiece and woodcut borders.
'Mourn all ye nobles! at that rigid fate'
The author intended is probably William Lloyd, bishop of Worcester, but the attributions of elegiac broadsides are unreliable; cf. 'Burnet, Gilbert'.
L(KTC.126.c.1/9).

Loyd, John, *minister of Gilden Sutton. See* Lloyd, John.

Lucanus, Marcus Annaeus.
Rowe, Nicholas: Lucan's Pharsalia. Translated into English verse, 1718, 1719, 1720, 1722. *See* R292–6.

Hughes, Jabez: The story of Sextus and Erichtho from Lucan's Pharsalia, book 6, 1714. *In* H368.

L313 Lucifer. Lucifer's defeat: or, the mantle-chimney. A Miltonic. Occasion'd by his majesty's grant of letters patent to Messieurs Fabené and Campbell for...curing smoky chimneys: and dedicated to ...the Duke of Devonshire. *London, printed for Lawton Gilliver,* 1729. (*MChr* 20 June)
2°: A–C²; *i–iv,* 1 2–8.
Bond 105.
'Kings, arms, and empire, common themes! The muse'
Dedicated to William Cavendish, second duke of Devonshire and patron of Fabené and Campbell, before his death on 4 June 1729.
LDW,O.

L314 — Leucifer's grand emesarys found out, or the Calves Head club discover'd, being an account of the apprehending and taking a gang of blasphemous and notorious persons who assembled together at the Golden Eagle in Suffolk Street near Chaering Cross on Thursday last the 30th of January...
[*London?* 1735?]
½°: 1 side, 2 columns.
Mourning borders; rough woodcuts at head.
A reference to the killing of Charles I as

Lucifer's grand emesarys

'eighty five years ago' suggests the date 1734, but 30 Jan fell on a Thursday in 1735.
'True churchmen all pray lend an ear'
A popular ballad.
L(1855.c.4/71).

Luck, Robert. A miscellany of new poems, on several occasions...To which are added poemata quaedam latina... *London, printed by Edward Cave, for the author, and subscribers,* 1736. (*GM* March)
8°: pp. vi, 192, 46.   L,O; CtY,MH.
There are variant states of the preliminaries; in some copies (ExP,LdU-B,ICN) there are no quotations on the title a1; c1 lists subscribers from Cambridge with errata on the verso; c2, a fly-title (sometimes bound as half-title), has a blank verso. In other copies quotations have been added to the title; Oxford subscribers have been added on a new leaf 'c2', and the errata transferred from c1 to the verso of the fly-title. Some copies contain a mixture of states, and a copy at C has an additional errata leaf.
—— Second edition, 1737. (*GM* May)
(Howes bookshop cat. 156 (1964) 340.)
Probably a reissue.

L315 — Abramis: carmen heroicum. Cui adjicitur ode, in resurrectionem Christi. *Londini, typis E. Say; veneunt apud J. Roberts, T. Worrall, E. Score Exoniæ, & J. Gaydon Barnastapulæ,* 1735.
4°: A–B⁴; *1–7 8–16.*
The ode is on pp. 14–16. *Abramis* was translated in *The art of life,* 1737.
'Uranie, puerum memora pietate parentis'
Ode: 'Heroa quem nunc, Uranie, canes?'
CT.

L316 Lucky. Luckie Gibson's latter-will, or comfort to her customers. [*Edinburgh,* 1718.]
½°: 1 side, 2 columns.
'Now do I find to death I'm near'
On the death of Lucky Gibson, the Edinburgh bawd.
E.

L317 — 'The lucky mistake: or, lady surpriz'd. A merry tale, in nine canto's. [*London*] *Printed for H. Goreham; sold by the booksellers of London & Westminster, and the persons who carry the news.* Price 6*d*.' [1742.]
'With a curious frontispiece.'
Possibly related to John Ellis, *The surprize,* 1739.
(*Haslewood,* newspaper advertisement of May 1742.)

— Lucky Spence's last advice, [1718.] *See* Ramsay, Allan.

Lucretius. Lucretius: a poem against the fear of death, 1709. *See* Dryden, John.

Lucretius Carus, T.

Lucretius Carus, Titus.
Marchetti, Alessandro: Di Tito Lucrezio Caro Della natura delle cose libri sei [Italian translation], 1717. *See* M93–4.

In imitation of Lucretius. Suave mari magno, &c., 1707. *See* I20.

Higgons, Bevil. A poem on nature: in imitation of Lucretius, 1736. *See* H183.

L318 Luctus. Luctus Aulæ Westmonasteriensis obitum invictissimi herois Joannis ducis Marlburiensis, &c. cui adjicitur epitaphium. *Londini, typis Pearsonianis,* 1722.
2⁰: *A*¹ B²; *i–ii,* 1–4.
   The copy seen probably lacks the final leaf with the epitaph.
'Vestros ante pedes, lacrymarum flumine largo'
   At foot of p. 4, 'P.M.S.': which may be the author's initials or (more probably) the catchword for the epitaph.
O.

L319 — Luctus Britannici, a poem, to the memory of Sir Roger L'Estrange. The late most ingenious refiner of the English tongue... By a gentleman of the university of Cambridge. *London, printed by R. Tookey, and are to be sold by S. Malthus,* 1705. (2 Jan)
4⁰: *A*² B⁴ C²; *i–ii* iii–iv, 1–'6' *12 blk* (9, 10, 11 as '3, 2, 6').
   Advertised in *PM* 4 Jan as published 'on Tuesday' [2 Jan].
'When great Apollo's learned fav'rites dye'
   Morgan H67 records this in error as by Sir Richard Bulkeley, possibly by confusion with his K67. Bulkeley was educated at Dublin and Oxford. Probably by the same author as *Albion's triumph,* 1705, who describes himself thus and uses the same printer and bookseller.
LDW,O; CLU-C,InU.

L320 Lucy. Lucy, a pastoral. Inscrib'd to the right honourable Philip, earl of Chesterfield... *London, printed for R. Dodsley; sold by M. Cooper,* 1747. (*GA* 17 Jan)
2⁰: *A*² < B²; 1–2 3–7 *8 blk.*
   Varying watermarks seen.
'My muse to Chesterfield directs her strains'
E; CSmH,ICN.

— Lucy and Colin, a song, 1725. *See* Tickell, Thomas.

L321 Lullaby. A lullaby for the d--n of St P-t-k's: or, the d--ct--r fed with his own spoon. To the tune of the Nurse's ballad. '*Brobdignagg, printed by Lamuel Hnhmyontrams, printer to his majesty of Laputa*' [Dublin, 1734?]
½⁰: 1 side, 1 column.

A lullaby for the d--n of St P-t-k's
   'O my sweet J——n——n, J——n——n'
      A satire on Swift.
CtY.

L322 — [column 1] A lullaby for the d--n of St. P--ks: or, the d--r fed with his own spoon. To the tune of the Nurse's ballad. [column 2] An huze: or, the d--n's answer to the lullaby. '*Brobdignagg, printed by Lamuel Hnhmyontrams, printer to his majesty of Laputa*' [Dublin, 1734?]
½⁰: 1 side, 2 columns.
   Teerink 1236; *Williams* 1135; *Ball* 290.
Huze: 'O my little F——y, sweet F——y'
   The answer is not by Swift and attacks a fellow of Trinity College.
C.

L323 Lumley, George. Frontello and Dorinda. A pastoral. *Newcastle upon Tyne, printed by Thomas Umfreville, and company, for the author,* 1737.
4⁰: π¹ A–D² E¹; *i–ii, 1–2* 3–⟨17⟩ *18 blk.* π1 hft.
'Frontello once the blithest of the swains'
NeP(mutilated).

L324 — The greatest statesman and the happiest fair, a pastoral humbly inscribed to the right honourable the Lady Walpole. *London, printed for the author; sold by the booksellers of London & Westminster,* 1738. (*GM,LM* April)
2⁰: *A*¹ B² C¹; 1–2 3–8.
   A1 and C1 have been seen to be conjugate.
'Great Walpole once the blithest of the train'
   In praise of Walpole's eventual marriage to Maria Skerret.
L(1959, uncut),O,C,DT,LdU-B+; CLU,CSmH, ICN,MH,TxU.

L325 — 'The royal hermitage. A poem. Humbly inscrib'd to her majesty. To which is prefix'd, an epistle to the right hon. the Earl of Scarborough. [*London*] *Printed for W. Mears; sold by Mr. Brindley, Mr. Jackson*... Price 1s.' (*DP* 21 March 1733)
   The author's name is spelt 'Lumbley' in the *DP* advertisement.

L326 Lunacy. [dh] The lunacy. A poem, address'd to the burroughs of Southwark and Bramber, against their next choice of members to serve in parliament. [col] *London printed, and sold by J. Baker,* [1710.] (*DC* 26 Sept)
8⁰: A⁸; 1–16.
'The times were come which bards of old'
   On the alleged lunacy of Joseph Edmonds of Hertfordshire.
L(164.k.33, Luttrell, 28 Sept); MB,OCU,TxU (uncut).

L327 Lunatic. 'The lunatick. A poem, inscrib'd to John Sh——r, esq; late one of the commisioners of stamp duties, upon his disaster at St. James's. To which is prefix'd, The Lincoln's-Inn 'squire: or, the protestant turn'd papist. A new ballad.

The lunatick

To the tune of King John and the abbot of Canterbury. [*London*] *Sold at the pamphlet shops.* Price 6d.' (*MChr* Dec 1730)

A poem on John Shorter; cf. *The Lincoln's-Inn 'squire*, [1730.]

'**Lunatus, Van Hugo Gasper.**' Homunculus: or, the character of Mezereon, 1715. *See* H293.

Lure. The lure of Venus, 1733. *See* Breval, John Durant (B427).

Lusus. Lusus poetici, [1722?]–. *See* Jortin, John.

— Lusus poetici olim conscripti, a T.B. e C.C.C. Oxon. discipulo, 1720. *See* Bisse, Thomas.

[**Lux, William.**] Poems on several occasions: viz. The garden... *Oxford, printed by Leon. Litchfield, for Stephen Fletcher, and are to be sold by James Knapton, London; and by Corn. Crownfield in Cambridge*, 1719.
8°: pp. 32.   O; CtY,IU.
Early ms. attribution in the O copy.

Luzara. Luzara. A pindarique ode, 170⅔. *See* Harris, Joseph.

'**Lydgate, John.**' The beasts in power, or Robin's song: with an old cat's prophecy. Taken out of an old copy of verses, suppos'd...by John Lidgate, 1709. *See* B125–6.

'**Lyrick, J.**' The re---cy, 1745. *See* R148.

Lyttelton, George, *baron Lyttelton.* Poems by the right honourable the late Lord Lyttelton. *Glasgow, printed by Robert & Andrew Foulis*, 1773.
12°: pp. 84.   L,O.
Gaskell, Foulis 556, recording fine-paper copies with the same watermark.

— The works of George lord Lyttleton, formerly printed separately, and now first collected together ... *London, printed for J. Dodsley*, 1774.
4°: pp. vii, 751.   L,O; MH,TxU.

L328 [—] Advice to a lady. *London, printed for Lawton Gilliver*, 1733. (*GSJ* 12 March)
2°: A² B²; *1–3* 4–8.
Reprinted with *A satyr on the New Tunbridge Wells*, 1733.
'The counsels of a friend, Belinda, hear'
Reprinted in Lyttelton's *Works*, 1774. Addressed to Lady Diana Spencer, subsequently duchess of Bedford.
L(1484.m.7/2; C.59.h.9/10, uncut),O,LdU-B; CSmH,CtY,ICN,MH,TxU(2)+.

L329 [—] — '*London, printed for Lawton Gilliver*' [*Edinburgh*], 1733.
8°: A⁴; *1–2* 3–8.

Lyttelton, G., *baron.* Advice to a lady

Printed by Ruddiman on the evidence of the ornaments.
L(1972); MH,NN,TxU.

L330 [—] Bleinheim. *London, printed for J. Roberts*, 1728. (*MChr* 23 April)
2°: A² B² C¹; *i–iv*, *1–6*.
'Parent of arts, whose skilful hand first taught'
Early ms. attribution in L copy; reprinted in Lyttelton's *Works*, 1774. On Blenheim Palace and the Churchills, dedicated to Lady Diana Spencer.
L(162.n.66),O(2),OW,BaP; CtY,ICU,IU,MH, TxU(2)+.

L331 [—] An epistle to Mr. Pope, from a young gentleman at Rome. *London, printed for J. Roberts*, 1730. (*DJ* 30 June)
2°: A² B¹; *1–2* 3–6.
'Immortal bard! for whom each muse has wove'
Printed in Lyttelton's *Works*, 1774.
O,OW(uncut); CSmH,CtY,IU,MH,TxU(2)+.

L332 [—] — *London printed*, 1730.
8°: a⁴; *1–2* 3–8.
Most copies seen were issued in *A collection of pieces...on occasion of the Dunciad*, 1732; it may well have been reprinted for the purpose, and should have no separate existence.
L(992.h.7/11),BaP; CLU-C,IU,MH.

[—] An epistle to William Pitt, 1746. *See* E434.

L333 [—] The progress of love. In four eclogues... *London, printed for L. Gilliver*, 1732. (*GSJ* 25 March)
2°: A¹ B–G²; *i–ii*, *1–23* 24. 24 advt.
Almost all copies have an errata slip on the verso of the title. The first two editions are discussed in *Williams, Points* 78.
'Pope, to whose reed beneath the beachen shade'
Reprinted in Lyttelton's *Works*, 1774.
L(11626.h.12/2; 163.n.25),O(2),OW(no errata), *MR*; CLU-C,CtY(2),MH,OCU(uncut),TxU(2, 1 no errata)+.

L334 [—] — *London, printed for L. Gilliver*, 1732.
2°: A² B–F²; *1–2* 3–24.
L(643.m.15/18),O(2),LdU-B; CSmH,ICN,MH, TxU(uncut).

L335 [—] — *London, printed for L. Gilliver*, 1732. (*GM* July)
8°: A² B–D⁴ E²; *i–iv*, *1–28*. A1 hft.
L(1488.c.35),LVA-D(Pope's copy),O,CT(2, –A1),*MR-C*; CtY(uncut),DFo,ICU,IU.

L336 [—] — *London printed. And, Dublin re-printed by George Faulkner*, 1732.
8°: A⁴ B–C⁴; *1–3* 4–22 *23–24 blk.*
Rothschild 1339.
DA; MH(–C4).

L337 [—] To the memory of a lady lately deceased. A monody. *London, printed for A. Millar; sold by M. Cooper*, 1747. (*DA* 30 Oct)

Lyttleton, G., *baron.* To the memory

2°: *A²* B–E²; *i–iv, 1* 2–15 *16 blk.* A1 hft.
Signature E under first a of 'again'. The order of editions is obscure. W. B. Todd in *PBSA* 44 (1950) 274f. proposed the opposite order of the first two to the present, but he did not know the 'second edition'; that appears to be closer to the following. All were printed by Samuel Richardson (*Sale* 348, 357). Horizontal chain-lines.
'At length escap'd from ev'ry human eye'
Reprinted in Lyttelton's *Works*, 1774. On the death of Lady Lyttelton.
L(11630.h.34),O,C,LdU-B; ICU,IU,MH,TxU.

L338 [—] [another edition]
Signature E under n of 'again'. Reset except for sheets B and E. Horizontal chain-lines.

L(643.m.16/15; 840.m.1/21,–A1),LVA-D,O(2, –A1),EU; CLU-C(uncut),CtY,ICN,MH,TxU.

L339 [—] — The second edition. *London, printed for A. Millar; sold by M. Cooper,* 1748 [1747]. (*DA* 1 Dec)
2°: *A²* B–E²; *i–iv, 1* 2–15 *16 blk.* A1 hft.
Apparently a reimpression of the preceding except for sheet C which corresponds to L337. Horizontal chain-lines.
L(11657.m.28; 11630.h.35,–A1),O(–A1),OW (uncut),E,LdU-B+; CU,CtY,IU,MH,TxU.

L340 —— By Mr. Lyttelton. *Dublin, printed by George Faulkner,* 1747.
8°: *A⁴* B⁴; *1–2* 3–15 *16.* 16 advt.
L(1960),O(2),DA(2),DG,DN(2); CtY,PP.

M

M., A. Fishery, a poem, 1714. *See* F151.

M., B. The planter's charity, 1704. *See* P477.

— Typhon: or the wars between the gods and giants, 1704. *See* Mandeville, Bernard.

— Wishes to a godson, with other miscellany poems, 1712. *See* Mandeville, Bernard.

M., C.W.A. The reformer's ghost, [1725/30.] *See* R151.

M., D. The apothecary in the sheet, [1726.] *See* A271.

M., J. Dionysius Cato his four books of moral precepts. Translated...by J.M., 1714. *See* D317.

— The doctors miscellany, 1731. *See* Doctors.

— An essay, to the pious memory of...Mr. George Trosse, 1713. *See* Mortimer, J.

— Heliocrene a poem in Latin and English, 1725–. *See* Merrick, John.

— A new poem in honour of the journey-men taylors, [1726?/27?] *See* N168.

— A poem on the taylor craft, 1733. *See* Morgan, John.

— The sine-cure, 1725. *See* Mitchell, Joseph.

M., J., *gent.* An ode: or elegy on the death of James the second, 1701. *See* O53.

M., J. *and* **P., W.,** *gents.* A whip for the Spaniards, 1701. *See* W401.

M., J., *S.S.S.* Scelus's ghost, 1748. *See* S132.

M., J., *S.T.C.D.* A paraphrase on part of the book of Joshua, 1724. *See* P51.

M., L. M. W. Six town eclogues, 1747. *See* Montagu, *Lady* Mary Wortley.

M., N. The Christian's exercise, 1712. *See* C169.

M., R. Ad virum ornatissimum...Jacobum Astley, [1710?] *See* Monsey, R.

— In diem illum auspicatissimum, 1719. *See* Monsey, R.

M., R., *præsb. Norfol.* Viro honoratissimo... Roberto Harley, 1711. *See* Monsey, R.

M., W. The countryman's true tale, [1714?] *See* Countryman.

— Dick, or devil, [1735.] *See* D300.

— Hesperi-neso-graphia, 1716–. *See* H162.

— Illia's plain, [1714?] *See* I5.

M., W., *an Oxford scholar.* The royal invitation, 1719. *See* R312.

M1 **M. M.** Ad----m's lamentation. For his being catch'd in bed with Mrs. A——rsh, and her sister, Miss —— and for several other crimes, as the m——dr, of Mr. M——ddle-b——rooke, &c. for which he is to be made an ex——mple. To the tune, of Chievy-chase. [*Dublin*, 1726.]
slip: 1 side, 1 column.
'Now ponder well my neighbours all'
    A satire on Mordecai Adam, caught in bed with two whores.
DN.

— M. Manlius Capitolinus, 1712. *See* Fenton, Elijah.

Mc.D., F., *student in the mathematicks.* Loyalty honour'd, 1711. *See* L309.

Mac-Dermot. Mac-Dermot: or, the Irish fortune-hunter, 1717. *See* Breval, John Durant.

McDermot, Murtagh.
It is not known whether this is the name of a real person. His name is related to the pseudonym 'Martin Gulliver' in A satyr. By way of reply, to Martin Guilliver, alias Murtagh Mc.Dermot, 1730. The prose work A trip to the moon, 1728 (copy at L) bears his name, but it is treated by L catalogue as a pseudonym. No person of this name is found in the registers of Trinity College Dublin. See 'Gulliver, Martin'.

'Mac-Dermot, Shane-baune.' Munster Juggy preferr'd or an answer to Molly Mogg, 1727. *See* M561.

'M'Doe-Roch, Patrick.' The sequel of Mr. Pope's law case, 1733. *See* S203.

M2 **Macdonald, Donald.** The apparition of Donald Macdonald's ghost, to a prisoner in the New-Goal, in Southwark. A poem, in the Ramsonian stile. *London, printed by and for R. Phillips, in West-Smithfield, and sold at the pamphlet shops in London & Westminster,* 1746.
$4°$: A^2($\pm$A1) B^2; *1–2* 3–8.
    Both copies seen were issued with *The saddle put on the right horse... The second edition,* 1746. In both copies, the price 6*d.* on the title is deleted; apparently this was the price for both parts together. There was probably an earlier separate issue.
'Before I in the widdy swang'
    Macdonald is not specifically named as author, but his authorship is clearly implied.
L(1488.d.16); IU.

Macdonald, D.

M3 — The saddle put on the right horse: or, Donald Macdonald's thoughts on the present times. A poem, in the stile of Allen Ramsay's poetical works. *London, printed by and for R. Phillips, in West-Smithfield, and sold at the pamphlet shops in London & Westminster,* 1746.
4°: *A*² B²; *1–2* 3–8.
'I have ten merks, nae mere, nor less'
    Macdonald's authorship is clearly implied; he was executed for treason in the Jacobite rebellion.
L(1488.d.15); *CLU-C*,CSmH,DLC,*MH*,OCU.

M4 —— The second edition. To which is subjoined, The apparition of his ghost, to a prisoner in the New-Goal, in Southwark. *London, printed by and for R. Phillips, in West-Smithfield, and sold at the pamphlet shops in London & Westminster,* 1746.
4°: *A*²(±A1) B², ²*A*²(±A1) B²; *1–2* 3–8, *1–2* 3–8.
    Apparently a reissue of the preceding with *The apparition*, recorded above.
L(1488.d.16); IU(pt. 2 separately bound).

M5 —— '*London, printed by and for R. Phillips*' [*Edinburgh?*], 1746.
4°: *A*²; *1* 2–4.
    A piracy.
E.

McEncroe, D.
An Irish writer of Latin verse, who used the name 'Demetrius de la Croix'. His poems appear to have been published in Paris between 1707 and 1728, and they are accordingly excluded from this catalogue. Compare Patrick St. John for another Irish Latinist in France.

Machiavelli, Niccolò.
[*Belfagor*] Belphegor: or the marriage of the devil, 1714. *See* B184.

M6 **Machine.** The machine: or, love's preservative. A poem in imitation of Homer and Virgil, and Dryden and Pope. *London, printed for T. Reynolds, in Fleet-street; 'and sold at the sign of the Scabbard in Ram-alley'*, 1744 [1743]. (13 Dec?)
4°: (frt+) *A*¹ B⁴ C²; *i–ii, 1* 2–12.
    Bond 173. The engraved frontispiece of the process of manufacture, seen only in a photograph, may have been conjugate with the title. The L copy, from Tom's Coffee House, appears to have been dated 13 Dec 1743.
'O all ye nymphs! who wait both day and night'
    A rewriting of [White Kennett] *Armour*, in heroic couplets. On the condom. Cf. E. J. Dingwall in *British Medical Journal*, 3 Jan 1953.
L(P.C.15.h.8, lacks frt, supplied by photograph; slightly cropt).

Mack-faux. Mack-faux the mock-moralist, 1705. *See* Forbes, William.

McKinstry, H.

M7 **McKinstry, H.** The glory of Spain subdu'd by British valour. A poetical narrative of the taking the Gloriosa Spanish man of war, by the Russel... *London, printed by H. Kent, for M. Cooper,* 1748. (*GM*,*LM* Oct)
4°: *A*² B–D⁴; *1–4* 5–27 *28* blk.
'Say, gods! how shall heroic souls behave'
    Dedication signed.
L(11630.c.8/14).

'Mac-Sturdy, Hercules.' A trip to Vaux-hall, 1737. *See* T494.

Mad. The mad dog, a tale, 1730. *See* Gay, John.

M8 **Madden, Samuel.** Boulter's monument. A panegyrical poem, sacred to the memory of... Dr. Hugh Boulter... *London, printed by S. Richardson, and are to be sold by M. Cooper, R. Dodsley, J. Brindley, A. Millar, T. Longman, J. Brotherton & H. Whitridge, J. Whiston, & J. Stagg,* 1745. (*GA* 25 Oct)
8°: *A*¹ B–L⁸ M⁴; *i–ii,* 1–168. ii err.
    No watermark. *Rothschild* 1355. The priority of editions is not certain, though the Dublin edition has additional errata. A copy at L (11632.e.42) has another setting of the title-page without errata on the verso; presumably the normal title-leaf is a cancel.
'Shall Boulter die, and no memorial shew'
    Dedication signed.
CT(contemporary morocco, ruled in red),DA; CtY,MH.

M9 — [fine paper]
    Watermark: Strasburg bend. All copies seen are in contemporary morocco bindings, but none has a presentation inscription.
L(11632.e.42; 78.i.23),O,C,DG.

M10 —— *Dublin, printed by George Faulkner,* 1745.
8°: *A*¹ B–G⁸; *i–ii,* 1–96. ii err.
    Copies at O,C,LdU-B,CSmH,CtY are in contemporary morocco bindings without presentation inscriptions.
L(11632.e.37),*LVA-D*,O,C,LdU-B; CSmH,CtY, IU,NN,PP.

M11 **Made.** ⟨   ⟩ made on the magnificent splendor and glory of the twenty four corporations of this honourable city of Dublin. Upon their riding the franchises. (Tune, First of August) [*Dublin,* 1725?/30.]
½°: 1 side, 2 columns.
    The copy seen forms part of a collection of Dublin half-sheets of 1725/30.
'All you that fain would jolly be'
L(C.121.g.8/17, cropt).

M12 **Madman.** The mad-mans hospital: or, a cure for the presbyterian itch, by an eminent doctor, that has lately cur'd many a thousand blind people in this nation. *London, printed in the year* 1710. (20 Sept, Luttrell)

The **madman**'s hospital

½º: 1 side, 2 columns.
'Since troops of mad-men are in Bedlam pent'
   Against the whigs, and in favour of Sacheverell.
O; MH(Luttrell).

M13 Madness. Madness: a poem... Written by a gentleman when under confinement for lunacy. *London printed, and sold by J. Roberts,* 1728. (*MChr* 16 Aug)
4º: *A*² B–E²; *1–5* 6–20. A1 hft.
'Pardon, good god! that I should lightly spend'
L(643.k.3/6); IU,OCU.

M14 Magdalen. Magdalen-grove: or, a dialogue between the doctor and the devil. Written in February in the year 1713. and found among the papers of a gentleman deceas'd. Humbly dedicated to the author and admirers of the Apparition, a poem. *London, printed by J. Carrett,* [1714.] (*MC* Oct)
8º: *A*⁴ B–C⁴; *1–5* 6–22 *23–24 blk.* A1 hft.
'When the sun darting gentle western light'
   A copy at LdU-B has a contemporary ms. note 'by N: G. Esqr', possibly Nehemiah Griffith. A satire on Sacheverell, suggested by [Abel Evans] *The apparition,* 1710.
L(1471.f.17,–C4),O,DT,LdU-B(–C4); CtY, DFo,MH(Luttrell, 1714).

M15 Magician. The magician, or bottle cungerer. *London, printed for B. Dickinson,* 1748/9. (5 March)
obl ½º: 1 side, 3 columns.
   Large engraving at head, bearing the above title and date of publication, 5 March 1748/9. Printed title 'English credulity; or ye're all bottled' heads text. Penultimate line reads '...Youth before, to...'.
'With grief, resentment, and averted eyes'
   On British credulity.
L(P&D 3022); NNP.

M16 — [another edition]
   Penultimate line reads '...Youth, before to...'
O-JJ.

M17 — [*idem*] English credulity; or ye're all bottled. *London, printed for B. Dickinson,* [1749.]
obl ½º: 1 side, 3 columns.
   The engraving in this state bears no title or date of publication; it may well be earlier than the others. The text is another setting.
L(P&D 3022).

M18 Magistrate. The magistrate. A poem. Inscrib'd to Sir John Barnard, knt. and Mr. Pope. *London, printed for T. Davies,* 1738. (*GM, LM* April)
4º: *A*² B–D²; *1–3* 4–15 *16 blk.*
'I grant th' enormous vices of the age'
   In praise of Sir John Barnard.
L(11630.e.16/1, Tom's Coffee House, 4 May),O, C; ICU,KU.

The **magistrate**

M19 — — The second edition. *London, printed for T. Davies,* 1738.
4º: *A*²(±A1) B–D²; *1–3* 4–15 *16 blk.*
   Reissue with cancel title.
O.

[**M20** = B80·5] **Magna.** Magna Britannia triumphans, 1702. *See* Barbon, —, *Dr.*

M21 Maiden. The maiden's dream. [*London?* 1725?/–.]
slip: 1 side, 1 column.
   Woodcut at head. Also printed with *The bachelor's dream,* 1725.
'One night extended on my downy bed'
C.

M22 Maids. The maids christmas box. [*London,* 1727?]
½º: 1 side, 2 columns.
   Rough woodcut at head. On the other side, *In answer to the Le H——p's ballad,* [1727.]
'Come my joy and hearts delight'
   An erotic song.
O.

M23 — The maids vindication: or, the fifteen comforts of living a single life. Being an answer to the Fifteen plagues of a maiden-head. Written by a gentlewoman. *London, printed for J. Rogers, in Fleet-street,* 1707.
8º: *A*⁴; *1–2* 3–8.
'Ye British maids with British beauty blest'
L(1076.1.22/9).

Maidwell, Lewis. Majestas imperij Britannici. The glories of Great Britain celebrated in Latin poems by Mr. Maidwell. Paraphras'd in English by Mr. Tate poet-laureat... Part I. *London, printed in the year* 1706.
4º: pp. 22.   O.
   No watermark.

— [fine paper]   L; CtY.
   Watermark: fleur-de-lys on shield.

———————

M24 — Comitia lyrica: sive carmen panegyricum. In quo, ad exornandas magni Godolphini laudes, omnes omnium odarum modi ab Horatio delegantur... Paraphras'd in English, by Mr. Tate... *London, printed by H.M.* [*H. Meere?*]; *sold by Timothy Child,* 1707. (*DC* 8 April)
2º: π¹ *A*² B–N²; *i–ii, 1–3* 4–52. π1 hft.
   With much additional prose on grammatical subjects.
'Ille ego sum Plutus, cujus moderamine justo'
'Behold the god of wealth, in whose just reign'
   Signed by Maidwell at end.
O(–π1),C,DT,LdU-B(–π1); CSmH(Luttrell, 8 April),CtY,TxU.

M25 — [reissue] Nova grammatices experimenta: or, some new essays of a natural and artificial grammar ... Design'd for the benefit of a noble youth, &c...

Maidwell, L. Nova grammatices

Celebrated with a parænetic poem, by Mr. Tate... *London printed, and sold by R. Burrough & J. Baker*, 1707.
2°: πA^2 b–c² A^2(−A1) B–N²(+folding plate); *i–xii*, 3 4–52.

With additional grammatical material and a prefatory poem by Tate.
L(66.e.17, contemporary morocco),GU(calf, gilt edges); CSmH(contemporary morocco),TxU.

[—] Vaticinium pacis. The prophecy of peace, 1706. *See* V21.

[**Mainwaring, Arthur.**] An address to our sovereign lady, [1704.] *See* A55.

M26 [—] An excellent new song, called, Credit restored, in the year of our lord god, 1711. To the tune of, Come prithee, Horace, hold up thy head. [*London*] *Printed in the year* 1711.
½°: 1 side, 2 columns.
17 rules above imprint, the eighth very short. The order of editions is uncertain.
'All Britains rejoyce at this turn of the state'
Reprinted in Mainwaring's *Life and posthumous works*, 1715. A satire on the profiteering under Harley's ministry. Listed in *Morgan* P430 as 'A new ballad upon the land bank' as [1713]. Answered by *Oxford and Mortimer's vindication*, 1711.
Rothschild; MH.

M27 [—] [another edition]
16 rules above imprint, the fifth short.
Herts CRO (Panshanger box 46); CSmH.

M28 [—] [another edition]
16 rules above imprint.
OCU.

M28·5 [—] [another edition]
22 rules above imprint, the eleventh and fifteenth very short.
MH,*MH-BA*.

M29 [—] [another edition]
Title misprinted 'To hte tune of...'; imprint 'Printetd...' An inferior piece of printing to the preceding editions.
L(1876.f.1/61),O,C; MH-BA,NN,TxU.

M30 [—] An excellent new song, called, Mat's peace, or the downfal of trade. To the good old tune of Green-sleeves. [*London*] *Printed in the year* 1711.
½°: 1 side, 2 columns.
Line of short rules above imprint.
'The news from abroad does a secret reveal'
Reprinted in Mainwaring's *Life and posthumous works*, 1715. A satire on Matthew Prior's peace mission to France.
L(1876.f.1/59),O,C,DA,DT; PPL,TxU.

M31 [—] [another edition]
No rules above imprint.
MH-BA.

[—] Fishery, a poem, 1714. *See* F151.

Mainwaring, A.

M32 [—] The history and fall of the conformity bill. Being an excellent new song, to the tune of the Ladies fall. [*London*, 1704.]
½°: 1 side, 2 columns.
'God bless our gracious sovereign Anne'
Crum G242. Partly reprinted in Mainwaring's *Life and posthumous works* (1715) 40 as specifically by him rather than other suspected authors; see F. H. Ellis in *POAS* VI (1970) 618.
MH.

M33 [—] The South Sea whim. To the tune of------To you fair ladies now at land, &c. [*London*] *Printed in the year* 1711.
½°: 1 side, 2 columns.
'To you fair traders now a shore'
Reprinted in Mainwaring's *Life and posthumous works*, 1715. A protest against the South Sea scheme.
O,Crawford; CSmH,MH-BA.

[—] When the cat's away, The mice may play, [1712.] *See* W384.

M34 Mainwario. Mainwario's welcome to Ophelia, on his meeting her in the shades. Inscrib'd to the honourable Mr. Mainwaring. *London, printed for W. Trott*, 1730. (*GSJ* 12 Nov)
2°: A–B²; *1–2* 3–8.
'Through dreary realms, and shores bereft of light'
Arthur Mainwaring's welcome to his former mistress, Anne Oldfield, celebrating their happiness together. Inscribed to their natural son, Arthur Mainwaring. Advertised as a sequel to *A pastoral elegy on the death of Calista*, 1730, in *Don Francisco's descent*, 1732.
LdU-B.

Maitland, Richard, *earl of Lauderdale.* The works of Virgil, translated into English verse. *London, printed for Bernard Lintott*, [1709.] (*DC* 1 Feb)
8°: pp. 32, 396.   L,O; CtY,MH.
I1–3 are cancels; the cancellanda are preserved in a copy at O. A copy at CLU-C is in contemporary morocco.

—— The second edition. *London, printed by W. Bowyer, for Bernard Lintott*, [1716.] (*MC* April)
12°: 2 vol.   L,LVA-D; CLU-C.
The trade sale of Richard Sare, 21 Sept 1726 (cat. at O-JJ), offered in both lots 40 and 41 an eighth share in the copyright and 100 books; both were purchased by John Osborn of Horsley Downs for £9. 5s. A fourth share formed part of lot 7 of the sale of Richard Williamson, 29 Nov 1737.

Maittaire, Michael. Senilia, sive poetica aliquot in argumentis varii generis tentamina. *Londini, anno salutis humanæ* 1742. (13 April?)
4°: pp. vi, 127.   L,O.
With a colphon of William Bowyer, dated

Maittaire, M.

'Idibus Aprilibus'; entered to Maittaire in Bowyer's ledgers, 500 copies printed; 100 proposals are also recorded.

M35 [—] [dh] Carmen epinicium augustissimæ Russorum imperatrici sacrum. [col] *Londini*, 1737, xvii. Cal. Octob. (15 Sept)
4°: *A²*; *1-4*.
Entered to Maittaire in Bowyer's ledgers under 15 Sept 1737, 52 copies printed.
'Qualem ministrum numinis alitem'
Ms. attribution to Maittaire in the L copy. On the Russian victory at Stavuchani in 1737.
L(837.k.11/76).

[Major, William.] Four satires: translated from the Latin, into English verse... To which are added, some occasional poems on various subjects. By a gentleman, late of Balliol College, Oxford. *London, printed for the author*, 1743.
8°: pp. 92.   CT; CtY(impft),TxHR.
The Latin satires were published as *Satyrae quatuor*, 1735. Ms. attribution in CtY copy.

M36 [—] The retirement. An ethic poem... By a gentleman, late of Balliol College, Oxford. *London, printed for the author*, 1747.
4°: *π²* A–B⁴ C²; *i-iv, 1 2-20*. π1 hft.
Vertical chain-lines.
'Tir'd with the busy follies of the town'
Ascribed to '— Major... of Baliol' by *Rawlinson*; there seems no doubt this is the author intended.
O(−π1),Forster.

M37 [—] [reissue] *London, printed for J. Swan, near St. Martin's Lane, in the Strand*, 1748. (*GM, LM* July)
4°: *π1* A–B⁴ C²; *i-ii, 1 2-20*.
Reissue with cancel title; no half-title seen.
L(11631.g.34/1).

M38 [Malden, —, Mr.] The Maldon ballad, or the naked truth. [*London*, 1733.] (27 Dec?)
2°: *A²*; *1-4*.
Printed on the two inner pages, the outer blank. On the left page, 'The vicar of Bray' with six verses; on the right, the imitation titled as above.
'In George the first and second's reign'
Ms. note in the copy seen '27 Dec. 1733. The author Mr. Malden the apothecary at Maldon'.
In praise of Walpole's ministry.
IU.

Maldon. The Maldon ballad, or the naked truth, [1733.] *See* Malden, —, *Mr.*

M39 Malet, Thomas. The soldier's religion: or, contemplations heroical-divine. *London, printed for Benj. Tooke*, 1705. (*TC* Easter)

Malet, T. The soldier's religion

8°: A⁴ B–D⁸; *i-ii iii-vii viii, 1-47 48*. 48 advt.
'When princes, charm'd with peace, enjoy the throne'
Dedication signed.
DA.

M40 Malice. Malice defeated. A pastoral essay. Occasioned by Mr. Pope's character of Lord Timon, in his epistle to the Earl of Burlington, and Mr. Welsted's answer. *London, printed for J. Millan*, 1732. (*DJ* 28 Jan)
½°: 2 sides, 2 columns.
'Good morrow Thyrsis. May Aurora prove'
In praise of Welsted's *Of dulness and scandal*, 1732.
CLU-C.

M41 — Malice's master-piece: or, an emblem of the ill treatment good men meet with from the bad. *London printed, and sold by several booksellers and picture-shops*, [1710.]
½°: 1 side, 2 columns.
Large emblematic woodcut at head.
'By kings and princes, god at first design'd'
Against Sacheverell.
Madan.

M42 Mall. The Mall: or, the reigning beauties. Containing the various intrigues of Miss Cloudy and her governante Madam Agility. *London printed, and sold by B. Bragg*, 1709. (23 May, Luttrell)
2°: *A²* B–D²; *1-2 3-16* (4 as '3').
The Luttrell copy is recorded in *Haslewood*; advertised in *DC* 25 May.
'Look here, immortal queen of beauty, rise'
TxU.

M43 — — *London, printed in the year* 1709.
8°: A⁴; *1-2 3-16*.
A piracy, resembling the poems published by Henry Hills.
L(11631.aaa.9),O.

Mallet, David. Poems on several occasions. *London, printed for A. Millar*, 1743. (*GM* Oct)
8°: pp. 182-275.   L,O; CtY,MH.
Usually bound as part of Mallet's *Works*, 1743, but also issued separately; so listed in *GM, LM*. Presentation copies at CtY,MH.

— Poems on several occasions. *London, printed for A. Millar*, 1762.
8°: pp. 80.   L,LVA-D; MH.
A new collection.

M44 [—] Amyntor and Theodora, or the hermit. A poem. In three cantos. *London, printed for Paul Vaillant*, 1747. (*SR* 27 April)
4°: *π²* A–M⁴ N²; [*4*] *i* ii-viii, *1-3 4-92*. π1 hft.
Listed in *GM* April. Deposit copies at L,E,EU,AdU,GU.
'Far in the watry waste, where his broad wave'

Mallet, D. Amyntor and Theodora

Subsequently reprinted with dedication signed by Mallet.

L(11630.d.12/1;11630.e.16/20;1465.i.6/3, −π1; 644.k.16/7),O(2),C,E,LdU-B+; CSmH(uncut), CtY(2),ICN,MH,TxU(3, 1 uncut)+.

M45 [—] — '*London, printed for Paul Vaillant*' [*Edinburgh*], 1747.

12°: π(5 ll) A–D⁶ E⁴; [2] *i* ii–viii, *1* 2–56.

π2.3 have been seen to be conjugate; the collation is perhaps π⁶(−π1). Copies at L,E are bound with collections of pamphlets largely of Edinburgh origin.

L(11643.aa.52/3),E,GM.

M46 [—] — *Dublin, printed by George Faulkner*, 1747.

12°: A–E⁶ F²; *i–ii* iii–xii, 13–64.

O.

M47 [—] — The third edition. *Dublin, printed by George Faulkner*, 1747.

12°: A–E⁶ F²; *i–ii* iii–xii, 13–64.

Apparently a reimpression with the exception of sheet B.

O.

M48 [—] — The second edition. *London, printed for Paul Vaillant*, 1748.

4°: π¹ A–M⁴ N²; [2] *i* ii–viii, *1–3* 4–92.

A reissue of M44 with a cancel title-leaf; no half-title in copies seen.

O,C,E; CtY,DFo,IU,*MH*.

M49 — — A new edition. Corrected by the author. *London, printed for Paul Vaillant*, 1748.

8°: A⁴ B–E⁸ F⁴; *i–iii* iv–viii, *1* 2–72.

Dedication signed.

L(992.h.11/5),O,CT; CtY.

M50 [—] The excursion. A poem. In two books. *London, printed for J. Walthoe*, 1728. (*MChr* 21 March)

8°: A² B–K⁴; *i–ii* iii–iv, *9* 10–80. iv err.

On p. 75, *William and Margaret*. Printed by Samuel Richardson (*Sale* 63). Readvertised in March 1731 at the time of Mallet's *Eurydice*.

'Fancy, creative power, at whose command'

Reprinted in Mallet's *Poems*, 1743.

L(992.h.7/7),O,E; CLU-C,CtY,ICN,ICU(uncut),MH+.

[—] An ode, to his royal highness on his birth-day [actually by Robert Nugent, earl Nugent], 1739. *See* N341.

M51 [—] Of verbal criticism: an epistle to Mr. Pope. Occasioned by Theobald's Shakespear, and Bentley's Milton. *London, printed for Lawton Gilliver*, 1733. (16 April?)

2°: A¹ B²(B1+χ1) C–D² E¹; *i–iv, 1–3* 4–14. A1 hft.

Harley's copy was received on 14 April; advertised in *LEP* 14 April for publication on 'Monday next', 16 April. All early advertisements give the title as 'An epistle to Mr. Pope...', which is the form of the drop-head

Mallet, D. Of verbal criticism

title on p. 3 and reappears in the 'second edition' below; presumably this was the original title. There are copies at L,O bound with collections of deposit copies, but no entry has been traced in *SR*. Also listed in *LM* June 1733 and in *GM*, *LM* March 1734 as 'Of verbal criticism'.

'Among the numerous fools, by fate design'd'

Harley's copy at O is annotated 'Sent by the author April. 14. 1733. By Mr Mallet a Scots gentleman'. Reprinted in Mallet's *Poems*, 1743.

L(643.m.14/4),LVA-D(−A1),O(2, 1−A1), LdU-B(−A1),*MR*; CSmH,CtY,ICN,MH(3, 2−A1),TxU(3, 1 uncut)+.

M52 [—] — '*London, printed for Lawton Gilliver*' [*Edinburgh*], 1733.

8°: A–B⁴; *1–3* 4–15 16.

Printed by Ruddiman on the evidence of the ornaments.

O,C,E; CSmH,CtY,ICU,MH,TxU+.

M53 [—] [*idem*] An epistle to Mr. Pope. Occasioned by Theobald's Shakespear, and Bentley's Milton. The second edition. *London, printed for Lawton Gilliver*, 1733.

2°: B(3 ll) C–D² E¹; *i–ii, 1–3* 4–14.

Apparently a reissue or reimpression of the first London edition; no half-title in the copy seen.

TxU.

M54 — [dh] A poem, in imitation of Donaides, by David Malloch, A.M. [*Edinburgh*, 1725.]

4°: A²; *1–3 4 blk*.

Watermark: grapes. Almost all copies are or were bound with John Ker's *Donaides*, 1725, of which it is a translation.

'In ancient times, e're wealth was learning's foe'

LVA-D,O,*ES*,AdU; MH.

M55 — [fine paper]

Watermark: fleur-de-lys on shield.

L(837.h.36),LVA-D,E,AdU; CtY.

M56 [—] A poem to the memory of Mr. Congreve. Inscribed to her grace, Henrietta, dutchess of Marlborough. *London, printed for J. Millan, and sold at his shop*, 1729. (*MChr* 9 May)

8°: A⁴ B⁴ C² D²; *1–6* 7–20 21–23; *24 blk*. A1 hft; D² advt.

The watermark apparently varies; sometimes a bird. C² and D² may have been printed together in this form for convenience in issuing the fine-paper copies without the advertisements of D².

'Oft has the muse, with mean attempt, employ'd'

Attributed to James Thomson by Peter Cunningham, who reprinted it in 1843. A. D. McKillop in *MLN* 54 (1939) 599 records advertisements in *LJ* 24 May 1729 'by the author of the Excursion' and in *DP* 9 March

Mallet, D. A poem to the memory

> 1730 'by the author of William and Margar-
> ate [!]'. Not collected in Mallet's poems, but
> almost certainly his.
> L(992.h.7/9, –A1),LDW,E,WcC(–D²); CLU-C
> (–D²),CtY,ICN,MH,NNC.

M57 [—] [fine paper] *London, printed in the year* 1729.
8⁰: *A*⁴ B⁴ C²; *1–6* 7–20. A1 hft.
> Watermark: Strasburg bend; no price on title.
> LVA-D(2, 1 Pope's copy),O; PSC.

M58 [—] Verses presented to his highness the Prince of
Orange. On his visiting Oxford. *London, printed for
Lawton Gilliver,* 1734. (*GSJ* 11 April)
2⁰: *A*² B²; *1–3* 4–8.
> Two sets of verses; those on pp. 3–6 'By the
> author of Eurydice' [David Mallet], on pp. 7–8
> signed 'W. Harte'.
> 'Receive, lov'd prince, the tribute of our praise'
> 'At length in pity to a nation's pray'r'
> L(11657.m.19),O; CtY,ICN.

M59 [—] [dh] William and Margaret, an old ballad.
[*Edinburgh,* 1723?]
8⁰: A²; *1–4*.
> Almost certainly published by Allan Ramsay;
> both copies seen are bound with pamphlet
> poems by him. Those at O are dated 1722–24,
> and this edition presumably precedes Mallet's
> departure from Edinburgh to London in
> August 1723. See Gordon F. Sleigh in *The
> library* V. 8 (1953) 121.
> 'When it was grown to dark mid-night'
> Subsequently revised by Mallet and printed
> with *The excursion,* 1728, and in his *Poems,*
> 1743. Translated into Latin by Vincent
> Bourne as *Thyrsis & Chloe,* 1728.
> L(11631.aaa.56/10),O.

M60 [—] — [*London,* 1723/24.]
½⁰: *1–2*, 1 column.
> The first stanza is also printed with six lines
> of typeset music before text. The text is
> printed in black-letter. At foot of p. 2 'N.B.
> This ballad will sing to the tune of Montrose's
> Lilt, Rothes's Lament, or the Isle of Kell'. The
> halfpenny tax stamp is printed in a state found
> between June 1723 and May 1724, but this
> edition appears to be authorized and probably
> precedes its publication in *The hive* I, Dec
> 1723. There are at least three early engraved
> editions with music, not listed here.
> 'When all was wrapt in dark mid-night'
> L(1876.f.1/107).

M61 [—] [*idem*] A lamentable ballad of the tragical
ends of William and Margaret. *Northampton,
printed by William Dicey,* [1723/–.]
obl ½⁰: 1 side, 4 columns.
> Printed in traditional ballad form, with two
> rough woodcuts at head. Apart from acci-
> dentals it follows the London text closely.
> L(L.R.31.b.19, vol. 2, ff. 36–7).

Mallet, D. William and Margaret

M62 [—] [*idem*] Margaret and William, a ballad. To the
tune of Fair Rosamond. [*Dublin,* 1723/30.]
½⁰: 1 side, 2 columns.
> The L copy is bound in a collection of Dublin
> half-sheets, mainly of 1725/30. A few textual
> changes have been made.
> 'Now all was wrapt in dark mid-night'
> L(C.121.g.8/115).

Malloch, David. *See* Mallet, David.

M63 **Man.** The man of honour. *London, printed in the
year* 1737.
4⁰: A–B⁴; *1–3* 4–13 *14–16 blk.*
> The three distinct editions are extremely
> similar, and their order is undetermined. First
> line on p. 9 reads 'I'd have a *Premier* satisfy'd,
> if clear'; no watermark in this edition.
> 'If fell corruption in each scene appears'
> An attack on the whig ministry. Cf. *The
> contrast to the Man of honour,* 1737.
> L(11631.f.23, –B4),O,CT,LdU-B(–B4),*MR-C*;
> CtY(–B4),KU,NjP(uncut, –B4),*TxU*(uncut).

M64 — [another edition]
> First line on p. 9 reads 'I'd have a *Premier*
> satisfy'd, if clear,'; watermark: star.
> CLU-C(–B4),IU,TxHR,TxU.

M65 — [another edition]
> First line on p. 9 reads 'I'd have a Premier
> satisfy'd, if clear,'; watermark: star.
> O; CSmH(–B4),NjP,TxU(–B4).

M66 — — 'London' [*Edinburgh*], *printed in the year*
1737.
8⁰: A⁴ B²; *1–3* 4–12.
> From the ornaments, apparently printed by
> William Cheyne.
> L(1488.c.37),O,E; IU,OCU.

M67 — — To which is added the Curious females, a
tale. '*London printed: and sold by the booksellers of
London & Westminster*' [*Dublin*], 'MDXXXVII'
[1737].
8⁰: A–B⁴ C²; *1–3* 4–18 *19; 20 blk.* 19 advt.
> *The man of honour* ends on B3ᵛ with the word
> 'Finis'; possibly copies were issued without
> the additional poem, which was published
> separately as *The curious females,* [172–?]
> *Curious females*: 'Four lovely lasses, gay and
> bright'
> L(1486.e.27, lacks B4, C²),DA(lacks B4, C²),
> DG(2, 1 uncut),DN.

— The man of honour: a poem, 1733. *See*
Montagu, Charles, *earl of Halifax.*

M68 — The man of honour, or the character of a true
country man. [*Edinburgh?*] *Printed in the year* 1706.
4⁰: *A*⁴; *1–2* 3–7 *8 blk.*
> 'Not all the threats or favours of a crown'
> A reworking of the poem by Charles Montagu,

The **man** of honour

Mandeville, B. Some fables

earl of Halifax, containing a section in praise of Scotland. Written against the Union?
L(11632.df.35),E(2),*MR-C*; CtY,InU.

— The man of taste, 1733. *See* Bramston, James.

M69 Man-midwife. The man-midwife unmasqu'd: being the case of a certain young lady, who apply'd to the noted Doctor D------ for his advice... *London printed, and sold by J. Dormer*, 1733. (*GM* Sept)
2°: *A*² B²; *1–2* 3–8.
In both copies seen the date has been altered to 1738.
'Tis needless the records of time to explore'
A satire against James Douglas. Answered by *The lady's decoy*, 1733, which has the date similarly altered to 1738.
L(163.n.30); Institute for Sex Research.

[**Mandeville, Bernard.**] Wishes to a godson, with other miscellany poems. By B.M. *London, printed for J. Baker*, 1712. (6 Nov, Luttrell)
8°: pp. 38. L; TxU.

M70 [—] The grumbling hive; or, knaves turn'd honest. *London, printed for Sam. Ballard; sold by A. Baldwin*, 1705. (*DC* 2 April)
4°: *A*⁴ B–C⁴ D²; *i–ii*, 1–26.
'A spacious hive well stock'd with bees'
An allegorical verse fable, reprinted as the nucleus of Mandeville's *Fable of the bees*.
O; NNC.

M71 [—] — [col] [*London*] *Printed in the year* 1705.
4°: *A*²; *1–4*, 2 columns.
Drop-head title only. A piracy.
L(11631.f.62; C.70.f.14),C.

M72 [—] The pamphleteers. A satyr. *London, printed in the year* 1703. (9 March, Luttrell)
2°: A–C²; *1–2* 3–12.
The Luttrell copy is recorded in *Haslewood*. A ninth of the copyright, the work being attributed to Mandeville, formed part of lot 32 of the trade sale of Charles Corbett, 22 Dec 1737 (cat. at O-JJ).
'Tho' William was the care of providence'
Advertised in *FP* 17 June as 'by the author of Some fables after the familiar method of Mr. de la Fontaine'; it advertises 'Francion's comical romance' below the imprint, as does Mandeville's *Some fables*, 1703.
L(11602.i.14/1),O,LdU-B; CSmH,CtY(uncut), DFo,MH,TxU.

[—] The planter's charity, 1704. *See* P477.

M73 [—] Some fables after the easie and familiar method of Monsieur de la Fontaine. *London, printed in the year* 1703. (*WL* May)
4°: A–L⁴ M²; *i–viii*, 1–81 *82–84*. 82–84 advt.
The advertisements on pp. 82–84 are those of

Richard Wellington, who was presumably the publisher.
'An honest country-man had got'
Reissued with Mandeville's name in 1704.
L(C.57.1.18; Ashley 3615),O; ICN,MH(–M2), OCU,TxU.

M74 — [reissue] Æsop dress'd or a collection of fables writ in familiar verse. By B. Mandeville, M.D. *London, printed for Richard Wellington*, 1704. (Jan?)
4°: A⁴(±A1) ˣB–C⁴ B⁴(–B1) C–N⁴; *i–viii*, 1–16 3–95 *96*.
The original M² has been cancelled to be replaced with additional fables. Listed in *PM* 18 Jan.
L(1967),DT; *OCU*,TxU.

M75 — — *London, sold [by John Peele] at Lock's-Head adjoyning to Ludgate*, [1727?]
8°: A² B–K⁴ L²; *i–iv*, 1–75 *76*.
Listed in *PM* 6 April 1727 with other works of Mandeville, and on 18 April as available bound with *The virgin unmask'd* (in prose).
L(G.16233/2); CtY,IU,MH,*OCU*,*PU*+.

M76 [—] Typhon: or the wars between the gods and giants: a burlesque poem in imitation of the comical Mons. Scarron. *London, printed for J. Pero, & S. Illidge; sold by J. Nutt*, 1704. (*DC* 15 April)
4°: A–G⁴; *i–viii*, 1–47 *48*. 47 err; 48 advt.
'I sing a base with topping voice'
Epistle dedicatory signed 'B.M.' The preface refers to Mandeville's *Some fables*, 1703.
L(11633.e.26; Ashley 3616); *CLSU*,TxU.

M77 Mandey, —, Captain. A modest occasional ode. By Captain Mandey. [*London*] '*Printed for Charles Trueman, near St. James's*', 1749. (*GM* Dec)
4°: A–C²; *1–2* 3–11 *12 blk.*
The publisher is clearly pseudonymous, despite the fact that the pamphlet was publicly advertised. The printing uses no identifiable ornaments.
'Shall every circling year'
A Jacobite poem in praise of the Young Pretender. In the circumstances one would expect the author to be pseudonymous, but one might suspect a link with Captain Richard Manley (*see* S785).
CtY,CU.

M78 Mandragora. Mandragora; or, the quacks: a poem, in two canto's. *London, printed in the year* 1717. (8 July)
8°: A–O⁴; *1–3* 4–111 *112 blk.*
Subscriptions invited in *PM* 27 June; advertised in *PM* 11 July as published on 8 July.
'Near Essex, fost'ring nurse of Lion'
L(1162.g.15); DNLM.

M79 — — The second edition. *London printed, and sold by John Morphew*, 1718. (*PB* 8 Feb)
8°: A⁴(±A1) B–O⁴; *1–3* 4–111 *112 blk.*

Mandragora

A reissue with cancel title-leaf.
DFo.

M80 — [reissue] The devil and the doctor; or, the tragi-comic consultation: an anthypochondriac satyr, for suppressing the turgent bile of the quacks. By Doctor Byfielde. *London printed, and sold by J. Bettenham*, 1719. (Feb, Luttrell)
8°: A⁴(±A1) B–O⁴; *1–3* 4–111 *112 blk.* 2 err.

Apparently reissued with this title to take advantage of the controversy caused by the publication of John Woodward's *State of physick*, 1718. The pseudonym 'Dr. Byfielde' was used by John Freind in his *Letter to the learned Dr. Woodward*, 1719, but this is almost certainly an unauthorized use of it, and it is doubtful whether the poem originally concerned Woodward.
L(1077.k.16; 161.l.19, Luttrell),CT,LdU-B.

[Manley, Richard.] A summer voyage to the gulph of Venice, 1750. *See* S785.

M81 **Manlius.** Manlius; or the brave adventurer. A poetical novel. '*Edinburgh, printed by Donald Murchieson, for Fergus Philabeg, near the Royal Exchange*' [*London?*], 1749.
4°: A² B–F²; *1–2* 3–24.

Almost certainly printed in London with a false imprint.
'Arms and the man renown'd, who last from — [France]'
A Jacobite poem, in praise of the Young Pretender.
E,GM,*LdU-B*(ms. notes).

Manners. The manners of the age, 1733. *See* Newcomb, Thomas.

M82 **Manners, Henry.** The linnet and goldfinch. A fable. Addressed to James Digges-Latouche, esq; *London printed: and, Dublin: re-printed by Richard James*, 1750. (April?)
8°: A⁴ B⁴; *1–2* 3–16.

No London edition traced.
'That man is made by nature free'
A eulogy of Digges-Latouche.
L(11631.bb.58),O,DA(ms. date, April),*LdU-B*.

Manning, Francis. Poems on several occasions and to several persons. *London, printed by G. Croom, for R. Tuckyr*, 1701.
8°: pp. 85, 68. EU,LdU-B; DFo,MH.
Watermark: ? grapes.

— [fine paper] E.
Watermark: fleur-de-lys; the copy seen is the dedication copy to Mary Chambers.

[—] Poems written at different times on several occasions, by a gentleman who resided many years abroad in the two last reigns with a publick character. *London, printed by John Watts*, 1752.
4°: pp. 267. L; CSmH,MH.

Manning, F.

Early ms. attribution to Manning in the L copy.

M83 [—] The adventures of Telemachus, son of Ulysses. The first book. Translated from the original French prose into English verse. *London, printed by J. Watts; sold by J. Roberts*, 1738.
4°: A–E⁴; *1–5* 6–39 *40 blk.*
'Ulysses fled, the darling of her breast'
Reprinted in Manning's *Poems*, 1752. Presumably from Fénelon's *Télémaque*.
MH(uncut).

M84 [—] The British hero; or the vision. A poem. Sacred to the immortal memory of John late duke of Marlborough... *London, printed for Fran. Clay; sold by J. Roberts*, 1733. (*GSJ* 22 May)
2°: a–b² A–L²; *i–viii, 1* 2–44.
Most copies have an errata slip on p. viii.
'What Europe owes to Marlborough's martial flame'
Reprinted in Manning's *Poems*, 1752.
C; CSmH,CtY,DFo(no errata),ICN.

M85 [—] An essay on the vicious bent and taste of the times. In an epistle to the right honourable Sir Robert Walpole. *London printed, and sold by J. Roberts*, 1737. (*GM,LM* May)
2°: A² B–E²; *1–3* 4–19 *20 blk.*
Rothschild 211.
'While now four lusters at the helm of state'
Reprinted in Manning's *Poems*, 1752.
CtY,NN-B,NjP.

M86 [—] The muse an advocate for injur'd merit. In an epistle to the right honourable Sir Robert Walpole. *London, printed for J. Roberts*, 1734. (*GSJ* 12 Jan)
2°: A² B–D² (D1 as 'C'); *1–2* 3–16.
'Whence comes it, Walpole, that a soul, like thine'
Reprinted in Manning's *Poems*, 1752.
CSmH,MH.

M87 [—] Of business and retirement. A poem. Address'd to the British Atticus. *London, printed for John Watts*, 'MDCXXXV' [1735]. (*GSJ* 24 Jan)
4°: A–F⁴; *1–3* 4–46 *47; 48 blk.* 47 err.
'Is there a man, whose genius and whose fate'
Reprinted in Manning's *Poems*, 1752.
L(11633.f.45; 11630.c.14/20; 11630.d.12/6, Tom's Coffee House, 24 Jan),O,CT,DT,LdU-B; CSmH(uncut),CtY,ICN,MH,NjP(uncut)+.

M88 [—] Of levity and steadiness. A poem. In an epistle to a friend, who was in doubt what course to take in difficult times. *London printed, and sold by J. Roberts*, 1735. (*GM* April)
4°: A⁴ B–C⁴ D²; *1–5* 6–27 *28 blk.*
The copy at CSmH is apparently variant, having no price after the imprint.
'When worth, like yours, with native candour join'd'
Reprinted in Manning's *Poems*, 1752.
L(840.k.3/3),O,EP; CSmH,CtY,IU,MH,OCU.

Manning, F.

M89 [—] On the late queen's sickness and death, an ode. Address'd to his grace the Duke of Newcastle... *London, printed for T. Cooper*, 1738. (*GM,LM* Jan)
4⁰: A–B⁴; *i–ii* iii–vi, 7–16.
'Say, muse, if sighs will give thee leave'
        Reprinted in Manning's *Poems*, 1752.
L(11630.d.12/15; 11631.g.30/4).

M90 — The shrine. A poem, sacred to the memory of King William III. *London, printed for Bernard Lintott*, 1702. (10 July, Luttrell)
4⁰: A–D⁴; *i–viii*, 1–23 *24 blk.*
        Listed in *WL* July.
'Farewel thou last and greatest of thy race'
L(161.1.83, Luttrell),LDW,O.

M91 [—] The two first odes of Horace imitated. With an introductory epistle to a friend. *London printed, and sold by J. Roberts*, 1738. (*GM,LM* Feb)
2⁰: *A*² B–D²; *1–3* 4–15 *16 blk.*
'Walpole, who com'st of ancient race'
'Of hail, and snow, and stormy rain'
        Reprinted in Manning's *Poems*, 1752.
O,LdU-B; CSmH,CtY,IU(uncut),MH,TxU.

Manning, Robert.
A letter of William Duckett to George Duckett, 11 Nov 1714, in The letters of Thomas Burnet to George Duckett *(1914) 238 refers to 'Rob. Manning's Collections of Songs' as recently published. They have not been traced, but were probably song-books with music, and hence outside the scope of this catalogue. Two ballads by Manning are referred to in a letter of 2 Aug 1713.*

M92 Mantua. The mantua-makers a poem. [*Dublin?* 172–?]
½⁰: 1 side, 1 column.
'Attend ye youths, with minds retentive'
        A bawdy piece on two sisters, Sarah and Nancy.
CLU-C.

Mantuan, Baptista Spagnuoli, *called.*
Bewick, William: Faustus, Fortunatus, and Amyntas: or, three eclogues of Baptist Mantuan, 1718. *See* B208.

— Alphus: or, the fourth eclogue of Baptist Mantuan, 1718. *See* B207.

M93 Marchetti, Alessandro. Di Tito Lucrezio Caro Della natura delle cose libri sei. Tradotti da Alessandro Marchetti... Prima edizione. *Londra, per Giovanni Pickard*, 1717.
8⁰: (frt+) A–Cc⁸ Dd⁴; *i–xvi*, 1–400 *401–408. 408* err.
        No watermark, countermark in corner.
'Alma figlia di Giove inclita madre'
        Marchetti was a Pisan who died in 1714. The dedication is signed 'P. Antinoo Rullo', pseudonym of Paolo Rolli.
L(998.1.11); CtY,IU.

Marchetti, A. Di Tito Lucrezio Caro

M94 — [fine paper]
        Watermark: Strasburg bend.
L(77.e.9,–frt),O.

Margaret. Margaret and William, [1723/30.] *See* Mallet, David [William and Margaret].

M95 — Margaret Dickson's penetential confession. [*Edinburgh*, 1724.]
½⁰: 1 side, 2 columns.
'What former friend may ease my troubled thought'
E(ms. date 1724).

Margarita. Margarita regina et diva Scotorum, [1713.] *See* Pitcairne, Archibald.

Maria. Maria Lodoix Stuarta, ad Alaricam Suecam, [1712/13.] *See* Pitcairne, Archibald.

[**M96** = M475·5] Maria or the picture of a certain young lady, 1730. See Morrice, Bezaleel [Astrea: or, the composition].

Marinda. Marinda. Poems and translations upon several occasions, 1716. *See* Monk, Mary.

M97 Markland, George. A divine poem, in memory of the late high wind. *London, printed for William Colson, bookseller in Winchester, and are to be sold by J. Nutt*, 1705. (15 Feb)
2⁰: *A*² B–D²; *i–iv*, 1–12.
        The Luttrell copy is recorded in *Haslewood* as '15 Jan'. Advertised in *PM* 17 Feb as published 'on Thursday last', i.e. 15 Feb.
'We slept: that was the hour th' almighty took'
O,*MR-C*; CtY.

M98 — Pteryplegia: or, the art of shooting-flying. A poem. *London printed, and sold by J. Roberts*, 1717. (*PM* 31 Jan)
8⁰: A–E⁴; [2] *i–v* vi, 1–32.
        There are variant states of sheet A, one with p. iii unnumbered, and without errata (CtY, TxU), the other with p. iii numbered and errata on p. vi (OW,CtY).
'Silent and grey the morning's dawn appear'd'
        Commonly ascribed to Abraham Markland (1645–1728), following *Nichols* VIII. 504, but clearly by his son George since he is described as 'Mr. Markland, A.B.'; Abraham was M.A. and D.D.
OW; CtY(2),TxU.

M99 —— *London, printed for Stephen Austen*, 1727. (*MC* Feb)
8⁰: *A*⁴ B–E⁴; [4] *i* ii–iv, *1* 2–32. A1ᵛ advt.
        Many copies have a four-leaf catalogue of Austen's books, signed A⁴, at end.
L(11631.e.40),O(–A1),E,DN(lacksA⁴),LdU-B+; CtY(2, 1 uncut).

M100 —— *London: printed, and Dublin reprinted by S. Powell, for Philip Crampton*, 1727.

Markland, G. Pteryplegia

8⁰: *A*⁴ B⁴ C²; [2] *i* ii–iii *iv*, *1* 2–14.
L(12274.e.1/3),C,DK; CtY,MiU.

M101 —— The second edition. *London, printed for T. Astley*, 1735. (*LM* July)
8⁰: *A*⁴(−A1,2 +A2) B–E⁴ *F*¹; [2] *i* ii–iv, *1* 2–32 [2]. F1 advt.

> A reissue of the London 1727 edition with a cancel title and an advertisement leaf. Ackers's ledger records 'printing 1000 title quarter sheets' under 24 July 1735. In the only copy seen which includes the advertisement leaf, it is bound after E4, and it has been assumed that this was the intention.

L(11631.d.34,−F1); CtY(2, 1−F1).

M102 — Pteryaplegia [!]... *Dublin, printed by and for Oliver Nelson, and for William Powell*, 1747.
12⁰: A–B⁶; [4] *i* ii–iv, *1* 2–15 *16 blk*. A1 hft.
DA,DN(2).

Markland, John.
This John Markland is probably to be identified with the John Markland who signs the dedication of Typographia: an ode on printing (*Williamsburg, printed by William Parks, 1730*) *and who is almost certainly the attorney of New Kent among the subscribers to the* Collected Acts of Virginia, *1733. See J. A. Leo Lemay,* A poem by John Markland of Virginia (*Williamsburg, 1965*).

[—] Cythereia: or, new poems upon love and intrigue... *London, printed for E. Curll, & T. Payne*, 1723. (*EvP* 6 April)
8⁰: pp. 112.   L; CtY,MH.

> *Griffith* 139. Although this may be considered a miscellany (*Case* 327), the first half was written by Markland; see Curll's receipt at L (Add. MS. 38728, fol. 141) for 'The Fryar's Tale, the Retaliation, & other poems...' Printed by Samuel Richardson (*Sale* 13).

———

M103 — An ode on the happy birth of the young princess. Humbly inscrib'd to his royal highness the prince. *London, printed for T. Payne*, 1723. (*MC* March)
2⁰: *A*² B–C²; *1–3* 4–11 *12 blk*.
'The godlike man who dares'
CSmH(Luttrell, March).

M104 [—] Three new poems. Viz. I. Family duty: or, the monk and the merchant's wife. Being the shipman's tale from Chaucer. Moderniz'd. II. The curious wife...by Mr. Fenton. Moderniz'd. III. Buckingham-house, a poem... *London, printed for E. Curll*, 1721. (*DP* 15 May)
8⁰: *A*¹ B–E⁴ F⁴(−F1?), ²B–D⁴; *i–ii*, *1* 2–37 *38 blk*, 1–24. 24 err.

> *Buckingham-house* occupies ²B–D⁴; it may previously have been separately published. Copies of the whole (less title-leaf) were reissued in *The altar of love*, 1727 (L,MH), and are recorded below.

Markland, J. Three new poems

Family duty: 'Whilome a merchant at St. Dennis liv'd'
Curious wife: 'There liv'd in Derby, near the Peak'
Buckingham-house: 'Of that fam'd British structure fain I'd write'

> A Curll advertisement in *A compleat key to the Dunciad... second edition*, 1728, attributed 'the tales from Chaucer' to Mr. Markland and *Buckingham-house* to William Bond. *Nichols* IV. 272f. wrongly identifies Markland as Jeremiah; a Curll receipt to John is recorded above under *Cythereia*, 1723.

L(1963, lacks A1),O(lacks ²B–D⁴); MH(lacks A1).

Marlborides. Marlborides, sive bellum Britannicum, 1707. *See* Harris, Joseph.

Marlborough. Marlborough, a poem in three cantos, 1722. *See* Cooke, Thomas.

M105 — Marlborough: a poem; occasion'd by the exploits of that famous general. *Dublin, printed by S. Powell, for Thomas Shepheard*, 1706.
2⁰: *A*² B–G²; *i–iv*, *1*–23 *24 blk*. A1 hft.
'The taking one poor town in ten years time'
C(uncut).

M106 — Marlborough remov'd, or, the down-fall of a great favourite. With a true list of all the new promotions and removals at court. *London printed and re-printed in Dublin*, 1711–12.
½⁰: 1 side, 1 column.
'When seventeen hundred is join'd to two ones'
DT.

M107 **Marquis.** The Marquis of Huntly's retreat from the battle of Sheriff Moor. [*Edinburgh*, 1715?]
½⁰: 1 side, 2 columns.
'From Bogie side to Bogie gight'
> A satire on the cowardice of the Jacobite Alexander Gordon, subsequently duke of Gordon.

Sotheby's 18 Oct 1961, lot 1328.

M108 — [another edition, title reads:] The Marquis of Huntlie's retreat... [*Edinburgh*, 1715?]
½⁰: 1 side, 2 columns.
L(1876.f.1/77).

Marriage. Marriage. A poetical essay, 1748. *See* Shiells, Robert.

M109 — Marriage; a satire: with two satires on love and old age. *London, printed for J. Roberts*, 1728. (*MChr* 2 July)
8⁰: *A*⁴ B–F⁴; *1–4* 5–47 *48 blk*. 37 err.
> A2 and E4 are fly-titles to the two sections, the second containing the two satires.

'What, dames, who so well the world has known'
> A satire against women.

L(1486.b.16),O; CSmH,*MB,MiU*.

M110 — Marriage a-la-mode: an humorous tale, in six canto's, in hudibrastic verse; being an explanation

Marriage a-la-mode

of the six prints lately published by the ingenious Mr. Hogarth. *London, printed for Weaver Bickerton,* 1746. (10 Feb)

8°: *A*² B–H⁴ I²; *i–iii* iv, *1–59* 60 blk.

> Horizontal chain-lines. R. E. Moore, *Hogarth's literary relationships* (1948) dates publication as 10 Feb; listed in *GM, LM* Feb.

'Social nuptial ties, 'tis said'

L(1489.pp.23); CtY(uncut),MH.

— Marriage dialogues, 1709. *See* Ward, Edward.

M111 — Marriage is honourable. Epithalamium, a wedding-poem upon the illustrious matrimony [blank] *Edinburgh, printed for the author,* 1738.

½°: 1 side, 2 columns.

> A printed form, bordered and divided by type flowers and with a small woodcut in the centre of the space for the title. The copy seen is completed in ms. for the marriage of James Smollet of Bonhill, advocate, and Jean Clerk, daughter of Sir John Clerk of Pennecuik, and dated 25 Jan 1740. There is a final note 'Let me know if this may be printed and published'.

Scottish Record Office (GD18/4417).

M112 — The marriage of Venus. *London, printed for M. Cooper,* 1750. (*GM* June)

8°: *A*¹ B–C⁴ ²C⁴; *1–3* 4–26.

'The heavenly contest, and award of Jove'

NjP.

M113 — — *Dublin, printed by S. Powell, for J. Hamilton,* 1750.

8°: A–C⁴; *1–3* 4–24.

DA,DK.

M114 **Marrow.** The marrow of the Tickler's works, or, three shillings worth of wit for a penny. In a ballad. (To the tune of Derry-down.) [*Dublin*] *Printed in the year* 1748.

8°: A⁸ (A1ᵛ as 'A2', A2ᵛ as 'A3'); *i* ii–xvi.

'Ye pedants, quacks, block-heads, and coffee-house smarts'

> The dedication signed 'Scriblerus'. A satire on Paul Hiffernan's *Ticklers* and his *Reflections on the structure and passions of man,* 1748.

L(11631.e.82),O,C.

M115 **Marsh, Charles.** 'A poem on Christmas-day. [*London*] *Sold by J. Roberts.* Price 6d.' (*LM* Dec 1736)

M116 — A poetical epistle. Humbly inscrib'd to —— anybody. *London, printed for Charles Marsh, at Cicero's Head in Round Court, in the Strand,* 1741. (*GM,LM* May)

2°: *A*² B–D²; *1–2* 3–16.

> Title in half-title form. Also listed in *GM,LM* Jan 1742. Printed by Samuel Richardson (*Sale* 278).

'Apollo's deity of verse'

CtY,DFo.

Martial

Martial. Martial reviv'd: or, epigrams, satyrical, panegyrical, political, moral, elegiacal, whimsical, and comical. Above one hundred in number... With a preface in defence of epigram, and merry fellows. *London, printed for Tho. Atkins,* [1722.] (*DJ* 26 Jan)

8°: pp. 31.   L,C; DFo.

M117 **Martin.** The martin and the oyster: or, the Alsatia amour. A ballad. By the author of L——p's ballad. *London, printed for A. Moore,* 1727. (Dec, Luttrell)

½°: 1 side, 2 columns.

'Tho' the martin is a summer bird'

> An erotic tale, possibly with reference to Le Heup's exploits. For 'L——p's ballad' see L94.3.

L(11602.i.6); MH(Luttrell).

Martin, Thomas. Imitations and translations of several odes of Horace: being an essay towards a translation of that part of the author's works. *London, printed for the author, and sold by the following booksellers, T. Astley; Mary & James Fletcher, in Oxon; B. Collins & E. Easton, in Sarum; and W. Pitt, in Blandford,* 1743. (*GM* May)

8°: pp. 52.   L.

— Poems on several occasions. *London, printed for and sold by J. Roberts; E. Easton at Sarum; W. Pitt at Blandford, and T. Langford at Warminster,* 1745.

8°: pp. 121.   O.

M118 [—] Captain John Peddie: an heroic poem...By a gentleman, late of Baliol College, in Oxford. *London, printed for the author,* 1741.

2°: *A*² B²; *1–3* 4–8.

> Horizontal chain-lines.

'While homeward bound brave Peddie makes his way'

> Ascribed to Martin by *Rawlinson,* 'on a sea fight between the said captain and a Spanish privateer which he took'.

L(1973); MH,IU.

M119 — A poem on the late action at Dettingen. Humbly inscribed to his majesty. *London, printed for Edward Easton, bookseller in Sarum; sold by James Roberts,* 1743. (*GM,LM* Dec)

4°: *A*² B–E²; *i–iv,* 1 *2*–14 15; 16 blk. A1 hft; 15 advt.

'The sacred nine, your aid once more impart'

MH,NjP.

M120 [—] A poem on the war in the West-Indies under Admiral Vernon. By a country curate. *London, printed for T. Astley,* [1742.] (*LEP* 19 Jan)

8°: A⁴ B(4 ll) C¹; *1–3* 4–18.

> The collation of B is irregular. In the copy at RPJCB B3 and B4 are said to be conjugate, while B1 and probably B2 are cancels. In the copy at L, B2 is clearly a cancel, but the relationship of the other leaves is obscure. Listed in *GM,LM* Jan; *LM* notes it is 'sold by B. Collins in Salisbury'.

Martin, T. A poem on the war

'Assist, my muse, brave Vernon's acts rehearse'
Reprinted in Martin's *Poems*, 1745.
L(11631.d.56, Tom's Coffee House, 19 Jan),O;
CtY,*RPJCB*.

'**Marvell, A.,** *junior*.' Satyrical and panegyrical
instructions to Mr. William Hogarth, 1740. *See*
S78.

M121 [**Marvell, Andrew.**] A dialogue between two noted
horses. *Dublin, printed in the year* 1736.
8°: *A*⁴; *1–2* 3–8.
'We read, in profane and sacred records'
According to Margoliouth's edition of Marvell
I. 317, 'ascribed to Marvell in all issues of
State Poems but in none of the manuscripts. It
is probably Marvell's'. Included here because
of its anonymity; it has been taken for an
eighteenth-century poem.
O,DA; PP.

M122 Mary. Mary Queen, of Scots dowary, when,
married to the Douphine of France. [*Edinburgh*,
1711.] (Feb?)
4°: *A*⁶; *1–2* 3–11 *12 blk*.
Wing M895 as [1700?], copying an error of
the L catalogue. Title in half-title form.
'What sudden heat inspires my lab'ring mind?'
A translation of George Buchanan's 'Francesci
Valesii et Mariae Stuartae regum Franciae &
Scotiae, epithalamium'.
L(11632.df.34),E(ms. date Feb 1711).

M123 Mason, William. Isis. An elegy. Written in the
year 1748, by Mr. Mason. *London, printed for
R. Dodsley; sold by M. Cooper*, 1749. (6 Feb)
4°: *A*⁴ B⁴; *1–6* 7–16. A1 hft.
Gaskell, Mason 2. Date from *Straus, Dodsley*.
A 'second edition' was advertised in *GA* 23
Feb; possibly it was an undifferentiated
impression.
'Far from her hallow'd grot, where mildly bright'
See *Cam and Isis*, 1749, and [Thomas Warton]
The triumph of Isis, [1750.]
L(11602.gg.24/17; 643.k.6/1; 161.m.3,–A1;
C.116.c.2/2),O(3),C(–A1),CT(–A1),E+;CSmH,
CtY(2),ICN(uncut),*MH*,TxU(2, 1–A1)+.

M124 [—] Musæus: a monody to the memory of Mr.
Pope, in imitation of Milton's Lycidas. *London,
printed for R. Dodsley; sold by M. Cooper*, 1747.
(*GA* 16 April)
4°: *A*⁴ B–C⁴; *1–4* 5–22 *23–24*. A1 hft; C4 advt.
Imprint reads 'M. Cooper in Pater-noster-
Row'; last line of p. 17 reads 'poetry'.
Gaskell, Mason 1; *Rothschild* 1393. Gaskell's
account was corrected by W. B. Todd in
PBSA 46 (1952) 397–8, and I follow his order
of editions here hesitantly; the evidence is
very slight and he was unaware that the
following was partly reset.
'Sorrowing I catch the reed, and call the muse'

Mason, W. Musaeus

Printed as Mason's in *Dodsley* III, and the
third edition published with Mason's name.
L(11632.g.61/2; 11641.g.59/1,–A1, C4),LdU-B;
CSmH,CtY,IU,MiU,TxU(2)+.

M125 [—] [another edition]
Imprint reads 'M. Cooper in Pater-noster-
Row'; last line of p. 17 reads 'Poetry'. The
inner forme of B and the outer of C are reset;
otherwise from standing type.
LVA-D,O; MH(–C4).

M126 [—] [another edition]
Imprint reads 'M. Cooper at the Globe'.
L(643.k.5/8,–A1, C4;   644.k.17/3,–A1, C4),
O,C;   ICN(–A1), ICU(–A1,C4),KU,MH(2, 1
uncut).

M127 —— By Mr. Mason. The third edition. *London,
printed for R. Dodsley; sold by M. Cooper*, 1748.
(*GA* 2 April)
4°: *A*⁴ B–C⁴; *1–5* 6–22 *23–24*. A1 hft; C4 advt.
L(12273.m.1/20,–A1),LVA-D(–C4),O(2,
1–A1),EU,*NeU*; CtY,ICU(2),KU,MH,TxU(2,
1–A1, 1–C4)+.

M128 [—] — *Dublin, printed for Edward & John Exshaw*,
1748.
8°: A–B⁴; *1–3* 4–15 *16 blk*.
DA; CSmH.

M129 — Ode performed in the Senate-house at Cam-
bridge July 1, 1749… *Cambridge, printed by J.
Bentham printer to the University*, 1749.
4°: π² < *⁴; *i–ii*, *1–2* 3–8 *9–10 blk*. π1 hft.
Gaskell, Mason 3; *Rothschild* 1394. Printed on
very good paper, presumably for presentation
at Cambridge.
'Here all thy active fires diffuse'
L(840.1.4/2,–π²),O(–π²),CT(–π²),BaP(–π²),
LdU(–π²)+; KU,PU,TxU(–π²).

M130 —— *Cambridge, printed by J. Bentham; sold by
W. Thurlbourn, Cambridge; and R. Dodsley, London*, 1749. (*GM,LM* July)
4°: π² < *⁴; *i–ii*, *1–2* 3–8 *9–10 blk*. π1 hft.
Rothschild 1395. Apparently another impression
for publication. In most copies Thurlbourn's
name in the imprint is set in full capitals; in a
variant state in two copies at L it is set in small
capitals.
L(11771.h.1/2,–π²; 11630.b.3/4,–π2; C.116.
c.2/3,–π²),O(–π²); CLU,CtY,ICN,MH(–π²),
TxU(–π²)+.

Masonry. Masonry: a poem, 1739. *See* Leslie,
Charles.

M131 Masquerade. The masquerade. A poem. *London,
printed for, and sold by J. Roberts*, 1724. (May,
Luttrell)
2°: *A*² B² C¹; *1–3* 4–10.
The Luttrell copy is recorded in Pickering &
Chatto cat. 284/499.
'Resolv'd to sing the midnight sport'
A satire on Heydegger's masquerades.
L(11661.dd.8); CSmH(uncut),IU,MH,OCU.

Masquerade

— The masquerade. A poem. Humbly inscribed to his grace the Duke d'Aumont, 1713. *See* Centlivre, Susanna.

— The masquerade. A poem. Inscrib'd to C—t H—d—g—r, 1728. *See* Fielding, Henry.

M132 — The masquerade plot. A ballad. [*London?* 1716?]
slip: 1 side, 1 column.
'Have ye heard of a plot to destroy the poor king'
A Jacobite satire on this false alarm.
CSmH.

M133 Massalina. Massalina: or; the town mistris in masquerade. *London, printed by John Still, 1707.*
8°: A⁸; *1–4* 5–16.
'Welcome to town, thou most esteem'd of friends'
CLU-C,OCU.

M134 — [another issue] The cloyster in Bartholomew Fair; or, the town-mistress disguis'd. A poem. *London, printed for A. Banks, 1707.*
8°: A⁸; *1–4* 5–16.
No sign of a cancel title in the copy seen, but the drop-head title on p. 5 'Massalina' suggests that was the original form.
ICN.

Massey, William. Musa paraenetica; or, a tractate of Christian epistles, on sundry occasions, in verse, *London, printed by the assigns of J. Sowle, 1717.*
8°: pp. xiv, 66.   L,LF; CtY,DFo.

—— The second edition... To which is added, an epistle of advice... *London printed, and sold by T. Sowle Raylton & Luke Hinde, 1746.*
8°: pp. xiv, 63.   LF; IU,MH.

———————

M135 — Synopsis sacerrima: or, an epitomy, of the holy scriptures, in English verse. Chiefly design'd for children, to be got by heart when they have learn'd to read. *London printed, and sold by the assigns of J. Sowle, 1719.*
8°: A⁸; *1–2* 3–16.
'The eternal god, at first by power divine'
LF(2, 1 uncut),C.

M136 [**Masters, George.**] A poem humbly inscribed to his royal highness the Duke of Cumberland, on his defeat of the rebels at Culloden, April 16, 1746. *London, printed for J. Hinton, 1747.* (*BM* April)
4°: π¹ A–H² I¹; *1–3* 4–36.
'The rout and slaughter of that savage band'
CtY.

M136·1 —— By George Masters. *London, printed for the author, 1747.*
4°: π¹ A–H² I¹; *1–3* 4–36.
Apparently an issue for private circulation, adding the author's name and changing the imprint; possibly on fine paper, though no watermark has been seen in either issue.
O.

Masters, M.

Masters, Mary. Poems on several occasions. *London, printed by T. Browne, 1733.*
8°: pp. 267.   L,O; CtY,MH.
Copy in presentation morocco, *Rothschild* 1402.

Match. The match, a poem, [1730?] *See* Dalacourt, James.

— A match at foot-ball, 1720–. *See* Concanen, Matthew.

[**Mather, John.**] Poverties coat turn'd by a taylor in Hamilton, [1702/14?] *See* P1008.

M137 [**Mathison, Thomas.**] The goff. An heroi-comical poem. In three cantos. *Edinburgh, printed by J. Cochran and company, 1743.* (*SM* May)
8°: π¹ A–B⁴ C⁴(–C1); *i–ii*, *1–2* 3–22. π1 hft.
Bond 180.
'Goff, and the man, I sing, who, em'lous, plies'
Attributed to Mathison by *Halkett & Laing* from E. A mock-heroic poem on golf.
L(11631. aaa. 56/20),O,E(with ms. key),GM(–π1); CtY.

Matrimonial. Matrimonial scenes, 1750. *See* Jackson, Andrew.

Matrimony. Matrimony; or, good advice to the ladies to keep single, 1739. *See* Good advice, 1702–.

M138 — Matrimony, pro and con: or, the resolve. *London, printed for M. Cooper, 1745.* (*DA* 24 April)
2°: A² B–D²; *i–iii* iv, *1* 2–12.
'Not marry! friend? why 'tis the life of life'
L(11631.k.5/10),O; ICN,KU,MH,TxU(uncut).

— Matrimony unmask'd, 1710. *See* Ward, Edward [Marriage dialogues].

M139 [**Maty, Matthew.**] Ode sur la rébellion de MDCCXLV. en Écosse. *A Amsterdam, chez Jean Joubert, 1746.*
8°: A⁸; *1–3* 4–15 *16 blk.*
'D'où partent ces coups de tonnerre'
Attributed to Maty by the L catalogue; since he was subsequently principal librarian, the attribution is presumably reliable. Maty was apparently domiciled in England by this date.
L(839.c.37).

M140 '**Maurus, Richardus.**' The Pretender's declaration, which was found amongst other papers on board the Salusbury; and since, at the request of a certain lord in the Tower, turn'd into verse, to gain new proselytes, by the most ingenious Richardo Mauro. *London, printed in the year 1708.*
8°: A⁴; *1–2* 3–7 *8 blk.*
'When we reflect what desolation'
'Richardus Maurus' is clearly intended for Sir Richard Blackmore; the attribution to him is satirical. Cf. F170.
LVA-F.

Mawer, J.

Mawer, John. Miscellaneous essays in verse and prose. With translations from the Greek, Latin, French, Italian, and Spanish poets. *Newcastle printed, and sold by Mess. J. & P. Knapton, London; Mr Crownfield in Cambridge; and Mr Hildyard in York,* [1743?]

12º: pp. 99, 92+.   NeA(lacks title); ICN.

A second edition of *The progress of language* dated 1743 and followed by miscellaneous poems, to which are added various reissues.

— [fine paper, in 8º]   O.

M141 — The coronation: a panegyrical poem to the queen. *London, printed in the year* 1727.

4º: A–B⁴; *1–3* 4–16.

Possibly not issued separately; see *An epistle to the king* below.

'As angels, in their first unsettled state'

L(1490.ee.56/2),O,DrU; KU.

M142 [—] An epistle humbly address'd to the right honourable the Earl of Oxford, &c. With a discourse on the usefulness, and some proposals, of a supplement to Bishop Walton's Polyglott Bible... To which is added, an address to the...University of Cambridge... *York, printed by Tho. Gent; sold by Mr. Hildyard, York; Mr. Prevost, Mr. Gyles, London; and by Mr. Ryles in Hull,* [1732?]

8º: A–H⁴; *1–2* 3–62 *63–64 blk.* 2 advt.

Watermark: GF. Pp. 3–41 are occupied by the proposals in prose; the 'Epistle' is on p. 43 and the 'Address' on p. 57. The work is included here because the verse epistle is mentioned first in the title. Listed in R. Davies *A memoir of the York press* (1868) 181 as 1735; but the epistle is dated 24 Nov 1731 and the advertisement is for *A layman's faith,* 1732.

Epistle: 'As when by some chance-thought, or force of wit'

Address: 'If right of birth is wont to name an heir'

Attributed to Mawer by Davies. A copy at YM is in a presentation volume with other tracts by Mawer.

L(4999.bb.17; G.20055),YM.

M143 [—] [fine paper]

Watermark: fleur-de-lys on shield.

YM(2).

M144 — An epistle to the king, on his majesty's most happy accession to the throne. *London, printed in the year* 1727.

4º: A–B⁴; *1–3* 4–16.

The copy at DrU is preceded by π²; π1 is blank except for a ms. note 'ex dono au⟨toris⟩', π2 is a half-title 'An epistle to the king... And, the coronation...'; it is followed by *The coronation.* Possibly all copies of both poems were thus issued together.

'Whilst Europe, waiting for the great event'

L(1490.ee.56/1),O,DrU(presentation copy); KU.

M145 [—] [dh] The happy reign. An eclogue. Imitated from Calpurnius Siculus, and inscrib'd to a person of honour. [*York?* 173–.]

8º: A⁴; *1–5* 6–7; *8 blk.*

Pp. 6–7 contain a Latin inscription for her majesty's grotto and an English translation of it. The two copies seen appear to be on different paper, the finer bearing the countermark IV.

'Why, Celadon, so museful and so still'

The copies at YM are bound in presentation volumes with other tracts by Mawer.

YM(2).

M146 — Liberty asserted: or, the siege of Gibraltar. A poem written as an essay in the spirit of Lucan. *London printed, and sold by J. Roberts, and W. Thurlbourn in Cambridge,* 1727. (*MC* Dec)

8º: A⁴ B–C⁸ D⁴ E¹; *i–viii, 1–3* 4–42.

'Indulgent pow'r! whose all-surveying eyes'

L(992.h.8/1, presentation copy),O.

M147 — Oppian's Cynegeticks. Translated into English verse. *York, printed by Thomas Gent; sold by T. Osborne, F. Gyles, & L. Gilliver, London; also by J. Hildyard, York,* 1736. (*GM* May)

8º: (frt+) π² A–H⁴; *i–vi, 1* 2–24, [2] *1–6, 1–4, 1–23, 1–3.* π1 hft.

Watermark: initials IK. The volume also includes 'A poem humbly inscrib'd to the queen' with title on D2, proposals for 'The book of psalms, and Solomon's song' on E2–3, a letter to Sir Robert Walpole beginning on E4, and the life of Oppian on H3ᵛ–H4.

'To thee, auspicious prince! I sing these lays'

To the queen: 'From scenes of blood, and war's destructive deeds'

Mawer's name is found in the proposals and elsewhere.

LVA-D(−π1),YM(2, 1 uncut, −π1); CtY.

M148 — [fine paper]

Watermark: fleur-de-lys on shield.

L(11335.c.31); MH.

M149 — The progress of language, an essay, wherein is prov'd the first language: occasion'd by his majesty's bounty and encouragement of modern languages. *London, printed for John Clarke,* 1726. (*MC* Sept)

2º: A² B–H²; *i–iv, 1* 2–27 *28 blk* (6,7 as '7,6'). iv err.

Reprinted in Mawer's *Miscellaneous essays,* [1743?] as 'The second edition'.

'When god first, temp'ring mortar, moulded man' Dedication signed.

AdU; MH,TxU.

M150 [—] Verses to the right reverend father in god, Edward, lord bishop of Durham. With an essay towards restoring the original texts of scripture... *London, printed for T. Payne,* 1731. (*GSJ* 1 May)

8º: A² B–D⁴ E²; *i–iv, 1–27 28 blk.* A1 hft.

Verse on pp. 1–12, prose essay pp. 13–27.

'As in some northern region wrapt in night'

M151–8

Mawer, J. Verses

> Attributed to Mawer in R. Davies, *A memoir of the York press* (1868) 182. The copies at YM are in presentation volumes with other Mawer tracts.
>
> *LdU-B,*YM(2).

Maximianus, Etruscus. The impotent lover describ'd in six elegies on old-age. In imitation of Cornelius Gallus [or rather Maximianus Etruscus], 1718. *See* I14.

Maxwell, James. Divine miscellanies; or, sacred poems. In two parts. *Birmingham, printed for the author, by T. Warren, jun.,* 1756.
12°.   BP.

> Some of the poems were clearly written in the seventeen-forties.

M151 Maxwell, John. The reflection. A poem. *York, printed by Thomas Gent,* 1743.
8°: A–D⁴; *1–2* 3–28 *29–32.*
> Subscribers list on pp. 29–32.

'When, at the first, good heav'n created man'
L(1346.e.21),YM,YP.

Maxwell, Stephen. The York miscellany: consisting of poems on several occasions. *London printed, and sold by J. Roberts, A. Dodd, and by the booksellers of York,* 1731. (*MChr* Aug)
8°: pp. 54.   L,O; CLU-C,ICU.

— A new miscellany in verse and prose. *York, printed by John White, for the author; sold by J. Osborn & T. Longman, J. Knapton & W. Innys, London; and by J. Hildyard, bookseller in York,* 1732. (*LM* Jan 1733)
8°: pp. 74.   L,PrP.

M152 — Eboracum. A poem. *York, printed by John White, for the author; sold by John Hildyard, and by the author at his house, also by Messieurs Chandler & Ward, Scarborough,* 1732.
4°: *A¹* B–D²; *1–2* 3–13 *14 blk.*
'Whilst Drake from darkness labours to retrieve'
YM; CtY.

M153 May-day. May-day: or, the original of garlands. A poem. *London, printed for J. Roberts,* 1720. (*DC* 2 May)
8°: A–D⁴ (C2 as 'C3'); [4] i–iii *iv, 1–24.* A1 frt.
'What tho' no fabl'd deities are found'
> On the mythical origins of London-Spaw.

L(164.1.57, Luttrell, May),LdU-B; MH.

Maynwaring, Arthur. *See* Mainwaring, Arthur.

M154 Mayor. The mayor and the mob. To which is added, a copy of the paper stuck up at the Royal Exchange...with the lord mayors complaint to the coutr [!] of aldermen. *London, printed for T.H.* [Thomas Harris], *in West-Smithfield,* [1742?]

The **mayor** and the mob

> ½°: 1 side, 2 columns.
> Only the first item is in verse.

''Twas in the town of London'
L(1876.f.1/125).

M155 Maypole. The maypole's new-years-gift, or thanks return'd to its benefactors... Written by a parishioner of St. Mary Savoy. *London, printed for J. Morphew,* 1714. (*PB* 19 Jan)
8°: A–C⁴; *1–4* 5–23 *24 blk.*
'Hail gen'rous masters all, I thus you greet'
> Preface signed 'Peter Penstrong'.

CtY,ICN,OCU.

M——'d. The M——'d c——b, 1704. *See* Et tu Brute? [1704.]

Means. The means of grace, [1742.] *See* Wesley, Charles.

'Meanwell, Timothy.' An epistle to MacD——d, 1730. *See* E401.

Medal. The medal. A satyr against sedition, 1709. *See* Dryden, John.

M156 Medallist. The medalist. A new ballad. *London, printed for J. Huggonson,* 1741. (*DP* 1 Dec)
2°: *A² < B²; 1–3* 4–8.
> *Percival* appendix 96. Reprinted in *No screen,* 1742.

'You merchants of Britain who've nothing to do'
> Wrongly ascribed to Horace Walpole in *Halkett & Laing;* cf. *Hazen, Walpole* p. 171. A satire on Walpole's administration.

L(11630.h.33),O; CSmH,ICN,MH,OCU,TxU.

M157 Meditation. The meditation, a cantata sung by Mrs. Margarita, and Mrs. Barbier, in the tragedy of the Lady Jane Grey. Set to musick by Dr. Pepusch. [*London,* 1715.]
½°: 1 side, 1 column.
'No, no, vain world, thy joys are frail'
> Rowe's play was first performed 20 April 1715, and this cantata was performed then, but no evidence for Rowe's authorship of it has been traced.

L(C.121.g.9/171).

M158 — A meditation in the fields, on seeing the herse [!] of that most illustrious prince the duke of Montagu, setting forward from his house in privy-garden, Whitehall, on tuesday July 18, 1749... [*London?* 1749.]
½°: 1 side, 1 column.
> The use of lower-case in the title is reminiscent of the style of John Hill's *The British magazine,* 1746–50.

'As when a furious tempest from on high'
LDW.

Meditations

M159 Meditations. Meditations on the fall of Bob and Harry. '*Printed for C. Cross near Westminster*', 1714. (16 Sept)
slip: 2 sides, 1 column.
> *The daily slip*, no. 4, for 16 Sept 1714. The imprint is fictitious; 'C. Cross' stands for Charing Cross. The copy seen was reissued in *State poems. Being a collection of choice private pieces*, 1715.

'Uncertainty of human fate'
> A satire on the fall of Harley and Bolingbroke.

Brett-Smith.

M160 Medlers. The medlers, or, a tale of four wise men. *London, printed in the year* 1710.
$\frac{1}{2}$°: 1 side, 1 column.
'When many shams and tricks beside'
> On a whig deputation to the queen led by Gilbert Heathcote after the dismissal of Sunderland.

CLU-C.

M161 Medley. A medley on the times. [*London?* 1729.]
$\frac{1}{2}$°: 1 side, 2 columns.
> *Percival* appendix 18.

'Attend ye good people, give ear to my ditty'
L(1876.f.1/118).

Melancholy. The melancholy muse, an elegy, [1723.] *See* Pennecuik, Alexander, *d. 1730.*

M162 — Melancholy sonnets. Being Fergusia's complaint upon Heptarchus...'*Elguze, printed for Pedaneous, and sold by Circumforaneous, below the zenith*' [*Edinburgh?*], 1741.
12°: A–C⁶; *1–3* 4–36.
'Fergusia once a sovereign free'
> Scotland's complaint against the Union.

E.

[M163 = H83] **Melazzo.** Melazzo, and it's brave defence, [1719.] *See* Harris, Timothy.

Meliora. Meliora's tears for Thyrsis, 1720. *See* Concanen, Matthew.

'Melissa.' Merlin: a poem, 1735. *See* Brereton, Jane.

M164 [Melmoth, William.] Of active and retired life, an epistle. *London, printed for T. Cooper*, 1735. (*GM* Jan)
2°: A² B–D²; *1–2* 3–16.
> Entered to Woodward in Bowyer's ledgers as 'Hawkins Poem' under 22 Jan, 4 sheets, 500 copies; this seems to correspond to the detailed printing accounts for 'Active Life Poem'. Possibly George Hawkins first accepted it for publication.

'Yes, you condemn those sages too refin'd'
> Early ms. attribution in the CtY copy; printed as Melmoth's in *Dodsley* I.

Melmoth, W. Of active and retired life

L(643.m.15/26),O,DG; CSmH,CtY,IU,MH, TxU(2)+.

M165 [—] Two epistles of Horace imitated. *London, printed for T. Cooper*, 1736. (7 April)
4°: A¹ B–G²; *i–ii*, 1–24.
> Listed in *LM* April.

'While bravely single in fair virtue's cause'
'You scorn, my Lollius, if I know thy heart'
> Early ms. attribution in the LdU-B copy. Epistles I.18 and II.1.

L(11630.c.10/5, Tom's Coffee House, 7 April), LdU-B; CSmH,DFo,MH,OCU,TxU+.

Members. The members to their soveraign, 1726. *See* Jacob, Hildebrand.

M166 Memorable. 'The memorable British sh——rs: or, characters of a select number of philosophers, astronomers, projectors, historians, poets, divines, &c. produc'd in Britain. An heroick satire. [*London*] *Printed for J. Wilford*. Price 1s.' (*MChr* 2 March 1730)
> Apparently a continuation of *A sequel to the Dunciad*, 1729, which dealt with poets' work as excrement.

M167 Memoriae. Memoriæ sacrum, reverendi admodum in Christo patris D. Gilberti Burnet, Salisburiensis episcopi fidelissimi, viri undiquaq; pietate, probitate, & eruditione omnigena clarissimi, non minus generis splendore, quam propria virtute perinclyti. [*London?* 1715.]
$\frac{1}{2}$°: 1 side, 1 column.
> Mourning borders.

'Isacidæ proles, si Mosem planxerat olim'
L(835.m.8/17).

M168 Men. Men and measures characterised from Horace. Being an imitation of the XVIth ode of his second book. *London, printed for T. Cooper*, 1739. (*LM* Aug)
2°: A² B² C¹; *i–ii*, 1–8.
'For quiet, friend, the sailor prays'
> Thomas Newcomb in his *Miscellaneous collection of original poems* (1740) 312 refers to this ode 'turn'd into a libel against the government by a Scotch poet'. It is indeed a satire against Walpole's ministry.

L(11661.dd.18),O,C,LdU-B(uncut); CSmH,CtY, IU,MH,TxU(uncut)+.

M169 — — '*London, printed for T. Cooper*' [*Edinburgh*], 1739. (*SM* Dec)
8°: A⁴; *1–2* 3–8.
MH.

M170 — — *Dublin, printed by and for E. Jones*, 1739.
12°: A⁴ B² (A3 as 'B'); *i–ii*, 1–8 *9–10* blk.
> The collation appears to be at variance with the signature.

C,DN(−B2).

Menalcas

M171 Menalcas. Menalcas, or a pastoral upon the death of a roman catholick clergy-man of distinction. Inscrib'd to a person of honour. By the Reverend F.L. *London, printed in the year* 1726.
8°: 11 pp.
> The copy recorded was bound with *A funeral oration* on the same subject, and it is not entirely clear that the two works were bibliographically distinct.
> The only suitable F.L. recorded in John Kirk, *Biographies of English catholics*, 1909, is Francis Lacy; but there is no further evidence for his authorship.
> (Pickering & Chatto cat. 265/8494.)

M172 [Mendez, Moses.] The Battiad. Canto the first. *London, printed for G. Smith*, 1750. (*GM,LM* Sept)
2°: *A*² B²; *1–3* 4–8. 8 advt.
'Awake, my muse, whate'er thy name may be'
> Authorship from *European magazine* 22 (1792) 251; *Nichols* IV. 606 suggests he was assisted by Paul Whitehead and Isaac Schomberg. A satire on the part taken by William Battie in the dispute between Schomberg and the College of Physicians.
L(1474.d.21, uncut),O; CtY,MH,TxU.

M173 [—] The Battiad. Canto the second. *London, printed for G. Smith*, 1750. (*LEP* 22 Nov)
2°: A–B²; *1–3* 4–8.
'O thou, great chief of physic and grimace'
O; CtY,TxU.

Mendico-hymen. Mendico-hymen, 1709–. *See* Thompson, William, *fellow of Trinity College, Dublin.*

— Mendico-hymen... The beggar's match, 1723–. *See* Fitzgerald, —, *Mr.*

Mentethus, R. *See* Monteith, Robert.

M174 Merchant. The merchant a-la-mode. To the tune of Which no body can deny. *London, printed by Rich. Newcomb*, 1713.
2°: *A*² < *B*¹; ff. *1* 2–3.
> Printed on one side of the leaf only, the third leaf on the verso. According to *Morgan* P405, Mrs. Boulter was imprisoned for publishing one edition.
'Attend and prepare for a cargo from Dover'
> *Crum* A1889. A satire against the Duke d'Aumont and the peace with France.
L(11602.i.12/7**).

M175 — — *London, printed by J. Read*, [1713.]
2°: *A*² < *B*¹; *1* 3 6.
> Printed on one side of the leaf only, as preceding; the pagination is therefore correct, curious as it may seem.
L(C.20.f.2/299),OW(uncut).

M176 — — [*London*] *Sold by E. Clayton in Goodman's-fields*, [1713.]
½°: 1 side, 2 columns.

The merchant a-la-mode

> Title reads: 'THE | MERCHANT | A-la-mode...'
PPL.

M177 — [variant]
> No imprint, but '(*Price Two Pence.*)' at foot of column one; it is printed on stamped paper.
O(price cropt),DT; MH.

M178 — — [*London*, 1713.]
½°: 1 side, 2 columns.
> Title reads: 'THE | MERCHANT | A-la-mode...' This and the two following editions are all by the same printer. Stanza 5 line 3 reads 'Warehouse' and line 3 of the final stanza 'Bauds'; these are also the readings of the preceding edition.
O,LLP; MH-BA.

M179 — [another edition]
> Stanza 5 line 3 reads 'Ware-house', the final stanza 'Bawds'; roman parentheses in stanza 1 line 3.
OW.

M180 — [another edition]
> Title reads: 'THE | MERCHANT | A-la-Mode...'; textual readings as the preceding, but italic parentheses in stanza 1 line 3.
InU,MB.

M181 — [another edition]
> Title reads: 'THE | MERCHANT, | A-LA-MODE...' An inferior piece of printing.
L(Lutt.II.141; 112.f.44/23),Crawford.

M182 — The merchant alamode... *London printed, and re-printed in Dublin*, 1714.
½°: 1 side, 2 columns.
> On the other side, *O raree show* (R125).
OCU.

M183 — The merchant a-la-mode, &c. [*London*, 1713.]
slip: 1 side, 1 column.
> Six stanzas only.
'Attend and prepare for a cargo from Dover'
> Apparently a tory ballad in praise of d'Aumont, in opposition to the preceding.
LSA.

M184 Merchants. The merchants advocate, a poem, in an imitation of Juvenals XIII. satyr. *London printed, and sold by most of the booksellers in London & Westminster*, [1708.] (*DC* 28 Jan)
2°: *A*² B–F²; *i–iv*, 1–20.
> The Luttrell copy, dated 28 Jan, was recorded in Pickering & Chatto cat. 247/13308.
'All evils, friend, whatever, great and small'
> The same author wrote *Great Britains hope*, [1708.]
LdU-B,*MR-C*; CtY.

M185 — The merchants and hammer-mens complaint against the taylors. Or, a hot goose for poet Davidson, the taylor; author of, The taylors vindication. [*Edinburgh*, 17–-?]

The **merchants** and hammer-mens complaint

$\frac{1}{2}^o$: 1 side, 3 columns.
'Come master taylor let us try'
 The taylor's vindication, [17––?] is entered
 under Davidson, —, *tailor*.
E(mutilated).

M186 Mercury. The mercury hawkers in mourning. An
elegy on the much lamented death of Edward
Jones, the famous Gazette printer of the Savoy;
who departed this life at his house at Kensington,
on Saturday the 16th day of February, 170$\frac{5}{6}$. in the
54 year of his age. *London, printed for T. Sawyer,
near Ludgate-hill*, 1706.
$\frac{1}{2}^o$: 1 side, 2 columns.
 Mourning headpiece and borders.
'Assist ye muses (all in number) nine'
LSA; CSmH,MH.

M187 [Meredith, Amos.] The prologue and epilogue to
the new tragi-comical-farcical opera, call'd Hurlo-
thrumbo: or, news from terra australis incognita.
London, printed for R. Walker, [1729.] (*MChr* 27
April)
2°: A–B^2; *1–2* 3–8.
'Rules were by coxcombs made to cramp the mind'
'Ladies and gentlemen, my lord of flame'
 The 1729 edition of the play, which is by
 Samuel Johnson, prints the prologue as by
 Amos Meredith, the epilogue as by Mr.
 Byrom.
OW; MH(uncut).

M188 Meredith, James. An essay on the divine attri-
butes; under the following heads, viz... *London,
printed for J. Hawkins*, 1738. (*GM* June)
2°: A^2 B–F^2; *i–iv*, 1–18 *19*; *20 blk.* F2 advt.
 The L copy has two errata in ms. on p. 18.
'Whence sprung this glorious frame? or whence
arose'
L(643.l.28/27),LdU-B; IU(–F2),KU.

M189 — Manners decypher'd. A reply to Mr. Whitehead, on his satire call'd Manners. *London, printed
for T. Cooper*, [1739.] (*GM,LM* March)
2°: π^1 A–C^2 D^1; *i–ii*, *1* 2–12 *13*; *14 blk.* D1 advt.
 π1 and D1 have been seen to be conjugate in
 the LdU-B copy, where D1 is bound before
 A1.
'Manners, a satire, stroling hawkers cry'
O(–D1),LdU-B; CtY,KU,MH(–D1),TxU(uncut).

M190 Merit. Merit. A satire. Humbly addressed to his
excellency the Earl of Chesterfield. *Dublin, printed
for the author; sold by Peter Wilson, and the rest of
the booksellers*, 1746.
8°: A–C^4; *1–2* 3–23 *24 blk.*
'While swarms of panegyricks on thee pour'
L(11631.e.59),DA,DN; CLU,CSmH,CtY,TxU.

M191 — Merit and gratitude conjoin'd: or, the Duke of
Marlborough's entry vindicated. Being a short
answer to the Republican procession; or, the

Merit and gratitude conjoin'd

tumultuous cavalcade, &c. [*London*] *Printed for
J. Johnson, near Charing-Cross, and sold by the
booksellers of London & Westminster*, 1715.
12°: A–C^6 D^6(–D6); *1–2* 3–46.
 D6 missing from the copy seen, possibly
 blank.
'As drowning men a straw will catch at'
 An answer to Edward Ward's poem.
NjP.

M192 Merits. The merites of piracie or, a new song on
Captain Green and his bloody crue: to the tune of,
My virgins treasure. [*Edinburgh?* 1705.]
$\frac{1}{2}^o$: 1 side, 2 columns.
 Rough woodcut at head.
'Of all the pirates I've heard or seen'
L(Rox.III.609).

Merlin. Merlin: a poem, 1735. *See* Brereton, Jane.

'Merlin.'
[Swift, Jonathan:] A famous prediction of Merlin,
the British wizard, 1709. *See* S849–53.

Merrick, James. Poems on sacred subjects...
Oxford, at the Clarendon Press, 1763. *Sold by R. &
J. Dodsley, London.*
4°: pp. 30. L,O; DLC,MH.

M193 — The destruction of Troy being the sequel of the
Iliad. Translated from the Greek of Tryphiodorus.
With notes. *Oxford, printed at the Theatre*, [1742?]
(*GM* Aug 1742)
8°: π^4 †^{4} ††^{4} a–l^4 A–T^4, ^{2}π^4 A–O^4; [*24*] i–lxxxviii,
1–151 *152 blk, i–viii*, 1–112. π1, ^{2}π1 hft; 148,104 err.
 The English text has imprimatur of 26 Oct
 1739; the Greek & Latin text of 6 Oct 1741.
 No evidence has been found of their having
 been published independently. Listed in *GM*
 Aug 1742 as 'pr. 5s. in sheets to subscribers.
 Birt and Rivington.'
'How conqu'ring Greece, by heav'n's assisting care'
L(76.d.27,–π1),O(2),RP(–π1),WgP; MH(–π1),
NBuG.

M194 — Messiah. A divine essay. Humbly dedicated to
the...vice-chancellor of the university of Oxford,
and the visitors of the free-school in Reading. By
James Merrick, ætat 14. senior scholar of the
school at their last triennial visitation, the 7th of
October, 1734. *Reading, printed by W. Ayres in the
Market-place*, [1734.]
4°: π^1 A^4; *i–ii*, *1* 2–7 *8 blk.*
 The watermark in the O copy is pro patria;
 in RP, Amsterdam arms. One is possibly fine
 paper, but neither appears of that quality.
'Ye who in constant hallelujahs join'
O,RP.

Merrick, John. [Festival hymns for the use of
charity schools, 1723.]

Merrick, John

— 'Festival hymns for the use of charity schools. Originally composed for the fraternity of the blue and green coat boys in the corporation of Reading. The third edition. *Reading, printed by J. Newbery & C. Micklewright,* 1742.'

Recorded by Charles Coates, *Supplement to the History and antiquities of Reading* (Reading, 1810; addition to p. 319) which also gives the date of the first edition.

M195 [—] Heliocrene a poem in Latin and English: on the chalybeate well at Sunning Hill in Windsor Forest. *Excudebat D. Kinnier, typographus Readingensis, anno dom.* 1725.
4°: *A*²(A1+χ¹) B² C²(±C1) D²; *1–2* [2] 3–16 (10 as '8'). 16 err.

χ1 is a Latin preface, the cancel C1 a dedication of the English translation to Mrs. Gr--y. According to Charles Coates, *Supplement to the History and antiquities of Reading* (Reading, 1810: addition to p. 319) the Latin text was separately published as a folio half-sheet in 1724.
'Barbaries patria quando expulit Hellade musas'
'When Greece, the muses native soil'
Preface by 'J.M.'; early ms. attribution in O copy.
O,RP.

M196 [—] — To which is added, by way of appendix, the author's case. *Reading, printed and sold by J. Newbery & C. Micklewright, and at the Bible and Crown without Temple-Bar, London,* 1744. (*GM, LM* June)
4°: A⁴ B⁴(±B1) C²; *1–2* 3–20.
Vertical chain-lines.
L(1961, uncut); KU.

M197 Merrivale, Thomas. The necromancer; or Harlequin Doctor Faustus: a poem; founded on the gentile theology. *London printed, and sold by J. Roberts,* 1724. (*MC* April)
8°: A–D⁴ (C2 as 'C3'); *i–viii, 1* 2–24. A1 hft.
'Of rival theatres the mighty fall'
Occasioned by John Rich's pantomime of this title.
L(1961, uncut); CtY,ICN,KU,MH,NN(–A1).

M198 Merry. Merrie Andrews remarks upon the months of the ensuing year one thousand seven hundred and sixteen. [*Edinburgh,* 1715.]
½°: 1 side, 2 columns.
'This month begins our year, god send it good'
E.

M199 — The merry campaign; or, the Westminster and Green-park scuffle. A new court ballad. *London, printed for B. Dickinson,* 1732. (*GSJ* 26 May)
2°: *A*² B²; *1–5* 6–8. A1 frt.
Percival appendix 45.
'God prosper long our noble peers'

The **merry** campaign

Ascribed to Sir Charles Hanbury Williams in his *Works* (1822) III. 43, in *DNB* and *CBEL*; there wrongly dated 1743. Williams's authorship at this date seems most unlikely. On a duel between Viscount Micklethwaite and Mr. Crowle of the Temple.
L(1959,–A1),O(2); CSmH(–A1),CtY(uncut), MH,OCU.

M200 — A merry dialogue, in the Tolbuith of Edinburgh; betwixt Tonny Ashton, and John Curry. [*Edinburgh,* 1728.] (16 April)
½°: 1 side, 1 column.
Ms. note in the E copy, 'Edr printed 16 Apr 1728'.
'Come, my couragious Jack, my metl'd Scot'
Tony Aston the actor and his son Walter were imprisoned for Walter's enticing and marrying Mrs. Joan Ker; John Curry was punished for forging banknotes. This is particularly directed against Tony Aston.
E.

M201 — A merry letter from the Ld. Bol----ke to a certain favourite mistress near Bloomsbury-square. *London printed, and sold by the pamphlet-sellers of London & Westminster,* 1715. (*MC* June)
8°: A–C⁴ (A2 as 'B'); *1–3* 4–24.
'Dear angel divine,/Who brighter doth shine'
A mock letter from Bolingbroke in Paris.
L(T.987/1),O,*AN*; CSmH,DFo,MH.

M202 —— *London printed, and sold by the pamphlet-sellers of London & Westminster,* 1715.
8°: *A*¹ B⁸ *C*¹ (B3 as 'B4'); *1–3* 4–20.
A1 and C1 have been seen to be conjugate.
LdU-B.

M203 — A merry new joke,|On Joseph's old cloak. [*Dublin,* 1729?]
slip: 2 sides, 1 column.
Rough woodcut of cloak at head. The DT copy is bound with half-sheets of 1729.
'This cloak was cut out in old Oliver's days'
A satire against the dissenters, applied to Richard Choppin. A sequel was *A comical sonnet,* [1729?].
L(1890.e.5/52; C.121.g.8/134, cropt),C,DT.

— The merry travellers, 1721–. *See* Ward, Edward.

'Merrypin, Margery.' The muse's vagaries, 1743. *See* Muse.

Merton. Merton walks, or the Oxford beauties, 1717. *See* Dry, John.

M204 Mess. A mess for the devil. Or an excellent new receipt to make a junto. [*London*] *Printed in the year* 1711.
½°: 1 side, 1 column.
'Two good-natur'd wou'd--be's (two state politicians)'
A satire on the new ministry.
L(1875.d.6/116, mutilated).

Messenger

M205 Messenger. The messenger defeated: or, the lawyer's escape. A new ballad. To the tune of, Hey boys up go we. [*London*] 1705.
½°: 1 side, 2 columns.
  Woodcut of an escape from a window.
'Scarce did the grey ey'd dawn appear'
  On Nicholas Lechmere's escape.
NNP,*Harding*.

M206 — — The third edition. [*London*] 1705. (*DC* 14 April)
½°: 1 side, 2 columns.
  On the other side, *The Coventry ballad* (H127).
L(1872.a.1/157*),Rothschild; CLU-C.

[Meston, William.] Old Mother Grim's tales, found in an old manuscript, dated 1527. Never before published. Decade I. '*London, printed, and sold by the booksellers in London & Westminster*' [*Edinburgh*], 1737.
8°: pp. xii, 88. L,O; CtY,ICN.
  Copies of a prospectus of eight leaves (E,TxU) have a half-title reading 'If the following swatch meets with a favourable reception... the publisher designs to print the whole collection...'

[—] Decadem alteram, ex probatissimis auctoribus ...admixtis subinde nonnullis, in gratiam pulchrioris sexus, vernaculis, subjunxit Jodocus Grimmus, anniculæ nostræ pronepos. '*Londinii, impensis editoris, & prostat venalis apud bibliopolas Londinenses & Westmonasterienses*' [*Edinburgh*], 1738.
8°: pp. 63. L,O; CtY,ICN.

— The poetical works...The sixth edition. *Edinburgh, printed by Wal. Ruddiman junior, for Francis Robertson*, 1767.
12°: pp. xiv, xvi, 227. L,O; ICU,MH.
  The account of the author's life here records that the two decades above 'underwent several impressions'; these have not been traced, but it is doubtless for this reason that this edition is called sixth.

———

M207 — Ad consulem Abredonensem. *Abredæis, exc. J. Chalmers, autore Gul. Meston A.M.* 1744.
½°: 1 side, 1 column.
  With a second poem in two columns below, 'In laudem inclytæ civitatis Abredoniæ somnium poeticum'.
'Quæ Paridi quondam spondebant numera divæ'
'Mane sub auroram, fessos complectitur artus'
  Meston's authorship in imprint.
AdU(2).

M208 [—] Cato's ghost. [1715?]
slip: 1 side, 1 column.
  Possibly printed in London, as other Jacobite slip songs seem to have been.
'From happy climes where vertue never dyes'
  Printed in Meston's *Decadem alteram*, 1738.

Meston, W. Cato's ghost

  Crum F693. A Jacobite poem in opposition to Addison's interpretation of Cato.
L(11626.i.11/5),O.

M209 [—] — [*Dublin?* 1715?]
½°: 1 side, 2 columns.
  Possibly printed in Dublin from the use of type flowers and the provenance of NN copy.
O; NN.

M210 [—] An elegy on the King of Sweden. [1718/19.]
½°: 1 side, 1 column.
'O who wou'd boast himself of royal birth?'
  Printed in Meston's *Decadem alteram*, 1738.
  On the death of Charles XII.
Harding.

M211 [—] The knight. [*Edinburgh*] *Printed in the year* 1723.
8°: †⁴ *² A–O⁴; [2] i–v vi–x, 1–111 *112 blk*.
  Bond 71. 'Canto, 1' in drop-head title and running-title.
'Come on thou muse who only dwells'
  Dedication signed 'Quidam'. Reprinted in Meston's *Poetical works*, 1767.
L(11632.b.45),O(uncut),E(3),AdU(2),GM; CtY, ICN,IU,MH.

M212 [—] [*idem*] The knight of the kirk: or, the ecclesiastical adventures of Sir John Presbyter... The second edition. *London, printed for M. Smith*, 1728. (*MChr* 24 April)
12°: A(3 ll) B–H⁶ I(3 ll) (D2 as 'D3'); i–vi, 1 2–89 90 blk.
  Possibly the leaves of A and I are conjugate and form a wrapper.
CtY,KU(uncut),TxU.

M213 [—] — The third edition. *London, printed for M. Smith*, 1728.
12°: A(3 ll) B–H⁶ I(3 ll) (D2 as 'D3'); i–vi, 1 2–89 90 blk.
  Apparently a press-variant title. Advertised in *A compleat key to the Dunciad* (May 1728).
E(2, 1 uncut).

M214 [—] Mob contra mob, or the rabblers rabbled. *Edinburgh printed, and sold at Mr. Freebairn's shop in the Parliament-closs*, [1714.] (March)
8°: A–D⁴ E²; 1–2 3–36.
  Bond 115. Entered in Ruddiman's ledger, both for case and press, between 13 and 27 March 1714.
'In pious all-reforming times'
  Reprinted in Meston's *Poetical works*, 1767. On the 'rabbling o' Deer', the riot caused by the installation of John Gordon as incumbent of Deer in 1711.
E,*GM*.

M215 [—] — *Edinburgh, printed in the year* 1731.
8°: A–D⁴; 1–2 3–32.
L(11631.aa.46/3).

M216 [—] — *Edinburgh, printed in the year* 1738.
8°: A⁴ B–D⁴; 1–2 3–32.

Meston, W. Mob contra mob

> Printed in the same format as *Old Mother Grim's tales*, 1737–38, and probably intended for issue with them.
> L(11631.aaa.56/2),O,E(2),AdU,GM(2); CtY, ICN,MH,OCU.

M217 [—] Phaethon: or the first fable of the second book of Ovid's Metamorphoses burlesqu'd. *Edinburgh, printed in the year* 1720.
8°: A–D⁴; *1–2* 3–32.
> *Bond* 64.
> 'Sol's mannor was a pretty good house'
> Reprinted in *Old Mother Grim's tales*, 1737.
> L(11355.b.15),E,AdU(2); ICN(uncut).

M218 [—] [dh] A tale of a man and his mare. Found in an old manuscript, never before printed. [1720/21.]
2°: *A*²; *1–4*.
> Well printed, on decent paper, probably at London or Edinburgh. *Morgan* R469 records what appear to be two editions printed with *A race at Sherrifmuir*; see R2.
> 'An honest man, once had a mare'
> Reprinted in *Old Mother Grim's tales*, 1737. A Jacobite satire on George I.
> L(C.121.g.9/187, ms. date 3 March 1720),E.

M219 [—] — The second edition, with additions. [*Edinburgh?*] *Printed in the year* 1721.
4°: A–E²; *1–2* 3–19 *20 blk.*
> L(11631.bbb.43),E(3).

M220 [—] A tale oe [!] a man and his mare... The second edition, with additions. *Printed in the year* 1721.
4°: A–E²; *1–2* 3–19 *20 blk.*
> A very poor piece of printing in comparison to the preceding; probably a piracy.
> ICN.

M221 [—] [dh] To the memory of the right honourable John earl of Strathmore, who was kill'd at the battle of Sheriffmuir, near Dunblain, November 13th, 1715. [*Edinburgh*, 1715/16?]
4°: A⁴; *1–8*.
> There are two different settings of the inner forme, which can be seen at E; in one, signature A2 is under the r and l of 'Eternal', in the other flanking the N of 'Night'.
> 'With gen'ral sadness Albion mourns'
> Early ms. note in the L copy 'supposed to be writ by the then Master of Stormount, afterwards Viscount...', but collected in Meston's *Decadem alteram*, 1738.
> L(11632.c.38),E(3).

M222 [—] [*idem*] [dh] In memory of the right honourable John earl of Strathmore, kill'd at the battle of Sheriffmuir, November the 13th, 1715. [*Edinburgh*, 1715/16?]
4°: A⁴; *1–8*.
> This is probably the later version; there are textual changes and footnotes recording classical parallels.
> E.

Meston, W. Viri humani

M223 [—] [dh] Viri humani, salsi, & faceti Gulielmi Sutherlandi, multarum artium & scientiarum, doctoris doctissimi, diploma. [*Edinburgh?* 1725?]
4°: *A*²; *1* 2–4.
> Reprinted in *The most wonderful wonder*, 1726, a prose work.
> 'Ubique gentium & terrarum'
> Printed in Meston's *Decadem alteram*, 1738.
> Doggerel verses in Latin and English.
> E,ES.

M224 Metamorphose. The metamorphose of a certain Dublin beau's-head, into a tea-kettle: a poem. By a lady. [*Dublin*] *Printed in the year* 1730.
½°: 1 side, 2 columns.
> 'S—n and the man I sing who forc'd by age'
> Cf. 'Philips, Ambrose', *The tea-pot; or, the lady's transformation*, [1725/30], and *The tea-kettle*, 1730.
> L(C.121.g.8/176),DT.

Metamorphosis. The metamorphosis: a poem, 1728. *See* Smedley, Jonathan.

— The metamorphosis of the town, 1730–. *See* Thomas, Elizabeth.

— 'The metamorphosis: or, the cit turn'd gentleman. In a congratulatory epistle to Mr. F.H. upon his late publick preferment, and poetical performance. By a gentleman of Cambridge. [*London*] *Printed for Tho. Bickerton*.' (*DC* 3 May 1721)
> It seems probable that this work is in verse, but it has not been traced. Probably an answer to *Love drowned in the South-Sea... By F.H. gent*, [1721.]

M225 Methodists. 'The methodists, a satirical poem, after the manner of Hudibras. In three canto's... By T.H. *Printed for D. Henry in Reading; sold in London by C. Corbett*.' (*LDP* 10 July 1739)
> Apparently a different work from *The methodists, an humorous burlesque poem*, 1739; that was published two months earlier.

M226 — The methodists, an humorous burlesque poem; address'd to the rev. Mr. Whitefield and his followers: proper to be bound up with his sermons, and the journals of his voyage to Georgia, &c. *London, printed for John Brett*, 1739. (*GM, LM* May)
8°: (frt+) *A*² B–D⁴; *1–2* 3–28.
> *Bond* 168.
> 'All men who 're not of sense bereav'd'
> L(11633.c.52),O,EN,*BU*,*MR*+; CtY,*DLC*,MH (–frt),NN(–frt),*NjR*+.

Mezentius. Mezentius on the rack, 1734. *See* Dunkin, William.

M227 Micah. Micah, vi. 8. Do justice, &c. To be wrote under the picture of justice, which is to be painted, with the verses under-written, by the special

Micah, vi. 8

order of Grandevus, a barrister at law...one of his majesty's justices of the peace, and of the quorum for the parts of Lindissi in Coritani. [*London?* 173–?]
½°: 1 side, 2 columns.

The motto is of six lines only; below is 'To the great Grandevus, on the foregoing piece'.
Motto: 'For in the word of god, by his command'
Reply: 'Genius of these aspiring times'

According to L, a satire on Justice Howgrave of Horncastle in Lincolnshire.
L(C.131.h.1/3).

M228 Michaelmas. Michaelmas term, or the battle of the loggerheads. Address'd to all the learned members of Rufus-Hall, and the Inns of C——t. A ballad to the tune of Dear catholic brother... *London, printed for T. Taylor*, [1742.] (*DP* 8 May)
4°: A–B⁴; *1–3* 4–15 *16 blk*.

The advertisement in *DP* notes four errata.
'On the very last day of last Michaelmas term'
L(11630.c.7/1; 11630.b.5/9),O,LdU-B(uncut); CtY,KU,MH.

Microscopium. Microscopium, [1716?] *See* Bisse, Thomas.

M229 Middlesex. The Middlesex patriots, a poem on the election at Brentford. *London, printed for T. Payne*, 1722. (13 April)
2°: *A*¹ B² C¹; *i–ii*, 1–6.

Advertised in *PB* 12 April for 'to-morrow', and *PB* 14 April as 'just publish'd'. *Thorn-Drury* records the Luttrell copy, dated April.
''Twas at a time when bribery bore the sway'
'On behalf of Mr Bertie & Sr John Austen & their friends', Luttrell.
O; CtY,InU.

M230 [Milbourne, Luke.] The moderate cabal. A satyr. *London printed, and sold by the booksellers*, 1710.
8°: A–H⁴; *1–2* 3–64.

Advertised in *PB* 15 Feb 1711, probably subsequent to publication.
'Must I be silent still, and still be teaz'd'
Early ms. attribution to Milbourne in the L copy.
L(11631.c.8),O(lacks A1),DN,DT,WcC; ICU, MB,MH,MiU,NjP.

[—] Tom of Bedlam: or, a mad poem, 1701. *See* T409.

Military. Military and other poems upon several occasions, and to several persons. By an officer of the army. *London, printed for the author, and sold by J. Browne*, 1716. (*MC* Jan)
8°: pp. 271.   L,O; ICN,TxU.

Attributed to J.D. Breval by Aitken in *DNB*, but many poems were written too early for this to be possible. I suspect the author was

Military and other poems

John Thornycroft, who published a poem in this year using this epithet.

M231 — The military prophet: or a flight from providence. Address'd to the foolish and guilty, who timidly withdrew themselves on the alarm of another earthquake, April 1750. [*London*, 1750.] (*GA* 12 April)
obl ½°: 1 side, 4 columns.

Large engraving at head. Advertised as sold by B. Dickinson.
'Sad stupid age! alike in church and state'
The false alarm of the earthquake was on 4 April.
L(P&D 3076).

M232 Miller. The miller of Essex, a new song, to the tune of, The miller of Mansfield. [*London?* 173–?]
slip: 1 side, 1 column.
'How happy a state did the miller possess'
Against a miller turned politician.
L(C.121.g.9/128).

M233 — The miller of Trompington: being an exercise upon Chaucer's Reeve's tale. *London, printed for Jonas Brown; sold by J. Roberts*, 1715. (*MC* May)
12°: A–K⁶; *1–9* 10–117 *118–20*.
'Pierian madams (no offence)'
L(1959),LdU-B; DFo,IU,MH.

Miller, James. Miscellaneous works in verse and prose... Volume the first. *London, printed by J. Watts*, 1741. (*LM* May)
4°: pp. 416.   O; MH,TxU.
Apparently only vol. I was published.

M234 [—] Are these things so? The previous question, from an Englishman in his grotto, to a great man at court. *London, printed for T. Cooper*, 1740. (*LDP* 23 Oct)
2°: *A*² B–D² E¹; *i–iv, 1* 2–14. A1 hft.

Pp. 5–11 have pagination in parentheses. The order of the early editions has not been finally established, but that presented here seems logical. The copyright was sold in a lot with other works by Miller in the trade sale of Francis Cogan (cat. at O-JJ) 10 July 1746, at 10s. 6d. to Corbett.
'Dead to the world's each scene of pomp or care'
Attributed to Miller in Baker's *Biographia dramatica*. Written as from Pope to Walpole. There are numerous replies; cf. [T. Newcomb] *A supplement*, 1740; [R. Morris] *Yes, they are*, 1740, and replies; *What of that*, 1740; G. Spiltimber, *The weather-menders*, 1740; *Pro and Con*, 1741. See also *What things?*, 1740, in prose. Miller himself wrote *The great man's answer*, 1740.
L(840.m.1/2,−A1),O(2, 1 lacks A², E1),C(2); CU,CtY(2,−A1),TxU.

Miller, J. Are these things so?

M235 [—] [another edition]
Pp. 5–8 have pagination in parentheses; floral headpiece to p. 1. A–C reimpressed, D–E reset.
L(643.l.28/19; C.131.h.1/11*),OA; ICN,IU, MH(–A1),NN-B,TxU(2,–A1)+.

M236 [—] [another edition]
Pp. 5–8 have pagination in parentheses; two small headpieces on p. 1. A–C reset in a different type face, D–E apparently reimpressed.
L(1973), OW,LdU-B; MiU,OCU,TxU(2).

M237 [—] — The second edition corrected: with the addition of twenty lines omitted in the former impressions. *London, printed for T. Cooper*, 1740. (*DP* 6 Dec)
2°: *A*² B–E²; *i–iv, 1* 2–15 *16 blk.* A1 hft.
Apparently in part a reimpression.
L(163.n.57),O,LdU-B(uncut); CLU-C,CtY,MH, MiU,TxU.

M238 [—] — '*London*' [*Edinburgh*], *printed in the year* 1740.
8°: A–B⁴; *1–2* 3–16.
Probably the edition listed in *SM* Oct; it follows the first edition text in omitting twenty lines at the end. The ornament is found in other Edinburgh piracies.
ICU,MH.

M239 [—] — '*London, printed for the perusal of all lovers of their country*', 1740.
8°: A–B⁴; *1–2* 3–16.
One of a series of piratical reprints with this imprint, including [R. Morris] *Yes, they are; They are not; What of that.* Copies are found in Scottish collections, but the printer's ornament has not been identified; possibly they are from Newcastle. Horizontal chain-lines. A variant copy at CtY has 'Fast-day' in the last line on p. 3 for 'Fast day', and the copy at PrP may have sheet B from the following.
O(lacks B4),AdU,PrP; CtY(2, variant),TxU.

M240 [—] [another edition]
Last line on p. 3 reads 'Fest day'. Vertical chain-lines.
C; National Library of Australia.

M241 [—] — By Alexander Pope, esq; *London: printed, and Dublin reprinted in the year* 1740.
8°: A–B⁴; *1–3* 4–16.
Signature A2 under 'my'. *Griffith* 520. The wrong attribution is not surprising.
L(11633.bbb.50),O,C(2),DA(2),DN+; CSmH, CtY,ICU,IU,TxU.

M242 [—] — By Alexander Pope, esq; *London; printed: and Dublin reprinted, in the year* 1740.
8°: A–B⁴; *1–3* 4–16.
Signature A2 under 'lolling'.
MH.

M243 [—] — By Alexander Pope, esq; *London: printed, and Dublin re-printed in the year* 1740.

8°: *A*⁴ B⁴; *1–3* 4–16.
A2 unsigned.
L(1488.bb.30).

M244 [—] — To which is added, Yes, they are... *London, printed in the year* One thousand seven hundred and forty.
8°: A–C⁴; *1–4* 5–24.
Presumably this is a piracy; the added poem is by Robert Morris.
LVA-D; CtY.

M245 [—] — By Alexander Pope, esq;... To which is added, the answer, Yes, they are! *London: printed, and Dublin re-printed in the year* 1740.
8°: *A*⁴ B¹; *1–2* 3–10.
The copy seen does not contain the answer, and has 'Finis' on p. 10; it was probably issued with one of the Dublin editions of *Yes, they are.*
L(1486.s.8).

M246 — The art of life. In imitation of Horace's Art of poetry. In two epistles. Epistle the first... *London, printed for J. Watts*, 1739. (*GM,LM* Oct)
4°: *A*² B–D⁴ E²; *i–iv, 1–3* 4–27 *28.* 28 advt.
No watermark: 'Price one shilling' on title. *Rawlinson* dates it as 2 Oct; this has not been confirmed, compare the dated copy below.
'Shou'd hum'rous Hogarth, from a knavish plan'
L(11630.c.10/1, ms. date 31 Oct; 11630.c.12/17, cropt; 840.k.3/10; 643.k.3/18),O; DFo,MH,NN, OCU,TxU.

M247 — [fine paper]
Watermark: crowned eagle; no price on title.
CSmH.

M248 — — The second edition. *London, printed for J. Watts*, 1739.
4°: *A*² B–D⁴ E²; *i–iv, 1–3* 4–27 *28.* 28 advt.
Apparently a reimpression or press-variant title.
ICN.

M249 [—] The great man's answer to Are these things so? In a dialogue brtween [!] his honour and the Englishman in his grotto... By the author of Are these things so? *London, printed for T. Cooper*, 1740. (*LEP* 18 Dec)
2°: *A*² B–D² E¹; *i–iv, 1* 2–13 *14 blk.* A1 hft.
There are variant positions of the signature 'D'; in the O copy it is misprinted 'E'. Possibly there was more than one impression. The copyright was sold in a lot with other works by Miller in the trade sale of Francis Cogan (cat. at O-JJ) 10 July 1746, at 10s. 6d. to Corbett.
'Hail blest Elizium! sweet, secure retreat'
Walpole's reply to Pope ends in the offer of a bribe.
L(11630.h.50),O,LdU-B; CLU-C,MH,NN-B, TxU(uncut).

M250 [—] — '*London, printed for T. Cooper*' [*Dublin*], 1740.

Miller, J. The great man's answer

8°: A–B⁴ (A2 as 'B2'); *1–3* 4–15 *16 blk*.
The LVA-D copy is bound with a Dublin edition of *Are these things so?* (M241).
L(1961),LVA-D; MH.

M251 [—] Harlequin-Horace: or, the art of modern poetry. *London, printed for Lawton Gilliver*, 1731. (*SR* 5 Feb)
8°: a² b⁴ B–H⁴ I²; *i–xii, 1* 2–59 *60*. a1 frt; 60 advt.
Bond 112. Title in red and black. There are three variant states of I²; with a wrong catchword 'Friend-' on p. 57, and p. 58 correctly numbered; with the right catchword, and p. 58 correctly numbered; and with the right catchword, and p. 58 misnumbered '57'. Listed in *GSJ* 9 Feb. Deposit copies at O,EU. Reissued in *A collection of pieces...on occasion of the Dunciad*, 1732; the copy of that issue at MH has a new setting of I², with 'Imperium pelagi' on p. 60 set in roman, not italic type.
'If some great artist in whose works conspire'
Subsequently published with Miller's name.
L(992.h.9/2; T.1056/13,−a1; T.902/14, lacks a², cropt),O(4),CT,E(2),DT+; CLU-C,CtY(2),ICU, MH(3),TxU(2, 1 uncut)+.

M252 [—] — *London: printed, and Dublin, re-printed and sold by George Faulkner*, [1731.]
8°: A⁴ *B*⁴ C–E⁴; *i–iii* iv–viii, *1* 2–32.
L(1966),DG,DN(2),DT; DFo,MiU.

M253 [—] — The third edition, corrected. With several additional lines and explanatory notes. *London, printed for Lawton Gilliver*, 1735.
8°: (frt+) a¹ b⁴ B–I⁴; *i–x, 1* 2–61 *62–63; 64 blk*.
61 err; 62–63 advt.
Title in red and black. 'Price 1s.' on title altered in ms. in all copies to 1s. 6d. No second edition has been identified.
L(11631.d.27,−I4),O(−frt),C(−frt); CSmH, CtY,*DFo*,ICU(−frt),NN+.

M254 — — The fourth edition, corrected. With several additional lines and explanatory notes. *London, printed for Lawton Gilliver*, 1735.
4°: (frt+) *A*² B–G⁴; *i–iv, 1–7* 8–47 *48 blk*.
Dedication signed.
CT(−frt); CSmH(−frt),ICU,IU,MH.

M254·5 [—] The H------r heroes: or, a song of triumph...By a H--n--r--n. Translated from the High German, into English verse, and the metre adapted to the tune of, The miller of Mansfield. *London, printed for W. Webb*, [1744.] (*GM, LM* Jan)
2°: *A*² B–D² *E*¹; *i–iv, 1* 2–17 *18 blk*. A1 hft.
Horizontal chain-lines. The copyright of 'Hanover heroes' was sold as one of 'seven articles by the reverend Mr. Miller' in a lot in the trade sale of Francis Cogan, 10 July 1746 (cat. at O-JJ), to Corbett for 10s. 6d.
'Shall the Englishman, Addison, sing a Campaign'
For Miller's authorship, see the copyright sale above. A satire on the conduct of the

Miller, J. The H------r heroes

Hanoverians and General Ilton in particular during the Dettingen campaign.
L(1482.f.40),O(2); OCU.

M255 [—] Of politeness. An epistle to the right honourable William Stanhope, lord Harrington. By the author of Harlequin Horace. *London, printed for L. Gilliver & J. Clark*, 1738. (*SR* 24 April)
2°: *A*² B–E²; *1–3* 4–20.
Horizontal chain-lines. Listed in *GM,LM* May. Deposit copies at L,O,E,AdU,GU.
'Politeness is my theme – to you I write'
Miller's authorship is revealed in the following edition.
L(644.m.14/22; C.131.h.1/10***),O(3),E,GU, LdU-B+; CSmH,CtY,DFo,ICN,TxU(2)+.

M256 — — The second edition. By the Rev. Mr. Miller author of Harlequin Horace, &c. *London, printed for L. Gilliver & J. Clark*, 1738.
2°: *A*² B–E²; *1–3* 4–20.
Apparently a reimpression.
O; KU(cropt),MH.

M257 — — The third edition. By the Revd. Mr. Miller... *Dublin, re-printed by George Faulkner*, 1738.
8°: *A*⁴ B⁴ C²; *1–3* 4–19 *20*. 20 advt.
L(1963),O.

M258 [—] Seasonable reproof, a satire, in the manner of Horace... To be continued occasionally as a poetical pillory... *London, printed for L. Gilliver*, 1735. (*SR* 12 Nov)
2°: *A*² B–H²; *i–iv, 1* 2–27 *28 blk*.
Sheets D and E are apparently cancels; cf. Powell Stewart in *The Library* V. 3 (1949) 295–8. Advertised in *GSJ* 13 Nov. Deposit copies at L,O,E,AdU,SaU.
'Ask Fa-ro-li, please your grace, to sing'
Reprinted in Miller's *Miscellaneous works*, 1741. Imitated from Horace satires I. 3, 4.
L(11602.i.11/1; 840.m.1/39; 643.m.14/6),O,E, DG(lacks H2),LdU-B+; CSmH,CtY,ICN,MH, TxU(3, 1 uncut)+.

M259 [—] — The second edition. *London, printed for L. Gilliver*, 1735.
2°: *A*² B–H²; *i–iv, 1* 2–27 *28 blk*.
Apparently a reissue with a new sheet A.
Forster.

M260 [—] — By the author of The man of taste. *London: printed, and Dublin, re-printed by George Faulkner*, 1736.
8°: A–B⁸ C²; *[2] i–iv, [2] 1* 2–27 *28*. 28 advt.
The attribution of authorship probably refers to Miller's play.
DK,DN,DT; CSmH,NN,NNC.

M261 [—] The year forty-one. Carmen seculare. *London, printed for Jacob Robinson*, 1741. (*GM,LM* Nov)
2°: *A*² B–E²; *i–iv*, 1–16.
Horizontal chain-lines. Probably the work described as 'Seventeen hundred forty-one, a poem', half the copyright of which was offered

Miller, J. The year forty-one

as part of a lot in a trade sale of Francis Cogan,
10 July 1746 (cat. at O-JJ), sold to Corbett for
10s. 6d. That lot specifically listed seven
works as by Miller, but this is entered
separately below them.

'It's finish'd – lo the long predicted year!'
The 'third edition' below attributed this to
'the author of Are these things so?' The
attribution has not apparently been recorded,
but it is made by the publisher of that poem,
and appears to be reliable. A political satire.
L(11630.h.53),O,C,LdU-B; CSmH,CtY,IU(uncut),MH,OCU+.

M262 [—] [reissue] The second edition. *London, printed
for J. Huggonson*, 1741.
2°: $A^2(\pm A_1)$ B–E²; *i–iv*, 1–16. ii advt.
The advertisement on p. ii lists Miller's *The
great man's answer* as 'this day...publish'd'
along with other works.
L(1482.f.38); CLU-C,CSmH,MH.

M263 [—] — [*Edinburgh*, 1741.]
8°: π^4 A–C⁴; *1–2* 3–7 *8 blk*, 1–24.
Title in half-title form. Printed by W. Cheyne
on the evidence of the ornaments.
L(1961),GU; MH.

M264 [—] — *Dublin, printed in the year* 1741.
12°: A⁸ B⁴; *i–v* vi–viii, *9* 10–24. A1 hft.
L(1488.bb.32),O,DG,DK,DN+ ; CtY,InU,TxU.

M265 [—] The yaer [!] forty-one. Carmen seculare.
Dublin, re-printed in the year 1741.
8°: A^4 B⁴; *i–iii* iv, *5* 6–15 *16 blk*.
L(1961).

M266 [—] — The third edition. By the author of Are
these things so? *London, printed for T. Cooper*,
1742.
2°: $A^2(\pm A_1)$ B–E²; *i–iv*, 1–16. ii advt.
A reissue of the London edition of 1741
(M262). The cancel retains the advertisement
for *The great man's answer* as 'this day...
published'; possibly this is merely a press
variant of that cancel title.
TxU(uncut).

'Miller, Richard.' 'The miller's tale. In hudi-
brastick verse. [*London*] *Printed for the author
Richard Miller, at the sign of the Miller's Thumb at
Mill-bank, being next door to a cook's shop.*' (*DP* 26
March 1722, 'in a few days')
No evidence of publication has been seen;
probably author and poem are fictitious and
publication day is 1 April.

Mills, A. An allusion to the third ode of the first
book of Horace, 1745. *See* A170.

Milton. Milton's epistle to Pollio, 1740. *See* King,
William, *principal of St. Mary Hall*.

M267 — Milton's sublimity asserted: in a poem.
Occasion'd by a late celebrated piece, entituled,

Milton's sublimity asserted

Cyder, a poem; in blank verse, by Philo-Milton.
*London, printed for W. Hawes; sold by J. Morphew,
and Stephen Fletcher, in Oxford*, 1709 [1708].
(*Observator* 25 Dec)
8°: A–D⁴; *i–ii* iii–xv *xvi*, 17–30 *31–32*. D4 advt.
The advertisement is for books printed for
Hawes. Reissued with remaindered poems of
Henry Hills in *A collection of the best English
poetry*, 1717 (*Case* 294).
'Long has the world impatient with desire'
L(11633.bb.1/2; 239.i.28, −D4; C.124.b.7/27),
O(2),C,EU,DN(−D4)+ ; CLU-C,CSmH,CtY,
DFo,MH.

Milton, John.
*Poems describing themselves as 'in imitation of
Milton' are usually merely written in his style; they
will be found in the subject index, but are not listed
here.*

[*Paradise lost*] Rolli, P.A.: Del paradiso perduto,
poema inglese di Giovanni Milton libri sei parte
prima tradotti di Paolo Rolli, 1729. *See* R255–6.

— Del paradiso perduto...traduzione di Paolo
Rolli, 1735, 1736. *See* R257–9.

Trapp, Joseph: Johannis Miltoni Paradisus amissus
latine redditus [2 vol], 1741–44. *See* T449–50.

Dobson, William: Paradisus amissus. Poema
Joannis Miltoni. Latine redditum [2 vol], 1750–53.
See D344–5.

[*book 1*] [Bold, Michael:] Paradisus amissa...
Nunc autem ex auctoris exemplari latine redditum... Liber primus, 1702, 1736. *See* B312–13.

Howard, W: A paraphrase in verse, on part of the
first book of Milton's Paradise lost, 1738. *See* H342.

[Jackson, Andrew:] Paradise lost: a poem. Attempted in rhyme. Book I, 1740. *See* J10.

[*book 4*] Theobald, John: Part of the fourth book
of Milton's Paradise lost, [1739/46.] *See* T132.

'Milton, John.' Miltonis epistola ad Pollionem,
1738. *See* King, William, *principal of St. Mary Hall*.

— Milton's epistle to Pollio, 1740. *See* King,
William, *principal of St. Mary Hall*.

— Mr. John Milton's satyre against hypocrites.
Written while he was Latin secretary to Oliver
Cromwell, 1710. *See* Phillips, John.

Miltonis. Miltonis epistola ad Pollionem, 1738.
See King, William, *principal of St. Mary Hall*.

M268 Minerva. Minerva to Phoebus. [*London*, 1710?]
$\frac{1}{2}^o$: 1 side, 1 column.
'With grace peculiar, and severely bright'
In praise of Harley.
MC.

— Minerva triumphans, 1701. *See* Settle, Elkanah.

M269 — [dh] Minerva's remonstrance to Great Britains
genius, for the encouragement of art and trade.

Minerva's remonstrance

Shewing the general abuses arising to the publick from banks and stocks. [*London?*] 1701. (7 April, Luttrell)
2°: A²; 1–4.
'The airy chariot breaks the azure roads'
ICN(Luttrell).

Minervae. Minervæ sacellum, 1722. *See* Settle, Elkanah.

M270 [**Minshull, —,** *Mr*.] The miser, a poem: from the first satire of the first book of Horace. Inscrib'd to Horatio Walpole, esquire. *London printed, and sold by A. Dodd, Mr. Penn, E. Nutt, and by the booksellers of London & Westminster*, 1735. (*LM* Feb)
2°: A² B–F² G¹; 1–3 4–25 26 blk. 25 err.
Latin and English text. Entered in Woodfall's ledgers under 19 Feb 1735 to 'Mr. Minshull'.
'Why rest the sons of fortune not content'
Authorship from the entry in Woodfall's ledgers, though it is just possible that Randal Minshull, bookseller of Chester, is intended.
L(643.1.25/21),O,LdU-B; CtY,KU,*MH*,NjP.

[**Minshull, Edward.**] To the E. of O----d; with the report of the committee of secrecy, 1715. *See* T368.

M271 Mirabello, *Comes de* 'De incarnatione. Auctore Comite de Mirabello ex Academia Atrebatensi. [*Edinburgh?*] 1746. (*SM* May) 8°: A⁴; 1–3 4–8.
'Quis puer obscuro jacet, hospes amabilis, antro?' L(1972).

Miraculous. The miraculous sheep's eye, 1743. *See* White, George.

M272 Mirth. Mirth in ridicule: or, a satyr against immoderate laughing. Containing the follies too often found in a sea-officer... *London printed, and sold by J. Morphew*, 1708. (*DC* 23 Jan)
4°: A² B–F²; 1–4 5–24.
'How sad of late is grown an author's case'
L(164.1.40, Luttrell, 23 Jan); CSmH,CtY,*MnU*.

Miscellanea. Miscellanea poetica: or, original poems upon several occasions; with translations. Never before printed. *London printed, and are to be sold by John Nutt*, 1706 [1705]. (*PM* 4 Dec)
8°: pp. 64. L.

Miscellaneous. A miscellaneous collection of original poems, consisting of odes, epistles, translations, &c, 1740. *See* Newcomb, Thomas.

M273 — A miscellaneous poem, inscribed to the right honourable the Earl of Oxford, lord high treasurer ... *London, printed for J. Morphew*, 1712. (5 April, Luttrell)
2°: A² B²; 1–2 3–8.
No watermark. Advertised in *Examiner* 10

A **miscellaneous** poem

April as 'just publish'd'. The fine paper copy below has a note of receipt 29 March 1712; probably presentation copies preceded public sale.
'Oxford, to you, my secret muse inclines'
On poetical method.
O(Luttrell); CtY,MH.

M274 — [fine paper]
Watermark: Amsterdam arms.
Chatsworth.

— 'Miscellaneous poems and translations. *Sold by J. Roberts*. Price 1s.' (*MC* Nov 1724)

— Miscellaneous poems. By a young gentleman. *London, printed for William Reason, bookbinder*, 1725.
8°: pp. 39. CLU-C.

M275 — Miscellanious [!] poetical novels or tales, relating many pleasing and instructive instances of wit and gallantry in both sexes... Adorn'd with sculptures. *London, printed for John Nutt*, 1705. (14 April, Luttrell)
2°: A¹ B–F² G¹; i–ii, 1–22.
Very fine engraved headpieces and initial letters. The Luttrell copy is recorded in Pickering & Chatto cat. 284/457.
'T"is never in list among miracles put'
Maurice Johnson's copy of both parts, sold at Sotheby's 23 March 1970, lot 99, was annotated 'after the Greek of Athenaeus, the Italian of Boccace, and the French of Monsr de la Fontaine – By Nahum Tate esquire...and Mons Peter Motteux...adorned with sculptures by Vn Hove [? F.H. van den Hove].'
L(11631.k.2),LVA-F; CLU-C,CSmH.

M276 — — The second collection. Adorn'd with sculptures. *London, printed for John Nutt*, 1705. (*WL* Sept)
2°: A¹ B–F²; i–ii, 1–19 20 blk.
'Oft have I deeply, and with wonder thought'
A continuation of the preceding, with three tales.
L(11631.k.2),LVA-F; CLU-C,CSmH,MH.

— Miscellaneous translations from Bion, Ovid, Moschus, and Mr. Addison. With an original poem on bowling. *Oxford, printed for E. Whistler; sold by R. Smith, J. Knapton, & J. Tonson, London*, 1716. (*MC* May)
8°: pp. 62. O,CT; CtY,IU.
A miscellany, not recorded by *Case* or *CBEL*; according to *Rawlinson*, by John Hart (who also wrote the poem on bowling), Thomas Tooly, and John Dry.

— Miscellaneous works, serious and humorous; in verse and prose. Design'd for the amusement of the fair sex, 1740. *See* Boyse, Samuel.

Miscellanies. Miscellanies in prose and verse, 1741. *See* Paget, Thomas Catesby, *baron Paget*.

Miscellanies

— Miscellanies in prose and verse. By a gentleman. *London printed, and sold by John Morphew, 1715.* 8°: pp. 16.   L,LdU–B; CtY,IU.

— Miscellanies in prose and verse, by a person of quality, 1725. *See* Howard, Edward, *8th earl of Sussex.*

— Miscellanies in prose and verse. (Viz.) I. The Bible in English verse... The second edition enlarged. *Dublin, printed by J. Carson, for S. Fuller, 1725.* 8°: pp. 106.   IU.

> Signed 'J.T.', possibly the author of *A prologue for his majesty's birth-day*, (Dublin, 1725). There are separate title-pages for each section, but the collation is continuous.

Miscellany. A miscellany of poems, [173–?] *See* Burton, John.

— Miscellany poems. By a gentleman of Oxford. *London, printed for the author; sold by J. Roberts, and W. Ratten, bookseller in Coventry, 1737. (SR 4 Aug)* 8°: pp. 68.   L,O.

> Entered in *SR* by James Roberts to 'The Author'; deposit copies at O,E,EU,AdU,SaU.

— Miscellany poems, on moral subjects. *Chester, printed by Eliz. Adams, for the author, 1750.* 4°: pp. 39.   L,EP; OCU.

— Miscellany poems on several occasions. By the author of the Choice, 1702. *See* Pomfret, John.

— Miscellany poems, on several occasions. Written by a lady, 1713. *See* Finch, Anne, *countess of Winchilsea.*

— Miscellany poems on several subjects, 1722. *See* Thomas, Elizabeth.

— Miscellany poems on several subjects. Viz. I. A disswasion... By T. B. gent. *London, printed by R. Janeway; sold by J. Nutt, 1702.* 2°: pp. 32.   OCU.

> The initials were perhaps intended to suggest Tom Brown, but the first poem is signed 'Tom B----r'. Baker, Barker, Brayer and Brewer have been privately suggested as possible candidates.

Miser. The miser, a poem, 1735. *See* Minshull, —, *Mr.*

[M277 = C548·5] The miser turn'd courtier, 1727. *See* Curry, J.

M278 Miseries. The miseries of England, from the growing power of her domestick enemies. A poem. *London, printed in the year 1702.* 4°: π¹ A–E² F¹; i–iv, 1–19 20 *blk.* (3–6 as '7–10'). π1 hft. 'Albion disclose thy drowsy eyes, and see'

> Opposing participation in the war of Spanish succession.

L(11645.e.56/1, –π1),DT; MH(–π1).

Mishap

M279 Mishap. The mishap. A poem. Written by the late rev. D. J.S. D.D. D.S.P.D. [*Dublin*, 1745/–.] ½°: 1 side, 2 columns.

> *Teerink* 990; *Williams* 1152.

'As youthful Strephon, t' other day'

> According to Williams, 'fathered upon the Dean after his death'.

L(1890.e.5/202).

M280 Miss. Miss Cadiere's case very handsomely handled. In metre. By a gentleman commoner. Calculated for the instruction of the ignorant, and proper to be read in all Christian families. *London, printed for J. Roberts, 1731. (GSJ 19 Nov)* 2°: A¹ B–C²; 1–2 3–10. 'What a bustle is here/About Madam Cadiere'

> Miss Cadière was seduced by her confessor, and many pamphlets about the case were published.

L(1973); PBL.

M281 — Miss Gall's, letter, to a certain c-o-l-l beau. [*Dublin*] *Printed by J. Durneene, in Pembroke-court, 1728.* *slip*: 1 side, 1 column. 'Dr. Sammy may I call you so'

> Signed 'Mon'key Gall', but a satire on her and her Trinity College keeper.

L(1890.e.5/121).

— Miss Prue in her tempting pinner, [1706?] *See* The city madam, 1702–.

M282 Missing, John. A poem to the memory of Isaac Watts, D.D. *London, printed for W. Owen, 1749. (GM May)* 4°: A–B⁴; 1–3 4–16.

> The DLC copy (not seen) is recorded as having an errata slip. Listed in *BM* May as, 'to which is added Titchfield...', the following poem.

'Shall Watts depart and quit the stage of life' LDW,O; *DLC.*

M283 — Titchfield, a poetical essay. *London, printed for W. Owen, 1749. (May?)* 4°: A–C⁴ D²; 1–3 4–16 25–36.

> Listed in *BM* May as issued with the preceding.

'Shall Titchfield yet remain a name unknown' O; TxU.

M284 [Missy, César de.] Bribery a satire. *London, printed for Francis Changuion; sold by M. Cooper, 1750. (GM,LM March)* 4°: A⁴ B–C⁴; 1–5 6–23 24. A1 hft.

> Vertical chain-lines.

'What! brib'ry still! What! brib'ry still your theme!'

> The L copy is signed in ms. 'C---r D-M---y'; cf. *Nichols* III. 309. It has the first line corrected in ms. to read 'What! bustling still, on brib'ry to declaim'.

L(11631.g.30/9, ms. corrections),O; IU(–A1, unopened),KU(uncut).

Missy, C. de

M285 [—] A dialogue between two free electors, Dick and Tim, on a certain day of the poll for L---d T—th—m and Sir G——e V—d--p--t... *London, printed for W. Owen*, 1749. (*BM* Dec)
4°: *A*⁴ B⁴; *i–iv* v–vii *viii*, 9–16. A1 hft.
Vertical chain-lines.
'O! how d'ye do? I'm glad to see you well'
The L copy has the preface signed in ms. 'C---r D. M---y'; cf. *Nichols* III. 309. A satire on Trentham and Vanderput in the Westminster election.
L(11631.g.40/8, ms. corrections).

M286 Mist. 'The mist clear'd up at the Nore: or, a versification of Fog's journal of Saturday, Aug. 17, 1734. [*London*] *Sold at the pamphlet shops*. Price 6*d*.' (*LM* Sept 1734)

M287 Mr. Mr. Addison's fine ode to Dr. Thomas Burnet, on his Sacred theory of the earth. Done into English by the author of a late tale call'd Coffee. *London, printed for T. Warner*, 1727. (*MC* Dec)
4°: *A*² B–C⁴; *i–iv*, *1* 2–15 *16 blk*. A1 hft.
Watermark: T.
'No usual flight of verse'
TxU(–A1).

M288 — [fine paper]
Watermarks: eagle, FM.
L(840.k.31).

— M. Ad----m's lamentation, [1726.] *See* M1.

M289 — Mr. Baron L------'s charge to the grand jury for the county of Devon, the 5th of April, 1710. At the castle of Exon... *London printed, and sold by the booksellers of London & Westminster*, 1710. (*EvP* 25 Nov)
8°: *A*⁸; *1–2* 3–16.
Teerink 841; *Williams* 1083. Williams refers to an advertisement in *DC* 14 April, but that is apparently the original speech which is here interspersed with the versification.
'From London to Exon/By special direction'
Attributed to Swift by Nichols and Scott; *Ball* (120) is doubtful and Williams rejects it. A skit on Sir Salathiel Lovell's speech.
E; NjP,MH.

M290 — [dh] Mr. Ba-- L---l's ch--ge to the grand-jury for the county of Devon... [col] [*London*] *Printed in the year* 1711.
8°: A–B⁴; *1–15 16 blk*.
This edition contains less of the original speech.
LLP,O,E; NN.

M291 — Mr. B-----ll's farewel to the ladies of Dublin, an excellent new ballad. To the tune of, To you fair ladies. *London printed, and sold by T. Griffiths, & J. Roberts*, [1719.] (*DC* 20 Feb)
½°: 1 side, 2 columns.
'To you fair ladies of Dublin'
Eustace Budgell left his Irish post on 11 Dec

Mr. B-----ll's farewel

1718; it is doubtful whether he is the author of this.
San Antonio College, Texas.

M292 — Mr. Bowman's sermon, preach'd at Wakefield, in Yorkshire, versify'd... By Christopher Crambo, esq; *London, printed for H. Cook*, 1731. (*GSJ* 19 Aug)
8°: A–D⁴; *1–2* 3–32.
'Of superstition such the case is'
L(11642.b.18),E,LdU-B; *CLU-C*,ICN,*TxU*.

M293 — — The second edition. *London, printed for H. Cook*, 1731. (Sept?)
8°: A–D⁴; *1–2* 3–32. 32 advt.
Published after 31 August on the evidence of the advertisement on p. 32. The copy at L is on very good paper, but no watermark has been identified.
L(1357.d.21/3),CT; CtY,*MnU*,OCU.

M294 — — The third edition. '*London, printed for H. Cook*' [*Edinburgh*], 1731.
8°: A–D⁴; *1–2* 3–32.
Printed by R. Fleming, from the ornament on p. 3. '[Price Six-pence.]' on title deleted, '4 Pence' in ms.
CtY.

M295 — — *Dublin, printed by S. Powell, for Abraham Bradley*, 1731.
8°: A–D⁴; *1–2* 3–32.
L(4455.b.28/2),C,DK(2).

— Mr John Milton's satyre against hypocrites, 1710. *See* Phillips, John.

M296 — Mr. Paul's speech turn'd into verse, and explain'd for the use of all lovers of the church, and the late Queen Ann. *London, printed in the year* 1716.
slip: 2 sides, 1 column.
'When the Reverend Paul'
William Paul the Jacobite was hanged, 13 July 1716; his speech is satirized here.
MH.

M297 — Mr. P-----d's elegy on the death of Mr. John Gadbury, the famous astrologer, who departed this life on Thursday the 30th of March, 1704. as he was sitting in the elbow-chair at his house in Brick-court in Westminster, aged 71 years. *London, printed for R. Longshaw, near Charing-Cross*, 1704.
½°: 1 side, 2 columns.
Mourning headpiece and borders.
'Arise ye long deceas'd astrologers'
The intended author is John Partridge the rival astrologer; but it is satirical of Partridge.
CSmH.

M298 — Mr. P—pe's picture in miniature, but as like as it can stare; a poem: with notes. *London, printed for G. Lion*, 1743. (*DP* 18 Feb)
2°: *A*² B²; *1–2* 3–7 *8 blk*.
'If C--bb--r's odes disgrace the laurel'd muse'
An attack on Pope.
LVA-D,O,LdU-B; CtY(uncut),DFo,MH,OCU.

Mr. Taste's tour

M299 — Mr. Taste's tour from the island of politeness, to that of dulness and scandal. *London, printed for S. Sloe; sold at the pamphlet-shops of London & Westminster, 1733. (DJ 31 May)*
2°: *A*² B*¹ B–D² E¹; *1–4* [2] 5–17 *18 blk.* A1 hft.
'Product of earth, by genial heat of sun'
    The introduction refers to *Ingratitude*, a prose pamphlet. For a discussion of Pope's implied authorship, see *TLS* 10 Jan, 14 Feb 1935.
O(−A1),GU,LdU-B; CtY,DLC,IU(uncut),MH, TxU+.

M300 — Mr. Whiston's erroneous principles and tenets fully expos'd. With a word of advice to Mr. Wolston. In a letter to a friend... *London printed, and sold by T. Warner, 1729.*
4°: *A*² B⁴ *C*²; *i–iv,* 1–11 *12 blk.*
'My six and twenty join as evidence'
    Each verse contains all the letters of the alphabet.
O.

M301 — Mr. Woods to all the people of Ireland. [*Dublin*] *Printed in the year 1727* [1724?].
½°: 1 side, 1 column.
'Ye people of Ireland, how comes it to pass'
    Since this is part of the propaganda against William Wood's coinage, Herbert Davis in his edition of the *Drapier's Letters* suggests that there is a misprint in the date.
Rothschild; InU.

M302 Mrs. Mrs. M'Leod's last farewel to John Gibson. [*Edinburgh, 1727.*]
½°: 1 side, 2 columns.
'Now John what makes thee look so shan'
    Margaret M'Leod was hanged for forgery, 8 March 1727; John Gibson was her accomplice.
E.

Mitchell, Joseph. Lugubres cantus. Poems on several grave and important subjects, chiefly occasion'd by the death of the late ingenious youth John Mitchell. In two parts... *London, printed for J. McEuen in Edinburgh, and for T. Cox, London, 1719. (PB 2 July, 'Monday next')*
8°: pp. 200.   L,O; CtY,DFo.
    Part 1 (to p. 104) by Mitchell; part 2 by J. Calender.

— Poems on several occasions. *London, printed for the author; sold by L. Gilliver, 1729* [1730?]. (*MC* Feb 1730)
8°: 2 vol.
    Watermark: fleur-de-lys. All copies seen are of the fine-paper issue, but the ordinary-paper copies were advertised in *MC* and used for the 1732 reissue.

— [fine paper]   L,O; MH,TxU.
    Watermark: T.

Mitchell, J.

— [reissue] *London, printed for Harmen Noorthouck, 1732.*
               L; CLU-C.
    Cancel titles; only ordinary paper copies seen.

M303 — The charms of indolence: a poem. *London, printed for T. Griffith; sold by J. Peele, [1721.] (PB 21 Nov)*
2°: π² *A¹* B–C²; *i–ii,* 1–3 *4–12.*
'Thy charms, O sacred indolence, I sing'
CSmH,TxU(3, 1 Luttrell, 5 Jan 1722).

— 'The cudgel.'
    Advertised as being subscribed for on the title-page of Mitchell's *The charms of indolence,* [1721]; no separate edition traced, but printed in his *Poems,* 1729.

M304 — The dolefull swains: a pastoral poem. Written originally in the Scotch dialect, with an English version. To which is prefix'd, a familiar epistle to Major Richardson Pack. *London, printed for T. Jauncy, 1720. (PB 4 Aug)*
8°: *A¹* B–E⁴ *F¹*; *1–3* 4–31 *32–33* '33'. 32 advt.
    There was clearly confusion about where the epistle to Pack on F1 should be bound; in the copy at OW it is bound after A1, with which it was presumably conjugate; this would agree with the title, but not with the pagination.
'Bellair, a lad, wha spent a hantle time'
'Bellair, a youth of the poetick train'
OW; MH.

M305 — An epistle to the right honourable John earl of Stairs; on the death of the right honourable Sir David Dalrymple bart. *London, printed for E. Bell, 1722* [1721]. (*DC* 18 Dec)
2°: *A*² B–C²; *1–4* 5–12. A1 hft.
    One leaf of A is possibly a cancel, presumably the title A2.
'A bard, whom no contending party sways'
L(11631.k.5/5),EU(lacks A2); TxU(2, 1 uncut, 1 Luttrell, Jan).

M306 — [dh] An epistle to the right honourable, the Earl of Stair... [col] *London printed, and Edinburgh reprinted, 1722.*
4°: *A*⁴; *1–8.*
E.

M307 — A familiar epistle to the right honourable Sir Robert Walpole; concerning poets, poverty, promises, places &c. To which are added congratulatory verses upon his taking possession...of the new house...in St James's Park... *London, printed for Alexander Cruden, 1735. (GM Oct)*
4°: A–B⁴; *1–3* 4–16.
    One copy seen has no price on title, the other 'Price Six-pence'. There appears to be no difference in the paper, but possibly the former was intended for presentation.
'Were I, Sir Robert, in your station'
'First noble master of this honour'd dome!'
L(1347.k.19; 11630.e.18/15).

Mitchell, J. A friendly epistle

[—] A friendly epistle to the author of the State dunces, 1733. *See* F269.

M308 — Gratulatory verses to Britannia. Upon occasion of the happy marriage of...the Prince of Wales, with...Augusta, princess of Saxe-Gotha. *London printed, and sold by T. Cooper*, 1736. (*GM,LM* May)
4°: *A*² B–C² ⟨D⟩²; *1–2* 3 iv 5–15 *16 blk.*
   Signature D probably cropped in the copy seen.
'Happy Britannia! Io pæan sing'
L(11632.e.39),*GM.*

M309 — Jonah: a poem. *London, printed by S. Palmer, for J. Roberts, & A. Dodd*, 1720. (*DC* 9 June)
8°: (frt+) A⁴ b⁴ B–G⁴ (+4 plates); [*8*] *i* ii–iv, *i* ii–iv, *1* 2–46 *47–48 blk.* b4ᵛ err.
   No watermark.
'Why righteous heav'n an angry face puts on'
   Dedication signed.
L(11631.e.31,–frt, G4); CSmH,CtY(Luttrell, June),ICN,MH,NN+.

M310 — [fine paper]
   Watermark: Strasburg bend. 'Price 1*s.*' on title as in the ordinary copies.
O.

M311 —— The second edition. *London, printed by S. Palmer, for J. Roberts, & A. Dodd*, 1720.
8°: (frt+) A⁴ b⁴ B–G⁴ (+4 plates); [*8*] *i* ii–iv, *i* ii–iv, *1* 2–46 *47–48 blk.* b4ᵛ err.
   Probably a variant title. Pickering & Chatto cat. 284/180 records a copy with the price deleted and 2*s.* 6*d.* added in ms. to the fly-leaf, and also a deletion in the title. Presumably this was a fine-paper copy of this issue with 'The second edition' deleted.
E(3, *1*–frt, *1*–G4); NN(–frt).

M312 — Jonah, a poetical paraphrase... The second edition, corrected and adorn'd with sculptures. To which are also added, poetical paraphrases on several other places of scripture. *London, printed for Aaron Ward, & John Oswald*, 1724. (*MC* Oct)
12°: (frt+) A⁴ B–G⁶ (+4 plates); *i–viii, 1* 2–72.
   A revised text, with variant first line:
'How heav'n, provok'd, an awful look assumes'
L(11631.c.5),O(2),*GM*,WcC.

M313 — The judgment of Hercules. A poem. *London, printed in the year* 1727. (*MC* June)
4°: A–C⁴ D²; *i–iii* iv–viii, *9* 10–28.
   No watermark. The imprint is that found on some fine-paper copies, where one would expect it; perhaps there was some confusion in the printing house.
'The conflict youthful Hercules endur'd'
   Dedication signed.
OCU.

M314 — [fine paper]
   Watermark: crowned eagle.
KU,MH(uncut).

Mitchell, J. The judgment of Hercules

M315 — [fine paper, variant imprint:] *London, printed for J. Roberts*, 1727.
   This is the imprint one would expect on ordinary-paper copies.
O,OW.

M316 — Melpomene: a poem to the memory of Mr. Joseph Foord, V.D.P. By Mr. Mitchel. S.T.S. *Edinburgh, printed by Mr. James M'Euen and Company, and sold at Mr. James M'Euen's shop*, 1719.
8°: π⁴ A⁸ B⁴; *i–ii* iii–vi *'vi' viii blk*, 1–24.
'That muse that lately sung, in mournful strains'
O,E(ms. corrections),*GM*; NN.

M317 — The monument: or, the muse's motion to the right honourable Sir Robert Walpole...upon occasion of the death of Sir Richard Steele, knt. *London, printed for J. Roberts*, 1729. (*MChr* 30 Sept)
2°: A–C²; *i–vi, 1* 2–5 *6 blk.* A1 hft.
'Crown'd with the wreath of universal praise'
   Mitchell's name appears in the penultimate line.
O(–A1); MH,TxU.

M318 — 'Ode on Buchanan. *London*, 1724.'
4°.
GM (missing 1967).

M319 — An ode on the power of musick. *London, printed for Thomas Jauncy*, 1721. (*DJ* 10 Feb)
2°: (frt+) *A*¹ B–E²; *i–vi, 1* 2–12. *12 advt.*
   The Luttrell copy, dated Feb, is recorded in *Haslewood.*
'When nature yet in embrio lay'
   Dedicated to Alexander Malcolm, author of a treatise on music.
L(841.m.26/3,–frt); CSmH,MH,TxU.

[—] An ode to Mr. Allan Ramsay, 1720. *In* R107.

M320 — 'The plea of Parnassus. An address to Sir John Williams, kt. lord mayor of London; concerning the place of city poet. [*London*] *Printed for S. Nevill.* Price 4*d.*' (*LM* Nov 1735)

M320·5 [—] Poltis king of Thrace; or the peace-keeper: a tale, from Plutarch, address'd to the powers of Europe, in the year, one thousand seven hundred and twenty six. *Dublin, printed in the year* 1726.
½°: 1 side, 2 columns.
   Reprinted in *A tale and two fables in verse*, 1727, which is entered below; this edition is possibly unauthorized.
'E'er Europe's peace is broken quite'
C.

M321 — The promotion, and the alternative: two poetical petitions to the right honourable Sir Robert Walpole. By the author of the Sine-cure and Equivalent. *Westminster, printed by A. Campbell, for J. Millan; sold by J. Roberts*, 1726. (*MC* April)
8°: π¹ A–D⁴ *E*¹; *i–ii, 1*–32 *33–34*. ii err; E1 advt.
   No watermark; 'Price 6*d.*' on title. The title to *The promotion* on A4 has imprint 'printed by

Mitchell, J. The promotion

J. Cluer & A. Campbell'; 'Finis' on p. 24 suggests a possible earlier issue of this poem alone. *The alternative* occupies pp. 25–32. π1 and E1 have been seen to be conjugate. Listed in *MC* as 'Two poetical epistles to...Sir Robert Walpole'.

'Twice has the muse to Walpole told my case'
'Wearied by continuous strife'

Prefatory verses addressed to Mitchell. The petitions continue *The sine-cure* and *The equivalent* (M344), proposing his appointment to the commission to superintend the next public lottery, or to the next general assembly of the church of Scotland.

L(11602.ee.22/2, lacks π1, E1; 11602.ee.22/4, lacks π1, D⁴, E1),*GM*; CtY,MH(−E1).

M322 — [fine paper] *Westminster, printed in the year 1726.*
Watermark: Strasburg bend in A; no price on title.
CLU-C.

M323 —— The second edition. *Westminster, printed by A. Campbell, for J. Millan; sold by J. Roberts, 1726.*
8°: π1 A–D⁴ E¹; *i–ii, 1–32 33–34.* ii err; E1 advt.
Apparently a reimpression or variant title.
E; InU(uncut).

M324 — Ratho: a poem to the king. *London, printed for John Gray, 1728.* (*MChr* 29 April)
8°: a⁴ b–c⁴ A–D⁴; *i–v* vi–xxiii *xxiv blk, 1* 2–32. a1 hft.
Watermark: initials GF.
'I sing of Ratho. Help me to relate'
GM(−a1); CSmH,CtY,*TxHR*.

M325 — [fine paper]
Watermark: fleur-de-lys on shield.
E(dedication copy to Charles earl of Lauderdale); ICN(presentation binding).

M326 — The royal hermitage or temple of honour: a poem to her majesty the queen-regent. To which is prefix'd, an epistle to...Sir Robert Walpole. *London, printed for J. Roberts, 1732.* (*GSJ* 30 Sept)
4°: A–B² C²; *1–3* 4–12.
'A bard, unvers'd in politicks, unhir'd'
L(11630.b.5/10); CtY(uncut),TxU.

M327 — The shoe-heel: a rhapsody. *London, printed for Tho. Astley, 1727.* (*MC* Aug)
8°: A⁴ a⁴ B–H⁴; *[8] i* ii–viii, *1* 2–56.
Bond 94. Copies at CLU-C,NjP have four leaves of advertisements added; that at DFo has two. Advertised in *MC* Sept 1728 as 'just re-printed', apparently in error. The copyright, with 126 books, formed lot 58 of the trade sale ascribed to 'Mr Astley & Conger', 11 Nov 1735 (cat. at O-JJ), apparently unsold.
'Ill fare the miscreant, who, to mischief prone'
L(11658.g.45),O,AdU; CSmH,DFo(uncut),ICU, MH,NjP+.

M328 — A sick-bed soliloquy to an empty purse: in Latin and English verse... To which is added a

Mitchell, J. A sick-bed soliloquy

curse upon punch; in imitation of the third epode of Horace... *London, printed for the author; sold by W. Mears,* [1735.] (*LM* April)
4°: A⁴ B⁴; *1–5* 6–16.
Bond 144.
'Perniciosa movet dum febris membra tumultus'
'While baleful fever, with progressive rage'
Curse: 'Is there a traitor, whoremonger, or thief'
L(840.k.3/4),O,LdU-B; MH.

M329 [—] The sine-cure. A poetical petition to the right honourable Robert Walpole, esq; for the government of Duck-Island, in St. James's-Park. *London, printed in the year 1725.*
4°: π1 A² B² C¹; *i–ii, 1–3* 4–10. π1 hft.
Reprinted in *Two poetical petitions,* 1725 (M344).
'Weary'd with vain pursuits, and humble grown'
Signed 'J. M.' See *The promotion* for further petitions.
L(11632.bb.57); TxU.

M330 [—] A tale and two fables in verse. With three prefaces, one postscript, and two nota-bene's, in prose. By the author of the Totness-address versify'd. *London, printed for J. Roberts, 1727.* (*MC* May)
8°: A⁴ B–D⁴; *1–5* 6–31 *32 blk.*
An earlier edition of the tale is entered above as *Poltis king of Thrace* (Dublin, 1726).
'E're Europe's peace is broken quite'
Fable 1: 'War happens not among the great'
Fable 2: 'Upon a time (ev'n so my nurse'
L(11633.e.36),O,OW,LdU-B; CSmH(cropt), CtY,DFo,ICN,MH+.

M331 — Three poetical epistles. To Mr. Hogarth, Mr. Dandridge, and Mr. Lambert, masters in the art of painting. *London, printed for John Watts, 1731.* (*GSJ* 13 Feb)
4°: A¹ B–C⁴; *i–ii, 1* 2–16.
'Hogarth, by merit of your own'
'Unskill'd in painting, vain were my essay'
'Hail, noble artist! nature's rival, hail!'
L(643.k.3/10),O; DFo,MH.

M332 — To their most excellent majesties, the humble address and petition of the water-drinking poets of Great-Britain. In Brobdingnagian verse. Presented at Kensington, by Mr. Mitchell. [*London*] *Printed for Tho. Astley,* [1727.] (*MC* Aug)
½°: 1 side, 1 column.
With a four-line answer at foot.
'Whereas, in late King George's reign, it was our fate to miss'
E.

M333 [—] The Totness address, versified. To which is annex'd, the original address, as presented to his majesty. *London, printed for H. Whitridge, 1727.* (*DJ* 16 March)
2°: A² B–C²; *1–2* 3–11 *12 blk.*
The first seven 'editions' are all impressions from the same setting of type; the 'second

Mitchell, J. The Totness address

edition' advertised in *DJ* 17 March may be concealed here. They were printed by Samuel Richardson (*Sale* 54).
'Among the many warm addresses'
Reprinted in Mitchell's *Poems*, 1729. A copy of the seventh edition at L has an early ms. attributing the versification to 'the E. of Chesterfeild', but there seem no grounds for this attribution.
O(2),OW(2),LdU-B; DLC,IU,MH,OCU(uncut), TxU.

M334 [—] — The third edition. *London, printed for H. Whitridge*, 1727.
2⁰: *A² B–C²; 1–2 3–11 12 blk.*
CtY(uncut).

M335 [—] — The fourth edition. *London, printed for H. Whitridge*, 1727. (*DJ* 18 March)
2⁰: *A² B–C²; 1–2 3–11 12 blk.*
L(163.m.62),O; ICU.

M336 [—] — The fifth edition. *London, printed for H. Whitridge*, 1727. (*DJ* 22 March)
2⁰: *A² B–C²; 1–2 3–11 12 blk.*
O.

M337 [—] — The sixth edition. *London, printed for H. Whitridge*, 1727. (*DJ* 24 March)
2⁰: *A² B–C²; 1–2 3–11 12 blk.*
L(1970),O; TxU.

M338 [—] — The seventh edition. *London, printed for H. Whitridge*, 1727.
2⁰: *A² B–C²; 1–2 3–11 12 blk.*
L(1476.dd.17/3),AdU.

M339 [—] — The eighth edition. With the addition of an angry Totnesian's letter to the author; and his answer thereto. *London, printed for H. Whitridge*, 1727. (Luttrell, May)
2⁰: *A² B–C²; 1 2–12.*
The letter and answer on pp. 11–12 are both in verse. The Luttrell copy is recorded in *Haslewood*. Listed in *MChr* 20 Dec 1729, no doubt because *The Oxford sermon versified* was published then.
O; MH.

M340 [—] The Totnes address, presented to his majesty, and printed in the London-gazette, March 2. 1726-7. versified. [*London*] *Printed for J. Williams, near the Strand*, [1727.]
½⁰: 1 side, 2 columns.
Verse only.
CLU-C.

M341 [—] [dh] The Totnes address versified. [*Edinburgh?* 1727.]
8⁰: *A²; 1 2–4.*
Probably a piracy; the Edinburgh origin is merely a plausible guess.
L(11659.c.66).

M342 [—] — *Dublin, printed by George Faulkner*, 1727.
½⁰: 2 sides, 2 columns.

Mitchell, J. The Totness address

On the verso, the original prose address.
L(C.121.g.8/160, mutilated).

M343 — Transportation: or, the tower. An ode to the right honourable Sir Robert Walpole... *London, printed for T. Warner*, 1732.
4⁰: *A–B⁴; 1–5 6–16. A1 hft.*
Half-title, 'Another ode to Sir Robert'.
'Seven years your levees I have haunted'
O.

M344 — Two poetical petitions to the right honourable Robert Walpole esq; I. The sine-cure. II. The equivalent. *London, printed for R. Francklin*, 1725. (*MC* June)
8⁰: *π² A⁴ B⁴(B1+χ²) C⁴ D²; i–iv, 1–3 4–31 32. π1 hft; 32 err, advt.*
Watermark: bird. χ² (pp. 11–14) contains congratulatory verses. Separate title-pages to the poems on A1, B2. The number of copies lacking π² suggests a possible earlier issue without the general title. *The sine-cure* was separately published; see M329.
Equivalent: 'Life of your country's hope! the bard, whose strain'
The second petition proposes the post of poet laureat in Scotland for Mitchell.
L(11602.ee.22/3),E(−π1, lacks D²),NwP(lacks π², χ²); DFo,MB,MH(lacks π²),NN(2, 1−π¹, 1 lacks π²,χ²).

M345 — [fine paper]
Watermark: MT (cf. *Heawood* 3089). The copy seen is without π²; possibly issued without the general title-leaf and half-title.
O(lacks π²).

M346 [—] Verses spoken after the performance of Mr. Otway's tragedy, called the Orphan: at a private meeting in Edinburgh, December 9th, 1719. By a boy in the university. [*Edinburgh*, 1719.]
½⁰: 1 side, 1 column.
'The beardless actors of this favourite play'
Early ms. attribution in the E copy 'Mr Mitchell'.
E.

M347 **Mitre.** The mitre. A tale. In hudibrastick verse. Describing three b-sh-ps in lawn-sleeves rowing to Lambeth for a see. *London, printed for E. Rayner; sold by the booksellers of London & Westminster*, [1731.] (*GSJ* 26 May)
2⁰: (frt+) *A² B¹; 1–2 3–6.*
Bond 114; *Percival* p. 54.
'Three mariners from diff'rent sees'
On the contention of Edmund Gibson, Benjamin Hoadly and Lancelot Blackburne for the see of Canterbury on Wake's illness. Cf. *First oars to L--m--th*, [1731.]
L(11602.i.16/2; 643.l.24/42, −frt),C(−frt); CLU-C.

M348 — — The second edition. *London, printed for E. Rayner; sold by the booksellers of London & Westminster*, [1731.]

The **mitre**

2⁰: (frt+) A^2 B^1; *1–2* 3–'7' (6 as '7').
CSmH,TxU(lacks frt).

M——k, W——m. The royal invitation, 1719. *See* R312.

'M---ky, Ann.' The taverners answer to the drunken wives lament, [1725?] *See* T100.

Mob. Mob contra mob, [1714.] *See* Meston, W.

M349 Mock. The mock campaign; or, English bravery: a poem. *London, published by C. Corbett*, 1740. (*DP* 7 July)
2⁰: A^2 $B–E^2$; *1–2* 3–19 *20 blk.*
'When foes obdurate grow, and treaties fail'
    A satire on military and naval preparations for the war with Spain.
L(1490.f.10),O; CSmH,CtY,OCU(cropt),TxU.

M350 —— '*London, published by C. Corbett*' [*Edinburgh*], 1740. (*SM* July)
8⁰: A^4 $B–C^4$ D^2; *1–2* 3–28.
    Printed by W. Cheyne, on the evidence of the ornament on p. 3.
L(1972),E,GU,MP; CSmH,MH(cropt).

M351 —— A mock epithalamium upon the fictitious marriage of the Pretender, with the Princess Sobieskie, now cloyster'd up at Isnpruck [!]. Inscribed to the tory wits and poets throughout Great-Britain. *London printed, and sold by J. Roberts*, 1718 [1719?]. (*DC* 9 Jan 1719)
8⁰: $A–D^4 E^2$ (A3 as 'A2'); *i–iv*, *1–30* 31–32 *blk.* A1 hft.
'Bright sons of Bacchus and Apollo'
    Macdonald, Dryden p. 49 tentatively suggests Nicholas Amhurst's authorship, apparently following Pickering & Chatto cat. 284/485; there is no concrete evidence for the attribution.
L(11631.d.30,–E2),O,E; CLU-C,CtY(–A1), DFo.

—— The mock magistrates, 1721. *See* P165.

M352 —— The mock marriage: or, a lady and no lady, a new ballad. Inscrib'd to a certain peer, and an Hibernian young lady; who were lately marry'd in jest, but bedded in earnest. To the tune of, Which no-body can deny. *London, printed for T. Reynolds*, 1733. (*GM* May)
2⁰: $A–B^2$; *1–2* 3–7 *8.* 8 advt.
'Ye beaux, and ye belles of the town and the city'
    Said to be about Thomas, baron Onslow and a trick played on him.
O(uncut); DLC,KU(cropt).

M353 —— The second edition. *London, printed for T. Reynolds*, 1733.
2⁰: $A–B^2$; *1–2* 3–7 *8.* 8 advt.
    Apparently a reimpression.
L(1480.d.11),O,OW,*LdU-B*; CtY,IU(uncut), KU,MH.

The **mock** marriage

M354 —— The third edition. *London, printed for T. Reynolds*, 1733.
2⁰: $A–B^2$; *1–2* 3–7 *8.* 8 advt.
    Apparently a reimpression.
NjP,OCU.

M355 —— Mock masonry: or the grand procession. [*London*] *Printed and published according to act of parliament*, 1741, *and sold by Mrs. Dodd, and at most booksellers and pamphlet-shops.* (*DG* 28 March)
1⁰: 1 side, 3 columns.
    Large engraving at head.
'Pray vat be dis vine show we gaze on?'
    On the mock procession to meet the masons, 19 March 1741, organized by Esq; Carey and Paul Whitehead. Cf. *LDP* 20 March 1741.
L(P&D 2494); NNP.

—— The mock mourners, 1702. *See* Defoe, Daniel.

M356 —— [dh] The mock-patron: or, an address from Grubstreet, to Dr. Cl---t----n. [*Dublin*, 1727?]
4⁰: A^2; *1* 2–4.
'As when a boy is passing thorough'
    Apparently a satire on Robert Clayton, subsequently bishop of Killala. He apparently promised a reward to the poets of Trinity College Dublin for poems in praise of King George, and then failed to pay. 1727 seems a likely time for the offer, and fits Clayton's career; cf. G267, T363.
LdU-B; CtY.

—— Mock poem: or, whiggs supplication, 1711. *See* Colvil, Samuel.

M357 —— [dh] The mock senator; a pleasant Arabian tale. Written originally in Arabick by Kara Mustapha Bashaw Reis Effendi, or clerk of the scribes of the Ottoman port, now faithfully rendred into English. [*London?* 1717/22?]
2⁰: A^2; *1* 2–4.
'When Sultan Mahomet Han the scepter sway'd'
    A satire on 'Mr P: Ha—n' (ms. note;? Hamilton), a Scot who curried favour at court and failed in his attempt to succeed Sir John Lauder of Fountainhall as lord of session.
E(ms. notes).

Mocking. Mocking is catching, [1726.] *See* Carey, Henry.

M358 Model. 'The model, or the modern gentleman, a new ballad. [*London*] Price 6d.' (*BM* April 1747)

Moderate. The moderate cabal, 1710. *See* Milbourne, Luke.

M359 —— The moderate man. [*London?* 1715/–.]
slip: 1 side, 1 column.
    Rough woodcut at head and foot.
'Pray lend me your ear, you who've any to spare'
    A satire on time-serving dissenters.
C.

The **moderate** man's advice

M360 — The moderate man's advice against extravagant drinking, or, enough is as good as a feast. To an excellent new tune. *Edinburgh printed, and sold by John Moncur*, 1707.
½°: 1 side, 2 columns.
'Come all you brave hearts of gold'
E.

M361 — The moderate man's confession. *Printed for and sold by William Yetts on the pier of Leith*, 173⟨ ⟩.
½°: 1 side, 1 column.
'I'm nor high church, nor low church, nor tory, nor whig'
E.

Moderation. Moderation display'd, 1704–. *See* Shippen, William.

M362 — Moderation display'd, the second part. Represented in the church of England's ghost. [*London*] *Printed in the year* 1705.
4°: π² A–E² (D2 as 'C2'); *i–viii*, 1–16. π1 hft.
''Twas night, as on my bed I waking lay'
A continuation of *Moderation display'd*, 1704, entered under William Shippen. There is no evidence that it is by the same author.
LVA–F,C.

— Moderation vindicated, in an answer, 1705. *See* Shippen, William.

[M363–4 = W46·2–5] **Modern.** The modern courtier, [1741.] *See* Ward, Edward [The ambitious father].

M365 — The modern Englishman. A satire. *London, printed for Daniel Farmer, & Jacob Robinson; sold by T. Cooper, & J. Graham*, 1738. (*GM, LM* May)
2°: *A*¹ B–E² F¹; *i–ii*, 1 2–18.
The priority of this and the undated variant below is not established; some dated copies may be included in error among those listed below.
'When luxury and lust cou'd once enslave'
A satire on contemporary manners and morals.
L(1482.f.29).

M366 — [variant, no date in imprint]
A second listing in *GM, LM* March 1739 may refer to this variant.
O,LdU–B; CSmH,CtY(2),ICU,MH,TxU+.

M367 — — By A.P. esq; '*London*' [*Dublin*], *printed in the year* 1739.
8°: A–B⁴ C²; *1–3* 4–20.
'By A.P.' is doubtless intended to suggest Pope's authorship.
DA.

M368 — [*idem*] The characters of the age; or the modern Englishman. A satire. *London, printed for J. Robinson*, 1743.
2°: *A*¹(±) B–E² F¹; *i–ii*, 1 2–18.
A reissue of the London edition.
CSmH.

The **modern** Englishman

M369 — — [*London*, 174–?]
2°: *A*¹(±) B–E² F¹; *i–ii*, 1 2–18.
Another reissue; the order of this and the preceding has not been determined. In place of the imprint there is a woodcut tailpiece.
MH.

M370 — The modern fanaticks characteriz'd. Being a lively description of a young fanatical pastor, an old schismatical elder, and a shining Christian widow, down in the north-country... *London, printed for J. Wilford*, 1732.
8°: *A*² B–C⁴ D²; *1–4* 5–24. A1 hft.
'A sister of old Levi's tribe'
A satire on Mr. R—f of Preston, an enthusiastic dissenting preacher.
O.

M371 — [reissue] The modern fanaticks characteriz'd. To which is added, a pathetick speech to the pious brethren in conventicle assembled... *London, printed for J. Cox*, 1735. (*LM* Feb)
8°: a⁴ B–C⁴ D²; *i–ii* iii–viii, 5–24.
The cancel preliminaries include the prose speech against the dissenters.
O.

M372 — ⟨Modern fashions. A poem, address'd to the ladies.⟩ ⟨*London, Cave & Dodd.*⟩ (*GM* Nov 1745)
2°: ⟨ ⟩ B–E²; ⟨ ⟩ 1 2–15 *16*. 16 advt.
The copy seen lacks the preliminary leaves; the title is supplied from the entry in *GM*. Horizontal chain-lines.
'Ye British fair! whose charms outshine'
CtY(imperfect).

— The modern fine gentleman, 1746. *See* Jenyns, Soame.

M373 — The modern fine lady. Or, a counterpart to a poem lately published, called, The modern fine gentleman. *London, printed for M. Cooper*, 1746. (*GA* 30 April)
2°: A⁴; *1–3* 4–8.
'At Hackney, or at Chelsea bred'
A sequel to Soame Jenyns's poem of 1746, by another hand; his *Modern fine lady* was not published until 1751.
CtY,MH,*OCU*.

[M374 = A365·5] — A modern inscription to the Duke of Marlborough's fame, 1706. *See* Atwood, William.

M375 — A modern Latin ode attempted in English. O qui recisæ finibus indicis, &c. [*London*] *Printed for J. Morphew*, 1707.
½°: 1–2, 1 column.
'Kind friend, with whom I sip, and smoke'
A translation of [John Philips] *Honoratissimo viro, Henrico St.-John*, 1707.
O,MC,*Crawford*,Rothschild; DFo.

M376 — Modern matrimony. A satire. To a young nobleman. *London, printed for T. Cooper*, 1737 [1736]. (*GM, LM* Nov)
2°: *A*² B²; *1–3* 4–8.

Modern matrimony

'A bard, to Phœbus and the world unknown'
O; CtY,OCU.

M377 — Modern patriotism, a poem. *London, printed for J. Brindley; sold by J. Roberts, J. Wilford, Mrs. Nutt, Cooke, & Charlton, A. Dodd, J. Chrichley, and by the booksellers of London & Westminster,* [1734.] (*GSJ* 3 May)
4⁰: A^4 B–G⁴; *1–2* 3–54 *55*; *56 blk.* 55 err.
Listed in *LM* April.
'Long waiting, when some poet's manly page'
L(1966); CSmH(uncut),CtY,ICN,KU.

M378 — [reissue] Modern patriotism, or faction display'd: a poem. Being a satire on political writers. *London, printed for J. Brindley, J. Jolliffe, O. Payne, A. Lyon, C. Corbett; sold by J. Roberts, J. Wilford, Mrs Nutt, Cooke, & Charlton, A. Dodd, J. Chrichley, and by the booksellers of London & Westminster,* [1734/–.]
4⁰: $A^4(\pm A1)$ B–G⁴; *1–2* 3–54 *55*; *56 blk.* 55 err.
CSmH,IU.

M379 — The modern patriots: a proper new ballad, humbly inscribed to the electors of members for the ensuing parliament of Great-Britain. To the tune of The cobler of Canterbury. [*London*] *Printed in the year* 1734.
½⁰: 1 side, 2 columns.
'The muse of good patriots now virtuously sings'
Against the tories.
MC.

M380 — The modern poet. A rapsody. *London, printed for C. Corbett,* 1735. (*GM* April)
2⁰: A^2 B–E²; *i–ii, 1–2* 3–18. A1 hft.
'In lofty verse, who would a master be'
Purporting to be by James Bramston, but rather a satire upon him, particularly against *The man of taste,* 1733.
L(1489.m.18; 1482.f.28,–A1),O,C; TxU(2).

M381 — — The second edition. *London, printed for A. Dodd,* 1736.
2⁰: $A^2(\pm A2)$ B–E²; *i–ii, 1–2* 3–18. A1 hft; 2 err.
Apparently reissued with a cancel title and the original half-title.
*CLU-C,*CSmH,IU,MH(–A1).

M382 — Modern quality. An epistle to Miss M---W--- on her late acquired honour. From a lady of real quality. *London, printed for J. Huggonson,* 1742. (*GM, LM* Feb)
2⁰: A^2 B–C²; *1–2* 3–12.
Drop-head title on p. 3, 'The modern countess'. Horizontal chain-lines.
'Shall British honour be insulted so'
An attack on the patent of precedence granted to Maria Walpole after Walpole's ennoblement.
L(643.l.28/18),O,C,LdU-B; CSmH,CtY,ICN, MH,TxU(2)+.

M383 — — The second edition, with additions. *London, printed for J. Huggonson,* 1742.

Modern quality

2⁰: A^2 B–C²; *1–2* 3–12.
Horizontal chain-lines.
O.

M384 — — *London printed, and Dublin re-printed in the year* 1742.
8⁰: A–B⁴; *1–2* 3–15 *16 blk.*
L(C.71.bb.15/2),C,DN.

— The modern reasoners, 1734. *See* Dodsley, Robert.

M385 — The modern turn-coats, or, Æsop at court. Being three select fables relating to the present changes. *London, printed in the year* 1710.
½⁰: 1 side, 2 columns.
'A certain oak of royal growth'
On the change of ministry.
CLU-C.

M386 — Modern virtue. A satire. *London, printed for M. Cooper,* 1746. (*GM, LM* June)
4⁰: A^4 B–C⁴; *1–5* 6–24. A1 hft.
'Let venal annals boast a Cæsar's reign'
L(11630.c.5/15,–A1, mutilated),O(–A1); CSmH,CtY,IU,KU,MH(2, 1 uncut).

M387 — The modern whig dictator: or, the exultation: a satyr. *London printed, and are to be sold by the booksellers of London & Westminster,* 1702. (19 Feb, Luttrell)
2⁰: A–D²; *i–iv, 1–12.*
The Luttrell copy is recorded in *Haslewood;* listed in *WL* Feb.
'Courage, my friends, 'tis now an equal lay'
O; CtY(uncut),IU,MH,TxU.

M388 — Modern wit; or twelve celebrated beauties, done into riddles. [*Dublin,* 1724?]
½⁰: 1 side, 2 columns.
'We are told of a sphinx who in ages of old'
C.

M389 **Modest.** A modest defence of Mr. Gr——n. Being an answer to the Censoriad. *Dublin, printed by James Hoey & George Faulkner,* 1730.
8⁰: A^4; *1–3* 4–8.
Reprinted as D⁴ of *Graffanio-mastix,* 1730.
'O what a sad age of corruption we live in'
A defence of Hugh Graffan.
DA,DT(2),*MR-C; CtY,*IU.

M390 — A modest enquiry, address'd to the bishop of Cloyne. *Dublin, printed in the year* 1736.
8⁰: A^2 B⁴; *1–2* 3–10 *11–12 blk* (10 as '01').
'To judge, my lord, from what you've writ'
A satire addressed to George Berkeley.
C,DK,DN; *MH.*

M391 — — address'd to the bishop of C--------e. *Printed in the year* 1738.
8⁰: A^4; *1–2* 3–8.
Possibly a piece of provincial Irish printing.
L(11643.bbb.24/1; C.71.bb.15/12),DN; *MH.*

M392 — The modest, loyal, and humble petition of the w--ggs... Almost to the tune of Last parliament

The **modest**, loyal, and humble petition

sate as snug as a cat. [*London*] *Printed in the year* 1710.
½°: 1 side, 2 columns.
'If Anne thou wilt but be so kind'
Harding.

M393 — A modest praise of pritty Miss Smalley. *Dublin, printed by and for James Hoey*, 1730.
8°: A⁴; *1–2* 3–8. 8 advt.
'Beauty's soft goddess on a day'
In praise of Molly Smalley.
L(11642.a.59).

Modish. 'Modish adultery: a congratulatory epistle to a great lady lately divorced. [*London*] *Printed for S. Slow; sold by all the pamphlet-sellers in town & country.* Price 6d.' (*LEP* 3 March 1744)
There is no evidence whether this is in prose or verse.

'Moffett, William.' Hesperi-neso-graphia, 1716–.
See H162.

M394 Mohocks. The Mohocks: a poem, in Miltonic verse: address'd to the Spectator. *London, printed in the year* 1712.
8°: A⁴; *1–2* 3–8.
    Advertisement for two poems published by Curll at foot of the title.
'Heroes, and dreadful arms, and bloody fields'
O,DT,*MR-C*; CtY,ICU,OCU,TxU(2).

M395 — The Mohocks revel. An excellent new ballad. To the tune of, The jovial beggars, &c. [*London?*] *Printed in the year* 1712.
½°: 1 side, 2 columns.
'We Mohocks rule the world by night'
    Against the whigs.
Rothschild; MH.

Mollineux, Mary. Fruits of retirement: or, miscellaneous poems, moral and divine... *London printed, and sold by T. Sowle*, 1702.
8°: pp. 174.   L,LF; CtY,MH.
    Mary Mollineux died in 1695.

— — The third edition. *London printed, and sold by the assigns of J. Sowle*, 1720.
8°: pp. 174.   L,LF.
    No second edition has been traced.

— — The fourth edition. *London printed, and sold by the assigns of J. Sowle*, 1739.
8°: pp. 174.   L,LF; PHC.

Molly. Molly Mog: or, the fair maid of the inn, [1726.] *See* Gay, John.

M396 Monarchy. Monarchy and church, as explain'd by Dr. Henry Sacheverel. By J. Distaff, cousin to Isaac Bickerstaff, esq; *London, printed for J. Baker*, 1710. (*SR* 26 Oct)
8°: *A⁴*; *1* 2–8.
    Entered in *SR* to Thomas Darrack; deposit copies at L,EU. Advertised in *PM* 28 Nov.

Monarchy and church

'Of all the cheats and shams that have of late'
    A revision of *A great noise about nothing*, 1705.
    'J. Distaff' is clearly a pseudonym.
L(698.h.13/8),E,EU; IU,InU,TxU.

M397 Moncrieff, Robert. Magnanimity. A poem. With the characters of some of the greatest men of the age. *London, printed for the author; sold at the booksellers and pamphlet shops of London & Westminster*, 1735. (*LM* Jan)
4°: π¹ a–b² χ¹ C–I²; [2] i–viii, 7–36. 36 err.
'O magnanimity! uplift my muse'
    Largely in praise of Eustace Budgell, and puffed by him in the *Bee*. Mrs. Lois Morrison suggests (privately) that Budgell was the author.
L(11631.f.24, lacks a1),LVA-F,O; MH.

Monimia. Monimia to Philocles: being a letter from an unfortunate lady, 1726–. *See* Hervey, John, *baron Hervey.*

Monk. The monk and the miller's wife, [1724/26.] *See* Ramsay, Allan.

[Monk, Mary.] Marinda. Poems and translations upon several occasions. *London, printed by J. Tonson*, 1716. (*SR* 13 June)
8°: pp. 156.   L,O; CtY,MH.
    Watermark: star. Deposit copy at O.

[—] [fine paper]   L.
    No watermark. Dedication copy in presentation morocco at L.

M398 Monkey. [dh] The monkey and the hounds. A fable. [173–?]
8°: A⁴; *1* 2–8.
'To cut the teeth, you use a coral'
    The L catalogue suggests this is a satire on Sir Robert Walpole.
LVA-F.

M399 — — [173–?]
8°: A⁴ (A2 as 'A'); *1* 2–8.
L(11632.df.18).

M400 Monmouth. 'Monmouth-street in tears: a sort of an elegy on the death of Country Jack the M——h—s——t banker... Dedicated to Mr. Henry Williams. [*London*] *Printed for M. Cooper, & John Harper.* Price 6d.' (*DA* 21 July 1743)

M401 Monody. A monody in commemoration of the 10th of September 1750. [*Edinburgh?* 1750?]
8°: *A²*; *1–3* 4.
    Title in half-title form.
'Hail, happy saint! from mortal woe set free!'
    Apparently written to commemorate a mother's death.
E.

M402 Monosyllable. The monosyllable If! A satire. *London, printed for H. Carpenter; sold at all the pamphlet-shops in London & Westminster,* 1748. (*GM, LM* Oct)
2°: A^1 B–C^2; *1–3* 4–10.
'If heav'nly truth on her etherial throne'
L(C.57.g.7/21),O,*DrU-U*,LdU-B; CLU,ICN, IU,MH(uncut),*OCU*(lacks A1).

M403 — — '*London, printed for H. Carpenter; sold at all the pamphlet-shops in London & Westminster*' [*Dublin, printed by Richard James*], 1748.
8°: A^4; *1–3* 4–8.
The printer's ornament on the title was used by Richard James in this year.
O,C(2),*LpU*; CtY,ICU.

M404 Mons. [dh] Mons Alexander, in Struani domini sui reditum. [*Edinburgh, printed by Thomas Ruddiman,* 1731/32.]
4°: A^2; *1* 2–4.
On p. 3, 'Mount Alexander's complaint... Imitated from the Latin ode'.
'Præda sui nuper Batavis ac hostibus Anglis'
'While my dear master, far frae hame'
The English imitation is printed from Allan Ramsay's ms. in Ramsay's *Works* III (1961) 191f. On Alexander Robertson of Struan's return from exile to his estate, Mount Alexander.
ICU.

M405 — [reissue] [*Edinburgh,* 1731/32.]
4°: A–B^2; *1* 2–8.
With two poems added, 'To the unknown author of the Latin ode' and 'The Latin ode imitated', first lines:
'With faint essay, I on the trembling string'
'To faithless English, and the Dutch a prey'
The additional poems are ascribed to 'S.B.' in the OCU copy below.
TxU.

M406 — [reissue] [*Edinburgh*] *Printed in the year* 1732.
4°: π^1 A–B^2 C^1; *i–ii, 1* 2–8, *1–2.*
π1 and C1 have been seen to be conjugate; π1 is title-leaf, C1 bears 'The Latin ode Mons Alexander imitated'. Both copies seen are followed by Robertson of Struan's *To the anonymous author of a Latin ode,* [1732?], probably issued with this.
'Of late a rude and helpless mass I lay'
The added poem is ascribed to 'Dr. W.' in the OCU copy.
E; OCU.

M407 [Monsey, R.] [dh] Ad virum ornatissimum totiq; clero summe observandum D. Jacobum Astley eq. barttum. et militem ad parliam. pro com. Norf. nuperrime electum. [*Norwich, printed by Henry Crossgrove,* 1710?]
2°: A^2; *i* ii–iii *iv blk.*
'Posthabitis, ultra quos non tulit Anna, duobus'

Signed 'R.M.' The authorship is clear from the following poems. Probably the author was Robert Monsey from Cambridge.
L(1870.d.1/100*).

M408 [—] [dh] In diem illum auspicatissimum Maii a vicessimo nono in quo bono reip. natus erat 1630, ab exilio redux [erat] 1660 R. Carolus a Carolo... epode. [col] *Norvici, excudebat Henricus Crossgrovus,* 1719.
2°: A^2; *1–4.*
'Huc, huc adeste, quotquot a sacris sibi'
Signed 'R.M.'
C('For the Revd. Mr. Martin of Thetford').

M409 — [dh] In obitum viri ornatissimi, & optime de me meriti, Clementis Herne, arm'...qui obiit die 17mo Sep. an. dom. 1720. ætat. suæ 84. elegia. [col] *Norvici, excudebat Henricus Crossgrovus,* 1720.
2°: A^2; *1* 2–3 *4 blk.*
Mourning woodcut on p. 1 with lettering 'CH | 1720 | Ætat | 84'.
'Huc inculta veni, qualem decet esse dolentis'
Signed 'R. Monsey, Pr. Norf.'
O.

M410 [—] [dh] Viro honoratissimo, doctorum Mecænati optimo, et patriæ suæ & seculi ornamento, Roberto Harley...Carmen 'euktikon. [col] *Norvici, excudebat Henricus Cross-grove,* 1711.
2°: A^2; *1–4.*
Ms. accents and corrections in the copy seen.
'Quod solium tandem inconcussum habet Anna, secundum'
Signed 'R.M. Præsb. Norfol.'
L(1870.d.1/99**).

Monsieur. Monsieur Boileau's epistle to his gardiner, 1712. *See* Southcott, Thomas.

M411 — Monsieur Pretendant, and Signioro Pretenderillo, a poem. *Dublin, printed* [*by George Faulkner*] *in the year* 1745.
8°: A^4; *1–2* 3–8.
Printer identified in *Bradshaw* 1132.
'Italian Mary's prayers were heard'
Signed 'H—. D—.' A satire against the Old and Young Pretenders.
C.

M412 — Monsieur Ragoo; or, a squib for the grand f-re-w-rks. A ballad. By Nahum Jews-harp, esq; *London, 'printed for Will. Wildfire, at the Powder-Mills near Temple-Bar',* 1749. (*BM* April)
2°: A^2 < B^1; *1–2* '4–5' 5–6.
'I am a man just come from Fraunce-e'
A satire on the fireworks celebrating the peace.
L(1959),O; CtY,KU.

— Monsieur Rapin's Latin heroick poem on Christ's-passion, 1717. *See* Beckingham, Charles.

M413 — Monsieur Thing's origin. [*London*] *Printed for R. Tomson, near Cheapside,* 1722. (*SR* 7 June)
4°: A–C^4; *1–2* 3–23 *24 blk.*
Large space on title of copies seen, apparently

Monsieur Thing's origin

intended for an engraved 'portrait'. Deposit copies at L,E,SaU. Advertised in *DP* 8 June 1722, 'Sold at the pamphlet shops of London and Westminster, excepting the French Hugonet's, who were so unnatural as to refuse their countryman room in their shops'; and see *DJ* 9 June for a female bookseller who 'sent constables to suppress the hawkers'.
'Astræa's kind, who taught me how to choose'
The E copy has an early ms. note on title, 'by A. Pope'. The attribution may readily be rejected. On the dildo.
L(841.i.21/5),E,SaU.

M414 Monster. The monster: or, the world turn'd topsy turvy. A satyr. *London printed, and sold by B. Bragg,* 1705. (*FP* 11 Jan)
4°: *A*² B–F²; *i–iv*, 1–19 *20 blk.* A1 hft; 19 advt.
'Search all the bright creation, you won't find'
Continued by *The Female monster,* 1705. A general satire on mankind, including prominent persons.
L(164.1.49, Luttrell, 11 Jan),O(3, 1 uncut),*MR*; CSmH,CtY(uncut),ICN,OCU.

Montagu, Charles, *earl of Halifax.* The works and life of the right honourable Charles, late earl of Halifax... *London, printed for E. Curll, J. Pemberton, & J. Hooke,* 1715. (*MC* Sept)
8°: pp. ii, 92, 264, viii.   L,O; CtY,MH.

— [reissue] The poetical works... With his lordship's life... The second edition. *London, printed for E. Curll, & J. Pemberton,* 1716.
     L,O; TxU.
Cancel title.

———

M415 [—] [The man of honour.] The honest man at court. A satyr. *London, printed by J. Read,* 1712.
4°: *A*⁴ B²; 1–2 3–12.
Previously published as *The man of honour,* 1690, and reprinted in *The dog in the wheel,* 1705. A reworking which adds a section in praise of Scotland is entered as *The man of honour,* 1706 (M68).
'Not all the threats and favours of a crown'
Crum N345. Printed with Montagu's poems in 1715.
OCU.

M416 [—] The man of honour: a poem. *London, printed for J. Wilford,* 1733. (*GSJ* 21 April)
2°: *A*² B²; 1–3 4–8.
Honour. A poem (Dublin, 1739) by John Ballard has the same first line and may be a fraudulent reprint.
O(uncut),LdU-B; CSmH,CtY,IU,MH,OCU +.

[Montagu, *Lady* Mary Wortley.] Court poems. Viz; I. The basset-table. An eclogue. II. The drawing-room. III. The toilet... *London, printed for J. Roberts,* '1706' [1716]. (26 March, Luttrell)

Montagu, *Lady* Mary Wortley

8°: pp. iii, 23.   L,O; CtY,MH.
Griffith 51. The authorship of these poems has been a problem ever since their publication, but the greatest share is Lady Mary's; see Robert Halsband in *PMLA* 68 (1953) 237–50. The collection later became a miscellany, but the subsequent forms are recorded here nevertheless.

[—] Court poems... [with] A copy of verses to the ingenious Mr. Moore... All four by Mr. Pope. To which is added W.T. [William Tunstall] to fair Clio. *Dublin, reprinted by S. Powell, for G. Risk,* 1716.
12°: pp. 24.   L,O; CtY,MH.
Griffith 64.

[—] Court poems. Part II. Viz, I. The dream... II. The Hyde-park ramble. With some other pieces. Written by a lady. To which are added, I. The worms a satire. II. A version of the first psalm... *London, printed for J. Roberts,* 1717 [1716]. (4 Sept, Luttrell)
8°: pp. 8+20+28.   L,O(impft); CLU-C,KU.
Griffith 59a. Largely a nonce collection; part 2 is *A tale of the finches,* 1716; part 3 is *State poems,* 1716. There is no evidence that Lady Mary was responsible for any of these poems. The first two were reprinted in the Dublin 1717 edition of Tickell's *An epistle from a lady.*

[—] [*idem*] Pope's miscellany. Viz. I. The basset-table... The second edition. *London, printed for R. Burleigh,* 1717. (*DC* 5 Jan)
12°: pp. 22.   L,O; CSmH,MH.
Griffith 90. Copies were reissued in *Court Poems,* 1719 (below).

[—] Pope's miscellany. The second part. Containing I. The Hyde-park ramble... *London, printed for R. Burleigh,* 1717. (*PB* 6 Aug)
12°: pp. 24.   O,LdU-B; MH,TxU.
Griffith 89. Copies were reissued in *Court Poems,* 1719 (below).

[—] Court poems in two parts compleat... *London, printed for R. Burleigh,* 1719 [1718]. (*EvP* 27 Nov)
12°: pp. 22+26.   LVA-D,O; MH,TxU.
Griffith 108. A reissue of the two preceding, with a final added leaf.

[—] Court poems. In two parts. By Mr. Pope, &c. *London, printed for E. Curll,* 1726.
12°.   L,EU; KU,MH.
Griffith 174–6, The contents vary. Apparently it should contain a new edition of part 1 (pp. 24) and the 1717 part 2, with five added leaves (pp. 25–34); but in typical Curll fashion it is often made up with other collections.

[—] Six town eclogues. With some other poems. By the rt. hon. L. M. W. M. *London, printed for M. Cooper,* 1747. (*GM* Nov)
4°: pp. 48.   L,O; CtY,MH.

Montagu, *Lady* **Mary Wortley**

[—] The poetical works of the right honourable Lady M—y W—y M—e. *London, printed for J. Williams,* 1768.
8°: pp. 109.   L,O; MH.

M416·5 [—] The Dean's provocation for writing the Lady's dressing-room. A poem. *London, printed for T. Cooper,* 1734. (*GSJ* 8 Feb)
2°: *A*² B²; *1–2* 3–8.
    Teerink 1310.
'The doctor, in a clean starch'd band'
    Ascribed to Lady Mary by R. Halsband in *The Augustan milieu. Essays presented to Louis A. Landa* (1970) 225–31. E. Green, *Bibliotheca Somersetensis* (1902) I. 443 attributes it to S. Robinson, author of *Cælia's revenge,* 1741; this is certainly an error. A satire on Swift as impotent and revengeful.
L(163.n.8),O; CLU-C,MH,TxU.

[—] An elegy to a young lady... By ------. With an answer: by a lady, author of the Verses to the imitator of Horace, 1733. *See* H21.

[—] To the imitator of the satire of the second book of Horace, 1733. *See* V46.

[—] Verses address'd to the imitator of the first satire of the second book of Horace. By a lady, [1733.] *See* V39.

[—] Virtue in danger: or Arthur Gray's last farewell to the world, [1722.] *See* V103.

'Monte Socio, Carlo.' An epistle to a certain dean, written originally in Italian, by Carlo Monte Socio, 1730. *See* E386.

'Monteego, *Count.'* The adventure of a German knight, 1733. *See* A64.

Monteith, Robert. The very learned Scotsman, Mr. George Buchanan's Fratres fraterrimi, three books of epigrams, and book of miscellanies, in English verse... By Robert Monteith. *Edinburgh, printed by the heirs and successors of Andrew Anderson,* 1708.
8°: pp. 76.   L,O; CtY,IU.

M417 — Augustissimæ, serenissimæ, lectissimæ, Annæ, D. G. Britanniarum &c. reginæ, fidei vindici, &c. Anna regina. Anagramma. Anna, I, regna... *Edinburgi, excudebant hæredes Andreæ Anderson,* 1702.
1°: 1 side, 2 columns.
    Acrostic verses in Latin and English.
'Alite perfausto, regnat, tu cœlitus orta'
'Auspiciously thou heav'n-born reigns; who by'
    Signed 'R. Mentethus', identified by E with Robert Monteith.
E,MC.

Monteith, R.

M418 — [another edition, title reads:]...Anagramma. Inania regna...
    First couplet of Latin and English changed.
'Alite perfausto regnas, O maxima, tu qua'
'Auspiciously thou, greatest, reignes; who by'
E.

M419 — Augustissimo, serenissimo, invictissimo, Georgio, D. G. Britanniarum monarchæ, &c. fidei defensori, &c. Georgius rex. Anagramma. Egregius Cæsar... *Edinburgi, excudebant hæredes Andreæ Anderson, anno dom.* 1714.
1°: 1 side, 2 columns.
    Acrostic verses in Latin and English.
'Grandia, magnanimis stipulantur fata Britannis'
'Great things, fates promise to th' brave British land'
    Signed 'R. Mentethus'.
E.

M420 [—] [An elegy] on the death of the incomparable Thomas Fisher, merchant in Edinburgh, and treasurer of George Heriot's hospital, who deceased 26th March 1711. [*Edinburgh,* 1711.]
½°.
'The debt which man by birth contracts, he must'
    Signed 'R.M.', i.e. Robert Monteith. Reprinted in his *Theater of mortality,* 1713.
(*Maidment* 185, from David Haig's copy.)

M421 — To the most noble, most illustrious, most honourable, and most renouned, Patrick, earl of Marchmount, lord high chancellar of the kingdom of Scotland, Sir Hugh Dalrymple of North-Berwick, lord president, and to the remanent lords, ordinary and extraordinary, senators of the colledge of justice: the address of Mr. Robert Monteith, sometime minister at Caringtoun. [*Edinburgh,* 170–?]
½°: 1 side, 1 column.
'Cretians and Grecians deemed were, to be'
    Signed 'R. Monteith'. Asking them to accept the dedication of his edition of Phocylides; he plans to go to London to print it. Apparently it was never published.
E.

M422 — To the very honourable, and right worshipful the dean and faculty of advocates. [*Edinburgh, printed by John Spottiswood,* 1706/10?]
½°: 1 side, 1 column.
    The last word of each line is a Latin word ending '-ela'. Spottiswood's printing is revealed in line 3.
'Patrons of men, my decus & tutela'
    Signed 'R: Monteith'.
EP.

Montrose, James Graham, *marquis. See* Graham, James, *marquis of Montrose.*

Monument. The monument, 1729. *See* Mitchell, Joseph.

Moore

M423 Moore. Moore' worms for the learned Mr. Curll, bookseller; who, to be reveng'd on Mr. Pope for his poisonous emetick, gave him a paper of worm-powder, which caused that gentleman to void a strange sort of worms. [*London*] *Printed for E. Smith, in Cornhill,* 1716. (17 May, Luttrell)
½⁰: *1–2,* 1 column.
'Oh learned Curll! thy skill excells'
> *Crum* O553. A satire on Curll in reply to his publication of Pope's 'Worms', i.e. *To the ingenious Mr. Moore,* 1716.

L(1871.e.1/2; 12273.m.1/7),O; ICN(Luttrell).

[**Moore,** —, *of Exeter College, Oxford.*] A poetical representation of the passion of our blessed saviour, [1747.] *See* P706.

Moore, Edward. Poems, fables, and plays. *London, printed by J. Hughs, for R. & J. Dodsley,* 1756.
4⁰: pp. xvi, 502.   L,O; CtY,MH.

M424 [—] Fables for the female sex. *London, printed for R. Francklin,* 1744. (*SR* 24 May)
8⁰: (frt+) *A⁴* B–M⁸ (+16 plates); *i–viii,* 1–173 *174–176 blk.*
> Watermark: fleur-de-lys. Title in red and black. A plate engraved after F. Hayman is prefixed to each book. Entered in *SR* to Moore by Francklin, but deposit copies have not been identified. Listed in *DA* 26 May.
'The moral lay, to beauty due'
> Subsequently printed as Moore's; he acknowledges the assistance of 'the author of Gustavus Vasa' (Henry Brooke) in the preface.

L(C.70.c.2),O; CSmH,CtY(−M8),*DFo*,IU, MH(−M8)+.

M425 [—] [fine paper]
> Watermark: Strasburg bend. A copy at Waddesdon Manor has Hayman's original drawings and different states of the plates.

CSmH(Mrs. Garrick's copy),MH.

M426 [—] — *Dublin, printed by George Faulkner,* 1744. (*Dublin Journal* 16 June)
12⁰: *A⁴* B–I⁸/⁴ K⁴; *1–8 9–112.*
> Apparently A⁴ and K⁴ were printed as octavo half-sheets.

L(C.71.bb.15/11),O.

M427 [—] — The second edition. *London, printed for R. Francklin,* 1746 [1745]. (*DA* 25 Oct)
8⁰: (frt+) A⁴ B–M⁸ (+plates); *i–viii,* 1–173 *174–176.* viii err; M8 advt.
> Title in red and black.

L(11643.h.24),O(lacks M2,−M8),E(−M8); InU(−M8).

M428 [—] — By Edward Moore. The third edition. *London, printed for R. Francklin,* 1749 [1748] (*DA* 31 Dec.)

Moore, E. Fables

8⁰: (frt+) *A²* B–M⁸ (+plates); *i–iv,* 1–173 *174–175; 176 blk.* M8 advt.
> Title in red and black.

L(11660.b.29),C,EU; CSmH(−frt),*DLC*,IU, MH,MiU.

M429 — — The fifth edition. *Dublin, printed by George Faulkner,* 1749.
12⁰: *A²* B–I⁸/⁴ K⁴; *1–4 5–108.*
C,DN; MH.

M430 [—] [*idem*] New fables invented for the amusement of young ladies. By the author of the Foundling. The third edition. *Printed in the year* 1749.
8⁰: A⁴(−A4) B–S⁴ T¹; *i–vi,* 1–137 *138 blk.*
> Clearly a piracy, possibly of Scottish origin. A 'fourth edition' of 1754 with this title is at CLU-C.

L(12304.d.33).

M431 [—] An ode to Garrick, upon the talk of the town. *London, printed for M. Cooper,* 1749. (*GM* June)
4⁰: A⁴ B²; *1–2 3–11 12 blk.*
> Vertical chain-lines. The genuine edition, advertised as forthcoming in *DA* 9 May.
'No, no; the left-hand box, in blue'
> A letter of Garrick to Lady Burlington, 3 Aug 1749, refers to 'Mr. Moore's verses'; printed in Moore's *Poems,* 1756. On Garrick's courtship of E. M. Violetti, whom he married 22 June 1749.

CtY,DFo(Kemble's copy),MH.

M432 [—] [*idem*] An ode to Mr. G--r--k. *London, printed for J. Bromage,* 1749. (*DA* 2 June)
2⁰: *A⁴; 1–2 3–8.*
OA; *CSmH*,DFo,IU(uncut).

[—] Solomon a serenata: taken from Canticles. Set to music by Mr. Boyce, and perform'd in the Academy of Music, 1742.
> Apparently an oratorio, the texts of which are outside the scope of this catalogue. Copy at CSmH; an edition of 1750 bearing Moore's name is at CtY.

[—] To Mrs. Cibber, 1742. *See* T351.

M433 [—] The trial of Selim the Persian, for divers high crimes and misdemeanours. *London, printed for M. Cooper,* 1748. (*DA* 26 May)
4⁰: *A²* B–F²; *i–iv, 1* 2–20. A1 hft.
'The court was met; the pris'ner brought'
> Early ms. attribution in the L copy; reprinted in Moore's *Poems,* 1756. In praise of George, Lord Lyttelton, occasioned by his *Observations on the conversion of St. Paul.*

L(11630.c.8/23, −A1; 11659.cc.1/5, cropt),O(2, 1−A1),E(2),LdU-B,*MR*(2); CtY(2),IU,MH(2, 1−A1),MiU,*TxU*+.

M434 [—] Yarico to Inkle. An epistle. *London, printed for Lawton Gilliver,* 1736. (*LM* Feb)
2⁰: *A²* B–E²; [2] *i* ii, 1–16.
> There is possibly a variant sheet B; the signature B in copies at L,DFo,MiU,OCU is under ea of 'Tear' rather than under T.

Moore, E. Fables

'From the sad place where sorrow ever reigns'
Early ms. attribution to Moore in the TxU
copy, also recorded (though not accepted) in
Dobell 2705. Not collected in Moore's *Poems*,
1756, and the attribution is unconfirmed.
Dedicated to Miss Arabella Saintloe.
L(1346.m.32),O,OA,LdU-B; CtY,DFo,ICU,
MH,TxU+.

M435 [—] [*idem*] The epistle of Yarico to Inkle. A poem.
*Glasgow, printed [by R. & A. Foulis] for John Ross,
Edinburgh*, 1750. (*SM* March)
8°: *A*⁴ B–D⁴; *1–3* 4–32.
> *Gaskell, Foulis* 157. Presumably the edition
> entered in *SR* to Andrew Millar, 25 April
> 1750; no deposit copies traced.
L(1465.f.61),O; InU,MH,*MiU*,NN.

[**Moore, John.**] Hell in epitome: or, a description
of the M--sh--sea, 1718. *See* H133.

M436 Moral. A moral poem on the middle state of life.
Shewing with what indifference the vulgar receive
Wood's coin, in a letter to the Drapier. [*Dublin*,
1724.] (Dec)
4°: *A*²; *1* 2–4.
'So many have for a dinner or half crown'
DT(ms. date Dec).

Morality. Morality in vice, 1733. *See* Breval, J. D.

Morando, Bernardo.
Samber, Robert: The paradox: being three poems,
from the Italian of...Bernardo Morando, 1721.
See S29.

More. More priestcraft, 1705. *See* Ward, Edward.

— More reformation. A satyr upon himself, 1703.
See Defoe, Daniel.

M437 — More to be done yet. Or; her majesty's most
gracious token to the right honourable the Earl of
Oxford. *London, printed for W. Brewer, near
Thames-street*, [1711.]
½°: 1 side, 1 column.
'High art thou rais'd (tho' short of thy desert)'
> On Harley's appointment as lord treasurer.
Crawford; MH(imprint cropt).

More, —, Mr.
*The following poems all claim to be by the same
author, and the first is attributed in a ms. note to 'Mr.
More'; he has not been identified.*

[—] The city madam, and the country maid, 1702.
See C207.

[—] The grand mistake; or all men happy if they
please, 1705. *See* G245.

[—] The pleasures of a single life, 1701–. *See* P488.

'**More, John,** *apothecary*.' An epistle from John
More, [1743.] *See* Dodington, George Bubb.

More, R.

'**More, Richard.**' *See* 'Maurus, Richardus'.

Morell, Thomas. Poems on divine subjects,
original and translated from the Latin of M. Hieron.
Vida... *London, printed by E. Owen; sold by
A. Bettesworth & C. Hitch, F. Fayram & T.
Hatchett, J. Osborn & T. Longman, C. Rivington,
J. Battley, S. Austen, & L. Gilliver*, 1732. (*GM*
June)
8°: pp. vi. 288.   L,O; CtY,MH.

— — The second edition, 1736.
> Copy seen at a dealer's; probably a reissue.

———————

M438 — The Christian's epinikion, or song of triumph.
A paraphrase on ch. XV. of St. Paul's 1st Epistle to
the Corinthians, attempted in blank verse. With
annotations... *London, printed for M. Cooper*, 1743.
(*GM,LM* June)
4°: *A*² B–I²; *1–3* 4–35 *36 blk*.
'Attend, ye busy mortals, much employ'd'
> Dedication signed.
L(1465.k.8); CtY.

M439 — Hope: a poetical essay on that Christian grace.
In three books. *London, printed for R. Dodsley*,
1745. (17 Feb)
4°: A(2 ll) B–D⁴ E(2 ll); *i–iv, 1* 2–26 *27–28*. E2
'Addenda, &c.'
> Apparently the leaves of A and E are conju-
> gate. Date from *Straus, Dodsley*; listed in
> *GM,LM* Feb.
'Look down, thou ever-chearful cherub, hope'
> Dedication signed.
L(11630.c.1/22; 11630.c.7/11; 643.k.5/7, lacks
A2; 161.m.12),C.

M440 [**Morgan, David.**] The country bard: or, the
modern courtiers. A poem. Inscrib'd to the prince.
Canto the first. *London, printed for the author*, 1739.
4°: *A*⁴ B–F²; *i–vi, 1* 2–21 *22 blk*.
'Since monarchs by prerogative are wise'
> The second canto was reissued with Morgan's
> name.
L(11630.c.9/2),O,PrP; CSmH,MH(uncut),OCU.

M441 [—] The country bard... Inscribed to his royal
highness the Prince of Wales. Canto the second.
Being a dissertation on Sir Martin Marrall's
coadjutors... *London, printed for the author*, 1741.
(*GM* May)
4°: *A*² B–I²; *i–iv, 1* 2–31 *32*. *32 err*.
'How high our reach, how far our talent goes'
O; CSmH,CtY,KU.

M442 — — By David Morgan...who was executed...
July 30, 1746. *London, printed for the author, in the
year 1741: reprinted in the year 1746; sold by Henry
Carpenter in Fleet-street*. (*LM* Aug)
4°: *π*² *A*²(−A1) B–I²; *i–vi, 1* 2–31 *32*. π1 hft; *32 err*.
> A reissue of the second canto. The copy at IU
> has no errata on p. 32.
E; IU(cropt).

Morgan, H.

M443 [**Morgan, H.**] Cynegetica; or, the force and pleasure of hunting: an heroi-comical poem, in two canto's... By a gentleman of the Inner Temple. *London, printed for William Chetwood*, 1718. (1 June?)

12°: A–D⁶ (C4 as 'C3'); *1–6* 7–46 *47–48 blk*. A1 frt.
Bond 61. The frontispiece is repeated on p. 30.
'Since disputations, wranglings, noise, and strife'
Morgan's name is added to the second edition. CtY(ms. date 1 June).

M444 — — The second edition, with additions. By H. Morgan, of the Inner-Temple, gent. *London, printed for W. Chetwood*, 1720. (*DP* 9 Feb)
The copy described has the same pagination as the preceding, and is possibly a reissue.
(*Bond* 61, describing a copy belonging to Mr. J. B. Keogh.)

[**Morgan, John.**] A new poem in honour of the journey-men taylors, [1726?/27?] *See* N168.

M445 — A poem on the taylor craft. Shewing the arise thereof from the first creation of the world, and progress ever since... By J. M. a well wisher of the said incorporations. *Edinburgh, printed by Robert Brown*, 1733.
8°: *A⁴* B–F⁴; *i–vi*, 1–41 *42 blk*.
Signature A2 possibly cropped in the copy seen.
'Much honoured trade, I greatly am to blame'
Dedication signed.
E.

[**Morgan, Macnamara.**] Remarkable satires. The Causidicade [*etc.*]...with notes variorum. *London, printed for Mrs. Newcomb*, 1760.
12°: pp. 51–171.   L; MH.
N&Q II. iv (1857) 94 notes that *The Causidicade*, which is often missing, is supplied in the L copy from *Poems on various subjects* (Glasgow, 1756). Probably the whole is a Scottish production. *DNB* records that copies in contemporary binding are frequently found lettered 'Morgan's Satires'. There is said to be another issue (?) titled 'Satires on several occasions'.

M446 [—] The Causidicade. A panegyri-satiri-serio-comic-dramatical poem. On the strange resignation, and stranger-promotion. *London, printed for M. Cooper*, 1743. (*GM,LM* July)
4°: π¹[=D4] A–C⁴ D⁴(–D4); *i–ii*, *1–2* 3–29 *30 blk.* π1 hft; 29 err.
'The inquisiter gen'ral resigning his place'
Authorship quoted by *N&Q* II. iv (1857) 94 from *European magazine* XXIII. 253. A satire on the appointment of William Murray as solicitor-general in Nov 1742.
L(11630.c.14/15,–π1),LdU-B; CtY,IU,MH, MiU,OCU+.

Morgan, M. The Causidicade

M447 [—] — By Porcupinus Pelagius... The second edition. *London, printed for M. Cooper*, 1743.
4°: π¹[=D4] A–C⁴ D⁴(–D4); *i–ii*, *1–2* 3–29 *30 blk.* π1 hft.
Minor changes to text, possibly reset.
L(T.669/1,–π1),O,E(–π1),*NeU*; CSmH(–π1), CtY,*NcU.*

M448 [—] — The third edition. *London, printed for M. Cooper*, 1743.
4°: π¹[=D4] A–C⁴ D⁴(–D4); *i–ii*, *1–2* 3–29 *30 blk.* π1 hft.
Apparently a reimpression.
L(643.k.5/4,–π1),O(–π1),LdU-B(–π1); ICN (–π1),IU.

M449 [—] — The fourth edition. *London, printed for M. Cooper*, 1743.
4°: π¹[=D4] A–C⁴ D⁴(–D4); *i–ii*, *1–2* 3–29 *30 blk.* π1 hft.
Partly reset. Some copies (e.g. L,C,CtY) appear to have a variant sheet B.
L(T.666/1,–π1),O(2, 1–π1),C(–π1),CT(2, 1–π1),PrP; CtY(2, 1–π1),KU,TxU(–π1).

M450 [—] The 'Piscopade: a panegyri-satiri-serio-comical poem. By Porcupinus Pelagius. *London, printed for W. Owen*, 1748. (*GM,LM* Feb)
4°: A⁴(±A1) B–D⁴; *i–iii* iv, *5* 6–32.
'The cabinet, summon'd, in council conven'd'
Attributed to Morgan on account of the pseudonym. A satire on the election of a successor to John Potter as archbishop of Canterbury.
L(11602.gg.24/14; 11630.c.6/14),O,C,*MR*; ICU,IU,MH,OCU(uncut),TxU.

M451 [—] — The second edition. *London, printed for W. Owen*, 1748. (25 Feb?)
4°: A–D⁴; *i–iii* iv, *5* 6–32.
Apparently a reimpression. Ms. note in the BaP copy, 'The Triumvirade & Processionade by the same author may be had of Mr. Owen'.
L(11631.f.58, ms. notes),O,BaP,LdU-B(ms. date 25 Feb & notes); CtY,IU.

M452 [—] — The third edition. *London, printed for W. Owen*, 1748.
4°: A–D⁴; *i–iii* iv, *5* 6–32.
Apparently reset, at least in part.
L(643.k.5/10),LDW,O,C; IU,KU,*MH.*

M453 [—] — The fourth edition. *London, printed for W. Owen*, 1748.
4°: A–D⁴; *i–iii* iv, *5* 6–32.
L(161.l.80, cropt); CtY,IU.

M454 [—] — The fifth edition. *London, printed for W. Owen*, 1748.
4°: A–D⁴; *i–iii* iv, *5* 6–32.
O,C,PrP; CtY,NN.

M455 [—] — 'London, printed for W. Owen' [*Dublin*], 1748.
12°: A–B⁶ C¹; *1–2* 3–26.

Morgan, M. The 'Piscopade

The order of this and the following variant has not been established.
DK,*MR*; CtY.

M456 [—] [variant title:] The 'Episcopade...
DA,DG.

M457 [—] The Processionade: in panegyri-satiri-serio-comi-baladical versicles... By Porcupinus Pelagius. *London, printed for M. Cooper*, 1745 [1746]. (12 Feb?)
2⁰: *A⁴*; *1–3* 4–8.
Listed in *BM,GM* Feb. An 'Advertisement' on p. 2 says that the author has published nothing since the *Triumvirade*, and that a former piece was published without authority and much changed; it has not been identified.
'There are few unacquainted with th' old Palace-hall'
A further satire on William Murray and other legal dignitaries.
L(1489.m.23, ms. notes),O(uncut),AdU,LdU-B (Tom's Coffee House, 12 Feb); CSmH,CtY,IU, MH.

M458 [—] — The second edition. *London, printed for M. Cooper*, 1745 [1746].
2⁰: *A⁴*; *1–3* 4–8.
Apparently a reimpression.
L(11630.e.16/2, cropt).

M459 [—] The Scandalizade, a panegyri-satiri-serio-comi-dramatic poem. By Porcupinus Pelagius, author of the Causidicade. *London, printed for G. Smith*, 1750. (*GM,LM* April)
4⁰: *A¹*[= *F₁*] B–E⁴ F⁴(– *F₁*); *i–ii*, 1–37 *38 blk.*
The copy at DFo has a printed key pasted on p. 37, frequently found in the second edition.
'Lo! westward the church which incumbers the street'
A satire on contemporary figures in the form of a contest between their portraits in a print-shop.
L(840.k.4/19),O,LdU-B; DFo,MH,OCU,TxU.

M460 [—] — The second edition. *London, printed for G. Smith*, 1750.
4⁰: *A¹* B–E⁴ F⁴(– *F₁*); *i–ii*, 1–37 *38 blk.*
Apparently a reissue or reimpression. Copies at O,CtY have a printed key pasted on p. 37.
O(3, 1 lacks F4, 1 ms. date 19 May),*MR*; CtY.

M461 [—] The sequel. Containing what was omitted in the Triumvirade, or broad-bottomry, at the asterisks... By Porcupinus Pelagius. *London, printed for M. Cooper*, [1745.] (*GM,LM* Feb)
4⁰: A⁴ B² *C¹*; *1–2* 3–13 *14 blk.*
'Then struck up a smart with a soldierly air'
Possibly not published under Morgan's direction, but probably by him. Collected in his *Remarkable satires*, 1760. Printed in Sir

Morgan, M. The sequel

Charles Hanbury Williams, *Works* (1822) II. 252, but it can scarcely be his.
L(11630.c.5/14; 11630.c.6/5, lacks C1),O(2, 1 ms. date 14 March); CSmH,ICN,KU,MH(2),NN+.

M462 [—] The Triumvirade: or, broad-bottomry. A panegyri-satiri-serio-comi-dramatical poem. By Porcupinus Pelagius, author of the Causidicade. [*London*] *Printed for M. Cooper*, [1745.] (*DA* 22 Jan)
4⁰: π¹ A–D⁴ *E¹*; *i–ii*, *1–2* 3–33 *34 blk.* π1 hft.
'When Grantown and Bathon, as story records'
Attributed to Morgan on account of the pseudonym. See *The sequel* above. A satire on the reconstruction of the ministry after the resignation of John Carteret, earl Granville, on 24 Nov 1744. Cf. *The Porcupinade*, 1745.
L(11630.c.6/4; 11630.d.12/3),O,LdU-B; CSmH,CtY(2),*DLC*,ICN(–π1),IU+.

M463 [—] — The second edition. [*London*] *Printed for M. Cooper*, [1745.]
4⁰: π¹ A–D⁴ *E¹*; *i–ii*, *1–2* 3–33 *34 blk.* π1 hft.
Apparently partly reset.
O(–π1),CT(2, 1 –π1, ms. notes),LdU-B(–π1), *MR*; CSmH(–π1),*CtY*,ICN,ICU,MH+.

M464 [—] — The third edition. [*London*] *Printed for M. Cooper*, [1745.]
4⁰: π¹ A–D⁴ *E¹*; *i–ii*, *1–2* 3–33 *34 blk.* π1 hft.
Half-title not in the copy seen, assumed from other editions. Apparently a reimpression.
MR; CtY(–π1).

M465 [—] — The fourth edition. [*London*] *Printed for M. Cooper*, [1745.]
4⁰: π¹ A–D⁴ *E¹*; *i–ii*, *1–2* 3–33 *34 blk.* π1 hft.
Apparently in part a reimpression.
L(1963),O(–π1); MH(–π1),TxU.

M466 [—] — The fifth edition. [*London*] *Printed for M. Cooper*, [1745.]
4⁰: π¹ A–D⁴ *E¹*; *i–ii*, *1–2* 3–33 *34 blk.* π1 hft.
Half-title not in the copies seen, assumed from other editions. Apparently a reimpression.
O(–π1); OCU(–π1, ms. notes).

M467 Morland, —, *Mr.* A poem to his majesty: on the fourth of November; being the anniversary of the birth of his late majesty King William... *London, printed for J. Roberts*, 1730. (*MChr* Nov)
2⁰: *A² B–C²*; *1–2* 3–12.
Listed in *GSJ* 10 Dec.
'To you, great sir, the humble muse presumes'
The author is possibly William Morland of Trinity College Oxford, who matriculated 17 Dec 1729, aged 20.
OW.

M468 Morley, R. 'A pindarick ode upon the death of that noble and virtuous Lady Anne, countess of Sunderland, who departed this life the 15th day of April, 1716. [*London*] *Printed for J. Roberts.*' (*MC* April 1716)

Morning

M469 Morning. The morning: or, judgment. An essay. *London, printed for H. Whitridge, & W. Owen,* 1748. (*GM, LM* Nov)
4°: π¹ A–D² E¹; *i–ii, 1 2–17 18 blk.*
'The night is past. – Once more I homage pay'
    A religious poem.
O; OCU.

M470 Morphett, Richard. The general loss, or the universal mourners. A poem, dedicated to the memory of...Sir Francis Hamilton, bart. *Dublin, printed by Samuel Fairbrother,* 1714.
4°: a² b¹ A–D² E¹ (A2 as 'B2'); *i–iii iv v–vi, 1–18.*
    The verses to the reader on b1 were possibly a later addition. On p.15, 'To the honourable the Lady Hamilton'.
'When men of high-rais'd merits are to die'
L(11631.bb.61, lacks b1),DT(2, 1 lacks b1, 1 with ms. verses to Theophilus Butler).

Morrice, Bezaleel. The muse's treat: or, a collation of wit and love. Being original poems on various occasions... *London, printed for Henry Morris,* 1702.
8°: pp. 166.   O.

— Miscellanies or amusements, in verse and prose. *London, printed for Daniel Brown,* 1712.
8°: pp. 87.   L,LdU-B; CtY,TxU.
    Some copies have a dedication to the Duke of Buckingham inserted.

— Poetical descriptions, natural and allegorical. *London, printed for W. Chetwood,* 1722.
8°: pp. 28.   O.

[—] The poetaster: containing, original poems, and songs, 1726. *See* Poetaster.

[—] Apollo: or a poetical definition of the three sister-arts, 1729. *See* Apollo.

[—] St. James's miscellany: or, the lover's tale. Being the amours of Venus and Adonis: or the disasters of unlawful love. With some curious poems on love and gallantry. *London, printed for J. Janeway,* 1732. (*GM* Nov)
8°: pp. 52.   Institute for Sex Research.
    The status of this volume is uncertain; it is not recorded as a miscellany by *Case* or *CBEL*, and the first poem is a reprint of Morrice's *The amour of Cytherea,* 1724.

— A miscellany in verse and prose. By Captain Morrice. *London, printed for the author; sold by J. Wilford,* 1739. (*GM* Jan)
8°: pp. 120.   L,WcC; CtY,TxU.

M471 — An address to Homer. *London, printed for T. Warner,* 1723. (*MC* June)
2°: B² C¹; *1–4 5–6.*
    The collation is tentative.
'Who can with thee, oh! bard immortal! joyn?'
CtY.

Morrice, B. The amour

M472 [—] The amour of Cytherea: a poem. Dedicated to the fair-sex. With the Dream, Composition, and a little epistle to a little lady, all monosyllables. *London printed, and sold by T. Warner,* 1724. (*PB* 9 Jan)
8°: *A*⁴(−A1?) B–G⁴; *[12] 1 2–41 42 blk.*
    A1 not seen, possibly half-title. Separate title on p. 29 for *The dream.* Reprinted in *St. James's miscellany,* 1732, entered above as a collection by Morrice.
'Listen ye fair! to love's prevailing sway'
Dream: 'Within a grove (the muses calm retreat'
Composition: 'Rise gracious muse! harmonious numbers find'
    Dedication signed 'Alexis', a pseudonym used by Morrice in *The present state of poetry,* 1726. 'The dream' and 'Composition' were previously published as *Astræa,* 1719, 1720.
L(1509/845),O; CU.

M473 — [*idem*] The amour of Venus: or, the disasters of unlicens'd love. A poem. In four parts. *London, printed for J. Janeway,* 1732.
8°: A–G⁴ H²; *1–3 4–8, 1 2–52.*
    With a preface on painting and poetry. Apparently an enlarged version.
L; DFo,MH,TxU.

M474 [—] Astræa: or, the dream, and Composition. *London, printed for Sam. Briscoe; sold by J. Roberts,* 1719. (*PM* 15 Dec)
2°: *A*¹ B² C¹; *i–ii, 1 2–6.*
    Two poems.
'Within a grove, the muses calm retreat'
Composition: 'Thou fair fore-runner! of the sun's up-rise'
    Composition was reworked and separately published (see following entry); both poems were reprinted in Morrice's *The amour of Cytherea,* 1724.
O; InU(Luttrell, Dec),TxU.

M475 [—] Astræa: or, the composition. *London printed, and sold by J. Roberts,* 1720. (*PM* 20 Sept)
2°: A² B¹; *1–2 3–5 6 blk.*
    The collation is tentative.
'Rise gracious muse! harmonious numbers find'
    A revision of the second poem in the preceding work. Reprinted in Morrice's *The amour of Cytherea,* 1724.
CtY,InU(Luttrell, undated).

M475·5 [—] [*idem*] Maria or the picture of a certain young lady. *Printed at Temple-Oge, anno dom.* 1730.
½°: 1 side, 1 column.
    Possibly printed at Dublin for sale at Temple-Oge. The text is slightly revised from M472, presumably by Morrice.
C.

M476 — The country-house. *Dublin, printed by and for J. Carson,* 1735.
4°: A⁴; *1–2 3–8. 8 advt.*
'Beyond a park's extensive limits, stands'
MH.

Morrice, B. Dissectio mentis

M477 — Dissectio mentis humanæ: or a satiric essay on modern critics, stage and epic poets... *London, sold by Tho. Warner, 1730. (MChr Oct)*
8°: A⁴(A3 + *a²) B–O⁴; *i–xvi, 1 2–100.*
'Oh reason, with thy well-discov'ring light'
Dedication signed. Erroneously ascribed to Defoe by *Halkett & Laing* on the grounds of a very tentative reference in W. Wilson, *Memoirs of...Defoe* (1830) III. 598.
ICN,*MB*,MH(lacks A4, B1),MiU.

M478 — [*idem*] Dissectio mentis: or a satyrical display of the faults and errors of human nature; as manifested in the knowledge and manners of the present time: a poem. *London, sold by T. Warner, 1731.*
8°: A⁴(A3 + *a²) B–O⁴; *i–xvi, 1 2–100.*
Apparently a variant title; no sign of cancellation in the copy seen.
InU.

M479 [—] An epistle to Mr. Pope, on reading his translations of the Iliad and Odyssy of Homer. To which are added, some examples of the variety of sound in verse... A short character of Virgil and Homer. And, an epistle to a young poet... Also the condition of a good poet. *London, printed for J. Wilford, 1731. (GSJ 9 Feb)*
4°: A–B⁴ C²; *1–6 7–20.*
'Who envies fair prosperity or fame'
Early ms. attribution to Morrice in the O copy. Attributed to Walter Harte in *CBEL* II. 318; the authority is not known, and the attribution erroneous. Dedicated to John Dennis.
LVA-D,LVA-F,O(uncut); MH.

M480 — An epistle to Mr. Welsted; and a satyre on the English translations of Homer... To which is added, an essay towards an encomium on the true merit of Homer. *London printed, and sold by Tho. Bickerton, 1721. (DJ 30 June)*
8°: *A⁴ B–D⁴; 1–7 8–30 31–32 blk.* A1 hft.
The satire 'On the English translations of Homer' was previously published in *Three satires*, and was reprinted separately in 1733 (M489).
'Oh supple bard! thy gentle muse delight's'
Satire: 'He's base who wou'd degrade what's truly fine'
Dedication to Prior signed.
L(T.1056/8,–D4),LdU-B; CLU-C,*CtY*,DFo (–A1, D4).

M481 [—] An essay on the poets. *London, printed for Daniel Brown; sold by A. Baldwin, 1712. (Spectator 3 Nov)*
8°: A⁸; *1–6 7–16.*
'Ye bards of small desert, but vast conceit'
Advertised in *Spectator* together with Morrice's *Miscellanies,* 1712; the two are bound together at LdU-B.
OW,LdU-B; CtY(uncut),*DLC*.

M482 [—] — *London, printed for Tho. Harbin; sold by J. Morphew, & N. Dodd, 1717. (DC 4 May)*

Morrice, B. An essay on the poets

2°: A–C²; *1–4 5–12.*
Advertised in *DC* 2 May for 'tomorrow'; N. Dodd's address is given as 'at the Peacock, without Temple-Bar'.
DN; ICU.

M483 — — *London, printed for T. Bickerton, 1721. (PB 24 Oct)*
8°: A–D⁴; *1–7 8–31 32 blk.*
Revised text.
'Ye bards! of shallow sence, but specious sound'
L(161.m.13, Luttrell, Nov),C.

M484 — An essay on the universe: a poem. *London printed, and sold by J. Roberts, N. Bland, J. Stagg, J. Graves, 1725. (MC Dec)*
2°: A² B–C²; *i–vi, 1 2–6.*
'Those stars, and this our elemental earth'
Dedication signed. Different first line from *An essay on the universe,* 1733, sometimes attributed to Morrice.
TxU(uncut).

M485 [—] Love and resentment: a pastoral. *London, printed for R. Burleigh, & Arrabella Morrice at the Black Lyon without Temple-Bar, 1717. (MC March)*
8°: π¹ A⁴ B² C–D⁴ E¹; *i–xiv, 1 2–18.* π1 hft.
In some copies page 17 is misnumbered '11', in others 18 is misnumbered '14'.
'Unkindly leaving the delightful plains'
Internal evidence suggests Morrice's authorship, and Arabella Morrice's name in the imprint tends to support it; it is unconfirmed.
L(164.1.55, Luttrell, April); *ICN*,IU(–π1),InU (–π1).

M486 [—] — The second edition. *London, printed for R. Burleigh, & Arrabella Morrice at the Black Lyon without Temple-Bar, [1717.]*
8°: π¹ A⁴(±A1) B² C–D⁴ E¹; *i–xiv, 1 2–18.* π1 hft.
A reissue. Date possibly cropped from title of copy seen.
O.

M487 [—] On rural felicity; in an epistle to a friend. *London printed, and sold by J. Wilford, 1733. (GSJ 19 Dec)*
2°: A² B–E²; *1–4 5–20.*
Rothschild 207. Engraving on p. 5, previously used in *Celadon,* 1708. Possibly previously published as *The felicity of a country life. In an epistle from the country,* [1732.]
'While you, my friend, the noisy town approve'
Reprinted with Morrice's name as *Rural felicity* below.
L(11626.h.11/1); CtY,IU,MH,OCU,TxU +.

M488 — [*idem*] Rural felicity; or, the delight and excellence of retirement: an epistle to a friend. Improv'd and enlarg'd by the author. *London printed, and Dublin re-printed by S. Powell, for Edward Exshaw, 1735.*
8°: *A⁴ B–C⁴; 1–5 6–24.*
Dedicated to John, archbishop of Dublin.
O,DN,DT; ICN.

Morrice, B. On the English translations

M489 [—] On the English translations of Homer: a satire... This satire was printed in the year 1721. (with the character of Homer) but is here improved and enlarged. *London, printed for John Oswald,* 1733. (*WM* 31 March)
8°: A^4 B–C^4; *1–4* 5–24.
    Previously printed with *An epistle to Mr. Welsted,* 1721.
'He's base, who wou'd degrade what's truly fine'
    The earlier edition was not anonymous. Dedicated to Lady Mary Wortley Montagu.
CLU-C,NN,OCU.

M490 — The present corruption of Britons; being a paraphrase on the latter part of Mr. P—e's first dialogue, entitled, One thousand seven hundred and thirty-eight. *London printed, and sold by Thomas Gray, and by the booksellers of London & Westminster,* [1738.] (*GM,LM* Nov)
2°: π^1 A–B^2 (A2 as 'A'); *1–7* 8–10.
    The collation is tentative.
'Virtue's the mind's direction – and defence'
    Dedication to Edward Young signed.
L(11602.i.16/7); ICU,OCU(cropt).

M491 [—] The present state of poetry. A satyr. Address'd to a friend. To which are added [3 poems]... By B.M. *London, printed for J. Roberts,* 1721. (*DP* 9 Jan)
8°: A^1 B–C^4 D^4(–D4); *i–ii, 1* 2–21 *22 blk.*
    The added poems occupy pp. 16–21.
'You wonder friend! that I, by nature mild'
    The following edition has dedication signed 'Alexis', a pseudonym of Morrice; it was advertised as Morrice's.
O.

M492 [—] — a satire; address'd to a friend, and dedicated to Mr. Welsted. *London printed, and sold by J. Roberts, and the booksellers of London & Westminster,* 1726 [1725]. (*SR* 21 Dec)
8°: A–C^4 D^2; *i–iii* iv–xi *xii, 13* 14–28.
    Entered in *SR* to John Millan by James Roberts; deposit copies at L,O,E,GU,SaU. Dedication signed 'Alexis'. Named as by Morrice in a Millan advertisement in J. Mitchell, *The promotion,* 1726.
L(993.f.51/4),O,E,GU,SaU + ; DFo(uncut),IU.

M493 [—] 'The religion of reason. A poem. [*London*] Printed for J. Wilford. Price 6d.' (*MChr* Dec 1730)
    Listed in *MChr* with *Dissectio mentis* 'by the same author'.

M494 [—] A satirical essay on modern poets. *London printed, and sold by J. Wilford,* 1734. (*LM* April)
2°: A^2 B–C^2 D^1; *i–iv, 1–9 10.* 10 advt.
'First – let us not, by reason's rules, intend'
    The advertisement is for 'Rural felicity' by the same author; clearly Morrice's *On rural felicity,* 1733.
O; CSmH(uncut),MH,TxU(2).

M495 — The successful fisher, or, all is fish, that comes to net. [*Dublin,* 1735.]

Morrice, B. The successful fisher

½°: 1 side, 1 column.
    At foot, advertisement for copies of the *London Magazine* imported by Edward Exshaw.
'The world's and heaven's eternal foe'
L(C.121.g.9/201, title cropt),C.

M496 [—] Three satires. Most humbly inscribed and recommended to that little gentleman, of great vanity, who has just published, a fourth volume of Homer. To which is added, a character of the nuns. A satire. *London, printed for J. Roberts,* 1719 [1718]. (*DC* 18 June)
8°: A^4 B–D^4; *1–5* 6–29 *30–32 blk.* A1 hft.
    The three satires are 'On the English translations of Homer'; 'To Mr. T--ck--ll, on the first appearance of Mr. P--pe's proposals...'; 'An epistle to Homer'. The second was previously published as *Verses to Mr. Tickell,* 1715.
'He's rash and base who do's at arts repine'
'Well then, th' expected hour is come at last'
'Oh worthy Homer! from the Stygian coast'
Nuns: 'Tho' wond'rous things the female saints pretend'
    A revised version of the first poem was printed in Morrice's *An epistle to Mr. Welsted,* 1721.
L(1489.t.49; C.133.c.2/5, –D4); ICU(–D4), MH(–D4).

M497 — To the falsely celebrated British Homer. An epistle. *London, printed for the author; sold by the booksellers of London & Westminster; and the pamphlet shops at the Royal-Exchange,* 1742. (*LEP* 6 April)
2°: A^2 B–E^2; *1–5* 6–20. 20 err.
'Both by the world and thee contemptuous made'
    Signed on p. 20. A satire on Pope.
O; DFo.

M498 [—] Two odes of Horace, with a description of Fame or Report from Virgil. Attempted in English verse, by the author of the Composition. *London, printed for T. Bickerton,* 1721 [1720]. (*DP* 26 Oct)
2°: (4 ll); *1–8.*
'While none more gratefully embrac'd'
    Advertised in *DP* 3 May 1721 as by the same author as *A voyage from Bengale,* which is Morrice's.
TxU.

M499 [—] The unequal enemies; being an essay in the stile of epick poesy. To which are added [5 translations]... *London printed, and sold by J. Peele,* 1722.
8°: A^4 B–D^4; *i–iv, 1* 2–26 *27–28 blk.*
    Listed in *MC* June 1723.
'In a tempestuous battle's raging heat'
    The O copy is bound between two of Morrice's poems; the preface speaks of his 'Reflections on our translators of Homer.'
O.

M500 [—] Verses on the king; occasion'd by his late danger and distress, at sea. *Westminster, printed by*

Morrice, B. Verses on the king

> *A. Campbell; sold by the booksellers of London &*
> *Westminster,* 1726. (*SR* 18 Jan)
> 2°: $A^2 <$ B¹; *1–3* 4–5 *6 blk.*
>> Entered in *SR* to B. Morrice; deposit copies
>> at L,O,E.
> 'Great Neptune, jealous of his rival's pow'r'
>> Morrice's authorship is clear from his copy-
>> right entry.
> L(643.m.13/25),O,E.

M500·5 [—] Verses to Mr. Tickell, on Mr. Pope's
translation of Homer. *London, printed for T. Baker;*
sold by all booksellers, 1715. (*MC* Oct)
2°: $A^1 B^2$; *1–2* 3–6.
'Well then th' expected hour is come at last'
> Reprinted in Morrice's *Three satires,* 1719.
L(12273.m.1/9); *NcD*(lacks A1).

M501 — A voyage from the East-Indies. By Capt.
Morrice. *London printed, and sold by J. Roberts,*
1716. (*MC* Dec)
8°: A^4 B–C⁴ D²; *1–7* 8–26 *27; 28 blk.* A1 hft; A2
frt; 27 advt.
> Advertised in *PB* 4 June 1717 as also sold by
> Arabella Morrice without Temple-Bar.
'Our anchors weigh'd, a fair auspicious gale'
L(11633.aaa.33,−A1),C,*MR; MH.*

M502 — [*idem*] A voyage from Bengale in the East
Indies. *London printed, and sold by Tho. Bickerton,*
& Tho. Edlin, ⟨1721.⟩ (*DP* 3 May)
2°: A^2 B–C² D¹; *1–3* 4–13 *14 blk.*
> The dedication to John Eccleston of the East
> India company is signed by Morrice.
CLU-C(title cropt).

[—] A walk from St. James's to Convent-Garden,
1717. *See* W12.

Morris, Peleg. Leisure hours well employ'd:
being, a collection of hymns and spiritual poems.
London, printed for the author, 1740.
12°: pp. 34.　　L,CT.

— Leisure hours well employ'd: being a collection
of hymns and poems. In two parts. Sacred I. to
the redeemer's humble and exalted state. II. to
piety and virtue. *London, printed for J. Oswald,* 1741.
12°: pp. 47.　　O.

— The favour'd moment: being a collection of
hymns and poems, I. sacred to deity. II. to piety
and virtue. *London, printed by J. Lewis,* 1745.
12°: pp. 48.　　L,O.

Morris, R. Divine poems on the sacred scriptures
... *London, printed for John Oswald,* [1730/37.]
8°: pp. 31.　　O.
> Probably by a relation of Peleg Morris above.

M503 [**Morris, Robert.**] The art of architecture, a poem.
In imitation of Horace's Art of poetry. Humbly
inscribed to the rt. honble the Earl of ---------.
London, printed for R. Dodsley; sold by T. Cooper,
1742. (25 Nov)

Morris, R. The art of architecture

> 4°: π¹[= E4] A^2 B–D⁴ E⁴(−E4); [2] *i–iii* 'iii', 5–34.
> π1 hft.
>> Engraving on title. Date from *Straus, Dodsley;*
>> listed in *LM* Nov.
> 'Should you, my lord, a wretched picture view'
>> Early ms. attribution to Morris in the IU
>> copy; advertised as by the same author in
>> Morris's *St Leonard's Hill,* 1743. Sometimes
>> attributed in error to John Gwynn.
> L(11656.r.7/11; 11630.e.7/1,−π1; 11602.gg.24/
> 7,−π1),O(−π1); CtY,ICU(−π1),IU,MH(−π1).

M504 [—] An enquiry after virtue: in a letter to a friend.
London, printed for C. Corbett, [173-.]
2°: A^2 B–E²; *1–3* 4–20.
'Health, happiness, contentment, to my friend'
> An advertisement in part II links this with
> Morris's *The art of architecture.*
O(uncut),LdU-B; CSmH,KU,MH(ms. correc-
tions),OCU,TxU+.

M505 [—] — The second edition. Contents... *London,*
printed for T. Cooper, 1740.
2°: A^2 B–E²; *1–3* 4–20.
> Apparently a reissue with new A^2, or a re-
> impression.
CtY.

M506 [—] An enquiry after virtue: in a letter to a friend.
Part II. being a proper appendix to the first part.
By the same author. *London, printed for T. Cooper,*
1743.
2°: A^4; *1–2* 3–8. 2 advt.
> The advertisement lists six books by the same
> author, including *The art of architecture,* 1742.
'While life rolls on, to chace dull cares away'
IU,TxU(2).

M507 [—] Have at you all: being a proper and distinct
reply to three pamphlets just published, intituled,
What of that? The Weather-menders, and They
are not. By the author of Yes, they are. *London,*
printed for T. Cooper, 1740. (*GM,LM* Dec)
2°: $A^2 B^2$; *1–3* 4–8.
'Once I had thought from writing to refrain'
> Advertised in Morris's *An enquiry after virtue,*
> part II, as by the same author. Answered by
> *Come on then,* 1740.
L (1973),O; CSmH,CtY,ICU,IU,MH.

M508 [—] — '*London, printed for the perusal of all lovers*
of their country', 1740.
8°: $A^4 B^4$; *1–4* 5–15 *16 blk.*
> A piracy; the copy seen is bound with
> Miller's *Are these things so?... To which is*
> *added, Yes they are,* 1740.
CtY.

M509 [—] Rupert to Maria. An heroic epistle. With
Maria's genuine answer. *London, printed for W.*
Webb, jun. near Temple-Bar, 1748. (*GM* May)
2°: π¹ A–C² D¹; *i–ii,* 1–14.
'Health, to his dear Maria, Rupert sends'
'Bless my dear Rupert for his ardent pray'r'

Morris, R. Rupert to Maria

Advertised in Morris's *The qualifications and duties of a surveyor*, 1752.

L(C.57.g.7/19),O; CSmH,CU,CtY,MH,TxU.

M510 — Saint Leonard's Hill: or, the hermitage. A poem. Humbly inscrib'd to -------. *London, printed for M. Cooper*, 1743. (*LDP* 17 Dec)

4°: *A*⁴ B–D⁴; *i–iii* iv, *5* 6–30 *31*; *32 blk*. 31 advt.

'While some in odes their tuneful tribute raise'

CtY,ICN.

M511 [—] Yes, they are: being an answer to Are these things so? The previous question from an Englishman in his grotto to a great man at court. *London, printed for T. Cooper*, 1740. (*LDP* 8 Nov)

2°: *A*¹ B–D² E¹; *i–ii*, *1* 2–13 *14 blk*.

Signature B under 'my'. The order of impressions has not been determined with certainty. A1 and E1 have been seen to be conjugate.

'Sir, in a garret near St. Martin's lane'

Advertised in Morris's *An enquiry after virtue*, part II (1743), as by the same author. The early ms. attribution to 'Mr. Love, comedian' in the Dublin edition below must be erroneous. An answer to James Miller's poem. Replied to in *They are not*, 1740, *What of that!* 1740, and G. Spiltimber, *The weather-menders*, 1740.

L(643.l.28/20),C,LdU-B; CLU-C,TxU(2).

M512 [—] — *London, printed for T. Cooper*, 1740.

2°: *A*¹ B–D² E¹; *i–ii*, *1* 2–13 *14 blk*.

Signature B under 'wish'. B reset, otherwise mainly a reimpression.

L(163.n.58),O(2),OA,OW,C; ICN(uncut),MH, MiU(2),OCU(2),TxU.

M513 [—] — *London, printed for T. Cooper*, 1740.

2°: *A*¹ B–D² E¹; *i–ii*, *1* 2–13 *14*. 14 advt.

Signature B under 'wish'. Apparently a reimpression with the addition of an advertisement on p. 14 for the second edition of *An enquiry after virtue*, 1740.

L(1960),O(uncut);ICU.

M514 [—] — '*London, printed for the perusal of all lovers of their country*', 1740.

8°: A–B⁴; *1–2* 3–16.

Horizontal chain-lines. A piracy, possibly of north-country origin; cf. James Miller, *Are these things so?* 1740 (M239).

O,C,AdU,*MR-C*,PrP; CtY,TxU.

M515 [—] — *London: printed, and Dublin re-printed in the year* 1740.

8°: A–B⁴; *1–3* 4–15 *16 blk*.

In this edition A2 is signed. One of these Dublin editions was probably issued with a Dublin edition of Miller's *Are these things so?* (M245) which listed it on the title, following an English printing of the two together.

O,DG; CSmH.

M516 [—] — *London, printed: and Dublin reprinted, in the year* 1740.

Morris, R. Yes, they are

8°: *A*⁴ B⁴; *1–3* 4–15 *16 blk*.

Early ms. note in the MH copy 'By Mr. Love, comedian'; clearly it is erroneous.

MH.

M517 [—] — *London: printed, and Dublin re-printed*, 1740.

12°: *A*⁴ B²; *1–3* 4–12.

L(1488.bb.31); CtY.

Mors. Mors triumphans: ode lyrica, 1744. *See* Belsham, James.

M518 [Mortimer, J.] An essay, to the pious memory of that late reverend divine, Mr. George Trosse, of the city of Exon... By J.M. *Exon, printed by Sam. Farley, for John Marsh*, 1713.

4°: A–B² C¹; *1–2* 3–10.

Early ms. note in the L copy 'Mortimere goldsmith of Exon'.

'Our parents first rebellious sin, gave death'

L(11631.e.39); CtY.

Morton, R., *A.M.*

Morton issued 'Proposals for printing by subscription, a translation of all the satires of Horace' dated 20 Dec 1739 (copy at O). The translation was apparently never published.

Moschus.

Cook, Thomas: The Idylliums of Moschus and Bion, translated from the Greek, 1724.

Moss, Robert. The belief of the divinity of Jesus Christ... The doctrines of transubstantiation... By Robert Moss. [The Latin texts translated into English verse], 1728. *See* B169.

M519 **Most.** [dh] A most gracious speech paraphras'd, in plain Englsh[!] meeter, for the benefit of vulgar readers, with something by way of introduction. [*London?* 1715.]

8°: *A*⁴; *1–8*.

'When royal Anne resign'd her breath'

Crum W1424. A vicious satire against George I and his first address to parliament, 21 March 1715.

L(11645.ee.44/1); CtY.

— A most pleasant description of Benwel village, 1726. *See* Ellison, Cuthbert.

M520 — The most renown'd history of Pope Joan. Collected from a postscript to a late eminent discourse. [*Dublin*] *Printed in the year* 1731.

8°: *A*⁴; *1–3* 4–8.

'As postscripts after sermons are'

A satirical versification of a postscript to a sermon.

DA,LdU-B,MR-C.

M521 **Mother.** Mother Gin, a tragi-comical eclogue: being a paraphrastical imitation of the Daphnis of Virgil. *London, printed for L. Gilliver & J. Clarke*, 1737. (*SR* 9 May)

Mother Gin

2°: *A–B² C–G²*; *3–7 8–29 30 blk*. 5 err.
  Bond 159. With the Latin text. Entered in *SR*
  to Gilliver; deposit copies at L,O,E,AdU,GU.
  Listed in *GM*, *LM* May.
'Since we, good fellows both, here haply meet'
L(644.m.14/21),O(2),C,E,LdU-B+ ; CSmH,
ICU,MH(uncut),NN,OCU.

M522 — Mother Hubbard's tale of the ape and fox,
abbreviated from Spencer. *London, printed in the
year* 1715.
2°: *A⁴* (A4 as 'B'); *1–2 3–8*.
'In days of old, when beasts in regal state'
  A Jacobite version.
L(C.115.i.3/17),O(uncut); OCU.

M523 — Mother Needham's elegy. Who died the 31st
of September 1730. Containing, an account of
Mother Needham's life and death, manner of lying
in state, her funeral, and epitaph; also P   y
P   m lamentation for her old acquaintance.
[*London*, 1730.]
½°: 1 side, 2 columns.
  Mourning headpiece.
'Ye ladies of Drury now weep'
  A false report of Elizabeth Needham's death
  appeared in *GSJ* 5 Oct 1730. She died on 3 May
  1731; cf. the following.
L(C.121.g.9/192).

— 'Mother Needham's lamentation, in an epistle
to a certain nobleman. [*London*] Price 6*d*.' (*GSJ*
8 May 1731)
  Listed in *MChr* May under 'plays, poetry,
  and books of entertainment'; it may be in
  prose.

M524 — Mother Osborne's letter to the protestant
dissenters faithfully rendered into English metre
from the London Journal of Saturday, September
8. 1733. By Mother Bunch, sister to the said
Mother Osborne. *London, printed for J. Roberts*,
1733. (*GSJ* 20 Sept)
8°: *A⁴* B–D⁴; *1–4 5–30 31–32 blk*. A1 hft.
'Troth, gentlemen, few know you better'
  A skit on the letter written by James Pitt under
  the pseudonym of F. Osborne.
L(1465.f.11,–D4; 161.l.18,–A1, D4); *CU*, MH
(–D4),OCU.

M525 Motion. The motion. [*London*] *Printed for T.
Cooper*, 1741. (*DP* 21 Feb)
obl 1°: 1 side, 3 columns.
  Large engraving at head. A 'new edition' was
  advertised in *DG* 16 March.
'Who be dat de box do sit on?'
  A satire on the motion for Walpole's dis-
  missal.
L(P&D 2479),O; CtY,NNP.

M526 — [*idem*] The patriots motion; or, the wise
men of Gotham. [*London*] *Printed for W. Webb;
sold by the booksellers of London and Westminster*,
1741.

The motion

obl ½°: 1 side, 3 columns.
  Large woodcut at head.
L(P&D 2483),LG; CtY.

Motteaux. *See* Mottoes.

Motteux, Peter Anthony. Britain's happiness, a
musical interlude. Perform'd at both the theatres.
Being part of the entertainment subscrib'd for by
the nobility, 1704.
  In theatrical form, and performed; accordingly
  outside the scope of this catalogue. There is a
  copy at L.

[—] Miscellanious [!] poetical novels or tales, 1705.
See M275–6.

M527 [—] [dh] A poem in praise of tea. [*London*, 1700?]
2°: *B–D²*; *1–12*.
  The copy seen may well lack the preliminary
  leaves. This edition prints a longer text than
  the following, with panegyrical references to
  William III; the couplet 'In a new century, it
  is decreed,/He shall reform the nations which
  he freed' suggests a date at the turn of the
  century. Possibly there is a connection with
  Nahum Tate's *Panacea: a poem upon tea*, 1700.
'Last night my hours on friendship I bestow'd'
  For Motteux's authorship see the editions
  below.
L(11633.h.10).

M528 — A poem upon tea. By Peter Motteux. *London,
printed for J. Tonson*, 1712. (26 Aug, Luttrell)
2°: *A² B–C²*; *i–iv, 1–8*.
  Drop-head title on p. 1, 'A poem in praise of
  tea'. Dedication to the *Spectator* dated 26 July
  1712.
MC; CLU-C(Luttrell),MiU,TxU(2, uncut).

M529 — — *London, printed for J. Tonson*, 1712.
8°: *A⁸*; *1–5 6–16*.
L(992.h.26),OW,LdU-B; ICN,MH-BA.

M530 — A poem in praise of tea. *London, printed for
J. Tonson*, 1712.
8°: *A⁸*; *1–5 6–16*.
  No sign of a cancel title in this or the pre-
  ceding; either a variant title or a reimpression.
MH.

M531 — A song perform'd at the post-office feast, on her
majesty's birth-day. [*London*] 1708.
½°: *1–2*, 1 column.
'Room room for the post, who, with zeal for the
queen'
Rothschild.

M532 — To the king on his majesty's landing in
Holland. [*London*, 1716?]
½°: *1–2*, 1 column.
'The, muse, who, near thy Britain's watry bounds'
  Signed 'Peter Motteux'.
TxU.

M533 — Words sung at the entertainment given by the
right honorable Sir Owen Buckingham, lord

Motteux, P. A. Words sung

mayor...to his grace the Duke of Marlborough, and other general officers, the 6th of January, 170⅘. Written by Mr Motteux. Set to musick by Mr Weldon. *London, printed by F.L. [Francis Leach?];* *sold by A. Baldwin,* 1705. (8 Jan, Luttrell)
½º: 1 side, 1 column.
'Welcome, the returning brave!'
Crawford; MH(Luttrell).

M534 — Words sung before her majesty on her birthday, Feb. 6. Set to music by Mr John Eccles. *London printed, and sold by A. Baldwin,* 1703.
½º: 1–2, 1 column.
'Inspire us, genius of the day'
LLP.

M535 Mottley, John. 'An epistle humbly address'd to the right honourable Sir Robert Walpole, on the treaty of peace being sign'd. *[London] Printed by J. Purser.* Price 6d.' (*MChr* 5 Dec 1729)

M536 — Verses addressed to the right honourable Sir Robert Walpole, on her majesty's being constituted regent of Great Britain. *London printed, and sold by T. Read, and by the booksellers of London & Westminster,* 1729. (*MChr* 31 May)
2º: (3 ll); 1–2 3–5 6 blk.
'Does thy great master, Walpole! for a while'
O.

M537 — 'Verses to the right honourable Sir Robert Walpole on his recovery. By Mr. Mottely [!]. *[London] Printed for J. Walthoe.* Price 2d.' (*MC* April 1727)

M538 Motto. The motto. An elegy on divine hereditary right. '*Printed for C. Cross near Westminster*', 1714.
slip: 1 side, 1 column.
The daily slip, no. 3, for 15 Sept 1714. The imprint is fictitious; 'C. Cross' stands for Charing Cross. The copy seen was reissued in *State poems. Being a collection of choice private pieces*, 1715.
'Come, ye Sachev'lites, lament and mourn'
On the disappointment of Sacheverell and his supporters on the coming of George I.
Brett-Smith.

M539 Mottoes. Motteaux before the eight copies of verses, by a gentleman at Bath, most humbly presented to their majesties, and the royal family. *Bath, printed by Felix Farley,* 1733.
½º: 2 sides, 1 column.
Woodcut headpiece of ladies bathing signed 'F Nixon F'. 8 mottoes, in Latin and English. The copies at O,BaP are bound with *To the fore-chairman that carried her majesty*, 1733; it is presumably by the same author and perhaps was issued with that work.
L(112.f.44/40),O,BaP.

— Motto's of the Wanderers; in Latin and English, 1718. *See* Fox, John.

Mouldy-Mowdiwart. Mouldy-Mowdiwart, [1724.] *See* Ramsay, Allan.

M540 Mountain. The mountain of miseries. From the Spectators, vol. VIII. no. 158, 159. Attempted in verse. *London printed, and sold by Josiah Graham,* 1739.
8º: *A*⁴ B–D⁴; *i*–*v* vi–viii, *9* 10–32. A1 hft; 32 advt. Ms. correction of title to read '558, 559'.
'O wondrous man! of all the works of nature'
The advertisement is for forthcoming 'Poems on several occasions' by the same author; they have not been identified.
MH.

Mountcashel, Edward Davys, *viscount. See* Davys, Edward, *viscount Mountcashel.*

M541 Mourner. The mourner. A funeral poem occasioned by the death of...Mr. James Brisbain, late minister of the gospel at Stirling; who died June 9. 1725. *Edinburgh, printed by Robert Brown,* 1725.
8º: A–B⁴; 1–2 3–16.
'Ah! news tormenting! is my father dead?'
L(11643.aa.37),E.

M542 Mournful. The mournful congress, a poem, on the death of the illustrious King William III. of glorious memory. By a sincere lover of his prince and country. *London, printed for John Nutt,* 1702. (14 March, Luttrell)
2º: A² B–D²; *i–iv,* 1–12.
Listed in *WL* March.
'When Gaul with force and fraud was making way'
O,LdU-B(lacks A²); CSmH,NjP(Luttrell).

M543 — A mournful copy of verses on the much lamented death of our late most glorious majesty Queen Anne, of ever-blessed memory. Who departed this life, August the first, 1713 [!]. *London, printed by E. Midwinter,* [1714.]
½º: 1 side, 1 column.
Royal arms at head and mourning woodcut borders.
'What joy did England once receive'
L(G.559/15).

M544 — [dh] The mournfull muse, an elegy on the much lamented death of King William IIId... [col] *London, printed for and sold by Tho. Parkhurst,* [1702.]
2º: B²; *1* 2–4.
Printed in mourning borders throughout. A copy at TxU with fleur-de-lys watermark is possibly on fine paper; other copies have crowned B.
'O heavens! inspire, O angels! now indite'
O; CtY,TxU.

M545 — The mournful muse or, a poem, upon the very much and universally, tho' never enough lamented death, and to the pious memory of that truely excellent and worthy patriot Lord Basil Hamilton,

The **mournful** muse

fifth lawful son to the deceast William duke of Hamiltoun, &c. *Edinburgh, printed by John Reid,* 1701.

1°: 1 side, 2 columns.

> Mourning borders.

'What sullen planet rul'd the direfull day'

E.

— A mournful poem on the never enough to be lamented death of his sacred and soveraign majesty King William, [1702.] *See* Williamson, David.

M546 — The mournful poem, on the royal funeral of King William the third, late of Great Britain, the preserver, defender, and hero; who was inter'd in King Henry the seventh's chappel, at Westminster, on Sunday night the twelfth of April, 1702. [*London*] *Printed by A. Milbourn,* [1702.]

½°: 1 side, 2 columns.

> Mourning borders. Printed in white ink on black paper.

'Mysterious fate how canst thou reconcile'

L(82.1.8/65); CSmH(mutilated).

M547 — A mournful song, upon the breach of national, and solemn league, and covenant: with some of the causes, and direfull effects thereof. [*Edinburgh?*] *Printed in the year* 1724.

8°: *A*⁴; *1* 2–8.

'I beg your attention for I design to write'

> A doggerel poem on the church.

E.

M548 Mourning. The mourning court: or, a tribute of tears, for the death of his royal highness Prince George: who departed this life on the twenty eighth of October, 1708 to the unspeakable grief of her sacred majesty, and all loyal and well disposed subjects. To the tune of Troy town, &c. [*London*] *Printed for B. Deacon & J. Walter,* [1708.]

½°: 1 side, 2 columns.

> Mourning headpiece and borders.

'Come let us mourn for well we may'

L(1876.f.1/44).

M549 — The mourning court; or, a tribute of tears, for the much lamented death of our pious Queen Anne: who departed this life at her court at Kingsington, on August the 1st. 1714. To the unspeakable grief of all loyal and obedient subjects. To the tune of, When Troy town for ten years wars, &c. [*London*] *Printed for J. Walter,* [1714.]

½°: 1 side, 2 columns.

> Mourning borders.

'With bleeding heart and weeping eyes'

L(1876.f.1/66).

— The mourning poet, 1703. *See* Brown, Thomas.

— The mourning prophet, 1714. *See* Ward, Edward.

M550 Mouse-trap. The mouse-trap. A new poem, translated from the Latin original... *Dublin,*

The **mouse-trap**

printed by E. Waters, and are to be sold by J. Henly, ⟨1710.⟩

8°: A–B⁴; *1–2* 3–16.

> The copy seen has the imprint shaved and is catalogued as 1719, but 1710 is probably correct.

'I sing the Briton mountain swain'

> A translation of Edward Holdsworth's *Muscipula,* [1708.]

DA.

M551 — The mouse trap, a poem, done from the original Latin in Milton's stile. *London, printed for R. Gosling,* 1715.

8°: *A*⁴(A1 + frt) B–C⁴; *1–4* 5–23 *24 blk.* A1 hft.

> *Bond* p. 219. The frontispiece is apparently that used for the Curll edition of *Muscipula,* 1709.

'The British mountaineer, who first uprear'd'

> A translation of Edward Holdsworth's *Muscipula,* [1708.]

O(−frt),LdU-B,WcC(2); CLU-C,CtY,ICN(Luttrell, no date),MH,TxU+.

— The mouse-trap: or, the Welsh engagement with the mice, 1709. *See* Quincy, John.

M552 — [dh] The mouse-trap: or, the Welshmen's scuffle with the mice. [col] *London, printed in the year* 1709.

8°: *A*⁴; *1–8*.

'A Britain, who on mountains liv'd'

> A translation of Edward Holdsworth's *Muscipula,* [1708.]

L(11408.e.60/2); InU,OCU.

M----r---n, Sh----ny, *Miss.* Advice to the ladies of Michael's parish, [1722.] *See* A95.

M----t, H----y, *esq.* The bawdy-house, [1723.] *See* B109.

Muff. The muff, or one good turn deserves another, 1740. *See* Lorleach, —, *Mr.*

Mulgrave, John Sheffield, *earl of. See* Sheffield, John, *duke of Buckingham.*

M553 Mullan, David. [dh] David Mullan's letter to Dean Swift. [col] *Dublin, printed in the year,* 1735.

4°: *A*²; *1–4*.

'To you in Pæan's fire and virtue's strong'

> Signed 'David Mullen'. See *The Dean's answer to David Mullan's letter,* 1735.

DA; CtY.

M554 — [dh] David Mullan's petition to the honble the counsellors, lawyers, &c. of the city of Dublin. From my garret in Back-lane, Dec. 11th, 1735. [col] *Dublin, printed in the year* 1735.

4°: *A*²; *1–3 4 blk.*

'Inspire my muse ye sons of sparkling wit'

CtY.

Mully

Mully. Mully of Mountown, 1704-. *See* King, William, *the gazetteer*.

Multa. Multa tulere tuæ, te, rex, absente, columbæ, [1710?/13.] *See* Pitcairne, Archibald.

Mum. Mum. A political ballad, for the present times, 1740. *See* Leslie, Charles.

[M555 = L115·2] Mum is the word, 1749. *See* Leslie, Charles.

M556 Mundus. Mundus delirans, or the infatuation. A poem. [*Edinburgh*] *Printed in the year* 1741.
4°: *A⁴*; *1–2* 3–8.
'Begin, my muse! and this strange truth unfold'
   A satire on Edinburgh politicians and academics.
L(643.k.5/1).

M557 Munns, Nathaniel. The great example, or, the way to conquest; a poem. Being considerations on the temptations and sufferings of the holy Jesus...
London, printed for and sold by F. Jefferies, 1735.
12°: (frt+) A⁶(±A1) B–L⁶ M²; *i–xxvi*, *1–94* 83–98. 98 err.
'When John the Baptist had prepar'd the way'
   Dedication signed.
L(1607/2349/3); ICN,NNUT(–frt),TxU.

M558 — Horneck's Fire of the altar versified: or, feasting on a sacrifice: a poem. Containing certain directions how to raise the soul into holy flames...
London, printed for, and sold by F. Jefferies, 1735.
(*GM* Aug)
12°: A⁴ B–H⁶ I²; *i–viii*, *1* 2–86 *87–88*.
   Copies at L, ICN have a frontispiece of the crucifixion, also found in *The great example*.
'Is it not meet, my soul, some time to pause'
   Dedication signed.
L(1607/2349/1); ICN,NNUT,TxU.

M559 Munster. The Munster and Conaught attorney's, a satyr. To which is added, the tripple plea; or, a grand dispute, between law, physick, and divinity, about superiority. [*Dublin?*] *Printed in the year* 1736.
½°: 1 side, 2 columns.
'Since sons of whores are noble men'
Crawford.

M560 — The Munster combat or the invasion of the Moors... *Dublin, printed by E. Needham & R. Dickson, next door to ⟨the Angel⟩ and Bible in Dames ⟨Street⟩*, [1725?]
½°: *1–2*, 1 column.
   Plomer dates this printing partnership at this address as 1725.
'To you my dear friend I this ballad indite'
   On the victory of Mr. Marshall over the Moore junto in the Clonmel election.
L(C.121.g.8/18, cropt); CSmH.

Munster

M561 — Munster Juggy preferr'd or an answer to Molly Mogg of the Rose. By Shane-baune Mac-Dermot. [*Dublin*] *Printed by J. Gowan*, 1727.
½°: 1 side, 2 columns.
'What a pother you keep about Molly'
MH.

M562 — The Munster wedding. To the tune of, Sawny's to be married to Moggy. [*Dublin*] *Printed in the year* 1722.
½°: 1 side, 1 column.
'Oh! there was a jovial wedding, a jovial wedding I trow'
L(C.121.g.8/14),DG(imprint cropt).

[**Murray, David,** *6th viscount Stormont.*] To the memory of the right honourable John earl of Strathmore [actually by William Meston], [1715/16?] *See* M221.

Musae. Musæ juveniles, 1732. *See* Cooke, William, *dean of Ely*.

Musaeus. Musæus: a monody to the memory of Mr. Pope, 1747-. *See* Mason, William.

Musaeus.
Catcott, A. S.: The poem of Musæus, on the loves of Hero and Leander, paraphras'd in English, heroick verse, 1715, 1716. *See* C70–1.

Sterling, James: The loves of Hero and Leander from the Greek of Musæus, 1728. *See* S754–5.

Bally, George: The loves of Hero and Leander. Translated from the Greek of Musæus, 1747. *See* B44.

Eusden, Laurence: Hero and Leander: a poem by Musaeus, translated from the Greek, 1750. *See* E490–1.

Musarum. Musarum deliciæ: containing essays upon pastoral, 1728. *See* Howard, Edward, *8th earl of Suffolk*.

Muschet. Muschet revived; or an elegy, [1723.] *See* Pennecuik, Alexander, *d. 1730*.

Muscipula. Muscipula: or, the mouse-trap, 1725. *See* Taswell, William.

— Muscipula: sive Cambro-muo-maxia, [1708]-. *See* Holdsworth, Edward.

Muse. The muse an advocate for injur'd merit, 1734. *See* Manning, Francis.

M563 — The muse in distress: a poem. Occasion'd by the present state of poetry; humbly address'd to the right honourable Sir William Yonge... *London, printed for T. Cooper*, 1733. (*GSJ* 3 Nov)
2°: *A²* B–D²; *1–3* 4–16.
'Amidst the great concerns, which fill thy mind'
O; CtY,DLC,IU,MH,TxU.

Muse

— A muse in livery. A collection of poems, 1732. *See* Dodsley, Robert.

M564 — [dh] The muse's address to the honourable house of commons, in behalf of insolvent prisoners for debt. [*London*, 1702/14.]
4°: *A*²; 1–4.
'Great Britain's worthy patriots will excuse'
IU.

M565 — The muse's flight. Reflections on a journey to the county of Cork... *Dublin, printed by and for S. Powell*, 1738.
8°: A⁸; 1–3 4–15 *16 blk.*
'O Strephon, (if that title please your ear)'
DN.

— The muse's treat: or, a collation of wit and love, 1702. *See* Morrice, Bezaleel.

— 'The muse's vagaries [: or the merry mortal's companion. By Sir Solomon Gundy, knt. and Margery Merrypin, spinster]. [*London*] *Printed for J. Robinson*. Price 6*d.*' (*GM,LM* April 1743)
A second part was issued before 15 Nov 1743 when both parts were advertised together in *LDP*. From an edition of both parts, 1745 (copy at DFo), it appears to be a miscellany. Compare *The poplar grove... By the author of the Muses vagaries*, 1743.

M566 Music. Musick. A poem. Inscrib'd to Mr. Robert Lympany, aged ninety, on his generous benefaction to the organ at Fulham, A.D. 1732. By an unknown author. *London, printed in the year* 1732.
4°: *A*⁴ B⁴; *i–iv*, 1 2–11 *12 blk.*
Possibly all copies seen are on fine paper, watermarked with a star; the copy at E has the gilt edges of a presentation copy.
'Hail! hoary'st of Apollo's sons; permit'
O,CT,E.

M567 — Music in good time. A new ballad. *London, printed for G. Lyon*, 1745. (*GM,LM* Sept)
2°: *A*⁴; 1–3 4–8.
Horizontal chain-lines.
'While threaten'd with ruin at home and abroad'
A satire on London's interest in music at the expense of military action.
L (1973),O; CSmH(cropt),KU.

Music in good time

M568 — — [*London?* 1745.]
½°: 1 side, 2 columns.
Three rough woodcuts at head.
L(1876.f.1/135).

M569 Musidora. Musidora; a pastoral elegy on the death of the honourable Mrs. Bowes. Inscrib'd to the right honourable the lord Viscount Killmorey. *London, printed for S. Bussey*, 1725. (*MC* Feb)
2°: *A*² B–C²; 1–3 4–12.
Printed by Samuel Richardson (*Sale* 34).
'Our flocks at feed, and we devoid of care'
CtY.

M570 Musidorus. Musidorus: a poem sacred to the memory of Mr. James Thomson. *London, printed for R. Griffiths*, [1748.] (*GM, LM* Oct)
4°: A–C⁴; 1–3 4–24.
'From lighter strains, to sing the tragic theme'
L(11630.c.8/15; 1465.i.12/13); OCU,PU.

M571 — — 'London, printed for R. Griffiths' [*Edinburgh?*], [1748.]
8°: *A*⁴ B⁴; 1–3 4–14 *15–16 blk.*
MH.

M572 M---y. M---y S----y's answer to her father's advice. [*Dublin*] *Printed in the year* 1730.
slip: 1 side, 1 column.
'Now C---b ceas'd and Molly rose'
A reply to *Advice from C----b S------y to his daughter*, 1730; Molly Smalley to her father Caleb.
CtY.

M573 Myrtillo. Myrtillo. A pastoral poem lamenting the death of Mr. Charles Shadwell, gratefully inscrib'd to all his friends. *Dublin, printed by William Wilmot*, 1726.
½°: 1 side, 2 columns.
'Ye weeping muses with sad pomp attend'
Reprinted in *Poems written occasionally by the late John Winstanley...interspers'd with many others*, II (1751).
DT(title cropt); CU.

Mytilopolis. Mytilopolis sive Musselburgi, oppidi antiquissimi, elogium, [1703?] *See* Denneston, Walter.

N

N., A. A conference concerning transubstantiation, 1730. *See* C338.

N., C. A poem on the happy union, 1707. *See* P619.

N., H., *bricklayer*. A new poem on the ancient and loyal society of journey-men taylors, 1725. *See* Nelson, Henry.

— A poem in the honour of the antient and loyal society of the journey-men taylors, 1726. *See* Nelson, Henry.

N., R. The invincible hero' Arthure Dillon's sword place'd amidst the stars, [1724.] *See* I55.

N., T. A miscellaneous collection of original poems, 1740. *See* Newcomb, Thomas.

— An ode, presented to his royal highness the Duke of Cumberland, 1746. *See* Newcomb, Thomas.

N., T., *Mr.* Pacata Britannia, 1713. *See* Newcomb, Thomas.

N., T., *philomath*. A famous prediction of Merlin, 1709. *See* Swift, Jonathan.

Namby. Namby Pamby: or, a panegyrick on the new versification, [1725.] *See* Carey, Henry.

'Namby Pamby.'
A nickname applied to Ambrose Philips, and here used in mockery of him. For other poems in the 'namby-pamby' style, see the subject index.

— Durgen, a satyr, to the celeberted [!] Mr. P--------pe, [1729.] *See* D554.

N1 — Namby Pamby's answer to Captain Gordon. [*Dublin*, 1725/26.]
½°: 1 side, 2 columns.
  Bond 84.
'Nymphlings three, and three, and three'
  Intended as a reply by Ambrose Philips to [Henry Carey] *Namby Pamby*, [1725], a Dublin edition of which attributes the authorship to Thomas Gordon; further satirizing Philips.
L(C.121.g.8/185),C,DT(2); TxU.

N2 — Namby Pamby's lamentation, for the departure of Mr, No-body. [*Dublin*, 1726.]
½°: 1 side, 2 columns.
  Bond 85.
'Must he then alass depart'
  A satire on Ambrose Philips's *To his excellency the Lord Carteret, &c. departing from Dublin,*

1726. Referred to in *Advice from fairyland*, 1726, as written by 'Ph—pps & Dun—can'.
L(C.121.g.8/184),O; NjP.

— A poem by Namby Pamby, [1725/–.] *See* P523.

Narration. A narration of the wonders of grace, 1734. *See* Dutton, Anne.

N3 Narrative. [dh] The narrative. [174–?]
4°: *A–B²*; 1–8.
  Bradshaw 5395 compares the rough printing to *The Hibernian politicians* (Isle-of-Man, 1740); it uses a different size of type.
'Whoever has a cause dependant'
  A satire on bribery and the law, possibly by the author of *The Hibernian politicians* and other works listed there.
C(uncut).

N4 — The narrative of high and low. [*Dublin*, 1710.]
½°: 1 side, 1 column.
  On the other side, *A late dialogue between Dr. Burgess and Daniel d'Foe*, [1710.]
'When sovereign commons princes made'
  In defence of Sacheverell.
DG.

N5 Nation. The nation run mad. [*London*, 1710.]
½°: 1 side, 2 columns.
'The nation had always some token'
  On the Sacheverell affair.
MH.

N6 National. The national alarm; or, seasonable admonition to the degenerate natives of the once formidable island of Great Britain... By J——H——, esq; *London printed, and sold by George Woodfall*, 1745.
2°: *A²* B–E² F¹; *1–5* 6–22. 22 err.
  Horizontal chain-lines.
'When we the tidings eagerly receiv'd'
CLU-C.

N7 Natural. The natural history of the arbor vitæ: or the tree of life; versify'd and explain'd. Addressed to the ladies, by a member of a society of gardeners. *London, printed for J. Wilkinson, near Charing-Cross; sold by the booksellers of London & Westminster*, 1732. (*DJ* 17 June)
8°: *A⁴* B–C⁴D²; *i–iv* v–vii, *viii blk.* 9 10–26 *27;28 blk.* A1 hft; D2 advt.
'Thou god, to whose great memory'
  A versification of the prose work with this title, published the same month in 4° (CSmH) and ½° (L). A phallic poem.
O.

N8 — — '*London, printed for J. Wilkinson...*' [*Dublin*, 1732?]
8°: *A⁸*; *i–ii* iii–iv, *5* 6–15 *16 blk.*
L(Cup.1000.aa.2).

Natural

N9 Natural. 'The natural philosophers: a tale. [*London*] *Printed for Samuel Prince, and sold at the Peacock without Temple-Bar*. Price 3*d*.' (*DC* 12 Feb 1723)

> The Peacock was Anne Dodd's address. The quotation in the advertisement suggests this is a bawdy tale in verse.

Nature. Nature, a poem, 1747–. *See* Fortescue, James.

— Nature display'd. A poem, 1727. *See* Collins, Richard.

N10 — Nature in perfection; or, the mother unveil'd: being a congratulatory poem to Mrs. Bret, upon his majesty's most gracious pardon granted to Mr. Richard Savage, son of the late Earl Rivers. *London, printed for T. Green; sold by J. Roberts*, 1728. (*MChr* 21 March)

2°: A² B² C¹; *1–2* 3–9 *10*. 10 advt.
'Let hireling poets ply their venal lays'

> Ascribed to Richard Savage by *Halkett & Laing*, quoting no authority; doubted by C. Tracy in his *Artificial bastard* (1953) 93, and not printed in his edition of the poems.

L(163.n.55); CSmH,MH,TxU(3).

N11 — The nature, necessity, use, and advantage of publick and private prayer. A poem. Humbly presented to the Lady Cowper. *London, printed for the author*, 1720.

4°: A¹ B–D²; *1–2* 3–13 *14 blk*.

> Probably issued with variant title-pages with alternative dedicatees.

'Prayer! thou vehicle of words, that shew'

> By the same author as *A divine poem on the creation*, 1718, and other poems listed there; possibly Henry Nevil was that author.

IU.

N12 — [reissue] Most humbly presented to the Lady Trumbal. *London, printed for the author*, 1723.

4°: A¹(±) B–D²; *1–2* 3–13 *14 blk*.

> With a cancel title-leaf; presumably issued with variants with alternative dedicatees.

L(1961).

— The nature of man. A poem, 1711. See Blackmore, *Sir* Richard.

— Nature will prevail, 1736. *See* Bancks, John.

Naumachius.

[Free, John:] Advice to the fair-sex. A poem translated from the Greek of Naumachius, 1736. *See* F235.

Naval. A naval panegyric, 1749. *See* Hudson, Thomas.

N13 Neale, Thomas. 'Ενυπνιον: or the vision, in imitation of the latter-part of the VIth book of Virgil. To which is annex'd an ode, occasion'd by the battle of Ramelies. In imitation of Horace

Neale, T. 'Ενυπνιον

lib. I. ode 37. Humbly dedicated to the Dutchess of Marlborough. *London, printed for W. Hawes*, 1706. (5 Dec, Luttrell)

2°: A–C²; *1–2* 3–12.

> The Luttrell copy is recorded in *Haslewood*.

'Say sacred goddess, say, for no retreat'
Ode: 'Fill up the glass, if ever, now's the time'
C.

N13·5 Near. [first line:] Near to the sacred and immortal frame... [*London*, 1712?]

½°: 1 side, 1 column.
No title.
'Near to the sacred and immortal frame'

> Reprinted in *Political merriment*, part 2 (1714) as 'Upon the Q——n's statue at Paul's. Written in June 1712. By the author of the Verses to the Duke of Marlborough upon his leaving England, lately printed and recommended to Sir Anthony Crabtree [i.e. V77]'. A variant text is printed with Garth's poems in *The works of celebrated authors* (1750) in association with [George Sewell] *To his grace the Duke of Marlborough, on the report of his going into Germany*, wrongly attributed to Garth. It is possible that the wrong set of verses to Marlborough were attributed to Garth, and that he wrote both the present poem and V77; but the problem needs further examination. Against Queen Anne's making peace with France, and France's ingratitude.

O,*Crawford*,Rothschild; NN.

Neck. Neck or nothing, 1716. *See* Wesley, Samuel, *the younger*.

N14 — Neck or nothing; or, the devil take the hindmost. An excellent new ballad, to the tune of A whim-wham's lately come over, &c. The words by a person of quality. [*London?* 1745.]

½°: 2 sides, 1 column.
'Young Perkin's lately come over'

> Ms. note in the O copy, 'Writ on Sir John Cope's defeat, 1745'.

O.

Needler, Henry. The works of Mr. Henry Needler. *London, printed for J. Watts*, 1724. (*MC* May)

8°: pp. xv, 320. L; DFo,PU.

> Mainly in prose. Listed in *MC* as sold by W. Hinchliffe.

— — The second edition. *London, printed for J. Watts; sold by A. Bettesworth, J. Pemberton, W. Hinchliffe, & A. Millar*, 1728. (*MChr* 1 Feb)

12°: pp. xi, 220.   L,O; CtY,MH.

— [reissue] The third edition. *London, printed for J. Watts; sold by J. Osborn*, 1735.

L; MH,PU.

N15 [—] The fifth ode of the fourth book of Horace imitated: and inscrib'd to the king. *London, printed*

Needler, H. The fifth ode

for William Hinchliffe; sold by John Morphew, 1714. (24 Aug, Luttrell)
2°: A(3 ll, second 'A2'); *1–2* 3–6.
Listed in *MC* Aug.
'Too long, illustrious prince, does Britain moan'
Reprinted in Needler's *Works*, 1724.
L(11631.h.19),*MR C*; CtY,ICU,IU,MH(Luttrell).

N16 Negative. The negative prophesy found under the ruins of White-hall. [*London*, 1704.] (5 April, Luttrell)
½°: 1 side, 1 column.
Line 4 ends with a semicolon. 'Price Two Pence' at end, deleted in ICN copy.
'I sing not of Jove's mighty thunder'
ICN(Luttrell),TxU.

N17 — [another edition]
Line 4 ends with a comma. Price deleted in all copies seen.
L(C.38.1.6/22),Crawford; MH.

N18 Negotiators. The negotiators. Or, Don Diego brought to reason. An excellent new ballad. Tune of Packington's pound. *London, printed for R. Thompson*, 1738. (*GM, LM* May)
2°: A² B²; *1–5* 6–7 *8 blk.* A1 frt.
'(Price Sixpence.)' on title. *Percival* XLII. Woodcut frontispiece. *Plomer* under 'Thompson' records a copy in the PRO with a ms. note suggesting alternative forms of legal action against those responsible for publishing it.
'Our merchants and tarrs a strange pother have made'
Crum O1305. Percival suspects William Pulteney's authorship on stylistic grounds. A satire on the Walpoles' negotiations with Spain. Don Diego is Sir Thomas FitzGerald, the Spanish envoy.
L(643.1.28/26),LU,O(2, 1 uncut),DT,MC; CSmH,CtY,ICN,MH(uncut),TxU(uncut)+.

N19 — [another impression]
'(Price Six-pence.)' on title; horizontal chain-lines.
MH(−A1),OCU(−A1).

'Neitherside, Neuter.' Raven and owl, 1739. *See* R134.

N20 [**Nelson, Henry.**] The Dublin-jubilee. a new poem, ascrib'd to the rt. honourable lord mayor of this city, on his rideing the franchises, August, the 12th. 1725. Accompanied by all the corporations. *Dublin, printed by E.N.* [*E. Needham*], 1725.
½°: *1–2*, 2 columns.
The sequence of editions here is highly tentative. The names of the corporations are printed in the margins.
'He who with Homer dares engage the field'

Nelon, H. The Dublin-jubilee

Nelson's authorship is revealed by the relationship of later versions to his *The order of the procession*.
L(C.121.g.8/54).

[N21 cancelled]

N22 [—] [*idem*] ⟨A⟩ second poem on the riding the franchises. [*Dublin*, 172–.]
½°: 1 side, 2 columns.
Only the introductory verses are new. The names of the corporations are printed in the margins.
'Ye tuneful nine, your poets mind inspire'
L(1890.e.5/79, cropt).

N23 [—] [*idem*] The cavalcade: a poem on the riding the franchises. [*Dublin*, 172–.]
½°: 1 side, 2 columns.
The names of the corporations are printed in the margins.
L(1890.e.5/77, cropt),Crawford.

N24 [—] [another edition]
The names of the corporations are indented.
Crawford(mutilated).

N25 [—] [*idem*] The new order and procession. of the riding the franchises. [*Dublin*, 172–?]
½°: 1 side, 2 columns.
With shorter introductory verses, identical with those of *The order of the procession*, N28 below. The names of the corporations in ms.
'Thou mighty Sol, who in the east ascend'
L(1890.e.5/78).

N26 [—] A new poem on the ancient and loyal society of journey-men taylors. Who are to dine at the King's-Inn's-Hall, this present Monday, being the 26th of this instant July, 1725. By H.N brick-layer, one of the brethren. *Dublin, printed by Corn. Carter, in the year* 1725.
½°: 1 side, 1 column.
'Assist my sacred muse, my pen inspire'
Answered by *A new London poem*, 1725.
L(1890.e.5/164; C.121.g.8/42).

N27 — A new poem on the procession of journey-men taylors; who are to dine at the King's Inns, on Tuesday the 25th of this instant July 1727. *Dublin, printed [by C. Hicks] at the Rein Deer in Montrath-street*, [1727.]
½°: 1 side, 2 columns.
'Aurora fair, who doth the skye adorn'
L(1890.e.5/166),DT(cropt).

N28 — The order of the procession of the journeymen builders, plaisterers, painters and free-masons. To which is added, a poem suitable to the occasion. [*Dublin*, 1728/29?]
½°: 1 side, 2 columns.
The order of the procession is printed above the poem. The date is suggested by the manuscript numeration of the L copy.
'Thou mighty Sol, who in the east ascend'
L(1890.e.5/209).

Nelson, H.

[—] A poem in praise of the journey-men taylors, [1725/30.] *See* P540.

N29 — A poem in praise of the loyal and charitable society of journeymen taylors, who are to dine at the King's-Inn's this present Monday being the 28th of July, 1729. *Dublin, printed by Nicholas Hussey*, [1729.]
½⁰: 1 side, 2 columns.
'What sight is this does every one behold?'
L(1890.e.5/167),DT.

N30 [—] A poem, in the honour of the antient and loyal society of the journey-men-taylors, who are to dine at the King's-Inns, on Monday the 25th inst, July, 1726. Written by H.N. bricklayer, one of the brethren. *Dublin, printed by C. Carter*, 1726.
½⁰: 1 side, 2 columns.
'You sacred sisters nine, my breast inspire'
L(1890.e.5/168).

N31 — ⟨A⟩ poem on the procession of journeymen smiths. On May the first, 1729. *Dublin, printed by and for Theophilis Musgrove in the year* 1729.
½⁰: 1 side, 2 columns.
'You sacred sisters nine my theme attend'
C.

N32 — ⟨A⟩ poem on the procession of journeymen taylors, July the 28th, MDCCXXIX. [*Dublin*, 1729.]
slip: 1 side, 1 column.
'Tho' Phæbus bright, ascended from the sea'
L(1890.e.5/170).

N33 — The speech of the first stone laid in the parliament-house, to the government, February 3d, 1728,9. [*Dublin*, 1729.]
½⁰: 1 side, 1 column.
'A rough unpolish'd formless lump I lay'
DT.

N34 **Neoptolemus.** Neoptolemus. Ode in nuperos rebelles devictos. *Londini, typis T. Gardner*, 1746.
4⁰: A–C²; *1–2* 3–12.
'Tutela nostræ, qua patet, insulæ'
O.

N35 **Neptune.** Neptune to Lord Carteret. [*Dublin*, 1725/30.]
½⁰: 2 sides, 1 column.
'The powerful monarch of the flood salutes'
    A plea on behalf of the 'admiral of the Irish ocean'.
CtY.

Nereides. Nereides: or, sea eclogues, 1712. *See* Diaper, William.

N36 **Nero.** Nero the second. [*London?* 1715.]
slip: 1 side, 1 column.
'As Nero laughing saw fierce fires consume'
    Crum A1611. A Jacobite satire against George

Nero the second

I, occasioned by a fire in Thames Street, 13 Jan 1715.
O.

N37 **Net.** A net for the d---l: or, the town display'd. A satyr. Written in a plain English style. *London, printed in the year* 1705. (Dec?)
4⁰: A–E² (A2 as 'B'); *i–ii*, 1–18.
    The printer is identified as 'Mr. Grantham' by Robert Clare; see below.
'Let those grave bards Apollo's aid demand'
    Attributed to Edward Ward by Robert Clare, one of Harley's informers, in Dec 1705; see H. L. Snyder in *The library* V. 22 (1967) 343. His attributions seem in many cases to be wild guesses.
L(11631.cc.1),DT; TxU.

N38 **Neuter.** The neuter: or, a modest satire on the poets of the age. By a lady. Dedicated to the right honourable Mary Wortley Montague. *London, printed for T. Osborne; sold by A. Dodd*, [1733.] (*GSJ* 29 May)
2⁰: A² B²; *1–5* 6–8.
'In this rude age, where vice triumphant reigns'
L(11621.k.2/65*),LdU-B.

N39 [**Nevil, Henry.**] A congratulatory poem, on the most auspicious birth-day of his majesty King George. Most humbly presented to Mr. Samuel Smithing. Goldsmith to his majesty. *London, printed for the author*, 1723.
2⁰: A¹ B–C²; *1–2* '4' 4–10.
    Probably issued with alternative titles for various dedicatees.
'O goddess! from whose name the month proceeds'
    The only evidence of Nevil's authorship is the subject and the personal presentation, but his authorship is at the least probable.
IU.

[—] A divine poem on the creation, 1718. *See* D341.

[—] Faith and practice, 1717. *See* F39.

N40 [—] The first of August, the anniversary of his majesty's happy accession to the throne of his ancestors. A poem. Humbly presented to Thomas Reynolds, esq;... *London, printed by H. Meere, for the author*, 1716.
2⁰: A⁴(±A1); *i–ii*, 1–6.
    Apparently issued with alternative titles for various dedicatees.
'Prepare, Britannia, now thy thoughts employ'
    Apart from the similarity with Nevil's poems, both 1716 and 1717 editions are printed by the printers of Nevil's other poems in those years.
CSmH.

Nevil, H. The first of August

N41 [—] [another edition] Humbly presented to... *London, printed by S. Palmer, for the author*, 1717. 2°: *A*⁴; *1–3* 4–8.
> Issued with alternative titles for various dedicatees: 'Nathaniel Collins, esq;' (OCU); 'Mr. Hinde' (CLU-C). Probably the title is a cancel.

CLU-C,OCU.

N42 [—] 'The first of August. A poem, in grateful remembrance of the dangers providentially escaped, and the blessings that happily supply'd their room, by his most gracious majesty King George's accession to the throne of Great Britain, 1714. Humbly dedicated to...the Duke of Newcastle... [*London*] *Printed for the author; sold by W. Boreham*. Price 6d.' (*DC* 1 Aug 1718)
> Nevil's authorship is presumed from the form of the title.

[—] A funeral poem, sacred to the memory of the most noble John Churchill, 1722. *See* F302.

[—] The Lord's day: or, the Christian sabbath, 1720–. *See* L263.

[—] The nature, necessity, use, and advantage of publick and private prayer, 1720–. *See* N11.

[—] On the creation of the world, 1719. *See* D342.

[—] On the nativity of our blessed lord and saviour Jesus Christ, 1717–. *See* O213.

N43 [—] A poem in honour of the birth-day of his most sacred majesty King George... Humbly presented to Sir Hans Sloane, baronet. *London, printed for the author*, 1720. 2°: *A*¹ B–C²; *1–2* 3–10.
> Probably issued with alternative titles for various dedicatees.

'Again the circling year its course has run'
> The L copy is bound with other birthday poems by Nevil.

L(643.1.24/41*).

N44 [—] A poem, occasion'd by the birth-day of his most sacred majesty King George. Most humbly inscrib'd to... *London, printed by H. Meere, for the author*, 1716. 2°: *A*² B–C²; *i–iv*, 1–8. A1 blk.
> Issued with alternative titles for various dedicatees: 'Sir Hans Sloane' (L); 'his grace Henry duke of Kent, &c.' (O); Christopher Montague, esq; (O); 'presented to Dr. Smart, physician to the royal hospital of Chelsea' (O); 'the right honourable Hugh earl of Loudoun' (ICU); 'Sir Richard Houblon' (IU). Some copies have A1 blank before title. The L copy has C1 unsigned.

''Twas at the joyful season of the year'
> Copies at L,O have a ms. letter from Nevil accompanying them.

L(643.1.24/33,–A1),O(3, 2–A1); ICU,InU (–A1).

Nevil, H.

N45 [—] A poem on the anniversary of his majesty's birthday. Humbly presented to... *London, printed for the author in the year* 1718. 2°: π¹ A–B²; *1–3* 4–10.
> Issued with alternative titles for various dedicatees: 'the honourable Sir Hans Sloan' (L); 'Gen. George Wade' (O).

'Attend, ye guardian angels of the state'
> The L copy is bound with other birthday poems by Nevil.

L(643.1.24/39*),O.

N46 [—] A poem on the anniversary of the birth-day of his majesty King George... Most humbly presented to... *London, printed for the author*, 1719. 2°: *A*¹ B–C²; *1–2* 3–10.
> Issued with alternative titles for various dedicatees: 'Sir Hans Sloane' (L); 'the most reverend father in god, William lord archbishop of Canterbury' (OC).

'When princes, fam'd for birth and merit, climb'
> The L copy is bound with other birthday poems by Nevil.

L(643.1.24/40*),OC(lacks C2).

N47 [—] [reissue] Humbly presented to John Duncomb esq; *London, printed for the author*, 1724. 2°: *A*¹(±) B–C²; *1–2* 3–10.

OCU.

N48 [—] A poem on the birth-day of her royal highness the Princess of Wales. Most humbly presented to the Lady Cottrel. *London, printed for the author*, 1717. 2°: *A*⁴ (A2 as 'A'); *1–3* 4–8.
> Probably issued with alternative titles for various dedicatees.

'Hail March! who, on thy downy wings, dost bring'
> For Nevil's authorship, compare the following poem addressed to Sir Clement Cottrell.

TxU.

N49 [—] A poem on the birth-day of his most sacred majesty King George. Humbly presented to... *London, printed by S. Palmer, for the author*, 1717. 2°: *A*⁴; *1–3* 4–8.
> Issued with alternative titles for various dedicatees (that at O is a cancel): 'Sir Hans Sloane' (L); 'Sir John Hartup' (O); 'the Reverend White Kennet' (CLU-C); 'Sir Clement Cottrell' (TxU).

'Britannia! highly favour'd from above'
> The L copy is bound with other birth-day poems by Nevil.

L(643.1.24/35),O; CLU-C,TxU.

N50 **New.** The new amour: or Volminia's complaint to her lord, occasion'd by his behaviour at a late interview with a certain lady... *London, printed for T. Robins; sold at the Royal Exchange, St. James's, Bond-street, and Charing-Cross*, 1740. (*LM* Oct) 8°: *A*² B–C⁴ D²; *1–4* 5–24. A1 hft.

The **new** amour

'She comes! the fair deluder charms our eyes'
Volminia, a politician's mistress, finds herself
displaced by the young Maria.
L(1486.s.20),O; CSmH,ICN.

N51 — A new and ingenious fortune book, for batchelors, maids, wives and widows: shewing, by
drawing cuts at cards, whether life long, or short...
London, printed by Edward Midwinter, 1710. (*SR*
19 Sept)
8°: *A*⁴; *1* 2–8.
   A verse chap-book. Deposit copy at E.
'Whatever person draws an ace'
E.

N52 — A new and mournful elegy, on the lamentable
death of the famous usurer, J—— S——wll, who
died raving mad on Sunday January the 19th
1728–9. *Dublin, printed by John Durneen, next door
to the Waly's head, in Patrick's-steet*[!], [1729.]
½°: 1 side, 1 column.
   'This indenture' in first line is printed by a
large ornamental woodcut presumably normally used for law stationery.
'Know all men by these presents, that this indhen-
ture'
DT.

N53 — A new ballad. [At James's...] [*London?* 1717/
18.]
slip: 1 side, 1 column.
   Printed with *An excellent new ballad on the
fall of guinea's,* [1717/18]; the O copy is not
divided.
'At James's house, is a damnable rout'
   A satire on the quarrel between King George
and the Prince of Wales at the christening of
his son George William.
O; CSmH.

— A new ballad. [Come listen...] *See* Wesley,
Samuel, *the younger.*

N54 — A new ballad. [I am a...] [*Dublin?* 1731?]
½°: 1 side, 2 columns.
   The band of type flowers at the head is
found in a number of Dublin broadsides.
'I am a famous scribbler'
   A satire on court and politics. A different and
shorter text is printed as *Percival XXXII.*
TxU.

N55 — A new ballad. [Oh! where art thou...] [*London?* 1715/–.]
slip: 1 side, 1 column.
   Printed with *The plagues of Nod,* [1715/–];
the MH copy is not divided.
'Oh! where art thou, St. Taffy?'
   Crum O955: 'A ballad to the tune of noble
race was Jenkin'. A Jacobite ballad addressed
to the Welsh.
CSmH,MH.

N56 — A new ballad. [motto: Sine me liber ibis in
urbem.] [*Dublin,* 1748/49.]
½°: *1*–2, 1 column.

A **new** ballad

'I sing of a hero, whose fame and repute'
   A satire on Charles Lucas.
C.

N57 — A new ballad, alluding to two modern vile
histories, the one of the staff, the other of the mitre
and purse. To the tune of Wou'd you have a
young virgin of fifteen year, &c. Humbly offer'd
to the consideration of... [*London,* 1714/15.]
slip: 1 side, 1 column.
'Staff, mitre, and purse, made a damnable rout'
   The secret history of the white-staff, 1714, is by
Defoe.
Harding.

N58 — An [!] new ballad by way of dialogue between a
kite, and a crow, on the quadrille. (Tune, A cobler
there, &c.) [*Dublin,* 1736.]
½°: 1 side, 1 column.
   Williams 823.
'How now Mr. Kite it is very well seen'
   Ascribed to Swift by *Ball* 291–2, but rejected
by Williams. Richard Bettesworth, who
quarrelled bitterly with Swift at the beginning
of 1734, was satirized by him as Sergeant
Kite (*Williams* 817). There was a new dispute
in 1736 over Josiah Hart's *New proposal for
the better regulation and improvement of
quadrille.*
C.

N59 — A new ballad, call'd the Greenwich hunting-
match. To the tune of Chevy-chace. [*London?*
1714.]
slip: 1 side, 1 column.
   Line 10 reads 'In *Drury Hundreds* bred'; line
25 misprints '*Wreenwich*'.
'God prosper long our noble king'
   A satire on Bolingbroke and the failure of his
Jacobite plans, here attributed to his wenching.
DA,Crawford.

N60 — [another edition]
   Line 10 reads 'In *Drury-Hundreds* bred';
line 25 misprints '*Wreenwich*'.
O.

N61 — [another edition]
   Line 10 reads 'In *Drury Hundreds* bred';
line 25 reads '*Greenwich*'.
C.

N62 — ⟨A⟩ new ballad, humbly inscrib'd to John
Higden of Hamstead, esq; Tune of, Ye commons
and peers. [*London,* 1722?]
¼°: 1 side, 2 columns.
'Come on, my brave boys'
   Possibly on the city of London election of
1722.
O.

N63 — A new ballad in praise of the ancient and loyal
city of Londonderry. *Dublin, printed by George
Faulkner,* 1726.
½°: 1 side, 1 column.

A **new** ballad in praise

On the other side, *A letter to the bishop of M.,* [1726.]

'Attend my good friends, and I'll give you a song'
PU.

N64 — A new ballad, inscrib'd to Polly Peachum. To the tune of Pretty parrot say. By the author of Leheup's ballad. *London, printed for A. Moore; sold at the pamphlet shops in London & Westminster,* [1728.] (*MChr* 22 March)
2°: A–B² C¹; *1–2* 3–10.
Pp. 9–10 contain Polly's answer (A242).
'Pretty Polly say,/When did Jo--y G--'
Answer: 'Pray sir who are you'
Sometimes attributed to Nicholas Amhurst, presumably because it appears in *The Twickenham hotch-potch,* 1728, by 'Caleb d'Anvers', a pseudonym in which Amhurst only had a share. A satire on Lavinia Fenton (who played Polly in the *Beggar's Opera*), her lovers, and Gay.
MH,TxU.

N65 —— The second edition. *London, printed for A. Moore; sold at the pamphlet-shops in London & Westminster,* [1728.]
2°: A–B²; *1–2* 3–8.
CtY(uncut).

N66 —— *London, printed for A. Moore,* [1728.]
½°: *1–2,* 2 columns.
A piracy.
O.

N67 — A new ballad inscripe'd [!] to Polly Peachum ... *London, printed in the year* 1728.
½°: *1–2,* 2 columns.
Possibly a Dublin reprint.
L(C.116.i.4/38),O; MH.

N68 — A new ballad inscrib'd to Polly Peachum... *Dublin, printed for Richard Norris,* 1728.
8°: *A⁴; 1–2* 3–8.
DA; MH.

N69 — A new ballad intituled the Freeman's advice to his fellow citizens: or, no butter box for me. (Tune of the Black joak) In the behalf of Alderman James Somervell. [*Dublin,* 1725/30.]
½°: 1 side, 2 columns.
The copy at L forms part of a collection of Dublin half-sheets of 1725/30.
'Come citizens all (that your country love)'
An Irish election ballad.
L(C.121.g.8/81).

N70 — 'A new ballad, most humbly inscrib'd to a most hon. m——te, who has lately shewn his fidelity in a true r—t—n of a m——r, for W——r. [*London*] "*Telltruth*". Price 6d.' (*BM* July 1750)
On the return of a member for Westminster.

N71 — A new ballad, occasion'd by the Pretenders declaration. To the tune of, Ye commons and peers, &c. *Dublin, printed by James Carson,* 1722.
½°: 1 side, 2 columns.

A **new** ballad, occasion'd

On the other side, *A poem occasioned by the funeral,* 1722.
'Ye commons and peers,/Ye've heard with your ears'
MH.

N72 — A new ballad, on a late drubbing. Tune, Ye gallants, come, &c. [*Dublin,* 1749?]
½°: 1 side, 2 columns.
'Ye gallants, come listen a while'
The victim of the drubbing was Charles Lucas.
C.

N73 — A new ballad on a late strolling doctor. To the old tune of, Hey boys! Up go we; or what other you please. [*London,* 1710.]
½°: 1 side, 2 columns.
'Good folks, I pray, have not you heard'
Against Sacheverell.
Rothschild.

N74 — A new ballad, on a mock duel between a lawyer and a certain physitian in this city. [*Dublin,* 1725/30.]
½°: 1 side, 2 columns.
Williams 1148. The copy at L forms part of a collection of Dublin half-sheets of 1725/30.
'All ye that good toping prefer to your rest'
Williams rejects the attribution to Swift in *Ball* 390.
L(C.121.g.8/82).

—— A new ballad on Lord D--n---l's altering his chapel, 1746. *See* Whitehead, Paul.

N75 — A new ballad on subsidy treaties. To the tune of Packington's pound. *London, printed for W. Webb,* [1750.]
2°: A⁴; *1–2* 3–7 *8 blk.*
'Hence courtiers and slaves, who no doubt are content'
Against the attempts of George II and Newcastle to influence the electors of the Holy Roman Empire to elect the Archduke Joseph.
L(11660.g.2); MH.

N76 — A new ballad on the battle of Drummossie-muir, near Inverness. To the tune of, The battle of Preston. [*Edinburgh,* 1746.]
½°: 1 side, 1 column.
'Duke William came, and, in a bang'
In praise of William duke of Cumberland's victory.
L(806.k.16/31; C.115.i.3/88),E.

N77 — A new ballad on the departure of Miss B——ll G——mb——ll. [*Dublin,* 1726?]
slip: 1 side, 1 column.
The date is suggested by the original ms. numeration of the copy seen.
'So the long absent winter-sun'
A ms. note in the L copy suggests the lady's name was Gamball.
L(1890.e.5/34).

A **new** ballad on the dispute

A **new** ballad, to an excellent old tune

N78 — A new ballad on the dispute between the quakers and anabaptists. [*Dublin*] *Printed for the benefit of the flying-stationers*, [1722.]
½°: 1 side, 1 column.
> On the other side, *A grand dispute between the anabaptists and quakers*, in prose.
'Ye dippers and quakers'
> A dispute between Oswald Edwards the anabaptist and John Dover the quaker. The prose account dates the dispute as Sunday 26 August, and *Smith, Anti-quakeriana* 36 dates as 1722.
L(1890.e.5/15).

N79 — A new ballad on the dissolution of the poorhouse, or, a hue and cry, after the same. Tune of, Commons and peers. *Dublin, printed in the year* 1725–6.
½°: 1 side, 2 columns.
'To the kingdom's content'
CtY.

N80 — A new ballad on the game of bragg, as it is now sung by Mr. Sullivan, at the New-gardens. [*Dublin?* 173–?]
½°: 1 side, 2 columns.
'Ye belles and ye beaus for a moment attend'
> The earliest occurrence of bragg mentioned in *OED* is 1734.
L(1890.e.5/35).

N81 — A new ballad on the taking of Porto-Bello, by Admiral Vernon. *London, printed for R. Dodsley; sold by the booksellers of London & Westminster,* 1740. (*LDP* 15 April)
2°: *A²* B²; *1–2* 3–7 *8 blk.*
> *Percival* LIV.
'Come attend British boys, / I'll make you rejoice'
> *Crum* C399: 'On Porto Bello, and the Convention'.
L(11633.i.8),O; CtY,ICN,MH,TxU.

N82 — A new ballad, or, the lamentation for Miss P——p, that run away with an Irish p——r. *Dublin printed* 1725.
½°: 1 side, 1 column.
'Good people draw near and lend me your ear'
L(C.121.g.8/56),Rothschild; MH.

N83 — A new ballad, shewing all shall be well one hundred years hence. To the tune of, The king shall enjoy his own again. [*London*] *Printed in the year* 1711.
½°: 1 side, 2 columns.
'Sad times! sad times! are coming on'
> A satire on politicians.
MH.

N83·5 — A new ballad. To an excellent French tune. [*London*, 1714.]
½°: 1 side, 1 column.
'When two forlorn st----tmen, by accident met'
> A satire on Harley and Bolingbroke.
TxU.

N84 — A new ballad, to an excellent old tune (Chevy Chace;) being a warning-piece to Englishmen in general, and to the land and sea-officers in particular. *London, 'printed for Thomas Standfast, at the Guardian Angel, near Westminster-Hall', and sold at the pamphlet shops,* 1749. (*GM* March)
4°: *A²* < B²; *1–3* 4–8.
'Britannia's guardian, liberty'
> Against the bills for martial law.
O.

N85 — A new ballad. To the old tune of Chevy-chase. *London, printed in the year* 1711.
½°: 1 side, 2 columns.
> Stanza 13 line 4 reads 'At-once...' The rule above the imprint is in one piece.
'God prosper long this free-born isle'
> Against a hasty peace.
L(82.l.8/64; 112.f.44/27); MH,NNP.

N86 — [another edition]
> Stanza 13 line 4 reads 'At once...' The rule above the imprint is in one piece.
Rothschild.

N87 — [another edition, title reads:]...Chevy-chace.
> Stanza 13 line 4 reads 'At-once...' The rule above the imprint is composed of 21 short rules.
Rothschild.

N88 — A new ballad. To the tune of, Chivy Chace. [*London*, 1708.]
½°: 1 side, 1 column.
'When good Queen Bess did rule this land'
> *Crum* W1113; quoted by Hearne 13 March 1708. On the relationship of Queen Elizabeth and Essex, implying that Queen Anne should dismiss Marlborough.
CSmH,MH,OCU.

N89 — A new ballad. To the tune of Dear catholick brother. [*London?* 1714/15?]
slip: 1 side, 1 column.
'Pray gentlemans come now and zee my vine zhow'
> *Crum* P335. A Jacobite satire against George I.
O(cut and mounted); *Harding.*

N90 — A new ballad. To the tune of Fair Rosamond. [*London*, 1710?]
½°: 2 sides, 2 columns.
> 16 stanzas on side 1.
'When as Qu---- A---- of great renown'
> On Abigail Masham's intrigues with Harley, attacking the latter.
L(162.m.70/11, mutilated),O; CSmH,InU,MH.

N91 — [another edition]
> 24 stanzas on side 1.
L(1850.c.10/12), Herts CRO (Panshanger box 46, 2 copies).

N92 — — [*London?* 1710?]
½°: 1 side, 2 columns.
> All 35 stanzas on one side.
L(Cup.645.e.1/26); NjP.

A **new** ballad. To the tune of Hey boys

N93 — A new ballad. To the tune of Hey boys up go
we. [*London?* 172–.]
½º: 1 side, 2 columns.
'Full thirty years and more we've seen'
A Jacobite ballad.
MH.

N94 — A new ballad, (To the tune of, Highland ladie,
bonnie ladie, &c.) [*Edinburgh,* 1745/46.]
½º: 1 side, 1 column.
'Of all that fought about the fire'
A satire on a Jacobite, 'Wadie'.
O,E.

N95 — A new ballad, to the tune of King John, and the
abbot of Canterbury. [*London,* 1719.]
½º: 1 side, 2 columns.
'As soon as the wind it came kindly about'
Crum A1670: 'A ballad. May 1719'. A
satirical dialogue between George I and the
Duchess of Kendal about the composition of
the council of regency.
Crawford; CSmH.

N96 — A new ballad. To the tune of, London is a
fine town, &c. *London, printed for J. Smith,* 1726
[1727?].
2º: A⁴; *1–2* 3–7 *8 blk.*
No price on title; no watermark. *Percival* IV.
'My lord m——r and his a--n and c--n c--l too'
Percival, quoting the poem from *The British
journal* 18 March 1727, relates it to the
banquet at court given to the lord mayor,
aldermen and common council of London on
their presenting an address to the king, 31 Jan
1727. The date in the imprint presumably
follows the legal year.
OW; CSmH(2, 1 uncut),CtY,MH,OCU,TxU.

N97 — [another impression]
'(Price Six Pence.)' on title; watermark:
Dutch lion.
DFo(uncut).

N98 — A new ballad, to the tune of Packington's
pound. [*London,* 1710.]
½º: 2 sides, 1 column.
'Packington's Pound' in title printed in
roman type.
'When the twenty brave pleaders, cull'd out of the
throng'
Against the bishops who voted against
Sacheverell.
O; OCU.

N99 — [another edition]
'Packington's Pound' printed in black letter.
O.

N100 — A new ballad. To the tune of, Packington's
pound. [*London,* 1710.]
½º: 1 side, 2 columns.
Line 5 misprints 'A Prelate *adorit*'.
L(Lutt.II.14); MH.

A **new** ballad, to the tune of Packington

N101 — — [*London,* 1710.]
1º: 1 side, 2 columns.
Line 5 reads correctly 'A Prelate *adroit*'.
The CtY copy is printed on the verso of a
legal form.
C,Chatsworth; CtY,MH.

N102 — A new ballad, to the tune of the Abbot of
Canterbury. [*Edinburgh?* 1735.] (Feb?)
½º: 1 side, 1 column.
Percival XXXVII.
'I'll tell you a story that happen'd of late'
On the petition presented to the house of
lords 13 Feb 1735 about the election of
Scottish peers.
L(11602.i.6/11, ms. date Feb 1735),O,E.

N103 — A new ballad, to the tune of the Black-smith.
[*London,* 1710.]
½º: 2 sides, 1 column.
Title reads '...TUNE of the|
BLACK-SMITH'.
'Since monarchs were monarchs, it never was
known'
Crum S570: 'On Dr. Sacheverell's tryal'. A
satire on the proceedings against Sacheverell.
L(Lutt.II.12),O.

N104 — [another edition]
Title reads '...TUNE of the|
BLACKSMITH'.
L(1850.c.10/17).

N105 — [another edition]
Title reads '...Tune of the|
BLACKSMITH'.
L(Add.MS 27408, fol. 101),Chatsworth.

N106 — A new ballad. To the tune of, To you fair
ladies now at land. [*London?* 17--.]
slip: 1 side, 1 column.
'Ye cucolds all of fam'd Cheapside'
Harding.

N107 — A new ballad. Tune of, To you fair ladies now
at land. [*London,* 1727/28.]
½º: 1 side, 2 columns.
'Let P——y speak, or Caleb write'
A satire on Horatio Walpole and Isaac Le
Heup.
L(C.20.f.2/316); CSmH.

N108 — [*idem*] The ladies skreen, a new ballad, tune of
To you fair ladies now at land. *London, printed for
A. More, near St. Paul's,* [1727/28.]
½º: 1 side, 2 columns.
Percival appendix 9. On the other side of one
L copy, *Account of a...duel,* in prose.
L(1872.a.1/160; C.116.i.4/42); MH(cropt).

N109 — — [*London?* 1727/28.]
½º: 1 side, 2 columns.
O.

N110 — A new bloody ballad on the bloody battle at
Dettingen: printed in bloody characters. To the

tune of Old Sir Simon the king. [*London*] *Printed for W. Webb*, 1743. (*LDP* 9 July)
2°: *A*⁴; *1–2* 3–8.
Printed in red.
'Of old Augustus the king'
Crum O139.
O,LdU-B; CSmH(uncut),IU,MH.

N111 —— [at foot:] Tune of, Old Sir Simon the king. [1743.]
½°: 1 side, 2 columns.
Printed in red.
O.

N112 — A new bloody ballad, on the late bloody battle at Dettingen... *London: printed. And Dublin, re-printed by C. Dickson*, 1743.
8°: *A*⁴; *1–2* 3–8.
Printed in red.
L(11633.bbb.58).

— A new book of the Dunciad, 1750. *See* Dodd, William.

N113 — The new b——p's complaint to his excellence, the L——L——t. A song. [*Dublin*, 1725?]
½°: 1 side, 1 column.
'When B—— perceiv'd the beautiful dames'
A reprint with slight modifications of 'The brawny bishop's complaint' of 1699, apparently applied to Hugh Boulter, archbishop of Armagh, addressing John Carteret on the distractions of women in church. See F. H. Ellis in *POAS* VI. 37–42.
L(C.121.g.8/132).

N114 — ⟨A⟩ new British prophecy, foretelling when the whole world will be in peace. [*Dublin*, 1727?]
½°: 1 side, 1 column.
The DT copy is bound with half-sheets of 1727.
'When Britains bulwarks humbles Britain's foes'
DT.

N115 — A new camp song. Tune of the King and the miller. [*London?* 1740.]
slip: 1 side, 1 column.
Rough cut of ship at head. *Percival* LVIII.
'All hail to old England so wise and so great'
A satire on the troops encamped in Hyde Park and on Hounslow Heath, and their inactivity against Spain.
C.

N116 — [variant]
Rough cut of fortified town at head.
C.

N117 — A new canto of Spencer's Fairy queen. Now first published. *London, printed for G. Hawkins*, 1747 [1746]. (*SR* 4 Dec)
4°: *A*² B–D⁴ E²; *i–iv, 1* 2–28. A1 hft.
Listed in *GM, LM* Dec 1746. Deposit copies at L,O,E,EU,GU.
'Unhappy man! whose ever changing mind'

Sometimes attributed to John Upton, apparently on the authority of a note in the O catalogue, 'This pretended new canto is attributed, with some degree of probability, to Mr. Upton'.
L(644.k.16/6),O(2),CT,E,LdU-B+; CtY(–A1), DFo,ICN,IU,MH(–A1).

— A new collection of miscellany poems, for the year, 1718. *See* Davis, George.

N118 — A new copy of verses compos'd on a certain young lady living near St. James's. The words by *⁎‡⁎* a foreign prince who is deeply smitten with her exquisite charms, and were lately enclosed in a letter to her. [*London*, 173–?]
slip: 1 side, 1 column.
Two woodcuts at head, one at foot; but apparently a sophisticated imitation of a popular ballad.
'Bright N---y the lovely, the charming, the fair'
Harding.

N119 — A new copy of verses concerning the late engagement, between Admiral Townsend, esq; and forty sail of Martenico ships out of which number he took, sunk and burnt upwards of thirty. *London, printed for J. Moore, near St Pauls*, [1745/46.]
½°: 1 side, 2 columns.
Rough woodcuts of ships at head. On the other side of the L copy, a proof sheet of a verse chap-book.
'Brave Admiral Townsend is now on the main'
In praise of Isaac Townsend's victory, 31 Oct 1745.
L(1876.f.1/132).

N120 — A new copy of verses, on the nativity, life and death of our blessed saviour. By S.C. *London, printed in the year* 1715. (26 Dec, Luttrell)
½°: 1 side, 2 columns.
'Let Christians all with one accord rejoice'
MH(Luttrell).

N121 — A new coppy of verses, on the present times. Tune. Come and listen to my ditty. [*London?* 1743/45.]
slip: 1 side, 1 column.
Rough woodcut of naval figure at head.
'God with us a glorious motto'
A militant song.
C.

N122 — A new copy of verses, or a true touch of the times. [*London?* 1739.]
slip: 1 side, 1 column.
Percival appendix 67. Rough woodcut of ship at head, of trophy at foot.
'The farmers of England say'
In favour of war with Spain.
C.

N123 — A new copy of verses, sung in triumph, for the joyful reception of the new dean and cannon, who

A **new** copy of verses

was install'd September 21, 1711. at Christ-Church College in Oxford. *London, printed by T. Gent, in Pye-Corner,* [1711.] (12 Nov?)
½°: 1 side, 1 column.
> Gent was employed by Edward Midwinter at Pye Corner from August 1710. On the other side, T. D'Urfey, *The authentick letter of Marshal de Boufflers,* [1709/10?].

'Oh! brave brother John, now it's plain'
> Francis Atterbury was the new dean of Christ Church and George Smalridge the new canon.

Chatsworth(ms. date 12 Nov 1711).

N124 — ⟨A new⟩ court ballad. [*London?* 1715.]
> The copy seen has been cut up and mounted, but was possibly a quarter-sheet, printed on one side, two columns.

'My country dear I have forsook,'
> *Crum* M610: 'A new court ballad upon the word grudge, and the last part of his maties. first speech to his parliamt. 20 March 1714/15'. Quoted by Hearne under 21 April 1715, and there attributed to 'Mr. Weever'. A Jacobite satire.

O(cropt).

N125 — The new court. To the tune of To you fair ladies now at land. [*London?* 1714/15.]
¼°: 1 side, 2 columns.
'To all you tories far from court'
> *Crum* T2894, 2897: 'A new court ballad for the year 1714...in imitation of...Lord Dorset's...' A Jacobite parody of Charles Sackville, earl of Dorset's song. The reference to Dorset in the following edition is ambiguous; there may be an allusion to Lionel, the seventh earl and subsequently duke of Dorset, who was a whig courtier.

MH.

N126 — [*idem*] The new court: being an excellent new song to an old tune, of To all you ladies now at land, &c. By the Earl of Dorset. [*London,* 1714/15.]
½°: 1 side, 2 columns.
> This edition leaves blanks for many of the names; the previous edition was clearly clandestine, this may be a later and more open publication.

L(C.121.g.9/169).

N127 — A new crop of blockheads: or, the poetical harvest-home. A court ballad. *London printed, and sold by J. Dormer,* 1733. (*GM* Sept)
2°: *A*² B²; *1-2* 3-8.
'I am a poet by my trade'
L(11657.m.34),O,LdU-B; MH,NNP.

— A new c-----t ballad, 1742. *See* Hervey, John, *baron Hervey* (H159).

N128 — A new dialogue, between a wolf, and shepherd's dog. [*Dublin,* 1727?]
½°: 1 side, 2 columns.
> *Morgan* M467, in error. The DT copy is

A **new** dialogue

bound with half-sheets of 1727; the NN copy has a Dublin collector's initial 'F'.
'As many persons now can tell'
DT; NN.

N129 — [dh] A new dialogue between the horse at Charing-Cross, and the horse at Stocks-market. [col] [*London*] *Printed in the year* 1703.
4°: A²; *1-4.*
'How many winters have I watch'd in vain?'
> On politics and religion.

L(C.121.g.9/138).

N130 — The new dozen at Westminster; or, Caleb's good men, and true. To the tune of, Which nobody can deny. *London, printed for A. Moore; sold by the booksellers of London & Westminster,* [1729.] (*MChr* 24 Dec)
2°: (3 ll); *1-2* 3-6.
> *Percival* appendix 22.

'A trial was lately in Westminster-hall'
> On the packed jury that acquitted Richard Francklin at the *Craftsman* trial.

L(11657.m.30),OW; MH,*OCl.*

N131 — A new elegy occasionly writ on the death of Dr. Traver's, who departed from this transitory world on Sunday the 17th of this instant September, 1727. [*Dublin,* 1727.]
½°: 1 side, 1 column.
> Printed within an ornamental arch.

'When heaven afflicts man must complain'
DT.

— A new elegy on John Tissey, [172–.] *See* A new L.E.G..., [172–.]

N132 — [dh] A new elegy on the death of trade. By the author of the True-born English-man. [col] *London, printed in the year* 1706.
4°: A²; *1* 2-4, 2 columns.
'A worthy old dame,/Mother Trade was her name'
> Not accepted by any Defoe bibliographer.

Rosenbach.

N133 — [*idem*] London in mourning: or, a new elegy upon the much lamented death of trade...Written by a relation of the deceas'd. [*London*] *Printed in the year* 1710.
8°: *A*⁴; *1* 2-8.
> Printed in chap-book style, with mourning borders on title.

Longleat.

N134 — A new elegy on the lamented death of Sir Cloudesly Shovel...who was cast away on the rocks of Scilly, on Wednesday the 22d of October, 1707. at 8 at night, as he was returning home from the Streights, in her majesty's ship the Association. *London, printed by J. Bradford,* 1707.
1°: 1 side, 2 columns.
> Mourning headpiece and woodcut borders.

'In sable weeds let widdow'd Albion mourn'
L(C.20.f.2/228),O.

A **new** elegy upon the death

N135 — A new elegy upon the death of Edward lord Griffin, who departed this life, a prisoner in the Tower of Londou[!], on Fryday the 10th of November, 1710. in the 76th year of his age. *London, printed by J. Dutton, near Fleet-street*, [1710.]
½°: 1 side, 2 columns.
    Mourning headpiece and borders.
'At length then death has set thee free from care'
L(Cup.645.e.1/29); CSmH.

N136 — A new elegy upon the death of Mr. Daniel Burgess, the famous dissenting teacher, who died at his house in Boswel-conrt,[!] on Monday the 26th of January, 1713, in the 65th year of his age. *London, printed by J. Read*, [1713.]
1°: 1 side, 2 columns.
    Mourning headpiece and woodcut borders.
'Why in complaints shou'd mortals wast their breath'
L(KTC.126.c.1/4); CSmH.

N137 — A new elegy upon the death of Sir Charles Duncomb, kt. formerly lord mayor of London; who departed this life, on Monday the 9th of April, 1711, at his house at Teddington, near Brentford in Middelsex, about the 60th year of his age. *London, printed by J. Read*, [1711.]
½°: 1 side, 2 columns.
    Mourning borders.
''Tis plain the great or rich no power have'
CSmH.

N138 — A new elegy upon the lamented death of that valiant and victorious general and soldier, the Lord Cuts, who departed this life at Dublin in Ireland, on the 29th of January last, 170⁶₇ ... *London, printed by J. Bradford*, 1707.
½°: 1 side, 2 columns.
    Mourning headpiece and borders.
'Something so mournful is in what I'd write'
MH.

N139 — The new epilogue spoke and sung by Polley Peachum at her benefit play: The way of the world. [*Dublin*] *Printed for J. Carr, in Silver Court in Castle-street, and sold by the stationers*, [1728/29.]
slip: 1 side, 1 column.
    The DT copy is bound with half-sheets of 1729. Three songs with a linking epilogue.
'A play, with scarce a song—— 'tis gross offence'
    Presumably a benefit for Mrs. Sterling, who originally played Polly in Dublin (*N&Q* 13 May 1905, p. 364); see N163–4 for 'opera-epilogues' by her.
DT.

N140 — A new epilogue to the Conscious lovers: spoken by Mrs. Knap. May the 13th. 1724. *Dublin, printed by J. Carson*, 1724.
½°: 1 side, 1 column.
    Reprinted with *A new prologue to the Conscious lovers*, 1724.

'I'm thinking, now the ceremony's over'
    L(C.121.g.8/30),Rothschild.

N141 — A new express from the dead, or the late D. W-h-t's hymn to the peace. *London, 'printed by A. Church in the Strand'*, [1731.]
½°: 1 side, 2 columns.
    On the other side of the O copy, The st-s-m-'s vision of h-ll, in prose.
'Hail! sacred peace, thrice happy are those climes'
    A satire on the treaties of Seville and Vienna.
L(1871.e.1/196),O.

N142 — A new extempore-prayer, fitted for the use of all conventicles; where rebellion has its rise, and loyalty its downfall. *London printed, and sold by J. Baker*, 1710. (*PB* 29 July)
8°: *A⁴ B–C⁴; 1–4 5–21 22–24 blk.* A1 frt.
    Entered in *SR* 29 July; deposit copies at C,AdU, probably O,E. The Luttrell copy, dated 29 July, is recorded in Dobell cat. 46/660.
'God grant us grace and courage to defend'
    A tory prayer for the state against the pope and the dissenters.
L(1078.1.16; 1078.m.6/5; 164.m.52,–C4), O(3,1–C4),C,E,AdU + ; CLU-C(–C4),CtY, ICN,IU(–C4),InU.

— New fables invented for the amusement of young ladies, 1749. *See* Moore, Edward [Fables for the female sex].

N143 — A new gingle | On Tom Dingle. [*Dublin*, 1726?]
slip: 1 side, 1 column.
    The DT copy is bound with half-sheets of 1726.
'Though Sh---d---n will / Be Sh---d--n still'
    A satire on Thomas Sheridan.
DT; CtY.

— 'A new hymn to the queen and parliament, for the use of the several prisons in England. (Verse.) 1712.'
    Morgan O493; not traced, possibly in ms.

N144 — The new idol, a poem. Dedicated to all true subjects . . . and inscrib'd to the unchristian author of the satyr, call'd, the Tripe club. [*Dublin?*] *Printed in the year* 1706. *And are to be sold by the booksellers.*
4°: A⁴ B²; 1–3 4–12.
    No Dublin edition of *The tripe club*, 1706, is certainly known, but the poem is of Dublin origin, and so is this reply.
'Long did Hibernia's isle in vain deplore'
LG,DA,DG(uncut); ICN.

N145 — The new Kilmainham ballad. To the tune of, Ye commons and peers. [*Dublin?* 1711/12.]
½°: 1 side, 2 columns.
    Teerink 854; Williams 1090. 16 unnumbered stanzas. Williams prints a manuscript text entitled 'The Whiggs lamentation' with 24 stanzas. The order of editions is obscure.
'At a sessions of late'

The **new** Kilmainham ballad

> *Ball* 115–16 suggested Swift's authorship, and Williams concedes that Swift 'may have had something to do with' it. On Francis Higgins who was presented as 'a common disturber of her majesty's peace' by the grand jury at Kilmainham, 5 Oct 1711.
>
> C; CtY,MH.

N146 — [*idem*] An excellent new ballad, or, The whigs lamentation; occasion'd by a sore of their own scratching. Tune of, Ye commons, &c. *Dublin, re-printed* 1711.
½⁰: 1 side, 2 columns.
> 24 numbered stanzas.
C; CSmH(cropt).

N147 — [*idem*] [dh] An Irish ballad, upon the revd Mr. Francis Higgins his tryal; before the lord lieutenant and council, in Dublin. To the tune of Ye commons and peers. [*London*, 1712.] (*PB* 19 July)
2⁰: A²; 1–4.
L(1850.c.10/18; 1876.f.1/56); CSmH,MH.

N148 — A new L.E.G on John Tissey, a late not able pun broker. [*Dublin*, 172–.]
½⁰: 1 side, 1 column.
'Merry was he, for whom we now are sad'
L(C.121.g.8/122).

— New light, [1728?] *See* A crutch for a lame conscience, [1728?]

N149 — 'A new Lilliputian ballad on the appearance of their majesties, and the court, upon the river Thames, July 15, 1727. [*London*] *Sold at the pamphlet shops.* Price 2d.' (*MC* July 1727)
> Possibly a half-sheet from the price. The title may be generalized. Cf. [Henry Carey] *A Lilliputian ode on King George the IId's and Queen Caroline's happy accession,* 1727.

N150 — A new litany. '*Cambridge*', *printed in the year* 1712.
½⁰: 1 side, 1 column.
> Probably printed at London.
'From a dozen of p— —s made all at a start'
Crum F639, as Dec 1711. A whig attack on the ministry.
L(1876.f.1/64),O,C,E; MH.

N151 — A new litany. To the tune of, An old courtier of the queen, &c. [*London*] *Printed in the year* 1710.
½⁰: 1 side, 1 column.
'From the fine Roman whore, or the Geneva slut'
> Against papists and presbyterians.
InU.

N152 — [*idem*] Samson's foxes, a new litany, to the tune of, An old courtier of the queen. *Edinburgh, printed by James Watson,* 1713.
½⁰: 1 side, 1 column.
E.

A **new** litany

N153 — A new litany very proper to be read by a merry society over a glass of good liquor. *Dubiln* [!], *printed by W.H.,* 1722.
½⁰: 1 side, 2 columns.
'From a poet that's proud of his wit and his parts'
Rothschild; MH.

N154 — A new London poem on the procession of the journey-men taylors of the city of Dublin, on St. James's day, and their behaviour at dinner. Or an answer to a poem publish'd by their authority. Written by a British author. *London printed, and re-printed in Dublin,* 1725.
½⁰: 1 side, 2 columns.
> Almost certainly there was no London edition.
'If I crave the assistance, of any one muse'
> A satire on the tailors, in answer to [Henry Nelson] *A new poem,* 1725 (N26).
L(C.121.g.8/39).

N154·5 — A new lord to the old lordship, or the D. of M----- turn'd out. To the tune of Forty one. *London, printed by W. Wilkins,* 1714.
½⁰: 1 side, 1 column.
> Printed on the reverse of the copy seen is a prose work, *Joy and sorrow intermixt* (printed for D. Brown, 1714), dealing with an accident at the coronation of George I.
'There was a great lord, came from a strange land'
TxU.

N155 — The new loyal health. To the tune of the Tackers. [*London*] *Printed for John Baker,* 1711 [1710]. (28 Nov, Luttrell)
½⁰: 1 side, 1 column.
'You brave loyal hearts ev'ry where'
> In praise of the tory victory in the elections.
L(C.121.g.9/162, Luttrell); MH.

N156 — The new loyal members of parliament's delight, or, the whigs mortification: it being in praise of the queen and church. To the tune of, Ye bold presbyterians, &c. *London, printed in the year* 1710.
½⁰: 1 side, 1 column.
'The disturbance we have in our nation of late'
> A tory election ballad.
CLU-C.

N157 — A new medley. [*London?* 1740.]
slip: 1 side, 1 column.
> *Percival* appendix 82. Rough woodcut at head.
'Cheer up your hearts you brave loyal Brittons'
C.

— 'New miscellaneous poems. With five love-letters from a nun, to a cavalier. Done into verse. [*London*] *Sold by J. Morphew.* Price bound in sheep, 1s. 2d. in calf 1s. 6d.' (*PB* 12 Feb 1713)
> Listed as a miscellany in *CBEL* II. 193–4, but it appears to be the work of a single author. Entered in *SR* 16 Feb 1713 to Morgan Kene or Keene (who was possibly the author); the deposit copies have not been traced. Probably the same author was responsible

New miscellaneous poems

for *The impotent lover describ'd*, 1718, and *Love-letters between a nobleman and his sister*, 1734, which are said to be 'by the author of the Letters from a nun to a cavalier'.

—— The second edition. *London, printed for W. Mears*, 1713. (*PB* 16 April)
12°: pp. 129.   J. R. Hetherington, Birmingham (lacks A3).

—— The third edition, with large additions. *London, printed for W. Mears*, 1714.
12°: pp. 160.   CSmH.

—— With the cavalier's answer. In two parts. Done into verse. The fourth edition, according to the original copy, with additions. *London, printed for Tho. Corbet*, 1716.
12°: pp. 132.   Harding.
From the title, both parts were intended to be issued together; they are entered separately here.

—— The fifth edition, according to the original copy, with additions. *London, printed for A. Bettesworth*, 1718.
12°: pp. 132.   OW; ICN.
The answer is not mentioned on the title. A note in this edition records that the second edition was altered by the printer and the additions to the third were made by another hand.

—— The seventh edition, according to the original copy, with additions. *London, printed for A. Bettesworth, & C. Hitch*, 1731.
12°: pp. 276.   (A. d'Aguiar, *Soror Marianna*, 1924.)
This edition contains both parts in one collation.

— New miscellaneous poems. With the cavalier's answers to the nun's five love-letters. In verse. *London, printed for Thomas Corbet*, 1716.
12°: pp. 136.   Harding.
Issued with the 1716 edition of the preceding. The preface records 'these letters and poems are made publick by the same hand'; it certainly seems to be a miscellany, as recorded in *CBEL* II. 193.

—— *London, printed for A. Bettesworth*, 1718.
12°: pp. 136.   CLU-C,ICN.

—— *London, printed for A. Bettesworth*, 1725.
12°: pp. 136.   OW.

— The new miscellany: consisting of poems and translations from Ovid and Horace; with a song most humbly inscrib'd to an old woman. *London, printed for T. Bickerton* 1720. (*SR* 20 Jan)
8°: pp. 36.   L,O.
Entered in *SR* to William Bray. The Luttrell copy at L is dated 'May'. Clearly by one author, though listed as a miscellany in *CBEL* II. 195. The running-title is 'Poems on several occasions'.

A **new** miscellany

— A new miscellany of poems and translations. Never before printed. By the author of the Smock race at Finglas, 1716. *See* Ward, James.

N158 — A new muster of Bays's troops. [*London*] *Sold at the print and pamphlet-shops*, 1745.
½°: 1 side, 4 columns.
Large engraving at head, with printed key.
'Ye rebels all, you're quite undone'
A satire on theatrical opposition to the Pretender at Drury Lane, led by Colley Cibber.
DFo.

N159 — A new Norfolk ballad, concerning the late Vienna treaty. Tune of, A trifling song you shall hear, &c. *London, printed for J. Dicks; sold by the booksellers of London & Westminster*, 1731. (*MChr* April)
2°: *A² B²; 1–4 5–8.*
Percival appendix 32.
'The town being full of confusion'
A satire on Sir Robert Walpole and the second Vienna treaty, signed March 1731.
O,OA; CSmH,CtY(uncut),IU(uncut),MH, TxU +.

N160 — 'A new Norfolk ballad. To the tune of Packington's pound. By Sir Francis Walsingham's ghost. [*London*] *Printed for A. Moore; sold by the booksellers of London & Westminster; and [by R. Walker] at the White-Hart over against Devereux Court.* Price 6d.' (*DJ* 17 Nov 1730, 'this morning at 10')
Percival XV.
'Good people of England give ear to my song'
Percival p. xlvii suggests William Pulteney's authorship on the evidence of style. A satire on Walpole's annual house-party at Houghton.

N161 —— By Sir Francis Walsingham's ghost. To the tune of Packington's pound. [*Dublin*] *Printed in the year* 1730.
½°: 1 side, 2 columns.
L(C.121.g.8/183),C.

N162 — A new ode, being a congratulatory poem on the glorious successes of her majesty's arms, under the command of the auspicious general his grace the Duke of Marlborough. Set to musick by Mr. Jer. Clark. To be perform'd by the best masters, on Friday the 20th of this instant, at seven a clock in York-buildings. *London printed, and sold by J. Morphew*, 1706. (19 Dec, Luttrell)
½°: 2 sides, 1 column.
At the foot of side 2, 'A new song, set by Mr. D. Purcell'.
'Hail happy queen! born to heal and to unite'
DG,MC; ICN(Luttrell).

— A new ode, to a number of great men newly made, [1742.] *See* Williams, *Sir* Charles Hanbury.

N163 — A new opera-epilogue, to the tragedy of Lady Jane Grey. Acted February 23d 172 9/30, for the

A **new** opera-epilogue

benefit of Mistress Sterling. Spoken and sung by Mrs. Sterling, representing the ghost of Lady Jane. *Dublin, printed in the year* 172⁹₃0.
½°: 1 side, 2 columns.
 Three songs with a linking epilogue.
'Ye tender fair, with streaming eyes'
L(1890.e.5/42),DT; CSmH,CtY.

N164 — A new opera-epilogue to the tragedy of Richard the third. Sung and spoken by Mrs. Sterling, who acted the part of Lady Anne. *Dublin, printed in the year* 1731.
½°: 1 side, 2 columns.
 Three songs with a linking epilogue.
'Brisk widows, in their sable'
CSmH.

— The new order and procession of the riding the franchises, [172–?] *See* Nelson, Henry (N25).

— A new poem ascrib'd to the honourable Miss Carteret, [1725.] *See* Philips, Ambrose (P224).

N165 — A new poem ascrib'd to the honble. the gentlemen of the late grand-jury. *Dublin, printed by G. Needham,* [1724.]
½°: 1 side, 1 column.
 Teerink 1169.
'As ship-wrack'd passengers when got to shore'
 In praise of the jury which refused to make a presentment of Swift's *Seasonable advice.*
L(C.121.g.8/78),LVA-F,C,DT,Rothschild; CtY.

N166 — A new poem ascrib'd to the lady who wrote the answer to Mr. Philips's poem on Miss C — t. [*Dublin,* 1725.]
½°: 1 side, 2 columns.
 Bond 86.
'The witling of the witty race'
 An 'advice to a painter' poem that he should paint the author of *A lady's answer to Mr. Ambrose Philips's poem,* [1725] in an indecent posture.
L(C.121.g.8/103),Rothschild.

N167 — A new poem, in commemoration of the 10th. of June, being the birth-day of the Chevalier d' St. George. [*Dublin,* 1726?]
½°: 1 side, 1 column.
 The DT copy is bound with half-sheets of June 1726.
'Ye furies dire who tread the Stygian sand'
 A satire against the Old Pretender.
DT.

N168 — A new poem in honour of the journey-men taylors: written by J.M. [*Dublin,* 1726?/27?]
½°: 1 side, 1 column.
'Grace this my theam, ye muses, and combine'
 Possibly by John Morgan; cf. his *A poem on the taylor craft* (Edinburgh, 1733).
L(1890.e.5/165),DT.

N169 — A new poem made on the safe arrival of the high, puissant and most noble prince Lionell

A **new** poem made

Cranfield Sacville, duke of Dorset...lord lieutenant general and general governour of Ireland. [*Dublin,* 1731.]
½°: 1 side, 1 column.
'Most noble prince, Hibernia welcomes thee'
DT.

— A new poem on a cract-pitcher, [1726/36?] *See* Whyte, Laurence.

— A new poem on the ancient and loyal society of journey-men taylors, 1725. *See* Nelson, Henry.

N170 — A new poem on the beauties of the universe. [*Dublin,* 1725/30.]
½°: 1 side, 2 columns.
 The copy at L forms part of a collection of Dublin half-sheets of 1725/30.
'Observe that arch, the firmament above'
L(C.121.g.8/129).

N171 — A new poem on the order of the procession, of the society of silk and worsted weavers... Written by J.S. a welwisher to the trade. [*Dublin,* 1728?/29?]
½°: 1 side, 2 columns.
 The date is suggested by the original ms. numeration of the L copy.
'Come all you jolly weavers'
L(1890.e.5/44).

N172 — A new proclamation cocerning[!] farthinggles, or old Mr. Fashoner shiting hoptpiticoats... [*Edinburgh,* 171–?]
½°: 1 side, 2 columns.
 Rough woodcut of devil excreting farthingales.
'All the inventions that ever was known'
 Possibly one of the satires which occasion'd *The lady's answer, to the sev'ral little satyres,* [171–?].
E.

— A new prologue, on the anniversary of his majesty K. George, 1725. *See* Arbuckle, James.

N173 — A new prologue relating to the Act at Oxford. With an epilogue, touching the model and form of the intended theatre in the Hay-market. Together with an epilogue spoken by a girl of four years old. *London, printed for B. Bragg,* [1703.] (15 July, Luttrell)
4°: A⁴ (A2 as 'A'); 1–2 3–8.
'Were tunes but such as in preceding days'
'And must this house your want of favour mourn'
'From Harry's daughter, and the Princess Bess'
L(164.m.33, Luttrell).

N174 — A new prologue spoke at the Theatre-royal before their graces the Duke and Dutchess of Grafton on Friday the 20th instant, being the anniversary of his majesty King George's coronation. By Mr. Elrington senior. *Dublin, printed by John Harding,* 1721.
½°: 1 side, 1 column.
'Ye grateful patriots, who this day revere'

A **new** prologue spoke

Presumably spoken by Thomas Elrington, not written by him.
TxU.

N175 — A new prologue spoken at the theatre in Lincoln's-Inn-fields, on Saturday, July the 8th, 1704. In praise of the wells. [*London*] *Printed for B. Lintott*, 1704. (12 July, Luttrell)
½°: A¹; *1–2*, 1 column.
Advertised in *DC* 13 July.
'Why is great Phœbus stil'd the god of lays'
Reprinted with commentary by E. L. Avery in *SEL* 5 (1965) 455f.
ICN(Luttrell).

— A new prologue spoken by Mr. Garrick, 1750. *See* Johnson, Samuel.

N176 — A new prologue to the Conscious lovers. Spoken by Mr. Husbands, May the 13th. 1724. *Dublin, printed by J. Carson*, 1724.
½°: 2 sides, 1 column.
On the verso, 'A new epilogue to the Conscious lovers: spoken by Mrs. Knap. May the 13th. 1724', which was previously printed separately by Carson.
'Long have the bards profan'd the British stage'
Epilogue: 'I'm thinking, now the ceremony's over'
CtY.

N177 — A new receipt to tame a shrew: a tale. *London, printed for D. Henry; sold by J. Griffiths*, 1749. (*SR* 30 Sept)
4°: A¹ B–C² D¹; *1–3* 4–11 *12 blk.*
Entered in *SR* to Henry New; deposit copies at O,GU,SaU.
'Shakespeare's receipt to tame a shrew'
O,GU,SaU.

N178 — The new revolution: or, the whigs turn'd Jacobites. A poem. *London printed, and sold by J. Baker*, 1710. (*SR* 2 Oct)
8°: A⁴ (A1ᵛ signed 'A2'); *1* 2–8.
Deposit copies at O,EU,AdU; advertised in *PM* 3 Oct.
'What a race were you running from bad into worse'
Tory verses on the Sacheverell affair.
LG,O,E,AdU,SaU + ; CSmH,CtY(2),ICU (uncut), MB(2),TxU(3) +.

N179 — — 'London: printed; and sold by J. Baker' [*Dublin?*], 171⟨0⟩.
8°: A⁴; *1–2* 3–7 *8 blk.*
The last figure of the date is mutilated in the copy seen, but is almost certainly o.
DA.

— A new rod for Tunbridge beaus, 1705. *See* A rod for Tunbridge beaus, 1701–.

N180 — A new satyr against the French king; with the true character of French-men in general... *London, printed in the year* 1701. (6 Oct, Luttrell)
½°: 2 sides, 1 column.

A **new** satyr against the French king

'Speak satyr quickly, we have theames enough'
ICN(Luttrell).

N181 — A new Scotch song, or a dialogue between two shepherds. [*Edinburgh?* 1715/–.]
½°: 1 side, 2 columns.
'Pray come you here the fight to shun'
On the battle of Sheriffmuir.
MH.

N182 — [*idem*] A dialogue, betwixt William Lick-ladle, and Thomas Clean-cogue, who were feeding their sheep upon the Ochel-hills, upon the 13th. of November 1715. Being the day the battle of Sheriffmoor was fought...to the tune of, The Cameronians march. [*Edinburgh,* 1715/–.]
½°: 1 side, 2 columns.
Printed together with *A race at Sheriff-muir,* [1715/–] (R5); the L copy is not divided. The order of editions has not been determined.
L(1876.f.1/75).

— A new simile for the ladies, 1732. *See* Sheridan, Thomas.

— A new song [Come ye Westminster boys...], [1741.] *See* The true English-boys song, [1741.]

N183 — A new song. [Two kings...] [*London?* 1739?]
slip: 1 side, 1 column.
Percival XLVII. Rough woodcut of ship at head.
'Two kings of great honour, Georgius and Phillip'
Crum T3463. In favour of war with Spain. Percival suggests it was occasioned by the royal proclamation of 10 July 1739.
C.

N184 — [another edition]
Rough woodcut of king at head.
C.

N185 — A new song. [What a cursed...] [*London?* 1715?]
slip: 1 side, 1 column.
'What a cursed crew have we got'
A Jacobite song.
L(C.121.g.9/173),O.

N186 — A new song. [When as Queen Robin...] [*London,* 1714?]
½°: 1 side, 2 columns.
Stanza 9, line 1 reads '...high Politics'.
'When as Queen Robin rul'd this land'
A satire on Harley.
L(112.f.44/35),MC.

N187 — [another edition]
Stanza 9, line 1 reads '...hight Politics'.
O.

N188 — A new song. [Ye lovers of physick...] [*Edinburgh,* 174–?]
½°: 1 side, 2 columns.
'Ye lovers of physick, come lend me your ear'
In defence of John Taylor the oculist against the attacks of an Edinburgh professor.
L(Rox.III.764, mutilated).

A **new** song. Being

N189 — A new song. Being a second part to the same tune of Lillibullero, &c. [*London*, 1711/12.]
½°: 1 side, 1 column.
    The rules in the title are composed of 13 and 18 small rules.
'A treaty's on foot, look about English boys'
    Crum A507. A second part to *An excellent new song to the memorable tune of Lillibullero*, 1711. Against a peace with France.
L(112.f.44/23),O,DT,Rothschild; NNP,PPL, TxU.

N190 — [another edition]
    The rules in the title are composed of 14 small rules each.
InU,MH.

N191 — [another edition]
    The rules in the title are continuous.
L(1850.c.10/5); MH-BA.

N192 — A new song, between Ormun and Malburor. [*London?* 1715?]
slip: 1 side, 1 column.
    Rough woodcut at head.
'Between Ormun and Malburor'
    A dispute between James duke of Ormonde and Marlborough; in the former's favour.
C.

N193 — A new song call'd Ireland's universal loss. Or, the lamentation of the poor inhabitants thereof, for the death of William King, late lord arch bishop of Dublin, and primate of Ireland; who departed this life on Thursday the 8th of this instant May 1729. at his house in Caven's Street, Dublin. Tune. Since Celia's my foe. [*Dublin*, 1729.]
½°: 1 side, 1 column.
    Mourning woodcut borders.
'Oh! what's this I hear, that disturbs my ear'
DT.

N194 — A new song. Call'd the Duke of Cumberland's victory over the Scotch rebels at Cullodon-moor, near Inverness. Made by a soldier who was in the engagement. To the tune of the Earl of Essex. *Sheffield, printed by Francis Lister, near the Shambles*, 1746.
½°: 1 side, 2 columns.
    Rough woodcut at head of column 1; column 2 contains 'England's glory; or, Duke William's triumph over the rebels in Scotland'.
'You subjects of Britton now you may rejoice'
England's glory: 'Brittons all your voices raise'
L(Rox.III.789).

N195 — A new song, call'd, the Observator of the times. [*London?* 1744?]
slip: 1 side, 1 column.
    Rough woodcut of chariot at head.
'O what is the matter? this noise and this clatter?'
    An attack on admiral Richard Lestock's conduct at Toulon.
O.

A **new** song, call'd

N196 — A new song call'd the Sorrowful lamentations of Anthony Bulger, James Costolow [and 15 others] ...who were taken on board a sloop at the bar of Dublin, on Fryday the 19th of this instant January 1721–22. who were supposed to be listed for the Pretender... Tune of, Sarsefield's lamentation. *Dublin, printed* 1721–22.
½°: 1 side, 2 columns.
'Good people all we pray give ear'
L(C.121.g.8/15).

N197 — A new song, call'd the Twitcher. Which was sung by Mr. Layfield, at the play-house the 29th of May last, 1721. *Dublin re-printed, by C. Carter*, 1721.
½°: 1 side, 2 columns.
    Two lines of woodcut music at head.
'A damsel I'm told,/Of delicate mold'
    Crum A93.
TxU.

N198 — A new song concerning the Westminster election. [*London*, 1749.] (Dec)
¼°: 1 side, 1 column.
'Tho' Trentham's exalted to be a fine lord'
    Against Lord Trentham.
L(1876.f.1/140, ms. date Dec 1749).

N199 — A new song, concerning two games at cards, play'd betwixt the King of England, King of France, and Queen of Spain; shewing the true honour and honesty of old England against the Pretender. To a good tune. [*London?* 1719?]
slip: 1 side, 1 column.
    Rough woodcut of king at head.
'Come jolly Brittons and play your game at whist'
    Against supporters of the Pretender.
L(Rox.III.400).

N200 — A new song entituled, the Warming-pan. [*Edinburgh?* 1745.]
slip: 1 side, 1 column.
'When Jemmy the second, not Jemmy the first'
    Against the Jacobites.
L(Rox.III.724).

N201 — [dh] A new song for Thursday the 17th of May 1750. (To the tune of the Cobler.) [*Edinburgh*, 1750.]
8°: *A*²; 1–4.
    At foot of p. 4, 'The end of the first part'.
'Whoever they be, they're the weakest of fools'
    In reference to the proceedings of the general assembly of the church of Scotland about a projected application to parliament for an augmentation of the stipends of the ministers. Answered by S584.
L(806.k.16/70*),E,*MR-C*.

— A new song, in praise of Molly Mogg, [1726/–.]
See Gay, John (G62).

N202 — A new song. Made on our late soverin [!] lord King George, who resign'd his breath at his sumtious palace in Hannover, on Wednesday the

A **new** song. Made on

14th of this instant June, 1727. Aged 68. To the tune of Ireland's lamentation. [*Dublin*, 1727.]
½°: 1 side, 2 columns.
　　Rough woodcuts after 'song' in title.
'What dismal tydings is this now I hear'
DT.

N203 — A new song, made on the intended invasion of the Spaniards in favour of the Pretender: or Great-Britain's triumph: or, the demolishers demolish'd, and the hopes of Prince Perkin's friends and abettors for ever extinguish'd. Tune, Now comes on the glorious year. [*London*? 1719?]
½°: 1 side, 2 columns.
'Chear up and sing ye loyal hearts'
MH(imprint cropt).

N204 — A new song made on the last speech, confession and dying words of Mr. John Porter, and Mr. Richard Johnson gentlemen, who were executed near St. Stephens Green, this present Saturday being the 12th of this instant December 1730. For the killing of Patrick Murphy the 21st of October last: whose deaths are much lamented. Tune, King Charles's martyrdom. [*Dublin*, 1730.]
½°: 1 side, 2 columns.
'Let disobedient youths I pray draw near'
DT.

N205 — A new song made on the right honourable Humphrey Parsons, esq, now our great and good lord mayer [!]. [*London*, 1730.]
½°: 1 side, 2 columns.
　　Percival appendix 27. Rough woodcut at head.
'You citizens of London'
　　Dated 1741 by *DNB*, but the reference to Parsons as a member of parliament shows that it belongs to his first term of office.
L(1872.a.1/170).

N206 — A new song made on the sumptious [!] procession of the noble and charitable society of scriblers; who walks to St. Cathrins Church to hear a sermon, and from thence to dine in Castle-street on Tuesday the first of August, 1727. Wherein is set forth the antiquity of their calling. To the tune of the First of August. [*Dublin*, 1727.]
½°: 1 side, 2 columns.
'Good people all I pray draw near'
L(C.121.g.8/164).

N207 — ⟨A⟩ new song of the warrs. [*London*? 1744?]
slip: 1 side, 1 column.
　　Rough woodcuts at head and foot; seven lines of verse above title. On the other side, *The loyal Britain*, [1744?].
'Come all loyal Britains come lssen[!] to me'
　　On the abortive Jacobite expedition from Dunkirk in Feb 1744.
L(Rox.III.753).

N208 — A new song. On Miss in her teens: or, the old squire out-witted by the young captain; taken from a celebrated farce, performed at the Theatre

A **new** song. On

Royal, in Covent-garden. Wrote by a principal actor. [*London*? 1747?]
½°: 1 side, 2 columns.
　　Small woodcut scene at head.
'Ye folk of the town,/From the peer to the clown'
　　The plot of Garrick's play versified.
L(1876.f.1/131).

N209 — A new song on St. George's day. And to the glorious memory of Queen Anne. With the restauration of K. Charles the 2d. To the tune of, Now now comes on the glorious year. *London, printed for R. Smith*, [1715?]
½°: 1 side, 2 columns.
　　Two rough woodcuts above text.
'You that are loyal churchmen smile'
　　A covertly Jacobite song.
L(1876.f.1/68).

N210 — A new song on the scrutiny for Sir George Vandeput. Tune – God save our noble king. [*London*? 1750/51.]
slip: 1 side, 1 column.
'God save brave Vandeput'
　　Signed 'B.Y. Poet'. In the hope that the election petition will invalidate Lord Trentham's election for Westminster.
O.

N211 — A new song, on the sharp and boody[!] battle fought the 16th. instant, between the English troops &c. on the Main in Germany, commande[!] by the King of Great Britain... (Tune, Glorious Charles of Sweeden.) *London, printed for E. Williams, near Chearing Cross*, [1743.]
½°: 1 side, 2 columns.
　　Rough woodcuts at head.
'Brave Briton's let your voices ring'
　　On the victory at Dettingen.
L(1876.f.1/127).

N212 — A new song, proper for the times, which may be sung to the tune of Derry down, or the Miller of Mansfield. *Salisbury, printed by Benjamin Collins*, 1745.
1°: 1 side, 2 columns.
'France, Spain, Rome, and devil (as always) of late'
　　Against the Jacobite uprising.
L(Cup.600.b.1/70).

N213 — A new song sung by a Spaniard before the C--r St. George, his lady, and the late D. of O--d. Tune Belinda. [*London*? 1719/20.]
½°: 1 side, 2 columns.
　　Two rough woodcuts at head.
'With crowns and orbs beneath your feet'
　　James Francis Edward, chevalier de St. George, married Maria Sobieski in May 1719; the Duke of Ormonde's expedition failed in the same year.
L(1872.a.1/1).

N214 — [variant title, adds:] Translated from the Spanish.
　　On the other side of the MH copy, *A full and*

A **new** song sung by a Spaniard

   true account of the apprending[!] . . . *Dr. Welton*,
[1720], in prose.
 MH.

N215 — 'A new song sung Wednesday Nov. 16, by a
society of loyalists. [*London*] "*Merryman*". Price
6*d*.' (*BM,LM* Nov 1750)

N216 — A new song to the honourable Miss C——
—— ——t. By L.B. *W.* [*Dublin*] *Printed in the year*
'MCCDXXVI' [1726].
 slip: 1 side, 1 column.
 'Why will Florella when I gaze'
  To Miss Carteret. *Crum* W2448, translated into Latin verse by William Jessop in a letter of
  4 Feb 1785; he says the English 'if I remember
  right, is by Soame Jennings' – but he is clearly
  wrong.
 DT.

— A new song. To the tune of, Come let us prepare, &c., [1741/42.] *See* The independent Westminster electors, [1741/42] (I35).

N217 — A new song. To the tune of Lilly bullaro, &c.
[*London*] *Printed in the year* 1708.
 ½º: 1 side, 2 columns.
 'In the reign of Queen Anne'
  An attack on the tory intrigues of Harley, St.
  John, and Harcourt(?) with Abigail Hill.
 O.

— A new song. Tune of Lochaber no more, [1723?]
See Ramsay, Allan.

N218 — A new song. To the tune of, Marlborough push
'em again. [*London*] *Printed in the year* 1713.
 ½º: 1 side, 2 columns.
 'Who mounts the loftiest dignitys'
  A whig song against Bolingbroke.
 O.

N219 — A new song, to the tune of To you, fair ladies,
now at land. [*London*? 1740/41.]
 ½º: 1 side, 1 column.
  Percival appendix 84.
 'To you, fine folks, at Marlbro' House'
  Crum T3226: 'To the D[uke] of M[arlbor-
  ough] from Enfield Chace', by 'C[olone]l G.',
  dated 1740–1. Against Walpole, and for the
  war with Spain.
 Harding.

N220 — [*idem*] A new song. Tune, To you fair ladies,
&c. [*London*? 1740/41.]
 slip: 1 side, 1 column.
  Rough woodcut at head.
 C.

N221 — [another edition, title reads:] To you fair ladys,
&c.
 C.

N222 — A new song: (To the tune of, To you, fair
ladies now at land, &c.) [*Edinburgh*? 174–?]
 ½º: 1 side, 2 columns.
 'Ye authors sage of every coat'

A **new** song. To the tune

  On the death of 'Salamander', a clerical
  controversialist, on 10 May.
 L(1876.f.1/101).

N223 — A new song. To the tune of, 'Twas when the
seas were roaring. [*London*? 1716?]
 slip: 1 side, 1 column.
 'When faction loud was roaring'
  A Jacobite song.
 O.

N224 — A new song. To the tune of, Which no body
can deny. [*London*, 1717/18?]
  The copy seen has been cut up and mounted,
  but was either a slip or a half-sheet, printed
  on one side.
 'A mighty great fleet the like was ne'er seen'
  Cf. *Crum* A287: 'England's triumph, in the
  year 1691 – To the tune of, the Blacksmith'.
  A Jacobite attack on a naval expedition against
  the Swedes.
 O.

— A new song. Tune of Packington's pound,
[1733.] *See* Britannia excisa: Britain excis'd. Part
II, [1733] (B463).

— A new song. Tune, To you fair ladies, [1740/
41.] *See* A new song, to the tune of To you, fair
ladies, [1740/41.]

N225 — A new song upon a new subject to be sung or
said as the maggot bites, calculated for all sorts of
sobriety or ebriety. By T.B, a rum duke. Tune of,
London is a fine town. [*London*? 1736.]
 slip: 1 side, 1 column.
  Rough woodcut at head.
 'God prosper long our king and queen, and the
 wise parliament'
  In praise of the Gin Act.
 L(C.116.i.4/24).

N226 — [another edition, adds after title:] You must sing
the chorus at the end of every verse.
 L(C.116.i.4/23).

N227 — A new song. Vote and be merry, or, Squire
Beavan's invitation. To the tune of the Marry'd
man's item. [*London*? 170–?]
 ½º: 1 side, 1 column.
 'Good people I say, / Come listen I pray'
  Possibly an election song in favour of Arthur
  Bevan, elected 1727, 1734; but the typography
  suggests an earlier date.
 InU.

N228 — A new song, warbled out of the oracular oven
of Tho. Baker, just after the D. of M------gh's
triumphal procession thro' the city of London...
To the tune of, Which no body can deny. [*London*,
1714.]
 slip: 1 side, 1 column.
  'Which no body can deny' is printed in
  italic. The order of editions has not been
  determined, but this is the better printed.
 'Hark, hark, brave boys do ye hear the report?'

Crum H221, dating the occasion of Marlborough's return as 4 Aug 1714. An attack on
him. Thomas Baker is treated as the author by
the L catalogue, but nothing is known of him
and the title is ambiguous.

Herts CRO (Panshanger box 46).

N229 — [another edition]
'Which no body can deny' is printed in
roman type.
L(C.121.g.9/165).

N230 — A new state picture. *London, printed for A.
More,* [1731.] (July, Luttrell)
$\frac{1}{2}$°: 1 side, 2 columns.
Woodcut portrait at head, 'The Anti-Crafts-
man unmask'd'.
'Britons behold! your petty tyrant here'
An attack on Walpole.
L(1872.a.1/167**; P&D 2558); ICN(Luttrell).

N231 — — *London, printed for A. Moore,* [1731.]
$\frac{1}{2}$°: 1 side, 2 columns.
Large woodcut portrait at head.
L(1872.a.1/167***).

N232 — A new system of rural politicks; or, the crafty
farmer's falsehood fitted... A humorous true tale,
in two canto's. By Swift junior. *London, printed for
G. Griffith,* 1746 [1747?].
8°: *A*¹[=F1] B–E⁴ F⁴(–F1); *1*–2 3–26 35–47
48 *blk*.
Both copies seen have the date altered in ms.
to 1747; listed in *BM* June 1748.
'Most authors chuse to celebrate'
L(11633.cc.2/5); OCU.

— The new theory of the orbs of heaven, [172–?]
See Hoffman, Francis.

N233 — A new toast: or, a ballad on the twenty-ninth of
May. To the tune of, Over the hills and far away.
[*London?* 1715.]
$\frac{1}{4}$°: 1 side, 2 columns.
''Tis the twenty-ninth of May'
Crum T2848: 'A new ballad on the 29 of
May...' A Jacobite toast.
O.

N234 — A new toast, to his grace James duke of
Ormond. *London, printed for J. Smith, in the
Strand,* [1715.]
$\frac{1}{2}$°: 1 side, 2 columns.
'Who durst have said some time agoe'
On the impeachment of Ormonde.
Crawford.

N235 — A new tory health: to the tune, Hark, hark, the
thundring cannons roar. [*London?* 1715.]
slip: 1 side, 1 column.
'Boast not of Bollingbroke's retreat'
Crum B472: 'The new toast', June 1715. A
Jacobite song, praising Bolingbroke and
Ormonde.
CSmH.

N236 — A new translation of Æsop. In a hundred select
fables, burlesqu'd. With a suitable new moral for
each fable. Never before printed. *London printed,
and sold by S. Malthus, & William Lucas,* 1705.
(*PM* 3 May)
8°: A–M⁴ (C1 as 'B'); [2] i–ii iii–vi, 1–48 59–98.
'A kite in a snare was unluckily taken'
It is not clear how far these fables are original.
DT(2); MH(uncut).

N237 — [reissue] The fables of Æsop, in English verse.
With suitable new morals, adapted to each fable.
Never before printed... [*London*] *Sold by A.
Baldwin,* [1705/10?]
8°: (frt+) A⁴(±A1) B–M⁴; [2] i–ii iii–vi, 1–48
59–98.
The woodcut frontispiece found in the O copy
is possibly not original, or it may be conjugate
with the cancel title A1.
O.

— A new translation of the first ode of Horace,
[1739/46.] *See* Theobald, John.

N238 — A new war between cakes and ale, and the tea
tables, &. [*Dublin,* 1727.]
slip: 1 side, 1 column.
According to a ms. note in the L copy,
printed with *An hoop for the broken mugg,*
1727.
'If tea tables, b' allow'd for summer's noise'
L(1890.e.5/48).

N239 — The new weather-cock's song, at the castle.
Dublin, printed by John Gowan, [1729?]
$\frac{1}{2}$°: 1 side, 2 columns.
The DT copy is bound with half-sheets of
1729.
'Erected at last,/To discover each blast'
DT.

N240 — The new Wife of Beath [!] much better re-
formed, enlarged, and corrected, than it was
formerly in the old uncorrect copy. With the
addition of many other things. *Glasgow, printed by
Robert Sanders,* 1705.
12°: *A*⁸ B⁴; *1*–3 '2' 5–23 *24 blk*.
Printed in black-letter. An earlier Glasgow
edition of 1700 (L,E) was not the first according to a ms. note in the E copy. P. 3, 'What
was papal or heretical in the former copy is
left out here in this second edition'.
'In Beath once dwelt a worthy wife'
On what happens to the Wife of Bath after
death, and how she gets into heaven. A moral
piece.
E(uncut).

N241 — The new wonder, or, a trip to St. Paul's. By
the author of the True born Englishman. [*London*]
Printed in the year 1710.
8°: A⁴; *1* 2–8.
'Now fame began abroad to spread'

The **new** wonder

Not accepted by any bibliographer of Defoe; recorded as doubtful in *Lowndes*.

MB.

N242 — The new-year's-gift; a poem. Address'd to a young lady. *London, printed for T. Cooper*, 1741. (*GM, LM* March)

2°: *A²* B–C²; *1–3* 4–12.

'My friend, (a privilege with pride I claim'

MH(uncut).

N243 — A new-years gift for the plunderers of the world: with an ancient prophecy. [*London*] *Printed by J. Jones at Temple-bar*, 1712.

½°: 1 side, 1 column.

'The sand-ridge baron now doth stand'

An attack on Marlborough.

C.

N244 — A new-years gift for the renegado and Hansel to his whiper. [*Edinburgh*] *Printed in the year* 1705.

4°: *A²*; *1–4*.

'Apollo was you in a lethargie'

Related to the Forbes/Allan controversy; an attack on Allan, but Forbes is also lightly touched.

OW,E(4); CSmH,DFo,TxU.

N245 — A new-years-gift: or, a respectful wish, from the hand of a stranger who (upon the 28th of November) was a sufferer by the fire which happened in the Canongate. To my lord Balmerino. [*Edinburgh*, 171–?]

½°: 1 side, 1 column.

The dedicatee's name is apparently stamped in by hand, enabling the author to solicit different patrons.

'May this years influence, the nation bless'

E.

Newcomb, Thomas. Sacred hymns: or, an attempt to discover and revive the original spirit... of some of the select psalms. To which is added, an ode on the agony of the Messiah. *London, printed for John Pemberton, & John Walthoe*, 1726. (*MC* March)

8°: pp. viii, 124. E; CLU.

Probably the work listed by *Nichols, Collection* VII. 162 as 'A paraphrase on some select psalms'.

[—] A miscellaneous collection of original poems, consisting of odes, epistles, translations, &c... *London, printed by J. Wilson*, 1740.

4°: pp. '388' [392]. L,O; CtY,MH.

Dedication signed 'T.N.' According to *DNB* there are large-paper copies, but all seen have watermark of a crowned eagle.

— 'A collection of odes and epigrams, &c. occasioned by the success of the British and confederate forces in Germany, 1743.'

Listed in *Nichols, Collection* VII. 162–3; possibly the same work as *Verses left in a grotto*, 1744.

Newcomb, T. Bibliotheca

N246 [—] Bibliotheca: a poem. Occasion'd by the sight of a modern library. With some very useful episodes, and digressions. *London printed, and are to be sold by J. Morphew*, 1712. (Jan?)

8°: *A⁴* B–I⁴; *i–viii*, 1–64.

No watermark. Advertised in *PB* 10 Jan 1712 for publication 'shortly'. A second edition was advertised in *PB* 24 Dec 1713, but has not been traced.

'The tea was sip'd, Ocella gone'

Wrongly ascribed to William King in *Nichols, Collection* III. 19; ascribed to Newcomb in IV. 355. Listed by Newcomb in *Rawlinson*.

L(1486.df.33), O(lacks A1), E; DLC,MH.

N247 [—] [fine paper] *London, printed in the year* 1712. Watermark: fleur-de-lys on shield.

CtY(in contemporary morocco),ICN.

N248 [—] Blasphemy as old as the creation: or, the Newgate divine. A satyr. Address'd to the modern advocates of irreligion, prophaneness, and infidelity. By a gentleman and a Christian. *London, printed for Lawton Gilliver*, 1730. (*GSJ* 25 June)

8°: *A²* B–D⁴ E²; *i–iv*, *1* 2–28. A1 hft.

'E'er yet the earth or heaven, or various frame'

Listed by Newcomb in *Rawlinson*. A satire on Thomas Woolston, the freethinker.

L(164.1.20),O,OW; OCU.

N249 [—] — *London: printed, and Dublin re-printed, and sold by George Faulkner*, 1730.

8°: *A⁴* B–C⁴; *1–5* 6–23 *24*. A1 hft; 24 advt.

DA(2); IU.

N250 — 'Carmen seculare, presented to the...king... Fol.' [1720?]

Advertised in Newcomb's *The consummation*, 1752, as 'presented to the late king on his accession to the British throne', but listed by Newcomb in *Rawlinson* as 'Presented to the late king, by the Ld Carteret then principal secretary of state'; while in a note on Rawlinson's description he dates it as 1720.

N251 — An epistle from the Duke of Burgundy to the French king. *London, printed for J. Tonson*, 1709. (7 April, Luttrell)

2°: A–C²; *i–iv*, 1–8.

The Luttrell copy is in the possession of R. D. Horn; listed in *DC* 13 April as 'just publish'd'.

'If yet unmindful of Ramillia's field'

O; MH(cropt),TxU(2, imperfect).

N252 — 'An [epistle/ode] to his royal highness the Duke of Cumberland on his voyage to Holland. 1746.'

Advertised in Newcomb's *The consummation*, 1752, as one of 'Two epistles to his royal highness...' but listed in *Nichols, Collection* VII. 162n. as one of 'Two odes...1746'.

— 'An [epistle/ode] to his royal highness the Duke of Cumberland on the victory obtained at Culloden, 1746.'

Newcomb, T. An epistle to

Advertised in Newcomb's *The consummation*, 1752, as one of 'Two epistles to his royal highness...' but listed in *Nichols, Collection* VII. 162n. as one of 'Two odes...1746'. Possibly the same work as N260 below.

— 'An epistle to the right honble. Sr. Rt. Walpole, occasioned by the peace of Sevile: and the influence of the British power in Europe. Oct.' '1732.'

Listed by Newcomb in *Rawlinson*, possibly by confusion with N262, written to the Duke of Newcastle on a similar subject; that, however, is a folio.

N253 — 'The happy rival or Venus mistaken a poem most humbly offer'd to the honourable Cecil Bishop esq; *Lond.* 1711. Fol.'
(*Rawlinson*.)

N254 — The last judgment of men and angels. A poem, in twelve books: after the manner of Milton. *London, printed for William Mears, & John Pemberton & John Hooke*, 1723. (*DP* 6 March)
2°: (frt+) π^1 A^2 a–e^2 B–4Y^2; *i–xxvi, 1 2–359 360 blk.* xxvi err.

Watermark: Amsterdam arms. The frontispiece is in mezzotint. Announced in *PB* 23 Feb as 'ready to be deliver'd to the subscribers'; there is a copy of the *Proposals*, 1722, at O-JJ.

'Oh! thou supreme of things, whose great command'

Dedication to the Earl of March.

O,LdU-B; CtY,ICN,MH,*NNUT*,TxU(–frt).

N255 — [fine paper]
Watermark: GF.
L(11641.1.6,–frt),OW.

N256 [—] The manners of the age: in thirteen moral satirs. Written with a design to expose the vicious and irregular conduct of both sexes... *London, printed for Jer. Batley*, 1733. (*GM,LM* June)
8°: π^2 B–Bb^8 Cc^2; *i–iv, 1–208 409–587 588.* $\pi2$ err; 588 advt.

Watermark: unicorn. The errata leaf, $\pi2$, is sometimes bound before the title. Apparently printed in two shops, which explains the mispagination.

'Forgive me, sacred bard, if I aspire'

Advertised as by the same author in Newcomb's *The consummation*, 1752; listed by Newcomb in *Rawlinson*.

L(1508/658); CLU-C,ICN,IU(–$\pi2$),MH(2, 1 uncut),*PU*+.

N257 [—] [another impression, in quarto] *London, printed for Jer. Batley*, 1733.
4°: π^2 B–Ccc^4 Ddd^2; *i–iv, 1–208 409–587 588.* $\pi2$ err; 588 advt.

Watermark: T; cut size $8\frac{1}{2} \times 6\frac{1}{2}$ in. The press-figures in the second half are identical with the preceding.

L(11631.cc.4),E.

Newcomb, T. The manners of the age

N257·2 [—] [fine paper]
Watermark: GAR crowned; the copy seen measures $10\frac{1}{4} \times 7\frac{1}{4}$ in.
TxU.

N258 — 'An ode inscribed to the memory of the late Earl of Orford, 1747 [1745?].'
(*Nichols, Collection* VII. 162n.)

N259 — 'An ode on the general conflagration; written in the plan of Dr Burnet. Inscrib'd to the rt. honble. the Ld. Carteret. Fol.' '1725.'

It is tempting to identify this with Newcomb's *The last judgment of men and angels*, 1723; he acknowledges his debt to Burnet in the preface of that work. But in addition to the different title and date, *The last judgment* is dedicated to the Earl of March.

(*Rawlinson*, confirmed by Newcomb.)

N260 — An ode, presented to his royal highness the Duke of Cumberland, on his return from Scotland. By the revd. Mr. Newcomb... *London, printed in the year* 1746. (*BM,GM* Aug)
4°: A^4 B^4 C^2; *1–4 5–19 20 blk.* A1 hft.

Copies recorded have watermark of fleur-de-lys on shield. Listed in *BM* as 'by T.N.' and sold by Cooper; that probably describes an ordinary-paper copy of which this is the fine-paper equivalent.

'Too well before thy arm has fought'

Possibly the same work as that listed in Newcomb's *Consummation*, 1752, as an 'epistle... on the victory gained at Culloden'.

AdU(presentation copy); *IU*.

N261 — An ode sacred to the memory of that truly pious and honourable lady, the Countess of Berkeley. Inscrib'd to the honourable the Earl of Berkeley. *London, printed for E. Curll*, 1717. (*PB* 23 July)
8°: A^1[=E4] B–D^4 E^4(–E4); *i–ii, 1–30.*

For the controversy between Edward Young and Curll over Curll's inclusion of Young's letter of recommendation in this edition, see Helen Leek in *PBSA* 62 (1968) 321f. Reissued in *The ladies miscellany*, 1718.

'As roses in their early bloom'

Presumably the same work as 'An ode to her grace the Duchess of Richmond; occasioned by the death of the Countess of Berkley', advertised in Newcomb's *Consummation*, 1752, and referred to with similar titles in *Rawlinson*; on one occasion there it is dated 1715, but listed as octavo.

O; CSmH,*CtY*,IU,KU,MH+.

— 'An ode to her grace the Duchess of Richmond; occasioned by the death of the Countess of Berkley.'

Probably the same work as N261 above.

N262 [—] An ode to his grace the Duke of Newcastle. Written on the present tranquillity of Europe, establish'd by the influence of British power.

Newcomb, T. An ode to his grace

London, printed for J. Batley, 1732. (*GSJ* 3 June)
2°: A² B²; *1–3* 4–8.
'While youth your poet once inspir'd'
> Printed in Newcomb's *Miscellaneous collection*, 1740, as 'An ode... Imitated from the French'. Possibly the work listed by Newcomb in *Rawlinson* as 'An epistle to the right honble. Sr. Rt. Walpole occasioned by the peace of Sevile...', though that is described as octavo.

NcD.

N263 [—] An ode to his grace the Duke of Richmond: occasion'd by his being elected governor of the Company of mine-adventurers in the principality of Wales. *London, printed for J. Pemberton,* [1720.] (*PB* 20 Sept)
2°: A² B²(B1 + 1); *i–ii*, *1–8*.
'Shall then the distant Indian coast'
> Advertised as 'By Thomas Newcomb'.

L(11661.dd.12),AN; *MH-BA*.

N264 [—] An ode to his grace the Duke of Richmond: occasion'd by some fine Italian paintings at Goodwood... *London, printed for Jer. Batley & J. Wood,* 1735.
4°: A–B⁴; *1–2* 3–16.
'While Rome, her genius to enflame'
> Printed in Newcomb's *Miscellaneous collection*, 1740, and listed by him in *Rawlinson* as 'Verses to his grace the Duke of Richmond'.

O.

N265 [—] An ode to Mr. Ellis, occasioned by a beautiful painting of the honourable Mr. Walpole, only son to the right hon. Lord Walpole. [*London,* 1737/8.]
4°: A⁴ B²; *1–3* 4–12.
> Watermark: fleur-de-lys on shield; possibly all copies are on fine paper.

'Whilst princes give thy art applause'
> Printed in Newcomb's *Miscellaneous collection*, 1740; listed by Newcomb in *Rawlinson* as 1737–8.

Lewis Walpole Library.

N266 [—] An ode to the queen. On the happy accession of their majesties to the crown. *London, printed for J. Walthoe,* 1727 [1728?]. (*MChr* 20 Feb)
8°: A² B–D⁴; *1–5* 6–28. A1 hft.
'Accept your Britain's smiles once more'
> Recorded as by Newcomb in *Nichols, Collection* VII. 162, and listed by Newcomb in *Rawlinson*.

L(992.h.7/5, title cropt),O(–A1),EtC.

N267 [—] An ode to the right honourable the E----l of O--------d, in retirement. *London, printed in the year* 1742.
4°: A–B⁴ C¹; *1–3* 4–17 *18 blk.*
> Watermark: fleur-de-lys on shield; possibly all copies are on fine paper.

'Whatever calm retreat you chuse'
> The copy seen has a presentation inscription from 'T.N.' Advertised as by the same author

Newcomb, T. An ode to the

in Newcomb's *The consummation*, 1752. To the Earl of Orford, Robert Walpole.
CtY (Osborn collection).

N268 [—] The oracle, an ode inscrib'd to Sir Edward Hawke, knight of the bath. *London printed, and sold by H. Kent,* 1747 [1748?]. (*BM, GM* Jan)
8°: A² B⁴ C²; *1–4* 5–15 *16 blk.* A1 hft.
'Amidst thy triumphs on the deep'
> Printed as Newcomb's in *Nichols, Collection* VII. 190ff.

L(11602.g.31/2),O.

N269 [—] Pacata Britannia. A panegyrick to the queen, on the peace, and the interest of the British nation. By Mr. T.N. *London, printed for R. Gosling,* 1713. (*PB* 21 July)
2°: A² B–C²; *1–2* 3–12. 12 advt.
'In ancient Rome thus great Augustus rose'
> Clearly the poem by Newcomb 'on the peace of Utrecht' referred to in *Jacob*.

O; CtY,MH(ms. date 11 Sept).

[—] Præ-existence and transmigration: or, the new metamorphoses, 1743. *See* P1019.

N270 [—] Scating: a poem. By Mr. Addison. *London, printed for E. Curll,* 1720. (*PB* 22 March)
8°: A⁴ B–C⁴; *i–vi*, *1–17 18 blk.* A1 hft, advt.
> Latin text by Philip Frowde on pp. 1–5; English translation by Newcomb on pp. 7–13; Pope's verses on Lady Mary Wortley Montagu on pp. 15–17. Sometimes issued with Addison's *Poems on several occasions*, 1719.

'Quæ nova naturæ facies, qui lumina terrent'
'See! Nature round a hoary prospect yields'
> Preface signed 'T.N'; reprinted in Addison's *Miscellanies in verse and prose*, 1725, as by Newcomb. The preface says the Latin 'Cursus glacialis' was published as Frowde's in *Musæ Anglicanæ* but was 'certainly written' by Addison; this is clearly incorrect.

L(161.l.2, Luttrell, May),O(uncut),CT(–A1); CtY,ICN(–A1),ICU,KU,MH+.

N271 [—] A supplement to a late excellent poem entitled, Are these things so? Address'd to the ****. *London, printed for J. Roberts,* 1740. (*LDP* 20 Dec)
4°: A–D²; *1–2* 3–16.
'While Europe's various realms your virtues own'
> Printed in Newcomb's *Miscellaneous collection*, 1740, from the same setting of type. Addressed to the king, satirizing the tories and their propagandists such as James Miller and James Ralph; occasioned by Miller's poem.

L(11630.e.14/8),OW; CtY(ms. notes).

N272 [—] A supplement to One thousand seven hundred thirty-eight. Not written by Mr. Pope. *London, printed for J. Roberts,* 1738. (*LDP* 24 Oct)
4°: A–D⁴ E² (A3 as 'A2'); *1–4* 5–35 *36 blk.* A1 hft.
No watermark.
'What! still intent on bus'ness, books, and rhimes?'
> The fine-paper copy below is bound with a

Newcomb, T. A supplement

presentation copy of Newcomb's *An ode to the...E----l of O--------d*, 1742.
L(11630.d.15/8; 840.k.2/2; 840.k.3,−A1),
LVA-D(−A1),O,OW(uncut),LdU-B(uncut);
CtY,IU,MH,NjP,TxU(−A1)+.

N273 [—] [fine paper] *London, printed by John Wilson, at the Turk's-Head, in Gracechurch-street*, 1738.
4°: A–D⁴ E²; *1–4* 5–35 *36 blk.*
Watermark: fleur-de-lys on shield.
CtY (Osborn collection).

N274 [—] — *Dublin: re-printed for the booksellers*, 1738.
8°: A–D⁴; *1–3* 4–32.
C(2),DK(2),DN; CSmH,CtY,MH.

N275 [—] Two poems viz. I. On the deluge, paradise, the burning of the world, and of the new heavens and new earth. An ode to Dr. Burnett. II. In praise of physic and poetry. An ode to Dr. Hannes. Written by Mr. Addison. *London, printed for E. Curll*, 1718.
12°: A–C⁴ (A3 as 'A2'); *1–9* '01' 11–24. A1 frt.
Addison's Latin texts on pp. 7–8, 17–18.
'No common height the muse must soar'
'While flying o'er the golden strings'
Reprinted as Newcomb's translations in Addison's *Miscellanies in verse and prose*, 1725; listed by Newcomb in *Rawlinson*.
L(11632.df.5),DG; CLU-C,CSmH,TxU.

N276 [—] Verses left in a grotto in Richmond Garden. To which are added, several odes on the battle of Dettingen. *London, printed for J. Roberts*, 1744.
(*GM, LM* Nov)
4°: A–D²; *1–3* 4–15 *16 blk.*
'While fame no more his bosom fires'
Printed as Newcomb's in *Nichols, Collection* VII. 181ff. In praise of George II.
L(11630.c.13/16),CT; CSmH.

N277 — 'Verses to his grace the Duke of Richmond; on his being installed knight of the garter along with Sr. Rt. Walpole. 4°.' [1726.]
Listed in *Rawlinson* by Newcomb; reprinted in *Nichols, Collection* VII. 170f. with first line:
'With every honour grac'd, thy youth appears'

N278 [—] Verses to the injur'd patriot. *London, printed for the author*, 1733.
2°: A² B²; *1–2* 3–8.
'If prudence were the parent of success'
Printed in Newcomb's *Miscellaneous collection*, 1740. Presumably addressed to Walpole.
MH.

N279 — Verses to the right honourable the Earl of Cadogan, occasion'd by the late funeral of the Duke of Marlborough. *London, printed for J. Roberts*, 1722.
8°: A² B–D⁴ E²; *i–iv*, *1–28.* A1 hft; iv err.
'Ye living heroes, who with grief o'erspread'
Horn(ms. corrections).

N280 [—] Vindicta Britannica: an ode, to the real patriot. Occasioned by the declaration of war

Newcomb, T. Vindicta Britannica

against Spain. *London, printed for C. Corbett*, 1740.
(*GM* Jan)
2°: A¹ B–C² D¹; *1–3* 4–12.
No watermark.
'Through the dark storm, and angry tide'
Printed in Newcomb's *Miscellaneous collection*, 1740. Presumably addressed to Walpole.
CtY,OCU,TxU.

N281 [—] [fine paper]
Watermark: fleur-de-lys on shield.
IU.

N282 [—] The woman of taste. Occasioned by a late poem, entitled, the Man of taste. By a friend of the author's. In two epistles, from Clelia in town to Sapho in the country. *London, printed for J. Batley*, 1733. (*GSJ* 2 June)
2°: A² B–F² G¹; *1–3* 4–26.
'If Sapho can believe her time well spent'
An advertisement in *GSJ* 13 Dec 1733 for Newcomb's *The manners of the age* lists this as by the same author, though they had previously been advertised together without this link. Not listed by Newcomb in *Rawlinson*, but he omitted satirical works of this kind. Newcomb's authorship seems probable, but it needs to be confirmed. Occasioned by James Bramston's poem.
L(11630.h.13),LVA-D,O,OW,GU; CSmH,ICU (uncut),MH,NjP,TxU(3)+.

N283 [—] — The second edition. *London, printed for J. Batley*, 1733.
2°: A² B–F² G¹; *1–3* 4–26.
L(1484.m.7/5),O(2, 1 lacks G1),C,LdU-B(2, 1 uncut); DLC,ICU,MH(2),NjP,TxU+.

N284 [—] — The third edition. *London printed, and, Dublin re-printed, by James Hoey*, 1733.
8°: A–C⁴; *1–2* 3–24. 24 advt.
CtY,MH.

N285 [—] The woman of taste. In a second epistle, from Clelia in town to Sappho in the country. *London, printed for J. Batley*, 1733. (*GSJ* 12 July)
2°: A² B–F²; *1–3* 4–23 *24 blk.*
'While still your rural scenes your eye delight'
Presumably by the same author as the preceding.
L(1484.m.7/4),O(2),LdU-B; CSmH,DLC,ICN, MH,TxU+.

N286 **Newgate.** 'A Newgate eclogue, in honour of the justly dignify'd Squire Ketch; being a midnight's conversation that pass'd between him and some of the apparitions of the departed rebels, which appeared to him in his cell after his condemnation and reprieve... [*London*] *Carpenter*. Price 6d.' (*BM,GM* June 1750)

N287 — Newgate in tears. Being an elegy on the much lamented death of Richard Murray, head hangman of England; who departed this life at his late dwelling house in Tyburn-road, on Saturday morning, being the 4th of this instant December,

Newgate in tears

1708. to the great grief of all the collegians in New-gate, New-prison, and Bridewel. *London, printed by J. Dutton, near Fleetstreet, 1708.*
½°: 1 side, 2 columns.
Mourning headpiece and borders.
'Each reverend whore and celebrated thief'
CSmH.

N288 — Newgate's garland: being a new ballad, shewing how Mr. Jonathan Wild's throat was cut, from ear to ear, with a penknife by Mr. Blake, alias Blueskin, the bold highwayman, as he stood at his trial at the Old-Bailey. To the tune of, The cutpurse. *[London, 1724/25.]*
obl ½°: 1 side, 2 columns.
Teerink 1168; *Williams* 1111f. Printed on the reverse of a postscript to *St. James's post* dated 28 Nov 1715, doubtless to use up the stamped paper. Williams's reference to a broadside with the imprint 'London: printed for J. Baker' is probably due to the fact that Baker published the *St. James's post*. Printed in *The weekly journal* 5 Dec 1724.
'Ye fellows of Newgate, whose fingers are nice'
Reprinted in the last volume of the Pope/Swift *Miscellanies*, 1727; in later editions asterisked as not by Swift. Usually ascribed to Gay; so *Faber* xxvi, suggesting that Swift added stanzas 6 and 7. Williams discusses the evidence in detail and argues in favour of Swift's authorship, but the case is weak.
L(515.l.2/223; 1876.f.1/74).

N289 — *[idem]* Blue-skin's ballad. To the tune of Packington's pound. *[Dublin] Printed in the year 1724–5.*
½°: 1 side, 2 columns.
Printed by John Harding on the evidence of the type. If the form of the date has its usual meaning, that the broadside was printed between 1 Jan and 25 March 1725, it is later than the poem's appearance in *The weekly journal* of 5 Dec 1724, which also gave the tune as Packington's pound. This weighs against Williams's argument for Swift's authorship.
L(C.121.g.8/31),*LVA-F*,Crawford; CtY.

N290 Newmarket. 'Newmarket. A satire. *[London] Newbery.* Price 1s.' (*BM,GM* Dec 1750)
Listed in *BM, GM* under the heading 'poetry'. Possibly the imprint is dated 1751.

N291 News. News. A burlesque poem. Humbly inscribed to the hon. William Pulteney, esq; *London, printed for T. Gyles in Holborn; sold by the pamphlet-shops in London & Westminster, 1733.* (*LaM* June)
4°: *A*⁴ B⁴; *1–4* 5–14 *15–16 blk.* A1 hft.
No watermark, greyish paper.
'Hail! busy motion, of a prating world'
L(11630.c.1/7, –B4),O(–B4).

News. A burlesque poem

N292 — *[fine paper]*
Watermark: fleur-de-lys.
IU(uncut).

N293 — News from Bathgate; a poem... The first part. *[Edinburgh] Printed in the year 1718.*
8°: A–D⁸ E⁴; *1–3* 4–69 *70–71; 72 blk.* 71 err.
Two Latin poems on pp. 61–70.
'No doubt, my readers, ye have heard at last'
A satire on the opposition to Thomas Laurie's appointment as minister.
L(1368.a.25/3),O,E(3),GM.

N294 — News from Borrowstounness. A burlesque poem. By J.H. Scriblerus secundus. *Edinburgh, printed for the author; sold by most booksellers in town & country, 1745.*
8°: *A*⁴ B⁴; *1–2* 3–16.
'Come, all ye muses, and display'
E; DLC.

— News from court. A ballad, 1719. *See* 'Pope, Alexander'.

— News from Parnassus, 1721. *See* Delany, Patrick.

N295 — News from Worcester, of verses round the eight bells at St. Hellens, cast in the year 1707. *[London? 1710?]*
½°: 1 side, 2 columns.
8 couplets. Followed by 'Abel's ring of high church bells', 10 couplets.
1. Blenheim: 'First is my note, and Blenheim is my name'
1. Sacheverell: 'Mine's the first note, I sound the whig's knell'
Crum F332, for the Blenheim verses.
CtY.

Newton, *Sir* **Henry.** Henrici Newton... Epistolæ, orationes, et carmina. *Lucæ, typis Dominici Ciuffeti,* 1710.
4°: pp. 205, 115.   L,O.

— Orationes quarum altera Florentiae anno MDCCV. altera vero Genuae MDCCVII. habita est. *Amstelodami,* 1710.
4°: pp. 51.   L,O.
With poems. There are variant states of this work at O.

N296 Nick. Nick and froth or, the bites of an ale-drapier. Being a comical dialogue between the sinful publicans and their drunken customers, on raising the price of ale. *[Dublin?] Printed for J.R. in the year 1725.*
½°: 1 side, 2 columns.
'Good-morrow, Guzzle, what, to work at five?'
L(C.121.g.8/87).

Nicol, Alexander. Nature without art: or, nature's progress in poetry. Being a collection of miscellany poems. *Edinburgh, printed by P. Matthie; sold by Alexander Beck, Perth,* 1739.
8°: pp. 115.   L.

Nicol, A.

— Nature's progress in poetry, being a collection of serious poems. *Edinburgh, printed by P. Matthie; sold by Alexander Beck, Perth*, 1739.
8°: pp. 68.   L.

— The rural muse: or, a collection of miscellany poems, both comical and serious. *Edinburgh, printed for the author*, 1753.
12°: pp. xii, 146, 30, 44.   L,O; MH.

— Poems on several subjects, both comical and serious. In two parts... *Edinburgh, printed for the author, and James Stark, Dundee*, 1766.
12°: pp. xvi, 335, 130.   L,O; MH.

N296·5 [Nicoll, J.] Hodge and the devil: a tale. [*London*, 1737.]
½°: 1 side, 2 columns.
> Engraving dated 1737 cut from head of copy seen.

'All is not gold, (the proverb says)'
> Reprinted as 'By Mr. J. Nicoll' in *A collection of miscellany poems, never before publish'd*, 1737.

LSA(mutilated).

N297 Nicols, William. De literis inventis libri sex. Ad illustrissimum principem Thomam Herbertum, Pembrokiæ comitem, &c. *Londini, apud Henricum Clementem*, 1711. (*DC* 17 May)
8°: (frt+) *A*² B–L⁸ M⁸(±M2) N–Bb⁸ Cc²; *i–iv*, *1 2*–385 *386–387*; *388 blk*. 386–387 err.
> The cancel leaf M2 names contemporary peers and politicians, doubtless changed after the fall of the whig ministry in Sept 1710.

'Sæpe revolvi animo, quis primus numine plenus'
L(1473.b.3,–Cc2),O,EU(2, 1–frt, lacks A²), DrU,WcC; *CtY,NN.*

N298 — [reissue] *Londini, apud Henricum Clementem*, 1716.
> Printed cancel slip over date in imprint. E1–4 are cancelled to introduce contemporary personalities; new cancel M2 with different names. A half-share of the copyright formed part of lot 32 in the trade sale of Henry Clements, 14 March 1720 (cat. at O-JJ), purchased by Knapton.

L(237.k.3, in presentation morocco).

N299 — Περι ἀρχων libri septem. Accedunt Liturgica. *Londini, typis & impensis J. Downing*, 1717.
12°: (frt+) *A*² B–S⁶ T⁴; *i–iv*, *1*–212. 212 err.
> There is a separate title to *Liturgica* (a collection of hymns and psalms) on p. 175. The frontispiece is often bound facing p. 1.

'Dic mihi, chare puer, patri dilecte supremo'
L(11409.bb.23; 1213.b.44,–frt; 843.e.19), O(2),EtC,WcC(–frt).

Night. The night-piece, 1719. *See* Foxton, Thomas.

— Night the second. On time, death, friendship, 1742–. *See* Young, Edward (Y32–5).

Night

— Night the third. Narcissa, 1742–. *See* Young, Edward (Y36–42).

N300 — A night's ramble: or, the unfortunate gallant. A mock-heroick poem. Humbly inscrib'd to the gentleman rakes in and about London. *London printed, and sold by S. Baker*, 1717. (*PB* 27 Aug)
8°: *A*⁴ B–D⁴ E²; *i–x*, *1*–26. A1 hft.
'The dire misfortunes of a youthful swain'
LdU-B; *MnU.*

N301 Nightingale. The nightingale. A tale. *London, printed for J. Peele*, 1721. (*DP* 19 Dec)
4°: *A*² B–D²; *1–3 4*–16.
'In Italy there is a town'
> An erotic tale in which the nightingale represents the penis. According to a ms. note in the O copy (below) from the *Decameron*, 5th day, 4th tale.

L(162.1.45, Luttrell, Jan 1722),C; CLU(cropt).

N302 —— '*London, printed for J. Peele*', 1721.
4°: A–B⁴; *1–3 4*–15 *16 blk*.
> Certainly a piracy; the rough printing and shortage of capitals suggests provincial printing, possibly Scottish.

O.

N302·5 Nihell, J. La bataille de Preston. Poëme. [1746.]
4°: A–B⁴; *1–5 6*–16.
> Clearly printed in France, and written by a Frenchman; accordingly outside the scope of this catalogue, but listed as a parallel to the other French Jacobite poems which have doubtfully found a place here; see A1, C131, I67, O22, O58, O172.

'Nos vœux sont accomplis: vous brillez, heureux jour'
> Dedication signed 'J. Nihell, médecin, à Vernon en Normandie, ce 20 Decembre 1745'.

E.

N303 Nine. Nine satyrs, or moral poems. Written by a plain, right down lover of truth and honesty. [*London*] '*Printed for no body but those that have a mind to read it*', 1703.
4°: *A*² B–I⁴; *i–iv*, *1*–64.
> The copies seen have ms. errata on p. 64.

'Silvius upon me call'd, not long ago'
L(1493.m.16/1),C.

'Ninnyhammer, Nickydemus.' Homer in a nutshell, 1715. *See* Tooly, Thomas.

N304 Ninth. The ninth ode of the third book of Horace, imitated. Ben——n and G——ge. [*London?* 1719.]
slip: 1 side, 1 column.
'Whilst I was darling of your breast'
> A satirical dialogue, between George I and the surveyor-general William Benson who worked at Herenhausen.

CSmH(ms. date 1719),*MH.*

Nixon, J.

N305 Nixon, John. Merlin. A poem. Humbly inscrib'd to the right honourable George, lord Lempster. *London, printed for T. Cooper; sold by the booksellers of London & Westminster*, 1736. (*GM, LM* Feb)
2°: *A*² B²; *1–2* 3–8.
'To charm the sense with beauteous scenes of art'
O; CSmH,MH(uncut),TxU(2).

N306 — An ode to the queen. On the prospect of peace. *London, printed for J. Roberts*, 1728. (*MChr* 26 March)
2°: *A*² B²; *1–3* 4–7 *8 blk.*
'Ye bards! who in immortal lays'
L(643.m.12/38),O; MH,NNC,TxU.

N——n, J——n. A funeral elegy on...Jonathan Swift, [1745.] *See* F290.

N307 No. No peace for the wicked: or wars broke out in the city. To the tune of, Under the greenwood tree. '*Oxford*', *printed in the year* 1749.
1°: 1 side, 3 columns.
 Large engraving at head. The imprint is probably false, and London the place of publication.
'Draw near, ye sober citizens'
 A satire on Alderman Behn who proposed 'in somewhat coarse terms' the health of the Pretender at a London city feast.
L(P&D 3071),O(2); MH,NNP.

N308 — No screen! or, the masque remov'd. Containing the following remarkable particulars; I. The sublime character of his excellency somebody... II. The medalist; a new ballad... III. The statesman's mirrour... *London, printed for T. Webster*, 1742.
8°: *A*⁴ B⁴ C(3 ll); *1–5* 6–21 *22 blk.*
 C4 probably lacking from the copy seen. The second and third poems were previously published separately.
'Read, sirs, away – I teach to kill dull time –'
CtY.

N309 — [dh] No----that's a mistake. To the author of a libel, entitled, No----this is the truth. [col] *Sold by Joseph West in the Groat-market, Newcastle*, [1741.]
2°: *A*²; *1–3; 4 blk.*
'A gnome sure presided o'er thy heavy lays'
 A reply to [Edward Chicken] *No; -- this is the truth*, [1741], satirizing Walter Blackett whose candidacy he was supporting in the Newcastle election.
NeA.

N310 — No thing and no body: being a cadet's opinion of our f---es in Ger---y. By a page of honor. *London, printed for J. Huggonson*, 1743.
4°: A–B⁴ C¹; *1–2* 3–18.
 Vertical chain-lines.
'Thorough Bruges and Ghent'
L(11630.c.13/8); CtY.

No

— No; -- this is the truth, [1741.] *See* Chicken, Edward.

N311 Nobilissimo. Nobilissimo domino Roberto domino Harley, comiti Oxonii & Mortimer, summo Magnæ Britanniæ thesaurario. De Dunquerca recepta. *Londini, apud Johannem Morphew*, 1712. (16 July, Luttrell)
½°: 1 side, 1 column.
'Magne Harlæe, tibi meritum gratamur honorem'
 Signed 'J.C.' Possibly by John Colme.
ICN(Luttrell),MH.

N312 — Nobilissimo & illustrissimo Jacobo comiti de Seafield, vicecomiti de Redhaven, domino Ogilvie, de Desford, Cullon, &c. comiti hæredi de Finlator. Nunc vero summo Scotiæ cancellario. Congratulatio. [*Edinburgh*, 1705?]
½°: 1 side, 1 column.
'Nobilis en ortu, ac illustris Ogilvius heros'
 Signed 'R: C:'
TxU.

N313 Noble. The noble duellists, or, Macario's welcome to the shades. A poem. *London, printed for A. Moore; sold by the booksellers of London & Westminster*, 1730. (*MChr* July)
2°: *A*² B²; *1–2* 3–8.
'Thro' those dread realms, encompass'd round with night'
 On the death of George MacCartney, with reference to his part in the fatal duel between Charles Mohun and James Douglas, duke of Hamilton.
O.

N314 Nobody. No-body turn'd some-body; or, the fair confession of M—— D——, esq; [*Dublin*] *Printed in the year* 1725.
½°: *1–2*, 1 column.
'From a beggarly off-spring, from dunghil and dirt'
 A ms. note in the CSmH copy identifies 'No-body' as Marcus Dowley.
L(C.121.g.8/52); CSmH,OCU.

'No Body.' Canterbury tales, 1701. *See* Pittis, William.

N315 Nocturnal. The nocturnal. A l----------n in defence of the ladies. By a young gentleman of Hampsted. *London, printed for Henry Whittridge; sold by A. Dodd, & N. Blandford*, 1726. (*MC* Nov)
8°: *A*² B–D⁴ E² (C2 as 'C3'); *i–v* vi–xii, *1* 2–19 *20 blk.* A1 hft.
 Watermark: initials.
'Thou merry muse, that didst of yore'
 A lampoon on Hampstead society.
L(992.h.7/3),WgP; IU(lacks A²),KU,MH.

N316 — [fine paper]
 Watermark: Strasburg bend.
O.

Noddell, J.

Noddell, Joseph. Christ's crucifixion: I. The strait and narrow way to Heaven [*etc.*]... in poems... Also a discription...of the church of Christ... *York, printed by John White for the author; sold by Thomas Hammond junior*, 1715.
8°: pp. 191.   L.
    With some sections in prose.

N317 Noise. A noise about nothing. Or, the Marshal Villars's letter to Major General Evans. [*London*] *Printed by Rich. Newcomb*, [1711.] (29 July?)
½°: 1 side, 1 column.
'Tho' my affairs, good Master Evans'
    A satire on Villars, complaining of false reports of his capture.
MH(2, 1 with ms. date 29 July 1711).

Nomina. Nomina quorundam e primariis olim regiæ grammaticalis scholæ Buriæ Sti Edmundi... illustrata, 1719. *See* Randall, John.

Non-con. 'Non con parson a poem.' [*London*, 1746?]
    Entered to Manby & Cox in Bowyer's ledgers, possibly on 16 Sept 1746; the dates are mutilated. The price of 7s. 6d. suggests it was a half-sheet. Conceivably it is the same work as *Dissenting piety*, [1747?].

N318 Norfolk. The Norfolk congress versified. To the tune of, King John and the abbot: or, the cobler's end. *London, printed for A. Moore*, [1728.] (Dec?)
2°: *A*² < B²; *1-3* 4-8.
    Percival appendix 14; pp. 7-8 contain a prose account.
'Old stories do tell, and the scripture does shew'
    A versification of the prose *Norfolk congress*, advertised in *MChr* 19 Nov 1728; satirizing Walpole. Cf. *Quadrille to perfection*, [1728], and *A supplement to the Norfolk congress*, [1728/29].
L(11641.h.10/11),O(uncut); MH.

N319 — The Norfolk gamester: or, the art of | Managing the whole pack, | Even king, queen, and jack. *London printed, and sold by J. Dormer*, 1734. (*LM* Jan)
2°: *A*² B-D²; *1-2* 3-15 *16 blk.*
    Percival p. 87. Title adds 'Price (with the fan) one shilling and six-pence'. The fan is not present in the copies listed, but was seen in the copy sold at Sotheby's 24 July 1961, lot 340. It consists of a folding plate with fan-shaped satirical engravings printed on each side in contrasting colours.
'Ye good Christian people, I pray you draw near'
    A satire on Walpole.
L(840.m.1/22),*MR-C*; CSmH,CtY,OCU,MH, TxU(uncut)+.

— The Norfolk garland, [1728?] *See* Yonge, *Sir* William.

Norfolk

— The Norfolk poetical miscellany, 1744. *See* Cowper, Ashley.

Normanby, John Sheffield, *marquis of. See* Sheffield, John, *duke of Buckingham*.

Norris, Henry. Poems on several occasions; with a farce, call'd, The deceit. *Dublin, printed by Edwin Sandys*, 1723.
8°.   LVA-F.

— Poems upon various subjects. *Hull, printed by J. Rawson*, 1740.
8°: pp. 24.   L,YM.
    It is not certain whether this collection is by the same author as the preceding, but it seems clear that a further collection printed at Taunton 1774 (copies at L,O) is by a different and younger author.

[Norris, Isaac.] A letter from a lady to her husband, [1740.] *See* L121.

North. The north-country-wedding, and the fire, 1722. *See* Brown, Nicholas.

N320 Northamptonshire. The Northamptonshire health. *London, printed in the year* 1705.
½°: 1 side, 1 column.
    With 'The Welch health' and 'A catch on the election for Middlesex'.
'Let's remember the men, that go with us again'
    Three tory election pieces.
DG,MC,Crawford.

Northern. The northern cuckold, 1721. *See* Ward, Edward.

N321 — The Northern monster, or Scotland's nurseling. A short poem, occasion'd by the precipitate flight of the rebels... *London, printed for J. Roberts*, 1746. (*BM* May)
4°: *A*² B-C²; *i-iv, 1* 2-8.
'Rebellion, offspring of the Romish whore'
CSmH.

N322 — — [*London*] *Printed for T. Johnson, in the Strand*, [1746.]
4°: *A*²; *1* 2-4.
    Vertical chain-lines; a cheap piracy.
O.

— The northern star, 1718-. *See* Hill, Aaron.

N323 Northumberland. The Northumberland miracle; or, the widows bewitch'd: a merry tale. *London, printed for G. Spavan*, 1743. (*LDP* 26 April)
8°: *A*⁴(-A1) B-D⁴; *3-4* 5-31 *32 blk.*
    The copy seen probably lacks A1, a frontispiece as in the following.
'In popish and illit'rate times'
    On the origin of a spa well near Melfield in Northumberland.
OCU.

The **Northumberland** miracle

N324 — [*idem*] The wanton widows; or the amorous priest. A humorous tale. *London, printed for E. Burgiss, in the Strand*, [1744.] (*GM* April)
8°: *A*⁴ B–D⁴; *1–4* 5–31 *32 blk*. A1 frt.
> Though this appears to be from the same setting of type as the preceding, the title A2 is not a cancel.
> E.

— The Northumberland prophecy, 1715. *See* Duckett, George.

Norton, Frances, *Lady*. A miscellany of poems, compos'd, and work'd with a needle, on the backs and seats &c. of several chairs and stools... *Bristol, printed by W. Bonny*, 1714.
4°: pp. 39. BrP.

N325 **Nostradamus.** Nostradamus's prophecy. [*London?* 1715?]
½°: 1 side, 1 column.
'For faults and follies London's doom shall fix'
> A Jacobite prophecy.

L(1484.g.5/30).

N326 **Notable.** The notable dialogue which passed yesterday, between the D--- of N-------'s great dog (Bounce) and the famous French dog, (le chiene savant) who is shewn to the gantry [!] at Chairing-Cross,) as he was coming in at the gate to be shewn to the D----ss. [*London*] '*Printed by J. Mastiff, in the Mint*', [1713?]
½°: 1 side, 2 columns.
'Bow, wow, oh, curse my collar'
> Apparently a satire against Louis d'Aumont and the Duchess of Northumberland.
> Crawford.

N327 [**Notcutt, William.**] The history of Joseph. In verse. To which is added, the Woman of Canaan ... *Ipswich, printed by J. Bagnall*, 1736.
8°: A–K⁴; *i–iv*, 1–76.
'While the amazing deeds my soul pursues'
> One L copy is bound with sermons by Notcutt in a volume previously owned by the Notcutt family. Intended for children.

L(11633.bb.22; 11633.bb.53/1).

N328 **Nothing.** Nothing but truth. A ballad. To the tune of A beggar of all trades is the best. [*London*, 1713.]
slip: 1–2, 1 column.
'There was once a glorious q——'
> A satire against the treaty of Utrecht.

Herts CRO (Panshanger box 46); OCU.

N329 **Nottinghamshire.** The Nottinghamshire ballade, an excellent new song, being the intended speech of a famous orator. [*London?*] *Printed in the year* 1711.
½°: 1 side, 1 column.
> One would expect this to be a London publi-

The **Nottinghamshire** ballade

cation, but its bad printing and the location of one copy at E suggests the possibility of a Scottish origin.
'An orator was found in Nottinghamshire'
> A rewriting of Swift's *An excellent new song, being the intended speech of a famous orator against peace*, [1711.] That was a satire on Daniel Finch, earl of Nottingham; this is in his defence, though it is in execrable verse.

E; IU.

Nova. Nova grammatices experimenta: or, some new essays of a natural and artificial grammar, 1707. *See* Maidwell, Lewis.

N330 **Novae.** Novæ bibliothecæ S.S. Trin. Coll. Dub. descriptio, poema. In duabus partibus. Ad calcem accesserunt nonnulla varii argumenti epigrammata ...Authore ******* A.M. *Dublinii, ex typographeo R. Reilly; impensis Thomæ Thornton*, 1735.
8°: π⁴(−π1) A⁴(−A1, 2) B–C⁴ D²; *i–ii, 1–2* 3–27 *28 blk*. 1 err.
> π1, not in copies seen, was possibly a half-title.
'Naturæ ambages, physicæ spectacula scenæ'

DA,DT(lacks π4).

N331 **Now.** Now is the time. A poem. By the author of the, True born English-man. *London, printed in the year* 1706.
½°: 1 side, 2 columns.
'If M——h would curb the king of France'
> The implied attribution to Defoe is surely false; stanza 12 suggests that Defoe and Tutchin are 'idle vagabonds' who should be pressed into the queen's service. A catalogue of desirable changes in the world.

CLU-C.

N332 — Now John's come, Robin must troop. [*London*] *Printed by B. Harris in Cornhil*, [1711.]
½°: 1 side, 1 column.
> After imprint, 'Price One Penny.'
'He's come! now tory ministers avaunt'
> Ironically suggesting that Marlborough's return will mean Harley's expulsion.

LLP.

N333 — [another edition]
> After imprint, 'Price One Peny.'

OCU.

N334 **N-rw-ch.** The N-rw-ch cav-lc-de and opposition; a satire: humbly addressed to the eight hundred twenty-nine uncorrupted freemen and freeholders, by a lover of liberty. *London, printed for the author, in the year* 1741.
8°: A–B⁴ C¹; *1–3* 4–17 *18 blk*.
'When the grand p——er arriv'd in town'
> A satire on Horatio Walpole's success in the Norwich election.

L(1485.tt.35),O,NwP.

Nugae

N335 Nugae. Nugæ canoræ: or, the taste of the town, in poetry and musick. *London printed, and sold by J. Morphew,* 1709.
8°: *A*⁴ B–C⁸; [*4*] i–iv, *1–31 32 blk.* A1 hft.
'By deathless Phœbus! 'tis not to be born'
    Against the Italian opera.
MB.

[**Nugent, Robert,** *earl Nugent.*] Odes and epistles. *London, printed for R. Dodsley,* 1739. (*GM* Feb)
8°: pp. *1–68 61–71.*   L,O; IU,MH.

[—] — The second edition. *London, printed for R. Dodsley,* 1739.
8°: pp. 79.   L,O.

———

[—] An epistle to the right honourable Sir Robert Walpole, 1739. *See* E426.

N336 [—] An essay on happiness. In an epistle to the right honourable the Earl of Chesterfield. *London, printed for J. Walthoe,* 1737. (*DG* 6 March)
2°: *A*² B–E²; *1–3 4–19 20 blk.*
    Rothschild 212. Printed by Samuel Richardson (*Sale* 204).
'Thro' the wild maze of life's stil-varying plan'
    Reprinted with Nugent's name in the Dublin edition of 1738, and collected in his *Odes,* 1739. The Rothschild copy has 13 lines of ms. notes in Lord Orrery's hand on the final blank, but the suggestion made under *Rothschild* 1497 that Orrery might be the author is clearly wrong.
L(643.m.15/28),O,E,LdU-B; CSmH,CtY,ICN, MH,TxU(2)+.

N337 [—] — 'London, printed for J. Walthoe' [*Edinburgh*], 1737.
8°: A–B⁴ C²; *1–2 3–20.*
    Printed by Ruddiman on the evidence of the ornament.
GU; CSmH,ICU,IU.

N338 —— By Robert Nugent, esq; *London: printed, Dublin: re-printed by Geo. Faulkner,* 1738.
8°: A–B⁴; *1–2 3–16.*
L(1963); TxU.

[—] Honour. A poem. Inscribed to the right honble the lord Viscount Lonsdale [actually by John Brown], 1743. *See* B504.

[—] H-----ss----y to Sir C--- H---- W----s: or, the rural reflection of a Welsh poet, 1746. *See* H346.

N339 [—] An ode on Mr. Pulteney. To which is added, a new epitaph. *London, printed by S. Osborn,* 1739. (12 Feb?)
2°: *A*² < B²; *1–3 4–5 6–7; 8 blk.*
    The relationship of this and the following has not been determined. The epitaph is printed in two columns on p. 7, headed 'Translation of the Latin epitaph, published in Old Common Sense, Feb. 3. 1738.'

Nugent, R., *earl.* An ode

'Remote from liberty and truth'
    Crum R143. Early ms. attribution to Nugent in the L,MH copies; reprinted in his *Odes,* 1739.
L(162.n.68, lacks A2),O,LdU-B; InU(lacks A2), MH(ms. date 12 Feb), OCU.

N340 [—] [*variant imprint:*] *London, printed in the year* 1739.
2°: *A*² < B²; *1–3 4–5 6–7; 8 blk.*
    Possibly another impression.
CLU(lacks A2),CtY,DLC,ICN,NjP.

N341 [—] An ode, to his royal highness on his birth-day. *London, printed for R. Dodsley,* 1739. (*GM,LM* Jan)
2°: *A*² < B²; *1–3 4–7 8 blk.*
'Fitly to hail this happy day'
    Reprinted in Nugent's *Odes,* 1739. A copy of the Edinburgh reprint at DLC has an early ms. attribution 'By Da: Maloch'; Mallet was tutor to Nugent's step-son, and often suspected of having a hand in Nugent's odes. To Frederick, prince of Wales.
L(11656.r.62; 1484.m.33; 163.n.49),O,C, LdU-B,*MR-C*; CSmH,ICN,MH,OCU,TxU (uncut)+.

N342 [—] — [*Edinburgh,* 1739.]
8°: *A*²; *1 2–4.*
    Drop-head title only. The copy at DLC is bound with *The Scots magazine.*
E,EN; DLC,MH.

N343 [—] An ode to mankind: address'd to the Prince of Wales. *London, printed for R. Dodsley; sold by T. Cooper,* 1741. (*DP* 8 Jan)
2°: π¹ *A*² B–C² D¹; *i–ii, 1–3 4–13 14 blk.* π1 hft.
'Is there, or do the schoolmen dream?'
    Reprinted with Nugent's poems in *Dodsley* II; wrongly attributed to Carey in *CBEL* II. 434. Satirized in [Ashley Cowper] *High boys up go we!,* 1741.
L(840.m.1/28,−π1),O,C(−π1),LdU-B,MR; CSmH,CtY,IU,MH(−π1),TxU(3, 1 uncut, 2−π1)+.

N344 [—] — 'London, printed for R. Dodsley; sold by T. Cooper' [*Edinburgh*], 1741.
8°: *A*⁴ B²; *1–3 4–11 12 blk.*
    Printed by Ruddiman on the evidence of the ornaments.
L(1970),E,LdU-B,MP; IU.

N345 [—] An ode to the right honourable lord Viscount Lonsdale. *London, printed for R. Dodsley; sold by M. Cooper,* 1745. (*GM,LM* July)
2°: *A*² < B²; *1–2 3–7 8 blk.*
    Also listed in *GM* Nov.
'Lonsdale! thou ever-honour'd name'
    Reprinted with Nugent's poems in *Dodsley* II. Wrongly ascribed to Sir Charles Hanbury Williams in *CBEL* and elsewhere.
L(1959),O(uncut); IU,*MH*,TxU.

Nugent, R., *earl*

N346 [—] Political justice. A poem. In a letter to the right hon. the Lord ****. *London, printed for J. Walthoe*, 1736. (*GM, LM* March)
2°: *A*² B–F²; *1–3* 4–24. 24 err.
Printed by Samuel Richardson (*Sale* 184).
'While you, my lord, amidst a chosen few'
Printed with Nugent's poems in *Dodsley* II. Inscribed to Henry Hyde, viscount Cornbury, on the evidence of the following edition and of *Dodsley*.
L(1482.f.31),O(uncut),C; CSmH,CtY,InU(uncut),MH,OCU+.

N347 — [*idem*] An essay on justice. A poem. In a letter to the right hon. the lord Viscount Cornberry. *London: printed, Dublin: re-printed by Geo. Faulkner*, 1737.
8°: *A*⁴ B⁴ C²; *1–2* 3–20.
DA(uncut).

Nundinae. Nundinæ Sturbrigienses, 1709. *See* Hill, Thomas.

Nuptial. A nuptial dialogue, between a pert young lady, 1735. *See* Ward, Edward [Nuptial dialogues].

— A nuptial dialogue, between a young libertine, 1735. *See* Ward, Edward [Nuptial dialogues].

Nuptial

— Nuptial dialogues and debates, 1710–. *See* Ward, Edward.

N348 **Nuptials.** The nuptialls of the lamb. A pindarick poem. 1701.
2°: π²(π1 + 1) A–H² (B2 as 'B'); *i–vi*, 1–32.
Probably printed on the continent.
'What bright empyreal scene is this!'
The dedication to Mary of Modena, queen of James II, by the editor is signed 'W.P.'; the preface is signed, 'Thy Christian well-willer NN'. Dedication, preface and notes of the following edition are signed 'J.S.', who is clearly the author. J. Gillow, *A literary and biographical history...of the English Catholics* V. 498 enters the 1707 edition of the poem under John Sergeant; though the attribution is not impossible, it has not been confirmed.
CtY (presentation copy to Lady Widdrington from Sister Petronilla Maria Tilden).

N349 — — [*London?*] *Printed in the year* 1707.
4°: A⁴(A1 + 1) B–E⁴ F²; *i–viii*, 1–38.
The inserted leaf in A bears the dedication to Anne, duchess of Richmond and Lennox. The CU copy has gilt edges and the original stabbing, but no wrappers.
O; CU.

O

O., P. An epistle to R--- W---, 1718. *See* E408.

— The woeful treaty, 1716. *See* W539.

O., S., *L.S.* A scourge for the author of the satyr, 1725. *See* Owens, Samuel.

O1 O. O raree show, O brave show! Who see my fine pretty show; or the new raree show ballad. To a new tune, much in request... *London, printed by Edw. Midwinter,* [1713?]
2°: *A² < B¹; 1 3 3.*
> Printed on one side of the leaf, the last on the verso, resulting in a confusion between pagination and foliation. 'Enter'd in the stamp-office according to the late act of parliament', rather than printed as a half-sheet on stamped paper. Wrongly dated as 1698 and attributed to Edward Ward by Pickering & Chatto cat. 269/12528 and *Wing* W752.

'Here be de ver pretty show, as ever was seen'
> A satire on the consequences of the Peace of Utrecht.

L(11602.i.12/32); InU,NjP.

— O raree show, O pritee show, [1713.] *See* The rare show, [1713] (R124).

— 'O tempora! O mores! A very new ballad, to a very old tune, calld the Old mans wish. Written by a person, who even in his own opinion never yet writ very much to the purpose, nor very much beside it.'
> Entered in *SR* 1 May 1710 to James Read as a half-sheet; there is no record of copies having been deposited. Possibly the same work as *O tempora!* below.

O2 — O tempora! or a satyr on the times; address'd to all the patrons of the good old cause, and asserters of resistance, of what denomination soever. *Sold by the booksellers of London & Westmenster* [!], [1710?]
8°: *A⁴; 1–2 3–8.*
> Possibly the same work as the half-sheet *O tempora! O mores!* above, entered in *SR* 1 May 1710 by James Read.

'What frantick madness has possest mankind'
> A high church satire, in favour of Sacheverell.

EU; CLU-C,ICN,MH,TxU.

Oak. The oak, and the dunghill, 1728. *See* Broome, William.

Oblectamenta. Oblectamenta pia: sive sacra modulamina, 1716. *See* Southcomb, Lewis.

O Brien, Terence. Poems upon several occasions. By Mr. Terence ô Brien. *Dublin, printed in the year* 1736.
8°: pp. 48.   LVA-F; CtY.

O3 O Brien, William. An epick poem. On the renowned and never to be forgotten William Leigh...who...invented the most misterious and most beneficial arts of stocking-frame-making... And also in praise of the loyal and charitable society of stocking-frame-knitters of the city and county of Dublin, who...hath a sermon preach'd at St Audeon's Church, in Dublin, on Monday being the 30th. of October, 1727... And most humbly dedicated to the Revd. Jonathan Swift, D.D. and dean of St. Patrick's, Dublin. *Dublin, printed by S. Powell,* 1727.
½°: 2 sides, 2 columns.
> *Teerink* 1659.

'Extoll my muse, our studious founder, Leigh'
DT.

O4 Observator. The Observator's, or, commonwealth-man's pedigree and coat of arms. *London, printed in the year* 1704. (9 Nov, Luttrell)
1°: 1 side, 4 columns.
> Large emblematic woodcut above text.

'Cease, cease, proud Jac--- to make a noise'
> A high church attack on whig dissenters and John Tutchin.

MH(Luttrell).

O5 — The Observator's recantation and confession, upon the proclamation issued out against him for his apprehension, with a reward of one hundred pounds to take him. *London, printed for Tho. Wilson,* 1704.
½°: 1 side, 2 columns.
'Well, now I see a man may be mislead'
> A mock confession of John Tutchin.

LLP.

'Observator.' An elegy on the death of the late famous Doctor Titus Oates... Written by the Observator, [1705.] *See* E203.

— A letter of advice to a friend, 1704. *See* L137.

O6 Occasional. An occasional poem. *London, printed for J. Roberts,* 1727. (*MC* Feb)
2°: *A² B² C¹; 1–2 3–10.*
'Soon as bright Phœbus with revolving light'
> Dedication to Lord Townshend signed 'J.T.'
> In praise of Walpole.

L(1959),O.

O7 — An occasional poem, upon the meeting of the Loyal Society, on the second of November; being the anniversary birthday of Edward Colston, esq; Written at Bristol, in the year 1711. [*Bristol,* 1711.]
4°: *A²; 1 2–4.*
> Probably printed by William Bonny.

'Since none have dar'd on this great theam to raise'
> In praise of Edward Colston.

BrP(2).

Occasional

— Occasional poems, very seasonable and proper for the present times, on the six following subjects: viz. I. Masquerades... *London printed, and sold by Joseph Downing,* 1726.
8°: pp. 31.   L; CtY.

— An occasional satyr, 1725. *See* Hatton, Henry Charles.

O8 Occasioned. Occasion'd by the lamentable death of the Lady Pryce, second wife of Sir John Pryce of Newtown-Hall in Montgomery-shire, bart. *London, printed by Henry Woodfall,* 1740.
4°: π¹ A² B–F⁴ G⁴(–G1); *i–ii* iii–v *vi blk, 1* 2–45 *46 blk.*
'Descend my muse, among the tuneful throng'
L(1485.r.18).

Ocean. Ocean. An ode, 1728–. *See* Young, Edward.

O9 'O Connor, Murroghoh.' A pastoral in imitation of the first eclogue of Virgil: inscrib'd to the provost, fellows, and scholars, of Trinity College, Dublin; by Murroghoh O Connor of Aughana-graun. *Dublin, printed by James Carson,* 1719.
4°: *A*⁴ B²; *1–3* 4–11 *12 blk.*
'My old acquaintance, and my dearest friend'
    'Murroghoh O Connor' is one of the participants in the pastoral, and is probably a pseudonym; the name is not found in the lists of T.C.D. A copy of O13, now at L, has a contemporary note that he 'pawn'd his College-Order, for a Reackoning, as he returned to Kerry & it was found in the Inn by Pierce Crosby Esqr.', but this is not necessarily inconsistent with an assumed name.
CLU-C.

O10 — — *Printed at Dublin; and reprinted at London for W. Boreham,* 1719.
8°: *A*⁴ B⁴ *C*²; *1–4* 5–17 *18–20 blk.* A1 hft.
O.

O11 — Poems, pastorals, and dialogues. I. A pastoral in imitation of the first eclogue of Virgil... II. Two facetious dialogues... III. A description of the county of Kerry... By Morgan O'Conner. *Dublin, printed by S. Powell, for J. Thompson,* 1726.
8°: A–C⁴; *i–ii, 1* 2–22. 22 err.
Dialogue 1: 'Tell me dear Owen what surprize of late'
Dialogue 2: 'Since we have shun'd the hurry of the court'
Kerry: 'Sure there are poets who never did dream'
    The last poem appears to be an imitation of Denham's *Coopers Hill.*
O,DK,DT,LdU-B.

O12 — — *Dublin, printed by E. Jones, for James Kelburn,* 1739.
12°: A–B⁶; *i–ii, 1* 2–22.
    The author's name reverts here to the form 'Murroghoh O Connor'.
L(C.71.bb.15/7),DN.

'O Connor, M.'

O13 — The petition of Morrough O Connor to the provost and senior fellows of Trinity College, near Dublin. To which are added, I. An eclogue, in imitation of the first eclogue of Virgil... II. Two dialogues... III. The county of Kerry. A poem. *Dublin, printed for the author,* 1740.
8°: A–C⁴ D²; *1–2* 3–28.
'Most learned and reverend, with humblest submission'
L(1970),DA(3),DG,DN.

October. October; a poem, 1717. *See* Churchill, William.

O14 Oculist. The oculist. A poem address'd to Sir William Read, knt. her majesties oculist in ordinary. *London printed, and sold by A. Baldwin,* 1705.
4°: A–C²; *1–2* 3–12.
'As the great founder, when he built his vast'
L(841.b.84/3).

Oculus. Oculus Britanniæ: an heroi-panegyrical poem on the university of Oxford, 1724. *See* Amhurst, Nicholas.

Odae. Odæ aliquot celebriores anglicanæ: latine redditæ, 1733. *See* Hay, Robert.

O15 Oddity. The oddity: a poem. Of near 250 lines in one continued rhyme. Being a letter from a sailor to his sweetheart. *London, printed for T. Robins,* 1740. (*GM, LM* Dec)
4°: *A*² B–C²; *1–2* 3–12.
'The great reputation/You have in this nation'
    Signed 'Frank Hopewell'.
L(11630.e.14/9),LdU-B; CtY,IU,*MH*,NNC.

O16 — — *Dublin, printed by James Carson,* ⟨1740/41.⟩
4°: *A*² B–C²; *1–2* 3–11 *12 blk.*
DA(date cut from title).

O17 Ode. Ode. [Carminum præses...] [*Oxford,* 1706?]
½°: 1 side, 1 column.
'Carminum præses citharæque Clio'
    In honour of the University of Frankfurt's jubilee.
O,Chatsworth,Herts CRO(Panshanger box 46).

— Ode [Ormond's glory...], [1702/03.] *See* Smith, Edmund.

O18 — Ode ad clarissimum virum Archibaldum Pitcarnium D.M. [*Edinburgh,* 1710?/13.]
½°: 1 side, 1 column.
'Vive, Pitcarni, columen camænis'
TxU.

— Ode ad honorabilem Thomam Parkyns, baro-nettum, 1724. *See* Bennison, J.

— Ode ad insignissimum virum, Matthæum Frampton, 1724. *See* Hannes, William.

O19 — [dh] An ode, address'd to all the freemen and freeholders of the city of Dublin. [*Dublin,* 1739?]

An **ode**, address'd to all the freemen

    4°: *A²*; *1* 2–4.
        Dated 1739 by DA.
    'How long must ye be deaf and blind?'
    DA.

O20 — An ode, addressed to his royal highness William duke of Cumberland. By a lady. [*Edinburgh?* 1746?]
    ½°: 1 side, 1 column.
        See *Gaskell, Foulis* 114.
    'Rejoice, brave prince! Perfection pure'
        Asking mercy for the Jacobite rebels.
    L(11602.i.5/6),E.

— An ode addressed to the author of the Conquered duchess, 1746. *See* Williams, *Sir* Charles Hanbury.

O21 — Ode after the manner of the first of Horace. Inscrib'd to the right honourable Horatio Walpole esq; *London, printed for T. Wooton*, 1732. (*GM* Oct)
    2°: A(3 ll); *1–3* 4–5 6 *blk*.
        A2 is signed.
    'Oh thou! who from an ancient race'
    TxU,*Lewis Walpole Library.*

O22 — Ode au prince conquerant d'Ecosse. '*A Edimbourg*', 1745.
    4°: *A⁴*; *1–2* 3–8.
        Almost certainly a piece of French printing.
    'Descens de la voute éthérée'
    E.

O23 — [dh] An ode compos'd in the year M.DCCXX. on the birth of a great prince. [*London?* 174–?]
    4°: *A²*; *1* 2–4.
        Dated by L as [*London*, 1721], but that copy
        is bound with pamphlets of 1747 to 1751.
    'Wrapt in one common wish three nations lay'
        On the birth of the Young Pretender.
    L(840.k.4/7),E,MP.

— Ode for musick, 1713–. *See* Pope, Alexander.

O24 — [dh] An ode for St. Cæcillia's day. Sett by Mr. Roseingrave. [*Dublin?* 1702/14.]
    2°: *A²*; *1–3; 4 blk.*
    'You, who can musick's charms inspire'
        Presumably set by Daniel Roseingrave, organist of St. Patrick's cathedral, Dublin.
    DG(2),MC.

— Ode for the thanksgiving day, 1706. *See* Walsh, William.

O25 — An ode for the thanksgiving day. To the tune of Derry down. By Titus Antigallicus, esq; *London, printed for W. Webb junior*, 1749. (*BM* April)
    2°: *A²* < B²; *1–3* 4–8.
    'Ye brave Britons all to my ditty attend'
        An attack on the peace of 1749.
    CLU-C(uncut),DFo,MH.

O26 — [dh] An ode for the thanksgiving day. By Titus Antigallicus, esq;... [*Edinburgh?* 1749.]
    8°: *A²*; *1–4.*
        Clearly a piracy, and probably from Edinburgh from the location of one copy. The

An **ode** for the thanksgiving day

    format is uncertain; possibly a quarto with vertical chain-lines.
    L(11633.bbb.53),O,E.

— An ode from the E---- of B---- to ambition, [1746.] *See* Williams, *Sir* Charles Hanbury.

O27 — An ode. Humbly inscribed to his grace Charles duke of Grafton lord lieutenant of Ireland, on his going for England. [*Dublin*, 1721/24.]
    4°: *A²*; *1–4.*
    'Thou azure god, that dost the trident guide'
    DG; DLC.

O28 — An ode humbly inscrib'd to his grace the lord archbishop of Canterbury on his majesty's happy accession. *London, printed for Bernard Lintott*, 1715 [1714]. (*MC* Dec)
    2°: *A²* B¹; *1–2* 3–6.
    'Thy long neglected voice, sweet Clio, raise'
        To Thomas Tenison.
    MH.

— An ode, humbly inscrib'd to his royal highness the Prince of Orange, 1733. *See* Barrett, M. & Rayner, W.

O29 — An ode, humbly inscribed to the honourable William Con—ly esq; [*Dublin*, 1724?]
    ½°: 1 side, 1 column.
    'A well dispos'd and virtuous heart'
        A satire on William Conolly's efforts in defence of Wood's halfpence.
    L(C.121.g.8/121).

O30 — An ode humbly inscribed to the king. *London, printed by W. Wilkins, for J. Peele*, 1723. (May, Luttrell)
    2°: *A²* B² C¹; *1–3* 4–9 10 *blk*.
    'When numerous prodigies prevail'
    OCU(Luttrell),TxU.

— An ode, humbly inscrib'd to the queen, 1706. *See* Prior, Matthew.

O31 — An ode. Humbly inscribed to the right reverend John, lord bishop of London. *London, printed for R. Gosling*, 1714. (*PB* 29 April)
    8°: *A²* B–C⁴ D²ㅤ(C as 'B'); *i–ii*, *1–2* 3–22. A1 hft.
    'Tho' long in rural shades retir'd'
        Inscribed to John Robinson.
    O,CT; InU.

— An ode, imitated from ode XI. book 2d. of Horace, 1745. *See* Pulteney, William, *earl of Bath.*

O32 — An ode, in honour of his majesty's birth-day. Performed at the Grandfestino room in Aungier-street, on the 31st of October 1748. Set to musick, by John Frederick Lampe... *Dublin, printed by Oli. Nelson*, 1748.
    4°: B–C² (B2 as 'B'); *1–3* 4–7 8 *blk*.
    'When the first sparks, at the creator's call'
    DT.

[**O33** = C56·7] — An ode. In imitation of the third ode of the third book of Horace, [1732.] *See* Carthy, Charles.

An **ode** in praise of musick

O34 — An ode in praise of musick. Composed by Mr Charles King, in five parts, for the degree of Batchelour of Musick, perform'd at the theatre in Oxford, on Friday the 11th of July, 1707. [*Oxford?* 1707.]
½°: 2 sides, 1 column.
'Musick soft charm of heav'n and earth'
   Presumably only the music is by King. Printed in *Nichols, Collection* IV. 64–6 as 'possibly written by Mr. Smith', i.e. Edmund Smith.
LG,OW,MC,Crawford.

— An ode inscribed to the memory of the late Earl of Orford, [1745?] *See* Newcomb, Thomas.

— An ode inscribed to the right honourable the Earl of Sunderland, 1720. *See* Tickell, Thomas.

— An ode, inscribed to the Royal Company of Archers, 1734. *See* Boyse, Samuel.

O35 — An ode, most humbly inscrib'd to his royal highness, the Prince of Wales, on his birth-day, Saturday, January 20th, 1738–9. *London, printed for J. Brindley; sold by Mrs. Dodd, and by the booksellers,* 1739.
2°: *A*² *B*²; *1–3* 4–8.
'Descend Polymnia! and sing'
C,LdU-B; CSmH,OCU.

— An ode. Occasion'd by rejecting the proposal, 1732. *See* Vaughan, John.

O36 — An ode occasion'd by some late successes at sea. Imitated from Horace. *London, printed for M. Cooper,* 1747. (*GM, LM* Aug)
2°: *A*⁴; *1–2* 3–7 *8 blk.*
   With the Latin text of Horace's book I, ode 15.
'Thames, when of late his swelling tide'
L(1474.d.5); CSmH(uncut).

O37 — An ode occasion'd by the battle of Rammelies. By Mr. B——y. [*London,* 1706.] (23 July, Luttrell)
½°: 1 side, 1 column.
   Copies at DG, ICN read 'recorded pillars' for 'recording pillars' in line 2. Advertised in *DC* 24 July.
'How will the grateful senate praise!'
DG; ICN(Luttrell),TxU.

— An ode on a distant prospect of Eton College, 1747. *See* Gray, Thomas.

— An ode on beauty, 1749. *See* Cooke, Thomas.

— An ode on Christmas day. By R.S. gent., 1716. *See* Samber, Robert.

[**O38 = S367**] — An ode on his majesty's happy arrival, 1720. *See* Sewell, George.

O39 — An ode on his majesty's return. *London, printed for J. Tonson,* 1720 [1719]. (*DC* 23 Nov)
½°: 1–2, 1 column.
'Safety attend the ship that brings'
ICN(Luttrell, Nov 1719).

— An ode on martial virtue, 1750. *See* Cooke, Thomas.

An **ode** on Mr. Pulteney

— An ode on Mr. Pulteney, 1739. *See* Nugent, Robert, *earl Nugent.*

— An ode on Saint Cæcilia's day, 1749. *See* Thornton, Bonnell.

O39·5 — 'An ode on Sir Robert Walpole's being created earl of Orford. [*London*] *Printed for T. Fullum.* Price 6*d*.' (*LM* March 1742)

O40 — 'An ode on the birth of the young prince. [*London*] *Printed for J. Roberts.* Price 3*d*.' (*PM* 10 Dec 1717)

O41 — An ode on the birthday of his royal highness the Duke of Cumberland. [*Edinburgh?*] *Printed in the year* 1747.
8°: *A*⁴; *1–2* 3–8.
   The printer's ornaments are of Edinburgh origin.
'Ye powers of song, my voice inspire'
MR-C; CtY,OCU.

O42 — An ode on the birth-day of his royal highness William duke of Cumberland. [*Edinburgh?* 1746.]
½°: 1 side, 2 columns.
'Of old, in April, martial Rome'
L(C.115.i.3/85).

— An ode on the coronation, 1727. *See* Watts, Isaac.

O43 — An ode on the death of King William III. *London, printed for John Nutt,* 1702. (13 March, Luttrell)
2°: *A*² *B*–*D*²; *i–ii,* 1–14.
   In the TxU copy B1 is signed 'A'.
'Great William, to the shades of death confin'd?'
LdU-B; ICN(Luttrell),IU,TxU.

O44 — An ode on the death of the late King James. Written originally in French at St. Germains... And now translated into English with very little alteration. [*London*] *Printed by D. Edwards; sold by the booksellers of London & Westminster,* 1701. (9 Oct, Luttrell)
2°: *A*² *B*–*D*²; *i–ii,* 1–14.
   The Luttrell copy was formerly in the possession of C. H. Wilkinson.
'My muse, let sacred truth be now thy guide'
E,AdU; CLU-C,NN,OCU.

O45 —— The second edition. [*London*] *Printed by D. Edwards; sold by the booksellers of London & Westminster,* 1701.
2°: *A*² *B*–*D*²; *i–ii,* 1–14.
   Apparently a reimpression, at least in part.
O,BaP; CtY,MH(uncut),NjP.

O46 — An ode on the Duke of Marlborough. *London, printed for Egbert Sanger,* 1706. (*PM* 1 June)
½°: 1–2, 1 column.
'What pow'r of words can equal thy renown'
DG,MC.

— An ode on the general conflagration, 1725. *See* Newcomb, Thomas.

An **ode** on the happy marriage

An **ode**: or elegy

O47 — An ode on the happy marriage of the learned and reverend Philip David Kræuter, D.D.... with Miss Eliz. Spellerberg... Composed and humbly exhibited by J.J.B. *London, printed by J. Haberkorn & J. Gussen, in Gerrard Street St. Ann's Westminster*, 1749.
4º: *A⁴*; *1–8*.
'Untaught and artless muse arise'
CtY.

— An ode on the incarnation, 1709. *See* Hughes, Jabez.

O48 — Ode on the incarnation of our lord and saviour Jesus Christ. By Theosebes. *London, printed for M. Cooper*, 1744. (*GM, LM* Jan)
4º: *A¹*[= C1] B⁴ C⁴(–C1); *i–ii, 1–13 14 blk.*
Vertical chain-lines.
'Awake, my song; and leave below'
L(1465.i.12/1); MH.

O49 — An ode on the marriage of his grace the Duke of Portland and the right honourable Lady Margaret Harley. *London, printed in the year* 1734.
4º: A⁴(–A4); *1–3 4–6.*
A4, possibly blank, missing from the copy seen.
'Leader of the nuptial band'
L(840.l.10/11).

O50 — 'An ode on the peace, inscribed to the hon. Sir Thomas Robinson, knight of the Bath, and second plenipotentiary at Aix-la-Chapelle. [*London*]*Corbett*. Price 6*d*.' (*BM, GM* Dec 1748)

— An ode on the present war with Spain, 1740. *See* Carthy, Charles.

O51 — An ode on the queen's birth-day, for the year, 170⁶⁄₇. Set by Mr. Ximenes, and performed at the castle of Dublin. *Dublin, printed by Edw. Sandys*, 1706 [1706/7].
½º: 1 side, 1 column.
'Hail happy day,/When thy beams thou dost display'
MH.

O52 — An ode on the success of his royal highness, the Duke of Cumberland. *London, printed for M. Cooper*, 1746. (*GA* 24 Feb)
2º: *A² B–C²; 1–2 3–11 12 blk.*
What is apparently the same poem is also listed in *GM, LM* May 1746.
'What generous warrior of distinguish'd fame?'
O; MiU,PU.

— An ode on the times, [1738.] *See* Sterling, James.

— An ode on the victory at Gladsmuir, [1745?] *See* Hamilton, William, *of Bangour*.

O53 — An ode: or elegy on the death of James the second, late king of England. Who departed this life at St. Germans, in France, on Wednesday the fourth of September, 1701. In the sixty seventh year of his age, 11 months., and a [!] 11 days. Written by J.M. gent. *London, printed for Robert Williams, near the Temple*, 1701.

1º: 1 side, 2 columns.
Mourning headpiece and borders.
'See how the wrangling world in fumes arise'
L(C.20.f.2/216).

O54 — An ode, perform'd on St. Cecilia's day, 1717. Set to musick by Mr. William Babel, and now perform'd in the new theatre in Lincoln's-Inn Fields. And a mad dialogue... *London, printed for Jonas Browne*, 1718.
4º: *A⁴ B⁴; i–iv, 1 2–11 12 blk.* A1 hft.
'Hail! great Cecilia! Hail, hail! patroness divine!'
Dialogue: 'Behold the man! that with gigantick might'
L(11631.bb.11).

O55 — An ode pindarick on Barbadoes. [*London?* 1702/14.]
½º: 2 sides, 1 column.
Although the text implies that the ode was performed in the Barbadoes, the use of a press-figure † on side 2 suggests a London printing.
'No more, great rulers of the sky, ye awful pow'rs, no more'
L(C.38.1.6/26).

— An ode, presented to his royal highness the Duke of Cumberland, 1746. *See* Newcomb, Thomas.

— An ode presented to the king, 1714. *See* Hinchliffe, William.

— 'An ode sacred to the memory of Dr. Francis Atterbury. With his picture. Written by a very near relation.'
Listed by *Straus, Curll* 300 from a Curll catalogue of 1735; the poem has not been traced, and the title may be generalized.

— An ode sacred to the memory of her grace Anne dutchess of Hamilton, [1724.] *See* Ramsay, Allan.

— An ode sacred to the memory of her late majesty, 1737. *See* Tomlinson, Matthew.

O56 — An ode sacred to the victorious return of his royal highness the Duke of Cumberland, from Scotland. *London, printed for M. Cooper*, [1746.] (*BM* July)
4º: A⁴ B²; *1–3 4–12.*
'Detesting flatt'ry's venal strain'
KU.

O57 — An ode, set to musick, and sung at the sheriffs-feast, before the nobility and gentry, by Mr. Hughes and Mr. Leveridge, at Merchant-Taylors-hall, March the 25th, 1712. [*London*] *Printed in the year* 1712.
½º: 1 side, 1 column.
'Descend Urania, haste descend'
MH.

— Ode sur la rébellion de MDCCXLV. en Ecosse, 1746. *See* Maty, Matthew.

O58 — [dh] Ode sur l'entreprise du Prince de Galles. [1745.]

Ode sur l'entreprise du Prince

4°: *A*²; *1–3 4 blk.*
    Probably printed in France.
'Où va cet aigle magnanime?'
E,*AdU*.

O59 — An ode, to Alexander Robertson of Strowan, esq; [*Edinburgh*, 173–?]
8°: *A*²; *1–2* 3–4.
    Title in half-title form.
'Mirror of wit! Mirror of loyalty!'
CSmH,CtY.

[O60 = S411·5] — An ode, to be perform'd at the castle in Dublin, on the 1st. of March 1729–30. Being the birth-day, 1730. *See* Sheridan, Thomas.

O61 — An ode, to be performed at the castle of Dublin, on the first of March, being the birth-day of... Queen Caroline... Set to musick by Mr. Matthew Dubourg... *Dublin, printed by S. Powell, for George Ewing*, 1732–3.
4°: *A*⁴; *1–3* 4–7 *8 blk.*
'Thou virgin, heav'nly train, descend and sing'
DN.

— An ode, to be performed at the castle of Dublin, on the 1st. of March, 1736. *See* Shepherd, Samuel.

O62 — An ode, to be performed at the castle of Dublin, on the 30th of October 1730. being the birth-day of...George II... Set to musick by Mr. Matthew Dubourg... *Dublin, printed by S. Powell, for George Ewing*, 1730.
4°: *A–B*²; *1–3* 4–7 *8 blk.*
'Guardian of our happy isle'
DLC.

O63 — An ode to be performed at the castle of Dublin, on the 30th of October, 1740, being the birth-day of...George II... Set to musick by Mr. Matthew Dubourg... *Dublin, printed by James Carson, for George Ewing*, 1740.
4°: A⁴; *1–2* 3–7 *8 blk.*
'Aurora quits her ouzy bed'
OW.

O64 — An ode to be performed at the castle of Dublin, on the 30th of October, being the birth-day of... George II... Set to musick by Mr. Matthew Dubourg...*Dublin, printed for George & Alexander Ewing*, 1746.
4°: A⁴; *1–3* 4–7 *8 blk.*
    A⁴ is composed of two half-sheets, one within the other, on the evidence of the watermarks.
'Ye hours that with the circling sun'
C.

O65 — An ode to evening. Translated into Latin verse. *London, printed for W. Owen*, 1749. (*BM, GM* April)
2°: (3 ll); *1* 2–5 *6 blk.*
    Both copies seen have apparently been cut down from folio to quarto size. Latin text on rectos, English on versos.
'Salve nympha oculos molles dejecta, humerosque'
    The English text is by Joseph Warton, pub-

lished in his *Odes*, 1746; presumably the Latin text is by another hand.
L(T·13*/5); CtY.

— An ode to Garrick, 1749. *See* Moore, Edward.

— An ode to his grace the Duke of Newcastle, 1732. *See* Newcomb, Thomas.

— An ode to his grace the Duke of Richmond: occasion'd by his being elected governor, [1720.] *See* Newcomb, Thomas.

— An ode to his grace the Duke of Richmond: occasion'd by some fine Italian paintings, 1735. *See* Newcomb, Thomas.

O66 — An ode to his royal highness, Charles, prince regent, &c. After the battle of Gladsmuir. [*Edinburgh*?] *Printed in the year* 1745.
8°: *A*²; *1–2* 3–4.
'Thy deeds are such, illustrious youth!'
E.

— An ode, to his royal highness on his birth-day, 1739. *See* Nugent, Robert, *earl Nugent*.

— An ode to mankind, 1741. *See* Nugent, Robert, *earl Nugent*.

— An ode to Mira, 1730. *See* King, William, *principal of St. Mary Hall*.

— An ode to Mr. Ellis, [1737/8.] *See* Newcomb, Thomas.

— An ode to Mr. G--r--k, 1749. *See* Moore, Edward.

O67 — An ode, to Mr. Handel. *London, printed for R. Dodsley*, 1745. (*GM, LM* May)
4°: *A*⁴ B⁴; *1–7* 8–16. A1 hft.
'While you, great author of the sacred song'
L(11630.c.4/18; 11630.c.6/2),O(uncut),*LdU-B*; MH(uncut),TxU.

— An ode to Mr. Tickell, [1720.] *See* Sewell, George.

— An ode to the creator of the world, 1713. *See* Hughes, John.

O68 — An ode to the Duke of Argyll. To which is added, one to the Earl of Marchmont. *London, printed for T. Cooper*, 1740. (*GM,LM* Dec)
2°: *A*⁴; *1–2* 3–8.
'Attend, O Cambel! nor refuse'
'Restrain thy tears! the pious son'
    Ascribed to Sir Charles Hanbury Williams in *CBEL* and *Halkett & Laing*, but not the 'Ode to the Duke of Argyll' printed in his *Works*, 1822.
O; CSmH(uncut),InU,MH,TxU(2, 1 uncut).

— An ode to the Earl of Chesterfield, 1737. *See* Hyde, Henry, *viscount Cornbury*.

O69 — An ode to the grand Khaibar. *London printed, and sold by J. Roberts*, 1726 [1725]. (*MC* Nov)
2°: *A*² B–C²; *i–ii, 1–9 10 blk.*

An **ode** to the grand Khaibar

'Some say their sires, the first made man'
A satire on masonry.
OA.

— An ode to the honourable H---y F--x, 1746.
See Williams, *Sir* Charles Hanbury.

— An ode to the hon. Philip Y--ke, esq; 1747. *See*
Jenyns, Soame.

O70 — An ode to the inhabitants of Great-Britain; in
imitation of Horace, book III. ode VI. *London,
printed for W. Owen*, 1747. (*GM, LM* June)
2°: *A*² B–C²; *1–4 5–11 12 blk*. A1 hft.
'What madness, Britons, to suppose'
Not to be confused with 'An ode to the people
of Great Britain. In imitation of the sixth ode of
the third book of Horace' by Robert Lowth,
originally published in Dodsley's *Museum* for
24 May 1746 (cf. *GM* 57 (1787) 1123f). As
reprinted in his *Sermons* (1834) 472, that has
a quite different text.
L(11631.h.6),E.

O71 — 'An ode to the late lord Viscount Townshend
on his retirement from court. [*London*] *Printed for
E. Cave*. Price 4*d*.' (*GM* July 1738)
Perhaps a reissue of a poem published on Lord
Townshend's retirement in 1730; he died 21
June 1738. Possibly the title is generalized.

— An ode to the most honourable the lord high-
treasurer, 1713. *See* Castleton, Nathaniel.

— An ode to the Pretender, 1713. *See* Reynardson,
Francis.

O72 — An ode to the queen, on the death of his royal
highness George, hereditary prince of Denmark,
&c... *London, printed by J.L.* [*John Leake?*] *for
John Morphew*, 1708. (17 Nov, Luttrell)
2°: *A*² B¹; *1–2 3–6*.
'Harmonious maid, whose tuneful ear'
Possibly the poem 'To the queen on the death
of his royal highness Prince George of Denmark' attributed to Joseph Trapp by *Rawlinson*; but there is no evidence that his poem was
separately published – the others listed with it
have not been identified.
O; CSmH,InU(Luttrell).

— An ode to the queen. On the happy accession,
1727. *See* Newcomb, Thomas.

O73 — Ode to the right honourable Anne countess of
Northesk. [*Edinburgh?* 1748.]
¼°: 1 side, 1 column.
'In vain did bounteous heaven bestow'
On her marriage.
CSmH.

— An ode to the right honourable lord viscount
Lonsdale, 1745. *See* Nugent, Robert, *earl Nugent*.

O74 — 'An ode to the right honourable Sir Peter
Warren, knight of the bath, occasioned by the late
signal successes of the British navy. [*London*] Kent.
Price 6*d*.' (*BM* Dec 1747; *GM* Jan 1748)

An **ode** to the right honourable

— An ode to the right honourable the Earl of
Cadogan, 1719. *See* Smedley, Jonathan.

— An ode to the right honourable the E----l of
O--------d, 1742. *See* Newcomb, Thomas.

— An ode to the sun, for the new-year, 1707. *See*
Fenton, Elijah.

O75 — An ode upon that execrable club of miscreants,
call'd the Blasters, in which their grand oracle,
lately arrived, is introduced as speaking in person
to his disciples... [*Dublin*, 1738?]
½°: 1 side, 2 columns.
The Rothschild copy is bound in a collection
of Lord Orrery's, with pieces of 1738.
'Hence all ye poor weak-minded fools'
Rothschild.

O76 — An ode upon the times. Humbly inscrib'd to
William Sloper, esq; member of parliament.
London printed, and sold by J. Roberts, 1720. (*DC*
19 Nov)
2°: (3 ll); *i–ii, 1 2–3 4 blk*.
'When Europe's peace was basely bought and sold'
InU(Luttrell, Dec),TxU.

— An ode, with a pastoral recitative, [1720.] *See*
Ramsay, Allan.

O77 **Ode-maker.** The ode-maker. A burlesque on the
Dean of Kil---a's Ode to the right honourable the
Earl of Ca----------n. *London, printed for T.
Warner*, 1719. (*DC* 2 April)
2°: A–B²; *1–3 4–8*.
Rothschild 2215; *Teerink* 1090; *Williams* 1100.
'Well! Sm-----y, since thou wilt expose'
A burlesque on Smedley's *Ode to the...Earl of
Cadogan*, 1719, regularly printed with that
ode, even in Smedley's own *Poems*, 1721, etc.
John Nichols (in his edition of Welsted)
suggested this was 'by one of the Irish wits
(probably Dr. Delany)'; but since it actually
satirizes Swift more than Smedley it may
conceivably be Smedley's own.
O; MH,TxU.

O78 —— *London, printed, and re-printed in Dublin*,
1719.
8°: *A*⁴ B⁴; *1–3 4–14 15–16 blk*.
Rothschild 2216.
DN; ICU,IU(–B4).

[**Odell, Thomas.**] Characters: an epistle to
Alexander Pope, esq; and Mr. Whitehead, 1739.
See C129.

[—] The London address: or, magistrates against
the muses, 1730. *See* L235.

O79 — An ode sacred to the nuptials of their highnesses
the Prince and Princess of Orange and Nassau, &c.
&c. *London, printed by J. Hughs; sold at most
pamphlet-shops*, 1733.
2°: *A*² B²; *1–2 3–8*.
'Nuptial joys the song inspire'
L(840.m.1/29; 162.n.16); CtY,ICN,NjP.

Odell, T.

O80 — An ode sacred to the nuptials of their royal highnesses the Prince and Princess of Wales. *Westminster, printed for Messieurs Fox, at the Half-moon and seven stars in Westminster-Hall*, 1736. (*GM,LM* April)
2°: *A*² B²; *1–3* 4–8.
'Strike, strike the lyre, the nuptial morn'
InU.

O81 —— *London. Printed, and reprinted in Dublin by Sylvanus Pepyat*, 1736.
4°: *A*⁴; *1–8*.
DA.

Odes. Odes and epistles, 1739. *See* Nugent, Robert, *earl Nugent.*

— 'Odes by a lady, inscribed to the Duke of Cumberland'. [*Glasgow, Foulis,* 1748?]
4°.
Advertised in Foulis books of 1748; see *Gaskell, Foulis* 114. A number of separate poems have been seen which might well have been collected under this title.

— The odes, epodes, and Carmen seculare of Horace, in Latin and English, 1713–. *See* Oldisworth, William.

— Odes on several subjects, 1745. *See* Akenside, Mark.

— Odes on various subjects, humbly address'd to the right honourable the Lord Walpole... By a gentleman of the Inner-Temple. *London printed, and sold by J. Roberts,* 1741 [1742?]. (*GM* Jan 1742)
4°: pp. 43.   IU.

'O Donald, Peregrine.' The toast, 1732–. *See* King, William, *principal of St. Mary Hall.*

Œconomy. *See* Economy.

Of. Of active and retired life, 1735. *See* Melmoth, William.

— Of business and retirement, '1635' [1735]. *See* Manning, Francis.

O82 — Of good nature. An epistle humbly inscrib'd to his g--ce the D-ke of C---s. *London, printed by J. Hughs, for T. Dormer,* 1732. (*GSJ* 22 Jan)
4°: *A*⁴ B⁴; *1–5* 6–15 *16 blk.* A1 hft.
'Accept, my lord, the tribute which I bring'
Ascribed in a well-annotated copy of *The Norfolk poetical miscellany,* 1744, at L to 'Dr: C—r'; in the context this is almost certainly Spencer Cowper, dean of Durham, though the Rev. John Cowper has also been suggested. To James Brydges, duke of Chandos, in answer to Pope's supposed attack on him as 'Timon' in *Of false taste,* 1732.
LVA-F,E,DK,*MR-C*; CSmH(uncut).

— Of legacy-hunting, 1737. *See* Ogle, George.

— Of levity and steadiness, 1735. *See* Manning, Francis.

O83 — Of modern wit. An epistle to the right honourable Sir William Young. *London, printed for Henry Lintot,* 1732. (*GSJ* 9 March)
2°: *A*² B² C¹; *1–2* 3–10.
'If Pope his muse to Burlington shou'd raise'
L(11631.k.4),O; CSmH,DFo,MH,OCU,TxU+.

— Of politeness, 1738. *See* Miller, James.

O84 — Of power. A moral poem. *London, printed for H. Lintot,* 1735. (*GM* March)
2°: *A*¹ B–E² F¹; *i–ii, 1* 2–18.
Printed by Samuel Richardson (*Sale* 159).
'Inform me, reason, what the cause may be'
O; CtY(uncut).

O85 — Of publick good. An epistle to the right honourable John earl of Stair. *London, printed for J. Wilford,* 1733. (*GSJ* 10 May)
4°: A–D²; *1–3* 4–16.
'Why those disputes about the publick good?'
DG,*MR*; CtY.

O86 —— 'London, printed for J. Wilford' [*Edinburgh*], 1733.
8°: A⁴ B²; *1–2* 3–12.
Printed by R. Fleming on the evidence of the ornaments.
L(1961); TxU.

— Of smoking. Four poems in praise of tobacco, 1736. *See* Browne, Isaac Hawkins (B524).

O87 — Of superstition: an epistle to a friend. *London, printed for J. Wilford,* 1734. (*LM* Oct)
4°: *A*² B–D² E¹; *1–3* 4–18.
'My friend! what can we do? with stubborn will'
L(1465.i.12/11, lacks E1); CtY,OCU.

O88 — Of the characters of men. An epistle to Ralph Allen, esq; *London, printed for M. Cooper,* 1750.
4°: A⁴(±A1) B–D⁴; *1–3* 4–32.
Vertical chain-lines. The title-leaf is found with chain-lines in alternative positions, but almost certainly is always a cancel.
'Oh! thou to shades of Prior Park attend'
L(11630.c.1/3; 164.l.44, cropt),O(uncut),BaP, *BrP*; DFo,IU(uncut).

— Of the knowledge and characters of men, 1734. *See* Pope, Alexander.

O89 — Of the use and improvement of the stage. An epistle to Charles Fleetwood, esq; *London, printed for T. Cooper,* 1737. (*GM, LM* June)
2°: *A*¹ B–D² E¹; *1–2* 3–16.
'While calmer C-bb-r ceases dire debate'
O(uncut); DFo,ICN(uncut).

— Of verbal criticism, 1733. *See* Mallet, David.

O90 — Of war. A poem. Being an encomium on the bravery of the English nation...With a particular description of the fleet. Written at the command of a person of honour. *London, printed for John Chantry; sold by John Nutt,* 1701. (24 May, Luttrell)
2°: *A*² B–C² D¹; *i–iv, 1*–10. *10 advt.*
Advertised in *PB* 24 May.

'Awake, ye lazy powers of peace, awake'
L(11631.i.15/6, uncut), LVA-D,O(Luttrell);
TxU.

[**Ogle, George.**] Basia Joannis Secundi Nicolai Hagensis: or the Kisses...in Latin and English verse. With a life of Secundus, and a critic upon his Basia... *London, printed for Henry Lintot*, 1731. (*MChr* Aug)
12°: pp. xxxvi, 98.   L; IU,NN.
> Ogle includes two earlier translations by James Ward and two by Fenton. Entered to Lintot in Bowyer's ledgers under 12 Aug, 500 copies printed. Apparently the text was ready before the introduction, for 20 copies were delivered to Lintot and 2 to the author on 28 May; the remainder (with the introduction) were delivered on 18 Aug.

— The Canterbury tales of Chaucer, modernis'd by several hands. Publish'd by Mr. Ogle. *London, printed for J. & R. Tonson*, 1741. (*GM* April)
8°: 3 vol.   L,O; CtY,MH.
> Ogle's contributions are proportionally small.

—— *Dublin, printed by and for George Faulkner*, 1742.
12°: 2 vol.   O; NN,TxU.

O91 — The eighth epistle of the first book of Horace imitated. *London, printed for R. Dodsley*, [1739.] (15 March)
4°: π¹ A⁴, ²π¹ A⁴; i–ii, 1–3 4–8, i–ii, 1–3 4–6 7–8. π1, ²π1 hfts; ²A4 advt.
> Issued with 'The ninth epistle of the first book of Horace imitated'; the half-title π1 lists both, and has been seen to be conjugate with ²π1. Date from *Straus, Dodsley*; listed in *GM,LM* March.

'Muse, thrice invok'd, to Celsus speed the verse'
Ninth: 'Candler has found, (and, doubtless, he alone)'
L(1972),DG(–²A4); TxU(–²A4).

O92 — The eleventh epistle of the first book of Horace imitated. *London, printed for R. Dodsley*, 1738. (*GM, LM* Feb)
4°: A¹ B⁴ C¹; i–ii, 1 2–10. 10 advt.
> Dated 25 April in *Straus, Dodsley*, presumably in error.

'Say, curious friend, who rome'st from pole to pole!'
L(11630.c.10/2, cropt),O; CSmH,MH,NjP.

O93 — Epistles of Horace imitated. And illustrated with gems and medals. *London, printed by W. Wilkins*, 1735. (*GSJ* 20 March)
4°: A⁴ B–D⁴; 1–3 4–32.
> Book 1, epistle 1 only. Engravings on pp. 3, 32.

'You! whom I chose, and whom I still wou'd chuse'
L(11631.g.33/1),O(2); DLC,MH,NN,TxU.

O94 — The fifth epistle of the first book of Horace imitated. *London, printed for R. Dodsley*, 1738.
4°: A⁸; i–iv, 1 2–10 11; 12 blk. A1 hft; A8 advt.
> Apparently printed as a quarto in eights.

'To lean on common oak cou'd Jocelyn bear'
L(1972); MH.

O95 — Gualtherus and Griselda: or the clerk of Oxford's tale. From Boccace, Petrarch, and Chaucer. To which are added [six small items]... *London, printed for R. Dodsley*, 1739. (*GM,LM* June)
4°: a–b⁴ B⁴ C–P⁴ (a2 as 'a'); i–iii iv–xvi, 1 2–109 110–112.

'Down at the foot of Vesulus the cold'
> The introductory letter says 'Chaucer was my chief guide'.

L(77.l.18),O,C; DLC,IU,MH,TxU(uncut).

O96 —— *Dublin, printed for George Faulkner*, 1741.
12°: A–N⁶; i–iii iv–xxxv xxxvi, 37 38–156.
L(11632.de.12),O,C,E,DN+; ICN,MH.

O97 [—] The Liffy: a fable. In imitation of the Metamorphosis of Ovid. Addrest to a young lady. With an epistle dedicatory...By ****** **** esq; *Dublin, printed by S. Powell, for George Risk*, 1726.
8°: A–D⁴; i–iii iv–xv 'xiv', 17 18–32.
> No watermark. Some ordinary-paper copies may be wrongly entered below.

'Joy of my life, whose wit my soul inspires'
> Ogle's authorship is suggested by DG; his translations in James Sterling's *Poems*, 1728, are printed as by ****** **** esq; and the attribution seems almost certain.

O,C,DG; MH.

O98 [—] [fine paper]
> Watermark: fleur-de-lys on shield.

LVA-F; CtY,DFo.

O99 [—] — *London, printed for Tho. Warner*, 1726. (*MC* Sept)
8°: A–D⁴; i–iii iv–xvi, 17 18–32.
> Listed in *MC* as 'Printed at Dublin, and reprinted at London, for T. Warner'.

O; NjP(uncut).

O100 — The miser's feast. The eighth satire of the second book of Horace imitated. A dialogue between the author and the poet laureat. *London, printed for R. Dodsley*, 1737. (1 Nov)
2°: A¹ B–F² G¹; 3–5 6–26.
> Date from *Straus, Dodsley*; listed in *GM,LM* Nov.

'Well, laureat, was the day in clover spent?'
L(840.m.1/9),O,DrU,SrS; CSmH,CtY,ICN,MH, TxU(2)+.

O101 [—] Of legacy-hunting. The fifth satire of the second book of Horace imitated. A dialogue between Sir Walter Raleigh, and Merlin the prophet. *London, printed for J. Brindley; sold by A. Dodd, and the rest of the pamphlet shops of London & Westminster*, 1737. (*GM,LM* June)
2°: A¹ B–E² F¹ G¹; 1–3 4–22. 22 advt.

Ogle, G. Of legacy-hunting

A1 and G1 have been seen to be conjugate.
'Indulge this favor, Merlin, and impart'
Ogle's authorship, stated in the Dublin edition below, seems very probable.
L(1490.f.9),O,E,LdU-B; OCU,TxU(uncut).

O102 —— By George Ogle, esq; *Dublin, printed by R. Reilly, for G. Risk,* 1737.
8°: A–B⁴ C²; *1–3* 4–20.
L(1963),O,DA.

O103 — The second epistle of Horace imitated. And illustrated with gems and medals. *London, printed by W. Wilkins,* 1735. (*LM* Nov)
4°: *A*² B⁴; *i–iv, 1* 2–8. A1 blk.
Engravings on pp. 1, 8. Blank A1 seen in the C copy only.
'Thou! the polite Tibullus of the age!'
The second epistle of the first book; the following is apparently a different version; the texts have not been compared.
L(11630.c.10/4, cropt,–A1),O(2,–A1),C; IU(–A1),MH(–A1).

O104 — The second epistle of the first book of Horace imitated. *London, printed for R. Dodsley,* 1738. (*GM,LM* April)
4°: *A*(2 ll) B–C⁴ *D*(2 ll); *i–iv, 1* 2–18 *19; 20 blk.*
A1 hft; D2 advt.
The two leaves of A are conjugate with those of D.
'While you on Liffy emulate Saint-James'
L(1972),OA(–A1, D2); CtY(–D2),KU(–D2), NN,NN-B(–D2).

O105 — The third epistle of the first book of Horace imitated. *London, printed for R. Dodsley,* 1738. (26 Oct)
4°: *A*⁸; *i–iv, 1* 2–10 *11; 12 blk.* A1 hft; A8 advt.
Apparently printed as a quarto in eights. Date from *Straus, Dodsley;* listed in *GM* Oct.
'Say, Orrery, for this I long to hear'
L(11630.c.10/3, cropt); TxU.

[—] Three odes from the second book of Horace imitated, 1739. *See* T255.

O106 — The twelfth epistle of the first book of Horace imitated. *London, printed for R. Dodsley,* [1739.] (12 Dec?)
4°: *A*² B–D⁴; *i–iv, 3* 4–24 *25; 26 blk.* A1 hft; D4 advt.
A copy from Tom's Coffee House at the Lewis Walpole Library is dated 12 Dec; advertised in *LDP* 15 Dec.
'With care what you collect, injoy with ease'
L(1972); MH.

O107 **Ogle, Margaret.** Mordecai triumphant: or, the fall of Haman, prime minister of state to King Ahasuerus: an heroic poem. *London, printed for and sold by the author, at the Golden Fleece, in Mount Street, near Grosvenor-square, & J. Leake, and most of the pamphlet shops in London & Westminster,* 1742. (*GM,LM* April)

Ogle, M. Mordecai triumphant

8°: A–E⁴; *1–2* 3–40.
'In those blest days, when Ahasuerus, the son'
The biblical narrative applied against Sir Robert Walpole.
L(161.m.16).

O108 **Old.** The old and new courtier. [*London?* 17––.]
slip: 1 side, 1 column.
Although this is a seventeenth-century poem, this edition appears to be an eighteenth-century production.
'With an old song made by an old ancient pate'
Crum W2541.
L(C.121.g.9/127).

— The old cheese, 1725. *See* King, William, *the gazetteer.*

— The old coachman, 1742. *See* Williams, *Sir* Charles Hanbury.

O109 — Old England's new triumph: or, the battel of Oudenard. A song. *London, printed for A. Baldwin,* 1708.
½°: *1–2,* 2 columns.
Reprinted with Henry Hills's editions of [John Gay] *Wine,* 1708, 1709.
'Ye Britons give ear/ To my story, and hear'
In praise of Marlborough.
CSmH,TxU.

O110 — An old fashion song, by a new fashion'd poet, found in an old fashion castle. *Dublin, printed for W. Bently, opposite the Sun in Pill-lane, where advertisements &c, are done reasonably, on copper-plate, &c.,* [1725/30.]
½°: 1 side, 2 columns.
The copy at L is bound with a collection of Dublin half-sheets of 1725/30.
'Of all the booby's call'd a beau'
A satire on Dublin beaus.
L(C.121.g.8/104); CtY.

O111 — The old fox and his son: or, the statesman's lecture. A fable. To Sir Watkin Williams Wynn, bart. *London, printed for T. Cooper,* 1742 [1743]. (*GM, LM* Feb)
8°: A–C⁴ D²; *31–33* 34–56 *57; 58 blk.* 57 advt.
The pagination continues *The emulation of the insects,* 1742; p. 49 is title to 'The mistake'; three remaining fables (not traced) are entered under *The eagle, falconer, and hawk.* Listed in *GM, LM* as 'Two political fables'.
'O be my son, the mother cries'
O; IU.

O112 — The old fox chas'd: a new court-ballad. Humbly inscribed to his grace the Duke of A-----l. By Humphry Doggrel, esq; *London, printed for the author; sold by T. Cooper,* 1742. (*GM, LM* June)
2°: *A*² < B²; *1–2* 3–7 *8 blk.*
Rothschild 230.
'I'll sing you a song of what happen'd of late'

The **old** fox chas'd

Apparently on the fall of Walpole and restoration of Argyll.
O(lacks B²); National Library of Australia (cropt).

O113 — The old fox his legacy left to his monsterous cat. *London, printed for A. More,* [1743?]
½°: 1 side, 2 columns.
Dated by LSA as 1743.
'In Sampson's days, the foxes they'
LSA.

O114 — An old maid's fortune: or, the bride at her wits-end. A burlesque poem, occasion'd by the reading of Hans Carvell. Humbly inscrib'd to the three sisters F----------ns. *London printed, and sold by John Applebee, & A. Dod,* 1727. (*MC* April)
8°: A–E⁴; *i–x, 1* 2–30.
Printed in Grover's scriptorial type.
'Sue Lackit, of the London mould'
The epistle signed 'T.R.' An erotic tale, occasioned by Prior's poem.
L(11631.bb.73),LdU-B; TxU.

O115 — The old man's legacy to his daughters. Wherein the hidden mysteries of faith and experience are briefly discussed and laid down. In a plain and familiar dialogue. In six several conferences... Written by N.T. deceased, when near ninety years of age...and made publick at the request of many. By an admirer of grace and truth. *London, printed for the author,* 1736.
8°: A–B⁴ ˣB⁴ C–M⁴ N²; *i–viii, 1* 2–99 *100 blk.*
Originally published by David Crosley in 1697 (*TC* Trinity).
'Seeing our leisure serves us now'
'To the reader' signed by the editor, David Crosley; N.T. was already dead on its first publication.
O.

— The old man's wish, [170–?]–. *See* Pope, Walter.

O116 — The old medal new struck or wh—gs at their witts end. [*London,* 1711.]
1°: 1 side, 1 column.
Engraved throughout, with medallions at the four corners. At foot, monogram 'S.T. [or T.S.] script'; 'Sutton Nicholls sculpt'.
'The clan being turn'd out of places of power'
Tory verses.
L(P&D 1572).

— Old Mother Grim's tales, found in an old manuscript, 1737. *See* Meston, William.

O117 — Old Mother-Money's farewell: in a country dialogue between Dick and Tom. *London printed, and sold by W. Boreham,* 1719. (Nov, Luttrell)
8°: A–D⁴; *1–2* 3–32.
'Why Tom, since thou cam'st last to town'
L(164.l.14, Luttrell),*BaP*; MH,NjP.

O118 — The old pack. [*London,* 1710.]
½°: 1 side, 2 columns.
12 stanzas; line 2 ends with a comma, line 3 with a semi-colon.

The **old** pack

'Come ye old English huntsmen that love noble sport'
A satire on the whigs' pursuit of Sacheverell.
O,LdU-B,MC; MH.

O119 — [another edition]
12 stanzas; line 2 ends with a semi-colon, line 3 with a comma.
L(Lutt.II.156),Chatsworth; NjP.

O120 — — With additions. [*London?* 1710.]
½°: 1 side, 2 columns.
With an additional stanza attacking John Dolben added as stanza 13.
Crawford.

O121 — — With additions. [*London,* 1710.]
½°: 1 side, 2 columns.
With the additional stanza as stanza 10. From the same typesetting as O119.
Madan; MH.

O122 — [another edition, title reads:] The old pack.
With the additional stanza as stanza 10.
L(1876.e.20/23).

O123 — [*idem*] The pack of bear-dogs. *Dublin, printed by E. Waters,* 1713.
½°: 1–2, 1 column.
13 stanzas, the additional one being stanza 9.
C(2),Crawford.

O124 — The old tack, and the new. *London, printed in the year* 1712.
½°: 1 side, 1 column.
Printed in italic type.
'The tack of old, /was thought as bold'
L(1876.f.1/62),O.

O125 — [another edition]
Printed in roman type. On the other side of the NN copy, a page of a prose pamphlet.
Crawford; NN.

O126 — Old Tom the tooper's last advice to his son or, the ale-wives, and tapsters usage to their customers. Publish'd for the benefit of the publick. *Dublin, printed in the year* 1725.
½°: 1 side, 2 columns.
'My son who now art in thy prime'
Beware of drunkenness.
L(C.121.g.8/62).

O127 — The old t---p m---'s letter to his son, concerning the choice of a new p-----t. With his son's answer. [*London?* 1722?]
¼°: 2 sides, 1 column.
Title on recto; letter and answer on verso.
'Deer Tom, pray lay aside your hoe'
Answer: 'Dear father, sure I hope you think'
Presumably a letter from the 'turnip man' or George I to the Prince of Wales, on occasion of the elections of 1722. A piece of tory propaganda.
LU.

The **old** t---p m--'s letter

O128 — [another edition, title reads:] Old t— m—'s letter...
InU.

O129 — The old wife's tale: or, E----d's wish. A satire. Humbly inscribed to her grace the Duchess dowager of M----------. By Aquila. *London, printed for T. Cooper; sold by the booksellers of London & Westminster, 1742. (GM, LM April)*
2⁰: A⁴; *1–2* 3–8.
'Ye gods! dear friend, where have you been?'
To the Duchess of Marlborough.
L(1973)O; CSmH,MH,NjP,OCU.

O130 — The old wives tales: a poem. Part I. *London printed, and sold by J. Morphew, 1712. (18 April, Luttrell)*
8⁰: A–C⁴ (A3 as 'A'); *i–iv, 1* 2–20.
The Luttrell copy is recorded in Dobell cat. 114/286; advertised in *PB* 22 April. Three tales; no continuation traced.
'Sol had just with-drawn his light'
L(11631.e.71); CtY,TxU.

O131 — The old woman and her bee hive. [*London? 1714/15?]*
¼⁰: 1 side, 2 columns.
'There was an old woman that had a bee-hive'
Jacobite propaganda.
L(1876.f.1/71).

O132 — The old woman and her goose. A tale. Devised on account of a certain late project. Inscrib'd to the Revd. Jonathan Swift... *Dublin, printed in the year 1736.*
8⁰: *A⁴; 1* 2–8.
Teerink 1317.
'There liv'd, no matter when, or where'
L(900.g.30/9),DA(2),DT; MH,PU.

O133 — The old woman spinning of thyme. [*London? 1715/–.]*
½⁰: 1 side, 2 columns.
'As I was a walking thro' fair London city'
A tory ballad.
(Copy seen, but not located.)

O134 — The old woman's tale. *London printed, and re-printed in Dublin, in the year 1725.*
½⁰: 2 sides, 1 column.
'As I thro' the city one morning was walking'
L(C.121.g.8/51); OCU.

'Old three.' Congratulatory verses to Edward Biddle... By the old three, 1718. *See* Amhurst, Nicholas.

[Oldisworth, William.] The odes, epodes, and Carmen seculare of Horace, in Latin and English; with a translation of Dr Ben-ley's notes. To which are added notes upon notes. In 24 parts complete. By several hands. *London, printed for Bernard Lintott, 1713.*
12⁰: 26 pt.   L,O; MH,NjP.
Published in 26 parts between 10 July 1712 and

Oldisworth, W.

28 March 1713 and consisting of *Dr. Bentley's dedication, The life of Horace,* and 24 parts of text. The preliminaries and the first 5 parts of text were reprinted at various dates up to 1725.

— — Translated from Dr. Bentley's Latin edition by Mr. William Oldisworth. The second edition. *London, printed for B. Lintot, 1719 [1718]. (PB 11 Nov)*
12⁰: pp. 138.   L,O; CLU-C,MH.
Without the Latin text. Entered to Lintot in Bowyer's ledgers under 24 Oct 1718, 2000 copies.

— [reissue] The third edition. *London, printed for John Osborn, 1737.*
O.

[—] State and miscellany poems...By the author of the Examiner, 1715.
This collection is attributed to Oldisworth by *DNB*, but it appears to be by Joseph Browne; the collection and the poems it reprints are entered under Browne.

[O135–41 = B527·1–7]

O142 **[—]** Callipædia: or, the art of getting pretty children. In four books. Translated from the original Latin of Claudius Quilletus. By several hands. *London, printed for Bernard Lintott, 1710. (DC 7 March)*
8⁰: (frt+) A–M⁴ (+4 plates); *i–xvi, 1–72* 73–80. 78–80 advt.
Case 253. All three copies at L are without the frontispiece and plates which were clearly issued with the copies at O,C; they were perhaps not ready when the poem was first published. Advertised as 'just publish'd' in *DC* 6 March, but that advertisement also says 'where may be seen the sheets already printed', suggesting it was incomplete. Lintot was competing with Morphew's translation, advertised in *PB* 7 March as 'just publish'd'. Entered to Lintot as 'old copy' in *SR* 22 May 1710. Re-advertised in *DC* 3 Aug 1711 and following dates as though new; and in *MC* Sept 1714 'for the use of schools'.
'What makes a happy bridal; from what seed'
The relationship between Oldisworth, who is credited with the authorship in the following editions, and the 'several hands' is not clear; it has seemed desirable to enter this as a separate edition, since it has caused confusion to *Case* and others.
L(1075.f.19; 1076.g.36; 11408.aa.9, all without plates),O,C(2),LdU-B; ICN.

O143 — — In four books, with cuts. Translated...by Mr. Will. Oldisworth. The second edition, corrected. *London, printed for Bernard Lintot, 1719 [1718]. (DC 2 Aug)*

Oldisworth, W. Callipaedia

12°: A–D¹² E⁶; *i–xviii*, *1–85* *86–90*. A1 frt.
The plates are included in the collation.
Entered to Lintot in Bowyer's ledgers under
29 July 1718, 2000 copies printed.
O,OW,EU; TxU.

O144 — — The third edition, corrected, with additions.
London, printed for Bernard Lintot, 1729. (*MChr* 21
Apr)
12°: A–E¹²; *i–xviii*, *1 2–96 97–102*. A1 frt; 102 advt.
The copyright formed part of lot 50 of a trade
sale attributed to Henry Lintot, 27 Nov 1739
(cat. at O–JJ); it is recorded as out of print,
and was bought in by Lintot.
L(11405.aa.35).

[O145–6 = B527·8–9]

[O147–55 = B530·1–6]

O156 [—] A pindarick ode, to the memory of Dr.
William King. Humbly inscrib'd to the rt. hon. the
Lady Theodosia Hyde. *London, printed by H.
Meere; sold by J. Morphew*, [1713.] (17 Jan?)
2°: *A*² B²; *1–2 3–8*. 8 advt.
'A widow'd friend invites a widow'd muse'
Reprinted as Oldisworth's in William King's
Original works, 1776.
CLU–C(Luttrell, 21 Jan),MH(ms. date 17 Jan),
PBL,TxU(2).

[O157–63 = B530·7–95]

— 'The temple of honour, a poem inscribed to
Matthew Prior esqr: fol°: by Will Oldisworth.'
Entered to Bernard Lintot in *SR* 14 Sept 1711;
no copies were deposited, and it may well have
not been published.

Oldmixon, John. Amores Britannici. Epistles
historical and gallant, in English heroic verse...in
imitation of the Heroidum epistolæ of Ovid...
London printed, and are to be sold by J. Nutt, 1703.
(*WL* Jan)
8°: pp. 173, 150.   L; CtY,MH.

_____

O164 — Britannia liberata. A poem. Humbly inscrib'd
to the right honourable Thomas earl of Clare.
London, printed for J. Pemberton, 1714. (*MC* Oct)
2°: *A*¹ B–C²; *1–2 3–9 10 blk.*
'The summer sun had half perform'd his race'
AdU.

O165 [—] [dh] The catholick poet; or, Protestant
Barnaby's sorrowful lamentation: an excellent new
ballad. To the tune of, Which no body can deny.
[col] *London, 'printed for J. Morphew, J. Roberts,
R. Burleigh, J. Baker, & S. Popping; and sold by all
the booksellers in England, dominion of Wales, and
town of Berwick upon Tweed'*, 1716. (26 May,
Luttrell)
2°: *A*(3 ll); *1–6.* 6 advt.
The imprint is probably false, and Curll the
publisher. In fact a miniature miscellany;
pp. 3–4 in prose. Advertised in *FP* 31 May.

Oldmixon, J. The catholick poet

'My song is of Sawny, the poet of Windsor'
Attributed by Pope in *The Dunciad*, 1729, to
'Mrs. Centlivre and others'; Curll in *The
Curliad* (1729) 31 claimed 'the whole by Mr.
Oldmixon, not one word by Mrs. Centlivre'.
A satire on Pope and Lintot.
O(lacks A2–3, Luttrell); CtY,TxU.

O166 — A funerall idyll, sacred to the glorious memory
of K. William III. *London, printed for Nich. Cox;
sold by J. Nutt*, 1702. (2 April, Luttrell)
2°: A–D²; *1–4 5–16.*
'Oh thou, who lately by this silver stream'
L(1346.m.49, uncut),E; CtY,ICN(Luttrell),
TxU(2).

[—] The grove: or, the rival muses [actually by
John Froud], 1701. *See* F275.

[—] Henriade. An epick poem... Translated from
the French into English blank verse [actually by
John Lockman], 1732. *See* L215.

O167 — Iberia liberata: a poem. Occasion'd by the
success of her majesties arms in Catalonia, Valentia,
&c. Under the command of the right honourable
Charles, earl of Peterborough and Monmouth...
*London, printed for Anthony Barker; sold by John
Nutt*, 1706. (*PB* 26 Jan)
8°: π¹ A–I⁴ K⁴(–K4); *i–x, 1–70.*
'Again, my muse! for lofty flights prepare'
Dedication to the Countess of Peterborough
signed.
O,DT; IU,MB.

O168 — A pastoral poem on the victories at Schellen-
burgh and Bleinheim; obtain'd by the arms of the
confederates, under the command of his grace the
Duke of Marlborough... With a large preface,
shewing the antiquity and dignity of pastoral
poetry. *London printed, and sold by A. Baldwin*,
1704 [1705?]. (*PM* 2 Jan 1705)
4°: π¹ a² A–F² H–O²; *i–xxx, 1–28.* ii err.
The preface occupies A–F².
'Oh father of the field! whose artful strains'
L(840. h. 2/4),LDW,O,DT; *InU*,NN.

O168·2 [—] [reissue] A chain of providence; or, the
successes of the Prince and Duke of Marlborough
on his forcing the French lines. *London printed, and
sold by A. Baldwin*, 1705. (*WL* Aug)
4°: ˣA–B² H²(–H1) I–O²; *i–ii, 1–6, 3–28.*
Without the preface, but with the addition of
five pages of introductory verse. Listed in *WL*
as sold by B. Bragg.
''Twas when the bright guide of day had driv'n'
O.

O169 Oldnall, Edward. Two essays, in verse. I. Union
of whig and tory, exemplify'd and recommended.
II. The folly of the protestant Jacobites display'd...
*Worcester, printed for the author, by T. Olivers; sold
by Messrs. Wilde, and Hodges, in Hereford; Mr.
Wilde, in Ludlow; Mr. Cotton, in Shrewsbury; Mr.
Haslewood, in Bridgnorth; Mr. Wilde, in Kidder-
minster, and Mr. Warren, in Birmingham*, [1745?]

Oldnall, E. Two essays

4º: A–B⁴; *1–2* 3–16.
'O wisdom! now thy helpful hands extend!'
''Tis strange that protestants of any sort'
O; CSmH.

Olive. The olive, an ode, [1713.] *See* Castleton, Nathaniel [An ode to the most honourable the lord high-treasurer].

— The olive: an ode. Occasion'd by the auspicious success, 1737. *See* Boyse, Samuel.

O170 Oliver. Oliver Cromwell's ghost's advice to his friends. [*London*] *Printed* 1705. (5 July, Luttrell)
½º: 1 side, 1 column.
'Ye sons of my church who were ever of such'
A tory poem.
Crawford; ICN(Luttrell),InU,MH.

O171 Olympic. The Olympick odes of Pindar, in English meetre. As they were lately found in an original manuscript of those sublime lyrick translators, Thomas Sternhold, John Hopkins, and others... *London, printed for E. Curll*, 1713. (*EvP* 12 Feb)
8º: A–E⁴ F²; *i–viii*, *1* 2–36.
'As water of all elements'
A translation of odes 1 and 2, parodying Sternhold and Hopkins's translation of the Psalms.
L(161.k.33, Luttrell, 14 Feb),O,LdU-B; KU,NN, OCU,TxU.

O172 Ombre. [dh] L'ombre de Jacques II. Ou le songe de George, roi d'Angleterre. Poème. [1745/46.]
4º: *A²*; *1–4*.
Probably printed in France.
'Dans le sein de Thétis, déposant sa lumiere'
A Jacobite poem.
E.

O173 Omega. Omega: a poem on the last judgment. Occasion'd from the words of St. Peter in his second epistle and third chapter, but especially those of the third and fourth verses. *London, printed for Edmund Parker*, 1708. (6 May, Luttrell)
8º: A⁴ B–C⁸; *1–2* 3–40. 2 advt.
Advertised as 'just publish'd' in *DC* 15 May.
'They're come, ----alas! those days are come, wherein'
L(11601.d.28/1; 164.k.71, Luttrell),O; CtY(lacks A1),NNUT.

On. On design and beauty, 1734. *See* Browne, Isaac Hawkins.

O174 — On Dr. Paul and Justice Hall, who were murder'd the 13th of July, 1716. by whigs, for the love of god and justice. [*London?* 1716.]
¼º: 1 side, 1 column.
'Divinity and justice hand in hand'
A poem on behalf of the executed Jacobites.
O.

On her majesty's grant

— On her majesty's grant of Woodstock park, [1704/05.] *See* Buckeridge, Bainbrigg.

O175 — [dh] On her majesty's inauguration-day. To the most honourable Robert earl of Oxford... [col] *London, printed for H. Clements*, [1711/14.]
2º: A²; *1–4*.
No watermark.
'Sacred to Britons be the happy day'
IU.

O176 — [fine paper]
Watermark: fleur-de-lys on shield.
Chatsworth.

— On his excellency the Earl of Cadogan's publick entry, [1718.] *See* Smedley, Jonathan.

[O177 = W576] — On his grace, the Duke of Marlborough, 1707. *See* Wycherley, William.

— On his grace the Duke of Marlborough, a poem, 1706. *See* Trotter, Catharine.

— On his grace the Duke of Marlborough going for Holland, 1707. *See* Harison, William.

O177·5 — On love, an elegy. [*London?*] *Printed in the year* 1745.
8º: *A⁴* B⁴; *1–3* 4–16.
On p. 13, 'Ode for the winter solstice, December 11th, 1740'.
'Too much my heart of beauty's power hath known'
Ode: 'Now to the utmost southern goal'
L(1969).

O178 — On man. A satyr. By a person of honour. [*London*, 1702/14.]
½º: 1 side, 1 column.
'To what intent and purpose was man made'
L(11602.i.5/5; Rox.III.837),O; DFo,MH,TxU.

O179 — On Miss Death. [*Dublin?* 174–?]
¼º: 1 side, 1 column.
'Poets have hitherto mistook'
DT.

— On Miss Forrester playing with her shadow, 1743. *See* Cobden, Edward.

O180 — On Miss Vane's f—t, in the Phillippick stile. To which is added, a meditation on a t—d, wrote in a place of ease. [*Dublin*] *Printed in the year* 1733.
8º: A⁴; *1–3* 4–8.
'Lovely babe of maid of honour'
Meditation: 'Since most agree, that 'tis a crime'
Namby-pamby verses on Anne Vane's fart.
DA.

O181 — On Mr. Walpole's recovery. [*London*, 1716.]
½º: *1–2*, 1 column.
'When sad Britannia fear'd of late'
Crum W1427.
O(cropt),E.

— On November 4. 1712. the anniversary of the birth of his late majesty, [1712.] *See* Hughes, Jabez.

On operas

O182 — On operas. These lines were written, during the dispute whether such entertainments ought to be exhibited, in a time of actual rebellion. [1745/46?]
½°: 2 sides, 1 column.
'Is it a time to melt at languid strains'
O.

— On Paddy's character of the Intelligencer, [1728/29.] *See* Swift, Jonathan.

O183 — On P—e and W—d. Occasion'd by their late writings... With advice to a modern poet. *London, printed for R.P.; sold by E. Nutt, A. Dodd, & J. Jollyffe, 1732.* (GSJ 8 Feb)
2°: A² B²; *1–2* 3–8.
'How greatly, by our modern poets rage'
    A satire on Pope and Welsted.
O; CtY,MH(uncut),TxU.

— On poetry: a rapsody, 1733–. *See* Swift, Jonathan.

— On pride. An epistle, [1724.] *See* Ramsay, Allan.

O184 — On reading a certain speech. [*London,* 1733.]
½°: 1 side, 1 column.
    The last line reads '...DESTRUCTION ...'. *Percival* XXX. Below, 'Sir Abr. Elton's speech alluding to the 27 of Ezek. ver. 35, 36. paraphras'd'.
'Go on, little captain, stick close to Sir Bob'
Elton's speech: 'Long hast thou reign'd, Sir R---n, uncontroul'd'
    Satires on Walpole; the first was occasioned by the king's speech, 11 June 1733.
L(1871.f.16/2).

O185 — [another edition]
    The last line reads '...DESTRUCTION ...'.
L(C.121.g.9/19, first poem only); CSmH.

O186 — — [and 12 other short satires]. [*London,* 1733.]
½°: 2 sides, 2 columns.
    A smaller version of this collection is entered under *The sturdy beggars garland,* [1733], S779.
O-JJ.

— On rural felicity, 1733. *See* Morrice, Bezaleel.

— On seeing the archers diverting themselves, [1724.] *See* Ramsay, Allan.

O187 — On seeing the prince's picture. [1745?]
obl ⅛°: 1 side, 1 column.
    Eight lines of verse, printed like a ticket within a border of type flowers.
'The Christian hero's martial looks here shine'
    In praise of the Young Pretender.
CSmH.

O188 — [*idem*] 'The Christian hero's martial looks here shine' [1745?]
¼°: 1 side, 1 column.
    No title; engraving above text of medallion

On seeing the prince's picture

bearing the Young Pretender's head and Britannia.
L(840.k.4/9),MC.

O189 — — [*Edinburgh?* 1745?]
¼°: 1 side, 1 column.
    No engraving; 21 lines of verse.
E.

O190 — On state affairs. Four fables. The pigeons. Fable the 1st... *Dublin, printed by Edward Waters,* 1728.
8°: A⁴; *1–3* 4–8. 8 advt.
    P. 8, 'Next Wednesday will be publish'd (Numb. 2.) of like state fables, by the printer hereof. And so on weekly.' No more seen.
'The hawks were once at mortal jars'
L(11631.a.63/10).

O191 — On the blessed day of our Saviours birth. 25th December 1705. [*Edinburgh,* 1705.]
½°: 1 side, 1 column.
'Eternal god, creator of all things!'
E.

— On the chief physitian Sir Archibald Stevenson, [1710.] *See* Pitcairne, Archibald (P381).

— On the creation of the world, 1719. *See* A divine poem on the creation, 1718–.

O192 — On the death of Dr. Alured Clarke. [1742.]
½°: 1 side, 1 column.
    On the other side, *The progress of charity,* [1742.]
'To lonely vales and deep sequester'd woods'
Crum T3011: 'On the death of the Rev. Dr. Clarke, late dean of Exeter. By a lady of that city. G[entleman's] Mag.'
DFo.

O193 — On the death of John Wagstaffe, an elegiac poem. [1736?]
1°: 1 side, 2 columns.
'The tears scarce dry'd, we for thy brother shed'
    Signed 'E.W.' Attributed by *Smith* II. 857 to Elijah Waring; but if the identification of John Wagstaffe with the quaker of Warborough is correct, he died in 1736 when Waring was only five. It seems more likely that this is written by a member of the Wagstaffe family.
LF(2).

O194 — [dh] On the death of King James. By a lady. [*London?* 1701?]
4°: A⁴; *1–8.*
    The order of editions is not determined.
'If the possession of imperial sway'
L(11631.e.35).

O195 — [*idem*] [dh] An elegy on the death of King James. By a lady. [1701?]
4°: A⁴; *1–8.*
NN.

— On the death of Lady Margaret Anstruther, [1728.] *See* Ramsay, Allan.

On the death of Mr. Brand

O196 — On the death of Mr. Brand, student of philosophy in the university of Edinburgh, who departed this life on the 10th December 1717, in the 17th year of his age. By J.C. one of his fellow students. [*Edinburgh*, 1717.]
½⁰: 1 side, 1 column.
'Must nature's vast profusion be in vain?'
> *Maidment* 218 tentatively suggests John Calender as author; but possibly by John Colme who was publishing half-sheets at this date, though the only recorded Edinburgh graduate of this name graduated in 1691.

E.

O197 — On the death of Mr. Edmund Smith, late student of Christ-Church, Oxon. A poem, in Miltonic verse. *London, printed for J. Morphew*, 1712. (8 Feb, Luttrell)
8⁰: *A*² B–D⁴ E²; *i–xii, 1* 2–20. A1 blank.
> *Rothschild* 200. Advertised in *PB* 7 Feb, 'to-morrow'.

'Shalt thou, O bard divine, who e'rewhile sung'
LVA-D(−A1),LLP(−A1),O(−A1),CT(−A1); CtY(−A1),DFo(−A1),ICU(Luttrell,−A1),MH, TxU+.

O198 —— 'a poem in Miltonick verse, with a preface containing some remarks upon Milton. The second edition. [*London*] *Printed for J. Morphew*. Price 6d.' (*PB* 1 July 1712)

O199 — On the death of Sir William Sharp of Stonniehill. [*Edinburgh*, 1706?]
½⁰: 1 side, 1 column.
> Mourning headpiece and woodcut borders.

'Two potent heraulds joyntly do proclaim'
> Signed 'R.D.'

E.

O200 — On the death of the honourable Colonel James Gardiner, who was slain in the battle at Preston-Pans, and the flight of the rebels at the approach of his royal highness the Duke; a poem. *London, printed for the author; sold by Jacob Robinson*, 1746. (*SR* 6 May)
2⁰: *A*² B²; *1–3* 4–8.
> Entered in *SR* by and for John Nourse; deposit copies at L,O. Listed in *GM*, *LM* May.

'Do thou, whom thy great death on earth renowns'
L(643.m.14/17),O,E,AdU; CSmH.

— On the death of the reverend Mr. Patrick Wotherspoon, 1732. *See* Preston, William.

O201 — On the dreadful fire, in the Land Market of Edinburgh; upon Tuesday the 28 day of October, 1701. [*Edinburgh*, 1701.]
½⁰: 1 side, 1 column.
'Great god almighty did at first decree'
O.

O202 — On the Duke of Marlborough's restoration. To the tune of, O London is a fine town &c. [*London?* 1714?]
slip: 1 side, 1 column.

On the Duke of Marlborough's restoration

'Come all ye anti-Perkinites'
Harding.

— On the English translations of Homer: a satire. 1733. *See* Morrice, Bezaleel.

O203 — [dh] On the excise-scheme being dropt in the house of commons. [*London*, 1733.]
2⁰: *A*²; *1–4*.
''Tis done!- - - - -Thou awful shade of Britain rise'
OCU.

— On the first fit of the gout, 1706. *See* Fenton, Elijah.

O204 — On the first of August, 1716. [*London?* 1716.]
slip: 1 side, 1 column.
'O gloomy day! O melancholly scene!'
> *Crum* O398: 'On Aug. 1. 1716'. A Jacobite lament on the anniversary of Queen Anne's death.

L(11626.i.11/2).

— On the happy situation of the British isle, [1707?] *See* Fowler, John.

O205 — On the jewel in the Tower. *London, printed in the year* 1712.
½⁰: 1 side, 2 columns.
> Two lines of typeset melody and two of flute accompaniment above the text.

'If what the Tower of London holds'
> A. T. Hazen in *A catalogue of Horace Walpole's library* (1969) no. 2446 records Horace Walpole's attribution of this work to Richard Estcourt. On Walpole's committal to the Tower.

L(1850.e.10/21),Herts CRO(Panshanger box 46); *Harding*.

O206 — On the ladies hoops and hats now worn. An epigram. *London, printed for J. Roberts*, 1719. (*DC* 10 Sept)
½⁰: 1 side, 1 column.
> An advertisement in *PB* 12 Sept denounces this as surreptitiously printed and shamefully incorrect; advertises as 'this day publish'd a neat edition, taken from the original. Sold by the bookseller[!] of London and Westminster'.

'Our granums of old were so piously nice'
> *Crum* O1276.

L(1872.a.1/159**),O; CLU-C.

O207 — On the late decease of the honourable John Spencer, esq; an elegiac essay... *London, sold by A. Dodd, G. Woodfall, & G. Steidel*, 1746. (*GM* July)
2⁰: *A*² B–C²; *i–iv, 1* 2–8.
'Thrice worthy Bedford, Roxborough, and Fane'
KU.

— On the late queen's sickness and death, 1738. *See* Manning, Francis.

O208 — On the marriage of the right honourable the lord-keeper to Mrs. Clavering. To the right honourable the Lady Cowper. [*London*] *Sold by B. Bragge*, 1707.

On the marriage

½°: 2 sides, 1 column.
'Apollo, angry that his sons so long'
William Cowper, subsequently earl Cowper, the lord-keeper, married Mary Clavering secretly in Sept 1706; the fact was made public 25 Feb 1707.
O.

O209 — 'On the modern incendiaries. A satire. *Sarum, sold by E. Easton & W. Collins; as likewise by A. Dodd & E. Nutt in London.* Price 6d.' (*MChr* Feb 1731)
The incendiaries demanded money under the threat of burning barns or houses.

O210 — On the most noble Lord Kenmure, humbly offered to his eternal memory. [*Edinburgh*, 1716.]
½°: *1–2*, 1 column.
'Long have I study'd for some mighty name'
Crum L544: 'On the death of the noble Wm. Gordon...who was made a sacrifice to usurpation and whiggish tyranny'. William Gordon, sixth viscount, was beheaded 24 Feb 1716 for his Jacobite command.
E(2).

O211 — On the much lamented death of the most pious and illustrious princess, her late majesty Queen Anne, who died 1. Aug. 1714. [*London, sold by T. Worrall*, 1737.] (*DP* 1 June 1737)
1°: 1 side, 2 columns.
Engraved throughout; the copy seen lacks the engraved portrait. Advertised in *DP* as 'Printed on a fine Genoa imperial paper, with the effigies of the late queen at the top... engraven in the most beautiful manner from a painting of Sir Godfrey Kneller's, by Mr. Vandergucht... Price 1s. in the sheet, 2s. fram'd, or 4s. 6d. in the best frame and glass.'
'From joyous songs, and from the vocal groves'
NjP(lacks the portrait).

O212 — On the much lamented death of the most serene & illustrious prince, James, VII. & II. king of Great Britain, France & Ireland, who departed this life in the royal palace of St. Germans en lay, the 3d. of September 1701. in the 68 year of his age. [*Edinburgh*, 1701.]
½°: 1 side, 1 column.
Mourning borders.
'All-conquering death, and even fortune too'
E(mutilated).

— On the much lamented death, of the most serene and illustrious prince, James VII. and II. late king of Scotland, [1701.] *See* An elegy on the death of the late King James, 1701 (E159).

O213 — On the nativity of our blessed lord and saviour Jesus Christ. A divine poem. Humbly presented to the Lady Sloane. *London, printed by S. Palmer, for the author*, 1717.

On the nativity

8° π¹ A⁴(−A4?); *1–2* 3–8.
Presumably issued with variant title-pages with different dedicatees.
'Whilst others think, more bright their numbers shine'
By the same author as *A divine poem on the creation*, 1718, and other poems recorded there. This imprint is also found in Henry Nevil's *The first of August*, 1717, which was also issued in this way; it is tempting to identify him as the author of these other poems.
L(11631.e.76).

O214 — [reissue] Humbly presented to the Lady Fletcher. *London, printed for the author*, 1718.
8°: π¹ A⁴(−A4?); *1–2* 3–8.
O.

O215 — [reissue] Humbly presented to the Lady Trumbal. *London, printed for the author*, 1722.
8°: π¹ A⁴; *1–2* 3–8 *9–10 blk.*
In the copy of this issue seen, A4 is apparently present and blank. At foot of p. 8, catchword 'ON'; apparently a variant state not seen elsewhere.
L(1489.t.4).

O216 — On the nature of the most ingenious arts, and the benefits of indulgence to the most curious things. A poem. *London, printed for C. Corbett*, [1747.] (*GM, LM* Nov)
8°: *A*(3 ll) B–H⁴; *i–vi, 1–52 53–54; 55–56 blk.*
A1 hft.
'Auspicious muse! to me thy aid dispense'
NN.

— On the passion of our blessed saviour, 1708–. *See* Samber, Robert.

O217 — On the peace proclaim'd in the year 1748, a poem. By the author of Kirkham Hunt. *Preston, printed by James Stanley & John Moon*, 1748.
8°: *A*⁴; *1–3* 4–8.
The words 'of Kirkham Hunt' are inked over on the title of the WgP copy, possibly because it was never published.
'Hail sacred peace! thrice welcome to our isle'
PrP,WgP.

— On the queens most glorious victories, [1707?] *See* Fowler, John.

O218 — On the rejoycings on the first of August: being the day of the queen's death, and of George's accession to the crown. [*London?* 1714?]
slip: 1 side, 1 column.
'Why shou'd the bells in merry peals thus roul?'
A Jacobite poem.
O(divided and mounted).

— On the Royal Company of Archers, shooting for the bowl, [1724.] *See* Ramsay, Allan.

On the Royal Company

— On the Royal Company of Scottish Archers, [1713?/14?] *See* Kincaid, Thomas (K43–4).

— On the scarcity of the copper coin, 1739. *See* Leslie, Charles.

O219 — On the sentence passed by the house of lords on Dr. Sacheverell. *London, printed in the year* 1710. (*PM* 1 June)
½⁰: 1 side, 1 column.
Advertised in *PM* by A. Baldwin.
'Hail pious days! Thou most propitious time'
A whig poem in praise of their clemency.
O,Crawford; *MH*,OCU.

O220 — ⟨   ⟩ on the sight of his majesty's picture. [*London?* 1716/20.]
The copy seen has been cut up and mounted, but was possibly a half-sheet printed on one side, two columns.
'Well fare the hand which to our humble sight'
Jacobite verses on the Pretender, apparently in imitation of Waller's 'To the queen, occasioned upon sight of her majesty's picture'.
O.

O221 — On the signal victory at Gladsmuir, gain'd by his royal highness Prince Charles, September 21. 1745. By a lady, extempore. [1745.]
½⁰: 1 side, 1 column.
'While Charles, with his youthful charms'
In praise of the Young Pretender.
L(C.38.g.14/12, cropt at foot); CSmH(cropt at head).

O222 — On the tenth of June, MDCCI. being the birthday of his royal highness the Prince of Wales; at which time he happily compleats the thirteenth year of his age. [*London?* 1701.]
½⁰: 2 sides, 2 columns.
'The lord of light, and charioteer of day'
A Jacobite poem.
L(8122.i.39/24).

O223 — On the thanksgiving-day. [*London?* 1715.]
¼⁰: 1 side, 2 columns.
Two poems, one in each column. The second poem was also published as *The blessings attending George's accession and coronation*, [1715.]
'Hail happy Albion! Thou art strangely blest'
'The golden age is now at last restor'd!'
Jacobite satires. The first is *Crum* H58a: 'On the day of thanksgiving, 20 Jan 1715'.
CSmH,*MH*.

O224 — [dh] On the 27th of January 17$\frac{29}{30}$, at the anniversary feast of...masons, after dinner the grand master bespoke the tragedy of the sequel of King Henry IV...to be acted on the 12th of February ...and order'd a new prologue and epilogue... [*London*, 1730.]
2⁰: *A²*; *1–4*.

On the 27th of January

'Prologue, spoken by Mr. Mills.' 'Epilogue, by way of dialogue between Mr. Mills and Mrs. Sherburn.' Below the text on p. 4, 'Order'd, that the above written prologue and epilogue be printed, for the benefit of Brother William Reid...' This edition has head and tail pieces to both prologue and epilogue, unlike the following. It seems possible that this is the earlier edition, though a reference to the reception of the performance makes it clear that it was not sold at the theatre on 12 Feb.
'As a wild rake that courts a virgin fair'
'Ladies and gentlemen – I beg you'd stay'
The deputy grand master was Nathaniel Blackerby; the performance took place at Drury Lane.
O.

O224·2 — [*idem*] Bl--ke--y's prologue and epilogue: or, the Theatre-royal in Drury-lane, the grand lodge for free masons. Order'd, that this prologue and epilogue be printed, for the benefit of Brother William Reid, secretary to the grand lodge... *Grub-street, printed by Andrew Trowel, and the assigns of W. Read, for the benefit of Brother William Ried* [!]; *sold by R. Walker*, 1729 [1730]. (*DJ* 14 Feb)
2⁰: A(3 ll); *1–2* 3–6.
A1 and A3 are conjugate; A2 is signed 'A2'.
The imprint is to some extent fictitious.
United Grand Lodge of England, London.

[O225 = S468·5] — On the twenty third day of April, [1713.] *See* Sinclair, *Sir* Archibald.

O226 — On the union of the two kingdoms, of England and Scotland as represented in one parliament. *London, sold by Benj. Bragge*, 1707. (8 Nov, Luttrell)
½⁰: *1–2*, 1 column.
'When Blenheim and Ramellies wond'rous fields'
MH(Luttrell).

O227 — On the very much lamented death of the truly noble, and universally respected, Lord Basil Hamiltoun...who was unfortunatly drown'd August 27. 1701. ætat: 29: by endeavouring to rescue his servant. *Edinburgh, printed by Mr. S.* [*Matthias Symson?*], [1701.]
1⁰: 1 side, 1 column.
Mourning borders, imprint engraved on lower border.
'Just as he liv'd, he dy'd: 'twas sympathy'
L(11633.i.9/4),E(imprint cropt).

O228 — On the victory at Ramelies. A pindaric. *London printed, and sold by Benj. Bragge*, 1706. (25 June)
2⁰: A–C² (A2 as 'A'); *1–2* 3–12.
Advertised in *DC* 26 June as 'yesterday'.
'Awake, awake, my lyre'
O,LdU-B,*MR*,MR-C; InU(Luttrell, 27 June).

On the works of Humpus

O229 — On the works of Humpus, town-poet. [*Dublin*] *Printed in the year* 1725.
½°: 1 side, 1 column.
'Dear Humpus will you still abuse'
The L catalogue tentatively suggests that 'Humpus' was Ambrose Philips; it seems unlikely.
L(C.121.g.8/55).

— On this great eclipse, 1715. *See* Ramsay, Allan.

— On Thursday next, sir, I expect, [1720.] *See* Watson, James.

O230 — On wisdom's defeat|In a learned debate. *Dublin, printed by Sarah Harding,* [1725.] (Sept)
½°: 1 side, 1 column.
Teerink 1172; *Williams* 1117. Burnt by the public hangman on 2 Oct following a resolution of the Irish house of lords.
'Minerva has vow'd since the bishops do slight her'
Signed 'Rose Common, shameless woman'. See *Williams* for details of the occasion and of Swift's possible authorship; William Nicolson, bishop of Derry, in a letter of 12 Oct 1725 clearly believed Swift was the author. See *The last speech of Wisdom's defeat,* 1725, on the burning of the poem and imprisonment of Sarah Harding.
L(1890.e.5/130; C.121.g.8/85),C,*DN*; CtY,MH, PU.

One. One epistle to Mr. A. Pope, 1730. *See* Welsted, Leonard & Smythe, James Moore.

O231 — One thousand, seven hundred, and forty-five. A satiric-epistle; after the manner of Mr. Pope. *London, printed for A. Dodd,* 1746. (*LM* March)
2°: A¹ B–D² E¹; *i–ii, 1–13 14 blk.*
Horizontal chain-lines.
'To thee, my Arcas, on the rural plain'
By the same author as *Past and present,* 1746.
O(cropt),C,AdU; CSmH(uncut),CtY,IU,MH, TxU(3)+.

O232 — — *London printed, and Dublin re-printed by J. Kinneir, & A. Long,* [1746.]
12°: A⁶; *1–3 4–12.*
O,DA(lacks A1).

O233 — One thousand seven hundred thirty nine. A rhapsody. By way of sequel to seventeen hundred thirty eight: by Mr. Pope. *London, printed for J. Cooper,* 1740 [1739]. (*LDP* 15 Nov)
2°: A⁴ (A3 as 'B'); *1–5 6–8.*
'Pope wrote a satire,---took it in his pate'
L(1890.c.1/6); CtY,ICU,TxU.

O234 — — The second edition. *London, printed for J. Cooper,* 1740.
2°: A⁴ (A3 as 'B'); *1–5 6–8.*

One thousand seven hundred thirty nine

Apparently a reimpression.
CtY(2),TxU.

O235 Onely, Richard. Cl. Alex. Popi Messiah, ecloga sacra. Latino carmine donata. *Londini, impensis M. Cooper,* 1749. (*GM,LM* Feb)
2°: A² B–D²; *1–5 6–15 16 blk.*
'Incipe virgineum, Solymæ chorus! incipe carmen!'
O; *CLU-C*,NN.

'O-Nephely, Dermot.' An answer to a scandalous poem, 1733. *See* Swift, Jonathan.

Oppian. Oppian's Cynegeticks, 1736. *See* Mawer, John.

O236 — Oppian's Halieuticks of the nature of fishes and fishing of the ancients in V. books. Translated from the Greek, with an account of Oppian's life ... *Oxford, printed at the Theater,* 1722.
8°: π⁴ A–2I⁴; *i–viii, 1–13 14–16, 1–232 [8].* π1 hft.
2I⁴ contains a list of subscribers.
'I sing the natives of the boundless main'
Dedication signed 'John Jones'. Books 1–2 were translated by William Diaper before his death in 1717 (*Crum* I478, Diaper's autograph); books 3–5 translated by Jones. The names of Diaper and Jones are given on the fly-titles to the two parts.
L(997.k.17; 76.c.2),O(presentation copy to the Bodleian); *CSmH*,CtY,PPL.

Oppianus.
Mawer, John: Oppian's Cynegeticks. Translated into English verse [book I], 1736. *See* M147 –8.

Oppian's Halieuticks of the nature of fishes and fishing... Translated [by William Diaper & John Jones], 1722. *See* O236.

O237 Opputtinomtompi. Opputtinomtompi: or, the parson married. A tale. *Dublin, printed in the year* 1728.
8°: A⁴; *1–3 4–8.*
'Tho' human pleasures finite are'
Apparently a true story of a henpecked husband.
L(12274.e.1/9),DN,*MR-C*.

O238 Optics. The optics: a poem. Inscrib'd to Roger Grant esq; oculist extraordinary to her majesty. On his opthalmic art. Written by a gentleman formerly of Trinity-College in Cambridge. *London, printed by Dryden Leach,* 1713.
8°: A⁸; *1–2 3–16.*
Morgan＊L311ᵃ records this title with description '1st ed., folio, L. (Baker), 1709'.
'When verdant honours crown a publick head'
O.

Oracle

Oracle. The oracle, 1747. *See* Newcomb, Thomas.

O239 Oracles. The oracles for war: or, Great Britain admonish'd to maintain our ancient rights by dint of sword. To a new play-house tune. [*London*] *Printed for S. Deacon, at the Angel in Gilt-spur-street*, [170–?]
½⁰: 1 side, 2 columns.
    Three lines of typeset music at head. Dated by L as [1690?]; but S. Deacon is not recorded as a bookseller until after 1700.
'To arms, to arms, to arms, to arms'
L(1876.f.1/137).

O240 Order. Order, a poem. *London, printed for J. Brindley; sold by Mrs Dodd, Mrs Nutt & Cook, and by the booksellers and pamphlet-shops of London & Westminster*, 1737. (*LM* May)
2⁰: *A²* B–E²; *1–5* 6–19 *20 blk.* 19 err.
    Rothschild 215. The TxU copy appears to have a variant sheet C.
'Unhappy man, thro' life's successive years'
L(643.m.15/27); CtY,IU,MH,OCU,TxU.

O241 — Order in government: the British plan. A poem. Inscribed to his royal highness the Prince of Wales... By a British subject. *London, printed for H. Jones*, 1741.
4⁰: *A⁴* B⁴(–B1) C–D⁴; *i–vi, 1* 2–23 *24 blk.*
'Whatever schemes in politicks arise'
L(1490.de.39, uncut); KU,OCU.

O242 Origin. [dh] The origin of the whale bone-petticoat. A satyr. Boston, August 2d. 1714. [1714.]
8⁰: *A⁴*; *1–8.*
    Evans 1709 and *Wegelin* 759, following the L catalogue, treat this as American printing; but it may be English.
'Rise gentle satyr, / In modest lines the mystery reveal'
L(11687.b.52).

O243 Original. The original and conduct of the Young Pretender. To the tune of, The broom of Cowden knows. [*Edinburgh*, 1746.]
½⁰: 1 side, 2 columns.
'All loyal Scots within our land'
    Probably by the same author as *A humble advice to the loyal Scots and English*, [1746] which it closely resembles. Against the Young Pretender.
E,*AdU.*

— An original canto of Spencer, 1714. *See* Croxall, Samuel.

O244 — The original of apparel: or, the ornaments of dress. Presented to Mr.   Vernum, taylor. *London, printed for the author*, 1732.
4⁰: π¹ A–C²; *i–ii, 1* 2–11 *12 blk.*
    Possibly issued with variant title-pages with different dedicatees.
'Had beauteous Eve, fair mother of mankind'

The original of apparel

    If this was issued with variant dedicatees, it might be attributed to W. Howard who used this technique at this period.
L(11641.bbb.27, slightly cropt).

O245 — The original of government, and duty of magistrats. A paraphrase on the LXXXII psalm. [*Edinburgh?* 17––.]
½⁰: 1 side, 1 column.
'The son of god, who rules the pregnant earth'
E.

— Original poems and translations on several occasions, 1723. *See* Lely, Richard.

O246 Origines. Origines Bathenses: or, the origin of the Bath, a burlesque. To which is added, the Wrinkle. Two curious pieces found among the papers of a very learned and ingenious gentleman deceas'd. *London, printed for T. Cooper; sold by the booksellers of London & Westminster*, 1736. (*LM* Nov; *GM* Dec)
8⁰: *A⁴* B–E⁴; *i–iii iv, 5* 6–39 *40 blk.*
'Philosophers, who peep and pore'
Wrinkle: 'Celia long had triumph'd o'er'
L(11602.f.23/1),BaP.

O247 Ormond. Ormond's vision. To the tune of – The children in the wood. [*London?*] *Printed in the year* 1715.
slip: 1 side, 1 column.
'As I from hunting came one night'
Harding.

O248 Ormondus. Ormondus redux. An heroick poem to his grace the Duke of Ormond, on his victorious expedition to Spain. His auspicious government of Ireland; and prosperous return to England. *London, printed for J. Nutt*, 1704. (22 April, Luttrell)
2⁰: *A¹ B²* C–E² (C1 as 'B'); *i–ii, 1*–16.
    The Luttrell copy is in the collection of R. D. Horn; advertised in *PM* 2 May.
'Illustrious prince! who best your martial race'
CtY,MH.

O249 Ormsbye, Robert. Carmen heroicum, compositum in memorabilem confæderatorum principum, contra Gallos & Bavaros libertatis Europæ, causa conflictum apud Blenheim... *Tipis per Edvardo Waters, Dublin*, 1708.
4⁰: A⁴ B⁴(±B2); *1–2* 3–15 *'12'* (13,16 as '11, 12').
    The copy at C has B2 uncancelled, with p. 12 misnumbered '10'. There are paste-on cancels for single words on pp. 7, 10, 16, and other corrections apparently stamped-in by hand.
'Carolus Hispaniæ rex Indorumque secundus'
O,OW,C,DA.

O250 — [*idem*] An heroic poem on the memorable battle fought at Bleinheim... This poem... is now re-printed for the benefit of the author's only son ...and at the request of his friends, translated into

Ormsbye, R. Carmen heroicum

English verse. By L.W. *Dublin, printed by Oliver Nelson*, 1741.
4°: *A²* B–E⁴; *i–iv, 1 2–32*.
Latin title on A1ᵛ, English on A2ʳ. The copy seen is on fine paper watermarked pro patria, with gilt edges.
'When death, great Charles the second's head, laid low'
L(11633.e.28).

O251 Orpheus. Orpheus and Hecate. An ode. Inscrib'd to the patroness of the Italian opera. *London, printed for W. Webb*, 1746. (*GA* 30 April)
2°: *A⁴; 1–5 6–7 8 blk.* A1 hft.
'When Orpheus, as old poets tell'
Printed in Sir Charles Hanbury Williams's *Collection*, 1763; Horace Walpole annotated his copy of that (now at L) 'Certainly not by Sr Ch. Williams'. An attack on Lady Margaret Cecil Brown.
L(C.57.g.7/14, Horace Walpole's),O,E(–A1); CtY(–A1)' DLC(cropt).

— Orpheus redivivus, [1723.] *See* 'Steele, *Sir* Richard'.

Orrery, John Boyle, *earl of. See* Boyle, John, *earl of Orrery.*

O——s, S., *L.S.* Trinity College vindicated, 1725. *See* Owens, Samuel.

Osiers. The osiers. A pastoral translated from the Latin of Sannazarius, 1724. *See* Bell, Beaupré.

Otia. Otia votiva: or, poems upon several occasions. *London printed, and sold by J. Nutt*, 1705. (*PM* 12 July)
8°: pp. 154. L; CLU-C,CtY.
The copy at CLU-C has ms. at end of preface 'T. Todderill'; he is perhaps the author.

Out. Out with 'em while you are about it, 1710. *See* Pittis, William.

O252 Overbury, *Sir* **Thomas.** The wife, a poem. Express'd in a compleat wife. With an elegy on the untimely death of the author... The seventeenth edition. *London printed, and sold by H. Hills*, 1709.
8°: A⁸; *1–2 3–16*.
First published in 1614. Reissued with other Hills poems in *A collection of the best English poetry*, 1717 (*Case* 294), and included here to complete the record of his reprints.
'Each woman is a brief of womankind'
L(C.124.b.7/41),O,WcC; CtY,IU,MH,TxU.

O253 Overton, John. 'David and Goliah. A poem. [*London*] *Printed for J. Clarke & R. Hett.* Price 6d.' (*MC* June 1727)

Ovid. Ovid in masquerade, 1719. *See* Breval, John Durant.

Ovid

O254 — Ovid's Tristia. Containing five books of mournful elegies...Newly translated into English by T.P. *London, printed for Arthur Bettesworth*, 1713. (*DC* 14 May)
12°: A⁸ B–L⁸ᐟ⁴ M⁴; *i–xvi, 1–125 126–128. 126–128* advt.
A1ᵛ is an emblematic woodcut title.
'My little book, go view imperial Rome'
L(11386.aa.26),LVA-D,O; CLU-C,CtY,IU, MiU.

O255 —— The fourth edition. *London, printed for A. Bettesworth*, 1726.
12°: A⁸ B–F¹² G⁴; *i–xvi, 1 2–125 126–128.* A1 frt; *126–128* advt.
No translator's initials in this edition; the frontispiece is engraved. No second or third edition has been traced.
L(11352.aa.29),LdU-B; CLU-C.

Ovidius Naso, Publius.

Ars amatoria

King, William, *gazetteer*: The art of love: in imitation of Ovid De arte amandi, [1708.] *See* K60–1.

Ars amatoria – burlesque

The art of love. Paraphrased from Ovid, 1701. *See* A323.

[reissue] The poet banter'd: or, Ovid in a visor. A burlesque poem on his Art of love, 1702. *See* A324.

Epistolae heroidum

Price, Henry: Laodamia to Protesilaus. Translated from Ovid, 1743. *See* P1041.

The epistles of Penelope to Ulysses, and Phyllis to Demophoon. Newly translated from Ovid, 1748. *See* E436.

Epistolae heroidum – burlesque

Radcliffe, Alexander: Ovid travestie, a burlesque upon Ovid's epistles, 1705. *See* R8.

Metamorphoses

[*book 1*] An imitation of Ovid Metamorphosis; inscribed to his excellency the Earl of Gallway, 1716. *See* I8.

[*book 2*] [Meston, William:] Phaethon: or the first fable of the second book of Ovid's Metamorphoses burlesqu'd, 1720. *See* M217.

[*book 8*] [Swift, Jonathan:] Baucis and Philemon, imitated from Ovid, 1709, 1710. *See* S800–3.

[*book 13*] Tate, Nahum: The celebrated speeches of Ajax and Ulysses, for the armour of Achilles... Essay'd in English verse, 1708. *See* T49.

[Breval, J. D:] Ovid in masquerade. Being, a burlesque upon the xiiith book of his Metamorphoses, containing the celebrated speeches of Ajax and Ulysses, 1719. *See* B430.

Ovidius Naso, P. *Metamorphoses*

[—] [reissue] The force of eloquence illustrated, in two witty orations, spoken before the nobles of Greece, 1721. *See* B431.

[Forbes, Robert:] Ajax his speech to the Grecian knabbs. From Ovid's Metam. lib. XIII... Attempted in broad Buchans, 1748. *See* F184.

Remedium amoris

Uvedale, Thomas: The remedy of love, in imitation of Ovid, 1704. *See* U33.

— [*idem*] A cure for love: a satyr. In imitation of Ovid, 1732. *See* U34.

Tristia

Ovid's Tristia. Containing five books of mournful elegies... Newly translated into English, 1713, 1726. *See* O254–5.

[**III.9**] An elegy on the death of Mr. Alexander Pope. Being an imitation of the ninth elegy in the third book of Ovid, 1744. *See* E218.

———————

Pack, Richardson: The nooning. A poem. Translated from Ovid, 1719. *See* P8.

O256 Owens, Samuel. An elegy on the much lamented death of Mr. John Lock, of Athyoe, who departed this life the second of November, 1747. [*Dublin*, 1747.]
½°: 1 side, 2 columns.
'Athyoe alas! who can thy grief express'
L(1890.e.5/30).

O257 — A petition humbly offer'd to his most gracious majesty King George; in behalf of his loyal subjects of Ireland: in relation to William Wood's esq; and others. [*Dublin*] *Printed by James Carson*, 1724.
½°: 1 side, 2 columns.
'What hurricanes disturb our isle?'
CtY.

O258 — A poem, or advice to the authors of a satyrical poem, upon Tom Punsibi and to the (form'd) dessenting teachers letters to Jett Black. *Dublin, printed in the year* 1724.
½°: 1 side, 2 columns.
'Ye sons of Levi, church divines'
Probably related to [William Tisdall] *Tom Pun-sibi metamorphosed*, 1724; 'Jet Black' was a nickname for Jonathan Smedley.
CtY.

O259 — Remarks on the young ladies petition, to the revnd. Dr. B—rk—y. [*Dublin*, 1725?]
½°: 1 side, 1 column.
'Fair lady your petition with care I did read'
In answer to *The humble petition of a beautiful young lady*, [1725?], asking to be allowed to accompany George Berkeley to his projected college in the Bermudas.
Crawford.

Owens, S.

O260 — Remarks upon the report of the committee of the lords of his majesty's most honourable privy-council, in relation to Mr. Woods's half-pence. [*Dublin*] *Printed in the year* 1724.
½°: 1 side, 2 columns.
'Vulcan my muse to me describe'
LVA-F,C; CSmH,CtY.

O261 [—] ⟨A⟩ scourge for the author of the satyr, gibing on Trinity College, and on the reverend Dean Swift, Hibernia's Apollo; presented to the reverend Dean Smedley, with remarks on his petition to the Duke of G—ft—n. Written by S. O. L. S. [*Dublin*] *Printed in the* ⟨*year*⟩ 1725.
½°: 1 side, 2 columns.
Teerink 1203.
'Most reverend dean, good Mr. Smedley'
An attack on Jonathan Smedley, occasioned by his *A satyr*, 1725, *An epistle to his grace*, 1724, and (apparently) an unidentified satire on Trinity College (possibly P1); but primarily against his defence of Wood's halfpence.
L(C.121.g.8/43).

O262 [—] Sr. Tubal Cain's advice to the free-holders and free-men, of the city of Dublin, concerning their setting up for candidate, and electing the hon. Sir William Fowns bart...member of parliament in the room of Alderman John Stoyte, lately deceas'd. [*Dublin*] *Printed in the year* 1729.
½°: 1 side, 1 column.
'To all freeholders now I write'
Signed 'S. O. L. S', for Samuel Owens Lock Smith. In favour of Sir William Fowns.
CtY.

O263 [—] Trinity Colledge vindicated, or a short defence, of the reverend Dean Swift. By S. O——s, L.S. *Dublin, printed by G.N.* [*Gwyn Needham*], 1725.
½°: 1 side, 2 columns.
Teerink 1202.
'Monsieur the revd. dean will write'
L(C.121.g.8/41),C; TxU.

O264 Ox. The ox roasted and the bull baited. On the Examiner's supporters, call'd ox and bull. [*London*, 1714.]
slip: 1 side, 1 column.
Below, 'On the late Examiner'.
'New revolutions, new alarms'
On the Examiner: 'O Jonathan of merry fame'
Satires on Harley, Bolingbroke, and Swift.
Crawford; CSmH.

O265 Oxenard. Oxenard reviv'd: or, a short account of his life: together with his late journey into hell, where he had a conference with Oliver Crumwell [!], who procur'd him a furlong to come back again into this world. [*Dublin*, 172–?]
½°: 2 sides, 1 column.
The L copy is bound with Dublin half-sheets of the 1720s.

'When I my exit from the world had made'
Oxenard was an Irish priest-catcher.
L(C.121.g.8/143); CtY.

O266 — Oxinards's lamentation e're he hung himself
naer [!] the cittadel. In a fit of despair being
abandoned by his friends, and his roguery and
cheating brought to light, which made him put a
final period to his wretched life. [*Dublin*, 171–.]
½°: 1 side, 2 columns.

Dated in *Rothschild* as 1724/25 on account of a
reference to 'Whartons fall the want of pelf';
but the reference must be to Thomas Wharton
and the whig defeat of 1710, for Oxenard
served under Wharton when lord lieutenant
of Ireland.

'What cursed planet rul'd when I was born'
Rothschild.

Oxford. Oxford. A poem, 1707. *See* Tickell,
Thomas.

— Oxford act: an epistle to a noble lord, 1714.
See Allett, Thomas.

O267 — Oxford and Mortimer's vindication: or, another new song, in answer to Credit restor'd. To
the tune, Come prithee, Horace, hold up thy head.
*London printed, and sold by the booksellers of London
& Westminster*, 1711.
½°: 1 side, 2 columns.
'Now high-church rejoyce at this turn of the
state'

A tory poem in defence of Harley against
[Arthur Mainwaring] *An excellent new song
called, Credit restored*, 1711.
Crawford; *Harding*.

O268 — The Oxford cricks. A satire. *London, printed
for J. Roberts*, 1719. (*PB* 5 Feb)
8°: π¹ A–C⁴ D¹; [2] *i–viii, 1* 2–17 *18 blk.* π1 hft.
'In Oxford bards there are most sad ones'

Nicholas Amhurst's authorship was suggested
in Pickering & Chatto cat. 284/12; one MH
copy is bound with a collection of Amhurst
pamphlets, and the attribution is plausible.
O(2); CSmH(−π1),MH(2,−π1).

— 'The Oxford loyalty.' [1720.]
*Copies taken from the records of the court of
King's bench* (1763) 23 records a warrant of
25 May 1720 beginning 'Whereas I have
received information, that a bale or large
parcel of seditious and treasonable ballads,
and other libels, particularly one, entitled, the
Oxford loyalty, directed to Mrs Elizabeth
Cole, alias Green, is bringing to town...'

— The Oxford oyster women, [1733.] *See* Sedition,
1733.

— 'The Oxford prophecy, fore-telling the late
sudden change at C[our]t. Verse. 1711.'
Morgan N469; not traced, possibly in ms.

O269 — The Oxford riddle, or, a key to Dr. Sa----l's
padlock. A poem. *London, printed by J. Read*,
[171–?]
2°: A² < B¹; *1–2* 3–6.
Printed on one side of the paper only, pp. 4–5
blank; presumably after the Stamp act of
1712.
'From heaven first my ancient lineage came'
On Sacheverell. The answer to the riddle is
the divine right of kings.
Madan.

O270 — The Oxford sermon versified. By Jacob
Gingle, esq; *London, printed for Timothy Atkins, at
Dr. Sacheverell's Head*, 1729. (*MChr* 20 Dec)
8°: A–H⁴; *i–ii* iii–vii *viii,* 9–63 *64 blk.* 63 advt.
The imprint is probably fictitious; see *Plomer*.
Possibly the 'Betty's Sermon, Verse', the
copyright of which, with 400 books, formed
lot 17 of the trade sale ascribed to 'Mr Astley
& Conger', 11 Nov 1735 (cat. at O-JJ), sold
to King for one guinea.
'Tho' dame religion's such a beauty'
'Jacob Gingle' is clearly a pseudonym. A skit
on Joseph Betty's sermon *The divine institution
of the ministry*, 1729.
L(1357.d.21/4),LVA-F,O,C,E+; CLU,CtY(uncut),ICN,IU(uncut),MH.

O271 — — Dedicated to the Revd. Joseph Betty, M.A.
By Jacob Gingle, esq; The second edition. *London
printed for Timothy Atkins*, 1730. (*MChr* 20 Jan)
8°: A² B–E⁴; *i–ii* iii–vi, 7–36. 36 advt.
L(T.1628/15; 164.l.61),LDW(lacks E4),O,
LdU-B; CtY(2),MH.

O272 — — The third edition. *London, printed for
Timothy Atkins*, 1730.
8°: A–D⁴ E²; *i–ii* iii–vi, 7–36. 36 advt.
L(11633.c.6),O; CU,CtY.

O273 — — *Dublin, printed by S. Powell, for George Risk,
George Ewing, & William Smith*, 1730.
8°: A–B⁸; *i–iii* iv–v, '7' 7–32.
L(11631.aa.5, title mutilated),O(2),C,DA,DK;
CtY.

— The Oxford shepherds, 1741. *See* The bench,
1741–.

O274 — The Oxford tragedy: or, the sorrowful lamentation of Sarah Sparrow, who was condemn'd for the
murther of her bastard child. To the tune of,
Near Tame a town in Oxford-shire. *London,
printed for B.M.*, 1716.
½°: 1 side, 2 columns.
'Good Christian people all, I pray'
In the O copy, Hearne has corrected the
lady's name to Jane in the title and Anna in
the text.
O.

O275 — The Oxford treatment of their Cambridge
friends, at the Act. In a dialogue between Eugenius
and Crites. *London printed, and sold by B. Bragg*,
1705. (10 July, Luttrell)

The **Oxford** treatment

2⁰: *A*² B–C²; *i–ii*, 1–10.
'Mother of arts, delight of men and gods'
'Writt by one of Cambridge, reflecting upon
Oxford', Luttrell.
L(11630.g.26),O,*MR-C*; CtY,MH,NjP(Luttrell).

O276 Oxfordshire. Oxfordshire. [*London*] *Printed in the*
year 1704 [1704/5?].
½⁰: 1–2, 1 column.
'Perusing the list of the tackers in print'
For a suggestion that the author was Charles
Darby, see the following entry. The same
authority identified Darby as the author of
The tackers, and in view of the similarity of
the subject there may have been a confusion
between the two poems. On the unanimous
Oxfordshire vote for the tack, 28 Nov 1704.
O.

O277 — [*idem*] The Oxfordshire nine. *London, printed*
in the year 1705. (April?)
½⁰: 1–2, 1 column.
The copy at PPL has a contemporary ms. note
'Sd to be writ by Mr Darby a Con: Minr in
Suffolk. Aprill 1705'.
L(C.121.g.9/143),LLP,DG,Crawford; PPL.

O278 — [another edition]
Pages not numbered.
DK.

O279 — The Oxfordshire election. *London, printed in the*
year 1710. (4 April, Luttrell)
½⁰: 1 side, 1 column.
The rule above the imprint is in two sections.
'We are told by the town, that a man of great note'
Crum W76: 'A ballad on Dr. Lancaster vice-
chancellor, and the Oxfordshire election
17[o]9/10'. He voted whig.
DG,*Chatsworth*; MH(Luttrell),OCU.

O280 — [another edition]
The rule above the imprint is composed of 17
short rules.
L(1876.f.1/49),O(2),DT,Rothschild.

— The Oxfordshire nine, 1705. *See* Oxfordshire,
1704 (O277).

Oxinards. *See* Oxenard.

O281 Oysters. 'Oysters. A poem. [*London*] *Sold by the*
booksellers. Price 6*d*.' (*GM* Dec 1733)
Possibly related to *The Oxford oyster women*,
[1733], S191.

O282 Ozell, John. Boileau's Lutrin: a mock-heroic
poem. In six canto's. Render'd into English verse.
To which is prefix'd some account of Boileau's
writings... *London, printed for R. Burrough & J.*
Baker, E. Sanger & E. Curll, 1708. (*DC* 1 June)
8⁰: (frt+) A⁸ *⁴(–*4) B–H⁸ I⁴ K¹; *i–xxii*, 1–122.
122 err, advt.
*⁴ contains the dedication.

Ozell, J. Boileau's Lutrin
'Arms and the priest I sing, whose martial soul'
Dedication signed.
L(11474.bbb.28),LVA-D,O(2, 1–frt),DT,
LdU-B; DFo,MH.

O283 — [reissue] *London, printed for E. Sanger & E.*
Curll, 1708.
8⁰: (frt+) A⁸(±A1) *⁴(–*4) B–H⁸ I⁴ K¹; *i–xxii*,
1–122. 122 err, advt.
OW,ExU; CSmH,KU.

O284 — [*idem*] The Lutrin: an heroi-comical poem. In
six cantos. By Monsieur Boileau... The third
edition, corrected and revis'd by the last Paris
edition. Adorn'd with cuts. *London, printed for E.*
Curll, & F. Burleigh, 1714. (*MC* July)
12⁰: A–D¹² E⁶; *i–v* vi–xxiv, 1–83 *84*. A1 frt.
The plates are included in the collation. In an
'advertisement' on p. 84 Ozell acknowledges
help from Samuel Cobb and [? Charles]
Johnson. The second edition formed part of
Boileau's *Works*, 1711–13.
L(240.e.3),O,OW; *CSmH,KU,MH*.

O285 — — The fourth edition, corrected and revis'd
by the last Paris edition. *Dublin, printed by S.*
Powell, for George Risk, George Ewing, & William
Smith, 1730.
12⁰: (frt+) A–F⁸/⁴; *1–2* 3–72.
No plates in this edition.
O,EN(–frt, lacks F4),DN(–frt),DT(2),AdU
(–frt).

O286 — La secchia rapita: the trophy-bucket. A mock-
heroic poem... by Signior Alessandro Tassoni...
Done from the Italian into English rhime, by Mr.
Ozell. To which is annex'd, a correct copy of
Tassoni's original... With historical cuts. Part I.
London, printed by J. D. [John Darby?] for Egbert
Sanger, 1710. (*DC* 10 July)
8⁰: A–D⁸ E⁴, ²A–C⁸ D⁴; *1–4* 5–70 *71–72*, *1–2*
3–54 *55–56 blk*. A1 frt; 70 err; 72 advt.
A translation of cantos I & II; the Italian text
has a separate title-leaf. A note on p. 71
records that 'it is intended, in the future parts
of this work, to sell [the English and Italian
texts] distinct'; but apparently no more were
published.
'How fierce a flame did Italy o'er-run'
O,OW,DT(–²D4),EtC; MH(–²D4),TxU(lacks
E4 and Italian text).

O287 — [reissue] La secchia rapita: the trophy bucket
... Made English from the original Italian, by
Mr. Ozell. To which is prefix'd, the judgment of
Mr. Dryden, and other learned men... With a
correct copy of Tassoni's original... *London,*
printed for E. Curll, 1713. (*PB* 6 June)
8⁰: A⁸(–A2+χ²) B–D⁸ E⁴, ²A–C⁸ D⁴; [6] 5–70
71–72, *1–2* 3–54 *55–56 blk*. A1 frt; 70 err; 72 advt.
χ1 is cancel title, χ2 contains Dryden's
judgment, etc. The Italian text retains the
1710 title-leaf.
L(1063.g.26, –²D4),DT(lacks Italian text).

Ozell, J. La secchia rapita

O288 — [reissue] The rape of the bucket. An heroi-
comical poem. The first of the kind. Made English
from the original Italian of Tassoni by Mr. Ozell.
The second edition. *London, printed for E. Curll,*
1715. (21 Aug)
8°: A⁸(±A2) B–D⁸ E⁴, ²A–C⁸ D⁴; *1–4* 5–70
71–72, 1–2 3–54 *55–56 blk*. A1 frt; 70 err; 72 advt.

With a new cancel title-leaf; the Italian text
still retains the 1710 title-leaf. Publication
date from *Straus, Curll.*
L(11426.d.86, stitched, uncut),O(2, 1–²D4, 1
lacks A1, Italian text),CT(–²D4, Italian bound
separately); CLU-C,DFo,TxU(lacks E4, Italian
text).

P

P——, —, *Mr.* The fairy-king, 1726. *See* F37.

P., A. *For Latin verses by* A.P., *see* Pitcairne, Archibald.

— A pastoral poem to the memory of...Lord Basil Hamiltoun, 1701. *See* P118.

— A satyr on the poets of the town, 1726. *See* S62.

P., A., *esq;* The modern Englishman, 1739. *See* M367.

P., A., *gent.* Corydon and Cochrania, 1723. *See* Pennecuik, Alexander, *d. 1730.*

P., J. Britanniæ lætantis exultatio, [1714.] *See* Perkins, Joseph.

— The glorious year, [1714/15.] *See* G183.

— To Robert earl of Oxford, [1714.] *See* T358.

P., J., *Sc.* A threnodie or the lamentations, 1702. *See* T265.

P., N. Weighley, alias Wild, 1725. *See* W277.

P., R. A poem on the thirtieth of October, [1726?] *See* P646.

P., S., *A.M.* The eleventh epistle of the first book of Horace, imitated, 1749. *See* Pullein, Samuel.

P., S., *ecclesiae presbyter.* Carmina sacra de omnibus festis ecclesiae anglicanae, 1748. *See* Pigott, Samuel.

P., S. *gent.* Britton's consort, 1703. *See* B482.

P., T. Ovid's Tristia...translated into English by T.P., 1713. *See* O254.

P., W. The nuptialls of the lamb, 1701. *See* N348.

P., W., *esq;* Quadrille to perfection as play'd at Soissons, [1728.] *See* Q3.

P., W., *gent.* A whip for the Spaniards, 1701. *See* W401.

————

P1 P——. ⟨The⟩ p—— and s—— fe——s of T——y C——e, Dublin, their a---s to the L--- C------, &c. —— —— versi. [*Dublin*, 1725?]
½°: 2 sides, 1 column.
'We loyal hearts of Dublin C-----e'
    The address of the provost and senior fellows of Trinity College to Lord Carteret satirized. Possibly the 'satyr, gibing on Trinity College' answered in [Samuel Owens] *A scourge for the*

author of the satyr, 1725, and there (apparently) ascribed to Smedley.
L(C.121.g.8/116); CSmH.

Pacata. Pacata Britannia, 1713. *See* Newcomb, Thomas.

P2 Pacific. The pacifick fleet: a new ballad. *London, printed for A. Moore,* 1729. (*MChr* 2 Aug)
2°: *A² B¹; 1–3 4–5 6 blk.*
    Percival appendix 17. Horizontal chain-lines. What is apparently another impression was issued with *Great Britain's glory,* 1729. A general warrant for the author, printer, and publisher was issued 12 Sept 1729.
'Good people, give ear, and I'll tell you a story'
    A satire on the inactivity of the fleet at Spithead.
L(1484.m.30),O; OCU,TxU.

P3 —— [1729.]
½°: 1 side, 1 column.
L(1875.d.6/12).

P4 —— [*Dublin?*] *Printed in the year* 1729. (Sept)
½°: 1 side, 1 column.
    The DT copy is bound with Dublin half-sheets; the Crawford has ms. note of 6 Sept 1729.
DT,Crawford.

Pack. The pack of bear-dogs, 1713. *See* The old pack, O123.

Pack, Richardson. Miscellanies in verse and prose. *London, printed for E. Curll,* 1719 [1718]. (*PB* 8 July).
8°: pp. iv, 127.   L,O; CtY,MH.

—— The second edition. *London, printed for E. Curll,* 1719. (*PB* 28 Feb)
8°: pp. vi, 190.   L,O; CtY,MH.
    Watermark: initials. An enlarged collection.

— [fine paper]   L; ICU.
    Watermark: Strasburg bend.

— [reissue] The second edition. *London, printed for E.C.; sold by John Hooke,* 1724.
        CLU-C,ViU.

— A new collection of miscellanies in prose and verse. *London, printed for E. Curll,* 1725. (24 June).
8°: pp. 34, 128.   L,O; CtY,MH.
    Watermark: initials.

— [fine paper]   L,E; ICU,KU.
    No watermark: cut copy measures 8¾ × 5½ inches. The L copy is in contemporary morocco.

— Miscellaneous works in verse and prose...In two parts... *Dublin, printed by S. Powell, for G. Risk,* 1726.
12°: pp. 283.   L,O.
    Apparently a reprint of both the previous collections.

Pack, R.

— The whole works...in prose and verse. Now collected into one volume: with some account of his life and writings... *London, printed for E. Curll,* 1729.
8°.   LVA-D; CtY,IU.
A nonce collection, including the two previous collections; the make-up of the volume varies from copy to copy.

— Major Pack's poetical remains... To which are added translations from Catullus, Tibullus, and Ovid. With an essay on the Roman elegiack poets, &c. *London, printed for E. Curll,* 1738. (*GM* Feb)
8°: pp. iv, iv, 40+.   O; CtY,KU.
Apparently intended to be followed by the second edition of Pack's *Miscellanies,* 1719, which included the translations and essay.

P5 — A congratulatory poem to his majesty George the IId upon his accession to the throne. To which are prefixed verses inscribed to...the Earl of Scarborough. *Cambridge, printed for Corn. Crownfield; sold by J. Knapton, London,* 1727. (*MC* Oct).
2°: A–B²; *1–2* 3–8.
Watermark: LC.
'While Cam and Isis at your royal feet'
C,*MR*; TxU.

P6 — [fine paper?]
Watermark: MT.
O.

P7 [—] An epilogue spoke to a play call'd the Alchymist. *Sold by the printsellers of London & Westminster,* [1721.] (*DP* 13 Dec)
½°: 1 side, 2 columns.
Engraved throughout; theatrical scene at head. Advertised as 'A new South-Sea epilogue'.
'Old surly Ben, to night, hath let us know'
Crum O1037: 'Epilogue to the Alchymist acted at Bury 1721 by Maj. Pack'.
L(P&D 1718).

P8 — The nooning. A poem. Translated from Ovid, at the request of a young lady at the last ball. By Major Pack. *London, printed for E. Curll,* 1719 [1718]. (*PB* 16 Dec)
2°: A² B¹; *1–2* 3–5 6. 6 advt.
''Twas summer, and, with sultry heat opprest'
DrU; MH.

P9 — Religion and philosophy: a tale. With five other pieces. *London, printed for E. Curll,* 1720. (*PB* 20 Feb)
8°: A² B–C⁴ D²; *i–ii* iii *iv,* 1–19 20. 20 advt.
Some copies (CSmH,ICN) add a catalogue of Curll's books signed A⁴.
'Iris, a tender soft believing maid'
L(11631.c.32),O; CSmH,ICN(Luttrell, April), IU,KU,MH+.

[—] To his grace the Duke of Argyle, upon his arrival at court, 1716. *See* T335.

Paget, T.C., *baron*

[**Paget, Thomas Catesby,** *baron Paget.*] Miscellanies in prose and verse. *London, printed in the year* 1741.
8°: pp. 374.   L,O; CtY,MH.
Some copies have a leaf of errata pasted to B5ᵛ.

P10 [—] An epistle to Mr. P— — in anti-heroicks. Written in MDCCXXXVI. *London, printed in the year* 1738 [1737?]. (28 Dec?)
8°: *A*⁴ B⁴(±B1) C⁴; *1–4* 5–24. A1 hft.
All copies are apparently on fine paper, watermarked with Strasburg bend. Entered twice in Bowyer's ledgers to Fletcher Gyles, first under 5 Dec 1737 and then as '2d Edit' under 28 Dec, *gratis.* The detailed accounts show that 15 copies were first printed, the work then reset and 18 copies printed, including the cancel leaf. It seems possible from the fact that the second edition was printed free that the first was faulty and suppressed. Probably for private circulation only.
'Disdain not, P—, my verse to hear'
Addressed to Pope; the dedication copy at LVA-D has note by Pope 'By Lord Paget'. Reprinted in Paget's *Miscellanies,* 1741.
LVA-D; CtY(−A1),DFo(presentation copy to Orrery),ICU.

P11 [—] An essay on human life. *London printed, and are to be sold by Fletcher Gyles,* 1734 [1735?]. (20 Jan?)
4°: *A*¹ B–D⁴ E¹; *i–ii,* 1–24 *25; 26* blk. E1 advt.
Entered to Gyles in Bowyer's ledgers under 6 Nov 1734, 250 copies printed. Probably circulated privately before publication. Listed in *GM* Jan 1735.
'Pleasure but cheats us with an empty name'
Reprinted in Paget's *Miscellanies,* 1741.
L(11630.e.6/11, Tom's Coffee House, 20 Jan, cropt; 1486.tt.2,−E1),O(−E1),OC(−E1),DT; CSmH(−E1),CtY,*MnU,PU,*TxU(−E1).

P12 [—] — '*London printed, and are to be sold by Fletcher Gyles*' [*Edinburgh*], 1735.
8°: A–B⁴ C²; *1–3* 4–20.
Printed by Ruddiman on the evidence of the ornaments.
L(993.e.51/6),O,E(2); CLU,CtY-M,ICU.

P13 [—] — The second edition. Corrected and much enlarg'd by the author. *London printed, and are to be sold by Fletcher Gyles,* 1736 [1735]. (*LM* Dec)
4°: π¹ A–D⁴ E⁴(−E4); *i–x,* 1–30.
Entered to Gyles in Bowyer's ledgers under 28 Nov 1735, 202 copies and 48 fine. Both qualities of paper have Strasburg bend watermark of differing design; fine paper copies have been distinguished by the imprint.
L(643.k.3/13),O,C,*MR*; CLU,MH,*OCU.*

P14 [—] [fine paper] *London, printed in the year* 1736.
L(1346.i.19); TxU.

Paget, T.C., *baron.* An essay on human life

P15 —— by the right honourable Lord Pagett[!]...
The third edition. Corrected and much enlarg'd
by the author. *London, printed for Fletcher Gyles,*
1736 [1737?]. (*GM* Feb)
8°: A⁴ a⁴ B–E⁴; *i–xvi,* 1–32. ii err.
> Watermark: GAR crowned. 'Price 1*s.*' on
> title. Entered to Gyles in Bowyer's ledgers
> under 1 Nov 1736, 500 copies and 6 royal.
> The detailed ledger under 13–27 Nov shows
> the setting and printing of 500 'Errata to
> Essay on Human Life', but what this means
> is uncertain. Since the errata are on the verso
> of the title-leaf, it could imply a cancel A1;
> this has not been observed. Copies were
> probably circulated privately before publica-
> tion.
L(11630.bbb.11),O; CtY,IU,MH,PU.

P16 [—] [fine paper] *London, printed in the year* 1736.
> Watermark: Strasburg bend. No price on
> title, no errata, Paget's name removed from
> title.
LVA-D(Pope's copy),LdU-B; DFo(presentation
copy to Orrery).

P17 [—] — By the author of the Essay on man. The
third edition. Corrected and much enlarg'd by the
author. '*London, printed for J. Witford,* 1736.'
8°: *A⁴* B–D⁴; *i–v* vi–xii, *1* 2–18 *19–20 blk.* A1 hft.
> A well-printed piracy; for the use of the false
> name 'Witford' (for Wilford) compare the
> piracies of Pope's *Essay on man.* By the analogy
> of that, the date may be later than 1736. The
> implied attribution to Pope has been corrected
> in ms. in the L copy.
L(11601.dd.11/3, −D4),*LVA-D,*O(−A1, D4);
KU(−A1),OCU(−D4).

P18 —— By the...Lord Paget. The third edition.
Corrected and much enlarg'd by the author.
*London: printed, and Dublin re-printed by George
Faulkner,* 1736.
8°: A–C⁴ D²; *i–x,* 1–16 *17–18.* D2 advt.
L(C136..aa.1/8),C(−D2),DA(2, 1−D2),DK;
CSmH.

P19 [—] An essay on human life. *London, printed by
J. Haberkorn,* [175–?]
8°: A⁴ B⁴ D⁴; *1–13* 14–23 *24 blk.*
> Horizontal chain-lines; possibly a duodecimo
> with three signatures. 'Advertisement' on p. 3
> speaks of 'the following poem being omitted
> in Mr. Pope's own edition'.
O(2); MH.

P20 [—] A kind of a dialogue in hudibrasticks. Design-
ed for the use of the unthinking and the unlearned.
London, printed for T. Cowper at the Globe, 1739.
(*GM, LM* Feb)
4°: π¹ A–B⁴ C¹; *i–ii,* 1–4 5–17 *18 blk.* π1 hft.
> Entered to Fletcher Gyles in Bowyer's
> ledgers under 23 Jan, 500 copies printed.
'Oft have we reason'd much and long'
Printed in Paget's *Miscellanies,* 1741.

Paget, T.C., *baron.* A kind of a dialogue

L(840.k.3/9, −π1; 11630.d.13/7, −π1, cropt),
MR; ICU,NjP,OCU(−π1, cropt),TxU.
[—] A satyr. In the manner of Persius [actually
by John, lord Hervey], 1730–. *See* H161·5.

P21 Paget, William. The humours of the Fleet. A
poem. By W. Paget, comedian. With a preface,
containing a sketch of the author's life. *Birmingham, printed by T. Aris, for the author,* [1745?]
8°: A–E⁴ (D2 as 'D3'); *i–iii* iv–viii, *1* 2–32.
> Dated from the preface which refers to pub-
> lishing *A voyage to Ipswich* 'four years since'.
'Ye sons of riot and imprudence come'
L(1419.e.32),BP.

P22 [—] — an humorous, descriptive poem. Written
by a gentleman of the college... With a preface...
London, printed for B. Dickinson, 1749. (*GM* Jan)
8°: A–E⁴; *i–iii* iv–vii *'vii',* 9–40.
> A folding engraving titled 'The humours of
> the Fleet' with imprint 'for B. Dickinson'
> and price 6*d.* is found as a frontispiece in most
> copies; it was probably issued separately.
L(11633.h.2, extra-illustrated),LG,LdU-B (extra-
illustrated); CSmH,CtY,DFo,ICN,OCU+.

P23 — A voyage to Ipswich, a narrative poem.
Interspersed with divers sentiments on happiness,
wealth, power... Including two prologues, one in
praise of commerce, the other in honour of
Admiral Vernon, spoken at the playhouse in
Ipswich, by the author...With a preface address'd
to the impartial. *Ipswich, printed by W. C. [William
Craighton] for the author,* 1741.
8°: *A¹* B–H⁴ I⁴(−I4); *i–iii* iv–xv *xvi,* 1–47 *48 blk.*
ii err.
> Advertised in the *Ipswich journal* 29 Aug as
> 'now in the press and will speedily be pub-
> lish'd by subscription, at 2*s.* 6*d.* each'.
'When Phæbus with enliv'ning warmth prevails'
L(11631.bb.3),IP; MH.

Pain. Pain and patience, 1742. *See* Dodsley,
Robert.

P24 Paine, James. Instructions to free-holders, or,
directions for the choice of a good parliament.
London, printed in the year 1715. (24 Jan?)
½°: 1 side, 1 column.
'Go now my muse, on thy allegiance go'
> Ms. note in the L copy 'January the 24th the
> day of election at Westminster'.
L(1876.f.1/78).

Palaemon. Palæmon; or, a pastoral imitation of
Mr. Pope's first pastoral, 1730. *See* Gahagan,
Usher.

— Palæmon to Cælia, at Bath, 1717. *See* Welsted,
Leonard.

Pallas. Pallas and Venus. An epigram, 1706. *See*
Prior, Matthew.

Pallas

— Pallas and Venus reconcil'd, 1731. *See* Shepherd, Samuel.

[**Palmer, Richard.**] Palmyra: or, poems on several subjects. Never before publish'd. *London printed, and sold by J. Morphew*, 1712 [1711]. (16 Nov, Luttrell)
8°: pp. 41.   L; CLU-C,TxU.
> The authorship is spelt out, one letter per page, on pp. 1–19. Reissued in *A new collection of miscellany poems for the year 1715.*

Palmyra. Palmyra: or, poems on several subjects, 1712. *See* Palmer, Richard.

P25 Pamela. Pamela: or, the fair impostor. A poem, in five cantos... By J---- W----, esq; *London, printed for E. Bevins; sold by J. Roberts*, 1744. (*GM, LM* Jan)
4°: π¹ B–F⁴ G⁴(–G1); *i–ii, 1–46.*
> Bond 186.
'Of female wiles I sing, their subtle art'
> The tale is a mock-heroic burlesque on Richardson's *Pamela.*
L(1962),O; ICN,MH.

P26 — — *Dublin, printed in the year* 1743 [1744?].
4°: A–G⁴; *1–3 4–56.*
> The regular collation suggests that this is the later edition despite the date, but it is unusual to find a Dublin reprint with more pages than the original.
L(1485.s.2),C(uncut).

Pamphleteers. The pamphleteers, 1703. *See* Mandeville, Bernard.

P27 Pancharilla. Pancharilla, from Bonefonius. A new ballad, ascrib'd to the honourable Miss C——t. By the honourable Mr. S——t. [*Dublin*, 1725/30.]
½°: 1 side, 1 column.
'I'll ne'er dissemble, 'tis in vain!'
> To Grace Carteret.
L(C.121.g.8/125); CtY.

P28 Pandemonium. Pandæmonium: or a new infernal expedition. Inscrib'd to a being who calls himself William Lauder. By Philalethes. *London, printed for W. Owen*, 1750. (*GM* Dec)
4°: A² B–D²; *1–3 4–15 16 blk.*
'By him they own'd their sov'reign when they fell'
> Listed by *Rawlinson* under John Douglas as part of the controversy between him and William Lauder. It is not clear whether he meant that Douglas was the author; it seems possible. A satirical attack on Lauder for his fraudulent essay on Milton's plagiarism.
L(11630.d.2/17; 840.l.39),LVA-D(ms. date 29 Dec); IU,MH.

P29 Pandora. Pandora's box: a satyr against snuff. *London printed, and sold by J. Bettenham*, 1718. (*PB* 9 Dec)

Pandora's box

8°: (frt+) A–D⁴; *1–3 4–32.*
'Of this lethargick age to lull the brain'
L(992.h.27; 164.k.50,–frt, Luttrell, Dec),O (uncut); NN-A.

P30 — — The second edition. *London printed, and sold by J. Bettenham*, 1719 [1718]. (*PB* 18 Dec)
8°: (frt+) A–D⁴; *1–3 4–32.*
> Apparently a variant title. *PB* 12 March 1720 advertises 'the third edition, corrected' as sold by Tho. Bickerton; but Bickerton appears to have been advertising invented new editions at this period.
NN-A.

P31 Panegyric. A panegyrick epistle, (wherein is given an impartial character of the present English poets) to S. R—— B—— on his most incomparable incomprehensible poem, call'd Advice to the poets. *London printed, and sold by B. Bragge*, 1706. (*DC* 10 Aug)
2°: *A²* B–C²; *i–iv, 1–8.* A1 hft.
'Permit an humble muse to sing thy praise'
> A reply to Sir Richard Blackmore's *Advice to the poets*, 1706. Identified in H. G. de Maar, *History of modern English romanticism* I (1924) 150 as the 'verses against Blackmore' by John Philips referred to in a letter of Elijah Fenton to Joseph Newton, 24 Jan 1707, but the attribution has not been generally accepted.
L(643.l.24/29; 643.l.25/10),O,*MR-C*; CLU-C (Luttrell, undated),MH,NjP,OCU,TxU+.

P32 — A panegyrick in answer to a lible [!] on the late famous D--------n of T.C. deceas'd. [*Dublin*] *Printed in the year* 1730.
8°: *A–B⁴*; *i–iv, 1–2 3–10 11–12 blk.* A1 blk.
'As Hudibrs[!] observes, inspite'
> Preface signed 'H—— G——n'; in fact a satire on Hugh Graffan, following *The Censoriad*, 1730.
DG(–A1); IU,MH(–A1, B4).

— A panegyric on a court, 1739. *See* Gilbert, Thomas.

P33 — [dh] A panegyrick on a noble peer and worthy patriot. [*Edinburgh*, 1704.]
4°: A²; *1–4.*
'Come sing my muse the noble prince's fame'
> A panegyric on James, duke of Hamilton.
E(2),ES(ms. date 1704).

P34 — A panegyrick on the fair-sex. *London, printed for M. Cooper*, 1747. (*BM* May; *GM* June)
4°: A–C⁴; *1–3 4–24.*
'And art thou then, dear lovely creature'
IU.

P35 — — *London printed: Dublin re-printed by R. James*, 1747.
8°: A–B⁴ C²; *1–2 3–20.*
L(11632.aa.61),DN.

Panegyric

P36 — A panegyric on the reverend D--n S----t. In answer to the Libel on Dr. D--y, and a certain great l--d. [*Dublin*] *Printed in the year* 1729–30.
8°: A⁴ (A2 as 'A'); *1–2* 3–8.
   Rothschild 2121; *Teerink* 691; *Williams* 491.
'Could all we little folks that wait'
   Attributed to James Arbuckle by Faulkner in 1768; *Ball* 252–3 attributed it to Swift on the evidence of his correspondence, and *Williams* agreed. A copy of the following edition at AN is bound in a collection of Arbuckle's published poems with additional ms. poems, which suggests the attribution to him was correct.
L(11631.a.63/8),LVA-F,DG,DN(2, 1 uncut), DT+; *CSmH*,CtY,ICN,MH.

P37 — A panegyric on the reverend Dean Swift. In answer to a Libel on Dr. Delany, and a certain great lord. Never before printed. *London, printed for J. Roberts, & N. Blandford,* 1730. (*MChr* 14 March)
4°: A–D² (A2 as 'B'); *1–3* 4–15 *16 blk.*
   Teerink 692.
L(11631.e.61),LVA-F,O,AN.

P38 — A panegyrick on the reverend father John Baptist Girard, Jesuit. Attempted in the namby-pambaick strain. By Timothy Flash, poetaster. *Dublin, printed in the year* 1731.
8°: A⁴; *1–2* 3–8.
'All ye searchers of the fair'
   Father Girard was involved in the scandalous case of Miss Cadière.
DK.

P39 — A panegyrick on the safe arrival of her grace Anna dutches of Buccleugh into the kingdom of Scotland her native countrey, September 16th. 1701. [*Edinburgh*, 1701.]
½°: 1 side, 1 column.
'Great princess welcome to your native land'
   Signed 'A vero Scoto'.
E.

P40 — A panegyrick on the vintners, by a blyth son of Bacchus. [*Edinburgh?* 1715/–.]
½°: 1 side, 2 columns.
'Let hakney poets draw their pen'
E; *Harding.*

P41 — A panegyrick upon the English Catiline. [*London?*] *Printed in the year* 1711.
½°: 1 side, 1 column.
'Hail mighty hero of the British race'
   Apparently an attack on Harley.
L(1850.e.10/8),DT,Crawford,Rothschild.

P42 Panegyrical. A panegyrical epigram. [*Dublin?* 1713?]
½°: 1 side, 1 column.
   On the other side, *Plot upon plot*, [1713?]; see that entry for the place of publication.
'Since antient fabulists this fancy had'

A **panegyrical** epigram

A whig poem comparing Marlborough and Harley.
L(1850.e.10/15),LLP,O,C,E.

— A panegyrical epistle to Mr. Thomas Snow, 1721. *See* Gay, John.

P43 — A panegyrical poem on the fair and celebrated beauties in and about the city of Canterbury... By T.H. gent. *Canterbury, printed for the author by J. Abree,* 1718.
2°: A² B²; *1–2* 3–8.
'Paphos, was once bright Citherea's court'
   The copy seen has an early ms. attribution to T. Harrison; from the other notes, the annotator seems to have been well informed. On the other hand J. R. Smith, *Bibliotheca Cantiana,* attributes the work to T. Hardres. The same author clearly wrote *A congratulatory poem, on the anniversary-day,* 1718. Answered by [John Goatley] *To the author of the panegyrick,* 1718.
L(11633.i.17/1, ms. notes).

P44 Panthea. Panthea. An elegy on the death of the right honourable the lady Viscountess Scudamore. Humbly inscrib'd to her grace the Dutchess of Beaufort. *London, printed for William Lewis,* 1729. (*MChr* 1 Nov)
2°: A² B¹; *1–3* 4–6.
'Pensive, where Vaga's current murm'ring glides'
L(11641.l.2/1),E; DFo,IU.

P45 Pantheon. The pantheon: a vision. *London, printed for R. Dodsley; sold by M. Cooper,* 1747. (17 April)
4°: A–D⁴ (A3 as 'A2'); *1–7* 8–32. A1 hft.
   Date from *Straus, Dodsley*; listed in *GM* April.
'Of mystic visions, and th' illusive scenes'
   Horace Walpole's copy at MH has his ascription to 'Blakiston'; the MH catalogue says 'sometimes ascribed to Henry Blackstone', but the correct attribution is still in doubt.
L(642.l.28/4),LdU-B; ICN,IU,MH(uncut),NjP.

P46 Pantin. The pantin. A new ballad. *London, 'printed for Henry Tinpan, near the Strand',* 1748. (*GM* May)
2°: A⁴; *1–2* 3–6 *7–8 blk.*
   Horizontal chain-lines.
'I sing not of battles that now are to cease'
L(C.57.g.7/24); MH.

P47 Paper. The paper kite, a fable: humbly submitted to the consideration of H.H. esq; [*Dublin*] *Printed in the year* 1729.
½°: 1 side, 2 columns.
'From dirty kennels and a jakes'
   An attack on Hartley Hutchinson.
DT.

P48 Parade. La parade des archers écossois, poeme dramatique, addressé au...prince Jacques duc

La **parade** des archers

d'Hamilton et Brandon...et à tous les officiers de la Compagnie royale des archers écossois. *Imprimé à Edinbourg, l'an 1734.*
4°: *A² B–C²; 1–2 3–12.*
'Quel bruit entends-je? Que veut dire cet appareil'
O.

Paradise. Paradise lost: a poem. Attempted in rhime, 1740. *See* Jackson, Andrew.

— Paradice regain'd: or, the art of gardening, 1728. *See* Zinzano, Nicholas.

Paradisus. Paradisus amissa, 1702–. *See* Bold, Michael.

P49 Paradox. A paradox. The best perfume. Or: a paradox in praise of farting. *Dublin, printed in the year 1723.*
½°: 1 side, 2 columns.
'I sing the praises of a fart'
MH.

P50 Parallel. The parallel: an essay on friendship, love, and marriage. *London, printed for M. Cooper, 1746* [1745]. (23 Oct)
2°: *A² B–E²; i–ii iii–iv, 1 2–16.*
     Listed in *GM* Oct 1745. First published in 1689, *Wing* P333.
'Of these, dear friend, you have enjoin'd'
L(1962, Tom's Coffee House, 23 Oct 1745),O;MH.

Paraphrase. A paraphrase in verse, on part of the first book of Milton's Paradise lost, 1738. *See* Howard, W.

— 'The paraphrase on Isaiah 14', 1742. *See* Wesley, Charles.

P51 — A paraphrase on part of the book of Joshua. In three canto's. By J.M. S.T.C.D. *Dublin printed, and sold by Pressick Rider & Thomas Harbin, & by William Smith, 1724.*
8°: *A⁴ B–C⁴; i–iv, 1 2–20.*
'Of martial tribes in arms, of growing fear'
L(993.e.49/8); ICN.

P52 — A paraphrase on part of the fourteenth chapter of Isaiah, in English verse. Written on occasion of the battle of Ramellies, and the following successes. By a person of honour. *London, printed for A. Baldwin, 1712.*
8°: *A⁴; 1–2 3–8.*
     Cf. *A paraphrase on the fourteenth chapter,* 1706, P56.
'The lord will yet on Jacob mercy show'
OCU,TxU.

P53 — 'A paraphrase on the book of Job in verse, with reflections: to which are added, poems on several subjects. [*London*] *Printed for Jacob Robinson.* Price 1s.' (*GA* 26 Aug 1748)

P54 — A paraphrase on the creation. By a young gentleman. *London, printed for the author; sold by M. Cooper, 1744.* (*GM, LM* April)

A **paraphrase** on the creation

4°: *A¹ B–E²; i–ii, 1 2–15 16 blk.*
     The copy seen possibly lacks a half-title. Entered in Strahan's ledger to Joseph Barnardiston under March 1744, 2000 copies. Under 22 June 1745 'Paid Mrs Cooper balance on Poem on the creation', 15s. 10½d.
'When all was wrapt in one continued night'
     Compare *Good nature,* [1744], also 'by a young gentleman' and published by Cooper. Strahan printed various works for Barnardiston, and it is unlikely that he was the author. In April 1744 Strahan also entered John Alney's translation of Callimachus to Barnardiston; possibly Alney was the author of this as well.
L(11630.c.7/8).

P55 — A paraphrase on the lxxxii psalm, ascrib'd to the r—— h——e. By —— L—— gent. [*Dublin,* 1725?]
½°: 1 side, 1 column.
     On the other side of the CSmH copy, a calendar, *Lent assizes, 172⁴₅.*
'Know all ye judges of the earth!'
     To the lord chief justice, William Whitshed.
L(C.121.g.8/75); CSmH.

P56 — 'A paraphrase on the fourteenth chapter of Isaiah, in English verse, on occasion of the battle of Ramilly and the following successes. [*London*] *Printed for Benj. Bragg.* Price 2d.' (*DC* 10 July 1706)
     Listed in *DC* 10 July as 'The fourteenth chapter...', but subsequently (e.g. *DC* 14 Nov 1706) as 'A paraphrase on the 4th [!] chapter ...' It is clear that the same work is intended in each case, and it is clearly related to *A paraphrase on part of the fourteenth chapter,* 1712, P52.

P57 — A paraphrase on the fourteenth chapter of Isaiah, only appropriating what is there meant of the King of Babylon to Oliver the Protector. A pindarique. Humbly dedicated to D——d P——ll, esq; For the use of the Kentish free-holders. *London, printed in the year 1710.*
8°: A–C⁴; *i–viii, 1–15 16 blk.*
'How is the great oppressor ceas'd?'
     Dedication signed 'Philo Dear-heart', addressed to D. Polhill.
L(11623.c.5),LG,LLP,O; ICU,IU,*NN.*

P58 — A paraphrase on the hundred and fourth psalm, in verse. By E.W. *London, printed for R. Dodsley; sold by T. Cooper, 1741.* (*LDP* 12 March)
4°: *A⁴ B–C⁴ D²; 1–3 4–28.*
'Despise, my soul, the pompous state'
L(1465.i.12/14); CLU.

P59 — A paraphrase on the CXXXIX psalm found in the pocket of Mr. Richard Johnston, lately executed at Steven's Green. *Dublin, printed by John Gowan, 1730.*

A **paraphrase** on the CXXXIX psalm

½°: 1 side, 2 columns.
'O lord I know, thou know'st me well'
DT.

P60 — A paraphrase on the seven penitential psalms, by the reverend Mr. R---d D---l, d. of A. Or Strephon to Belinda. [*Dublin*, 1727?]
½°: *1–2*, 1 column.
'Hear, fair Belinda, hear thy suppliant's cry'
> A skit on Richard Daniel's *The royal penitent*, 1727.

L(1890.e.5/56).

— A paraphrase on the Song of the three children, 1724. *See* Le Pla, Mark.

P61 — A paraphrase on the XXIXth psalm, occasioned by the prospect of peace. Inscribed to Joseph Addison, esq; *London, printed for Bernard Lintott*, 1713. (*SR* 13 Jan)
2°: A–B²; *i–iv*, *1–3* 4. 4 advt.
> Deposit copies at L,LSC,O,EU,AdU; advertised in *PM* 17 Jan.

'Arise O Israel, know the lord'
L(643.1.26/7),LSC,O,EU,AdU; CSmH(Luttrell, 13 Jan),MH,MiU,*OCU*,TxU.

P62 — A paraphrase upon the golden verses of Pythagoras. *London, printed for George Sawbridge*, 1704.
8°: A–E⁴; *i–xii*, 1–20 25–31 *32 blk*. A1 blk.
'First worship god th' eternal three and one'
GM.

P63 Parent, Daniel. Serious thoughts on death: or, a visit to the dead. A poem. To which is added, an essay on reason, with an universal prayer, in imitation of Mr. Pope... *London, printed for J. Swan*, [1750.] (*GM* Nov)
4°: A⁴ B–C⁴; *1–4* 5–24.
'I follow fancy through her wanton maze'
> Dedication signed.

E.

P64 Paris. The Paris gazeteer: or, a dialogue between the English and Paris Gazette. To a play-house tune. [*London*] *Printed for C. Bates*, [1706.]
½°: 1 side, 2 columns.
> 5 lines of typeset music with first 2 verses.

'Paris Gazette say/tho' 'tis not your way'
> On the battle of Ramillies.

CSmH,*MH*.

P65 Paris, John. Ramillies. A poem, humbly inscrib'd to his grace the Duke of Marlborough. Written in imitation of Milton. By Mr. Paris of Trinity-College Cambridge. *London, printed for Jacob Tonson*, 1706. (*LG* 14 Oct)
2°: A–C²; *i–ii*, 1–10.
'Of Britons second conquest, and the man'
> Answered by *The taylor turn'd poet*, 1706; the suggestion that the author was a tailor has not been explained.

O,*MR-C*; CtY,ICN,MH,NNC,TxU(2).

Parish

Parish. The parish gutt'lers, 1722–. *See* Ward, Edward.

— The parish priest, 1732. *See* Wesley, Samuel, *the younger*.

P66 Park, Henry. The mourning curat: a poem occasion'd by the death of our late renowned soveraign, William III. of glorious memory. *London printed, and are to be sold by A. Baldwin*, 1702. (8 May, Luttrell)
2°: A² B²; *1–2* 3–8.
'Since William's gone into the bright abodes'
LdU-B(Luttrell); MH,TxU.

[—] The sylvan dream or, the mourning muses, 1701. *See* S943.

P67 Parker, Benjamin. Money. A poem. In imitation of Milton. Humbly inscrib'd to the right honourable, the Earl of Chesterfield. *London, printed for the author, at Sir Isaac Newton's Head, the corner of Lincoln's-Inn-fields, next Great Turn-stile, & T. Cooper*, 1740. (6 Feb)
4°: A⁴ B⁴; *1–2* 3–15 *16*. 16 advt.
> Ms. correction on p. 10 line 6. The advertisement on p. 16 is for patent medicines prepared by Parker. Listed in *GM,LM* Feb.

'Ye muses now assist my vent'rous pen'
L(11630.c.13/2, Tom's Coffee House, 6 Feb); MH (uncut),PU.

[**Parker, George.**] The impeachment, 1710. *See* I11.

[**Parkman, John.**] The priest turn'd poet, [1709.] *See* P1053.

Parliament. The parliament of birds, 1712–. *See* Stacy, Edmund.

P68 — The parliament of hell; or the marriage of the devil. [*Dublin*] *Printed in the year* 1728.
8°: A⁸; *i*, *1–2* 3–14 *15 blk*.
'Once on a time as ancient stories tell'
L(12274.e.1/7),*MR-C*.

P69 Parnassus. Parnassus to be sold: or, the poetical estate. *London, printed by T. Dormer, for the author; sold at the pamphlet-shops of London & Westminster*, 1735. (*GM* May)
2°: A² B–D²; *1–4* 5–16.
'Well met, old friend! Time was when thou and I'
L(1482.f.43); MH,TxU(2).

Parnell, Thomas. Poems on several occasions. Written by Dr. Thomas Parnell...and published by Mr. Pope. *London, printed for B. Lintot*, 1722 [1721]. (*WEP* 7 Dec)
8°: pp. 221.   L,O; CtY,MH.
> *Griffith* 130. Entered in *SR* 14 Dec; deposit copies at O, EU. *Nichols* VIII. 300 records that Lintot paid Pope £15 on 13 Dec 1721 for the copyright.

Parnell, T. *Collections*

—— *Dublin, printed by A. Rhames, for J. Hyde, R. Gunne, R. Owen, & E. Dobson, 1722.*
8°: pp. vi, 159.   L; NNP.

—— *London, printed for Bernard Lintot, 1726.* (*DC* 16 June)
8°: pp. 221.   L,O; CtY,MH.
The copy at MH is in contemporary morocco.

—— *The sixth edition. Dublin, printed by R. Reilly, for R. Gunne, & R. Owen, 1735.*
12°: pp. 185.   C,DN.

—— *To which is added, the life of Zoilus: and his remarks on Homer's Battle of the frogs and mice. London, printed for H. Lintot, 1737.* (*GM* Aug)
8°: pp. 221+xii, 64.   L,O; CLU-C,ICU.
Some copies (e.g. O,CLU-C) have both the title quoted and a separate title to the poems alone in red and black.

—— *The seventh edition with additions. Dublin, printed by A. Reilly, for R. Gunne & R. Owen, 1744.*
12°: pp. 185.   L,O; MH.
Without the added prose.

—— *To which is added the life of Zoilus... London, printed for H. Lintot, J. & R. Tonson & S. Draper, 1747.*
8°: pp. 279.   L,O; CtY,MH.

—— *Glasgow, printed by Robert Urie, and sold by the booksellers in town & country, 1748.*
12°: pp. 247.   L,O; MH.
Without the added prose. Reprinted in 1752.

— *The works in verse and prose...Enlarged with variations and poems, not before publish'd. Glasgow, printed and sold by R. & A. Foulis, 1755.*
8°: pp. 232.   O; MiU,PU.

———————

P70 [—] An essay on the different stiles of poetry. *London, printed for Benj. Tooke, 1713.* (*PB* 26 March)
8°: A–E⁴ F²; *i–viii*, 1–36.
Watermark IM. *Rothschild* 1512. Entered in *SR* 26 March to Tooke by John Morphew; deposit copies at O,E,EU,AdU,SaU. Reprinted in Dublin, 1715, with John Philips's *Cyder.*
'I hate the vulgar with untuneful mind'
A presentation copy signed by Parnell is recorded in *Rothschild.*
L(1078.m.6/6),O(2),C(2, 1 uncut),E,DT(2)+; CtY,ICN,IU,MH,TxU(2)+.

P71 [—] [fine paper]
Watermark: fleur-de-lys on shield.
LdU-B.

P72 [—] 'The hermit, a poem, by the rev. Dr. P——l. [*London*] Price 3d.' (*BM* April 1748)
Listed in *LM* May (for April and May) as 'The hermit. Reprinted, from the Dublin

Parnell, T. The hermit

edition, pr. 3d. *Dodd.*' No Dublin edition has been identified.
'Far in a wild, unknown to public view'
The poem was published in Parnell's *Poems,* 1722.

P73 [—] Homer's Battle of the frogs and mice. With the remarks of Zoilus. To which is prefix'd, the life of the said Zoilus. *London, printed for Bernard Lintot, 1717.* (*PB* 16 May)
8°: A–F⁸; *i–xlii*, *1* 2–30 *31–54.* A1 hft; 54 advt.
No watermark. *Griffith* 74. Listed in *MC* April; probably that number was published in May. Entered in *SR* 17 May; deposit copies at O,E,EU,AdU.
'To fill my rising song with sacred fire'
Presentation copy to Pope from Parnell below. Gay received a payment of fifteen guineas for Parnell, 4 May 1717 (*Nichols* VIII. 296).
O(2, 1 uncut),C(−A1),E,DT,LdU-B+; CLU-C, CSmH,DFo,InU,TxU.

P74 — [fine paper]
8°: A⁸ B⁸(±B1) C⁸(±C6) D⁸ E⁸(±E5) F⁸; *i–xlii*, *1* 2–30 *31–54.* A1 hft; 54 advt.
Watermark: Strasburg bend. B1, C6 and E5 have been cancelled to substitute engraved headpieces; the engraved headpiece on A3 is printed normally.
L(C.133.c.2/1),O,C(in presentation calf, 'No. 22' in ms. on free endpaper); MH(2, 1 Pope's presentation copy from Parnell).

P75 [—] Homer's battle of the frogs and mice. *Dublin, printed by Thomas Hume, for George Grierson, 1717.*
8°: A–C⁴; *1–3* 4–24.
L(832.b.15/1),DN; ICN.

P76 [—] — *Dublin printed, and sold by Gwyn Needham, 1717.*
8°: A–B⁴; *1–2* 3–16.
DN.

P77 [—] The horse and the olive: or, war and peace. [*London*] *Printed for John Morphew,* [1713.] (9 April)
½°: 2 sides, 1 column.
Advertised in *Examiner* 10 April as published 'yesterday'. Halfpenny tax stamp on the copy seen.
'With moral tale let ancient wisdom move'
Early ms. attribution to Parnell in the CLU-C copy.
CLU-C,*MH.*

Parody. A parody on Pope's prologue to Cato. Address'd to the late Mr. Henry Bridges, constructor of that elaborate piece of mechanism, the Microcosm.
Wiley 320, quoting Pickering & Chatto cat. 288/339, dates it as [*c*.1740]; but Henry Bridges's will is dated 19 April 1754. Copy at IU.

Parratt, W.

P78 Parratt, William. Carmen seculare, for the year 1735. To the king, on his going to Hanover. *London printed, and sold by J. Roberts*, 1735 [1736?]. (*GM,LM* Jan 1736)
4°: π² A–C⁴ D²; *i–xii, 1 2–19 20 blk.* π1 hft.
'Before bright Phœbus, with his pompous train'
L(11630.c.4/2),O(−π1); CSmH,PU.

P79 — An ode, to the right honourable Sir Robert Walpole, on his majesty's birth-day, October the 30th, 1739. *London, printed for C. Corbet,* 1739. (6 Nov)
4°: *A⁴* B⁴; *1–4 5–15 16 blk.*
Listed in *LM* Nov.
'Whilst you, great Walpole, bare the weight'
L(11630.d.12/17, Tom's Coffee House, 6 Nov),O.

— 'A panegyrical poem on the right honourable Sir Robert Walpole.'
Referred to in Parratt's *Carmen seculare*, 1735, as published 'some months since'; it has not been traced, and may not have been published separately.

P80 Parrot. The parrot and the owl. A fable. *London, printed for J. Roberts,* 1729. (*MChr* 17 March)
2°: π1 A–B² C¹; *i–ii, 1–3 4–10.* π1 hft.
'The baneful yew erects its head'
L(162.n.48),O; IU(−π1).

P81 Parson. The parson and his clerk. Occasion'd by a pamphlet entitl'd, a Letter to the rev. Dr. Codex, on the subject of his modest instruction to the crown, &c. *Dublin printed: London re-printed, for M. Pike,* 1734. (*LM* June).
2°: *A²* B–D²; *1–3 4–16.*
There was probably no Dublin edition.
'Not light from darkness differs more'
Dedication signed 'Philalethes'. A versification of that part of William Arnall's letter to Edmund Gibson (attacking him for interfering in Thomas Rundle's appointment to the see of Gloucester) which suggests he shielded a priest guilty of sodomy with his clerk.
L(1482.f.27); IU,MH.

P82 — The parson and his maid, a tale. *London, printed for T. Payne,* 1722. (*PB* 6 Dec)
8°: π1 A–B⁴ C²; *i–ii, 1–2 '1' 4–19 20 blk.* π1 hft.
C1–2 add 'Venus enrag'd'; it is possible that this and the half-title were later additions, in which case the copy at OCU represents the earlier state.
'Some score of miles from town, as stories tell'
Venus enrag'd: 'Thus, Venus once bespoke her son'
L(164.l.54, Luttrell, Dec); CtY(−π1),OCU (−π1, lacks C1–2).

P83 — — To which is added, Venus enrag'd, a poem. The second edition. *London, printed for T. Payne,* 1722.
8°: *A⁴* B–C⁴; *i–iv, 1–17 18–20 blk.* A1 hft.
Advertised in *PB* 20 Dec as 'last week'

The **parson** and his maid

[9–15 Dec]. *DJ* 14 Jan 1723 advertised 'The 3d edition'.
L(11633.e.45,−C4); MH(−A1,C4),Institute for Sex Research.

P84 — The parson bewitch'd: or, a word to the wise. A political ballad. To the tune of the Irish trot... [*Dublin*] *Printed in the year* 1730.
8°: *A⁴; 1–2 3–8.* 4 advt.
'Where lillies were growing'
The epistle signed 'The Patriot'. An amorous, not a political ballad. The advertisement is for *The state of the nation* by the same hand; it has not been identified.
DT; IU.

P85 — The parson hunter. A poem. *London, printed for A. Dodd, & E. Nutt,* 1731. (*GSJ* 11 Feb)
2°: A–C²; *1–2 3–12.*
'Hail! holy tribe, nor let the impious brood'
L(1484.m.26); TxU.

P86 — 'Parson Paul's speech, translated into English metre. [*London*] *Printed for J. Roberts, Price 6d.*' (*PM* 26 July 1716)
William Paul was executed for high treason on 23 July 1716. Compare *Mr. Paul's speech turn'd into verse,* 1716.

P87 — The parson preferred. A poem. *London, printed for E. Withers,* 1750. (*LM* March)
8°: A–B⁴ C²; *i–iii iv–vi, 7 8–20.*
'When arts and sciences look low'ring down'
L(906.k.7/2),LdU-B.

— The parson's daughter, 1717. *See* Wyvill, Christopher.

P88 Parsoniad. The Parsoniad; a satyr. Inscribed to Mr. Pope. *London, printed for Charles Corbet,* 1733. (*GSJ* 6 Nov)
2°: *A²* B–D²; *1–2 3–15 16.* 16 advt.
'Shall Temple beaus, or college smarts maintain'
O; CLU-C,CtY,IU,MH,TxU(2)+.

P89 Parsons. The parsons compassion, or, the clergys conduct in their late petition against the quakers affirmation. A poem. *London, printed in the year* 1722.
8°: A–D⁴; *1–2 3–32.*
'Some say the weapons Levi wears'
In praise of the quakers, against the church of England clergy. Cf. *The London clergy's petition,* 1722.
L(11633.bb.31),LF,O.

P90 — Parsons's triumph. *London, printed by J. Thompson,* 1731.
½°: 1 side, 2 columns.
Percival appendix 31. Large rough woodcut at head.
'Why whigs can't you be easy'
On Humphrey Parsons, lord mayor of London.
L(C.20.f.2/243).

P91 Part. Part of the XLI psalm, to be sung by the British charity-children, on Tuesday, March 1, 1725–6, being St. David's day, at Christ-church, near Newgate-street... [*London*, 1726.]
½°: 1 side, 1 column.
'The man is blest that doth provide'
O.

— Part of the fourth book of Milton's Paradise lost, [1739/46.] *See* Theobald, John.

P92 — Part of the CXXXVIIIth psalm, the new version, to be sung by the charity-children of St. George the martyr in the county of Middlesex, upon the first Sunday after the Epiphany, January 9th, 1742... [*London*, 1743.]
½°: 1 side, 1 column.
'With my whole heart, my god and king'
Crawford.

P93 — Part of the 112th psalm, taken out of the new version, to be sung by the charity-children of St. Dunstan's in the west. On Sunday, the 18th of February, 1727. [*London*, 1728.]
½°: 1 side, 2 columns.
        The accounts of the schools are given below.
'The soul that's fill'd with virtue's light'
Crawford.

P94 — Part of the CXIIth psalm...to be sung by the charity-boys belonging to Billingsgate-ward, on Sunday the 31st of March, 1734... [*London*, 1734.]
½°.
(LG copy destroyed by enemy action.)

— Part of the seventh epistle of the first book of Horace imitated, 1713. *See* Swift, Jonathan.

P95 — Part of the song of Deborah and Barak para-phras'd, from Judges V. As set to musick by Dr. Greene. *London, printed for B. Barker*, 1732. (*LM* Sept)
2°: *A*² B¹; *1–3* 4–6.
'Attend, ye princes, and ye kings, give ear'
TxU(uncut).

P96 — Part of the 23d psalm taken out of the new version, to be sung by the charity children of Cordwainers and Breadstreet wards, on Sunday, March 12. 17³¹₃₂. at the parish-church of St Mary le Bow... [*London*, 1732.]
½°: 1 side, 1 column.
'The lord himself, the mighty lord'
LG.

Parvish, Samuel. A poem in defence of free enquiry in matters of religion; occasioned by the general clamour raised against the author of a book, intitled, an Enquiry into the Jewish and Christian revelations... *London printed, and sold by T. Cooper*, 1740.
        There is a copy at O collating 8°: *4; Parvish's name is revealed on p. 3. Copies were included in the second edition of Parvish's *An enquiry*,

1740, and this may well have been extracted from that work, though the possibility of separate issue cannot be excluded.

P97 Pasquin. Pasquin at Paul's. [*London*, 1712/13?]
short slip: 1 side, 1 column.
'Anna was once the wise, the great, the good'
        Against the peace with France.
CSmH.

P98 — Pasquin to the queen's statue at St. Paul's, during the procession, Jan. 20. 1714. [*London?* 1715.]
¼°: 1 side, 2 columns.
        Title over both columns, single rule between them.
'Behold he comes to make thy people groan'
        Crum B202. A Jacobite satire against George I.
O; CSmH,MH, *Harding*.

P99 — [another edition]
        Title over the first column only; double rule between columns.
Herts CRO (Panshanger box 46).

Passion. The passion of Sappho, 1711. *See* Harison, William.

Passions. The passions of man, 1746. *See* Ruff-head, James.

P100 Past. Past and present, or, times compared: a satire. By the author of One thousand seven hundred and forty-five. *London, printed for A. Dodd*, 1746. (*GM*, *LM* April)
2°: *A*¹ B–D² E¹; *i–ii*, 1–13 *14 blk.* 13 advt.
'In April, when the vernal skies, serene'
DT; CSmH(uncut),CtY,IU,OCU,TxU.

P101 — Past and present; or, times compared: a satire. Part II. Which concludes the poem. By the author of One thousand... *London, printed for M. Cooper*, 1746. (*GA* 9 July)
2°: *A*¹ B–D² E¹; *i–ii*, 1–14.
        Horizontal chain-lines.
'Now tete a tete, prepar'd for chearful chat'
CtY,KU.

P102 Pastora. Pastora's lament for Adonis; being the mournful complaints of my Lady Craighall, upon the death of her lovely darling child John Carstairs, who died the 14th. of February 1708, ætat 8. [*Edinburgh*, 1708.]
obl 1°: 1 side, 2 columns.
'Adonis dies! the lovely boy expires'
E.

P103 Pastoral. A pastoral elegy: being a florist's lamentation for the loss of his flowers, destroy'd by birds. Inscrib'd to the right hon. the Lady Lux-borough, by a clergyman of Warwickshire. With an advertisement to florists. *Birmingham, printed for the author; sold by T. Aris & T. Warren, in*

A **pastoral** elegy: being

> *Birmingham; and J. Keating, at his shops at Stratford, Shipston, and Alcester,* 1749.
> 8⁰: *A*⁴ B⁴; *1–5* 6–16.
> 'A florist, ever seeking something new'
> BP.

— A pastoral elegy on the death of a lady's canary bird, 1725. *See* Pilkington, Matthew.

P104 — A pastoral elegy on the death of Calista. Humbly inscrib'd to the honourable Col. C -------rchill. *London, printed for W. Trott,* 1730. (*MChr* Nov)
2⁰: A–B²; *1–2* 3–8.
> GS*J* 12 Nov 1730 advertised 'The second edition', not traced.
'Stay, friendly swain, and hear a lover's woe'
> On the death of Anne Oldfield, inscribed to Charles Churchill, her lover. Cf. *Mainwario's welcome to Ophelia,* 1730, advertised in *Don Francisco's descent,* 1732, as a sequel. The author also wrote a poem to the memory of Barton Booth in his *Life,* 1733.
CtY,MH(uncut).

P105 — A pastoral elegy on the death of Christian Riddel, lady Dean younger. *Edinburgh, printed by James Watson,* 1706. (6 Aug?)
4⁰: A⁴; *1–8*.
'I ask not, lovely virgins, why you weep?'
CtY(ms. date 6 Aug).

— A pastoral elegy on the death of the Lady Hilaretta, [1729/30.] *See* Campbell, Archibald, *duke of Argyll.*

— A pastoral elegy on the death of the right honourable the Earl of Burlington, 1704. *See* Pix, Mary.

P106 — A pastoral elegie, on the death of the right honourable, the Earl of Cromarty, who departed this life, the 27th of August 1714. [*Edinburgh?* 1714.]
1⁰: 1 side, 2 columns.
> Mourning borders.
'As I in Rosian plains my flocks did feed'
E.

P107 — A pastoral elegy on the much lamented death of the reverend and celebrated Mr. Peter Finall, who belong'd to the choirs of St. Patrick's and Christ-church, and departed this mortal life on Friday the eighth of this instant March, 1727–8. *Dublin, printed by George Faulkner & James Hoey,* 1727–8. (March)
½⁰: 1 side, 1 column.
'Weep ev'ry eye, and ev'ry tongue deplore'
L(11602.i.1/26).

P108 — A pastoral elegy upon the death of Mr. Allan Ramsy[!]. *Dublin, printed by William-Shaw Anburey,* 1727.
½⁰: 1 side, 2 columns.
'Allan is dead!——Ye listing mountains hear!'
> A false alarm; Ramsay did not die until 1758.

A **pastoral** elegy upon

> Ramsay wrote a poem 'To my kind and worthy friends in Ireland' on this occasion.
DT.

P109 — A pastoral essay lamenting the death of the honourable Mr. Coke of Norfolk. Humbly inscrib'd to his lady. *London, William Turner,* 1707. (8 July, Luttrell)
2⁰: 10 pp.
(Pickering & Chatto cat. 247/13328, Luttrell.)

P110 — A pastoral in imitation of Virgil's first eclogue. *Edinburgh, printed in the year* 1730.
4⁰: π¹ A–B⁴ C¹; *i–viii*, 1–12. π1 hft.
'Thrice happy swains! stretch'd in this silvan cave'
> Dedication signed 'T.J.'
EP; *OCU.*

P111 — A pastoral lamenting the death of the right honourable Scroope lord viscount Howe, governour of Barbados... *Cambridge, printed at the University-press,* 1736.
2⁰: *A*² B–E²; *1–7* 8–20. A1 hft.
'Why when the spring renews the rising year'
O(uncut); CtY,IU,OCU.

P112 — A pastoral letter. The tune, To all ye ladies, &c. [*London?* 1719.]
slip: 1 side, 1 column.
> Stanza 10, line 1 reads '...Catholick indeed'. Printed with *Forty-one,* [1719]; the L copy is not divided.
'To all the clergy in this land / Eleven bishops write'
> An attack on the bishops who voted for the repeal of the schism act and the act against occasional conformity, Jan 1719.
L(1876.f.1/83); MH.

P113 — [another edition]
> Stanza 10, line 1 reads '...Catholick, indeed'. Printed with *Forty-one,* [1719]; the O copy is not divided.
O,Herts CRO(Panshanger box 46); CSmH.

P114 — A pastoral on St. Patick's-day [!]. Damon and Thirsis. *Dublin, printed by C.C.* [*Cornelius Carter*], 1725–6.
½⁰: 1 side, 1 column.
'Begin my muse, inspire your poets lays'
DT.

P115 — 'A pastoral poem. [*London*] *Printed for W. Mears.* Price 6d.' (*LM* Oct 1733)
> Possibly a generalized title.

P116 — [dh] A pastoral poem, sacred to the memory of his late majesty King George. [*Edinburgh,* 1727?]
4⁰: *A*²; *1–4*.
'Young Tityrus, thoughtful, mus'd along the plain'
L(11630.b.8/5),EP(uncut).

P117 — A pastoral poem to a lady in St. P--- parish, on the death her lover, occasion'd by her cruelty. *Dublin, printed by S. Powell,* 1728–9.
½⁰: 1 side, 1 column.

A **pastoral** poem to a lady

'While my sad lines in mournful numbers flow' DT.

P118 — A pastoral poem to the memory of the honourable Lord Basil Hamiltoun... By A.P. *Edinburgh, printed in the year* 1701.
4°: A⁴; *1–3* 4–8.
'Wandring I went alongst a river side'
> Ascribed to Alexander Pennecuik (d. 1730) by Aitken in *DNB*; William Brown (*Papers of the Edinburgh Bibliographical Society* 6 (1906) 117f.) queries the attribution, which is highly improbable, since Pennecuik's first poem is otherwise 1718. The attribution was doubtless made on the strength of the initials 'A.P.'; Alexander Pennecuik (1652–1722) would seem a more likely candidate, but it is not collected in his poems.

L(11626.c.44/2).

P119 Pastorella. ⟨Pastorella; or, the sylvan muse.⟩ ⟨*London, sold by M. Cooper.*⟩ (*GM, LM* July 1746)
8°: ⟨*A²*⟩ B–D⁴ E² (+5 plates); ⟨*1–4*⟩ 5 6–32.
> The copy seen lacks the preliminary leaves and is bound up in *A banquet of the muses*, 1746; the title is supplied from the entry in *LM*. 'Pastorella' is followed on p. 21 by 'The shepherd's day: in four pastoral dialogues'.

'Aspiring Phoebus, who alone can warm'
First dialogue: 'Just o'er the eastern hills the blushing morn'
L(12314.ee.4/1, imperfect).

Patch. The patch, 1724. *See* Hauksbee, Francis.

P120 — Patch work or the comprehension in four canto's. '*Printed by Mark'em Merry Wise for Serious Seeker and Company at the sign of the Looking Glass opposite to the Cameleon in Little Britain*', [1720?]
8°: ã⁴ ẽ⁴ õ² A–Z⁴; *i–xx*, 1–184.
> Certainly printed abroad; the L catalogue suggests St Omer's, 1718, but a reference to *Robinson Crusoe*, published April 1719, suggests a later date. The CtY copy has an errata slip on p. 184.

'When pious spleen, and godly jar'
> A Roman catholic satire on the Bangorian controversy.

L(1077.c.14); CtY,OCU.

Patie. Patie and Roger, [1720.] *See* Ramsay, Allan.

P121 Patience. Patience. A present to the Press-yard. A poem. *London, printed in the year* 1706.
4°: B–D⁴; *i–iv*, 1–20.
'In a dark corner of a silent grove'
> Dedicated to Major B——, who had been ten years in prison; expressing Jacobite sentiments.

O(uncut),E; CLU-C,OCU.

Patricius

P122 Patricius. Patricius to Manlius. *London, printed by H. Meere, for the author*, 1720.
8°: A–D⁴; *1–8* 9–32. 5 err; 8 advt.
> The advertisement records two poems 'design'd for the press'.

'Whether, possess'd of Circe's art'
> Preface signed 'Patricius'; 'To the author' signed 'J.F.' i.e. John Fox, with whose *Wanderers* the IU copy is bound.

L(1969); IU,OCU.

P123 Patriot. The patriot. A poem, humbly dedicated to his grace the Duke of Bolton... *London, printed for J. Roberts*, 1715. (16 Aug, Luttrell)
2°: A² B² C–D²; *i–vi*, 1–9 *10 blk*.
> Listed in *MC* Aug 1715.

'Amongst the numerous crouds, that daily press'
L(11602.i.14/5); CLU-C(Luttrell),CSmH,MH.

P124 — The patriot, an ode. Addressed to the right honourable Henry Boyle, esq; in imitation of the 9th of the 4th book of Horace. *Dublin, printed by James Hoey*, 1734.
8°: A⁴; *1–2* 3–8.
'If from the beauteous Bandon's side'
C.

'Patriot.' The parson bewitch'd, 1730. *See* P84.

Patriotic. Patriotic love, 1737. *See* Jacob, Hildebrand.

P125 Patriotism. Patriotism. A satire. *London, printed for T. Cooper*, [1741.] (*GM, LM* May)
2°: A¹ B–C²; *i–ii*, *1* 2–8.
'To live secure from party rage and want'
> In defence of Walpole.

MH.

Patriots. The patriots. A poem, 1702. *See* Pittis, William.

— The patriots, a satyr, written on the 12th of October, 1734. *See* Forbes, William.

— The patriots are come, [1742.] *See* Hervey, John, *baron Hervey*.

— The patriots motion, 1741. *See* The motion, 1741.

— The patriots of Great Britain, 1707. *See* Browne, Joseph.

P126 — The patriots triumph: a new hymn for the eleventh day of April. Humbly inscrib'd to those glorious protectors of liberty who voted against the excise... *London, printed for P. Holder; sold by the booksellers of London & Westminster*, 1734. (*GM* April)
2°: A² B²; *1–2* 3–8.
'Ye bards that glow with sacred fire'
L(162.n.76),LU,O; ICN,NNC(uncut).

P127 — — *Edinburgh, printed by W. Cheyne; sold by A. Symmer, G. Hamilton, J. Traill, and other booksellers*, 1734.

The **patriots** triumph

8°: *A*⁴; *1–2* 3–8.
GM; MH-BA.

Pattern. The pattern of piety, 1734. *See* Gent, Thomas.

Pattison, William. The poetical works of Mr. William Pattison... *London, printed for H. Curll,* 1728 [1727]. (9 Sept)
8°: pp. viii, 60, 248.   L,O; CtY,MH.
> The list of subscribers records a few copies on 'super-fine paper'; all copies seen have watermark A. The portrait frontispiece was advertised separately, 16 Sept 1727, and also with the following volume. Publication date from *Straus, Curll.*

— Cupid's metamorphoses... Being the second and last volume of the poetical works... *London, printed in the year* 1728. (*MChr* 4 April).
8°: pp. iv, 312.   L; IU,TxU.
> All copies seen are watermarked with horse in circle. Listed in *MC, MChr* as printed for E. Curll, and with the portrait.

P128 — An epistle to his majesty, on his accession to the throne. *London, printed for H. Curll,* 1727. (*EvP* 18 July)
8°: (frt+) *A*⁴ B⁴ C²; *1–4* 5–18 *19–20*. A1 hft; C2 advt.
'My sacred liege, if sorrow cease to flow'
> A note in *Cupid's metamorphoses* (1728) 171 records 'The author died on the day, he was to have been introduced to the king, with this poem, viz. July 10th, 1727'.

O; InU(−frt),KU.

P129 Paul. [dh] Paul Diack: or, the chat of the gods at their tea-table. To be said or sung. [*London,* 1701.] (3 Jan, Luttrell)
4°: *A*²; *1–4*.
'To a hussar no room was by Charon allow'd'
> Against the French.
LLP,LVA-F(Luttrell); OCU.

P130 Paul, William. 'A pindarique ode sacred to the memory of her late most excellent majesty Queen Anne. *Lond.* 1715 – fol.'
(*Rawlinson.*)

Pax. Pax in crumena: or, the trooper, turn'd poet, 1713. *See* Rands, Thomas.

P131 Peace. A peace, a peace, a glorious peace, in spite of the D--ch memorial. *Printed in the year* 1712.
½°: 1 side, 2 columns.
> First line misprinted 'Tow...'
'Now things are to the last decision bent'
TxU.

P132 —— *London printed, and Edinburgh re-printed by John Moncur,* 1712.
½°: 1 side, 2 columns.
E.

Peace

P133 — Peace. A poem. Humbly inscribed to his majesty King George II. *London, printed by R. Walker; sold by the booksellers of London & Westminster,* 1731. (*GSJ* 5 May)
2°: *A*² B²; *1–2* 3–8.
'Pensive, in sable weeds, Britannia sat'
> In praise of George and the whigs gaining peace.
WrP.

— Peace. A poem: inscribed to...Viscount Bolingbroke, 1713. *See* Trapp, Joseph.

P134 — The peace: a poem. Most humbly inscribed to the right hon. the Earl of Sandwich, &c... By a student of Christ-Church College, Oxford. *London, printed for G. Woodfall,* [1748.] (*GM, LM* Oct)
4°: A–C⁴; *1–2* 3–24.
> Also listed in *BM* May 1749.
'Welcome, O welcome, thou celestial maid'
L(11630.c.8/13),O(2, 1 uncut).

— Peace and Dunkirk, 1712. *See* Swift, Jonathan.

P135 — The peace-haters: or, a new song, for the illumination of those that won't see. To the tune of the Catholick ballad. *London, printed in the year* 1711. (*SR* 30 Oct)
8°: *A*⁴; *1–2* 3–8.
> Entered in *SR* to John Baker; deposit copies at E,EU,SaU.
'Was ever a nation besotted like this'
> A tory poem in favour of a reasonable peace.
L(164.m.54, Luttrell, 10 Dec),O,E,EU,SaU; TxU.

P136 [Pearson, Thomas.] Hester, a poem. *London, printed for H. Clements,* 1714. (*Examiner* 14 May)
8°: *A*² B–E⁸ F⁶; *i–iv,* 1–73 *74–76 blk.* A1 blk.
'Say, muse, what pow'r unseen does vertue guide'
> Attributed to Pearson by *Rawlinson*; a copy at ICN has ms. note 'by Mr Henley of Cambridge', but in fact a quite different work from John Henley's *Esther* of the same year.
L(11631.bbb.39/1),O,LdU-B; CtY(−A1,F6), ICN(−A1,F6),IU(−A1,F6),KU(−A1,F6),OCU (−A1,F6).

P137 [Peck, Francis.] Sighs upon the never enough lamented death of Queen Anne. In imitation of Milton. By a clergyman of the church of England. *London, printed for Henry Clements,* 1719. (*PB* 1 Aug)
8°: *A*² B–K⁴ M²; *i–v* vi–xx, *21* 22–88. A1 frt.
> In the OW copy, B1 is signed 'A'. Second title, 'Poems by the same author' on p. 65. Engraved head and tailpieces in first part.
'What Anna and the Stuarts were? Their names'
> Early ms. attribution to Peck in L copy; see also *Rawlinson.*
L(1466.i.8),O(2, 1 – frt),OW,LdU-B,*MR-C*; CSmH,*DLC*,MH.

Pedlar

[P138 cancelled]

P139 **Pedlar.** The pedlar: being an excellent new song. To the old tune of King John, and the abbot of Canterbury. [*London*] *Sold by J. Baker*, [1713.]
½°: 1 side, 2 columns.
'Ye lads and ye lasses that live in Great Britain'
    A whig attack on Louis d'Aumont.
Crawford.

P140 — [*idem*] The French pedlar. Being an excellent new song. To an old tune. [*London?* 1713.]
½°: 1 side, 1 column.
    Variant first line:
'Ye ladies and lasses that live in Great Britton'
PPL.

P141 **Peeper.** The peeper: being a sequel to the Curious maid. *London, printed for Thomas Edlin*, 1721. (*DP* 23 Feb)
2°: A² B¹; *1-2* 3-6.
    'The 2d edition' advertised in *DP* 13 March; 'the 3d edition' in *DP* 13 April. These may have been fictitious editions, or may represent concealed reimpressions.
'And is this all? No, curious maid'
    This has been attributed to Prior and to Hildebrand Jacob as the suspected and true author of *The curious maid*, 1720; there is no reason to believe either attribution. A bawdy poem.
L(Ashley 4982),O(uncut),OW; CLU-C,CSmH, DFo,IU(Luttrell, March).

P142 — [*idem*] The whole discover'd: or, a certain lady's secrets found out. *Dublin, printed in the year* 1736.
8°: A⁴; *1-3* 4-7 *8 blk.*
DA.

P143 **Peg.** Peg T-------------m's invitation to the two shilling voters of Westmnster [!]. [*London*] '*Printed for E. Wink-a-pinka*', [1750.]
½°: 1 side, 2 columns.
    Column 1 contains a prose address, signed 'A.B.'; column 2, 'The French strollers bit, or, a vote for Peg T------m.'
'Ye pert buffoons of France'
    A Westminster election pamphlet against Granville Leveson-Gower, lord Trentham.
L(1876.f.1/139).

P144 — Peg Trim Tram in the suds, or, no French strolers. A new ballad. [*London*, 1750.]
½°: 1 side, 1 column.
'I sing you a song, of a right noble -----'
    A Westminster election ballad against Granville Leveson-Gower, lord Trentham.
L(1876.f.1/137, cropt),Crawford.

P145 — Peg Trim-tram's defeat; a new ballad. With the downfall of my l--d's sur-loin of beef, which was kick'd and cuff'd out of half the publick houses in Westminster... Tune of, When she was

Peg Trim-tram's defeat

brought before my lord mayor. *London*, '*printed for Mr. Merryman*', [1750.]
½°: 1 side, 2 columns.
    The second column is in prose.
'False Britons who favour the measures of France'
L(1876.f.1/138),Crawford.

P146 **Pellieux,** —, *Monsieur.* Panegyrique de son altesse royale Monseigneur le duc de Cumberland. Par Monsieur Pellieux. *A Londres, chez Moise Chastel, dans Compton-street, Soho*, 1746.
4°: *⁴; *1-2* 3-8.
'Cumberland, couronné des mains de la victoire'
L(1490.bb.37).

Pennecuik, Alexander, *1652-1722.* A geographical, historical description of the shire of Tweeddale. With a miscelany [!] and curious collection of select Scotish poems. By A.P. M.D. *Edinburgh, printed by John Moncur*, 1715.
4°: pp. 40, 142.   L,O; CtY,MH.
    The description on pp. 1-40 is a prose work.

— [*idem*] A collection of curious Scots poems, on the following subjects... *Edinburgh, printed in the year* 1762.
4°: pp. 142.   L,E; ICN.
    The prose description is omitted. Pp. 49-142 appear, in the copy compared, to be a reissue of the preceding; and possibly the earlier portion of the volume had been reprinted early in the century, for the typography is homogeneous.

P147 [—] An address to his majesty King George. By the author of the Lintoun-address. *Edinburgh, printed by James Watson*, 1714.
1°: 1 side, 2 columns.
'Thrice glorious sir, our sov'reign, lord, and king'
    Reprinted in Pennecuik's *Collection*, 1715.
L(1881.c.6/15),E(mutilated); NNP,TxU.

P148 [—] Lintoun-address to his highness the Prince of Orange. *Edinburgh, printed by James Watson*, 1714.
1°: 1 side, 2 columns.
    The address is preceded and followed by a prologue and epilogue; previously published [1689].
Prologue: 'Victorious Sir, still faithful to thy word'
    Reprinted in Pennecuik's *Collection*, 1715.
L(806.k.1/142, mutilated),O-JJ,E(2).

[—] A pastoral poem to the memory of the honourable Basil Hamilton, 1701. *See* P118.

Pennecuik, Alexander, *d. 1730.* Streams from Helicon: or, poems on various subjects. In three parts. *Edinburgh, printed by John Mosman & company. Anno* 1721.
8°: pp. 199.   E; CLU-C,DFo.
    Apparently the titles of this and the two following issues are all press-variants, and despite the date this is probably intended as the

Pennecuik, A., *d. 1730.* Collections

'first edition'. I suspect it may be a fine-paper issue for presentation.

— [another issue] The second edition. *Edinburgh printed by John Mosman & company for the author,* 1720.

> L,E; CtY,NN.

— [another issue] The second edition. *London, printed for the author. Anno* 1720.

> L,E; ICU,MH.

— 'Entertainments for the curious. *Edinburgh,* 1726.'

> Apparently six numbers were published; probably the 'weekly paper' of which a list of recipients is included in the Pennecuik ms. with the date 9 June 1726. This is the drop-head title on p. 3 of *A compleat collection.*

— 'Flowers from Parnassus. *Edinburgh*', [1727?]

> Recorded in *DNB,* apparently from *Allibone;* both date it 1726. This heading is used on p. 4 of *A compleat collection,* 'Ex musæo nostro, primo Junii, 1727'.

— 'Poems revived, the blythe man's banquet, or an entertainment for the curious. *Edinburgh,* 1734. 8º.' (*Lowndes.*)

— A compleat collection of all the poems wrote by that famous and learned poet Alexander Pennecuick. To which are annexed some curious poems by other worthy hands. *Edinburgh printed, and sold by R. Drummond, and at most booksellers shops in town & country,* [1743?/44?]

8º: pp. 136+.   L.

> Published in parts, of which only two survive; there is a catchword for the third. An advertisement on p. 2 records fine-paper copies at 8*d.* a part (against 6*d.*) but they have not been identified. The date is suggested by Drummond's known publications.

— A collection of poet Pennicuike's satires on kirkmen &c... [*Edinburgh?*] *Printed in the year* 1744.

12º: pp. 12.   L.

> Although 'Finis' appears on p. 12, there are works listed on the title which are not included. Possibly part 1 of another series.

— A collection of Scots poems on several occasions, by the late Mr. Alexander Pennecuik, gent. and others. *Edinburgh, printed for James Reid, Leith,* 1756.

8º: pp. [156].   O.

> Reprinted in 1769, 1787. This is really a miscellany, and appears to contain as much of Ramsay as of Pennecuik.

[—] Amyntar, a pastoral elegy bewailing the death...of...John earl of Rothes, [1722.] *See* A219.

Pennecuik, A. An ancient prophecy

P149 — An ancient prophecy concerning stock-jobbing, and the conduct of the directors of the South-Sea-company. Written, a thousand years ago, in the form of a parable, by the famous Avian: translated from the Greek into Latin, by Romulus of Athens: and now rendred into English, with additions, by Mr. Pennecuik. *Edinburgh, printed by John Mosman & company; and are to be sold at William Brown's shop,* 1721.

4º: A⁴ B²; *1–2* 3–12.

> Drop-head title on p. 5 'The fable of the tortoise and the birds'.

'On th' oozie bed among the scaly fry'

E.

P150 — Britannia triumphans: in four parts; Part I. Pan a pastoral. Part II. Magnalia. Part III. Panegyrick on the royal family. Part IV. Genethliacons; or the Saphick muse. Sacred to XXVIII May... *Edinburgh, printed by John Mosman & William Brown for the author, and sold by the said William Brown & John Martin,* 1718.

8º: π¹ *A*⁸ B⁴(−B1); *i–ii, 1–4* 5–21 *22 blk.* A1 hft.

> The half-title reads 'Poems on the royal family'; separate title on p. 13, 'A panegyrick on the royal family'. The first part was rewritten as *A poem on the birth-day of his most sacred majesty King George* (Dublin, 1725), probably by another hand.

'Hail happy day, on which pleas'd heav'n doth smile'

'O were my muse, inspir'd with sacred flame'

'Angels and saints, salute the blissful morn'

'Britains blessing, faiths defender'

L(11631.c.34),O,C,E(−π1),GM(−π1).

P151 [—] Burnbank's farewel to Edinburgh, at his departure for the Indies, with his last will and testament. [*Edinburgh,* 1722?]

½º: 1 side, 2 columns.

'Waes me, auld Reikie, we man part'

> In the Pennecuik ms. at E. On James Campbell's transportation.

E; CSmH.

P152 [—] Corydon and Cochrania, a pastoral on the nuptials of... James duke of Hamiltoun...with the lady Anne Cochran... Solemniz'd February 14, 1723. By A.P. gent. *Edinburgh, printed by William Adams junior,* 1723.

4º: A² B–C²; *1–2* 3–11 *12 blk.*

> A colophon on p. 11 reads 'Printed and sold by William Adams junior, at his printing house in Carubber's Close'.

'Of late our fields wore sick and pallid looks'

> Pennecuik's authorship is clear from the initials; it also forms part of the Pennecuik ms.

O,GM; TxU(date cropt).

P153 [—] The criminal stirling imprisoned for the crime of high treason. [*Edinburgh,* 172–?]

½º: 1 side, 1 column.

Pennecuik, A. The criminal stirling

'A zealous brother of the canting crew'
Attributed to Pennecuik in Robert Chambers'
History of Edinburgh, new edition [1880] 42,
dating the event (surely wrongly) as 1735.
Reprinted in *A compleat collection*, [1743?]
and probably by Pennecuik. The starling
offended against an act of presbytery, 29 April
1719, for keeping the Sabbath.
E(cropt).

P154 — Dialogue betwixt a Glasgow malt-man and an
English excise-m⟨an⟩at the commencement of
the malt-tax. [*Edinburgh*, 1724/25.]
½°: 1 side, 2 columns.
'Flush'd with a double draught of double strong'
E(mutilated).

[—] Elegie on John Pringle, town-piper of Lauder,
[172–?] *See* E220.

P155 [—] Elegy on the death of Nicol Muschet of
Boghall: written, at the desire of his friends.
[*Edinburgh*, 1721.]
½°: 1 side, 2 columns.
'The highest pitch of sorrow swells my heart'
In the Pennecuik ms. Muschet was hanged
for the murder of his wife, 6 Jan 1721.
E(2); OCU.

[—] Elegy on the deplorable death of Margaret
Hall, [1720.] *See* E136.

P156 — Elegy on the deplorable death of the right
honourable, John lord Belhaven, who was lost at
sea, on the 10th of Nov. 1721. [*Edinburgh*, 1721/
22.]
½°: 1 side, 1 column.
Mourning borders.
'Let Scotia's sons in sable weeds appear'
E.

P157 [—] Elegy on the much lamented death of merry
Maggie Wilson, poultry-wife in Edinburgh. (Done
by Rorie Pringle drawer in the Tolbooth.) [*Edin-
burgh*, 172–.]
½°: 1 side, 2 columns.
'Walliwafaw your fingers, death'
In the Pennecuik ms. at E.
E.

P158 [—] The faithful sheepherd, a funeral poem, to the
memory of that pious and learned pastor, the
reverend Mr. Thomas Paterson, minister of the
gospel at St. Cuthbert's, who dropt mortality
Sabbath 22. May 1726. [*Edinburgh*, 1726.]
½°: 1 side, 1 column.
Mourning borders. The 'd' in 'sheepherd'
was omitted in the original printing and was
stamped in subsequently.
'Jesus the faithful sheepherd of the flock'
In the Pennecuik ms. at E.
E.

[—] The flight of religious piety from Scotland,
[1736?] *See* F169.

Pennecuik, A. Groans from the grave

P159 [—] [dh] Groans from the grave: or, complaints
of the dead, against the surgeons for raising their
bodies out of the dust. [*Edinburgh*, 1725.] (13
March)
4°: *A*²; 1–4.
According to a letter from W. D. D. Turnbull
to James Maidment inserted in the latter's
copy now at L, his copy substituted 'a blank
line' for the word 'surgeon' in p. 4 line 9 –
apparently a press variant.
'Last even'ing toil'd with dull fatigue of life'
The letter referred to above describes a ms.
note in Turnbull's copy, 'This was published
at Edr 13 Mar. 1725 by Alexr Pennycook'.
L(11630.b.8/3).

[—] An habbiack elegy on the untimely and
deplorable death of Robert F------s, [1724.]
See H1.

P160 [—] A huy and cry after Sir John Barlycorn,|A
base rebel denounc'd at the horn,|Fled from the
country where he was bred and born. [*Edinburgh*,
1725.] (Aug?)
½°: 1 side, 2 columns.
'We all the drunkards of the nation'
Contemporary ms. note in the E copy, 'Done
by Alexr Pennycook when the brewers in Edr
disisted to brew & were therefor a part of them
imprisoned for not complying with the malt
tax Augst 1725.'
E,MC.

P161 [—] Huy and cry for apprehending George
Fachney professor of gaming, and one of the
subaltern officers in Collonel Caldwells's new levied
regiment of robbers. By John Dalgliesh, lockman
of Edinburgh. [*Edinburgh*, 1721/22.]
½°: 1 side, 2 columns.
Both copies seen are cut close at head, possibly
cropping an introductory 'A'.
'O yes, O yes, both young and old'
Included in the Pennecuik ms. at E. Dalgleish
was hangman of Edinburgh, and this versified
offer of a reward for Fachney is appropriately
attributed to him; it is signed 'John Dalglish'.
E(2).

P162 [—] ⟨The last⟩ speech and dying words of
John Dalgliesh, lock man alias hang-man of
Edinburgh. [*Edinburgh*, 172–.]
½°: 1 side, 2 columns.
'When Hangie saw death drawing near'
In the Pennecuik ms. at E, with the title as
given above.
E(cropt?).

P163 [—] A lecture to the ladies, by a disobliged admirer
of the fair sex. [*Edinburgh*, 1726.] (Aug?)
½°: 1 side, 1 column.
'Satan, to ruin mankind in the root'
Ms. note in the E copy 'said to be Penni-
cook Aug. 1726.' Reprinted in *A compleat*

Pennecuik, A. A lecture to the ladies

collection, [1743?] as 'A satyr on the tea table.' Pennecuik's authorship is not certain.

E.

[—] A letter from Doctor Dalgleish to his patient Mrs. M'Leod, [1727.] *See* L125.

P164 [—] 'The melancholy muse, an elegy, occasioned by the death of...Robert Calder.' [*Edinburgh?* 1723.]
$\frac{1}{2}$°.
'Ah is the matchless man the charmer dead?'
Maidment 239 prints the text from ms, but records a printed copy (with the same title?) in David Haig's possession. In the Pennecuik ms. at E.
(*Maidment* 239.)

P165 [—] The mock magistrates: a Dutch tale, written originally in High Dutch, by the exquisite pen of Hermanus Van Huff, now faithfully rendred into English. '*Amsterdam, printed in the year 1720, by Weybran Swart bookseller at the Crown'd Bible: and London reprinted*' [*Edinburgh*], 1721.
4°: A⁴ B²; *1–2* 3–12.
The whole imprint is probably false.
'Four mushroom merchants, insolent and proud'
In the Pennecuik ms. at E. Apparently a satire on the attempt of four Edinburgh magistrates to form an oligarchy. Their election was invalidated by parliament.
ES; DFo.

P166 — The mournfull sheepherds, a pastoral sacred, to the memory of Sir Francies Grant of Cullen, one of the senators of the college of justice, who died 23. March 1726. [*Edinburgh*, 1726.]
$\frac{1}{2}$°: 1 side, 2 columns.
Mourning borders.
'Gibbie, sin a' the hirstle's fled the field'
MH.

P167 [—] Muschet revived; or an elegy on the deplorable death of Elizabeth Murray...barbarously murdered by her husband Thomas Kincaid younger of Gogar-Mains, March 29th 1723. [*Edinburgh*, 1723.]
$\frac{1}{2}$°: 1 side, 2 columns.
'As there are fatal times when Nature's sighs'
In the Pennecuik ms. at E.
E.

P168 — Old-Reekie's loud and joyful acclamation, | For Sir John Barleycorn his restoration. [*Edinburgh*, 1725/26.]
$\frac{1}{2}$°: 1 side, 2 columns.
'Welcome, dear friend, the joy of ev'ry heart'
Apparently on the breaking of the brewers' combination against the malt tax.
E.

P169 — A panegyrick on Philip king of Spain, upon his renouncing his crown and kingdoms, to live in a hermitage. [*Edinburgh*, 1724?]
$\frac{1}{2}$°: 1 side, 1 column.

Pennecuik, A. A panegyrick

'Hail miracle of monarchs who resigns'
Dated as 1724 in the Pennecuik ms. at E.
E.

[—] A pastoral poem to the memory of the honourable Lord Basil Hamiltoun, 1701. *See* P118.

P170 — [dh] Rome's legacy, to the kirk of Scotland, a saty'r on the stool of repentance. By Mr. Pennicuik. [*Edinburgh*, 172–?]
8°: A⁴; 1–8.
A very rough publication which may well be later than the edition below.
'When pop'ry was pull'd down in days of yore'
L(11631.aaa.56/15).

P171 [—] Rome's legacy to the kirk of Scotland: or the rise and progress of stools of repentance. A satyr. The second edition with various additions... By an eminent hand. [*Edinburgh*] *Printed for the author,* 1724.
8°: A⁶; *1–2* 3–11 *12 blk.*
E(2, 1 cropt).

P172 [—] The shepherds tears: a pastoral sacred to the memory of that excellent gentleman, and noble patriot, William Nisbet of Dirleton esq;, who died October 20th, 1724. [*Edinburgh*, 1724.]
$\frac{1}{2}$°: 1 side, 1 column.
Mourning borders.
'Why weeps Melindor in this sullen grove?'
In the Pennecuik ms. at E.
E.

[—] The women's indictment against Burnbank, and George Fachney, 1721. *See* W550.

Pennyman, Margaret, *Lady.* Miscellanies in prose and verse... *London, printed for E. Curll,* 1740.
12°: pp. viii, 112.   L, O.
Mainly in prose.

Penshurst. Penshurst. Inscribed to William Perry, esq, 1750. *See* Coventry, Francis.

'Penstrong, Peter.' The maypole's new-years-gift, 1714. *See* M155.

'Pentweazle, Ebenezer.' The Horatian canons of friendship, 1750. *See* Smart, Christopher.

Pepusch, John Christopher. Dr. Pepusche's song perform'd for his exercise in the Theatre, [1713.] *See* D355.

— An ode for the second of March next [by John Hughes], [1719?] *See* H379.

P173 [**Percival, William,** *barrister.*] The college-examination. A poem. *Dublin, printed by S. Powell, for John Watson,* 1731.
8°: A⁸; *1–4* 5–16. A1 hft.
No watermark; no dedication in this issue.
'Examination's ever-dreaded toils'
The fine-paper issue below has the dedication to Kean O Hara signed 'William Percival'.

Percival, W. The college-examination

The dedication makes it clear that this was the son of the dean of Emly, admitted to Trinity College, Dublin, on 3 Oct 1727.

C(−A1),DA,DG,DN,DT(4)+; CSmH,OCU.

P174 — [fine paper]

8°: *A*⁸; *1–4* 5–16.

Watermark: fleur-de-lys on shield. Apparently reimposed so that A1 becomes title, A2 dedication to Mr. Kean O Hara.

L(11632.c.44, ms. note),LdU-B(presentation copy in marbled wrappers).

P175 [**Percival, William,** *dean of Emly.*] A description in answer to the Journal. *Dublin, printed in the year* 1722.

½°: 1 side, 2 columns.

Teerink 627.

'Near St. Sepulchres stands a building'

For Percival's authorship see *Williams* 277.

An answer to Swift's *The journal* [1721/22.]

L(C.121.g.8/26),C,DT.

P176 [—] — [*Dublin,* 1722.]

½°: 1 side, 2 columns.

On the other side, Swift's *The journal*, [1722.]

DN,Rothschild.

P177 [—] Elegia. In obitum reverendi Henrici Alderich S.T.P. Ædis Christi in Academia Oxoniensi nuper decani, qui ex hac vita emigravit Decemb. 14. & in sacello ecclesiæ cathedralis Ædis Christi honorifice inhumatus fuit Decemb. 22. 1710. [*Dublin?* 1710/11.]

½°: 2 sides, 1 column.

Title in woodcut mourning block at head, possibly intended for funeral-tickets.

'Lux tua splendescat latum, reverende per orbem'

Ms. note on the O copy, 'Made by Mr Percivall'.

O(MS. Ballard 50, fol. 68).

P178 Perils. The perils of false brethren: set forth in the fable of the boy and wolf. *London, printed in the year* 1710. (*Observator* 17 May)

8°: A⁴; *1* 2–7 '7'.

Advertised in *Observator* by B. Bragge.

'In days of yore as Æsop tells'

A fable against Sacheverell.

L(164.m.56),LG,CT,DK,MP+; CtY.

P179 Perkin. Perkin redivivus: to the tune of Lillibullero. [*London?*] *Printed in the year* 1715.

slip: 1 side, 1 column.

'The papists and tories do openly boast'

An attack on the Pretender.

L(C.121.g.9/172), Herts CRO (Panshanger box 46).

P180 — Perkin's-cabal, or the mock ministry characterized. *London, printed for A. Boulter, & S. Popping; sold by the booksellers of London & Westminster,* 1714. (15 Sept, Luttrell)

4°: *A*² B–C²; *1–2* 3–12.

Perkin's cabal

Listed in *MC* Sept 1714.

'Satyrick muse, who knows so well'

An attack on the tories.

L(164.n.3, Luttrell),C,*MR*; CLU-C,CtY,IU, MH.

P181 — — '*London, printed for A. Boulter...*' [*Dublin*], 1714.

8°: *A*⁴; *1–2* 3–8.

DA.

P182 — Perkin's farewel to all his faithful friends in Great-Britain. [*London*] *Printed by Tho. Vernon, near the Temple,* [1714?]

slip: 1 side, 1 column.

'Altho', my dear friends, my eggs are all addle'

A satire on the fall of the tory Jacobites.

O.

— 'Perkins last adventure, or, a trip through the back door.'

One of 'Three loyal songs...Price one penny each' advertised in *Rebellious fame,* 1717.

P183 Perkinite. The Perkinite Jacks: or, a new ballad on the tackers. *London, printed in the year* 1705. (11 May, Luttrell)

½°: 1 side, 2 columns.

'We have no great cause to be vaunting'

A whig poem against the tackers.

L(C.121.g.9/144, imprint cropt, Luttrell),LLP, Rothschild.

Perkins, Joseph. Poematum miscellaneorum, a Josepho Perkins. Liber primus. *Londini, prostant venales apud B. Bragg,* 1707. (8 April, Luttrell)

4°: pp. 28. L,O; CtY.

A frontispiece found in the Luttrell copy (at CtY) is clearly original.

_____

P184 — Ad serenissimam Annam, D. G. Mag. Brit. &c. reginam, ad Thermas iter facientem. *Exeter, printed by Sam. Farley, over against the New-Inn in the Forestreet,* 1704.

½°: 1 side, 2 columns.

Four sets of verses in Latin and English; the English verses in column 2 headed '⟨To the⟩ queen's most excellent majesty, resorting to the Bath'.

'Ad thermas graditur victrix regina calentes'

'To Bath the queen a golden charriot draws'

Each column signed 'J. Perkins.'

Crawford(title cropt).

P185 [—] Britanniæ lætantis exᵘₐltatio, ob felicem Georgii regis clarissimi, in Britanniam adventum, ejusdemque splendidum in Londinum introitum; nec non coronandi eucharisticon. [1714.]

½°: 1 side, 1 column.

Probably a piece of provincial printing, perhaps from Bristol. The copy at LDW appears to be conjugate with *Octostichon eucharisticon,* a series of acrostics.

Perkins, J. Britanniæ lætantis exultatio

'Exhilarent alacres Britonum jam gaudia vultus!'
A long list of dedicatees at foot addressed by
'J.P.'; almost certainly by Joseph Perkins.
L(835.m.8/16),LDW.

P186 — Elegia in obitum celsissimi, potentissimi,
illustrissimiq; principis, Henrici ducis de Beaufort marcionis Vigorniæ: dom. Herbert de Ragland... Qui ex hac vita emigravit Jan. 20. die
anno 1699... A. Jos. Perkins. *Bristoliæ, excudebat
G. Bonny, 1701.*
4°: A⁴; *1–2* 3–7 *8 blk.*
Many of the side-notes are in English.
'Stemmata quid faciunt? Quid prodest sanguine
longo'
O(2),BrP.

P187 — [another impression, title reads:] Elegia in
obitum... Henrici ducis de Beaufort marcionis &
comitis Vigorniæ: comitis Glamorgan: dom.
Herbert de Ragland...
Four lines are omitted from p. 3, many
changes are made to the text, and the side-
notes are all in Latin but one.
L(1415.f.9/8),BrP.

P188 — [reissue]
4°: (frt+) π¹ A⁴ ²A² B¹; [2] *1–2* 3–7 *8 blk, 1–4*
[*2 blk*].
A reissue with the addition of a portrait of
Perkins; a Latin verse dedication to the
Duchess of Beaufort on π1, verso blank; and
an English translation in ²A² headed 'An
elegy on the death... Being a translation of
the Latin-copy. By J. Perkins'. B1, blank, is
conjugate with π1.
'What profit is in parentage? what good'
Longleat; CtY(slightly cropt).

P189 — An elegy on the death of the reverend and
honourable William Grahme, S.T.P. Late dean of
Wells, and clerk of the closet to her sacred majesty,
&c. Who departed this life, Feb. 5. 17¹¹⁄₁₂, and was
interr'd in the parish-church at Kensington. Being
a translation of the Latin copy, by Joseph Perkins.
London, printed for the author, 1712.
½°: 1 side, 2 columns.
Mourning borders.
'As I pass'd o'er Parnassus shady hills'
It is not clear whether this translation is also
by Perkins; the Latin original has not been
traced.
MH.

[—] Phœnix moriendo revixit: or Britain's great
mourning for the late King William's death,
[1702?] *See* P263.

P190 — A poem (both in English and Latin) on the
death of the rt. reverend father in god, Thomas
Kenn, sometime lord bishop of Bath and Wells,
who died March the 19th, 1710... *Bristol, printed
by W. Bonny, 1711.*
4°: A⁴; *1–3* 4–8.

Perkins, J. A poem...on the death

Copies at L,NjP are watermarked with
Amsterdam arms; that at O, with pro patria.
'Pluck'd from an angel's wing give me a pen'
'Porrigat ætheras, mihi porrigat angelus alas'
L(11626.c.28),O; NjP.

P191 — The poet's fancy: in a love letter to Galatea,
or any other fair lady. In English and Latin.
*London, printed for [Samuel Bunchley] and sold at
the publishing office, in Dove-court, near Bearbinder-lane, 1707.* (*TC* Trinity)
4°: A⁴; *1–2* 3–8.
'Read o'er these lines, O fairest of the graces!'
'Perlege versiculos, charitum pulcherrima, nos-
tros'
L(11642.e.43),DT.

Persian. Persian eclogues, 1742. *See* Collins,
William.

Persius Flaccus, Aulus.
[Brewster, Thomas:] The satires of Persius, trans-
lated into English verse [in 5 parts], 1741–42. *See*
B432–6.

[*Satire 1*] D'Anvers, G. M.: Persius Scaramouch
... In imitation of the first satire of Persius, 1734.
See D42.

Dudley, *Mr*: The first satire of Persius, translated
into English verse, 1739. *See* D487.

Loveling, Benjamin: The first satire of Persius
imitated, 1740. *See* L291.

[*Satire 2*] Brewster, Thomas: A translation of the
second satyr of Persius, 1733. *See* B437.

[*Satire 4*] Advice to an aspiring young gentleman
of fortune. In imitation of the fourth satyr of
Perseus, 1733. *See* A77.

Perspective. The perspective, or Calista dissected,
1731. *See* Chamberlen, Paul.

P192 Peter. Peter. A tale. *London, printed in the year*
1744.
4°: B–D⁴ E²; *1–3* 4–27 *28 blk.*
'Ye nine of Hippocrenes streams'
A satire on Francis Larwood, recorder of Nor-
wich.
L(1490.de.35, ms. notes),O,LdU-B,*MR*; CSmH,
CtY,ICN,NjP,OCU(uncut)+.

Petition. A petition to his g——e the D——e of
G——n, 1724. *See* Smedley, Jonathan (S499).

P193 — ⟨A⟩ petition to the ladies of Dublin, from
Dunlary. Writen by the old wash-women. [*Dublin,
172–.*]
½°: 1 side, 1 column.
'Ye famales [!] of Dublin make haste, and repair'
In praise of the sea bathing at Dunleary.
DT(imprint cropt).

— A petition to the right hon. Mr. —— , 1750.
See Bentley, Richard.

P194 — The petition. To the tune of, Which no body
can deny. [*London? 1718?*]
slip: 1 side, 1 column.
Title reads, 'To the TUNE of...'. Printed
with *King Theodore's defeat*, [1718?] to the
right (undivided copy at L) and *An excellent
new ballad. To the tune of Chivy Chace*,
[1718?] to the left (undivided copy at O);
possibly these represent two different impressions.
'To you, German sir, a petition I bring'
Crum T3227: 'The petition from Tyburn'.
A Jacobite song. The scaffold at Tyburn begs
for whig victims.
L(C.116.i.4/5),O; MH.

P195 — [another edition]
Title reads, 'To the Tune of...'. Printed with
*An excellent new ballad. To the tune of Chivy
Chace*; the NjP copy is not divided.
O; NjP.

'Petronius Arbiter.'
The Richardiad. A satire. Translated from a
Greek fragment of Petronius Arbiter, 1743, 1744.
See R192–3.

P196 Petticoat. The pettycoat. A poem. In four canto's.
Written by —— , late of Westminster School,
a king's scholar: and now published by a lady.
Dublin, printed by George Faulkner, 1738.
4°: A^2 A^{*2} $B–K^2$; *i–viii*, *1–36*.
Bond 165. List of subscribers, pp. iv–vi.
'In strains-majestic, and with heavenly fire'
'Wrote by a young gentleman of about sixteen
years of age... Published by a lady who was
sister to the author'. Dedication to Miss
Susannah Wandesford signed 'Mary Broggin'.
L(11643.bbb.20/2),MR-C.

— The petticoat, an heroi-comical poem, 1716–.
See Chute, Francis.

P197 Pettifoggers. The pettifoggers. A satire. In
hudibrastick verse. Displaying the various frauds,
deceits, and knavish practices, of the pettifogging
counsellors, attornies, solicitors and clerks...
London, printed for A. Dodd, 1723. (*MC* March)
8°: $A–D^4$; *1–2* 3–30 *31–32* blk.
Bond 75.
'In ancient days, when times were good'
L(164.1.26, Luttrell, March, –D4),O(–D4),C;
CLU-C(–D4),MH.

Phaedrus.
[Browne, Joseph:] The singing-bird's address to
the eagle... Imitated from an old fable of Phædrus;
not in any edition, 1707. *See* B530–9.

A fable translated out of Phædrus. Humbly inscribed to the directors and members of the South-
Sea Company, 1714. *See* F19.

Phaenix, J.

Phaenix, John. *See* Phoenix, John.

Phaethon. Phaethon: or the first fable of the
second book of Ovid's Metamorphoses burlesqu'd,
1720. *See* Meston, William.

P198 Phantom. The phantom. *London, printed for J.
Stagg*, 1725. (*MC* Feb)
2°: A^2 $B–C^2$; *1–3* 4–12.
Listed in *MC* as sold by J. Roberts.
'To these our days, from days of old'
O; MH,OCU.

Pheasant. The pheasant and the lark. A fable,
1730. *See* Delany, Patrick.

P199 Phelips, Paulin. Of man's chief happiness: a
poetical essay. *Northampton, printed by William
Dicey*, 1735.
4°: $A–C^2$; *1–2* 3–12. 12 err.
'Some poets court the airy praise of men'
LdU-B.

P200 Phelps, J. The human barometer: or, living
weather-glass. A philosophick poem. *London,
printed for M. Cooper*, 1743. (*GM* April).
4°: A^4 $B–C^4$ D^2; *1–9* 10–28.
'When on my mind I turn my studious eye'
'The influence of atmosphere on the human
frame.'
L(11630.d.15/9),O; CSmH,ICN.

'Philalethes.' An excise elegy, 1733. *See* E599.

— Pandæmonium: or a new infernal expedition,
1750. *See* P28.

— The parson and his clerk, 1734. *See* P81.

Philander. Philander and Cydippe, 1727. *See*
Cooke, Thomas.

P201 — Philander and Sacharissa. A novel. To which is
added, an elegy on Mr. Addison. *London, printed
for John Noon*, 1724. (*MC* April)
8°: $A–C^4$; *1–3* 4–23 *24*. 24 advt.
'Under a myrtle, by fair Isis side'
Elegy: 'Is then, alas! Britannia's genius fled'
L(11633.e.45/6); CtY.

Philanglus. Philanglus and Astræa, 1712. *See*
Kirkham, Charles.

'Philanthropos.' The Temple-Oge ballad, 1730.
See Poekrich, Richard.

'Phileirene.' Loyalty triumphant in bonds, 1749.
See L311.

'Phileleutherus Britannus.' A short trip into
Kent, 1743. *See* S451.

'Philemon.' The lover's miscellany, 1719. *See*
Jacob, Giles.

Philibert

'Philibert.' A poem, compos'd the second of November, [1747.] *See* P525.

P202 [**Philips, —, Captain.**] The romance of the rose. Imitated from Chaucer. *London, printed for Jonah Bowyer,* 1721. (*PB* 21 Feb)
2°: A–G² H¹; *1–2* 3–30.
> The copy at OW was perhaps presented before publication.

'Howe're, some men accounted wise'
> The OW copy has a ms. note by George Clarke, 'by Captain Philips'.

O,OW(presentation copy, 16 Feb); CSmH,ICN, IU,MH,TxU(uncut).

Philips, Ambrose. Pastorals, epistles, odes, and other original poems, with translations from Pindar, Anacreon, and Sappho. *London, printed for J. & R. Tonson & S. Draper,* 1748. (*GM* May)
12°: pp. 147.   L,O; CtY,TxU.

For poems by 'Namby Pamby' in which Philips's authorship is mockingly intended, see 'Namby Pamby'.

[—] Durgen, a satyr, to the celeberted [!] Mr. P--------pe, on his Dunciad. By Namby Pamby, [1729.] *See* D554.

P203 — An epilogue spoke by Mr. Griffith, to their graces the Duke and Dutchess of Grafton. At the Theatre-royal in Dublin. Written by Ambrose Philips, esq; *Dublin, printed by Thomas Hume, in Smock-alley,* [1721.] (Oct?)
½°: 1 side, 1 column.
> Also printed in the *Dublin courant* 4 Oct 1721; see W. S. Clark, *The early Irish stage* (1955) 177.

'Illustrious pair! the blessing of this isle'
CtY.

P204 — An epistle to the honourable James Craggs, esq; secretary at war: at Hampton-Court. *London, printed for Jacob Tonson,* 1717. (*PB* 22 Oct)
2°: *A²* B–C²; *i–iv, 1* 2–8. A1 hft.
> Watermark: O. Entered in *SR* 22 Oct; deposit copies at L,LSC,O,E,EU.

'Though Britain's hardy troops demand your care'
L(643.m.13/14),LVA-F,O(–A1),C,E+; CtY(–A1),IU,MH,PU,TxU+.

P205 — [fine paper]
> Watermark: monogram PH.

CLU-C,NjP.

P206 — An epistle to the right honourable Charles lord Halifax, one of the lords justices appointed by his majesty. *London, printed for J. Tonson,* 1714. (1 Sept, Luttrell)
2°: *A²* B² *C¹; i–iv,* 1–5 *6 blk.* A1 hft.
> Watermark: post-horn on shield. Listed in *MC* Sept. Entered in *SR* on 3 Sept to Tonson by Tho. Glenister; deposit copies at L,LSC, O,EU,AdU,SaU.

Philips, A. An epistle

'Patron of verse, O Halifax, attend'
L(643.m.13/3),O,EU,DT,AdU+; CSmH,CtY, IU,MH(Luttrell),TxU(2)+.

P207 — [fine paper]
> Watermark: O.

LVA-F; DFo.

[—] The fairy-king, a poem. By Mr. —— P. ——, 1726. *See* F37.

P208 [—] The following poems, writen [!] by Mr. P——s, and but now come to our hands, claim a sort of right to be communicated to the lovers of poetry, who always find an agreeable entertainment in what flows from the pen of that ingenious gentleman; who we hope, will therefore forgive a publication, of which he is wholly unappriz'd. *Dublin, printed by George Faulkner,* 1725.
½°: 1 side, 2 columns.
> The poems are 'A supplication for Miss Carteret, in the small-pox' and 'To Miss Georgina, youngest daughter of the Lord Carteret'.

'Power, o'er ev'ry power supreme'
'Little charm, of placid mien'
> Both poems were reprinted in Philips's *Pastorals, epistles, odes,* 1748, and dated 31 July and 10 Aug 1725. They are listed separately in *CBEL*, apparently in error.

L(C.121.g.8/68).

P209 '—' A new poem by Mr. Philipps. [*Dublin*] *Printed by J. Tompson in Highstreet,* 1726.
slip: 1 side, 1 column.
'Dapper spark tho' dwarf in size'
> Written in 'namby-pamby' verse; the attribution to 'Philipps' is presumably a joke. Not included in M. G. Segar's edition, 1937. On Patrick Walsh, 'the little beau' (cf. *Williams* 424f.). *Capt. Wel—he's answer to Miss Molly War-rt-on,* [1726/28] is perhaps intended as a reply.

L(1890.e.5/43),DT; CtY,MH.

P210 — An ode (in the manner of Pindar) on the death of the right honourable William, earl Cowper. *London, printed for T. Woodward, J. Walthoe, & J. Peele,* 1723. (*MC* Dec)
2°: *A²* B–C²; *i–iv, 1* 2–8. A1 hft.
'Wake the British harp, again'
L(643.l.24/46; 162.n.17),O(–A1),OA; CLU-C, IU,MH,NjP,TxU+.

P211 — Pastorals, by Mr. Philips. *London printed, and sold by H. Hills,* 1710.
8°: A⁸ B⁴; *1* 2–24.
> Title vignette is a Tudor rose; '(Price Twopence.)' on title. The order of editions is uncertain. Previously printed in Tonson's *Poetical miscellanies: the sixth part,* 1709. An offprint from that volume, with the word 'Finis' added on p. 48, is at NjP.

'If we, O Dorset, quit the city throng'
L(1486.aaa.5),O,CT,AdU,*LpU*; CtY,ICN,MH.

Philips, A. Pastorals

P212 — [another edition]
Title vignette is a bowl of flowers; price on title. P. 9, line 33 reads 'Menalcas'.
O; MH,TxU.

P213 — [another edition]
Title vignette is a bowl of flowers; price on title. P. 9, line 33 reads 'Menalcus'. There appear to be two settings of p. 5, possibly caused by an accident in printing; in one p. 5, line 17 ends 'yet show', in the other 'Yet show'. Both states can be seen at O,MH. Reissued with other Hills piracies in *A collection of the best English poetry, 1717 (Case 294)*.
L(C.124.b.7/55),LVA-F,O(2),C,LdU-B; CLU-C,CSmH,CtY,MH(2),TxU.

P214 — [another edition]
Title vignette is a bowl of flowers; no price on title. The copy seen is bound with pamphlets of around 1720; it is possibly a later piracy.
O.

P214·5 — Six pastorals by Mr. Philips. '*London printed, and sold by H. Hills, 1710*' [172–?].
12°: π² B–C⁶; *1–7 8–27 28 blk.* π1 hft.
Type flowers only on title; '(Price Fourpence.)' The date and place of printing are undetermined, but the price suggests a comparatively late piracy. It was originally bound with works of 1726 and 1728.
L(1970).

P215 — Pastorals, by Mr. Philips. '*London printed, and sold by H. Hills, 1710*' [173–?].
8°: A–C⁴; *1–2 3–24*.
A piracy, well printed and on good paper. From the printer's ornaments it appears to be a London production of the 1730s.
LG.

P216 — — [*Edinburgh*] *Printed in the year 1731*.
8°: A–C⁴; *1 2–24*.
Another piracy; the ornament formerly belonged to James Watson in Edinburgh.
L(1972),EU; CtY.

P217 — Poems by Mr. Philips, &c. *Dublin, printed by Pressick Rider & Thomas Harbin, 1725*.
½°: 1 side, 2 columns.
The poems are 'To Miss Charlotte Pulteney in her mother's arms', 'To Miss Peggy Pulteney in the nursery', and 'On the death of my Lord Halifax'.
'Timely blossom, infant fair'
'Dimply damsel, sweetly smiling'
'Weeping o'er thy sacred urn'
The poems are dated 1 May 1724, 27 April 1727, and 30 June 1718 in Philips's *Pastorals, epistles, odes, 1748*. The second date is presumably erroneous; that poem is listed separately with the date 1727 in *CBEL*, apparently in error.
L(C.121.g.8/89, mutilated),Rothschild; CSmH.

[—] A satyr on the poets of the town... Writ by A.P., 1726. *See* S62.

Philips, A. The tea-pot

P218 '—' The tea-pot; or, the lady's transformation. A new poem. By Mr. Philips. [*Dublin*, 1725/30.]
½°: 1 side, 2 columns.
The copy at L forms part of a collection of Dublin half-sheets of 1725/30.
'Soft Venus, love's too an anxious queen'
Ambrose Philips is presumably intended as the author, but his authorship seems unlikely. M. G. Segar in her edition of Philips's poems (1937) 184 suggests there is no doubt of its authenticity, but gives no evidence. Cf. *The metamorphose of a certain Dublin beau's-head, into a tea-kettle, 1730*.
L(C.121.g.8/107); CSmH,MH.

P219 — [dh] To his excellency the Lord Carteret, &c. departing from Dublin. [col] *Dublin, printed by George Grierson, 1726*.
2°: A²; *1–4*.
'Behold, Britannia waves her flag on high'
CtY.

P220 — — *Dublin, printed by A. Rhames, 1726*.
½°: 2 sides, 1 column.
Possibly a piracy, though it is well printed.
L(C.121.g.8/148),DT; CtY.

P221 — To the honourable Miss Carteret. [col] *Dublin, printed by George Grierson*, [1725.]
2°: A⁴; *1–3 4–7 8 blk.*
Title in half-title form.
'Bloom of beauty, early flow'r'
See [*A lady's answer*] *To Mr. Ambrose Philips*, 1725, L21. There were numerous parodies of Philips's 'namby-pamby' verse, of which this was the classic example; see also *A poem upon R——r*, [1725], and 'Edward Young', *A poem by Doctor Young, on Miss Harvey*, [1725.]
L(840.m.1/20),O; TxU.

P222 — — *London, printed for J. Roberts, 1725.* (*MC* May)
2°: A² B–C²; *i–iv, 1 2–6 7–8 blk.* A1 hft.
L(643.1.24/48, –C2),O(–C2),BaP(–C2); CSmH(–C2),CtY,ICU,NjP(–C2),TxU.

P223 [—] [*idem*] A poem ascrib'd to the honourable Miss Carteret. [*Dublin*] *Printed by E. Needham & R. Dickson, 1725.*
½°: 1 side, 2 columns.
L(C.121.g.8/73); CSmH.

P224 [—] [*idem*] A new poem ascrib'd to the honourable Miss Carteret. [*Dublin*, 1725.]
½°: 1 side, 1 column.
On the other side, *A lady's answer to Mr. Ambrose Philips's poem*, [1725.]
L(C.121.g.8/127),Rothschild; CtY,NjP.

[—] Toasts elected by the Hanover-club, for the year 1713.
A half-sheet (copy at MH) listing 31 names and ending with eight lines of verse. Philips was secretary of the club, and the verses are probably those attributed to him by *Jacob* as

Philips, A. Toasts

'Upon the toasts of the Hanover Club'. It is excluded from this catalogue as primarily a prose work.

P225 Philips, Erasmus. 'A pindarique ode on the birth-day of his majesty King George. [*London*] *Printed for R. Baldwin.*' (*MC* May 1715)

Philips, John. The works of Mr. John Philips... To which is prefix'd, his life and character. *London printed, and sold by E. Curll,* 1712 [1713?]. (14 Jan, Luttrell)

8°.   L,OW,CK.

A nonce collection, consisting of *The life and character of Mr. John Philips,* 1712 (with his *Ode,* dated 1713), and the 1709 Hills editions of *Bleinheim* and *Cyder.*

— [reissue] *London, printed and sold by E. Curll,* 1714.

LVA-D; PU.

Cancel title. With the 1710 Hills edition of Ambrose Philips's *Pastorals* added.

— Poems by Mr. John Philips... To which is prefix'd his life. *London, printed in the year* 1715.

12°: pp. 36+28+*37-43*.   L,O; CLU-C,CSmH.

This edition is composed of the *Life* with Curll's imprint; *The splendid shilling* (second edition) and *Bleinheim* (fourth edition) with Clements's imprint; and the *Ode* (third edition) with Curll's imprint.

— Poems on several occasions... The third edition. *London, printed for J. Tonson, E. Curll, & T. Jauncy,* 1720.

12°: pp. 36+12+28+71.   L,O; CtY,MH.

A similar edition to the preceding; a Curll edition of the *Life* and the *Ode* with P249 and P242. Some copies (L,IU) use a later reprint of *The splendid shilling* and *Bleinheim* with no title (pp. 23). The copyright of these two works formed lot 9 of the trade sale of Henry Clements, 14 March 1720, bought by Jauncy for £17 10s. (cat. at O–JJ).

— The whole works of Mr. John Philips... *Loldon* [!], *printed for J. Tonson, & T. Jauncy,* 1720.

8°: pp. xxxix, 60+89+13.   L,O; CtY,MH.

This edition includes a reissue of the first edition of *Cyder,* 1708.

— Poems on several occasions... The fourth edition. *London, printed for E. Curll, & T. Astley,* 1728.

12°: pp. 46+23+72.   L; IU.

— [reissue] *London printed, and sold by Thomas Astley,* 1728. (*MChr* 3 Sept)

L,O; CtY,MH.

Most copies contain a new edition of *The splendid shilling* and *Bleinheim* with 24 pp.

— Poems on several occasions... *Dublin, printed by S. Powell, for A. Bradley,* 1730.

12°: pp. 144.   L,O; IU.

Philips, J.

— Poems, viz... The sixth edition. *Glasgow, printed by R. Urie & company, for J. Gilmour,* 1744.

12°: pp. '110' [130].   L,E.

— Poems attempted in the style of Milton... The tenth edition. *London, printed for E. Curll,* 1744 [1745?]. (*LM* Jan)

12°: pp. xxx, 42+72.   L,O; CtY,MH.

Cyder (P243) has a separate title-leaf with Tonson & Draper's imprint.

— Poems: viz. An ode... *Glasgow, printed by R. Urie, for J. Gilmour,* 1750.

8°: pp. 122.   O,E; MH.

———

P226 [—] Bleinheim, a poem, inscrib'd to the right honourable Robert Harley, esq; *London, printed for Tho. Bennet,* 1705. (*DC* 2 Jan)

2°: *A*¹ B–F² G¹; *i–ii,* 1–22. 22 err.

No watermark. *Thomas* 1b. Some copies, asterisked below, read 'Army, Death' in p. 8 line 12; the other reading 'Army Death,' is found in the fine-paper copies and later editions. The Luttrell copy, dated 2 Jan, is in the possession of J. R. B. Brett-Smith.

'From low and abject themes the grov'ling muse' The late L. W. Hanson informed me that the secret service receipt books record under 16 May 1705 the payment of £100 royal bounty to Philips 'for writing a poem in blank verse of the battle of Bleinheim'.

L*(11630.g.5),O*,OW*(2, 1 uncut),C*(ms. date 3 Jan),DT+; CSmH*(2),CtY,ICU,MH,TxU+.

P227 [—] [fine paper]

Watermark: B.

L(1962, 'Donum authoris Johannis Philips'); IU.

P228 — — By Mr. Philips, of Christ-Church, Oxon. *London, printed for Tho. Bennet,* 1705.

2°: *A*¹ B–F² G¹; *i–ii,* 1–22.

Thomas 1a. No errata on p. 22. A fine-paper copy with sheet A/G in a different state. The copy seen has no sign of presentation and this may be a proof state. On the other hand the existence of a Dublin and possibly an Edinburgh reprint with this form of title suggests that this form may have been used for government circulation.

OC.

P229 [—] — The second edition. *London, printed for Tho. Bennet,* 1705. (*PM* 16 Jan)

2°: *A*¹ B–F² G¹; *i–ii,* 1–22.

Thomas 2. A1 and G1 have been seen to be conjugate. Apparently reset and corrected.

L(11631.k.17; 1960),O,C,EU,LdU-B+; CU, ICU,KU,*MH*,TxU(2, 1 uncut)+.

P230 [—] — The third edition. *London, printed for Tho. Bennet,* 1705. (*LG* 1 March)

2°: *A*¹ B–F² G¹; *i–ii,* 1–22.

No watermark. *Thomas* 3. An aberrant copy

Philips, J. Bleinheim

at L (1489.m.31) has sheet A/G of the preceding edition bound with B–F of this. Apparently reset and corrected.

L(11630.g.23; 11602.i.10/2; 1489.m.31),OW, LdU-B; ICU,MH,TxU.

P231 [—] [fine paper?]
Watermark: grapes.

O.

P232 —— By Mr. John Philips, of Christ-Church, Oxon. *London, printed for Tho. Bennet*, 1705.
4⁰: *A*⁴ B⁴; *1–2* 3–16.
The status of this edition is undetermined. It is tempting to hypothesize an Edinburgh reprint, possibly government sponsored, parallel to the following Dublin edition.

NN.

P233 —— By Mr. John Philips of Christ-Church, Oxon. '*London, printed for Tho. Bennet*' [*Dublin*] 1705.
8⁰: *A*⁴ B⁴; *1–2* 3–16.
Printed by John Brocas on the evidence of faulty titling capitals, according to Miss Mary Pollard. Apparently reprinted from the named issue of the London first edition, possibly circulated by the English government.

DT.

P234 [—] — *London, printed by H. Hills; sold by the booksellers of London & Westminster*, 1709.
8⁰: A⁸; *1–2* 3–16.
Title rules 27 mm apart; p. 5 misnumbered '4' in most copies (correct in OA,ICN,TxU). *Thomas* 4, not distinguishing editions. Reissued in Philips's *Works*, 1712.

L(11631.c.6; 1077.k.23/2), O(2), E, C, CT(4)+; ICN,IU,MH(3),OCU,TxU.

P235 [—] [another edition]
Title rules 38 mm apart. Reissued with other Hills piracies in *A collection of the best English poetry*, 1717 (*Case* 294).

L(C.124.b.7/30),LDW,O,EU,WcC+; CtY,MH, TxU.

P236 [—] — *London: printed; and reprinted in Dublin by S. Powell, for John Henly*, 1713.
12⁰: A–B⁶; *1–2* 3–22 *23–24* blk.
Thomas 5. Copies usually form part of *A select collection of modern poems* (Dublin, 1713), reissued as *Poetical miscellanies* (Dublin, 1714; copy at CtY). Whether it was sold separately is not known.

O,DN,DT; CtY(2),MH.

[—] Cerealia: an imitation of Milton [actually by Elijah Fenton], 1706. *See* F104.

P237 [—] Cyder. A poem. In two books. *London, printed for Jacob Tonson*, 1708. (*LG* 29 Jan)
8⁰: *A*² B–F⁸ G⁴ H²; *i–vi*, *1* 2–89 *90* blk. A1 frt; B1 fly-title.
Watermark: X, with corner counter-mark.

Philips, J. Cyder

Rothschild 1535; *Williams, Points* 92. *Thomas* xxvn. quotes the terms of Philips's agreement with Tonson, made 27 Nov 1707; Philips was paid forty guineas on 24 Jan 1708 and also received one hundred copies on large paper and two dedication copies bound in Turkey leather. Reissued in *The annual miscellany*, 1708, and in Philips's *Works*, 1720.
'What soil the apple loves, what care is due'
Cf. *Milton's sublimity asserted*, 1709.

L(1077.h.2),O(2),C,EU,DT+; CLU-C,CSmH (uncut),IU,MH.

P238 [—] [fine paper]
No watermark. *Rothschild* 1534. P. 74 misnumbered '47'. In most copies sheet D is reset and does not have the press-figures 44–*, 46–* present in ordinary copies; but copies at WcC, TxU have the original setting. There are a number of corrections and the sheet may have been reprinted to make them. The two copies at WcC (containing the two states) are in identical calf bindings; possibly Philips's one hundred copies were supplied bound.

L(11631.f.40),*BU*,WcC(2); CSmH,MH,*NN-A*, NjP(–A1),TxU.

P239 [—] — With the Splendid shilling. Paradise lost, and two songs, &c. *London printed, and sold by H. Hills*, 1708.
8⁰: A–C⁸; *1* 2–48. 48 advt.
The splendid shilling occupies pp. 41–45, the three minor poems (not by Philips) pp. 45–47.

L(11643.bb.31/1),O(2),CT(3),E,DT+; CtY, ICN,IU,MH.

P240 [—] — *London printed, and sold by H. Hills*, 1709.
8⁰: A–C⁸; *1* 2–48. 48 advt.
Signature A3 under 'oft the'. Reissued in Philips's *Works*, 1712.

L(11631.c.10),O(2),C(uncut),E,LdU-B+; CtY, ICN,MH,TxU.

P241 [—] [another edition]
Signature A3 under 'and oft'. Reissued in *A collection of the best English poetry*, 1717 (*Case* 294).

L(C.124.b.7/28),WcC(2); CtY,IU,MH,TxU.

P241·5 [—] — With an essay on the different stiles of poetry. *Dublin, printed by Edwin Sandys, for George Grierson*, 1715.
12⁰: A–I⁶; *1–2* 3–52, [4] 1–18, *1–2* 3–34.
The *Essay* (by Parnell) and *A key to the Lock* (in prose) each has a separate title as well as pagination, but the collation does not seem well adapted to their separate issue, despite the state of the recorded copies. *Cyder* ends on E2.

L(1966, *Cyder* only),DA(*Cyder* only),DN.

P242 [—] — *London, printed for J. T. [Jacob Tonson] and sold by Thomas Jauncy*, 1720. (*PM* 9 Feb)
12⁰: A–F⁶; *1–7* 8–71 *72*. A1 frt; A2 hft; 72 advt.

Philips, J. Cyder

Usually found issued in Philips's *Poems*, 1720; those copies are not noted here.
L(1484.bb.10),E(–A1); IU.

P243 [—] — The fourth edition. *London, printed for J. & R. Tonson & S. Draper*, 1744. (*GM* July)
12°: A–C¹²; *1–5* 6–72. A1 frt.
Usually found issued in Philips's *Poems*, 1744; those copies are not noted here. The third edition is found in *Poems*, 1728.
CtY,DFo,MH.

P244 [—] [dh] Honoratissimo viro, Henrico St.--John, armigero. Ode. [col] *Londini, impensis J. Bowyer*, 1707. (*PB* 13 March)
2°: A²; *1–3 4 blk.*
P. 3, line 14 has what appears to be the correct reading, 'Ornat! labellis...'
'O qui recisæ finibus Indicis'
Reprinted in Philips's collected poems. Translated as *A modern Latin ode attempted in English*, 1707.
L(835.m.8/15),O,*CJ*; CLU-C,CtY,MH.

P245 [—] [another impression?]
P. 3, line 14 reads 'O! labellis...' Apparently p. 3 is from a different setting of type, while the pagination and rules on pp. 1, 2 are new.
O; ICN.

[—] A panegyrick epistle...to S. R—— B——, 1706. *See* P31.

[—] A poem on the memorable fall of Chloe's p--s pot, attempted in blank verse, 1713. *See* P627.

P246 [—] The splendid shilling. A poem, in imitation of Milton. By the author of Bleinheim. *London printed, and sold by B. Bragg*, 1705. (29 Jan)
2°: A⁴; *i–ii*, 1–6.
An unauthorized edition, probably reprinted from one of the miscellanies in which it was published in 1701. Advertised in *FP* 30 Jan as published 'yesterday'; the Luttrell copy dated 29 Jan is in the possession of J. R. B. Brett-Smith.
'Happy the man, who void of cares and strife'
L(1959),O,OW,*CJ*,DG+; CSmH,DFo,MH, NN-A.

P247 [—] The splendid shilling. An imitation of Milton. Now first correctly publish'd. *London, printed for Tho. Bennet*, 1705. (*DC* 8 Feb)
2°: A² B–C²; *i–iv*, 1–8. A1 hft.
The order of these Bennet editions has not been finally established; here the pagination is enclosed in 9 mm. brackets. Line 24 reads '...Kings,', line 31 'Eclips'd'.
L(1855.c.4/18,–A1; 1962, uncut),O(2),C,LdU-B,WcC(–A1)+; CLU-C,*DLC*,IU,NjP,TxU+.

P248 [—] [another edition]
The pagination is enclosed in 7 mm. brackets. Only sheet B is reset. Line 24 here reads '...Kings', and line 31 'Eclip'd'. An aberrant

Philips, J. The splendid shilling

copy at TxU has the first state of sheet B and the second of C. Reprinted in Hills's editions of *Cyder*, 1708, 09, and in the Dublin edition of Pope's *Essay on criticism*, [1711?].
O,C(uncut),DT; CtY(–A1),ICU,KU(uncut, –A1).

P249 —— The third correct edition. *London, printed by G. J. for Hen. Clements*, 1719.
12°: A–B⁶ C²; *1–3* 4–28.
A5 is title to 'Bleinheim... The fifth edition'. Usually found in Philips's *Poems*, 1720; those copies are not listed, nor are the editions of 1715, 1720, 1728 found in collections.
O(uncut); DFo.

P250 —— *Dublin, printed by James Hoey, & George Faulkner*, 1728.
8°: A⁴; *1–3* 4–8. 8 advt.
L(993.e.49/7, slightly cropt).

[—] The sylvan dream or, the mourning muses, 1701. *See* S943.

P251 **Phillips, Edward.** 'An ode on the birth-day. [*London*] *Printed for H. Lintott; sold by J. Roberts.* Price 6*d.*' (*DP* 6 Nov 1732)

P252 — On the nuptials of his highness the Prince of Orange, to her highness the Princess Royal of England. An irregular ode. *London, printed for Richard Wellington*, 1734. (*GM* March)
2°: *A*² B–C² D¹; *1–3* 4–14.
'When Britannia, bright and gay'
CtY.

[—] The players: a satire, [1733.] *See* P484.

P253 [**Phillips, John.**] Mr John Milton's satyre against hypocrites. Written while he was Latin secretary to Oliver Cromwell. *London, printed for E. Powell; sold by J. Morphew*, 1710. (*PB* 15 Aug)
8°: A–C⁴; *i–ii*, 1–6 9–24.
Originally published in 1655.
'Tedious have been our fasts, and long our pray'rs'
For Phillips's authorship see the edition by Leon Howard in *Augustan Reprint Society* 38 (1953).
L(161.k.21, Luttrell, 15 Aug),O,CT(2),E,EU+; CtY,ICN,IU.

P254 [—] The vision of Mons. Chamillard concerning the battle of Ramilies: and the miraculous revolution in Flanders... A poem. Humbly inscrib'd to the right honourable John lord Somers. By a nephew of the late Mr. John Milton. *London, printed for Wm Turner*, 1706. (6 Aug, Luttrell)
2°: π¹ A–C² D¹; *i–iv*, 1–12. π1 hft.
π1 and D1 have been seen to be conjugate. Listed in *WL* August.
'One ev'ning e'rst the moon unveil'd her light'
O(Luttrell, –π1),*MR-C*; CtY,InU(–π1),TxU, *ViU*.

Phillips, S.

[**Phillips, Samuel.**] Britton's consort: or, the musick-meeting. A satyr. Written by S.P. gent., 1703. *See* B482.

P255 — England's glory: a congratulatory poem on the coronation, and happy accession of her majesty to the crown. *London printed, and are to be sold by John Nutt,* 1702. (22 April, Luttrell)
2°: *A*² B–D²; *1–4* 5–16.
The Luttrell copy is recorded in *Haslewood.*
'Soon as Aurora 'd left old Tithon's bed'
NN.

P256 — England's happiness. A panegyrick, on the present parliament. *London printed, and sold by John Nutt,* 1702. (16 March, Luttrell)
2°: *A*² B–C²; *1–4* 5–12.
'Let fair Augusta raise her drooping head'
CSmH,CtY(Luttrell),MH.

P257 — The German Cæsar. A panegyrick on Prince Eugene of Savoy, relating to the present posture of affairs in Italy, especially before Mantua. *London printed, and are to be sold by John Nutt,* 1702. (*WL* May)
2°: A–C² (A2 as 'A'); *i–iv,* 1–8.
'What! durst the Frenchman such a sentence breathe'
MC; MH.

P258 — The grove, or, muse's paradice: a dream. Wherein are describ'd the pleasures that attend a colledge-life. *London printed, and are to be sold by J. Nutt,* 1702. (19 June, Luttrell)
2°: *A*² B–D²; *1–4* 5–16.
The Luttrell copy is recorded in *Haslewood;* listed in *WL* June.
'When scorching Phœbus had half run his course'
CtY,TxU.

P259 Phillips, Thomas. To the right reverend & religious Dame Elizabeth Phillips on her entering the religious order of St. Benet in the convent of English dames of the same order at Gant. [1731.]
4°: A⁴; *1–8.*
Clearly a piece of continental printing; the L catalogue suggests [Ghent?]. The date is taken from J. Gillow, *A literary and biographical history...of the English Catholics,* V. 306.
'When gracefull Judith, conscious of her charms'
The poem is signed.
L(1346.k.18),BrP,LdU-B.

'**Philometrius.**' The country vicar's address, 1707. *See* C460.

'**Philo-Milton.**' Milton's sublimity asserted, 1709. *See* M267.

'**Philo-musus.**' Oculus Britanniae, 1724. *See* Amhurst, Nicholas.

'**Philonactos Rossendaliensis.**' A poem on the late rebellion, [1746?] *See* P624.

Philopatriae

'**Philopatriae.**' South Britain, 1731. *See* S609.

'**Philo-patris.**' Liberty: or the meeting of the parliament, 1728. *See* L172.

— A Scots poem, 1707. *See* S145.

P260 Philosophic. A philosophic ode on the sun and the universe. *London, printed for J. Payne, & J. Bouquet,* 1750. (*GM* April)
4°: *A*⁴ B–C⁴ D²; *i–viii,* 1 2–18, 1 2. A1 hft; D2 advt.
'Radiant sovereign of the day!'
L(11631.g.2/3, —A1),O(—A1, D2); CSmH,IU, OCU,TxU(—D2).

Philosophical. 'A philosophical hymn to the sun, on his majesty's birth-day, set to musick by a gentleman. [*London*] Cooper. Price 3*d*.' (*BM* Oct 1746)
Possibly an engraved half-sheet with music. Listed in *GM* as 'A hymn to the sun'.

Philosophy. Philosophy. A poem address'd to the ladies who attend Mr. Booth's lectures, 1746. *See* Jones, Henry, *the bricklayer.*

P261 Phino-Godol. Phino-Godol. A poem. In hudi-brastick verse. In two canto's. *London, printed for J. Towers; sold by the booksellers of London & Westminster,* 1732. (*GSJ* Aug)
2°: *A*² B–D²; *1–2* 3–16.
Bond 124.
'How oft from trifles, hints we take'
On the second Duchess of Marlborough's breaking the wax image of her lover William Congreve.
LdU-B(uncut); CLU-C,CtY,MH.

P262 — [reissue] The amorous d---h--ss: or, her g--- grateful. A true tale... In two canto's. *London, printed for N. Holloway; sold by the booksellers of London & Westminster,* 1733.
2°: *A*²(±) B–D²; *1–2* 3–16.
Apparently both leaves of A² are cancelled.
L(163.n.33); CSmH(uncut).

Phocylides.
Hart, J.: Ποιημα νουθετικον: or, the preceptive poem of Phocylides, translated into English, 1744. *See* H92.

P263 Phoenix. Phœnix moriendo revixit: or Britain's great mourning for the late King William's death, turned into rejoycing, by the happy succession of Queen Anne on the throne. The second edition, with additions. *Bristol, printed and sold by W.B.* [*William Bonny*], [1702?]
4°: *A*⁴ B¹; *1–2* 3–9 *10 blk.*
The additional short poems are by various hands. No first edition has been traced.
'I sang the exit of the best of kings'

Phoenix moriendo revixit

> Probably by Joseph Perkins, who published poems of this sort from Bristol.
> O(slightly cropt),*BrP*.

P264 — The Phœnix of Claudian. Translated into English verse (in Milton's manner.) Being a colledge exercise, anno 1714. Now first published, and inscrib'd to...Lord George Sackville. *Dublin, printed for Robert Owen*, 1731.
8º: *A*⁸; *i–iv* v–vi, 7–15 *16 blk*. A1 hft.
'A lovely grove, dress'd in perpetual green'
> The inscription signed 'A.B.'
LVA-F(−A1),DN; NjP.

— Phœnix Paulina, 1709. *See* Wright, James.

Phoenix, John. 'A song on the bill preferred in parliament for suppressing of players and playhouses. By John Phænix, commedian[!]. [*London*] Price 3*d.*' (*GM* May 1735)
> Possibly an engraved half-sheet with music.

P265 Phosphorus. Phosphorus. Or, the church of England the best of all protestant churches. In an essay to the nonconformists of all sorts. *London, printed for J. Nutt*, 1704 [1703]. (18 Dec, Luttrell)
2º: *A*² B–H²; *i–iv*, 1–27 *28 blk*.
'An honest heathen (no fanatick hears!)'
O,E; IU,NjP(Luttrell).

P266 —— The second edition. *London, printed for J. Nutt*, 1704.
2º: *A*² B–H²; *i–iv*, 1–27 *28 blk*.
> Apparently a reimpression.
LdU-B.

P267 Physic. Physick. A poem. *London, printed for George Sawbridge*, 1712.
4º: *A*⁴ B⁴; *1–2* 3–16.
> 'Price 6*d*.' on title overprinted with fleurons and 'Price 4*d*.' below. Vertical chain-lines.
'When first omnipotence his pow'r display'd'
L(1963, slightly cropt),O; CtY-M.

P268 Pibrach. Pibrach Chonald Dui: or Gard'ner's revenge. [*Edinburgh?*] *Sold at the printing-house in the Fish-market* [*by J. Robertson & T. Lumisden?*], 1746.
½º: 1 side, 1 column.
'Gard'ner, thy blood for vengeance cry'd'
> In praise of the victory of William, duke of Cumberland, at Culloden; in revenge for the death of James Gardiner at Prestonpans.
KU.

P269 Picture. The picture and history of W-----m F-----ce, Comi the second, son to Comus Cassaw the first. [*Edinburgh*, 17––.]
½º: 1 side, 1 column.
'Poor Comi Willie, that good father's son'
> The subject of the satire is unidentified; a ms. note in the E copy reads 'Lynes on N.M.'
E.

Picture

— The picture of a church militant, 1711. *See* Stacy, Edmund.

P270 — The picture of a female favourite. *London, printed in the year* 1708.
8º: *A*⁴; *1* 2–8.
'In that most pious and as happy time'
> On Elizabeth and Essex; with reference to Anne and Marlborough?
CLU-C.

— The picture of love, 1731. *See* Hill, Aaron.

P271 — The picture of pictures; or, look upon him, and know him. *London, printed for C. Hill, Cheap-side*, [1726/30?]
½º: 1 side, 2 columns.
> Large wood engraving above text.
'When poignant satire lash'd a guilty age'
> In praise of 'Caleb d'Anvers's' attacks on Walpole in *The Craftsman*.
L(1850.e.10/57; C.116.i.4/45; P&D 2556).

P272 — [dh] The picture of the first occasional conformist (Job I. 6.) drawn in little. [*London*, 1705?]
2º: *A*²; *1–4*, 2 columns.
'A picture I must paint, but yet'
L(C.121.g.9/145); MH.

P273 — The picture of the Observator drawn to the life. *London, printed in the year* 1704. (27 July, Luttrell)
4º: *A*²; *1* 2–4.
> Page numbers in roman parentheses. Woodcut of Tutchin in the pillory on title.
'His aim (as by his notions plain appears'
> A satire on John Tutchin. Answered by *Tutchin defended*, 1704.
LVA-F(Luttrell).

P274 —— ⟨*London*, 1704.⟩
4º: *A*²; *1* 2–4.
> Page numbers in italic parentheses.
AdU(cropt).

Pierce, Allan.
This form of name is found in modern catalogues for the author known in Scotland as either Allan or Pierce; his real name was perhaps J. Pierce. For his works, see Allan,—.

P275 Piers, Sarah, *Lady.* George for Britain. A poem. Written by the Lady Piers. *London, printed for Bernard Lintott*, 1714. (11 Sept?)
8º: A² B–C⁸ D⁶; *i–iv*, 1–44.
> Watermark: ? VC; cut copies measure 7¼ × 4¾ in. Entered to Lintot in Bowyer's ledgers under 11 Sept, 300 copies, 'with margin altered for fine paper'. Listed in *MC* Sept.
'Long had Britannia mourn'd her native isle'
L(1346.g.3; 161.m.20, Luttrell, 1 Oct),DT, LdU-B; DFo,MH,*NjR*.

P276 — [fine paper]
> No watermark; cut copies 8¼ × 5½ in.
O(original gilt edges),LVA-D; TxU(presentation copy).

Pig. The pig. A tale, 1735. *See* Wesley, Samuel, *the younger* (W352).

— The pig, and the mastiff, 1725–. *See* Wesley, Samuel, *the younger*.

[Pigott, Samuel.] Carmina sacra de omnibus festis ecclesiae anglicanae. Autore S.P. ejusdem ecclesiae presbytero. *Londini, ex officina J. Hinton*, 1748.
8°: pp. 24.   MH,OU.
    Ms. attribution in the OU copy.

P277 Pigs. The pigs petition against Bartholomew Fair; with their humble thanks to those unworthy preservers of so much innocent blood. Humbly inscrib'd to the illustrious C------n C-----l. [*London*, 1712?]
½°: 1–2, 1 column.
'May't please your wors—ps, craving your permission'
    Possibly ironically inscribed to Colonel Cardonnel.
Harding.

P278 Pike. The pike: a tale. *London, printed for J. Penn*, 1733. (*GM,LM* Dec)
2°: *A*¹ *B*²; *i–ii, 1 2–4*.
'In London liv'd, some years ago'
MH.

Pilgrim. The pilgrim's progress, 1706. *See* Hoffman, Francis.

P279 [Pilkington, Laetitia.] The statues: or, the trial of constancy. A tale for the ladies. *London, printed for T. Cooper*, 1739. (*GM, LM* April)
2°: *A*² B–E²; *1–5 6–18 19–20 blk.* A1 hft.
    Rothschild 223.
'In a fair island, in the southern main'
    Printed in Mrs. Pilkington's *Memoirs*, 1749.
L(840.m.1/40, −A1, E2),O(3, 1 uncut, 2−A1, E2),LdU-B(−E2); CSmH(−E2),CtY(−E2), MH,NN-B,TxU(2, 1 uncut)+.

[—] To the reverend Doctor Swift...on his birth-day, 1732. *See* T390.

Pilkington, Matthew. Poems on several occasions. *Dublin, printed by George Faulkner*, 1730.
8°: pp. iv, 189.   L,O; CtY,ICN.
    There are presentation copies in morocco at C,BlL,CtY. All copies seen are on heavy paper, watermarked with fleur-de-lys.

—— With several poems not in the Dublin edition... Revised by the reverend Dr. Swift. *London, printed for T. Woodward, Charles Davis, & W. Bowyer*, 1731. (*GSJ* 20 March)
8°: pp. xiv, 184.   L,O; CtY,MH.
    S3–4 were cancelled and not replaced, though the pagination remains continuous; the cancellanda were recorded in Stonehill cat. 154 (1967) 238. Entered in Bowyer's ledgers to 'Partners' under 13 March, 750 copies.

Pilkington, M.

    It appears from the detailed ledgers that 500 copies of the half-sheet H were printed in April as an 'imperfection'. 205 copies were delivered to subscribers, 94 to Faulkner in Dublin. A third share of the copyright formed part of lot 22 of Woodward's trade sale, 12 March 1752 (cat. at O-JJ).

***

P280 — An ode to be performed at the castle of Dublin, on 30th of October, being birth-day of...George II... Set to musick by Matthew Dubourg... [*Dublin*] *Printed for George Ewing*, 1734.
4°: A⁴; *1–3 4–7 8 blk.*
'Great, inexhausted source of day'
L(11642.bbb.50); CSmH.

P281 [—] A pastoral elegy on the death of a lady's canary bird: inscrib'd to the fair mourner. *Dublin printed, and sold by Pressick Rider & Thomas Harbin*, 1725.
8°: *A*⁴; *1–3 4–8.*
    Reprinted in *The progress of musick in Ireland*, below.
'The greyish dawn had scarce o'ercome the night'
    Printed in Pilkington's *Poems*, 1731.
DN(2).

P282 [—] The progress of musick in Ireland, a poem. Together with a pastoral elegy on the death of a lady's canary bird. And a poem on Mr. Pope's works... The second edition revis'd and corrected by the author. *Dublin printed, and sold by Pressick Rider, & Thomas Harbin*, 1725.
12°: A–D⁴ᐟ²; [2] *i ii, 1 2–20.*
    A pastoral elegy, 1725, which was printed separately, is perhaps considered as the first edition.
'By thee enjoin'd th'obsequious muse obeys'
    Printed in Pilkington's *Poems*, 1731.
LVA-F,DA,DN.

Pill. A pil for pork-eaters, 1705. *See* Forbes, William.

P283 — A pil to Tonny Ashton or the play-house puld down. [*Edinburgh*, 1728.] (10 April)
½°: 1 side, 1 column.
    Ms. note in the E copy, 'Edr printed 10 Apr 1728'.
'O my blood boiles, my spirit's all in fire'
    An attack on Anthony Aston and his Edinburgh playhouse.
E.

P284 Pillory. The pillory scuffle; or, the bloody battle at Charing-Cross. [*London*, 1721.]
½°: 1 side, 2 columns.
    Rough woodcut at head.
'There's never scarce a party-martyr'
    On the struggle at Charing Cross when Nathaniel Mist was put in the pillory, 23 Feb 1721, for his Jacobite publishing.
MH.

Pillo-tisanus

'**Pillo-tisanus.**' An epistle to Ge--ge Ch--ne, 1725. *See* E398.

Pindar.
West, Gilbert: Odes of Pindar. With several other pieces in prose and verse, translated from the Greek, 1749.

————————

The Olympick odes of Pindar, in English meetre [odes 1 & 2, in imitation of Sternhold and Hopkins's style], 1713. *See* O171.

Cruttenden, Robert: Pindar's ode to Proserpina. Translated from the French of Monsieur De la Motte, 1738. *See* C534.

Harte, Walter: Part of Pindar's first Pythian ode, paraphrased, 1749, [1755/–.] *See* H99–100.

P284·5 Pindaric. A pindaric essay on the arrival of his majesty King George. Address'd to the king. *London, printed by W. Wilkins, 1714.*
2⁰: *A*² *B*²; *1–3* 4–8.
'I'll tell ye all'
MR–C.

P285 — A pindaric ode dedicated to the lasting memory of the most illustrious and pious King William III. As it relates unto the occasion of his famous expedition into England, his excellent reign, his illustrious character, and his most lamented death. *London, printed for A. Baldwin, 1702.* (24 April, Luttrell)
2⁰: A–D²; *1–2* 3–16.
'Ye great divinities above!'
NjP(Luttrell),TxU.

P286 — [dh] A pindarick ode, occasioned by the death of the late lord chief justice Treby. [col] *London printed, and are to be sold by A. Baldwin, 1701.*
2⁰: *A*²; *1–4.*
'As Indians when a valu'd hero dies'
BlU,MC.

P287 — A pindarick ode on his excellency John duke of Marlborough... With a view of the three last glorious and memorable campaigns. *London printed, and sold by A. Baldwin,* [1706?]
4⁰: *A*² B–D⁴ E²; *i–iv, 1–27 28 blk.*
'Apollo and the muses lend your aid'
 Dedication signed 'W.L.' Early ms. note in the MR copy 'probably by Wm. Lauder. A.' I know of no evidence that Lauder (MA 1695; *d.*1771) published verse in England at this period.
MR.

P288 — [dh] A pindarique ode on the arrival of his excellency Sir Nicholas Lawes, governor of Jamaica, &c...The second edition. [col] *Jamaica, printed by R. Baldwin in Church-street in Kingston,* 1718.
2⁰: *A*²; *1–4.*
 Reproduced in D. C. McMurtrie, *The first*

A pindaric ode on the arrival

printing in Jamaica, (Evanston, 1942). No first edition traced.
'Hark how the voice of joy breaks through the air'
MC.

P289 — A pindarick ode, on the resurrection of our saviour Jesus Christ, on Easter-Sunday. *Dublin, printed by S. Powell, for T. Benson, 1728.*
4⁰: *A*⁴; *1–3* 4–8.
'Sing all ye sacred heavenly choir'
L(11633.e.20),DT.

— A pindarique ode sacred to the memory of her late most excellent majesty Queen Anne, 1715. *See* Paul, William.

— A pindarick ode, to the memory of Dr. William King, [1713.] *See* Oldisworth, William.

— A pindaric ode upon the death of her late majesty Queen Anne, 1714. *See* Turner, Purbeck.

— A pindaric on the nativity of the son of god, 1712. *See* Williams, David.

— A pindaric poem, on the propagation of the gospel in foreign parts, 1711. *See* Settle, Elkanah.

P290 Pinkeman. Pinkeman's company in mourning: or, an elegy on the much unlamented death of John Edwards, the horse-doctor and Merry-Andrew, who departed this life on Saturday the 16th of this instant November, at his seat in Castle-street, in the parish of sweet St. Giles's in the fields. *London, printed for T. Goodall, near Castle-street, 1706.*
½⁰: 1 side, 2 columns.
 Mourning headpiece and borders.
'Alas what sudden news flies o'er the town'
L(Harley 5931, fol. 251).

P291 Pious. 'Pious exhortation of Sir Samuel Goodere when under confinement. [1741?] *leaflet.*'
 Listed under 'poetry' in *Bristol bibliography,* 1916, a catalogue of books in the Central Reference Library. Probably a popular chapbook or broadside.
 Sir Samuel Goodere was executed on 15 April 1741 for the murder of his brother.
BrP (missing since 1950, probably a war loss).

P292 — The pious youth: a poem. Humbly addressed to the reverend Mr. Whitefield. *London, printed for J. Roberts, 1739.* (*GM, LM* July)
4⁰: *A*² B–E²; *i–iv, 1 2–15 16 blk.* iii err.
'The gloomy horrors of the night'
 A eulogy of George Whitefield.
L(11602.ff.25/3),LDW(2).

————————

Pipe. A pipe of tobacco, 1736–. *See* Browne, Isaac Hawkins.

Piscatory. Piscatory eclogues, 1729. *See* Browne, Moses.

'Piscopade. The 'Piscopade: a panegyri-satiri-serio-comical poem, 1748. *See* Morgan, Macnamara.

P293 Piss-pot. The piss-pot. A copy of verses on a silver chamber-pot sent to the Tower to be coyned, occasion'd by the Lady —— at St. James's unlucky hand at basset, which forc'd her to sell her plate. [*London*] *Printed for Robert Barnham*, 1701.
½°: *1–2*, 1 column.
'A beauteous gamester at court end of town'
L(C.20.f.2/214); MH.

[**Pitcairne, Archibald.**] Poemata selecta. 9ab5c2d 8eg2h14i3l8m1on5o4p7r6s7t6v. [*Edinburgh*, 1709?]
4°: pp. 16.   L,O; CtY,TxU.
Early ms. attribution to Pitcairne in the copy at CtY; the cipher has not been broken. Most copies add an errata leaf.

— Selecta poemata, Archibaldi Pitcarnii... Gulielmi Scot...Thomæ Kincadii...et aliorum. *Edinburgi, excusa anno* 1727.
12°: pp. 12, 145.   L,E; CtY,MH.
No watermark.

— [fine paper]   L,O.
Watermark: fleur-de-lys on shield.

— [reissue] Editio secunda. *Londini, apud A. Millar*, 1729 [1728]. (*MChr* 28 Aug).
L.
Cancel title.

Almost all of Pitcairne's ephemeral Latin verse which was printed on half-sheets or slips of different sizes seems to be later than his little collection of Latin verse [1709?]; those which can be precisely dated fall mainly in the years 1712 and 1713, immediately before his death. The many variant editions and states, as well as the frequent Jacobite verses, suggest private and occasional printing. Robert Freebairn, whose imprint appears twice, was a close friend, and Pitcairne's protégé Thomas Ruddiman set up a printing house in 1712 in association with Freebairn; Ruddiman's brother Walter had been apprenticed to Freebairn in 1706. Ruddiman's accounts for 1712–13 (at E, MS 763) record the printing of some of these poems, and it seems likely that the others were printed by Freebairn.

A few of the verses collected here may be by Pitcairne's friends (the situation is complicated by his occasional use of their names), but the material is so homogeneous both in its nature and the collections in which it is found that it seemed desirable to keep it all together. Evidence of Pitcairne's authorship is given where it is available; where there is none, it may still be considered very probable.

Many of the verses are printed on pieces of paper which vary in size and shape from copy to copy, making formal description impossible. Collations are

therefore omitted in most cases; these items are all printed in one column on one side of the paper, which is usually oblong in shape.

P294 [—] Ad Annam britannam. [*Edinburgh*, 1712?/13.]
'Anna Stuartorum decus et spes altera regum'
E.

P295 [—] Ad Annam Pitcarniam. [*Edinburgh*, 1710?/13.]
'Anna mihi genuit te Margaris Haia, nulli'
E(2).

P296 [—] Ad Archibaldum Reidium Joannis Reidij typographi optimi filium. [*Edinburgh*, 1713.]
Dated '23 Junij, 1713'.
'Vive diu felix, et laetos redde parentes'
E.

P297 — Ad Bertramum Stotum equitem anglum. [*Edinburgh*, 1712?/13.]
Also printed with *Pythagora jactat Samius*, [1710?/13.]
'Stote tuae moerens astat Pitcarnius urnae'
Printed in Pitcairne's *Poemata*, 1727.
E.

P298 [—] Ad Calvini discipulos. [*Edinburgh*, 1712.]
Dated above title 'IV. Nov. M.DCC.XII.'
Printed with alternative second half as *Ad Johannem Calvinum*, [1712.]
'Quod non quinta dies potuit patrare Novembris'
TxU.

P299 [—] Ad Cyclopas alpinos. Virgilius AEneidos libro octavo. [*Edinburgh*, 1712?/13.]
'Tollite cuncta ---- caeptosque auferte labores'
E.

P300 — Ad Elisam Ramisaeam Archibaldi Stevensoni medicorum principis conjugem, Archibaldus Pitcarnius. [*Edinburgh*, 1712?/13.]
'Magnanimis Scotisque atavis dignissima vixti'
E.

P301 [—] Ad G. B. [*Edinburgh*, 1710.] (11 Oct?)
Two rules above title; line 2 reads 'Atque diu in patrios bella ciere deos'. The copy seen is noted 'Edenburgh' and endorsed '11 Oct 1710'.
'Juppiter est hominis facie te fallere passus'
An attack on Gilbert Burnet.
O(MS Ballard 50, fol. 175).

P302 [—] [variant]
Line 2 reads 'Impiaque in patrios fundere verba deos'.
TxU.

P303 [—] Ad G. B. [*Edinburgh*, 1710/13.]
No rules above title; the text follows the preceding version.
E.

P304 [—] [*idem*] Ad Gilb. Burnet. scotum, A.P. scotus. [*Edinburgh*, 1710/13.]
Variant text.
'Vejovis est hominis facie te fallere passus'
E.

Pitcairne, A. Ad Georgium Kirtonum

P305 [—] Ad Georgium Kirtonum, Proserpinæ a potione. [*Edinburgh*, 1708?/13.]
½°: 1 side, 1 column.
'Nuper Hamiltonus vacuæ pertœsus Edinæ'
E.

[—] Ad Georgium Makenzium, regium, olim, apud Scotos, advocatum, Roberti Hepburnij, scoti, carmen sapphicum, [1711?] *See* H148.

P306 — Ad Gulielmum Benedictum equitem auratum, Grubetii agri dominum, Archibaldus Pitcarnus. [*Edinburgh*, 1713.] (Oct)
> An entry in Ruddiman's ledger for the week ending 3 Oct 1713 reads 'A Poem of Dr Pitcairn ad Bened. Equitem, Case... Another of ditto ad Gulielmum Benedictum, Case... Press of both ditto.' Possibly one poem or a variant edition is lost.

'Hunc, Benedicte, tuo cineri Pitcarnus honorem'
Printed in Pitcairne's *Poemata*, 1727.
E(2); TxU.

P307 [—] Ad Haium comitem Kinulium. *Edinburgi, apud Robertum Freebairn*, [1712?/13.]
> Possibly the poem 'to the Viscount of Duplin, thrice wrought at the press' entered in Ruddiman's ledger for the week ending 15 Nov 1712.

'Felix Dupplinio, nuruque felix'
> Printed in Pitcairne's *Poemata*, 1727. A congratulatory poem to Thomas Hay, earl of Kinnoul, on his son (Viscount Dupplin) and daughter-in-law.

O,E.

P308 [—] [variant, without imprint.]
TxU.

P309 [—] Ad Homerum, Catulli carmen ex Græco Sapphus versum, & Albæ Græcæ repertum, anno vulgaris æræ 1711. [*Edinburgh*, 1711.]
½°: 1 side, 1 column.
'Te poetarum coluere regem'
To the Old Pretender.
TxU.

P310 [—] Ad Hugonem Dalrimplium, supremi senatus juridici in Scotia præsidem. [*Edinburgh*, 1712?/13.]
'Consultissime juris, atque rite'
Printed in Pitcairne's *Poemata*, 1727.
TxU.

P311 [—] Ad Jacobum Andraeas Pitcarnius Archibaldi filius, et agri Pitcarnii dominus. [*Edinburgh*, 1712?/13.]
'Septem Pitcarni pro te cecidere lubentes'
To the Pretender.
E.

P312 — Ad Jacobum Dromondum, dominum Stobhallum, Archibaldus Pitcarnius scotus. [*Edinburgh*, 1713.] (May)
> Note at foot, 'Natus est Jacobus Stobhallus undecimo Maii, anni M.DCC.XIII.' Entered in Ruddiman's ledger for the week ending

Pitcairne, A. Ad Jacobum Dromondum

> 16 May, 'Poem of Dr. Pitcairn's on my Lord Drummond's son 4 times wrought'.

'Salve, dignus avis, exoptatusque Dromondis'
E; TxU.

P313 [—] Ad Jacobum gallovidium equitem, caledonium. [*Edinburgh*, 1712?/13.]
'Quis fuero, cum tu Jacobe redibis in urbem'
To the Pretender.
E.

P314 [—] [another edition, title reads:] Ad Jacobum gallovidium, equitem caledonium.
The text of the last two lines is rewritten.
E.

P315 [—] Ad Jacobum Magnum. [*Edinburgh*, 1711?]
'Quarta dies abijt te salvo, Magne, Novembris'
> At foot 'On George Main's son James, born on the 7th of November 1711'; but referring to the Pretender.

O.

P316 — Ad Januarium anni MDCCXIII, Archibaldus Pitcarnius anno aetatis suae LXI. [*Edinburgh*, 1712/13.]
'Jane, senex optat Pitcarnius esse velitis'
E.

P317 — [*idem*] Ad Janum, Archibaldus Pitcarnius... [*Edinburgh*, 1712/13.]
E.

P318 [—] Ad Janum. [*Edinburgh*, 1712?]
Title reads 'AD *JANUM*.'
'Jane, tui sexto mihi filia prodijt Agnes'
Printed in Pitcairne's *Poemata*, 1727.
E.

P319 [—] [another edition, title reads:] 'Ad Janum,'
TxU.

P320 — Ad Jesum Christum dei filium, Archibaldus Pitcarnius scotus. [*Edinburgh*, 1713.] (April)
> Entered in Ruddiman's ledger for the week ending 4 April, 'Poem of Dr Pitcairn's to Jesus Christ 5 times wrought 600 copies'.

'Natali vestro, lacrymis jejunia pascunt'
E; TxU.

P321 [—] Ad Joanetam Pitcarniam, decimo Junij natam. [*Edinburgh*, 1712?/13.]
Printed in a large type face.
'Te placidus vidit sol nasci, filia, luce'
E.

P322 [—] [another edition]
Printed in a small type face.
E.

P323 [—] Ad Johannem Calvinum. [*Edinburgh*, 1712.]
Printed with alternative second half as *Ad Calvini discipulos*, [1712.]
'Quod non quinta dies potuit patrare Novembris'
TxU.

P324 [—] Ad Jonathanem ----------- ------ Novembris anni MDCCXII. [*Edinburgh*, 1712.]

Pitcairne, A. Ad Jonathanem

'Davidis fautor Jonathan fuisti'
E.

P325 [—] Ad Josephum Scaligerum. Decimo nono Maij 1710. [*Edinburgh*, 1710.]
½°: 1 side, 1 column.
    Below, 'Ad Elisam Pitcarniam. Decimo Junij 1710.'
'Scaliger, quo nil voluere musae'
Ad Elisam: 'Te quoque sol vidit nascentem, filia, luce'
    'Ad Elisam' is printed in Pitcairne's *Poemata*, 1727.
E; TxU.

P326 [—] [another edition, title reads:] Ad Josephum Scaligerum 29 Maij 1710.
O.

P327 [—] Ad Junium anni MDCCXII. [*Edinburgh*, 1712.]
'Juni te regem nunc annis esse jubemus'
    Printed in Pitcairne's *Poemata*, 1727.
E(2).

P328 [—] [*idem*] Ad Junium. [*Edinburgh*, 1712?]
    Another version, with first line:
'Juni, te regem jam mensibus esse fatetur'
E; TxU.

P329 [—] Ad Lodoicam Stuartam, ipso suo natali, die decimo septimo Junii 1710. [*Edinburgh*, 1710?]
'Risit Apollo tuo felici fidere fratri'
    A variant text (P385) was printed in Pitcairne's *Poemata*, 1727.
O.

P330 [—] Ad Margaritam Pitcarniam. [*Edinburgh*, 1712?/13.]
    Title reads 'AD|MARGARITAM PIT CARNIAM,'
'Octavus Martis te jussit, filia, nasci'
    Printed in Pitcairne's *Poemata*, 1727.
E.

P331 [—] [another edition, title reads:] 'AD|Margari tam Pitcarniam,'
E; TxU.

P332 [—] Ad Phoebum. [*Edinburgh*, 1710?/13.]
'Phoebe pater, manes non hic vexare sepultos'
    Printed in Pitcairne's *Poemata*, 1727.
E.

P333 [—] [variant title] Ad Phæbum.
TxU.

P334 [—] Ad Phoebum Apollinem. [*Edinburgh*, 1712?/13.]
'Dic mihi qui medicae mortalibus auctor es artis'
    Printed in Pitcairne's *Poemata*, 1727.
O,E.

P335 [—] Ad Robertum Lindesium. [*Edinburgh*, 1710?/13.]
'Vidimus hæc pueri, juvenes hæc vidimus arva'
E.

Pitcairne, A. Andraeae Flechero

P336 — Andraeae Flechero regulo Saltonio. Archibaldus Pitcarnius s.d. [*Edinburgh*, 1712?/13.]
    Printed in a small type face.
'Quod repetita sequi nollet Proserpina matrem'
    Printed in Pitcairne's *Poemata*, 1727.
E.

P337 — [another edition]
    Printed in a large type face.
TxU.

P338 — Annae reginae Archibaldus Pitcarnius scotus, s.d. [*Edinburgh*, 1712?/13.]
    Last line reads '...linquite, diva, tuo.'
'Anna Caledoniae quae nunc felicior orae'
TxU.

P339 — [variant]
    Last line reads '...linquite grata, suo.'
O.

P340 [—] [first line:] Arbiter Europae, mandato Brittonis Annae. [*Edinburgh*, 1712?]
'Arbiter Europae, mandato Brittonis Annae'
    Apparently addressed to a plenipotentiary at the peace negotiations: possibly to Prior.
E.

P341 [—] Archibaldo Pitcarnio Gualterus Dannistonus εὐχαιρειν. [*Edinburgh*, 1710?/13.]
    At foot, 'Dabam ex Horatii villa Tiburis Elysii.'
'Me vis Dupplinii divinas dicere laudes'
    Printed in Pitcairne's *Poemata*, 1727; Pitcairne used Walter Danniston's name on several occasions.
E.

P342 [—] [variant]
    At foot, 'Dabam ex Horatii villa Tiburte Elysia.'
E.

P343 — Archibaldo Stevensono equiti, scotorum archiatrorum comiti, octogenario, socero suo, Archibaldus Pitcarnius s. [*Edinburgh*, 1709/10.]
½°: 1 side, 1 column.
'Pallidi vivis bene spretor Orci'
    Sir Archibald Stevenson died on 16 Feb 1710 just before his eightieth birthday.
E; TxU.

P344 [—] Archimedes regi Geloni, s. [*Edinburgh*, 1712?/13.]
    Three Latin quotations below text.
'Hanno nos visit Syracusis nuper amice'
TxU.

P345 [—] Calderus Visharto qui se moderatorem, hoc est, vel deum aut regem vocat: sacerdos spurius ex infima fanaticaque plebe. [*Edinburgh*, 1713?]
    Below, two lines headed 'Vishartus moderator.'
'Proclamas omnes papistas esse fugandos'
    Probably written by Pitcairne in the guise of Robert Calder; William Wishart became

Pitcairne, A. Calderus Visharto

moderator for the second time on 30 April 1713.

E.

— Archibaldi Pitcarni scoti. Carmen, [1712.] *See* P368.

P346 [—] [first line:] Carole Gothorum longe fortissime ductor. [*Edinburgh*, 1711?]
'Carole Gothorum longe fortissime ductor'
   Printed in Pitcairne's *Poemata*, 1727, with title 'Ad Carolum XII Suecorum regem'.
E; TxU.

P347 [—] [*idem*] Carole Gothorum ductor fortissime, solus. [*Edinburgh*, 1712?/13.]
   Revised first line:
'Carole Gothorum ductor fortissime, solus'
E.

P348 [—] [first line:] Carole, si similis fratris, similisve parentis. [*Edinburgh*, 1711?]
   Ornamental initial C in first line.
'Carole, si similis fratris, similisve parentis'
   To Charles VI of Austria, who succeeded in 1711.
E.

P349 [—] [another edition]
   Plain initial C set to the left of text.
E.

P350 [—] [another edition]
   Plain initial C indented in text.
E.

P351 [—] [another edition] [*Edinburgh*, 1712?/13.]
   No large initial C in first line.
TxU.

P352 [—] [first line:] Credidimus terras Hydram liquisse Britannas. [*Edinburgh*, 1710.]
'Credidimus terras Hydram liquisse Britannas'
   Printed in Pitcairne's *Poemata*, 1727, with title 'Ad Annam reginam'; on the defeat of the whigs.
O,E; TxU(ms. date 1710).

P353 [—] [first line:] Cur tibi natalem felix Heriote quotannis. [*Edinburgh*, 1712?/13.]
   A series of short verses under the names of Heriotus, Pitcarnius, and Robertus Calderus. The heading to the first is possibly cropped from the copy seen.
'Cur tibi natalem felix Heriote quotannis'
E.

P354 [—] Dannistonus Pitcarnio s.d. [*Edinburgh*, 1710?/13.]
½°: 1 side, 1 column.
   With 'Pitcarnius Dannistono s.d.' and 'Maecenati Duplinio Robertus Fribarnus s.d.'
Pitcarnio: 'Pitcarni quereris quod nullo carmine laudem'
Dannistono: 'Dannistone jubes me digno dicere versu'
Maecenati: 'Maecenas volui grates tibi solvere, musa'

Pitcairne, A. Dannistonus Pitcarnio

All three poems printed as Pitcairne's in his *Poemata*, 1727; Pitcairne used Walter Danniston's name on several occasions.
TxU.

P355 [—] David Veneri. [*Edinburgh*, 1710?/13.]
½°: 1 side, 1 column.
   Below, 'Venus Davidi'.
'Militis infesti me vis urgebat inermem'
'Deliciae generis nostri, mihi rebus in arctis'
   Printed in Pitcairne's *Poemata*, 1727.
E; TxU.

P356 — Davidi Dromondio jurisconsulto Archibaldus Pitcarnius s. [*Edinburgh*, 1708.]
½°: 1 side, 1 column.
   Dated at foot, '25 Decemb. 1708. st. vet.'
'Me brevis mimum peragente vitæ'
E,AdU; TxU.

P357 — [first line:] Delphinis quanto balaena britannica fertur. [*Edinburgh*, 1710?/13.]
'Delphinis quanto balaena britannica fertur'
   Pitcairne's name appears in the last line.
E.

P358 [—] Die XXV. Decembris anni MDCCXII. [*Edinburgh*] *Apud Robertum Freebairn*, 1712.
   Entered in Ruddiman's ledger for the week ending 20 Dec, 'Poem on Christmas by Dr Pitcairn 5 times wrought. Press'.
'Hac Christus jussit se nostram sumere formam'
   Signed 'A.P.' Printed in Pitcairne's *Poemata*, 1727.
E(2); CtY.

P359 [—] [another edition, title reads:] Die XXV. Decembris, anni . . .
E.

P360 [—] Die XXX Novembris, anni MDCCXII. Ad Andream Christi apostolum. Qui Scotis dedit esse Christianis. A.P. [*Edinburgh*, 1712.]
'Andraea vixti Jacobo semper amicus'
E.

P361 — [first line:] Dum tibi laudatur Maij vigesima nona. [*Edinburgh*, 1713.]
   Dated on the feast of the Ascension, 1713.
'Dum tibi laudatur Maij vigesima nona'
   Jacobite verses, also praising Sacheverell.
E.

P362 [—] Elisae Havartae principi Gordoniae, A.P. scotus s,d. [*Edinburgh*, 1712.] (Nov)
   Entered in Ruddiman's ledger for the week ending 15 Nov, 'A poem of Dr Pitcairn's to the Dutchess of Gordon twice wrought'.
'Quantus erat Mariae vindex Havartus, Elisae'
   Printed in Pitcairne's *Poemata*, 1727.
E; TxU.

P363 [—] [first line:] Goddolphine Stygem potas et Averna fluenta. [*Edinburgh*, 1712?]
'Goddolphine Stygem potas et Averna fluenta'
   Sidney Godolphin died in 1712.
O.

Pitcairne, A. Gualteri Dannistoni

P364 [—] Gualteri Dannistoni ad Georgium Buchananum epistola, conscripta anno æræ christianæ M.DCC.VI. [*Edinburgh, printed by James Watson,* 1706?]
8°: *A*⁸; *i–ii, 1–2 3–12 13–14 blk.* A1, A8 blk.
'Dexteram læti canimus Jovemque'
　　A copy at E has a ms. note on the title 'Archibald Pitcarne M:D:', and an inscription on A1, 'A. Campbell from Dr Gray'; the last two letters of the date in the title are deleted, and the foot of the title-leaf cut away.
E(2, 1 – A1.8).

P365 [—] [*idem*] Gualteri Dannistoni ad Georgium Buchananum epistola, et Buchanani responsum. MDCC. *Edinburgi, typis Jacobi Vatsoni,* [1706?]
8°: *A*⁸; *1–2 3–15 16 blk.*
　　A new edition, closely following the preceding, and adding on p. 13 'Ad Georgium Buchananum' and on p. 15 Buchanan's reply (possibly also written by Pitcairne). One copy at E adds a leaf of *corrigenda* and *mutanda,* verso blank; it was probably an afterthought.
Reply: 'Dannistone meæ quid turbas otia vitæ'
E(2, 1 + errata),WcC.

P366 [—] Gualterus Dannistonus ad amicos. [*and*] Walter Danniston, Ad amicos. Imitated by Mr. Prior. [*Edinburgh,* 1710?]
2°: *A*²; *1–2.*
　　Latin and English text on facing inner pages; outer pages blank. This is the form of the Latin text reprinted by Prior in his *Poems;* his imitation is dated 1710 in the Lansdowne ms.
'Dum studeo fungi fallentis munere vitæ'
'Studious, the busy moments to deceive'
O,E(2, and 1 Latin only),Chatsworth.

P367 [—] Gualterus Dannistonus ad amicos. [*Edinburgh,* 1710?]
½°: 1 side, 1 column.
　　A very similar setting of the Latin text to the preceding, but with altered first line and with an added couplet after line 18 which is preserved in the later edition below.
'Dum prudens utor redituræ munere vitæ'
O,E.

P368 — [*idem*] Archibaldi Pitcarnii scoti. Carmen. Anno aetatis suae LX. [*and*] Imitated by Mr. Prior. [*Edinburgh,* 1712.]
2°: *A*²; *1–2.*
　　Latin and English text on facing inner pages; outer pages blank. Another revision of the Latin text; quotation from St. Paul in Latin and English at the foot of the pages. Reprinted with yet further changes as 'Joannis Sylvii de seipso carmen' in Pitcairne's *Selecta poemata,* 1727.
'Dum moriens laetor redeuntis munere vitae'
L(Ashley 4973),O,E.

P369 [—] Gualterus Danistonus, scotus, Sannazario veneto propriam quietem gratulatur. [*Edinburgh,* 170–?]

Pitcairne, A. Gualterus Danistonus

　　With a variant version headed 'Aliter' below. 'Tellurem fecere dii, sua littora Belgæ'
　　Pitcairne used Walter Danniston's name on several occasions, as in P364–6.
O,E(2); TxU.

P370 [—] [first line:] Hac Jovis Hammonis cineres conduntur in urna. [*Edinburgh,* 1710?/13.]
'Hac Jovis Hammonis cineres conduntur in urna'
E(2, 1 with ms. variants).

P371 [—] [first line:] Hectoris exuvias indutum cernite Mosen. [*Edinburgh,* 1712?/13.]
　　With an English translation below.
'Hectoris exuvias indutum cernite Mosen'
'Lo! Moses wrapt in Hector's skin'
E; TxU.

P372 [—] Horatius ad Luciferum. [*Edinburgh,* 1712?/13.]
'Lucifer, nam te docilis magistro'
E.

P373 [—] In Barbaram & Margaritam Caroli Stuarti comitis Traquarij filias gemellas. [*Edinburgh,* 1712?/13.]
'Tertia Septembris vos orbi misit ovanti'
　　Printed in Pitcairne's *Poemata,* 1727.
E.

P374 [—] In Jacobum principem Hamiltonium. Virum fortissimum, parricidio foedissimo trucidatum, Londini die quindecimo Novembris anni MDCCXII. [*Edinburgh,* 1712.] (Dec)
　　Entered in Ruddiman's ledger for the week ending 6 Dec 1712, 'A poem of Dr Pitcairn's on D. Hamilton 3 times wrought press'.
'Dum patriae servire studes patriaeq; parenti'
　　Printed in Pitcairne's *Poemata,* 1727.
E.

P375 [—] [another edition, title punctuated:] In Jacobum principem Hamiltonium virum fortissimum, parricidio foedissimo trucidatum, Londini, die quinto decimo Novembris, anni MDCCXII. [*Edinburgh,* 1712.]
　　Variant text, signed 'A.P.'
TxU.

P376 [—] In Jacobum secundum, Britanniae regem. [*Edinburgh,* 1710?/13.]
'Barbarus exclusit tumulo me Nassus avito'
E.

P377 [—] [another edition, with no title.] [*Edinburgh,* 1712?/13.]
TxU.

P378 [—] In Maij vigesimam nonam, anno MDCCXII. [*Edinburgh,* 1712.]
　　Six lines, the third beginning 'Hac justos voluit...'
'Hac Christus voluit patrio se reddere coelo'
　　Printed in Pitcairne's *Poemata,* 1727; on the Pretender's birthday.
E.

Pitcairne, A. In Maij vigesimam nonam

P379 [—] [another edition]
Third line begins 'Hac jus cuique...'
E.

P380 [—] [*idem*] In Maii XXIX, sive Juni X, anni
MDCCXII. [*Edinburgh*, 1712.]
Variant text, divided into two and four lines.
E.

P381 [—] In undecimum Martii, quo ante annos
octoginta natus est Archibaldus Stevensonus...
[*and*] On the chief physitian Sir Archibald Stevenson. [*Edinburgh*, 1710.]
2°: A²; *1–2*.
Latin and English texts on facing inner pages;
outer pages blank.
'Lux optata nitet, quæ soles noctibus æquat'
'Fancy the great Hippocrates's art'
Reprinted in Pitcairne's *Selecta poemata*,
1727. Stevenson's birthday was 11 March; he
died on 16 Feb 1710.
E.

P382 — An inscription on John Bell. [*Edinburgh*, 1712?/
13.]
½°: 1 side, 1 column.
Below the text of the inscription, 'Imitated by
Archibald Pitcairn...' and two Latin ver-
sions.
'I Jocky Bell o' Braiken-brow lyes under this
stane'
'Hoc saxum mihi filij induerunt'
'Hic Belus abscondor caput objectare periclis'
E; TxU.

P383 [—] Jacobo septimo ejus nominis, Scotiae regi, die
Octobris decimo quarto. [*Edinburgh*, 1712?/13.]
'Hic est ille tuus natalis, septime, qui te'
A Jacobite poem.
O.

P384 [—] [first line:] Jam te, dive, tenent Homius,
sapiensque Stevinus. [*Edinburgh*, 1712?]
'Jam te, dive, tenent Homius, sapiensque Stevinus'
Printed in Pitcairne's *Poemata*, 1727, titled
'Ad Gulielmum Kethium, magnum Scotiæ
mariscallum, anno 1712'; a different (but
unidentified) ms. dedicatee in the TxU copy.
E; TxU.

P385 [—] Lodoix Maria Stuarta. [*Edinburgh*, 1712?]
'Fratre tuo viso derisit Apollo Gradivum'
Printed in Pitcairne's *Poemata*, 1727, titled
'Ad Mariam Lodovicam Teresam, ipso suo
natali die xvii. Junii, MDCCX.' Cf. P329.
E.

P386 [—] Margarita regina et diva Scotorum, ad Maij
vigesimam nonam anni MDCCXIII. [*Edinburgh*,
1713.]
Four lines only.
'Sacra dies olim Marti Caroloque fuisti'
On the Pretender's birthday.
E.

Pitcairne, A. Margarita regina

P387 [—] — [*Edinburgh*, 1713.]
Extended to six lines; partly from the same
setting of type.
E.

P388 [—] Maria Lodoix Stuarta, ad Alaricam suecam.
[*Edinburgh*, 1712/13.]
Four lines of verse.
'Juppiter arripuit sibi me, Junone relicta'
Louisa Maria, the daughter of James II,
persuading Ulrica (later queen of Sweden) to
marry the Pretender.
E.

P389 [—] — [*Edinburgh*, 1712/13.]
Six lines of verse, largely rewritten.
E.

P390 [—] [*idem*] Maria Lodoix britanna ad Alaricam
suecam. [*Edinburgh*, 1712/13.]
Eight lines of verse.
E.

P391 [—] [first line:] Multa tulere tuæ, te, rex, absente,
columbæ. [*Edinburgh*, 1710?/13.]
Line 2 begins 'Impius &...'. Large initial M
aligned with top of line 1.
'Multa tulere tuæ, te, rex, absente, columbæ'
To the Pretender.
E.

P392 [—] [variant state, first line:] Multa tulere sacræ,
te, rex, absente, columbæ.
Line 2 begins 'Atque impune...'
O.

P393 [—] [another edition]
Line 2 begins 'Atque impune...' Large
initial M aligned with bottom of line 1.
E.

P394 [—] [another edition, first line:] Multa tulere
tuae, te, rex, absente, columbae. [*Edinburgh*,
1712?/13.]
No large initial M to line 1; printed in a
larger type face.
E.

P395 [—] Presbyteri scoti Petro. [*Edinburgh*, 1713.]
Below, 'Respondet Sanctus Petrus. 29 Junij,
1713.'
'Esse tibi notum Christum ter Petre negasti'
'Mox me poenituit, sed vos non poenitet esse'
E.

P396 [—] [first line:] Prisca redit virtus, pietasque
refulget avita. [*Edinburgh*, 1710?/13.]
'Prisca redit virtus, pietasque refulget avita'
O.

P397 [—] [first line:] Pythagora jactat Samius se fundus
alumno. [*Edinburgh*, 1710?/13.]
Below, 'In Bertramum Stotum equitem
anglum', printed separately as *Ad Bertramum
Stotum*, [1712?/13.]
'Pythagora jactat Samius se fundus alumno'
Printed in Pitcairne's *Poemata*, 1727.
MC.

Pitcairne, A. Pythagora jactat

P398 — [*idem*] Pythagoras samius et Isaacus Neutonus anglus. [*Edinburgh*, 1712?/13.]
At foot, 'Scribebat Archibaldus Pitcarnius scotus'. A revised text, also printed with *Thomae Boero, scoto*, [1710?/13], titled 'Isaaco Neutono anglo...'
E.

P399 — Q. Horatio Flacco. Archibaldus Pitcarnius caledonius. [*Edinburgh*, 1708?/13.]
½°: 1 side, 1 column.
'Dive, dic vatem medicumve Phœbo'
E; TxU.

P400 [—] Ricardio Stilio anglo, viro hujus sæculi maximo, Robertus Hepburnius scotus. S. D. [*Edinburgh*, 1713?]
½°: 1 side, 1 column.
Possibly the 'Poem for Dr Pitcairn A. R. S.' entered in Ruddiman's ledger for the week ending 28 March 1713 for setting and 'Press thrice wrought'.
'Dicite heroem sociumve, musæ'
Robert Hepburn produced an imitation of Steele's *Tatler* in Edinburgh, Jan–May 1711; he is said to have died in 1712, though the set at EU has a ms. note 'Ex dono authoris 3 July 1713'. Almost certainly written by Pitcairne under Hepburn's name. On the assistance of wine to an author.
EU; TxU.

P401 — Roberto Fribarnio typographo regio, et in certamine Sagittariorum Regiorum victori, Archibaldus Pitcarnius sagittarius s.d. [*Edinburgh*, 1713.]
'Prisca pharetratis quae fulsit gloria Scotis'
Freebairn won the Musselburgh arrow, 1713.
O; TxU.

P402 — Roberto Graio scoto Londini medicinam profitenti, Archibaldus Pitcarnius scotus. S. [*Edinburgh*, 1708?/13.]
½°: 1 side, 1 column.
Misprint in line 14, 'raqtos'.
'Ille qui terris latitat britannis'
E.

P403 — [another edition]
Misprint in line 14 corrected, 'raptos'.
L(Cup. 645.e.1/29),E; TxU.

P404 [—] [first line:] Saxonas ac Anglos olim Germania fudit. [*Edinburgh*, 1712?/13.]
'Saxonas ac Anglos olim Germania fudit'
TxU.

P405 — Thomae Boero, scoto, matheseos et medicinae professori, Archibaldus Pitcarnius scotus, s.d. [*Edinburgh*, 1710?/13.]
½°: 1 side, 1 column.
Below, 'Isaaco Neutono anglo, mathematicorum omnis aevi principi, Archibaldus Pitcarnius scotus, plusquam Nestoreos annos, hoc est, plusquam Samios optat'; other editions of this entered as *Pythagora jactat*...
'I salutatum propere virorum'

Pitcairne, A. Thomae Boero

Printed in Pitcairne's *Poemata*, 1727. Possibly a Thomas Bower is intended, but he has not been identified.
TxU.

P406 [—] To the tune of James Anderson my jo. [*Edinburgh*, 1712?/13.]
'Come, good Father Bacchus, astride on your butt'
E.

P407 [—] Vaticinum in sepulcro Caroli quinti repertum 1710. [*Edinburgh*, 1710/13.]
Printed in a small type face.
'Teutonicas acies, supremaque Cæsaris arma'
TxU.

P408 [—] [another edition]
Printed in a large type face; misprint in line 1, 'Tutonicas'.
O.

P409 [—] XXV Julii MDCCXIII. [*Edinburgh*, 1713.]
'Quam te prisca cupit gens Grampia, sancte, redire!'
E.

Pitcarnium. Pitcarnium morientem, [1713.] *See* Ker, John, *d. 1741.*

Pitt, Christopher. Poems and translations. *London, printed for Bernard Lintot, & Arthur Bettesworth*, 1727. (*MC* Feb)
8°: pp. xv, 192.   L,O; CtY,MH.
Copy in presentation morocco at CLU-C. Entered in *SR* 9 March; deposit copy at O.

[—] Poems by the celebrated translator of Virgil's Æneid. Together with the Jordan, a poem: in imitation of Spenser, by ------ -------, esq; *London, printed for M. Cooper*, 1756. (*LM* Oct)
4°: pp. 32.   L; CtY.

———

P410 — An essay on Virgil's Æneid. Being a translation of the first book. *London, printed for A. Bettesworth, & W. Hinchliffe*, 1728. (*MChr* 30 April)
8°: A–I⁴; *1–3* 4–71 *72.* 72 advt.
Printed by Charles Ackers on the evidence of the ornaments.
'Arms and the man I sing, the first who bore'
L(11355.bb.5),LVA-D,O(2),OW,CT; CLU-C, CtY,*DFo*,IU,NjP.

P411 — Virgil's Æneid translated by Mr. Pitt. Vol. I. *London, printed for A. Bettesworth & C. Hitch, W. Hinchliffe, & L. Gilliver*, 1736. (*LM* April)
8°: ᵖA⁴ A⁴(−A1 ± A2) B–G⁴ H⁴(−H2−4+H2) I–2F⁴ 2G¹; *i–v* vi–viii, *3* 4–230. ᵖA1 blk; viii err.
Books 1–4; book 1 is a reissue of P410.
IU.

P412 — The Æneid of Virgil. Translated by Mr. Pitt. In two volumes. *London, printed for R. Dodsley; sold by Mr. Hitch, Mr. Hinchliffe; Mr. Clements at Oxford; Mr. Crownfield & Thurlbourne at Cambridge; and Mr. Leake at Bath*, 1740. (22 April)

Pitt, C. The Aeneid of Virgil

4°: A^4 B–2O⁴ 2P⁴(−2P4), ²A⁴ 2Q–4K⁴; *i–iii* iv–viii, *1* 2–294, *i–ii* iii *iv–vi*, *295* 296–623 *624 blk.* A4ᵛ, ²A1ᵛ err.

>Watermark: eagle. Publication date from *Straus, Dodsley.* 2G1, 3D1, 3F2, 3L2, 3M3, 3Q2, 3Z2, 4A3 are cancels; six cancellanda are preserved in a fine-paper copy at O.

LdU-B(2); CtY,ICU,*MH*,NjP.

P413 — [fine paper]
>Watermark: Φ.

L(76.h.3,4, probably the dedication copy to Frederick, prince of Wales),O(2, 1 impft); IU.

P414 —— *London, printed by J. Hughs, for Robert Dodsley,* 1743 [1744?]. (*LM* March 1744)
12°: A–I¹² K¹²(K2+χ²) L–S¹² T⁶ U²; [2] *i–ii* iii–vi, *1*–212 [4] 213–439 *440*. A1 hft; 440 advt.

>χ² is the half-title and title to vol. 2. Advertised in *LM* as in two volumes; the CtY copy is bound in one volume omitting χ².

L(1473.b.21); CtY(no χ²),IU.

P414·5 [—] The plague of Marseilles: a poem. By a person of quality. *London, printed for J. Bateman, & J. Nicks,* 1721. (*DP* 6 Feb)
8°: A^4 B–D⁴; *1*–7 8–30 *31; 32 blk.* A1 hft; D4 advt.
'Why with such care will poor deluded man'

>Clearly the work by Pitt referred to in *Cibber* V. 298; the publishers are the same as the following poem by Pitt, printed in the same year.

L(1490.pp.74),LG,O; ICN,IU,MH,OCU(−A1), TxU(−D4)+.

P415 — A poem on the death of the late Earl Stanhope. Humbly inscrib'd to the Countess of Stanhope. *London, printed for J. Bateman, & J. Nicks,* 1721. (*DP* 13 March)
8°: A^4 B–C⁴; *i–iv*, *1*–19 *20 blk.* A1 hft.
'Now from thy riot of destruction breathe'
L(11633.bb.1/4),LDW; CSmH,CtY,MH.

P416 — Vida's Art of poetry, translated into English verse, by the reverend Mr. Christoph. Pitt... *London, printed by Sam. Palmer, for A. Bettesworth,* 1725. (*SR* 26 Feb)
12°: A^2 B–L⁶ (I2 as 'I3'); *i–iv*, *1* 2–118 *119–120.* L6 advt.

>Entered in *SR* to Bettesworth; deposit copy at O and ? L. Listed in *MC* Feb.

'Give me, ye sacred muses, to impart'
L(1213.e.30; 237.f.37),O,C,LdU-B,WcC; CSmH,IU,InU,*MH*,TxU+.

P417 —— *Dublin, printed by J. Watts, for J. Thompson,* 1726.
8°: A^4 B–I⁴; *1*–5 6–72.

>Printed in such a way that each book starts a new signature with a separate title-page; possibly each book was sold separately.

L(11630.aaa.45/2),O(2),DA,DK,DN; PU.

P418 —— The second edition. *London, printed by John Hughs, for Robert Dodsley,* 1742 [1743?]. (*GM, LM* Jan 1743)

Pitt, C. Vida's Art of poetry

12°: A–G⁶; *1–4* 5–82 *83–84.* G6 advt.
L(1213.e.38),LVA-D,O,WcC; CLU-C,CtY.

P419 —— The second edition. *London, printed for C. Hitch,* 1743.
12°: A^2 B–L⁶ (I2 as 'I3'); *i–iv*, *1* 2–118 *119–120.* L6 advt.

>A reissue of the London edition of 1725 with either cancel A1 or A².

IaU.

P420 [—] Vida's Art of poetry, translated into English verse, after the manner of Mr. Pope. In three books. *Printed in the year* 1750.
8°: A^2 B–M⁴; *i–iv*, *1* 2–88.

>Apparently a piracy; Pitt's name is suppressed.

CtY; *Otago University, N.Z.* (microfilm at L).

P421 Pitt, Henry. Verses, humbly address'd to his majesty: occasion'd by his majesty's royal bounty to the town of Blandford... *London printed, and sold by J. Jackson, & J. Roberts,* [1731.] (*MChr* Aug)
2°: A^2 B²; *1–2* 3–8.
'Oh, born to chasten, and to banish pain!'
ICN(uncut).

Pittis, William.
Several groups of fables which might be considered as collected works are entered separately below. The attribution of some of them to Pittis is new; while his connection with them seems clear, it is not impossible that others took a hand. The attribution of individual fables to Pittis because they appeared in these collections should therefore be received with some caution.

P422 [—] Æsop at Oxford: or, a few select fables in verse, under the following heads... *London, printed in the year* 1709, *and sold by the booksellers* [1708]. (*Observator* 15 Nov)
8°: A^2 B–K⁴ L²; *i–iv*, *1*–76.
Fable 1: 'Æsop, grown weary of the trade'

>Dedication to Thomas Lewis signed 'Æsop'. Lewis disclaimed all knowledge of the author and the book in *DC* 2 Dec 1708, and in a similar advertisement in *LG* 9 Dec Pittis is specifically named as author. Six fables were reprinted in *Æsop at the Bell-tavern,* 1711, and five of these reappeared in *Æsop in masquerade,* 1718.

L(164.1.7, Luttrell, 16 Nov),O(4, 1 uncut),E,DT, DrU; CSmH,ICN,IU,MH.

P423 [—] —— [*London?* 1709?]
4°: A^4; *1*–8, 2 columns.

>Drop-head title only; a piracy. Signatures possibly cropped from copy seen.

O(cropt).

P424 [—] [reissue] Bickerstaff's Æsop: or the humours of the times, digested into fables. Humbly dedicated to those flourishing sisters, the two universities... *London printed, and sold by B. Bragge,* [1709.] (*DC* 7 Dec)

Pittis, W. Aesop at Oxford

8°: A(3 ll) B⁴(−B1) C–I⁴ K⁴(−K4) L⁴; *i–iv*, *1–78*.
The preliminary leaves of the first edition are cancelled, and four new fables added at the end, the original L² being cancelled. Dedication signed 'Is. Bickerstaff'. Three of the new fables are taken from *Canterbury tales*, 1701.
O; CLU-C,IEN,MH,TxU.

P425 [—] Æsop at the Bell-tavern in Westminster, or, a present from the October-club, in a few select fables from Sir Roger L'Estrange, done into English verse... *London, printed in the year* 1711. (*Review* 23 June)
8°: A² B–F⁴; *i–iv*, *1–40*.
Drop-head title on p. 1, 'Select fables, from Sir Roger L'Estrange's Æsop...' Entered in *SR* 23 June to John Baker; deposit copies at O,SaU.
Fable 1: 'A drolling sort of fellow made'
T. F. M. Newton in *MP* 33 (1935–6) 292 suggests that William Pittis was the author. Fifteen of the seventeen fables are reworked from Pittis's *Æsop at Oxford*, 1709, from *Chaucer's whims*, 1701, and from *Canterbury tales*, 1701. The preface suggests that one author was responsible for the whole work, which makes Pittis the obvious candidate. *Æsop in masquerade*, 1718, reprints ten fables from this collection.
L(1474.b.38),O,E,LdU-B,SaU+; CtY(2),MH.

P426 [—] Æsop in masquerade: or some state-lessons for certain courtiers, in a few select fables in verse. Written by a person of quality... *London, printed for W. Boreham, and sold by the booksellers*, 1718. (*PB* 20 May)
8°: A–G⁴; *1–2 3–54 55–56*. G4 advt.
Fable 1: 'A drolling sort of fellow made'
Ten of these sixteen fables are taken from *Æsop at the Bell-tavern*, 1711 (five of these had previously appeared in Pittis's *Æsop at Oxford*, 1709), and three from *Chaucer's whims*, 1701; like them it is probably by Pittis.
L(11631.d.3),O(−G4); CtY,DFo,ICU,MH(uncut),TxU(−G4)+.

[—] The ballad, or some scurrilous reflections in verse, on the proceedings of the honourable house of commons: answered stanza by stanza, 1701. *See* B34.

P427 [—] Canterbury tales, rendred into familiar verse, viz... Written by no body. *London, printed in the year* 1701 [1700]. (*PB* 12 Nov)
8°: A⁴ B–E⁴; *i–viii*, *1–31 32 blk*. A1 hft.
Tale 7 (p. 16) is titled 'The Revolution'.
Tale 1: 'The lion having held the reins'
T. F. M. Newton in *MP* 33 (1935–6) 292 reports that three of these twelve tales were reprinted in Pittis's *Bickerstaff's Æsop*, 1709; eight were incorporated in *Æsop at the Bell-tavern*, 1711, which was probably by him.

Pittis, W. Canterbury tales

Pittis's authorship of this collection is therefore likely.
L(1508/1529),LVA-F(−A1),O(−A1).

P428 [—] — *London, printed in the year* 1701.
8°: A⁴ B–E⁴; *i–viii*, *1–31 32 blk*. A1 hft.
The title on p. 16 is 'Resolution', and a note on p. viii records that 'some part of the impression of the 7th tale...went by the name of the *Revolution*'. This edition is apparently reset except for sheets A and E.
O(2, 1 uncut, 1 −A1); OCU(−A1).

P429 [—] — To which is added, the author's case. *London, printed for the author*, 1701.
8°: A⁴ B–E⁴; *i–viii*, *1–32*. A1 hft.
This edition omits the words 'Written by no body' from the title.
CT(−A1); DFo,IU.

P430 [—] — Written by no body. *London, printed in the year* 1701.
8°: A⁸; *1 2–16*.
A piracy, priced at 2d. as opposed to 6d.
CtY(cropt),MH.

P431 [—] Chaucer's whims: being some select fables and tales in verse, very applicable to the present times... *London, printed by D. Edwards; sold by the booksellers of London & Westminster*, 1701. (*PB* 31 July)
8°: A² B–E⁴ F²; *i–iv*, *1–35 36 blk*.
Fable 1: 'In times of old, when beasts were wondrous wise'
Three of these political fables were reprinted in *Æsop in masquerade*, 1718, which was probably by Pittis; one had previously appeared in *Æsop at the Bell-tavern*, 1711. This is probably by Pittis also.
L(11631.d.9),O; CLU-C,DFo,IU,MH,NN+.

P432 [—] [reissue] Jest and earnest: being a bundle of fables, tales and whims, in verse, (some old, some new,) but all very applicable to the present times. Written by Tom. Teltroth, under discontent in the late reign, but now somewhat recover'd. *London, printed in the year* 1703 [1702]. (*WL* Sept)
8°: A–C⁴, ²A² B–E⁴ F²; *i–iv*, *1–20*, *i–iv*, *1–35 36 blk*.
Four verse fables, followed by a reissue of *Chaucer's whims*, 1701, including its original title; they are linked by a catchword on p. 20. One of the added tales reappeared in *Æsop at the Bell-tavern*, 1711.
Fable 1: 'The dolphin's race had govern'd long'
MH.

P433 [—] [idem] The London Æsop; or jest and earnest on the present times. Written by Tom. Teltroth. *London, printed in the year* 1702.
8°: A⁴; *1 2–8*.
The four new fables only; probably a piracy.
O.

P434 [—] An elegy on the lamented death of poor Truth and Honesty; who departed this life, with

Pittis, W. An elegy

the renowned paper call'd the London-post, on Monday the 11th day of June, 1705. *London, printed in the year* 1705.
½°: 1 side, 2 columns.
Mourning borders.
'All humane things are subject to decay'
T. F. M. Newton in *MP* 33 (1935–6) 290n. records Dunton's attribution to Pittis. On the end of Benjamin Harris's newspaper.
Crawford (with proof corrections).

P435 [—] The fable of the cods-heads: or, a reply to the Dutch-men's answer to the resolutions of the house of commons. *London, printed in the year* 1712. (*PB* 26 Feb)
½°: 1 side, 1 column.
'The beasts with indignation warm'd'
Printed in Pittis's *Æsop at Oxford*, 1709. Against the Dutch.
L(11602.i.12/7*; 1875.d.6/10; G.1390/15), LLP; ICN(Luttrell, 27 Feb),MH.

P436 [—] 'Fire and faggot or the city bonfire.' [*London*, 1705.]
½°.
Recorded by T. F. M. Newton, 'William Pittis and Queen Anne journalism', *MP* 33 (1935) 175 as reprinted from Pittis's *Whipping-post* for 18 Sept 1705. Reprinted in *Poems on affairs of state* IV (1707) 35–7.
'She's dead! thanks to the jury's pious care'
Luttrell under 11 Oct 1705 records 'Pettis's' committal for writing 'a half sheet call'd *Fire and faggot*, being a reflection upon burning *The memorial*'. Pittis claimed in *The whipping-post* of 2 Oct 1705 that it 'was sent him by the penny-post', and he may be innocent. Attacking the grand jury which on 31 Aug 1705 presented *The memorial of the church of England* and ordered it to be burnt the following day. Cf. *An elegy on the burning of the Church memorial*, 1705.

P437 [—] [dh] The fox unkenell'd: or, the sham memorial. By the author of the Seven extinguishers. [*London*, 1710.] (*SR* 15 Aug)
4°: A⁴; 1–8.
Watermark: fleur-de-lys, poor paper. Entered in *SR* to Pittis; deposit copies at LSC,E,EU, SaU. Advertised in *EvP* 19 Aug as sold by J. Baker.
'A fox of quality that long'
On Godolphin's dismissal.
L(11631.e.23),LSC,E,EU,SaU; CtY.

P438 [—] [fine paper]
Watermark: fleur-de-lys on shield.
O(uncut).

P439 — A funeral poem sacred to the immortal memory of the deceas'd Sir Cloudesly Shovel, kt... In which is inserted, a short description of the procession at his interment in Westminster-Abbey.

Pittis, W. A funeral poem

London printed, and sold by J. Morphew, 1708 [1707]. (24 Dec, Luttrell)
2°: A² B–C²; 1–4 5–11 12 blk.
No watermark. An advertisement in *DC* 31 Dec lists errata on pp. 8, 9, 10.
''Tis true! Great losses for amazement call'
LdU-B,WgP(Luttrell).

P440 — [fine paper]
Watermark: Dutch lion.
EU('Ex dono authoris Xber 25: 1707').

P441 — — *London, printed by Henry Hills*, 1708.
8°: A⁴; 1 2–8.
A piracy.
DFo.

[—] The generous muse. A funeral poem, in memory of his late majesty K. James the II, 1701. See G105.

P442 [—] A hymn to confinement. Written by the author of the Case of the church of England's Memorial fairly stated, &c. while in durance. Fit to be stitch'd up with the said pamphlet. To which is added, a poem on the same subject by the famous Sir Roger L'Estrange, when in New-gate, in the days of Oliver's usurpation. *London, printed in the year* 1705, *and sold by the booksellers.* (*DC* 22 Nov, 'just published')
4°: a² A–D²; i–iv, 1–16.
Advertised in *DC* as sold by B. Bragge. The printer is identified as 'Mr. Brudenel, or Meeres' by Robert Clare, one of Harley's informers; see H. L. Snyder in *The library* V. 22 (1967) 339. The reliability of these identifications is uncertain.
'Hail, bless'd abode! thou mansion of repose'
L'Estrange: 'Beat on, proud billows, Boreas blow'
Pittis was convicted in April 1706 for writing *The case of the church of England's Memorial.* The added poem is from a manuscript, 'said to be Sir Roger L'Estrange's'.
L(11645.e.56/2),O,DT,LdU-B; CSmH,CtY,MB.

P443 [—] A hymn to Neptune; occasion'd by the late glorious victory obtain'd in the height of Malaga by her majesty's royal navy... *London, printed for R. Basset*, 1705 [1704]. (*PM* 23 Nov)
4°: A–F⁴; i–viii, 1–40. viii err, advt.
No watermark. Advertised in *FP* 1 March 1705 as 'newly published'.
'No, 'tis in vain, not all their factious arts'
The fine-paper copy below has the dedication to Sir George Rooke signed.
O(A⁴ only); CSmH,NjP.

P444 — [fine paper]
Watermark: initials (? LC); dedication signed.
NN.

P445 [—] Kiss me if you dare or a royal faverit turn'd out. *London, printed in the year* 1710.
½°: 1 side, 2 columns.
'Four sisters once a pretty handsome brood'

Pittis, W. Kiss me if you dare

Printed in Pittis's *Æsop at Oxford*, 1709. A satire against dissenting piety.
L(Cup.645.e.1/21); CLU-C.

P446 [—] The last new prologues and epilogues, relating to the life of the Observator and the death of the Royal-Oak lottery, as they were spoken at the new theatre in Little Lincoln's Inn Fields, with what was then left out. Publish'd in opposition to some spurious copies that have crept abroad. *London printed, and sold by J. Nutt*, 1703. (2 Oct, Luttrell)
4°: A–C⁴ (A3 as 'A'); *i–iv*, 1–20.
'The prologue, by way of dialogue; between Heraclitus Ridens, the Observator, and his country-man'; p. 12, 'The prologue, on the death of the Royal-Oak lottery'; p. 16, 'The epilogue upon the Observator'. The first prologue appears to have been spoken on 28 Sept; the earliest record of the other prologue and epilogue is 5 Oct, but if Luttrell's date is correct, there was an earlier performance; the records of performances at Lincoln's Inn Fields are incomplete.
'Well – since we are met, our business is to try'
'As when some tyrant dies that long has made'
'The stage has been, and yet improv'd shall rise'
T. F. M. Newton in *MP* 33 (1935–6) 182 quotes the *Observator*'s sarcasms in reply, clearly referring to Pittis.
L(164.m.28, Luttrell),O,C; CLU-C,CtY,MH.

P447 [—] The l---d t——rs out at last, and diliver'd up his s--ff. *London, printed for J. Smith*, 1710.
½°: 1 side, 1 column.
'A certain fox had stole a neighboors goose'
Printed in *Canterbury tales*, 1701, and subsequently in *Æsop at the Bell*, 1711. A fable applied to the dismissal of Godolphin from the post of lord treasurer.
L(Cup.645.e.1/6).

[—] The loyalist: a funeral poem in memory of William III, 1702. *See* L305.

P448 — Nereo. A funeral-poem sacred to the immortal memory of Sir George Rooke, kt. lately deceas'd...
London printed, and sold by B. Bragge, 1709. (17 May, Luttrell)
2°: *A*² B–D²; *1–4* 5–16.
'When loud-tongu'd vertue calls for our applause'
DN; MH(Luttrell),TxU.

P449 [—] Out with 'em while you are about it. [*London?*] *Printed in the year* 1710.
½°: 1 side, 1 column.
'There was a fellow hard at work a sowing'
Printed in Pittis's *Æsop at Oxford*, 1709. A fable, presumably on the fall of the whigs.
L(Cup.645.e.1/26); *Harding*.

P450 [—] [variant title, adds:] or a great change at court.
L(Cup.645.e.1/26).

P451 [—] The patriots. A poem, in vindication of several worthy members of the late parliament.

Pittis, W. The patriots

Dedicated to the honourable Robert Harley...
London, printed for R. Basset, 1702. (6 Jan, Luttrell)
2°: A–D²; *i–iv*, 1–11 *12 blk.*
Watermark: London arms. The Luttrell copy is recorded in Pickering & Chatto cat. 247/13331.
'Once more, my muse, a generous offring make'
Pittis's name is printed on the title of the fine-paper copy below.
L(1972)O,LdU-B; CSmH,MH,TxU(2).

P452 — [fine paper] By William Pittis...
Watermark: Dutch lion; Pittis's name added to title.
O.

P453 [—] The seven extinguishers, a poem. *London, printed in the year* 1710. (*SR* 4 July)
4°: A⁴ (A2 as 'A3'); *1–3* 4–8.
Entered in *SR* to Pittis; deposit copies at LSC,E,EU,SaU. Advertised in *DC* 5 July; a 'second edition' advertised in *PB* 5 Aug has not been identified.
'The Calv's-head brawny c—— leads the van'
Copyright entered to Pittis. A satire on the seven bishops who voted against Sacheverell.
L(11631.f.12),LVA-F(Luttrell, 6 July),O,E,DN +; CSmH,ICU.

P454 [—] A story to the purpose, or, nothing in the warming pan but the coals of sedition. *London, printed in the year* 1710.
½°: 1 side, 1 column.
'The lyon having held the reins'
Apparently the first poem of *Canterbury tales*, 1701; also printed in *Æsop at the Bell*, 1711, and *Æsop in masquerade*, 1718.
Harding.

P455 [—] The Sunderland tale. [*London*, 1710.] (*SR* 30 June)
½°: 1 side, 1 column.
Entered in *SR* to Richard Newcomb by Ann Newcomb; deposit copy at E.
'A knot of fellows out upon the pad'
Printed in Pittis's *Æsop at Oxford*, 1709; also in *Æsop at the Bell*, 1711, and *Æsop in masquerade*, 1718. On the fall of Sunderland.
L(1876.f.1/100),E.

P456 [—] The true-born-Hugonot: or, Daniel de Foe. A satyr. By a True-born-Englishman. *London, printed in the year* 1703. (24 Aug, Luttrell)
4°: π1 A–C⁴ D¹; *i–ii*, *1–2* 3–25 *26 blk.* π1 hft.
'Are we then lost to sense as well as shame'
According to T. F. M. Newton in *MP* 33 (1935–6) 182 Pittis revealed his authorship in his *Heraclitus ridens*.
L(1077.k.30, −π1),LU(−π1),O,C; MB(D1 mutilated),NNP,Rosenbach(Luttrell).

P457 [—] [dh] The true-born-Hugonot: or, Daniel de Foe. A satyr. [*London*, 1703.]

Pittis, W. The true-born-Hugonot

4°: *A*²; *1–4*, 2 columns.
A piracy.
C; CtY,MB.

P458 [—] Vulpone's tale. [*London*] *Printed in the year* 1710.
½°: 1 side, 1 column.
On the other side of the L copy, *The high church spectakles*, 1710.
'A fox was out upon the pilfering lay'
Printed in Pittis's *Æsop* at Oxford, 1709; also in *Æsop at the Bell*, 1711, and *Æsop in masquerade*, 1718. Against Godolphin and the whigs.
L(Cup 645.e.1/22); CLU-C,*Harding*.

P459 [—] ⟨The⟩ Windsor prophecy. [*London*] *Printed in the year* 1712.
½°: 1 side, 1 column.
'There was a fig-tree on a rising ground'
Printed in Pittis's *Æsop* at Oxford, 1709.
L(1850.e.10/19).

P460 [—] [*idem*] A tale of a disbanded courtier. [*London?* 1712?]
½°: 1 side, 1 column.
This version has 12 lines of 'Application' at end, and may be the earlier.
OCU(imprint cropt).

P461 Pix, Mary. A pastoral elegy on the death of the right honourable the Earl of Burlington. *London, printed in the year* 1704.
2°: A–C² (C1 as 'B'); *i–iv, 1–8*.
'Welcome my Thyrsis to thy native plains'
Dedication signed.
Chatsworth.

P461·5 [—] A poem, humbly inscrib'd to the lords commissioners for the union of the two kingdoms. *London printed, and are to be sold by J. Morphew*, 1707. (Luttrell, 1 May)
2°: A–C² (A2 as 'A3'); *i–ii, 1–8 9–10 blk*.
Watermark: three circles.
'Hail, fragrant May, thou glory of the spring'
A copy of the fine-paper issue below at MR-C has a letter of presentation from Mary Pix to Lord Somers. The other copy, at CSmH, has a printed dedication signed 'John Fowler', but this properly belongs to his *On the queens most glorious victories*, [1707?], and was not originally bound with the copy.
Horn(Luttrell, –C2).

P461·6 [—] [fine paper]
Watermark: Dutch lion.
MR-C(–C2); CSmH.

P462 — To the right honourable the Earl of Kent, lord chamberlain of her majesties houshold, &c. This poem is humbly address'd, by your lordship's most obedient and most humbly servant. Mary Pix. [*London*, 1704/06.]
2°: A–B²; *1–2 3–8*.
Title in form of a dedication. Dated by

Pix, M. To the…Earl of Kent

Macdonald, Dryden p. 297n. as *c*.1701; but the recipient must be Henry Grey the 22nd earl, created marquess in 1706, who was lord chamberlain from 1704 to 1710.
'Dark chaos reign'd e're green the earth o'respread'
CLU-C(in original wrappers),ICU.

P463 [—] Violenta, or the rewards of virtue: turn'd from Boccace into verse. *London, printed for John Nutt*, 1704.
8°: A⁴ B–I⁸; *i–viii, 1–128*. vii err.
'Begin my muse, the wondrous tale reherse'
The copy at CLU-C is a presentation copy from Mrs. Pix to May Wallis; see also the following. From the eighth tale of the second day.
L(1478.aa.17),O; CLU-C(presentation copy), DFo,OCU.

P464 — [another issue]
The dedication is signed 'Mary Pix' in type, but it is not apparently printed on fine paper.
LVA-D.

P465 Place. The place-bill, a ballad. To the tune of Which no body can deny. *London, printed for John Cooper*, 1740. (*GM* Feb)
2°: *A*¹ B²; *1–3 4–6*.
Percival LII.
'Since so very impatient to hear of the doom'
The motion to introduce the bill was defeated by a very small majority on 29 Jan 1740.
L(11630.h.36),O; CtY(uncut),*ICN*,MH.

P466 — — [*Edinburgh*, 1740.]
8°: A²; *1–4*.
Drop-head title only.
AdU.

— Place-book for the year seventeen-hundred, forty-five, 1744–5. *See* Williams, *Sir* Charles Hanbury.

— The place of the damn'd, 1731. *See* Swift, Jonathan.

[**P467** = **P414·5**] **Plague.** The plague of Marseilles, 1721. *See* Pitt, Christopher.

P468 Plagues. The plagues of Ægypt. A poem. In two parts. *London printed, and sold by John Morphew*, 1708. (*WL* May)
4°: *A*² B–F²; *1–4 5–23 24 blk*. 23 advt.
'Where Memphian tombs their royal mummies keep'
IU,NN.

P469 — The plagues of Nod. [*London?* 1715/–.]
slip: 1 side, 1 column.
Printed with *A new ballad*, (N55); the MH copy is not divided.
'The scourge of heav'n, the prophet's lifted rod'
Crum T1287, dated 1715. A Jacobite satire.
CSmH,MH.

Plaid

P470 Plaid. The plaid hunting. A ballad. By no puff. *London, sold by William Owen,* [1747.] (13 Nov?)
2°: *A²* < B¹; *1–2* 3–6.
   Listed in *GM, LM* Nov 1747.
   'When Charly of late in a damnable fright'
      On the Jacobites who wore plaid waistcoats for hunting as a safe gesture.
L(1346.m.43, uncut),O,AdU; CLU-C,CtY,IU (cropt),MH(ms. date 13 Nov).

P471 — — A ballad. To the tune of Packington pounds. [*Edinburgh?* 1747.]
8°: *A²*; *1* 2–4.
   Drop-head title only.
E.

P472 Plain. 'A plain hymn to our redeemer; containing the substance of Christian religion, more particularly recommended to the charity schools. *London* (*J. Wyatt*), 1707, (*3d.*).'
(*Morgan* J372.)

— Plain thoughts in plain language, 1743. *See* Williams, *Sir* Charles Hanbury.

P473 — 'The plain truth. A poem. [*London*] *Sold by R. Burleigh.* Price 2*d.*' (*MC* Nov 1715)
   Probably a half-sheet from the price.

P474 — Plain truth: a satire. Humbly inscribed to the right honourable J--- e--- of G. *London, printed for M. Cooper,* 1747. (*GM* Feb)
4°: A–C⁴; *1–2* 3–24.
   'Yes, I will write. And let them laugh who will'
      A satire on society, inscribed to John, earl of Granville.
L(1961),O(2),C,LdU-B,*MR*; CLU,CtY,IU,MH (uncut),TxU+.

P475 — Plain truth, or downright Dunstable. A poem. Containing the author's opinion of the sale of poetic and prose performances. With some critical thoughts concerning Horace and Virgil. Together with a few hints on the author's amours... *London, printed for J. Roberts,* 1740. (25 March?)
4°: *A²* B–D⁴ E²; *i–iv*, *1–28*.
   Entered in Woodfall's ledgers (*N&Q* I. 9 (1855) 420) under 22 March 1740 to 'Dr. Kennedy'. Listed in *GM* May 1740.
   'Now, honest friend, would'st thou, I shew'
      The other works entered with this in Woodfall's ledger are attributed by the L catalogue to Dennis de Coetlogon, but it seems possible that they are all by the unidentified Dr. Kennedy.
L(11630.c.13/1, ms. date, 25 March),O(2); CSmH.

P476 — [reissue] A short critical poem on poets and poetry. With that call'd Plain truth on poetry, gallantry, and politicks. *London, printed for W. Owen,* 1750. (*BM* Feb; *LM* March)
4°: A(3 ll) B–D⁴ E²; *i–ii*, 1–4, 1–28.
   Cancel preliminaries A. The added 'short critical poem' occupies the first pp. 1–4.

Critical poem: '''Tis said Poeta nascitur non fit' MH.

'**Plain-Truth, Peter.**' The Litchfield squabble, 1747. *See* L175.

P477 Planter. The planter's charity. *London, printed in the year* 1704.
4°: *A²* B²; *1–2* 3–8.
   Variations in the position of pagination in the copies seen suggest a possible reimpression or variant.
'You that oppress the captive African'
   Preface signed 'B.M.' Ascribed to Mandeville by *Lowndes* and *DNB*; but F. B. Kaye in *JEGP* 20 (1921) 446f. considered the attribution unproved.
LLP; DFo,MH.

P478 Platonic. The platonic. A tale. *London, printed for W. Boreham,* 1721. (*DP* 20 March)
2°: *A²* B²; *1–3* 4–8.
'Young Damon, once upon a time'
   A bawdy tale about wooing the muses.
CSmH.

— The platonic lovers, 1732. *See* Fowke, Martha.

P479 [**Plaxton, William.**] Advice to new-married husbands, in hudibrastick verse. By the author of the York-shire horse-racers. [*London*] *Printed for John Morphew,* 1712. (*PB* 22 May)
8°: A⁸; *1–4* 5–16. A1 hft.
'Tom, when the heat of battle's over'
   Ascribed to Plaxton on account of the following. In praise of wine and tobacco, against the insatiability of women.
O(−A1),*DrU*; CtY,OCU,TxU.

P480 [—] The Yorkshire-racers. A poem. In a letter from H---- S---------ton, to his friend T----- P---------n. *London, 'printed for the use of all sorts of jockeys, whether north, south, east, or west',* [1709.] (*DC* 19 April)
4°: A–F²; *1–2* 3–23 *24 blk.*
'Fret not, dear Tom, that thou ha'st lost the race'
   Crum F606, ascribing the poem to 'Mr. Plaxton'; William Plaxton seems the probable identification. A letter from Henry Singleton to Tom Pullen on the successful Yorkshire candidates in the election of 1708.
L(11601.ddd.6/4, lacks B²),LdU-B; NN(ms. notes).

P481 [—] — *London, 'printed for the use of all sorts of jockeys, whether north, south, east, or west',* [1709.]
8°: A⁸; *1–2* 3–15 *16*. 16 advt of Hills's poems.
   A piracy. Reissued with poems published by Henry Hills in *A collection of the best English poetry,* 1717 *Case* 294).
L(C.124.b.7/21),LVA-F,O,DN,YM(2)+; CtY, ICU,MH,OCU,TxU+.

P482 Player, Henry. Tobacco: a poem in two books. Translated from the Latin of Raphael Thorius. *London, printed by W. H.; sold by J. Noon & T. Sharpey, & S. Popping*, 1716. (Jan?)
12°: A² B–D⁶ E²; *i–iv*, 1–40.
'I sing the potent herb, and sweet repast'
Dedication signed.
O; *DNLM*,MH(ms. date, Jan),NN-A,*OCl*,*RPB*.

P483 — — The second edition. *London, sold by J. Roberts, J. Wyat, S. Ballard, J. Downing, & J. Noon*, [1718.] (*DC* 18 Nov)
12°: A²(±) B–D⁶ E²; *i–iv*, 1–40.
A reissue with cancel preliminaries. Frank Cundall, *A history of printing in Jamaica* (Kingston, 1935) records an advertisement in *The weekly Jamaica courant* 15 April 1719 for an edition 'Reprinted by R. Baldwin, in Church Street, Kingston, price 2*s*. 6*d*. stitch'd in blew paper, 6 ryals bound in marble paper'; no copy traced.
L(1972); MH.

P484 Players. The players: a satire. *London, printed for the author; sold by J. Wilford, and the booksellers of London & Westminster*, [1733?]
8°: A–C⁸; *1–46; 47–48 blk.*
'Well! I confess it, I have said the play'rs'
Attributed to Edward Phillips in a ms. note of *c.* 1800 in the MH copy of the following issue; his authorship is considered doutbful by *DNB*, *CBEL*.
CSmH,DFo,ICU(–C8).

P485 — [reissue] *London, printed for W. Mears*, 1733. (*DJ* 16 March)
8°: A⁸(±A1) B–C⁸; *1–46; 47–48 blk.*
L(T. 1056/16, –C8),LdU-B(2); MH.

P486 — The players turn'd academicks: or, a description (in merry metre) of their translation from the theatre in Little Lincolns-Inn-Fields, to the Tennis-court in Oxford. With a preface relating to the proceedings of the university the last act: as also the Wadhamite prologue that was spoken there, with a prologue and epilogue, by way of answer to it, at the Theatre Royal. *London, printed in the year* 1703. (11 Nov, Luttrell)
2°: A–D²; *i–iv*, 1–12.
Drop-head title on p. 1. 'The Oxford expedition'. The prologues and epilogue are reprinted from *A prefatory prologue...* [1703.]
'When mony, and manners, were both a decaying'
A banter on Betterton's visit to Oxford. The 'Wadhamite prologue' was by Joseph Trapp.
L(11630.f.34; 11795.k.31/2),*MR-C*; CtY(uncut), DFo(Luttrell),MH,TxU.

P487 Playhouse. The play-house scuffle, or, passive obedience kickt off the stage. Being a true relation of a new tragi-comedy, as it was acted last week at the play-house in Drury-lane; by several notorious actors, frequently call'd her majesties servants, but of late turn'd their own masters. In two canto's. *London, printed for J. Bethel; sold by John Morphew*, 1710. (1 July, Luttrell)
8°: A⁸; *1–2* 3–16.
'How strange an aukward thing is man'
'Of the quarrel between Mr Rich the master & the players', Luttrell.
L(11631.e.87, Luttrell),*MR*; MH.

P488 Pleasures. The pleasures of a single life, or, the miseries of matrimony. Occasionally writ upon the many divorces lately granted by parliament. *London printed, and are to be sold by J. Nutt*, 1701. (5 Aug, Luttrell)
2°: A–D²; *i–ii*, 1–13 *14 blk.*
Last line of p. 3 reads 'Heav'n'; the order of editions is undetermined. The Luttrell copy is recorded in *Haslewood*; listed in *WL* Aug.
'Wedlock, oh! curss'd uncomfortable state'
The same author apparently also wrote *The city madam*, 1702, and *The grand mistake*, 1705; a copy of the former is attributed to 'Mr More', not further identified. It has also been attributed to Edward Ward and to Dillon (see P501 below), and there is an incomplete (and therefore doubtful) entry for it in *Rawlinson* under Thomas Brown. Cf. *An answer to the Pleasures*, 1701; *The ladies choice*, 1702; *Wedlock a paradice*, 1701.
NN,TxU.

P489 — [another edition]
Last line of p. 3 reads 'Heavn'.
CLU-C.

P490 — — *London, printed for Richard Briggs*, 1701.
8°: *A⁴*; *1* 2–8.
Part printed in two columns; a piracy.
Institute for Sex Research.

P491 — — [col] *Printed, and sold by the booksellers of London & Westminster*, 1701.
4°: A²; *1–4*, 2 columns.
Drop-head title only; another piracy.
L(11631.f.26).

P492 — — The second edition. *London printed, and are to be sold by J. Nutt*, 1702.
2°: A–C²; *i–ii*, 1–10.
CSmH,CtY,IU.

P493 — — The second edition. [*London?*] *Printed in the year* 1705.
8°: *A⁴*; *1* 2–8.
Smaller type on pp. 7–8; presumably a piracy.
O.

P494 — — With the Choice, or, the pleasures of a country-life... *London printed, and sold by H. Hills*, [1708/09.]
8°: A⁸; *1* 2–16.
This is probably the earliest Hills edition; the CtY copy is bound with other Hills poems,

The **pleasures** of a single life

mainly of 1708. *The choice* is Pomfret's poem, previously pirated alone by Hills.
O,CT(2); CSmH,CtY,*MH*.

P495 —— With the Choice... *London printed, and sold by H. Hills*, 1709.
8°: A⁸; *1* 2–16.
P. 2, line 17 reads 'noisy sound'; p. 3, line 24 'Samaites'.
L(11631.aa.53),E,EU; CLU-C,ICN,MH,NN.

P496 — [another edition]
P. 2, line 17 reads 'noisy sound'; p. 3, line 24 'Samnites'.
O,CT,AdU.

P497 — [another edition]
P. 2, line 17 reads 'noisey sound'; p. 3, line 24 'Samnites'. This edition was reissued in *A collection of the best English poetry*, 1717 (*Case* 294).
L(C.124.b.7/9),O,LdU-B; CtY,ICU,MH.

P498 —— With the Choice... *London, printed by J. Read near Fleet-street*, [1709/–.]
8°: A⁸ C²; *1–2* 3–20.
Presumably the linking of these two poems is copied from Hills's editions.
DG.

P499 —— [col] *London, printed in the year* 1709.
4°: A²; *1–4*, 2 columns.
Drop-head title only. Without *The choice*.
L(163.1.45).

P500 —— With the Choice: or, the pleasures of a country-life. Dedicated to the beaus against the next vocation [!]. *Dublin, printed by E. S. [Elizabeth Sadleir] in School-house-lane*, [1715/26.]
8°: A⁸; *1–3* 4–16.
A2 is the title; A1 not in copy seen.
C(lacks A1).

P501 —— With the Choice...Dedicated to the beaus ... *Dublin, printed by C. Hicks, at the Rein-Deer in Montrath Street, where country chapmen may be furnished*, [1726/36.]
8°: A⁸; *1* 2–16.
No cut on title. The order of these chap-book editions is uncertain.
DN.

P502 —— *Dublin, printed by C. Hicks at the Rein Deer in Montrath Street, where country chapmen may be furnished*, [1726/36.]
8°: A⁸; *1* ⟨2⟩ 3–16.
With *The choice*, but the large cut on the title-page leaves no room for its mention there.
O(cropt).

P503 —— To which is added, the pleasures of a country life. By John Dillon, kt. [col] *Dublin, printed and sold [by C. Hicks?] at the Rein Deer*, [1726/36?]
8°: A⁸; *1* 2–16.
Large woodcut on title. The attribution to Dillon seems completely spurious, though it

The **pleasures** of a single life

has achieved some currency. *The pleasures...* was reprinted with *Love's invention* (London, 1746).
LVA-F.

P504 —— And further to acquaint all persons of either sex, that labours under unhappy affairs in a marriage state, may get relief, by being unmarried at the chapple, near Hide-park, for one guinea only. Together with the sweet entertainment, of the most charming pleasures of a country life... [*London?*] *Printed for a bold clergy-man*, 1747.
12°: A⁴ B²; *1* 2–12.
Vertical chain-lines.
L(Tab.603.a.51/2).

— The pleasures of imagination. A poem, 1744–. *See* Akenside, Mark.

— The pleasures of melancholy, 1747. *See* Warton, Thomas, *the younger*.

P505 — The pleasures of piety. *London, printed for J. Roberts; sold by J. Harrison*, 1716. (23 June, Luttrell)
8°: A–C⁴; *1–3* 4–24.
'Of piety's unfeign'd delights I sing'
LDW; CSmH,MH(Luttrell),OCU.

— The pleasures of the Bath, 1721. *See* Aston, Anthony.

P506 **Plot.** A plot discover'd against the trade and industry of Great-Britain. By B.F. gent. [*London*, 1714?]
slip: 2 sides, 1 column.
'Since all the world's turn'd up-side down'
A satire on Harley's South Sea company, comparing it with Aaron Hill's beech-nut oil project of 1714.
L(11602.i.12/30).

P507 — The plot discover'd: or, a trick to bring in the Pretender. *London, printed for E. Smith*, 1713.
2°: A²...; *1–2* 3– .
The copy seen lacks all after p. 4, probably only one leaf since the price is 2*d*.
'A lyon whose disputed blood'
O(A² only).

— The plot discover'd or, the man with horns, 1738. *See* 'Rattle, John'.

P508 — A plot or no plot. *London, printed in the year* 1712. (15 May, Luttrell)
½°: 1 side, 1 column.
The rule above the imprint is composed of 10 short rules.
'The summons were sent, and without more ado'
A satire on a whig scheme against Harley.
OW,Crawford; ICN(Luttrell),MH,TxU.

P509 —— *London, printed in the year* 1712.
½°: 1 side, 1 column.
The rule above the imprint is in one piece. The copies at E suggest a possible Edinburgh origin.
E(2); MH.

Plot

P510 — Plot or no plot, or Sir W---m and his spy foil'd. A new ballad. *London, printed for H. Carpenter*, 1747. (*GM* May)
2°: $A^2 < B^1$; *1–3* 4–6.
In the MH copy, leaf B has horizontal chain-lines.
'Ye lords, and ye commons, give ear to my ditty'
A satire on exaggerated fears of the Jacobites.
O,E; MH,OCU,TxU.

P511 — — [1747.]
obl ¼°: 1 side, 2 columns.
O.

P512 — [*idem*] Plot, or no plot. A new ballad. [*London?* 1747.]
½°: 1 side, 1 column.
Tailpiece with winged head at foot.
L(1890.c.1/3; G.559/5).

P513 — — [*Edinburgh?* 1747.]
½°: 1 side, 1 column.
Tailpiece of bowl of flowers at foot.
E.

P514 — Plot upon plot: a ballad. To the tune of Heigh boys up go we. [*Dublin?* 1713?]
½°: 1 side, 1 column.
On the other side, *A panegyrical epigram*, [1713?]. The Dublin origin, suggested by C, fits the Dublin practice of reprinting two broadsides on opposite sides of one sheet; but the location of copies argues against it. Previously printed in *Two poems*, 1713.
'Oh wicked whigs! what can you mean?'
L(1850.e.10/15),LLP,O,C,E.

P515 Plotters. The plotters; a satire. Occasion'd by the proceedings of the Earl of Or----y; the lord b. of R. the Lord N. and G. and others. Containing a true description of all the statesmen belonging to the Chevalier's court... *London, printed for A. Moore*, 1722. (*DP* 9 Oct)
8°: A^1 B–E⁴ F^1; *i–ii*, *1* 2–34. 34 err.
'He who his freedom cou'd, by wit command'
A satire on the Jacobite court. Luttrell expands names in title as the Earl of Orrery, the lord bishop of Rochester, the Lord North and Grey.
L(164.n.22, Luttrell, Oct),E; CtY,MH,NN,OCU (uncut).

'Plowden, Pilgrim.' Farrago, 1733. *See* Farewell, George.

Plutarch.
[Mitchell J:] Poltis king of Thrace; or the peace-keeper: a tale, from Plutarch, 1726. *See* M320·5.

Poekrich, Richard. The miscellaneous works of Richard Poekrich, esq; *Dublin, printed for the author, by James Byrn*, 1755.
12°: pp. 119.　　L.

Poekrich, R.

P516 [—] The Temple-Oge ballad. *Rathfarnam, printed, at the Cherry-tree*, 1730.
8°: A^4; *1–3* 4–8.
Possibly printed at Dublin by James Hoey and George Faulkner who used this address.
'Ye Dublin ladies that attend'
Dedication signed 'Philanthropos'; early ms. attributions in copies at L,DG. Characters of the society at Temple-Oge.
L(11631.a.36, ms. notes; 993.e.49/4),DA,DG.

Poem. A poem [I sing the man...], 1716. *See* Keinton, Martha.

— A poem [Ye true-born Englishmen proceed ...], [1701.] *See* Ye true-born Englishmen proceed, [1701.]

[**P517** = R139·2] — A poem addressed to all persons of the Roman catholic religion in Ireland, [1749?] *See* Reason's tribunal, 1735–.

P518 — A poem address'd to the Quidnunc's, at St. James's coffee-house London. Occasion'd by the death of the Duke of Orleans. [*Dublin*] *Printed in the year* 1724. (Jan?)
½°: 1 side, 2 columns.
Teerink 919; *Williams* 1118. From the typography, probably printed by James Carson.
'How vain are mortal man's endeavours'
Reprinted in the Pope-Swift *Miscellanies*, 1727, and variously ascribed to Gay or Swift by subsequent editors. L. M. Beattie in *MP* 30 (1933) 317–20 quotes letters from William Stratford to Edward Harley of 4 and 10 Feb 1724 which clearly imply Harley's belief that Arbuthnot was the author. Williams favours Arbuthnot's authorship, but the Dublin origin of the broadside has not been taken into account. Cf. *A letter from the Quidnunc's*, [1724?].
L(C.121.g.8/34); CSmH.

P519 — A poem, address'd to the right honourable William Pulteney, esq; occasion'd by some late court writings. *London, printed for E. Rayner*, 1731. (*GSJ* 24 June)
2°: A^2 B^2; *1–3* 4–8.
'While Pult'ney still the publick cause sustains'
A eulogy of Pulteney.
L(643.m.15/13, uncut),O; CSmH,KU,MH.

— A poem ascrib'd to the honourable Miss Carteret, 1725. *See* Philips, Ambrose (P223).

P520 — A poem being an answer to the Ladies libraries in general. *Dublin, printed by S. Powell*, 1722.
½°: 2 sides, 1 column.
'Forgive th' audacious man, ye injur'd fair'
The *Ladies libraries* were a series of prose broadsides giving the characters of Dublin ladies in the form of book titles.
L(C.121.g.8/23).

P521 — A poem by a lady on seeing his royal highness the prince regent. [*Edinburgh?* 1745?]

A **poem** by a lady

$\frac{1}{2}$°: 1 side, 1 column.
    Printed within a border of type-flowers.
'O glorious youth! 'tis evidently plain'
    In praise of the Young Pretender.
L(C.115.i.3/76),E.

P522 — A poem by D—— S——. On the scheme propos'd to the people of Ireland. Humbly address'd to the skilfull and ingenious Mr. Maculla ... *Dublin, printed by Thomas Walsh*, [1729.]
8°: A^4; *1–3* 4–8.
    Teerink 944. Advertised as just published in *Walsh's Dublin Post-Boy*, 10 March 1729.
'Thou, furnish'd with a great sagacious mind'
    Not in *Williams*; the implied attribution to Swift is apparently false. On James Maculla's proposals for establishing a mint in Ireland.
C,DN.

P523 — A poem by Namby Pamby. [*Dublin*, 1725/–.]
$\frac{1}{2}$°: 1 side, 2 columns.
'Fie fie Dick,/To take chick'
    In imitation of Ambrose Philips's style, but attacking someone else.
Crawford.

P524 — A poem. Canto I. *London, printed in the year* 1742.
$\frac{1}{2}$°: *1–2*, 1 column.
    Above imprint, 'Canto II. The remedy, &c.'; heading, but no text.
'God prosper long our noble king'
    Against George II and Hanover.
L(806.k.16/63),E.

P525 — [dh] A poem, compos'd the second of November, 1747. the day the honourable Archibald Stuart, esq; was assoilzied from his second trial. [*Edinburgh*, 1747.]
4°: A^2; *1* 2–4.
'While Scota's tribes, on hills, in glens complains'
    Signed 'Philibert'. A Jacobite poem.
O,E,*DrU*,GM; CSmH(ms. notes).

— A poem dedicated to the memory of the late learned and eminent Mr. William Law, [1728?] *See* Blair, Robert.

P526 — A poem dedicated to the queen, and presented to the congress at Utrecht, upon declaration of the peace. Writ in Latin, that foreigners might more easily understand and celebrate the transcendent virtues of her Britannic majesty. *London, printed by H. Meere, for R. Gosling; sold by J. Morphew*, 1713. (*PB* 23 April)
2°: A^2 B^1; *1–2* 3–6.
'Si vati faveas optima principum'
'O best of sovereigns! if you kindly hear'
    The Latin verses use each of Horace's 25 metres. Conceivably the poem by 'Dr. Adams' advertised in *PB* 7 July 1713 (A24).
O; CLU-C(Luttrell, 24 April),CtY,OCU.

— A poem delivered to the reverend Doctor Swift, [1725.] *See* Davys, Edward, *viscount Mountcashel*.

A **poem**. French and English

— A poem. French and English, [1749?] *See* A satyr: in French and English, 1749.

P527 — A poem humbly address'd to his highness the Prince of Orange, and the Princess Royal of Great Britain. Consisting of I. An epistle to Nassau... II. On that prince's sickness. III. On his recovery. IV. Liberty and religion flourishing... *London, printed for J. Roberts*, 1734. (*DJ* 13 March)
2°: A^2 B^2; *1–3* 4–8.
'My subject's too sublime for common pen'
    Possibly the work listed in *GM* March as 'A poem on the same occasion [the royal nuptials]. By Wm. Collins'. I. A. Williams in *Seven eighteenth-century bibliographies* (1924) 107 suggested that this was a misprint for William Collier. There is no evidence to support the attribution, but the suggestion is plausible; the only poem known to be by him was also published by Roberts.
O.

P528 — A poem humbly dedicated to the right honourable William lord Cowper, &c. *London printed, and sold by John Morphew*, 1711 [1710?].
$\frac{1}{2}$°: A^1; *1–2*, 1 column.
'Since Britains seals to other hands are gone'
    In praise of his period as lord chancellor.
L(Cup.645.e.1/21),LLP,OW,Crawford, Rothschild; TxU.

P529 — — '*London printed, and sold by John Morphew*' [*Dublin*], 1710.
$\frac{1}{2}$°: 1 side, 2 columns.
    On the other side, *To Mr. Stanhope*, 1710.
DG(mutilated).

— A poem humbly inscrib'd to his grace the Duke of Marlborough, 1709. *See* Churchill, William.

[**P530** = **M136**] — A poem humbly inscribed to his royal highness the Duke of Cumberland, on his defeat of the rebels, 1747. *See* Masters, George.

P531 — 'A poem humbly inscrib'd to Sir John Norris, on his preparing to sail. [*London*] *Printed for W. Chetwood, & J. Roberts*. Price 4d.' (*DC* 17 March 1720)

P532 — A poem humbly inscrib'd to the gentlemen of the Oxfordshire society. *London, printed for E. Moore*, 1723.
4°: A^2 B–D^2; *1–3* 4–16.
'This once the grateful muse presumptive sends'
L(643.k.3/1).

P533 — A poem humbly inscribed to the honourable Thomas Tickell, esq; *Dublin, printed in the year* 1726.
$\frac{1}{2}$°: 2 sides, 1 column.
'Why sleeps the bard? Why hangs the lyre unstrung'
    In praise of George I and Carteret.
DN,DT; CSmH,OCU.

— A poem, humbly inscrib'd to the lords commissioners for the union, 1707. *See* Pix, Mary.

A **poem** humbly offer'd

— A poem humbly offer'd to the pious memory of
...King William III, 1702. *See* Harris, Joseph.

P534 — A poem in a letter from a young lady in Mary's
parish, to a certain young lady in Andrew's; for the
loss of her maiden-head, being a warning to all her
sex. [*Dublin?* 172–?]
½°: 1 side, 1 column.
'Madam, to you I send these lines'
    Signed 'Rus'.
CLU-C.

P535 — A poem in answer to a lampoon, which was
wrote on the Cambridge ladies. *London, printed for
J. Wilford*, 1731. (*MChr* Jan)
2°: A² B²; *1–2* 3–8.
'E'er Lucifer dispers'd the shades of night'
    In praise of various Cambridge ladies. The
    same author's works were apparently collected
    as *A collection of poems. By the author of a poem
    on the Cambridge ladies*, 1733, and *Poems on
    several occasions. By the author of the poem on
    the Cambridge ladies*, 1736.
O,C.

536 — A poem in defence of the church of England, in
opposition to the Hind and panther, written by Mr.
John Dryden. *London printed, and sold by H. Hills*,
1709.
8°: A⁸ B⁴; *1–2* 3–24.
    First published in 1688 (*Macdonald, Dryden*
    253). This edition was reissued in *A collection
    of the best English poetry*, 1717 (*Case* 294), and
    is included here to complete the tally of Hills's
    piracies.
'If we into our selves, or round us look'
L(C.124.b.7/38),O(2),EU,WcC; CtY,ICN,MH,
TxU.

— A poem in honour of the birth-day of his most
sacred majesty King George, 1720. *See* Nevil,
Henry.

P537 — A poem in Latin, on the wonderful conversion
of Dr. Shea, ὑμνολογια. [*Dublin?* 170–?]
½°: 1 side, 1 column.
'Nequiter, ut medicam praxen, temerare suesti'
    On Dr. Nicholas Shea.
DG.

P538 — A poem in memory of Robert Nelson, esquire.
London, printed by Geo. James, for Richard Smith,
1715. (30 April, Luttrell)
8°: A–C⁴; *1–3* 4–21 22–24. 21 err; 24 advt.
    The errata are to Nelson's *An address to per-
    sons of quality and estate*, 1715. Listed in *MC*
    April 1715 as printed for R. Sare.
'Hail, saint triumphant, in whom earth did see'
L(11602.ee.22/1),LDW,O; CLU-C,CU,IU(Luttrell).

P539 — A poem in praise of nastiness. To Cindercola
scrub. [*Dublin*] *Printed in the year* 1724.
½°: 1 side, 2 columns.
'O! goddess of the dirty hue!'

A **poem** in praise of nastiness

    Cf. *Crum* O452, apparently a later version of
    1757.
MH.

— A poem in praise of tea, [1700?]–. *See* Motteux,
Peter Anthony.

— A poem in praise of the horn-book, 1728–. *See*
Tickell, Thomas.

P540 — A poem in praise of the journey-men taylors.
[*Dublin*, 1725/30.]
½°: 1 side, 1 column.
    The copy at L forms part of a collection of
    Dublin half-sheets of 1725/30.
'Soft Milton's charms in verse assist my pen'
    Possibly by Henry Nelson, who wrote other
    poems for the tailors. Cf. *The butchers answer
    to the taylors poem*, [1725/30.]
L(C.121.g.8/139).

— A poem, in the honour of the antient and loyal
society of the journey-men-taylors, 1726. *See*
Nelson, Henry.

P541 — 'A poem, inscrib'd and dedicated to Mrs.
Deane, oculist, in New-street, by Fleet-street,
London, on her great judgment and performances
on the various distempers incident to the eyes.
Written by a gentleman, with gratitude for the
great cure she perform'd on him. [*London*] *Printed
for the author; sold by Mr. Stagg, Mr. Strahan, Mr.
Brindley, Mr. Bathurst, & Mr. Rivington. Price
6d.*' (*LEP* 18 Feb 1744)

P542 — [dh] A poem inscrib'd to his excellency the
Lord Carteret. By a gentleman from England.
[col] *Dublin, printed by Pressick Rider, & Thomas
Harbin*, 1725.
2°: A²; *1* 2–4.
'Detesting flatt'ry, and to art unbred'
L(1890.e.5/97; C.121.g.8/69); TxU.

P543 — A poem inscrib'd to Lieut. gen. Ingoldsby,
occasioned by his going to Ireland. On the glorious
successes of her majesties arms and councils.
London printed, and sold by John Morphew, 1708.
(29 Jan, Luttrell)
2°: A¹ B–E² F¹; *1–2* 3–19 *20 blk*.
    The Luttrell copy is in the collection of R. D.
    Horn.
'As by some wond'rous sympathy appears'
LdU-B,*MR-C*; CtY,IU,OCU.

P544 — A poem inscrib'd to the author of The birth of
manly virtue. *Dublin, printed in the year* 1725.
½°: 1 side, 1 column.
    Teerink 1201.
'Hail! happy bard, who durst explore'
    In praise of Carteret. *The birth of manly virtue*
    was probably by Swift.
L(C.121.g.8/45).

P545 — A poem inscrib'd to the memory of our late
glorious deliverer, King William. *Dublin, printed by
John Whalley*, 1722.
½°: 1 side, 2 columns.

A **poem** inscrib'd to the memory

'Assist, with aid united, all ye nine'
CSmH.

— A poem inscrib'd to the right honourable Col. Boyle, [1733.] *See* Verses inscrib'd..., 1733.

P546 — A poem. Inscrib'd to the right honourable Sir Robert Walpole, on the success of his majesty's arms in America. By C——H——. *London, printed for the author; sold by J. Hazard & J. Wright, 1741.* (*GM, LM* June)
2°: *A² B²*; *1–5* 6–8. A1 hft.
'Hail faithful pilot of the British state'
On the naval victories against Spain.
RPJCB.

P547 — A poem, inscribed to the right honourable the Earl of Orford. *London, printed for T. Cooper, 1742.* (*GM, LM* June)
4°: *A² B–F²*; *1–5* 6–23 *24 blk*. A1 hft.
'When party-rage o'er silent truth prevails'
L(C.118.c.2/11).

— A poem inscribed to the right honourable the Lord Tullamoore, 1740. *See* Shepherd, Samuel.

P548 — A poem occasioned by a view of Powers-court House, the improvements, park, &c. Inscribed to Richard Wingfield, esq; *Dublin, printed by George Faulkner, 1741.*
8°: A⁸ (A2–5 as 'A' to 'A4'); *i–ii, 1* 2–13 *14 blk.*
'The muse forgetting, by the muse forgot'
The copy at LVA-F has a reference to a ms. index as by the 'Revd Walt. Chamberlain'; *Aubin* 320 lists it as by 'Rev. —— Chamberlayne'. The copy at O has a ms. note 'by the Revd Doct Towers', possibly John Towers, prebendary of St. Patrick's, Dublin. The conflict has not been resolved.
L(11631.e.52),LVA-F,O,DA; CtY,MH.

P549 — 'A poem; occasion'd by reading Shaftsbury's Characteristicks. Referr'd to the consideration of the author of a book, intitled, The scheme of literal prophesy consider'd, &c. Dedicated to the bishop of Lichfield and Coventry. [*London*] *Sold by J. Roberts.* Price 6*d*.' (*MC* Oct 1727)
The author of *The scheme of literal prophecy* was Anthony Collins; it is related to works by Edward Chandler, the bishop of Lichfield and Coventry.

— A poem, occasion'd by the birth-day of his most sacred majesty, 1716. *See* Nevil, Henry.

P550 — A poem occasion'd by the city of Dublin's repairing the statue of William the IIId. of ever glorious and immortal memory. Humbly inscrib'd to the right honourable the lord-mayor and the city of Dublin. *Dublin, printed for M. Gunne, [1702/14.]*
½°: 2 sides, 1 column.
'Whilst Troy's defensive arms Minerva crown'd'
Cf. *A poem on the late King William... occasioned by the defacing and breaking some part of his statue, 1710.*
NjP.

A **poem** occasion'd by the death

P551 — 'A poem occasion'd by the death of Charles Talbot, lord high chancellor of Great Britain. [*London*] *Printed for C. Corbet.* Price 1*s*.' (*LM* Feb 1737) Possibly the title is generalized.

P552 — A poem occasioned by the death of Mr. Dent, who was lately murder'd in Covent-garden. Addressed to his friends. [*London,* 1709.] (7 April, Luttrell)
½°: 1 side, 1 column.
'Cleansing th'Augean stable help'd to raise'
John Dent was a constable who met his death executing the laws against profaneness and immorality.
L(C.121.g.9/152, Luttrell).

P553 — A poem occasioned by the death of Mr. John Pryer, late minister of the gospel, who departed this life, Nov. 4th, 1740. in the 40th year of his age. [*London?* 1740.]
1°: 1 side, 3 columns.
Mourning borders.
'John Pryer's dead; dead! oh the cutting sound!'
LDW,O.

P554 — A poem, occasioned by the death of the persons unfortunately killed and wounded in the Grass-market of Edinburgh, April 14. 1736. after the execution of Andrew Wilson. [*Edinburgh,* 1736.]
½°: 1 side, 1 column.
'Shall innocence by fatal rashness bleed'
The beginning of the Porteous riots.
EP.

P555 — A poem occasioned by the funeral of the glorious and invincible, John duke of Marlborough. *Dublin, printed by James Carson, 1722.*
½°: 1 side, 2 columns.
'Whence this sad pomp? the mighty cause declare'
Possibly a poem of London origin; it is quoted, as previously incorrectly published, in Thomas Lediard, *The life of John, duke of Marlborough* (1736) III. 429–32.
L(C.121.g.8/20).

P556 — [variant title, adds:] By R.S.
On the other side of the MH copy, *A new ballad occasion'd by the Pretenders declaration,* 1722.
MH.

P557 — A poem, occasioned by the hangings in the castle of Dublin, in which the story of Phaeton is express'd. [*Dublin?* 1701?]
½°: *1–2*, 1 column.
Teerink 829; Williams 1072.
'Not asking, nor expecting ought'
Crum N349. Reprinted as by Swift by successive editors, following Malone, but Williams regards the attribution as 'little more than a guess'. The date of 1701 rests on the assumption of Swift's authorship when he was at Dublin Castle in that year; the subject matter is very generalized. C dates it as *c.* 1730.
C(2),Rothschild.

A **poem** occasion'd by the late thanksgiving

[P558 = G10·5] — A poem occasion'd by the late thanksgiving, 1707. *See* Gardiner, *Mrs.* E.

P559 — A poem occasion'd by the lord mayor's reducing the price of coals, &c. Written by a fellow-sufferer in the hardships of the times, and humbly inscrib'd to his lordship. *Dublin, printed in the year* 1729.
½°: 1 side, 1 column.
'Go on O worthy prætor, nor refuse'
DT.

P560 — A poem occasioned by the present war with Spain. *London, printed for M. Steen*, 1740. (*GM, LM* Jan)
2°: A^2 B^2 C^1; *1–3* 4–9 *10 blk*. 9 err.
  288 copies were sold as lot 28 of the quire stock in the trade sale of Meshach Steene, 11 May 1742 (cat. at O-JJ), to Waller for 10s. 6d.
'War, horrid war, his brazen throat extends'
O; CLU-C,CSmH.

P561 — A poem occasion'd by the rise and fall of South Sea stock... By J.B. gent. *London printed, and sold by Samuel Chapman, & John Williams*, 1720. (*DP* 8 Nov)
8°: π^1 A–C^4 D^1; *i–ii, 1–3* 4–26. π1 hft.
'While the amazed world, admiring, sees'
L(164.n.21, Luttrell, Nov),OW(−π1).

P562 — A poem of condolance on the loss of Sir Cloudesley Shovel... Humbly inscribed to the officers of her majesty's navy. *London printed, and are to be sold by J. Philips*, 1707. (*DC* 31 Oct)
2°: A^2; *i, 1–3*.
'Dilate your breasts, brave souls, and scorn to weep'
MH(Luttrell, 6 Nov).

— A poem of Hugo Grotius on the holy sacrament, 1732. *See* Lauder, William.

P563 — A poem on a lady's bed. [*Dublin*] *Printed by J. Gowan*, 1726.
½°: 1 side, 1 column.
'As when the business of the day is done'
NN.

P564 — A poem on Captain F-rr--r's travelling in the highlands of Scotland in winter. [*Dublin*, 172–?]
½°: 1 side, 1 column.
'O'er Calydonia's ruder alps'
  A satire on Captain Forrester, a beau.
CtY.

P565 — A poem on Dr C——d, and the three rival sisters... *Dublin, printed in the year* 1730.
12°: A^4; *1–5* 6–8.
'Love, like a tyrant with superior sway'
LVA-F.

P566 — A poem on Dr. Taylor. Addressed to the ladies, or Celia, by a young gentleman, who heard the doctor's lecture to the ladies in woman's habit. [*Edinburgh*, 1744.]
½°: *1–2*, 1 column.

A **poem** on Dr. Taylor

'Madam, you're right, the q——'s a knowing man'
  John Taylor the oculist gave lectures for ladies in Edinburgh in 1744; see *SM* (1744) 295.
L(1865.c.8/147),AdU.

— A poem on her sacred majesty Q. Anne, 1703. *See* Symson, David.

— A poem on his grace the Duke of Marlborough's return from his German expedition, 1705. *See* Trotter, Catharine.

P567 — A poem on his grace the D. of Or---d. [*London?* 1714/15?]
½°: 1 side, 1 column.
'Sweet charming muses, teach me how to raise'
  In praise of James Butler, duke of Ormonde, hoping for his reconciliation with George I.
LLP.

P568 — 'A poem on his royal highness the Duke of Cumberland. [*London*] *Sold by S. Birt*. Price 6d.' (*LEP* 10 Sept 1748)
  'Written when a congress was propos'd to be held at Aix-la-Chapelle, to treat of a general peace', *LEP*.

P569 — A poem on his royal highness the Prince of Wales's birth-day. October the 30th, 1722. To A.S. esq; [*Dublin?* 1722.]
½°: 1 side, 1 column.
'All sing our monarch's praise, nor must his son'
  Probably by the author of P638.
C.

P570 — A poem, on Miss Bellamy. *Dublin, printed in the year* 1748.
8°: A^4; *1–3* 4–8.
'While beauty claims the love-resounding shell'
  The author wants to take her away to Leixlip.
O,DA.

P571 — A poem on Mr. Paul. [*London*, 1716.]
slip: 1 side, 1 column.
'The man that fell by faction's strife'
  In praise of William Paul the Jacobite, executed 13 July 1716.
O(2).

P572 — A poem on Mr. Sheridan and Mr. Barry. *Dublin, printed by Kinneir & Long*, 1746.
8°: A^4; *1–2* 3–8.
'Come from your garrets Grubstreet bards'
  On Thomas Sheridan and Spranger Barry, the actors.
DA.

P573 — A poem on Mrs. M——t A——s. By a young gentleman. [*Dublin*] *Printed in the year* 1726.
½°: 1 side, 1 column.
'Love like a tyrant whom no laws constrain'
CtY,NN.

P574 — 'A poem on our war in Flanders dedicated to the Prince of Wales. [*London*] *Cooper, Dod*. Price 3d.' (*BM,GM* Feb 1747)

A **poem** on Prince Charles

— A poem on Prince Charles, [1745.] *See* A poem on the prince, [1745?]

P575 — [dh] A poem on Prince Charles's victory at Gladsmuir. [*Edinburgh*, 1745.]
8°: A²; 1–4.
'Hail happy Scotland! Bless the long'd for day'
A Jacobite poem.
AdU.

— A poem on Prince Eugene, 1712. *See* Cobb, Samuel.

— A poem on regeneration, 1746. *See* Dowie, Thomas.

P576 — A poem on self-denial and resignation, written by a young lady. Address'd to the prisoners and their friends. [*Edinburgh*, 1716.]
½°: 1 side, 1 column.
'When passions sleep, and every care's at rest'
L(C.115.i.3/24),E(ms. date 1716); *Harding*.

— A poem on the anniversary of his majesty's birthday, 1718. *See* Nevil, Henry.

— A poem on the anniversary of the birth-day of his majesty King George, 1719. *See* Nevil, Henry.

P577 — A poem on the anniversary of the birth-day of his majesty King George. Humbly inscrib'd to his majesty. By an officer in the army. *London, printed for J. Wilcox; sold by T. Warner*, 1717. (*DC* 30 May)
2°: *A*¹ B–C² *D*¹; *i–ii, 1* 2–9 *10 blk.* 9 err.
A1 and D1 have been seen to be conjugate. The date of the O copy has been altered in ink to 1718.
'I that e'erwhile, from lonely cottage sprung'
The epithet suggests the possibility of an attribution to John Thornycroft.
L(11631.k.5/3),O.

P578 — A poem on the approaching coronation. [*Dublin*] *Printed by J. Gowan*, 1727.
½°: 1 side, 1 column.
'Behold! at length the joyful days return'
DT.

P579 — 'A poem on the approaching nuptials of Anne, princess royal of Great Britain, with his highness William, prince of Orange. [*London*] *Printed for J. Wilford*. Price 6d.' (*DC* 11 March 1734)
Possibly a generalized title.

P580 — A poem on the arrival of his majesty King George. *London, printed for S. Popping; sold by the booksellers of London & Westminster*, 1714. (1 Oct, Luttrell)
4°: A⁴ B²; 1–4 5–12.
'Now night retires, and, glorious, breaks the day'
L(164.n.2, Luttrell).

P581 — A poem on the arrival of his royal highness Prince Frederick. *London printed, and sold by J. Roberts*, 1728. (*MChr* 23 Dec)
2°: A–C²; *i–iv, 1* 2–8.
Below imprint, 'Price one shilling'; watermark, circular snake (cf. *Heawood* 3786–92).

A **poem** on the arrival of his royal highness

'From royal tombs, we change the awful scene'
IU.

P582 — [fine paper]
No price on title; watermark, fleur-de-lys.
CtY.

P583 — — *London printed and reprinted in Dublin* [*by A. Rhames*], 1728.
8°: A⁴; *1–2* 3–8.
O,C,DA(3).

P584 — A poem on the arrival of the king. Address'd to his majesty. *London, printed by W. Wilkins; sold by J. Morphew*, 1714. (21 Sept, Luttrell)
4°: *A*² B–C²; *1–3* 4–11 *12.* 12 advt.
Listed in *MC* Sept.
'While we to Anna's urn the tribute bring'
Possibly by Theophilus Dorrington; p. 12 advertises books written by him and published by different booksellers.
L(163.m.54, Luttrell; C.118.c.2/1),DT; OCU.

— A poem on the arrival of the right honourable William earl Cowper, 1730. *See* Boyd, Elizabeth.

P585 — A poem on the art of printing. [*Dublin*, 1728.] (8 Aug?)
¼°: 1 side, 2 columns.
Printed on a quarter-sheet of fine large paper, probably royal. In column 2, 'Verses added to the former by another hand'. Ms. note in the L copy, '⟨riding⟩ the franchises, in the street upon the frame drawn along by 6 horses, on Thursday 8 Augst 1728'.
'Hail sacred art! thou gift of heaven, design'd'
Added verses: 'Say, Cadmus, by what ray divine inspir'd'
Crum H97. This first poem may well be that said to have been written on this occasion by Constantia Grierson. The added poem is by James Sterling, reprinted in his *Poetical works*, 1734.
L(1890.e.5/59); CSmH,MH.

P586 — — [*Dublin*] *Printed before the Company of Stationers*, August the eighth, 1728.
½°: 1 side, 2 columns.
Engravings of Fust and Coster at head, copied from those used by Moxon. Text printed in red. Reproduced in *Proceedings of the Royal Irish Academy* 27 (1909) 401–3.
DA(title cropt).

P587 — — which was wrought at the printing machine carry'd before the corporarion [!] of stationers, cutlers and painters, on Thursday the 8th of this instant August 1728, the day appointed for riding the franchises of this city. [*Dublin*, 1728.]
½°: 1 side, 2 columns.
L(C.121.g.8/169).

P588 — A poem, on the associate synods procedure, against the defenders of the religious clause of some burgess oaths... *Printed for, and sold by Walter Smith chapman in Balfron*, [1749.]

A **poem** on the associate synods procedure

8⁰: *A⁴* B⁴; *1–3* 4–16. 16 err.
Dated at end, 9 Dec 1749.
'When covenanted reformation'
L(11631.a.51).

P589 — A poem on the banks of Forth. [*Edinburgh?*]
Printed in the year 1737.
8⁰: *A⁴*; *1* 2–8.
'Near the silver sands wher Forth doth pass'
L(1078.k.26/12).

P590 — A poem on the battle of Dettingen. Inscrib'd to
the king. *London, sold by A. Dodd,* 1743. (*DA* 1
Aug)
2⁰: *A⁴*; *1–4* 5–7 *8 blk.* A1 hft.
'Inscrib'd to thee, and to eternal fame'
L(1850.c.10/67, –A1); *Lewis Walpole Library*
(Tom's Coffee House, 3 Aug).

— A poem on the birth-day of her royal highness
the Princess of Wales, 1717. *See* Nevil, Henry.

— A poem on the birth-day of his most sacred
majesty King George, 1717. *See* Nevil, Henry.

P591 — ⟨A⟩ poem on the birth-day of his most sacred
majesty King George, being the 28th of May.
Dublin, printed by Thomas Hume, 1725.
½⁰: 1 side, 1 column.
A rewriting of 'Pan a pastoral' from Alexander
Pennecuik (d.1730), *Britannia triumphans,*
1718.
'Hail happy day! on which pleas'd heaven doth
smile'
L(C.121.g.8/50).

P592 — A poem on the birth-day of his royal highness
the Prince of Wales. *London, printed for A. Dodd;
sold at the pamphlet shops by the Royal-Exchange,*
1741. (*DP* 20 Jan)
2⁰: *A²* B–D²; *1–2* 3–16.
Pp. 10–16 contain specimens of a translation
of Cicero.
'In times when dire Erinnys only reigns'
O.

— A poem on the blessed nativity, 25th December,
1717, [1717.] *See* Colme, John.

P593 — A poem on the charitable society of journeymen
shoemakers of the city of Dublin and liberties
thereof. Who walk in procession this day being the
25th of Oct. 1734. [*Dublin*] *Printed by Christopher
Dickson, a member of the society,* [1734.]
½⁰: 1 side, 2 columns.
'Thou tuneful choir whose province 'tis to sing'
CtY.

P594 — A poem on the civil-wars of the Old-Baily;
occasion'd by a late dispute, between the sheriffs
and students of the law. *London printed, and are to
be sold by J. Baker,* 1713. (10 Jan, Luttrell)
2⁰: *A²* B¹ (A2 as 'A3'); *1–2* 3–6.
'A nobler theme my feeble muse invites'
L(162.n.61),O; CSmH(Luttrell),MH(uncut, ms.
date 10 Jan).

A **poem** on the coronation

P595 — 'A poem on the coronation of his majesty King
George II. and his royal consort, Oct. 11. 1727.
Written by a free-mason. [*London*] *Printed for J.
Pemberton.* Price 6*d*.' (*MC* Nov 1727)

P596 — A poem on the dean of St. Patrick's birth-day,
Nov. 30th being St. Andrew's-day. [*Dublin*]
Printed by J. Gowan, 1726.
½⁰: 1 side, 2 columns.
Teerink 1214.
'Between the hours of twelve and one'
In praise of Swift.
Rothschild.

P597 — A poem on the death of his highness the Duke
of Gloucester. Written by a gentleman in New-
England. *London, printed by J. Darby; sold by B.
Lintot,* 1701.
2⁰: *A²*; *1–2* 3–4.
'The publisher to the reader' on p. 2 explains
the delay involved, and records that this is the
author's 'first essay in poetry'.
'With the sad tidings of the day opprest'
MH.

P598 — A poem on the death of Mr. Peter Molineux.
London, printed in the year 1712.
½⁰: *1–2*, 1 column.
'Mourn all who do the use of numbers know'
Molineux was an arithmetician and writing
master.
MH.

P599 — A poem on the death of Mr. Rich Shales, of
Hatfield Broadoak in Essex... The second edition.
Corrected. *London, printed for R. Walker, & E.
Nutt,* [1729?] (*MChr* 17 April 1729)
2⁰: (3 ll); *1–2* 3–6.
MChr gives a specific date for this second
edition; the ms. date in the OCU copy may
refer to Mr. Shales's death, or to the untraced
first edition.
'Long thy return thy Hatfield wish'd in vain'
OCU(ms. date 1728).

— A poem on the death of our most gracious
sovereign Queen Anne, 1715. *See* Smalridge,
George.

P600 — A poem on the death of Robert Keck, esq; of
the Inner-Temple, who died at Paris, Sept. 16.
1719. By a friend... *London, printed in the year*
1720.
2⁰: *A²* B²; *i–ii, 1* 2–6.
'I heedless bless'd the flatt'ring wind and tide'
L(643.m.12/31).

P601 — A poem on the death of the Countess of Sunder-
land. By F.C. gent. *London printed, and sold by J.
Roberts,* 1716. (28 April, Luttrell)
2⁰: *A²* B–C²; *i–iv, 1–8.* A1 hft.
Listed in *MC* April 1716.
'Be present to my aid, ye heav'nly quire!'
L(11602.i.26/5); DFo(Luttrell).

A **poem** on the death

P602 — A poem on the death of the honourable the Lady Elizabeth Hastings. *London, printed for John Hildyard, bookseller, in York; sold by J. & P. Knapton, T. Longman, & A. Dodd,* 1740. (*GM* April)
2°: *A*² B²; *1-2* 3-8.
'Away with tears, the cypress, and the yew'
CtY,ICN,MH.

[**P603** = H85] — A poem on the death of the king of Sweden, 1719. *See* Harris, Timothy.

P604 — A poem on the death of the late Duke of Devonshire. *London, printed for J. Roberts,* 1729. (*MChr* 21 June)
2°: *A*² B¹; *1-3* 4-5 *6 blk.*
'Great Devonshire is dead!---How dire the sound?'
IU.

P605 — A poem on the death of the reverend Mr. Mordecai Andrews... *London, printed for George Keith,* [1750.] (*BM,GM* March)
Copy acquired by O, 1971.

P606 — A poem on the death of the right honourable William earl Cowper. *London, printed for J. Roberts,* 1724.
2°: *A*² B²; *1-2* 3-8.
'Shall poets drive a mercenary trade'
L(1347.m.43),C; CSmH,IU.

P607 — A poem on the death of Tho. Cholmondeley of Vale Royal esquire. Who dyed February 26. 170½. *London, printed in rhe* [!] *year* 1702.
2°: *A*¹ B² C² D¹; *i-ii,* 1-10.
''Twould seem a little strange, I must confess'
O,OW.

P608 — 'A poem on the defeat of the French army at the river Schelde, and raising the siege of Brussels. [*London*] *Printed for Wm. Harvey, and are to be sold by him and John Morphew.*' (*DC* 11 Dec 1708)
Probably a folio edition, of which the following is a piracy.
'A muse in arms inspire my willing pen'
On the battle of Oudenard.

P609 — A poem on the defeat of the French army at the river Scheld, and raising the siege of Brussels, by his grace the Duke of Marlborough and Prince Eugene. *London, printed by J. Read,* [1708?]
8°: A⁴; *1-2* 3-8.
Presumably a piracy.
O-JJ.

P610 — A poem on the Drapiers birth-day. Being November the 30th. *Dublin, printed by C.C.* [*Cornelius Carter*], 1725.
½°: 1 side, 1 column.
'O born by heaven's providential care'
In praise of Swift.
DT; CtY.

P611 — A poem on the drawing room: together with three epilogues: one as design'd to have been spoke

A **poem** on the drawing room

by Mrs Cross to a comedy, call'd, The way of the world. The second, as spoke by her to the Provok'd wife, March the 22d 17$\frac{15}{16}$, for her own benefit. And the third, as spoke by Mrs Thurmond to the Pilgrim, April the 24th 1716. By T. B. gent. *London, printed for James Roberts,* 1716. (19 May, Luttrell)
8°: *A*² B–C⁴ D²; *i–iv,* *1* 2-20. A1 hft.
'As rash hot youths, impatient of delay'
'In various forms, we ladies of the stage'
'Stripp'd now of ev'ry vain, fantastick air'
'Some fourscore years ago, we plainly see'
CtY suggests Thomas Baker the dramatist as author, but there is no apparent evidence to support the attribution except Baker's stage connections.
L(164.1.30, Luttrell),O(−A1); CtY.

P612 — A poem on the earthquake. By the author of Age in distress. [*London,* 1750.]
¼°: 2 sides, 1 column.
Copies seen are bound with *Age in distress,* 1750, and possibly were issued with it.
'By various means we lose the vital breath'
O; OCU.

P613 — [dh] A poem on the election of a knight of the shire of Edinburgh. [*Edinburgh,* 1744.]
4°: *A*²; *1* 2-4.
On p. 3, 'Old England's Te deum' by Sir Charles Hanbury Williams, not in verse.
'The day is come, and freedom is betrayed'
The poem is signed 'Scoticus'. On the re-election of Sir Charles Gilmour in Jan 1744.
L(11647.e.1/120; 11630.b.8/9),E(2),GM.

P614 — A poem on the erecting a groom-porter's-house adjoining to the chapple, in the castle of Dublin. [*Dublin,* 1725?]
slip: 1 side, 1 column.
Williams 1124.
'A purgatory is a jest'
Included in Nichols's edition of Swift's *Works* but rejected by subsequent editors, including Williams.
L(1890.e.5/65; C.121.g.8/137).

P615 — A poem on the glorious atchievements of Admiral Vernon in the Spanish West-Indies. *London, printed for T. Cooper,* 1740. (*GM, LM* Dec)
2°: *A*² B–D²; *1-3* 4-16.
'What! shall one man the nation's genius raise'
L(1870.d.1/83); CLU-C,CSmH,MH,NN-B.

— 'A poem on the glorious peace of Utrecht, inscribed in the year 1713 to the Earl of Oxford. L., 1713.'
Listed by *Morgan* P476 in this form, but the title suggests that it was published subsequently; it has not been traced, and I suspect that it may be quoted in a generalized form from a later authority.

A poem on the great Mr. Law

P616 — [dh] A poem on the great Mr. Law. Done by a lady. [*Edinburgh*, 1719/20.]
2°: *A*²; *1–3 4 blk.*
   Watermark: Dutch lion.
'Could the great Lewis from death's shades advance'
   On John Law (1671–1729).
E(3).

P617 — [*idem*] [dh] A poem on the truly great Mr. Law. Done by a lady. [*Edinburgh*, 1719/20.]
2°: *A*²; *1–3 4 blk.*
   No watermark; textual changes throughout, probably reset.
E.

— A poem on the happy reconciliation of his most excellent majesty, 1720. *See* Jacob, Giles.

P618 — A poem on the happy return of his most sacred majesty King George. Humbly inscrib'd to his royal highness the Prince. *London, printed for W. Chetwood, & W. Boreham*, 1719. (Nov, Luttrell)
½°: 2 sides, 1 column.
'Britons rejoice! your Io-pæans sing!'
MH(Luttrell).

P619 — A poem on the happy union between England and Scotland. Perfected May the first, 1707... By C.N. *Dublin, printed* 1707.
4°: *A*¹ B–F² *G*¹; *1–2 3–23 24 blk.*
'Britannia's bards, who rival Greece and Rome'
LDW,O(cropt),E(cropt),DT(cropt).

— A poem on the high-church champion Dr. Sacheverell, [1710?] *See* Ellis, William.

P620 — 'A poem on the intended nuptials of Anne princess royal of Great Britain with his highness Frederick, prince of Orange. [*London*] *Printed for J. Jackson, & J. Wilford.* Price 6d.' (*DJ* 9 Nov 1733)
   Possibly the same work as *A poem on the nuptials*... (P632) printed at Dublin in 1733; what is clearly this poem was listed with that form of the title in *LM* Nov 1733.

P621 — A poem on the journeymen sheermen, and dyers. *Dublin, printed by M. Wilmot*, 1727.
½°: 1 side, 2 columns.
'Behold the ruddy morn springs from afar'
   Similar in style to the verses by Robert Ashton and Henry Nelson.
L(1890.e.5/66),DT.

P622 — A poem on the late glorious success of his grace the Duke of Ormond at Vigo. By the authors of Britannia's loss. *London printed, and are to be sold by J. Nutt*, 1702. (19 Nov, Luttrell)
2°: *A*² B–C²; *i–ii, 1–9 10 blk.*
   The Luttrell copy is in the collection of R. D. Horn; listed in *WL* Nov.
'Near Albion's clifts a pleasant vale there lies'
O; CtY,TxU(2).

P623 — A poem on the late King William, (of glorious and immortal memory) occasioned by the defacing and breaking some part of his statue erected on

A poem on the late King William

College-green. *Dublin, printed by S. Powell*, Monday, July 10, 1710.
½°: 2 sides, 1 column.
'Ill fate, thou wandering, unseen, shapeless foe'
DK.

P624 — A poem on the late rebellion, giving an account of the rise and progress thereof, from the Young Pretender's first landing in the Isle of Skie, to his defeat at the battle near Culloden. By Philonactos Rossendaliensis. *Manchester, printed by R. Whitworth, for the author*, [1746?]
8°: A–C⁴; *i–iii iv–v, 6–24.*
'Thou heav'nly muse, who kind assistance lent'
E,EP,MP; CtY.

P625 — A poem on the late violent storm, the 26th of November. 1703. By S.W. gent. *London, printed for B. Bragg*, 1703.
½°: *A*¹; 2 sides, 1 column.
'O great Jehovah! Lord of heav'n and earth'
MH.

P626 — A poem on the marriage of the right honourable lord Viscount Mountjoy. [*Dublin*, 1734.]
½°: 1 side, 1 column.
'Since you're resolv'd this dangerous state to try'
   William Stewart, third viscount, married Eleanor FitzGerald on 10 Jan 1734.
CtY.

P627 — A poem on the memorable fall of Chloe's p--s pot, attempted in blank verse. *London printed, and sold by A. Baldwin, & W. Chetwood*, 1713. (*SR* 2 Feb)
2°: *A*¹ B²; *i–ii, 1–4.*
   Teerink 878; *Bond* 34; *Rothschild* 2207. Entered in *SR* by Richard Palmer to W. Mears; deposit copies at L,LSC,O,EU,SaU. Advertised in *PB* 3 Feb.
'Of wasteful havock, and destructive fate'
   There are no grounds for an attribution to Swift; not discussed in *Williams*. Printed as by John Philips in *The poetical calendar* (2d ed, 1764) IV. 107, and ascribed to him in *CBEL*; but he died in 1709. Discussed by *Thomas* xxviii–ix.
L(643.1.26/11; Ashley 5064),O,EU,DN,LdU-B+; MH(lacks A1).

P628 — A poem on the modern Arians. By a gentleman of Oxford. *London, printed for the author, in the year* 1721–2.
4°: *π*¹ A–B² *C*¹; *1–2 3–12.*
'As at the moon each dog will bark, when bright'
ICU.

P629 — A poem on the much to be lamented death of Captain Chiesly and Lieutenant Moody, with a particular account how they were slain. [*Edinburgh*, 171–?]
½°: 1 side, 1 column.
'O! now my muse dramatick stand aside'
E.

A **poem** on the nativity

P630 — A poem on the nativity of our blessed saviour. *London, printed by T. Howlatt in Silver Street Bloomsbury, for the author,* 1719.
2°: *A*¹ B–E²; *i–ii,* 1–16.
'The sun full half his daily course had run'
L(1484.m.5); CLU,DFo,MH.

P631 — A poem on the new lord chancellor. [*Dublin,* 1725.] (22 July?)
½°: 1 side, 1 column.
'To thee great West our isle this tribute send'
Richard West was appointed lord chancellor of Ireland 29 May, and landed there at the end of July.
L(C.121.g.8/141, ms. date 22 July).

— A poem on the new method of treating physic, 1726. *See* Bowden, Samuel.

P632 — A poem on the nuptials of Anne, princess-royal of Great-Britain, with his highness Frederick, prince of Orange. *Dublin, printed by S. Powell, for Edward Exshaw,* 1733.
8°: *A*⁴; *1–2* 3–8.
'The gods, one day, to heaven's imperial court'
L(11774.aaa.19).

P633 — A poem on the peace, sung by the children of the charity schools in Bath, on the 7th of July, 1713. Being the thanksgiving day for the peace. [*Bath,* 1713.]
½°: 1 side, 2 columns.
'While some their spoils from battle bring'
Compare *An hymn to be sung by the charity-children at Bath,* [1713.]
BaP.

P634 — [dh] A poem on the Pretender's birth-day. [col] *Dublin, printed by Thomas Hume,* 1718.
4°: *A*²; *1* 2–4.
'What means this secret, yet insulting pride'
Against the Pretender.
L(C.38.f.39),DN(cropt).

P635 — — [col] *Dublin, printed by Thomas Hume,* 1726.
4°: *A*²; *1* 2–4.
DT.

P636 — A poem on the prince. [1745?]
½°: 1 side, 1 column.
Probably printed in Scotland.
'Aloud I heard the voice of fame'
In praise of the Young Pretender.
LdU-B.

P637 — [*idem*] A poem on Prince Charles. [*Edinburgh?* 1745.]
¼°: 1 side, 1 column.
On the other side, *Prince Charles his welcome to Scotland,* [1745]; originally conjugate with *A poem upon the 29th of May.*
L(C.38.g.14/10),E; CSmH.

P638 — A poem on the Princess of Wales's birth-day. Being the first day of March, 1722–3. [*Dublin?* 1723.]
½°: 1 side, 1 column.

A **poem** on the Princess of Wales

'My tow'ring muse, by his great actions fir'd'
Probably by the author of *A poem on his royal highness the Prince of Wales's birth-day,* [1722.]
NN.

P639 — A poem on the proceedings, at the annual meeting of the journeymen taylors, on the 25th of July 1726. [*Dublin,* 1726.]
½°: 1 side, 2 columns.
On the other side of the DT copy, ⟨*An elegy*⟩ *on the lamented death of the right hon. William Cadogan,* 1726.
'Come you taylors from your houses'
The Rothschild copy has a contemporary ms. note 'By John Dunkan of T.C.D.' but no such person is known in their records. Cf. *Heltskelter,* [1726/27?] ascribed in the same hand to 'John Duncan'. Possibly Jacob Duncan (matriculated 1725) or William Dunkin (B.A. 1729) is intended.
DT(title cropt),Rothschild.

P639.5 — A poem on the queen's birth-day. *London,* 1710.
½°.
(*Christie's* 1 July 1965, lot 84.)

P640 — A poem on the race of Leith, October, twenty second. To the praise of the Highland ladie. [*Edinburgh,* 171–?]
½°: 1 side, 1 column.
'I hear a horse race lately run'
E.

— A poem on the recovery of the honble. Mrs. Eliz. Courtenay, 1743–. *See* Kennicott, Benjamin.

P641 — A poem on the Royal Company of Scottish Archers. [*Edinburgh,* 1713/–.]
½°: 1 side, 1 column.
This translation was also printed with the original Latin in *A list of the Royal Company,* 1715.
'Can any be with envy so possest'
A translation of Thomas Kincaid's *In Regiam Sagittariorum Scotorum cohortem,* [1713?]. Another English version which uses most of the same rhymes and is perhaps an earlier state by the same author was published in two editions of that work (K43–4).
E; CSmH.

— A poem on the South-Sea, 1720. *See* Ramsay, Allan [Wealth].

P642 — A poem on the South-Sea: or, the jobbers fate. *Edinburgh printed, and sold by John Moncur,* 1723.
8°: *A*⁴; *1* 2–8.
'When travelling up and down my lane'
GM(uncut).

— A poem on the taylor craft, 1733. *See* Morgan, John.

P643 — [dh] A poem on the taking St. Mary's. [*London,* 170–.]

A **poem** on the taking St. Mary's

8⁰: A⁴; *1* 2–8.
> Woodcut ornament at the head of p. 1. A copy at MB is bound with pamphlets of *c.*1710; though it was printed in *Letters from the living to the living*, 1703, this edition may be some years later than that.

'When Lewis strove as all agree'
> A witty poem on the raping of the nuns at Puerto de Santa Maria opposite Cadiz, captured by the English 20 Aug 1702.

DT; DFo,MB,OCU.

P644 — — [*London, Henry Hills,* 1709/10.]
8⁰: A⁴; *1* 2–8.
> Type flowers at the head of p. 1. This edition was certainly published by Hills; reissued with other remaindered Hills poems in *A collection of the best English poetry,* 1717 (*Case* 294). The edition advertised by Hills in 1709 may be this or the preceding. Reprinted with Lord Hervey's *Monimia to Philocles,* 1728.

L(C.124.b.7/39),LVA-F,WcC; CtY,*ICN*,MH.

P645 — [*idem*] The amorous soldiers; or, a battle with the nuns. A poem on the taking of St. Mary's by the English. *London, printed for A. More, near St. Paul's,* 1741.
8⁰: A⁴; *1*–2 3–8.
LdU-B.

— A poem on the 30th of January 1716, [1716.] *See* Colme, John.

P646 — A poem on the thirtieth of October, being his royal highness George prince of Wales's birth day. By R.P. [*Dublin,* 1726?]
½⁰: 1 side, 1 column.
> The DT copy is bound with half-sheets of 1726.

'Welcome to us great prince, welcome I say'
DT.

— 'A poem on the triumphs of the coronation, with a copper cut of the glorious procession. [*London*] *Sold by J. Marshal, & R. Minors.* Price 6d.' (*MC* Oct 1727)
> Possibly a generalized title; no copy has been traced.

— A poem on the truly great Mr. Law, [1719/20.] *See* A poem on the great Mr. Law, [1719/20.]

— A poem on the war in the West-Indies under Admiral Vernon, [1742.] *See* Martin, Thomas.

P647 — A poam [!] on Tom Pun----bi, on occasion of his late death, and in vindication of some verses written, entitled Sheridan's resurrection. *Dublin, printed* 1722.
½⁰: 1 side, 1 column.
'Alas! ye bards the elegy's you've made'
> A reply to a mock *Elegy on the deplorable death of Mr. Thomas Sheridan,* [1722], and a lost poem on his resurrection, satirizing him. Cf. *Tom Pun-sibi's resurrection disprov'd,* [1722.]

CSmH,CtY.

A **poem,** sacred to the birth-day

[P648 = O90]

P649 — A poem, sacred to the birth-day of his most august majesty, George, king of Great Britain. *London, printed for the author,* 1727.
8⁰: A⁸; *1*–4 5–15 *16 blk.*
> A1 not seen, possibly half-title.

'While crouds of nobles fill the royal dome'
IU(–A1).

P650 — A poem sacred to the immortal memory of her most excellent majesty, Anne, late queen of Great-Britain... Written by a lady of quality. *London printed, and sold by A. Dodd,* 1715.
8⁰: B–C⁴; *1*–3 4–15 *16 blk.*
'What mean these horrid visions of the night?'
> *Crum* W597: 'To the immortal memory...'

L(11646.aa.27).

P651 — A poem sacred to the memory of her late majesty, Caroline, queen consort of Great-Britain. By a gentleman of Exeter. *London, printed for S. Birt, & E. Score, bookseller in Exeter,* 1737. (*GM, LM* Dec)
2⁰: A–C²; *1*–2 3–12.
'Let solemn grief in every face appear'
L(1959),OA; OCU.

P652 — — The second edition. *London, printed for S. Birt, & E. Score, bookseller in Exeter,* 1737.
2⁰: A–C²; *1*–2 3–12.
L(603.k.28/3),O,LdU-B; NjP,TxU(uncut).

P653 — 'A poem sacred to the memory of that most worthy patriot the hon. Dan. Poulteney, esq; By the author of the Duel. [*London*] *Sold at the pamphlet shops.* Price 6d.' (*MChr* Sept 1731)
> The author also wrote *A collection of poems,* 1731.

P654 — A poem sacred to the memory of the honourable the Lady Aber——ny. Humbly inscrib'd to the quality of Great-Britain, &c. *Westminster, printed by A. Campbell; sold by Mrs. Nutt, Mrs. Dodd, and the pamphlet-sellers in London & Westminster,* 1729. (*MChr* 11 Dec)
2⁰: *A²* < B¹ (B1 as 'B2'); *1*–3 4–6.
'Ye muses all, and pitying virgins come'
> Printed in Sir Charles Hanbury Williams, *Odes,* 1775, as 'On the death of Lady Abergavenny: by a lady'; clearly not by Williams.

L(163.m.60; G.559/2, uncut),O,OW,LdU-B; ICN,MH,TxU.

P655 — A poem, sacred to the memory of the Lady Harriot Boyle. *Dublin, printed by Halhed Garland,* 1747.
4⁰: *A⁴* < B–C⁴; *1*–4 5–24.
'If yet, oh gen'rous Boyle! the tide of grief'
L(11631.f.2, 'The gift of the author'),DK.

P656 — A poem sacred to the memory of the reverend and learned Isaac Watts, D.D. who departed this life November 25th, 1748, in the 75th year of his age. *London, printed for J. Oswald & W. Dilly, J. Buckland, & E. Gardner,* [1749.] (*BM* April)

A **poem** sacred to the memory

8°: *A*⁴ B⁴ C²; *i–iii* iv, *5* 6–20.
The dedication is dated 11 March 1748–9.
'Upon the mossy grave I sat reclin'd'
L(T.1697/5),LDW,O; CSmH.

P657 — A poem, sacred to the memory of the reverend, Mr. James Smith, principal of the university of Edinburgh... *Edinburgh, printed by T. & W. Ruddimans, 1736.*
8°: *A*⁴; *1–3* 4–7 *8 blk.*
'Whilst streaming tears thro' half a nation flow'
The O copy has the name 'Hewgh Blair' written between title and imprint; possibly an ownership inscription, but also possibly indicating Blair's authorship.
O,E,*LdU-B.*

P658 — A poem, shewing a plain and short way to be happy. Being some remarks on a paper lately publish'd, call'd, The true intelligence. Written on the occasion of a dream... Done by a venerable person to recommend the said paper for the general good of all. [*London*] *Sold by J. Morphew,* [1708.] (24 Jan, Luttrell)
½°: 1 side, 2 columns.
'We are of new false prophets warn'd'
In praise of *The true intelligence*, an unidentified religious tract advertised below the imprint.
L(C.20.f.2/302); MH(Luttrell).

—A poem (the fox and monkey), [1740.] *See* Gibbons, Thomas.

P659 — A poem to a widow, upon a fly geting [!] into her eye. [*Dublin*] *Printed by J. Gowan, 1726.*
½°: 1 side, 1 column.
'That pretty little gaudy fly'
Reprinted in *Poems occasionally written by the late John Winstanley...interspers'd with many others,* II (1751).
L(C.121.g.8/149),DT; NN.

P660 — A poem to D-------- S---------. *Dublin, printed in the year 1724–5.*
½°: 1 side, 1 column.
Teerink 1207. From the type the printer appears to be John Harding.
'As joyful sailors when the tempest's o'er'
In praise of Swift's *Drapier's Letters.*
L(C.121.g.8/28),DG.

P661 — A poem to Francis Bindon, esq; on a picture of his grace...Dr Hugh Boulter...set up in the work-house near Dublin... *London, printed in the year 1742.* (*GM, LM* Dec)
8°: *A*² B–C⁴ D²; *1–5* 6–22 *23–24 blk.* A1 hft.
'Your pencil, Bindon, like the poet's quill'
CSmH(uncut),CtY(−A1),OCU(−D2).

P662 — A poem to her grace the Dutchess of Marlborough. Occasion'd by the late glorious victory obtain'd by his grace the Duke of Marlborough, over the French and Bavarians at Hochstet. Written by a lady. *London, printed for Abel Roper, 1704.* (16 Sept, Luttrell)

A **poem** to her grace

2°: A–C²; *i–ii*, *1–9* '01'.
The Luttrell copy is in the possession of R. D. Horn; advertised in *PM* 21 Sept.
'Pardon me, madam, if in humble strain'
MR-C; NN,*OCU.*

[P663 = T336]

— A poem to his grace the Duke of Marlborough, on the glorious successes of the last campaign, 1705. *See* Geree, John.

— A poem to the author of the Scots answer to the Brittish vision, 1706. *See* Defoe, Daniel (D150).

— A poem to the Earl of Godolophin, 1710. *See* Garth, *Sir* Samuel.

— A poem to the king, 1717. *See* Crabb, John.

P664 — 'A poem to the king. [*London*] *Printed for M. Cooper, A. Dodd, & G. Woodfall.* Price 6*d.*' (*LEP* 2 April 1747)

— A poem to the memory of his late majesty William the third, 1702. *See* Stennett, Joseph.

— A poem to the memory of Mr. Congreve, 1729. *See* Mallet, David.

P665 — A poem to the memory of Mr. Hugh Murray-Kynnynmound of Melgum and Kynnynmound, advocate. *Edinburgh, printed by T. W. & T. Ruddimans, 1742.*
4°: A–C² D¹; *1–2* 3–14.
'Sad turn! when these, whom noblest passions join'd'
GM.

—A poem to the memory of Mr. Nathanael Taylor, 1702. *See* Stennett, Joseph.

P666 — A poem to the memory of Mrs. Oldfield. Inscrib'd to the honourable Brigadier Churchill. *London, printed for J. Roberts, 1730.* (*MChr* Oct)
4°: *A*² B–C²; *i–ii*, *1* 2–9 *10 blk.*
'Oldfield's no more! ------ And can the muse forbear'
Ascribed to Richard Savage in Chetwood's *History of the stage* (1749) 204, which is followed by most authorities despite Johnson's explicit statement that Savage 'did not celebrate her in elegies'. *MChr*, presumably following a newspaper advertisement, lists it as 'By a gentleman commoner of Oxford', which certainly excludes Savage.
ICN,ICU.

P667 —— *London: printed, and Dublin re-printed, and sold by George Faulkner, 1731.*
8°: *A*⁴; *1–3* 4–8. 2 advt.
L(1961),DA.

— A poem to the memory of the famous Archibald Pitcairn, [1713.] *See* Ramsay, Allan.

— A poem to the memory of the incomparable Mr. Philips, 1710. *See* Welsted, Leonard.

P668 — ⟨A⟩ poem to the memory of the late honourable Colonel Henry Piercy. [*Dublin, 1725/30.*]

A **poem** to the memory of the late

½°: 1 side, 1 column.
The copy at L forms part of a collection of
Dublin half-sheets of 1725/30.
'The victor death, who will no mortal spare'
L(C.121.g.8/114).

P669 — A poem to the memory of the late reverend Mr.
Joseph Stennett. *London, printed by John Darby,
and are to be sold by Andrew Bell, & John Baker,*
1713. (28 Sept?)
2°: *A*² B–C²; *1–2* 3–12.
Horizontal chain-lines, with a foolscap watermark on its side. An unidentified advertisement dated 28 Sept is in *Haslewood.*
'Is there but one so grateful as to tell'
LDW,ICU.

— A poem to the memory of the right reverend
father in god, Dr. Thomas Rattray, 1743. *See*
Drummond, Thomas.

P670 — A poem to the memory of Thomas late marquiss
of Wharton, lord privy-seal. *London, printed for
Jacob Tonson,* 1716. (*SR* 12 April)
2°: A–C² D¹; *i–iv,* 1–10.
Deposit copies at L,LSC,O,EU,AdU; listed
in *MC* April. The Luttrell copy, dated 18
April, is in the collection of J. R. B. Brett-
Smith.
'Vain are these pomps, thy funeral rites to grace'
L(643.m.13/12),LVA-F,O,EU,AdU+; CtY,
OCU,PPL,TxU(2).

P671 — A poem, to the most ilustrious [!] hero George
Lewis…now by the laws human and divine, and
by the voice of the people, king of Great Britain,
France and Ireland. [*Edinburgh,* 1714.]
½°: 1 side, 1 column.
'Hail mighty Brunsuick, in whose glorious veins'
E.

P672 — A poem to the pious memory of the most
reverend father in god, Alexander, &c. and late lord
bishop of Edinburgh. [*Edinburgh*] *Printed in the
year* 1720.
2°: A–C²; *1–2* 3–11 *12 blk.*
'No common sorrow swells our brimful eyes'
E.

P673 — [dh] A poem to the praise of his majesty King
George, or his farewell. [*London?* 1716?]
8°: A⁴; 1–8.
Imprint suggested by the MB catalogue.
'Farewel great George, not only great but good'
MB.

P674 — A poem to the praise of the Voluntier company.
[*Edinburgh,* 1715?]
½°: 1 side, 1 column.
'Wellcome October, wellcome twenty day'
E.

— A poem, to the victory at Glenshiel in Scotland,
1719. *See* A hymn to the victory in Scotland,
[1719.]

A **poem** to the whole people

P675 — A poem to the whole people of Ireland, relating
to M.B. drapier. By A.R. hosier. [*Dublin*] *Printed
by Elizabeth Sadlier* [!], 1726.
½°: 1 side, 2 columns.
'Once on a time, when the ague was brief'
DT(cropt).

P676 — ⟨A⟩ poem upon a lady's being offered a purse
by one of the late directors of ⟨the⟩ South Sea
company. By a lady. *Edinburgh, printed by William
Adams junior, an. dom.* 1719 [1720?].
½°: 1 side, 1 column.
'Curse on thy bribes! shall female love be stain'd'
E.

— A poem upon his majesties accession, 1714. *See*
Sewell, George.

— A poem, upon his sacred majesty King George,
1715. *See* Comberbach, Roger, *junior.*

[**P677** = D44·5] — A poem upon our unhappy loss of
Sir Cloudesly Shovel, 1708. *See* Darby, Charles.

P678 — A poem upon R—r a lady's spaniel. [*Dublin,*
1725.] (June?)
½°: 1 side, 2 columns.
Bond 88; *Teerink* 652; *Williams* 1124. Some
copies (L,CSmH,TxU) have italic capital *L*s
in place of roman in the last two lines. Reprinted in *Mist's weekly journal,* 3 July 1725.
'Happiest of the spaniel-race'
Early ms. attribution to Swift in the L copy,
and reprinted as his in *Whartoniana,* 1727; not
accepted by Williams. A parody of Ambrose
Philips's *To the honourable Miss Carteret,* 1725.
L(C.121.g.8/123); CSmH,PU,TxU(2).

P679 — A poem upon the bright, auspicious day of his
majesty's coronation. *London printed, and are to be
sold by S. Popping,* 1714. (*FP* 6 Nov)
4°: π¹ *A*² B² C¹; *i–ii,* 1–2 3–9 *10 blk.* π1 *hft.*
'Welcome, thrice welcome most illustrious day'
IU.

P680 — [dh] A poem upon the happy arrival of his most
serene majesty King George. [col] *Dublin, printed
by Elizabeth Dickson,* 1714.
4°: A⁴; 1–8.
'When sable fame great Anna's death declar'd'
C.

— A poem upon the late glorious successes, 1707.
See Conduitt, John.

— A poem upon the law, 1707. *See* Hawke,
Edward.

P681 — A poem upon the most potent prince James
dnke [!] of Hamilton; anent the union, of Great
Britain. [*Edinburgh,* 1707.] (Feb)
½°: 1 side, 2 columns.
Ms. note in one E copy 'Edinburgh printed
Febr. 1707', and under the title 'To the tune
of the Merchants daughter of Bristol town'. In
the other copy the two middle letters of 'duke'
have failed to print.

A **poem** upon the most potent prince

> 'All you brave noble men, give ear'
> E(2).

P682 — A poem upon the most serene and potent Prince William of glorious memory, late of Great-Britain, France and Ireland, king. [*Edinburgh*, 1702.]
½°: 1 side, 2 columns.
'Long had Britannia, plung'd in vice and ease'
E.

P683 — A poem upon the news of his excellency the Lord Carteret's return for Ireland. [*Dublin*] *Printed in the year* 1727.
½°: 1 side, 1 column.
'The vast extent of empire is too large'
L(C.121.g.8/162),DT,Rothschild.

P684 — ⟨A⟩ poem upon the noble company of young archers, belonging to the High-school, Edinburgh. To the honourable Mr. John Maitland, brother-german to the right honourable, the Earl of Lauderdale, one of the brigadeers of the Royal company of young archers. [*Edinburgh*, 171–?]
½°: 1 side, 1 column.
'The heav'n doth now put forth her smiling flag'
> Signed 'G.H.'
E.

P685 — A poem upon the tragedy of Thorn. *Edinburgh, printed in the year* 1725.
8°: A⁸; *1–3 4–13 14–16 blk.*
'All tender-hearted protestants'
> The publisher's introduction signed 'I.P.', i.e. John Paton?
TxU.

P686 — A poem upon the 29th of May, the day of King Charles II. his birth and happy restoration. [*Edinburgh?* 1745.]
¼°: 1 side, 1 column.
> On the other side, *June 10th, 1745. Being the anniversary...*; originally conjugate with *Prince Charles his welcome.*
'No voice more soft than thunder can express'
> A Jacobite poem.
L(C.38.g.14/11),E; CSmH.

P687 — A poem upon the union. [*Edinburgh*, 1706.] (19 Dec?)
½°: 1 side, 1 column.
> Variant readings 'independence' and 'independency' in the last line but two.
'Before the thistle with the roses twin'd'
> An attack on the union.
E(2, 1 ms. date 19 Dec 1706).

P688 Poema. Poema in Richardum Sadlerum, collegii Dublinensis proto pincernam. *Dublinii, typis Jacobi Hoey,* 1731.
8°: A⁴ B⁴; *1–4 5–15 16 blk.* A1 hft.
'Musæ, noster amor, Lilliputides hoc mihi carmen'
DG(2),DK(2).

Poemata. Poemata selecta, [1709?] *See* Pitcairne, Archibald.

Poems

Poems. Poems. [motto: Amicis candidisque legenda.] [*London?* 1745/–.]
8°: pp. 16.   L,O; CtY.
> A copy at L has a ms. note 'written in the years 1743, 1744, & 1745', as well as ms. corrections to the text. It includes two prologues for 'young gentlemen'; the author was presumably a schoolmaster.

— Poems; amorous, moral, and divine, 1718–. *See* Hinchliffe, William.

— Poems and odes, after the manner of Anacreon, 1746. *See* Brecknock, Timothy.

— Poems by a relation of Sir John Denham. *London, printed for Jacob Ilive,* 1742. (*GM* June)
8°: pp. 42.   L,O.
> The L copy is in a presentation binding inscribed to 'the Lady Finch', signed 'M. Winchilsea'; there are copious ms. corrections. The author has not been identified.

— Poems divine, moral, and philosophical. To which is annex'd, an appendix of divine and philosophical subjects... *Gloucester, printed* [*by Robert Raikes*] *for the author,* 1746.
8°: pp. 55.   O,GlP.
> The preface is signed 'M.C.'

— Poems miscellaneous, mostly divine. [*London*] *Sold by A. Baldwin.* Price 6d. (*TC* Michaelmas 1708/Trinity 1709)

— Poems occasion'd by reading the Travels of Captain Lemuel Gulliver, 1727. *See* Several copies of verses, 1727.

— Poems of love and gallantry. Written in the Marshalsea and Newgate, by several of the prisoners taken at Preston. *London, printed by J. Grantham,* 1716.
8°: pp. 24.   L,O; CtY,MH.
> *Case* 289(b); reprints of poems by William Tunstall and Charles Wogan. Enlarged as Tunstall's *Ballads and some other occasional poems,* 1716.

— Poems on divers subjects... By a young gentleman. *London, printed in the year* 1718. (*PB* 4 Feb)
8°: pp. 47.   L.

P689 — Poems on her sacred majestie. [*Edinburgh,* 1702?]
½°: 2 sides.
> On side 1, 'An accrostick and anagram, Anne Stewart anag. new treaswre'; on side 2, 'An accrostick anacreontique, on her majesty'.
'Anne the new treasure of our Albion'
E.

— Poems on several occasions. *London, printed in the year* 1714.
8°: pp. 1–24 29–32.   LdU-B (ms. corrections).

— Poems on several occasions, 1721, 1723. *See* Smedley, Jonathan.

— Poems on several occasions, [1724?] *See* Haywood, Eliza.

— Poems on several occasions. *London, printed by S.G.; sold by J. Roberts, 1727.*
8°: pp. 23.   CSmH.

— Poems on several occasions, 1728. *See* Ray, T.

— Poems on several occasions, 1740. *See* Dixon, Sarah.

— Poems on several occasions, 1743. *See* Gibbons, Thomas.

— Poems on several occasions. *Dublin, printed by S. Powell for the author, 1748.*
8°: pp. 102.   L,C; CSmH,DFo.
By a female author. Most copies include a list of subscribers.

— Poems on several occasions, 1748–. *See* Hamilton, William, *of Bangour.*

— Poems on several occasions. By a gentleman. *London, printed for W. Mears, 1733.* (*LM* July)
8°: pp. 87.   O.

— Poems on several occasions, by a lady, 1726. *See* Thomas, Elizabeth.

— Poems on several occasions. By a young gentleman. *London, printed for W. Mears, 1724.* (*MC* April)
12°: pp. 57.   O.
The copy seen is printed on a heavy paper, but with no watermark, and priced at 1*s.* 6*d.* as opposed to 1*s.* in *MC.* There is a frontispiece.

— Poems on several occasions. By H.G. *London, printed for M. Cooper, 1748.* (*GM* July)
8°: pp. 29.   L,O.

— Poems on several occasions. By the author of the poem on the Cambridge ladies. *Norwich, printed by William Chase, 1736.*
8°: pp. viii, 40.   O,C; DFo.
The same author wrote *A collection of poems. By the author of a poem on the Cambridge ladies,* 1733, and see P535 for the poem on the Cambridge ladies. For a ms. version of 'Stirbitch fair', the main poem in the collection, see G. C. Moore Smith in the *Library* IV. 3 (1922) 35–48, and cf. *Bond* 154.

— Poems on several occasions: containing I. Fancy and reason... By a lady. *London, sold by J. Roberts, 1728.*
8°: pp. 38.   LdU-B; CLU-C.
Despite the title, this appears to be by several authors.

— Poems on several occasions: never before printed. *Shrewsbury, printed by Tho. Durston, for the author, 1727.*
8°: pp. 88.   L,AN.
The copy at AN is in a contemporary morocco binding.

— Poems on several occasions. Never before printed. *London, printed for J. Penn, and sold by the booksellers of London & Westminster, 1733.*
12°: pp. 84.   IU.
A very faint pencil note in the copy at IU perhaps reads 'by Edward ⟨Ho⟩skins'.

— Poems on several occasions. Published by subscription. *Manchester, printed for the author, by R. Whitworth, 1733.*
8°: pp. *1*–36 51–138.   L,MP; NNC,OCU.
A note in a copy seen recorded that C. W. Sutton decided this was the production of a Staffordshire parson.

— Poems on several occasions. To which is added, A letter to Mr. Law. By a student of Oxford, 1720. *See* Amhurst, Nicholas.

— Poems on several occasions, together with a pastoral. By Mrs. S. F., [1703.] *See* Egerton, Sarah Fyge.

— Poems on several occasions: together with some odes in imitation of Mr. Cowley's stile and manner. *London, printed for Luke Stokoe, & George Harris, 1703.*
8°: pp. 120.   L,O; CtY.

— [reissue] Poems on variety of subjects; together with the character of a trooper, and some odes, on several occasions. *London, printed for J. Woodward, 1710.* (*SR* 30 June)
L,O.
Cancel preliminaries include 'The character of a trooper'. Entered in *SR* to George Harris as 'new' copy; deposit copies at L,LSC,O,C,E, EU,AdU.

— Poems on several occasions. Together with the apparition: a merry tale. *London, printed for J. Duick, 1722.* (*PB* 23 Jan)
2°: pp. 20.   IU,TxU.

— Poems on several occasions: viz. The garden..., 1719. *See* Lux, William.

— Poems on several occasions. With Anne Boleyn to King Henry VIII. An epistle. *London, printed for John Clarke, 1724.* (*MC* Aug/Sept)
12°: pp. 84.   L; CtY.
The copy at CtY appears to have A5 and G6 cancels, though they have not been identified in the copy at L.

— Poems on several occasions... Written by a lady, 1727. *See* Thomas, Elizabeth.

— 'Poems on several occasions. Written by a soldier. [*London*] *Sold by W. Graves. Price 3d.*' (*DC* 20 Oct 1718)

— Poems on several occasions. Written by a young lady, 1747. *See* Ramsay, Charlotte.

— Poems on several subjects, addrest to the Lancashire ladies. *Printed in the year 1737.*
8°: pp. 48.   MP.

— Poems on several subjects. By a land-waiter in the port of Poole, 1741. *See* Price, Henry.

Poems on several subjects

— Poems on several subjects. Formerly written by an under-graduate at the university. *London, printed for T. Caldecott; sold by J. Roberts*, 1714. (*MC* Nov)
8⁰: pp. 38.   L,O; CtY,IU.
    Listed in *MC* as 'Poems on several subjects, in imitation of some odes of Horace'. A copy at GM has a pencil note in the contents leaf of the volume attributing this collection to Robert Samber; other works by him are bound in the volume, but this note appears to be in a later hand, and the attribution needs confirmation.

P690 — Poems on the death of her late majesty Queen Mary of blessed memory. *London printed, and sold by H. Hills*, 1710.
8⁰: A⁸; *1–2* 3–15 *16*. 16 advt.
    Two poems; 'A pindarick poem, &c.' and 'A pindarick ode, &c.' Reissued with other remaindered Hills poems in *A collection of the best English poetry*, 1717 (*Case* 294), and included here to complete the list of his piracies.
'Desolate Albion, mourn thy cruel fate'
'She's dead, alas! beyond recov'ry dead'
L(11632.de.26; C.124.b.7/53),LVA-F,O,E; *ICN,IU*,InU,MH+.

P691 — Poems on the death of the right honourable Henrietta Hamilton, countess of Orrery, who died at Cork in Ireland, August the twenty second, 1732. Inscrib'd to the...Earl of Orrery. [1732.]
4⁰: A–C² D¹; *1–2* 3–18.
    Two poems, probably by the same author. The copies seen are on fine paper, watermarked with fleur-de-lys on shield; possibly all were for presentation.
'While the full breast swells with unutter'd woe'
'It must be so – on terms so slight'
DA,DN; CSmH.

— Poems on the four last things: viz. I. Death. II. Judgment. III. Hell. IV. Heaven. *London printed, and sold by A. Betsworth*, 1706. (*TC* Hilary).
8⁰: pp. 122.   CU.
    A collection of short pieces. The copyright formed part of lot 52 in the trade sale of Benjamin Sprint, 11 April 1738 (cat. at O-JJ).

— [variant imprint:] *London printed, and sold by Thomas Ballard*, 1706.
             L.

— Poems on variety of subjects; together with the character of a trooper, 1710. *See* Poems on several occasions: together with some odes, 1703.

—Poems, paraphrases and translations, 1736. *See* Crackanthorp, John.

— Poems upon particular occasions, 1738. *See* Carter, Elizabeth.

— Poems upon several occasions, chiefly publick; and on some important subjects. By a gentleman, 1745. *See* Hanway, William.

Poems upon several occasions

— Poems upon several occasions. With the British enchanters. A dramatick poem. Lately revis'd and enlarg'd by the author. *Dublin, S. Powell*, 1732.
8⁰.   (Pickering & Chatto cat. 261/4689.)

— Poems upon various occasions. Written for the entertainment of the author, 1737. *See* Shenstone, William.

— Poems written upon several occasions, and to several persons. To which are added, three essays, I. On pride. II. Contempt. III. Solitude. By E.W. *London, printed for J. Baker*, 1711.
8⁰: pp. 128.   L.

Poet. The poet, 1739. *See* Hiffernan, Paul.

P692 — The poet and the muse. *London printed, and sold by R. Amy, Mrs. Dodd, and by the booksellers of London & Westminster*, 1737. (*GM, LM* June)
2⁰: π¹ A² B–D² E¹; *i–ii*, *1–3* 4–16 *17–18*. π1 hft; 16 err; E1 advt.
    π1 and E1 are conjugate, sometimes bound as π²; π1 has imprint 'Dublin: printed, and re-printed in London...'.
'Rouse, drowsy muse, how you provoke me'
L(1961),LVA-D,*LVA-F*,O(uncut, −π1); CSmH −π1, E1),CtY(−π1, E1),MH(−π1, E1),NjP, TxU(uncut, −π1, E1)+.

— The poet banter'd, 1702. *See* The art of love, 1701.

P693 — The poet's address to his majesty King William. Occasion'd by the insolence of the French king, in proclaiming the sham Prince of Wales, king of England... *London, printed for A. Baldwin*, 1702.
4⁰: A–B⁴; *1–2* 3–15 *16 blk*.
'What! are the muses dumb, when 'tis agreed'
CSmH,CtY,InU.

P694 — [dh] The poet's address to the ensuing parliament. [col] [*London*] Printed in the year 1702.
4⁰: A⁴; *1–7* 8. 8 advt.
'Whereas the nation has address'd'
L(11631.bb.69).

P695 — The poet's dream. *Dublin, printed by S. Powell, for Joseph Cotter*, 1747.
4⁰: A² B–C²; *1–3* 4–12.
'Dublin, that breeds the poet, breeds the dun'
C(cropt); MH.

P696 — A poet's impartial reply, to a poem, entitled the Impartial: an address without flattery. Being a poet's free thoughts, on the situation of our public affairs, an' 1744. *London, printed for M. Cooper*, 1744. (10 May?)
2⁰: A⁴; *1–4* 5–8.
'Awake, my muse; to the Impartial sing'
    Dedication signed 'Antiquæ'. A reply to Aaron Hill's poem.
L(162.n.49); OCU(uncut, ms. date 10 May).

P697 — The poet's paradise: or the art of contentment. *London printed, and sold by John Morphew*, 1708. (5 June, Luttrell)

The **poet's** paradise

2°: A^2 B–C^2 (B1 as 'C'); *1–2* 3–12.

    The verse is imbedded in prose, but the overall intention appears to be poetic, even if no first line can be quoted. The Luttrell copy is recorded in Pickering & Chatto cat. 247/13398.
IU,OCU.

— The poet's prayer, 1734. *See* Dunkin, William.

— The poet's ramble after riches, 1701–. *See* Ward, Edward.

Poetae. Poetæ rusticantis literatum otium, 1713. *See* Boureau Deslandes, André François.

Poetaster. The poetaster: containing, original poems, and songs. Never before printed. *Dublin, printed by S. Powell, for Richard Norris*, 1726.
8°: pp. 27.   L,C; CtY.

    The preface records 'many of 'em writ at Sea; some in the East, and some in the West-Indies...' Cf. Bezaleel Morrice for a similar naval poet.

Poetess. The poetess, a satyr, [1706.] *See* Gould, Robert.

P698 Poetic. 'A poetic epistle, addressed to Sir George Vandeput. [*London*] *Needham*. Price 6d.' (*GM* Dec 1749)

    Listed in *LM* Dec as 'An epistle to Sir George Vandeput'.

— Poetic essays, on nature, men, and morals, 1750. *See* Thompson, Isaac.

— The poetick sermon, [1724.] *See* Ramsay, Allan.

Poetical. A poetical abridgement both in Latin and English, 1749. *See* King, William, *principal of St Mary Hall*.

P699 — A poetical and critical essay on Homer, and Lucretius. By the author of the Essay on the soul of man. *London printed, and sold by J. Robinson*, 1744. (*GM, LM* April)
2°: A^2 B–C^2; *1–3* 4–11 *12 blk.*

    Two poems: 'A bold censure on Homer' and 'Against the general assertion of Lucretius...'.
'When Homer's gods together fight'
'Tell me, Lucretius! was it chance that made'
O; TxHR.

P700 — 'A poetical description of the life, pranks, and practice of that noted actress Melissa and her confidant Grimaria. [*London*] *Printed for S. Slow*. Price 6d.' (*GM, LM* Nov 1733)

    GM has an apparent misprint, 'Valissa' for 'Melissa'.

[P701 = M116] Poetical. A poetical epistle, 1741. *See* Marsh, Charles.

P702 — A poetical epistle to Miss C––h––y: occasioned by her appearing in the character of Iphigenia, at the late jubilee ball at Ranelagh: with a digression

A **poetical** epistle to Miss C – – h – – y

on the d––ke, and the celebrated Mrs. C––b––r. *London, printed for Tom Andrew, jun.*, 1749. (*GM, LM* Aug)
4°: A^1 B–C^2 D^1; *3–5* 6–14.
'Curse on the times! for satire reigns o'er all'

    On Elizabeth Chudleigh (later accepted as countess of Bristol) and her flirtation with George II.

L(1962).

P703 — A poetical essay on physick. Inscrib'd to Dr. Pellet, president of the College of Physicians and F.R.S. *London, printed for T. Cooper*, [1740.] (*GM, LM* Jan)
2°: A^2 B–D^2; *1–5* 6–16.
'The muse an exile from her once lov'd lyre'

    To Thomas Pellett.
L(643.m.15/8),O,*DrU-U*; CtY,MH,OCU,TxU.

P704 — A poetical essay on the equal distribution of happiness among mankind. In which several eminent characters are touch'd. Address'd to his royal highness the Duke of Cumberland. *London, printed for M. Cooper*, [1746.] (26 Jan)
2°: A^2 B–C^2 D^1; *1–4* 5–14.

    Listed in *GM* Jan.
'To take a superficial view of things'

    Possibly by James Fortescue, whose poems on *Nature*, 1747, 1748, are closely related in subject, and who also addressed himself to Cumberland; it is not, however, recorded in *Rawlinson*.

L(1962, Tom's Coffee House, 26 Jan),O,C; DFo.

— A poetical essay on the Te Deum, twelve select psalms, with arguments prefix'd, and the third chapter of Habakkuk. *London, printed for John Clark & Richard Hett*, 1728. (*MChr* 6 Feb)
4°: pp. viii, 48.   O.

P705 — A poetical essay on vulgar praise and hate; in which is contain'd, the character of a modern patriot. *London, printed for T. Cooper*, 1733. (*GSJ* 8 June)
4°: A^4 B^4; *1–5* 6–15 *16 blk.* A1 hft.
'He who attempts to sing the glorious deeds'

    A satire on William Pulteney.

MR.

— A poetical paraphrase on part of the book of Job, 1726–. *See* Thompson, William, *fellow of Trinity College, Dublin*.

— A poetical paraphrase on the universal hymn of praise to the creator, 1727. *See* Foxton, Thomas.

— Poetical recreations, 1705. *See* Spooner, Lawrence.

P706 — A poetical representation of the passion of our blessed saviour. By a young gentleman of Oxford. *London, printed for C. Corbett*, [1747.] (*GM* April)
2°: A^2 < B^1; *1–3* 4–6.
'No more, O muse! delight in trifling strains'

    Entered on an otherwise blank slip in *Rawlinson*

A **poetical** representation

to 'Moore, of Exeter college'; no appropriate person of this name has been traced.
L(11631.k.7/2).

P707 — A poetical thought on the creation. *London, printed for James Brackstone*, 1743. (*GM, LM* Nov)
2°: *A² B–E²; 1–3 4–20.*
'See a young muse extend her callow wing'
IU.

P708 Poets. 'The poets address. [*London*] *Printed, and sold by Messieurs Smith & Moore. Price 6d.*' (*DJ* 28 March 1727)
Possibly related to [Joseph Mitchell] *The Totness address, versified*, first published 16 March 1727.

P709 — The poets petitions; an essay on modern wit. Inscribed...to the poetical ladies of the three kingdoms. *Dublin printed, and sold by the flying stationers*, 1747.
8°: *A⁴; 1–3 4–8.*
'To Sol's bright temple paved with gold'
O(2),DN.

P710 Politic. The politic j-------ge, or, he would be a colonel. A ballad. (To the tune of a Cobler there was, &c.) *London, printed for J. Trott*, 1745. (*GM* Dec)
2°: *A¹ B–C²; i–ii, 1 2–7 8 blk.*
Horizontal chain-lines.
'I'll tell you a story of lawyers right stout'
On the lawyer volunteers for the forty-five.
AdU; CtY,ICN.

Political. Political justice, 1736. *See* Nugent, Robert, *earl Nugent*.

P711 — Political madness. A new ballad. Humbly inscrib'd to the sage politicians of Grubstreet... *London, printed for T. Buck, in the Strand*, 1739.
2°: (3 ll); *1–3 4–6.*
'A convention of late was concluded at Pardo'
CtY.

P712 — The political padlock, and the English key, a fable. Translated from the Italian of Father M-----r S----ini... With explanatory notes. *London, printed for W. Webb*, 1742. (*GM* Aug)
8°: *π¹[=D4?] A–C⁴ D⁴(–D4); i–ii, 1–2 3–29 30 blk. π1 hft.*
'The Samian sage, who first maintain'd'
The English key is naval victory.
L(11631.d.47),O(–π1); *ICN,OCU*.

P713 — [column 1] The political pair; or, the state gossip. A song. To the tune of, Gossip Joan. [column 2] A knave at the bottom. Or, the dealer sure of a trump. To the tune of, Hey boys up go we. *London, printed by J. Wright behind the Cchange* [!], [1727/–.]
½°: 1 side, 2 columns.
'Good morrow gossip Will'
'Quoth Hal to Will the other day'

Two satires against Bolingbroke and Pulteney. For another poem with the same title as the second, see Laurence Price.
O.

— Political poems. Viz. I. Protestant popery... Written by a student at Oxford, 1719. *See* Amhurst, Nicholas.

P714 — A political touch of the times. [*London?* 1739.] *slip:* 1 side, 1 column.
Percival XLVI. Woodcut at head.
'How happy a state did Britain once enjoy'
Against Walpole's unwillingness to fight with Spain.
C.

P715 Politics. The politicks and patriots of Jamaica. A poem. *London printed, and sold by T. Warner*, 1718.
8°: *A–B⁴ C²; 1–3 4–19 20. 20 advt.*
'Mad actions to describe, lo! I prepare'
On p. 13 the author refers to the A. Wagstaffe who signed *A true account of the late pyracies of Jamaica*, 1716; this is advertised as by the same author on p. 20. In *A true account* 'Wagstaffe' describes himself as secretary and clerk of the council, a post held from 1714–1729 by William Congreve. It seems clear that Wagstaffe is a pseudonym, and there is no reason to credit the poem to Congreve. A satire on the struggle between the governor, Archibald Hamilton, and the assembly, which led to the removal of Congreve's deputy, Samuel Page; apparently in support of Hamilton.
L(T.1541/2); *RPJCB*.

P716 Polly. Polly Peachum on fire, the Beggars opera blown up, and Capt. Macheath entangled in his bazzle-strings... Wherein also are contained, I. Polly's description of a terrible hairy monster... II. A dialogue between Polly and Punch... *London, printed for A. Moore; sold by the booksellers of London & Westminster*, 1728. (*MChr* 20 June)
8°: *π¹ A–C⁴ D⁴(–D1); i–ii, 1–29 30 blk.*
'Polly's description...' is a reprint of [Edward Ward] *The riddle. Or, a paradoxical description...*; the dialogue is in prose.
'When Poll first mounted on the stage'
MH.

P717 Polsted, Ezekiel. Cambria triumphans, or, a panegyrick upon Wales. A pindarick poem. The 2d edition. *London printed, and sold by J. Mayos, & J. Nutt*, 1703 [1702]. (Dec)
4°: *π⁴ A–C⁴ (A1 as 'A2'); i–viii, 1–24. π1 hft.*
The first edition has not been identified; it may not have been separately published. There is a problem about the date of publication, since the 'Epistle to the reader' is dated 20 Dec 1702, while Luttrell dated his copy 9 Dec 1702.
'The nume'rous rhimers of the age'
L(161.m.22, Luttrell),*MR*.

Poltis

[P718 = M320·5] **Poltis.** Poltis, king of Thrace; or the peace-keeper, 1726. *See* Mitchell, Joseph.

P719 Polygamist. The polygamist: or, the lustful priest. Giving an account of one James Christie... With original letters that pass'd on both sides. Written by an Irish laureat. *London, printed for A. More,* [1741?] (*GM* April 1741)
8°: (frt+) A¹ B–D⁴ E⁴(–E1); *i–ii*, *1* 2–30.
> Both copies seen have a ms. date '1738' added; but these are probably later additions, based on the date of the legal proceedings.
'At a late Derby assizes came forth'
L(1078.1.14); Institute for Sex Research (lacks frt).

P720 Polymnia. Polymnia: or, the charms of musick. Being an ode, sacred to harmony. Occasion'd by Mr. Handel's oratorio, and the Harmonia sacra... By a gentleman of Cambridge. *London, printed for T. Game, & D. Gardner, 1733.* (*LM* April)
2°: A² B²; *i–iv*, *1–4*.
'Awake! awake! my silent, sleeping lyre'
> MH suggests a possible attribution to John Taylor on grounds of similarity to his *The music speech*, 1730.
MH(uncut).

P721 Polyphemus. Polyphemus's farewel: or, a long adieu to Ireland's eye. A poem. *Dublin, printed by E. Waters, 1714.*
½°: 1 side, 1 column.
'Whilst on the crowded beach the rabble stand'
> A satire on Charles Talbot, duke of Shrewsbury and lord lieutenant of Ireland, on his departure.
L(1890.e.5/140); MH.

[**Pomfret, John.**] Miscellany poems on several occasions. By the author of the Choice. *London, printed for John Place, 1702.*
8°: pp. 179. L,O; ICN,TxU.

— Miscellany poems... By Mr. Pomfret, deceas'd, author of the Choice. The second edition with additions. *London, printed for Edward Place, 1707.*
8°: pp. 186. L,O; CtY,MH.

— Poems on several occasions. By Mr. Pomfret, deceas'd... The third edition with additions. *London, printed for Edward Place, 1710.*
8°: pp. 186. L,LVA-D; CtY.

— Poems upon several occasions. By the late revd. Mr. Pomfret... The fourth edition, corrected. *London, printed for E. Curll, & W. Taylor, 1716.*
12°: pp. 148. L,O; KU.

—— The fifth edition, corrected. *London, printed for E. Curll, & J. Hooke, & W. Taylor, 1720.*
12°: pp. 4, 144. LVA-D,O; NjP.

—— The sixth edition, corrected. To which are added, his remains. *London, printed for A. Bettesworth, & W. Taylor, E. Curll, & J. Hooke, 1724.*

Pomfret, J. *Collections*

12°: pp. 132+vi, 17. LVA-D.
> The 'Remains' are described as 'second edition' on their title and bear Curll's imprint; he had previously published 'Reason' and 'Dies novissima' which make up the addition.

— [reissue] The sixth edition, corrected. With some account of his life and writings. To which are added, his remains. *London, printed for D. Brown, J. Walthoe, A. Bettesworth, & E. Taylor, & J. Hooke, 1724.*
12°: pp. 132+vi, 17. C; IU.
> Cancel title. In the trade sale of W. Taylor, 3 Feb 1726 (cat. at O-JJ), lot 64 consisting of the rights to 750 in 2000 copies was sold to Mears for £12.

—— To which are added, poems: by Mr. Tickell... *Dublin, printed by S. Powell, for George Risk, 1726.*
12°: pp. 144. L,DN; CtY,ICU.
> Tickell's poems occupy pp. 130–144.

—— The seventh edition, corrected... To which are added his remains. *London, printed for D. Brown, J. Walthoe, A. Bettesworth, W. Mears, & J. Hooke, 1727.*
12°: pp. 132+vi, 17. L,O; IU.
> Lot 11 of the trade sale of J. Hooke, 31 May 1731 (cat. at O-JJ), containing the rights to 375 copies in 2000 was sold to Birt for £13.5s.

—— The eighth edition, corrected... *London, printed for J. Walthoe, A. Bettesworth & C. Hitch, W. Mears, S. Birt, & D. Brown, 1731.*
12°: pp. xi, 132+vi, 17. L,O; CtY.
> Printed by Samuel Richardson (*Sale* 100).

—— The ninth edition, corrected... *London, printed for A. Bettesworth & C. Hitch, W. Mears, S. Birt, D. Brown, & F. Cogan, 1735.*
12°: pp. xii, 132+vi, 17. L,O.
> Lot 49 of a trade sale ascribed to 'Mr Astley & Conger' of 11 Nov 1735 (cat. at O-JJ), contained an eighth share, sold to Cox for £15. Subsequent sales offer at most a sixty-fourth share until Birt's sale of 5 Feb 1756.

—— The tenth edition, corrected... 'London, printed by Ed. Cook; sold by the booksellers in town & country, 1736.'
> A piracy; there are at least seven distinct editions with this title and imprint, of various origins; their relationship has not been determined but they probably span a period of at least twenty years.

—— The tenth edition, corrected... *London, printed for S. Birt, D. Brown, C. Hitch, J. Hodges, & F. Cogan, 1740.*
12°: pp. xii, 132+vi, 17. L,O.
> Entered in Strahan's ledger to Hitch under 16 June 1740, 3000 copies.

—— Poems on several occasions... 'London, printed by Ed. Cook; sold by the booksellers in town & country, 1746.'

Pomfret, J. *Collections*

12⁰: pp. 144.   L,C; ICN.
    A piracy, related to those of '1736'; the date is perhaps false.

—— [The eleventh edition... 1748.]
    An edition of Pomfret's poems is entered in Strahan's ledger to Charles Hitch under May 1748, 2000 copies. An eleventh edition of 1749, recorded at MWA, is possibly another piracy; there are also 'eleventh editions' of 1751, 1755.

P722 [—] The choice. A poem... By a person of quality. The fourth edition corrected. *London printed, and are to be sold by J. Nutt*, 1701. (*TC* Hilary)
    2⁰: *A*² B–C²; *i–ii, 1–2 3–9 10*. A1 hft; 10 advt.
        The first edition has imprint dated 1700, but is dated by Luttrell 1 Dec 1699 in the MH copy; second and third editions 1700.
    'If heav'n the grateful liberty wou'd give'
    L(1347.m.36),O(uncut); TxU.

P723 [—] The choice, or wish; a poem. Written by a person of quality. *Edinburgh, printed in the year* 1701.
    4⁰: *A*⁴; *1–3 4–8*.
        Monogram (probably of Matthias Symson) on title.
    L(11633.bbb.7),E,ES,GM(ms. date 7 Nov 1701); ICN.

P724 [—] — *Edinburgh, printed in the year* 1701.
    8⁰: *A*⁴ (A2, 3 as 'A, A2'); *1–3 4–8*.
        Thistle ornament on title; an inferior production to the preceding.
    E.

P725 [—] The choice. A poem. By a person of quality. *Norwich, reprinted by Fr. Burges*, 170½.
    2⁰: *A*¹ B–C² *D*¹; *i–ii, 1–8 9–10* blk.
        Title A1 and blank D1 have been seen to be conjugate.
    NwP(uncut); ICU(–D1).

P726 [—] [*idem*] [dh] The town despis'd; or, the pleasures of a country-life. Dedicated to the beaus against the next vacation. [col] *London, printed by H. Hills*, [170–.]
    4⁰: *A*²; *1–4*.
        A piracy; Hills and other chap-book printers subsequently reprinted the poem with *The pleasures of a single life*.
    NN.

P727 [—] The choice. A poem. By a person of quality. *Edinburgh, printed by James Watson, and sold at his shop*, 1709.
    4⁰: *A*⁴; *1–2 3–8*. 2 advt.
        The advertisement on p. 2 announces Watson's intention of publishing 16 poems by Pomfret to be bound together. Only the five listed as published have been seen, consisting of this and P732, P731, P737.
    E,EP.

Pomfret, J. The choice

P728 —— By the late reverend Mr. Pomfret. *Edinburgh printed, and sold by Robert Brown*, 1718.
    8⁰: *A*⁴; *1–2 3–8*.
    O.

P729 —— *Edinburgh printed, and sold by Robert Brown*, 1721.
    8⁰: *A*⁴; *1–2 3–8*.
    E.

P730 — Dies novisima [!]: or, the last epiphany. A pindarick ode, on Christ's second appearance to judge the world. *London, printed for E. Curll*, 1722 [1721]. (*DP* 4 Nov)
    8⁰: *A*⁴(–A4) B–C⁴; *[4] i–ii, 1–16*. A1 hft.
        Reissued without the preliminaries in *The altar of love*, 1727 (*Case* 340) and Addison's *The Christian poet*, 1728. The poem formed part of Pomfret's 'Remains' added to his collected poems in 1724.
    'Adieu, ye toyish reeds, that once cou'd please'
    LVA-D; TxU.

P731 [—] [dh] The fortunate complaint. A poem. By the author of the Choice. [col] *Edinburgh, printed by James Watson, and sold at his shop*, 1709.
    4⁰: *A*⁴; *1–8*.
        Part 3 of Watson's collection of Pomfret's poems.
    'As Strephon in a wither'd cyprus shade'
        Printed in Pomfret's *Miscellany poems*, 1702, but sometimes wrongly attributed to Thomas Hamilton, sixth earl of Haddington.
    E,EP; CtY,ICN.

P732 [—] Love triumphant over reason. A poem. By the author of the Choice. *Edinburgh, printed by James Watson; and sold at his shop*, 1709.
    4⁰: A–C⁴; *1–2 3–24*.
        Part 2 of Watson's collection of Pomfret's poems.
    'Tho' gloomy thoughts disturb'd my anxious breast'
        Printed in Pomfret's *Miscellany poems*, 1702, but sometimes wrongly attributed to Thomas Hamilton, sixth earl of Haddington.
    E(2),EP; CtY.

P733 [—] A prospect of death: a pindarique essay. Written by the right honourable the late Earl of Roscommon. *London, printed by J. Gardyner; sold by John Nutt*, 1704 [1703]. (16 Dec, Luttrell)
    2⁰: *A*² B–C²; *i–iv, 1–8*. iv advt.
        The Luttrell copy is recorded in Pickering & Chatto cat. 245/12197. Reprinted in F141.
    'Since we can dye but once, and after death'
        Wrongly ascribed to Roscommon; printed in Pomfret's *Miscellany poems*, 1702. The 1724 introduction by 'Philalethes' to his 'Remains' specifically refers to this misattribution.
    L(1347.m.26; 11632.i.7, lacks A²),O(uncut); CLU-C.

P734 [—] A prospect of death, a pindarick essay. *Printed for and sold by Mary Morris*, 1721.

Pomfret, J. A prospect of death

4⁰: *A⁴*; *1* 2–8.
> *Smith* II. 185 records this edition and says 'I cannot believe it to have been written by M. M'.

LF.

P735 [—] Quae rara, chara. A poem on Ponthea's [!] confinement. By the author of the Choice. *London, printed for Tho. Atkinson, 1707. (PM* 1 May)
8⁰: *A⁸*; *1–4* 5–15 *16*. A1 hft; 16 advt.
> 'Panthea' is correctly spelt on the half-title and elsewhere.

'As choicest oar in deepest caves is hid'
> This poem was not apparently collected in Pomfret's works, and though it is listed by *CBEL* as his, some confirmation would be welcome.

L(1481.aaa.2),CT,EU; NjP.

— Reason, a satire [first published 1 July 1700]. *In* Three poems viz. I. Reason, 1720.

P736 [—] Two love poems. I. Strephon's love to Delia. Justified; in a letter to Celadon. II. Strephon's address to Delia. By the author of the Choice. *London, printed for J. Place, and are to be sold by J. Nutt*, 1701. (19 July, Luttrell)
2⁰: *A¹* B–D²; *1–2* 3–14.
> Listed in *WL* July.

'All men have follies, which they blindly trace'
'As those, who hope hereafter heav'n to share'
> Reprinted in Pomfret's *Miscellany poems*, 1702.

O(Luttrell); TxU.

P737 [—] [*idem*] [dh] Strephon's love for Delia, justify'd: in an epistle to Celadon: and an epistle to Delia. By the author of the Choice. [col] *Edinburgh, printed by James Watson, and sold at his shop*, 1709.
4⁰: A⁴ B²; *1–12*.
> Part 4 of Watson's collection of Pomfret's poems. Sometimes wrongly attributed to Thomas Hamilton, sixth earl of Haddington.

E,EP; CtY.

Pomfret, Samuel. *There is a partial collection of Samuel Pomfret's 'annual hymns' in Edward Lodge, A funeral poem, [1722.] They may have been distributed before the date each bears.*

P738 — Mr. Pomfret's hymn at the sacrament. January 2d. 1709. [*London, 1708/09.*]
½⁰: 1 side, 1 column.
'Lord, in this parable, I see'
LDW.

P739 — Mr. Pomfret's hymn at the sacrament. January the first, 1710. [*London, 1709/10.*]
½⁰: 1 side, 1 column.
'While at thy table, lord, I sup'
LDW.

P740 — Mr. Pomfret's hymn at the sacrament. January the sixth 1712. [*London, 1711/12.*]
½⁰: 1 side, 1 column.
'Did once the morning stars admire'
LDW.

Pomfret, S.

P741 — Mr. Pomfret's hymn at the sacrament. January the 4th 1713. [*London, 1712/13.*]
½⁰: 1 side, 1 column.
'Upon this mountain, lord, of thine'
LDW.

P742 — Mr. Pomfret's hymn at the sacrament. January the 3d 1714. [*London, 1713/14.*]
½⁰: 1 side, 1 column.
'Ye daughters of Jerusalem'
LDW.

P743 — Mr. Pomfret's hymn at the sacrament. January the 2d, 1715. [*London, 1714/15.*]
½⁰: 1 side, 1 column.
'In this inspired sacred text'
LDW.

P744 — Mr. Pomfret's hymn at the sacrament. January the first, 1716. [*London, 1715/16.*]
½⁰: 1 side, 1 column.
'In paradise, by one man's sin'
LDW.

P745 — Mr. Pomfret's hymn at the sacrament. January the 6th 1717. [*London, 1716/17.*]
½⁰: 1 side, 1 column.
'In Eden's garden Adam fell'
LDW.

P746 — Mr. Pomfret's hymn at the sacrament. January the 5th. 1718. [*London, 1717/18.*]
½⁰: 1 side, 1 column.
'When first the law of god was given'
LDW.

P747 — Mr. Pomfret's hymn at the sacrament. January the 4th, 1719. [*London, 1718/19.*]
½⁰: 1 side, 1 column.
'Behold the lamb of god, who came'
LDW.

P748 — Mr. Pomfret's hymn at the sacrament. January the 3d. 1720. [*London, 1719/20.*]
½⁰: 1 side, 1 column.
'Ah lord! the wound that I had got'
LDW.

P749 — Mr. Pomfret's hymn at the sacrament. January the first, 1721. [*London, 1720/21.*]
½⁰: 1 side, 1 column.
'Come, lord, at this solemnitie'
LDW.

P750 — Mr. Pomfret's hymn at the sacrament. January the 7th, 1722. [*London, 1721/22.*]
½⁰: 1 side, 1 column.
'My lord, my love upon the stage'
LDW.

P751 — Mr. Pomfret's hymn, sung after his sermon preach'd to young people, on new-years day, 1718. [*London, 1718?*]
½⁰: 1 side, 1 column.
> Below, 'The following hymn was sung on Easter monday, after a sermon preach'd from the aforesaid text'.

Pomfret, S.

'This new-years day, lord, take away'
'Renowned Jesus, hast thou stood'
LDW.

Pomp. The pomp of death, 1722. *See* Harris, Timothy.

P752 [**Poole, —,** *Alderman.*] Advice to the ladies. A poem: with an elegiac complaint on the death of the inimitable Alexander Pope esq. By a Norfolk gentleman. *London, printed for M. Cooper; sold by the booksellers in town & country,* 1745. (*GM, LM* June)
4°: *A*¹[= F4] B–E⁴ F⁴(–F4); *i–ii,* 1–38. 38 advt.
Entered to Cooper in Bowyer's ledgers under 10 [May?], 1000 copies printed.
'On Twit'nham's banks the nine now pensive sit'
Ms. attribution to 'Alderman Poole' in one copy at NwP; he has not been identified, but is perhaps James Poole, grocer, who became a freeman 12 March 1747, alderman 1762, and mayor 1765.
L(11630.c.4/10),NwP(2, 1 uncut); MB,MH.

[**Poole, Robert.**] The Christian muse: or, second gift of Theophilus Philanthropos, student in physick... The second edition, greatly enlarg'd. *London, printed ann. dom.* 1740. *and are to be had at Mr. Duncomb's,* 1740.
8°: pp. iv, vi, 46.   L; CtY-M.
Gifts 1, 2–6 were in prose. No first edition has been traced. The priority of these editions is uncertain.

[—] — The second edition, with large additions. *London, printed ann. dom.* 1740. *and are to be had at Mr. Duncomb's,* 1740.
8°: pp. iv, vi, 50.   L.

P753 Poor. [dh] The poor client's complaint. Paraphrased out of Buchanan. [*Edinburgh, printed by W. Cheyne,* 173–?]
8°: A⁴; *1* 2–8.
There is a folio half-sheet edition at E which has a ms. date 1698.
'Colin, by promise, being oblig'd to pay'
E; DFo.

P754 — Poor England bob'd at home and abroad. By N.F.G. gent. [*London*] *Printed in the year* 1712.
½°: 1 side, 1 column.
'To get a good peace and a flourishing trade'
A tory manifesto, in praise of Harley and John Robinson, bishop of London and plenipotentiary at Utrecht.
L(11602.i.12/7); MH.

P755 — Poor land's ruin;|Is it Robin's doing?|An excellent new ballad. To an excellent old tune. To which is added, the Freeholder's complaint. *London, printed for E. Holloway, near Hungerford-market,* 1734. (*LM* Jan)
2°: *A*² B²; *1–2* 3–8.

Poor land's ruin

'Some people have pretended to talk of Sir William Butler's as the best colt in the town'
CSmH,InU(uncut).

P756 — Poor Robin's song; or a dialogue between poor robbin and the hawk. *London, printed for A. Hynde near Fleet-street,* 1716.
8°: *A*⁴; *1* 2–8.
'In Æsop's days, when birds and beasts could speak'
A political satire.
AdU.

P757 — Poor Teague: or, the faithful Irishman's joy, for the Duke of Ormond's happy deliverance. Tune of, Catholick brother. *London, printed for William White, near Fleet-street,* [1715.]
½°: 1 side, 2 columns.
Two rough woodcuts at head.
'Ab ab bue, by my shoul I was quite almost mad'
Tory propaganda.
L(1876.f.1/72).

P758 — The poor widows mite in seven meditations... All very comfortable, and useful for the people of god, and which may be sung with the tune of any psalm... [*Edinburgh?*] *Printed in the year* 1714.
12°: A⁶; *1–2* 3–12.
'Ah helpless wretch, what shall I do?'
Cf. *Crum* A774: 'A sinners complaint', set to music by Ravenscroft.
L(11630.aa.10).

P759 —— [*Edinburgh?*] *Printed in the year* 1717.
12°: A⁴ B²; *1–2* 3–12.
L(4403.bb.25).

P760 Pope. The Pope and Pretender in a quandary, or King George in triumph. Tune, Moggy's lamentation. [*London?* 1746?]
slip: 1 side, 1 column.
'You Englishmen draw near a while'
L(1875.d.16).

P761 — Pope's ghost: a ballad. To the tune of William and Margaret. *London, printed for W. Lewis; sold by the booksellers of London & Westminster,* 1744. (*GM* Oct)
2°: *A*² < B²; *i–ii,* '*3*' 2–6.
The wrong page number '3' has been overprinted with a '1'. Horizontal chain-lines.
'When midnight's silent, solemn hour'
Pope's ghost visits Colley Cibber and attacks him for his epitaph on Pope.
L(1962),O; CtY,DFo,IU,MH.

Pope, Alexander.
Because of the complexity of the editions of Pope, the belief that a revision of Griffith's bibliography could not long be delayed, and the frequency with which copies of his poems occur, the account given here has been somewhat abbreviated. No attempt has been made to list the collections of Pope's works, whether large or small, or his translations of the Iliad *and* Odyssey.

Pope, A.

The records of American copies of some of his works like the Dunciad, *where the determination of their state is a difficult task, are incomplete.*

'—' Are these things so? [actually by James Miller], 1740. *See* M241.

[—] A ballad on the battle of the two dukes, [1720?] *See* D506.

[—] Bounce to Fop. An heroick epistle from a dog at Twickenham to a dog at court. By Dr. S——t, 1736. *See* B326.

— Bucolica Alexandri Popii...latine reddita: interprete S. Barrett, 1746. *See* B88.

P762 — The court ballad... To the tune of, To all you ladies now at land, &c. [*London*] *Printed for R. Burleigh*, [1717.] (*PM* 31 Jan)
½°: 1–2, 1 column.
    Griffith 67. Advertisement for 'Pope's *Miscellany*' after imprint.
'To one fair lady out of court'
L(Ashley 4931, ms. notes); TxU.

P763 —— The second edition, corrected. [*London*] *Printed for A. Smith in Cornhill*, [1717.] (*PB* 2 Feb)
½°: 1–2, 1 column.
    Griffith 69. A reimpression, with at least one textual revision; the imprint and advertisement are reset. Advertised in *EvP* 9 Feb as sold by E. Berrington.
L(12273.m.1/5),O.

[—] Court poems... By Mr. Pope, 1716–. *See* Montagu, *Lady* Mary Wortley.

[—] The discovery: or, the squire turn'd ferret, 1727. *See* D328.

[—] Duke upon duke, an excellent new play-house ballad, 1720, 1723. *See* D502–7.

Because of the difficulty of determining the state of early editions of the Dunciad, *the records of American copies are incomplete. Editions of the* Dunciad *which formed a volume of Pope's* Works *in octavo are omitted.*

P764 [—] The Dunciad. An heroic poem. In three books. *Dublin, printed, London re-printed for A. Dodd,* 1728. (*MChr* 18 May)
12°: A–E⁶ F²; [2] *i–iii* iv–viii *ix–x*, 1–51 *52*. A1 frt; A6 fly-title; 52 advt.
    Griffith 198; *Rothschild* 1596. There was no earlier Dublin edition. The duodecimo appears to have been printed before the octavo below; see Foxon in *TLS* 24 Jan 1958. Mrs. Dodd did not own the copyright, but may have acted as distributor.
'Books and the man I sing, the first who brings'
    No attempt has been made here to note the replies to the *Dunciad*; see the index.
L(C.59.ff.13/4, uncut; Ashley 1304, uncut); CLU-C(frt inlaid),CSmH,CtY(uncut, F supplied), ICN(frt from 8°),TxU+.

Pope, A. The Dunciad, 1728

P765 [—] — *Dublin, printed, London re-printed for A. Dodd,* 1728. (8 June?)
8°: *a*⁴ b² B–G⁴ H²; [2] *i–iii* iv–viii *ix–x*, 1–51 *52 blk.* a1 frt; b2 fly-title.
    Griffith 199; *Rothschild* 1594 (stitched, uncut), 1595. A reimpression with changed format which corresponds to a fine-paper issue, though printed on the same paper stock as the duodecimo. Probably printed immediately after the duodecimo; though copies may have been privately distributed at an earlier stage, publication seems to have been delayed. Entered by James Bettenham, the printer, in *SR* 30 May; deposit copies at L,O,EU,SaU. Listed in *Mist's Journal* 8 June.
L(C.59.ff.12/1; Ashley 1303),LVA-D,O(2),OW ('D. D: Autoris'),EU+; CSmH,CtY,MH(frt supplied).

P766 [—] — The second edition. *Dublin, printed; London, re-printed for A. Dodd,* 1728. (*DP* 24 May)
12°: A–E⁶ F²; [2] *i–iii* iv-viii *ix–x*; 1–51 *52 blk.* A1 frt; A6 fly-title.
    Griffith 202. Copies with a variant title-page, reading 'Dudlin,...' (*Griffith* 201) are asterisked. A reimpression with sheet B and most of C reset.
L(1077.e.33/1,–A6; Ashley 1306, uncut; Ashley 1305*),O(2, 1*),CT,BaP(stitched, uncut, –A1), *DrU*; CSmH*(uncut),CtY*,IU(variant title inserted),MH(uncut),TxU*+.

P767 [—] — The third edition. *Dublin, printed; London, re-printed for A. Dodd,* 1728. (*Mist* 8 June)
12°: A–E⁶ F²; [2] *i–iii* iv-viii *ix–x*, 1–51 *52 blk.* A1 frt; A6 fly-title.
    Griffith 203. Press-figures iv-3, 2-2, 24-3, 26-4. Apparently a reimpression with sheets E, F and part of D reset.
L(Ashley 1307, A1 supplied),O,BaP(stitched, uncut); CSmH,CtY(2),IU,MH,TxU.

P768 [—] — The third edition. *Dublin, printed; London, re-printed for A. Dodd,* 1728.
12°: A–E⁶ F²; [2] *i–iii* iv-viii *ix–x*, 1–51 *52 blk.* A1 frt; A6 fly-title.
    Griffith 204. Press figures iv-2, 2-4, 26-4, 48-4. Apparently a reimpression with corrections.
L(Ashley 1308),O,CT(lacks F2),BaP(stitched, uncut); CtY,MH,TxU.

P769 [—] — 'Dublin, printed, London re-printed for A. Dodd' [*Edinburgh*?], 1728.
12°: (frt+) A–E⁶; *i–iii* iv-viii, 1–51 *52*. 52 advt.
    Griffith 200. A piracy of the first edition, known as the 'Gold chains' edition from a misprint in line 76 noted by Pope in the quarto of 1729. Copies at LdU-B, CtY are bound with Edinburgh piracies, and it was apparently advertised as 'The Dunciad, small edition, 6d.' in a catalogue of piracies in the Edinburgh reprint of Pope's *Sober advice*, [1735.]

Pope A. The Dunciad, 1728

L(Ashley 1310),O,*LdU-B*; CSmH,CtY,IU(−frt), MH,TxU.

P770 —— Written by Mr. Pope. *London: printed, and Dublin re-printed by and for G. Faulkner, J. Hoey, J. Leathley, E. Hamilton, P. Crampton, & T. Benson, 1728.*
8⁰: *A⁴ B–E⁴ G⁴; i–iii iv–vi, 7 8–47 48 blk.*
Griffith 206. Published before Swift's letter to Pope of 16 July.
L(12274.e.1/1; Ashley 1309),O,C; CSmH,CtY (title from Dublin 1729),TxU.

P771 [—] The Dunciad, variorum. With the prolegomena of Scriblerus. *London, printed for A. Dod,* 1729. (13 March)
4⁰: (engraved title +) a–b⁴ B–I⁴ K⁴(−K1,2 +K1.2)
L–O⁴ P² Q–X⁴; *1–2 3–16, [2] 1 2–6 9–29 30–32, 1 2–118, cxix–cxxiv.*
Watermark: S. *Griffith* 211, not distinguishing fine-paper copies. The cancel leaves K1.2 were printed with P²; they are thus bound in the EU copy. The title-page is engraved, and includes a vignette of an ass. Printed by John Wright. Presented to the king and queen by Sir Robert Walpole 12 March; then privately distributed by Lord Oxford, Lord Bathurst, Edward Digby and others. A letter of Pope to Oxford, 13 March, gives permission for distribution to begin. Since this differs from P773 only in lacking the leaf of addenda, copies may easily be sophisticated.
L(11633.g.56),O,LdU-B(2); CtY,IU,MH(2, 1 uncut in wrappers),TxU.

P772 [—] [fine paper]
Watermark: phoenix. The fine-paper copies seen are all without the addenda of P773.
LUC(uncut),LVA-F(presentation copy to Swift), C; CtY,TxU.

P773 [—] [reissue] *London, printed for A. Dod,* 1729. (*SR* 12 April)
4⁰: (engraved title +) a–b⁴ B–I⁴ K⁴(−K1,2 +K1.2)
L–O⁴ P² Q–X⁴ Y¹;
Watermark: S. *Griffith* 212; *Rothschild* 1597. Added leaf Y1 headed 'Addenda. M. Scriblerus lectori' at end. Entered in *SR* to Lawton Gilliver; deposit copies are apparently of this issue at L,O,C,SaU. (A copy at EU, apparently deposit, lacks Y1; perhaps a binder's error.) This edition was published through the normal channels by 8 April (Pope to Caryll) and advertised in *DP* 10 April as printed for Lawton Gilliver and A. Dodd, but it is not certain whether Y1 was added at that time.
L(642.k.2/1; Ashley 3773),LVA-D,O(2),C,SaU; CSmH,CtY,IU(2),TxU.

P774 [—] — *London, 'printed for A. Dob',* 1729. (*DP* 22 April, 'tomorrow')
8⁰: (engraved title +) A–P⁴ a–d⁴ e² (e1 as 'c'); *i–iii iv–xxxvii xxxviii–xl, 1 2–80, i–ii iii–xxx xxxi–xxxvi.*
Griffith 216. A piracy, reprinted from the

Pope, A. The Dunciad, 1729

quarto. The titlepage is engraved, and includes the vignette of an ass. Gilliver brought a suit in chancery against the publishers on 6 May (J. R. Sutherland in *MLR* 31 (1936) 347–53); they are listed as James Watson, printer, Thomas Astley, John Clarke and John Stagg, booksellers. James Watson was subsequently (1732) involved in the efforts to print with Ged's stereotype plates at Cambridge; in 1737 he pirated Pope's *Letters*, using the name T. Johnson (*Griffith* 470).
O(title mutilated),E; CLU-C,CtY(2),MH.

P775 [—] [reissue] *London, 'printed for A. Dob',* 1729. (25 April)
8⁰: (engraved title +) A–P⁴ a–d⁴ e² f¹.
Griffith 217. 'Addenda' added as f1. Gilliver in *DP* 24 April had attacked this edition as lacking the additions made in the octavo (P779, published on 17 April); the additional leaf supplying these was advertised in *DP* 25 April; it would be given to any who had purchased the original state.
L(12274.i.11; 11632.df.41),LVA-D,O,C,LdU-B +; CLU-C,CSmH(uncut),CtY,IU(2),MH(2).

P776 [—] — *London, printed for A. Dod,* 1729.
8⁰: A⁴(A1+Ass frt) B–Gg⁴ (A3 as 'A2'); *1–6 7–24, 17–18 19–221, ccxxii–ccxxxii. A1 blk.*
Griffith 213. The three states recorded as P776–8 were almost certainly never intended for publication, and may well be the result of binders' errors. They have been separately listed by earlier authorities, and may help to clarify the changes that were made.
In the copy seen the title-leaf with Dod's imprint has been slit for cancellation and repaired with the blank A1.
L(12274.i.10).

P777 [—] — *London, printed for Lawton Gilliver,* 1729.
8⁰: A⁴(A1+Ass frt; ±A2) B–Gg⁴ (A3 as 'A2'); *1–6 7–24, 17–18 19–221, ccxxii–ccxxxii. A1 blk.*
Griffith 214. Title cancelled to substitute Gilliver for Dod in imprint. No cancel Bb3 or errata leaf.
LVA-D(−A1).

P778 [—] — *London, printed for Lawton Gilliver,* 1729.
8⁰: A⁴(A1+Ass frt; ±A2) B–Aa⁴ Bb⁴(±Bb3) Cc–Gg⁴ Hh¹ (A3 as 'A2'); *1–6 7–24, 17–18 19–221, ccxxii–ccxxxii [2]. A1 blk; Hh1 err.*
Griffith 215. The cancel Bb3 (pp. 189–90) expands a two-line note on *Mist's weekly journal* to eight lines; it was printed conjugate with Hh1, the added leaf of errata headed 'M. Scriblerus lectori'. In the copy seen, both are bound together at the end; in a copy described by Griffith they were bound together between the uncancelled Bb2 and Bb3. These errors suggest that this state represents copies of P780 below, lacking the Owl plate.
CtY(−A1),*TxU*.

Pope, A. The Dunciad, 1729

P779 [—] — *London, printed for Lawton Gilliver, 1729.* (*DP* 17 April)
8°: A⁴(−A2, A1+χ²) B–Aa⁴ Bb⁴(±Bb3) Cc–Gg⁴ Hh¹ (A3 as 'A2'); [8] 7–24, *17–18* 19–221, ccxxii–ccxxxii [2]. A1 blk; χ1 Owl frt; Hh1 err.

> *Griffith* 218. The cancelled title is replaced by two conjugate leaves bearing an Owl frontispiece and the Gilliver title. The title is from the same setting of type as the cancel in the preceding. In almost all copies a half-title is printed on the recto of the frontispiece. I believe this to be the first published form of the octavo. Some copies (e.g. L,CtY) have a catalogue of Gilliver's books at the end.

L(12274.i.8: 12274.i.9,−A1),O(3, 2−A1, 1−Hh1),AdU(uncut),BaP(uncut, stitched in blue wrappers),LdU-B(−A1)+; CtY(−A1),*TxU.*

P780 [—] [another issue]

> *Griffith* 219. This issue contains both the Ass and the Owl frontispieces, bound in various ways. Normally the Ass is bound as the frontispiece, the Owl facing p. 51 or 87 (the opening of book 1 or 2). In some copies the Owl has the half-title printed on its recto, as in the preceding.

L(G.19019,−A1; Ashley 1311,−A1),LVA-D(2, 1−A1),O(2, 1 stitched, uncut); CSmH(2, 1 with separate hft),CtY(2, 1−A1),MH.

P781 [—] — *The second edition with some additional notes. London, printed for Lawton Gilliver, 1729.* (*DP* 24 Nov)
8°: A⁴ B–C⁴ D⁴(±D3) E⁴(±E2) F–O⁴ P⁴(±P3) Q–Gg⁴, ²A⁴ B¹; *1–6* 7–24, *17–18* 19–232, *1–6* 7–10. A1 frt; ²A1–3 err; ²A4 blk; ²B1 additional errata.

> *Griffith* 224–227, treating copies with some uncancelled leaves and without ²B1 as variants. The cancels for D3 and E2 were probably printed together; in all copies where they are not present (O,C,E,GU) the cancellanda are slit. Cancel P3 and errata leaf ²B1 were certainly printed together; they are bound together after uncancelled P3 in a copy at O. P3 is not cancelled and not slit in copies at L,O,DT,CtY,MH, and elsewhere, although ²B1 is present; this may be because cancel P3 was wrongly printed. Deposit copies apparently have one pair of leaves or the other, which suggests they were not part of the same half sheet and were therefore printed at different times, though before publication. The errata ²A⁴ are often bound before A4 or B1; blank ²A4 is often discarded. Entered in *SR* by Gilliver 21 Nov, recording the assignment by Burlington, Bathurst and Oxford (which was dated 16 Oct); deposit copies apparently at L,O,C,E,AdU,GU,SaU.

L(991.h.26,−²A4, ²B1; Ashley 1312,−²A4),O(4, 3−²A4),C(2),E,DT(−²A4)+; CtY(3, 1−²A4, 1−²A4, ²B1),IU(−²B1),MH(2, 1−²A4).

Pope A. The Dunciad, 1729

P782 [—] The Dunciad, with the prolegomena of Scriblerus in three books, from the new quarto edition, done at London. *London: printed, and Dublin re-printed by and for James Hoey, and George Faulkner, 1729.*
8°: π¹ A⁴ B–F⁴ G²; [2] *1–3* 4–15 *16*, 13–38, *1* 2–4, *1* 2, *1* 2–4. π1 hft.

> *Griffith* 220. The half-title reads 'The new Dunciad... To which is added, the Martiniad. By Mr. Theobald. In answer to the Dunciad'. 'The Martiniad' was originally published in *Pope Alexander's supremacy and infallibility examin'd*, 1729, which Pope ascribed to Duckett and Dennis; possibly Lewis Theobald also had a hand in it. The volume also includes 'A dialogue between Hurlothrumbo and death' and 'Mr. Congreve's fine epistle to Lord Cobham'. The prose apparatus to the *Dunciad* is omitted from this edition.

Martiniad: 'At Twickenham, chronicles remark' DA(−π1); CSmH(−π1),*TxU.*

P783 [—] The Dunciad, variorum. With the prolegomena of Scriblerus. *London: printed and re-printed, for the booksellers in Dublin, 1729.*
12°: (engraved title+) A–Q⁸′⁴ R⁸ S⁴(−S4); *1–2* 3–192 185–204 '105' 206 blk.

> *Griffith* 221. The Grolier catalogue (1911) recorded the presence of S4 'blank and genuine'; no such copy has been seen and Griffith suggested the collation S²+addenda leaf. The watermarks seen are not inconsistent with S⁴(−S4), and Falkner Greirson cat. 16 (1970) 365 recorded a copy where 'the printed title-page is the last leaf S4'. In some copies (e.g. O) S2 is signed 'R2'; in others it is unsigned.

LUC,O,C,DN(2),AdU; CLU-C,CSmH,CtY,IU, MH.

P784 [—] [another issue]
12°: (engraved title+) π¹ A–Q⁸′⁴ R⁸ S⁴(−S4).

> *Griffith* 222. Letterpress title-leaf added to the engraved title. Griffith rightly suggests that copies of the preceding issue are not merely imperfect. It seems possible that the letterpress title was printed as S4 in case the engraved title was not ready in time, and that it was frequently discarded by the binders.

L(12274.f.3; 11630.b.43),O; CSmH,CtY,IU, MH.

[—] The Dunciad, in three books, written in the year 1727. [*London*, 1735.]

> *Griffith* 373 records an offprint from Pope's *Works* II, 1735, and on p. 287 quotes Gilliver's advertisement from the *Grub-street journal* 24 April 1735 offering 'any part separate of the folio already publish'd'. These are excluded from this catalogue, but there appear to be copies of the *Dunciad* from the large-paper folio at L,TxU; from the ordinary folio at CSmH; and from the quarto at O.

Pope, A. The Dunciad, 1735

P785 [—] The Dunciad. With notes variorum, and the prolegomena of Scriblerus. Written in the year, 1727. *London, printed for Lawton Gilliver*, [1735.] (*GSJ* 18 Sept)

8°: (frt+) A–Q⁸ R⁴ (A3 as 'A4'); *1–4* 5–263 *264 blk* (23 as '22').

> *Griffith* 392–4, recording variants. A copy at MH has 'Pride' on p. 225 printed in gothic, not roman type, and the page misnumbered '125'; other copies (L,O,CtY) have the changed reading but the page still misnumbered. The frontispiece is usually the Owl plate, but some copies (O,CtY) have the Ass. Advertised in *GSJ* 31 July 1735 for 'to-morrow', in *DJ* 31 July as 'speedily', but not recorded as published until 18 Sept.

L(12274.e.11; 11633.aa.36),O(4, 1 – frt),AdU (– frt),GU,LdU-B(uncut) + ; CSmH,CtY,ICU(3), MH(3),TxU + .

P786 [—] [reissue] The Dunciad. An heroic poem. To Dr. Jonathan Swift. With the prolegomena of Scriblerus, and notes variorum. *London, printed for Lawton Gilliver*, 1736 [1735]. (18 Nov?)

8°: (frt+) A⁸(±A1) B–N⁸ O⁸(±O7) P–Q⁸ R⁴; *1–4* 5–263 *264 blk* (23 as '22'). 2 err.

> *Griffith* 405. Normally issued with the Owl frontispiece. *Griffith* 406 records an issue with the Ass frontispiece; the only copy traced (at MH) forms volume IV of the octavo edition of Pope's *Works*, 1736. Copies used thus are found with binder's title 'Pope's Works' and numbered 4 (or 7); the use of the Ass frontispiece may be an error. Publication date from *Griffith*, based on Pope's letter to Broome of 18 Nov.

L(12274.f.51),LUC,O(2),C,AdU; CSmH,CtY, IU(3),MH.

P787 [—] The new Dunciad: as it was found in the year 1741. With the illustrations of Scriblerus, and notes variorum. *London, printed for T. Cooper*, 1742. (*Craftsman* 20 March)

4°: *A*⁴ B–F⁴; *i–viii*, *1* 2–39 *40 blk*. A1 hft; 39 err.

> Engraved headpiece on p. 1. *Griffith* 546–7; *Rothschild* 1598, both describing large-paper copies, apparently on the authority of T. J. Wise's *Catalogue of the Ashley Library* IV (1923) 27f. All copies seen have a Strasburg bend watermark. Entered to Pope by John Wright in *SR* 18 March, possibly before publication; deposit copies at L,O,E,EU,GU, SaU.
>
> 'Yet, yet a moment, one dim ray of light'

L(11630.e.3/11; 11642.h.43/3; Ashley 4934), LVA-D(3, 1 uncut, 2 – A1),O,CT,E(2) + ; CLU-C,ICU,IU,KU,MH + .

P788 [—] [another edition]

> Woodcut headpiece on p. 1. (Not recorded in *Griffith*.) This corresponds in all other respects with the description of the preceding, but the

Pope, A. The new Dunciad, 1742

> signature positions differ from that. It may be another impression.

IU.

P789 [—] — *London, printed for T. Cooper*, 1742. (25 March?)

4°: *A*⁴ B–F⁴ G²; *i–viii*, *1* 2–44. A1 hft.

> *Griffith* 549. Slight revisions to text and notes. Apparently the edition entered to Pope in Bowyer's ledgers under 25 March, 6½ sheets 4°, 2000 copies printed; 1000 titles were reprinted, presumably for the following issue.

L(11632.g.61/1; 11630.f.17, – A1),LVA-D,LUC (uncut),O(– A1),BaP(stitched, uncut); CLU-C, CtY,IU,MH(2),TxU(2, 1 – A1).

P790 — [reissue] The Dunciad: book the fourth. By Mr. Pope... The second edition. *London, printed for T. Cooper*, 1742. (*LEP* 24 April)

4°: *A*⁴(– A1–3 + A2) B–F⁴ G²; *i–iv*, *1* 2–44.

> *Griffith* 556. Cancel title; half-title and 'To the reader' omitted. A4 (the argument) is retained, contrary to the description in *Griffith*.

O,*MR*; CtY(2),ICU,KU,TxU.

P791 [—] The new Dunciad: as it was found in the year 1741... *London, printed for J. H. Hubbard, in the Old-Bailey*, 1742. (March?)

8°: A² B–E⁴; *i–ii* iii–iv, *5* 6–36.

> *Griffith* 548. A piracy, based on the first quarto edition. In most copies the date appears as 'MDCCXIII' with the second I very faint; it might possibly be a raised space. The O copy has no date, possibly because of frisket bite, and the copy at CtY represents an intermediate stage.

L(T.1057/1),O; CtY,MH,TxU(uncut).

P792 — The new Dunciad: by Mr. P·····o·····p ·····e... The second edition. *London, printed for J. H. Hubbard*, 1742.

8°: A² B–E⁴; *i–ii* iii–iv, *5* 6–36.

> *Griffith* 550. Another piracy, including the expansion of lines 39–40 to 39–42, introduced in P789 above. *Griffith* suggests a date early in April, but perhaps the piracy which was the subject of Pope v. Ilive (see H. P. Vincent in *PQ* 18 (1939) 287–9); that was not published until October.

O,*MR*; CtY,TxU.

P793 [—] The new Dunciad: as it was found... '*London, printed for T. Cooper*' [*Edinburgh*], 1742. (*SM* March)

8°: *A*² B–E⁴ F²; *i–iv*, *1* 2–36.

> *Griffith* 551. Copies at MP, National Library of Australia are bound with Edinburgh piracies. The *SM* for March may have been published about the middle of April.

L(11633.e.11),O,GU,MP; ICU,IU.

P794 [—] — *Dublin: re-printed by and for George Faulkner*, 1742.

8°: A–C⁸ D²; *1–9* 10–51 *52 blk*.

Pope, A. The new Dunciad, 1742

> *Griffith* 552. A reprint of the first quarto edition.
> L(11633.cc.2/7),O,DA(3),DG,DN+; CLU-C, CtY,TxU.

P795 [—] — *Dublin, printed by A. Reilly, for G. Ewing, 1742.*
12°: A–E⁶; *1–7* 8–58 *59–60* blk.
> *Griffith* 553. Reissued as part of *The Dunciad, in four books,* 1744 (P799).
> L(11774.aaa.10/2; 1962),O(–E6),DA(–E6); CSmH(–E6).

P796 [—] The Dunciad, in four books. Printed according to the complete copy found in the year 1742... To which are added several notes... *London, printed for M. Cooper,* 1743. (29 Oct?)
4°: πA⁴ χ² A–U⁴ X⁴(±X3) Y–Ff⁴ Gg² Dd⁴ Ee²; *i–iv* v–vi [4] ix–x, *i* ii–xxxvii *xxxviii,* 39 40–235 *236–248.* πA1 hft; πA2ᵛ advt.
> Watermark: fleur-de-lys. *Griffith* 578; *Rothschild* 1599, not distinguishing fine-paper copies. The binding of the preliminaries varies. The date of 29 Oct is quoted by *Griffith* from Cibber; entered in *SR* 28 Oct by Mary Cooper, possibly before publication; deposit copies at O,AdU,GU,SaU, and possibly C. Listed in *LM* Oct. Entered to Pope in Bowyer's ledgers under 2 Oct 1743, 1500 copies Demy and 100 Royal; 500 copies were delivered to Cooper on 14 Oct.
> L(Ashley 3774/2),O,C(2, 1 uncut),E,LdU-B+; CtY,IU,KU,MH(2, 1 uncut),TxU+.

P797 [—] [fine paper]
> Watermark: Strasburg bend. X3 is not cancelled in the copies seen. Bowyer's ledgers suggest that X3 was printed with the title of *An essay on man,* 1743, 'without Royal'. His paper ledger records that 17 copies were delivered to Pope between Nov 1743 and April 1744, 5 to Brindley and 3 to Knapton.
> L(641.l.17/1); CtY(presentation copy from Warburton).

P798 — The Dunciad, as it is now changed by Mr. Pope. In four books. *Dublin, printed for Philip Bowes,* 1744.
12°: *A¹* B–E⁶ F¹; *i–ii,* 1–49 *50.*
> The copy at DT has date 'MDCCXLIV'; that at L, 'MDCCXLIII' followed by what is apparently a damaged piece of type.
> L(1966),DT.

P799 [—] The Dunciad, in four books... *London printed, and Dublin re-printed for G. & A. Ewing,* 1744. (25 Feb?)
12°: A–Q⁶ R², ²A⁶(–A1,2) B–D⁶ E⁶(–E5,6) F⁴ G–K⁶; *i–ii* iii–liv, *55–56* 57–196, *5–7* 8–97 *98–112.* ii advt.
> *Griffith* 605a. ²A–E are reissued from Reilly's edition of *The new Dunciad,* 1742 (P795).
> L(1959, ms. date 25 Feb),DT; MH.

Pope, A. The Dunciad, 1749

P800 — The Dunciad, complete in four books, according to Mr. Pope's last improvements... Published by Mr. Warburton. *London, printed for J. & P. Knapton,* 1749 [1750]. (*GM* Jan)
8°: (frt+) π² a⁸(–a1) b⁸(–b4–8) B–Q⁸ R² d⁸(–d1) e⁴; [4] xix–xxi xxii–xxxviii, *1–3* 4–163 *164–166,* 1 2–78, *lxvii* lxviii–lxxxvii *lxxxviii.* e4ᵛ err.
> *Griffith* 638. Title in red and black. Sheets a,b,d,e and B–L are reissued from the octavo edition of Pope's *Works* III. i, 1743 (*Griffith* 586); B1,6,8, D4–6, E2,5, H4–5 are cancels as in that edition. Possibly the new sheets are those entered to Knapton in Bowyer's ledgers under 10 Nov [1749?] 'A cancelled Leaf of Dunciad 8° reprinted' and 22 Nov 'Dunciad Book IV in 8° 5 sh & ½ Titles Red', both 1000 copies. See [W. Dodd] *A new book of the Dunciad: occasion'd by Mr. Warburton's new edition,* 1750.
> L(12274.f.1),LVA-D,O,BaP; CLU-C,CtY,MH, TxU.

— [Elegy to the memory of an unfortunate lady] Elegeia Popi in memoriam infelicis nymphæ, in latinum versum reddita, 1744. *See* E34.

P801 — Eloisa to Abelard. Written by Mr. Pope. The second edition. *London, printed for Bernard Lintot,* 1720 [1719]. (*DC* 13 Oct)
8°: A–D⁸ (B3 as 'F3'); *1–5* 6–63 *64.* A1 frt.
> *Griffith* 109. Pp. 27–34 contains Pope's 'Verses to the memory of an unfortunate lady'; poems by other authors on pp. 35–64. The first edition was in Pope's *Works,* 1717. Entered in *SR* 27 Oct; deposit copies at O,E, EU. Entered to Lintot in Bowyer's ledgers under 9 Oct 1719, 2500 copies printed; 500 were delivered to Roberts on 9 Oct, 1999 to Lintot on 14 Oct.
> 'In these deep solitudes and awful cells'
> Answered by [James Dalacourt] *Abelard to Eloisa,* 1730.
> L(1465.f.26; 991.h.25/3; C.59.ff.13/3),LVA-D, O,E,EU+; CSmH,ICU(2),IU,MH(2),TxU+.

P802 — An epistle from Mr. Pope, to Dr. Arbuthnot. *London, printed by J. Wright, for Lawton Gilliver,* 1734 [1735]. (*LEP* 2 Jan)
2°: *A*² B–F²; *i–iv,* *1* 2–19 *'30'.*
> *Griffith* 352; *Rothschild* 1623. Entered in *SR* to Gilliver 2 Jan; deposit copies at L,SaU.
> 'Shut, shut the door, good John! fatigu'd I said'
> L(1484.m.7/11; 644.m.14/5; 162.n.24; C.131. h.1/4*; Ashley 5221),O(4, 1 Harley's copy, dated 2 Jan),C(2),E,LdU-B+; CLU-C(2),CtY(5),IU, MH(4),TxU(4, 1 uncut)+.

P803 —— *'London, printed by J. Wright, for Lawton Gilliver'* [Edinburgh], 1734 [1735].
8°: A–C⁴ D²; *1–5* 6–27 *28.* 28 advt.
> *Griffith* 353. Printed by Ruddiman on the evidence of the ornaments. Advertisement on p. 28 for *Liberty: a poem* 'By our countryman

Pope, A. An epistle to Dr. Arbuthnot

Mr. James Thomson... To be sold by A. Millar and Allan Ramsay, at their shops in London and Edinburgh'.
L(11630.bbb.42/4; 993.e.51/4),O(2, 1 lacks D²), E,*MP*; CtY,ICU(2),MH,TxU.

P804 —— *London: printed. And Dublin re-printed by George Faulkner, 1735.*
8⁰: *A*⁴ B–C⁴; *i–iv, 1 2–20.*
Griffith 354.
O(2),DK(2),DN; CtY,IU,TxU(4, 1 uncut).

P805 —— *London: printed. And Dublin re-printed by George Faulkner, 1735.*
8⁰: *A*⁴ B–C⁴; *1–5 6–24.*
Apparently from the same setting of type as the preceding, but with changed pagination. Possibly a reimpression. A copy at CSmH apparently has sheet A of the preceding and B–C from this issue, but there p. 9 is numbered '6'.
L(11630.aaa.45/10); MH.

— An epistle to the right honourable Richard, earl of Burlington. *See below* Of false taste (P908).

— An epistle to the right honourable Richard lord visct. Cobham. *See below* Of the knowledge and characters of men (P920).

P806 [—] An essay on criticism. *London, printed for W. Lewis; sold by W. Taylor, T. Osborn, & J. Graves, 1711. (DC 15 May)*
4⁰: π¹ A–E⁴ F² G¹; *i–ii, 1–3 4–43 44–45; 46 blk.* π1 hft; G1 advt.
Griffith 2; *Rothschild* 1562. No watermark. π1 and G1 have been seen to be conjugate; from the evidence of uncut copies this half-sheet was separate from F², though they may have been printed together and divided before collation. That this half-sheet was part of the original issue is shown by its presence in deposit copies. Entered in *SR* to Will. Lewis by John Morphew on 11 May, possibly before publication; deposit copies at LSC,E,EU.
''Tis hard to say, if greater want of skill'
L(161.m.24,–G1, Luttrell 17 May; C.57.i.49, –π1, G1; Ashley 3765,–π1, G1; Cup.402.f.4, stabbed, uncut), O(? made-up by T. J. Wise), C(–π1, G1, uncut),E(–G1),DT(–π1, G1)+; CLU-C,InU,MH(–π1, G1),NNP,TxU(**–π1,** G1)+.

P807 [—] [variant imprint:] *London, printed for W. Lewis, 1711.*
No watermark. *Griffith* 3, not recording fine-paper copies. Copies with this imprint were presumably Lewis's own stock; the change in imprint was apparently made at press.
CSmH(–G1, ? π1 in facsimile),CtY,IU(made-up copy),TxU.

P808 [—] [fine paper] *London, printed for W. Lewis, 1711.*
Apparently there are different watermarks in

Pope, A. An essay on criticism, 1711

A–C, D–G; the latter is a monogram, ? PHL, resembling *Heawood* 2935.
NN-B(stabbed, in remains of marbled wrappers).

P809 [—] —— *Dublin, printed by A. Rhames, for George Grierson, [1711?]*
12⁰: A–C⁶; *1–3 4–36.*
Griffith Add. 27a. John Philips, *The splendid shilling,* on pp. 33–36. Dated as probably 1713 by *Griffith,* on the supposition that it was a part of a larger work. It now seems reasonable to see it as a reprint of the anonymous first edition.
L(1958, lacks C3–4); MH(lacks C5–6).

P810 —— Written by Mr. Pope... The second edition. *London, printed for W. Lewis, 1713 [1712]. (Spectator 27 Nov)*
8⁰: A–B⁸ C⁴; *i–iv, 1 2–36.* A1 hft.
Griffith 8. Two different watermarks are found; presumably printed on mixed stock. Advertised in *Spectator* 22 Nov for 'Tuesday next' [25 Nov].
L(11631.bbb.45),LVA-D(2, uncut),O,C,DK+; CtY,ICU,IU,MH,TxU.

P811 —— The third edition. *London, printed for W. Lewis, 1713. (EvP 28 Nov)*
12⁰: A⁸ B⁴ C⁶; *1–5 6–35 36 blk.* A1 hft.
Griffith 26. Copies at O have variant head-pieces on p. 5; one is a floral pattern on a black ground, the other a bowl with floral pattern on a white ground.
L(1346.d.31),LVA-D(2),O(2),AdU,*MR*; CLU-C, ICU,MH(2),TxU.

P812 —— The fourth edition. *London, printed for W. Lewis, 1713.*
12⁰: A⁸ B⁴ C⁶; *1–5 6–35 36 blk.* A1 hft.
Griffith 27. Apparently a press-variant title of the preceding; certainly from the same setting of type.
L(11868.d.9/1),O,DT; ICN,ICU,MH,NjP,TxU (uncut).

P813 —— The fifth edition. *London, printed for Bernard Lintot, 1716. (July?)*
12⁰: A⁸ B⁴ C⁶; *1–5 6–35 36 blk.* A1 hft.
Griffith 71, dating it before 16 May 1717 when it was listed in Parnell's *Homer's Battle*... Lintot paid Pope £15 for the copyright on 17 July 1716 (*Nichols* VIII.300), and it seems reasonable to associate this edition with that payment.
L(1346.d.33/3),O(uncut); CtY,MH,TxU.

P814 —— The fifth edition. 'London' [The Hague], *printed for T. Johnson, 1716.*
8⁰: A–C⁸ D²; *1–3 4–51 52 blk.*
B6 is a title-leaf to *The temple of fame,* which occupies pp. 27–51. Reissued with D² cancelled by D⁸ E² (adding *Windsor Forest* and the *Ode for...St. Cecilia's day*) in Johnson's piracy of Pope's *Works,* 1718. *Griffith* 63 records that form (copies at L,TxU), not

Pope, A. An essay on criticism, 1716

knowing this; but it possibly had no existence apart from that collection.
MH.

P815 [—] — Written in the year 1709. *London, printed: Dublin, re-printed, for George Grierson, 1717.*
8°: A–D⁴ E¹; *1–3* 4–34.
Also issued in Grierson's reprint of Pope's *Works*, 1718. Other sections of that reprint may have been issued separately, but have not been listed here; the copy here recorded was certainly issued separately.
L(832.b.15/2).

P816 — — The sixth edition, corrected. *London, printed for Bernard Lintot, 1719.* (*WEP* 2 May)
8°: A–C⁸ (A3 as 'A5'); *1–5* 6–48. A1 frt.
Griffith 107. The corrections are those introduced in Pope's *Works*, 1717.
L(11634.b.3),LVA-F,O,CT; CtY(uncut),*ICN*, ICU,IU,MH(2).

P817 — — The seventh edition, corrected. *London, printed for Bernard Lintot, 1722 [1721].* (*PB* 5 Oct)
8°: A–C⁸; *1–5* 6–48. A1 frt.
Griffith 129. Entered to Lintot in Bowyer's ledgers under 29 [Sept], 1000 copies.
L(991.h.25/1),O,LdU-B; CtY(2),ICU(2),IU,MH.

P818 — — The seventh edition. *London, printed for Bernard Lintot, 1728.*
12°: A–C⁶; *1–4* 5–35 *36*. A1 hft; 36 advt.
ICU.

P819 [—] — With the commentary and notes of W. Warburton... [*London, printed for M. Cooper, 1744.*] (*GM, LM* Feb)
4°: A² B–H⁴ I²; *i–iv, 1* 2–60.
Watermark: fleur-de-lys. *Griffith* 590, not recording fine-paper copies. Title in half-title form; issued with *An essay on man*, 1743, and so listed in *GM, LM. An essay on man* was entered in *SR* by Mary Cooper 17 Feb 1744, and deposit copies at E,AdU,GU (and probably L,O,C) also contain *An essay on criticism*. Entered to Pope in Bowyer's ledgers (together with *An essay on man*) under 18 Feb 1744, 1500 copies and 100 Royal; the ledger records 'reprinted a line through the impression', probably the last line of the note on p. 20.
L(642.k.2/3); 643.k.4/1; C.59.e.1/3),O,C,E, GU+; IU,MH(2),NjP,*TxU*.

P820 [—] [fine paper]
Watermark: Strasburg bend.
CtY(in presentation volume from Warburton).

P821 — — With notes by Mr. Warburton. *London, printed for Henry Lintot, 1749.* (*GM* Nov)
8°: π¹ A–E⁸ F⁴ G²; *i–ii, 1–2* 3–89 *90–92 blk.*
Griffith 635; π1 is the title, A1 a fly-title; in some copies (e.g. O) the title is inserted after A1, making A1 into a half-title. Horizontal chain-lines.
LVA-F,O(–G2); CtY(–G2),MH(2).

Pope, A. An essay on criticism

Translations

[Robethon, John:] Essai sur la critique; imité de l'anglois de Mr. Pope, 1717. *See* R228–9.

Kirkpatrick, James: Celeberrimi Popii Tentamen de modis criticis scripta dijudicandi, [1745.] *See* K88.

Gahagan, Usher: Tentamen de re critica, 1747. *See* G6.

Verse translations published abroad (e.g. G. E. Müller, Versuch über die Critik, *Dresden, 1745) and prose translations published in England (e.g. E. de Silhouette,* Essais sur la critique et sur l'homme, *1737, 1741) are excluded, although they reprint the English text.*

———————

[—] An essay on human life... By the author of the Essay on man [in fact by T. C. Paget, baron Paget], 1736. *See* P17.

P822 [—] An essay on man. Address'd to a friend. Part I. *London, printed for J. Wilford,* [1733.] (*DJ* 20 Feb)
2°: A² B–E²; *1–5* 6–19 *20 blk.*
Griffith 294; *Rothschild* 1613. For the order of the early impressions see Foxon in *TLS* 24 Jan 1958. The small-paper issue (*Griffith* 295) is apparently a ghost.
'Awake my Lælius! leave all meaner things'
See William Ayre, *Truth. A counterpart to Mr. Pope's Essay on man*, 1739; [Bridges] *Divine wisdom and providence*, 1736; Dodsley, *An epistle to Mr. Pope*, 1734.
L(C.59.h.9/2; Ashley 5212),LSC,O(Harley's copy, dated Feb),OW,C+; CSmH,CtY,IU,MH(2, 1 uncut),TxU(2, 1 uncut).

P823 [—] — *London, printed for J. Wilford,* [1733.] (*DJ* 9 March)
2°: A² B²(–B2) B–D²; *1–5* 6 *9–20.*
Griffith 304, not recording fine-paper copies. Watermark: London arms. Pp. 1–6 (and presumably cancelled B2) are reimpressed; the remainder is from standing type revised and rearranged. Entered in *SR* 10 March; deposit copies at L,LSC,O,AdU,SaU.
L(644.m.14/2, title only; Ashley 5211, all but title from preceding copy),LSC(uncut),O,OW(uncut), SaU(uncut)+; CLU-C(uncut),MH(2),TxU(2).

P824 [—] [fine paper]
No watermark. *Rothschild* 1614.
L(Ashley 4935),LVA-D; CtY.

P825 [—] — In epistles to a friend. The second edition. Part I. *London, printed for J. Wilford,* [1733]. (*DJ* 22 March)
4°: A⁴ B⁴ C⁴(–C4); *1–7* 8–21 *22 blk.* A1 hft.
Griffith 305, not recording fine-paper copies. No watermark. The collation of C is apparently as given here, though in the fine-paper copies it is clearly C⁴(–C1). A reimpression of the preceding, B–C probably printed concurrently

Pope, A. An essay on man I, 1733

with that; A printed subsequently, with pp. 7–8 reset.
L(1346.i.25,–A1; 11630.e.5/16,–A1, lacks A2), O,C(–A1); IU(–A1),TxU.

P826 [—] [fine paper]
Watermark: Strasburg bend.
L(Ashley 5213); CtY.

P827 [—] — In epistles to a friend. Epistle I. Corrected by the author. *London, printed for J. Wilford,* [1733.] (23 April?)
2°: *A²*(A1 + a²) B–D² *E¹; 1–7 8, 5–17 18 blk* (12 as '11').
> *Griffith* 307; *Rothschild* 1615. In some copies (e.g. O,MH) p. 16 is misnumbered '10'; there are variant press-figures. a² contains an epistle to the reader and the contents of epistles I–III. Listed in *LM* April, 'with the contents of three parts'. *Griffith* 312 (following Aitken) records a reissue with epistles II & III; they were advertised together in *GSJ* 17 May, and I have seen a copy where the three were stabbed together, but it is not a distinct issue.
L(12273.m.1/3; Ashley 5214, uncut),O(2, 1 Harley's copy 'publisht April. 23. 1733'),DT, BaP(stitched, uncut),LdU-B+; CSmH,CtY,IU, MH(4),TxU(2, 1 uncut).

P828 [—] — Address'd to a friend. Part I. '*London, printed for J. Wilford*' [*Edinburgh*], 1733.
8°: A–B⁴ C²; *1–5 6–19 20 blk.*
> *Griffith* 296. Printed by Ruddiman on the evidence of the ornaments.
L(011641.ee.130),O,CT,E,AdU; CSmH,CtY,IU, MH(2),TxU(2)+.

P829 [—] — '*London, printed for J. Wilford*' [*Edinburgh*], 1733.
8°: A–B⁴; *1–3 4–16.*
> *Griffith* 299. Also printed by Ruddiman. Possibly a reprint later than the date it bears.
O; ICU,TxU.

P830 [—] — *Dublin, printed by S. Powell, for George Risk, George Ewing, & William Smith,* 1733.
8°: A–B⁴ C²; *1–5 6–19 20 blk.*
> *Griffith* 297; *Rothschild* 1616. In some copies (e.g. DT,TxU) B1 and 2 are signed 'C, C2'.
L(11630.aaa.45/6),O,DN,DT(stitched, uncut); CSmH,CtY,IU,TxU.

P831 [—] — The second edition. *Dublin, printed by S. Powell, for George Risk, George Ewing, & William Smith,* 1734.
8°: A–B⁴ C²; *1–5 6–19 20 blk.*
> *Griffith* 349.
L(11631.aa.47/1),O(2),DK,DN; CtY(ms. note 'Dublin Decembr. 17th 1734'),MH.

P832 [—] — In epistles to a friend. Epistle I. Corrected by the author. The second edition. *London, printed for J. Wilford,* 1735.
2°: *A² B–E² F¹; i–iv, 1–3 4–17 18 blk.*
> *Griffith* 409. *Griffith* 314, which has the same title but no date, is almost certainly a ghost

Pope, A. An essay on man I, 1735

which originated with Aitken in the *Athenaeum.* Doubtless reprinted to complete sets of the folio edition.
LUC,LVA-D,O; CtY,ICU,MH(uncut),TxU.

P833 [—] An essay on man. In epistles to a friend. Epistle II. *London, printed for J. Wilford,* [1733.] (*DJ* 29 March)
2°: *π¹ A² B–D² E¹; i–ii, 1–5 6–18. π1 hft.*
> *Griffith* 300; *Rothschild* 1613–15. The lines are numbered (erroneously); rules on half-title are spaced about 160 mm. π1 and E1 have been seen to be conjugate in the copy at BaP. Entered in *SR* 29 March; deposit copies at LSC,O,AdU,SaU. Harley's copy dated 23 April was apparently received with the corrected edition of Epistle I, P827.
'Know then thyself, presume not god to scan'
L(12273.m.1/3,–π1; C.59.h.9/2, uncut; Ashley 4935; Ashley 5215, uncut),O(2, 1 Harley's 'publisht April. 23. 1733',–π1),C(–π1),EU, DT+; CSmH,CtY,IU,MH(6, 1 uncut, 3–π1), TxU(3).

P834 [—] [another edition]
> *Griffith* 311. Lines unnumbered except for 175 on p. 13; printer's flowers instead of rules on half-title. π1 and E1 have been seen to be conjugate in the copy at CtY. The precise date is uncertain, but copies are usually bound with the early editions of epistles I and III.
L(Ashley 5216),LVA-D(–π1, lacks A²),O(–π1), GU,LdU-B; CSmH,CtY,IU(–π1),MH(–π1), TxU(2).

P835 [—] — '*London, printed for J. Wilford*' [*Edinburgh*], 1733.
8°: D–E⁴; *21–23 24–36.*
> *Griffith* 301. Signature D2 under 'or dis-'. Printed by Ruddiman on the evidence of the ornaments; intended to be bound after the first Edinburgh piracy of Epistle I, P828. In some copies (e.g. L,TxU) E2 is signed 'E3'.
L(011641.ee.130),O,CT,AdU; CSmH,CtY,IU, MH(2),TxU(3)+.

P836 [—] — [*Edinburgh,* 1733/–.]
8°: D⁴(–D1) E⁴; *23 24–36.*
> Signature D2 under 'd, or'. No title-leaf in copies seen; clearly intended for binding-up with the other parts of *Essay on man.* The copy at TxU forms part of a nonce-collection, *Poems, a chosen collection,* dated as 1736 by *Griffith* 441 but possibly 1735; could D1 have been printed as the general title for that when stock of epistle II was replenished?
ICU,TxU.

P837 [—] — *London: printed. Dublin, re-printed, by and for George Faulkner,* 1733.
8°: *A⁴ B⁴ C²; 1–5 6–18 19; 20 blk. 19 advt.*
> *Griffith* 302 (not seen); *Rothschild* 1616. In some copies (L,IU) p. 18 is numbered '15'.
L(11630.aaa.45/7),O,DN; CtY,IU.

Pope, A. An essay on man II, 1734

P838 [—] — The second edition. *Dublin: printed by S. Powell, for George Risk, George Ewing, & William Smith,* 1734.
8°: A–B⁴; *1–3* 4–16.
Griffith 350. The words 'The second edition' were perhaps carried over from epistle I, P831, reprinted at this time.
L(11631.aa.47/1),O,DK; MH,TxU.

P839 [—] — *London, printed for J. Wilford,* [1734/35.]
2°: π¹ A² B–D² E¹; *i–ii, 1–5* 6–18.
Griffith 313, dating it 1733. Lines unnumbered; rules on half-title spaced about 190 mm. π1 and E1 have been seen to be conjugate. Copies are frequently found with the 1735 edition of epistle I, P832; it was clearly reprinted to complete sets.
L(Ashley 5217),LUC(−π1),CK(uncut); CtY, ICU,IU,MH,TxU.

P840 [—] An essay on man. In epistles to a friend. Epistle III. *London, printed for J. Wilford,* [1733.] (*DJ* 8 May)
2°: A² B–E²; *1–5* 6–20. A1 hft; 20 advt.
Griffith 308; *Rothschild* 1613–15. 2 line advertisement on p. 20; lines misnumbered as 323. Entered in *SR* 9 May; deposit copies at L, LSC,O,AdU,SaU. Harley's copy at O, dated 4 May, was probably presented before publication.
'Learn Dulness, learn! "The universal cause'
L(12273.m.1/3,−A1; 644.m.14/2; C.59.h.9/2, uncut; Ashley 4935; Ashley 5218), O(2, 1 Harley's 'R. May 4. 1733'),C(2, 1 cropt),GU,DT+; CSmH,CtY,IU,MH(4, 2−A1),TxU(3).

P841 [—] — '*London, printed for J. Wilford*' [*Edinburgh*], 1733.
8°: F–G⁴ H²; *37–38* 39–55 *56 blk*. 55 advt.
Griffith 309. Printed by Ruddiman on the evidence of the ornaments; intended to be bound after the Edinburgh piracies of epistles I & II.
L(011641.ee.130),O,CT; CtY,ICU(2),IU,MH(2), TxU(3).

P842 [—] — *London: printed. Dublin, re-printed, by and for George Faulkner,* 1733.
8°: A–B⁴ C²; *1–3* 4–18 *19–20*. 18, C2 advt.
Griffith Add. 310a. One copy at O is a variant, with C1 unsigned.
O(2),DN; CtY.

P843 [—] — *Dublin, printed by S. Powell, for George Risk, George Ewing, & William Smith,* 1733.
8°: A⁴ B⁴ C²; *1–5* 6–20. A1 hft.
Griffith 310; *Rothschild* 1616. *Griffith* 318 records 'The second edition' from the Lefferts catalogue (no. 14); this is apparently a ghost. Epistles I, II, IV in Powell's edition bear these words, but not epistle III.
L(11630.aaa.45/8; 11631.aa.47/1*),O(2),DK, DN; IU,MH,TxU.

Pope, A. An essay on man III

P844 [—] — *London, printed for J. Wilford,* [1734/35.]
2°: A² B–E²; *1–5* 6–20. A1 hft; 20 advt.
Griffith 315, dating it 1733. Advertisement on p. 20 in one line. In most copies seen, the penultimate line is correctly numbered 315; variant, misnumbered 320 (as described in *Griffith*), at CK. Copies are frequently found with the 1735 edition of epistle I (P832); it was clearly reprinted to complete sets.
L(Ashley 5219),LUC(−A1),CK(uncut); CtY, ICU,MH(uncut),TxU.

P845 [—] An essay on man. In epistles to a friend. Epistle IV. *London, printed for J. Wilford,* [1734.] (*DJ* 24 Jan)
2°: A² B–F²; *i–iv, 1* 2–18 *19; 20 blk* (17 as '71'). F2 advt.
Griffith 331; *Rothschild* 1613–15. *Griffith* 332 claims the existence of fine-paper copies; all seen have watermark T. Entered in *SR* 25 Jan; deposit copies at L,O,AdU,SaU. Harley's copy at O, dated 22 Jan, was probably presented before publication.
'Oh Happiness! our being's end and aim'
L(12273.m.1/3; 644.m.14/2; C.59.h.9/2, uncut; Ashley 4935; Ashley 5220),O(2, 1 Harley's 'R. Janu. 22. 1733/4'),C(2, 1 cropt),GU,LdU-B+; CSmH,CtY,IU,MH(uncut),TxU(4).

P846 [—] — '*London, printed for J. Wilford*' [*Edinburgh*], 1734.
8°: A⁴ I–K⁴; *57–60* 61–80.
Griffith 333. Printed by Ruddiman on the evidence of the ornaments; intended to be bound after the Edinburgh piracies of epistles I–III.
L(011641.ee.130),O,CT; CtY,ICU(2),IU,MH, TxU.

P847 [—] — *London: printed. And re-printed in Dublin, by George Faulkner,* 1734.
8°: A⁴ B–C⁴; *1–5* 6–22 *23–24*. C4 advt.
Griffith 334; *Rothschild* 1616.
L(11631.a.63/1; 11631.aa.47/1**); IU,TxU.

P848 [—] — The second edition. *Dublin, printed by S. Powell, for George Risk, George Ewing, & William Smith,* 1734.
8°: A–C⁴; *1–5* 6–23 *24*. 24 advt.
Griffith 351. The words 'The second edition' were perhaps carried over from epistle I, P831, reprinted at this time.
L(11630.aaa.45/9),O(3),DK,DN; CtY,MH,TxU.

———

P849 [—] An essay on man. In epistles to a friend. *Dublin, printed by S. Powell, for George Risk, George Ewing, & William Smith,* 1733 [1734].
8°: A–F⁴ G⁴(−G4); *1–3* 4–54.
Presumably printed immediately after the publication of epistle IV and before the end of the legal year on 24 March 1734.
O.

Pope, A. An essay on man, 1734

P850 [—] An essay on man, being the first book of ethic epistles. To Henry St. John, L. Bolingbroke. *London, printed by John Wright, for Lawton Gilliver,* 1734. (*LEP* 20 April)
2°: πA–B² A–B² B–I² K²(−K2) L–Q²; *i–viii, 1–7* 8–66. πA1 hft.
Griffith 340; *Rothschild* 1617. Watermark: royal arms; small folio. Copies in quarto, large and small folio were all advertised together, but the folios represent the earlier printing; epistle IV is printed from standing type of the separate edition, which was revised for the quarto. Priority between large and small folios has not been determined. The quarto seems to have been the version generally sold; the folios were reissued in Pope's *Works*, 1735, and those copies are not recorded here. L1 is a cancel for K2, but caused many errors in binding; K2 is present in the copies seen.
O(2, 1−A1, 1 lacks L1).

P851 [—] [large folio]
Griffith 339. No watermark; large folio. Reissued in Pope's *Works*, 1735.
ICU(+K2, lacks L1),MH.

P852 [—] — *London, printed by John Wright, for Lawton Gilliver,* 1734. (*LEP* 20 April)
4°: π^4 A–H⁴ I⁴(±I2) K¹ (F2 as 'D2'); *i–viii, 1–7* 8–74 (54 as '45'). π1 hft.
Griffith 336. No watermark, except in π. Title in red and black. The cancel I2 and final leaf K1 are on thicker paper. Possibly K1 should be considered a cancel for the final K² described in the following entry; it is from a different setting of type.
L(1486.d.3),LUC,O,C,SaU; CtY,IU,MH(−π1), TxU.

P853 [—] [fine paper]
4°: π^4 A–H⁴ I⁴(±I2) K² (F2 as 'D2'); *i–viii, 1–7* 8–74 *75; 76 blk.*
Griffith 337/338. Watermark: Strasburg bend. Griffith lists both fine and superfine copies, but no authority is given. The copy seen bears on K2 'Index to the Ethic epistles'; Spence (ed. Osborn, 1966, I. 132) records: 'the most exact account of his plan as it stood then will best appear from a leaf which he annexed to about a dozen copies of the poem, printed in that year, and sent as presents to some of his most particular friends. Most of these were afterwards called in again...' K2 seems to be conjugate with the final leaf of text K1; they are reproduced in the Scolar Press facsimile, 1969. In ordinary copies K² may have been cancelled by a new K1. Other copies (IU,MH) were issued in special presentation copies of Pope's *Works* II, with title-page date 1737; there the half-title to the following 'Ethic epistles' is signed K2 but is not conjugate with K1; the index leaf has again been cancelled.
Forster.

Pope, A. An essay on man, 1734

P854 [—] — *London, printed: and, re-printed in Dublin, by George Faulkner,* 1734.
8°: A–H⁴; *1–13* 14–64.
Griffith Add. 351b.
DA,GU(lacks A1); MH.

Piracies
The following piracies, although mainly dated 1736, undoubtedly have varying origins and dates; they probably represent only some versions of what was clearly the standard piratical format. 'Witford' is a deliberate variation on Wilford's name. Griffith 420 quotes an advertisement from LEP 8 May 1736 for 'a beautiful Elzevir edition of Mr. Pope's Essay on Man. In four epistles. Pr. 1s. This edition was sold, ready printed (as his Letters were) to Mr. Curll...' This probably represents the earliest of the piracies, but is has not been possible to arrange the editions chronologically. It will be seen that the Verses on the death of Dr. Swift became part of the standard volume. See Teerink in SB 4 (1951) 183–8 and SB 7 (1955) 238–9, and also A. H. Scouten in SB 15 (1962) 243–7.

P855 [—] An essay on man. In four epistles to a friend. Corrected by the author. The seventh edition. '*London, printed for J. Witford,* 1736.'
8°: A⁴(−A1) B–E⁴ F⁴(−F4); *i–vi, 1* 2–37 *38 blk.*
Griffith 419. The irregular collation suggests the possibility that this is an early edition; but perhaps a half-title and advertisement leaf are missing from this copy and that described in *Griffith*.
LUC.

P856 [—] — The seventh edition. '*London, printed for J. Witford,* 1736.'
12°: A⁶ B–C⁶ D(3 ll); *1–7* 8–42.
The same printer (on the evidence of the ornaments) was responsible for a piracy of 1747 (P862), and for a 1744 piracy of Akenside's *Pleasures of imagination*. A possible Newcastle origin has been suggested.
CtY.

P857 [—] — The seventh edition. '*London, printed for J. Witford,* 1736.'
12°: A–C⁶ D¹; *i–iii* iv–vi, 7 8–38.
Watermark: fleur-de-lys. *Griffith* 420. Apparently D2–6 should contain *Verses on the death of Dr. Swift,* as in P859 below; it is strange that they are missing from all copies.
O(uncut); TxU(2).

P858 [—] [another edition]
No watermark.
L(11805.bb.40/1); MH.

P859 [—] — The seventh edition. '*London, printed for J. Witford,* 1736.'
12°: A–D⁶; *i–iii* iv–vi, 7 8–⟨48⟩.
Teerink 775. With *Verses on the death of Dr. Swift,* beginning on p. 39.
L(1970); *Bibliothèque Mazarine, Paris*(lacks D6; ms. date '1756').

Pope, A. An essay on man (*Piracies*)

P860 [—] An essay on man. With some humourous verses on the death of Dean Swift, written by himself. '*Dublin printed, & sold by the booksellers of London & Westminster, 1736.*'
12°: π(2 ll) B–D⁶ E², (frt+) ²E⁶; [2] *i–iii* iv–vi, *1* 2–36, *1–2* 3–12. π1 frt, π2 engraved title.

> Teerink 1605. The engraved title π2 is not apparently conjugate with the frontispiece. ²E1 is the title to Swift's *Verses*, with imprint 'Dublin, printed: London: re-printed, and sold by the booksellers...' According to A. H. Scouten in *SB* 15 (1962) 243–7, the text was probably based on Bathurst's 1742 edition of the Pope/Swift *Miscellanies*.

C(uncut).

P861 [—] — '*Dublin: printed, & sold by the booksellers of London & Westminster, 1736.*'
12°: π² B–D⁶, (frt+) E⁶; [2] *i–iii* iv–vi, *1* 2–32, *1–2* 3–12. π1 frt, π2 engraved title.

> Sheets B and C resemble those of the preceding edition. The copy at C has sheet C from a different edition, resulting in the omission of the beginning of Epistle II.

O(−π1),C.

P862 — An essay on man. By Alexander Pope, esq; '*London*', *printed in the year 1747.*
8°: π¹ †⁴ A–B⁸ C⁴ D¹; *i–iii* iv–ix *x*, *1* 2–41 *42 blk*.
By the same printer as P856 above.

CtY.

P863 — An essay on man. In four epistles. By Alexander Pope, esq; '*London*', *printed and sold by the book-sellers in town and country,* [175–?]
12°: A–E⁶; *1–60.*

> Griffith 612. Apparently a piracy; its appearance suggests a Scottish origin.

TxU.

P864 [—] An essay on man. In four epistles to a friend. Corrected by the author. A new edition. *London, printed for, and sold by the booksellers, in town and country,* [1750/–.]
8°: *A*⁴ B–D⁸; *i–v* vi–viii, *1* 2–47 *48 blk*. A1 frt.

> Griffith 412; Teerink 1607. According to Teerink in *SB* 4 (1951) 183–8, printed from Teerink 775, P859 above; like that it contains *Verses on the death of Dr. Swift*. It appears to be considerably later than 1750; the L copy has a note of ownership dated 11 April 1775.

L(11631.bb.25); ICU(lacks D3–8).

P865 [—] An essay on man: being the first book of ethic epistles to H. St. John L. Bolingbroke. With the commentary and notes of W. Warburton, A. M. *London, printed by W. Bowyer, for M. Cooper,* 1743 [1744]. (*LEP* 23 Feb)
4°: π²(π1+title) A–O⁴; *i–vi*, *1* 2–111 *112 blk*. π1 hft.

> Griffith 589; Rothschild 1618, not recording fine-paper copies. Watermark: fleur-de-lys.

Pope, A. An essay on man, 1744

> The title is normally inserted between π1 (half-title) and π2; but there are exceptions. Entered in *SR* to Mary Cooper 17 Feb 1744; deposit copies at E,AdU,GU (and probably L,O,C) also contain *An essay on criticism* which was advertised in *GM*, *LM* Feb as issued with it. Entered to Pope in Bowyer's ledgers (together with *An essay on criticism*) under 18 Feb 1744, 1500 copies and 100 Royal. A copy was delivered to Pope on 13 Nov 1743 and 250 to Mrs. Cooper on 20 Jan 1744. An obscure entry to Knapton in Bowyer's ledgers under 29 April and 26 Sept [1749?] records 'Titles. Essay on Man 4° 12. & 50 more', suggesting a new issue, not traced.

L(642.k.2, lacks π², title; C.59.e.1, lacks π²; Ashley 3774/1),O,C,E,GU+; IU,MH(lacks title), NjP,*TxU.*

P866 [—] [fine paper]
4°: π² A–O⁴; *i–iv*, *1* 2–111 *112 blk*. π1 hft.

> Watermark: Strasburg bend. No title in copy seen; probably this is the intended form for fine-paper copies. Bowyer's ledgers suggest that the title was printed with a cancel leaf of the *Dunciad*, 1743 'without Royal'. Only 7 fine-paper copies had been delivered by 17 Sept 1745.

CtY(presentation copy from Warburton).

P867 — — Enlarged and improved by the author. With notes by William Warburton, M.A. *London, printed for John & Paul Knapton,* 1745. (*GM* Feb)
8°: (frt+) a–b⁴ c² d⁴ A–H⁴ I²; *i–iii* iv–vi 7–20 *xxi* xxii–xxviii, *1*–66 *67–68*. I2 advt.

> Griffith 607, not distinguishing this and the following. Press-figures 24–2, 32–1. The foot of p.v reads 'Inscriptions, have all the force...' Titlepage in red and black. For an account of this and following editions, see K. I. D. Maslen in *PBSA* 62 (1968) 177–88. Entered in Bowyer's ledgers under 11 Feb 1744 [/5], 1500 copies and 20 fine with margins altered; the entry also records a cancelled half-sheet (perhaps not printed off) and later 'reprinted 100 titles red' (possibly for another edition). No fine-paper copies have been identified.

L(1471.df.21),LVA-F,O(uncut); CSmH,CtY,IU, MH(−I2),TxU+.

P868 — — *London, printed for John & Paul Knapton,* 1745. (April?)
8°: (frt+) a–b⁴ c² d⁴ A–H⁴ I²; *i–iii* iv–vi 7–20 *xxi* xxii–xxviii, *1*–66 *67–68*. I2 advt.

> Rothschild 1619. Press-figures 15–3, xxvii–3, 50–3. The foot of p. v reads 'Inscriptions on the fastidious ruins of Rome...', a change not preserved in subsequent editions. Partly from standing type (including all the preliminary leaves), with revisions which were included in later editions. Entered in Bowyer's ledgers as '2d. edition' under 6 April 1744 [!], 2000 copies printed.

Pope, A. An essay on man, 1745

> L(11632.aaa.39, annotated by Michael Lort); IU(2),NjP,TxU(uncut).

P869 —— *London, printed for John & Paul Knapton*, 1745.
> 8°: (frt+) π¹ A–L⁴ M²; *i–iii* iv–vi, 7–20 *xxi* xxii–xxviii, 29–94.
>> *Griffith* 608. Title in red and black. No press-figures; frontispiece and vignette recut. Although this edition is very well produced, the new plates would suggest a piracy, were it not for the possibility that it is a parallel edition printed by Wright; cf. Pope's letter to Bowyer, 23 Feb 1744, referring to 'the *little* Essay on Man' as completed by Wright 'but possibly a title leaf may be wanting'.
> O; CtY,TxU.

P870 —— *Dublin, printed by George Faulkner*, 1745.
> 12°: (frt+) a⁸ c⁴ D–i⁸/⁴ (D2 as 'B2', D5 as 'B5'); *i–iii* iv–v 6–18 *xix* xx–xxiv, 25–94 *95–96*. i4 advt.
>> The four-leaf gatherings are signed in lower-case, in the form 'e2' on E1.
> L(1966),O; MH.

P871 —— With notes by Mr. Warburton. *London, printed for John & Paul Knapton*, 1746. (Sept?)
> 8°: (frt+) a–b⁴ c² d⁴ A–H⁴ I²; *i–iii* iv–xxviii, 1–67 *68*. 68 advt.
>> *Griffith* 620. Title in red and black. Variable press-figures on pp. 13, 56. An aberrant copy at O apparently has a⁴ of this edition prefixed to sheets of P872. There are some additions to the notes. Entered in Bowyer's ledgers as '3d. edit.' under 23 Aug 1746, 1500 copies and 30 fine with margins altered; no fine-paper copies have been identified.
> L(11632.aaa.40),BaP,EN; CtY,MH.

P872 —— With notes by Mr. Warburton. *London, printed for John & Paul Knapton*, 1748. (Feb?)
> 8°: (frt+) a–b⁴ c² d⁴ A–H⁴ I²; *i–iii* iv–xxviii, 1–67 *68*. 68 advt.
>> Entered in Bowyer's ledgers as '4th. edit.' under 8 Feb 1748, 2000 copies printed.
> L(11634.b.13; 1484.bbb.13); CtY.

P873 —— With the commentary and notes of Mr. Warburton. *London, printed for J. & P. Knapton*, 1748.
> 8°: (frt+) a⁴(−a1) B–K⁸ L⁸(−L8) M⁴; *i–ii* iii–vi, 1–5 6–165 *166*. 166 advt.
>> *Griffith* 631. The n of 'An' in the title usually fails to print. Sheets D–L have horizontal chain-lines, and are possibly by another printer since they contain no press-figures. Warburton's commentary is substantial.
> L(11631.c.36, made-up),LVA-D,O; CLU-C,IU, MH.

P874 —— With notes by William Warburton, A.M. *Dublin, printed by George Faulkner*, 1749.
> 12°: (frt+) A–D¹²; *i–ii* iii–v, 6–96.
>> *Griffith* 637.
> L(1960); *TxU*(−frt).

Pope, A. An essay on man, 1750

P875 —— An essay on man. In four epistles. By Alexander Pope. *Glasgow, printed and sold by R. & A. Foulis*, 1750. (*SM* Jan)
> 8°: a⁴ A–G⁴; *i–viii*, 1 2–57 *58–63*; *64 blk*.
> MH.

> *Verse translations of the* Essay on man *published abroad* (e.g. B. H. Brockes, Versuch vom Menschen, Hamburg, *1740*) *and prose translations published in England* (e.g. E. de Silhouette, Essais sur la critique et sur l'homme, *1737, 1741*) *are excluded, although they reprint the English text.*

[—] An excellent old ballad, called Pride will have a fall, [1720?] *See* D505.

P876 —— [dh] First chorus. Of Athenian philosophers. Written at the command of his grace, by Mr. Pope. [*London*, 1723.] (Jan)
> 4°: A⁴; *1–8*.
>> Four choruses for John Sheffield, duke of Buckingham's *Brutus*; the first two by Pope (previously published in his *Works*, 1717), the second two by Buckingham. This is a reprint of the words for a performance of the setting by Bononcini given at Buckingham House on 10 or 11 Jan 1723. Entered to Alderman Barber in Bowyer's ledgers under 14 Jan 1723, 200 copies printed.
> 'Ye shades, where sacred truth is sought'
> *Duke of Portland* (ms. notes by Lady Harley and Wanley, photocopy at O), *Thomas Cottrell-Dormer.*

P877 —— The first epistle of the first book of Horace imitated. *London, printed for R. Dodsley; sold by T. Cooper*, 1737 [1738]. (7 March)
> 2°: A¹ B–F²; *i–ii*, 1–3 4–17 '20–21' *20 blk*. B1 fly-title.
>> *Griffith* 480; *Rothschild* 1640. 'Price 1s.' on title. Publication date from *Griffith*; entered to Dodsley by Cooper in *SR* 6 March; deposit copies at L,O,AdU,GU.
> 'S * * whose love indulg'd my labours past'
> L(644.m.14/8; 162.n.41; C.57.g.7/4,−A1; Ashley 5224),O(4, 1−A1),C,EU,DT+; CLU-C, CtY(2),ICN,MH,TxU(2)+.

P878 —— *London, printed for R. Dodsley; sold by T. Cooper*, 1737 [1738].
> 2°: A¹ B–F²; *i–ii*, 1–3 4–19 *20 blk*. B1 fly-title.
>> *Griffith* 481. 'Pric 1s.' on title; pp. 18–19 correctly numbered. Apparently reset except for sheet E and part of F.
> L(1486.g.14),LVA-D(uncut),O; MH,NN-B.

P879 —— '*London, printed for R. Dodsley; sold by T. Cooper*' [*Edinburgh*], 1738.
> 8°: π¹ A–B⁴ C⁴(−C4); *i–ii*, 1–2 3–21 *22 blk*. π1 hft.
>> *Griffith* 482. The E copy is bound with Edinburgh piracies.
> O,E,EN(2, 1−π1); CtY(−π1),MH(−π1),TxU.

P880 —— *Dublin: re-printed by Geo. Faulkner*, 1738.
> 8°: A⁴ B⁴ C²; *1–5* 6–19 *20*. 20 advt.

Pope, A. The first epistle of the first book

> Griffith 483. Advertisement on p. 20 dated 23 May.
>
> L(1963),DK,DN; ICU,TxU.

P881 [—] The first epistle of the second book of Horace, imitated. *London, printed for T. Cooper,* 1737. (*DA* 20 May)

2°: A^2 B–G^2; *i–iii* iv, *1* 2–23 *24 blk.*

> Griffith 458/467. No watermark. See W. B. Todd in *Book collector* 5 (1956) 51–2. Some variant press-figures, probably representing an apprentice at work. The early state of p. 21 has catchword '[37]Charles'; the later state (in copies asterisked) '[38]Charles'. Woodfall's ledger under 12 May records 2000 copies and 150 fine for Dodsley.
>
> 'While you, great patron of mankind, sustain'
>
> L(835.m.29; Ashley 5226*),LVA-D(4, 3*),O(3, 2*),C,EU+; CLU-C*,CtY(2, 1*),ICU(2, 1*), MH*,TxU(5, 2*)+.

P882 — [fine paper] The second book of the epistles of Horace, imitated. By Mr. Pope. *London, printed for T. Cooper,* 1737.

2°: A^2(A1+title) B–G^2; [*2*] *i–iii* iv, *1* 2–23 *24 blk.* A1 hft.

> Watermark: H. Catchword on p. 21 '[38]Charles'. A1 is changed to a half-title and a general title (entered in Woodfall's ledger 18 May) is added. See Foxon in *Book collector* 5 (1956) 277–8. This issue was entered in *SR* to Dodsley, 17 May; deposit copies at L,O,AdU, GU,SaU.
>
> L(644.m.14/11),O(lacks title),AdU,GU(lacks title),SaU.

P883 [—] The first epistle of the second book... *London, printed for T. Cooper,* 1737. (*DA* 28 July)

2°: A^2 B–G^2; *i–iii* iv, *1* 2–23 *24 blk.*

> See Todd in *Book collector* 5 (1956) 51–2. Largely reset: press-figures 3–1, 6–2, 20–1, 22–†. Catchword on p. 21 '[28]Charles'. Entered in Woodfall's ledger under 21 July; 500 copies printed for Dodsley.
>
> L(1485.dd.1),O(2, 1 uncut),OA,E,LdU-B(uncut); ICN,*ICU*,MH,*NjP*.

P884 [—] — '*London, printed for T. Cooper*' [*Edinburgh*], 1737.

8°: A–C^4 D^2; *i–ii* iii–iv, *5* 6–27 *28 blk.*

> Griffith 459. Printed by Ruddiman on the evidence of the ornaments.
>
> O(2),E,EN; CtY-M,IU,MH,TxU.

P885 [—] — *London: printed. Dublin: reprinted by and for George Faulkner,* 1737.

8°: A^4 B–C^4; *i–iv* v–vi, *1* 2–18.

> Griffith 460.
>
> DK,DN; ICU,TxU.

P886 — The first satire of the second book of Horace, imitated in a dialogue between Alexander Pope of Twickenham in com. Midd. esq; on the one part, and his learned council on the other. *London, printed by L.G.* [*Lawton Gilliver*]*; sold by A. Dodd,*

Pope, A. The first satire of the second book

> E. Nutt, and by the booksellers of London & Westminster, 1733. (*GSJ* 15 Feb)

2°: A^2 B–E^2; *1–5* 6–19 *20 blk.*

> Griffith 288; *Rothschild* 1608–9. No price on title; no comma after Pope; press-figure 15–1. Entered to Gilliver in *SR* 14 Feb; deposit copies at L,LSC,EU,SaU.
>
> 'There are (I scarce can think it, but am told)' Answered by *A just imitation of the first satire,* 1733, and *The sequel of Mr. Pope's law-case,* 1733.
>
> L(644.m.14/7; 162.n.38; Ashley 5206),O(lacks E^2),OW,C,EU+; CSmH,CtY,IU,MH,TxU.

P887 — — *London, printed by L.G.* [*Lawton Gilliver*]*; sold by A. Dodd, E. Nutt, and by the booksellers of London & Westminster,* 1733.

2°: A^2 B–E^2; *1–5* 6–19 *20 blk.*

> Griffith 290/291. No price on title; comma after 'Pope' in title; no press-figure. Incorrect catchword 'In' on p. 13 corrected to 'Whether' in copies asterisked. Sheet A is reset, together with part of pp. 9, 10.
>
> L(C.59.h.9/5*; Ashley 5207; Ashley 5208*), LVA-D*,O(4, 3*),OW,C+; CLU-C,CtY(2, 1*), IU*,MH,TxU(3, 2*, 1 uncut)+.

P888 — [reimpression]

> Griffith 292. 'Price One Shilling.' added to title; catchword 'Whether' on p. 13.
>
> L(1484.m.7/9, lacks A1; Ashley 5209),LSC, LVA-D,O(3),BaP(stitched, uncut); CtY,IU,MH (2, 1 lacks A1),NN-B,TxU+.

P889 — [another edition]

> Griffith 293. Reset throughout, and probably the '2nd edition' recorded under *Griffith* 328 as listed on 17 (for 16) Jan 1734. On p. 9, line 2, 'Laureat' lacks the final e, present in all other folio printings.
>
> L(Ashley 5210),O,LdU-B; CtY,IU,TxU.

P890 — — '*London, printed by L.G; sold by A. Dodd, E. Nutt, and by the booksellers of London & Westminster*' [*Edinburgh*], 1733.

8°: D–E^4 F^2; *25* 26–43 *44 blk.*

> Griffith 289. Printed by Ruddiman on the evidence of the ornaments. Pagination and signatures are intended to follow the Edinburgh piracy of *Of the use of riches,* P927.
>
> L(993.e.51/2),O,LdU-B; CLU-C,CtY,IU,MH, TxU+.

P891 — — *London: printed. Dublin, re-printed by and for George Faulkner,* 1733. (March?)

8°: A^4 B–C^4; *1–3* 4–24. C3–4 advt.

> Griffith 298; *Rothschild* 1610. Advertisement on p. 21 dated 2 March.
>
> L(11601.cc.38/12),C,DK(2),DN,DT; ICU,IU, TxU(−C3–4).

P892 — — *London: printed. Dublin, re-printed by and for George Faulkner,* 1733. (May?)

8°: A^4 B–C^4; *1–3* 4–24. C3–4 advt.

Pope, A. The first satire of the second book

> *Griffith* 306. Advertisement on p. 21 dated 30 April. *Griffith* erroneously reports that pp. 21–24 are unnumbered.
>
> O(uncut); MH.

P893 — — To which is added, the second satire of the same book. By the same hand. Never before printed. *London, printed for L.G. [Lawton Gilliver] in Fleetstreet,* 1734. (*GSJ* 4 July)

> 4°: π¹ A–E⁴; *i–ii,* 1–3 4–40. ii err.
>
> *Griffith* 341; *Rothschild* 1620. Issued in various formats; the order of printing has not been determined. This has engraved ornaments on pp. 18, 19, 40; no watermark except on π1. Entered in *SR* 3 July; deposit copies at E, SaU, probably L,O. *Griffith* Add. 341a records a thick paper copy, lacking the title, in his own collection. It cannot at present be traced at TxU.
>
> *Second satire*: 'What, and how great, the virtue and the art'
>
> L(11642.h.43/1; 11630.c.10/6, cropt; 12273.m.1/4),O(2),OW(2, 1 uncut in wrappers),E(2),SaU + ; CtY,IU,MH,TxU.

P894 — [another impression, in folio] *London, printed for L.G.,* 1734. (*GSJ* 4 July)

> 2°: π¹ A–I²; *i–ii,* 1–3 4–36. ii err.
>
> *Griffith* 343. Small (pot) folio; watermark: royal arms. The second satire, E2–I2, was also issued separately, probably as advertised by Gilliver in *GSJ* 12 Sept; see *The second satire*, P961.
>
> L(1489.f.40; Ashley 4937, uncut),LdU-B(uncut); CtY,TxU.

P895 — [fine paper]

> *Griffith* 342. Large folio, no watermark; probably demy, measuring 14 × 9 in. when trimmed. Gilliver in *GSJ* 4 July advertised 'This edition may be had with copper ornaments in quarto and folio, of the same sizes with Mr. Pope's Homer and Works', but there are no engravings in the copy seen.
>
> O(ms. notes by Harley).

[—] Horace, epod. IV. imitated, by Sir James Baker, kt. to Lord Cad – – – –n, [1717?] *See* B15.

P896 — Horace his ode to Venus. Lib. IV. ode I. Imitated by Mr. Pope. *London, printed for J. Wright; sold by J. Roberts,* 1737. (*DP* 9 March)

> 2°: A¹ B–C²; *i–ii,* 1–3 4–7 8 blk. B1 fly-title.
>
> *Griffith* 443; *Rothschild* 1629–30. Assigned to Wright by Pope 25 Feb 1737, and entered by Wright in *SR* 8 March; deposit copies at L,O, AdU,SaU.
>
> 'Again? new tumults in my breast?'
>
> L(644.m.14/4; Ashley 4942),O(2),C,E,LdU-B + ; CLU-C,CtY,IU,MH,TxU(4).

P897 — — '*London, printed for J. Wright; sold by J. Roberts*' [*Edinburgh*], 1737.

> 8°: π¹[= C4] A–B⁴ C⁴(– C4); *i–ii,* 1–3 4–22. π1 hft.
>
> *Griffith* 444. Copies at IU,NN are bound with

Pope, A. Horace his ode to Venus

> Edinburgh piracies. Half-title reads 'Two odes of Horace imitated'. The Latin text and Pope's imitation occupy pp. 2–7; 8–14 contain another imitation of this ode, and 15–22 contain book I ode 24 and an imitation, with fly-title 'Horace his ode to Virgil, lib. I. ode xxiv. imitated'. Their author is William Hamilton of Bangour; they are collected in his *Poems*, 1748.
>
> 'Venus! call'st thou once more to arms?'
>
> 'What measures shall affliction know?'
>
> O,E(uncut); CLU-C,IU,MH(– π1),NN,TxU.

— The Iliad of Homer, translated by Mr. Pope, 1715–.

> Excluded from this catalogue.

P898 [—] The impertinent, or a visit to the court. A satyr. By an eminent hand. *London, printed for John Wileord* [!], *behind the Chapter-house near St. Paul's,* 1733. (*GSJ* 5 Nov)

> 4°: π¹ A² B–C² D¹; *1–4* 5–16. π1 hft.
>
> *Griffith* 317.
>
> 'Well, if it be my time to quit the stage'
>
> L(840.k.3/1, – π1; Ashley 3775),O(– π1),OW,C (– π1); CSmH,CtY(– π1),DFo(– π1),MH(– π1), TxU(– π1).

P899 — — By Mr. Pope. The second edition. *London, printed for E. Hill,* 1737. (*GM* June)

> 2°: A² B–E²; *i–iv,* 1–15 16 blk.
>
> *Griffith* 463. This edition adds verses 'To the author of the following satire' on A2.
>
> L(11630.h.40),O,LdU-B(uncut),*MR*; CtY,*ICN,* IU,MH,TxU.

P900 — — The third edition. *London, printed for E Hill,* 1737.

> 2°: A² B–C² D¹; *1–3* 4–14.
>
> *Griffith* 465. Without the added verses.
>
> L(11630.h.39; Ashley 5690),LVA-D,LVA-F,O, BaP; CtY(2),*ICN,*MH(2).

P901 — — The third edition. *London, printed for E. Hill,* 1737.

> 4°: A⁴ B⁴; *i–iv,* 1–12.
>
> Not in *Griffith*; possibly a piracy. The price is 6d. as opposed to 1s. for the preceding editions. CLU-C.

P902 — — The second edition. *London: printed. Dublin: re-printed by and for George Faulkner,* 1737.

> 8°: A⁴ B⁴ C²; *1–2* 3–20.
>
> *Griffith* 464. Apparently reprinted from the London second edition, P899.
>
> L(1963),LVA-D,DA,DK,DN; DFo,ICU,MH, TxU.

— Messiah...translated into Latin. *In* Gahagan, Usher: Mr. Pope's Temple of fame, 1748. *See* G4.

— Cl. Alex. Popi Messiah, ecloga sacra. Latino carmine donata. By...Richard Onely, 1749. *See* O235.

[—] Monsieur Thing's origin, 1722. *See* M413.

40-2

Pope, A. News from court

P903 '—' News from court. A ballad. To the tune of, To all ye ladies now at land. By Mr. Pope. *London, printed for S. Huddleston*, 1719. (Jan?)
½°: 2 sides, 1 column.
    Griffith Add. 110a; *Rothschild* 1652. Advertisement for 10 books below imprint. Listed in *PB* 31 Jan, advertising 'An answer to Mr. Pope's Ballad'. *Straus, Curll* notes a second edition advertised in *PB* 28 Feb, but this is part of *The court miscellany*, 1719.
'Ye ladies fair who live remote'
    Pope's authorship is doubted by all authorities; in Curll's *The court miscellany*, 1719, it is attributed to 'Mr. Caley'. Cf. *An answer to Mr. Pope's ballad*, 1719.
MC,Rothschild; *NN-B*.

P904 — Ode for musick. *London, printed for Bernard Lintott*, 1713. (16 July)
2°: *A²* B–C²; *i–iv, 1–8*. A1 hft.
    Griffith 20; *Rothschild* 1568. Publication date from *Griffith*. Entered to Lintot in *SR* 16 July; deposit copies at L,LSC,O,EU,SaU. Lintot paid Pope £15 for the copyright, 23 July (*Nichols* VIII.300).
'Descend ye nine! descend and sing'
    Pope's name on half-title only. Translated into Latin by Christopher Smart, *Carmen cl. Alexandri Pope in S. Cæciliam*, 1743, 1746.
L(643.1.26/5; Ashley 4919),LVA-D(uncut), O(uncut),EU,DT+; CLU-C,CtY(2, 1 lacks A²), MH(–A1).

P905 — Ode for musick on St. Cecilia's Day... The third edition. *London, printed for Bernard Lintot*, 1719. (EvP 15 Oct)
8°: *A⁸*; *i–ii, 1–3 4–12 13–14*. A1 frt; A8 advt.
    Griffith 110. The second edition is probably represented by Pope's *Works*, 1717.
L(11634.b.4),LVA-F,O,CT(–A8);CtY,ICU,IU, MH,TxU+.

P906 — — The fourth edition. *London, printed for Bernard Lintot*, 1722 [1721?])
8°: *D⁸*; *i–ii, 1–3 4–12 13–14*. D1 frt; D8 advt.
    Griffith 136; *Rothschild* 1569. Presumably intended to be bound with the seventh edition of *An essay on criticism*, 1722, and (like that) probably published by 5 Oct 1721.
L(991.h.25/4,–D8),O,LdU-B; CLU-C(–D8), CtY,MH(–D8),TxU.

P907 — [*idem*] An ode compos'd for the publick commencement, at Cambridge: on Monday July the 6th. 1730. At the musick-act. The words by Alexander Pope... The musick by Maurice Greene... [*Cambridge*, 1730.] (July)
2°: *A²*; *1–2 3–4*.
    Rothschild 1600. The copy at C is bound with another pair of leaves containing the anthems for 5 July. Also printed as a quarter-sheet octavo, bound at the end of *Quæstiones, una cum carminibus*, 1730 (*Griffith* 240); I doubt if

Pope, A. Ode for musick

that form was separately issued, though it is sometimes found by itself; the copies seen were previously bound with *Quæstiones*.
C; CSmH(uncut),CtY,MH.

[—] An ode for the new year. Written by Colley Cibber, [1731?] *See* C195.

— The Odyssey of Homer, 1725–.
Excluded from this catalogue.

P908 — [Of false taste] An epistle to the right honourable Richard earl of Burlington. Occasion'd by his publishing Palladio's designs of the baths, arches, theatres, &c. of ancient Rome. *London, printed for L. Gilliver*, 1731. (13 Dec?)
2°: *A²* B–D²; *1–4 5–14 15; 16 blk*. A1 hft; D2 advt.
    Griffith 259; *Rothschild* 1602. See W. B. Todd in *Book collector* 5 (1956) 48–50 for these editions. Watermarks: star & R. 'Price 1s.' on title; 10 books advertised on p. 15. Half-title 'Of taste...' Entered in *SR* 7 Dec; deposit copies at LSC,EU,AdU,SaU. Date of publication from Harley's note; advertised in *GSJ* 14 Dec.
''Tis strange the miser should his cares employ'
    Compare *Of good nature*, 1732; L. Welsted, *Of dulness and scandal*, 1732; [J. Turner] *An epistle to Mr. Pope*, 1732; *Malice defeated*, 1732; [J. Bramston] *The man of taste*, 1733.
L(162.n.18; Ashley 5203),O(4, 1–A1, 1–D2, 1 Harley's, 'first edition was publisht Dec. 13'),C, E(stitched, uncut),LdU-B(ms. date 17 Dec)+; CLU-C,CtY,IU,MH(3),TxU+.

P909 — [fine paper]
    Watermark: fleur-de-lys on shield. No price on title.
L(1485.f.3); ICN,MH.

P910 — [reimpression]
    12 books advertised on p. 15. Sheet B reset. Todd's B edition.
L(12273.m.1/1,–A1,D2),LSC; *CtY,IU,NN-B, NjP*.

P911 — — The second edition. *London, printed for L. Gilliver*, 1731 [1732]. (EvP 6 Jan)
2°: *A²* B–D²; *1–4 5–14 15; 16 blk*. A1 hft; D2 advt.
    Griffith 265. A reimpression. Half title 'Of false taste...' Todd's C edition.
O(2, 1–A1),OA,BaP(2, 1 stitched, uncut, 1–A1, D2); CtY,IU(uncut).

P912 — [*idem*] Of false taste. An epistle to...Richard earl of Burlington... The third edition. *London, printed for L. Gilliver*, 1731 [1732]. (15 Jan)
2°: *A²* B–D²; *1–4 5–14 15; 16 blk*. D2 advt.
    Griffith 267, not distinguishing the following editions. All have dedicatory epistle by Pope on A2 instead of half-title. 'Price 1s.' on title; p. 11, line 19 reads 'Cielings'. Todd's D edition. A reimpression of the preceding. Publication date from *Twickenham Pope* III. ii.124.

Pope, A. Of false taste

L(162.n.19; C.59.h.9/3),LVA-D,O,GU,
LdU-B; CLU-C,CtY,IU,MH,TxU+.

P913 — [another edition]
'Price 1s.' on title; p. 11, line 19 reads 'Ceil-
ings'. Todd's E edition. Another setting,
probably printed to meet the demand caused
by the publication of the later ethic epistles.
L(Ashley 5204),LVA-D,O,DT,WcC; CtY,ICU,
MH,NN-B,TxU+.

P914 — [another edition]
'(Price 1s.)' on title; p. 11 line 19 reads 'Ceil-
ings'. Press-figures 6–2, 8–2, 11–2. Todd's F
edition. Possibly printed as late as 1735 to
complete sets of the ethic epistles.
ICU.

P915 — [idem] Of taste, an epistle to...Richard earl of
Burlington... [Edinburgh] Printed in the year 1732.
8°: A⁸; 1–2 3–15 16 blk.
Griffith 264. Printed in Edinburgh on the
evidence of the ornaments.
L(11630.bbb.42/1),E; CSmH,ICU,MH,TxU.

P916 —— London: printed. And, Dublin re-printed by
George Faulkner, 1732.
4°: A² B⁴; 1–3 4–12.
Griffith 277. Also reprinted by Faulkner with
[Gilbert West] Stowe, 1732.
L(11632.bb.55),LdU-B; DLC,MH.

P917 — Of the characters of women: an epistle to a lady.
London, printed by J. Wright, for Lawton Gilliver,
1735. (7 Feb?)
2°: A² ˣB¹ B–D² E¹; 1–4 [2] 5 6–16 17; 18 blk. A1
hft; E1 advt.
Griffith 360–1; Rothschild 1624–5. Some
copies, asterisked below, have a misprint in the
imprint, 'Flettstreet'; the corrected reading is
found in Harley's pre-publication copy. ˣB¹
and E¹ have been seen to be conjugate.
Entered in SR 7 Feb; deposit copy at L.
Harley annotated his copy 'Publisht. Feb. 7.';
the earliest advertisement seen is in LEP 8
Feb.
'Nothing so true as what you once let fall'
L(1484.m.7/10; 644.m.14/5,–A1; 162.n.25;
Ashley 4939*; Ashley 4940, made-up, –E1),O(6,
1*, 1 Harley's 'R. Feb. 6.'),C,E*,LdU-B(3, 1*)+;
CLU-C,CtY(4, 1* uncut),ICU(3),MH(2, 1 uncut),
TxU(3, 1* lacks ˣB/E)+.

P918 —— 'London, printed by J. Wright, for Lawton
Gilliver' [Edinburgh], 1735.
8°: A⁴ B⁴; 1–5 6–15 16 blk.
Griffith 362. Printed by Ruddiman on the
evidence of the ornaments.
L(993.e.51/5),O,E; CtY(uncut),CtY-M,ICU,
TxU.

P919 —— London: printed. Dublin: re-printed by George
Faulkner, 1735.
8°: A⁸ (A2 as 'A3'); 1–5 6–15 16 blk.
Griffith 363.
O,DK; CSmH,MH,TxU.

Pope, A. Of the knowledge

P920 — [Of the knowledge and characters of men] An
epistle to the right honourable Richard lord visct.
Cobham. London, printed for Lawton Gilliver, 1733
[1734]. (GSJ 16 Jan)
2°: A² B–E²; i–iv, 1 2–13 14–15; 16 blk. A1 hft; E2
advt.
Griffith 329; Rothschild 1611–12. Half-title
'Of the knowledge and characters of men...'
Entered in SR 5 Feb; deposit copies at L,O,
EU,AdU,SaU.
'Yes, you despise the man to books confin'd'
L(644.m.14/6, –E2; 162.n.23, –A1, E2; C.59.
h.9/6, uncut; Ashley 4936),O(6, 1 –A1, E2,
1 –E2),C,EU,LdU-B(uncut)+; CSmH,CtY,
ICU(3),MH(4),TxU(7)+.

P921 [—] — 'London' [Edinburgh], printed in the year
1734.
8°: A⁴ B²; 1–2 3–12.
Griffith 330. Printed by Fleming on the
evidence of the ornaments.
L(11630.bbb.42/10),O; CLU-C,ICU(uncut),
MH,TxU.

P922 —— London: printed. And re-printed in Dublin, by
George Faulkner, 1734.
8°: A² B–C⁴; 1–5 6–20. A1 hft.
Griffith 335. In some copies (e.g. 3 at O) C2
and C4 appear to be cancels; apparently the
sheet was first wrongly imposed so that C1 and
C3 were conjugate, and the other leaves had to
be pasted in. No change of text has been seen.
L(11631.aa.47/6; 1963),O(4),DA(2, –A1),DN,
DT+; CtY,DFo,IU,TxU.

P923 — Of the use of riches, an epistle to the right honorable Allen lord Bathurst. London, printed by J.
Wright, for Lawton Gilliver, 1732 [1733]. (15 Jan)
2°: A²(–A2) B² C²(±C2[=A2]) D–F²; i–ii, 1–20.
20 err.
No watermark. Griffith 280–2, recording
variants but not fine-paper copies; Rothschild
1605–6. Most copies read 'ypon' in p. 13, line
13, for 'yon'; the error is noted in the erratum
on p. 20. The copies with the corrected reading
(Griffith 281) are asterisked below; they may
represent a reimpression. No copies have been
identified with the erratum on p. 20 removed
(Griffith 282, not seen). Advertised in DJ 16
Jan 'yesterday'; entered in SR 13 Jan; deposit
copies are fine-paper.
'Who shall decide, when doctors disagree'
L(1484.m.7/12; 1485.f.7*; 162.n.20; C.59.h.
9/4; Ashley 5205),O(5, 1*),C(2, 1*),EU,LdU-B+;
CLU-C(2, 1*),CtY(2, 1*),IU(2, 1*),MH(3, 1 ms.
date 16 Jan),TxU(3, 1 uncut, 1*)+.

P924 — [fine paper]
Watermark: fleur-de-lys on shield. All copies
seen are deposit copies. Misprint 'ypon' in
p. 13, line 13.
L(644.m.14/3),LSC,O,EU,SaU.

Pope, A. Of the use of riches

P925 — — The second edition. *London, printed by J. Wright, for Lawton Gilliver*, 1733. (16 Jan?)

2⁰: A^2 B–D^2 F^2 *F^2; *1–2* 3–22 *23; 24 blk*. *F_2 advt.
Griffith 324. See W. B. Todd in *Book collector* 5 (1956) 50; he dates this edition as 16 Jan with a reference to the *Evening-post*, but it has not been traced in Berrington's *Evening post*. 14 books advertised on p. 23.
L(1485.dd.7; 12273.m.1/2, title with P923 text), LVA-D(− *F_2),O,LdU-B; CtY,MH(2),NcD, TxU.

P926 — — The second edition. *London, printed by J. Wright, for Lawton Gilliver*, 1733.

2⁰: A^2 B–F^2; *1–2* 3–22 *23; 24 blk*. F_2 advt.
Griffith 323. 16 books advertised on p. 23, including Bramston's *Man of taste*, published 8 March. Todd's B edition. Possibly a later reprint to complete sets of the ethic epistles.
L(11657.m.24),LVA-F,O,EU,LdU-B; CLU-C, CtY,ICU,IU,TxU(2).

P927 — — '*London, printed by J. Wright, for Lawton Gilliver*' [*Edinburgh*], 1732 [1733].

8⁰: A–C^4; *1–2* 3–24.
Griffith 283. Printed by Ruddiman on the evidence of the ornaments.
L(11630.bbb.42/6),O,E(2),GM,LdU-B; CtY, ICU,MH,TxU.

P928 — — *London: printed, and re-printed in Dublin, by Sylvanus Pepyat*, 1733.

4⁰: π^1 A–D^2 E^1 (A1 as 'A2'); *i–ii*, 1–17 *18 blk*.
Griffith 325. π1 and E1 have been seen to be conjugate.
DT; MH.

P929 — — *Dublin, printed by S. Powell, for George Risk, George Ewing, & William Smith*, 1733.

8⁰: A^4 B–C^4; *i–iv*, 1–20. A1 hft.
Griffith 326; Rothschild 1607.
L(1963),O,DA,DK; CSmH,IU,MH,TxU.

P930 — — *Printed at London: Dublin, re-printed by and for George Faulkner*, 1733.

8⁰: A^4 B–C^4; *1–3* 4–22 *23–24 blk*.
Griffith 327. The order of this and the following (not recorded in *Griffith*) has not been determined. C4 is blank.
L(11630.aaa.45/5),DA(uncut),DN(2); TxU.

P931 — — *London: printed. Dublin, re-printed, by and for George Faulkner*, 1733.

8⁰: A^4 B–C^4; *1–3* 4–22 *23–24*. C4 advt.
C4 bears advertisements.
L(11631.aa.47/4),O.

P931·5 — 'On Charles earl of Dorset, in the church of Knolle in Kent.' [*London*, 1731?]

1⁰.
The title and first line are taken from Pope's *Works* II, 1735. H. G. Pollard reports having seen a framed copy of this poem at Knole, but it cannot now be traced. The errata to the *Works* change the title to 'in the church of

Pope, A. On Charles earl of Dorset

Withyham in Sussex'; see *Twickenham Pope* VI.334–6. Compare P977 for this type of publication.
'Dorset, the grace of courts, the muse's pride'

P932 — One thousand seven hundred and thirty eight. A dialogue something like Horace. *London, printed for T. Cooper*, [1738.] (16 May)

2⁰: A^2 B–D^2; *i–iv*, 1 2–10 *11; 12 blk*. A1 hft; D2 advt.
Griffith 484; Rothschild 1642. '(Price ONE SHILLING.)' on title. Publication date from *Griffith*; entered in *SR* to Pope by John Wright, 12 May; deposit copies at L,O,AdU, GU.
'Not twice a twelvemonth you appear in print'
Cf. *August the second, one thousand seven hundred and thirty eight*, 1738; *A dialogue on one thousand seven hundred and thirty-eight*, 1738; Bezaleel Morrice, *The present corruption of Britons; being a paraphrase*, [1738]; [T. Newcomb] *A supplement to One thousand seven hundred thirty-eight*, 1738; *One thousand seven hundred thirty nine*, 1740.
L(643.1.28/24,−A1; 644.m.14/13,−A1; 162.n. 21; Ashley 5229),O,C(2, 1 uncut),E,DG(−A1, D2)+; CLU-C,CtY,ICU,IU,MH+.

P933 — [reimpression]
Griffith 485. '(Price One Shilling.)' on title; signature D under 'her'.
L(11630.h.41; Ashley 5230),LVA-D(uncut),O, BaP; CLU-C(uncut),CtY(uncut),IU(uncut),MH, TxU.

P934 — [reimpression]
Griffith 486. '(Price One Shilling.)' on title; signature D under 'behind'. Title in part reset.
LVA-D; CtY,TxU.

P935 — — *London, printed for T. Cooper*, 1738.
2⁰: A^2 B–D^2; *i–iv*, 1 2–10 *11; 12 blk*. A1 hft; 10 err; D2 advt.
Griffith 498. '(Price 1s.)' on title. Reset throughout. *Griffith* suggests this is listed in *LM* August, but the entry is for D286.
L(Ashley 5231),O; CLU-C,CtY.

P936 — — '*London, printed for T. Cooper*' [*Edinburgh*], 1738.
8⁰: π^1 A^4 B^1; *1–3* 4–12.
Griffith 487. Printed by Ruddiman on the evidence of the ornaments. π1 and B1 have been seen to be conjugate.
L,O,EN; CtY,ICU(2, 1 uncut),MH,MiU,TxU.

P937 — — *Dublin: re-printed by Geo. Faulkner*, 1738.
8⁰: A^4 B^2; *1–3* 4–12.
Griffith 488.
L(11602.bb.33/6),O,C(2),DN,DT+; CtY,ICU, MH,TxU.

P938 — One thousand seven hundred and thirty eight. Dialogue II. *London, printed for R. Dodsley*, 1738. (18 July)

Pope, A. One thousand... Dialogue II

2°: A^2 B–D^2; *1–3* 4–16.
　　Griffith 494; *Rothschild* 1643. Some copies (asterisked below) have misprint 'Fools' for 'Tools' in the last line on p. 10; see W. B. Todd in *Book collector* 1 (1952) 127. Publication date from *Griffith*; entered in *SR* to Pope by Dodsley 17 July; deposit copies at L,O, AdU,GU (all in the correct state).
'Tis all a libel – P-xt-n (Sir) will say'
L(1476.dd.29*); 644.m.14/13; 162.n.22; Ashley 5232*),O(4, 1*),C(2, 1*),E(2, 1* uncut), DG+; CtY(2, 1*),ICU,IU,MH,TxU(3, 1*)+.

P939 — — '*London, printed for R. Dodsley*' [*Edinburgh*], 1738.
8°: A–B^4; *1–3* 4–16.
　　Griffith 495. Printed by Ruddiman on the evidence of the ornament.
O,E,EN; ICU(2, 1 uncut),MH(2),TxU.

P940 — — *Dublin, printed by R. Reilly, for G. Risk, G. Ewing, W. Smith, & G. Faulkner*, 1738.
8°: A–B^4; *1–3* 4–16.
　　Griffith 496.
L(1963),O,C(2),DN,DT+; CtY,ICU,MH,TxU.

— [Pastorals] Bucolica Alexandri Popii...latine reddita: interprete S. Barrett, 1746. *See* B88.

[—] A poem by Doctor Young, on Miss Harvey a child of a day old, [1725.] *See* Y108.

[—] Poems occasion'd by reading the travels of Captain Lemuel Gulliver, 1727. *See* S358.

[—] 'Prologue & epilogue [to Addison's Cato].' Pope wrote to Caryll, 30 April 1713, 'the prologue & epilogue are cry'd about the streets by the common hawkers'; there is no other evidence for a separate edition. Conceivably the reference is to publication in periodicals such as the *Guardian* of 18 April.

P941 — The rape of the lock. An heroi-comical poem. In five canto's. *London, printed for Bernard Lintott*, 1714. (*PB* 4 March)
8°: (frt+) A^4 B–D^8 (+5 plates); *i–viii, 1* 2–48 (29 as '26', 44, 45 as '45, 44').
　　Griffith 29. Watermark: IM; uncut copies $8\frac{1}{8}\times5$ in. Title in red and black; engraved ornaments. Entered to Lintot in *SR* 2 March; deposit copies at LSC,E,EU,AdU. First published in *Miscellaneous poems and translations*, 1712, in two cantos; Lintot paid Pope £15 for additions, 20 Feb 1714 (*Nichols* VIII.300). According to Pope's correspondence, 3000 copies were sold in four days.
'What dire offence from am'rous causes springs'
L(C.70.bb.1/1; C.59 ff.13/1,–1 plate; Ashley 1297),O,C(2, 1 made-up),E,DG+; CSmH(uncut), CtY,IU,MH(3),TxU(2)+.

P942 — [fine paper]
　　Griffith 30. No watermark; cut copies measure $8\frac{1}{2}\times5\frac{1}{2}$ in. The inner margins are enlarged.

Pope, A. The rape of the lock

　　PB 28 Jan 1714 advertised fine-paper copies as being printed to order only.
L(1958, 'ex dono authoris'),LVA-D,O; CSmH,IU, MH,TxU.

P943 — — The second edition. *London, printed for Bernard Lintott*, 1714. (*PB* 11 March)
8°: (frt+) A^4 B–D^8 (+5 plates); *i–viii, 1* 2–48.
　　Griffith 34. Title in red and black.
L(11659.aaa.90),O,C,DT,LdU-B+; CtY, ICU (3, 1–frt),IU(2),MH(2, 1 uncut),TxU+.

P944 — — The third edition. *London, printed for Bernard Lintott*, 1714. (27 July?)
8°: A–D^8; *i–x, 1* 2–52 *53–54*. A1 frt; D8 advt.
　　Griffith 35. In this and subsequent London editions the plates are included in the collation. Presumably the edition entered to Lintot in Bowyer's ledgers under 13 July 1714, 1000 copies printed. Advertised in *DC* 27 July, but also in *MC* May; since the latter was published by Lintot, he probably anticipated the publication date.
L(11631.bbb.39/2),O(–D8),CT(–D8),*MR*; CtY,ICU(2),MH,TxU.

P945 — — The third edition. With additions. *Dublin, printed for J. Henly*, 1714.
12°: A–C^6; *1–4* 5–36.
　　Griffith Add. 35b (the CtY copy).
DN(2),DT; CtY.

P946 — — The fourth edition corrected. *London, printed for Bernard Lintott*, 1715. (*MC* Sept)
8°: A–D^8; *i–x, 1* 2–52 *53–54*. A1 frt; D8 advt.
　　Griffith 43. Entered to Lintot in Bowyer's ledgers under 6 Sept, 1000 copies printed.
L(12274.h.10),O; CtY,ICU(4),IU,MH,TxU (–D8).

P947 — — The fifth edition. '*London*' [*The Hague*] printed for T. Johnson, 1716.
8°: A–B^8; *1–4* 5–30 *31–32*. B8 advt.
　　Griffith 62. The only copies seen form part of Johnson's piracy of Pope's *Works*, 1718; but it was clearly issued separately.
L(12274.e.12); TxU.

P948 — — The fifth edition corrected. *London, printed for Bernard Lintot*, 1718.
8°: A–D^8; *i–x*, 1–53 *54*. A1 frt; 54 advt.
　　Griffith 100.
L(12274.h.3/1),LVA-F,O(2),AdU; CtY(uncut), ICU,IU,MH.

P949 — — The sixth edition corrected. *London, printed for Bernard Lintot*, 1723. (2 Feb?)
8°: A–D^8; *i–x*, 1–53 *54*. A1 frt; 54 advt.
　　Griffith 140. Entered to Lintot in Bowyer's ledgers together with the *Key* under 17 Jan, 1000 copies printed; the paper ledger records delivery on 2 Feb.
L(11634.b.5/1),O,C,LdU-B; CLU-C,CtY,MH, TxU(–A1, D3).

Pope, A. The rape of the lock

P950 — — *Dublin, printed for J. Thompson, 1729.*
8°: A–D⁴; *1–3* 4–32.
The title of the copy seen appears to be a cancel; no earlier issue has been traced.
L(11630.aaa.45/3).

P951 — — Written in the year 1712... And dedicated to Mrs. Arabella Fermor. *Dublin, printed in the year 1750.*
8°: (2 ll) C–E⁴; [*4*] 9–32.
The collation is irregular; the leaf after the title, which bears the first two pages of text, is numbered '48' on the verso. Possibly a reissue of an earlier unrecorded edition.
Bibliothèque nationale, Paris.

[—] A receipt for cuckolding. By a female physician, 1726. *In* D208.

P952 — A receipt to make a soop. By Mr. Pope to D----n S----t. [1726/–.]
slip: 1 side, 1 column.
The typography is quite good, but gives no indication of place or date. It is not inconsistent with a date of 1726.
'Take a nuckle of veal'
For a discussion of the authorship see *Twickenham Pope* VI. 253–5 and references. Originally written in a composite letter to Swift from Pope, Gay and others.
O.

P953 — A Roman catholick version of the first psalm, for the use of a young lady. *London, printed for R. Burleigh, 1716.* (*FP* 30 June)
½°: 1–2, 1 column.
Griffith 58. Advertisements below imprint. Possibly published before the date given here; Pope writing to Swift on 20 June refers to the 'wicked...who have printed a scandalous [psalm] in my name'.
'The maid is blest that will not hear'
See T. Brereton's *An English psalm*, 1716.
L(Ashley 5202).

P954 — — *Dublin, printed, and sold, by S. Powell, 1716.*
½°: 1 side, 1 column.
Rothschild 1583.
Rothschild.

— The second book of the epistles of Horace, imitated. *See* P882.

P955 — The second epistle of the second book of Horace, imitated by Mr. Pope. *London, printed for R. Dodsley, 1737.* (*LDP* 28 April)
2°: A² B–E²; *1–3* 4–19 *20 blk.*
Griffith 447, not distinguishing editions and issues. See W. B. Todd in *Book collector* 5 (1956) 50–1 and Foxon *ibidem* 277–9. Variable press-figures on pp. 6, 9, 10, 13, 14, 18. No watermark. Some copies (asterisked below) have footnote on p. 12 misnumbered '16' (for 15). Entered in *SR* to Dodsley on 28 April; deposit copies are fine-paper except for GU.
'Dear Col'nel! Cobham's and your country's friend!'

Pope, A. The second epistle of the second book

L(Ashley 4941*),LVA-D(2),O(3, 2*),C*,EU+;
CLU-C,CtY(2, 1*),ICU,MH*,TxU+.

P956 — [fine paper]
Watermark: H. Footnote on p. 12 corrected in these copies. All copies seen are deposit copies.
L(644.m.14/11),O,AdU,SaU.

P957 — — *London, printed for R. Dodsley, 1737.* (20 May?)
2°: A² B–E²; *1–3* 4–19 *20 blk.*
Press-figures 12–1, 14–2, 18–1; pp. 3–12 reset, the remainder reimpressed. Publication date suggested by Todd, to accompany P881.
L(1959),LVA-D(2, 1 uncut),O,C,E; CtY,ICN, MH,*NN-B.*

P958 — — To Colonel ***** [*Edinburgh*] *Printed in the year 1737.*
8°: π¹ A–B⁴ C¹; *1–3* 4–19 *20 blk.*
Griffith 448. The copy at E is bound with Edinburgh piracies.
L(1509/88),O,E,EN(2); ICU,MH(2),TxU.

P959 — — *London: printed, Dublin: reprinted by and for George Faulkner, 1737.*
8°: A–B⁴ C¹; *1–3* 4–18.
Griffith 449, suggesting copies lack one leaf.
DN; ICU,TxU.

P960 — — *Dublin, printed by and for Sylvanus Pepyat, 1737.*
8°: A–C⁴; *1–3* 4–24.
Griffith 450.
C,DG(uncut); TxU.

P961 [—] The second satire of the second book of Horace paraphrased. [*London*, 1734.] (12 Sept?)
2°: E2 F–I²; *19–21* 22–36.
Half-title only; a reissue of the second part of the small folio issue of *The first satire... To which is added the second*, P894. That was published 4 July 1734; this issue is probably that advertised by Gilliver in *GSJ* 12 Sept, quoted in *Griffith* 344.
'What, and how great, the virtue and the art'
LVA-D,O,C,WcC(uncut).

P962 [—] — 'London, printed for L.G. in Fleetstreet' [*Edinburgh*], 1734.
8°: A–B⁴ C²; *1–4* 5–20.
Griffith 344. Printed by Ruddiman on the evidence of the ornaments. The form of the imprint suggests it was reprinted from the edition of the two satires together.
L(993.e.51/3),O; MH,TxU.

P963 — — *Dublin: re-printed by and for J. Carson, 1734.*
8°: A⁴ B⁴; *1–3* 4–16.
DT.

P964 [—] The second satire of the second book of Horace praprhased [!]. By the author of the first. *London, printed by J. Wright, for Lawton Gilliver, 1735* [1734?]. (3 Oct?)
2°: A¹ B–E² F¹; *i–ii, 1–3* 4–18.
Griffith 410 (not seen by him). Probably the

Pope, A. The second satire of the second book

edition advertised in *GSJ* 3 Oct 1734, as quoted under *Griffith* 345.
L(1484.m.7/8),LdU-B; CtY,IU(uncut).

[—] A sermon against adultery, [1738.] *See* P973.

[—] Several copies of verses on occasion of Mr. Gulliver's travels, 1727. *See* S356.

P965 — The sixth epistle of the first book of Horace imitated. *London, printed for L. Gilliver, 1737 [1738].* (23 Jan?)
2°: *A*² B–E²; *i–iv, 1–3 4–15 16 blk.* A1 hft.
Griffith 476; *Rothschild* 1638–9. Publication date from *Griffith*; listed in *GM, LM* Jan. Entered by Pope in *SR* 14 Jan as 'speedily to be published'; Gilliver is authorized to print and publish the first edition; deposit copies at L,O,AdU,GU.
'"Not to admire, is all the art I know'
L(644.m.14/9; Ashley 5225),O(3, 1–A1),C,E, LdU-B(2, 1 uncut)+; CLU-C,CtY,ICU,MH(3), TxU(3)+.

P966 — — '*London, printed for L. Gilliver*' [*Edinburgh*], 1738.
8°: A–B⁴; *1–3 4–15 16 blk.*
Griffith 477. The E copy is bound with Edinburgh piracies.
O,E,*MP*; CtY(uncut in wrappers),IU,MH,TxU.

P967 — The sixth epistle of the first book of Horace. *Dublin, printed by and for J. Jones, 1738.*
12°: A⁶ B²; *1 2–15 16 blk.*
Griffith 478. The collation differs from that in *Griffith*, but has been clearly seen in the copy at O.
O; TxU.

P968 [—] Sober advice from Horace, to the young gentlemen about town. As deliver'd in his second sermon. Imitated in the manner of Mr. Pope. Together with the original text, as restored by the Revd. R. Bentley... And some remarks on the version. *London, printed for T. Boreman; sold by the booksellers of London & Westminster,* [1734.] (*LEP* 21 Dec)
2°: π¹ *A*² B–E² F¹; *i–iii, 1 2–10* (both Latin & English) [*1 blk*].
Griffith 347; *Rothschild* 1621. P. 5, line 3 reads 'amiss'. π1 and F1 have been seen to be conjugate.
'The tribe of templars, play'rs, apothecaries'
L(840.m.1/18; 643.m.16/13; 162.n.43; Ashley 5223, uncut),O(6, 1 Harley's 'R. Dec. 20'),OW(2), C(3),LdU-B+; CSmH,CtY(2),ICU(5),MH,TxU (2, 1 uncut)+.

P969 [—] [another edition]
Griffith 356. P. 5, line 3 reads 'amise'; sheets A–C are reset, the rest reimpressed. Publication date of Jan 1735 suggested by *Griffith*.
L(Ashley 5222),O,LdU-B; IU,TxU.

P970 [—] — '*London, printed for T. Boreman; sold by the booksellers of London & Westminster*' [*Edinburgh*], [1735.]

Pope, A. Sober advice from Horace

8°: *A*⁴ B–C⁴; *i–iii, 1 2–10* (twice) [*1*]. C4ᵛ advt.
Griffith 348 & 355, apparently describing the same book. Printed by Ruddiman on the evidence of the ornament; advertisement of piracies on C4ᵛ.
LVA-D,O,*MP*; ICU(2),MH,TxU.

P971 [—] — *London: printed. And, Dublin re-printed by George Faulkner, 1735.*
8°: *A*⁴ B–C⁴; *i–iii, 1 2–10* (twice) [*1 blk*].
L(T.902/10),DA; IU(cropt).

P972 [—] — *London: printed for T. Boreman; and Dublin re-printed, 1737.*
8°: *A*⁸; *i–iii, 2 3–7* (twice) [*1 blk*].
Griffith 475b, suggesting it might be a London piracy; the location of copies in Dublin suggests it is a true Dublin edition.
DA,DK; MH,TxU.

P973 [—] [*idem*] A sermon against adultery: being sober advice from Horace, to the young gentlemen about town. As delivered in his second sermon. Imitated in the manner of Mr. Pope... *London, printed for T. Cooper; sold by the booksellers of London & Westminster,* [1738.] (*LDP* 26 May)
2°: π¹(±) *A*² B–E² F¹; *i–iii, 1 2–10* (twice) [*1 blk*].
Griffith 489. A reissue of P969 with a cancel title. *Sober advice from Horace,* the earlier state, was advertised by Cooper on 16 May 1738; see *Griffith.* '200 Sober advice from Horace, by Mr. Pope, and his fourth share of the copy' formed lot 4 of an anonymous trade sale (probably of C. Corbett) on 23 Dec 1742 (cat. at O-JJ), sold to Lintot for 16s. od.
L(11602.i.20/2; Ashley 4938),LVA-D,O; IU, MH,TxU(2).

P974 — The temple of fame: a vision. *London, printed for Bernard Lintott, 1715.* (1 Feb)
8°: *A*⁴ B–G⁴; *1–6 7–52 53–56.* A1 hft; G3–4 advt.
Griffith 36. Publication date from *Griffith*; listed in *MC* Jan. Entered in *SR* 1 Feb; deposit copies at LSC,O,E,EU. Lintot paid Pope 30 guineas for the copyright on 1 Feb (*Nichols* VIII.300). There is an uncut copy in the original blue wrappers at LVA-D. Reprinted with his Latin translation by Usher Gahagan, *Mr. Pope's Temple of fame,* 1748.
'In that soft season when descending showers'
See — Preston, *Æsop at the bear-garden...In imitation of the Temple of fame,* 1715.
L(C.59.ff.13/2),O(3),C(2),E,DT+; CLU-C, CSmH,IU(2),MH(3),TxU(4)+.

P975 — — The second edition. *London, printed for Bernard Lintott, 1715.* (*DC* 8 Oct)
8°: *A*⁴ B–G⁴; *1–6 7–52 53–56.* A1 hft; G3–4 advt.
Griffith 45. Apparently the edition entered to Lintot in Bowyer's ledgers under 1 Oct 1715, 1000 copies printed. The majority of copies have a frontispiece inserted after A1, with matching stab-holes. *Griffith* suggests this was

Pope, A. The temple of fame

a later addition of about 1718 and refers to it as first advertised in 1720.

L(12274.h.8,+frt),LVA-D,LVA-F(−G3–4),O(2, 1+frt),LdU-B(+frt); CLU-C(+frt),CtY(+frt), IU,MH,TxU(2, 1+frt,−G3–4)+.

P976 —— *Dublin: re-printed by Edw. Sandys, for George Grierson, 1715.*

12°: A–B⁶ C¹ (A3 as 'A2'); *1–2* 3–25 *26 blk.*

DA,DN,DT.

P977 — To Sir Godfrey Kneller, on his painting for me the statues of Apollo, Venus, and Hercules. [*London*, 1719?]

obl ¼°: 1 side, 1 column.

Collected in *Poetical miscellanies...published by Sir Richard Steele*, 1727 (cf. *Twickenham Pope* VI. 213). The date is suggested in Pope's *Correspondence* ed. Sherburn II (1956) 17–18n.

'What god, what genius did the pencil move'

Below the verse, 'A. Pope.'

Herts CRO (Panshanger box 46).

P978 — To the ingenious Mr. Moore, author of the celebrated worm-powder. *London, printed for E. Curll*, 1716. (*PB* 1 May)

½°: 1–2, 1 column.

Griffith 53; *Rothschild* 1578. Advertised in *PB* as 'The worms, a satyr.'

'How much, egregious Moore, are we'

For a reply see *Moore' worms for the learned Mr. Curll*, 1716, not mentioned in standard accounts of the Pope–Curll quarrel.

L(12273.m.1/6; Ashley 5201),O,E,*Rothschild*; CtY,*ICN*(Luttrell, 2 May),MH,TxU.

P979 —— The second edition. *London, printed for E. Curll*, 1716. (*PM* 5 May)

½°: 1–2, 1 column.

Griffith 57. Apparently a reimpression.

MH.

P980 —— [*London?* 1716/–.]

slip: 1 side, 1 column.

Griffith Add. 53a. Rough woodcuts at head and foot; apparently a hawker's song. There are various engraved versions with music which are not included here.

MH.

P981 [—] To the ingenious Mr. John Moor, author of the celebrated worm-powder. [*Dublin?* 1716?]

½°: 1 side, 1 column.

Rothschild 1580. The footnote to the penultimate line 'Burttons[!] Coffee-House London' makes it clear that this is not a London edition; it is almost certainly Dublin.

Rothschild.

P982 [—] The universal prayer. By the author of the Essay on man. *London, printed for R. Dodsley*, 1738. (*LEP* 22 June)

2°: A–B²; *1–3* 4–7 *8 blk.*

Griffith 492; *Rothschild* 1644. According to *Rothschild*, 'some copies have sig. B on p. 5': none has been seen.

Pope, A. The universal prayer

'Father of all! in every age'

Translated into French by J. J. Le Franc de Pompignan as *La prière universelle*, [1740.]

L(C.57.g.7/5; C.131.h.1/4***; Ashley 5233),O, OW(uncut),C,LdU-B(2)+; CLU-C,CtY(2),ICU, MH,TxU(2)+.

P983 [—] — '*London, printed for R. Dodsley*' [*Edinburgh*], 1738.

8°: A⁴; *1–3* 4–7 *8 blk.*

Griffith 493. Printed by Ruddiman on the evidence of the ornament.

O(2); CtY(uncut),IU,MH,TxU.

— Verses on the grotto at Twickenham... Attempted in Latin and Greek [by Robert Dodsley], 1743. *See* D390.

P984 [—] Verses upon the late D——ss of M——. By Mr. P——————. *London, printed for W. Webb*, 1746. (*GA* 22 Feb)

2°: A² B¹; *1–2* 3–5 *6.*

Griffith 613; *Rothschild* 1647. (*Griffith* 614 is a ghost, based on misdescription of the L copy.) There appear to be three impressions distinguishable by the letter spacing between V,E,R in 'Verses' at head of p. 3; no priority has been established. This has spacing 12·5 and 12 mm. Sheet B was printed (by half-sheet imposition) 'at one pull'; it has a point-hole in the margin.

'But what are these to great Atossa's mind?'

A suppressed passage from Pope's *Of the characters of women*, probably published on the initiative of Bolingbroke. The suggestion that they refer to Sarah, duchess of Marlborough is probably wrong; it is now considered virtually certain that Katherine, duchess of Buckingham was intended.

CSmH,CtY,MH(uncut).

P985 [—] [another impression]

Spacing of 14 and 10 mm. between V,E,R on p. 3.

L(Ashley 4946),O; CLU-C.

P986 [—] [another impression]

Spacing of 11 and 13·5 mm. between V,E,R on p. 3. In this impression sheet A was also printed 'at one pull'.

L(11631.h.15); IU,MH(2).

P987 — Windsor-Forest. To the right honourable George lord Lansdown. *London, printed for Bernard Lintott*, 1713. (*DC* 7 March)

2°: A–E²; *i–ii*, 1–18.

No watermark. *Griffith* 9; *Rothschild* 1567, not noting fine-paper copies. Entered to Lintot in *SR* 5 March; deposit copies at L,LSC,O,EU, AdU,SaU. The Luttrell copy, dated 7 March, is recorded in *Haslewood*. Lintot paid Pope 30 guineas for the copyright on 23 Feb (*Nichols* VIII.300).

'Thy forests, Windsor! and thy green retreats'

L(643.l.26/6; Ashley 4918),O(2, 1 uncut),EU, DT(2),LdU-B+; CSmH,CtY,ICU,MH,TxU+.

Pope, A. Windsor-Forest

P988 — [fine paper]
Watermarks: O in B,C,E; C in A,D.
L(C.131.h.1/1).

P989 — — The second edition. *London, printed for Bernard Lintott,* 1713. (*DC* 9 April)
2°: A–E²; *i–ii,* 1–18.
Griffith 10, describing it as a reissue with A1 cancelled. However, A2 is also reset, though the rest of the text is unchanged. It may be a reissue with cancel A² or a reimpression.
O,C,DN,BaP; CSmH,ICU,MH(2),TxU.

P990 — — To which is added, The rape of the locke: an heroi-comical poem. *Dublin, printed by S.P. [Stephen Powell] for G. Grierson,* 1713.
12°: A–D⁶ (B3 as 'B4', C3 as 'C4'); *1–2* 3–48.
Griffith Add. 28a. *The rape of the locke* is the early version in two cantos; Sir Robert Howard's *The duel of the stags* is also included. A copy at CtY has the Dublin 1714 edition of the enlarged *Rape* bound in place of the earlier version (cf. *Griffith* Add. 35b); this appears to be the work of a collector, not a bookseller, for the stab-holes do not match.
L(1488.de.46/4); CtY.

P991 — — The fourth edition. *London, printed for Bernard Lintot,* 1720 [1719?]. (Dec?)
8°: A–D⁸; *1–5* 6–58 *59–64.* A1 frt; D6–8 advt.
Griffith 125. This also reprints Pope's 'Messiah'; the third edition is no doubt represented by Pope's *Works,* 1717. Entered to Lintot in Bowyer's ledgers under 2 Dec 1719, 1000 copies printed. Advertised in *DC* 26 Oct 1720, but Griffith (who quotes this advertisement) suggests it may have been issued earlier.
L(991.h.25/2),LVA-F,O,LdU-B; IU,MH,TxU.

P992 **Pope, Thomas.** The Stamford toasts: or panegyrical characters of the fair-ones, inhabiting the good town of Stamford... With some other poetical amusements. By Mr. Pope; not the undertaker. *London, printed for the author; sold by E. Curll, J. Jackson, and E. Palmer & W. Thompson at Stamford,* 1726 [1725]. (*MC* Nov)
8°: A² B–G⁴ H²; *i–iv,* 1–52.
Other poems on pp. 15–52. Reissued in *The altar of love,* 1727.
'Forbear, ye criticks, to chastise my muse'
O; CtY(2),ICU.

P993 [**Pope, Walter.**] The old man's wish... To a pleasant new play-house tune. [*London*] *Printed by W.O. [William Onley] for B. Deacon, at the Angel in Guilt-spur-street,* [170–?]
obl ½°: 1 side, 4 columns.
Printed in black-letter in traditional broadside style. Two rough woodcuts above text in columns 1 & 2. Bridget Deacon apparently took over the business of Jonah Deacon who was dead by 1704. First published separately in 1693.

Pope, W. The old man's wish

'If I live to grow old,/(for I find I go down)'
Translated into Latin verse by Vincent Bourne as *Votum Dris Gualteri Pope,* 1728.
L(Rox.II.386).

P994 — [*idem*] The wish. Written by Dr. W. Pope, fellow of the Royal Society... The third edition, being the only correct and finish'd copy. *London, printed for Tho. Horne,* 1710. (*Tatler* 16 Sept)
8°: A–E⁴ F²; *i–x,* 1–32 *33–34.* A1 hft; F2 advt.
Entered in *SR* to Horne on 26 Aug 1710 as 'old copy'. Some copies (asterisked below) have the date changed in ms. to 1719. This authorized text has variant first line:
'If I live to be old'
L(11626.d.65,—A1),LVA-D(2, 1 uncut),O(2, 1–A1),OW,E(2, 1*–A1, 1–A1,F2); CLU-C, CSmH,ICU(–A1, F2),MH*(—A1),TxHR(—A1).

P995 [—] The old man's wish... To a pleasant new play-house tune. *London, printed by and for T. Norris at the Looking-glass on London-bridge; sold by J. Walter,* [171–?]
obl ½°: 1 side, 4 columns.
Two rough woodcuts before text in columns 1 & 2. Printed in popular broadside style, though not in black-letter.
Rothschild.

P996 [—] — *London, printed for J. Hodges, at the Looking-glass, on London-bridge,* [173–?]
obl ½°: 1 side, 4 columns.
Rough woodcuts before text. Printed in popular broadside style.
DFo.

Popish. The popish impostor, [1740]–. *See* Fra Cipolla, 1737.

Poplar. 'The poplar grove; or, the amusements of a rural life. Containing a variety of poems, &c... By the author of the Muses vagaries. [*London*] *Printed for J. Robinson. Price 6d.*' (*DA* 15 Nov 1743)
Possibly a miscellany despite the apparent statement of authorship, for *The muse's vagaries* appears to be a miscellany.

P997 **Popular.** The popular convention. A poem. By the Dutchess of Puddledock. *London, printed for T. Cooper; sold by the pamphlet-shops of London & Westminster,* 1739.
2°: (4 ll); *1–3* 4–8.
'Good people! flock here in a throng'
NjP,TxU.

P998 **Porch.** The porch and academy opened, or Epictetus's manual newly turn'd into English verse, with notes. By J.W. late of Exon College in Oxford, student. To which is added, Cebes's table never before translated into English verse. By a lady. *London, printed for J. Goudge,* 1707. (*PB* 20 March)
8°: A⁸ B–C⁴ D–M⁸ N²; *i–xxxii,* 1–147 *148 blk.*
'Some things beyond our reach without us stand'

The **porch** and academy open'd

Cebes: 'Walking in Saturn's goodly fane one morn'
L(11633.bbb.13),O; IU.

P999 — [*idem*] Epictetus: a poem, containing the maxims of that celebrated philosopher... Done from the original Greek of Arrian, with notes. Being an epitome of the Morals of Epictetus, translated from the Greek by Dr. Stanhope. To which is added, the table of Cebes. *London printed, and are to be sold by B. Bragge*, 1709. (*PB* 14 April)
8°: *A*⁴ B–C⁴ D–M⁸ N²; [*24*] *1*–*147* *148 blk*.
Apparently a reissue with cancel *A*⁴.
MeWC.

P1000 **Porcupinade.** The Porcupinade, a very poetical poem. To which is prefixed, a copy of smooth commendatory rhymes to the author, from Porcupinus Pelagius, author of the Triumvirade... By Quidnuncius Profundus. *London, printed for W. Webb*, 1745. (*GM, LM* March)
4°: *A*⁴ B–C⁴ D²; *i–v* vi–viii, *9* 10–28. A1 hft.
All copies seen have a ms. correction to p. 15, line 1.
'O Phœbus, Phœbus, whether now employ'd'
A satire on heroic verse.
L(11630.c.5/11; 11630.c.6/17),O; NjP.

'Porcupinus Pelagius.' *See* Morgan, Macnamara.

P1001 **Porterfield, James.** God's judgements against sin: or a relation of three dreadful fires happening in the city of Edinburgh. Poematized by James Porterfield, schoolmaster in Edinburgh. *Edinburgh, printed by James Watson*, 1702.
4°: *A*⁴ B–D⁴; *i–iv*, *1–26* *27–28 blk*.
Introduction and three separate poems.
Introduction: 'No kingdom's free from scourge where sin abounds'
The fires were those of 6 Nov 1696, 3 Feb 1700, and 28 Oct 1701.
L(1485.t.27,–D4),ES.

[—] The practical atheist: or blasphemous clubs taxed [actually by James Clark], 1721. *See* C228.

P1002 — A relation of the late misfortune at Leith, happening the third of July, 1702. Being an appendix to a lamentable poem, called Gods judgement against sin... Composed by the same author. *Edinburgh, printed by George Jaffrey, and are to be sold at his shop*, 1702.
4°: *A*¹ B²; *1–2* ⟨*3–6*⟩.
'Stay, stay a while my faithful servant yet'
Dedication signed.
ES(pagination cropt).

P1003 **Portraiture.** The portraiture of Oliverus secundus, the modern protector in body and conscience. [*London*] *Printed in the year* 1712.
½°: 1 side, 1 column.
'Of birth obscure, his soul ingrate, uncouth'
A tory attack on Marlborough.
C; MH.

Potter, R.

P1004 **Potter, Robert.** A farewell hymne to the country. Attempted in the manner of Spenser's Epithalamion. *London, printed for R. Manby & H. S. Cox*, 1749. (*GM* May)
4°: *A*¹[=D1] B–C⁴ D⁴(–D1); *1–2* 3–23 *24 blk*.
Probably the 'Hymn 3 sh 4°' entered to Manby & Cox in Bowyer's ledgers, no date, 500 copies printed.
'Sweet poplar shade, whose trembling leaves emong'
L(11630.b.3/1; 840.k.4/11),O(2),OW,LdU-B, NwP; DFo,ICN,MH.

P1005 — — The second edition. *London, printed for R. Manby & H. S. Cox*, 1750.
4°: *A*² B–C⁴ D⁴(–D1); *i–ii*, *1–2* 3–23 *24 blk*. A1 hft; A2ᵛ err.
A reissue with cancel half-title and title substituted for A1 title.
L(643.k.5/14,–A1, lacks D4),O,*MR*; CtY, TxU(2).

P1006 — Retirement: an epistle. *London, printed for Paul Vaillant*, 1748 [1747]. (*GM, LM* Dec)
4°: *A*² B–C⁴ D²; *1–4* 5–23 *24*. A1 hft; 24 advt.
'When on the stage Bayes bids th' eclipse advance'
L(11630.c.14/11; 11630.d.18/10; 11602.gg.24/16,–A1; 161.m.25),O(4, 3–A1),LdU-B,*NeU*; CLU,ICN,MH,TxU.

P1007 **Pound.** The pound for the Hereford freemen, an excellent new ballad: to the tune of the, Tippling philosophers. [*Hereford?* 1741.]
½°: 1 side, 1 column.
'In the Milk-lane a house to be let is'
Verses on the Hereford city election.
O.

P1008 **Poverty.** Poverties coat turn'd by a taylor in Hamilton. To the tnne [!] of Poultrane poverty. [*Edinburgh?* 1702/14?]
obl 1°: 1 side, 3 columns.
'Never was creature plagued so'
The E copy has ms. 'John Mather' after title: he may well be the author of this begging poem.
E.

P1009 **Powell, James.** A poem on the Earl of Peterborow and Monmouth; humbly address'd to his lordship. *London printed, and sold by John Morphew*, 1708. (4 March, Luttrell)
2°: A–C²; *1–2* 3–11 *12 blk*.
'Invading fleets affright us now no more'
In praise of Charles Mordaunt, 3rd earl of Peterborough's military campaign in Spain.
O,OW; CtY(Luttrell).

P1010 **Power.** Power and patriotism: a poetical epistle, humbly inscribed to the right honourable H.P. esq; To which an introduction is prefixed, shewing the occasion. *London, printed for J. Hinton*, 1746. (22 Feb)

Power and patriotism

2°: A^2 B–D^2; *1–2* 3–16.
Listed in *GM* Feb.
'Sure there are times when bards may venture praise'
A panegyric on Henry Pelham.
L(1962, Tom's Coffee House, 22 Feb); CSmH (uncut),CtY(cropt),TxU.

P1011 — The power of beauty: a poem. *London, printed for J. Payne & J. Bouquet, 1750.* (*GM* Feb)
4°: A^2 B–D^4 E^2 (B4 as 'B2'); *i–iv, 3* 4–30. iv err; 30 advt.
'Come, fair Dorinda, and, while beauty glows'
Reprinted in *Pearch* I.172 as 'By ——'.
O,*MR*; DFo,TxHR.

— The power of harmony: a poem, 1745. *See* Cooper, John Gilbert.

— The power of love, 1728–9. *See* Welsted, Leonard.

P1012 [**Powney, Richard.**] The stag chace in Windsor Forest. A poem. *London, printed for J. Shuckburgh,* 1739. (*GM, LM* July)
2°: A^1 B–E^2 F^1; *i–ii, 1* 2–17 *18 blk.*
No watermark. A1 and F1 have been seen to be conjugate.
'Let others paint the terrors of the plain'
Subsequently printed with Powney's name.
L(643.m.16/7),O,OW(uncut); CSmH,MH(3, 1 ms. corrections),NjP.

P1013 [—] [fine paper]
Watermark: fleur-de-lys on shield.
O.

P1014 [—] — The second edition. *London, printed for J. Shuckburgh,* 1740. (April?)
2°: A^1 B–E^2 F^1; *i–ii, 1* 2–17 *18 blk.*
Either another issue (with cancel title?) or a reimpression. Advertisement of April 1740 in *Haslewood.*
O,*MR*; CLU-C,CSmH,CtY(uncut),NjP.

P1015 — — By Richard Powney, esq; *London, printed for T. Cooper,* 1742. (*GM, LM* March)
2°: A^1 B–E^2 F^1; *i–ii, 1* 2–17 *18 blk.*
L(1486.g.3),O,LdU-B(uncut); CtY.

P1016 — Templum harmoniæ. Carmen epicum. *Londini, apud Carolum Bathurst,* 1745. (*LM* April)
4°: A^2 a^2 B^2(±B1) C(2 ll) D–M^2; *[4]* i–iv, 1–44. A1 hft.
The collation is obscure; presumably one leaf of C is a cancel. Some copies (CtY,MH) have an errata slip on p. 44. Also listed in *GM, LM* Oct 1745.
'Quis fidibus sociæ monstravit munera vocis'
Dedication signed.
L(11409.gg.1),OW,SrS; CSmH(–A1),CtY,MH.

Practical. The practical atheist, 1721. *See* Clark, James.

Praehonorabili

Praehonorabili. Praehonorabili domino, ——————, [1749.] *See* Cooper, William.

P1017 Prat, Daniel. An ode to Mr. Handel, on his playing the organ. *London, Jacob Tonson,* 1722.
2°: 6 ll.
(*Dobell* 1404.)

P1018 Prediction. A prediction, said to have its rise from Scotland; which is attested to have been in the hands of a person in York for near this 20 years, and affirmed by some, to have heard it in the time of King Charles the second: as follows, The good man of the whiggs. *York, printed and sould by John White,* [170–?]
$\frac{1}{2}$°: 1 side, 1 column.
'But he foresees with prophetick unction'
CLU-C.

Pre-existence. Præ-existence. A poem, in imitation of Milton, 1714–. *See* Evans, Abel.

P1019 — Præ-existence and transmigration: or, the new metamorphoses. A philosophical essay... A poem, something between a panegyrick, and a satire. *London, printed for M. Cooper,* 1743. (*GM* April)
4°: A^4 B–D^4; *1–3* 4–31 *32 blk.*
Watermark: fleur-de-lys.
'See Mira here, how atoms change'
Tentatively attributed to Thomas Newcomb in *Nichols, Collection,* VII. 163, 'I have reason to think that he was the author'.
L(11630.e.11/9),O(uncut),*MR*; CSmH(uncut), CtY,ICU,IU,NjP.

P1020 — [fine paper]
Watermark: fleur-de-lys on shield.
ICN,OCU.

P1021 — — *Dublin, printed by and for George Faulkner,* 1743.
12°: A^{12}; *1–2* 3–23 *24.* 23–24 advt.
DA,DN.

P1022 Prefatory. [dh] A prefatory prologue, by way of introduction, to one spoken by Mr. Betterton at Oxford, on Monday the 5th of July. Spoken by Mr. Mills...on Friday the 16th of July, 1703. [*London,* 1703.] (26 July, Luttrell)
4°: A^4; *1–7; 8 blk.*
On p. 3 'A prologue to the University of Oxford...' and on p. 5 'The epilogue, by way of answer...' Reprinted in *The players turn'd academicks,* 1703.
'As paupers who on charity are fed'
'Once more our London muses pleas'd repair'
'Had Athens all the Grecian sence engross'd'
The second prologue was by Joseph Trapp.
L(164.n.72, Luttrell),O.

P1023 Preparative. A preparative address to a certain great man. Adapted to the present times and posture of affairs. *Dublin printed, and London reprinted, for J. Millan,* 1741. (*GM, LM* Feb)

A preparative address

8⁰: *A² B–G⁴ H²*; *i–iv, 1 2–47 48–52.* A1 hft; H²
advt.

   The Dublin edition is probably fictitious. H²
is a list of Millan's publications.
'Imperial jugler of the state!'
   An attack on Walpole.
L(1509/1433, – H²),O; KU(–A1).

P1024 Presbyter. The presbyter unmask'd. A tale. By
H.K. gent. *Dublin, printed in the year 1724.*
8⁰: A⁴; *1–3 4–8.*
'In elder times when vice was young'
   A bawdy tale.
DA.

Presbyteri. Presbyteri Scoti Petro, [1713.] *See*
Pitcairne, Archibald.

Present. The present corruption of Britons, [1738.]
See Morrice, Bezaleel.

— The present state of poetry, 1721–. *See* Morrice,
Bezaleel.

P1025 Press. The press restrain'd: a poem, occasion'd by
a resolution of the house of commons... *London,
printed for John Morphew, 1712.* (23 Feb, Luttrell)
8⁰: A⁸; *1–5 6–16.* A1 hft.
'Mourn all ye wits, who suck the purer air'
   An attack on whig writers.
L(1078.m.6/7; 164.m.60, Luttrell); CSmH,
CtY(–A1),IU,MH,TxU +.

Preston. The Preston prisoners to the ladies about
court and town, 1716. *See* Wogan, Charles.

P1026 'Preston, —, Mr.' Æsop at the bear-garden: a
vision. By Mr. Preston. In imitation of the Temple
of fame, a vision, by Mr. Pope. *London, sold by John
Morphew, 1715.* (PB 10 March)
8⁰: *A⁴ B–E⁴; 1–8 9–38 39–40 blk.* A1 hft.
   Bond 40.
'In that soft season when each hedge and field'
   Listed in *MC* as 'by Mr. Preston, master of
the bears'; a mock attribution. A mock-heroic
poem on the bear garden, satirically imitating
Pope.
L(C.116.b.1/4, Pope's copy),O(–A1, E4),C(uncut),BaP(–A1, E4); CSmH(–E4),CtY,IU,MH
(uncut),TxU +.

P1027 [Preston, William.] An epistle to the heritors of
the West-kirk parish; occasioned by the poem on
the death of the reverend Mr. Wotherspoon.
*Edinburgh, printed for and sold by A. Davidson,
1732.*
8⁰: A⁴; *1–2 3–8.*
'Ye who by merit, love and duty sway'd'
   Preston's authorship is implied by this defence
of his poem on Mr. Wotherspoon, which is
entered below.
E,GM(uncut).

Preston, W.

P1028 [—] On the death of the reverend Mr. Patrick
Wotherspoon, minister of the West-Kirk; a poem.
*Edinburgh, printed for and sold by Alexander
Davidson, 1732.*
8⁰: A⁴; *1–2 3–8.*
'Oh Wotherspoon! just object of regret'
   Preston's authorship seems tolerably certain.
Davidson advertised other poems by the same
author in *To the divine majesty*, and appears
to have published no other poet.
L(11631.c.46, title cropt),E.

P1029 — 'The saints rich treasure. *Edinburgh, 1717.*'
12⁰.
GM (missing 1967).

P1030 — To the divine majesty, a poem. *Edinburgh,
printed for, and sold by Alexander Davidson...
where are to be had several of the author's poems,
1733.*
8⁰: *π¹ A⁴ B¹; [2] i–ii iii–iv, 5–10.* π1 hft.
   π1 and B1 have been seen to be conjugate.
'Whilst other poets female charms admire'
   Dedication signed.
E,GM; DLC(–π1).

P1031 Pretended. The pretended Prince of Wales's
lamentation for the small pox. [*London, 1708.*] (12
March, Luttrell)
½⁰: A¹; *1–2,* 1 column.
'Cruel disease! must now thy spite be shewn'
ICN(Luttrell).

P1032 Pretender. The Pretender is coming: a new ballad.
To the tune of You commons and peers. [*London*]
Printed in the year 1715.
½⁰: 1 side, 1 column.
'Run, tell my lord mayor'
   A loyal ballad.
Herts CRO (Panshanger box 46).

P1033 — The Pretender routed: or, his majesty King
George's conquest over the rebels in Scotland.
Dublin, printed by E. Waters, 1716.
½⁰: *1–2,* 1 column.
'Assist, O muse! a youthful bard inspir'd'
CtY.

P1034 — The Pretender. To the tune called Daniell
Cooper and his man. [*London? 1717/18.*]
slip: 1 side, 1 column.
   Printed with *The falling out,* [1717/18]; the
NjP copy is not divided.
'Wee have too kinges; the one is true'
   A Jacobite poem.
O; CSmH,NjP.

P1035 — The Pretender's declaration, explain'd in verse.
By H.B. poet-laureat, and one of his master's
principal secretaries of state. *London, printed for
James Roberts, 1716.* (25 Jan, Luttrell)
2⁰: A⁴; *1–2 3–8.*
   The Luttrell copy is recorded in *Haslewood*;
listed in *MC* Jan.

The **Pretender**'s declaration

'James, by the grace of Mar, the thing'
    The initials 'H.B.' stand satirically for Henry Bolingbroke. On the Pretender's declaration of 25 Oct 1715.
L(643.1.25/17),O,E; CtY,OCU,PPL.

P1036 — The Pretender's declaration. In imitation of Hudibras. [*London*] '*Printed for C. Cross near Westminster*', [1714.]
slip: 1 side, 1 column.
    The imprint is fictitious; 'C. Cross' stands for Charing Cross. Advertisement at foot. The copy seen was reissued in *State-poems. Being a collection of choice private pieces*, 1715.
'Long I depended with full hope'
    Against the Pretender.
Brett-Smith.

— The Pretender's declaration, which was found ..., 1708. *See* 'Maurus, Richardus'.

P1037 — The Pretender's letter to the tories. To the tune of To you, dear Ormond, cross the seas, &c. [*London*? 1716?]
slip: 1 side, 1 column.
'To his dear vassals of the north'
O(cut and mounted).

[**Priaulx**, —, *Mr*.] Faction display'd. A poem [actually by William Shippen], 1704. *See* S427.

P1038 Price, Francis. Wales: a poem. *London, printed for John Hooke*, 1714. (16 June, Luttrell)
8°: *A*⁴ B–C⁴ (C1 as 'E'); *i–viii*, 1–16. A1 hft.
    The Luttrell copy is recorded in Dobell cat. 51/482. The copyright with 12 books formed part of lot 37 in the trade sale of Hooke, 31 May 1731 (cat. at O-JJ), sold to Osborn.
'When good old Saturn banished from above'
AN.

Price, Henry. 'Poems on several occasions. [*London*] *Printed for T. Payne. Price 6d.*' (*DJ* 27 Feb 1723)

— Poems on several subjects. By a land-waiter in the port of Poole. *London, printed for T. Astley*, 1741.
8°: pp. 206.   L,O; CLU-C,CtY.
    Dedication to 'Shalum and Hilpa' signed.

— Poems. Never published together before. *London*, 1749. (*BM, LM* Feb)
8°: 14 ll.   (Dobell 1451.)
    The publisher is given in *LM* as R. Baldwin, jun.

_____

P1039 — Batrachomuomachia: or the battle of the frogs and mice. Translated from Homer. By a land-waiter in the port of Poole. With some additional poems by the same hand. *London, printed for J. Wilford*, 1736. (*LM* Sept)
8°: π² A–C⁴ D²; *i–iv*, 1–28.
    Other poems on pp. 20–28.

Price, H. Batrachomuomachia

'O may the nine from Helicon inspire'
    Dedication signed.
L(900.h.23/4); *CLU-C*,CtY.

P1040 — 'A copy of verses occasioned by the death of the late right revd father in god George lord bishop of Bristol, humbly inscribed to the reverend Robert Clavering, D.D. 1720. fol.'
    Printed in Price's *Poems*, 1741, with title 'To the right reverend father in god, Robert, lord bishop of Peterborough'; in this form the first line reads:
'When Bion, gentlest bard! resign'd his breath'
(*Rawlinson*.)

P1041 — Laodamia to Protesilaus. Translated from Ovid; and address'd to Mrs. Vernon. By a land-waiter in the port of Poole. *London printed, and sold by H. Kent, and by the booksellers and pamphlet shops of London & Westminster*, 1743. (*LDP* 14 April)
4°: *A*² B–F²; *1–4* 5–23 *24 blk*.
    Vertical chain-lines.
'Health to my spouse, and may that health I send'
    Dedication signed.
LdU-B(uncut).

P1042 [—] – Risum teneatis? amici: or, a true and diverting account of a late battle between a priest and a porter. In hudibrastick verse... To which is added, the fat vicar's race... Wrote by a gentleman, who saw the race perform'd. [*London*] *Printed for J. Roberts*, 1732. (*LM* Nov)
2°: B–C² D¹ (B2 as 'B'); *1–3* 4–10.
'Of kicks and cuffs, of wounds and wars'
'I'll tell you a story, a story so merry'
    The first poem was reprinted in Price's *Poems*, 1741; the second, on Parson Vaughan, is probably by another hand.
L(643.m.15/17; C.131.h.1/3**),OW(uncut); MH(uncut).

P1043 — Shalum and Hilpa. Done from the Spectator. Volume VIII. Number 584. *Bristol printed, and sold by S. Farley, W. Cossley, & M. Lewis*, 1731.
4°: *A*² B–F²; *i–iv*, *1* 2–19 *20 blk*.
'E'er that the flood, with unresisted sway'
CtY.

P1044 — [*idem*] The antediluvian novel; or, the entertaining story of the loves of Shalum and Hilpa. Done into verse from the Spectator... To which is annexed, an ode, to the honourable Sir Charles Wager... *London, printed for Richard Chandler; sold by J. Roberts*, 1733. (*Bee* 22 Feb)
2°: *A*² B–C²; *1–5* 6–11 *12*. 2, 4 advt.
    The ode to Wager is on p. 12.
Ode: 'Dear to thy country and thy king'
L(643.m.15/20, uncut).

P1045 — The spectre: or, Admiral Hosier's ghost. To which is added, Admiral Vernon's answer to Admiral Hosier's ghost. By a land-waiter in the port of Poole. *Lynn, W. Garratt*, [1740]. (July?)
4°.

Price, H. The spectre

> Dated by Pickering & Chatto as [1749?], but certainly 1740; *Percival* appendix 83 records that 'Vernon's answer' was reprinted in *LM* July 1740.
> *Vernon's answer*: 'Hosier! with indignant sorrow'
> 'The spectre' is presumably Richard Glover's poem; only the answer is included in Price's *Poems*, 1741.
> (Pickering & Chatto cat. 219/7481.)

P1046 Price, John. Christmas day. A poem. *Salisbury, printed for the author, by B. Collins*, 1745.
8°: A⁸; *1–4* 5–16.
'Hail sacred day, distinguish'd by the birth'
L(1962).

P1047 — 'A protestant king and the Bible. A poem. [*London*] *Sold by J. Rivington*. Price 6*d*.' (*GM, LM* Dec 1745)

P1048 [Price, Laurence.] Win at first, lose at last: or, the game at cards which were shuffled by President Bradshaw, cut by Colonel Hewson the cobler, and play'd by Oliver Cromwell and Ireton... *London, printed in the year* 1707.
8°: A⁴; *1* 2–8.
'Ye merry hearts that love to play'
> Originally published in 1680 (*Wing* P3390), signed 'L.P.'; by Laurence Price.
OW,DA.

P1049 [—] [*idem*] Win first, lose last, or, a new game at cards. [*Dublin*, 1710.]
½°: 1 side, 2 columns.
> On the other side, *The dissenters triumph*, 1710.
OCU.

P1050 [—] [*idem*] A knave at the bottom, the dealer's sure of a trump. *London, printed by J. Ranger*, [17––.]
½°: 1 side, 2 columns.
> A line of printed music above text. The imprint is possibly fictitious. Dated by L catalogue '[1720?]'. *Applebee's weekly journal* 21 April 1733 records that 'On Saturday last [14 April] several hawkers were taken into custody for dispersing... *The dealer's sure of a trump, when the knave's at the bottom*'; whether that had the same text as this is uncertain.
L(112.f.44/50, imprint mutilated).

P1051 Pride. Pride's exchange broke up: or Indian calicoes and silks expos'd. Written by R.L. gent. *London, printed in the year* 1703.
½°: 1 side, 2 columns.
'Can man forbear to check such jilts as you'
> A satire against those who neglect English weaving.
L(C.121.g.8/1).

Prière. La prière universelle, [1740.] *See* Le Franc de Pompignan, Jean-Jacques.

Priest

P1052 Priest. The priest and the widow, a tale. *London, printed for E. Comyns, J. Robinson, J. Jackson, & A. Dodd*, 1741. (*GM, LM* Oct)
2°: A¹ B–E² F¹; *i–ii, 1* 2–17 *18*. 18 advt.
'In Lombardy there dwelt a wealthy knight'
L(1962),O; CSmH,ICN,*MH*,NjP,TxU+.

P1053 — The priest turn'd poet: or, the best way of answering Dr. Sacheverel's sermon, preached at St. Paul's, Nov. the 5th. 1709... Being his discourse paraphras'd in burlesque rhime. *London, printed for the booksellers of London & Westminster*, [1709.] (*Supplement* 23 Dec)
8°: A⁸; *i–ii*, 1–14.
Bond 26.
'Now let me begin with a noise and a pother'
> Dedication signed 'J.P.' A copy at InU has a ms. note on the title 'By John Parkman' in what appears to be a nineteenth-century hand. No confirmation of this attribution has been found. A burlesque version of Sacheverell's sermon *The perils of false brethren*.
L(E.1991/3; 164.m.46),LVA-F,CT,E,AdU+; CSmH,CtY,ICN,*InU*(3),TxU+.

P1054 Priestcraft. Priest-craft and lust: or, Lancelot to his ladies. An epistle from the shades. *London, printed for W. Webb*, 1743. (*GEP* 30 April)
2°: A¹ B–C² D¹; *1–2* 3–12.
Rothschild 241. Horizontal chain-lines.
'Since charitable B---l---r's dead and gone'
> A satire on Lancelot Blackburne, archbishop of York, recently deceased.
O; CtY,IU.

P1055 — Priestcraft: or, the way to promotion: a poem address'd to the inferior clergy of England. Being wholesome advice, how to behave at the approaching election. *London, printed for J. Wilford*, 1734. (*LM* April)
2°: A² B–D²; *i–ii, 1–3* 4–13 *14*. A1 hft; 14 advt.
> A second edition was advertised in *The connoisseur*, [1735.]
'Let men of wit and foplings of the town'
L(C.131.h.1/11); CSmH,TxU.

P1056 Prince. The prince. An epigram, originally written by George Buchanan to Thomas Randolph, in a better language, and with more art, but upon a less occasion. *London, printed for Bernard Lintott*, 1711. (27 June, Luttrell)
½°: *1–2*, 1 column.
> Advertised in *DC* 25 July 1711.
'At your request, sir! which to me's command'
> In praise of Queen Anne.
Rothschild, DT; ICN(Luttrell).

P1057 — A prince and no prince. Or, Mother Red-cap's strange and wonderful prophecy. [*London*] *Printed for J. Reed*, [1714.] (14 May, Luttrell)
½°: 1 side, 2 columns.
'Once on a time some old wives met'
> Apparently suggesting that the Pretender will

A **prince** and no prince

come and exile the Duke and Duchess of Marlborough.
L(C.121.g.9/168, Luttrell).

P1058 — Prince Charles his welcome to Scotland. [*Edinburgh*? 1745.]
$\frac{1}{4}$°: 1 side, 1 column.
On the other side, *A poem on Prince Charles*, [1745]; originally conjugate with *A poem upon the 29th of May*.
'Welcome to Scotia's plains, dear injur'd youth'
A Jacobite poem.
L(C.38.g.14/10),E; CSmH.

P1059 — [dh] Prince Eugene; a pindarique. Written by the author of the Muses-treat. [col] [*London*] *Printed for Jo. Senex; sold by J. Nutt*, 1702.
2°: A²; 1–4. 4 advt.
'Wake! m' ambitious soul awake!'
LLP,*MR-C*.

— Prince Eugene: an heroic poem on the victorious progress of the confederate arms, 1707. *See* Bolton, J.

P1060 — Prince Eugene's welcome. *London, printed for Bernard Lintott*, [1712.] (*DC* 21 Feb)
$\frac{1}{2}$°: 1–2, 1 column.
'Great-Britain, styl'd from military deeds'
O,DT,Rothschild; ICN(Luttrell, 21 Feb),MH.

P1061 — The Prince of Wales: a poem. *London, printed for A. Baldwin*, 1702 [1701]. (27 Nov, Luttrell)
2°: A–C²; 1–2 3–12. 12 advt.
Many copies (e.g. O,AdU,CLU-C,InU) add 'erreta' on p. 12. Listed in *WL* Nov 1701, and again in *WL* Oct 1702; J. R. B. Brett-Smith has another Luttrell copy dated 23 Oct [1702].
'Kings without scepters, a pretended heir'
Against the proclamation of James Francis Edward, the Old Pretender, as prince of Wales, and in praise of King William.
LDW,LG,O,AdU; CLU-C,InU(Luttrell),TxU.

P1062 — Prince Perkin the 2d. Or, Æsop on this juncture. *London, printed in the year* 1702. (*WL* Jan)
8°: A⁴ B–E⁴; i–xvi, 1–23 24 blk.
A1 bears a mock advertisement relating to Perkin Warbeck.
''Twas in the midst of night, when Joan'
On the Pretender; a collection of fables.
C(–A1),DrU; IU,MH(–A1),NjP,OCU(–A1).

P1063 Princess. The princess's lock: a merry tale. [*London*? 1715?]
slip: 1 side, 1 column.
'The princess somewhat in disorder'
A bawdy Jacobite tale, apparently directed at Caroline, princess of Wales.
O(divided and mounted).

'**Pringle, Rorie**, *drawer in the Tolbooth*.' Elegy on the much lamented death of merry Maggie Wilson, [172–.] *See* Pennecuik, Alexander, d. *1730*.

Printers

P1064 Printers. The printers petition to the poetical senate assembled in Grub-street. [*Dublin*, 1726?]
$\frac{1}{2}$°: 1 side, 1 column.
The DT copy is bound with half-sheets of 1726.
'Apollo and the poets meeting'
DT.

Prior, Matthew. Poems on several occasions: consisting of odes, satyrs and epistles... *London, printed for R. Burrough & J. Baker, & E. Curll*, 1707. (*DC* 31 Jan)
8°: pp. 128.   L,O; CtY,MH.
An unauthorized collection.

— Poems on several occasions. *London, printed for Jacob Tonson*, 1709 [1708]. (*LG* 2 Dec)
8°: pp. xxiv, 328.   L,O; CtY,MH.
No watermark: size of cut copy 7$\frac{1}{2}$ × 5 in.

— [fine paper]   L,LVA-D; CtY.
No watermark; size of cut copy 8$\frac{1}{2}$ × 5$\frac{1}{2}$ in.; presentation copies at LVA-D,CtY.

—— The second edition. *London, printed for Jacob Tonson*, 1709.
8°: pp. xxiv, 328.   L,O; CLU-C,MH.

—— *London, printed for Jacob Tonson*, 1711.
12°: pp. 248.   L,O; MH.

—— *London, printed for Jacob Tonson*, 1713.
12°: pp. 248.   L,O; IU,MH.

—— *London, printed for Jacob Tonson*, 1717.
12°: pp. 248.   O; IU.

———————

— A second collection of poems on several occasions. *London, printed for J. Roberts*, 1716. (13 March, Luttrell)
8°: pp. 71.   L,O; CLU-C,MH.
Repudiated in *LG* 24 March, but the poems are Prior's.

———————

— Poems on several occasions. *London, printed for Jacob Tonson, & John Barber*, 1718 [1719].
2°: pp. 506.   L,O.
Watermark: London arms; the trade issue. For details of the bibliography of this edition see H. Bunker Wright in *MP* 49 (1952). Entered in *SR* to Tonson & Barber 24 Dec 1718, but not ready for delivery to subscribers until 17 March 1719 (*DC*). The agreement between Prior and Tonson (including the cost of recomposing 73 sheets) dated 20 Feb 1718 [/19?] was offered in Dobell cat. 66 (1941) 28.

— [fine paper]   L,O; CLU-C,IU.
Watermark: Strasburg bend. The subscribers' edition. Many sheets, at least up to 3D, were reset and reprinted to meet an increased demand.

— [superfine paper]   CJ; DLC.
Watermark: fleur-de-lys on shield.

—— *Dublin, printed for J. Hyde, R. Gunne, R. Owen, & E. Dobson,* 1719.
8°: pp. 378.   L,O.

—— 'London' [*The Hague*], *printed for T. Johnson,* 1720.
8°: pp. xx, 456.   L,O; IU.
Fine-paper copies are advertised on Hh3ᵛ, but have not been identified.

—— *London, printed for J. Tonson, & J. Barber,* 1721.
12°: 2 vol.   L,O; CtY,MH.

—— To which are added, memoirs...with a supplement... *Dublin, printed by and for George Grierson,* 1723.
8°: 2 vol.   L,O.
This edition adds the poems of Curll's *Supplement,* 1722. Vol. 2 of both copies seen has this title added to a 1732 edition.

—— *London, printed for J. Tonson, & J. Barber,* 1725.
12°: 2 vol.   L,O; CtY,MH.

—— *Dublin, printed by and for George Grierson,* 1732.
8°: vol. 2.   L,O.
Only vol. 2 seen, with a 1723 title as well. It is not known whether the first volume was reprinted at this time.

—— The fifth edition. *London, printed for R. Knaplock, J. Round, & J. Tonson,* 1733.
12°: pp. 231.   L,O; IU,MH.
Two sixteenth shares of the copyright, probably Knaplock's, formed lots 102–3 of a trade sale, 9 Dec 1740 (cat. at O-JJ); both were bought by Lintot at £23 each.

— [reissue] *London, printed for S. Birt, & W. Feales,* 1734.
CtY.
This must be in some way related to the unauthorized 'Volume the third' published by these booksellers in 1733.

—— With a supplement of several poems... *Dublin, printed by and for George Grierson,* 'MDCCXXVIII' [1738?].
12°: 2 vol.   O,C.
Vol. 2 is octavo, with title dated 1738. Both titles are cancels, and appear to have been printed at the same time.

—— The sixth edition. *London, printed for H. Lintot, and J. & R. Tonson,* 1741.
12°: pp. 402.   L,O; IU,MH.

— A supplement to Mr. Prior's poems. Consisting of such pieces as are omitted in the late collection of his works... *London, printed for E. Curll,* 1722 [1721]. (*DP* 13 Nov)
8°: pp. 71.   O,C.
Also issued with *Some memoirs of the life,* 1722.

— A new collection of poems on several occasions. By Mr. Prior, and others. Adorned with cuts. *London, printed for Tho. Osborne,* 1725. (*MC* Aug)
12°: pp. 32, 129+34.   L,O; CtY,IU.
There are two variant titles (possibly both cancels) which are distinguished by the ornaments; one represents a face with scroll-work, the other a face with trumpets. A miscellany (*Case* 334), but, as subsequent editions show, intended to accompany the 12° editions of Prior.

— [*idem*] Poems on several occasions, by Matthew Prior esq; &c. Volume III. The second edition. Adorned with cuts. *London, printed in the year* 1727.
12°: pp. xii, 129+54.   L,O; CLU-C,IU.
In most copies the dedication is unsigned, but in one copy at O it is signed 'E. Curll'.

—— Volume the third and last. The third edition. To which is prefixed the life... *London printed, and sold by S. Birt, & W. Feales,* 1733.
12°: pp. xlii, 203.   L,O; CtY.
The right to 92 copies out of 1500 formed part of lot 21 of the trade sale of John Pemberton, 8 Jan 1741 (cat. at O-JJ), sold to Astley.

—— Volume the second. The fourth edition... *London, printed for C. Hitch, & J. Hodges,* 1742.
12°: pp. lxxii, 236+120.   L; CtY,MH.
Much expanded, and intended to accompany the one volume *Poems* of 1741. Subsequently reprinted in 1754, 1767.

— Miscellaneous works...consisting of poems on several occasions...copied fair for the press by Mr. Adrian Drift... *London, printed for the editor,* 1740 [1739]. (Oct?)
8°: pp. iv, 380, xcv.   L,O.
This became the second volume of two, but appears to have been issued before the first volume was ready. Both volumes were listed in *GM* Oct 1739. The added title referring to two volumes was normally prefixed to vol. 1, Prior's *History of his own time.*

— [reissue] The second edition. *London, printed for the editor,* 1740.
L,O.
Cancel title.

—— *Dublin, printed by S. Powell, for G. Risk, G. Ewing, W. Smith, & G. Faulkner,* 1739.
12°: pp. 308.   O.

— [reissue] Miscellaneous works... In two volumes. *Dublin, printed by S. Powell, for G. Risk, G. Ewing, W. Smith, & G. Faulkner,* 1740.
O.
Apparently the title for vol. 1 substituted for the preceding.

[—] An answer to the Curious maid, [1721.] *See* A247.

Prior, M. A ballad

[—] A ballad on the battle of the two dukes, [1720?] *See* D506.

[—] Carmen sæculare to the king [Prior's poem of 1700 reprinted with a Latin translation by Thomas Dibben], 1701. *See* D295.

P1065 [—] Colin's mistakes. Written in imitation of Spenser's style. *London, printed for Jacob Tonson,* 1721. (*DC* 13 Feb)
2°: *A*² B–C²; *i–iv, 1 2-6 7–8 blk.* A1 hft.
Watermark: WVL. *Rothschild* 1683.
'Fast by the banks of Cam was Colin bred'
Reprinted in Prior's *A new collection,* 1725. Wrongly attributed to Samuel Croxall in *Nichols, Collection* VII.345n.
L(C.131.h.1/4***; Ashley 4983),OW; CLU-C (Luttrell, March),CtY(–C2),DFo(–C2),ICU (–A1),NjP(–C2)+.

P1066 [—] [fine paper]
Watermark: fleur-de-lys.
L(163.n.27),LVA-F,O(marbled wrappers, gilt).

P1067 [—] [another edition?]
Watermark: cursive I. It has not been possible to collate this with the preceding, but I suspect that it is a reprint.
ICN,MH,TxU.

P1068 [—] The conversation. A tale. *London, printed for Jacob Tonson,* 1720. (*DC* 16 Feb)
2°: *A*² B²; *1–3 4-7 8 blk.*
No watermark. *Rothschild* 1682. Entered in *SR* 15 Feb; deposit copies at L,LSC,O,E,EU, SaU.
'It always has been thought discreet'
Reprinted in Prior's *A new collection,* 1725.
L(643.m.13/16; Ashley 4979),OW(uncut),C,E, DT+; CSmH,CtY,ICN,MH,*TxU*+.

P1069 [—] [fine paper]
Watermark: fleur-de-lys on shield.
IU.

[—] The curious maid. A tale [actually by Hildebrand Jacob], 1720–. *See* J34.

[—] The curious maid, continu'd. A tale, 1721. *See* C547.

P1070 [—] The dove. A poem. *London, printed for J. Roberts,* 1717. (*DC* 15 Jan)
2°: *A*² B–C²; *i–iv, 1–7 8 blk.* A1 hft.
Rothschild 1680.
'In Virgil's sacred verse we find'
Reprinted in Prior's *Poems,* 1718.
L(163.n.14,–A1; Ashley 4977),O(2, 1 –A1),OW, LdU-B; CSmH(3),CtY(–A1),MH,NjP(uncut, –A1),TxU(2, 1 uncut, –A1)+.

P1071 [—] — *Dublin, printed by T. Hume, for G. Grierson,* 1717.
12°: *A*⁴ B²; *1–2 3–11 12 blk.*
DN.

P1072 — Down-Hall: a poem. By the late Mr. Prior. *London, printed for J. Roberts,* 1723. (*PB* 5 March)
4°: *A*² B–C⁴; *i–iv, 1 2–15 16 blk.*

Prior, M. Down-Hall

CBEL lists an edition of 1727, apparently in error.
'I sing not old Jason, who travell'd thro' Greece'
L(161.m.26, Luttrell, April),O,OW,LdU-B; CLU-C,CSmH,CtY,ICN,MH.

[—] Duke upon duke, an excellent new play-house ballad, 1720. *See* D502.

P1073 [—] Earl Robert's mice. A poem in imitation of Chaucer, &c. By M——w P——r, esq; *London, printed for A. Baldwin,* 1712. (2 Oct, Luttrell).
2°: A(3 ll); *i–ii, 1–4.*
Rothschild 1678. A1 and A3 are conjugate; A2, inset, is signed 'A'. An unauthorized edition. Advertised in *PB* 7 Oct.
'Twa mice, full blythe and amicable'
L(11631.i.11, uncut; Ashley 4974),LLP,LVA-F, C,LdU-B(uncut)+; CSmH(uncut),CtY(uncut), MH,TxU(2, 1 uncut, Luttrell).

P1074 [—] Erle Robert's mice. A tale, in imitation of Chaucer, &c. By M——w P——r, esq; Corrected from the errors of a spurious edition. *London, printed for John Morphew,* 1712. (14 Oct, Luttrell)
2°: A(3 ll); *i–ii, 1 2-4.*
Watermark: post-horn on shield. Collation as the preceding edition. The Luttrell copy is recorded in *Haslewood;* advertised in *DC* 16 Oct.
L(C.59.h.13; Ashley 5237),O,LdU-B; CLU-C, CtY,IU,NjP,TxU(2, uncut).

P1075 [—] [fine paper?]
No watermark.
MH.

— Emma, carmen...latine redditum, 1748. *See* E305.

P1076 [—] An English padlock. *London, printed for Jacob Tonson,* 1705.
½°: *1–2,* 1 column.
'Miss Danae, when fair and young'
Reprinted in Prior's *Poems,* 1718, and with his name in *Cloe convinc'd,* 1733.
L(Ashley 4967),O,OW,CJ,DG; CLU-C,CSmH, MH.

P1077 [—] — *London, 'printed for Jocab Tompson',* 1705.
½°: *1–2,* 1 column.
A piracy, with imprint deliberately mis-spelt.
L(C.20.f.2/220; Ashley 4966).

[—] An epistle from the Elector of Bavaria to the French King [actually by Stephen Clay], 1706. *See* C233.

[—] Et tu Brute? or, the m--'d c--l, [1704.] *See* E479.

[—] A fable of an old woman and her doctor, [1718/19.] *See* F1.

[—] The fable of the lyon and the fox, 1712. *See* F9.

Prior, M. Faction display'd

[—] Faction display'd. A poem [actually by William Shippen], 1704–. *See* S427.

— The female Phaeton, [1718.] *See* P1094.

[—] For the new year: to the sun.
First published in 1694. A second edition of 1707 is recorded by T. J. Wise in the *Ashley Catalogue* IV.70, probably by confusion with Fenton's *An ode to the sun, for the new-year,* 1707.

[—] A genuine epistle from M——w P——r, esq; at Paris, to the reverend J——n S——t, D.D. at Windsor, 1714. *See* G125.

— 'Hans Carvel of Monsr. de la Fountaine imitated by Mr. Prior.'
Entered to Jacob Tonson in *SR* 26 March 1701, but apparently not separately published.

P1078 [—] Horace lib. I. epistle the ninth... To the right honourable R--- H---, esq; [*London*] *Printed for Bernard Lintott,* [1711.] (*PB* 6 March)
½°: 2 sides, 1 column.
Reprinted in an unrecorded miscellany, *Horace's epistle to Claudius Nero...imitated... By several hands* (Edinburgh, 1719; copy at EU).
'Dear Dick, howe'er it comes into his head'
Collected in Prior's *Poems* 1718. Addressed to Harley.
L(Cup.645.e.1/22),C,Chatsworth,Crawford; MH(2).

[—] An impossible thing. A tale [actually by Congreve], 1720. *See* C372.

[—] Jack Frenchman's lamentation. An excellent new song, 1708. *See* J1.

P1079 [—] A letter to Monsieur Boileau Depreaux; occasion'd by the victory at Blenheim. *London, printed for Jacob Tonson,* 1704. (*PM* 30 Sept)
2°: A–C²; *i–ii,* 1–10.
Watermark: DP. The Luttrell copy, dated 30 Sept, was sold in the Christie Miller sale, 1926.
'Since hir'd for life, thy servant muse must sing'
Reprinted in Prior's *Poems,* 1718.
L(11632.i.1; Ashley 4965),O(2),OW(uncut),DG, DrU + ; CSmH,CtY,MH,MiU,TxU(2) + .

P1080 [—] [fine paper]
Watermark: star. Inner margins enlarged.
OW(George Clarke's copy, 'Donum e autori 29° Sept: 1704'); ICN,IU.

[—] The m——'d c——b: or, the L——th consultation, 1704. *See* E480.

[—] The members to their soveraign [actually by Hildebrand Jacob], 1726. *See* J45.

[—] Ode for the thanksgiving day [actually by William Walsh], 1706. *See* W35.

P1081 [—] An ode, humbly inscrib'd to the queen. On the late glorious success of her majesty's arms. Written in imitation of Spencer's stile. *London, printed for Jacob Tonson,* 1706. (*DC* 6 July)

Prior, M. An ode

2°: π¹ A–E² F¹ (A2 as 'A'); *i–vi,* 1–18. π1 hft.
Rothschild 1674.
'When great Augustus govern'd ancient Rome'
Reprinted in Prior's *Poems,* 1718. Attacked in the preface to William Atwood's *A modern inscription,* 1706.
L(840.m.1/24, –π1; Ashley 5236, uncut),O(4, –π1),C(cropt, –π1),EU(–π1),DG(cropt, –π1) + ; CSmH,CtY,ICN(–π1),MH,TxU(3, 2–π1) +.

P1082 [—] Pallas and Venus. An epigram. *London, printed for John Nutt,* 1706.
½°: 1–2, 1 column.
'The Trojan swain had judg'd the great dispute'
Reprinted in Prior's *Poems,* 1718.
L(C.38.1.6/23; Ashley 4969).

[—] The peeper: being a sequel to the Curious maid, 1721. *See* P141.

P1083 [—] Prologue, spoken at court before the queen, on her majesty's birth-day, 170¾. *London, printed for Jacob Tonson,* 1704. (12 Feb, Luttrell)
½°: 1–2, 1 column.
Apparently previously published by 10 Feb in a four page folio headed 'Overture. Prologue.' which also contains the songs in the performance. Luttrell's copy at CtY is dated 10 Feb and has the note 'gratis'.
'Shine forth, ye planets, with distinguish'd light'
Reprinted in Prior's *Poems,* 1718.
L(C.121.g.9/140; Ashley 4964); CLU-C,CSmH, *Ct Y,*ICN(Luttrell).

P1084 [—] Prologue to the Orphan. Represented by some of the Westminster-scholars at Hickford's dancing-room, the 2d of February, 1720. Spoken by the Lord Duplin, who acted Cordelio. *London, printed for Jacob Tonson,* 1720. (*DC* 10 March)
½°: *1–2,* 1 column.
'What wou'd my humble comrades have me say?'
Reprinted in Prior's *A new collection,* 1725.
L(Ashley 5241),OW(uncut); *CtY,*TxU.

P1085 [—] [*idem*] A prologue spoken by the right honble the Lord Duplyn, (aged 9 years and 7 months.) On the acting of a play, call'd The orphan; by the Westminster-scholars, on the 3d 5th and 6th of February, 1719. [*London,* 1720.]
½°: 1 side, 1 column.
The status of this edition is uncertain; from its inferior production it may be a piracy.
LWS.

[—] The silent flute, a poem [actually by Hildebrand Jacob], 1729. *See* J46.

— Solomon de mundi vanitate... latine redditum, per Guil. Dobson [3 books], 1734, 1735, 1736. *See* D346–8.

— Solomon de mundi vanitate, liber secundus... latine traductum...a Georgio Bally, 1743. *See* B45.

Prior, M. The squirrel

P1086 [—] The squirrel. A poem. *London, printed for Bernard Lintott, 1706.* (*DC* 14 Jan)
½°: A¹; 1–2, 1 column.
 Reproduced in F. H. Ellis & D. F. Foxon, 'Prior's *Simile*' *PBSA* 57 (1963) 337–9.
'Dear William, didst thou never pop'
 Reprinted in Prior's *Poems*, 1718 as 'A simile'.
Crawford.

P1087 [—] [*idem*] A simile. *London, printed for Bernard Lintott, 1706.* (*DC* 19 Jan)
½°.
(Danielson cat. 41 (1937) 248.)

P1088 [—] To a young gentleman in love. A tale. [*London*] *Printed for J. Tonson, 1702.* (16 June?)
½°: 1–2, 1 column.
 Copies at O, Crawford have variant catchword 'A' (incorrect, for 'Contempt'). In print by 16 June, when Prior wrote of it to G. Stepney.
'From publick noise and factious strife'
 Reprinted in Prior's *Poems*, 1718.
L(11602.i.12/3; Ashley 4963),O,Crawford; CLU-C,TxU.

P1089 [—] To the right honourable Mr. Harley, wounded by Guiscard. *London, printed for Jacob Tonson, 1711.* (*Spectator* 10 April)
½°: 1–2, 1 column.
 Entered in *SR* 9 April to Tonson by John Watts; apparently no copies were deposited.
'In one great now, superior to an age'
L(Ashley 4970),O,Chatsworth,Crawford; CLU-C, CSmH(Luttrell, 13 April),MH,*NcD*,TxU(2).

P1089·1 [—] — *London, printed by John Barber; sold by John Morphew, 1711.*
½°: 2 sides, 1 column.
 Variant first line:
'In one short now, superior to an age'
CtY.

P1090 — The turtle and the sparrow. A poem. By the late Matthew Prior, esq; *London, printed for J. Roberts, 1723.* (*MC* May)
2°: A² B–E²; i–iv, 1–15 *16 blk.* A1 hft; 15 err.
 Rothschild 1684. In some copies (e.g. LVA-D, MH) A1 is bound as a fly-title after the title.
'Behind an unfrequented glade'
L(1347.m.32; Ashley 4984),LVA-D(uncut), LWS,O(uncut),LdU-B; CSmH,CtY,DFo,MH, TxU(2, 1 uncut)+.

P1091 — — The second edition. *London, printed for J. Roberts, 1723.* (May, Luttrell)
2°: A² B–E²; i–iv, 1–15 *16 blk.* A1 hft; 15 err.
 Either a press-variant title or a reimpression; the errata have not been corrected. A second edition was advertised by Thomas Osborn, 20 Sept 1723 (cutting in *Haslewood*), and is recorded by *Wright & Spears* p. 986. No such edition has been traced, and it may have no separate existence.
O(2, 1 Luttrell),OW(uncut); ICU(mutilated), TxU(uncut, made-up).

Prior, M. The turtle and the sparrow

P1092 — — The third edition. *London printed, and Dublin re-printed by Elizabeth Sadleir, for Dominick Roach, 1723.*
8°: A⁸ B²; 1–2 3–20.
O.

— Two imitations of Chaucer, 1712. *In* C245.

P1093 ['—'] Upon Lady Katherine H-de's first appearing at the play-house in Drury-lane. By M——w P——r, esq; [*London*] *Sold by W. Graves & W. Chetwood, 1718.* (*DC* 8 April)
½°: 2 sides, 1 column.
'Thus Kitty, beautiful and young'
 For the problem of authorship, see *Wright & Spears* 1073–5. The weight of evidence suggests that Simon Harcourt rather than Prior was the author. Since they were friends, it may be that Prior lent his assistance to Harcourt. See also *Three poems*, 1720.
L(Ashley 4978); CSmH.

P1094 '—' [*idem*] The female Phaeton. By Mr. Prior. [*London*] *Printed for E. Curll; sold by T. Warner,* [1718.] (*SJEP* 10 April)
½°: 2 sides, 1 column.
 Below imprint, 'N.B. The copy, before publish'd, has not one stanza printed right.' The copy at L has the title and Prior's name deleted in ink and a new title substituted in contemporary ms., 'Upon Lady Kitty Hide's first appearing in publick'.
L(1850.c.10/59); CSmH.

P1095 ['—'] [*idem*] Kitty: or the female Phaeton, a new song sung by Mr. Beard. [*London?* 174–?]
slip: 1 side, 1 column.
 Rough woodcut at head. Two stanzas of the original are omitted. If the singer was John Beard (1716?–1791), it probably dates from the 1740s; cf. W563.
C.

P1096 — Verses spoke to the Lady Henrietta-Cavendish Holles Harley, in the library of St. John's College, Cambridge, November the 9th. An. 1719. *Cambridge, printed for Cornelius Crownfield; and are to be sold by Jacob Tonson, bookseller in London,* [1719.]
½°: 1 side, 1 column.
 Rothschild 1681.
'Since Anna visited the muses seat'
L(Ashley 5239),O(imprint mutilated),CT(uncut); CSmH(uncut),CtY,TxU.

P1097 — [variant: no imprint]
 Presumably a presentation issue.
MH(uncut).

P1098 — — *London, printed for Jacob Tonson, 1720* [1719?]. (27 Nov?)
½°: 1 side, 1 column.
 A new edition, and conceivably the one advertised in *DC* 27 Nov as 'for Jacob Tonson'.
OW(uncut),CJ; CLU-C.

Prior, M. Walter Danniston

— Walter Danniston, Ad amicos. Imitated by Mr. Prior, [1710?] *In* P366.

[—] When the cat's away,|The mice may play, [1712.] *See* W384.

[—] Yarhell's kitchen: or, the dogs of Egypt, 1713. *See* Y5.

Prisca. Prisca redit virtus, [1710?/13.] *See* Pitcairne, Archibald.

P1099 Prison. The prison groans and sorrowful lamentation of Elizabeth Forister, for the murder of Mr. Pimlot, attorney, in Chancery Lane. [*London*] *Printed for E. Sharp, in Holborn*, [172–?]
½°: 1 side, 2 columns.
   Popular woodcut at head.
'A warning take young women all'
L(1876.f.1/97).

Prisoner. The prisoner's ballad: or, welcome, welcome, brother debtor, 1748. *See* Wilkes, Wetenhall.

P1100 — The prisoner's petition to his patron. *Dublin, printed by George Faulkner*, 1726.
½°: 1 side, 2 columns.
'Your honour I court/For a timely support'
DT.

Prisons. The prisons open'd, 1729. *See* Wesley, Samuel, *the younger*.

P1101 Pritz, Johann Georg. De serenissima atque potentissima principe, Anna...poemation; cui subnecitur in expeditionem gloriosissimi ducis de Marlborough, qua fossas Brabanticas feliciter perrupit, elegia. Auctore Io. Georgio Pritio, Lipsiensi... *Londini, prostant apud Ionam Bowyer*, 1705.
4°: A⁴; i–ii, 1–6.
'Anna tuæ mater patriæ, primaria mundi'
'Continuat nostras coeli clementia palmas'
LLP.

P1101·5 [—] Antonii Varisci Elogium Annae, Magnae Britanniae reginae; una cum elegia in felicissimam expeditionem invictissimi belli ducis, Ioannis de Malberough, anno cIↃ Iↄccv susceptam, Londini editum; nunc conversis animis atque rebus cum duobus aliis poematiis de praesenti rerum statu recusum. *Amstelodami, apud Io. Petri*, 1713.
2°:)(²)()(²)()()(¹; 1–2 3–10.
   The original poems are printed as 1 and 3; added poems on the changed state of affairs as 2 and 4. Dedication to Franciscus Alemannus by the editor and reviser, 'Philuraeus Hermundurus'.
O.

P1102 Pro. Pro and Con. *London, printed for J. Roberts*, 1741. (*LDP* 8 Jan)
2°: A² B² C¹; 1–2 3–10.
'Pro met with Con:-----says Con to Pro'

Pro and con

On the political satires of 1740, [James Miller] *Are these things so?* and the answers to it.
L(162.n.55),O; CtY,IU,MH,OCU,TxU(uncut).

Processionade. The Processionade, 1745. *See* Morgan, Macnamara.

P1103 Proclamation. A proclamation, a poem. *London, printed for W. Webb; sold by the booksellers in London & Westminster*, 1750. (*GM, LM* March)
2°: A² < B¹; 1–2 3–6.
'Whereas good learning was design'd'
   A call to all the wits to join against Warburton.
L(C.57.g.7/27, Horace Walpole's),O,LdU-B; CU,CtY,DFo,OCU.

— A proclamation from Parnassus, 1734. *See* 'Dunkin, William'.

Proctor. The proctor's banquet, 1731. *See* 'Gulliver, Martin'.

Prodicus.
[Shenstone, William:] The judgment of Hercules, a poem [from the abstract of Prodicus in Xenophon's *Memorabilia*]. Inscrib'd to George Lyttelton, 1741. *See* S394.

[Lowth, Robert:] The judgment of Hercules, a poem, 1743. *See* L293–4.

[—] [*idem*] The judgement of Hercules, from Xenophon's Memoirs of Socrates, lib.ii. Tat. no.97, 1746. *See* L295.

Layng, Peter: The judgment of Hercules, imitated from the Greek of Prodicus, 1748. *See* L79.

P1104 Prodigal. 'The prodigal son return'd, a poem, address'd to all parents and youth. [*London*] Cooper. Price 6d.' (*BM, GM* June 1750)

Prodigy. The prodigy, [1726?] *See* Barber, Mary.

P1105 Progress. The progress of a harlot. In six canto's. With an introduction to each, never before publish'd. Adorn'd with six copper cuts. *London, printed for T. Reynolds*, 1733.
12°: A¹ B–C⁶ D(3 ll) (+6 folding plates); 1–2 3–14 17–28 25–30.
'Here an old bawd a girl draws in'
   Based on Hogarth's prints.
MnU.

P1106 — The progress of a rake: or, the templar's exit. In ten cantos, in hudibrastick verse... By the author of the Harlot's progress. *London, printed for B. Dickinson, & R. Montague; sold by E. Nutt, & J. Brotherton, A. Dodd, J. Brindly, J. Jolliff, Mr. Critchly, J. Stagg*, 1732. (*DJ* 11 May)
8°: (frt+) A–H⁴; 1–2 3–61 62–63; 64 blk. 63 advt.
'There liv'd i' th' west a squire, so great'
   Sometimes attributed in error to J. D. Breval who wrote a verse account of Hogarth's *Harlot's progress* as *The lure of Venus*, 1733,

The **progress** of a rake

under the pseudonym of Joseph Gay. This is by the author of *The harlot's progress*, 1732. L(P&D, – H4),O; CSmH(– H4),CtY,MH,OCU (– H4).

— The progress of beauty. A poem, 1732. *See* Dalacourt, James.

P1107 — The progress of charity. A poem. Occasioned by reading the proposals for the establishment of a county hospital at Northampton. [1742.]
½°: 1 side, 2 columns.
On the other side, *On the death of Dr. Alured Clarke*, [1742.]
'Mild charity - - - - - best blessing of the blest'
The county infirmary was instituted in 1743.
DFo.

P1108 — 'The progress of divine love; a poem. Written by a young lady of fifteen, in the year 1731. [*London*] *Printed for N. Cholmondeley*. Price 6d.' (*GSJ* 18 July 1732; *GM* July)
Presumably the edition entered in Ackers's ledger 14 July 1732, 500 copies 'containing 3 sheets' for 'Cholmondeley...declared a bankrupt'.

P1109 — The progress of glory: an irregular ode, address'd to his majesty, on the happy suppression of the rebellion... *London, printed by Daniel Browne, for Richard Wellington*, 1746. (*BM*, *GM* Aug)
2°: A¹ B–D² E¹; *i–ii, 1 2–14*.
Horizontal chain-lines.
'Away with ev'ry trifling theme'
E; CSmH.

— The progress of honesty, 1739. *See* D'Urfey, Thomas.

— The progress of love, 1732. *See* Lyttelton, George, *baron Lyttelton*.

P1110 — The progress of methodism in Bristol: or, the methodist unmask'd. Wherein the doctrines, discipline, policy...are...display'd, in hudibrastick verse. By an impartial hand. To which is added, by way of appendix, the paper-controversy ... *Bristol, printed by J. Watts*, 1743.
8°: A⁴ B–I⁴; *1–5 6–71 72. 72* err.
Horizontal chain-lines, with watermark normally placed. Pp. 43–71 contain the prose appendix.
'That many gross deceits are rife'
L(4374.b.26/5).

— The progress of musick in Ireland, 1725. *See* Pilkington, Matthew.

P1111 — The progress of patriotism: a poem. Humbly inscribed to that worthy patriot John Howe esq; knight of the shire for the county of Wilts. *London, printed for L.B.; sold by A. Dodd, and the booksellers of London & Westminster*, 1731. (*GSJ* 18 Feb)
2°: B² C²; *1–3 4–8*.
'Sing muse, the progress of the patriot flame'
L(643.m.15/15),O,DrU.

The **progress** of physic

— The progress of physic, 1743. *See* Cowper, Ashley.

P1112 — The progress of the war, from the first expedition at Spithead; to the late memorable one to and from Torbay. A poem in hudibrastick verse. *London, printed for Thomas Robins, and sold at the Royal Exchange, St. James's, Bond-street, and Charing-Cross*, 1740. (*GM*, *LM* Oct)
8°: A⁴ B–C⁴; *1–5 6–23 24 blk.* A1 hft.
'I feel an impulse from the muse'
A satire on the inactivity of the fleet.
L(164.n.26, – A1),O; CtY(– A1).

P1113 — The progress of time; or, an emblematical representation of the four seasons and twelve months, as marching in procession round their annual circle. In imitation of Spencer's Fairy queen. N. Dove scr. Tho. Gardner scu. *London, printed for the editors*, 1743.
4° size, 19 leaves, engraved and printed on one side only.
'The bloom of youth upon his cheek is seen'
TxU.

P1114 — [reissue] *London, printed for, and sold by Thomas Gardner engraver, John King printseller, & William Reeve bookseller*, 1749.
L(11642.eee.28).

P1115 — The progress of valour, humbly inscrib'd to his grace the Duke of Marlborough. *London, printed for A. Baldwin*, 1709. (*PB* 7 April)
8°: A⁸; *1–4 5–16*.
'Whilst Saturn rul'd the awful world in peace'
CT,DrU; CSmH,CtY,InU.

— The progress of wit, 1730. *See* Hill, Aaron.

P1116 — The progress: or, the unfortunate knight. By the author of the sermon in praise of cuckoldom. *London printed, and sold by Doctor Gaylard, in Great Carter-lane near Doctors-Commons*, [172–?]
8°: A⁴ B–C⁴; *1–4 5–24*. A1 hft.
'When George with all his noble train'
The 'sermon' has not been traced.
Brett-Smith.

P1117 **Projector.** The projector in the dumps: or the Grand Schemifl's lamentation for the downfall of his last scheme. A new ballad. *London, printed by J. Jenkins near the Strand*, [1733.]
½°: 1 side, 2 columns.
'My scheme's turn'd topsy turvy'
A satire on the failure of Walpole's excise scheme.
Harding.

P1118 — The projector, or Remarker remark'd, a poem in burlesque, occasion'd by a just resentment the author conceiv'd at the Remarker's pirating Mr. Bickerstaff's works, and mixing such bright thoughts with his own trumpery. [*London*] *Printed in the year* 1710. (*British Apollo* 3 March)
2°.

The **projector**

Advertised in *The British Apollo* as 'To be had of our servants in their walks, Mr. Carter, Mr. Bickerton, or at the printer hereof [J. Mayo]'. The copy recorded was bound with a file of *The British Apollo*, and the background is revealed in no. 104 for 23 Feb 1710.

An attack on Charles Povey who pirated *The Tatler* in his periodical *The general remark*.

(Lowe Bros. cat. 1204 (1963) 177.)

P1119 — The projector's looking-glass, being the last dying words and confession of Sir Robert Marral, &c. &c. in an epistle to his associates, wherein he makes a confession of some notorious crimes... *London printed, and sold by T. Tibbitt, 1733. (LM April)*

2⁰: A⁴; *1–2* 3–8. 8 advt.

> *Percival* XXVIII. Title in mourning border. Note after imprint, 'The picture may be had of Mr. Aldam, stationer, near Weaver's Hall'.

'With heavy heart and trembling hand'

> A satire on Walpole.

L(11657.m.35),LU,O,C,LdU-B; CSmH,CtY, KU,MH,NjP.

P1120 Prologue. The prologue and epilogue of George Barnwell, the London merchant: to be spoke this night in the play-house. The prologue spoke by Mr. Elrington. [*Dublin*, 1731?]

½⁰: 1 side, 1 column.

> Below, 'Epilogue. Spoken by Mrs. Sterling'. The DT copy is bound with half-sheets of 1731.

'The tragick muse, sublime, delights to show'
Epilogue: 'Since fate has robb'd me of the hapless youth'

> The epilogue is attributed to Colley Cibber in the editions of Lillo's play; the prologue may well be by Lillo himself.

DT.

— Prologue and epilogue, spoken at the opening of the theatre in Drury-lane, 1747. *See* Johnson, Samuel.

P1121 — [dh] The prologue and epilogue to the last new play of the Albions queens, or, the death of Mary queen of Scotland. Printed as they were written, but not permitted to be spoken. [col] [*London*] *Sold by J. Nutt, 1704. (DC 13 March)*

4⁰: A²; *1–4*.

> Pagination and signature are possibly cropped from the copies seen.

'As when the dreadful sessions time draws near'
Epilogue: 'Now sirs y'ave seen this bug-bear of a play'

> The play was by John Banks, who may well have written the prologue and epilogue.

L(806.k.16/68),LLP.

— The prologue and epilogue to the new...opera, call'd Hurlothrumbo, [1729.] *See* Meredith, Amos.

P1122 — Prologue, and epilogue, to the Orphan. As it was acted at a private school at Isleworth, April 25,

Prologue, and epilogue, to the Orphan

1728. *London, printed for L. Gilliver, 1728. (MChr 1 May)*

2⁰: A¹ B²; *1–2* 3–6. 2 advt.

'Wond'rous the bard, whose happy tragic vein'
Epilogue: 'My birthright's privilege is sure but small'

> *Rawlinson* records that the epilogue is by Joseph Trapp, 'spoke by his son Joseph'; possibly the prologue is also his.

OW.

— The prologue at the opening of the Theatre-Royal, 1714. *See* Steele, *Sir* Richard.

— A prologue design'd for the play of Oedipus, [1723.] *See* Sheridan, Thomas.

P1123 — A prologue for his majesty's birth-day, May 28th, 1725. To be spoken at the play-house. Written by J.T. lately one of his majesty's servants; and dedicated to his excellency the Lord Carteret. *Dublin, printed in the year 1725.*

½⁰: 1 side, 1 column.

'To heaven altars, men most justly raise'

> Possibly by the author of *Miscellanies in prose and verse* (Dublin, 1725).

L(C.121.g.8/46).

P1124 — Prologue for the musick, spoken on Tuesday, January the 4th, 1703. [*London*] *Printed for J. Tonson, 1704. (DC 7 Jan)*

½⁰: A¹; 2 sides, 1 column.

> On side 2, 'Epilogue to the ladies'.

'Such is, yee fair, your universal sway'
Epilogue: 'With joy we see this circle of the fair'

Crawford; CSmH,MH,TxU.

P1125 — [dh] A prologue, sent to Mr. Row, to his new play, call'd, The fair penitent. Design'd to be spoken by Mr. Betterton; but refus'd. [*London*, 1703.]

4⁰: A²; *1–4*.

'Quacks set out bills, Jack-Pudding makes harangues'

> Rowe's play was first performed in May 1703.

L(806.k.16/69),LVA-F; MH.

P1126 — A prologue, spoke at Mr. Smith's mugg-house in St. Jones's, on the anniversary of the king's coronation. October the 20th, 1716. [*London?*] *Printed in the year 1716.*

½⁰: *1–2*, 1 column.

'Oft as the sun returns the circling year'

C.

P1127 — A prologue, spoke at Mr. Smith's mugg-house in St. Jones's, on the birth-day of his royal highness the Prince of Wales. October the 20th, 1716. [*London?*] *Printed in the year 1716.*

½⁰: *1–2*, 1 column.

> Date in title corrected in ms. to 'October the 30th'.

'New scenes of pleasure now your joys invite'

L(1850.e.10/47),C.

Prologue spoke

— Prologue spoke at the Theatre-Royal, [1720.] *See* Sheridan, Thomas.

— A prologue, spoke by Mr. Elrington, [1720.] *See* Sheridan, Thomas.

— Prologue. Spoke by one of the young gentlemen, [1720.] *See* Ramsay, Allan.

— Prologue, spoken at court before the queen, 1704. *See* Prior, Matthew.

— Prologue spoken at the first opening of the Queen's new theatre, 1705. *See* Garth, *Sir* Samuel.

P1128 — A prologue, spoken at the opening of the new play-house, in Ransford-street, before the rt. hon. the Earl of Meath. *Dublin, printed at Dick's-Coffee-House, in Skinner-row,* [1732.]
½°: 1 side, 1 column.
'While factious feuds, loud strife and fierce debate'
CtY.

— Prologue spoken before a Greek play, 1728. *See* Sheridan, Thomas.

P1129 — A prologue spoken by F---ny L--e, of the new play-house, on a dray-horse, in answer to Will. P--k---m--n's on an ass. [*London*] *Printed in the year* 1704. (20 July, Luttrell)
½°: 1-2, 1 column.
On p. 2, 'An epilogue, in answer to Mr. L--'s prologue spoken by Jubilee Dicky on foot'.
'Since joking epilogues for current pass'
Epilogue: 'The business of the drama being done'
Pinkethman spoke his epilogue on an ass at Drury-lane 1 July 1704; this reply was spoken by Francis Leigh. Reprinted with commentary by E. L. Avery in *SEL* 5 (1965) 455ff.
ICN(Luttrell).

— A prologue, spoken by Mr. Elrington, 1725. *See* Coffey, Charles.

P1130 — The prologue spoken by Mrs. Babb, at her first appearance in the play-house in Dorset-garden, the 24th of October, 1706. [*London,* 1706.] (26 Oct, Luttrell)
½°: 1 side, 1 column.
'Bless me! An audience here! I'm all surprize!'
Reprinted with commentary by E. L. Avery in *SEL* 5 (1965) 455ff.
ICN(Luttrell),MH.

— A prologue spoken by Mrs. Bracegirdle, 1709. *See* Congreve, William.

— A prologue spoken by the right honble the Lord Duplyn, [1720.] *See* Prior, Matthew.

P1131 — A prologue spoken December 9, 1745, at the Theatre-Royal in Drury-lane, when the whole receipt of the house was apply'd to the veteran scheme, for giving to our soldiers, in the North, flannel-waistcoats, &c. [*London,* 1745.]
⅛°: 1 side, 1 column.
'Methinks I see Britannia's genius here'
Crum M340.
L(Add. MS. 30012, fol. 159),E.

The prologue that was spoke

— The prologue that was spoke at the Queen's theatre in Dublin, 1712. *See* Garth, *Sir* Samuel.

— A prologue to Julius Caesar, [1732.] *See* Sheridan, Thomas.

P1132 — [dh] A prologue to Peace-triumphant, for the sixteenth of June 1713. Being the day appointed of thanksgiving for her majesty's most glorious peace. Spoke by Mr. Griffith . . . [col] *Dublin, printed by Edward Waters,* 1713.
4°: A²; 1 2-4.
On p. 3 'The epilogue spoke by Mr. Leigh'.
'Long time had discord reign'd thro' all the world'
Epilogue: 'Long had th' affrighted world with loud alarms'
InU.

P1133 — A prologue to the Conscious lovers: spoken the 7th. of this instant March, 1722. By the ghost of Sir Fopling Flutter. On occasion of it's being play'd at the request of the young gentlemen of the College, Dublin. [*Dublin*] *Printed by J. Carson,* 1723.
½°: 1-2, 1 column.
At foot of p. 2, 'Epilogue'.
'Ladies, ye stare as if ye knew me not——'
Epilogue: 'Ye gen'rous fair by whom our house is grac'd'
Blanchard 122 refutes an attribution to Steele, and suggests the author was Concanen or one of his circle.
L(C.121.g.8/27).

— Prologue to the court; on the queen's birthday, 1705. *See* Congreve, William.

— Prologue to the Orphan, 1720. *See* Prior, Matthew.

P1134 — A prologue upon the beaus, for Mrs. Davis's benefit, but none of the players wou'd venture to speak it, for fear of disobliging that formidable party. [*Dublin,* 1728/29?]
½°: 1 side, 1 column.
'When lust and rage usurp'd the human breast'
DT; CtY.

Prometheus. Prometheus, a poem, 1724. *See* Swift, Jonathan.

Promotion. The promotion, and the alternative, 1726. *See* Mitchell, Joseph.

Proper. A proper new ballad, to the tune of I'le never love thee more, [17--.] *See* Graham, James, *marquis of Montrose*.

P1135 — A proper reply to a lady, occasioned by her Verses address'd to the imitator of the first satire of the second book of Horace. By a gentleman. *London, printed for T. Osborne,* [1733.] (*GSJ* 3 April)
2°: A² B²; 1-3 4-8.
Some copies (at O,IU,NN-B) have an early state of p. 6 with ms. corrections.

A **proper** reply to a lady

    'What lust of malice, what malicious spite'
      The same author wrote *The classic quarrel*,
      [1733.] A satire on Lady Mary Wortley
      Montagu, assuming her to be the author of
      the *Verses*.
    L(1346.m.38),O(2),LdU-B; CSmH,CtY(2),IU,
    MH,TxU(2)+.

P1136 Prophecy. A prophecy. [*London?* 1714/–.]
    obl ⅛⁰: 1 side, 1 column.
    'When dames of Britain shall espouse'
      A Jacobite prophecy.
    O.

P1137 — A prophecy, by Merlyn, the famous British
    prophet; found written upon an old wall in Saxon
    characters; dated the year 482. about the time of
    the restoration of King Vortigern, to the British
    throne; faithfully transcrib'd from the original.
    [*London?* 1715?/18?]
    slip: 1 side, 1 column.
    'When savage Goths from Rhine return'
      Crum W1435: 'Merlyn's prophecy dated in
      the year 482...' A Jacobite satire.
    CSmH.

    — The prophecy, or an imitation of the 15th. ode
    of the first book of Horace, 1714. *See* Welsted,
    Leonard.

    — The prophesy: or, M——m's lamentation for
    H——y, 1710. *See* Abigail's lamentation, [1708.]

P1138 Prophetic. A prophetick congratulatory hymn to
    his sacred Britannick majesty King James the III.
    February the 3d. 1718. By G—— F—— gent.
    [*London?* 1718/19.]
    ½⁰: *1–2*, 2 columns.
    'Sound the shril trumpet, fill it's silver womb'
      A Jacobite welcome.
    CSmH.

P1139 — The prophetic physician. An heroi-comic poem,
    address'd to the physicians. *London, printed for T.*
    Cooper, 1737. (*GM, LM* April)
    2⁰: A¹ B² C² D¹; *1–3* 4–12.
      Bond 162.
    'Ye learn'd adepts, in wond'rous secrets skill'd'
    L(11642.i.10/4),WcC(uncut); CtY-M,OCU,*TxU*.

P1140 Prophets. The prophets: an heroic poem. In three
    cantos. Humbly inscrib'd to the illumin'd assembly
    at Barbican. *London printed, and are to be sold by A.*
    Baldwin, [1707/08.]
    8⁰: A–C⁸; [2] i–xiv *xv–xviii*, 1–28.
    'Thrice holy lanthorns, whose transcendent light'
      On the 'Prophets of the Cevennes'. With an
      epistle congratulatory to Sir Richard Bulkeley.
    L(11631.aaa.32),EN,EU; CLU-C,CtY,TxU.

P1141 Proposals. Proposals for the erecting a protestant
    nunnery, in the city of Dublin. Utterly rejecting
    and renouncing the new game of quadrille, by the
    ladies. *Dublin printed, and sold by E. Waters, 1736.*

Proposals for the erecting

    8⁰: *A⁴*; *1–2* 3–8.
      In some copies the 3 of 1736 is damaged and
      resembles a 2.
    'A circle of ladies, more bright than their pewter'
    L(11631.a.48),DA(2).

P1142 Prosodia. Prosodia Alvariana quibusdam in locis
    aucta & emendata, et in usum scholarum edita per
    J.W. *Londini, apud Joannem Clark, & Aaronem*
    Ward, 1719.
    8⁰: A–B⁴; *1* 2–15 *16 blk.*
      Text on rectos, notes on versos. Ms. errata on
      p. 16 of the copy seen.
    'Vocalem breviant alia subeunte Latini'
      The *Prosodia* of Emmanuel Alvarez was
      originally in prose, though mnemonic verses
      are found in a Dublin edition of 1729. It is not
      clear whether J.W. was the versifier. Cf. Louis
      Vaslet, *Emmanuelis Alvari Regulæ de syllabarum*
      quantitate, 1730.
    L(625.c.26/6).

P1143 — Prosodia Alvariana (quatenus ad syllabarum
    quantitatem spectat) aucta & emendata ab J.W. In
    usum scholarum iterum edita. Accedit huc appendix
    de patronymicis... *Londini, apud Joannem Clark &*
    Richardum Hett, & Aaronem Ward. Venit [!] *etiam*
    a Samuele Chandler, 1726. (*MC* June)
    8⁰: A–C⁴; *1* 2–24. 24 err.
    L(625.c.26/7),LDW.

P1144 Prospect. The prospect: a divine poem. On
    humane life, and its depravity...death, judgment,
    heaven, and hell. In two parts. *London printed, and*
    sold by the booksellers, and at the pamphlet-shops,
    1735. (*GM* Oct)
    8⁰: A–K⁴; *i–ii* iii–vi, 7–79 *80.* 80 err.
      An errata slip is pasted over the errata list on
      p. 80.
    'Warm'd by th' ethereal ray th' indulged muse'
    L(11633.bb.37); ICU.

    — A prospect of death, 1704–. *See* Pomfret, John.

    — The prospect of plenty, 1720. *See* Ramsay,
    Allan.

    Prosperity. Prosperity to Houghton, [1728/29?]
    See Floyd, Philip.

P1145 Protest. The protest. [*London*] *Published,* April the
    7th 1741, *and sold by J. Tinney, and at the print and*
    pamphlet-shops.
    obl 1⁰: 1 side, 3 columns.
      Large engraving at head.
    'Who be de noble lady dere'
      A satire against Walpole.
    L(P&D 2488),O,*MC*.

P1146 Protestant. Protestant divisions; or, party against
    party. With a view of the old buildings at West-
    minster. *London, printed in the year 1702.* (14 Feb,
    Luttrell)

Protestant divisions

2°: A–G²; *i–ii*, 1–26.
'When all the kingdom wanted grace'
    On the statues and paintings in Westminster Hall.
LdU-B; CSmH,CtY,IU,InU(Luttrell),TxU+.

P1147 — The protestant knock: or, the Boulogn fray. A ballad. To the tune of, The abbot of Canterbury. *London printed, and sold by C. Corbett*, [1740.] (*GM, LM* April)
2°: *A² B²*; *1–3* 4–8.
'Of religion and broils, and bold hardy deeds'
CSmH.

— Protestant popery: or, the convocation, 1718. *See* Amhurst, Nicholas.

P1148 — The protestant queen: or, the glorious proclaiming her royal highness Princiss [!] Ann of Denmark, queen of England, Scotland, France and Ireland, on the 8th. of March. 1702. on the joy and satisfaction of all loyal and loving subjects. To the tune of, Did you not here of a gallaut [!] sailor. *London, printed for John Alkin, near Fleet street,* [1702.]
½°: 1 side, 2 columns.
    Woodcut at head.
'I must confess that we all lamented'
CM-P.

P1149 — — Tune of, Did you not hear of a gallant sailor. Licensed according to order. [*London*] *Printed for B. Deacon, & C. Bates,* [1702.]
½°: 1 side, 2 columns.
    Rough woodcut at head.
CM-P.

P1150 — — To the tune of Gallant sailor. Licensed according to order. [*London?* 1702.]
½°: 1 side, 2 columns.
    Two rough woodcuts at head. The Crawford copy has a modern ms. note 'Printed by B. Deacon', but the authority has not been traced.
Crawford.

— The protestant session, a poem, 1719. *See* Amhurst, Nicholas.

P1151 — The protestant toasts. To the tune of, Ye commons and peers. [*London*] *Printed for J. Harrison; sold by R. Burleigh,* [1717.] (*DC* 22 May)
½°: 2 sides, 1 column.
'Fill the glasses all round'
    Whig verses.
MC.

P1152 Provisions. 'Provisions for the convent, a poem. [*London*] *Printed for and sold by B. Dickenson, J. Jolliffe, and at the book, print, and pamphlet-shops in town & country.* Price 6d.' (*GA* 4 April 1748)
    'To which is prefix'd a large humorous frontispiece, very neatly engrav'd, and fit for framing, representing a friar going into a cloyster, with a beautiful young girl, in the middle of a sheaf

Provisions for the convent

of wheat on his back.' 'The cut lively colour'd one shilling.' Possibly the text forms the lower half of an engraved sheet.

P1153 Prude. The prude, a tale. In two canto's. *Dublin printed, and sold by Tho. Hume,* 1722.
8°: A⁸ (A3 as 'A2'); *1–5* 6–16. A1 hft.
'Clara, a prude in early bloom'
    The same author also wrote *The lady's watch,* [1722?].
DN.

P1154 — — *Printed at Dublin; and re-printed in London, for J. Roberts, J. Harison, A. Dodd, S. Huddleston, & E. Griffith,* 1722. (*PB* 23 June)
8°: *A⁴ B–D⁴*; *1–4* 5–29 *30–32 blk.* A1 hft.
O; OCU.

— The prude's purgatory, 1736. *See* Jacob, Hildebrand.

'**Prudentia.**' An epistle to the most learned Doctor W--d----d, 1723. *See* E416.

P——s, *Mr.* The following poems, writen by Mr. P——s, 1725. *See* Philips, Ambrose.

Psalm. A psalm of thanksgiving to be sung by the children of Christ's Hospital, 1703–13. *See* Cobb, Samuel.

— — 1716–18. *See* Crow, Isaac.

— — 1729–36. *See* Hetherly, Seawell.

Psalmi. Psalmi Davidis quinquaginta priores, 1723. *See* Hanway, John.

P1155 Psychomachia. Psychomachia; the war of the soul: or, the battle of the virtues, and vices. Translated from Aur. Prudentius Clemens. *London, printed in the year 1743.*
8°: *A¹ B–K⁴*; *i–ii*, 1–72.
'In Abram's life we see a plan'
L(1466.i.7),LdU-B.

Public. The publick spirit, 1718. *See* Fox, John.

'**Public Credit.**' The stocks: or, high change in 'Change-alley, [1734?] *See* S767.

Publius. 'Publius Lentulus his account concerning the person and character of Jesus Christ. A poem.'
    Entered in *SR* 25 Aug 1710 to Thomas Slater as 'a broad sheet'; none of the deposit copies has been traced. It was possibly engraved throughout, like a version dated [*c.* 1680] at CtY.

'**Puddledock,** *Dutchess of.*' The popular convention, 1739. *See* P997.

P1156 Pugna. [dh] Pugna navalis inter Anglos & Gallos, anno 1692. Carmine heroico celebrata. Ad illustris-

Pugna navalis

simum dominum Edouardum Orfordiæ comitem
... [col] *Londini, apud A. Baldwin*, 1702.
2°: A²; 1-4.
'Magna quidem, non grata tamen, phantasmata
Morpheus'
CtY.

P1157 [**Pullein, Samuel**.] The eleventh epistle of the
first book of Horace, imitated, and addressed to a
young physician then on his travels. By S.P. A.M.
Dublin, printed by George Faulkner, 1749.
8°: A⁴ B⁴; 1-3 4 5 6-15 16 blk. A1 hft.
Text in Latin and English.
'Prithee, dear Harry, be sincere'
Ascribed to Pullein by *O'Donoghue*.
L(1486.ee.19),O,DG,DN,DT(uncut); CtY.

P1158 — Scacchia, ludus: a poem on the game of chess.
Written by Marcus Hieronymus Vida. And trans-
lated into English verse by the Rev. Samuel
Pullein, A.M. *Dublin, printed by S. Powell, for the
author*, 1750.
8°: A⁴ B⁴(−B1) C−N⁴; i−ii iii-vi, 1 2-95 96 blk.
Text in Latin and English. Engraving on A4ʳ.
Apparently also published in England; listed
in *GM* May 1750 as published by Whiston.
'How mimic realms, and pageant hosts engage'
L(1466.d.24),O,C,DA; *DLC*,MH,NN,*NjP*.

P1159 — The silkworm: a poem. In two books. Written
by Marcus Hieronymus Vida, and translated into
English verse by the Reverend Samuel Pullein...
Dublin, printed by S. Powell, for the author, 1750.
8°: (frt+) a² A−P⁴ R⁴(±R2) S⁴(±S4); [4] i ii-x,
11-13 14-141 142-144. S4 err.
S4, which bears 'Some observations', is some-
times bound after B1.
'What pow'rs of nature, and what wond'rous arts'
L(11405.g.29),O(2, 1−S4),C(2, 1 uncut, 1−frt),
DA,DN+; CtY,MH-BA,NN,TxU.

Pulpit. The pulpit-fool. A satyr, 1707. *See* Dunton,
John.

— Pulpit-war, 1710. *See* Ward, Edward.

[**Pulteney, William**, *earl of Bath*.] Britannia
excisa: Britain excis'd, 1733. *See* B459-65.

[—] The congress of excise-asses, [1733.] *See*
C368.

[—] The convention. An excellent new ballad,
1739. *See* C402.

[—] The discovery: or, the squire turn'd ferret,
1727. *See* D328.

P1160 [—] An epistle from L---l to Lord C---d. By
Mr. P----. *London, printed for T. Cooper*, 1740.
(*GM, LM* Dec)
2°: A⁴; 1-2 3-8.
'O Hol---m! blest, belov'd abode!'
Early ms. attribution to Pulteney (who is
clearly intended) in the TxU copy. Ascribed
to Pulteney in Walpole (ed. Park) *Royal &*

Pulteney, W., *earl*. An epistle

noble authors (1806) IV.278. Written as from
Thomas Coke, baron Lovel and subsequently
earl of Leicester, to Lord Chesterfield.
L(162.n.56),O(2),LdU-B(uncut); CSmH,CtY,
ICN,MH(2),TxU(2)+.

P1161 [—] The honest jury; or, Caleb triumphant. A
new ballad. To the tune of Packington's pound.
*London, printed for the author, and sold by the book-
sellers and pamphletsellers*, 1729. (*MChr* 12 Dec)
2°: A² < B¹; 1-2 3-6.
Percival XI. Listed in *MChr* as printed for
R. Walker.
'Rejoyce ye good writers, your pens are set free'
Attributed to Pulteney in *N&Q* I.ii.147, and
see *Percival*. Celebrating the release of Richard
Francklin, printer of *The craftsman*, 3 Dec 1729.
L(1972),SrS(uncut); ICN,TxU.

P1162 [—] — The second edition. *London, printed for the
author, and sold by the booksellers and pamphlet-
sellers*, 1729.
2°: A² < B¹; 1-2 3-6.
O,BaP; CtY(uncut),MH,OCU.

P1163 [—] The honest jury; or, Caleb triumphant. To
the tune of Packington pound. [*London?* 1729.]
(Dec)
½°: 1 side, 2 columns.
Rule above and below 'To the tune of...' On
the other side of the L copy, *The distiller's
petition*, in prose.
L(C.116.i.4/31); MH(ms. date 'Decr. 1729').

P1164 [—] — [*Edinburgh*, 1729/30.]
½°: 1 side, 2 columns.
No rules or ornaments in title.
L(Rox.III.637).

P1165 [—] — [*Dublin?* 1729/30.]
½°: 1 side, 2 columns.
Row of type-ornaments above and below 'To
the tune of...' The typography suggests a
Dublin edition.
TxU.

[—] The negotiators. Or, Don Diego brought to
reason, 1738. *See* N18.

[—] A new Norfolk ballad. To the tune of Packington's pound. By Sir Francis Walsingham's ghost,
1730. *See* N160.

P1166 [—] An ode, imitated from ode XI. book 2d. of
Horace. From P---l F----y to N----s F---y,
esq; By a person of honour. *London, printed for W.
Webb*, 1745. (*GM, LM* April)
2°: A⁴; 1-3 4-8.
'Never, dear Faz, torment thy brain'
Ms. note by Horace Walpole in the L copy
'Lord Bath'. Included in Sir Charles Hanbury
Williams, *Poems*, 1763, and thence ascribed to
him (as in *CBEL*); Horace Walpole again
annotated his copy of that printing 'By Lord
Bath'. From Paul Foley to Nicholas Fazakerly.

Pulteney, W., *earl*. An ode

> L(C.57.g.7/10, Horace Walpole's copy),O,E,
> LdU-B(uncut); CSmH,CtY,InU,MH,TxU+.

> [—] Quadrille to perfection as play'd at Soissons,
> [1728.] *See* Q3.

P1167 Punch. Punch's petition to the ladies. [*Dublin*,
1724.]
½°: 1 side, 2 columns.
> *Teerink* 1146; *Williams* 1108. With spaces
> between the paragraphs of verse.
'Fair ones! to you who hearts command'
> Signed, 'Punch cum sociis'. Scott (Swift's
> *Works*, 1814, X. 558) suggested Sheridan's
> authorship; there is no evidence for Swift's.
> Occasioned by Edward Hopkins who as
> master of the revels refused to let Stretch
> act without the payment of a large sum of
> money.
CSmH.

P1168 — [another edition]
> No spaces between paragraphs of verse.
CSmH.

> **'Punsibi, Tom.'** *Nickname of Thomas Sheridan;
> for satirical works such as* Tom Punsibi's farewell to
> the muses, *1725, see* Tom.

> — A trip to Temple-Oge, Stephen's-green and the
> Bason, 1730. See T489.

P1169 Puppet. The puppet-show, a poem. *Dublin,
printed by John Harding*, [1721.] (April?)
½°: 1 side, 2 columns.
> *Williams* 1102.
'The life of man to represent'
> Included in Faulkner's edition of Swift's
> *Works* (1762) VIII.175 and subsequent
> collections, but rejected by *Williams* on the
> evidence of a letter of Swift to Ford of 15
> April 1721; 'we cannot find the author, and it
> is not Delany'. Occasioned by a puppet-show
> arranged by Sheridan.
CSmH.

P1170 — The puppet shew: a poem humbly inscribed to
H—— P——. *London, printed for M. Cooper*,
1748. (*GM* May)
2°: *A*² B–E²; *1–2* 3–20.
> Horizontal chain-lines. Entered in Strahan's
> ledger to Andrew Millar, May [1748], 250
> copies. After an entry for Fielding's *Joseph
> Andrews* in June, there are entries for 'Adver-
> tisements for F's Puppet shew, no. 50 with
> paper' and 'Receipts for Miss F's Octavia &c.',
> 600 on fine paper.
'I've often heard an antient story'
> The ledger entries for June suggest the name
> of Fielding; 'Octavia' probably refers to Sarah
> Fielding's *Lives of Cleopatra and Octavia*, later
> published by subscription. The poem is a poor
> political satire on recent politics, ironically
> addressed to Henry Pelham, whom it satirizes;

The **puppet** shew

> Fielding on the other hand was currently
> writing in defence of Pelham. It is possible
> that the advertisements were not for this poem
> but for the real puppet show that Fielding held
> in Panton Street between 28 March and 2 June;
> see M. Battestin in *PQ* 45 (1966) 191–208.
> Strahan printed *Clio*, 1748, for Millar in
> February and that is 'by T---- F----'; so
> there is another possible author with the same
> initial.
L(C.57.g.7/23, Horace Walpole's copy),O; CtY,
MH,OCU.

P1171 [Purney, Thomas.] The Chevalier de St. George:
an heroi-comick poem. In six canto's. *London,
printed for W. Chetwood*, 1718. (Oct)
12°: a⁴ B–E⁶ F²; *i–viii*, *1–52*. a1 frt.
> The publication date is suggested in H. O.
> White's edition of Purney, 1933.
'Th' heroick youth, whose spear and batter'd helm'
> Ascribed to Purney by *Jacob*.
LVA-F,E.

P1172 — Pastorals. After the simple manner of Theocritus. *London, printed for J. Brown, & R. Burleigh*,
1717 [1716]. (*PB* 16 Nov)
8°: A–D⁸; *1–10* 11–63 *64*.
> Two pastorals. Luttrell's copy, dated Dec, was
> listed in Dobell cat. 114/329.
'A gentle swain yfed in Kentish mead'
L(11630.bb.2),O,OW; MnU,NjP.

P1173 — — The second edition corrected. *London,
printed by H. Parker, for J. Brown, & R. Burleigh*,
1717 [1716]. (*EvP* 26 Dec)
8°: A–D⁸; *1–10* 11–63 *64*.
> Apparently from the same setting of type as
> the preceding; probably a reimpression.
WgP; DFo.

P1174 — — The third edition. *London, printed by H.
Parker, for J. Brown, & R. Burleigh*, 1717.
8°: A–D⁸; *1–10* 11–63 *64*.
> Apparently another reimpression.
DFo.

P1175 — Pastorals. Viz. The bashful swain: and beauty
and simplicity. *London, printed by H.P.* [*H. Parker*]
for Jonas Brown, 1717. (*PM* 14 Feb)
8°: A–E⁸ (D2 as 'A2'); *i–xxiv*, *1–54* 55; *56 blk*. E8
advt.
> Listed in *MC* as 'Part 2d.'
'Paplet lov'd (ah lov'd too well!)'
O; CLU-C(−E8),CtY(−E8),DFo,ICN,MH.

P1176 Purver, Anthony. Counsel to Friends children.
*London printed, and sold at the Bible in George-yard,
Lombard-street*, [1737/–.]
1°: 1 side, 3 columns.
> The footnotes reveal that the poem was
> written at Coggeshal in Essex '22d of the 5th
> month', i.e. 22 July, 1737. The address is that
> of T. Sowle Raylton.

Purver, A. Counsel to Friends children

'Dear little Friends, not tainted yet with ill'
Signed 'Anthony Purver'.
L(imprint cropt),LF(2),O-JJ; *PHC*.

P1177 — — The third edition. Price 1d. [col] *London printed, and sold at the Bible in George-yard, Lombard-street,* [1737/–.]
8°: *A*⁴; 1–8.
Drop-head title only.
LF; *PHC*.

P1178 — A poem to the praise of god. Written by Ant. Purver, schoolmaster at Frenchay near Bristol, to his wife. *Bristol, printed by S. & F. Farley,* 1748.
½°: 1 side, 2 columns.
Dated from Frenchay, 18 Dec 1747. Note at foot, 'This poem that has been printed with part of the title, and without my name, was done so unknown to me, and contrary to my mind, being imperfect and obscure'.
'While wanton love to others is a theme'
LF.

[—] Psalm XXIII. versified.
A half-sheet (copy at LF), is attributed to Purver by *Smith* I.60, and dated there as [1740]; from the appearance of paper and type, the date appears to be considerably later.

P1179 Pygmaïogeranomachia. Pygmaïogeranomachia: or, the battel of the pygmies and cranes. Done from the Latin original. *London, printed for J. Roberts,* 1715. (*MC* Dec)
8°: A–B⁴ C²; *i–iv,* 1–15 *16 blk*. A1 hft.
Bond p. 210.
'I sing a winged army, and the train'
The Latin original is by Addison. A different

Pygmaïogeranomachia

translation from that printed in Addison's *Miscellanies in prose and verse,* 1725.
O(–A1); OCU.

P1180 Pyramid. A pyramid to the immortal memory of William the second & third, king of Great Britain, France and Ireland, prince of Orange... [*Edinburgh,* 1702.]
½°: 1 side, 1 column.
Printed in pyramidal form, with the title below.
'E-/rected/to him elected'
E.

P1181 Pyrrha. Pyrrha a cantata: being an imitation of the fifth ode of the first book of Horace. Not by John earl of Orrery. With a preface address'd to his lordship. *London, printed for J. Huggonson,* 1741 [1742?]. (*DP* 22 Jan)
2°: *A*² B–C²; *1–3* 4–11 *12 blk*.
'On beds of roses, Pyrrha, say'
Occasioned by Orrery's *Pyrrha,* 1741.
CSmH,NN(lacks C2).

Pythagora. Pythagora jactat Samius se fundus alumno, [1710?/13.] *See* Pitcairne, Archibald.

Pythagoras.
A paraphrase upon the golden verses of Pythagoras, 1704. *See* P62.

Rowe, Nicholas: The golden verses of Pythagoras. Translated from the Greek, 1732, 1740, 1750. *See* R288–90.

———————

A fragment on tranquility of mind, from Pythagoras. *In* Human wisdom displayed, 1731. *See* H388.

Q

Q., P. The vulture and eagle, [1727?] *See* V124.

Q1 Quack. The quack-doctor. A poem. As originally spoke at the Free Grammar School in Manchester. With notes... To which is added, a declamation, spoke at the same time...December 13. 1744. *London, printed for J. Roberts, 1745.*
4°: *A*⁴ B–C⁴ D²; *i–xii, 1–15 16 blk.* A1 hft.
 An edition 'Preston: printed and sold by W. Sergent' (copy at MP) with an additional poem by 'Tim Bobbin' has been thought to precede this London edition, but is probably a reprint of 176–.
'As I was walking up and down'
 The poem is attributed to Henry Brooke, master of Manchester Grammar School, in *DNB* and refs.; the dedication is addressed to him as reputed author, and the Latin declamation is certainly by him (printed separately at Manchester, 1744, copy at MP). But the preface and notes are highly ironic at his expense, and the poem itself may well not be his.
L(11633.cc.18),MP; DFo,KU.

Q2 — The quack triumphant: or, the N--r----ch cavalcade. A new ballad. *London printed, and sold by J.D.* [*J. Dormer?*] *and at the pamphlet shops,* 1733. (*GM* Aug)
2°: *A*¹ B–C²; *1–2 3–9 10 blk.*
 Percival XXXI. Issued with a folded broadsheet bearing an engraved plate and 'The history of Sir Sidrophel, and his man Whaccum' in prose.
'Attend, ye Britons, and give ear'
 A satire on the reception of Sir Robert and Horatio Walpole at Norwich in July 1733.
CtY,DLC(lacks broadsheet),MH(lacks broadsheet).

— The quack-vintners, 1712. *See* Ward, Edward.

Quadriennium. Quadriennium Jacobi, 1722. *See* Crabb, John.

Q3 Quadrille. Quadrille to perfection as play'd at Soissons: or, the Norfolk congress pursu'd, versify'd and enliven'd. By the hon. W.P. esq; *London, printed for the author,* [1728.] (*MChr* 18 Dec)
2°: *A*² < *B*¹; *1–3 4–6.*
'Come give me the cards, let me try this new game'
 The initials suggest an attribution to Pulteney. Occasioned by the prose *Norfolk congress*, advertised in *MChr* 19 Nov 1728, satirizing Walpole's visit to Houghton after the congress of Soissons. A different work from *The Norfolk congress versified,* [1728.]
L(Burney 267, uncut),O,*LdU-B*; CLU(uncut), CtY(uncut).

Q4 — [*idem*] A supplement to the Norfolk congress. Or, the game of quadrille, as now play'd at Soissons. *London, printed for A. More,* [1728/29.]

½°: 1 side, 1 column.
 A piracy, on bluish paper.
(Copy seen in private hands.)

Quae. Quae rara, chara, 1707. *See* Pomfret, John.

Q5 Quaker. The quaker's petition, to the h------ of c----. [*Dublin,* 1723/30?]
½°: 2 sides, 1 column.
'Since we have gain'd what we attempted'
 A satire on the quakers' attempts to be exempted from paying tithes.
L(1890.e.5/216).

Q6 — The quaker's song, sung by Mrs. Willis, at the theatre in Lincolns-Inn-Fields. [*London,* 1705?]
½°: 1 side, 1 column.
 Some music editions are entitled 'sung by Mrs Willis at the New Theatre', i.e. the Queen's theatre, Haymarket, to which the company transferred in October 1705.
'Amongst the pure ones all, which conscience doth profess'
Crawford.

Quarendon, George Henry Lee, Lord. *See* Lee, George Henry, *earl of Lichfield.*

Q7 Quarrel. The quarrel between Venus and Hymen: an heroi-satyrical mythological poem, in imitation of the antients: in VI. cantos. Found among the papers of a very learned antiquarian... *London, printed for M. Cooper,* 1750–1 [1750]. (*SR* 7 Nov)
8°: A–C⁸ D² (A2, 3 as 'A3, 4'); *1–3 4–51 52 blk.*
 Deposit copy at L; advertised in *GA* 8 Nov.
'The cruel taunts, the dire revengful flame'
L(992.h.12/4),O.

Quatrième. Quatrième dialogue entre deux freres, [1707.] *See* Dialogue entre deux freres, 1707.

Q8 Queen. Queen Elizabeth's day: or, the down-fall of the devil, pope, and pretender. To the tune of Bonny Dun-dee. [*London?* 1711.] (Nov)
½°: 1 side, 1 column.
'Let us sing to the mem'ry of glorious Queen Bess'
 A satire against the tories, on their seizing the effigies to be burnt by the whigs on 17 Nov 1711.
L(C.20.f.9/557),O(ms. date Nov 1711); DFo, MH.

— The queen of Great Brittain's royal bounty to the distressed Palatines, 1709. *See* Ellis, William.

Q9 — The queen's and my lord of Oxford's new toast. [*London*] *Printed by R. Newcomb,* [1711.] (*SR* 1 June)
½°: 1 side, 1 column.
 Teerink 872; *Williams* 1097. Deposit copies at L,E.
'Here's a health to the queen and her faithful adviser'

The **queen**'s and my lord of Oxford's new toast

> *Ball* 126 suggested Swift's authorship; not accepted by Williams. Tory verses.
> L(C.20.f.2/232),O,E,Crawford; TxU.

Q10 — — *London, printed by T. Jones, near Fleetstreet,* [1711.]
½⁰: 1 side, 1 column.
TxU.

Q11 — — [*Dublin, printed by C. Carter,* 1711.]
½⁰: 1 side, 1 column.
> On the other side, *Scotch cloath,* [1711.]
C,DG,DT.

Q12 — The queen's and the Duke of Ormond's new toast. [*London*] *Printed by Rich. Newcomb,* 1712.
½⁰: 1 side, 1 column.
> *Teerink* 872; *Williams* 1097.
'Here's a health to the queen, who in safety does sit on'
> *Ball* 126 suggested Swift's authorship; not accepted by Williams. Welcoming Marlborough's dismissal and Ormonde's appointment in his place.
L(11602.i.12/6).

Q13 — [variant imprint:] [*London*] *Printed in the year* 1712.
L(Cup 645.e.1/23); MH.

Q14 — The queen's thanksgiving hymn, in St. Paul's church, for the glorious victory obtained at Blenheim... *London, printed for William Turner, & J. Nutt,* 1704.
4⁰: A⁴; *1–2* 3–7 *8 blk.*
> Vertical chain-lines.
'O magnifie the lord of hosts with me'
InU.

Quevedo Villegas, Francisco Gomez de.
The visions of Dom Francisco de Quevedo Villegas ...Made English by Sir R. Lestrange, and burlesqu'd by a person of quality, 1702. *See* V107.

'Quidam.' The knight, 1723. *See* Meston, William.

'Quidnuncius Profundus.' The Porcupinade, 1745. *See* P1000.

Quillet, Claude.
Callipædiæ; or, an art how to have handsome children, 1710, 1718. *See* C4–5.

Quillet, C.
[Oldisworth, William:] Callipædia: or, the art of getting pretty children, 1710. *See* O142.

— — Translated by Mr. Will. Oldisworth, 1719, 1729. *See* O143–4.

Rowe, Nicholas: Callipædia. A poem. In four books, 1712. *See* R280–1.

— [*idem*] Callipædia: or, the art of getting beautiful children, 1720, 1728, 1733. *See* R282–4.

Q15 [**Quincy, John.**] The mouse-trap: or, the Welsh engagement with the mice. *London, printed for Edward Pool, & J. Morphew,* 1709. (*DC* 12 Feb)
8⁰: A⁴ B–C⁴; *1–3* 4–23 *24 blk.* A1 hft.
> *Bond* p. 218. Latin title 'Muscipula...' on A1ᵛ; Latin and English texts.
'Muse sing the British mountaneer, who told'
> Quincy's authorship is acknowledged in the edition of 1714; the Latin is by Edward Holdsworth.
L(11626.bbb.15; 11626.bbb.26/2),O(2, 1–A1), EU,DT,WcC+; CLU-C,CSmH,CtY,MiU,NN.

Q16 — The mouse-trap, a poem: written in Latin by Mr. E. Holdsworth...done into English by John Quincy. The second edition: whereunto are added some short remarks upon a translation...by Mr. Samuel Cobb... *London, printed for J. Phillips, & J. Baker,* 1714.
8⁰: π² A⁴(A2 + *⁴) C–E⁴; *i–xx, 1–22* 23–24 *blk.* π1 hft.
O(–E4),C,CT(–π1, E4),WcC(–π1, E4); CtY (–π1, E4).

Q17 — A poem to the memory of the reverend Mr. Joseph Stennett. *London printed, and sold by A. Baldwin, J. Noon, & T. Harrison,* 1713. (*SR* 1 Aug)
2⁰: A² B–C²; *1–2* 3–12. *12 advt.*
> Entered in *SR* to Quincy; deposit copies at L,LSC,O,EU.
'To mourn the loss of a departed friend'
L(643.1.26/12),LDW(2),LSC,O(uncut),EU; CtY, TxU.

'Quintinus Plagosus.' The school-master's letter, [1749.] *See* S137.

R., A. An elegy on Patie Birnie, [1721.] *See* Ramsay, Allan.

— Fy gar rub her o'er wi' strae, [172–.] *See* Ramsay, Allan.

— An ode sacred to the memory of her grace Anne dutchess of Hamilton, [1724.] *See* Ramsay, Allan.

— On the death of Lady Margaret Anstruther, [1728.] *See* Ramsay, Allan.

— On this great eclipse, 1715. *See* Ramsay, Allan.

— To the honourable, Sr. John Clerk, [1722.] *See* Ramsay, Allan.

— The young laird and Edinburgh Katy, [1720.] *See* Ramsay, Allan.

R., A., *hosier.* A poem to the whole people of Ireland, 1726. *See* P675.

R., E. The fair sex turn'd amazons, [172–?] *See* F32.

R., I. The passions of man, 1746. *See* Ruffhead, James.

R., J., *A.M. Coll. Christi Cantab.* Nomina quorundam e primariis olim regiæ grammaticalis scholæ Buriæ Sti Edmundi...illustrata, 1719. *See* Randall, John.

R------, L------. A tale of an ass, [1718.] *See* Tale.

R., N. Æsop in Europe, 1706. *See* A113.

R., R. Epinikion Marlburiense Bleinhemianum, 1704. *See* E356.

R., R., *B.D.* Carmen coronarium, 1727. *See* Roach, Richard.

R., T. An old maid's fortune, 1727. *See* O114.

— The true state of mortality, 1708. *See* T531.

R., T., *esquire.* An epistolary poem to a lady, 1740. *See* Rogers, Thomas.

R., T., *gent.* Eternity: a poem, 1716. See E482.

R., W., *M.D.R.* Britannia invicta, 1745. *See* B466.

R1 R------. R------P------'s complaint of his hard fate, or the town officer's lament for the loss of his coat. To the tune of The bonny boat man. [*Edinburgh,* 1727/–.]
½°: 1 side, 2 columns.
'I pray draw near and you shall hear'
    According to a ms. note in the E copy, on

Robert Penman, who was a town officer from 3 May 1727 to 28 March 1753. The occasion of this disgrace is not clear.
E.

R2 Race. A race at Sheriff-muir, fairly run on the 13th of November 1715. To the tune of the Horseman's port[!]. [*Edinburgh*? 1715/–.]
½°: 1 side, 2 columns.
    17 stanzas. The text is printed in roman type with proper names and refrain in italic. For its possible publication with Allan Ramsay's *Elegy on Lucky Wood,* see R48. *Morgan* R469 records editions, with [William Meston] *A tale of a man and his mare* added, as '8 pp., 8°, [1715?]'; another ed., 4°, [E.?, 1715?]'; they have not been seen, but cf. *Case* 476 for a collection beginning with this poem.
'There's some say that we wan, some say that they wan'
    A satire on the Jacobite defeat.
L(1876.f.1/76).

R3 — ... Horseman's sport. [1715/–.]
½°: 1 side, 2 columns.
    21 stanzas. Woodcut at head; text printed in italic type. The additional four stanzas on Lowrie the traitor suggest a later date.
E.

R4 — fairly run on the thirteenth day of November 1715. To the tune of The horseman's sport. [1715/–.]
½°: 1 side, 2 columns.
    21 stanzas. The text is printed in roman type throughout.
MC.

R5 — fairly run, on the 13th. November, 1715... [1715/–.]
slip: 1 side, 1 column.
    14 stanzas. Printed with *A dialogue betwixt William Lick-ladle,* N182.
L(1876.f.1/75).

R6 — fairly run on the 17th November. 1717... [1717?]
slip: 1 side, 1 column.
    13 stanzas. The wrong date in the title suggests a possible date of printing.
NjP.

R7 — A race for Canterbury: or, Lambeth ho! A poem, describing the contention for the metropolitan see. *London, printed for B. Dickinson,* 1747. (17 Oct)
4°: *A*² B–D²; *1–4* 5–16. A1 frt.
    The engraved frontispiece copies the design in *First oars to L--m--th,* [1731.] Listed in *BM* Oct.
'The doctrines which our Saviour taught'
    A satire on the competition after Archbishop Potter's death – the candidates were Thomas

A **race** for Canterbury

The **rake's** progress

Sherlock, Benjamin Hoadly, Matthias Mawson and Edmund Gibson.
L(11630.b.6/14, Tom's Coffee House, 17 Oct, lacks A1),O,E.

Radcliffe, Alexander.
There is no evidence that Radcliffe was alive after 1700, so editions of his collected works are excluded.

[—] A bowl of punch upon the peace, 1713. *See* B336.

R8 — Ovid travestie, a burlesque upon Ovid's epistles. The fourth edition. *London, printed for J.T. [Jacob Tonson?] and are to be sold by Richard Wellington*, 1705. (*DC* 27 Sept)
8°: A–I⁸; *i–xvi*, 1–126 *127–128*. I8 advt.
First published in 1680. *Macdonald* 195d.
'When these my doggrel rhimes you chance to see'
L(11355.b.14),O(−I8); CLU–C,MH.

R9 Rake. The rake in fetters: or, the marriage mouse trap. [*Edinburgh?* 17——.]
½°: 1 side, 1 column.
The E copy is bound with Edinburgh half-sheets of *c.* 1720, but there is no other indication of origin.
'Of all the simple things I know'
E.

— The rake of taste, [1735.] *See* Dorman, Joseph.

— The rake reform'd, 1718. *See* Glanvill, Abraham.

R10 — The rake's progress; or, the humours of Drury-lane. A poem. In eight canto's. In hudibrastick verse. Being the ramble of a modern Oxonian; which is a compleat key to the eight prints lately published by the celebrated Mr. Hogarth... *London, printed for J. Chettwood, and sold at Inigo Jones's head*, 1735. (*DA* 24 July)
8°: A¹ B–G⁴ H⁴(−H4) (H2 as 'H3'); *i–ii*, 1 2–54.
The copy at NN has an earlier state of D2, but no cancel has been identified in other copies.
'With muse invok'd, and solemn proem'
Ascribed to J. D. Breval by *CBEL*, probably by confusion with *The progress of a rake*, 1732, which is itself wrongly ascribed to Breval by the confusion of his *The lure of Venus*, 1733, with *The harlot's progress*, 1732. A very free low-life poem.
L(P&D); NN,OCU,*PP*.

R11 — — The second edition with additions, particularly an epistle to Mr Hogarth. *London, printed for J. Chettwood, and sold at Inigo Jones's head*, 1735.
8°: (frt+) A⁴ B–G⁴ H¹; *1–5* 6–58.
'Price 1s. 6d. with cuts'; no plates in the copy seen, but presumably there should be eight.
O(lacks plates).

R12 — — The second edition with additions, particularly an epistle to Mr. Hogarth. *London, printed for J. Chettwood, and sold at Inigo Jones's head*, [1735/42.]

8°: (frt+) A⁴ B–G⁴ (+8 plates); *1–5* 6–56.
Presumably this new edition should have a frontispiece and eight plates.
LG(lacks plates); CtY(lacks frt and 3 plates).

R13 — — The third edition, with additions, particularly an epistle to Mr. Hogarth. *London, printed for J.L. and to be had at the pamphlet shops in London & Westminster*, 1742.
12°: (frt+) A(3 ll) B–E⁶ (+8 plates); *1–3* 4–54.
The TxU copy has misprint 'Oxonion' for 'Oxonian' in title. There are a number of editions after 1750.
IU,TxU.

Ralph, James. Miscellaneous poems, viz. Night... *London, printed by C. Ackers, for W. Meadows, S. Billingsley, & J. Gray*, 1729. (*LEP* 22 April)
8°. L(impft),WcC; NN.
A nonce collection of previously published poems.

———————

R14 [—] Clarinda: or the fair libertine. A poem. In four cantos. *London, printed for John Gray*, 1729. (*MChr* 27 Jan)
8°: A⁴ B–I⁴; *i–viii*, 1 2–64. A1 hft.
Bond 101.
'Would Denham's muse revisit earth again'
Reissued in Ralph's *Miscellaneous poems*, 1729.
L(992.k.15/3),O,C; CtY,DFo,NN(2),NjP,OCU.

R15 — The muses' address to the king: an ode. *London, printed for W. Meadows*, 1728. (*MChr* 21 Aug)
8°: A⁴a⁴ B–F⁴ G²; [*10*] *i* ii–v *vi*, 1 2–43 *44 blk*. A1 hft.
Watermark: fleur-de-lys. Reissued in Ralph's *Miscellaneous poems*, 1729.
'Peace is the joy of heav'n, the happiness'
L(992.k.15/4),LDW; CSmH,CtY(−A1),DFo, ICN,NN(2)+.

R16 — [fine paper].
No watermark, very heavy paper.
O.

R17 — — *London: printed, and Dublin re-printed, and sold by George Faulkner & James Hoey*, 1729 [1728?].
8°: A–B⁸ C²; [*6*] *i* ii–iv, 1 2–24 25–26. C2 advt.
A Dublin 'third edition' was advertised in Hoey & Faulkner's edition of John Philips's *Splendid shilling* (Dublin, 1728), P250.
O,DA,DK.

R18 — Night: a poem. In four books. *London, printed by C. Ackers, for S. Billingsley*, 1728. (*MChr* 31 Jan)
8°: A–E⁸ F⁸(−F7, 8); [*6*] *i* ii–x, *1–3* 4–75 *76 blk*. x err.
'Lo! sable night ascends the dusky air'
L(1466.h.16),O,OW,E,*MR*; CSmH,CtY(lacks A⁸), ICN,MH(cropt),NjP+.

R19 — — *Dublin, printed by S. Powell, for George Risk, George Ewing, & William Smith*, 1728.

Ralph, J. Night

8°: A–D⁸; [6] *i* ii–x, *1* 2–47 *48.* 48 advt.
L(12274.e.1/10),DK,DN,DT; *CSmH,CtY,DLC*
(title cropt).

R20 — — The second edition. *London, printed by C. Ackers, for W. Meadows, & S. Billingsley,* 1729 [1728]. (*MChr* 21 Nov)
8°: A–L⁴ M²; [6] *i* ii–xi *xii–xvi,* *1* 2–68 *69–70.* M2 advt.
    Reissued in Ralph's *Miscellaneous poems,* 1729.
L(992.k.15/1); CU,NN(2),*RPJCB.*

R21 [—] Sawney. An heroic poem. Occasion'd by the Dunciad. Together with a critique on that poem address'd to Mr. T---d, Mr. M---r, Mr. Eu---n, &c. *London printed, and sold by J. Roberts,* 1728. (*MChr* 26 June)
8°: π¹[=G4] A⁴ a⁴ B–F⁴ G⁴(–G4) (A2 as 'a2'); [2] *i* ii–xvi, *1* 2–45 *46 blk.*
'Sawney, a mimick sage of huge renown'
    Attributed to Ralph by Pope in his *Dunciad,* 1729.
L(11643.c.18; C.116.b.2/7, Pope's copy),LVA-D (uncut),O(uncut),C(lacks π1),LdU-B; DFo,ICU, MH,*NN,*TxU(2)+.

R22 — The tempest: or, the terrors of death. A poem in blank verse. *London, printed for W. Meadows,* 1727. (*MC* Feb)
8°: *A²* B–D⁴ E²; [2] *i–ii,* *1* 2–27 *28 blk.*
    Reissued in Ralph's *Miscellaneous poems,* 1729.
'When blooming youth, and rosy health combine'
L(992.k.36, uncut),O; ICN,IU(lacks A2),MH,NN (2),NjP+.

R23 — Zeuma: or the love of liberty. A poem. In three books. *London, printed by C. Ackers, for S. Billingsley,* 1729 [1728]. (*MChr* 16 Oct)
8°: A⁴ a² b⁴ B–S⁴ (b2 as 'a2'); [12] *i* ii–vi *vii–viii,* *1* 2–136. a2ᵛ, b4ᵛ err.
    Reissued in Ralph's *Miscellaneous poems,* 1729.
''Tis hard for man, bewilder'd in a maze'
L(992.k.15/2); CSmH,CtY,ICN,MH,NN(2)+.

R24 **Ramble.** A ramble thro' Hyde-Park; or, the humours of the camp, a poem. *London, printed for T. Payne,* 1722. (*PB* 3 July)
8°: *A¹* B–E⁴; *i–ii,* 1–24 17–24.
'When kind informers new chimeras start'
L(11633.e.45/3; 164.l.10, Luttrell, Aug),LG; ICU,NjP,TxU.

R25 — — The second edition. *London, printed for T. Payne,* 1722. (*DJ* 15 Sept)
8°: *A¹* B–E⁴; *i–ii,* 1–24 17–24.
    Probably a reissue.
TxHR.

Rambling. The rambling fuddle-caps, 1706–. *See* Ward, Edward.

Ramelies. Ramelies. A poem, 1706. *See* Johnson, Charles.

Ramondon, L.

R26 **Ramondon, Lewis.** In Heriot's-Walks, &c. A new song, compos'd by Mr. Ramondon, senior. To it's own proper tune. *Edinburgh, printed and sold by John Reid,* 1715.
½°: 1 side, 2 columns.
    Two rough Edinburgh woodcuts at head.
'In Heriot's-Walks as I was roving'
E.

R27 — A new song, by Mr. Ramondon, senior. To the tune of, I am a silly old man. [*Edinburgh,* 171–.]
½°: 1 side, 2 columns.
    Edinburgh headpiece above title.
'Since fancy's in pleasure so strong'
L(C.121.g.9/180); NjP.

R28 — A new song, to an Irish coranoch; the words by Mr. Ramondon, senior. [*London?* 171–?]
½°: 1 side, 2 columns.
'Remember, Damon, you did tell'
O.

R29 — A new song to the tune of, Peggie I must love thee. The words, by Mr. Ramondon, senior. [*Edinburgh,* 171–.]
½°: 1 side, 2 columns.
    Two rough Edinburgh woodcuts at head.
'Adieu, my Cælia, oh adieu!'
L(C.121.g.9/179),E.

R30 — Victory and beauty, a new song by Mr. Ramondon, senior; to the good old tune of Catharine Ogie. [*Edinburgh,* 171–.]
½°: 1 side, 2 columns.
    Edinburgh headpiece above title.
'I sing not of affairs of states'
L(C.121.g.9/183).

R31 **Rams.** Rams all. A new ballad. Addressed to the satirists of a late contention. To the tune of, Sing tanterarara fools all. [*London*] *Printed for A. Moore,* 1750. (*LM* Feb)
2°: (3 ll); *1–3* 4–6.
'Ye satirical wits, who can make a great joke'
    On cuckoldry.
L(C.57.g.7/29, Horace Walpole's); CtY(uncut).

Ramsay, Allan. Poems. *Edinburgh, printed for the author,* 1720.
8°.

See *Martin* 41 and references. Late in 1719, (if not before) Ramsay seems to have issued collections of his poems in a standard octavo format; about April 1720 he provided preliminary leaves with the title noted above. Later poems were added as they were printed, and as the constituent parts were reprinted an attempt was made to give continuous pagination to the volume. The process of piecemeal reprinting continued under the title-pages of the third and fourth editions of 1723 and 1727; the result is that copies vary in their constituent parts. The latest part seen is *Tartana,* 1732.

The history of the collections issued before the 1720 titlepage is fragmentary, since copies have been broken up by booksellers in recent times. Only a collection at GM and that described by R.W. Chapman in *RES* 3 (1927) 343–6 survive intact, both with remains of blue paper wrappers; the latter is now at O (Don. f.14). There are substantial remains of an intermediate collection at C (S 721.d.71/13–18 & S 721.d.72/7, 9); all eight parts have matching stab-holes, showing that they were issued together.

An advertisement, in *DP* 10 March 1721, for 'A collection of poems, by Mr. Allan Ramsay' for T. Jauncy, 4s.6d., suggests that copies were sold in London. Copies may be tabulated thus:

1 With *The scriblers lash'd*, 1718, and the first edition of *Content*, 1719.   GM.
2 With the second editions of *The scriblers lash'd*, 1720, and *Content*, 1719.   C(fragmentary, described above).
3 With *Tartana* and *Scots songs* reprinted with continuous pagination, 1720.   O(Don. f. 14, Chapman's copy).
4 With 1720 prelims, ending with *Patie and Roger*. (April?)   OW.
5 Adding *Edinburgh's salutation.* (May?)   CLU-C, CSmH.
6 Adding *Wealth.* (July?)   E(NG.1170. c. 15).
7 Adding *To the royal...* and *Scots songs, viz...* with pagination 229–60. (Nov?)   E(Glen 124).
8 Completed volume, ending with a glossary and including 1721 reprints.   E(F.5.b.13); MH.
9 *Christ's kirk* a 1722 reprint.   L,O(12 Θ 1435), OW,E(Glen 106, impft).

— Poems. *Edinburgh, printed by Mr. Thomas Ruddiman, for the author,* 1721. (*Edinburgh Courant* 27 July)
4°: pp. xxviii, 400.   L,E; MH.
Watermark: fleur-de-lys. There are proposals dated 1720 at E. Entered to Ramsay in *SR* 18 Sept; deposit copy at O. Reissued in 1728.

— [fine paper]   O; CLU-C,CSmH.
Watermark: Strasburg bend.

— — The third edition. *Edinburgh, printed by Mr. Thomas Ruddiman, for, and sold by the author, and by Mr. Taylor, London, by Mr. James M'Euen in Glasgow, by Martin Bryson in Newcastle, and by Mr. Farquhar in Aberdeen,* 1723.
8°.   L,E; ICU.
A collection of parts of various dates, continuing the series started in 1720.

— Miscellaneous works of that celebrated Scotch poet, Allan Ramsay. *Dublin, printed by S. Powell, for George Risk,* 1724.
8°: pp. xix, 464, 23.   L,O; ICN,MH.

— Poems... The fourth edition. *Edinburgh, printed by Mr. Thomas Ruddiman, for and sold by the author,*

by Mr. Longman, London, and by Martin Bryson in Newcastle, 1727.
8°.   L,O; IU,MH.
A collection of parts of various dates, continuing the series started in 1720.

— Poems... Volume I. *Edinburgh, printed by Mr. Thomas Ruddiman, for the author,* 1728.
4°.   CtY,NN.
A reissue of the 1721 edition with a cancel title.

— [fine paper]   EU.
Watermark: Strasburg bend.

—————

— Poems... Volume II. *Edinburgh, printed by Mr. Thomas Ruddiman, for the author,* 1728. (*Caledonian Mercury,* 6 June)
4°: pp. xii, 420.   L,O; CtY,MH.
No watermark. According to *Martin* 98, some copies omit the words 'Volume II'; this appears to be an error. Listed in *MChr* 29 June as sold by J. Osborn & T. Longman, and W. Lewis.

— [fine paper]   EU; CSmH.
Watermark: Strasburg bend. A letter of Ramsay to Sir John Clerk of May 1728 records that only two dozen were printed.

— Poems... Volume II. *Edinburgh, printed by Mr. Thomas Ruddiman, for the author,* 1729.
12°: pp. iv, 307.   O,E; IU.
An advertisement at the end refers to the separate publication of parts of this 'and the former volume' at sixpence each.

—————

— Poems... In two volumes. *London, printed for J. Clarke, A. Millar, F. Cogan, R. Willock, and S. Palmer & J. Huggonson,* 1731 [1730].(*MChr* Oct)
8°: 2 vol.   L,O; CSmH,MH.
A fifth share of the copyright, with 80 books, formed lot 55 of the trade sale of 'Mr Astley & Conger', 11 Nov 1735, sold to J. Osborn for seven guineas; a fifth with 10 books in Mrs. Bowyer's sale of 11 Jan 1737, sold to G. Hawkins for £2. 4s.; a fifth without any books was in the sale of Francis Cogan, 10 July 1746. A tenth share appeared in the sale of Weaver Bickerton, [1737?]. (Copies of all sale catalogues at O-JJ.)

— Poems... With new additions and notes... *Dublin, printed by S. Powell, for George Risk,* 1733.
12°: pp. xii, 436.   L,O; NN.

—————

— Fables and tales. *Edinburgh, printed for the author, at the Mercury, opposite to Niddry's Wynd,* 1722.
8°: pp. iv, 36.   L; CtY.
Martin 63. *Martin* 63a records a copy at E with this address but with the addition of F⁴ like the following; it is sophisticated.

Ramsay, A. *Collections*

— [reissue] *Edinburgh, printed for the author, at the Mercury, opposite to the Cross Well,* 1722.
8°: pp. iv, 44 + .   O.

The copy seen adds F⁴, containing *Bagpipes no musick* (R33), and seven other Ramsay publications of 1722–24 with separate collations. This appears to be a collection similar to those which preceded *Poems,* 1720.

[—] [*idem*] Collection of thirty fables. *Edinburgh, printed for the author, and sold at his shop,* 1730.
12°: pp. 61–132.   L.

A separate issue with a new title-leaf of part of Ramsay's *Poems... Volume II,* 1729. Collections like this are advertised in that volume. Variant contents from the preceding.

———

— Health: a poem. *Edinburgh, printed for the author,* 1724.
8°: pp. 24 + .   L,O.

As well as being issued separately with collation *A*⁴ B–C⁴ (R57), it was also issued with additional poems in D–K⁴ (pp. 25–80) published at separate times, apparently building up a collection similar to that which preceded *Poems,* 1720. That at O (pp. 56) probably represents the first stage of additions as advertised on p. 24; the copy at L (pp. 80) adds further poems.

[—] Health: a poem. To which are added, The fair assembly... *Edinburgh, printed for the author, and sold at his shop,* 1730.
12°: pp. 1–60.   L.

A separate issue with a new title-leaf of part of Ramsay's *Poems... Volume II,* 1729. The added poems are not those found in the collection described above. An advertisement in *Volume II* lists sixpenny collections such as this; there were clearly others, not traced.

———

Ramsay's habit, described above, of issuing the same editions of his poems both individually and in collections causes difficulty to the bibliographer. The copies which formed part of collections have naturally been the ones to survive, but the habit of booksellers in this century of breaking up the collections to produce separate editions has obscured his publishing practices. I have tried below to list those poems for which there is evidence of separate publication, while noting that most copies have been extracted from collections; copies which form part of unbroken collections have not been listed, though they are usually comparatively common.

After a poem was admitted to one of Ramsay's collections it was reprinted when stocks became low, and pagination appropriate to its place in the volume was supplied if it was not present in its original publication. These reprints were probably available for separate purchase, but no such copies have been

Ramsay, A.

seen; they would have the appearance of imperfect fragments and would doubtless have been discarded. I have considered them as offprints from Ramsay's works and excluded them from my list; a full account may be found in Martin.

R32 [—] An address of thanks from the Society of rakes, to the pious author of An essay upon improving and adding to the strength of Great Britain and Ireland by fornication. To which is added, an epistle to the said author by another hand. *Edinburgh, printed, and sold at Allan Ramsay's shop,* 1735. (May?)
8°: A–B⁴; *1–2* 3–16.
        Martin 117.
'Thanks and renown be ever thine'
'How much, O pastor, do we owe'
        A copy was enclosed in a letter of Ramsay to Sir John Clerk, 27 May 1735; there is a rough draft in Ramsay's hand at L. Addressed to 'Philosarchus', i.e. David MacLauchlan, who wrote the *Essay.*
L(11631.c.35),O,E; MH.

R33 [—] [dh] Bag-pipes no musick: a satyre on Scots poetry. An epistle to Mr. Stanhope. [*Edinburgh,* 1722.]
8°: F⁴; 37–44.
        Three poems, the first by 'John Couper' (the first edition of which is entered under that name). Pp. 38–40 reprint *Grubstreet nae satyre* signed 'Pate Birnie', and pp. 41–44 'Ramsay's reasons for not answering the hackney scriblers, his obscure enemies'. The only copy seen is bound with the second issue of *Fables and tales,* 1722, at O; it continues the collation of that collection. It was advertised as separately available in *Health,* 1724 (though the advertisement leaf was perhaps cancelled), under the title 'Pate Birny to John Cowper. With a general answer to the hackneys'.
Reasons: 'These to my blyth indulgent friends'

R34 [—] The battel: or, morning-interview. An heroi-comical poem. *Edinburgh, printed for George Stewart,* 1716.
8°: A⁸ B⁴; *1–2* 3–24.
        Gibson 3; *Martin* 3; *Rothschild* 1705. The 'advertisement' on pp. 3–4 is printed in Grover's scriptorial type. Gibson identifies the printer as William Adams junior. In some copies (e.g. ICU) p. 5 is numbered '3'.
'When silent show'rs refresh the pregnant soil'
        Reprinted with Ramsay's name, below.
L(11645.e.46/1),*Bl*U; ICU,MH.

R35 — [*idem*] The morning-interview. An heroi-comical poem. By Allan Ramsay. The second edition. *Edinburgh, printed by William Adams junior, for the author,* 1719.
8°: A–C⁴; *1–2* 3–24.
        Gibson 12; *Martin* 23. Pp. 19–24 reprint *Edinburgh's address* (R44). Copies were probably issued in rudimentary collections pre-

Ramsay, A. The battel

dating Ramsay's *Poems*, 1720. Subsequently reprinted with additions and title-pages dated 1720, 1721, 1724, and 1731 for *Poems*, 1720, and subsequent issues.

L(1486.ee.22; 1078.h.24, lacks A1),O,E,EP, GM(2)+; MH,TxU(uncut).

R36 [—] Bessy Bell and Mary Gray. [*Edinburgh?* 1720?] *slip*: 1 side, 2 columns.

The copy described is a mutilated oblong slip measuring 6½×8 in., with the two columns divided by a row of type flowers; it is well printed, but the format is unusual. Possibly it is an imperfect copy of a half-sheet bearing two poems. The use of type-flowers suggests that it is an Edinburgh edition printed by Ruddiman or James Watson, and it could be an authorized first edition.

'Bessy Bell and Mary Gray'
B*l*U(mutilated).

[—] — [*Edinburgh*, 1720.]
½⁰: '26'–'25'.

Gibson 23; *Martin* 28. This leaf, conjugate with *Prologue*, [1720], is found both in a rudimentary collection predating Ramsay's *Poems*, 1720, and in early states of that volume; its separate issue is unproved, though there are copies apparently extracted from collections at CLU-C,CtY. Gibson suggested that *The young laird* (paged 1–4) was intended to follow *Scots songs... The second edition*, 1719 (paged 1–20), and that this should have been paged 25–26 to follow that. The existence of a half-sheet edition of *The young laird* with this poem (R109) supports the idea that they were published about the same time, and they appear together in Ramsay's collections.

R37 — Christ's kirk on the green in two canto's. *Edinburgh, printed by William Adams junior, for the author of the second canto, at the Mercury opposite to Nidderie's Wynd*, 1718.
8⁰: A–D⁴; *1-2* 3–32.

Gibson 5; *Martin* 4. There was a series of half-sheet editions of the first canto, 'composed (as was supposed) by King James the fifth' published in the late seventeenth and early eighteenth century. They are not included here, but may be seen at C,E,MC.

Canto I: 'Was ne'er in Scotland heard nor seen'
Canto II: 'But there had been mair blood and skaith'

Dedication signed 'Allan Ramsay', making clear his authorship of the second canto; the first is ascribed in traditional fashion to King James V, corrected in subsequent editions to James I. In Ramsay's *Poems*, 1721, he ascribes the composition of canto II to 1715.

E,EP,B*l*U; CLU-C,CSmH,MH(uncut).

R38 — — [*Edinburgh*, 1718?]
obl 1⁰: 1 side, 6 columns.

Ramsay, A. Christ's kirk

Martin 5. A broadside containing canto one on the left half and canto two on the right, headed by Ramsay's dedication and advertisement. Almost certainly a piracy.

E.

R39 — — [*Newcastle on Tyne, printed by John White?* 1718/–.]
obl ½⁰: 1 side, 6 columns.

Martin 6. Rows of type-flowers between columns; 'Canto II. by Allan Ramsey' but without his dedication and advertisement. The NeU copy is in a collection of ballads printed by John White; it may well be late in date, though Martin assigns it to 1718 without being aware of its Newcastle connection.

L(L.R.31.b.19, fol. 478–80; C.20.f.9/706–7), MC,NeU; MH.

R40 — Christ's-kirk on the green, in three cantos. *Edinburgh, printed for the author*, 1718.
8⁰: A–B⁸; *1-4* 5–31 *32*.

Gibson 10; *Martin* 7; *Rothschild* 1710. Ramsay's name appears at the beginning of cantos II & III; canto I is here ascribed to James I. Copies were usually issued in early states of Ramsay's *Poems* 1720; many copies listed here have been extracted thence. Subsequent editions of 1720, 1722 and 1726, paged [89]–120, appear in later states of *Poems*.

Canto III: 'Now frae east-nook of Fife the dawn'
L(1078.h.21; Ashley 1351, uncut),C,E,GM(2), LdU-B; CLU-C,CtY,MH,NjP,TxU+.

R41 — Content. A poem. *Edinburgh, printed for the author*, 1719.
8⁰: A–C⁴ D² (B3 as 'B5'); *1-2* 3–28.

Gibson 16; *Martin* 16; *Rothschild* 1714. A copy at L has apparently been extracted from a rudimentary collection of Ramsay's poems, and there is an unbroken collection containing it at GM; others probably came from similar collections.

'When genial beams wade thro' the dewy morn'
L(C.71.b.47; Ashley 1353, uncut),O,E,GM, LdU-B+; CLU-C,MH.

R42 — — The second edition. *Edinburgh, printed for the author*, 1719.
8⁰: A–C⁴ D² (B3 as 'B5'); *1-2* 3–28.

Gibson 17; *Martin* 17. Copies were apparently issued both in rudimentary collections predating Ramsay's *Poems*, 1720, and in that volume; most of the copies listed here have been extracted from them. Subsequently reprinted with pagination [133]–160 and with title-pages dated 1721, 1723, and 1728 for later issues of the octavo *Poems*.

O(sheet B from preceding),C,E,EP,GU; ICN,IU, MH.

R43 — — *London, printed for E. Curll*, 1720. (16 July?)
8⁰: π¹ A–D⁴ E¹; *i–ii*, *1-2* 3–34. π1 hft.

Martin 30. Publication date from *Straus, Curll*.

Ramsay, A. Content

Advertised in advance by Curll in *PB* 9 July as a specimen of a proposed edition of Ramsay's complete works which will include 'a small number...on superfine royal paper'. Reissued in *The altar of love*, 1727.
L(11631.d.43),O; CtY(lacks A1, −π1),KU(−π1), TxU.

R44 [—] Edinburgh's address to the country. [*Edinburgh*, 1718.] (Nov?)
8°: A⁴; *1–2* 3–8.
Gibson 4; *Martin* 8. Title in half-title form. Advertised in *Elegies*, 1718. Printed by William Adams jr. according to Gibson. Subsequently reprinted with *The morning interview*, 1719 (R35).
'From me Edina, to the brave and fair'
Reprinted in Ramsay's *Poems*, 1721, as written in Nov 1718.
L(11631.e.18),EP,*BlU*.

R45 — [dh] Edinburgh's salutation to the most honourable, my lord marquess of Carnarvon. [*Edinburgh*, 1720.] (May?)
8°: A²; *1–4*.
Gibson 27; *Martin* 31; *Rothschild* 1722. Copies were issued in some states of Ramsay's *Poems*, 1720 & 1723; most of the copies listed here were probably extracted from those volumes. Reprinted with pagination 213–216 for subsequent issues of the octavo *Poems*.
'Welcome, my lord, heav'n be your guide'
Signed 'A. Ramsay' and dated 17 May 1720.
O,E(2, uncut),*LdU*-B; CLU-C,CtY,MH.

R46 — Elegies on Maggy Johnston, John Cowper, and Lucky Wood... Second edition corrected and amended. *Edinburgh, printed for the author*, 1718.
8°: A–B⁴ C²; *1–2* 3–20. 20 advt.
Gibson 6; *Martin* 9. Printed by William Adams on the evidence of the ornament. No previous edition has been traced, though the elegy on Maggy Johnston was originally written in 1711 and revised 1713; Lucky Wood, on the other hand, died in May 1717. An earlier edition would presumably have been limited to one or two elegies. There was a separate edition of *Elegy on Lucky Wood*.
'Auld Reeky mourn in sable hue'
'I wairn ye a' to greet and drone'
'O Cannigate! poor elrich hole'
L(1078.h.20),*BlU*.

R47 [—] [*idem*] [dh] Elegy on Maggy Johnston. Who died anno 1711. [*Edinburgh*, 1719/20.]
8°: A–B⁴; *1–16*.
Gibson 13; *Martin* 18; *Rothschild* 1712. A new edition with *Lucky Spence* added. Copies were apparently issued in rudimentary collections of Ramsay's works, predating his *Poems*, 1720; copies at L,O,C and doubtless elsewhere have been extracted from these collections. They were subsequently reprinted with pagination

Ramsay, A. Elegies on Maggy Johnston

25–40 to follow *The morning interview* in octavo editions of the *Poems*.
L(C.71.b.46; Ashley 1350, uncut),O,C,E(2), GM+; CLU-C,NjP.

R48 [—] Elegy on Lucky Wood. [*Edinburgh*, 1718?]
½°: 1 side, 2 columns.
Martin 10. The text is corrupt, and Martin considered it a piracy of the text in *Elegies on Maggy Johnston...*1718. Its appearance is consistent with a date of 1718. One copy at E is endorsed 'Luckie Woods Elegie & the Batle of Shirrif Muire'; possibly it was printed with *A race at Sherrifmuir*. A volume sold at Sotheby's 16 Oct 1961, lot 1328, contained both this edition and the 17 stanza version of that poem.
'O Cannygate poor ellritch hole'
E(2).

R49 [—] An elegy on Patie Birnie,|The famous fiddler of Kinghorn;|Wha gart the lieges gawff and girn ay,|Aft till the cock proclaim'd the morn... [*Edinburgh*, 1721.] (Jan?)
½°: 1 side, 2 columns.
Martin 379. Probably the authorized first edition; it has a good text and is well printed.
'In sonnet slee the man I sing'
Signed 'A.R.' and dated 24 Jan 1721.
E.

R50 — The fair assembly, a poem. *Edinburgh printed, and sold at the Mercury, opposite to the Cross-Well*, 1723. (July?)
8°: a⁴ B⁴; *1–4* 5–16.
Martin 68; *Rothschild* 1728.
'Awake, Thalia, and defend'
Dedication signed and dated 28 June 1723.
L(11631.aa.46/1),O(2),E.

R51 [—] [dh] Familiar epistles between W--H--- and A--R--. [*Edinburgh*, 1719.] (Sept?)
8°: A–C⁴; *1–24*.
Gibson 19; *Martin* 20; *Rothschild* 1717. In some copies (e.g. GM) C4 is signed 'C2'. Six epistles, the last dated 2 Sept 1719. Most copies have apparently been extracted from rudimentary collections predating Ramsay's *Poems*, 1720.
'O fam'd and celebrated Allan!'
Verse epistles between William Hamilton of Gilbertfield and Allan Ramsay, entered here since they were published in Ramsay's works.
L(C.71.b.45; Ashley 1355),O,E,*BlU*,GM; MH.

R52 [—] [*Edinburgh*, 1719/20.]
8°: A–C⁴ D²; *1–28*.
Gibson 19–21; *Martin* 21–2. Additional stanza 'Before a lord and eek a knight' added on p. 5. D² contains an added epistle from Ramsay dated 19 Dec 1719 which may have been issued separately to purchasers of the preceding edition. Copies were apparently issued both in rudimentary collections predating Ramsay's

Ramsay, A. Familiar epistles

Poems, 1720, and in early states of that volume; most of the copies listed here have been extracted from them. Subsequently reprinted with pagination 173–196 for later issues of the octavo Poems.

C,E,EP,GM; CLU-C,CtY(lacks D²),MH.

R53 [—] Fy gar rub her o'er wi' strae. An Italian canzone (of seventeen hundred years standing) imitated in braid Scots. [*Edinburgh, printed by Thomas Ruddiman, 172–*.]
obl ½°: 1 side, 2 columns.

> Printed within a border of type flowers, and with a factotum belonging to Ruddiman; clearly an authorized edition, and possibly the first. Printed as 4 eight-line stanzas, with no refrain.

'Gin ye meet a bonny lassie'
> Signed 'A.R.'. A version containing 15 four-line stanzas in imitation of Horace's ode I. ix is printed in Ramsay's Poems, 1721; this version, which omits the first eight stanzas, is printed in *The tea-table miscellany* I, 1723.

E.

R54 [—] [*idem*] An excellent song intituled Fy gar rub her o're wi strae. An Italian canzone... [*Edinburgh, 172–*.]
½°: 1 side, 2 columns.

> Two rough woodcuts at head, found in other Edinburgh half-sheets. The text is divided into 8 four-line stanzas, and the refrain is printed after each verse.

E.

R55 [—] The general mistake... [*Edinburgh, 1725/26*.]

> Advertised in Ramsay's reprint of Swift's *Cadenus and Vanessa*, 1726, as 'The general mistake, a satyr; and the Lure, a tale, &c. Price 3d.'

'The finish'd mind in all its movements bright'
> Reprinted in Ramsay's Poems II, 1728.

R56 [—] Grubstreet nae satyre: in answer to Bag-pipes no musick. An epistle to the umquhile John Cowper late kirk-treasurer's man of Edinburgh; now his ghaist studying poetry at Oxford, for the benefit of Ethert Curll. [*Edinburgh, 1720?*] (Nov?)
½°: 1 side, 1 column.

> *Martin* 394. Reprinted in a supplement to Ramsay's *Fables and tales*, 1722, entered above under the title *Bagpipes no musick* (R33).

'Dear John, what ails ye now? ly still'
> Signed 'Pate Birnie' and dated from Kinghorn 16 Nov 1720. Allan Ramsay wrote an elegy on the fiddler Patie Birnie in January 1721; presumably he is here using his name as a pseudonym in reply to 'John Couper', *Bag-pipes no musick*, [1720?], C463.

E.

R57 — Health: a poem. *Edinburgh, printed for the author*, 1724.
8°: *A*⁴ B–C⁴; *1–2* 3–22 *23; 24 blk*. C4 advt.

Ramsay, A. Health

Martin 76. The collation given and copies recorded refer to the separate edition; it was also issued with other poems printed in sections D–K⁴, advertised on p. 23 as separately available; the only copies of these parts seen have continuous pagination 25–80. Copies of *Health* containing them are listed with Ramsay's collections above. The fact that C4, the advertisement leaf, is missing from all separate copies suggests it may have been cancelled.

'Be 't mine the honour, once again to hear'
O(uncut, – C4),E(2, – C4, 1 uncut); CLU-C(– C4), MH(– C4).

R58 [—] [dh] The highland laddie. [*Edinburgh, 1723?*]
8°: A⁴; 1–8.

> Four songs. The copy seen is bound in a collection of Ramsay's publications which appears to be chronologically arranged; the date given is that suggested by that arrangement.

'The Lawland lads think they are fine'
> Reprinted in Ramsay's Poems II, 1728.

O.

R59 — Jenny and Meggy. A pastoral, being a sequel to Patie and Roger. *Edinburgh, printed for the author*, 1723.
8°: A⁴ B²; *1–2* 3–12.

> *Martin* 69.

'Come, Meg, let's fa to wark upo' this green'
L(11631.aaa.56/9),O,E.

[—] The loyal Britain: or, George for ever, [1744?]
See L297.

R60 [—] [dh] Lucky Spence's last advice. [*Edinburgh, 1718*.]
8°: A²; 1–4.

> *Gibson* 9; *Martin* 11. The half-sheet editions below may precede this edition. The copy at L was originally bound after *Elegies*, 1718, with which it was subsequently reprinted. *Gibson* suggests that the printer was William Adams junior.

'Three times the carline grain'd and rifted'
L(1078.h.23),BlU.

R61 [—] — [*Edinburgh, 1718*.]
½°: 1 side, 2 columns.

> *Martin* 395, not knowing the existence of two half-sheet editions. Line 4 of the first stanza reads 'when now she fawn'. Both editions are similar in typography though with minor variants in spelling and punctuation; there seems a probability that they are both early editions, and they may precede the octavo for the text is a good one. Ms. note on verso of a copy at E 'Luckie Spences Last Advyce 1718'.

OW,E(2).

R62 [—] [another edition]
> Line 4 of the first stanza reads 'whan now she

Ramsay, A. Lucky Spence

fawn'. Ms. note on verso of the L copy 'Luckie Spence the bawd her last advyce. 1718.'
L(C.121.g.9/131),E.

R63 [—] [dh] The monk and the miller's wife; or, all parties pleas'd. A unco tale! [*Edinburgh*, 1724/26.]
Martin 78. With 'Advice to Mr. -------- on his marriage' on pp. 78–80. Advertised in Ramsay's reprint of Swift's *Cadenus and Vanessa*, 1726, as separately published. The only copy seen (at L) was issued as part of a series of pamphlets continuing *Health*, 1724, and has collation I–K⁴; 65–80.
'Now lend your lugs, ye benders fine'

— The morning interview, 1719. *See* R35.

R64 [—] [dh] Mouldy-Mowdiwart: or the last speech of a wretched miser. [*Edinburgh*, 1724.]
Martin 80. Advertised in *Health*, 1724, as separately published (though that advertisement was possibly cancelled). The only copies seen (at L,O) were issued with *Health* and have collation E⁴; 33–40.
'O dool! and am I forc'd to die'
Reprinted in Ramsay's *Poems* II, 1728.

[—] Mount Alexander's complaint ... Imitated from the Latin ode, [1731/32.] *In* M404.

R65 [—] A new song. Tune of Lochaber no more. [*Edinburgh*, 1723?]
½°: 1 side, 1 column.
Martin 402. Rough woodcut at head. Probably a piracy. The date is suggested by another edition reprinted with *An account of the life... of Alaster Mackalaster, who was hanged...31st of May 1723* (copy at E).
'Farewel to Lochaber, and farewell my Jean'
Reprinted in Ramsay's *Poems* II, 1728.
E.

R66 — The nuptials: a masque on the marriage of his grace James duke of Hamilton, and Lady Anne Cochran. *Edinburgh, printed in the year* 1723.
2°: A–C²; *1–2* 3–12.
Martin 70. A note on p. 3 records its performance on 14 Feb 1723; it falls outside the proper scope of this catalogue.
'Joy to the bridegroom, prince of Clyde'
E.

R67 — — To which is prefix'd, an introduction concerning masques. *London, printed for J. Pemberton*, 1723. (*MC* April)
8°: π¹ A–C⁴; i–ii, *1–3* 4–23 24 blk.
Martin 71.
E,C; MH.

R68 [—] [dh] An ode sacred to the memory of her grace Anne dutchess of Hamilton. [*Edinburgh*, 1724.]
2°: A²; *1* 2–4.
'Why sounds the plain with sad complaint?'
Signed 'A.R.' Reprinted in Ramsay's *Poems* II, 1728.
NN.

Ramsay, A. An ode

R69 — [dh] An ode. To the memory of Sir Isaac Newton; inscrib'd to the Royal Society of London, for the improving of natural knowledge. [*Edinburgh*, 1727.]
2°: A²; *1–4*.
'Great Newton's dead, – full ripe his fame'
MH.

R70 — An ode, with a pastoral recitative on the marriage of the right honourable James earl of Weemy.s, and Mrs. Janet Charteris. Edinburgh 17th September, 1720. [*Edinburgh*, 1720.] (Sept?)
2°: A²; *1–4*.
Martin 403.
'Last morn young Rosalind, with laughing een'
Signed 'Allan Ramsay'.
E(mutilated),EU.

R71 [—] [dh] On pride. An epistle to -----------. [*Edinburgh*, 1724.]
Martin 82. Three poems, the others being 'Fable of the twa books' and 'Spoke to Æolus one night...' Advertised in *Health*, 1724, as separately published (though that advertisement was possibly cancelled). The only copies seen (at L,O) were issued with *Health* and have collation G⁴; *49–56*.
'Shut in a study six foot square'
Reprinted in Ramsay's *Poems* II, 1728. The epistle is to Duncan Forbes.

R72 [—] [dh] On seeing the archers diverting themselves at the butts and rovers, &c. At the desire of ——. [*Edinburgh*, 1724.]
Martin 83. Advertised in *Health*, 1724, as separately published (though that advertisement was possibly cancelled). The only copies seen (at L,O) were issued with *Health* and have collation D⁴; *25–32*.
'The rovers and the butts you saw'
Reprinted in Ramsay's *Poems* II, 1728; written at the desire of Sir William Bennet.

R73 [—] [dh] On the death of Lady Margaret Anstruther. [*Edinburgh*, 1728.]
8°: A²; *1–4*.
Rothschild 1733.
'All in her bloom the graceful fair'
Signed 'A.R.' Reprinted in Ramsay's *Poems* II, 1728.
L(1969).

R74 [—] [dh] On the Royal Company of Archers, shooting for the bowl, July 6th 1724; on which day, his grace, James duke of Hamilton was chosen their captain general... [*Edinburgh*, 1724.]
8°: H⁴; *57–64*.
See *Martin* 83. With 'On the Royal Company of Archers marching...August 4th 1724' on pp. 61–64. Not advertised as separately published, but all the other pamphlets added to *Health*, 1724 were so advertised. The copy listed here appears to have been issued

Ramsay, A. On the Royal Company

separately; it is bound in a volume with pamphlets of 1724 and 1725.
'Again the year returns the day'
'Now like themselves again the archers raise'
EN.

R75 [—] On this great eclipse. A poem by A.R. *Edinburgh, printed by James Watson, and sold at his shop, 1715.*

Gibson 2; *Martin* 2. Printed on a single sheet to the right of *A scheme and type of the great and terrible eclipse of the sun on the 22nd of April, 1715.* One copy formed part of the ms. journal of the Easy Club; another was described in a Pickering & Chatto catalogue of 1901, quoted by Gibson.
'Now do I press amongst the learned throng'
Reprinted in Ramsay's *Poems, 1721.*
(*Gibson* 2.)

R76 [—] [dh] Patie and Roger: a pastoral inscribed to Josiah Burchet esq; secretary of the admiralty. [*Edinburgh,* 1720.]
8°: A⁴ B²; 1–12.

Gibson 26; *Martin* 37. Verses to Burchett on pp. 1–3. Copies were issued in early states of Ramsay's *Poems,* 1720; most of the copies listed here were probably extracted from that volume. Reprinted with pagination '200–211' for later issues of the octavo *Poems.*
'Beneath the south-side of a craigy bield'
See *Jenny and Meggy,* 1723 (R59) for a sequel.
L(11659.df.37),E(uncut); CLU-C,CtY,MH.

R77 — — a pastoral, by Mr. Allan Ramsay, in the Scots dialect. To which is added, an imitation of the Scotch pastoral: by Josiah Burchett esq; *London, printed for J. Pemberton, & T. Jauncy,* 1720. (*PB* 2 Aug)
8°: A–D⁴; *i–ii* iii–vii *viii blk, 1* 2–23 24. 24 advt.

Martin 38; *Rothschild* 1720. Without Ramsay's verses to Burchett, but with a preface by George Sewell encouraging subscriptions to Ramsay's *Poems, 1721.*
Imitation: 'Skreen'd by a mountain, on the southern side'
O(uncut),E; CSmH,CtY,IU,MH,TxU+.

— A poem on the South-Sea, 1720. *See* R106.

R78 [—] A poem to the memory of the famous Archbald Pitcairn, M.D. By a member of the Easy Club in Edinburgh. [*Edinburgh,* 1713.]
4°: (4 ll); *i–iv,* 1–4.

Gibson 1; *Martin* 1. The only copy known formed part of the ms. journal of the Easy Club; it cannot now be traced. The poem was ordered to be printed 18 Nov 1713; subsequent entries suggest Andrew Hart was their printer. Dedicatory epistle (in verse) signed 'Gawin Douglass', Ramsay's name within the club.
(*Gibson* 1.)

R79 [—] [dh] The poetick sermon: to R---- Y---- esquire. [*Edinburgh,* 1724.]

Ramsay, A. The poetick sermon

Martin 81. Advertised in *Health,* 1724, as separately published (though that advertisement was possibly cancelled). The only copies seen (at L,O) were issued with *Health* and have collation F⁴; 41–48.
'Frae north'ren mountains clad with snaw'
Reprinted in Ramsay's *Poems* II, 1728; to Robert Yarde.

[—] Prologue. Spoke by one of the young gentlemen, who...acted the Orphan, and Cheats of Scapin, the last night of the year 1719. [*Edinburgh,* 1720.]
⅛°: 1–2.

Gibson 22; *Martin* 42; *Rothschild* 1721. This leaf, conjugate with *Bessy Bell,* [1720], is found both in a rudimentary collection predating Ramsay's *Poems,* 1720, and in early states of that volume; its separate issue is unproved, though there are copies apparently extracted from collections at CLU-C,CtY,DFo,MH.

R80 — [The prospect of plenty] To the royal burrows of Scotland, the following poem is humbly dedicated, by Allan Ramsay. [*Edinburgh,* 1720.] (Oct?)
8°: A–B⁴; *1–2* 3–16.

Gibson 38; *Martin* 44. Dedication leaf instead of title, dated 18 Oct 1720. Drop-head title on p. 3 'The prospect of plenty: a poem on the North Sea'. There is another state (Gibson 39; *Martin* 45) with pagination 229–244, intended for inclusion in Ramsay's *Poems,* 1720. The variant pagination makes it clear that the poem was intended to be issued separately but almost all copies of this state form part of *Poems,* 1723, and are therefore not listed here. Clearly they were used when the proper state was exhausted.
'Thalia anes again in blythsome lays'
EN.

R81 — The prospect of plenty: a poem on the North-Sea fishery. To which is added, an explanation of the Scotch words used in this poem. Inscribed to the royal burrows of Scotland. *London, printed for T. Jauncy,* 1720. (*DP* 31 Oct)
8°: *A²* B–D⁴; *i–iv,* 1–24. A1 hft, advt.

Martin 43. The advertisement on A1ᵛ is for the proposals for Ramsay's *Poems, 1721.*
L(161.k.23, Luttrell, Oct),OW,GM,*GU*; MH.

R82 — [dh] Richy and Sandy, a pastoral on the death of Mr. Joseph Addison. [*Edinburgh,* 1719.]
8°: A²; 1–4.

Gibson 18; *Martin* 24; *Rothschild* 1715. This is probably the first edition, though Ramsay's remarks about Lucky Reid's piracy below could imply that that was printed (from ms.) before his own. Copies were apparently issued in rudimentary collections preceding Ramsay's *Poems,* 1720; most of the copies listed here have been extracted from them. Subsequently issued with pp. 5–12 added (R86).
'What gars thee look sae dowf, dear Sandy say'

Ramsay, A. Richy and Sandy

Richy and Sandy in this pastoral represent Steele and Pope.
L(C.71.b.44; Ashley 1354, uncut),O,C,GM(3), GU+; CLU-C.

R83 — — [*Edinburgh, printed by Margaret Reid, 1719.*]
The town council of Edinburgh on 26 Aug 1719 granted Allan Ramsay's petition against the piracy of his poems, and in Ramsay's poetical address 'To the right honourable, the town-council of Edinburgh' (printed in his *Poems*, 1721) he makes it clear that *Richy and Sandy* was pirated by 'Lucky Reid', and thence reprinted by Lintot in London with the corrupt text of that edition.

R84 — — a pastoral on the death of the right honourable Joseph Addison, esq; By Allan Ramsey. *London, printed for Bernard Lintot*, 1720 [1719]. (*DC* 30 July)
2⁰: *A*² *B*²; *1-3* 4-8.
Entered to Lintot in Bowyer's ledgers under 29 July 1719, 250 copies printed. Apparently reprinted from the corrupt piracy by Margaret Reid. A correct version with Josiah Burchett's 'explanation' or English paraphrase and with his poem to Ramsay was printed in Pope's *Eloisa to Abelard*, 1720 (published 13 Oct 1719).
E.

R85 — [*idem*] A pastoral elegy on the death of Mr. Joseph Addison. In a dialogue, between Sir Richard Steel, and Mr. Alexander Pope. By Mr. Alan Ramsey. *Nottingham, printed by John Collyer*, [1719/20?]
4⁰: *A*²; *1-4*.
Title in half-title form. The history and origins of this unrecorded edition are obscure, but it is presumably an early edition.
L(1973),LDW.

R86 — [dh] Richy and Sandy, a pastoral... [*Edinburgh, 1720?*]
8⁰: *A*² *B*⁴ (B1 as 'A3'); *1-12*.
Gibson 25; *Martin* 25. A reissue of the 1719 Edinburgh edition (R82) with the addition of Josiah Burchett's 'explanation', his epistle to Ramsay, and Ramsay's reply. Copies with the added verses are found in early issues of Ramsay's *Poems*, 1720, which suggests they were not printed until 1720; the copies listed here were probably extracted from that collection. Subsequently reprinted with pagination 161-172 for later issues of the octavo *Poems*.
Explanation: 'What makes thee look so sad? Dear Sandy say'
To Ramsay: 'Well fare thee, Allan, who in mother tongue'
To Burchett: 'Thirsting for fame, at the Pierian spring'
O,E,EP; CtY,MH.

Ramsay, A. The rise and fall

R87 — The rise and fall of stocks, 1720. An epistle to the right honourable my Lord Ramsay, now in Paris. To which is added the satyr's comick project for recovering a bankrupt stockjobber. *Edinburgh, printed for the author, and sold by T. Jauncy, London*, 1721.
8⁰: *A*⁴ *B*⁴; *261-262 263-276*.
Martin 58. Copies were issued in late states of Ramsay's *Poems*, 1720; one of the copies listed has been extracted from that volume. Subsequently reprinted without title-page for later issues of that collection.
'Withoutten preface or preamble'
Satyr: 'On the shore of a low ebbing sea'
The first poem is signed and dated 25 March 1721.
E(2).

R88 — Robert, Richy and Sandy. A pastoral on the death of Matthew Prior, esq; Dedicated to the right honourable person design'd by the Old Shepherd. *London, printed by S. Palmer, for Bernard Lintot; sold by J. Roberts*, 1721. (*DP* 11 Oct)
8⁰: *A*⁴ *B*⁴ *C*²; *1-7* 8-19 *20 blk*. A1 hft.
Martin 59. In some copies (e.g. MH) A4 is signed 'A2'.
'Robert the douse, by a' the swains rever'd'
L(11631.d.44),O(-A1),E; MH(uncut).

R89 — A Scots ode, to the British Antiquarians. [*Edinburgh*, 1726.] (Feb?)
8⁰: *A*⁴; *1-2* 3-8.
Martin 90. Title in half-title form.
'To Hartford, and his learned friends'
Signed on p. 8 and dated 21 Feb 1726. A ms. version dated 4 Jan 1726 is among the Clerk of Pennycuik papers in the Scottish Record Office, together with a letter from Ramsay to Sir John Clerk of 8 March 1726 which refers to sending about thirty copies to 'such of the Society as I knew to be members of parliament'.
L(1077.h.13),C; MH.

R90 — Scots songs. *Edinburgh, printed for the author*, 1718.
8⁰: A-*B*⁴; *1-2* 3-16.
Gibson 8; *Martin* 12. Seven songs. Gibson suggests that the printer was William Adams junior.
'The last time I came o'er the moor'
L(1078.h.19),E,*BlU*.

R91 — — The second edition. *Edinburgh, printed for the author*, 1719.
8⁰: *A*⁴ *B*² *C*⁴; *1-2* '1' 4-20.
Gibson 15; *Martin* 26; *Rothschild* 1716. Three songs added. Copies were apparently issued in rudimentary collections of Ramsay's works, predating his *Poems*, 1720; copies at O,C,E, and doubtless elsewhere, have been extracted from these collections. Subsequently reprinted

Ramsay, A. Scots songs

with pagination *65–84* and title-page dated 1720 to form part of *Poems*, 1720.
O(2),C,E,*BlU*,GM(2); CtY,MH,TxU(uncut).

R92 [—] Scots songs, viz. Mary Scot... *Edinburgh, printed for the author; and sold by T. Jauncy, London,* [1720/21.]
8°: π^2 A–B⁴; *i–iv*, 245–260. $\pi2^r$ advt.
> *Gibson* 40; *Martin* 47. A second collection. $\pi2$, the advertisement leaf for *Poems*, 1721, which is paged '245' on the recto (verso blank) was perhaps intended to be bound after the text as described in *Gibson*. This state is clearly intended for separate issue, while without π^2 it was intended for inclusion in issues of Ramsay's *Poems*, 1720; but it is found in both states in that collection. It was re-printed with pagination 245–260 for later issues of *Poems*.

'How sweet's the love which meets return'
BlU($-\pi2$); MH.

R93 [—] The scriblers lash'd. *Edinburgh, printed anno dom.* 1718.
4°: A–B⁴; *1–2* 3–16.
> *Martin* 13.

'That I thus prostitute the muse'
> Subsequently printed with Ramsay's name. An attack on the writers of such verse as *Edinburgh's Observator*, [171–.]

E.

R94 — — *Edinburgh, printed anno dom.* 1718.
8°: A⁸ (A5, 6 as 'B, B2'); *1–2* 3–16.
> *Gibson* 11; *Martin* 14; *Rothschild* 1707–9. A copy at GM forms part of a rudimentary collection predating Ramsay's *Poems*, 1720, and others may have been extracted from similar collections.

L(1078.h.18, lacks A8; Ashley 1352, uncut),O,*BlU*, GM,*LdU-B;* CtY,ICN.

R95 — — The second edition. *Edinburgh, printed for the author,* 1720.
8°: A⁴ B² (A2 as 'A'); *1–2* 3–12.
> *Gibson* 24; *Martin* 48. Copies were apparently issued both in rudimentary collections pre-dating Ramsay's *Poems*, 1720, and in that volume; many copies listed here have been extracted from them. Subsequently reprinted with pagination *121–132* and title-pages dated 1721, 1723, and 1728 to form part of later octavo issues of *Poems*.

O(2),C,E,GM,GU; *ICN*,IU,MH.

R96 [—] A tale of three bonnets. [*Edinburgh*] *Printed in the year* 1722.
8°: A–B⁸ C²; *1–2* 3–36.
> *Martin* 65. In dramatic form.

'When men of mettle thought it nonsense'
> The copy at L has early ms. on title 'By Sir Willm Bennet of Grubbet'. Reprinted in Ramsay's duodecimo *Poems* II, 1729, but not

Ramsay, A. A tale

elsewhere; his authorship is perhaps uncertain. It was advertised in Ramsay's *Health*, 1724.
L(11623.a.49),O,E,*BlU*; CtY(2),TxU.

R97 — Tartana: or, the plaid. *Edinburgh, printed for the the author,* 1718.
8°: A–D⁴; *1–2* 3–31 *32 blk.*
> *Gibson* 7; *Martin* 15. Gibson suggests that the printer was William Adams junior.

'Ye Caledonian beauties, who have long'
L(1078.h.17, cropt),EP,*BlU*,GM(lacks D⁴); CtY.

R98 — — The second edition. *Edinburgh, printed for the author,* 1719.
8°: *A*⁴ B–C⁴; *1–2* 3–24.
> *Gibson* 14; *Martin* 27; *Rothschild* 1711. Copies were apparently issued in rudimentary collec-tions predating Ramsay's *Poems*, 1720; some copies listed here (e.g. at C) have been ex-tracted from them. Subsequently reprinted with pagination *41–64* (*Martin* 49) for *Poems*, 1720, and with title-pages dated 1721, 1724, and 1732 for subsequent issues.

L(1487.aa.5),O,C,E,GM+; CtY,MH,TxU.

R99 — To Mr. Law. *Edinburgh, printed for the author,* 1720.
2°: A–B²; *1–2* 3–8.
> *Martin* 35. Title in a border of type-flowers.

'O could my muse in nervous numbers draw'
> Signed on p. 8 'Alan Ramsay'.

OW,E(uncut).

R100 — [dh] To the honourable, Duncan Forbes of Culloden, lord president of the session, and all our other good judges, who are careful of the honour of the government, and the property of the sub-ject; the address of Allan Ramsay. [*Edinburgh,* 1737.] (Aug?)
2°: *A*²; *1* 2–4.
> *Martin* 120. Dated on p. 4, 25 July 1737; reprinted in *GM* Aug.

'To you, my lords, whase elevation'
> A protest to the lords of session against the closing of Ramsay's playhouse.

EP.

R101 [—] [dh] To the honourable, Sr. John Clerk of Pennycuik bart. one of the barons of exchequer. On the death of his most accomplish'd son, John Clerk esqr. who died the 20th year of his age, August 1722. [*Edinburgh,* 1722.]
4°: A²; *1–4.*
> Watermark: small fleur-de-lys.

'If tears can ever be a duty found'
> Signed on p. 4 'A.R.'

NN-B.

R102 — [fine paper?]
2°: *A*²; *1–4.*
> Watermark: London arms. Another impres-sion in folio. Two rules are added between the page number 1 and the title; the poem is

Ramsay, A. To the honourable

signed 'A. Ramsay' no p. 4, and a tailpiece is added below that.

Scottish Record Office(GD18/4313).

[—] To the memory of Mr. David Drummond [actually by Thomas Drummond], [1741.] *See* D443.

— To the royal burrows of Scotland, [1720.] *See* R80.

R103 [—] The vision compylit in Latin be a most lernit clerk, in time of our hairship and oppression, anno 1300, and translatit in 1524. [*Edinburgh*] *Printed in the year* 1748.

8°: *A⁴ B⁴; 1-2 3-15 16 blk.*

> *Martin* 128. First published in *The ever green*, 1724. Reprinted in the *Scots magazine* Aug 1748, perhaps from this edition.

'Bedoun the bents of Banquo brae'
> Printed as by 'Ar. Scot', and widely accepted as an old poem; for Ramsay's authorship, see Chalmers's edition of Ramsay's *Poems* (1800) I. cx. A Jacobite lament.

L(11621.b.52; 11632.df.11),E(2).

R104 — [dh] Wealth, or the woody. [*Edinburgh*, 1720.] (June?)

8°: *A⁴; 1-8.*

> *Gibson* 28; *Martin* 50; *Rothschild* 1723.

'Thalia, ever welcome to this isle'
> Signed 'A. Ramsay'. Dated as June 1720 in *Poems*, 1721.

E(unopened).

R105 — [reissue]

8°: *A⁴ B²; 1-12.*

> *Gibson* 29; *Martin* 51. B² adds 'An epistle to Anthony Hammond esq; with the foregoing poem. By Dr. Sewell', dated July 1720, and probably reprinted from the London edition below. Copies were issued in an early state of Ramsay's *Poems*, 1720; the copies seen may have been extracted from that volume. Reprinted without Sewell's poem and with pagination 217-'228' or 217-224 for later issues of the octavo *Poems*.

Epistle: 'If, Hammond, I know who, and what you are'

O,GM; MH.

R106 — [*idem*] A poem on the South-Sea. By Mr. Alexander [!] Ramsay. To which is prefix'd, a familiar epistle to Anthony Hammond esq; By a friend. *London, printed for T. Jauncy*, 1720. (*DP* 4 July)

8°: *π¹[= C4] A–B⁴ C⁴(−C4); 1-2 3-23 24. 24 advt.*

> *Martin* 40; *Rothschild* 1724. Title on A4, 'Wealth: or, the woody', with imprint 'Printed at Edinburgh, and reprinted at London'.

LDW,OW,C,E,GM + ; CLU-C,CSmH(uncut), ICN(impft),InU(uncut),MH(2, 1 uncut).

R107 — Wealth, or the woody: a poem on the South-Sea. By Mr. Allan Ramsay. To which is prefix'd, a

Ramsay, A. Wealth

familiar epistle... By Mr. Sewell. The second edition corrected. *London, printed for T. Jauncy*, 1720. (July)

8°: *π¹ A⁴ a⁴ B⁴ C⁴(−C4); 1-2 3-8 9-10 11-18 11-23 24. 24 advt.*

> *Martin* 52; *Rothschild* 1725. Apparently a re-impression with a revised title; A4 (the second title) also corrects Ramsay's christian name to Allan, substitutes imprint 'London, printed for T. Jauncy', and adds a commendatory poem signed 'C.B.' on the verso. a⁴ contains 'An ode to Mr. Allan Ramsay' signed 'J.M.' (for Joseph Mitchell). (*Martin* 53 is surely a ghost caused by mis-binding, as he suggested.) *DP* 7 July advertises this title, but not until *DP* 21 July is the 'second edition' or the added ode (which is there ascribed to Mitchell) mentioned. It may be that there is an intermediate issue which has not been identified.

O(2),E(lacks π1, A4 substituted),GM(2, 1−π1), NeU; CSmH,CtY.

R108 [—] [dh] The young laird and Edinburgh Katy. [*Edinburgh*, 1720.]

8°: *A²; 1-4.*

> *Martin* 54; *Rothschild* 1713. Copies were issued both in a rudimentary collection pre-dating Ramsay's *Poems*, 1720, and in early states of that volume; copies listed here were probably extracted from them. Subsequently added to the *Scots songs* in that collection with pagination 85-88.

'Now wat ye wha I met yestreen'
> Signed on p. 4 'A.R.'

CtY,MH.

R109 [—] [column 1:] The young laird and Edinburgh Katy. [column 2:] An excellent new ballad intituled, Bessy Bell and Mary Gray. [*Edinburgh*, 1720?]

½°: 1 side, 2 columns.

> *Martin* 410. Probably a piracy.

E.

Ramsay, Andrew Michael. Some few poems composed by the Chevalier Ramsay, author of the celebrated Travels of Cyrus. *Edinburgh, printed by John Catanach, and sold by most booksellers in town*, 1728.

4°: pp. 38.   L,E; CtY,ICN.
> Watermark: three circles.

— [fine paper]   CLU-C.
> Watermark: fleur-de-lys.

Ramsay, Charlotte. Poems on several occasions. Written by a young lady. *London, printed for, and sold by S. Paterson*, 1747. (*SR* 3 Nov)

8°: pp. 88.   L,EU; CtY,ICU.
> The dedication is signed.

[Randall, John.] Nomina quorundam e primariis olim regiæ grammaticalis scholæ Buriæ Sti Edmundi, inter icenos celeberrimæ carminibus illustrata.

Randall, J. Nomina quorundam

(Miscellaneis quibusdam adjectis.) Edita ab J.R. A.M. Coll. Christi Cantab... *Londini, impensis authoris, 1719.*
8°: pp. 8, iv, 111.   L.

> Apparently the original title A2 has been cancelled and a preliminary gathering substituted including a dedication leaf to Edward and Robert Wood. Clearly issued in various states with various dedicatees; compare the following.

— [another issue] Edita a Joan. Randall... *Londini, impensis authoris, 1719.*
8°: pp. 4, iv, 111.   O.

> This issue has a leaf of presentation before the title with space for the recipient's name in ms. The general dedication to Thomas Maynard has been altered.

R110 Randolph, —, *Mrs.* [dh] On the much lamented death of that incomparable lady the honourable the Lady Oxenden. A pindarique ode. By Mrs. Randolph. [*London?* 1735.]
2°: A²; *1* 2–3 *4.*

> Printed with an 'endorsement title' on p. 4.

'Ah! 'tis too much, relentless fate!'

> The same poem, with some changes, as Timothy Harris, *A pindarique ode, on the much lamented death of...Madam Howland,* 1719.

L(11621.k.2/79); CtY.

R111 Randolph, Herbert. [dh] Chichlæus. [*Oxford,* 1716?]
2°: A–B²; *1* 2–8.

> No watermark. Printed in Oxford on the evidence of the ornament on p. 8. A copy at O notes that it was composed at the time he was soliciting the fellowship at All Souls to which he was appointed in 1716, and he records in *Rawlinson* 'a few copies [were] printed to present to the Warden & Fellows of All Souls College when he stood candidate'.

'Dum lustro, celebris quas Dorovernia jactat'

> Dedication signed, 'H. Randolph, A.B. ex Æde Christi.' In praise of Henry Chichele.

L(11409.h.39),O(2, 1 presentation to Jo. Bowles, 1721),OW; CtY,DFo,ICN.

R112 — [fine paper]

> Watermark: Amsterdam arms.

O(presentation copy to the library).

R113 [—] Commercium ad mare australe. *Londini* [*Oxford?*], *et prostant venales apud bibliopolas Lond. & Westm.* 1720. (6 Dec?)
2°: A–C²; *1–2* 3–12.

> Ms. correction to p. 7, line 3 in all copies seen. Hearne is quoted by *Bradner* 255 as recording publication on 6 Dec: 'It is said to have been printed at the Theatre in Oxford, and the author is said to be Mr. Randolph of All Souls'.

'Scire velim quare tota trepidatur in urbe'

Randolph, H. Commercium

> Early ms. attribution to Randolph in the copy at O.

O,EtC; CtY,DLC,MH,MH-BA(Luttrell, Dec), TxU+.

R114 [—] — Editio secunda. *Londini* [*Oxford?*], *et prostant venales apud bibliopolas Lond. & Westm.* 1720.
2°: A–C²; *1–2* 3–12.

> Apparently the same sheets as the preceding; the same ms. correction to p. 7, line 3. No cancel title seen; possibly a press-variant title.

L(1970); ICN.

Rands, Thomas. Pax in crumena: or, the trooper turn'd poet... *London, printed for the author, Thomas Rands; sold by the booksellers of London & Westminster,* 1713.
8°: pp. 136.   C; CLU-C.

> Dedicatory epistle signed.

— [reissue] By Thomas Rands, of the late Lieutenant General Wood's regiment of horse. *London printed, and sold by John Morphew,* 1714.
      L,O; DFO,TxU.

> Cancel title.

R115 Rann, —, *Mr, forester at Windsor.* A new song, by Mr Rann one of his majestys forresters at Windser [!]. Tune King Georges march. [1746?]
slip: 1 side, 1 column.

> Woodcut at head.

'From London to Scotland'

> *Crum* F711. In praise of William Augustus, duke of Cumberland.

O.

R116 Rap. A rap at the rapsody. *London, printed for J. Roberts,* 1734. (*GM* Jan)
2°: *A²* B²; *1–3* 4–8.

> *Teerink* 1311.

'Doctor, I thank you, for your inkling'

> A reply to Swift's *On poetry: a rapsody.*

L(11633.i.10),O; CtY,MH,TxU(3, 1 uncut).

R117 Rape. The rape. An epistolary poem. Addressed to Colonel Francisco. *London, printed by J. Read; sold by the booksellers of London & Westminster,* [1730.] (*MChr* 2 March)
2°: A–B²; *1–2* 3–8.

'When, fir'd by novelty, and beauty's eyes'

> Listed in *Waller* as attributed to Prior; rejected in *Wright & Spears* 811. A satire on Francis Charteris.

IU,TxU.

R118 — The rape of Helen. Translated from the Greek of Coluthus Thebæus: and illustrated with the notes of Michael Nicander... *London, printed for and sold by J. Roberts, and by the booksellers & pamphletsellers of London,* 1731.
4°: (frt+) *A²* a–b² B–K²; [*4*] *i* ii–viii, *1* 2–34 *35–36.*
A2ᵛ err.

The **rape** of Helen

Title in red and black.
'Ye Trojan nymphs and goddesses, who bring'
L(11340.c.2, –frt),LDW,O(uncut).

R119 — The rape of the bride; or, marriage and hanging go by destiny...A poem hudibrastick, in 4 canto's. With an epistle dedicatory to the fair sex. *London printed, and sold by J. Peele*, 1723. (*DP* 21 Jan)
12°: (frt+) A–H⁴ᐟ²; *i–iii* iv–vi, 7–48.
   Bond 76.
'I sing the rape of an old woman'
L(1507/459); ICU(lacks D²),MH(–frt),NN.

R120 — — The second edition. *London printed, and sold by J. Peele*, 1723. (*DP* 6 Feb)
12°: (frt+) A–H⁴ᐟ²; *i–iii* iv–vi, 7–48.
   Apparently a reimpression or press-variant title.
L(11632.bb.37); CSmH(uncut).

— The rape of the smock, 1717–. *See* Jacob, Giles.

Rapin, René.
[*Christus patiens*] Bragge, Francis: The passion of our saviour... In imitation of Rapin, [1703/–.] *See* B378–9.

[Beckingham, Charles:] Monsieur Rapin's Latin heroick poem on Christ's passion, 1717. *See* B140.

— [*idem*] Christus patiens: or the sufferings of Christ, 1720, 1737. *See* B141–2.

[*Hortorum*] Gardiner, James: Rapin of gardens, [1706]–1728. *See* G11–14.

Bragge, Francis: Two odes from the Latin of the celebrated Rapin, 1710. *See* B380–1.

Rapsody. *See* Rhapsody.

Rare. Rare feasting at H——, [1740?] *See* Horace, book IV. ode V. imitated, 1740.

R121 — A rare new song, shewing the bravery of his grace the Duke of Argile. To the tune of the Caping-trade. [*Edinburgh?* 1709.]
½°: 1 side, 1 column.
'Now, now comes on the glorious year'
E.

R122 Raree-show. The rare show. [*London*, 1713.]
slip: 1 side, 1 column.
   The order of editions is uncertain, and the texts they print are so various that they are probably taken from various manuscript sources. This is the text imitated by the tory *Raree show*, R126 below.
'Here be de var pretty show just come from Parrie'
A whig satire on the peace with France. See *The second part of the rare show*, [1714.]
L(Rox.III.817, mutilated),Herts CRO (Panshanger box 46).

R123 — [*idem*] A rare show, a fine show. '*Switzerland, printed in the canton of Bern*' [*London?*], 1713.
½°: 1 side, 1 column.

The **raree-show**

Bradshaw 4146, 'apparently Dublin'; but the copies at DT,PPL are bound with London half-sheets. The variant text gives all names in full; the first line reads:
'Here be my pretty show just come from Paree'
C,DT; PPL.

R124 — [*idem*] O raree show, O pritee show. Will you see my fine show. [*London*] *Sold by Tom. Johnson, on Tower-hill*, [1713.]
½°: 1 side, 2 columns.
   Another variant text, with first line:
'Here be de ver pritte show, just come from Parry'
L(Lutt.II.155, cropt),DT; CSmH.

R125 — O raree show, O pratee show, will you see my finee show. *London printed; and re-printed in Dublin*, 1714.
½°: 1 side, 2 columns.
   On the other side, *The merchant alamode*, 1714.
OCU.

R126 — [dh] The raree show. [col] *London, printed by R. Newcomb*, 1713.
2°: *A² < B¹*; ff. 1–3.
   Printed on one side of the leaf only, the third on the verso.
'Here be de var pretty show just come from Parrie'
   A tory imitation of the preceding, following the text of R122; the early verses repeat the first line of each couplet and change the second.
OW.

R127 — The raree show ballad: or, the British Missisippi. In broken English. [*Edinburgh?* 1720?]
½°: 1 side, 2 columns.
   4 lines of woodcut music at head; the text printed in Grover's scriptorial type.
'Here first come de Zew, who did bite all de varle'
   Although written in terms of the Mississippi company, this is apparently a satire on the South Sea bubble.
E(mutilated).

R128 — A rary--show: lately brought from the flaming isle of moderation, all alive. *London, printed [by Richard Newcomb] in the year* 1710. (*SR* 3 July)
½°: 1 side, 2 columns.
   Entered in *SR* by Newcomb, deposit copy at E.
'Good people all, both low and high'
   A satire on Gilbert Burnet.
LSA,E.

R129 — [*idem*] The Whitson-fair: rary-show. Lately brought from the flaming isle of moderation, all alive. [1710?]
½°: 1 side, 1 column.
   The NN copy has a variant reading in the title, 'Whison-fair'.
O; NN,*Harding*.

The **raree-show** man

R130 — The raree-show-man. Or, his box and magick lanthorn expos'd to pubilick [!] view. [*London?* 1740.]
slip: 1 side, 1 column.
Percival appendix 79.
'Who'll see my gallantee show?'
Crum W2249a. A satire on the ministry's unwillingness for war.
C.

R131 '**Rattle, John.**' The plot discover'd or, the man with horns a new poem. By John Rattle, bellows maker. *Dublin, printed in the year* 1738.
8º: *A*⁴; *1–2* 3–8.
'The sacred nine despise a cuckold's name'
'John Rattle' is presumably a pseudonym.
MC; OCU.

Rattlesnake. The rattle-snake, or, a bastonado for a whig, 1712–13. *See* Forbes, William.

R132 Raunce, John. A few words to all people, concerning the present and succeeding times. [*London*] *Printed in the year 1662, and reprinted in the year 1684. again reprinted 1706.*
1º: 1 side, 4 columns.
'Whoso is wise amongst the people'
Signed 'John Raunce'; he died in 1705.
LF.

R133 — — [*London*] *Printed in the year 1662, and reprinted in the year 1684. again reprinted in 1706. and* 1707.
1º: 1 side, 4 columns.
LF.

R134 Raven. Raven and owl: a politico-polemico-sarcastico-historical dialogue. By Neuter Neitherside, of No-land, esq; *London, printed for J. Jones; sold by the booksellers & pamphlet-shops of London & Westminster,* 1739. (GM, LM Jan)
2º: *A*² B–D² ˣD² E²; *i–iv, 1* 2–19 20 *blk.*
'Near a fair, ancient, rural seat'
A political fable.
L(162.n.15),O,LdU-B; CtY,NjP,OCU,TxU.

Raw, James. ⟨A⟩ new miscellany of songs, compos'd by James Raw, a blind man. *Printed by subscription at York,* 1741.
8º: pp. 42.   YM.

[**Ray, T.**] Poems on several occasions. *London, printed for J. Roberts,* 1728.
8º: pp. viii, 23.   Harding.
Ms. attribution in the copy recorded.

Rayner, William. An ode, humbly inscrib'd to his royal highness the Prince of Orange, 1733. *See* B86.

R135 R--b--n. R--b--n in the suds, or, a hue and cry after the bill of excise. [*London*] *Printed for J. Jenkens in the Strand,* [1733.]

R--b--n in the suds

½º: 1 side, 2 columns.
'O yes! O yes! thrice and again – O yes!'
On the failure of Walpole's excise bill.
L(1850.e.10/65; 1875.d.6/12, cropt).

R136 — R--b--n's progress; in eight scenes; from his first coming up from Oxford to London, to his present situation. With Mr. Frank Lyn's remark. *London printed, and sold by T. Dormer,* 1733.
2º: (frt+) *A*² B²; *1–2* 3–8.
The 'frontispiece' is an engraved plate of eight scenes folded to make two folio leaves.
'Simple and plain, nor yet impress'd by vice'
A satire on Walpole.
L(162.n.70),O,LdU-B; CSmH,IU,InU,MH, NN+.

R137 Reason. The reason. [*London*] *Printed for T. Cooper,* 1741. (23 Feb?)
obl 1º: 1 side, 3 columns.
Large engraving at head with coach driving to the right. An edition was advertised in *LDP* 23 Feb 1741.
'Who be dat de box do sit on?'
Occasioned by *The motion,* 1741, on the motion for Walpole's dismissal.
L(P&D 2492).

R138 — [another edition]
Large engraving at head with coach driving to the left; engraved date 'March the 2 1740'.
L(P&D 2491),O; NNP.

R139 — Reason's tribunal. A poem. Address'd to all persons of the Romish persuasion in Ireland... By a member of the catholic church. *Dublin, printed by S. Powell, for William Heatly,* 1735.
8º, in 8 parts: each A–B⁴ except VIII, A–C⁴ D². I.16 advt.
Only parts I–III have title-leaves, and those of II–III were frequently cancelled when the parts were bound; they are preserved at O,DA. A 'second' extract was published as *A friendly admonition,* 1745.
'For true religion with a zeal inspir'd'
L(1959),O(I–VI),C(lacks II.A1–3),DA,DK(I,II, IV); CtY(I–IV),OCU.

R139·2 — — [*London,* 1749?]
8º: (only B–D⁴; *1* 2–24 in copy seen).
The copy seen appears to be a fragment, though possibly it is the first instalment of an edition intended for publication in parts. No title-page is present; B1–2 bear a list of the contents of all eight parts; B3–D4 contain part 1 only, with the drop-head title 'A poem addressed to all persons of the Roman Catholic religion in Ireland.' A revised text. The date is suggested by a reference on p. 13 to *A dialogue between Archibald and Timothy,* which was published in Oct 1748.
'Hibernia's sons unprejudiced attend'
L(1465.f.63, imperfect).

Reasons

R140 Reasons. Reasons for writing verse: an epistle to a friend. *London, printed for T. Cooper,* 1741. (*GM* Feb; *LM* March)
2°: *A*² *B*²; *1–3* 4–8.
'In me, my friend, you'll call it madness quite'
MH,OCU.

R141 Rebel. 'The rebel Scot. A poem. [*London*] *Printed for J. Collyer.* Price 6*d*.' (*GA* 18 Nov 1745)

Rebellion. Rebellion. A poem, 1745. *See* Weeks, James Eyre.

R142 Rebellious. Rebellious fame: a poem occasion'd by the many lies and scandals dispers'd against the government, since the late rebellion. *London, printed for Bezaleel Creake; sold by R. Burleigh, & J. Harrison,* 1717 [1716]. (*MC* Nov)
8°: *A*² B–C⁴; *i–iv*, *1–4* 5–13 *14–15*; *16 blk*. A1 hft; C4 advt.
The copyright and 36 books formed part of lot 16 of the trade sale of B. Creake, 21 April 1727 (cat. at O-JJ); it was apparently unsold.
'When the rebellious rout their god assail'd'
L(164.n.11, Luttrell, Dec 1716; 11631.bbb.13, –A1),O,DT,AdU,*MR-C*; CLU,CtY(–A1),DFo, MH(–A1),NjP+.

R143 Rebels. The rebels bold march into England, with their shameful retreat. Dedicate to the truly loyal the wights in and about Ormiston and Cousland, for unmerited favours. [*Edinburgh?* 1746.]
½°: 1 side, 2 columns.
'A Roman bird to Scotland flew'
Against the Jacobites.
E.

R144 Rebus. A rebus written by a lady, on the rev. D---n S----t. With his answer. [*Dublin,* 1724?]
½°: *1–2*, 1 column.
Teerink 632; Williams 715. The answer begins at the foot of p. 1. The half-sheets with which the CSmH copy is bound suggest a date around 1724. Reprinted with Warner's edition of *Cadenus and Vanessa,* 1726 (S826).
'Cutt the name of the man who his mistress deny'd'
Answer: 'The nymph who wrote this in an amorous fit'
The rebus was early attributed to Esther Vanhomrigh ('Vanessa'), though Williams apparently regards it as doubtful. The answer is clearly by Swift.
CSmH.

Recantation. The recantation, 1703. *See* Burridge, Richard.

R145 Receipt. A receipt to dress a parson after the newest fashion; said to be laid under a gentleman's plate at a publick entertainment, instead of a bill of fare. [*London*] *Printed by Rich. Newcomb,* 1710. (*SR* 28 June)

A **receipt** to dress a parson
½°: 1 side, 1 column.
Deposit copy at E.
'When you have a fat parson that's fleshy and new'
Advice to Sir Peter King for roasting Sacheverell. Cf. R223.
LSC,E.

R146 — [another impression, title reads:] ...laid under Sir P--- K---'s plate... [*London*] *Printed in the year* 1710.
O; InU,MH,OCU.

R147 — — [*Dublin?* 1710.]
½°: 1 side, 1 column.
The Dublin origin is suggested by the provenance of associated half-sheets at NN.
NN.

Record. The record of a famous action upon the case, 1727. *See* Brome, Alexander.

R148 Re---cy. The re---cy. A poem. Inscribed to W.P. esq; by his loving kinsman, and humble servant, J. Lyrick, esq; *London, printed in the year* 1745.
2°: *A*¹ *B*² *C*¹ (C1 as 'B'); *1–2* 3–8.
A1 and C1 have been seen to be conjugate.
'How shall I paint the man my soul doth love?'
A satire on the regency.
OCU.

R149 Reflections. Reflections upon the glorious victory over the French. [*London,* 170–.]
½°: 1 side, 2 columns.
'Chear up Calliope, good news rehearse'
Harding.

R150 Reformation. [dh] The reformation: a satyre. [*Dublin?* 172–?]
4°: *A*²; *1–4*.
'Let rakes for ever rail at rules'
MH.

— Reformation of manners, a satyr, 1702. *See* Defoe, Daniel.

R151 Reformer. The reformer's ghost, to his quondam friends at the Custom-house coffee-house, by W.C.A.M. [*Dublin,* 1725/30.]
½°: 1 side, 1 column.
The copy at L forms part of a collection of Dublin half-sheets of 1725/30.
'Banish'd by fates decree from lightsome earth'
From the text, the ghost was apparently that of Edward Briton.
L(C.121.g.8/113).

R152 Regular. The regular physician: or make hay while the sun shines. A poem, by the man in the moon. *London printed, and sold by Edm. Powell,* 1715.
4°: *A*² B–C²; *i–ii*, *1–9* *10 blk*.

The **regular** physician

'Justice and honour, who have taken wing'
  Tory propaganda.
L(11631.bb.65).

Relation. A relation of the late misfortune at Leith,
1702. *See* Porterfield, James.

R153 **Religio.** Religio poetæ: or, a satyr on the poets.
London, printed in the year 1703. (*TC* Mich)
2⁰: *A*² B–D²; *i–iv*, *1–12*. 12 err.
'In various shapes religion has been drest'
CtY.

Religion. The religion of reason, [1730.] *See*
Morrice, Bezaleel.

— 'Religion tos't in a blanckit. Broadside poem,
L. (J. Smith near Fleet-street), 1710.'
  Morgan M544, recording that it has an 'engraving of the Pretender and the French king
  being tossed in a blanket by the church,
  ministers, and dissenters'. Possibly engraved
  throughout. There is a related cut recorded at
  L (P&D 1559).

Religious. A religious ode, 1745. *See* Cobden,
Edward.

— The religious turn-coat, [1711.] *See* Ward,
Edward.

Reliquiae. Reliquiæ Eboracenses, 1743. *See*
Dering, Heneage.

Relph, Josiah. A miscellany of poems, consisting
of original poems, translations, pastorals in the
Cumberland dialect, familiar epistles... *Glasgow,
printed by Robert Foulis for Mr. Thomlinson in
Wigton,* 1747.
8⁰: pp. xlix, 168.   L,O; CtY,MH.
  Gaskell, Foulis 96.

Remark. A remark upon the baths, in the city of
Bath, 1715. *See* Ashby, Richard.

R154 **Remarks.** [dh] Remarks on the author of the
Hymn to the pillory. With an answer to the Hymn
to the funeral sermon. [col] *London, printed in the
year* 1703. (9 Oct, Luttrell)
4⁰: A²; *1–4*.
'Forbear thou great destroyer of mens fame'
Answer: 'Let's see the wondrous charge fix'd on
Lorrain'
  The first poem is a satire on Defoe.
L(164.m.34, Luttrell).

R155 — Remarks on the life of Japhet Crook, alias Sir
Peter Stranger. In three several ballads... *London,
printed for M. Head, and sold by the booksellers of
London & Westminster,* 1731. (*GSJ* 3 June)
2⁰: *A–B*²; *1–2* *3–8*.
  Listed in *GSJ* as 'Some account of the life...'
'When great Anna rul'd the nation'
OCU.

Remarks

R156 — Remarks upon remarks, on a certain lady, and
her sparks. [*Dublin*, 1725/30.]
½⁰: 2 sides, 1 column.
  The copy at L forms part of a collection of
  Dublin half-sheets of 1725/30.
'Among the various presentations'
  A satire on Sally, a whore from Shrewsbury.
L(C.121.g.8/96).

R157 **Remonstrance.** The remonstrance. A poem, to his
G*₄*₄*₄*₄ the D*₄*₄*₄ of D*₄*₄*₄*₄*₄*₄.
London: printed. And, Dublin re-printed in the year
1732.
8⁰: *A*⁸; *1–5* *6–16*. A1 hft.
  The address to the reader refers in great detail
  to the London edition and its authenticity; but
  it is probably fictitious.
'While, D*₄*₄*! here you prop our falling state'
  A satire addressed to the lord-lieutenant, the
  Duke of Dorset.
L(1966),DA,DK,DN(2); MH,OCU,TxU.

Renegado. The renegado whip't, 1704. *See* Forbes,
William.

Renny, —, *Mr.* 'Poem on Doctor Pitcairn.'
[*Edinburgh*, 1713.]
  Entered in Ruddiman's ledger for the week
  ending 28 Nov 1713 as one page, 100 copies
  printed.

Reply. A reply to the Scots answer to the British
vision, 1706. *See* Defoe, Daniel.

R158 **Report.** The report or a hymn to the tories. Set to
musick. *London printed, and sold by the booksellees*
[!] *of London & Westminster,* 1715. (*MC* June)
½⁰: 1 side, 2 columns.
  Listed in *MC* as printed for R. Burleigh.
'Oh! what fine stories/Display the gay tories'
  A satire against the tories.

O.

R159 **Reports.** The reports of Sir Edward Coke, kt. in
verse. Wherein the name of each case, and the
principal points, are contained in two lines... *In
the Savoy, printed by Henry Lintot (assignee of Edw.
Sayer, esq;) for J. Worrall,* 1742. (*SR* 29 June)
8⁰: A² a⁴ B–K⁴; *1–84*. 84 advt.
  Entered in *SR* to John Worrall; deposit copies
  at E,EU.
'**Buckhurst,** Such deeds as warranty deraign'
  'The bookseller's preface' signed 'John
  Worrall'. Legal mnemonics.
L(1465.f.29; 8005.d.46/2),O,CT,E(2),EU.

Repos. Le repos, 1737. *See* Brodie, Joseph.

R160 **Reprieve.** The reprieve: an epistle from J---ck
K---ch to C-----l C--------s. *London, printed
for A. Moore,* 1730. (*MChr* April)

The **reprieve**

2°: A^2 B²; 1–3 4–7 8 blk.
'Since fate deceiv'd us both, in fear and hope'
   Signed 'J--ck K--ch'; Jack Ketch to Colonel
   Charteris.
CSmH,CtY,IU,MH,TxU.

Reproof. Reproof: a satire, 1747. *See* Smollett,
Tobias.

Republican. The republican procession, 1714–.
See Ward, Edward.

R161 Resolution. The resolution of a layman in times of
peril. Written by a country gentleman. *London
printed, and sold by John Morphew,* 1715. (*MC*
March)
2°: A^2 < B1; 1–2 3–5 6 blk.
'All in amaze at what is past, I stood'
CLU-C(Luttrell, July),MH.

R162 Restoration. The restoration of famous Cathcart
from death to life: or, a poem upon a false elegy,
published by an unjust, scandalous scribler un-
known, to the detriment and ruin of the famous
Mr. James Cathcart, physician, astrologer...
[*Edinburgh,* 172–?]
½°: 1 side, 2 columns.
'Now for these forty years in Great Britain's land'
   A reply to a false elegy on Cathcart, E79.
E.

R163 — The restauration; or: a change for the better.
Being a paper of verses in memory of the citizens of
London's gratitude, in chusing Sir William
Pritchard, Sir John Fleet, Sir Francis Child, and
Gilbert Heathcot, esq; for their members to serve
in parliament. *London, printed by D. Edwards; sold
by Benj. Brag,* 1702.
½°: 1–2, 1 column.
'Calvin lament, thy conquer'd champions mourn'
LG,LVA-F.

R164 —— *London, printed for B.D. in Fleet-street,* 1702.
½°: 1 side, 2 columns.
Crawford.

Resurrection. The resurrection. A poem, 1718.
See Amhurst, Nicholas.

R165 — The resurrection of the potatoes; being an
answer to the elegy on their death. *Dublin, printed by
Edward Waters,* 1739 [1739/40].
½°: 1 side, 2 columns.
'Saint Patrick, guardian of this isle'
   A reply to *Elegy on the much lamented death of
   those excellent patriots...the potatoes,* 1739–40.
Crawford.

[R166 = W566·7] **Retirement.** Retirement: a divine
soliloquy, 1722. *See* Wren, John.

R167 — The retirement. A poem. *London, printed for
Tim. Goodwin,* 1712. (24 May, Luttrell)

The **retirement**

2°: A^2 < B²; i–ii, 1–6.
'Happy the man, who, free'd from vain desires'
O(Luttrell); CLU(uncut),TxU.

— Retirement: a poem, occasioned by seeing the
palace and park of Yester, 1735. *See* Boyse, Samuel.

— The retirement. An ethic poem, 1747–. *See*
Major, William.

R168 Retrievement. The retrievement: or a poem, distinguishing between the late and the present
administration. Being an offering of thanksgiving
for the glorious progress of her majesty's forces by
sea and land. *London, printed for John Nutt,* 1703
[1702]. (27 Nov, Luttrell)
2°: A^1 B–C² D¹; i–ii, 1–10.
   On p. 8, 'To the queen'. The Luttrell copy is
   in the collection of R. D. Horn; listed in *WL*
   Dec 1702.
'Pamper'd in Kentish meads with pickled feed'
To the queen: 'Your shining conquests, madam,
still maintain'
DT,*MR*; CtY.

Return. A return to the author of a Letter to the
author of a Character, 1717. *See* Bockett, Elias.

Revels. The revels of the gods, 1701. *See* Ward,
Edward.

R169 Reverend. The revd. Dr. S---- answer to the
distress'd maids petition,|Being a state of the case,
setting forth the plaintiffs condition.|Ditto, in
imitation of Frances Harris's petition. [*Dublin,*
172–?]
½°: 1 side, 1 column.
'Whereas you were never marry'd, tho' come to the
years of five and twenty'
   An answer to *The distress'd maid's petition,*
   [172–?], which was addressed to Swift. Both
   poems are in the style of his 'Petition of
   Frances Harris' (*Williams* 68).
C; CtY.

R170 Review. The review. A poem. Inscrib'd to the
right honourable the Earl of Litchfield. *London,
printed for A. Webb, near St. Paul's Church,* 1744
[1745?]. (*GM, LM* Jan 1745)
2°: A^1 B–C² D¹; 1–2 3–12.
   There is a variant state of sheet B (MH,TxU)
   which may represent another impression.
'Review, my Litchfield, with regret mankind'
   A satire on politicians, and particularly Pope's
   patrons.
L(1962),O(uncut); MH,OCU,TxU.

R171 —— '*London, printed for A. Webb*' [*Edinburgh*],
1745.
8°: A–B⁴ C²; 1–2 3–19 20 blk.
   Printed by R. Fleming on the evidence of the
   ornaments.
O; CtY,KU.

Revolution

R172 Revolution. Revolution upon revolution: an old song made in the year 1688, revised in the year 1715. [*London*? 1715.]
slip: 1 side, 1 column.
'Come, come, great monarch, come away'
> *Crum* C430. A Jacobite welcome to the Pretender.

O(divided and mounted).

R173 Reward. The reward of ambition: exemplified in Æsop's fable of the courtier; with reflections. [*London*] *Printed in the year* 1712.
½°: 1 side, 1 column.
'A milk-white rogue, immortal and unhang'd'
> A satire in imitation of Dryden's *The hind and the panther*; probably referring to Walpole's disgrace rather than that of Marlborough, though the L catalogue suggests the latter.

L(1876.f.19/25),O,DT.

R174 — [*idem*] The courtier. [*Edinburgh*? 1712?]
½°: 1 side, 1 column.
> The E copy is bound with Edinburgh publications of 1707, but is probably a reprint of the preceding.

E.

Reynardson, Francis. Poems on several occasions. *London, printed for E. Curll*, 1714.
8°: pp. 32+26+? O; DFo,NN.
> A reissue of 'Mr. Webster', *The stage*, 1713, with A² cancelled and this title supplied. It must, however, have had additional material, since *The stage* cost 6*d*. and this 1*s*. 6*d*. The copy at NN is still bound with *Sacred miscellanies*, 1713 (*Case* 267), in which the longest poem, 'An ode on divine vengeance', is known from *Rawlinson* to be by Reynardson; but there must have been some other addition to make up the price of 1*s*. 6*d*. Probably it was *An ode to the Pretender*, 1713.

R175 [—] An ode to the Pretender. Humbly inscrib'd to Mr. Lesley, and Mr. Pope. To which is added Earl Mortimer's fall. *London, printed for Mark Foster*, 1713. (25 April, Luttrell)
8°: A² B–C⁴ D² (D1 as 'C'); i–iv, 1–19 *20 blk*. A1 hft.
> A new edition, collating A⁴ B⁴(–B1) was issued with *A genuine epistle from M—w P—r*, 1714, and is sometimes disbound separately. The copies of the present edition lacking A² may have had a similar history; those at LLP,DT are still bound with *A genuine epistle*.
'Attend, you loyal Britons, to my lays'
> A whig satire on the Jacobites; 'Mortimer his fall' is from Ben Jonson. Almost certainly 'An ode to the Pretender' attributed by *Rawlinson* to Reynardson; he wrote in favour of the whigs, and the next item mentioned by *Rawlinson*, 'satyr agt Earl of Oxford', may well refer to 'Earl Mortimer's fall'.

Reynardson, F. An ode

L(164.m.69, Luttrell,–A1; 994.c.47,–A²), LDW,LLP(–A²),C,DT(–A²); CtY(–A²),IU, MH(–A1),TxU(uncut).

R176 [—] The stage: a poem. Inscrib'd to Joseph Addison, esq; by Mr. Webster, of Christ-Church, Oxon. *London, printed for E. Curll*, 1713. (5 April?)
8°: A² B–E⁴; i–iv, 1 2–32. i hft; ii advt; iv err.
> Publication date from F. W. Bateson in *MLN* 45 (1930) 27–9. Reissued with *Sacred miscellanies*, 1713, as *Poems on several occasions by Mr. Reynardson*, 1714, and also in Curll's *Collection of original poems*, 1714 (copy at L).
'Since all the din of war begins to cease'
> Ascribed to Reynardson by Luttrell in the CLU-C copy; see also the article by Bateson above.

L(701.d.12/3,–A1; T.1056/4,–A1),O,DK; CLU-C(Luttrell, 28 April),CSmH,DFo,KU, MH+.

R177 [**Reynolds, John.**] Death's vision represented in a philosophical, sacred poem. *Shrewsbury, printed and sold by John Rogers, bookseller in the High-street*, 1709.
4°: π² A–C², ²A–T², a–k²; i–ii, 1–13 *14*, 1–73 '47', 1–22 33–52. C2ᵛ advt.
> Apparently issued with variant imprints. The advertisement is for John Rogers's publications in all copies. Printed on a mixed stock of paper; the copy of the following issue at NNC has a Strasburg bend watermark in the early sheets of the text, only occasionally seen elsewhere, but does not seem to be on fine paper throughout.
'Come gentle ghost that's lanch'd & gone'
> Reissued in 1716 with Reynolds's name.

LDW.

R178 [—] [variant imprint:] *London, printed for Thomas Parkhurst, John Lawrance, John Clerk, & William Taylor*, 1709.
L(11630.bbb.2); NNC.

R179 [—] [variant imprint:] *London, printed for Thomas Guy*, 1709.
L(11630.bbb.25),O; CSmH(presentation inscription to Thomas Pudsey, signed 'J.R.').

R180 [—] [reissue] Writ at the request of the famous Mr. John Lock... The second edition. *London, printed for Tho. Varnam, & John Osborn*, 1713.
4°: π²(±π1) A–C², ²A–T², a–k²; i–ii, 1–13 *14*, 1–73 '47', 1–22 33–52. C2ᵛ advt.
> Cancel title. Entered in *SR* as 'old copy', 27 Jan 1713, to John Rogers by John Osborn.

L(11631.c.13),LDW,O(2); MH.

R181 — [reissue] Death's vision represented in a philosophical sacred poem. *London, printed for John Clark*, 1716.
4°: π² A–C², ²A–T², a–k²; i–ii, 1–13 *14*, 1–73 '47', 1–22 33–52. C2ᵛ advt.

Reynolds, J. Death's vision

Cancel title not seen; possibly both leaves of π are new.
ICN.

R182 — [*idem*] A view of death: or, the soul's departure from the world. A philosophical sacred poem... *London, printed for John Clark & Richard Hett, & W. Hinchliffe,* 1725. (*MC* June)
4°: A² a⁴ B⁴(±B4) C–R⁴; *i–xii, 1* 2–128.
Cancel B4 has not been identified in all copies.
L(11631.c.37; 11630.c.7/10; 11631.cc.12/2; 840.h.10),O,E,WcC; CSmH,CtY,ICU,InU,MH.

R183 — A view of death... With a copious body of explanatory notes, and some additional composures, never before printed. The third edition. *London, printed for R. Ford, R. Hett, J. Oswald, & J. Gray,* 1735.
8°: a⁸(–a1.8) B–I⁸ K(3 ll) L⁴; *iii–vi* vii–xiv, 1–141 *142.* a2 frt.
The collation of the preliminary leaves is tentative; the copy seen may be imperfect, and the frontispiece may not be a conjugate leaf a2. It is not clear whether the lack of a8 is an imperfection.
NN.

R184 —— The third edition. To which is added, some account of the life of the author... *London, printed for R. Ford, & R. Hett,* 1735.
8°: π*a*–1⁸, a⁸(–a1–3, 8) B–I⁸ K(3 ll) L⁴; *i–ii* iii–viii, 9–176, vii–xiv, 1–141 *142.*
A reissue, with the addition of the life of Reynolds. The copies seen may lack the frontispiece found in the copy above.
EN(lacks a⁸); DLC.

R185 [—] Jesus. A poem. In blank verse. *London, printed for S. Rivington,* 1745. (*GM,LM* April)
8°: A¹[=E4] B–D⁴ E⁴(–E4); *i–ii, 1* 2–30.
Ms. correction to imprint, J. for S. Rivington; other ms. corrections to text of the ICN copy.
'Long I continued mute, and fear'd to sing'
Attributed to Reynolds by Moses Browne in a ms. note in the CSmH copy of Reynolds's *A view of death,* 1725.
ICN,IU.

R186 **Rhapsody.** Rhapsody by John Baptist Felix Zappi ...To which is added, a ludicrous epitaph. By the same author. *London, printed for W. Owen,* 1749. (*BM,GM* May)
4°: A–B² C–F²; *1–7* 8–23 *24 blk.* A1 hft.
Italian title on A1ᵛ, 'Canzone di Giovanne Battista Felice Zappi... Aggiuntovi, epitaffio jocoso. Da l'istesso autore'. Listed again in *BM* Jan 1750 under the Italian title.
'Spieghiamo i vanni, io dissi al alma un giorno'
'Spread forth thy wings, I to my soul once said'
Zappi died in 1719; the author of the translation has not been identified.
O,CT.

Rhapsody

R187 — A rapsody on the army. *Dublin, printed [by Edward Waters] in the year* 1736.
8°: A² B–C⁴; *1–2* 3–20.
The printer is identified by *Bradshaw* 624.
'All officers would fain appear'
By the same author as *An essay on preferment,* 1736.
C,DA(2, 1 uncut).

— A rhapsody on virtue and pleasure, 1738. *See* Cooke, Thomas.

R187·5 — ⟨A rhapsody upon the marvellous.⟩ ⟨*London,* 173–?⟩
4°: A–C⁴ D²; *1–3* 4–28. 28 err.
The copy seen lacks the title-leaf; the title is quoted here from the drop-head title on A2. A2 is also mutilated, affecting the first line.
'Fame, by your leave! ⟨   ⟩ worth'
L(11630.d.2/16, lacks A1, mutilated).

Rhodomontado. Rhodomontado's garland, or, the jubilee ring in limbo. [*Dublin*] *Printed in the year* 1745.
8°: pp. 7.   DA,DT; OCU.
A small collection of epigrammatic verse, probably by one author.

R188 **Rhyme.** [dh] Rime and reason: or, a word in season. A satyr. By the author of the Great noise about nothing. [col] [*London*] *Printed by H. Hills,* [1705/–.]
4°: A²; *1–4.*
Dated 1704 by ICU, but later than *The great noise,* 1705.
'Who could believe the town should prove so witty!'
L(1972); ICU,IU.

Ricardio. Ricardio Stilio anglo..., [1713?] *See* Pitcairne, Archibald.

Rich, Edward Pickering. Original poems on several occasions. *London, printed for J. Roberts,* 1720.
8°: pp. xii, 52.   O,GlP; CLU-C,MH.

— [reissue] The second edition. *London, printed for the booksellers of London & Westminster,* 1721.
O; TxHR.
Cancel title. *Rawlinson* records 'proposals for miscellaneous poems (dedicated to his maj. K. G.)', which cannot be earlier than 1747.

R189 — A poem on Cheltenham beauties. [1750.]
½°: 1 side, 1 column.
Dated 'Cheltenham, Aug. 11, 1750.'
'To-morrow (heav'n permit) I'll steal away'
GlP; MH.

R190 — A poem on the Bath beauties. *Printed in the year* 1750.
2°: A²; *1* 2–3 *4 blk.*

Rich, E. P. A poem on the Bath beauties

'Inspire me every muse, and every grace'
DFo.

R191 — Stinchcomb-Hill, a poem: or, the prospect. *London, printed by Robert Brown for the author; sold by C. Bathurst, T. Trye, & R. Dodsley,* 1747. (*GM* April)
2°: *A*² B–C²; *1–4* 5–12. A1 hft.
'If you, ye virtuous fair, will fire my breast'
O; MH(−A1, ms. corrections and additions).

R192 Richardiad. The Richardiad. A satire. Translated from a Greek fragment of Petronius Arbiter, by Theodorus Gratian. With notes variorum. [*Dublin*] *Printed in the year* 1743.
8°: A⁴; *1–2* 3–8.
'Satan's first-born, vers'd in his parent's skill'
An attack on Richard Annesley, 6th earl of Anglesey.
L(11631.aa.23),O,DA,DN.

R193 — — *Dublin printed: London reprinted for John Warner, and sold by the booksellers,* 174⟨4⟩. (7 Jan?)
4°: *A*⁴ B⁴; *1–5* 6–16. A1 hft.
Entered to 'Hitch, Davis & self, partners' in Bowyer's ledgers under 7 Jan 1744, 500 copies: in one place the entry is repeated, suggesting that there were two impressions, but this may be merely an error.
L(11630.c.9/7, cropt).

R194 Richards, Thomas. Cambriæ [!] suspiria in obitum desideratissimæ reginæ Carolinæ. Ad reverendum in Christo patrem, Isaacum, episcopum Asaphensem. *Salopiæ, excudit R. Lathrop,* 1738.
2°: *A*² *B*²; *1–2* 3–8.
A letter of Richards dated 20 Sept 1740 in *Rawlinson* records 'it was never publish'd, only I printed some copies of it for the use of my friends, to save myself the trouble of transcribing'.
'Cæsarei cladem thalami, viduumque cubile'
L(11409.i.14).

R195 [—] Χοιροχωρογραφια: sive, Hoglandiæ descriptio. *Londini, anno domini* 1709. (6 July?)
8°: A–C⁴; *i–ii* iii–vi, 1–16 *17*; *18 blk.* C4 advt.
Engraving of hog on title. Mock catalogue of books on p. 17. Advertised in *DC* 5 July for 'tomorrow', and in *Tatler* 14 July as published.
'Sylvestrem qui primus aprum mira arte subegit'
Attributed to Richards in *Rawlinson*; apparently the poem was planned by Edward Lhuyd. Dedication to 'H-- S--' (Henry Sacheverell) and preface by 'Maredydius Caduganus Plymlymmonensis', signed 'M.C.' A reply to [Edward Holdsworth] *Muscipula*, [1708]. Translated into English as *The* (*Latin*) *description of Hogland,* 1711, and *Hog-land,* 1728.
L(1078.m.6/2),OW,C,CT(2, 1−C4); CSmH (−C4),CtY,ICN,KU,TxU(2, 1 uncut).

Richards, T. Χοιροχωρογραφια

R196 [—] — *Londini, anno domini* 1709.
8°: A⁸; *i–ii* iii–iv, 1–10 *11*; *12 blk.* A8 advt.
Apparently a piracy. Engraving of hog on title; mock advertisement on p.11.
L(1490.pp.77),C,EU,WcC.

R197 [—] — *Londini, anno domini* 1709.
8°: A–B⁴; *i–ii* iii–vi, 7–15 *16.* 16 advt.
A piracy by Henry Hills; his books advertised on p. 16. Woodcut hog on title.
L(1973),O(3),AdU; CSmH,DFo(2),IU,KU.

R198 Richardson, Laurence. The transfiguration. A poem. *Dublin, printed by and for James Hoey,* 1732.
8°: A–B⁴; *1–2* 3–16.
'The son of man transfigur'd, and the light'
LVA-F.

R199 Richmond. Richmond. A vision. By a lodger. *London, printed for Charles Corbett,* [1747.] (*GM, LM* Nov)
2°: *A*² < *B*¹; *1–3* 4–6.
'In that soft season, when the blushing rose'
L(643.m.15/1; C.57.g.7/20, Horace Walpole's); CSmH,KU,MH.

[**R200** = **H114·5**] — The Richmond beauties, 1730. *See* Hawling, Francis.

R201 — The Richmond maidenhead, a tale. *London, printed for J. Roberts,* [1722.] (*DJ* 3 March)
2°: *A*² *B*¹; *1–3* 4–6.
'A young conceited fop, a cit'
L(11661.dd.3),LdU-B(Luttrell, March); CLU-C, TxU.

R202 — Richmond or Richmount. A poem, humbly inscribed to his grace Charles duke of Richmond, &c. *London, printed for J. Wilcox, S. Chapman; sold by J. Peele,* 1721. (*DP* 26 May)
2°: *A*² < *B*²; *i–ii*, *1* 2–5 *6 blk.* 5 err.
'Phoebus descend, on thy own Richmond shine'
On Richmond in Yorkshire.
L(11661.dd.11); MH.

R203 — Richmond Park: a poem. *London, printed for T. Cooper,* 1734. (*LM* Aug)
2°: *A*² B–D²; *1–3* 4–16.
'Since you, my friend, desire I should apply'
LG; CSmH,IU,TxU.

Riddel, —, '*Maggie Riddel's son*'. Elegie on John Pringle, town-piper of Lauder, [172–?] *See* E220.

Riddle. A riddle by Doctor R——e, [1725/30.] *See* Swift, Jonathan.

R204 — A riddle by Dr, S——t, to my lady Carteret. [*Dublin,* 1725/30.]
½°: 1 side, 1 column.
Teerink 482; *Williams* 911. Reply below, headed 'Answer'd by Dr, S— —g'. See Swift's *A riddle by Doctor R— —e,* [1725/30] for a companion piece. The copy at L forms part of a collection of Dublin half-sheets of

A riddle by Dr. S——t

1725/30; possibly it dates from 1726 when Delany's riddles were printed.
'From India's burning clime I'm brought'
Answer: 'Your house of hair and lady's hand'
The riddle first appeared in *The muses mercury* April 1707 as 'Ænigma. By Mr. S.T.' and was answered in May 'By Mr. S.W.' They were reprinted in Faulkner's edition of Swift's *Works* (1762) VIII. 171, the answer as by Sheridan. The riddle may have been Swift's, but the answer cannot have been Sheridan's.
L(C.121.g.8/135).

— A riddle by the reverend Dean S——y, [1726/27?] *See* Smedley, Jonathan.

— A riddle by the revd. Doctor D-----y, inscrib'd to the Lady C--------t, 1726. *See* Delany, Patrick.

R205 — A riddle, in answer to the Hairy monster, by a young lady. [*Dublin*, 172–.]
½⁰: 1 side, 1 column.
'Tho' by birth I'm a slave, yet I'm seldom confin'd'
A reply to W167, a Dublin reprint of the following.
L(1890.e.5/69).

— The riddle, or a paradoxical character of a hairy monster, 1706–. *See* Ward, Edward.

Ridgway, E. 'Sacramental hymns. [*London*] Sold by *Jos. Marshal, & J. Roberts*. Price 2d.' (*PM* 8 April 1718).

R206 [**Ridley, Glocester.**] Jovi eleutherio: or, an offering to liberty. *London, printed for R. Dodsley; sold by M. Cooper*, 1745. (12 Dec)
4⁰: A–C⁴ D²; *1–3* 4–27 *28 blk.*
Engraved roundel on title. Date from *Straus*.
'Hail liberty! whose presence glads th' abode'
Listed in *BM* Jan/Feb 1746 as 'by Ridley'.
L(11630.c.4/15; 840.l.7/6),O(2),LdU-B,*NeU*; *DLC*,ICN,MH(2, 1 uncut),*NcU*.

R207 Ridotto. 'Ridotto al fresco. [*London*] Printed for *J. Roberts*. Price 4d.' (*DJ* 23 June 1732)
Also printed in *The ladies delight*, 1732 (copy at O).
'What various arts attempt the am'rous swain'
A satire on Heidegger's ridottos at Spring Gardens, Vauxhall.

R208 — Ridotto: or, downfall of masquerades; in commendation of the suppos'd author of the poem, lately publish'd, call'd, The bawdy-house: a poem. *London, printed for A. Moore*, 1723. (*DP* 4 March)
4⁰: A¹ B⁴ C²; *1–4* 5–13 *14 blk.*
'Auspitious bard! whose late successful lays'
The dedication signed 'Moses Statute', addressed to 'H----y M-----t', the alleged author of *The bawdy-house*. Against Heidegger changing masquerades to ridottos. See *The first of April: a blank poem*, [1723.]
LdU-B,*MR.*

Ridout, T. H.

Ridout, Thomas Hollier. Poems and translations. *London, printed by W. Wilkins, for W. Hinchliffe*, 1717. (*PM* 4 May)
4⁰: pp. vi, 72.   L; ICN.
Presentation copy at ICN. A copy at NjP is dated 1716; whether this is a deliberate variant has not been determined. The copyright with 38 books formed lot 5 of the trade sale of W. Hinchliffe & J. Carter, 2 Dec 1742 (cat. at O-JJ); it was apparently unsold.

R209 Right. Right Brunswick-mum, a safe and speedy remedy, to remove the unnatural heat of the stomach, and giddiness in the head, contracted by drinking French brandy. Or King George's welcome to London, being the white-hair'd gentlemen's congratulation of his sovereign majesty upon his happy arrival... By J. C. Whitelock, one of their society. *London, printed for the author, and are sold by the booksellers of London & Westminster*, 1715.
4⁰: A² B–C²; *1–2* 3–12.
'Welcome great hero to our British shore'
The author is presumably pseudonymous, but the poem is not a satirical one. Compare C353, *A congratulatory poem... By the company of grey-headed gentlemen*, 1724.
L(161.m.58),LDW,O.

R210 — Right triumphant, or the devil to pay; being might overcome: a poem on a strange war, &c. exemplify'd in the conduct of a late **:***. *London, printed for the author; and sold at the first house in Elliot's-court, Little Old-Bailey; and at the pamphlet-shops of London & Westminster*, 1742. (*LEP* 16 Feb, 'just publish'd')
2⁰: A² B–C²; *1–2* 3–12.
''Tween Britain's wall and Troy's huge wall around'
CtY.

R211 Rightful. Rightful monarchy, and revolution tyranny discuss'd. A poem. With the characters of the thirteen pilots, who at present steer the helm of a ship-wrack't nation. *London, printed in the year* 1719.
8⁰: A–D⁴ E²; *1–2* 3–35 *36 blk.*
'When royal James in long process'
L(164.n.18),C(2, 1 lacks A1).

R212 — Rightful monarchy: or, revolution tyranny. A satyr: being a dialogue between High-Dutch illustrious, and Low-Dutch glorious. *Printed in the year* 1722.
8⁰: A–E⁴; *1–2* 3–39 *40 blk.*
'Long had usurping George in council sate'
Crum L536: 'A satyr on the times' by J.W.
A very outspoken Jacobite poem: a dialogue between George I and William III.
L(11631.e.43),OC(uncut),DrU(Horace Walpole's); MH.

Rime. *See* Rhyme.

Risdale, —, Mr.

[**Risdale, —, Mr.**] Congratulatory verses to the reverend Mr. Thomas Wharton, 1722. *See* C365.

Rise. The rise and fall of stocks, 1721. *See* Ramsay, Allan.

R213 — The rise and progress of sacerdotal sanctity: to cure men of incredulity. A poem. To which is prefixed, the French original, as handed about at the Hague. *London, printed for the author, and to be had at the pamphlet shops in London & Westminster,* [1747.] (*LEP* 6 Jan)
4°: *A–B² C² D¹; 1–3* 4–14. 14 err.
    Advertised in *LEP* as 'sold by J. Oldcastle, near St. Paul's'.
'Dans le temps ancien où l'ignorance florissoit'
'In days of old, when ignorance prevail'd'
    The advertisement in *LEP* reads 'the French original of M. Voltaire, as handed about...'; Voltaire's authorship has not been confirmed.
IU,OCU.

Risum. – Risum teneatis? amici, 1732. *See* Price, Henry.

R214 Rival. The rival lap dog and the tale, | (as ladys fancys never fail;) | that little rival to the great: | So odd, indeed, we scarce dare say't. *London, printed for W. Smith, at Corelli's Head, (a musick shop) against Norfolk-street, in the Strand, & — G. Greg,* 1730. (*SR* 2 April)
8°: *π¹ *² A⁴(–A1) B–H⁴; i–vi, 3–5* 6–60 *61–63; 64* blk. 61 err, 63 advt.
    Rothschild 885. *π*1 is a cancel title-leaf; *²* has a discussion of the weaknesses of copyright protection and says that each copy will be 'number'd, sign'd and seal'd, on the page fronting the title page' (cf. *The fidler's fling at roguery,* 1730). Copies at L(11631.bb.50) and OCU are signed 'S. Fox' and numbered 94, 142 respectively. Entered in *SR* to Susannah Fox; deposit copies at L(992.h.8/3),O(?), EU are unnumbered; listed in *MChr* April.
'What monsters nature does afford!'
    The author is probably Susannah Fox, cf. *The fidler's fling at roguery,* 1730. *Rothschild* interprets her signature as that of Stephen Fox, lord Ilchester.
L(11631.bb.50, uncut; 992.h.8/3, lacks *²),O,EU; OCU.

R215 — [fine paper]
    Printed in quarto form, watermarks: Royal arms, London arms. The copies seen are unnumbered; deposit copies at E,SaU.
E,SaU(lacks *²); MH.

R216 — The rival politicians: or, the biter bitten. A fable, betwixt a lion, a wolf, and a fox. *Oxford, printed by L. Lichfield, for Sam Wilmot, and are to be sold by J. Knapton, R. Knaplock, W. Meeres, & J. Roberts, London,* 1723. (Aug, Luttrell)
8°: *π² A–B⁴ C²; 1–4* 5–21 *22–24. π*1 hft; C2 advt.

The **rival** politicians

    Listed in *MC* Aug/Sept 1723.
'A grim old lion sicken'd in his cave'
L(164.n.24, Luttrell, – C2),OW; CtY(–π1, C2), ICN(– C2),MH.

R217 — The rival wives. Or, the greeting of Clarissa to Skirra in the Elysian shades. *London, printed for W. Lloyd; sold by the booksellers of London & Westminster,* 1738. (*LM* June)
2°: *A¹ B–E²; 1–2* 3–18.
    It seems clear that there are several impressions associated with re-setting of the type, but copies may contain mixed sheets. The suggested order is:
1 L(840.m.1/12),O(Vet.A4 c.325/9); CSmH.
2 L(11633.i.3). B outer reset.
3 LVA-D,O(G.P.1665/27; G.P.1670/21); OCU. All B and C outer reset.
4 CtY. D and E also reset.
'Scarce had the ghosts of Pluto's gloomy shade'
    A satire on Walpole's wives, Catherine Shorter and Maria Skerret.
L(840.m.1/12; 11633.i.3),LVA-D,O(3); CSmH, CtY,OCU.

R218 — — *London, printed for W. Lloyd; sold by the booksellers of London & Westminster,* 1738.
2°: *A¹ B–E²; 1–2* 3–17 *18 blk.*
    A new edition, title reads 'The rival wives: or...'
LdU-B; OCU,TxU.

R219 — The rival wives answer'd: or, Skirra to Clarissa. *London, printed for W. Lloyd; sold by the booksellers of London & Westminster,* 1738. (*GM, LM* Aug)
2°: *A¹ B² C–E²; 1–2* 3–17 *18 blk.*
    Rothschild 217.
'Clarissa ended---and the dæmons round'
    In praise of Walpole and against both his wives.
L(840.m.1/13),O(uncut); CSmH,CtY,MH,OCU.

R220 Rivals. The rivals. A poem. Occasion'd by Tom Punsibi, metamorphos'd, &c. [*Dublin,* 1724.]
½°: 2 sides, 1 column.
    Teerink 1628.
'Men who are out, hate those in play'
    A reply to [William Tisdall] *Tom Pun-sibi metamorphosed,* 1724, defending Sheridan and Swift.
DT,Rothschild; CSmH(2),MH.

R221 [**Roach, Richard.**] Carmen coronarium: or a gratulatory poem on the coronation of King George II. and Queen Caroline. By R.R. B.D. *London, printed for N. Blandford,* 1727. (*MC* Oct)
2°: *A² B²; 1–3* 4–7 *8.* 8 advt.
'Welcome, great monarch, to th' imperial crown'
    Ascribed to Roach by *Rawlinson*; the advertisement is for his *The great crisis* (in prose). *Crum* W219, Roach's autograph copy.
O,WcC(uncut).

Roast

Roast. The roast beef of Old England, [1749/–.] *See* Forrest, Theodosius.

R222 — A roast for a Scots parson. A new song, to some tune. With a word to the reader... By the fool. *London, printed for B. Dickinson,* 1749. (*BM* Dec)
8°: *A*⁴ B–C⁴; *1*–4 5–21 22–24 blk. A1 hft.
'I sing of a parson, and Archy by name'
    A satire on an unidentified Scottish parson in England.
L(11632.df.15).

R223 Roasting. The roasting of a parson. A ditty, that may be sung by the high-church and said by the low. In imitation (and to the tune of) Chevy Chace. *London printed, and sold by the booksellers of London & Westminster,* 1710. (*SR* 11 Dec)
8°: *A*⁴; *1* 2–8.
    Entered in *SR* to Henry Hills; no deposit copies traced.
'May heav'n preserve our good Queen Anne'
    A fanciful account of Sacheverell's trial.
CLU-C,*CtY*,ICU,*MH*.

R224 Robert. Robert the rymer's hue and cry after the flying man, for non-performance. [*Edinburgh,* 1721?]
½°: 1 side, 2 columns.
'What thing is this I see and hear'
    A satire on the 'flying man' who gave performances by sliding down a stretched rope.
E.

R225 Roberts, —, *Captain.* England's glory. Or the French king strip'd, being a new song, compos'd by Capt. Roberts, in praise of those bold sailors belonging to the Prince Frederick, and Duke privateers, who took the two French ships, with forty five waggon loads of money on board, which was brought thro' the city, in triumph to the Tower. Tune of A vast! honest mess-mate. [1745?]
slip: 1 side, 1 column.
'Come all you jolly seamen'
L(1876.e.20/11).

Robertson, Alexander, *baron of Struan.* Poems on various subjects and occasions...mostly taken from his own original manuscripts. *Edinburgh, printed for Ch. Alexander, and sold at his house,* [1751/52.]
8°: pp. 360.   L,E; DFo,ICN.
    Usually dated 1751, but a copy at L (now missing) had ms. date 1752.

R226 [—] [dh] Str-------'s farewell to the hermitage, sitting on the top of Mount Alexander. [*Edinburgh?* 1716/–.]
8°: *A*²; *1*–4.
'With this diversity of view'
    Reprinted in Robertson's *Poems,* [1751/52]; on his exile.
L(11631.e.60),E.

Robertson, A., *baron*

R227 [—] [dh] To the anonymous author of a Latin ode, &c. [*Edinburgh,* 1732?]
4°: *A*⁴; *1*–7 *8* blk.
    On p. 3, 'To himself against disquietude and despair'. Probably issued with *Mons Alexander, in Struani domini sui redditum,* 1732; both copies seen are bound after that collection.
'A picture drawn so full of grace, there's none'
'Let fortune do whate'er she will'
    Reprinted in Robertson's *Poems,* [1751/52.]
E; OCU.

R228 [**Robethon, John.**] Essai sur la critique; imité de l'Anglois de Mr. Pope. *A Londres, par J. Delage, et se vend par P. Dunoier,* 1717. (*DC* 3 June)
4°: A–E² (B2 as 'B3'); *1*–2 3–19 *20* blk.
'Oui, Damis, il est vrai, pour dix méchans auteurs'
    Early ms. attribution to 'Robeton' in the E copy.
E; IU.

R229 [—] — *Amsterdam, chez l'Honoré & Chatelain,* 1717.
4°: A–C⁴ D²; *1*–2 3–27 *28* blk.
    In this edition the poem is divided into five books, and is said (cf. E. Audra, *Les traductions françaises de Pope,* 1931) to be a longer text. The priority of the two editions has not been established.
L(1489.s.11).

R230 Robin. The robin. A poem. *London, printed for J. Roberts,* 1730. (*MChr* 31 Jan)
2°: *A*⁴; *1*–2 3–8.
    Also listed in *MChr* June 1730.
'When circling time more sprightly grows'
    In praise of Walpole.
L(1959),O; CtY,MH(cropt),OCU.

R231 — Robin and Will. Or, the millers of Arlington. A new ballad. *London, printed for W. Webb; sold by the booksellers of London & Westminster,* 1733. (*GSJ* 10 Sept)
2°: *A*² B²; *1*–4 5–8. A1 frt.
    Percival appendix 53.
'Come listen a while, and a tale I will tell'
    Against Walpole and his excise bill; in favour of Pulteney.
O(uncut).

R232 — Robin-Hood and the Duke of Lancaster. A ballad. To the tune of The abbot of Canterbury. *London, printed for J. Roberts; sold by the booksellers of London & Westminster,* 1727. (*WEP* 21 Jan)
2°: *A*² < B¹; *1*–3 4–6.
    Percival II.
'Come listen, my friends, to a story so new'
    A satire on Lord Lechmere complaining to the king against Walpole. Cf. *Little-John's answer,* [1727.]
L(1959),O(2),O-*JJ*,DT,MP; CSmH,CtY,IU,MH, TxU+.

Robin-Hood and the Duke of Lancaster

R233 —— *London, printed by T. White,* [1727.]
2⁰: *A²*; *i–ii, 1 2.*
The TxU copy has A2ᵛ numbered 4; it is
either a variant or another impression.
L(1872.a.1/170*); CSmH,TxU.

R234 —— *London, printed for J. Jones; sold by the booksellers of London & Westminster,* 1727.
2⁰: *A²* < *B¹*; *1–3 4–6.*
Horizontal chain-lines. A piracy, priced at 2*d.*
against 4*d.* for the preceding editions.
L(C.116.i.4/17); MH(uncut).

R235 — Robin red-breast and the wren; or Robin's complaint on the vanity of the times... Compyled
above sixty years ago. *Edinburgh, printed by John
Reid junior,* 1709.
8⁰: *A⁸*; *1–2 3–16.*
'In the last of October, the first of November'
E.

R236 —— *Edinburgh, printed by John Reid,* 1715.
8⁰: *A⁸*; *1 2–16.*
E.

R237 — The robin-red-breast, or the shepherd's tale.
A poem. By M.P. *Dublin, printed by John Harding,*
1722.
8⁰: *A⁴*; *1–2 3–8.*
''Twas when the swains, to shun the scorching
beam'
The initials are perhaps intended to suggest
Prior's authorship; it is a good poem, but not
Prior's.
DA.

R238 — Robin-red-breast's answer to the Black-bird's
song. *London, printed in the year* 1715.
4⁰: *A⁴ B²*; *1–2 3–12.*
'A dismal song is sung of late'
A reply to [Edmund Stacy] *The blackbird's
song,* 1715; against Harley.
L(11631.bb.75).

R239 — Robin's pathetick tale, an heroic poem. Written
by Glubech Digbeye, gent. *London, printed for A.
Moore,* 1727. (*MC* June)
2⁰: *A–C²*; *1–3 4–12.*
'Unhappy me amongst the birds of prey'
A mock elegy supposedly written by Walpole
on the death of George I.
L(1959); CSmH,ICN,OCU.

'Robin-Hog.' A hue and cry after Daniel de Foe,
1711. *See* H352.

R240 **Robins, Jasper.** The hero of the age: or, Duke of
Marlborough. In three parts. I. Pindarick. II.
Heroick. Being a description of the late battel at
Bleinheim. III. An ode. *London printed, and sold by
Benjamin Bragg,* 1705 [1704]. (*FP* 21 Dec)
4⁰: *A² B–G²*; *i–iv, 1–24.*
'When Europe's sav'd, in silence can we sit?'
'The feilds [!] no longer husbandry confess'
'Sing! O Britannia! do not cease!'

Robins, J. The hero of the age

Dedication to Lady Henrietta Godolphin
(subsequently duchess of Marlborough) signed
by Robins.
LDW.

R241 **Robinson, —,** *Mr.* A poem occasion'd by the
king's arrival; humbly inscrib'd to his grace the
Duke of Newcastle. *London, printed for J. Tonson,*
1717. (*PM* 31 Jan)
2⁰: *A² B–C²*; *1–2 3–12.*
'O were an ancient bard to raise his voice'
L(643.l.24/36); NjP.

Robinson, Nicholas. The Hertfordshire spy...
London, printed for B. Bragg, 1707. (22 March,
Luttrell)
4⁰: pp. 27.   O(Luttrell).
Pp. 18–27 are in verse.

R242 **Robinson, S.,** *Mrs.* Cælia's revenge. A poem. Being
an answer to the Lady's dressing-room: said to be
wrote by D—n S—t. By Mrs. S. Robinson, late
chamber-maid at an inn in Bath. To which is
added, the Lady's dressing room. *London, printed
for T. Cooper, and sold by the booksellers in town &
countrey,* 1741. (*GM, LM* May)
8⁰: A–D⁴; *i–ii iii–vi vii–viii,* 1–22 *23–24 blk.*
'Cælia return'd from visiting'
LG(lacks C4–D4),C,BaP(–D4),BrP.

[**Robinson, William,** *of Kendal.*] The intriguing
milliners and attornies clerks. A mock-tragedy...
With the lace-women, a satire; and poems on
several occasions. *London, printed by J. Hughs, for
W. Smith,* 1738 [1737]. (*GM* Dec)
12⁰: pp. xxix, 136.   L,O; DFo,ICN.
The play was reprinted without the poems in
1740.

R243 **Roch, William.** The Christians A.B.C. or a lesson
for sinners, being an alphabetical poem, wherein is
contained choice precepts, and good instructions for
young and old to observe and follow... [*Edinburgh*]
Printed by John Reid, 1714.
obl 1⁰: 1 side, 5 columns.
'All people the which in'
Signed 'William Roch'.
E.

R244 **Rochester.** The Rochester pad, relating to the dis-
pute between Balaam and his ass, whose cunnings
be – in some things very different. – *London
printed, and sold by T. Warner, A. Dodd, and at the
Court of requests,* 1719. (*PB* 17 Feb)
½⁰: *1–2, 1* column.
'An ass well drubb'd with sturdy oak'
On a dispute between Francis Atterbury and
Thomas Coningsby, earl Coningsby in the
house of lords, Dec 1718.
L(1850.c.10/53; 1871.e.1/220),O,Herts CRO
(Panshanger box 46); CSmH,ICN(Luttrell, 16
March).

Rockall, J.

[**Rockall, John.**] Fables and tales for the ladies, 1750. *See* Fables.

R245 **Rod.** A rod for Tunbridge beaus, bundl'd up at the request of the Tunbridge ladies, to jirk fools into more wit, and clowns into more manners. A burlesque poem. To be publish'd every summer, as long as the rakes continue their rudeness, and the gentry their vertue. *London printed, and are to be sold by the booksellers of London & Westminster,* 1701. (18 Sept, Luttrell)
2°: A–H²; *i–ii, 1–30.*
  Bond 8. The Luttrell copy is at CtY (Osborn collection); listed in *WL* Sept, and advertised in *PB* 2 Oct.
'In the dull time of long vacation'
  Cf. [John Dunton] *Bumography,* 1707, for a similar title.
L(11660.c.12/1; 163.n.10),O,*MR-C*; *CLU-C,* CtY,ICN,MH.

R246 —— *London printed, and are to be sold by the booksellers of London & Westminster,* 1701.
4°: A–B²; *1 2–8,* 2 columns.
  A piracy.
CtY(cropt).

R247 —— *London printed, and are to be sold by the booksellers of London & Westminster,* 1701.
4°: A–B²; *1 2–8,* 2 columns.
  Note below imprint, 'The *Post-Boy* lyes, for there's nothing here omitted in the 8 sheet book'. Probably a reimpression of the preceding.
L(11660.c.12/2); TxU.

R248 — [*idem*] A new rod for Tunbridge beaus, bundl'd up at the request of the Tunbridge ladies... *London printed, and are to be sold by the booksellers of London & Westminster,* 1705.
4°: A⁴; *1 2–8,* 2 Columns.
DT(uncut).

R249 — A rod in piss for the a---m-n: an election song. To the tune of, By Jove I'll be free. *Dublin, printed in the year* 1749.
½°: 1 side, 2 columns.
'The time of elections is now drawing near'
  In praise of Charles Lucas against the aldermen.
C.

'**Roger.**' An epistle to the Rev'd. --- occasioned by a long sermon, 1734. *See* E419.

'**Roger,** *the Observator's country-man.*' An epilogue to the court, on the queen's birth-day, 1705. *See* E355.

Rogers, Thomas.
The identity of the Rogers intended here has not been established, but he is presumably a different author from the following.

Rogers, T.

[—] Eternity: a poem. By T.R. gent., [1716.] *See* E482.

[—] The true state of mortality... By T.R., 1708. *See* T531.

R250 **Rogers, Thomas.** Disease: or, the vanity and misery of human life. A poem. Humbly inscrib'd to the right honourable Arthur Onslow, esq; *London, printed for J. Roberts; sold at the pamphlet-shops in Westminster-Hall, at Temple-Bar, & the Royal Exchange,* [1741.] (*LM* March)
2°: A² B–E²; *1–3 4–20.*
  Four elegies. Advertisement at foot of title. Ms. corrections in copies at CSmH,IU.
'If human ills, which thou too well hast known'
O; CSmH,IU.

R251 [—] An epistolary poem to a lady, on the present expedition of Lord Cathcart. By T.R. esquire. *London, printed for and sold by O. Payne,* 1740. (26 Sept)
2°: A–C²; *1–2 3–12.*
  Listed in *GM* Sept/Oct.
'Accept once more, my Celia, e'er we part'
  Ms. attribution to Thomas Rogers in the copy recorded; advertised in Rogers's *Disease,* [1741.]
Lewis Walpole Library (Tom's Coffee House, 26 Sept).

R252 — The royal pattern. Or, advice to the fair sex. *London, printed for J. Roberts; sold at the pamphlet-shops in Westminster-Hall, at Temple Bar, & the Royal Exchange,* [1741.] (*GM* March)
2°: A–B²; *1–2 3–8* (5 as '8').
  Advertisement at foot of title. The copy from Tom's Coffee House in the Lewis Walpole Library is dated 25 April (? in error for March).
'Trust not, fond maids! those who adore'
CLU,MH.

Rolli, Paolo Antonio. Rime di Paolo Antonio Rolli dedicate dal medesimo all'eccellenza di my lord Bathurst. *Londra, per Giovanni Pickard,* 1717.
8°: pp. 158. L,O; CLU-C,ICN.
  Watermark: fleur-de-lys on shield in copies seen; possibly all are on fine paper.

— Rime di Paolo Rolli. *Londra, per Carlo Bennet,* 1735.
8°: pp. 262.
  A reissue of an enlarged collection published in Verona, 1733 (copies at L,MH); recorded in A. Salza, *Note biografiche e bibliografiche intorno a Paolo Rolli* (1915) 48n.

— Di canzonete e di cantate libri due... *Londra, presso Tommaso Edlin,* 1727.
8°: pp. 124. L,O; CLU-C,ICN.

— Delle ode d'Anacreonte Teio traduzione. *Londra,* 1739.
8°: pp. 108. L,O.

Rolli, P. A.

R253 — All'augusta imperadrice Elisabetta Cristina canzone. Dedicata all'eccellenza del signor conte Cristoforo Volkra... *In Londra, per Giovanni Darby,* 1716.
4°: pp. 6.
  Recorded by A. Salza, *Note biografiche e bibliografiche intorno a Paolo Rolli* (1915) 41.
Biblioteca Estense, Modena.

R254 — La Bucolica di Publio Virgilio Marone, all'altezza serenissima di Giorgio...da Paolo Rolli... *Londra,* 1742.
8°: (frt+) A^1 B–E^8 F^4 G^1; *i–ii, 1* 2–73 *74 blk.*
Italian translation only.
'Titiro, tu d'un faggio ampio al coperto'
L(1000.i.13),O(–frt),C.

R255 — Del paradiso perduto, poema inglese di Giovanni Milton libri sei parte prima tradotti di Paolo Rolli. *Londra, presso Samuel Aris,* 1729. (Dec?)
2°: (frt+) π^1 A^2 a–f^2 B–3F^2; *i–xxx, 1* 2–204.
  Watermark: GF. Dedication to Cardinal, Fleury dated Dec 1729. Reprinted at Verona 1730 (copies at CLU-C,MH).
'Dell'uom la prima trasgressione e il frutto'
L(C.59.h.11); NjP.

R256 — [blue paper]
IU.

R257 — Del paradiso perduto, poema inglese di Giovanni Milton, traduzione di Paolo Rolli. *Londra, presso Carlo Bennet,* 1735.
2°: (frt+) π^1 A^2 a–f^2 B–5K^2 (+2 plates); [2] *i* ii–iv *v–xxviii, 1* 2–397 *398, 1* 2–4.
  The first six books are a reissue of the preceding. Colophon on p. 397 dated 19 Jan 1735. 5K^2 contains emendations to the first six books. Mezzotint of Frederick prince of Wales (the dedicatee of this issue) facing dedication, and of Rolli facing p.1 of text; engraving of Milton as frontispiece as in the preceding.
L(643.m.3); *MH.*

R258 — [fine paper]
  Watermark: Strasburg bend; additional mezzotints in the copy seen.
L(74.i.14); *TxU.*

R259 — [reissue] *Londra, presso Carlo Bennet,* 1736.
  Cancel title.
L(642.m.3); *CLU-C,IU,MH,NN.*

R260 Rolt, Richard. Cambria. A poem, in three books: illustrated with historical, critical & explanatory notes. Humbly inscribed to his royal highness Prince George. *London, printed for W. Owen,* 1749. (*GM* May)
4°: A^4 B–H^4 I^2; *1–4* 5–66 *67–68.* I2 advt.
  Title in red and black. The size of the type page is octavo; see the following entry.
'Shall other climes incite poetic strains'
L(161.m.31,–I2),O,LdU-B,PrP; CtY,IU(–I2).

R261 — — The second edition. *London, printed for W. Owen,* 1749.

Rolt, R. Cambria

8°: A^4 B–H^4 I^2; *1–4* 5–66 *67–68.* I2 advt.
  Apparently another impression in octavo.
MH(uncut).

[—] An elegy on the much lamented death of Sir Watkin Williams Wynn, 1749. *See* E287.

R262 — A poem, sacred to the memory of the late Sir Watkins Williams Wynne, bart. *London, printed for W. Owen,* 1749. (*LM* Oct)
4°: A^2 B–D^4; *1–4* 5–26 *27–28.* D4 advt.
'When the bright flame, that fires the patriot heart'
L(11630.f.48),C(–D4),CT(–D4),PrP; MH.

R263 Roman. 'Roman courage display'd in English bravery. With the praise of love and beauty. A poem. Inscribed to Mrs. Sally Salisbury. [*London*] *Printed for W. Ellis.* Price 6*d.*' (*MC* March 1723)
  Sarah Priddon, alias Salisbury, was tried for an assault with a knife on her lover John Finch, 24 April 1723.

— 'The Roman relique.'
  The Edinburgh cuckolds, 1722, is said to be 'Written by the author of the Roman relique'; it has not been traced, and may not be in verse. William Forbes has been suggested as the author.

Romance. The romance of the rose, 1721. *See* Philips, —, *Captain.*

Rome. 'Rome in an uproar and the pope in armour: a poem. S. sh. folio, L (sold by J. Morphew), 1705, (3*d.*)'
  Morgan H385, recording it as 'with engraving, depicting the pope mounted on an ass with clerical followers'. Possibly engraved throughout.

— Rome's legacy to the kirk of Scotland, 1724. *See* Pennecuik, Alexander, *d.1730.*

Ronksley, William. The child's weeks-work: or, a little book, so nicely suited to the genius and capacity of a little child...that it will infallibly allure and lead him on into a way of reading... *London, printed for G. Conyers & J. Richardson,* 1712 [1711]. (*SR* 19 Dec)
12°: pp. 60. L,E; NNC.
  Four weeks' work, almost entirely in verse form; cf. William Jole's *The father's blessing,* [170–?]. Deposit copy at E. The copyright was sold as lot 9 in the trade sale of Conyers, 14 Feb 1740 (cat. at O-JJ), with 200 books to Ward for £2.15*s.*; probably several editions are lost. 'Ronksley's Spelling', of which shares appear in other sales, is perhaps his *Reading made more easie,* listed in *TC* Easter 1699.

Rooke, John. Select translations from the works of Sannazarius, H. Grotius [and others]... To which is prefix'd, some account of the authors. *London, printed for J. Millan; sold by G. Strahan, A. Bettes-*

Rooke, J.

worth, *T. Woodward, J. Stagg, S. Harding, J. Jackson, & N. Blandford*, 1726. (*MC* April)
8°: pp. xliii, 63 + 62 + 80.   O,WcC; IU,NN.
    Each of the three parts has a separate title dated 1725; they may have been issued separately, but only *The silk-worms* is a single poem and accordingly entered here.

— [reissue?] The second edition. *London, printed for J. Millan*... [*as preceding*], 1726.
8°: pp. xliii, 63 + 62 + 80.   DLC.

R264 — The silk-worms. A poem. In two books. Translated from the Latin of M. Hieronymus Vida, bishop of Alba. *London, printed in the year* 1725.
8°: A⁴(−A4) B–L⁴; *i–vi, 1* 2–80.
    All copies seen were issued in Rooke's *Select translations*, 1726; it may never have been separately published.
'What well-wrought webs the reptile race infold'
    Dedication to Richard Mead signed.
O,WcC; *CLU-C*,IU,*NN,TxU.*

R264·5 [—] A true ecclestical history, from Moses, to the time of Martin Luther, in verse. By Thomas Hobbes of Malmesbury. Made English from the Latin original. *London, printed for E. Curll*, 1722 [1721]. (*DP* 14 July)
8°: *A*⁴ B–Bb⁴; *i–viii, 1* 2–187 *188–192*. 192 err.
    The LdU-B and O copies have a 16 page catalogue of Curll's publications, signed A⁸, at the end.
'What news, my friend, from your serene retreat'
    There is a record of payment by Curll to Rooke for the translation, dated 6 Oct 1721, at L(Add. MS. 38728, fol. 185). A copy at DrU has a contemporary ms. note 'By Dr. Dillingham master of Emanuel Col. in Camb.'; its significance is obscure. A translation of Hobbes's *Historia ecclesiastica carmine elegiaco concinnata*, 1688.
L(1123.d.7; G.18951),LDW,O,DrU,LdU-B; *CSmH,CtY,DFo,MH,TxU* +.

R265 Rooks. The rooks and crows: or, the song of a bird in the park. Written by a gentleman of Magdalen College in Oxford, for the use of the parishioners of St. Andrews-Holborn. *London, printed for J. Roberts*, 1715. (*MC* May).
8°: A–C⁴; *1–4* 5–23 *24*. A1 hft; 24 advt.
'Whilst early larks soar'd up on high'
    On Sacheverell.
DrU; CtY(2),IU,KU,*MH*,OCU(−A1).

R266 Rosalind. Rosalind, a pastoral. To the memory of the right honourable the Countess Granville. Inscrib'd to his lordship. *London, printed for M. Cooper*, 1745. (23 Dec?)
2°: *A*² < B²; *1–2* 3–7 *8* blk.
    Watermark: pro patria. Listed in *GM* Feb 1746.

Rosalind, a pastoral

'Accept, oh Granville! this my rural lay'
L(1962, Tom's Coffee House, ⟨23⟩ Dec 1745); *CLU-C*,CtY,PU.

R267 — [fine paper]
    Watermark: fleur-de-lys on shield.
MH.

R268 Rosciad. The Rosciad. A poem. *London, printed for J. Robinson*, 1750. (*GM* Nov)
4°: π² A–F²; *i–iv, 1* 2–24. π1 hft.
'Ceres, with each autumnal scene, was fled'
    A discussion of actors, particularly in Shakespearean roles.
L(840.k.4/20, −π1),LVA-D,O(−π1),*MR*; CtY(−π1),DFo(−π1),NjP(cropt).

Roscommon, Wentworth Dillon, *earl of. See* Dillon, Wentworth, *earl of Roscommon.*

R269 Rose, William. The history of Joseph. A poem in six books. With cuts proper to each book. *London, printed for James Knapton*, 1712. (*DC* 13 Oct)
8°: (frt +) A⁴ a² B–M⁸ N² (+5 plates); *i–xii, 1*–179 *180*. xii err; 180 advt.
    No watermark.
'I sing the youth, by envying brothers scorn'
L(11631.c.38),C,WgP(−frt); CSmH,IU.

R270 — [fine paper]
    Watermark: star.
CLU-C(in contemporary morocco).

R271 Rosse, Andrew. Andreæ Rossæi, professoris Glasgoviensis Glottiades, carmen regi in Britanniam reduci gratulatorium. *Londini, impensis R. Ford*, 1720.
2°: *A*² B–D²; *1–4* 5–16.
'Lætitia plausuque urbem populumque frementem'
L(1972),LDW,EU.

R272 — — Editio secunda. *Edinburgi, in ædibus Thomæ Ruddimani*, 1720.
4°: A–B⁴; *1–4* 5–16.
    The copy seen has fleur-de-lys watermark and is perhaps on fine paper.
E.

Rowe, Elizabeth. Philomela: or, poems by Mrs. Elizabeth Singer, (now Rowe,)... The second edition. *London, printed for E. Curll*, 1737 [1736]. (*LM* Oct)
8°: pp. xviii, 184. L; CtY,MH.
    First published anonymously in 1696.

— — The third edition. *Dublin, printed by S. Powell, for Edward Exshaw*, 1738.
8°.
(Dobell, *Literature of the Restoration* (1918) 855.)

— The miscellaneous works in prose and verse... To which are added, poems on several occasions, by Mr. Thomas Rowe... *London, printed for R. Hett, & R. Dodsley*, 1739. (*SR* 8 March)

Rowe, E. *Collections*

8°: 2 vol.   L,O.
The second volume was printed by Samuel Richardson (*Sale* 251); some copies are dated 1738. Deposit copies at L,O.

—— The second edition, corrected. *London, printed for Henry Lintot*, 1749.
12°: 2 vol.   L.

— [reissue] The third edition, corrected. To which is now first added, The history of Joseph... *London, printed for Henry Lintot; sold by S. Birt & B. Dod, J. Ward, & W. Johnston*, 1750.
L.
Cancel titles; *The history of Joseph* is added at the beginning of vol. 2.

R273 [—] An expostulatory epistle to Sir Richard Steele upon the death of Mr. Addison. By a lady. *London, printed for W. Hinchliffe*, 1720. (Feb, Luttrell)
8°: A⁴; *1–3* 4–8.
'If I, O Steele, presumptuous shall appear'
The copy at IU has 'Mrs Elizabeth Singer' written in capitals below 'a lady' on the title. Not collected in her *Miscellaneous works*, 1739, and confirmation of her authorship is desirable.
IU,MH(Luttrell).

R274 [—] The history of Joseph. A poem. In eight books. By the author of Friendship in death. *London, printed for T. Worrall*, 1736. (*GM, LM* July)
8°: (frt+) A¹ B–E⁸ F⁸(–F8); *i–ii, 1* 2–78.
'Celestial muse, that on the blissful plain'
Later editions bear Mrs. Rowe's name.
L(992.h.9/10,–frt),LVA-D,O,*MR*; CSmH,ICN, MH.

R275 [—] — In ten books. By the author of Friendship in death. The second edition. *London, printed for T. Worrall*, 1737.
8°: (frt+) A¹(±) B–E⁸ F⁸(–F7, 8) G⁸ H⁴(–H4); *i–ii, 1* 2–98.
A reissue with two additional books added in G⁸ H1–3.
O; CSmH(–frt),CU,IU,PU.

R276 [—] — The second edition. *London, printed for B.D. [Benjamin Dod]; sold by S. Birt, S. Harding, & T. Worrall*, 1738.
8°: (frt+) A¹(±) B–E⁸ F⁸(–F7, 8) G⁸ H⁴(–H4); *i–ii, 1* 2–98.
A reissue with a new cancel title. Reprinted by Franklin in Philadelphia, 1739.
L(11632.e.34,–frt),OW; *CLU-C*,DFo.

R277 —— The third edition. *London, printed for B. Dod*, 1741.
8°: (frt+) A¹(±) B–E⁸ F⁸(–F7, 8) G⁸ H⁴(–H4); *i–ii, 1* 2–98. ii advt.
Another reissue, with the author's name on the title.
CU,CtY.

Rowe, E. The history of Joseph

R278 —— *Dublin, printed for Cor. Wynne*, 1742.
12°: A–F⁶; *1–3* 4–70 *71; 72 blk*. F6 advt.
CtY,MH.

R279 —— The fourth edition. *London, printed for B. Dod*, 1744.
8°: (frt+) A¹ B–F⁸ G⁸(–G8); *i–ii, 1* 2–94.
L(11632.e.54),O(2); NNC.

Rowe, Nicholas. Poems on several occasions. *London, printed for E. Curll*, 1714.
4°: pp. 37.   L,O; CLU-C,CtY.
Some copies (e.g. L,O,CLU-C) have an added leaf at end, 'The exceptionable passages left out in...Jane Shore'.

—— The third edition. *London, printed for E. Curll*, 1714. (20 July)
12°: pp. 32.   L,O; CU,MH.

— The poetical works of Nicholas Rowe, esq; *London, printed for E. Curll*, 1715.
8°:   L,O; IU,MH.
Title to nonce collection; the contents vary, but the basis is *Callipædia* and *Poems on several occasions* (apparently reprinted for this edition).

—— The second edition. *London, printed for J. Tonson, E. Curll, T. Jauncy, A. Bell [and 10 others]*, 1720. (*PB* 12 July)
12°.   L,O; IU.
The constituent parts vary from copy to copy. Reissued as vol. 1 of *The works*, 1728 (copies at O,MH). A half share in 'Rowe's Poems and Life' appears in lot 6 of the trade sale of Jauncy, 25 May 1721 (cat. at O-JJ), and a fourth in lot 103 of T. Woodward's sale, 12 March 1752 (cat. at O-JJ).

— [*idem*] The miscellaneous works... The third edition. *London printed, and sold by W. Feales*, 1733.
12°: pp. xvii, 100+36+162.   L,O; MH.
All parts appear to have been reprinted for this edition, but they were also issued separately. The contents appear to be somewhat different from the preceding.

— The works of Nicholas Rowe... *London, printed for J. Darby [and 15 others]*, 1728.
12°: 3 vol.   O; MH.
Essentially a series of reissues.

—— *London, printed for H. Lintot, J. & R. Tonson & S. Draper*, 1747.
12°: 2 vol.   L,O.

R280 — Callipædia. A poem. In four books. With some other pieces. Written in Latin by Claudius Quillet, made English by N. Rowe, esq; To which is prefix'd, Mr. Bayle's account of his life. *London, printed for E. Sanger, & E. Curll*, 1712. (23 June?)
8°: (frt+) π¹ a⁴ B⁴ ²a⁴ b(3 ll), B⁸ C–F⁴ G², ²A–F⁴, ³π¹ A–F⁴, ⁴A–M⁴, ⁵A–D⁴; *i–xxxii, 1* 2–51 *52 blk, 1–3*

Rowe, N. Callipædia

4–48, *i–ii, 1 2–48, 1–3 4–95 96 blk, 1–2 3–29 30–32.*
⁵D4 advt.
    'Price 4s.' on title. The collation given appears to be the intended order of the preliminary leaves; there is a separate title to each book. ⁵A–D⁴ contains 'An epistle to Eudoxus' and 'A panegyrical elegy on the death of Gassendus'. *Haslewood* records an advertisement of 23 June 1712; also advertised in *PB* 3 July. Reissued in *The poetical works,* 1715, with a cancel title. *PB* 19 Nov 1717 advertises it as 'republished' at the same prices; *Craftsman* 2 Sept 1727 again advertises it as re-published, price 5s., under the title 'The art of getting beautiful children'.
'What crowns the fruitful marriage bed with joy'
    Book I only is translated by Rowe; the remainder is by Sewell, Cobb, and Diaper.
L(11643.c.12),O,OW,AdU; CSmH,KU,MH (lacks π1, general title).

R281 — [fine paper]
    No price on title; advertised as on a superfine royal paper, price 7s. 6d. The fine-paper copies were still advertised in 1727.
DT; CSmH(lacks *b,* ⁵D4),DFo,DLC.

R282 — Callipædia: or, the art of getting beautiful children... *London, printed for A. Bell, J. Darby, A. Bettesworth, E. Curll, J. Pemberton, C. Rivington, J. Hooke, R. Cruttenden, T. Cox, F. Clay, J. Battley, and E. Symon,* 1720.
12°: A¹²(A1+A*¹²) B–G¹² (+4 plates); *1–2, i–xxiv, 3–166 167–168 blk.*
    Reprinted to form part of *The poetical works,* 1720. It is not clear whether it was intended to be issued separately. A fourth share of the copyright formed part of lot 6 of the trade sale of T. Jauncy, 25 May 1721 (cat. at O-JJ).
NeU; CSmH,KU.

R283 — — The third edition. *Dublin printed, and sold by Tho. Hume,* 1728.
12°: A–H⁶ I⁶(–I6); *i–iii iv, 5 6–106.*
    The copy seen probably lacks I6.
DN.

R284 — — The third edition. *London printed, and sold by W. Feales,* 1733 [1732]. (Dec)
12°: A–G¹² H⁶ (+4 plates); *i–xxiv, 7 8–162.*
    Copies are usually found in *The miscellaneous works...The third edition,* 1733, published by Feales; those are not recorded here. Entered to 'Partners in Rowe's Callipaedia' in Bowyer's ledgers under 14 and 27 Nov 1732, 2000 copies printed. 6 copies were delivered to Feales on 15 Nov and 950 on 2 Dec; 1000 were delivered to Woodward on 28 April 1733. A fourth share of the copyright formed part of lot 103 in the trade sale of Woodward, 12 March 1752 (cat. at O-JJ). The copyright of 'Quillet's Callipaedia' sold in Mrs. Bowyer's sale 18 May 1736, resold 11 Jan 1737 to Woodward, and

re-appearing in lot 104 of Woodward's sale perhaps refers to the Latin text.
L(1081.f.10),EN,AdU; CLU-C,CSmH.

R285 — [*idem*] 'The pleasures and mysteries of the marriage bed modestly unveil'd. An instructive poem for young brides... Translated by the late ingenious Nicholas Rowe, esq; Ann. 1712. [*London*] *Printed, and sold by Mrs. Nutt, Mrs. Dodd, J. Jolliffe, & E. Curll. Price 1s. 6d.'* (*DJ* 8 June 1733)
    'The two first books are now offered, and the two last will be publish'd in a month.' Apparently an answer to Feales's edition. It is not clear whether this is a reissue of an earlier Curll edition or a new edition of which the second part perhaps never appeared.

R286 [—] Colin's complaint, for his mistress unkindness. By Mr. Addison [!]. To its own proper tune. [*London?* 171–?]
slip: 1 side, 1 column.
    A different text from that printed in Rowe's works. There are engraved editions with music, not recorded here.
'By the side of a murmuring stream'
    Translated into Latin by Vincent Bourne as *Corydon querens,* 1722.
L(1871.f.3/24).

R287 [—] Epilogue spoken by Mrs. Barry, April the 7th, 1709. At a representation of Love for love: for the benefit of Mr. Betterton at his leaving the stage. *London, printed for E. Sanger, & E. Curll,* 1709. (*DC* 13 April)
8°: A⁴; *1–3 4–6 7–8.* A4 advt.
    Also printed as a half-sheet with Congreve's *A prologue spoken by Mrs. Bracegirdle,* 1709.
'As some brave knight who once with spear and shield'
    Reprinted in *Poetical miscellanies: the sixth part* (1709) as 'By Mr. Rowe'.
L(11634.bbb.13/1,–A4),CT; CSmH,DFo,KU, MB.

R288 — The golden verses of Pythagoras. Translated from the Greek, by N. Rowe, esq; With a poem on the late glorious successes, &c. And an ode for the new-year, MDCCXVI. By the same hand. *London, printed for J. Tonson; sold by W. Feales,* 1732.
12°: A¹² B⁶; *1–5 6–36.*
    Copies are usually found in *The miscellaneous works... The third edition,* 1733, published by Feales; those copies are not recorded here. Previously published in editions of Rowe's works.
'First to the gods thy humble homage pay'
LDW; ICU,MnU.

R289 — — [*Edinburgh*] *Printed in the year* 1740.
8°: A⁴ B²; *1–3 4–12.*
    The golden verses only. Printed by Ruddiman on the evidence of the ornaments.
L(1968),E; CU.

Rowe, N. The golden verses

R290 — — To which is added, the Universal prayer, by Alexander Pope esq; *Glasgow, printed and sold by Robert & Andrew Foulis, 1750.*
8°: π¹ A⁴ B⁴(−B1.4); *i–ii*, 1–8 11–13 *14 blk.*
>No watermark; 'Price three-pence' on title. *Gaskell, Foulis* 165 suggests there was also a fine-paper issue. 'The Universal prayer' occupies pp. 11–13; the collation is obscure, and the copies seen possibly incomplete.

'First to the gods thy humble service pay'
EN,GM(lacks B).

R291 [—] Horace, lib. II. ode IV. imitated. Ne sit ancillæ, tibi amor pudori, &c. The Lord G—— to the E. of S——. *London printed, and sold by J. Nutt,* [1705/07?]
½°: A¹; 1–2, 1 column.
'Do not, most fragrant earl, disclaim'
>*Crum* D366. Printed in Rowe's *Poetical works,* 1720. A ms. version in O (MS. Ballard 50, fol. 81) is titled '...my Lord Granville...to the Earl of Scarsdale'; the printed version in Johnson's *Poets* improbably suggests Lord Griffin. On Robert Leke, earl of Scarsdale's love for Mrs. Bracegirdle.

L(1850.e.10/45),O.

R292 — Lucan's Pharsalia. Translated into English verse by Nicholas Rowe, esq; *London, printed for Jacob Tonson, 1718* [1719]. (*DC* 10 March)
2°: π² A² a–g² h¹ B–2I² ᵡK² 2K–5U² 5X¹ 6A–6O² (+map); [8] i–xxv *xxvi–xxx,* 1–3 4–126 [3] 126–446, 1–55 *56 err.* π1 frt.
>No watermark. List of subscribers on pp. xxvi–xxx. Engraved ornaments. Entered in *SR* 5 March 1719; deposit copies at L, ?O.

'Emathian plains with slaughter cover'd o'er'
L(11352.i.7),O,*LdP,LdU-B*; CSmH,CtY,IU, MH,*PU*+.

R293 — [fine paper]
>Watermark: Strasburg bend. The copy at L has an additional A² containing the dedication in French.

L(74.k.9, in presentation morocco); DFo.

R294 — — *Dublin, printed by James Carson for Joseph Leathley, 1719.*
8°: A⁸ b–c⁸ d⁸(d4+χ¹; d5 as 'e'; d8 blk) A–2A⁸ 2B⁶, ²A–D⁸ E⁴; [6] i–x xvii–lv *lvi blk* [10], *1* 2–469 *470 blk,* 1–72.
>The list of subscribers begins on the inserted leaf after d4 and continues on d5–7 (d5 signed as 'e'). The blank leaf d8 was probably intended to be cancelled.

O(2, 1−d8),C,DN(−d8); IU,NjP(−d8).

R295 — — 'London' [*The Hague*], *printed for T. Johnson,* 1720.
8°: A⁸ b–c⁸ A–O⁸ P⁶ χ¹ Q–2K⁸ 2L⁶; *i–iii* iv–xlviii, 1–236 [2, vol. 2 title] 237–488.
L(1000.d.7),O; CLU-C,*PU.*

R296 — — The second edition. *London, printed for J. Tonson, 1722.*

Rowe, N. Lucan's Pharsalia

>12°: 2 vols: A¹² a–b¹² B–N¹² (+map); ²A–N¹²; [8] i–lxiv, *1–3* 4–287 *288 blk;* 1–5 6–310 *311–12.* A1 frt; ²N12 advt.

L(1000.d.4,5),O(2),*LdP; IaU*,MH,NjP.

R297 — Mecænas. Verses occasion'd by the honours conferr'd on the right honourable the Earl of Hallifax. *London, printed for Bernard Lintott,* 1714. (15 Oct?)
2°: A² B¹; *i–iv,* 1–2. A1 hft.
>Entered to Lintot in Bowyer's ledgers under 15 Oct, 500 copies printed. Listed in *MC* Oct.

'Phœbus and Cæsar once conspir'd to grace'
O; CLU-C(lacks A²),MH.

[—] The meditation, a cantata sung...in the tragedy of the Lady Jane Grey, [1715.] *See* M157.

R298 — Ode for the new year MDCCXVI. *London, printed for J. Tonson, 1716.* (*SR* 3 Jan)
2°: A² B–C²; *i–iv,* 1–7 *8 blk.* A1 hft.
>Listed in *MC* Jan. Deposit copies at L,LSC, O,EU,AdU,SaU.

'Hail to thee glorious rising year'
L(643.m.13/11),LVA-F,O,EU,LdU-B+; CSmH(Luttrell, 10 Jan),CtY(uncut),ICU,MH, TxU+.

R299 — — *London, printed for J. Tonson, and reprinted in Dublin, by S. Powell, for G. Risk,* 1716.
4°: B⁴; *1–2* 3–8. 2 advt.
>Watermark: Amsterdam arms.

DA.

R300 — [fine paper?]
>Watermark: Strasburg bend.

CtY.

R301 — A poem upon the late glorious successes of her majesty's arms, &c. Humbly inscrib'd to the right honourable the Earl of Godolphin... *London, printed for Jacob Tonson, 1707.* (*LG* 6 Jan)
2°: A² B–F²; *i–iv,* 1–20. A1 hft.
>Watermark: WC.

'While kings and nations on thy counsels wait'
L(1487.d.2; Ashley 5243),O,OW,EU,DG+; CSmH(uncut),CtY,ICN(Luttrell, 6 Jan),MH, TxU(2)+.

R302 — [fine paper]
>Watermark: monogram HD,ID.

LdU-B; IU(−A1),TxU.

R303 '—' 'The tory's downfall, an excellent new ditty. To the tune of the King shall enjoy his own again. Made by Mr. Rowe, esq; on his being elected a member of the Constitution Club in Oxford. [*London*] *Printed for E. Curll.* Price 2*d.*' (*EvP* 14 July 1715)
>Probably a half-sheet, possibly anonymous. The attribution to Rowe is surely satiric.

R304 [—] Unio. *London, printed for Egbert Sanger, 1707.* (*PB* 12 June)
½°: 2 sides, 1 column.
>Latin text on recto; on verso 'The same in English'.

Rowe, N. Unio

'Dum rosa purpureo suffunditur ora rubore'
'Whilst rich in brightest red the blushing rose'
Contemporary ms. note after title on verso of the copy seen, 'Mr Row:' Advertised in *PB* as 'By N. Row esq;' Printed in Rowe's *Poems*, 1714; both Latin and English versions are his.
Chatsworth.

R305 Rowland, David. A true copy of David Rowland, the Welshman's most strange and wonderful prophesy, foretelling many things, already past, now present, and which are to come, found in my Lord Powis's house, being left there 60 years since: together with Dr. Wheatstone's explanation thereof. [*London*] *Printed for F. Clifton*, 1716.
$\frac{1}{2}$°: 1 side, 2 columns.
Dr. Wheatstone's explanation is indistinguishable from the prophecy.
'About the time that one shall be'
L(1876.f.1/79).

R306 Royal. The royal conqueress, a poem, in honour of the late signal victory over the French and Bavarians, in the empire of Germany, by our sovereign lady Queen Ann's forces...under...his grace the Duke of Marlborough, &c. *Bristol, printed by W. Bonny for the author*, 1704.
4°: *A*² B–C²; *i–ii*, 1–10.
'I stood amaz'd at first, I could not bear'
Dedication to the mayor and aldermen of Bristol signed 'your most humble servant, and daily orator, N.B.' and dated 7 Sept 1704.
O,*BrP*.

— The royal conquest, or, the happy success against a potent enemy, [1705.] *See* Betterton, Thomas.

R307 — The royal court in mourning, for the death of our gracious King William, who left this earthly crown the 8th. of March 170$\frac{1}{2}$. for one more glorious in heaven, or protestants lamentation for the loss of so good and gracious a prince, who was the defender of all good protestants. Tune of, Aim not too high. [*London*] *Printed for J. Blare*, [1702.]
$\frac{1}{2}$°: 1 side, 2 columns.
Rough woodcuts at head; mourning borders.
'England, thy sun have shined many years'
CM-P.

— 'The royal effigies and character of her sacred majesty Queen Ann &c.'
Entered in *SR* 19 Feb 1711 to Josephus Sympson as 'A poem & cutt in an half-sheet'; none of the deposit copies has been traced. Probably engraved throughout.

R308 — [dh] The royal gamsters; or the old cards new shuffled, for a conquering game. [col] *London, printed by E.B. near Ludgate*, [1706.]

The **royal** gamsters

4°: A²; 1–4.
'Er'e we to play this match prepare'
On European politics 1702–6 as a card game.
L(C.121.g.9/146).

R309 — — newly shuffled; for a conquering game, there is one card more to be played yet. [*Dublin?*] *Printed in the year* 1749.
$\frac{1}{2}$°: 1 side, 2 columns.
The NN copy is in a collection of half-sheets largely of Dublin origin. The text is identical with the preceding, except that the dates of 1702–1706 are omitted. Probably reprinted on account of the peace of Aix-la-Chapelle, signed in Oct 1748.
NN.

— The royal guardian. A poem, 1732. *See* Bancks, John.

R310 — The royal health, drank by the loyal Brittains, to the tune of, Let Ceaser [!] live long, &c. [*London?*] *Printed and sold by T. Moore*, 1706.
$\frac{1}{2}$°: 1 side, 2 columns.
Rough woodcuts at head.
'Heres a health to Queen Anne boys'
DG.

R310·5 — The royal hero. A poem. Sacred to the glorious memory of his late majesty, William III. king of England, &c. *London printed, and are to be sold by the booksellers*, 1702.
4°: A–B⁴; *1–2* 3–15 *16 blk*.
'In clouds let sorrow sit, on ev'ry brow'
MR-C.

R311 — The Royal Hunters, or, Chevy-chace revived. *London, printed for J. Jones, near St. Paul's*, 1746. (*GM*, *LM* Jan)
2°: *A*⁴; *1–3* 4–8.
Previously published in *The York journal*, no. 1, 26 Nov 1745.
'God prosper long our noble king'
A mock ballad on the campaign against the Jacobites. The Royal Hunters were a regiment of horse raised in Yorkshire.
O; CSmH,InU,OCU.

R312 — The royal invitation: or, Britannia's glory. A poem. By W.M. an Oxford scholar. *London, printed for J. Morris*, 1719. (*PB* 8 Aug)
8°: A–D⁴ E⁴(–E4); *i–viii*, 1–38.
E4 not seen, possibly blank.
'Hail sacred majesty: serene and great'
Dedication signed 'W——m M——k'; not identified. A panegyrick to George I.
L(11649.d.42/1),O; MH.

R313 — The royal martyr. Or, a poem on the martyrdom of King Charles I. *London, printed for the author; sold by S. Noble*, 1715.
8°: A⁴; *1–2* 3–7 *8 blk*.
'Ye sacred muses! now inspire my quill'
O; PU.

The **royal** martyr

R314 — The royal martyr: or, fanatick piety. A poem. *London printed, and sold by John Morphew*, 1718. (*PB* 28 Jan, 'tomorrow')
8°: A–D⁴; *1–3* 4–31 *32 blk*.
'The ancient poets, when they undertook'
E; TxU.

R315 — — The second edition. *London printed, and sold by J. Bettenham*, 1719. (*PB* 27 Jan)
8°: A⁴(±A1) B–D⁴; *1–3* 4–31 *32 blk*.
   A reissue. Engraved portrait on title. The copy seen is bound with A⁴ of advertisements dating from 1732. 'The 3d edition' was advertised in *PB* 28 Jan 1720.
ICN.

R316 — The royal martyr: or, the bloody tragedy of King Charles the first... To the tune of, The king shall enjoy his own again. *London, printed by Thomas Gent, near West-Smithfield*, 1711.
½°: 1 side, 2 columns.
   Rough woodcut of execution at head.
'The cunning wiles of all the saints'
   Against the dissenters.
MH.

R317 — The royal progress: or, the universal joy of her majesty's subjects, at Oxford, and other places in her passage with her prince to the town of Bath, where they were received with all the demonstrations of joy. To the tune of, The Oxfordshire lady. *London, printed for B. Deacon*, [1702.]
½°: 1 side, 2 columns.
'You loyal subjects now draw near'
O.

— The royal prophetess, 1706. *See* Browne, Joseph.

R318 — The royal shuffler, or, a new trick at cards: shewing how the French king has been playing a game at picket with the allies, and had like to have won the set, but that P----- E----- and the D--- of M---------h finding the cheat, are resolv'd to begin the game again. *London, printed in the year* 1709.
½°: 1 side, 2 columns.
'Monsieur so long the cards had play'd'
   On the abortive peace negotiations at the Hague.
TxU.

R319 — [another edition, title reads:]...P---E----and the D--- of M------h...
CLU-C.

R320 — The royal sin: or, adultery rebuk'd in a great king: or, the history of David and Bathsheba, moderniz'd in verse. By a Romish priest, lately converted to the protestant religion. *London, printed for, and sold by William Lloyd*, 1738. (*GM, LM* Aug)
8°: (frt+) A² B–D⁴; *i–iv*, *1* 2–23 *24 blk*.
'This sentence, which I introduce'

The **royal** sin

Occasioned by Joseph Trapp's sermon of this title.
CLU,CtY(uncut).

R321 — The royal strangers ramble, or, the remarkable lives, customs, and character of the four Indian kings: with the manner of their daily pastimes, humours and behaviours since their first landing in England. Render'd into pleasant and familiar verse. Written by a person of quality. ⟨*London, printed*⟩ *by W. Wise, in Fetter-lane, Fleetstreet*, 1710. (*SR* 28 April)
½°: 1 side, 2 columns.
'Four monarchs of worth'
Crawford (imprint mutilated).

R322 — The royal triumph: a poem. To her most excellent majesty Queen Anne, on her going in state, to St. Paul's cathedral, to return thanks to god, for the success of her majesties arms, in conjunction with the allies. *London, printed by R. Tookey; sold by S. Malthus*, [1704.] (7 Sept, Luttrell)
½°: *1–2*, 1 column.
'Hail Britain's queen, and empress of the sea!'
MH(Luttrell).

R323 R-----r. The r-----r's s-----ch explain'd. *Dublin, printed by Edward Waters; publish'd by Edward Lloyd*, [1711.]
½°: 1 side, 1 column.
   Teerink 851; *Williams* 1089.
'An antient metropolis, famous of late'
   Attributed to Swift by Scott (*Works* 1814, X. 438); Williams considers it not impossible, but Swift was not at this time in Ireland. A parody of the speech of John Foster, recorder of Dublin, welcoming the Duke of Ormonde who arrived on 4 July 1711.
L(C.121.g.8/2),C,DT.

R324 — [another edition, title reads:] The r------r's s----ch explain'd.
Rothschild; MH.

R325 — [another issue]
   On the other side, *The recorder's speech to the Lord Wharton*, in prose.
C,DK,DT; *CtY*.

'R——se, *Doctor*.' A riddle by Doctor R——se, [1725/30.] *See* Swift, Jonathan.

R326 **Rudd, Sayer.** An elegiac essay on the death of the reverend Mr. John Noble, who deceased the 12th of June, 1730. in the 71st year of his age... *London, printed for J. Roberts, A. Ward, H. Whithridge*, 1730. (*MChr* June)
8°: A–E⁴; *1–2* 3–38 *39–40 blk*.
'Now Zion bid thy lucid fountains flow'
L(1418.e.43; 1418.e.44; 161.k.24),LG(−E4), LDW; MH.

Rudd, S.

R327 — A poem on the death of the late Thomas Hollis, esq; Humbly inscrib'd to Mr. John Hollis, brother of the deceased. *London printed, and sold by A. Ward, & T. Cox,* 1731. (*GSJ* 11 March)
8°: *A*² B-E⁴ F²; *i-iv,* 1-36. A1 hft; iv err.
'Hollis, tho' long the conscious muse has stay'd'
L(1416.i.40; 161.k.25, -A1),LDW(-A1),*MR*;
CtY,MH.

R328 — Zara. An elegiac pastoral on the death of Mrs. Sarah Abney, daughter of the late Sir Thomas Abney, knight... *London, printed for J. Roberts,* 1732. (*GSJ* 22 June)
2°: A-C²; *1-2* 3-12.
'Myra, reverse thy suit; it cannot be'
O; CtY.

R329 Ruddiman, Thomas. In obitum Archibaldi Pitcarnii scoti, medicorum sui seculi facile principis, qui fatis concessit X. Kalend. Novemb. anno ærae Christianæ vulgaris M. DCC. XIII. ætatis suæ LXI. [*Edinburgh,* 1713.] (Nov)
½°: 1 side, 1 column.
   Entered in Ruddiman's ledger for the week ending 7 Nov 1713, 340 copies printed.
'Quid frustra erepti fatis quæramus, amici'
Signed 'Thomas Ruddimanus'.
E(2); TxU.

R330 — [variant] In obitum Archibaldi Pitcarnii scoti, medici præstantissimi...
   Title reset; signed 'Thomas Ruddiman'.
L(1185.k.2/23).

Rudimentum. Rudimentum grammaticæ latinæ metricum, 1702-. *See* Busby, Richard.

R331 [Ruffhead, James.] The passions of man. A poem. In four epistles. *London, printed for the author,* 1746 [1747?]. (*GM,LM* Jan 1747)
8°: A-B⁴ S⁴ C-R⁴ (+4 plates); *i-iii* 'vi'-xv *xvi, 1* 2-5 *6-8, 1-3* 4-112.
   S⁴, which is sometimes bound at the end, contains a list of subscribers and a description of the plates.
'Pierian daughters of immortal Jove'
   A signed copy is recorded by *Dobell* 1563.
O(-plates),C,*HU*; ICN,*IEN*,IU,MH(uncut).

R332 [—] — *London, printed for the author,* 1746 [1747?].
12°: *A*⁶ B-L⁶ M² (+4 plates) (D1 as 'E'); *i-iii* iv-xiv, *1-2* 3-28 [2] 1-29 [3] 1-27 [3] 1-28.
   Dedication signed 'I. R.' Possibly an edition for non-subscribers.
L(11633.c.38).

Ruins. The ruins of Rome, 1740. *See* Dyer, John.

R332·5 Rules. 'Rules for a Christian life versified.' [*London,* 1745.] (Dec)

Rules for a Christian life

   Entered in Strahan's ledger to Richard Hett under Dec [1745], 'no. 2000... Do. 500 more... Do. recomposed, and 1500 more'. The price of 15*s.* for 2000 suggests it was a half-sheet.
(Strahan's ledger.)

Rump. The rump: or, a touch at the lady's tails, 1708. *See* Dunton, John [Bumography].

Run. Run upon the bankers, [1720.] *See* Swift, Jonathan.

Rupert. Rupert to Maria, 1748. *See* Morris, Robert.

Rus. Rus. Satira nata ex tertia Juvenalis, [1724.] *See* Earle, Jabez.

'Rus.' A poem in a letter from a young lady in Mary's parish, [172-?] *See* P534.

R333 [Russell, Richard.] The impeachment: or, the church triumphant. A poem. *London, printed in the year* 1712 [1711]. (*PB* 8 Dec)
8°: *A*¹[= G4] B-F⁴ G⁴(-G4); *i-ii,* 1-46.
   Advertised in Nahum Tate's *An epigram on the Spectator,* 1712, which was published by E. Curll & R. Gosling.
'When men of parts, with indignation fir'd'
   Attributed to Russell by *Rawlinson*; it is ascribed to a non-existent 'David Russell' of University College, Oxford in an early ms. note in the WcC copy and by *Jacob.* A copy of the reissue as *The junto* at MH has a ms. note 'By John Gill Esq'; the source and Gill's identity are equally obscure. Apparently written by April 1710, and discussed by Hearne; a tory piece on the Sacheverell affair.
L(164.m.65, Luttrell, 8 Dec),O,EU,AdU,WcC; CLU-C,CtY,ICU,OCU(uncut),TxU+.

R334 [—] — *Dublin, re-printed for John Hyde,* 1712.
8°: A-C⁴; *i-ii,* 1-22.
L(1974),C,DA(uncut),DN; CtY(2).

R334·5 [—] [*idem*] The junto. A poem. *London, printed in the year* 1712.
8°: A⁴ B⁴(-B1) C-F⁴ G⁴(-G4) (A4 as 'B'); *i-vi, 1* 2-46. A1 hft.
   A reissue of the London edition, R333.
L(164.m.62),O(2,-A1),DrU; CSmH(-A1),CtY, IU,MH,OCU(-A1)+.

R335 [Rutter, John.] Bethlem Hospital. A poem in blank verse. *London, printed for E. Smith in Cornhill,* 1717.
4°: *A*² B-F²; *i-ii,* 1-22.
'Whilst rude of numbers, artless I attempt'

Rutter, J. Bethlem hospital

> Early ms. attribution in the O copy, 'By John
> Rutter M.A. of the University of Dublin'.
> L(C.118.c.2/3),O.

R336 Ryall, Charles. The mourner: a sacred poem. In
imitation of the lxxviith psalm. *Sherborne, printed
for the author, in the year 1740.*
8°: *A*⁴ B–C⁴; *i–v* vi, 7 8–22 23–24 blk. 22 err.
'Ye Solymean muses change the strain'
BlU; CtY.

Rymer, T.

Rymer, Thomas. Some translations from Greek,
Latin and Italian poets: with other verses and songs
on several occasions... *London printed, and sold by
D. Browne, W. Mears, & J. Browne, 1714.* (*MC*
Oct)
12°: pp. 133–192.   L,O; NjP.
> Part of *Curious amusements: fitted for the
> entertainment of the ingenious of both sexes,*
> 1714.

S

S., A., *philophilus.* Unio politico-poetico-joco-seria, 1706. *See* Symson, Andrew.

S——, D——. A poem by D—— S——. On the scheme propos'd to the people of Ireland, [1729.] *See* P522.

S., E. Æsop's fables, with morals and reflections, 1720. *See* Stacy, Edmund.

— Spes Hunsdoniana, 1702. *See* Settle, Elkanah.

'S., F., *Cantabrigiensis.*' Miltonis epistola ad Pollionem, 1738. *See* King, William, *principal of St. Mary Hall.*

S., G. Carmen seculare, for the year 1720, 1720. *See* Sewell, George.

— Epitaphium viri reverendissimi D. Georgii Meldrumii, [1709.] *See* Scott, *Sir* William.

— An ode to Mr. Tickell, [1720.] *See* Sewell, George.

— The statesman, 1740. *See* Spiltimber, George.

S., J. An exelent [!] new ballad ascrib'd to the ladies of Munster, [173–?] *See* E542.

— A familiar epistle to his excellency Charles earl of Sunderland, 1720. *See* Smedley, Jonathan.

— The innocent epicure, 1713–. *See* I41.

— A new poem on the order of the procession [1728?/29?] *See* N171.

— The nuptialls of the lamb, 1701–. *See* N348.

— A poem to the memory of his late majesty, 1702. *See* Stennett, Joseph.

— A poem to the memory of Mr. Nathanael Taylor, 1702. *See* Stennett, Joseph.

S., J., *D.D. D.S.P.D.* The place of the damn'd, 1731. *See* Swift, Jonathan.

S., J., *D.S.P.* The beasts confession to the priest, 1738. *See* Swift, Jonathan.

S., L. Poetical recreations, 1705. *See* Spooner, Lawrence.

S., M. The beau in a wood, 1701. *See* B127.

S., P.M. Luctus Aulæ Westmonasteriensis, 1722. *See* L318.

S., R. The Counter scuffle, [170–?]–. *See* Speed, Robert.

— A poem occasioned by the funeral, 1722. *See* P556.

S., R., *AB, lately of St. John's College Cambridge.* A translation of Mr. Hill's Nundinae Sturbrigienses, 1709. *See* T442.

S., R., *gent.* An ode on Christmas day, 1716. *See* Samber, Robert.

— On the passion of our blessed saviour, 1708. *See* Samber, Robert.

S——, T. The Scheld, [1709.] *See* S133.

S., W. Britons thanksgiving, 1723. *See* B481.

— The life and actions of W.S., 1750. *See* L179.

S., W., a *brother of the quill.* Fools have fortune, 1707. *See* F180.

S1 S——. S——'s master piece or, Tom Pun——sibi's folly compleat, Alexanders overthrow, or the downfall of Babylon as it was acted at Mr. Lyddals in Damestreet, Decemb. 11th. 1721. [*Dublin,* 1721.] (Dec)
½°: 1 side, 1 column.
At foot, 'Note: there will soon be published a collection, of this famous authors works fit for country chapmen.'
'What man are you that dares to come this way sir?'
A satire on Thomas Sheridan.
C,Rothschild(cropt).

S2 Sacheverell. Sacheverell, and Hoadly, or; a dialogue between high-church, and low-church. *London printed, and sold by the booksellers of London, & Westminster,* 1710.
8°: A⁸; *1* 2–16. 16 advt.
'Here drawer, bring us t'other quart'
Compare [Edward Ward] *Helter skelter,* 1704, which has the same first line.
LG.

S3 — — [col] *London printed, and sold by the booksellers of London & Westminster,* 1710.
4°: A²; 1–4, 2 columns.
Drop-head title only. Probably a piracy.
Madan.

S4 [Sacheverell, John.] The tempest: a poem. Written at sea. *London, printed for R. Willock,* 1741. (*GM, LM* March)
4°: π¹ A–B² C–H² I¹; [2] *i–ii* iii–iv, 5–34. π1 hft, advt.
Entered in Strahan's ledger to Willock under 17 March 1741, number of copies not recorded.
'Of æther pure, and distant spheres of light'
For Sacheverell's authorship, see the following entry.
L(11630.d.12/19; 163.1.42,–π1); OCU,TxU (–π1).

Sacheverell, J. The tempest

S4·1 — [fine paper?] *London, printed for the author,* 1741.
> The variant imprint suggests that this was a fine-paper copy, possibly printing the author's name.
(Pickering & Chatto cat. 219/7271.)

'Sackbut, Fustian.' An ode on Saint Cæcilia's day, adapted to the ancient British musick, 1749. *See* Thornton, Bonnell.

Sackville, Charles, *earl of Dorset.* The new court, [1714/15.] *See* N126.

Sacred. Sacred and moral poems... By a Cambridge gentleman, 1716. *See* Williams, John.

— Sacred hymns for the children of god in the days of their pilgrimage, 1741–. *See* Cennick, John.

S4·5 — A sacred ode on the passion. To be performed the 3d of April next. The musick composed by Mr. Lampe. [*London,* 173–?]
4°: *A*⁴; *1–2* 3–8.
> Divided into acts, and possibly outside the scope of this catalogue. Dedicated to the Countess of Hertford.
'Earth trembled, the sun blush'd a crimson red'
MR-C.

S5 — The sacred parallel of royal martyrdom. A poem for the thirtieth of January. *London printed, and sold by J. Morphew,* 1709.
4°: *A*² B–C²; *1–2* 3–11 *12 blk.*
'Say, heav'n born muse, (for who can better tell'
> On the martyrdom of Charles I.
OCU.

S6 Sad. Sad pretext: or, divine love ill-requited. A satyr. Wherein is consider'd the great love of Christ, in a view of the wonders of his birth, life, and exit... *London, printed for T. Cox,* 1733. (*LM* Feb)
8°: A–B⁴ C⁴(−C4); *1–3* 4–21 *22 blk.*
> C4 not in copy seen, possibly blank. Ackers's ledger records the printing of 150 copies for Cox, 19 Jan 1733.
'Rouze satyr, take thy pen, nor dormant lie'
LDW.

Saddle. The saddle put on the right horse, 1746. *See* Macdonald, Donald.

S7 Sadler, John. Loyalty, attended with great news from Drake's and Raleigh's ghosts. Presenting the true means whereby Britain may be recovered from her maladies, and obtain a lasting happiness, honour, and renown. In an heroick poem. *London, printed for the author,* 1705.
4°: 16 pp.
'Had not the sov'reign of the globe took care'
> The dedication to the queen is signed.
(*Harleian miscellany* ed. Park, II (1809) 557.)

Sage, C.

S7·5 Sage, Charles. The loyalists. A poem, on the meeting of the Loyal Society in Bristol, Nov. 2. 1712. being the anniversary birth-day of Edward Colston, esq; *London, printed by H. Meere, for Richard Standfast,* 1713.
2°: *A*² B²; *1–4* 5–8.
'Hail, noble sirs! may mirth your banquet crown'
> Dedicated to Henry Somerset, duke of Beaufort.
TxU.

S8 Sailor. The sailor: or a sketch of the seaman's art in working a ship. In a dialogue between a captain and his two mates... To which is added a description of ships...in imitation of Dryden. *London, printed for J. Roberts,* 1733. (*LaM* May)
2°: *A*² B² C¹; *1–2* 3–10.
'Ye jolly ladds! how fair do's now the sky appear?'
L(163.n.42).

S9 — The sailor turn'd pyrate: or; a scourge for a press gang. Written by a gentleman who was unlawfully detain'd in custody by those merciless soul-hawlers. *London, printed for the author,* 1705. (6 Feb, Luttrell)
½°: A¹; *1–2,* 1 column.
'O assist me, ye powers that have rhimes at command'
Crawford; MH(Luttrell).

S10 — The sailor's lementation [!]. [*London?* 1736.] (23 Dec?)
slip: 1 side, 1 column.
> Rough woodcut at head.
'Come all you valiant sailors, of courage, stout and bold'
> Crum C390. On the sufferings of the Canterbury in a storm in the bay of Biscay.
C(ms. date 23 Dec 1736).

S11 Sailors. The sailors account of the action at Vigo. *Exon, printed by Sam. Farley,* 1702.
½°: 1 side, 2 columns.
'Muse will have her song; hark! she merrily sings'
> On Sir George Rooke's victory at Vigo, 12 Oct 1702.
Crawford.

S12 — The saylors address to his majesty. *London, printed for B. Smith near the Exchange,* 1727.
2°: *A*² < B¹; *1–2* 3–5 *6 blk.*
> Drop-head title, 'The humble address of his majesty's ship the Orford'. A variant text was printed with *The humble address of the people, called quakers, to the king,* [1727] (copy at LF).
'Most gracious sovereign lord, may it please'
L(C.116.i.4/68),O; CtY.

S13 — [*idem*] An humble address to his majesty, from the Orford man of war. [*London?* 1727.]
½°: 1 side, 1 column.
> Variant text, first line reads:
'Most gracious sovereign lord our king'
O(ms. date 1727).

The **sailors** address

S14 — [*idem*] ⟨?⟩ The following humble address of the officers and sailors, of his majesty's ship the Orford, to be presented to the king. *Dublin, printed by Christopher Dickson, 1727.*
½°: 1 side, 1 column.
DT(cropt).

S15 — The sailors pleasure before the mast, or the October fight at sea. [*London? 1747?*]
slip: 1 side, 1 column.
'What is greater joy and pleasure'
　　Crum W517, dated 1747. On the capture of a French man of war near Lisbon.
C.

S16 — The saylors song, or, Dunkirk restored. A new ballad. To the tune of To all you ladies now at land; &c. *London, printed for J. Jackson, 1730.* (*MChr* 19 Feb)
2°: *A¹ B²*; *1–6*.
　　Percival XIII. Some copies (e.g. CSmH) have horizontal chain-lines, possibly representing another impression.
'To all ye merchants now at land'
　　On the political struggle over the French fortification of Dunkirk.
L(1959, lacks A1),*LVA-D*,OW(2, 1 lacks A1); CSmH,CU(lacks A1),CtY(uncut),MH.

S17 —— or D-nk--k restored... *London, printed by J. Jackson, 1730.*
4°: *A²*; *1–2 3–4.*
　　A piracy.
L(11621.h.1/90).

S18 **Saint.** St. A-d-è's miscarriage: or, a full and true account of the rabbet-woman. *London, printed for E. Nutt & M. Smith, A. Dodd, & N. Blandford, 1727.* (*MC* Feb)
2°: *A⁴*; *1–3 4–7 8 blk.*
'Physicians, and surgeons, and midwives draw near'
　　Crum P185. A satire on Mary Toft and Nathanael St André.
L(1178.h.4/15); MH,NjP.

— St. Cyprian's Discourse to Donatus, 1716–. *See* Tunstall, William.

S19 — The St. James's beauties: or the real toast. A poem. *London, printed for J. Robinson, 1744.* (*LEP* 24 April)
2°: *A² B–D²*; *1–4 5–16.* A1 hft.
　　Horizontal chain-lines. Hannas cat. 17/633 recorded a copy with the date altered in ink to 1747.
'Friends and companions, servants of the fair'
　　The real toast, Virtue, compared with modern ladies.
L(1489.m.3),O(–A1); CSmH,CtY,DFo(uncut, –A1),KU,MiU.

— St. James's miscellany: or, the lover's tale, 1732. *See* Morrice, Bezaleel.

— St. James's Park, 1708–. *See* Browne, Joseph.

Saint

S20 — Saint Patrick's well: a tale. *Dublin, printed in the year 1733.*
8°: *A⁴*; *1–2 3–7 8 blk.*
'Near winding Boyn, a chapel stands'
IU.

S21 — St. Paul's cathedral, a poem. In two parts. Part I. Relating to the cathedral. Part II. The prospect from the gilded gallery. *London, printed for the author; sold by George Keith, 1750.* (*GM* April)
4°: *A¹ B–H⁴ I²*; *3–5 6–64.*
　　Half-title, A1 of *A²*, possibly missing from copies seen.
'While thy epistles, to reform the age'
L(11630.b.7/2; 164.k.25),O.

— St. Paul's church, 1716. *See* Ward, Edward.

S22 — St. Taffy's day: or, the Cambro-British gamboles. In three merry canto's... By C.L. a true-Briton. *London, printed for T. Warner, 1724.*
8°: *A–F⁴ G¹*; *i–ii, 1–44 45–47; 48 blk.* F4 blk; G1 err.
'O Clio, shou'dst thou think to mount'
L(11602.ee.1/3),O(uncut); CtY(–F4, G1).

Sainte-Marthe, Scévole de.
Pædotrophiæ...written in Latin by Monsieur St. Marthe... Now done into English verse, 1710, 1718. *In* C4–5.

St. Jean, P. de. *See* St. John, Patrick.

St. John, Patrick.
St. John, who described himself as 'Hibernus' and 'Poeta regius', appears to have been attached to the court of the Pretender. Fourteen Latin and two French poems by him with dates from 1704 to 1721 are listed in the catalogue of the Bibliothèque nationale, Paris; two are preserved among the Carte papers at O. Apparently all were printed abroad, some at least in France, and they are accordingly excluded from this catalogue. Compare D. McEncroe for another Irish Latinist in France.

— [*Invicti herois Arthur Dillon, etc. ensis*] The invincible hero' Arthure Dillon's sword place'd amidst the stars, [1724.] *See* I55.

S23 **Saints.** The saints congratulatory address: or Th---s B---dbury's speech in the name of all the prot—nt diss—rs to the b---p of B---r's jesuit; with that r—d father's answer. In hudibrastick verse. Humbly dedicated to the right worshipful Sir Rich--d St--le, knt. *London, printed for J. Cuxon; sold by the booksellers of London & Westminster, 1718.*
8°: *A–E⁴*; *i–viii, 1 2–31 32 blk.* viii err.
　　Bond 56.
'When church was prov'd to have no pow'r'
　　A travesty of Thomas Bradbury's *The primitive tories,* 1717. The 'bishop of Bangor's jesuit'

The **saints** congratulatory address

was F. de la Pillonière. Against the whigs and dissenters.
L(T.1056/5; 164.n.13); OCU.

'Sallust.'
The speech of Memmius to the people of Rome. Translated into blank verse from the Latin of Sallust, 1728. *See* S630.

Salvini, Antonio Maria.
Taubman, Nathaniel: The British nations tribute of loyalty and duty ['being a translation of a poem wrote in Italian by Sign: Ant. Maria Salvini'], 1718. *See* T92.

[**Samber, Robert.**] Poems on several subjects. Formerly written by an undergraduate at the university, 1714. *See* Poems.

S24 — Cassandra. A pastoral eclogue, on the death of the Duchess of Chandos. *London, E. Gardner*, 1735.
2°: 10 pp.
Dedicated to the Duke of Chandos. There is an autograph ms. at O (MS. Rawl. poet. 11) from which the first line is taken.
'Far in a lonely vale where poplars spread'
(Pickering & Chatto cat. 266/9563)

S25 — Epithalamium on the marriage of the right honourable the Lord Brudenel, and the Lady Mary, daughter to his grace the Duke of Montagu. *London, printed in the year* 1730. (*MChr* Aug)
2°: *A*² B–C²; *i–iv*, *1* 2–8.
'What diff'rent subjects diff'rent poets move!'
L(1484.m.34).

S26 [—] An ode on Christmas-day. By R.S. gent. *London, printed for R. Palmer; sold by J. Roberts*, 1716 [1715]. (29 Dec, Luttrell)
8°: π¹ A² B⁴ C²; *i–vi*, *1* 2–12. π1 hft.
Listed in *MC* Dec 1715.
'Awake, my soul, thou drowsy power, awake'
Attributed to Samber in *N&Q* II. 11 (1861) 503; it is dedicated to his friend Francis Browne.
GM(−π1); MH(Luttrell)

S27 [—] On the passion of our blessed saviour. An essay. By R.S., gent. *London, printed for S. Battersby*, 1708.
8°: (frt+) A–D⁴; *i–iv*, *1*–28.
Prose introduction on pp. 1–4, changing to verse.
'Thus said, /The son of god bows down his awful head'
A copy of the following edition at AN has an early ms. note 'By Mr. Sambre'.
ViU.

S28 [—] — *London, printed for John Sackfield; sold by John Morphew*, 1717.
8°: *A*⁴ B–D⁴; *i–viii*, *1* 2–23 *24 blk*. A1 hft.

Samber, R. On the passion

A revised version; the dedication signed 'R.S.'
''Tis done, 'tis finish'd. – This he scarce had said'
AN,GM,WcC(−A1); MH.

S29 — 'The paradox: being three poems, from the Italian of signior cavallero Bernardo Morando, a noble Genovese. With several other miscellaneous tracts. [*London*] *Printed for W. Boreham*. Price 1s.'
(*DP* 11 Jan 1721)
There is an autograph ms. at O (MS. Rawl. poet. 11) from which the first line is taken.
'Ye beauteous youths to happiness design'd'

S30 — To the memory of Edward Russel, late earl of Orford, from his character by Anthony Hammond, esq; An essay. *London, printed for J. Roberts; sold by the booksellers of London & Westminster*, 1731. (April?)
8°: A–B⁴ C²; *i–iii* iv–vii *viii*, *1* 2–12.
'The bold attempt, and vain, perhaps, essay'
Dedication to the Duke of Bedford, dated 12 April 1731, signed by Samber.
L(11631.d.48).

S31 [**Sampson, John.**] The intrigue. A college eclogue. By a gentleman of Oxford. *London, printed for R. Griffiths*, 1750. (*GM, LM* March)
4°: π¹[=B1] A⁴ B⁴(−B1); *i–ii*, *1*–2 3–14. π1 hft.
'Tom solemn toll'd-----the college bells around'
Sampson's authorship is recorded by *Rawlinson*. A heavily annotated copy in the possession of John Sparrow records that it was 'suppos'd to be wrote' by Thomas Warton, Sampson, and Bonnell Thornton; but Sampson may have played the leading part.
L(11630.c.14/3),O; CSmH,CtY(2),ICU.

Samson. Samson's foxes, 1713. *See* A new litany, 1710–.

Samuel, Keimer. *See* Keimer, Samuel.

S32 Sanderson, Thomas. Three odes. The royal hero; to the king. The royal nuptials; to the queen. Religion and liberty triumphant; to the prince. *Cambridge printed, and sold by J. Wilford, London*, 1733. (*GSJ* 22 Nov)
4°: *A*⁴ B–C⁴; *1*–5 6–24. A1 hft.
'Awake my soul! From Jove begin the song'
L(11631.h.10); MH(uncut).

Sanguine. Sanguine lovers, or the Irish cry, 1733. *See* Hamilton, Thomas, *chaplain to his majesty*.

[**S33** = W29·5] **Sannazarius.** Sannazarius on the birth of our saviour, 1736. *See* Walpole, Edward.

Sannazaro, Jacopo.
[Rooke, John:] Eclogues, written originally, by Actus Syncerus Sannazarius. And now translated into English, 1725.

[Bell, Beaupré:] The osiers. A pastoral translated from the Latin of Sannazarius, 1724. *See* B173.

Sannazaro, J.

[Walpole, Edward:] Sannazarius on the birth of our Saviour. Done into English verse, 1736. *See* W29·5.

S34 Sappho. 'Sappho to Adonis, after the manner of Ovid. [*London*] *Printed for L. Gilliver.* Price 1s.' (*GM, LM* March 1733)

> Possibly a reference to the quarrel between Lady Mary Wortley Montagu and Pope is intended.

Sappho.
The odes, fragments, and epigrams of Sappho. *In* Addison, John: The works of Anacreon, 1735.

S35 Sappho-an. The Sappho-an. An heroic poem of three cantos, in the Ovidian stile, describing the pleasures which the fair sex enjoy with each other . . . Found amongst the papers of a lady of quality, a great promoter of Jaconitism. *London, printed for Cha. Brasier, in Fleet-street,* [1749.] (*LEP* 11 April)
8°: A^1 B–F^4; [2] 9–48.

> The copy seen lacks some preliminary leaves; the advertisement in *LEP* describes it as 'adorn'd with a neat frontispiece'.

'Swains of Britannia's happy, gladsome isle'
Institute for Sex Research (−frt).

Sarah. Sarah, the quaker, to Lothario, 1728–. *See* Beckingham, Charles.

S36 — Sarah's farewel to c-----t: or, a trip from St. James's to St. Albans. To the tune of, Farewel joy and farewel pleasure. *London, printed in the year* 1710.
$\frac{1}{2}$°: 1 side, 2 columns.
'Farewel c——t and farewel pleasure'

> On the Duchess of Marlborough's dismissal.

L(Cup.645.e.1/18),Crawford.

S37 Sarah-ad. The Sarah-ad: or, a flight for fame. A burlesque poem in three canto's, in hudibrastic verse. Founded on An account of the conduct of the dowager Du——ss of M——gh... Proper to be bound up therewith. *London, printed for T. Cooper,* 1742. (*GM, LM* April)
8°: A–D^4; *1–3* 4–32.
> *Bond* 177.

'Stiff as I am, worn out with age'
> A travesty of the Duchess of Marlborough's *An account of the conduct,* 1742.

L(1077.h.60/2),O,C,AdU,LdU-B + ; CSmH,CtY, ICN,MH,TxU+.

S38 Satira. Satira in poetastros O–c---enses. *Londini, anno dom.* 1702. (4 July, Luttrell)
4°: A^4 B–C^4; *i–viii,* 1–16. A1 hft.
> Listed in *WL* July.

'Non merito irascar cum tot prurigine famæ'
> In poetastros Oxcantenses.

L(161.n.39, Luttrell, −A1),O.

Satirae

S39 Satirae. Satyrae quatuor. Auctore D.G. *Londini excudebat J. Hughs,* 1735. (*GM* March)
2°: π^1 A–D^2; *i–ii,* 1–15 *16 blk.*
'Quantum possideat quivis, cognoscere ferme'
> Translated by William Major as *Four satires,* 1743; there said to be by a native of Holland.

L(644.m.14/19).

Satire. A satyr, 1725. *See* Smedley, Jonathan.

S40 — A satire. *London, printed for T. Cooper,* 1734. (*GM, LM* March)
2°: A–D^2; *1–2* 3–16.
'While, Walpole, thou'rt engag'd in Britain's cause'
> Addressed to Walpole, on his opponents.

L(840.m.1/32),LdU-B; CSmH,KU,MH,OCU, TxU(2).

— A satyr against confinement, 1702. *See* Hopkins, Charles.

S41 — A satyr against dancing. By a person of honour. *London, printed for A. Baldwin,* 1702. (18 June, Luttrell)
2°: A^2 B–C^2; *i–ii, 1* 2–9 *10 blk.* 9 advt.
> Listed in *WL* June 1702.

'Sure of all arts that ever were invented'
CSmH,CtY,*MH*,OCU(Luttrell).

S42 — [dh] A satyr against hypocrites, with the character of a true-church-man. [*London?* 1702/14.]
4°: A^4 (A1 as 'B'); *1–8.*
'To sing of those blest days when providence'
C; OCU.

— A satyr against ingratitude, 1706. *See* Against ingratitude, 1706.

S43 — A satyr against love. Revis'd and corrected by Mr. Congreve. *London, printed in the year* 1703. (26 June, Luttrell)
2°: A–D^2; *i–ii,* 1–11 '8–9' *14 blk.*
'After the rebel Lucifer was driv'n'
> Congreve denied any part in this in *The tears of Amaryllis,* 1703. See John Barnard in *Bulletin of NYPL* (May 1964).

CLU-C(Luttrell),TxU.

— A satyr against wine, 1705–. *See* Ward, Edward.

S44 — ⟨A⟩ satyr. Ascrib'd to his excellency, L—— C——t. [*Dublin,* 1725.]
$\frac{1}{2}$°: 1 side, 2 columns.
'Long time the scriblers of the town have try'd'
> A satire on the bad verse endured by Lord Carteret, apparently with particular reference to [Charles Coffey] *A prologue spoken by Mr. Elrington,* 1725.

DT.

S45 — A satyr. By way of reply, to Martin Guilliver, alias Murtagh Mc.Dermot. Occasion'd by his letter to ------. *Dublin, printed in the year* 1730.
$\frac{1}{2}$°: 1 side, 2 columns.
'What silly Murtagh wrap't in livid gloom?'
> The pseudonymous letter of Mc.Dermot has not been identified; the only obvious candidate

A **satire**. By way of reply

is *A letter from Martin Gulliver, to George Faulkner*, 1730 (G317).
DT.

S46 — A satyr: in French and English. '*Paris*' [*London?*], *printed* April, 1749.
4°: *A*⁴; *1* 2–7 *8 blk.*
Vertical chain-lines.
'Quel est le triste sort des malheureux François'
'Hard fate! O Gauls! how soon our triumphs cease!'
On the expulsion of the Young Pretender from France.
L(840.k.4/5),O.

S47 — [*idem*] A poem. French and English. [*Edinburgh*, *1749?*]
8°: *A*⁶; *1–3* 4–11 *12 blk.*
Title in half-title form.
E.

[S48–9 = H161·5–6] — A satyr. In the manner of Persius, 1730–. *See* Hervey, John, *baron Hervey.*

— 'A satire in verse on Drs. Cheyne, Helsham, and the medical profession. Dublin (?), 1725, folio sheet.'
Listed by *O'Donoghue* under Anonymous; his records are usually reliable, but this sounds very much like a generalized title.

S50 — A satyr, on a true-born Dutch-skipper; with some remarks on his character, and qualifications. *London, printed in the year* 1701.
½°: 2 sides, 1 column.
'Begot on board some fly-boat, ship or hoy'
The title is accurate; there is no satire on Defoe.
CLU-C,Rosenbach.

— A satire on all parties: a poem, 1749. *See* Gilbert, Thomas.

— A satire on Dr. D—ny, 1730. *See* Swift, Jonathan (S880).

— A satyr on F---s of D---r, [1704.] *See* Allan, —.

— A satyr on Lincolnshire, 1736. *See* Lincolnshire. A poem, 1720–.

S51 — A satyr on Madam Cut-A—e, or the h---y m-----r. [*Dublin?* 172–?]
½°: 1 side, 2 columns.
'When female fury reunites it's force'
On an alleged assault with a knife on the fundament of Madam B—ns.
NN.

S52 — [dh] A satyr on mankind: with a word of advice in this critical juncture. [col] [*London*] *Published by John Nutt*, 1701. (5 Dec, Luttrell)
2°: *A*²; *1*–4.
'When power divine, the earth and sea had fram'd'
ICN(Luttrell),OCU.

S53 — A satyr on Miss Ga—fny by the Little Beau, in imitation of Mr. Philipis. [*Dublin*, 1725/30.]
slip: 1 side, 1 column.

A **satire** on Miss Ga—fny

Bond 89. Dated by the L catalogue as [1728?], but more likely 1726.
'Proper, slender, not too tall'
Signed 'B.W.', doubtless intended for Patrick Walsh, known as 'the Little Beau', but surely satirizing him. Written in imitation of Ambrose Philips's 'namby-pamby' verse.
L(1890.e.5/71).

S54 — A satyr on the author of She would if she could. *Dublin, printed in the year* 1726.
½°: 1 side, 1 column.
On the other side of the DN copy, *She wou'd if she cou'd*, [1726.]
'In striving sir her to expose'
In defence of Margaretta.
DN.

S55 — A satyr on the author of the Ladies-library. By a young lady. [*Dublin*, 1722.]
½°: 1 side, 1 column.
'What silly numbskull was't that did indite'
There were at least nine parts of the *Ladies library* published in 1722; there are copies of parts 1 and 9 at DN.
NN.

— A satyr on the journey-men taylors, [172–.] *See* Ashton, Robert.

S56 — A satyr on the Kentish-men and T--te, the poet. By Andrew Dothat, gent. *London printed, and sold by the booksellers of London & Westminster*, 1701. (23 Sept, Luttrell)
2°: A–C²; *1–2* 3–11 *12 blk.*
The Luttrell copy is recorded by *Thorn-Drury*; listed in *WL* Sept.
'Shall British senators permit the bays'
On the Kentish petitioners and Nahum Tate.
L(1346.m.22),LdU-B,MR-C; CLU-C.

S57 — A satyr on the lawyers concerning two clowns and an oyster. [*Dublin*] *Printed in the year* 1727.
½°: 1 side, 1 column.
The MH copy has a Dublin collector's initial, F.
'In Cornwall once, or somewhere else'
MH.

S58 — A satyr on the Mall in Great Britain-street. [*Dublin*] *Printed in the year* 1733.
4°: *A*² B² *C*²; *1–2* 3–10 *11; 12 blk.*
Woodcuts of courtiers on pp. 2, 11. A perfect copy is in the possession of J. R. B. Brett-Smith.
'Hail! sacred nymphs, whose influence inspires'
A satire on the ladies.
O(−C2).

S59 — A satyr on the New Tunbridge Wells. Being a poetical description of the company's behaviour... Occasion'd by...Islington: or, the humours of New Tunbridge Wells... To which is added, Advice to an aspiring young lady. *London, printed for J. Iorns; sold at the pamphlet-shops of London & Westminster*, 1733. (*LaM* June)

A **satire** on the New Tunbridge Wells

2⁰: *A¹ B² C¹*; *1–3 4–7 8 blk.*
>The added poem is a reprint of Lyttelton's
>*Advice to a lady*, 1733, printed in 2 columns.

'At six this morn, disturb'd from pleasing rest'
>*Islington; or the humours of New-Tunbridge-Wells*, 1733, is a prose pamphlet (copy at L).

IU(uncut).

S60 —— To which is added, The state dunces; with notes. *London, printed for J. Iorns; sold at the pamphlet-shops of London & Westminster, 1733.*
2⁰: *A¹ B² C²*; *1–3 4–6, 1 2–3 4 blk.*
>*The state dunces* is printed in 2 columns.

DLC.

[S61 = H387]

S62 — A satyr on the poets of the town... Writ by A.P. *Dublin, printed in the year 1726.*
½⁰: 1 side, 1 column.
>*Bond p. 118n.*

'In aged times when nations waged war'
>Although the initials suggest that the author is Ambrose Philips, he is the chief object of the satire.

C; CtY.

S63 — [variant, no imprint]
L(C.121.g.8/112).

S64 — A satyr on the stabbing of the right honourable Robert Harley esq; one of her majesty's privy counsellors, &c. by the barbarous hand of the Marquis de Guiscard, on the 8th of March, being the day of her majesty's happy aeccssion [!] to the throne. [*London*] *Sold by J. Morphew*, 1711.
½⁰: 1 side, 1 column.
'Are these then, France, the arts which you imploy'
>Against Guiscard and France.

MH.

S65 — [another edition, title reads:] ...ac-|cession to the throne.
CLU-C.

S66 — A satyr on the taylors procession, July the 28th, 1729. *Dublin, printed in the year 1729.*
½⁰: 1 side, 2 columns.
'My tender muse pray don't be in a rage'
DT(cropt).

S67 — A satyr, on the town-poet's, in a letter to the Revd. Dean Swift. [*Dublin, 1725/30?*]
slip: 1 side, 1 column.
'Good sir, in such a leaden age as this'
>According to this satire, the price of an elegy was half a crown.

C.

S68 — A satyr satiris'd, an answer to a satyr on the reverend D—n S—t. [*Dublin, 1725.*]
½⁰: 1 side, 1 column.
>*Teerink 1204.*

'What will the world at length come to'
>A reply to [Jonathan Smedley] *A satyr*, 1725; in defence of Swift.

L(C.121.g.8/133),DT,Rothschild; TxU.

A **satire**: shewing

S69 — [dh] A satyr: shewing, the nature and proceedings of the church of En : : : : : : : :d, &c. [*171–?*]
8⁰: *A⁴*; 1–8.
'You people of zeal that love your poor souls'
>*Crum* Y322: 'The nature and proceedings of sectaries, from their original, to the present times.' Apparently a Roman catholic satire on the church of England.

O(presentation copy from Rawlinson to Hearne).

S70 — A satyr. To Miss M——y W——t——n. By an admirer. *Dublin, printed by John Ware, 1726.*
slip: 1 side, 1 column.
'Were I dear madam, who am none'
>Molly W—t—n is referred to as Patrick Walsh's neglected love in *The Little Beau's lamentation*, [1727?].

C.

S71 — A satyr. To the author of Namby Pamby, address'd to Amb. P—p's esq; By a lady. [*Dublin*] *Printed in the year 1726.*
½⁰: 1 side, 2 columns.
>*Teerink 923.*

'All ye poets of the age'
>An attack on the author of *Namby Pamby*; in defence of Ambrose Philips. There is no sign that the author knew that Henry Carey wrote *Namby Pamby*.

DT.

S72 — A satyre upon a monstrous peruke gown and band. Written by a k——e. [*Dublin, 173–.*]
½⁰: 1 side, 1 column.
'The excrements which they void all men are dust'
>Ascribed by *Ball* 291 to Swift; rejected by *Williams* 823. The author is intended to be 'a kite' or lawyer; the suggestion is that it represents Richard Bettesworth, satirized by Swift as Sergeant Kite. It is, however, a quite general satire on the pains of the law.

C.

S73 — A satyr upon Allan Ramsay, occasioned upon a report of his translating Horace. [*Edinburgh, 172–?*]
½⁰: 1 side, 1 column.
'D----d brazen face, how could you hope'
E.

— 'A satyr upon drunkeness. [*London*] *Sold by J. Morphew*.' (*WL* Aug 1706)
>No work with this title has been traced; the title may be generalized, or it may be in prose.

S74 — A satyr upon musty-snuff. [*London, 1707.*] (31 May, Luttrell)
½⁰: 1–2, 1 column.
'To all nice beauxs, and nicer ladies, who'
Crawford; ICN(Luttrell).

S75 — A satyr upon old maids. *London, printed by W. Denham, for the author; and are to be sold by J. Morphew, 1713 [1712].* (*PB* 11 Dec)
4⁰: *A² B–C²*; 1–2 3–12.
'When satyrs daily lash with honest rage'

A **satire** upon old maids

> An advertisement on the title is for *Memoirs of the Mint and Queen's Bench* by Marshall Smith; they are advertised together in *PB* and this may also be by Smith.
>
> L(163.1.44, Luttrell, 12 Dec); CLU-C.

S76 —— The second edition. [*London*] *Printed by T. Moore near St. George's Church* S⟨*outhwark*, 1714.⟩
4°: *A*²(±A1) B–C²; *1–2* 3–12.
> A reissue.

ViU(title cropt).

S77 — A satyr upon the present times. *London printed, and sold by J. Morphew*, 1717. (*EvP* 24 Jan)
8°: *A*² B–C⁴; *1–5* 6–19 *20 blk.*
> 'Fixt in the spacious main there lays an isle'

L(164.n.10),MP; CSmH,MH.

> — A satyr upon thirty seven articles, 1701. *See* English men no bastards, 1701.

Satires. The satires of Persius, 1741. *See* Brewster, Thomas.

S78 Satirical. Satyrical and panegyrical instructions to Mr. William Hogarth, painter, on Admiral Vernon's taking Porto Bello with six ships of war only. By A. Marvell, junior. *London, printed for H. Goreham*, 1740. (*GM* May)
2°: *A*² B–E²; *1–3* 4–20. *20 err.*
> 'Hogarth to virtue and to truth a friend'

CLU-C,CtY,DFo,*NN*,TxU.

> — A satirical epistle to Mr. Pope, 1740. *See* Lorleach, —, *Mr.*

> — A satirical essay on modern poets, 1734. *See* Morrice, Bezaleel.

S79 — A satyrical poem on the society of journey-men taylors. [*Dublin*, 172–.]
slip: 1 side, 1 column.
> 'You sorry lousy taylors all'

L(1890.e.5/169).

S80 — A satyrical poem: or, the Beggar's-opera dissected. *London, printed by E. Berington, for J. Wilford*, [1729.] (*MChr* 1 April)
2°: *A*–*B*²; *1–3* 4–8.
> 'Had I the power to will or to indite'

OW; MH.

S81 Satirist. The satirist: in imitation of the fourth satire of the first book of Horace. *London, printed for L.G.* [*Lawton Gilliver*]; *sold by Mrs. Dodd, Mrs. Nutt, and the booksellers of London & Westminster*, 1733. (*GSJ* 7 June)
2°: *A*² B–F²; *1 2–23 24. 24 advt.*
> Latin and English text.
> 'When awful Johnson on th' improving stage'

L(11631.k.5/8),O(3),OW,DT,LdU-B(uncut);
CSmH,CtY,IU,MH(2),TxU+.

S82 —— *Dublin, printed by S. Powell, for George Risk, George Ewing, & William Smith*, 1733.
8°: A–C⁴; *1 2–23 24 blk.*

L(11630.aaa.45/4),O,C,DA,DN+; MH,CtY.

S83 Satirists. The satirists: a satire. Humbly inscrib'd to his grace the Duke of Marlborough. *London, printed for C. Corbett; sold by the pamphlet-sellers of London & Westminster*, [1739.] (*GM, LM* Dec)
2°: *A*² B–D²; *1–3* 4–16.
> No watermark.
> 'A while to satire we have seen a truce---'
> A satire on Pope, Swift, and others.

L(643.m.15/6),LdU-B; CSmH,CtY,ICN(uncut), MH,TxU+.

S84 — [fine paper]
> Watermark: fleur-de-lys.

NjP.

S85 Satirizer. The satyrizer satyriz'd: or a defence of Mr. Britton's musick-meeting. By a lover of musick. *London printed, and are to be sold by the booksellers of London & Westminster*, 1703. (21 April, Luttrell)
2°: 8 pp.
> A reply to *Britton's consort*, 1703.

(*Thorn-Drury.*)

S86 [**Saunders,** —, *Mr.*] An essay on calumny. Humbly inscribed to his royal highness the Prince of Wales. *London, printed for J. Roberts*, 1744. (*GM* June)
2°: *A*¹ B–H² I¹; *i–ii, 1* 2–29 *30 blk.*
> Horizontal chain-lines, no watermark.
> 'Britannia, queen of isles, whose glorious name'
> Early ms. attribution to 'Mr Saunders' in the BaP copy.

L(11602.i.17/9),BaP; OCU.

S87 [—] [fine paper]
> Watermark: fleur-de-lys.

IU.

S88 [**Savage, John.**] Horace to Scaeva. Epist. XVII. book I. imitated. *London, printed for John Brindly*, 1730. (13 May?)
8°: *A*⁴ B–D⁴ E²; *1–5* 6–36. A1 hft.
> Fine engraving of horse in red-brown ink on title. Entered in Bowyer's ledgers under 13 May, 750 copies printed. Listed in *MChr* May.
> 'Savage, I blame not your ambition'
> Listed among his works by Savage in a letter in *Rawlinson*. Dedicated to Lord Malpas.

L(11659.b.67),O,C,E,LdU-B+; CtY,IU(–A1), MH(2),MiU,OCU+.

S89 [**Savage, Richard.**] The authors of the town; a satire: inscribed to the author of the Universal passion. *London, printed for J. Roberts*, 1725. (*MC* June)
2°: *A*² B–E²; *i–iv, 1*–16. A1 hft.
> 'Bright arts, abus'd, like gems, receive their flaws'
> Savage's authorship is clear from his use of certain passages in subsequent poems; see *Poetical works* ed. Tracy (1962) 66f.

L(11602.i.20/1, –A1),O(2, –A1),*HU*,WrP;
CSmH,ICN(–A1),MH(2),TxU(2, 1 uncut).

Savage, R. The bastard

S90 — The bastard. A poem, inscribed with all due reverence to Mrs. Bret, once countess of Macclesfield. *London, printed for T. Worrall*, 1728. (*MChr* 18 April)
2°: *A*² B–C²; *i–vi*, 1–6. A1 hft, advt.
    Rothschild 1815.
'In gayer hours, when high my fancy ran'
L(C.57.h.4),O,OW,EtC,LdU-B(–A1); CSmH, MH,TxU(2, 1–A1).

S91 — — The second edition. *London, printed for T. Worrall*, 1728. (*Mist* 11 May)
2°: *A*² B–C²; *i–vi*, 1–6. A1 hft, advt.
    Apparently a reimpression.
TxU.

S92 — — The third edition. *London, printed for T. Worrall*, 1728. (*Mist* 8 June)
2°: *A*² B–C²; *i–vi*, 1–6. A1 hft, advt.
    Apparently a reimpression.
C,LdU-B.

S93 — — The fourth edition. *London, printed for T. Worrall*, 1728. (*Mist* 3 Aug)
2°: *A*² B–C²; *i–vi*, 1–6. A1 hft, advt.
    Apparently a reimpression. The previous 'editions' have a fool's cap watermark; this and the following have pro patria. Though some 'editions' may merely be the result of variant titles, the change in paper shows there was some reprinting.
BaP; CtY.

S94 — — The fifth edition. *London, printed for T. Worrall*, 1728.
2°: *A*² B–C²; *i–vi*, 1–6. A1 hft, advt.
    Apparently a reimpression. '16 Bastard, a poem, the whole of the copy' formed lot 61 of the trade sale of Thomas Worrall, 10 Nov 1737 (cat. at O-JJ), sold to Birt for 13s. 0d.
TxU.

S95 — — *Dublin, printed by S. Harding*, 1728.
8°: *A*⁴; 1–4 5–8.
L(12274.e.1/4),DA; CLU-C.

S96 — — *Dublin, printed by S. Powell, for T. Benson, & P. Crampton*, 1728.
8°: *A*⁸; *i–vi*, 1 2–9 10. A1 hft; 10 advt.
O,DA,DN(2, 1–A1),MR-C; CtY.

S97 — — *Dublin, printed by Edw. Bate, for James Kelburn*, 1743.
8°: *A*⁴ B⁴; 1–7 8–15 16. A1 hft; 16 advt.
O,C,DA; CLU-C.

S98 — The convocation: or, a battle of pamphlets. A poem. *London, printed for E. Young; sold by J. Morphew*, 1717. (*PB* 27 Aug)
8°: *A*¹ B–E⁴ F¹; *i–ii*, 1–33 34 blk. 33 err.
    Rothschild 1813.
'When vertue's standard ecclesiasticks bear'
L(161.m.33); PP,TxU.

S99 — An epistle to the right honourable Sir Robert Walpole, knight of the most noble order of the garter. *London, printed for J. Roberts*, 1732. (*GSJ* 28 Aug)
2°: *A*² B–D²; 1–4 5–16. A1 hft; 16 err.
    Advertised in *Volunteer laureat* II & IV as 'Religion and liberty: an epistle...'; no copy seen with that title.
'Still let low wits, who sense nor honour prize'
CSmH(uncut),KU,MH(–A1),NjP,TxU(uncut).

S100 — London and Bristol compar'd. A satire: written in Newgate, Bristol, by the late Richard Savage, esq; *London, printed for M. Cooper*, 1744 [1743]. (*GM* Dec)
2°: *A*² < B²; 1–3 4–8.
    Horizontal chain-lines.
'Two sea-port cities mark Britannia's fame'
L(162.n.26); CSmH,MH.

S101 — — The second edition. *London, printed for M. Cooper*, 1744.
2°: *A*² < B²; 1–2 3–8.
    Apparently a reimpression.
O(title cropt).

[—] Nature in perfection; or, the mother unveil'd, 1728. *See* N10.

S102 — Of public spirit in regard to public works. An epistle to his royal highness Frederick, prince of Wales. *London, printed for R. Dodsley*, 1737. (25 June)
2°: *A*–B² C–E² F¹; *i–iv*, 1 2–18.
    Rothschild 1818. Publication date from *Straus, Dodsley*; listed in *LM* June. A revision, greatly enlarged, of *A poem on the birth-day*, [1736.]
'Great hope of Britain! – Here the muse essays'
L(643.m.15/29),O; CSmH,ICU,IU,MH,TxU.

S103 — — *Dublin, printed by James Hoey*, 1738.
8°: *A*⁸; *i–iv*, 1 2–12. 12 advt.
GU.

S104 — — The second edition. *London, printed for R. Dodsley*, 1739. (*LDP* 21 May)
2°: *A*–B²(–A1, B²+A1.B1) C²(–C1+ˣC²) D–E² F¹; *i–iv*, 1 2–18.
    A reissue with revisions; the cancel A1 and first leaf of text B1 are conjugate, surrounding the original A2; two leaves of text signed 'C' replace the original C1.
O.

S105 — On the departure of the Prince and Princess of Orange. A poem. *London, printed for Lawton Gilliver*, 1734. (*GM*, *LM* July)
2°: *A*² B² C¹; 1–5 6–10.
'Mild rose the morn, the face of nature bright'
L(643.m.15/22); MH.

S106 — A poem on the birth-day of the Prince of Wales. Humbly inscribed to his royal highness. *London, printed for J. Roberts*, [1736.] (*LM* Jan)
2°: *A*² < B²; 1–2 3–8.
    In the L copy, B1 is unsigned. Revised and greatly enlarged as *Of public spirit*, 1737.

Savage, R. A poem on the birth-day

'Awake, my muse! awake! expand thy wing!'
L(643.m.15/25); CSmH.

S107 — A poem, sacred to the glorious memory of our late most gracious sovereign lord King George. Inscribed to the right honourable George Dodington, esq; *London, printed for Samuel Chapman; sold by J. Roberts,* 1727. (*MC* June)
2°: A–B²; *1–2* 3–8.
'Let gaudy mirth, to the blithe carrol-song'
TxU(2).

S108 — — *Dublin, printed by S. Powell, for G. Risk, G. Ewing, & W. Smith,* 1729.
8°: *A*⁴; *1–3* 4–8.
L(12274.e.1/6),DN,DT.

[—] A poem to the memory of Mrs. Oldfield, 1730. *See* P666.

S109 — The progress of a divine. A satire. *London, printed for the author; sold by the booksellers of London & Westminster,* 1735. (*SR* 17 April)
2°: *A*(2 ll) B–F² G¹; *1–3* 4–26. 2, 26 err.
Rothschild 1817. Apparently the two leaves of A are conjugate in some copies; a copy at LdU-B has no errata on A1ᵛ. A possible explanation would be that the enlarged list of errata was added in the course of printing A², and additional cancel title-leaves with the errata were then printed; the LdU-B copy escaped cancellation. Entered in *SR* by Savage; deposit copies at L,O,E,AdU,SaU. Listed in *GM* April.
'All priests are not the same, be understood!'
L(643.m.14/7),O(2),E,AdU,LdU-B+; CSmH, CtY(uncut),ICN,MH,TxU(3)+.

S110 — To his most sacred majesty, this poem is humbly inscrib'd by his majesty's most obedient, dutiful, and loyal subject to command, R. Savage. [*London?* 1714/15.]
⅛°: 1 side, 1 column.
The copy seen is cut and mounted; it may possibly have been printed with another short poem.
'Had I with Plato's eloquence been fill'd'
Addressed to the Pretender.
O (MS. Rawl. poet. 203, fol. 90ᵇ).

S111 — Verses, occasion'd by the right honourable the lady Viscountess Tyrconnel's recovery at Bath. *London, printed for A. Millar; sold by J. Roberts,* 1730. (*MChr* May)
2°: *A*² B²; *1–2* 3–8.
'Where Thames with pride beholds Augusta's charms'
L(643.m.15/10); CSmH,MH,TxU(2).

S112 — The volunteer laureat. A poem. Most humbly address'd to her majesty on her birth-day. *London, printed for John Watts,* 1732. (*GSJ* 1 March)
4°: A–B² C²; *1–5* 6–9 *10–12 blk.* A1 hft.
According to *GM* (1738) 210 Savage received fifty pounds each year from Queen Caroline for these birthday poems.

Savage, R. The volunteer laureat

'Twice twenty tedious moons have roll'd away'
L(643.k.3/11,—A1, C2),O(—C2); CSmH(uncut), DLC(cropt,—A1, C2),MH(—C2),TxU(2, *1*—C2, *1*—A1, C2).

S113 — The volunteer-laureat. Most humbly inscribed to her majesty, on her birth-day... Number II. For the year 1733. To be continued annually. *London, printed for L. Gilliver,* 1733. (*Bee* 8 March)
2°: *A*² B² C¹; *1–4* 5–10. A1 hft.
'Great princess, 'tis decreed!--once ev'ry year'
CSmH,TxU.

S114 — 'The voluntier-laureat. [*London*] Printed for L. Gilliver. Price 6d.' (*GM* March 1734)

S115 — The volunteer-laureat. Most humbly inscribed to her majesty, on her birth-day... Number IV. For the year 1735. To be continued annually. *London, printed for L. Gilliver,* 1735. (*GM* March)
2°: *A*² B²; *1–3* 4–8. 2 advt.
'In youth no parent nurs'd my infant songs'
L(643.m.15/24); CSmH(uncut).

S116 — The volunteer laureat. A poem. On her majesty's birth-day. For the year 1736. *London, printed for R. Dodsley,* 1736.
2°: *A*² B¹; *1–2* 3–5 *6 blk.*
'Lo! the mild sun salutes the opening spring'
CSmH,*NN-B.*

S117 — The volunteer laureat: an ode on her majesty's birth-day... Numb. VI. for the year 1737. Continued annually by permission. [*London,* 1737.]
8°: *A*²; *1–3; 4 blk.*
Title in half-title form.
'Ye guardian pow'rs! that ether rove'
L(643.k.3/16).

S118 — Volunteer laureat, number VII. For the first of March, 1738. A poem sacred to the memory of the late queen. Humbly address'd to his majesty. [*London*] *Printed by E. Cave, for R. Dodsley,* 1738. (*LDP* 2 March)
2°: π² A² B¹; *i–ii, 1–3* 4–7 *8 blk.* π1 hft.
In *CBEL* as 'A poem sacred to the memory of her majesty'.
'Oft has the muse, on this distinguish'd day'
CSmH,TxU.

S119 — The wanderer: a poem. In five canto's. *London, printed for J. Walthoe,* 1729. (*MChr* 4 Jan)
8°: A⁴ B–K⁸ L⁴; *i–iii* iv–viii, *1* 2–149 *150–152.* 149 err; 150–152 advt.
Watermark: bird; 'Price two shillings' on title. Rothschild 1816. D7 appears to be a cancel, and there seem to be more in sheet E not fully identified; certainly E6, 7 are replaced by conjugate E6.7. Printed by Samuel Richardson (*Sale* 80).
'Fain wou'd my verse, Tyrconnel, boast thy name'
L(11633.bbb.32/2),O(2, 1 lacks A2–4),EU(uncut), LdU-B,*NeU;* CSmH,CtY,ICN,IU,MH+.

S120 — [fine paper]
No watermark: no price on title.
LVA-D; CU,TxU.

Save-alls

S121 Save-alls. The save-alls. [*London*, 1710.] (8 May, Luttrell)

½°: 2 sides, 1 column.

Title in capitals and lower-case.

'While faction with its baleful breath proclaims'

'Upon the bishops that were for Dor Sachevrel, for them', Luttrell. Cf. *An answer to the Six save-alls*, 1710.

L(1872.a.1/163),O,MC; MH(Luttrell),NN,OCU, *Harding.*

S122 — [*idem*] The six save-alls. [*London*, 1710.]

½°: 2 sides, 1 column.

Printed from the same type as the preceding, but with some censorings, e.g. 'H—ly' for 'Hoadly' (line 4), 'A—A' for 'ANNA' (line 9). Since all other editions print these in full, this may be the earliest state.

L(1871.f.3/21).

S123 — The save-alls. [*London?* 1710.]

½°: 2 sides, 1 column.

Title in capitals throughout.

Rothschild.

S124 — — [*London?*] *Printed in the year* 1710.

½°: 1 side, 2 columns.

O(cropt).

S125 — — Or, the bishops who voted for Dr. Sacheverell. *Edinburgh, printed by James Watson, and sold at his shop*, 1710.

½°: 2 sides, 1 column.

This edition omits the first 28 lines.

OW,E,AdU; CLU-C.

Sawney. Sawney. An heroic poem. Occasion'd by the Dunciad, 1728. *See* Ralph, James.

S126 — Sawney and Colley, a poetical dialogue: occasioned by a late letter from the laureat of St. James's, to the Homer of Twickenham. Something in the manner of Dr. Swift. *London, printed for J.H.* [*Huggonson*] *in Sword and Buckler Court, on Ludgate-Hill*, [1742.] (*DP* 31 Aug)

2°: π¹ A–E² F¹; i–ii, 1 2–21 22 blk.

All copies have a ms. correction on p. 12, line 15.

'One morning, in his Twickenham grott'

Occasioned by *A letter from Mr. Cibber to Mr. Pope*, 1742, in prose.

L(643.l.28/5),LVA-D; DFo,ICN,TxU.

Saxonas. Saxonas ac Anglos olim Germania fudit, [1712?/13.] *See* Pitcairne, Archibald.

Say, Samuel. Poems on several occasions: and two critical essays... *London, printed by John Hughs*, 1745.

4°: pp. xxiv, 174.   L,O; CtY,MH.

Scaffold. The scaffold lately erected in Westminster-Hall, 1701. *See* Settle, Elkanah.

Scalled

S127 Scalled. ⟨The⟩ scall'd crow's nest. A very old tale. [*Dublin*, 1734/35.]

½°: 2 sides, 1 column.

Teerink 974; *Williams* 1134. Before 1736, when it was reprinted in *S—t contra omnes*.

'In antient days, as sages write'

Ascribed to Swift by *Ball* 290, but questioned by Williams, who relates it to the verse war between Charles Carthy and William Dunkin which broke out in 1734.

C(cropt).

S128 — — a tale. *London, printed: and Dublin: re-printed in the year* 1748. (May?)

½°: 1 side, 2 columns.

There is no evidence of a London edition at this time.

DN(ms. date, May); CtY.

Scamnum. Scamnum, ecloga, 1740. *See* King, William, *principal of St. Mary Hall.*

— Scamnum, ecloga: or, the pastoral politicians, 1744. *See* The bench, 1741–.

S129 Scamperer. The scamperer; or, Gambol's gallop to France to save him from the ax in Great Britain. With his diary... To which is added a true copy of my Lord Bolingbroke's letter from Dover. *London printed, and sold by S. Keimer, A. Boulter, & J. Harrison*, 1715. (6 April, Luttrell)

2°: (3 ll); 1–5; 6 blk. 5 advt.

'Not many days since'

A satire on Bolingbroke.

OCU(Luttrell).

Scandalizade. The Scandalizade, 1750. *See* Morgan, Macnamara.

S130 Scandalous. Scandalous Fuller rewarded, or; the impostures doom. With Fuller's lamentation and confession, &c. To the tune of, Down with 'em, &c. *London, 'printed for Whitherington and Jones, two statues in Rome'*, 1702.

½°: 1 side, 2 columns.

On the other side a piece of prose, obscured by the pasting of the half-sheet to the album.

'Let knaves and fools lament'

On William Fuller the impostor, who was fined, pilloried, and sent to Bridewell in 1702.

CM-P.

S131 Scandalum. Scandalum magnatum; or, the general wrong'd. [*London*] *Printed in the year* 1712.

½°: 1 side, 2 columns.

'With indignation let my muse exclaim'

In defence of Marlborough.

MH(cropt),NjP.

Scarronides. Scarronides: or, Virgil travestie, 1717. *See* Smith, John.

Scating. Scating: a poem, 1720. *See* Newcomb, Thomas.

S132 **Scelus.** Scelus's ghost: or, the lawyer's warning piece. A ballad, to the tune of William and Margaret. By J.M. S.S.S. *London, printed for W. Owen,* 1748. (*GM* June)
4°: B–C⁴ (B2 as 'B'); *1–3* 4–16.
''Twas at the dark and silent hour'
L(11630.c.8/22; 11602.gg.24/13); NjP,OCU.

'Scheffer, Frederick.' The toast, an epic poem. . . Written in Latin by Frederick Scheffer, 1732–. *See* King, William, *principal of St. Mary Hall.*

S133 **Scheld.** The Scheld: a poem on the late glorious victory, obtain'd by his grace the Duke ⟨of⟩ Marlborough, and Prince Eugene of Savoy, over the French forc⟨es⟩ in Flanders, together with the notable advantages, concomitant a⟨nd⟩ subsequent thereunto, viz. the raising of the siege of Brussels t⟨he⟩ surrender of the citadel of Lisle, the taking of Ghent and Bruges, &c. *London, printed for the author T. S—,* [1709.]
½°: 1 side, 2 columns.
The imprint has been inked over in the copy seen.
'Heroes like stars when single radient shine'
Probably by 'T------s S---------on' who wrote *A condolatory poem. . .to her most sacred Britannick majesty,* 1708.
L(C.121.g.9/150).

'Schethrum, Andrew.' The Northumberland prophecy, 1715. *See* Duckett, George.

[**Schomberg, Isaac.**] The Battiad, 1750. *See* M172.

S134 **Schomberg, Ralph.** An ode on the present rebellion dedicated to her royal highness the Princess of Orange. *Rotterdam,* 1746.
4°: A–B⁴ C⁴(–C4); *1–5* 6–21 *22 blk.*
The imprint is apparently correct; it is not clear whether this is the edition listed in *BM, LM* June without any publisher named.
'Do thou, fair liberty, descend'
DG.

S135 —— *Rotterdam, printed 1746. Edinburgh, re-printed by R. Fleming,* 1747.
8°: π¹ *A*⁴ B⁴ C¹; *1–5* 6–19 *20 blk.* π1 hft.
E,AdU,MP.

S136 **Schoolboy.** A school-boy's elegy upon the death of the right honourable the Earl of Sunderland; with an epitaph. *London, printed for T. Payne,* 1722. (May)
2°: A² B¹; *1–2* 3–6.
Drop-head title on p. 3 'The Earl of Sunderland's eleygy[!]'. Advertised for publication 'next week' in *PB* 28 April.

'Cælestial pow'rs, that rule all earthly things' *CtY.*

S137 **Schoolmaster.** The school-master's letter: or, a rod for the author of the Election. [*Dublin*] *Printed for Halhed Garland,* [1749.]
½°: 2 sides, 2 columns.
A series of booksellers' advertisements occupy the last column and a quarter.
'Well! – has your spite broke out at length?'
Introductory letter signed 'Quintinus Plagosus'. On Charles Lucas and a satirical play, *The election.*
C.

Schoolmistress. The school-mistress, a poem, 1742. *See* Shenstone, William.

Schopper, Hartmann.
The crafty courtier: or the fable of Reinard the fox: newly done into English verse, from the antient Latin iambics of Hartm. Schopperus, 1706. *See* C493.

Science. Science: an epistle on it's decline and revival, 1750. *See* Fortescue, James.

S137·5 **Scipio.** 'Scipio Britannicus: the scourge of France. An heroick poem, inscrib'd to the immortal glory of his grace John duke of Marlborough. . . Also a Latin poem annex'd, to the Christian Hannibal the most illustrious Prince Eugene of Savoy, &c. [*London*] *Sold by B. Bragge.* Price 6*d.*' (*DC* 8 March 1709)
Advertised in *The supplement* 7 March (for publication 'tomorrow') as 'By T. G. Physician in Essex'. The same author wrote 'Ελεοθριαμβος: *being England's triumphs,* 1698 (*Wing* G61).

'Scot, Ar.' The vision compylit in Latin be a most lernit clerk, 1748. *See* Ramsay, Allan.

S138 **Scotch.** Scotch-cloath, or occasional-conformity. *London, printed in the year* 1711. (11 July, Luttrell)
½°: 1 side, 2 columns.
Teerink 855; *Williams* 1096.
'Occasionally as we discourst'
Crum O9, recording its printing in *Poems on affairs of state* III (1704) 390. Attributed to Swift by Ball, who suggested it was the verse referred to in the *Journal to Stella,* 23 Dec 1711. Williams did not accept the attribution, which is negated by Luttrell's dating. An attack on occasional conformists, perhaps reprinted with reference to the bill before parliament.
L(1876.f.19/20),LLP; ICN(Luttrell),MH.

S139 —— *Dublin re-printed [by C. Carter] at the Old-Post-office in Fishamble-street,* [1711.]
½°: 1 side, 2 columns.

On the other side, *The queen's and my lord of Oxford's new toast*, [1711.]
C,DG,DT.

S140 — The Scotch lords welcome to England: or the union dialogue, between a Scotch-man and an English-man, on the coronation of Queen Anne. To the tune of, Over the hills, and far away. [*London?* 1707?]
½°: 1 side, 2 columns.
    Two rough woodcuts at head. On the other side of the Crawford copy (now split and mounted) was *When we shall have peace...* (London, printed by D. Brown, 1711).
'Come let us joyful anthems raise'
    In praise of the union.
DG(cropt); Crawford.

S141 — The Scotch mist clearing up: or, England will not be wet to the skin. A timely new test ballad... *London, printed for W. Bickerton*, 1745. (*GM* Oct)
2°: *A*² C²; *1–3* 4–8.
'Friends, Britons, and countrymen, hark ye draw near'
GM; CSmH.

— The Scotch prophecy, 1716. *See* Tickell, Thomas [An imitation].

— Scotch tast[!] in vista's, [1741/42.] *See* Bramston, James.

'Scoticus.' A poem on the election of a knight of the shire of Edinburgh, [1744.] *See* P613.

S142 Scotland. Scotland's tears. An elegy, lamenting the death of the honourable Sir David Dalrymple of Hailes... who died at London December 3. 1721. *Edinburgh printed, and sold by Alexander Davidson*, 1721.
4°: *A*⁴; *1–2* 3–7; *8 blk.*
    Title in mourning borders.
'Complaints like ours thro' Tyber's vales did fly'
EP(uncut).

S143 — ⟨Scot⟩lands tears, or Scotland bemoaning the loss of her antient priviledges upon consideration that the house ⟨of⟩ commons have past the bill discharging all ⟨foreign⟩ liquors &c. to be exported into England after the first of May. [*Edinburgh*, 1707.]
½°: 1 side, 2 columns.
    Mourning borders.
'What dismal news? what sad allarms do sound?'
    An excuse for a complaint against the union.
L(8142.k.1/19, mutilated).

'Scoto-Britannus.' An epistle to Mr. Pope, 1716. *See* E404.

Scots. A Scots answer to a British vision, [1706.] *See* Hamilton, John, *baron Belhaven*.

S144 — A Scots excise-man described. [*Edinburgh*, 1707/–.]

½°: 1 side, 1 column.
'Whence did this dreadfull monster come?'
E.

— A Scots ode, to the British Antiquarians, [1726.] *See* Ramsay, Allan.

S145 — A Scots poem: or a new-years gift, from a native of the universe, to his fellow-animals in Albania. *Edinburgh, printed anno dom.* 1707. (Jan?)
8°: A–B⁸ C²; *i–vi*, 1–30.
    Moore 137.
'Now are our noble representers met'
    Epistle to the reader signed 'Philo-patris'. Ascribed to Defoe on internal evidence by C. E. Burch, *PQ* 22 (1943) 51, who dates it between 1–14 Jan. Accepted by Moore. Replied to in *A short satyre on that native of the universe, the Albanian animal*, [1707], one copy of which has a ms. note suggesting it is answering Defoe. The attribution seems plausible.
E(2).

— Scots songs, [1720/21.] *See* Ramsay, Allan.

S146 [**Scott, Thomas.**] England's danger and duty, represented in a copy of verses on the present rebellion in Scotland. *London printed, and sold by J. Waugh, and also sold at the pamphlet-shops in London & Westminster*, 1745. (*GM* Nov)
2°: *A*² B²; *1–2* 3–8.
'Treason too long contriv'd, too late believ'd'
    Early ms. note in the MH copy 'By the revd Mr. Scott dissenting minister at Ipswich'.
AdU; MH.

S147 — A father's instructions to his son. *London, printed for R. Dodsley; sold by M. Cooper*, 1748. (21 Jan)
4°: *A*⁴ B–C⁴ D²; *1–4* 5–27 *28 blk.* A1 hft.
    Publication date from *Straus, Dodsley*.
'Attend, my son; while a fond father's care'
    Dedication signed.
L(11632.g.39; 11630.c.8/12,—A1; 162.l.49,—A1); CSmH(—A1),CU,ICN,NjP.

S148 — Reformation a poem. *London printed, and sold by J. Waugh*, 1746. (*LM* April)
4°: *A*⁴ B–C⁴ D¹; *1–2* 3–26.
    Listed in *LM* as sold by A. Dodd.
'Has earth no judge? Or has that judge no rod'
LDW,O; PU.

S149 [**Scott, Sir William.**] Epitaphium viri reverendissimi D. Georgii Meldrumii...qui multo cum bonorum luctu decessit XII cal. Martias anno æræ Christianæ MDCCIX. [*Edinburgh*, 1709.]
1°: 1 side, 1 column.
    Mourning borders.
'Melleus hic situs est Meldrumius, ore disertus'
    At foot, 'P. dolens G.S.' Almost certainly by Sir William Scott, the only Edinburgh Latinist with these initials.
E(2).

Scourge

Scourge. A scourge for the author of the satyr, 1725. *See* Owens, Samuel.

S150 — A scourge for the incendiary. *Dublin, printed for Joseph Cotter,* 1749.
12°: A⁶ (A2–4 as 'A, A2, A3'); *1–3* 4–11 *12 blk.*
'Fraught with rebellions, feuds, and murthers fell'
On Charles Lucas?
O(3); MH.

'**Scrawl, Ned.**' Godly Sarah, or, the sighing sister, 1737. *See* G206.

S151 **Screen.** The screen. A simile. [*London,* 1742.] (March)
½°: 1 side, 2 columns.
Large engraving at head, titled 'A new screen for an old one or the screen of screens' and dated 'March 18. 1741/2'. Advertised in *LEP* 16 March; the verses were printed in *LEP* 11 March.
'Dear William, did'st thou never go'
Ms. note in the O copy, 'supposed to be written by Ld Quarendon', i.e. George Henry Lee, subsequently earl of Lichfield. An imitation of Prior's *Simile*: although Walpole is out of office, he still pulls the strings.
L(P&D 2540),O; NNP.

S152 **Screw.** The screw-plot discover'd: or, St. Paul's preserv'd. *London, printed in the year* 1710.
8°: A⁸; *1–2* 3–16.
'No more I write of war and arms'
LG,EtC; InU,MB.

'**Scribble, Timothy.**' The faction, a tale, 1740. *See* Cowper, Ashley.

—– High boys up go we!, 1741. *See* Cowper, Ashley.

— The Norfolk poetical miscellany, 1744. *See* Cowper, Ashley.

— The progress of physic, 1743. *See* Cowper, Ashley.

Scribblers. The scriblers lash'd, 1718. *See* Ramsay, Allan.

Scribimus. Scribimus indocti doctique poemata passim, [1737.] *See* Brodie, Joseph.

S153 **Scribleriad.** The Scribleriad. Being an epistle to the dunces, on renewing their attack upon Mr. Pope, under their leader the laureat. By Scriblerus. *London, printed for W. Webb,* 1742. (*LEP* 2 Oct)
8°: A⁴(±A1) B–C⁴ D⁴(–D4); *1–2* 3–29 *30.* 30 advt.
In some copies (e.g. CtY) there is a period, not a comma, in the title after 'Pope'.
'The wits are jarring, and the witlings strive'
LVA-D,BaP; CtY,DFo,IU,TxU(2).

'**Scriblerus**'

'**Scriblerus.**' The marrow of the Tickler's works, 1748. *See* M114.

— The Scribleriad, 1742. *See* S153.

'**Scriblerus, Erasmus.**' The Tamiad, 1733. *See* T35.

'**Scriblerus Maximus.**' The art of scribling, 1733. *See* A326.

'**Scriblerus Quartus.**' The Bays miscellany, or Colley triumphant, [1730.] *See* Cooke, Thomas, *1703–1756.*

'**Scriblerus Tertius.**' The candidates for the bays, 1730. *See* Cooke, Thomas, *1703–1756.*

— The hard-us'd poet's complaint, [1750.] *See* H48.

S154 **Scriptural.** The scriptural history of Joseph and his brethren, turn'd into heroick verse: wherein the whole narration of his life is declared in the following arguments… *London printed, and sold by J. Bradford,* [1703.] (30 April, Luttrell)
1°: 1 side, 4 columns.
In twelve sections, each headed with an illustrative woodcut.
'In Canaan dwelt one Jacob call'd by name'
MH(Luttrell).

S155 **Scrub.** Scrub, scrub: a poem in praise of the itch: with a word or two in favour of brimstone. *London printed, and sold [by Samuel Bunchley?] at the publishing-office in Bearbinder-lane,* 1707.
½°: *1–2,* 1 column.
A ms. correction in line 11 changes 'Putaneous monarch!' to 'Cutaneous…'
'Hail subtile heat! which pleasure brings'
DG; DFo,*TxU.*

S156 —— *London, printed by R. Wilson, near Ludgate-hill,* 1707.
½°: 1 side, 2 columns.
Line 11 reads 'Lutaneous monarch'.
L(C.121.g.9/148).

'**Scrubb, Timothy,** *of Ragg-Fair.*' Desolation: or, the fall of gin, 1736. *See* Budgell, Eustace.

S157 **Scrutiny.** The scrutiny: with a further dissertation upon Horace, the first ode. Inscrib'd to the right honourable the Lord Hallifax. *London, printed for R. Burrough & J. Baker; sold by E. Sanger,* 1708.
8°: A–B⁴; *1–2* 3–16.
The dissertation occupies pp. 3–12.
'Some in the ring delight to guide the rein'
L(841.i.21/4, lacks B4); TxU.

S158 — The scrutiny: with the second ode, first satyr, and a short dissertation upon Horace. The satyr, inscrib'd to the right honourable the Lord Hallifax. *London, printed for R. Burrough & J. Baker, & E. Sanger,* 1708.

The scrutiny

8°: C–E⁴ (C2 as 'C'); *i–ii,* 17–25 *26 blk,* 1–12.
A continuation of the preceding.
Ode 2: 'Long has the dreadful tempest rag'd'
Satire 1: 'Whence is't, Mæcenas, that so few approve'
Longleat.

Sea. The sea piece, 1749. *See* Kirkpatrick, James.

Seagrave, Robert. Hymns for Christian worship, partly composed and partly collected from various authors. *London, printed in the year* 1742. (*GM* Jan)
8°: pp. 82.
Recorded in the reprint of 1860.

— — The second edition; with additions. *London, printed in the year* 1742.
8°: pp. 90.   L.
Original poems on pp. 1–46.

— — The third edition. *London, printed in the year* 1744.
12°: pp. iv, 112.   DT.
A fourth edition of 1748 (12°: pp. 156) is recorded in the reprint of 1860.

S159 — The peace of Europe. A congratulatory poem. Inscrib'd to the right honourable Sir Robert Walpole. *London, printed for J. Roberts,* 1732. (*GSJ* 11 Jan)
2°: *A*² B–C²; *i–iv, 1* 2–8.
'Whilst guardful Britain with majestic care'
L(11646.w.16); CLU-C,CtY,ICU.

S160 — — The second edition. *London, printed for J. Roberts,* 1732.
2°: *A*² B–C²; *i–iv, 1* 2–8.
Apparently a reimpression or press-variant title.
WcC.

S161 — The state of Europe, an occasional poem. *London, printed by J. Bettenham,* 1728. (*MChr* 29 May)
2°: *A*² B² *C*¹; *i–ii, 1–9 10 blk.*
'Whilst British council, steer'd with arduous care'
NjP.

S162 Seamen. The seamen's sorrow, an elegy, on the much lamented death of Admiral John Benbow, who died of his late wounds at Port Royal in Jamaica on the 4th of November. 1702. *London, printed for J. Wilkins,* [1702/03.]
½°: 1 side, 2 columns.
Mourning headpiece and borders.
'England lament at Benbows fate severe'
CSmH.

S163 Search. A search after honesty a poem. [*Edinburgh?*] *Printed in the year* 1706.
4°: π² < A⁴; *1–2* 3–12.
The collation is tentative. Pp. 3–4 print 'By a friend on the following poem'.

A search after honesty

'In silent shades, upon the bank of Thames'
EN,GM.

S164 Seasonable. Seasonable admonitions. A satire. Most humbly address'd to the right honourable ****** *******. *London, printed for J. Roberts,* 1740. (*GM, LM* May)
2°: *A*¹ B–D² *E*¹; *1–2* 3–15 *16 blk.*
'Satire's my verse; my lord, a friendly ear'
L(1489.m.13),O,LdU-B; MH,OCU.

S165 — A seasonable advice, to all who encline to go in pirrating; drawn from what has happ'ned to Captain Green, as it were from his own mouth, one of that rank. To the tune of, To the weaver if ye go, &c. [*Edinburgh,* 1705.]
½°: 1 side, 2 columns.
'My countrymen who do intend'
Thomas Green was executed for piracy at Leith, 11 April 1705.
E.

S166 — A seasonable rebuke to the playhouse rioters, contained in two new prologues... To which is prefixed, a petitionary dedication to the fair members of the Shakespear-club. *London, printed for C. Corbett,* 1740. (3 March?)
4°: *A*⁴ B⁴; *1–9* 10–16.
'Attend, illustrious wights, whose favourite joy'
'Friends! Britons! Countrymen! I pray from whence'
After the riot at Drury Lane, 23 Jan 1740.
L(11630.c.13/20, ms. date ⟨3?⟩ March); TxU.

— Seasonable reproof, a satire, in the manner of Horace, 1735–. *See* Miller, James.

— A seasonable sketch of an Oxford reformation, 1717. *See* Ward, Edward.

S167 Second. A second defence of the Scotish vision. [*Edinburgh,* 1706.] (Dec?)
½°: 1 side, 1 column.
'How stronge's thy sense! How charming are thy strains!'
In answer to [Defoe] *A reply to the Scots answer to the British vision,* [1706.]
L(8142.k.1/18),E(6); InU,MH.

S168 — A second dialogue between G--s E-e and B--b D-----n. *London, printed for W. Webb,* 1743. (*DP* 3 May)
2°: *A*² < B²; *1–2* 3–8.
Rothschild 2579.
'When last we met, you sir, thro' manly pride'
Giles Earle to Bubb Dodington, in imitation of [Sir Charles Hanbury Williams] *A dialogue between G--s E----e and B--b D---n,* 1741.
L(11630.h.19),O(2),LdU-B; CSmH,CtY,MH, NjP,OCU+.

— Second dialogue entre deux freres, [1707.] *See* Dialogue entre deux freres, 1707.

S169 — A second elegy on the much lamented death of the reverend and worthy Mr. David Blair, minister

A **second** elegy...on David Blair

of the gospel in Edinburgh who died the 10th of June 1710. [*Edinburgh, 1710.*]
½°: 1 side, 1 column.
 Mourning borders.
'Hence goes a lamp of light, a son of thunder'
E.

S170 — A second elegy upon the most lamentable death of the right honourable Sir James Stewart of Goodtrees, her majesty's advocat, who departed this life, May 1st. 1713. In the 78 year of his age. [*Edinburgh, 1713.*]
½°: 1 side, 1 column.
 Mourning borders.
'Let Scotland mourn, the state and church have lost'
E(2).

— A second epistle to Mr. Tickell, [1718.] *See* Burnet, *Sir* Thomas.

— The second part of Absalom and Achitophel, 1709. *See* Tate, Nahum.

S171 — The second part of King Edward and the cobler. To the tune of the Abbot of Canterbury. [*London? 1712?*]
slip: 1 side, 1 column.
'King Edward, who lately at Windsor had been'
 Apparently a sequel to [James Craggs] *King Edward's ghost*, [1712?].
Harding.

S172 — The second part of the Apparition. A poem. *London printed, and sold by the booksellers of London, and Mrs. Dod at Westminster,* 1710.
8°: *A*⁴ B–C⁴; *1–5* 6–24. A1 hft.
'No sooner Satan in the mist withdrew'
 A satirical continuation of [Abel Evans] *The apparition*, 1710.
O(–A1),*OM*,DT(–A1); CtY(2,–A1),ICN (–A1),NN(–A1),*PU*.

S173 — The second part of the Fair quakers: a poem. *London printed for John Morphew,* 1714 [1713]. (*PB* 12 Dec)
2°: *A*² B–D²; *i–iv,* 1–11 *12 blk.*
Rothschild 392.
'Begin, O grateful muse, a second strain'
 A continuation of [John Bingley] *The fair quakers,* 1713; internal references and an advertisement in *PB* 15 Jan 1714 make it clear that this is by another hand.
L(1481.f.19/10, uncut).

— The second part of the Locusts, 1704. *See* The locusts, 1704.

— The second part of the Pulpit-fool, 1707. *See* Dunton, John.

S174 — The second part of the Rare show. [*London? 1714.*]
slip: 1 side, 1 column.
'Since, shentlemans, my rare show hit so pat'
 In praise of the fall of tories and Jacobites. A

The **second** part of the Rare show

sequel to (rather than a second part of) *The rare show,* [1713.]
O(imprint cropt?).

— The second part of the Totness address, [1735.] *See* The speech englished, [1735.]

— A second poem on the riding the franchises, [172–.] *See* Nelson, Henry (N22).

S175 — A second poem, to Dr. Jo——n S——t. *Dublin, printed in the year* 1725.
½°: 1 side, 1 column.
Teerink 1208.
'When mighty chiefs, for mighty deeds renown'd'
 In praise of Swift and his campaign against Wood's halfpence.
L(C.121.g.8/44),Rothschild.

— The second satire of the second book of Horace paraphrased, 1735. *See* Pope, Alexander.

S176 — 'Second thoughts... [*London*] *Printed for John Baker.*' [1713/14.]
 An advertisement in *PB* 15 Jan 1714 for John Bingley's *The fair quakers* and for the second part by another hand ends 'N.B. A poem call'd, Second thoughts, printed for John Baker, is spurious, and not writ by either of the authors'.

— A second volume of the writings of the author of the True-born Englishman, 1705–. *See* Defoe, Daniel.

S177 **Secret.** The secret history of an old shoe. Inscribed to the most wondrous-wonderful of all wonderful men and lovers. *Dublin, printed: London, reprinted by J. Dickenson; sold at the pamphlet-shops,* 1734. (*GM* April)
2°: *A*¹ B–E² F¹; *3–5* 6–22. 22 err.
 Verse mixed with prose. Probably there was no Dublin edition.
'Despising all the idle cant'
 A satire on Walpole, Maria Skerret and Lady Mary Wortley Montagu.
L(11631.k.18),O,OW,E; CSmH,MH,OCU,TxU.

— The secret history of bubbies, 1733. *See* 'Jones, Jasper.'

S178 **Secretary.** Secretary Janus, a dialogue between Simon lord Frazer of Lovat, and J. M--r--y, secretary to the late Pretender. *London, printed for, and sold by G. Foster,* 1747. (*BM* April)
2°: *A*² < B¹; *1–3* 4–6.
'As sly old Lovat to the Tow'r was led'
 On Sir John Murray, who turned king's evidence against Lord Lovat.
L(1959),*DrU-U*; CSmH,MH.

S179 **Secrets.** The secrets of a woman's heart. An epistle from a friend to Signior F-----lli. Occasion'd by the epistle of Mrs C--- P-----ps, to the angelick signior F-----lli. *London, printed for E. Cook; sold at the pamphlet shops,* 1735. (*GM, LM* May)

The **secrets** of a woman's heart

> 2°: *A*² B–D²; *1–2* 3–15 *16 blk.*
> Engraving on title.
> 'To thee, sweet songster, my advice I send'
>> An epistle to the castrato Farinelli, on Constantia Phillips; occasioned by *The happy courtezan*, 1735. Cf. *The fate of courtezans*, 1735.
> KU,MH(uncut),OCU(cropt).

Secundus, Joannes.
[Ogle, George:] Basia Joannis Secundi Nicolai Hagensis: or the Kisses...in Latin and English verse, 1731.

S180 Sedgwick, Ralph. [dh] A cheirological essay on the royal family, nobility, gentry, and commonalty of Great Britain. By Ralph Sedgwick, M.A. a blind clergyman, living at the reverend Mr. Patterson's, in Bell-Savage Yard, Ludgate-hill. [*London*, 1734?]
8°: *A*²; *1–4*.

> A variant (and probably incorrect) form of the title in the L copy reads 'A keirological essay' and omits the 'a' before 'blind clergyman'. The order of the two addresses found in Sedgwick's poems has not been determined.
'Sublime attempts above our strength receive their value still'
L(1078.m.23),O.

S181 — [dh] A divine poem: or, a paraphrase on the Lord's prayer. By Ralph Sedgwick, M.A. a blind clergyman, living at the reverend Mr. Patterson's, in Bell-Savage Yard, Ludgate-hill. [*London*, 173–?]
8°: *A*²; *1–4*.
'Our father, which in heav'n art, most high'
L(1465.f.33).

S182 — — living at No 7. in College-court near Dean's Yard, Westminster. [*London*, 173–?]
8°: *A*²; *1–4*.
ICU.

S183 — An epithalamium on the marriage of his highness the Prince of Orange, and her royal highness the Princess Anne. Humbly dedicated to the society of Ancient Britons. *London, printed for the author*, 1733.
4°: *A*⁴; *1–2* 3–8.
'Hymen, Minerva, and celestial choir'
L(840.h.7/6).

S184 — [dh] A metaphisical essay: or, a divine poem on the creation of the heavens &c. By Ralph Sedgwick ...living at the reverend Mr. Patterson's in Bell-Savage Yard, Ludgate-hill. [*London*, 173–?]
8°: *A*²; *1–4*.
'Should the nine sisters from Parnassus high'
L(1076.m.11).

S185 — — living at No 7. in College-court near Dean's Yard, Westminster. [*London*, 173–?]
8°: *A*²; *1–4*.
ICU.

Sedgwick, R.

S186 — [dh] A paraphrase, or, an explanation of the apostles creed: in a divine poem. [*London*, 173–?]
8°: *A*⁴; *i* ii–iv, 5–8.
> No address is given in these three paraphrases.
'Bearing record in heaven there are three'
ICU.

S187 — [dh] A paraphrase, or, an explanation of the ten commandments: in a divine poem. [*London*, 173–?]
8°: *A*²; *1* 2–4.
'If we look back with retrospective eye'
ICU.

S188 — [dh] A paraphrase on the second table of the ten commandments: in a divine poem. [*London*, 173–?]
8°: B²; *1* 2–4.
'Of all morality these are best plan'
ICU.

S189 Sedition. Sedition: a poem, humbly inscribed to the right hon. Sir Robert Walpole... *London, printed for the author; sold by E. Nutt, A. Dodd, and at the rest of the pamphlet-shops of London & Westminster*, 1736. (*LM* April)
2°: π¹ A–C² D¹; *i–ii, 1–3* 4–14. π1 hft.
> π1 and D1 have been seen to be conjugate. Engraving on p. 3.
'All hail! great sir! Behold an infant muse'
L(1487.d.3).

S190 — Sedition. A poem. To which are added, I. An hymn to the moon. II. The oyster woman... *London, printed for J. Roberts*, 1733. (*GSJ* 16 April)
8°: *A*¹[=D1] B–C⁴ D⁴(–D1) (D2 as 'C'); *i–ii, 1–21* 22 blk.
'Sedition first and most accursed crime!'
Hymn: 'Hail, Cynthia, silent empress of the night'
Oyster-woman: 'From loftier subjects the heroick muse'
CSmH,MH,*MnU*.

S191 — [reissue] The Oxford oyster women. A poem. To which is prefix'd, a hymn to the moon. *Sold by the booksellers in Oxford, and at the pamphlet-shops in London*, [1733.] (*GSJ* 7 July)
8°: *A*¹(±) B–C⁴ D⁴(–D1) (D2 as 'C'); *i–ii, 1–21 22 blk.*
WcC; CCC,CtY(2).

S192 Seditious. The seditious insects: or, the levellers assembled in convocation. A poem. *London printed, and sold by B. Bragg*, 1708. (*Observator* 7 Feb)
2°: π¹ *A*² B–G² H¹; *i–ii, 1–2* 3–30. π1 hft.
> The Luttrell copy, dated 7 Feb, is recorded in *Haslewood*.
'Near the cool verge of that delightful strand'
> Against the high church tories and convocation.
L(11602.i.26/2, –π1),LLP,OC(uncut),DT, LdU-B(ms. notes, –π1); OCU(uncut, –π1).

Sedley, *Sir* Charles. The miscellaneous works.. *London printed, and sold by J. Nutt*, 1702.
8°: pp. 213, 24, 64.   LVA-D,O; CtY,DFo.

Sedley, *Sir* **C.**

— [*idem*] The poetical works...with large additions never before made publick... With a new miscelany of poems by several of the most eminent hands. And a compleat collection of all the remarkable speeches in both houses of parliament... *London, printed for Sam Briscoe; sold by B. Bragg,* 1707.

8°: pp. 224+175.   L,O; CtY,MH.

— [*reissue*] The second edition... *London, printed for Sam. Briscoe; sold by James Woodward, & John Morphew,* 1710.

8°: pp. 224+178.   L,O; DLC.
> Cancel title and addition at end.

— The works... Containing his poems, plays, &c... *London, printed for S. Briscoe,* 1722.

12°: 2 vol.   L,O; CtY,NN.

S193 — The happy pair: or, a poem on matrimony. *London, printed for John Nutt,* 1702. (7 Jan, Luttrell)

2°: A–D²; *1–2* 3–16.
> The Luttrell copy is recorded in Pickering & Chatto cat. 238/8287; listed in *WL* Jan.
> 'When first the world from the black chaos rose'
> CLU-C,CSmH,MH,NN.

S194 — — The second edition, corrected. *London, printed for John Chantry; sold by Benj. Brag,* 1705. (7 Oct, Luttrell)

2°: A–C²; *1–2* 3–12. 12 advt.
> Listed in *WL* Oct.
> O(uncut); *MH*,NjP(Luttrell).

S195 Seguin, James. An acrostick upon the name of Mrs Elizabeth Ball. [17––.]

½°: 1 side, 1 column.
> Possibly printed with the following.
> 'Even as the dew within a rose'
> Signed 'James Seguin'.
> L(1875.d.6/10).

S196 — To Mrs Elizabeth Ball. [17––.]

½°: *1–2*, 1 column.
> 'For heaven's sake, what d' you mean to do?'
> Signed 'James Seguin'.
> L(1875.d.6/10).

S197 Selbey, William. The temple of Venus. A poem. In five cantos. *London, printed in the year* 1727.

12°: A–E⁶; *1–3* 4–58 *59–60*. E6 advt.
> Separate title on p. 31 (C4) to 'Two novels... By Mrs. Arabella Plantin'; they are in prose.
> 'Say, Maija's son, by whose intriguing aid'
> L(11631.b.41, lacks all after C3),EU,DA(lacks all after C3); KU(uncut),*MB*,MH(–E6).

S198 Selden, Ambrose. Love and folly. A poem. In four canto's. *London, printed for W. Johnston,* 1749. (*GM* April)

8°: π² A⁴ a⁴ B–Pp⁴; [2] *i–iii* iv–xvii *xviii*, *1* 2–296. π1 hft; xviii err.

Selden, A. Love and folly

> Engraving on title. Most copies have an errata slip pasted over the errata on p. xviii; they are marked with an asterisk below.
> 'Fond to record to future times'
> Dedication signed.
> L(1486.b.8),LVA-D*,O,E*(–π1);   CLU*,CtY*(–π1),DFo*,ICN*,IU(–π1)+.

S199 — — The second edition. *London, printed for W. Johnston,* 1749.

8°: π²(±) A⁴ a⁴ B–Pp⁴; [2] *i–iii* iv–xvii *xviii*, *1* 2–296. π1 hft; xviii err.
> Apparently another issue of the same sheets with cancel π². No errata slip in copies seen.
> L(991.h.42),C; IU.

S200 — — The third edition. With many corrections and additions, by the author, not in either of the London editions. *Dublin, printed by Richard James,* 1750.

12°: A⁶ B–G¹²; *i–iii* iv–x *xi–xii*, *1* 2–143 *144 blk.* A6 advt.
> E(–A6); DFo.

'Semper Anonimus.' The dream, a poem, 1715. *See* D430.

Senilia. Senilia, 1742. *See* Maittaire, M.

S201 Sephalissa. Sephalissa to Sylvius: being a letter from a lady in the country to her lover in town... To which is prefix'd, a copy of verses to Mr. Pope ... By the author of the Epistle to Mrs. N--v--l. *London, printed for J. Duncan,* 1743. (*GM, LM* Oct)

2°: A² B–F²; *1–2* 3–24.
> Horizontal chain-lines. Listed in *GM, LM* as printed for W. Bickerton.
> *To Pope*: 'I'll read no more, but catching from his lays'
> 'Yes, I will write. O would the muse inspire'
> O; DFo(2),IU,KU,OCU.

Sequel. The sequel. Containing what was omitted in the Triumvirade, [1745.] *See* Morgan, Macnamara.

S202 — The sequel of Arms and the man. A new historical ballad. *London, printed for W. Webb,* 1746. (*GM, LM* April)

2°: A⁴; *1–2* 3–8.
> 'Ye whigs sing Te Deum, ye Jacobites fret'
> L(C.57.g.7/17),O,EU; CSmH,CU,DLC,MH,OCU.

S203 — The sequel of Mr. Pope's law-case: or, farther advice thereon: in an epistle to him. With a short preface and postscript. By a Templer... With notes ... By another hand... The second edition, revised and corrected, and the notes enlarged. *London, printed by Anth. Gibbons, for the benefit of the author,* 1733. (*DJ* 6 March)

2°: A² B–C²; *1–2* 3–11 *12 blk.* 4 err.
> Below title, 'Price 2s. 6d. i.e. for Verse 6d. for Notes 1s. and for Mr. Pope's Law-case 1s.' No first edition has been traced, but the prose

The **sequel** of Mr. Pope's law-case

Achilles dissected by Alexander Burnet is listed in *LM*, *LaM* (March) as 'with the Sequel of Mr. Pope's Law case'. 'Mr Pope's Law-case' is not found with copies seen; apparently the intention was that this should be bound with Pope's *The first satire of the second book of Horace imitated in a dialogue between Alexander Pope...and his learned council*, 1733.
'An opinion, single, is of no weight'
    Preface signed 'Patrick M'Doe-Roch'. Occasioned by Pope's *The first satire of the second book of Horace*, 1733 (15 Feb). Pope's letter to Fortescue of 8 March 1733 refers to 'another thing, wherein Pigott is abused as my learned council, written by some Irish attorney'.
O(uncut); CtY(2),MH.

— The sequel: or moderation further display'd, a poem, 1705. *See* Shippen, William.

S204 — A sequel to Britannia excisa. A new political ballad. To the tune of, Ye commons and peers. *London, printed for T. Cooper*, 1733. (*GM, LM* Jan)
2°: *A*² B²; *1–2* 3–8.
    Percival appendix 47. Printed by Samuel Richardson (*Sale* 119).
'Good people draw near,/To my ballad give ear'
L(162.n.71),LU,O; CSmH(uncut),InU,NNC (uncut).

S205 — — [*London*, 1733.]
½°: 1 side, 2 columns.
L(C.116.i.4/19).

S206 — A sequel to the Dunciad; being the famous British sh——rs. A satire. *London, printed for A. Moore; sold at the pamphlet-shops*, 1729. (*MChr* 6 June)
2°: *A*² B–F²; *1–2* 3–24.
    Listed in *MC* May, possibly in error.
'Happy the man, who, when he goes to stool'
    The work of British poets discussed as excrement. Apparently continued by *The memorable British sh——rs*, 1730.
L(163.n.6),WcC; NjP,TxU.

S207 Serenade. A serenade to be represented on the birth-day of his most sacred majesty George...king of Great Britain, &c. at the castle of Dublin the 28th of May, 1719... Compos'd by Mr. John Sigismond Cousser... *Dublin, printed by Thomas Hume*, 1719.
4°: A⁴; *1–3* 4–8.
'All hail! thou most auspicious day'
O.

S208 — A serenade to be represented on the birth-day of his most sacred majesty George...at the castle of Dublin the 28th of May, 1724... Compos'd by Mr. John Sigismond Cousser... *Dublin, printed by Thomas Hume*, 1724.
4°: *A*⁴; *1–3* 4–8.
'As to the birth of worlds in boundless spaces'
DT.

Serenade

S209 — A serenade to be represented on the birth-day of his most sacred majesty George...at the castle of Dublin, the 28th of May, 1725... Compos'd by Thomas Hume, 1725.
4°: *A*⁴; *1–3* 4–8.
'With more than usual brightness'
DT.

S210 — A serenade to be represented on the birth-day of his most sacred majesty George...at the castle of Dublin, the 28th of May, 1726... Compos'd by Mr. John Sigismond Cousser... *Dublin, printed by George Faulkner*, 1726.
4°: *A*⁴; *1–3* 4–8.
'Tho' my almighty hand sustains in being'
DT.

S211 Serenata. A serenata da camera, to be represented on the birth-day of his most supreme majesty George...at the castle of Dublin the 28th. of May, 1717... Prepared by Mr. John Sigismond Cousser... *Dublin, printed by Thomas Hume*, 1717.
4°: A⁴ B²; *1–3* 4–11 *12 blk*.
'Ye hov'ring zephirs/To climes etherial'
L(1875.d.6/173),DT.

S212 — A serenata theatrale to be represented on the birth-day of Anne queen of Great Britain at the castle of Dublin 6 February 1712. *Dublin*, 1712.
4°.
    Recorded by Hans Scholz, *J. S. Kusser* (Leipzig, 1911).
Library of the dean & chapter of Cashel.

S213 — A serenata theatrale, to be represented on the birth-day of his most serene majesty George... king of Great Britain, &c. at the castle of Dublin the 28th. of May, 1716... Set by Mr. John Sigismond Cousser... *Dublin, printed by E. Waters*, 1716.
4°: ⟨A²⟩ B² ⟨C²⟩; *1–3* 4–12.
'All hail! All hail! Thou happy land'
O(slightly cropt).

S214 — A serenata theatrale, to be represented on the birth-day of his most serene majesty George the second...at the castle of Dublin the 30th of October 1727... Prepared by Mr. John Sigismond Cousser... *Dublin, printed by George Faulkner*, [1727.]
4°: *A*⁴; *1–2* 3–8.
'Wanton loves, around me sporting'
DT.

S215 — A serenata. To be represented on the birth-day of the most serene Anne...at the castle of Dublin. The sixth day of February, 1710... Set by Mr. John Sigismond Cousser. *Dublin, printed by Edwin Sandys*, 1710.
4°: A⁴; *1–2* 3–8.
'Let's melt the sullen world with sounds harmonious'
DK.

Serenata

S216 — A serenata. To be represented on the birth-day of the most serene Anne... queen of Great Britain, &c. at the castle of Dublin, the sixth day of February, 1714... Set by Mr. John Sigismond Cousser... *Dublin, printed by Corn. Carter,* [1714.]
4°: ⟨A⁴⟩; *1–2* 3–8.
'Sing great Anna's matchless name'
L(11631.bb.2, cropt).

S217 Serenissimae. Serenissimæ Magnæ Britanniæ, Hiberniæque, reginæ; post gravissimum ab ea confectum bellum...epinicium. *Londini, impensis Gulielmi Redmayne, pro authore,* 1713. (*PB* 4 April)
4°: A–B⁴; *i–iv,* 1–12.
'Telorum siluere minæ, redivivaque terris'
L(161.n.32, Luttrell, 6 April),DA; MH.

Serenissimo. Serenissimo et clementissimo principi Georgio, 1723. *See* Ker, John, *chaplain to the fleet.*

— Serenissimo et invictissimo principi...Georgio, [1718/20?] *See* Ker, John, *chaplain to the fleet.*

[Sergeant, John.] The nuptialls of the lamb, 1701–. *See* N348.

S218 Serio-comical. 'A serio-comical elegy, on the much lamented death of Matthew Buckinger, the famous little man, without arms or legs; who departed this life at Cork, Sept. 28, 1722. With an epitaph, and a sketch of his most surprizing performances... By the author of the Benefit of farting explain'd. [*London*] *Printed for J. Roberts.* Price 4*d.*'
(*DP* 16 Nov 1722)
> Probably the same work as *An elegy on the much lamented death of Matthew Buckinger,* [Dublin, 1722.] The author of *The benefit of farting* has not apparently been identified, though T318 suggests that it was Thomas Sheridan.

S219 Serious. A serious address to Mr. Cinnick's followers. Occasioned by his attempting to revive certain dangerous and long-exploded errors. *Dublin, printed by and for Edward Bate,* 1746.
8°: A⁸; *1* 2–16.
'To fabled deities, the dreams of men'
> To the followers of John Cennick, the preacher.
DN.

— A serious poem upon William Wood, [1724.] *See* Swift, Jonathan.

— Serious thoughts on death, [1750.] *See* Parent, Daniel.

Sermo. Sermo pedestris, 1739. *See* King, William, *principal of St. Mary Hall.*

Sermon. A sermon against adultery, [1738.] *See* Pope, Alexander [Sober advice].

Services

S220 Services. Services and sufferings; or, the three cuckoos. *London, printed for J. Roberts,* 1726. (*MC* May)
4°: A² B–D²; *1–2* 3–15 *16 blk.*
'With what impatience merit waits'
> A satirical fable on politicians.
O,GM; CSmH,KU,OCU(uncut).

S221 —— *London printed, and at Dublin re-printed, by, and for, J. Gowan,* [1726.]
4°: A² B² C¹; *1–3* 4–10.
DT.

S222 Servitor. The servitour: a poem. Written by a servitour of the university of Oxford, and faithfully taken from his own original copy, &c. *London printed, and sold by H. Hills,* 1709. (Oct?)
8°: A⁸; *1–4* 5–16. A1 hft.
> *Bond* 24. Hearne records the poem as just published on 11 Oct 1709.
'When Phebus shon with warmest rays'
> By the same author as *The gentleman commoner,* 1716, which gives the author as J.L. A.B.
O(2, 1–A1),C,CT,E,AdU+; CtY,ICN,MH(2), OCU(–A1),TxU+.

Servitude. Servitude: a poem, [1729.] *See* Dodsley, Robert.

S223 Session. The session of musicians. In imitation of the Session of poets. *London, printed for M. Smith,* 1724. (*MC* May)
2°: A² B–C²; *1–3* 4–12.
> Reissued in *A collection of original poems,* 1724 (*Case* 329).
'Apollo, (the god both of musick and wit)'
> On contemporary musicians.
L(841.m.26/1),BaP; CSmH,CtY,IU,MH,TxU+.

S224 — A session of painters, occasion'd by the death of the late Sir Godfrey Kneller, inscrib'd to his widow, the Lady Kneller. *London, printed for J. Roberts,* 1725. (*MC* Nov)
2°: A² B²; *1–2* 3–8.
'Mourn, England, mourn, since Kneller is no more'
> A satire on contemporary painters.
L(1347.m.47); *PBL,*TxU(uncut).

S225 — The session of the critics: or, the contention for the nettle. A poem. To which is added, a dialogue between a player and a poet... *London printed, and sold by T. Cooper, and by the booksellers of London & Westminster,* [1737.] (*LM* March)
2°: A² B–D²; *1–2* 3–16.
> With 16 other short poems, probably by various authors.
'Old Zoilus, the sourest Dame Critice bore'
O; MH,NN-B,OCU,TxU.

Settle, Elkanah.
Most of Settle's poems in this period were produced for presentation to individuals and not for public sale; this

Settle, E.

list is undoubtedly very incomplete, and other poems must still remain in private hands.

Presentation copies were almost always in characteristic bindings which are said to be by Settle himself; the presence of these bindings is not noted here. They make Settle's authorship so immediately apparent that some anonymous poems may erroneously have been entered as though they bore Settle's name.

Poems with the same general title are arranged chronologically. Between 1714 and 1723 the same basic poem Thalia triumphans was issued with alternative additions applying it to various persons. Some other poems have a common basic text, but they are apparently all distinct editions.

Many poems were printed as large quartos and cut down to folio shape in binding; they are described as quarto here. Some were mounted on large paper with gilt and coloured borders; these are described as 'illuminated'.

S226 — 'Augusta lacrimans a funeral poem to the memory of the honourable Sr Thomas Crisp kt. *London, printed for the author, 1704. fol.'*
(*Rawlinson.*)

S227 — Augusta lacrymans. A funeral poem to the memory of the honourable Sr Charles Thorold, kt. *London, printed for J. Reade, 1709.*
2°: *B*² C–D²; *1–2* 3–12.
'Now great Augusta, whilst within thy walls'
L(C.67.f.16/4),LG; MH.

S228 — Augusta lacrimans. A funeral poem to the memory of Heneage Fetherston esq; *London, printed for the authour, 1711.*
4°: π¹ A–B² C¹; *i–ii*, *1–9 10 blk.*
'Oe'r some dead worthy's grave the sweets to strow'
        For the first line, cf. S230, S237, S297.
LVA.

S229 — 'Augusta lacrimans. A funeral poem to the memory of Sir Joseph Wolfe, kt. *London, printed for the author, 1711.'*
(*Sotheby's 8 April 1918, lot 269.*)

S230 — Augusta lacrimans. A funeral poem, to the memory of the honoured Charles Baynton esq; *London, printed for the author, 1712.*
4°: *A*¹ B–C²; *1–2* 3–10.
'O'er some dead worthy's grave our sweets to strow'
        For the first line, cf. S228.
L(C.66.f.19).

S231 — Augusta lacrimans. A funeral poem to the memory of the honourable Sir Henry Furnesse, kt. and baronet. *London, printed for the author, 1712.*
4°: *A*² B–C²; *1–2* 3–12.
''Twas near his Sandwich, in his rural seat'
LG.

S232 — 'Augusta lacrimans a funeral poem to the memory of the honourable Sir Wm Hodges bart. *London, 1714. fol.'*
(*Rawlinson.*)

S233 — Augusta lacrimans. A funeral poem to the memory of the honoured John Seale esq; *London, printed for the author, 1714.*
4°: *A*² B²; *1–2* 3–8.
'Jersey and Guernsey, who so near the Gaul's'
CSmH,CtY.

S234 — 'Augusta lacrimans a funeral poem to the memory of the honour'd Caesar Chambrelan esqr. *London, printed for the author, 1716. fol.'*
(*Rawlinson.*)

S235 — Augusta lacrimans. A funeral poem to the memory of the honourable Sir Sam. Moyer, bar. *London, printed in the year 1716.*
4°: *A*² B¹ C² (C2 as C); *i–ii*, *1–8.*
'For th' off'rings paid at some dead worthy's urn'
OC.

S236 — Augusta lacrimans. A funeral poem to the memory of the honourable Sir James Bateman, kt. *London, printed for the author, 1718.*
4°: π¹ *A*² B–C² D¹; *1–2 [4]* 3–12.
    The dedication in A² to the governors and directors of the South-Sea company is apparently an addition to the original design. π1 and D1 have been seen to be conjugate.
'Her watry walls, a barrier all her own'
        For the first line, cf. S238.
LVA; DLC.

S237 — Augusta lacrimans. A funeral poem to the memory of the honourable Sir Daniel Wray, kt. *London, printed for the author, 1719.*
4°: *A*¹ B² C¹; *1–2* 3–8.
'O'er some dead worthy's grave the sweets to strow'
L(11630.f.69).

S238 — Augusta lacrimans. A funeral poem to the memory of the honourable Sir William Ashurst, kt. *London, printed for the author, 1720.*
4°: *A*¹ B–C² D¹; *i–ii*, *1–10.*
'Her watry walls, a barrier all her own'
        For the first line, cf. S236.
LG.

S239 — Augusta lacrimans. A funeral poem to the memory of the honourable Sir Thomas Abney, kt. *London, printed for the author, 1721 [1722].*
2°: B–C² (B2 as 'B'); *1–2* 3–8.
'To worthies dead for offrings at their urn'
LG.

S240 — Augusta triumphans. Ramilly and Turin, or a hymn to victory. In a panegyrical address to the honourable city of London... *London, printed for the author, 1707.*
2°: *A*–B² C–E²; *1–4* 5–20.
    No watermark.
'Hail, fair Augusta, thro' the world renown'd'
    Dedication signed.
LG.

S240·2 — [fine paper]
        Watermark: London arms.
ICN.

Settle, E. Augusta triumphans, 1711

S241 — Augusta triumphans. To the lieutenancy of the honourable city of London a congratulatory poem. *London printed anno* 1711.
4°: *A*(2 ll) B–D²; *i–iv*, 1–11 *12 blk*.
    Title on A2; dedication faces on A1ᵛ, with different dedicatees stamped in by hand: 'Iohn Amy' (LG); 'Samuel Benson' (MH); 'William Lightfoot' (LG).
'An outly of the globe fair Albion reigns'
LG(2); MH.

S242 — Augusta triumphans. A congratulatory poem to the lieutenancy of the honourable city of London. *London, printed anno* 1714.
4°: *A–B² C¹*; *1–5 6–10*.
'When some illustrious nuptial Gordian's tyed'
L(C.66.f.21).

S243 — Carmen irenicum. The happy union of the two East-India companies. An heroick poem. *London, printed for John Nutt*, 1702. (23 March, Luttrell)
2°: *A² B² C²*(±C1); *1–2 3–12*.
    Watermark: London arms. Cancel not seen in the LVA-D copy. The Luttrell copy is in the possession of J. R. B. Brett-Smith.
'Poets, when they some glorious theme design'
LVA-D; TxU.

S244 — [fine paper]
    Watermark: Amsterdam arms.
Broxbourne Library; CSmH.

S245 — Carmen irenicum. The union of the imperial crowns of Great Britain. An heroick poem. *London, printed for the author*, 1707.
2°: *A–B² C–E² ˣE² F–L²*; *1–7 8–47 48 blk*.
    Watermark: dagger. Latin title on A1ᵛ, with Settle's name (which is not on the English title). Latin and English texts. In some copies, asterisked below, the date is altered in ms. to 1708.
'Hac volvente die, quanto pæane, Britannos'
'For aiding pow'rs this task to undertake'
L(C.66.f.8; C.67.f.12; C.67.f.13), LVA(5, 2*), OW,C,E+; CSmH,CtY,ICN,ICU*,MH*+.

S246 — [variant imprint:] *London, printed by J. Brudenell in Little-Britain, for the author*, 1707.
L(C.67.f.16/2),LVA-D,O; MH.

S247 — [fine paper] *London, printed for the author*, 1707.
    Watermark: fleur-de-lys on shield; in quarto.
L(75.h.16, dedication copy to Queen Anne?)

S248 [—] Carmen natalitum. A congratulatory poem to the right honourable Thomas lord Pelham. *London, printed anno* 1714.
4°: *A² B² C¹*; *1–2 3–10*.
'The ever shining charioteer of heav'n'
NcD.

S249 — Carmen natalitum. A congratulatory address to the right honourable the lord Viscount Townshend on the happy birth of a son, honoured by his majesty for his godfather. *London, printed in the year* 1715.

Settle, E. Carmen natalitum, 1715

4°: *A*(2 ll) *B²*; *1–2 3–8*.
'When on the royal head the crown devolv'd'
LG.

S250 — Carmen natalitum. A congratulatory address to the right honourable Brownloe, earl of Exeter, on his lordship's anniversary birthday. *London, printed for the author*, 1722.
2°: *A² B²*; *1–2 3–8*.
'The everlasting charioteer of heav'n'
Burleigh House, Stamford.

S251 — The eucharist. Or the holy sacrament of our lord's supper. A divine poem. *London, printed for the author*, 1717.
4°: *A² B–D²*; *1–4 5–16*.
    The copy at MH has the date altered in ms. to 1718, and an autograph note of presentation. See S252·2 for a reissue.
'So much the creature his creator's care'
L(Ashley 5015),LG; CLU-C(2),CSmH,CtY,ICU, MH.

S252 — — *London, printed for the author*, 1721.
8°: *A–B⁴*; *1–4 5–16*.
O; ICU.

S252·2 [—] — *London, printed for the author*, 1717 [1725].
4°: *A² B–D²*; *1–4 5–16*.
    A copy of the edition of 1717 with Settle's name cut from the title and the date altered in ms. to 1725. The copy at KU is bound with Timothy Harris, *An hymn on Christ's nativity*, 1722 (altered in ms. to 1724); it seems likely that Harris was exploiting remainder stock after Settle's death, as he did with Joseph Harris's *An Indian pastoral eclogue*, 1717.
KU.

S253 — Eusebia triumphans. The Hannover succession to the imperial crown of England, an heroick poem. *London, printed for John Nutt*, 1702.
2°: *A² B–N²*; *1–5 6–51 52 blk*. A1 hft.
    Watermark: post-horn on shield. Latin title on A1ᵛ, with Settle's name. Latin and English texts. Most copies, asterisked below, have the date altered in ms. to 1703. Some copies (e.g. LVA,CLU-C,ICU) have errata slips pasted over individual words; the number present varies, but they have been seen on pp. 8, 10, 12, 16, 32, 36, 42, 48 in the ICU copy.
'Insuper immensi myrias cum subdita regni'
'When 'midst the myriads of his angel train'
LVA(3, 1*),*OA*,AdU*; CLU-C(2, 1*),DFo*, ICU*,TxU*.

S254 — [fine paper]
    Watermarks: Dutch lion and Amsterdam arms. Copies with date altered to 1703 in ms. are asterisked. Copies at CtY,NjP have a few errata slips.
L(837.l.4/2*, ms. corrections; C.66.f.25),LG,O, C,LdU-B*+; CLU-C,CSmH(dedicatory poem in ms.),CtY*,MH*,NjP*.

Settle, E. Eusebia triumphans, 1704

S255 — — The Hanover succession... *London, printed for the author,* 1704.
  2°: *A*² B–C² †² D–O²; *i–iv, 1–9* 10–55 *56 blk.* A1 hft. Watermark: London arms. Latin title on A1ᵛ with Settle's name. Some copies (LVA,CSmH, MiU) have misprint 'Hanoner' in title.
  L(C.128.g.3),LG,LVA(4),O,NwP; CSmH,InU (in contemporary marbled wrappers),MWiW-C, MiU.

S256 — [fine paper?]
  Watermark: Dutch lion. The copy seen is not in a Settle binding.
  OW.

S257 — [reissue]
  2°: *A*² ˣB² D–O²; *1–5* 6–8, 13–55 *56 blk.* A1 hft. This issue cancels the preface by replacing B–C² †² with a new B². Watermark: London arms.
  ICN.

S258 — — *London, printed for the author,* 1705.
  2°: *A*² B–P²; *1–13* 14–57 '59' '58' *60 blk.* A1 hft. Watermark: Dutch lion. Latin title on A1ᵛ with Settle's name.
  L(C.67.f.14; C.67.f.16/1),LVA-D(with autograph dedicatory poem to John Morris), OC (congratulatory poem to John Evelyn); DFo (in contemporary wrappers).

S259 — [fine paper]
  Watermark: Amsterdam arms.
  LVA-D.

S260 — — The protestant succession as now establish'd, and inviolably secur'd, by the happy union of the imperial crowns of Great Britain. An heroick poem. *London, printed for the author in the year* 1709.
  2°: *A*²(±) B–O² P²(–P2) Q–T²; *1–13* 14–73 *74 blk.* (58 as '59').
  A reissue with additional text. The words 'The end' on P1ᵛ are covered by a blank slip in L, stamped over in MH.
  L(C.66.f.23),LG,LVA,O,AdU; CLU-C,MH.

S260·5 — — The Hanover succession to the imperial crown of Great Britain. An heroick poem. *London, printed for the author in the year* 1711.
  2°: *A*²(±A2) B²(±B1) C–O² P²(–P2) Q–T²; *1–13* 14–73 *74 blk.* (58 as '59').
  Another reissue; date of Latin title (A1ᵛ) altered in ms. The cancels A2, B1 are apparently conjugate.
  CLU-C.

S261 — [reissue]
  2°: *A*²(±A1; ±A2) B²(±B1) C–P²; *1–13* 14–57 '59' '58' *60 blk.*
  In the copy seen the Latin title is also cancelled, but the additional text after P is not present.
  L(C.67.f.15).

S262 — — To the most happy inauguration of the Hanover succession in the most august prince,

Settle, E. Eusebia triumphans, 1715

George... A congratulatory poem. *London, printed, anno* 1715.
  2°: *A*(2 ll) B–M²; *1–13* 14–45 *46–48.*
  Latin title on A1ᵛ. Without Settle's name on the titles, but with the dedication signed. The copy at NN, which lacks B1 and has A2 and B2 stuck together, is possibly intended as another issue with the dedication cancelled.
  LG,O,*OC*; CLU-C(3),ICN,ICU,MH(with autograph poem to William Norcliffe),NN(lacks B1).

S263 — [reissue] With the addition of a new postscript on the present state of affairs. *London, printed, anno* 1715.
  A2 is a cancel with horizontal chain-lines; the postscript on M² is unchanged.
  LVA-D.

S264 — A funeral tear, to the memory of the right honourable Charles, earl of Burlington. *London, printed for the author,* 1704.
  2°: *A*² B–C²; *1–2* 3–11 *12 blk.*
  The running-title is 'Memoriæ fragranti'. Ms. corrections in the copy seen.
  'When the whole sacred choir, the virgin nine'
  MH.

S265 [—] Honori sacellum. A funeral poem, to the memory of William duke of Devonshire... *London printed, and sold by A. Baldwin,* 1707 [1708]. (*DC* 2 Feb)
  2°: *A*¹ B–I² K¹; *i–ii, 1–33* 34 blk.
  Advertised in *DC* as 'A funeral poem...'.
  'When in the rites to the great dead we joyn'
  Brett-Smith (Luttrell, 3 Feb 1708).

S266 — 'Honori sacellum. A funeral poem to the memory of the right honourable Robert earl of Scarsdale. *London,* 1708. fol.'
  (*Rawlinson.*)

S267 [—] Honori sacellum. A funeral poem to the memory of the honourable Henry Thynne, esq; *London, printed for Tho. Bickerton,* 1709.
  2°: B–D²; *1–2* 3–12.
  'On their Castalian banks, the sacred nine'
  L(C.67.f.16/4).

S268 [—] Honori sacellum. A funeral poem. To the memory of the most noble John duke of Rutland. *London, printed for John King,* 1711.
  4°: *A*¹ B–D² E¹; *1–2* 3–16.
  'Ye sacred nine, can sorrow tune your choir'
  For poems with similar first line, see S270, S339 below.
  LG.

S269 — Honori sacellum. A funeral poem, to the memory of the right honourable Thomas earl of Coventry. *London, printed for the author,* 1712.
  4°: *A*² B–D²; *1–2* 3–16.
  'Near that proud dome where Mars his worn-out race'
  L(C.66.f.18).

Settle, E. Honori sacellum, 1714

S270 — Honori sacellum. A funeral poem to the memory of the most noble Henry duke of Beaufort, &c. *London, printed for the author,* 1714.
4°: *A*² B–C² D¹; *1–2* 3–13 *14 blk.*
'Ye sacred nine, can sorrows tune your choir'
For poems with similar first line, see S268, S339.
L(1479.d.21/15).

S271 — Honori sacellum. A funeral poem to the memory of the right honourable Robert ld. Tamworth. *London, printed for the author,* 1714.
4°: *A*² B² C¹; *1–2* 3–10.
'The noble Tamworth dead, th' harmonious nine'
CSmH.

S272 — Honori sacellum. A funeral poem to the memory of the honoured Clement Pettit, esq;...
London, printed for the author, 1717.
4°: *A*¹ B–D²; *1–2* 3–13 *14 blk.*
The copy at O has a ms. note by Rawlinson criticizing the Pettit family for distributing this poem to their friends.
'What tho' but rais'd from dust, thou human mould'
For other poems by Settle with the same first line, see S323 below.
LG,LVA,O.

S273 — 'Honori sacellum. A funeral poem to the memory of the honourable Sr John Shaw bart. late collector of the port of London. *London,* 1721. fol.'
(*Rawlinson.*)

S274 — Honori sacellum. The muses congratulatory address, to the right honourable William lord North and Grey; on his happy arrival from Holland. *London, printed for the author,* 1721.
2°: B–C² (B2 as 'B'); *1–2* 3–8.
'The fam'd Columbus his proud sails unfurl'd'
CLU-C.

S275 [—] Irene triumphans. The British muse's congratulatory poem, on the peace. Humbly addrest to his excellency the most noble Duke D'Aumont; embassador from the most Christian king, &c. *London, printed for the author,* 1713.
2°: *A*–D²; *1–3* 4–15 *16 blk.*
Watermark: London arms. Latin title on A1ᵛ; Latin and English texts.
'Cum primum immensi deus unus, trina potestas'
'When the great three, the highest heav'ns dread lord'
L(C.66.f.15).

S276 [—] [fine paper]
Watermark: pro patria.
LVA; MH(2, 1 dedication copy, illuminated),NNP.

S277 — [reissue] Irene triumphans. The address of the British muse to the peace-makers. An heroick poem. By E. Settle. *London, printed for the author,* 1713.
2°: π¹ *A*²(±) B² C²(± C2) D²(±); [5] 4–15 *16 blk.*
Watermark: London arms. Original titles A² cancelled, removing the references to Louis

Settle, E. Irene triumphans, 1713

d'Aumont because of his disgrace; A2 dedication 'To the patriots of Great Britain'; other cancels remove d'Aumont's name from the text.
LG,LVA(3),LdU-B; CLU-C,CSmH.

S277·2 — [fine paper]
Watermark: pro patria.
L(C.64.f.5).

S278 — Memoriæ fragranti. A funeral poem to the memory of the right honourable the lady Viscountess Fitzharding. *London, printed for Tho. Bickerton,* 1708.
2°: B–D²; *1–2* 3–12.
'On the Castalian banks the sacred nine'
L(C.67.f.16/5).

S279 — Memoriæ fragranti. A funeral poem, to the pious memory of the honourable Sr. E: Waldo kt. *London, printed for the author,* 1708.
2°: *A*¹ B² C²; *1–2* 3–10.
'To worthies dead, for off'rings at their urne'
LG.

S280 — 'Memoriæ fragranti. A funeral poem to the memory of the honourable Sir Richard Levet, kt. *London,* 1711.'
2°.
(*Nichols* VIII. 300n.)

S281 — Memoriæ fragranti. A funeral poem, to the memory of the honourable Ldy. Margaret Woolfe. *London, printed for the author,* 1713.
4°: *A*–B²; *1–2* 3–8.
'The call when to consummate virtue given'
L(C.66.f.17).

S282 [—] Minerva triumphans. The muses essay, to the honour of that generous foundation the Cotton Library at Westminster, as it is now given to the publick, confirm'd by act of parliament. *London, printed for J. Nut,* 1701. (4 July, Luttrell)
2°: *A*² B–C²; *i–ii,* 1–10.
Watermark: garlanded shield. Row of type flowers below title in place of Settle's name found in the fine-paper copies. The Luttrell copy is recorded in *Haslewood*; listed in *WL* July.
'Hail learning's Pantheon, thou, the lovely prize'
LG,O; CLU-C,OCU.

S283 — [fine paper]
Watermark: Amsterdam arms. Settle's name added to title.
L(Huth 154),LWS; CSmH,TxU.

S284 — [superfine paper]
Watermark: fleur-de-lys on shield; printed as a quarto.
CLU-C.

S285 [—] Minervæ sacellum. The muses address to the right honourable Richard, earl of Burlington, on the erecting the new dormitory for the king's scholars at Westminster. '*London, printed for T. Payne.*'
(*PB* 8 Dec 1722)

Settle, E. Minervæ sacellum

Ordinary paper issue of the following, adver-
tised in *PB* as 'By an Oxonian, formerly of
that foundation'. The ms. account book of the
Earl of Burlington's steward (at Chatsworth)
records payment of ten guineas to Settle 25
July 1722 'for his poem on the dormitory'.
Burlington was the architect of the building.
'From thy own Westminster's Castalian spring'

S286 — [fine paper] *London, printed for the author*, 1722.
2°: *A*¹ B² C¹; *1–2* 3–8.
The copy seen was printed on one side of the
paper and then mounted on heavy paper.
LWS(illuminated).

S287 — 'Musa triumphans. To his grace the Duke of
Newcastle on the happy recovery of the Lady
Henrietta Holles, a congratulatory poem. *London*,
1708. fol.'
(*Rawlinson*.)

S288 [—] A pindaric poem, on the propagation of the
gospel in foreign parts. A work of piety so zealously
recommended and promoted by her most gracious
majesty. *London, printed for the author*, 1711.
2°: *A*²(A1 + a²) B–E² F¹; [2] *i* ii–vi, *1* 2–18.
Various watermarks. Dedication to the queen
on pp. i–vi. Paste-on cancels for individual
words on pp. ii, 5 in some copies.
'Thou evangelic glory quickly dawn'
L(C.66.f.24),LG,LVA(3),EU,WcC; CLU-C(2),
CSmH(2),CtY,MH,TxU+.

S289 [—] [fine paper]
4°: *A*²(±A2) B–E² F¹; *i–iv*, *1* 2–18.
Printed as a quarto except for the title; A2 is a
dedication to the archbishop of Canterbury
and other members of the society.
LLP.

S290 — Rebellion display'd: or, our present distractions
set forth in their true light. An heroick poem.
London, printed for the author, 1715.
4°: *A*¹ B–E² F¹; *1–3* 4–20.
In some copies (e.g. at L,CLU-C) F1 is unsigned; A1 and F1 have been seen to be conjugate.
'As thro' that lordliest of the creatures, man'
L(643.m.12/26, dedicatory note in ms.; C.66.
f.22),LVA-D,AdU; CLU-C(2),CSmH,ICU,MH.

S291 [—] The scaffold lately erected in Westminster-
Hall. A poem. *London printed, and are to be sold by
the booksellers of London & Westminster*, 1701.
(4 Sept, Luttrell)
2°: *A*² B–D²; *1–2* 3–16.
Watermark: London arms. Listed in *WL* Sept.
'What riddles are the favours of a crown?'
Ascribed to Settle in *Rawlinson*. Luttrell
annotated his copy, 'In behalf of the late
impeached lords' i.e. Somers, Orford, Portland, and Haversham.
L(11657.m.18),O,*LdU-B,MR-C*; CLU-C(Luttrell),CtY,ICN,MH,TxU+.

Settle, E. The scaffold

S292 [—] [fine paper]
Watermark: Amsterdam arms.
LLP.

S293 [—] [superfine paper]
Watermark: fleur-de-lys on shield; printed as
a quarto.
MH,OCU.

S294 [—] Spes Hunsdoniana: a poem on the anniversary
birth-day of the incomparable youth, Mr. Matthew
Bluck, son and heir to the worshipful Matthew
Bluck, esq; of Hunsdon-House in Hartfordshire.
By E.S. *London, printed for A. Baldwin*, 1702. (16
March, Luttrell)
2°: A–C²; *i–ii*, 1–9 *10 blk.*
Watermark: twin spiral on shield with suppor-
ters. Luttrell's copy is in the possession of
J. R. B. Brett-Smith.
'Just as my restless mind began to please'
Settle's authorship is deduced from the initials
and style of the work.
O.

S295 [—] [fine paper]
Watermark: Dutch lion.
L(1346.m.20).

S296 — Thalia lacrimans. A funeral poem to the
memory of the honoured Lytton Lytton esq;
London, printed for the authour, 1710.
4°: *A*² B–D²; *1–2* 3–16.
'In these sad rites assist ye sacred nine'
L(C.66.f.20).

S297 — Thalia lacrimans. A funeral poem, to the
memory of the honoured Edward Godfrey esq;
London, printed for the author, 1713.
4°: *A*¹ B–C²; *i–ii*, 1–8.
'O'er some dead worthy's grave the sweets to
strow'
LG.

S298 — Thalia lacrimans. A funeral poem to the memory of the right honourable Baptist earl of Gains-
borough. *London, printed for the author*, 1714.
4°: *A*² B–C² D¹; *1–2* 3–14.
'The call when to consummate virtue given'
L(G.19057), Broxbourne Library.

S299 — 'Thalia triumphans to the hond Saml. Barker
esqr. on his happy marriage a congratulatory poem.
Lond. 1706. fol.'
(*Rawlinson*.)

S300 [—] Thalia triumphans. To the right honourable
James earl of Salisbury, on his happy marriage. A
congratulatory poem. *London, printed for J. Wilcox*,
1709.
2°: B–D²; *1–2* 3–12.
'On their Pernassus brow the sacred nine'
IU.

The following editions of Thalia triumphans
*(1714–1723) are typically paged 1–2 3–8; pp. 3–6
are a standard congratulatory poem to which are
added differing title-leaves and a final leaf of text*

Settle, E. Thalia triumphans, 1714

containing personal references. The standard text is normally printed on a pair of conjugate folio leaves, though the signatures are often misleading; seven editions have been distinguished as A–G.

In many copies the text is 'illuminated' by being mounted on larger sheets of heavy paper with decorative borders in colour and gilt. In some cases the text is printed on one side of the leaf and some copies (probably fine-paper) are printed as quartos; but it has often been impossible to verify these details.

S301 —— Thalia triumphans. A congratulatory poem on the happy marriage of the right honourable the Lord Dunkellin. *London, printed anno* 1714.
2⁰: A^1 B^2 C^1 (B2 as 'B'); *1–2* 3–8.
Edition A; signature B under r of 'consecrate'. 'When the great founder this vast pile began' LG(illuminated).

S301·5 —— A congratulatory poem on the happy marriage of the honoured William Smith esq; *London, printed anno* 1714.
Edition A.
William Smyth of Drumcree House, Collinstown (xerox at DN; illuminated).

S302 —— To the right honourable the Lord Cobham, on his happy marriage. A congratulatory poem. *London, printed in the year* 1715.
2⁰: A^1 B^2 C^1 (B2 as 'B'); *1–2* 3–8.
Edition B; signature B under n of 'consecrate.' The words 'printed in the' on title are on a cancel slip.
CSmH(illuminated).

S303 —— To the honoured David Mitchel esq; on his happy marriage. A congratulatory poem. *London, printed in the year* 1715.
Edition B; the copy seen is printed as a quarto.
L(1489.f.27).

S304 —— A congratulatory poem on the happy marriage of the honourable Sir George Skipwith, bart. *London, printed anno* 1715.
Edition B.
LVA(illuminated).

S305 —— To the worthy Mr William Westfield on his happy marriage. A congratulatory poem. *London, printed in the year* 1715.
Edition B; the copy seen has sheet B printed as quarto, the rest as folio, and is printed on one side of the paper.
L(C.66.i.7, illuminated).

S306 —— To the right honourable Arthur earl of Donegal. On his happy marriage. A congratulatory poem. *London, printed in the year* 1716.
Edition B; the copy seen is mixed quarto and folio as the preceding.
LG(illuminated).

S307 —— To the honoured Mr Joshua Ironmonger, on his happy marriage. A congratulatory poem. *London, printed in the year* 1716.
2⁰: π^1 A^2 B^1; *1–2* 3–8.

Settle, E. Thalia triumphans, 1716

Edition C. The penultimate line of p. 4 reads 'Reins'.
CtY(illuminated).

S308 —— To the honoured Richard Morgan esq; on his happy marriage. A congratulatory poem. *London, printed in the year* 1716.
Edition C. Described in H. M. Nixon, *Styles and designs of bookbindings* (1956) 167.
Broxbourne Library (illuminated).

S309 —— To the honoured Walter Cary esq; on his happy marriage. A congratulatory poem. *London, printed in the year* 1717.
Edition C. Printed as a quarto.
TxU.

S310 —— To the right honourable Henry, earl of Lincoln, on his happy marriage. *London, printed in the year* 1717.
2⁰: π^1 A^2 B^1; *1–2* 3–8.
Edition D. The penultimate line of p. 4 reads 'Reigns'. Described in G. D. Hobson, *English bindings 1490–1940 in the library of J. R. Abbey* (1940) 71.
Brett-Smith (illuminated).

S311 —— a congratulatory poem, to the honoured Richard Price, esq; on his happy marriage. *London, printed for the author*, 1717.
Edition D.
LVA-D(illuminated).

S312 —— a congratulatory poem, to the reverend Mr. Croxall, on his happy marriage. *London, printed for the author*, 1718.
Edition D.
LG(illuminated).

S313 —— a congratulatory poem, to the honourable Sir Edm. Littleton, bar. on his happy marriage. *London, printed for the author*, 1718.
Edition D.
CLU-C(illuminated).

S314 —— a congratulatory poem, to the honoured Montague-Gerard Drake, esq; on his happy marriage. *London, printed for the author*, 1719.
2⁰: π^1 A^2 B^1; *1–2* 3–8.
Edition E. Some copies have a cancel slip on p. 3, line 10. In many issues B1 is not signed.
CSmH(illuminated).

S315 —— 'a congratulatory poem to the honourable Sir Fran. Hen. Drake, bt. on his happy marriage. *London, printed for the author*, [1720.]'
Edition not determined; described in *Some unpublished papers relating to the family of Sir Francis Drake*, edited by the Rev. Thomas Hervey (Colmer, 1887).

S316 —— A congratulatory poem to the honoured John Green, esq; on his happy marriage. *London, printed for the author*, [1720?]
Edition E.
TxU(illuminated).

Settle, E. Thalia triumphans, 1720

S317 —— a congratulatory poem. To the honoured William Heathcote, esquire. On his happy marriage. *London, printed for the author,* [1720.]
  Edition E.
CtY(illuminated, ms. 'in April 1720').

S318 —— a congratulatory poem. To the honoured John Watts, esq. On his happy marriage. *London, printed for the author,* 1720.
  Edition E.
LG(illuminated).

S319 —— A congratulatory poem to the honoured Edmund Morris, esq; on his happy marriage. *London, printed for the author,* 1721.
  Edition E. π1 and B1 are printed as a quarto.
CLU-C(illuminated).

S320 —— A congratulatory poem to the right honourable William lord Craven, on his happy marriage. *London, printed for the author,* [1721.]
2°: *A*¹ B² *C*¹; *1–2* 3–8.
  Edition F.
NjP.

S321 —— A congratulatory poem to the honoured John Buissiere, esq; on his happy marriage... *London, printed for the author,* 1722.
2°: *A*¹ B² *C*¹ (B2 as 'B'); *1–2* 3–8.
  Edition G.
MH.

S322 —— A congratulatory poem to the honourable Sr Thomas Lowther, brt. on his happy marriage. *London, printed for the author,* 1723.
  Edition G.
Chatsworth (illuminated).

S323 [—] Threnodia apollinaris. A funeral poem, to the memory of the right honourable Laurence earl of Rochester. *London, printed for John King,* 1711.
4°: *A*² B–D²; *1–2* 3–15 *16 blk.*
'What though but rais'd from dust, thou human mould'
  A similar first line is found in S272, S324, S327, S341, S347. It has not been possible to establish how far the texts are identical.
NNP.

S324 —— Threnodia apollinaris. A funeral poem, to the memory of Dr. Martin Lister, late physician to her majesty. *London, printed for the author,* 1712.
4°: *A*–*C*²; *1–2* 3–12.
'What tho' but raised from dust, thou human-mould'
  Compare first line with the preceding.
L(11631.f.39).

S325 —— Threnodia apollinaris. A funeral poem to the memory of the right honourable Charles E. of Hallifax... *London, printed for the author,* 1715.
4°: *A*² B–C²; *1–2* 3–12.
''Twas on their own Castalian flowry plain'
CSmH.

Settle, E. Threnodia apollinaris, 1719

S326 —— Threnodia apollinaris. A funeral poem to the memory of the right honourable Joseph Addison, esq; *London, printed for the author,* 1719.
4°: *A*¹ B–D²; *1–2* 3–6 5–12.
''Twas at their own Apollo's rising dawn'
L(11630.ff.1),LVA-D.

S327 —— Threnodia apollinaris. A funeral poem, to the memory of the right honourable William earl Cowper, &c. *London, printed for the author,* 1723.
2°: *A*–*C*²; *1–2* 3–12.
  Cancel slip with initial S on p. 8, line 11.
'What tho' but rais'd from dust, thou humane mould'
  For the first line, compare S323.
LG; CLU-C,MH.

S328 —— Threnodia apollinaris. A funeral poem to the memory of the honourable Sir Christopher Wren, kt. &c. *London, printed for the author, in the year* 1723.
2°: *A*² B²; *1–2* 3–8.
'To pay a glorious subject its just right'
O.

S329 —— Threnodia britannica. A funeral poem to the memory of our late soveraign lady Anne queen of Great Britain, &c. *London, printed for the author,* 1714.
4°: *A*² B–D²; *1–4* 5–16.
  Dedication to the 'Ladies of her late majesty's bed-chamber'.
'Urania, fairest of the sacred nine'
  Dedication signed.
Chatsworth; CSmH.

S330 —— [reissue]
  With cancel dedication A2 to the 'Officers of her late majesty's household'.
L(C.128.g.2),LVA.

S331 —— Threnodia britannica. A funeral oblation to the memory of the most noble prince John duke of Marlborough. *London, printed by S. Gilbert, for the author,* 1722.
2°: *A*² B–D²; *1–2* 3–16.
'As the great dead, by lawful tenure, claim'
CSmH.

S332 —— [reissue]
2°: *A*²(A1+χ1) B–D²; *i–iv,* 3–16.
  Added χ1 'To the reader' criticises other funeral poems on Marlborough.
LG.

S333 [—] Threnodia hymenæa. A funeral tear to the memory of the honourable Thomas Thynne esq; *London, printed for J. King,* 1710.
4°: *A*² B–D²; *1–2* 3–15 *16 blk.*
'In these sad rites assist ye sacred nine'
  For the first line, compare S338.
Longleat.

S334 —— 'Threnodia hymenæa, a funeral poem to the memory of the hon. Sir Henry Atkins, bart. *London, printed for the author,* 1712.'
(*Sotheby's* 4 April 1913, lot 373.)

Settle, E. Threnodia hymenæa, 1712

S335 — Threnodia hymenæa. A funeral poem, to the memory of the honoured George Carter esq. *London, printed for the author*, 1712.
4°: A–B²; *1–2* 3–8.
'The verdant Hackney with her rural bow'rs'
LVA; MH.

S336 — Threnodia hymenæa. A funeral poem, to the memory of the honoured Mrs. Anna Raymond. *London, printed for the author*, 1712.
4°: *A*(2 ll) B–C²; *i–ii*, 1–10.
'For whom is it we weep, and whence arise'
LG.

S337 — Threnodia hymenæa. A funeral poem, to the memory of the right honourable Frances viscss. Weymouth. *London, printed for the author*, 1712.
4°: *A*¹ B–C² D¹ (D1 as 'D2'); *i–ii*, 1–10.
    A1 and D1 have been seen to be conjugate.
'This silver head call'd t' an immortal crown'
Longleat.

S338 — Threnodia hymenæa. A funeral poem, to the memory of the right honourable William earl of Kingston. *London, printed for the author*, 1713.
4°: *A*¹ B–D² (D1 as 'C'); *i–ii*, 1–12.
'In these great rites assist ye sacred nine'
    For the first line, compare S333.
MH.

S339 — Threnodia hymenæa. A funeral poem, to the memory of the right honourable the Lady Mary Chamber. *London, printed for the author*, 1714.
4°: B² C² D² E¹; *1–2* 3–14.
'Ye sacred nine, can sorrows tune your choir?'
LG,LVA-D.

S340 — Threnodium apollinare. A funeral poem to the memory of the right honourable Henry Hare baron of Colerane. *London, printed for Tho. Bickerton*, 1708.
2°: *A*¹ B–C² D² E¹ (B1 as 'A2'); *1–2* 3–15 *16 blk.*
    The collation given is tentative; some signatures are possibly cropped in the copy seen.
'To the great dead we shrines and altars give'
L(C.67.f.16/2).

S341 — Threnodium apollinare. A funeral poem to the memory of Dr. Edward Tyson late physician to the hospitals of Bethlem and Bridewel. *London, printed for Tho. Bickerton*, 1708.
2°: *A*¹ B–C² D¹; *i–ii*, 1–10.
'What tho' but rais'd from dust, thou human-mould'
    For the first line, compare S323.
L(643.m.12/23, cropt; C.67.f.16).

[—] Trophaea marina. To Sir Charles Wager, rear admiral, *1710. See* T507·5.

S342 — Trophæa marina. To the honourable Captain Ogle, on his happy return from his glorious services on the coast of Guinea. *London, printed for the author*, 1723.
2°: *A*² B²; *1–2* 3–7 *8 blk.*
'Poets when they some glorious theme design'
LG.

Settle, E. Virtuti sacellum, 1707

S343 — Virtuti sacellum: a funeral poem, to the pious memory of the honourable Sir Robert Clayton, kt. *London, printed for the author*, 1707.
2°: A–E²; *1–2* 3–19 *20 blk.*
'When Clayton, call'd to an immortal crown'
L(C.67.f.16/6).

S344 — Virtuti sacellum. A funeral poem to the memory of the honourable Sr. John Buckworth, kt. and bt. *London, printed for J. King at the Bible and Crown in Little-Britain*, 1709.
2°: B² C–D²; *1–2* 3–12.
'A dome of honour, Richmond's neighbouring pride'
L(C.67.f.16/3),WcC.

S345 — Virtuti sacellum: a funeral poem to the memory of the honourable Sir Edmund Harrison kt. *London, printed for the author*, 1712.
4°: *A*¹ B–D²; *1–2* 3–14.
    Cancel slip pasted over catchword on p. 6.
'The call when to consummate virtue given'
LG.

S346 — Virtuti sacellum. A funeral poem, to the memory of Mrs. Kath. Richards, widow. *London, printed for the author*, 1713.
4°: *A*¹ B² C¹; *1–2* 3–8.
'When honour'd heads call'd t' an immortal crown'
LVA-D.

S347 — Virtuti sacellum. A funeral poem to the memory of the right honourable Sir Charles Hedges. *London, printed for the author*, 1714.
4°: A–B² C¹; *1–2* 3–10.
'What tho' but rais'd from dust, thou human mould'
    For the first line, compare S323.
LG.

S348 — Virtuti sacellum. A funeral poem to the memory of the honourable Sir Stephen Fox, kt. *London, printed for the author*, 1716.
4°: *A*¹ B–D²; *1–2* 3–14.
'Whenever the all-gracious providence'
LG.

S349 — Virtuti sacellum. A funeral poem to the memory of the right honourable John earl of Dundonald. *London, printed for the author*, 1720.
4°: *A*¹ B–C² D¹; *1–2* 3–12.
    Childish pencil note in the L copy, 'Anne Cochrane my book sent me from London by Mr. E. Settle of the 16 of Novbr – 1720.'
'Some darling worthy t' an immortal crown'
L(C.66.f.16),LG.

Seven. The seven extinguishers, *1710. See* Pittis, William.

S350 — The seven wise men. From a correct copy. *London, printed in the year* 1704.
4°: *A*⁴; *1–2* 3–8.
    This is presumably the first edition; the changes are analysed by F. H. Ellis in *POAS* VI. 792f.

The **seven** wise men

'Seven sages in our happy isle are seen'
'Upon the committee of seven lords appointed
to enquire into the Scotch plot', Luttrell's
note on the following edition.
OCU.

S351 —— From a correct copy. *London, printed in the
year* 1704. (18 May, Luttrell)
2⁰: *A*² *B*²; *1–2* 3–8.
'Seven sages in these latter times are seen'
O,AdU(Luttrell, ms. notes),*MR-C*; CLU-C,
CSmH,CtY,IU.

S352 — The seven wise-men of England. To the tune of,
To all you ladies, &c. [*London*, 1719.]
½⁰: 1 side, 2 columns.
The politicians' names are given in full in this
edition.
'Seven planets they do grace the skies'
Crum S315. A satire on a meeting of the whig
ministry with the Prince of Wales, June 1719.
O-JJ.

S353 —— *London, printed in the year* 1719.
½⁰: 1 side, 2 columns.
The politicians' names are disguised by blanks
and dashes in this edition.
L(C.20.f.2/240; C.116.i.4/47, cropt),O,E,
Rothschild; MH.

S354 **Seventeen.** Seventeen hundred and thirty-nine.
Or, the modern p––––s. A satire. Most humbly
inscrib'd to the right honourable Philip earl of
Chesterfield. *London, printed for T. Reynolds; sold
by the booksellers of London & Westminster*, 1739.
(*GM* Feb)
2⁰: *A*¹ *B*² *C*¹; *1–2* 3–8.
Rothschild 221–2. A1 and C1 have been seen
to be conjugate.
'When virtue in her infancy appear'd'
Britannia's precaution, [1741] claims to be by
the author of this and *The Hibernian politicians*,
1740, who was possibly named Gardiner. On
the modern peers.
L(11630.h.47),O(2),LdU-B,WrP; CLU,CtY,DFo
(uncut),MH,TxU+.

S355 **Seventh.** The seventh satyre of Juvenal imitated.
London, printed for C.B. [*Charles Bathurst*]; *sold by
A. Dodd*, 1745. (*DA* 31 Jan)
2⁰: π² A–D² (A1 as 'A2'); *i–ii*, *1–3* 4–18. π1 hft.
On p. 4, line 15, the last word is added in ms.
A copy from Tom's Coffee House has been
seen with date 31 Jan.
'From Cæsar, now, each poet hopes reward'
L(1959, uncut, −π1),O(uncut); CSmH,CtY,MH,
OCU.

S356 **Several.** Several copies of verses on occasion of
Mr. Gulliver's travels. Never before printed.
London, printed for Benj. Motte, 1727. (*SR* 4 May)
8⁰: *A*⁴ B–D⁴; *1–4* 5–30 *31–32 blk*. A1 hft.
Griffith 187; *Rothschild* 1592; *Teerink* 1224.

Several copies of verses

First published with four poems only. Advertised in *SJEP* 6 May. Deposit copies at
LSC,E,EU,SaU, probably at L,O. The verses
were simultaneously published in the 'second
edition' of *Gulliver's travels*, and there also
copies are found with and without the fifth
poem, printed as *². Entered after *Gulliver*
in Bowyer's ledgers under 3 May as '2 sheets
& ¼', 1000 copies printed.
'In amaze/Lost, I gaze!'
Crum I1237. Usually attributed to Pope (cf.
Twickenham ed. VI.266–7 and references);
but see Sherburn in *Texas studies in language
and literature* 3 (1961) 3–7 arguing for a joint
production of Pope, Gay and Arbuthnot.
L(992.h.7/6,−D4),O(−D4),E(−D4),DN(−D4),
SaU+; CLU-C,CSmH(−D4),CtY(−D4),PU
(−A1,D4).

S357 — [*reissue*]
8⁰: *A*⁴ B⁴ *² C–D⁴; *1–4* 5–17 14–30 *31–32 blk*. A1 hft.
Griffith 188. Added poem 'The words of the
king' on *². Bowyer's paper ledger records
delivery to Motte on 11 May of '500 of a
quarter sheet in verse annex'd to Gulliver';
whether this represents the additions to the
pamphlet or to the volume, the date probably
indicates the time the addition was made.
L(Ashley 1302,−D4),O(−A1,D4),OW,DN;
CSmH,CtY(−A1,D4),IU,MH(2,−D4),TxU
(−D4).

S358 — [*idem*] Poems occasion'd by reading the Travels
of Captain Lemuel Gulliver, explanatory and
commendatory. *Dublin, printed by and for J. Hyde*,
1727.
8⁰: A⁸; *1–3* 4–16.
Griffith 189; *Rothschild* 1593. Four poems only.
L(12274.e.1/8),C,DT; CSmH,CtY.

S359 —— [*Dublin*, 1727.]
½⁰: 1 side, 3 columns.
Four poems only, reprinting the Dublin text.
L(1872.a.1/11, mutilated),DT.

S360 — The several qualities of the British court,
characteris'd. D. of Marlborough, E. of Godolphin
[and 19 more]... *London, printed in the year* 1707.
(*DC* 22 May)
8⁰: *A*⁴; *1* 2–8.
'Brave Marlbro' who preserves our Capitol'
A general eulogy.
L(1078.l.18).

S361 **Seward, Benjamin.** A hymn. Compos'd by Mr.
Benjamin Seward. [17––.]
slip: 1 side, 1 column.
'Come, blessed Jesus, quickly come'
Harding.

Sewell, George. Miscellanies in verse and prose.
Written by Mr. Sewell. *London, printed for E. Curll*,
1714. (*PB* 4 Feb)
8⁰.   O(impft); ICN.

Sewell, G. *Collections*

Title for a nonce collection (price 4*s*.); the contents appear to vary in the way typical of Curll's collections.

— Poems on several occasions. *London, printed for E. Curll & J. Pemberton*, 1719. (*PB* 29 Jan)
8⁰: pp. vii, 76.   L,O; CtY,MH.

— A new collection of original poems, never printed in any miscellany. By the author of Sir Walter Raleigh. *London, printed for J. Pemberton, & J. Peele*, 1720. (March)
8⁰: pp. 87.   L,O; CtY,MH.
  Entered in Bowyer's paper ledger, 750 copies printed, first delivered on 25 and 26 March.

— Posthumous works of Dr. George Sewell... To which are added, Poems on several occasions, published in his life-time. *London, printed for Henry Curll*, 1728.
8⁰: pp. xxiv, 56 + 76.   L,O; ICU,MH.
  The second part is a reissue of *Poems*, 1719. Half the copyright in 'Sewell's Poems, 2 parts' formed part of lot 24 in the trade sale of John Pemberton, 8 Jan 1741 (cat. at O-JJ).

— Callipædia. A poem [in part translated by Sewell], 1712–. *See* R280.

S362 [—] Carmen seculare, for the year 1720. An ode humbly inscribed to the king, on his return from Hannover. *London, printed for John Pemberton, & Thomas Jauncy*, 1720. (*DP* 12 Dec)
2⁰: A² B–H²; i–iii iv, 1 2–28.
  Advertised in *DP* as 'presented yesterday to the king' and as printed for J. Roberts.
'Hail! sacred name! who kindly live'
  Preface signed 'G.S.' Almost certainly by Sewell; other poems of his were published this year by Pemberton, Jauncy, and Roberts.
L(1347.m.42, lacks all but B²); OCU,TxU.

S363 — An epistle from Hampstead, to Mr. Thornhill in Covent-Garden. *London, printed for J. Pemberton, & J. Watts*, 1719. (*DC* 11 May)
2⁰: A² B–C²; i–iv, 1 2–7 8 blk.
'Thornhill, what miracles are to be wrought'
L(1962); *CU*,DFo,MH,TxU(2).

S364 [—] An epistle from London, to Richardson Pack, esq; at St. Edmond's-Bury. Written at the decline of the South-Sea. *London, printed for Jacob Tonson*, 1722 [1721]. (*DC* 27 Nov)
2⁰: A² B²; i–ii, 1 2–5 6 blk.
'Wrapt in the pleasures of a country seat'
  Early ms. attribution to 'Sewel' in the TxU copy; advertised in *DC* as by him.
O; TxU.

[—] An epistle from Sempronia to Cethegus, 1713. *See* E375.

— An epistle to Anthony Hammond esq; [1720.] *In* R105.

Sewell, G. *An epistle*

S365 [—] An epistle to Joseph Addison, esq; occasioned by the death of the right honourable Charles, late earl of Halifax. *London, printed for J. Roberts*, 1715. (*PB* 25 Aug)
2⁰: A² B–C²; i–ii, 1–9 10 blk.
'And shall great Halifax resign to fate'
  Advertised in *PB* by Curll as by Sewell; reprinted in his *Poems*, 1719.
DT; CSmH,CU,CtY,TxU.

S366 [—] The favourite, a simile. *Etonæ, typis Savilianis, anno* 1712. (*PPB* 26 Feb)
½⁰: 1–2, 1 column.
'When boys at Eton once a year'
  Reprinted in Sewell's *Poems*, 1719. Advertised in *PPB* as 'on Mr. Walpole's being sent to the Tower'.
DT,MC,Crawford; MH,TxU.

S367 [—] An ode on his majesty's happy arrival. Humbly inscrib'd to the right honourable James Craggs, esq;... *London, printed for J. Pemberton, & T. Jauncy*, 1720. (7 Nov?)
2⁰: A² B¹; 1–3 4–6.
  The relation between this and the following is obscure. The poem was advertised in *DP* 7 Nov with Sewell's name, and there is no evidence from watermarks to suggest that the state bearing his name is on fine paper.
'He lands––––the pious fears Britannia bore'
OCU.

S367·1 — [variant title:] By Mr. Sewell.
ICN(cropt).

S368 [—] An ode to Mr. Tickell, occasion'd by his ode to the right honourable the Earl of Sunderland, at Windsor. *London, printed for J. Pemberton; sold by T. Jauncy, & J. Roberts*, [1720.] (3 June, Luttrell)
½⁰: 2 sides, 1 column.
  Advertised in *PB* 4 June as 'by Mr. Sewell'.
'Tickell, whose muse ambitious sings'
  Signed 'G.S.', 28 May 1720.
O; CLU-C(Luttrell).

S369 — The patriot. A poem, inscrib'd to the right honourable Robert earl of Oxford, &c... *London, printed for E. Curll*, 1712. (27 June?)
2⁰: A¹ B–C² D¹; i–ii, 1–10.
  Watermark: O. A1 and D1 have been seen to be conjugate. Publication dated 28 June by *Straus, Curll*; advertised in *PB* 1 July.
'A patriot soul by nature is design'd'
  Printed in Sewell's *Posthumous works*, 1728, as 'Walpole: or, the patriot'!
L(11631.i.15/9),O(2),DrU,*LdU-B*; CSmH,CtY, ICN,KU(uncut),MH(uncut, ms. date 27 June?)+.

S370 — [fine paper]
  Watermark: IM.
O; TxU.

S371 [—] A poem upon his majesties accession. Inscrib'd to his grace John duke of Marlborough. By the

Sewell, G. A poem upon his majesties accession

author of the verses upon his grace's retiring into Germany. *London, printed for J. Roberts, 1714.* (8 Oct, Luttrell)
2º: *A²* B–C²; *1–2* 3–11 *12 blk.*
Listed in *MC* Oct.
'What? are at length the doubtful nations freed?'
   Early ms. attributions in copies at CtY,TxU; reprinted in Sewell's *Poems*, 1719. Attributed to Garth in a ms. note in the CtY-M copy because Sewell's *To his grace the Duke of Marlborough*, 1713, was wrongly ascribed to Garth.
LDW(2),O(2),AdU; CtY,CtY-M(uncut),InU (Luttrell),TxU(2, 1 uncut).

S372 — The proclamation of Cupid: or, a defence of women. A poem from Chaucer. *London, printed for W. Meares, J. Brown, & F. Clay, 1718 [1717].* (*DC* 18 Nov)
2º: *A²* a¹ B–F²; *i–vi, 1* 2–20.
   Advertised in DC 15 Nov for 'to-morrow'. A third share of the copyright formed part of lot 13 in the trade sale of Francis Clay, 12 Sept 1738 (cat. at O-JJ).
'We Cupid, king, whose arbitrary sway'
L(11631.k.5/4); CSmH(uncut),ICN,ICU,IU, TxU(2)+.

[—] Protestant popery: or, the convocation [actually by Nicholas Amhurst], 1718. *See* A200.

S373 [—] To his grace the Duke of Marlborough, on the report of his going into Germany. *[London] Printed for E. Curll, & J. Pemberton, 1713 [1712].* (10 Nov, Luttrell)
½º: *1–2*, 1 column.
   Four books advertised below imprint. Copies bear the halfpenny tax stamp. The Luttrell copy is recorded by *Thorn-Drury*; his copy appears to have subsequently been at MH, disposed of as a duplicate in 1947.
'Go, mighty prince, and those great nations see'
   Reprinted in Sewell's *Poems*, 1719. Wrongly ascribed to Garth; see A. Rosenberg in *N&Q* (1956) 429–30.
L(1850.c.10/40; 1871.e.1/221),OA,MC,Crawford; CtY,MH.

S374 [—] [reimpression] To his grace the Duke of Marlborough, upon his going into Germany. *[London] Printed for E. Curll, & J. Pemberton, 1713.*
   Five books and six lives advertised below imprint; two lines have been moved back to p. 1 to make room for them.
C.

S375 [—] Verses to her royal highness the Princess of Wales. Occasion'd by the death of the young prince. *London, printed for E. Curll, 1718.* (*PB* 18 Feb)
8º: *A⁴* B⁴ *C¹*; *1–10* 11–17 *18 blk. A1 hft.*
'Fair royal mourner! hear the pious muse'
   Reprinted in Sewell's *Poems*, 1719.
LDW(–A1),O; KU.

Sewell, G. Verses to his grace

S376 [—] Verses to his grace the Duke of Marlborough, upon the present rebellion. *London, printed for J. Roberts, 1715.* (27 Sept, Luttrell)
½º: *1–2*, 1 column.
   Listed in *MC* Sept; also in *MC* Oct as 'by Mr. Sewell', printed for J. Baker.
'Once more, great prince, in shining arms appear'
   Reprinted in Sewell's *Poems*, 1719.
MH.

S377 — Verses to the right honourable the Lord Carteret, principal secretary of state. *London, printed for Jacob Tonson, 1721.* (*PB* 25 March)
2º: *A²* B²; *i–ii, 1* 2–6.
   Watermark: ? script J.
'Sure there's a fate in excellence too strong'
LVA-F; CtY,ICU(Luttrell, April),MH.

S378 — [fine paper]
   Watermark: fleur-de-lys.
TxU.

S379 [—] Verses written on the morning of the Duke of Marlborough's funeral. By the author of those on his grace's going into Germany. *[London] Printed for John Pemberton, 1722.*
½º: *1–2*, 1 column.
'The sun appears to take a farewell view'
   Sewell's authorship is clear from the reference to *To his grace the Duke...*, 1713.
L(1876.f.1/93, cropt); MH.

S380 [**Seymour, Frances,** *duchess of Somerset.*] The story of Inkle and Yarrico. A most moving tale from the Spectator. Attempted in veres [!] by the right hon. the Countess of ****. *London, printed for J. Cooper, in Fleetstreet, 1738.* (*GM,LM* May)
2º: *A²* B–D²; *1–5* 6–10 *11–13* 14–16. *1 hft; 2 errata slip.*
   On p. 11 there is a second title-page 'An epistle from Yarrico to Inkle, after he had left her in slavery', followed by the poem on pp. 13–16.
'A youth there was possess'd of every charm'
Epistle: 'If yet thou any memory retain'
   For the authorship see H. S. Hughes, *The gentle Hertford* (1940) 419.
L(840.m.1/41),O; CLU-C,CSmH,KU,MH(–A1).

S381 [**Shadwell, Charles.**] A second song, sung at the club at Mr. Taplin's the sign of the Drapier's-head in Truck-street. *Dublin, printed in the year 1725.*
½º: 1 side, 1 column.
'Since the Drapier's set up, and Wood is cry'd down'
   Attributed to Shadwell in the *Hibernian patriot*; cf. Swift, *Drapier's letters* ed. H. Davis (1935) 382. In praise of Swift.
LVA-F.

S382 **Sham.** The sham author; or, the English rap, explained... Written by Patrick-Vanmattersculpt. *London printed: and re-printed at the request of the several societies of artists in Dublin, 1735.*

8º: *A–B⁴*; *1–2* 3–16.
There was probably no London edition.
'A captain once to Britain sail'd'
DA.

S383 Sharp, Joseph. ⟨The⟩ lawyer's tears. A mourning elegy occasioned by the sudden, and much lamented death of Francis Bernard, esq; one of the judges of his majesty's court of common pleas, on Wednesday July 30, 1731. [*Dublin*] *Printed* [*by Richard Dickson?*] *in Silver-Court in Castle-street*, 1731.
½º: 1 side, 1 column.
'O Bernard! could these notes of mourning lays'
DT.

S384 She. She put her hand upon his scull, | With this prophetick blessing, Be thou dull, &c. [*Edinburgh*, 1706?]
½º: 1 side, 1 column.
'Ye coblers, and taylors draw near'
A satire against Lord Belhaven and his attacks on the union with England, particularly *A Scots answer to a British vision*, [1706.]
E(3),ES; MH.

S385 — She wou'd if she cou'd, or a poem on a certain young widow. [*Dublin*, 1726.]
½º: 1 side, 1 column.
On the other side of the DN copy, *A satyr on the author of She would if she could*, 1726.
'Widows all of Dublin town'
On Margaretta, in namby-pamby verses.
DN; NN,OCU.

S386 — She's her own woman again. [*London*] *Sold by J. Baker*, 1710. (Sept, Luttrell)
½º: 2 sides, 1 column.
A long prose introduction on side 1. Baker's name has been deleted in ink in the copy seen.
'A woman grown lousey for want of due care'
In praise of Queen Anne appointing the tory ministry.
MC(Luttrell).

S387 Sheeres, Peregrine. A new year's gift: intitul'd Sacred contentment, to her sacred majesty Queen Anne. From her dutiful, and loyal subject, Perigrine Sheeres. [170–.]
4º: *a–b² c¹, A² B–C²; i–x, 1 blk 2–11 12 blk*. a1 woodcut frt; b1 blank.
The collation of the preliminary leaves is tentative. The copy seen had only the stub of a1, but had offset of a woodcut bust of Queen Anne, printed sideways, on the title a2. b2 is the dedication leaf with the dedicatee's name stamped in; 'Sir Stephen Fox' in the copy seen. c1 (with vertical chain-lines) bears 'An acrostick upon the name of her most sacred majesty'.
'Sacra coronatum præit Autarcheia monarcham'
'Content transcends a crown, 'tis wisdom's mark'
Sotheby's 16 May 1962, lot 557(–a1).

Sheffield, John, *duke of Buckingham*. The works of...John Sheffield... Published, by his grace, in his life time. *London, printed for E. Curll*, 1721. (12 Dec).
8º: pp. 151.   L,O; DLC,KU.

— The works of John Sheffield... *London, printed by John Barber, alderman of London*, 1723. (*DC* 25 Jan)
4º: 2 vol.   L,O; CtY.
Watermark: Strasburg bend. Seized by a warrant of 26 Jan. Two prose essays in vol. 2 (pp. 69–102, 159–172) were suppressed; the original sheets are not uncommon, and the omissions were subsequently reprinted on unwatermarked paper and inserted in other copies. Vol. 1 was entered to Alderman Barber in Bowyer's ledgers under 13 Dec 1722, 500 copies and 100 fine. Entered in *SR* to Barber by John Wright, 15 Jan; deposit copy at O. Republished 29 Feb 1724 (*EvP*); sold by W. Taylor, J. Bowyer, and W. & J. Innys.

— [fine paper]   L.
Watermark: Strasburg bend over LVG; the copy seen is in contemporary morocco.

— [reissue?] *London, printed for John Barber; sold by the booksellers of London & Westminster*, 1723.
L,O; CtY,MH.
Cancel title, possibly for booksellers', as opposed to subscribers' copies.

— — 'Printed for John Barber, alderman of London' [*T. Johnson, The Hague*], 1726.
8º: 2 vol.   L,O; CSmH,DLC.
On half-title to vol. 1, 'A new edition, with several additions, and without any castrations'.

— — The second edition corrected. *London, printed for J.B.* [*James Barber*]; *sold by Aaron Ward, T. Wotton, D. Browne, R. Williamson, T. Astley, & J. Stagg*, 1729. (*MChr* 14 Feb)
8º: 2 vol.   L,O; MH.

— — The third edition, corrected. *London, printed for T. Wotton, D. Browne, T. Astley, A. Millar, J. Stagg, & S. Williamson*, 1740.
8º: 2 vol.   L,O; MH.

S388 — An essay on poetry: by the right honourable the Earl of Murlgrave. *London printed, and sold by H. Hills*, 1709.
8º: A⁸; *1–2* 3–16.
Signature A2 under 'is by'. First published in 1682.
'Of things in which mankind does most excel'
O,CT; CtY,IU,OCU.

S389 — [another edition]
Signature A2 under 'by all'. Reissued with other remaindered Hills poems in *A collection of the best English poetry*, 1717 (*Case* 294).
L(C.124.b.7/43),LG,O(uncut),E(2),WcC+;
CLU-C(uncut),CtY,MH,TxU.

Sheffield, J., *duke*

S390 — The temple of death, a poem, by the right honourable the Marquis of Normanby: a translation out of French. With an ode in memory of her late majesty Queen Mary. By a person of quality. *London printed, and sold by H. Hills,* 1709.
8°: A⁸; *1–2* 3–16.
Signature A2 under 'which it'.
'In those cold climates, where the sun appears'
Ode: 'Long our divided state'
Translated from P. Habert, *Le temple de la mort.*
L(11601.d.20/2),O(2),CT,EU,AdU; CtY,MH, TxU.

S391 — [another edition]
Signature A2 under first letters of 'which'. Reissued with other remaindered Hills poems in *A collection of the best English poetry,* 1717 (*Case* 294).
L(C.124.b.7/5),O,C; CtY,IU,MH.
[—] Third chorus. Of Roman senators. – Fourth chorus. Of Roman soldiers, [1723.] *In* P876.

Sheilds, Alexander. *See* Shields, Alexander.

S392 **Shelvocke, George.** 'Divine love; being a brief rehearsal of some particular instances of god's goodness, extracted from holy writ. A pindarick poem. Part the first. [*London*] *Printed for James Mills; sold by W. Boreham.*' (*PB* 29 April 1718)
'Adorn'd with a curious frontispiece', *PB.*

S393 **'Shenkin ap Morgan.'** The true-born Welshman. Written by Shenkin ap Morgan, and published on St. Taffy's day, for the honour of hur country. *London, printed for Shon ap Rice, at the sign of the Goat in Rixham Row,* 1701. (1 March, Luttrell)
½°: *1–2,* 1 column.
'Cot-splut-hur-nails! Shall hur sit dumb and mute'
The author and imprint are probably both pseudonymous.
CLU-C,MH(Luttrell).

[**Shenstone, William.**] Poems upon various occasions. Written for the entertainment of the author, and printed for the amusement of a few friends, prejudic'd in his favour. *Oxford, printed by Leon Lichfield,* 1737.
8°: pp. vii, 69.   L,O; CtY,MH.
Watermark: pro patria. There are variant forms of the imprint, with and without a colon after 'Oxford'. Presentation copy at MH.

— [another issue] By William Shenstone, gent.
O.
There is no evidence that the title is a cancel; the quotation it bears is different from the preceding. Though the watermark is identical, the paper in the copy seen may possibly be finer than the preceding.

— [fine paper]   CtY.
Watermark: fleur-de-lys.

Shenstone, W.

— The works in verse and prose... *London, printed for R. & J. Dodsley,* 1764.
8°: 2 vol.   L,O; MH.
A third volume was printed in 1769.

———

S394 [—] The judgment of Hercules, a poem. Inscrib'd to George Lyttelton esq; *London, printed for R. Dodsley; sold by T. Cooper,* 1741. (23 April)
8°: *A*² B–C⁸ D²; *i–ii, 1–2* 3–35 *36–37;* 38 blk. A1 hft; D2 advt.
Rothschild 1837. Publication date from *Straus, Dodsley;* listed in *GM,LM* April.
'While blooming spring descends from genial skies'
Reprinted in Shenstone's *Works,* 1764. Based on the abstract of Prodicus in Xenophon's *Memorabilia.*
L(11631.f.16,–A1; Ashley 1682),LVA-F,O(2, 1 uncut, –A1, D2),OW,LdU-B; CLU-C,CSmH (–A1, D2),ICN,MH,TxU(–A1).

S395 [—] The school-mistress, a poem. In imitation of Spenser. *London, printed for R. Dodsley; sold by T. Cooper,* 1742. (*LEP* 15 May)
8°: π² A⁸ B⁴; [*28*]. π1 blk; π2 hft.
Watermark: GM garlanded. *Bond* 178; *Rothschild* 1838. Title in red and black.
'Ah me! full sorely is my heart forlorn'
An earlier version was printed in Shenstone's *Poems,* 1737; reprinted in his *Works,* 1764.
L(11631.d.49, –π²; 164.l.17, –π²; Ashley 4237, uncut),LVA-D,O(–π²),CT(–π²); CSmH,CtY, MH(–π1),NNP(–π²),TxU(–π1)+.

S396 [—] [fine paper]
Watermark: Strasburg bend.
LVA-F(presentation copy, 1752, –π1); MH(–π1).

S397 **Shepheard, James.** An hymn to the holy and undivided trinity; written by James Shepheard, during his imprisonment. Printed from the copy which he wrote and gave to his mother two hours before his execution. *London, printed for J. Bettenham,* 1718. (*PB* 22 March)
2°: A¹ B²; *i–ii, 1* 2–4.
Entered to William & John Innys in Bowyer's ledgers under 22 March 1718, 2000 copies printed; 1900 were delivered to Bettenham, 100 to Innys.
'All creating father, all sustaining'
L(1851.c.19/29, uncut; C.116.i.4/70, lacks A1); NcU.

S398 — An hymn to the holy and undivided trinity. [*London,* 1718.]
½°: 1 side, 1 column.
Signed, 'Newgate March, 17. 1718.' This edition may possibly be the earlier.
Harding.

———

Shepherd. The shepherd's tears: a pastoral, [1724.] *See* Pennecuik, Alexander, *d. 1730.*

Shepherd, S.

Shepherd, Samuel. Part of the poetical works of the late Rev. Samuel Shepherd... *Dublin, printed by Sleater,* 1790.
8°: pp. viii, 247.   L,O; ICU.

S399 [—] Chloe surpriz'd: or, the second part of the Lady's dressing-room. To which are added, Thoughts upon reading the Lady's dressing-room, and the Gentleman's study. The former... by D----n S----t, the latter by Miss W— —. *London, printed, and Dublin, reprinted,* 1732.
8°: *A*⁴; *1–3* 4–8.
   Teerink 961. There was probably no London edition.
'One morning as Chloe the prude lay a-bed'
   Printed in Shepherd's *Poetical works,* 1790; it has no real relation to Swift's poem.
L(11632.aa.67),LVA-F,DA; CtY,PU.

S400 — Leixlip: a poem. Inscribed to the right honourable William Conolly, esq; *Dublin, printed by George Faulkner,* 1747.
8°: *A*⁴ B⁴; *1–5* 6–15 *16*. 16 advt.
'Leixlip! thy devious walks, thy vary'd views'
L(11632.c.51),O(2),C,DA(2),DN(3); CSmH,CtY, ICN,NNC.

S401 [—] An ode, to be performed at the castle of Dublin, on the 1st. of March, being the birth-day of...Queen Caroline... Set to musick by Mr. Matthew Dubourg... *Dublin, printed by S. Powell, for George Ewing,* 1736.
4°: *A*⁴; *1–3* 4–7 *8 blk.*
'Where-e'er Hibernia's tuneful lyre is strung'
   Printed in Shepherd's *Poetical works,* 1790.
CSmH.

S402 [—] Pallas and Venus reconcil'd. A poem. Inscrib'd to a young lady on her birth-day. [*Dublin*] *Printed in the year* 1731.
8°: *A*⁴; *1–2* 3–8.
   Rothschild 203.
'In ancient days (as authors speak'
   Early ms. attribution to 'the revd. Mr. Sheppard' in the DN copy; reprinted in his *Poetical works,* 1790. To Kitty, his future wife.
DK,DN; IU,MH,TxU.

S403 [—] A poem inscribed to the right honourable the Lord Tullamoore. Occasioned by the late charity. *Dublin, printed by George Faulkner,* 1740.
8°: *A*⁴; *1–2* 3–6 *7–8*. A4 advt.
'While thousands, crowding with a grateful strife'
   Note in LVA-F copy that it was attributed to Shepherd in 'the ms. index', presumably to the volume from which it was extracted. Reprinted in his *Poetical works,* 1790.
LVA-F(−A4),O(−A4),DA(−A4),DT(uncut), LdU-B.

[**Sherborne, —,** *Mr.*] John and Betty. A tale, 1746. *See* J68.

Sherburn, W.

S404 **Sherburn, William.** The fourth book of Virgil's Æneid... Translated into English verse. To which are added the following poems, viz.... *London, printed for J. Pemberton,* 1723.
8°: *A*² B–H⁴; *i–iv, 1* 2–55 *56 blk.*
Four added poems on pp. 47–55.
'But long had wasting cares the queen opprest'
L(1103.c.18/10); CtY.

Sheridan. 'Sheridan's resurrection.' [1722.]
   Referred to in *A poam* [!] *on Tom Pun----bi ...in vindication of some verses written, entitled Sheridan's resurrection,* 1722; see also *Tom Pun-sibi's resurrection disprov'd,* [1722.] No copy has been traced, and the exact title remains in doubt.

[**Sheridan, Thomas.**] An answre [!] to the Christmas-box, 1729. *See* A246.

S405 [—] 'Ballyspellin.' [*Dublin?* 1728.]
   Williams 437, quoting Swift's letter of 28 Sept 1728 saying that Sheridan 'sent us in print a ballad upon Ballyspelling'. The printed edition is untraced.
'All you that wou'd refine your blood'

S406 [—] The Drapier's ballad. To the tune of the London 'prentice. *Dublin, printed by John Harding,* 1724–5.
½°: 1 side, 2 columns.
   Rothschild 1853; *Teerink* 1175.
'Of a worthy Dublin Drapier'
   Attributed to Sheridan in *The Hibernian patriot,* 1730.
L(C.121.g.8/36),LVA-F,DT,Rothschild.

[—] Epilogue. Designed to be spoken by Alonzo, at the acting of the Revenge by some school-boys, [1727?] *See* E346.

S407 [—] The invitation in imitation of Horace's epistle to Torquatus... Written by Mr. T. S--- to D---r S---. *Dublin, printed* 1720.
½°: 1 side, 1 column.
   Rothschild 1850; *Teerink* 1094.
'Dear Doctor – Being you're so kind'
   Clearly an invitation from Sheridan to Swift is intended, and his authorship is accepted by *Rothschild.*
Rothschild; TxU.

S408 — Mr. Sheridan's prologue, to the Greek play of Phædra and Hyppolitus; design'd to have been spoke by a boy of six years old. *Dublin, printed in the year* 1721.
½°: 1 side, 1 column.
'Under the notion of a play you see'
   This is the prologue that was to have been spoken by the six-year-old Tom Putland; Richard Helsham persuaded him to substitute his own, printed as *D—n S—t's prologue,* 1720; see *Williams* 1023n.
Rothschild; TxU.

Sheridan, T. A new simile

S409 [—] A new simile for the ladies, with useful annotations. *Dublin, printed in the year 1732.*
8°: A⁴; *1–2* 3–8.
> *Teerink* 960; *Williams* 612. *Teerink* 1615 records that the copy of an edition of this poem with Swift's *An answer to a scandalous poem,* 1733, seen and noted by Williams as 1733, pp. 8+8, lacked the first and last leaves. Apparently it might have been an imperfect copy of this with Swift's poem added.
'I often try'd in vain to find'
> For Sheridan's authorship see *Williams* and refs.

LVA-F,DN; IU,TxU.

S410 [—] [*idem*] The simile: or, woman a cloud. A poem. *London, printed for W. Owen,* 1748. (*BM, GM* April)
2°: A² B²; *1–3* 4–8.
> Variant first line:
'In vain I oft have try'd to find'
L(11602.i.26/7).

S411 — An ode to be performed at the castle of Dublin, March the 1st, 1728–9. Being the birth-day of her most serene majesty Queen Caroline... The musick compos'd by Matthew Dubourg... *Dublin, printed in the year* 1728–9.
4°: A⁴; *1–2* 3–7 *8 blk.*
'Early queen of light arise'
DT; DLC.

S411·5 [—] An ode, to be perform'd at the castle of Dublin, on the 1st. of March 1729–30. Being the birth-day of...Queen Caroline... Set to musick for this day, by Mr. Matthew Dubourg... *Dublin, printed for George Ewing,* 1730.
4°: A⁴; *1–2* 3–7 *8 blk.*
> Wrongly ascribed to William Dunkin by the L catalogue by confusion with his ode of 1734; although the text has not been collated with the preceding, the ode has the same first line.
L(11633.bbb.6).

S412 [—] A prologue design'd for the play of Oedipus. Written in Greek, and perform'd by Mr. Sheridan's scholars, at the King's-Inn's-hall, on Tuesday the 10th of December, 1723. [*Dublin,* 1723.]
½°: 1 side, 1 column.
'To day before a learn'd audience comes'
> There is no proof of Sheridan's authorship of this and the other prologues to his school's plays below. In view of their consistent satire upon his discipline, they must at the very least have been written with his connivance, and it seems desirable to bring them together. W. R. Wilde, *The closing years of Dean Swift's life* (1849) 159 wrongly identifies this with Richard Helsham's burlesque prologue of 1720.
CSmH.

S413 [—] Prologue spoke at the Theatre-royal in behalf of the poor weavers of the city of Dublin, April,

Sheridan, T. Prologue spoke

1st. 1720. By Mr. Elrington. *Dublin, printed by J. Carson,* [1720.]
½°: 1 side, 1 column.
'Great cry and little wool – is now become'
> Reprinted as Sheridan's in Concanen's *Miscellaneous poems,* 1724; see *Williams* 273–4. The PU copy of the following edition has early ms. note 'I believe this was written by Dr. Delany', but there is no support for this attribution.
L(C.121.g.8/11),DG.

S414 [—] [*idem*] A prologue, spoke by Mr. Elrington at the Theatre-royal on Saturday the first of April. In the behalf of the distressed weavers. *Dublin, printed by John Harding,* [1720.]
½°: 1 side, 1 column.
> The copy at DA has verso blank; all other copies print Swift's *An epilogue as it was spoke by Mr. Griffith* (S839) on the other side.
L(1850.c.10/4; 1890.e.5/67),C,DA; PU,TxU.

S415 [—] Prologue spoken before a Greek play, at the reverend Dr. Sheridan's school, at the breaking-up of his scholars for Christmas, 1728. *Dublin printed, and sold at the pamphlet-shop opposite the Tholsel in Skinner-row,* 1729.
½°: 2 sides, 1 column.
> 'Epilogue' at foot of side 1.
'Come out my lads, make haste, come out and play'
Epilogue: 'Grand-mothers, mothers, aunts, and sisters dear'
> For Sheridan's authorship, compare *A prologue design'd for...Oedipus* above.
DT.

S416 [—] A prologue to Julius Cæsar, as it was acted at Madam Violante's booth, December the 15th, 1732, by some of the young gentlemen in Dr. Sheridan's school. *Dublin, printed by S. Hyde,* [1732.]
½°: 1 side, 1 column.
'Ladies, our master chose a dreadful play'
> For Sheridan's authorship, compare *A prologue design'd for...Oedipus* above.
DFo.

[—] Punch's petition to the ladies, [1724.] *See* P1167.

[—] A riddle by Doctor R—e, [1725/30.] *See* S899.

[—] A riddle by Dr, S—t, [1725/30.] *See* R204.

[—] A riddle by the reverend Dean S—y, [1726/27?] *See* S508.

[—] To the honourable Mr. D.T., 1725. *See* T373.

S417 [—] To the right honourable the lord Viscount Mont-Cassel: this fable is most humbly dedicated by a person who had some share in his education. *Dublin, printed by S. Harding,* 1727.
8°: A⁴; *1–2* 3–8.
'A peacock nobly born, and bred'
> Ms. attribution to Sheridan in the L copy;

Sheridan, T. To the right honourable

> Mountcashel certainly went to Sheridan's school, and the attribution is very plausible.
> L(12304.c.12).

S418 [—] Tom Punsibi's letter to Dean Swift. [*Dublin*] *Printed in the year* 1727.
½°: 1 side, 2 columns.
'When to my house you come dear Dean'
> The nickname is Sheridan's, and the poem has always been accepted as his; compare *Williams* 1045.

L(1890.e.5/227; C.121.g.8/158),C,DT.

[—] A trip to Temple-Oge, Stephen's-green and the Bason, 1730. *See* T489.

S419 [—] [A true and faithful inventory...] A letter. Sir, there having been some editions of Dean Swift's Cadenus and Vanessa publish'd before the following little copy was added to it; you are desired to give it the publick in a single paper... A true and faithful inventory of the goods belonging to D. Sw—t, vicar of Lara Cor; upon lending his house to the Bishop of M—, till his own was built. [*Dublin*, 1726.]
½°: 1 side, 1 column.
> *Teerink* 931, *Williams* 1034–5, 1044. Reprinted with Blandford's fourth edition of Swift's *Cadenus and Vanessa*, 1726.
'An oaken broken elbow chair'
> For the attribution to Sheridan, see *Williams* and refs.

DT.

S419·5 [**Sherman, Thomas.**] Youth's tragedy, a poem. Drawn up by way of dialogue... For the caution, and direction of the younger sort. *London printed, and sold by Nath. Hillier*, 1707.
8°: A–D⁴; *1*–2 3–31 *32 blk*.
> First published in 1671 (*Wing* S3392) as 'By T.S.'
'How pleasant is it, when the sun displays'
O.

S419·6 [—] [*idem*] Youth undone: a tragick poem: compos'd by way of discourse... For the caution and direction of young people. *London, printed by T. Ilive, for Jonathan Robinson*, 1709.
4°: A² B–D⁴; *1*–4 5–28.
O; DFo.

S420 Shields, Alexander. An elegie upon the death of that famous and faithful minister, and martyr, Mr. James Renwick. By...Master Alexander Shiels. [*Edinburgh?*] *Printed in the year* 1711.
8°: A–B⁴; *1*–2 3–15 *16*.
> First published 1688 (*Wing* S3430; copy at L).
'Here's work, alas! for mourners, to deplore'
E.

S421 —— composed immediately after his execution at Edinburgh, 17th February, 1688. [*Edinburgh?*] *Printed in the year* 1688, *reprinted, anno* 1723.

Shields, A. An elegie

8°: A–B⁴; *1*–3 4–16.
L(C.53.k.4/4, mutilated),E(3); CSmH.

S422 Shiells, Robert. Marriage: a poetical essay. *London, printed for R. Griffiths*, 1748. (*GM, LM* Feb)
4°: *A*¹ B–E⁴ F⁴(−F4); *i*–ii, *1* 2–37 *38 blk*.
'Rehearse, my muse, the solemn rites of love'
L(11630.c.8/4, mutilated),O; ICN,MH,*RPB*.

S423 [—] —— '*London, printed for R. Griffiths*', 1748.
8°: π² A–B⁴ C²; *i*–iv, *1* 2–20. π1 hft.
> Possibly an Edinburgh piracy; a space between rules on the title suggests that the author's name was suppressed.

AdU.

S424 —— *Dublin, printed by George Faulkner*, 1747 [1748].
12°: A¹² (A3 as 'B3'); *1*–2 3–23 *24 blk*.
L(C.71.bb.15/3),DT; CtY.

S425 Shining. The shining sisters. Written at Tunbridge. *London, printed for Bernard Lintot*, 1712. (*PB* 2 Sept)
½°: *1*–2, 1 column.
> Copies bear the new halfpenny tax stamp.
'Now, happy spring, retrieve thy sinking name'
> In praise of Marlborough and the beauties of his daughters.

Herts CRO (Panshanger box 46),Crawford; OCU, TxU,Brett-Smith.

S426 Ship. The ship's mate and the parson, a poem to his grace the lord arch-bishop of Dublin. [*Dublin*] *Printed by Rich. Dickson*, [1725/29.]
½°: 1 side, 2 columns.
'Prithee! adventrous Jac——n stay'
> A satire on Jackson, the chaplain (?) to William King, archbishop of Dublin.

L(C.121.g.8/94).

S427 [**Shippen, William.**] Faction display'd. A poem ... From a correct copy. *London, printed in the year* 1704.
4°: *A*² B–C⁴ D²; *i*–iv, *1*–20.
> Last line on p. iv reads 'Government'; two rules at head of p. iv. This and the two following entries represent one basic setting of type; this impression has the top rule on p. 1 in one piece.

'Say, goddess muse, for thy all-searching eyes'
> Attributed to Shippen by *Jacob* and also by Pope (a friend of Shippen) in his copy of *A new collection*, 1705 (*Case* 237) at L. Also attributed, together with *Moderation display'd*, to Bertram Stote in [William Pittis], *The proceedings of both houses of parliament*, 1710; to Mr. Priaulx in Hearne, *Remarks & Collections* I.31; and to 'Mr. D--' in [Defoe?] *The experiment*, 1705. See F. H. Ellis in *POAS* VI.649f. Believed by many contemporaries (including the author of *Faction display'd...answer'd*) to

Shippen, W. Faction display'd

be by Prior; he explicitly denied it in a letter of 28 April 1704. *Faction display'd. The second part,* 1704, is by another hand. See also *Faction display'd, in answer to Faction display'd,* 1704.

L(164.m.38),LLP,O(2),C,DT+; CSmH,CtY, DFo,InU,MH+.

S428 [—] [reimpression]
This impression has both rules at head of p. 1 broken. The inner forme of B is apparently reset.

O,OW,DG,*DT*,LdU-B(almost uncut); DFo,ICN, TxU.

S429 [—] [reimpression]
Note added at foot of title, 'A counterfeited edition is lately published, it may be discovered by being printed in old letter, hardly legible, and full of errors, no lines over *To the Reader* [i.e. p. iv]; and particularly in page 18, after line 9, one verse run so into another as makes it nonsense'.

O,C,E,AdU,LdU-B.

S430 [—] — *London, printed in the year,* 1704.
4°: *A*² B–C⁴ D²; *i–iv,* 1–20.
Last line on p. iv reads 'Destroy the Government'; no rules at head of p. iv. In most copies D2 is unsigned, but it is signed in the LDW copy. This is clearly the counterfeit copy referred to in the preceding.

L(11631.e.21),LDW,DrU; CLU-C,ICU,TxU.

S431 [—] — 'London' [Edinburgh?], *printed in the year* 1704.
4°: *A*² B–C⁴ D²; *i–iv,* 1–20.
Last line on p. iv reads 'stroy the Government'; no rules at head of p. iv. From the copies at E apparently an Edinburgh edition; the L copy is also bound in a Scottish collection of tracts.

L(11626.c.44/7),E(3); IU,KU,NjP.

S432 [—] Faction display'd. A poem. Answer'd paragraph by paragraph. *London, printed in the year* 1704. (*WL* April)
4°: *A*² B–G²; *i–iv,* 1–22 '22' 24 blk.
Signature B under 'his In'. The order of impressions is uncertain. Text reprinted with a prose rejoinder.

LLP,LVA-F,C; CLU-C,DFo.

S433 [—] [another impression?]
Signature B under 'with his'; apparently largely from standing type.

L(1960); InU.

S434 [—] Faction display'd... Now first correctly published, with large amendments, and the addition of several characters omitted in former editions. *London, printed in the year* 1705.
8°: *A*⁸ B–F⁴, ²*A*⁸ B–D⁴ E²; *i–xvi,* 1–38 *39–40, i–xvi,* 1–28. F4 hft to *Moderation*.
²A1 is title 'Moderation display'd... By the same author. Now first correctly published'.

The bookseller's preface makes it clear that the two were published together.

L(1077.1.22; G.13508/1, lacks *Moderation*),O, LdU-B; CtY,DFo,ICU,MH.

S435 [—] — From a corrected copy. *London printed, and sold by H. Hills,* 1709.
8°: *A*⁸; *1–3* 4–16.
The words of the imprint 'near the Waterside' are set to the left of the page.

L(1485.w.33),O(2),OW,CT(2); CtY,ICN,OCU, TxU.

S436 [—] [another edition]
The words of the imprint 'near the Waterside' are centred. Reissued with other remaindered Hills poems in *A collection of the best English poetry,* 1717 (*Case* 294).

L(11631.e.22; C.124.b.7/33),O(2),CT,E,AdU, LdU-B+; CLU-C,MH,TxU.

S437 [—] Moderation display'd: a poem... By the author of Faction display'd. *London, printed in the year* 1704.
4°: *A*² B–C⁴ D² (C2 as 'B2'); *i–iv,* 1–20.
In some copies (e.g. LVA-F,ICN) C2 is correctly signed. Reprinted with *Faction display'd,* 1705.
'Again, my muse – nor fear the steepy flight'
No evidence has been traced for Shippen's authorship except the statement of the title, which should perhaps be regarded with caution. A copy at DrU has an early ms. note 'By Bertram Stote esqr. Member of Parliament for Northumberland'. A continuation was published as *Moderation display'd, the second part,* 1705.

L(11659.c.13; 164.m.39),O(uncut),C(2),E,DG+; CSmH,CtY,ICN,MH,TxU+.

S438 [—] — 'London' [Edinburgh?], *printed in the year* 1705.
4°: A–B⁴; *1–4* 5–16.
Apparently an Edinburgh piracy, judging from the location of copies.

L(11626.c.44/4),E(3),ES.

S439 [—] Moderation display'd: a poem... Answer'd paragraph by paragraph. *London printed, and sold by B. Bragg,* 1705 [1704]. (*FP* 21 Dec)
4°: A⁴ B² C⁴ D²; *i–vi,* 1–18.
The answer is in verse.
Answer: 'Once more my muse these dark designs declare'

O,AdU; InU(uncut),MiU.

S440 [—] [*idem*] Moderation vindicated, in an answer, paragraph by paragraph, to a late new poem, intituled, Moderation display'd. *London, printed in the year* 1705.
4°: *A*⁴ B–C⁴; *1–4* 5–23 24. A1 hft.
Moderation display'd reprinted with a prose commentary interspersed.

LLP,LVA-F.

Shippen, W.

S441 [—] Moderation display'd: a poem... By the author of Faction display'd. *London printed, and sold by H. Hills*, 1709.
8°: A⁸; *1–4* 5–16.
> Reissued with other remaindered Hills poems in *A collection of the best English poetry*, 1717 (*Case* 294).
L(C.124.b.7/13),O,OC(uncut),CT,E(2)+; CSmH,CtY,IU,MH,TxU+.

S442 [—] The sequel: or moderation further display'd, a poem. By the author of Faction display'd. [*London*] *Printed in the year* 1705.
4°: *A*² B–C⁴ D²; *i–iv*, 1–20. 20 err.
'Satyr once more my towring muse sustain'
> No evidence for Shippen's authorship has been traced except the statement of the title; it should be regarded with caution. The reissue below has not been previously noted, but does nothing to confirm the authorship; the implied attribution to Defoe in S442·6 can probably be ignored.
LDW,LLP,O,C,*MR*; CSmH,CtY(uncut),ICN, InU,MH+.

S442·2 [—] [reissue] The devil upon dun: or, moderation in masquerade. A poem. [*London*] *Printed in the year* 1705. (*DC* 7 July 'yesterday')
4°: A²(±) B⁴(–B1, 2) C⁴ D²; *1–2* 3–20. 20 err.
> A reissue with cancel title-leaf and first leaf of text with variant first line:
'While yet expecting the returning day'
OW,C,DA,DT,*MR*; OCU,TxU.

S442·4 [—] — [col] [*London?*] *Printed in the year* 1705.
4°: A²; *1–4*, 2 columns.
> Drop-head title only. A piracy.
O(uncut).

S442·6 [—] — By the author of the True born English-man. [1705.]
4°: ⟨A²⟩; *1–4*. 2 columns on pp. 1, 2 and top of 3.
> The cropping of the copy seen may have removed a colophon.
L(806.k.16/67, cropt).

S443 '—' Tyburn's courteous invitation to William Wood, esq; Written by Mr. Shippen. [*Dublin*, 1725.]
½°: 2 sides, 1 column.
> At foot of side 1, 'Wood's melancholly complaint. Written by Sir R——d S——le'.
'Oh name it once again, will William come?'
Wood's: 'I was the man, oh! cruel change of fate'
> Shippen's authorship of the first poem may be considered as dubious as Steele's authorship of the second.
L(C.121.g.8/120).

S444 Shooting. Shooting flying, a poem: to which are annexed, some remarks on the woodcock. *London, printed by G.D. in the year* 1735.
4°: A–B⁴; *1–3* 4–15 *16 blk*.
> Ms. correction to p. 5, line 7.

Shooting flying

'Long was this art to Britain's sons unknown'
LdU-B; CtY.

S445 Short. [dh] A short account of the expiring parl--m--nt. [col] *London, printed by R. Newcomb*, 1713. (*SR* 24 Feb)
2°: *A*² < *B*¹; ff. 1–3.
> Printed on one side of the leaf only, the third leaf on the verso. Entered in *SR* by Michael Holt to John Baber (? for Barber) and Richard Newcomb; deposit copies at L,O,EU.
'Some mighty genius now my breast inspire'
L(C.20.f.2/239),O(2, 1 lacks B1),E,EU(uncut).

S446 — A short answer to a late scurrilous libel, entitul'd, a Trip to Balli---re Loghsun----d: or, Crispin kick'd into good manners. Under the same characters, or names. [*Dublin*] *Printed in the year* 1714.
8°: *A*⁴; *1* 2–8.
''Twas not the talent of the sot'
> A ms. note in the DA copy expands 'Ballimore Loghsunderld[!]'; the libel has not been traced.
DA.

— A short answer to a short paper entitled a Short way to a bishoprick, [1722?] *See* Via ad episcopatum, [1722?]

— A short critical poem on poets and poetry, 1750. *See* Plain truth, or downright Dunstable, 1740–.

S447 — A short dehortatory poem to a claret-prone kinsman and godson of mine, against immoderate drinking. [*London?* 170–?]
¼°: 1 side, 2 columns.
'Pass by a tavern-door, my son'
DFo.

S448 — [dh] A short hint of the life of Al--------r Scl-----r. [*Edinburgh?* 174–?]
8°: A⁴; *1*–8.
> The copy seen is bound in a volume of pamphlets mainly of Edinburgh origin *c.* 1740.
'I sing a man of merit great'
> An attack on a landowner's villainous agent, apparently Alexander Sclater.
L(1078.k.26/11).

— 'Short reflections on vice and riches: a poem. 4°, E., 1709.'
Morgan L375; not traced, and possibly in ms.

S449 — A short satyre on that native of the universe, the Albanian animal, author of the new-year's gift, or Scots poem upon the union. [*Edinburgh*, 1707.]
½°: 1 side, 1 column.
'Sir, 'mong your gifts your candour's not the least'
> A satire against Defoe, assuming his authorship of *A Scots poem*, 1707.
E(2).

S450 — A short state of the case, | To the vicar of N—. [*Dublin*, 1725/30.]
½°: 1 side, 2 columns.

A **short** state of the case

The copy at L forms part of a collection of Dublin half-sheets of 1725/30.
'From this small text the furious priests take pains'
In favour of religious toleration. The vicar of Naas has not been identified.
L(C.121.g.8/110),C,DN; MH.

S451 — A short trip into Kent, containing the occurrences of four summer days... In hudibrastick verse. By Phileleutherus Britannus. *London, printed for the author*, 1743. (*GM* Feb)
8°: A–D⁴; *1–2* 3–30 *31–32*. D4 advt.
D4 contains 'a catalogue of prints and books sold by George Bickham'; listed as published by Bickham in *GM*.
'Life's but a burden when confin'd'
The work has similarities to William Gostling's 'An account of...five days peregrination' written in 1732 and reprinted in *Hogarth's perambulation*, 1952.
O(uncut).

S452 — Short verses, in imitation of long verses: in an epistle to W---m P--tt, esq; *London, printed for M. More, near St. Paul's*, 1746. (*LM* March)
2°: A⁴; *1–2* 3–7 *8 blk.*
'Since one hath writ,/To thee, O P-tt!'
Printed in Sir Charles Hanbury Williams, *A collection of poems*, 1763; but Horace Walpole noted in his copy (now at L) 'not by Sr Ch. W.' A parody in 'namby-pamby' verse of *An epistle to William Pitt esq;* 1746, suggesting the author of that was 'Ly——n', or George Lyttelton.
L(11657.m.11),O; CSmH,MH,NN.

— 'A short way with St. Paul and Sacheverell: a poem [of 15 stanzas]. 12°, L., 1710.'
Morgan M606; not traced, and possibly in ms.

S453 Shorter. A shorter and truer advertisement by way of supplement, to what was published the 7th instant: or, Dr. D--g--l--s in an extasy, at Lacey's Bagnio, December the 4th, 1726. *London, printed in the year* 1727.
2°: A²; *1–2* 3–4.
'Have I my fingers? and have I my eyes?'
Signed 'Flamingo'. *Crum* H313. A satire on Dr. James Douglas and Mary Toft.
L(1178.h.4/13).

S454 —— *London, printed in the year* 1727. (*MC* Feb)
2°: A¹ B²; *1–2* 3–5 *6 blk.*
With textual revisions and three additional stanzas.
L(1178.h.4/13, lacks A1; C.20.f.2/242).

S455 Shortest. The shortest way to peace: or, an answer to a prologue that was to be spoke at the Queen's theatre in Dublin, on Monday the 5th of November, 1711. [*Dublin*, 1711.]
½°: 1 side, 1 column.
Reprinted in 1712 with Garth's *The prologue*

The **shortest** way to peace

that was spoke at the Queen's theatre in Dublin on Tuesday the 4th of November, *1712.*
'When Bajazet was quell'd by Tamerlane'
A tory answer to Garth's prologue.
C.

Shrewsbury. Shrewsbury Quarry, 1747. *See* Warter, Thomas.

S456 Shute, James, *1663–1688.* A sacred poem of the glory & happiness of heaven. By James Shute, M.A., sometime rector of Tymsborough... *London printed, and sold by Joseph Downing*, 1712.
8°: A⁴ B–H⁴ I²; [*4*] *i–iv*, 1–58 *59–60.* A1 hft; I2 advt.
'Above the tallest most exalted view'
LDW(–A1, I2),O(–A1, I2),BrP(–A1, I2); NN, TxU(–A1, I2).

S457 Shute, James. A pindarick ode, upon her majesties sending his grace the Duke of Marlborough to command the English forces in Holland... *London, printed for the author; sold by J. Nutt*, 1703. (15 Jan, Luttrell)
2°: A–C²; *i–iv*, 1–8.
The Luttrell copy is in the possession of R. D. Horn.
'Hear O celestial hosts that shine so bright'
This author has not been identified, but is clearly a different man from the preceding.
O(lacks A2); CSmH,MH,NjP,TxU.

[—] A poem to the memory of his late majesty William the third [actually by Joseph Stennett], 1702. *See* S741.

[—] A poem to the memory of Mr. Nathanael Taylor [actually by Joseph Stennett], 1702. *See* S745.

Shuttlecock. The shuttlecock, 1736. *See* Whistler, Anthony.

Sick. The sick lyon and the ass, 1725. *See* To the honourable Mr. D.T., 1725.

S458 Siege. The siege of Cales. [*London?* 1715/–.]
slip: 1 side, 1 column.
Rough woodcut at head.
'O brave England's forces!'
In praise of James Butler, duke of Ormonde's campaigns in Spain against Cadiz and Vigo; after his banishment.
C.

S459 — The siege of Carlisle. A poem. With a dedication to all men of sense, &c. *London, printed for M. Cooper*, 1746. (*GM, LM* Jan)
2°: A² B² C¹; *1–5* 6–10.
'Of Carlisle siege, that dreadful scene'
Dedication signed 'Charles Easy', probably a pseudonym.
L(1959),O.

S460 Sighs. The sighs of Albion: or the universal mourner. An ode sacred to the memory of... Caroline, queen-consort of Great-Britain. Inscrib'd to...the Lord Harvey, vice-chamberlain of his majesty's household. *London printed, and sold by Charles Jephson; also by J. Wilcox, L. Gilliver, J. Jolliffe, R. Dodsley, Mrs. Nutt, & Mrs. Dodd,* 1737. (*GM, LM* Dec)
2°: *A²* B–C²; *i–iv, 1* 2–8.
> In the copy seen, 'Caroline' in the title has been painted over in red.

'When youth or beauty perish e'er they bloom'
LDW.

— Sighs upon the never enough lamented death of Queen Anne, 1719. *See* Peck, Francis.

Sight. The sights retreat, [171–?] *See* Waring, Henry [The dark penitent's complaint].

Signal. The signal; or, a satyr against modesty, 1727. *See* Hawling, Francis.

S461 Signior. The signior in fashion: or the fair maid's conveniency. A poem on Nicolinis's musick-meeting. Humbly dedicated to the subscribers. [*Dublin*] *Printed in the year* 1711.
4°: *A²; 1* 2–4.
> The ornament on the title is found in other Dublin books of the period.

'All hail ye soft mysterious pow'rs, which charm'
> Reprinted in *A new collection of miscellany poems, for the year, 1718,* edited and perhaps written by George Davis. A satire on the castrato Nicolini (Nicolino Grimaldi), with an attack on Ireland for her pliancy.

L(11631.bb.33); DFo.

Silent. The silent flute, 1729. *See* Jacob, Hildebrand (J46).

S462 Silk-worms. Silk-worms: a poem. In two books. Written originally in Latin, by Marc. Hier. Vida... And now translated into English. With a preface, giving an account of the life and writings of Vida. *London, printed for J. Peele,* 1723. (*MC* May)
8°: A² a⁴ B–F⁴ G²; *i–xii, 1* 2–43 *44 blk.* xii err.
'What curious webs the well-fed worms enclose'
L(78.c.42),O(2),LdU-B; CSmH,CtY,IU.

S463 Silva. Silva to Strephon, or Miss Dolly Workits letter, to the Little Beaue, Dublin, March 28, 1728. [*Dublin*] '*Printed by John Toybow, in Sheep-street, opposite the Bulls-head*', 1728.
slip: 1 side, 1 column.
'Dear Captain may I call you so'
> A letter from a discarded mistress to Patrick Walsh.

L(C.121.g.8/165).

'Silva, Bestia de.' The congress of beasts, [1728.] *See* C367.

Silver. 'The silver piss-pot.'
> *The way of the town,* 1716, is said to be 'By the author of the Silver piss-pot'; the text is included in a reissue of the former with the first line 'In days of yore there liv'd a stately dame'. No trace of a separate edition has been found.

Silvester, Tipping. Original poems and translations. Consisting of the Microscope, Piscatio or angling, the Beau and academic. With a poem on the approaching marriage of the Princess Royal... *London, printed for J. Wilford,* 1733 [1734]. (*GM* Feb)
8°: pp. viii, 60. L,O; CtY,MH.
> Some copies have an errata slip on p. 60. The first three poems are translations from the Latin.

S464 — Piscatio. Or, angling. A poem. Written originally in Latin by S. Ford... Translated from the Musæ Anglicanæ by Tipping Silvester. *Oxford, printed by Leon. Litchfield, and are to be sold by the Widow Fletcher, and by Mr. Thurlburne, bookseller in Cambridge,* 1733.
8°: π² A–C⁸; *i–iv, 1*–23 *24 blk.* π1 hft.
> Watermark: fleur-de-lys: 'Price six-pence' on title.

'Th' insidious art, and the alluring snare'
OW,LdU-B; CSmH,CtY,MH(2).

S465 — [fine paper]
> Watermark: Strasburg bend; no price on title.

L(162.e.62, –π1),O,WcC; NjP.

Silvia. Silva [!] to Strephon, 1728. *See* Silva.

Simile. A simile, 1706. *See* Prior, Matthew [The squirrel].

— The simile; or, woman a cloud, 1748. *See* Sheridan, Thomas [A new simile].

S466 Simmonds, James. The Wandsworth campaign. A poem. By a brother volunteer. *London, printed in the year* 1748.
8°: *A⁸; 1*–3 'ii', 5 6–16.
'Awake my muse from thy lethargick dream'
> Dedication signed.

L(1961).

Simson, Andrew. *See* Symson, Andrew.

S467 [Simson, Patrick.] The Song of Solomon, called the Song of songs. In English meeter. Fitted to be sung with any of the common tunes of the psalms. Very necessary to be taught children at school. *In the Gorbals, printed by James Watson, and sold at his house in Craig's-Closs, Edinburgh,* 1701.
8°: A–C⁴; *1*–2 3–24.
'This is the song most excellent'
> Previously printed in Simson's *Spiritual songs,* 1685.

E,*ES*; NN.

Simson, P. The Song of Solomon

S468 [—] — *Glasgow, Sanders, 1716.*
(W. J. Couper, 'A Gorbals imprint' in *Records of the Glasgow Bibliographical Society* 6 (1920) 11n.)

S468·5 [Sinclair, *Sir* Archibald.] On the twenty third day of April 1713, the queen's coronation-day. [*Edinburgh*, 1713.] (May)
½°: 1 side, 1 column.
Ruddiman's ledger for the week ending 16 May 1713 records printing 150 copies of 'Sir Arbd Sinclair's poem on the Queen's Coronation'.
'This day, with joy may Brittish hearts abound'
This poem is the only one that fits Ruddiman's description, and the authorship seems to be established by that evidence.
E.

S468·7 [—] To the queen, on the happy conclusion of the peace. [*Edinburgh*, 1713.] (April)
½°: 1 side, 1 column.
Ruddiman's ledger for the week ending 25 April 1713 records printing 500 copies of a half-sheet 'Sir Archbald Sinclair's poem on the peace'.
'Hail mighty Anne! may thou be ever blest'
With a prayer for the succession of Stuarts.
E(2).

Sinecure. The sine-cure, 1725. *See* Mitchell, Joseph.

Singing. The singing bird's address, 1707. *See* Browne, Joseph.

S469 **Sion.** Sion comforted; and the methodist reprov'd: or, vice, immorality, and a neglect of divine service, prov'd to be the real causes of schism and enthusiasm. A poem. By a layman of the church of England. *London, printed for the author; sold by J. & R. Swan*, 1750. (*SR* 12 Feb)
4°: *A*¹ B–F² G¹; *3–5* 6–26. 26 err.
Entered in *SR* to J. & R. Swan; deposit copies at L,E,GU,SaU. Listed in *BM* Feb.
'Hail Sion's friends, to you glad news I bring'
L(C.70.f.1/10),O,E,GU,SaU.

S470 **Sir.** Sir Billy Tinsel: an excellent new ballad, to the tune of The abbot of Canterbury. [*London*, 1748/49.]
½°: *1–2*, 1 column.
'A story I'll tell you, a story so merry'
A satire on Sir William Calvert's election as lord mayor of London.
L(C.121.g.9/206),O-JJ.

S471 — Sir Blue blu'd: or, t'other squeak for the 'squire. Tune of, King John and the abbot. *London, printed in the year* 1731.
2°: *A*² B²; *1–3* 4–7 *8 blk.*
'Come all ye that love laughing, and like not Sir Blue'

Sir Blue blu'd

A satire on Walpole.
L(1972),O-JJ; CtY,OCU.

— Sir Humphry Mackworth's real vindication, 1705. *See* The university answer, 1705.

S472 — Sir John Leake's fight with Admiral Ponty. Being a bloody fight between the confederate fleet, & the French fleet, in the bay of Gibraltor on the 20th of March last... Tune of, Oh rare popery, &c. [*London*] *Printed by T. Moore*, 1705.
½°: 1 side, 2 columns.
Three rough woodcuts of ships at head.
'Here is news upon news boys come from Giblatore [!]'
O-JJ.

— Sir Lowbred O---n, [1748.] *See* Byrom, John.

S473 — Sir R----- triumphant. A song. Address'd to his friends. To the tune of To all you ladies now at land. *London, printed for J. Cooper*, 1739. (12 Jan)
2°: *A*² B–C²; *1–2* 3–12.
Percival LI. The copy from Tom's Coffee House in the Lewis Walpole Library is dated 12 Jan; listed in *GM* Jan.
'This song of triumph now I send'
A satire on Sir Robert Godschall's election victory in Bishopsgate ward.
L(1484.m.32),O,NwP; CSmH,CtY(uncut),DFo, MH.

S474 — Sir Robert Brass: or, the knight of the blazing star. A poem. After the manner of Hudibras. Canto I. *London, printed for A. Moore; sold by the booksellers in town & country*, 1731. (*GSJ* 9 Feb)
2°: *A*² B–F²; *1–3* 4–23 *24.* 24 advt.
Bond 118.
'While peace, and war, and turns of state'
A satire on Walpole.
O; CtY,ICN,IU,MH,TxU(uncut).

S475 — [reissue] Sir Robert Brass: or, the intriegues, serious and amorous, of the knight of the blazing star. *London, printed for A.M.; sold by J. Davis*, 1731. (*MChr* Feb)
2°: *A*²(±A1) B–F²; *1–3* 4–23 *24.* 24 advt.
Some copies (MH, NjP) have F unsigned, possibly due to frisket-bite.
L(162.n.65),O(lacks A1),LdU-B; MH,NjP,OCU.

S476 — — or, the intrgues[!], serious and amorous; of the knight of the blazing-star. In hudibrastick verse. '*London: printed by A. Moore, and sold by the booksellers*' [*Dublin*], 1731.
8°: *A*⁴ B–C⁴; *1–3* 4–24.
Some copies (DG, AdU) have corrected reading 'intrigues' in title. Advertised by George Faulkner in *Bœoticorum liber*, 1732.
DG,DT,AdU; CtY(lacks A1),MB,TxU.

S477 — Sir Roger's speech to his mercenary troops, at W—. [*London*, 1713.]
slip: 1 side, 1 column.
'Welcome my bosom-friends, once more we're met'

Crum W227, dated 1713. A satire against the
Jacobite tories.
OCU,*Harding*.

S478 — Sir * * * speech upon the peace. To the tune of
the Abbot of Canterbury. *London, printed for Jacob
Lock, 1739. (DP* 6 Feb)
2°: *A*⁴; *1–3* 4–8.
Percival XLIV.
'I'll tell you a story, how lately Sir Blue'
A satire on Walpole's speech of 1 Feb 1739 on
the peace with Spain.
L(162.n.58),O,LdU-B; CSmH,CtY(uncut),InU,
MH,TxU+.

S479 — [*idem*] Sir *'s speech upon the peace with Sp - - n.
To the tune of the Abbot of Canterbury. *London,
printed for Jacob Lock*, 1739.
2°: *A*⁴; *1–3* 4–8.
Apparently a reimpression with revisions. Most
copies are on unwatermarked paper, but some
(L,11630.g.37; OCU) are watermarked, sug-
gesting a further reimpression.
L(11657.m.17; 11630.g.37; 1486.g.2),O,OA,
MC; CLU-C,CtY(uncut),ICN,MH(mutilated),
OCU+.

S480 — [*dh*] Sir * * * speech upon the peace... [*Edinburgh*, 1739.]
8°: *A*²; *1–4*.
Copies seen are bound in volumes of Edinburgh origin.
E(2); DLC.

S481 — [*idem*] A song in praise of the late convention,
to the good old tune, of the Abbot of Canterbury,
or, the Honest-cobler. *Printed in the year* 1738–9.
½°: 1 side, 1 column.
Possibly a Dublin edition from the provenance
of the copy seen.
NN.

— Sr. Tubal Cain's advice to the free-holders and
free-men, of the city of Dublin, 1729. *See* Owens,
Samuel.

S482 Sirs. Sirs, are ye mad? or, caution to the cits.
[*London*, 1733.] (*GM* March)
2°: *A*²; *1–2* 3 '6'.
Title in half-title form. Listed in *GM* as
printed for W. Mears.
'In the court of requests, I was yesterday walking'
On the excise bill.
OCU.

Six. The six save-alls, [1710.] *See* The save-alls,
[1710.]

— Six town eclogues, 1747. *See* Montagu, *Lady*
Mary Wortley.

Sixième. Sixième dialogue entre deux freres,
[1707.] *See* Dialogue entre deux freres, 1707.

S483 Sixteenth. The sixteenth epode of Horace imi-
tated; and addressed to the people of England.
London, printed for J. Standen, 1739. (*GM* May)
2°: *A*² B–C²; *1–2* 3–12.
'Briton's awake! and bravely make a stand'
In favour of war against Spain.
L(840.m.1/8),O,LdU-B; OCU.

S484 — The sixteenth ode of Horace, book III. [!]
imitated. Address'd to the right hon. the lord
Viscount Percival. *London, printed for J. Huggenson*,
1741. (*GM, LM* Dec)
2°: B–C² (B2 as 'B'); *1–3* 4–8.
The copy at IU has a cancel slip over imprint,
'London: printed for T. Cooper'; traces of the
slip remain in the L copy. Listed in *GM, LM*
as published by Cooper.
'For rest, my lord, the sailor prays'
It seems clear that this is the sixteenth ode of
Horace's book II.
L(1959); IU,MH.

Sixth. The sixth satire of the first book of Horace
imitated, 1738. *See* Walpole. Edward.

Skating. Scating: a poem, 1720. *See* Newcomb,
Thomas.

S485 Skene, Robert. Immobilia sanctorum festa, cum
in ecclesia anglicana, tum etiam alibi, per totum
annum observata: or the immoveable feasts or
holy-days...described briefly in Latine verse...
Also an English translation of the Latine account...
Edinburgh, printed by William Adams junior, 1716.
4°: π¹ A–C² D¹; *i–ii*, *1–2* 3–14.
The English text is in prose.
'Principio Jani fit circumcisio Christi'
Dedication signed.
L(11409.g.8).

S486 Slight. A slight sketch of some insignificant
characters deservedly address'd to that very wise
and loyal society the Anti-Georgians. By an impartial hand. *London, printed in the year* 1749.
4°: B–C⁴ (B2 as 'B'); *1–3* 4–16.
Below imprint, 'To be deliver'd gratis'.
'The clock had struck – and eager to be drunk'
MH.

S487 Smallpox. The small-pox. A poem. In five cantos.
Form'd on the plan of Dr. Mead's prose on that
subject. After the manner of Mr. Prior, in his
Alma mater. Canto I. By Andrew Tripe, M.D.
*London, printed for Jeremiah Reason, in Flower de
Luce Court, Fleet-street*, 1748.
8°: *A*⁴ B–C⁴; *i–vi*, *1* 2–18.
'Old Homer sounds Achilles' rage'
The same pseudonymous author wrote *Dr.
Woodward's ghost*, 1748, and a footnote on p.
18 refers to 'my poem on the plague', doubt-
less satirizing that treatise of Mead's. A

The **small-pox**

travesty of Richard Mead's *Treatise on the small-pox*, 1747.
L(1174.d.46/23).

S488 [**Smallwood, James.**] A congratulatory poem to his grace the Duke of Marlborough, &c. upon his safe return to England, after the glorious victory obtain'd by the English and Germans, under his conduct, over the French and Bavarians at the battel of Hockstet in Germany, A.D. 1704. *London, printed by R. Janeway, for John Isted; sold by B. Bragg*, 1704. (*DC* 28 Dec)
2°: *A*² B–D²; *i–iv, 1–12.* A1 hft.
'As Cæsar at the end of each campaign'
> Early ms. attributions to Smallwood in DrU, MH copies; advertised as by him in *DC*. See R. D. Horn in *Huntington Library Quarterly* 24 (1961) 4.

LDW(–A1),DrU(uncut),*MR-C*; CSmH,MH (–A1),PBL.

[—] A congratulatory poem to his grace the Duke of Marlborough, on his glorious success and victories over the French and Bavarians, 1704. *See* C361.

S489 **Smalridge, George.** A poem on the death of our most gracious sovereign Queen Anne; and the accession of his most excellent majesty, King George. *London, printed for E. Curll*, 1715 [1714]. (27 Nov)
8°: *π*⁴ A–B⁴; *i–viii, 1–3 4–15 16.* π1 hft; 16 err, advt.
> Latin and English text. Some copies (L,O,CtY) have an eight-page catalogue of Curll's books. Publication date from *Straus, Curll*.

'Cum suus exanimem populus ploraret Elisam'
'When her Britannia wept Eliza's doom'
> According to the 'advertisement', Smalridge's poem is from the 'Oxford Verses'; the English translation is probably by another hand.

L(12301.b.12),LVA-D(2, 1 lacks π⁴),O,*MR*; *CLU-C*,CtY,ICN,MH,TxU(lacks π⁴) +.

Smart, Christopher. Poems on several occasions. *London, printed for the author, by W. Strahan; sold by J. Newbery*, 1752. (*LM* June/July)
4°: pp. 230.   L,O; MH.

———

S490 — Carmen cl. Alexandri Pope in S. Cæciliam latine redditum a Christophero Smart... *Cantabrigiæ, typis academicis excudebat J. Bentham, impensis authoris*, 1743.
2°: *π*¹ A–C² *D*¹; *i–ii, 1–3 4–13 14 blk.*
> *Griffith* 581; *Rothschild* 1862. English and Latin text. Some copies (DFo,MH) have ms. errata on p. 13.

'Descende cœlo, spiritu quæ melleo'
L(11409.k.1; 837.1.4/17),O(uncut),C,EU; CSmH,CtY,IU,MH,TxU +.

Smart, C. Carmen cl. Alexandri Pope

S491 — — Editio altera. To which is added Ode for musick on Saint Cecilia's day, by Christopher Smart... *Cambridge, printed by J. Bentham; sold by R. Dodsley, London*, 1746. (21 Aug)
4°: *π*¹ A–D⁴ E² *F*¹; *i–ii, 1 2–36 37; 38 blk.* F1 advt.
> Watermark: bird. *Griffith* 618; *Rothschild* 1864. π1 and F1 have been seen to be conjugate. Publication date from *Straus, Dodsley*.
Ode: 'From your lyre-enchanted tow'rs'
L(11602.gg.24/11),C(–F1),EU,LdU-B; CLU-C (–F1),CSmH,CtY(–F1),IU(–F1),MH(–F1).

S492 — [fine paper?]
> Watermark: initials. Even with the two issues at IU side by side, I have been unable to judge which is the better paper, but I have treated this as the fine paper because of its comparative rarity. It is possible that it is another impression on different stock.
O; IU(–F1),KU.

S493 [—] The Horatian canons of friendship. Being the third satire of the first book of Horace imitated. With two dedications; the first to...William Warburton... By Ebenezer Pentweazle, of Truro in the county of Cornwall, esq; *London, printed for the author; sold by J. Newbery*, 1750. (*GEP* 18 June)
4°: *π*² a–b² B–F²; *[4] i–viii, 1–19 20.* π1 hft; 20 advt.
> *Rothschild* 1867.
'Nay, 'tis the same with all th' affected crew'
> Smart used this pseudonym in other works. Reprinted in his *Poems*, 1791.

L(11630.d.18/6,–π1; T.666/10,–π1),LVA-D, O,C(–π1),LdU-B; DFo,*DLC*,ICU(–π1),KU (–π1),MH.

S494 [—] — The second edition. *London, printed for the author; sold by J. Newbery*, 1750.
4°: *π*² a–b² B–F²; *[4] i–viii, 1–19 20.* π1 hft; 20 advt.
> Apparently a reissue or reimpression.
O; CtY(2),*DLC*,IU,NjP.

S495 — On the eternity of the supreme being. A poetical essay. *Cambridge, printed by J. Bentham; sold by W. Thurlbourn in Cambridge; C. Bathurst, R. Dodsley, London; and J. Hildyard in York*, 1750. (27 April)
4°: *A*⁴ B⁴; *1–5 6–13 14–16.* B4 advt.
> Watermark: fleur-de-lys. Publication date from *Straus, Dodsley*; listed in *GM* April.
'Hail wond'rous being, who in pow'r supreme'
L(11602.gg.24/21; 840.k.2/5; 840.k.4/15),O, *MR*; ICN(–B4),ICU,IU(–B4),MH(lacks A2), NjP.

S496 — [fine paper]
> Watermark: fleur-de-lys on shield.
CtY,TxU.

[**Smedley, Jonathan.**] Poems on several occasions. *London, printed by S. Richardson, for the author*, 1721.
8°: pp. xv, 176.   O; MH.
> Both copies seen are on fine paper, watermark:

Smedley, J. *Collections*

Strasburg bend; possibly only presentation copies were circulated at this time.

[—] [reissue] *London, printed in the year* 1723. 8°: pp. 210.   L.

No watermark. Cancel title and no other preliminaries in the copy seen; substantial additions at end.

— [reissue] By Jonathan Smedley... *London, printed in the year* 1730. 8°: pp. iv, 210.   L.

New preliminaries, consisting of title, contents, and epistle to the reader.

———————

[—] Advice from fairyland. An imitation of our present Irish poetry, 1726. *See* A71.

S497 [—] [dh] A Christmas invitation to the Lord Carteret. [col] *Dublin, printed in the year* 1725. 2°: *A*²; *1–4*.

A proof copy at C is printed on one side of the paper.

'The muse, tho' late, to thee, the muse's friend'

Early ms. note in the C copy (which has Dublin collector's mark 'F'), 'By Dean Smedley'. Reprinted in *Gulliveriana*, 1728. Smedley's authorship has been universally accepted.

L(C.121.g.8/67),C(proof copy).

S498 [—] An epistle to his grace the Duke of Grafton, lord lieutenant of Ireland. *Dublin, printed by J. Carson*, 1724. 2°: *A*¹ *B*²; *1–3* 4–6. *Williams* 357–61.

'It was, my lord, the dextrous shift'

Smedley's authorship is clearly revealed in the poem. Answered by Swift, *His grace's answer to Jonathan*, 1724, and referred to in [Samuel Owens] *A scourge for the author of the satyr...* 1725.

C.

S499 [—] [*idem*] A petition to his g—ce the D—e of G——n. *Dublin, printed in the year* 1724. ½°: 1 side, 2 columns.

This edition was presumably for popular sale while the preceding was for private circulation; blanks are left for the names that were printed there in full.

L(1966),DN; CSmH(2).

S500 [—] A familiar epistle to his excellency Charles earl of Sunderland, one of the lords justices of England. *London, printed for, and sold by J. Roberts, and by J. Graves, & T. Griffith*, 1720. (*DP* 30 Aug) 2°: *A*² B–C² (C1 as 'B'); *1–5* 6–12. A1 hft.

No watermark. *Rothschild* 1888; *Teerink* 902. The Luttrell copy, dated Sept, is recorded in Pickering & Chatto cat. 248/13743.

'Loaded, my lord, with cares of state'

Signed at end 'J.S.' Early ms. attribution to Smedley in the MH copy below; reprinted in

Smedley, J. A familiar epistle

Smedley's *Poems*, 1721. See *A familiar answer to a familiar letter*, 1720.

L(11661.dd.7); TxU.

S501 [—] [fine paper]

Watermark: Amsterdam arms.

MH.

S502 [—] — *London, printed for J. Roberts, and reprinted by E. Waters* [*Dublin*], 1720. 4°: *A–B²*; *1–3* 4–8. *Rothschild* 1889.

DT; CLU-C,CSmH.

S503 [—] A familiar epistle to the right reverend the ld. bp. of Bangor. *London, printed for W. Chetwood*, 1720. (Feb, Luttrell) 2°: *A*² B²; *1–3* 4–8.

'Since epic strains no more are heard'

Reprinted in Smedley's *Poems*, 1721. A friendly letter of congratulation to Benjamin Hoadly.

L(1471.k.26),O,EtC,LdU-B; CSmH,InU(Luttrell),MH,TxU.

S504 [—] The metamorphosis: a poem. Shewing the change of Scriblerus into Snarlerus: or, the canine appetite: demonstrated in the persons of P-p-e and Sw—t. *London, printed for A. Moore*, 1728. (*MChr* 18 July) 2°: A–B²; *1–2* 3–8.

'Jove once, in humour, fix'd an hour'

Early ms. note in the L copy, 'This was writ by Dean Smedley'. A satire on Pope and Swift.

L(12273.m.1/11),LVA-D; TxU(3).

[—] The ode-maker. A burlesque on the Dean of Kil---a's Ode to the right honourable the Earl of Ca----------n, 1719. *See* O77.

S505 [—] An ode to the right honourable the Earl of Cadogan. *London, printed by W. Wilkins; sold by J. Roberts, & T. Griffiths*, 1719. (*DC* 23 March) 2°: *A*² B²; *1–3* 4–8.

'Hero! sprung from antient blood!'

Reprinted in Smedley's *Poems*, 1721. See *The ode-maker*, 1719, which in the form of a reply satirizes Swift more than Smedley. It was reprinted in Smedley's poems, and may conceivably also be by him.

CtY.

S506 [—] — *Dublin, printed*, 1719. 8°: *A*⁴; *1–3* 4–8.

DN.

S507 [—] On his excellency the Earl of Cadogan's publick entry at the Hague, this present May the 28th, 1718... *London, printed by W.W.* [*William Wilkins*]; *sold by W. Graves, at the Black-spread-eagle in Pater-noster-row, & J. Graves, in St. James's-street*, [1718.] (*DC* 28 May) ½°: 2 sides, 1 column.

'Aurora, goddess of the purple morn'

Reprinted in Smedley's *Poems*, 1721.

O.

Smedley, J.

[—] The p— and s— fe—s of T—y C—e, Dublin, [1725?] *See* P1.

S508 [—] A riddle by the reverend Dean S——y, to the Countess of N——g. [*Dublin*, 1726/27?]
½°: 1 side, 1 column.
    Below, 'A riddle by T—m. Pun—i address'd to D—h'. On the other side of the DT copy, *Epilogue designed to be spoken by Alonzo*, [1727?] The DT copy is bound with half-sheets of 1727; early ms. numeration in the L copy suggests 1726.
'The sun was my mother, and bore me at night'
'There's a thing in the east, that inhabits the south'
    Smedley and Sheridan are clearly intended as the authors, but it is impossible to tell whether the attributions are correct.
L(1890.e.5/68),DT.

S509 [—] A satyr. [motto: Canit, ante victoriam triumphum.] [*Dublin*] *Printed in the year* 1725.
½°: 1 side, 2 columns.
    Rothschild 1890; *Williams* 369–71. The copy at CSmH is an early state, possibly proof, with uncorrected text: the imprint reads 'Printed in year'. Reprinted in *Gulliveriana*, 1728, in an abridged text.
'Most reverend dean, pray cease to write'
    Smedley's authorship of this attack on Swift is made clear by Swift's answer *A letter from D. S—t. to D. S—y*, [1725.] See also *A satyr satiriz'd*, [1725], [S. Owens] *Trinity Colledge vindicated*, 1725, and his *A scourge for the author of the satyr*, 1725.
L(C.121.g.8/59),Rothschild; CSmH,TxU.

S510 [—] Smoke the doctor: or, an excellent new ballad, call'd, The school-master of Eaton. To the tune of Packington's pound. *London, printed in the year* 1717.
slip: 1 side, 1 column.
'My masters, and friends, and good people give ear'
    Printed in Smedley's *Poems*, 1721. A satire on Andrew Snape, occasioned by his attack on Benjamin Hoadly.
E.

S511 [—] Smoke the doctor, or the the [!] school-master of Eaton. [*London?*] *Printed in the year* 1717.
½°: 1 side, 2 columns.
MH.

[—] Tom Pun-sibi metamorphosed: or, the giber gibb'd, 1724. *See* T318.

S512 **Smith, —, Mr.** The invitation. In honour of the birth-day of his royal highness the Prince of Wales ... By Mr. Smith. *London, printed for J. Roberts*, 1728.
2°: (3 ll); *1–3* 4–5 *6 blk.*
    The copy seen, with watermark LC, is possibly on fine paper.
'Here poesy – O lend thy aid divine'

Smith, —, Mr. The invitation

    The author has not been identified; possibly he was Joseph Smith.
O.

S513 **Smith, Dorothy.** The shepherds jubilee, or, a pastoral welcome to his excellency the Earl of Rochester, &c. on his arrival in Ireland. *Dublin, printed by John Brocas*, 1701.
4°: *A*² B–E²; *i–iv*, 1–16.
'Come forth, ye swains, forsake your herds and flocks'
DA,DN(2).

Smith, Edmund, *1672–1710.* The works of Mr. Edmund Smith... *London, printed for Bernard Lintott*, 1714. (*MC* Dec)
12°: pp. 101.   L,O; CtY,TxU.

—— The third edition, corrected. *London, printed for Bernard Lintot*, 1719.
12°: pp. 103.   L,O; DFo,ICU.

—— The fourth edition. *London, printed for Bernard Lintot*, 1729. (*MChr* 15 May)
12°: pp. xxiv, 103.   L,O; IU,MH.

[—] Charlettus Percivallo suo [actually by Anthony Alsop], 1706. *See* A177.

S514 [—] [first line:] Janus, did ever to thy wond'ring eyes. [*London*, 1704/05.]
½°: 2 sides, 1 column.
'Janus, did ever to thy wond'ring eyes'
    Reprinted in Smith's *Works*, 1714, as 'Ode for the year 1705'.
Crawford; MH,PBL.

S515 [—] Ode. [Ormond's glory...] [*London*, 1702/03.]
½°: 1 side, 1 column.
'Ormond's glory, Marlbrough's arms'
    Attributed to Smith in *Nichols, Collection* IV. 62, 'The odes here printed were published anonymously at the time they were written, and are now ascribed to Mr. Smith on the authority of a note in ms. by one of his contemporaries'. *Crum* O1232: 'Theatre musick' for Oxford. On the recovery from illness of George, prince of Denmark.
Crawford.

[—] An ode in praise of musick. Composed by Mr. Charles King, [1707.] *See* O34.

S516 — A poem on the death of Mr. John Philips, author of the Splendid shilling, Blenheim and Cyder. *London, printed for Bernard Lintott*, [1710.] (*SR* 22 May)
2°: *A*¹ B–D² *E*¹; *i–ii*, 1–13 *14 blk.*
    The Luttrell copy, dated 23 May, is in the possession of J. R. B. Brett-Smith; advertised in *DC* 25 May. Deposit copies at L,LSC,O,E, EU. *Morgan* K378 records another edition as '8°, 1712', probably referring to the reprint in Philips's *Works*.

Smith, E. A poem on the death

'Sir, since our Isis silently deplores'
L(11630.d.1/1, cropt; 643.1.26/1),O(4),E,DG,
LdU-B+; CSmH,CtY,ICU,MH,TxU(3)+.

Smith, John, *1662–1717.* Poems upon several
occasions. *London, printed for H. Clements, 1713.*
8°: pp. viii, vi, 384.   L,O; CtY,IU.
      Watermark: AR. Errata slip in some copies.

— [fine paper]   LVA-D,LdU-B; CtY.
      Watermark: IH.

S517 [—] Scarronides: or, Virgil travestie. A mock-
poem... The second edition. *London, printed by
J.H. for Chr. Coningsby, 1717. (PM 22 Jan)*
8°: *A*⁸(±*A*2) B–F⁸ G(3 ll); *i–xvi, 1–86.*
      A reissue of the first edition of 1692; A1 is the
      original license leaf dated 1691. The copyright
      appeared in lot 11 of the trade sale of Conings-
      by, 11 Aug 1721 (cat. at O-JJ).
'The Trojan tongues now, after feast'
      For Smith's authorship see *DNB* and
      references.
ICN.

      [—] Worcester dumb-bells; a ballad, [1710.] *See
      W561.*

S518 [Smith, Joseph.] The British worthies. A poem.
*London, printed for J. Pemberton & J. Shuckburg,
B. Creake, & J. Jackson, and sold by the other book-
sellers of London & Westminster, [1729.] (MChr 8
May)*
2°: *A*² B–D²; *i–ii iii–iv, 5–16.*
      Watermark: T; 'Price One Shilling' on title.
'Satire! be mute, decline thy baneful views'
      Ascribed to Smith in *MC* May. A eulogy of
      various peers.
LDW,O(uncut); MH,OCU,TxU(2).

S519 [—] [fine paper]
      Watermark: fleur-de-lys; no price on title.
CSmH,NN.

Smith, Marshall.
*The works of this author always give his name as 'M.
Smith gent.'; the identification with Marshall Smith
is suggested by the MH catalogue. Marshall Smith
was a contributor to, and then proprietor of, the
periodical* The British Apollo, *1708–11, which bears
many similarities to the later poetical periodicals* The
monitor, *1713 (written with Nahum Tate in the
Queen's Bench prison) and* The daily oracle, *1715.
Both of these are by 'M. Smith gent.'.*

S520 — On the peace: a poem. Humbly inscrib'd to the
most honourable the Earl of Oxford and Mortimer
... *London, printed for the author; sold by the booksellers of London & Westminster, [1713.] (PB 28
April)*
4°: *A–E*²; *1–2 3–20.*
      No watermark; 'Price Six Pence' on title.

Smith, M. On the peace

'At length the work is done, a work so great'
MH.

S521 — [fine paper]
      Watermark: fleur-de-lys on shield; no price
      on title.
DrU.

S522 — 'A pastoral sacred to the glorious memory of her
late majesty Queen Anne, inscrib'd to his excellency
the Earl of Pembroke, &c. [*London*] *Sold by B.
Lintott.* Price 3*d.*' (*DC* 6 Aug 1714)
'Kind heav'n, avert the threatned stroke, and
take'

S523 — — The second edition. *London, printed for the
author; sold by Bernard Lintott, and the other booksellers of London & Westminster, [1714.]*
4°: *A*⁴ B²; *1–2 3–11 12 blk.*
ICU.

S524 — A pindarique poem sacred to the glorious
memory of King William III. *London, printed for
Andrew Bell, 1702. (13 March, Luttrell)*
2°: *A*² B–C²; *1–2 3–12.*
      In some copies (e.g. L, O), p. 12 is mis-
      numbered '4'.
'Come all you mournful Britains, you who know'
L(643.1.24/23),LDW,O(2, 1 uncut); CtY,*NjP*
(Luttrell).

      [—] A satyr upon old maids, 1713. *See S75.*

S525 — The vision, or a prospect of death, heav'n and
hell. With a description of the resurrection and the
day of judgment. *London, printed for Andrew Bell,
1702. (April?)*
8°: (frt+) *A*⁸ *a*² B–L⁸ M⁴; *i–xx, 1–166 167–168.* xx
err; M4 advt.
      Horizontal chain-lines; no watermark seen.
      A2–3 contain a dedication 'To the right
      honourable the Lady Olimpia Roberts'. One of
      four supplementary dedications, each on a
      pair of leaves, was bound after a² in some copies;
      copies of all four are bound in copies at L,
      National Library of Australia. The supple-
      mentary dedicatees were 'Mrs. St. John' (O),
      'the honourable Mrs. Jandrau daughter to...
      the late Lord Fitzharding' (MH), 'Mrs.
      Walpole', and 'My dear sister Mrs. Harvy'.
      Advertised in *FP* 29 April 1704 and 15 Dec
      1705; abridged in *WL* April 1702.
'In the cool ev'ning of a summers day'
L(11623.c.19/2),O(–frt, to Mrs. St. John);
CLU-C,MH(to Mrs. Jandrau).

S526 — [fine paper]
      Watermark: fleur-de-lys on shield. In the copy
      seen A1 and A2 appear to be conjugate,
      suggesting a pair of cancel leaves.
IU.

Smith, Robert, *schoolmaster at Glenshee.* Smith's
poems of controversy betwixt episcopacy and
presbytry...as also several poems and merry songs

Smith, R.

...with some funeral elegies... [*Edinburgh?*] *Printed in the year* 1714.
8°: pp. 119.   L,E; MH.
A copy is recorded in the reprint of 1869 with ms. corrections and printed lines, 'To William Seton' pasted at the foot of p. 119.

S527 — The Assembly's shorter catechism, in metre. For the use of young ones. *Edinburgh, printed by Thomas Lumisden & John Robertson, at the Fishmarket,* 1727.
8°: A–C⁴; *1–2* 3–23 *24 blk.*
'The chief and highest end of man'
E.

S528 —— *Edinburgh, printed by Thomas Lumisden & John Robertson, and sold at their printing-house,* 1729.
8°: A⁸ B⁴; *1–3* 4–24.
L(1018.i.38),E(3).

S529 — An elegie upon the never enough to be lamented death of the illustrious and noble John marquis of Tullibardine; who departed this life at the battle near Mons, the first of September 1709. [*Edinburgh,* 1709.]
1°: 1 side, 2 columns.
'What sighs, what groans, are those I hear always?'
At end 'Posuit Mr. Robert Smith'.
E.

S530 Smithfield. [dh] Smithfield groans: or, an humble remonstrance to the magistrates of London, concerning the horrid wickedness committed and conniv'd at, in Bartholomew-Fair... [col] *London printed, and sold by B. Bragg,* 1707 [1706]. (23 Sept, Luttrell)
4°: A²; *1–3* 4 *blk,* 2 columns.
'Hear now, O heavens, and thou, O earth, give ear'
LVA-F(Luttrell).

Smock. The smock race at Finglas, 1716. *See* Ward, James.

Smoke. Smoke the doctor, 1717. *See* Smedley, Jonathan.

S531 [Smollett, Tobias.] Advice: a satire. *London, printed for M. Cooper,* 1746. (*GM, LM* Aug)
2°: A² B–D²; *1–2* 3–16.
Rothschild 1903. Horizontal chain-lines in A and B.
'Enough, enough; all this we knew before'
Smollett's authorship is recorded in the 1751 sale of copyright under S533.
L(840.m.1/37; 643.l.25/26),O,C,BaP; CSmH, CtY,MH,MiU,TxU.

S532 [—] [variant imprint:] *London, printed for George Freer,* 'MDCCXVI' [1746].
Possibly a reimpression. The L copy contains a reprinted sheet B of which at least the inner forme is reset; signature B is under 'that'.
L(11630.h.3); MH.

Smollett, T. Advice

S533 [—] Advice, and Reproof: two satires. First published in the year 1746 and 1747. *London, printed for W. Owen,* 1748. (*BM* March)
4°: π¹ B–D⁴ E(3 ll); *1–3* 4–32.
The collation of E is extremely obscure; possibly it was wrongly imposed and copies assembled from the separated leaves. Entered in Strahan's ledger, apparently to John Osborn and before Jan 1748, 750 copies. The copyright of the two, with 566 books, formed lot 1 of the trade sale of John Osborn, 19 Nov 1751 (cat. at O-JJ); they were bought by Millar for £1. 5s.
L(11631.g.30/2; 11631.g.31/14),O(2, 1 ms. date 24 March),E,LdU-B; CtY,ICU,IU,MH,*NjP.*

S534 [—] Reproof: a satire. The sequel to Advice. *London, printed for W. Owen, & M. Cooper,* 1747. (*GM, LM* Jan)
2°: A¹ B–D²; *i–ii, 1–12.*
Rothschild 1904. Reprinted in 1748 with *Advice.*
'Howe'er I turn, or whersoe'er I tread'
Smollett's authorship is recorded in the 1751 sale of copyright under S533.
L(840.m.1/38),O,E,*DrU-U;* CtY,MH.

[—] A sorrowful ditty; or, the lady's lamentation for the death of her favourite cat, 1748. *See* S602.

S535 [—] [dh] The tears of Scotland. [*Edinburgh?* 1746/50?]
8°: A²; *1–4.*
The typography appears to be Scottish; it has a good text and may be authorized. Apparently the poem was first published (set to music by James Oswald) in *The land of cakes,* advertised in *GA* 3 Dec 1746.
'Mourn, hapless Caledonia, mourn'
For Smollett's authorship see William Scott, 'Smollett's *The tears of Scotland*' in *RES* n.s. 8 (1957) 38–42; in a letter of [1747] printed in *TLS* 24 July 1943 Smollett refers to his 'paternal concern' for this poem, *Advice,* and *Reproof.* The subject is further discussed by J. D. Short in *N&Q* 213 (1968) 453–6.
O,E,AdU,GM; CSmH,CtY,MH,*NN.*

S536 Smut. Smut's epistle to the whigs. [*London,* 1714.]
slip: 1 side, 1 column.
Stanza 2, line 2 reads 'Paul'.
'Ye waggish whigs, who raise your heads'
A satire on Swift and the fall of the tories.
L(C.121.g.9/182).

S537 — [another edition]
Stanza 2, line 2 reads '*Paul*'. The copy seen was reissued in *State-poems. Being a collection of choice private pieces,* 1715.
Brett-Smith.

Smythe, J. M.

[S538-9 = W302·5-6] [**Smythe, James Moore.**] One epistle to Mr. A. Pope, occasion'd by two epistles lately published, [1730.] *See* Welsted, Leonard & Smythe, J. M.

Snuff. Snuff: a poem, 1732. *See* Arbuckle, James.

S540 Soames, *Sir* **William.** The art of poetry, written in French by the Sieur de Boileau... Made English, by Sir William Soames. Since revis'd by John Dryden, esq; *London printed, and sold by H. Hills,* 1710.
8°: A–B⁸ C⁴; *1–2* 3–40.
> Previously published in 1683. Reissued with other remaindered Hills poems in *A collection of the best English poetry,* 1717 (*Case* 294), and included here to complete the record of his reprints.
'Rash author, 'tis a vain presumptuous crime'
L(11475.d.8; C.124.b.7/45),O,CT,WcC; CSmH, CtY(2),MH,TxU.

S541 — The art of poetry, in four cantos. By Monsieur Boileau. The second edition, revis'd and compar'd with the last Paris edition. *London, printed for E. Curll, & F. Burleigh,* 1715 [1714]. (*PB* 27 July)
12°: A⁴ B–C¹² D⁶ ²D²; *i–iv* v *vi–viii,* 1–59 *60 blk* [*4*]. A1 frt; A4, ²D² advt.
> B7 and C1 are blank leaves between the cantos. The Curll advertisement leaves ²D² found in some copies probably form part of the original collation. It is not known who was responsible for this revised text. Soames's name is revealed in the 'advertisement'.
L(11475.aa.10; 1076.g.39, cropt, – C1),O(– ²D²); CLU-C(– C1, ²D²),KU,*MH.*

S542 — [reissue] The true περι βαθους: or, the art of sinking in poetry, and rising again. In four cantos. By Monsieur Boileau. The third edition, revised and compared with the Dunciad. *London, printed for E. Curll,* 1728. (*MChr* 17 Sept)
12°: A⁴(±A2) B–C¹² D⁶ ²D²; *i–iv* v *vi–viii,* 1–59 *60 blk* [*4*]. A1 frt; A4, ²D² advt.
KU.

Sober. Sober advice from Horace, [1734]–. *See* Pope, Alexander.

S543 Sodom. Sodoms catasthrophe [!], a poem, with the addition of other pieces of poetry. *London, printed for Jacob Robinson,* 1748.
8°: A–L⁴; *1–2* 3–85 *86; 87–88 blk.* 86 err.
'Near Jordans fertile streams in grandure stood'
> Dobell cat. 145 (1955) 15, recording the copy now at L bound with works attributed to J. Basset, suggested he was the author and that this might have been printed at Birmingham. The former is quite likely, the latter less certain.
L(11661.b.18/1),O.

Soldier. A soldier and a scholar, 1732. *See* Swift, Jonathan.

Soldier

S544 — The soldier's loyalty: in a congratulatory poem on his majesty's safe return to his British dominions. In Latin and English. *London, printed for R. Burleigh,* 1717. (*MC* Jan)
4°: A² B–C²; *1–3* 4–11 *12 blk.*
'Dum tua bellator, princeps, vexilla secutus'
'Your soldier, taking courage from his coat'
OCU.

— The soldier's religion, 1705. *See* Malet, Thomas.

S545 Soldiers. The soldiers elegy on the much lamented death of John, duke of Marlborough. Who departed this life on Saturday the 16th of this instant June, 1722, at Windsor Lodge, in the 72d year of his age. *Written by and printed for a gentleman volunteir in the camp,* [1722.]
½°: 1 side, 2 columns.
> Mourning headpiece and woodcut borders.
'Amidst those troops, who've put their stables on'
O.

S546 — The soldiers lamentation for the loss of their general. In a letter from the recruiters in London, to their friends in Flanders. To the tune of, To you fair ladies, &c. [*London*] *Printed in the year* 1712.
½°: 2 sides, 2 columns.
'To you, dear brothers, who in vain'
> A lament for the dismissal of Marlborough.
L(162.m.70/12),MC,Herts CRO (Panshanger box 46).

S547 — — In a letter from the officers in Ireland, to their friends in Flanders. [*Dublin?* 1722.]
½°: 1 side, 2 columns.
> The L copy is bound with Dublin half-sheets. Revised first line:
'To you, dear brothers, we complain'
> A revision of the preceding on the occasion of Marlborough's death. A further revision for William Augustus, duke of Cumberland was published in 1757 or 1765 (copy at C).
L(C.121.g.8/24); MH,TxU.

S548 — The soldiers praise of Duke William. [*London?* 1746?]
slip: 1 side, 1 column.
> Royal arms at head.
'Good news is arrived/Duke William the glorious'
> *Crum* G404. On the victory of William Augustus, duke of Cumberland, at Culloden.
O.

S549 Solemnity. The solemnity of the muses, at the funeral of King William III. By the author of an elegy from the Dut⟨ch.⟩ *London printed, and sold by Benj. Harris, and V. Harris, in Windstreet, Bristol,* 1702. (21 April, Luttrell)
2°: A² B–D²; *i–ii,* 1–14.
> Engraving on title.
'Methinks I see, beneath an arbor's shade'
> By the 'author' (translator?) of *Batavia in tears,* 1702.
O; NjP(Luttrell).

Soliloquy. A soliloquy, [1746.] *See* Hamilton, William, *of Bangour*.

S550 — The soliloquy of a great man. A new ballad. To the tune of, Down, down, down, derry down. *London, printed for Tom Robins in Fleet-street,* [1740.] (22 Feb)
2°: A⁴; *1–3* 4–8.
> *Percival* appendix 78. The copy from Tom's Coffee House in the Lewis Walpole Library is dated 22 Feb. Listed in *PSGB* Feb.

'As R***** one morning, in cogit'ive mood'
> A satire against Walpole.

L(11661.dd.14; 1484.m.16),O,MC; CLU–C (uncut),CtY,ICN,OCU(uncut),TxU +.

S551 **Solitary.** 'The solitary. An ode. Inscrib'd to Ralph Allen esq; of Bath. [*London*] *Hawkins, Cooper.* Price 6d.' (*BM, GM* Aug 1747)

S552 **Solitude.** Solitude. An irregular ode, inscribed to a friend. *London, printed for L. Gilliver & J. Clark,* 1738. (*SR* 12 Dec)
2°: A¹ B–E²; *i–ii, 1–15* 16 blk.
> Deposit copies at L,O,E,GU,SaU; listed in *GM, LM* Dec.

'Nor war's alarms, nor raging pow'r'
L(643.m.14/13),O(2, 1 uncut),E,GU,SaU; CSmH(uncut),CtY,NN.

Solomon. Solomon a serenata, 1742. *See* Moore, Edward.

S553 — Solomon and Abra; or, love epistles. *London, printed for R. Griffiths,* 1749. (*GM* June)
8°: A⁸ B–C⁸ D⁴; *1–8* 9–56. A1 hft.
> Also listed in *BM* Jan 1750.

'Soon as these lines salute thy piercing eye'
L(11633.cc.2/6),O; IU,MH,OCU(–A1).

S554 **Some.** Some bold truths out at last, or,| Un-natural jars,| Is the cause of wars. *London, printed, and re-printed in Dublin,* 1711.
½°: 2 sides, 1 column.
> Above imprint, an advertisement for the re-capture of Captain Christopher Dolston.

'Influenced by the vile unchristian jars'
C.

— Some fables after the easie and familiar method, 1703. *See* Mandeville, Bernard.

— Some fruits of solitude, 1705. *See* Thompson, William, *schoolmaster of Nottingham*.

— 'Some poems on the welcome arrival, entry, and coronation of the most illustrious Elector of Brunswick, George-Lewis... [*London*] *Printed for J. Marshal.* Price 4d.' (*MC* Jan 1715)
> No collection answering to this description has been traced; possibly the title is generalized.

— Some pressing motives, [1718?] *See* Cheyn, William.

S555 — Some seasonable advice to Doctor D——n——y. [*Dublin*] *Printed in the year* 1730.
½°: 1 side, 2 columns.
> *Teerink* 951.

'My friend D——y be not vain'
> An attack on Patrick Delany, answering Swift's *To Doctor D—l—y,* 1730.

L(1890.e.5/158; C.121.g.8/182).

— Some verses composed upon the insurrection of the Jacobites, 1746. *See* Turnbull, Walter.

S556 — Some verses inscrib'd to the memory of the much lamented John Dolben, esq; who departed this life the 29th of May 1710. [*London,* 1710.]
½°: 1 side, 1 column.
> Mourning borders.

'Come all the managers, come forth and moan'
> Tory verses on his death.

O,AN,Chatsworth.

S557 — Some verses occasion'd by the late death of an Irish nobleman, in France. *London printed, and sold by R. Burleigh,* 1715. (1 Dec, Luttrell)
8°: A–C⁴; *1–2* 3–23 24 blk.
> Listed in *MC* Nov.

'When sorrows in the soul tempestuous rage'
L(164.n.7, Luttrell),O,DN; MB(cropt).

S558 — Some verses on the advantages of a fishery. Formerly published, now reprinted, and address'd to Mr. George James, on his scheme for a national fishery. [*c.* 1720.]
'2°: 4 pp. broadsheet.'
> The date is that suggested by Pickering & Chatto. Possibly related to *Fishery, a poem,* 1714.

(Pickering & Chatto cat. 259/3732.)

S559 — Some verses on the death onr [!] late sovereign King William of blessed memory, with an epitaph, made by a young English maid... as also some verses encouraging believers... [*London?*] *Printed in the year* 1702.
8°: A⁴; *1* 2–8.
'The crown is fallen from our head'
CtY.

S560 — Some verses on the king's going to Hanover. Humbly inscrib'd to the right honourable Robert Walpole, esq;... *London, printed for J. Roberts,* 1716. (*PM* 12 July)
2°: A² B² C²; *1–2* 3–12.
> 'Price Six-pence' on title; mixed paper. On p. 9, 'To the right honourable Robert Walpole, esq; upon his first coming to the Treasury...'.

'Fair Albion's brightest, but abating joys'
DFo,MH.

S561 — [fine paper]
> No price on title; watermark: star.

TxU.

— Some verses sent to the right honourable the Earl of Oxford, 1712. *See* Crispe, Henry.

Somerset, F. S., *duchess*

Somerset, Frances Seymour, *duchess of. See* Seymour, Frances, *duchess of Somerset.*

Something. Something for every body, 1729. *See* The Welchman-s last will and testament, 1719–.

Somervile, William. Occasional poems, translations, fables, tales, &c. *London, printed for Bernard Lintot,* 1727 [1726]. (*MC* Dec)
8º: pp. vi, 392. L; CtY,MH.
    According to *Nichols* VIII. 301, Lintot paid Somervile £35. 15s. for the copyright on 14 July 1727.

— The poetical works... *Glasgow, printed for Robert Urie,* 1766.
8º: 2 vol. L.

_____

S562 — The chace. A poem. *London, printed for G. Hawkins; sold by T. Cooper,* 1735. (*SR* 13 May)
4º: (frt+) A⁴ a² B–O⁴ P²; *i–xii, 1-2* 3-106 *107; 108 blk.* 107 err.
    Entered to Somervile in *SR* by George Hawkins; deposit copies at L, EU and probably O, SaU. Entered in Bowyer's ledgers to Hawkins under 3 May, 750 copies printed; 500 copies of a quarter-sheet 'Proposals for Poem on Hunting on royal paper' had been entered to Woodward on 3 Feb 1735. For a detailed study of the printing see J. D. Fleeman in *PBSA* 58 (1966) 1-7. Listed in *GM, LM* May. A presentation copy with the errata corrected in ms. is at Waddesdon Manor.
'The chace I sing, hounds, and their various breed'
    A rewriting in heroic verse by another hand is entered as *The chace,* 1735.
L(78.g.28; C.70.f.1/3),O(2, 1 uncut),C,EU, DT+; CSmH(uncut),CtY(presentation copy), ICN(–frt),MH,TxU+.

S563 —— *London, printed for G. Hawkins; sold by T. Cooper,* 1735. (*DC* 26 June)
8º: A⁸(±A7, 8) B–I⁸ K⁴; *i–xx, 1-131 132 blk.*
    The cancel leaf A8 bears press-figure 8, not seen in copies at WrP,CU,IU; these may have uncancelled leaves. Entered in Bowyer's ledgers under 23 June, 1000 copies printed; the 'two cancelled leaves' were not entered until 7 July.
L(11659.c.77),LVA-D,O,LdU-B,WrP; CSmH (uncut),CU,ICN,MH,TxU+.

S564 —— The third edition. *London, printed for G. Hawkins; sold by T. Cooper,* 1735. (*DG* 20 Aug)
8º: A–I⁸ K⁴; *i–xx, 1-131 132 blk. 131* err.
    Entered in Bowyer's ledgers under 5 Aug, 1500 copies printed.
L(993.e.51/1; T.1678/1),LVA-D,O(3, 1 uncut), C,EU; CtY,IU,MH,*NN,TxU.*

S565 —— The fourth edition. '*London, printed for G. Hawkins; sold by T. Cooper*' [Edinburgh?], 1735.
12º: A–G⁶; *i–xiv, 1-70.*

Somervile, W. The chace

    A piracy; the copy at EN is bound with Edinburgh piracies. The title of that copy is altered in ms. to read 'The tenth edition' and the date to 1738.
EN; DFo.

S566 —— *Dublin, printed by R. Reilly, for R. Gunne & R. Owen,* 1735.
12º: A–D¹² E²; *i–iii* iv–x, *11* 12-99 *100 blk.*
L(993.e.49/1),O,C(lacks A1),DA(2),DN(3)+; CtY.

S567 —— The fourth edition. *London, printed for J. Stagg, G. Hawkins; sold by M. Cooper,* 1743.
8º: A–I⁸ K⁴; *i–xx,* 1-131 *132.* 132 advt.
L(1960); CtY,InU,MH,*NN,*TxU.

S568 —— To which is added, Hobbinol... The fourth edition. *London, printed for G. Hawkins; sold by M. Cooper,* 1749.
8º: A–M⁸; *i–iv* v–xv *xvi,* 1-176.
L(1960),O,*MR;* CU,CtY,DFo,IU,*NjP.*

S569 — Field sports. A poem. Humbly address'd to his royal highness the prince. *London, printed for J. Stagg,* 1742. (*DP* 16 Jan)
2º: π¹ A–D² E¹ (A1 as 'A2'); *i–vi, 1* 2-14. 14 advt.
    Horizontal chain-lines. Entered to Stagg in Bowyer's ledgers under 15 Jan 1742, 1500 copies printed.
'Once more, great prince, permit an humble bard'
L(162.n.27),LVA-D,O,OW(uncut),LdU-B+; CSmH,CtY(uncut),ICN,MH(2),TxU+.

S570 —— *Dublin, printed by S. Powell, for George Ewing,* 1742.
12º: *A⁴* B² C⁴ D²; *i–v* vi–vii *viii, 9* 10-23 *24.* A1 hft; 24 advt.
L(993.e.49/2),O,C,DT; CtY,MH.

S571 — Hobbinol, or the rural games. A burlesque poem, in blank verse. *London, printed for J. Stagg,* 1740. (*SR* 4 Feb)
4º: a⁴ b² B–I⁴; [4] i–vii *viii blk, 1-2* 3-64.
    Bond 172. Entered to Somervile in *SR;* deposit copies at L,O,E,EU,AdU,GU. Entered to Stagg in Bowyer's ledgers under 2 Feb, 600 copies printed. Listed in *GM* Feb.
'What old Menalcas at his feast reveal'd'
L(11631.g.30/1; 840.k.3/12; 840.l.3/3, uncut; 840.l.7/2; C.70.f.1/6),O(2, 1 uncut),CT,EU(2, 1 uncut in wrappers),LdU-B+; CSmH,CtY,ICN, MH,TxU(2, 1 uncut)+.

S572 —— The second edition. *London, printed for J. Stagg,* 1740. (12 Feb?)
4º: a⁴ b² B–I⁴; [4] i–vii *viii blk, 1-2* 3-64.
    Almost entirely reset. Apparently the edition entered in Bowyer's ledgers under 12 Feb 1740, 750 copies printed.
L(643.k.4/2, lacks b²),O,OW; CLU-C,IU,KU, MH,*NNC.*

S573 —— The third edition. *London, printed for J. Stagg,* 1740. (*GM, LM* April)
8º: A–F⁸; [4] i–xi *xii blk, 1-2* 3-80.

Somervile, W. Hobbinol

Apparently entered in error as 'The Chace' to Stagg in Bowyer's ledgers under 22 March, '8° 6 Sh. No 1000'. Reprinted with *The chace*, 1749.

L(11632.c.54),O,BaP(stitched, uncut),GU,WrP + ; CU,ICN,MH,*OO*.

S574 —— The third edition. '*London, printed for J. Stagg*' [*Edinburgh?*], 1740.

8°: *A*⁴ B–E⁴ F¹; *1–3* 'i–iv' *8* 9–42.

A piracy. In the copy at NN, page 42 is numbered '28'; pp. ii–iv are numbered at the inner margin.

E; CtY,NN.

S575 —— *Dublin: re-printed by and for George Faulkner*, 1740.

8°: π¹ A–G⁴ H⁴(–H4) (A1 as 'A2'); [4] *i* ii–vi, *1–2 3–53 54.* 54 advt.

L(1962),O(2),C,DG(2),DN(2)+ ; CLU-C,PP.

S576 —— The fourth edition. *Dublin: re-printed by and for George Faulkner*, 1740.

8°: π¹ A–G⁴ H⁴(–H4) (A1 as 'A2'); [4] *i* ii–vi, *1–2 3–53 54.* 54 advt.

Possibly a reimpression.

TxU.

S577 [—] An imitation of the ninth ode of the fourth book of Horace. Inscribed to the right honourable James Stanhope, esq;... *London, printed for J. Tonson*, 1715. (*MC* Jan)

2°: A–C²; *i–ii*, *1–9 10 blk.*

'Born near Avona's winding stream'

Printed in Somervile's *Occasional poems*, 1727.

LVA-F,O; CtY(cropt),NN,OCU.

S578 — The two springs, a fable. Occasion'd by his majesty's late bounty to the universities, and inscrib'd to the right honourable the Earl of Halifax. *London, printed for J. Roberts*, 1725.

2°: *A*² B–C²; *1–2 3–12.*

'Two sister springs, from the same parent hill'

O; CSmH(uncut),MH,TxU.

S--------on, T------s. A condolatory poem humbly inscrib'd to her most sacred Britannick majesty, 1708. *See* C333.

S579 **Song.** A song. [In a council of state...] [*London?* 1715.]

slip: 1 side, 1 column.

'In a council of state,/Was a mighty debate'

A Jacobite satire against George I's choice of the motto 'Dieu et mon droit'.

Herts CRO (Panshanger box 46).

— A song compos'd by Mr. Henry Purcell, [1707.] *See* Brady, Nicholas.

S580 — The song. Doctor Higgins's deliverance: or, the Rose t---n cabal defeated. [*Dublin*, 1712?]

½°: 2 sides, 1 column.

'Since the business is over I'm glad there's an end on't'

The **song.** Doctor Higgins's deliverance

On Francis Higgins's second trial for seditious preaching.

L(C.121.g.8/6).

S581 — A song entitl'd a satyr on a trades, song by Mr. Harper and Mrs. Kavana, at Salsbury, Winchester, Southampton, and Portsmouth, with great aplause [!]. [172–?]

½°: 1 side, 2 columns.

Apparently a provincial publication.

'There's ne're a thriving trader'

O.

S582 — Song for his majesty's birth-day. [*London?* 1715?]

slip: 1 side, 1 column.

'Freedom, goddess frank and fair'

Listed in *Blanchard* 114 as possibly by Steele; it was printed as 'An ode to freedom' in Steele's *Town-talk* 6 Jan 1716, describing the entertainment at his Censorium on 28 May 1715.

L(C.121.g.6/31; C.121.g.9/177).

S583 — A song, for the thanksgiving night. Tune of, Bumper 'Squire Jones. [*London?* 1746?]

slip: 1 side, 1 column.

'Ye friends of the state'

L(1875.d.16).

S584 — A song, in answer to the first part on the 17th May 1750. (To the same tune of the Cobler.) [*Edinburgh*, 1750.]

½°: 1 side, 1 column.

'The schemes of our kirk are much better supported'

On the Church of Scotland's resolution for augmenting stipends, in answer to N201.

E.

S585 — Song in commemoration of royal Nann. *London, printed by T. Jones, in Fleetstreet*, [1715?]

½°: 1 side, 2 columns.

Two rough portraits at head.

'My Nan she was good'

Lamenting the death of Queen Anne, against the Pretender.

L(1876.f.1/67).

— 'A song in praise of begging, or the beggars rival'd. 1 p., 1710.'

Morgan M657, 'The theme is that native beggars are being ruined by lazy foreigners (Palatines)'. Not traced, and possibly in ms.

— A song in praise of the late convention, 1738–9. *See* Sir * * * speech upon the peace, 1739.

— The Song of Solomon, called the Song of songs, 1701–. *See* Simson, Patrick.

S586 — The song of the robin-redbreast turn'd canary-bird. To the tune of, Chivy-chace. *London printed, and sold by J. Roberts*, 1715. (*MC* June)

8°: A–C⁴; *1–2 3–23 24 blk.*

'In Æsop's days when birds could prate'

The **song** of the robin-redbreast

A satire on Harley.
L(11631.bb.80),O,CT; CSmH,CtY,IU,MH.

S587 — A song on his grace the Duke of Marlborough's happy return into England; which is to be sung this day, being Thursday the 23d of January 1707; by Mr. Abel in the Tennis-court. [*Edinburgh?* 1707.]
½°: 1 side, 1 column.
The E copy is bound with Edinburgh half-sheets. The Crawford copy is a proof with ms. corrections.
'Fame thy loudest blast prepare'
E,Crawford.

S588 — A song on the battle of Dettingen near the Main, June 16th, 1743. To the tune of, Charles of Sweden. [*London?* 1743.]
½°: 1 side, 1 column.
'Come Britton's now, with joy be fill'd'
OCU.

S589 — A song, on the confession and dying words of William Stevenson, merchant, late of North-Allerton...who was executed at Durham on Saturday the 26th of August, 1727, for the barbarous murder of Mary Fawden, near Hartlepool ... To the tune of, Since Celia's my foe. [1727?]
½°: 1 side, three columns.
Two woodcuts below title.
'Good lord! I'm undone, thy face I would shun'
Harding.

S590 — A song on the king's birth-day, 1701. Compos'd by Mr. Leveridge. [1701.] (Nov)
½°: 1 side, 1 column.
'Welcome genial day!'
DG(imprint cropt?).

S591 — A song on the late Duke of Ormond. [*London?* 1715/–.]
slip: 1 side, 1 column.
Rough woodcuts at head and foot.
'I am Ormond the brave, did you never hear of me?'
On Ormonde's banishment.
C.

S592 — A song sung before King Charles the IId, and the whole court, on May-day, upon Edmund the gardiner, getting Rose, the milk-maid, with child. By the poet laureat. *London, printed for J. Roberts,* 1733. (*GSJ* 1 May)
2°: *A*² < B¹; *1–2* 3–6.
The collation is tentative.
'Let wine turn a spark, and ale huff like a Hector'
On the virtues of milk, with bawdy overtones.
L(1484.m.15).

S593 — A song to the Old Britons, on St. Taffy's day. To the tune, Of noble race was Shinkin. [*London?* 1717/18.]
slip: 1 side, 1 column.
In the last line of the penultimate stanza, 'STUART' is spelt with a swash U.

A **song** to the Old Britons

'How are the mighty fallen!'
A Jacobite song addressed to the Welsh.
O,C; CSmH.

S594 — [another edition]
'STUART' spelt with an ordinary U. Printed with *A song. To the tune of, Dear catholick brother,* [1717/18]; the NjP copy is not divided.
NjP.

S595 — [dh] A song, to the tune of Auld lang syne. [*Edinburgh?* 1746/–.]
8°: *A*²; 1–4.
'O Caledon, O Caledon/How wretched is thy fate'
A Jacobite lament.
AdU; *CSmH*,DFo.

S596 — [*idem*] An excellent new song, to the tune of, Old long syne. [*Edinburgh?* 1746/–.]
½°: 1 side, 2 columns.
L(Rox.III.608),E(2).

S597 — A song. To the tune of, Dear catholick brother, or, The Irish dear-joy. [*London?* 1717/18.]
slip: 1 side, 1 column.
First line ends 'Changelings/I sing'.
'Of quarrels, and changes, and changelings I sing'
A Jacobite satire on the quarrel between George I and the Prince of Wales at the christening of Prince George William.
O,C.

S598 — [another edition]
First line ends 'Change-/lings I sing'. Printed with *A song to the Old Britons,* [1717/18]; the NjP copy is not divided.
NjP.

S599 — A song to the tune of the Abbot of Canterbury, &c. [*Edinburgh?* 1745.]
½°: 1 side, 1 column.
Horizontal chain-lines.
'What child has not heard of a conquering tour'
A satire on Louis XV and the Young Pretender.
L(Rox.III.710).

S600 — A song upon the late victory at Culloden. By a lady. To the tune of To you fair ladies all at land. [1746.]
½°: 1 side, 2 columns.
'See where our glorious William comes'
O.

S601 Sophron. Sophron: a poem. Occasion'd by the death of the late revd. Mr. Robert Wright. *London, printed for J. Buckland,* 1744. (*GM, LM* April)
2°: π¹ *A*² B–D²; *i–ii, 1–2* 3–15 *16 blk.* π1 hft.
Horizontal chain-lines. Ms. correction to line 3 in copies at L,LdU-B.
'O thou supreme, whom gods their god confess!'
L(1959),LdU-B; IU(–π1).

S602 Sorrowful. A sorrowful ditty; or, the lady's lamentation for the death of her favourite cat. A parody. *London, printed for J. Tomlinson,* 1748. (*GM* May)

A sorrowful ditty

2°: *A*¹ B–C² D¹; *1–2* 3–12.
>> *Bond* 199; *Rothschild* 1907. A1 and D1 have been seen to be conjugate.

'Well! thanks to my stars! I'm at last all alone'
>> Sometimes ascribed to Smollett, who wrote a similar burlesque on George lord Lyttelton's monody *To the memory of a lady*, 1747. Cordasco in *N&Q* (1948) 428 appears to confuse the two, and L. M. Knapp, *Tobias Smollett* (1949) 129 rightly says the attribution is made 'without any real evidence'.

L(C.57.g.7/22),O,C,LdU-B; CSmH,CtY,MH (uncut).

S603 — The sorrowful lamentation and confession of Daniel Damere, the queen's waterman: who was convicted for high treason at the Old-Baily, on Thursday the 20th of April, 1710... To the tune of, Forgive me if your looks I thought, &c. *London, printed for W. Walker, near Holbourn*, 1710.
½°: 1 side, 2 columns.
>> Rough woodcuts at head.

'Dear friends and countrymen give ear'
L(Cup.645.e.1/29).

S604 — The sorrowful lamentation and last farewel, of John Price, alias Jack Ketch, who was executed at Bun-hill-fields, for the cruel and most barbarous murder of Mrs. White. [*London*] *Printed by Henry Lingard, in Fleet-street*, [1718.]
½°: 1 side, 2 columns.
>> Two rough woodcuts at head.

'Behold a wicked harden'd wretch'
L(1876.f.1/82).

S605 — The sorrowful lamentation of Herrie Ormistoun late hang-man in Edinburgh, for the loss of his post. [*Edinburgh*, 1715?/22.]
½°: 1 side, 2 columns.

'All people that hears my complaint for my sake'
E(cropt).

S606 — The sorrowful lamentation, of James Campbell of Burnbank. Who is banished to the West Indians...with his last farewell to Scotland. [*Edinburgh*, 1722?]
½°: 1 side, 2 columns.
>> Two rough woodcuts at head.

'They call me Bourn-bank/A bloody murthering cheet'
E.

S607 — The sorrowfull lamentation of Nicol Mucshet [!] of Boghall. Who was execute in the Grass-market of Edinburgh, on the 6th. of January, 1721. For murdering of his wife: with his last dying speech, and farewell to the world. [*Edinburgh*, 1721.]
½°: 1 side, 2 columns.

'All people now both far and near'
E.

S608 Sorsoleil, John B. Columna votiva regi. Inscribendum tradebat Johannes B. Sorsoleil, E. A. presb. *Londini, anno d.* 1702.

Sorsoleil, J. B. Columna votiva

2°: *A*² B²; *i–ii*, 1–6.
'Auspicor regi pangere carmen'
>> A funeral poem on William III.

L(11409.i.9).

'Sou Ma Quang.' A Chinese tale, [1740.] *See* C151.

'Soundbottom, Tim.' Wit, a poem, 1745. *See* W536.

S609 South. South Britain: a poem. Describing its situation, product and trade, civil and religious liberty, and the bravery and beauty of the inhabitants. By Philopatriæ. *London, printed for J. Wilford; sold by A. Holbeche, and by the booksellers of London & Westminster*, 1731. (*GSJ* 29 May)
8°: A–D⁴ E²; *1–5* 6–36.
'In northern climes, where tides uncertain roll'
O,LdU-B; NjP.

S610 — A South-Saxon ode. [*London?* 1741.]
½°: 1 side, 2 columns.
>> *Percival* appendix 100.

'Upon a time, not long ago'
>> Election propaganda for Thomas Sergison, candidate for Sussex.

L(1890.c.1/4).

— A South-Sea ballad: or, merry remarks upon Exchange-alley bubbles, [1720.] *See* Ward, Edward.

S611 — The South Sea ballad, set by a lady. [*Edinburgh?* 1720.]
½°: 1 side, 2 columns.
>> The Edinburgh origin is suggested by the two copies at E.

'Change Alley's so thin that a man may now walk'
L(C.20.f.9/402),E(2); MH-BA.

S612 — [another edition, with no title]
>> Text in italic throughout.

CSmH(cropt?).

— The South Sea whim, 1711. *See* Mainwaring, Arthur.

S613 South, Robert. Musica incantans, sive poema exprimens musicæ vires... *Londini, typis & impensis H. Hills*, [1708/10.]
8°: A⁸; *1–2* 3–14 *15–16*. A8 advt.
>> Signature A2 under 'connubia'. First published in 1655, and included here to complete the list of Hills reprints.

'Non, ego, Cæsareas acies; non arma virumq;'
CT; ICN,TxU.

S614 — [another edition]
>> Signature A2 under '-bia gaudet'. Reissued with other remaindered Hills poems in *A collection of the best English poetry*, 1717 (*Case* 294).

L(C.124.b.7/12),O; CSmH,CtY,*ViU*.

Southampton. Southampton; a poem, 1748. *See* Freeman, Byam.

Southcomb, L.

[**Southcomb, Lewis.**] Oblectamenta pia: sive sacra modulamina... Editio altera... Ab ecclesiæ catholicæ sacerdote, anachoreta. *Iscæ Dunmoniorum [Exeter], excudebat, & venales prostant apud Philippum Bishop,* 1716.
8°: pp. *1*–96 91–138.   L,O.
    The first edition has not been identified.

S615 [**Southcott, Thomas.**] [dh] Monsieur Boileau's epistle to his gardiner. [col] *London, printed for W. Lewis,* 1712.
2°: A²; *1*–4.
'Say drudging slave, the happiest of thy kind'
    Attributed to Southcott by *Dobell* 1723; the evidence is not known.
LVA-F,*MR-C*; MH(uncut).

S616 **Spanish.** The Spanish armada, an ode. *London, printed for J. Oswald,* 1745. (*GM, LM* Dec)
2°: *A*² B¹; *1*–3 4–6.
'Hail happy morn! Auspicious day'
NN.

S617 — Spanish courage. A satire. In an epistle from Don Blass to Admiral Vernon on his taking Carthagena. [*London*] *Printed for A. Dodd; sold at the Royal Exchange, St. James's, Bond-street, and Charing-Cross.* Price 6*d.*' (*DP* 6 June 1741)

— The Spanish descent, 1702. *See* Defoe, Daniel.

S618 — A Spanish farst[!]. *London printed, and reprinted in Dublin,* 1727.
½°.
(Dobell cat. 105/308).

S619 **Speak.** Speak truth, and shame the devil. In a dialogue between his cloven-footed highness, of sulphurious memory, and an occasional conformist ... *London, printed in the year* 1708.
4°: *A*²; *1* 2–4.
'Mortal, thou art betrayed to us'
    Against occasional conformists.
L(164.m.45).

S620 **Speaker.** [dh] The speaker. A poem inscrib'd to Alan Brodrick, esq; speaker to the honourable house of commons, met at Dublin, November the 25th, 1713... [*Dublin,* 1713.]
4°: *A*²; *1*–4.
'Lately I walkt towards the Colledge-green'
    Cf. *A letter to the author of the Speaker,* [1713/14.]
L(11631.bb.8),C,DK,DT; ICU.

Spectre. The spectre; or, Admiral Hosier's ghost, [1740.] *See* Price, Henry.

S621 **Speech.** A speech deliver'd by the High-German speaking-dog, when he had audience at Kensington: introduced by his grace the Duke of N-w-c---le. [*London?* 1718?]
slip: 1 side, 1 column.

A speech deliver'd

Line 6 reads 'Belles without smocks...'
'From dreary realms where cold and famine reign'
    A Jacobite satire.
CSmH.

S622 — [another edition]
Line 6 reads 'Bellies without smocks'. Italic exclamation mark in line 14.
NN.

S623 — [another edition]
Line 6 reads 'Bellies without smocks'. Roman exclamation mark in line 14.
L(C.121.g.9/181, cropt).

S624 — The speech englished, a new ballad. [*London,* 1735.]
½°: 1 side, 1 column.
Percival XXXVI; *Teerink* 1250.
'O ye c—s and p—s, who are bound by your pay'
    Crum O984, dated in the ms. '1734' [1734/5]. Teerink suggests it was a satire on George II's speech to parliament of 1 Feb 1739; but Percival quotes extensive parallels to his speech of January 1735.
L(1876.f.1/116),E.

S625 — [*idem*] The second part of the Totness address. [*London,* 1735.]
½°: 1 side, 1 column.
    From the same setting of type as the preceding, with slight changes.
L(1876.f.1/117).

S626 — [another edition, no title] [*London,* 1735.]
slip: 1 side, 1 column.
'Ye commons and peers, who are bound by your pay'
L(1871.f.3/27),O,LdU-B; MH.

S627 — The speech of his grace, the Duke of M---, which was verily and indeed spoken to the first regiment of foot-guards, June 2, 1715. [*London?* 1715.]
slip: 1 side, 1 column.
'I am very much concern'd to find'
    Crum I52. A satire on Marlborough's speech placating the mutinous foot-guards.
LSA; CSmH.

S628 — [another edition, title reads:] The speech of his grace, the Duke of M----------...
MH.

S629 — The speech of John Curry, to be delivered on the Tron 10th Apr. 1728. [*Edinburgh,* 1728.]
½°: 1 side, 2 columns.
'Altho my lug's nail'd, to the Tron'
    Curry was exposed at the Tron for forging banknotes.
E.

S630 — 'The speech of Marius [!] to the people of Rome. Translated into blank verse from the Latin of Sallust; with an introductory essay comparing the manners of the Romans... [*London*] *Printed by J. Stephens.* Price 1*s.*' (*MChr* 1 May 1728)

The **speech** of Marius

Apparently a versification of a work claiming to be 'from Sallust' and published with the imprint 'Amsterdam, 1656', under the titles *The speech of Caius Memmius*... (*Wing* S410) and *The true patriot's speech*... The catalogue of L suggests they were printed at London in 1708.

S631 — The speech of Oliver's ghost to the protesters against a peace. [*London*] *Printed by R.N.* [*Richard Newcomb*] *in Fleetstreet*, 1712.
½°: 1 side, 1 column.
'Forth from the silent mansions of the dead'
A tory poem.
MC.

S632 — [dh] The speech of the most illustrious... George I. to her majesty, Queen Anne...on the almost unanimous vote of the university of Cambridge, for keeping her place in their senate-house, in January term 1748–9. [*Cambridge? 1749.*]
2°: *A²*; *1–4*.
P. 3, 'Her sacred majesty Queen Anne's most gracious answer'.
'Hail, all-victorious sister! we rejoice'
Answer: 'I thank you, sire, and triumph much to see'
O(2).

S633 — The speech of the p——st of T——y C——ge, to his royal highness George prince of Wales. [*Dublin*] *Printed in the year* 1716.
½°: 1 side, 2 columns.
Teerink 890; *Williams* 1099.
'Illustrious prince we'r come before you'
Attributed to Swift by Scott (Swift's *Works* 1814, X. 451) but rejected by Williams and others. A satire on the speech delivered by Benjamin Pratt, provost of Trinity College, 11 April 1716.
CSmH,MH.

S634 [**Speed, John.**] Batt upon Batt. A poem upon the parts, patience, and pains of Barth. Kempster... By a person of quality. To which is annexed the Vision... The fifth edition. Dedicated to the gentry of Hampshire... *London, printed for Samuel Crouch*, 1706. (*DC* 2 May)
8°: A–B⁴ (B2 as 'B3'); *1–4* 5–14 *15–16*. B4 advt.
First published in 1680.
'Had I! O had I! Batt, thy face and throat'
For Speed's authorship, see *DNB* and references. Early ms. attribution in the C copy of the seventh edition below.
L(11631.d.31,–B4),LVA-F,O(3),CT,EU+; ICU,IU,MH,NN,NjP+.

S635 [—] — The fifth edition... *Dublin, printed for R. Gunne*, 1709.
8°: A⁸; *1–2* 3–14 *15; 16 blk*. 15 advt.
DA(uncut).

S636 [—] — The sixth edition... *London, printed by J.H., for Samuel Crouch*, 1711. (*DC* 16 June)

Speed, J. Batt upon Batt

8°: A–B⁴; *1–4* 5–15 *16 blk*.
L(11632.c.31),O(2),CT,DA; CtY,MH.

S637 [—] — The seventh edition... *London, printed by E.S.* [*Edward Say?*] *for Mary Fifield in Southampton*, 1733.
8°: A–B⁴; *1–4* 5–15 *16 blk*.
C,CT; CU.

S638 [—] — A poem, by a person of quality. The seventh edition. *London, printed for M. Cooper*, [174–?]
8°: *A⁴* B–D⁴; *i–iii* iv–vii *viii*, 1–24.
The added preface has a reference to Garrick.
L(992.h.3/4),O(2); CSmH,MH(cropt).

S639 [**Speed, Robert.**] The Counter scuffle. Whereunto is added, the Counter ratt. Written by R.S. *London, printed for R. Chiswell, M. Wotton, G. Conyers, J. Walthoe, & J. Innys*, [170–?]
8°: A–F⁴; *1–4* 5–26, [*4*] 1–16 *17–18*. A1 woodcut frt; F4 advt.
Apparently first published in 1647. Recorded here on account of the added poems. Parts of shares in the copyright, formerly belonging to Tho. Basset and Rich. Chiswell, formed part of lots 5 and 7 in the trade sale of John Nicholson, 3 April 1718 (cat. at O-JJ); another share appeared in lot 55 of the sale of George Conyers 14 Feb 1740 (cat. at O-JJ).
'Let that majestick pen that writes'
Counter rat: 'Of knights and squires of low degree'
On the Wood-street compter, or debtor's prison.
L(11626.bb.54).

S640 [—] — whereunto is added, a duel, between two doctors. With an elege on the ld. ch. bar. Hen's Connaught pig. *Dublin, printed by E. Waters, for M. Gunne*, 1708.
12°: A–B⁶ C²; *1–28*.
The duel is on p. 25 and the elegy on p. 27; see *Teerink* 835 and *Williams* 1055, 1075f describing what is apparently a detached copy of C².
Duel: 'Ye high commissioners of death'
The duel relates to a contest between Sir Patrick Dun and Sir Ralph Howard for the office of physician to the army. It was ascribed to Swift by Wilde, but not accepted by Williams.
DA.

S641 [—] — A poem. *London printed, and sold by the booksellers of London & Westminster*, 1710.
12°: A⁸ B⁴; *1–2* 3–24.
Apparently one of Henry Hills's piracies. Most copies have no watermark, but those at LdU-B,NN have a fleur-de-lys; they are not, apparently, on fine paper, and probably represent a mixed paper stock.
L(11601.dd.11/1),DK,DT,LdU-B; IU,NN,TxU (uncut).

Speed, R. The Counter scuffle

S642 [—] — Written by R.S. Whereunto is added, The Irish entertainment. Written by W. and G. *Dublin, printed by Edward Waters*, 1716.
8⁰: A–B⁸; *1–32*.
Irish entertainment: 'From Carrick, where the noble Ormond met'
L(11631.a.50),DT; *CSmH*,TxU.

S643 [—] — Whereunto is added, the Irish entertainment. With an elegy on the Connaught-pig. *Dublin, printed by E. Waters*, 1727.
8⁰: *A⁴ B⁴ C² D⁴*; *1–28*.
LVA-F.

S644 [—] — To which is added a Dutchman's proverb: and other new additions. *Dublin printed, and sold by E. Waters in Dames' Street*, [173–?]
8⁰: π¹ *A⁴ B⁴ C¹*; *1–20*.
The additional poems are all on p. 20.
C,DA.

S645 [—] — written by R.S. Whereunto is added the Irish entertainment. Written by W. & G. *Belfast, printed by and for Samuel Wilson & James Magee*, 1740.
8⁰: A–D⁴; *1–3 4–30 31–32 blk*.
DN.

S646 [—] The Compter scuffle: or, the prisoners in an uproar. *London, printed for Thomas Baron; and are to be had at the Boar's-Head in Fleet-street, and of the persons who carry the news*, 1741.
12⁰: A–B⁶; *1–3 4–24. 24 advt*.
The date in the L copy is corrected in ms. to 1751; this may be the true publication date.
L(1485.w.35).

S647 **Spencer, Beckwith.** The benefactress. A poem, occasion'd by her grace the Dutchess of Newcastle's giving five hundred pounds, towards the repairing the collegiate church of Southwell... *London, printed for W. Ward, bookseller in Nottingham*, 1713.
2⁰: *A² < B¹*; *i–ii, 1 2–4*.
Ms. corrections in the copies seen.
'Not far from Trent's fair stream, and fruitful soil'
L(11630.h.63),O; PBL.

S648 **Spencer, Richard.** A congratulatory line: to the right honourable the Lord North and Grey; being made a collonel of a regiment; for his great gallantry and valorous conduct. Humbly presented by Ri. Spencer. [1703?]
4⁰: *A¹ B²*; *i–ii, 1–4*.
Title in the form of a dedication, with vertical chain-lines. A generalized text, doubtless intended to be issued with variant titles for various dedicatees. Very primitive printing.
'When England's peace was threatened with a war'
O.

S649 — A congratulatory poem on the birth-day of her royal highness Wilhelmina Cherlotta princess of Wales. Most humbly inscrib'd to the right hon. Scroop earl of Bridgwater...[1714/20.]

Spencer, R. A congratulatory poem

4⁰: *A¹ B²*; *i–ii, 1–4*.
Possibly issued with variant titles in the form of a dedication.
'Assemble loyal Britains, meet with joy'
CSmH.

S650 — An epithalamium upon the happy marriage of the...Earl of Orrorey, with...the lady Elizabeth Cecil. Humbly presented by Rich. Spencer. [1706.]
4⁰: π¹ A–B²; *i–ii, 1–8*.
Title in the form of a dedication. A generalized text, issued with different titles for various dedicatees; another copy for the marriage of Sir Thomas Twysden, 1700, is at L.
'No greater comfort to well-minded men'
L(11631.c.39).

'Spenser, Edmund.'
[Croxall, Samuel:] An original canto of Spencer: design'd as part of his Fairy queen, but never printed, 1714. *See* C522–6.

[Croxall, Samuel:] Another original canto of Spencer, 1714. *See* C527.

[West, Gilbert:] A canto of the Fairy queen. Written by Spenser. Never before published, 1739. *See* W357.

A new canto of Spencer's Fairy queen. Now first published, 1747. *See* N117.

———————————

Mother Hubbard's tale of the ape and fox, abbreviated from Spencer, 1715. *See* M522.

Spes. Spes Hunsdoniana, 1702. *See* Settle, Elkanah.

Sphinx. Sphinx: a poem, 1724–5. *See* Swift, Jonathan.

S651 **Spiltimber, George.** On public virtue; a poem. In three books. Book I. Inscrib'd to the right honourable Henry Pelham, esq; *London, printed for W. Bickerton*, 1745. (2 Dec)
4⁰: *A¹ B–C⁴ D⁴(–D4)*; *3–5 6–26*.
'On publick virtue if the lyre be strung'
L(11630.c.4/14, Tom's Coffee House, 2 Dec),O.

S652 [—] The statesman: a poem. Humbly inscrib'd to the right honourable Sir Robert Walpole. By a gentleman of Gray's Inn. *London, publish'd by Charles Corbett*, 1740. (LM Sept)
2⁰: *A² B–E²*; *1–5 6–20*.
'The man for senates and for councils form'd'
Dedication signed 'G.S.' Advertised as 'by the same author' in Spiltimber's *To the king*.
L(1959, uncut),O; MH,OCU.

S653 — To the king, on his majesty's happy return. An ode. *London, printed for Charles Corbett*, [1740.] (*LM* Oct)
2⁰: *A² B²*; *1–3 4–8*.
Presentation inscription to Philip Yorke, lord

Spiltimber, G. To the king

Hardwicke, on the fly-leaf of the MH copy, and dedicatory Latin verses dated 1 Dec.
'Awake, Thalia! sweep thy string'
MH(presentation copy),OCU(important ms. notes, deleted).

S654 — The weather-menders: a tale. A proper answer to Are these things so? *London, printed for J. Roberts*, 1740. (*LDP* 18 Nov)
2°: *A*² B²; *1-2* 3-8.
Reprinted in a piratical edition of *He has kept his word*, 1740.
'Saunt'ring in an ev'ning's walk'
Occasioned by [James Miller] *Are these things so?*, 1740. Answered by [Robert Morris] *Have at you all*, 1740.
O,LdU-B; CU,CtY(uncut),MH,OCU,TxU.

S655 **Spiritual.** Spiritual fornication. A burlesque poem. Wherein the case of Miss Cadiere and Father Girard are merrily display'd. In three canto's. By Jeremy Jingle, esq; *London, printed for H. Cooke*, 1732 [1731]. (*GSJ* 19 Nov)
8°: *A*² B-D⁴ (+1 plate); *1-5* 6-28. A1 hft.
Also printed in *The ladies miscellany*, [1731.]
'Physicians hold evacuation/Is very proper on occasion'
L(1964).

S655·5 — [*idem*] Spiritual amours. A burlesque poem... The second edition. *London, printed for H. Cooke*, 1732.
8°: *A*² B-D⁴; *1-4* 5-28. A1 hft.
The half-title reads 'To which are prefix'd, as an ornament, several curious copper-plates, done from the French originals'; they are not in the copies described.
L(1973); *MR*.

S656 — — The third edition. *London, printed for H. Cooke*, 1732.
(Pickering & Chatto cat. 202/11628.)

— Spiritual life. Poems on several divine subjects, 1727. *See* Craig, James.

— A spiritual poem: or Christian counsel to youth, 1728. *See* Besse, Joseph.

S657 **Spite.** Spite and spleen: or the doctor run mad. To the worthy Dr. T----s----n. [*London*, 1701.] (28 May, Luttrell)
½°: 2 sides, 1 column.
'Sir, to your care we timely would commit'
Addressed to Edward Tyson, physician to Bethlehem hospital; satirically committing Samuel Garth, run mad with envy of Sir Richard Blackmore and others.
Rothschild; MH(Luttrell).

Spleen. The spleen, a pindarique ode, 1709. *See* Finch, Anne, *countess of Winchilsea*.

S658 — The spleen: a poem. Humbly inscrib'd to a certain dean. [*Dublin*] *Printed in the year* 1732.

The **spleen**: a poem

½°: *1-2*, 2 columns.
Teerink 1303.
'Black wayward power, who o'er the discontent'
Inscribed to Dean Swift, but not directly referring to him.
Rothschild(mutilated).

Splendid. The splendid shilling, 1705-. *See* Philips, John.

S659 **Splitter.** 'Splitter of freeholds. A satyr. [*London*] *Printed for the booksellers*. Price 6*d*.' (*WL* Dec 1705) 4°.
Listed in *TC* Michaelmas as a quarto. It is possibly identical with Joseph Browne's poem with this title, printed in 1708.

— The splitter of freeholds, 1708. *See* Browne, Joseph.

S660 **Sponge.** 'The spunge. A new song on the times. To the tune of London is a fine town. [*London*] *Printed for A. Moor*. Price 2*d*.' (*DJ* 16 Feb 1722)
Possibly a half-sheet from the price.

S661 **Spooner, Lawrence.** A looking-glass for smokers: or, the dangers of the needless or intemperate use of tobacco... A poem. *London, printed for A. Baldwin*, 1703. (8 Sept, Luttrell)
8°: A-F⁸ G⁴; *i-iv* v-xv *xvi*, 17-104. A1 hft.
'When at the first I step'd upon the stage'
L(161.k.27, Luttrell, —A1); CSmH,MH(—A1, lacks F1).

S662 [—] Poetical recreations: or pleasant remarks on the various rumours upon the publication of my poem call'd, A looking-glass for smokers... *London, printed for A. Baldwin*, 1705. (15 March, Luttrell)
8°: A-D⁸; *1-2* 3-63 *64 blk*.
Two poems, both with title 'Poetical recreations'; the second is a dialogue.
'When first this doubtful task I did engage'
'Upon the evening of a summers day'
The author's apology signed 'L.S.'
L(164.k.49, Luttrell).

S663 **Sprat, Thomas.** The plague of Athens, which hapned in the second year of the Peloponnesian war. First described in Greek by Thucydides; then in Latin by Lucretius. Since attempted in English. By...Thomas lord bishop of Rochester. *London, printed for Charles Brome*, 1703.
8°: A-B⁸ C⁴; *i-vi*, 1-34.
First published in 1659.
'Unhappy man! by nature made to sway'
O,EtC; CLU-C,*DNLM*.

S664 — The plague of Athens, which hapened in the second year of the Peloponnesian war... *London printed, and sold by H. Hills*, 1709.
8°: A⁸ B⁴; *1* 2-24.

Sprat, T. The plague of Athens

The order of these 1709 editions has not been determined.

L(11633.df.51),LG,O(2),C,E + ; CtY,*DFo*,IU (uncut),MH,TxU(uncut) +.

S665 — [another edition, title reads:] The plague of Ahtens [!]...

8⁰: A⁸ B⁴; *1-2* 3-24.

Page 15 is blank except for note, 'Reader, through mistake of the press, a page being transpos'd, you are desir'd to turn over leaf'.

L(473.a.36/3),O,C,CT(3),EU; CSmH,CtY,ICN, OCU,TxU +.

'Sprightly, Phil.' Love verses, 1716. *See* L286.

S666 **Spuddy.** Spuddy's lamentation for the loss of her collar, who was deprived of it the 12th of April, 1728. [*Dublin*, 1728.]

½⁰: 2 sides, 1 column.

Teerink 936; *Williams* 1131.

'A creature I, of flesh and blood'

Ball 239 suggested Swift was 'probably responsible' for these lines; Williams rejects the attribution. Spuddy is a dog that laments the death of her mistress Dorothea Gorges and her master Richard Gorges in April 1728.

L(1890.e.5/160),DT.

S667 **Squib.** The squib. An epistle from a gentleman in the country to his friend in town. *Isle-of-Man, printed in the year* 1743.

4⁰: A² B-F²; *1-2* 3-24.

Catchword p. 4, 'VVhere'. The imprint may be false.

'Far from the town remov'd, that faithless den'

This is closely related to *The Hibernian politicians*, 1740-, and probably by the same author, possibly Mr. Gardiner. A satire on Dublin town life and politicians.

O,DA,DG; DFo.

S668 — [another edition]

Catchword p. 4, 'Where'.

DA.

S669 **Squire.** The squire and the cardinal: an excellent new ballad. Tune of, King John and the abbot. *London, printed for A. Moore,* 1730. (*MChr* Dec)

2⁰: A¹ B²; *1-3* 4-5 *6 blk.*

Percival XVII.

'I'll tell you a story, a story so merry'

A satire against Horatio Walpole's negotiations with Cardinal Fleury about France raising troops in Ireland.

O(2, 1 lacks A1),C(lacks A1); CSmH,MH,OCU, TxU.

S670 — — *London, printed by A.M. near St. Pauls,* 1730.

4⁰: A²; *1-2* 3-4.

A piracy.

L(1876.f.1/104).

Squire

— The 'squire and the parson, [1749.] *See* Jenyns, Soame.

S671 — Squire Bickerstaffe's elegy on the much-lamented death of John Dolben, esq; manager in chief against Dr. Sacheverell. [*London*] *Printed for John Baker,* 1710. (8 June, Luttrell)

½⁰: 1 side, 1 column.

'Weep, all you schismaticks, since he is gone'

Against Dolben.

MC(Luttrell); MH.

[**Squire, John.**] The Lilliputian widow. A poem addressed to the Chester-ladies, 1729. *See* L182.

Squire, Joshua. Select psalms of David. Translated anew into English meter. Fitted to all the old tunes. *London, printed for J. Baker, J. Round, Nath. Cliff, & B. Bragg,* 1707. (*DC* 2 Jan)

8⁰: pp. 95. O,AdU.

S672 **Squirelin.** The squirelin. A tale. *Dublin, printed in the year* 1726.

8⁰: A⁴; *1-2* 3-8.

'A rev'rend parson of the gown'

CtY.

Squirrel. The squirrel. A poem, 1706. *See* Prior, Matthew.

S—s. S—s and J—l. A new ballad, 1743. *See* Williams, *Sir* Charles Hanbury.

S------t, D------n. D-----n S------t's prologue to Hyppolitus, 1721. *See* Helsham, Richard.

S—t, *Dr.* Annoque domini 1732. The Irish bishops, 1732. *See* Swift, Jonathan.

— Bounce to Fop, 1736. *See* B326.

— Cadenus and Vanessa, 1726-. *See* Swift, Jonathan.

— The lady's dressing room, 1732. *See* Swift, Jonathan.

— A letter from D. S—t to D. S—y, [1725.] *See* Swift, Jonathan.

— The life and genuine character of the rev. Dr. S—t, 1733. *See* Swift, Jonathan.

— A riddle by Dr. S—t, to my lady Carteret, [1725/30.] *See* R204.

S—t, *the honourable Mr.* Pancharilla, from Bonefonius. A new ballad, [1725/30.] *See* P27.

S673 **Stacie,** —, *Mr.* Consolatory verses to a lady upon her lover's being displac'd... By Mr. Stacie. *London, printed for J. Roberts,* 1727. (*MC* Oct)

2⁰: A² B²; *1-3* 4-7 *8 blk.*

'When grief intrusive does thy peace invade'

Possibly the author should be identified with Edmund Stacy.

O(impft); NjP.

Stacy, E.

Stacy, Edmund. Sir Roger L'Estrange's fables, with morals and reflections, in English verse. *London, printed by M. Jenour, for Tho. Harbin, 1717* [1716]. (*MC* Nov)
12°: pp. 316.   L.

[—] [reissue] Æsop's fables, with morals and reflections, as improved by Sir Roger L'Estrange, done into variety of English verse... The fourth edition. *London, printed for Edmund Parker, 1720.*
12°: pp. 315.   O.
> Cancel title, a4, and final P², the latter two removing references to a second volume. Dedication signed 'E.S.'.

The attribution of the poems below rests on the entry of The tale of the robin-red-breast, 1710, *to 'Stacey' in* SR; *the other poems are related to that by authorship statements of the form 'By the author of the Black-bird's tale', and by links in advertisements, particularly in* The way of the town, 1717. *These attributions are new, and confirmation of them is desirable.*

S674 [—] Assassination display'd in the fable of the robin red-breast and vulture. By the author of the Black-bird's tale. *London printed, and sold by J. Morphew, 1711.* (*PB* 10 April, 'tomorrow')
8°: A⁸; *i–ii*, 1–14. 14 advt.
'Near to the ruines of an ancient seat'
> A tory poem ascribing the stabbing of Harley by Guiscard to a whig plot.
LLP,O; CtY,MH,*NN*,TxU.

S675 [—] The blackbird's song. [*London*] *Printed for J. More, near St. Paul's, 1715.* (25 March, Luttrell)
8°: A⁴ B–C⁴; *1–4* 5–24. A1 hft.
> Listed in *MC* March.
'The blackbird who had waited long'
> Crum T340. An advertisement in *The way of the town*, 1717, lists *The black-bird's tale* as by the same author; the link is also seen in the reissue of *The picture of a church militant* (S698). It seems reasonable to identify the author as Stacy, though confirmation is desirable.
L(164.n.5, Luttrell,–A1),O; CtY,ICN,InU,MH, OCU+.

S676 [—] — The second edition. [*London*] *Printed for J. More, 1715.*
8°: A⁴ B–C⁴; *1–4* 5–24. A1 hft.
CSmH,CtY.

S677 [—] — *London, printed by D. Brown, 1715.*
8°: A² B⁸; *1–4* 5–19 20 blk. A1 hft.
> The AdU copy has variant punctuation of the imprint, 'London: Printed: by D. Brown'. Presumably this is a piracy; the paper and print are poor.
E,AdU; TxU.

S678 [—] [*idem*] The blackbird's winter song. [*London?*] *Printed for the author,* [1715/–.]
8°: A⁸; *1–2* 3–16.

Stacy, E. The blackbird's song

> The text of this edition has not been collated with the preceding, but the first line is the same.
DFo.

S679 [—] The black-bird's tale. A poem. *London, printed in the year 1710.* (*SR* 13 May)
8°: A⁸; *i–ii*, 1–13 14 blk.
> Entered in *SR* to Edmund Powell; deposit copies at O,C,E,EU,AdU. Listed in *WL* May.
'A good old blackbird, whose retreat'
> *The tale of the robin-red-breast*, 1710, which appears to be by Stacy, is 'By the author of the Black bird's tale'. Against the whigs.
O(4, 1 uncut),C,CT(2),E,AdU+; CtY,IU,MH.

S680 [—] — The second edition, corrected and enlarged by the same author. *London, printed by E. Powell, and sold by the booksellers,* [1710.] (1 July, Luttrell)
8°: A⁸; *i–ii*, 1–14.
> Misprint in line 1, 'Blacbird'. The order of the two 'second editions' has not been determined.
L(164.k.34, Luttrell),LdU-B; InU,MH,OCU.

S681 [—] — The second edition corrected and enlarged by the same author. *London, printed by E. Powell, and sold by the booksellers,* [1710.]
8°: A⁸; *i–ii*, 1–14.
> Apparently a different edition; line 1 correctly, 'Blackbird'.
O(2),C,E; DFo,ICN,IU,NjP,TxU+.

S682 [—] — *London, printed in the year 1710.*
8°: A⁴; *1–2* 3–8.
> Presumably a piracy.
OCU.

S683 [—] — [col] *Edinburgh, printed by James Watson, and sold at his shop, 1710. From the London copy printed by E. Powell.*
4°: A⁴; *1–8*.
> Drop-head title only.
E(ms. date, Aug).

S684 [—] — In two parts... The third edition corrected and enlarged. *London, printed by E. Powell, and sold by the booksellers,* [1710/11.]
8°: A⁸; *1–2* 3–16.
> This is the first edition to refer to 'two parts'; it was advertised 'with the addition of the whole second part' in *The hermit* 8 Sept 1711, but may well be earlier.
CSmH(uncut).

S685 [—] The black-bird's second tale. A poem. By the author of the first. *London, printed for, and sold by Ed. Lewis, 1710.* (*SR* 6 July)
8°: A⁴; *i–ii*, 1–6. 6 advt.
> The advertisement on p. 6 announces that this poem will be published every Thursday in half-sheets. Entered in *SR* to Edward Lewis; deposit copies at O,C,E,EU,AdU.
'The blackbird whose incessant care'
'Endeavouring to persuade the queen to

Stacy, E. The black-bird's second tale

quitt the whigg interest & stick to the church',
Luttrell.
L(164.k.35, Luttrell, 18 July),O,C,E,AdU+;
CtY,IU(2),InU,MH,OCU.

S686 [—] The black-bird's third tale. A poem. By the
author of the first. *London printed, and sold by John
Morphew*, 1710.
8°: A⁴; *i–ii*, 1–6. 6 advt.
The advertisement on p. 6 repeats that of the
second tale. All copies seen have a ms. correc-
tion in p. 1, last line, 'Ears' to 'Cares'.
'As on a bough the blackbird sat'
Against the whigs.
LLP,O(uncut); IU,MH,OCU.

S687 [—] Britannia's memorial... By the author of the
Blackbird's song. [*London*] *Printed for J. Baker*,
1715. (*MC* July)
8°: *A*⁴ B–C⁴; *1–4* 5–24. A1 hft; 24 advt.
'Upon the fruitful banks of Thame'
A high church lament for the state of Britain.
CT; CSmH,InU.

S688 [—] — [*London?*] *Printed in the year* 1715.
slip: *1–2*, 1 column.
MH.

S689 [—] An elegy, sacred to the memory of Dr.
Thomas Kenn, the depriv'd bishop of Bath and
Wells. *London, printed for and sold by John Mor-
phew*, [1711.] (*PM* 31 March 1711, 'just publish'd')
½°: *1–2*, 1 column.
'When great men dy'd the custom was of old'
Listed in an advertisement in *The way of the
town*, 1717, as by the author of *The blackbird's
song*.
O; MH.

S690 [—] The parliament of birds. *London, printed for
John Morphew*, 1712. (*PB* 13 Nov)
8°: A⁸ B⁴; *1–2* 3–24.
Entered to Morphew in *SR* 22 Nov 1712;
deposit copies at O,E,EU,AdU,SaU.
'An eagle, that long time had been'
Advertised in *The way of the town*, 1717, as
by the author of *The blackbird's song*. A
political allegory.
L(11631.b.32),O(2),CT,E,DT+; CSmH,CtY,
ICU,MH,TxU(uncut)+.

S691 [—] — *London, printed by J. Bradford*, 1712.
8°: A⁸ B⁴; *1–2* 3–24.
Probably a piracy; no price on title, inferior
paper.
CtY,TxU.

S692 [—] — *Edinburgh, re-printed by Mr. Robert
Freebairn, and sold at his shop*, [1712.] (Nov)
8°: A⁸; *1–2* 3–16.
Entered in Ruddiman's ledger for the week
ending 6 Dec 1712 'a sheet Crown Engl.' for
both setting and printing; an entry in the
following week records 'wrought of new 8

Stacy, E. The parliament of birds

quairs press'. The impressions have not been
distinguished.
E(2, 1 ms. date Nov 1712); DLC,ICN,NjP.

S693 [—] — with an account of the late and present
ministry. *London: printed for John Morphew and
reprinted in Dublin by C. Carter*, 1713.
8°: *A*⁴ B⁴; *1* 2–16.
The 'account' is the poem itself.
C.

S694 [—] — The third edition. *London: printed for John
Morphew and reprinted in Dublin by C. Carter*, 1713.
8°: *A*⁴ B⁴; *1* 2–16.
NjP(uncut).

S695 [—] The parliament of birds. The second part.
By the author of the first part. *London, printed by
J. Bradford*, [1712?]
8°: A⁸ B⁴ (A4 as 'A3'); *1–2* 3–24.
'The day was come, and all the birds'
It is strange that this continuation is so scarce,
and is published by Bradford rather than
Morphew; the latter published the authorized
edition of the first part. The facts might
suggest that this is an unauthorized second
part by another hand.
TxU.

S696 [—] The picture of a church militant. An original,
after the modern manner. For the use of St
Stephen's Chapel... By the author of the Black-
bird's tale. *London, printed for S.B.* [*Samuel
Briscoe*]; *sold by J. Morphew*, 1711. (22 Feb,
Luttrell)
8°: A⁸; *i–ii*, 1–13 *14 blk*.
Entered in *SR* to Samuel Briscoe, 23 Feb;
deposit copies at E,EU,AdU.
'Great god of truth, direct my muse'
L(164.m.59, Luttrell; 698.h.14/6),O,E,EU,AdU;
DLC,IU.

S697 [—] — The second edition, with additions...
London, printed for S.B.; sold by J. Morphew, 1711.
8°: A⁸; *i–ii*, 1–14.
Apparently largely a reimpression.
O.

S698 [—] [reissue] The former, present, and future
state of the church of England... By the author
of the Blackbird's song. The second edition, with
additions. *London printed, and sold by J. Morphew*,
1715.
8°: A⁸(−A1, 2 +A1.2; −A8 +B²); *i–ii*, 1–16.
IU(ms. date 25 Oct 1716).

S699 [—] — The third edition, with additions. *London
printed, and sold by J. Morphew*, 1715.
8°: A⁸(−A1, 2 +A1.2; −A8 +B²); *i–ii*, 1–16.
Another reissue, possibly with press-variant
cancel.
O.

[—] The tale of my lord the owl, told by the black-
bird, 1718. *See* T24.

Stacy, E. The tale of the raven

S700 [—] The tale of the raven and the blackbird. By the author of the Blackbird's song. *London, printed for R. Barnham; sold by J. Morphew*, 1715. (*SR* 15 June)
8°: A–C⁴; *1–2* 3–23 *24 blk.*
Entered in *SR* to Samuel Briscoe; deposit copies at E,EU,AdU,SaU. Listed in *MC* June.
'As on a bough the blackbird sate'
A political fable against the Jacobites.
L(11631.e.62),O,CT,E,LdU-B+ ; CtY,IU,TxU.

S701 [—] — The second edition. *London, printed for R. Barnham; sold by J. Morphew*, 1715.
8°: A–C⁴; *1–2* 3–23 *24 blk.*
Apparently a reimpression.
AdU; MH.

S702 [—] The tale of the robin-red-breast, a poem. By the author of the Black bird's tale. *London printed, and sold by most booksellers of London & Westminster*, 1710. (10 Nov, Luttrell)
8°: A⁸; *1–2* 3–15 *16. 16 advt.*
Entered in *SR* 30 Oct (possibly before publication) to 'Stacey' by Geo. Parker for the author. The AdU copy of this and the E copy of the second edition are possibly deposit copies.
'Robin-red breast, that long'
The entry in *SR* suggests the author's name is Stacey; Edmund Stacy is revealed as a tory propagandist by H. L. Snyder in *The library* V.22 (1967) 328, and it seems safe to identify him as the author of these tory poems. This is an attack on the late whig ministry.
L(164.k.36, Luttrell; 11601.dd.17/7),O,AdU, *MR-C*; CtY,ICN,OCU.

S703 [—] — The second edition. *London printed, and sold by most booksellers of London & Westminster*, 1710.
8°: A⁸; *1–2* 3–15 *16. 16 advt.*
Apparently a reimpression or press-variant title.
E,CT; IU.

Stafford, P. Poems on several occasions. *London, printed for Tho. Atkins*, 1721. (*DJ* 28 Sept)
8°: pp. 72.   L,WcC; ICN,MH.

— [? variant, imprint undated]
L; CtY,DFo.

Stag. The stag chace in Windsor forest, 1739–. *See* Powney, Richard.

S704 [**Stammers, William.**] Liberty. A poem. To the queen. *London, printed for J. Roberts*, 1729. (*MChr* 1 Oct)
2°: A¹ B–C²; *1–3* 4–10.
'To thee, blest guardian of the British world'
Listed in *MChr* as 'lately presented to her majesty by William Stammers'.
L(1489.d.32),OW; MH,OCU.

Standfast, R.

Standfast, Richard. A dialogue between a blind man and death.
Standfast died in 1684, so this work falls outside the scope of this catalogue. I have noted an Edinburgh edition of 1702 at O, and further editions which add John Bunyan's 'The great assize' of [170–?] at LDW; [1710] at E, EU; 1713 at L; Edinburgh [171–?] at E; and Edinburgh 1735 at E.

S705 '**Standfast, Tho.**' The trinitarin [!] combat: or, Calvins instruction to the young academicks: in a discourse lately deliver'd at Salters-Hall. By their old friend Tho. Standfast. *London, printed in the year* 1719.
8°: A⁴(–A1?) B–C⁴ D²; *3–4* 5–27 *28 blk* (15 as '51').
The copies seen probably lack A1, half-title.
'To view this wretched town, what man can live'
'Tho. Standfast' is almost certainly a pseudonym.
C; MH.

Stanhope, Hugh.
'*H. Stanhope' is usually considered to be a pseudonym for William Bond since Curll in* The Curliad (*1729*) *24–5 links them as responsible for* The progress of dulness, *1728. Further clarification seems desirable since presentation poems like those below are rarely pseudonymous. S714 gives his name as Hugh; elsewhere he is* 'Mr. Stanhope'.

S706 — An epistle to his royal highness the Prince of Wales; occasion'd by the state of the nation. Presented on his birth-day. *London, printed for E. Curll*, 1720. (*DP* 31 Oct)
8°: A² B–C⁴; *i–iv*, *1*–15 *16 blk.* A1 hft.
No watermark identified; 'Price 6d.' on title. Entered in *SR* 1 Nov; deposit copies at O,E, EU,SaU are of the 'third edition'. All the London 'editions' are from the same setting of type, and they may be no more than pressvariant titles. Some copies (e.g. L) have A⁴ containing Curll's advertisements at end.
'Pardon, illustrious prince, if in these times'
See Arundell, *The directors...addressed to Mr. Stanhope*, 1720.
L(161.m.38, Luttrell, Oct); *MH-BA,MnU*.

S707 — [fine paper]
Watermark: Strasburg bend; no price on title. The inner margins have been enlarged.
O.

S708 — — The second edition. *London, printed for E. Curll*, 1720. (*DP* 2 Nov)
8°: A² B–C⁴; *i–iv*, *1*–15 *16 blk.* A1 hft.
From the same type as the preceding; possibly a press-variant title. All copies seen have added A⁴ of Curll advertisements.
O; CSmH,CtY,KU,*NN*.

S709 — — The third edition. *London, printed for E. Curll*, 1720. (*DP* 4 Nov)

Stanhope, H. An epistle

8°: *A*² B–C⁴; *i–iv*, *1–15 16 blk*. A1 hft.
The copies deposited at Stationers' Hall for the entry of 1 Nov are of this 'edition'; possibly a press-variant title.
L(11601.ddd.7/1),O(2, 1 – A1),E,EU,SaU;
CLU-C.

S710 — — The fourth edition. *London, printed for E. Curll*, 1720. (*PB* 15 Nov)
8°: *A*² B–C⁴; *i–iv*, *1–15 16 blk*. A1 hft.
Apparently from the same setting of type; A⁴ o Curll advertisements added to the copy at C.
C; *CU*,KU,MH-BA.

S711 — — *Dublin: re-printed, and sold by Thomas Hume*, 1720.
8°: *A*⁴; *1 2–8*.
Signature possibly cropped from the copy seen.
DN.

S712 — The governour, a poem on the present posture of affairs: presented to the king. *London, printed for E. Curll*, 1720. (*PB* 26 Nov)
8°: *A*⁴ B–C⁴ D²; *1–4 5–28*. A1 hft, advt.
Added A⁴ of Curll advertisements at KU, MH-BA. An advertisement in *DP* 28 Nov reports 'Presented (on Friday last [25 Nov]) to the king'.
'Loud, and more loud, ye Britons shout, – 'tis he'
CtY,KU,MH-BA.

S713 — — The second edition. *London, printed for E. Curll*, 1720. (*DP* 30 Nov)
8°: *A*⁴ B–C⁴ D²; *1–4 5–28*. A1 hft, advt.
From the same setting of type; possibly a variant title.
L(1964, – A1),LdU-B; *CU*,DLC,KU(– A1).

S714 — The patriot: an epistle to the most noble Philip earl of Chesterfield... *London, printed for T. Cooper; sold at the pamphlet shops of London & Westminster*, 1733. (*GSJ* 4 May)
2°: *A*² B²; *1–2 3–8*.
'Let other bards another subject chuse'
L(11642.i.9, uncut); CtY,TxU.

S715 — Verses sacred to the memory of the right honourable James earl Stanhope... *London, printed for E. Curll*, 1721. (17 Feb?)
2°: *A*² B¹; *1–3 4–6*.
Advertised in *DP* 15 Feb for 'next Friday', 17 Feb.
'When patriots fall, the most degen'rate age'
DFo.

S716 [**Stanhope, Philip,** *earl Stanhope.*] The state screen display'd; or, the projector at his last shift. In which the vicissitudes of his fortune, and the virtues of his gilded pacificks are fully delineated. *London, printed for, and sold by S. Slow in the Strand, and also by the booksellers in town & country*, 1734. (*GM* Feb)
4°: (frt+) *A*² B–D²; *1–2 3–12* '*11 12 10*' *16 blk*.
Folding engraved plate as frontispiece.

Stanhope, P., *earl.* The state screen

'The sages, lest you might their meaning find'
Early ms. note in the O copy 'By Ld Stanhope'; the attribution has been accepted by *Halkett & Laing*, but no confirmation has been found. The verse is a commentary on the engraving, satirizing Walpole's policies.
O(– frt); CtY.

S717 [**Stanhope, Philip Dormer,** *earl of Chesterfield.*] The Cambro Briton robb'd of his bauble. To which is annex'd, Bob and Harry: a new occasional song. *London printed, and sold by J. Smith, & A. Moore*, 1727. (*SJEP* 23 March)
2°: *A*² B²; *1–3 4–8*.
Percival III.
'Hear, all ye friends to knighthood'
Bob & Harry: 'As scriblers poor, who write to eat'
Early ms. note on title of the CSmH copy 'By the Earl of Chesterfield'; printed in Chesterfield's *Works* III (1778) 197. A satire on the theft of the order of the Bath from Sir William Morgan in Nov 1726. It is not clear whether 'Bob and Harry' is also by Chesterfield; Percival suggests it is probable, and (for what it is worth) the ms. ascription in the CSmH copy follows 'Bob and Harry' on the title.
AdU; CLU,CSmH,MH.

[—] The Gymnasiad [actually by Paul Whitehead], 1744. *See* W413.

[—] The Totness address, versified [actually by Joseph Mitchell], 1727. *See* M333.

S718 **Stanzas.** Stanza's on King Charles the martyr: and the loyal peers, and others, in Mr. Playford's printed sheet. *London printed, and sold by H. Hills*, [1710.] (16 Feb, Luttrell)
1°: 1 side, 3 columns.
Printed in red and black, within mourning borders; engraved portrait of Charles I in centre. 20 separate stanzas. Wrongly dated by *Wing* (S5253) as 1649, by L as 1660.
The King: 'Enthron'd in center of the planets bright'
An edition 'printed for F. Playford, in the Strand' at O is perhaps a seventeenth-century edition; it has a woodcut portrait. Possibly this is a republication occasioned by the Sacheverell affair.
L(C.20.f.2/19); MH(Luttrell).

— Stanza's on the marriage of his royal highness the Prince of Wales with the Princess of Saxe-Gotha, [1736.] *See* An epistle to his grace the Duke of Grafton, 1736.

S719 — Stanzas sacred to the spotless memory, of the very reverend Mr. David Blair, who died the 10 of June 1710, and in the 74 year of his age. [*Edinburgh*, 1710.]

Stanzas sacred to...David Blair

½º: 1 side, 2 columns.
'Forbear ye bold rapacious worms, forbear'
E.

— Stanza's to my Lady Sunderland, 1712. *See* Watts, Isaac.

— Stanza's to the lord treasurer, upon the peace, 1713. *See* Hinchcliffe, William.

S720 Star. The star-gazer: or, latitude for longitude. A poem. *London, printed by J. Jones; sold by the booksellers and pamphlet shops of London & Westminster,* 1739. (*GM* Feb)
2º: *A*² B–C²; *1–3* 4–12.
    Horizontal chain-lines. On pp. 10–12. 'The lamentable ballad of the rampant Jesuit and deluded virgin', on Father Girard and Miss Cadière.
'Authors report, there's to be found'
Ballad: 'Now maidens all, pray lend an ear'
    An erotic tale.
O,LdU–B; CLU–C,DLC,OCU.

S721 Starrat, William. A pastoral in praise of Allan Ramsay. [*Dublin*] *Printed by J. Gowan,* 1726.
½º: 1 side, 2 columns.
'Æ wonny day, last ouk, I'll ne'er forget'
E.

State. State and miscellany poems; compos'd occasionally, 1715. *See* Browne, Joseph.

S722 — The state bell-mans collection of verses for the year 1711... *London printed, and sold by John Morphew,* 1710 [1711]. (*PB* 24 Feb)
8º: A–C⁴; *1–2* 3–22 *23–24 blk.* 22 advt.
    12 short satirical poems, possibly by one author, though *CBEL* II. 189 suggests it is a miscellany.
Introduction: 'My masters tho' my muse be dull'
L(164.k.18, Luttrell, 24 Feb, –C4),O,NeU(–C4); CtY,NN,OCU(–C4).

S723 — *London, printed by John Morphew: and Edinburgh re-printed in the year* 1711.
8º: *A*⁸; *1–2* 3–15 *16 blk.* 15 advt.
E; CLU–C(uncut),CSmH.

— The state dunces, 1733. *See* Whitehead, Paul.

S724 — The state gamesters; or, the old cards new pack'd and shuffl'd. *London, printed for J. Brookes, near Fleetstreet,* 1714. (18 Oct, Luttrell)
½º: *1–2,* 1 column.
'A set of gamesters all together met'
    An allegory on political intrigues about the succession.
L(11602.i.12/8), ICN(Luttrell).

S725 — The state of Rome, under Nero and Domitian: a satire. Containing, a list of nobles, senators, high priests, great ministers of state, &c. &c. &c. By Messrs. Juvenal and Persius. *London, printed for C. Corbett,* 1739. (*GM, LM* June)
2º: *A*² B–D² *E*¹; *1–3* 4–17 *18 blk.*

The state of Rome

Rothschild 2551.
'What! still be plagu'd and never take the scourge,' *Crum* W692. A copy at L has an early ms. note 'by Paul Whitehead'. First ascribed to Whitehead in *CBEL*, possibly from this authority, but not previously mentioned or included in his works. A satire on Walpole's convention with Spain.
L(11352.h.7; C.131.h.1/10****),O,C,WrP; IU, MH,*NNC*,OCU,TxU.

S726 — — The second edition, corrected. *London, printed for C. Corbett,* 1739.
2º: *A*² B–D² *E*¹; *1–3* 4–17 *18 blk.*
    Apparently a reimpression with some revisions.
L(1346.m.15; 840.m.1/35); IU,MH,OCU.

S727 — — '*London, printed for C. Corbett*' [*Edinburgh*], 1739. (*SM* June)
8º: A–C⁴; *1–3* 4–24.
    Copies (e.g. at C,E) are found bound in collections of Edinburgh piracies.
L(11658.f.26),O,C,E,GU; ICN,IU,MH,NN.

— 'The state of the nation.'
    Advertised in *The parsons bewitch'd* (Dublin, 1730) as by the same hand; possibly in prose.

— The state screen display'd, 1734. *See* Stanhope, Philip, *earl Stanhope.*

S728 — The state weather-cocks. *London printed, and sold by J. Dormer,* 1734. (*GM* March)
2º: *A*² B–D²; *1–2* 3–16.
    Engraving on title.
'Let great men loll ingloriously in state'
L(11630.h.48),O,LdU–B; CSmH,CtY,MH, OCU,TxU.

S729 — The state weather-cocks: or, no side the better for false-brethren. *Dublin, re-printed by E. Waters,* 1712.
½º: *1–2,* 1 column.
    No London edition has been traced.
'Since Dismal became low, and D-----et high'
    Against the whigs.
Rothschild.

S730 Statesman. The statesman. A new court ballad. Tune of, A begging we will go, &c. *London, printed for S. Slow; sold by the booksellers of London & Westminster,* [1731.] (*GSJ* 18 June)
2º: *A*² B²; *1–2* 3–8.
    Percival appendix 33.
'Some years ago from Norfolk'
    A ballad biography of Walpole.
CtY,DLC,KU,MH.

S731 — [another issue] *London, printed by R. Walker; sold by the booksellers of London & Westminster,* [1731.]
2º: *A*² B²; *1–2* 3–8.
    No cancel seen; probably another impression or a variant title.
ICN.

The statesman

S732 —— *London, printed for L. Sow*[!]; *sold by the booksellers of London & Westminster*, [1731.]
4°: *A*²; *1* 2–4.
A piracy. The imprint is perhaps deliberately misspelt.
L(C.40.m.10/177).

—— The statesman: a poem, 1740. *See* Spiltimber, George.

S733 —— The statesman's mirrour: or, friendly advice to a certain great minister to retire from court. A poem. *London, printed for J. Huggonson*, 1741. (*GM, LM* Dec)
2°: *A*² B–C²; *1–5* 6–12. A1 hft.
Reprinted in *No screen*, 1742.
'Great wretched man, whom cares of state distress'
Addressed to Walpole.
L(1959),O(uncut),LdU-B; CSmH(–A1),CtY, IU,MH,TxU+.

Statues. The statues: or, the trial of constancy, 1739. *See* Pilkington, Laetitia.

S734 **Statutarian.** The statutarian. A poem. *London, printed for J. Morphew*, 1714 [1713]. (*PB* 10 Nov)
8°: *A*² B–C⁴ *D*²; *i–iv, 1* 2–17 *18–19; 20 blk.* A1 hft; D2 advt.
'Britannia's heroes, who still dauntless stood'
On the upholders of the statutes at Oxford, Cambridge and elsewhere against innovators.
L(164.m.75,–A1); CtY(–A1, D2),OCU(–A1), TxU.

'Statute, Moses.' Ridotto, 1723. *See* R208.

Stayley, George. 'Poems on several occasions. [*London*] *Shuckburgh.* Price 2s.' (*GM, LM* Dec 1748)

S---te. The s---te m—r's are come, [1742.] *See* Hervey, John, *baron Hervey* (H161).

S735 [**Stearne, John.**] The death and burial of John Asgill, esq;: with some other verses occasion'd by his books. *Dublin, printed in the year* 1702.
4°: *A*⁴ B–F² G¹; *i–vi, 1–24.*
Some copies are printed on paper watermarked with grapes throughout; others on mixed stock.
'Will not the fi'ery chari'ot come'
A copy at DA has a contemporary ms. note 'By Dr. Sterne'. John Stearne, subsequently bishop of Dromore and friend of Swift, is clearly intended, and his authorship seems probable. A satire on John Asgill.
L(11631.bbb.42),O,*C*,DN(3),DT(3)+; CLU-C, ICN,ICU,IEN,InU.

[**Steddy, John.**] An epistle to Mr. Pope. By the author of the letter to the patron of the Trip to Barleduc, 1716. *See* E404.

Steddy, J.

S736 — A trip to Bar-le-Duc. A poem. *Edinburgh, printed for William Dickie*, 1715.
2°: A–D²; *i–ii* iii–iv, 1–11 *12 blk.*
Title in red and black. Copies at L, AdU have a ms. correction in p. 11, line 15.
'As poets in the days of yore'
Dedication signed.
L(1959),E,AdU(uncut).

[**Steele, Sir Richard.**] Female folly: or, the plague of a woman's riding-hood and cloak, 1713. *See* F94.

S737 [—] An imitation of the sixth ode of Horace, apply'd to his grace the Duke of Marlborough. With a prologue design'd for the first day of Mr. Estcourt's acting, but forbid to be spoke by Mr. Rich, who thought himself reflected on in one of the verses, which seems to compare his present circumstances with those of the king of France. *London, printed in the year* 1704. (31 Oct, Luttrell)
2°: *A*²; *1–4.*
'Shou'd Addison's immortal verse'
Prologue: 'Since Churchill's fame has thro' our regions run'
Printed by *Blanchard* 14f from *The diverting post* 4 Nov 1704, 'suppos'd to be made by Capt. R.S.' Also printed as Steele's in other eighteenth-century collections. The prologue has not been collected, and may be by another hand.
IU,MH(Luttrell).

S738 '—' Orpheus redivivus: a poem on the Irish harp, with an encomium on the famous Mr. Morphy's performance thereon. By Sir Richard Steel. *Corke, printed by A. Welsh*, [1723.] (26 March)
½°.
Printed in red.
'By learned antiquarians we are told'
Blanchard 122 rejects the attribution, quoting an anonymous letter to Steele of 26 March 1723 which refers to the broadside as published 'this day...under too great name for such poetry...'
(Maggs cat. 457 (1924).)

S739 [—] The prologue at the opening of the Theatre-Royal, the day after his majesty's publick entry. Spoken by Mr. Wilks. [*London*] *Printed for J. Tonson*, 1714. (*DC* 24 Sept)
½°: *1–2*, 1 column.
'At length, Britannia, rescu'd from thy fears'
Reprinted in Steele's *Poetical miscellanies*, 1727, and considered as probably Steele's by *Blanchard* 106f.
Crawford; MH(Luttrell, 25 Sept).

[—] A prologue to the Conscious lovers, 1723. *See* P1133.

[—] A prologue to the town... With an epilogue on the same occasion, by Sir Richard Steele, 1721. *See* W310.

Steele, *Sir* R.

Steele, *Sir* R.

S740 — Prologue to the University of Oxford. Written by Mr. Steel, and spoken by Mr. Wilks. *London, printed for Bernard Lintott,* 1706. (*DC* 4 July)
½°: 1 side, 1 column.
'As wandring streams by secret force return'
MC,Crawford; ICN(Luttrell, 8 Aug).

[—] Song for his majesty's birth-day, [1715?] *See* S582.

[—] To the queen, upon the death of his royal highness [actually by Charles Dive], 1709. *See* D339.

[—] Wood's melancholly complaint. Written by Sir R—d S—le, [1725.] *In* S443.

Stennett, Joseph. Hymns in commemoration of the sufferings of our blessed saviour Jesus Christ. Compos'd for the celebration of his holy supper... The second edition enlarged. *London printed, and sold by W. & J. Marshal, A. Bell, & J. Baker,* 1705. (*TC* Easter 1705)
8°: pp. xl, 64.   L,EN.
The copy at L appears to be on fine paper; it is ruled in red and bound in morocco. First published in 1697.

— — The second edition enlarged. *London printed, and sold by J. Marshall,* 1705 [1707?]. (*TC* Michaelmas 1707)
8°: pp. xl, 64.   L; NNUT.
The imprints quoted in *TC* correspond with this ordering of the editions.

— — The third edition enlarged. *London, printed by J. Darby, for John Baker,* 1709. (*LG* 18 April)
8°: pp. xli, 68.   O,DT; NN.

— [reissue] *London, printed by J. Darby, for N. Cliff, & D. Jackson,* 1713.
L; NNUT.
Cancel title. Reprinted in 1720 with Tate & Brady's psalter.

— Hymns compos'd for the celebration of the holy ordinance of baptism. *London, printed by J. Darby; sold by J. Baker, & J. Clark,* 1712.
12°: pp. 16.   L,DT; NN.

— [reissue] The second edition. *London, printed for John Marshall,* [171–?]
L; ICN,NN.
Cancel title.

— — The second edition. *London, printed by J. Darby; sold by J. Clark & R. Ford, E. Matthews, & A. Ward,* 1722.
8°: pp. 16.   L.

S741 [—] A poem to the memory of his late majesty William the third. By J.S. *London, printed for D. Brown, A. Bell, & J. Baker,* 1702. (14 May, Luttrell)
2°: *A*² B–D²; *i–iv*, 1–11 *12 blk.*
Rules at head of p. 1 are 2 mm. apart. Water-

Stennett, J. A poem to the memory

mark: Dutch lion. A copy at TxU has an early state of p. 7, line 18, containing no italicized words. The Luttrell copy is recorded by *Thorn-Drury.* Reprinted in a shortened form at the request of a friend in Leonard Howard's *Miscellaneous pieces,* 1765; possibly it was also reprinted by Howard as *A poem sacred to the immortal memory of King William III,* [1728], of which no copy has been traced.
'Where is the tuneful tribe that sang so well'
Advertised in Stennett's *Hymns in commemoration...,* 1705. Sometimes attributed in error to James Shute, on account of the initials; an imperfect copy at O has been attributed to John Tutchin, and the entry has thence found its way to *CBEL.*
O,LdU-B; CLU-C,MH,TxU(2).

S742 [—] [fine paper]
Watermark: fleur-de-lys.
Chatsworth; DFo.

S743 [—] [reimpression]
Rules at head of p. 1 are 5 mm. apart.
L(11641.h.10/10); ICN.

S744 [—] — The third edition. *London, printed for D. Brown, A. Bell, & J. Baker,* 1702.
2°: *A*² B–D²; *i–iv*, 1–11 *12 blk.*
Another reimpression, with corrections.
LDW,O-*JJ*; CSmH,CtY,TxU.

S745 [—] A poem to the memory of Mr. Nathanael Taylor, late minister of the gospel. By J.S. *London, printed for John Lawrence, & Andrew Bell,* 1702.
2°: *A*² B–C²; *i–ii*, 1–10.
'Attempt, O muse, the pious task, and shed'
Attributed to Stennett by the catalogue of LDW. Sometimes attributed in error to James Shute, like the preceding, but Stennett is clearly the author.
LDW,Chatsworth; CSmH,MH.

S746 — A version of Solomon's Song of songs. Together with the XLVth psalm. The second edition, corrected. *London, printed by J. Darby, for John Baker,* 1709.
8°: A⁸ a⁸ C–D⁸; *i–ii* iii–xxiv, 25–64.
First published in 1700.
'O let him seal his lips on mine'
L(3440.f.4/3; 844.e.22/3),EN,DT; NN,*NNUT.*

S747 Step. [dh] A step to the d---l's exchange: or, the humours of the Wells, &c. [*London,* 170–?]
4°: A²; 1–4.
'When nature had drest up the trees alamode'
Compare *A trip to the devil's summer-house,* 1704.
TxU.

S748 — A step to the lobby. *London, printed in the year* 1704. (*Review* 4 April)
4°: π¹ A–B⁴ C–E² F¹; *1–2* 3–32.
Re-advertised in *PB* 25 July 1717.
'Term-time at hand, I, hit or miss it'

A **step** to the lobby

A satirical trip from the country to Westminster.
O,DT,EtC; CtY,DFo,TxU.

[**Stephens, —, 'a young parson'.**] Chivalrie, no trifle --- or, the knight and his lady, 1746. *See* C152.

Stephens, Edward. Miscellaneous poems. *Cirencester, printed for the author by Tho. Hill & comp.,* 1747.
8°: pp. 56.　GlP; CtY,MH.

— Poems on various subjects. *London, printed for R. & J. Dodsley,* 1759.
8°: pp. 179.　L,O; CtY,MH.

— The birth-day, a pastoral, with other poems. *Ipswich, printed for the author; sold by W. Keymer in Colchester, J. Shave in Ipswich, and T. Toft & R. Lobb in Chelmsford,* 1765.
4°: pp. 39.　L.

_____

S749　— The dying heathen. A poem. Compos'd by Edward Stephens, and translated into Latin by James Brown. Moribundus ethnicus... [*Cirencester,* 1745?]
4°: *A*⁴; *1–3 4–7 8 blk.*
Probably printed at Cirencester; the type and paper resemble Stephens's poem of 1748 below.
'Tell me, thou unknown something, that resid'st'
'Pande, anima, ignotas causas cui mystica sedes'
O,CT(ms. date 1745 and notes).

S750　— A poem on the park and woods of the right honourable Allen lord Bathurst. The second edition. *Cirencester, printed for the author,* 1748.
4°: *A*⁴ *B*¹; *1–5 6–10.*
The first edition was possibly in Stephens's *Miscellaneous poems,* 1747.
'Bear me, auspicious, O ye rural pow'rs'
L(1490.e.29),O,LdU-B.

S751 **Stephens, Henry.** An epistle to his royal highness Frederick, prince of Wales. *London, printed for N. Blandford,* 1729. (*MChr* 18 Aug)
2°: *A–B*²; *1–3 4–7 8 blk.*
'Young heroe, whose fair virtues early rise'
MH.

Stephens, Zach. Poems on several occasions. [*London*] *Printed for the author,* 1742.
8°: pp. viii, *9–32 41–48.*　L; CtY.

Sterling, James. The poetical works... Vol. I. *Dublin, printed by and for George Faulkner,* 1734.
8°: pp. 282.　O,DN; CLU-C,IU.

_____

S752 [—] The alderman's guide; or, a new pattern for a lord-mayor. A ballad. To the tune of Ye commons

Sterling, J. The alderman's guide

and peers, &c. Written by a craftsman of the city of Dublin. [*Dublin,* 1732.]
½°: 1 side, 2 columns.
Teerink 965; *Williams* 1133.
'Kind heav'n has granted'
Reprinted in Sterling's *Poetical works,* 1734. In praise of Humphry French's election as lord mayor of Dublin. Attributed to Swift by *Ball* 280–1; not accepted by Williams.
L(C.121.g.8/111),C; CtY.

[—] A friend in need is a friend in deed, 1737. *See* F266.

S753 [—] A funeral poem on the death of the right honourable William Conolly, esq; *Dublin, printed by A. Rhames,* 1729.
1°: 1 side, 2 columns.
''Tis done! – and fate has giv'n the final blow! – '
Reprinted in Sterling's *Poetical works,* 1734.
L(1872.a.1/12),DT.

S754　— The loves of Hero and Leander from the Greek of Musæus... By Mr. Sterling. To which are added, some new translations from various Greek authors... By ****** **** esq; *Dublin, printed by Andrew Crooke,* 1728.
8°: *A–B*⁴ **₊**⁴ *C–L*⁴ *M*²; *1–10 11–15 16 blk [8], 1–74 75–76 blk.*
₊⁴ contains the list of subscribers.
'Sing, muse, the conscious torch; whose friendly light'
Dedicated to George Ogle, who translated the additional poems.
O(–M2),C,DA(–M2),DG(2),DN(–M2); MH (cropt, –**₊**⁴, M2),NNC(–M2).

S755　——　To which are added, some new translations ...by another hand. *London, printed for J. Walthoe,* 1728. (*MChr* 21 Aug)
12°: *A–F*⁶ *G*² (A2 as 'A'); *1–3 4–76.*
L(1467.b.4/2); IU.

S756 [—] An ode on the times. Address'd to — the hope of Britain. *London, printed for R. Doddesley; sold at the pamphlet shops,* [1738.] (*SR* 28 Feb)
2°: *A*² *B–C*² *D*¹; *1–3 4–13 14 blk.*
Entered in *SR* to Thomas Gardner; deposit copies at L,O,E,AdU,GU. Listed in *GM,LM* March, and dated 1 March by *Straus, Dodsley.*
'Ye bold offenders, quick atone'
Printed in Sterling's *Poetical works,* 1734. To Frederick, prince of Wales.
L(644.m.14/17),O,E,GU,LdU-B+; CSmH,CtY, IU,MH,OCU+.

[—] A poem on the art of printing, [1728.] *See* P585.

[**Stevens, —, 'a young parson'.**] Chivalrie, no trifle --- or, the knight and his lady, 1746. *See* C152.

Stevens, Alexander. A small collection of original poems, &c. never before printed. *London, printed by W.H. for the author,* [172–?]

Stevens, A.

8⁰: pp. 23.   CtY.
> There is a modern ms. note '1720' in the copy seen, but the date may well be later.

Still. Still more advice, [1728.] *See* The tale of a nettle, 1710–.

S757 [**Stillingfleet, Benjamin.**] An essay on conversation. *London, printed for L. Gilliver & J. Clarke*, 1737. (*GM, LM* Feb)
2⁰: π¹ A–E²; *i–ii, 1* 2–19 *20 blk.*
> *Rothschild* 210. The headpiece on p. 1 is found in slightly varying relationship to the type, but this appears to be the sole variant.
> 'The art of converse, how to sooth the soul'
> The second edition bears Stillingfleet's name.
L(840.m.1/48; *Ashley* 5184),O,OW(uncut),BaP, LdU-B+; CSmH,CtY,IU,MH(2),TxU+.

S758 [—] — '*London, printed for L. Gilliver and J. Clarke*' [*Edinburgh*], 1737.
8⁰: A–B⁴ C²; *1–3* 4–20.
> Printed by Ruddiman on the evidence of the ornament.
E; ICN,MH,NN(mutilated).

S759 [—] — *Dublin: re-printed, and sold by George Faulkner*, 1737.
8⁰: A–C⁴; *1–3* 4–24.
DA,DK,DN; CSmH.

S760 — — By Benj. Stillingfleet... The second edition. *London, printed for W. Wilkins*, 1738.
2⁰: A² B–E²; *1–3* 4–20.
O; MH,TxU.

S761 — Some thoughts occasioned by the late earthquakes. A poem. *London, printed for J. Brindley; sold by M. Cooper*, 1750. (*LM* May)
4⁰: A² B–C²; *1–4* 5–12.
> 'Yes, glorious being, humbly I adore'
L(11630.c.8/20; 1465.i.12/10; 643.k.5/13),OW; MH,*NcU.*

S762 **Stilton.** The Stilton hero: a poem. *London, printed for M. Cooper*, 1745. (*GM* May)
4⁰: π(2 ll) A⁴ B(2 ll); *i–ii, 1–2* 3–14. π1 hft.
> π and B are composed of a single sheet: π1 and B2, π2 and B1 are conjugate. Entered to Cooper in Bowyer's ledgers, no details given.
> 'Steeds and the man I sing; the man'
> A satire on Mr. Thornhill's ride from Stilton to London and back in fifteen hours.
L(11630.c.4/17, –π1),O; OCU.

Stinking. Stinking fish, 1708. *See* Dunton, John.

S763 **Stirling, John.** A system of rhetoric, in a method entirely new: containing all the tropes and figures ...The whole is divided into two parts; in the first of which the rules are given in English, in the second in Latin verse... For the use of schools. *London, printed for Thomas Astley*, 1733. (*LM* Nov)

Stirling, J. A system of rhetoric

8⁰: π¹ A² B–C⁴ D⁴(–D1); *i–vi, 1* 2–21 22. 21–22 advt.
> 'A metaphor, in place of proper words'
> 'Dat propriæ similem translata metaphora vocem'
O; *ICU,IU.*

S764 — — The second edition. *London, printed for Thomas Astley*, 1736. (*LM* Nov)
8⁰: A² B–D⁴ E²; *i–iv, 1–5* 6–28. A1 hft; 25–28 advt.
L(1965),O(–A1); *PPL*(lacks C⁴).

S764·5 — — The third edition. *London, printed for Thomas Astley*, 1740. (*LM* Sept)
8⁰: A¹ B–D⁴ E²; *i–ii, 1–5* 6–25 *26–28.* 26–28 advt.
> The copy seen probably lacks a half-title, A1 of A².
L(117.b.33),*HU*; *CtY,ICU.*

S765 — — The fourth edition. *Dublin, printed by Joseph Rhames*, 1744.
8⁰: A² B–D⁴ E¹; *i–iv, 1–5* 6–25 *26 blk.* A1 hft.
L(11824.d.10).

S766 — — The fifth edition. *London, printed for Thomas Astley; sold by R. Baldwin, jun.*, 1750.
8⁰: A² B–D⁴ E²; *i–iv, 1–5* 6–25 *26–28.* A1 hft; 25–28 advt.
ICU,NN,TxU.

S767 **Stocks.** The stocks: or, high change in 'Change-alley. To those honourable gentlemen the bulls and bears, this plate is inscribed, by their very humble servant, Public Credit. *Sold by all the print and pamphlet-sellers in London & Westminster*, [1734?]
½⁰: 1 side, 2 columns.
> Engraving at head.
> 'Here you see, without delusion'
> Probably related to the bills against stock-jobbing introduced in 1733–35.
L(P&D 2016),O; MH.

S768 **Stockton, W.** Cursus venaticus leporinus: carmen heroicum, inscriptum Gulielmo Huet de comitatu Leicestriensi armigero. *London, printed by J. Tilly, for Steph. Austen*, 1735. (*GM* Aug)
4⁰: A¹ B–C⁴ D(3 ll); *i–ii, 1* 2–22.
> The 'r' in 'carmen' is a one-letter paste-on cancel. Listed in *GM* as sold by Ward and Chandler.
> 'Sunt quos Pelidis stomachum cecinisse juvabit'
L(1970).

Stogdon, Hubert. Poems and letters of the late reverend Mr. Hubert Stogdon, collected from his original papers. *London, printed for J. Noon, & S. Billingsley*, 1729. (*MChr* 20 May)
8⁰: pp. xxxiii, 75.   L; CtY.

S769 **Stoppage.** Stoppage no payment: or, a tale upon Dunkirk. '*Holland*' [*London*], *printed in the year* 1712. (25 June, Luttrell)
½⁰: 1 side, 1 column.
> 'Old stories tell how Hercules'
CtY,ICN(Luttrell).

Stormont, D. M., *viscount*

Stormont, David Murray, *6th viscount. See* Murray, David, *6th viscount Stormont.*

Story. The story of Inkle and Yarrico, 1738. *See* Seymour, Frances, *duchess of Somerset.*

— The story of Susanna, 1730. *See* Free, John.

S770 — The story of Typhon. *London, printed for John Morphew,* 1711. (*PM* 22 May)
½°: 1-2, 2 columns.
'To British ancestry I trow'
The story is clearly intended to have political intentions, possibly against Marlborough.
O,C; CLU-C,MH,OCU.

— A story to the purpose, 1710. *See* Pittis, William.

[**Stote, Bertram.**] Faction display'd. A poem [actually by William Shippen], 1704–. *See* S427.

[—] Moderation display'd: a poem... By the author of Faction display'd [i.e. William Shippen], 1704–. *See* S437.

Stowe. Stowe, the gardens of the right honourable Richard lord viscount Cobham, 1732. *See* West, Gilbert.

Str -------. Str -------'s farewell to the hermitage, [1716/-.] *See* Robertson, Alexander.

S771 **Strahan, Alexander.** The first Æneid of Virgil, translated into blank verse. *London, printed for George Strahan,* 1739. (*GM, LM* Dec)
8°: *A*⁴ B–D⁸ E⁴; *i–iv* v–viii, *1* 2–55 *56 blk.* A1 hft.
Watermark: sun.
'Arms, and the hero who from Trojan shores'
L(1068.m.19,–A1),O(–A1); NN,PU.

S772 — [fine paper]
Watermark: Strasburg bend.
L(237.f.1),O.

S772·5 **Strange.** Strange news from St. James's: or, the beef-eaters last supper. [*London*] *Printed for J. Smith in Cornhil,* [1714?]
½°: 1 side, 2 columns.
'When men were taking pains to please their wives'
Hoping that King George will dismiss the beefeaters, though the significance of the term here is not necessarily the obvious one.
TxU.

Strephon. Strephon's love for Delia, 1709. *See* Pomfret, John.

— Strephon's revenge: a satire on the Oxford toats, 1718–. *See* Amhurst, Nicholas.

Strolling. The strolling hero, 1744. *See* 'Butler, Jemmy'.

S773 **Stubbes, George.** The laurel, and the olive: inscrib'd to George Bubb, esq; *London, printed for Egbert Sanger,* 1710. (2 May, Luttrell)

Stubbes, G. The laurel
2°: A–D²; *i–ii* iii–iv, 1–12.
Watermark: Dutch lion.
'E'er bright Aurora streak'd with rose the east'
O,WcC(uncut); CLU-C(Luttrell),*DLC*,IU,MH.

S774 — [fine paper]
Watermark: London arms.
L(11630.ff.2/15),EtC; TxU.

Study. The study[!] beggars, [1733.] *See* S777.

S775 **Stumbling.** [dh] The stumbling-block. From Claudian against Rufinus. [col] *London, printed for Bernard Lintott,* 1711. (*PB* 18 Aug)
2°: A²; 1–4.
Entered in Bowyer's ledgers under 9 Aug, 250 copies printed.
'Twenty conundrums have o'-late'
A parody of bk. 1, lines 1–23.
L(1876.f.19/19),LLP,DT.

S776 — The stumbling-horse. Ascrib'd by a friend to the right h—e — — — — — —. [*Dublin,* 1725/30.]
½°: 1 side, 1 column.
The copy at L forms part of a collection of Dublin half-sheets of 1725/30.
'Here lies a horse beneath this stone'
L(C.121.g.8/97).

S777 **Sturdy.** The study[!] beggars. [*London?* 1733.]
slip: 1 side, 1 column.
Rough woodcut at head. *Percival* XXIX.
'Of all the trades of London'
Against Walpole's excise bill.
C.

S778 — The sturdy beggars garland. [*London,* 1733.]
½°: 1 side, 2 columns.
Below 'The sturdy beggars', five short poems headed 'On the hermitage at Richmond'.
L(C.121.g.9/196).

S779 — [reimpression?]
Three additional short poems added on the verso. An enlarged version of this collection is entered under *On reading a certain speech,* [1733], O186.
CtY.

S780 **Subscribers.** The subscribers, an excellent new song: to the tune of Chevy-chace. *London, printed for John Noon,* 1722. (Sept, Luttrell)
4°: *A*² B–C²; *1–4* 5–11 *12 blk.* A1 hft.
'God prosper long our noble king'
On the attempt to enforce a religious test on the doctrine of the trinity. Answered (in prose) by [Philemon Collier] *The ballad intituled the Subscribers censured,* 1722 (copy at CtY).
L(164.n.23, Luttrell),LDW,OW(–A1).

S781 **Succession.** The succession. A poem. Humbly inscrib'd to his sacred majesty, King George.

The **succession**

London printed, and sold by A. Boulter, and the rest of the booksellers of London & Westminster, 1714.
2°: A² B²; *1–3* 4–8.
'Illustrious monarch, but permit my song'
O.

S782 Suffolk. Suffolk and Norfolk: or, two prodigies in nature. *London, printed for P. Monger; sold at the pamphlet shops in London & Westminster, 1735.*
2°: A² B²; *1–2* 3–8.
'Ancient philosophers declare'
A political satire, on Walpole and an unidentified politician.
O; KU,MH,OCU.

S783 — The Suffolk health. [*London,* 1705.]
½°: 1 side, 1 column.
With an additional untitled poem below.
'Here's a health to the tackers, about let it pass'
'The commons once destroy'd the church'
A tory poem in praise of the tackers and against the house of lords.
Crawford.

Suffolk, Edward Howard, *earl of. See* Howard, Edward, *earl of Suffolk.*

S784 Suffragium. Suffragium: or, the humours of the electors in chusing members for parliament. A poem. *London printed, and sold by J. How, & B. Bragg,* 1702. (23 July, Luttrell)
2°: A² B–C²; *1–2* 3–12.
The Luttrell copy is recorded in *Haslewood.*
'Should England's worthies from Elysium slide'
O,LdU-B,MR-C; NcU.

S784·5 Sugar. 'The sugar plantation a poem.' [*London,* 1746.] (Aug)
Entered in Strahan's ledgers to Andrew Millar under August 1746, 3 sheets, no. 250.
(Strahan's ledgers.)

S785 Summer. A summer voyage to the gulph of Venice, in the Southwell frigate, captain Manly, junr. commander. An irregular ode. The first poetical present ever made by the author to the right honourable the E— of C—d. *London, printed for Lloyd, well known for...ship news; sold by A. More, and at the pamphlet shops in London & Westminster,* 1750. (*GM, LM* July)
4°: A¹ B–F² G¹; *i–ii,* 1 2–21 22 blk.
Vertical chain-lines.
'Wellcome ye zephyrs from your southern shores!'
Pp. 18–19 clearly suggest that the author is the captain of the Southwell, possibly the Richard Manley whose lieutenancy dates from 1744.
L(11630.c.1/14),O; DLC,MH,OCU.

Summum. 'The summum bonum.'
The accomplish'd leader, 1733, is 'by the author of the Summum bonum'; it is advertised on

The **summum** bonum

p. 24 with other books printed for Aaron Ward, but there is no evidence whether it is in verse or not.

Sunday. A sunday evening's conversation at Benwell, 1726. *See* Thirkeld, Taylor.

— Sunday thoughts, 1749–. *See* Browne, Moses.

Sunderland. The Sunderland tale, [1710.] *See* Pittis, William.

Supplement. A supplement to a late excellent poem entitled, Are these things so?, 1740. *See* Newcomb, Thomas.

— A supplement to One thousand seven hundred thirty-eight, 1738. *See* Newcomb, Thomas.

S786 — A supplement to the Norfolk congress. Containing a full and true account of the table-talk: which the master of the feast entertain'd his guests with after dinner... *London, printed by A. Moore,* [1728/29.]
4°: A² B¹; *1–3* 4–6.
'Now, after the Norfolk dinner was over'
A satire on Walpole at Houghton, occasioned by the prose *Norfolk congress,* [1728], and *The Norfolk congress versified,* [1728.]
San Antonio College, Texas.

— A supplement to the Norfolk congress. Or, the game of quadrille, as now play'd at Soissons, [1728/29.] *See* Quadrille to perfection, [1728.]

S787 — A supplement to the verses, entitul'd, The duties of servants to their masters which children (as is herein shewn) are likewise bound to pay to their parents... This begins with number 30, because it has a reference to the former verses, printed under 29 heads in plain verse... *Worcester, printed by S. Bryan, for E. Robinson in Ludlow,* [171–?]
1°: 1 side, 4 columns.
The first set of verses has not been traced.
30. Thankfulness: 'If master prove much kinder than his word'
LG.

S788 Supplication. The supplication and lamentation of George Fachney, an officer in Caldwell's regiment of robbers, to Rob Roy in the Highlands, with Rob Roy's answer. [*Edinburgh,* 1721/22.]
½°: 1 side, 2 columns.
'A lawland robber in distress'
CSmH.

Surprise. The surprize: or, the gentleman turn'd apothecary, 1739. *See* Ellis, John.

S789 Sutherland. Sutherland's lament, for the loss of his post. With his advice to John Daglees his successor. [*Edinburgh,* 1722.]
½°: 1 side, 2 columns.
'I think Auld Reikie's now grown daft'

Sutherland's lament

Sutherland was the Edinburgh executioner, supplanted by John Dalgleish in July 1722. E(2).

S790 Swaddling. Swaddling John's address to the publick. To the tune of, Ye commons and peers... *Dublin, printed in the year* 1728.
½°: 2 sides, 1 column.
'All people draw near;/Cit, rustick, and peer'
A satire on a dissenting sect, probably the 'new light'; compare *A crutch for a lame conscience,* [1728?].
L(1890.e.5/162).

Swan. The Swan tripe-club, 1706-. *See* The tripe club, 1706.

S791 Swans. The swans: a fable on the fall and rise of credit. *Dublin, printed by S. Powell,* 1747.
8°: *A*⁴; *1-2* 3-8.
'A stately swan, all white and fair'
DN; NN.

S792 Swedish. The Swedish lamentation. To the tune of Chivey-chace. [*London?* 1718?]
slip: 1 side, 1 column.
'Oh all you statesmen now at court'
Harding.

S793 Sweet. [dh] The sweet William. [*Edinburgh,* 1746?]
8°: *A*²; *1-4.*
Also printed in *The compliment,* 1746.
'The pride of France is lilly-white'
On William duke of Cumberland, victorious over the Jacobites.
E.

— Sweet William's farewell to black-ey'd Susan, [1719.] *See* Gay, John.

'**Swift** *junior.*' A new system of rural politicks, 1746. *See* N232.

Swift, Jonathan.
No attempt has been made here to list collected editions of Swift's poems, most of which form part of the various editions of his Works; *see the account in* Teerink.

[—] The alderman's guide; or, a new pattern for a lord-mayor [actually by James Sterling], [1732.] *See* S752.

S794 [—] Annoque domini 1732. The Irish bishops, a satyr. By an honest whig curate. Dr. S—t. *London, printed for T. Bray,* 1732. (*GM, LM* Aug)
2°: (3 ll, the third as 'C'); *1-2* 3-6.
Teerink 962; *Williams* 801-5. Previously printed in *GM* June 1732 with the title 'A poor Ir—sh parsons prayer'.
'Old Latimer preaching did fairly describe'
Reprinted in Faulkner's edition of Swift's *Works* (1735) II. 426.
CtY(uncut),TxU.

Swift, J. An answer

S795 [—] An answer to a scandalous poem, wherein the author most audaciously presumes to cast an indignity upon their highnesses the clouds, by comparing them to a woman. Written by Dermot O-Nephely, chief cap. of Howth. *Dublin, printed in the year* 1733.
8°: (4 ll).
Teerink 1615, describing an imperfect copy seen by Williams containing Sheridan's *A new simile for the ladies* and this reply. *Williams* 612 describes the copy as pp. 8+8; it lacked the first and last leaves. Possibly the two poems were issued separately.
'Presumptuous poet, could you dare'

S796 [—] An answer to Dr. D-----y's fable of the pheasant and the lark. [*Dublin*] *Printed in the year* 1730.
8°: *A*⁴; *1-2* 3-7 *8 blk.*
Rothschild 2123; *Teerink* 695; *Williams* 507.
'In antient times the wise were able'
Reprinted in Faulkner's edition of Swift's *Works* (1765) XIII. 342. A reply to Delany's *The pheasant and the lark,* 1730.
L(11601.ccc.38/6; Ashley 1832),LVA-F,DA(2), DN,DT; *CSmH,*CtY,MH.

S797 [—] An answer to the Ballyspellin ballad. *Dublin, printed by George Faulkner,* 1728.
½°: 1 side, 2 columns.
Williams 437.
'Dare you dispute/You sawcy brute'
Reprinted in Faulkner's edition of Swift's *Works* (1762) VIII. 163-7. A reply to a poem by Sheridan which was separately published though no copy has been traced.
L(1966).

S798 [—] 'Apollo outwitted, a poem, by Rev. D. S[wif]t. *Dublin (by Gwyn Needham)* [c. 1720].'
½°.
Teerink 523A; *Williams* 119. Recorded in the catalogue of DG, but now missing. The poem was written in 1709; *Williams* xix n. suggests the broadside may have been of later date, as is confirmed by the imprint.
'Phœbus now shortning every shade'
(*Catalogue of the books & manuscripts composing the library of the late Sir John T. Gilbert* (1918) 807.)

[—] Apollo's edict [actually by Mary Barber], [1725?] *See* B75.

S799 [—] An apology to the Lady C—r—t. On her inviting Dean S--f--t to dinner; he came accordingly, but, her ladyship being abroad, went away ...he went to make an apology, for his going away, but my lady wou'd accept of none but in verse. [*Dublin*] *Printed in the year* 1730.
8°: *A*⁴; *1-2* 3-8.
Rothschild 2124; *Teerink* 696; *Williams* 374. Some copies (L,DT,Rothschild) have a double rule above the ornament on the title and a single rule below; others have the single rule

Swift, J. An apology

above and the double rule below. They are possibly press-variants.

'A lady, wise as well as fair'
Reprinted in Swift's *Miscellanies* (1742) VIII. 327. A ms. copy at Longleat attributes the poem to Delany.

L(Ashley 1831),LVA-F,DA(2),DT; *CSmH*,MH.

[—] The bank thrown down. To an excellent new tune, [1721.] *See* B60.

S800 [—] [dh] Baucis and Philemon, imitated from Ovid. [col] [*Oxford*] *Printed* [*by Leonard Lichfield*] *an. dom.* 1709.

4°: *A*⁴; *1* 2–8.
Rothschild 2004; *Teerink* 516/17; *Williams* 110. Hearne's copy at O has his ms. note above colophon, 'Oxon by Leon. Lichfield'. There are variant states of both inner and outer forme. Copies at L,O,C have 'Price Two-Pence.' below colophon; Rothschild, PU have none. In the inner forme, copies at L,O read 'godly Yeoman' in p. 2 line 1; C, Rothschild, PU read 'honest Yeoman'.

'In ancient times, as story tells'
Reprinted in Faulkner's edition of Swift's *Works* (1735) II. 21.

L(11633.e.56),O,C; PU.

S801 [—] — a poem on the ever lamented loss... Together with Mrs. Harris's earnest petition. By the author of the Tale of a tub. As also an ode upon solitude. By the Earl of Roscommon. *London printed, and sold by H. Hills,* 1709.

8°: A⁸; *1–2* 3–16.
Rothschild 2005; *Teerink* 521. The 'ode upon solitude' is actually by Anthony Hammond and reprinted in his *A new miscellany,* 1720, with a note on this misattribution.

Ode: 'Hail, sacred solitude! from this calm bay'

L(11659.b.66),O(2),OW,C,LdU-B(2); CSmH, CtY,IU,MH,PU+.

S802 [—] — As also an ode upot [!] solitude... *London printed, and sold by H. Hills,* 1710.

8°: A⁸; *1–2* 3–16.
Teerink 522, as another state of the following; it is a different edition.

LVA-F,O(2).

S803 [—] [another edition, title reads:]...ode upon solitude...
Rothschild 2006–7; *Teerink* 522. Reissued with other remaindered Hills poems in *A collection of the best English poetry,* 1717 (*Case* 294).

L(11659.b.65; C.124.b.7/51),O,C(2),DN,AdU+; CSmH,CtY,ICN,MH(2),TxU(2)+.

S804 [—] The beasts confession to the priest, on observing how most men mistake their own talents. Written in the year 1732. *Dublin, printed by George Faulkner,* 1738.

8°: A–C⁴; *1–8* 9–22 *23–24 blk* (3–6 as 'i–iv').
Rothschild 2163; *Teerink* 758; *Williams* 599.

'When beasts could speak, the learned say'

Swift, J. The beasts confession

Reprinted in Faulkner's edition of Swift's *Works* (1746) VIII. 123.

LLP(uncut),C; *CSmH*,MH(–C4).

S805 [—] — The second edition. *Dublin, printed by George Faulkner,* 1738.

8°: A–C⁴; *1–8* 9–22 *23–24 blk* (3–6 as 'i–iv').
Rothschild 2164. Apparently a reimpression.

C(–C4),E,DK(2).

S806 [—] — By J.S. D.S.P. *Dublin, printed: London, re-printed: and sold by T. Cooper,* 1738. (*SR* 15 Dec)

8°: *A*⁴ B–C⁴; *1–7* 8–22 *23–24 blk.* A1 hft.
Teerink 759. Entered in *SR* to John Shuckburgh; deposit copy at AdU. Listed in *GM,LM* Dec.

L(1465.f.42,–C4),O(2, *1*–A1, C4),C(2, *1*–A1, C4),DN,GU(–C4)+; CSmH,*MB*(–A1),MH, PU.

S807 [—] — The second edition. *Dublin, printed: London, re-printed: and sold by T. Cooper,* 1738.

8°: *A*⁴ B–C⁴; *1–7* 8–22 *23–24 blk.* A1 hft.
A reimpression.

L(11659.b.79),LVA-F,O,E,EtC; CtY,ICN,MH (2),PU(2, *1*–A1, *1*–C4).

S808 [—] — The second edition. '*Dublin, printed: London, re-printed: and sold by T. Cooper*' [*Edinburgh*], 1738.

8°: A–B⁴; *1–3* 4–16.
Teerink 760. Printed by Ruddiman on the evidence of the ornaments.

C,E(2),GM; TxU.

S809 [—] A beautiful young nymph going to bed. Written for the honour of the fair sex... To which are added, Strephon and Chloe. And Cassinus and Peter. *Dublin printed: London reprinted for J. Roberts,* 1734. (*GSJ* 5 Dec)

4°: A–D⁴; *1–2* 3–31 *32.* 32 advt.
Rothschild 2149; *Teerink* 744; *Williams* 580. There was apparently no separate Dublin edition. Entered in Bowyer's ledgers under 13 Nov, 750 copies printed.

'Corinna, pride of Drury-Lane'
'Of Chloe all the town has rung'
'Two college sophs of Cambridge growth'
Reprinted in Faulkner's edition of Swift's *Works* (1735) II.312.

L(840.k.3/2),C,LdU-B; TxU(2).

[—] The birth of manly virtue from Callimachus, [1725.] *See* B221.

[—] Blue-skin's ballad. To the tune of Packington's pound, 1724–5. *See* N289.

[—] Bounce to Fop. An heroick epistle from a dog at Twickenham to a dog at court. By Dr. S—t, 1736. *See* B326.

[—] The broken mug. A poem [actually by Laurence Whyte], [1725?] *See* W447.

S810 [—] The bubble: a poem. *London, printed for Benj. Tooke; sold by J. Roberts,* 1721. (*SR* 2 Jan)

8°: *A*⁴ B–C⁴; *1–4* 5–23 *24 blk.* A1 hft.

Swift, J. The bubble

Rothschild 2068; *Teerink* 623; *Williams* 248.
Entered in *SR* to Tooke; deposit copies at
L,O,E,EU,SaU. Advertised in *DC* 3 Jan.
'Ye wise philosophers explain'
Reprinted in Faulkner's edition of Swift's
Works (1735) II.147. On the South Sea bubble.
L(993.f.51/3, mutilated; 164.1.75, Luttrell, Jan),
O(2, 1 – A1),E(2),EU,SaU; CSmH,NN-B.

S811 [—] — '*London, printed for Benj. Tooke*': *and are
to be sold at John Paton's shop* [*Edinburgh*], 1721.
4°: A⁴ B²; *1–2* 3–12.
C; CtY(uncut),MH.

S812 [—] — *London, printed for Benj. Tooke; sold by
J. Roberts: and re-printed in Dublin*, 1721.
8°: *A*⁴ B⁴; *1–3* 4–15 *16 blk.*
Teerink 624. No motto on title. This Dublin
edition adds two stanzas after the eighth.
DG; *CSmH.*

S813 [—] — [reimpression?]
Motto from Virgil added to title. This issue
appears to be from the same setting of type,
but the fact that the copy seen is on paper with
a different watermark (Amsterdam arms) from
the preceding suggests another printing.
C.

S814 [—] Cadenus and Vanessa. A poem. From the
original copy. *Dublin, printed in the year* '2726'
[*1726*]. (April?)
8°: A–D⁴; *1–2* 3–32.
Rothschild 2098–9; *Teerink* 657; *Williams* 683.
A letter of Swift dated 19 April suggests the
imminence of this Dublin edition.
'The shepherds and the nymphs were seen'
Reprinted in Faulkner's edition of Swift's
Works (1735) II.53.
L(11659.c.74, lacks A1),C,DT; CLU-C,CSmH,
MWiW-C,PU.

S815 [—] — The second edition. *Dublin, printed in the
year* 1726.
8°: A–D⁴; *1–2* 3–32.
Ten lines added (818–27).
L(11661.aa.40),DA; CtY,MH.

S816 [—] Cadenus and Vanessa. A poem. *London
printed, and sold by J. Roberts*, 1726. (*DC* 19 May)
8°: *A*⁴ B–E⁴; *1–5* 6–37 *38–40 blk.* A1 hft.
Teerink 659. A copy at TxU has an errata slip
(reprinted in *Teerink*, 1963). This edition includes the ten lines added above.
L(C.71.h.10, – E4; Ashley 1829, – E4),O(– E4),
C(– E4); CLU-C(– A1, E4),CSmH(2, 1 – E4),IU,
MH(– A1, E4),TxU(3, – E4).

S817 [—] Cadenus and Vanessa: or, the judgment of
Venus, a poem. Written by Dr. Sw—ft, upon himself and Mrs. Vanh---y... The second edition.
*London, printed for J. Roberts; sold by the booksellers
in town & country*, 1726.
8°: A–D⁴; *1–2* 3–32.

Swift, J. Cadenus and Vanessa

This edition follows the text of the Dublin
first edition and omits the additional ten lines.
C.

S818 [—] — To which is added, The birth of manly
virtue... The third edition. *London, printed for J.
Roberts; sold by the booksellers in town & country*,
1726.
8°: A–D⁴; *1–3* 4–32.
This edition restores the additional ten lines
and adds *The birth of manly virtue* on pp.
27–32.
C; PU.

S819 [—] Cadenus and Vanessa. A poem. By Dr. S—t.
London, printed for N. Blandford; sold by J. Peele,
1726. (19 May?)
8°: A–D⁴; *1–3* 4–31 *32 blk.*
Rothschild 2100; *Teerink* 658. This edition
omits the additional ten lines, and an advertisement for the Roberts edition in *DC* 20
May says 'the other which was published
yesterday was printed from an imperfect copy,
wanting several lines'. This edition was
advertised in *LJ* 21 May, 'on a superfine
paper'.
L(992.i.30),C; CSmH(2),CtY,ICN,PU(uncut),
TxU+.

S820 [—] — The second edition. *London, printed for N.
Blandford; sold by J. Peele*, 1726.
8°: A–D⁴; *1–3* 4–32.
This edition (according to *Williams*) adds the
extra ten lines. Probably in part a reimpression.
L(11659.c.75),C; IU.

S821 [—] — The third edition. *London, printed for N.
Blandford; sold by J. Peele*, 1726. (*LJ* 4 June)
8°: A–D⁴; *1–3* 4–32.
Apparently a reimpression.
ICN,MH,PU.

S822 [—] — To which is added, a true and faithful
inventory of the goods belonging to Dr. S—t...
By Dr. S—t. The fourth edition. *London, printed
for N. Blandford; sold by J. Peele*, 1726. (*DP* 16
June)
8°: A–D⁴; *1–3* 4–31 *32.*
Rothschild 2101. Mainly a reimpression; pp.
29–31 have two lines extra per page to make
room for the *Inventory* (by Sheridan) on p. 32.
That was also printed in *LJ* 25 June with a note
that it was omitted in the early editions.
L(11633.cc.2/3),LVA-F,O,C(2),E+ ; CtY,IU,
MH,PU,TxU.

S823 [—] — The fifth edition. *London, printed for N.
Blandford; sold by J. Peele*, 1726. (*LJ* 9 July)
8°: A–D⁴; *1–3* 4–31 *32.*
Rothschild 2102. A reimpression.
C(uncut).

S824 [—] — The sixth edition. *London, printed for N.
Blandford; sold by J. Peele*, 1726. (*LJ* 13 Aug)
8°: A–D⁴; *1–3* 4–31 *32.*

Swift, J. Cadenus and Vanessa

A reimpression.
L(11660.e.40),O,OW,C,DN; CLU-C,MH,PU.

S825 [—] — By Dr. Sw—t. The seventh edition. *London, printed for N. Blandford; sold by J. Peele,* 1726.
8°: A–D⁴; *1–3* 4–31 *32.* 32 advt.
The type has been reset.
L(1488.c.40),O; IU,MH,PU.

S826 — Cadenus and Vanessa, a law case. By Dean Swift. *London, printed for T. Warner,* 1726. (*DP* 13 June)
12°: A–C⁶ *²; *1–4* 5–36 *37–40.*
Teerink 661A, and see Teerink in *Harvard library bulletin* 2 (1948) 254–7. Three short poems added in *². Apparently from the same setting of type as pp. 88–119 of *Miscellanea* I, 1727 (*Teerink* 24). A1 not in the copy seen, possibly a half-title.
CLU-C(−A1),MH(*² only).

S827 [—] Cadenus and Vanessa. A poem. *London, printed and sold by J. Roberts, and in Edinburgh by Allan Ramsay,* 1726.
8°: A–D⁴ E²; *1–2* 3–34 *35; 36 blk.* E2 advt.
Rothschild 2103; *Teerink* 658A.
C(−E2); MH.

S828 [—] [another issue] [*Edinburgh*] *Printed in the year* 1726.
8°: L–O⁴ P²; *81–82* 83–114 *115; 116 blk.* P2 advt.
Teerink 661; see Teerink in *Harvard library bulletin* 3 (1949). Changed signatures and pagination to follow the Edinburgh piracy of Young's *Universal passion,* 1726; they are bound together in the CtY copy.
L(992.h.7/4); CtY(−P2),MH(−P2).

S829 [—] Cadenus and Vanessa... To which is added, a true and faithful inventory... By Dr. Sw—t. The eighth edition. *London, printed for J. Peele, & N. Blandford,* 1729.
8°: A–D⁴; *1–3* 4–31 *32.* 32 advt.
A reprint of Blandford's seventh edition of 1726, S825.
CtY.

[—] A Christmas box for Namby Pamby, [1725.] *See* C170.

S830 [—] [first line:] Confondant du passé le leger souvenir... [*London?* 1731?]
¼°: 1 side, 1 column.
Teerink 706; *Williams* 539. Eight lines of French verse followed by fourteen lines of English headed 'Imitated in English'. For the date, see *Williams*; a copy in Maggs *Mercurius* 101 (1947) 187 was attributed to 1728.
'With favour and fortune fastidiously blest'
A ms. of the imitation, which attacks Walpole, appears to have been included in a letter of Swift to the Countess of Suffolk, 26 Oct 1731.
C.

[—] The cur and the lap-dog, a poem, 1737. *See* C542.

Swift, J. The Dean's answer

[—] The Dean's answer to David Mullan's letter, 1735. *See* D78.

[—] The description of Dunkirk with Squash and Dismal's opinion, 1712. *See* D235.

[—] A dialogue between the cities of London and Paris, in relation to the present posture of affairs, 1701. *See* D267.

[—] D-----n S------t's prologue to Hyppolitus, spoken by a boy of six years old [actually by Richard Helsham], [1721.] *See* H138.

[—] A duel between two doctors, 1708. *In* S640.

[—] The E—l of G—d—n to D—ct—r G—th, upon the loss of Miss Dingle, 1711. *See* E28.

S831 [—] An elegy on Dicky and Dolly, with the Virgin: a poem. To which is added the narrative of D. S. when he was in the north of Ireland. *Dublin, printed by James Hoey,* 1732.
8°: A⁴; *1–3* 4–7 *8.* 8 advt.
Teerink 966; *Williams* 429.
'Under this stone, lies Dicky and Dolly'
'The things that make a virgin please'
'The Dean wou'd visit Market-hill'
The first and third poems are by Swift; the first, written in 1728 on the death of Richard Gorges and his wife Dorothea, countess of Meath, was collected by Deane Swift in 1765; the third was previously printed in 1730 as *Lady A—s—n weary of the Dean.*
C(2),DN; CtY(cropt),MH(lacks A1).

S832 [—] An elegy on Mr. Patrige, the almanack-maker, who died on the 29th of this instant March, 1708. *London, printed in the year* 1708. (30 March?)
1°: 1 side, 2 columns.
Teerink 496; *Williams* 97. Mourning headpiece and borders. Publication date from *Teerink.*
'Well, 'tis as Bickerstaff has guest'
Part of Swift's satirical campaign against John Partridge. For another elegy on the same occasion, see *An elegy upon the death of the famous Dr. John Partridgd* [!], 1708.
L(C.40.m.11/74; Harley 5931, fol. 85),C, Chatsworth.

S833 [—] — *Edinburgh, re-printed in the year* 1708.
½°: 1 side, 2 columns.
Teerink 497.
L(12350.m.18/4),E; CtY.

S834 [—] [*idem*] An elegy on Dr. John Whalley, who departed the 17th. of this inst. Jan. 1724. [*Dublin,* 1724.]
½°: 1 side, 2 columns.
Mourning borders. A revision of the preceding, omitting lines 95–102. Swift is not known to have been responsible for this adaptation.
'Well 'tis as learned Coats has guest'
CSmH.

Swift, J. An elegy

S835 [—] — who departed this life, on the 17th, of January, 1724, in the 71st year of his age. [*Dublin?* 1724.]
½°: 1 side, 2 columns.
 Teerink 1647. Mourning borders. A very inferior piece of printing to the preceding, but not necessarily subsequent to it.
Rothschild.

[—] Elegy on the much-lamented death of John Harding printer, [1725.] *See* E143.

[—] An elegy on the much lamented death of Matthew Buckinger, [1722.] *See* E67.

S836 [—] An elegy on the much lamented death of Mr. Demar, the famous rich man, who died the 6th of this inst. July, 1720. [*Dublin,* 1720.] (July)
½°: 1 side, 1 column.
 Teerink 611; *Williams* 232. Mourning borders.
'Know all men by these presents, death the tamer'
 Reprinted in Faulkner's edition of Swift's *Works* (1735) II. 137. Apparently this may be a joint production of Swift, Sheridan, Stella and others; see *Williams*.
L(11602.i.1/1),DT.

S837 [—] — Mr. Joseph Demar, the famous rich man, who died in Dublin the 6th of this inst. July, 1720. [*Dublin?* 1720.]
½°: 1 side, 1 column.
 Rothschild 2060; *Teerink* 1662. Mourning borders. An inferior piece of printing to the preceding, but not necessarily later in date.
Rothschild.

[—] Elegy on the much lamented death of those excellent patriots and lovers of their country the family of the potatoes, 1739–40. *See* E219.

[—] An elegy upon Tiger; her dear lady's joy and comfort, [1727.] *See* E254.

S838 [—] An epilogue, to be spoke at the Theatre-royal this present Saturday being April the 1st. In the behalf of the distressed weavers. *Dublin, printed by J.W.,* [1721.]
½°: 1 side, 1 column.
 Teerink 625; *Williams* 273.
'Who dares affirm this is no pious age'
 Reprinted in London as Swift's in *SJP* 12 April 1721; collected in Faulkner's edition of his *Works* (1735) II.172.
L(C.121.g.8/10, cropt),DG; CtY.

S839 [—] [*idem*] An epilogue, as it was spoke by Mr. Griffith at the Theatre-royal on Saturday the first of April... [*Dublin,* 1721.]
½°: 1 side, 1 column.
 Teerink 626. The text appears to be from the same setting of type as the preceding, though with changes. On the other side, Sheridan's *A prologue, spoke by Mr. Elrington,* [1721], with imprint 'Dublin, printed by John Harding'.
L(1850.c.10/4; 1890.e.5/67),C; PU,TxU.

Swift, J. An epilogue

S840 [—] [*idem*] The encouragement of the ladies of Ireland to the woollen manufactury. And the downfall of callicoes. An epilogue: spoke at the Theatre-royal... *Limerick, printed by Andrew Welsh, at the sign of the Globe in Key-lane,* [1721.]
½°: 1 side, 1 column.
 Rothschild 2066; *Teerink* 1650. The Rothschild copy has a misplaced pull of the same text on the other side of the half-sheet.
Rothschild.

S841 [—] An epistle to a lady, who desired the author to make verses on her, in the heroick stile. Also a poem, occasion'd by reading Dr. Young's satires, called, The universal passion. *Dublin, printed: and reprinted at London for J. Wilford,* 1734 [1733]. (15 Nov?)
2°: A^1 B–E^2 F^1; *i–ii,* 1 2–18 (13 as '16').
 Rothschild 2146; *Teerink* 745; *Williams* 628. There was no Dublin edition. Publication date from *Teerink*. Wilford was taken into custody (11 Jan 1734) on account of the satirical passages upon Walpole, and subsequently the printer, Lawton Gilliver, Matthew Pilkington, Benjamin Motte, and Mary Barber were also arrested.
'After venting all my spight'
'If there be truth in what you sing'
 Reprinted in Faulkner's edition of Swift's *Works* (1746) VIII.323.
L(11602.i.13/4; Ashley 5066),LVA-D(uncut),O (3),C(2),DT+; CSmH,CtY,IU,MH,TxU(2)+.

S842 [—] An epistle upon an epistle from a certain doctor to a certain great lord: being a Christmas-box for D. D---ny. *Dublin, printed in the year* 1730.
8°: A^4; *1–3* 4–8.
 Rothschild 2117; *Teerink* 684; *Williams* 470. Possibly to be dated as Dec 1729. Reprinted in one Dublin edition of Delany's *An epistle to his excellency John lord Carteret,* 1730 (D198).
'As Jove will not attend on less'
 Reprinted in Cogan's *Supplement to the Works of Dr. Swift* (1752) 140. A satire on Delany's epistle to Lord Carteret. See *An answer to the Christmas-box,* 1729.
LVA-F,C,DA(3),DG,DT(3)+; MH,TxU.

[—] An exelent [!] new ballad ascrib'd to the ladies of Munster. By the h---- J. S., [173–?] *See* E542.

[—] An excellent new ballad: being the second part of the Glorious warriour, [1710.] *See* E543.

S843 [—] An excellent new ballad: or, the true En---sh d---n to be hang'd for a r-----pe. [*Dublin,* 1730.]
½°: 2 sides, 1 column.
 Teerink 701; *Williams* 516.
'Our brethren of E----nd who love us so dear'
 Early ms. attribution to Swift in the CSmH copy; reprinted in Faulkner's edition of Swift's *Works* (1735) II.273. A satire on

Swift, J. An excellent new ballad

Thomas Sawbridge, dean of Ferns, who was indicted for a rape at Chester in June 1730.
L(C.121.g.8/178),C; CSmH.

S844 [—] An excellent new song, being the intended speech of a famous orator against peace. [*London*, 1711.] (6 Dec?)
½°: 2 sides, 1 column.
    Rothschild 2023; *Teerink* 554; *Williams* 141. First line of title in roman type. *Ball* 118 suggested that *The Earl of Nottingham's speech*, 'printed by J. Tomson, 1711', which was proceeded against 15 Dec 1711 (see Lords' *Journals*) was an untraced edition of this work.
'An orator dismal of Nottinghamshire'
    Referred to in Swift's letter to Stella 5 Dec 1711. A satire against Daniel Finch, earl of Nottingham, who went over to the whigs. Answered by *The Nottinghamshire ballade*, 1711.
L(1876.f.19/43; Ashley 5060),LLP,O,C,Crawford, Chatsworth (ms. date 6 Dec), Rothschild (ms. date 7 Dec); MH,TxU(2).

S845 [—] [another edition]
First line of title in black letter.
LU,DT.

[—] An excellent new song, call'd the Trusty and true English-man, [1712.] *See* E584.

[—] An excellent new song, to a good old tune, 1726. *See* E589.

S846 [—] An excellent new song upon his grace our good lord archbishop of Dublin. By honest Jo. one of his grace's farmers in Fingal. To the tune of . *Dublin, printed by John Harding*, 1724. (Nov?)
½°: 1 side, 1 column.
    Rothschild 2093; *Teerink* 1153; *Williams* 340. Publication date from *Teerink*.
'I sing not of the Draper's praise, nor yet of William Wood'
    Reprinted as Swift's in *Whartoniana*, 1727; first collected in Swift's poems by Scott in 1814. The external evidence for Swift's authorship is slight. In praise of William King's opposition to Wood's halfpence.
L(C.121.g.8/29, mutilated),C,DG,Rothschild; NNP,TxU.

[—] An excellent new song upon the declarations of the several corporations of the city of Dublin, [1724.] *See* E593.

[—] An excellent new song upon the late grand-jury, 1724. *See* E594.

[—] An excellent old ballad, made at the restauration of K. Charles II., 1711. *See* E595.

S847 [—] The fable of Midas. [*London*] *Printed for John Morphew*, 1712. (14 Feb, Luttrell)
½°: 2 sides, 1 column.
    Rothschild 2038; *Teerink* 558; *Williams* 155.
'Midas, we are in story told'
    Referred to in Swift's letter to Stella of 14 Feb 1712; early ms. attribution to Swift in the

Swift, J. The fable of Midas

TxU copy of the following. A satire on Marlborough.
Crawford, Rothschild (ms. date 16 Feb); ICN (Luttrell),MH.

S848 [—] [variant imprint:] [*London*] *Printed in the year*, 1711.
    Possibly copies with this imprint were intended for presentation, not for sale.
L(1876.f.19/17),LLP,C(2),Chatsworth(ms. date 14 Feb),Crawford; TxU.

[—] A fable of the housewife and her cock, 1712. *See* F8.

[—] A fable of the widow and her cat, 1712. *See* F13.

[—] A familiar answer to a familiar letter, 1720. *See* F53.

S849 [—] A famous prediction of Merlin, the British wizard; written above a thousand years ago, and relating to this present year. With explanatory notes. By T. N. Philomath. *London printed, and sold by A. Baldwin*, 1709. (21 Feb, Luttrell)
½°: 2 sides, 1 column.
    Rothschild 2002; *Teerink* 499; *Williams* 101. Short black-letter text with prose commentary; woodcut portrait at head, titled 'Merlinus Verax'. In this edition, line 5 of the introduction reads 'Year.'; it is placed first on account of Luttrell's dating.
'Seven and ten addyd to nyne'
    Reprinted in Swift's *Miscellanies*, 1711.
Rothschild; MH(Luttrell).

S850 [—] [another edition]
In this edition, line 5 of the introduction reads 'for the present Year.'
L(Ashley 5250); CSmH,CtY,TxU.

S851 [—] — *London, printed in the year* 1709.
½°: 2 sides, 1 column.
    Apparently a piracy; the woodcut at head has been copied from the preceding.
MH.

S852 [—] — *London printed, and sold by H. Hills*, 1708 [1709].
½°: 2 sides, 1 column.
    Teerink 500. Another piracy, with a different copy of the woodcut at head.
C,Chatsworth.

S853 [—] — *London, printed by A. Baldwin: Edinburgh re-printed by James Watson*, 1709.
½°: 2 sides, 1 column.
    Teerink 501. No woodcut at head.
E(2).

[—] A farewel to the world. By the honourable D— [actually by Sir Henry Wotton], 1725. *See* W565.

S854 [—] The first ode of the second book of Horace paraphras'd: and address'd to Richard St--le, esq; *London, printed for A. Dodd*, 1714. (*DC* 7 Jan)

Swift, J. The first ode

4°: A⁴ B²; *1–2* 3–11 *12 blk.* 11 advt.
> *Rothschild* 2052; *Teerink* 594; *Williams* 179.
> Some copies (O,DrU) have variant date in
> imprint '1713'; in some copies the catchword
> on p. 3 fails to print. Entered in *SR* to John
> Barber, 21 Jan; deposit copies at L,O,E,SaU.
> 'Dick, thour't resolv'd, as I am told'
>> First collected in Nichols's *Supplement* to
>> Swift's *Works*, 1776; accepted by *Williams*,
>> though *Ball* 140 is a little sceptical. An attack
>> on Steele's forthcoming *The crisis*.

L(841.a.21/1; Ashley 4341),O(2),C,E,DN+;
CtY(2, 1 uncut),IU,MH,PU,TxU(2)+.

S855 [—] — [col] *Dublin, reprinted for John Henly*, 1714.
4°: *A²*; *1* 2–4.
> *Rothschild* 2053; *Teerink* 595. Drop-head title
> only.

DK,DT,LdU-B; ICN.

S856 [—] The first of April: a poem. Inscrib'd to Mrs.
E.C. [*Dublin*, 1723/24?]
½°: 1 side, 2 columns.
> *Teerink* 917; *Williams* 320. The copy at CSmH
> is bound with half-sheets of 1724; Ball suggests
> the date 1723.
> 'This morn the god of wit and joke'
>> First ascribed to Swift by *Ball* 171 and accepted
>> by *Williams*; addressed to the second wife of
>> Robert Cope whom Swift used to visit at his
>> seat at Loughall.

E,DA; CSmH,CtY.

[—] A funeral apotheosis on the Tribunes, 1729–30.
See F286.

S857 — The furniture of a woman's mind. Written by
Dr. Swift. [*London?* 1735/–.]
¼°: 1 side, 2 columns.
> *Teerink* 988; *Williams* 415. Fine engraving
> printed in sepia at head. The poem was printed
> in collections of 1735; this is certainly a later
> edition, and probably later than 1750. Line 59
> substitutes 'Bickerstaff' in place of 'Mrs.
> Harding', and a footnote describes him as
> 'The printer, at the Black-Boy in Fleet-lane'.
> 'A set of phrases learnt by rote'
> L(C.121.g.9/212).

[—] The garden plot, 1709. *See* G10.

[—] Good advice to beaus and batchelours... By
the author of, A tale of a tub, 1705. *See* G218.

[—] The grand question debated, 1732. *See* S908.

[—] Helter skelter, or the hue and cry after the
attornies, going to ride the circuit, [1726/27?] *See*
H139.

S858 [—] His grace's answer to Jonathan. *Dublin,
printed in year* 1724.
¼°: 1 side, 2 columns.
> *Rothschild* 2096; *Teerink* 634; *Williams* 357.
> 'Dear Smed I read thy brilliant lines'
>> Reprinted in Faulkner's edition of Swift's
>> *Works* (1762) X. 137. A reply to Smedley's

Swift, J. His grace's answer

> *An epistle to his grace the Duke of Grafton*, 1724.
C,Crawford,Rothschild; CSmH(2),CtY.

S859 [—] Horace book I. ode XIV. O navis, referent, &c.
Paraphrased and inscribed to Ir—d. [*Dublin*]
Printed in the year 'MDCDXXX' [1730].
8°: *A⁴*; *1–3* 4–7 *8 blk.*
> *Teerink* 705; *Williams* 769. Reprinted in *The
> grand question debated*, 1732 (S908).
> 'Unhappy ship, thou art return'd in vain'
>> Reprinted in Faulkner's edition of Swift's
>> *Works* (1735) II. 250.

C,DG,DN,DT(2); CSmH,DFo.

S860 — An imitation of the sixth satire of the second
book of Horace... The first part done in the year
1714, by Dr. Swift. The latter part now first added
... *London, printed for B. Motte & C. Bathurst,
and J. & P. Knapton*, 1738. (*SR* 28 Feb)
2°: *A–B² C–G²*; *i–iv, 1–3* 4–23 *24 blk.* A1 hft.
> *Griffith* 479; *Rothschild* 2162; *Teerink* 757;
> *Williams* 197. Entered in *SR* to Motte,
> Bathurst, and Knaptons; deposit copies at
> L,O,AdU,GU. Listed in *GM,LM* March, and
> publication date given in *Griffith* as 1 March.
> 'I've often wish'd that I had clear'
>> Originally published in the Pope-Swift *Miscel-
>> lanies*, 1727; most of the additions made here
>> are by Pope.

L(643.m.14/12),O(2, 1 – A1),C(2),GU,LdU-B+;
CLU-C,CtY(3, 1 uncut),IU,MH(2),TxU(2)+.

[—] Ireland's warning, being an excellent new
song, upon Woods's base half-pence, [1724.] *See*
I66.

[—] Jack Frenchman's lamentation. An excellent
new song, 1708. *See* J1.

[—] Jack Presbyter's downfal: or, the church in
glory, 1710. *See* J6.

[—] The Jacks put to their trumps. A tale of King
James's Irish shilling, 1714. *See* J8.

[—] John Dennis, the sheltring poet's invitation to
Richard Steele, 1714. *See* J69.

S861 [—] The journal. [*Dublin*, 1721/22.]
½°: 1 side, 2 columns.
> Title in two lines. *Teerink* 627; *Williams* 276.
> 'Thalia, tell in sober lays'
>> Early ms. attribution to Swift in a copy at C;
>> reprinted in Faulkner's edition of Swift's
>> *Works* (1735) II. 174. A description of the
>> house-party at Gaulstown House in 1721.
>> Answered by [William Percival] *A description
>> in answer to the Journal*, 1722.

L(C.121.g.8/24),C(2); CtY,MH,NNP.

S862 [—] — [*Dublin*, 1722.]
½°: 1 side, 2 columns.
> Title in one line. *Rothschild* 2072; *Teerink* 628.
> On the other side of the copies seen, [William
> Percival] *A description in answer to the Journal*,
> [1722.]

DN(cropt),Rothschild.

Swift, J. The journal of a Dublin lady

S863 [—] [dh] The journal of a Dublin lady; in a letter to a person of quality. [col] *Dublin, printed by S. Harding,* [1729.] (Jan?)
8⁰: *A*⁴; *1* 2–8.
> *Teerink* 669; *Williams* 443. Sent by Swift for Mrs. Harding, 13 Jan 1729; reprinted in London in *Fog's weekly journal,* 15 Feb.
> 'It was a most unfriendly part'
>> Reprinted in Faulkner's edition of Swift's *Works* (1735) II. 224. Answered by *The journal of a Dublin beau,* 1728–9.
L(11631.aa.11),DA.

S864 [—] — The second edition carefully corrected and amended. *Dublin, re-printed by Nicholas Hussey,* 1729.
8⁰: *A*⁸; *1–2* 3–16.
> *Teerink* 669A.
O.

S865 [—] [*idem*] The journal of a modern lady. In a letter to a person of quality. By the author of Cadenus and Vanessa. *First printed at Dublin; and now reprinted at London; for J. Wilford,* 1729. (*MChr* 1 April)
8⁰: A–C⁴; *1–3* 4–23 *24.* 24 advt.
> *Teerink* 671. Subsequently reprinted with Elizabeth Thomas's *The metamorphosis of the town,* 1730–.
L(11631.e.33),O(uncut),C; CLU-C,CtY,MH, TxU.

S866 [—] — *London, printed by George Gorden,* [1729/–.]
½⁰: *1–2,* 3 columns.
> *Teerink* 670. The imprint immediately follows the last line of the middle column on p. 2. A piracy.
L(1872.a.1/169*).

S867 — — Written by Dean Swift. *London printed, and sold by W. Parker,* 1740.
12⁰: *1–12.*
(*Teerink* 674.)

[—] Jove's ramble: a tale shewing how the moon was made of a green cheese, 1723. *See* J105.

S868 [—] Lady A——s——n weary of the Dean. [*Dublin*] *Printed in the year* 1730.
½⁰: 1 side, 2 columns.
> *Teerink* 700; *Williams* 859. Reprinted with *An elegy on Dicky and Dolly,* 1732 (S831).
> 'The Dean wou'd visit Market-hill'
>> Reprinted in Faulkner's edition of Swift's *Works* (1762) X. 319. On a visit of Swift to Sir Arthur Acheson's house at Market Hill.
C; CtY.

S869 [—] The lady's dressing room. To which is added a poem on cutting down the old thorn at Market Hill. By the rev. Dr. S—t. *London, printed for J. Roberts,* 1732. (*GSJ* 17 June)
4⁰: A–B⁴ C²; *1–3* 4–20. 20 err.
> *Rothschild* 2132–3; *Teerink* 720; *Williams* 524. This edition contains the same three additional poems as the following. Entered in Bowyer's

Swift, J. The lady's dressing room

> ledgers to 'WB & partners' under 10 June, 750 copies printed.
> 'Five hours, (and who can do it less in?)'
>> Reprinted in Faulkner's edition of Swift's *Works* (1735) II. 305. Reprinted and answered in S. Robinson, *Cælia's revenge,* 1741. See also *The gentleman's study, in answer to the Lady's dressing room,* 1732, [S. Shepherd] *Chloe surpriz'd,* 1732, and [Lady M. Wortley Montagu] *The dean's provocation for writing the Lady's dressing-room,* 1734.
L(11630.c.5/2),LVA-F,C(2); CSmH,IU.

S870 [—] — To which is added, I. A poem... II. Advice to a parson. III. An epigram... By the rev. Dr. S—t. The second edition. *London, printed for J. Roberts,* 1732. (*LM* July)
4⁰: A–B⁴ C²; *1–3* 4–19 20.
> *Teerink* 720. Entered in Bowyer's ledgers under 1 July, though not apparently delivered until 5 July; 750 copies printed.
L(11631.cc.9),C; KU,PU.

S871 [—] The lady's dressing-room. A poem. By *.*.*.*.*.*. *London, printed, and Dublin, re-printed, in the year* 1732.
8⁰: *A*⁴; *1–2* 3–8.
> *Rothschild* 2134; *Teerink* 721. The text of the Dublin editions varies from the London editions.
C,DG,DK,DT; TxU.

S872 [—] — The second edition. *London, printed, and Dublin, reprinted, in the year* 1732.
8⁰: *A*⁴; *1–2* 3–8.
> *Rothschild* 2135. A reimpression with corrections.
LVA-F; CtY,MH,TxU.

S873 [—] — By D–n S-----t. From the original copy. The third edition. *Dublin, printed and sold by George Faulkner,* 1732.
8⁰: *A*⁴; *1–3* 4–8.
> *Teerink* 722.
L(11632.aa.43); TxU.

S874 [—] The lady's dressing-room, discover'd; a poem. By D--n S--t. *Corke: printed and sold by Andrew Welsh, next door but one to the Corke-Arms, near the Corn-market,* 1732–3.
8⁰: *A*⁴; *1–2* 3–8.
(Sir Harold Williams's copy recorded as *Teerink* 722A; not with his books now at C.)

S875 [—] — From the original copy. The third edition. *Corke: printed and sold by Andrew Welsh,* 1732–3.
8⁰: *A*⁴; *1–2* 3–8.
(*Rothschild* 2136.)

S876 [—] A letter from D. S—t. to D. S—y. [*Dublin,* 1725.]
½⁰: 1 side, 2 columns.
> *Teerink* 651; *Williams* 369.
> 'Dear Dean, if e're again you write'
>> Accepted by *Ball* as Swift's; *Williams* writes

Swift, J. A letter from D. S—t

that it 'hardly admits of a doubt'. A reply to
Smedley's *A satyr*, 1725.

L(C.121.g.8/76).

[—] A letter to the bishop of M. by Dr. Sw—t,
[1726.] *See* L155.

S877 [—] A libel on D-- D-----, and a certain great
lord. [*Dublin*] *Printed in the year* 1730. (2 Feb?)
4⁰: *A*⁴ B²; *1–3* 4–12.

Teerink 689A; *Williams* 479, not knowing this
edition, which from its format is probably the
first. A letter of Marmaduke Coghill 3 Feb
1730 (quoted *Williams* 474) refers to this poem
being 'cry'd about the streets' the preceding
night; but that was perhaps the following
edition. Reprinted in 'Martin Gulliver', *The
Censoriad*, 1730 (G315), and in William Dunkin's *A vindication of the libel*, 1730 (D531).

'Deluded mortals, whom the great'

Reprinted in Faulkner's edition of Swift's
Works (1735) II. 255. Originally occasioned by
Delany's *An epistle to his excellency John lord
Carteret*, [1729]. Answered in *An epistle to
D—n S—t*, 1730; Swift's *To Doctor D-l---y,
on the libels writ against him*, 1730; *A panegyric
on the reverend D--n S----t*, 1729–30. See also
[Dunkin, William] *A vindication of the libel*,
1729–30.

CSmH.

S878 [—] A libel on D— D—. and a certain great lord.
[*Dublin*] *Printed in the year* 1730.
8⁰: *A*⁴; *1–2* 3–8.

Rothschild 2118; *Teerink* 688. Some copies
(O,DA,TxU) have type-flowers instead of a
headpiece above the text on p. 2; they perhaps
only represent a press-variant.

L(11601.ccc.38/3),O,DA(6),DN(2),DT(2)+;
CSmH,CtY,MH,TxU.

S879 [—] A libel on D-------- D---------- and a
certain great lord. [*Dublin?*] *Printed anno* 1730.
8⁰: *A*⁴; *1–2* 3–8.

Teerink 687.

PU.

S880 [—] [*idem*] A satire on Dr. D—ny. By Dr. Sw—t.
To which is added, the poem which occasion'd it.
*Printed at Dublin: and re-printed at London, for A.
Moore*, 1730. (*MChr* 9 Feb)
8⁰: *A*² B–D⁴; *1–5* 6–27 *28 blk.* A1 hft.

Rothschild 2120; *Teerink* 689. With Delany's
An epistle to his excellency . . .

L(11633.cc.2/12),O(−A1),OW,C(2, 1 uncut),E+;
CLU-C,CtY(−A1),ICN,MH.

S881 [—] [*reissue*] A libel on Dr. D—ny, and a
certain great lord. By Dr. Sw—t . . . To which is
added, I. An epistle to his excellency John lord
Carteret, by Dr. D—ny. II. An epistle on an
epistle; or a Christmas-box for Dr. D—ny. *Printed
at Dublin: and re-printed at London, for A. Moore*,
1730.
8⁰: *A*¹ B–D⁴ E⁴(−E4); *3–5* 6–34.

Swift, J. A libel on Dr. D—ny

Teerink 689B. A reissue of the preceding with
a cancel title and the added poem in sheet E.
No half-title seen in this issue; presumably the
cancel A1 was printed as E4.

O,CK; *DLC,MWiW-C,TxU.*

S882 [—] — To which is added, I. An epistle to his
excellency . . . II. An epistle on an epistle . . . III. Dr.
Sw—t's proposal for preventing the children of
poor people being a burthen . . . The second edition.
*Printed at Dublin: and re-printed at London, for A.
Moore*, 1730. (before 19 Feb)
8⁰: A–D⁴ (A2 as 'B2', C3 as 'E2'); *1–3* 4–32.

Teerink 689C. C2–4 are printed from the same
type as E1–3 of the preceding; in some copies
(e.g. L) B4 is signed 'D2', representing its
position in the preceding. Some copies lack
D⁴, containing Swift's *Modest proposal*. The
advertisement for the following edition in *GSJ*
19 Feb refers to this as spurious, 'first published under the title of *A satire, &c.* and since
twice altered . . . pretended to be a second
edition, contains the errors of the first'.

L(11601.d.28/3, lacks D⁴),O,OW,DN; CSmH,
CtY,IU(lacks D⁴),PU(lacks D⁴),TxU(lacks D⁴)+.

S883 [—] — *Dublin: printed, London: reprinted 'for Capt.
Gulliver near the Temple'*, 1730. (*MChr* 12 Feb)
8⁰: A–D⁴ (D1, 2 as 'B, B2'); *1–3* 4–32.

Teerink 36. The imprint is clearly false.

O,C,DA; CLU-C,DFo.

S884 — The life and genuine character of Doctor Swift.
Written by himself. *London, printed for J. Roberts;
sold at the pamphlet shops, &c.*, 1733. (12 April?)
2⁰: *A–B*² C–E²; *1–9* 10–19 *20 blk.* A1 hft.

Rothschild 2143; *Teerink* 727; *Williams* 541.
Dedication to Pope signed 'L. M.' and dated
1 April 1733. Nearly as much mystification
surrounds the publication of the poem as its
authorship; Harley's copy received on 12
April appears to precede the newspaper
advertisements (*DJ* 20 April) in the same way
as with some of Pope's poems, supporting
T. J. Wise's theory that Pope was concerned
in the publication.

'Wise Rochefoucault a maxim writ'

For the problem of Swift's authorship see
Williams and references; Swift disclaimed the
poem in his correspondence and in *Dublin
Journal* 15 May 1733, but it has resemblances
to his *Verses on the death of Dr. Swift*, 1739,
and was accepted as his by some well-informed
contemporaries. If it be spurious, a good case
could be made out for Pope's authorship.

L(840.m.1/16, −A1; 162.n.28, −A1; Ashley
5068),O(3, 1 Harley's copy 'R. April 12', −A1),
C(2, 1 −A1),EU,DT(uncut)+; CSmH,CtY,ICN,
MH,PU(2)+.

S885 [—] The life and genuine character of the rev. Dr.
S--t, D.S.P.D. Written by himself. '*London,
printed for J. Roberts; sold by the booksellers, &c.*'
[*Dublin*], 1733.

Swift, J. The life and genuine character

8°: A^4 B^4 C^2; *1–8* 9–20.
> *Rothschild* 2144; *Teerink* 728. Printed by Faulkner on the evidence of the ornaments.

L.VA-F(2),C,DT.

S886 [—] — *London: printed, and re-printed and sold by Edward Waters, Dublin, 1733.*

8°: A^2 B^4; *1–4* 5–12.
> *Teerink* 729.

L(1963, cropt),O(cropt),DA(2),DN.

[—] The London tale. By the author of the Tale of a nettle, 1710. *See* L241.

[—] The loyal address of the clergy of Virginia, 1702. *See* L296.

[—] The mishap. A poem. Written by the late rev. D. J.S. D.D. D.S.P.D., [1745/–.] *See* M279.

[—] Mr. Baron L------'s charge to the grand jury for the county of Devon, 1710. *See* M289.

[—] A new ballad by way of dialogue between a kite, and a crow, on the quadrille, [1736.] *See* N58.

[—] The new Kilmainham ballad, [1711/12.] *See* N145.

[—] Newgate's garland: being a new ballad, [1724/25.] *See* N288.

S887 [—] On Paddy's character of the Intelligencer. [*Dublin, 1728/29.*]

½°: 1 side, 1 column.
> *Teerink* 683; *Williams* 457.

As a thorn-bush, or oaken-bough'
> Reprinted in Cogan's *A supplement to the Works of Dr. Swift* (1752) 126 and subsequently; there seems no strong authority for Swift's authorship, plausible though it is. As noted in *Williams*, this appears to be an answer to Delany's attacks on *The intelligencer*; but it specifically replies to 'Pady Drogheda', *The true character of the Intelligencer*, 1728, which is in fact by William Tisdall.

L(C.121.g.8/173).

S888 [—] On poetry: a rapsody. *Printed at Dublin, and re-printed at London: and sold by J. Huggonson, and at the booksellers and pamphlet-shops, 1733.* (*GSJ* 31 Dec)

2°: A^1 $B–G^2$ H^1: *1–3* 4–28. 28 err.
> *Rothschild* 2147; *Teerink* 741; *Williams* 639. There are minor movements in the type, and particularly in the position of the headpiece on p. 3, which suggest the possibility of concealed impressions; they can be seen in the copies at C,CtY,ICN,MH,TxU.

'All human race wou'd fain be wits'
> Reprinted in Faulkner's edition of Swift's *Works* (1735) II. 433. Certain passages of political satire omitted from the printed text are quoted in *Williams*. See *A rap at the rapsody*, 1734.

L(11630.h.37; Ashley 5056),O(5, 1 uncut),C(3),DT,LdU-B+; CSmH,CtY(2),ICN(2),MH(3),TxU(4, 1 uncut)+.

Swift, J. On poetry

S889 [—] — '*Printed at Dublin, and re-printed at London, and sold by J. Huggonson...*' [*Edinburgh, 1734.*]

8°: A^4 $B–C^4$; *1–2* 3–22 23–24 blk.
> *Rothschild* 2148; *Teerink* 742. Printed by R. Fleming on the evidence of the ornaments. The position of signature B varies, suggesting the possibility of a variant sheet.

L(11630.bbb.42/9),LVA-F,O,C(2),GU(2); CtY(– C4),CtY-M,IU(– C4),MH(– C4),PU.

S890 [—] — *London printed, and Dublin re-printed, by and for S. Hyde, 1734.* (Jan)

8°: A^4 $B–C^4$ D^2; *1–3* 4–26 27–28. D2 advt.
> *Teerink* 743. See *Williams* 640 for the arrest of printers and publishers on 28 Jan for publishing this poem.

L(11631.aa.47/2),O(2, 1 – D2),C,DA(2),DT+; CtY(2),PU.

[—] On wisdom's defeat|In a learned debate, [1725.] *See* O230.

[—] A panegyric on the reverend D--n S----t. In answer to the Libel on Dr. D--y, 1729–30. *See* P36.

S891 [—] Part of the seventh epistle of the first book of Horace imitated: and address'd to a noble peer. *London, printed for A. Dodd, 1713.* (*Examiner* 23 Oct)

4°: A^4 B^2; *1–2* 3–12.
> *Rothschild* 2047; *Teerink* 589; *Williams* 169. Entered in *SR* 23 Oct to John Barber by John Morphew; deposit copies at O,E,SaU.

'Harley, the nation's great support'
> Reprinted in Faulkner's edition of Swift's *Works* (1735) II. 100.

L(11385.f.15),O,C(2),E,DT+; CSmH,CtY,MH,PU,TxU(uncut)+.

S892 [—] — The second edition. *London, printed for A. Dodd, 1713.*

4°: A^4 B^2; *1–2* 3–12.
> Apparently a reimpression.

L(11602.ff.25/2; 841.c.9/14),O,C,DG,GU; CtY(uncut),ICN,MH.

S893 [—] — The third edition. *London, printed for A. Dodd, 1713 [1714?].*

4°: A^4 B^2; *1–2* 3–12.
> Apparently a reimpression. Advertised in *Examiner* 8 Jan 1714, but possibly published before that date.

OC,C,LdU-B; ICU,IU,MH,PU.

S894 [—] [*idem*] [dh] The seventh epistle of the first book of Horace imitated. And address'd to a noble lord. [col] *Dublin: reprinted for John Henly, 1713.*

4°: A^2; *1* 2–4.

L(11621.h.1/3),O,DA,DN,DT(2)+; CSmH,CtY.

S895 [—] Peace and Dunkirk; being an excellent new song upon the surrender of Dunkirk to General Hill. To the tune of, The king shall enjoy his own again. *London, printed in the year 1712.* (*Examiner* 10 July)

½°: 1 side, 1 column.

Swift, J. Peace and Dunkirk

Line 3 of the title in italic type. *Rothschild* 2043; *Teerink* 581; *Williams* 167.
'Spight of Dutch friends and English foes'
Early ms. attribution to Swift in the LLP copy; mentioned in his *Journal to Stella* under 17 July.
L(11602.i.12/5*; 1850.c.10/13; Ashley 5063), LLP,C,Chatsworth,Rothschild; MH.

S896 [—] [another edition]
Line 3 of the title in roman type; probably a piracy.
O.

S897 [—] The place of the damn'd: by J.S. D.D.D.S.P.D. [*Dublin*] *Printed in the year* 1731. (Nov?)
½°: 1 side, 1 column.
Teerink 711; *Williams* 575. Reprinted in *Fog's weekly journal* 4 Dec.
'All folks who pretend to religion and grace'
Reprinted in Faulkner's edition of Swift's *Works* (1735) II. 278.
L(C.121.g.8/189).

[—] A poem address'd to the Quidnunc's, at St. James's Coffee-house, London, 1724. *See* P518.

[—] A poem by D— S—. On the scheme propos'd to the people of Ireland, [1729.] *See* P522.

[—] A poem, occasioned by the hangings in the castle of Dublin, in which the story of Phaeton is express'd, [1701?] *See* P557.

[—] A poem on the erecting a groom-porter's-house adjoining to the chapple, in the castle of Dublin, [1725?] *See* P614.

[—] A poem on the memorable fall of Chloe's p--s pot, attempted in blank verse, 1713. *See* P627.

'—' A poem to his majesty King George, II. on the present state of affairs in England... By the rev. Dr. J. Swift, dean of St. Patrick's [or rather, by Henry Carey]. In Lilliputian verse, 1727. *See* C46.

[—] A poem upon R—r a lady's spaniel, [1725.] *See* P678.

S898 [—] Prometheus, a poem. *Dublin, printed in the year* 1724. (Nov?)
½°: 1 side, 2 columns.
Rothschild 2090; *Teerink* 1154; *Williams* 343. Possibly printed by John Harding on the evidence of the typography. Publication date from *Williams*.
'When first the 'squire, and tinker Wood'
Early ms. attribution to Swift in the CSmH copy; reprinted in Faulkner's edition of Swift's *Works* (1735) IV. 385. Occasioned by Wood's halfpence.
L(C.121.g.8/32),LVA-F,C(2),DG,DN,DT, Crawford,Rothschild; CSmH,CtY(cropt).

[—] Punch's petition to the ladies, [1724.] *See* P1167.

Swift, J. The puppet-show

[—] The puppet-show, a poem, [1721.] *See* P1169.

[—] The queen's and my lord of Oxford's new toast, [1711.] *See* Q9.

[—] The queen's and the Duke of Ormond's new toast, 1712. *See* Q12.

[—] A rebus written by a lady, on the rev. D---n S----t. With his answer, [1724?] *See* R144.

[—] The revd. Dr. S---- answer to the distress'd maids petition, [172–?] *See* R169.

S899 [—] A riddle by Doctor R——fe, [*Dublin*, 1725/30.]
½°: 1 side, 1 column.
Williams 971. Below, another poem headed 'Answer'd by Mr, S—g'. Clearly printed at the same time as *A riddle by Dr, S—t, to my Lady Carteret*, [1725/30], which is entered as anonymous. The copy at DT is bound with half-sheets of 1727, that at L with half-sheets of 1725/30; possibly it dates from 1726 when Delany's riddles were printed.
'In reading your letter alone in my hackney'
Answer: 'Dear Sir since in cruxes and puns, you and I deal'
Both the text and the names are confused. What is printed here as the riddle is actually Swift's answer to Sheridan's riddle; the answer is a conflation of Sheridan's riddle and a third poem by him replying to Swift. They apparently date from Sept 1718; see *Williams* and references.
L(C.121.g.8/100),DT.

[—] A riddle by Dr, S—t, to my lady Carteret, [1725/30.] *See* R204.

[—] A riddle by the revd. Doctor D-----y ['Answered by the reverend Dean S----t'], 1726. *See* D205.

[—] The r-----r's s-----ch explain'd, [1711.] *See* R323.

S900 [—] [dh] Run upon the bankers. [*Dublin*, 1720.]
4°: *A*²; *1* 2–3 *4 blk.*
Teerink 611A; *Williams* 238. Ms. date 1720 in the CSmH copy.
'The bold encroachers on the deep'
Reprinted in Faulkner's edition of Swift's *Works* (1735) II. 208.
CSmH.

S901 [—] The run upon the bankers, and, the South-Sea detected. *Cork, printed by Samuel Terry, in Cock-Pit-lane,* 1721.
½°: 1 side, 2 columns.
Rothschild 2067; *Teerink* 611B. One poem to each column, with titles at head. *South-Sea detected* is a reprint of [Edward Ward] *A South-Sea ballad*, [1720.]
Rothschild.

[—] A satire on Dr. D—ny, 1730. *See* S880.

[—] A satyre upon a monstrous peruke gown and band. Written by a k—e, [173–.] *See* S72.

Swift, J. A serious poem

S902 [—] A serious poem upon William Wood, brasier, tinker, hard-ware-man, coiner, counterfeiter, founder and esquire. *Dublin, printed by John Harding,* [1724.] (17 Sept?)
½°: 2 sides, 1 column.
> *Rothschild* 2086; *Teerink* 1148; *Williams* 333.
> Advertised in Harding's *News letter* of 15 Sept for publication on 17 Sept.

'When foes are o'ercome, we preserve them from slaughter'
> Reprinted in Faulkner's edition of Swift's *Works* (1762) IV. 351; there seems no other evidence for Swift's authorship.

LVA-F,C,DT,Rothschild; CSmH,CtY(cropt).

S903 [—] — [*Edinburgh*] *Reprinted from the Dublin copy,* [1724.]
½°: 1 side, 2 columns.
> This edition follows the text printed in the London papers, omitting 52 lines and the word 'counterfeiter' from the title.

E.

[—] The seventh epistle of the first book of Horace, 1713. *See* S894.

S904 [—] A soldier and a scholar: or the lady's judgment upon those two characters in the persons of Captain —— and D—n S—t. *London, printed for J. Roberts,* 1732. (*GSJ* 12 Jan)
4°: A–E²; *1–3* 4–19 20. 20 advt.
> *Rothschild* 2128–9; *Teerink* 713; *Williams* 863. The relationship between the London and Dublin editions is not clear; apparently they were from different mss. Faulkner may have supplied copy for the London edition, but it is probably earlier nevertheless. Entered in Bowyer's ledgers to 'Partners' (of which he was probably one) under 11 Jan; 300 and 200 copies printed. The detailed account of the printing shows a single impression of 500 copies. Press-figures 4–1, 8–2, 11–1, 14–1.

'Thus spoke to my lady the knight full of care'
> Reprinted in Faulkner's edition of Swift's *Works* (1735) II. 238. Cf. *An answer to Hamilton's Bawn*, [1732.]

L(C.116.g.20),O,C,*MR*; CtY,ICN,MH(uncut).

S905 [—] — The second edition. *London, printed for J. Roberts,* 1732.
4°: A–E²; *1–3* 4–19 20. 20 advt.
> With the same press-figures as the preceding; probably a press-variant title for the 200 copies noted above.

E; MH,MiU,TxU(2).

S906 [—] — The third edition. *London, printed for J. Roberts,* 1732. (22 Jan?)
4°: A² B–E²; *1–3* 4–19 20. 20 advt.
> Entered in Bowyer's ledgers under 22 Jan, 750 copies printed, probably including the following. The detailed accounts record that three half-sheets (probably A–C) were recomposed. Press-figures 8–2, 9–3, 13–3, 20–7.

Swift, J. A soldier and a scholar

L(11632.g.51; G.5181/2),O,C(uncut),DN(uncut), LdU-B; CtY,MH,PU.

S907 [—] — The fourth edition. *London, printed for J. Roberts,* 1732.
4°: A² B–E²; *1–3* 4–19 20. 20 advt.
> With the same press-figures as the preceding; probably a press-variant title.

O,C; MH(uncut),PU.

S908 [—] [*idem*] The grand question debated: whether Hamilton's Bawn should be turn'd into a barrack, or a malt-house. According to the London edition, with notes. *London printed by A. Moore. And, Dublin re-printed by George Faulkner,* 1732.
8°: A⁴ B⁴ C²; *1–3* 4–18 *19–20*. C2 advt.
> *Rothschild* 2130; *Teerink* 714. Watermark: grapes (not always seen). Pp. 13–18 contain *Horace book I. ode XIV*. There was no London edition with the (fictitious) imprint of A. Moore.

L(11601.d.28/5),DA,DG,DT(2),GU+; CLU-C, MH(cropt),PU.

S909 [—] [fine paper]
> Watermark: fleur-de-lys.

PU.

[—] The speech of the p—st of T—y C—ge, to his royal highness George prince of Wales, 1716. *See* S633.

S910 — Sphinx: a poem, ascrib'd to certain anonymous authors. By the rev'd Dean S—t. *Dublin, printed in the year* 1724·5.
8°: A⁸; *1–2* 3–14 *15–16 blk.*
> *Teerink* 468; *Williams* 13. First published in *The supplement to the fifth volume of the Athenian gazette,* [1692], as 'An ode to the Athenian Society', and apparently also issued separately (cf. *Teerink* 467).

'As when the deluge first began to fall'
> Signed on p. 14.

L(C.71.bb.15/6, –A8),LVA-F(lacks A1, –A8), DA(–A8),DN; CSmH,CtY(–A8),MH(–A8).

[—] Spuddy's lamentation for the loss of her collar, [1728.] *See* S666.

[—] 'The storm; Minerva's petition.' [1722.]
> *Teerink* 913; *Williams* 301. The first known publication took place in a collection of 1749, but *Ball* 167, 176 suggests the existence of a broadside edition at the time of its writing. It is not known whether this is purely hypothetical.

[—] A tale in allusion to a certain tale, 1731. *See* T9.

[—] The tale of a nettle. Written by a person of quality, 1710. *See* T13.

[—] Tea. A poem. Or, ladies into china-cups; a metamorphosis, 1729. *See* T109.

[—] There's but one plague in England. D—— M——, [1711.] *See* T148.

Swift, J. T--l--nd's invitation

S911 [—] T--l--nd's invitation to Dismal, to dine with
the Calves-Head Club. Imitated from Horace,
epist. 5. lib. 1. [*London*, 1712.] (*Examiner* 26 June,
'lately publish'd')
½°: 1 side, 1 column.
   Rothschild 2040; *Teerink* 580; *Williams* 161.
   'Dismal' in line 1 is in black-letter. Williams
   suggests 'it was almost certainly printed by
   Morphew, who published *The examiner*.'
'If, dearest Dismal, you for once can dine'
   Referred to in Swift's *Journal to Stella* 1 July
   1712; reprinted in Faulkner's edition of
   Swift's *Works* (1765) XIII. 357. A lampoon on
   Daniel Finch, earl of Nottingham.
L(11602.i.12/32**; 1850.c.10/42; Ashley 5062),
LLP,O(2),C(2, 1 uncut),MC,LdU-B,Chatsworth,
Rothschild; CLU-C,CSmH,CtY,ICN(Luttrell,
26 June),IU,*InU*,MH,TxU(3).

S912 [—] — [*Edinburgh?* 1712.]
½°: 1 side, 1 column.
   'Dismal' in line 1 is in italic capitals.
E; MH.

S913 [—] To Doctor D-l---y, on the libels writ against
him. *London: printed. And, Dublin reprinted in the
year* 1730.
8°: *A*⁸; *1–5* 6–16. A1 hft.
   Rothschild 2122; *Teerink* 693; *Williams* 499.
   There was no London edition.
'As some raw youth in country bred'
   Reprinted in Faulkner's edition of Swift's
   Works (1735) II. 265. Addressed to Delany.
L(11601.ccc.38/5),LVA-F,DA,DT(2); MH,TxU.

[—] To his excellency John, lord Carteret... An
imitation of Horace, ode IX. lib. IV., 1729. *See* T332.

[—] To his grace the arch-bishop of Dublin, a
poem, [1724.] *See* T334.

[—] To the citizens, 1724. *See* T362.

[—] To the honourable Mr. D.T. great pattern of
piety, 1725. *See* T373.

S914 [—] Traulus. The first part. In a dialogue between
Tom and Robin. [*Dublin*] *Printed in the year* 1730.
(April?)
8°: *A*⁴; *1–3* 4–8.
   Teerink 699; *Williams* 794. The order of
   editions has not been determined; in this the
   last line of p. 3 reads '...Draper?' Publication
   date from *Williams*.
'Say, Robin, what can Traulus mean'
   Reprinted in the fifth volume of *Miscellanies*
   (1735). An attack on Joshua, viscount Allen for
   his actions against *A libel on Dr. D—*, 1730.
L(11601.ccc.38/11),DA(2),DN,DT,*MR*+; CtY,
IU,TxU.

S915 [—] [another edition]
   The last line of p. 3 reads '...Draper:'
L(Ashley 1834).

S916 [—] Traulus. The second part. [*Dublin*] *Printed in
the year* 1730.

Swift, J. Traulus. The second part

8°: *A*⁴; *1–3* 4–7 *8 blk*.
   Headpiece on p. 3 is a military trophy with
   cupids. The stop after 'Traulus' on the title is
   not always seen. Reprinted as 'Thersites' with
   Thomas Tickell's *A poem in praise of the horn-
   book*, 1732.
'Traulus of amphibious breed'
L(1963),DA(2),DK,DN; IU,TxU.

S917 [—] [reimpression?]
   Headpiece on p. 3 represents crossed cornu-
   copias. Clearly from the same setting of type
   as the preceding, and possibly a mere variant;
   but the association of the only copy seen with
   an equally rare edition of the first part suggests
   a lapse of time.
L(Ashley 1834).

[—] A trip to Dunkirk: or, a hue and cry after the
pretended Prince of Wales, 1708. *See* T484.

[S918–19 = H13·2–5] '—' Ub-bub-a-boo: or, the Irish-
howl, 1735. *See* Hamilton, Thomas, *chaplain to his
majesty.*

[—] Upon the fringes, commonly so call'd by the
vulgar, 1722. *See* U20.

S920 — Verses on the death of Doctor Swift. Written by
himself: Nov. 1731. *London, printed for C. Bathurst*,
1739. (*DA* 19 Jan)
2°: *A*¹ B–E² F¹; *i–ii, 1* 2–18. 18 advt.
   Rothschild 2166–8; *Teerink* 771; *Williams* 551.
   This edition was prepared for the press by
   William King (1685–1763) in association with
   Pope; he wrote to Swift on 5 Jan 1739 to say
   it had gone to press. Apparently two thousand
   copies were printed; see *Williams* 552. Entered
   in *SR* 17 Jan; deposit copies at L,O,AdU,GU.
'As Rochfoucault his maxims drew'
L(643.m.14/14; 840.m.1/17),O(3),C(2),DG,
LdU-B+; CSmH,CtY(uncut),ICU,MH(2),TxU
+.

S921 — — The second edition. *London, printed for C.
Bathurst*, 1739.
2°: *A*² B–E²; i–ii, *1* 2–18. 18 advt.
   Teerink 1600. Vignette of fame with trumpet on
   title. A second edition was advertised in *DA*
   9 Feb, but that may have been the following.
L(11657.m.33),LVA-D,LVA-F,O; CtY,IU,MH,
PU,TxU.

S922 — — The second edition. *London, printed for C.
Bathurst*, 1739. (12 Feb?)
2°: *A*² B–E²; *1–3* 4–20. 20 advt.
   Teerink 1601. Vignette of bust on title.
L(643.1.28/22, cropt),LVA-F(2),O(ms. date, 12
Feb),BaP,LdU-B; CSmH(ms. adds.),ICN,PU,
TxU.

S923 — — The third edition. *London, printed for C.
Bathurst*, 1739. (29 March?)
2°: *A*² B–E²; *1–3* 4–20. 20 advt.
   Teerink 1602. Vignette of flowers on title.

Swift, J. Verses on the death

Partly from the same type as the preceding. A 'third edition' was advertised in *DA* 29 March.
L(11657.m.26),C,BaP(uncut); CtY,MH(ms. adds.),TxU.

S924 — — The third edition. *London, printed for C. Bathurst,* 1739 [1740?].
2º: *A*² B–E²; *1–3* 4–20. 20 advt.
Teerink 1603. Vignette on title has head in centre. An entirely different edition from the preceding, and possibly a later reprint, like the Edinburgh piracy of 1741. It is tempting to identify it with an otherwise incomprehensible entry, 'Poem on the Death of Dr. Swift D.P. Fol' for Bathurst in Bowyer's ledgers under 20 March 1740, 500 copies.
CSmH,IU,MH,MiU,PU(2, 1 uncut).

S925 — — '*London, printed for C. Bathurst*' [*Edinburgh*], 1739.
8º: A–C⁴; *1–2* 3–22 *23–24 blk.*
Teerink 772. Printed by Ruddiman on the evidence of the ornaments.
L(11659.c.76, uncut),EN; CSmH,CtY,IU(2), MH(2),PU+.

S926 [—] Verses on the death of Dr. S----, D.S.P.D. Occasioned by reading a maxim in Rochefoulcault ... Written by himself, November 1731. *London printed: Dublin: re-printed by George Faulkner,* 1739. (Feb?)
8º: *A*⁴ B–F⁴; *1–4* 5–44 *45–48.* 48 advt.
Rothschild 2169; Teerink 774. A more complete text than the preceding. According to William King's letter of 6 March 1739, copies of the Dublin edition had already reached London.
L(11631.bb.82; 11601.d.28/7),LVA-F(ms. adds.),C(2, 1 ms. adds.),DK(2, 1 ms. adds.),DT+; CSmH,CtY,ICN(ms. adds.),PU(–F3, 4),TxU(ms. adds.).

S927 — Verses on the death of Dr. Swift, D.S.P.D... The second edition. *London printed: Dublin: re-printed by George Faulkner,* 1739.
8º: *A*⁴ B–F⁴; *1–4* 5–44 *45–48.* 48 advt.
Rothschild 2170. A reimpression. Minor changes are made through the successive impressions. According to a note in *Teerink,* sheets from the various impressions are sometimes mixed.
LVA-F,GU; TxU.

S928 — — The third edition. *London printed: Dublin: re-printed by George Faulkner,* 1739.
8º: *A*⁴ B–F⁴; *1–4* 5–44 *45–48.* 48 advt.
A reimpression.
C,E; PU.

S929 — — The fourth edition. *London printed: Dublin: re-printed by George Faulkner,* 1739.
8º: *A*⁴ B–F⁴; *1–4* 5–44 *45–48.* 48 advt.
A reimpression.
MH,PU.

S930 — — The fifth edition. *London printed: Dublin: re-printed by George Faulkner,* 1739.
8º: *A*⁴ B–F⁴; *1–4* 5–44 *45–48.* 48 advt.
A reimpression.
O,C(ms. adds.); MH.

S931 — — The sixth edition. *London printed: Dublin: re-printed by George Faulkner,* 1741.
8º: *A*⁴ B–F⁴ (E2 as 'E'); *1–4* 5–41 *42–47; 48 blk* (40 as '38'). 46–47 advt.
L(1966); PU.

S932 — — Written by himself: Nov. 1731. '*London, printed for C. Bathurst*' [*Edinburgh*], 1741.
8º: A–C⁴; *1–2* 3–22 *23–24 blk.*
Teerink 773. Printed by Ruddiman on the evidence of the ornaments; cf. S925.
LVA-F,E; MH.

S933 — — Occasioned by reading the following maxim in Rochfoucault... *Dublin, printed: London: re-printed, and sold by the booksellers of London & Westminster,* [174–?]
12º: (frt+) A⁴ B²; *1–2* 3–12.
Teerink 1608. One of a series of piratical reprints (*Teerink* 1604–8), most of which were added to piracies of Pope's *Essay on man.* See that, and also the note in *Teerink* (1963) p. 372 and references.
C.

S934 — ⟨—⟩
12º: A⁶; *1–2* 3–12.
Teerink 1604. First reported by H. Teerink in *SB* 4 (1951) 184; the only known copy lacks the title-leaf A1. A piracy, probably after 1740.
DN(–A1).

S935 [—] The virtues of Sid Hamet the magician's rod. *London, printed for John Morphew,* 1710. (*SR* 7 Oct)
½º: 2 sides, 1 column.
Rothschild 2009; Teerink 524; Williams 131. Entered in *SR* to Benj. Motte; deposit copy at E. Sent to the printer on 4 Oct (*Williams* 132).
'The rod was but a harmless wand'
Reprinted in Faulkner's edition of Swift's *Works* (1735) II. 44. A satire on Sidney Godolphin.
L(1876.f.1/50, cropt; Ashley 5251),LLP,O,OA,C, E(2),DA,Chatsworth,Crawford,Rothschild; CLU-C,CSmH,CtY,MH,MiU,PU.

S936 [—] — *London printed: and re-printed at Edinburgh by James Watson, and sold at his shop,* 1710.
½º: 2 sides, 1 column.
E.

S937 [—] — *London printed, and re-printed in Dublin,* 1710.
½º: 1 side, 2 columns.
On the other side, *The devil a barrel better herring,* [1710.]
O; CSmH,TxU.

Swift, J. The W--ds-r prophecy

S938 [—] The W--ds-r prophecy. [*London*] *Printed in the year* 1711. (24 Dec?)
½°: 1 side, 1 column.
  Rothschild 2024; *Teerink* 555; *Williams* 145.
  First line of introduction reads '*W--nd--r*'.
  Text in black-letter and roman type. According to *Williams* it was printed on 24 Dec, and on 4 Jan 1712 Swift wrote 'it is not published here, only printed copies given to friends'; but this may be an equivocation.
'When a holy black Suede, the son of Bob'
  Reprinted in Faulkner's edition of Swift's *Works* (1762) X. 266. A satire on Elizabeth Seymour, duchess of Somerset.
L(1871.f.3/22; C.20.f.2/235; Ashley 5061),C, MC,Chatsworth(ms. date 25 Dec),Rothschild; CLU-C,CtY,MH,*NN-B*,NNP,PU,TxU.

S939 [—] — [*London?*] *Printed in the year* 1711.
½°: 1 side, 1 column.
  Teerink 556. First line of introduction reads '*W--nd-r*'. Text in black-letter and roman type. Printed in a different type-face from the preceding, and probably a piracy.
L(G.1390/10),O,C; TxU.

S940 [—] — '*London*' [*Edinburgh*], *printed in the year* 1711.
½°: 1 side, 1 column.
  No black-letter in text.
E,DN.

S941 [—] — [*Dublin?*] *Printèd* [!] *in the year* 1711.
½°: 1 side, 1 column.
DA.

[—] Whiggism laid open: and the loyal churchman's health, [1712.] *See* W391.

[—] Wit upon crutches, or, the biter bitten, 1725. *See* W537.

[—] A young lady's complaint for the stay of Dean Swift in England, 1726. *See* Y22.

Sw—t, *Dr.* A libel on Dr. D—ny, 1730. *See* Swift, Jonathan.

— A satire on Dr. D—ny, 1730. *See* Swift, Jonathan [A libel on D— D—].

S—y, *Dean.* A riddle by the reverend Dean S—y, [1726/27?] *See* Smedley, Jonathan.

S942 **Syllabus.** 'A syllabus of the animal œconomy, in hudibrastick verse. By Dr. Umbraticus. [*London*] *Willock.* Price 1*s.*' (*GM, LM* July 1748)

S943 **Sylvan.** The sylvan dream or, the mourning muses. A poem. *London, printed for Joseph Turner, bookseller in Sheffield, Yorkshire; and are to be sold by A. Baldwin*, 1701. (20 Aug, Luttrell)
2°: *A*² B–F²; *i–iv, 1–19 20 blk.*
'Th' immortal youth had newly left the day'

The **sylvan** dream

An early ms. note on the title of the L copy reads 'by John Philips', but its Sheffield associations and unsophisticated introduction make the attribution most implausible; it may result from a reference in Leonard Welsted, *A poem to the memory of the incomparable Mr. Philips*, 1710, to a 'Mourning Muse' of his. W. T. Freemantle, *A bibliography of Sheffield and vicinity* (1911) 153 says 'There is every reason to believe...[it] is by Henry Park'; but the preface explicitly states that it is the author's first poem, whereas Henry Park published his first in 1695; Freemantle's annotated copy of his bibliography in Sheffield City Libraries withdraws the attribution.
L(11631.h.4),LdU-B; TxU(Luttrell).

Sylvia. Sylvia's revenge, 1707–. *See* Ames, Richard.

Symson, Andrew. [A small collection, with drop-head title to first poem:] On the horrid murder committed upon the sacred person of...James late lord arch-bishop of Saint Andrews... [*Edinburgh*, 1705?]
8°: pp. 32.   L,O; DFo.
  Commonly called 'Elegies'; usually found accompanying Symson's *Tripatriarchicon*, 1705.

———————

S944 — Tripatriarchicon; or, the lives of the three patriarchs Abraham, Isaac & Jacob. Extracted forth of the sacred story, and digested into English verse. *Edinburgh, printed by the author: and are to be sold by Mr. Henry Knox, Mr. David Freebairn, Mr. Robert Freebairn, and other booksellers*, 1705.
8°: π¹ ⁿA⁴ a–b⁴ A–Z⁸ Aa⁴(−Aa4) (a3 as 'a2'); [2] 1–8 [16], 1–374. π1ᵛ err.
'Betwixt the banks of pleasant Euphrates'
L(994.b.30; G.18871/1),O,E(3),GU(2),SaU+; *CLU-C*,DLC.

S945 [—] Unio politico-poetico-joco-seria. Written in the latter end of the year 1703; and afterwards, as occasion offered, very much enlarged, in severall paragraphs. By the author of Tripatriarchicon. *Edinburgh, printed by the author*, 1706.
4°: A–D⁴ (A2 as 'A'); *1–2 3–32.*
'Some say, our states men now are very willing'
  Signed on p. 32 'A.S. philophilus, philopatris'. On the union with England.
L(1077.h.11),E(2),EN(uncut),AdU,*MR-C*; CSmH,*InU*.

S946 [—] [another impression in 8°]
  The copy at EN is bound with *Tripatriarchicon* and the collection of elegies, that at DFo with the elegies. It is possible that this impression was produced to range with those works.
O,EN; DFo.

S947 [**Symson, David.**] A poem on her sacred majesty Q. Anne, occasioned by her majesty's gracious

Symson, D. A poem on her sacred majesty

letter to her honourable privy council; and her act of indemnity to all her good subjects of the kingdom of Scotland. *Edinburgh, printed in the year* 1703. 4°: A⁴; *1–2* 3–8.

The initial 'A' of the title not seen in the copy at DFo, possibly as a result of frisket-bite.

'Hail sacred princess! Hail Great Britain's glory!' Early ms. attribution in the DT copy to ' Mr David Symson, brother to Mr Matthias Symson'.
L(11626.c.44/3),E,DT,AdU; DFo,InU.

T

T., F. The Welsh mouse-trap, 1709. *See* W283.

T., J. An occasional poem, 1727. *See* O6.

— Miscellanies in prose and verse, 1725. *See* Miscellanies.

T., J., *late of Cambridge.* Winter, an ode, 1747. *See* Tattersal, John.

T., J., *lately one of his majesty's servants.* A prologue for his majesty's birth-day, 1725. *See* P1123.

T., N. The old man's legacy to his daughters, 1736. *See* O115.

T., W. From W.T. in the Marshalsea, 1716. *See* Tunstall, William.

T----, W----. St. Cyprian's discourse to Donatus, 1716. *See* Tunstall, William.

T., W. Some fruits of solitude, 1705. *See* Thompson, William, *schoolmaster of Nottingham.*

— W.T. to fair Clio, 1716. *See* Tunstall, William.

— W.T. to Mrs. M.M. in answer to a song, 1716. *See* Tunstall, William.

Table. Table-talk, 1747–. *See* Kidgell, John.

T1 Tacker. The tacker's ghost. In answer to the Geneva ballad. To the tune of, A hundred and thirty four. *London, printed in the year* 1705.
½º: 1 side, 2 columns.
'Behold a poor ghost from below'
    A whig poem against the tackers, answering the 1705 reprint of *The Geneva ballad.*
Rothschild.

Tackers. The tackers. By a church of England minister, 1705. *See* Darby, Charles.

T2 Tacking. The tacking-club: or, a satyr on Doctor S——ll, and his bulleys. [*London?*] *Printed in the year* 1710.
8º: A⁴; *1–2* 3–8.
'Attend you fools, your character is such'
    An attack on Sacheverell.
L(164.k.47),E; MB.

T3 Taffy. Taffi's master-piece: or, the Cambro-British invention. A mock poem. Being the Muscipula Oxoniensis translated... By a Cantab. *London printed, and sold by John Morphew,* 1709. (*Tatler* 1 Sept)
8º: A–C⁴ D²; *i–ii, 1* 2–26.
'Muse, sing the mountaineer, the Briton'
    A translation of Edward Holdsworth's *Muscipula.* Pickering & Chatto cat. 204/13207a

ascribes the translation to Charles Cholmondeley, but the evidence for the attribution is not known.
L(11409.aaa.21),*DrU*,WcC; OCU.

— Taffy's triumph: or, a new translation of the Cambro-muo-maxia, 1709. *See* Bellamy, Daniel.

T4 Taffydeis. The Taffydeis. An heroic poem. In honour of St. David, and the leek... By Hywgi ap Englyn Margonwe, son, in the ninth score degree, of Camber ap Brute the Trojan. *London, printed for M. Cooper,* 1746. (*GA* 6 March)
8º: A¹ B–G⁴ H¹; *i–ii, 1* 2–49 *50 blk.* 49 err.
'Sing muse, the glorious day, consign'd to fame'
O; CtY.

T5 —— An humorous heroic poem. In honour of St. David and the leek. Dedicated to Bumbalio... *London, printed for M. Cooper,* 1747. (Feb?)
8º: A¹(±) B–G⁴ H¹(±); *i–ii, 1* 2–49 *50 blk.*
    A reissue, with cancel title and H1; dedication to Bumbalio on A1ᵛ, no erratum on p. 49. *Old England* 28 Feb 1747 discusses the poem and refers to a 'second edition'. Later listed in *BM* March 1748 and *GM* March 1750.
L(161.m.64); CtY.

'Tagg, Timothy.' A dialogue in burlesque verse, 1731. *See* D285.

Tail. A tail [!] of J—n and S—h, 1711. *See* Tale.

T6 Tailor. The taylor turn'd poet. An inscription sacred to the memory of the author of a late poem (intitl'd Rammillies.) Written in imitation of Milton. [*London*] *Printed for J. Morphew,* 1706. (26 Oct, Luttrell)
½º: *1–2,* 1 column.
    Advertised in *DC* 30 Oct.
'Nine taylors make a man, the muses nine'
    Apparently a satire on John Paris, *Ramillies,* 1706; but the reference to the tailor is obscure, for Paris was in the middle of his academic career at Cambridge.
DG; MH(Luttrell),TxU.

— The taylor's vindication, [17––?] *See* Davidson, —, *tailor.*

T7 Tailors. The taylors answer to Vulcan's speech, address'd to the right honourable the Lady Carteret. [*Dublin, printed by George Faulkner,* 1725.]
½º: 1 side, 1 column.
    On the other side, *Vulcan's speech,* 1725.
'So great your honour, so deserv'd your fame'
    A reply to the smiths in the dispute about their precedence.
L(C.121.g.8/70); TxU.

Taking. The taking of Jericho, 1742. *See* Wesley, Charles.

Tale. A tale, and no tale, 1715. *See* Crabb, John.

— A tale and two fables in verse, 1727. *See* Mitchell, Joseph.

— A tale being an addition to Mr. Gay's Fables, 1728. *See* Barber, Mary.

T8 — A tale from St. James's. *London, printed in the year* 1710.
½°: 1 side, 1 column.
'Near to a parks delightful grove'
    An allegory on the fall of Godolphin.
O.

T9 — A tale in allusion to a certain tale. [*Dublin*] *Printed in the year* 1731.
½°: 1 side, 2 columns.
'Good people, I pray ye attend and draw near'
    On the Duke of Dorset's speech to both houses of the Irish parliament, 5 Oct 1731. Answered by *An explanation of a tale of a tale*, 1731, which apparently takes Swift to be the author; this suggestion does not seem to have been considered by Swift's editors.
C(2),DG,DT; CSmH.

T10 — A tale of a bottomless tub. *London, printed for J. Roberts*, 1723. (*DJ* 28 Feb)
2°: *A² B–C²; 1–3* 4–12.
    The Luttrell copy, dated March, is recorded in Pickering & Chatto cat. 336/635. Reissued in *A collection of original poems*, 1724 (*Case* 329).
'If bards of old we may believe'
    By the same author as *The longitude discover'd*, 1726. On the insatiability of women.
L(11631.k.5/6),O; CtY,TxU.

— 'A tale of a cow and her keepers.'
    Answered by *A cure for the cow*, [173–?]; it may be in verse.

— The tale of a disbanded courtier, [1712?] *See* Pittis, William [The Windsor prophecy].

T11 — The tale of a disbanded officer. *London, printed in the year* 1711.
½°: 1 side, 1 column.
'The birds reduc'd once to a pop'lar state'
    On the debate about the dismissal of Marlborough.
L(Cup.645.e.1/16).

T12 — The tale of a dolphin. *London, printed in the year* 1710.
½°: 1 side, 1 column.
'A dolphin of note with a whale did agree'
    Against Godolphin's dismissal.
Herts CRO (Panshanger box 46); CLU-C,IU.

— A tale of a man and his mare, [1720/21.] *See* Meston, William.

T13 — The tale of a nettle. Written by a person of quality. '*Cambridge*', *printed in the year* 1710. (1 March, Luttrell)
½°: 1 side, 1 column.

Last couplet in roman type. *Rothschild* 2196; *Teerink* 842; *Williams* 1084. The Cambridge imprint is almost certainly false. A copy in an early state (possibly proof) at MH omits the words 'Written by a person of quality' in the title and is leaded throughout.
'A man with expence of wonderful toil'
    Printed in Swift's *Works* by Scott, 1814, but considered 'very doubtful' by *Williams*. A fable against the repeal of the test act. See *The London tale. By the author of the Tale of a nettle*, 1710, and *An answer to The tale of a nettle. Written by D. D'Foe*, 1710.
L(1870.d.1/99); C.116.i.4/36, cropt),C,MC (Luttrell),Crawford,Rothschild; CtY,MH(2), TxU.

T14 — [another edition]
    Last couplet in italic type.
L(Ashley 5059),O.

T15 — [*idem*] An explanation of the Tale of a nettle, paragraph by paragraph. From the best edition, printed at Cambridge, at the request of several of the university. [*London?*] *Printed in the year* 1710.
8°: *A⁴; 1–2* 3–8.
    The verse reprinted with a prose commentary.
L(C.116.i.4/37),C; NN,TxU.

T16 — The tale of a nettle... '*Camdidge* [!]' [*Dublin?*], *printed in the year* 1712.
½°: 1 side, 1 column.
DG(cropt).

T17 — [*idem*] Still more advice. A tale of a nettle. [1727–8.]
½°: 2 sides, 1 column.
    A reprint, slightly altered and with the addition of a six-line moral. The copy seen has ms. date '1727–8'.
C.

T18 — Tale of a Newcastle-salmon. *London, printed in the year* 1711.
½°: 1 side, 1 column.
'A salmon of a lord like size'
Harding.

T19 — Tale of a tarr. A new ballad. *London, printed for A. Baldwin*, 1710. (*DC* 12 May)
½°: 1 side, 2 columns.
    Stanza 2 ends with a period. Advertised as 'The tale...'; all copies seen are perhaps cropt. Entered in *SR* 12 May to John Darby, – possibly referring to the following edition.
'A tight and trim vessel'
    Against Sacheverell, disturbing the ship of state.
O; MH,PPL(cropt).

T20 — [another edition, no imprint seen]
    Stanza 2 ends with a colon.
L(C.121.g.9/174, imprint cropt?).

T21 — Tale of a tub bottled off and moraliz'd. Or, an heroi-comick oration. With a touch upon the

Tale of a tub bottled off

times. *London, printed for J. Roberts*, 1736. (*LDP*
24 June)
2°: *A*² B² C¹; *1–3* 4–10.
'At th' oratory near 'Tower-hill'
WcC(uncut); CtY,ICU,IU,PU,TxU(2).

— 'A tale of an ass; or, the boar of Cullen: by
L------ R------. [*London*] *Printed for S.
Popping*. Price 3*d*.' (*PB* 29 Nov 1718)
There is no evidence that this is in verse.

T22 — A tail [!] of J–n and S–h or, both turnd out of
c——t at last. [*London*] *Printed for John Arbor, in
Fleetstreet*, 1711.
½°: 1 side, 1 column.
'Alas, the warlike hero seems to grieve'
In favour of the dismissal of John and Sarah
Churchill, the duke and duchess of Marl-
borough.
L(Cup.645.e.1/16); TxU.

— A tale of Midas the king, 1714. *See* Tomkins,
T.

T23 — A tale of my L--d Wh--on: upon his going
for Ir----nd. [*London*] *Printed in the year* 1710.
½°: 1 side, 1 column.
Horizontal chain-lines.
'Gone, with a paunch stuff'd out with arrogance'
A satire against Thomas, marquis of Wharton,
lord-lieutenant of Ireland.
CtY,MH.

T24 — The tale of my lord the owl, told by the black-
bird. *London, printed in the year* 1718.
2°: π¹ *A*² B–E² F¹; *i–ii*, *1–2* 3–22. π1 hft.
'Near to an ancient country seat'
Satirical verses on the whigs. Possibly
Edmund Stacy, author of *The blackbird's tale*,
1710, is intended as the author.
L(11660.g.1, cropt, −π1),O(−π1); CtY,MH(ms.
notes),TxU(−π1).

T25 — A tale of Sir John Cass, kt. and alderman; one
of the members of parliament for the city of
London. *London, printed by Mich. Holt in Fleet-
street*, 1713.
2°: *A*² < B¹; ff. *1 2 3*.
Printed on one side of the paper only; the
collation is tentative.
'As Rome of old. by tyranny oppress'd'
MR-C; OCU.

T26 — The tale of the cock-match fought near Sir
O---n B-----m's in Berk-shire. *London, printed
for T. Smith, in Fleetstreet*, [1710?]
½°: 1 side, 2 columns.
'The world I don't question has heard of the trial'
The cocks represented Daniel Burgess and
Sacheverell.
MH,*Harding*.

T27 — A tale of the finches. *London, printed for J.
Roberts*, 1716. (18 April, Luttrell)
8°: *A*² B–C⁴ D²; *i–iv*, *1–20*. A1 hft.

A tale of the finches

Reissued without A² in *Court poems. Part II*,
1717 (*Case* 295(2a)).
'In ancient days when birds cou'd speak'
A political fable.
L(164.k.37, Luttrell),LVA-F(lacks A²),O(lacks
A²),DK,LdU-B; MH(lacks A²),OCU.

T28 — A tale of the lady's bodkin. A poem. By T.H.
gent. *London printed, and sold by the booksellers
of London & Westminster*, [1721.] (Sept, Luttrell)
2°: (3 ll); *1–2* 3–6.
'Florinda, whose enchanting face'
OCU(Luttrell).

T29 — A tale of the mag-pies and jack-daws. *London,
printed for J. Baker*, 1713.
2°: *A*² B¹; *1–2* 3–6. 2 advt.
'Long had the mag-pies and the daws'
A fable on low and high church.
L(163.m.63),LLP; TxU(uncut).

— The tale of the raven and the blackbird, 1715.
See Stacy, Edmund.

T30 — The tale of the robbin, and the tom-titt,|Who
all the birds in the air have bitt. *London, printed by
K. Clifton, in Hanging-sword Court, in Fleet
Street*, [1725?]
½°: 1 side, 2 columns.
Woodcut at head.
'In the days of Æsop, as we do hear'
On the dismissal of Thomas Parker, earl of
Macclesfield, the lord chancellor.
L(P&D 1839).

— The tale of the robin-red-breast, 1710. *See*
Stacy, Edmund.

— 'The tale of the two bridges. A merry poem.
[*London*] *Printed for Sam Briscoe*. Price 6*d*.' (*DP*
5 June 1722)
Listed in *DP* with poems by Edward Ward
after an advertisement for *Whipping-Tom*. I
suspect it is the same work as *The Westminster
bubble*, 1722, which was published by Briscoe
in March 1722.

— A tale of three bonnets, 1722. *See* Ramsay,
Allan.

T31 — A tale of two tubs: or, the b——rs in querpo.
Being a humorous and satirical description of
some principal characters... *London, printed for
A. Price, jun.*, 1749. (*BM* March)
8°: (frt +) *A*² B–H⁴; *i–iv*, *1–55* 56 blk. A1 hft.
'In some far country, now unknown'
A satire on two brothers, the Duke of New-
castle and Henry Pelham.
L(T.1057/2),LdU-B; CSmH(−A1),CtY,KU,
MH(lacks frt),NN.

T32 — — 'London' [*Dublin*] *Printed in the year* 1749.
8°: (frt +) A–F⁴; *1–3* 4–47 *48 blk*.
L(11632.df.29),LVA-F(lacks frt),O(lacks frt),
DG,DK; CLU-C(lacks frt),*MH*,OCU.

A **tale**. Robin's tame pidgeons

T33 — A tale. Robin's tame pidgeons turn'd wild. *London, printed for J. Baker, 1713.*
2°: *A*² B¹; *1–2* 3–6.
 All copies seen except that at OCU have ms. correction of 'Price 3*d*.' to 2*d*.
'Robin, by some misterious fate'
 A political fable on Harley.
L(1481.f.19/7, uncut),O,OW; CLU-C,MH,OCU.

T34 — — The second edition. *London, printed for J. Baker, 1713.*
2°: *A*² B¹; *1–2* 3–6.
 Apparently a reimpression, with printed 'Price 2*d*.'
L(1484.m.1),LLP,O; TxU(uncut).

T35 Tamiad. The Tamiad: an heroic poem. Publish'd by Erasmus Scriblerus, cousin-german to the learned and witty Martinus. *London, printed for T. Astley, 1733. (GSJ 14 Aug)*
8°: A–H⁴ (E2 as 'E3'); *i–iii* iv–vii *viii, 1* 2–56.
viii err.
 Ackers's ledger records the printing of 500 copies, 27 June 1733, for Astley.
'O thou, whose wings, by night, by day'
O; TxU.

T36 Tankerville, E. An elegiack poem, on the death of a lady's sparrow: humbly inscrib'd to a young gentleman. *Dublin, printed in Dame-street, opposite Eustace-street, 1731.*
8°: *A*⁴; *1–2* 3–8.
'While poets sing of doves, and Philomel'
MH.

Tans'ur, William.
The collections of verse by Tans'ur are omitted here since they are set to music.

T37 — Poetical meditations on the four last things. Viz. on death and judgment, heaven and hell... *London, printed for Charles Corbett; sold by the author at Barns in Surrey, 1740. (GM March)*
8°: *A*⁴ B–C⁴; *1–5* 6–24. A1 frt.
 Reissued in *The diverting jumble* II (1748) edited by 'Obadiah Bookworm', copies at O, CtY.
'Death, as a king, does all the world engage'
O(2); *CU*,CtY,*DLC*,MH.

Taperell, John. A new miscellany: containing the art of conversation, and several other subjects. *London, printed for the author, 1731.*
8°: pp. 40.   O; CtY.
 Only 'the art of conversation', pp. 5–12, is in prose. *Rawlinson* records 'A new miscellany of poems... To which is added the art of conversation...1739'; possibly there was another issue or edition.

— Poems on several occasions, viz... *London, printed for E. Withers, 1748.*
8°: pp. iv, 84.   L,O.

Taperell, J.

— [reissue?] The second edition. Vol. 1. *London, printed for E. Withers, 1750.*
  LdU-B; MH,DFo.
 Probably a cancel title.

— A new miscellany. Containing several subjects in verse, and the same in prose, in imitation of sermons... *London, printed for the author, 1763.*
8°: pp. iv, 92.   L; CtY.

———

T38 — 'A pastoral in memory of ⟨ ⟩ dedicated to the muse's friend. *Lond.* 1730 – oct.'
(*Rawlinson.*)

T39 Tar. Tar water, a ballad, inscribed to the right honourable Philip earl of Chesterfield: occasioned by reading a narrative on the success of tar water, dedicated to his lordship by Thomas Prior, esquire. *London, printed for W. Webb, 1747. (GM,LM Jan)*
2°: A⁴; *1–3* 4–7 *8 blk.*
 Printed by Samuel Richardson (*Sale* 349).
'Since good master Prior,/The tar water 'squire'
Crum S537. Printed in Sir Charles Hanbury Williams, *A collection of poems*, 1763; Horace Walpole annotated his copy (now at L) 'Not by Sr Ch. W.' The verses were commonly ascribed to Williams. The reprint of the poem in *The foundling hospital for wit* IV (1747) 12 is ascribed in ms. in the CtY copy to Soame Jenyns, possibly by confusion with his poem in defence of Chesterfield against Williams, *The embarrass'd knight*, 1748.
L(1959),OA; CtY,NjP,OCU.

T40 — — The second edition. *London, printed for W. Webb, 1747.*
2°: A⁴; *1–3* 4–7 *8 blk.*
E,EU.

T41 — — The third edition. '*London, printed for W. Webb*' [*Edinburgh*], 1747.
8°: A⁴; *1–3* 4–8.
E,MP; CtY-M.

T42 — — *Dublin, printed for R. James, 1747.*
½°: 1 side, 2 columns.
L(1890.e.5/163),DT.

Tarillon, François. 'Pulvis pyrius carmen. Auctore Francisco Tarillon. S.J. [*London*] *Imp. John Morphew.*' (*MC* Jan 1717)
 It is not certain that this advertisement represents a separate English edition. An edition with precisely this title (in half-title form) and no imprint at DLC collates 12°: A⁸ B⁴; *1–3* 4–21 *22–24 blk*; it appears to be of continental origin, and may be the edition listed here.

T43 Tartarean. A Tartarean tale... By W.C. A.M. *Dublin, printed by and for S. Powell, 1746.*
8°: *A*⁴; *1–2* 3–8.
'Once on a day, for so report'

A **Tartarean** tale

Bradshaw 452 quotes a letter of 1910 from D. J. O'Donoghue suggesting Walter Chamberlaine as the author. The attribution is plausible, but apparently only rests on the initials.
C,DA(2, 1 uncut).

Tasso, Torquato.
[*Gerusalemme liberata*, books 1–3] Brooke, Henry: Tasso's Jerusalem, an epic poem. Translated from the Italian, 1738. *See* B488–490.

[book 1] Hooke, Thomas: The Jerusalem of Torquato Tasso, 1738. *See* H302.

[book 3] Bond, William: The third book of Tasso's Jerusalem. Written originally in Italian. Attempted in English, 1718. *See* B319.

[books 15, 16] Layng, Henry: Tasso's xv. [and xvi.] book of Jerusalem deliver'd. *In* his *Several pieces in prose and verse*, 1748.

Tassoni, Alessandro.
Ozell, John: La secchia rapita: the trophy-bucket. A mock-heroic poem... by Signior Alessandro Tassoni... Done from the Italian into English rhime [cantos 1, 2], 1710, 1713. *See* O286–7.

— [reissue] The rape of the bucket, 1715. *See* O288.

T44 Taste. Taste. A satire. In an epistle to a friend. *London*, [1746?]
2⁰: ⟨A–B² C¹⟩; *1–2* ⟨*3*⟩–10.
'Yes, G----n! when once virtue quits the earth'
  A political satire.
MH(cropt).

T45 — Taste and beauty. An epistle to the right honourable the Earl of Chesterfield. *London, printed for J. Roberts*, 1732. (*GSJ* 16 March)
2⁰: *A*² B–C²; *1–3* 4–12.
'Pardon th' officious muse, my lord, whose strain'
DT; CSmH,CtY(uncut),IU,MH,OCU.

[**Taswell**, —, *Mr.*] The Deviliad. An heroic poem, 1744. *See* D252.

T46 Taswell, E. Miscellanea sacra, consisting of three divine poems; viz. The song of Deborah and Barak. The lamentation of David over Saul and Jonathan. The prayer of Solomon at the dedication of the Temple. With a proposal for publishing a large collection...in two volumes octavo. *London, printed for the author; sold by J. Morphew*, 1718. (*PB* 13 Sept)
8⁰: A–E⁴; *i–viii*, *1–31* *32* blk.
  Errata slip in copies at L,O,OC, either on A1ᵛ or A4ᵛ. Note below imprint 'Given gratis to the subscribers'. The large collection was never apparently published.
'Let Israel now her grateful trophies raise'
'A sad and melancholy tale'

Taswell, E. Miscellanea sacra

'By thee, eternal god of truth, I reign'
L(11602.ee.1/1),O(uncut),OC(uncut),C; CSmH (uncut),CtY,ICN,ICU(Luttrell, 19 Jan 1719), MH.

T47 [**Taswell, William.**] Muscipula: or, the mousetrap. Attempted in English burlesque. *London printed, and sold* [*by John Peele*] *at Lock's Head adjoyning to Ludgate*, 1725.
8⁰: π¹ *A*⁴ B–D⁴ E¹; *i–ii*, *1* 2–33 *34* blk. π1 hft.
  Latin and English text. The copy at CLU-C has a variant reading of the title, 'in English verse.'
'Come sing, my muse, that ancient Briton'
  Ms. cipher attribution in L copy, 'B6 W377318 T1zw277', or 'By William Tazwell'. A translation of Holdsworth's poem.
L(11408.aaa.36, ms. corrections),LdU-B; CLU-C (−π1, lacks E1).

Tate, Nahum. Majestas imperij Britannici. The glories of Great Britain celebrated in Latin poems by Mr. Maidwell. Paraphras'd in English by Mr. Tate, 1706. *See* Maidwell, Lewis.

T48 — Britannia's prayer for the queen. *London, printed for John Chantry*, 1706. (23 May, Luttrell)
½⁰: *1–2*, 1 column.
'How justly now might I aspire'
  Translated from the Latin of Lewis Maidwell; collected in his *Majestas imperij Britannici*, 1706.
L(C.38.1.6/24, cropt),MC; MH(Luttrell).

T49 — The celebrated speeches of Ajax and Ulysses, for the armour of Achilles... Essay'd in English verse by Mr. Tate...and Aaron Hill... *London, printed for William Keble, & Tho. Bickerton*, 1708. (May?)
4⁰: A–D⁴ E²; *i–viii*, *1–28*.
  Listed in *DC* 22 May, probably after publication.
'The captains take their seats, the soldiers stand'
CSmH,TxU.

— Comitia lyrica: sive carmen panegyricum [by Lewis Maidwell]... Paraphras'd in English, by Mr. Tate, 1707. *See* M24.

T49·5 — A congratulary poem, to the right honourable Richard earl Rivers, upon his lordship's expedition. *London printed, and sold by B. Bragge*, 1706. (*PM* 5 Nov)
4⁰: *A*² B²; *1–2* 3–8.
  Vertical chain-lines. 'Price Two Pence' on title.
'The modest muse presumes not to enquire'
TxU.

T49·6 — [fine paper?] *London, printed in the year* 1706.
2⁰: *A*² B²; *1–2* 3–8.
  No price on title; horizontal chain-lines. It is

Tate, N. A congratulary poem

not certain that these two are from the same setting of type.
MR-C.

T50 — A congratulatory poem, on her majesties happy recovery, and return to meet her parliament. *London, printed for James Holland; sold by John Morphew, 1714. (PB 16 March)*
2°: A–C²; *i–ii*, 1–10.
    Watermark: Amsterdam arms.
'A mourning muse, with wrongs and years de-clin'd'
MR-C; MH,TxU(2, 1 uncut).

T51 — [fine paper]
    Watermark: Dutch lion.
CtY.

T52 — A congratulatory poem on the new parliament assembled on this great conjuncture of affairs. *London, printed for W. Rogers, 1701. (18 Feb, Luttrell)*
2°: A–C²; *1–2* 3–12.
    Watermark: fool's cap. Advertised in *PM* 20 Feb.
'You ancient bards, who Britain's glory wrote'
L(1347.m.11),LDW,O,*MR-C*; CLU-C,CSmH (Luttrell),MB,MH,TxU(2).

T53 — [fine paper]
    Watermark: Dutch lion.
CtY,NjP.

T54 — — With an humble address from the muses to the king... The second edition. *London, printed for W. Rogers, 1701. (20 May, Luttrell)*
2°: π² χ² A²(−A1) B–C²; *i–iv*, 1–4 3–12.
    A reissue with new title and preface π², and with the addition of *The humble address of the muses to his majesty*, 1701, previously published separately. The Luttrell copy is recorded in *Haslewood*; advertised in *PB* 22 May.
LLP; NcU.

T55 — A congratulatory poem to his royal highness Prince George of Denmark... Upon the glorious successes at sea. *London, printed by H. Meere for J.B.; sold by R. Burrough & J. Baker, & J. Morphew, 1708. (Aug?)*
4°: A–E²; *1–3* 4–18 '17–18'.
    No watermark. Listed in *WL* July 1708 which was published late (see A173); advertised in *LG* 2 Sept.
'Bless'd prince! in whom the graces seem com-bin'd'
C; InU,MiU.

T56 — [fine paper]
    Watermark: Strasburg bend.
L(79.h.13, in presentation morocco).

T57 — — To which is added A happy memorable song, on the fight near Audenarde, between the Duke of Marlborough and Vendome, &c. *London, printed by Henry Hills, 1708.*

Tate, N. A congratulatory poem

8°: A⁸; *1* 2–16.
    A piracy, with a reprint of *A happy memorable ballad*, [1708.] Reissued with other remain-dered Hills poems in *A collection of the best English poetry*, 1717 *(Case* 294).
L(C.124.b.7/6),O,CT(2),E,EU(2); CSmH,CtY, IU(lacks A2),MH(2),TxU+.

[T58 = T49·5] — A congratulary [!] poem, to the right honourable Richard earl Rivers, 1706.

T59 — A consolatory poem to the right honourable John lord Cutts, upon the death of his most accomplish'd lady. *London, printed by R.R. for Henry Playford, 1708. (19 March, Luttrell)*
2°: A–C²; *i–ii*, 1–9 *10 blk.*
'Stretch'd in a lonesome vale (where spring decays'
CSmH(Luttrell).

T60 [—] An epigram on the Spectator. *[London] Printed for E. Curll, & R. Gosling, 1712.*
½°: 2 sides, 1 column.
    Advertisements at foot of recto and on verso.
'When first the Tatler to a mute was turn'd'
    Crum W1063, ascribed to Tate. Contempor-ary ms. attribution to Tate in the O copy.
O; KU.

[—] An epistle to the right honourable Charles Montague, 1707. *See* E420.

T61 [—] [dh] The humble address of the muses to his majesty. *[col] London printed, and sold by A. Baldwin, 1701.*
2°: A²; 1–4.
    Reissued in the 'second edition' of Tate's *A congratulatory poem on the new parliament*, 1701 (T54).
'While Britain's monarch does her state support'
O; OCU.

[—] An hymn to be sung by the charity-children of the parish of St. Bride's, [1712.] *See* H447.
    A number of other hymns entered anony-mously may well be by Tate; no attempt to determine their authorship has been made, since it seemed desirable that they should be entered together under Hymn.

T62 — [dh] The Kentish worthies. A poem. *[col] London, printed for A. Baldwin, 1701. (1 Aug, Luttrell)*
2°: A²; 1–4.
    Watermark: London arms.
'Shall Britain and applauding nations round'
    Answered by *A satyr on the Kentish-men and T--te, the poet*, 1701.
MR-C; CLU-C,MH(Luttrell).

T63 — [another impression?]
    Watermark: unicorn. The page numbers are in a different position relative to the text, but whether this is a sign of a new edition, a new impression, or merely the printing of fine-paper copies with changed margins, has not

Tate, N. The Kentish worthies

been determined. The latter is perhaps most probable.

TxU.

[—] Miscellanious [!] poetical novels or tales, 1705. *See* M275–6.

T64 — A monumental poem in memory of the right honourable Sir George Treby kt. late lord chief justice of his majesty's court of common-pleas: consisting of his character and elegy. *London, printed for Jacob Tonson*, 1702 [1701]. (25 Nov, Luttrell)

2°: π² A–C²; *i–iv*, *1–12* (6, 7 as '2, 3').

   Watermark: fool's cap. Listed in *WL* Nov 1701.

Character: 'Indulge one labour more, my drooping muse'

Elegy: 'With pleasure, muse, did we the picture view'

O,*CJ,MR-C*; CLU-C,CSmH(Luttrell),MH.

T65 — [fine paper]

   Watermark: Strasburg bend.

CLU-C.

T66 — The muse's bower, an epithalamium on the auspicious nuptials of the...Marquis of Caermarthen, with the Lady Elizabeth Harley... *London, printed for the author; sold by J. Morphew*, 1713. (*PB* 6 Jan)

4°: *A*² B–D²; *1–2 3–15 16*. 16 advt.

'Love's queen, yet not the Cyprian Venus sprung'

L(162.1.18, Luttrell, 8 Jan); CtY,ICN,MH.

T67 — The muse's memorial of the happy recovery of the right honourable Richard earl of Burlington ... A congratulatory poem. With an account of the present state of poetry. *London, printed for Tho. Osborne; sold by B. Bragge*, 1707. (*DC* 5 March)

4°: *A*² B–F²; *1–3 4–24*. 24 advt.

   The 'account of the present state of poetry' occupies pp. 19–24.

'In sorrow's gloomy vale, where mournful yew'

CSmH.

T68 — The muse's memorial, of the right honourable Earl of Oxford, lord high treasurer of Great Britain. *London, printed by E. Berington; sold by J. Baker, & B. Berington*, 1712. (1–6 Sept)

2°: *A*² B–D²; *1–2 3–16*.

   Listed in *DC* 6 Sept as 'this week was published'. A second edition was advertised in *The muse's bower*, 1713, and *Morgan* O675 records a Dublin reprint of 1715, possibly in error.

'A lawrel'd bard, with wrongs and years oppress'd'

L(11630.g.29),O; CLU-C,*DLC*,MH,TxU.

T69 — [dh] An ode upon the assembling of the new parliament. Sung before his majesty on new-years-day. 1702. [*London*, 1702.] (Jan?)

4°: *A*²; *1–4*.

'Wake Britain, 'tis high time to wake'

Tate, N. An ode upon the assembling

The ode was set by John Eccles; parliament assembled on 30 Dec 1701.

LLP; CLU-C,MH,TxU.

T70 — [dh] On a new copy-book, entitl'd the Penman's magazine, &c. A poem. [*London*, 1705.]

2°: B²; *1–4*. 4 advt.

   An offprint of B² of *The penman's magazine*, 1705, which is advertised on p. 4. Probably printed as publicity for that publication; cf. Stuart L. Astor in *SB* 21 (1968) 261–6. Horizontal chain-lines.

'As Adam once, with more than royal state'

LSA; NNC.

T71 — A poem sacred to the glorious memory of her late majesty Queen Anne. [*London*] *Printed in the year* 1716.

8°: *A*² B⁸ C²; *i–iv*, *1–20*.

   Apparently a posthumous publication.

'Her self half dead, to find her queen expir'd'

L(11631.e.63).

T72 — A poem upon tea: with a discourse on its sov'rain virtues; and directions in the use of it for health. Collected from treatises of eminent physicians... Also a preface concerning beau-criticism. *London, printed for J. Nutt*, 1702.

8°: A–D⁸; *i–xvi*, *1–47 48 blk*.

   Watermark: ? F. Apparently the frontispiece was not included in the ordinary-paper copies. First published as *Panacea: a poem upon tea*, 1700, which was possibly published in 1701; it is listed in *WL* April 1701.

'By Avon's stream (the muses calm retreat)'

L(1971),O,DT,GU; CSmH,MH,NN.

T73 — [fine paper]

   Watermark: fleur-de-lys on shield. Frontispiece of the plant prefixed.

LLP; CLU-C,DLC,DFo(contemporary morocco).

T74 — Portrait-royal. A poem upon her majesty's picture set up in Guild-hall by order of the lord mayor and court of aldermen of the city of London. Drawn by Mr. Closterman. *London, printed by J. Rawlins, for J. Nutt*, 1703. (*WL* Feb)

4°: A–D⁴; *i–viii*, *1–24*.

   Watermark: X.

'Come, where's this wonder? This surprising piece!'

   Dedicated to Prince George of Denmark.

LDW,LG,LSC,O,*DrU*; CSmH(cropt),CtY,MH.

T75 — [fine paper]

   Watermark: Strasburg bend.

L(79.h.11, in presentation morocco),AdU.

T76 — [—] [dh] The second part of Absalom and Achitophel. A poem. [col] *London printed, and sold by J. Read*, 1709. *Where you may have the first part.*

4°: A⁴; *1–8*, 2 columns.

   First published in 1682. This is apparently a continuation of the piracy of the first part entered under Dryden (D448, D448.5).

Tate, N. The second part

'Since men like beasts each other's prey were made'
   Written by Nahum Tate with Dryden's assistance.
DFo.

T77 — [dh] The song for her majesty's birth-day, February the 6th, 171$\frac{10}{11}$[!]. Set by Mr. Eccles... the words by Mr. Tate... [*London*, 1711.]
4°: *A*²; 1–4.
'Fair as the morning, as the morning early'
MH.

T78 — [dh] The song for new-year's-day, 1703. Perform'd before her majesty. Set by Mr. Eccles... The words by Mr. Tate... [col] [*London*] *Printed for J. Nutt,* 1703. (*FP* 2 Jan)
4°: *A*²; 1–3 *4*. 4 advt.
'Heark, how the muses call aloud'
L(161.m.47, Luttrell, 2 Jan),LVA-F,MC.

T79 — [dh] The song for new-year's-day, 1706. Perform'd to musick before her majesty, at St. James's. The words by Mr. Tate... [*London*, 1706?]
4°: *A*²; *1* 2–4. 4 advt.
   A ms. copy at O dates this ode as 1706/7, but the date 1706 is the right one by analogy with other odes. Watermark of fleur-de-lys on shield seen in the copy at C, initials WR at DFo. The former is probably fine-paper, but one may be the countermark of the other.
'O harmony where's now thy pow'r'
C; DFo.

T80 — The song for the new-year 1708. Set by Mr. Eccles master of her majesty's musick. The words by Mr. Tate poet-laureat to her majesty. [*London*, 1708?]
$\frac{1}{2}$°: 1 side, 1 column.
'See how the new-born season springs!'
Crawford; MH.

T81 — The triumph of peace. A poem, on the magnificent public entry of his excellency the illustrious Duke of Shrewsbury...and the magnificent public entry of his excellency the illustrious Duke D'Aumont... With the prospect of the glorious procession for a general thanksgiving at St. Paul's. *London, printed for James Holland; sold by J. Morphew,* 1713. (*PB* 16 July)
2°: *A*² B–C²; *1*–4 5–12.
'What, shall Bellona bid her thunder cease'
O,DA(uncut); CLU-C(uncut, ms. date 24 July), MH,TxU.

T82 — The triumph of union: with the muse's address for the consummation of it in the parliament of Great Britain. *London, printed in the year* 1707.
4°: *A*² B–D²; *1*–2 3–16.
   No watermark.
'The glorious day is past for which we pray'd'
LLP,O,*MR*.

Tate, N. The triumph of union

T83 — [fine paper]
   Watermark: fleur-de-lys on shield.
L(11630.c.5/7),LDW.

T84 — The triumph, or warriours welcome: a poem on the glorious successes of the last year. With the ode for new-year's day. 1705. *London, printed by J. Rawlins for J. Holland; sold by J. Nutt,* 1705. (*PM* 18 Jan)
4°: *A*² B–E⁴; *i–iv*, 1–29 '22' '30' '30'.
   No watermark. Possibly published before 18 Jan; listed in *WL* Dec 1704, but that was probably published late.
'O for a muse of flame, the daring fire'
Ode: 'From fate's dark cell to empire call'd'
L(1465.i.12/5),LDW,LVA-F,O,*MR*+ ; CtY,MH.

T85 — [fine paper]
   Watermark: fleur-de-lys on shield.
LLP,*DrU*; DLC.

T86 —— The second edition. *London, printed by J. Rawlins for J. Holland; sold by J. Nutt,* 1705. (*LG* 5 March)
4°: A–D⁴; *i–iv*, 1–28. 28 advt.
   Normal horizontal chain-lines, watermark O in A.
C; CLU-C,InU,MH,NN.

T87 — [fine paper?]
   Vertical chain-lines.
TxU.

T88 — 'The Windsor muse's address, presaging the taking of Lisle; presented to her majesty at the court's departure from the castle, September 28, 1708, 4to.'
(*Cibber* III.260.)

Tatersal, Robert. The bricklayers miscellany: or, poems on several subjects... The second edition. *London, printed for the author; sold by J. Wilford,* 1734.
8°: pp. vi, 32.   L,O; MH.
   What was possibly the first edition (or perhaps another issue) was listed in *GSJ* 23 May 1734.

—— The second part. Containing poems on several subjects. *London, printed for the author; sold by J. Wilford,* 1735.
8°: pp. v, 23.   L,O; MH.
   Ackers's ledger records the printing of 500 copies for Wilford, 5 June 1735.

T89 [**Tattersal, John.**] Winter, an ode: to a friend at Oxford. A translation of Mr. Thomson's Ode brumalis, &c. By J.T. late of Cambridge. *London, printed for T. Waller,* 1747. (*GM, LM* June)
4°: A⁴ B²; *1*–2 3–11 *12 blk.*
   The order of this and the following have not been determined.
'Alas! no longer now appear'
   A translation of William Thompson's *Ode brumalis,* 1747. Ascribed to Tattersal in a

Tattersal, J. Winter

> letter of Thompson in *Rawlinson*; reprinted as his in Thompson's *Poems*, 1757.

NjP.

T90 [—] — A translation from the Latin of Mr. Thompson. By J.T. late of Cambridge. *London, printed for T. Waller*, 1747.

4°: A⁴ B²; *1–2* 3–11 *12 blk.*

> Apparently from the same setting of type, at least in part.

L(1966),LdU-B.

'Tattle, Tom.' The turn-coats, [1714.] *See* T558.

T91 **Tattoo.** The tattoo: a poem. Occasioned by the darkness which happened at our saviour's crucifixion... By a gentleman of Oxford. *London printed, and are to be sold by J. Aylward*, 1736.

4°: *A*² B–C²; *1–5* 6–12.

'O thou, who on thy flaming chariot rid'st'

L(C.118.c.2/9).

T92 **Taubman, Nathaniel.** 'The British nations tribute of loyalty and duty, express'd upon the occasion of their celebrating the festival of their most august monarchs coronation George I. in Leghorn November 27. 1714. *Lond.* 1718.'

> 'Single sheet dedicated to James earl Stanhope, being a translation of a poem wrote in Italian by Sign: Ant. Maria Salvini, a learned man of Florence.'

(*Rawlinson*.)

T93 — Virtue in distress: or, the history of Mindana. *London, printed for Bernard Lintott*, 1706.

4°: A⁴ B–D⁴; *i–vi*, *1–25 26 blk.* vi err.

'Of all terrestrial kingdoms and abodes'

> Based on Boccacio's *Decameron*, day 2, tale 6.

L(11631.e.64).

T94 **Tauronomachia.** Tauronomachia or a description of a terrible and bloody fight between two champions, Taurus and Onos, at Gresham-College. *London, printed for Tho. Bickerton*, 1719. (*PB* 16 June)

2°: *A*¹ B²; *1–2* 3–6.

> *Bond* 59. The Luttrell date of 13 June possibly originates with an advance advertisement in *PB* 13 June.

'Tho' the fam'd errant bard of old'

> A satire on the quarrel between Richard Mead and John Woodward.

L(C.20.f.2/311); IU(Luttrell, 13 June),MH.

T95 **Taurus.** Taurus in circo. The bull-baiting. A poem, in Latin and English. To which are prefixed, some thoughts concerning the usefulness of publick sports... *London, printed for J. Baker*, 1716. (14 April, Luttrell)

8°: A–C⁴; [2] i–v, 1–16 *17 blk.*

> Latin text and English translation on facing pages. Listed in *MC* April. The copyright

Taurus in circo

> was offered as lot 6 in the trade sale of Thomas Warner, 15 [Oct, 1734] (cat. at O-JJ).

'The muse a brutall battle shall recite'

> The Latin text by Francis Knapp is from *Musæ Anglicanæ.*

L(161.m.79, Luttrell; 11658.e.53),O.

T96 **Tavern.** The tavern hunter; or, a drunken ramble from the Crown to the Devil. *London printed, and are to be sold by the booksellers of London & Westminster*, 1702. (12 March, Luttrell)

2°: A–D²; *1–2* 3–16.

> The Luttrell copy is recorded in *Thorn-Drury*.

'When th' world was so wicked that drinking and roaring'

> Pickering & Chatto cat. 269/12530 ascribes it to Edward Ward; it is written in his manner, but there is no external evidence for his authorship.

L(10350.g.12/10),LG,O; CLU-C,CtY(lacks D²), ICN,NjP,OCU.

T97 — — *London printed, and are to be sold by the booksellers of London & Westminster*, 1702.

8°: A⁸; *1–2* 3–16.

> Apparently a piracy.

LG,O(largely uncut).

T98 — — [*London? 1702?*]

4°: A²; *1–4*, 2 columns.

> Drop-head title only. A piracy; page 4 is in smaller type.

NN.

T99 — The tavern query, or the loyal health, to the tune of, Jolly Bacchus, or I am the Duke of Norfolk. *London, printed for S.P. near Charing-Cross,* [1702.]

½°: 1 side, 2 columns.

> Two rough woodcuts at head.

'True English boys be merry'

> A high church health to Queen Anne.

CM-P.

T100 **Taverners.** The taverners answer to the drunken wives lament,|With reflections on the brewers for their new stent;|A curious new ballad fou witty and paky,|Made in the salt-beef office by drunken Ann M---ky. [*Edinburgh, 1725?*]

½°: 1 side, 2 columns.

'Ann, fou as cap or stoup cou'd make her'

> A reply to *The lamentation of the fruit wives over their bicker*, [1725?].

E.

T101 **Taylor, C.** Britannia: a poem, inscribed to his royal highness the Duke of Cumberland, on his expedition against the Scots... *Preston, printed by J. Stanley & J. Moon*, 1750.

8°: *A*⁴ B⁴; *1–2* 3–16.

'Great Albion's genius, from her ease profound'

PrP.

Taylor, C.

T102 — The scale, or, woman weigh'd with man. A poem; in three canto's. By C. Taylor. Author of the Britannia. [*Preston?* 1750/–.]
8°: *A*⁴ B⁴ C¹; *1–2* 3–18.
'Begin my muse, with bold unborrow'd praise'
    Ms. note in the O copy, 'This gentⁿ was born in Finsthwaite'.
O.

T103 Taylor, John. The music speech at the public commencement in Cambridge, July 6... To which is added, an ode designed to have been set to music on that occasion. *London, printed by William Bowyer, jun.; sold by W. Thurlbourn in Cambridge, R. Clements in Oxford, and the booksellers of London & Westminster,* 1730. (*SR* 14 July)
8°: *A*⁴ B–C⁴ D²; *1–5* 6–26 *27; 28 blk.* A1 hft; D2 advt.
    The speech starts in prose, then changes into verse. Entered in *SR* to Bowyer; deposit copies at O,EU,AdU,SaU. Entered in Bowyer's ledgers under 15 July, 2500 copies printed. The detailed accounts suggest that there were two impressions of 2000 and 500 which have not been distinguished. Listed in *MChr* July; listed again in *LM* July 1749 for Cooper.
'And now awhile let sterner science rest'
Ode: 'Goddess of the brave and wise'
    Compare the third edition of Roger Long, *The music speech,* published in the preceding month.
L(1042.h.6/3; 557*.d.43/1),O(5, 1–A1, 1–D2), C(4, 1 uncut),EU,SaU+; CLU-C,CSmH,CtY (3),ICN,MH+.

[—] Polymnia: or, the charms of musick. Being an ode, sacred to harmony, 1733. *See* P720.

T104 T--ch--n. [dh] T--ch--n touch'd to the quick: or; faction's secretary whipp'd at the carts-arse. [*London,* 1704.] (14 Aug, Luttrell)
4°: *A*²; *1* 2–4.
    Woodcut of the cart above text.
'From pillory, describ'd with wondrous art'
    A satire on John Tutchin.
LVA-F(Luttrell).

Te. The Te deum, 1702. *In* B80·5.

T105 — A Te deum for Lewis le Grand. *London, printed for A. Baldwin,* 1704. (27 Dec, Luttrell)
½°: 1 side, 2 columns.
    Stanza 1, line 4 reads '...Monsieur's fate'.
    Advertised in *PM* 28 Dec.
'Ye princes, that on thrones do dwell'
CLU-C,MH(Luttrell).

T106 — [another edition]
    Stanza 1, line 4 misprinted '...Mousieur's fate'.
LLP.

Te deum

T107 — Te deum, ou, actions de graces a dieu pour les glorieux succez des armes de sa majesté britannique, la reine Anne, tant par mer que par terre, & de ses hauts alliez. *A Londres, par J. Delage,* 1702.
½°: 1 side, 2 columns.
'O dieu, dont tous les cieux racontent les louanges'
NN(title cropt).

T108 Tea. Tea, a poem. In three cantos. *London, printed for Aaron Ward; sold by M. Cooper,* 1743. (*DA* 6 July)
4°: *A*² B–N²; *i–iv, 1* 2–47 *48.* A1 hft; 48 advt.
    Bond 182.
'While bards renown'd dire feats of arms rehearse'
L(11630.c.6/3; 11630.c.7/12,–A1).

T109 — Tea. A poem. Or, ladies into china-cups; a metamorphosis. *London, printed for J. Roberts,* 1729. (*MChr* 27 Sept)
2°: *A*² B–C²; *1–3* 4–11 *12 blk.*
    Subsequently reprinted as 'The female metamorphosis' in Elizabeth Thomas, *The metamorphoses of the town,* 1743, with a group of poems by Swift.
'In Homer's Iliad, and Odysses'
    A satire on tea-drinking. The fact that the poem was reprinted with works by Swift as noted above, and reprinted at Cork like his *The lady's dressing room,* suggests that it was thought to be by Swift.
BaP,LdU-B; TxU.

T110 — [*idem*] ⟨The ladies exercise at tea...⟩ ⟨*Dublin, printed by Richard Dickson,* 1729?⟩
8°: *A*⁴; *1–2* 3–8.
    The only copy seen lacks the title, but the title and imprint probably correspond to the Cork reprint.
DN(lacks A1).

T111 — The ladies exercise at tea. With the rise and progress thereof, or the metamorphosis of a set of ladies into a set of china tea-cups. *Dublin, printed by Rich Dickson, and re-printed in Corke,* [1729?]
8°: *A*⁴; *1* 2–8.
IU.

T112 — The tea-kettle a poem humbly inscrib'd to Miss H-----lt. *Dublin, printed in the year* 1730.
8°: *A*⁴; *1–2* 3–7 *8 blk.*
'Assist me now ye sacred nine'
    A pencil note of unknown authority in the copy at LVA-F ascribes the poem to James Dalacourt. Cf. *The metamorphose of a certain Dublin beau's-head, into a tea-kettle,* 1730.
LVA-F,DA.

Teague. Teague-root botanically considered, [174–?] *See* Wisdom revealed, [1732.]

— Teague's ramble, [1719.] *See* Gent, Thomas.

T113 Teakel, John. An excellent new song, to the excellent old tune of God prosper long our noble king, &c. *Edinburgh, printed in the year* 1746.

Teakel, J. An excellent new song

8°: A^4; *1–2* 3–8.
'Heaven bless great George, long may he be'
AdU; DFo.

Tears. The tears of Scotland, [1746/50?] *See* Smollett, Tobias.

— The tears of the muses: a poem, 1736. *See* Boyse, Samuel.

— The tears of the muses; in a conference, 1737–. *See* Hill, Aaron.

Technethurambeia. Τεχνηθυραμβεια. Sive poema in Patricium Murphæum, 1728, 1730. *See* Dunkin, William.

— Τεχνηθυραμβεια or, a poem upon Paddy Murphy, 1728, 1730. *See* Cowper, Joseph.

Teft, Elizabeth. Orinthia's miscellanies: or, a compleat collection of poems, never before published. *London, printed in the year* 1747.
8°: pp. 159.   L; DFo.

Tell. The tell tale; or, the patriot's defeat, 1741. *See* Tibal, Peter.

'Teltroth, Tom.' Jest and earnest, 1703. *See* Pittis, William [Chaucer's whims].

— The London Æsop, 1702. *See* Pittis, William [Chaucer's whims].

[T114 = S4] **Tempest.** The tempest: a poem. Written at sea, 1741. *See* Sacheverell, John.

Temple. The temple of fame, a poem occasion'd by the late success of the Duke of Ormond, 1703–. *See* Bryan, —.

T115 — The temple of war. To which is annex'd the Birth-day, an ode; and an ode congratulating his present majesty's late safe arrival from Holland... By the author of the Hebrew campaign, and Review. *London, printed for the author; sold by J. Jolliffe, and by Joseph Smith*, 1731.
8°: $A^4(-A4)$ B–D^4 E^1; *i–vi, 1* 2–26.
List of subscribers on pp. iii–vi.
'Tremendous Mars! thou awful source of war'
The same author also wrote *The bed of honour*, 1732.
L(1964, cropt),O; CtY.

— The Temple-Oge ballad, 1730. *See* Poekrich, Richard.

T115·5 — The Temple-Oge ballad. Tune, The lad's a dunce. [*Dublin*, 1725/30.]
½°: 1 side, 1 column.
The L copy forms part of a collection of Dublin half-sheets of 1725/30.
'Ye fops of light heels without one grain of sense'
A satyr on the company at the wells. A different work from Richard Poekrich's ballad with this title.
L(C.121.g.8/79).

Temple

— Temple-Oagg: or, the spaw-well, 1723. *See* Coffey, Charles.

T116 **Templer.** The Templer's bill of complaint; to the right honourable the lord high chancellor. *London, printed for J. Walthoe*, 1727. (*MC* July)
8°: A–C^4; *1–2* 3–23 24. 24 advt.
'Plaints, unattempted yet in bill or court'
L(11633.bbb.38),LDW; CtY,ICU,MH,OCU.

T117 **Temples.** The temples of virtue and pleasure. A poem. *London, printed for W. Sandby, and Stephen Fox, bookseller in Darby*, 1742. (*GM*, *LM* July)
2°: A^1 B–E^2 F^1; *i–ii, 1* 2–18.
Some copies (DFo,IU,OCU) read 'Samuel Fox' in imprint; Samuel is the form recorded in *Plomer* for 1755, but there may have been two booksellers in the family.
'The silent night her sable robe had spread'
CU,DFo,IU,MH,OCU+.

Templum. Templum harmoniæ, 1745. *See* Powney, Richard.

— Templum libertatis, 1742, 1743. *See* King, William, *principal of St. Mary Hall*.

Ten commandments.
Sedgwick, Ralph: A paraphrase, or, an explanation of the ten commandments, [173–?] *See* S187.

— A paraphrase on the second table of the ten commandments, [173–?] *See* S188.

T118 **Ter-Horst, Joannes Hermannus.** Augustissimo atque potentissimo principi, ac domino domino Georgio secundo...in ipsa novi anni festivitate hos paucos votivos elegos demissime offert Joannes Hermannus Ter-Horst. *Londini, anno domini* 1734. (Jan?)
2°: A^2; *1–2* 3–4.
Probably the poem variously listed in Bowyer's ledgers as 'Hermans poem' and 'Lat. poem to K. George fol: sheet'; 250 copies were printed before 12 Jan 1734.
'Dum novus annus adest: tibimetque secunde Georgi'
O.

T118·5 **Terpsicore.** 'Terpsicore à Londres.' [*London*, 1734.] (May?)
8°.
Entered in Bowyer's detailed ledgers for May 1734, pica 8° sheet 'with many alterations', 150 copies printed. One entry refers to it as 'The French Gent^m Poem'.
(Bowyer's ledgers.)

Test. The test of love. A poem, 1737. *See* Amhurst, Nicholas.

Thalia. Thalia: or the sprightly muse. Poems on several occasions, 1705. *See* Grimston, William, *viscount Grimston*.

Thalia

— Thalia triumphans. To the right honourable James earl of Salisbury, 1709. *See* Settle, Elkanah.

T119 Thanksgiving. The thanksgiving: a new protestant ballad. To an excellent Italian tune. *London, printed in the year* 1711.
½°: 1 side, 2 columns.
> The rules in the title and above the imprint are continuous.

'Let's sing the new m——y's praise'
> Against the new ministry, on the occasion of their seizing effigies of the Pope, Pretender and others which were to have been burnt by the whigs on 17 Nov 1711.

L(Rox.III.556),DT; DFo,MB,MH,TxU.

T120 — [another edition]
> The rules are made up of short rules.

L(112.f.44/28),O,Crawford; NNP.

T121 —— [*London?*] *Printed in the year* 1711.
½°: 1 side, 2 columns.
OCU.

T122 —— *London printed, and reprinted in Dublin,* 1711–12.
½°.
(Dobell cat. 105/309.)

T123 — The thanksgiving. A poem. By a late officer in the army. *London printed, and sold by Benjamin Bragge,* 1705. (*PM* 8 Sept, 'just published')
4°: A–C⁴; *1–2* 3–23 *24 blk.*
'Madam, attending providence, we do'
> Robert Clare, one of Harley's informers, reported that the author was 'supposed Mr. Ward'; see H. L. Snyder in *The library* V. 22 (1967) 334. His attributions seem in many cases to be wild guesses. Thanksgiving for Marlborough's victories.

O.

— Thanksgiving for the colliers, 1742. *See* Wesley, Charles.

T124 — A thanksgiving, or the elect-lady upon the war. Much in the words and ancient manner, (before rules;) of the royal and other sacred poets. [*London?*] *Printed in the year* 1710 [1709]. (21 Nov?)
8°: A⁸; *1–2* 3–15 *16 blk.*
> Ms. corrections throughout the L copy and ms. note 'For Doctor Gastrell' dated 21 Nov 1709.

'Awake, rejoyce, O my soul'
L(104.a.70).

T125 — The thanksgiving song: or the horse and foot-race at Oudenard. *London, printed for J. Morphew,* 1708.
½°: 1 side, 2 columns.
'As I told you before/You would never give o'er'
L(1876.f.1/43).

T126 Theatre. The theatre turned upside down: or, the mutineers. A dialogue, occasioned by a

The **theatre** turned upside down

pamphlet, called, The theatric squabble. *London printed, and sold by A. Dodd,* 1733. (*LM* Oct)
2°: A² B²; *1–2* 3–8.
'With what amusement shall we crown the day'
> On the dispute between players and patentees at Drury Lane.

CtY,DLC.

T127 Theatric. The theatric squabble: or, the p---n-tees. A satire. *London, printed for E. Nutt, & A. Dodd,* 1733. (*GSJ* 2 July)
2°: A² B²; *1–3* 4–8.
'Of mighty deeds, by doughty heroes done'
> On the dispute between the players and patentees at Drury Lane. Cf. *The theatre turned upside down,* 1733.

LSC,*MR*; CSmH,CtY,DFo.

T128 Theatrical. The theatrical volunteer; or, impartial bard. A poetical essay, occasioned by part of the laureat's apology... Part the first. Humbly inscrib'd to...John Spencer, esq; By J. Altior, esq; some time governor of the province of Histrionesia. *London, printed for T. Taylor; sold by the booksellers of London & Westminster,* 1741.
2°: A² B–G²; *1–7* 8–27 *28 blk.* 27 err.
'Thy volume, Cibber, Iv'e [!] perus'd with care'
> On Cibber's *Apology,* 1740; the author is clearly pseudonymous.

L(1347.m.18).

Theobald, John. Poems on several occasions. *London, printed for John Morphew,* 1719.
8°: pp. 117.   CtY,MH.

— Miscellaneous poems and translations. *London printed, and sold by J. Roberts,* 1724.
8°: pp. 118.   CLU-C.

— Joannis Theobald, novo ineunte anno, musa gratulatoria. *Londini, anno domini* 1747.
4°.   L.
> A collection of congratulatory poems to various persons, one to a page. The copy seen has a letter of presentation to Sir Hans Sloane.

— Joannis Theobald, medicinæ doctoris, musa panegyrica. *Londini, impensis authoris,* 1753.
8°: pp. 80.   L.
> A similar collection of congratulatory poems, some in English; there was another edition in 1756 (copy at L).

T129 — Albion, a poem. *Oxford, printed in the year* 1720 [1721]. (*DJ* 22 March)
8°: A⁴(−A3, 4 + 'A2'.1) B–G⁴; [*2 blk*] *1–9* 10–51 *52*; 53–54 *blk.*
> All copies are watermarked with Strasburg bend, but ordinary paper copies are apparently on crown paper, approximately 7½ × 5 in. when cut. A1 blank normally vanishes with the

Theobald, J. Albion

cancellation of A3, 4; the stub of title A2 normally follows the revised dedication to Lord Kinsale on 'A2'.1. Engraving of the Clarendon building on title. The copy at CSmH apparently has variant sheets C and D. 'Phoebe pater, tremulis qui primus carmina nervis' 'Phoebus! great sire! from whom harmonious sprung' Dedication signed. CT(−A1); CSmH(−A1, G4),CtY(−A1),ICU (−A1).

T130 — [fine paper] Copies advertised in *DJ* 22 March 1721 as 'on superfine imperial paper', approximately 9 × 5½ in. when cut. The copy at MH has sheet A in the original uncancelled state. L(C.27.f.10, dedication copy to Lord Kinsale, −A1),O(−A1, G4); MH(A⁴ uncancelled).

T131 — A new translation of the first ode of Horace, agreeably to its original pointing, now first restored. With remarks. *London, printed by B. Milles,* [1739/46.] 4°: D–E⁴; *i–iii* iv, 5–16. The collation suggests that this is not an independent work; possibly it should continue *Part of the fourth book* below. The date is suggested by the dedication to George Ogle, who died in 1746. 'Mæcenas! sprung from royal blood!' Dedication signed. O; *MnU.*

T132 — Part of the fourth book of Milton's Paradise lost. Translated into Latin verse. *London, printed by B. Milles,* [1739/46.] 4°: *A⁴* B–C⁴; *1–2 3–24.* Engraving on title. Latin and English texts. Dates established from the dedicatees, John Huxham and Clement Kent. Possibly intended to be issued with *A new translation* above. 'Humanæ gentis fundebat talia pulchra' Dedicatory poems signed. L(11623.g.6).

T133 — 'A poem sacred to the king. [*London*] *Printed for Jacob Robinson.* Price 1s.' (*DA* 8 May 1744)

T134 — The second book of Virgil's Æneid. In four cantos, with notes. [*London*] *Printed by J. Hughs, for the author,* [1736.] 4°: (frt+) π¹ a⁴ B–K⁴ M² (+4 plates); [2] *i* ii–viii, *1 2–84.* Watermark: ? FM. Title in red and black. Unsigned engraved headpieces to each canto in copies seen. The plate to each canto bears an individual dedication. L(P&D) has what appears to be a part of G1 with a headpiece engraved by Gravelot, but the setting of type is different. Probably this is taken from a later prospectus for the complete *Aeneid.* Ackers's ledger under 22 Oct 1737 charges to Theobald '2 sheets of his translation...4to

Theobald, J. The second book

no. 600 coarse and 400 fine...4 sheets of ditto in folio, no. 200...250 receipts'. This would seem to refer to a prospectus. 'Attentive all in solemn silence wait' Dedication signed. L(11656.r.7/1; 833.l.3, ms. date 1736),O(lacks a4); *CtY,ICU,NcU.*

T135 — [fine paper] Watermark Φ with corner countermark of CMT. Probably the 'large imperial paper' referred to in the prospectus mentioned below; cut copies are over 12 × 9 in. a4, missing from two copies, bore the preface, perhaps suppressed when further books were planned. L(11630.g.19/9),O,OW(lacks a4); MH(lacks a4), NjP(−frt, plates).

T136 — The fourth book of Virgil's Æneid. In four cantos, with notes. [*London*] *Printed by T. Aris, for the author,* [1739.] 4°: *A¹* B–L⁴; *i–ii, 1 2–80.* All copies seen are watermarked with Strasburg bend, possibly used on both sizes of paper referred to in the prospectus; fine-paper copies have not been identified. Engraved ornaments by Gravelot dated 10 May 1739, 'publish'd by J. Theobald'. Title in red and black. A prospectus of 2 Nov 1739 (copy at O) offers books 2 & 4 at 8s. 6d., delivered in blue covers, and books 1 & 3 at the same price by 2 March 1740; thereafter a book would be published every three months at 4s. 3d. Copies on large imperial paper cost 6s. 3d. per book. Apparently no more were published. 'But now the queen, long seized with fest'ring pains' Theobald's name appears only on the engravings. O(uncut); *CtY,ICN.*

T137 Theobald, Lewis. The cave of poverty, a poem. In imitation of Shakespeare. *London, printed for Jonas Browne; sold by J. Roberts,* [1715.] (*MC* March) 8°: *A⁴* B–G⁴ (D2 as 'C2'); *i–viii, 1 2–48.* A1 hft. Title in red and black. 'In barren soil, and damp unwholsome air' L(11764.cc.19,−A1),O,C,DA(−A1),LdU-B+; CSmH,CtY,DFo,IU,TxU+.

T138 — [variant title with date] 1715. L(1962,−A1); CSmH,CtY(−A1),ICN,*MH,* TxU(2, 1−A1)+.

T139 — An epistle humbly addressed to the right honourable John, earl of Orrery. *London, printed for W. Mears,* 1732. (*GSJ* 9 May) 2°: *A² B² C¹; 1–3 4–10.* 10 advt. 'If grief, or dear respect, have made me slow' CSmH,MH.

Theobald, L.

'—' The Martiniad. By Mr. Theobald, 1729. *In* P782.

T140 — The mausoleum. A poem. Sacred to the memory of her late majesty Queen Anne. *London, printed for Jonas Brown; sold by J. Roberts,* 1714. (24 Aug, Luttrell)
2°: *A*² B–G²; *i–iv, 1 2–22 23–24.* G2 advt.
Listed in *MC* Aug.
'Mourn, Albion, mourn; Astræa's now no more'
L(162.n.29, – G2),LDW(– G2),LVA-F(– G2), O(2, 1 uncut),LdU-B; CSmH,CtY,DFo,ICN (Luttrell, – G2),MH(uncut).

T141 — — The second edition. *London, printed for Jonas Brown; sold by J. Roberts,* 1714.
2°: [*A*² B–G²; *i–iv, 1 2–22 23–24.* G2 advt.]
No copy seen, but clearly another issue like the following.
(*Dobell* 3061.)

T142 — — The third edition. *London, printed for Jonas Brown; sold by J. Roberts,* 1714.
2°: *A*² B–G²; *i–iv, 1 2–22 23–24.* G2 advt.
Clearly from the same setting of type, and probably a reimpression or a press-variant title.
IU.

T143 — — *Dublin: re-printed by E. Sandys, for George Grierson,* 1714.
12°: A–B⁶ (A2 as 'A3'); *i–iv, 1–20.*
L(1958).

T144 — Naufragium britannicum. A panegyrical poem, dedicated to the memory of Sr Cloudesly Shovel, kt. *London, printed for Tho. Chapman,* 1707.
4°: A–C⁴; *i–viii, 1–16.* A1 hft.
''Twas at the dawn, when dreams are sacred held'
CtY,ICN.

T145 — The Odyssey of Homer. Book I. Translated from the Greek; with notes. By Mr. Theobald. *London, printed for J. Roberts,* 1717 [1716]. (*PM* 20 Nov)
12°: A(3 ll) B¹² C(3 ll) (A2 as 'B2'); *i–ii iii–vi, 1 2–30.*
Possibly the leaves of A and C are conjugate and wrapped around B¹². Apparently the 'Theobalds Homer Odysses a sheet & ½' entered to Lintot in Bowyer's ledgers under 20 Jan 1716, 500 copies printed. The discrepancy in the dates has not been explained. See *Nichols* VIII. 302 for articles of 21 April 1714 between Theobald and Lintot for translating the Odyssey into blank verse at £2. 10s. for 250 Greek verses; the original is at L (Add. MS 38729, fol. 235).
'Muse, sing the man, for various wiles renown'd'
NcD.

T146 — A pindarick ode on the union. *London, printed for T.C.; sold by J. Morphew,* 1707. (17 May, Luttrell)
2°: *A*² B–C²; *i–iv, 1–8.*

Theobald, L. A pindarick ode

Watermark: crown.
'Haste, Polyhymnia, haste; thy shell prepare'
O,LdU-B,MC(ms. date 17 May); CLU-C(Luttrell),CtY,TxU.

T147 — [fine paper?]
Watermark: fool's cap.
L(1490.f.13),C(uncut); ICN.

'**Theophilus Philanthropos**, *student in physick.*' The Christian muse, 1740. *See* Poole, Robert.

'**Theophylus Phylanglus.**' The church of England's new hymn, 1710. *See* H466.

'**Theosebes.**' Ode on the incarnation, 1744. *See* O48.

T148 There. There's but one plague in England. D——M——. [*London*] *Printed by A. Hinde,* [1711.] (*SR* 12 July)
½°: 1 side, 1 column.
Teerink 845. Deposit copy at L.
'People may make reflections on a whore'
Ball 113 suggested Swift's possible authorship; Williams rightly ignores the attribution. A tory poem, against marriage; possibly directed against the Duchess of Marlborough.
L(C.20.f.2/231).

T149 They. They are all mad and bewitch'd: or, the devil to do at Westminster, and at St. James's. *London, printed for Hugh Montgomery near Ludgate,* 1712.
½°: 1 side, 2 columns.
Prose introduction below title.
'Yes, cries John Calvin's Boanerges'
Harding.

T150 — They are not. *London, printed for J. Roberts,* 1740. (Nov?)
2°: *A*² B²; *1–2 3–8.*
'Of all the torments, cares and plagues that wait'
A reply to [Robert Morris] *Yes, they are,* 1740, occasioned by [James Miller] *Are these things so?,* 1740. Answered by [Robert Morris] *Have at you all,* 1740; this author then wrote *Come on then,* 1740.
O; MH,OCU(uncut).

T151 — — The second edition. *London, printed for T. Cooper,* 1740.
2°: *A*² B²; *1–2 3–8.*
O; IU.

T152 — — The third edition. *London, printed for T. Cooper,* 1740 [1741?]. (*DP* 23 Jan)
2°: *A*² B²; *1–2 3–8.*
CSmH.

T153 — — '*London, printed for the perusal of all lovers of their country*', 1740.
8°: *A*⁴ B⁴; *1–4 5–16.* A1 hft.
Horizontal chain-lines. A piracy, probably

They are not

from the north; cf. James Miller, *Are these things so?* (M239).
CtY,MH.

Thief. The thief slain, [175–?] *See* Jacob, Giles (J26).

Thimble. The thimble, 1743–. *See* Hawkins, William.

Third. The third ode, of the third book of Horace, imitated, 1740. *See* Carthy, Charles.

— The third part of the Humours, &c. or, the satyrist, 1737. *See* Wilkes, Wetenhall.

— A third riddle, 1725–6. *See* Delany, Patrick.

T154 [Thirkeld, Taylor.] ⟨A Sunday evening's conversation at Benwell, or a pastoral between Corydon and Thyrsis; occasion'd by a book lately published, intituled, A Sunday's trip to Benwell. By a lover of the clergy.⟩ ⟨*Newcastle upon Tyne, printed and sold by J. White*, 1726.⟩
2°: A^2 B^2 C^1; *i–ii* iii–x.
>The copy seen lacks the title A1; it is here supplied from the reprint in Robert Robinson's *Collectanea curiosa*, 1892.

'This evening, Thyrsis, with it's sultry heat'
>Ms. note in the L copy 'Written by the Revd. Mr. Thirkeld, curate of Whickham...in opposition to Ellison's Trip to Benwell, which was thought to be a work of too much levity...' Robinson's tentative ascription to Edward Chicken is clearly erroneous.

L(G.19071, lacks A1).

T155 Thirteenth. The thirteenth satyre of Juvenal imitated. *London, printed for, and sold by Charles Bathurst*, 1745. (18 June?)
2°: π^2 A–D^2; *1–5* 6–20. π1 hft; 20 err slip.
>Listed in *GM* July.

'Is there on earth a torment can exceed'
L(1962, Tom's Coffee House, 1⟨8⟩ June); DFo, MH,OCU(−π1).

T156 This. This is to give notice to all gentlemen, ladies and others, that there is to be seen at the roiting [!] house of the late famous Don Parabocka; a new and diverting puppet shew, call'd the Burlesque upon magistracy; or, Punch out of humour... *London, printed: and Dublin: re-printed in the year* 1736.
8°: A^4; *1* 2–8.
>Probably there was no London edition.

'By all the gods, I'll fret my guts'
>A political satire.

DA.

T157 Thomas. Thomas redivivus: or, a compleat history of the life and marvellous actions of Tom Thumb. In three tomes. Interspers'd with that

Thomas redivivus

ingenious comment of the late Dr. Wagstaff... *London, printed for R. Walker*, 1729.
2°: A^2 B–G^2; *1–2* 3–28.
>*Teerink* 947.

'In Arthur's court Tom Thumb did live, a man of mickle might'
ICN,PU(uncut).

[Thomas, Elizabeth.] Miscellany poems on several subjects. *London, printed for Tho. Combes*, 1722. (*DC* 5 Feb)
8°: pp. 295.   L,O; CLU-C,DFo.

[—] [reissue] Poems on several occasions, by a lady. *London, printed for T. Combes*, 1726.
    L,LVA-D.
Cancel title.

[—] [reissue] Poems on several occasions... Written by a lady... The second edition. *London, printed for Tho. Astley*, 1727 [1726]. (*MC* Nov)
    LVA-D,O; CtY,DFo.
Cancel title.

———

T158 [—] The metamorphosis of the town: or, a view of the present fashions. A tale: after the manner of Fontaine. *London, printed for J. Wilford*, 1730. (*MChr* June)
8°: A^2 B–D^4 E^2; *i–iv, 1* 2–28. A1 hft.
'A knight long absent from the town'
>Subsequently reprinted with Mrs. Thomas's name.

O,LdU-B,MP(−A1); CSmH,CU,IU(−A1), MH(2),TxU(2, 1 uncut)+.

T159 [—] — The second edition. To which is added, the Journal of a modern lady... By Dr. Swift. *London, printed for J. Wilford*, 1730. (*MChr* Nov)
8°: A–E^4; *1–3* 4–40.
L(11631.e.37; 994.c.44),LG,O,C,LdU-B+; CLU-C,CtY,*DLC*,ICN.

T160 [—] The metamorphoses of the town... The third edition... To which is added, the Journal of a modern lady. By Dean Swift. *London, printed for J. Wilford*, 1731. (*MChr* July)
8°: A–E^4; *1–3* 4–40.
>There are two very similar editions, one of which is possibly some years later; their order has not been determined. This has signature B under r of 'another' and signature E under e of 'cheap'.

L(T.1056/14),O(lacks A1),BaP,SrS; CLU-C, *CtY*,MH,TxU.

T161 [—] [another edition]
>Signature B under c of 'Scene'; signature E under p of 'cheap'.

O,DN; ICU.

T162 [—] — *Dublin, printed by James Hoey*, 1732.
8°: A–C^4; *1–2* 3–24.
DN(uncut),LdU-B; CSmH.

Thomas, E. The metamorphoses

T163 —— To which are added, I. The female meta-morphosis... II. The journal of a modern lady. III. The furniture of a woman's mind. IV. An inventory of a lady's dressing-room. The fourth edition. *London, printed for J. Wilford*, 1743. (*GM, LM* Jan)

8°: A–H⁴; *1–3* 4–62 *63–64*. A1ᵛ, H4 advt.

'The female metamorphosis' is a reprint of *Tea. A poem*, 1729; the other additions are by Swift.

L(11632.cc.23),O(–H4); IU.

T164 —— To which are added, I. A new touch upon the ladies capuchins. II. The female metamor-phosis... The fifth edition. *London printed, and sold by J. Wilford*, 1744.

8°: π² A⁴(–A1) B–H⁴; [2] *1–3* 4–62 *63–64*. π1ᵛ, H4 advt.

A reissue with cancel title π1 and introduction π2. 'A new touch upon the ladies capuchins' was included in the preceding but not listed; it is a short poem on p. 24.

IU,MiU.

Thompson, Isaac. A collection of poems, occa-sionally writ on several subjects. *Newcastle upon Tyne, printed by John White, for the author; sold by the booksellers*, 1731.

8°: pp. xiv, 176.   L,O; CtY,ICN.

T165 [——] Poetic essays, on nature, men, and morals. Essay I. To Dr Askew, of Newcastle. *Printed for R. Akenhead, jun. in Newcastle upon Tyne, and C. Hitch, in London*, 1750. (*GM, LM* April)

4°: π² a² A–G²; *i–viii*, *1* 2–28. π1 hft.

Engraving on title.

'While you with lenient hand, around impart'

Early ms. ascription to Thompson recorded in Murray Hill cat. 30 (1949) 705; he was a close friend of Askew.

L(11630.d.13/2; 11630.d.7/1,–π1; 840.k.4/23, –π1),O,LdU-B,*NeP*; CSmH,CtY,MH(–π1), NjP,OCU.

T166 [**Thompson, William,** *fellow of Trinity College, Dublin.*] Mendico-hymen: seu tuphlo-pero-gamia. *Dublinii, typis A. Rhames, impensis Jer. Pepyat*, 1709.

8°: A–B⁴; *1–3* 4–16.

'Dic mihi mitis Hymen, cui sunt connubia curæ'

Ms. attribution to Thompson in a DN copy of the following edition. Translated into English by a Mr. Fitzgerald under the same title, 1723.

L(C.136.aa.1/17, lacks A1); IU.

T167 [——] *Dublinii, typis Georgii Faulkner, impensis ejusdem, & prostant venales in vico dicto Essex-street*, 1730.

8°: A⁴ B⁴; *1–3* 4–15 '15'.

L(11631.a.34/1),O,C,DA(2),DN(2)+.

Thompson, W., *fellow of T.C.D.*

T168 — A poetical paraphrase on part of the book of Job: in imitation of the style of Milton. *Dublin, printed by and for J. Hyde*, 1726.

2°: A² B–F²; *i–viii*, *1*–15 *16*. 16 err.

Watermark: Dutch lion.

'Job silent stood, when from a thick'ning cloud' Dedication signed.

O,C(uncut),DA; TxU.

T169 — [fine paper]

Watermark: fleur-de-lys on shield.

MH.

T170 —— *London, printed for Tho. Worrall*, 1726. (*MC* May)

4°: π² A–E² F¹; *i–viii*, *1* 2–18.

L(643.k.3/2; 11630.e.5/2, cropt),O,OC,OW, LdU-B; CSmH,CtY,NN(cropt).

Thompson, William, *M.A. of Queen's College, Oxford.* Poems on several occasions, to which is added Gondibert and Birtha, a tragedy. *Oxford, printed at the theatre*, 1757.

8°: pp. 444.   O; MH.

Errata and errata slip in copy at O.

T171 — An hymn to May. *London printed, and sold by R. Dodsley, T. Waller, & M. Cooper*, [1746.] (28 April?)

4°: π¹ A⁴ B–D⁴ E¹; [2] *i–iii* iv–v *vi*, *7* 8–33 *34 blk*. π1 and E1 have been seen to be conjugate. Publication date from *Straus, Dodsley*; listed in *GM,LM* June.

'Ethereal daughter of the lusty spring'

L(11630.e.5/5,–π1),O(2, *1*–π1),OW,CT(–π1), LdU-B; CtY(–π1),DFo,ICN(–π1),NjP,TxU (–π1)+.

T172 — Ode brumalis: ad amicum oxoniensem. A Gulielmo Thompson, A.M. e Coll. Reg. Oxon. *Londini, apud T. Waller*, 1747. (*GM, LM* March)

4°: π¹ A⁴ B¹; *i–ii*, *1*–2 3–8 *9*; *10 blk*. π1 hft.

π1 and B1 have been seen to be conjugate; the latter bears 'Allusions'.

'Eheu! sereni mollia tempora'

Translated into English by John Tattersal as *Winter, an ode: to a friend at Oxford*, 1747.

O(2, *1*–π1, lacks B1),OW.

T173 — Sickness. A poem. In three books. Book I. *London, printed for R. Dodsley; sold by M. Cooper*, 1745. (*SR* 26 Feb)

4°: A⁴ B–G⁴; *i–iv* v–viii, *1*–47 *48 blk*. A1 hft; viii err.

Publication dated as 27 Feb by *Straus, Dodsley;* listed in GM,LM March. Deposit copies at L,E,EU,AdU,GU.

'Of days with pain acquainted, and of nights'

L(11630.e.5/3; 644.k.16/3),O,C(–A1),E, LdU-B+; CSmH,DLC,ICN,KU,TxU(uncut)+.

T174 — Sickness. A poem. Book the second. *London, printed for R. Dodsley; sold by M. Cooper*, 1745. (12 April)

Thompson, W., *M.A.* Sickness, bk. 2

4º: H–O⁴; *49–50* 51–104.
Publication date from *Straus, Dodsley*; listed in *GM,LM* April. Entered in *SR* 24 April; deposit copies at L,E,EU,AdU,GU.
'The fair, the bright, the great, alas! are fall'n'
L(11630.e.5/3; 644.k.16/3),O,C,E,LdU-B+; DLC,ICN,KU,TxU(uncut).

T175 — Sickness. A poem. Book the third and last. *London, printed for R. Dodsley; sold by M. Cooper,* 1746. (14 Feb)
4º: P–X⁴; *105–106* 107–159 *160 blk.*
Publication date from *Straus, Dodsley*; listed in *GM,LM* Feb. Entered in *SR* 14 Feb; deposit copies at L,E,EU,AdU,GU.
'Swift too, thy tale is told: a sound, a name'
L(644.k.16/3),O,C,E,LdU-B+; ICN,TxU(uncut).

T176 [**Thompson, William,** *schoolmaster of Nottingham.*] Some fruits of solitude: in reflections and maxims relating to the conduct of humane life. Done into verse, by W.T. *London printed, and sold by T. Sowle,* 1705.
8º: A–G⁸ (A3 as 'B3'); *1–4* 5–111 *112 blk.*
In some copies (e.g. LF,MH), G3 is signed 'F3'.
''Tis strange to think what multitudes of men'
Attributed to Thompson in *Smith* II. 740. A verse adaptation of William Penn's *Fruits of solitude.*
LF(3); CtY,MH,*PHC.*

Thomson, James. The works of Mr. Thomson. Volume the second. Containing, Liberty, a poem, in five parts: Sophonisba, a tragedy. *London, printed for A. Millar,* 1736.
4º.   L,O; MH,NN-B.
A reissue of the fine-paper copies of *Liberty,* with a new edition of *Sophonisba.* The place of the first volume is taken by the quarto edition of *The seasons,* 1730. The date is obscure; *DA* 11 Feb 1736 announced the publication of *Sophonisba* to complete the volume 'in a few days', but the whole was only listed in *GM, LM* Jan 1738. *A poem to...Lord Talbot,* 1737, is found in some copies.

— The works of Mr. Thomson. In two volumes. *London, printed for A. Millar,* 1738. (*SR* 24 June)
8º: 2 vol.   L,O; MH,NNC.
Deposit copy at O. Volume 1 contains a reissue of the play *Sophonisba,* 1730, in octavo; in a copy at L this is the quarto issue cut down to size. Volume 2 usually contains a reissue of *Agammemnon,* 1738; in some copies (e.g. CtY) *Edward and Eleonora,* 1739, is added; in what are probably later copies still, issued in 1744 and 1749 (e.g. O), the plays are reprinted to provide continuous signatures throughout.

Thomson, J.

— The works of Mr. Thomson... Vol. I. With additions and corrections. *London, printed for A. Millar,* 1744.
8º: pp. 323+79.   L,O; NNC,PSC.
Issued with volume 2 of 1738.

— The works of Mr. Thomson. Vol. III. *London, printed for A. Millar,* 1749.
8º.   O; MH,NNC.
A nonce collection.

— The works of James Thomson. In four volumes ... *London, printed for A. Millar,* 1750. (*GM* Feb)
12º: 4 vol.   L,O; CtY,MH.
In some copies, volume 1 is a reissue of *The seasons,* 1746; others have a 1752 edition with a preface dated 1 Oct 1751. 'Thomson's Works vols 2d, 3d and 4th. 34 sheets no. 2000' were entered in Strahan's ledger to Millar, Sept 1749. The *Works* were not entered in *SR* until 12 Oct 1751; the deposit copies at L, O have both sets of preliminaries and the 1752 text of vol. 1.

— Poems on several occasions. *London, printed for A. Millar,* 1750.
8º: pp. 24.   L,O; NNC,PSC.
Entered in Strahan's ledger to Millar under May 1750 as 'Thomson's additional poems, 3 half sheets no. 750'. Some copies were issued with *The works* III, 1749.

———

— Antient and modern Italy compared, 1735. *See* T186.

— Autumn, a poem, 1730. *See* T233.

— Britain: being the fourth part of Liberty, 1736. *See* T196.

T177 [—] Britannia. A poem. *London, printed for T. Warner,* 1729. (*MChr* 21 Jan)
2º: *A*¹ B–D² E¹; *1–2* 3–16.
Rothschild 2422. A1 and E1 have been seen to be conjugate. Printed by Samuel Richardson (*Sale* 81).
'As on the sea-beat shore Britannia sat'
L(1347.m.56),O,E,BaP,LdU-B+; CtY(2),ICN, MH,PSC,TxU(uncut)+.

T178 —— By Mr. James Thomson... *Dublin, printed for George Faulkner & James Hoey,* 1729.
8º: A⁸; *1–3* 4–15 *16 blk.*
C,DN,DT(2); NNC.

T179 [—] — The second edition corrected. *London, printed for John Millan,* 1730.
4º: A–B⁴; *1–2* 3–16.
This edition was apparently published to add to the quarto edition of *The seasons,* 1730; it was so listed at the end of the third edition of *Summer,* 1730. All copies seen are bound thus.
L(1480.d.2; 641.l.13),O,CT,E,GU+; MH,MiU, NN-B,NNC,PSC+.

Thomson, J. Britannia

T180 [—] — The third edition. *London, printed by N. Blandford, for J. Millan*, 1730.
8°: A⁸ B²; *1–3* 4–19 20. 20 advt.
> Apparently the same setting of type as the preceding, reprinted to add to *Winter*, 1730, in octavo collections of *The seasons*, 1730; all copies seen are so bound. Also reprinted without title-page and with collation A–B⁴ C² to be bound with the octavo edition of *The seasons*, 1730 (T240).

L(1465.f.37; 1486.b.29; 992.h.7/13),O(3),C, EU,DT; CtY,IU,PSC.

T181 — The castle of indolence: an allegorical poem. Written in imitation of Spenser. *London, printed for A. Millar*, 1748. (*SR* 6 May)
4°: A¹ B⁴(±B1) C–L⁴ M(2 ll); *i–ii, 1* 2–81 *82–84*.
> R. W. Chapman in *RES* 3. 456 reported that title A1 and M2 (which bears an 'Advertisement') were conjugate, as were cancel B1 and M1. A1 and M2 have certainly been seen to be conjugate in some copies (e.g. at OW,CtY, TxU), and so may B1 and M1 have been; but in a number of copies the watermarks are only consistent with binders having divided the sheets and assembled the leaves at random. See also W. B. Todd in *Book collector* 1 (1952) 192. Deposit copies at L,E,EU,AdU,GU. Advertised in *GA* 7 May.

'O mortal man, who livest here by toil'
L(644.k.16/4),LVA-D(2),O,E(2),LdU-B+; CSmH,CtY,ICN,MH,TxU(2)+.

T182 — — By James Thompson. The second edition. *London, printed for A. Millar*, 1748. (*GA* 21 Sept, 'to-morrow')
8°: A⁴(−A4) B–F⁸ G¹[=A4]; *i–iii* iv–v *vi, 1* 2–81 *82 blk* (75 as '77').
> Apparently an incorrect state of sheet A with Thomson's name mis-spelt on title and p. 82 blank.

L(11633.c.44; 161.m.51),LVA-D,C,CT,E(2); CLU,CtY,PSC.

T183 — [variant:] By James Thomson. The second edition.
> Apparently the corrected state of sheet A, with Thomson's name correctly spelt on title and advertisements on p. 82.

O(lacks A2.3),C,*MR*; CLU-C,NNC,PSC.

T184 — — 'London', printed in the year 1748.
8°: π¹[=C1] A–B⁸ C⁸(−C1); *i–ii, 1–5* 6–45 *46 blk*. π1 hft.
> A Scottish piracy; all copies seen are in pamphlet volumes of Edinburgh and Glasgow editions.

L(1346.d.32/3,−π1); ICU,MiU(−π1).

T185 — — Dublin, printed for George & Alexander Ewing, & Richard James, 1748.
8°: π¹ A⁸(A1+χ¹) B–C⁸ D⁸(−D8); [6] *5* 6–60 61–63; *64 blk*. π1 hft; D6–7 advt.

Thomson, J. The castle of indolence

χ1, usually found after title A1, contains the 'Advertisement' and glossary.
L(1961,−χ1),C(2, *1*−π1, D6–7, *1*−π1,χ1),DA, DN(2); CtY.

— Greece: being the second part of Liberty, 1735. *See* T191.

Liberty, a poem

T186 — Antient and modern Italy compared: being the first part of Liberty, a poem. *London, printed for A. Millar*, 1735. (*SR* 11 Jan)
4°: A² B–K²; *i–v* vi–vii *viii, 9* 10–37 *38–39; 40 blk*. A1 hft; K2 advt.
> No watermark. *Rothschild* 2425. 'Price one shilling' on title. The half-title has the general title 'Liberty. A poem.' Entered in Woodfall's ledger under 8 Jan 1735; 3000 copies and 250 fine. Entered in *SR* 11 Jan 1735; deposit copies (fine-paper) at O,E,EU,SaU. The register under 9 Jan transcribes Thomson's agreement with Millar assigning the whole of *Liberty* to him for £250. Advertised in *DA* 7 Jan 1735 for 'Friday next [10 Jan]' and in *DA* 10 Jan for 'Monday next [13 Jan]'.

'O my lamented Talbot! while with thee'
L(11602.gg.24/4,−A1; 840.k.3/5,−A1; Ashley 4561),O(2, *1* uncut),C(−A1),E,DT+; ICU,MH, PSC(uncut),TxU(2).

T187 — [fine paper]
> Watermark: MT, with corner countermark CMT (cf. *Heawood* 3089).

O(−A1, K2),E,EU,LdU-B('Ex dono authoris perquam amicissimi, J. Thomson Alexandro Pope', −K2),SaU; CSmH,NNC.

T188 — [reissue] *London, printed for A. Millar*, 1735 [1736].
4°: A²(±A2) B–K²; *i–v* vi–vii *viii, 9* 10–37 *38–39; 40 blk*. A1 hft; K2 advt.
> Fine-paper copies with cancel title, removing price from title and adding contents on the verso. Woodfall's ledger records printing 100 of these titles under 29 Jan 1736. Copies of this issue are usually found in Thomson's *Works* II, 1736, but not all those are recorded here.

O; ICN,MH,PSC(−A1, K2).

T189 — — Edinburgh, re-printed by W. Cheyne, 1735.
8°: A⁴ B–C⁴; *i–ii* iii–iv, 5–24.
> Douglas Grant, *James Thomson* (1951) 147 quotes the *Daily Post-boy* 24 Feb 173[5], 'We are assured from Edinburgh that by the care and diligence of the worthy magistrates of that city, a pirated edition of Mr. Thompson's *Liberty* has been seized there, and the offender committed to jail'. It is interesting to note that an Edinburgh piracy of *Autumn*, 1730, was possibly suppressed; that an Edinburgh piracy of Pope's *An epistle...to Dr. Arbuthnot*, 1734 [1735], advertises 'Speedily will be published, beautifully printed, on a

Thomson, J. Liberty, pt. 1

fine paper, Liberty: a poem. By our country-
man Mr. James Thomson... To be sold by
A. Millar and Allan Ramsay, at their shops
in London and Edinburgh'; and if this is a
piracy, it is unique of its class in giving away
both its Edinburgh origin and its printer.
E,EU; CtY-M.

T190 — — *Dublin, printed by S. Powell, for J. Leathley,
A. Bradley, & T. Moore, 1735.*
8⁰: A–C⁴ D²; *i–iii* iv–vi, *7* 8–27 *28 blk.*
DN.

T191 — Greece: being the second part of Liberty, a
poem. *London, printed for A. Millar, 1735.* (*SR*
6 Feb)
4⁰: π¹ *A*² B–E⁴ F¹; [6] *9* 10–42. π1 hft.
Watermark: H; 'Price one shilling' on the
title. Half-title 'Liberty. A poem.' π1 and F1
have been seen to be conjugate. Entered in
Woodfall's ledger under 1 Feb, 2000 copies
and 250 fine. Deposit copies (fine-paper) at
O,E,EU,SaU. Listed in *GM* Feb; A. D.
McKillop in *MLQ* 11 (1950) 307–16 gives the
publication date as 7 Feb, perhaps from *DA*.
'Thus spoke the goddess of the fearless eye'
L(840.k.3/5,−π1; Ashley 4561),O(2, 1 uncut),
OW,C,E+; ICU,MH,PSC(−π1),TxU(2).

T192 — [fine paper]
Watermark: MT, with corner countermark
CMT; no price on title. Also found in
Thomson's *Works* II, 1736.
O(−π1),E,EU,LdU-B(−π1),SaU; CSmH(uncut),
ICN,NNC(−π1),PSC(−π1).

T193 — — *Dublin, printed by S. Powell, for J. Leathley,
A. Bradley, & T. Moore, 1735.*
8⁰: *A*⁴ B–D⁴; *1–5* 6–31 *32 blk.*
DN.

T194 — Rome: being the third part of Liberty, a poem.
London, printed for A. Millar, 1735. (*SR* 23 March)
4⁰: *A*² B–F⁴; [4] *9* 10–48. A1 hft.
Watermark: H; 'Price one shilling' on title.
Half-title 'Liberty. A poem.' Entered in
Woodfall's ledger under 12 March, 2000
copies and 250 fine. Deposit copies (fine-
paper) at O,E,EU,SaU. Listed in *LM* March;
McKillop gives the date of publication as
24 March, perhaps from *DA*.
'Here melting mix'd with air th' ideal forms'
L(840.k.3/5,−A1; Ashley 4561),O(2, 1 uncut),
OW,C,E+; ICU(−A1),MH,PSC(−A1),TxU(2).

T195 — [fine paper]
Watermark: MT, with corner countermark
CMT; no price on title. Also found in
Thomson's *Works* II, 1736.
O(−A1),E,EU,LdU-B(−A1),SaU; CSmH,ICN,
NNC(−A1),PSC(−A1).

T196 — Britain: being the fourth part of Liberty, a
poem. *London, printed for A. Millar, 1736.* (*SR*
15 Jan)
4⁰: *A*² B–H⁴ I²; *1–5* 6–63 *64.* A1 hft; 64 advt.

Thomson, J. Liberty, pt. 4

Watermark: H; 'Price one shilling and six-
pence' on title. Half-title 'Liberty. A poem.'
Entered in Woodfall's ledger under 13 Jan,
1000 copies and 250 fine. Listed in *GM,LM*
Jan. Deposit copies (fine-paper) at O,E,
EU,SaU.
'Struck with the rising scene, thus I amaz'd'
L(840.k.3/5,−A1; Ashley 4561),O,OW,C,SaU
+; ICU,MH,PSC,TxU.

T197 — [fine paper]
Watermark: MT, with corner countermark
CMT; no price on title. Also found in Thom-
son's *Works* II, 1736.
O(−A1),E,EU,LdU-B(−A1),SaU; CSmH,ICN,
NNC(−A1),PSC(−A1).

T198 — The prospect: being the fifth part of Liberty.
A poem. *London, printed for A. Millar, 1736.* (*SR*
10 Feb)
4⁰: *A*² B–E⁴ F²; *1–5* 6–38 *39–40.* A1 hft; F2 advt.
Watermark: H; 'Price one shilling' on title.
Half-title 'Liberty. A poem.' Entered in
Woodfall's ledger under 29 Jan, 1000 copies
and 250 fine. Listed in *GM,LM* Feb. Deposit
copies (fine-paper) at O,E,EU,SaU.
'Here interposing, as the goddess paus'd, − '
L(840.k.3/5,−A1; Ashley 4561),O,OW,C,SaU+;
ICU,MH(2),PSC,TxU.

T199 — [fine paper]
Watermark: MT, with corner countermark
CMT; cancel title A2 with no price. Also
found in Thomson's *Works* II, 1736.
O(−A1),E,EU,LdU-B(−A1),SaU; CSmH,ICN
(−A1, F2),NNC,(−A1),PSC(−A1, F2).

— 'Liberty, a poem, 1738.'
So listed by *CBEL*, probably referring to the
revised text printed in Thomson's *Works*,
1738.

_____

T200 — A poem sacred to the memory of Sir Iasac
Newton. *London, printed for J. Millan, and sold
at his shop, 1727.* (*SR* 8 May)
2⁰: A–D²; *1–5* 6–15 *16 blk.*
Watermark: circular snake (cf. *Heawood*
3786–92). *Rothschild* 2420. Entered in *SR* to
Millan by James Roberts; deposit copies at
L,O,EU. Listed in *MC* May. Misprints in
p. 15, lines 5, 11 are corrected in the second
edition; a copy at O with the corrected lines
probably has sheet D from T202.
'Shall the great soul of Newton quit this earth'
Dedication to Sir Robert Walpole.
L(643.m.14/1),O(2, 1 lacks A2),OW(2),EU;
CSmH,CtY,MH,PSC,TxU+.

T201 — [fine paper]
Watermark: Strasburg bend; the margins
have apparently been enlarged.
NjP.

T202 — — The second edition. *London, printed for J.
Millan, and sold at his shop, 1727.* (*LJ* 13 May)

Thomon, J. A poem sacred

2°: A–D²; *1–5* 6–15 *16 blk.*
A reimpression with corrections.
DT; CtY,IU,PSC.

T203 —— The third edition. *London, printed for J. Millan, and sold at his shop, 1727.*
2°: A–D²; *1–5* 6–15 *16 blk.*
Apparently a reimpression or press-variant title.
L(11630.g.33),C; CU,CtY,MH,NNC.

T204 —— The fourth edition. *London, printed for J. Millan, and sold at his shop, 1727.* (*LJ* 8 July, 'just published')
2°: A–D²; *1–5* 6–15 *16 blk.*
Apparently a reimpression or press-variant title. Also listed in *MChr* 25 March 1728.
CtY,NNC.

T205 —— The fifth edition. *London, printed for J. Millan, and sold at his shop, 1727.*
2°: A–D²; *1–5* 6–15 *16 blk.*
Apparently a reimpression or press-variant title. Reprinted with *Winter*, 1730, and also in octavo, without title and collating A–B⁴, for binding with the edition of *The seasons*, 1730, with continuous pagination (T240).
C; CtY,ICN(sheet D from T200).

T206 —— *Dublin, printed by S. Powell, for Richard Norris, 1727.*
8°: A–B⁴; *1–5* 6–15 *16.* 16 advt.
L(11631.aa.44/2),DT.

T207 —— inscrib'd to the right honourable Sir Robert Walpole. *London, printed for Andrew Millar, 1741.*
4°: π¹ *A² B–D²; i–ii, 1–2* 3–15 *16 blk.* π1 hft.
There is no dedication to Walpole in this edition, only the title-page reference to him.
E.

T208 — A poem to the memory of the right honourable the Lord Talbot... *London, printed for A. Millar, 1737.* (*SR* 17 June)
4°: *A² B–D⁴; i–iv, 1–23* 24. A1 hft; 24 advt.
No watermark; 'Price 1s.' on title. *Rothschild* 2426. The half-title is often bound after the title as a fly-title, and this was perhaps intended. Entered in Woodfall's ledger under 16 June, 1000 copies and 156 fine. Entered in *SR* to Thomson by Millar; deposit copies (all of the fine-paper issue) at L,O,E,EU,AdU, GU,SaU. Listed in *GM,LM* June.
'While, with the public, you, my lord, lament'
L(11630.b.8/8,–A1; 840.k.3/6; Ashley 4562), LVA-D,OW,LdU-B(uncut); CSmH,*CtY*,ICN, MH,PSC(3, 1 uncut)+.

T209 — [fine paper]
Watermark: Strasburg bend; no price on title. Advertised as 'on a fine royal paper'. Sometimes (e.g. at MH) bound with Thomson's *Works* II, 1736, as was the intention.
L(643.k.3/15),O,E,GU,SaU+; CSmH(uncut), PSC.

Thomson, J. A poem to the memory

T210 —— 'London, printed for A. Millar' [*Edinburgh*], 1737.
8°: π² A–B⁴; *i–iv, 1–16.* π1 hft.
Printed by Fleming on the evidence of the ornaments.
CT; TxU(uncut).

— The prospect: being the fifth part of Liberty, 1736. *See* T198.

— Rome: being the third part of Liberty, 1735. *See* T194.

The seasons

Winter, Spring, *and* Summer *were each published separately in octavo;* Autumn *was added in the collected quarto edition of 1730, and also published separately in octavo to complete sets. Some of these octavo sets were doubtless assembled and bound by individuals, others by the publisher or booksellers; some of these collections have more recently been broken up by booksellers. A set of four engraved frontispieces was issued for sets in octavo but is not always present. Many of the copies recorded below form part of these collections, and the record of copies is incomplete. The collected editions are listed as T236–46.*

T211 — Winter. A poem. *London, printed for J. Millan; sold by J. Roberts, & N. Blandford, 1726.* (*SR* 29 April)
2°: A–E²; *i–iv, 1* 2–16. ii err.
Entered in *SR* to Millan by James Roberts; deposit copies at L,O,E,SaU. Listed in *MC* April as sold by Roberts.
'See! Winter comes, to rule the varied year'
L(643.m.13/26),LVA-D,O,E,SaU+; CSmH, CtY,MiU,PSC(cropt).

T212 —— The second edition. *London, printed by N. Blandford, for J. Millan, 1726.* (*LJ* 16 July?)
8°: π¹ A–B⁴ C² D–G⁴ H¹; *3–5* 6–19 *20–25* 26–56 *57–58.* H1 advt.
π1 and H1 apparently conjugate. Some copies (LVA-D,CtY,MH) have variant reading on p. 15, 5 lines from foot, 'how gay' for 'How gay'.
LVA-D(–H1),O,C(–H1),E; CtY(2),IU(–H1), MH(–H1),PSC(–H1).

T213 —— The third edition. *London, printed by N. Blandford, for J. Millan, 1726.* (*MC* Sept)
8°: π¹ A–B⁴ C² D–G⁴ H¹; *3–5* 6–19 *20–25* 26–56 *57–58.* H1 advt.
Either a reimpression or a press-variant title.
L(992.1.28,–H1),O(uncut),C(–H1); MH (–H1),PSC(2).

T214 —— The fourth edition. *London, printed by N. Blandford, for J. Millan, 1726.*
8°: π¹ A–B⁴ C² D–G⁴ H¹; *3–5* 6–19 *20–25* 26–56 *57–58.* H1 advt.
Either a reimpression or press-variant title.
L(11630.bbb.42/8,–H1),LVA-D,O(2,–H1), OW(–H1); CtY(–H1),PSC(–H1).

Thomson, J. The seasons. Winter

T215 — — *Dublin: re-printed by Thomas Hume, for William Smith,* 1726.
8°: *A*⁴ B–C⁴ D²; *i–iii* iv–vi, 7 8–27 *28 blk.*
DA,DK; CtY,DLC.

T216 — — The fifth edition. *London, printed for J. Millan,* 1728. (*MChr* 25 March)
8°: *A*¹ B–E⁴ F²; *1–3* 4–38.
A new edition, omitting all preliminaries except dedication, and with textual revisions. The listing in *MChr* is possibly subsequent to publication.
O; CtY(2, 1 stitched, uncut),MH,PSC,TxU.

T217 — Winter, a poem, a hymn on the seasons, a poem to the memory of Sir Isaac Newton, and Britannia, a poem. *London, printed for J. Millan,* 1730. (June?)
8°: A–D⁸ E⁴(–E4), ²A⁸ B²; *1–6* 7–69 *70 blk,* *1–3* 4–19 20. A2 fly-title; ²B2ᵛ advt.
Almost all copies seen form part of *The seasons,* 1730 (T239); the collective title for that volume was probably printed as E4. ²A⁸ B² contain *Britannia... The third edition,* 1730. The frontispiece found in some copies is one of four added to complete sets. Listed as a new edition with additions and corrections after *Autumn* in *MChr* June 1730.
L(992.h.7/13; 1465.f.37; 1486.b.29),O(3),C, EU,DT+; CtY,IU,PSC.

T218 — Winter, a poem. With large additions and amendments... To which is added... A hymn... To the memory of Sir Isaac Newton. And Britannia. *Dublin, printed by S. Powell, for George Risk, George Ewing, & William Smith,* 1730.
8°: A–B⁸ E⁴(–E4); *1–5* 6–70. A2 fly-title.
Published like the London edition to form part of a collected edition with title *Poems. Viz. Spring...,* 1730 (T241); the general title was printed as E4.
L(1489.i.17),O(2),DN; CtY,MH,PSC.

T219 — Winter, a poem; a hymn... a poem to the memory... and Britannia, a poem. *London, printed for J. Millan,* 1734.
8°: A–E⁸; *1–2* 3–79 *80.* 80 advt.
Printed to complete sets; usually found in *The four seasons, and other poems,* 1735 (T242). Printed by Samuel Richardson (*Sale* 150).
L(11630.bbb.13),LVA-D,O,E; CtY,*MH*,*MiU*, NNC,PSC.

T220 — Summer. A poem. *London, printed for J. Millan,* 1727. (*SR* 20 Feb)
8°: A–L⁴; *i–iii* iv–vi *vii–viii,* 9 10–88. viii err.
The errata on A4ᵛ are headed 'N.B.'; in a copy at TxU they are found on A1ᵛ headed 'Errata', and A4 is cancelled. See T. R. Francis in *The book collector* 5 (1956) 383; he suggests that this change represents two issues, but I would consider it merely a state of sheet A. Entered in *SR* to John Millan by James

Thomson, J. The seasons. Summer

Roberts; deposit copies at O,E,EU. Listed in *MC* Feb.
'From southern climes, where unremitting day'
L(1162.h.36),O,C(2, 1–A4),CT(uncut),E+; CSmH,CtY(2),IU,MH,TxU(2, 1–A4)+.

T221 — — *Dublin, printed by S. Powell, for Richard Norris,* 1727.
8°: A–G⁴ H²; *1–7* 8–59 *60 blk.*
L(11631.aa.44/1),DN(2); ICN,*NNC*,TxU.

T222 — — The second edition. *London, printed for J. Millan,* 1728. (*MChr* 25 March)
8°: A⁴(±A1) B–L⁴; *i–iii* iv–vi *vii–viii,* 9 10–88. viii err.
A reissue of T220 with cancel title. The copy seen has a four-leaf catalogue of Thomas Astley's books at end. The listing in *MChr* is possibly subsequent to publication.
CtY(uncut).

T223 — — The third edition with additions. *London, printed by N. Blandford, for J. Millan,* 1730. (June?)
8°: π² A–D⁸ E²; *1–5* 6–71 *72.* π2 fly-title; 72 advt.
Almost all copies seen form part of *The seasons,* 1730 (T239). The frontispiece found in some copies is one of four added to complete sets. Listed as a new edition with additions and corrections after *Autumn* in *MChr* June 1730.
L(11632.df.16; 1465.f.37; 1486.b.29),O(4),C, EU,DT+; CtY,IU,MH,PSC.

T224 — — With large additions. *Dublin, printed by S. Powell, for George Risk, George Ewing, & William Smith,* 1730.
8°: A–C⁸ D⁶ E²; *1–5* 6–60 *61–64.* A2 fly-title; E² advt.
Published like the London edition to form part of a collected edition with title *Poems. Viz. Spring...,* 1730 (T241). The advertisement leaves E² were printed as D4.5 of the original D⁸; they are so bound in the L copy, and at CtY they are bound at the end of the collected volume. The latter is perhaps what was intended.
L(1489.i.17),O,DN; CtY,MH,PSC.

T225 — — The fourth edition, with additions. *London, printed for J. Millan,* 1735.
8°: A–D⁸; *1–2* 3–64.
Printed to complete sets; usually found in *The four seasons, and other poems,* 1735 (T242). Printed by Samuel Richardson (*Sale* 179).
L(11630.bbb.13),O; PSC.

T226 — — *Dublin, printed by S. Powell, for George Risk, George Ewing, & William Smith,* 1740.
8°: π¹ E⁴ F–H⁸; *1–3* 4–58.
Printed with *Spring,* 1740, to complete sets.
O.

T227 — Spring. A poem. *London printed, and sold by A. Millar, & G. Strahan,* 1728. (*MChr* 5 June)

Thomson, J. The seasons. Spring

8º: A⁴ a² B–D⁸ E⁴ F²; *i–xii, 1 2–57 58–59; 60 blk.*
A1 hft; 58 err; F2 advt.

> *Rothschild* 2421. A copy at MH lacks the price on the title, apparently a variant. Some copies (e.g. O,TxU) add two leaves advertising Millar's books. Entered to Millar in *SR* 23 Jan 1729; deposit copies at O,E,EU,SaU.
> 'Come, gentle spring, ætherial mildness, come' Dedication to the Countess of Hertford.
> L(C.58.d.28),O,C(–F2),E(2),LdU-B+; CSmH(uncut),CtY(2, 1 stitched, uncut),MH, PSC,TxU+.

T228 — — *Dublin, printed by S. Powell, for George Risk, George Ewing, & William Smith,* 1728.

8º: A–C⁸ D⁴; *i–ii, 1 2–53 54. 54* advt.

> Copies are usually found in the Dublin collection *Poems. Viz. Spring*..., 1730 (T241).
> L(1489.i.17),O(2); CtY,MH,PSC.

T229 — — The second edition. *London, printed for A. Millar,* 1729.

8º: A⁴(±A2) a² χ¹ B–D⁸ E⁴ F²; *i–xii* [2], *1 2–57 58–59; 60 blk.* A1 hft; 58 err; F2 advt.

> A reissue of T227, with cancel title and χ1 (contents) printed together (so bound at PSC). J. E. Wells in *The library* IV. 22 (1942) 223–43 styles this 'second edition' A. Some copies (L,EU,CtY) entirely omit the original preliminaries; this may have been intended when copies were bound in collections, as with the following edition.
> L(1485.h.7; 1465.f.37, lacks A⁴ a²),O(lacks A1, 2),C,EU(lacks A⁴ a²); CtY(2, 1–F2, 1 lacks A⁴ a²),ICU(–F2),PSC(–A1).

T230 — — The second edition. *London, printed for A. Millar,* 1731.

8º: A–E⁸; *1–4 5–77 78–80.* A1 hft; 78–80 advt.

> Wells's second edition B. Almost all copies seen form part of *The seasons,* 1730 (T239); it is possibly post-dated. Press-figures 12–1, 30–3, 38–2, 48–2... Wells records a copy (now at PSC) with the general title to *The seasons,* 1730, in 'contemporary wrappers'; these are almost certainly a modern addition to a broken-up set. The frontispiece found in some copies is one of four added to complete sets.
> L(1486.b.29),O(2),C,DT; CtY,IU,MH,PSC.

T231 — — The second edition. *London, printed for A. Millar,* '1731' [1734]. (Oct)

8º: A–E⁸; *1–4 5–77 78–80.* A1 hft; 78–80 advt.

> Wells's 'second edition' C. No press-figures. Reprinted to complete sets of T242; Woodfall's ledger records an edition of 250 copies under 14 Oct 1734.
> L(11630.bbb.13),O,E; PSC.

T232 — — *Dublin, printed by S. Powell, for George Risk, George Ewing, & William Smith,* 1740.

8º: A–C⁸ D⁴(–D4); *1–3 4–54.*

> Printed with *Summer,* 1740, to complete sets; D4 provided the title of *Summer* (T226).
> O.

Thomson, J. The seasons. Autumn

T233 — Autumn. A poem... The second edition. *London, printed by N. Blandford, for J. Millan,* 1730. (*MChr* June)

8º: A–D⁸ E⁴; *1–5 6–72.* A2 fly-title.

> The first edition was in the quarto *Seasons,* 1730; this was printed to complete octavo sets. Some copies (e.g. PSC) have pp. 42, 43 misnumbered '40, 41'. The frontispiece found in some copies is one of four added to complete sets.
> 'Crown'd with the sickle, and the wheaten sheaf'
> L(11630.bbb.13; 1465.f.37; 1486.b.29),O(4), C,E,DT+; CtY(2, 1 stitched, uncut),IU,MH, PSC(3),TxU+.

T234 — — The second edition. '*London, printed by N. Blandford, for J. Millan*' [Edinburgh], 1730.

8º: A⁴ B–H⁴; *1–5 6–62 63–64 blk.* A2 fly-title.

> Printed by R. Fleming on the evidence of the ornaments. This piracy was perhaps suppressed out of consideration for a Scots poet and a Scots publisher; compare T189.
> E(uncut); MH(lacks A1).

T235 — — *Dublin, printed by S. Powell, for George Risk, George Ewing, & William Smith,* 1730.

8º: A–D⁸ *1–5 6–60 61–64.* A2 fly-title; D7–8 advt.

> Copies are usually found in the Dublin collection *Poems. Viz. Spring*..., 1730 (T241).
> L(1489.i.17,–D7, 8),O(2); CtY,MH,PSC.

T236 — The seasons. *London, printed in the year* 1730. (June)

4º: π⁴ *A²* B–Ii⁴ Kk² (+5 plates); *i–xii, 1–252.* A1ᵛ err.

> Title in red and black. A subscription edition; the subscribers' names on pp. iii–ix. The prospectus is recorded in *MChr* 26 Jan 1728. Listed in *MChr* June 1730 as 'delivered to subscribers by A. Millar, and J. Brindley'. This issue includes 'A hymn on the seasons' and 'A poem to the memory of Sir Isaac Newton', but not *Britannia.* Printed by Samuel Richardson (*Sale* 87). See J. E. Wells in *N&Q* 180 (1941) 350.
> LVA-D,C,DT,LdU-B; CSmH,CtY,IU,PSC(uncut).

T237 — [reissue]

> This issue adds *Britannia... The second edition corrected,* 1730, which was apparently not in the original issue. An advertisement of 21 Nov 1730 in *Haslewood* advertises supernumary unsubscribed sets with *Britannia* 'not delivered to the subscribers' at one guinea bound and gilt.
> L(641.l.13),O,CT,E,EU(said to be presentation copy to Earl of Buchan, with mss.)+; MiU,NN-B, NNC.

T238 — [reissue]

> This issue adds A⁴ containing four additional poems previously published in J. Ralph's

Thomson, J. The seasons

Miscellaneous poems by several hands, 1729, with drop-head title 'A paraphrase on the latter part of the sixth chapter of St. Matthew'. Separate copies of that have been seen at O,MH; their origin is obscure. This quarto edition was also issued in fortnightly parts; proposals are advertised in *DA* 8 Jan 1733, and publication was to start on 22 Jan. When *Works* II was published in 1736, this became volume I, but without any new title.

L(1480.d.2); CtY,*MH*,NNC,PSC.

T239 — The seasons, a hymn, a poem to the memory of Sir Isaac Newton, and Britannia, a poem. *London, printed for J. Millan, & A. Millar*, 1730. (*MChr* June)

The collective title (in red and black) to the separate octavo editions, probably printed as E4 of *Winter*, 1730 (T217). Some sets (e.g. PSC) include A⁴ containing four additional poems like the preceding, doubtless issued subsequently. Listed in *MChr* at '1s. 6d. each, or 7s. a set bound'.

L(1465.f.37; 1486.b.29),O(2),C,EU,DT; CtY, IU,PSC(3).

T240 — The seasons, a poem. *London, printed for J. Millan, & A. Millar*, 1730.
8°: π^2 A–Qq⁴, ²A–B⁴, ³A–B⁴ C²; *i–iv*, 1–311 *312 blk*, 1–15 *16 blk*, 1–20.
GU; CtY,*MH*(3),NNC,PSC(2).

T241 — [*idem*] Poems. Viz. Spring. Summer. Autumn. Winter. A hymn... To the memory... And Britannia. *Dublin, printed by S. Powell, for George Risk, George Ewing, & William Smith*, 1730.
A general title, printed as E4 of the Dublin edition of *Winter*, 1730 (T218), for sets of Dublin editions.

L(1489.i.17),O(2); CtY,MH,PSC.

T242 — The four seasons, and other poems. *London, printed for J. Millan, & A. Millar*, 1735.
A general title for sets of the separate London editions.

L(11630.bbb.13),LVA-D,O,E; MH,MiU,NNC, PSC.

T243 — The seasons. *London, printed for A. Millar*, 1744. (*GM* July)
8°: *A*(3 ll) B–Q⁸ R²; *i–vi*, 1–2 3–243 *244 blk*.
Press-figures 34–3, 68–2, 91–1, 102–1... Described by J. E. Wells in *The library* IV. 22 (1942) 236–40 as '1744 A'. Title in red and black. Entered in Woodfall's ledger under 19 June, 1500 copies printed of 16¼ sheets; this total suggests that there were 5 cancel leaves. L2.3 and L5.6 have been seen to be conjugate in the copy at O and must be cancels; a stub is found either between K6 and K7 or K7 and K8, which suggests the remaining cancel was K7. 1500 copies of an errata slip were also printed; they are usually pasted on

Thomson, J. The seasons

R2. The plates to each book are included in the collation.

L(1465.b.38; 1481.d.44),LVA-D,O,E('from the author'),WcC(Joseph Spence's copy 'from the author'); CtY(–err),MH,NNC(–err),PSC(3).

T244 — — *London, printed for A. Millar*, '1744' [1745]. (June?)
8°: *A*(3 ll) B–Q⁸ R¹; *i–vi*, 1–2 3–242.
Press-figures 88–3, 104–3, 150–3, 194–3. Wells '1744 B'. Title in red and black. Entered in Woodfall's ledger under 26 June 1745, 500 copies printed.

L(11630.aa.7); CtY,PSC.

T245 — — *London, printed for A. Millar*, 1746.
12°: *A*² B–K¹² L¹⁰; *i–iv*, 1–4 5–230 *231–236*. L8–10 advt.
Sheet B has press-figure 22–3. See J. E. Wells in *The library* IV. 17 (1937) 214–20 calling this 'type A'. Woodfall's ledger records this edition under 9 May 1746, 4000 copies, and charges for 'recomposing the first sheet'. Wells argued that this edition of sheet B, which is manifestly inaccurate, was reset to complete an edition which had been enlarged in size. Copies are, however, so scarce that it seems equally likely that this incorrect sheet was suppressed.

O; PSC.

T246 — [variant sheet B]
Sheet B has press-figure 15–3; Wells 'type B'. Copies were reissued with a cancel sheet H (press-figures 165–3, 166–3) as volume 1 of *Works*, 1750; a copy issued separately with the cancel sheet is at O. Strahan's ledger enters 'Letter H. of the Seasons no. 2000' to Millar under Feb 1750.

L(1465.b.39),E; CtY,ICN,MH,PSC(3).

— Spring, 1728. *See* T227.

— Summer, 1727. *See* T220.

— Winter, 1726. *See* T211.

T247 Thomson, John. Sir Solomon Gundi, with her highness the punch-bowl; with wine a-bun-dan-di. A miscellaneous poem: or the tarantula turning, or metamorphosed into a pope... [*Dublin*] *Pinted* [!] *for, and sold by the author*, 1738.
8°: *a*⁴ b–d⁴ B–G⁴ H²; *i–ii* 'ii' *iv* v–vi, 5–30, 1–48 *49; 50–52 blk*. d2ᵛ err.
The pagination is irregular. Long list of subscribers up to d2, pp. 5–26; miscellaneous poems by Thomson from D1 onwards.
'By novels from the Irish strand'
The author describes himself as 'High Germanick Doctor'.

L(993.e.49/6),O(–H2),DG(2, 1–H2); MH (–H2).

T248 — A specimen of thought upon the gloomy region: or, Polyphemus evaporated: or, a satiri-

Thomson, J. A specimen of thought

tragi-comi-poetick hodge-podge and miscellaneous poem, upon the Wooden-man in Essex-street... *Dublin, printed for the author, 1732.*
8°: π¹[=E4] A⁴ χ¹ a–d⁴ e² B–D⁴ E⁴(–E4) (+1 plate); *[2] i–viii vii–xliv, 1–30.*
> List of subscribers begins on χ1. The plate is a folding woodcut, bound as frontispiece in the L copy. Despite the title, this is really a collection of poems with some prose pieces added.
'Trudging once thro' Temple-Bar'
L(11631.a.53),LVA-F(–χ1).

Thorius, Raphael.
Player, Henry: Tobacco: a poem in two books. Translated from the Latin of Raphael Thorius, 1716, [1718.] *See* P482–3.

Bewick, William: A poem on tobacco, from the original Latin of Raphael Thorius, 1725. *See* B209.

[Thornton, Bonnell.] The intrigue. A college eclogue, 1750. *See* S31.

T249 [—] An ode on Saint Cæcilia's day, adapted to the ancient British musick. As it was performed on the twenty-second of November. *London, printed for J. & J. Rivington, & C. Corbet, 1749. (GM April)*
4°: π¹ A² B–C² D¹; *[2] i–iii iv–vi, 7–14.* π1 hft.
> Bond 203. The publication date has sometimes been questioned, apparently by confusion with the edition of 1763.
'Be dumb, be dumb, ye inharmonious sounds'
> Preface signed 'Fustian Sackbut'. Published with Thornton's name in 1763. Early ms. attribution 'by —— Lloyd' in the copy at LWS.
L(11630.e.5/11; 840.k.2/4; 840.k.4/10,–π1), LWS,O,C(–π1),LdU-B; CLU-C(uncut),CSmH, CtY,MH.

[Thornycroft, John.] Military and other poems upon several occasions, and to several persons. By an officer of the army, 1716. *See* Military.

———

[—] Love verses, by an officer in the Duke of Argyle's army, 1716. *See* L286.

[—] A poem on the anniversary of the birth-day of his majesty King George... By an officer in the army, 1717. *See* P577.

T250 — A poem on the complete victory gain'd over the Turks at Peterwaradin, by the most serene Prince Eugene of Savoy. Inscrib'd to his grace, John duke of Marlborough. By John Thornycroft, officer in the army. *London printed, and sold by R. Burleigh, 1716. (MC Sept)*
2°: A–B²; *1–2 3–8.*
'To heights untower'd, through paths untrod before'
O.

Thoughts

T251 Thoughts. Thoughts in sickness. *London, printed for M. Cooper, 1743. (GM Nov)*
4°: A⁴ B–D⁴; *1–5 6–29 30–32 blk.* A1 hft.
> Four poems.
'Too long I have delay'd, most patient god'
L(1970),LdU-B; KU,NjP.

— Thoughts upon the four last things, 1734–. *See* Trapp, Joseph.

T252 Three. Three Belgic fables; or hieroglyphic riddles. Containing I. The fable of the crafty statesman and subtle cardinal. II. The passive goose. III. The —— bull-dog and tooth-drawer. Illustrated with proper cutts. *London, printed for A. More, 1729. (MChr 15 Aug)*
2°: A–B²; *1–7; 8 blk.*
> Printed on one side of the leaf only; large woodcut to each fable. Horizontal chain-lines.
'Britons, behold! what medly virtues meet?'
> Tory propaganda.
L(11631.k.5/7); MH,OCU(uncut).

T253 — The three champions. *London, printed for J. Baker, [1709.]*
½°: 1 side, 2 columns.
> Engraved plate at head with portraits of Isaac Bickerstaff, the Review and the Observator.
'View here three brethren in iniquity'
> An attack on whig journalists, and particularly on the *Tatler*. The portraits are said to be those of Steele, Defoe, and Tutchin, but the last died in 1707. The text suggests that George Ridpath was intended, though he is not known to have written the *Observator*.
L(P&D 1512),LLP.

T254 — Three epistles in the ethic way. From the French of M. de Voltaire. Viz. I. Happiness. II. Freedom of will. III. Envy. *London, printed for R. Dodsley, 1738. (LDP 21 Sept)*
8°: A² B–G⁴; *i–iv, 1 2–46 47; 48 blk.* 46 err; 47 advt.
> With a separate title-page to each poem.
'O thou, with temper form'd to bless mankind'
> A different translation from that by William Gordon, 1738.
L(992.h.10/3),O; CSmH,IU.

— Three new poems, 1721. *See* Markland, John.

— Three odes, 1739. *See* Hamilton, William, *of Bangour.*

T255 — Three odes from the second book of Horace imitated. *London, printed for C. Corbett, 1739. (GM, LM May)*
4°: A⁴ B⁴; *1–3 4–15 16 blk.*
'Happy the people, who, tho' keen'
> Attributed in the DG catalogue to George Ogle; that copy is bound with two of his translations from Horace, but the association may be fortuitous; they were published within two months of each other. Ogle's normal publisher was Dodsley.
DG; CtY,MH,TxU.

Three

— Three original poems; being the posthumous works of Pendavid Bitterzwig, [1751.] *See* Berkenhout, John.

T256 — Three poems, Mahanaim, or, strivings with a saviour...Peniel, or, the combatant triumphing ...and the Triumph consummat... By an experienced admirer of sanctified afflictions. [*Edinburgh*] *Printed in the year* 1706.
4°: A–D² (A2 as 'A3'); *1–2* 3–16.
'How now, sad soul! what means this constant moan'
>Dedication to Viscountess Stormont and Lady Æmilia Murray signed 'J.W.', 7 Feb 1706. Attributed by *Halkett & Laing* to John Wilson and James Webster. The attribution to Wilson comes from a ms. note in the L copy, probably by James Maidment, 'John Wilson an episcopal minister'. This attribution seems the more probable.

L(11632.e.72),E.

— Three poems, viz. I. Reason, a satire. By the reverend Mr. Pomfret... II. The female Phaeton. By Mr. Harcourt. III. The judgment of Venus. By the same. *London, printed for E. Curll,* 1720. (*PB* 27 Feb)
8°: pp. 18.   L,LdU-B; CtY,KU.
>Listed as a miscellany by *CBEL*. Pomfret's *Reason* was separately published in 1700, and added (as 'his remains') to his *Poems upon several occasions*, 1724.

T257 — The three politicians: or, a dialogue in verse between a patriot, a courtier, and their friend. Concluding with an exhortation to Admiral Vernon. *London, printed for T. Cooper,* 1741. (*GM, LM* March)
2°: A² B–D²; *i–iv, 1* 2–11 *12 blk.* A1 hft.
Horizontal chain-lines.
'Preach concord to the winds. – I plainly see'
L(163.n.3); CtY,IU,KU,MH,OCU.

— Three satires, 1719. *See* Morrice, Bezaleel.

— Three songs in English and Latin, [1746.] *See* Bourne, Vincent.

— The three travellers, 1733. *See* Chamberlaine, Walter.

T258 — Three verses of the 78th psalm, in the new translation; with an addition of four lines on the blessed effects of the charity-schools: to be sung by the charity-children, belonging to the Tabernacle in Petticoat-lane, at the parish-church of St. Dunstan's Stepney, on Sunday the 25th of April... [*London,* 1714?]
½°: 1 side, 1 column.
'For Jacob he this law ordain'd'
MC(ms. note).

T259 Threnodia. Threnodia. A funeral poem, to the memory of the late, learned, pious and reverend, Mr. James Webster...who died May 17. 1720. To which are added other three, all done by differ-

Threnodia

ent hands, none know[ing] of another. *Edinburgh, printed in the year* 1720.
8°: π² A–E⁴ F²; *i–iv,* 1–44.
>The added elegies occupy pp. 29–44.

'Melpomene assist my doleful song'
L(1368.a.25/4),E,GM.

— Threnodia apollinaris, 1711–. *See* Settle, Elkanah.

— Threnodia britannica, 1714. *See* Settle, Elkanah.

T260 — Threnodia Cestriensis: a poem sacred to the memory of the right reverend father in god Francis late ld bishop of Chester. *London, printed for J. Roberts,* 1726.
2°: *A*² B–C²; *i–ii,* 1–10.
'Could virtue, learning, and religion, all'
L(11630.g.30),O,LdU-B(uncut); CSmH,MH, OCU.

— Threnodia hymenæa, 1710–. *See* Settle, Elkanah.

— Threnodia: or, an elegy on the unexpected and unlamented death of the Censor, 1730. *See* 'Gulliver, Martin'.

T261 — Threnodia virginea: or, the apotheosis. A poem, occasion'd by the much lamented death of Mrs. Elizabeth Buckworth, only daughter of Sir John Buckworth, kt. and bar. *London, printed for John Lawrence; sold by A. Baldwin,* 1708.
2°: *A*² B–C²; *1–4* 5–12.
'Clogg'd with a mournful gloom, arose the day'
>Dedication signed 'C.G.' Attributed by *Morgan* *K179ᵃ to Charles Gildon. The attribution is plausible, but apparently only rests on the initials.

MH,TxU.

T262 — — *London, printed by H. Hills,* 1708.
8°: A⁸; *1–3* 4–16.
>The title reads 'Mrs. Hester Buckworth'.

L(12331.ee.31/5),O,OW,GM,NwP; CSmH,DFo, OCU.

T263 Threnodiae. Threnodiæ Britannicæ; or, England in tears. [*London?* 1716/20.]
slip: 1 side, 1 column.
'We're a nation of fools, who are govern'd by knaves'
>A Jacobite satire.

O; CSmH.

T264 — [another edition]
>First line misprinted '...govean'd by knaves'.

MH.

T265 Threnody. A threnodie or the lamentations of Scotland, England, France, Ireland, Orange, and the souldiers of Britain, on the decease of...William king of Great Britain... By J.P. Sc. *Edinburgh, printed in the year* 1702.
4°: A⁴ (A2 as 'A'); *1–2* '1' 4–8.
'Tears must succumb, where sullen grief abounds'
L(11632.df.6),O,E.

Thresher

Thresher. The thresher's miscellany: or, poems on several subjects, written by Arthur Duck, 1730. *See* 'Duck, Arthur'.

T266 Thundering. A thundering poem to the swearer: or, a dreadful warning to all wicked and presumptious blasphemers; with a lively description of divine vengeance, prepar'd for the punishment of such impenitent and obstinate sinners. *London printed, and sold by H. Hills,* [1707.] (12 Dec, Luttrell)
1°: 1 side, 3 columns.
　　Large emblematic woodcut at head. Advertisement for patent medicines above imprint.
'Bold swearer stop, no farther progress make'
MH(Luttrell).

T267 Thura. Thura Britannica. A congratulatory poem to her sacred majesty Queen Anne and the whole realm, for the late signal and happy success of her majesty's forces both by sea and land. By W.H. *London, printed for Benj. Tooke,* 1702. (30 Dec, Luttrell)
2°: *A–B² C² D¹; i–iv, 1–9 10 blk.* A1 hft.
　　Listed in *WL* Jan 1703.
'Fair Albion's sons your tuneful notes advance'
O,*MR-C*; *CSmH*,TxU(Luttrell).

Thurston, Joseph. Poems on several occasions. *London, printed by W.P. for Benj. Motte,* 1729. (*MChr* 28 Feb)
8°: pp. 77.　　L,E; ICN,MH.

—— The second edition. *London, printed for B. Motte, & C. Bathurst,* 1737. (*SR* 24 March)
12°: pp. 143.　　LVA-D,O; MH,NjP.
Deposit copies at AdU,SaU.

T268 —— The fall. In four books. *London, printed for B. Motte,* 1732. (*GM* 26 Feb)
8°: *A² B–H⁴ I²; i–ii, 1–3 4–61 62.* i blk; ii, 62 advt.
Bond 120. Entered in *SR* 26 Feb; deposit copies at LSC,O,EU,AdU.
'Nor wars alarms, nor falling states I sing'
　　On the fall of Florella; a mock-heroic poem.
L(993.f.43/3),O(−A1),EU,AdU,BaP(stitched, uncut)+; CU,CtY,ICN(2),IU,MH.

T269 —— The toilette. In three books. *London, printed for Benj. Motte,* 1730. (*MChr* May)
8°: π² A⁴(−A1) B–E⁴ F⁴(±F3); [2] *1–3 4–47 48 blk.* π1 frt.
　　The cancel title π2 is in red and black.
'What mystic arts support a female reign'
L(11658.g.99,−π1),O,CT,BaP(uncut),MP+; CSmH,CtY,DFo,*ICN*,MH(−π1)+.

T270 —— The second edition. *London, printed for Benj. Motte,* 1730. (*MChr* Oct)
8°: (frt+) A–F⁴; *1–3 4–47 48 blk.*
L(993.f.43/2),SrS; ICN,IU,MH,*NN*.

Thyrsis

Thyrsis. Thyrsis & Chloe, 1728. *See* Bourne, Vincent.

T271 [Tibal, Peter.] The tell tale; or, the patriot's defeat. A satire... By a gentleman of Christ-Church, Oxford. *London, printed for J. Roberts; sold by Sackville Parker, bookseller, in Oxford,* 1741. (*GM, LM* March)
2°: *A² B² C¹; 1–4 5–10.* A1 hft.
'What news from London, says my friend?'
　　Attributed to Tibal by *Rawlinson.* On the motion to remove Walpole, defeated Feb 1741.
L(1959),O(−A1); CLU-C,CSmH,CU(uncut, −A1),KU,NjP.

Tibullus, Albius.
Dart, John: The works of Tibullus, containing his four books of love-elegies, 1720.

T272 [Tickell, Thomas.] An epistle from a lady in England; to a gentleman at Avignon. *London, printed for J. Tonson,* 1717. (*PM* 15 Jan)
2°: *A¹ B–C² D¹; i–ii, 1–10.*
　　Watermark: TH. Entered in *SR* 15 Jan; deposit copies at L,LSC,O,EU,SaU.
'To thee, dear rover, and thy vanquish'd friends'
　　Subsequently published with Tickell's name.
L(643.m.13/13),LSC,O,C,EU+; CtY(uncut), NjP,TxU.

T273 [—] [fine paper]
　　Watermark: star.
LdU-B; *CLU-C*,DFo,MH,TxU.

T274 [—] —— The second edition. *London, printed for J. Tonson,* 1717.
2°: *A¹ B–C² D¹; i–ii, 1–10.*
　　A reimpression.
OW,AdU,BaP,*MR*; ICN,NN-B,NjP,TxU.

T275 —— By Mr. Tickell. The third edition. *London, printed for J. Tonson,* 1717. (*PM* 19 Jan)
2°: *A¹ B–C² D¹; i–ii, 1–10.*
　　Watermark: TH (and other initials). A reimpression, with a couplet omitted from p. 3.
L(643.l.25/18),O(3),DN; CtY,IU,TxU(2, 1 uncut).

T276 —— [fine paper]
　　Watermark: O.
C.

T277 —— The fourth edition. *London, printed for J. Tonson,* 1717. (*PM* 2 Feb)
2°: *A² B–C²; 1–2 3–12.*
O; PPL(lacks C²),TxU.

T278 —— The fifth edition. *London, printed for J. Tonson,* 1717. (*PB* 23 Feb)
2°: *A² B–C²; 1–2 3–12.*
　　A reimpression of the fourth edition.
L(11631.h.13),O(2),DT; IU,KU,TxU(uncut).

Tickell, T. An epistle from a lady

T279 [—] — *London printed, and Edinburgh re-printed by William Brown & John Mosman, and sold by the said Wil. Brown, and Alexander Mathie, Glasgow,* 1717.
4°: A⁴ B²; *1–2* 3–12.
E(3, 1 uncut); MH(uncut).

T280 [—] — *To which is added, Court-poems. Part II. The second edition. London printed; and reprinted in Dublin, by S. Powell, for G. Risk,* 1717.
12°: A–B⁶; *1–2* 3–24.
C,DN.

T281 — The first book of Homer's Iliad. Translated by Mr. Tickell. *London, printed for J. Tonson,* 1715. (*SR* 7 June)
4°: A–F⁴ G¹; *i–viii*, 1–41 *42 blk*.
Engraved ornaments. Publication dated 8 June by Sherburn in his edition of Pope's correspondence I. 295n. Listed in *MC* June. Entered in *SR* to Tonson by T. Glenister; deposit copy at SaU, possibly at L,O.
'Achilles' fatal wrath, whence discord rose'
It was widely believed that Addison had a hand in this translation; see Spence's *Anecdotes*, ed. J. M. Osborn (1966) I. 70.
L(11630.d.1/2; 652.c.4, mutilated; 75.g.21), O(3, 1 ms. notes after Pope),C(2, 1 lacks A1),DT, LdU-B+; CLU-C,CSmH,IU(2),MH.

T282 — — [and] The poem of Musæus, on the loves of Hero and Leander, paraphras'd in English, heroick verse. *London printed; and reprinted in Dublin, by S. Powell, for G. Risk,* 1716.
12°: A–C⁶; *1–6* 7–36.
Issued with Catcott's Musaeus, which is entered separately.
O,CT,DK,DT.

— The horn-book, a poem, [1739.] *See* T302.

T283 [—] An imitation of the prophecy of Nereus. From Horace book I. ode XV. *London, printed for J. Roberts,* 1715. (*MC* Nov)
2°: A–B²; *i–ii*, 1–5 *6 blk*.
'As Mar his round one morning took'
Early ms. attributions to Tickell in the copies at AdU, CSmH; ascribed to him by *Jacob* and printed as his in *Dodsley*. R. E. Tickell considered its authenticity doubtful, but the external evidence is very strong.
LVA-F,O,DT,AdU; CLU,CSmH,NjP.

T284 [—] — The second edition. *London, printed for J. Roberts,* 1715.
2°: A–B²; *i–ii*, 1–6.
This edition (or, more probably, impression) adds the Latin text on p. 6.
CtY,ICN,MH,NjP,TxU.

T285 [—] — The third edition. *London, printed for J. Roberts,* 1716.
2°: A–B²; *i–ii*, 1–6.
L(1970),OW.

Tickell, T. An imitation

T286 [—] — from Hor. l. 1. od. 15. [*Edinburgh,* 1715/16.]
½°: 1 side, 2 columns.
L(C.115.i.3/18),E(mutilated, ms. date 7 Jan 1716), Rosebery.

T287 [—] [*idem*] [dh] The Scotch prophecy, being an imitation of the prophecy of Nereus. From Horace book I. ode XV. [col] *Dublin: re-printed, and sold by Thomas Humes,* 1716.
4°: A²; *1–4*.
DN,DT; OCU.

T288 [—] Kensington Garden. *London, printed for J. Tonson,* 1722 [1721]. (*DC* 25 Nov)
4°: A–E⁴; *i–iv*, 1–32 *33–36*. A1 hft; E3–4 advt.
Rothschild 2433. E2 is signed. Engraving on title. Entered in *SR* 24 Nov; deposit copies at E,EU.
'Where Kensington high o'er the neighb'ring lands'
Advertised in *DC* and listed in *SR* as by Tickell.
L(163.m.2, Luttrell, Feb, –A1),O,OC,OW,E (cropt)+; CLU-C,CSmH(–A1),CtY(2),DFo (–A1).

T289 [—] [fine paper]
4°: A–D⁴ E²; *i–iv*, 1–32.
Inner margins enlarged, advertisements omitted; in this issue E2 is not signed.
LG,OW('Donum autoris', gilt edges),LdU-B; NjP.

T290 [—] Lucy and Colin, a song. Written in imitation of William and Margaret. *Dublin, printed by Pressick Rider & Thomas Harbin,* 1725.
½°: 1 side, 2 columns.
'Of Leinster, fam'd for maidens fair'
Reprinted with Tickell's name in *The musical miscellany* I, 1730; the ms. is among Tickell's papers. Tickell was in Dublin at this time.
O.

T291 [—] An ode inscribed to the right honourable the Earl of Sunderland at Windsor. *London, printed for Jacob Tonson,* 1720. (*PB* 26 May)
2°: *A*² B² C¹; *i–iv*, *1* 2–5 *6 blk*. A1 hft.
Watermark: script J.
'Thou dome, where Edward first enroll'd'
Advertised in *PB* as by Tickell. See George Sewell's *An ode to Mr. Tickell occasion'd by his ode to…the Earl of Sunderland,* [1720.]
LVA-F,O(–A1),OW,*LdU-B*; CSmH,CtY,ICN, *InU*.

T292 [—] [fine paper]
Watermark: fleur-de-lys.
L(840.m.1/31,–A1); IU.

T293 — An ode. Occasioned by his excellency the Earl Stanhope's voyage to France. *London, printed for Jacob Tonson,* 1718. (*PB* 17 June)
2°: *A*² < B¹; *1–3* 4–5 *6 blk*.
Watermark: script J. Entered in *SR* 19 June; deposit copies at L,LSC,EU,AdU. A 'second

Tickell, T. An ode

edition' was advertised in *DC* 4 July; it has not been seen, and may be an undifferentiated reimpression.

'Fair daughter once of Windsor's woods!'
Satirized by [Sir Thomas Burnet] *The tickler tickell'd*, 1718, and *A second epistle to Mr. Tickell*, [1718.]

L(643.m.13/15),LDW,O,EU,AdU+; CSmH, CtY,ICU,MH,TxU+.

T294 — [fine paper]
Watermark: fleur-de-lys on shield.
LVA-F,OW; NjP.

T295 — [*idem*] An ode, on his excellency the Earl Stanhope's voyage to France. By Mr. Tickell, June 1718. [*London*] 1718.
1°: 1 side, 2 columns.
Large engraving at head, with engraved text below. A copy listed by Grinke & Rogers cat. 3 (1969) 396 has the imprint 'Engraven and sold by Clark & Pine...'; it is not clear whether this is another issue or if these words are cropped from the L copy.
L(P&D 1608).

T296 — On her majesty's re-building the lodgings of the Black Prince, and Henry V, at Queen's-College Oxford. *London, printed for J. Tonson*, 1733. (*GM* Aug)
2°: *A⁴*; *1–5* 6–7 *8 blk.* A1 hft.
No watermark.
'Where bold and graceful soars, secure of fame'
O(−A1),OW(2); CSmH(−A1),CU,TxU(−A1).

T297 — [fine paper]
Watermark: post-horn on shield.
L(162.n.30,−A1); TxU.

T298 — [superfine paper?]
Watermarks: unicorn in A1.4, fleur-de-lys on shield in A2.3.
O.

T299 [—] Oxford. A poem. Inscrib'd to the right honourable the Lord Lonsdale. *London, printed for Egbert Sanger*, 1707 [1706]. (*DC* 14 Nov)
2°: A–C²; *i–ii*, 1–10.
'Whilst you, my lord, adorn that stately seat'
Early ms. attribution to Tickell in the LdU-B copy; referred to as his in Hearne's papers under 26 Nov.
L(11602.i.16/1),O,LdU-B; CLU-C(Luttrell, 14 Nov),CtY,MH,OCU,TxU(2)+.

T300 [—] A poem in praise of the horn-book: written by a gentleman in England, under a fit of the gout. *Dublin, printed by and for J. Gowan*, 1728.
8°: *A⁴*; *i–ii*, 1–6.
'Hail ancient book, most venerable code'
First published anonymously in *Miscellaneous poems, by several hands. Published by D. Lewis*, 1726. Subsequently issued with Tickell's name, T302.
L(C.58.cc.14, cropt),C,DN.

Tickell, T. A poem in praise

T301 [—] — *London, printed for J. Wilford*, 1732. (*GM* 22 Feb)
2°: *A² B²*; *1–2* 3–8.
With an additional poem 'Thersites' on pp. 7–8; it is a reprint of Swift's *Traulus. The second part*, 1730.
LdU-B(uncut); TxU(uncut).

T302 — [reissue] The horn-book, a poem. By Thomas Tickle, esq; [*London*] *Printed for Charles Corbet*, [1739.] (*DP* 31 Dec)
2°: *A²*(±A1) B²; *1–2* 3–8.
A reissue of the preceding with a cancel title.
O; CtY,MH.

T303 — A poem, to his excellency the lord privy-**seal**. on the prospect of peace. *London, printed for J. Tonson*, 1713 [1712]. (28 Oct?)
2°: A–F²; *i–iv*, 1–20.
No watermark. Entered in *SR* 30 Oct 1712; deposit copies at L,LSC,O,EU,AdU,SaU. Publication date from newspaper advertisement in *Haslewood*; advertised as 'just publish'd' in *PB* 1 Nov 1712.
'The haughty Gaul, in ten campaigns o'erthrown'
L(643.1.26/2),LSC,O(3),EU,LdU-B+; CtY, ICN,ICU,MH,TxU(3).

T304 — [fine paper]
Watermark: O.
OW.

T305 — — The second edition. *London, printed for J. Tonson*, 1713. (5 Nov?)
2°: A–F²; *i–iv*, 1–20.
Publication date from newspaper advertisement in *Haslewood*.
L(11631.h.11),O; CSmH.

T306 — — The third edition. *London, printed for J. Tonson*, 1713. (10 Nov?)
2°: A–F²; *i–iv*, 1–20.
A reimpression or press-variant title. Publication date from newspaper advertisement in *Haslewood*; listed as 'just publish'd' in *PB* 11 Nov.
L(11631.k.16),LVA-F,O; CLU-C,KU,TxU(uncut).

T307 — — The fourth edition. *London, printed for J. Tonson*, 1713. (3 Dec?)
2°: A–F²; *i–iv*, 1–20.
Publication date from newspaper advertisement in *Haslewood*.
L(1482.h.1/1, uncut),O,CJ,AN; IU(uncut),KU, TxU.

T308 — — The fifth edition. *London, printed for J. Tonson*, 1713.
2°: A–F²; *i–iv*, 1–20.
Reprinted with its own title-page reading 'The fifth edition' and dated 1713 as A–B⁶ of *Poetical miscellanies* (Dublin, 1714), copies at DN,CtY.
PPL.

Tickell, T. A poem to his excellency

T309 — — The sixth edition. *London, printed for J. Tonson,* 1714. (*PB* 15 May)
12°: A–B⁶ C²; *1–9* 10–27 *28 blk.* A1 blk.
O(–A1),OW; *CLU-C*,DFo,KU,MH(uncut), NjP+.

T310 — The prologue to the university of Oxford. Written by Mr. Tickell. Spoken by Mr. Cibber. [*London*] *Printed for J. Tonson,* 1713. (3 Aug?)
½°: *1–2,* 1 column.
'What kings henceforth shall reign, what states be free'
L(Ashley 5662/9, ms. date 3 Aug),O,OW; CSmH.

T311 [—] To Sir Godfrey Kneller, at his country seat. *London, printed for Jacob Tonson,* 1722.
2°: *A² B²; i–iv, 1 2–3 4 blk.* A1 hft.
The copy seen, with fleur-de-lys in A and fleur-de-lys on shield in B is almost certainly on fine paper.
'To Whitton's shades, and Hounslow's airy plain'
Reprinted with Tickell's poems in *Dodsley.*
L(840.m.1/14).

Tickler. The tickler tickell'd, 1718. *See* Burnet, *Sir* Thomas.

T312 Tilly, William. Beata Maria virgo ab angelo Gabriele salutata: carmen heroicum sacrum; aliquot ante annis conditum, nunc vero primum editum. *Londini, apud J. Roberts,* 1729.
4°: *A⁴ B⁴; i–vi, 1–9 10 blk.*
'Magna sequor tenuis, tenerisque per æthera nitor'
Dedication signed.
L(11409.h.24, B4 mutilated).

T313 Time. Time and eternity, or the present and future state. Humbly presented to the right honourable Charles Butler, earl of Arran... *London, printed for the author,* 1738.
4°: *π¹ A–C² D¹; i–ii, 1 2–13 14 blk.*
π1 and D1 have been seen to be conjugate.
'Our present state, and all things we survey'
IU.

Timely. A timely caution, 1727–. *See* Good advice to the ladies, 1702–.

T314 Tin. The tinn-plate-workers complaint of the ab⟨use⟩ of their trade. Address'd to their fellow-citizens, the masters, wardens, &c. of all the corporations of the city of Dublin. [*Dublin,* 1711?]
½°: 1 side, 2 columns.
The DT copy is bound with half-sheets of 1711.
'Honoured friends, we are undone'
DT.

Tippling. The tipling philosophers, 1710. *See* Ward, Edward.

'Tis

T315 'Tis. Tis high time to make hast or, never let your noble courage be cast-down, a new copy of verses, being the valiant souldiers resolution to use expedition, to fight their enemys, who they question not but to conquer, and take the traytorous Pretender alive, and bring him to condign punishment. Tune of, Valiant Jockey's march'd away. [*London*] *Printed for E. Jackson,* [1708.] (March?)
½°: 1 side, 2 columns.
Three rough woodcuts at head.
'Come brave souldiers hast away'
Against the Pretender's attempt at invasion. Rothschild.

T316 — 'Tis pity they shou'd be parted: or the fable of the bear and the fox. *London, printed in the year* 1712.
½°: 1 side, 2 columns.
'Bruin and Reynard who had made'
On the disgrace of Marlborough and Walpole.
L(1850.c.10/30); MH.

T317 — [*idem*] Where's your impeachment now? Or, the D--- safe delivery. [*London*] *Printed by John Bill in the Strand,* 1712.
½°: 1 side, 2 columns.
With an added stanza on Marlborough's delivery.
L(G.1390/16).

[**Tisdall, William.**] An answer to Hamilton's Bawn: or, a short character of Dr. S——t, [1732.] *See* A237.

T318 [—] Tom Pun-sibi metamorphosed: or, the giber gibb'd. *Dublin, printed in the year* 1724. (25 March?)
½°: 1 side, 2 columns.
Rothschild 2435; *Teerink* 1198; *Williams* 1123.
'Tom was a little merry grig'
Reprinted in *Gulliveriana* (1728) 260 as by Tisdall; the CSmH copy has a ms. note at the end 'Sheridan, Swift, Tisdall', presumably as the subjects of the satire and its author. Answered by *The rivals,* [1724], which refers to his authorship and his jealousy of Sheridan; see also Samuel Owens, *A poem, or advice to the authors,* 1724. Sometimes ascribed to Smedley, but with no valid evidence.
L(Cup.600.a.1/63),C,DT,Rothschild; *CSmH* (ms. date 25 March).

T319 [—] [*idem*] The true character of the Intelligencer. Written by Pady Drogheda. [*Dublin*] *Printed in the year* 1728.
½°: 1 side, 1 column.
Teerink 1295. Although this only omits 13 lines of the preceding it has been treated by Teerink as a different work. Because Swift's reply *On Paddy's character of the Intelligencer,* [1728], appears to be directed against Patrick Delany, Delany has been thought to be the author; Swift himself may have believed it.
CSmH.

Tit

T320 Tit. The tit-bit. A tale. *London, printed for T. Cooper*, 1738. (*GM, LM* March)
2º: *A*² B²; *1-3* 4-8.
'A waggish jest, if cleanly told'
Attributed to Hildebrand Jacob in the O catalogue, but no evidence for the attribution has been found. An erotic tale.
L(11602.i.17/6; Ashley 5194; Ashley 5662/10), O,LdU-B; CSmH(uncut),MH,OCU,TxU(2).

T321 — Tit for tat: or an answer to the Dublin ballad. *Dublin, printed by Edward Waters*, 1714.
½º: 1 side, 2 columns.
'Come listen, good people, and I will relate'
On the disputes concerning the election of the lord mayor of Dublin, in answer to *The Dublin ballad*, [1713/14.]
C; MH.

T322 — Tit for tat. Or an answer to the Epistle to a nobleman. *London, printed for T. Cooper*, 1734. (*DJ* 26 Jan)
2º: *A*² B²; *1-3* 4-8.
An edition printed for W. Rayner was advertised in *DJ* 4 Dec 1733 for publication 'next week'; it never appeared. This edition has a more complete text than the Reynolds edition below, and corresponds to the 'suppressed edition' quoted by Lord Ilchester, *Lord Hervey and his friends* (1950) 300-1.
'Sweet, pretty pratler of the c---t'
A reply to Lord Hervey's *An epistle from a nobleman to a doctor of divinity*, 1733.
L(11631.k.3),O; CLU-C,CSmH,IU,InU,TxU+.

T323 — — To which is added, an Epistle from a nobleman to a doctor of divinity. In answer to a Latin letter in verse... *London printed, and sold by J. Dormer*, 1734. (*GSJ* 14 Feb)
2º: *A*⁴; *1-2* 3-8.
Advertised in *GSJ* as 'the only book printed from the original copies'; the title denounces a shilling piracy, presumably the Reynolds edition below which alone bore this price.
MR-C; CSmH,CtY,DLC.

T324 — — To which is annex'd, an Epistle from a nobleman to a doctor of divinity. In answer to a Latin letter in verse. Also the Review; or, the case fairly stated on both sides... *London, printed for T. Reynolds; sold by the booksellers in town & country*, 1734. (*LM* Feb)
2º: *A*² B-C²; *1-2* 3-12.
Review: 'When grave divinity thought fit'
L(11602.i.22; 840.m.1/3, omissions supplied in ms; 163.n.32; C.59.h.9/9),O,LdU-B(uncut); CSmH,CtY,IU(2, 1 cropt),MH,TxU+.

T325 — — The second edition. With the additional lines...of Tit for tat that were omitted in the former impression... *London, printed for T. Reynolds; sold by the booksellers in town & country*, 1734.
2º: *A*² B-C²; *1-2* 3-12.

Tit for tat

At least one couplet is still omitted.
L(1961),OW(uncut); CSmH,IU,OCU,TxU.

T326 — — To which is annex'd, an Epistle from a nobleman to a doctor of divinity... Also the Review... '*London, printed for T. Reynolds; sold by the booksellers in town & country*' [*Edinburgh*], 1734.
8º: *A*-B⁴ C²; *1-2* 3-19 *20 blk.*
Printed by R. Fleming on the evidence of the ornaments.
L(1962),O,E; CU,ICU.

T327 — — To which is annex'd, an Epistle... Also the Review... *London printed, and Dublin re-printed, by and for S. Hyde*, 1734.
8º: *A*-B⁴ C²; *1-2* 3-20.
O,C,DK.

T328 — Tit for tat. Part II. By the author of the first part... To which is added, the Latin letter from a doctor of divinity to a noble lord, burlesqu'd. With proper references to the doctor's original Latin... *London, printed for P. Monger, in the Strand; sold at the pamphlet-shops of London & Westminster*, 1735. (*LM* March)
2º: *A*² B-D²; *1-2* 3-16.
'When lordly witlings bounce and chatter'
Letter: 'No more as pædagouge [!], but friend'
Dr. William Sherwin's original Latin letter has apparently not been identified.
L(1482.f.34),O; CSmH.

'**Titus Antigallicus.**' An ode for the thanksgiving day, 1749. *See* O26.

T--l--nd. T--l--nd's invitation to Dismal, [1712.] *See* Swift, Jonathan.

To. To a lady on her passion for old china, 1725. *See* Gay, John.

— To a young gentleman in love. A tale, 1702. *See* Prior, Matthew.

T329 — To arms: or, the British lyon rouz'd. A poem. Occasion'd by the present armaments against the Spaniards. *London, printed for George Brett; sold at the pamphlet-shops in London & Westminster*, 1739. (*GM, LM* Sept)
2º: *B*² C²; *i-ii, 1* 2-6.
'At last the long expected day is come'
DT; CtY.

T330 — To be sung by the children of the Blew Coat school, at the new church in Westminster, on Sunday the 23d of December, 1711 in the morning ...an hymn. [*verso:*] In the afternoon...an hymn. [*London*, 1711.]
½º: 2 sides, 1 column.
'The day draws near, the joyful day'
'On this returning happy day'
MC.

T331 — To be sung on Wednesday Feb. 6. 171½ before

To be sung on Wednesday

her majesty, being the birth-day. *London, printed for Bernard Lintott*, [1712.] (*PB* 5 Feb)
½°: 1 side, 1 column.
Advertised in *PB* as sold by J. Morphew.
'Hail happy day! that bless'd the earth'
LLP; ICN(Luttrell, 5 Feb),MH.

— To Doctor D-l---y, on the libels writ against him, 1730. *See* Swift, Jonathan.

— To her grace the Dutchess of Buckingham, 1743. *See* Lockman, John.

— To her royal highness the Princess of Wales, 1716. *See* Addison, Joseph.

T332 — To his excellency John, lord Carteret; lord lieutenant of Ireland. An imitation of Horace, ode IX. lib. IV. *Dublin, printed by James Carson*, 1729.
½°: 1 side, 2 columns.
Teerink 681; *Williams* 1132.
'Patron of the tuneful throng'
Swift's authorship is rejected by Ball and Williams; the latter records a revised version addressed to Humphry French, which has been ascribed to Charles Carthy as well as to Swift.
L(C.121.g.8/174); CtY.

— To his excellency Jonathan Belcher, 1730. *See* Watts, Isaac.

— To his excellency the Lord Carteret, 1725. *See* Barber, Mary.

T333 — To his grace, James, duke of Perth, &c. [*Edinburgh?* 1746.]
½°: 1 side.
The dedication is in one column, in prose; below, in two columns and in verse, 'To the memory of Sir William Wallace'.
'Inspir'd with your applause, the daring muse'
E(2, 1 with verse only, probably cropt).

T334 — To his grace the arch-bishop of Dublin, a poem. *Dublin, printed by John Harding*, [1724.]
½°: 1 side, 1 column.
Teerink 1152; *Williams* 339.
'Great, good and just was once apply'd'
First printed as Swift's by Scott in 1814, apparently on the strength of Harding's imprint; Williams says 'it is very probable... that it should be attributed to Swift'. In praise of William King's opposition to William Wood.
L(C.121.g.8/118),LVA-F,C; CtY.

T335 — To his grace the Duke of Argyle, upon his arrival at court, after the defeat of the northern rebellion, March the 6th, 1715. *London, printed for Jacob Tonson*, 1716. (*SR* 12 April)
2°: A-B²; *i-ii*, 1-6.
The Luttrell copy, dated 18 April, is recorded in *Haslewood*; listed in *MC* April. Deposit copies at L,LSC,O,EU,AdU,SaU.
'Eternal Phœbus! whose propitious ray'

To his grace the Duke of Argyle

Listed by *Waller* as attributed to Prior; rejected by *Wright & Spears* 804, who suggest Richardson Pack as author since *Jacob* refers to a poem of his to Argyll; but two poems to Argyll by Pack are in his *Miscellanies*, 1719, and neither is this. Possibly the poem by Samuel Croxall on his victory, recorded in *Cibber* V. 292.
L(643.m.13/9),O,EU,AdU,SaU+; PPL,TxU.

T336 — To his grace the Duke of Marlborough. [*London*, 1707.] (23 Oct, Luttrell)
½°: 1 side, 1 column.
Doubtless the work advertised in *DC* 23 Oct as 'A poem to his grace the Duke of Marlborough'.
'Haste, great commander, to our longing isle'
MH(Luttrell).

T337 — To his grace the Duke of Marlborough, a poem. By a clergy-man of the church of England. [*London*, 1712.]
½°: 2 sides, 1 column.
'May't please your grace, in your recess'
On Marlborough's dismissal. Prof. R. D. Horn privately suggests that the author was Richard Chapman.
L(1850.c.10/41),LSA; MH(2).

T338 — To his grace the Duke of Marlborough on his late successes in Flanders. *London, printed for Egbert Sanger*, 1706. (5 Sept, Luttrell)
½°: 1-2, 1 column.
'While you, my lord, with an extensive hand'
MH(Luttrell).

— To his grace the Duke of Marlborough, on the report of his going into Germany, 1713. *See* Sewell, George.

— To his grace the Duke of Marlborough, upon his going into Germany, 1713. *See* Sewell, George.

T339 — To his grace the Duke of Ormond: upon his second accession to the government of Ireland. *London, printed for John Morphew*, 1711. (14 June, Luttrell)
½°: 2 sides, 2 columns.
The order of editions is uncertain. Advertised in *Examiner* 26 July.
'What means this mingled pomp on sea and land?'
MR; ICN(Luttrell).

T340 — — [*Dublin?* 1711.]
2°: A²; 1-4.
Both copies seen are bound with collections of Dublin half-sheets, but it may have been imported from England.
C,DT.

— To his most excellent majesty James III. [1710?/16.] *See* Berington, Simon.

T341 — To his m----y, the loyal address of the tories. [*London*] *Printed by W. Davis*, [1714/15?]
slip: 1 side, 1 column.

To his m----y

'Accept, mighty monarch, our duty at last'
Satirizing the tories' attitude to George I.
O.

T342 — To his royal highness, Charles, prince of Wales, &c. regent of the kingdoms of Scotland, England, France and Ireland. [*Edinburgh?*] *Printed in the year* 1745.
4°: A–D²; *1–2* 3–16.
'Hail glorious youth! the wonder of the age'
L(1093.d.108; C.38.g.14/19),E,AdU; CSmH, IU,OCU.

T343 — [first line:] To John Caswal esquire, so brisk and so bold. [*Hereford?* 1741.]
½°: 1 side, 1 column.
'To John Caswal esquire, so brisk and so bold'
A Leominster election ballad in favour of John Caswell.
MC.

— To Mr. Law, 1720. *See* Ramsay, Allan.

T344 — To Mr. Philips, on his late poetry in Ireland. [*Dublin*, 1725/27?]
½°: 1 side, 1 column.
'Gentle poet, brother swain'
A satire on Ambrose Philips's namby-pamby verses.
CSmH.

T345 — [dh] To Mr. S-------- M-----, on his turning evidence. [col] *London*, '*printed for T. Cooper*', 1747.
8°: *A²*; *1–4*.
The imprint is false; Thomas Cooper died in 1743. Possibly an Edinburgh edition. A slightly different text from the following.
'To all that virtue's holy ties can boast'
A satire on Sir John Murray of Broughton, secretary to the Young Pretender, who turned king's evidence.
L(1489.gg.1/16),O,*AdU,LdU-B*.

T346 — [*idem*] Lord Lovat's last legacy, to his particular friend secretary M----y. *London*, *printed for W. Webb*, [1748.] (*GM* April)
2°: *A² < B¹*; *1–2* 3–6.
L(515.l.11/6, uncut),AdU; ICN,InU.

T347 — To Mr. Stanhope, one of the managers of the house of commons, and general of her majesty's forces. *London*, *printed for and sold by H. Hills*, & *John Baker*, 1710. (*SR* 4 Oct)
½°: 1 side, 1 column.
Roman colon after 'London' in imprint. Deposit copy at E.
'Whene'er you fought the haughty foes were broke'
O,E; MH(Luttrell, 5 Oct).

T348 — [another edition]
Italic colon after 'London' in imprint.
LLP,Rothschild; InU,OCU.

T349 — — '*London*, *printed for and sold by H. Hills*, & *John Baker*' [*Dublin*], 1710.

To Mr. Stanhope

½°: 1 side, 1 column.
On the other side, *A poem humbly dedicated to...William lord Cowper*, 1710.
DG.

T350 — [dh] To Mr. Thomas Murray, on a celebrated picture drawn by him, representing George Granville, Henry St. John, and Thomas Cook esquires. [*London*, 170–?]
4°: *A²*; *1–4*.
'Inform me, Murray, by what wondrous skill'
LVA-F.

T351 — To Mrs. Cibber, a poem. *Dublin*, *printed by and for George Faulkner*, 1742.
8°: *A⁶*; *1–3* 4–10 *11–12*.
Stub only of A6 seen.
'O thou, to whom thy poet pays'
Possibly by Edward Moore.
LVA-F(–A6).

— 'To modern poverty: a satirical poem. 5 pp., 1705.'
Listed by *Morgan* H439, possibly from ms.

T352 — [dh] To my friend Dr. Tho. Clark, physician and oculist, on his great skill in the opticks, and successful cures. [*London?* 1705.]
4°: *A²*; *1–4*.
'When deeds like thine our just encomiums raise'
Provoked by the knighthoods conferred in July 1705 on Edward Hannes and William Read (who are attacked here).
O.

T353 — To my lord bishop of R— — on his noble, and constant behaviour against time-servers, courtiers, and trimmers. [*London?* 1709?]
2°: *A²*; *1–2* 3–4.
Title in half-title form. Despite the location of the only copy seen, it appears to be a London edition. The order of editions is uncertain.
'Great soul! who no disguise, no changes knows'
Addressed to John Pooley, bishop of Raphoe, who was committed to Dublin castle in June 1709 for a protest he made in the Irish house of lords.
DT.

T354 — To my lord bishop of Raphoe... [*Dublin?* 1709?]
½°: 2 sides, 1 column.
DG.

T355 — To my worthy friend T--- S--- D.D. on his incomparable translation of, and notes on Persius. [*Dublin*, 1728?]
½°: 1 side, 1 column.
The DT copy is bound with half-sheets of 1727.
'Hail bard triumphant! whose poetick fire'
On Thomas Sheridan's *Persius*, 1728.
DT.

To Nicholas Harding

T356 — To Nicholas Harding, esq; on his being appointed law-reader to his royal-highness the duke. *London, printed for J. Roberts*, 1732. (*LM* Dec)
2°: *A*² B²; *1–2* 3–8.
'In your proceedings with the royal-youth'
OCU.

T357 — To Robert Ch-ster, esq; in imitation of the first ode of Horace. *London, printed for J. Morphew*, [1720.] (*PB* 23 Aug)
4°: A–C² (A2 as 'A'); *1–2* 3–10 *11–12 blk*.
'Ch-ster, my patron and my aid'
  To Robert Chester.
L(162.1.21, Luttrell, Aug, –C2),O.

T358 — To Robert earl of Oxford, late lord treasurer, on his excess of mirth at the proclaiming of his majesty King George. To the tune of, Ye commons and peers. By J.P. [*London*, 1714.]
slip: 1 side, 1 column.
  The rule between title and text is in one piece. The order of editions has not been determined, but the printing of this is superior.
'I thought to have sent/My due compliment'
Herts CRO (Panshanger box 46); CSmH.

T359 — [another edition]
  The rule between title and text is in two parts.
L(C.121.g.9/147),O.

— To Sir Godfrey Kneller, at his country seat, 1722. *See* Tickell, Thomas.

T360 — To Sylvia, a poem. Occasion'd by her commending the epistles of the platonick lovers, Clio and Strephon. *London, printed in the year* 1738.
4°: *A*² B–C⁴ D²; *1–4* 5–21 *22–24 blk*.
'Grant me, great love, that gen'rous fire to know'
  Occasioned by *The epistles of Clio and Strephon*, 1720–, by Martha Fowke and William Bond.
IU.

— To the anonymous author of a Latin ode, [1732?] *See* Robertson, Alexander.

T361 — To the author of a late lampoon. *Dublin, printed in the year* 1729.
½°: 1 side, 1 column.
'While your dul lines in senseless numbers flow'
  Against a satirist of the ladies.
DN.

— To the author of the panegyrick on the Canterbury ladies, 1718. *See* Goatley, John.

T362 — To the citizens. *Dublin, printed by G. Needham*, 1724. (Oct?)
½°: 1 side, 1 column.
  Teerink 1151; *Williams* 1110.
'And shall the patriot who maintain'd your cause'
  Signed 'M.B.', and accordingly ascribed to Swift by Scott (*Works*, 1814, X. 579). Rejected by Williams. The last line was quoted by Tickell in a letter of 1 Nov 1724. Conceivably

To the citizens

by Mary Barber who published half-sheets with these initials at this period.
L(C.121.g.8/33),*LVA-F*,DT,Crawford; *CtY*.

T363 — To the college poets who are encourag'd to write on his majesty's birth-day. [*Dublin*, 1727?]
½°: 1 side, 1 column.
'Let the aspiring few, who pant for fame'
  A prize was offered by Robert Clayton to the members of Trinity College, Dublin; cf. G267, M356.
L(C.121.g.8/187, imprint cropt).

— To the divine majesty, a poem, 1733. *See* Preston, William.

— To the Dutchess of Grafton, 1723. *See* Delany, Patrick.

T364 — To the Duke of Marlborough, on the taking of Bouchain. *London, printed for W.H.; sold by S. Popping*, 1711.
½°: 1 side, 1 column.
'Great, glorious man! Thus after clouds more bright'
L(G.1390/18),LLP,LSA,DT; MH.

T365 — — [*Dublin?* 1711?]
½°: 1 side, 1 column.
  On the other side of copies at L,LSA,CtY, *To the most illustrious hero George Lewis*, [1713?].
L(C.121.g.8/5),LSA; CtY,MH.

T366 — To the Duke of Marlborough, upon the late victory at Blaregnies. *London, printed by E. Berington, for E. Sanger*, 1709.
½°: 2 sides, 1 column.
'Tho' bold the muse, yet scarce she dares assay'
L(Cup.645.e.1/12),Crawford.

[T367 cancelled]

T368 — To the E. of O----d; with the report of the committee of secrecy. *London, printed for John Baker*, 1715. (9 Aug, Luttrell)
2°: *A*¹ B²; *1–2* 3–6.
  The Luttrell copy was once in the possession of Messrs. Dobell.
'O thou great patron of mysterious fame'
  Morgan R378 attributes to Edward Minshull, but quotes no evidence. To Robert Harley, earl of Oxford.
NjP,OCU.

T369 — — *Dublin, re-printed and sold by Thomas Humes*, 1715.
4°: (2 ll).
(*Dobell* 2675.)

T370 — [dh] To the Earl of Essex, on his instalment, June the 15th, 1738. [*London*, 1738.]
4°: *A*²; *1* 2–3 *4 blk*.
'The prize which worth deserves, when worth receives'
  On his installation as knight of the garter.
CSmH.

To the falsely celebrated

— To the falsely celebrated British Homer, 1742. *See* Morrice, Bezaleel.

T371 — To the fore-chairman that carried her majesty, February ------, 1732. By a gentleman at Bath. *Bath, printed [by Felix Farley] in the year* 1733. 2°: $A^2 < B^2$; *3–5* 6–9 *10* blk.

> Text of p. 9 on cancel slip pasted over the original. *Motteaux before the eight copies of verses...* 1733, is bound with the O,BaP copies of this, and perhaps belongs with it.
> 'Unhappy man! Traitor, I dare not say'
> The chairman dropped her majesty.

L(162.n.72, presentation copy to Viscount Torrington),O(with ms. Latin translation by Thomas Dibben),BaP; OCU.

T372 — To the honourable Master Henry Barry, son to the right honourable the Lord Santry, on his birth-day. By one of his school-fellows. [*Dublin*, 1725/30.] ½°: 1 side, 1 column.

> The copy at L forms part of a collection of Dublin half-sheets of 1725/30.
> 'My master, sir, I must obey'
> Ms. date '7br. 3th.' in the L copy is in the same hand as the date on Edward Davys, lord Mountcashel's *To his excellency our Lord Carteret*, [1725.] Probably both were written at Thomas Sheridan's school, and this may also be by Mountcashel.

L(C.121.g.8/131).

T373 — To the honourable Mr. D.T. great pattern of piety, charity, learning, humanity, good nature, wisdom, good breeding, affability, and one most eminently distinguished for his conjugal affection. *Dublin, printed by S. Harding*, 1725. ½°: *1–2*, 1 column.

> *Teerink* 921; *Williams* 1126. Above imprint, 'This paper will be continued weekly, if due encouragement be given.'
> 'What strange disorder often springs'
> This and the following were ascribed to Swift by Ball, but rejected by Williams, who records a copy once in the possession of Messrs. Pickering & Chatto with a contemporary ms. attribution to 'T. Sherridon, D.D.' A satire against Richard Tighe.

L(1890.e.5/229; C.121.g.8/63),C,Rothschild; CSmH,MH,PU.

T374 — Numb. II. The following fable is most humbly inscribed to the honourable Mr. D.T.... The sick lyon and the ass. *Dublin, printed by Sarah Harding*, 1725. ½°: 1 side, 1 column.

> *Teerink* 921; *Williams* 1127.
> 'A lyon sunk by time's decay'
> Reprinted in *Poems written occasionally by the late John Winstanley... interspers'd with many others*, II (1751).

L(C.121.g.8/63),C,DN,Rothschild; CSmH, CtY,MH,PU.

To the honourable Sr. John Clerk

— To the honourable, Sr. John Clerk of Pennycuik, [1722.] *See* Ramsay, Allan.

T375 — To the honoured Cavendish Weedon, esq; upon his excellent and pious entertainment of divine musick, perform'd at Stationers-hall. *London printed, and sold by John Nutt*, 1702. (16 Feb, Luttrell) ½°: 1 side, 1 column. 'Your sacred anthems, pious hymns, and psalms' MH(Luttrell).

T376 — To the immortal memory of that renowned manager, and hero, who obtain'd a signal victory over the Spanish forces... An epigram. [*London*, 1710.] (*SR* 9 Oct) ½°: 1 side, 1 column.

> Engraved throughout; a military trophy above text. Entered in *SR* by Jane Simson to Symon Sympson.
> 'Large is the fame, great hero, thou hast won'
> On the victory of James Stanhope at Saragossa.

L(1876.f.1/51; P&D 1530),O.

— To the ingenious Mr. John Moor, [1716?] *See* Pope, Alexander.

T377 — To the k---g's most excellent m——y, the humble address of the Tower of London, presented by the committee of secrecy, June the 10th, 1715. introduced by his grace the D. of M------. [*London?* 1715.] *slip*: 1 side, 1 column.

> 'Let England's church her sinking state deplore'
> *Crum* L171. Jacobite verses, suggesting that George I as tyrant will need the help of the Tower.

L(11626.i.11/1).

T378 — [another edition, title reads:]...presented by the secret committee... CSmH.

T379 — To the king. [*London*, 1714.] ½°: 1 side, 1 column. 'As a fond mother anxious for her son' Welcoming George I's first landing in England. O,Crawford.

T380 — To the ladies of Dublin, a poem. To which is added, Ierne's answer to Albion. By a lady. *Dublin, printed by James Esdall*, 1745. 8°: A^4; *1–3* 4–7 *8* blk. 'Tell me unthinking giddy nymphs' *Ierne*: 'Sister, I sometimes have complain'd' L(11631.bb.48),DN,DT; CtY.

— To the memory of a lady lately deceased. A monody, 1747–. *See* Lyttelton, George, *baron Lyttelton*.

T381 — To the memory of Alexander Robertson of Strowan. [*Edinburgh?* 1749?] 8°: A^2; *1–4*. Title in half-title form.

To the memory of Alexander Robertson

'Shall Strowan fall without the warrior's bays'
NjP.

— To the memory of Edward Russel, late earl of Orford, 1731. *See* Samber, Robert.

— To the memory of Mr. David Drummond, [1741.] *See* Drummond, Thomas.

T382 — To the memory of Sir James Steuart elder, her majesty's advocate. [*Edinburgh*, 1713.]
½⁰: 1 side, 1 column.
'Speak, grieved muse, alarm the world, and read'
E(3),Rosebery.

— To the memory of Sir William Wallace, [1746.] *See* To his grace, James, duke of Perth, &c, [1746.]

— To the memory of the late reverend Mr. John Anderson, 1721. *See* Boyse, Samuel.

— To the memory of the revd. Mr. Mordecai Andrews, 1750. *See* Cole, John.

— To the memory of the right honourable John earl of Strathmore, [1715/16?] *See* Meston, William.

— To the memory of the right honourable William, late earl of Kintore, 1719. *See* Harvey, John.

— To the memory of the right reverend father in god, Francis Gastrell, 1726. *See* Wesley, Samuel, *the younger*.

T383 — [dh] To the memory of the singularly accomplish'd Mr. William Dunlop, regius professor of divinity...who died October 29. 1720. [*Edinburgh*, 1720.]
4⁰: *A*⁴; 1–7 8 blk.
'Just so the beauteous flow'r'
E.

— To the memory of the truly pious Sir George Freeman, [171–/22.] *See* Bonwick, Ambrose.

T384 — To the memory of the very reverend and truly pious George Meldrum...who died the 18th day of February 1709, in the 75th year of his age. A pindarick ode. *Edinburgh, printed by the heirs and successors of Andrew Anderson*, 1709.
4⁰: *A*⁴; ⟨i–iv, 5⟩–8.
'Awake my muse, go to'
L(11622.bb.1/2, slightly cropt).

T385 — [dh] To the ministers and elders met at Edinburgh April 26, 1710. The just complaint and remonstrance of the national covenant of Scotland, and the solemn league and covenant of the three kingdoms... [*Edinburgh*, 1710.]
8⁰: A⁴; 1 2–8.
'That whereas your petitioners forlorn'
   Complaining of their betrayal of the reformation.
L(11630.aaa.1),O.

T386 — To the most illustrious hero George Lewis... duke of Brunswick, and Lunenburg...presumptive heir by laws humane and divine, to the crown

To the most illustrious hero

of Great Britain, France and Ireland. [*Dublin?* 1713?]
½⁰: 1 side, 1 column.
   On the other side, *To the Duke of Marlborough, on the taking of Bouchain*, [1711?]. The L copy is bound with a collection of Dublin half-sheets. Printed at London in *Two poems*, 1713.
'I sing the prince, the scourge of Gallick power'
L(C.121.g.8/5),LSA; CtY.

T387 — — *Dublin, printed by Elizabeth Dickson*, [1713.]
½⁰: 1 side, 1 column.
(Dobell cat. 105/310.)

T388 — To the most serene and potent princess, Ann of Scotland, England, France and Ireland queen. The humble and hearty address, of a great many of your majesties subjects presbyterians, of the church of Scotland, whose maxims are known to be consistent with monarchy, contrary to the false aspersions of their enemies. [*Edinburgh*, 1702.]
½⁰: 1 side, 2 columns.
'With floods of tears we cannot but deplore'
L(11602.i.6/9).

— To the queen, on her coronation day, 1706. *See* Walsh, William [Horace lib. III. ode III. imitated].

[**T389** = S468·7] — To the queen, on the happy conclusion of the peace, [1713.] *See* Sinclair, *Sir* Archibald.

T390 — [dh] To the reverend Doctor Swift, dean of St. Patrick's. With a present of a paper-book, finely bound, on his birth-day, November 30, 1732. [col] *Dublin, printed by George Faulkner*, 1733.
4⁰: *A*²; 1 2 3–4.
   Teerink 1307. With two other poems, 'Verses left with a silver standish...' and 'Sent with a quill...'
'To thee, dear Swift, these spotless leaves I send'
'Hither from Mexico I came'
'Shall then my kindred all my glory claim'
   The first two poems are ascribed to John Boyle, earl of Orrey, and Patrick Delany in Faulkner's edition of Swift; the third is printed by Laetitia Pilkington in her *Memoirs*, 1748.
C; MH.

— To the right honourable Arthur, earl of Anglesey, [1721.] *See* Delany, Patrick.

T390·5 — To the right honourable Lady Mary, vis. T——y. On wishing to have an acrostick wrote on her name. Supposed by B. B——m, esq; *Dublin, printed by James Hoey*, 1732–3.
½⁰: 1 side, 1 column.
'Restraint and fear alike destroy'
C.

— To the right honourable Mr. Harley, 1711. *See* Castleton, Nathaniel.

To the right honourable Mr. Harley

— To the right honourable Mr. Harley, on his first appearing in publick, 1711. *See* Trapp, Joseph.

— To the right honourable Mr. Harley, wounded by Guiscard, 1711. *See* Prior, Matthew.

— To the right honourable Sir George Rooke, 1702. *See* Tooke, Charles.

T391 — To the right honourable the Earl of Oxford and Mortimer, lord high-treasurer of Great Britain: after his recovery of the wounds given him by Guiscard. *London, printed for J. Morphew,* 1711. (15 June, Luttrell)
2°: *A²*; *1–2* 3–4.
　　Advertised in *DC* 15 Sept.
'Since you, my lord, did Europe's fate support'
LLP,O(Luttrell); TxU(2).

T392 — To the right honourable the Earl of Oxford, upon his not appearing at St. James's. [*London,* 1727?]
½°: 1 side, 2 columns.
'Whilst thick to court transported tories run'
　　To Edward Harley, second earl of Oxford, reminding him of his father's virtues and George I's treatment of him.
L(C.121.g.9/191, cropt); OCU.

T393 — [dh] To the right honourable the Lady Aubrey Beauclerk. In memory of her lord. [*London,* 1741.]
4°: **⁴; *1* 2–8.
'Shall so much worth in silence pass away'
　　Lord Aubrey Beauclerk was killed in the attack on Boca Chica, 1741.
L(11657.m.3).

— To the right honourable the Lady Elizabeth Boyle, 1733. *See* Barber, Constantine.

— To the right honourable the Lord Harley, on the promotion, 1711. *See* Castleton, Nathaniel.

T394 — To the right honourable the lord high treasurer of Great Britain. *London printed, and sold by J. Morphew,* 1711. (11 Oct, Luttrell)
½°: 1 side, 1 column.
'When from his breast, brave Harley drew the knife'
　　To Harley after the attack by Guiscard.
ICN(Luttrell).

T395 — To the right honourable the Lord P---m, at the H---r c--b. *London, printed for Ferd. Burleigh,* [1714.] (8 April?)
½°: 2 sides, 1 column.
　　With the halfpenny tax stamp.
'When Horace so divinely sings'
　　Inviting Thomas Pelham, subsequently duke of Newcastle, to act the part of Maecenas to the poet.
CSmH(ms. date 8 April).

— To the right honourable the lord Viscount Mont-Cassel, 1727. *See* Sheridan, Thomas.

— To the right honourable William lord Harrington, 1730. *See* Boyd, Elizabeth.

To the right reverend

— To the right reverend & religious Dame Elizabeth Phillips, [1731.] *See* Phillips, Thomas.

T396 — To the soldiers of Great Britain. Upon passing an act which enables the court martial to punish mutiny and desertion with death. [*London?* 1717/18.]
slip: 1 side, 1 column.
　　Printed with *An elegy upon the young prince,* [1717/18], E288; the NjP copy is not divided.
'Let the soldiers beware/How they're caut in a snare'
　　A Jacobite song addressed to the army.
O; NjP.

T397 — To the truely noble, James marquess of Montrose, on his auspicious marriage, with the very vertuous lady, Lady Christian Carnagie, daughter to the right honourable, the late Earl of North-Esk. On Easter-Munday, Apr. 6. 1702. [*Edinburgh,* 1702.]
½°: 1 side, 1 column.
'Permit, my lord, me to congratulate'
E.

— To the tune of James Anderson my jo, [1712?/13.] *See* Pitcairne, Archibald.

T398 — To the worshipful, cordners of the West-port,| A humble petition is enter'd in court|For apprentice boys, who would fain take a drink,|Be blyth like their masters, but want ready clink. [*Edinburgh,* 1725.] (8 May)
½°: 1 side, 1 column.
　　Printed date above title, '(May 8th, 1725.)'.
'Ye sons of old Crispian, a saint and a king'
　　The apprentices ask for a drink at the cordwainers' incorporation celebration.
E.

T399 — To Venus, upon the charms of music: occasion'd by a musical assembly of gentlemen and ladies. [*Canterbury?* 1722?]
½°: 1 side, 1 column.
　　The O copy was given to Thomas Hearne 25 June 1722 with two other half-sheets, one certainly, the other probably, printed at Canterbury.
'Goddess of beauty, have a care'
　　Given to Hearne by Thomas Allen, rector of Thurston, who may possibly be the author.
O.

Toast. The toast, an epic poem, 1732–. *See* King, William, *principal of St. Mary Hall.*

T400 — A toast for A--------e and Robbin, in the French wine. *London, printed for John Turnham, near St. Paul's church-yard,* 1711. (8 Dec, Luttrell)
½°: 1 side, 1 column.
'Great A—— be cautious and beware'
　　In praise of Anne and Harley, in hope of peace.
L(1850.e.10/10; G.1390/113); ICN(Luttrell).

Toast

T401 — A toast for all true hearts. [*London*] *Printed in the year* 1710. (*SR* 22 May)

½°: 1 side, 1 column.

> Entered in *SR* to Richard Newcomb. No lines run over.

'Long life to the queen, and a prosperous reign'

> *Crum* L549: 'A new health...' In praise of Sacheverell.

LSA.

T402 — [another edition]

> Most of the lines run over.

Rothschild.

T403 — [*idem*] The church of England's new toast. [*London*?] *Printed in the year* 1710.

½°: 1 side, 1 column.

> An expansion from 12 to 26 lines, probably for use as election propaganda.

O.

T404 **Toasts.** The toasts. A new ballad. Tune, To all you ladies now at land. [*London*? 1731/35.]

½°: 1 side, 2 columns.

'To toast the fair of Britain's isle'

> To seven named beauties.

L(C.121.g.9/203).

T404·5 **Tobacco.** Tobacco, a poem. [*London*, 1733.] (Feb)

½°: *1–2*, 1 column.

> Two engraved coats of arms of John Lacy and Thomas Lacy flank the title. Two paragraphs of advertisement at the foot of p. 2, 'The *History of tobacco*...by J. Lacy, merchant, will be given away next week, at the corner of Spring-Gardens... At the same place, is sold all sorts of pigtail tobacco...' The 'History of tobacco' is almost certainly *Observations on the nature, use and trade of tobacco*, 1733, which is signed 'J. Lacy' and dated 1 March. Misdated [1671] by the L catalogue.

'Hail thought inspiring plant! Thou balm of life!'

> Clearly published by Lacy as part of the campaign against Walpole's excise act; and if he wrote the *Observations* himself, it is possible that he wrote this poem as well. Lacy's Christian name is variously given as John and Joseph; a Joseph Lacy who was a tobacco merchant published a defence of his bankruptcy at Dunkirk in 1729, and *Watt* assumes their identity.

L(C.121.g.9/20).

T404·6 — [another impression]

> This impression has only the first paragraph of advertisement at the foot of p. 2, which refers to the forthcoming *History of tobacco* (it is here signed 'Lacy'); the second paragraph advertising the sale of tobacco is omitted. The order of impressions has not

Tobacco, a poem

> been determined. The copy seen does not bear the engraved coats of arms.

L(1968).

— Tobacco: a poem in two books, 1716–. *See* Player, Henry.

[Todderill, T.] Otia votiva: or, poems upon several occasions, 1705. *See* Otia.

Tollet, Elizabeth. Poems on several occasions. With Anne Boleyn to King Henry VIII. an epistle. *London, printed for John Clarke*, 1755.

12°: pp. 238. L; CSmH,DLC.

— [reissue] The second edition. *London, printed for T. Lownds*, [176–?]

> L.

Cancel title.

T405 **Tolson, Francis.** Hermathenæ, or moral emblems, and ethnick tales, with explanatory notes; vol. I. [*London*, 174–.]

8°: (engraved title+) *a⁴ b² A–K⁸ L⁸(L7+χ¹)*; *i–xii, 1–173 174–177; 178 blk. χ1, L8 err.*

> The title-page is engraved; there is an engraved emblem to each poem. Proposals were issued in Sept 1739 (copy at L) and 8 Oct 1739 (copy at GU); they offer fine-paper copies on imperial paper, but all copies seen have fleur-de-lys watermark. Subscribers' list on pp. vi–xi.

'When dawning nature in the world's first age'

L(12304.f.8,–L8,χ1),O,EU,GU(2); *DFo,MH*.

T406 — Octavius prince of Syra, or, a lash for Levi. A poem. *London, printed for T. Warner*, 1719.

8°: *B–E⁴ (B3 as 'B'); 1–4 5–31 32 blk.* B1 hft.

'In ancient honest days, e'er factious pride'

> A political and religious satire.

L(11633.bb.1/5),O(–B1),LdU-B; CtY,IU,MH (ms. annotations).

T407 — A poem on his majesty's passing the South-Sea bill. *London, sold by J. Morphew*, 1720.

2°: *A² B–C²; i–iv, 1–7 8 blk.*

'Ye heav'ns! To what a boundless theam'

MH-BA.

[T408 = B514·5] Tom. Tom. Brown's letter from the shades, [1713?] *See* Brown, Thomas.

— Tom in the suds, 1737–. *See* Wilkes, Wetenhall.

— Tom K----g's: or, the Paphian grove, 1738–. *See* Barber, James.

T409 — Tom of Bedlam: or, a mad poem, writ by a mad author. Reflecting on the madness of some persons, who make all people mad that have any thing to do with them. *London printed, and are to be sold by the booksellers of London & Westminster*, 1701. (1 Sept, Luttrell)

2°: *π¹ A² B–C² D¹; i–iv, 1–12. π1 hft.*

> The Luttrell copy is recorded in *Haslewood*; listed in *WL* Sept.

Tom of Bedlam

'So ho, who's there? Alas, where am I got?'
Luke Milbourne's authorship has been proposed by Dawson's cat. 167 (1966) 657 on the parallel of his *Tom of Bedlam's answer*, 1709; it seems unlikely. 'A satyr on a priest statesman, 5 Kentish petitioners and the Society of Reformation', Luttrell.
L(163.n.11,−π1),LG,O(2,−π1),C*J*,LdU-B
(−π1)+; CtY,ICN,MH,OCU,TxU+.

[T410 = H145·5] — Tom o' Bedlam's Dunciad: or, Pope Alexander the pig, 1729. *See* Henley, John.

T411 — Tom of Bedlam's new medley. *London, printed by F. Clifton*, [1720.]
½°: 1 side, 2 columns.
Two rough woodcuts at head. On the other side of the L copy, the 'dying speech' of Mr. Davis, 1720.
'Ye tories of Britain, if you think it fitting'
L(1872.a.1/160*).

— Tom Pun-sibi metamorphosed, 1724. *See* Tisdall, William.

T412 — Tom Punsibi's farewel to the muses. *Dublin, printed in the year* 1725.
½°: 1 side, 1 column.
'This is to give notice, I Tom the great scribler'
A satire on Thomas Sheridan.
L(1890.e.5/226).

— Tom Punsibi's letter to Dean Swift, 1727. *See* Sheridan, Thomas.

T413 — Tom Pun-sibi's resurrection disprov'd. [*Dublin*, 1722.] (June?)
½°: *1–2*, 2 columns.
'Well Ralph, howe'er your pleas'd to strive'
A reply to a mock *Elegy on the deplorable death of Mr. Thomas Sheridan*, [1722], and a lost poem on his resurrection. Cf. *A poam on Tom Pun----bi*, 1722.
DN; CSmH(ms. date June 1722),TxU.

T414 Tomkins, T. A tale of Midas the king. Dedicated to Ar----r Tariff, one of my lords footmen. *London, printed for J. Baker*, 1714. (May, Luttrell)
8°: *A*⁴ B–C⁴; *i–xii, 1 2–9 10–11; 12 blk*. A1 hft; 10–11 advt.
'Ye sisters nine, assist my quill'
Dedication signed 'T. Tomkins', probably a pseudonym; the MH catalogue relates it to the pseudonymous Timothy Tomkins who wrote *A letter to Mr. Steele*, 1714. A skit on Arthur Moore, the economist and politician.
L(164.l.45, Luttrell),O; CLU-C,CSmH,CtY
(−A1, C4),DFo,MH(uncut,−C4).

T415 Tomlinson, Matthew. An ode sacred to the memory of her late majesty. *London, printed in the year* 1737.
4°: *A*⁴; *1–5 6–8*. A1 hft.
'Begin my muse, and strike the adventrous string'
Signed at the end from Blyth, 24 Dec 1737.
Rosenbach.

Tomlinson, M.

T416 — The trinity. A poem. *London, printed for R. Dodsley*, 1745. (*GM*, *LM* May)
4°: A–C⁴; *i–ii iii–iv, 5–24*.
'Beyond the vast circumf'rence of the skies'
CSmH.

T417 — — The second edition, corrected and very much enlarged. *London, printed for R. Dodsley; sold by M. Cooper*, 1750.
4°: *A*⁴ B–C⁴ D²; *1–2 3–28*.
L(11630.d.9/11).

T418 [**Tooke, Charles.**] To the right honourable Sir George Rooke, vice admiral of England &c. at his return from his glorious enterprize near Vigo. 1702. *London, printed for Benj. Tooke*, 1702 [1703]. (15 Jan, Luttrell)
2°: *A*² B–D²; *i–iv, 1–11 12 blk*. A1 hft.
Watermark: Amsterdam arms. Listed in *WL* Jan 1703.
'Amidst the loud applause, which fills the ears'
R. W. Chapman in *RES* 1 (1925) 92 quotes a ms. attribution to Tooke; it is reprinted as his in *A collection of poems*, 1716 (*Case* 151g).
L(11630.h.61),O(−A1),EtC(−A1),*MR-C*; CSmH(−A1),MB,TxU(Luttrell).

T419 [—] [fine paper]
Watermark: D.
NN.

[**Tooly, Thomas.**] Miscellaneous translations from Bion, Ovid, Moschus, and Mr. Addison, 1716. *See* Miscellaneous.

[—] Basia: or, the charms of kissing. Translated from the Latin of Catullus and Secundus, and the Greek of Menage. *London printed, and sold by T. Bickerton*, 1719. (*SR* 28 Nov)
8°: pp. 38. O,EU; CSmH.
Attributed to Tooly by *Rawlinson*. Entered in *SR* to William Bray; deposit copies at O,EU. Advertised in *PB* 8 Dec.

[—] — The second edition. *London printed, and sold by T. Bickerton*, 1719. (*PB* 24 Dec)
8°: pp. 38. L.
A 'third edition' was advertised in *PB* 5 Jan 1720.

According to Tooly's account of himself in Rawlinson, *'He printed also some hundreds of other pieces in verse and prose'; but none has been identified.*

T420 [—] Homer in a nutshell: or, the Iliad of Homer in immortal doggrel. By Nickydemus Ninnyhammer, F.G. *London, printed for W. Sparkes over against the Golden Lyon in Fetter-lane in Fleet-street*, 1715. (*PB* 16 July)
12°: A–C¹² D⁴; *i–xii, 1 2–68*.
Bond 43. Some copies have misprint 'Aledt-street' in imprint. The Nichol Smith copy (now at the National Library of Australia,

Tooly, T. Homer in a nutshell

Canberra) had a folding frontispiece stabbed round A, not seen elsewhere.
'I sing the rancour of a knight'
Attributed to Tooly by *Rawlinson* (who gives the publication date as 1717). W. H. Irving, *John Gay*, very tentatively suggested Gay's authorship; the O copy of the reissue is bound in late nineteenth-century cloth, lettered as by 'J. Bridges'.
L(832.c.43),O; *CLU-C*,CtY,IU(uncut),OCU, TxU(uncut).

T421 [—] [reissue] Homer travestie: being a new translation of that great poet. With a critical preface and learned notes. Shewing how this translation excells Chapman, Hobbes, Ogilby, Dryden, Pope, and all other pretenders. *London, printed for W. Boreham*, 1720. (*DP* 16 Nov)
12°: A¹²(−A1–6 +A1.2) B–C¹² D⁴; *i–iv, 1 2–68*.
The copyright of 'Homer in a Nutshell' formed part of lot 22 in the trade sale of T. Woodward, 12 March 1752 (cat. at O-JJ).
L(1962),O; IU.

T422 Torbay. The Torbay expedition: a satire. *London, printed for T. Robins; sold at the Royal Exchange, St. James's, Bond-street, and Charing-Cross*, 1740. (*GM, LM* Oct)
4°: A⁴ B⁴; *1–5 6–15 16 blk*.
The copy recorded lacks A1, doubtless a half-title as in the following.
'Stout Jason's golden fleece, the sacking Troy'
PU(−A1).

T423 —— The second edition. *London, printed for T. Robins; sold at the Royal Exchange, St. James's, Bond-street, and Charing-Cross*, 1740.
4°: A⁴ B⁴; *1–5 6–15 16 blk*. A1 hft.
Apparently a reimpression.
CSmH(uncut).

T424 Tories. The tories address to King G——e. A satirical poem... By a well-wisher to his king and country. *London, printed for R. Burleigh*, 1716. (14 Feb, Luttrell)
8°: A–E⁴; *1–8 9–40*.
Listed in *MC* Feb.
'Your duteous subjects, sir, and loyal'
A satire on the tories.
L(164.k.17, Luttrell).

—— The tories looking-glass: a congratulatory poem in commemoration of his majesty's birth-day, May 28, 1718. *See* Gaynam, John.

T425 —— The tories triumph on the news of the Pretender's expedition to Switzerland, alias England. Being a new song to a merry old tune, made in the year 1641. reviv'd in 1683. and lately perform'd at the Bell-tavern in W——r. [*London*] Printed in the year 1711.
½°: 1 side, 2 columns.
'Now, now the whigs shall all go down'

The **tories** triumph

A satire on the tories.
O,Crawford.

T426 Tory. The tory hero: or, the run-away general. To the tune of How happy are we, &c. *London printed, and sold by A. Boulter*, 1715.
slip: 1 side, 1 column.
'Ye tories for shame,/Give over your game'
Possibly referring to James Butler, duke of Ormonde, who fled to France 8 Aug 1715.
Harding.

—— The tory's downfall, 1715. *See* 'Rowe, Nicholas'.

T427 Totnes. The Totness address transversed. By Captain Gulliver... To which is added, somewhat beside. *London, printed for H. Curll*, 1727.
8°: A⁴; *1–2 3–8*.
Teerink 1226. The only copies seen have been issued in *The altar of love*, 1727 (*Case* 340); these apparently contain the *Totness address* as a self-contained unit, but it may have been originally issued with some other poems.
'We loyal subjects, may it please ye'
L(1490.d.59); *MH*.

—— The Totness address, versified, 1727. *See* Mitchell, Joseph.

T428 Touch. A touch of the times. A new ballad. To the tune of, Oh! London is a fine town. *London, printed for T. Cooper*, 1740 [1739]. (*GM, LM* Nov)
2°: A⁴; *1–3 4–8*.
Percival LIII. Entered to George Hawkins in Bowyer's ledgers under 15 Nov, 500 copies printed.
'Good people all, I pray attend'
A satire on the behaviour of the common council of London.
L(162.n.54); CtY,MH,OCU(uncut),TxU(2).

T429 — [dh] A touch of the times. A new ballad. [*Edinburgh*, 1740.]
8°: A²; *1–4*.
Printed by Ruddiman on the evidence of the ornament.
L(806.k.16/129).

T430 — A touch of the times: an allusion to our good Samaritan King George. With the Jacobites purgatory and prayer. *London, printed for the author; sold by J. Marshal⟨l⟩*, 1717.
12°: A⁶ B²; *1–2 3–16*.
'England of late has fell among the thieves'
CSmH.

T431 — A touch to the wheedlers. Or,|What high and low|Must all pass through|at last. *London printed and re-printed in Dublin*, 1711.
½°: 1 side, 1 column.
On the other side, [Edward Ward] *The religious turncoat*, [1711.]

A **touch** to the wheedlers

'May such be crost, if not be curs'd who's zeal'
Against the dissenters.
C.

Tower. The tower, 1727. *See* Foxton, Thomas.

— The tower of Babel, 1718. *See* Ward, Edward.

[**Towers, John.**] A poem occasioned by a view of Powers-court House, 1741. *See* P548.

T432 Town. The town assemblies. A satyr. *London, printed for S. Baker*, 1717. (*PB* 21 Nov)
8º: *A*⁴ B–D⁴; *i–viii*, 1–24. A1 hft; viii err.
'When flagrant scandals o'er the world prevail'
LG,*LdU-B*; CtY,*DFo*.

— The town despis'd, [170–.] *See* Pomfret, John (P726).

T433 — The town display'd, in a letter to Amintor in the country. *London, printed in the year* 1701. (10 July, Luttrell)
2º: A–D²; *1–2* 3–16.
'My dear Amintor, on a summer's day'
'Reflects upon the women of the town, the men, divines & poets', Luttrell.
LG,LLP,O,*CY*,LdU-B; CLU-C(2),CtY(Luttrell), IU,MH,TxU(2).

T434 — A town eclogue in allusion to part of the fifth eclogue of Virgil: on the death of the celebrated Matthew Prior, esq; *London, printed for T. Bickerton*, 1721. (*DJ* 28 Sept)
2º: *A*⁴; *1–3* 4–8.
'Dear Dick! since thus conveniently we meet'
O; TxU.

T435 — A town eclogue: or, a poetical contest between Toby and a minor-poet of B-tt-n's Coffee-house ...being an imitation after the new mode of the 3d eclogue of Virgil. Inscrib'd to the author of the Tale of a tub. *London, printed for Ferdinando Burleigh, & A. Dodd*, [1714.] (*MC* June)
8º: *A*⁴ B–C⁴; *i–iv*, 1–18 *19–20 blk*. A1 hft.
Teerink 1035.
'Hah! young sedition: how does treason sell?'
A contest between Swift and Dunton at Lintot's.
LG(–C4),O(–C4),LdU-B(–A1, C4); CU, CtY(–C4),ICN(–A1, C4),IU(–A1, C4),MiU (–A1, C4)+.

T436 Towzer. Towzer, a tale. *Dublin, printed by Thomas Walsh*, [1729?]
½º: 1 side, 2 columns.
The DT copy is bound with half-sheets of 1729.
'In William's reign, when faction raged'
A tale, suggesting that the cause of political anxiety is not foreign powers but the noise made by politicians out of office.
DT.

T——r, R.

T——r, R——t, *A.M. Εἰς τὴν τοῦ Χριστου σταυρωσιν μονοστροφικα*, 1742. *See* E27.

T437 Tracey, Michael. The critical minute: a poem of the epick kind. In two books. Inscrib'd to the reverend Dr. S. *Dublin, printed by and for James Hoey*, 1731.
8º: *A*⁴; *1–3* 4–8. 2 advt.
'In antient times, a prince of matchless fame'
A curious mythological poem on the Irish invention of the chamber-pot. The intended dedicatee is apparently Sheridan, not Swift.
DK,DN; ICN,MH.

T438 Tradesman. The tradesman's hue and cry after the bumb-bailiffs and setters. [*Dublin*, 1725/30.]
½º: 1 side, 1 column.
On the other side, *The butchers answer*, [1725/30.] The copy at L forms part of a collection of Dublin half-sheets of 1725/30.
'Good people give attention, and hear the bailiffs praise'
L(C.121.g.8/91).

Tragi-comic. A tragi-comic dialogue, between the ghost of an a-----l, and the substance of a g-----l... [*London*] *Printed in the year* 'M.DCC. XLIX'.
The date is a misprint for M.DCC.LIX; there are copies at CtY,MH.

— A tragicomic, heroical, satyrical burlesque poem...on the hyperbole, [1748.] *See* Harrison, H.

'Tranquilla.' The triumphs of bigotry, 1749. *See* T506.

T439 Transactions. The transactions of the Pretender's son, and his company of rebels. *Printed in the year* 1746.
8º: *A*⁴; *1* 2–8.
A chap-book.
'A whelp of Cerbrus is come here'
DFo.

T440 Translation. A translation of Horace's epistle to Augustus, in imitation of Lord Roscommon's stile in the Art of poetry. Most humbly inscrib'd and dedicated, to...Lord Carteret... *Dublin, printed by A. Rhames*, 1730.
2º: A–D²; *1–2* 3–16.
Watermark: Dutch lion.
'While you, alone, the reins of empire hold'
L(1972),DA,DT.

T441 — [fine paper]
Watermark: fleur-de-lys.
C.

T442 — A translation of Mr. Hill's Nundinae Sturbrigienses. Essay'd by RS. AB. lately of St. John's College Cambridge. *London printed, and sold by J. Morphew*, 1709. (11 May, Luttrell)

T443–51

A **translation** of Mr. Hill

2°: A–B²; *1–2* 3–8.

The Luttrell copy is recorded in *Haslewood*; advertised in *PM* 12 May.

'Near Grant's fair walls a stately city reign'd' C(uncut).

Trapp, Joseph. The works of Virgil: translated into English blank verse... *London, printed for J. Brotherton, J. Hazard, W. Meadows [and 6 others]*, 1731. (*MChr* Feb)

12°: 3 vol.   L,O.

The *Aeneid* was published alone in 1718, 1720, and is entered below.

—— The second edition, corrected, and in the notes much enlarged. *London, printed for J. Brotherton, J. Hazard, W. Meadows [and 6 others]*, 1735. (*LM* July)

12°: 3 vol.   O; CLU-C,MH.

— [variant titles:] The third edition, corrected..., 1735.

LVA-D,O; MH.

—— The fourth edition, corrected... *Dublin, printed for G. Risk, G. Ewing, & W. Smith*, 1737.

12°: 3 vol.   O,DN.

T443 — Ædes Badmintonianæ: a poem most humbly presented to his grace Henry duke of Beaufort, &c. and to her grace Mary dutchess dowager of Beaufort, &c. upon their magnificent and delightful seat in Gloucester-shire. [*London?*] *Printed in the year* 1701.

2°: a² b–c²; *i–iv*, 1–8.

'Blest heav'nly mind, which from thy native skys' Dedication signed.

O(uncut),*MR-C*; CLU-C,TxU(uncut).

T444 — The Æneis of Virgil, translated into blank verse... Volume the first. *London, printed in the year* 1718. (*PB* 15 July)

4°: π² *4 **4 a⁴(±a2) b–g⁴ B–3N⁴ 3O²; [20] i ii–lvi, 1 2–467 468 blk.* π1 frt.

Title in red and black. Engraved head and tail pieces to each book. Advertised in *PB* as ready for delivery to the subscribers. Subsequently reprinted in Trapp's edition of Virgil's *Works*, 1731–.

'Arms, and the man I sing, who first from Troy' L(1349.k.1,−π1),O,LdU-B; *NjP,TxU*.

T445 —— Volume the second. *London, printed in the year* 1720. (*PB* 26 May)

4°: π⁴ 3P–6H⁴; *[8] 469 470–971 972.* π1 frt; *972* err.

L(1349.k.2),O,LdU-B; *NjP,TxU*.

T446 [—] The church and monarchy secur'd, by the return of his grace the Duke of Ormonde, and the change of the late ministry. *Dublin printed, and sold by Edward Waters*, [1711.]

½°: 2 sides, 1 column.

Trapp, J. The church and monarchy

'Our tongues are loos'd, and our restorer's come' Ascribed to Trapp in a contemporary ms. note on the Chatsworth copy of the London edition below. In praise of Ormonde, Harley, and the tories.

C.

T447 [—] — *Printed at Dublin, and reprinted at London; and sold by John Morphew*, 1711. (20 June, Luttrell)

½°: 1–2, 1 column.

Chatsworth; ICN(Luttrell),OCU.

T448 [—] Dr. Crofts's exercise perform'd in the Theatre at Oxford, July 10. 1713. [*Oxford?* 1713.]

½°: 2 sides, 1 column.

Latin text headed 'Ode' on recto; English text headed 'Ode' on verso.

'Laurus cruentas, & faciles nimis'

'With noise of cannon, and of rattling drums' Ms. attribution to Trapp in the MH copy.

O; CtY,MH.

T449 — Johannis Miltoni Paradisus amissus latine redditus. Interprete Josepho Trapp, S.T.P. Vol. I. *Londini, typis J. Purser. Impensis L. Gilliver, J. Wood & C. Woodward*, 1741 [1740]. (*SR* 22 Dec)

4°: A⁴(−A4) B–2P⁴ 2Q¹ (2Q1 as 'Q'); *i–vi, 1 2–294. vi* err.

Entered to Trapp in *SR*; deposit copies probably at L,O,E. Possibly the 'Specimen of Paradisus amissa over again' referred to in Bowyer's ledgers in Aug 1738 is related to this translation.

'Primum hominis lapsum, vetitaque ex arbore fructus'

L(641.1.7),O,E.

T450 —— Vol. II. *Londini, typis J. Purser. Prostant venales apud S. Austen*, 1744. (*GM, LM* June)

4°: π¹ 2R–4E⁴ 4F¹; *[2] 295–575 576.* 576 err.

O.

[—] An ode to the queen, on the death of his royal highness George, hereditary prince of Denmark, 1708. *See* O72.

T451 [—] Peace. A poem: inscribed to the right honourable the lord Viscount Bolingbroke. *London, printed for John Barber, & Henry Clements*, 1713. (*DC* 9 April)

2°: A¹ B–F² G¹; *i–ii, 1–22.*

Watermark: AC. Some copies (e.g. O,LdU-B) have an incorrect state of the last two lines of p. 19 covered by a cancel slip; other copies have the revised reading. The Luttrell copy dated 10 April is recorded in *Haslewood*.

'Then it is done! the wond'rous work compleat!' Early ms. attribution to Trapp in the ICN copy; on 1 April 1713 Swift would not dine with Bolingbroke because he was expected to 'look over a dull poem for Parson Trapp upon the Peace'.

L(11661.dd.13),O(2),OW(2),C(2, 1 uncut), LdU-B(uncut); CtY,ICN,MH,NjP,TxU(2)+.

Trapp, J. Peace

T452 [—] [fine paper]
Watermark: star.
ICU.

T453 [—] — The second edition. *London, printed for J. Barber, & H. Clements*, 1713. (*Examiner* 18 May)
8°: *A*⁴ B–E⁴; *1–4* 5–39 *40 blk*. A1 hft.
A half-share of the copyright formed part of lot 3 of the trade sale of Henry Clements, 14 March 1720 (cat. at O-JJ), purchased by Bowyer. It was re-sold as lot 26 of Mrs. Bowyer's sale, 18 May 1736, in lot 1 on 11 Jan 1737, and the whole was in lot 23 of Joseph Hazard's sale, 20 June 1738 (cats. at O-JJ).
LVA-D,O(2, 1 – A1),DT,*MP*,WcC(–A1); CLU-C(–A1),CtY(–A1),NN(2, –A1).

T454 [—] — *Dublin: reprinted by S.P.* [*Stephen Powell*] *for J. Hyde*, 1713.
12°: *A*¹²; *1–2* 3–24.
L(11633.a.39),DN.

[—] Prologue, and epilogue, to the Orphan. As it was acted at a private school at Isleworth, 1728. *See* P1122.

T455 [—] A prologue to the University of Oxford. Spoke by Mr. Betterton. [*London?* 1703.]
½°: 1 side, 1 column.
Reprinted in *The players turn'd academicks*, 1703, and in *A prefatory prologue*, [1703]. The date 5 July in the L copy apparently refers to the date it was spoken.
'Once more our London muses pleas'd, repair'
Early ms. attribution to Trapp in the L copy.
L(1347.m.38, ms. date 5 July),O; MH.

T456 [—] Thoughts upon the four last things: Death; Judgment; Heaven; Hell. A poem in four parts. Part I. Death. *London, printed for Lawton Gilliver*, 1734. (*LM* Dec)
2°: *A*² B–G²; *1–3* 4–28. *28 err*.
The order of these two editions has not been determined; presumably one was a reprint to complete sets of the poem. This edition has signature C under B of 'Body'.
'Dark to futurity, in doubt, and fear'
Subsequently reprinted with Trapp's name.
L(11630.h.57/2; 643.m.15/21),O('a present from Dr. Trapp'),OA,C,LdU-B; CtY(2).

T457 [—] — [another edition]
Signature C under t of 'the'.
CLU-C,CtY,IU,MH,TxU +.

T458 [—] — Part II. Judgment. *London, printed by J. Wright, for Lawton Gilliver*, 1734 [1735]. (*LM* Feb)
2°: *A*² B–G²; *1–3* 4–28. *28 err*.
'O thou Eternal! (hallow'd, wond'rous name!)'
L(11630.h.57/2),O,OA,C,LdU-B; CLU-C,CtY, IU,MH,TxU +.

T459 [—] — Part III. Heaven. *London, printed by J. Wright, for Lawton Gilliver*, 1735. (*LM* Aug)
2°: *A*² B–F² *G*¹; *1–3* 4–25 *26*. *25 err*; *26 advt*.

Trapp, J. Thoughts

'The great apostle, in his ravish'd breast'
L(11630.h.57/2),O,LdU-B; CtY,IU,MH,TxU.

T460 [—] — Part IV. Hell. *London, printed by J. Wright, for Lawton Gilliver*, 1735. (*SR* 12 Dec)
2°: *A*² B–I² *K*¹; *1–3* 4–25 *26* [*12*]. G1ᵛ err; K1ᵛ advt.
G2 and H² ('Advertisement' and contents) are 'to be placed after the title-page of the first part'; I² and K1 (the notes) 'at the end of the fourth'. Listed in *GM* Dec. Deposit copies at L,O,E,AdU.
'Tremble, ye guilty! Tremble, ev'n the good!'
L(11630.h.57/2; 644.m.14/15),O(2),E,AdU, LdU-B; CLU-C,CtY,IU,MH.

T461 [—] — Part I. Death. *London: printed. And, Dublin re-printed by George Faulkner*, 1735.
8°: *A*⁴ B–C⁴ D²; *1–2* 3–28.
The *Dublin journal* for 23 March 1736 advertises all four parts as 'to be published tomorrow'.
L(T.902/9),O,DN.

T462 [—] — Part II. Judgment. *London: printed. And Dublin re-printed by George Faulkner*, 1735.
8°: *A*⁴ B–C⁴; *1–2* 3–'7' 24.
L(T.902/9).

T463 [—] — The second edition. To which are added, the I, CIV, and CXXXVII psalms paraphras'd. *London, printed for W. Russel*, 1745. (*SR* 10 April)
8°: A⁴ B–I⁸ K²; *i–ii* iii–vii *viii*, 1–132.
Horizontal chain-lines. Listed in *LM* April. Deposit copies at O,AdU.
L(852.g.23),O,AdU(uncut); NNUT.

T464 — — By Joseph Trapp, D.D. The second edition ... *London, printed for W. Russel*, 1748.
8°: π² A⁴(–A1) B–I⁸ K²; [2] *i–ii* iii–vii *viii*, 1–132.
A reissue with cancel title π2; π1 has an extract from Trapp's will bequeathing a copy of the book to all heads of families in certain parishes.
NNUT.

T465 — — The third edition... *London, printed for W. Russel*, 1749.
8°: A⁴ B–I⁸ K⁴; *i–ii* iii–vii *viii*, 1–132 *133–136*. K3–4 advt.
L(11632.aa.46),E.

T466 [—] To the right honourable Mr. Harley, on his first appearing in publick, after the wound given him by Guiscard. *London, printed for John Morphew*, 1711. (*PM* 22 May)
½°: 2 sides, 1 column.
'At last dispelling his lov'd country's fears'
Subsequently printed with Trapp's name.
L(1958),O,C,Chatsworth,Crawford; MH,TxU.

T467 — — By Jos. Trapp, M.A. *London, printed for Bernard Lintott*, [1711.] (*DC* 5 June)
½°: *1–2*, 1 column.
Listed in Bowyer's ledgers under 2 June, 1,000 copies for Lintot.

Trapp, J. To the rt. hon. Mr. Harley

L(1850.c.10/43),O; *MB*,TxU(2, 1 Luttrell, 5 June).

T468 [—] — *Edinburgh: reprinted by James Watson,* 1711.
½°: 1 side, 1 column.
E(2).

Traulus. Traulus, 1730. *See* Swift, Jonathan.

Travers, Henry. Miscellaneous poems and translations. *London, printed for Benj. Motte,* 1731. (*GSJ* 16 Feb)
8°: pp. 202.   L,O; CtY,MH.
Watermark: crowned initials. Many copies have no frontispiece.
— [fine paper]   CT.
Watermark: fleur-de-lys on shield. The presentation copy at CT has a cancel A2.
—— *York, printed by C. Ward & R. Chandler,* 1740.
8°: pp. xxix, 366.   L,O; CtY,MH.

T469 **Treason.** Treason against the ladies. A poem. *Dublin, printed in the year* 1731.
8°: *A²; 1–4 5–8.*
'Tell me no more of purling streams'
Preface signed 'A.B.C.D.T.W.'. A satire against women.
DA.

T470 **Tres.** Tres libri Solomonis, scilicet, Proverbia, Ecclesiastes, et Cantica, carmine latino redditi. Per G.B. *Londini, typis E.P.* [Edmund Powell?] *Prostant venales apud Maur. Atkins,* 1708.
8°: A⁴ B⁸ C⁸(±C8) D–G⁸ H⁴; *1–6 7–8, 1–101 102–104.*
Ms. corrections throughout the L copy.
Proverbia: 'Inclytus hæc fudit Solomon Proverbia, natus'
Eccles.: 'Aurea dicta sacri præconis, & inclyta, nati'
Cantica: 'Inclyta doctiloqui Solomonis cantica regis'
L(3165.de.13).

T471 —— 'Editio secunda. [*London*] *Prostant venales apud M. Atkins.*' (*PB* 8 Feb 1709, 'lately published')
'The second edition, with amendments, for the use of schools', *PB*. Also listed in *TC* Michaelmas/Hilary, 1708/09.

Trial. The trial and condemnation of John duke of Marlborough, 1715. *See* An excellent new song, call'd The full tryal...[1712.]

T472 — The trial of Roger, for an accident that happened at a game of romps with Esther. *London, printed for G. Lyon,* 1744 [1743]. (*LDP* 28 Nov)
8°: *A⁴(–A4) B–H⁴ I¹[=A4]; i–vi, 1–57 58 blk.*
A1 hft.
'The judges sat, and jury call'd'
The preface says (jokingly?) 'The following

The **trial** of Roger

...poem, was brought from America'. A trial for rape.
L(C.131.f.6, uncut); Institute for Sex Research (−A1).

— The trial of Selim the Persian, 1748. *See* Moore, Edward.

T473 — A tryal of skill between a court lord, and a Twickenham 'squire. Inscrib'd to Mr. Pope. *London printed, and sold by J. Dormer,* 1734. (*GSJ* 14 Jan)
2°: *A² B–D²; 1–2 3–16.*
Engraving on title.
'A pretty, smock-fac'd, prattling boy'
A satire on John, lord Hervey and his quarrel with Pope.
L(11602.i.17/3),LVA-D,O; DLC,ICN,MB,MH, TxU.

T474 — The tryal of skill between 'Squire Walsingham and Mother Osborne. An eclogue, in imitation of Virgil's Palæmon. To which are added, Horace to Fannius, and an apology for printing a certain nobleman's Epistle to Dr. S--w--n. *London printed; sold by J. Huggonson,* 1734. (*GSJ* 17 Jan)
2°: *A² B–F² G¹; 1–3 4–25 26 blk.*
'So slave! who owns those ragged journals there?'
To Lord Fanny: 'If, for thy breach of sense and truth'
Apology: 'As in the gay circle Lord Fanny recited'
On Francis Walsingham (pseudonym of William Arnall, editor of the *Free Briton*) and F. Osborne (pseudonym of James Pitt, editor of the *London Journal*). The other poems are satires on John, lord Hervey, the third occasioned by his *Epistle from a nobleman,* 1733.
L(11630.h.51; 163.m.5; 1963),O(2),BaP, LdU-B; CSmH,CtY,IU,MH,TxU(2)+.

T475 — The tryal of skill: or, a new session of the poets. Calculated for the meridian of Parnassus, in the year, MDCCIV. *Printed for the booksellers of London & Westminster,* 1704. (*DC* 8 Aug)
2°: A–F² G¹; *i–iv, 1–21 '20'.*
The Luttrell copy in the possession of J. R. B. Brett-Smith is dated 8 Aug.
'Apollo perplext with poetical duns'
CtY,DFo.

T476 **Tribe.** 'The tribe of Levi: a satire. [*London*] *Printed for T. Wildbore.* Price 6d.' (*LM* Aug 1736)
Possibly related to Tutchin's poem with this title, published in 1691.

T477 **Tribute.** A tribute of tears: or, the loyal subjects sorrowful lamentation for the death of William the third, king of England, Scotland, France, and Ireland, &c... Tune of, My bleeding heart. *London, printed for E. Tracy,* [1702.]
obl ½°: 1 side, 3 columns.
Rough woodcut and title above first two columns.

A **tribute** of tears

'With bleeding heart and melting eyes'
CM-P.

T478 — The tribute of the muses: a pindaric-ode, addressed to his excellency Philip earl of Chesterfield, on his arrival from Ireland. *London, printed for Richard Wellington, 1746. (GM, LM* May)
2°: *A*² B–*D*²; *1–2* 3–15 *16 blk.* 15 err.
'While Stanhope's praise I try to sing'
O; DFo,OCU.

T479 Trick. Trick for trick; or, the hasty cuckold. Dedicated to the greatest in christendom. [*London*] *Printed for J. Cramphorne, near Snow-hill,* [1714.] (14 Oct, Luttrell)
½°: *1–2,* 2 columns.
'A certain man, (no matter who'
    A tale apparently aimed at George I's divorce from Sophia Dorothea.
L(11602.i.12/33; C.121.g.9/123),LLP; ICN (Luttrell).

T479·5 — 'Trick upon trick.' [*London,* 1732.] (16 Nov?)
½°.
    Entered in Bowyer's ledgers to Mr. Emerson as 'A Dialogue in Verse' under 16 Nov 1732; a half sheet, 25 copies printed. The title given is found in the record for setting the poem; it appears in the record of printing as 'Verses for Mr Emerson'.
    Mr. Emerson, who may well be the author, is recorded as the person for whom the 'Hymns for St. George's Chapel' were printed on 20 Jan 1731; probably he was the incumbent there.
(Bowyer's ledgers.)

T480 Trifle. The trifle, a new song. To the tune of Winchester wedding; or, Old Sir Simon the king. [*London*] *Printed for B—— A—— by Temple-Bar,* 1714.
½°: 1 side, 1 column.
    On the other side, *A great overthrow at court,* [1714.]
'A trifling song ye shall hear'
    Cf. *Crum* A509, 'The triffle', 1703, attributed in L (Add. MS. 28101, fol. 186) to Farquhar.
Harding.

T481 Trimmer. The trimmer trimm'd; or, the washball and razor used to some purpose. By a real barber. [*Oxford?*] *Printed in the year* 1749.
4°: *A*⁴ B⁴; *1–2* 3–15 *16 blk.*
'Be kind my muse, assist my lays'
    A reply to *An address to the worshipful company of barbers,* 1749. A heavily annotated copy of [John Sampson] *The intrigue,* 1750, in the possession of John Sparrow refers to 'Bilstone's Answer to the Address to the Oxford Barber's suppo⟨sed⟩to be wrote by Web the Barber'. Bilstone has not been identified, but presumably this is the work referred to.
L(11630.d.4/19, lacks B⁴),O(2).

Trinitarian. The trinitarin [!] combat, 1719. *See* 'Standfast, Tho.'

Trinity. Trinity Colledge vindicated, 1725. *See* Owens, Samuel.

T482 Trip. A trip from Westminster-hall to Oxford. *London, printed for A. Hinde,* 1710.
½°: 1 side, 1 column.
'Quite tired with the projects of the town'
    In favour of Sacheverell.
L(Cup.645.e.1/21),DG(cropt).

T483 — A trip lately to Scotland. With a true character of the country and people: also reflections on their proceedings to disturb the present reign: to which are added several remarks, on the late barbarous execution of Capt. Green... *London printed, and sold by S. Malthus,* 1705. (12 June, Luttrell)
2°: A–*D*² (A2 as 'A'); *i–ii,* 1–13 *14 blk.*
    The Luttrell copy is recorded in *Haslewood.*
'Equipt for journey, mounted on a steed'
L(11626.i.23),O,DrU.

— A trip to Bar-le-Duc, 1715. *See* Steddy, John.

T484 — [dh] A trip to Dunkirk: or, a hue and cry after the pretended Prince of Wales. Being a panegyrick on the descent. [col] *London printed, and sold by the booksellers of London & Westminster,* 1708.
4°: *A*²; *1–4.*
    Bond 205; *Teerink* 837; *Williams* 1078.
'Why, hark ye me, sirs, – if the rumour holds true'
    Attributed to Swift in the *Harleian Miscellany* and elsewhere, but rejected by Williams. A satire on the Pretender.
L(11631.bb.43); NN.

T485 — [dh] A trip to Germany: or, the D. of M------h's farewel to England. Who with his d---hess is going to live in Germany as a prince of the Empire. [col] *London, printed by J. Read,* [1712/13.]
2°: A² B¹; *1–5 6 blk.*
'Are all my lawrels come to this?'
    On the Duke of Marlborough leaving England in Nov 1712.
L(11602.i.12/32*; C.116.i.4/67),MC,*MR-C*; CtY(uncut).

— A trip to Germany: or, the poet turn'd carbineer, [1705.] *See* Ward, Edward.

T486 — [dh] A trip to Kensington: or, that town drawn to the life. [col] *London, printed in the year* 1710. (9 May, Luttrell)
4°: A²; *1–4.*
'Where Kensington's inviting structures lie'
L(162.l.30),LVA-F(Luttrell).

— A trip to Leverpoole, 1706. *See* Lenthall, William.

T487 — A trip to Litchfield. With a character of the French officers there. By the author of the Trip to Nottingham. *London, printed in the year* 1705. (*DC* 1 March)

A **trip** to Litchfield

2°: A^2 B–C^2; *i–ii*, '*1*' *4–12*.
'Now muse, grown acquainted with country air'
L(11602.i.10/3; 193.d.14/48),LG; CLU-C
(Luttrell, 1 March),CSmH.

T488 — A trip to Nottingham. With a character of Mareschal Tallard and the French-generals. *London, printed in the year* 1705. (1 Feb, Luttrell)
2°: A–D^2; *1–2 3–4 3–14*.
   Listed in *FP* 3 Feb as just published.
'Half tir'd with drinking, dull-plays, and the rest'
   The same author wrote *A trip to Litchfield*, 1705.
L(193.d.14/47),O,DG,DT; CLU-C(Luttrell), CtY.

T489 — A trip to Temple-Oge, Stephen's green and the Bason: or, an election of Dublin beauties. A poem. By Thom. Pun—sibi, D.D. *Dublin, printed in the year* 1730.
½°: 2 sides, 1 column.
'Since bailiffs and mayors, to evade all objection'
   The implied attribution to Thomas Sheridan does not seem plausible.
L(C.121.g.8/177).

T490 — A trip to the devil's summer-house: or, a journey to May-fair. *London, printed for Joseph Hughes, and are to be sold by the booksellers of London & Westminster,* 1704. (*FP* 6 July)
2°: A^2 B–D^2; *1–2 3–15 16 blk.*
   The advertisement in *FP* records it as 'lately publish'd...having been delay'd thus long by an unhappy accident, but is now made publick. Sold by B. Bragg'.
'When the spring of the year had arriv'd at its prime'
   The title is reminiscent of Edward Ward's poems, but there is no evidence for his authorship. Compare *A step to the d---l's exchange*, [170–?].
CtY(Luttrell, 7 July),TxU(cropt).

T491 — [dh] A trip to the d----l's summer-house: or, a journey to the Wells: with the old preaching quaker's sermon to the London-mobb. [*London?* 1704?]
4°: A^2; *1–4*, 2 columns.
   Wrongly dated by *Wing* 2285A as [1695]; apparently a piracy of the preceding.
MH.

T492 — [dh] A trip to the masquerade, or, a journey to Somerset-House. [col] *London, printed by J. Read,* 1713.
2°: $A^2 < B^1$; *1–6*.
   Printed on one side of the leaf only, the third on the verso. Horizontal chain-lines in sheet A.
'Battles no more 'twixt us and France I sing'
O.

T493 — A trip to the pillory. In two parts. Being an excellent new ballad. To a pleasant new tune.

A **trip** to the pillory

London, printed for J. Smith; sold by the booksellers of London & Westminster, 1727.
2°: A^4; *1–2 3–8*.
'In London late a person did'
   On a man sentenced to the pillory for sexual offences.
L(1964, uncut).

T494 — A trip to Vaux-hall: or, a general satyr on the times. With some explanatory notes. By Hercules Mac-Sturdy, of the county of Tiperary, esq; *London, printed for A. Moore; sold at the pamphlet-shops of London & Westminster,* 1737. (*GM, LM* Aug)
2°: (frt+) A^1 B–C^2; *1–3 4–10*.
'To please two punks, who freely share their bounties'
L(840.m.5),LG(–frt),WcC; CtY(lacks frt, A1), MH(–frt).

T495 Tripe. The tripe club. A satyr. Dedicated to all those who are true friends to her present majesty ... By the author of the Tale of a tub. *London, printed for Jacob Tonson; sold by the booksellers of London, & Westminster,* 1706.
4°: A^1 B–E^2 F^1; *1–3 4–20*.
   Teerink 836; *Williams* 1077. In most copies E1 is signed 'D'; the watermark varies. The collation suggests that this is the earlier edition, as does the form of the title; it might possibly be of Dublin origin. The two editions correspond page-for-page, but that which follows has normalized spelling and accidentals.
'How this fantastick world is chang'd of late'
   Swift's authorship, suggested by the reference to *A tale of a tub*, is generally rejected; the suggestion first made by Nichols in his *Supplement* to Swift's works that William King (1663–1712) was the author is plausible. Cf. *The new idol*, 1706.
L(11631.d.55),LG,DG,DK,DT; CSmH,CtY, DLC,MH.

T496 — [*idem*] The Swan tripe-club in Dublin... *Printed at Dublin, and sold by the booksellers in London & Westminster,* 1706. (*DC* 15 Jan)
4°: A^2 B–C^4; *1–2 3–20*.
   It is clear that this is the edition advertised in *DC*, and it was probably printed in London, not Dublin.
L(1481.c.42; 840.h.7/5),LLP,DG,DN,DT+; ICN,PU,TxU.

T497 — The Swan tripe-club: a satyr, on the high-flyers; in the year 1705. *London printed, and sold by the booksellers of London & Westminster,* 1710.
8°: A^8 (A2 as 'A3'); *1–2 3–16*.
   Probably printed by Henry Hills; reissued with other remaindered Hills poems in *A collection of the best English poetry,* 1717 (*Case* 294). Apparently a revised text.

The **tripe** cl ub

L(1481.d.22; C.124.b.7/52; Ashley 1821),O,CT, DN,LdU-B+; CSmH,CtY,IU,MH,TxU+.

'**Tripe, Andrew.**' Dr. Woodward's ghost, 1748. *See* D357.

— The small-pox. A poem, 1748. *See* S487.

T498 Triple. The triple alliance. [*London?* 1724/27.]
slip: 1 side, 1 column.
   Printed as 'Ay and No: a fable' in the Pope/Swift *Miscellanies. The last volume,* 1727, where the introductory couplet (here printed in italic and ignored) is amalgamated with the text.
'Once on a time, near Channel-row'
   Crum O1141. A ms. was among the papers for the *Craftsman* seized from Francklin on 3 Sept 1730, now Cholmondeley (Houghton) MS 74 (29). Included in editions of Gay, but his authorship doubted by *Faber* xxv. Also attributed to Philip, duke of Wharton. Bought votes 'Ay' and 'No' as Walpole's allies.
O-JJ; *Harding.*

T499 Triumph. The triumph of beauty: or, the prude metamorphos'd. *London, printed for C. Corbett; sold by the booksellers of London & Westminster,* 1740. (*GM, LM* April)
2⁰: *A*² B–E²; *1–3* 4–20.
'While some for int'rest plough the foaming deep'
L(1482.f.36),O; CSmH(uncut),CtY,TxU.

— The triumph of Isis, 1750. *See* Warton, Thomas, *the younger.*

T500 — The triumph of monarchy: or, defeat of anarchy. To an excellent loyal tune, viz. There's no hopes of peace, and the war will never cease till, &c. By N.F.G. gent. *London, printed by and for H. Hills,* [1710.]
½⁰: 1 side, 2 columns.
'When proud fanaticks bore the sway'
   On the defeat of the whigs.
L(1876.f.19/46); MH.

T501 — The triumph of the great L——d S——. *London printed, and sold by the booksellers of London & Westminster,* 1701. (16 Sept, Luttrell)
2⁰: *A*² B–D²; *i–iv,* 1–12.
   Listed in *WL* Sept.
'Thus in the triumphs of my pow'r I reign'
   On John, baron Somers. 'Upon him & his party, making him speak in a fustian romantick way', Luttrell.
L(11630.f.52),LLP,O(2),E,*LdU-B*; CLU-C(2, 1 Luttrell),CtY,MH,OCU,TxU(2).

T502 — The triumph of virtue: a poem upon the peace, inscribed to the Earl of Oxford and Mortimer... Written by a gentleman of North-Britain. *London, printed by J. Grantham, for the author,* 1713.
2⁰: A–D²; *i–iv,* 1–12. iv err.
'Now sing, my muse, the noble patriots fame'

The **triumph** of virtue

   Probably by the same author as *An essay upon friendship... By a gentleman of Scotland,* 1714, which has a dedication signed 'W.F.'
O.

T503 — The triumph of wisdom, a poem. Inscribed to his excellency the Earl of Chesterfield, lord lieutenant of Ireland. *Dublin, printed by George Faulkner,* 1745.
8⁰: *A*⁴ B⁴ C²; *1–4* 5–20.
'Whilst the bold muse, by great examples taught'
O,C,DA; CtY,NjP,PP.

T504 Triumphant. The triumphant taylors: or the vanquished lice. A satyr, on the taylors procession July the 25th, 1726. [*Dublin,* 1726.]
½⁰: 1 side, 2 columns.
'Should I invoke the antient Romans muse'
L(1890.e.5/173).

T505 Triumphs. [dh] The triumphs & excellency of faith, as described by the apostle Paul, Heb. xi. versified. [*London,* 174–?]
8⁰: *A*⁴; *1*–8.
'Faith is the gift of god, and 'tis the scope'
LF(uncut).

T506 — The triumphs of bigotry. A poem, sacred to the peaceful memory of Charistes. Inscribed to the reverend Mr. Thomas Bradbury. By a lady. *London, printed for M. Cooper,* 1749. (*GM* Nov)
4⁰: *A*⁴ B² C¹; *1–2* 3–14.
'Farewell the great, the good!----this all may cry'
   Dedication signed 'Tranquilla'.
L(1962).

T507 — The triumphs of the lady of the ocean. *London, printed in the year* 1712.
4⁰: A⁴; *1–2* 3–8.
'Anna, lady of the ocean'
CtY.

Triumvirade. The Triumvirade: or, broadbottomry, [1745.] *See* Morgan, Macnamara.

Troisième. Troisième dialogue entre deux freres, [1707.] *See* Dialogue entre deux freres, 1707.

T507·5 Trophaea. 'Trophaea marina. To Sir Charles Wager, rear admiral... *London, A. Baldwin,* 1710.'
2⁰.
   Listed by *Morgan* M378. There is no evidence that it is in verse, but the similarity of the title to Elkanah Settle's *Trophaea marina. To the honourable Captain Ogle,* 1723, and the fact that a poem of his for general circulation (S265) was published by Abigail Baldwin in 1708 suggest that it may be a poem by Settle.
(*Morgan* M378.)

'**Trot, John.**' The bellman of St. James's verses extraordinary, 1746. *See* B181.

Trotter, C.

Trotter, Catharine (*married Patrick Cockburn, 1708*). The works of Mrs. Catharine Cockburn... *London, printed for J. & P. Knapton, 1751.*
8°: 2 vol.   L.
> The L copy has been mislaid, so the watermark of ordinary paper copies has not been established; their existence is clear from the list of subscribers. The poems are in vol. 2, pp. 556–576.

— [fine paper]   L.
> Watermark: Strasburg bend. Two different editions of the list of subscribers have been seen in the copies at L.

—————

T508 [—] On his grace the Duke of Marlborough, a poem. *London, printed for John Morphew, 1706.*
½°: 1–2, 1 column.
'Durst thou attempt to sing of Blenheim's plain'
> Reprinted in her *Works*, 1751.

LSA,Longleat; CLU-C.

T509 [—] A poem on his grace the Duke of Marlborough's return from his German expedition. *London, printed for B. Bragg, 1705.*
4°: A⁴; 1–2 3–8.
'Assist me sacred muse, the man I sing'
> Reprinted in her *Works*, 1751.

L(11641.bb.19),DG.

—————

[**Trotter, Robert.**] Εἰς την του Χριστου σταυρωσιν μονοστροφικα. An ode on the crucifixion of Christ, 1742. *See* E27.

T510 Trouat, Louis. The best discovery in a new-year's gift. [*London*, 1730?]
slip: 1 side, 1 column.
> At the foot of the slip are printed the words 'By the same Louis Trouat', which suggests that this was previously conjugate with another work. The copy seen is among the papers seized in a search of Richard Francklin's house, 3 Sept 1730; among the papers is a letter from Trouat to Francklin dated 1 Jan 1730 which suggests he had been courting prosecution by publishing works in Latin, and enclosing a work in English that may have been this.

'Longitude, in the world, it's she that bears the sway'
> The verses (as, indeed, the letter referred to above) appear to be the work of someone mentally deranged; there are parallels with the work of Christopher Smart.

Cholmondeley (Houghton) MS 74/16 (at C).

T511 True. The true and genuin[!] ⟨e⟩legy of Matthew Gun bookseller, who departed, &c. [*Dublin*, 1724.]
½°: 1 side, 1 column.
> Mourning borders. At foot, 'From my death

The true and genuine elegy

bed, January 20th 1723–4. This is my true elegy and no other. Matthew Gun.'
'Gun is discharg'd of life, death was much quicker'
> A witty elegy, but possibly occasioned by the real death of Matthew Gunne. He is not recorded after 1710 by *Plomer*.

L(11602.i.1/7).

T512 — True blue will never stain. A ballad. [*London*, 175–?]
½°: 1 side, 1 column.
'Let those that love Helicon sip at the stream'
> In praise of the 'true-blue order', which here seems as much social as political.

MH.

T513 — The true-born Britain. Written by the author of the True-born Englishman. *London, printed in the year 1707.*
8°: A⁴; 1 2–8.
> *Moore* 147. P. 8 is printed in smaller type.
'Hail! mighty genius of this fruitful isle,'
> Attributed to Defoe by *Moore*, 'from internal evidence certainly his'; but the half-sheet chap-book format resembles other poems falsely attributed to Defoe. A panegyric on Queen Anne and the Union.

O.

— The true-born Englishman, 1700–. *See* Defoe, Daniel.

— The true-born-Hugonot, 1703. *See* Pittis, William.

— The true-born Welshman. Written by Shenkin ap Morgan, 1701. *See* S393.

T514 — The true Briton's thought. [*London*? 1740?]
slip: 1 side, 1 column.
> Cut of bearded head above title, of fortified town at foot.
'In full flowing bowls while the liquor does smile'
> *Crum* I1322: 'To the tune of the Miller of Mansfield'. In support of the attacks of John Campbell, duke of Argyll, on the government's inactivity against Spain.

C.

T515 — [variant]
> Cut of bearded head above title, of canting coat of arms at foot.

C.

T516 — The true Britons. A poem. *London, printed for F. Adams; sold by the booksellers of London & Westminster, 1735.*
4°: A–D⁴; 1–2 3–30 31–32 blk.
> The copy at OCU has errata on p. 31.
'Where patriot-hearts once naked to your sight'
CSmH(uncut),InU(presentation copy, –D4), OCU(uncut).

T517 — A true caracter[!] of the Bread-street tatlers; or, a satyr against impudence. *London, printed for T. Jones, near Smithfield, 1707.*
½°: 1 side, 2 columns.

A **true** character

'A person that's devoted to his ease'
MH.

— The true character of the Intelligencer, 1728.
See Tisdall, William.

T518 — A true character of the Prince of Wales's poet,
with a discription [!] of the new erected folly at
White-hall. *London, printed in the year* 1701.
½°: A¹; 1–2, 1 column.
'I sing the man, who n'ere distinction knew'
A satire on Sir John Vanbrugh as dramatist,
homosexual, and builder of his 'goose-pie'
house in Whitehall.
CtY.

T519 — A true character of the wooden monster, arch
enemy to Ireland. By no friend to William Woods.
Dublin, printed by R. Dickson, 1724.
½°: 1–2, 1 column.
'To draw a tinker, esquire and an ape'
A satire against Wood's halfpence.
LVA-F(mutilated); CtY.

T520 — The true Christian's jubile[!]: or, a divine
poem, on the birth of our saviour. Tune of The
pious Christians exhortations. *London, printed by
J. Read,* 1705.
½°: 1 side, 2 columns.
'Let Christians now with joyful mirth'
DG.

— A true collection of the writings of the author
of the True born English-man, 1703–. *See* Defoe,
Daniel.

T521 — The true copy of a paper stuck upon the D. of
M------'s gate at St. James's, on Saturday last,
being the day of her majesty's accession to the
crown. [*London*] *Printed by R. Mott, in Alders-
gatet*[!]*-street,* 1712. (11 March, Luttrell)
½°: 1 side, 1 column.
'A German prince of noble race'
A satire against Marlborough.
LSA,*Chatsworth*; ICN(Luttrell).

T522 — [another edition, title reads:]...D. of M----'s
gate...
Crawford; MH.

T523 — — *London, printed by D. Davis in Fleetstreet,*
[1712.]
½°: 1 side, 1 column.
The title reads, 'The true coppy...'
Harding.

T524 — [*idem*] Copy of the paper stuck upon the D. of
M--'s gate at St. James's, on the 8th of March
instant... [*Edinburgh?* 1712.]
½°: 1 side, 1 column.
The location of the copy seen and the quality
of the printing suggest the possibility of an
Edinburgh origin.
E.

— A true ecclesiastical history, 1722. *See* Rooke,
John.

The **true** emblem

— The true emblem of a sot, [171–?] *See* Ellis,
William.

T525 — The true English-boys song, to Vernon's glory.
Occasioned by the birth-day of that brave admiral.
To be sung round the bonfires of London and
Westminster. To the tune of, Come let us prepare,
&c. [*London,* 1741.] (Nov?)
½°: 1 side, 2 columns.
Percival appendix 97.
'Ye Westminster boys,/All sing and rejoice'
In praise of Edward Vernon (whose birthday
was 12 Nov) after the Westminster election of
1741.
L(8133.i.33).

T526 — [*idem*] A new song. [*London,* 1741.]
½°: 1 side, 2 columns.
Percival LXXI. Rough woodcut at head.
A slightly variant text.
'Come ye Westminster boys/All sing and rejoice'
L(8133.i.33).

T527 — The true great man. A poem sacred to the
memory of the right honourable Charles lord
Talbot, baron of Hensol... *London, printed for
Ward & Chandler, booksellers, at the Ship without
Temple Bar; and at York and Scarborough,* 1737.
(*GM, LM* Feb)
2°: A² B–C²; 1–5 6–12.
'When crowding thoughts no utterance can find'
Dedication signed 'C.C.'
CSmH(uncut),MH,MiU,NN-B,OCU.

— A true history of the honest whigs, 1710. *See*
Ward, Edward [The dissenter].

T528 — The true patriot. A ballad. To the air of, Ye
commons and peers. [*Dublin*] *Printed in the year*
1749.
½°: 2 sides, 2 columns.
There are only advertisements on the verso.
'Ye freemen so wise/Now open your eyes'
In praise of Charles Lucas.
C.

— The true περι βαθους, 1728. *See* Soames, *Sir*
William.

T529 — 'True popery no foppery; or, the pope as
infallible as Mess. John. A burlesque poem.
In hudibrastick verse. [*London*] *Sold at the pamphlet shops. Price* 1s.' (*LM* March 1735)

— The true Scots genius, reviving, 1704. *See*
Forbes, William.

T530 — The true Scots mens lament for the loss of the
rights of their ancient kingdom. *Edinburgh, printed
and sold by John Reid,* 1718.
½°: 1 side, 2 columns.
On the other side, *An excellent new song
entituled, the distracted sailor,* excluded as not
topical. *Morgan G479* records an edition as
'Folio, [E.?, 1704]', probably in error.

The **true** Scots mens lament

'Shall monarchy be quite forgot'
Against the union with England.

E.

T531 — The true state of mortality... By T.R. *London printed, and sold by B. Bragge*, 1708. (12 Aug, Luttrell)

2⁰: A¹ B–C² D¹; *i–ii*, 1–10.

Listed in *WL* Aug. Reprinted with [Jabez Hughes] *An ode on the incarnation*, 1709.

'Weary of life, with restless thoughts opprest,'

A modern pencil note in the ViU copy expands the initials as T.R'ogers A.M. Oxfd'. ViU tentatively identifies him with the rector of Slapton of this name, but according to *DNB* he died in 1694. Cf. *Eternity: a poem. By T.R. gent,* [1716.]

NjP(Luttrell),*ViU.*

T532 — True taste: or, female philosophy. Being an epistle from Sylvia to Libertina. *Dublin printed: London re-printed, and sold by Mrs. Nutt, Mrs. Cook, & Mrs. Charlton, at the Royal Exchange; Mrs. Dodd, Mrs. Charlton, & Mr. Slow; Mr. Taylor; and at the pamphlet-shops at Charing-Cross, and Westminster-Hall,* 1735. (*GM* Nov)

2⁰: A² B–E²; *1–4* 5–20. A1 frt.

There was probably no Dublin edition.

'In vain, fair libertine, with wit misplac'd'

A reply to [Joseph Dorman] *The female rake,* [1735.]

O; DLC,IU,OCU(lacks A1).

T533 — A true touch of the times, or, the free-thinker's confession. Written by the author of the Hymn to the victory in Scotland. *London, printed by A. Hinde,* 1719.

½⁰: 1 side, 2 columns.

Horizontal chain-lines.

'I never meddl'd with intreagues'

A general satire, apparently suggesting that freethinkers are better than whig dissenters.

L(11626.i.11/3, title cropt); MH.

T534 **Trumpeter.** The trumpeter. A fable. Humbly inscrib'd to the lower house of convocation. *London, printed for J. Baker,* 1710. (*WL* Jan)

8⁰: A⁴; *1–2* 3–8.

'In days of yore, when old folks tell us'

A satire on Sacheverell at his trial.

CT,DT; CSmH,MH.

T535 **Tr——us.** The tr——us treaty: exemplified in the fable of the wolves and sheep. [*London*] *Printed in the year* 1712.

½⁰: 1 side, 1 column.

'The wolves, as 'tis said, in politicks deep'

A whig poem against the peace with France.

L(1876.f.19/22),DT,Crawford; MH,*Harding.*

Trusty. The trusty and true Englishman, [1712.] *See* An excellent new song, call'd the Trusty and true Englishman, [1712.]

Truth

T536 **Truth.** 'The truth. A poem.' [*London*] 6d. (*GSJ* 17 May 1735)

The price is given as 1s. in *GM* May.

— Truth, a poem. Address'd to the right honourable William lord Harrington, 1740. *See* Boyd, Elizabeth.

T537 — Truth and moderation. [*London*] *Sold by John King, John Tinney, and at the print and pamphlet shops,* April the 21, 1741.

obl 1⁰: 1 side, 3 columns.

Large engraving at head; three short poems. The date of publication is engraved.

''Midst home-bred feuds and foreign nurtur'd jars'

The third poem is followed by initials 'C.P.G.' In favour of Walpole.

L(P&D 2489),O(title cropt).

T538 — The truth at last. To the tune of, Which nobody can deny. [*London*] *Printed in the year* 1711.

½⁰: 1 side, 2 columns.

'Come all ye brave boys, and high-churchmen, draw near'

A satire on the tories.

L(112.f.44/30),O,E,DA,MC,Rothschild; MH.

T539 — The truth found out at last, or the whig prov'd worse than the tory. *London, printed by W. Richardson,* [1720?]

½⁰: 1 side, 2 columns.

'As 'tother day I chanc'd to walk'

On the South Sea speculation.

MH.

T540 — Truth in disguise: or, the tale of the lady and her huntsman. *London, printed in the year* 1712.

½⁰: 1 side, 2 columns.

'In ancient times (as stories tell)'

A whig poem, against Anne's dismissal of Marlborough.

L(112.f.44/34).

— Truth in rhyme, 1732. *See* Ward, Edward [The parish gutt'lers].

T541 — Truth on all sides. A new masquerade ballad, as it is intended to be sung the next ball night, at the K---g's theatre in the H--ym----t. To the tune of Tantararara, masks all, masks all. *London, printed for H. Carpenter,* 1750. (*GM* Jan)

2⁰: A⁴; *1–2* 3–8.

'Ye courtiers and patriots, ye statesmen and wits'

CtY,KU,MH,OCU.

T542 — — *Printed in the year* 1750.

8⁰: A⁴; *1* 2–8.

A piracy, possibly of provincial origin. Horizontal chain-lines.

O.

T542·5 — Truth's champion or an elegie. On the much to be lamented death of that pious and godly minister of the gospel. Mr. Alexander Shields. [*Edinburgh,* 1700/01.]

½⁰: 1 side, 1 column.

Truth's champion

> Mourning borders.
> 'Invoke no muse, but the cœlestial king'
> Shields died at Port Royal, Jamaica, on 14 June 1700.
> MB.
> — 'The truth's come out at last: or, the downfall of a great favourite. Tune of O brave popery. 1711.'
> Morgan N624; not traced and possibly recorded from ms.

Tryphiodorus.
Merrick, James: The destruction of Troy being the sequel of the Iliad. Translated from the Greek of Tryphiodorus, [1742?] *See* M193.

T543 Tub. The tub and pulpit, or, a dialogue between an old cloak of forty one, and a rusty gown of eighty eight. Written by the man in the moon. *London, printed in the year* 1710.
½°: 1 side, 2 columns.
'Grave sir, if I am not mistaken'
> A dialogue between church and dissenters, inspired by the Sacheverell controversy.
OW,Rothschild; CtY,MH.

T544 Tucker, Nicholas. A new poem on the ratification of the safe and honourable peace, with Spain as well as France... Also on the blessed art of cultivating peace at home... *London, printed by E. Everingham, at the Seven Stars, in Ave-Mary-lane, near Ludgate.* September the 9th, 1713.
2°: A² B¹; *1–2* 3–6.
'Glory to god, author of Britains peace'
'Most happy day, the glorious peace is sign'd'
LLP(title crop't),LdU-B(uncut).

Tunbridge. The Tunbridge prodigy, 1706. *See* Finch, Anne, *countess of Winchilsea.*

Tunbridgiale. Tunbridgiale, a poem, 1726. *See* Byrom, John.

T545 Tunstall, —, *Mr.* Carmen genethliacum: humbly dedicated to the honourable Sir Thomas Parkyns bart. [*Nottingham, printed by John Collyer,*] 1723.
4°: 24 pp.
(W. J. Clarke, *Early Nottingham printers and printing* (1953) 47.)

Tunstall, William. Ballads and some other occasional poems: by W----- T---- in the Marshalsea. *London, printed by E. Berington, for the benefit of the author,* 1716. (*MC* Aug)
8°: pp. 53.   L,O; CtY,MH.
> Treated as a miscellany by *Case* (289); it includes poems by Charles Wogan and others. An enlarged version of *Poems of love and gallantry*, 1716 (*Case* 289b).

— [*idem*] A collection of ballads and some other occasional poems... To which is added, Saint

Tunstall, W.

> Cyprian's discourse to Donatus... *London, printed for John Wilford,* 1727 [1726]. (*MC* Sept)
> 8°: pp. 40+39.   L,O; DFo,ICU.
> *Saint Cyprian's discourse* is a reissue of the fifth edition, 1725.

T546 [—] From W.T. in the Marshalsea, to C.W. in Newgate. Tune, To all ye ladies. *London, printed for J. Roberts,* 1716.
½°: 1 side, 2 columns.
'From me, dear Charles, inspir'd with ale'
> *Crum* F713. To Tunstall's fellow-prisoner Charles Wogan; answered by his *The Preston prisoners*, 1716.
MH.

T547 [—] From W.T. to C.W. The second part. To the same tune. *London, printed for J. Roberts,* 1716.
½°: 1 side, 2 columns.
'Whilst impotent, tho' fill'd with rage'
> *Crum* W1206. In answer to [Charles Wogan] *The Preston prisoners*, 1716.
L(C.121.g.9/178).

T548 [—] St. Cyprian's discourse to Donatus. Done into English metre, by W---- T---- in the Marshalsea. The second edition corrected. *London, printed for the author, by E. Berington at the Cross-keys without Temple-Bar,* 1716. (*SR* 19 July)
8°: A–F⁴; *i–viii,* 1–39 *40 blk.* 39 err.
> The first edition has not been identified; it was perhaps not separately published. Some copies (L,CtY,MH) have an early state of A2 without the footnote '*My muse'. Entered in *SR* to Tunstall by John Morphew; deposit copies at L,O,E,EU,SaU.
'Donatus, you as opportunely ask'
> Tunstall's authorship is clear from the entry in *SR*.
L(992.h.6/5; T.1541/1),O(2),E,LdU-B(presentation copy),SaU+; CtY(2),MH.

T549 [—] — The third edition corrected. *London, printed for the benefit of the author, by E. Berington,* 1716.
8°: A–F⁴; *i–viii,* 1–38 '29' *40 blk.*
> Possibly in part a reimpression.
L(1960),LG,O,C,LdU-B; CSmH,CtY,MH (lacks A1),NN.

T550 [—] — The fourth edition corrected. *London, printed for the benefit of the author, by E. Berington,* 1717. (*PB* 6 July)
8°: A–F⁴; *i–viii,* 1–39 *40 blk.*
L(1973); KU.

T551 — [reissue] St. Cyprian's description of the pagan age. In a discourse to his friend Donatus. Render'd into English metre from the Latin original. By William Tunstal, gent... The fifth edition. *London, printed for John Wilford,* 1725. (*MC* Nov)
8°: A⁴(±A1) χ¹ B–F⁴; *i–x,* 1–39 *40 blk.*
> A reissue; χ1, the contents leaf, has been seen

Tunstall, W. St. Cyprian's discourse

to be conjugate with the cancel title A1. Also reissued with another cancel title, without imprint, in Tunstall's *A collection of ballads*, 1727.

L(161.m.66).

T552 [—] W.T. to fair Clio; who, the first time he had the honour to see her, sung a ballad of her own composing, in compliment to one he had writ before. To the tune of, To all ye ladies, &c. *London, printed for J. Roberts*, 1716.

½°: 1 side, 2 columns.

Reprinted in the Dublin 1716 edition of Lady Mary Wortley Montagu's *Court poems*.

'Ah! Clio, had thy distant lays'

L(C.121.g.9/178).

T553 [—] W.T. to Mrs. M.M. in answer to a song she sent him, which ends with this stanza... *London, printed in the year* 1716.

½°: 1 side, 2 columns.

'Believe me, nymph, whilst you contend'

Crum B271, identifying the author as Tunstall.

O.

T554 Turco-judaeo-machia. Turco-judæo-machia, being a full and true account of a memorable battle fought upon a summer's-day between a Jew and a Turk. *Dublin, printed in the year* 1733.

8°: *A*⁴ *B*⁴; *1-2* 3-16.

'Say, goddess, for 'tis you can tell'

A fight between Ben J——h (who taught Hebrew at Trinity College, Dublin and sold coffee) and F——y.

DA(imprint cropt),DK.

T555 Turkish. The Turkish paradise or Vaux-hall gardens. Wrote at Vaux-hall last summer. The Prince and Princess of Wales...being in the gardens. *London, printed for T. Cooper*, 1741. (*GM, LM* May)

2°: *A*² *B*²; *1-2* 3-8.

'Why dies the trumpets sound? strike every string'

O; IU.

T556 Turnbull, Walter. Some verses composed upon the insurrection of the Jacobites...from their first rise to the present time. To the tune of, Balhaven's voyage... *Newcastle upon Tyne, printed for the author*, 1746.

8°: A-D⁴; *1-3* 4-32.

'The Jacobites, their insurrections'

Dedication signed.

L(11631.bb.87).

T557 Turncoat. The turncoat. To the tune of John Anderson my jo. [*Edinburgh?* 1712/14.]

½°: 1 side, 2 columns.

'I lov'd no king in forty one'

Based on [Edward Ward] *The religious turncoat*, [1711]; *Crum* I324. The verses have some echoes of *The vicar of Bray*. Further

The **turncoat**

adapted as *An excellent new ballad, intituled the New way of the turn coat*, [1715.]

L(1489.gg.1/15),E.

T558 Turncoats. The turn-coats. A new speech. By Tom. Tattle. [*London*] '*Printed for T. Caution at Guild-hall*', [1714.]

slip: 1 side, 1 column.

Stanza 1, line 3 reads 'Almanacks'. The Brett-Smith copy was reissued in *State poems. A collection of choice private pieces*, 1715.

'To change! What is it but to live?'

A satire on the tories.

O; Brett-Smith.

T559 — [another edition]

Stanza 1, line 3 reads 'Almonacks'.

L(C.121.g.9/193),LSA.

T560 Turned. The **** turn'd into English: to render it more intelligible to the merchant-man and country free-holder. [*London?* 1739.]

½°: 1 side, 1 column.

'My lords and gentlemen, I meet you again'

The king's speech to parliament on the convention with Spain, satirized.

L(11626.i.11/30),LG.

Turner, Daniel. Divine songs, hymns and other poems. *Reading printed, and sold by S. Blackman, Reading; and A. Ward, London*, 1747.

8°: pp. xii, 44. L,O; IU.

The copy at IU has ms. additions.

———

T561 — 'A poem to the memory of the late reverend Mr. Samuel Wilson, who died Oct. 6, 1750. In the 48th year of his age. [*London*] *Printed for John Ward*. Price 4d. or 3s. 6d. per dozen.' (*LEP* 27 Nov 1750)

T562 [**Turner,** *Sir* **Edward.**] An imitation of Horace's 16th epode. *London, printed for T. Cooper*, 1739. (28 June?)

2°: *A*¹ *B*² *C*¹; *i-ii*, *1-6*.

A1 and C1 have been seen to be conjugate. Entered in Bowyer's ledgers under 28 June, 500 copies printed. Listed in *GM, LM* July.

'England again, by civil discord torn'

Early ms. attribution to Turner in the O copy.

L(1490.f.11, uncut),O; TxU(2).

T563 Turner, Joseph. Almeria. *London, printed for J. Roberts, & J. Jackson*, 1730. (*MChr* Sept)

2°: *A*² *B*²; *1-2* 3-8.

Drop-head title on p. 3, 'Almeria. A poem. Inscrib'd to the right honourable Viscountess Castlemain'.

'What stile, what language, suits the poet's lays'

Apparently in praise of Emma Child.

LdU-B; TxU.

Turner, J.

T564 [—] An epistle to Dr. Young. *London, printed for W. Mears*, [1734.] (*GM, LM* June)
2°: A^2 B–E^2; *i–iv, 1–16.* A1 hft.
The half-title reads 'On the depravity of human nature: to Dr. Edward Young.'
'Rare virtue, who forsook the town with you'
Reissued with Turner's name below.
O,LdU-B,WcC(uncut); CSmH,CU(–A1),CtY (lacks A2),OCU,TxU(ms. corrections).

T565 —— By Mr. Turner... The second edition. *London, printed for W. Mears; sold by J. Roberts,* 1738.
2°: A^2($\pm$A2) B–E^2; *i–iv, 1–16.* A1 hft.
A reissue.
O; IU,NN-B.

T565·5 [—] An epistle to Mr. Pope. *London, printed for H. Whittridge*, 1732. (*GM* 27 Jan)
2°: A^2 B^2 C^1; *1–2 3–10.*
'Superiour qualities alike will raise'
J. V. Guerinot, *Pamphlet attacks on Alexander Pope* (1969) 332 refers to *Mr. Pope's literary correspondence* II (1735) 39–40 which prints a short poem 'To the author of an epistle to Mr. Pope; occasion'd by his Epistle to the Earl of Burlington'; a footnote identifies the author as Mr. Jos. Turner and records that the epistle was published in folio in 1732. This appears to be the only poem that meets this description. In praise of Pope and against Welsted, occasioned by the latter's *Of dulness and scandal*, 1732.
O(uncut),OW,WcC; CtY,ICU,MH,TxU(2).

T566 — The first epistle of the first book of Horace imitated. *London, printed for J. Roberts*, 1738. (*GM, LM* March)
2°: A^2 B–E^2; *1–4 5–19 20 blk.* A1 hft.
'Thou! the bright judge of learning, and the friend'
O(–A1); CSmH,CtY,MH(uncut).

T567 Turner, Naphtal. The heathen's conversion, in seven parts. The life of Jehosaphat, the son of king Avernio of Barma in India... By Naphtal Turner, a blind man. *Printed and sold in Aldermary Church Yard, London*, [174–?]
12°: A^6; *1 2–12.*
Vertical chain-lines. A chap-book. This imprint was used by Cluer Dicey and Richard Marshall from 1764 (cf. *Plomer*), but the typography suggests an earlier date.
'Good Christian people, now be pleas'd to mind'
L(1078.k.23/1); *MH*(2).

T568 —— *London printed by L. How, in Petticoat-lane*, [174–?]
12°: A^6; *1 2–12.*
Apparently from the same press as the preceding; the priority between the two has not been established. Vertical chain-lines.
MH.

Turner, P.

T569 Turner, Purbeck. Augustus. A poem on the accession of his majesty King George. Humbly dedicated to the right honourable Charles, lord Hallifax... *London, printed by W. Wilkins; sold by Ferd. Burleigh*, 1714. (1 Sept, Luttrell)
2°: A^2 B–C^2; *i–ii, 1–3 4–10.*
Horizontal chain-lines. Listed in *MC* Sept.
'Close by where Camus moves his languid streams'
LDW,O,DT; CLU-C(Luttrell),CtY,MH.

T570 [—] A pindaric ode upon the death of her late majesty Queen Anne, of blessed memory. *London printed, and sold by J. Morphew*, 1714. (*EvP* 14 Aug)
2°: A^2 B^2; *1–2 3–7 8 blk.*
'The sable mantle of the low'ring night'
Advertised in *EvP* as by Turner; early ms. attribution in the CtY copy.
CLU-C(Luttrell, Aug),CtY,InU,TxU.

T571 Turnip. The turnip song: a georgick. To the tune of, A begging we will go. [*London?* 1715/20.]
slip: 1 side, 1 column.
'Of all roots of H——r'
Crum O29. A Jacobite song against the Hanoverians.
O.

T572 Tutchin. Tutchin defended: or, an answer to the Picture of the Observator. *London printed, and sold by B. Bragg*, 1704. (4 Aug, Luttrell)
$\frac{1}{2}$°: *1–'3'* [i.e. 2], 1 column.
'Reading the sordid lines that you have writ'
MH(Luttrell).

T573 — Tutchin's everlasting monument; or, John drawn to the life. An epitaph in memory of John Tutchin, to be inscribed in letters of brass upon the triangle monument near Padington. Humbly recommended to the Calves Head clubb. Subscriptions are taken in by his wife. [*London*, 1707?]
$\frac{1}{2}$°: 1 side, 1 column.
'Here lies stoick John,/Born since forty and one'
An attack on Tutchin, probably on his death in 1707, though the Crawford copy has been dated 1704 by a modern hand, doubtless in reference to his prosecution then.
Crawford.

T574 [**Tutchin, John.**] The apostates. A poem. Written by the author of the Foreigners. *London, printed for M. Fabian*, 1701. (20 Aug, Luttrell)
2°: A–C^2; *1–2 3–12.* 12 advt.
The Luttrell copy is recorded in *Haslewood*; listed in *WL* Aug.
'Art thou, dear Israel! still the butt of fate?'
Tutchin's *The foreigners* was published in July 1700.
O,*MR-C*; CLU-C,CSmH.

T575 [—] The apostates: or, the revolters. A poem. Against foreigners. Written by the author of the Foreigners. *London, printed in the year* 1701.

Tutchin, J. The apostates

4°: A^2; *1* 2–4, 2 columns.
A piracy.
CtY.

T576 [—] The apostates: or the noble cause of liberty deserted. A satyr. With the character of a late l---d li-----nt. And a comparison between the fate of Troy and that of Israel. *London, printed for Eliz. Mallet,* 1702. (31 Jan, Luttrell)
2°: A^2($\pm$A1) B–C^2 D^1; *1–2* 3–12 *13; 14 blk.*
12, 13 advt.
A reissue of T574 with a cancel title and added advertisement leaf for Mallet's books.
L(11630.ff.2/12,–D1),LLP,O; *CU*,CtY(–D1), ICU(Luttrell),IU(–D1),OCU(–D1).

T577 [—] The British muse: or tyranny expos'd. A satyr, occasion'd by all the fulsom and lying poems and elegies, that have been written on the occasion of the death of the late King James. *London, printed for Eliz. Mallet; sold by the booksellers of London & Westminster,* 1702 [1701]. (15 Nov, Luttrell)
2°: A–C^2; *1–2* 3–12.
The Luttrell copy is recorded in *Haslewood.*
'For tyrants dead no statues we erect'
Ascribed to Tutchin by *Jacob* II. 309.
LG,E,DK,AdU,*MR-C*; ICN.

T578 [—] — To which is added, a smart poem on the generous articles of Limerick and Galway. *London, printed for Eliz. Mallet, and sold by the Williamite book-sellers of London and Dublin, who are haters of tyranny and slavery,* [1701/02.]
4°: A^4 B^2; *1–2* 3–12.
Almost certainly a Dublin reprint; the 'smart poem' (of twelve lines) is on p. 12.
L(11633.e.3),O,DN(2),DT(2),LdU-B+; DFo, DLC,MH,MiU.

[—] An elegy on the death of the late famous Doctor Titus Oates… Written by the Observator, [1705.] *See* E203.

[—] A letter of advice to a friend in London: written by the Observator, 1704. *See* L137.

T579 — A poem in the praise of folly and knavery. *London, printed for Sam. Ballard,* 1704. (*DC* 6 March)
4°: A^2 B–F^2; *1–6* 7–22 *23–24 blk.*
'My humble muse no hero sings'
MH(slightly cropt).

[—] A poem to the memory of his late majesty William the third [actually by Joseph Stennet], 1702. *See* S741.

[—] The tackers. By a church of England minister [i.e. Charles Darby], 1705. *See* D45.

[—] The tribe of Levi, 1736. *See* T476.

T580 **Twelve.** The twelve blessings of a scolding wife. [*London*] *Printed by R.N.* [*Richard Newcomb*] *in Wine-office-court, Fleetstreet,* 1711. (*SR* 15 March)
$\frac{1}{2}$°: 1 side, 2 columns.

The twelve blessings

'Ye marry'd men, who think ye lead sad lives'
E.

T581 **Twentieth.** The XX Plalm [!], imitated from Buchanan. [*Edinburgh,* 1711.]
$\frac{1}{2}$°: 1 side, 1 column.
'Tho' the ungodly senate has decreed'
In favour of the Pretender.
E(ms. date 1711).

T582 — The 20th psalm imitated from Buchanan. [*Edinburgh,* 1711?/–.]
$\frac{1}{2}$°: 1 side, 1 column.
E.

Twenty-six. Twenty six chosen psalms of thanksgiving and praise, love and glory (out of the whole book) for the use of a country parish church; to be sung, in order, all over, several times in the year, constantly. All of an equal length. By the rector. *At Exon, printed by Andrew Brice, for Nath. Thorn,* 1725.
12°. ExI.

Two. Two elegies on the much to be lamented death of Mathew Buckingher, the famous little man expos'd for a German show. Who died at Cork in Ireland, Sept. 28. 1722. The former, written by Counsellor Burk at Dublin; the other, suppos'd to be done by the reverend Dr. Swift. To which is subjoin'd, Buckingher reviv'd… *Edinburgh, printed by William Adams,* 1723.
4°: pp. 16. C.
A miscellany, not known to *Case* or *CBEL.* The editor's preface, signed (pseudonymously?) 'Matthew Slow' records that the elegies were sent to Scotland by 'Ar—e', presumably by James Arbuckle. One of the additional poems is by Alexander Pennecuik, and the others are probably of Scots origin.

T583 — Tow [!] elegys, the first, on wanton Watty M'Aulay, the famous piper in Port-glasgow. The second, on George Rollance, king's boatman… *Edinburgh, printed in the year* 1730.
8°: A–B^4; *1–2* 3–16.
'Portglasgow thou's e'en left a lean'
'Superior powers that bieds aboon'
L(11631.a.68).

— Two epistles of Horace imitated, 1736. *See* Melmoth, William.

— Two epistles to Mr. Pope, 1730. *See* Young, Edward.

T584 — Two excellent new ballads, viz. I. The Uxbridge duplicate: or, the j--dge justify'd. II. On Colonel Francisco, rape-master general of Great Britain. *London, printed in the year* 1730.
2°: A^4; *1–2* 3–8.
Percival XIV and appendix no. 23. These poems and two more were reprinted in an octavo half-sheet, pp. 1–8 (copies at DK,

Two excellent new ballads

NjP), apparently to accompany the collection *Robin's panegyrick*.
'Come ye ministers all so courtly'
'Good people, come heark, and a story I'll tell'
Satires against Walpole.
OW; MH,TxU.

— The two first odes of Horace imitated, 1738. *See* Manning, Francis.

T585 — Two kingdoms made one, in a dialogue between St. George and St. Andrew; occasioned by the union, that commenced on Thursday, the first of May, 1707. [*London*] *Printed, and sold by J. Morphew*, 1707.
½°: 1–2, 1 column.
'Long have our arms each others arms withstood'
L(C.20.f.2/227).

T586 — Two Lilliputian odes: the first, on the famous engine with which Captain Gulliver extinguish'd the flames in the royal palace... The second, inviting a bookseller, to a coffee-house, where the author was. *London*, '*printed by S. Pigmy, for Tom. Thumb near St. Paul's*', 1727. (May, Luttrell)
8°: A⁴ B–C⁴; 1–5 6–24. A1 hft.
Teerink 1227. Separate title on p. 13 to the second ode. Listed in *MC* June.
'Engine strong, / Thick and long!'
'––––––, wou'd / You be good?'
L(164.1.73, Luttrell),LVA-F,C; CtY,KU.

— Two love poems, 1701. *See* Pomfret, John.

— 'The two lurchers.'
The compliment, 1746, is 'by the author of the Two lurchers, &c'; this work has not been traced, and may possibly be in prose.

T587 — Two new ballads. [*London*, 1728.] (10 March?)
½°: 1 side, 2 columns.
Percival VIII and appendix 10, recording a copy in PRO endorsed 10 March 1727–8. The ballads are 'The L——ds address to K.G. II.' and 'A new ballad'.
'Thank ye, most great and martial sir'
'Hither from farthest east to west'
The first ballad parodies the lords' address to the king of January 1728; the second is *Crum* H1243: 'A new ballad on the Jews getting liberty to purchase land in England'.
LPR,O; OCU.

— Two odes from the Latin of the celebrated Rapin, 1710. *See* Bragge, Francis.

— Two odes of Horace, with a description of Fame or Report from Virgil, 1721. *See* Morrice, Bezaleel.

Two poems

T588 — Two poems: one on the royal family, and the other on Mr. Addison's being made one of the lords commissioners of trade. *London printed, and sold by J. Harrison, A. Boulter, S. Boulter, J. Fox, & R. Burleigh*, 1716. (24 March, Luttrell)
2°: A² B–C²; 1–2 3–12.
Listed in *MC* March.
'Children like these, made Niobe compare'
'Next to those men, who, with their lutes, did call'
CtY(Luttrell).

— Two poems viz. I. On the deluge, 1718. *See* Newcomb, Thomas.

T589 — Two poems. Viz. I. Plot upon plot. II. To the most illustrious hero George Lewis, duke of Brunswick and Lunenburg, &c. *London, printed by R. Janeway*, 1713.
2°: A² B¹; 1–2 3–6.
Each poem was printed separately as a Dublin half-sheet. Both poems are sometimes found detached, resembling half-sheet editions except for the pagination.
'Oh wicked whigs! what can you mean?'
'I sing the prince the scourge of Gallick power'
The first poem is particularly concerned with the 'band-box plot' and Swift.
O,C,DA(uncut); OCU(uncut).

T590 — Two poems. Viz. The retreat, and The aspiration. *London, printed in the year* 1717.
8°: A⁸; 1–2 3–16.
'Full twenty years exper'ence have I had'
'Why am I limited to place'
Religious poems.
L(11659.aaa.86).

— Two tales, [1722?] *See* Congreve, William.

Typhon. Typhon: or the wars between the gods and giants, 1704. *See* Mandeville, Bernard.

T591 [**Tyrwhitt, Thomas.**] An epistle to Florio, at Oxford. *London, printed for J. Robinson*, 1749.
4°: A⁴ B–C⁴; 1–4 5–24. A1 hft.
Vertical chain-lines. The copy seen, with uncancelled title, may be the result of a binder's error rather than a separate issue.
''Tis true, my friend, what busy fame has told'
For Tyrwhitt's authorship see *Nichols* III. 147n.
LVA-D.

T592 [—] — *London, printed for J. Brindley; sold by J. Robinson*, 1749. (*LM* June)
4°: A⁴(±A2) B–C⁴; 1–4 5–24. A1 hft.
Cancel title.
L(840.k.4/12, –A1),LVA-D,O; CtY(2).

U

U., Fr., *coll. Exon socius.* In laudem Edvardi Vernoni, 1742. *See* Upton, Francis.

Ub-bub-a-boo. Ub-bub-a-boo: or, the Irish-howl, 1735. *See* Hamilton, Thomas, *chaplain.*

'Umbraticus, *Dr.*' A syllabus of the animal œconomy, 1748. *See* S942.

'Umbritius Cantianus.' Umbritii Cantiani poemata, 1729. *See* Earle, Jabez.

U1 Unbiassed. The unbyassd patriot. A poem on his grace James duke of Hamilton. [*Edinburgh*, 170–.]
½°: 2 sides, 1 column.
    On side 2, 'An accrostick'.
'All men of renown give ear'
    In praise of James Douglas, fourth duke of Hamilton.
E.

U2 Unembarrassed. The unembarassed countenance, a new ballad. To the tune of a Cobler there was, &c. &c. *London, printed for Henry Carpenter,* 1746. (*GM, LM* April)
2°: *A*² <*B*²; *1–3* 4–6 '8' *8 blk.*
'To a certain old chapel well known in the town,'
    Printed in Sir Charles Hanbury Williams, *A collection of poems,* 1763; Horace Walpole annotated his copy (now at L) 'Not by Sr C.W.' A satire on William Pitt.
L(11626.h.12/4),O,AdU,LdU-B; ICN,MH,MiU, TxU(2).

Unequal. The unequal enemies, 1722. *See* Morrice, Bezaleel.

— The unequal match, 1737. *See* Jacob, Hildebrand.

U3 Unfortunate. The unfortunate family: in four parts... To which is added, a notable poem upon the uncertainty of man's life. [*London*] *Printed for E. Blare on London-Bridge,* [1706/12?]
8°: *A*⁴; *1* 2–8.
    A chap-book. Compare *Wing* U51.
'Not long ago in Dorsetshire'
L(1076.l.26/5).

U4 — The unfortunate fortunate marry'd-man. [*London*, 170–?]
½°: 1 side, 1 column.
    At end of verse, 'The author of this has a very compleat collection of matrimony-stories, and intends if this meets with a favourable reception, to oblige the publick with 253 more'.
'Jack met his friend Dick, and some compliments past'

The advertisement could be considered as satirical of John Dunton or Edward Ward. MH,TxU.

U5 — The unfortunate lovers: or, the history of Girolamo and Sylvestra. A tragical tale. *London, printed by J. How, for the author; sold by B. Bragge,* 1706. (29 June, Luttrell)
2°: *A*² B–H²; *i–iv,* 1–28. 28 err.
'In Florence, far renown'd about those times'
ICU(Luttrell),TxU.

U6 — The unfortunate ramble: or, the Bread-street adventurers. Written by Timothy Goosequil of the Custom-house. *London, printed in the year* 1709. (20 Sept, Luttrell)
8°: *A*⁴; *1–2* 3–8.
'Speak, goddess muse, in soft description tell'
    A tale of three city prentices in a St. James's brothel.
L(161.k.14, Luttrell).

U7 Ungrateful. The ungrateful world, or; the hard case of a great g-----l. [*London,* 1712.]
½°: 1 side, 1 column.
'A village swain secure from wants'
    Against Marlborough.
L(1850.e.10/14).

U8 Unhappy. The unhappy voyage. Giving an account of the Royal Anne galley, Captain Willis commander, which was split to pieces on the Stag rocks on the Lizzard the 10th of November, 1721. having on board the Lord Belhaven, who was going as governor to Barbadoes... To the tune of, Womens work is never done, &c. [*London?* 1721/22.]
½°: 1 side, 3 columns.
    Rough woodcut at head. Mourning borders.
'Oh! the sad and dismal story'
L(Rox.III.593).

Unio. Unio, 1707. *See* Rowe, Nicholas.

— Unio politico-poetico-joco-seria, 1706. *See* Symson, Andrew.

[U9 = D46·5] Union. The union, a poem humbly dedicated to the queen, 1707. *See* Darby, Charles.

U10 — Union. A poem humbly inscrib'd to all true patriots, on the meeting of the parliament... By a hearty well-wisher to the welfare of Great Britain. [*London?*] *Printed in the year* 1722.
8°: *A*⁸; *1–5* 6–16. A1 hft.
'Assist you tuneful genius of our isle'
MP; DFo.

U11 — The union, a poem. Humbly inscrib'd to her royal highness the Princess Ann. *London, printed for J. Roberts,* 1733. (*GSJ* 1 Nov)
2°: *A*¹ B² C¹ D¹; *1–3* 4–9 *10 blk.*
    The collation is obscure; possibly there should

The **union**

be a half-title, and the pamphlet then be composed of three sheets within one another.
'Hail, royal maid! divinely good and great!'
On the marriage of Princess Anne to Prince William of Orange.
TxU.

U12 — [dh] The union topknot: or, advice to the semptress[!] a-la-mode. [col] *London printed, and sold by B. Bragge*, 1707.
4°: A²; 1–4.
'Ladies, since you the knot of union wear'
A satire on women, with reference to the Scots.
OCU.

U13 — — [col] *London, printed for B. Braggs* [!], 1707.
4°: A²; 1–4.
Possibly a piracy, with the imprint deliberately mis-spelt.
CtY.

U14 — — [col] *London, printed for B. Breggs* [!], 1707.
4°: *A²*; 1–4.
Title reads 'semptriss'; another piracy?
LG.

U15 Universal. The universal applause of Mount Parnassus, a serenata da camera, to be represented on the birthday of the most serene Anne...at the castle of Dublin, the sixth day of February, 1711 ... Set by Mr. John Sigismond Cousser... *Dublin, printed by Edwin Sandys*, 1711.
4°: A⁴; 1–2 3–8.
'Such harmony, as crowns th' Olympick revels'
DT.

— Universal beauty a poem, 1735. *See* Brooke, Henry.

U16 — The universal coquet: a fable. Inscribed to a certain young l--y in Dublin. By W.W. esqr; *Dublin, printed by James Hoey*, 1749.
8°: *A⁴*; 1–3 4–8.
'Fatigued with granting mortal pray'rs'
The initials suggest Wetenhall Wilkes as author, but there is no confirmation for the attribution.
C,DT.

— The universal doom, 1732–. *See* Howard, W.

— The universal passion, 1725–. *See* Young, Edward.

— The universal prayer, 1738. *See* Pope, Alexander.

U17 University. The university answer to the pretended University ballad. *London, printed in the year* 1705.
½°: 1 side, 2 columns.
21 stanzas.
'We receiv'd your advice as good daughters should do'
A tory reply in favour of Sir Humphry Mackworth.
O,AdU,Crawford.

The **university** answer

U18 — [*idem*] Sir Humphry Mackworth's real vindication, or the true University answer to the pretended University ballad. *London, printed in the year* 1705; *and sold by Ben: Bragg.*
½°: 2 sides, 2 columns.
26 stanzas. After imprint, 'The reader is desir'd to distinguish this from the Scoto-Cambrian edition, lately set forth in a broadside, which was publish'd contrary to the author's intentions, and has very little in it that comes up to his meaning, as may be seen by the perusal.'
L(C.121.g.9/142).

U19 — The university ballad, or, the church's advice to her two daughters, Oxford and Cambridge. First part. [*London*, 1705.]
½°: 2 sides, 2 columns.
'I have heard my dear daughters, a story of late'
Advice on their choice of members of parliament, against the whigs. Cf. *The university answer*, 1705.
L(C.40.m.11/82),O(2),AdU,Crawford.

Upon. Upon Lady Katherine H-de's first appearing at the play-house in Drury-lane, 1718. *See* 'Prior, Matthew'.

— Upon the anniversary held at Preston, [1738.] *See* Hall, David.

U20 — Upon the fringes, commonly so call'd by the vulgar. *Dublin, printed in Molesworth's Court*, Aug. 3d, 1722.
½°: 1 side, 2 columns.
Teerink 911; *Williams* 1107.
'O Dublin is a fine town,/And a gallant city'
Ball 166 suggested that 'the mind of Swift is seen' in this ballad, but Williams rejects it. On the unveiling of a statue of George I at Essex Bridge in Dublin.
L(C.121.g.8/21).

U21 — Upon the happy and glorious reign and memory of King William the III. [*Dublin?* 1702.]
1°: 1 side, 1 column.
'William was he whom god's decree did send'
DT.

U22 — [*idem*] Upon the glorious memory of King William the III. who dy'd the 8th of March 170½. Dedicated to those honourable and worthy gentlemen of Ireland, who commemorate his birth-day, Novmber [!] 4th. *Dublin, printed for M. G.* [*Gunne*] *at Essex-street-gate*, [1702.]
½°: 2 sides, 1 column.
CtY.

U23 — Upon the poet laureat's being expelled the house of lords. *London, printed for J. Jenkins, near Ludgate*, [1733.] (*LM* June)
½°: 1 side, 1 column.
After imprint, 'Price (on stamp'd paper) 2d.'
'C——r (the wonder of a brazen age)'

Upon the poet laureat

A satire on Colley Cibber.
Crawford; MH.

U24 — [another issue]
No imprint or price at foot; printed on un-
stamped paper.
OW.

Upper. The upper gallery, 1733. *See* Lawson,
John.

U25 **Upstart.** The upstart. A satyr. *London, printed anno*
1710.
8°: A⁴; *1–2* 3–8.
Reissued with poems published by Henry
Hills in *A collection of the best English poetry*,
1717 (*Case* 294).
'Northward a county lyes (in which does stand'
A satire on Francis Taylor, a Yorkshire lawyer;
cf. *Don Francisco Sutorioso*, 1710.
L(11601.dd.17/8; C.124.b.7/57),O,O-JJ,
LdU-B,YM+; CSmH,CtY,ICN,MH,TxU+.

U26 [**Upton, Francis.**] In laudem Edvardi Vernoni,
apud insulas Americanas classis Britannicæ præfecti. *London, Sam Birt*, 1740. (*GM, LM* Oct)
2°: 8 pp.
'Unde novus vates deserta per ardua Pindi'
(Pickering & Chatto cat. 219/7228a.)

U27 [—] — Impressio altera. *Londini, excudebatur*
impensis Sam. Birt; & Tanoduni [Taunton] apud
Sar. Chauklin prostat venale, 1742.
2°: A⁴; *1–2* 3–8.
Signed on p. 8 'Fr. U. coll. Exon. socius';
Upton was elected a fellow of Exeter in 1741.
His authorship (and this second edition title)
is recorded in *Rawlinson*.
RPJCB.

[**Upton, James.**] Discontent the universal misery.
In an epistle to a friend, 1734. *See* D324.

[**Upton, John.**] A new canto of Spencer's Fairy
queen. Now first published, 1747. *See* N117.

Upton, Robert. Poems on several occasions...
London, printed for the author; sold by W. Reeve,
D. Job, A. Dodd, & E. Cooke, 1750.
8°: pp. 63.   L,LG.

[U28–9 = G162·5–6] **Useful.** Useful and delightful
instructions, by way of dialogue, 1712–. *See* Gill,
Thomas.

Usurer

U30 **Usurer.** ⟨The⟩ usurer. To the tune of, Such a
parcel a rogues in a nation. By a cabal of young
ladies. [*Edinburgh*, 171–?]
½°: 1 side, 2 columns.
'O happy time!/'Tis no more a crime'
According to a ms. note in the E copy, on Sir
James Nicolson.

E.

Utopia. Utopia: or, Apollo's golden days, 1747.
See Young, Lewis.

U31 **Uvedale, Thomas.** The death-bed display'd: with
the state of the dead. A sacred poem. *Westminster,*
printed by A. Campbell, for the author, and to be had
only of him, at Mr. Coulan's in St. Martin's Court,
1727.
4°: A⁴(−A4) a² B–G⁴; *i–iii* iv–ix *x, 1* 2–48. x err.
Various watermarks.
'Fond of applause, let other poets raise'
L(643.k.3/4),O; ICN,MH.

U32 — [fine paper]
4°: A⁴(−A4) a² B–G⁴ H¹; *i–iii* iv–ix *x, 1* 2–48 *49;*
50 blk. H1 err.
Watermark: Strasburg bend. The errata
appear on the added leaf H1 instead of on a2ᵛ.
L(11630.c.7/9, lacks a²); KU.

U33 — The remedy of love, in imitation of Ovid. A
poem. *London, printed for Nich. Cox*, 1704. (*DC*
10 April)
8°: A⁴ a⁴ b¹[=O4] B–N⁴ O⁴(−O4); *i–xviii, 1*–100
101–102. xviii err; O3 advt.
Because of the use of half-sheets it is difficult
to be certain of the watermarks; most copies
have fleur-de-lys, but the only watermark seen
in a copy at ICU is a fleur-de-lys on shield; it
is possibly on fine paper.
'Rejoyce successless youths, and love-sick swains'
L(11386.e.3),O; CSmH,CtY,DFo(2),ICN,MH+.

U34 — [*idem*] A cure for love: a satyr. In imitation of
Ovid... The second edition, corrected. *London,*
printed for T. Warner, 1732. (*LM* July)
8°: A² a⁴ B–G⁴ H²; *i–iii* iv–xi *xii, 1* 2–51 *52 blk.*
O; CLU-C,DFo,ICN.

U35 **Uzziah.** Uzziah and Jotham. A poem. *London*
printed, and sold by J. Roberts, 1719.
12°: *A*⁴ C⁶ E⁶ G⁶; *i–viii, 1* 2–36. A1 hft.
Apparently a reprint of the edition of 1690
(*Wing* U232).
'In dubious times, when plots so num'rous grew'
E,DT.

V

V., L. Emanuelis Alvari Regulae de syllabarum quantitate, 1730. *See* Vaslet, Louis.

V., R. A commendatory poem to the honourable city of Dublin, [1727.] *See* C316.

V1 Vacation. The vacation ramble: or, a view of Westminster. *London, printed in the year* 1711.
½⁰: 1 side, 2 columns.
'Now that the days go smoothly on'
  A satire on Westminster lechers.
NN.

V2 Vade-mecum. A vade mecum for malt-worms: or, a guide to good-fellows: being a description of the manners and customs of the most eminent publick houses, in and about the cities of London and Westminster... *London printed, and sold by T. Bickerton at the Crown in Paternoster-row,* [1720.] (*DP* 17 June)
8⁰: *A*⁴ B–G⁴; *1–2* 3–56.
  Entered in *SR* to John Cluer, 18 June; deposit copies of the issue below at O,EU. A series of short poems with woodcuts of the inn signs; since Cluer described himself as 'engraver on wood' (H435) the book may have originated with the cuts.
Dedication: 'To you, right worshipful the brewers!' Ascribed to Edward Ward by Aitken in *DNB* and by *CBEL*; *Troyer* rightly doubts the attribution. Possibly written by several hands, like the continuation below.
L(C.39.b.18).

V3 — [reissue] Illustrated with proper cuts... *London printed, and sold by T. Bickerton,* [1720.]
8⁰: *A*⁴(±A1) B–G⁴; *1–2* 3–56.
  The cancel title-leaf adds the reference to illustrations.
O,EU; CSmH.

V4 — — The second edition. Illustrated with proper cuts... *London printed, and sold by T. Bickerton,* [1720.] (Sept, Luttrell)
8⁰: π² *A*⁴(−A1) B–G⁴; *i–iv,* 3–56. π1 hft.
  A reissue with cancel title-leaf and half-title; the title appears to be from standing type of the preceding.
LG(uncut); CSmH(Luttrell).

V5 — A guide for malt-worms. The second part... Done by several hands. Illustrated with proper cuts. [*London*] *Sold by T. Bickerton in Pater-noster-row,* [1720.] (*PB* 22 Sept)
8⁰: *A*⁴ B–F⁴; *1–2* 3–48.
'Now for a landlord, who to let us know'
L(C.39.b.19),LG(lacks F1),O(lacks F4); CSmH (Luttrell, Sept).

V6 Vagabond. The vagabond tories. To a well-known tune. [*London,* 1714/15?]
½⁰: 2 sides, 1 column.
'What a racket is here'
  Probably the same work as 'A mug-house song. Written by T.B. minister of the gospel', printed as 'by an eminent presbyterian teacher' in [Sir Humphrey Mackworth] *Down with the mug,* 1717.
Harding.

V7 Valiant. The valliant souldiers and sailors loyal subjects health, to the queen, prince and noble commanders: to a new trumpet tune. [*London?* 1705/07.]
½⁰: 1 side, 2 columns.
  Two rough woodcuts at head.
'Now now the queens health'
DG(cropt).

'Vane, Anne.' Vanella: or an elegy, [1736.] *See* V12.

V8 Vanella. Vanella in the straw. A poem, inscrib'd to a certain lady in St. James's-street. *London, printed for W. James; sold by the book-sellers & pamphlet-sellers of London & Westminster,* 1732. (*GSJ* 12 June)
4⁰: A⁴ B–C²; *1–2* 3–16.
  Copies seen have no frontispiece, which was possibly only added to later editions.
'Hail! royal maid, divinely fair and good'
  On Anne Vane's delivery of the child of Frederick, prince of Wales.
L(C.118.c.2/7),*MR*; DFo.

V9 — A poem, inscrib'd to a certain lady in St. James's-street, lately deliver'd of a fine boy... The third edition. *London, printed for W. James; sold by the book-sellers & pamphlet-sellers of London & Westminster,* 1732.
4⁰: (frt+) A⁴ B–C²; *1–2* 3–16.
  Apparently a reimpression. No second edition traced.
L(1489.t.6).

V10 — — The fourth edition. *London, printed for W. James; sold by the book-sellers & pamphlet-sellers of London & Westminster,* 1732.
4⁰: (frt+) A⁴ B–C²; *1–2* 3–16.
O.

V11 — — '*London, printed for W. James; sold by the booksellers & pamphlet-sellers of London & Westminster*' [*Dublin*], 1732.
8⁰: *A*⁴; *1–3* 4–8.
DT; IU,MH.

V12 — Vanella: or, an elegy on the death of Miss V------e, writ by herself at the Bath, some few hours before her decease. [*Dublin,* 1736.]
8⁰: *A*⁴; *1–3* 4–7 *8 blk.*

Vanella: or, an elegy

Rough mourning woodcuts.
'With streaming eyes, and with dejected mien'
   On the death of Anne Vane, but probably not
   written by herself.
DG(uncut).

V13 — Vanella's progress. In eight scenes. *London,
printed for D. Ashburn, near Fleetstreet,* 1736.
4°: A^2 B^2 (+plates); *1–2* 3–7 *8 blk.*
   Text to eight engraved scenes.
'As yet unconscious of the latent snare'
   The history of Anne Vane.
CSmH,CtY,DFo,KU,MH(lacks plates)+.

[**Vanhomrigh, Esther.**] A rebus written by a lady,
[1724?] *See* R144.

V14 Vanière, Jacques. Jacobi Vanerii e Societate Jesu
Apes. *Londini, apud F. Gyles, Woodman & Lyon,
& C. Davis,* 1729 [1728]. (*SR* 16 Oct)
8°: A–F^4; *i–vi,* 1–10 17–46 *47–48.* F4 advt.
   Entered in *SR* (to all three booksellers) 16 Oct
   1728; deposit copies at O,EU,SaU. Entered in
   Bowyer's ledgers to Gyles, Woodman, &
   Davis, 500 copies printed, delivered 15 Oct.
   Listed in *MC* Oct. The earliest edition traced
   is *Tolosæ,* 1727; it subsequently became book
   14 of Vanière's *Prædium rusticum.*
'Artifices cano mellis apes, quas arva secutus'
L(972.i.28),O,OW,C,EU+; CSmH,CtY(2),MH.

V15 — Columbæ. Jacobo Vanierio tolosano authore,
poetarum hujus sæculi nulli secundo. *Londini, anno*
1725.
4°: A–F^4; *1–5* 6–47 *48 blk.*
'Quæ juvet, & lætas faceat quæ cura columbas'
'Je consacre, Daphnis, ma verve, & mon repos'
   The French translation is that published earlier
   in French editions as 'Gallicis versibus redditæ ab illustrissimo senatore'.
L(837.e.46),OW,C.

V16 Vanity. The vanity of free-thinking, expos'd in a
satyr. Dedicated to Mr. C—ns, proprietor, and the
rest of the thoughtless members of the Kitt-katt
Club. *London, printed for J. Morphew,* 1713.
8°: A^4 B–C^4; *1–6* 7–23 *24 blk.* A1 hft.
'Forbear, fond man, to think that thou canst live'
ICN.

— The vanity of the life of man, 1708–. *See*
Crouch, Nathaniel.

— The vanity of upstarts, 1709–. *See* Ward,
Edward.

'**Vanmattersculpt, Patrick.**' The sham author,
1735. *See* S382.

Variety. Variety: a poem, in two cantos, 1727. *See*
Boyd, Elizabeth.

[**V17** = P1101·5] '**Variscus, Antonius.**' Antonii Varisci
Elogium Annae, 1713. *See* Pritz, Johann Georg.

Vaslet, L.

V18 Vaslet, Louis. Emmanuelis Alvari Regulae de
syllabarum quantitate, cultiores multo & auctiores
quam antea editae. His accedit ars metrica...
Quibus adjungere visum est lusus aliquot poeticos
... Cum indice... Opera & studio L.V. *Londini, ex
typographia regia. Venales prostant apud Gul. Innys
& Nic. Prevost,* 1730. (*MChr* May)
8°: π^1 A^2 B–M^8 N^2; *i–vi,* 1 2–176, 1 2–4. 176 err.
   No watermark. N^2 adds a Latin ode, 'In
   impios'.
'Vocalem breviant alia subeunte Latini'
   Dedication of 'Ludovicus Vaslet' dated from
   Fulham '8° Id. Maij, 1730'. Rewritten from
   Prosodia Alvariana (P1142), which is related to
   the grammatical works of Emmanuel Alvarez.
   Despite common first lines and arrangement
   of topics, the works seem very different.
O.

V19 — [fine paper]
   Watermark: Strasburg bend.
L(982.g.23),O.

Vaticinium. Vaticinum in sepulcro Caroli quinti
repertum 1710, [1710/13.] *See* Pitcairne, Archibald.

V20 — Vaticinium, or the prophecy, occasion'd by the
dedication of the Voyage to the South-Sea, and
round the world, to the rt. honble Robert earl of
Oxford and Mortimer... [*London*] *Sold by John
Baker,* 1712.
½°: 1 side, 1 column.
   Text in Latin and English.
'Jure dicat tibi navis iter, qui cinxerat orbem'
'The voyage round the world is thought your due'
   Occasioned by the dedication of Edward
   Cooke's book.
O,Crawford; MH.

V21 — Vaticinium pacis. The prophecy of peace spoke
in a dream, to a Westminster scholar. *London
printed, and sold by B. Bragge,* 1706.
½°: 2 sides, 1 column.
   Text in Latin and English, the verso headed,
   'In English thus attempted next morning'.
'Quatuor Europæ charissima flumina cœlo'
'Four belov'd river gods, move Jove by prayer'
   A longer and variant version of the Latin is
   found in Lewis Maidwell's *Majestas imperii
   Britannici,* 1706, with a different English
   translation.
L(Add.MS 22267, fol. 92).

V22 [**Vaughan, John.**] An ode. Occasion'd by rejecting
the proposal for erecting a statue of King William
III. in the city of London; and by its being receiv'd
in the cities of Bristol and Dublin. Dedicated to Sir
Nicholas Williams... *London, printed for J. Roberts;
sold by the booksellers of London & Westminster,*
1732. (*GM* 7 Feb)
2°: A^2 B–F^2; *1–5* 6–24. 24 err.
   Listed in *LM* June 1732, with the asterisk

Vaughan, J. An ode

indicating a new edition, as printed for T. Read.

'Rise, lawrell'd shade, from peaceful seats'

Ascribed to Vaughan by *Rawlinson* who records he 'printed a great number of coppys, by J. Roberts'.

LG; CSmH,DFo,IU,KU.

'**V——e, Miss.**' Vanella: or, an elegy, [1736.] *See* V12.

V23 Veillée. Veillée a la campagne: or the simnel. A tale. *London, printed for R. Manby & H. S. Cox,* 1745. (22 April?)

2°: *A*² B–D²; *1-6* 7–16. A1 hft; 16 err.

Entered to Manby in Bowyer's ledgers under 22 April, 500 copies printed. Listed in *GM, LM* May.

'The cushion dance had clos'd the ball'

On the mystic virtues of simnel cake.

L(1962,–A1),O; KU,OCU(–A1).

V24 Vel, Simon. [dh] The troopers elogy. On the account here, of the much lamented death, of Mr. Jones, the soldiers advocate. By Simon Vel, late trooper in Catherlogh. [*Dublin,* 1725.]

4°: *A*²; *1-4*.

A covering letter on p. 4 is dated from Catherlogh, 1 Feb 1724-5.

'Shall all the battles, great Marlborough fought'

DT.

Veneer, John.

Rawlinson records 'he hath publish'd a few pamphlets both in prose and verse, but for some prudential reasons of a private nature hath thought fit to leave the world to guess at the author'.

Venture. The venture: being a collection of poems on several occasions. *London, printed for J. Penn,* 1731. (*MChr* Aug)

8°: pp. iv, 60.   NN-A.

V25 Venus. Venus and Ardelia, a tale. By a gentleman of Oxford. *London, printed for R. Dodsley,* 1748.

4°: *A*² B–F²; *1-2* 3–24.

'Retiring to a cool retreat'

In praise of Ardelia, Miss P------n.

L(11630.d.16/4).

V26 — Venus reveng'd: or, Cloe triumphant. A poem. [*Dublin,* 1730?]

8°: A⁴; *1-2* 3–7 *8 blk*.

Title in half-title form.

'As Cupid was dispos'd to view'

LVA-F,DK.

V27 Verax. Verax to Adamia. An epistle in Ovid's manner. *London, printed for H. Chapelle; sold by M. Cooper,* 1747. (*GM, LM* June)

2°: *A*² <B²; *1-2* 3–8.

Verax to Adamia

Entered in Strahan's ledger to Chapelle, 500 copies.

'Oh you! at once my Venus, and my muse'

L(1850.c.10/69); CSmH.

V28 Verney, Richard, *baron Willoughby de Broke.* Dunces out of state. A poem. Addressed to Mr. Pope. By the right honourable the Lord Willoughby de Broke. *London, printed in the year* 1733.

2°: π¹ *A*² B¹; *i-ii,* *1-2* 3–6. π1 hft.

The order of editions has not been determined.

'If wanton leisure, and a cool recess'

Presumably occasioned by Paul Whitehead's *State dunces,* 1733.

MH.

V29 — [*London*] *Printed in the year* 1733.

½°: 1 side, 2 columns.

Horizontal chain-lines; a very badly printed half-sheet. Ms. note in the C copy 'This poem was sold by L. Willoughby himself in the court of requests for half a crown.'

C.

V30 — A poem on the safe arrival of the Prince of Orange to England. Together with the celebration of the nuptials of her royal highness Anne, with his serene highness William prince of Orange. *London, printed in the year* 1733.

2°: *A*² B²; *1-2* 3–7 *8 blk*.

'Hail Belgian prince, we joy to see you in our isle'

L(C.57.g.7/1),O,O-*JJ*; MH.

V31 Vernon. Vernon's glory: or, the king of Spain in a consumption. [*London?* 1741.]

slip: 1 side, 1 column.

Verses 2 & 3 printed in italic type. *Percival* LXIX.

'Brave Britton's hear my story'

C.

V32 — [another edition]

Printed in roman type throughout, with the exception of proper names.

C.

V33 — Vernon's glory: or, the Spaniards defeat. Being an account of the taking of Carthagena by Vice-admiral Vernon, Rear-admiral Ogle, and Commodore Lestock on the first of April last. Written by a sailor on board the Shrewsbury, and brought over by the Spence sloop. (Tnne [!] of, Brave Vernon's triumph.) [*London?* 1741.]

½°: 1 side, 2 columns.

Percival appendix 94. Two rough woodcuts at head; no divider between columns.

'Once more brave boys let us proclaim'

One of a number of premature celebrations of the fall of Cartagena.

L(Rox.III.873).

V34 — [another edition]

Two rough woodcuts at head; columns divided by type flowers.

L(1876.f.1/123).

Vernon's glory

V35 — [another edition]
    Large woodcut at head; columns divided by
    type flowers.
    L(1876.f.1/122).

V36 [**Vernon**, —, *Rev. Mr.*] Corona civica. A poem, to
the right honourable the lord-keeper of the great
seal of England. *London printed, and sold by John
Nutt*, 1706. (30 April, Luttrell)
2°: π¹ A–C² D¹; *i–iv*, 1–12. π1 hft.
    Signature B under d of 'Weldon'. Watermark
    not seen throughout; in most copies there is a
    crowned P in sheet B, sometimes in C, but the
    copy at O appears to have a serpent watermark
    in sheets B and C; it is possibly on fine paper.
    Perhaps this would explain the presence of the
    half-title, which is missing elsewhere.
    'When on some antique medal's dimmer brass'
    See R. W. Chapman in *RES* 1 (1925) 92 for a
    ms. attribution to Vernon (also found in a copy
    at MR-C); he has not been further identified.
    In praise of William Cowper, earl Cowper.
L(1959, −π1),LLP(−π1),O,DG(−π1),LdU-B
(−π1)+; CLU-C(Luttrell, ms. notes, −π1),
CtY(−π1),KU(−π1),MH(−π1),TxU(−π1).

V37 [—] — *London printed, and sold by John Nutt*, 1706.
2°: A–C² D¹; *i–ii*, 1–12.
    Signature B under h of 'with'. The text makes
    substantial changes, and includes satirical
    passages; it may be the earlier state.
OCU.

V38 — The union. A poem, inscrib'd to the right
honourable lord Marquis of Granby, one of her
majesty's commissioners for the Scotch union.
London printed, and sold by John Morphew, 1707.
(27 March, Luttrell)
2°: A–C²; *i–iv*, 1–8.
    'O my Mecænas, sprung of royal race'
E,LdU-B; CLU-C(Luttrell),CSmH,CtY,MH.

Vernoniad. The Vernon-iad, 1741. *See* Fielding,
Henry (F120).

Verres. Verres and his scribblers, 1732. *See*
Budgell, Eustace.

V39 **Verses.** Verses address'd to the imitator of the first
satire of the second book of Horace. By a lady.
*London, printed for A. Dodd, and sold at all the
pamphlet-shops in town*, [1733.] (*DP* 8 March)
2°: A² B²; *1–2* 3–8.
    P. 4, last line 'distinction'; 14 lines on p. 8.
    This edition apparently precedes its rival *To
    the imitator* below by one day; an advertise-
    ment in *DP* 10 March denounced that as a
    'spurious and piratical edition...printed from
    a very bad copy' while Roberts replied in *DP*
    12 March that it was 'the genuine and correct
    edition'. It seems possible that this edition
    originated with Lady Mary and *To the
    imitator* with Lord Hervey.

Verses address'd to the imitator

    'In two large columns, on thy motly page'
    Crum I1601. Almost certainly a joint produc-
    tion; Harley annotated his copy (at O) 'The
    authors of this poem are Lady Mary Wortley,
    Lord Harvey, & Mr Windham'. Hervey re-
    vised a copy of *To the imitator* (now at Ick-
    worth) for a 'second edition corrected by the
    author, with a preface'. Lady Mary Wortley
    Montagu was generally credited with the
    authorship. Cf. *Advice to Sappho*, 1733, and
    A proper reply to a lady, [1733]. A satire against
    Pope.
L(162.n.39),O(Harley's copy),OW,LdU-B;
CSmH,ICU,IU,MH,TxU.

V40 — [another edition]
    P. 4, last line 'Distinction'; 14 lines on p. 8.
    Apparently sheet A and the outer forme of B
    are reset.
L(11641.1.1/1; C.59.h.9/11, uncut),O,OW,
LdU-B; CSmH,CtY(2),DLC,TxU(2).

V41 — [another edition] (*LEP* 20 March)
    16 lines on p. 8, two lines having been added
    on p. 5; motto from Juvenal added to title.
    Largely reset and corrected.
LVA-D,O,DT; CtY(lacks B²),ICU(2),MH(2),
MiU,TxU.

V42 — — '*London, printed for A. Dodd, and sold at all
the pamphlet-shops in town*' [Edinburgh], 1733.
8°: A⁴; *1–2* 3–8.
    Printed by Ruddiman on the evidence of the
    ornament. No motto on title.
CLU-C,ICN,ICU,MH,TxU.

V43 — — *London: printed for A. Dodd; Dublin: reprinted by Christopher Dickson*, 1733.
8°: A⁴; *1–2* 3–8.
L(11630.aaa.45/11; 11642.a.59/1); IU.

V44 — — The fifth edition corrected. *London, printed
for A. Dodd, and sold at all the pamphlet-shops in
town*, [1735.] (*LEP* 16 Jan)
2°: A² B²; *1–2* 3–8.
    A new edition; motto from Juvenal on title.
    The O copy is annotated by Harley, 'This wch
    is called the fifth edition is not true but a sham
    of the booksellers upon Mr Popes printing his
    Epistle to Dr Arbuthnot [2 Jan 1735] where
    these works are mentioned they supposed
    that some copies would be called for.' Adver-
    tised in *LEP* as printed for A. Dodd and J.
    Fisher.
L(1484.m.7/7; 11641.1.1/3),O(Harley's copy),
WcC; CtY(2),MH,TxU(2).

V45 — — The sixth edition. *London, printed for A.
Dodd, and sold at all the pamphlet-shops in town*,
[1735/–.]
2°: A² B²; *1–3* 4–8.
    A new edition; motto from Proverbs on title.
TxU.

Verses address'd to the imitator

V46 — [*idem*] To the imitator of the satire of the second book of Horace. *London, printed for J. Roberts,* 1733. (*DJ* 9 March)
2°: *A*² B–C²; *i–iv, 1 2–7 8 blk.* A1 hft.
   A rival edition to the preceding, possibly originating with John lord Hervey. His copy (at Ickworth) is revised in his hand for a second edition, never printed.
LSC,O(2),OA,LdU-B; CLU-C,CtY,ICU,MH, TxU(2, 1–A1)+.

[**V47** = B354] — Verses by a young nobleman, on the death of his grace the Duke of B——, [1736?] *See* Boyle, John, *earl of Orrery.*

— Verses humbly address'd to Sir Thomas Hanmer, 1743. *See* Collins, William.

V48 — Verses humbly inscrib'd to his majesty, on his glorious victory at the battle of Dettingen; and on his safe and happy arrival in his British dominions. By a true-born English man. *London, printed for H. Chapelle; sold by Jacob Robinson,* 1744 [1743]. (*DA* 18 Nov)
2°: *A*⁴; *1–5 6–8.* A1 hft.
   Entered in Strahan's ledger to H. Chapelle under 12 Dec [1743], 500 copies.
'Beam on me, god of wit, seraphick fire'
O; MH(–A1),OCU(–A1).

V49 — Verses inscrib'd to the right honourable Col. Boyle; on his being chosen speaker to the house of commons of Ireland. *Dublin, printed by S. Powell, for T. Thornton,* 1733.
8°: *A*⁴; *1–3 4–8.*
'Accept a muse that strives her voice to raise'
L(11631.a.63/14).

V50 — [*idem*] A poem inscrib'd to the right honourable Col. Boyle; on his being chosen speaker to the house of commons of Ireland. *Dublin: printed, and re-printed in Corke by Andrew Welsh,* [1733.]
8°: *A*⁴; *1–2 3–8.*
DN.

V51 — Verses inscribed to the right honourable Humphry Parsons, esq; lord mayor elect... by his most devoted, humble servant, J.W. *Westminster, printed by A. Campbell, for the author; sold by A. Dodd, and all the other pamphlet shops,* 1730. (*MChr* Oct)
2°: B⁴; *1–3 4–8.*
'To genuine worth, to Parsons let the muse'
L(1476.d.24).

— Verses left in a grotto in Richmond Garden, 1744. *See* Newcomb, Thomas.

V52 — Verses occasioned by seeing proposals for founding an hospital for incurables in the city of Dublin... Humbly inscribed to...the Dutchess dowager of Marlborough. *London, printed for R. Dodsley; sold by M. Cooper,* 1744. (*DA* 3 May)
2°: *A*⁴; *1–2 3–8.*
   The order of editions has not been determined.
'When heav'n incens'd with-held his rain'
CSmH.

Verses occasioned by seeing proposals

V53 — — *Dublin, printed by and for George Faulkner,* 1744.
8°: *A*⁴; *1–2 3–8.*
C,DA,DG,DK(2).

— Verses occasion'd by seeing the captives, [1734/35.] *See* Barber, Mary.

— Verses occasioned by seeing the palace and park of Dalkeith, 1732. *See* Boyse, Samuel.

V54 — Verses occasioned by the college examinations, and the scheme for distributing premiums, first contrived and promoted by Samuel Madden, D.D. *Dublin, printed by George Faulkner,* 1747.
8°: *A*⁴ B⁴ C²; *1–4 5–20.*
'While gloomy winter the sad muse forbids'
O,C,DN,DT; OCU.

V55 — [*dh*] Verses occasioned by the judgment passed on John Ward of Hackney, in Westminster-Hall, and in both houses of parliament. [*London,* 1726.]
2°: *A*²; *1 2–3 4 blk.*
'When spoil, corruption, every nameless lust'
   Ward was expelled from the commons in May 1726 after his conviction.
L(1487.k.26/1); CSmH.

V56 — Verses occasion'd by the present rebellion. *London, printed in the year* 1745.
2°: *A*²; *i–ii, 1–2.*
'Whence this tumultuous noise? these dire alarms?'
   Patriotic verses.
AdU.

V57 — Verses, occasion'd by the sight of a chamera [!] obscura. *London, printed for John Cuff, optical instrument maker; sold by Mrs. Cooke,* 1747. (*GM, LM* Nov)
4°: A–B⁴; *1–2 3–15 16.*
   Advertisement for Cuff's instruments on p. 16.
'Say, rare machine, who taught thee to design?'
L(11626.e.56),C; IU,NN.

V58 — Verses on a certain young lady who by overturning of a coach, had her coats behind flung up, and what was under shewn to the view of the company. Out of Voiture. *Dublin, printed in the year* 1735.
8°: *A*⁴; *1–2 3–7 8 blk.*
'Phillis, 'tis own'd, I am your slave'
DA.

[**V59** = F279] — Verses on her majesty's birth-day, [1728.] *See* Frowde, Philip.

[**V60** = S507]

— Verses on Miss C-----s and W-----t, 1749. *See* Warton, Thomas, *the younger.*

V61 — Verses on the death of Dr. Samuel Clarke. *London, printed for Weaver Bickerton; sold by J. Roberts,* 1729. (*MChr* 19 June)
2°: *A*² B–C²; *i–iii iv, 1–8.*
'When purpled monarchs fall, the sons of verse'
LDW; CSmH,MH.

Verses on the death

V62 — Verses on the death of her late most excellent majesty Queen Caroline, of blessed memory; who departed this life, Novemb. 20. MDCCXXXVII. *London, printed for Richard Hett,* 1738.
2°: π¹ A–B² C¹; *i–ii, 1–2* 3–10. π1 hft.
'Muse, bid the verse in plaintive numbers flow'
L(603.k.28/5); MH(−π1),OCU,TxU.

— Verses on the death of Mrs. Morice, 1730. *See* Wesley, Samuel, *the younger.*

— Verses on the grotto at Twickenham, 1743. *See* Dodsley, Robert.

— Verses on the king, 1726. *See* Morrice, Bezaleel.

V63 — Verses on the king's return. *London, printed for B. Lintot,* 1720. (*DC* 12 Nov)
2°: (3 ll).
The Luttrell copy, dated Nov, is described in *Haslewood,* and the first line quoted thence.
'What strange impetuous storms of state'
(Pickering & Chatto cat. 247/13373, Luttrell.)

V64 — Verses on the late earthquakes: address'd to Great Britain. *London, printed for J. Payne & J. Bouquet,* 1750. (*GM, LM* March)
4°: *A*² B–D²; *1–2* 3–15 *16 blk.*
Entered in Strahan's ledger to Payne & Bouquet, 500 copies.
'Earth shakes again, and Britain cries'
Possibly by Moses Browne, whose *Sunday thoughts* were printed and published by the same hands this month.
L(1465.i.12/15),LdU-B.

V65 — 'Verses on the much lamented death of her sacred majesty Queen Caroline. [*London*] Printed for A. Dodd. Price 3d.' (*GM, LM* Dec 1737)

— Verses presented to his highness the Prince of Orange, 1734. *See* Mallet, David.

V66 — Verses sacred to the memory of the honourable Alexander Stuart, master of Gairlies: inscrib'd to the right honourable Lord Boyle... By a young student at the university. *Glasgow-College, printed in the year* 1739.
8°: *A*⁴; *1–2* 3–8.
Presumably printed by Alexander Miller, the university printer.
'Tho' sable woe o'ercast the mournful soul'
E(2).

— Verses sacred to the memory of the most noble Henrietta, late duchess of Grafton, 1727. *See* Bond, William.

— Verses, sacred to the memory of the right honourable Charles, earl of Peterborough, 1735. *See* Boyse, Samuel.

— Verses spoken after the performance of Mr. Otway's tragedy, [1719.] *See* Mitchell, Joseph.

— Verses to a lady of quality, insulted by the rabble of writers, 1741. *See* Lockman, John.

— Verses to her royal highness the Princess of Wales, 1718. *See* Sewell, George.

Verses to his grace

— Verses to his grace the Duke of Marlborough, upon the present rebellion, 1715. *See* Sewell, George.

— Verses to his grace the Duke of Richmond; on his being installed knight of the garter, [1726.] *See* Newcomb, Thomas.

[**V67** = M500·5] — Verses to Mr. Tickell, 1715. *See* Morrice, Bezaleel.

— Verses to the injur'd patriot, 1733. *See* Newcomb, Thomas.

V68 — Verses to the Lord Carteret, occasioned by the present conspiracy. By a gentleman of Cambridge. *London, printed for Jacob Tonson,* 1722. (*DC* 16 Nov)
2°: *A*² B–C²; *i–iv, 1* 2–7 *8 blk.* A1 hft.
The Luttrell copy, dated Nov, is in the collection of R. D. Horn.
'Since senates safe in legal rights rejoice'
L(11651.m.85),O(−A1); IU,MH(−A1).

V69 — Verses to the memory of John Roydon Hughes, esq; captain of foot, in General Pultney's regiment. *London, printed for C. Hitch,* 1750. (*BM* May)
4°: *A*² B–C²; *1–3* 4–11 *12 blk.*
'Vain were the task to give the soul to glow'
LVA-D,O.

V70 — Verses to the memory of Matthew Prior, esq. Inscrib'd to the right honourable Edward lord Harley. By a gentleman of Cambridge. *London, printed for J. Roberts,* 1721. (Dec, Luttrell)
4°: *A*² B–D²; *1–3* 4–16.
No watermark.
'Shall Harley's sorrows then no limits know?'
L(163.m.49, Luttrell),O,C; NN.

V71 — [fine paper]
Watermark: fleur-de-lys.
CtY(in original marbled wrappers).

V72 — Verses to the memory of Mrs. Elizabeth Frankland. [*London,* 1736.]
4°: A⁴ B²; *1–2* 3–12.
Title in half-title form.
'Silence, ye plaintiff instruments of woe!'
L(840.1.3/5); MH.

V73 — Verses to the memory of the honourable James Peadie of Ruch-hill esquire, lord provost of Glasgow. [*Glasgow?* 1728.] (7 June?)
½°: 1 side, 2 columns.
Mourning borders.
'Shall blazing-stars, drop from their spheres'
E(ms. date 7 June 1728).

V74 — Verses to the memory of the late illustriously pious Christian, the right honourable, the Lady Elizabeth Hastings. *London, printed for T. Cooper,* 1740. (16 May)
2°: *A*² B–F²; *1–5* 6–24.
The copy from Tom's Coffee House in the Lewis Walpole Library is dated 16 May; listed in *GM, LM* May.

Verses to the memory

'While many a bard of Phœbus' warbling throng'
O.

[V75 = B537] — Verses to the right honourable the Earl
of Scarborough, 1727. *See* Browne, Moses.

— Verses to the right reverend father in god,
Edward, 1731. *See* Mawer, John.

V76 — Verses upon Dr. G--'s verses to the E. of
G---n. [*London?* 1710/11.]
½°: 1 side, 1 column.
'To be discarded is indeed an evil'
   A reply to Garth's *A poem to the Earl of
   Godolphin*, 1710.
O,Chatsworth.

— Verses upon the late D——ss of M——, 1746.
See Pope, Alexander.

— Verses upon the much-lamented death of her
sacred majesty Queen Caroline, 1737. *See* Hawling,
Francis.

— Verses written on the morning of the Duke of
Marlborough's funeral, 1722. *See* Sewell, George.

V77 — Verses written to the Duke of Marlborough
upon his leaving England. Now first printed, and
recommended to Sir Anthony Crabtree, who is
best able to supply what's wanting in them.
London, printed for R. Burleigh, 1715 [1714]. (*MC*
Nov)
2°: *A*² *B*¹; *i–iv*, *1–2*. A1 hft.
'Farewell, great man; th' ungrateful land forgive'
   According to *Political merriment*, part 2 (1714)
   the same author wrote 'Upon the Q——n's
   statue at Paul's' (N13·5). That was subsequently printed as by Garth, so this work
   may also be by him.
LdU-B(uncut); CtY,MH,OCU(– A1),TxU.

Versus. Versus inopes rerum, nugæque canoræ.
Commonly call'd Poems on several occasions.
London, printed for J. Peele, [1729.] (*MChr* 10 July)
8°: pp. xii, 106.   L,LdU-B.

Vertumnus. Vertumnus. An epistle to Mr. Jacob
Bobart, 1713. *See* Evans, Abel.

V78 Vestry. The vestry: a poem. *London, printed in the
year* 1701. (5 Feb, Luttrell)
2°: *A*² *B–D*²; *1–4* 5–16.
   The Luttrell copy is recorded in *Haslewood*;
   advertised in *PB* 6 Feb.
'At a time when the church was much out of repair'
   A satire on the vestry of St. Clement Dane's.
LDW,O; CLU-C,CSmH,DFo,MB,MH.

V79 Vézian, Antoine. L'anniversaire de la naissance du
roy. *A Londres, chés Jacob Tonson*, 1720.
4°: A–C⁴; *i–ii*, *1* 2–22.
'Par quel pouvoir divin se ranime ma voix?'
CSmH.

Vézian, A.

V80 — Ode au roi sur son avenement a la couronne.
A Londres, chez Jacob Tonson, 1727.
4°: A² B–C⁴; *i–iv*, *1* 2–16. A1 hft.
'Quel bruit étonnant nous menace?'
KU,PU.

V81 — Vers a Monsieur Pelham, secrétaire des guerres
et conseilleur privé, sur la naissance de son fils.
London, Jacob Tonson, 1729.
4°.
(Pickering & Chatto cat. 204/13132.)

V82 Via. Via ad episcopatum. *Dublin, printed by John
Harding*, [1722?]
½°: 1 side, 1 column.
   Text in Latin and English, the latter titled 'A
   short way to a bishoprick'.
'Si ad præsulatum velles ascendere'
'Unto prelatick order you'd ascend'
OC(Wake letters XIV.62),C; MH.

V83 — [another issue, adding transversely on verso:]
A short answer to a short paper entitled a Short way
to a bishoprick. *Dublin printed ut ante*.
Answer: 'Let news-boys cry the scandal through
the crowd'
OC(Wake letters XIV.63),Rothschild.

V84 Vicar. The vicar of Bray. [*London?* 1714/–.]
slip: 1 side, 1 column.
   This and the following edition resemble early
   Jacobite slip songs.
'In Charles the second's golden reign'
   Crum I1332. Clearly inspired by [Edward
   Ward] *The religious turncoat*. A ms. version at
   O (*Crum* O75), probably dating from the
   1730s and adding a verse on George II and
   Prince Frederick, is ascribed to 'Saml
   Westley'. This text apparently only lists
   variants from 'the former ballad', and it is
   not clear which is claimed for Wesley. His
   authorship is not improbable.
Crawford.

V85 — [another edition, with variant text]
'In Charles the second's golden days'
L(C.121.g.9/186).

V86 — [another edition]
   Rough woodcut at head. This and the following edition are popular slip-songs of
   indeterminate date.
C.

V87 — [another edition, with variant text]
   Rough woodcut at head.
'In good King Charles's golden days'
L(1876.e.20/27).

— The vicar of Bray, [1733.] *In* M38.

Vice. Vice triumphant, 1719. *See* Cockburn,
Robert.

Vices

V88 Vices. The vices of the town. A satire. *London, printed for W. Webb*, [1747.] (*GM, LM* Feb)
2°: A¹ B–D² E¹; *i–ii*, 1–13 *14 blk*.
> Most copies have ms. corrections, presumably by the printer.

'O thou, whose soul with ev'ry virtue fraught'
O; CtY,IU,KU,OCU,TxU.

Vicesimo. XXV Julii MDCCXIII, [1713.] *See* Pitcairne, Archibald.

V89 Victor, Benjamin. An ode, to be performed at the castle of Dublin, on the 30th of October, being the birth-day of...George II... By B. Victor. Set to musick by Mr. Matthew Dubourg... *Dublin, printed by S. Powell, for George Ewing*, 1735.
4°: A⁴; *1–3* 4–7 *8 blk*.
'Bright Sol, thy purest beams display'
DG.

V90 Victory. The victory a poem. In two parts. I. To the queen. II. To the Duke of Marlborough. *London printed, and sold by Benjamin Bragg*, 1704. (18 Sept, Luttrell)
2°: A–C²; *1–2* 3–12.
> The Luttrell copy is in the possession of R. D. Horn.

'Inspir'd by you, what can our thoughts restrain?'
CtY,MH.

Vida. Vida's art of poetry, 1750. *See* Pitt, Christopher.

Vida, Marco Girolamo.
[*Bombyx*] Silk-worms: a poem. In two books. Written originally in Latin, by Marc. Hier. Vida... And now translated into English, 1723. *See* S462.

Rooke, John: The silk-worms. A poem. In two books. Translated from the Latin of M. Hieronymus Vida, 1725. *See* R264.

Pullein, Samuel: The silkworm: a poem. In two books. Written by Marcus Hieronymus Vida, and translated into English verse, 1750. *See* P1159.

[*De arte poetica*] Pitt, Christopher: Vida's Art of Poetry, translated into English verse, 1725, 1726, 1742, 1743, 1750. *See* P416–20.

[*Scacchia ludus*] Erskine, William: Scacchia ludus: or, the game of chess. A poem. Written originally in Latin by Marcus Hieronymus Vida... Translated into English [with three pastoral eclogues, translated by Mr. Craig], 1736. *See* E460.

Jeffreys, George: Chess: a poem. Translated into English from Vida, 1736. *In* J57.

Pullein, Samuel: Scacchia, ludus: a poem on the game of chess...translated into English verse, 1750. *See* P1158.

V91 [Vievar, Alexander.] What is man? An ode, in pindaric verse. In fifteen stanzas. *London, printed*

Vievar, A. What is man?
for J. Buckland; sold by W. Meadows, & R. Dodsley, 1738. (*GM, LM* March)
2°: A² B–D² E¹; *1–5* 6–18. A1 hft.
> *Dobell* 2697 records a copy with a final blank leaf, possibly in error. Entered in Ackers's ledger 13 March 1738, 5 sheets, 500 copies printed, to Buckland.

'Assist me, heavn'ly muse, in lofty verse'
> Early ms. attribution to Vievar in the copy at TxU.

C; IU(–A1),MH(–A1),OCU,TxU.

V92 View. [first line:] View here the pourtrait of a factious priest... '*Engrav'd, and printed at Amsterdam*' [*London*], 1710.
½°: 1 side, 1 column.
> Engraving of Hoadly with devils at head. Text in roman and italic type.

'View here the pourtrait of a factious priest'
> An attack on Hoadly, quoting Shippen's *Faction display'd*.

L(806.k.16/45; P&D 1533).

V93 — [another edition]
> Text printed in roman and black letter, with an inferior engraving.

L(P&D 1534).

— A view of life in its several passions, 1749. *See* Fortescue, James.

— A view of the Duke of Marlborough's battles, 1717. *See* Amhurst, Nicholas.

V94 — A view of the Irish bar. To the free-mason tune, Come let us prepare, &c. *Dublin, printed in the year* 1729–30.
½°: 1 side, 2 columns.
'There's M——y the neat'
> Satirical verses on individual members of the bar.

L(C.121.g.8/172),C; CSmH(ms. indentifications).

— A view of the town, 1735. *See* Gilbert, Thomas.

V95 'Vigaeus, Tranquillus.' Actum fidei, sive de vi in re religionis adhibenda, sermo. Tranquilli Vigaei. *Londini, impensis S. Chandler*, 1725. (*MC* Apr)
4°: A⁴ ⟨B⟩⁴; *i–iii* iv, 5 6–16.
'Ad sacrum incumbas toto quod pectore verum'
> The author is probably pseudonymous; the poem is dedicated to 'H. Bagwelio'.

MH(cropt).

V96 Vigo. The Vigo victory; or, the happy success of the Duke of Ormond, in the taking, of several French men of war and galleons, together with much plate, which crowns him with immortal fame and glory. To the tune of, Did not you hear of a gallant sailor. [*London?* 1702.]
½°: 1 side, 2 columns.
'Come listen now to the nations glory'
L(1871.f.3/16).

Villiers, J. de

Villiers, Jacob de.
[*L'apoticaire devalisé*] [Ellis, John:] The surprize: or, the gentleman turn'd apothecary. A tale written originally in French prose; afterwards translated into Latin; and from thence now versified in hudibrastics, 1739. *See* E290–1.

V97 Vindication. A vindication of the Duke of Marlborough. *Printed in the year* 1712.
½°: 1 side, 2 columns.
    On the other side, *A Bob for the court*, 1712; possibly printed in Dublin.
'Fir'd with just resentment I will write'
Harding.

V98 — A vindication of the Duke of Wh——n's answer to the Quaker's letter. [*Dublin*] *Printed in the year* 1726.
½°: 1 side, 2 columns.
'Pray isn't it queer / That a wild peer'
    A satire on Philip duke of Wharton becoming a Roman catholic. The *Quaker's letter* and Wharton's answer have not been identified.
L(C.121.g.8/151),DT; CSmH,NN.

— A vindication of the libel on Dr. Delany, 1730. *See* Dunkin, William.

V99 Vindiciae. Vindiciæ publicæ: an ode to the real patriot. *London, printed for* T. Cooper, 1741. (19 March)
4°: π1 A⁴ B⁴(−B1); i–ii, 1–3 4–13 14 blk. π1 hft.
'Say, Lælius, by what power you claim'
    In praise of Walpole.
L(11630.c.6/13, Tom's Coffee House, 19 March; 11630.c.12/9); CtY(−π1),MH(−π1).

V100 — Vindiciæ secundum Joannem Despauterium datæ. [*Edinburgh*, 171–?]
1°: 1 side, 2 columns.
    Below, in one column, 'In Vacerram'.
'Iambe noster, sive tarde, seu celer'
In Vacerram: 'Romanæ scabies linguæ, teterrima Pindi'
E.

Vindicta. Vindicta Britannica, 1740. *See* Newcomb, Thomas.

'Vinegar, Hercules.' The cudgel, or a crab-tree lecture, 1742. *See* Ward, Edward [*Durgen*].

Violenta. Violenta, or the rewards of virtue, 1704. *See* Pix, Mary.

V101 Virasel, Samuel. An ode to the right honourable Philip earl of Chesterfield. Upon his being appointed one of his majesty's principal secretaries of state. *Dublin, printed by George Faulkner*, 1747.
8°: A⁴ B²; 1–2 3–12.
'Illustrious peer, whose friendly mind'
DA,DN(2); ICN.

Virasel, S.

V102 — Philander and Aspasia. A poem. *Dublin, printed by George Faulkner*, 1749.
8°: A⁴; 1–3 4–8.
'Aspasia's to an angel half refin'd'
L(11633.c.48),O,C(2, 1 uncut),DA,DN; ICU.

Virgil. Virgil's husbandry, or an essay on the Georgics, 1724–. *See* Benson, William.

Virgilius Maro, Publius.

Works

Maitland, Richard, *earl of Lauderdale*: The works of Virgil, translated into English verse, [1709, 1716.]

Trapp, Joseph: The works of Virgil: translated into English blank verse [3 vols], 1731, 1735, 1737.

Aeneid

Brady, Nicholas: Proposals for publishing a translation of Virgil's Æneids in blank verse, 1713. *See* B374.

— Virgil's Æneis translated into blank verse [book I], 1714. *See* B375.

— Virgil's Æneis translated into blank verse [books I–VI], 1716–17. *See* B376–7.

Trapp, Joseph: The Æneis of Virgil, translated into blank verse [2 vols], 1718–20. *See* T444–5.

Pitt, Christopher: An essay on Virgil's Æneid [book I], 1728. *See* P410.

— Virgil's Æneid translated by Mr. Pitt. Vol. I [books I–IV], 1736. *See* P411.

— The Æneid of Virgil, 1740, 1743. *See* P412–14.

[*book I*] Strahan, Alexander: The first Æneid, translated into blank verse, 1739. *See* S771–2.

[*book II*] Theobald, John: The second book of Virgil's Æneid. In four cantos, [1736.] *See* T134–5.

[*book IV*] Sherburn, William: The fourth book of Virgil's Æneid, 1723. *See* S404.

Theobald, John: The fourth book of Virgil's Æneid. In four cantos, [1739.] *See* T136.

[*book IV*] Neale, Thomas: Ἐνύπνιον: or the vision, in imitation of the latter-part of the VIth book of Virgil, 1706. *See* N13.

Georgics

Rolli, Paolo Antonio: La Bucolica [Italian translation], 1742. *See* R254.

[*book I*] The Georgics of Virgil attempted in English verse, 1750. *See* G129.

[*books I, II*] [Benson, William:] Virgil's husbandry, or an essay on the Georgics, 1724–25. *See* B195–7.

[*book III*] Hallam, Isaac: The cocker: a poem. In imitation of Virgil's third Georgic, 1742. *See* H6.

Eclogues

[*1, 4*] An introduction of the ancient Greek and Latin measures into British poetry, 1737. *See* I49.

Virgilius Maro, P. *Eclogues*

[1] 'O Connor, Murroghoh': A pastoral in imitation of the first eclogue, 1719. *See* O9–10.

A pastoral in imitation of Virgil's first eclogue, 1730. *See* P110.

The happy marriage: an eclogue. In imitation of Virgil's Tityrus, 1733. *See* H44.

Lonergan, Edward: The dean and the country parson. An imitation of the first eclogue of Virgil, 1739. *See* L242.

[3] A town eclogue...being an imitation after the new mode of the 3d eclogue, [1714.] *See* T435.

The tryal of skill between 'Squire Walsingham and Mother Osborne. An eclogue, in imitation of Virgil's Palæmon, 1734. *See* T474.

[4] The golden age from the fourth eclogue of Virgil, 1703. *See* G211–13.

[5] A town eclogue in allusion to part of the fifth eclogue of Virgil, 1721. *See* T434.

Mother Gin, a tragi-comical eclogue: being a paraphrastical imitation of the Daphnis of Virgil, 1737. *See* M521.

[6] A brush to the Curry-comb of truth... An eclogue in imitation of Virgil's Silenus, 1736. *See* B550.

Viri. Viri humani, salsi, & faceti Gulielmi Sutherlandi, [1725?] *See* Meston, William.

Viro. Viro honoratissimo, doctorum Mecænati optimo...Roberto Harley, 1711. *See* Monsey, R.

V103 **Virtue.** Virtue in danger: or Arthur Gray's last farewell to the world. Written by a gentleman at St. James's; (Tune, of Chivy Chase.) [*London?* 1722.]
½°: 1 side, 2 columns.
'Now ponder well you ladies fair'
    A squib on the attempted rape by Arthur Gray on Mrs. Griselda Murray, 14 Oct 1721. Mrs. Murray believed Lady Mary Wortley Montagu (who wrote a serious poem on the subject) to be the author, and so did Horace Walpole; but Robert Halsband, *Lady Mary Wortley Montagu* (1956) 106f. considers it still in doubt.
CSmH.

Virtues. The virtues of Sid Hamet, 1710. *See* Swift, Jonathan.

V104 **Vision.** The vision. *London, printed for B. Bragg,* 1705.
4°: A–F²; *1–2* 3–20 '*17–19*' *24*. 24 advt.
''Twas in that welcome quarter of the year'
    An allegorical dream.
DT.

— The vision, a poem, [1706.] *See* Defoe, Daniel.

— The vision compylit in Latin, 1748. *See* Ramsay, Allan.

Vision

— The vision of Mons. Chamillard concerning the battle of Ramilies, 1706. *See* Phillips, John.

V105 — The vision of the two brothers, Ebenezer and Ralph. To which is subjoin'd a French prophecy by Mrs. Desmarets... *Glasgow, printed in the year* 1737.
4°: *A*² B–C²; *1–3* 4–11 *12 blk.*
    The imprint is probably false; the printers' ornaments are those of W. Cheyne of Edinburgh.
'Ne'er more is Satan pleas'd, malicious toad'
    On the brothers Ebenezer and Ralph Erskine in relation to the act for bringing to justice the murderers of John Porteous.
L(11630.b.8, lacks C2),GM.

V106 — The vision: or, virtue in danger, a poem. Humbly address'd to a lady in St. Mary's parish. *Dublin, printed in the year* 1734.
8°: *A*⁴; *1–2* 3–8.
'In that still hour of calm delight'
DT; OCU.

V107 **Visions.** The visions of Dom Francisco de Quevedo Villegas. Knight of the order of St. James. Made English by Sir R. Lestrange, and burlesqu'd by a person of quality. *London printed, and sold by B. Harris,* 1702 [1701]. (*PM* 15 Nov 'yesterday')
8°: A–S⁸; *i–iv*, 1–284.
'Going to mass the other day'
    The epistle to the reader says it is 'performed by a celebrated hand'. L'Estrange's translation was first published in 1667.
L(11623.aaa.15),EN; *MiU.*

V108 **Visit.** The visit. Or, the lady in the lobster: a poem. *Dublin printed, and sold by E. Waters,* 1733.
8°: *A*⁴; *1–2* 3–8.
'In days of yore, when maiden-heads'
    A satire on a female author.
DA.

V109 **Voice.** A voice from the north or an answer to the voice from the south, writen by the presbyterians of Scotland, to the dissenters in England, a poem. [*Edinburgh,* 1706/07.]
½°: 2 sides, 2 columns.
'There is no cause why ye so much admire'
    Against the union with England.
E(2); MH.

— The voice of liberty; or, a British philippic, 1738. *See* Akenside, Mark (A134).

Voiture, Vincent de.
Verses on a certain young lady... Out of Voiture, 1735. *See* V58.

V110 **Volpone.** Volpone disappointed, a chronical apologue. Humbly inscribed to T.R.H.T.L.H.C. O.G.B. By Æsop Horncastle, esq; of the Inner-Temple. *London, printed in the year* 1746. (Jan)

Volpone disappointed

2⁰: *A*² <B²; *1–3* 4–8.

 Ms. imprint added to most copies 'Sold by J. Jackson, at the Golden Lion near St. Paul's'.
'Be none employ'd to guard the weal'
 'Horncastle' is clearly a pseudonym. To (and about) 'The right honourable the Lord Hardwicke, chancellor of Great Britain'.
L(1962, Tom's Coffee House, Jan); CSmH,CU, ICN,OCU.

V111 — Vulpoon in the snare; or, a hue and cry after eight and twenty millions sunk by the Hawkubite crew. Written by Fr---- H---n, gent. [*London*] *Printed in the year* 1712.
½⁰: 1 side, 2 columns.
 A different text with the same first stanza was published as *An excellent new song call'd Loyalty restored*, 1711.
'All Britains rejoyce / With a general voice'
 A tory attack on Godolphin and the whigs.
C(mutilated),Chatsworth.

— Volpone, or the fox, 1706. *See* Browne, Joseph [The fox].

— Vulpone's tale, 1710. *See* Pittis, William.

V112 **Voltaire, François Marie Arouet,** *called.* La Henriade. De Mr. de Voltaire. *A Londres,* 1728.
4⁰: (frt+) *π*¹ *A*²)(⁴][¹ B–Cc⁴ Dd¹ (+ 10 plates); [*16*] *1* 2–202.

)(⁴][¹ contain the list of subscribers. Engraved head and tail pieces. There are apparently cancels, not noted here. This edition was reissued in 1741. First surreptitiously printed as *La Ligue,* 1723.
'Je chante ce héros, qui régna dans la France'
L(84.h.9; 640.l.4, both in contemporary morocco, no list of subscribers),O; Ct*Y,DLC,ICN,NN,NjP*.

V113 — — Seconde edition revûe, corrigée, & augmentée de remarques critiques sur cet ouvrage. *A Londres, chez Woodman & Lyon,* 1728. (*SR* 20 March)
8⁰: *π*A⁴ A⁸ a⁴ B–T⁸ (*π*A2 as 'A3'); [*8*] *i* ii–xxiii *xxiv blk, 1* 2–287 *288 blk.*

 Listed in *MChr* 20 March. Entered in *SR* to James Woodman, David Lyon, and Tho. Woodward; deposit copies at L,O,EU. Probably the edition of which the Bowyer ledgers record printing 3½ sheets for Woodward & Woodman under 18 March 1728, 650 copies and 100 large. The large-paper copies have not been distinguished, but may well be represented by the deposit copies which are all that have been seen. In the trade sale of James Woodman, 19 July 1731 (cat. at O-JJ) lot octavo 51 consisted of 40 copies and half the copyright, purchased by Gyles for £1. 6s.
L(1065.k.3),O,EU; *CLU-C,CtY,NjP.*

V114 — — Seconde edition. *A Londres,* 1728. (March?)
8⁰: A⁴ B–L⁸ M⁸(±M3) N–Q⁸ R⁴; viii, 243.
 The cancellandum M3 is preserved in the copy at CtY. Probably the edition listed in *MChr*

Voltaire. La Henriade

18 March, 'With a criticism on the whole work. Printed for N. Prevoust and Company; and P. Coderc. Price 5s.' Bengesco I. 484 records a '*Nouvelle édition non châtiée. Londres, Prévost et Coderc,* 1728. In 8⁰ de viii, 243 pp. et xvi pp. pour la *Critique de la Henriade*'; it is clearly related to this edition. There were subsequent continental editions of 1730, 1734, 1737 with false London imprints. *CtY,TxU.*

V115 — — Avec des remarques, & les differences qui se trouvent dans les diverses editions de ce poëme. '*A Londres*' [*Paris, Gandouin*], 1741.
4⁰: (frt+) *(3 ll) *A*² *** **** a–f⁴ g² h⁴ i(2 ll) k¹ l–r⁴, B–Cc⁴ Dd¹; *iii–v* vi–viii [*4*] *ix* x–xxiv, *i* ii–cxxii, *1* 2–202.
 A reissue of V112 with an added commentary, the whole published in Paris by Gandouin.
L(C.68.d.20, in a French presentation binding with the royal arms); *MH.*

V116 — Lettre au roi de Prusse par Mons. Voltaire de Paris. *Londres, imprimée pour G. Steidel, a l'ensigne de la Bible et Couronne, en New-Bond-street, et chez M. Cooper,* 1744–5. (*DA* 15 Jan)
2⁰: *A*⁴; *1–3* 4–7 *8 blk.*
'Du heros de la Germanie'
L(11482.m.20; 1962, Tom's Coffee House, 16 Jan); *MH.*

Translations

[*Discours en vers sur l'homme*] Gordon, William: Epistles translated from the French of Mr. Voltaire. On happiness, liberty and envy, 1738. *See* G229.

Three epistles in the ethic way. From the French of M. de Voltaire, 1738. *See* T254.

[*Henriade*] [Lockman, John:] Henriade. An epick poem. In ten canto's. Translated from the French into English blank verse, 1732. *See* L215.

———

The rise and progress of sacerdotal sanctity: to cure man of incredulity. A poem. To which is prefixed, the French original, as handed about at the Hague, [1747.] *See* R213.

Votum. Votum Dris Gualteri Pope, 1728. *See* Bourne, Vincent.

V117 — Votum pro pace. [*London?* 1710.]
½⁰: 1 side, 1 column.
 Dated at head, '10 Junij 1710'.
'Quid juvat densis glomerata turmis'
Rothschild.

Vowler, John. An essay for instructing children on various useful and uncommon subjects: being a collection of plain composures in verse... By an aged person who takes a pleasure in conversing with and teaching children... *Exon, printed for the author, by Andrew and Sarah Brice in Gandy's-lane* 1743.

Vowler, J. An essay

8°: pp. xvi, 144.   L; MH.
　　　One hundred verse lessons on various subjects.

V118 Vox. Vox britannica: or, the state of Europe. An heroic poem: in four parts... *London printed, and are to be sold by J. Nutt, and the booksellers of London & Westminster*, 1701. (8 Dec, Luttrell)
2°: *A*² B–F²; *1–2 3–24.*
Listed in *WL* Dec.
'When swift wing'd time his circle had begun'
LG,LVA-D; ICN(Luttrell),MH,*RPJCB.*

V119 — Vox populi or; the general cry. [*Edinburgh*, 1721.] (May)
½°: 1 side, 1 column.
'In vain Great Britain sues for Knight's discharge'
　　　A wish that Robert Knight, cashier of the South Sea company, should be extradited from Antwerp and reveal the corruption of politicians.
E(2, 1 dated in ms. May 1721).

V120 — Vox populi, or, the general cry of England. *Dublin, re-printed by John Harding*, 1721.
½°: 2 sides, 1 column.
　　　With 10 additional lines and a prose note.
OCU.

Voyage. A voyage from Bengale in the East Indies, 1721. *See* Morrice, Bezaleel.

V121 — A voyage from the East-Indies. *London, printed by R. Reilly; sold by T. Cooper*, 1736. (*GM, LM* July)
2°: *A*² B–E² *F*¹; *i–iv, 1 2–17 18 blk.*
'Oh daring Industry! inspire my muse'
WcC(uncut); TxU.

V122 — A voyage to the court of Neptune. *London, printed for J. Roberts*, 1714.

A voyage to the court of Neptune

8°: A–D⁴; *i–viii, 1–22 23–24 blk*. A1 hft.
　　　The drop-head title on p. 1 is 'The floating islands, &c.'
'From low and abject themes the soaring muse'
　　　A poem in imitation of Milton with references to the dismissal of Marlborough and other political themes.
O(uncut); *IU*,NN,TxU.

V123 Vulcan. Vulcan's speech spoken the 12th of August 1725, to his excellency the Lord Carteret, on occasion of the contest between the smiths and taylors, about precedency in their march. [*Dublin*] *Printed by George Faulkner*, 1725.
½°: 1 side, 1 column.
　　　On the other side of the TxU and one L copy, *The taylors answer to Vulcan's speech.*
'So great, my lord, your worth, so bright your fame'
L(1890.e.5/200; C.121.g.8/70); TxU.

Vulgus. Vulgus britannicus, 1710–. *See* Ward, Edward.

Vulpone. *See* Volpone.

Vulpoon. *See* Volpone.

V124 Vulture. The vulture and eagle. A poem humbly inscrib'd to Counsellor H——d. Written by P.Q. [*Dublin*, 1727?]
½°: 1 side, 1 column.
　　　The DT copy is bound with half-sheets of 1727.
'Within a grove, whose trees and fruitful soil'
　　　In favour of Counsellor Howard.
DT.

W

W., *Dr.* Mons Alexander, 1732. *See* M406.

W., *Miss.* The gentleman's study, 1732. *See* G123.

'W., *Mr.*' The muff, 1740. *See* Lorleach, —, *Mr.*

W., A.B.C.D.T. Treason against the ladies, 1731. *See* T469.

W., B. A satyr on Miss Ga—fny, [1725/30.] *See* S53.

W., C. The Preston prisoners, 1716. *See* Wogan, Charles.

W., C., *A. M.* The reformer's ghost, [1725/30.] *See* R151.

W., E. The mourning prophet, 1714. *See* Ward, Edward.

— On the death of John Wagstaffe, [1736?] *See* O193.

— A paraphrase on the hundred and fourth psalm, 1741. *See* P58.

— Poems written upon several occasions, and to several persons, 1711. *See* Poems.

— The sixth satire of the first book of Horace imitated, 1738. *See* Walpole, Edward.

W., G. Christianity without persecution, 1719. *See* Waldron, George.

W-----, G., *M.A., minister of the church of England.* The miraculous sheep's eye, 1743. *See* White, George.

W., H., *gent.* The access or permitted approach, 1703. *See* Waring, Henry.

— The access to virtue, 1704. *See* Waring, Henry.

— The coronation, or, England's patroness, 1702. *See* Waring, Henry.

— The dark penitent's complaint, 1712. *See* Waring, Henry.

— The divine or hypostatical union, 1707. *See* Waring, Henry.

W., J. The beau-thief detected, 1729. *See* B128.

— The courtship, 1748. *See* C471.

— Dotage. A poem, inscrib'd to a gentleman, 1728-. *See* D410.

— The glorious works of creation, 1707. *See* G182.

— On Thursday next, sir, I expect, [1720.] *See* Watson, James.

— Prosodia Alvariana...edita per J.W., 1719-. *See* P1142.

— Rightful monarchy: or, revolution tyranny, 1722. *See* R212.

— Three poems, 1706. *See* T256.

— Verses inscribed to the right honourable Humphry Parsons, 1730. *See* V51.

— A welcome to victory, 1704. *See* Wine, John.

W—, J—, *esq.* Pamela: or, the fair impostor, 1743-. *See* P25.

W., J., *late of Exon College.* The porch and academy open'd, 1707. *See* P998.

W., J.E. The cobler's poem, 1745. *See* Weekes, James Eyre.

W., L. An heroic poem on the memorable battle fought at Bleinheim, 1741. *See* Ormsbye, Robert.

W., L.B. A new song to the honourable Miss C——t, 1726. *See* N216.

W., R. The Christian priest, 1729. *See* C167.

W., R., *M.D.R.* Britannia invicta, 1745. *See* B466.

W., S., *gent.* A poem on the late violent storm, 1703. *See* P625.

W.T. W.T. to fair Clio, 1716. *See* Tunstall, William.

— W.T. to Mrs. M.M. in answer to a song, 1716. *See* Tunstall, William.

W., T., *an enemy to faction.* The K-ntish spy, 1712. *See* K104.

W., T., *gent.* The country priest, 1746. *See* C457.

W., W. The eclipse, 1715. *See* E14.

— Elegie on the death of the right honourable Sir James Falconer of Phesdo, [1705.] *See* Whyte, William.

— The humours of the Black-dog, 1737. *See* Wilkes, Wetenhall.

W., W., *esqr.* The universal coquet, 1749. *See* U16.

W1 **Wagstaff, Humphry.** The Dullardiad; or, the author of the Heraldiad satyriz'd. *Dublin, printed in the year* 1730.
8°: A⁴; *1-2* 3-7 *8 blk.*
'Ill nature strange reigns in this age'
    'Wagstaff' is probably a pseudonym; *The Heraldiad,* 1730, is by 'Martin Gulliver'.
IU.

'**Wagstaffe, A.**' The politicks and patriots of Jamaica, 1718. *See* P715.

Wagstaffe, J.

W2 Wagstaffe, John. A choice of life, composed by J. Wagstaffe; in the nineteenth year of his age. *London, printed for T. Eldridge, who frames and sells all sorts of map, prints, and almanacks,* [1746/–.]
½°: 1 side, 3 columns.
　　Smith II. 845.
'Could but success attend my wish'
LF.

W3 Wagstaffe, William. Ramelies: a poem, humbly inscrib'd to his grace, the D. of Marlborough. *London, printed for T. Atkinson,* 1706. (*DC* 4 July)
2°: A–C²; *1–2* 3–12.
　　The Luttrell copy, dated 4 July, is in the possession of Robert H. Taylor.
'Bleinheim e're while at ev'ry turn appear'd'
LdU-B,*MR*; MH(uncut).

Waldron, George. The compleat works, in verse and prose. [*London*] *Printed for the widow and orphans,* 1731.
2°: pp. xvi, 191.　　L,O; DLC,MH.

———

W4 [—] Christianity without persecution: or a congratulatory poem, on the late act for strengthening the protestant religion... *London, printed in the year* 1719.
8°: *A*⁴ B–C⁴; [*4*] *i* ii–iv, 1–16. A1 hft.
'When to retrieve the glory of our crown'
　　Dedication signed 'G.W.' Reprinted in Waldron's *Compleat works,* 1731.
L(1163.b.14/1),LDW; ICU.

W5 — 'An occasional poem on the death of the rt honble Anne countess of Sunderland...humbly inscribed to the rt honble the Earl of Sunderland. *Lond.* 1716 – 4to.'
　　Reprinted in Waldron's *Compleat works,* 1731, with first line:
'All creatures date their birth since ancient time'
(*Rawlinson.*)

W6 — An ode on the 28th of May, being the anniversary-day of his majesty's happy nativity... [*London?*] *Printed in the year* 1723.
8°: A⁴; *1–2* 3–8.
'Genius of harmony arise!'
L(11631.e.75),O; InU.

W7 — A poem, humbly inscrib'd to the illustrious and heroic prince, his royal highness, George, prince of Wales. [*London?*] *Printed in the year* 1717.
2°: *A*² B² C¹; *1–2* 3–10.
'When first Britannia's slavish chain was broke'
L(643.1.24/34; 162.n.31),O(marbled wrappers).

W8 — A poem on the parliament. *London, printed in the year* 1718.
8°: *A*² B⁴ C²; *i–iv, 1* 2–12. A1 hft.
'When daring poets would encomiums raise'
O,E,EtC; CSmH,CtY(–A1),ICU.

Waldron, G.

W9 — [dh] The regency and return. A poem. [*London?* 1717?]
2°: A²; *1–4.*
　　The L copy is bound with Waldron's *A poem humbly inscrib'd,* 1717, and the date is suggested by that.
'As tender wives their husbands absence mourn'
L(643.1.24/35),OC,LdU-B.

W10 Waldron, John. A poem upon musick. *Dublin, printed by James Hoey,* 1733.
8°: A–C⁴ D¹; *i–iii* iv–vi *vii–viii,* 9–24 '23–24'.
　　Teerink 1248. With 'The hoop-peticoat, in Lilliputian verse', dedicated to Swift by Waldron, on pp. 21–'24'.
'When bright Aurora shone with ruddy hue'
Hoop-petticoat: 'My muse / Infuse'
LVA-F(uncut).

W11 — A satyr against tea. Or, Ovington's essay upon the nature and qualities of tea, &c. dissected, and burlesqu'd. *Dublin, printed by Sylvanus Pepyat,* 1733.
8°: A⁸; *1–3* 4–14 *15; 16 blk.* 15 advt.
'Famale [!] Ovington, how poor, and thin'
　　John Ovington's *Essay* was first published in 1699, and now reprinted by Pepyat.
L(11631.a.63/6).

W12 Walk. A walk from St. James's to Convent-Garden, the back way, through the Meuse. In imitation of Mr. Gay's Journey to Exeter. In a letter to a friend. *London printed, and sold by James Roberts, & Arabella Morice, next to the Rose-Tavern without Temple-Bar,* 1717.
2°: *A*² B–C²; [*2*] i–ii, 1–8.
　　Listed in *PB* 4 June as in print.
'While you with Lady Betty drank Bohee'
　　Possibly by Bezaleel Morrice, whose poems were sold by Arabella Morrice (presumably a relation) in 1717. His *Voyage from the East-Indies,* 1716, was listed with this poem in the advertisements for [Giles Jacob] *A journey to Bath and Bristol,* 1717. The 'Journey to Exeter' is the first of Gay's *Two epistles,* [1717.]
LG,LVA-F.

— A walk to Islington, 1701. *See* Ward, Edward.

W13 Walker, Ellis. Epicteti Enchiridion made English. In a poetical paraphrase. *London, printed for Sam. Keble,* 1701. (*TC* Michaelmas)
12°: A⁶ b⁶ c⁴ B–I⁶ K² (A3 as 'B4'); *i–xxxii,* 1–98 *99–100.* A1 frt; xxxii advt.
　　First published 1692.
'Respecting man, things are divided thus'
L(1485.aaa.30),O; *CU,*IU,*MH.*

W14 —— *Dublin, printed by J. Ray, for P. Campbell, M. Milner, & J. Gill,* 1702.
12°: A–E¹² F⁶ (B2 as 'A2'; F3,4 as 'I3,4'); *i–v* vi–xxxi *xxxii blk,* 1–98 *99–100.* A1 license leaf.
O,C(–A1),DG,DN; IU(–A1).

Walker, J. Epicteti Enchiridion

W15 —— *London, printed for Sam. Keble,* 1702 [1703?]. (*TC* Hilary 1703).
12°: A⁶ b⁶ c⁴ B–I⁶ K²; *i–xxxii,* 1–98 *99–100.* A1 frt; xxxii advt.
L(1067.d.12),O,OC; CSmH,*CtY*,IU,*MH,MnU.*

W16 —— *London, printed for Sam. Keble,* 1708.
12°: A–L⁶; *i–xxxii,* 1–98 *99–100.* A1 frt.
L(1385.a.25).

W17 — [reissue] *London, printed for Sam. Keble; sold by Jonah Bowyer,* 1709. (May?)
12°: A⁶(±A2) B–L⁶; *i–xxxii,* 1–98 *99–100.* A1 frt.
Advertised in *PM* 19 May 1709 'for Jonah Bowyer'. Entered in *SR* 4 May 1710 to Sam. Keble as 'old' copy.
O(–A1); CLU-C,*PPL.*

W18 — Epicteti Enchiridion. The morals of Epictetus made English, in a poetical paraphrase. *London, printed by W. Bowyer, for S. Keble, & R. Gosling,* 1716.
12°: A–D¹²; *i–xxx,* 1–63 *64–66.* A1 frt; 66 advt.
A fourth share of the copyright was sold in the trade sale of Jonas Brown, 21 Oct 1718 (cat. at O-JJ) to Gosling for £2.5s.
L(11632.a.13),O; *MH,OCU.*

W19 —— *Dublin, printed by and for Sam. Fairbrother,* 1724.
12°: A–E¹² F²; *i–iii* iv–xxviii, 1–92 *93–96.* F2 advt.
L(11632.a.14),DA(lacks F²).

W20 — [*idem*] The morals of Epictetus; made English, in a poetical paraphrase... *London, printed for R. Gosling,* 1737. (27 Aug?)
12°: (frt+) A–D¹²; *i–xxii,* 1 2–69 *70–72; 73–74 blk* (17 as '15').
Entered to Gosling in Bowyer's ledgers under 27 Aug 1737, 2000 copies printed. Apparently the edition listed in *GM, LM* July 1738. The copyright formed part of lot 5 in the trade sale of Robert Gosling, 27 Oct 1741 (cat. at O-JJ); it was purchased by his son Francis at a guinea for the lot.
L(11630.a.10),O(uncut, –frt, D12).

[Walker, *Sir* **Hovenden.]** The impotent lover describ'd in six elegies on old-age. In imitation of Cornelius Gallus, 1718. *See* I14.

W21 Wall, Thomas. An ode for an entertainment of musick on her majesty's birth-day, and, the success of her majesty's arms... The night performance before her majesty at St. James's. The words by Mr. Wall. Set to musick by Mr. Abell. *London, printed for J. Nutt,* 1703. (*PB* 6 Feb)
4°: A⁴ B–C⁴; *i–viii,* 1–13 *14–15; 16 blk.* A1 hft; C4 advt.
Title to the second ode on p. 7, text on pp. 9–13. The copy at MH appears to have a variant sheet B with textual changes.
'Hark, Britain, hark! The loudest trump of fame'
'Conquest and triumph the glories proclaim'
L(11602.f.24/3, Luttrell, 8 Feb); MH.

Wallace, J.

[Wallace, John.] The wanderer and traveller. In form of a dramatick composition [actually by John Hunter], 1733. *See* H407.

W22 Waller. Waller's ghost to the modern poets: occasion'd by some Dutch and German reflections on the English beauties. *London, printed in the year* 1719.
2°: *A²* B–C²; *1–3* 4–12.
'From the blest mansions of eternal joy'
On the Hanoverians' choice of women.
CLU-C,CtY.

W23 Waller, Edmund. A panegyrick on Oliver Cromwell, and his victories... With three poems on his death. Written by Mr. Dryden, Mr. Sprat, and Mr. Waller. *London, printed by H. Hills; sold by the booksellers of London & Westminster,* 1709.
8°: A⁸ B⁴; *1–2* 3–24.
First published 1655; included here to complete the tally of piracies by Hills.
'While with a strong, and yet a gentle hand'
L(11626.e.59),O,C,CT(2),E+; CSmH,CtY,IU, MH,TxU+.

W24 Waller, William. On the death of King William IIId. of ever blessed memory. A pindarique poem. *Norwich, printed by Francis Burges, for Samuel Oliver,* 1702.
4°: A⁴ (A3ᵛ as 'A2'); *1–2* 3–8.
'What means this solemn damp quite thro' the land'
O(uncut, unopened).

W25 — Peace on earth. A congratulatory poem. *London, printed for John Morphew,* 1713.
2°: A–C²; *i–iv,* 1–8.
'Most justly now 'tis ev'ry muse's theme'
CSmH,CtY(uncut).

W26 —— To which is added, a poem on her majesty's birth-day. *Dublin: re-printed by E. Sandys, for G. Grierson,* 1713.
12°: A–B⁶; *i–iv,* 1–20.
With 'An essay upon unnatural flights in poetry' on pp. 17–20.
Poem: 'Auspicious day! to which we owe'
L(1488.de.46/3),DN,DT.

Wallin, Benjamin. Evangelical hymns and songs, in two parts... [*London*] *Printed for John Ward; sold by Ebenezer Gardiner, & George Keith,* 1750.
8°: pp. xii, 260.   L,E.

Wallis, John. The occasional miscellany in prose and verse... *Newcastle upon Tyne, printed by John Gooding,* 1748.
8°: 2 vol.   L,NeP.
In spite of the title, this contains only one poem.

W27 [—] The history of David's troubles: or, human frailty delineated. A sacred poem. *Oxford, printed*

Wallis, J. The history of David's troubles

by Leonard Litchfield, for Sackville Parker, 1741.
(March?)
2°: *A*² B–E²; *1–4* 5–20. A1 hft; 4 err.
    Imprimatur on p. 4 'Mart. 11. 1740'.
'I sing the causes of a troubled reign'
    Wallis's authorship is recorded in *Rawlinson*;
    the poem was reprinted in his *Occasional
    miscellany*, 1748, as 'The royal penitent'.
O; CSmH,TxU.

W28 — Reflections on a candle, in an irregular ode.
*Newcastle upon Tyne, printed by John Gooding, on
the Side. Sold by the booksellers of Newcastle, Durham, Hexham, Morpeth, and Alnwick*, 1745.
4°: *A*² B²; *1–5* 6–8. 4 advt.
    The copy at DrU, which belonged to the
    dedicatee, Thomas Sharp, archdeacon of
    Northumberland, has the advertisement (for
    Wallis's academy at Wallsend) crossed out.
'Light of my solitude, I see'
O,DrU(presentation copy),NeL.

W29 **Walpole.** Walpole redivivus: or, a new excise. A
ballad. [*London?* 1744?]
slip: 1 side, 1 column.
'Come, all ye jolly fellows'
    An attack on Henry Pelham, possibly occa-
    sioned by his attempt to impose an extra duty
    on sugar, 1744.
C.

W29·5 [**Walpole, Edward.**] Sannazarius on the birth of
our saviour. Done into English verse, and...
inscrib'd to the gentlemen of the learned society of
Spalding. *London, printed for W. Lewis*, 1736. (*LM*
July)
8°.
    Errata slip on verso of title. Entered to Lewis
    in Bowyer's ledgers under 16 April 1736, 5
    sheets octavo, 500 copies printed; there was an
    extra charge of 3s. for 'errata'. Maurice
    Johnson's copy, sold as recorded below, was
    the gift of the translator whom he identified in
    ms. He also noted that it was 'perused &
    corrected by Alexr Pope esqr'.
(*Sotheby's*, 23 March 1970, lot 132.)

W30 [—] The sixth satire of the first book of Horace
imitated. Inscribed to Sir Richard Ellis, bart.
London, printed for J. Hawkins, 1738. (*GM, LM*
May)
2°: *A*² B–C²; *i–iv*, *1–7* 8. 8 advt.
'Tho' great of birth, tho' none can higher trace'
    Dedication signed 'E.W.' Early ms. attribu-
    tion to Edward Walpole of Dunstan in a copy
    at L; see also *Nichols* VI.119.
L(11642.i.10/6; C.131.h.1/10**, ms. note),O;
CLU,KU,MH,TxU(uncut).

W31 [**Walpole, Horace,** *subsequently 4th earl of Orford.*]
The beauties. An epistle to Mr. Eckardt, the
painter. *London, printed for M. Cooper*, 1746. (*SR*
25 Sept)

Walpole, H. The beauties

2°: *A*² <B²; *1–2* 3–8.
    Hazen 2. Horizontal chain-lines. Deposit copy
    at L. Listed in *GM* Sept.
'Desponding artist talk no more'
    Walpole's ms. is printed in the Yale edition of
    Walpole's *Correspondence* XXX.324ff.
L(643.m.14/15),O,WrP; DLC,*MH*,MiU,NN,
OCU.

W32 [—] Epilogue to Tamerlane, on the suppression of
the rebellion. Spoken by Mrs. Pritchard, in the
character of the comic muse, Nov. 4. 1746. *London,
printed for R. Dodsley; sold by M. Cooper*, [1746.]
(5 Nov)
2°: *A*⁴; *1–3* 4–7 8 blk.
    Hazen 3. Publication date from *Hazen*.
'Britons, once more in annual joy we meet'
    Early ms. attribution to Walpole in the L copy.
L(1347.m.33); MH.

[—] The medalist. A new ballad, 1741. *See* M156.

[**Walsh, Patrick.**] A satyr on Miss Ga-fny by the
Little Beau, [1725/30.] *See* S53.

Walsh, William. The works in prose and verse...
London, printed for E. Curll, 1736.
8°: pp. ii, xii, 86+.   L,O; ICN,MH.
    Different copies are variously constructed.
    Reissued in vol. 5 of *Mr. Pope's literary
    correspondence*, 1737.

[—] Abigail's lamentation for the loss of secretary
H-----y, [1708.] *See* A3.

[—] The golden age from the fourth eclogue of
Virgil, 1703. *See* G211.

W33 [—] Horace, lib. III. ode III. imitated. *London,
printed for J. Tonson*, 1706. (*DC* 3 May)
½°: *1–2*, 1 column.
'The man that's resolute and just'
    Crum T1000. Printed in Walsh's *Works*, 1736;
    wrongly ascribed to Fenton in *Nichols,
    Collection* IV.43, but ascribed to Walsh in the
    errata, VIII.296.
CSmH,ICN(Luttrell, no date),TxU.

W34 [—] [*idem*] To the queen, on her coronation-day.
1706. Horace lib. 3. ode 3. imitated. *London,
printed for J. Tonson*, 1706. *Dublin, printed for M.
Gunne.*
½°: 2 sides, 1 column.
MH.

W35 [—] Ode for the thanksgiving day. *London, printed
for Jacob Tonson*, 1706 [1707?]. (*DC* 1 Jan 1707)
2°: *A*¹ B–D² E¹; *i–ii*, *1–14*.
    No watermark except WC in A in some copies.
'Begin, my muse, and strike the lyre!'
    Early ms. attributions to Walsh in copies at
    Longleat, ICU, TxU. Wrongly attributed to
    Prior and to Tate.
L(11631.i.15/8),O,*MR-C*; CSmH,CtY(2),ICU,
MH,TxU(2)+.

Walsh, W. Ode for the thanksgiving day

W36 [—] [fine paper]
    Watermarks ID, HD.
LLP,C,LdU-B; IU.

W37 Walter, Thomas. A poem dedicated to the memory and lamented death of his late sacred majesty, William the third, king of England. *London printed, and sold by B. Harris*, 1702. (16 April, Luttrell)
2°: A–B²; *i–ii*, 1–6.
'So Orange fell, so Glo'ster went before'
NjP(Luttrell).

Wandering. The wand'ring spy, 1722. *See* Ward, Edward [The merry travellers].

Wandsworth. The Wandsworth campaign. A poem, 1748. *See* Simmonds, James.

W38 Wanton. The wanton baker of Westminster. Or, the cook's two leg timpany. Being a pleasant and comical copy of verses on a certain baker in Westminster, who having a mind to a sop in the cook-maid's dripping pan, gave her so of his half-penny rowles, that her belly swell'd as big as a peck loaf, which at last prov'd a two legg'd tympany, to her sad vexation, and the bakers sorrowful repentance. To the tune of, Clack, clack. [*London*, 171–?]
½°: 1 side, 2 columns.
    With two woodcuts, but not like the usual street ballads.
'In Westminster lived a baker by trade'
    Possibly a satire on Marlborough is intended.
Harding.

— The wanton widows, [1744.] *See* The Northumberland miracle, 1743–.

W39 War. 'War. A poem. In blank verse. [*London*] *Printed for J. Roberts.* Price 6d.' (*DA* 2 Aug 1745)

— War, an epic satyr, 1747. *See* Barrett, Stephen.

W40 — War with priestcraft: or, the free-thinkers Iliad. A burlesque poem, in three canto's... Dedicated to the celebrated author of Christianity as old as the creation. *London, printed for J. Roberts; sold by the booksellers in town & country*, 1732. (*GM* 20 Jan)
8°: A⁴ a⁴(−a4) B–F⁴ G¹[= a4] (A3 as 'A'); [*4*] *i* ii–iv *ix* x–xiv, *1* 2–42. A1 hft.
    Bond 127. Many copies have a four-leaf section of advertisements added.
'Since all the learned world agree'
    Dedication signed 'Diagoras'; to Matthew Tindal.
L(11632.aaa.17),O(−A1); CSmH(−A1),CtY (−A1),ICN(stitched, uncut),IU(−A1),NN (−A1)+.

W41 — — The second edition. *London, printed for J. Roberts; sold by the booksellers in town & country*, 1732.

War with priestcraft

8°: A⁴ a⁴(−a4) B–F⁴ G¹[=a4] (A3 as 'A'); [*4*] *i* ii–iv *ix* x–xiv, *1* 2–42. A1 hft.
    Probably a variant title-page.
C,LdU-B.

Warburton, William. Miscellaneous translations, in prose and verse, from Roman poets, orators, and historians. *London, printed for Anthony Barker; sold by G. Strahan, A. Bettesworth, & J. Isted*, 1724 [1723]. (*MC* Dec)
12°: pp. 125.   L,O; CtY,MH.

— [reissue] *London, printed for W. Reeve*, 1745.
    O.

W42 Ward. Ward's downfal: or, the plot detected. A poem. Being a full and true account of a most horrid, barbarous, and bloody plot, to undermine the Hanover succession... *London, printed for the author; sold by the booksellers of London & Westminster*, 1734. (*HM* Dec)
2°: (4 ll); *1–2* 3–8.
'All Britons, attend,/And an ear to me lend'
    Preface signed 'A.B.' A satire on the quack-doctor Joshua Ward and on Lady Gage who helped distribute his pill. The *Daily Courant* 28 Nov 1734 had claimed that his pill was part of a Jacobite plot against England.
O.

Ward, Edward.
Ward's collected works were pieced together in such a way that it has seemed best to deal with each volume separately, including the prose London-spy *which formed the first volume. Some of the 'editions' listed below may be reissues.*

[—] The London-spy compleat, in eighteen-parts. By the author of the Trip to Jamaica. *London printed, and sold by J. How*, 1703.
8°: pp. 437.   L; ICU,MH.

[—] — The first volume of the authors writings. The second edition much enlarged and corrected. *London printed, and sold by J. How*, 1704.
8°: pp. 439.   L; DLC.

[—] — The third edition. *London printed, and sold by J. How*, 1706.
8°: pp. 439.   L,O; CLU-C,MH.

[—] — The fourth edition. *London printed, and sold by J. How*, 1709.
8°: pp. 439.   L,O; ICN,MiU.

— — Being the first volume of the writings of Mr. Edward Ward. The fifth edition. *London, printed for A. Bettesworth*, 1718.
8°: pp. 439.   CSmH,TxU.

[—] The second volume of the writings of the author of the London-spy... *London printed, and sold by J. How*, 1703.
8°: pp. 372.   L,O; CLU-C,TxU.

Ward, E. *Collections*, vol. 2

[—] — The second edition. *London printed, and sold by J. How*, 1704.
8°: pp. 401.   L; DLC,ICU.

[—] — The third edition. *London printed, and sold by J. How*, 1706.
8°: pp. 401.   O; ICN,MH.

[—] — The fourth edition. *London printed, and sold by J. How*, 1709.
8°: pp. 401.   L,O; CtY,MiU.

— A collection of the writings of Mr. Edward Ward... Vol. II. The fifth edition. *London, printed for A. Bettesworth*, 1717.
8°: pp. 401.   CLU-C,MH.

[—] The third volume, consisting of poems on divers subjects... By the author of the London-spy. *London printed, and sold by B. Bragg*, 1706. (*DC* 19 April)
8°: pp. 383.   L,O; ICN,MH.

— [*idem*] Miscellaneous writings, in verse and prose... By Mr. Edward Ward. Vol. III. The second edition, with large additions and amendments. *London, printed by W.D.; sold by J. Woodward*, 1712 [1711]. (*DC* 26 Oct 'tomorrow')
8°: pp. 336, 94.   O,E; CLU-C.
Entered in *SR* to W. Downing and administrators of B. Bragge, 13 Nov 1711; deposit copies at O,E.

— — Vol. III. The third edition. *London, printed by W.D.; sold by A. Bettesworth*, 1718.
8°: pp. 336, 98.   CtY,TxU.

[—] The fourth volume of the writings of the author of the London-spy. Prose and verse. *London, printed for George Sawbridge*, 1709 [1708]. (*DC* 10 Sept)
8°.   L; CLU-C,TxU.

A nonce collection, including six numbers of *The London Terraefilius*, 1707–08, and of *The diverting muse*, 1707. For a '*fourth volume*' of 1729, see the sixth volume below.

[—] Satyrical reflections on clubs... Vol. V. *London, printed for J. Phillips*, 1710.
8°: pp. 392.   MH.
A reissue of *The secret history of clubs*, 1709. Replaced by the following.

[—] A collection of historical and state poems, satyrs, songs, and epigrams. Being the fifth volume of miscellanies. By the author of the London-spy. *London, printed in the year* 1717. *And sold by A. Bettesworth.* (*PB* 1 Aug)
8°.   L,WcC; CtY,MH.
A nonce collection; in some copies the original titles survive. The contents vary slightly.

— The wandering spy: or, the merry observator. Consisting of the following... Being the sixth

Ward, E. *Collections*, vol. 6

volume of miscellanies by Ed. Ward. *London, printed for the author; sold by A. Bettesworth*, 1724. (*MC* Dec)
8°.   L,WcC; CtY,ICU.
A nonce collection.

— [reissue] *London, printed for the author and sold at his own house; likewise by A. Bettesworth*, 1727.
CLU-C.
The copy seen has a blank slip pasted over the line of the title referring to the 'sixth volume'.

— [reissue] Being the fourth volume of miscellanies by Edward Ward. *London, printed for the author; sold by A. Bettesworth*, 1729.
O.
Possibly the 'Mr. E. Ward's Works, 4th vol.' which formed part of lot 8 of the copyrights in Wilford's trade sale, 24 Feb 1736 (cat. at O-JJ), sold to Rivington.

[—] Æsop at Paris, his letters and fables. Translated from the original French, 1701.
A series of letters, each of which is followed by a verse fable; since the verse follows the prose, the editions are excluded from this catalogue. There are two editions, one collating 8°: A–E⁴ at L, DrU, and a piracy collating 8°: A–B⁴ at TxU.

W43 [—] All men mad: or, England a great Bedlam. A poem. *London, printed in the year* 1704. (14 Sept, Luttrell)
4°: A–C⁴ D²; *1–2* 3–27 *28 blk.*
Troyer 232. Listed in *WL* Sept.
'The muses now send forth their sonnets'
Reprinted in Ward's *Third volume*, 1706.
L(164.1.67, Luttrell),LLP,O,DT; CLU-C, CSmH,InU,MH.

W44 [—] — [*Reading?* 1737?]
4°: A²; *1–4*, 2 columns.
Drop-head title only. Probably a later reprint. *The Reading mercury: or, the London spy* was issuing Ward's works as a supplement in 1736–37 (see R. M. Wiles, *Serial publication* (1957) 63); the copy at LSA has a ms. note 'G. Burton Cath: Hall 1737'. Compare *Helter skelter*, [1737?], W79.
LSA; CtY(cropt).

W45 [—] The ambitious father: or, the politician's advice to his son. *London, printed by E. Shaw for the author*, [1730?/31.]
8°: A–I⁴; *i–ii*, *1*–69 *70 blk.*
Troyer 278 dates as [1730].
'My son, if to a courtier's life inclin'd'
Listed in *Cibber* as by Ward; Troyer doubts it on the evidence of the style. Cibber clearly follows the advertisements for the issue below, e.g. *MChr* Jan 1732 'By Mr. Edward Ward. Being the last work he left finished in his

Ward, E. The ambitious father

life-time'. It is admitted here solely on the strength of that unequivocal statement.

LdU-B; OCU,*ViU*.

W46 [—] — *London, printed for T. Warner,* [1732.] (*GM* 17 Jan)

A reissue with a cancel slip pasted over the imprint.

CtY.

W46·2 [—] [*idem*] The modern courtier: or the ambitious statesman's advice to his son. In order to his advancement at c------t... Written by a noble l----d to his son. *London printed, and sold by J. Torbuck, and by the booksellers and publishers in town & country,* [1741.] (*LM* May; *GM* June)

8°: π² A–G⁴ H²; *i–iv, 1*–60. π1 hft.

The text has not been collated with the preceding, but an identical first line and similar length make the identification justifiable.

L(1487.aaa.2,−π1),O; InU(−π1),OCU.

W46·5 [—] — '*London printed, and sold by J. Torbuck, and by the booksellers and publishers in town & country*' [*Edinburgh?*], [1741.]

8°: A⁴ B–G⁴; *1–2 3*–56.

The copies at E,GU are bound in volumes with Edinburgh piracies.

E,GU; CtY,MH,NN.

W47 [—] Apollo's maggot in his cups: or, the whimsical creation of a little satyrical poet. A lyrick ode... Merrily dedicated to Dicky Dickison, the witty, but deform'd governour of Scarborough-spaw. *London printed, and sold by the booksellers of London & Westminster,* 1729. (7 Aug?)

8°: A–G⁴ H⁴(−H1); *i–xiv, 1*–48.

Troyer 232. This issue is probably the result of a binder's error in not cancelling the title; the copy at L has the title listed below bound at the end and apparently conjugate with H4 (H2, 3 are signed 'H, H2'). The publication date is inferred from the following.

'In a calm season of the year'

Ward's authorship is revealed in the postscript. An attack on Pope's *Dunciad*. Richard Dickinson is portrayed, with satirical verses on him, in an engraved sheet at O-JJ.

L(1969),O.

W48 [—] — *London printed, and sold by T. Warner, and the booksellers of London & Westminster,* 1729. (*MChr* 7 Aug)

8°: A⁴(±A1) B–G⁴ H⁴(−H1); *i–xiv, 1*–48.

The cancel title has not been clearly seen, but is assumed from the preceding. The copy at ICN contains the receipt for 8*s.* pamphlet duty paid at the stamp-office, 16 Sept.

CLU-C,CtY,ICN,IU,TxU.

[—] The ball; or, un passo tempo, 1723. *See* B19.

W49 [—] Battel without bloodshed: or, martial discipline buffoon'd by the City-train-bands. *London printed, and sold by John How,* 1701. (27 Aug, Luttrell)

Ward, E. Battel without bloodshed

2°: A² B–D²; *1–2 3*–16. 2 advt.

Troyer 233. The Luttrell copy was recorded in Pickering & Chatto cat. 248/14122. Listed in *WL* Aug. An edition of 1710 is referred to by C. E. Jones in *N&Q* 6 April 1946.

'Dub, dub, dubbadub, says the drum in the morning'

Reprinted in Ward's *Second volume,* 1703.

L(1344.n.63, Luttrell),LG,*MR-C*; CLU-C(uncut),ICU,MH.

W50 [—] Bribery and simony; or, a satyr against the corrupt use of money. By the author of the London spy. *London, printed for C.C.; sold by John Nutt,* 1703 [1702]. (23 Nov, Luttrell)

2°: A² B–D²; *1–2 3*–16.

Troyer 233. Listed in *WL* Nov. Reprinted in the Bury St. Edmunds editions of *Honesty in distress,* [172–.]

'Money, thou universal Indian curse'

Reprinted in Ward's *Third volume,* 1706, as 'A satyr against...'

MR-C; CSmH(Luttrell),CtY,MH,TxU(2).

W51 [—] Britannia: a poem. With all humility inscrib'd to the fifty two (not guilty) lords. *London, printed for John Morphew,* 1710. (6 April, Luttrell)

2°: A² B–C²; *1–2 3*–12.

Advertised in *PB* 8 April. The Luttrell copy is recorded in *Haslewood*.

'O fair Britannia! lovliest of the sea'

Early ms. attribution in the CLU-C copy 'By Ned: Ward. The London spy'. It has not previously been attributed to Ward, and confirmation is needed.

L(1481.f.19/6),O(2),C; CLU-C,ICU,MH(cropt), MiU,OCU.

W52 [—] — [col] *London, printed for John Morphew,* 1710. (20 April, Luttrell)

8°: A⁴; *1*–8.

Drop-head title only; possibly a piracy.

L(164.m.57, Luttrell),O,LdU-B; CSmH,MH.

W53 [—] British wonders: or, a poetical description of the several prodigies and most remarkable accidents that have happen'd in Britain since the death of Queen Anne. *London printed, and sold by John Morphew,* 1717. (*DC* 20 April)

8°: A–E⁴; *i–ii, 1*–38.

Bond 51; *Troyer* 233. Reissued in Ward's *Fifth volume of miscellanies,* 1717.

'In wretched times, when men were given'

L(164.1.60, Luttrell, April),O,C,LdU-B; CLU-C, CtY,DFo,ICN,OCU+.

W54 [—] [reimpression]

8°: A–H⁴; *i–ii, 1*–61 *62*. 62 advt.

A reimpression of the preceding with the type heavily leaded and reimposed. Clearly the equivalent of a fine-paper issue; 'Price one shilling' on title, whereas the preceding bore no price. One copy of this issue was reissued in Ward's *Fifth volume* (at MH).

L(1489.pp.2),O,AdU; CtY,ICU.

Ward, E. The character

W55 [—] The character of a covetous citizen, or, a ready way to get riches. A poem. *London printed, and are to be sold by the booksellers of London & Westminster*, 1702 [1701]. (*WL* Nov)
2⁰: A²(±) B–D²; *1–2* 3–16.
    Troyer 273. A reissue of *The wealthy shop-keeper*, 1700, with new title and revised version of the opening lines.
'The man who dotes on gold, how curs'd his fate!'
    Reprinted in Ward's *Third volume*, 1706. Listed in *Waller* as attributed to Prior; rejected by *Wright & Spears* who are unaware of Ward's authorship.
L(11630.h.60),LG; CLU-C,MH,TxU.

[—] The complete vintner, 1734. *See* W61.

[—] The contending candidates, 1722. *In* W122.

[—] The cudgel, 1742. *See* W67.

W56 [—] The dancing devils: or, the roaring dragon. A dumb farce. As it was lately acted at both houses, but particularly at one, with unaccountable success. *London printed, and sold by A. Bettesworth, J. Bately, & J. Brotherton*, 1724.
8⁰: A–B⁴ C⁴(±C4) D–H⁴ I⁴(–I4) (H2 as 'H3'); *1–2* 3–70.
    Troyer 235. In some copies (LdU-B,CtY, TxU) C4 is uncancelled, and reads in p. 24, line 8 'King Hector', sometimes (e.g. TxU) corrected in ms. to 'Prince Paris'; the cancel (which has an asterisk in the direction-line of p. 23) reads 'Young Paris'. Reissued in Ward's *Sixth volume of miscellanies*, 1724.
'Near barren fields, where honour dwells'
L(11633.e.45/9),O(2),LdU-B; CLU-C,CtY(2), ICN,MH,TxU(2)+.

W57 [—] The delights of the bottle: or, the compleat vintner... To which is added, A South-Sea song upon the late bubbles. By the author of the Cavalcade. *London, printed for Sam. Briscoe*, 1720. (*PB* 1 Sept)
8⁰: (frt+) A–G⁴; *1–2* 3–54 *55–56*.
    Troyer 235. The 'South-Sea song' is on G4; see W177 below. Entered to Sam. Briscoe in *SR* 30 Aug; deposit copies at O,E,EU.
'O Bacchus, with thy noble juice'
    'The author of the Cavalcade' refers to *The republican procession*, 1714.
L(164.l.21, Luttrell, Sept),O(3, 1–frt),E(–frt), EU(–frt); DLC,*NN*.

W58 [—] [variant imprint?] *London, printed by W. Downing*, 1720.
8⁰: (frt+) A–G⁴; *1–2* 3–54 *55–56*.
    No cancel title has been seen; presumably it is a press-variant. Copies with this imprint were reissued in Ward's *Sixth volume of miscellanies*, 1724.
O,LdU-B; CLU-C(2,–frt),CtY(–frt),ICN,NjP (–frt).

W59 [—] — The second edition. *London, printed for Sam. Briscoe*, 1721 [1720]. (*PM* 20 Oct)

Ward, E. The delights of the bottle

8⁰: (frt+) A–G⁴; *1–2* 3–54 *55–56*.
    The copy seen has sheet B from the first edition and no frontispiece.
O(–frt).

W60 [—] — The third edition. *London, printed for Sam. Briscoe*, 1721 [1720]. (*PB* 8 Nov)
8⁰: (frt+) A–G⁴; *1–2* 3–54 *55–56*.
    Probably a press-variant title. Reissued with *The northern cuckold*, 1721.
NN(–frt).

W61 [—] [*idem*] The complete vintner; or, the delights of the bottle... To which is added, a song extempore over a bowl of punch. By the author of the Cavalcade. *London, printed for Alex. Smyth; sold by Francis Jefferies*, 1734. (*LM* March)
8⁰: A–G⁴; *1–2* 3–*55 56*.
S. H. Ward, Letchworth (xerox of title at L).

W62 [—] [*reissue*] The delights of the bottle; or, the complete vintner... To which is added, a song extempore... By the author of the Cavalcade... The third edition. *London printed, and sold by R. Baldwin & J. Jefferys*, 1743. (*DP* 12 April)
8⁰: A⁴(±A1) B–G⁴; *1–2* 3–*55 56*.
L(11643.b.9).

[—] A dialogue between a depending courtier, 1735. *See* W133.

[—] A dialogue between a surly husband, [172–?] *See* W132.

W63 [—] The dissenter. *London, printed in the year* 1704. (*DC* 16 Aug)
4⁰: π² A⁴(–A1) B–G⁴ H²; *i–ii*, *1–2* 3–60.
'What wild opinions have possest mankind'
    Advertised with Ward's *Hudibras redivivus* as early as 1706, and subsequently as specifically by him (e.g. *PB* 25 July 1717). Also attributed to him in an advertisement in *Hudibras redivivus*, [1722]; confirmation of the attribution is desirable.
O(part cropt),E(part cropt),DT(part cropt); InU (part cropt),MH,TxU(uncut).

W64 [—] [*idem*] A true history of the honest whigs. A poem. In answer to the Thoughts of an honest tory. *London, printed in the year* 1710.
8⁰: A⁸; *1–2* 3–16. 16 advt.
    The order of variants has not been determined. Reprinted in answer to Benjamin Hoadly's *Thoughts of an honest tory*. The text has not been collated, and may be abridged.
LG,AdU,WcC,*WgP*; CSmH,IU(2).

W65 [—] [variant title:] A true history of the honest whigs. A poem.
    This may be another impression.
MB(2),*MH*,OCU.

[—] The dissenting hypocrite, 1704. *See* W97.

W66 [—] Durgen. Or, a plain satyr upon a pompous satyrist... Amicably inscrib'd, by the author, to those...gentlemen misrepresented in a late invec-

Ward, E. Durgen

tive poem, call'd, the Dunciad. *London, printed for T. Warner*, 1729 [1728]. (*MChr* 12 Dec)
8°: A–H⁴; *i–viii*, *1–56*.
> *Troyer* 237. There are variant readings in the last line on p. 56. The copyright formed part of lot 16 of the trade sale of John Wood, 15 June 1742; it was purchased by Gosling and re-sold in lot 15 of his sale, 5 Oct 1742 to A. Ward (copies of the catalogues at O-JJ).

'From sultry regions, in the road to hell'
Acknowledged by Ward in the postscript to *Apollo's maggot*, 1729. A satire on Pope.
L(12274.h.2/6),LVA-D,O,*BP*;   CLU-C,CtY,IU, MH,TxU+.

W67 [—] [reissue] The cudgel, or, a crab-tree lecture. To the author of the Dunciad. By Hercules Vinegar, esq; *London, 'printed for the author, and sold at his house, the Crab-tree, in Vinegar-yard, near Drury-lane'*, 1742. (*DP* 26 July)
8°: *A¹* B⁴(±B1) C–H⁴; *1–2* 3–4 3–56.
> Cancel title A1 and B1 are conjugate; the other preliminaries are suppressed. The imprint is apparently fictitious. This issue has been erroneously attributed to Henry Fielding on account of the pseudonym he used in *The Champion*.

L(11643.b.4),BaP; CtY,IU,MH(2),TxU.

W68 [—] A fair shell, but a rotten kernel: or, a bitter nut for a factious monkey. *London printed, and sold by B. Bragge*, 1705. (20 Oct?)
4°: A–H⁴; *1–8* 9–63 *64 blk*.
> *Troyer* 279. Advertised in *DC* 22 Oct 1705 as published 'Saturday last', 20 Oct. The printer is identified as 'Mr. Meeres' by Robert Clare, one of Harley's informers; see H. L. Snyder in *The library* V. 22 (1967) 337. The reliability of these identifications is uncertain.

'Bless'd was Utopia, when her soveraign's care'
Attributed to Ward by Aitken in *DNB*; listed as doubtful by Troyer who had failed to locate a copy. It was advertised as Ward's in *PB* 25 July 1717 and subsequent advertisements as late as 1723; also in *Hudibras redivivus*, [1722.] A tory satire.
L(11631.e.58),O,C,DA(lacks A1),DT(uncut); CLU-C,CSmH,CtY,*DFo*,IU(lacks A2–4, A1 supplied).

[—] The fidler's fling at roguery, 1730–. *See* F117.

W69 [—] The field-spy: or, the walking observator. A poem. By the author of the London-spy. *London printed, and sold by J. Woodward, & J. Morphew*, 1714 [1713]. (*PB* 20 Oct)
8°: A–E⁴; *i–ii*, *1–38*.
> *Troyer* 238. Entered to Woodward in *SR* 19 Oct 1713; deposit copies at L,E,EU,AdU.

'When wordly cares my pensive soul opprest'
Ward's authorship is clear from the reference to the *London-spy*; his works in four volumes are advertised in the imprint.

Ward, E. The field-spy

L(992.h.6/1; Crach.1.Tab.4.b.4/1),O(2),E,DG, AdU+;   CLU-C,CU,CtY,MH.

W70 [—] The forgiving husband, and adulterous wife: or, a seasonable present to the unhappy pair in Fenchurch-street... By the author of the London-spy. *London, printed by H. Meers; sold by J. Woodward, & J. Morphew*, 1709. (*Observator* 12 Feb)
8°: G⁸; *79–80* 81–94. *80 advt*.
> *Troyer* 239, not seen. Printed to add to *Marriage dialogues*, 1709; reissued with that as *Matrimony unmask'd*, 1710 (M115). Drop-head title on p. 81, 'Dialogue the seventh.' A catchword on p. 94 'Dialogue' suggests an intention of continuing the series.

'My dear Lavinia, once the only joy'
CT.

W71 [—] — *London printed, and sold by H. Hills*, [1709.]
8°: A(6 ll); *1–2* 3–12.
> Although signed on A2, A3, A4, the collation is actually A² B⁴. A piracy; reissued with other remaindered Hills poems in *A collection of the best English poetry*, 1717 (*Case* 294). A Bury St. Edmunds edition is advertised in Ward's *Honesty in distress*, [172–?] (W89).

L(1075.m.14, stitched, uncut; 164.k.57; C.124.b.7/46),LVA-F,O,E,LdU-B+;   CSmH, CtY,ICN,MH(2),TxU(2)+.

W72 [—] Fortune's bounty: or, an everlasting purse for the greatest cuckold in the kingdom. *London printed, and are to be sold by B. Bragge*, [1705.] (12 July?)
4°: A–C⁴ D²; *1–2* 3–28.
> *Troyer* 239. Advertised in *DC* 13 July as published 'yesterday'.

'In wicked times, when wanton wives'
Reprinted in Ward's *Third volume*, 1706.
L(11626.e.26, lacks C3),O,DT(2),*DrU*; CSmH.

W73 [—] — [col] [*London?*] *Printed in the year* 1705.
4°: A²; *1–4*, 2 columns.
> Drop-head title only. A piracy.

InU.

W74 [—] The galloper: or, needs must when the devil drives. A poem. *London, printed for John Morphew*, 1710. (*SR* 8 Aug)
4°: A² B–D⁴; *i–iv*, *1–23* *24 blk*.
> Entered to Abel Roper in *SR*; deposit copies at LSC,E,EU,SaU. Advertised in *PB* 10 Aug as 'by the author of the Quaker's vision'.

'What a bustle we make about high-church and low-church?'
I believe Ward to have been the author of *Aminadab, or the quaker's vision*, 1710; it was frequently advertised in his works, and *Matrimony unmask'd*, 1714, is said to be 'By the author of Aminidab'. On the evidence of the advertisement in *PB* above, this should be equally attributed to Ward, though confirmation is desirable. It is a satire on the whigs.

Ward, E. The galloper

L(11631.bb.19; 11631.f.9),LLP,O,E(2),SaU+; DFo,IU,InU,MH,OCU(Luttrell, 8 Aug, uncut).

W75 [—] A Good-Friday ramble: or, the sermon hunters. *London printed, and sold [by Samuel Bunchley] at the publishing-office in Bearbinder ⟨Lane, 1707?⟩*
½⁰: 1–2, 1 column.
'On Good-Friday last (which the learned have told'
Ward's *Humours of a coffee-house*, 1707, was published with this imprint (Samuel Bunchley seems to have been there for this year only); the style and subject are so typical of Ward that the attribution seems tolerably certain.
CSmH(imprint cropt).

W76 [—] Helter skelter: or, the devil upon two sticks: a comedy, as it is spitefully acted between high-church and low-church, in most taverns about London. By the author of, All men mad, &c. *London, printed in the year 1704.* (FP 7 Nov)
4⁰: A–C⁴ D²; 1–2 3–27 28. 28 advt.
Troyer 239.
'Here drawer, bring us t'other quart'
Reprinted in Ward's *Third volume*, 1706. Compare *Sacheverell, and Hoadly*, 1710, which has the same first line and may be a reprint.
L(11631.bb.53),O,E,MR; CLU-C,CtY(uncut), DLC,InU,MH(uncut).

W77 [—] — In a comical dialogue between high-church and low-church, relating to the times... [col] *London: printed [1704/05.]*
4⁰: A²; 1–4, 2 columns.
Drop-head title only. A piracy; 'Price one penny' after imprint.
ICU.

W78 [—] — *[Edinburgh, 1704/05.]*
2⁰: A²; 1–4, 2 columns.
Drop-head title only. Both copies are bound in collections of Edinburgh printing.
L(12350.m.18/2),E.

W79 [—] — *[Reading? 1737?]*
4⁰: A²; 1–4, 2 columns.
Probably a later reprint. *The Reading mercury: or, the London spy* was issuing Ward's works as a supplement in 1736–37 (see R. M. Wiles, *Serial publication* (1957) 63); the copy at LSA has a ms. note 'G. Burton Cath: Hall 1737'. Compare *All men mad*, [1737?], W44.
LG,LSA; TxU.

W80 [—] The history of the grand rebellion; containing, the most remarkable transactions from the beginning of the reign of King Charles I... Digested into verse. Illustrated with about a hundred heads... In three volumes... To which is added an appendix of several valuable tracts... *London, printed for J. Morphew, 1713.*
8⁰: 3 vol; A⁶ a⁸ B–O⁸; 2π² P–2F⁸ 2G²; 2G⁴ 2H–3G⁸ (+ plates); [2] i–x [16], 1–207 208 blk; [2] 207–451 452 blk; [8] 453–628 679–862 863–868; 869–870 blk. a7ᵛ err; a8 advt.

Ward, E. The history of the...rebellion

Troyer 240. The first two volumes were advertised in *DC* 2 Feb, with the third said to be in the press.
'When popish priestcraft in a cruel reign'
Reissued with Ward's name in 1715; *Troyer* refers (apparently in error) to a dedicatory epistle to John Cass signed by him. A versification of Edward Hyde, earl of Clarendon's *History*.
L(1078.m.7–9, lacks a4–7; G.11515, 6,–3G8),O (lacks a1–4),C,LdU+; CSmH,CtY,IU,MH,NN.

W81 — [reissue] By Edward Ward, gent. *London, printed for John Nicholson; sold by J. Morphew, 1715.*
Cancel title seen in vol. 1 only, but *Troyer* records a vol. 3 title as *The Lord Clarendon's History of the grand rebellion compleated*, with imprint 'London, printed for John Nicholson, 1715'. The copy described by him is apparently complete, but that at L only contains the plates and appendix of documents.
CLU-C.

[—] Hob turn'd courtier. A satyr, 1703. *See* H263.

W82 [—] Honesty in distress, but reliev'd by no party. A tragedy, as it is basely acted by her majesty's subjects upon god's stage the world. *London printed, and are to be sold by B. Bragge, 1705.* (DC 9 Jan)
4⁰: A² B–D⁴; i–iv, 1–24.
Troyer 242. Since it is written in dramatic form, copies that have been classified with plays have doubtless escaped me.
'From anch'rites lonely caves, from hermites cells'
Reprinted in Ward's *Third volume*, 1706.
L(11778.c.15),O,MR; CLU-C(uncut),CSmH, CtY.

W83 [—] — A tragedy: as it is acted on the stage, &c... *London printed, and sold by J. Morphew, 1708.* (16 Jan, Luttrell)
8⁰: A⁴ B–D⁴ E²; 1–4 5–34 35–36.
Listed in *WL* Dec 1707 with this imprint; advertised in *DC* 24 Jan 1708 and subsequently as sold by J. Morphew and T. Norris. The date of publication may well be Jan 1708; *WL* was frequently published late in the following month.
L(163.k.57, Luttrell),DT; CLU-C.

W84 [—] — *London printed, and sold by Hen. Hills, 1708.*
8⁰: A⁸; 1 2–15 16.
'Price 1d.' on title; *Troyer* records copies with 'Price 4d.' but this is probably a misreading of a dirty or damaged figure. A piracy.
EU; DFo,DLC,MH,TxU.

W85 [—] — *London printed, and sold by M. Edwards in Fetter-lane, 1708.*
8⁰: A⁸; 1 2–16.
A piracy.
CSmH,ICN,IU.

W86 [—] — *London, printed for, and sold by H. Hills, 1710.*
8⁰: A⁸; 1 2–15 16.

Ward, E. Honesty in distress

> A piracy. The price 1d. has been altered to 2d. in ms. in the copy at MH.
> L(11775.c.57; 12330.f.26/2),O,E,AdU; CLU-C, CtY,*DFo,ICN*,MH(ms. corrections).

W87 [—] — Enter'd persuant to the late act of parliament. *London printed, and sold by Mary Edwards*, 1710. (June?)
8°: *A*⁴ B–D⁴; *1–4* 5–32.
> *Honesty in distress* was entered to Will. Heathcott in *SR* 7 June 1710; the relation of that entry to this edition remains obscure.
> L(1508/724); CLU-C.

W88 [—] — To which is added, a satyr against the corrupt use of money. *Bury St. Edmunds, Suffolk. Printed by Thomas Baily & William Thompson*, [1721?]
8°: *A*⁴ B–C⁴ D²; *1–2* 3–28. 2 advt.
> Signature B2 under 'weave them'. The books advertised include a sermon of 20 April 1721. The 'satyr' is a reprint of *Bribery and simony*, 1703. A prose version became a popular chap-book; there is a copy at O, and a Dublin edition is advertised in *The ladies choice* (L10).
> L(11775.c.58).

W89 [—] [another edition]
> Signature B2 under 'Exub'rance'. Other poems by Ward advertised on p. 2; this is probably the later edition.
> CLU-C.

W90 [—] Hudibras redivivus: or, a burlesque poem on the times. Part the first. *London printed, and sold by B. Bragge*, 1705. (*DC* 29 Aug)
4°: *A*² B–D⁴; *i–iv*, *1–24*.
> The first volume was published in 12 parts, issued at monthly intervals; parts 2–12 have collation A–C⁴ D²; *1–2* 3–28. Their dates are as follows (Luttrell's dates are not given when they coincide with the advertisements):
> 2 1705. (*DC* 3 Oct 'tomorrow'; *DC* 4 Oct 'yesterday'; 6 Oct, Luttrell)
> 3 1705. (*DC* 8 Nov)
> 4 1706 [1705]. (*DC* 7 Dec)
> 5 1706. (*DC* 16 Jan)
> 6 1706. (6 Feb, Luttrell)
> 7 1706. (*DC* 12 March)
> 8 1706. (27 April, Luttrell)
> 9 1706. (22 May, Luttrell)
> 10 1706. (13 June, Luttrell; *DC* 15 June)
> 11 1706. (25 June, Luttrell; *DC* 26 June)
> 12 1707 [1706]. (*DC* 27 July for 'next Tuesday' [30]; 30 July, Luttrell)
> Only complete sets of first editions are listed below.
> 'In pious times, when soul-physicians'
> Ward's authorship is clear not only from numerous references, but from his being taken into custody (Hearne, 7 Feb 1706), arrested again 13 June 1706, and sentenced to the pillory 14 Nov 1706.

Ward, E. Hudibras redivivus

> L(G.18957, Luttrell); CSmH,CtY,MH,*NNC*, TxU+.

W91 [—] Hudibras redivivus: or, a burlesque poem on the various humours of town and country. Part the first. Vol. II. *London printed, and sold by Benj. Bragge*, 1707 [1706]. (13 Aug, Luttrell)
4°: 2A⁴–2C⁴ 2D²; *1–2* 3–28.
> The second volume was published in twelve parts, issued at monthly intervals; each was paged as *1–2* 3–28, but with successive signatures. Their dates and collation are as follows:
> 2 2E–2G⁴ 2H² 1707 [1706]. (*DC* 29 Aug; 31 Aug, Luttrell)
> 3 2I–2L⁴ 2M² 1707 [1706]. (14 Sept, Luttrell; *DC* 20 Sept)
> 4 2N–2P⁴ 2Q² 1707 [1706]. (21 Sept, Luttrell; *DC* 5 Oct 'on Thursday [3] was published')
> 5 2R–2T⁴ 2U² 1707 [1706]. (25 Oct, Luttrell)
> 6 2X–2Z⁴ 3A² 1707 [1706]. (23 Dec, Luttrell)
> 7 3B–3D⁴ 3E² 1707. (*DC* 24 Feb 'just publish'd')
> 8 3F–3H⁴ 3I² 1707. (13 March, Luttrell; *DC* 15 March)
> 9 3K–3M⁴ 3N² 1707. (10 April, Luttrell)
> 10 3O–3Q⁴ 3R² 1707. (9 May, Luttrell)
> 11 3S–3U⁴ 3X² 1707. (*DC* 29 May)
> 12 3Y–4A⁴ 4B² 1707. (*DC* 13 June)
> L(G.18957, Luttrell); CSmH,CtY,MH,*NNC*, TxU+.

W92 [—] — or, a burlesque poem on the times. Part 1. Vol. I. The second edition. To which is added, an apology, and some other improvements throughout the whole. *London printed, and sold by the booksellers of London & Westminster*, 1708 [1707]. (*DC* 2 Aug)
4°: A–C⁴ D²; *1–6* 7–28.
> A note below the imprint offers the complete work at 12s. or by single parts. This title formed the title of the complete work; the part titles were sometimes cancelled when the work was bound. Parts 2 & 3 were also reprinted as 'the second edition' with date 1709; in the absence of titles they can be identified by having 13 and 19 lines respectively on p. 28. Parts 4–6 were also reprinted without titles and with 24 pages; part 4 was advertised in *DC* 11 Nov 1710 for 'next week'. Copies listed here have all 24 parts; the number reprinted is noted.
> L(11631.e.31, pt. 1–6),LG(2, 1 pt. 1, 1 pt. 1–3), EU(pt. 1–3),AdU(pt. 1–6),LdU-B(pt. 1–3)+; CtY(pt. 1–6),ICU(pt. 1–3),MH(2, 1 pt. 1, 1 pt. 1–6),*NNC,OCU*.

W93 [—] — In two volumes. The third edition. To which is added an apology, and some other improvements... *London, printed for George Sawbridge*, 1715 [1714]. (*PB* 16 Nov)

Ward, E. Hudibras redivivus

A reissue with cancel title and added frontispiece; the part titles are cancelled. It includes the reprint editions of pt. 1–6.

C,E.

W94 —— In twenty four parts. With an apology... The fourth edition. To which is now added. The rambling fuddle-caps... *London, printed for John Wilford,* [1722.] (June?)

Another reissue with cancel title (advertisement on verso) and with the addition of *The rambling fuddle-caps,* 1706; all part titles cancelled. Advertised in *DJ* 30 June 1722 as 'newly publish'd' at 10s.; in *DJ* 9 Oct 1722 the price is 7s. 6d.; in the copy at MH the price 'ten shillings' on title is altered in ms. to 'six shillings'. It was advertised again by Wilford in *GSJ* July 1734 at 12s. The copyright formed part of lot 8 of the trade sale of Wilford, 24 Feb 1736 (cat. at O-JJ), sold to Rivington.

L(1609/699); MH.

W95 —— *London, printed for John Wren, near Great Turnstile, High Holborn,* [175–?]

Yet another reissue, dated by *Troyer* as [1710] and by MH as [1725?], but Wren appears to have been active in the 1750s.

MH.

W96 [—] The Hudribrastick [!] brewer: or, a preposterous union between malt and meter. A satyr upon the suppos'd author of the Republican procession; or, the tumultuous cavalcade. *London, printed for John Morphew,* 1714. (21 Sept?)

8⁰: A–D⁴ E²; *1–3* 4–36.

Bond 36; *Troyer* 244. The Luttrell copy (at L) has the date 21 Sept, but not in Luttrell's usual hand; listed in MC Sept. Reissued in Ward's *Fifth volume,* 1717.

'I sing the bard, whose merry strains'

Apparently a satire by Ward on himself.

L(11631.bbb.19; 164.k.45, Luttrell),LG(part uncut),O,EN; CLU-C,CtY,ICN,ICU,NjP+.

W97 [—] In imitation of Hudibras. The dissenting hypocrite, or occasional conformist; with reflections on two of the ring-leaders, &c. Viz... *London, printed in the year* 1704 [1703]. (*TC* Mich 1703)

8⁰: A⁴ a⁴ B–L⁴; *i–xvi,* 1–78 *79–80 blk.* xvi err.

Bond 9; *Troyer* 236. In some copies (e.g. InU) C1 is signed 'B'.

'When scribes to reason said good night'

First attributed to Ward by Wilson, *Memoirs of the life and times of Defoe,* 1830. No external evidence has been presented, but it has been generally accepted on internal style; the attribution should be received with caution, plausible though it is.

*LL,*O(lacks A1,–L4); CLU-C,CtY(–L4),ICN (–L4),InU(–L4),MH.

W98 [—] The insinuating bawd: and the repenting harlot... *London printed, and are sold by most booksellers,* [1701/–.]

Ward, E. The insinuating bawd

2⁰: *A²* B–D²; *i–iv,* 1–12.

Troyer 244–5. What is apparently the first edition (copies at L,O,MH,NNC) has imprint reading '...booksellers' and advertisements on the verso of the title; it was clearly published in 1700, and was listed in *TC* Mich. This edition, with A1ᵛ blank, may be the one that was advertised in *Observator* 29 Aug 1702, but it was probably intended to complete sets of Ward's *A collection of the writings,* 1701 (mainly in prose, and not listed above).

'Happy was I, before I knew to sin'

CtY.

W99 [—] —— To which is added, Love. An ode to a lady. By a marry'd gentleman. [*London?* 173–/4–?]

8⁰: B–C⁴ D⁴; *i–ii* iii–vii *viii blk,* 9–24.

Dated [1755?] by L catalogue, but the typography suggests a rather earlier date. The added poem 'Love' is on pp. 23–24.

L(1346.b.42).

W100 [—] A journey to h–ll: or, a visit paid to the d----l. A poem. Part III. By the author of the first and second parts. *London printed, and are to be sold by the booksellers of London & Westminster,* 1705 [1704]. (*DC* 2 Nov)

2⁰: A–D²; *1–2* 3–16.

Troyer 245. Parts I & II were published in 1700, dated by Luttrell 12 Feb and 7 May.

'After some short retirements from the bench'

Reprinted in Ward's *Third volume,* 1706.

CSmH(Luttrell, 2 Nov),MH.

W101 [—] The libertine's choice: or, the mistaken happiness of the fool in fashion. *London, printed in the year* 1704. (*Observator* 5 Feb)

4⁰: A–C⁴ D²; *1–2* 3–27 *28 blk.*

Troyer 246. Advertised in *Observator* as sold by B. Bragg. An edition of 1707 is referred to by C. E. Jones in *N&Q* 6 April 1946.

'Let holy guides prevail on tim'rous fools'

Reprinted in Ward's *Third volume,* 1706.

L(163.1.47, Luttrell, 5 Feb); CLU-C,MH.

W102 [—] —— *London printed, and sold by H. Hills,* 1709.

8⁰: A⁸; *1–2* 3–15 *16.* 16 advt.

A piracy. Reissued with other remaindered Hills poems in *A collection of the best English poetry,* 1717 (*Case* 294).

L(1077.c.46; C.124.b.7/25),LG,O(3),LdU-B; CSmH,CtY,DFo,ICN,MH+.

W103 —— The life and notable adventures of that renown'd knight, Don Quixote de la Mancha. Merrily translated into hudibrastick verse. Part I. For the month of October. To be continued till the whole history is compleated. *London, printed for T. Norris, & A. Bettesworth; sold by J. Woodward,* [1710.] (*SR* 23 Nov)

8⁰: *A⁴* B–K⁴; *i–vi,* 1–73 *74 blk.* A1 frt.

Volume 1 was published in monthly parts as listed here. The structure of A is uncertain; the frontispiece may have been a later addition.

Ward, E. The life...of Don Quixote

Entered in *SR* to Norris, Bettesworth and Woodward; deposit copies at O,C,E.
'In jealous regions where the heat'
O(−A1),C(−A1),E; CLU-C(−A1).

W104 — — Part II. For the month of November...
London, printed for T. Norris, & A. Bettesworth; sold by J. Woodward, [1710.]
8°: L–U⁴; *75–76* 77–152. 76 advt.
L1 is the title, cancelled when copies were bound. In some copies (e.g. O) L2 is signed 'L'. No entry in *SR* has been traced, though the copies recorded are all deposit.
O,C,E.

W105 — — Part II [ink correction 'III']. For the month of December... *London, printed for T. Norris, & A. Bettesworth; sold by J. Woodward, B. Lintott, & W. Taylor,* [1711.] (*SR* 16 Jan).
8°: π1 X–2G⁴ π2 (Z1 as 'Y'); [2] 153–232 [2] (161–176 as '159–174', 193–200 as '137–144'). π1ᵛ, π2 advt.
The two leaves of π have been seen to be conjugate and formed a disposable wrapper. Entered in *SR* by Bettesworth and Woodward to the five booksellers named in imprint, in fifths.
O,C,E(−π2).

W106 — — Part IV. For the month of January... *London printed for T. Norris, & A. Bettesworth; sold by J. Woodward, B. Lintott, & W. Taylor,* [1711.] (*SR* 26 Feb)
8°: π1 2H–2R⁴ π2; [2] 233–312 [2]. π1ᵛ, π2 advt.
Entered in *SR* by Woodward to Norris, Bettesworth and Woodward.
O,C,E(−π2).

W107 — — 'Part V. For the month of February...' [*London*, 1711.] (*PM* 24 March)
8°: 2S–3D⁴; 313–392.
No separate copy seen; presumably a wrapper with title was added. Advertised in *PM* 24 March 1711 as 'Part IV [!]' and with the same imprint as the preceding.

W108 — — 'Part VI. For the month of March.' [*London*, 1711.] (*PM* 5 May as 'yesterday')
8°: πA⁸ 3E–3O⁴ 3P²; *i–xvi*, 393–456 '456–471' '72–75' [= 476] (441–448 as '437–444').
No separate copy seen; the collation is uncertain; a table of contents and two advertisement leaves found at the end of the collected volume were probably issued with this part, as well as a part title. Advertised as 'Printed for T. Norris, & A. Bettesworth; sold by J. Woodward, & J. Harding'.

W109 — — Vol. I. *London, printed for T. Norris, & A. Bbttesworth* [!], *J. Harding; sold by J. Woodward,* 1711.
8°: (frt=A1+) πA⁸ A4 B–K⁴ L⁴(−L1) M–3O⁴ 3P² (+3 ll); [*18*] 1–73 *74 blk* 77–456 '456–471' '72–75' [=476] [+6].
The collation given here is for the completed volume, which varies according to the binder's

whim. The frontispiece and first leaf of text, A1 & A4, are from the separate issue of pt. 1. The three leaves at end are a leaf of contents, a leaf advertising *Nuptial dialogues*, and a leaf advertising books printed for T. Norris; the contents leaf is frequently bound after πA8, while the conjugate advertisement leaves are often omitted.
L(1078.h.8; Cerv.249; G.18961),O(2),E,LdU-B; *CU*,CtY(−frt),KU,MH,*OCU*+.

W110 — — Vol. II. *London, printed for T. Norris, & A. Bettesworth, J. Harding, J. Woodward, E. Curl, & R. Gosling,* 1712 [1711]. (*PB* 20 Nov)
8°: A⁴(−A1) B–Hh⁸; *i–vi*, 1–477 *478–480*. 478–480 advt.
No part issue of volume 2 has been seen. A half-share of the copyright of vols. 1 & 2, together with 'About 20 copies of this author, the parts and shares doubtful' formed lot 6 of the trade sale of Timothy Hatchett, 26 April 1737 (cat. at O-JJ), sold to J. & T. King for £1.12s.
L(1078.h.8; Cerv.249; G.18962),O,E,LdU-B; *CU*,ICU,KU,MH(lacks A3),*OCU*.

W111 — — Vol. III. Part the 1ˢᵗ. By Edward Ward. To be continued till the whole is compleated. With covers to keep it clean in order to be bound up. *London, printed for Eben. Tracey; sold by J. Morphew, & J. Woodward,* 1714 [1713]. (*SR* 14 Nov)
8°: π² A–E⁴; *i–iv*, 1–40. π1ᵛ, π2 advt.
π2 was probably intended to follow the text to form a wrapper, as in some parts of vol. I. Entered in *SR* to Tracey and Woodward, 'a moiety' each; deposit copies at O,E,EU. Advertised in *PB* 26 Nov.
'Scarce had the curate made an end'
O,E,EU.

W112 [—] [dh] The Lord Whiglove's elegy: to which is added a pious epitaph upon the late bishop of Addlebury. [col] *London, printed in the year* 1715.
8°: A⁴; 1–8.
Troyer 253. Reissued in Ward's *Fifth volume*, 1717. An edition of 1714 is referred to by C. E. Jones in *N&Q* 6 April 1946.
'Farewell, old bully of these impious times'
'Here Scotus lyes, of late as wise'
Ward's authorship is established by its reissue in his works. Satires on Thomas, marquis of Wharton and Bishop Gilbert Burnet. Possibly 'the Bishop of Ailsbury's [!] Elegy, written either by Mr. Cary or some other hand' referred to in Pope's letter to Parnell, 18 March 1715.
L(1490.d.46),O; MH.

W113 [—] Marriage-dialogues: or, a poetical peep into the state of matrimony... With moral reflexions on every dialogue. Together with, The wars of the elements... To which are added [13 poems] ... By the author of the London-spy. [*London*]

Ward, E. Marriage-dialogues

Sold by J. Woodward, & J. Morphew, 1709 [1708]. (*Observator* 22 Sept)
8⁰: A–K⁴ (B2 as 'A2'), ²A⁴(–A1, +ᵗA²) B–I⁴ K²; *1–8* 9–80, *i–ii*, *1–2* 3–76. A1ᵛ advt.
　　Troyer 253. The second part is a reissue of *The wars of the elements,* 1708, complete with title.
'Sometimes you tell me I am pert and proud'
　　Subsequently incorporated into Ward's *Nuptial dialogues,* 1710.
L(1077.k.45); MH,*MnU.*

W113·5 [—] [dh] Marriage-dialogues... With moral reflexions on every dialogue. [col] *London, printed in the year* 1708.
4⁰: A⁴; *1–8,* 2 columns.
　　A piracy. 3 columns on pp. 7–8.
TxU.

W114 [—] Marriage-dialogues: (to be publish'd weekly) or, a poetical peep into the state of matrimony. With moral reflections on every dialogue. Numb. 1[–5]. *Edinburgh, printed by James Watson, and sold at his shop,* 1709.
4⁰: A⁴; *1–2* 3–8.
　　Five numbers have been seen; no. 2–5 have drop-head title 'Marriage-dialogues: (publish'd weekly)...' with the numeration implied by the subheading 'Dialogue the second [etc]'. They all collate A⁴; *1–8.*
L(11631.aaa.56/17, no. 3),EP(no. 1–5, uncut).

W115 [—] [*idem*] Matrimony unmask'd, in seaven dialogues... With moral reflexions on every dialogue. By the author of the London-spy. *London, printed for A. Bettesworth; sold by J. Morphew,* 1710. (15 July, Luttrell)
8⁰: A⁴(±A1.4) B⁴(±B1) C–K⁴, ²G⁸(–G1); *1–8* 9–94.
　　A reissue of *Marriage dialogues,* W113, with the addition of *The forgiving husband,* 1709, less title. Advertised in *PM* 28 Nov.
S. H. Ward, Letchworth; *TxU*(Luttrell).

W116 [—] Matrimony unmask'd; or the comforts and discomforts of marriage display'd. By the author of Aminidab... *London, printed by H. Meere, for J. Woodward, T. Norris, & A. Bettesworth,* 1714. (*MC* June)
12⁰: (frt+) A⁴ B–D¹² E²; *i–iv,* 1–80.
CLU-C,KU(stitched, uncut).

W117 [—] The merry travellers: or, a trip upon ten-toes, from Moorfields to Bromley. An humorous poem. Intended as the Wandering spy. Part I. By the author of the Cavalcade. *London, printed by W. Downing, and sold by the booksellers of London & Westminster,* 1721. *Also to be had at the Bacchus-tavern in Moorfields.*
8⁰: (frt+) A–B⁴ ˣC² C–K⁴ L² (E2 as 'F2'); *i–ii,* 1–17 14–81 *82 blk.*
　　Troyer 256.
'In that dull time of recreation'
　　'The author of the Cavalcade' refers to *The republican procession,* 1714.
LdU-B; CtY,MH(–frt),TxU.

Ward, E. The merry travellers

W118 [—] [*idem*] The wandering spy: or, the merry travellers... The second edition. Part I. By the author of the Cavalcade. *London, printed for Sam. Briscoe; also at the Sun against John's Coffee-house in Swithen's Alley, in Cornhill,* 1723.
8⁰: A–G⁴; *1–2* 3–55 *56.* 56 advt.
　　'The second part' is advertised in the imprint.
CLU-C.

W119 [—] — The third edition. Part I. By the author of the Cavalcade. *London, printed for Sam. Briscoe; also at the Sun against John's Coffee-house in Swithen's Alley, in Cornhill,* 1723.
8⁰: A–G⁴; *1–2* 3–55 *56.* 56 advt.
　　Apparently a press-variant title.
DLC.

W120 [—] The merry travellers: or, a trip upon ten-toes... Intended as the Wandering spy. Part I. By the author of the Cavalcade. The second edition. *London, printed for the author; sold by A. Bettesworth,* 1724.
8⁰: A–K⁴; *i–ii,* 1–78.
　　Reissued in Ward's *Sixth volume,* 1724.
L(11659.aaa.89/1),LG,O; CLU-C,CSmH,ICN, MH(lacks A1).

W121 [—] — *London, printed for Sam. Briscoe, & E. Pollard at the Queen's-Head Inn on St. Margaret's Hill, Southwark,* 1726.
8⁰: A⁴(±A1) B–G⁴; *1–2* 3–55 *56.* 56 advt.
　　A reissue of Briscoe's edition of 1723 (W118–19); the words 'The end of part one' have been erased from p. 55 in the copy seen. No statement of edition or part on title.
LVA-D.

W122 [—] [part 2] The wand'ring spy: or, the merry travellers. Part II. To which is added, The contending candidates... By the author of the Cavalcade. *London printed, and are to be sold by A. Bettesworth & J. Batley, J. Hook, S. Briscoe, M. Hotham, and at the Bacchus Tavern in Finsbury, against the middle of Middle-Moorfields,* 1722. (*PB* 30 Aug)
8⁰: A–I⁴, ²A–E⁴; *i–ii,* 1–3 6–71 *72,* 1–40.
　　Troyer 256. No separate title to *The contending candidates.* An advertisement on p. 72 disclaims the authorship of *Whipping Tom;* one on p. 40 of part 2 recommends Ward's public house. Reissued in Ward's *Sixth volume,* 1724.
'The sun now chasing from our sight'
'When some by fraud and some by stealth'
L(11659.aaa.89/2; 1078.h.12/2; 992.h.6/2, lacks pt. 2); CLU-C,CtY,TxU.

[—] The modern courtier, [1741.] *See* W46·2.

W123 [—] More priestcraft: being a new whip for an old whore, or, a protestant scourge for a popish jacket. A poem. *London printed, and are to be sold by B. Bragge,* 1705. (*PM* 29 Nov)
4⁰: A–C⁴ D²; *1–2* 3–27 *28 blk.* 27 err.
'In slavish times when Peter rul'd the roast'

Ward, E. More priestcraft

> Reprinted in Ward's *Third volume*, 1706, as 'The protestant scourge'.
> L(164.m.40, Luttrell, 29 Nov),DT.

W124 [—] — [*London?* 1705?]
4°: *A*²; *1–4*, 2 columns.
> Drop-head title only. A piracy.
> OCU.

W125 [—] The mourning prophet: or, drooping faction reviv'd, by the death of Queen Anne. A poem. By E.W. *London, printed for J. Woodward*, 1714. (*SR* 13 Sept)
4°: A–D²; *1–2* 3–16.
> *Troyer* 259. Listed in *MC* Sept. Deposit copies at L,E.
> 'Early one Sunday, when Aurora's dawn'
> Ward's authorship is attested by his initials, publisher, and subject-matter.
> L(993.f.51/1),E(uncut),GU(uncut),*MR*; ICN, MH,TxU(2, 1 uncut).

[—] A net for the d---l: or, the town display'd, 1705. *See* N37.

W126 — News from Madrid. The Spanish beauty: or, the tragicomical revenge. Interspers'd with the humours of a merry tinker, in conveying off the bodies of three murder'd fryars. A poem. *London, printed for the author; sold by A. Bettesworth*, 1726.
8°: A–G⁴ (A2 as 'B2'); *1–2* 3–55 *56 blk*.
> *Troyer* 259.
> 'At Madrid, where the kings of Spain'
> O,BaP,LdU-B; MH,TxU.

W127 [—] The northern cuckold: or, the gardenhouse intrigue. *London, printed in the year* 1721.
8°: A–D⁴; *i–ii*, 1–28 *29–30 blk*.
> *Troyer* 259. Reissued in Ward's *Sixth volume*, 1724.
> 'Far north from London may be seen'
> L(164.k.56),O; CLU-C(−D4),CSmH(−D4), IU(−D4),MH,MiU.

W128 [—] — With an addition to the Delights of the bottle...With the South-Sea song...as likewise the Spitle-Fields ballad on the calico's. By the author of the Cavalcade. *London, printed for Sam. Briscoe*, 1721. (*PB* 13 April)
8°: π¹ A–D⁴, ²A–G⁴, H⁴(−H4); *i–iv*, 1–28 *29–30 blk*, *1–2* 3–54 *55–56*, 1–6.
> A reissue with the addition of *The delights of the bottle*, 1721 (the third edition in copies seen) and with the ballad in H⁴. The L copy has the frontispiece to *The delights* placed before the general title; the copy at E has none.
> *Ballad*: 'In the ages of old,/When of silver and gold'
> L(11631.e.72/3),E.

W129 — Nuptial dialogues and debates: or, an useful prospect of the felicities and discomforts of a marry'd life... In two volumes. By the author of the London-spy. *London, printed by H. Meere, for T. Norris, & A. Bettesworth; sold by J. Woodward*, 1710. (*SR* 16 Dec)

Ward, E. Nuptial dialogues

8°: 2 vol; (frt+) A–Cc⁸; ²A² B–Ee⁸; *i–xvi*, 1–352 349–396; *i–iv*, 1–430 *431–432*. Cc8ᵛ, ²Ee8 advt.
> *Troyer* 254. The pagination of both volumes is irregular. Entered in *SR* to Norris, Bettesworth & Woodward; deposit copies at O,E,EU,AdU. Possibly only volume 1 was deposited, for vol. 2 was advertised in *PB* 11 Jan 1711 and the deposit copy at E has vol. 1 only.
> 'Here, wife, let's see my slippers, cap, and gown'
> Dedication signed. This work incorporates the poems in *Marriage dialogues*, 1709.
> L(11643.c.54; 1078.h.7/2, vol. 1 only; G.18959, 60),O(−frt),E(2, 1−²Ee8, 1 vol. 1 only),AdU, LdU-B(−frt)+; CLU-C,CtY(lacks A2–3),ICN, MH,TxU+.

W130 —— *London, printed for T. Norris, A. Bettesworth, & F. Fayrham*, 1723. (*DP* 4 Feb)
12°: 2 vol; A¹⁰ B–N¹² O²; ²A² B–N¹² O⁴ (+ plates); *i–xx*, 1–292; *i–iv*, 1–296.
> An edition of 1724 is recorded by *CBEL* and one of 1729 by C. E. Jones in *N&Q* 6 April 1946; they are probably ghosts. Four eighth-shares of the copyright, 'out of print', formed lots 14–17 of the trade sale of Timothy Hatchett, 26 April 1737 (cat. at O-JJ); they were purchased at five guineas each by Hodges, Ware, Comyns, and J. Osborn.
> L(11632.df.26),LG(vol. 1 only),E(vol. 2 only), *BP*; CLU-C(vol. 2 only),CSmH,CtY(vol. 1 only), DLC,OCU.

W131 —— The third edition, adorn'd with cuts. *London, printed for Mess. Bettesworth, & Hitch, Ware, & Osborn, Hodges, Baily, & Cummins*, 1737. (*GM,LM* Sept)
12°: 2 vol; A¹²(−A6.7) B–N¹² O²[= A6.7]; ²A² B–N¹² O⁴ (+ plates); *i–xx*, *1* 2–292; *i–iv*, *1* 2–296.
> An eighth-share of the copyright formed lot 24 of the trade sale of Edmund Comyns, 20 June 1758, and three sixth-shares were lots 179*–81* in the sale of Arthur Bettesworth, 18 Jan 1759, sold for a guinea each to Hitch, Davey, & Wren. Reprinted in 1759.
> L(11631.aa.40, 41),LG(vol. 2 only),O; DLC(vol. 2 only).

Single dialogues

W132 [—] A dialogue between a surly husband, and a condescending wife. *Dublin, printed by Gwyn Needham*, [172–?]
½°: 2 sides, 2 columns.
> A reprint of vol. 1, dialogue 1.
> 'Here, wife, let's see my slippers, cap, and gown'
> L(C.121.g.8/142).

W133 [—] A dialogue between a depending courtier, who would have sacrific'd the chastity of his wife to a certain great man, in hopes of preferment, and his virtuous lady, who was avers'd to a compliance. To which is added, moral reflections thereon. *Dublin, printed by and for George Gowan*, 1735.
8°: A⁸; *1–3* 4–16.

Ward, E. Nuptial dialogues

A reprint of vol. 1, dialogue 12.
'My dear, what makes my lord his visits pay'
L(11601.aa.48/1).

W134 [—] A nuptial dialogue, between a pert young lady, and an old fumbling libertine. To which is added, moral reflections thereon. *Dublin, printed by and for George Gowan*, 1735.
12°: A⁶; *1–2* 3–12.
A reprint of vol. 1, dialogue 3.
'Tis to your credit much, my dear, to praise'
DN.

W135 [—] A nuptial dialogue, between a young libertine, and an old canting rich widow, whom he had marry'd for her money. To which is added, moral reflections thereon. *Dublin, printed by and for George Gowan*, 1735.
12°: A⁶; *1–3* 4–12.
A reprint of vol. 1, dialogue 27.
'Prithee, old granny, hold thy jarring tongue'
L(1078.i.24/5).

———————

W136 [—] The parish gutt'lers: or, the humours of a select vestry. *London, printed in the year* 1722. (*DP* 30 March)
8°: A–H⁴; *1–2* 3–64.
Bond 70; *Troyer* 260. Advertised in *DP* as printed for Sam. Briscoe; see the following issue. Also reissued in Ward's *Sixth volume*, 1724.
'As nations oft by cunning knaves'
Troyer argues for Ward's authorship on internal evidence, not knowing of its reissue in his works. On the dispute in the parish of St. Botolph's; the relevant vestry book is at LG.
L(1480.aaa.14),O(2, 1 impft),LdU-B; CSmH,CtY, ICU,MH(2),TxU +.

W137 [—] — or, the humours of a vestry. A merry poem. *London, printed for Sam. Briscoe; also at the Sun against John's Coffee-House in Swithin's-Alley, Cornhill*, 1722.
8°: A⁴(±A1) B–H⁴; *1–2* 3–64.
A reissue, with cancel title.
CtY.

W138 [—] — or, the humours of a select vestry. *Dublin, printed by Pressick Rider & Thomas Harbin, for P. Dugan*, 1725.
12°: A–E⁶ F⁴; *1–2* 3–66 *67–68 blk.*
DA; IU.

W139 [—] — or, the humours of a vestry. A merry poem. *London, printed for John King*, 1732. (*GSJ* 23 Oct)
8°: A–H⁴; *1–2* 3–64.
LG; CLU-C,ICN.

W140 [—] [reissue] Truth in rhyme, | To suit the time, | or, the parish guttlers. A merry poem. As it is acting every day with great applause near the Poors house, Gray's-Inn-lane... *London, printed in the year of guttling* 1732.

Ward, E. The parish gutt'lers

8°: A⁴(±A1) B–H⁴; *1–2* 3–64.
L(11643.g.13),LG,O,BaP(stabbed, uncut, traces of marbled wrapper).

[—] The pleasures of a single life, 1701–. *See* P488.

W141 [—] The poet's ramble after riches: with reflections upon a country corporation. Also the author's lamentation in the time of adversity. By the author of the Trip to Jamaica. The third edition. *London printed, and sold by J. How*, 1701.
2°: *A²* B–D²; *1–2* 3–16.
Troyer 261. First published in 1691. Also issued in Ward's *Collection*, 1701, which is mainly in prose, and not listed above.
'I sing of neither Hogan Mogan'
L(11632.i.8/8); CLU-C,CSmH,NNC,TxU.

W142 [—] — *London printed, and sold by J. How*, 1710.
8°: A–B⁴ C²; *1–2* 3–19 20. 2, 20 advt.
No statement of authorship on title.
O,E; CSmH,ICN,MH.

W143 [—] — *London printed, and sold by J. How*, [171–?]
8°: A–B⁴ C²; *1–2* 3–19 20. 2, 20 advt.
Apparently another issue with a different A⁴; it may be earlier than the preceding.
L(11632.aaa.65).

W144 [—] — *London printed, and sold by J. How*, [171–?]
8°: A⁸; *1–2* 3–15 16. 2, 16 advt.
A chap-book version, though still priced at 3*d.* like the preceding editions.
O-JJ.

W145 [—] — *Dublin, printed by J. Carson, for W. Smith*, 1724.
8°: A–B⁴ C⁴(–C4); *1–2* 3–21 22. 22 advt.
O,DA(lacks A1).

W146 [—] The poet's ramble after riches. A poem. By the author of the London spy. *Dublin, printed for George Golding at the Blew Anchor in High Street*, [173–?]
8°: *A⁸*; *1–2* 3–16.
DT; MH.

W147 [—] [another issue] *Dublin, printed, at the Rein Deer in Montrath Street, by C. Hicks*, [173–?]
8°: *A⁸*; *1–2* 3–16.
Apparently a variant imprint; listed in DG catalogue as [1737?].
L(11631.a.63/12),DA(lacks A4.5),DG(uncut); CtY,DFo.

W148 [—] Pulpit-war: or, Dr. S——ll, the high church trumpet, and Mr. H——ly, the low-church drum, engaged. By way of dialogue between the fiery dragon, and aspiring grasshopper. *London printed, and sold by J. Baker*, 1710. (*WL* Jan)
8°: A⁸ (A3 as 'A4'); *1–2* 3–16.
Also advertised by Henry Hills among his chap-book poems.
'Tell me, proud insect, since thou can'st not fly'
A reprint of Ward's *Ecclesia et factio*, 1698, applied to Sacheverell and Hoadly.
L(474.b.29/23),O,C,E,DT +; MH,TxU.

Ward, E. The quack-vintners

W149 [—] The quack-vintners: or, a satyr against bad wine. With directions where to have good. Inscrib'd to B—ks and H—r. [*London*] *Sold by the booksellers of London & Westminster*, 1712. (7 Feb, Luttrell)
8°: A⁴ B–C⁴; *1–4* 5–24. A1 hft.
  Troyer 262. Entered in *SR* to John Morphew, 9 Feb; deposit copies at E,EU,AdU.
  'Let B—ks and H—r vend their cloudy wines'
  In favour of the wines of Truby, Witham, Tash, and other wine-merchants, against the wines of Brooke and Hellier praised in *Brooks and Hellier, a poem*, 1712. Replied to by *Brooke and Hellier, a satyr*, 1712, which refers to Ward writing for the vintners. Ward's authorship seems very probable, but not finally confirmed.
L(1078.m.6/10; 164.k.67, Luttrell),E,EU,AdU (uncut); CtY,DFo,MH,TxU(uncut).

W150 [—] The rambling fuddle-caps: or, a tavern struggle for a kiss. By the author of Hudibras redivivus. *London printed, and are to be sold by B. Bragge*, 1706. (14 March?)
4°: A–C⁴ D²; *1–2* 3–27 *28 blk*.
  Troyer 262. Advertised in *DC* 12 March for 'Thursday' [14 March]. Reissued in the 'fourth edition' of *Hudibras redivivus*, [1722.]
  'Tho' fuddl'd o'er night, the next morning we found'
CLU-C.

W151 [—] — [col] *London, printed by E.B. near Ludgate*, [1706?]
4°: A²; *1–4*, 2 columns.
  Drop-head title only. A copy in the Turnbull Library, N.Z., has the first N in London in the imprint turned on its side; see W. J. Cameron in *N&Q* (1953) 284f.
DG.

W152 [—] — By the author of Hudibrass redivivus. *London printed, and sold by H. Hills*, 1709.
8°: A⁸; *1–2* 3–16.
  Signature A2 under 'm w'.
L(11601.dd.17; 11633.bbb.56),CT; ICU,MH, TxU.

W153 [—] [another edition]
  Signature A2 under 'h m'. Reissued with other remaindered Hills poems in *A collection of the best English poetry*, 1717 (*Case* 294).
L(C.124.b.7/24),O(2),LdU-B; CtY,IU,MH.

W154 [—] The religious turn-coat, or, the triming observator. [*Dublin*, 1711.]
½°: 1 side, 2 columns.
  Originally printed in 1693; see *Wing* R912–4. On the other side, *A touch to the wheedlers*, 1711.
  'I lov'd no king in fourty one'
  Crum I324. A revised version of the 1693 edition was printed in Ward's *Third volume* (1706) 375. This version substitutes a final stanza applying it to the Sacheverell affair. Another version adapted to Scottish affairs

Ward, E. The religious turn-coat

is entered as *The turncoat* [Edinburgh, 1712/14]. A fore-runner of *The vicar of Bray*.
C.

W155 [—] The republican procession; or, the tumultuous cavalcade. A merry poem. [*London*] *Printed in the year* 1714.
8°: A–E⁴ F²; *1–2* 3–44.
  Bond 38; Troyer 263. The order of the first two editions has not been determined; some copies (DrU,CtY) have mixed sheets. In this edition page 44 is numbered.
  'In times of libelling and squabbling'
  The 'second impression' was reissued in Ward's *Fifth volume*, 1717. An attack on Marlborough and his followers. Answered by *Merit and gratitude conjoin'd*, 1715.
L(11643.b.10),O,DN,DrU,LdU-B; ICU,MH, *NN*,NjP.

W156 [—] — [*London*] *Printed in the year* 1714.
8°: A–E⁴ F²; *1–2* 3–43 44.
  In part another impression; sheets B, C, and the outer forme of D are reset. In this edition page 44 is unnumbered.
E; CLU-C,CSmH,CtY,MH.

W157 [—] — The second impression, with additional characters. [*London*] *Printed in the year* 1714.
8°: A–E⁴ F²; *1–3* 4–43 *44 blk*.
  Although called an impression, this is apparently a new edition, though standing type may have been used in it. Reissued in Ward's *Fifth volume*, 1717.
L(164.m.74),O,AdU,LdU-B; CLU-C,CtY,IU, KU,MH.

W158 [—] — The second impression, with additional characters. [*London?*] *Printed in the year* 1714.
8°: A⁴ B–E⁴ F²; *1–3* 4–43 *44 blk*.
  Apparently a piracy; the ornaments on pp. 1, 43 are imitations of those in the preceding. It is printed on inferior paper.
L(11631.b.40),O(lacks F²),C; CtY(impft),DFo (uncut),MB,TxU.

W159 [—] — The second impression, with additional characters. [*London*] *Printed for W. Wilkins, near Fleetstreet. This small volume contains the whole original.* [1714.]
12°: A⁴ B² C⁴ D²; *1–2* 3–24.
  A piracy.
LG.

W160 [—] — The second impression, with additional characters. [*Dublin?*] *Printed in the year* 1714.
12°: A–D⁴ E²; *1–3* 4–36.
  The copy at L is in a volume of Irish tracts though the copies at E, AdU might suggest a Scottish origin. The following related edition appears to be of Dublin origin.
L(1963),E,AdU; ICN,KU.

W161 [—] — The third imression [!], with additional characters. [*Dublin?*] *Printed in the year* 1714.

Ward, E. The republican procession

8°: A–D⁴ E²; *1–3* 4–35 *36 blk.*
DT.

W162 [—] — To which is added, an answer, by the same author; being a satyr against himself. *London printed, and are to be sold by the booksellers of London & Westminster,* 1727.
8°: A–F⁴; *1–2* 3–48.
> No answer is found in any copy seen; one would expect it to be *The hudibrastick brewer.* Reissued with *The wars of the elements,* 1730. An edition of 1744 is referred to by C. E. Jones in *N&Q* 6 April 1946.
L(11601.d.20/5); MH,NjP,TxU.

W163 [—] The revels of the gods: or, a ramble thro' the heavens. By the author of the Trip to Jamaica. *London printed, and sold by J. How,* 1701. (14 Oct, Luttrell)
2°: A² B–D²; *1–2* 3–16. 2 advt.
> Troyer 264. Listed in *WL* Oct. A Bury St. Edmunds edition was advertised in *Honesty in distress,* W89; possibly the same edition advertised in *The curiosity: or, gentlemen and ladies repository* (Lynn, 1740; copy at O).
'When punch, that inspires us with wit and with gladness'
> Reprinted in Ward's *Second volume,* 1703.
AN; CSmH,DFo,ICN(Luttrell),MH,TxU(2)+.

W164 [—] 'The riddle, or a paradoxical character of a hairy monster often found in Holland. To which is added, a merry musical entertainment to be perform'd before a grave assembly of cornuted citizens, consisting of the following songs... [*London*] *Sold by B. Bragg.* Price 6*d*.' (*DC* 6 July 1706)
> Listed by *Morgan* K148 as 'The Dutch riddle: or a character of a h—y monster, 1708.'
'When full 'tis round, when empty long'
> Advertised by Bragg in some parts of Ward's *Hudibras redivivus,* 1706–07; specifically advertised as by Ward in *PB* 25 July 1717 and subsequently, and in the [1722] edition of *Hudibras redivivus.* Confirmation of his authorship is desirable. A genital riddle.

W165 [—] A riddle: or, a paradoxical character of an hairy monster, often found under Holland. *London, printed for A. Moore; sold at most of the pamphlet-shops in London & Westminster,* [172–?]
2°: A–B² C¹; *1–2* 3–10.
> Reprinted in *Polly Peachum on fire,* 1728. What is probably a provincial edition, perhaps originally published at Bury St. Edmunds, is advertised in *The curiosity: or, gentlemen and ladies repository* (Lynn, 1740; copy at O).
O.

W166 [—] — The second edition. *London, printed for A. Moore; sold at most of the pamphlet-shops in London & Westminster,* [172–?]
2°: A² B²; *1–2* 3–8.
L(P.C.31.1.24).

Ward, E. A riddle

W167 [—] — [*Dublin,* 172–.]
½°: 1 side, 3 columns.
> Answered by *A riddle, in answer to the Hairy monster,* [172–.]
MH.

W168 [—] — To which is added, Little Merlin's cave... The third edition. *London, printed for T. Read,* 1737.
2°: A¹ B–C²; *1–3* 4–10.
> The additional poem is presumably not by Ward.
Little Merlin's cave: 'As blue-ey'd Kate, sweet-blooming buxom maid'
CSmH.

W169 [—] [*idem*] Little Merlin's cave. As it was lately discover'd, by a gentleman's gardener, in maidenhead thicket. To which is added, a riddle: or, a paradoxical character of an hairy monster often found under Holland... The fourth edition. *London, printed for T. Read,* 1737.
2°: A¹ B–C²; *1–3* 4–10.
> With an engraved erotic landscape on p. 4. The riddle was subsequently printed in *The harlot's progress,* 1740.
L(P.C.31.1.23),WcC.

W170 [—] St. Paul's church; or, the protestant ambulators. A burlesque poem. *London, printed for John Morphew,* 1716. (14 July, Luttrell).
8°: A–D⁴; *1–2* 3–32.
> Bond 49; Troyer 264. 'Price 6*d*.' on title. Listed in *MC* Aug. Reissued in Ward's *Fifth volume,* 1717.
'Amidst a city much decay'd'
L(164.k.26, Luttrell),LG; CLU-C(uncut),CtY.

W171 [—] [reimpression]
8°: A–F⁴; *1–2* 3–47 *48 blk.*
> A reimpression of the preceding with the type heavily leaded and reimposed. Clearly the equivalent of a fine-paper issue; 'Price 1*s*.' on title.
L(G.18423/1),C.

W172 [—] A satyr against wine. With a poem in praise of small beer. Written by a gentleman in a fever, occasion'd by hard drinking. *London printed, and sold by B. Bragg,* 1705 [1704]. (*FP* 21 Nov)
2°: A–D²; *1–2* 3–16.
> Troyer 264.
'Bacchus be damn'd, and all his drunken brood'
> Reprinted in Ward's *Third volume,* 1706.
CLU-C(Luttrell, 21 Nov),MH,OCU.

W173 [—] — *London, printed: and sold by M. Gunne, in ⟨Dublin,* 1706.⟩
8°: ⟨A–B⁴⟩; *1–2* 3–16. 16 advt.
> Advertisement on p. 16 for [Richard Daniel] *The British warrior,* which is dated 1706 and in its turn advertises this as 'lately published'.
DN(cropt).

W174 [—] — The second edition. *Printed at St. Edmund's-Bury in Suffolk; and Stamford, Lincolnshire; by W. Thompson, and T. Baily,* [172–?]

Ward, E. A satyr against wine

    4°: A–B⁴; *1–2* 3–16.
        Advertised in Ward's *Honesty in distress*,
        [172–?] (W89).
    DLC.

W175 [—] A seasonable sketch of an Oxford reformation.
Written originally in Latin by John Allibond, D.D.
And now reprinted, with an English version...
London printed, and sold by John Morphew, 1717.
(*PB* 23 May)
    8°: *A*⁴ B–D⁴; [*5*] 1–13 (twice) [*1 blk*].
        'Price 6*d*.' on title. *Troyer* 265. Separate Latin
        and English titles on A2ᵛ, A3ʳ, 'Rustica
        Academiæ Oxoniensis...' and 'A rustical
        description...' Reissued in Ward's *Fifth
        volume,* 1717.
    'Whilst out of town, strange news alarm'd'
    L(T.902/1, title mutilated),O(2),CT,DrU,LdU-B;
    CtY,ICN.

W176 [—] [fine paper]
        'Price 12*d*.' on title.
    CCC,MH.

W177 [—] A South-Sea ballad: or, merry remarks upon
Exchange-alley bubbles. To a new tune, call'd, The
grand elixir: or, the philosopher's stone discover'd.
[*London?* 1720.]
    ½°: 1 side, 2 columns.
        Troyer 268, quoting *The weekly packet*, 22 Oct.
        Two rough woodcuts at head. Previously
        printed in *The delights of the bottle*, 1720 (1
        Sept).
    'In London stands a famous pile'
    L(1876.f.1/88, imprint cropt).

W178 [—] — [*Edinburgh,* 1720.]
    ½°: 1 side, 2 columns.
        No type-flowers between columns; no wood-
        cuts at head.
    E; MH-BA.

W179 [—] — [1720.]
    ¼°: 1 side, 2 columns.
        Row of type flowers between columns;
        possibly a Dublin edition.
    L(1876.f.1/89); NN.

W180 [—] — *Dublin, re-printed* 1720.
    ½°: 1 side, 2 columns.
        No reference to the tune in the title; first verse
        set to woodcut music; row of type-flowers
        between columns.
    CSmH,MH.

W181 [—] — *Dublin, re-printed* 1720.
    ½°: 1 side, 2 columns.
        Apparently composed from the preceding
        edition; the first verse is set out as though to
        music; but with type-flowers in its place. On
        the other side, [Thomas Durfey] *The hue and
        cry after the South-Sea,* [1720]. Also reprinted
        at Cork, 1721, with Swift's *The run upon the
        bankers.*
    TxU.

Ward, E. A South-Sea ballad

W182 [—] [*idem*] A ⟨lo⟩oking-glass for England: or, the
⟨ ⟩ess of stock-jobbing explain'd. W⟨ritt⟩en
by a true-born Englishman, and recommended to
the serious consideration of his loving countrymen.
Bristol, reprinted by S. Farley, 1720.
    ½°: 1 side, 2 columns.
    MH-BA(mutilated).

    [—] The tavern hunter; or, a drunken ramble from
    the Crown to the Devil, 1702. *See* T96.

    [—] The thanksgiving. A poem. By a late officer
    in the army, 1705. *See* T123.

W183 [—] The tippling philosophers. [*London?* 17––.]
slip: 1 side, 1 column.
        Rough woodcut at head, geometrical figure at
        foot. From its appearance an early printing,
        possibly c. 1710. Six stanzas.
    'Diogenes surly and proud'
        The original state of Ward's text, which was
        set by Richard Leveridge (early engraved
        editions with music at L,CtY) and printed in
        Ward's *Wars of the elements,* 1708.
    L(1876.e.20/27).

W184 [—] The tipling philosophers, set by Mr. Leveridge, and sung at the theatre in Dublin. *Dublin,
printed by Tho. Hume,* 1720.
    ½°: 2 sides, 1 column.
        At the foot of the recto 'This addition in
        Dublin by subscription', followed by eight
        more stanzas. It was probably this version that
        provoked *The ancient philosophers vindicated
        against tipling* (Dublin, 1721). Reprinted with
        [Anthony Aston] *The pleasures of the Bath,*
        1721.
    CtY,TxU.

W185 [—] The tipling philosophers. A lyrick poem.
To which is subjoin'd, a short abstract of their lives
and most memorable actions. *London printed, and
sold by J. Woodward,* 1710. (*SR* 16 Aug)
    8°: A–F⁴; *i–viii,* 1–40. A4 advt.
        Troyer 269. Entered in *SR* to Woodward;
        deposit copies at O,C,E,EU,AdU. In some
        copies (CLU-C,ICN,IU) the date is changed
        in ms. to 1719.
    'Wise Thales the father of all'
        Originally published in six stanzas, as above,
        in *The wars of the elements,* 1708.
    L(1078.m.6/11),O,C,E,LdU-B+; CLU-C(uncut),
    CtY,ICN,MH,TxU(−A4)+.

W186 [—] [reissue] Wine and wisdom: or, the tipling
philosophers. A lyrick poem. To which are subjoin'd, the most remarkable memoirs of the following ancients... *London printed, and sold by J.
Woodward,* 1710.
    8°: A⁴(±A1) B–F⁴; *i–viii,* 1–40. A4 advt.
        Some copies (CSmH,IU,TxU) preserve the
        original title as well as the cancel. In some
        copies (O,CSmH,IU,MH,TxU) the date is
        changed in ms. to 1719, as in the preceding.

Ward, E. The tipling philosophers

> L(11631.b.50),O,DT; CSmH,CtY,IU,MH,
> TxU+.

W187 [—] — *Edinburgh, printed in the year* 1721.
8º: *A*⁴ B–C⁴ D²; *i–iv, 1–23 24 blk.*
> Without the notes.
> E; CLU-C.

W188 — To the right honourable Humphrey Parsons lord mayor of the city of London. A congratulary poem upon his lordship's accession to the chair. *London, printed by J. W. and publish'd by John Wilford,* 1730. (*MChr* Oct)
4º: A–D⁴; *1–7 8–32.*
> *Troyer* 269.
'Since great Apollo, with his harp in hand'
CLU-C,DFo,MH,TxU.

W189 [—] The tower of Babel: an anti-heroic poem. Humbly dedicated to the B----p of B----r. *London, printed for J. Morphew,* 1718 [1717]. (*DC* 29 Oct)
8º: A–D⁴; *1–2 3–32.*
'As, when a fire with dreadful blaze'
> Early ms. note in an O copy, 'Written by Mr. Edward Ward'. Confirmation is desirable. A satire on Benjamin Hoadly, bishop of Bangor.
> L(164.1.69),O(2, 1 lacks A1),C,EN,*LdU-B*; CLU-C(uncut),*CtY*,DFo,MH,OCU.

[—] 'A trip to Germany: or, the poet turn'd carbineer. Being a relation of several comical intrigues and diverting adventures: with an impartial character of the country. By the author of, the Step to the Bath. [*London*] Sold by B. Bragg.' (*FP* '21' [for 22] May 1705)
> It is clear that the author intended is Ward, and the work is listed by *Troyer* 270. Until a copy is traced, it is impossible to say whether or not it is in verse.

[—] A trip to the devil's summer house: or, a journey to Mayfair, 1704. *See* T490.

[—] A true history of the honest whigs, 1710. *See* W64.

[—] Truth in rhyme, 1732. *See* W140.

W190 [—] The vanity of upstarts: or, an honest enquiry into ignoble greatness. An ode. [*London*] *Printed in the year* 1709. *and sold by the booksellers.* (*DC* 19 April)
8º: A–B⁴; *1–2 3–15 16 blk.*
> *Troyer* 271, recording its reissue in Ward's *Fifth volume*, 1717; it is not in any copy I have examined.
'What is it to be rich and great?'
> Advertised as by Ward in *Hudibras redivivus*, [1722.]
> L(161.b.12, Luttrell, 20 April),O,CT; *CU.*

W191 [—] — *London, printed in the year* 1709. *and sold by the booksellers.*
8º: A⁴; *1–2 3–8.*

Ward, E. The vanity of upstarts

> Apparently a piracy.
> *MR-C*; MH.

W192 [—] — To which is prefix'd an epistle to a noble lord. *London, printed for J. Roberts,* 1721.
8º: πA⁴ A⁴(–A1) B⁴; *1–3 4–8, 3–15 16 blk.*
> A reissue of the first edition of 1709, with new preliminaries; the dedicatory verses are dated 29 Sept 1720. Listed in *DJ* 17 March 1721 with other works 'just publish'd'.
> CSmH,CtY,MH(Luttrell, April).

W193 [—] Vulgus britannicus: or, the British Hudibrass. [Part 1] *London, printed for James Woodward, & John Morphew,* 1710. (*SR* 26 April)
8º: *A*² B–G⁴ H²; *i–iv, 1–51 52.*
> Entered to Samuel Briscoe in *SR* 26 April 'in six parts'; deposit copies at O,C,E,EU,AdU; only part 1 was deposited. The separate parts listed here are those which have their form as first issued, even though they may have been bound together. Advertised in *DC* 29 April as 'just publish'd'.
'In spiteful times when humane folly'
> Later titles attribute the work to 'the author of the London spy'.
> L(11631.d.28; 1078.m.6/3; G.18958/1),O(3),C, E,DT+; CLU-C(uncut),CtY,IU,TxU.

W194 [—] — Part the second. *London, printed for James Woodward, & John Morphew,* 1710. (*DC* 11 May)
8º: π² I–M⁴; *i–iv, 53–84.*
> According to a ms. note by F. F. Madan, there are two states of p. 77, one with 12 lines, one with 14; only the latter has been observed.
> L(11631.d.28; G.18958),LdU-B; CLU-C(uncut), CtY,IU,TxU.

W195 [—] — Part the third. *London, printed for James Woodward, & John Morphew,* 1710. (*PB* 6 June)
8º: π² N–Q⁴; *i–iv, 85–116. 116 err.*
> L(11631.d.28; G.18958),LdU-B; CLU-C(uncut), CtY,*TxU.*

W196 [—] The fourth part of Vulgus britannicus: or, the British Hudibras... Written by the author of the London spy. *London printed, and sold by James Woodward, & John Morphew,* 1710. (July?)
8º: π² R–U⁴; *i–iv, 117–147 148.* π1 frt.
> L(11631.d.28; G.18958),LdU-B; CtY,IU,*TxU.*

W197 [—] The fifth and last part of Vulgus britannicus... Written by the author of the London spy. *London printed, and sold by James Woodward, & John Morphew,* 1710. (*PB* 5 Aug)
8º: π² X–2A⁴; *i–iv, 149–180.* π1 frt.
> L(11631.d.28; G.18958),LdU-B; CtY,*TxU.*

W198 [—] Vulgus britannicus: or, the British Hudibras. In fifteen cantos. The five parts compleat in one volume. Containing the secret history of the late London mob... The second edition, adorn'd with cuts... *London, printed for Sam. Briscoe; sold by James Woodward, & John Morphew,* 1710. (*EvP* 19 Aug)

Ward, E. Vulgus britannicus

A reissue in one volume. Copies vary slightly in their construction, but apparently new conjugate frontispieces and titles were issued for parts 1–3. The contents leaves to parts 2 & 3 are often cancelled in error, and the extent to which other leaves are cancelled varies.

O,C,BaP; CLU-C,CSmH,CtY,ICU,MH+.

W199 [—] — The third edition, adorn'd with cuts... *London, printed for Sam. Briscoe; sold by James Woodward, & John Morphew, 1711 [1710].* (PB 23 Nov)
8°: (frt+) A–H⁴ K–2A⁴ (+4 plates); *i–iv, 1–4* 5–180.
A–H⁴ K⁴ are a new edition; the remainder is a reissue without the part titles.
L(1960),LG,AdU,*DrU*; CLU-C,CtY,*NN*,MiU.

W200 [—] A walk to Islington: with a description of New Tunbridge-Wells, and Sadler's Musick-house. By the author of the Poet's ramble after riches. The second edition. *London, printed in the year 1701.*
2°: *A² B–C²; 1–2* 3–12.
Troyer 272. First published in 1699.
'In holiday-time, when the ladies of London'
L(11632.i.8/9); CLU-C,CSmH.

[—] The wandering spy, 1722, 1723. *See* W118, W122.

[—] A warning to lovers... By the author of the London spye, 1709. *See* W241.

W201 [—] — The wars of the elements: or, a description of a sea storm. To which are added [13 poems]... By the author of the London-spy. *London printed, and publish'd by John Morphew, 1708.*
8°: ᵖA² A⁴(–A1) B–I⁴ K²; *i–ii, 1–2* 3–76.
Troyer 272. Title apparently cancelled to insert dedication. Reissued with *Marriage dialogues,* 1709.
'When by the help of canvas wings I'd flown'
MH,*MnU*.

W202 [—] — [col] *London, printed in the year 1709.*
4°: A–B²; *1–8,* 2 columns.
Drop-head title only. A piracy. There are three columns on p. 8.
CtY.

W203 — — To which are added, the Contemplative angler, and the Republican procession, &c. All originally written, and now reviv'd by Edward Ward. *London printed, and are to be sold by the booksellers of London & Westminster, 1730.*
8°: A–D⁴, ²A⁴(–A1) B–F⁴; *1–2* 3–31 *32 blk,* 3–48.
'The contemplative angler' is on pp. 25–31; *The republican procession* is a reissue of the edition of 1727, without its title.
Angler: 'How beauteous does the azure skies appear!'
LG,*CQ*; CtY,DFo,MH.

[—] Wedlock a paradice: or, a defence of woman's liberty against man's tyranny, 1701. *See* W267.

Ward, E. The Welsh-monster

[—] The Welsh-monster: or, the rise and downfal of... Innuendo Scribble, [1708.] *See* W282.

[—] Wine and wisdom, 1710–. *See* W186.

Ward, Henry. The works of Mr. Henry Ward, comedian. Consisting of dramatick pieces, poems, prologues... The third edition, with additions. *London, printed for the author, by T. Gardner, 1746.*
8°: pp. 128.   L; CtY,MH.
Perhaps 'The dramatic works', listed in *GM, LM* Feb 1746 as sold by M. Cooper.

[Ward, James.] A new miscellany of poems and translations. Never before printed. By the author of the Smock race at Finglas. *Dublin, printed by Thomas Humes, for George Grierson, 1716.*
12°: pp. 34.   MH.
The smock race, included here, was previously published with Gay's *The fan,* Dublin, 1714.

[—] [another issue] The smock race, at Finglas: with some other poems and translations. By the same hand. *Dublin, printed by Thomas Humes, for George Grierson, 1716.*
O.
With a different (and possibly later) title.

W204 **[Ward, John.]** An address humbly inscribed to his grace, the Duke of Devonshire, lord lieutenant of Ireland... By the author of Happiness. *Dublin, printed by S. Powell, for William Smith, 1737.*
2°: *A² B–E²; 1–3* 4–20.
'While you, my lord, from Britain's coasts retire'
Ms. attribution to Ward in the CSmH copy.
L(11633.h.24),OW; CSmH,CtY.

W205 — Happiness: a poem. *London, printed for J. Wilford, 1737.* (*LM* March; *GM* April)
8°: *A⁴ B–G⁴; i–viii, 1–47 48.* A1 hft; 48 advt.
'To warm the mind by virtue's brightest fires'
Dedication signed.
L(11631.d.58,–A1); ICN,ICU(–A1),TxHR, *TxU*.

W206 — — *Dublin, printed by R. Reilly, for Edward Exshaw, 1739.*
12°: A–D⁴ᐟ²; *1–5* 6–24. 24 advt.
DA,DN; CtY.

W207 **Ward, Thomas.** Englands reformation from the time of King Henry the VIIIth to the end of Oates's plot. *Printed at Hambourgh, 1710.*
4°: π² A⁴ B⁴(±B3) C–R⁴, ²A–I⁴ χ² K–O⁴, ³A–G⁴, ⁴A–O⁴ (A2 as 'B2'); *i–iv, 1–136, 1–72* (73)–(76) 73–112, 1–56, 1–110 *111–112 blk.*
B3 is apparently uncancelled in copies at CSmH,TxU. Most copies add a leaf of errata, bound either before A1 or at the end. Reissued in 1731 (W211).
'When old King Harry youthful grew'
L(840.l.1,–err, ⁴O4),O(2,–⁴O4); CLU-C, CSmH(–err),CtY,MH(lacks π², –⁴O4),TxU.

Ward, T. England's reformation

W208 — — A poem in four cantos. *London, printed for John Baker*, 1715. (*MC* April)
12⁰: 2 vol; π² A⁴ B–O¹², ²*A*¹ B–I¹² K⁶ L(3 ll); *i–xii*, 1–312, *i–ii*, 1–209 *210 blk.*

> Vol. 2 has imprint, 'London, printed in the year 1715'. Listed in *Straus, Curll* under 28 July 1715 as 'advertised in Curll's lists'.

L(11631.b.45, 46),O,E,LdU-B; CLU-C,ICN, *MB*,NN.

W209 — — With large marginal notes, according to the original. *London, printed for W.B. [William Bray]; sold by Thomas Bickerton*, 1716. (*SR* 11 Jan)
8⁰: a² b⁴ B–Cc⁸ Dd²; *i–xii*, 1–402 *403–404.* Dd2 advt.

> Title in red and black. b⁴ contains the editor's preface which is absent from the deposit copies (O,EU,SaU) among others; it may have been a later addition. Dd2 refers to the addition of John Bramhall's *The consecration and succession of protestant bishops justified* which was entered with it in *SR* and is frequently bound with it; in the deposit copy at O, Dd2 appears to be the title to Bramhall.

L(79.c.18, lacks Dd2),O(lacks b⁴, Dd2),EU(lacks b⁴, Dd2),DrU,LdU-B+; CLU-C(lacks b⁴, Dd2), CtY(lacks b⁴, Dd2).

W210 — — *London printed, and sold by E. More*, 1719.
12⁰: 2 vol; *A*² B–O¹², ²*A*¹ B–S⁶; *i–iv*, 1–312, *i–ii*, 1–204.

> A trade sale containing shares of Curll's copyrights, [c. 1721] (cat. at O-JJ) has as lot 18 'Ward's England's Reformation, 2 vols. 12⁰. one 6th, being 332 in 2000, going to the press', sold to Mears for £2. 2s.

L(11607.b.25, lacks ²B–C⁶),O(lacks ²A1),LdU-B, *MR*; CLU(vol. 2 only),CtY,DFo,IU(vol. 1, with vol. 2 of 1715),MH(vol. 1 only)+.

W211 — — *London, printed in the year of our lord* 1731.
4⁰: πA–B⁴ D², A–R⁴, ²A–I⁴ χ² K–O⁴, ³A–G⁴, ⁴A–O⁴; *1–2* 3–20, 1–136, 1–72 (73)–(76) 73–112, 1–56, 1–110 *111–112 blk.*

> A reissue of the edition of 1710 with a life of the author and textual notes on the poem. The copy seen has the original leaf of errata added.

LdU-B.

W212 — — Adorn'd with copper plates. *London, printed in the year* 1747.
8⁰: 2 vol; (frt+) A² B–Y⁸, ²*A*² B–O⁸(+plates);*i–iv*, 1–336, *i–iv*, 1–207 *208 blk.* ²A1 hft.

> Horizontal chain-lines.

L(239.d.7; G.18873,74),O,E,AdU,*LdU-B*; CLU-C,DFo,ICU,IU.

W213 [**Wardlaw, Elizabeth,** *Lady.*] Hardyknute, a fragment. *Edinburgh, printed by James Watson*, 1719.
2⁰: A–C²; *1–2* 3–12.

> Printed within borders of type flowers.
> 'Stately stept he east the wa'
> > Published as a fragment of an ancient ballad, but generally ascribed to Lady Wardlaw at the

Wardlaw, E., *Lady.* Hardyknute

> time; see Chalmers's edition of Ramsay's *Poems* (1800) I. xxxf.

L(1876.e.26/1),O,*E.*

W214 [—] [dh] Hardiknute. A fragment of an old heroick ballad. [*Edinburgh*, 1724?]
8⁰: A⁴; 1–8.

> The copy seen is bound with a collection of Ramsay's poems of c. 1724, and was probably published by him; it introduces certain variants, and omits three stanzas. Ramsay also reprinted it in *The Ever green*, 1724, in a text which was probably archaized and augmented by his own hand.

O.

W215 [—] Hardyknute: a fragment. Being the first canto of an epick poem; with general remarks, and notes. *London, printed for R. Dodsley*, 1740. (3 May)
4⁰: A–D⁴ E²; *1–2* 3–36.

> Publication date from *Straus, Dodsley*; listed in *GM, LM* May. The introduction and notes are probably by John Moncrief; see Chalmers's edition of Ramsay's *Poems* (1800) I. xxxn.

L(11630.c.4/8; 1876.e.26/2),OW,E; CtY,ICU, MH.

W216 [—] Hardyknute. A fragment of an antient Scots poem. *Glasgow, printed and sold by Robert Foulis*, 1745.
4⁰: *A*² B–G²; *1–2* 3–27 *28 blk.*

> Watermark: London arms; 'Price four-pence' on title. *Gaskell, Foulis* 69.

L(11623.c.20).

W217 [—] [fine paper]

> Watermark: royal arms; 'Price six-pence' on title. Asterisk before each signature in these fine-paper copies.

O,GM.

W218 [—] — *Glasgow, printed and sold by Robert Foulis*, 1748.
4⁰: *A*² B–G²; *1–2* 3–27 *28.* 28 advt.

> Watermark: royal arms; 'Price four-pence' on title. *Gaskell, Foulis* 121. Since both issues are on paper with the same watermark, some copies have probably been mis-assigned.

GM; DLC,*MB.*

W219 [—] [fine paper]

> Watermark: royal arms; 'Price six-pence' on title.

L(T.969/8, presentation copy from Foulis; C.117.bb.22/5),O,GM,SaU; CSmH(uncut), OCU.

W220 **Ware, Henry.** An eligiaick song. On the death of the late celebrated beauty, Mrs. Mary Wall, who died at her country-seat, the 14th inst. June, 1729 ... Tune, How hapy could I be &c. *Dublin, printed in the year* 1729.
½⁰: 1 side, 2 columns.
'Ye beaus, who all hear my sad ditty'

Ware, H. An eligiaick song

A note below, signed 'I.G.', alludes to the death of Henry Ware and quotes his epitaph on himself.

L(1890.e.5/27); CSmH,CtY.

[Waring, Elijah.] On the death of John Wagstaffe, an elegiac poem, [1736?] *See* O193.

Waring, Henry.

Nothing appears to be known of Henry Waring except his books, and since he also used the names of Henry Anderson, Henry Audley, Henry Wingar and Henry Wentworth, one cannot even be certain of his true name. Since The rule of charity, *1690, and* The dark penitent's complaint, *1712, bear the name of Waring, it may be said to appear more consistently than any other, and it has become the generally accepted form.*

Waring produced almost all his poems for presentation in the hope of reward, like Elkanah Settle but on a more modest scale; the dedication leaves have spaces for various dedicatees to be stamped or written in. The printing of his poems is primitive and often clearly provincial, but apart from one printed in Bristol in 1703, and another in Edinburgh in 1712, they bear no place of origin. The bindings are rough and unusual, frequently over scabbard (with a vertical grain) rather than pasteboard; the L copy of The court convert, *1698, is bound in sealskin and in others the leather resembles continental rather than English bindings.*

— Miscellanies: or, a variety of notion and thought. Being a small treatise of many small matters, consisting of things both moral and divine. By H.W. gent. *Printed for the author,* 1708.

4°: pp. 28. O; ICU,IU.

Prose thoughts followed by verse comment. The dedication leaf A2 has a blank at head for the insertion of dedicatees.

W221 [—] The coronation, or, England's patroness: being a small poem dedicated to her sacred majesty Queen Anne. By H.W. gent. *Printed in the year* 1702.

4°: A^4 B–D^4; *1–8* 9–32.

'If in this world, where dangers daily spring'

Preface signed 'Henry Wentworth'; the same poem as the following.

L(1973); TxU.

W222 — [*idem*] The access or permitted approach of a court penitent to the divine Astrea. By H.W. gent. *Printed* 1703.

4°: $A^4(\pm A2)$ B–C^4 D^4; *[4]* 9–36.

A2 is dedication, signed 'Henry Waring', with stamped-in addressee; the ICU copy, lacking A2, has the addressee on p. 9.

L(11631.b.47, to 'Mr. Francis Williams'); ICU(to 'Edmund Alblaster esq.', lacks A2).

W223 — [*idem*] The access to virtue: or, permitted approach of a court penitent to the divine Astrea. By H.W. gent. *Printed* 1704.

Waring, H. The coronation

4°: A–D^4; *1–5* 6–32.

The dedication leaf A2 is a cancel in the DM copy; the names of addressees are stamped in. DK(lacks A2),DM('To his grace the lord archbishop of Armagh', lacks A3); CLU-C(to 'reverend Mr. Moore').

W224 [—] The court convert: or, a sincere sorrow for sin, faithfully travers'd: expressing the dignity of a true penitent. Drawn in little, by one, whose manifold misfortunes abroad; have render'd him necessitated, to seek for shelter here; by dedicating himself, and the said small poem, to the divine Astrea. By H.A. gent. *Printed in the year* 1698.

8°: A^4 χ^1 B–D^4 (A3 as 'A2'); *1–8* [2] 9–32. A1 hft.

This edition is included here despite its date because it is apparently the first of the series. A3–4 is addressed to Princess Anne of Denmark, subsequently Queen Anne, signed 'Henry Audley'. χ^1 is an additional dedication with stamped-in addressee.

'Deluding world, which hath so long amus'd'

L(C.108.aa.21, to 'The Lady Poultney'); CLU-C (to 'Dr. Bird').

W225 [—] — *Printed for the author,* [170–?]

8°: π^2 'A2' B–D^4; [6] 9–32. π^1 hft.

'A2' is the dedication leaf, signed 'Henry Audley'; it appears with variant texts and with stamped-in addressees.

L (C.108.aa.18, dedicatee deleted), LdU-B; CLU-C (to 'Joh. Holbeach, esq.'), CSmH(to 'Mr Lawrence Renaut'),IU(to 'Samuel Pitt of Keir esq.'),MH(2, 1 to 'Sir Francis Jerningham', 1 to 'Edward Villiers, earl of Jersey').

W226 — [reissue]

The dedication leaf 'A2' is reprinted and signed 'Henry Waring'; there may be more than one setting of the type. The addressees' names are stamped in.

LDW(to 'reverend Mr. Williams'); IU(to 'Henry Lloyd esq.', $-\pi^1$).

W227 [—] — *Printed for the author,* [170–?]

8°: A(3 ll) B–D^4; [6] 9–32. A1 hft.

A3, the dedication leaf, is signed 'Henry Anderson' with the addressee inserted in ms. The order of the following editions, which all have inserted dedications signed 'Henry Anderson' with ms. addressees, has not been finally established; this has signature B under A of 'Ashes', D under o of 'account'.

O(lacks A2, 3); CLU-C (2, to 'Mrs Nales' and 'Benjamin Warren esqr.'), MH(to 'Mrs Ann Gostwick').

W228 [—] [another edition, title reads:]...dedicating himself and this small poem. By H.A. gent. *Printed for the author,* [171–?]

8°: A^1 χ^1 B–D^4; [4] 9–32.

This edition has signature B under o of 'of', D under c of 'Account'. The omission of reference to Astrea in the title suggests the

Waring, H. The court convert

possibility that these editions are after the death of Queen Anne.

L(238.e.47, to 'George Thorold esq.')

W229 [—] — *Printed for the author*, [171–?]

8°: A^2 χ^1 B–D⁴; [6] 9–32. A1 blk.

Signature B under f of 'of', D under e of 'the'.

MH(to 'William Stukeley esqr').

W230 [—] — *Printed for the author*, [171–?]

8°: A^1 χ^1 B–D⁴; *1–4* 5–28.

Signature B under f of 'of', D under e of 'the'. Note the change in pagination.

O(to 'Mr John Chancler'); ICN(to 'John Jones, esqr.'),MH(to 'Joseph Boyeck esqr.').

W231 [—] — *Printed for the author*, [171–?]

8°: A^1 χ^1 B–D⁴; *1–4* 5–28.

Signature B under As of 'Ashes', D under ou of 'Account'.

O(to 'Sr. John Marshall br.'); CLU-C(to 'Sr. William Windham, sr.'),CtY(to 'Mathew Lister esqr.').

W232 [—] — *Dublin, printed for J.C.* [*James Connor of Drogheda*] *in the year* 1727–8.

12°: A–B⁶ C⁸; *1–2* 3–39 *40. 40 advt.*

The title reverts to its mention of 'the divine Astrea'. The status of this edition is obscure; it may have been authorised by Waring. Pp. 14–24 contain elegies and hymns; C⁸, which is printed in octavo in a different type, adds 'A poem on the real presence and the rule of faith'; the advertisement on p. 40 is for James Connor of Drogheda.

Poem: 'Friend, finding some weary of more rugged prose'

DN.

W233 — The dark penitent's complaint: or a hue and cry after charity. Dedicated in particular [!] to the honourable and reputed charitable   . By H.W. gent. *Eristol* [!], *printed by W. Bonny*, 1712.

4°: A²(A1 + χ1) B–C²; [4] 3–12.

The order of these editions has not been determined. The space on the title is apparently left for insertion of the dedicatee's name. χ1 is a dedication leaf, with stamped-in addressee. The copy seen has note on title 'Wm Jones: cost: o: 2: o Dec: the 12 1712'.

'Dark in a closet all alone'

Dedication signed 'Henry Waring'.

O(to 'Esquire Iones').

W234 — [*idem*] The sights retreat a poem by H.W. gent. [171–?]

8°: A(2 ll) B⁴ C⁴(−C4); ⟨ −20⟩.

A1 is an improvised title-page, apparently hand-stamped like the dedicatee on A2. The dedication is signed 'Henry Waring'.

L(1076.g.37, to 'Dr. Sloane', pagination cropt).

W235 [—] [*idem*] Light extinguish'd. A poem intitul'd the Sight's retreat; or, the true light at last made manifest. By H.W. gent. *Printed for the author*, [171–?]

Waring, H. The dark penitent's complaint

8°: A^4 B–C⁴; *1–4* 5–24.

Dedication leaf A2 has stamped-in dedicatee. This is better printed than Waring's other poems, but it is still very provincial. Variant first line:

'Dark in my closet all alone'

Dedication signed 'Hen. Wingar', an anagram of Waring.

L(11631.d.63, no dedicatee); CLU-C(to 'Countess of Dalkyth'),CtY(to 'Lady Parker').

W236 — The divine or hypostatical union: being a small poem, upon the life and death of the blessed Jesus: beginning with the advent. By H.W. gent. *Edinburgh, printed in the year* 1707.

4°: π^1 χ^1 A–D⁴; [4] 9–39 *40 blk.*

χ1 is a dedication leaf, with stamped-in addressee.

'As when a mighty monarch, with renown'

Dedication signed 'Henry Waring'.

L(11631.b.48, to 'Mr Thomas Weims advocat').

W237 Warning. Warning; once warning. A poem. *Dublin, printed by Edward Waters*, [1713?]

4°: A⁴; *1–2* 3–7 *8 blk.*

Note on p. 7, 'N.B. This paper is to be continu'd'. The copy at DA is bound with a memorandum of 23 Jan 1713.

'Nay whigs since you're resolv'd you'll ne'er be wise'

An attack on the whigs for their lack of respect for the divine right of kings.

O,DA,DN; DFo.

W238 — A warning piece. *London, printed by J. Sowle*, 1709.

1°: 1 side, 3 columns.

Smith I. 49 also records an octavo of 1709, possibly in error.

'Awake! rouse up, shake off your lethargy'

A moral warning, calling England to repentance.

LF.

W239 — Warning to coucolds. A new ballad on the whipping-club, held at Rings-End, this present year of our lord, 1727. The tune is, Which no-body can deny, brave boys, &c. [*Dublin*, 1727.]

½°: *1–2*, 1 column.

Rough woodcut at head.

'Ye husbands, draw near, while I sing you a ditty'

L(C.121.g.8/163).

W240 — A warning to Ireland, or its deplorable condition, occasion'd by the late flood and storm which happened on the first of January, 1725–6... *Dublin, printed in the year* 1725–6.

obl 1°: 1 side, 4 columns.

Two big cuts at head.

'Who can keep silence that doth see'

DT.

W241 — A warning to lovers. Or a new way to make a man wiser than his grand-father. To which is added the widdow's answer... As also the danger of going to law. By the author of the London spye. [*London*] *Printed for J. Bagnall, near Fleet-street*, 1709.

8°: A^4; *1* 2–8.

A chap-book.

'Take (if you please) for nothing my advice'
The implied attribution to Edward Ward is almost certainly false, unless the poem is an extract from one of his larger works.

L(1076.1.22/32).

Wars. The wars of the elements, 1708–. *See* Ward, Edward.

W242 [**Warter, Thomas.**] Shrewsbury Quarry: a poem. In imitation of Mr. Pope's Windsor Forest. Inscrib'd to the rev. Mr. Leonard Hotchkis. *Salop, printed by R. Lathrop*, 1747.

4°: A–C²; *i–ii*, *1–10*.

'Salopian plains, those shady green retreats'
Ms. note in the MH copy 'E dono autoris Tho: Warter ex Æd. Ch. Ox.'

MH.

Warton, Joseph. Odes on various subjects. *London, printed for R. Dodsley; sold by M. Cooper*, 1746. (*GA* 4 Dec)

4°: pp. 47.   L,O; CtY,MH.

— — The second edition. *London, printed for R. Dodsley; sold by M. Cooper*, 1747. (*GA* 9 Jan)

4°: pp. 47.   L,O; CtY,MH.

W243 [—] The enthusiast: or, the lover of nature. A poem. *London, printed for R. Dodsley; sold by M. Cooper*, 1744. (*LEP* 8 March)

2°: A^2 B–D²; *1–4* 5–16. A1 hft.

'Ye green-rob'd dryads, oft' at dusky eve'
Printed as Warton's in *Dodsley* III.

L(11626.h.11/5),O,C(lacks A²); CSmH,DFo,IU.

W244 [—] Fashion: an epistolary satire to a friend. *London, printed for R. Dodsley; sold by T. Cooper*, 1742. (*LDP* 16 Nov)

2°: A–C²; *1–2* 3–11 *12* blk.

Rothschild 227.

'Yes, yes, my friend, disguise it as we will'
A copy belonging to H. B. Forster has a ms. attribution to Warton; it was collected as his by Chalmers. However, when it was printed in *Dodsley* III (1748) 250 it was not ascribed to Warton, and some doubt may remain.

L(1347.m.54),O(2),OA,C; CSmH,CtY,DFo, ICN,TxU(2)+.

W245 — An ode occasion'd by reading Mr. West's translation of Pindar. *London, printed for W. Owen*, 1749. (*LM* July)

2°: A^4 (A3 as 'B'); *1–2* 3–8.

'Albion rejoice! thy sons a voice divine have heard'
O(2),C,LdU-B(uncut); CtY,TxU.

[—] An ode to evening. Translated into Latin verse [from Warton's *Odes*], 1749. *See* O65.

Warton, Thomas, *the elder, 1688?–1745.* Poems on several occasions. *London, printed for R. Manby & H. S. Cox*, 1748. (*GM* March)

8°: pp. 228.   L,O; MH,NN.

[—] An excellent new ballad. To the tune of, A begging we will go, &c., [1715/20.] *See* E558.

[—] Worcester dumb-bells; a ballad, [1710.] *See* W561.

Warton, Thomas, *the younger, 1728–1790.* Poems. A new edition, with additions. *London, printed for T. Becket*, 1777. (14 March)

8°: pp. iii, 83.   L,O.

No previous collected edition had appeared; the additions are those poems not previously published. Dates from *Public Advertiser*.

— — A new edition. *London, printed for T. Becket*, 1777. (12 July)

8°: pp. iii, 83.   O.

With textual changes found in the later editions of 1779 and 1789.

W245·5 [—] Five pastoral eclogues: the scenes of which are suppos'd to lie among the shepherds, oppress'd by the war in Germany. *London, printed for R. Dodsley*, 1745. (*GM*, *LM* March)

4°: A^4 B–D⁴; *1–2* 3–32.

'Arise, my Lycas: in yon' woody wilds'
For some reason the attribution to Warton has been long disputed, and Warton's family disclaimed the poems. The presence of various drafts among Warton's papers at Trinity College, Oxford clearly demonstrates his authorship.

L(11630.c.4/16; 11630.c.6/19),O; CtY,IU,TxU.

[—] The intrigue. A college eclogue, 1750. *See* S31.

W246 [—] The pleasures of melancholy. A poem. *London, printed for R. Dodsley; sold by M. Cooper*, 1747. (*GM* April)

4°: A–C⁴; *1–3* 4–24.

Most copies have a ms. correction on p. 4.

'Mother of musings, contemplation sage'
Reprinted as Warton's in *Dodsley* IV, and collected in his poems.

L(11630.e.6/6),O(2),BrP(lacks A1),LdU-B; CSmH,CtY,ICN,MH,TxU(3, 1 uncut)+.

W247 [—] The triumph of Isis, a poem. Occasioned by Isis, an elegy. *London, printed for W. Owen*, [1750.] (*GA* 12 March)

4°: A–B⁴; *1–2* 3–16.

Usually dated 1749, but the advertisement in *GA* and the references in *GM*, *LM* March seem to refer to this edition.

Warton, T. The triumph of Isis

'On closing flow'rs when genial gales diffuse'
Early ms. attribution in a copy at O; collected
in Warton's *Poems*, 1779. Occasioned by
Mason's *Isis*, 1749.
L(11630.d.12/5; 840.k.4/18),O(2); *DLC*,IU,
MH(uncut).

W248 [—] — The second edition corrected. *London,
printed for W. Owen, and sold by J. Barrett in
Oxford*, 1750. (*GA* 23 March)
4°: A–B⁴; *1–2* 3–16.
Apparently a new edition, though some
standing type may be used.
L(11602.gg.24/19, ms date 24 March; 11630.d.
16/3),O(3); CLU-C,CSmH.

W249 [—] — The third edition. *London, printed for W.
Owen, and sold by J. Barrett in Oxford*, 1750.
4°: A–B⁴; *1–2* 3–16.
Apparently a reimpression.
L(C.116.c.2/2),O(3); CtY,IU.

W250 [—] — [*Edinburgh?*] *Printed in the year* 1750.
8°: A–B⁴; *1–3* 4–16.
Probably an Edinburgh piracy.
O,E; NjP,OCU.

W251 [—] Verses on Miss C-----s and W-----t.
London, printed for W. Owen, 1749. (*GM* July)
4°: A⁴ B²; *1–2* 3–12.
Two poems.
On Miss C—s: 'To trivial nymphs while Oxford's
tasteless swains'
On Miss W--------t: 'O'er Isis blooming banks
with busy care'
Early ms. note in the DLC copy 'Both by
Tho. Warton, scholar of Trinity College,
Oxford'; ascribed to him by *Rawlinson*.
Signed at end from 'Trin. Coll. A.B.C.R.';
ms. note, 'In 1747 &c this Junior Common
Room annually elected a Lady Patroness'.
The ladies are identified in ms; 'Miss Cotes
was the eldest daughter of Digby Cotes
publick orator, & Miss Wilmot the beautiful
daughter to Wilmot the bookseller, now a
widow'.
DLC (xerox at O).

W252 [**Watson, James.**] [first line:] On Thursday next,
sir, I expect... [*Edinburgh, printed by James
Watson*, 1720.]
½°: 1 side, 1 column.
'On Thursday next, sir, I expect'
Signed 'J.W.'; the ornament at head was used
by James Watson, who is clearly the signer, if
not the author. An invitation to the wedding
breakfast of a Dutch type-setter called Adrian,
headed 'Edinburgh, May [ms. correction
'June'] 15th. 1720.'
E.

Watts, Isaac. Horæ lyricæ. Poems chiefly of the
lyric kind... *London, printed by S. & D. Bridge,*

Watts, I. *Collections*

for John Lawrence, 1706 [1705]. (*DC* 21 Dec)
8°: pp. 267.   L,O; CtY,MH.

—— The second edition, altered and much
enlarged. *London, printed by J. Humfreys, for N.
Cliff*, 1709. (*DC* 19 May)
8°: pp. xxviii, 343.   L,O; CtY,MH.

—— The third edition. *London, printed by W.
Wilkins, for S. Cliff*, 1715.
12°: pp. xxxi, 314.   L,O; IU,MH.

—— The fourth edition corrected. *London, printed
for John Clark*, 1722.
12°: pp. xxxv, 299.   LDW,O; IU.

—— The fifth edition corrected. *London, printed
for John Clark & Richard Hett*, 1727. (*MC* July)
12°: pp. xxxv, 299.   O,EN; IU,MH.

—— The sixth edition corrected. *London, printed
for Richard Hett*, 1731.
12°: pp. xxxii, 299.   L,E; IU,NNUT.

—— The seventh edition corrected. *London,
printed for Richard Hett*, 1737.
12°: pp. xxxii, 299.   L,O; IU,MH.
Errata slip in O copy.

—— The eighth edition, corrected. *London,
printed for James Brackstone*, 1743.
12°: pp. xxxii, 299.   L,O; IU,MB.

—— Hymns and spiritual songs. In three books...
With an essay towards the improvement of
Christian psalmody... *London, printed by J.
Humfreys, for John Lawrence*, 1707. (*DC* 24 July)
12°: pp. xxiv, 276.   L; CtY,MB.
The title is a cancel.

—— The second edition, corrected and much
enlarged. *London, printed by J.H. for John Lawrence*, 1709. (*DC* 12 May)
12°: pp. xxiv, 344.   L; NN.
The additions were separately printed as
*Hymns and spiritual songs...added by way
of supplement to the first edition*, 1709 (copy at
NN). The essay is omitted from this and subsequent editions.

—— The third edition. *London, printed by J.H.
for John Lawrence*, 1712 [1711]. (*DC* 28 Dec)
12°: pp. xxiv, 344.   BaP; NNP.

—— The fourth edition. *London, printed by S.
Keimer, for John Lawrence*, 1714.
12°: pp. xxiv, 344.   CtY.

—— The fifth edition, corrected and much
enlarged. *London, printed by J.H. for M. Lawrence*,
1716.
12°: pp. xxiv, 344.   L.

—— [reissue] The fifth edition, corrected. *London,
printed by J.H. for M. Lawrence*, 1716.
L,LVA-D.
Cancel title and A7 removing references to the
additions and to their being separately
available.

— — The sixth edition. *London, printed by J.H. for R. Ford,* 1718.
Stoke Newington Public Library.

— — The seventh edition. *London, printed by J.H. for R. Ford,* 1720.
12°: pp. xxiv, 344.　　L,LVA-D.

— — The eighth edition. *London, printed for Richard Ford,* 1723.
12°: pp. xxiv, 344.　　L.

— — The ninth edition. *London, printed for Richard Ford,* 1725. (*MC* May)
12°: pp. xxviii, '129' [329].　　LdU; IU.

— [fine paper]　　L.
No watermark traced, but the copy seen is clearly one on 'fine large paper for the curious', as listed in *MC*.

— — The tenth edition. *London printed by J.H. for Richard Ford,* 1728. (*MChr* 29 July)
12°: pp. xxviii, '129' [329].　　L,O; IU.

— — The eleventh edition. *London, printed for Richard Ford,* 1731.
NeP.

— — The twelfth edition. *London, printed for Richard Ford,* 1734.
12°: pp. xxviii, 329.　　L,DT.

— — The fourteenth edition. *London, printed for D. Midwinter, A. Ward, T. Longman, R. Hett, C. Hitch, J. Hodges, & J. Davidson,* 1740.
12°: pp. xxviii, 331.　　L,EN.

— — The fifteenth edition. *London, printed for A. Ward, T. Longman, R. Hett, C. Hitch, J. Hodges, J. Davidson, T. Harris, & M. Cooper,* 1744.
12°: pp. xxvi, 331.　　L,EN.

— — The sixteenth edition. *London, printed for R. Ware, T. Longman, C. Hitch, J. Hodges, J. Oswald, J. Davidson, J. Buckland, J. Ward, & M. Cooper,* 1748.
12°: pp. xxvi, 331.　　L; MH.
As the imprints show, the copyright of Watts's hymns became much divided. At the trade sale of Richard Ford, 14 Nov 1738 (cat. at O-JJ), lots 23–6 each consisted of a twelfth share and were all bought by Richard Hett for a total of £70. The assignment from Catherine Ford to Hett, dated 20 Dec 1738, was listed in Dobell cat. 66 (1941) 44. Hett assigned one twentieth and one hundred-and-twentieth (together with a quarter of Foxton's *Moral songs*) on 19 Dec 1738 to Aaron Ward for £14. 15s. (Dobell cat. 66/46). At Midwinter's sale, 4 Aug 1743 (cat. at O-JJ), lots 177–80 contained further shares which were bought by Davidson, Davis, and Harris at similar prices. At Hett's sale, 9 May 1745 (cat. at O-JJ), shares

formed part of lots 35 and 38 and were purchased by Ware. There must also have been other private transfers.

— Divine songs attempted in easy language for the use of children. *London, printed for M. Lawrence,* 1715. (*MC* Aug)
LDW; NNP (presentation copy).
Copies of all editions are so scarce that no attempt has been made to give collations. References to *Stone* are to W. M. Stone's edition (New York, 1918).

— — The second edition. *London, M. Lawrence,* 1716.
CSmH.

— — The third edition. *London, R. Ford,* 1719.
(*Stone*: Sotheby's, April 1911)

— — The fourth edition. *London, R. Ford,* 1720. (*PB* 3 May)
(*Stone*: Maggs, 1909)

— — 'The sixth edition, with the addition of a cradle hymn. *London, R. Ford.*' (*MC* May 1724)

— — 'The seventh edition. *London, R. Ford.*' (*MC* Jan 1726)

— — The eighth edition. *London, Richard Ford,* 1727. (*MC* Feb)
CSmH.

— — The ninth edition. *London, Richard Ford,* 1728.
L; CSmH.

— — The tenth edition. *London, R. Ford,* 1729.
(*Stone*: Sotheby's, Feb 1900)

— — The twelfth edition. *London, R. Ford,* 1733.
CSmH.

— — The thirteenth edition. *London, Richard Ford,* 1735.
O; TxU.

— — The fourteenth edition. *London, Richard Ford,* [1737?]
(advertised in Foxton, *Moral songs,* 1737)

— — The fifteenth edition. *London, R. Hett & J. Brackstone.* [1737/-.]
(*Stone*: advertised in *The art of reading and writing English,* 1740)

— — The sixteenth edition, with some additional composures. *London, J. Brackstone,* 1740.
(*Stone*: Bull & Auvache, 1905)

— — The seventeenth edition... *London, James Brackstone,* 1740.
(*Gumuchian* 5789)
A note on the last page records that the added songs can be separately purchased for one penny. The next recorded edition is the twenty-first, 1752.

Watts, I. *Collections*

— The psalms of David imitated in the language of the new testament, and apply'd to the Christian state and worship. *London, printed for J. Clark, R. Ford, & R. Cruttenden, 1719.*
12°: pp. xxxii, 399.   L,O; CtY,NNUT.
Dedication copy at L. Editions were published in almost regular alternation in large or small duodecimo, with or without the preface and notes.

— — The second edition. *London, printed for J. Clark, R. Ford, & R. Cruttenden, 1719.*
12°: pp. viii, 318.   L,E; CtY-D,MH.
Presentation copy, ruled in red, at L.

— — The third edition, with the preface and notes. *London, printed for John Clark, & Richard Ford, 1722.*
12°: pp. xxx, 381.   L,LDW; CtY-D,MH.

— — 'The fifth edition. [*London*] *Printed for J. Clark & R. Hett, & R. Ford.*' (*MC* Jan 1725)

— — 'The sixth edition. [*London*] *Printed for J. Clark & R. Hett, & R. Ford.*' (*MC* Nov 1727)

— — The seventh edition. *London, printed for John Clark & Richard Hett, & Richard Ford, 1729.*
12°: pp. viii, 319.   L,O.

— — The ninth edition. *London, printed for Richard Ford, & Richard Hett, 1734.*
12°: pp. viii, 319.   L,DT; CtY.

— — The tenth edition, with the preface and notes. *London, printed for Richard Ford, & Richard Hett, 1736.*
12°.   O(impft).

— — The eleventh edition. *London, printed for Richard Ford, & Richard Hett, 1737.*
12°: pp. viii, 319.   L.

— — The eleventh edition, with the preface and notes. *London, printed for T. Longman, & J. Brackstone, 1744.*
12°: pp. xxx, 381, 18.   O.
Apparently the edition number is a misprint.

— — The fourteenth edition. *London, pinted* [!] *for J. Oswald, & J. Buckland, 1747.*
12°: pp. viii, 8, 318.   LDW,DT.

— — The fifteenth edition. With the preface and notes. *London, printed for J. Oswald, & J. Buckland, 1748.*
12°: pp. xxx, 381, 18.   L,AdU.
There is said to be a Limerick reprint of 1750.

———

— Reliquiæ juveniles: miscellaneous thoughts in prose and verse, on natural, moral, and divine subjects... *London, printed for Richard Ford, & Richard Hett, 1734.* (*GM* April)
12°: pp. xx, 350.   L,O; CLU-C,MH.

— — The second edition. *London, printed for Richard Ford, & Richard Hett, 1737.* (*GM* Sept)
12°: pp. xvi, '168' [350].   L; IU.

Watts, I.

— — The third edition. *London, printed for James Brackstone, 1742.*
12°: pp. xvi, 350.   L,OQ; IU,MH.

———

W253 [—] An ode on the coronation of their majesties King George II. and Queen Caroline. October the 11th, 1727. *London, printed for J. Roberts, 1727.* (*MC* Oct)
2°: *A*² B²; *1-3* 4-8.
'Rise happy morn, fair sun arise'
   Printed in Watts's *Reliquiæ juveniles, 1734.*
L(1959),LDW,AdU; CSmH,CtY,IU,InU,PPL.

W254 [—] Ode on the coronation of their majesties King George II. and Queen Caroline. [*Dublin, 1727.*]
½°: 1 side, 2 columns.
DT.

W255 [—] Stanza's. To my Lady Sunderland at Tunbridge-Wells. 1712. *London, printed for E. Curll, and sold at his shop on Tunbridge-Walks, 1712.* (*PB* 2 Sept)
½°: 1-2, 1 column.
   Ms. correction to last line of p. 1 in all copies. Copies bear the new halfpenny tax stamp.
'Fair nymph, ascend to beauty's throne'
   Ms. ascription to Watts in the PPL copy; advertised as his in [G. Sewell] *To his grace the Duke of Marlborough, on the report of his going to Germany, 1713.*
O,C,Crawford; PPL.

W256 — [dh] To his excellency Jonathan Belcher, esq; in London, appointed by his majesty King George II. to the government of New-England, and now returning home. [col] *Boston, printed for J. Phillips and T. Hancock, 1730.* (*Weekly news-letter* 18 June)
4°: A²; *i* ii–iii *iv blk.*
   W. C. Ford, *Broadsides, ballads &c. printed in Massachusetts, 1639–1800* (1922) no. 589 records the advertisement but not the poem. Included here despite its American origin.
'Go, favourite man; spread to the wind thy sails'
   Signed on p. 3 and dated 31 March.
E.

W257 Way. 'The way of the town; or, the Covent-Garden heiress. A burlesque poem. By the author of the Silver piss-pot; being a satyr on the ladies of pleasure, and beaux of the town. [*London*] *Sold by J. Morphew.*' (*MC* Nov 1716)
'The country 'squire that wants to be undone'

W258 — — The second edition. *London printed, and sold by John Morphew, & A. Dodd, 1716.*
12°: A–E⁶; *i–xii, 1* 2–36. A1 frt.
   Both copies seen are aberrant, containing also the additions of the following issue; the collation is therefore conjectural. The frontispiece appears to be A1, but its conjugacy has not been confirmed.
L(1078.1.34); CtY.

Way

W259 — [reissue] The way of the town: or, the sham heiress. A burlesque poem. Being a satyr on the ladies of pleasure and the beaux's [!] of the town. With the fable of the lady's silver piss-pot. *London printed, and sold by J. Morphew, & A. Dodd, 1717* [1716]. (*MC* Dec)

12°: A⁶(±A2) B–E⁶ F⁴; *i–xii*, 1 2–40 41–44. A1 frt; F3, 4 advt.

 The cancel title A2 is followed by a conjugate leaf bearing a small advertisement for the pamphlet, set in duplicate and clearly meant to be detached; offset shows these leaves to have been printed with F4.

Fable: 'In days of yore there liv'd a stately dame' L(1078.1.34); CtY.

W260 — The way to heaven in a string: or, Mr. A——'s argument burlesqu'd. A poem. Canto I. *Re-printed in the year 1701.*

8°: A⁸; *1–4* '1' 6–16.

 A reprint of the original folio edition of Sept 1700.

'There are some things are counted real'

 A burlesque of John Asgill's *An argument*, 1700.

L(1078.f.6).

W—d, *Mr.* The bridegroom at his wit's end, [1727.] *See* B440.

W--ds-r. The W--ds-r prophecy, 1711. *See* Swift, Jonathan.

W261 We. We've lost it at last. [*London?* 171–?]

½°: 2 sides, 1 column.

'In vain were all the forts we w——s could use'

 Apparently a tory poem in praise of Sir W——, put in the mouth of the whigs; the occasion and characters have not been identified. L dates it as [1730?], but an earlier date seems more plausible.

L(C.121.g.9/194).

Wealth. Wealth, or the woody, [1720.] *See* Ramsay, Allan.

W262 Weaver. The weaver turn'd devil: or, a new copy of verses, on a baker in Spitle-fields, who was frighted by a weaver in the shape of a devil... To the tune of, the Royal forester. *London, printed for T.C. near Spitle-fields, 1701.*

½°: 1 side, 2 columns.

'You bakers of England both country and citty'

Crawford.

W262·5 — 'The weaver's new ballad on the S—h-Sea. To the tune of To you fair ladies now at land, &c. [*London*] *Printed, and sold by the booksellers of London & Westminster*. Price 2*d*.' (*DP* 15 Sept 1720)

 Possibly a half-sheet from the price. The title

The **weaver**'s new ballad

may be generalized, but compare Samuel Wilde's *The weaver's humble offering*, [1721]; perhaps he also wrote this.

[**Web, —,** *barber in Oxford*.] An address to the worshipful company of barbers in Oxford... By a barber, 1749. *See* A57.

W263 Webb, George. Batchelors-Hall. A poem. By George Webb, native of Philadelphia. *Philadelphia: printed and re-printed in Dublin, for James Hoey,* ⟨1731?⟩

8°: A⁸(−A8); *1–2* 3–14.

 The American edition was published in 1731 (*Wegelin* 418). The copy seen probably lacks A8.

'O spring, thou fairest season of the year'

L(11631.a.58, slightly cropt).

'**Webster, —,** *Mr., of Christ-Church, Oxon*.' The stage: a poem, 1713. *See* Reynardson, Francis.

[**Webster, James,** *minister of the Tolbooth church, Edinburgh*.] Three poems, Mahanaim, or, strivings with a saviour, 1706. *See* T256.

W264 Wedding. The wedding song of Gibbie and Marjorie; who were married in Edinburgh, on the 13th of June 1718; their ages one hundred and sixty years: to the tune of, The old woman poor and blind. [*Edinburgh*, 1718.]

½°: 1 side, 2 columns.

 Two rough woodcuts at head.

'Come all good people, give an ear'

E.

W265 — A wedding song, on the marraige [!] of John Brown, merchant in Holland, and Margaret Hepburn, daughter to the Laird of Bairfoot, solemnized 28 of July 1714. [*Edinburgh,* 1714.]

slip: 1 side, 1 column.

'The beauty new of Edinburgh town'

L(Rox.III.669),E.

W266 — A wedding song upon the famous Tincklarian Doctor William Mitchel, and Ann Stewart. Who was married upon the 2d of April 1717. [*Edinburgh,* 1717.]

½°: 1 side, 1 column.

'Who can sufficiently approve'

 Satirizing William Mitchel's search for a second wife.

E.

W267 Wedlock. Wedlock a paradice; or, a defence of woman's liberty against man's tyranny. In opposition to a poem, entitul'd, The pleasures of a single life, &c. *London printed, and are to be sold by J. Nutt, 1701.* (4 Dec, Luttrell)

2°: A–D² (A2 as 'B2'); *i–ii*, 1–14.

 The Luttrell copy is recorded in *Haslewood*; listed in *WL* Dec.

'When time had freed me from my childish years'

Wedlock a paradice

Listed in *Waller* as attributed to Prior; rejected in *Wright & Spears*. Mr. S. H. Ward privately suggests Edward Ward's authorship. L(163.n.17),O,LdU-B; CSmH,CtY,DFo(uncut), ICN,TxU+.

W268 — Wedlock vindicated: or, the ladies answer, to the (pretended) good advice to them... Written by a young lady. *London, printed for C.M. in Fleet-street*, 1702.
8°: *A⁴*; *1* ⟨ ⟩8.
'What contradictious notions now are spent'
The preface, which is signed 'R.B.', is perhaps not the author's. A reply to *Good advice to the ladies*, 1702.
MH(cropt).

Weeks, James Eyre. Poems on several occasions. *Corke, printed by Thomas Pilkington, for the author*, 1743.
8°: pp. 153.   DA,DN; MH.

W269 — The Amazon or female courage vindicated... Address'd to the ladies of Great-Britain...and humbly inscribed to the Countess of Chesterfield. *Dublin, printed by James Esdall*, 1745.
8°: A⁴; *1–2* 3–8.
'Oh Chesterfield! to thee an Irish muse'
L(11631.bb.89),DG,DT.

W270 [—] The cobler's poem. To a certain noble peer. Occasioned by the brick-layer's poem... After the manner of Dean Swift. To which is added the Exception. *Dublin, printed by James Hoey*, 1745.
8°: *A⁴*; *1–3* 4–8.
'The exception' is on p. 8.
'While brick-layers hail thee, in the throng'
Signed 'J.E.W.' on p. 7; early ms. attribution to Weeks in the LVA-F copy. Listed on the title of his *A rhapsody*, 1746. Occasioned by Henry Jones's poem to the lord lieutenant.
LVA-F,C,DG,DK.

W271 [—] [variant title:] The cobler's poem... To which is added the Exception. After the manner of Dean Swift. [in place of imprint:] Just publish'd, Home clenches being a new set of conundrums, &c.
C.

W272 [—] Rebellion. A poem. Humbly inscribed to his excellency Philip, earl of Chesterfield, lord lieu-tenant...of Ireland. *Dublin, printed for Peter Wilson*, 1745.
8°: A⁴; *1–3* 4–8.
'While wild ambition dictates lawless claim'
Listed on the title of *A rhapsody*, 1746, as by the same author. On the Jacobite rebellion.
L(1486.s.17),O; CtY.

W273 — The resurrection. A poem. Most humbly inscribed to the Reverend John Blachford, D.D... *Dublin, printed by James Esdall*, 1745.
8°: A⁴ (A2 as 'A3'); *1–2* 3–8.

Weeks, J. E. The resurrection

'The vocal picture, and the pencil's speech'
DG,DT,LdU-B; CtY.

W274 — A rhapsody on the stage or, the art of playing. In imitation of Horace's Art of poetry. Humbly addressed to...Philip, earl of Chesterfield... *Dublin, printed for the author; sold by James Esdall*, 1746.
4°: A⁴ B–H² (A2 as 'A'); *i–iii* iv–v, [2] 4–32.
From the evidence of the watermarks, A⁴ is composed of two separate half-sheets.
'Scipio and Lelius by the muse rever'd'
DA; DFo,*MiU*.

W275 **Weeping.** The weeping church-men: being a mourning copy of verses on the departure of our late soveraign Queen Anne, who departed this life, August the first, 1714. Tune of, Troy town. *London, printed by Tho. Norris*, [1714.]
½°: 1 side, 2 columns.
Rough woodcuts at head.
'You loyal church-men far and near'
L(1876.f.1/70).

[**Weever**, —, *Mr.*] A new court ballad, 1715. *See* N124.

W276 **Weichmann, Christian Friedrich.** [dh] Etwas Teutsches zur Verteidigung der Teutschen über die am 7den Oct. 1727. vollzogene Verehligung (S.T.) Herrn Lueders mit (S.T.) Jungfer Voguells aufgesetzt von Weichmann. [col] *London, gedruckt durch James Bettenham*, 1727.
2°: *A²*; *1* 2–4.
'In London Teutsch? – Verhasste Muse, still!'
L(C.20.f.2/241).

W277 **Weighley.** Weighley, alias Wild. A poem, in imitation of Hudibras. To which is annex'd, a... account in prose... Also Jonathan's last farewel and epitaph, with a song, never before printed. By N.P. many year his intimate acquaintance. *London, printed for J. Roberts*, 1725. (*MC* July)
8°: A–F⁴; *1–2* 3–48.
The prose text begins on p. 26.
'I sing a prig, read it who list'
An account of Jonathan Wild.
O; NN.

Welchman. *See* Welshman.

W278 **Welcome.** A welcome to the medal; or an excellent new song; call'd the constitution restor'd, in 1711. To the tune of Mortimer's-Hole. '*Oxford, at the Theatre*' [*London*], 1711. (Sept?)
½°: 1 side, 2 columns.
The numbers to each stanza are followed by a period. A warrant against Henry Hills and Thomas Harrison for publishing this was signed by St. John, 28 Sept 1711.
'Let's joy in the medal with James the IIId's face'

A **welcome** to the medal

A satire on the tories as Jacobites. Replied to in *Loyalty display'd*, 1711.
O,DT,Crawford,Rothschild; TxU.

W279 — [another edition]
No period after stanza numbers.
LSA; NNP.

W280 — The welcome. Two congratulatory poems, the first, humbly inscrib'd to the most august monarch George... The other to his grace the Duke of Marlborough, on his return to England. By different hands. *Nottingham, printed by J. Collyer, and sold by Hen. Allestree, bookseller in Derby*, 1714.
4°: A⁴ B¹ (A2 as 'A'); *1–3* 4–9 *10 blk.*
'Great sir, a welcome, equal to your joy'
'We saw great sir, when every year you wore'
L(164.m.72).

W281 Well-timbered. A well-timber'd poem, on her sacred majesty; her marble statue, and its wooden enclosure in Saint Paul's church-yard. *London printed, and sold by H. Hills, and the booksellers of London & Westminster*, 1712.
8°: A⁴; *1–2* 3–8. *2 advt.*
'Some Eastern princes to be counted great'
Using the covering of the statue as an allegory. A tory poem.
O.

W282 Welsh. The Welsh-monster: or, the rise and downfal of that late upstart, the r--t h--ble Innuendo Scribble. *London, printed in the year of grace, and sold by the booksellors*, [1708.]
8°: A² B–F⁴; *i–iv*, 1–40. *40 advt.*
On p. 40, 'The end of the first part'. *Observator* 8 Jan 1709 advertised a 'second edition'.
'In a wild corner of the world'
A satire on Harley and his relations with Tutchin and Defoe. Mr. S. H. Ward privately suggests Edward Ward's authorship.
L(11601.d.20/1),O(2, 1 lacks F2–4),EU,DT,AN, *CdP*; IU,MB,NN.

W283 — The Welsh mouse-trap. Translated from the Latin. By F.T. *London printed, and sold by the booksellers of London & Westminster*, 1709.
8°: A⁴; *1–2* 3–8.
Bond p. 217.
'Muse sing the Brittain, who on mountains liv'd'
A translation of Edward Holdsworth's *Muscipula*, 1709.
O,C,CT,LdU-B,WcC; CtY,DFo,OCU.

W284 Welshman. The Welchman-s last will and testament. *London printed, and sold by Tho. Bickerton*, 1719.
8°: A–C⁴; *1–3* 4–24.
The text of the following editions has not been collated, but all are apparently the same poem.

The **Welshman**'s last will

'A Welchman, that long,/With a scythe and a prong'
L(1966); OCU.

W285 — [*idem*] Something for every body: or, the last will and testament of a Welch man, lately deceased. *London, printed for W. Rayner; sold by the booksellers of London & Westminster*, 1729. (*MChr* 16 Aug)
4°: A¹ B⁴ C⁴(−C4); *1–3* 4–16.
L(1077.k.29/5).

W286 — [*idem*] Humorous reflections of an antient Briton in a fit of sickness. *London, printed by R. Walker, without Temple-Bar; sold by the booksellers of London & Westminster*, [1731.] (*MChr* March)
4°: A² B–D² (A2 as 'B'); *1–2* 3–16.
O(uncut).

W287 — The Welchman's tales concerning the times. Viz. The parson's progress. The fox and lamb. The shepherd and wolves. The lyon and dogs. The rook and cock. The mag-pye and black-bird. *London, printed in the year* 1710. (*SR* 23 May)
8°: A⁴; *1* 2–8.
Entered in *SR* to Will Wise; deposit copies at O,C,EU.
Fable 1: 'I'll tell you a fine tale of note'
Satires on the Sacheverell trial.
LLP,O,C,CT,EU; IU.

Welsted, Leonard. Epistles, odes, &c. written on several subjects... *London, printed for J. Walthoe, & J. Peele*, 1724. (*MC* March)
8°: pp. lxiv, 255.   L,O; DFo,TxU.
No watermark.

— [fine paper]   CtY,TxU.
Watermark: Strasburg bend. Presentation copy at MH-BA.

— — The second edition. *London, printed for J. Walthoe, & J. Peele*, 1725. (*MC* April)
12°: pp. lii, 101.   L,O; CtY.
The title appears to be a cancel. The copy at O was presented by Welsted to his daughter Frances.

———

[—] Apple-pye. A poem, by Dr. King [!], 1717. *In* B418.

W288 — The Duke of Marlborough's arrival. A poem. Humbly inscribed to the right honourable Lionel, earl of Dorset and Middlesex, &c. *London, printed for J. Gouge, and are to be sold by A. Baldwin*, 1709. (*PB* 28 April)
2°: A–C²; *i–iv*, 1–7 *8 blk.*
'Soon as bleak northern winds had froze the air'
Dedication signed.
O; CLU-C(Luttrell, 28 April).

W289 — An epistle to his grace the Duke of Chandos. *London, printed for W. Chetwood*, 1720. (*PB* 23 Jan)
2°: A² B²; *1–3* 4–7 *8 blk.*
'While over arts unrivalled you preside'
O,WcC; TxU.

Welsted, L. An epistle to...Duke of Chandos

W290 — — The second edition. *London, printed for
W. Chetwood,* 1720. (*DP* 13 Feb)
2°: A^2 B^2; *1–3* 4–7 *8 blk.*
Apparently a reimpression.
MH.

W291 — An epistle to Mr. Steele, on the king's accession
to the crown. *London, printed for Tim. Childe,* 1714.
(*SR* 20 Nov)
2°: A–C^2; *i–ii, 1–9 10 blk.*
Listed in *MC* Nov. Deposit copies at
L,LSC,O,EU,AdU,SaU.
'O generous Varus, happy and admired!'
L(643.m.13/4),LSC,O(2),EU,AdU + ; CLU-C,
CSmH(uncut),CtY,MH,TxU(2, 1 uncut).

W292 — An epistle to the late Dr. Garth, occasion'd by
the death of the Duke of Marlborough. *London,
printed for J. Peele,* 1722. (*DP* 14 Dec)
2°: A^2 B–C^2; *1–3* 4–12.
The Luttrell copy, dated Dec, is in the
possession of R. D. Horn.
'From the fair banks of Thame this verse I send'
CtY,MH,TxU(2).

W293 — An epistle to the right honourable the Earl of
Cadogan. *London, printed for B. Lintott,* 1722. (*PB*
10 May)
2°: A–B^2; *1–2* 3–7 *8 blk.*
'Whilst careful crowds your levees wait'
TxU.

W294 — The genius, an ode, written on occasion of the
Duke of Marlborough's first apoplexy, and reserv'd
not to be publish'd till after his death. With a
prefatory epistle to Dr. Chamberlen. *London,
printed for Bernard Lintot; sold by J. Roberts,* 1722.
(*DP* 3 July)
2°: A^2 B^1; *i–iv, 1* 2.
'Awful hero, Marlborough, rise'
A ms. copy at Herts CRO (Panshanger box 46)
is endorsed 'On the D. of Marlb. in his decay
sent by Mr. Jn. Hughes Aug. 1718 & said to be
wrote by Mr. Welsted a parson who had
before wrote some verses but not much
known'.
Horn(Luttrell, Nov).

W295 [—] A hymn to the creator. Written by a gentleman, on the occasion of the death of his only
daughter. *London, printed for J. Walthoe,* 1727
[1726?]. (*MC* Dec 1726)
2°: A^2 B^2; *1–3* 4–8.
'Creator! genial source of day!'
Advertised in Welsted's *Of false fame,* 1732.
ICU,IU,MH(uncut).

W296 — An ode on the birthday of his royal highness the
Prince of Wales. To the Princess. To the Earl of
Clare, on his being created duke of Newcastle.
Amintor and the nightingale. *London, printed for
J. Tonson,* 1716. (*MC* Jan)
2°: A–B^2; *i–iv,* 1–4.
Four poems.
'When Churchill on Onarda's plain'

Welsted, L. An ode on the birthday

'O born for nations! Britain's joy confest!'
'When fair Astræa to the earth descends'
'As in a blowing jasmyn bower'
LVA-F; CtY.

W297 — An ode to the honourable Major-general Wade,
on occasion of his disarming the highlands.
Imitated from Horace. To which is added, the
fourth ode, translated from the fourth book of the
same author. *London, printed by W. Wilkins, for
J. Peele,* 1726. (*MC* Feb)
2°: A^2 B–D^2; *1–3* 4–16.
'Some future Garth, brave chief, shall sing'
Fourth ode: 'Like to the thunder-bearing bird'
O,*AdU*; TxU.

W298 — Of dulness and scandal. Occasion'd by the
character of Lord Timon. In Mr. Pope's epistle to
the Earl of Burlington. *London, printed for T.
Cooper,* 1732. (*GSJ* 3 Jan)
2°: A^2 B^2; *1–2* 3–8.
Printed by Samuel Richardson (*Sale* 114).
'While strife subsists 'twixt Cibber and the pit'
Answered by [J. Turner] *An epistle to Mr. Pope,*
1732; see also *Malice defeated,* 1732, and *On
P—e and W—d,* 1732.
L(162.n.32),O; CLU-C,CtY,ICN,MH(uncut),
TxU(2, 1 uncut).

W299 — — The second edition. *London, printed for T.
Cooper,* 1732. (6 Jan?)
2°: A^2 B^2; *1–2* 3–8.
Apparently a reimpression. An advertisement
of 6 Jan is inserted in *Haslewood.*
L(11631.i.20),O,WcC(uncut); CtY(2),DFo,ICU,
MB,TxU.

W300 — — The third edition. *London, printed for T.
Cooper,* 1732. (Jan)
2°: A^2 B^2; *1–2* 3–8.
A reimpression with some minor corrections.
The second and third 'editions' were noticed
in *GSJ* 13 Jan.
OW; CSmH,ICU(uncut),IU,TxU.

W301 — Of false fame. An epistle to the right honourable
the Earl of Pembroke. *London, printed for T.
Cooper,* 1732. (*DJ* 3 Feb)
8°: A^4 B–C^4; *1–4* 5–21 *22–23; 24 blk.* A1 hft; C4
advt.
Printed by Samuel Richardson (*Sale* 116).
'Amidst the factions, that the world enrage'
L(992.h.9/7, –C4),LG,O,DrU(uncut); DFo,
ICN(–A1, C4),MH(–A1, C4),*NN.*

W302 — Oikographia: a poem, to his grace the Duke of
Dorset. *London, printed for T. Woodward, J.
Walthoe, & J. Peele,* 1725. (*MC* Dec)
2°: A^2 B–D^2; *1–3* 4–16.
'At length, O Dorset, not to raise'
L(643.m.12/33),O; CtY,IU,MH,NN-B,TxU.

W302·5 [— & **Smythe, James Moore.**] One epistle to
Mr. A. Pope, occasion'd by two epistles lately

Welsted, L. One epistle to Mr. A. Pope

published. *London, printed for J. Roberts,* [1730.] (*DJ* 28 April)
4°: *A*⁴ B–C⁴; *i–iv* v–viii, *9* 10–24. A1 hft.
Printed by Samuel Richardson (*Sale* 89).
'Of noble B——m, in metre known'
Originally announced as in preparation by Smythe and Welsted in the *Universal spectator* for 1 Feb 1729. Pope in the appendix to the *Dunciad* writes of Welsted's *Labeo* 'which after came into *One epistle*, and was publish'd by James Moore'. It is advertised in Welsted's *Of false fame*, 1732, as 'by Mr. Welsted, and Mr. Moore Smythe'. Whatever the nature of the collaboration, and whether or not others had a hand in it, this joint authorship must be accepted.
L(12273.m.1/12),LVA-D(–A1),O; CSmH,CtY, ICN,MH(–A1),TxU+.

W302·6 [—] — The second edition. *London, printed for J. Roberts,* [1730.]
4°: *A*⁴ B–C⁴; *i–iv* v–viii, *9* 10–24. A1 hft.
Apparently a reimpression or a press-variant title. There is an advertisement of 29 Aug in *Haslewood*, but publication may well have preceded this.
L(1959).

W303 [—] Palæmon to Cælia, at Bath; or, the triumvirate. *London printed, and sold by J. Roberts,* 1717. (*PM* 7 March)
2°: *A*(2 ll) B–C² D¹; *1–2* 3–14.
The watermarks in the copies seen suggest that the two leaves of A are neither conjugate with each other nor with D1; possibly there is a cancel leaf in A.
'Cælia, you rule with such despotick sway'
Ascribed to Welsted in *Jacob* II. 227 and by Pope in *The Dunciad,* 1729. A satire on Pope, Gay, and Arbuthnot's *Three hours after marriage*.
L(643.m.12/27),LVA-F,*BrP*; MH(2),NNC.

W304 [—] — The second edition. *London printed, and sold by J. Roberts,* 1717. (*DC* 13 March)
2°: *A*² B–C² D¹; *1–2* 3–14.
A and B are reset, C and D reimpressed.
L(643.m.12/28),O,*BrP*; IU,MH.

W305 — A poem, occasioned by the late famous victory of Audenard. Humbly inscrib'd to the honourable Robert Harley, esq; *London, printed for Benjamin Barker; sold by J. Morphew,* 1709 [1708]. (*DC* 16 Nov)
2°: A–C²; *i–ii,* 1–10.
Morgan L441 records 'another edition', probably in error.
'O for that heav'nly voice, that pierc'd so high'
CLU-C(Luttrell, 16 Nov),CtY(uncut),IU(uncut), *PBL*.

W306 — A poem to her royal highness the Princess of Wales. Occasioned by her late happy delivery, and

Welsted, L. A poem to her royal highness

the birth of a princess. *London, printed for J. Walthoe,* 1737. (*GM, LM* Aug)
2°: *A*² B²; *1–3* 4–7 *8 blk.*
No watermark.
'Strike the deep note, the concent swell'
O(2, 1 uncut).

W307 — [fine paper]
Watermark: fleur-de-lys on shield.
MH.

W308 — A poem to the memory of the incomparable Mr. Philips, humbly inscrib'd to the right honourable Henry St. John esq; *London, printed for Daniel Browne; sold by A. Baldwin,* 1710. (12 July)
2°: *A*² B–D²; *i–iv,* 1–12.
Advertised in *PB* 11 July for 'tomorrow'; the Luttrell copy, dated 12 July, is in the Osborn collection at CtY.
'Forgive my crime, forgive it, gentle shade'
Dedication signed.
O(2, 1 uncut); CLU-C,DFo,*DLC*,TxU(uncut).

W309 [—] The power of love. A tale. Writ on a young lady in M——'s parish. [*Dublin*] *Printed in the year* 1728–9.
½°: 1 side, 2 columns.
'Thyrsis, the darling of the fair'
Printed in Welsted's *Epistles,* 1724.
DT.

W310 — A prologue to the town, as it was spoken at the theatre in Little Lincoln's-Inn-Fields... With an epilogue on the same occasion, by Sir Richard Steele. *London printed, and sold by J. Brotherton & W. Meadows, J. Roberts, A. Dodd, W. Lewis, & J. Graves,* 1721. (*DP* 3 Feb)
2°: *A*² B²; *1–8.*
'At length the phrenzy of the realm is o'er'
'What could our young dramatic monarch mean'
Intended for a performance of *Measure for measure* on 23 Jan 1721, but not spoken.
L(643.m.12/32); CLU-C(uncut),CtY,DFo(Luttrell, Feb).

W311 [—] The prophecy, or an imitation of the 15th. ode of the first book of Horace. Address'd to Mr. Steele. *London, printed for J. Baker,* 1714.
8°: *A–B*⁴ C⁴; *1–5* 6–19 *20–22: 23–24 blk.* A1 hft; C3 advt.
'When Mago, learn'd in deep deceit'
Welsted's authorship is recorded in Nichols's edition of his *Works* (1787) xvii. A satire on Harley, prophesying the failure of a Jacobite invasion.
L(1485.pp.13),O(2, 1–C4, 1–C3, 4); NjP,TxU (–C3, 4).

W312 — The summum bonum; or, wisest philosophy. In an epistle to a friend. *London, printed for T. Cooper,* 1741. (*GM, LM* Feb)
2°: *A*¹ B–D² E¹: *i–ii, 1* 2–14.
Printed by Samuel Richardson (*Sale* 288).
'Smile, my Hephestion, smile; no more be seen'
L(Cup.600.b.1/17),O; CLU,CtY,ICU,TxU.

Welton, J.

[Welton, James.] The art of beauty: a poem. Humbly address'd to the Oxford toasts, 1719. *See* A317.

'**Wentworth, Henry.**' The coronation, 1702. *See* Waring, Henry.

Wesley, Charles.
Most of the hymns by Charles Wesley were printed with those of his brother John; see the joint heading of John & Charles below, and the note there.

— Hymns and sacred poems. In two volumes. *Bristol, printed and sold by Felix Farley, 1749. (SR 12 July)*
8°: 2 vol.   L,O; MH,NN.
     Entered to Charles Wesley in *SR*. There are proposals of 18 Dec 1748 at LMA (entered in Strahan's ledger under Dec 1748, 2000 copies).

W313 — An elegy on the death of Robert Jones, esq; of Fonmon-Castle in Glamorganshire, South-Wales. *Bristol, printed by Felix Farley, and sold at his shop in Castle Green, & by John Wilson: in London by Thomas Trye, & Thomas Harris, and at the Foundery, 1742.*
4°: A–G²; *1–3 4–26 27; 28 blk.* 26 err; G2 advt.
     Green 39.
'And is he gone to his eternal rest!'
L(11631.e.70),BrP(uncut); *NcD*.

W314 [—] — The second edition. *Bristol, printed by Felix Farley, 1748.*
12°: A–B⁶; *1–3 4–22 23–24 blk.*
L(11632.b.32,−B6),BrP(uncut),MR(−B6); *NcD*,OCU(−B6).

W315 [—] [dh] A hymn at the sacrament. [1744/45.]
12°: A²; *1 2–4.*
     Green 61. The format is uncertain.
'God of truth and power and grace'
     Charles Wesley's authorship rests on the poem's inclusion among his manuscripts.
LMA; Victoria University, Toronto.

W316 [—] 'A hymn for Christmas day.' [*London*, 1743.] (Dec)
     Baker 47C. Entered in Strahan's ledger to John & Charles Wesley under 23 Dec 1743, 1000 copies. Clearly a quarter-sheet from the paper used, and possibly a four-page pamphlet. The hymn has not been identified, and the attribution to Charles rests on the fact that the other separately published hymns were by him and not by John.
(Strahan's ledger.)

W317 [—] 'A hymn for condemned prisoners.' [*London*, 1742.] (Dec)
     Baker 41B. Entered in Strahan's ledger to John & Charles Wesley under Dec 1742, 1000 copies. Clearly a quarter-sheet from the paper used, and possibly a four-page pamphlet.
'O thou that hangedst on the tree'

Wesley, C. A hymn for condemned prisoners

     Baker's identification of the hymn in Charles Wesley's *Hymns and sacred poems*, 1749, is tentative.
(Strahan's ledger.)

W318 — [dh] The life of faith, exemplified in the eleventh chapter of St. Paul's epistle to the Hebrews. [*London*, 1740.] (May)
12°: B⁶; *1 2–12.*
     Baker 18A; entered in Strahan's ledger to Charles Wesley, 2000 copies on 24 May, '1000 more' on 2 June. Apparently there were two impressions from the same setting. A paraphrase in the form of sixteen hymns.
'Author of faith, eternal Word'
O(lacks B6),*CQ,NeP; GEU,NNUT,NcD*.

W319 [—] 'The means of grace.' [*London*, 1742.] (Oct)
     Baker 18B. Entered in Strahan's ledger to John & Charles Wesley under 4 Oct 1742, 1000 copies. Clearly a quarter-sheet from the paper supplied, and possibly a four-page pamphlet. Baker also records a 1740 edition, apparently from Strahan's ledgers, but I have not been able to find the entry.
'Long have I seem'd to serve thee, lord'
     Reprinted from *Hymns and sacred poems*, 1740; noted as by Charles in John Wesley's diary.
(Strahan's ledger.)

[W320 cancelled.]

W321 [—] 'The paraphrase on Isaiah 14.' [*London*, 1742.] (Sept)
     Baker 19.i. Entered in Strahan's ledger to John & Charles Wesley after 1 Sept 1742, 1500 copies; clearly a quarter-sheet from the paper used, and possibly a four-page leaflet. Presumably Strahan's entry is an error for 'Isaiah lxiv'; an edition with this drop-head title is found at the end of John Wesley's *A serious answer to Dr. Trapp's four sermons* (Cork, 1748) at Victoria University, Toronto, but it is not perhaps bibliographically distinct.
'O that thou would'st the heavens rend!'
     Previously published in John & Charles Wesley's *Hymns and sacred poems*, 1740.
(Strahan's ledger.)

W322 [—] 'The taking of Jericho.' [*London*, 1742.] (March)
     Baker 32A. Entered in Strahan's ledger to John & Charles Wesley after 23 March, 1000 copies and under 31 March '2000 more'. Clearly printed on a quarter sheet from the paper supplied, possibly as a four-page leaflet; from the costs, the second impression was from standing type.
'And shall we now turn back'
     Reprinted in Charles Wesley's *Hymns and sacred poems*, 1749.
(Strahan's ledger.)

W323 [—] 'Thanksgiving for the colliers.' [*London*, 1742.] (Oct)

Wesley, C. Thanksgiving for the colliers

    Baker 40D. Entered in Strahan's ledger to John & Charles Wesley under 13 Oct 1742, 1000 copies. Clearly a quarter-sheet from the paper supplied, and possibly a four-page leaflet.

'Ye neighbours and friends of Jesus draw near'
    Baker's identification of the hymn in Charles Wesley's *Hymns and sacred poems*, 1749, is tentative.
    (Strahan's ledger.)

W324 [—] The whole armour of god. Ephesians VI. [*London?* 1742?]
$\frac{1}{2}°$: 1 side, 2 columns.
    Baker 33A. Double row of type flowers between columns. Dated in the L catalogue as [1749?]; arranged in *Baker* with poems of 1742.

'Soldiers of Christ, arise'
L(C.121.g.9/205).

Wesley, John. A collection of psalms and hymns. *Charles-town, printed by Lewis Timothy,* 1737.
8°: pp. 74.   LMA; NN.
    Green 6.

—— *London, printed in the year* 1738. (24 May?)
8°: pp. 81.   LLP.
    Green 7. Entered to John Hutton in Bowyer's ledgers under 24 May, 500 copies printed. For the collection of 1741, see the joint heading below.

Wesley, John & Charles.
The works of these two brothers have never been satisfactorily distinguished, and I list all anonymous collections of hymns under this heading, though a few may be the work of Charles alone.
References are given to Richard Green, The works of John and Charles Wesley, a bibliography, *1896. Frank Baker's* A union catalogue of the publications of John and Charles Wesley (*Durham, N.C., 1966*) *keeps Green's numeration; where he has distinguished new works I have referred to his number; e.g. 'Baker 18B'. Further locations of copies will be found in his catalogue; I have normally confined my lists to the major libraries.*

—— Hymns and sacred poems. Published by John Wesley...and Charles Wesley... *London, printed by W. Strahan; sold by James Hutton; and at Mr. Bray's,* 1739.
12°: pp. x, 223.   L,O; MH,NN.
    Green 15.

—— The second edition. *London, printed by W. Strahan; sold by James Hutton, and at Mr. Bray's,* 1739. (July)
12°: pp. viii. 160.   LMA,MR; GEU,NcD.
    Entered to Charles Wesley in Strahan's ledger under 20 July, 1500 copies.

—— The third edition. *London, printed by W. Strahan; sold by James Hutton; and at Mr. Bray's,* 1739. (*GM* Aug)

Wesley, J. & C. *Collections*

12°: pp. x, 223.   L,O; GEU,NcD.
    Entered in Strahan's ledger immediately after the preceding, 1000 copies.

—— The fourth edition. *Bristol, printed by Felix Farley; sold by the booksellers of Bristol, Bath, Newcastle upon Tyne, and Exeter; – as also by A. Bradford, in Philadelphia,* 1743.
12°: pp. vi, 316.   LDW,LMA; MH,NcD.
    This edition incorporates the following collection.

———————

— Hymns and sacred poems. *London, printed by W. Strahan; sold by James Hutton, and at the Foundery,* 1740. (July)
12°: pp. xi, 207.   O,MR; MH,NcD.
    Green 19. A second collection, incorporated with the fourth edition of the preceding. Entered in Strahan's ledger under 14 July.

———————

— Hymns and sacred poems. *Bristol, printed and sold by Felix Farley, J. Wilson, and at the Schoolroom: in Bath, by W. Frederick: and in London, by T. Harris; also at the Foundery,* 1742.
12°: pp. 304.   L,O; MH,NN.
    Green 40. A third collection.

—— The second edition. *Bristol, printed by Felix Farley; sold by the booksellers of Bristol, Bath, London, Newcastle upon Tyne, and Exeter; as also by A. Bradford, in Philadelphia,* 1743.
12°: pp. v, 300.   L,LMA; GEU.

—— The second edition. *Bristol, printed by Felix Farley,* 1745.
12°: pp. v, 300.   LMA,EN; MH,NcD.

———————

— Hymns and sacred poems. *Dublin, printed in the year* 1747.
12°: pp. 60.   L,LMA; GEU,NcD.
    Green 106. A small selection from the previous collections.

———————

— A collection of psalms and hymns. Published by John Wesley... *London, printed by W. Strahan; sold at the Foundery, at James Hutton's, and at John Lewis's,* 1741.
12°: pp. 126.   LMA,MR; NNP,NcD.
    Green 30.

—— Published by John Wesley...and Charles Wesley... The second edition, enlarged. *London, printed by W. Strahan; sold at the Foundery,* 1743.
12°: pp. 138.   LMA,MR; NcD.

—— The third edition, enlarged. *London, printed by W. Strahan; sold by T. Trye, and at the Foundery.* 1744.
12°: pp. 136.   L,O; NcD.

— — The fourth edition, enlarged. *Bristol, printed by Felix Farley; sold by T. Trye, and at the Foundry, London,* 1748.
12°: pp. 144.　L,O; NcD.

— A collection of hymns published by John Wesley...and Charles Wesley... *London, printed by W. Strahan; sold by Thomas Harris, T. Trye, and at the Foundery,* 1742. (Nov)
12°: pp. 36.　O,CT; GEU.
　　Green 41. A selection from the first collection of 1739. Entered in Strahan's ledger under 6 Nov 1742, 3000 copies.

— — Extracted from the first volume of Hymns and sacred poems... *London, printed by W. Strahan; sold by Thomas Harris, T. Trye, and at the Foundery,* 1743. (Oct)
12°: pp. 36.　O.
　　Entered in Strahan's ledger under 15 Oct 1743, 1500 copies.

— — *Dublin, printed by S. Powell,* 1749.
12°: pp. 36.　LMA,MR; NcD.

— [*idem*] A collection of hymns. By the reverend Mr. John Westley... *Belfast, printed by James Magee,* 1750.
8°: pp. 36.　LMA; NcD.

Smaller collections, arranged alphabetically

[—] Funeral hymns. [*London,* 1746.] (Feb)
12°: pp. 24.　LMA,MR; NcD.
　　Green 96. Entered in Strahan's ledger under Feb 1746, 1500 copies. Half-title only. The catalogue of O suggests Charles was the sole author.

[—] — The second edition. [1746/47?]
12°: pp. 24.　L,O; MH,NcD.

[—] — The third edition. *Dublin, printed by S. Powell; sold at Mr. Verney's, by Mrs. Crump, and Mr. Watts,* 1747.
12°: pp. 24.　LMA; NcD.

[—] Gloria patri, &c. or hymns to the trinity. *London, printed in the year* 1746. (Oct)
12°: pp. 11.　O,MR; NNP,NcD.
　　Green 93. Entered in Strahan's ledger under 5 Oct, 1500 copies. The catalogue at O suggests Charles was the sole author.

[—] — The second edition. *Bristol, printed by Felix Farley; sold at the School-room. Also by T. Trye, and at the Foundry, London,* 1749.
12°: pp. 12.　LMA,EN; CtY-D,MH.

[—] [dh] Graces before meat. [*London?* 1746?]
12°: pp. 12.　LMA,EN; NNUT,NcD.
　　Green 98. There are a number of undifferentiated editions, but the earliest appears to be that with a double rule above the drop-head title (later editions use a row of printers' flowers). A copy of this edition at EN is bound in a volume with pamphlets of 1746–7.

There are apparently two impressions, distinguished as *Baker* 98A (a) & (b); one has the misprint '*Festival·s*' for '*Festivals.*' in the note on p. 1.

[—] Graces before and after meat. To which is added, Gloria patri; or, hymns to the trinity. *Dublin, printed by S. Powell; sold at Mr. Verney's, by Mrs. Crump, and Mr. Watts,* 1747.
12°: pp. 23.　LMA,MR; GEU.

[—] Hymns for ascension-day. *Bristol, printed by Felix Farley,* 1746.
12°: pp. 12.　LMA,MR; MH,NNP.
　　Green 91.

[—] — The second edition. *Bristol, printed by Felix Farley,* 1747.
12°: pp. 12.　L,O; GEU,NcD.

[—] — The third edition. *Dublin, Powell,* 1747.
12°: pp. 12.　GEU,NcD.

[—] [dh] Hymns for children. [1746?]
12°: pp. 12.　LMA.
　　Green 99. *Baker* distinguishes copies as A or B; the headpiece above the drop-head title in A has a shell in the centre, and p. 4, line 3 reads '...hath'; in B the headpiece has an apple in the centre, and p. 4, line 3 reads '...hast'. These are from the same setting of type and probably represent different impressions.

[—] 'Hymns for Christmas day.' *See* Hymns for the nativity of our lord.

[—] Hymns for new year's day, M.DCC.L. *Bristol, printed by Felix Farley,* [1749.]
12°: pp. 11.　LMA.
　　Green 147.

[—] — M.DCC.LI. *Bristol, printed by Felix Farley,* [1750.]
12°: pp. 11.　LMA,MR.

[—] Hymns for our lord's resurrection. *London, printed by W. Strahan; sold by T. Trye, Henry Butler, and at the Foundery,* 1746. (March)
12°: pp. 20.　O,EN; NNP,NcD.
　　Green 90. Entered in Strahan's ledger under 17 March, 1500 copies.

[—] — The second edition. *Bristol, printed by Felix Farley; sold at the School-room. Also by T. Trye, Henry Butler, and at the Foundery, London,* 1746.
12°: pp. 24.　LMA; GEU,NcD.

[—] — The third edition. *Dublin, printed by S. Powell; sold at Mr. Verney's, by Mrs. Crump, and Mr. Watts,* 1747.
12°: pp. 24.　L,LMA; MH,NcD.
No ornament on p. 24.

[—] [another edition]　LMA; NcD.
Ornament on p. 24. In the copy at LMA, A⁶ is from the same setting as the preceding, B⁶ reset.

[—] — The third edition. *Bristol, printed by Felix Farley; sold at the School-room. Also by T. Trye, Hen. Butler, and at the Foundry, London,* 1748.
12°: pp. 24.   O,EN; CtY-D,NNUT.

[—] Hymns for the festivals, and on other solemn occasions, 1748. *See* Hymns.

[—] Hymns for the nativity of our lord. [*London,* 1745?]
12°: pp. 24.   L,O; GEU,NcD.
Green 84; *Baker* quotes Strahan's ledger, 20 Dec 1744, for 1500 copies of 'Hymns for Christmas day' on a ream and a half of paper, and so apparently referring to a 12-page and not the 24-page pamphlet seen. He ignores a further entry under 17 Dec 1745 for 3000 copies in six reams which may correspond to this edition. Half-title only.

[—] — The second edition. *Bristol, printed by Felix Farley,* 1745.
12°: pp. 24.   LMA; NcD.

[—] — The third edition. *Dublin, printed by S. Powell; sold at Mr. Verney's, by Mrs. Crump, and Mr. Watts,* 1747.
12°: pp. 24.   LMA; NcD.

[—] — The fourth edition. *Bristol, printed by Felix Farley,* 1750.
12°: pp. 24.   LMA,O; NcD.

—— The tenth edition. *London, printed by Henry Cock; sold at the Foundery, by T. Trye, and by George Englefield. – In Bristol, by J. Wilson, and at the School-room. – In Newcastle upon Tyne, by R. Akenhead. And in Exeter, by Mr. Thorn,* 1750.
12°: pp. 24.   LMA,O; GEU.
Baker also records an undated edition, without title and adding *Gloria patri* on pp. 18–24, as c. 1750 (copy at LMA).

[—] Hymns for the public thanksgiving-day, October 9, 1746. *London, printed in the year* 1746. (Oct)
12°: pp. 12.   L,MR; CtY-D,NcD.
Green 95. Entered in Strahan's ledger under 5 Oct 1746, 1500 copies.

[—] — [*Bristol*] *Printed in the year* 1746.
12°: pp. 12.   LMA,MR; NNP,NNUT.

[—] [dh] Hymns for the watch-night. [*London, Strahan,* 1749?]
12°: pp. 12.
Green 97, suggesting the date 1746; *Baker* thinks the poems are reprinted from Charles Wesley's *Hymns and sacred poems,* 1749. There are numerous editions, of which the earlier have four stanzas on p. 1. I suspect the first to be *Baker* B, printed by Strahan on the evidence of the ornament; there is a double rule above the drop-head title, and a press figure 2 on p. 6 (copies at LMA,O).

[—] Hymns for those that seek, and those that have redemption in the blood of Jesus Christ. *London, printed by W. Strahan; sold by Thomas Trye, and at the Foundery,* 1747. (July)
12°: pp. 70.   LMA,MR; GEU,NcD.
Green 105. Entered in Strahan's ledger, July 1747, 1500 copies.

[—] — The second edition. *Bristol, printed by Felix Farley; sold at the School-room: also by T. Trye, and at the Foundry, London. – And at the several societies in England and Ireland,* 1747.
12°: pp. 72.   O,MR; NcD.

[—] — *Dublin printed by S. Powell; sold at Mr. Verney's, by Mrs. Crump, and Mr. Watts,* 1747.
12°: pp. 72.   LMA.

[—] — The third edition. *Bristol, printed by Felix Farley; sold at the School-room: also by T. Trye, and at the Foundery, London,* 1749.
12°: pp. 72.   LMA; NcD.

[—] — *Dublin, printed by S. Powell,* 1750.
12°: pp. 72.   LMA,EN; NcD.
Baker records a 64-page edition at the Wesley Historical Society Library, Belfast, with a cropped imprint reading 'Dublin printed, Corke ⟨   ⟩'; he suggests it was reprinted by Harrison from the Dublin 1747 edition.

[—] Hymns for times of trouble. [*London,* 1744.] (March?)
12°: pp. 12.   L,O; NNP,NcD.
Green 60; Baker tentatively identifies it with 'Hymns for the year 1744' of which Strahan printed 3000, 1 March 1744, and a further 3000 on 17 March; he suggests both were from the same type, though the fact that the cost was the same for each batch suggests the opposite. No distinguishing feature has been noted. Added to the 1756 edition of *Hymns for times of trouble and persecution.*

[—] Hymns for times of trouble and persecution. *London, printed in the year* 1744. (April)
12°: pp. 47.   L,O; MH.
Green 59. Entered in Strahan's ledgers under April, 1500 copies.

—— The second edition, enlarged. *London: printed in the year* 1744. *Reprinted at Bristol, by Felix Farley,* 1745.
12°: pp. 69.   O,MR; NcD.
Adds 'Hymns for times of trouble, for the year 1745'.

[—] 'Hymns in times of trouble.' [*London,* 1745.] (Dec)
Baker 60[C]. Entered in Strahan's ledgers under 17 Dec 1745 'one half sheet no. 3000'. It must surely be the fifteen 'Hymns for times of trouble, for the year 1745' added to the second edition of *Hymns for times of trouble and persecution* (Bristol, 1745) above.

Wesley, J. & C. *Smaller collections*

[—] 'Hymns from Jeremiah.' [*London*, 1745.] (Oct)

> *Baker* 84C from Strahan's ledger under Oct 1745, 2000 copies on two reams of paper; possibly a 12-page pamphlet rather than the 8-page pamphlet suggested by Baker.

[—] Hymns occasioned by the earthquake, March 8, 1750. *London, printed in the year* 1750.

12°: pp. 12.   O,MR.

> *Baker* 148, identifying the printer as Strahan.

[—] — The second edition. *London, printed in the year* 1750.

12°: pp. 12.   LMA.

[—] Hymns occasioned by the earthquake... Part II. *London, printed in the year* 1750.

12°: pp. 23.   LMA,MR; NN,NcD.

> *Baker* 148A, identifying the printer as Strahan.

— Hymns of petition and thanksgiving for the promise of the Father. *Bristol, printed by Felix Farley*, 1746.

12°: pp. 36.   LMA,MR; NNP,NcD.

> *Green* 92.

— — The second edition. *Bristol, printed by Felix Farley*, 1747.

12°: pp. 36.   L,EN; GEU,NcD.

— — The third edition. *Dublin, printed by S. Powell; sold at Mr. Verney's, by Mrs. Crump, and Mr. Watts*, 1747.

12°: pp. 36.   LMA; NcD.

[—] Hymns on god's everlasting love. To which is added, the cry of a reprobate. *Bristol, printed by S. & F. Farley*, 1741.

12°: pp. 36.

> *Green* 31. There are several apparent editions of which the following have been clearly distinguished:
> 1. dh on p. 3 'A collection of hymns'; vignette of head on title (*Baker* B).   NeP; NNP.
> 2. dh on p. 3 'Hymns on god's everlasting love'; vignette of head on title (*Baker* A). GEU.
> 3. Title adds 'and the horrible decree'; dh on on p. 3 'Hymns on god's everlasting love'; vignette of cherubs on title (*Baker* D). NcD.

[—] Hymns on god's everlasting love. *London, printed by W. Strahan; sold by T. Harris, and at the Foundery*, [1742.] (March)

12°: pp. 60.   LMA,MR; NNP,NcD.

> *Green* 32; a different collection. The two were combined in 1756. Entered in Strahan's ledger under 23 March 1742, 1500 copies.

[—] Hymns on the great festivals, and other occasions. *London, printed for M. Cooper; sold by T. Trye, Henry Butler, the booksellers of Bristol, Bath, Newcastle upon Tyne, and Exeter, and at the musick-shops*, 1746.

4°: pp. 66.   L,O; DLC,NcD.

Wesley, J. & C. *Smaller collections*

> *Green* 94. Interleaved with engraved music. A selection from other collections.

— Hymns on the lord's supper... With a preface... *Bristol, printed by Felix Farley*, 1745.

12°: pp. 32, 141.   L,O; NNP,NcD.

> *Green* 83.

— — The second edition. *Bristol, printed by Felix Farley*, 1747.

12°: pp. 32, 129.   O,MR; NcD.

[**Wesley, Samuel,** *the elder, 1662–1735.*] An elegy on the royal family of France, [1712.] *See* E120.

W325 — The history of the new testament, representing the actions and miracles of our blessed saviour and his apostles, attempted in verse: and adorn'd with CLII. sculptures... The cuts done by J. Sturt. *London, printed for Cha. Harper*, 1701.

8°: A–X⁸; *i–xvi, 1* 2–305 *306–320.* A1 frt; A2 engraved title; 316–320 advt.

> Title quoted from the letterpress title in red and black, A3; the engraved title A2 reads 'The history of the new testament attempted in verse...' with imprint 'London, printed for C. Harper, 1701'. Subsequently intended to be issued with the *Old testament* of 1704.

'Christ's line and birth St. Matthew first relates' O(2); CLU-C,CSmH,*DFo*,ICU(lacks A3),NNUT.

W326 — [reissue] *London, printed for Benj. Cowse, & John Hooke*, 1715. (*MC* Feb)

> Cancel letterpress title A3, but with the original 1701 engraved title. Intended for issue with the 1715 *Old testament.*

L(1163.b.6),E; *DLC*.

W327 — — The third edition. *London, printed by R.B., for Thomas Ward*, 1717.

8°: A–X⁸; *i–xvi, 1* 2–305 *306–320.* A1 frt; A2 engraved title; 316–320 advt.

> Title quoted from the letterpress title A3; the imprint of the engraved title A2 has been altered to 'London; printed for T. Ward', no date. The copyright of 'Wesley's History of the Bible 3 vol. 8vo. with all the plates' was sold as lot 3 of the trade sale of Thomas Ward, 8 March 1720 [1721] to Mears for £12. A third share re-appeared in the sale of John Hooke, 31 May 1731, sold to Lintot, and another in the sale of Richard Wilkin, 7 Feb 1738 (cats. at O-JJ).

L(1411.c.5; 11643.bb.37; G.19995),O; CLU-C, CtY,MH,NN.

W328 — The history of the old testament in verse: with one hundred and eighty sculptures: in two volumes. Dedicated to her most sacred majesty... The cuts done by J. Sturt. *London, printed for Cha. Harper*, 1704 [1703]. (*TC* Michaelmas 1703)

8°: 2 vol; π² A⁴ B–Y⁸ Z⁸(±Z8); 2π² 2A–2T⁸ 2V–3A⁴ (B3, 4 as' B4, B3'); [*4*] *i–viii, 1* 2–351 *352*; [*2*] *351* 352–709 *710–712.* π1 frt; π2 engraved title;

Wesley, S., *elder*. The history

352 err; 2π1 engraved title; 2π2 fly-title; 662 err; 663–665, 711–712 advt.

Title quoted from the letterpress title A1; the engraved title π2 reads 'The history of the old and new testament attempted in verse' with imprint 'London, printed for C. Harper, 1704'. Letterpress fly-title to vol. 2 on 2π2; the engraved title on 2π1 reads 'The history of the holy Bible from the revolt of the ten tribes...' with imprint 'Printed for C. Harper', no date. Clearly intended to be issued with the *New testament* of 1701, and so advertised in *TC*. Title in red and black. Vol 2 contains a signature W⁴.

'In the beginning did th' all-high create'
L(1163.b.4,5),O(−π1),E; CSmH(−3A4),DFo.

W329 — [reissue] *London, printed for Benj. Cowse, & John Hooke, 1715.* (*MC* Feb)

Cancel letterpress title A1, but with the same engraved titles as the preceding.
CSmH,ICU.

W330 — [reissue] The history of the old and new testament attempted in verse... *London, printed for John Hooke, 1716.*

Title and imprint quoted from the revised engraved title π2; the engraved title to vol. 2 has its imprint changed to 'Printed for John Hooke', no date. The original 1704 printed title to vol. 1 (A1) was presumably intended to be cancelled, but survives in copies at CLU-C, MH; the cancel title of 1715 is found in a copy at L. The copy at O has the Harper state of the engraved title to vol 2. Copies are usually found with the 1717 edition of the *New testament*.
L(11643.bb.37; G.19993, 4),O; CLU-C,CSmH, MH,NN,NjP +.

W331 — An hymn on peace. To the prince of peace. *London, printed by J. Leake, for Benj. Barker & Charles King, 1713.*
2°: *A*² B–C²; *1–2* 3–12.
'Once more, O saviour prince, thy bard inspire'
L(1960),O; CSmH,CtY,MH(uncut),TxU.

W332 — Marlborough; or, the fate of Europe: a poem. Dedicated to the right honourable Master Godolphin. *London, printed for Charles Harper, 1705.* (19 Jan, Luttrell)
2°: *A*¹ B–D²; *1–2* 3–10 9–12.
Advertised in *PM* 25 Jan. The copyright formed part of lot 14 of the trade sale of Thomas Ward, 8 March 1721 (cat. at O-JJ), sold to Hooke, and was sold in his sale, 31 May 1731 (cat. at O-JJ) in lot 43 to Wilford.
'Th' Eternal, who the fates of empires weighs'
L(11632.h.28),LDW,O,E,WgP(ms. corrections) +; CLU-C(Luttrell),CSmH,ICN,NjP.

Wesley, Samuel, *the younger, 1691–1739.* Poems on several occasions. *London, printed for the author, by E. Say; sold by S. Birt, 1736.* (*GM* Feb)

Wesley, S., *younger*

4°: pp. 412.   L,O; CtY,MH.
The title appears to be a cancel in copies at CtY,MH. The additions and life of Wesley included in the following were issued separately to bind up with this edition as 'Some account of the life and character...1743' (copies at L,O).

— — The second edition, with additions. *Cambridge, printed by J. Bentham, for J. Brotherton, & S. Birt, London, 1743 [1744].* (*GM* March)
12°: pp. iv, ix, 332.   L,AN; IU,MH.

W333 [—] The battle of the sexes: a poem. *London, printed for J. Roberts, 1723 [1724?].*
8°: A–E⁴; *1–2* 3–38 *39–40 blk.*
Entered in *SR* 27 April 1724 to John Brotherton, possibly on a transfer of copyright; deposit copies at O,E,EU,SaU. A listing in *MC* March 1724 'for J. Brotherton' may be similarly explained; if so, the original publication date is not known.
'Thou, for whose view these numbers are design'd'
Reprinted in Wesley's *Poems*, 1736; the preface is by Thomas Cooke, which has caused it to be credited to him by some authorities. Translated into Latin by Glover Denny as *Sexus invicem depraeliantes*, 1740.
L(1490.p.83),O(2, 1−E4),E,EU(−E4),SaU; CtY(−E4),DFo(Luttrell, undated),IU,MH, TxU +.

W334 [—] — The second edition. *London, printed for J. Brotherton; sold by J. Roberts, 1724.* (July?)
8°: A⁴ a⁴ B⁴(−B1) C–E⁴ (a4 as 'B'); *i–ii* iii–xiii *xiv, 1* 2–32. xiv advt.
Listed in *MC* July as 'just publish'd... To which is added two stanza's, and the whole corrected by the author; with a preface of his own writing'.
L(11633.cc.2/2),OW,CT,E(2),MR; CSmH(uncut),CtY,ICN,MH,TxU +.

W335 [—] — *London printed, and re-printed in Dublin, for William Smith, 1724.*
8°: A–E⁴; *1–2* 3–38 *39–40.* E4 advt.
L(1959),O,C(−E4),DA(2, 1−E4),LdU-B(−E4); PHC.

W336 [—] — *London, printed, and re-printed in Dublin, 1724.*
8°: A² B–C⁴ (C1 as 'B'); *5–9* 10–24.
DN.

W337 [—] — [Bath] *Printed in the year 1738.*
8°: π¹ A–C⁴ D¹; [2] *i–iii* iv–vi, 7 8–25 *26 blk.* π1 hft.
Ms. note in the L copy 'This book was reprinted and bound at Bath in the year 1738'.
L(11644.ee.28).

W338 [—] — The third edition. *Dublin, printed by George Faulkner, 1740.*

Wesley, S., *younger.* The battle of the sexes

8^0: A–D^4; *i–iii* iv–viii, *1* 2–21 *22–23; 24 blk.* 22–23 advt.

L(1960),C,DA(–D4),DG,GU; CSmH,NNUT.

W339 [—] [reissue]

8^0: A–D^4; *i–iii* iv–viii, *1* 2–24.

The edition of Edward Waters (below) commented on changes in the text of Faulkner's edition; this issue (possibly created by cancelling D3–4) compares the changed passages with the original on p. 22 and quotes the *Guardian* no. 152 on pp. 23–24. It presumably followed Waters's edition.

DG.

W340 [—] — *Dublin, printed by Edward Waters,* 1740.

8^0: *A*^{4} B–D^4; *i–ii* iii–x, *1–20 21; 22 blk.*

A postscript on p. 21 discusses the text of Faulkner's edition above.

DA.

[—] The bridge of life, an alegorical poem, 1724. *See* B441.

W341 [—] [dh] The cobler, a tale. [*Dublin, Edward Exshaw,* 173–.]

12^0: *A*^{4}; *1* 2–7 *8.* 8 advt. of Exshaw books.

'Your sage and moralist can show'
Printed in Wesley's *Poems,* 1736.

LVA-F.

[—] Georgia, a poem, 1736. *See* G128.

W342 — The Iliad in a nutshell: or Homer's Battle of the frogs and mice. Illustrated with notes. *London, printed for B. Barker; sold by J. Roberts,* 1726. (*MC* May)

8^0: A^2 B–I^4; *i–iv, 1–61 62; 63–64 blk.* 62 err.

'Your aid, ye heav'n-born muses, hither bring'
Dedication signed.

L(T.854/1,–I4),LG,O(–I4),CT(–I4),E(–I4) +; CSmH,CtY,IU,MH,TxU+.

W343 [—] Neck or nothing: a consolatory letter from Mr. D-nt-n to Mr. C--rll upon his being tost in a blanket, &c. [*London*] *Sold by Charles King in Westminster-Hall,* 1716.

8^0: A^8; *1–4* 5–16. A1 frt.

Copies usually show a 1*d.* tax stamp called for on pamphlets of one sheet or less.

'Lo! I that earst the glory spread'
Early ms. attribution in the CT copy; reprinted in Wesley's *Poems,* 1736. A mock letter from John Dunton to Edmund Curll.

L(1481.aaa.1; 164.m.8),LVA-D,O(2, 1 lacks A1.8),OW,CT+; CtY,ICN,MH,NjP,TxU+.

W344 [—] A new ballad. [Come listen...] [*London,* 1723.]

$\frac{1}{2}^0$: 1 side, 1 column.

'Come listen ye tories and Jacobites now'
Crum C529: 'On the Bishop of Rochester's plot. – By Mr. Westley'. Samuel Wesley is known to have been a writer of Jacobite ballads. A satire on the whigs for inventing the Atterbury plot.

O; MH(dated in ms. 1723).

Wesley, S., *younger*

[—] An ode for the new year. Written by Colley Cibber [!], [1731?] *See* C195.

W345 [—] The parish priest. A poem, upon a clergyman lately deceas'd. *London, printed for J. Roberts,* 1731. (*GSJ* 9 Nov)

4^0: A–B^4 C^2; *1–3* 4–20.

Entered to himself (as 'WB') in Bowyer's ledgers under 4 Nov 1731, 300 copies printed. The paper ledger records that the copies were delivered to Roberts on 4 Nov; 25 received of him for Wesley on 6 Nov, followed by 50 more; and 12 more 'stitcht in black' on 8 Nov.

'Accept, dear sire, this humble tribute paid'
Reprinted in Wesley's *Poems,* 1736. The clergyman was identified by Maurice Johnson (in his copy sold at Sotheby's, 23 March 1970, lot 164) as John Berry, vicar of Walton in Norfolk.

C.

W346 [—] — The second edition. *London, printed for J. Roberts,* 1732 [1731]. (21 Dec?)

4^0: A–B^4 C^2; *1–3* 4–20.

Entered in Bowyer's ledgers under 21 Dec 1731, 500 copies printed.

L(840.k.2/1),O; NN(ms. notes).

W347 [—] The pig, and the mastiff. Two tales. *London, printed for J. Brotherton; sold by J. Roberts,* 1725. (*MC* April)

8^0: *A*^{2} B–D^4 E^2; *i–iv, 1* 2–28. i hft; ii advt.

Pig: 'Some husbands on a winter's day'
Mastiff: 'Your deep observers of mankind'
Reprinted in Wesley's *Poems,* 1736.

L(1960,–A1),O(–A1),LdU-B; CSmH(–A1), CtY,DFo,IU(–A1),MH(cropt)+.

W348 [—] — *Dubdin* [!], *printed by J. Watts, for W. Smith,* 1725.

8^0: A–C^4; *1–2* 3–23 *24.* 24 advt.

Advertisement on p. 24 for books 'sold opposite the Watch-House', apparently Watts's address (see *Plomer*).

DA,DN.

W349 [—] — The third edition. *Dublin, printed by J. Watts, and sold opposite the Watch-House,* 1725.

8^0: A–C^4; *1–2* 3–23 *24.* 24 advt.

DN,DT.

W350 [—] — *London, printed by J. Stephens, for J. Brotherton,* 1727.

8^0: *A*^{2} B–D^4 E^2; *i–iv, 1* 2–28. i blk; ii advt.

O(–A1),MR; NNC,TxU(–A1).

W351 [—] — The fourth edition. *Dublin, printed by and for James Hoey,* 1735.

8^0: A–C^4; *1–3* 4–23 *24.* 24 advt.

A copy at DA has an incorrect state of the date, 'MDCCXXVV'.

L(11602.bb.33/7),LVA-F,DA(2, 1 uncut),DN.

W352 [—] The pig. A tale. *Dublin, printed by S. Powell, for Edward Exshaw,* 1735.

Wesley, S., *younger.* The pig

8°: A^4; *1–3* 4–8. 2 advt.
A reprint of the first tale only.
DA.

W353 [—] The prisons open'd. A poem occasion'd by the late glorious proceedings of the committee appointed to enquire into the state of the goals of this kingdom. *London, printed for J. Roberts,* 1729. (*MChr* 15 May)
4°: A^2 B–D^4; *i–iv, 1* 2–24.
Entered to Wesley in Bowyer's ledgers under 14 May, 500 copies printed; the ledgers also record stitching 100 in marble paper and 'a dozen in marble paper & gilt'.
'Let arms and warriors other poets fire'
Reprinted in Wesley's *Poems,* 1736.
L(11642.f.47),O; MH,NjP.

— The song of the three children paraphras'd. By Marc Le Pla.... Revis'd and publish'd by S. Wesley, 1728. *See* L107.

W354 [—] To the memory of the right reverend father in god, Francis Gastrell; doctor in divinity...and ...lord bishop of Chester. *London printed, and sold by J. Roberts,* 1726 [1727?]. (*MC* March 1727)
4°: A–B^4; *1–2* 3–16.
'I sing a prelate good, unbodied now'
Reprinted in Wesley's *Poems,* 1736.
L(840.h.4/10),OW(uncut).

W355 [—] Verses on the death of Mrs. Morice. *London, printed in the year* 1730.
4°: A^1 B–C^2 D^1; *1–2* 3–11 *12 blk.*
A1 and D1 have been seen to be conjugate.
'No fabling song, my mournful heart, essay'
Reprinted in Wesley's *Poems,* 1736; a letter from Pope to Wesley, 24 April 1730, thanks him for a copy. On the death of Mary Morice, daughter of Francis Atterbury, who died on the way to see her father in exile at Montpellier.
L(11631.f.38),C; OCU.

W356 [—] Verses on the death of Mrs. Morrice, late wife to Mr. Morrice, high-bailiff of Westminster, and daughter to the late bishop of R–ch––––r, now in exile. *London: printed, and Dublin re-printed, and sold by George Faulkner,* 1730.
8°: A^4; *1–3* 4–8.
DT; IU.

[—] The vicar of Bray, [1714/–.] *See* V84.

West, Gilbert. Odes of Pindar. With several other pieces in prose and verse, translated from the Greek. To which is prefixed a dissertation on the Olympic games. *London, printed for R. Dodsley,* 1749. (*GA* 11 May)
4°: pp. ccvi, 315.   L,O; CtY,MH.

—————

W357 [—] A canto of the Fairy queen. Written by Spenser. Never before published. *London, printed for G. Hawkins,* 1739. (*GM, LM* May)
2°: A^2 B–D^2; *i–iv,* 1–12.

West, G. A canto of the Fairy queen

'Wise was that Spartan lawgiver of old'
Printed as West's in *Dodsley* II, titled 'On the abuse of travelling. A canto in imitation of Spenser'.
L(641.m.13/2),O,C(uncut),EU,DG+; CLU, CtY,ICN,MH(2),TxU(2, 1 uncut).

W358 [—] The institution of the order of the garter. A dramatick poem. *London, printed for R. Dodsley,* 1742. (23 Feb)
4°: A–H^4; *1–5* 6–64.
Watermark: fleur-de-lys. Written in the form of a masque, but not apparently intended for performance. Publication date from *Straus, Dodsley;* listed in *GM* Feb.
'Hither, all ye heav'nly pow'rs'
Ascribed to West in *Dodsley* II.
L(11630.d.6/1; 605.e.8; 162.m.11),O,CT,DT, LdU-B; CLU-C(uncut),CSmH,ICN,NjP,TxU+.

W359 [—] [fine paper]
Watermark: crowned eagle.
CtY,MiU.

W360 [—] Stowe, the gardens of the right honourable Richard lord viscount Cobham. Address'd to Mr. Pope. *London, printed for L. Gilliver,* 1732. (*GSJ* 17 March)
2°: A^1 B–F^2 G^1; *i–ii,* 1–22.
Watermark: circular snake (cf. *Heawood* 3786–92). A1 and G1 have been seen to be conjugate.
'To thee, great master of the vocal string'
Ms. note in Harley's copy at O 'By mr West nephew to my Lord Cobham'.
O(4),OW,BaP(uncut),LdU-B; CSmH,DFo(uncut),IU,MH,TxU(3, 2 uncut)+.

W361 [—] [fine paper]
Watermark: fleur-de-lys on shield.
L(12273.m.1/13; 163.n.48).

W362 [—] — *London, printed by J. Wright, for Lawton Gilliver,* 1732.
8°: A^2 B–E^4; *i–iv,* 1–31 *32.* A1 hft; 32 advt.
L(992.h.9/5),LVA-D,O; CtY,DFo,MH(−A1).

W363 [—] — To which is added, Taste. A poem. By Mr. Pope. *London: printed. And, Dublin, re-printed by George Faulkner,* 1732.
8°: A^4 B–D^4; *1–3* 4–32.
O,DA,GU; CtY,IU,MH,TxU.

Westminster. Westminster Abbey: a poem, 1721. *See* Dart, John.

W364 — The Westminster bubble. A merry tale. In a dialogue between an old bridge and a new. By a water poet. *London, printed for J. Peele,* 1722. (*DP* 21 Feb)
8°: A^4 B–D^4; *1–4* 5–31 *32 blk.* A1 frt.
The frontispiece is an early wood-engraving.
'Good people draw near,/And a tale you shall hear'
L(1959),LG,O,EtC,LdU-B; InU,MH,NN.

W365 — — The second edition. *London, printed for J. Peele,* 1722.

The **Westminster** bubble

8°: $A^4(\pm A2)$ B–D^4; 1–4 5–31 32 blk. A1 frt.
  A reissue with cancel title. The copy seen is aberrant, containing also the preliminaries of the following issue.
O.

W366 — [reissue] To which is prefixed, a short history of screening and screeners: or, seasonable advice to the electors of the city of London... The second edition. *London, printed for Sam. Briscoe, & J. Peele*, 1722. (*DP* 15 March)
  8°: $^\pi$A^4 $A^4(-A2)$ B–D^4; 1–2 3–8, [2] 5–31 32 blk. The additions, in prose, occupy $^\pi$A2–4. The cancel title A2, present in the copy seen, should doubtless be absent and the frontispiece A1 placed before $^\pi$A. Possibly the work listed by Briscoe as *The tale of the two bridges* in *DP* 5 June 1722 along with poems by Edward Ward.
O.

W367 — The Westminster combat. [*London*, 1710.] (9 May, Luttrell)
  $\frac{1}{2}$°: 1 side, 2 columns.
  Title in roman type, two lines.
  ''Tis odd to conceive what a war has been wag'd'
    Against the managers at Sacheverell's trial.
  L(112.f.44/22); MH(Luttrell).

W368 — [another edition]
  Title in roman type, one line.
  Crawford.

W369 — [another edition]
  Title in black-letter, centre rule in three sections.
  O; MH.

W370 — [another edition]
  Title in black-letter, centre rule in one piece.
  L(1876.e.20/34).

W371 — The Westminster election. Tune of, Diogenes sur⟨l⟩y and proud. [*London*, 1741.]
  slip: 1 side, 1 column.
  Percival LXX. Rough woodcut at head.
  'You that wish your country's peace'
    In support of Edward Vernon.
  C.

W372 — 'The Westminster justice. A tale. *London, printed for Patrick Coram; sold at the pamphlet-shops in London & Westminster*. Price 4d.' (*DG* 16 Jan 1741)
  Listed in *LM* Jan 1741 under 'poetry'. The publisher's name is printed in *DG* with a space between the o and r; there is possibly a misprint there.

W373 — Westminster tryumphant in their choice of Englands glory. [*London*, 1741.]
  slip: 1 side, 1 column.
  'You Westminster boys so hearty and tight'
    A Westminster election ballad in favour of Edward Vernon and Charles Edwin.
  NNP.

Weston, J.

W374 [**Weston, James.**] The assembled patriots; or, the meeting of the parliament. A poem, dedicated to his majesty. *London, printed for T. Dormer*, 1732. (*GSJ* 13 Jan)
  4°: A^4 B^4; 1–5 'ii' 7–15 16 blk. A1 hft.
  'Again Great-Britain's sons auspicious meet'
    The dedication of the L copy is signed in pencil 'James Weston'; that copy belonged to a member of the Weston family in Nottingham. The L catalogue identifies the author with the stenographer of this name.
  L(11631.cc.7).

Whaley, John. A collection of poems. *London, printed for the author, by John Willis, & Joseph Boddington; sold by Messrs Innys, & Manby, Messieurs Bettesworth & Hitch, & T. Astley*, 1732.
  8°: pp. '287' [289].   L,O; CtY,IU.
  In addition to poems by 'S.D.' (Sneyd Davies), Lord Lyttelton's *Bleinheim* and *An epistle to Mr. Pope* are printed as though by Whaley; possibly in part a miscellany. Presentation copy at L.

— A collection of original poems and translations. *London, printed for the author; sold by R. Manby, & H. S. Cox*, 1745. (*GM* Aug)
  8°: pp. viii, 335.   L,O(impft); CtY,MH.
  Entered to Manby in Bowyer's ledgers under ⟨July?⟩ 30, 750 copies printed; 1000 proposals are entered under 2 March 1745, and a copy dated 1 March 1745 is at L. Dedication copy to Walpole at LVA-D.

W375 **Whalley, John.** A decree of the stars for Cornelius Carter. *Dublin, printed by John Whalley*, [1714.]
  $\frac{1}{2}$°: 1 side, 2 columns.
  'You that pretend my friend to be'
    A reply to *Advice from the stars*, 1714.
  C.

Wharton, Philip, *duke of Wharton.* The poetical works of Philip late duke of Wharton; and others of the Wharton family, and of the duke's intimate acquaintance, [1731?]
  A reissue of *Whartoniana*, 1727, which is a miscellany. See *Case* 347.

W376 ['—'] The drinking match, a new ballad in imitation of Chevy Chace. By a person of quality. *Dublin, printed by Thomas Hume*, 1722.
  $\frac{1}{2}$°: 1 side, 2 columns.
  Bond 93 (not knowing this early edition).
  'God prosper long our noble king'
    Printed in *Whartoniana*, 1727, as 'By the Duke of Wharton'; hence the attribution in the copy below. Wharton's authorship has been generally accepted, but it seems improbable. On a drinking match between the Duke of Wharton and 'Earl Harold' (usually identified as the

Wharton, P., *duke.* The drinking match

> Earl of Thanet) at Sir Christopher Musgrave's house, Eden Hall.
> NN,TxU.

W377 '—' The drinking match. An imitation of Chevy Chace. By the Duke of Wharton. *Edinburgh printed, and sold by several booksellers in town,* 1728.
8°: A⁴; *1–2* 3–8.
L(11631.aaa.56/11); CtY.

W378 ['—'] The drinking match, a new ballad... By a person of quality. *Dublin, re-printed by James Hoey & George Faulkner,* 1729.
½°: 1 side, 2 columns.
L(C.121.g.8/170),DT.

[—] An epistle from Jack Sheppard to the late l—d c—ll--r of E--d, 1725. *See* E369.

W379 '—' The fear of death. An ode. By the late Duke of Wharton. *London, printed for and sold by John Brett,* 1739. (*GM, LM* Nov)
2°: *A*² B²; *i–iv, 1* 2–4. A1 hft.
'Say, sov'raign queen of awful night'
> Referred to in Park's edition of Walpole's *Noble authors* (1806) IV.127 where it is said to have been advertised as 'communicated to the public by a merchant lately arrived from Spain'; it is ignored by subsequent writers, and its authenticity is perhaps questionable.
LdU-B; CU,CtY(−A1),KU,MH,TxU(3).

[—] The triple alliance, [1724/27.] *See* T498.

What. What is man?, 1738. *See* Vievar, Alexander.

W380 — What of that! Occasion'd by a pamphlet, intitled, Are these things so? and its answer, Yes, they are. *London, printed for T. Cooper; sold by the pamphlet shops of London & Westminster,* 1740. (*DG* 15 Nov)
2°: A–D²; *1–3* 4–16.
'To fill the realm with fears of coming woe'
> Part of the controversy started by [James Miller], *Are these things so?*, 1740. Replied to by [Robert Morris] *Have at you all*, 1740.
L(1484.m.23),O,OW,LdU-B; CLU-C,CSmH, ICN(uncut),OCU(2),TxU(2)+.

W381 — The second edition. *London, printed for T. Cooper; sold at the pamphlet shops of London & Westminster,* 1740. (*DP* 6 Dec)
2°: A–D²; *1–3* 4–16.
> Apparently a reimpression.
L(163.n.59); ICU,MH,NN-B(uncut).

W382 — — '*London, printed for J. Hooper; and to be had of all true hearts and sound bottoms*', 1740.
8°: A–B⁴; *1–2* 3–16.
> A piracy, probably printed in the north; cf. James Miller, *Are these things so*, 1740 (M239). The publisher's name is perhaps a deliberate misspelling of 'T. Cooper'. Horizontal chain-lines.
C,*MR-C*,PrP; CtY,MH.

Wheedling

W383 Wheedling. The wheedling gilts of White-Cross-street: or, a poem on the two dripping-pan scrapers, and my Lady Lu---y, receiver of the stuff. *London, printed in the year* 1710.
½°: 1 side, 2 columns.
'Rouse now my muse, surely in such a cause'
Harding.

W384 When. [dh] When the cat's away,|The mice may play.|A fable, humbly inscrib'd to Dr. Sw——t. [col] *London, printed for A. Baldwin,* [1712.] (*Spectator* 31 Jan)
2°: A²; *1–4.*
> Teerink 1299; *Rothschild* 1690. Entered in *SR* 31 Jan; deposit copies at L, ?E.
'A lady once (so stories say)'
> Tentatively ascribed to Prior in *Nichols, Collection* IV.50, probably following a ms. attribution in the LLP copy; conclusively rejected in *Wright & Spears* 801, following C.H. Firth in *RES* 1 (1925) 456. Firth suggested the author might have been Arthur Mainwaring, but there is no evidence for his authorship. A reply to *A fable of the widow and her cat*, 1712; Swift's authorship of that, implied here, is uncertain.
L(644.m.14/20; Ashley 4976, uncut),LLP,O,E, DT+; ICN,MH,TxU(corrected as printer's copy).

W385 — When we shall have peace, the Lord of Oxford knows. *London, printed by D. Brown, near Fleet-street,* 1711.
½°: 1 side, 1 column.
> On the other side of the Crawford copy (now split and mounted) was *The Scotch lords welcome to England*, [1707?].
'The old whiggish sages, we plainly do see'
> A tory poem.
Crawford.

W386 — [variant imprint:] *London, printed by David Walkwood, near Fleet-street,* 1711.
> This imprint is possibly fictitious. On the other side of the C copy, Samuel Wilde, *The weavers humble offering*, [1721?].
C.

Where. Where's your impeachment now?, 1712. *See* 'Tis pity they shou'd be parted, 1712.

W387 Whig. Whig and tory. [*London?* 1714?]
½°: 2 sides, 1 column.
'Good-morrow Tom; if not in haste'
> Whig and tory reconciled in welcoming George I as king.
L(C.121.g.9/176, cropt).

W388 — A whig-ballad: called, A safe peace, or none. To an excellent new tune. [*London*] *Printed and sold by T.H. in Black-fryars,* [1711/12.]
½°: 1 side, 2 columns.
'At Reswick Monsieur gave us peace'
DT,Rothschild.

Whiggery

W389 Whiggery. Whiggery display'd; or, the principles, practices, erudition and religion of our modern whiggs... By a true son of the church of England. *London, printed in the year* 1719.
8°: A–D⁴ (A3 as 'A'); *i–iv*, 1–27 *28 blk.* A1 hft.
    An omitted line is added in ms. on p. 11 in all copies seen.
'Since men unite for to infect'
L(11632.bb.46,–A1),O(–A1); MH.

W390 Whiggish. The whiggish fair warning to the q---n, upon the late change of the ministry; with the tory's fair answer. [*London*] Printed in the year 1711.
½°: 1 side, 1 column.
    In lower half of the sheet, 'The answer, by N.F.G.'. The original was printed as *Fair warning*, 1710.
'Madam, look out, your title is arraign'd'
Answer: 'Monarchs beware, your titles they disown'
MH.

W391 Whiggism. Whiggism laid open: and the loyal church-man's health. To the tune of Old Simon the king. [*London*, 1712.] (17 July)
½°: 1 side, 2 columns.
    Teerink 868. Advertised in *PB* 19 July.
'Now the whigs and their friends are confounded'
    Ball 145 suggested that Swift and Arbuthnot might have had a hand in it; not discussed by Williams.
L(1876.f.1/53),LLP(ms. date 17 July 1712); MH(title cropt).

W392 Whigs. The whigs address to his majesty. *London, printed by R. Ward, in the Strand*, [1714.]
½°: 1 side, 1 column.
'We who were never yet at quiet'
    Crum W164, 166. A tory satire on the whigs.
L(1876.f.1/31); MH(2),OCU.

— 'Whigs' coat of arms: or the thirteen plagues of a usurper. Folio broadside, poem (p. by John Monk), [ca. 1716].'
    Morgan S475, who records 'An engraving of "coat of arms" shows the devil supporting the Pretender, and shield with quarterings of Popish atrocities'. Possibly engraved throughout; but compare *The Jacobites coat of arms*, [1710?].

W393 — The whigs new toast to the b--- of S----y. [*London*] Printed by Rich. Newcomb, 1711. (*SR* 6 June)
½°: 1 side, 1 column.
    Woodcut at head. Deposit copies at L,E.
'Here's a health to the p-----te, whose excellence reaches'
    To Gilbert Burnet, bishop of Salisbury; apparently ironic.
L(C.20.f.2/238),C,E; TxU.

Whigs

W394 — The whigs no plunderers. [*London*, 1710/11.]
½°: 1 side, 1 column.
'If running the nation in debt'
    A tory attack on Godolphin and the whigs' financial policies.
C.

W395 — — [*London?*] *Printed in the year* 1710.
½°: 1 side, 2 columns.
Harding.

W396 — — '*London*' [*Dublin*], *printed in the year* 1711.
½°: 1 side, 2 columns.
    On the other side of the DT copy, *The Scotch truth at last*, in prose.
DT.

W397 — The whigs scandalous address answered stanza by stanza. By one who thinks it an honour to be called a high-flyer. [*London*] Printed in the year 1704.
8°: A–D⁴ E(3 ll); *i–viii*, 1–30. A1 hft.
    A reprint of *The address*, 1704, with a verse answer.
Address: 'Ye men of might and muckle power'
Reply: 'Ye senseless mutineering crew'
O; CtY,MH(–A1).

— Whiggs supplication, 1702. *See* Colvil, Samuel.

W398 Whimsical. The whimsical age, or the political juglers. [*London?* 1740.] (13 Nov?)
slip: 1 side, 1 column.
    Percival LXV. Two small cuts at head.
'I pray now come listen to me'
C(ms. note '1740 Nov. 13. on the quarrel at court').

W399 — [another edition]
    Woodcut at head.
C.

W400 Whip. A whip and a bell. [*London*] Printed by Rich. Smith at Charing-Cross, 1712.
½°: 1 side, 2 columns.
    On the other side of the Harding copy, a prose account of Adam de Cardonel's trial.
'A gentlewoman once of high renown'
    A tale relating to Marlborough's dismissal.
Harding.

W401 — A whip for the Spaniards, and a scourge for the French. In two satyrs. Written by J.M. and W.P. gents. *London, printed in the year* 1701. (*PB* 22 May)
2°: A–C²; *i–iv*, 1–8.
    The Luttrell copy, dated 22 May, is recorded in *Haslewood.*
'When conquering Spain before the Indians stood'
'If violated leagues for vengeance call'
LVA-D,O; CSmH,InU,TxU.

W402 — — *London, printed in the year* 1701.
8°: *A*⁸; *i–iv*, 1 ⟨2⟩–12.
O(slightly cropt).

W403 — — *London: printed in the year*, 1701. *and are to be sold at the printing-house in the Post-Office Coffee-house* [*Dublin*], 1701.

A **whip** for the Spaniards

8°: A–B⁴; *i–iv, 1–11 12 blk.*
DA.

W404 — A whip for the whiggs. '*Buckinghamshire. Printed at the Catherine-wheel, for the right worshipful the mayor of Chipping Wiccomb*', 1705.
4°: *A²; 1 2–4.*
The imprint is presumably false.
'We may reasonably fear a sad turn in the nation'
Longleat (cropt).

W405 — — [col] '*Buckinghamshire. Printed at the Catherine-wheel, for the right worshipful the mayor of Chipping Wiccomb*', 1705.
4°: *A²; 1–4.*
No title-page, drop-head title only.
MH,TxU.

Whison-fair. The Whison-fair: rary-show, [1710.]
See A rary-show, 1710. (R129)

W406 [**Whistler, Anthony.**] The shuttlecock. An heroi-comical poem. In four canto's. *Oxford, printed by L. Lichfield*, 1736.
8°: π⁴ A–E⁴; *i–viii, 1–39 40 blk.* π1 hft.
Bond 153. π3 is signed '*⁎⁎⁎*'.
'When female virtues make the world admire'
Ms. signature at end of dedication in the L copy.
L(11643.bbb.13/2),O; MH.

[**Whiston, William.**] The eclipse, a poem… By W.W., 1715. *See* E14.

W407 **White.** The white regiment's lament for the death of Captain Sarah. [*Edinburgh,* 1718.]
½°: 1 side, 2 columns.
'As dandering on the shoar of Leith'
E.

W408 [**White, George.**] The miraculous sheep's eye, at St. Victor's in Paris. A poem. In two canto's. By G.W----, M.A. minister of the church of England. *London, printed for Mary Marshall*, 1743. (*GM, LM* March)
8°: A⁸; *1–5 6–16.* A1 hft.
'Where Paris boasts her polite scrapes'
Early ms. note in the O copy 'Revd. Geo: White minister of Colne'. A satire on Roman Catholic practices.
L(1485.pp.12),O; MH.

W409 **Whiteacre.** Whiteacre's glory: or, the drubbing of Seignior Stopha. At Figg's amphitheatre in London. To the tune of the Protestant flail. *Dublin, printed in the year* 1725.
½°: *1–2,* 1 column.
'All you that to true English blood do belong'
On a boxing match between an Englishman and an Italian.
L(C.121.g.8/60),DG(cropt).

Whitehall

W410 **Whitehall.** The White-hall prophecy, lately found under the ruins of that royal chapel. [*London*] *Printed in the year* 1712.
½°: 1 side, 1 column.
'When two brother starlings shall piss in a quill'
A tory attack on the peculations of the whig ministry.
Crawford.

W411 **Whitehaven.** The Whitehaven garters. A ballad. *Dublin, printed by G. Faulkner*, 1734.
½°: *1–2,* 1 column.
'If e'er I forget/How much I'm in debt'
L(C.121.g.9/200).

Whitehead, Paul. Satires written by Mr. Whitehead. Viz. I. Manners… II. The state dunces… *London, printed in the year* 1739.
8°: pp. 38.
The title is quoted from the half-title; each poem has a separate title-page with the imprint quoted. Three editions have been seen, possibly all piratical, (i) at L,CSmH,KU, (ii) at CtY, (iii) at O.

— — III. Honour… *Islington, printed near the three pumps, in the year* 1748.
8°: pp. 52.   L,O; DFo,MH.
A similar production to the preceding.

— Poems and miscellaneous compositions… *London, printed for G. Kearsley, & J. Ridley*, 1777.
4°: pp. lxiii, 185.   O.

— [reissue?]   L,O.
Cancel leaves add pp. lxiii–lxv to the Life; the words 'Entered at Stationers Hall' are on the verso of the titles of the copies seen.

——————

[—] The Battiad, 1750. *See* M172.

[—] The green-cloth: or, the verge of the court… By Mr. Wh----d, 1739. *See* G276.

W412 [—] The Gymnasiad, or boxing match. A very short, but very curious epic poem. With the prolegomena of Scriblerus Tertius, and notes variorum. *London, printed for M. Cooper*, 1744. (*GM, LM* June)
4°: π¹ A⁴ B–D⁴ E¹; *[2] i–iii iv–xi xii, 13 14–33 34 blk.* π1 hft.
Bond 185. Vertical chain-lines.
'Sing, sing, O muse, the dire contested fray'
Dedication signed in ms. in the MH copy; collected in Whitehead's *Poems*, 1777.
L(11630.b.5/12; 11630.c.13/13; 643.k.5/5, uncut, − π1),O(− π1),CT,*MR,WgP*; CSmH,CtY, ICU(lacks A1),MH,TxU(uncut).

W413 [—] — An epic poem. With the prolegomena… Written by the E—l of C————d. *Dublin, printed for Thomas Butler*, 1744.
8°: A–B⁴ D–E⁴; *i–iii iv–xii, 13 14–31 32. 32 advt.*

Whitehead, P. The Gymnasiad

The reason for the implied attribution to the Earl of Chesterfield is not known.

DA,DK.

[—] The hard-us'd poet's complaint... By Scriblerus Tertius, [1750.] *See* H48.

W414 — Honour. A satire. *London, printed for M. Cooper,* 1747. (*GM, LM* June)
4⁰: π¹[= C1] A–B⁴ C⁴(– C1); *i–ii, 1–2* 3–22. π1 hft.
'"Load, load the pallet, boy!" hark! Hogarth cries'
L(840.k.4/1,–π1),O,C(–π1),E(3,–π1),LdU-B (uncut)+; CSmH(uncut),CtY,IU(uncut),NN, TxU(–π1)+.

W415 — — '*London, printed for M. Cooper*' [*Edinburgh?*], 1747.
8⁰: A⁴ B⁴; *1–3* 4–16.
There is no direct evidence for an Edinburgh origin, but it is suggested by a copy at Glasgow and by its general resemblance to Edinburgh piracies.
L(1488.c.38),GU(lacks A1); MH.

W416 — — *Dublin, printed by and for S. Powell, and sold by all the booksellers,* 1747.
8⁰: A⁴ B⁴ C²; *1–5* 6–19 *20 blk.* A1 hft.
L(C.71.bb.15/10),O,DA(–A1),DN.

W417 — Manners: a satire. *London, printed for R. Dodsley,* 1739. (*LDP* 31 Jan)
2⁰: π¹ A² B–D² E¹; *i–ii, 1–3* 4–17 *18 blk.* π1 hft.
Williams, Points 102. Band of type flowers between title and text on p. 3. Dodsley was summoned before the house of lords on 12 Feb 1739 for publishing this poem.
'Well--of all plagues which make mankind their sport'
For a reply, see James Meredith, *Manners decypher'd,* [1739]; see also *Characters: an epistle,* 1739.
L(11631.i.21,–π1; 840.m.1/36,–π1; 643.1.28/ 21; 643.m.16/8; 162.n.35,–π1),LG,O(2, 1 uncut),LdU-B(–π1)MR; CSmH,CtY,DLC(–π1), ICN,TxU(–π1)+.

W418 — [reimpression]
No type flowers between title and text on p. 3. Some minor textual changes. π1 and E1 have been seen to be conjugate.
L(1489.m.30),O(uncut),OW,C(–π1),DT; CtY (2),MH(2),MiU(–π1),NjP,TxU.

W419 — — [*London?* 1739.]
2⁰: A² B–D²; *1–3* 4–16.
Bust in vignette on title. Probably a clandestine London edition.
L(11657.m.25; 11657.m.32),LVA-F,O,OA, LdU-B; CtY,IU,KU,NjP,TxU+.

W420 — — [1739?]
2⁰: A² B–D²; *1–3* 4–16.
Vignette of sun, moon, and stars on title. An inferior piece of printing, possibly as a result of clandestine work in a small shop.
L(1960),EU,BaP.

Whitehead, P. Manners

W421 — — *London, printed by J. Hodgson in Fleetstreet,* 1739.
8⁰: A¹ B–C⁴ D¹; *3–5* 6–22. 4, 22 advt.
A1 and D1 have been seen to be conjugate. Both advertisements are for *The state dunces* 'next week'; no edition corresponding to this advertisement has been seen. The copy at L has a preliminary leaf with an acrostic, probably from another work.
L(1486.b.61); CtY(crop't).

W422 — — *London, printed in the year* 1739.
8⁰: A–B⁴ C²; *1–2* 3–20.
Probably a London piracy.
CT(2, 1 crop't).

W423 — — '*London, printed for R. Dodsley*' [*Edinburgh*], 1739.
8⁰: π¹ A–B⁴ C¹; *1–2* 3–20.
There appear to be two states of sheet A, one with signature A under a of 'darkling' (L,CtY), one with A under e of 'the' (LVA-D, C,IU). Copies at LVA-D,C,IU are bound with other Edinburgh piracies.
L(11631.c.44),LVA-D,C,EN; CtY,IU.

W424 — — '*London, printed for R. Dodsley*' [*Edinburgh*], 1739.
8⁰: A⁴ B⁴ C²; *1–3* 4–20.
Printed by Ruddiman on the evidence of the ornaments.
E,EN; DLC,KU.

W425 [—] A new ballad on Lord D--n---l's altering his chapel at Gr----e into a kitchen. *London, printed for M. Moore,* 1746. (*BM, GM* April)
2⁰: A⁴; *1–2* 3–8.
'By Ovid, 'mongst many more wonders were told'
Printed in Whitehead's *Poems,* 1777. A different text was added to Sir Charles Hanbury Williams's *Odes,* 1768, along with other poems not by him; that attribution is commonly accepted. The attribution to Whitehead seems more authoritative, but it is not unquestionable. On Lord Doneraile's house at Grove.
L(11626.h.11/6),O,OA,DT,LdU-B; CSmH(uncut),CtY,DLC,MH,TxU.

W426 [—] The state dunces. Inscribed to Mr. Pope. *London, printed for W. Dickenson in Witch-street,* 1733. (*DP* 7 June)
2⁰: A¹ B–E² F¹; *i–ii, 1* 2–18.
Williams, Points 101; the tentative order of editions adopted here varies from that incomplete account. A note by W. B. Todd in *Book collector* 9 (1960) 195 is also limited to two of the three folio editions. This edition contains 24 lines not in the J. Dickenson editions; it is better produced; and it is the one copied by Edinburgh and Dublin piracies, the former published by 19 June. On the other hand, the advertisements in *DP* 7 June and following give 'J. Dickson' as the publisher. A1 and F1 have been seen to be conjugate. The ornament

Whitehead, P. The state dunces

on the title is upside-down in about half the copies seen. Some copies (L,O,CtY,TxU) have a ms. correction to p. 11, line 11. Reprinted with *A satyr on the New Tunbridge Wells*, 1733. 'While cringing crowds at faithless levees wait' Reprinted in Whitehead's *Poems*, 1777. See *The counterpart of the State-dunces*, 1733; *A friendly epistle to the author of the State dunces*, 1733; Richard Verney, *Dunces out of state*, 1733.
L(1484.m.7/15; 163.n.1; C.59.h.9/8, uncut), O,OW(2),C,LdU-B(2)+; CSmH,CtY(2),IU,MH, TxU(3, 1 uncut)+.

W427 [—] — *London, printed for J. Dickenson in Witch-street*, 1733.
2°: *A*¹ B–E² F¹; *i–ii, 1 2–17 18 blk.*
Another edition, omitting twenty-four lines. P. 18 is blank and F1 is signed. The accidentals of this edition correspond more closely to the W. Dickenson edition than do those of the following.
L(840.m.1/45; G.19070),O(4, 1–A1),C,DT,BaP (uncut)+; CSmH,CtY,ICN,MH(2),TxU(2)+.

W428 [—] — *London, printed for J. Dickenson*, 1733.
2°: *A*¹ B–E² *F*¹; *i–ii, 1 2–17 18 blk.*
Another edition; p. 18 is blank and F1 unsigned.
L(643.m.15/19),LdU-B; CLU-C,CtY,IU,TxU.

W429 [—] — '*London, printed for W. Dickenson*' [*Edinburgh*], 1733. (19 June?)
4°: A–E²; *1–2 3–20.*
Printed by W. Cheyne on the evidence of the ornaments.
L(11634.c.3/1),E,EP,LdU-B(uncut, ms. notes); CtY('Edinbr 19th June 1733. 6d.'),MH,TxU.

W430 [—] — '*London, printed for W. Dickenson*' [*Dublin*], 1733.
8°: A–B⁴ C²; *i–ii, 1 2–18.*
Printed by S. Powell on the evidence of the ornaments.
L(11631.aa.47/5),O,CT,DA,DK; CU,IU,KU, MH,TxU.

W431 [—] The state dunces. Inscribed to Mr. Pope... Part II. Being the last. *London, printed for J. Dickenson*, 1733. (*GSJ* 6 July)
2°: *A*² B–E²; *1–2 3–19 20 blk.*
'Once more, O Pope, I take the pen in hand' This second part is not reprinted in Whitehead's *Poems*, 1777 or elsewhere; his authorship must be regarded as questionable.
L(1484.m.7/14),LVA-D(2),LVA-F,O(2),BaP(uncut); CSmH,CtY,ICN,MH(uncut),TxU+.

W432 [—] — '*London, printed for J. Dickenson*' [*Edinburgh*], 1733.
4°: *A*² B–E²; *1–2 3–18 19–20 blk.*
Printed by W. Cheyne on the evidence of the ornaments.
L(11602.gg.24/4,–E2; 11634.c.3/2); ICU (–E2),MH.

W433 [—] — In two parts. '*London, printed for J. Dickenson*' [*Edinburgh*], 1733.
8°: π¹ A–C⁴ D⁴(–D4); *i–ii, 1–29 30 blk.*
Printed by Fleming on the evidence of the ornaments.
E(3); CtY,ICU,TxU.

[—] The state of Rome, under Nero and Domitian ... By Messrs. Juvenal and Persius, 1739. *See* S725.

Whitehead, William. Poems on several occasions, with the Roman father, a tragedy. *London, printed for R. & J. Dodsley*, 1754.
12°: pp. 266.   O; MH.

———

W434 — Ann Boleyn to Henry the eighth. An epistle. *London, printed for R. Dodsley; sold by M. Cooper*, 1743. (5 May)
2°: *A*² B–D²; *1–3 4–16. 2 advt.*
Rothschild 2556. Ann Boleyn's original letter on A2. Publication date from *Straus, Dodsley*, which records an assignment of copyright of 28 April. Listed in *GM, LM* May.
'If sighs could soften, or distress cou'd move'
L(643.1.28/15),O(2, 1 lacks A2),OA,C,LdU-B(2); CSmH,CtY,ICN,MH,TxU(2, 1 uncut)+.

W435 — Atys and Adrastus, a tale in the manner of Dryden's fables. *London, printed for R. Manby; sold by M. Cooper*, 1744 [1743]. (*GM, LM* Dec)
2°: *A*¹ B–E² F¹; *i–ii, 1 2–18. 18 advt.*
A1 and F1 have been seen to be conjugate.
'Where Hermus' waters wash the Lydian strand'
L(840.m.1/44; 162.n.34),O,C,DT,BaP; CSmH, CtY,IU,MH,TxU(2)+.

W436 —— The second edition. *London, printed for R. Manby; sold by M. Cooper*, 1744.
2°: *A*¹ B–E² F¹; *i–ii, 1 2–18. 18 advt.*
Apparently a reimpression.
L(11657.m.27),O,LdU-B; DFo,ICN,TxU.

W437 —— The fourth edition. '*London, printed for R. Manby; sold by M. Cooper*', 1749.
8°: A⁴ B–C⁴; *1–3 4–23 24 blk.*
The copy seen is bound in a volume containing some Edinburgh piracies; this may well be piratical too. The title omits the words 'in the manner of...'.
GM.

W438 — The danger of writing verse: an epistle. *London, printed for R. Dodsley; sold by T. Cooper*, 1741. (*LDP* 22 Jan)
2°: *A*² B–D²; *1–2 3–16.*
'You ask me, Sir, why thus by phantoms aw'd'
L(1489.d.30),LG,O,C,LdU-B+; CtY,DFo,ICN, MH,TxU(2)+.

W439 — An essay on ridicule. *London, printed for R. Dodsley; sold by M. Cooper*, 1743. (19 Feb)
2°: *A*² B–E²; *1–3 4–20.*
Rothschild 2555. Publication date from *Straus, Dodsley*. Listed in *GM, LM* Feb.

Whitehead, W. An essay on ridicule

'''Twas said of old, deny it now who can'
L(11630.h.52),LVA-D,O,C,LdU-B+; CSmH,
CtY,IU,MH(2),TxU(2)+.

[—] The green-cloth: or, the verge of the court...
By Mr. Wh----d, 1739. *See* G276.

W440 — On nobility: an epistle to the right honble. the
Earl of ******. *London, printed for R. Dodsley;
sold by M. Cooper,* 1744. (26 April)
2°: *A¹* B–D² *E¹*; *1–3* 4–14 *15; 16 blk.* EI advt.
In many copies the advertisement leaf, here
called EI, follows the title; the collation given
here seems intended. AI and EI have been
seen to be conjugate. Publication date from
Straus, Dodsley; listed in *GM, LM* May.
'Poets, my lord, by some unlucky fate'
L(643.m.16/14; 162.n.36),O,LdU-B(−EI);
CSmH,CtY(−EI),IU,MH(−EI),TxU(2)+.

'Whitelock, J. C.' Right Brunswick-mum, 1715.
See R209.

Whitsun. The Whitson-fair: rary-show, [1710.]
See R129.

W441 Whittington. Whittington reviv'd, or the city in
triumph: on Alderman Parson's being chose twice
lord-mayor of the city of London, (Tune of,
Glorious Charles of Sweeden). [*London,* 1740.]
½°: 1 side, 2 columns.
Percival appendix 88. Rough portrait at head.
'Great Alderman Parsons now is chose'
L(1876.f.1/120).

W442 Who. Who's afraid now, or, a dialogue between the
King and Queen of Spain. [*London,* 1739?]
slip: 1 side, 1 column.
Percival XLVIII. Rough woodcut at head.
'Come hither my queen, and if we must agree'
A satire on Queen Elizabeth of Spain bullying
Philip V to fight England.
C.

Whole. The whole armour of god, [1742?] *See*
Wesley, Charles.

— The whole discover'd, 1736. *See* P142.

W443 — The whole duty of a Christian, both in faith and
practice: succinctly explain'd in familiar verse: by
way of question and answer... Done into English
from the Latin catechism of Hugo Grotius. *London
printed, and sold by John Morphew,* 1711. (*SR* 10
Sept)
8°: A–B⁴; *1–2* 3–16.
Entered in *SR* by Benjamin Motte to Anne
Motte; deposit copy at E.
'Knowst thou, my child, thou wert baptiz'd of old'
From Grotius's *Baptizatorum puerorum institutio.*
L(161.m.68, Luttrell, no date),LLP,E.

W444 — The whole tryal, examination, and conviction of
the turnip-man, before the judges of the king's
bench bar at Westminster Hall, on Monday the

The **whole** tryal

30th of November, 1719. [*London*] *Printed by
R. Thomas, in Fleet-street,* [1719.]
½°: 1 side, 2 columns.
Two rough woodcuts at head.
'The hue and cry we had of late'
A tory ballad; the turnip-man's name appears
from a pun to have been Huggett, his crime
speaking against King George.
L(C.116.i.4/46).

W445 Whores. The whores and bawds answer to the
Fifteen comforts of whoring. [*London*] *Printed in
the year* 1706.
8°: *A⁴; i–ii,* 3–8.
'No sooner does a maid arrive to years'
CLU-C.

W446 — The whores of Edinburgh's lament for want of
Luckie Spence. [*Edinburgh,* 1718.]
½°: 1 side, 1 column.
'Twice sixteen years hath over past'
Lucky Spence was an Edinburgh bawd.
E.

Whyte, Laurence. Poems on various subjects,
serious and diverting, never before published...
*Dublin, printed by S. Powell; sold by L. Dowling,
T. Brown, & Ed. Hamillton, Mr. J. Hoey & Oli.
Nelson, G. Falkiner, and by the author at his house,*
1740.
12°: pp. xx, 236.   L,DN.

— [reissue] Original poems on various subjects...
To this edition, are added the following poems...
The second edition. *Dublin, printed by S. Powell,
and are to be sold by the author, and by most of the
booksellers in Dublin,* 1742.
12°: pp. xx, 236+42.   DA.
The additions have a separate title-page
reading 'Original poems... Part the second...'
and dated 1742.

W447 [—] The broken mug a poem. *Dublin, printed by
John Harding,* [1725?]
½°: 2 sides, 1 column.
Teerink 992; *Williams* 1102. The copy at L
forms part of a collection of Dublin half-
sheets of 1725/30; Harding died in 1725.
'How shall I the nine invoke'
An enlarged version was printed in Whyte's
Poems, 1740, which records that it was started
in 1720, 'handed about and printed here
[Dublin] without my knowledge or direction,
'twas in some time after printed in London...'
The London printing by Curll in his *Mis-
cellanea,* 1727, attributed it to Swift. Cf. *A
hoop for the broken mugg,* 1727.
L(C.121.g.8/83).

W448 [—] [*idem*] A new poem on a cract-pitcher, or
broken-mug. By L.W. gent. *Dublin, printed at the
Rein-deer in Montrath-street,* [1726/36?]

Whyte, L. The broken mug

8°: *A*⁴; *1–3* 4–8.
A chap-book edition, probably published by
C. Hicks.
'How shall I now the nine invoke'
LVA-F.

[—] Elegy on the much lamented death of his
excellency Richard West, 1726. *See* E270.

[—] Hibernia in universal mourning: or, a royal
funeral elegy on...King George, [1727.] *See* H172.

W449 Whyte, William. Elegy on the never enough to be
lamanted death of Lord John Hamilton of Bal-
haven, &c. who depated this life, (at London,) 21.
June 1708. *Edinburgi, excudebat Joan. Rheædus,
1708.*
½°: 1 side, 1 column.
Mourning borders.
'Melpomonie, come and inspyre my quile'
Signed 'Gulielmus Candidus'.
L(11633.i.9/12),E.

W450 [—] Elegie on the death of the right honourable
Sir James Falconer of Phesdo, one of the lords of
the colledge of justice, &c. Who dyed the 9th of
June 1705. [*Edinburgh*, 1705.]
½°: 1 side, 1 column.
Mourning borders.
'I need no art to set a' needless gloss'
Signed 'W.W.' *Maidment* 151 suggests
Whyte's authorship, which seems extremely
probable.
E.

W451 Wicksted, —, *Mr.* An ode for the year
MDCCXVII. To the king. *London, printed for
Bernard Lintot, 1717.* (*DC* 23 July)
2°: *A*² B–E²; *i–iv*, *1–15* *16 blk*.
'Whom now, of all the world calls great'
L(840.m.1/26); MH.

Widow. The widows address, 1725. *See* Barber,
Mary.

W452 Widows. ⟨The⟩ widows and orphans triumph: or,
the projector defeated. Tune of, The glorious 29th
of May. [*London?* 1737.]
slip: 1 side, 1 column.
Percival XL. Below, 'The true-blue. A new
song'.
'John the quaker, did invent'
True-blue: 'I hope there's no soul/Met over this
bowl'
On the defeat of Sir John Barnard's three per
cent. scheme, 29 April 1737.
O.

W453 Wife. A wife and no wife, a tragi-comi-canonical-
farcical ballad. [*London*] *Printed for Joseph Collyer,*
[1744.] (*GM* April)
2°: B–C² (B2 as 'B'); *1–2* 3–7 *8 blk*.
'O teach me, my muse, a strange tale to rehearse'

A wife and no wife

Rawlinson records under Thomas Hilman that
the poem was occasioned by his marriage to
Dr. Barrow's daughter; she insisted on preserving her virginity.
MC; IU.

W454 — — *London, printed for W. Williams near St.
Paul's,* [1744?]
4°: *A*²; *1–4*.
A hawkers' reprint.
O(MS Rawl. J fol. 6, fol. 260); CLU-C.

W455 — — ... Derry down. [*Dublin*, 1744?]
½°: 1 side, 2 columns.
L(1890.e.5/85),C.

W456 — A wife and no wife; or, the mad gallant. An
humorous tale of lunacy, love and cuckoldom.
Wherein are contained the following letters; I.
From Donna Hanmerina to her husband, accusing
him of impotency. II. From Don Furioso Harvides
to Don Hanmerio... III. From Hanmerio to
Harvides. Concluding with a caution to all hus-
bands. *London, printed for J. Huggonson,* 1742.
(*GM*, *LM* May)
8°: A–D⁴; *1–2* 3–30 *31*; *32 blk*. D4 advt.
'Women, e'er since their mother Eve'
A satirical poem on the elopement of Sir
Thomas Hanmer's wife with the honourable
Thomas Hervey, and the ensuing pamphlet
war.
Institute for Sex Research; *National Library of
Australia*.

— The wife and the nurse, 1743. *See* Williams, *Sir*
Charles Hanbury.

W457 Wigglesworth, Michael. The day of doom: or, a
poetical discription [!] of the great and last
judment [!]; with a short discourse about eternity.
*Newcastle upon Tyne, printed by John White, in the
Close,* 1711.
12°: *A*⁶ B–F⁶ G⁶(– G6); *i–ix*, *1–51* 51–72.
First published in 1666 (*Wing* W2100);
Wigglesworth died in 1705.
'Still was the night, serene and bright'
L(1163.b.28); CSmH,DLC,*MB*.

W458 Wild, John. [Nottingham printing perfected,
spelling consummate, grammar complete, July 31.
1710. For John Wild of Little-leak... The happiness of death; a satire of life, letters and learning.]
[*Nottingham, printed by William Ayscough,* 1710?]
½°: 1 side, 1 column.
Printed in a phonetic alphabet contrived from
conventional letters, with a tune noted in the
same way. See R. C. Alston, *A bibliography of
the English language* 6 (1969) 113–14, where it
is also reproduced.
['Our selves we're all deceiving']
MC(cropt at foot).

W458·5 Wild, Robert. Dr. Wild's humble thanks for his
majesty's gracious declaration for liberty of

Wild, R. Dr. Wild's humble thanks

conscience. March 15. 1672. *London printed, and sold by H. Hills,* 1710.
8⁰: A⁴; *1–2* 3–8.
　First published 1672; reprinted on account of the Sacheverell affair. Included here to complete the tally of cheap reprints by Hills.
'No, not one word, can I of this great deed'
EU.

[—] Elegy on the much lamented death of the right honourable William Whitshed, [1727.] *See* E278.

W459 Wilde, Samuel. The weavers humble offering and hearty thanks to our gracious king and parliament. Composed by Samuel Wilde, weaver. To the tune of, Ah how happy is he, that's from business free. [*London,* 1721?]
½⁰: 1 side, 2 columns.
　On the other side of C copy, *When we shall have peace,* 1711.
'Since the blissing fates'
　Apparently inspired by the act to preserve and encourage the woollen and silk manufactures (7 Geo.I.c.7).
C.

[—] The weaver's new ballad on the S—h-Sea, [1720.] *See* W262·5.

[**Wilkes, Israel.**] A British philippic: a poem, in Miltonic verse [actually by Mark Akenside], 1738. *See* A133.

W460 Wilkes, Thomas. The golden farmer a poem. Humbly inscrib'd to the right honourable William lord Craven. *London, printed for T. Payne,* 1723. (*MC* May)
2⁰: *A*² B–C²; *i–iv,* 1–8. A1 hft.
　Presentation copies at L,O,CLU-C,CSmH, ICN,TxU have ms. corrections and additions.
'Near Wantage, where our learned king'
L(C.61.e.9),O,GlP; CLU-C,CSmH,ICN,MH, TxU(2)+.

W461 [**Wilkes, Wetenhall.**] Hounslow-Heath, a poem ... Inscribed to a nobleman. *London, printed for C. Corbett; sold at the booksellers in London & Westminster,* 1747 [1748?]. (*GM, LM* Jan 1748)
4⁰: *A*¹ B–F² G¹; *i–ii, 1* 2–21 22. 22 err.
　Vertical chain-lines.
'Let plodding cits, my lord, indulge their vein'
　Subsequently printed with Wilkes's name.
L(11630.b.3/2).

W462 [—] [variant date:] 1748.
L(11630.c.1/19); OCU.

W463 — — The second edition. Carefully corrected and enlarged. *London, printed for the author; sold by T. Gardner,* 1748. (Dec?)
4⁰: *a–b*² c–d² B–H²; *i–iii* iv–xvi, *1* 2–27 28. 28 advt.
　Dedication dated 29 Nov. Vertical chain-lines.
　Variant first line:

Wilkes, W. Hounslow-Heath

'Let plodding cits, great sir, indulge their vein'
L(11602.ff.25/4),O,*MR*; ICN,MH(lacks b2).

W464 [—] The humours of the Black-dog, in a letter to the R. *J.S. D.D.D.S.P.D.* By a gentleman in confinement. A new poem... The first edition. *Dublin printed, and sold in the Four-Courts-Marshalsea,* 1737.
8⁰: A⁴; *1–3* 4–8.
'Afraid to set so great a name as thine'
　Dedication to Swift signed 'W.W.' Advertised by Wilkes in *Hounslow-Heath,* 1748. The Black-dog was the Sheriff's or debtor's prison in Dublin.
DG.

W465 [—] — The second edition, corrected. *Dublin printed, and sold in the Four-Courts-Marshalsea,* 1737.
8⁰: A⁴; *1–3* 4–8.
　A new edition was advertised as 'ready for the press' in *Hounslow-Heath,* 1748: 'the 10th edition, after seventeen thousand being sold'. A similar note, recording that 'I sold 17,000 copies in two months' appeared in Wilkes's *An essay on...female literature,* 1741.
C,DG(uncut).

W466 [—] ⟨The⟩ humours of the Black-dog continued. By the same hand: in hudibrastick verse. Part the second... To which is added a short view of the humours of the Four-Courts-Marshalsea. *Dublin: compiled and printed, at the request of several gentlemen of taste and fortune; and to be sold at the Four-Courts-Marshalsea,* 1737.
8⁰: A⁴; *1–2* 3–⟨8⟩.
'Descending, whether right or wrong'
C(slightly cropt).

W467 [—] The third part of the Humours, &c. or, the satyrist. In four parts... By the author of the Humours of the Black-dog. *Dublin printed, and sold in the Four-Courts-Marshalsea,* 1737.
8⁰: A⁴; *1–2* 3–8. 8 advt.
　A small collection of poems. No fourth part has been traced.
'Not a mile from an oak in the island of Coss'
ICN.

W468 — The mourning muse or, verses sacred to the memory of the revd. Mr. Robert Craighead...who died on the 30th. day of July 1738... In a friendly manner inscrib'd to the revd. Mr. Francis Iredal, and the rd. Mr. John Abernethy... [*Dublin*] *Printed by Samuel Dalton, in Warburgh-street,* [1738.]
8⁰: *A*⁴; *1–2* 3–7 *8 blk.*
'Look round, Alexis, see the gloomy shade'
C.

W469 [—] The prisoner's ballad: or, welcome, welcome, brother debtor, &c. The true copy of which was never printed before. Sent to the press by the author. *London, printed in the year* 1748.
4⁰: A²; *1–2* 3–4.

Wilkes, W. The prisoner's ballad

Vertical chain-lines. According to the 'advertisement' on p. 2, it was written in Dublin in 1737 and pirated by shorthand when performed at a concert.

'Welcome, welcome, brother debtor'

Early ms. attribution to Wilkes in the C copy. Advertised in his *Hounslow-Heath*, 1748.

C.

— 'Rural felicity compared with public life; a Doric poem, ready for the press.'

So advertised in Wilkes's *Hounslow-Heath*, 1748; there is no evidence for its publication at this time. It was previously appended to Wilkes's *A letter of genteel and moral advice to a young lady*, 1740.

W470 [—] Tom in the suds; or, the humours of Newgate: a new poem. In four canto's most humbly dedicated to the members of the honourable house of commons; by the author of the Humours of the Black-dog. *Dublin printed, and sold in the Four-Courts-Marshalsea*, 1737. (Oct?)

8°: A⁴; *1* 2–8.

A prefatory letter dated 3 Oct 1737 and addressed to 'Tom', the Newgate gaoler, refers to the projected publication of this poem 'next week'.

'Speak satire for by thee alone'

Largely an attack on 'Tom', the gaoler both of Newgate and the Black-dog.

C,DA; CtY.

W471 [—] [dh] Tom in the suds: or, the humours of Newgate. Canto the second; containing, 1st. The preamble... [*Dublin*, 1738.]

8°: B⁴; *9* 10–15 *16* (11 as '3').

'Number 2' above title. An 'advertisement' on p. 16 apologizes for several months' delay in publishing the second part.

'Dread not, my muse, the task pursue'

C,DA,DN; CtY.

W472 [—] [dh] Tom in the suds... Canto the third; containing, 1st. A sketch of Tom's extraction... [*Dublin*, 1738.]

8°: C⁴; *17* 18–24.

'Number 3' above title.

'Tom is a fellow to be sure'

C; CtY.

W473 [—] [dh] Tom in the suds... Canto the fourth containing: 1st. A description of the several appartments... [*Dublin*, 1738.]

8°: D⁴; *25* 26–30 *31–32*. 32 advt.

'Number 4' above title. Pp. 31–32 contain 'An address to the honourable house of commons', a verse dedication of the poem.

'Whores, cutpurses and men of fashion'

C; CtY.

[—] The universal coquet: a fable, 1749. See U16.

Wilkinson, J.

Wilkinson, John. Poems on several occasions. *London, printed in the year* 1725.

8°: pp. 40. MH.

Wilkinson, Thomas. 'Musick, a pindaric ode. To Signor Cavalier Nicolini Grimaldi. By Tho: Wilkinson, gent.'

Entered to Wilkinson in *SR* 5 March 1712, but no copies were deposited; possibly it was not published.

William. William and Margaret, [1723?]–. *See* Mallet, David.

Williams, Anna. Miscellanies in prose and verse. *London, printed for T. Davies*, 1766.

4°: pp. 184. O; CtY,MH.

W474 Williams, Bartholomew. Congratulatio Roffensis. Or, the salutation. A pindarick poem, on the arrival of his excellency Lawrence earl of Rochester, lord lieutenant of Ireland. *Dublin, printed by John Brocas*, 1701.

4°: *A*² B–F²; *i–iv*, 1–20.

'Fame, the charming'st girl on earth'

Dedication signed.

DA.

Williams, *Sir* **Charles Hanbury.** A collection of poems, principally consisting of the most celebrated pieces of Sir Charles Hanbury Williams... *London, printed for Lynch*, 1763.

8°: pp. 73. L; CSmH,CtY.

Horace Walpole annotated his copy (at L) 'This is a bookseller's collection in which many pieces were not written by Sr C. Williams, and all have been printed before'.

— The odes of Sir Charles Hanbury Williams... *London, printed for D. Lynch*, 1768.

8°: pp. 132. O; CSmH.

An enlarged collection. Reissued with cancel title-leaves by D. Culver (Lynch's successor) undated, and by S. Vandenbergh, 1775. The price was reduced from six shillings, to four, to three.

___

The canon of Sir Charles Hanbury Williams presents many difficulties. A collection of poems, 1763, contains 'many pieces...not written by Sr. C. Williams' as Horace Walpole noted in his copy (at L); others were added to the enlarged collection Odes, 1768; and further poems by other authors were included in his Works, 1822, possibly from Williams's own mss. (now in the Lewis Walpole Library). The biography of Williams by Lord Ilchester and Mrs. Langford Brooke tends to accept his authorship of all the poems in 1822, while CBEL includes a number of poems which do not appear to have been separately published. It has seemed inevitable that poems which have been thus accepted should be listed here unless evidence against Williams's authorship can be adduced; but the

Williams, *Sir* **C. H.**

attribution of those not vouched for by Horace Walpole in his annotated copy of A collection of poems, *1763, or in his ms. life of Williams (printed in the Yale edition of his correspondence, vol. XXX) should be sceptically regarded.*

[—] 'The capuchin, [1742.]'
Listed in *CBEL* as separately published, but according to Horace Walpole's ms. life it was published in the newspapers; it also appeared in *The new ministry,* 1742.

[—] A congratulatory ode, most humbly inscribed to the statesman on his travels, 1748. *See* C347.

W475 [—] The country girl: an ode. *London, printed for W. Webb,* 1742. (3 Aug)
2°: *A*⁴; *1–2* 3–7 *8 blk.*
Williams, Points 106; W. B. Todd in *PBSA* 47 (1953) 159. 'Price sixpence' on title, in many copies (L,O,TxU,MH) altered in ms. to 'threepence'. A copy from Tom's Coffee House, dated 3 Aug, now in the Lewis Walpole Library, makes it clear that this is the first edition. Advertised in *DA* 4 Aug at 3*d.*
'The country girl that's well inclin'd'
Attributed to Williams in Horace Walpole's ms. life of Williams, printed in the Yale edition of Walpole's correspondence, vol. XXX. A satire on William Pulteney, lord Bath.
L(1484.m.18),O,*LdU-B*; CSmH,ICN,MH,TxU.

W476 [—] — [another edition]
'Price threepence' on title. Possibly in part a reimpression.
OA; NjP.

W477 [—] — [1742.]
4°: *A*²; *1–4.*
Drop-head title only. A piracy, possibly of Edinburgh origin.
CtY,TxU.

W478 [—] A dialogue between G--s E---e and B--b D---n. *London, sold by T. Taylor at the Rose in Exeter Exchange, or at his house in Burleigh-street in the Strand,* 1741. (27 June)
2°: A–B²; *1–2* 3–8.
Signature B under 'Green'. A copy from Tom's Coffee House in the Lewis Walpole Library is dated 27 June.
'My dear Pall-Mall, I hear you're got in favour'
Attributed to Williams in Walpole's life. A dialogue between Giles Earle and Bubb Dodington. Imitated in *A second dialogue between G--s E-e and B--b D-----n,* 1743.
L(162.n.64),LG,O(2),C,*LdU-B*; CSmH,CtY, DFo,IU,TxU(2)+.

W479 [—] [another edition]
Signature B is under the space between 'Cloth to'. Possibly in part a reimpression.
MH.

[—] An epistle to the right honourable William Pultney, esq; upon his late conduct in publick affairs, 1742. *See* E429.

Williams, *Sir* **C. H.** An epistolary letter

[—] An epistolary letter from T----- H----- to Sr H-----s S------e, 1729. *See* E437.

W480 [—] Esq; S---ys's budget open'd; or, drink and be d--d. A new ballad, to the tune of, A begging we will go. *London, printed for W. Webb,* 1743. (28 Jan)
2°: *A*⁴; *i–v* vi–viii. A1 hft.
Rothschild 2573. In some copies (L,CtY) p. vi is mis-numbered 'v'; it is not clear whether this is a press-variant or a sign of reimpression. A copy from Tom's Coffee House, dated 28 Jan, is in the Lewis Walpole Library; listed in *GM, LM* Feb.
'Attend, my honest brethren'
Not in the early collections of 1763, 1768, but collected in Williams's *Works* (1822) III.192; the authorship is perhaps questionable. On the proposal for repealing the gin act.
L(1484.m.31; 011653.o.71),O(uncut),OA, LdU-B,MC; CtY,MH.

W481 [—] The heroes: a new ballad. To the tune of ---- Sally in our alley. *London, printed for M. Moore, near St. Paul's,* 1745. (*GM* Dec)
2°: *A*⁴; *1–2* 3–7 *8 blk.*
Price on title in square brackets.
'Of all the jobbs that e'er have past'
Reprinted in Williams's *Collection,* 1763; Walpole notes, 'on the fifteen new regiments' which were raised by various noblemen and then turned over to the government at its expense.
L(11626.h.13/8),O,AdU,LdU-B,*DrU-U*; CSmH, CtY,IU,NjP,TxU+.

W482 [—] [another edition, title reads:]...To the tune of --- Sally in our alley.
Price on title in parentheses.
MH.

W483 [—] — [*Edinburgh,* 1745/46.]
8°: *A*²; *1–4.*
Drop-head title only. The copy seen is bound in a volume of Edinburgh piracies.
E.

[—] H----ss----y to Sir C--- H---- W----s: or, the rural reflections of a Welch poet, 1746. *See* H346.

[—] The merry campaign; or, the Westminster and Green-park scuffle, 1732. *See* M199.

[—] A new ballad on Lord D--n---l's altering his chapel at Gr----e into a kitchen [actually by Paul Whitehead], 1746. *See* W425.

W484 [—] A new ode, to a number of great men, newly made... By the author of the Country maid. *London, printed for J. Carpenter,* [1742.] (*DA* 3 Sept)
2°: *A*⁴; *i–ii,* 1–5 *6 blk.*
'See a new progeny descends'
Reprinted in Williams's *Collection,* 1763; referred to in Walpole's life.
O(2, 1 cropt); CSmH.

Williams, *Sir* **C. H.** A new ode

W485 [—] — [*Edinburgh?* 1742.]
   8º: *A*²; 1–4.
      Drop-head title only. A piracy.
   MH(cropt).

W486 [—] An ode addressed to the author of the
Conquered duchess. In answer to that celebrated
performance. *London, printed for A. Moore,* 1746.
(*GM* Sept)
   2º: *A*² <*B*²; 1–2 3–8.
      In some copies (L,MH,MiU) there is no
      period after 'rul'd' on p. 7, stanza 9 line 3.
      This may be the mark of another impression.
   'What clamour's here about a dame'
      Reprinted in Williams's *Collection*, 1763, and
      referred to in Walpole's life. Reprinted in *The
      new foundling hospital for wit* (1786) III.47 as
      by Robert Nugent, earl Nugent, but that
      attribution has less authority. A reply to
      Williams's own *Ode to the honourable H---y
      F--x*, 1746, on Edward Hussey marrying the
      Duchess of Manchester.
   L(11602.i.14/9; 1486.g.17),O,OA,LdU-B; CtY,
   DFo,DLC,MH,MiU.

W487 [—] An ode from the E---- of B---- to ambition.
London, printed for A. Moore, [1746.] (*BM* March)
   2º: *A*⁴; 1–2 3–7 *8 blk*.
      Printed on paper with varying watermarks,
      possibly representing different impressions.
   'Away, ambition, give me rest'
      Reprinted in Williams's *Collection*, 1763;
      referred to in Walpole's life, 'on the revolution
      of three days 1746'. The pretended author is
      William Pulteney, earl of Bath.
   L(1959),O,C,LdU-B(uncut); CSmH(uncut),CtY,
   MH,OCU.

[—] 'An ode humbly inscribed to the right
honourable W— e— of B—, [1742?]'
      Listed in *CBEL* as separately published, but
      apparently it appeared in *GM* Oct 1742;
      possibly it was reprinted there from a news-
      paper.

[—] An ode, imitated from ode XI. book 2d. of
Horace [actually by William Pulteney], 1745. *See*
P1166.

[—] An ode to the Duke of Argyll. To which is
added, one to the Earl of Marchmont, 1740. *See*
O68.

W488 [—] An ode to the honourable H---y F--x, on
the marriage of the Du---s of M------r to
H---s---y, esq; *London, printed for A. Moore,*
1746. (23 Aug)
   2º: *A*² <*B*²; 1–2 3–8.
      Williams, Points 107f; W. B. Todd in *PBSA*
      47 (1953) 160. This edition has vignette of
      fisherman on title. P. 4, line 1 reads '...be-
      gun'; p. 5, line 8 'C-b-r-y'. I follow Todd's
      order of editions, but reverse the order of
      impressions ('states' in Todd); the order given

Williams, *Sir* **C. H.** An ode to the honourable

      here is tentative. Publication date from Todd;
      listed in *GM* Aug.
   'Clio, behold this charming day'
      Walpole's life notes that this was written in
      July 1746 and published in August through the
      carelessness of Lord Lincoln. On the marriage
      of the Duchess of Manchester to Edward
      Hussey, addressed to Henry Fox.
   L(11602.i.14/10; 11602.i.10/9),DT; CtY,IU,
   MH,NN,TxU.

W489 [—] [another impression?]
      Vignette of fisherman on title. P. 4, line 1 reads
      '...began'; p. 5, line 8 'C--b-r-y'. I have
      a note of a copy seen in private hands with the
      mixed readings 'began' and 'C-b-r-y', but I
      cannot confirm this.
   LVA-F,O(2, 1 uncut),E,LdU-B; CSmH,DLC.

W490 [—] [another edition]
      Vignette of fruit flanked by eagles; the readings
      on pp. 4, 5 follow the preceding. Reset in part,
      but probably some standing type is used.
   OA; *CtY*.

W491 [—] [*idem*] Irish legs a match for English brains.
[*Dublin*] *Printed in the year* 1746.
   ½º: 1 side, 2 columns.
      Column 1 headed 'An ode to H---y F-x,
      esq; on the marriage of the Dutchess of
      M——r, to E----d H----y, esq;' column 2
      'An ode, in answer thereto'.
   Answer: 'Clio, behold this dreadful day'
      The answer is possibly that recorded by
      Horace Walpole in his ms. life of Williams:
      'One Soame Jennings a paltry poet wrote an
      abusive parody on Williams's ode, without his
      name'.
   DT.

[—] An ode to the right honourable lord Viscount
Lonsdale [actually by Robert Nugent, earl Nugent],
1745. *See* N345.

W492 — An ode to the right honourable Stephen Poyntz,
esq; &c. &c. &c. *London, printed for R. Dodsley;
sold by M. Cooper,* 1746. (27 Sept)
   2º: *A*² <*B*²; 1–2 3–7 *8 blk*.
      The penultimate line on p. 5 reads 'Fond
      Virtue'. Publication date from *Straus, Dodsley*.
   'Whilst William's deeds and William's praise'
      Translated into Latin by Samuel Bishop as
      Ode...ad honoratissimum Stephanum Poyntz,
      [1746/50.]
   L(11602.i.14/11),O,E,LdU-B,*DrU-U*; CSmH,
   CtY,MH,MiU.

W493 — [reimpression?]
      The penultimate line on p. 5 has correct
      reading 'Found Virtue'. A change in the rules
      on the title suggests that, though the setting of
      type is the same, this is a reimpression.
   L(1471.k.25),DT; DFo.

Williams, *Sir* **C. H.** The old coachman

W494 [—] The old coachman: a new ballad. To which is added, Labour in vain. *London, printed for W. Webb*, 1742. (30 July)
2°: *A*⁴; *1–2* 3–7 *8 blk.*
> *Williams, Points* 104; W. B. Todd in *PBSA* 47 (1953) 160. On p. 3, line 3 of stanza 1 reads 'chear'; ornament of small basket with scroll-work on title. This text was followed in *GM, LM* Aug. Publication date from Todd.
'Wise Caleb and C--t, two birds of a feather'
Labour: 'Ye patriots, who twenty long years'
> Not included in the collections of 1763 and 1768, but printed in Williams's *Works* (1822) II.186. Lord Ilchester mistakes a note of Horace Walpole, but quotes a letter to Fox which suggests Williams's authorship. On the travels of Pulteney and Carteret to Clermont. *Labour in vain* is attributed to Richard, baron Edgcumbe by Walpole and in Williams's *Works* (1822) II.50.
OA; TxU(uncut).

W495 [—] [another edition]
> *Rothschild* 2575. On p. 3, line 3 of stanza 1 reads 'cheer'; ornament of large basket with butterflies on title.
L(1484.m.29),O; CtY,MH(uncut).

W496 [—] — *London, printed for J. Jones*, 1742.
4°: *A*²; *1* 2–4.
> Cut of coach and horses on title; vertical chain lines. A piracy.
LG; CSmH.

[—] Old England's Te deum, [1743.]
> Usually listed among Williams's poems, but not in a poetical form. Only versifications are included in this catalogue.

[—] Orpheus and Hecate. An ode, 1746. *See* O251.

[—] 'Peter and my lord Quidam, 1743.'
> Listed in *CBEL*, but there is no evidence of its separate publication.

W497 [—] Place-book for the year seventeen-hundred, forty-five. A new ballad. *London, printed for W. Webb*, 1744–5. (*GM, LM* Jan)
2°: *A*⁴; *1–5* 6–8. A1 hft.
'Since with the new year a new change hath begun'
> Not included in the collections of 1763 and 1768, but printed in Williams's *Works* (1822) III.23. The attribution should be accepted with caution.
L(C.57.g.7/8),O(2, 1 – A1),E(uncut),*DrU-U*, LdU-B; CSmH(– A1),CtY,TxU(uncut, – A1).

W498 [—] — [*London*? 1745.]
½°: 2 sides, 1 column.
> Woodcut at foot of the verso.
C; CtY,KU(cropt).

W499 [—] — A new court ballad. [*London*? 1745.]
½°: 1 side, 2 columns.
> Woodcut of hawkers at head.
L(1876.f.1/130); MH,OCU.

Williams, *Sir* **C. H.** Place-book

W500 [—] [dh] Place-book a new ballad, &c. [*Edinburgh*, 1745.]
4°: *A*²; *1* 2–4.
> Copies at L,E, are bound with Edinburgh publications. With an additional final verse.
L(C.38.g.14/3),O,E(2),AdU,*LdU-B*.

W501 [—] Plain thoughts in plain language. A new ballad. *London, printed for W. Webb*, 1743.
2°: *A*⁴; *i–v* vi–viii. A1 hft.
> *Rothschild* 2577.
'Attend, ye brave Britons'
> Not included in the collections of 1763 and 1768, but printed in Williams's *Works* (1822) III.18. The attribution should be accepted with caution.
L(1484.m.17; 011653.0.72,–A1),O(2, 1 uncut), LdU-B; CtY,ICN,InU(–A1).

W502 [—] — '*London, printed for W. Webb*' [*Edinburgh*], 1743.
8°: *A*⁴; *1–2* 3–7 *8 blk.*
> Printed by R. Fleming on the evidence of the ornament.
CtY,MH(cropt).

[—] A poem sacred to the memory of the honourable the Lady Aber—ny, 1729. *See* P654.

[—] Short verses, in imitation of long verses, 1746. *See* S452.

[—] 'Sir C. H. W. to E—d H—y esq, [1743?]'
> Listed in *CBEL*, apparently in error for *H------ss----y to Sir C--- H---- W----s*, 1746, which is almost certainly not by Williams.

[—] 'Solomon's porch S—s and W—r, 1743.'
> Listed in *CBEL*, but there is no evidence of its separate publication.

W503 [—] S——s and J——l. A new ballad. *London, printed for W. Webb*, 1743. (*GM, LM* Feb)
2°: *A*⁴; *1–2* 3–8.
''Twas at the silent solemn hour'
> Reprinted in Williams's *Works*, 1822; noted in Walpole's life. A parody of Mallet's *William and Margaret*; the ghost of Sir Joseph Jekyll appears to Samuel, baron Sandys. Against Sandys's gin act. Answered by *J---l's wife*, 1743.
L(11626.h.13/7; 162.n.63),O(2, 1 uncut); CSmH(uncut),CtY(uncut),DFo,TxU.

W504 [—] — The second edition. *London, printed for W. Webb*, 1743.
2°: *A*⁴; *1–2* 3–8.
> *Rothschild* 2574. A reimpression.
L(1484.m.21); MH.

W505 [—] — The third edition. *London, printed for W. Webb*, 1743.
2°: *A*⁴; *1–2* 3–8.
> A reimpression. Type flowers only on title.
L(1482.d.32),O,*OA*; CtY,MH,TxU.

W506 [—] S-----s and J----l...The third edition. *London, printed for W. Webb*, 1743.

Williams, *Sir* **C. H.** S——s and J——l

2⁰: *A*⁴; *1–2* 3–8.
>Vignette on title; probably a new edition.
LdU-B.

W507 [—] — The second edition. '*London, printed for W. Webb*' [*Edinburgh*], 1743.
8⁰: *A*⁴ *B*²; *1–2* 3–12.
>Printed by Ruddiman on the evidence of the ornament.
E; CtY.

W508 [—] S--nd--s and J--k--l... '*London, printed for W. Webb*' [*Dublin?* 1743].
½⁰: 1 side, 2 columns.
>The copy seen is in a collection of Dublin half-sheets.
C.

W509 [—] S----s and J----l... [*London?* 1743.]
½⁰: 1 side, 2 columns.
O.

W510 [—] [*idem*] A full and true account of the ghost of Sir J....h J...l, late master of r..lls, appearing to Esquire S..ds... [*London?* 1743.]
½⁰: 1 side, 2 columns.
L(1850.e.10/61),O.

[—] Tar water, a ballad, inscribed to...Philip earl of Chesterfield, 1747. *See* T39.

[—] The unembarassed countenance, a new ballad, 1746. *See* U2.

W511 [—] The wife and the nurse: a new ballad. *London, printed for W. Webb*, 1743. (*GM, LM* Jan)
2⁰: *A*⁴; *1–3* 4–8.
>*Rothschild* 2576. The lowest point of the ornament on the title is over D of 'London'.
'Vice once with virtue did engage'
>Not in the collections of 1763, 1768, but reprinted in Williams's *Works* (1822) III.9. Williams's authorship should be accepted with caution.
L(163.n.20),O(2, 1 uncut),*LdU-B*; NjP,TxU(2, 1 uncut).

W512 [—] [another impression?]
>The lowest point of the ornament on the title is over a break in the rule above the imprint.
L(C.57.g.7/6),LdU-B; CSmH,CtY,IU,MH.

W513 [—] — '*London, printed for W. Webb*' [*Edinburgh*], 1743.
8⁰: *A*⁴; *1–2* 3–8.
>Printed by Ruddiman on the evidence of the ornaments.
E; CtY,MH.

W514 [**Williams, David.**] A pindaric on the nativity of the son of god. *London, printed for St. John Baker at Thavies-Inn-gate in Holborn*, 1712 [1711]. (*PB* 27 Nov)
8⁰: *A–B*⁴; *1–2* 3–14 *15–16 blk.*
>Entered in *SR* 27 Nov by John Morphew for St. John Baker; deposit copy at EU.
'Prepare th' harmonious lyre'

Williams, D. A pindaric

>Attributed to Williams by *Rawlinson*.
L(161.a.69, Luttrell, 1 Dec, —B4),LLP,EU, *LpU*; DFo(—B4).

[**Williams, John.**] Sacred and moral poems... By a Cambridge gentleman. *London, printed for the author*, 1716. (*SR* 12 Sept)
8⁰: pp. 40.   L,O.
>Entered to Williams in *SR*; deposit copies at O,E,EU,SaU.

— Sacred and moral poems on the most important duties of common life. *London, printed for the author. A.D.* 1723.
8⁰: pp. 120.   L.

W515 **Williams, William.** A poem on the piety and prosperity of her most sacred and serene majesty Anne... *Dublin, printed by E. Waters, for the author*, 1709.
4⁰: ᵖ*A*² *A–B*² *D–E*²; *i–iv*, ⟨*1–16*⟩.
'If muses may direct the mind of man'
O(pagination cropt).

W516 [**Williamson, David.**] A mournful poem on the never enough to be lamented death of his sacred and soveraign majesty King William of ever blessed and glorious memory. [*Edinburgh*, 1702.]
1⁰: 1 side, 2 columns.
>Mourning borders.
'Opprest with grief, distrest with mournful groans'
>Ms. attribution to Williamson in the E copy.
E.

Willison, John. 'One hundred gospel hymns, in memory of redeeming love... *Edinburgh, printed by T. Lumisden & J. Robertson*.' (*SM* Aug 1747)

Willoughby de Broke, Richard, *baron. See* Verney, Richard, *baron Willoughby de Broke*.

W517 [**Wilmot, George.**] Carmen rhythmicum, monachicum, Momo dicatum, a rusticante Oxoniensi in honorem literatissimi ********* conscriptum... *Londini, impensis W. Owen* [?], 1749. (*LEP* 6 July)
8⁰: *A–C*⁴ (A2 as 'B2'); *1–2* 3–24.
>*Rawlinson* notes the Owen imprint and adds '[anglice Jac. Fletcher Oxon]'.
'Mi rure detento/Ah! cursu quam lento'
>Attributed to Wilmot by *Rawlinson*. Two copies at O are bound with tracts by William King; it is clearly related to his attack on Edward Bentham, and it is also listed by *Rawlinson* under King on one occasion; he may have had a hand in it.
O(3),CT; CtY(presentation copy),*DLC*,MH.

W518 [**Wilson, Bernard.**] Aldenardum carmen Duci Malburiensi, datum, donatum, dedicatumque anno salutis humanæ, 1708. *Londini, impensis H. Clements*, [1708.] (7 Dec, Luttrell)
8⁰: *A–C*⁴; *1–2* 3–23 *24 blk.*

Wilson, B. Aldenardum carmen

> Watermark: post-horn on shield. Listed in *WL* Jan 1709.
> 'Vandomus Gallorum acies, arma arma frementes'
> L(161.b.62, Luttrell),O,CT,EU; ICN.

W519 — [fine paper]
> Watermark: fleur-de-lys on shield; author's name added to title.
> L(1967).

W520 [—] — *Londini, impensis J. Read*, 1709.
> 8°: A⁴; *1* 2–8.
> Probably a piracy.
> L(1964),CT; ICN.

[**Wilson, John.**] Three poems, Mahanaim, or, strivings with a saviour, 1706. *See* T256.

W521 — To Dr. David Dickson, lamenting the death of his learned friend Dr. Archbald [!] Pitcairn. [*Edinburgh*, 1713.]
> ½°: 1 side, 1 column.
> 'Ah! cease, dear sir, cease to lament his fate'
> Signed 'John Wilson'.
> E.

W522 '**Wimble, William.**' The character of a certain f——w of T——y C——e, illustrated with curious notes and comical remarks. By William Wimble, esq; [*Dublin*, 1725/30.]
> ½°: *1*–2, 2 columns.
> The copy at L forms part of a collection of Dublin half-sheets of 1725/30.
> 'Blush not, my muse, (unworthy tho' the theme)'
> The fellow of Trinity College satirized is apparently Lambert Hughes. William Wimble is presumably a pseudonym.
> L(C.121.g.8/119),DT.

Win. Win at first, lose at last, 1707. *See* Price, Laurence.

— Win first, lose last, or, a new game at cards, [1710.] *See* Price, Laurence.

Winchilsea, Anne Finch, *countess of. See* Finch, Anne, *countess of Winchilsea.*

W523 **Wind.** The wind in the east: or pri'thee friend keep back. An ominous warning. A humorous ballad. By a sailor on board the S---ness fleet. *London, printed for W. Webb*, 1743. (4 May)
> 2°: A⁴ (A3 as 'B'); *1*–3 4–8.
> Rothschild 242. The copy from Tom's Coffee House, dated 4 May, is in the Lewis Walpole Library; listed in *LM* May.
> 'To dupes I write that stay home'
> An attack on the ministry.
> CSmH,CtY,KU(uncut),MH,OCU.

W524 — — *London, printed for A. Moore*, 1743.
> 4°: A²; *1* 2–4, 2 columns.
> Vertical chain-lines. Apparently a piracy.
> O(2).

Windsor

W525 **Windsor.** Windsor Castle: a poem. Inscrib'd to the immortal honour of our most gracious soveraign, Anne. *London printed, and are to be sold by B. Bragge*, 1708. (*DC* 31 July)
> 2°: A–C²; *1–2* 3–12.
> 'After great Nassaw taught this nation war'
> Sotheby's, 27 March 1961, lot 1157 (Luttrell, 31 July).

W526 — — To which is added, Britain's jubilee; a new congratulatory song, &c. *London printed, and sold by H. Hills*, 1708.
> 8°: A⁸; *1* 2–16.
> 'Britain's jubilee' occupies pp. 15–16; it is by Richard Estcourt and was separately printed [1707?]. Reissued in *A collection of the best English poetry*, 1717 (Case 294).
> L(C.124.b.7/7; G.1390/2; G.18914/3),O(2, 1 lacks A8),CT,EU,LdU-B; CSmH,CtY,IU,MH, TxU+.

— The Windsor prophecy, 1712. *See* Pittis, William.

W527 — The Windsor prophecy, found in a Marlborough rock. *London, printed in the year* 1711.
> ½°: 1 side, 1 column.
> No price in imprint. *Teerink* 857.
> 'In an old rock, as stories go'
> DT; PU.

W528 — [variant]
> 'Price one penny' in imprint.
> L(G.1390/7).

Wine. Wine a poem, 1708. *See* Gay, John.

— Wine and wisdom, 1710–. *See* Ward, Edward [The tipling philosophers].

W529 [**Wine, John.**] A welcome to victory: a congratulatory poem on the success of her majesty's forces in Germany, under the command of his grace, the Duke of Marlborough. With an after-thought on the late engagement at sea. *London, printed in the year* 1704. *Sold by S. Malthus.* (*PM* 28 Nov)
> 4°: π² A–L²; *i–iv*, 1–42 *43–44 blk*.
> Watermark: London arms.
> 'Who can be silent, when the jovial round'
> *After-thought*: 'To what exalted heights doth heav'n intend'
> Dedication to Queen Anne signed 'J.W.'
> C(uncut).

W530 — [fine paper] *London, printed in the year* 1704.
> Watermark: fleur-de-lys. Dedication signed in full.
> O(−L2); DFo(in presentation morocco).

'**Wingar, Henry.**' *See* Waring, Henry.

Winstanley, John. Poems written occasionally by John Winstanley…interspers'd with many others, by several ingenious hands. *Dublin, printed by S. Powell, for the author*, 1742.

Winstanley, J.

8°: pp. xiv, 320.   L,O; CtY,MH.
No watermark. Essentially a miscellany (*Case 437*); Winstanley's poems are not distinguished from the rest.

— [fine paper]   CtY.
Watermark: AB.

— — Vol. II. Published by his son. *Dublin, printed by S. Powell, for the editor,* 1751.
8°: pp. 320.   O; CLU-C,CtY.

———

The following separately printed Irish poems are included in the volumes of Poems *above; there is no evidence that any particular one is by Winstanley:*
An elegy on the much lamented death of Jenny the fish, [1718.] E163.
The imperious beauty, 1730. I13.
A letter to the bishop of M., [1726.] L155.
Myrtillo. A pastoral poem, 1726. M573.
A poem to a widow, upon a fly, 1726. P659.
Poltis king of Thrace, 1726. M320·5.
To the honourable Mr. D.T. (Numb. II), 1725. T374.

W531 **[Winter, John.]** Bury, and its environs, a poem, written in the year MDCCXLVI. *London, printed for W. Owen,* 1747 (*GM, LM* Jan)
2°: *A*² B² C¹; *i–ii, 1–2* 3–6 '6' *8 blk.*
Horizontal chain-lines.
'Hail Bury! loveliest spot I ever found'
Early ms. note in the L copy 'By Dr. Winter'.
Dedicated to the Duke of Grafton.
L(1890.b.2/6),O,E; CSmH.

W532 **Wisdom.** The wisdom of religion, and the folly of vice, display'd. In two alphabets in verse. *Newcastle, printed in the year* 1740.
8°: *A*⁸; *1–2* 3–15 *16 blk.*
'A wicked will, alas! who can persuade?'
'A disregard, where care is most requir'd'
CLU-C.

W533 — Wisdom revealed; or, the tree of life discover'd and describ'd, a tale. By a studious enquirer into the mysteries of nature. To which is added, the Crab-tree: or Sylvia discover'd. *London, printed for W. Shaw; sold at all the pamphlet-shops in London & Westminster,* [1732.] (*GM, LM* Dec)
8°: *A*² B–D⁴ E²; *i–iv, 1–27* 28 blk.
The crab-tree was published separately, [172–?]
'Phoebus, whose charriot ne'er stands still'
Largely based on the prose *Natural history of the arbor vitae,* 1732. A phallic poem.
L(P.C.22.b.18).

W534 — [*idem*] [dh] Teague-root botanically considered. The tree of life; or, Chloe convinced. [*Dublin?* 174–?]
8°: *A*⁴; *1* 2–8.
The copy seen is bound with Dublin tracts of the 1740s.
O.

Wise

Wise. The wise or foolish choice, 1703. *See* Clark, James.

Wishes. Wishes to a godson, with other miscellany poems, 1712. *See* Mandeville, Bernard.

W535 **Wishing.** The wishing-maid. A Christmas-trick. *Dublin, printed in the year* 1735.
8°: *A*⁴ (A1ᵛ as 'A2'); *1* 2–8.
'It happen'd on a winter's night'
The virgin succeeds in losing her virginity.
DN.

W536 **Wit.** Wit, a poem most humbly inscribed to the right honourable the Earl of Orford. *London, printed for J. Robinson,* 1745. (*GM* April)
4°: *A*² B–H²; *1–2* 3–32.
'Yes – you, my lord, can stand the test of wit'
Listed in *GM* as 'By Tim. Soundbottom'.
L(11630.c.8/7; 11630.e.3/10); ICN,MH.

W537 — Wit upon crutches, or, the biter bitten, most humbly dedicated to the ingenious Mr. Arbuckle author of the Dublin weekly journal. *Dublin, printed in the year* 1725.
½°: 1 side, 2 columns.
Williams 1127.
'A writer held in great renown'
Ball 203 seems to ascribe this satire on Arbuckle to Swift, but Williams regards that as purely conjectural.
L(C.121.g.8/65),Rothschild; OCU,TxU.

[Witheral, —, Mr.] A new song sung at the club at Mr. Taplin's, 1724. *In* D428.

W538 **Withers, John.** An epistle to the right honourable Robert Walpole, esq; upon his majesty's arrival. By Mr. Withers. *London, printed for Jacob Tonson,* 1723 [1724?]. (4 Jan 1724, Luttrell)
2°: *A*² B–C²; *i–iv, 1*–6 *7–8 blk.* A1 hft.
The Luttrell copy was formerly in the possession of C. H. Wilkinson; that copy had the blank leaf C2 included in the collation, though it may have resulted from imperfect perfecting of a half-sheet.
'With longing arms, while grateful Albion stands'
The identification of the author as John Withers by the L catalogue seems plausible.
L(11630.h.56,–C2; 163.m.14, lacks A², –C2), O(–A1, C2); DLC(–C2).

With—rs, Peggy. The fairy-king a poem. By Mrs. Peggy With—rs, 1726. *See* F38.

W539 **Woeful.** The woeful treaty: or the unhappy peace. An ode. In the measure of the celebrated song of Chevy-chase... With a dedication to the E——l of Ox——d. *London printed, and are to be sold by J. Harrison & J. Billingsley, J. Baker, & A. Boulter,* 1716 [1715]. (*MC* Nov)
4°: A–C⁴; *i–viii, 1* 2–16.

The **woeful** treaty

'God prosper long our noble king'
Dedication signed 'P.O.' The same author wrote *An epistle to R--- W--*, 1718. An attack on Harley and the tories.
L(1486.i.4; 164.n.6, Luttrell, 28 Dec); IU(2).

W540 —— The second edition. *London printed, and are to be sold by J. Harrison & J. Billingsley, J. Baker, & A. Boulter*, 1716.
4°: A–C⁴; *i–viii, 1* 2–16.
Apparently in part a reimpression.
AdU; OCU.

W541 —— The third edition. *London printed, and are to be sold by J. Harrison & J. Billingsley, J. Baker, & A. Boulter*, 1716.
4°: A–C⁴; *i–viii, 1* 2–16.
Apparently a reimpression. Advertised in *DC* 2 May 1717, probably subsequent to publication.
L(11631.g.30/3),O; MH.

W542 —— *Dublin: re-printed, and sold by Tho. Humes*, 1716.
8°: A⁸; *i* ii–vi, 7–16.
CtY.

Wogan, Charles. *Poems by Wogan are included in William Tunstall's* Ballads and some other occasional poems, *1716–*.

W543 [—] The Preston prisoners to the ladies about court and town. By way of comfort, from C.W. to W.T. *London, printed for J. Roberts*, 1716. (*MC* Jan)
½°: 1 side, 2 columns.
The rule above the imprint is composed of 17 short rules.
'You fair ones all at liberty'
Crum Y253. In reply to William Tunstall, *From W.T. in the Marshalsea*, 1716; answered by his *From W.T. . . . The second part*, 1716.
O(cropt),OC; MH.

W544 [—] [another edition]
The rule above the imprint is in two pieces.
MC.

W545 **Wolf.** The wolf stript of his shepherd's clothing, address'd to Dr. Sacheverell. By a Salopian gentleman. *London, printed for J. Baker*, 1710. (*Review* 3 June)
8°: A⁴; *1–2* 3–8.
Listed in *WL* May, but since it was often published late the date of 3 June may still be correct.
'Of all the jolly sights the town has shown'
An attack on Sacheverell and his followers.
L(E.1990/6; E.1991/11),O,*OM*,CT; CLU-C, ICN,IU,InU,OCU.

W546 **Woman.** Woman in miniature. A satire. . . By a student of Oxford. *London, printed for J. Huggonson*, 1742. (*LM* March)

Woman in miniature

8°: A–D⁴; *1–3* 4–32.
'Fetch! fetch the paper! in my rage I said'
L(11631.bb.92),O; CtY,ICN(uncut),NN(lacks B2),OCU,TxU+.

—— The woman of taste, 1733. *See* Newcomb, Thomas.

—— Woman unmask'd, and dissected, 1740. *See* Female chastity, *1734–*.

W547 —— The woman's man. A poem. *London, printed for T. Flower; sold at the booksellers and pamphlet shops of London & Westminster*, 1735. (*GSJ* 21 March)
4°: A² B–C²; *i–ii* iii–iv, 5–12.
'Price sixpence' on title. Listed in *LM* March with this price and imprint as '. . . A poem, dedicated to the pretty young fellows and rakes of the town', but in *LM* April with title as given here 'Printed for M. Harris, pr. 1s.'
'To win the fair, whom most the fair approve'
L(1972); OCU.

[W548 = C472] —— Woman's prerogative, 1736. *See* Cousteil, Isaac.

W549 **Women.** The women-hater's lamentation: or a new copy of verses on the fatal end of Mr. Grant, a woollen-draper, and two others that cut their throats or hang'd themselves in the Counter; with the discovery of near hundred more that are accused for unnatural dispising the fair sex, and intriguing with one another. To the tune of, Ye pretty sailors all. *London, printed for J. Robinson*, 1707.
½°: 1 side, 2 columns.
Three rough woodcuts at head. On the other side of the LG copy, *A full and true account of a dreadful fire*, 1708, in prose.
'Ye injur'd females see'
LG.

W550 —— The women's indictment against Burnbank, and George Fachney. . . [*Edinburgh*] *Printed in the year* 1721.
4°: A⁴; *1–2* 3–8.
'Pannels, you are indicted as rascals'
Reprinted in Alexander Pennecuik (d. 1730) *A compleat collection*, [174–], and probably by him, though that collection includes poems by other hands. A mock trial.
E.

W551 **Wonder.** The wonder of wonders; or, a rich vintner, and no cuckold. To which is added some remarks upon marriage. *Dublin, printed by Christopher Dickson*, 1730.
8°: A⁴; *1* 2–8.
'Oh! happy F——ck, thou alone art he'
The remarks on pp. 4–8 are in prose.
DA.

W552 —— The wonder: or, the devil outwitted. *Dublin, printed in the year* 1736.
8°: A⁴; *1–3* 4–8.
'To thee, dear Dick, this tale I send'

The **wonder**: or, the devil outwitted

> An imitation of La Fontaine; the same tale as Congreve's *An impossible thing*, 1720.
> O,DN(title mutilated).

W553 Wonderful. The wonderful bard. Or, a character of a certain d—n. [*Dublin*] *Printed in the year* 'MDCCCXXXVI' [1736].
½°: 1 side, 2 columns.
> At the foot of column 2, six lines titled 'Concerning the same'.
> 'To suit this worthy and judicious age'
> 'His good performance let no mortal boast'
> Satires on Swift.
> *CtY*(mutilated).

— The wonderful bonnet, [1729?] *See* A comical sonnet, [1729?]

W554 — The wonderfull man: part the third: inscrib'd to the right honourable M.C. [*Dublin*, 1724?]
½°: 1 side, 1 column.
> The DT copy is bound with half-sheets of 1727, but is dated in ms. on the verso as 1724.
> 'I sing a subject sung by no man'
> A satire on Marmaduke Coghill. The previous parts have not been identified, but may well be in prose; a note refers to 'some papers upon the wooden man in Essex-street, under the title of the *Wonderfull Man*'.
> C,DT; *CtY*.

W555 — A wonderful new prophecy: giving a certain and true account when the church ills will be great again... Written by an acquaintance of Dr. Eems. [*London*] *Printed in the year* 1711.
½°: 1 side, 2 columns.
> 'When the best of all queens that e're fill'd a throne'
> A tory song.
> C,Chatsworth.

W556 — [dh] The wonderful pentecost, on occasion of the thundrings and lightnings on Whit-Sunday last. [col] *London, printed for the author*, 1703. (5 June, Luttrell)
2°: A²; 1–4.
> With 'Messiah triumphant. To the Jews.'
> 'What! Sinai's thunders on our pentecost?'
> ICN(Luttrell).

W557 — The wonderful works of providence, shown to the widow and fatherless, being a true and well-attested relation of one Mary Blake in Newport... [*Edinburgh*] *Printed and sold in the Swan-close* [*by R. Drummond?*], 1744.
8°: A⁴; 1 2–8.
> A chap-book. After imprint, 'Done from the original. Licensed.' No earlier edition has been traced.
> 'Come all you poor distressed souls'
> L(1078.k.26/3).

W557·5 Wonders. Wonders upon wonders. In answer to the Age of wonders. To the tune of Chivy Chase.

Wonders upon wonders

[*London*] *Sutton Nicholl excudit*, [1710.]
½°: 1 side, 3 columns.
> Engraved throughout; satirical print at head; 29 stanzas of verse below. Included here on account of the amount of verse present.
> 'The year of wonders is arriv'd'
> In praise of the tories and Sacheverell after their election victory.
> L(P&D 1549; C.121.g.9/160, imprint cropt).

[**Wood, Thomas,** *of Hardwick.*] The K-ntish spy: or, a memorial of the C--ves H--d club, 1712. *See* K104.

W558 Wooden. The wooden age. A satyrical poem. Humbly inscrib'd to William Pulteney, esq; *London, printed for L. Gulliver; sold by the booksellers in St. Paul's Church-yard, and at the pamphlet shops of London & Westminster*, 1733. (*GSJ* 23 Aug)
2°: A¹ B–C²; 1–4 5–10.
> 'Since the metallick ages all are past'
> L(11630.h.43),LdU-B; DLC,ICN,IU,KU,MH.

W559 Woodman, John. The rat-catcher at Chelsea College. A tale... With letters from John Samford, esq;... As, also, a scheme to pay the out-pensioners of Chelsea... *London, printed for the author; sold by the booksellers of London & Westminster*, 1740.
8°: A–H⁴; *i–ii* iii–viii, 5–59 *60 blk*. 59 err.
> Some copies (L,O) add engraved plates and copious ms. material by Woodman. The verse, on pp. 5–17, is only a small part of the set of proposals.
> 'Upon a time there was a lord'
> L(1485.t.12; 79.b.25),LG,O(2); *MH*.

Woodward, —, *Mr.* The Kingston Atalantis: or, Woodward's miscellany, viz... *London printed, and sold by J. Wilford*, 1731.
8°: pp. 60.   L.
> The dedication makes it clear that Woodward was the sole author; about half the volume is in verse.

Woodward, George. Poems on several occasions. *Oxford, printed at the Clarendon printing-house*, 1730.
8°: pp. '140' [240].   L,O; CtY,DFo.

———

[—] Merton walks, or the Oxford beauties [actually by John Dry], 1717. *See* D446.

W560 — A poem to the glorious memory of his sacred majesty King George I. *London, printed for J. Roberts*, 1727. (*MC* Nov)
8°: A⁴ B–D⁴; *i–viii*, 1 2–23 *24 blk*.
> ''Tis done! the glorious lamp of Britain's fled'
> CT(cropt).

W561 Worcester. Worcester dumb-bells; a ballad. To the tune of All in the land of Essex. [*London*,

Worcester dumb-bells

printed by William Bowyer, for Henry Clements, 1710.] (Sept?)
½°: 1 side, 2 columns.
    Entered in Bowyer's ledgers for Mr. Clements under 23 Sept 1710, 1 ream, and on 6 Oct 'again 1 R more'. Presumably there were two impressions or editions which have not been distinguished.
'I sing the famous city'
    Crum I470. Early ms. note in the O copy, 'By Mr Tho: Warton poetical lecturer', but collected in John Smith's *Poems upon several occasions* (1713) 261–71. Possibly it was a joint production. A satire on William Lloyd, bishop of Worcester, prohibiting the ringing of bells.
L(Cup 645.e.1/20),O,Chatsworth; *InU*,NNP.

W562 Word. A word of advice to the male-contents. *London, sold by J. Nutt,* 1700 [1701]. (20 Feb, Luttrell)
½°: 1–2, 1 column.
    Not in *Wing*.
'What nation e'er can hope for happiness'
ICN(Luttrell).

W563 World. The world in disguise: or masks all. A new ballad, sung by Mr. Beard, at the ball (after the Venetian manner) at Ranelagh House. To the tune of Sing tantararara fools all. *London, printed for R. Dodsley; sold by M. Cooper,* [1749.] (*GA* 19 May)
2°: *A*² <B²; *1–2* 3–8.
'Ye medley of mortals that make up this throng'
L(1482.ee.6); CSmH,CtY(uncut).

— The world unmask'd. A satire, 1738. *See* Gilbert, Thomas.

W564 Worlidge, Edward. The resurrection: a poem in three canto's. *London, printed for John Morphew,* 1716. (26 May, Luttrell)
8°: *A*⁴ B–E⁴; *1–8* 9–40. A1 hft.
    Listed in *MC* May.
'While tow'ring bards the fate of heroes sing'
O,GM; CSmH,*CtY*(Osborn collection, Luttrell), ICN,IU.

W565 [Wotton, *Sir Henry.*] A farewel to the world. By the honourable D——. *Dublin, printed in the year* 1725.
½°: 1 side, 2 columns.
    Teerink 921; *Williams* 1127.
'Farewel ye gilded follies pleasing troubles'
    For Wotton's authorship, see *Crum* F216; it is still uncertain. Attributed to Swift by Ball; rejected by Williams. The MH copy expands the author's name in ms. to 'Dick'.
L(1890.e.5/7); MH.

Wr., Ja. Burley on the Hill, [170–?] *See* Wright, James.

W566 [Wren, John.] The country life; or an invitation of the soul to retirement. Being a poetical soliloquy on

Wren, J. The country life

Cant. vii. 11. *London, printed for W. Taylor,* 1717. (May, Luttrell)
8°: *A*² B–C⁴ D²; *i–iv, 1* 2–19 20 *blk.* iv err.
'Haste, O my soul, and wing thy course away'
    According to the preface, 'a trial of skill in imitation of Mr. Arwaker's *Pia desideria*'.
CtY,IU(Luttrell),OCU.

W566·2 — [another issue]
    Apparently a variant state of the title, adding 'By John Wren, A.M.'
L(11601.dd.10/2).

W566·5 [—] — The second edition. *London, printed for John Bateman,* 1721.
8°: *A*¹ B–C⁴ D²; *i–ii, 1* 2–19 20 *blk.*
    A reissue with a cancel title replacing the original A².
O.

W566·7 [—] Retirement: a divine soliloquy. *London, printed for J. Bateman,* 1722.
8°: *A*¹ B–D⁴ E¹ (E1 as 'D'); *i–ii, 1* 2–26.
'Haste, O my soul, and let thy winged speed'
    The text has not been compared with the preceding, but the unusual publisher they have in common makes Wren's authorship almost certain.
MH,OCU.

W567 [Wright, James.] Burley on the Hill. A poem, dedicated to the right honourable the Earl of Nottingham. By Ja. Wr. [170–?]
4°: *A*⁴; *i–ii,* 1–6.
    The copy at CSmH is bound with poems of 1702, 05. It also occupies the greater part of the *Farther additions* (1714) to Wright's *The history and antiquities of the county of Rutland,* 1684 (copy at O).
'Hail, happy fabrick, whose auspicious view'
    Attributed to Wright in *DNB*. Burley House, near Oakham, was the seat of Daniel Finch, earl of Nottingham, after his retirement in 1704.
O; CSmH.

W568 [—] Phœnix Paulina. A poem on the new fabrick of St. Paul's cathedral. *London, printed by G. J. for Arthur Collins,* 1709. (*PB* 29 Jan)
4°: A–C⁴; *1–4* 5–23 24 *blk.*
'I, he whose infant muse did heretofore'
    Early ms. attribution to Wright by Hearne in the O copy.
L(1973, Luttrell, 29 Jan),*LVA-D*,O.

Wright, John. 'The best mirth: or, the melody of Sion, being a collection of hymns on divers occasions. [*London*] *Joseph Marshal.*' (*PPB* 4 March 1712)

—— The second edition corrected. *London, printed for Aaron Ward,* 1745.
12°.   NNUT.

Wright, J.

— Spiritual songs for children: or, poems on several subjects and occasions. *London, printed for and sold by Joseph Marshal, 1727.*
12⁰: pp. 70.   L.

—— '*London, printed for J. & J. Marshall, 1738.*' Ms. title to an imperfect copy at MH.

—— '3rd edn corrected, 1750.' (*CBEL* II. 130)

W569 Wright, Samuel. A hymn to the incarnation. A pindaric poem on our saviour's nativity. *London, printed for J. Clark, 1705.* (12 Jan, Luttrell)
2⁰: *A*² B–D² E¹; *i–iv*, 1–14. 14 err.
Advertised in *PM* 13 Jan.
'God did his throne forsake'
L(1875.d.6/176),*MR-C*; CLU-C(Luttrell),TxU.

W570 Wright, Thomas, *B.A., of St. John's.* Four pastorals, entitled Spring, Summer, Autumn, and Winter. *London, printed for T. Waller, 1749.* (*GM, LM* Feb)
8⁰: *A*⁸ B–C⁸; *1–4* 5–46 *47–48 blk.*
Spring: 'Stretch'd on the plain I grasp the slender reed'
L(11631.d.65,–C8),OW,CT(–C8),DT; ICN, NN,TxHR.

W571 Wright, Thomas, *M.A., physician.* Bruma, et vespera brumalis, Roystoniæ agitata. Poema. Authore Tho. Wright, artium magistro, & medico. *Londini, impensis Guil. Carter, 1710.*
8⁰: A–C⁸; *i–ii*, 1–44 *45–46.* C8 advt.
The pagination of sheet C is irregular.
'Hactenus æstatis brumæq; reciprocus ordo'
L(1213.m.16/3,–C8),O; CtY(–C8),MH(–C8).

W572 Wrongheads. The wrongheads: a poem. Inscrib'd to Mr. Pope. By a person of quality. *London, printed for T. Astley; sold by R. Wellington, 1733.* (*GSJ* 31 May)
2⁰: *A*² B–C²; *1–3* 4–12.
Also listed (in error?) in *GSJ* as 28 June. Ackers's ledger under 29 May 1733 records the printing of 250 copies for Astley.
'Shall knaves and fools command the world's applause'
A satire in emulation of Pope.
L(11657.m.38),LVA-D,O,OA; CtY,IU,MH, OCU(uncut),TxU(2)+.

W573 —— *London printed, and, Dublin re-printed, by James Hoey, 1733.*
8⁰: *A*⁴ *B*²; *1–3* 4–12.
L(1963),O,DN.

Wycherley, William. Miscellany poems: as satyrs, epistles, love-verses, songs, sonnets, &c. *London, printed for C. Brome, J. Taylor, & B. Tooke, 1704.* (*DC* 28 March)
2⁰: pp. xlvi, 438.   L; CLU-C,MH.

Wycherley, W. *Collections*

Watermark: fool's cap. Proposals were issued as early as 1696.

— [fine paper]   O; CLU-C.
Mixed watermarks, largely D.

— The posthumous works…in prose and verse … In two parts… *London, printed for A. Bettesworth, J. Osborn, W. Mears, W. & J. Innys, J. Peele, T. Woodward, & F. Clay, 1728* [1729?]. (*MChr* 9 Sept 1729)
8⁰: pp. 14, 80+240.   L,O; CtY,MH.
Drop-head title to the second part, 'Miscellaneous poems… Vol. II.'

— The posthumous works… Vol. II… *London, printed for J. Robetrs* [!], *1729.* (*DP* 4 Nov 1729)
8⁰: pp. 51+44.   O; NN-B.
Edited by Pope, and apparently suppressed. See V. A. Dearing in *PMLA* (1953) 223–36.

———————

W574 [—] The folly of industry: or, the busy man expos'd. A satyr, address'd to a friend. *London, printed for A. Baldwin, 1704.* (16 March, Luttrell)
2⁰: *A*² B–D²; *1–4* 5–15 *16 blk.*
The Luttrell copy was in the possession of John Fleming in 1960. Advertised in *FP* 28 March as 'just publish'd'.
'Your man of bus'ness is your idlest ass'
CLU-C,CSmH,CtY,MH.

W575 — [reissue] The idleness of business: a satyr. Address'd to one who said, a man shewed his spirit, industry, and parts, by his love of business… The second edition. *London, printed for Benj. Bragg, 1705.* (*PM* 20 Jan)
2⁰: *A*¹ B–D²; *3–4* 5–15 *16 blk.*
Cancel title; preface A2 omitted.
LDW; MH.

W576 [—] [dh] On his grace, the Duke of Marlborough. [col] *London, printed for John Morphew, 1707.* (2 Jan, Luttrell)
2⁰: *A*²; *1–4.*
Watermark: Amsterdam arms.
'Swift as his fame, o'er all the world he flies'
Early ms. attribution to Wycherley in copies at O,CSmH,CtY. Reprinted in Wycherley's *Posthumous works, 1728.*
O,DG,DT,LdU-B(Luttrell); CLU-C,CSmH, CtY,MB.

W577 [—] [fine paper]
Watermark: fleur-de-lys.
OW,Blickling Hall ('ex dono autoris').

[Wyndham, William.] Verses address'd to the imitator of the first satire of the second book of Horace, [1733.] *See* V39.

[Wynne, John.] Eubulus Oxoniensis discipulis suis, 1720. *See* E483.

Wynter, J.

> **Wynter, John.** Les badinages de Monsieur Wynter, feu medecin, aux bains chauds. Or Wynter's whims... *London, printed for the author,* 1744.
> 8⁰: pp. 84.   L,O; CLU-C,ICN.
> > Largely in verse.

W578 [**Wyvill, Christopher.**] The parson's daughter. A tale. For the use of pretty girls with small fortunes... To which are added, epigrams, and the Court ballad, by Mr. Pope. From correct copies.

Wyvill, C. The parson's daughter

> *London, printed for J. Harris near St. James's Bagnio,* 1717. (*PM* 21 Feb)
> 8⁰: π¹ A⁴ C⁴ D⁴(−D4); i–ii, 1–22.
> > Griffith 70.
> 'Cloe, a country vicar's daughter'
> > Wyvill's authorship is revealed in a Curll catalogue found in *The altar of love,* 1731; see also *Twickenham Pope* VI. 421.

L(11632.bb.33),O,LdU-B; CLU-C(uncut; ms. note 'Pack & Young: gift'),CtY,KU(uncut), MH(2).

X

Xantippe. Xantippe, or the scolding wife, 1724.
See Forbes, William.

Y

Y., B. A new song on the scrutiny for Sir George
Vandeput, [1750/51.] *See* N210.

Y., S. 'Εωσφορος: or, the morning star, 1746.
See H147·5.

Y1 [**Yalden, Thomas.**] Æsop at court. Or, state
fables. Vol. I. *London printed, and sold by J. Nut,*
1702. (*WL* Jan)
8°: *A⁴* B-E⁴ F²; *1-4* 5-43 *44 blk.* A1 hft.
Fable 1: 'A river insolent with pride'
    Attributed to Yalden in *Cibber* IV. 345.
L(12305.e.18),LLP,O,DrU,LdU-B; CLU-C,
CtY,IU,MH,OCU+.

Y2 — An essay on the character of Sir Willoughby
Aston, late of Aston in Cheshire. A poem. *London,
printed for Jacob Tonson,* 1704. (4 July, Luttrell)
2°: *A²* B-C²; *i-iv,* 1-8.
    A faint watermark of initials has been seen in
most but not all copies. Probably they are all
on the same paper. Advertised in *PM* 26 Aug.
'What man renown'd! what British worthy's
praise'
    Dedication signed.
L(11630.h.64),O,MP; CtY(Luttrell),ICU,NjP
('for Sr. Robt Cotton'),TxU(2).

Y3 — 'A poem on the mines late of Sir Carbery Price,
dedicated to Sir Humphry Mackworth. [*London*]
Published by John Nutt.' (*PB* 21 Oct 1701)
    Much advertised as part of a publicity cam-
paign by the Company of Mine Adventurers.
'What spatious veins inrich the British soil'

Y4 — — The second edition. *London, printed for J.
Nutt,* 1701.
4°: *π¹* A-C²; *i-ii,* *1* 2-11 *12 blk.*
C.

Y5 **Yarhell.** Yarhell's kitchen: or, the dogs of Egypt.
An heroic poem. *London, printed for Bernard
Lintott,* 1713. (*DC* 12 Jan)
2°: *A²* B-F²; *i-iv,* 1-19 20. 20 advt.
    Entered in *SR* 13 Jan; deposit copies at
LSC,O,EU,AdU,SaU. The Luttrell copy,
dated 12 Jan, was in the collection of C. H.
Wilkinson.
'In ancient times, and long before the flood'
    Listed by *Waller* as attributed to Prior;
Faber xxxii–iii argues for his authorship.

Conclusively rejected by *Wright & Spears*
803. The ICN copy has an early ms. note
'A very extraordinary piece written on state
affairs, by Dr. King', but Dr. King's name has
been deleted. In praise of Harley and against
the whigs.
L(11602.i.15/1),O(uncut),C,EU,SaU+ ; ICN,
IU,MH,*PBL*,TxU.

Y6 — — The second edition. *London, printed for
Bernard Lintott,* 1713. (*PB* 5 May)
2°: *A²* B-F²; *i-iv,* 1-19 20. 20 advt.
    Apparently a reimpression.
O; CLU-C,MH,OCU,TxU.

Yarico. Yarico to Inkle, 1736. *See* Moore, Edward.

Ye. [first line:] Ye commons and peers, who are
bound by your pay, [1735.] *See* The speech
englished, [1735.]

Y7 — [first line:] Ye true-born Englishmen proceed
... [*London,* 1701.]
4°: *A²*; 1-4, 2 columns.
    Moore 36. These editions are without a title;
their order has not been established. This alone
has the correct reading 'neglected' in the
last line on p. 1. Reprinted with a verse answer
as *The ballad, or some scurrilous reflections in
verse...answered stanza by stanza,* 1701; the
answer is possibly by Pittis.
'Ye true-born Englishmen proceed'
    Defoe's authorship, suggested as doubtful in
Bohn's edition of *Lowndes,* seems probable;
Defoe twice quoted it in subsequent writings.
For the authorship and the relation of the
various editions see F. H. Ellis in *POAS*
VI. 319, 768f.
MB.

Y8 — [another edition]
    This and the two following editions read
'neglelcted' in the last line on p. 1. The
signature A comes under the space between
the words 'Nation lies' in this line.
LDW,MC; CtY,InU(2),MB,MH.

Y9 — [another edition]
    Signature A under 'Nation'. Stanzas 31-33
all numbered '31'.
L(11631.e.88, cropt; 11633.e.54/1, mutilated),
O(uncut); *MB*.

Y10 — [another edition]
    Signature A under 'Nation'. Stanzas 31-34
correctly numbered.
L(C.116.i.4/34; 11621.h.1/6).

Y11 — [*idem*] You true born-English-men proceed...
[*Dublin?* 1701.]
4°: *A²*; 1-4, 2 columns.
    This edition adds 'The second part' on p. 3
and 'A dialogue between the old horse at
Charing Cross, London, and the young one

Ye true-born Englishmen proceed

over against the Trustee's Court on Colledge-Green, Dublin' on p. 4.
Second part: 'No wonder P——s, F——ch and Sh——r'
Dialogue: 'Dear brother or sire, for I'm sure we're a kin'
O; CSmH.

Y12 — [*idem*] A coppy of verses, expressing the peoples dissatisfaction with the proceedings of the house of commons. ⟨*Edinburgh?* 1701.⟩
obl 1°: 1 side, 4 columns.
E(imprint cropt).

Y13 — [*idem*] A poem. [1701.]
½°: 2 sides, 2 columns.
Possibly an Edinburgh reprint, from the location of one copy.
L(C.121.g.9/121),E; MH.

Yea. The yea and nay stock-jobbers, 1720. *See* Bockett, Elias.

Year. The year forty-one, 1741. *See* Miller, James.

Y14 — The year of wonders. Being a literal and poetical translation of an old Latin prophecy, found near Merlin's Cave. By S——n D——k.
London printed, and sold by J. Johnson, and the booksellers of London & Westminster, 1737. (*LM* March)
2°: A⁴; *1–3* 4–6 *7–8 blk.*
'When a true son of church, and Tom-a-Becket'
The author intended is Stephen Duck; satirically ascribed to him.
O(ms. notes),LdU-B; CSmH,ICN(–A4),IU,MH (–A4),*MnU*+.

Y15 —— '*London printed, and sold by J. Johnson, and the booksellers of London & Westminster*' [*Edinburgh*], 1737.
4°: *A⁴*; *1–2* 3–6 *7–8 blk.*
Printed by William Cheyne on the evidence of the ornaments.
AdU(–A4); TxU.

Y15·2 —— *Dublin, re-printed by George Faulkner*, 1737.
8°.
DN.

Y16 **Yellow.** The yellow sash, or, H—————r beshit. An excellent new ballad, to the old tune of Lillibullero.
London, printed for B———— C———— [*Cowse*], *in Pater-noster Row*, 1743. (*LDP* 26 Oct)
2°: A⁴; *1–5* 6–8. A1 hft.
Advertised in *LDP* as printed for B. Cowse.
'Ye Dettingen heroes, regard what I say'
A satire on the cowardice of the Hanoverians and their general, Baron Ilton, at Dettingen.
L(162.n.46,–A1),O(2),AdU(uncut); CSmH, CtY,TxU(uncut).

Y17 —— *London, printed J.S. near St. Paul's*, [1743.]
½°: 1 side, 2 columns.

The yellow sash

A piracy. Copies appear to be printed on various papers, some with horizontal chain-lines.
L(1890.c.1/8; 1876.f.1/129; G.559/13).

Y18 — The yellow sash. Or, H—————r beshit. To the old tune of Lillibullero. [*Edinburgh?* 1743.]
8°: *A²*; *1–3* 4.
Title in half-title form.
AdU.

Yes. Yes, they are, 1740. *See* Morris, Robert.

Y19 [**Yonge, Sir William.**] The Norfolk garland: or, the death of Reynard the fox. To the tune of, A begging we will go, &c. [*London*, 1728/29?]
½°: 1 side, 2 columns.
Percival appendix 19.
'Come all ye Sussex fox hunters'
Attributed to Yonge by Horace Walpole; his authorship is also revealed in a related poem, *Houghton hare-hunting*, [1729?].
L(1876.f.1/113); Lewis Walpole Library (Horace Walpole's copy).

Yorkshire. The Yorkshire-racers, [1709.] *See* Plaxton, William.

You. [first line:] You true born-English-men proceed...[1701.] *See* Ye true-born Englishmen proceed, [1701.]

Young. The young club a congratulatory poem to his excellency John lord bishop of Bristol, [1713.] *See* Dibben, Thomas.

Y20 — A young distracted lady. A song. [*London*] '*Printed for A.B.*', [1732.]
½°: 1 side, 2 columns.
Printed in black-letter as if it were a popular ballad, which it is not.
'You lovers that are passing by'
Anne Vane's lament for her seduction by Frederick, prince of Wales.
MH.

Y21 — A young Frenchman's lampoon upon his mistress's nose as long and as yellow as a parsnip. [*Dublin*, 1729?]
½°: 2 sides, 2 columns.
The DT copy is bound with half-sheets of 1729. Although printed as verse, it is in prose except for the valentine at the end.
'La passion dans laquelle je me trouve...'
To Mlle Suzanne Riottau.
DT.

Y22 — A young lady's complaint for the stay of Dean Swift in England. *Dublin, printed by George Faulkner*, 1726.
½°: 1 side, 1 column.
Teerink 655; *Williams* 1128.
'Blow ye zephyrs gentle gales'

A **young** lady's complaint

Young, E. The complaint, I.

Originally included in Swift's works by Nichols, 1775, but dismissed by Williams. DT.

— The young laird and Edinburgh Katy, [1720.] *See* Ramsay, Allan.

Y23 — The young senator. A satyre. With an epistle to Mr. Fielding, on his studying the law. *London, printed for David Jones*, 1738. (*GM, LM* March)
2°: *A*¹ B–E² *F*¹; *1–2* 3–19 20.

With a separate title to the epistle on p. 13, and an 'Epigrammatical postscript on standing armies' on p. 20. Printed by Samuel Richardson (*Sale* 226).
'Who wou'd be proud of being made a tool?'
Epistle: 'Or who the writer? or whence comes th' address?'
O(uncut),LdU-B,YU; CSmH,CtY,ICN,MH, TxU(2, uncut)+.

Young, Edward. Poems on several occasions. *Dublin, printed by S. Powell, for George Risk, George Ewing, & William Smith*, 1730.
8°.   DT; DLC.
Title for a nonce collection.

— The works... *Dublin, printed by S. Powell, for George Risk, George Ewing, & William Smith*, 1730.
8°: 2 vol.   C; CSmH.
New titles, for a larger collection.

— The poetical works of the Reverend Edward Young... *London, printed for Messieurs Curll, Tonson, Walthoe, Hitch, Gilliver, Browne, Jackson, Corbett, Lintot & Pemberton*, 1741. (*LM* Jan)
8°: 2 vol.   L,O; CtY,IU.

— The works... *Dublin, printed for George & Alexander Ewing*, 1751.
8°: 2 vol.   O.
Titles for nonce collections of Dublin reprints, excluding *Night thoughts*.

— The poetical works... *London, printed in the year* 1752.
12°: 2 vol.   L.
Vol. 2 contains *Night thoughts*, also issued separately. Possibly a piratical edition.

—— *Printed in the year* 1755.
12°: 3 vol.   MH.
Vol. 3 contains *Night thoughts*, perhaps also issued separately.

[—] The works of the author of the Night thoughts ... Revised and corrected by himself. *London, printed for D. Browne, C. Hitch & L. Hawes [and 10 others]*, 1757. (*LEP* 21 May)
12°: 4 vol.   O; CtY,TxU.
A supplementary fifth volume (titled 'a new edition') was issued by other publishers to accompany the duodecimo reprint of 1767 (copies at L,IU); a six volume edition appeared in 1778–79 (copies at L,CtY).

Y24 [—] The complaint: or, night-thoughts on life, death, & immortality. *London, printed for R. Dodsley*, 1742. (*DP* 31 May)
2°: *A*² B–E²; *1–3* 4–20.
Pettit 1a; *Rothschild* 2619.
'Tir'd nature's sweet restorer, balmy sleep!'
L(C.116.h.5; Ashley 5280),LVA-D,O(ms. annotation),LdU-B; CLU-C,CSmH,CtY(2),MH, TxU(2).

Y25 [—] The complaint... Night the first. Humbly inscrib'd to...Arthur Onslow, esq; speaker of the house of commons. The second edition. *London, printed for R. Dodsley*, 1742. (*LEP* 31 July)
4°: A–D⁴; *1–3* 4–30 *31; 32 blk*. D4 advt.
Pettit 1b. Press-figures 4–1, 12–2, 15–1, 18–1, 20–2, 26–2; title reads 'House of COMMONS'. Pettit records D4 as a cancel, suggesting it was made to add the advertisement for Night the second; its existence has not been confirmed, and in some copies (C,BaP) there is certainly no cancel. The order of editions proposed by Pettit (see *Library* V. 3 (1949) 299f.) is followed with some hesitation; the changes in accidentals recorded by him provide ambiguous evidence, since the 'third edition' (Y29) follows this text in some respects. The wrappers on the copy at C are printed with four pages of advertisement for Dodsley's books.
LVA-D,O,C(original blue printed wrapper),BaP, GU(uncut,–D4)+; ICU,MH,TxU(2).

Y26 [—] — The second edition. *London, printed for R. Dodsley*, 1742.
4°: A–D⁴; *1–3* 4–30 *31; 32 blk*. D4 advt.
Pettit 1c. Press-figure 14–1; title reads 'House of COMMONS'. Sheets B (inner forme) and D are from the same type as the preceding.
L(11656.r.7; 841.k.15,–D4; Ashley 5145, uncut,)LVA-F(lacks A1),E; CSmH,CtY,ICU,MiU, TxU+.

Y27 [—] — The third edition. '*London, printed for R. Dodsley*' [*Edinburgh*], 1742 [1743?].
8°: A–C⁴ D²; *1–2* 3–25 *26–27; 28 blk*. D2 advt.
Pettit 1d. The copy at CtY-M is bound in a volume of Edinburgh piracies, and the others are bound with later Nights with Edinburgh printers' ornaments. A date of 1743 is suggested by the use of the words 'The third edition'.
O; CtY(–D2),CtY-M,MH.

Y28 [—] — The second edition. *London, printed for R. Dodsley*, 1743.
4°: A–D⁴; *1–3* 4–30 *31–32 blk*.
Pettit 1e. Press-figures 8–3, 11–3, 20–3, 28–3. I wonder whether that this may be a later reprint since it omits the numeration of lines found in the other second and third editions.
L(11660.c.13/1),O(–D4); TxU.

Y29 [—] — The third edition. *London, printed for R. Dodsley*, 1743.

Young, E. The complaint, I.

4°: A–D⁴; *1–2* 3–31 *32*. D4 advt.
    Pettit 1f, not recording D4. Press-figures 4–1, 15–1, 16–2, 23–1, 26–1.
LVA-D,O(−D4); CtY,MH.

Y30 [—] — The fourth edition. *London, printed for R. Dodsley,* 1743.
    4°: A⁴(±A1) B–D⁴; *1–2* 3–31 *32*. D4 advt.
        Pettit 1g. A reissue, with the same press-figures as the preceding.
    H. Pettit.

Y31 [—] — The fifth edition. *London, printed for R. Dodsley,* 1744.
    4°: A–D⁴; *1–3* 4–30 *31–32 blk.*
        Pettit 1h. Entered to Dodsley by Ben. Cowse in *SR* 30 July 1744; deposit copies at L,C,E, GU,SaU. That entry was made along with *Night the sixth*; this part had not previously been entered.
    L(642.k.4/1),O,C,E,GU+; MH(−D4),TxU (−D4).

Y32 [—] Night the second. On time, death, friendship. Humbly inscrib'd to the right honourable the Earl of Wilmington. *London, printed for R. Dodsley, & T. Cooper,* 1742. (*LEP* 30 Nov)
    4°: *A*⁴ B–E⁴ F²; *1–4* 5–44. A1 hft, advt.
        Pettit 2a. Possibly more than one impression is concealed here, though the press-figures remain unchanged. Entered to Dodsley in *SR* 3 Dec; deposit copies at L,C,E,GU,SaU.
    '"When the cock crew, he wept" – Smote by that eye'
    L(841.k.15; 642.k.4; 11656.r.7/3; Ashley 5146, uncut),O(3),C,E(2),GU(2, 1 uncut)+; CSmH,CtY (2),ICU,MH,TxU(3)+.

Y33 [—] — The third edition. '*London, printed for R. Dodsley, & T. Cooper*' [*Edinburgh*], 1742 [1743?].
    8°: π¹ A–D⁴ E¹; *i–ii, 1–2* 3–34. π1 hft, advt.
        Pettit 2b. Copies seen are bound with Edinburgh piracies of Nights 3 & 4. A date of 1743 is suggested by the use of the words 'The third edition'.
    O(−π1); CtY(−π1),MH.

Y34 [—] — The third edition. *London, printed for R. Dodsley, & T. Cooper,* 1743.
    4°: *A*⁴ B–E⁴ F²; *1–4* 5–44. A1 hft.
        Pettit 2c. No second edition has been seen. Pettit suggests a publication date of Jan or Feb 1743 since Thomas Cooper died on 9 Feb 1743.
    L(11660.c.13/2); CtY,MH(−A1).

Y35 [—] — *London, printed for R. Dodsley, & M. Cooper,* 1744.
    4°: A–E⁴; *1–3* 4–40.
        Pettit 2d. Presumably printed to complete imperfect sets. No edition statement on title.
    MH.

Y36 [—] Night the third. Narcissa. Humbly inscrib'd to her grace the Dutchess of P------. *London,*

Young, E. The complaint, III.

printed for R. Dodsley, & T. Cooper, 1742. (*LEP* 16 Dec)
    4°: *A*⁴ B–D⁴ E²; *1–4* 5–34 *35–36 blk.* A1 hft, advt.
        Pettit 3a, not distinguishing this and the following. Press-figures 7–2, 12–3, 15–3, 20–1, 23–1, 26–3, 28–3, 33–1. P. 7, line 15 reads 'merry'; an advertisement in *DP* 16 Dec records the correct reading 'mazy'. Entered to Dodsley in *SR* 15 Dec; deposit copies at L,C,E,GU,SaU.
    'From dreams, where thought in fancy's maze runs mad'
    L(642.k.4),O,C,E,GU(2, 1 uncut, −A1, E2)+; CtY(2),ICU,MH(−E2),MiU,TxU(3).

Y37 [—] [reissue?]
    A4 has been altered, omitting press-figure 7–2 and correcting p. 7, line 15 to read 'mazy'. Pettit suggests that A4 only was cancelled, but this can be seen to be erroneous in the Ashley copy at L. Either the change to A4 is a press variant, or *A*⁴ has been reimpressed.
    L(841.k.15; Ashley 5147, uncut),O; CSmH,ICU, IU.

Y38 [—] [reissue?] The second edition. *London, printed for R. Dodsley, & T. Cooper,* 1742.
    4°: *A*⁴ B–D⁴ E²; *1–4* 5–34 *35–36 blk.* A1 hft, advt.
        Pettit 3c. The title A2 has been altered, but the rest of the text is identical with the preceding, including the press-figures.
    L(11656.r.7/4),O; MH.

Y39 [—] — '*London, printed for R. Dodsley, & T. Cooper*' [*Edinburgh*], 1742 [1743?].
    8°: π¹ A–C⁴ D¹; *i–ii, 1–2* 3–26. π1 hft, advt.
        Pettit 3b. An Edinburgh piracy on the evidence of the printers' ornaments.
    O(−π1); CtY(−π1),MH.

Y40 [—] — The third edition. *London, printed for R. Dodsley, & T. Cooper,* 1743.
    4°: *A*⁴(±A2) B–D⁴ E²; *1–4* 5–34 *35–36 blk.* A1 hft, advt.
        Pettit 3d. The title is reported to be a cancel; presumably a reissue of the second edition. Probably published before 9 Feb when Thomas Cooper died, though his name appears in imprints as late as 8 March.
    H. Pettit.

Y41 [—] — The fourth edition. *London, printed for R. Dodsley, & M. Cooper,* 1743.
    4°: *A*⁴ B–D⁴ E²; *1–4* 5–34 *35–36 blk.* A1 hft.
        Pettit 3e. Sheet E is possibly from standing type.
    L(11660.c.13); CtY(−E2).

Y42 [—] — *London, printed for R. Dodsley; sold by M. Cooper,* 1744.
    4°: A⁴(−A4) B–D⁴ E¹; *1–2* 3–6 9–32 31–32.
        Pettit 3f. Presumably reprinted to complete imperfect sets. No edition statement on title.
    LVA-F; MH,TxU.

Young, E. The complaint, IV.

Y43 [—] The complaint: or, night-thoughts on life, death, & immortality. [Night the fourth.] *London, printed for R. Dodsley; sold by M. Cooper,* 1743. (10 March)

4°: *A² B⁴* C–G⁴; [2] i–ii, *1–3* 4–47 *48*. B1 fly-title; 48 advt.

> *Pettit* 4a, not distinguishing this and the following. Sheaf at centre of ornament on p. i; basket of flowers on p. ii. The title is printed in red and black; this and the preface on A2 were intended to be bound before Nights 1–4. B1 is fly-title, 'Night the fourth. The Christian triumph. Containing our only cure for the fear of death... Humbly inscrib'd to the honourable Mr. York.' In most copies, p. 5, line 17 reads 'stars up' for 'starts up'; the correct reading has been seen in a copy at CtY. Entered to Dodsley in *SR* 9 March; deposit copies at L,C,E,SaU,GU. Advertised in *DP* 9 March for 'tomorrow'.

'A much indebted muse, O York! intrudes'

L(11660.c.13/4; 642.k.4/4; Ashley 5148, uncut), LVA-D(2),O(3),C,GU+; CSmH,CtY(2),MH, TxU(3).

Y44 [—] [another issue?]

> Head at centre of ornaments on p. i and ii; A² is from a different setting of type. Possibly A² was set in duplicate at the first impression, since this state is found in what is apparently the deposit copy at E. The remainder of the text is apparently identical with the preceding, for the erroneous reading in p. 5 line 17 is found in most copies.

L(11656.r.7/5),E,GU; CtY,ICU(2),MH,MiU, TxU+.

Y45 [—] — '*London, printed for R. Dodsley; sold by M. Cooper*' [*Edinburgh*], 1743. (*SM* March)

8°: *a⁴* B–E⁴; [2] i–ii, 1–36.

> *Pettit* 4b. An Edinburgh piracy on the evidence of the printers' ornaments.

O; CtY.

Y46 [—] — Night the fourth. *London, printed for R. Dodsley; sold by M. Cooper,* 1744.

4°: *A² B⁴* C–G⁴; [2] i ii, *1–3* 4–47 *48 blk*.

> *Pettit* 4c. Pettit reports a cancel B1 which has not been identified in the copies seen. Presumably reprinted to complete imperfect sets. No edition statement on title.

MH,TxU.

Y47 [—] The complaint... Night the fifth. *London, printed for R. Dodsley; sold by M. Cooper,* 1743. (*DP* 16 Dec)

4°: *A⁴* B–G⁴ H²; *1–7* 8–60. A1 frt; A3ʳ fly-title, A3ᵛ err.

> *Pettit* 6a. Fly-title A3 reads 'Night the fifth. The relapse. Humbly inscrib'd. To the right honourable the Earl of Litchfield'. Possibly this part was intended to begin a second volume. Some copies have an early state of A3ᵛ, blank, lacking the errata; the copy at

Young, E. The complaint, V.

> CtY reported by Pettit cannot now be found, but there is one at TxU. Entered to Dodsley in *SR* 23 Dec; deposit copies at L,C,E,GU, SaU. Young sold the copyright of Nights 1–5 to Dodsley on 24 Nov 1743 for 160 guineas (*Straus, Dodsley,* 326).

'Lorenzo! to recriminate is just'

L(841.k.16; 642.k.4, lacks G–H⁴; 11656.r.7/6; Ashley 5149, uncut),O(2),C,E,GU(2, 1 uncut)+; CSmH,CtY(2),ICU,MH,TxU(4)+.

Y48 [—] — *London, printed for R. Dodsley; sold by M. Cooper,* 1744.

4°: *A⁴* B–G⁴ H²; *1–7* 8–60. A1 frt; A3 fly-title.

> Not recorded in *Pettit*. Presumably reprinted to complete imperfect sets.

LVA-F; ICU,MH.

Y49 [—] Night the sixth. The infidel reclaim'd. In two parts. Containing, the nature, proof, and importance of immortality. Part the first... Humbly inscrib'd to the right honourable Henry Pelham... *London, printed for R. Dodsley,* 1744. (*DG* 30 March)

4°: *A⁴* B–F⁴ G²; [2] *i–iii* iv–v *vi*, *1* 2–42 *43–44*. A1 hft; G2 advt.

> *Pettit* 7a. Entered in *SR* to Dodsley by Ben. Cowse, 30 July 1744, together with *Night the first*; deposit copies at L,C,E,GU,SaU. Young sold the copyright to Dodsley for 60 guineas, 26 Jan 1745 (*Straus, Dodsley,* 326).

'She (for I know not yet her name in heaven)'

L(841.k.16/2; 642.k.4/6; 11656.r.7/7,–G2; Ashley 5150, uncut),O(2, –G2),C,E,GU(2, 1 uncut, –A1, G2); CSmH,CtY(3, 2–G2),ICU(2), MH(2),TxU(4)+.

Y50 [—] The complaint... [Night the seventh.] *London, printed for G. Hawkins; sold by M. Cooper,* 1744. (*DG* 23 July)

4°: *A⁴* B–K⁴; *i–iv* v–vii *viii*, *1* 2–72. A2 fly-title.

> *Pettit* 9a. No watermark. Fly-title A2 reads 'Night the seventh. Being the second part of the Infidel reclaimed...' Printed by Samuel Richardson (*Sale* 323). A letter of Young to Richardson dated 29 July 1744 suggests the existence of a piracy 'which, as to letter and ornaments, mimics your's'; it has not been identified. The press-figures, 2–6, 4–6, 16–3, 22–4, 28–1, 30–3..., vary slightly from copy to copy. Pettit suggests a publication date of 16 July, based on a letter of Young to the Duchess of Portland, but that referred to ordering a presentation copy for her. Entered to Mary Cooper by Ben. Cowse in *SR* 30 July; deposit copies at L,C,E,GU,SaU.

'Heav'n gives the needful, but neglected, call'

L(841.k.16/2; 642.k.4/7; 11656.r.7/8; Ashley 5151, uncut),O(2),C,E,GU(2, 1 uncut, lacks A1) +; CSmH,CtY,ICU,MH(2),TxU(4)+.

Y51 [—] [fine paper]

> Watermark: Strasburg bend.

LVA-D.

Young, E. The complaint, VIII.

Y52 [—] The complaint... Night the eighth. Virtue's apology: or, the man of the world answer'd... *London, printed for G. Hawkins; sold by M. Cooper,* 1745. (7 March?)
4°: A^1 B–I^4 K^4(–K4); *i–ii, 1 2–70*.
> *Pettit* 10a. Watermark: fleur-de-lys. In some copies the watermarks are inconsistent with A1 being K4 folded back, but it may have been so printed. Printed by Samuel Richardson (*Sale* 332). Publication date from a copy quoted by R. W. Chapman in *RES* 4 (1928) 330; advertised in *Old England* 9 March. Entered to Mary Cooper in *SR* 26 March; deposit copies at L,C,E,GU,SaU.
'And has all nature, then, espous'd my part?'
L(841.k.16/4; 642.k.4/8; Ashley 5152),O(3),C, E,GU(2, 1 uncut)+; CSmH,CtY,ICU,MH(2), TxU(3)+.

Y53 [—] [fine paper]
Watermark: Strasburg bend.
LVA-D.

Y54 [—] [Night the ninth.] The consolation. Containing, among other things, I. A moral survey of the nocturnal heavens... To which are annex'd, some thoughts, occasioned by the present juncture: humbly inscribed to his grace the Duke of Newcastle... *London, printed for G. Hawkins; sold by M. Cooper,* 1745 [1746]. (*SR* 21 Jan)
4°: A^1 B–P^4 Q^4(±Q4) R^4 S^4(±S4) T^4 U^1; *i–ii, 1 2–146. ii err.*
> *Pettit* 11a, recording the second cancel as S1 rather than S4. There are ms. corrections in most copies on pp. 12, 75, 129, 131, 144. Printed by Samuel Richardson (*Sale* 333). Entered in *SR* to Hawkins; deposit copies at L,C,E,GU,SaU. Advertised in the *True Patriot*, 28 Jan.
'As when a traveller, a long day past'
L(642.k.4; 11630.e.10*/9; Ashley 5153),O(2), C,E,GU(2, 1 uncut)+; CSmH,CtY,ICU,MH(2), TxU(3)+.

Collected editions

Y55 [—] The complaint... The fifth edition. [Nights 1–4] *London, printed for R. Dodsley; sold by M. Cooper,* 1743. (*Craftsman* 11 June)
8°: A^8(A4+χ^1) B–K^8 L^4(–L4); *i–iv* v–viii [2], 9–165 *166 blk*. A1 hft; χ1 fly-title.
> *Pettit* 5a.
L(11658.bb.46),O.

Y56 [—] — The fourth edition. [Nights 1–4] *Dublin, printed for Peter Wilson,* 1743.
8°.
(*Bibliotheca Lindesiana* (1910) I. 1944.)

Y57 [—] — The sixth edition. [Nights 1–4] *London, printed for R. Dodsley; sold by M. Cooper,* 1743.
8°: A–K^8 L^4; *i–iv* v–viii, 9–10 11–167 *168 blk*. A1 hft.
> *Pettit* 5b. The copies seen have Nights 5–6 added and are entered under Y58.
H. Pettit.

Young, E. The complaint

Y58 [—] — The sixth edition. [Nights 1–6] *London, printed for R. Dodsley; sold by M. Cooper,* 1743 [1746]. (*GA* 15 March)
8°: (frt+) A–K^8 L^4, M–S^8 T^4 (N as 'L'); *i–iv* v–viii, 9–10 11–167 *168 blk*, [2] 169–214 '225–239' *230–236* 237–284 *285–286 blk*. A1 hft.
> A reissue of the preceding. *Pettit* 8a. M–S^8 T^4 add Nights 5 and 6. Pettit records no frontispiece, but adds Aa^4 of Dodsley advertisements, not in the copies seen. The advertisement in *GA* records 'Those who have the first four in octavo, may have the fifth and sixth alone'.
LVA-D(–frt),O,C(–T4); IU.

Y59 [—] — The seventh edition. [Nights 1–6] *London, printed for R. Dodsley,* 1747.
8°: (frt+) A–K^8 L^4, M–S^8 T^4 (N as 'L'); *i–iv* v–viii, 9–10 11–'168' *168 blk*, [2] 169–214 '225–239' *230–236* 237–284 *285–286 blk*. A1 hft.
> *Pettit* 8b. Apparently a new edition of A–K^8 L^4, Nights 1–4, with the same addition as the preceding.
L(11633.df.21); CLU-C,CtY(–T4).

Y60 [—] — The eighth edition. [Nights 1–6] *London, printed for R. Dodsley,* 1749. (*GA* 19 April)
8°: A^2 B–N^8 O^4; *i–iv, 1–2* 3–199 *200 blk*. A1 frt.
> *Pettit* 8c.
LVA-D,O,C.

Y61 [—] The complaint... Vol. II. [Nights 7–9] To which is added, a paraphrase on part of the book of Job. *London, printed for G. Hawkins; sold by M. Cooper,* 1748. (*Jacobite's journal* 30 Jan)
8°: A^8(±A1) C–Z^8 (A6 as 'B'); *i–iv* v–viii ix–x, *1 2–340 341–342 blk*.
> *Pettit* 12a. A copy at IU has the cancelland title-leaf which was dated 1747 and had no reference to the *Paraphrase*. Printed by Samuel Richardson (*Sale* 363).
L(11633.df.21,–Z8),O(–Z8); CLU-C,IU (–Z8).

Y62 [—] — *London, printed for G. Hawkins,* 1749.
8°: A–Q^8 R^4; *i–iv* v–viii ix–x, *11 12–263 264 blk*.
> *Pettit* 12b. Printed to accompany Dodsley's first volume (Y60) by Samuel Richardson (cf. *Sale* 363).
LVA-D,O,C.

Y63 [—] The complaint... The seventh edition. [Nights 1–9] *Dublin, printed for Peter Wilson,* 1747.
12°: A–C^{12} D^6 E–F^{12} G^6 H–O^{12} P^6; *i–ii* iii–iv, *5 6–321 322–324*. 84, 116, 322–324 advt.
> The signatures are arranged so that the book may be divided after Night 4 or Night 6; there are advertisements at the end of Night 5, but in the middle of what appears to be a normal gathering.
O,DT.

Y64 [—] The complaint... To which is added, a paraphrase on part of the book of Job. *London,*

Young, E. The complaint

printed for *A. Millar, & R. Dodsley,* 1750. (*GA* 30 Jan)

12°: *A*² B–O¹² P⁸ Q²; *i–iv, 1–2* 3–326 *327–332.* A1 frt; P8–Q2 advt.

> *Pettit* 13a, not recording Q2. Printed by Samuel Richardson (*Sale* 383A). Millar had purchased the rights to Nights 7–9 from Young on 7 April 1749; publication of this edition was withheld until the octavo edition (in two volumes?) was exhausted (cf. *Sale* 363).

L(11634.b.12),LDW,SaU; CtY(−Q2),TxU.

Y65 [—] — *London, printed for A. Millar, & R. Dodsley,* 1750.

8°: A–Bb⁸ Cc²; *1–4* 5–404. A1 frt.

> *Pettit* 13b. The *Paraphrase* is included, though not mentioned on the title.

O; ICU,*NNUT.*

Piracies
The following collections, in spite of the dates they bear, were almost certainly published after 1750.

Y66 [—] The complaint: or, night-thoughts... '*London, printed in the year* 1743' [1746/–].

12°: A–Mm⁶; *1–6* 7–420.

> *Pettit* 14a. Presumably a piracy; Pettit is in error in saying it uses the shortened preface introduced in 1750, but it may well be later than 1750.

H. Pettit.

Y67 [—] — '*London, printed in the year* 1746' [175–?].

12°: A–R¹² S⁶; *i–ii* iii–iv, *5–6* 7–420 (251 as '151').

> *Pettit* 14b.

CSmH.

Y68 [—] — '*London, printed in the year* 1746' [175–?].

12°: 2 vol; A–D¹² E⁶, A–H¹² I⁴ K–O¹²; *i–ii* iii–iv, *5–6* 7–108, *1–4* 5–318 *319–320 blk.*

> Despite the difference in collation, the early sheets of this edition are very closely related to the preceding. Their priority has not been established.

GU.

———

Y69 [—] Cynthio. *London, printed for J. Roberts,* 1727. (*MC* June)

2°: *A*¹ B–C² D¹; *i–ii, 1* 2–9 *10 blk.*

> No watermark. A1 and D1 have been seen to be conjugate.

'I hate the spring, I turn away'

> Presentation copy at L (below) signed by Young. On the death of the Marquis of Carnarvon.

CSmH.

Y70 [—] [fine paper]

Watermarks: various initials.

L(643.m.12/37, presentation copy to Mr. Victor); TxU.

Y71 [—] [dh] An epistle to the lord Viscount Bolingbroke, sent with a poem on the last day. [col] *London, printed in the year* 1714.

Young, E. An epistle to...Bolingbroke

2°: A²; *1* 2–4.

'While you, my lord, for others welfare born'

> Dated from All-Souls College, 7 March. The reference to *The last day* makes Young's authorship clear. See C. K. Firman in *N&Q* (1963) 218f.

CCC.

Y72 — An epistle to the right honourable the Lord Lansdown. *London, printed for Bernard Lintott,* 1713. (*DC* 10 March)

2°: A–E²; *1–2* 3–19 *20. 20 advt.*

> No watermark. *Rothschild* 2606. Entered in *SR* 11 March; deposit copies at L,LSC,O, EU,AdU,SaU. The Luttrell copy, dated 19 March, is recorded in *Haslewood.*

'When Rome, my lord, in her full glory shone'

> On the peace with France.

L(643.l.26/3),O(uncut),EU,BaP,LdU-B+; CLU-C(uncut),CtY,IU,MH,TxU(3)+.

Y73 — [fine paper]

> Watermark: Φ; it is very faint, and some examples may have been missed.

OW('Donum autoris').

Y74 — The force of religion; or, vanquish'd love. A poem. In two books. *London, printed for E. Curll & J. Pemberton,* 1714. (*PB* 25 May)

8°: *A*⁴ B–F⁴; *i–x, 1*–38. A1 frt; D3 plate.

> 'Price 1*s*.' on title. In some copies (e.g. CtY,KU,TxU) C1.3 have been seen to be conjugate and C2, 4 arranged round them, presumably due to an error of imposition; all copies may suffer this defect. Some fine-paper copies may be wrongly entered here.

'From lofty themes, from thoughts that soar'd on high'

L(161.m.63),*OQ*,C,E,WcC; CSmH,CtY,IU,MH, TxU+.

Y75 — [fine paper]

> No price on title. *Rothschild* 2608 (presentation copy from Young to Pope). No watermark, but 'a small number on superfine paper for such as are curious' were advertised for future publication in *PB* 23 March. The copies at O,LdU-B have the same accident to sheet C as the ordinary issue. A copy at LG has no price on title, but does not appear to be on fine paper.

O('Donum autoris', frt and plate supplied from ordinary-paper copy),OW,LdU-B.

Y76 —— The second edition. *London, printed for E. Curll & J. Pemberton,* 1715 [1714]. (*PB* 28 Aug)

8°: A⁴(±A2) B–F⁴; *i–x, 1*–38. A1 frt; D3 plate.

> A reissue with a cancel title. Some copies (O,MH) have two unsigned leaves of advertisement added. Large paper copies at 1*s*. 6*d*. 'neatly cover'd and gilt' are advertised in *PB,* but have not been seen with this title.

L(11631.bbb.39/4; 011650.ee.70/1),O,CT (−frt),DT,WcC; MH,PU.

Young, E. The force of religion

Y77 —— Founded upon the story of the Lady Jane Gray... The third edition. *London, printed for E. Curll, & J. Pemberton*, 1715.
8⁰: $A^4(\pm A2)$ B–D⁴ E⁴($\pm$E1) F⁴; *i–x, 1–38*. A1 frt; D3 plate.
Another reissue.
O,C(–A1),E; CLU-C,CtY.

Y78 —— *Dublin, printed by S. Powell, for Thomas Whitehouse*, 1725.
8⁰: A–D⁴; *i–iv, 1 2–28*.
O,DA,DN; IU,PU.

Y79 —— *Dublin, printed by S. Powell, for Thomas Whitehouse*, 1728.
8⁰: A–D⁴; *i–iv, 1 2–28*.
Some copies were reissued in a Dublin collection of Young's *Works*, 1730.
O,DA,DT; DLC.

Y80 —— *Dublin, printed by S. Powell, for George Ewing*, 1735.
8⁰: A–D⁴; *i–iv, 1 2–28*.
Some copies were issued in collections of Young's *Works* with titles dated 1730 and 1751.
L(1606/1509),O,C,DN,DT; CSmH.

Y81 [—] The foreign address: or, the best argument for peace. Occasion'd by the British fleet, and the posture of affairs when the parliament met, 1734 ... By a sailor. *London, printed for Lawton Gilliver*, 1735. (*LM* Jan)
4⁰: A–D²; *1–2 3–16*.
'Ye guardian gods! who wait on kings'
Collected in Young's *Poetical works*, 1741.
L(11630.c.13/9),E,DT.

Y82 [—] Imperium pelagi. A naval lyrick: written in imitation of Pindar's spirit. Occasion'd by his majesty's return, Sept. 1729. and the succeeding peace. *London, printed for Lawton Gilliver*, 1730. (*SR* 2 April)
8⁰: $\pi^1 a^2$ A⁴(–A1) B–G⁴ H² I¹; *i–vi, 3 4–60 61–62*. 60 err; I1 advt.
Watermark: MT. *Rothschild* 2615. π1 and I1 have been seen to be conjugate. Originally intended for publication as 'The merchant. A naval lyrick'; that is the head-title on A2, and A1 was presumably a cancelled title with those words. Advertised for publication 'in a few days' with that title in *GSJ* 2 April, but entered in *SR* on the same date with this title; deposit copies at L,O,EU,AdU,SaU.
'Fast by the surge my limbs are spread'
Reprinted in Young's *Poetical works*, 1741.
L(992.h.8/2),O(2, 1–I1),C(–I1),EU,LdU-B (–I1)+; ICN,MH(–I1),NN.

Y83 [—] [fine paper]
Watermark: monogram OT. *Rothschild* 2616, reporting that the leaf of advertisement I1 is not conjugate with π1.
LVA-D,O(–I1),OW('Donum autoris', –I1), DA(–I1); CSmH,CtY.

Young, E. Imperium pelagi

Y84 — [*idem*] The merchant. A naval lyrick: written in imitation of Pindar's spirit. On the British trade, and navigation. *Dublin, printed by S. Powell, for George Risk, George Ewing, & William Smith*, 1730.
8⁰: A–D⁸; *1–6 7–64*.
Ornaments on pp. 3, 7. Presumably reprinted from an advance copy of the London edition with uncancelled title. Some copies recorded were issued in collections of Young's *Works*, 1730.
L(1960),C(2),DN,DT(2); CSmH,CtY,DLC.

Y85 —— *Dublin, printed for George Risk, George Ewing, & William Smith*, '1730'.
8⁰: A–D⁸; *1–7 8–64*.
No ornaments; probably a later reprint. The copy at O is issued in a collection of Young's *Works*, 1751.
O,DA.

Y86 — The instalment. To the right honourable Sir Robert Walpole, knight of the most noble order of the garter. *London, printed for J. Walthoe*, 1726. (*MC* July)
2⁰: A² B–C²; *1–2 3–11 12*. 12 advt.
Watermark: BF.
'With invocations some their breasts inflame'
L(840.m.1/1; Ashley 5279),O,OW(2); CLU-C, CSmH,CtY,ICN,NjP.

Y87 — [fine paper?]
2⁰: A² B–C²; *1–2 3–11 12 blk*.
No advertisement on p. 12. Watermark: BF; apparently a fine paper with the same watermark as the preceding. The DT copy is bound with another fine-paper copy of a poem by Young, Y133.
DT,LdU-B; MH.

Y88 —— *Dublin, printed by S. Powell, for Thomas Whitehouse*, 1726.
8⁰: A⁴ B²; *1–2 3–11 12*. 12 advt.
Reissued in a collection of Young's *Works*, 1730; such a collection is announced on p. 12.
L(1490.m.50/3),O,DT(2); CLU-C,DLC.

Y89 —— *Dublin, printed for George Ewing*, 1738.
8⁰: A⁴ B²; *1–3 4–11 12 blk*.
Copies seen are issued in Young's *Works* with title-pages of 1730 and 1751.
L(1607/3766),O,C; CSmH.

Y90 — A letter to Mr. Tickell. Occasioned by the death of the right honourable Joseph Addison, esq; *London, printed for Jacob Tonson*, 1719. (*DC* 18 July)
2⁰: π^1 A–B² C¹; *i–ii, 1–3 4–10*. π1 hft.
No watermark. Entered in *SR* 18 July; deposit copies at L,LSC,E,EU,SaU.
'O long with me in Oxford-groves confin'd'
L(643.m.13/24),O(–π1),OW,E,LdU-B+; CSmH,CLU-C,IU,*NjP*,TxU(2, 1–π1).

Young, E. A letter to Mr. Tickell

Y91 — [fine paper]
Watermark: fleur-de-lys.
L(840.m.1/19); CtY,ICU.

Y92 — — The second edition. *London, printed for Jacob Tonson,* 1719.
2°: π¹ A–B² C¹; *i–ii, 1–3* 4–10. π1 hft.
Apparently a reimpression. π1 and C1 have been seen to be conjugate.
L(1489.m.20,–π1),LVA-F,O(–π1); CSmH (Luttrell, Dec),ICN,MH(–π1),TxU(crop).

Y93 — — — The third edition. *London printed, and reprinted in Dublin for Pat. Dugan,* [1719.]
8°: *A*⁴ B⁴; *1–3* 4–14 *15–16 blk.*
O,DG.

[—] Love of fame, the universal passion. *See below:* The universal passion.

— The merchant, 1730. *See* Y84.

Y94 [—] Ocean. An ode. Occasion'd by his majesty's late royal encouragement of the sea-service. To which is prefix'd, an ode to the king: and a discourse on ode. By the author of the Universal passion. *London, printed for Tho. Worrall,* 1728. (*MChr* 8 June)
8°: *A*² B–H⁴; [4] *i* ii, *3* 4–55 *56 blk.* A1 hft, advt.
Watermark: fleur-de-lys. *Rothschild* 2613.
Some copies (e.g. IU,MH,TxU) have 'Price one shilling' on the half-title; others have none. Entered in *SR* 13 June; deposit copies (fine paper) at O,EU,AdU and (?)C. The copyright was sold as part of lot 60 of the trade sale of Worrall, 10 Nov 1737 (cat. at O-JJ) to Lintot.
'Sweet rural scene!/Of flocks, and green!'
To the king: 'Old Ocean's praise/Demands my lays'
Reprinted in Young's *Works,* 1757.
LVA-D,O(–A1),DA(lacks A²),LdU-B,WcC (–A1); CSmH,CtY,ICN,MH,TxU +.

Y95 [—] [fine paper]
Watermark: Strasburg bend; no price on half-title in those few copies where it has been seen.
L(11633.bb.29),LVA-D(Pope's copy,–A1),O(2, –A1),C(–A1),WcC(contemporary morocco with royal arms,–A1) +; CtY(–A1),DFo,TxU (–A1).

Y96 — — *London: printed, and Dublin re-printed and sold by George Faulkner & James Hoey,* 1728.
8°: *A*⁴ B–D⁸ (B2 as 'C2'); [2] *i* ii, *3* 4–54.
L(T.902/5; 12274.e.1/2),O,DN.

Y97 — — *Dublin, printed by S. Powell, for George Risk, George Ewing, & William Smith,* 1730.
8°: A–B⁸ C⁴; *i–iv, 1* 2–35 *36. 36 advt.*
Some copies were issued in a collection of Young's *Works,* 1730.
O,DT(2); DLC.

Y98 — — *Dublin, printed by S. Powell, for George Risk,* 1743.

Young, E. Ocean

8°: A–B⁸ C⁴; *1–5* 6–39 *40. 40 advt.*
Copies recorded were issued in collections of Young's *Works* with title-pages dated 1730 or 1751.
L(1607/3752),O,C; CSmH.

Y99 — On the late queen's death, and his majesty's accession to the throne. Inscribed to Joseph Addison, esq;... *London, printed for J. Tonson,* 1714. (*DC* 17 Sept)
2°: A–C²; *i–ii, 1–10.*
Rothschild 2609.
'Sir, I have long, and with impatience, sought'
L(643.m.12/25),LLP,O,C,DN +; CSmH,CtY, ICU,MH,TxU +.

Y100 — A paraphrase on part of the book of Job. *London, printed for Jacob Tonson,* 1719. (*DC* 10 Feb)
4°: A–E⁴; *i–viii, 1* 2–26 *27–32.*
Watermark: London arms. Entered in *SR* 11 Feb to Tonson by Robt. Fayram; deposit copy at O.
'Thrice happy Job long liv'd in regal state'
O,CT,E,DK; CSmH,IU.

Y101 — [fine paper]
Watermark: fleur-de-lys on shield.
L(3050.d.25),OW('Donum autoris'),LdU-B (lacks A2–4, dedication),WcC(contemporary morocco); CtY.

Y102 — — The second edition. *London, printed for Jacob Tonson,* 1719. (*DC* 9 March)
4°: A–E⁴; *i–viii, 1* 2–26 *27–32.*
No watermark.
LDW(heavily annotated by Isaac Watts),WcC (with ms. by Young?); CLU-C,CtY,MH,NjP.

Y103 — [fine paper]
Watermark: fleur-de-lys.
O(notes by Aaron Hill).

Y104 — — *Dublin, printed by J. Carson, for Richard Norris,* 1719.
8°: *A*⁴ B–D⁴; *i–iii* iv–vi, *7* 8–24 *25–31; 32 blk.*
O,DG,DK,DT(2); CSmH.

Y105 [—] — The third edition. *London, printed by W. Wilkins,* 1726.
4°: *A*² B–E⁴; *i–iv, 1* 2–26 *27–31; 32 blk.* A2 fly-title.
The title is taken from the fly-title A2; the title on A1 is 'A specimen for subscribers' and is followed by the imprint; the verso bears proposals for a quarto edition of Young's prose and verse in three volumes.
OW('Donum autoris', gilt edges, lacks A1); CSmH.

Y106 — — *Dublin, printed by S. Powell, for Thomas Whitehouse,* 1726.
8°: A–D⁴; *1–3* 4–24 *25–32.*
Reissued in a Dublin collection of Young's *Works,* 1730.
L(1490.m.50/6),O(2),DN,DT; DLC.

Young, E. A paraphrase

Y107 — — *Dublin, printed by S. Powell, for G. Risk, G. Ewing, & W. Smith,* 1732.
8⁰: A–D⁴; *1–3* 4–24 *25–32.* 32 advt.
    Copies were issued in collections of Young's *Works* with title-pages dated 1730 or 1751.
L(1607/3783),O,C,DT; CSmH,MH.

Y108 '—' A poem by Doctor Young, on Miss Harvey a child of a day old, in imitation of Mr. Philips's poem on Miss C——t. [*Dublin,* 1725.] (Nov?)
slip: 1 side, 1 column.
    Bond 87; *Teerink* 1655.
    'Little girl in swadling cloaths'
    A letter of Swift to Pope, 26 Nov 1725, says 'we say and think it is yours'; Pope's reply of 14 Dec is a possibly equivocal denial.
L(C.121.g.8/108).

Y109 — A poem on the last day. *Oxford, printed at the Theatre for Edward Whistler,* 1713. (*PB* 14 July)
8⁰: A⁴ B–L⁴; *i–xii,* 1–74 *75–76 blk.* A1 hft.
    Rothschild 2607. No watermark has been seen. A copy at OW in presentation morocco, formerly belonging to George Clarke and annotated 'Donum autoris', is almost certainly on fine paper; since no distinguishing feature has been observed, fine-paper copies are not separately entered. The imprimatur is dated 19 May 1713. Advertised in *PB* as sold by Henry Clements and John Morphew.
    'While others sing the fortune of the great'
L(11631.c.47, uncut),O,OW('Donum autoris'), C,LdU-B+; CSmH(–A1, L4),CtY(–A1, L4), ICN,MH,TxU(2)+.

Y110 — — The second edition. *Oxford, printed at the Theatre for Edward Whistler,* 1713 [1714?]. (*PB* 20 Feb 1714)
8⁰: A⁴ B–L⁴; *i–xii,* 1–74 *75–76 blk.* A1 hft.
    Apparently a press-variant title. The date of publication is obscure; it was also listed in *MC* May 1714 under 'books reprinted' as 'sold by H. Clements'.
L(11631.bbb.39/5),O,DA,LdU-B,WcC+; CtY, MH(–A1, L4),MiU(–A1, L4),TxU(2).

Y111 — — The third edition corrected. Adorn'd with cuts. *London, printed for A. Bettesworth, E. Curll, & J. Pemberton,* 1715. (*PB* 26 Nov)
12⁰: A–F⁶; *i–iv* v–xii, 1–56 *57–60.* A1 frt; F5–6 advt.
    The plates are included in the collation.
L(11632.aa.55, lacks B3; 11868.d.9/4),O(2),OW, C(–F5–6),LdU-B; CLU-C,MH,NjP.

Y112 — — The fourth edition. *London, printed for A. Bettesworth, & E. Curll,* 1725. (*EvP* 22 June)
12⁰: A–E⁶; *i–v* vi–xii, *1* 2–47 *48.* A1 frt; 48 advt.
L(992.a.40; 11601.ccc.38/1, –A1),O(uncut); CLU-C,DFo,MH.

Y113 — — The fifth edition. *Dublin, printed by Pressick Rider & Thomas Harbin, for Thomas Whitehouse,* 1725.

Young, E. A poem on the last day

8⁰: A⁴ B–I⁴; *i–iii* iv–x, 1–60 *61–62.* 62 advt.
L(11630.aaa.45/1),O,DN(2); CSmH,DLC,*MH.*

Y114 — — The sixth edition. *Dublin, printed by S. Powell, for George Risk, George Ewing, & William Smith,* 1730.
8⁰: (frt+) A–D⁸; *1–6* 7–63 *64.*
    Most copies were issued in collections of Young's *Works* with title-pages dated 1730 or 1751. When thus issued, the frontispiece was transferred to the beginning of the volume; it is not present in some copies recorded here, doubtless because they were extracted from those volumes.
L(1607/3768),O(2),C,DA,DT(2); CSmH,DLC.

Y115 — — The fifth edition. *London, printed for E. Curll, & C. Hitch,* 1741.
8⁰: (frt+) A–D⁸ E⁴; *i–iii* iv–vi, *7–13* 14–72.
L,WcC; IU(2, 1–frt),KU,PU.

Y116 — — The tenth edition. '*London, printed for J. Watts, and sold by B. Dod,* 1750.'
8⁰: a⁴ b² A–D⁴; *i–iii* iv–vii *vii–xii, 1* 2–32.
    A Scottish piracy; compare *Love of fame... The tenth edition,* 1750 (Y176). Possibly printed after 1750.
EN,AdU; MH(lacks A1).

Y117 [—] Two epistles to Mr. Pope, concerning the authors of the age. *London, printed for Lawton Gilliver,* 1730. (*MChr* 26 Jan)
8⁰: A–F⁴; *1–3* 4–44 *45–48.* 44 err; F3–4 advt.
    Rothschild 2617. Entered to Gilliver in *SR* 24 Jan 1730, with a note of the copyright having been assigned to him by the author; deposit copies at L,O,EU,SaU. Reissued in *A collection of pieces...on occasion of the Dunciad,* 1732.
    'Whilst you at Twick'nam plan the future wood'
    'All write at London; – shall the rage abate'
    Reprinted in Young's *Works,* 1757.
L(C.59.ff.12/3),O,CK,E,LdU-B(–F3–4)+; CSmH(uncut),CtY(–F3–4),ICN,MH(–F3–4), TxU(2)+.

Y118 — — By E. Young... *London: printed, and Dublin re-printed, by James Hoey & George Faulkner,* 1730.
8⁰: A⁸ B⁴; *1–3* 4–24.
    Rothschild 2618.
O; CtY.

Y119 [—] — By the author of the Universal passion. *Dublin: re-printed by and for James Hoey,* 1730.
8⁰: A⁸ B⁴(–B4); *1–3* 4–21 *22.* 22 advt.
    B4 probably missing from the copy seen. Presumably published after the partnership between Faulkner & Hoey was dissolved in 1730.
L(C.136.aa.1/6),DK.

Y120 [—] — *Dublin, printed by S. Powell, for George Risk, George Ewing, & William Smith,* 1730.
8⁰: A–D⁴; *1–3* 4–32.

Young, E. Two epistles to Mr. Pope

Some copies were issued in Young's *Works*, 1730.
L(11631.aa.47/3; T.902/6),O,C,DN,DT(3)+;
CtY,DFo,DLC,TxU.

Y121 [—] — *Dublin, printed for George Risk, George & Alexander Ewing, & William Smith*, 1748.
8⁰: A–D⁴; *1–3* 4–32.
Copies recorded were issued in collections of Young's *Works* with title-pages dated 1730 or 1751.
L(1607/3774),O,C; CSmH.

Y122 [—] The universal passion. Satire I. To his grace the Duke of Dorset. *London, printed for J. Roberts*, 1725. (*DP* 25 Jan)
2⁰: *A² B–E²*; *i–iv, 1* 2–15 *16 blk*. A1 hft; 15 advt.
No watermark. Press-figures 2–4, 8–4, 14–2. Entered to Jacob Tonson by James Roberts in *SR* 9 April 1725, at the same time as Satire 2; deposit copies at L,O,E,EU,SaU.
'My verse is satire; Dorset, lend your ear'
L(643.m.13/21; C.59.h.9/1),O,E,GU,SaU+; CLU-C(uncut),CtY(3, 1 uncut),MH,NjP,TxU+.

Y123 [—] [fine paper]
Watermark: fleur-de-lys.
NjP.

Y124 [—] — *London, printed for J. Roberts*, 1725.
2⁰: *A² B–E²*; *i–iv, 1* 2–15 *16 blk*. A1 hft; 15 advt.
Press-figure 11–4. Reset except for sheet A. A copy at OW from George Clarke's collection is noted 'Donum autoris – Feb: 8⁰ – 1725'; this refers to a gift of Satires 1–4 and 'last' in the year 1725/6.
L(643.1.25/20,–A1),OW(3),BaP,LdU-B; CLU-C,CSmH.

Y125 [—] — Satire II. *London, printed for J. Roberts*, 1725. (*DC* 2 April)
2⁰: *π¹ A² B–D² E¹*; *i–ii, 1–3* 4–17 *18 blk*. π1 hft.
No watermark. Press-figure 14–4. π1 and E1 have been seen to be conjugate. Entered to Jacob Tonson by James Roberts in *SR* 9 April; deposit copies at L,O,E,EU,SaU. Listed in *MC* April.
'My muse, proceed, and reach thy destin'd end'
L(643.m.13/21; C.59.h.9/1),O(–π1),E,GU, BaP(stitched, uncut)+; CSmH,CtY(uncut),KU, MH,TxU+.

Y126 [—] [fine paper]
Watermark: fleur-de-lys.
ICN.

Y127 [—] — *London, printed for J. Roberts*, 1725.
2⁰: *π¹ A² B–D² E¹*; *i–ii, 1–3* 4–17 *18 blk*. π1 hft.
No press-figure. Reset, with the exception of the title and half-title.
L(643.1.25/20),OW,BaP,LdU-B; CLU-C,NjP.

Y128 [—] — Satire III. To the right honourable Mr. Dodington. *London, printed for J. Roberts*, 1725. (*MC* April)
2⁰: *A² B–E²*; *i–iv, 1* 2–15 *16 blk*. A1 hft.

Young, E. The universal passion, III.

No watermark. Entered to Jacob Tonson by James Roberts in *SR* 7 May; deposit copies at L,O,E,EU,SaU.
'Long, Dodington, in debt, I long have sought'
L(643.m.13/21; 643.1.25/20; C.59.h.9/1),O(–A1),E,BaP(2, 1 stitched, uncut),LdU-B+; CSmH, CtY(uncut),MH,NjP,TxU(3, 1 uncut)+.

Y129 [—] [fine paper]
Watermark: fleur-de-lys.
DFo,NjP.

Y130 [—] — Satire IV. To the right honourable Sir Spencer Compton. *London, printed for J. Roberts*, 1725. (*SR* 18 June)
2⁰: *A² B–E²*; *i–iv, 1* 2–14 *15–16 blk*. A1 hft.
No watermark. Press-figure 4 on p. 8 missing from copies at L,EU,TxU, possibly due to damage. Entered to Jacob Tonson by James Roberts in *SR* 18 June; deposit copies at L,O,E,EU,SaU. Listed in *MC* June.
'Round some fair tree th' ambitious woodbine grows'
L(643.m.13/21,–E2; C.59.h.9/1,–E2),O (–A1),E,BaP(2, 1 stitched, uncut),LdU-B+; CLU-C,CtY(uncut),MH,NjP,TxU(3, 1 uncut, 2–E2)+.

Y131 [—] [fine paper]
Watermark: fleur-de-lys. No press-figure on p. 8.
NjP.

Y132 [—] — Satire the last. To the right honourable Sir Robert Walpole. *London, printed for J. Roberts*, 1726. (*SR* 21 Jan)
2⁰: *A² B–D²*; *i–iv, 1* 2–12. A1 hft.
No watermark. Entered to Jacob Tonson in *SR* 21 Jan; deposit copies at L,O,E,EU, SaU. Listed in *MC* Jan.
'On this last labour, this my closing strain'
L(643.m.13/21; 643.1.25/20*; 840.m.1/34, –A1),O(–A1),E,BaP(2, 1 stitched, uncut), LdU-B+; CSmH,CtY(uncut),MH,NjP,TxU (2, 1 uncut)+.

Y133 [—] [fine paper]
Watermark: fleur-de-lys.
DT; ICN.

Y134 [—] — Satire V. On women. *London, printed for J. Roberts*, 1727. (*MC* Feb)
2⁰: A–H²; *i–iv, 1* 2–28. A1 hft.
No watermark. Presentation copy to George Clarke at OW dated 3 Feb, possibly before publication.
'Nor reigns ambition in bold man alone'
L(643.m.15/7, lacks A²; C.59.h.9/1),OW(2), GU,BaP,LdU-B+; CSmH,CtY(uncut),MH, NjP,TxU(3, 2 uncut)+.

Y135 [—] [fine paper]
Watermark: GF.
O; NjP.

Young, E. The universal passion, VI.

Y136 [—] — Satire VI. On women. Inscrib'd to the right honourable the Lady Elizabeth Germain. *London, printed for J. Roberts, 1728.* (*MChr* 24 Feb)
2°: *A*¹ B–H² I¹; *i–ii, 1 2–30.* 30 err.
> No watermark. A1 and I1 have been seen to be conjugate. All copies (apparently) have the top two lines of p. 28 deleted in ms.
'I sought a patroness, but sought in vain'
L(840.m.1/33; C.59.h.9/1),O,OW,BaP(stitched, uncut); CtY,DFo,MH,TxU(uncut).

Y137 [—] [fine paper]
> Mixed watermarks: fleur-de-lys, fleur-de-lys on shield, and post-horn.
L(163.n.56).

Edinburgh piracies

The following editions, intended for binding up together, were all printed in Edinburgh by Thomas Ruddiman. An advertisement in an Edinburgh piracy of Swift's Cadenus and Vanessa, *1726, shows that they were sold by Allan Ramsay.*

Y138 [—] The universal passion. Satire I... [Edinburgh] *Printed in the year 1725.*
8°: A–B⁴; *1–2 3–16.* 16 advt.
MH(2).

Y139 [—] — '*London*' [Edinburgh], *printed in the year 1726.*
8°: A–B⁴; *1–2 3–16.*
O(2),EN; CtY.

Y140 [—] — Satire II. [Edinburgh] *Printed in the year 1725.*
8°: C–D⁴; *17–18 19–32.*
O,EN; MH.

Y141 [—] — [Edinburgh] *Printed in the year 1728.*
8°: C–D⁴; *17–18 19–32.*
O; CtY.

Y142 [—] — Satire III. [Edinburgh] *Printed in the year 1725.*
8°: E–F⁴; *33–34 35–48.*
> The rule above the imprint is 74 mm. long.
O,EN; MH.

Y143 [—] — [Edinburgh] *Printed in the year '1725'.*
8°: E–F⁴; *33–34 35–48.*
> The rule above the imprint is 71 mm. long. Judging by the editions with which it is found, this is a later reprint.
O; CtY.

Y144 [—] — Satire IV... [Edinburgh] *Printed in the year 1725.*
8°: G–H⁴; *49–50 51–64.*
> The ornament on p. 51 contains mermaids.
O,EN; MH.

Y145 [—] — [Edinburgh] *Printed in the year '1725'.*
8°: G–H⁴; *49–50 51–64.*
> The ornament on p. 51 represents flowers. Judging by the editions with which it is found, this is a later reprint.
O; CtY.

Young, E. The universal passion

Y146 [—] — Satire the last... [Edinburgh] *Printed in the year 1726.*
8°: I–K⁴; *65–66 67–80.*
O(2),EN; CtY,MH.

Y147 [—] — Satire VI. On women. [Edinburgh] *Printed in the year 1727.*
8°: Q–T⁴; *123–124 125–154.*
> This corresponds to Satire 5 of the London edition. The gap in pagination from p. 80 of the preceding is partly filled by an Edinburgh piracy of Swift's *Cadenus and Vanessa*, 1726, which was issued with pagination *81–114*.
O(2),EN; CtY.

Y148 [—] — Satire VII. On women... [Edinburgh] *Printed in the year 1728.*
8°: U–Z⁴; *155–156 157–185 186 blk.*
> This corresponds to Satire 6 of the London edition.
O; CtY.

Dublin reprints

Y149 [—] The universal passion. Satire I... *Dublin, printed by S. Powell, for George Ewing, 1725.*
8°: A–B⁴; *i–ii, 1 2–14.* 14 advt.
L(1490.m.1),DT.

Y150 [—] — The second edition. *Dublin, printed by S. Powell, for George Ewing, 1725.*
8°: A–B⁴; *i–ii, 1 2–14.*
O(3),DN(2).

Y151 [—] — *Dublin, printed by S. Powell, for George Ewing, 1727.*
8°: A⁸; *1–3 4–16.*
> Most of the copies recorded here were issued in collections of the whole work, 1728 (Y168, Y170).
L(11632.a.26; 1490.m.50/1),DA,DN,DT,GU; CSmH,DLC,MH.

Y152 [—] — Satire II. *Dublin, printed by S. Powell, for George Ewing, 1725.*
8°: A–B⁴; *1–3 4–16.*
> Signature A2 under a and d of 'and'.
DT.

Y153 [—] — *Dublin, printed by S. Powell, for George Ewing, 1725.*
8°: A–B⁴; *1–3 4–16.*
> Signature A2 under n and space after 'and'.
O(2),DN(3).

Y154 [—] — *Dublin, printed by S. Powell, for George Ewing, 1726.*
8°: A–B⁴; *1–3 4–16.*
L(1490.m.50),O,GU.

Y155 [—] [idem] Love of fame, the universal passion. Satire II. *Dublin, printed by S. Powell, for George Ewing, 1728.*
8°: B⁸; *17–18 19–32.*
> Most of the copies recorded here were issued in collections of the whole work, 1728 (Y168, Y170) as the collation suggests was intended.
L(11632.a.26),DA,DT; CSmH,DLC,MH.

Young, E. The universal passion

Y156 [—] The universal passion. Satire III... *Dublin, printed by S. Powell, for George Ewing, 1725.*
8°: A–B⁴; *1–3* 4–15 *16 blk.*
　Apparently the earlier edition, from its association with the first Dublin edition of Satire 1 at DT.
DA(uncut),DN,DT.

Y157 [—] — *Dublin, printed by S. Powell, for George Ewing, 1725.*
8°: A–B⁴; *1–3* 4–16.
O(2),DN(2).

Y158 [—] — The third edition. *Dublin, printed by S. Powell, for George Ewing, 1726.*
8°: A–B⁴; *1–3* 4–16.
L(1490.m.50),GU.

Y159 [—] [*idem*] Love of fame, the universal passion. Satire III... *Dublin, printed by S. Powell, for George Ewing, 1728.*
8°: C⁸; *33–34* 35–47 *48 blk.*
　Most of the copies recorded here were issued in collections of the whole work, 1728 (Y168, Y170) as the collation suggests was intended.
L(11632.a.26),DA,DT; CSmH,DLC,MH.

Y160 [—] The universal passion. Satire IV... *Dublin, printed by S. Powell, for George Ewing, 1725.*
8°: A–B⁴; *i–ii,* *1* 2–13 *14.* 14 advt.
O(2),DN(3),DT,GU.

Y161 [—] — *Dublin, printed by S. Powell, for George Ewing, 1727.*
8°: A⁸; *i–ii,* *1* 2–13 *14 blk.*
　Some copies were issued in a collection of the whole work, 1728.
L(11632.a.26; 1490.m.50); CSmH.

Y162 [—] [*idem*] Love of fame, the universal passion. Satire IV... *Dublin, printed by S. Powell, for George Ewing, 1728.*
8°: D⁸; *49–51* 52–63 *64 blk.*
　Most of the copies recorded here were issued in collections of the whole work, 1728 (Y168, Y170) as the collation suggests was intended.
DA,DN,DT; CtY,DLC,MH.

Y163 [—] The universal passion. Satire the last... *Dublin, printed by S. Powell, for George Ewing, 1726.*
8°: A–B⁴; *1–2* 3–15 *16.* 16 advt.
　Some copies were issued in a collection of the whole work, 1728.
L(1490.m.50),O(2),DN(2),DT,GU.

Y164 [—] [*idem*] Love of fame, the universal passion. Satire the last... *Dublin, printed by S. Powell, for George Ewing, 1728.*
8°: A–B⁴; *1–2* 3–14 *15–16 blk.*
　Most of the copies recorded here were issued in collections of the whole work, 1728 (Y168, Y170).
L(11632.a.26),O,DA,DT; CSmH,DLC,MH (−B4).

Young, E. The universal passion

Y165 [—] The universal passion. Satire V. On women. *Dublin, printed by S. Powell, for George Ewing, 1727.*
8°: A–C⁴ D²; *i–ii,* 1–26.
　Some copies were issued in a collection of the whole work, 1728.
L(11632.a.26; 1490.m.50),GU; CSmH.

Y166 [—] [*idem*] Love of fame, the universal passion. Satire V. On women. *Dublin, printed by S. Powell, for George Ewing, 1728.*
8°: E⁸ F⁴ G²; *65–66* 67–92.
　Most of the copies recorded here were issued in collections of the whole work, 1728 (Y168, Y170) as the collation suggests was intended.
DA,DN,DT; DLC,MH.

Y167 [—] Love of fame, the universal passion. Satire VI. On women... *Dublin, printed by S. Powell, for George Ewing, 1728.*
8°: A⁸ B⁸(−B8); *1–3* 4–30.
　B8 was printed as a general title, 'The universal passion, in seven satires compleat', 1728; it is still found in this position in a copy at DT. Most of the copies recorded here were issued in that collection.
L(11632.a.26; 1490.m.50),DN,DT; CSmH, DLC,MH.

Collected editions

Y168 [—] The universal passion, in seven satires compleat. Satire I. and II... III... IV... V... VI... VII... *Dublin, printed by S. Powell, for George Ewing, 1728.*
　A general title for the Dublin reprints above, printed as B8 of Satire 6, Y167. Also issued with added preliminaries as Y170.
L(11632.a.26),DT.

Y169 [—] [*idem*] Love of fame, the universal passion. In seven characteristical satires... The second edition corrected, and alter'd. *London, printed for J. Tonson, 1728.* (*MChr* 19 March)
8°: A⁴ a² B–M⁸; *i–xii,* *1–3* 4–175 *176 blk.*
　Rothschild 2612. A presentation copy to George Clarke at OW, dated 14 March, was perhaps presented before publication.
L(C.45.c.18, ms. notes by Horace Walpole),LG, O,C,GU+; CLU-C,CtY,IU,MH,TxU+.

Y170 [—] — The second edition corrected. *Dublin, printed by S. Powell, for George Ewing, 1728.*
8°: a⁴; *i–viii.*
　Preliminary leaves for the Dublin collection of the satires, previously issued as *The universal passion, in seven satires compleat,* 1728 (Y168). The whole was also reissued in Young's *Works,* 1730.
L(11632.a.26; 1490.m.50),DA,DT; DLC,MH.

Y171 [—] — The third edition. *London, printed for J. Tonson, 1730.*
8°: A⁴ a² B–M⁸; *i–xii,* *1–3* 4–175 *176 blk.*
　The 'third edition' was listed in *MChr* July 1731 as printed for J. Tonson and sold by

Young, E. The universal passion

> A. Bettesworth & C. Hitch. Presumably it was also this 'third edition' that was listed in *GM, LM* Aug 1737 as printed for Bettesworth & Hitch.
> L(11633.bb.26),O,C,AdU,LdU-B+; CSmH, CtY,ICN,MH,*TxU*+.

Y172 [—] — The third edition corrected. *Dublin, printed by S. Powell, for George Ewing*, 1731.
8°: π⁴ A–L⁴ M² N–Q⁴ R² S⁴; *i–viii*, *1–3* 4–136.

> A collection of the satires, each with a separate title dated 1731, which were doubtless also available separately but are not so entered here. In those copies of Satire 6 intended to be issued separately (copies at O,DA) Q4 is blank; in others it bears the title for *Satire the last*. Copies were also issued in collections of Young's *Works* with title-pages dated 1730 and 1751.
> L(11632.aa.33),O(3),C(2),DN(lacks π1); CSmH.

Y173 [—] — The fourth edition. *London, printed for J. & R. Tonson*, 1741.
8°: A⁴ a² B–M⁸; *i–xii*, *1–3* 4–175 *176 blk.*
L(11633.e.28),*LVA-D*,O,E,BaP; CtY,ICU,IU, MH,*PU*.

Y174 — — *Glasgow, printed and sold by Robert & Andrew Foulis*, 1750. (*SM* Oct)
8°: a⁴ b² A–M⁴; *i–iii* iv–xii, *1* 2–96.
> Watermark: Royal arms. *Gaskell, Foulis* 176, not recording variant papers.
> DT,GM.

Y175 — [fine paper?]
> Watermark: Dutch lion.

> O.

Y176 — — The tenth edition. '*London, printed for J. Watts; sold by B. Dod*, 1750.'
8°: π⁴ A–I⁴; *i–viii*, *1* 2–71 *72 blk.*
> A piracy of Scottish origin; the copy at NN is bound with a collection of Scottish publications. Compare *A poem on the last day... The tenth edition*, 1750. Possibly printed after 1750.
> L(1486.df.24),O,AdU; NN.

Y177 [**Young, Lewis.**] Utopia: or, Apollo's golden days. *Dublin, printed by George Faulkner*, 1747.
8°: A⁴(±A2) B–C⁴ D²; [2] *i–ii*, *1–24*.
> The cancel leaf A2 bears a preface.
'All curious poets keep a muse'
> Early ms. attribution to Young in one DN copy. On Lord Chesterfield in Ireland.
> L(1959),O(2, 1 lacks A2),C,DN(3),DT(uncut)+; CLU-C(lacks A2),CSmH,NjP.

Y178 Younger. The younger brother's garland. To the tune of Packington's pound. [*London?* 1740?]
slip: 1 side, 1 column.
> *Percival* LXIII, printing a text from the *Craftsman* 25 Oct 1740.

The **younger** brother's garland

'No more our proud neighbours shall tell us with scorn'
> A satire on Walpole's conduct as ruining English trade.

C.

Youth. Youth's divine pastime, [1710?]–. *See* Crouch, Nathaniel.

[Y179 = S419·5] — Youth's tragedy, a poem, 1707. *See* Sherman, Thomas.

[Y180 = S419·6] — [*idem*] Youth undone: a tragick poem, 1709. *See* Sherman, Thomas.

Z

Z., C. Hymns composed for the use of the brethren, 1749. *See* Zinzendorf, N. L. von, *count*.

'**Z., Q.**, *late commoner of Oxon.*' A most pleasant description of Benwel village, 1726. *See* Ellison, Cuthbert.

Zappi, Giovanni Battista Felice.
[*Canzone*] Rhapsody by John Baptist Felix Zappi, 1749. *See* R186.

Zara. Zara, at the court of Annamaboe, 1749. *See* Dodd, William.

Z1 Zealous. [dh] The zealous country-mens lament for the absence of Mr. George Whitefield, with a deep concern of the schism... By a well wisher of the ministry. [*Edinburgh*, 1742.] (Oct)
8°: *A⁴*; *1* 2–8.
> Above title, '(Edinburgh October 11th 1742.)'.
'October one day, with mournful tune'
L(1078.k.26/10).

Z2 [**Zinzano, Nicholas.**] Paradice regain'd: or, the art of gardening. A poem. *London, printed for G. Strahan; sold by J. Roberts*, 1728. (*MChr* 30 March)
8°: *A²* B–H⁴ I²; *i–iv*, *1–59* *60 blk.*
'When weekly bills increase, and here, and there'
> Ascribed to Zinzano by *Rawlinson*. Also ascribed to John Laurence (d. 1732) in an early pencil note on the O copy, but that attribution has long been doubted; cf. G. O. Bellowes in *Antiquities of Sunderland* IV (1905).
> L(966.f.20/3),O,CK; MH,TxU.

[**Zinzendorf, Nicholas Ludwig von**, *count*.] Hymns composed for the use of the brethren. By the right reverend, and most illustrious C.Z.

Zinzendorf, N. L. von, *count*

[*London*] *Published for the benefit of all mankind.*
In the year 1749.
12°: pp. 12.   L,CT.
   Apparently the 'Moravian hymns' entered to
John & Charles Wesley in Strahan's ledger
under Feb 1749, 1500 copies. *Green* 137;

edited by John Wesley. A selection of the
more absurd specimens from the Moravian
A collection of hymns . . . Part III, 1748, which
is apparently a compilation of the work of
various authors and hence excluded from this
catalogue.